SPANISH-ENGLISH
ENGLISH-SPANISH
THE IDEAL COMPANION FOR
ALL LEARNERS OF SPANISH

BBC

SPANISH

D1638492

LEARNER'S DICTIONARY

ISBN 0-563-40086-2

Published by BBC Books, a division of BBC Worldwide Ltd,
Woodlands, 80 Wood Lane, London W12 0TT
First published 1997

Printed and bound in Great Britain by Mackays of Chatham
Cover printed by Belmont Press Ltd, Northampton

Introduction

The BBC *Spanish Learner's Dictionary* is the result of a collaboration between the BBC and the Larousse Language Reference team. It is aimed at all learners of Spanish and can be used either independently or alongside the BBC's best-selling *Sueños World Spanish* course.

Containing over 78,000 translations, the dictionary provides thorough coverage of everyday Spanish, wide coverage of Latin American Spanish and detailed coverage of GCSE word lists, along with business terms and computing vocabulary. There are also handy cultural notes throughout, giving a useful insight into the language as well as into Spanish-speaking countries and their traditions.

Whether you are reading, writing, listening or speaking, the dictionary makes communication simpler as each word is clearly divided, where appropriate, into its different meanings and parts of speech, while there is essential guidance on Spanish pronunciation.

Up-to-date and easy to use, this dictionary is the ideal companion for all learners, whether at school, at home or travelling abroad.

Abbreviations

Abreviaturas

abbreviation	*abbr/abrev*	abreviatura
adjective	*adj*	adjetivo
adjective only used in feminine form	*adj f*	adjetivo femenino
administration, administrative	ADMIN	administración
adverb	*adv*	adverbio
aeronautics, aviation	AERON	aeronáutica, aviación
agriculture, farming	AGR	agricultura
American English	Am	inglés americano
Latin American Spanish	Amer	español latinoamericano
anatomy	ANAT	anatomía
before noun	*antes de sust*	antes de sustantivo
– indicates that the translation is always used directly before the noun which it modifies		– indica que la traducción siempre se utiliza en inglés antepuesta al sustantivo al que modifica
archeology	ARCHEOL	arqueología
architecture	ARCHIT/ARQUIT	arquitectura
article	*art*	artículo
astrology	ASTROL	astrología
astronomy	ASTRON	astronomía
automobile, cars	AUT(OM)	automovilismo, coches
biology	BIOL	biología
botany	BOT	botánica
British English	Br	inglés británico
Canadian English	Can	inglés canadiense
chemistry	CHEM	química
cinema, film-making	CIN(EMA)	cine
commerce, business	COM(M)	comercio, negocios
compound	*comp*	sustantivo antepuesto a otro
comparative	*compar*	comparativo
computers, computer science	COMPUT	informática
conjunction	*conj*	conjunción
construction, building	CONSTR	construcción
continuous	*cont*	continuo
culinary, cooking	CULIN	cocina
definite	*def*	determinado
demonstrative	*demos*	demostrativo
sport	DEP	deporte
juridical, legal	DER	derecho, jurídico
pejorative	*despec*	despectivo, peyorativo
dated	*desus*	desusado
ecology	ECOLOG	ecología
economics	ECON	economía
school, education	EDUC	educación
electricity	ELEC(TR)	electricidad
electronics	ELECTRON/ELECTRÓN	electrónica
especially	*esp*	especialmente
exclamation	*excl*	interjección
feminine noun	*f*	sustantivo femenino

informal	*fam*	familiar
pharmacology, pharmaceutics	FARM	farmacología, farmacia
railways	FERROC	ferrocarril
figurative	*fig*	figurado
finance, financial	FIN	finanzas
physics	FÍS	física
formal	*fml*	formal, culto
photography	FOT	fotografía
soccer	FTBL	fútbol
inseparable	*fus*	inseparable

– shows that a phrasal verb is 'fused', i.e. inseparable, e.g. **look after** where the object cannot come between the verb and the particle, e.g. I *looked after him* but not **I looked him after*

– indica que una locución verbal o 'phrasal verb' (verbo + preposición o adverbio) es inseparable y el objeto no puede aparecer entre el verbo en sí y la partícula, p. ej. en **look after** se dice I *looked after him* no **I looked him after*

generally, in most cases	*gen*	generalmente, en general
geography, geographical	GEOGR	geografía
geology, geological	GEOL	geología
geometry	GEOM	geometría
grammar	GRAM(M)	gramática
history	HIST	historia
humorous	*hum*	humorístico
industry	IND	industria
indefinite	*indef*	indeterminado
informal	*inf*	familiar
infinitive	*infin*	infinitivo
computers, computer science	INFORM	informática
exclamation	*interj*	interjección
invariable	*inv*	invariable
ironic	*iro/irón*	irónico
juridical, legal	JUR	derecho, jurídico
linguistics	LING	lingüística
literal	*lit*	literal
literature	LITER	literatura
phrase(s)	*loc*	locución, locuciones
adjectival phrase	*loc adj*	locución adjetiva
adverbial phrase	*loc adv*	locución adverbial
conjunctival phrase	*loc conj*	locución conjuntiva
prepositional phrase	*loc prep*	locución preposicional

– adjectives, adverbs etc. consisting of more than one word, e.g. **a pesar de, a horcajadas**

– construcciones fijas de más de una palabra con función adjetiva, adverbial, etc.; p. ej. **a pesar de, a horcajadas**

masculine noun	*m*	sustantivo masculino
mathematics	MAT(H)	matemáticas
mechanical engineering	MEC	mecánica
medicine	MED	medicina
metallurgy	METAL	metalurgia
weather, meteorology	METEOR	meteorología
very informal	*mfam*	muy familiar

military	MIL	militar
mining	MIN	minería
mythology	MITOL	mitología
music	MUS/MÚS	música
mythology	MYTH	mitología
noun	*n*	sustantivo
nautical, maritime	NAUT/NÁUT	náutica, marítimo
numeral	*num/núm*	número
oneself	*o.s.*	
pejorative	*pej*	peyorativo, despectivo
personal	*pers*	personal
pharmacology, pharmaceutics	PHARM	farmacología, farmacia
photography	PHOT	fotografía
phrase(s)	*phr*	locución, locuciones
physics	PHYS	física
plural	*pl*	plural
politics	POL(ÍT)	política
possessive	*poss/poses*	posesivo
past participle	*pp*	participio pasado
press, journalism	PRENS	periodismo, prensa
preposition	*prep*	preposición
pronoun	*pron*	pronombre
psychology, psychiatry	PSYCH/PSICOL	psicología
past tense	*pt*	pasado, pretérito
chemistry	QUÍM	química
registered trademark	®	marca registrada
railways	RAIL	ferrocarril
relative	*relat*	relativo
religion	RELIG	religión
someone, somebody	*sb*	
school, education	SCH	educación
Scottish English	*Scot*	inglés escocés
separable	*sep*	separable

– shows that a phrasal verb is separable, e.g. **let in**, where the object can come between the verb and the particle, e.g. I *let her in*

– indica que una locución verbal o 'phrasal verb' (verbo + preposición o adverbio) es separable y el objeto puede aparecer entre el verbo en sí y la partícula, p. ej. en **let in**, se dice I *let her in*

singular	*sg*	singular
slang	*sl*	argot
sociology	SOCIOL	sociología
stock exchange	ST EX	bolsa
something	*sthg*	
subject	*subj/suj*	sujeto
superlative	*superl*	superlativo
bullfighting	TAUROM	tauromaquia
theatre	TEATR	teatro
technology, technical	TECH/TECN	tecnología, técnico
telecommunications	TELEC(OM)	telecomunicaciones
television	TV	televisión
printing, typography	TYPO	imprenta

uncountable noun – i.e. an English noun which is never used in the plural or with 'a'; used when the Spanish word is or can be a plural, e.g. **infighting** n (U) disputas fpl internas, **balido** m bleat, bleating (U)	U	sustantivo 'incontable' – esto es, sustantivo inglés que jamás se usa en plural o con el artículo 'a'; utilizado cuando la palabra española es o puede ser plural, p. ej. **infighting** n (U) disputas fpl internas, **balido** m bleat, bleating (U)
university	UNIV	universidad
usually	usu	normalmente
auxiliary verb	vaux	verbo auxiliar
verb	vb/v	verbo
veterinary science	VETER	veterinaria
intransitive verb	vi	verbo intransitivo
impersonal verb	v impers	verbo impersonal
very informal	v inf	muy familiar
pronominal verb	vpr	verbo pronominal
transitive verb	vt	verbo transitivo
vulgar	vulg	vulgar
zoology	ZOOL	zoología
cultural equivalent	≃	equivalente cultural

Trademarks

Words considered to be trademarks have been designated in this dictionary by the symbol ®. However, neither the presence nor the absence of such designation should be regarded as affecting the legal status of any trademark.

Marcas registradas

El símbolo ® indica que la palabra en cuestión se considera marca registrada. Hay que tener en cuenta, sin embargo, que ni la presencia ni la ausencia de dicho símbolo afectan a la situación legal de ninguna marca.

Spanish alphabetical order

As this dictionary follows international alphabetical order, the Spanish letter combinations **ch** and **ll** are *not* treated as separate letters. Thus entries with **ch** appear after **cg** and not at the end of **c.** Similarly, entries with **ll** appear after **lk** and not at the end of **l.** Note, however, that **ñ** *is* treated as a separate letter and follows **n** in alphabetical order.

English compounds

A compound is a word or expression which has a single meaning but is made up of more than one word, e.g. **point of view**, **kiss of life**, **virtual reality**, **West Indies** and **Confederation of British Industry**. It is a feature of this dictionary that English compounds appear in the A–Z list in strict alphabetical order. The compound **blood poisoning** will therefore come after **bloodhound** which itself follows **blood group**.

La ordenación alfabética en español

En este diccionario se ha seguido la ordenación alfabética internacional; por lo tanto, las consonantes **ch** y **ll** *no* se consideran letras aparte. Esto significa que las entradas con **ch** aparecerán después de **cg** y no al final de **c**; del mismo modo las entradas con **ll** vendrán después de **lk** y no al final de **l**. Adviértase, sin embargo, que la letra **ñ** *sí* se considera letra aparte y sigue a la **n** en orden alfabético.

Los compuestos en inglés

En inglés se llama compuesto a una locución sustantiva de significado único pero formada por más de una palabra; p. ej. **point of view**, **kiss of life**, **virtual reality**, **West Indies** o **Confederation of British Industry**. Uno de los rasgos distintivos de este diccionario es la inclusión de estos compuestos con entrada propia y en riguroso orden alfabético. De esta forma **blood poisoning** vendrá después de **bloodhound**, el cual sigue a **blood group**.

Phonetic Transcription

English vowels

[ɪ] **p**it, b**i**g, r**i**d
[e] **p**et, t**e**nd
[æ] **p**at, b**a**g, m**a**d
[ʌ] r**u**n, c**u**t
[ɒ] **p**ot, l**o**g
[ʊ] **p**ut, f**u**ll
[ə] m**o**ther, s**u**ppose
[iː] b**ea**n, w**ee**d
[ɑː] b**a**rn, c**a**r, l**au**gh
[ɔː] b**o**rn, l**a**wn
[uː] l**oo**p, l**oo**se
[ɜː] b**u**rn, l**ea**rn, b**i**rd

English diphthongs

[eɪ] b**ay**, l**a**te, gr**ea**t
[aɪ] b**uy**, l**i**ght, **ai**sle
[ɔɪ] b**oy**, f**oi**l
[əʊ] n**o**, r**oa**d, bl**ow**
[aʊ] n**ow**, sh**ou**t, t**ow**n
[ɪə] p**ee**r, f**ie**rce, **i**dea
[eə] p**ai**r, b**ea**r, sh**a**re
[ʊə] p**oo**r, s**u**re, t**ou**r

Semi-vowels

you, span**i**el	[j]
wet, **wh**y, t**w**in	[w]

Consonants

pop, **p**eople	[p]
bottle, **b**i**b**	[b]
	[β]
train, **t**ip	[t]
dog, **d**i**d**	[d]
come, **k**itchen	[k]
ga**g**, **g**reat	[g]
	[ɣ]
chain, wre**tch**ed	[tʃ]
jet, fri**dge**	[dʒ]
fib, **ph**ysical	[f]
vine, li**v**e	[v]
think, fif**th**	[θ]
this, wi**th**	[ð]
seal, pea**ce**	[s]
zip, hi**s**	[z]
sheep, ma**ch**ine	[ʃ]
u**s**ual, mea**s**ure	[ʒ]
	[x]
how, per**h**aps	[h]
metal, com**b**	[m]
night, di**nn**er	[n]
su**ng**, parki**ng**	[ŋ]
	[ɲ]

Transcripción Fonética

Vocales españolas

[i] p**i**so, **i**magen
[e] t**e**la, **e**so
[a] p**a**ta, **a**migo
[o] b**o**la, **o**tro
[u] l**u**z, **u**na

Diptongos españoles

[ei] l**ey**, p**ei**ne
[ai] **ai**re, c**ai**ga
[oi] s**oy**, b**oi**na
[au] c**au**sa, **au**la
[eu] **Eu**ropa, d**eu**da

Semivocales

h**i**erba, m**i**edo
ag**u**a, h**u**eso

Consonantes

papá, **c**ampo
vaca, **b**om**b**a
cur**v**o, ca**b**allo
toro, pa**t**o
donde, cal**d**o
que, **c**osa
grande, **gu**erra
a**gu**ijón, buld**og**
o**ch**o, **ch**usma

fui, a**f**án

cera, pa**z**
ca**d**a, par**d**o
solo, pa**s**o

gemir, **j**amón
madre, ca**m**a
no, pe**n**a
ba**n**co, e**n**canto
ca**ñ**a

little, help	[l]	ala, luz
right, carry	[r]	atar, paro
	[rr]	perro, rosa
	[ʎ]	llave, collar

The symbol ['] indicates that the following syllable carries primary stress and the symbol [,] that the following syllable carries secondary stress.

Los símbolos ['] y [,] indican que la sílaba siguiente lleva un acento primario o secundario respectivamente.

The symbol [ʳ] in English phonetics indicates that the final 'r' is pronounced only when followed by a word beginning with a vowel. Note that it is nearly always pronounced in American English.

El símbolo [ʳ] en fonética inglesa indica que la 'r' al final de palabra se pronuncia sólo cuando precede a una palabra que comienza por vocal. Adviértase que casi siempre se pronuncia en inglés americano.

Since Spanish pronunciation follows regular rules, phonetics are only provided in this dictionary for loan words from other languages, when these are difficult to pronounce. All one-word English headwords have phonetics. For English compound headwords, whether hyphenated or of two or more words, phonetics are given for any element which does not appear elsewhere in the dictionary as a headword in its own right.

Las palabras españolas no llevan transcripción fonética en este diccionario; sólo algunos préstamos lingüísticos procedentes de otras lenguas y de difícil pronunciación aparecen transcritos. Todas las entradas inglesas que constan de una palabra llevan transcripción fonética. En el caso de los compuestos ingleses (ya sea cuando lleven guiones o cuando no) se proporciona la transcripción fonética de todo aquel elemento que no aparezca en alguna otra parte del diccionario como entrada en sí misma.

Spanish Verbs

Key: *pr ind* = present indicative, *imperf* = imperfect, *pret* = preterite, *fut* = future, *cond* = conditional, *pr subj* = present subjunctive, *imperf subj* = imperfect subjunctive, *imperat* = imperative, *ger* = gerund, *pp* = past participle

N.B. All forms of the *imperfect subjunctive* can also take the endings: -se, -ses, -se, -semos, -seis, -sen

acertar: *pr ind* acierto, acertamos, etc., *pr subj* acierte, acertemos, etc., *imperat* acierta, acertemos, acertad, etc.

adquirir: *pr ind* adquiero, adquirimos, etc., *pr subj* adquiera, adquiramos, etc., *imperat* adquiere, adquiramos, adquirid, etc.

AMAR: *pr ind* amo, amas, ama, amamos, amáis, aman, *imperf* amaba, amabas, amaba, amábamos, amabais, amaban, *pret* amé, amaste, amó, amamos, amasteis, amaron, *fut* amaré, amarás, amará, amaremos, amaréis, amarán, *cond* amaría, amarías, amaría, amaríamos, amaríais, amarían, *pr subj* ame, ames, ame, amemos, améis, amen, *imperf subj* amara, amaras, amara, amáramos, amarais, amaran, *imperat* ama, ame, amemos, amad, amen, *ger* amando, *pp* amado, -da

andar: *pret* anduve, anduvimos, etc., *imperf subj* anduviera, anduviéramos, etc.

asir: *pr ind* asgo, ase, asimos, etc., *pr subj* asga, asgamos, etc., *imperat* ase, asga, asgamos, asgad, etc.

avergonzar: *pr ind* avergüenzo, avergonzamos, etc., *pret* avergoncé, avergonzó, avergonzamos, etc., *pr subj* avergüence, avergoncemos, etc., *imperat* avergüenza, avergüence, avergoncemos, avergonzad, etc.

caber: *pr ind* quepo, cabe, cabemos, etc., *pret* cupe, cupimos, etc., *fut* cabré, cabremos, etc., *cond* cabría, cabríamos, etc., *pr subj* quepa, quepamos, cabed, etc., *imperf subj* cupiera, cupiéramos, etc., *imperat* cabe, quepa, quepamos, etc.

caer: *pr ind* caigo, cae, caemos, etc., *pret* cayó, caímos, cayeron, etc., *pr subj* caiga, caigamos, etc., *imperf subj* cayera, cayéramos, etc., *imperat* cae, caiga, caigamos, caed, etc., *ger* cayendo

conducir: *pr ind* conduzco, conduce, conducimos, etc., *pret* conduje, condujimos, etc., *pr subj* conduzca, conduzcamos, etc., *imperf subj* condujera, condujéramos, etc., *imperat* conduce, conduzca, conduzcamos, conducid, etc.

conocer: *pr ind* conozco, conoce, conocemos, etc., *pr subj* conozca, conozcamos, etc., *imperat* conoce, conozca, conozcamos, etc.

dar: *pr ind* doy, da, damos, etc., *pret* di, dio, dimos, etc., *pr subj* dé, demos, etc., *imperf subj* diera, diéramos, etc., *imperat* da, dé, demos, dad, etc.

decir: *pr ind* digo, dice, decimos, etc., *pret* dije, dijimos, etc., *fut* diré, diremos, etc., *cond* diría, diríamos, etc., *pr subj* diga, digamos, etc., *imperf subj* dijera, dijéramos, etc., *imperat* di, diga, digamos, decid, etc., *ger* diciendo, *pp* dicho, -cha.

discernir: *pr ind* discierno, discernimos, etc., *pr subj* discierna, discernamos, etc., *imperat* discierne, discierna, discernamos, discernid, etc.

dormir: *pr ind* duermo, dormimos, etc., *pret* durmió, dormimos, durmieron, etc., *pr subj* duerma, durmamos, etc., *imperf subj* durmiera, durmiéramos, etc., *imperat* duerme, duerma, durmamos, dormid, etc., *ger* durmiendo

errar: *pr ind* yerro, erramos, etc., *pr subj* yerre, erremos, etc., *imperat* yerra, yerre, erremos, errad, etc.

estar: *pr ind* estoy, está, estamos, etc., *pret* estuve, estuvimos, etc., *pr subj* esté, estemos, etc., *imperf subj* estuviera, estuviéramos, etc., *imperat* está, esté, estemos, estad, etc.

HABER: *pr ind* he, has, ha, hemos, habéis, han, *imperf* había, habías, había, habíamos, habíais, habían, *pret* hube, hubiste, hubo, hubimos, hubisteis, hubieron, *fut* habré, habrás, habrá, habremos, habréis, habrán, *cond* habría, habrías, habría, habríamos, habríais, habrían, *pr subj* haya, hayas, haya, hayamos, hayáis, hayan, *imperf subj* hubiera, hubieras, hubiera, hubiéramos, hubierais, hubieran, *imperat* he, haya, hayamos, habed, hayan, *ger* habiendo, *pp* habido, -da

hacer: *pr ind* hago, hace, hacemos, etc., *pret* hice, hizo, hicimos, etc., *fut* haré, haremos, etc., *cond* haría, haríamos, etc., *pr subj* haga, hagamos, etc., *imperf subj* hiciera, hiciéramos, etc., *imperat* haz, haga, hagamos, haced, etc., *pp* hecho, -cha

huir: *pr ind* huyo, huimos, etc., *pret* huyó, huimos, huyeron, etc., *pr subj* huya, huyamos, etc., *imperf subj* huyera, huyéramos, etc., *imperat* huye, huya, huyamos, huid, etc., *ger* huyendo

ir: *pr ind* voy, va, vamos, etc., *pret* fui, fue, fuimos, etc., *pr subj* vaya, vayamos, etc., *imperf subj* fuera, fuéramos, etc., *imperat* ve, vaya, vayamos, id, etc., *ger* yendo

leer: *pret* leyó, leímos, leyeron, etc., *imperf subj* leyera, leyéramos, etc., *ger* leyendo

lucir: *pr ind* luzco, luce, lucimos, etc., *pr subj* luzca, luzcamos, etc., *imperat* luce, luzca, luzcamos, lucid, etc.

mover: *pr ind* muevo, movemos, etc., *pr subj* mueva, movamos, etc., *imperat* mueve, mueva, movamos, moved, etc.

nacer: *pr ind* nazco, nace, nacemos, etc., *pr subj* nazca, nazcamos, etc., *imperat* nace, nazca, nazcamos, naced, etc.

oír: *pr ind* oigo, oye, oímos, etc., *pret* oyó, oímos, oyeron, etc., *pr subj* oiga, oigamos, etc., *imperf subj* oyera, oyéramos, etc., *imperat* oye, oiga, oigamos, oíd, etc., *ger* oyendo

oler: *pr ind* huelo, olemos, etc., *pr subj* huela, olamos, etc., *imperat* huele, huela, olamos, oled, etc.

parecer: *pr ind* parezco, parece, parecemos, etc., *pr subj* parezca, parezcamos, etc., *imperat* parece, parezca, parezcamos, pareced, etc.

PARTIR: *pr ind* parto, partes, parte, partimos, partís, parten, *imperf* partía, partías, partía, partíamos, partíais, partían, *pret* partí, partiste, partió, partimos, partisteis, partieron, *fut* partiré, partirás, partirá, partiremos, partiréis, partirán, *cond* partiría, partirías, partiría, partiríamos, partiríais, partirían, *pr subj* parta, partas, parta, partamos, partáis, partan, *imperf subj* partiera, partieras, partiera, partiéramos, partierais, partieran, *imperat* parte, parta, partamos, partid, partan, *ger* partiendo, *pp* partido, -da

pedir: *pr ind* pido, pedimos, etc., *pret* pidió, pedimos, pidieron, etc., *pr subj* pida, pidamos, etc., *imperf subj* pidiera, pidiéramos, etc., *imperat* pide, pida, pidamos, pedid, etc., *ger* pidiendo

poder: *pr ind* puedo, podemos, etc., *pret* pude, pudimos, etc., *fut* podré, podremos, etc., *cond* podría, podríamos, etc., *pr subj* pueda, podamos, etc., *imperf subj* pudiera, pudiéramos, etc., *imperat* puede, pueda, podamos, poded, etc., *ger* pudiendo

poner: *pr ind* pongo, pone, ponemos, etc., *pret* puse, pusimos, etc., *fut* pondré, pondremos, etc., *cond* pondría, pondríamos, etc., *pr subj* ponga, pongamos, etc., *imperf subj* pusiera, pusiéramos, etc., *imperat* pon, ponga, pongamos, poned, etc., *pp* puesto, -ta

predecir: se conjuga como **decir** excepto en la segunda persona del singular del *imperat* predice

querer: *pr ind* quiero, queremos, etc., *pret* quise, quisimos, etc., *fut* querré, querremos, etc., *cond* querría, querríamos, etc., *pr subj* quiera, queramos, etc., *imperf subj* quisiera, quisiéramos, etc., *imperat* quiere, quiera, queramos, quered, etc.

reír: *pr ind* río, reímos, etc., *pret* rió, reímos, rieron, etc., *pr subj* ría, riamos, etc., *imperf subj* riera, riéramos, etc., *imperat* ríe, ría, riamos, reíd, etc., *ger* riendo

saber: *pr ind* sé, sabe, sabemos, etc., *pret* supe, supimos, etc., *fut* sabré, sabremos, etc., *cond* sabría, sabríamos, etc., *pr subj* sepa, sepamos, etc., *imperf subj* supiera, supiéramos, etc., *imperat* sabe, sepa, sepamos, sabed, etc.

salir: *pr ind* salgo, sale, salimos, etc., *fut* saldré, saldremos, etc., *cond* saldría, saldríamos, etc., *pr subj* salga, salgamos, etc., *imperat* sal, salga, salgamos, salid, etc.

sentir: *pr ind* siento, sentimos, etc., *pret* sintió, sentimos, sintieron, etc., *pr subj* sienta, sintamos, etc., *imperf subj* sintiera, sintiéramos, etc., *imperat* siente, sienta, sintamos, sentid, etc., *ger* sintiendo

SER: *pr ind* soy, eres, es, somos, sois, son, *imperf* era, eras, era, éramos, erais, eran, *pret* fui, fuiste, fue, fuimos, fuisteis, fueron, *fut* seré, serás, será, seremos, seréis, serán, *cond* sería, serías, sería, seríamos, seríais, serían, *pr subj* sea, seas, sea, seamos, seáis, sean, *imperf subj* fuera, fueras, fuera, fuéramos, fuerais, fueran, *imperat* sé, sea, seamos, sed, sean, *ger* siendo, *pp* sido, -da

sonar: *pr ind* sueno, sonamos, etc., *pr subj* suene, sonemos, etc., *imperat* suena, suene, sonemos, sonad, etc.

TEMER: *pr ind* temo, temes, teme, tememos, teméis, temen, *imperf* temía, temías, temía, temíamos, temíais, temían, *pret* temí, temiste, temió, temimos, temisteis, temieron, *fut* temeré, temerás, temerá, temeremos, temeréis, temerán, *cond* temería, temerías, temería, temeríamos, temeríais, temerían, *pr subj* tema, temas, tema, temamos, temáis, teman, *imperf subj* temiera, temieras, temiera, temiéramos, temierais, temieran, *imperat* teme, tema, temamos, temed, teman, *ger* temiendo, *pp* temido, -da

tender: *pr ind* tiendo, tendemos, etc., *pr subj* tienda, tendamos, etc., *imperat* tiende, tendamos, etc.

tener: *pr ind* tengo, tiene, tenemos, etc., *pret* tuve, tuvimos, etc., *fut* tendré, tendremos, etc., *cond* tendría, tendríamos, etc., *pr subj* tenga, tengamos, etc., *imperf subj* tuviera, tuviéramos, etc., *imperat* ten, tenga, tengamos, tened, etc.

traer: *pr ind* traigo, trae, traemos, etc., *pret* traje, trajimos, etc., *pr subj* traiga, traigamos, etc., *imperf subj* trajera, trajéramos, etc., *imperat* trae, traiga, traigamos, traed, etc., *ger* trayendo

valer: *pr ind* valgo, vale, valemos, etc., *fut* valdré, valdremos, etc., *cond* valdría, valdríamos, etc., *pr subj* valga, valgamos, etc., *imperat* vale, valga, valgamos, valed, etc.

venir: *pr ind* vengo, viene, venimos, etc., *pret* vine, vinimos, etc., *fut* vendré, vendremos, etc., *cond* vendría, vendríamos, etc., *pr subj* venga, vengamos, etc., *imperf subj* viniera, viniéramos, etc., *imperat* ven, venga, vengamos, venid, etc., *ger* viniendo

ver: *pr ind* veo, ve, vemos, etc., *pret* vi, vio, vimos, etc., *imperf subj* viera, viéramos, etc., *imperat* ve, vea, veamos, ved, etc., *ger* viendo, etc., *pp* visto, -ta

Numbers

Cardinal numbers are used for counting. The most important ones are:

0	cero	21	veintiuno (ƒveintiuna)	60	sesenta
1	uno (ƒuna)	22	veintidós	70	setenta
2	dos	23	veintitrés	80	ochenta
3	tres	24	veinticuatro	90	noventa
4	cuatro	25	veinticinco	100	ciento
5	cinco	26	veintiséis	101	ciento uno (ƒuna)
6	seis	27	veintisiete	102	ciento dos
7	siete	28	veintiocho	110	ciento diez
8	ocho	29	veintinueve	200	doscientos
9	nueve	30	treinta		(ƒdoscientas)
10	diez	31	treinta y uno (ƒuna)	201	doscientos uno
11	once	32	treinta y dos		(ƒ doscientas una)
12	doce	33	treinta y tres	202	doscientos (ƒ -as) dos
13	trece	34	treinta y cuatro	300	trescientos (ƒ -as)
14	catorce	35	treinta y cinco	400	cuatrocientos (ƒ -as)
15	quince	36	treinta y seis	500	quinientos (ƒ -as)
16	dieciséis	37	treinta y siete	600	seiscientos (ƒ -as)
17	diecisiete	38	treinta y ocho	700	setecientos (ƒ -as)
18	dieciocho	39	treinta y nueve	800	ochocientos (ƒ -as)
19	diecinueve	40	cuarenta	900	novecientos (ƒ -as)
20	veinte	50	cincuenta		

1 000	mil	10 000	diez mil
1 001	mil uno (ƒuna)	100 000	cien mil
1 002	mil dos	1 000 000	un millón
1 100	mil ciento	2 000 000	dos millones
1 200	mil doscientos (ƒ -as)	1 000 000 000	mil millones
2 000	dos mil	1 000 000 000 000	un billón
3 000	tres mil		

NOTES:

– the numeral **uno** and its compounds (41, 101) are shortened to **un** if they precede a masculine noun or an adjective plus masculine noun: **cuarenta y un coches**, **un pequeño error**. **Ciento** is shortened to **cien** if it precedes a noun or an adjective plus noun, and also if it is followed by **mil**, **millones** or **billones**: **cien mil libras**.

– **uno**, compound numerals ending in **-uno** and the words for 200, 300, 400 etc. and their compounds (1 200, 2 300) agree with the nouns they precede: **veintiuna mujeres**, **cuarenta y una mujeres**, **quinientas mujeres**.

– all other numbers are invariable: **diez semanas**, **mil habitantes**.

– the following compound numbers are written with an accent: **dieciséis**, **veintiún**, **veintidós**, **veintitrés**, **veintiséis**.

– both **millón** and **billón** have a plural form (**millones**, **billones**) which is used after a plural number: **cuatro millones**, **nueve billones**. They are followed by **de** if used with another noun: **dos millones de parados**, **tres billones de pesetas**.

Contrary to English usage, Spanish uses a comma to mark the decimal part of a number: **6,5** (**seis coma cinco** = 6 point 5). Numbers like one thousand (**1.000**) and 40 million (**40.000.000**) are written with a full stop not a comma.

Ordinal numbers are used for putting things in order. From 1 to 10 they are:

1st	primero(ra)	5th	quinto(ta)	8th	octavo(va)
2nd	segundo(da)	6th	sexto(ta)	9th	noveno(na)
3rd	tercero(ra)	7th	séptimo(ma)	10th	décimo(ma)
4th	cuarto(ta)				

NOTE:

- **primero** is shortened to **primer** and **tercero** is shortened to **tercer** before a noun which is masculine singular: **el primer libro**, **mi tercer marido**.

From 'eleventh' onwards, the ordinal numbers are usually replaced in everyday written or spoken Spanish by the cardinal numbers: **el treinta aniversario**, **el capítulo veintiuno**. Ordinals are preferred in formal Spanish.

The ordinal numbers behave like adjectives and always agree with the noun they precede: **la primera vez**, **el cuarto hombre**. They can be shortened to **6º** or **6ª** (**sexto**, **sexta**).

For more information on numbers, look at the entries for **seis** and **sexto** on the Spanish-English side of your dictionary, and at the entries for **six** and **sixth** on the English-Spanish side.

Dates

The most usual ways of asking the date are: **¿qué día** or **fecha es hoy?**, **¿a cuánto(s)** or **a cómo estamos hoy?** The reply will follow the pattern **es cinco de julio** or **estamos a cinco de julio**.

Remember that the cardinal numbers are used in dates in Spanish: **el diez de enero**, **el veinticinco de febrero**. The first of the month can be expressed using **uno** or **primero**: **el primero** or **el uno de marzo**.

To say the date in Spanish use **de** before both the month and the year: 13 September 1997, for example, is **el trece de setiembre de mil novecientos noventa y siete**.

The days of the week are:

Monday	**lunes**
Tuesday	**martes**
Wednesday	**miércoles**
Thursday	**jueves**
Friday	**viernes**
Saturday	**sábado**
Sunday	**domingo**

The months of the year are:

January	**enero**
February	**febrero**
March	**marzo**
April	**abril**
May	**mayo**
June	**junio**
July	**julio**
August	**agosto**
September	**se(p)tiembre**
October	**octubre**
November	**noviembre**
December	**diciembre**

Note that the days of the week and the months of the year start with a small letter in Spanish.

For more information on days and months, look at the entries for **sábado** and **se(p)tiembre** on the Spanish-English side of your dictionary, and at **Saturday** and **September** on the English-Spanish side.

The Time

The most usual way of asking the time is: **¿qué hora es?** or **¿qué hora tienes?** Here are some possible answers:

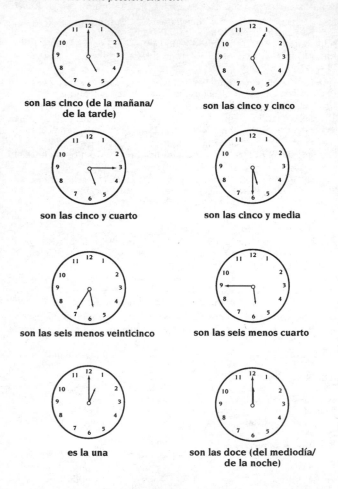

son las cinco (de la mañana/ de la tarde)

son las cinco y cinco

son las cinco y cuarto

son las cinco y media

son las seis menos veinticinco

son las seis menos cuarto

es la una

son las doce (del mediodía/ de la noche)

In Spanish you may find times expressed using the 24-hour clock: **el tren de las catorce veinte**, for example, would leave at 2.20 p.m.

a¹ (*pl* aes), **A** (*pl* Aes) *f* (*letra*) a, A.

a² *prep* (*a* + *el* = **al**) **1.** (*periodo de tiempo*): **a las pocas semanas** a few weeks later; **al día siguiente** the following day. **2.** (*momento preciso*) at; **a las siete** at seven o'clock; **a los 11 años** at the age of 11; **al caer la noche** at nightfall; **al oír la noticia se desmayó** on hearing the news, she fainted. **3.** (*frecuencia*) per, every; **40 horas a la semana** 40 hours per o a week; **tres veces al día** three times a day. **4.** (*dirección*) to; **voy a Sevilla** I'm going to Seville; **me voy al extranjero** I'm going abroad; **llegó a Barcelona/la fiesta** he arrived in Barcelona/at the party. **5.** (*posición*): **a la puerta** at the door; **está a la derecha/izquierda** it's on the right/left. **6.** (*distancia*): **está a más de cien kilómetros** it's more than a hundred kilometres away. **7.** (*con complemento indirecto*) to; **dáselo a Juan** give it to Juan; **dile a Juan que venga** tell Juan to come. **8.** (*con complemento directo*): **quiere a sus hijos/su gato** she loves her children/her cat. **9.** (*cantidad, medida, precio*): **a cientos/miles/docenas** by the hundred/thousand/dozen; **a ... kilómetros por hora** at ... kilometres per hour; **¿a cuánto están las peras?** how much are the pears?; **ganaron tres a cero** they won three nil. **10.** (*modo*): **lo hace a la antigua** he does it the old way; **a lo Mozart** in Mozart's style; **a escondidas** secretly. **11.** (*instrumento*): **escribir a máquina** to use a typewriter; **a lápiz** in pencil; **a mano** by hand. **12.** (*después de verbo y antes de infin*) (*finalidad*) to; **entró a pagar** he came in to pay; **aprender a nadar** to learn to swim. **13.** (*después de sust y antes de infin*) (*complemento de nombre*): **temas a tratar** matters to be discussed. **14.** (*en oraciones imperativas*): **¡a la cama!** go to bed!; **¡a comer!** let's eat!

abad, -desa *m y f* abbot (*f* abbess).

abadía *f* abbey.

abajo ◆ *adv* **1.** (*posición - gen*) below; (*- en edificio*) downstairs; **vive (en el piso de) ~** she lives downstairs; **está aquí/allí ~** it's down here/there; **más ~** further down. **2.** (*dirección*) down; **ve ~** (*en edificio*) go downstairs; **hacia/para ~** down, downwards; **calle/escaleras ~** down the street/stairs; **río ~** downstream. **3.** (*en un texto*) below. ◆ *interj*: **¡~ la dictadura!** down with the dictatorship! ▶ **abajo de** *loc prep* Amer (*debajo de*) underneath, under. ▶ **de abajo** *loc adj* bottom.

abalanzarse *vpr*: **~ sobre** to fall upon; **~ hacia** to rush towards.

abalear *vt* Amer to shoot.

abalorio *m* (*gen pl*) (*bisutería*) trinket.

abanderado *m lit & fig* standard-bearer.

abandonado, -da *adj* **1.** (*desierto*) deserted. **2.** (*desamparado*) abandoned. **3.** (*descuidado - jardín, casa*) neglected.

abandonar *vt* **1.** (*gen*) to abandon; (*lugar, profesión, cónyuge*) to leave. **2.** (*desatender - obligaciones, estudios*) to neglect. ▶ **abandonarse** *vpr* (*a una emoción*) **~se a** (*desesperación, dolor*) to succumb to; (*vicio*) to give o.s. over to.

abandono *m* **1.** (*acción - gen*) abandonment; (*- de lugar, profesión, cónyuge*) leaving; (*- de obligaciones, estudios*) neglect. **2.** (*estado*) state of abandon. **3.** (DEP): **ganar por ~** to win by default.

abanicar *vt* to fan.

abanico *m* (*para dar aire*) fan.

abaratar vt to reduce the price of.
▶ **abaratarse** vpr to become cheaper.
abarcar vt (incluir) to cover, to take in.
abarrotado, -da adj: ~ **(de)** (teatro, autobús) packed (with); (desván, baúl) crammed (with).
abarrotar vt: ~ algo **(de o con)** (teatro, autobús) to pack sthg (with); (desván, baúl) to cram sthg full (of).
abarrotería f Amer grocer's (store).
abarrotes mpl Amer groceries.
abastecer vt: ~ algo/a alguien (de) to supply sthg/sb (with).
abastecimiento m supply, supplying.
abasto m: no dar ~ a algo/para hacer algo) to be unable to cope (with sthg/ with doing sthg).
abatible adj folding.
abatido, -da adj dejected.
abatir vt **1.** (derribar - muro) to knock down; (- avión) to shoot down. **2.** (desanimar) to depress. ▶ **abatirse** vpr: ~se **(sobre)** to swoop (down on).
abdicación f abdication.
abdicar vi to abdicate.
abdomen m abdomen.
abdominal adj abdominal.
abecé m lit & fig ABC.
abecedario m (alfabeto) alphabet.
abedul m birch (tree).
abeja f bee.
abejorro m bumblebee.
aberración f perverse o evil thing.
abertura f opening.
abertzale [aβer'tʃale] adj, m y f Basque nationalist.
abeto m fir.
abierto, -ta ◆ pp → **abrir**. ◆ adj (gen) open; **dejar el grifo** ~ to leave the tap on; **bien** o **muy** ~ wide open.
abigarrado, -da adj multi-coloured; fig motley.
abismal adj vast, colossal.
abismo m (profundidad) abyss.
abjurar vi culto: ~ **de algo** to abjure sthg.
ablandar vt (material) to soften. ▶ **ablandarse** vpr (material) to soften.
abnegación f abnegation, self-denial.
abochornar vt to embarrass. ▶ **abochornarse** vpr to get embarrassed.
abofetear vt to slap.
abogacía f legal profession.
abogado, -da m y f (DER) lawyer; ~ **defensor** counsel for the defence; ~ **del estado** public prosecutor.

abogar vi fig (defender): ~ **por algo** to advocate sthg; ~ **por alguien** to stand up for sb.
abolengo m lineage.
abolición f abolition.
abolir vt to abolish.
abolladura f dent.
abollar vt to dent.
abominable adj abominable.
abonado, -da m y f (a telefónica, revista) subscriber; (al fútbol, teatro) season-ticket holder.
abonar vt **1.** (pagar - factura etc) to pay; ~ **algo en la cuenta de alguien** to credit sb's account with sthg. **2.** (tierra) to fertilize. ▶ **abonarse** vpr: ~se **(a)** (revista) to subscribe (to); (fútbol, teatro) to buy a season ticket (for).
abono m **1.** (pase) season ticket. **2.** (fertilizante) fertilizer. **3.** (pago) payment. **4.** Amer (plazo) instalment.
abordar vt **1.** (embarcación) to board. **2.** fig (tema, tarea) to tackle.
aborigen adj (indígena) indigenous; (de Australia) aboriginal.
aborrecer vt to abhor, to loathe.
abortar vi (MED - espontáneamente) to have a miscarriage; (- intencionadamente) to have an abortion.
aborto m (MED - espontáneo) miscarriage; (- intencionado) abortion.
abotonar vt to button up. ▶ **abotonarse** vpr to do one's buttons up; (abrigo, camisa) to button up.
abovedado, -da adj arched, vaulted.
abrasar vt **1.** (quemar - casa, bosque) to burn down; (- persona, mano, garganta) to burn. **2.** (desecar - suj: sol, calor, lejía) to scorch; (- suj: sed) to parch.
abrazadera f (TECN) brace, bracket; (en carpintería) clamp.
abrazar vt (con los brazos) to hug, to embrace. ▶ **abrazarse** vpr to hug o embrace (each other).
abrazo m embrace, hug; **un (fuerte)** ~ (en cartas) best wishes.
abrebotellas m inv bottle opener.
abrecartas m inv paper knife.
abrelatas m inv tin opener Br, can opener Am.
abreviar vt (gen) to shorten; (texto) to abridge; (palabra) to abbreviate; (viaje, estancia) to cut short.
abreviatura f abbreviation.
abridor m **1.** (abrebotellas) (bottle) opener. **2.** (abrelatas) (tin) opener Br, (can) opener Am.

abrigado, -da adj (lugar) sheltered; (persona) well wrapped up, warm.

abrigar vt **1.** (arropar - suj: persona) to wrap up; (- suj: ropa) to keep warm. **2.** fig (albergar - esperanza) to cherish; (- sospechas, malas intenciones) to harbour. ▶ **abrigarse** vpr (arroparse) to wrap up.

abrigo m **1.** (prenda) coat, overcoat. **2.** (refugio) shelter.

abril m April; ver también **septiembre**.

abrillantar vt to polish.

abrir ♦ vt **1.** (gen) to open; (alas) to spread; (melón) to cut open. **2.** (cerradura) to unlock, to open; (pestillo) to pull back; (grifo) to turn on; (cremallera) to undo. **3.** (túnel) to dig; (canal, camino) to build; (agujero, surco) to make. ♦ vi (establecimiento) to open. ▶ **abrirse** vpr **1.** (sincerarse): **~se a alguien** to open up to sb. **2.** (cielo) to clear.

abrochar vt to do up; (cinturón) to fasten. ▶ **abrocharse** vpr to do up; (cinturón) to fasten.

abrumar vt (agobiar) to overwhelm.

abrupto, -ta adj (escarpado) sheer; (accidentado) rugged.

absceso m abscess.

absentismo m (de terrateniente) absentee landownership.

ábside m apse.

absolución f **1.** (DER) acquittal. **2.** (RELIG) absolution.

absoluto, -ta adj (gen) absolute; (silencio, obediencia) total. ▶ **en absoluto** loc adv (en negativas) at all; (tras pregunta) not at all; **¿te gusta? – en ~** do you like it? – not at all; **nada en ~** nothing at all.

absolver vt: **~ a alguien (de algo)** (DER) to acquit sb (of sthg); (RELIG) to absolve sb (of sthg).

absorbente adj **1.** (que empapa) absorbent. **2.** (actividad) absorbing.

absorber vt **1.** (gen) to absorb. **2.** (consumir, gastar) to soak up.

absorción f absorption.

absorto, -ta adj: **~ (en)** absorbed o engrossed (in).

abstemio, -mia adj teetotal.

abstención f abstention.

abstenerse vpr: **~ (de algo/de hacer algo)** to abstain (from sthg/from doing sthg).

abstinencia f abstinence.

abstracción f (gen) abstraction.

abstracto, -ta adj abstract.

abstraer vt to consider separately.

abstraído, -da adj lost in thought.

absuelto, -ta pp → **absolver**.

absurdo, -da adj absurd. ▶ **absurdo** m: **decir/hacer un ~** to say/do something ridiculous.

abuchear vt to boo.

abuelita f fam granny, grandma.

abuelo, -la m y f (familiar) grandfather (f grandmother). ▶ **abuelos** mpl grandparents.

abulia f apathy, lethargy.

abúlico, -ca adj apathetic, lethargic.

abultado, -da adj (paquete) bulky; (labios) thick.

abultar ♦ vt **1.** (hinchar) to swell. **2.** (exagerar) to blow up. ♦ vi (ser difícil de manejar) to be bulky.

abundancia f **1.** (gran cantidad) abundance; **en ~** in abundance. **2.** (riqueza) plenty, prosperity.

abundante adj abundant.

abundar vi (ser abundante) to abound.

aburguesarse vpr to adopt middle-class ways.

aburrido, -da ♦ adj **1.** (harto, fastidiado) bored; **estar ~ de hacer algo** to be fed up with doing sthg. **2.** (que aburre) boring. ♦ m y f bore.

aburrimiento m boredom.

aburrir vt to bore. ▶ **aburrirse** vpr to get bored; (estar aburrido) to be bored.

abusado, -da adj Amer astute, shrewd.

abusar vi **1.** (excederse) to go too far; **~ de algo** to abuse sthg; **~ de alguien** to take advantage of sb. **2.** (forzar sexualmente): **~ de alguien** to sexually abuse sb.

abusivo, -va adj (trato) very bad, appalling; (precio) extortionate.

abuso m (uso excesivo): **~ (de)** abuse (of); **~ de confianza** breach of confidence; **~s deshonestos** sexual abuse (U).

abyecto, -ta adj culto vile, wretched.

a/c abrev de **a cuenta**.

a. C. (abrev de **antes de Cristo**) BC.

acá adv **1.** (lugar) here; **de ~ para allá** back and forth. **2.** (tiempo): **de una semana ~** during the last week.

acabado, -da adj **1.** (completo) perfect, consummate. **2.** (fracasado) finished. ▶ **acabado** m (de producto) finish; (de piso) décor.

acabar ♦ vt **1.** (concluir) to finish. **2.** (consumir - provisiones, dinero) to use up; (- comida) to finish. ♦ vi **1.** (gen) to finish, to end; **~ de hacer algo** to finish doing sthg. **2.** (haber hecho recientemente): **~ de hacer algo** to have just done sthg; **acabo de llegar** I've just arrived. **3.** (ter-

minar por - persona): **~ por hacer algo**, **~ haciendo algo** to end up doing sthg. **4.** (*destruir*): **~ con** (*gen*) to destroy; (*salud*) to ruin; (*paciencia*) to exhaust; (*violencia, crimen*) to put an end to. ▶ **acabarse** *vpr* **1.** (*agotarse*) to be used up; **se nos ha acabado la gasolina** we're out of petrol; **se ha acabado la comida** there's no more food left, all the food has gone. **2.** (*concluir*) to finish, to come to an end. **3.** *loc*: **¡se acabó!** (*¡basta ya!*) that's enough!; (*se terminó*) that's it, then!

acabóse *m fam*: **¡es el ~!** it really is the limit!

academia *f* **1.** (*colegio*) school, academy. **2.** (*sociedad*) academy. ▶ **Real Academia Española** *f* institution that sets lexical and syntactical standards for Spanish.

académico, -ca *adj* academic.

acaecer *v impers culto* to occur.

acallar *vt* to silence.

acalorado, -da *adj* **1.** (*por calor*) hot. **2.** (*apasionado - debate*) heated.

acalorar *vt* (*excitar*): **~ a alguien** to make sb hot under the collar. ▶ **acalorarse** *vpr* (*excitarse*) to get aroused o excited.

acampanado, -da *adj* flared.

acampar *vi* to camp.

acanalado, -da *adj* (*columna*) fluted; (*tejido*) ribbed; (*hierro, uralita*) corrugated.

acantilado *m* cliff.

acaparar *vt* **1.** (*monopolizar*) to monopolize; (*mercado*) to corner. **2.** (*guardarse*) to hoard.

acápite *m Amer* paragraph.

acaramelado, -da *adj fig* (*afectado*) sickly sweet.

acariciar *vt* **1.** (*persona*) to caress; (*animal*) to stroke. **2.** *fig* (*idea, proyecto*) to cherish.

acarrear *vt* **1.** (*transportar*) to carry; (*carbón*) to haul. **2.** *fig* (*ocasionar*) to bring, to give rise to.

acaso *adv* perhaps; **¿~ no lo sabías?** are you trying to tell me you didn't know?; **por si ~** (just) in case. ▶ **si acaso** ◆ *loc adv* (*en todo caso*) if anything. ◆ *loc conj* (*en caso de que*) if.

acatar *vt* to respect, to comply with.

acatarrarse *vpr* to catch a cold.

acaudalado, -da *adj* well-to-do.

acaudillar *vt* to lead.

acceder *vi* **1.** (*consentir*): **~ a algo/hacer algo** to agree (to sthg/to do sthg).

2. (*tener acceso*): **~ a** to enter. **3.** (*alcanzar*): **~ a** (*trono*) to accede to; (*poder*) to come to; (*grado*) to obtain.

accesible *adj* (*gen*) accessible.

accésit *m inv* consolation prize.

acceso *m* **1.** (*entrada*): **~ (a)** entrance (to). **2.** (*paso*): **~ (a)** access (to). **3.** (*carretera*) access road. **4.** *fig* (*ataque*) fit; (*de fiebre, gripe*) bout.

accesorio, -ria *adj* incidental. ▶ **accesorio** *m* (*gen pl*) accessory.

accidentado, -da ◆ *adj* **1.** (*vida*) turbulent. **2.** (*viaje - en coche, tren, avión*) bumpy. **3.** (*terreno, camino*) rough, rugged. ◆ *m y f* injured person, victim.

accidental *adj* (*imprevisto*) accidental; (*encuentro*) chance.

accidentarse *vpr* to be involved in o have an accident.

accidente *m* **1.** (*desgracia*) accident; **~ de avión/coche** plane/car crash; **~ de tráfico** road accident. **2.** (*gen pl*) (*del terreno*) unevenness (U).

acción *f* **1.** (*gen*) action. **2.** (*hecho*) deed, act. **3.** (*FIN*) share; **~ ordinaria/preferente** ordinary/preference share.

accionar *vt* to activate.

accionista *m y f* shareholder.

acechar *vt* **1.** (*vigilar*) to keep under surveillance; (*suj: cazador*) to stalk. **2.** (*amenazar*) to be lying in wait for.

acecho *m*: **estar al ~ de** to lie in wait for; *fig* to be on the lookout for.

aceite *m* oil; **~ de colza/girasol/oliva** rapeseed/sunflower/olive oil.

aceitera *f* oil can. ▶ **aceiteras** *fpl* cruet (*sg*).

aceitoso, -sa *adj* oily.

aceituna *f* olive.

aceleración *f* acceleration.

acelerador, -ra *adj* accelerating. ▶ **acelerador** *m* accelerator.

acelerar ◆ *vt* (*avivar*) to speed up; (*TECN*) to accelerate. ◆ *vi* to accelerate. ▶ **acelerarse** *vpr* to hurry up.

acelga *f* chard.

acento *m* **1.** (*gen*) accent. **2.** (*intensidad*) stress, accent.

acentuación *f* accentuation.

acentuar *vt* **1.** (*palabra, letra - al escribir*) to put an accent on; (*- al hablar*) to stress. **2.** *fig* (*realzar*) to accentuate. ▶ **acentuarse** *vpr* (*intensificarse*) to deepen, to increase.

acepción *f* meaning, sense.

aceptable *adj* acceptable.

aceptación *f* **1.** (*aprobación*) acceptance. **2.** (*éxito*) success, popularity.

aceptar vt to accept.

acequia f (reguero) irrigation channel; Amer (canal) canal.

acera f (para peatones) pavement Br, sidewalk Am.

acerbo, -ba adj culto (mordaz) caustic.

acerca ▸ **acerca de** loc adv about.

acercar vt to bring nearer o closer; ¡acércame el pan! could you pass me the bread? ▸ **acercarse** vpr (arrimarse - viniendo) to come closer; (- yendo) to go over.

acero m steel; ~ **inoxidable** stainless steel.

acérrimo, -ma adj (defensor) diehard (antes de sust); (enemigo) bitter.

acertado, -da adj 1. (con acierto - respuesta) correct. 2. (- comentario) appropriate. 2. (oportuno) good, clever.

acertar ◆ vt 1. (adivinar) to guess (correctly). 2. (el blanco) to hit. 3. (elegir bien) to choose well. ◆ vi 1. (atinar): ~ **(al hacer algo)** to be right (to do sthg). 2. (conseguir): ~ **a hacer algo** to manage to do sthg. 3. (hallar): ~ **con** to find.

acertijo m riddle.

acervo m (patrimonio) heritage.

achacar vt: ~ **algo a alguien/algo** to attribute sthg to sb/sthg.

achantar vt fam to put the wind up. ▸ **achantarse** vpr fam to get the wind up.

achaparrado, -da adj squat.

achaque m ailment.

achatado, -da adj flattened.

achicar vt 1. (tamaño) to make smaller. 2. (agua - de barco) to bale out. 3. fig (acobardar) to intimidate.

achicharrar vt (chamuscar) to burn. ▸ **achicharrarse** vpr 1. fig (de calor) to fry. 2. (chamuscarse) to burn.

achicoria f chicory.

achuchado, -da adj fam hard, tough.

achuchar vt fam (abrazar) to hug.

achurar vt Amer 1. (acuchillar) to stab to death. 2. (animal) to disembowel.

aciago, -ga adj culto black, fateful.

acicalar vt (arreglar) to do up. ▸ **acicalarse** vpr to do o.s. up.

acicate m fig (estímulo) incentive.

acidez f 1. (cualidad) acidity. 2. (MED): ~ **(de estómago)** heartburn.

ácido, -da adj 1. (QUÍM) acidic. 2. (bebida, sabor, carácter) acid, sour. ▸ **ácido** m (QUÍM) acid.

acierto m 1. (a pregunta) correct answer. 2. (habilidad, tino) good o sound judgment. 3. (éxito) success.

aclamación f (ovación) acclamation, acclaim; **por ~** unanimously.

aclamar vt to acclaim.

aclaración f explanation.

aclarar vt 1. (ropa) to rinse. 2. (explicar) to clarify, to explain. 3. ~ **la voz** (carraspeando) to clear one's throat. ▸ **aclararse** vpr 1. (entender) to understand. 2. (explicarse) to explain o.s.

aclaratorio, -ria adj explanatory.

aclimatación f acclimatization.

aclimatar vt 1. (al clima): ~ **algo/a alguien (a)** to acclimatize sthg/sb (to). 2. (a ambiente): ~ **algo/a alguien a algo** to get sthg/sb used to sthg. ▸ **aclimatarse** vpr 1. (al clima): ~**se (a algo)** to acclimatize (to sthg). 2. (a ambiente) to settle in; ~**se a algo** to get used to sthg.

acné m acne.

acobardar vt to frighten, to scare. ▸ **acobardarse** vpr to get frightened o scared; ~**se ante** to shrink back from.

acodarse vpr: ~**se (en)** to lean (on).

acogedor, -ra adj (país, persona) welcoming, friendly; (casa, ambiente) cosy.

acoger vt 1. (recibir) to welcome. 2. (dar refugio) to take in. ▸ **acogerse a** vpr (inmunidad parlamentaria etc) to take refuge in; (ley) to have recourse to.

acogida f 1. (de persona) welcome. 2. (de idea, película etc) reception.

acolchar vt to pad.

acometer ◆ vt 1. (atacar) to attack. 2. (emprender) to undertake. ◆ vi (embestir): ~ **contra** to hurtle into.

acometida f 1. (ataque) attack, charge. 2. (de luz, gas etc) (mains) connection.

acomodado, -da adj (rico) well-off.

acomodador, -ra m y f usher (f usherette).

acomodar vt 1. (instalar - persona) to seat, to instal; (- cosa) to place. 2. (adaptar) to fit. ▸ **acomodarse** vpr (instalarse) to make o.s. comfortable; ~**se en** to settle down in.

acomodaticio, -cia adj (complaciente) accommodating, easy-going.

acompañamiento m (CULIN & MÚS) accompaniment.

acompañante m y f companion.

acompañar vt 1. (ir con): ~ **a alguien** (gen) to go with o accompany sb; (a la puerta) to show sb out; (a casa) to walk sb home. 2. (estar con): ~ **a alguien** to keep sb company. 3. (adjuntar) to enclose. 4. (MÚS) to accompany.

acompasar vt: ~ **algo (a)** to synchronize sthg (with).

acomplejar *vt* to give a complex.
▶ **acomplejarse** *vpr* to develop a complex.

acondicionado, -da *adj* equipped.

acondicionador *m* (air) conditioner.

acondicionar *vt* 1. (*reformar*) to convert, to upgrade. 2. (*preparar*) to prepare, to get ready.

acongojar *vt* to distress.

aconsejable *adj* advisable.

aconsejar *vt* (*dar consejos*): ~ **a alguien (que haga algo)** to advise sb (to do sthg).

acontecer *v impers* to take place, to happen.

acontecimiento *m* event; **adelantarse o anticiparse a los** ~**s** to jump the gun; (*prevenir*) to take preemptive measures.

acopio *m* stock, store.

acoplar *vt* 1. (*encajar*) to attach, to fit together. 2. (FERROC) to couple. 3. *fig* (*adaptar*) to adapt, to fit.

acorazado, -da *adj* armour-plated.
▶ **acorazado** *m* battleship.

acordar *vt*: ~ **algo/hacer algo** to agree on sthg/to do sthg. ▶ **acordarse** *vpr*: ~**se (de algo/de hacer algo)** to remember (sthg/to do sthg).

acorde ◆ *adj* (*en consonancia*): ~ **con** in keeping with. ◆ *m* (MÚS) chord.

acordeón *m* accordion.

acordonar *vt* (*cercar*) to cordon off.

acorralar *vt lit & fig* to corner.

acortar *vt* 1. (*falda, pantalón etc*) to take up; (*cable*) to shorten. 2. (*tiempo*) to cut short. 3. (*extensión*) to shorten. ▶ **acortarse** *vpr* (*días*) to get shorter; (*reunión*) to end early.

acosar *vt* 1. (*hostigar*) to harass. 2. (*perseguir*) to pursue relentlessly.

acoso *m* (*hostigamiento*) harassment; ~ **sexual** sexual harassment.

acostar *vt* (*en la cama*) to put to bed. ▶ **acostarse** *vpr* 1. (*irse a la cama*) to go to bed. 2. (*tumbarse*) to lie down. 3. *fam* (*tener relaciones sexuales*): ~**se con alguien** to sleep with sb.

acostumbrado, -da *adj* 1. (*habitual*) usual. 2. (*habituado*): **estar** ~ **a** to be used to.

acostumbrar ◆ *vt* (*habituar*): ~ **a alguien a algo/a hacer algo** to get sb used to sthg/to doing sthg. ◆ *vi* (*soler*): ~ **a hacer algo** to be in the habit of doing sthg, usually to do sthg. ▶ **acostumbrarse** *vpr* 1. (*habituarse*): ~**se a algo/a hacer algo** to get used to doing

sthg. 2. (*ser costumbre*): **así se acostumbra por aquí** that's the way things are done round here.

acotación *f* (*nota*) note in the margin.

acotar *vt* 1. (*terreno, campo*) to enclose; *fig* (*tema etc*) to delimit. 2. (*texto*) to write notes in the margin of.

acrecentar *vt* to increase.

acreditado, -da *adj* 1. (*médico, abogado etc*) distinguished; (*marca*) reputable. 2. (*embajador, representante*) accredited.

acreditar *vt* 1. (*certificar*) to certify; (*autorizar*) to authorize. 2. (*confirmar*) to confirm. 3. (*embajador*) to accredit. 4. (FIN) to credit.

acreedor, -ra ◆ *adj*: **hacerse** ~ **de algo** to earn sthg, to show o.s. to be worthy of sthg. ◆ *m y f* creditor.

acribillar *vt* (*herir*): ~ **(a)** to pepper o riddle (with).

acrílico, -ca *adj* acrylic.

acrimonia = **acritud**.

acristalar *vt* to glaze.

acritud, acrimonia *f* 1. (*de olor*) acridity, pungency; (*de sabor*) bitterness. 2. *fig* (*mordacidad*) venom. 3. (*desavenencia*) acrimony.

acrobacia *f* (*en circo*) acrobatics (*pl*).

acróbata *m y f* acrobat.

acta *f* (*el*) 1. (*de junta, reunión*) minutes (*pl*); **levantar** ~ to take the minutes. 2. (*de defunción etc*) certificate; ~ **notarial** affidavit. ▶ **actas** *fpl* minutes.

actitud *f* (*disposición de ánimo*) attitude.

activar *vt* 1. (*gen*) to activate. 2. (*explosivo*) to detonate.

actividad *f* activity.

activo, -va *adj* 1. (*gen & GRAM*) active. 2. (*trabajador*) hard-working. 3. (*abogado, médico*): **en** ~ practising. ▶ **activo** *m* (FIN) assets (*pl*).

acto *m* 1. (*acción*) act; **hacer** ~ **de presencia** to show one's face; ~ **de solidaridad** show of solidarity. 2. (*ceremonia*) ceremony. 3. (TEATR) act. ▶ **en el acto** *loc adv* on the spot.

actor, -triz *m y f* actor (*f* actress).

actuación *f* 1. (*conducta, proceder*) conduct, behaviour. 2. (*interpretación*) performance.

actual *adj* 1. (*existente*) present, current. 2. (*de moda*) modern, up-to-date. 3. (*de actualidad*) topical.

actualidad *f* 1. (*momento presente*) current situation; **de** ~ (*moderno*) in fashion; (*de interés actual*) topical; **en la** ~ at the present time, these days. 2. (*noticia*) news (U); **ser ~** to be making the news. ▶ **actualidades** *fpl* (*temas de actualidad*) current affairs.

actualizar *vt* to update; (*tecnología, industria*) to modernize.

actualmente *adv* (*hoy día*) these days, nowadays; (*en este momento*) at the (present) moment, now.

actuar *vi* (*gen*) to act; **~ de** to act as.

acuarela *f* watercolour.

acuario *m* aquarium. ▶ **Acuario** ◆ *m* (*zodiaco*) Aquarius. ◆ *m y f* (*persona*) Aquarius.

acuartelar *vt* 1. (*alojar*) to quarter. 2. (*retener*) to confine to barracks.

acuático, -ca *adj* aquatic.

acuchillar *vt* 1. (*apuñalar*) to stab. 2. (*mueble, parquet*) to grind down.

acuciar *vt culto* (*suj: persona*) to goad; (*suj: necesidad, deseo*) to press.

acuclillarse *vpr* to squat (down).

acudir *vi* 1. (*ir*) to go; (*venir*) to come. 2. (*recurrir*): **~ a** to go o turn to. 3. (*presentarse*): **~ (a)** (*escuela, iglesia*) to attend; (*cita, examen*) to turn up (for); *fig* (*memoria, mente*) to come (to).

acueducto *m* aqueduct.

acuerdo *m* agreement; **de ~** all right, O.K.; **de ~ con** (*conforme a*) in accordance with; **estar de ~ (con alguien/en hacer algo)** to agree (with sb/to do sthg); **llegar a un ~, ponerse de ~** to reach agreement.

acumular *vt* to accumulate.

acunar *vt* to rock.

acuñar *vt* 1. (*moneda*) to mint. 2. (*palabra*) to coin.

acuoso, -sa *adj* (*gen*) watery.

acupuntura *f* acupuncture.

acurrucarse *vpr* to crouch down; (*por frío*) to huddle up; (*por miedo*) to cower; (*en sitio agradable*) to curl up.

acusación *f* (*inculpación*) charge.

acusado, -da ◆ *adj* (*marcado*) marked. ◆ *m y f* (*procesado*) accused, defendant.

acusar *vt* 1. (*culpar*) to accuse; (DER) to charge; **~ a alguien de algo** (*gen*) to accuse sb of sthg; (DER) to charge sb with sthg. 2. (*mostrar*) to show.

acusativo *m* accusative.

acuse ▶ **acuse de recibo** *m* acknowledgement of receipt.

acústico, -ca *adj* acoustic. ▶ **acústica** *f* (*de local*) acoustics (*pl*).

a.D. (*abrev de* anno Domini) AD.

adagio *m* (*sentencia breve*) adage.

adaptación *f* 1. (*aclimatación*): **~ (a)**

adjustment (to). 2. (*modificación*) adaptation.

adaptar *vt* 1. (*acomodar, ajustar*) to adjust. 2. (*modificar*) to adapt. ▶ **adaptarse** *vpr*: **~se (a)** to adjust (to).

adecentar *vt* to tidy up.

adecuado, -da *adj* appropriate, suitable.

adecuar *vt* to adapt. ▶ **adecuarse a** *vpr* 1. (*ser adecuado*) to be appropriate for. 2. (*adaptarse*) to adjust to.

adefesio *m fam* (*persona fea*) fright.

a. de JC., a.JC. (*abrev de* **antes de Jesucristo**) BC.

adelantado, -da *adj* advanced; **llevo el reloj ~** my watch is fast; **por ~** in advance.

adelantamiento *m* (AUTOM) overtaking.

adelantar ◆ *vt* 1. (*dejar atrás*) to overtake. 2. (*mover hacia adelante*) to move forward, to advance; (*pie, reloj*) to put forward. 3. (*en el tiempo - trabajo, viaje*) to bring forward; (*- dinero*) to pay in advance. ◆ *vi* 1. (*progresar*) to make progress. 2. (*reloj*) to be fast. ▶ **adelantarse** *vpr* 1. (*en el tiempo*) to be early; (*frío, verano*) to arrive early; (*reloj*) to gain; **~se a alguien** to beat sb to it. 2. (*en el espacio*) to go on ahead. 3. (*predecir*): **~se a** to anticipate.

adelante ◆ *adv* forward, ahead; (**de ahora**) **en ~** from now on, in future; **de 18 años en ~** from 18 (years of age) upwards; **más ~** (*en el tiempo*) later (on); (*en el espacio*) further on. ◆ *interj* **¡~!** (*¡siga!*) go ahead!; (*¡pase!*) come in!

adelanto *m* advance; **~ de dinero** advance.

adelgazar ◆ *vi* to lose weight, to slim. ◆ *vt* to lose.

ademán *m* (*gesto - con manos etc*) gesture; (*- con cara*) face, expression; **en ~ de** as if to.

además *adv* moreover, besides; (*también*) also; **~ de** as well as, in addition to.

adentrarse *vpr*: **~ en** (*jungla etc*) to enter the heart of; (*tema etc*) to study in depth.

adentro *adv* inside; **tierra ~** inland; **mar ~** out to sea.

adepto, -ta *m y f*: **~ (a)** follower (of).

aderezar *vt* (*sazonar - ensalada*) to dress; (*- comida*) to season.

aderezo *m* (*aliño - de ensalada*) dressing; (*- de comida*) seasoning.

adeudar *vt* 1. (*deber*) to owe. 2. (COM)

to debit. ▶ **adeudarse** *vpr* to get into debt.

adherir *vt* to stick. ▶ **adherirse** *vpr* 1. (*pegarse*) to stick. 2. (*mostrarse de acuerdo*): ~se a to adhere to.

adhesión *f* (*apoyo*) support.

adhesivo, -va *adj* adhesive. ▶ **adhesivo** *m* (*pegatina*) sticker.

adicción *f*: ~ (a) addiction (to).

adición *f* addition.

adicional *adj* additional.

adicto, -ta ♦ *adj*: ~ (a) addicted (to). ♦ *m y f*: ~ (a) addict (of).

adiestrar *vt* to train; ~ a alguien en algo/para hacer algo to train sb in sthg/to do sthg.

adinerado, -da *adj* wealthy.

adiós ♦ *m* goodbye. ♦ *interj*: ¡~! goodbye!; (*al cruzarse con alguien*) hello!

adiposo, -sa *adj* fatty, adipose.

aditivo *m* additive.

adivinanza *f* riddle.

adivinar *vt* 1. (*predecir*) to foretell; (*el futuro*) to tell. 2. (*acertar*) to guess (correctly).

adivino, -na *m y f* fortune-teller.

adjetivo *m* adjective.

adjudicación *f* awarding.

adjudicar *vt* (*asignar*) to award. ▶ **adjudicarse** *vpr* (*apropiarse*) to take for o.s.

adjuntar *vt* to enclose.

adjunto, -ta ♦ *adj* (*incluido*) enclosed; ~ le remito ... please find enclosed ... ♦ *m y f* (*auxiliar*) assistant.

administración *f* 1. (*suministro*) supply; (*de medicamento, justicia*) administering. 2. (*gestión*) administration. 3. (*gerentes*) management; (*oficina*) manager's office. ▶ **Administración** *f* (*gobierno*) administration; **Administración local** local government; **Administración pública** civil service.

administrador, -ra *m y f* 1. (*de empresa*) manager. 2. (*de bienes ajenos*) administrator.

administrar *vt* 1. (*gestionar - empresa, finca etc*) to manage, to run; (- *casa*) to run. 2. (*país*) to run the affairs of. 3. (*suministrar*) to administer.

administrativo, -va *adj* administrative.

admirable *adj* admirable.

admiración *f* 1. (*sentimiento*) admiration. 2. (*signo ortográfico*) exclamation mark.

admirador, -ra *m y f* admirer.

admirar *vt* 1. (*gen*) to admire. 2. (*sor-* prender) to amaze. ▶ **admirarse** *vpr*: ~se (de) to be amazed (by).

admisible *adj* acceptable.

admisión *f* 1. (*de persona*) admission. 2. (*de solicitudes etc*) acceptance.

admitir *vt* 1. (*acoger, reconocer*) to admit; ~ a alguien en to admit sb to. 2. (*aceptar*) to accept.

ADN (*abrev de* **ácido desoxirribonucleico**) *m* DNA.

adobar *vt* to marinate.

adobe *m* adobe.

adobo *m* (*salsa*) marinade.

adoctrinar *vt* to instruct.

adolecer ▶ **adolecer de** *vi* 1. (*enfermedad*) to suffer from. 2. (*defecto*) to be guilty of.

adolescencia *f* adolescence.

adolescente *adj, m y f* adolescent.

adonde *adv* where; la ciudad ~ vamos the city we are going to, the city where we are going.

adónde *adv* where.

adopción *f* (*de hijo, propuesta*) adoption; (*de ley*) passing.

adoptar *vt* (*hijo, propuesta*) to adopt; (*ley*) to pass.

adoptivo, -va *adj* (*hijo, país*) adopted; (*padre*) adoptive.

adoquín (*pl* **adoquines**) *m* cobblestone.

adorable *adj* (*persona*) adorable; (*ambiente, película*) wonderful.

adoración *f* adoration; sentir ~ por alguien to worship sb.

adorar *vt* 1. (*reverenciar*) to worship. 2. (*pirrarse por*) to adore.

adormecer *vt* (*producir sueño*) to lull to sleep. ▶ **adormecerse** *vpr* to nod off.

adormilarse *vpr* to doze.

adornar *vt* to decorate.

adorno *m* decoration.

adosado, -da *adj* (*casa*) semi-detached.

adquirir *vt* 1. (*comprar*) to acquire, to purchase. 2. (*conseguir - conocimientos, hábito, cultura*) to acquire; (- *éxito, popularidad*) to achieve; (- *enfermedad*) to catch, to get.

adquisición *f* 1. (*compra, cosa comprada*) purchase. 2. (*obtención*) acquisition.

adquisitivo, -va *adj* purchasing (*antes de sust*).

adrede *adv* on purpose, deliberately.

adrenalina *f* adrenalin.

adscribir *vt* 1. (*asignar*) to assign. 2. (*destinar*) to appoint o assign to. ▶ **adscribirse** *vpr*: ~se (a) (*grupo, par-*

tido) to become a member (of); (*ideología*) to subscribe to.

adscrito, -ta ♦ *pp* → **adscribir.** ♦ *adj* assigned.

aduana *f* (*administración*) customs (*pl*).

aducir *vt* to adduce.

adueñarse ► **adueñarse de** *vpr* 1. (*apoderarse*) to take over. 2. (*dominar*) to take hold of.

adulación *f* flattery.

adulador, -ra *adj* flattering.

adular *vt* to flatter.

adulterar *vt* (*alimento*) to adulterate.

adulterio *m* adultery.

adúltero, -ra ♦ *adj* adulterous. ♦ *m y f* adulterer (*f* adulteress).

adulto, -ta *adj, m y f* adult.

adusto, -ta *adj* dour.

advenedizo, -za *adj, m y f* parvenu (*f* parvenue).

advenimiento *m* advent; (*al trono*) accession.

adverbio *m* adverb.

adversario, -ria *m y f* adversary.

adversidad *f* adversity.

adverso, -sa *adj* adverse; (*destino*) unkind; (*suerte*) bad; (*viento*) unfavourable.

advertencia *f* warning; **servir de ~** to serve as a warning.

advertir *vt* 1. (*notar*) to notice. 2. (*prevenir, avisar*) to warn; **te advierto que no deberías hacerlo** I'd advise against you doing it; **te advierto que no me sorprende** mind you, it doesn't surprise me.

adviento *m* Advent.

adyacente *adj* adjacent.

aéreo, -a *adj* 1. (*del aire*) aerial. 2. (AERON) air (*antes de sust*).

aerobic [aeˈroβik] *m* aerobics (U).

aeroclub (*pl* **aeroclubs**) *m* flying club.

aerodeslizador *m* hovercraft.

aerodinámico, -ca *adj* 1. (FÍS) aerodynamic. 2. (*forma, línea*) streamlined.

aeródromo *m* airfield, aerodrome.

aeroespacial *adj* aerospace (*antes de sust*).

aerógrafo *m* airbrush.

aerolínea *f* airline.

aeromoza *f* Amer air hostess.

aeronauta *m y f* aeronaut.

aeronaval *adj* air and sea (*antes de sust*).

aeronave *f* (*gen*) aircraft; (*dirigible*) airship.

aeroplano *m* aeroplane.

aeropuerto *m* airport.

aerosol *m* aerosol.

aerospacial = **aeroespacial.**

aerostático, -ca *adj* aerostatic.

aeróstato *m* hot-air balloon.

aerotaxi *m* light aircraft (*for hire*).

afabilidad *f* affability.

afable *adj* affable.

afamado, -da *adj* famous.

afán *m* 1. (*esfuerzo*) hard work (U). 2. (*anhelo*) urge.

afanador, -ra *m y f* Amer cleaner.

afanar *vt fam* (*robar*) to pinch. ► **afanarse** *vpr* (*esforzarse*): **~se (por hacer algo)** to do everything one can (to do sthg).

afanoso, -sa *adj* 1. (*trabajoso, penoso*) demanding. 2. (*que se afana*) eager.

afear *vt* to make ugly, to scar.

afección *f* (MED) complaint, disease.

afectación *f* affectation.

afectado, -da *adj* 1. (*gen*) affected. 2. (*afligido*) upset, badly affected.

afectar *vt* 1. (*gen*) to affect. 2. (*afligir*) to upset, to affect badly.

afectísimo, -ma *adj* (*en cartas*): **suyo ~** yours faithfully.

afectivo, -va *adj* 1. (*emocional*) emotional. 2. (*cariñoso*) affectionate.

afecto *m* affection, fondness; **sentir ~ por alguien, tenerle ~ a alguien** to be fond of sb.

afectuoso, -sa *adj* affectionate, loving.

afeitar *vt* (*pelo*) to shave. ► **afeitarse** *vpr* to shave.

afeminado, -da *adj* effeminate.

aferrarse *vpr*: **~ a** lit & fig to cling to.

Afganistán Afghanistan.

afianzamiento *m* (*en cargo, liderazgo*) consolidation.

afianzar *vt* (*objeto*) to secure. ► **afianzarse** *vpr* to steady o.s.; **~se en algo** (*opinión etc*) to become sure o convinced of sthg; (*cargo, liderazgo*) to consolidate sthg.

afiche *m* Amer poster.

afición *f* 1. (*inclinación*) fondness, liking; **por ~** as a hobby; **tener ~ a algo** to be keen on sthg. 2. (*aficionados*) fans (*pl*).

aficionado, -da ♦ *adj* 1. (*interesado*) keen; **ser ~ a algo** to be keen on sthg. 2. (*amateur*) amateur. ♦ *m y f* 1. (*interesado*) fan; **~ al cine** film fan. 2. (*amateur*) amateur.

aficionar *vt*: **~ a alguien a algo** to make sb keen on sthg. ► **aficionarse** *vpr*: **~se a algo** to become keen on sthg.

afilado, -da *adj* (*fino*) sharp; (*dedos*) pointed.

afilar vt to sharpen.
afiliado, -da m y f: ~ (a) member (of).
afiliarse vpr: ~ a to join, to become a member of.
afín adj (semejante) similar, like.
afinar vt 1. (MÚS) (instrumento) to tune; ~ la voz to sing in tune. 2. (perfeccionar, mejorar) to fine-tune. 3. (pulir) to refine.
afinidad f (gen & QUÍM) affinity.
afirmación f statement, assertion.
afirmar vt 1. (confirmar) to confirm. 2. (decir) to say, to state. 3. (consolidar) to reaffirm. 4. (CONSTR) to reinforce.
afirmativo, -va adj affirmative.
aflicción f suffering, sorrow.
afligir vt to afflict; (causar pena) to distress.
aflojar ◆ vt (destensar) to loosen; (cuerda) to slacken. ◆ vi 1. (disminuir) to abate, to die down. 2. fig (ceder) to ease off. ▶ **aflojarse** vpr (gen) to come loose; (cuerda) to slacken.
aflorar vi fig (surgir) to (come to the) surface, to show.
afluencia f stream, volume.
afluente m tributary.
afluir ▶ **afluir a** vi 1. (gente) to flock to. 2. (sangre, fluido) to flow to.
afonía f loss of voice.
afónico, -ca adj: quedarse ~ to lose one's voice.
aforo m (cabida) seating capacity.
afortunadamente adv fortunately.
afortunado, -da adj 1. (agraciado) lucky, fortunate. 2. (feliz, oportuno) happy, felicitous.
afrenta f (ofensa, agravio) affront.
África Africa.
africano, -na adj, m y f African.
afrontar vt (hacer frente a) to face.
afuera adv outside; por (la parte de) ~ on the outside. ▶ **afueras** fpl: las ~s the outskirts.
afuerita adv Amer fam right outside.
afusilar vt Amer fam to shoot.
agachar vt to lower; (la cabeza) to bow. ▶ **agacharse** vpr (acuclillarse) to crouch down; (inclinar la cabeza) to stoop.
agalla f (ZOOL) gill. ▶ **agallas** fpl fig guts.
agarradero m 1. (asa) hold. 2. fam fig (pretexto) pretext, excuse.
agarrado, -da adj 1. (asido): ~ (de) gripped (by); ~s del brazo arm in arm; ~s de la mano hand in hand. 2. fam (tacaño) tight, stingy.
agarrar vt 1. (asir) to grab. 2. (pillar - ladrón, enfermedad) to catch. 3. Amer

(tomar) to take. ▶ **agarrarse** vpr (sujetarse) to hold on.
agarrón m (tirón) pull, tug.
agarrotar vt (parte del cuerpo) to cut off the circulation in; (mente) to numb. ▶ **agarrotarse** vpr 1. (parte del cuerpo) to go numb. 2. (mecanismo) to seize up.
agasajar vt to lavish attention on.
ágata f (el) agate.
agazaparse vpr 1. (para esconderse) to crouch. 2. (agacharse) to bend down.
agencia f 1. (empresa) agency; ~ matrimonial marriage bureau; ~ de viajes travel agency. 2. (sucursal) branch.
agenda f 1. (de notas, fechas) diary; (de teléfonos, direcciones) book. 2. (de trabajo) agenda.
agente ◆ m y f (persona) agent; ~ de policía o de la autoridad policeman (f policewoman); ~ de aduanas customs officer; ~ de cambio (y bolsa) stockbroker; ~ secreto secret agent. ◆ m (causa activa) agent.
ágil adj (movimiento, persona) agile.
agilidad f agility.
agilizar vt to speed up.
agitación f 1. (intranquilidad) restlessness. 2. (jaleo) racket, commotion. 3. (conflicto) unrest.
agitar vt 1. (mover - botella etc) to shake; (- líquido) to stir; (- brazos) to wave. 2. (inquietar) to perturb, to worry. 3. (alterar, perturbar) to stir up. ▶ **agitarse** vpr (inquietarse) to get worried.
aglomeración f build-up; (de gente) crowd.
aglomerar vt to bring together. ▶ **aglomerarse** vpr to amass.
agnóstico, -ca adj, m y f agnostic.
agobiado, -da adj: ~ (de) (trabajo) snowed under (with); (problemas) weighed down (with).
agobiar vt to overwhelm. ▶ **agobiarse** vpr to feel overwhelmed, to let things get one down.
agobio m 1. (físico) choking, suffocation. 2. (psíquico) pressure.
agolparse vpr (gente) to crowd round; (sangre) to rush.
agonía f 1. (pena) agony. 2. (del moribundo) death throes (pl).
agonizante adj dying.
agonizar vi (expirar) to be dying.
agosto m 1. (mes) August; ver también septiembre. 2. loc: hacer su ~ to line one's pockets.
agotado, -da adj 1. (cansado): ~ (de) exhausted (from). 2. (producto) out of

stock, sold out. **3.** (*pila, batería*) flat.

agotador, -ra *adj* exhausting.

agotamiento *m* (*cansancio*) exhaustion.

agotar *vt* (*gen*) to exhaust; (*producto*) to sell out of; (*agua*) to drain. ▶ **agotarse** *vpr* **1.** (*cansarse*) to tire o.s. out. **2.** (*acabarse*) to run out; (*libro, disco, entradas*) to be sold out; (*pila, batería*) to go flat.

agraciado, -da *adj* **1.** (*atractivo*) attractive, fetching. **2.** (*afortunado*): ~ **con algo** lucky enough to win sthg.

agraciar *vt* (*embellecer*) to make more attractive o fetching.

agradable *adj* pleasant.

agradar *vt* to please; **¿te agrada?** do you like it?

agradecer *vt* (*suj: persona*): ~ **algo a alguien** (*dar las gracias*) to thank sb for sthg; (*estar agradecido*) to be grateful to sb for sthg.

agradecido, -da *adj* grateful.

agradecimiento *m* gratitude.

agrado *m* (*gusto*) pleasure; **ésto no es de mi** ~ this is not to my liking.

agrandar *vt* to make bigger.

agrario, -ria *adj* (*reforma*) agrarian; (*producto, política*) agricultural.

agravante ◆ *adj* aggravating. ◆ *m o f* **1.** (*problema*) additional problem. **2.** (DER) aggravating circumstance.

agravar *vt* to aggravate; (*impuestos etc*) to increase (the burden of). ▶ **agravarse** *vpr* to get worse.

agraviar *vt* to offend.

agravio *m* **1.** (*ofensa*) offence, insult. **2.** (*perjuicio*) wrong.

agredir *vt* to attack.

agregado, -da *m y f* **1.** (EDUC) assistant teacher. **2.** (*de embajada*) attaché; ~ **cultural** cultural attaché. ▶ **agregado** *m* (*añadido*) addition.

agregar *vt*: ~ **(algo a algo)** to add (sthg to sthg).

agresión *f* (*ataque*) act of aggression, attack.

agresividad *f* aggression.

agresivo, -va *adj lit & fig* aggressive.

agresor, -ra *m y f* attacker, assailant.

agreste *adj* (*abrupto, rocoso*) rugged.

agriar *vt* (*vino, leche*) to (turn) sour. ▶ **agriarse** *vpr lit & fig* to turn sour.

agrícola *adj* agricultural; (*pueblo*) farming (*antes de sust*).

agricultor, -ra *m y f* farmer.

agricultura *f* agriculture.

agridulce *adj* bittersweet; (CULIN) sweet and sour.

agrietar *vt* **1.** (*muro, tierra*) to crack. **2.** (*labios, manos*) to chap. ▶ **agrietarse** *vpr* (*la piel*) to chap.

agrio, agria *adj* **1.** (*ácido*) sour. **2.** *fig* (*áspero*) acerbic, bitter.

agronomía *f* agronomy.

agropecuario, -ria *adj* farming and livestock (*antes de sust*).

agrupación *f* (*asociación*) group.

agrupamiento *m* (*concentración*) grouping.

agrupar *vt* to group (together). ▶ **agruparse** *vpr* **1.** (*congregarse*) to gather (round). **2.** (*unirse*) to form a group.

agua *f* (el) water; ~ **mineral sin gas/con gas** still/sparkling mineral water; **venir como** ~ **de mayo** to be a godsend. ▶ **aguas** *fpl* **1.** (*manantial*) waters, spring (*sg*). **2.** (*de río, mar*) waters; ~**s territoriales** o **jurisdiccionales** territorial waters. **3.** (*de diamantes, telas*) water (U). ▶ **agua de colonia** *f* eau de cologne. ▶ **agua oxigenada** *f* hydrogen peroxide. ▶ **aguas residuales** *fpl* sewage (U).

aguacate *m* (*fruto*) avocado (pear).

aguacero *m* shower.

aguachirle *f* dishwater (U), revolting drink.

aguado, -da *adj* (*con demasiada agua*) watery; (*diluido a propósito*) watered-down.

aguafiestas *m y f inv* spoilsport.

aguafuerte *m* etching.

aguamarina *f* aquamarine.

aguanieve *f* sleet.

aguantar *vt* **1.** (*sostener*) to hold. **2.** (*resistir - peso*) to bear. **3.** (*tolerar, soportar*) to bear, to stand; **no sé cómo la aguantas** I don't know how you put up with her. **4.** (*contener - risa*) to contain; (*- respiración*) to hold. ▶ **aguantarse** *vpr* **1.** (*contenerse*) to restrain o.s. **2.** (*resignarse*): **no quiere** ~**se** he refuses to put up with it.

aguante *m* **1.** (*paciencia*) self-restraint. **2.** (*resistencia*) strength; (*de persona*) stamina.

aguar *vt* **1.** (*mezclar con agua*) to water down. **2.** *fig* (*estropear*) to spoil.

aguardar *vt* to wait for, to await.

aguardiente *m* brandy, *clear spirit distilled from fermented fruit.*

aguarrás *m* turpentine.

agudeza *f* (*gen*) sharpness.

agudizar *vt fig* (*acentuar*) to exacerbate. ▶ **agudizarse** *vpr* (*crisis*) to get worse.

agudo, -da *adj* 1. (*gen*) sharp; (*crisis, problema, enfermedad*) serious, acute. 2. *fig* (*perspicaz*) keen, sharp. 3. *fig* (*ingenioso*) witty. 4. (MÚS) (*nota, voz*) high, high-pitched.

agüero *m*: **de buen/mal ~** that bodes well/ill.

aguijón *m* 1. (*de insecto*) sting. 2. *fig* (*estímulo*) spur, stimulus.

aguijonear *vt* 1. (*espolear*): **~ a alguien para que haga algo** to goad sb into doing sthg. 2. *fig* (*estimular*) to drive on.

águila *f* (*el*) 1. (*ave*) eagle. 2. *fig* (*vivo, listo*) sharp o perceptive person.

aguileño, -ña *adj* aquiline.

aguilucho *m* eaglet.

aguinaldo *m* Christmas box.

aguja *f* 1. (*de coser, jeringuilla*) needle; (*de hacer punto*) knitting needle. 2. (*de reloj*) hand; (*de brújula*) pointer; (*de iglesia*) spire. 3. (FERROC) point. 4. (*de tocadiscos*) stylus, needle. ▶ **agujas** *fpl* (*de res*) ribs.

agujerear *vt* to make a hole o holes in.

agujero *m* hole.

agujetas *fpl*: **tener ~** to feel stiff.

aguzar *vt* 1. (*afilar*) to sharpen. 2. *fig* (*apetito*) to whet; (*ingenio*) to sharpen.

ah *interj* **¡~!** (*admiración*) ooh!; (*sorpresa*) oh!; (*pena*) ah!

ahí *adv* there; **vino por ~** he came that way; **la solución está ~** that's where the solution lies; **¡~ tienes!** here you are!, there you go!; **de ~ que** (*por eso*) and consequently, so; **está por ~** (*en lugar indefinido*) he/she is around (somewhere); (*en la calle*) he/she is out; **por ~, por ~** *fig* something like that; **por ~ va la cosa** you're not too far wrong.

ahijado, -da *m y f* (*de padrinos*) godson (*f* goddaughter).

ahijuna, aijuna *interj Amer fam*: **¡~!** wow!

ahínco *m* enthusiasm, devotion.

ahíto, -ta *adj culto* (*saciado*): **estar ~** to be full.

ahogar *vt* 1. (*asfixiar - en el agua*) to drown; (- *cubriendo la boca y nariz*) to smother, to suffocate. 2. (*estrangular*) to strangle. 3. (*extinguir*) to extinguish, to put out. 4. *fig* (*dominar - levantamiento*) to quell; (- *pena*) to hold back. ▶ **ahogarse** *vpr* 1. (*en el agua*) to drown. 2. (*asfixiarse*) to suffocate.

ahogo *m* 1. (*asfixia*) breathlessness. 2. *fig* (*económico*) financial difficulty.

ahondar *vi* (*profundizar*) to go into detail; **~ en** (*penetrar*) to penetrate deep into; (*profundizar*) to study in depth.

ahora ◆ *adv* 1. (*en el presente*) now; (*hoy día*) today, nowadays; **y ~ tú** it's your turn now; **~ mismo** right now; **por ~** for the time being. 2. (*pronto*) in a second o moment. ◆ *conj* (*pero*) but, however; **~ que** but, though; **~ bien** but, however.

ahorcar *vt* to hang. ▶ **ahorcarse** *vpr* to hang o.s.

ahorita, ahoritita *adv Amer fam* right now.

ahorrador, -ra ◆ *adj* thrifty, careful with money. ◆ *m y f* thrifty person.

ahorrar *vt* to save. ▶ **ahorrarse** *vpr*: **~se algo** to save o spare o.s. sthg.

ahorro *m* 1. (*gen*) saving. 2. (*gen pl*) (*cantidad ahorrada*) savings (*pl*).

ahuecar *vt* (*poner hueco - manos*) to cup.

ahuevado, -da *adj Amer fam* (*tonto*) daft.

ahumado, -da *adj* smoked.

ahumar *vt* 1. (*jamón, pescado*) to smoke. 2. (*habitación etc*) to fill with smoke.

ahuyentar *vt* 1. (*espantar, asustar*) to scare away. 2. *fig* (*apartar*) to drive away.

aijuna = **ahijuna**.

airado, -da *adj* angry.

airar *vt* to anger, to make angry. ▶ **airarse** *vpr* to get angry.

aire *m* 1. (*fluido*) air; **al ~** exposed; **al ~ libre** in the open air; **estar en el ~** to be in the air; **tomar el ~** to go for a breath of fresh air. 2. (*viento*) wind; (*corriente*) draught; **hoy hace (mucho) ~** it's (very) windy today. 3. *fig* (*aspecto*) air, appearance. ▶ **aires** *mpl* (*vanidad*) airs (and graces). ▶ **aire (acondicionado)** *m* air-conditioning.

airear *vt fig* (*contar*) to air (publicly). ▶ **airearse** *vpr* to get a breath of fresh air.

airoso, -sa *adj* 1. (*garboso*) graceful. 2. (*triunfante*): **salir ~ de algo** to come out of sthg with flying colours.

aislado, -da adj 1. (gen) isolated. 2. (TECN) insulated.

aislar vt 1. (gen) to isolate. 2. (TECN) to insulate.

ajá interj: ¡~! (sorpresa) aha!; fam (aprobación) great!

ajar vt (flores) to wither, to cause to fade; (piel) to wrinkle; (colores) to make faded; (ropa) to wear out. ▶ **ajarse** vpr (flores) to fade, to wither; (piel) to wrinkle, to become wrinkled.

ajardinado, -da adj landscaped.

a.JC. = a. de JC.

ajedrez m inv chess.

ajeno, -na adj 1. (de otro) of others; **jugar en campo ~** to play away from home. 2. (extraño): **~ a** having nothing to do with; **~ a nuestra voluntad** beyond our control.

ajetreo m 1. (tarea) running around, hard work. 2. (animación) (hustle and) bustle.

ají m Amer chilli (pepper).

ajiaco m Amer (estofado) stew.

ajillo ▶ **al ajillo** loc adj (CULIN) in a sauce made with oil, garlic and chilli.

ajo m garlic; **andar** o **estar en el ~** fig to be in on it.

ajustado, -da adj (ceñido - ropa) tight-fitting; (- tuerca, pieza) tight; (- resultado, final) close.

ajustadores mpl Amer bra (sg).

ajustar vt 1. (arreglar) to adjust. 2. (apretar) to tighten. 3. (encajar - piezas de motor) to fit; (- puerta, ventana) to push to. 4. (pactar - matrimonio) to arrange; (- pleito) to settle; (- paz) to negotiate; (- precio) to fix, to agree.

ajuste m (de pieza) fitting; (de mecanismo) adjustment; (de salario) agreement; **~ de cuentas** fig settling of scores.

al → **a**.

ala f (el) 1. (POLÍT & ZOOL) wing. 2. (parte lateral - de tejado) eaves (pl); (- de sombrero) brim. 3. (DEP) winger, wing. ▶ **ala delta** f (aparato) hang glider.

alabanza f praise.

alabar vt to praise.

alabastro m alabaster.

alacena f recess for storing food.

alacrán m (animal) scorpion.

alado, -da adj (con alas) winged.

alambique m still.

alambrada f (cerco) wire fencing.

alambrado m Amer (cerco) wire fencing; (ELECTR) wiring.

alambre m wire; **~ de espino** o **púas** barbed wire.

alameda f 1. (sitio con álamos) poplar grove. 2. (paseo) tree-lined avenue.

álamo m poplar.

alano m (perro) mastiff.

alarde m: **~ (de)** show o display (of); **hacer ~ de algo** to show sthg off.

alardear vi: **~ de** to show off about.

alargador m extension lead.

alargar vt 1. (ropa etc) to lengthen. 2. (viaje, visita, plazo) to extend; (conversación) to spin out. ▶ **alargarse** vpr (hacerse más largo - días) to get longer; (- reunión) to be prolonged.

alarido m shriek, howl.

alarma f (gen) alarm; **dar la ~** to raise the alarm.

alarmante adj alarming.

alarmar vt 1. (avisar) to alert. 2. fig (asustar) to alarm. ▶ **alarmarse** vpr (inquietarse) to be alarmed.

alarmista m y f alarmist.

alazán, -ana adj chestnut.

alba f (el) (amanecer) dawn.

albacea m y f executor (f executrix).

albahaca f basil.

albanés, -esa adj, m y f Albanian. ▶ **albanés** m (lengua) Albanian.

Albania Albania.

albañil m (gen) construction worker; (que pone ladrillos) bricklayer.

albañilería f (obra) brickwork.

albarán m delivery note.

albaricoque m apricot.

albedrío m (antojo, elección) fancy, whim; **a su ~** as takes his/her fancy; **libre ~** free will; **a su libre ~** of his/her own free will.

alberca f 1. (depósito) water tank. 2. Amer (piscina) swimming pool.

albergar vt 1. (personas) to accommodate, to put up. 2. (odio) to harbour; (esperanzas) to cherish. ▶ **albergarse** vpr to stay.

albergue m accommodation (U), lodgings (pl); (de montaña) shelter, refuge; **~ de juventud** o **juvenil** youth hostel.

albino, -na adj, m y f albino.

albis ▶ **in albis** loc adv: **estar in ~** to be in the dark; **quedarse in ~** not to have a clue o the faintest idea.

albóndiga f meatball.

alborada f (amanecer) dawn.

alborear v impers: **empezaba a ~** dawn was breaking.

albores mpl: **los ~ de** the dawn of.

albornoz m bathrobe.

alborotar ◆ vi to be noisy o rowdy.

♦ vt (amotinar) to stir up, to rouse.
▶ **alborotarse** vpr (perturbarse) to get worked up.
alboroto m 1. (ruido) din. 2. (jaleo) fuss, to-do.
alborozar vt to delight.
alborozo m delight, joy.
albufera f lagoon.
álbum (pl **álbumes**) m album.
alcachofa f (BOT) artichoke.
alcahuete, -ta m y f (mediador) go-between.
alcalde, -desa m y f mayor (f mayoress).
alcaldía f (cargo) mayoralty.
alcance m 1. (de arma, misil, emisora) range; **de corto/largo ~** short-/long-range. 2. (de persona): **a mi/a tu** etc **~** within my/your etc reach; **al ~ de la vista/mano** within sight/reach; **fuera del ~ de** beyond the reach of. 3. (de reformas etc) scope, extent.
alcanfor m camphor.
alcantarilla f sewer; (boca) drain.
alcantarillado m sewers (pl).
alcanzar ♦ vt 1. (llegar a) to reach. 2. (igualarse con) to catch up with. 3. (entregar) to pass. 4. (suj: bala etc) to hit. 5. (autobús, tren) to manage to catch. 6. (lograr) to achieve. ♦ vi 1. (ser suficiente): **~ para algo/hacer algo** to be enough for sthg/to do sthg. 2. (poder): **~ a hacer algo** to be able to do sthg.
alcaparra f caper.
alcayata f hook.
alcázar m fortress.
alce m elk, moose.
alcoba f bedroom.
alcohol m alcohol.
alcohólico, -ca adj, m y f alcoholic.
alcoholímetro m (para la sangre) Breathalyzer® Br, drunkometer Am.
alcoholismo m alcoholism.
alcohotest (pl **alcohotests**) m Breathalyzer® Br, drunkometer Am.
alcornoque m 1. (árbol) cork oak. 2. fig (persona) idiot, fool.
aldaba f (llamador) doorknocker.
aldea f small village.
aldeano, -na m y f villager.
aleación f (producto) alloy.
aleatorio, -ria adj (número) random; (suceso) chance (antes de sust).
aleccionar vt to instruct, to teach.
alegación f allegation.
alegar vt (motivos, pruebas) to put forward; **~ que** to claim (that).

alegato m 1. (DER & fig) plea. 2. (ataque) diatribe.
alegoría f allegory.
alegórico, -ca adj allegorical.
alegrar vt (persona) to cheer up, to make happy; (fiesta) to liven up. ▶ **alegrarse** vpr (sentir alegría): **~se (de algo/por alguien)** to be pleased (about sthg/for sb).
alegre adj 1. (contento) happy. 2. (que da alegría) cheerful, bright. 3. fam (borracho) tipsy.
alegría f 1. (gozo) happiness, joy. 2. (motivo de gozo) joy.
alegrón m fam pleasant surprise.
alejamiento m 1. (lejanía) remoteness. 2. (distancia) distance. 3. (separación - de objetos etc) separation; (- entre personas) estrangement.
alejar vt 1. (poner más lejos) to move away. 2. fig (ahuyentar) to drive out. ▶ **alejarse** vpr: **~se (de)** (ponerse más lejos) to go o move away (from); (retirarse) to leave.
aleluya interj: **¡~!** Hallelujah!
alemán, -ana adj, m y f German. ▶ **alemán** m (lengua) German.
Alemania Germany.
alentador, -ra adj encouraging.
alentar vt to encourage.
alergia f lit & fig allergy; **tener ~ a algo** to be allergic to sthg.
alérgico, -ca adj lit & fig: **~ (a)** allergic (to).
alero m 1. (del tejado) eaves (pl). 2. (DEP) winger, wing.
alerta ♦ adj, m y f & adv alert. ♦ f alert.
alertar vt to alert.
aleta f 1. (de pez) fin. 2. (de buzo, foca) flipper. 3. (de coche) wing.
aletargar vt to make drowsy. ▶ **aletargarse** vpr to become drowsy o sleepy.
aletear vi to flap o flutter its wings.
alevín m 1. (cría de pez) fry, young fish. 2. fig (persona) novice, beginner.
alevosía f (traición) treachery.
alfabetizar vt 1. (personas) to teach to read and write. 2. (palabras, letras) to put into alphabetical order.
alfabeto m alphabet.
alfalfa f alfalfa, lucerne.
alfarería f (técnica) pottery.
alféizar m window-sill.
alférez m ≃ second lieutenant.
alfil m bishop.
alfiler m 1. (aguja) pin; **~ de gancho** Amer safety pin. 2. (joya) brooch, pin.

alfombra f carpet; (*alfombrilla*) rug.
alfombrar vt to carpet.
alfombrilla f 1. (*alfombra pequeña*) rug.
2. (*felpudo*) doormat. 3. (*del baño*) bathmat.
alforja f (*gen pl*) (*de caballo*) saddlebag.
alga f (*el*) (*de mar*) seaweed (U); (*de río*) algae (*pl*).
algarroba f (*fruto*) carob o locust bean.
algarrobo m carob tree.
álgebra f (*el*) algebra.
álgido, -da adj (*culminante*) critical.
algo ♦ pron 1. (*alguna cosa*) something; (*en interrogativas*) anything; **¿te pasa ~?** is anything the matter?; **~ es ~** something is better than nothing; **por ~ lo habrá dicho** he must have said it for a reason. 2. (*cantidad pequeña*) a bit, a little; **~ de** some, a little. 3. *fig* (*cosa importante*) something; **se cree que es ~** he thinks he's something (special). **♦** adv (*un poco*) rather, somewhat.
algodón m cotton; **~ (hidrófilo)** (FARM) cotton wool Br, absorbent cotton Am.
algoritmo m (INFORM) algorithm.
alguacil m (*del juzgado*) bailiff.
alguien pron 1. (*alguna persona*) someone, somebody; (*en interrogativas*) anyone, anybody; **¿hay ~ ahí?** is anyone there? 2. *fig* (*persona de importancia*) somebody; **se cree ~** she thinks she's somebody (special).
alguno, -na ♦ adj (*antes de sust masculino* **algún**) 1. (*indeterminado*) some; (*en interrogativas*) any; **¿tienes algún libro?** do you have any books?; **algún día** some o one day; **ha surgido algún (que otro) problema** the odd problem has come up. 2. (*después de sust*) (*ninguno*) any; **no tengo interés ~** I have no interest, I haven't any interest. **♦** pron 1. (*persona*) someone, somebody; (*pl*) some people; (*en interrogativas*) anyone, anybody; **¿conocisteis a ~s?** did you get to know any?; **~s de, ~s (de)** entre some o a few of. 2. (*cosa*) the odd one; (*pl*) a few; (*en interrogativas*) any; **me salió mal ~** I got the odd one wrong; **~ de** some o a few of.
alhaja f (*joya*) jewel.
alhelí (*pl* alhelíes) m wallflower.
aliado, -da adj allied.
alianza f 1. (*pacto, parentesco*) alliance. 2. (*anillo*) wedding ring.
aliar vt (*naciones*) to ally. ▶ **aliarse** vpr to form an alliance.
alias ♦ adv alias. **♦** m inv alias; (*entre amigos*) nickname.

alicaído, -da adj (*triste*) depressed.
alicates mpl pliers.
aliciente m 1. (*incentivo*) incentive. 2. (*atractivo*) attraction.
alienación f 1. (*gen*) alienation. 2. (*trastorno psíquico*) derangement.
aliento m (*respiración*) breath; **cobrar ~** to catch one's breath; **sin ~** breathless.
aligerar vt 1. (*peso*) to lighten. 2. (*ritmo*) to speed up; (*el paso*) to quicken. 3. *fig* (*aliviar*) to relieve, to ease.
alijo m contraband (U).
alimaña f pest (*fox, weasel etc*).
alimentación f 1. (*acción*) feeding. 2. (*comida*) food. 3. (*régimen alimenticio*) diet.
alimentar vt (*gen*) to feed; (*motor, coche*) to fuel. ▶ **alimentarse** vpr (*comer*): **~se de** to live on.
alimenticio, -cia adj nourishing; **productos ~s** foodstuffs.
alimento m (*gen*) food; (*valor nutritivo*) nourishment.
alineación f 1. (*en el espacio*) alignment. 2. (DEP) line-up.
alinear vt 1. (*en el espacio*) to line up. 2. (DEP) to select. ▶ **alinearse** vpr (POLÍT) to align.
aliñar vt (*ensalada*) to dress; (*carne*) to season.
aliño m (*para ensalada*) dressing; (*para carne*) seasoning.
alioli m garlic mayonnaise.
alisar vt to smooth (down).
alistarse vpr to enlist.
aliviar vt 1. (*atenuar*) to soothe. 2. (*aligerar - persona*) to relieve; (*- carga*) to lighten.
alivio m relief.
aljibe m (*de agua*) cistern.
allá adv 1. (*espacio*) over there; **~ abajo/arriba** down/up there; **más ~** further on; **más ~ de** beyond. 2. (*tiempo*): **~ por los años cincuenta** back in the 50s; **~ para el mes de agosto** around August some time. 3. *loc*: **~ él/ella** *etc* that's his/her *etc* problem.
allanamiento m forceful entry; **~ de morada** breaking and entering.
allanar vt 1. (*terreno*) to flatten, to level. 2. (*irrumpir en*) to break into.
allegado, -da m y f 1. (*familiar*) relative. 2. (*amigo*) close friend.
allí adv there; **~ abajo/arriba** down/up there; **~ mismo** right there; **está por ~** it's around there somewhere.
alma f (*el*) 1. (*gen*) soul. 2. (*de bastón, ovillo*) core.

almacén m 1. (*depósito*) warehouse. 2. Amer (*tienda*) shop. ▶ **grandes almacenes** mpl department store (*sg*).

almacenar vt 1. (*gen & INFORM*) to store. 2. (*reunir*) to collect.

almendra f almond.

almendro m almond (tree).

almíbar m syrup.

almidón m starch.

almidonar vt to starch.

almirantazgo m (*dignidad*) admiralty.

almirante m admiral.

almirez m mortar.

almizcle m musk.

almohada f pillow.

almohadilla f (*gen, TECN & ZOOL*) pad; (*cojín*) small cushion.

almorrana f (*gen pl*) piles (*pl*).

almorzar ◆ vt (*al mediodía*) to have for lunch. ◆ vi (*al mediodía*) to have lunch.

almuerzo m (*al mediodía*) lunch.

aló interj Amer (*al teléfono*) hello.

alocado, -da m y f crazy person.

alojamiento m accommodation.

alojar vt to put up. ▶ **alojarse** vpr 1. (*hospedarse*) to stay. 2. (*introducirse*) to lodge.

alondra f lark.

alpargata f (*gen pl*) espadrille.

Alpes mpl: **los ~** the Alps.

alpinismo m mountaineering.

alpinista m y f mountaineer.

alpiste m (*semilla*) birdseed.

alquilar vt (*casa, TV, oficina*) to rent; (*coche*) to hire. ▶ **alquilarse** vpr (*casa, TV, oficina*) to be for rent; (*coche*) to be for hire; **'se alquila'** 'to let'.

alquiler m 1. (*acción - de casa, TV, oficina*) renting; (*- de coche*) hiring; **de ~** (*casa*) rented; (*coche*) hire (*antes de sust*): **tenemos pisos de ~** we have flats to let Br, we have apartments to rent Am. 2. (*precio - de casa, oficina*) rent; (*- de televisión*) rental; (*- de coche*) hire charge.

alquimia f alchemy.

alquitrán m tar.

alrededor adv 1. (*en torno*) around; **mira a tu ~** look around you; **de ~** surrounding. 2. (*aproximadamente*): **~ de** around, about. ▶ **alrededores** mpl surrounding area (*sg*). ▶ **alrededor de** loc prep around.

alta → **alto**.

altanero, -ra adj haughty.

altar m altar.

altavoz m (*para anuncios*) loudspeaker; (*de tocadiscos*) speaker.

alteración f 1. (*cambio*) alteration. 2. (*excitación*) agitation. 3. (*alboroto*) disturbance; **~ del orden público** breach of the peace.

alterado, -da adj (*enojado*) angry; (*trastornado*) upset.

alterar vt 1. (*cambiar*) to alter. 2. (*persona - enojar*) to annoy; (*- trastornar*) to upset. 3. (*orden público*) to disrupt. ▶ **alterarse** vpr (*perturbarse*) to get agitated o flustered.

altercado m argument, row.

alternar ◆ vt to alternate. ◆ vi 1. (*relacionarse*): **~ (con)** to mix (with), to socialize (with). 2. (*sucederse*): **~ con** to alternate with. ▶ **alternarse** vpr 1. (*en el tiempo*) to take turns. 2. (*en el espacio*) to alternate.

alternativa → **alternativo**.

alternativamente adv (*moverse*) alternately.

alternativo, -va adj 1. (*movimiento*) alternating. 2. (*posibilidad*) alternative. ▶ **alternativa** f 1. (*opción*) alternative. 2. (*TAUROM*): **tomar la alternativa** to become a professional bullfighter.

alterno, -na adj alternate; (*ELECTR*) alternating.

alteza f fig (*de sentimientos*) loftiness. ▶ **Alteza** f (*tratamiento*) Highness; **Su Alteza Real** His Royal Highness (f Her Royal Highness).

altibajos mpl fig (*de vida etc*) ups and downs.

altiplano m high plateau.

altisonante adj high-sounding.

altitud f altitude.

altivez f haughtiness.

altivo, -va adj haughty.

alto, -ta adj 1. (*gen*) high; (*persona, árbol, edificio*) tall; (*piso*) top, upper. 2. (*ruidoso*) loud. 3. (*avanzado*) late; **a altas horas de la noche** late at night, in the small hours. ▶ **alto** ◆ m 1. (*altura*) height; **mide dos metros de ~** (*cosa*) it's two metres high; (*persona*) he's two metres tall. 2. (*interrupción*) stop. 3. (*lugar elevado*) height; **en lo ~ de** at the top of. 4. (*MÚS*) alto. 5. loc: **pasar por ~ algo** to pass over sthg. ◆ adv 1. (*arriba*) high (up). 2. (*hablar etc*) loud. ◆ interj: **¡~!** halt!, stop! ▶ **alta** f (el) (*del hospital*) discharge; **dar de alta** o **el alta a alguien** to discharge sb (from hospital).

altoparlante m Amer loudspeaker.

altramuz m lupin.

altruismo m altruism.

altura f 1. (*gen*) height; (*en el mar*)

depth; **tiene dos metros de ~** (gen) it's two metres high; (persona) he's two metres tall. **2.** (nivel) level; **está a la ~ del ayuntamiento** it's next to the town hall. **3.** (latitud) latitude. ▶ **alturas** fpl (el cielo) Heaven (sg); **a estas ~s** fig this far on, at this stage.

alubia f bean.

alucinación f hallucination.

alucinado, -da adj **1.** (MED) hallucinating. **2.** fam (sorprendido) gobsmacked.

alucinante adj **1.** (MED) hallucinatory. **2.** fam (extraordinario) amazing.

alucinar ◆ vi (MED) to hallucinate. ◆ vt fam fig (seducir) to captivate.

alud m lit & fig avalanche.

aludido, -da m y f: **el ~** the aforesaid; **darse por ~** (ofenderse) to take it personally; (reaccionar) to take the hint.

aludir vi: **~ a** (sin mencionar) to allude to; (mencionando) to refer to.

alumbrado m lighting.

alumbramiento m (parto) delivery.

alumbrar vt **1.** (iluminar) to light up. **2.** (instruir) to enlighten. **3.** (dar a luz) to give birth to.

aluminio m aluminium.

alumnado m (de escuela) pupils (pl); (de universidad) students (pl).

alumno, -na m y f (de escuela, profesor particular) pupil; (de universidad) student.

alunizar vi to land on the moon.

alusión f (sin mencionar) allusion; (mencionando) reference.

alusivo, -va adj allusive.

aluvión m **1.** (gen) flood. **2.** (GEOL) alluvium.

alza f (el) rise; **en ~** (FIN) rising; fig gaining in popularity.

alzamiento m uprising, revolt.

alzar vt **1.** (levantar) to lift, to raise; (voz) to raise; (vela) to hoist; (cuello de abrigo) to turn up; (mangas) to pull up. **2.** (aumentar) to raise. ▶ **alzarse** vpr **1.** (levantarse) to rise. **2.** (sublevarse) to rise up, to revolt.

a.m. (abrev de **ante meridiem**) a.m.

ama → **amo**.

amabilidad f kindness; **¿tendría la ~ de ...?** would you be so kind as to ...?

amable adj kind; **¿sería tan ~ de ...?** would you be so kind as to ...?

amaestrado, -da adj (gen) trained; (en circo) performing.

amaestrar vt to train.

amagar ◆ vt **1.** (dar indicios de) to show signs of. **2.** (mostrar intención) to threaten; **le amagó un golpe** he threatened to

hit him. ◆ vi (tormenta) to be imminent, to threaten.

amago m **1.** (indicio) sign, hint. **2.** (amenaza) threat.

amainar vi lit & fig to abate.

amalgama f (QUÍM & fig) amalgam.

amalgamar vt (QUÍM & fig) to amalgamate.

amamantar vt (animal) to suckle; (bebé) to breastfeed.

amanecer ◆ m dawn. ◆ v impers: **amaneció a las siete** dawn broke at seven.

amanerado, -da adj (afectado) mannered, affected.

amansar vt **1.** (animal) to tame. **2.** fig (persona) to calm down.

amante m y f **1.** (querido) lover. **2.** fig (aficionado): **ser ~ de algo/hacer algo** to be keen on sthg/doing sthg; **los ~s del arte** art lovers.

amañar vt (falsear) to fix; (elecciones, resultado) to rig; (documento) to doctor.

amaño m (gen pl) (treta) ruse, trick.

amapola f poppy.

amar vt to love.

amarar vi (hidroavión) to land at sea; (vehículo espacial) to splash down.

amargado, -da adj (resentido) bitter.

amargar vt to make bitter; fig to spoil.

amargo, -ga adj lit & fig bitter.

amargoso, -sa adj Amer bitter.

amargura f (sentimiento) sorrow.

amarillento, -ta adj yellowish.

amarillo, -lla adj (color) yellow. ▶ **amarillo** m (color) yellow.

amarilloso, -sa adj Amer yellowish.

amarra f mooring rope o line.

amarrar vt **1.** (NÁUT) to moor. **2.** (atar) to tie (up); **~ algo/a alguien a algo** to tie sthg/sb to sthg.

amarre m mooring.

amarrete adj Amer mean, tight.

amasar vt **1.** (masa) to knead; (yeso) to mix. **2.** fam fig (riquezas) to amass.

amasia f Amer mistress.

amasijo m fam fig (mezcla) hotchpotch.

amateur [ama'ter] (pl **amateurs**) adj, m y f amateur.

amatista f amethyst.

amazona f fig (jinete) horsewoman.

Amazonas m: **el ~** the Amazon.

amazónico, -ca adj (gen) Amazon (antes de sust); (cultura, tribu) Amazonian.

ambages mpl: **sin ~** without beating about the bush, in plain English.

ámbar m amber.

ambición f ambition.

ambicionar vt to have as one's ambition.

ambicioso, -sa adj ambitious.

ambidextro, -tra ◆ adj ambidextrous. ◆ m y f ambidextrous person.

ambientación f 1. (CIN, LITER & TEATR) setting. 2. (RADIO) sound effects (pl).

ambientador m air freshener.

ambiental adj 1. (físico, atmosférico) ambient. 2. (ECOLOG) environmental.

ambiente m 1. (aire) air, atmosphere. 2. (circunstancias) environment. 3. (ámbito) world, circles (pl). 4. (animación) life, atmosphere. 5. Amer (habitación) room.

ambigüedad f ambiguity.

ambiguo, -gua adj (gen) ambiguous.

ámbito m 1. (espacio, límites) confines (pl); **una ley de ~ provincial** an act which is provincial in its scope. 2. (ambiente) world, circles (pl). 3. (campo) field.

ambivalente adj ambivalent.

ambos, -bas ◆ adj pl both. ◆ pron pl both (of them).

ambulancia f ambulance.

ambulante adj travelling; (biblioteca) mobile.

ambulatorio m state-run surgery o clinic.

ameba f amoeba.

amedrentar vt to scare, to frighten.

amén adv (en plegaria) amen. ▶ **amén de** loc prep 1. (además de) in addition to. 2. (excepto) except for, apart from.

amenaza f threat; **~ de bomba** bomb scare; **~ de muerte** death threat.

amenazar vt to threaten; **~ a alguien con hacerle algo** to threaten to do sthg to sb; **~ a alguien con hacer algo** to threaten sb with doing sthg; **amenaza lluvia** it's threatening to rain.

amenidad f (entretenimiento) entertaining qualities (pl).

ameno, -na adj (entretenido) entertaining.

América America; **~ del Sur** South America.

americana → americano.

americano, -na adj, m y f American. ▶ **americana** f (chaqueta) jacket.

ameritar vt Amer to deserve.

amerizar vi (hidroavión) to land at sea; (vehículo espacial) to splash down.

ametralladora f machine gun.

ametrallar vt (con ametralladora) to machinegun.

amianto m asbestos.

amígdala f tonsil.

amigdalitis f inv tonsillitis.

amigo, -ga ◆ adj 1. (gen) friendly. 2. (aficionado) **~ de algo/hacer algo** keen on sthg/doing sthg. ◆ m y f 1. (persona) friend; **hacerse ~ de** to make friends with; **hacerse ~s** to become friends. 2. fam (compañero, novio) partner; (amante) lover.

amigote, amiguete m fam pal.

amiguismo m: **hay mucho ~** there are always jobs for the boys.

aminoácido m amino acid.

aminorar vt to reduce.

amistad f friendship; **hacer o trabar ~ (con)** to make friends (with). ▶ **amistades** fpl friends.

amistoso, -sa adj friendly.

amnesia f amnesia.

amnistía f amnesty.

amo, ama m y f 1. (gen) owner. 2. (de criado, situación etc) master (f mistress). ▶ **ama de casa** f housewife. ▶ **ama de llaves** f housekeeper.

amoblar etc Amer= amueblar.

amodorrarse vpr to get drowsy.

amoldar vt (adaptar): **~ (a)** to adapt (to). ▶ **amoldarse** vpr (adaptarse): **~se (a)** to adapt (to).

amonestación f 1. (reprimenda) reprimand. 2. (DEP) warning.

amonestar vt 1. (reprender) to reprimand. 2. (DEP) to warn.

amoníaco, amoniaco m (gas) ammonia.

amontonar vt 1. (apilar) to pile up. 2. (reunir) to accumulate. ▶ **amontonarse** vpr 1. (personas) to form a crowd. 2. (problemas, trabajo) to pile up; (ideas, solicitudes) to come thick and fast.

amor m love; **hacer el ~** to make love; **por ~ al arte** for the love of it. ▶ **amor propio** m pride.

amoral adj amoral.

amoratado, -da adj (de frío) blue; (por golpes) black and blue.

amordazar vt (persona) to gag; (perro) to muzzle.

amorfo, -fa adj (sin forma) amorphous.

amorío m fam (romance) fling.

amoroso, -sa adj (gen) loving; (carta, relación) love (antes de sust).

amortajar vt (difunto) to shroud.

amortiguador, -ra adj (de ruido) muffling; (de golpe) softening, cushioning. ▶ **amortiguador** m (AUTOM) shock absorber.

amortiguar vt (ruido) to muffle; (golpe) to soften, to cushion.

amortización f (ECON) (de deuda, préstamo) paying-off; (de inversión, capital) recouping; (de bonos, acciones) redemption; (de bienes de equipo) depreciation.

amortizar vt 1. (sacar provecho) to get one's money's worth out of. 2. (ECON - deuda, préstamo) to pay off; (- inversión, capital) to recoup; (- bonos, acciones) to redeem.

amotinar vt to incite to riot; (a marineros) to incite to mutiny. ▶ **amotinarse** vpr to riot; (marineros) to mutiny.

amparar vt 1. (proteger) to protect. 2. (dar cobijo a) to give shelter to. ▶ **ampararse** vpr 1. fig (apoyarse): ~se en (ley) to have recourse to; (excusas) to draw on. 2. (cobijarse): ~se de o contra to (take) shelter from.

amparo m (protección) protection; **al ~ de** (persona, caridad) with the help of; (ley) under the protection of.

amperio m amp, ampere.

ampliación f 1. (aumento) expansion; (de edificio, plazo) extension. 2. (FOT) enlargement.

ampliar vt 1. (gen) to expand; (local) to add an extension to; (plazo) to extend. 2. (FOT) to enlarge, to blow up.

amplificación f amplification.

amplificador m (ELECTRÓN) amplifier.

amplificar vt to amplify.

amplio, -plia adj 1. (sala etc) roomy, spacious; (avenida, gama) wide. 2. (ropa) loose. 3. (explicación etc) comprehensive; **en el sentido más ~ de la palabra** in the broadest sense of the word.

amplitud f 1. (espaciosidad) roominess, spaciousness; (de avenida) wideness. 2. (de ropa) looseness. 3. fig (extensión) extent, comprehensiveness.

ampolla f 1. (en piel) blister. 2. (para inyecciones) ampoule. 3. (frasco) phial.

ampuloso, -sa adj pompous.

amputar vt to amputate.

Amsterdam Amsterdam.

amueblado, -da, amoblado, -da Amer adj furnished.

amueblar, amoblar Amer vt to furnish.

amurallar vt to build a wall around.

anacronismo m anachronism.

anagrama m anagram.

anal adj (ANAT) anal.

anales mpl lit & fig annals.

analfabetismo m illiteracy.

analfabeto, -ta adj, m y f illiterate.

analgésico, -ca adj analgesic. ▶ **analgésico** m analgesic, painkiller.

análisis m inv analysis; ~ **de sangre** blood test.

analizar vt to analyse.

analogía f similarity; **por ~** by analogy.

analógico, -ca adj (INFORM & TECN) analogue, analog.

análogo, -ga adj: ~ (a) analogous o similar (to).

ananá, ananás m Amer pineapple.

anaquel m shelf.

anarquía f 1. (falta de gobierno) anarchy. 2. (doctrina política) anarchism.

anárquico, -ca adj anarchic.

anarquista adj, m y f anarchist.

anatema m (maldición) curse.

anatomía f anatomy.

anca f (el) haunch; ~s **de rana** frogs' legs.

ancestral adj ancestral; (costumbre) age-old.

ancho, -cha adj (gen) wide; (prenda) loose-fitting; **te va o está** ~ it's too big for you; **a mis/tus** etc **anchas** fig at ease; **quedarse tan** ~ not to care less. ▶ **ancho** m width; **a lo** ~ crosswise; **cinco metros de** ~ five metres wide; **a lo** ~ **de** across (the width of); ~ **de vía** gauge.

anchoa f anchovy (salted).

anchura f 1. (medida) width. 2. (de ropa) bagginess.

anciano, -na ◆ adj old. ◆ m y f old person, old man (f old woman). ▶ **anciano** m (de tribu) elder.

ancla f (el) anchor.

anclar vi to anchor.

andadas fpl: **volver a las** ~ fam fig to return to one's evil ways.

andadura f walking.

ándale, ándele interj Amer fam: ¡~! come on!

Andalucía Andalusia.

andaluz, -za adj, m y f Andalusian.

andamio m scaffold.

andanada f (MIL & fig) broadside.

andando interj: ¡~! come on!, let's get a move on!

andante adj (que anda) walking.

andanza f (gen pl) (aventura) adventure.

andar ◆ vi 1. (caminar) to walk; (moverse) to move. 2. (funcionar) to work, to go; **las cosas andan mal** things are going badly. 3. (estar) to be; ~ **preocupado** to be worried; ~ **tras algo/alguien**

fig to be after sthg/sb. **4.** (*antes de gerundio*): ~ **haciendo algo** to be doing sthg; **anda echando broncas a todos** he's going round telling everybody off. **5.** (*ocuparse*): ~ **en** (*asuntos, líos*) to be involved in; (*papeleos, negocios*) to be busy with. **6.** (*hurgar*): ~ **en** to rummage around in. **7.** (*alcanzar, rondar*): **anda por los 60** he's about sixty. ♦ *vt* **1.** (*recorrer*) to go, to travel. **2.** *Amer* (*llevar puesto*) to wear. ♦ *m* gait, walk. ▶ **andarse** *vpr* (*obrar*): ~**se con cuidado/misterios** to be careful/secretive. ▶ **andares** *mpl* (*de persona*) gait (*sg*). ▶ **¡anda!** *interj*: ¡anda! (*sorpresa, desilusión*) oh!; (¡*vamos!*) come on!; (¡*por favor!*) go on!; **¡anda ya!** (*incredulidad*) come off it!

ándele = **ándale**.

andén *m* (FERROC) platform.

Andes *mpl*: los ~ the Andes.

andinismo *m* *Amer* mountaineering.

andinista *m* y *f* *Amer* mountaineer.

Andorra Andorra.

andorrano, -na *adj*, *m* y *f* Andorran.

andrajo *m* (*harapo*) rag.

andrajoso, -sa *adj* ragged.

andrógino, -na *adj* androgynous.

androide *m* (*autómata*) android.

anduviera *etc* → **andar**.

anécdota *f* anecdote.

anecdótico, -ca *adj* **1.** (*con historietas*) anecdotal. **2.** (*no esencial*) incidental.

anegar *vt* (*inundar*) to flood. ▶ **anegarse** *vpr* **1.** (*inundarse*) to flood; **sus ojos se anegaron de lágrimas** tears welled up in his eyes. **2.** (*ahogarse*) to drown.

anejo, -ja *adj*: ~ (**a**) (*edificio*) connected (to); (*documento*) attached (to). ▶ **anejo** *m* annexe.

anemia *f* anaemia.

anémona *f* anemone.

anestesia *f* anaesthesia.

anestésico, -ca *adj* anaesthetic. ▶ **anestésico** *m* anaesthetic.

anexar *vt* (*documento*) to attach.

anexión *f* annexation.

anexionar *vt* to annex.

anexo, -xa *adj* (*edificio*) connected; (*documento*) attached. ▶ **anexo** *m* annexe.

anfetamina *f* amphetamine.

anfibio, -bia *adj lit* & *fig* amphibious.

anfiteatro *m* **1.** (CIN & TEATR) circle. **2.** (*edificio*) amphitheatre.

anfitrión, -ona *m* y *f* host (*f* hostess).

ángel *m lit* & *fig* angel; ~ **custodio** o **de la guarda** guardian angel; **tener ~** to

have something special.

angelical *adj* angelic.

angina *f* (*gen pl*) (*amigdalitis*) sore throat; **tener ~s** to have a sore throat. ▶ **angina de pecho** *f* angina (pectoris).

anglicano, -na *adj*, *m* y *f* Anglican.

anglosajón, -ona *adj*, *m* y *f* Anglo-Saxon.

Angola Angola.

angora *f* (*de conejo*) angora; (*de cabra*) mohair.

angosto, -ta *adj culto* narrow.

angostura *f* (*extracto*) angostura.

anguila *f* eel.

angula *f* elver.

angular *adj* angular. ▶ **gran angular** *m* (FOT) wide-angle lens.

ángulo *m* **1.** (*gen*) angle. **2.** (*rincón*) corner.

anguloso, -sa *adj* angular.

angustia *f* (*aflicción*) anxiety.

angustiado, -da *adj* (*preocupado*) worried; (*trastornado*) upset.

angustiar *vt* to distress. ▶ **angustiarse** *vpr* (*agobiarse*): ~**se** (**por**) to get worried (about).

angustioso, -sa *adj* (*espera, momentos*) anxious; (*situación, noticia*) distressing.

anhelante *adj*: ~ (**por algo/hacer algo**) longing (for sthg/to do sthg), desperate (for sthg/to do sthg).

anhelar *vt* to long o wish for; ~ **hacer algo** to long to do sthg.

anhelo *m* longing.

anhídrido *m* anhydride; ~ **carbónico** carbon dioxide.

anidar *vi* (*pájaro*) to nest.

anilla *f* ring.

anillo *m* (*gen* & ASTRON) ring; ~ **de boda** wedding ring.

ánima *f* (*el*) soul.

animación *f* **1.** (*alegría*) liveliness. **2.** (*bullicio*) hustle and bustle, activity. **3.** (CIN) animation.

animado, -da *adj* **1.** (*con buen ánimo*) cheerful. **2.** (*divertido*) lively. **3.** (CIN) animated.

animador, -ra *m* y *f* **1.** (*en espectáculo*) compere. **2.** (*en fiesta de niños*) children's entertainer. **3.** (*en béisbol etc*) cheerleader.

animadversión *f* animosity.

animal ♦ *adj* **1.** (*reino, funciones*) animal (*antes de sust*). **2.** *fam* (*persona - basto*) rough; (- *ignorante*) ignorant. ♦ *m* y *f fam fig* (*persona*) animal, brute. ♦ *m* animal; ~ **doméstico** (*de granja etc*) domestic animal; (de compañía) pet.

animar vt 1. (estimular) to encourage. 2. (alegrar - persona) to cheer up. 3. (avivar - fuego, diálogo, fiesta) to liven up; (comercio) to stimulate. ▶ **animarse** vpr 1. (alegrarse - persona) to cheer up; (- fiesta etc) to liven up. 2. (decidir): ~se (a hacer algo) to finally decide (to do sthg); ¿te animas? will you have a go?

ánimo ◆ m 1. (valor) courage. 2. (aliento) encouragement; dar ~s a alguien to encourage sb. 3. (humor) disposition. ◆ interj (para alentar): ¡~! come on!

animoso, -sa adj (valiente) courageous; (decidido) undaunted.

aniñado, -da adj (comportamiento) childish; (voz, rostro) childlike.

aniquilar vt to annihilate, to wipe out.

anís (pl anises) m 1. (grano) aniseed. 2. (licor) anisette.

aniversario m (gen) anniversary; (cumpleaños) birthday.

ano m anus.

anoche adv last night, yesterday evening; antes de ~ the night before last.

anochecer ◆ m dusk, nightfall; al ~ at dusk. ◆ v impers to get dark.

anodino, -na adj (sin gracia) dull, insipid.

anomalía f anomaly.

anómalo, -la adj anomalous.

anonadado, -da adj (sorprendido) astonished, bewildered.

anonimato m anonymity; permanecer en el ~ to remain nameless.

anónimo, -ma adj anonymous. ▶ **anónimo** m anonymous letter.

anorak (pl anoraks) m anorak.

anorexia f anorexia.

anormal adj (anómalo) abnormal.

anotación f (gen) note; (en registro) entry.

anotar vt 1. (apuntar) to note down. 2. (tantear) to notch up.

anquilosamiento m 1. (estancamiento) stagnation. 2. (MED) paralysis.

anquilosarse vpr 1. (estancarse) to stagnate. 2. (MED) to become paralysed.

ansia f (el) 1. (afán): ~ de longing o yearning for. 2. (ansiedad) anxiousness; (angustia) anguish.

ansiar vt: ~ hacer algo to long o be desperate to do sthg.

ansiedad f 1. (inquietud) anxiety; con ~ anxiously. 2. (PSICOL) nervous tension.

ansioso, -sa adj 1. (impaciente) impatient; estar ~ por o de hacer algo to be impatient to do sthg. 2. (preocupado) anxious, uneasy.

antagónico, -ca adj antagonistic.

antagonista m y f opponent.

antaño adv in days gone by.

antártico, -ca adj Antarctic. ▶ **Antártico** m: el **Antártico** the Antarctic; el océano Glacial Antártico the Antarctic Ocean.

Antártida f: la ~ the Antarctic.

ante¹ m 1. (piel) suede. 2. (animal) elk.

ante² prep 1. (delante de, en presencia de) before. 2. (frente a - hecho, circunstancia) in the face of. ▶ **ante todo** loc adv 1. (sobre todo) above all. 2. (en primer lugar) first of all.

anteanoche adv the night before last.

anteayer adv the day before yesterday.

antebrazo m forearm.

antecedente ◆ adj preceding, previous. ◆ m (precedente) precedent. ▶ **antecedentes** mpl (de persona) record (sg); (de asunto) background (sg); poner a alguien en ~s de (informar) to fill sb in on.

anteceder vt to precede.

antecesor, -ra m y f (predecesor) predecessor.

antedicho, -cha adj aforementioned.

antelación f: con ~ in advance, beforehand; con dos horas de ~ two hours in advance.

antemano ▶ **de antemano** loc adv beforehand, in advance.

antena f 1. (RADIO & TV) aerial, antenna; ~ parabólica satellite dish. 2. (ZOOL) antenna.

anteojos mpl desus o Amer (gafas) spectacles.

antepasado, -da m y f ancestor.

antepenúltimo, -ma adj, m y f last but two.

anteponer vt: ~ algo a algo to put sthg before sthg.

anterior adj 1. (previo): ~ (a) previous (to). 2. (delantero) front (antes de sust).

anterioridad f: con ~ beforehand; con ~ a before, prior to.

anteriormente adv previously.

antes adv 1. (gen) before; no importa si venís ~ it doesn't matter if you come earlier; ya no nado como ~ I can't swim as I used to; lo ~ posible as soon as possible. 2. (primero) first; esta señora está ~ this lady is first. 3. (expresa preferencia):

~ ... **que** rather ... than; **prefiero la sierra ~ que el mar** I like the mountains better than the sea; **iría a la cárcel ~ que mentir** I'd rather go to prison than lie. ▶ **antes de** *loc prep* before; ~ **de hacer algo** before doing sthg. ▶ **antes (de) que** *loc conj* before; ~ **(de) que llegarais** before you arrived.

antesala *f* anteroom; **estar en la ~ de** *fig* to be on the verge of.

antiadherente *adj* nonstick.

antiaéreo, -a *adj* anti-aircraft.

antibala, antibalas *adj inv* bullet-proof.

antibiótico, -ca *adj* antibiotic. ▶ **antibiótico** *m* antibiotic.

anticiclón *m* anticyclone.

anticipación *f* earliness; **con ~ in** advance; **con un mes de ~** a month in advance; **con ~ a** prior to.

anticipado, -da *adj* (*elecciones*) early; (*pago*) advance; **por ~** in advance.

anticipar *vt* 1. (*prever*) to anticipate. 2. (*adelantar*) to bring forward. 3. (*pago*) to pay in advance. ▶ **anticiparse** *vpr* 1. (*suceder antes*) to arrive early; **se anticipó a su tiempo** he was ahead of his time. 2. (*adelantarse*): **~se a alguien** to beat sb to it.

anticipo *m* (*de dinero*) advance.

anticonceptivo, -va *adj* contraceptive. ▶ **anticonceptivo** *m* contraceptive.

anticongelante *adj, m y f & m* antifreeze.

anticonstitucional *adj* unconstitutional.

anticorrosivo, -va *adj* anticorrosive.

anticuado, -da *adj* old-fashioned.

anticuario, -ria *m y f* (*comerciante*) antique dealer; (*experto*) antiquarian.

anticuerpo *m* antibody.

antidepresivo, -va *adj* antidepressant. ▶ **antidepresivo** *m* antidepressant (drug).

antidisturbios *mpl* (*policía*) riot police.

antidopaje *m* doping tests (*pl*).

antidoping [anti'ðopin] *adj* doping (*antes de sust*).

antidoto *m* antidote.

antier *adv* Amer *fam* the day before yesterday.

antiestético, -ca *adj* unsightly.

antifaz *m* mask.

antigás *adj inv* gas (*antes de sust*).

antigualla *f* despec (*cosa*) museum piece; (*persona*) old fogey, old fossil.

antiguamente *adv* (*hace mucho*) long ago; (*previamente*) formerly.

antigubernamental *adj* anti-government.

antigüedad *f* 1. (*gen*) antiquity. 2. (*veteranía*) seniority. ▶ **antigüedades** *fpl* (*objetos*) antiques.

antiguo, -gua *adj* 1. (*viejo*) old; (*inmemorial*) ancient. 2. (*anterior, previo*) former.

antihéroe *m* antihero.

antihigiénico, -ca *adj* unhygienic.

antihistamínico *m* antihistamine.

antiinflamatorio *m* anti-inflammatory drug.

antílope *m* antelope.

antinatural *adj* unnatural.

antiniebla *adj inv* → **faro**.

antioxidante *m* rustproofing agent.

antipatía *f* dislike, antipathy; **tener ~ a alguien** to dislike sb.

antipático, -ca *adj* unpleasant, disagreeable.

antípodas *fpl*: **las ~** the Antipodes.

antiquísimo, -ma *adj* ancient.

antirreglamentario, -ria *adj* (DEP) illegal, against the rules.

antirrobo *m* (*en coche*) antitheft device; (*en edificio*) burglar alarm.

antisemita *adj* anti-Semitic.

antiséptico, -ca *adj* antiseptic. ▶ **antiséptico** *m* antiseptic.

antiterrorista *adj* anti-terrorist.

antítesis *f inv* antithesis.

antitetánico, -ca *adj* anti-tetanus (*antes de sust*).

antivirus *m inv* (INFORM) antivirus system.

antojarse *vpr* 1. (*capricho*): **se le antojaron esos zapatos** he fancied those shoes; **se le ha antojado ir al cine** he felt like going to the cinema; **cuando se me antoje** when I feel like it. 2. (*posibilidad*): **se me antoja que ...** I have a feeling that ...

antojitos *mpl* Amer snacks, tapas.

antojo *m* 1. (*capricho*) whim; (*de embarazada*) craving; **a mi/tu** *etc* ~ my/your *etc* (own) way. 2. (*lunar*) birthmark.

antología *f* anthology.

antónimo *m* antonym.

antonomasia *f*: **por ~** par excellence.

antorcha *f* torch.

antracita *f* anthracite.

antro *m* despec dive, dump.

antropófago, -ga *m y f* cannibal.

antropología *f* anthropology.

anual *adj* annual.

anualidad *f* annuity, yearly payment.

anuario *m* yearbook.

anudar *vt* to knot, to tie in a knot.

anulación *f* (*cancelación*) cancellation; (*de ley*) repeal; (*de matrimonio, contrato*) annulment.

anular¹ *m* → **dedo**.

anular² *vt* 1. (*cancelar - gen*) to cancel; (*- ley*) to repeal; (*- matrimonio, contrato*) to annul. 2. (DEP *- gol*) to disallow; (*- resultado*) to declare void.

anunciación *f* announcement. ▶ **Anunciación** *f* (RELIG) Annunciation.

anunciador, -ra *m y f* (*de publicidad*) advertiser.

anunciante *m y f* advertiser.

anunciar *vt* 1. (*notificar*) to announce. 2. (*hacer publicidad de*) to advertise. 3. (*presagiar*) to herald. ▶ **anunciarse** *vpr*: ~**se en** to advertise in, to put an advert in.

anuncio *m* 1. (*notificación*) announcement; (*cartel, aviso*) notice; (*póster*) poster. 2. ~ (**publicitario**) advertisement, advert; ~**s por palabras** classified adverts. 3. (*presagio*) sign, herald.

anverso *m* (*de moneda*) head, obverse; (*de hoja*) front.

anzuelo *m* (*para pescar*) (fish) hook.

añadido, -da *adj*: ~ (**a**) added (to).

añadidura *f* addition; **por ~** in addition, what is more.

añadir *vt* to add.

añejo, -ja *adj* 1. (*vino, licor*) mature; (*tocino*) cured. 2. (*costumbre*) age-old.

añicos *mpl*: **hacer o hacerse ~** to shatter.

añil *adj, m y f & m* (*color*) indigo.

año *m* year; **en el ~ 1939** in 1939; **los ~s 30** the thirties; ~ **académico/escolar/fiscal** academic/school/tax year; **bisiesto/solar** leap/solar year; ~ **nuevo** New Year; **¡Feliz Año Nuevo!** Happy New Year! ▶ **años** *mpl* (*edad*) age (*sg*); **¿cuántos ~s tienes? – tengo 17 ~s** how old are you? – I'm 17 (years old); **cumplir ~s** to have one's birthday; **cumplo ~s el 25** it's my birthday on the 25th.

añoranza *f*: ~ (**de**) (*gen*) nostalgia (for); (*hogar, patria*) homesickness (for).

añorar *vt* to miss.

apabullar *vt* to overwhelm.

apacentar *vt* to graze.

apacible *adj* (*gen*) mild, gentle; (*lugar, ambiente*) pleasant.

apaciguar *vt* 1. (*tranquilizar*) to calm down. 2. (*aplacar - dolor etc*) to soothe. ▶ **apaciguarse** *vpr* 1. (*tranquilizarse*) to

calm down. 2. (*aplacarse - dolor etc*) to abate.

apadrinar *vt* 1. (*niño*) to act as a godparent to. 2. (*artista*) to sponsor.

apagado, -da *adj* 1. (*luz, fuego*) out; (*aparato*) off. 2. (*color, persona*) subdued. 3. (*sonido*) muffled; (*voz*) quiet.

apagar *vt* 1. (*extinguir - fuego*) to put out; (*- luz*) to put off; (*- vela*) to extinguish. 2. (*desconectar*) to turn o switch off. 3. (*aplacar - sed*) to quench. 4. (*rebajar - sonido*) to muffle. ▶ **apagarse** *vpr* (*extinguirse - fuego, vela, luz*) to go out; (*- dolor, ilusión, rencor*) to die down; (*- sonido*) to die away.

apagón *m* power cut.

apaisado, -da *adj* oblong.

apalabrar *vt* (*concertar*) to make a verbal agreement regarding; (*contratar*) to engage on the basis of a verbal agreement.

apalancar *vt* (*para abrir*) to lever open; (*para mover*) to lever.

apalear *vt* to beat up.

apañado, -da *adj fam* (*hábil, mañoso*) clever, resourceful.

apañar *vt fam* 1. (*reparar*) to mend. 2. (*amañar*) to fix, to arrange. ▶ **apañarse** *vpr fam* to cope, to manage; **apañárselas** (**para hacer algo**) to manage (to do sthg).

apaño *m fam* 1. (*reparación*) patch. 2. (*chanchullo*) fix, shady deal. 3. (*acuerdo*) compromise.

aparador *m* (*mueble*) sideboard.

aparato *m* 1. (*máquina*) machine; (*de laboratorio*) apparatus (U); (*electrodoméstico*) appliance. 2. (*dispositivo*) device. 3. (*teléfono*): **¿quién está al ~?** who's speaking? 4. (MED *- prótesis*) aid; (*- para dientes*) brace. 5. (ANAT) system. 6. (POLÍT) machinery. 7. (*ostentación*) pomp, ostentation.

aparatoso, -sa *adj* 1. (*ostentoso*) ostentatious. 2. (*espectacular*) spectacular.

aparcamiento *m* 1. (*acción*) parking. 2. (*parking*) car park Br, parking lot Am; (*hueco*) parking place.

aparcar ◆ *vt* (*estacionar*) to park. ◆ *vi* (*estacionar*) to park.

aparcero, -ra *m y f* sharecropper.

aparear *vt* (*animales*) to mate. ▶ **aparearse** *vpr* (*animales*) to mate.

aparecer *vi* 1. (*gen*) to appear. 2. (*acudir*): ~ **por** (**un lugar**) to turn up at (a place). 3. (*ser encontrado*) to turn up.

aparejado, -da *adj*: **llevar ~** (*acarrear*) to entail.

aparejador, -ra *m y f* quantity surveyor.

aparejo *m* 1. (*de caballerías*) harness. 2. (MEC) block and tackle. 3. (NÁUT) rigging. ▶ **aparejos** *mpl* equipment (U); (*de pesca*) tackle (U).

aparentar ◆ *vt* 1. (*fingir*) to feign. 2. (*edad*) to look. ◆ *vi* (*presumir*) to show off.

aparente *adj* (*falso, supuesto*) apparent.

aparición *f* 1. (*gen*) appearance. 2. (*de ser sobrenatural*) apparition.

apariencia *f* (*aspecto*) appearance; **guardar las ~s** to keep up appearances; **las ~s engañan** appearances can be deceptive.

apartado, -da *adj* 1. (*separado*): **~ de** away from. 2. (*alejado*) remote. ▶ **apartado** *m* (*párrafo*) paragraph; (*sección*) section. ▶ **apartado de correos** *m* PO Box.

apartamento *m* apartment.

apartar *vt* 1. (*alejar*) to move away; (*quitar*) to remove. 2. (*separar*) to separate. 3. (*escoger*) to take, to select. ▶ **apartarse** *vpr* 1. (*hacerse a un lado*) to move to one side. 2. (*separarse*) to separate; **~se de** (*gen*) to move away from; (*tema*) to get away from; (*mundo, sociedad*) to cut o.s. off from.

aparte ◆ *adv* 1. (*en otro lugar, a un lado*) aside, to one side; **bromas ~** joking apart. 2. (*además*) besides; **~ de fea ...** besides being ugly ... 3. (*por separado*) separately. ◆ *m* 1. (*párrafo*) new paragraph. 2. (TEATR) aside. ▶ **aparte de** *loc prep* (*excepto*) apart from, except from.

apasionado, -da ◆ *adj* passionate. ◆ *m y f* lover, enthusiast.

apasionante *adj* fascinating.

apasionar *vt* to fascinate; **le apasiona la música** he's mad about music. ▶ **apasionarse** *vpr* to get excited.

apatía *f* apathy.

apático, -ca *adj* apathetic.

apátrida *adj* stateless.

apdo. *abrev de* **apartado**.

apeadero *m* (*de tren*) halt.

apear *vt* (*bajar*) to take down. ▶ **apearse** *vpr* (*bajarse*): **~se de** (*tren*) to alight (from), to get off; (*coche*) to get out (of); (*caballo*) to dismount (from).

apechugar *vi*: **~ con** to put up with, to live with.

apedrear *vt* (*persona*) to stone; (*cosa*) to throw stones at.

apegarse *vpr*: **~ a** to become fond of o attached to.

apego *m* fondness, attachment; **tener/tomar ~ a** to be/become fond of.

apelación *f* appeal.

apelar *vi* 1. (DER) to (lodge an) appeal; **~ ante/contra** to appeal to/against. 2. (*recurrir*): **~ a** (*persona*) to go to; (*sentido común, bondad*) to appeal to; (*violencia*) to resort to.

apelativo *m* name.

apellidarse *vpr*: **se apellida Suárez** her surname is Suárez.

apellido *m* surname.

apelmazar *vt* 1. (*jersey*) to shrink. 2. (*arroz, bizcocho*) to make stodgy. ▶ **apelmazarse** *vpr* 1. (*jersey*) to shrink. 2. (*arroz, bizcocho*) to go stodgy.

apelotonar *vt* to bundle up. ▶ **apelotonarse** *vpr* (*gente*) to crowd together.

apenado, -da *adj* Amer ashamed.

apenar *vt* to sadden.

apenas *adv* 1. (*casi no*) scarcely, hardly; **~ me puedo mover** I can hardly move. 2. (*tan sólo*) only; **~ hace dos minutos** only two minutes ago. 3. (*tan pronto como*) as soon as; **~ llegó, sonó el teléfono** no sooner had he arrived than the phone rang.

apéndice *m* appendix.

apendicitis *f inv* appendicitis.

apercibir *vt* (*amonestar*) to reprimand. ▶ **apercibirse de** *vpr* to notice.

aperitivo *m* (*bebida*) aperitif; (*comida*) appetizer.

APERITIVO

Before their main midday meal, Spanish people often go to a bar, where they sit outside and have a glass of vermouth, wine or some other drink and some 'tapas', to whet their appetite. It is also common for them to have an aperitif at home, whilst finishing the cooking.

apero *m* (*gen pl*) tool; **~s de labranza** farming implements.

apertura *f* 1. (*gen*) opening; (*de año académico, temporada*) start. 2. (POLÍT) (*liberalización*) liberalization (*especially that introduced in Spain by the Franco regime after 1970*).

aperturista *adj, m y f* progressive.

apesadumbrar *vt* to weigh down. ▶ **apesadumbrarse** *vpr* to be weighed down.

apestar *vi*: **~ (a)** to stink (of).

apetecer vi: ¿**te apetece un café?** do you fancy a coffee?; **me apetece salir** I feel like going out.

apetecible adj (comida) appetizing, tempting; (vacaciones etc) desirable.

apetito m appetite; **abrir el ~** to whet one's appetite; **perder el ~** to lose one's appetite; **tener ~** to be hungry.

apetitoso, -sa adj (comida) appetizing.

apiadar vt to earn the pity of. ▶ **apiadarse** vpr to show compassion; **~se de** to take pity on.

ápice m 1. (pizca) iota; **no ceder un ~** not to budge an inch. 2. (punto culminante) peak, height.

apicultura f beekeeping.

apilar vt to pile up. ▶ **apilarse** vpr to pile up.

apiñar vt to pack o cram together. ▶ **apiñarse** vpr to crowd together; (para protegerse, por miedo) to huddle together.

apio m celery.

apisonadora f steamroller.

aplacar vt to placate; (hambre) to satisfy; (sed) to quench. ▶ **aplacarse** vpr to calm down; (dolor) to abate.

aplanar vt to level.

aplastante adj fig (apabullante) overwhelming, devastating.

aplastar vt 1. (por el peso) to flatten. 2. (derrotar) to crush.

aplatanar vt fam to make listless.

aplaudir vt & vi to applaud.

aplauso m 1. (ovación) round of applause; **~s** applause (U). 2. fig (alabanza) applause.

aplazamiento m postponement.

aplazar vt to postpone.

aplicación f (gen & INFORM) application.

aplicado, -da adj (estudioso) diligent.

aplicar vt (gen) to apply; (nombre, calificativo) to give. ▶ **aplicarse** vpr (esmerarse): **~se (en algo)** to apply o.s. (to sthg).

aplique m wall lamp.

aplomo m composure; **perder el ~** to lose one's composure.

apocado, -da adj timid.

apocalipsis m o f inv calamity. ▶ **Apocalipsis** m o f Apocalypse.

apocarse vpr (intimidarse) to be frightened o scared; (humillarse) to humble o.s.

apodar vt to nickname.

apoderado, -da m y f 1. (represen-

tante) (official) representative. 2. (TAUROM) agent, manager.

apoderar vt (gen) to authorize; (DER) to grant power of attorney to. ▶ **apoderarse de** vpr 1. (adueñarse de) to seize. 2. fig (dominar) to take hold of, to grip.

apodo m nickname.

apogeo m fig height, apogee; **estar en (pleno) ~** to be at its height.

apolillar vt to eat holes in. ▶ **apolillarse** vpr to get moth-eaten.

apolítico, -ca adj apolitical.

apología f apology, eulogy.

apoltronarse vpr 1. (apalancarse): **~ (en)** to become lazy o idle (in). 2. (acomodarse): **~ en** to lounge in.

apoplejía f apoplexy.

apoquinar vt & vi fam to fork out.

aporrear vt to bang.

aportación f (contribución) contribution.

aportar vt 1. (proporcionar) to provide. 2. (contribuir con) to contribute.

aposentar vt to put up, to lodge. ▶ **aposentarse** vpr to take up lodgings.

aposento m 1. (habitación) room. 2. (alojamiento) lodgings (pl).

apósito m dressing.

aposta, apostas adv on purpose.

apostar ◆ vt 1. (jugarse) to bet. 2. (emplazar) to post. ◆ vi: **~ (por)** to bet (on). ▶ **apostarse** vpr (jugarse) to bet; **~se algo con alguien** to bet sb sthg.

apostas = aposta.

apostilla f note.

apóstol m lit & fig apostle.

apóstrofo m (GRAM) apostrophe.

apoteósico, -ca adj tremendous.

apoyar vt 1. (inclinar) to lean, to rest. 2. fig (basar, respaldar) to support. ▶ **apoyarse** vpr 1. (sostenerse): **~se en** to lean on. 2. fig (basarse): **~se en** (suj: tesis, conclusiones) to be based on, to rest on; (suj: persona) to base one's arguments on. 3. (respaldarse) to support one another.

apoyo m lit & fig support.

apreciable adj 1. (perceptible) appreciable. 2. fig (estimable) worthy.

apreciación f (consideración) appreciation; (estimación) evaluation.

apreciar vt 1. (valorar) to appreciate; (sopesar) to appraise, to evaluate. 2. (sentir afecto por) to think highly of. 3. (percibir) to tell, to make out.

aprecio m esteem.

aprehender vt (coger - persona) to apprehend; (- alijo, mercancía) to seize.
aprehensión f (de persona) arrest, capture; (de alijo, mercancía) seizure.
apremiante adj pressing, urgent.
apremiar ◆ vt (meter prisa): ~ a alguien para que haga algo to urge sb to do sthg. ◆ vi (ser urgente) to be pressing.
apremio m (urgencia) urgency.
aprender ◆ vt 1. (estudiar) to learn. 2. (memorizar) to memorize. ◆ vi: ~ (a hacer algo) to learn (to do sthg).
aprendiz, -za m y f 1. (ayudante) apprentice, trainee. 2. (novato) beginner.
aprendizaje m 1. (acción) learning. 2. (tiempo, situación) apprenticeship.
aprensión f: ~ (por) (miedo) apprehension (about); (escrúpulo) squeamishness (about).
aprensivo, -va adj 1. (miedoso) apprehensive. 2. (hipocondríaco) hypochondriac.
apresar vt (suj: animal) to catch; (suj: persona) to capture.
aprestar vt 1. (preparar) to prepare, to get ready. 2. (tela) to size.
▶ **aprestarse a** vpr: ~se a hacer algo to get ready to do sthg.
apresto m size.
apresurado, -da adj hasty, hurried.
apresurar vt to hurry along, to speed up; ~ a alguien para que haga algo to try to make sb do sthg more quickly.
▶ **apresurarse** vpr to hurry.
apretado, -da adj 1. (gen) tight; (triunfo) narrow; (esprint) close; (caligrafía) cramped. 2. (apiñado) packed.
apretar ◆ vt 1. (oprimir - botón, tecla) to press; (- gatillo) to pull; (- nudo, tuerca, cinturón) to tighten; el zapato me aprieta my shoe is pinching. 2. (estrechar) to squeeze; (abrazar) to hug. 3. (comprimir - ropa, objetos) to pack tight. 4. (juntar - dientes) to grit; (- labios) to press together. ◆ vi (calor, lluvia) to intensify.
▶ **apretarse** vpr (agolparse) to crowd together; (acercarse) to squeeze up.
apretón m (estrechamiento) squeeze; ~ de manos handshake.
apretujar vt 1. (gen) to squash. 2. (hacer una bola con) to screw up. ▶ **apretujarse** vpr (en banco, autobús) to squeeze together; (por frío) to huddle up.
apretujón m fam (abrazo) bearhug.
aprieto m fig fix, difficult situation; poner en un ~ a alguien to put sb in a difficult position; verse o estar en un ~ to be in a fix.
aprisa adv quickly.
aprisionar vt 1. (encarcelar) to imprison. 2. (inmovilizar - atando, con camisa de fuerza) to strap down; (- suj: viga etc) to trap.
aprobación f approval.
aprobado, -da adj (aceptado) approved. ▶ **aprobado** m (EDUC) pass.
aprobar vt 1. (proyecto, moción, medida) to approve; (ley) to pass. 2. (comportamiento etc) to approve of. 3. (examen, asignatura) to pass.
apropiación f (robo) theft.
apropiado, -da adj suitable, appropriate.
apropiar vt: ~ (a) to adapt (to).
▶ **apropiarse de** vpr lit & fig to steal.
aprovechable adj usable.
aprovechado, -da adj 1. (caradura): es muy ~ he's always sponging off other people. 2. (bien empleado - tiempo) well-spent; (- espacio) well-planned.
aprovechamiento m (utilización) use.
aprovechar ◆ vt 1. (gen) to make the most of; (oferta, ocasión) to take advantage of; (conocimientos, experiencia) to use, to make use of; (recursos, tierra) to exploit. 2. (lo inservible) to put to good use. ◆ vi (ser provechoso) to be beneficial; ¡que aproveche! enjoy your meal!
▶ **aprovecharse** vpr: ~se (de) to take advantage (of).
aprovisionamiento m supplying.
aproximación f 1. (acercamiento) approach. 2. (en cálculo) approximation.
aproximadamente adv approximately.
aproximado, -da adj approximate.
aproximar vt to move closer.
▶ **aproximarse** vpr to come closer.
aptitud f ability, aptitude; tener ~ para algo to have an aptitude for sthg.
apto, -ta adj 1. (adecuado, conveniente): ~ (para) suitable (for). 2. (capacitado - intelectualmente) capable, able; (- físicamente) fit. 3. (CIN): ~/no ~ para menores suitable/unsuitable for children.
apuesta f bet.
apuesto, -ta adj dashing.
apuntador, -ra m y f prompter.
apuntalar vt lit & fig to underpin.
apuntar vt 1. (anotar) to note down; ~ a alguien (en lista) to put sb down. 2. (dirigir - dedo) to point; (- arma) to aim; ~ alguien (con el dedo) to point at sb;

(con un arma) to aim at sb. **3.** (TEATR) to prompt. **4.** fig (indicar) to point out. ▶ **apuntarse** vpr **1.** (en lista) to put one's name down; (en curso) to enrol. **2.** (participar) **~se (a hacer algo)** to join in (doing sthg).

apunte m (nota) note. ▶ **apuntes** mpl (EDUC) notes.

apuñalar vt to stab.

apurado, -da adj **1.** (necesitado) in need; **~ de** short of. **2.** (avergonzado) embarrassed. **3.** (difícil) awkward.

apurar vt **1.** (agotar) to finish off; (existencias, la paciencia) to exhaust. **2.** (meter prisa) to hurry. **3.** (preocupar) to trouble. **4.** (avergonzar) to embarrass. ▶ **apurarse** vpr **1.** (preocuparse): **~se (por)** to worry (about). **2.** (darse prisa) to hurry.

apuro m **1.** (dificultad) fix; **estar en ~s** to be in a tight spot. **2.** (penuria) hardship (U). **3.** (vergüenza) embarrassment; **me da ~ (decírselo)** I'm embarrassed (to tell her).

aquejado, -da adj: **~ de** suffering from.

aquejar vt to afflict.

aquel, aquella (mpl **aquellos**, fpl **aquellas**) adj demos that, (pl) those.

aquél, aquélla (mpl **aquéllos**, fpl **aquéllas**) pron demos **1.** (ése) that (one), (pl) those (ones); **este cuadro me gusta pero ~ del fondo no** I like this picture, but I don't like that one at the back; **~ fue mi último día en Londres** that was my last day in London. **2.** (nombrado antes) the former. **3.** (con oraciones relativas) whoever, anyone who; **~ que quiera hablar que levante la mano** whoever wishes o anyone wishing to speak should raise their hand; **aquéllos que ...** those who ...

aquella → **aquel**.

aquélla → **aquél**.

aquello pron demos (neutro) that; **~ de su mujer es una mentira** all that about his wife is a lie.

aquellos, aquellas → **aquel**.

aquéllos, aquéllas → **aquél**.

aquí adv **1.** (gen) here; **¡~ está!** here it is!, it's here! **~ abajo/arriba** down/up here; **~ dentro/fuera** in/out here; **~ mismo** right here; **por ~** over here. **2.** (ahora) now; **de ~ a mañana** between now and tomorrow; **de ~ a poco** shortly, soon; **de ~ a un mes** a month from now, in a month.

ara f (el) culto (altar) altar. ▶ **en aras de** loc prep culto for the sake of.

árabe ◆ adj Arab, Arabian. ◆ m y f (persona) Arab. ◆ m (lengua) Arabic.

Arabia Saudí, Arabia Saudita Saudi Arabia.

arábigo, -ga adj **1.** (de Arabia) Arab, Arabian. **2.** (numeración) Arabic.

arado m plough.

arancel m tariff.

arándano m bilberry.

arandela f (TECN) washer.

araña f **1.** (animal) spider. **2.** (lámpara) chandelier.

arañar vt (gen) to scratch.

arañazo m scratch.

arar vt to plough.

arbitraje m **1.** (DEP - en fútbol etc) refereeing; (- en tenis, críquet) umpiring. **2.** (DER) arbitration.

arbitrar ◆ vt **1.** (DEP - en fútbol etc) to referee; (- en tenis, críquet) to umpire. **2.** (DER) to arbitrate. ◆ vi **1.** (DEP - en fútbol etc) to referee; (- en tenis, críquet) to umpire. **2.** (DER) to arbitrate.

arbitrariedad f (cualidad) arbitrariness.

arbitrario, -ria adj arbitrary.

arbitrio m (decisión) judgment.

árbitro m **1.** (DEP - en fútbol etc) referee; (- en tenis, críquet) umpire. **2.** (DER) arbitrator.

árbol m **1.** (BOT) tree. **2.** (TECN) shaft; **~ de levas** camshaft. **3.** (NÁUT) mast. ▶ **árbol genealógico** m family tree.

arboleda f wood.

arbusto m bush, shrub.

arca f (el) (arcón) chest. ▶ **arcas** fpl coffers; **~s públicas** Treasury (sg).

arcada f **1.** (gen pl) (de estómago) retching (U); **me dieron ~s** I retched. **2.** (ARQUIT - arcos) arcade; (- de puente) arch.

arcaico, -ca adj archaic.

arce m maple.

arcén m (de autopista) hard shoulder; (de carretera) verge.

archiconocido, -da adj fam very well-known.

archiduque, -quesa m y f archduke (f archduchess).

archipiélago m archipelago.

archivador, -ra m y f archivist. ▶ **archivador** m filing cabinet.

archivar vt (guardar - documento, fichero etc) to file.

archivo m **1.** (lugar) archive; (documentos) archives (pl); **imágenes de ~** (TV) library pictures. **2.** (informe, ficha) file. **3.** (INFORM) file.

arcilla f clay.

arco m 1. (GEOM) arc. 2. (ARQUIT) arch; ~ **de herradura** horseshoe arch; ~ **triunfal** o **de triunfo** triumphal arch. 3. (DEP, MIL & MÚS) bow. ▶ **arco iris** m rainbow.

arcón m large chest.

arder vi to burn; (sin llama) to smoulder; ~ **de** fig to burn with; **está que arde** (persona) he's fuming; (reunión) it's getting pretty heated.

ardid m ruse, trick.

ardiente adj (gen) burning; (líquido) scalding; (admirador, defensor) ardent.

ardilla f squirrel.

ardor m 1. (quemazón) burning (sensation); ~ **de estómago** heartburn. 2. fig (entusiasmo) fervour.

arduo, -dua adj arduous.

área f (el) 1. (gen) area; ~ **metropolitana/de servicio** metropolitan/service area. 2. (DEP): ~ **(de castigo** o **penalti)** (penalty) area.

arena f 1. (de playa etc) sand; ~s **movedizas** quicksand. 2. (para luchar) arena. 3. (TAUROM) bullring.

arenal m sandy ground (U).

arenga f harangue.

arenilla f (polvo) dust.

arenoso, -sa adj sandy.

arenque m herring.

arete m earring.

argamasa f mortar.

Argel Algiers.

Argelia Algeria.

Argentina: (la) ~ Argentina.

argentino, -na adj, m y f Argentinian.

argolla f 1. (aro) (large) ring. 2. Amer (alianza) wedding ring.

argot m 1. (popular) slang. 2. (técnico) jargon.

argucia f sophism.

argüir ◆ vt culto 1. (argumentar) to argue. 2. (demostrar) to prove. ◆ vi (argumentar) to argue.

argumentación f line of argument.

argumentar vt 1. (teoría, opinión) to argue. 2. (razones, excusas) to allege.

argumento m 1. (razonamiento) argument. 2. (trama) plot.

aria f (MÚS) aria.

aridez f (gen) dryness; (de zona, clima) aridity.

árido, -da adj (gen) dry; (zona, clima) arid. ▶ **áridos** mpl dry goods.

Aries ◆ m (zodiaco) Aries. ◆ m y f (persona) Aries.

ariete m (HIST & MIL) battering ram.

ario, -ria adj, m y f Aryan.

arisco, -ca adj surly.

arista f edge.

aristocracia f aristocracy.

aristócrata m y f aristocrat.

aritmético, -ca adj arithmetic. ▶ **aritmética** f arithmetic.

arma f (el) 1. (instrumento) arm, weapon; ~ **blanca** blade, weapon with a sharp blade; ~ **de fuego** firearm; ~ **homicida** murder weapon. 2. fig (medio) weapon.

armada → **armado.**

armadillo m armadillo.

armado, -da adj 1. (con armas) armed. 2. (con armazón) reinforced. ▶ **armada** f (marina) navy; (escuadra) fleet.

armador, -ra m y f shipowner.

armadura f 1. (de barco, tejado) framework; (de gafas) frame. 2. (de guerrero) armour.

armamentista, armamentístico, -ca adj arms (antes de sust).

armamento m (armas) arms (pl).

armar vt 1. (montar - mueble etc) to assemble; (- tienda) to pitch. 2. (ejército, personas) to arm. 3. fam fig (provocar) to cause; ~**la** fam to cause trouble. ▶ **armarse** vpr 1. (con armas) to arm o.s. 2. (prepararse): ~**se de** (valor, paciencia) to summon up. 3. loc: **se armó la gorda** o **la de San Quintín** o **la de Dios es Cristo** fam all hell broke loose.

armario m (para objetos) cupboard; (para ropa) wardrobe; ~ **empotrado** fitted cupboard/wardrobe.

armatoste m (mueble, objeto) unwieldy object; (máquina) contraption.

armazón f (gen) framework, frame; (de avión, coche) chassis; (de edificio) skeleton.

armería f 1. (museo) military o war museum. 2. (depósito) armoury. 3. (tienda) gunsmith's (shop).

armiño m (piel) ermine; (animal) stoat.

armisticio m armistice.

armonía f harmony.

armónico, -ca adj harmonic. ▶ **armónica** f harmonica.

armonioso, -sa adj harmonious.

armonizar ◆ vt 1. (concordar) to match. 2. (MÚS) to harmonize. ◆ vi (concordar): ~ **con** to match.

arnés m armour. ▶ **arneses** mpl (de animales) harness (U).

aro m 1. (círculo) hoop; (TECN) ring; **los** ~s **olímpicos** the Olympic rings. 2. Amer (pendiente) earring.

aroma m aroma; (de vino) bouquet; (CULIN) flavouring.

aromático, -ca adj aromatic.

arpa f (el) harp.

arpía f fig (mujer) old hag.

arpillera f sackcloth, hessian.

arpón m harpoon.

arquear vt (gen) to bend; (cejas, espalda, lomo) to arch. ▶ **arquearse** vpr to bend.

arqueología f archeology.

arqueológico, -ca adj archaeological.

arqueólogo, -ga m y f archaeologist.

arquero m (DEP & MIL) archer.

arquetipo m archetype.

arquitecto, -ta m y f architect.

arquitectónico, -ca adj architectural.

arquitectura f lit & fig architecture.

arrabal m (barrio pobre) slum (on city outskirts); (barrio periférico) outlying district.

arrabalero, -ra adj 1. (periférico) outlying. 2. (barriobajero) rough, coarse.

arracimarse vpr to cluster together.

arraigado, -da adj (costumbre, idea) deeply rooted; (persona) established.

arraigar vi lit & fig to take root. ▶ **arraigarse** vpr (establecerse) to settle down.

arraigo m roots (pl); **tener mucho ~** to be deeply rooted.

arrancar ♦ vt 1. (desarraigar - árbol) to uproot; (- malas hierbas, flor) to pull up. 2. (quitar, separar) to tear o rip off; (cable, página, pelo) to tear out; (cartel, cortinas) to tear down; (muela) to pull out; (ojos) to gouge out. 3. (arrebatar): **~ algo a alguien** to grab o snatch sthg from sb. 4. (AUTOM & TECN) to start; (INFORM) to start up. 5. fig (obtener): **~ algo a alguien** (confesión, promesa, secreto) to extract sthg from sb; (sonrisa, dinero, ovación) to get sthg out of sb; (suspiro, carcajada) to bring sthg from sb. ♦ vi 1. (partir) to set off. 2. (suj: máquina, coche) to start. 3. (provenir): **~ de** to stem from.

arranque m 1. (comienzo) start. 2. (AUTOM) starter motor. 3. fig (arrebato) fit.

arrasar vt to destroy, to devastate.

arrastrar ♦ vt 1. (gen) to drag o pull along; (pies) to drag; (carro, vagón) to pull; (suj: corriente, aire) to carry away. 2. fig (convencer) to win over; **~ a alguien a algo/a hacer algo** to lead sb into sthg/ to do sthg; **dejarse ~ por algo/alguien** to allow o.s. to be swayed by sthg/sb. 3. fig (producir) to bring. ♦ vi (rozar el suelo)

to drag (along) the ground. ▶ **arrastrarse** vpr to crawl; fig to grovel.

arrastre m 1. (acarreo) dragging. 2. (pesca) trawling. 3. loc: **estar para el ~** to have had it, to be done for.

arre interj: **¡~!** gee up!

arrear vt 1. (azuzar) to gee up. 2. fam (propinar) to give.

arrebatado, -da adj 1. (impetuoso) impulsive, impetuous. 2. (ruborizado) flushed. 3. (iracundo) enraged.

arrebatar vt 1. (arrancar): **~ algo a alguien** to snatch sthg from sb. 2. fig (cautivar) to captivate. ▶ **arrebatarse** vpr (enfurecerse) to get furious.

arrebato m 1. (arranque) fit, outburst; **un ~ de amor** a crush. 2. (furia) rage.

arrebujar vt (amontonar) to bundle (up). ▶ **arrebujarse** vpr (arroparse) to wrap o.s. up.

arreciar vi 1. (temporal etc) to get worse. 2. fig (críticas etc) to intensify.

arrecife m reef.

arreglado, -da adj 1. (reparado) fixed; (ropa) mended. 2. (ordenado) tidy. 3. (bien vestido) smart. 4. (solucionado) sorted out. 5. fig (precio) reasonable.

arreglar vt 1. (reparar) to fix, to repair; (ropa) to mend. 2. (ordenar) to tidy (up). 3. (solucionar) to sort out. 4. (MÚS) to arrange. 5. (acicalar) to smarten up; (cabello) to do. ▶ **arreglarse** vpr 1. (apañarse): **~se (con algo)** to make do (with sthg); **arreglárselas (para hacer algo)** to manage (to do sthg). 2. (acicalarse) to smarten up.

arreglo m 1. (reparación) mending, repair; (de ropa) mending. 2. (solución) settlement. 3. (MÚS) (musical) arrangement. 4. (acuerdo) agreement; **llegar a un ~** to reach agreement.

arrellanarse vpr to settle back.

arremangar, remangar vt to roll up. ▶ **arremangarse** vpr to roll up one's sleeves.

arremeter ▶ **arremeter contra** vi to attack.

arremetida f attack.

arremolinarse vpr 1. fig (personas): **~ alrededor de** to crowd around. 2. (agua, hojas) to swirl (about).

arrendamiento, arriendo m 1. (acción) renting, leasing. 2. (precio) rent, lease.

arrendar vt 1. (dar en arriendo) to let, to lease. 2. (tomar en arriendo) to rent, to lease.

arrendatario, -ria m y f leaseholder, tenant.

arreos *mpl* harness (U).

arrepentido, -da ◆ *adj* repentant. ◆ *m y f* (POLÍT) person who renounces terrorist activities.

arrepentimiento *m* regret, repentance.

arrepentirse *vpr* to repent; ~ de algo/ de haber hecho algo to regret sthg/having done sthg.

arrestar *vt* to arrest.

arresto *m* (*detención*) arrest.

arriar *vt* to lower.

arriba ◆ *adv* 1. (*posición - gen*) above; (- en edificio) upstairs; **vive (en el piso de)** ~ she lives upstairs; **está aquí/allí** ~ it's up here/there; ~ **del todo** right at the top; **más** ~ further up. 2. (*dirección*) up; **ve** ~ (en edificio) go upstairs; **hacia/para** ~ up, upwards; **calle/escaleras** ~ up the street/stairs; **río** ~ upstream. 3. (en un texto) above; **el** ~ **mencionado ...** the above-mentioned ... ◆ *loc*: **de** ~ **abajo** (cosa) from top to bottom; (persona) from head to toe o foot; **mirar a alguien de** ~ **abajo** (con desdén) to look sb up and down. ◆ *prep*: ~ **(de)** Amer (encima de) on top of. ◆ *interj*: **¡~ ...!** up (with) ...!; **¡~ los mineros!** up (with) the miners!; **¡~ las manos!** hands up! ▶ **arriba de** *loc prep* more than. ▶ **de arriba** *loc adj* top; **el estante de** ~ the top shelf.

arribar *vi* to arrive; (NÁUT) to reach port.

arribeño, -ña *m y f* Amer fam highlander.

arribista *adj, m y f* arriviste.

arriendo → **arrendamiento**.

arriesgado, -da *adj* (peligroso) risky.

arriesgar *vt* to risk; (hipótesis) to venture, to suggest. ▶ **arriesgarse** *vpr* to take risks/a risk.

arrimar *vt* (acercar) to move o bring closer; ~ **algo a** (pared, mesa) to move sthg up against. ▶ **arrimarse** *vpr* (acercarse) to come closer o nearer; ~**se a algo** (acercándose) to move closer to sthg; (apoyándose) to lean on sthg.

arrinconar *vt* 1. (apartar) to put in a corner. 2. (abandonar) to discard, to put away. 3. *fig* (persona - dar de lado) to coldshoulder; (- acorralar) to corner.

arrodillarse *vpr* to kneel down; *fig* to go down on one's knees, to grovel.

arrogancia *f* arrogance.

arrogante *adj* arrogant.

arrojar *vt* 1. (lanzar) to throw; (con violencia) to hurl, to fling. 2. (despedir - humo) to send out; (- olor) to give

off; (- lava) to spew out. 3. (echar): ~ **a alguien de** to throw sb out of. 4. (resultado) to produce, to yield. 5. (vomitar) to throw up. ▶ **arrojarse** *vpr* to hurl o.s.

arrojo *m* courage, fearlessness.

arrollador, -ra *adj* overwhelming; (belleza, personalidad) dazzling.

arrollar *vt* 1. (atropellar) to run over. 2. (tirar - suj: agua, viento) to sweep away. 3. (vencer) to crush.

arropar *vt* (con ropa) to wrap up; (en cama) to tuck up. ▶ **arroparse** *vpr* to wrap o.s. up.

arroyo *m* 1. (riachuelo) stream. 2. (de la calle) gutter.

arroz *m* rice; ~ **blanco** boiled rice; ~ **con leche** rice pudding.

arruga *f* 1. (en ropa, papel) crease. 2. (en piel) wrinkle, line.

arrugar *vt* 1. (ropa, papel) to crease, to crumple. 2. (piel) to wrinkle. ▶ **arrugarse** *vpr* 1. (ropa) to get creased. 2. (piel) to get wrinkled.

arruinar *vt lit & fig* to ruin. ▶ **arruinarse** *vpr* to go bankrupt, to be ruined.

arrullar *vt* to lull to sleep. ▶ **arrullarse** *vpr* (animales) to coo.

arrumar *vt* Amer to pile up.

arsenal *m* 1. (de barcos) shipyard. 2. (de armas) arsenal. 3. (de cosas) array.

arsénico *m* arsenic.

art. (abrev de **artículo**) art.

arte *m o f* (en sg gen m; en pl f) 1. (gen) art; ~ **dramático** drama. 2. (habilidad) artistry. 3. (astucia) artfulness, cunning; **malas** ~**s** trickery (U). ▶ **artes** *fpl* arts; **bellas** ~**s** fine arts.

artefacto *m* (aparato) device; (máquina) contraption.

arteria *f lit & fig* artery.

artesa *f* trough.

artesanal *adj* (hecho a mano) handmade.

artesanía *f* 1. (técnica) crasftsmanship, handicraft; **de** ~ (producto) handmade. 2. (artículos) handmade articles (pl).

artesano, -na *m y f* craftsman (*f* craftswoman).

ártico, -ca *adj* arctic. ▶ **Ártico** *m*: **el Ártico** the Arctic; **el océano Glacial Ártico** the Arctic Ocean.

articulación *f* 1. (ANAT & TECN) joint. 2. (LING) articulation.

articulado, -da *adj* articulated.

articular ◆ *adj* (enfermedad, dolor) articular, of the joints. ◆ *vt* (palabras, piezas) to articulate.

artículo m (gen) article; ~ **de fondo** editorial, leader; ~ **de primera necesidad** basic commodity.

artífice m y f fig architect.

artificial adj artificial.

artificio m fig (falsedad) artifice; (artimaña) trick.

artificioso, -sa adj fig (engañoso) deceptive.

artillería f artillery.

artillero m artilleryman.

artilugio m gadget, contrivance.

artimaña f (gen pl) trick, ruse.

artista m y f 1. (gen) artist. 2. (de espectáculos) artiste.

artístico, -ca adj artistic.

artritis f inv arthritis.

arveja f Amer pea.

arzobispo m archbishop.

as m 1. (carta, dado) ace. 2. (campeón): un ~ **del volante** an ace driver.

asa f (el) handle.

asado, -da adj (al horno) roast; (a la parrilla) grilled. ► **asado** m roast.

asador m 1. (aparato) roaster. 2. (varilla) spit.

asaduras fpl offal (U); (de pollo, pavo) giblets.

asalariado, -da m y f wage earner.

asalmonado, -da adj salmon (pink).

asaltante m y f (agresor) attacker; (atracador) robber.

asaltar vt 1. (atacar) to attack; (castillo, ciudad etc) to storm. 2. (robar) to rob. 3. fig (suj: dudas etc) to assail.

asalto m 1. (ataque) attack; (de castillo, ciudad) storming. 2. (robo) robbery. 3. (DEP) round.

asamblea f assembly; (POLÍT) mass meeting.

asar vt (alimentos - al horno) to roast; (- a la parrilla) to grill.

ascendencia f 1. (linaje) descent. 2. (extracción social) extraction. 3. fig (influencia) ascendancy.

ascender ♦ vi 1. (subir) to go up, to climb. 2. (aumentar, elevarse) to rise, to go up. 3. (en empleo, deportes): ~ **(a)** to be promoted (to). 4. (totalizar - precio etc): ~ **a** to come o amount to. ♦ vt: ~ **a alguien (a)** to promote sb (to).

ascendiente m y f (antepasado) ancestor.

ascensión f ascent. ► **Ascensión** f (RELIG) Ascension.

ascenso m 1. (en empleo, deportes) promotion. 2. (ascensión) ascent.

ascensor m lift Br, elevator Am.

ascético, -ca adj ascetic.

asco m (sensación) revulsion; **siento** ~ I feel sick; **¡qué ~ de tiempo!** what foul weather!; **me da** ~ I find it disgusting; **¡qué ~!** how disgusting o revolting!; **hacer** ~**s a** to turn one's nose up at; **estar hecho un** ~ fam (cosa) to be filthy; (persona) to be a real sight.

ascua f (el) ember.

aseado, -da adj (limpio) clean; (arreglado) smart.

asear vt to clean. ► **asearse** vpr to get washed and dressed.

asediar vt to lay siege to; fig to pester.

asedio m siege; fig pestering.

asegurado, -da m y f policy-holder.

asegurar vt 1. (fijar) to secure. 2. (garantizar) to ensure. 3. (prometer) to assure; **te lo aseguro** I assure you; ~ **a alguien que** ... to assure sb that ... 4. (COM): ~ **(contra)** to insure (against); ~ **algo en** (cantidad) to insure sthg for. ► **asegurarse** vpr (cerciorarse): ~**se de que** ... to make sure that ...

asemejar ► **asemejarse** vpr to be similar o alike; ~**se a** to be similar to, to be like.

asentamiento m (campamento) settlement.

asentar vt 1. (instalar - empresa, campamento) to set up; (- comunidad, pueblo) to settle. 2. (asegurar) to secure; (cimientos) to lay. ► **asentarse** vpr 1. (instalarse) to settle down. 2. (sedimentarse) to settle.

asentir vi 1. (estar conforme): ~ **(a)** to agree (to). 2. (afirmar con la cabeza) to nod.

aseo m (limpieza - acción) cleaning; (- cualidad) cleanliness. ► **aseos** mpl toilets Br, restroom (sg) Am.

aséptico, -ca adj (MED) aseptic.

asequible adj 1. (accesible, comprensible) accessible. 2. (razonable - precio, producto) affordable.

aserradero m sawmill.

aserrar vt to saw.

asesinar vt to murder; (rey, jefe de estado) to assassinate.

asesinato m murder; (de rey, jefe de estado) assassination.

asesino, -na m y f murderer (f murderess); (de rey, jefe de estado) assassin.

asesor, -ra m y f adviser; (FIN) consultant; ~ **fiscal** tax consultant.

asesorar vt to advise; (FIN) to provide with consultancy services. ► **asesorarse** vpr to seek advice; ~**se de** to consult.

asesoría f (oficina) consultant's office.
asestar vt (golpe) to deal; (tiro) to fire.
aseveración f assertion.
asfaltado m (acción) asphalting, surfacing; (asfalto) asphalt, (road) surface.
asfalto m asphalt.
asfixia f asphyxiation, suffocation.
asfixiar vt (ahogar) to asphyxiate, to suffocate. ▶ **asfixiarse** vpr (ahogarse) to asphyxiate, to suffocate.
así ♦ adv (de este modo) in this way, like this; (de ese modo) in that way, like that; **era ~ de largo** it was this/that long; **~ es/era/fue como ...** that is how ...; **~ se dice en castellano** that's how you say it in Spanish; **~ ~** (no muy bien) so so; **algo ~** (algo parecido) something like that; **~ es** (para asentir) that is correct, yes; **y ~ todos los días** and the same thing happens day after day; **~ como** (también) as well as, and also; (tal como) just as, exactly as. ♦ conj **1.** (de modo que): **~ que** so. **2.** (aunque) although. **3.** (tan pronto como): **~ que** as soon as. **4.** Amer (aun si) even if. ♦ adj inv (como éste) like this; (como ése) like that. ▶ **así y todo, aun así** loc adv even so.
Asia Asia.
asiático, -ca adj, m y f Asian, Asiatic.
asidero m (agarradero) handle.
asiduidad f frequency.
asiduo, -dua adj, m y f regular.
asiento m (mueble, localidad) seat; **tomar ~** to sit down.
asignación f **1.** (atribución) allocation. **2.** (sueldo) salary.
asignar vt **1.** (atribuir): **~ algo a alguien** to assign o allocate sthg to sb. **2.** (destinar): **~ a alguien** to send sb to.
asignatura f (EDUC) subject.
asilado, -da m y f person living in an old people's home, convalescent home etc.
asilo m **1.** (hospicio) home; **~ de ancianos** old people's home. **2.** fig (amparo) asylum; **~ político** political asylum. **3.** (hospedaje) accommodation.
asimilación f (gen & LING) assimilation.
asimilar vt (gen) to assimilate.
asimismo adv (también) also, as well; (a principio de frase) likewise.
asir vt to grasp, to take hold of.
asistencia f **1.** (presencia - acción) attendance; (- hecho) presence. **2.** (ayuda) assistance; **~ médica** medical attention; **~ sanitaria** health care; **~ técnica** technical assistance. **3.** (afluencia) audience. **4.** (DEP) assist.

asistenta f cleaning lady.
asistente m y f **1.** (ayudante) assistant, helper; **~ social** social worker. **2.** (presente) person present; **los ~s** the audience (sg).
asistido, -da adj (AUTOM) power (antes de sust); (INFORM) computer-assisted.
asistir ♦ vt (ayudar) to attend to. ♦ vi: **~ a** to attend, to go to.
asma f (el) asthma.
asmático, -ca adj asthmatic.
asno m lit & fig ass.
asociación f association; **~ de vecinos** residents' association.
asociado, -da ♦ adj (miembro) associate. ♦ m y f (miembro) associate, partner.
asociar vt (relacionar) to associate. ▶ **asociarse** vpr to form a partnership.
asolar vt to devastate.
asomar ♦ vi (gen) to peep up; (del interior de algo) to peep out. ♦ vt to stick; **~ la cabeza por la ventana** to stick one's head out of the window. ▶ **asomarse a** vpr (ventana) to stick one's head out of; (balcón) to come/go out onto.
asombrar vt (causar admiración) to amaze; (causar sorpresa) to surprise. ▶ **asombrarse** vpr: **~se (de)** (sentir admiración) to be amazed (at); (sentir sorpresa) to be surprised (at).
asombro m (admiración) amazement; (sorpresa) surprise.
asombroso, -sa adj (sensacional) amazing; (sorprendente) surprising.
asomo m (indicio) trace, hint; (de esperanza) glimmer.
aspa f (el) X-shaped cross; (de molino) arms (pl).
aspaviento m (gen pl) furious gesticulations (pl).
aspecto m **1.** (apariencia) appearance; **tener buen/mal ~** (persona) to look well/awful; (cosa) to look nice/horrible. **2.** (faceta) aspect; **en todos los ~s** in every respect.
aspereza f roughness; fig sourness.
áspero, -ra adj **1.** (rugoso) rough. **2.** fig (desagradable) sharp, sour.
aspersión f (de jardín) sprinkling; (de cultivos) spraying.
aspersor m (para jardín) sprinkler; (para cultivos) sprayer.
aspiración f **1.** (gen & LING) aspiration. **2.** (de aire - por una persona) breathing in; (- por una máquina) suction.
aspiradora f, **aspirador** m vacuum cleaner; **pasar la ~ por** to vacuum.
aspirante m y f: **~ (a)** candidate (for);

(*en deportes, concursos*) contender (for).

aspirar ♦ *vt* (*aire - suj: persona*) to breathe in, to inhale. ♦ *vi*: ~ **a algo** (*ansiar*) to aspire to sthg.

aspirina® *f* aspirin.

asquear *vt* to disgust, to make sick.

asqueroso, -sa *adj* disgusting, revolting.

asta *f* (*el*) 1. (*de bandera*) flagpole, mast. 2. (*de lanza*) shaft; (*de brocha*) handle. 3. (*de toro*) horn.

asterisco *m* asterisk.

astigmatismo *m* astigmatism.

astilla *f* splinter.

astillero *m* shipyard.

astringente *adj* astringent.

astro *m* (ASTRON) heavenly body; *fig* star.

astrofísica *f* astrophysics (U).

astrología *f* astrology.

astrólogo, -ga *m y f* astrologer.

astronauta *m y f* astronaut.

astronomía *f* astronomy.

astrónomo, -ma *m y f* astronomer.

astroso, -sa *adj* (*andrajoso*) shabby.

astucia *f* 1. (*picardía*) cunning, astuteness. 2. (*gen pl*) (*treta*) cunning trick.

astuto, -ta *adj* (*ladino, tramposo*) cunning; (*sagaz, listo*) astute.

asueto *m* break, rest; **unos días de ~** a few days off.

asumir *vt* 1. (*gen*) to assume. 2. (*aceptar*) to accept.

asunción *f* assumption. ▶ **Asunción** *f*: **la Asunción** (RELIG) the Assumption.

Asunción (GEOGR) Asunción.

asunto *m* 1. (*tema - general*) subject; (*- específico*) matter; (*- de obra, libro*) theme; **~s a tratar** agenda (*sg*). 2. (*cuestión, problema*) issue. 3. (*negocio*) affair, business (U); **no es ~ tuyo** it's none of your business. ▶ **asuntos** *mpl* (POLÍT) affairs; **~s exteriores** foreign affairs.

asustado, -da *adj* frightened, scared.

asustar *vt* to frighten, to scare. ▶ **asustarse** *vpr*: **~se (de)** to be frightened o scared (of).

atacar *vt* (*gen*) to attack.

atadura *f* lit & *fig* tie.

atajar ♦ *vi* (*acortar*): **~ (por)** to take a short cut (through). ♦ *vt* (*contener*) to put a stop to; (*hemorragia, inundación*) to stem.

atajo *m* 1. (*camino corto, medio rápido*) short cut; **coger** o **tomar un ~** to take a short cut. 2. *despec* (*panda*) bunch.

atalaya *f* 1. (*torre*) watchtower. 2. (*altura*) vantage point.

atañer *vi* 1. (*concernir*): **~ a** to concern. 2. (*corresponder*): **~ a** to be the responsibility of.

ataque *m* 1. (*gen* & DEP) attack. 2. *fig* (*acceso*) fit, bout; **~ cardíaco** o **al corazón** heart attack.

atar *vt* 1. (*unir*) to tie (up). 2. *fig* (*constreñir*) to tie down.

atardecer ♦ *m* dusk. ♦ *v impers* to get dark.

atareado, -da *adj* busy.

atascar *vt* to block (up). ▶ **atascarse** *vpr* 1. (*obstruirse*) to get blocked up. 2. *fig* (*detenerse*) to get stuck; (*al hablar*) to dry up.

atasco *m* 1. (*obstrucción*) blockage. 2. (AUTOM) traffic jam.

ataúd *m* coffin.

ataviar *vt* (*cosa*) to deck out; (*persona*) to dress up. ▶ **ataviarse** *vpr* to dress up.

atavío *m* (*indumentaria*) attire (U).

atemorizar *vt* to frighten. ▶ **atemorizarse** *vpr* to get frightened.

Atenas Athens.

atenazar *vt* 1. (*sujetar*) to clench. 2. *fig* (*suj: dudas*) to torment, to rack; (*suj: miedo, nervios*) to grip.

atención ♦ *f* 1. (*interés*) attention; **llamar la ~** (*atraer*) to attract attention; **poner** o **prestar ~** to pay attention. 2. (*cortesía*) attentiveness (U). ♦ *interj*: **¡~!** (*en aeropuerto, conferencia*) your attention please! ▶ **atenciones** *fpl* attentions.

atender ♦ *vt* 1. (*satisfacer - petición, ruego*) to attend to; (*- consejo, instrucciones*) to heed; (*- propuesta*) to agree to. 2. (*cuidar de - necesitados, invitados*) to look after; (*- enfermo*) to care for; (*- cliente*) to serve; **¿le atienden?** are you being served? ♦ *vi* (*estar atento*): **~ (a)** to pay attention (to).

atenerse ▶ **atenerse a** *vpr* 1. (*promesa, orden*) to stick to; (*ley, normas*) to abide by. 2. (*consecuencias*) to bear in mind.

atentado *m*: **~ contra alguien** attempt on sb's life; **~ contra algo** crime against sthg.

atentamente *adv* (*en cartas*) Yours sincerely o faithfully.

atentar *vi*: **~ contra (la vida de) alguien** to make an attempt on sb's life; **~ contra algo** (*principio etc*) to be a crime against sthg.

atento, -ta adj 1. (pendiente) attentive; **estar ~ a** (explicación, programa, lección) to pay attention to; (ruido, sonido) to listen out for; (acontecimientos, cambios, avances) to keep up with. 2. (cortés) considerate, thoughtful.

atenuante m (DER) extenuating circumstance.

atenuar vt (gen) to diminish; (dolor) to ease; (luz) to filter.

ateo, -a ♦ adj atheistic. ♦ m y f atheist.

aterciopelado, -da adj velvety.

aterrador, -ra adj terrifying.

aterrar vt to terrify.

aterrizaje m landing.

aterrizar vi (avión) to land.

aterrorizar vt to terrify; (suj: agresor) to terrorize.

atesorar vt (riquezas) to amass.

atestado m official report.

atestar vt 1. (llenar) to pack, to cram. 2. (DER) to testify to.

atestiguar vt to testify to.

atiborrar vt to stuff full. ▶ **atiborrarse** vpr fam fig: **~se (de)** to stuff o.s. (with).

ático m penthouse.

atinar vi (adivinar) to guess correctly; (dar en el blanco) to hit the target; **~ a hacer algo** to succeed in doing sthg; **~ con** to hit upon.

atingencia f Amer (relación) connection.

atípico, -ca adj atypical.

atisbar vt 1. (divisar, prever) to make out. 2. (acechar) to observe, to spy on.

atisbo m (gen pl) trace, hint; (de esperanza) glimmer.

atizar vt 1. (fuego) to poke, to stir. 2. fam (puñetazo, patada) to land, to deal.

atlántico, -ca adj Atlantic. ▶ **Atlántico** m: **el (océano) Atlántico** the Atlantic (Ocean).

atlas m inv atlas.

atleta m y f athlete.

atlético, -ca adj athletic.

atletismo m athletics (U).

atmósfera f lit & fig atmosphere.

atmosférico, -ca adj atmospheric.

atolladero m (apuro) fix, jam; **meter en/sacar de un ~ a alguien** to put sb in/get sb out of a tight spot.

atolondrado, -da adj 1. (precipitado) hasty, disorganized. 2. (aturdido) bewildered.

atómico, -ca adj atomic; (central, armas) nuclear.

atomizador m atomizer, spray.

átomo m lit & fig atom.

atónito, -ta adj astonished, astounded.

atontado, -da adj 1. (aturdido) dazed. 2. (tonto) stupid.

atontar vt (aturdir) to daze.

atormentar vt to torture; fig to torment.

atornillar vt to screw.

atorón m Amer traffic jam.

atorrante adj Amer lazy.

atosigar vt fig to harass.

atracador, -ra m y f (de banco) armed robber; (en la calle) mugger.

atracar ♦ vi (NÁUT): **~ (en)** to dock (at). ♦ vt (banco) to rob; (persona) to mug. ▶ **atracarse** vpr: **~se de** to eat one's fill of.

atracción f 1. (gen) attraction. 2. (espectáculo) act. 3. fig (centro de atención) centre of attention. 4. (gen pl) (diversión infantil) fairground attraction.

atraco m robbery.

atracón m fam feast; **darse un ~** to stuff one's face.

atractivo, -va adj attractive. ▶ **atractivo** m (de persona) attractiveness, charm; (de cosa) attraction.

atraer vt (gen) to attract.

atragantarse vpr: **~ (con)** to choke (on).

atrancar vt 1. (cerrar) to bar. 2. (obturar) to block. ▶ **atrancarse** vpr 1. (atascarse) to get blocked. 2. fig (al hablar, escribir) to dry up.

atrapar vt (agarrar, alcanzar) to catch.

atrás adv 1. (detrás - posición) behind, at the back; (- movimiento) backwards; **quedarse ~** fig to fall behind. 2. (antes) earlier, before. ▶ **atrás de** loc prep Amer (detrás de) behind.

atrasado, -da adj 1. (en el tiempo) delayed; (reloj) slow; (pago) overdue, late; (número, copia) back (antes de sust). 2. (en evolución, capacidad) backward.

atrasar ♦ vt to put back. ♦ vi to be slow. ▶ **atrasarse** vpr 1. (demorarse) to be late. 2. (quedarse atrás) to fall behind.

atraso m (de evolución) backwardness. ▶ **atrasos** mpl fam arrears.

atravesar vt 1. (interponer) to put across. 2. (cruzar) to cross. 3. (traspasar) to penetrate. 4. fig (vivir) to go through. ▶ **atravesarse** vpr (interponerse) to be in the way.

atrayente adj attractive.

atreverse vpr: ~ **(a hacer algo)** to dare (to do sthg).

atrevido, -da adj (osado) daring; (caradura) cheeky.

atrevimiento m 1. (osadía) daring. 2. (insolencia) cheek.

atribución f 1. (imputación) attribution. 2. (competencia) responsibility.

atribuir vt (imputar): ~ **algo a** to attribute sthg to. ▶ **atribuirse** vpr (méritos) to claim for o.s.; (poderes) to assume.

atributo m attribute.

atril m (para libros) lectern; (MÚS) music stand.

atrocidad f (crueldad) atrocity.

atropellado, -da adj hasty.

atropellar vt 1. (suj: vehículo) to run over. 2. fig (suj: persona) to trample on. ▶ **atropellarse** vpr (al hablar) to trip over one's words.

atropello m 1. (por vehículo) running over. 2. fig (moral) abuse.

atroz adj atrocious; (dolor) awful.

ATS (abrev de **ayudante técnico sanitario**) m y f qualified nurse.

atte. abrev de **atentamente**.

atuendo m attire.

atún m tuna.

aturdido, -da adj dazed.

aturdir vt (gen) to stun; (suj: alcohol) to fuddle; (suj: ruido, luz) to bewilder.

audacia f (intrepidez) daring.

audaz adj (intrépido) daring.

audición f 1. (gen) hearing. 2. (MÚS & TEATR) audition.

audiencia f 1. (público, recepción) audience. 2. (DER - juicio) hearing; (- tribunal, edificio) court.

audífono m hearing aid.

audiovisual adj audiovisual.

auditivo, -va adj ear (antes de sust).

auditor, -ra m y f (FIN) auditor.

auditorio m 1. (público) audience. 2. (lugar) auditorium.

auge m (gen & ECON) boom.

augurar vt (suj: persona) to predict; (suj: suceso) to augur.

augurio m omen, sign.

aula f (el) (de escuela) classroom; (de universidad) lecture room.

aullar vi to howl.

aullido m howl.

aumentar ◆ vt 1. (gen) to increase; (peso) to put on. 2. (en óptica) to magnify. 3. (sonido) to amplify. ◆ vi to increase; (precios) to rise.

aumento m 1. (incremento) increase; (de sueldo, precios) rise; **ir en ~** to be on the increase. 2. (en óptica) magnification.

aun ◆ adv even. ◆ conj: ~ **estando cansado, lo hizo** even though he was tired, he did it; **ni ~ puesta de puntillas logra ver** she can't see, even on tiptoe; ~ **cuando** even though.

aún adv (todavía) still; (en negativas) yet, still; **no ha llegado ~** he hasn't arrived yet, he still hasn't arrived.

aunar vt to join, to pool. ▶ **aunarse** vpr (aliarse) to unite.

aunque conj 1. (a pesar de que) even though, although; (incluso si) even if. 2. (pero) although.

aúpa interj: ¡~! (¡levántate!) get up!; ¡~ el Atleti! up the Athletic!

aupar vt to help up; fig (animar) to cheer on. ▶ **auparse** vpr to climb up.

aureola f 1. (ASTRON & RELIG) halo. 2. fig (fama) aura.

auricular m (de teléfono) receiver. ▶ **auriculares** mpl (cascos) headphones.

aurora f first light of dawn.

auscultar vt to sound with a stethoscope.

ausencia f absence; **brillar por su ~** to be conspicuous by one's/its absence.

ausentarse vpr to go away.

ausente ◆ adj 1. (no presente) absent; **estará ~ todo el día** he'll be away all day. 2. (distraído) absent-minded. ◆ m y f 1. (no presente): **criticó a los ~s** he criticized the people who weren't there. 2. (DER) missing person.

auspicio m (protección) protection; **bajo los ~s de** under the auspices of.

austeridad f austerity.

austero, -ra adj (gen) austere.

austral ◆ adj southern. ◆ m (moneda) austral.

Australia Australia.

australiano, -na adj, m y f Australian.

Austria Austria.

austríaco, -ca adj, m y f Austrian.

autarquía f 1. (POLÍT) autarchy. 2. (ECON) autarky.

auténtico, -ca adj (gen) genuine; (piel, joyas) genuine, real; **un ~ imbécil** a real idiot.

auto m 1. fam (coche) car. 2. (DER) judicial decree.

autoadhesivo, -va adj self-adhesive.

autobiografía f autobiography.

autobús m bus.

autocar m coach.

autocontrol *m* self-control.

autóctono, -na *adj* indigenous.

autodefensa *f* self-defence.

autodeterminación *f* self-determination.

autodidacta *adj* self-taught.

autoescuela *f* driving school.

autoestop, autostop *m* hitch-hiking; **hacer ~** to hitch-hike.

autoestopista, autostopista *m y f* hitch-hiker.

autofoco *m* autofocus, automatic focus.

autógrafo *m* autograph.

autómata *m lit & fig* automaton.

automático, -ca *adj* automatic. ▶ **automático** *m* (*botón*) press-stud.

automatización *f* automation.

automóvil *m* car Br, automobile Am.

automovilismo *m* motoring; (DEP) motor racing.

automovilista *m y f* motorist, driver.

automovilístico, -ca *adj* motor (*antes de sust*); (DEP) motor-racing (*antes de sust*).

autonomía *f* (POLÍT - *facultad*) autonomy; (- *territorio*) autonomous region.

autonómico, -ca *adj* autonomous.

autónomo, -ma ◆ *adj* 1. (POLÍT) autonomous. 2. (*trabajador*) self-employed; (*traductor, periodista*) freelance. ◆ *m y f* self-employed person; (*traductor, periodista*) freelance.

autopista *f* motorway Br, freeway Am.

autopsia *f* autopsy, post-mortem.

autor, -ra *m y f* 1. (LITER) author. 2. (*de crimen*) perpetrator.

autoridad *f* 1. (*gen*) authority. 2. (*ley*): **la ~** the authorities (*pl*).

autoritario, -ria *adj, m y f* authoritarian.

autorización *f* authorization.

autorizado, -da *adj* 1. (*permitido*) authorized. 2. (*digno de crédito*) authoritative.

autorizar *vt* 1. (*dar permiso*) to allow; (*en situaciones oficiales*) to authorize. 2. (*capacitar*) to allow, to entitle.

autorretrato *m* self-portrait.

autoservicio *m* 1. (*tienda*) self-service shop. 2. (*restaurante*) self-service restaurant.

autostop = **autoestop**.

autostopista = **autoestopista**.

autosuficiencia *f* self-sufficiency.

autovía *f* dual carriageway Br, state highway Am.

auxiliar ◆ *adj* (*gen & GRAM*) auxiliary. ◆ *m y f* assistant; **~ administrativo** office

clerk. ◆ *vt* to assist, to help.

auxilio *m* assistance, help; **primeros ~s** first aid (U).

av., avda. (*abrev de avenida*) Ave.

aval *m* 1. (*persona*) guarantor. 2. (*documento*) guarantee, reference.

avalancha *f lit & fig* avalanche.

avalar *vt* to endorse, to guarantee.

avance *m* 1. (*gen*) advance. 2. (FIN) (*anticipo*) advance payment. 3. (RADIO & TV - *meteorológico etc*) summary; (- *de futura programación*) preview; **~ informativo** news (U) in brief.

avanzado, -da *adj* advanced.

avanzar ◆ *vi* to advance. ◆ *vt* 1. (*adelantar*) to move forward. 2. (*anticipar*) to tell in advance.

avaricia *f* greed, avarice.

avaricioso, -sa *adj* avaricious.

avaro, -ra *adj* miserly, mean.

avasallar *vt* (*arrollar*) to overwhelm.

avatar *m* (*gen pl*) vagary.

avda. = **av**.

ave *f* (*el*) (*gen*) bird; **~ rapaz** o **de rapiña** bird of prey.

AVE (*abrev de alta velocidad española*) *m* Spanish high-speed train.

avecinarse *vpr* to be on the way.

avellana *f* hazelnut.

avemaría *f* (*el*) (*oración*) Hail Mary.

avena *f* (*grano*) oats (*pl*).

avenencia *f* (*acuerdo*) compromise.

avenida *f* avenue.

avenido, -da *adj*: **bien/mal ~s** on good/bad terms.

avenirse *vpr* (*ponerse de acuerdo*) to come to an agreement; **~ a algo/a hacer algo** to agree on sthg/to do sthg.

aventajado, -da *adj* (*adelantado*) outstanding.

aventajar *vt* (*rebasar*) to overtake; (*estar por delante de*) to be ahead of; **~ a alguien en algo** to surpass sb in sthg.

aventura *f* 1. (*gen*) adventure. 2. (*relación amorosa*) affair.

aventurado, -da *adj* risky.

aventurero, -ra ◆ *adj* adventurous. ◆ *m y f* adventurer (*f* adventuress).

avergonzar *vt* 1. (*deshonrar*) to shame. 2. (*abochornar*) to embarrass. ▶ **avergonzarse** *vpr*: **~se (de)** (*por remordimiento*) to be ashamed (of); (*por timidez*) to be embarrassed (about).

avería *f* (*de máquina*) fault; (AUTOM) breakdown.

averiado, -da *adj* (*máquina*) out of order; (*coche*) broken down.

averiar *vt* to damage. ▶ **averiarse**

vpr (*máquina*) to be out of order; (AUTOM) to break down.
averiguación *f* investigation.
averiguar *vt* to find out.
aversión *f* aversion.
avestruz *m* ostrich.
aviación *f* 1. (*navegación*) aviation. 2. (*ejército*) airforce.
aviador, -ra *m* y *f* aviator.
aviar *vt* (*comida*) to prepare.
avicultura *f* poultry farming.
avidez *f* eagerness.
ávido, -da *adj*: ~ de eager for.
avinagrado, -da *adj* lit & *fig* sour.
avío *m* 1. (*preparativo*) preparation. 2. (*víveres*) provisions (*pl*). ▶ **avíos** *mpl fam* (*equipo*) things, kit (U).
avión *m* plane; **en ~** by plane; **por ~** (*en un sobre*) airmail; **~ a reacción** jet.
avioneta *f* light aircraft.
avisar *vt* 1. (*informar*): ~ **a alguien** to let sb know, to tell sb. 2. (*advertir*): ~ **(de)** to warn (of). 3. (*llamar*) to call, to send for.
aviso *m* 1. (*advertencia, amenaza*) warning. 2. (*notificación*) notice; (*en teatros, aeropuertos*) call; **hasta nuevo ~** until further notice; **sin previo ~** without notice.
avispa *f* wasp.
avispado, -da *adj fam* sharp, quick-witted.
avispero *m* (*nido*) wasp's nest.
avituallar *vt* to provide with food.
avivar *vt* 1. (*sentimiento*) to rekindle. 2. (*color*) to brighten. 3. (*fuego*) to stoke up.
axila *f* armpit.
axioma *m* axiom.
ay (*pl* ayes) *interj*: ¡~! (*dolor físico*) ouch!; (*sorpresa, pena*) oh!; ¡~ **de tí si te cojo!** Heaven help you if I catch you!
aya → **ayo.**
ayer ◆ *adv* yesterday; *fig* in the past; ~ **(por la) noche** last night; **~ por la mañana** yesterday morning. ◆ *m fig* yesteryear.
ayo, aya *m* y *f* (*tutor*) tutor (*f* governess).
ayuda *f* help, assistance; (ECON & POLÍT) aid; **~ en carretera** breakdown service.
ayudante *adj, m* y *f* assistant.
ayudar *vt* to help; ~ **a alguien a hacer algo** to help sb (to) do sthg; **¿en qué puedo ~le?** how can I help you? ▶ **ayudarse** *vpr*: **~se de** to make use of.
ayunar *vi* to fast.
ayunas *fpl*: **en ~** (*sin comer*) without having eaten; *fig* (*sin enterarse*) in the dark.

ayuno *m* fast; **hacer ~** to fast.
ayuntamiento *m* 1. (*corporación*) ≃ town council. 2. (*edificio*) town hall.
azabache *m* jet; **negro como el ~** jet-black.
azada *f* hoe.
azafata *f*: **~ (de vuelo)** air hostess Br, air stewardess.
azafate *m* Amer (*bandeja*) tray.
azafrán *m* saffron.
azahar *m* (*del naranjo*) orange blossom; (*del limonero*) lemon blossom.
azalea *f* azalea.
azar *m* chance, fate; **al ~** at random; **por (puro) ~** by (pure) chance.
azorar *vt* to embarrass. ▶ **azorarse** *vpr* to be embarrassed.
azotar *vt* (*suj: persona*) to beat; (*en el trasero*) to smack; (*con látigo*) to whip.
azote *m* 1. (*golpe*) blow; (*en el trasero*) smack; (*latigazo*) lash. 2. *fig* (*calamidad*) scourge.
azotea *f* (*de edificio*) terraced roof.
azteca *adj, m* y *f* Aztec.
azúcar *m* o *f* sugar; **~ blanquilla/moreno** refined/brown sugar.
azucarado, -da *adj* sweet, sugary.
azucarero, -ra *adj* sugar (*antes de sust*). ▶ **azucarero** *m* sugar bowl.
azucena *f* white lily.
azufre *m* sulphur.
azul *adj & m* blue; **~ marino** navy blue.
azulejo *m* (glazed) tile.
azuzar *vt* (*animal*) to set on.

B

b, B *f* (*letra*) b, B.
baba *f* (*saliva - de niño*) dribble; (*- de adulto*) saliva; (*- de animal*) foam.
babear *vi* (*niño*) to dribble; (*adulto, animal*) to slobber; *fig* to drool.
babero *m* bib.
babi *m* child's overall.
bable *m* Asturian dialect.
babor *m* port; **a ~** to port.
baboso, -sa *adj* Amer fam (*tonto*) daft, stupid. ▶ **babosa** *f* (ZOOL) slug.
babucha *f* slipper.
baca *f* roof o luggage rack.
bacalao *m* (*fresco*) cod; (*salado*) dried

salted cod; **partir** o **cortar el ~** *fam fig* to be the boss.

bacanal *f* orgy.

bache *m* **1.** (*en carretera*) pothole. **2.** *fig* (*dificultades*) bad patch. **3.** (*en un vuelo*) air pocket.

bachiller *m y f* person who has passed the 'bachillerato'.

bachillerato *m* (*former*) Spanish course of secondary studies for academically orientated 14-16-year-olds.

bacinica *f Amer* chamber pot.

bacon ['beikon] *m inv* bacon.

bacteria *f* germ; **~s** bacteria.

badén *m* (*de carretera*) ditch.

bádminton *m inv* badminton.

bafle (*pl* **bafles**), **baffle** (*pl* **baffles**) *m* loudspeaker.

bagaje *m fig* background; **~ cultural** cultural baggage.

bagatela *f* trifle.

Bahamas *fpl*: **las ~** the Bahamas.

bahía *f* bay.

bailaor, -ra *m y f* flamenco dancer.

bailar ◆ *vt* to dance. ◆ *vi* (*danzar*) to dance.

bailarín, -ina *m y f* dancer; (*de ballet*) ballet dancer.

baile *m* **1.** (*acción*) dancing. **2.** (*danza*) dance; **~ clásico** ballet. **3.** (*fiesta*) ball.

baja → **bajo**.

bajada *f* **1.** (*descenso*) descent; **~ de bandera** (*de taxi*) minimum fare. **2.** (*pendiente*) (*downward*) slope. **3.** (*disminución*) decrease, drop.

bajamar *f* low tide.

bajar ◆ *vt* **1.** (*poner abajo - libro, cuadro etc*) to take/bring down; (*- telón, ventanilla, mano*) to lower. **2.** (*descender - montaña, escaleras*) to go/come down. **3.** (*precios, inflación, hinchazón*) to reduce; (*música, volumen, radio*) to turn down; (*fiebre*) to bring down. **4.** (*ojos, cabeza, voz*) to lower. ◆ *vi* **1.** (*descender*) to go/come down; **~ por algo** to go/come down sthg; **~ corriendo** to run down. **2.** (*disminuir*) to fall, to drop; (*fiebre, hinchazón*) to go/come down; (*Bolsa*) to suffer a fall. ▶ **bajarse** *vpr*: **~se (de)** (*coche*) to get out (of); (*moto, tren, avión*) to get off; (*árbol, escalera, silla*) to get/come down (from).

bajeza *f* **1.** (*cualidad*) baseness. **2.** (*acción*) nasty deed.

bajial *m Amer* lowland.

bajo, -ja *adj* **1.** (*gen*) low; (*persona, estatura*) short; (*piso*) ground floor (*antes de sust*); (*planta*) ground (*antes de sust*); (*sonido*) soft, faint. **2.** (*territorio, época*)

lower; **el ~ Amazonas** the lower Amazon. **3.** (*pobre*) lower-class. **4.** (*vil*) base. ▶ **bajo** ◆ *m* **1.** (*gen pl*) (*dobladillo*) hem. **2.** (*piso*) ground floor flat. **3.** (MÚS - *instrumento, cantante*) bass; (*- instrumentista*) bassist. ◆ *adv* **1.** (*gen*) low. **2.** (*hablar*) quietly. ◆ *prep* **1.** (*gen*) under. **2.** (*con temperaturas*) below. ▶ **baja** *f* **1.** (*descenso*) drop, fall. **2.** (*cese*): **dar de baja a alguien** (*en una empresa*) to lay sb off; (*en un club, sindicato*) to expel sb; **darse de baja (de)** (*dimitir*) to resign (from); (*salirse*) to drop out (of). **3.** (*por enfermedad - permiso*) sick leave (U); (*- documento*) sick note; **estar/darse de baja** to be on/to take sick leave. **4.** (MIL) loss, casualty.

bajón *m* slump; **dar un ~** to slump.

bajura → **pesca**.

bala *f* **1.** (*proyectil*) bullet. **2.** (*fardo*) bale.

balacear *vt Amer* (*tirotear*) to shoot.

balada *f* ballad.

balance *m* **1.** (COM - *operación*) balance; (*- documento*) balance sheet. **2.** (*resultado*) outcome; **hacer ~ (de)** to take stock (of).

balancear *vt* (*cuna*) to rock; (*columpio*) to swing. ▶ **balancearse** *vpr* (*en cuna, mecedora*) to rock; (*en columpio*) to swing; (*barco*) to roll.

balanceo *m* **1.** (*gen*) swinging; (*de cuna, mecedora*) rocking; (*de barco*) roll. **2.** *Amer* (AUTOM) wheel balance.

balancín *m* **1.** (*mecedora*) rocking chair; (*en el jardín*) swing hammock. **2.** (*columpio*) seesaw.

balanza *f* **1.** (*báscula*) scales (*pl*). **2.** (COM): **~ comercial/de pagos** balance of trade/payments.

balar *vi* to bleat.

balaustrada *f* balustrade; (*de escalera*) banister.

balazo *m* (*disparo*) shot; (*herida*) bullet wound.

balbucear, balbucir *vi & vt* to babble.

balbuceo *m* babbling.

balbucir = **balbucear**.

Balcanes *mpl*: **los ~** the Balkans.

balcón *m* (*terraza*) balcony.

balde *m* pail, bucket. ▶ **en balde** *loc adv* in vain.

baldosa *f* (*en casa, edificio*) floor tile; (*en la acera*) paving stone.

baldosín *m* tile.

balear ◆ *vt Amer* to shoot. ◆ *adj* Balearic.

Baleares *fpl*: **las (islas)** ~ the Balearic Islands.
baleo *m* Amer (*disparo*) shot.
balido *m* bleat, bleating (U).
balín *m* pellet.
balístico, -ca *adj* ballistic.
baliza *f* (NÁUT) marker buoy; (AERON) beacon.
ballena *f* (*animal*) whale.
ballesta *f* 1. (HIST) crossbow. 2. (AUTOM) (suspension) spring.
ballet [ba'le] (*pl* **ballets**) *m* ballet.
balneario *m* (*con baños termales*) spa; Amer (*con piscinas, etc*) ≃ lido.

BALNEARIO

In South America, a 'balneario' is a place where there are several open-air swimming pools and cheap facilities for sunbathing, eating and drinking etc.

balompié *m* football.
balón *m* (*pelota*) ball.
baloncesto *m* basketball.
balonmano *m* handball.
balonvolea *m* volleyball.
balsa *f* 1. (*embarcación*) raft. 2. (*estanque*) pond, pool.
bálsamo *m* 1. (FARM) balsam. 2. (*alivio*) balm.
Báltico *m*: **el (mar)** ~ the Baltic (Sea).
baluarte *m* 1. (*fortificación*) bulwark. 2. *fig* (*bastión*) bastion, stronghold.
bambolear *vi* to shake. ▶ **bambolearse** *vpr* (*gen*) to sway; (*mesa, silla*) to wobble.
bambú (*pl* **bambúes** o **bambús**) *m* bamboo.
banal *adj* banal.
banana *f* Amer banana.
banca *f* 1. (*actividad*) banking. 2. (*institución*): **la** ~ the banks (*pl*). 3. (*en juegos*) bank.
bancario, -ria *adj* banking (*antes de sust*).
bancarrota *f* bankruptcy; **en** ~ bankrupt.
banco *m* 1. (*asiento*) bench; (*de iglesia*) pew. 2. (FIN) bank. 3. (*de peces*) shoal. 4. (*de ojos, semen etc*) bank. 5. (*de carpintero, artesano etc*) workbench. ▶ **banco de arena** *m* sandbank. ▶ **Banco Mundial** *m*: **el Banco Mundial** the World Bank.
banda *f* 1. (*cuadrilla*) gang; ~ **armada** terrorist organization. 2. (MÚS) band. 3. (*faja*) sash. 4. (*cinta*) ribbon. 5. (*franja*) stripe. 6. (RADIO) waveband. 7. (*margen*) side; (*en billar*) cushion; (*en fútbol*) touchline. ▶ **banda magnética** *f* magnetic strip. ▶ **banda sonora** *f* soundtrack.
bandada *f* (*de aves*) flock; (*de peces*) shoal.
bandazo *m* (*del barco*) lurch; **dar** ~**s** (*barco, borracho*) to lurch; *fig* (*ir sin rumbo*) to chop and change.
bandear *vt* to buffet.
bandeja *f* tray; **servir** o **dar algo a alguien en** ~ *fig* to hand sthg to sb on a plate.
bandera *f* flag; **jurar** ~ to swear allegiance (to the flag).
banderilla *f* (TAUROM) banderilla, *barbed dart thrust into bull's back*.
banderín *m* (*bandera*) pennant.
bandido, -da *m y f* 1. (*delincuente*) bandit. 2. (*granuja*) rascal.
bando *m* 1. (*facción*) side; **pasarse al otro** ~ to change sides. 2. (*edicto - de alcalde*) edict.
bandolero, -ra *m y f* bandit. ▶ **bandolera** *f* (*correa*) bandoleer; **en bandolera** slung across one's chest.
bandurria *f small 12-stringed guitar*.
banjo ['banjo] *m* banjo.
banquero, -ra *m y f* banker.
banqueta *f* 1. (*asiento*) stool. 2. Amer (*acera*) pavement Br, sidewalk Am.
banquete *m* (*comida*) banquet.
banquillo *m* 1. (*asiento*) low stool. 2. (DEP) bench.
bañada *f* Amer (*acción de bañarse*) bath.
bañadera *f* Amer (*bañera*) bath.
bañador *m* (*for women*) swimsuit; (*for men*) swimming trunks (*pl*).
bañar *vt* 1. (*asear*) to bath; (MED) to bathe. 2. (*sumergir*) to soak, to submerge. 3. (*revestir*) to coat. ▶ **bañarse** *vpr* 1. (*en el baño*) to have o take a bath. 2. (*en playa, piscina*) to go for a swim.
bañera *f* bathtub, bath.
bañista *m y f* bather.
baño *m* 1. (*acción - en bañera*) bath; (*en playa, piscina*) swim; **darse un** ~ (*en bañera*) to have o take a bath; (*en playa, piscina*) to go for a swim. 2. (*bañera*) bathtub, bath. 3. Amer (*servicio*) toilet. 4. (*capa*) coat.
baqueta *f* (MÚS) drumstick.
bar *m* bar.
barahúnda *f* racket, din.
baraja *f* pack (of cards).

BARAJA ESPAÑOLA

The Spanish deck contains 48 cards divided into 4 suits of 12 cards each.

The symbols of the four suits are gold coins, wooden clubs, swords and goblets. In each suit, the cards called 'sota', 'caballo' and 'rey' correspond roughly to the jack, queen and king in a standard deck.

---

barajar vt **1.** (*cartas*) to shuffle. **2.** (*considerar - nombres, posibilidades*) to consider; (*- datos, cifras*) to marshal, to draw on.

baranda, barandilla f handrail.

baratija f trinket, knick-knack.

baratillo m (*tienda*) junkshop; (*mercadillo*) flea market.

barato, -ta adj cheap. ▶ **barato** adv cheap, cheaply.

barba f beard; ~ **incipiente** stubble; **por** ~ (*cada uno*) per head.

barbacoa f barbecue.

barbaridad f **1.** (*cualidad*) cruelty; **¡qué** ~**!** how terrible! **2.** (*disparate*) nonsense (U). **3.** (*montón*): **una** ~ **(de)** tons (of); **se gastó una** ~ she spent a fortune.

barbarie f (*crueldad - cualidad*) cruelty, savagery; (*- acción*) atrocity.

barbarismo m **1.** (*extranjerismo*) foreign word. **2.** (*incorrección*) substandard usage.

bárbaro, -ra ♦ adj **1.** (HIST) barbarian. **2.** (*cruel*) barbaric, cruel. **3.** (*bruto*) uncouth, coarse. **4.** fam (*extraordinario*) brilliant, great. ♦ m y f (HIST) barbarian. ▶ **bárbaro** adv fam (*magníficamente*): **pasarlo** ~ to have a wild time.

barbecho m fallow (land); (*retirada de tierras*) land set aside.

barbería f barber's (shop).

barbero, -ra m y f barber.

barbilampiño, -ña adj beardless.

barbilla f chin.

barbo m barbel; ~ **de mar** red mullet.

barbotar vi & vt to mutter.

barbudo, -da adj bearded.

barca f dinghy, small boat.

barcaza f lighter.

barco m (*gen*) boat; (*de gran tamaño*) ship; **en** ~ by boat; ~ **cisterna** tanker; ~ **de guerra** warship; ~ **mercante** cargo ship; ~ **de vapor** steamer, steamboat; ~ **de vela** sailing ship.

baremo m (*escala*) scale.

bario m barium.

barítono m baritone.

barman (*pl* barmans) m barman.

barniz m (*para madera*) varnish; (*para loza, cerámica*) glaze.

barnizar vt (*madera*) to varnish; (*loza, cerámica*) to glaze.

barómetro m barometer.

barón, -onesa m y f baron (f baroness).

barquero, -ra m y f boatman (f boatwoman).

barquillo m (CULIN) cornet, cone.

barra f **1.** (*gen*) bar; (*de hielo*) block; (*para cortinas*) rod; (*en bicicleta*) crossbar; **la** ~ (*de tribunal*) the bar; ~ **de labios** lipstick; ~ **de pan** baguette, French stick. **2.** (*de bar, café*) bar (*counter*). ~ **libre** unlimited drink for a fixed price. **3.** (*signo gráfico*) slash, oblique stroke.

barrabasada f fam mischief (U).

barraca f **1.** (*chabola*) shack. **2.** (*caseta de feria*) stall. **3.** (*en Valencia y Murcia*) thatched farmhouse.

barranco m, **barranca** Amer f ravine.

barraquismo m shanty towns (*pl*).

barrena f drill.

barrenar vt (*taladrar*) to drill.

barrendero, -ra m y f street sweeper.

barreno m **1.** (*instrumento*) large drill. **2.** (*agujero - para explosiones*) blast hole.

barreño m washing-up bowl.

barrer vt **1.** (*con escoba, reflectores*) to sweep. **2.** (*suj: viento, olas*) to sweep away.

barrera f **1.** (*gen*) barrier; (FERROC) crossing gate; (*de campo, casa*) fence; ~**s arancelarias** tariff barriers. **2.** (DEP) wall.

barriada f neighbourhood, area.

barricada f barricade.

barrido m **1.** (*con escoba*) sweep, sweeping (U). **2.** (TECN) scan, scanning (U). **3.** (CIN) pan, panning (U).

barriga f belly.

barrigón, -ona adj paunchy.

barril m barrel; **de** ~ (*bebida*) draught.

barrio m (*vecindario*) area, neighborhood Am; ~ **residencial** suburb.

barriobajero, -ra despec adj low-life (*antes de sust*).

barrizal m mire.

barro m **1.** (*fango*) mud. **2.** (*arcilla*) clay. **3.** (*grano*) blackhead.

barroco, -ca adj (ARTE) baroque. ▶ **barroco** m (ARTE) baroque.

barrote m bar.

bartola ▶ **a la bartola** loc adv fam: **tumbarse a la** ~ to lounge around.

bártulos mpl things, bits and pieces.

barullo m fam **1.** (*ruido*) din, racket; **armar** ~ to raise hell. **2.** (*desorden*) mess.

basar vt (*fundamentar*) to base.

▶ **basarse en** *vpr* (*suj: teoría, obra etc*) to be based on; (*suj: persona*) to base one's argument on.

basca *f* (*náusea*) nausea.

báscula *f* scales (*pl*).

bascular *vi* to tilt.

base *f* **1.** (*gen, MAT & MIL*) base; (*de edificio*) foundations (*pl*). **2.** (*fundamento, origen*) basis; **sentar las ~s para** to lay the foundations of. **3.** (*de partido, sindicato*): **las ~s** the grass roots (*pl*), the rank and file. **4.** *loc:* **a ~ de** by (means of); **me alimento a ~ de verduras** I live on vegetables; **a ~ de bien** extremely well. ▶ **base de datos** *f* (*INFORM*) database.

básico, -ca *adj* basic; **lo ~ de** the basics of.

basílica *f* basilica.

basta *interj:* **¡~!** that's enough!; **¡~ de chistes/tonterías!** that's enough jokes/of this nonsense!

bastante ♦ *adv* **1.** (*suficientemente*) enough; **es lo ~ lista para ...** she's smart enough to ... **2.** (*considerablemente - antes de adj o adv*) quite, pretty; (*- después de verbo*) quite a lot; **me gustó ~** I quite enjoyed it, I enjoyed it quite a lot. ♦ *adj* **1.** (*suficiente*) enough; **no tengo dinero ~** I haven't enough money. **2.** (*mucho*): **éramos ~s** there were quite a few of us; **tengo ~ frío** I'm quite o pretty cold.

bastar *vi* to be enough; **basta con que se lo digas** it's enough for you to tell her; **con ocho basta** eight will be enough. ▶ **bastarse** *vpr* to be self-sufficient.

bastardilla → **letra.**

bastardo, -da *adj* **1.** (*hijo etc*) bastard (*antes de sust*). **2.** *despec* (*innoble*) mean, base.

bastidor *m* (*armazón*) frame. ▶ **bastidores** *mpl* (*TEATR*) wings; **entre ~es** *fig* behind the scenes.

basto, -ta *adj* coarse. ▶ **bastos** *mpl* (*naipes*) = clubs.

bastón *m* **1.** (*para andar*) walking stick. **2.** (*de mando*) baton. **3.** (*para esquiar*) ski stick.

basura *f* *lit & fig* rubbish *Br*, garbage *Am*; **tirar algo a la ~** to throw sthg away.

basurero *m* **1.** (*persona*) dustman *Br*, garbage man *Am*. **2.** (*vertedero*) rubbish dump.

bata *f* **1.** (*de casa*) housecoat; (*para baño, al levantarse*) dressing gown. **2.** (*de trabajo*) overall; (*de médico*) white coat; (*de laboratorio*) lab coat.

batacazo *m* bump, bang.

batalla *f* battle; **de ~** (*de uso diario*) everyday.

batallar *vi* (*con armas*) to fight.

batallón *m* (*MIL*) batallion.

batata *f* sweet potato.

bate *m* (*DEP*) bat.

batear ♦ *vt* to hit. ♦ *vi* to bat.

batería *f* **1.** (*ELECTR & MIL*) battery. **2.** (*MÚS*) drums (*pl*). **3.** (*conjunto*) set; (*de preguntas*) barrage; **~ de cocina** pots (*pl*) and pans.

batido, -da *adj* **1.** (*nata*) whipped; (*claras*) whisked. **2.** (*senda, camino*) well-trodden. ▶ **batido** *m* (*bebida*) milkshake. ▶ **batida** *f* **1.** (*de caza*) beat. **2.** (*de policía*) combing, search.

batidora *f* (*para batir*) electric beater; (*para mezclar*) food processor.

batín *m* short dressing gown.

batir *vt* **1.** (*gen*) to beat; (*nata*) to whip; (*récord*) to break. **2.** (*suj: olas, lluvia, viento*) to beat against. **3.** (*derribar*) to knock down. **4.** (*explorar - suj: policía etc*) to comb, to search. ▶ **batirse** *vpr* (*luchar*) to fight.

batuta *f* baton; **llevar la ~** *fig* to call the tune.

baúl *m* **1.** (*cofre*) trunk. **2.** *Amer* (*maletero*) boot *Br*, trunk *Am*.

bautismo *m* baptism.

bautista *m y f* (*RELIG*) Baptist.

bautizar *vt* **1.** (*RELIG*) to baptize, to christen. **2.** *fam* *fig* (*aguar*) to dilute.

bautizo *m* (*RELIG*) baptism, christening.

baya *f* berry.

bayeta *f* **1.** (*tejido*) flannel. **2.** (*para fregar*) cloth.

bayo, -ya *adj* bay.

bayoneta *f* bayonet.

baza *f* **1.** (*en naipes*) trick. **2.** *loc:* **meter ~ en algo** to butt in on sthg; **no pude meter ~ (en la conversación)** I couldn't get a word in edgeways.

bazar *m* bazaar.

bazo *m* (*ANAT*) spleen.

bazofia *f* **1.** (*comida*) pigswill (*U*). **2.** *fig* (*libro, película etc*) rubbish (*U*).

bazuca, bazooka *m* bazooka.

beatificar *vt* to beatify.

beato, -ta *adj* **1.** (*beatificado*) blessed. **2.** (*piadoso*) devout. **3.** *fig* (*santurrón*) sanctimonious.

bebe *m* *Amer* *fam* baby.

bebé *m* baby; **~ probeta** test-tube baby.

bebedero *m* (*de jaula*) water dish.

bebedor, -ra *m y f* (*borrachín*) heavy drinker.

beber ♦ *vt* (*líquido*) to drink. ♦ *vi* (*tomar líquido*) to drink.

bebida *f* drink.

bebido, -da *adj* drunk.

beca *f* (*del gobierno*) grant; (*de organización privada*) scholarship.

becar *vt* (*suj: gobierno*) to award a grant to; (*suj: organización privada*) to award a scholarship to.

becario, -ria *m y f* (*del gobierno*) grant holder; (*de organización privada*) scholarship holder.

becerro, -rra *m y f* calf.

bechamel [betʃa'mel], **besamel** *f* béchamel sauce.

bedel *m* janitor.

befa *f* jeer; hacer ~ de to jeer at.

begonia *f* begonia.

beige [beis] *adj inv & m inv* beige.

béisbol *m* baseball.

belén *m* (*de Navidad*) crib, Nativity scene.

belfo, -fa *adj* thick-lipped.

belga *adj*, *m y f* Belgian.

Bélgica *f* Belgium.

Belgrado Belgrade.

Belice Belize.

bélico, -ca *adj* (*gen*) war (*antes de sust*); (*actitud*) bellicose, warlike.

belicoso, -sa *adj* bellicose; *fig* aggressive.

beligerante *adj*, *m y f* belligerent.

bellaco, -ca *m y f* villain, scoundrel.

belleza *f* beauty.

bello, -lla *adj* beautiful.

bellota *f* acorn.

bemol ♦ *adj* flat. ♦ *m* (MÚS) flat; **tener (muchos) ~es** (*ser difícil*) to be tricky; (*tener valor*) to have guts; (*ser un abuso*) to be a bit rich o much.

bendecir *vt* to bless.

bendición *f* blessing.

bendito, -ta *adj* 1. (*santo*) holy; (*alma*) blessed; **¡~ sea Dios!** *fam fig* thank goodness! 2. (*dichoso*) lucky. 3. (*para enfatizar*) damned.

benefactor, -ra *m y f* benefactor (*f* benefactress).

beneficencia *f* charity.

beneficiar *vt* to benefit. ► **beneficiarse** *vpr* to benefit; **~se de algo** to do well out of sthg.

beneficiario, -ria *m y f* beneficiary; (*de cheque*) payee.

beneficio *m* 1. (*bien*) benefit; **a ~ de** (*gala, concierto*) in aid of; **en ~ de** for the good of; **en ~ de todos** in everyone's interest; **en ~ propio** for one's own good. 2. (*ganancia*) profit.

beneficioso, -sa *adj*: ~ (**para**) beneficial (to).

benéfico, -ca *adj* 1. (*favorable*) beneficial. 2. (*rifa, función*) charity (*antes de sust*); (*organización*) charitable.

Benelux (*abrev de* **België-Nederland-Luxembourg**) *m*: **el ~** Benelux.

beneplácito *m* consent.

benevolencia *f* benevolence.

benevolente, benévolo, -la *adj* benevolent.

bengala *f* 1. (*para pedir ayuda, iluminar etc*) flare. 2. (*para fiestas etc*) sparkler.

benigno, -na *adj* 1. (*gen*) benign. 2. (*clima, temperatura*) mild.

benjamín, -ina *m y f* youngest child.

berberecho *m* cockle.

berenjena *f* aubergine Br, eggplant Am.

Berlín Berlin.

bermejo, -ja *adj* reddish.

bermellón *adj inv & m* vermilion.

bermudas *fpl* Bermuda shorts.

Berna Berne.

berrear *vi* 1. (*animal*) to bellow. 2. (*persona*) to howl.

berrido *m* 1. (*del becerro*) bellow, bellowing (U). 2. (*de persona*) howl, howling (U).

berrinche *m* *fam* tantrum; **coger** o **agarrarse un ~** to throw a tantrum.

berro *m* watercress.

berza *f* cabbage.

besamel = **bechamel**.

besar *vt* to kiss. ► **besarse** *vpr* to kiss.

beso *m* kiss.

bestia ♦ *adj* 1. (*ignorante*) thick, stupid. 2. (*torpe*) clumsy. 3. (*maleducado*) rude. ♦ *m y f* (*ignorante, torpe*) brute. ♦ *f* (*animal*) beast; **~ de carga** beast of burden.

bestial *adj* 1. (*brutal*) animal, brutal; (*apetito*) tremendous. 2. *fam* (*formidable*) terrific.

bestialidad *f* 1. (*brutalidad*) brutality. 2. *fam* (*tontería*) rubbish (U), nonsense (U). 3. *fam* (*montón*): **una ~ de** tons (*pl*) o stacks (*pl*) of.

best-seller [bes'seler] (*pl* **best-sellers**) *m* best-seller.

besucón, -ona *fam adj* kissy.

besugo *m* 1. (*animal*) sea bream. 2. *fam* (*persona*) idiot.

besuquear *fam vt* to smother with kisses. ► **besuquearse** *vpr fam* to smooch.

bético, -ca adj (andaluz) Andalusian.

betún m 1. (para calzado) shoe polish. 2. (QUÍM) bitumen.

bianual adj 1. (dos veces al año) twice-yearly. 2. (cada dos años) biennial.

biberón m (baby's) bottle; **dar el ~ a** to bottle-feed.

Biblia f Bible.

bibliografía f bibliography.

biblioteca f 1. (gen) library. 2. (mueble) bookcase.

bibliotecario, -ria m y f librarian.

bicarbonato m (FARM) bicarbonate of soda.

bicentenario m bicentenary.

bíceps m inv biceps.

bicho m 1. (animal) beast, animal; (insecto) bug. 2. (pillo) little terror.

bici f fam bike.

bicicleta f bicycle; **ir en ~** to cycle.

bicolor adj two-coloured.

bidé m bidet.

bidimensional adj two-dimensional.

bidón m drum (for oil etc); (lata) can, canister; (de plástico) (large) bottle.

biela f connecting rod.

bien ◆ adv 1. (como es debido, adecuado) well; **has hecho ~** you did the right thing; **habla inglés ~** she speaks English well; **cierra ~ la puerta** shut the door properly; **hiciste ~ en decírmelo** you were right to tell me. 2. (expresa opinión favorable): **estar ~** (de aspecto) to be nice; (de salud) to be o feel well; (de calidad) to be good; (de comodidad) to be comfortable; **está ~ que te vayas, pero antes despídete** it's all right for you to go, but say goodbye first; **oler ~** to smell nice; **pasarlo ~** to have a good time; **sentar ~ a alguien** (ropa) to suit sb; (comida) to agree with sb; (comentario) to please sb. 3. (muy, bastante) very; **hoy me he levantado ~ temprano** I got up nice and early today; **quiero un vaso de agua ~ fría** I'd like a nice cold glass of water. 4. (vale, de acuerdo) all right, OK; **¿nos vamos? – ~** shall we go? – all right o OK. 5. (de buena gana, fácilmente) quite happily; **ella ~ que lo haría, pero no la dejan** she'd be happy to do it, but they won't let her. 6. loc: **¡está ~!** (bueno, vale) all right then!; (es suficiente) that's enough; **¡ya está ~!** that's enough!; **¡muy ~!** very good!, excellent! ◆ adj inv (adinerado) well-to-do. ◆ conj: **~ ... ~** either ... or; **dáselo ~ a mi hermano, ~ a mi padre** either give it to my brother or my father. ◆ m good; **el ~ y el mal** good and evil; **por el**

~ de for the sake of; **lo hice por tu ~** I did it for your own good. ▶ **bienes** mpl 1. (patrimonio) property (U); **~es inmuebles** o **raíces** real estate (U); **~es gananciales** shared possessions; **~es muebles** personal property (U). 2. (productos) goods; **~es de consumo** consumer goods. ▶ **más bien** loc adv rather; **no estoy contento, más ~ estupefacto** I'm not so much happy as stunned. ▶ **no bien** loc adv no sooner, as soon as; **no ~ me había marchado cuando empezaron a ...** no sooner had I gone than they started ... ▶ **si bien** loc conj although, even though.

bienal f biennial exhibition.

bienaventurado, -da m y f (RELIG) blessed person.

bienestar m wellbeing.

bienhechor, -ra m y f benefactor (f benefactress).

bienio m (periodo) two years (pl).

bienvenido, -da ◆ adj welcome. ◆ interj: **¡~!** welcome! ▶ **bienvenida** f welcome; **dar la bienvenida a alguien** to welcome sb.

bies m inv bias binding; **al ~** (costura) on the bias; (sombrero etc) at an angle.

bife m Amer steak.

bífido, -da adj forked.

biftec = **bistec**.

bifurcación f fork; (TECN) bifurcation.

bifurcarse vpr to fork.

bigamia f bigamy.

bígamo, -ma ◆ adj bigamous. ◆ m y f bigamist.

bigote m moustache.

bigotudo, -da adj with a big moustache.

bikini = **biquini**.

bilateral adj bilateral.

biliar adj bile (antes de sust).

bilingüe adj bilingual.

bilis f inv lit & fig bile.

billar m 1. (juego) billiards (U). 2. (sala) billiard hall.

billete m 1. (dinero) note Br, bill Am. 2. (de rifa, transporte etc) ticket; **~ de ida y vuelta** return (ticket) Br, round-trip (ticket) Am; **~ sencillo** single (ticket) Br, one-way (ticket) Am. 3. (de lotería) lottery ticket.

billetera f, **billetero** m wallet.

billón núm billion Br, trillion Am; ver también **seis**.

bingo m 1. (juego) bingo. 2. (sala) bingo hall. 3. (premio) (full) house.

binóculo m pince-nez.

biodegradable adj biodegradable.
biografía f biography.
biográfico, -ca adj biographical.
biógrafo, -fa m y f (persona) biographer.
biología f biology.
biológico, -ca adj biological.
biólogo, -ga m y f biologist.
biombo m (folding) screen.
biopsia f biopsy.
bioquímico, -ca ◆ adj biochemical. ◆ m y f (persona) biochemist. ➤ **bioquímica** f (ciencia) biochemistry.
biorritmo m biorhythm.
biosfera f biosphere.
bipartidismo m two-party system.
bipartito, -ta adj bipartite.
biplaza m two-seater.
biquini, bikini m (bañador) bikini.
birlar vt fam to pinch, to nick.
Birmania Burma.
birra f mfam beer.
birrete m 1. (de clérigo) biretta. 2. (de catedrático) mortarboard.
birria f fam (fealdad - persona) sight, fright; (- cosa) monstrosity.
bis (pl **bises**) ◆ adj inv: viven en el 150 ~ they live at 150a. ◆ m encore.
bisabuelo, -la m y f great-grandfather (f great-grandmother); ~s great-grandparents.
bisagra f hinge.
bisección f bisection.
bisectriz f bisector.
biselar vt to bevel.
bisexual adj, m y f bisexual.
bisiesto → año.
bisnieto, -ta m y f great-grandchild, great-grandson (f great-granddaughter).
bisonte m bison.
bisoño, -ña m y f novice.
bistec, biftec m steak.
bisturí (pl **bisturíes**) m scalpel.
bisutería f imitation jewellery.
bit [bit] (pl **bits**) m (INFORM) bit.
biter, bitter m bitters (U).
bizco, -ca adj cross-eyed.
bizcocho m (de repostería) sponge.
bizquear vi to squint.
blanco, -ca ◆ adj white. ◆ m y f (persona) white (person). ➤ **blanco** m 1. (color) white. 2. (diana) target; **dar en el** ~ (DEP & MIL) to hit the target; fig to hit the nail on the head. 3. fig (objetivo) target; (de miradas) object. 4. (espacio vacío) blank (space). ➤ **blanca** f (MÚS) minim; **estar** o **quedarse sin blanca** fig to

be flat broke. ➤ **blanco del ojo** m white of the eye. ➤ **en blanco** loc adv 1. (gen) blank; **se quedó con la mente en** ~ his mind went blank. 2. (sin dormir): **una noche en** ~ a sleepless night.
blancura f whiteness.
blandengue adj lit & fig weak.
blandir vt to brandish.
blando, -da adj 1. (gen) soft; (carne) tender. 2. fig (persona - débil) weak; (- indulgente) lenient, soft.
blandura f 1. (gen) softness; (de carne) tenderness. 2. fig (debilidad) weakness; (indulgencia) leniency.
blanquear vt 1. (ropa) to whiten; (con lejía) to bleach. 2. (con cal) to whitewash. 3. fig (dinero) to launder.
blanquecino, -na adj off-white.
blanqueo m 1. (de ropa) whitening; (con lejía) bleaching. 2. (encalado) whitewashing. 3. fig (de dinero) laundering.
blanquillo m Amer egg.
blasfemar vi (RELIG): ~ **(contra)** to blaspheme (against).
blasfemia f (RELIG) blasphemy.
blasfemo, -ma adj blasphemous.
bledo m: **me importa un** ~ **(lo que diga)** fam I don't give a damn (about what he says).
blindado, -da adj armour-plated; (coche) armoured.
bloc [blok] (pl **blocs**) m pad; ~ **de dibujo** sketchpad.
bloque m 1. (gen & INFORM) block. 2. (POLÍT) bloc. 3. (MEC) cylinder block.
bloquear vt 1. (gen & DEP) to block. 2. (aislar - suj: ejército, barcos) to blockade; (- suj: nieve, inundación) to cut off. 3. (FIN) to freeze.
bloqueo m 1. (gen & DEP) blocking; ~ **mental** mental block. 2. (ECON & MIL) blockade. 3. (FIN) freeze, freezing (U).
blues [blus] m inv (MÚS) blues.
blusa f blouse.
blusón m smock.
bluyín m, **bluyines** mpl Amer jeans (pl).
boa f (ZOOL) boa.
bobada f fam: **decir** ~s to talk nonsense.
bobina f 1. (gen) reel; (en máquina de coser) bobbin. 2. (ELECTR) coil.
bobo, -ba ◆ adj 1. (tonto) stupid, daft. 2. (ingenuo) naïve. ◆ m y f 1. (tonto) idiot. 2. (ingenuo) simpleton.
boca f 1. (gen) mouth; ~ **arriba/abajo** face up/down; **abrir** o **hacer** ~ to whet one's appetite; **se me hace la** ~ **agua** it

makes my mouth water. **2.** (*entrada*) opening; (*de cañón*) muzzle; **~ de metro** tube o underground entrance Br, subway entrance Am. ▶ **boca a boca** *m* mouth-to-mouth resuscitation.

bocacalle *f* (*entrada*) entrance (*to a street*); (*calle*) side street; **gire en la tercera ~** take the third turning.

bocadillo *m* (CULIN) sandwich.

bocado *m* **1.** (*comida*) mouthful. **2.** (*mordisco*) bite.

bocajarro ▶ **a bocajarro** *loc adv* point-blank; **se lo dije a ~** I told him to his face.

bocanada *f* (*de líquido*) mouthful; (*de humo*) puff; (*de viento*) gust.

bocata *m fam* sarnie.

bocazas *m y f inv fam despec* big mouth, blabbermouth.

boceto *m* sketch, rough outline.

bocha *f* (*bolo*) bowl. ▶ **bochas** *fpl* (*juego*) bowls (U).

bochorno *m* **1.** (*calor*) stifling o muggy heat. **2.** (*vergüenza*) embarrassment.

bochornoso, -sa *adj* **1.** (*tiempo*) muggy. **2.** (*vergonzoso*) embarrassing.

bocina *f* **1.** (AUTOM & MÚS) horn. **2.** (*megáfono*) megaphone, loudhailer.

boda *f* wedding.

bodega *f* **1.** (*cava*) wine cellar. **2.** (*tienda*) wine shop; (*bar*) bar. **3.** (*en buque, avión*) hold.

bodegón *m* (ARTE) still life.

bodrio *m fam despec* (*gen*) rubbish (U); (*comida*) pigswill (U); **¡qué ~!** what a load of rubbish!

body [ˈboði] (*pl* **bodies**) *m* body (*garment*).

BOE (*abrev de* **Boletín Oficial del Estado**) *m* official Spanish gazette.

bofetada *f* slap (in the face).

bofetón *m* hard slap (in the face).

bofia *f fam:* **la ~** the cops (*pl*).

boga *f:* **estar en ~** to be in vogue.

bogavante *m* lobster.

Bogotá Bogotá.

bohemio, -mia *adj* **1.** (*vida etc*) bohemian. **2.** (*de Bohemia*) Bohemian.

boicot (*pl* **boicots**), **boycot** (*pl* **boycots**) *m* boycott.

boicotear, boycotear *vt* to boycott.

boina *f* beret.

boîte [bwat] (*pl* **boîtes**) *f* nightclub.

boj (*pl* **bojes**) *m* (*árbol*) box.

bol (*pl* **boles**) *m* bowl.

bola *f* **1.** (*gen*) ball; (*canica*) marble; **~s de naftalina** mothballs. **2.** *fam* (*mentira*) fib.

bolada *f* Amer *fam* opportunity.

bolea *f* (DEP) volley.

boleadoras *fpl* bolas, *sling consisting of three balls strung on leather cords, used for hunting.*

bolear *vt* Amer to shine, to polish.

bolera *f* bowling alley.

boletería *f* Amer box office.

boletero, -ra *m y f* Amer box office attendant.

boletín *m* journal, periodical; **~ noticias** o **informativo** news bulletin; **~ meteorológico** weather forecast; **~ de prensa** press release.

boleto *m* **1.** (*de lotería, rifa*) ticket; (*de quinielas*) coupon. **2.** Amer (*billete*) ticket.

boli *m fam* Biro®.

boliche *m* **1.** (*en la petanca*) jack. **2.** (*bolos*) ten-pin bowling. **3.** (*bolera*) bowling alley. **4.** Amer (*tienda*) small grocery store.

bólido *m* racing car.

bolígrafo *m* ballpoint pen, Biro®.

bolívar *m* bolivar.

Bolivia Bolivia.

boliviano, -na *adj, m y f* Bolivian.

bollo *m* **1.** (*para comer - de pan*) (bread) roll; (*- dulce*) bun. **2.** (*abolladura*) dent; (*abultamiento*) bump.

bolo *m* **1.** (DEP) (*pieza*) skittle. **2.** (*actuación*) show. **3.** Amer (*borracho*) drunk. ▶ **bolos** *mpl* (*deporte*) skittles.

bolsa *f* **1.** (*gen*) bag; Amer (*de mujer*) handbag; **~ de aire** air pocket; **~ de aseo** toilet bag; **~ de basura** bin liner; **~ de deportes** holdall, sports bag; **~ de plástico** (*en tiendas*) carrier o plastic bag; **~ de viaje** travel bag. **2.** (FIN): **~ (de valores)** stock exchange, stock market; **la ~ ha subido/bajado** share prices have gone up/down; **jugar a la ~** to speculate on the stock market. **3.** (MIN) pocket. **4.** (ANAT) sac. **5.** Amer (*saco de dormir*) sleeping bag. ▶ **bolsa de trabajo** *f* job vacancies.

bolsillo *m* pocket; **de ~** pocket (*antes de sust*); **lo pagué de mi ~** I paid it out of my own pocket.

bolso *m* bag; (*de mujer*) handbag.

boludo, -da *m y f* Amer *mfam* prat Br, jerk Am.

bomba ◆ *f* **1.** (*explosivo*) bomb; **~ atómica** atom o nuclear bomb; **~ de mano** (hand) grenade. **2.** (*máquina*) pump. **3.** *fig* (*acontecimiento*) bombshell. **4.** Amer (*gasolinera*) petrol station Br, gas station Am. **5.** *loc:* **pasarlo ~** *fam* to have a great time. ◆ *adj inv fam* astounding.

bombachas *fpl* Amer (*pantalones*) baggy trousers; (*ropa interior*) knickers.

bombachos *mpl* baggy trousers.

bombardear *vt* lit & *fig* to bombard.

bombardeo *m* bombardment.

bombardero *m* (*avión*) bomber.

bombazo *m fig* (*noticia*) bombshell.

bombear *vt* (*gen* & DEP) to pump.

bombero, -ra *m y f* 1. (*de incendios*) fireman (*f* firewoman). 2. Amer (*de gasolinera*) petrol-pump Br o gas-pump Am attendant.

bombilla *f* light bulb.

bombillo *m* Amer light bulb.

bombín *m* bowler (hat).

bombo *m* 1. (MÚS) bass drum. 2. *fam fig* (*elogio*) hype; **a ~ y platillo** with a lot of hype. 3. (MEC) drum.

bombón *m* (*golosina*) chocolate.

bombona *f* cylinder; **~ de butano** (butane) gas cylinder.

bonachón, -ona *fam adj* kindly.

bonanza *f* 1. (*de tiempo*) fair weather; (*de mar*) calm at sea. 2. *fig* (*prosperidad*) prosperity.

bondad *f* (*cualidad*) goodness; (*inclinación*) kindness; **tener la ~ de hacer algo** to be kind enough to do sthg.

bondadoso, -sa *adj* kind, good-natured.

boniato *m* sweet potato.

bonificar *vt* 1. (*descontar*) to give a discount of. 2. (*mejorar*) to improve.

bonito, -ta *adj* pretty; (*bueno*) nice. ▶ **bonito** *m* bonito (tuna).

bono *m* 1. (*vale*) voucher. 2. (COM) bond.

bonobús *m* multiple-journey ticket.

bonoloto *m* Spanish state-run lottery.

BONOLOTO

In this Spanish state-run lottery, participants try to guess a combination of six numbers between one and forty-nine. A ticket contains eight grids of forty-nine boxes, each grid being equivalent to one entry. The 'bonoloto' is drawn four times a week.

---

boñiga *f* cowpat.

boquerón *m* (fresh) anchovy.

boquete *m* hole.

boquiabierto, -ta *adj* open-mouthed; *fig* astounded, speechless.

boquilla *f* 1. (*para fumar*) cigarette holder. 2. (*de pipa, instrumento musical*) mouthpiece. 3. (*de tubo, aparato*) nozzle.

borbotear, borbotar *vi* to bubble.

borbotón *m*: **salir a borbotones** to gush out.

borda *f* (NÁUT) gunwale. ▶ **fuera borda** *m* (*barco*) outboard motorboat; (*motor*) outboard motor.

bordado, -da *adj* embroidered. ▶ **bordado** *m* embroidery.

bordar *vt* (*coser*) to embroider.

borde ◆ *adj mfam* (*antipático*) stroppy, miserable. ◆ *m* (*gen*) edge; (*de carretera*) side; (*del mar*) shore, seaside; (*de río*) bank; (*de vaso, botella*) rim; **al ~ de** *fig* on the verge o brink of.

bordear *vt* (*estar alrededor de*) to border; (*moverse alrededor de*) to skirt (round).

bordillo *m* kerb.

bordo *m* (NÁUT) board, side. ▶ **a bordo** *loc adv* on board.

borla *f* tassel; (*pompón*) pompom.

borrachera *f* 1. (*embriaguez*) drunkenness (U). 2. *fig* (*emoción*) intoxication.

borracho, -cha ◆ *adj* (*ebrio*) drunk. ◆ *m y f* (*persona*) drunk. ▶ **borracho** *m* (*bizcocho*) ~ rum baba.

borrador *m* 1. (*escrito*) rough draft. 2. (*goma de borrar*) rubber Br, eraser Am.

borrar *vt* 1. (*hacer desaparecer - con goma*) to rub out Br, to erase Am; (- *en ordenador*) to delete; (- *en casete*) to erase. 2. (*tachar*) to cross out; *fig* (*de lista etc*) to take off. 3. *fig* (*olvidar*) to erase.

borrasca *f* thunderstorm.

borrego, -ga *m y f* (*animal*) lamb.

borrón *m* blot; *fig* blemish; **hacer ~ y cuenta nueva** to wipe the slate clean.

borroso, -sa *adj* (*foto, visión*) blurred; (*escritura, texto*) smudgy.

Bosnia Bosnia.

Bosnia Herzegovina Bosnia Herzegovina.

bosnio, -nia *adj, m y f* Bosnian.

bosque *m* (*pequeño*) wood; (*grande*) forest.

bosquejar *vt* (*esbozar*) to sketch (out).

bosquejo *m* (*esbozo*) sketch.

bostezar *vi* to yawn.

bostezo *m* yawn.

bota *f* 1. (*calzado*) boot; **~s de agua** o **de lluvia** wellingtons. 2. (*de vino*) *small leather container in which wine is kept.*

botana *f* Amer snack, tapa.

botánico, -ca ◆ *adj* botanical. ◆ *m y f* (*persona*) botanist. ▶ **botánica** *f* (*ciencia*) botany.

botar ◆ *vt* 1. (NÁUT) to launch. 2. *fam* (*despedir*) to throw o kick out. 3. (*pelota*) to bounce. 4. Amer (*tirar*) to throw away.

◆ *vi* 1. (*saltar*) to jump. 2. (*pelota*) to bounce.

bote *m* 1. (*tarro*) jar. 2. (*lata*) can. 3. (*botella de plástico*) bottle. 4. (*barca*) boat; ~ **salvavidas** lifeboat. 5. (*salto*) jump; **dar ~s** (*gen*) to jump up and down; (*en tren, coche*) to bump up and down. 6. (*de pelota*) bounce; **dar ~s** to bounce.

botella *f* bottle.

botellín *m* small bottle.

boticario, -ria *m y f* desus pharmacist.

botijo *m* earthenware jug.

botín *m* 1. (*de guerra, atraco*) plunder, loot. 2. (*calzado*) ankle boot.

botiquín *m* (*caja*) first-aid kit; (*mueble*) first-aid cupboard.

botón *m* button. ▶ **botones** *m inv* (*de hotel*) bellboy, bellhop Am; (*de oficinas etc*) errand boy.

boutique [bu'tik] *f* boutique.

bóveda *f* (ARQUIT) vault.

box (*pl* **boxes**) *m* 1. (*de coches*) pit; **entrar en ~es** to make a pit stop. 2. Amer (*boxeo*) boxing.

boxeador, -ra *m y f* boxer.

boxear *vi* to box.

boxeo *m* boxing.

bóxer (*pl* **bóxers**) *m* boxer.

boya *f* 1. (*en el mar*) buoy. 2. (*de una red*) float.

boyante *adj* 1. (*feliz*) happy. 2. (*próspero - empresa, negocio*) prosperous; (*- economía, comercio*) buoyant.

boycot *etc* = **boicot**.

bozal *m* (*gen*) muzzle.

bracear *vi* (*nadar*) to swim.

braga *f* (*gen pl*) knickers (*pl*).

bragueta *f* flies (*pl*) Br, zipper Am.

braille ['braile] *m* Braille.

bramar *vi* 1. (*animal*) to bellow. 2. (*persona - de dolor*) to groan; (*- de ira*) to roar.

bramido *m* 1. (*de animal*) bellow. 2. (*de persona - de dolor*) groan; (*- de ira*) roar.

brandy, brandi *m* brandy.

branquia *f* (*gen pl*) gill.

brasa *f* ember; **a la ~** (CULIN) barbecued.

brasero *m* brazier.

brasier, brassier *m* Amer bra.

Brasil: (**el**) ~ Brazil.

brasileño, -ña *adj, m y f* Brazilian.

brasilero, -ra *adj, m y f* Amer Brazilian.

brassier = **brasier**.

bravata *f* (*gen pl*) 1. (*amenaza*) threat. 2. (*fanfarronería*) bravado (U).

braveza *f* bravery.

bravío, -a *adj* (*salvaje*) wild; (*feroz*) fierce.

bravo, -va *adj* 1. (*valiente*) brave. 2. (*animal*) wild. 3. (*mar*) rough. ▶ **bravo** ◆ *m* (*aplauso*) cheer. ◆ *interj*: ¡~! bravo!

bravuconear *vi* despec to brag.

bravura *f* 1. (*de persona*) bravery. 2. (*de animal*) ferocity.

braza *f* 1. (DEP) breaststroke; **nadar a ~** to swim breaststroke. 2. (*medida*) fathom.

brazada *f* stroke.

brazalete *m* 1. (*en la muñeca*) bracelet. 2. (*en el brazo*) armband.

brazo *m* 1. (*gen* & ANAT) arm; (*de animal*) foreleg; **cogidos del ~** arm in arm; **en ~s** in one's arms; **luchar a ~ partido** (*con empeño*) to fight tooth and nail; **quedarse o estarse con los ~s cruzados** *fig* to sit around doing nothing; **ser el ~ derecho de alguien** to be sb's right-hand man (*f* woman). 2. (*de árbol, río, candelabro*) branch; (*de grúa*) boom, jib. ▶ **brazo de gitano** *m* ≃ swiss roll.

brea *f* 1. (*sustancia*) tar. 2. (*para barco*) pitch.

brebaje *m* concoction, foul drink.

brecha *f* 1. (*abertura*) hole, opening. 2. (MIL) breach. 3. *fig* (*impresión*) impression.

bregar *vi* 1. (*luchar*) to struggle. 2. (*trabajar*) to work hard. 3. (*reñir*) to quarrel.

breña *f* scrub.

breve ◆ *adj* brief; **en ~** (*pronto*) shortly; (*en pocas palabras*) in short. ◆ *f* (MÚS) breve.

brevedad *f* shortness; **a o con la mayor ~** as soon as possible.

brezo *m* heather.

bribón, -ona *m y f* scoundrel, rogue.

bricolaje, bricolage *m* D.I.Y., do-it-yourself.

brida *f* (*de caballo*) bridle.

bridge *m* bridge.

brigada ◆ *m* (MIL) ≃ warrant officer. ◆ *f* 1. (MIL) brigade. 2. (*equipo*) squad, team; **~ antidisturbios/antidroga** riot/drug squad.

brillante ◆ *adj* 1. (*reluciente - luz, astro*) shining; (*- metal, zapatos, pelo*) shiny; (*- ojos, sonrisa, diamante*) sparkling. 2. (*magnífico*) brilliant. ◆ *m* diamond.

brillantina *f* brilliantine, Brylcreem®.

brillar *vi* lit & *fig* to shine.

brillo *m* 1. (*resplandor - de luz*) brilliance; (*- de estrellas*) shining; (*- de zapatos*) shine. 2. (*lucimiento*) splendour.

brilloso, -sa adj Amer shining.

brincar vi (saltar) to skip (about); ~ **de alegria** to jump for joy.

brinco m jump.

brindar ◆ vi to drink a toast; ~ **por algo/alguien** to drink to sthg/sb. ◆ vt (regalo) to offer. ▶ **brindarse** vpr: ~**se a hacer algo** to offer to do sthg.

brindis m inv toast.

brío m (energía, decisión) spirit, verve.

brisa f breeze.

británico, -ca ◆ adj British. ◆ m y f British person, Briton; **los ~s** the British.

brizna f 1. (filamento - de hierba) blade; (- de tabaco) strand. 2. fig (un poco) trace, bit.

broca f (drill) bit.

brocha f brush; ~ **de afeitar** shaving brush.

brochazo m brushstroke.

broche m 1. (cierre) clasp, fastener. 2. (joya) brooch.

broma f (ocurrencia, chiste) joke; (jugarreta) prank, practical joke; **en ~** as a joke; **gastar una ~ a alguien** to play a joke o prank on sb; **ni en ~** fig no way, not on your life.

bromear vi to joke.

bromista m y f joker.

bronca → **bronco**.

bronce m (aleación) bronze.

bronceado, -da adj tanned. ▶ **bronceado** m tan.

bronceador, -ra adj tanning (antes de sust), suntan (antes de sust). ▶ **bronceador** m (loción) suntan lotion; (leche) suntan cream.

broncear vt to tan. ▶ **broncearse** vpr to get a tan.

bronco, -ca adj 1. (grave - voz) harsh; (- tos) throaty. 2. fig (brusco) gruff. ▶ **bronca** f 1. (jaleo) row. 2. (regañina) scolding; **echar una bronca a alguien** to give sb a row, to tell sb off.

bronquio m bronchial tube.

bronquitis f inv bronchitis.

brotar vi 1. (planta) to sprout, to bud. 2. (agua, sangre etc): ~ **de** to well up out of. 3. fig (esperanza, sospechas, pasiones) to stir. 4. (en la piel): **le brotó un sarpullido** he broke out in a rash.

brote m 1. (de planta) bud, shoot. 2. fig (inicios) sign, hint.

broza f (maleza) brush, scrub.

bruces ▶ **de bruces** loc adv face down; **se cayó de ~** he fell headlong, he fell flat on his face.

bruja → **brujo**.

brujería f witchcraft, sorcery.

brujo, -ja adj (hechicero) enchanting. ▶ **brujo** m wizard, sorcerer. ▶ **bruja** f 1. (hechicera) witch, sorceress. 2. (mujer fea) hag. 3. (mujer mala) (old) witch. ◆ adj inv Amer fam (sin dinero) broke, skint.

brújula f compass.

bruma f (niebla) mist; (en el mar) sea mist.

bruñido m polishing.

brusco, -ca adj 1. (repentino, imprevisto) sudden. 2. (tosco, grosero) brusque.

Bruselas Brussels.

brusquedad f 1. (imprevisión) suddenness. 2. (grosería) brusqueness.

brutal adj (violento) brutal.

brutalidad f (cualidad) brutality.

bruto, -ta ◆ adj 1. (torpe) clumsy; (ignorante) thick, stupid; (maleducado) rude. 2. (sin tratar): **en ~** (diamante) uncut; (petróleo) crude. 3. (sueldo, peso etc) gross. ◆ m y f brute.

Bta. abrev de **beata**.

Bto. abrev de **beato**.

bubónica → **peste**.

bucal adj oral.

Bucarest Bucharest.

bucear vi (en agua) to dive.

buceo m (underwater) diving.

bucle m (rizo) curl, ringlet.

Budapest Budapest.

budismo m Buddhism.

buen → **bueno**.

buenas → **bueno**.

buenaventura f (adivinación) fortune; **leer la ~ a alguien** to tell sb's fortune.

bueno, -na (compar **mejor**, superl m **el mejor**, superl f **la mejor**) adj (antes de sust masculino: **buen**) 1. (gen) good. 2. (bondadoso) kind, good; **ser ~ con alguien** to be good to sb. 3. (curado, sano) well, all right. 4. (apacible - tiempo, clima) nice, fine. 5. (aprovechable) all right; (comida) fresh. 6. (uso enfático): **ese buen hombre** that good man; **un buen día** one fine day. 7. loc: **de buen ver** good-looking; **de buenas a primeras** (de repente) all of a sudden; (a simple vista) at first sight; **estar ~** fam (persona) to be a bit of all right, to be tasty; **estar de buenas** to be in a good mood; **lo ~ es que ...** the best thing about it is that ... ▶ **bueno** ◆ m (CIN): **el ~** the goody. ◆ adv 1. (vale, de acuerdo) all right, O.K. 2. (pues) well. ◆ interj Amer (al teléfono): **¡~!** hello. ▶ **¡buenas!** interj: **¡buenas!** hello!

Buenos Aires Buenos Aires.
buey (*pl* **bueyes**) *m* ox.
búfalo *m* buffalo.
bufanda *f* scarf.
bufar *vi* (*toro, caballo*) to snort.
bufé (*pl* **bufés**), **buffet** (*pl* **buffets**) *m* (*en restaurante*) buffet.
bufete *m* lawyer's practice.
buffet = **bufé**.
bufido *m* (*de toro, caballo*) snort.
bufón *m* buffoon, jester.
buhardilla *f* (*habitación*) attic; (*vivienda*) attic flat.
búho *m* owl.
buitre *m* *lit* & *fig* vulture.
bujía *f* (AUTOM) spark plug.
bulbo *m* (ANAT & BOT) bulb.
buldozer (*pl* **buldozers**), **bulldozer** (*pl* **bulldozers**) [bul'doθer] *m* bulldozer.
bulevar (*pl* **bulevares**) *m* boulevard.
Bulgaria Bulgaria.
búlgaro, -ra *adj, m y f* Bulgarian.
▶ **búlgaro** *m* (*lengua*) Bulgarian.
bulla *f* racket, uproar; **armar ~** to kick up a racket.
bulldozer = **buldozer**.
bullicio *m* (*de ciudad, mercado*) hustle and bustle; (*de multitud*) hubbub.
bullicioso, -sa *adj* 1. (*agitado - reunión, multitud*) noisy; (- *calle, mercado*) busy, bustling. 2. (*inquieto*) rowdy.
bullir *vi* 1. (*hervir*) to boil; (*burbujear*) to bubble. 2. *fig* (*multitud*) to bustle; (*ratas, hormigas etc*) to swarm; (*mar*) to boil; **~ de** to seethe with.
bulto *m* 1. (*volumen*) bulk, size; **escurrir el ~** (*trabajo*) to shirk; (*cuestión*) to evade the issue. 2. (*abombamiento - en rodilla, superficie etc*) bump; (- *en maleta, bolsillo etc*) bulge. 3. (*forma imprecisa*) blurred shape. 4. (*paquete*) package; (*maleta*) item of luggage; (*fardo*) bundle; **~ de mano** piece o item of hand luggage.
bumerán (*pl* **bumeráns**), **bumerang** (*pl* **bumerangs**) *m* boomerang.
bungalow [buŋga'lo] (*pl* **bungalows**) *m* bungalow.
búnquer (*pl* **búnquers**), **bunker** (*pl* **bunkers**) *m* (*refugio*) bunker.
buñuelo *m* (CULIN - *dulce*) = doughnut; (- *de bacalao etc*) = dumpling.
BUP *m academically orientated secondary-school course taught in Spain for pupils aged 14-17.*
buque *m* ship; **~ nodriza** supply ship.
burbuja *f* bubble; **hacer ~s** to bubble.
burbujear *vi* to bubble.
burdel *m* brothel.

burdo, -da *adj* (*gen*) crude; (*tela*) coarse.
burgués, -esa *adj* middle-class, bourgeois.
burguesía *f* middle class; (HIST & POLÍT) bourgeoisie.
burla *f* 1. (*mofa*) taunt; **hacer ~ de** to mock. 2. (*broma*) joke. 3. (*engaño*) trick.
burlar *vt* (*esquivar*) to evade; (*ley*) to flout. ▶ **burlarse de** *vpr* to make fun of.
burlesco, -ca *adj* (*tono*) jocular; (LITER) burlesque.
burlón, -ona *adj* (*sarcástico*) mocking.
burocracia *f* bureaucracy.
burócrata *m y f* bureaucrat.
burrada *f* (*acción, dicho*): **hacer ~s** to act stupidly; **decir ~s** to talk nonsense.
burro, -rra *m y f* 1. (*animal*) donkey; **no ver tres en un ~** *fam* to be as blind as a bat. 2. *fam* (*necio*) dimwit.
bursátil *adj* stock-market (*antes de sust*).
bus (*pl* **buses**) *m* (AUTOM & INFORM) bus.
busca ◆ *f* search; **en ~ de** in search of; **la ~ de** the search for. ◆ *m* → **buscapersonas**.
buscapersonas, busca *m inv* bleeper.
buscar ◆ *vt* 1. (*gen*) to look for; (*provecho, beneficio propio*) to seek; **voy a ~ el periódico** I'm going for the paper o to get the paper; **ir a ~ a alguien** to pick sb up. 2. (*en diccionario, índice, horario*) to look up. 3. (INFORM) to search for. ◆ *vi* to look. ▶ **buscarse** *vpr* (*personal, aprendiz etc*): '**se busca camarero**' 'waiter wanted'.
buscón, -ona *m y f* (*estafador*) swindler.
búsqueda *f* search.
busto *m* 1. (*pecho*) chest; (*de mujer*) bust. 2. (*escultura*) bust.
butaca *f* 1. (TEATR) seat. 2. (*mueble*) armchair; (*en barco, tren*) reclining seat.
butano *m* butane (gas).
butifarra *f* type of Catalan pork sausage.
buzo *m* 1. (*persona*) diver. 2. *Amer* (*chandal*) tracksuit.
buzón *m* letter box; **echar algo al ~** to post sthg.
byte [bait] (*pl* **bytes**) *m* (INFORM) byte.

C

c, C *f* (*letra*) c, C.

c., c/ (*abrev de* **calle**) St.

c/ 1. (*abrev de* **cuenta**) a/c. 2. = **c**.

cabal *adj* 1. (*honrado*) honest. 2. (*exacto*) exact; (*completo*) complete. ▶ **cabales** *mpl*: **no estar en sus ~es** not to be in one's right mind.

cábala *f* (*gen pl*) (*conjeturas*) guess.

cabalgar *vi* to ride.

cabalgata *f* cavalcade, procession.

caballa *f* mackerel.

caballería *f* 1. (*animal*) mount, horse. 2. (*cuerpo militar*) cavalry.

caballeriza *f* stable.

caballero ◆ *adj* (*cortés*) gentlemanly. ◆ *m* 1. (*gen*) gentleman; (*al dirigir la palabra*) sir; **ser todo un ~** to be a real gentleman; **'caballeros'** (*en aseos*) 'gents'; (*en grandes almacenes*) 'menswear'. 2. (*miembro de una orden*) knight.

caballete *m* 1. (*de lienzo*) easel. 2. (*de mesa*) trestle. 3. (*de nariz*) bridge.

caballito *m* small horse, pony. ▶ **caballitos** *mpl* (*de feria*) merry-go-round (*sg*).

caballo *m* 1. (*animal*) horse; **montar a ~** to ride. 2. (*pieza de ajedrez*) knight. 3. (*naipe*) = queen. 4. (MEC): **~ (de fuerza o de vapor)** horsepower.

cabaña *f* 1. (*choza*) hut, cabin. 2. (*ganado*) livestock (U).

cabaret (*pl* **cabarets**) *m* cabaret.

cabecear *vi* 1. (*persona - negando*) to shake one's head; (*- afirmando*) to nod one's head. 2. (*caballo*) to toss its head. 3. (*dormir*) to nod (off).

cabecera *f* 1. (*gen*) head; (*de cama*) headboard. 2. (*de texto*) heading; (*de periódico*) headline. 3. (*de río*) headwaters (*pl*).

cabecilla *m y f* ringleader.

cabellera *f* long hair (U).

cabello *m* hair (U).

caber *vi* 1. (*gen*) to fit; **no cabe nadie más** there's no room for anyone else; **no me cabe en el dedo** it won't fit my finger. 2. (MAT): **nueve entre tres caben a tres** three into nine goes three (times). 3. (*ser posible*) to be possible; **cabe destacar que ...** it's worth pointing out that ...

cabestrillo ▶ **en cabestrillo** *loc adj* in a sling.

cabestro *m* (*animal*) leading ox.

cabeza *f* 1. (*gen*) head; **por ~** per head; **obrar con ~** to use one's head; **tirarse de ~ (a)** to dive (into); **venir a la ~** to come to mind; **~ (lectora)** (*gen*) head; (*de tocadiscos*) pickup. 2. (*pelo*) hair. 3. (*posición*) front, head; **a la o en ~** (*en competición etc*) in front; (*en lista*) at the top o head. 4. loc: **andar o estar mal de la ~** to be funny in the head; **se le ha metido en la ~ que ...** he has got it into his head that ...; **sentar la ~** to settle down. ▶ **cabeza de ajo** *f* head of garlic. ▶ **cabeza de turco** *f* scapegoat.

cabezada *f* 1. (*de sueño*) nod, nodding (U); **dar ~s** to nod off. 2. (*golpe*) butt.

cabezal *m* (*de aparato*) head.

cabezón, -ona *adj* (*terco*) pigheaded, stubborn.

cabida *f* capacity.

cabina *f* 1. (*locutorio*) booth, cabin; **~ telefónica** phone box Br, phone booth. 2. (*de avión*) cockpit; (*de camión*) cab. 3. (*vestuario - en playa*) bathing hut; (*- en piscina*) changing cubicle.

cabinera *f* Amer air hostess.

cabizbajo, -ja *adj* crestfallen.

cable *m* cable.

cablegrafiar *vt* to cable.

cabo *m* 1. (GEOGR) cape. 2. (NÁUT) cable, rope. 3. (MIL) corporal. 4. (*trozo*) bit, piece; (*trozo final*) stub, stump; (*de cuerda*) end. 5. loc: **llevar algo a ~** to carry sthg out. ▶ **cabo suelto** *m* loose end. ▶ **al cabo de** *loc prep* after.

cabra *f* (*animal*) goat; **estar como una ~** fam to be off one's head.

cabré → **caber**.

cabrear *vt* mfam: **~ a alguien** to get sb's goat, to annoy sb.

cabría → **caber**.

cabriola *f* prance; **hacer ~s** to prance about.

cabrita *f* Amer popcorn.

cabrito *m* (*animal*) kid (goat).

cabro, -bra *m y f* Amer fam kid.

cabrón, -ona *vulg* ◆ *adj*: **¡qué ~ eres!** you bastard! ◆ *m y f* bastard (*f* bitch).

cabuya *f* Amer rope.

caca *f* fam 1. (*excremento*) pooh. 2. (*cosa sucia*) nasty o dirty thing.

cacahuate *m* Amer peanut.

cacahuete *m* (*fruto*) peanut.

cacao *m* 1. (*bebida*) cocoa. 2. (*árbol*) cacao.

cacarear *vi* (*gallo*) to cluck, to cackle.

cacatúa *f* (*ave*) cockatoo.

cacería *f* hunt.

cacerola *f* pot, pan.

cachalote *m* sperm whale.

cacharro *m* 1. (*recipiente*) pot; **fregar los ~s** to do the dishes. 2. *fam* (*trasto*) junk (U), rubbish (U). 3. (*máquina*) crock; (*coche*) banger.

cachear *vt* to frisk.

cachemir *m*, **cachemira** *f* cashmere.

cacheo *m* frisk, frisking (U).

cachet [ka'tʃe] *m* 1. (*distinción*) cachet. 2. (*cotización de artista*) fee.

cachetada *f* Amer fam smack.

cachete *m* 1. (*moflete*) chubby cheek. 2. (*bofetada*) slap.

cachirulo *m* (*chisme*) thingamajig.

cachivache *m fam* knick-knack.

cacho *m* 1. *fam* (*pedazo*) piece, bit. 2. Amer (*asta*) horn.

cachondearse *vpr fam*: **~ (de)** to take the mickey (out of).

cachondeo *m fam* 1. (*diversión*) lark. 2. *despec* (*cosa poco seria*) joke.

cachondo, -da *adj* 1. (*divertido*) funny. 2. (*salido*) randy.

cachorro, -rra *m y f* (*de perro*) puppy; (*de gato*) kitten; (*de león, lobo, oso*) cub.

cacique *m* 1. (*persona influyente*) cacique, local political boss. 2. (*jefe indio*) chief.

caco *m fam* thief.

cacto, cactus (*pl* **cactus**) *m* cactus.

cada *adj inv* 1. (*gen*) each; (*con números, tiempo*) every; **~ dos meses** every two months; **~ cosa a su tiempo** one thing at a time; **~ cual** each one, everyone; **~ uno de** each of. 2. (*valor progresivo*): **~ vez más** more and more; **~ vez más largo** longer and longer; **~ día más** more and more each day. 3. (*valor enfático*) such; **¡se pone ~ sombrero!** she wears such hats!

cadalso *m* scaffold.

cadáver *m* corpse, (dead) body.

cadena *f* 1. (*gen*) chain; **en ~** (*accidente*) multiple. 2. (TV) channel. 3. (RADIO - *emisora*) station; (- *red de emisoras*) network. 4. (*de proceso industrial*) line; **~ de montaje** assembly line. 5. (*aparato de música*) sound system. 6. (GEOGR) range. ▶ **cadena perpetua** *f* life imprisonment.

cadencia *f* (*ritmo*) rhythm, cadence.

cadera *f* hip.

cadete *m* cadet.

caducar *vi* 1. (*carnet, ley, pasaporte etc*) to expire. 2. (*medicamento*) to pass its use-by date; (*alimento*) to pass its sell-by date.

caducidad *f* expiry.

caduco, -ca *adj* 1. (*viejo*) decrepit; (*idea*) outmoded. 2. (*desfasado*) no longer valid.

caer *vi* 1. (*gen*) to fall; (*diente, pelo*) to fall out; **dejar ~ algo** to drop sthg; **~ bajo** to sink (very) low; **estar al ~** to be about to arrive. 2. (*al perder equilibrio*) to fall over o down; **~ de un tejado/caballo** to fall from a roof/horse. 3. *fig* (*sentar*): **~ bien/mal (a alguien)** (*comentario, noticia etc*) to go down well/badly (with sb). 4. *fig* (*mostrarse*): **me cae bien/mal** I like/don't like him. 5. *fig* (*estar situado*): **cae cerca de aquí** it's not far from here. 6. *fig* (*recordar*): **~ (en algo)** to be able to remember (sthg). ▶ **caer en** *vi* 1. (*entender*) to get, to understand; (*solución*) to hit upon. 2. (*coincidir - fecha*) to fall on; **cae en domingo** it falls on a Sunday. 3. (*incurrir*) to fall into. ▶ **caerse** *vpr* 1. (*persona*) to fall over o down. 2. (*objetos*) to drop, to fall. 3. (*desprenderse - diente, pelo etc*) to fall out; (- *botón*) to fall off; (- *cuadro*) to fall down.

café (*pl* **cafés**) *m* 1. (*gen*) coffee; **~ solo/con leche** black/white coffee; **~ instantáneo** o **soluble** instant coffee. 2. (*establecimiento*) cafe.

CAFÉ

Spanish coffee is usually of the strong, expresso variety, served in very small cups. A small cup of black coffee is called 'un solo'. A 'solo' with a tiny amount of milk added is called 'un cortado'. 'Un carajillo' is a black coffee with a dash of liqueur. 'Café con leche' is a large cup filled half with coffee and half with hot milk and is usually drunk at breakfast. In South America, 'café de olla', which contains sugar, cinnamon and other spices, is also common.

cafebrería *f* (*Amér*) *cafe cum bookshop.*

CAFEBRERÍA

The South American 'cafebrería' is a cafe which, in addition to serving drinks and snacks, also sells books, magazines and records. 'Cafebrerías' are often the venue for 'tertulias', poetry readings, conferences and concerts.

cafeína *f* caffeine.

cafetera → **cafetero**.

cafetería *f* cafe.

cafetero, -ra *m y f* 1. (*cultivador*) coffee grower. **2.** (*comerciante*) coffee merchant. ▶ **cafetera** f **1.** (*gen*) coffee pot. **2.** (*en bares*) expresso machine; (*eléctrica*) percolator, coffee machine.

cafiche m Amer fam pimp.

cagar vulg vi (*defecar*) to shit. ▶ **cagarse** vpr vulg lit & fig to shit o.s.

caído, -da adj (*árbol, hoja*) fallen. ▶ **caída** f **1.** (*gen*) fall, falling (U); (*de diente, pelo*) loss. **2.** (*de paro, precios, terreno*): **caída (de)** drop (in). **3.** (*de falda, vestido etc*) drape. ▶ **caídos** mpl: **los ~s** the fallen.

caiga etc → **caer**.

caimán m **1.** (*animal*) alligator, cayman. **2.** fig (*persona*) sly fox.

caja f **1.** (*gen*) box; (*para transporte, embalaje*) crate; **una ~ de cervezas** a crate of beer; **~ de cartón** cardboard box; **~ torácica** thorax. **2.** (*de reloj*) case; (*de engranajes etc*) housing; **~ de cambios** gearbox. **3.** (*ataúd*) coffin. **4.** (*de dinero*) cash box; **~ fuerte** o **de caudales** safe, strongbox. **5.** (*en tienda, supermercado*) till; (*en banco*) cashier's desk. **6.** (*banco*): **~ (de ahorros)** savings bank. **7.** (*hueco - de chimenea, ascensor*) shaft. **8.** (IMPRENTA) case. **9.** (*de instrumento musical*) body. ▶ **caja negra** f black box. ▶ **caja registradora** f cash register.

cajero, -ra m y f (*en tienda*) cashier; (*en banco*) teller. ▶ **cajero** m: **~ (automático)** cash machine, cash dispenser.

cajetilla f **1.** (*de cigarrillos*) packet. **2.** (*de cerillas*) box.

cajón m **1.** (*de mueble*) drawer. **2.** (*recipiente*) crate, case. ▶ **cajón de sastre** m muddle, jumble.

cajuela f Amer boot Br, trunk Am.

cal f lime.

cala f **1.** (*bahía pequeña*) cove. **2.** (*del barco*) hold.

calabacín m courgette Br, zucchini Am.

calabaza f pumpkin, gourd.

calabozo m cell.

calada → **calado**.

calado, -da adj soaked. ▶ **calado** m (NÁUT) draught. ▶ **calada** f (*de cigarrillo*) drag.

calamar m squid.

calambre m **1.** (*descarga eléctrica*) (electric) shock. **2.** (*contracción muscular*) cramp (U).

calamidad f calamity; **ser una ~** fig to be a dead loss.

calaña f despec: **de esa ~** of that ilk.

calar ◆ vt **1.** (*empapar*) to soak. **2.** fig (*persona*) to see through. **3.** (*gorro, sombrero*) to jam on. **4.** (*fruta*) to cut a sample of. **5.** (*perforar*) to pierce. ◆ vi **1.** (NÁUT) to draw. **2.** fig (*penetrar*): **~ en** to have an impact on. ▶ **calarse** vpr **1.** (*empaparse*) to get soaked. **2.** (*motor*) to stall.

calavera f (*cráneo*) skull. ▶ **calaveras** fpl Amer (AUTOM) rear lights.

calcar vt **1.** (*dibujo*) to trace. **2.** (*imitar*) to copy.

calce m **1.** (*cuña*) wedge. **2.** Amer (DER) footnote.

calceta f stocking; **hacer ~** to knit.

calcetín m sock.

calcificarse vpr to calcify.

calcinar vt (*quemar*) to char.

calcio m calcium.

calco m **1.** (*reproducción*) tracing. **2.** fig (*imitación*) carbon copy.

calcomanía f transfer.

calculador, -ra adj lit & fig calculating. ▶ **calculadora** f calculator.

calcular vt **1.** (*cantidades*) to calculate. **2.** (*suponer*) to reckon.

cálculo m **1.** (*operación*) calculation. **2.** (*ciencia*) calculus. **3.** (*evaluación*) estimate. **4.** (MED) stone, calculus.

caldear vt **1.** (*calentar*) to heat (up). **2.** fig (*excitar*) to warm up, to liven up.

caldera f **1.** (*recipiente*) cauldron. **2.** (*máquina*) boiler.

caldereta f stew.

calderilla f small change.

caldero m cauldron.

caldo m **1.** (*sopa*) broth. **2.** (*caldillo*) stock. **3.** (*vino*) wine.

calefacción f heating; **~ central** central heating.

calefactor m heater.

calendario m calendar; **~ escolar/laboral** school/working year.

calentador m **1.** (*aparato*) heater. **2.** (*prenda*) legwarmer.

calentar ◆ vt (*subir la temperatura de*) to heat (up), to warm (up). ◆ vi (*entrenarse*) to warm up. ▶ **calentarse** vpr (*por calor - suj: persona*) to warm o.s., to get warm; (*- suj: cosa*) to heat up.

calentura f **1.** (*fiebre*) fever, temperature. **2.** (*herida*) cold sore.

calesitas fpl Amer merry-go-round (sg).

calibrar vt **1.** (*medir*) to calibrate, to gauge. **2.** (*dar calibre a - arma*) to bore. **3.** fig (*juzgar*) to gauge.

calibre m **1.** (*diámetro - de pistola*) calibre; (*- de alambre*) gauge; (*- de tubo*) bore.

2. (*instrumento*) gauge. **3.** *fig* (*tamaño*) size.

calidad *f* **1.** (*gen*) quality; **de ~** quality (*antes de sust*); **~ de vida** quality of life. **2.** (*clase*) class. **3.** (*condición*): **en ~ de** in one's capacity as.

cálido, -da *adj* warm.

caliente *adj* **1.** (*gen*) hot; (*templado*) warm; **en ~** *fig* in the heat of the moment. **2.** *fig* (*acalorado*) heated.

calificación *f* **1.** (*atributo*) quality. **2.** (EDUC) mark.

calificar *vt* **1.** (*denominar*): **~ a alguien de algo** to call sb sthg, to describe sb as sthg. **2.** (EDUC) to mark. **3.** (GRAM) to qualify.

calificativo, -va *adj* qualifying. ▶ **calificativo** *m* epithet.

caligrafía *f* **1.** (*arte*) calligraphy. **2.** (*rasgos*) handwriting.

cáliz *m* (RELIG) chalice.

calizo, -za *adj* chalky. ▶ **caliza** *f* limestone.

callado, -da *adj* quiet, silent.

callar ♦ *vi* **1.** (*no hablar*) to keep quiet, to be silent. **2.** (*dejar de hablar*) to be quiet, to stop talking. ♦ *vt* **1.** (*ocultar*) to keep quiet about; (*secreto*) to keep. **2.** (*acallar*) to silence. ▶ **callarse** *vpr* **1.** (*no hablar*) to keep quiet, to be silent. **2.** (*dejar de hablar*) to be quiet, to stop talking; **¡cállate!** shut up! **3.** (*ocultar*) to keep quiet about; (*secreto*) to keep.

calle *f* **1.** (*vía de circulación*) street, road; **~ arriba/abajo** up/down the street; **~ de dirección única** one-way street; **~ peatonal** pedestrian precinct. **2.** (DEP) lane. **3.** *loc*: **dejar a alguien en la ~** to put sb out of a job; **echar a alguien a la ~** (*de un trabajo*) to sack sb; (*de un lugar público*) to kick o throw sb out.

callejear *vi* to wander the streets.

callejero, -ra *adj* (*gen*) street (*antes de sust*); (*perro*) stray. ▶ **callejero** *m* (*guía*) street map.

callejón *m* alley; **~ sin salida** cul-de-sac; *fig* blind alley, impasse.

callejuela *f* backstreet, side street.

callista *m y f* chiropodist.

callo *m* (*dureza*) callus; (*en el pie*) corn. ▶ **callos** *mpl* (CULIN) tripe (U).

calma *f* **1.** (*ausencia de ruido o movimiento*) calm; **en ~** calm. **2.** (*sosiego*) tranquility; **con ~** calmly; **tómatelo con ~** take it easy. **3.** (*apatía*) sluggishness, indifference.

calmante ♦ *adj* soothing. ♦ *m* sedative.

calmar *vt* **1.** (*mitigar*) to relieve. **2.** (*tranquilizar*) to calm, to soothe. ▶ **calmarse** *vpr* to calm down; (*dolor, tempestad*) to abate.

caló *m* gypsy dialect.

calor *m* (*gen*) heat; (*tibieza*) warmth; **entrar en ~** (*gen*) to get warm; (*público, deportista*) to warm up; **hacer ~** to be warm o hot; **tener ~** to be warm o hot.

caloría *f* calorie.

calumnia *f* (*oral*) slander; (*escrita*) libel.

calumniar *vt* (*oralmente*) to slander; (*por escrito*) to libel.

calumnioso, -sa *adj* (*de palabra*) slanderous; (*por escrito*) libellous.

caluroso, -sa *adj* **1.** (*gen*) hot; (*templado*) warm. **2.** *fig* (*afectuoso*) warm.

calva → **calvo**.

calvario *m fig* (*sufrimiento*) ordeal.

calvicie *f* baldness.

calvo, -va *adj* bald. ▶ **calva** *f* (*en la cabeza*) bald patch.

calza *f* (*cuña*) wedge, block.

calzado, -da *adj* (*con zapatos*) shod. ▶ **calzada** *f* road (surface).

calzar *vt* **1.** (*poner calzado*) to put on. **2.** (*llevar un calzado*) to wear; **¿qué número calza?** what size do you take? **3.** (*poner cuña a*) to wedge. ▶ **calzarse** *vpr* to put on.

calzo *m* (*cuña*) wedge.

calzón *m* (*gen pl*) *desus* (*pantalón*) trousers (*pl*). ▶ **calzones** *mpl* *Amer* (*bragas*) knickers (*pl*).

calzoncillo *m* (*gen pl*) underpants (*pl*).

cama *f* bed; **estar en** o **guardar ~** to be confined to bed; **hacer la ~** to make the bed; **~ individual/de matrimonio** single/double bed.

camada *f* litter.

camafeo *m* cameo.

camaleón *m lit & fig* chameleon.

cámara ♦ *f* **1.** (*gen & TECN*) chamber; **~ alta/baja** upper/lower house; **~ de aire/gas** air/gas chamber. **2.** (CIN, FOT & TV) camera; **a ~ lenta** *lit & fig* in slow motion. **3.** (*de balón, neumático*) inner tube. **4.** (*habitáculo*) cabin. ♦ *m y f* (*persona*) cameraman (*f* camerawoman).

camarada *m y f* (POLÍT) comrade.

camarero, -ra *m y f* (*de restaurante*) waiter (*f* waitress); (*de hotel*) steward (*f* chambermaid).

camarilla *f* clique; (POLÍT) lobby.

camarón *m* shrimp.

camarote *m* cabin.

cambiante *adj* changeable.

cambiar ◆ *vt* **1.** (*gen*) to change; **~ libras por pesetas** to change pounds into pesetas. **2.** (*canjear*): **~ algo (por)** to exchange sthg (for). ◆ *vi* **1.** (*gen*) to change; **~ de** (*gen*) to change; (*casa*) to move; **~ de trabajo** to move jobs. **2.** (AUTOM) (*de marchas*) to change gear. ▶ **cambiarse** *vpr*: **~se (de)** (*ropa*) to change; (*casa*) to move; **~se de vestido** to change one's dress.

cambio *m* **1.** (*gen*) change. **2.** (*trueque*) exchange; **a ~ (de)** in exchange o return (for). **3.** (FIN - *de acciones*) price; (*- de divisas*) exchange rate; **'cambio'** 'bureau de change'. **4.** (AUTOM): **~ de marchas** o **velocidades** gear change; **~ de sentido** U-turn. ▶ **cambio de rasante** *m* brow of a hill. ▶ **libre cambio** *m* **1.** (ECON) (*librecambismo*) free trade. **2.** (FIN) (*de divisas*) floating exchange rates (*pl*). ▶ **en cambio** *loc adv* **1.** (*por otra parte*) on the other hand, however. **2.** (*en su lugar*) instead.

camelar *vt fam* (*seducir, engañar*) to butter up, to win over.

camelia *f* camellia.

camello, -lla *m y f* (*animal*) camel. ▶ **camello** *m fam* (*traficante*) drug pusher o dealer.

camellón *m Amer* central reservation.

camerino *m* dressing room.

camilla ◆ *f* (*gen*) stretcher; (*de psiquiatra, dentista*) couch. ◆ *adj* → **mesa**.

caminante *m y f* walker.

caminar ◆ *vi* **1.** (*a pie*) to walk. **2.** *fig* (*ir*): **~ (hacia)** to head (for). ◆ *vt* (*una distancia*) to travel, to cover.

caminata *f* long walk.

camino *m* **1.** (*sendero*) path, track; (*carretera*) road; **abrir ~ a** to clear the way for; **abrirse ~** to get on o ahead. **2.** (*ruta*) way; **a medio ~** halfway; **estar a medio ~** to be halfway there; **quedarse a medio ~** to stop halfway through; **~ de** on the way to; **en el** o **de ~** on the way. **3.** (*viaje*) journey; **ponerse en ~** to set off. **4.** *fig* (*medio*) way.

camión *m* **1.** (*de mercancías*) lorry Br, truck Am; **~ cisterna** tanker; **~ de la mudanza** removal van. **2.** *Amer* (*autobús*) bus.

camionero, -ra *m y f* lorry driver Br, trucker Am.

camioneta *f* van.

camisa *f* **1.** (*prenda*) shirt. **2.** *loc*: **meterse en ~ de once varas** to complicate matters unnecessarily; **mudar** o

cambiar de ~ to change sides. ▶ **camisa de fuerza** *f* straitjacket.

camisería *f* (*tienda*) outfitter's.

camiseta *f* **1.** (*ropa interior*) vest. **2.** (*de verano*) T-shirt. **3.** (DEP - *de tirantes*) vest; (*- de mangas*) shirt.

camisola *f* **1.** (*prenda interior*) camisole. **2.** *Amer* (DEP) sports shirt.

camisón *m* nightdress.

camorra *f* trouble; **buscar ~** to look for trouble.

camote *m Amer* sweet potato.

campamento *m* camp.

campana *f* bell; **~ extractora de humos** extractor hood.

campanada *f* **1.** (*de campana*) peal. **2.** (*de reloj*) stroke. **3.** *fig* (*suceso*) sensation.

campanario *m* belfry, bell tower.

campanilla *f* **1.** (*de la puerta*) (small) bell; (*con mango*) handbell. **2.** (*flor*) campanula, bellflower.

campanilleo *m* tinkling (U).

campante *adj fam*: **estar** o **quedarse tan ~** to remain quite unruffled.

campaña *f* (*gen*) campaign; **de ~** (MIL) field (*antes de sust*).

campechano, -na *adj fam* genial, good-natured.

campeón, -ona *m y f* champion.

campeonato *m* championship; **de ~** *fig* terrific, great.

campero, -ra *adj* country (*antes de sust*); (*al aire libre*) open-air. ▶ **campera** *f* **1.** (*bota*) ≃ cowboy boot. **2.** *Amer* (*chaqueta*) short leather jacket.

campesino, -na *m y f* farmer; (*muy pobre*) peasant.

campestre *adj* country (*antes de sust*).

camping ['kampin] (*pl* **campings**) *m* **1.** (*actividad*) camping; **ir de ~** to go camping. **2.** (*terreno*) campsite.

campito *m Amer* property, estate.

campo *m* **1.** (*gen* & INFORM) field; **~ de aviación** airfield; **~ de batalla** battlefield; **~ de tiro** firing range; **dejar el ~ libre** *fig* to leave the field open. **2.** (*campiña*) country, countryside; **a ~ traviesa** cross country. **3.** (DEP - *de fútbol*) pitch; (*- de tenis*) court; (*- de golf*) course. ▶ **campo de concentración** *m* concentration camp.

camuflaje *m* camouflage.

cana → **cano**.

Canadá: **(el) ~** Canada.

canadiense *adj, m y f* Canadian.

canal *m* **1.** (*cauce artificial*) canal. **2.** (GEOGR) (*estrecho*) channel, strait. **3.** (RADIO & TV) channel. **4.** (ANAT) canal, duct. **5.** (*de agua, gas*) conduit, pipe. **6.** *fig* (*medio, vía*) channel.

canalizar *vt* **1.** (*territorio*) to canalize; (*agua*) to channel. **2.** *fig* (*orientar*) to channel.

canalla *m y f* swine, dog.

canalón *m* (*de tejado*) gutter; (*en la pared*) drainpipe.

canapé *m* **1.** (CULIN) canapé. **2.** (*sofá*) sofa, couch.

Canarias *fpl*: **las (islas) ~** the Canary Islands, the Canaries.

canario, -ria ◆ *adj* of the Canary Islands. ◆ *m y f* (*persona*) Canary Islander. ▶ **canario** *m* (*pájaro*) canary.

canasta *f* (gen & DEP) basket.

canastilla *f* **1.** (*cesto pequeño*) basket. **2.** (*de bebé*) layette.

canasto *m* large basket.

cancela *f* wrought-iron gate.

cancelación *f* cancellation.

cancelar *vt* **1.** (*anular*) to cancel. **2.** (*deuda*) to pay, to settle.

cáncer *m* (MED & *fig*) cancer. ▶ **Cáncer** ◆ *m* (*zodiaco*) Cancer. ◆ *m y f* (*persona*) Cancer.

cancerígeno, -na *adj* carcinogenic.

canceroso, -sa *adj* (*úlcera, tejido*) cancerous; (*enfermo*) suffering from cancer.

canciller *m* **1.** (*de gobierno, embajada*) chancellor. **2.** (*de asuntos exteriores*) foreign minister.

canción *f* song; **~ de amor** love song; **~ de cuna** lullaby.

cancionero *m* songbook.

candado *m* padlock.

candela *f* **1.** (*vela*) candle. **2.** *Amer* (*fuego*) fire.

candelabro *m* candelabra.

candelero *m* candlestick; **estar en el ~** *fig* to be in the limelight.

candente *adj* **1.** (*incandescente*) red-hot. **2.** *fig* (*actual*) burning (*antes de sust*).

candidato, -ta *m y f* candidate.

candidatura *f* (*para un cargo*) candidacy.

candidez *f* ingenuousness.

cándido, -da *adj* ingenuous, simple.

candil *m* **1.** (*lámpara*) oil lamp. **2.** *Amer* (*araña*) chandelier.

candilejas *fpl* footlights.

canelo, -la *adj* *fam* *fig* (*inocentón*) gullible. ▶ **canela** *f* cinnamon.

canelón *m* (CULIN) cannelloni (*pl*).

cangrejo *m* crab.

canguro ◆ *m* (*animal*) kangaroo. ◆ *m y f* *fam* (*persona*) babysitter; **hacer de ~** to babysit.

caníbal *m y f* cannibal.

canica *f* (*pieza*) marble. ▶ **canicas** *fpl* (*juego*) marbles.

caniche *m* poodle.

canijo, -ja *adj* sickly.

canilla *f* **1.** (*espinilla*) shinbone. **2.** *Amer* (*grifo*) tap. **3.** *Amer* (*pierna*) leg.

canillita *m* *Amer* newspaper seller.

canino, -na *adj* canine. ▶ **canino** *m* (*diente*) canine (tooth).

canjear *vt* to exchange.

cano, -na *adj* grey. ▶ **cana** *f* grey hair.

canoa *f* canoe.

canódromo *m* greyhound track.

canon *m* **1.** (*norma*) canon. **2.** (*modelo*) ideal. **3.** (*impuesto*) tax. **4.** (MÚS) canon.

canónigo *m* canon.

canonizar *vt* to canonize.

canoso, -sa *adj* grey; (*persona*) grey-haired.

cansado, -da *adj* **1.** (gen) tired; **~ de algo/de hacer algo** tired of sthg/of doing sthg. **2.** (*pesado, cargante*) tiring.

cansador, -ra *adj* *Amer* boring.

cansancio *m* tiredness.

cansar ◆ *vt* to tire (out). ◆ *vi* to be tiring. ▶ **cansarse** *vpr*: **~se (de)** *lit* & *fig* to get tired (of).

Cantábrica → cordillera.

Cantábrico *m*: **el (mar) ~** the Cantabrian Sea.

cantaleta *f* *Amer* nagging.

cantante ◆ *adj* singing. ◆ *m y f* singer.

cantaor, -ra *m y f* flamenco singer.

cantar ◆ *vt* **1.** (*canción*) to sing. **2.** (*bingo, línea, el gordo*) to sing. ◆ *vi* **1.** (*persona, ave*) to sing; (*gallo*) to crow; (*insecto*) to chirp. **2.** *fam* *fig* (*confesar*) to talk.

cántaro *m* large jug, pitcher; **llover a ~s** to rain cats and dogs.

cante *m*: **~ (jondo** o **hondo)** flamenco singing.

cantera *f* (*de piedra*) quarry.

cantero *m* *Amer* flowerbed.

cantidad *f* **1.** (*medida*) quantity. **2.** (*abundancia*) abundance, large number; **en ~** in abundance; **~ de** lots of. **3.** (*número*) number. **4.** (*suma de dinero*) sum (of money).

cantilena, cantinela *f*: **la misma ~** *fig* the same old story.

cantimplora *f* water bottle.

cantina *f* (*de soldados*) mess; (*en fábrica, colegio*) canteen, cafeteria; (*en estación de tren*) buffet.

cantinela = cantilena.

canto m 1. (acción, arte) singing. 2. (canción) song. 3. (lado, borde) edge; **de ~** edgeways. 4. (de cuchillo) blunt edge. 5. (guijarro) pebble; **~ rodado** (pequeño) pebble; (grande) boulder.

cantor, -ra m y f singer.

canturrear vt & vi fam to sing softly.

canuto m 1. (tubo) tube. 2. fam (porro) joint.

caña f 1. (BOT) cane; **~ de azúcar** sugarcane. 2. (de cerveza) small glass of beer. 3. Amer (bebida) rum. ▶ **caña de pescar** f fishing rod.

cañabrava f Amer kind of cane.

cáñamo m hemp.

cañería f pipe.

caño m (de fuente) jet.

cañón m 1. (arma) gun; (HIST) cannon. 2. (de fusil) barrel; (de chimenea) flue; (de órgano) pipe. 3. (GEOGR) canyon.

caoba f mahogany.

caos m inv chaos.

caótico, -ca adj chaotic.

cap. (abrev de capítulo) ch.

capa f 1. (manto) cloak, cape; **andar de ~ caída** to be in a bad way; **de ~ y espada** cloak and dagger. 2. (baño - de barniz, pintura) coat; (- de chocolate etc) coating. 3. (estrato) layer; (GEOL) stratum; **~ de ozono** ozone layer. 4. (grupo social) stratum, class. 5. (TAUROM) cape.

capacidad f 1. (gen) capacity; **con ~ para 500 personas** with a capacity of 500. 2. (aptitud) ability; **no tener ~ para algo/para hacer algo** to be no good at sthg/at doing sthg.

capacitación f training.

capacitar vt: **~ a alguien para algo** (habilitar) to qualify sb for sthg; (formar) to train sb for sthg.

capar vt to castrate.

caparazón m lit & fig shell.

capataz m y f foreman (f forewoman).

capaz adj 1. (gen) capable; **~ de algo/ de hacer algo** capable of sthg/of doing sthg. 2. (espacioso): **muy/poco ~** with a large/small capacity; **~ para** with room for.

capazo m large wicker basket.

capellán m chaplain.

caperuza f (gorro) hood.

capicúa adj inv reversible.

capilla f chapel; **~ ardiente** funeral chapel.

cápita ▶ **per cápita** loc adj per capita.

capital ◆ adj 1. (importante) supreme. 2. (principal) main. ◆ m (ECON) capital. ◆ f (ciudad) capital.

capitalismo m capitalism.

capitalista adj, m y f capitalist.

capitalizar vt 1. (ECON) to capitalize. 2. fig (sacar provecho) to capitalize on.

capitán, -ana m y f captain.

capitanear vt (DEP & MIL) to captain.

capitel m capital.

capitoste m y f despec big boss.

capitulación f capitulation, surrender.

capitular vi to capitulate, to surrender.

capítulo m 1. (sección, división) chapter. 2. fig (tema) subject.

capó, capot [ka'po] m bonnet Br, hood Am.

caporal m (MIL) ≈ corporal.

capot = capó.

capota f hood Br, top Am.

capote m 1. (capa) cape with sleeves; (militar) greatcoat. 2. (TAUROM) cape.

capricho m whim, caprice; **darse un ~** to treat o.s.

caprichoso, -sa adj capricious.

Capricornio ◆ m (zodiaco) Capricorn. ◆ m y f (persona) Capricorn.

cápsula f 1. (gen & ANAT) capsule. 2. (tapón) cap.

captar vt 1. (atraer - simpatía) to win; (- interés) to gain, to capture. 2. (entender) to grasp. 3. (sintonizar) to pick up, to receive.

captura f capture.

capturar vt to capture.

capucha f hood.

capuchón m cap, top.

capullo, -lla vulg m y f (persona) prat. ▶ **capullo** m 1. (de flor) bud. 2. (de gusano) cocoon.

caqui, kaki adj inv (color) khaki.

cara f 1. (rostro, aspecto) face; **~ a ~** face to face; **de ~** (sol, viento) in one's face. 2. (lado) side; (GEOM) face. 3. (de moneda) heads (U); **~ o cruz** heads or tails; **echar algo a ~ o cruz** to toss (a coin) for sthg. 4. fam (osadía) cheek; **tener (mucha) ~, tener la ~ muy dura** to have a cheek. 5. loc: **de ~ a** with a view to; **echar en ~ algo a alguien** to reproach sb for sthg; **romper o partir la ~ a alguien** to smash sb's face in; **verse las ~s** (pelearse) to have it out; (enfrentarse) to fight it out.

carabela f caravel.

carabina f 1. (arma) carbine, rifle. 2. fam fig (mujer) chaperone.

Caracas Caracas.

caracol m 1. (animal) snail. 2. (concha) shell. 3. (rizo) curl.

caracola f conch.

carácter (pl **caracteres**) m character; **tener buen/mal ~** to be good-natured/bad-tempered; **una reunión de ~ privado/oficial** a private/official meeting; **caracteres de imprenta** typeface (sg).

característico, -ca adj characteristic. ▶ característica f characteristic.

caracterización f 1. (gen) characterization. 2. (maquillaje) make-up.

caracterizar vt 1. (definir) to characterize. 2. (representar) to characteristic. 3. (maquillar) to make up. ▶ **caracterizarse por** vpr to be characterized by.

caradura fam adj cheeky.

carajillo m coffee with a dash of liqueur.

carajo mfam interj: **¡~!** damn it!

caramba interj: **¡~!** (sorpresa) good heavens!; (enfado) for heaven's sake!

carambola f cannon (in billiards). ▶ **¡carambolas!** interj Amer: **¡~s!** good heavens!

caramelo m 1. (golosina) sweet. 2. (azúcar fundido) caramel.

cárate = **kárate**.

carátula f 1. (de libro) front cover; (de disco) sleeve. 2. (máscara) mask.

caravana f 1. (gen) caravan. 2. (de coches) tailback. ▶ **caravanas** fpl Amer (pendientes) earrings.

caray interj: **¡~!** (sorpresa) good heavens!; (enfado) damn it!

carbón m (para quemar) coal.

carboncillo m charcoal.

carbonilla f (ceniza) cinder.

carbonizar vt to char, to carbonize.

carbono m carbon.

carburador m carburettor.

carburante m fuel.

carca fam despec adj old-fashioned.

carcajada f guffaw; **reír a ~s** to roar with laughter.

carcamal m y f fam despec old crock.

cárcel f prison.

carcelero, -ra m y f warder, jailer.

carcoma f 1. (insecto) woodworm. 2. (polvo) wood dust.

carcomer vt lit & fig to eat away at.

carcomido, -da adj (madera) worm-eaten.

cardar vt 1. (lana) to card. 2. (pelo) to backcomb.

cardenal m 1. (RELIG) cardinal. 2. (hematoma) bruise.

cardiaco, -ca, cardíaco, -ca adj cardiac, heart (antes de sust).

cárdigan, cardigán m cardigan.

cardinal adj cardinal.

cardiólogo, -ga m y f cardiologist.

cardo m (planta) thistle.

carecer vi: **~ de algo** to lack sthg.

carencia f (ausencia) lack; (defecto) deficiency.

carente adj: **~ de** lacking (in).

carestía f (escasez) scarcity, shortage.

careta f 1. (máscara) mask; **~ antigás** gas mask. 2. fig (engaño) front.

carey m (material) tortoiseshell.

carga f 1. (acción) loading. 2. (cargamento - de avión, barco) cargo; (- de tren) freight. 3. (peso) load. 4. fig (sufrimiento) burden. 5. (ataque, explosivo) charge; **volver a la ~** fig to persist. 6. (de batería, condensador) charge. 7. (para mechero, bolígrafo) refill. 8. (impuesto) tax.

cargado, -da adj 1. (abarrotado): **~ (de)** loaded (with). 2. (arma) loaded. 3. (bebida) strong. 4. (bochornoso - habitación) stuffy; (- tiempo) sultry, close; (- cielo) overcast.

cargador m 1. (de arma) chamber. 2. (ELECTR) charger.

cargamento m cargo.

cargante adj fam fig annoying.

cargar ◆ vt 1. (gen) to load; (pluma, mechero) to refill. 2. (peso encima) to throw over one's shoulder. 3. (ELECTR) to charge. 4. fig (responsabilidad, tarea) to give, to lay upon. 5. (producir pesadez - suj: humo) to make stuffy; (- suj: comida) to bloat. 6. (gravar): **~ un impuesto a algo/alguien** to tax sthg/sb. 7. (importe, factura, deuda): **~ algo (a)** to charge sthg (to). ◆ vi (atacar): **~ (contra)** to charge. ▶ **cargar con** vi 1. (paquete etc) to carry away. 2. fig (coste, responsabilidad) to bear; (consecuencias) to accept; (culpa) to get. ▶ **cargarse** vpr 1. fam (romper) to break. 2. fam (matar - persona) to bump off; (- animal) to kill. 3. (por el humo) to get stuffy.

cargo m 1. (gen, ECON & DER) charge; **correr a ~ de** to be borne by; **hacerse ~ de** (asumir el control de) to take charge of; (ocuparse de) to take care of; (comprender) to understand; **tener (uno) algo a su ~** to be responsible for sthg. 2. (empleo) post.

cargosear vt Amer to annoy, to pester.

carguero m cargo boat.

Caribe m: **el (mar) ~** the Caribbean (Sea).

caribeño, -ña adj Caribbean.

caricatura f caricature.

caricia f caress; (a perro, gato etc) stroke.
caridad f charity.
caries f inv tooth decay.
cariño m 1. (afecto) affection; **tomar ~ a** to grow fond of. 2. (cuidado) loving care. 3. (apelativo) love.
cariñoso, -sa adj affectionate.
carisma m charisma.
carismático, -ca adj charismatic.
Cáritas f charitable organization run by the Catholic Church.
caritativo, -va adj charitable.
cariz m look, appearance; **tomar mal/buen ~** to take a turn for the worse/better.
carmesí (pl carmesíes) adj & m crimson.
carmín ◆ adj (color) carmine. ◆ m 1. (color) carmine. 2. (lápiz de labios) lipstick.
carnada f lit & fig bait.
carnal adj 1. (de la carne) carnal. 2. (parientes) first (antes de sust).
carnaval m carnival.
carnaza f lit & fig bait.
carne f 1. (de persona, fruta) flesh; **ser de ~ y hueso** fig to be human. 2. (alimento) meat; **~ de chancho** Amer o **de cerdo** pork; **~ de cordero** lamb; **~ de res** Amer o **de vaca** beef; **~ de ternera** veal. ▶ **carne de gallina** f gooseflesh.
carné (pl carnés), **carnet** (pl carnets) m (documento) card; **~ de conducir** driving licence; **~ de identidad** identity card.
carnicería f 1. (tienda) butcher's. 2. fig (masacre) carnage (U).
carnicero, -ra m y f lit & fig (persona) butcher.
carnívoro, -ra adj carnivorous. ▶ **carnívoro** m carnivore.
carnoso, -sa adj fleshy; (labios) full.
caro, -ra adj (precio) expensive. ▶ **caro** adv: **costar ~** to be expensive; **vender ~ algo** to sell sthg at a high price; fig not to give sthg up easily; **pagar ~ algo** fig to pay dearly for sthg.
carozo m Amer stone (of fruit).
carpa f 1. (pez) carp. 2. (de circo) big top; (para fiestas etc) marquee; Amer (tienda) tent.
carpeta f file, folder.
carpintería f 1. (arte) carpentry; (de puertas y ventanas) joinery. 2. (taller) carpenter's/joiner's shop.
carpintero, -ra m y f carpenter; (de puertas y ventanas) joiner.
carraca f (instrumento) rattle.

carraspear vi (toser) to clear one's throat.
carraspera f hoarseness.
carrera f 1. (acción de correr) run, running (U). 2. (DEP & fig) race; **~ armamentística** o **de armamentos** arms race; **~ de coches** motor race; **~ de obstáculos** steeplechase. 3. (trayecto) route. 4. (de taxi) ride. 5. (estudios) university course; **hacer la ~ de derecho** to study law (at university). 6. (profesión) career. 7. (en medias) ladder.
carreta f cart.
carrete m 1. (de hilo) bobbin, reel; (de alambre) coil. 2. (FOT) roll (of film). 3. (para pescar) reel. 4. (de máquina de escribir) spool.
carretera f road; **~ de circunvalación** ring road; **~ comarcal** ≃ B road Br; **~ de cuota** Amer toll road; **~ nacional** ≃ A road Br, state highway Am; **~ principal** main road.
carretilla f wheelbarrow.
carril m 1. (de carretera) lane; **~ bus** bus lane. 2. (de vía de tren) rail.
carrillo m cheek; **comer a dos ~s** fig to cram one's face with food.
carrito m trolley.
carro m 1. (vehículo) cart; **~ de combate** (MIL) tank. 2. (de máquina de escribir) carriage. 3. Amer (coche) car; **~ comedor** dining car.
carrocería f bodywork Br, body.
carromato m (carro) wagon.
carroña f carrion.
carroza f (coche) carriage.
carruaje m carriage.
carrusel m (tiovivo) carousel.
carta f 1. (escrito) letter; **echar una ~** to post a letter; **~ de recomendación** reference (letter). 2. (naipe) playing card; **echar las ~s a alguien** to tell sb's fortune (with cards). 3. (menú) menu. 4. (mapa) map; (NÁUT) chart. 5. (documento) charter; **~ verde** green card. 6. loc: **jugarse todo a una ~** to put all one's eggs in one basket. ▶ **carta blanca** f carte blanche. ▶ **carta de ajuste** f test card.
cartabón m set square.
cartapacio m (carpeta) folder.
cartearse vpr to correspond.
cartel m (anuncio) poster; **la obra estuvo dos años en ~** the play ran for two years; **'prohibido fijar ~es'** 'billposters will be prosecuted'.
cártel m cartel.
cartelera f 1. (tablón) hoarding, bill-

board. **2.** (PRENS) listings (pl); **estar en ~** (película, obra) to be showing; **lleva un año en ~** it's been running for a year.

cárter m (AUTOM) housing.

cartera f **1.** (para dinero) wallet. **2.** (para documentos) briefcase; (sin asa) portfolio; (de colegial) satchel. **3.** (COM, FIN & POLÍT) portfolio; (pedidos atrasados) backlog. **4.** Amer (bolso) bag.

carterista m y f pickpocket.

cartero, -ra m y f postman (f postwoman).

cartílago m cartilage.

cartilla f **1.** (documento) book; **~ (de ahorros)** savings book. **2.** (para aprender a leer) primer.

cartón m **1.** (material) cardboard; **~ piedra** papier mâché. **2.** (de cigarrillos) carton.

cartucho m (de arma) cartridge.

cartujo, -ja adj Carthusian.

cartulina f card.

casa f **1.** (edificio) house; **~ adosada** semi-detached house; **~ de campo** country house; **~ rodante** caravan Br, trailer Am; **~ unifamiliar** house (usually detached) on an estate; **echar o tirar la ~ por la ventana** to spare no expense; **ser de andar por ~** (sencillo) to be simple o basic. **2.** (hogar) home; **en ~** at home; **ir a ~** to go home; **pásate por mi ~** come round to my place. **3.** (empresa) company; **~ de huéspedes** guesthouse. **4.** (establecimiento): **~ de cambio** bureau de change; **~ Consistorial** town hall; **~ de socorro** first-aid post. **5.** (restaurante, bar): **especialidad de la ~** speciality of the house; **vino de la ~** house wine.

CASA ROSADA

The Casa Rosada, just off the Plaza de Mayo in Buenos Aires, is the official residence of the Argentinian president and the seat of the Argentinian government. It is here that the president holds cabinet meetings and receives State visits.

---

casaca f frock coat.

casado, -da adj: **~ (con)** married (to).

casamiento m wedding, marriage.

casar ◆ vt **1.** (en matrimonio) to marry. **2.** (unir) to fit together. ◆ vi to match. ▶ **casarse** vpr: **~se (con)** to get married (to).

cascabel m (small) bell.

cascada f (de agua) waterfall.

cascado, -da adj **1.** fam (estropeado)

bust; (persona, ropa) worn-out. **2.** (ronco) rasping.

cascanueces m inv nutcracker.

cascar vt **1.** (romper) to crack. **2.** fam (pegar) to thump. ▶ **cascarse** vpr (romperse) to crack.

cáscara f **1.** (de almendra, huevo etc) shell. **2.** (de limón, naranja) skin, peel.

cascarilla f husk.

cascarón m eggshell.

cascarrabias m y f inv grouch.

casco m **1.** (para la cabeza) helmet; (de motorista) crash helmet. **2.** (de barco) hull. **3.** (de ciudad): **~ antiguo** old (part of) town; **~ urbano** city centre. **4.** (de caballo) hoof. **5.** (envase) empty bottle.

caserío m (casa de campo) country house.

casero, -ra ◆ adj **1.** (de casa - comida) home-made; (- trabajos) domestic; (- reunión, velada) at home; (de la familia) family (antes de sust). **2.** (hogareño) home-loving. ◆ m y f (propietario) landlord (f landlady).

caserón m large, rambling house.

caseta f **1.** (casa pequeña) hut. **2.** (en la playa) bathing hut. **3.** (de feria) stall, booth. **4.** (para perro) kennel.

casete, cassette [ka'sete] ◆ f (cinta) cassette. ◆ m (magnetófono) cassette recorder.

casi adv almost; **~ me muero** I almost o nearly died; **~ no dormí** I hardly slept at all; **~, ~** almost, just about; **~ nunca** hardly ever.

casilla f **1.** (de caja, armario) compartment; (para cartas) pigeonhole. **2.** (en un impreso) box. **3.** (de ajedrez etc) square. ▶ **casilla postal** f Amer PO Box.

casillero m **1.** (mueble) set of pigeonholes. **2.** (casilla) pigeonhole.

casino m (para jugar) casino.

caso m **1.** (gen, DER & GRAM) case; **el ~ es que** the fact is (that); **en el mejor/peor de los ~s** at best/worst. **2.** (ocasión) occasion; **en ~ de** in the event of; **en ~ de que** if; **(en) ~ de que venga** should she come; **en cualquier o todo ~** in any event o case. **3.** loc: **hacer ~ a** to pay attention to; **no hacer o venir al ~** to be irrelevant.

caspa f dandruff.

casquete m (gorro) skullcap.

casquillo m **1.** (de bala) case. **2.** (de lámpara) socket, lampholder.

cassette = casete.

casta f **1.** (linaje) lineage. **2.** (especie, calidad) breed. **3.** (en la India) caste.

castaña → castaño.

castañetear vi (dientes) to chatter.

castaño, -ña adj (color) dark brown. ► **castaño** m 1. (color) dark brown. 2. (árbol) chestnut (tree). ► **castaña** f (fruto) chestnut.

castañuela f castanet.

castellano, -na adj, m y f Castilian. ► **castellano** m (lengua) (Castilian) Spanish.

castidad f chastity.

castigador, -ra fam adj seductive.

castigar vt 1. (imponer castigo) to punish. 2. (DEP) to penalize. 3. (maltratar) to damage.

castigo m 1. (sanción) punishment. 2. (sufrimiento) suffering (U); (daño) damage (U). 3. (DEP) penalty.

Castilla-La Mancha Castile and La Mancha.

Castilla-León Castile and León.

castillo m (edificio) castle.

castizo, -za adj pure; (autor) purist.

casto, -ta adj chaste.

castor m beaver.

castrar vt (animal, persona) to castrate; (gato) to doctor.

castrense adj military.

casual adj chance, accidental.

casualidad f coincidence; **dio la ~ de que ...** it so happened that ...; **por ~** by chance; **¡qué ~!** what a coincidence!

casualmente adv by chance.

casulla f chasuble.

cataclismo m cataclysm.

catacumbas fpl catacombs.

catador, -ra m y f taster.

catalán, -ana adj, m y f Catalan, Catalonian. ► **catalán** m (lengua) Catalan.

catalejo m telescope.

catalizador, -ra adj fig (impulsor) catalysing (antes de sust). ► **catalizador** m 1. (QUÍM & fig) catalyst. 2. (AUTOM) catalytic converter.

catalogar vt 1. (en catálogo) to catalogue. 2. (clasificar): **~ a alguien (de)** to class sb (as).

catálogo m catalogue.

Cataluña Catalonia.

catamarán m catamaran.

cataplasma f (MED) poultice.

catapulta f catapult.

catar vt to taste.

catarata f 1. (de agua) waterfall. 2. (gen pl) (MED) cataract.

catarro m (resfriado) cold; (mucosidad) catarrh.

catastro m land registry.

catástrofe f catastrophe; (accidente de avión, tren etc) disaster.

catastrófico, -ca adj catastrophic.

catch [katʃ] m (DEP) all-in wrestling.

catchup ['ketʃup], **ketchup** m inv ketchup.

catear vt fam to fail.

catecismo m catechism.

cátedra f 1. (cargo - en universidad) chair; (- en instituto) post of head of department. 2. (departamento) department.

catedral f cathedral.

catedrático, -ca m y f (de universidad) professor; (de instituto) head of department.

categoría f 1. (gen) category. 2. (posición social) standing; **de ~** important. 3. (calidad) quality; **de (primera) ~** first-class.

categórico, -ca adj categorical.

catequesis f inv catechesis.

cateto, -ta despec m y f country bumpkin.

catolicismo m Catholicism.

católico, -ca ◆ adj Catholic. ◆ m y f Catholic.

catorce núm fourteen; ver también **seis**.

catorceavo, -va, **catorzavo, -va** núm fourteenth.

catre m (cama) camp bed.

catrín, -trina m y f Amer fam toff.

cauce m 1. (AGR & fig) channel. 2. (de río) river-bed.

caucho m (sustancia) rubber.

caudaloso, -sa adj 1. (río) with a large flow. 2. (persona) wealthy, rich.

caudillo m (en la guerra) leader, head.

causa f 1. (origen, ideal) cause. 2. (razón) reason; **a ~ de** because of. 3. (DER) case.

causalidad f causality.

causante adj: **la razón ~** the cause.

causar vt (gen) to cause; (impresión) to make; (placer) to give.

cáustico, -ca adj lit & fig caustic.

cautela f caution, cautiousness; **con ~** cautiously.

cauteloso, -sa adj cautious, careful.

cautivador, -ra ◆ adj captivating, enchanting. ◆ m y f charmer.

cautivar vt 1. (apresar) to capture. 2. (seducir) to captivate, to enchant.

cautiverio m, **cautividad** f captivity.

cautivo, -va adj, m y f captive.

cauto, -ta adj cautious, careful.

cava ◆ m (bebida) Spanish champagne-

type wine. ◆ *f* (*bodega*) wine cellar.

cavar *vt* & *vi* (*gen*) to dig; (*con azada*) to hoe.

caverna *f* cave; (*más grande*) cavern.

cavernícola *m* y *f* caveman (*f* cavewoman).

caviar (*pl* caviares) *m* caviar.

cavidad *f* cavity; (*formada con las manos*) cup.

cavilar *vi* to think deeply, to ponder.

cayado *m* (*de pastor*) crook.

cayera *etc* → **caer.**

caza ◆ *f* 1. (*acción de cazar*) hunting; **salir** o **ir de ~** to go hunting. 2. (*animales, carne*) game. ◆ *m* fighter (plane).

cazabombardero *m* fighter-bomber.

cazador, -ra *m* y *f* (*persona*) hunter. ► **cazadora** *f* (*prenda*) bomber jacket.

cazalla *f* (*bebida*) aniseed-flavoured spirit.

cazar *vt* 1. (*animales etc*) to hunt. 2. *fig* (*pillar, atrapar*) to catch; (*en matrimonio*) to trap.

cazo *m* saucepan.

cazoleta *f* 1. (*recipiente*) pot. 2. (*de pipa*) bowl.

cazuela *f* 1. (*recipiente*) pot; (*de barro*) earthenware pot; (*para el horno*) casserole (dish). 2. (*guiso*) casserole, stew; **a la ~** casseroled.

cazurro, -rra *adj* (*bruto*) stupid.

c/c (*abrev de* **cuenta corriente**) a/c.

CC OO (*abrev de* **Comisiones Obreras**) *fpl* Spanish communist-inspired trade union.

CD *m* 1. (*abrev de* **club deportivo**) sports club; (*en fútbol*) FC. 2. (*abrev de* **compact disc**) CD.

CDS (*abrev de* **Centro Democrático y Social**) *m* Spanish political party at the centre of the political spectrum.

CE *f* (*abrev de* **Comunidad Europea**) EC.

cebada *f* barley.

cebar *vt* 1. (*sobrealimentar*) to fatten (up). 2. (*máquina, arma*) to prime. 3. (*anzuelo*) to bait. ► **cebarse en** *vpr* to take it out on.

cebo *m* 1. (*para cazar*) bait. 2. *fig* (*para atraer*) incentive.

cebolla *f* onion.

cebolleta *f* 1. (BOT) spring onion. 2. (*en vinagre*) pickled onion; (*muy pequeña*) silverskin onion.

cebollino *m* 1. (BOT) chive; (*cebolleta*) spring onion. 2. *fam* (*necio*) idiot.

cebra *f* zebra.

cecear *vi* to lisp.

ceceo *m* lisp.

cecina *f* dried, salted meat.

cedazo *m* sieve.

ceder ◆ *vt* 1. (*traspasar, transferir*) to hand over. 2. (*conceder*) to give up. ◆ *vi* 1. (*venirse abajo*) to give way. 2. (*destensarse*) to give, to become loose. 3. (*disminuir*) to abate. 4. (*rendirse*) to give up; **~ a** to give in to; **~ en** to give up on.

cedro *m* cedar.

cédula *f* document; **~ (de identidad)** *Amer* identity card.

CEE (*abrev de* **Comunidad Económica Europea**) *f* EEC.

cegar *vt* 1. (*gen*) to blind. 2. (*tapar - ventana*) to block off; (*- tubo*) to block up. ► **cegarse** *vpr lit* & *fig* to be blinded.

cegato, -ta *fam adj* short-sighted.

ceguera *m lit* & *fig* blindness.

CEI (*abrev de* **Confederación de Estados Independientes**) *f* CIS.

ceja *f* (ANAT) eyebrow; **se le metió entre ~ y ~** *fam* he got it into his head.

cejar *vi*: **~ en** to give up on.

celda *f* cell.

celebración *f* 1. (*festejo*) celebration. 2. (*realización*) holding.

celebrar *vt* 1. (*festejar*) to celebrate. 2. (*llevar a cabo*) to hold; (*oficio religioso*) to celebrate. 3. (*alegrarse de*) to be delighted with. 4. (*alabar*) to praise. ► **celebrarse** *vpr* 1. (*festejarse*) to be celebrated; **esa fiesta se celebra el 24 de Julio** that festivity falls on 24th July. 2. (*llevarse a cabo*) to take place.

célebre *adj* famous, celebrated.

celebridad *f* 1. (*fama*) fame. 2. (*persona famosa*) celebrity.

celeridad *f* speed.

celeste *adj* (*del cielo*) celestial, heavenly.

celestial *adj* celestial, heavenly.

celestina *f* lovers' go-between.

celibato *m* celibacy.

célibe *adj, m* y *f* celibate.

celo *m* 1. (*esmero*) zeal, keenness. 2. (*devoción*) devotion. 3. (*de animal*) heat; **en ~** on heat, in season. 4. (*cinta adhesiva*) Sellotape®. ► **celos** *mpl* jealousy (U); **dar ~s a alguien** to make sb jealous; **tener ~s de alguien** to be jealous of sb.

celofán *m* cellophane.

celosía *f* lattice window, jalousie.

celoso, -sa *adj* 1. (*con celos*) jealous. 2. (*cumplidor*) keen, eager.

celta ◆ *adj* Celtic. ◆ *m* y *f* (*persona*) Celt. ◆ *m* (*lengua*) Celtic.

céltico, -ca adj Celtic.

célula f cell. ▶ **célula fotoeléctrica** f photoelectric cell, electric eye.

celular m Amer (teléfono portátil) mobile phone.

celulitis f inv cellulitis.

celulosa f cellulose.

cementerio m 1. (de muertos) cemetery, graveyard. 2. (de cosas inutilizables) dump; ~ **de automóviles** o **coches** scrapyard.

cemento m (gen) cement; (hormigón) concrete; ~ **armado** reinforced concrete.

cena f dinner, supper; **dar una** ~ to give a dinner party.

cenagal m bog, marsh.

cenagoso, -sa adj muddy, boggy.

cenar ◆ vt to have for dinner o supper. ◆ vi to have dinner o supper.

cencerro m cowbell; **estar como un** ~ fam fig to be as mad as a hatter.

cenefa f border.

cenicero m ashtray.

cenit = **zenit**.

cenizo, -za adj ashen, ash-grey. ▶ **cenizo** m 1. (mala suerte) bad luck. 2. (gafe) jinx. ▶ **ceniza** f ash. ▶ **cenizas** fpl (de cadáver) ashes.

censar vt to take a census of.

censo m 1. (padrón) census; ~ **electoral** electoral roll. 2. (tributo) tax.

censor, -ra m y f (funcionario) censor.

censura f 1. (prohibición) censorship. 2. (organismo) censors (pl). 3. (reprobación) censure, severe criticism.

censurar vt 1. (prohibir) to censor. 2. (reprobar) to censure.

centavo, -va núm hundredth; **la centava parte** a hundredth.

centella f 1. (rayo) flash. 2. (chispa) spark.

centellear vi to sparkle; (estrella) to twinkle.

centelleo m sparkle, sparkling (U); (de estrella) twinkle, twinkling (U).

centena f hundred; **una** ~ **de** a hundred.

centenar m hundred; **un** ~ **de** a hundred.

centenario, -ria adj (persona) in one's hundreds; (cifra) three-figure (antes de sust). ▶ **centenario** m centenary; **quinto** ~ five hundredth anniversary.

centeno m rye.

centésimo, -ma núm hundredth.

centígrado, -da adj Centigrade.

centigramo m centigram.

centilitro m centilitre.

centímetro m 1. (medida) centimetre. 2. (cinta) measuring tape.

céntimo m (moneda) cent.

centinela m sentry.

centollo m spider crab.

centrado, -da adj 1. (basado): ~ **en** based on. 2. (equilibrado) stable, steady. 3. (rueda, cuadro etc) centred.

central ◆ adj central. ◆ f 1. (oficina) headquarters, head office; (de correos, comunicaciones) main office; ~ **telefónica** telephone exchange. 2. (de energía) power station; ~ **nuclear** nuclear power station.

centralista adj, m y f centralist.

centralita f switchboard.

centralización f centralization.

centralizar vt to centralize.

centrar vt 1. (gen & DEP) to centre. 2. (arma) to aim. 3. (persona) to steady. 4. (atención, interés) to be the centre of. ▶ **centrarse** vpr 1. (concentrarse): ~se **en** to concentrate o focus on. 2. (equilibrarse) to find one's feet.

céntrico, -ca adj central.

centrifugadora f (para secar ropa) spin-dryer.

centrifugar vt (ropa) to spin-dry.

centrista adj centre (antes de sust).

centro m 1. (gen) centre; **ser de** ~ (POLÍT) to be at the centre of the political spectrum; ~ **de cálculo** computer centre; ~ **de planificación familiar** family planning clinic; ~ **de salud** health centre; ~ **social** community centre; ~ **de veraneo** (summer) holiday resort. 2. (de ciudad) town centre; **me voy al** ~ I'm going to town. ▶ **centro comercial** m shopping centre. ▶ **centro de mesa** m centrepiece.

centrocampista m y f (DEP) midfielder.

ceñir vt 1. (apretar) to be tight on. 2. (abrazar) to embrace. ▶ **ceñirse** vpr 1. (apretarse) to tighten. 2. (limitarse): ~se a to keep o stick to.

ceño m frown, scowl; **fruncir el** ~ to frown, to knit one's brow.

CEOE (abrev de **Confederación Española de Organizaciones Empresariales**) f Spanish employers' organization, ≈ CBI Br.

cepa f lit & fig stock.

cepillar vt 1. (gen) to brush. 2. (madera) to plane.

cepillo m 1. (para limpiar) brush; ~ **de dientes** toothbrush. 2. (de carpintero) plane.

cepo m 1. (para cazar) trap. 2. (para vehículos) wheel clamp. 3. (para sujetar) clamp.

cera f (gen) wax; (de abeja) beeswax; ~ **depilatoria** hair-removing wax.

cerámica f 1. (arte) ceramics (U), pottery. 2. (objeto) piece of pottery.

ceramista m y f potter.

cerca ◆ f (valla) fence. ◆ adv near, close; **por aquí** ~ nearby; **de** ~ (examinar etc) closely; (afectar, vivir) deeply. ► **cerca de** loc prep 1. (en el espacio) near, close to. 2. (aproximadamente) nearly, about.

cercado m 1. (valla) fence. 2. (lugar) enclosure.

cercanía f (cualidad) nearness. ► **cercanías** fpl (lugar) outskirts, suburbs.

cercano, -na adj 1. (pueblo, lugar) nearby. 2. (tiempo) near. 3. (pariente, fuente de información): ~ (a) close (to).

cercar vt 1. (vallar) to fence (off). 2. (rodear, acorralar) to surround.

cerciorar vt to assure; ~**se (de)** to make sure (of).

cerco m 1. (gen) circle, ring. 2. (de puerta, ventana) frame. 3. (asedio) siege.

cerdo, -da m y f 1. (animal) pig (f sow). 2. fam fig (persona) pig, swine. ► **cerda** f (pelo - de cerdo, jabalí) bristle; (- de caballo) horsehair. ► **cerdo** m (carne) pork.

cereal m cereal; ~**es** (breakfast) cereal (U).

cerebro m 1. (gen) brain. 2. fig (cabecilla) brains (sg). 3. fig (inteligencia) brains (pl).

ceremonia f ceremony.

ceremonial adj & m ceremonial.

ceremonioso, -sa adj ceremonious.

cereza f cherry.

cerezo m (árbol) cherry tree.

cerilla f match.

cerillo m Amer match.

cerner, cernir vt (cribar) to sieve. ► **cernerse** vpr 1. (ave, avión) to hover. 2. fig (amenaza, peligro) to loom.

cernícalo m 1. (ave) kestrel. 2. fam (bruto) brute.

cernir = cerner.

cero ◆ adj inv zero. ◆ m 1. (signo) nought, zero; (en fútbol) nil; (en tenis) love. 2. (cantidad) nothing. 3. (FÍS & METEOR) zero; **sobre/bajo** ~ above/ below zero. 4. loc: **ser un** ~ **a la izquierda** fam (un inútil) to be useless; (un don nadie) to be a nobody; **partir de** ~ to start from scratch; ver también **seis.**

cerrado, -da adj 1. (al exterior) closed, shut; (con llave, pestillo etc) locked. 2. (tiempo, cielo) overcast; (noche) dark. 3. (rodeado) surrounded; (por montañas) walled in. 4. (circuito) closed. 5. (curva) sharp, tight. 6. (vocal) close. 7. (acento, deje) broad, thick.

cerradura f lock.

cerrajero, -ra m y f locksmith.

cerrar ◆ vt 1. (gen) to close; (puerta, cajón, boca) to shut, to close; (puños) to clench; (con llave, pestillo etc) to lock. 2. (tienda, negocio - definitivamente) to close down. 3. (apagar) to turn off. 4. (bloquear - suj: accidente, inundación etc) to block; (- suj: policía etc) to close off. 5. (tapar - agujero, hueco) to fill, to block (up); (- bote) to put the lid o top on. 6. (cercar) to fence (off). 7. (cicatrizar) to heal. 8. (ir último en) to bring up the rear of. ◆ vi to close, to shut; (con llave, pestillo etc) to lock up. ► **cerrarse** vpr 1. (al exterior) to close, to shut. 2. (incomunicarse) to clam up; ~**se a** to close one's mind to. 3. (herida) to heal, to close up. 4. (acto, debate, discusión etc) to (come to a) close.

cerrazón f fig (obstinación) stubbornness, obstinacy.

cerro m hill.

cerrojo m bolt; **echar el** ~ to bolt the door.

certamen m competition, contest.

certero, -ra adj 1. (tiro) accurate. 2. (opinión, respuesta etc) correct.

certeza f certainty.

certidumbre f certainty.

certificación f 1. (hecho) certification. 2. (documento) certificate.

certificado, -da adj (gen) certified; (carta, paquete) registered. ► **certificado** m certificate; ~ **médico** medical certificate.

certificar vt 1. (constatar) to certify. 2. (en correos) to register.

cerumen m earwax.

cervato m fawn.

cervecería f 1. (fábrica) brewery. 2. (bar) bar.

cervecero, -ra m y f (que hace cerveza) brewer.

cerveza f beer; ~ **de barril** draught beer; ~ **negra** stout; ~ **rubia** lager.

cesante adj 1. (destituido) sacked; (ministro) removed from office. 2. Amer (parado) unemployed.

cesantear vt Amer to make redundant.

cesar ♦ *vt* (*destituir*) to sack; (*ministro*) to remove from office. ♦ *vi* (*parar*): ~ **(de hacer algo)** to stop o cease (doing sthg); **sin** ~ non-stop, incessantly.

cesárea *f* caesarean (section).

cese *m* **1.** (*detención, paro*) stopping, ceasing. **2.** (*destitución*) sacking; (*de ministro*) removal from office.

cesión *f* cession, transfer.

césped *m* (*hierba*) lawn, grass (U).

cesta *f* basket. ▶ **cesta de la compra** *f fig* cost of living.

cesto *m* (*cesta*) (large) basket.

cetro *m* **1.** (*vara*) sceptre. **2.** *fig* (*reinado*) reign.

cf., cfr. (*abrev de* **confróntese**) cf.

cg (*abrev de* **centígramo**) cg.

ch, Ch *f* ch, Ch.

ch/ *abrev de* **cheque.**

chabacano, -na *adj* vulgar. ▶ **chabacano** *m Amer* apricot.

chabola *f* shack; **barrios de ~s** shanty town (*sg*).

chacal *m* jackal.

chacarero, -ra *m y f Amer* farmer.

chacha *f* maid.

chachachá *m* cha-cha.

cháchara *f fam* chatter, nattering; **estar de ~** to have a natter.

chachi *adj inv fam* cool, neat Am.

chacolí (*pl* **chacolís**) *m* light wine from the Basque country.

chacra *f Amer* farm.

chafar *vt* **1.** (*aplastar*) to flatten. **2.** *fig* (*estropear*) to spoil, to ruin. ▶ **chafarse** *vpr* (*estropearse*) to be ruined.

chaflán *m* (*de edificio*) corner.

chagra *Amer* ♦ *m y f* peasant, person from the country. ♦ *f* farm.

chal *m* shawl.

chalado, -da *fam adj* crazy, mad.

chalar *vt* to drive round the bend.

chalé (*pl* **chalés**), **chalet** (*pl* **chalets**) *m* (*gen*) detached house (with garden); (*en el campo*) cottage; (*de alta montaña*) chalet.

chaleco *m* waistcoat, vest Am; (*de punto*) tank-top; **~ salvavidas** life jacket.

chalet = **chalé.**

chamaco, -ca *m y f Amer fam* nipper, lad (*f* lass).

chamarra *f* sheepskin jacket.

chamiza *f* (*hierba*) thatch.

chamizo *m* **1.** (*leña*) half-burnt wood (U). **2.** (*casa*) thatched hut.

champán, champaña *m* champagne.

champiñón *m* mushroom.

champú (*pl* **champús** o **champúes**) *m* shampoo.

chamuscar *vt* to scorch; (*cabello, barba, tela*) to singe. ▶ **chamuscarse** *vpr* (*cabello, barba, tela*) to get singed.

chamusquina *f* scorch, scorching (U); **me huele a ~** *fam fig* it smells a bit fishy to me.

chance *f Amer* opportunity.

chanchada *f Amer* dirty trick.

chancho *m Amer* pig.

chanchullo *m fam* fiddle, racket.

chancla *f* (*chancleta*) low sandal; (*para la playa*) flip-flop.

chancleta *f* low sandal; (*para la playa*) flip-flop.

chándal (*pl* **chandals**), **chandal** (*pl* **chandals**) *m* tracksuit.

changarro *m Amer* small shop.

chanquete *m* tiny transparent fish eaten in Málaga.

chantaje *m* blackmail; **hacer ~ a** to blackmail.

chantajear *vt* to blackmail.

chanza *f* joke.

chao *interj fam*: **¡~!** bye!, see you!

chapa *f* **1.** (*lámina - de metal*) sheet; (*- de madera*) board; **de tres ~s** three-ply. **2.** (*tapón*) top, cap. **3.** (*insignia*) badge. **4.** (*ficha de guardarropa*) metal token o disc. **5.** *Amer* (*cerradura*) lock. ▶ **chapas** *fpl* (*juego*) children's game played with bottle tops.

chapado, -da *adj* (*con metal*) plated; (*con madera*) veneered; **~ a la antigua** *fig* stuck in the past, old-fashioned.

chaparro, -rra ♦ *adj* short and squat. ♦ *m y f* (*persona*) short, squat person.

chaparrón *m* downpour; *fam fig* (*gran cantidad*) torrent.

chapopote *m Amer* bitumen, pitch.

chapotear *vi* to splash about.

chapucear *vt* to botch (up).

chapucero, -ra ♦ *adj* (*trabajo*) shoddy; (*persona*) bungling. ♦ *m y f* bungler.

chapulín *m Amer* grasshopper.

chapurrear, chapurrar *vt* to speak badly.

chapuza *f* **1.** (*trabajo mal hecho*) botch (job). **2.** (*trabajo ocasional*) odd job.

chapuzón *m* dip; **darse un ~** to go for a dip.

chaqué (*pl* **chaqués**) *m* morning coat.

chaqueta *f* jacket; (*de punto*) cardigan.

chaquetón *m* long jacket.

charanga *f* (*banda*) brass band.

charca *f* pool, pond.

charco *m* puddle.

charcutería *f* 1. (*tienda*) shop selling cold cooked meats and cheeses, = delicatessen. 2. (*productos*) cold cuts (*pl*) and cheese.

charla *f* 1. (*conversación*) chat. 2. (*conferencia*) talk.

charlar *vi* to chat.

charlatán, -ana ◆ *adj* talkative. ◆ *m y f* 1. (*hablador*) chatterbox. 2. (*mentiroso*) trickster, charlatan.

charlotada *f* (*payasada*) clowning around (U).

charlotear *vi* to chat.

charnego, -ga *m y f pejorative term referring to immigrant to Catalonia from another part of Spain*.

charol *m* 1. (*piel*) patent leather. 2. *Amer* (*bandeja*) tray.

charola *f Amer* tray.

chárter *adj inv* charter (*antes de sust*).

chasca *f Amer* mop of hair.

chascar ◆ *vt* 1. (*lengua*) to click. 2. (*dedos*) to snap. ◆ *vi* 1. (*madera*) to crack. 2. (*lengua*) to click.

chasco *m* (*decepción*) disappointment; **llevarse un ~** to be disappointed.

chasis *m inv* (AUTOM) chassis.

chasquear ◆ *vt* 1. (*látigo*) to crack. 2. (*la lengua*) to click. ◆ *vi* (*madera*) to crack.

chasquido *m* (*de látigo, madera, hueso*) crack; (*de lengua, arma*) click; (*de dedos*) snap.

chatarra *f* 1. (*metal*) scrap (metal). 2. (*objetos, piezas*) junk.

chateo *m* pub crawl; **ir de ~** to go out drinking.

chato, -ta ◆ *adj* 1. (*nariz*) snub; (*persona*) snub-nosed. 2. (*aplanado*) flat. ◆ *m y f fam* (*apelativo*) love, dear. ▶ **chato** *m* (*de vino*) small glass of wine.

chau, chaucito *interj Amer fam*: **¡~!** see you later!

chauvinista = **chovinista**.

chaval, -la *m y f fam* kid, lad (*f* lass).

chavo *m fam* 1. (*dinero*) **no tener un ~** to be penniless. 2. *Amer* (*hombre*) guy, bloke.

checo, -ca *adj, m y f* Czech. ▶ **checo** *m* (*lengua*) Czech.

che, ché *interj*: **¡~!** hey!

checoslovaco, -ca *adj, m y f* Czechoslovak, Czechoslovakian.

Checoslovaquia Czechoslovakia.

chef [ʃef] (*pl* **chefs**) *m* chef.

chelín, schilling ['ʃilin] *m* shilling.

chelo, -la *adj Amer* blond (*f* blonde).

cheque *m* cheque Br, check Am; **exten-** der un ~ to make out a cheque; **~ cruzado o barrado** crossed cheque; **~ (de) gasolina** petrol voucher; **~ nominativo** cheque in favour of a specific person; **~ al portador** cheque payable to the bearer; **~ de viajero** *Amer*, **~ de viaje** traveller's cheque.

chequear *vt* 1. (MED): **~ a alguien** to examine sb, to give sb a checkup. 2. (*comprobar*) to check.

chequeo *m* 1. (MED) checkup. 2. (*comprobación*) check, checking (U).

chequera *f* chequebook Br, checkbook Am.

chévere *adj Amer fam* great, fantastic.

chic *adj inv* chic.

chica *f* 1. (*joven*) girl. 2. (*tratamiento*) darling. 3. (*criada*) maid.

chicano, -na *adj, m y f* Chicano, Mexican-American. ▶ **chicano** *m* (*lengua*) Chicano.

chicarrón, -ona *m y f* strapping lad (*f* strapping lass).

chícharo *m Amer* pea.

chicharra *f* (ZOOL) cicada.

chicharro *m* (*pez*) horse mackerel.

chicharrón *m* (*frito*) pork crackling. ▶ **chicharrones** *mpl* (*embutido*) cold processed meat made from pork.

chichón *m* bump.

chicle *m* chewing gum.

chiclé, chicler *m* (AUTOM) jet.

chico, -ca *adj* (*pequeño*) small. ▶ **chico** *m* 1. (*joven*) boy. 2. (*tratamiento*) sonny, mate. 3. (*recadero*) messenger, office-boy.

chicote *m Amer* whip.

chifla *f* (*silbido*) whistle.

chiflado, -da *fam adj* crazy, mad.

chiflar ◆ *vt fam* (*encantar*): **me chiflan las patatas fritas** I'm mad about chips. ◆ *vi* (*silbar*) to whistle.

chiflido *m Amer* whistling.

chile *m* chilli (pepper).

Chile Chile.

chileno, -na *adj, m y f* Chilean.

chillar ◆ *vi* 1. (*gritar - personas*) to scream, to yell; (- *aves, monos*) to screech; (- *cerdo*) to squeal; (- *ratón*) to squeak. 2. (*chirriar*) to screech; (*puerta, madera*) to creak; (*bisagras*) to squeak. ◆ *vt fam* (*reñir*) to yell at.

chillido *m* (*de persona*) scream, yell; (*de ave, mono*) screech; (*de cerdo*) squeal; (*de ratón*) squeak.

chillón, -ona *adj* 1. (*voz*) piercing. 2. (*persona*) noisy. 3. (*color*) gaudy.

chilpayate, -ta *m y f Amer* kid.

chimenea f 1. (*hogar*) fireplace. 2. (*tubo*) chimney.

chimpancé m chimpanzee.

china → chino.

China : (**la**) ~ China.

chinchar vt fam to pester, to bug. ▶ **chincharse** vpr fam: **ahora te chinchas** now you can lump it.

chinche ◆ adj fam fig annoying. ◆ f (*insecto*) bedbug.

chincheta f drawing pin Br, thumbtack Am.

chinchín m (*brindis*) toast; **¡~!** cheers!

chinchón m strong aniseed liquor.

chingar ◆ vt 1. fam (*molestar*) to cheese off. 2. mfam (*estropear*) to bugger up. 3. Amer vulg (*fornicar con*) to fuck. ◆ vi vulg (*fornicar*) to screw. ▶ **chingarse** vpr mfam (*beberse*) to knock back.

chino, -na adj, m y f Chinese. ▶ **chino** m (*lengua*) Chinese. ▶ **china** f (*piedra*) pebble.

chip (pl **chips**) m (INFORM) chip.

chipirón m baby squid.

Chipre Cyprus.

chipriota adj, m y f Cypriot.

chiquillo, -lla m y f kid.

chiquito, -ta adj tiny. ▶ **chiquito** m (*de vino*) small glass of wine.

chiribita f (*chispa*) spark.

chirimbolo m fam thingamajig.

chirimoya f custard apple.

chiringuito m fam (*bar*) refreshment stall.

chiripa f fam fig fluke; **de** o **por** ~ by luck.

chirivía f (BOT) parsnip.

chirla f small clam.

chirona f fam clink, slammer; **en** ~ in the clink.

chirriar vi (*gen*) to screech; (*puerta, madera*) to creak; (*bisagra, muelles*) to squeak.

chirrido m (*gen*) screech; (*de puerta, madera*) creak; (*de bisagra, muelles*) squeak.

chis = chist.

chisme m 1. (*cotilleo*) rumour, piece of gossip. 2. fam (*cosa*) thingamajig.

chismorrear vi to spread rumours, to gossip.

chismoso, -sa ◆ adj gossipy. ◆ m y f gossip, scandalmonger.

chispa f 1. (*de fuego, electricidad*) spark; **echar** ~s fam to be hopping mad. 2. (*de lluvia*) spot (of rain). 3. fig (*pizca*) bit. 4. fig (*agudeza*) wit.

chispear ◆ vi 1. (*chisporrotear*) to spark.

2. (*relucir*) to sparkle. ◆ v impers (*llover*) to spit (with rain).

chisporrotear vi (*fuego, leña*) to crackle; (*aceite*) to splutter; (*comida*) to sizzle.

chist, chis interj: **¡~!** ssh!

chistar vi: **me fui sin** ~ I left without a word.

chiste m joke; **contar** ~s to tell jokes; ~ **verde** dirty joke.

chistera f (*sombrero*) top hat.

chistorra f type of cured pork sausage typical of Aragon and Navarre.

chistoso, -sa adj funny.

chistu m Basque flute.

chita ▶ **a la chita callando** loc adv fam quietly, on the quiet.

chitón interj: **¡~!** quiet!

chivar vt fam to tell secretly. ▶ **chivarse** vpr fam: ~**se** (**de/a**) (*niños*) to split (on/to); (*delincuentes*) to grass (on/to).

chivatazo m fam tip-off; **dar el** ~ to grass.

chivato, -ta m y f fam (*delator*) grass, informer; (*acusica*) telltale.

chivo, -va m y f kid, young goat; **ser el** ~ **expiatorio** fig to be the scapegoat.

choc (pl **chocs**), **choque**, **shock** [tʃok] m shock.

chocante adj startling.

chocar ◆ vi 1. (*colisionar*): ~ (**contra**) to crash (into), to collide (with). 2. fig (*enfrentarse*) to clash. ◆ vt fig (*sorprender*) to startle.

chochear vi (*viejo*) to be senile.

chocho, -cha adj 1. (*viejo*) senile. 2. fam fig (*encariñado*) soft, doting.

choclo m Amer corn Br, maize Am.

chocolate m (*para comer, beber*) chocolate; ~ (**a la taza**) thick drinking chocolate; ~ **blanco** white chocolate; ~ **con leche** milk chocolate.

chocolatina f chocolate bar.

chófer (pl **chóferes**), **chofer** Amer m y f chauffeur.

chollo m fam (*producto, compra*) bargain; (*trabajo, situación*) cushy number.

chomba, chompa f Amer jumper.

chongo m Amer (*moño*) bun.

chopo m poplar.

choque m 1. (*impacto*) impact; (*de coche, avión etc*) crash. 2. fig (*enfrentamiento*) clash. 3. = choc.

chorizar vt fam to nick, to pinch.

chorizo m 1. (*embutido*) highly seasoned pork sausage. 2. fam (*ladrón*) thief.

choro m Amer mussel.

chorrada f mfam rubbish (U); **decir** ~s to talk rubbish.

chorrear vi 1. (gotear - gota a gota) to drip; (- en un hilo) to trickle. 2. (brotar) to spurt (out), to gush (out).

chorro m 1. (de líquido - borbotón) jet, spurt; (- hilo) trickle; **salir a ~s** to spurt o gush out. 2. fig (de luz, gente etc) stream; **tiene un ~ de dinero** she has loads of money.

choteo m fam joking, kidding; **tomar algo a ~** to take sthg as a joke.

choto, -ta m y f 1. (cabrito) kid, young goat. 2. (ternero) calf.

chovinista, chauvinista [tʃoβi'nista] ◆ adj chauvinistic. ◆ m y f chauvinist.

choza f hut.

christmas = **crismas**.

chubasco m shower.

chubasquero m raincoat, mac.

chúcaro, -ra adj Amer fam wild.

chuchería f 1. (golosina) sweet. 2. (objeto) trinket.

chucho m fam mutt, dog.

chufa f (tubérculo) tiger nut.

chulear fam vi (fanfarronear): **~ (de)** to be cocky (about).

chulería f (valentonería) cockiness.

chuleta f 1. (de carne) chop. 2. (en exámenes) crib note.

chulo, -la ◆ adj 1. (descarado) cocky; **ponerse a ~** to get cocky. 2. fam (bonito) lovely. ◆ m y f (descarado) cocky person. ► **chulo** m (proxeneta) pimp.

chumbera f prickly pear.

chumbo → **higo**.

chungo, -ga adj fam (persona) horrible, nasty; (cosa) lousy. ► **chunga** f fam: **tomarse algo a chunga** to take sthg as a joke.

chupa f fam coat.

chupachup® (pl chupachups) m lollipop.

chupado, -da adj 1. (delgado) skinny. 2. fam (fácil): **estar ~** to be dead easy o a piece of cake. ► **chupada** f (gen) suck; (fumando) puff, drag.

chupar vt 1. (succionar) to suck; (fumando) to puff at. 2. (absorber) to soak up. 3. (quitar): **~le algo a alguien** to milk sb for sthg.

chupe m Amer stew.

chupete m dummy Br, pacifier Am.

chupi adj fam great, brill.

chupón, -ona m y f fam (gorrón) sponger, cadger. ► **chupón** m Amer (chupete) dummy Br, pacifier Am.

churrería f shop selling 'churros'.

churro m (para comer) dough formed into sticks or rings and fried in oil.

churrusco m piece of burnt toast.

churumbel m fam kid.

chusco, -ca adj funny. ► **chusco** m fam crust of stale bread.

chusma f rabble, mob.

chut (pl **chuts**) m kick.

chutar vi (lanzar) to shoot. ► **chutarse** vpr mfam to shoot up.

chute m mfam fix.

CIA (abrev de **Central Intelligence Agency**) f CIA.

cía., Cía. (abrev de **compañía**) Co.

cianuro m cyanide.

ciático, -ca adj sciatic. ► **ciática** f sciatica.

cibercafé m cybercafe.

ciberespacio m cyberspace.

cibernética f cybernetics (U).

cicatero, -ra adj stingy, mean.

cicatriz f lit & fig scar.

cicatrizar ◆ vi to heal (up). ◆ vt fig to heal.

cicerone m y f guide.

cíclico, -ca adj cyclical.

ciclismo m cycling.

ciclista m y f cyclist.

ciclo m 1. (gen) cycle. 2. (de conferencias, actos) series.

ciclocrós m cyclo-cross.

ciclomotor m moped.

ciclón m cyclone.

cicuta f hemlock.

ciego, -ga ◆ adj 1. (gen) blind; **a ciegas** lit & fig blindly. 2. fig (enloquecido): **~ (de)** blinded (by). 3. (pozo, tubería) blocked (up). ◆ m y f (invidente) blind person; **los ~s** the blind.

cielo m 1. (gen) sky. 2. (RELIG) heaven. 3. (nombre cariñoso) my love, my dear. 4. loc: **como llovido del ~** (inesperadamente) out of the blue; (oportunamente) at just the right moment; **ser un ~** to be an angel. ► **¡cielos!** interj: **¡~s!** good heavens!

ciempiés m inv centipede.

cien = **ciento**.

ciénaga f marsh, bog.

ciencia f (gen) science. ► **ciencias** fpl (EDUC) science (U). ► **ciencias económicas** fpl economics (U). ► **ciencia ficción** f science fiction. ► **a ciencia cierta** loc adv for certain.

cieno m mud, sludge.

científico, -ca ◆ adj scientific. ◆ m y f scientist.

ciento, cien núm a o one hundred; **~ cincuenta** a o one hundred and fifty; **cien mil** a o one hundred thousand; **~s**

de hundreds of; **por ~** per cent; **~ por ~,**
cien por cien a hundred per cent.

cierne ▶ **en ciernes** *loc adv*: **estar en ~s**
to be in its infancy; **una campeona en ~s**
a budding champion.

cierre *m* **1.** (*gen*) closing, shutting; (*de*
fábrica) shutdown; (RADIO & TV) close-
down; **~ patronal** lockout. **2.** (*mecanismo*)
fastener; **~ metálico** (*de tienda etc*) metal
shutter; **~ relámpago** *Amer* zip.

cierto, -ta *adj* **1.** (*verdadero*) true;
estar en lo ~ to be right; **lo ~ es que ...**
the fact is that ... **2.** (*seguro*) certain,
definite. **3.** (*algún*) certain; **~ hombre** a
certain man; **en cierta ocasión** once, on
one occasion. ▶ **cierto** *adv* right, certainly. ▶ **por cierto** *loc adv* by the
way.

ciervo, -va *m y f* deer, stag (*f* hind).

CIF (*abrev de* **código de identificación fiscal**) *m* tax code.

cifra *f* (*gen*) figure, number.

cifrar *vt* **1.** (*codificar*) to code. **2.** *fig* (*centrar*) to concentrate, to centre.
▶ **cifrarse en** *vpr* to amount to.

cigala *f* Dublin Bay prawn.

cigarra *f* cicada.

cigarrillo *m* cigarette.

cigarro *m* **1.** (*habano*) cigar. **2.** (*cigarrillo*) cigarette.

cigüeña *f* stork.

cigüeñal *m* crankshaft.

cilantro *m* coriander.

cilindrada *f* cylinder capacity.

cilíndrico, -ca *adj* cylindrical.

cilindro *m* (*gen*) cylinder; (*de imprenta*)
roller.

cima *f* **1.** (*punta - de montaña*) peak,
summit; (*- de árbol*) top. **2.** *fig* (*apogeo*)
peak, high point.

cimbrear *vt* **1.** (*vara*) to waggle.
2. (*caderas*) to sway.

cimentar *vt* **1.** (*edificio*) to lay the foundations of; (*ciudad*) to found, to build.
2. *fig* (*idea, paz, fama*) to cement.

cimiento *m* (*gen pl*) (CONSTR) foundation; **echar los ~s** *lit & fig* to lay the foundations.

cinc, zinc *m* zinc.

cincel *m* chisel.

cincelar *vt* to chisel.

cincha *f* girth.

cinco *núm* five; **¡choca esos ~!** *fig* put it
there!; *ver también* **seis**.

cincuenta *núm* fifty; **los (años) ~** the
fifties; *ver también* **seis**.

cincuentón, -ona *m y f* fifty-year-old.

cine *m* cinema; **hacer ~** to make films.

cineasta *m y f* film maker o director.

cineclub *m* **1.** (*asociación*) film society.
2. (*sala*) club cinema.

cinéfilo, -la *m y f* film buff.

cinematografía *f* cinematography.

cinematográfico, -ca *adj* film (*antes
de sust*).

cinematógrafo *m* (*local*) cinema.

cínico, -ca ◆ *adj* cynical. ◆ *m y f* cynic.

cinismo *m* cynicism.

cinta *f* **1.** (*tira - de plástico, papel*) strip,
band; (*- de tela*) ribbon; **~ adhesiva** o
autoadhesiva adhesive o sticky tape; **~
métrica** tape measure. **2.** (*de imagen,
sonido, ordenadores*) tape; **~ magnetofónica**
recording tape; **~ de vídeo** videotape.
3. (*mecanismo*) belt; **~ transportadora**
conveyor belt. **4.** (*película*) film.

cintura *f* waist.

cinturilla *f* waistband.

cinturón *m* **1.** (*cinto*) belt. **2.** (AUTOM)
ring road. **3.** (*cordón*) cordon. ▶ **cinturón de seguridad** *m* seat o safety
belt.

ciprés *m* cypress.

circo *m* (*gen*) circus.

circuito *m* **1.** (DEP & ELECTRÓN) circuit.
2. (*viaje*) tour.

circulación *f* **1.** (*gen*) circulation.
2. (*tráfico*) traffic.

circular ◆ *adj* & *f* circular. ◆ *vi* **1.**
(*pasar*): **~ (por)** (*líquido*) to flow o circulate (through); (*persona*) to move o walk
(around); (*vehículos*) to drive (along).
2. (*de mano en mano*) to circulate; (*moneda*) to be in circulation. **3.** (*difundirse*) to
go round.

círculo *m* *lit & fig* circle. ▶ **círculos** *mpl*
(*medios*) circles. ▶ **círculo polar** *m*
polar circle; **el ~ polar ártico/antártico**
the Arctic/Antarctic Circle. ▶ **círculo
vicioso** *m* vicious circle.

circuncisión *f* circumcision.

circundante *adj* surrounding.

circundar *vt* to surround.

circunferencia *f* circumference.

circunloquio *m* circumlocution.

circunscribir *vt* **1.** (*limitar*) to restrict,
to confine. **2.** (GEOM) to circumscribe.
▶ **circunscribirse a** *vpr* to confine o.s.
to.

circunscripción *f* (*distrito*) district;
(MIL) division; (POLÍT) constituency.

circunscrito, -ta ◆ *pp* → **circunscribir.**
◆ *adj* restricted, limited.

circunstancia *f* circumstance; **en estas
~s** under the circumstances; **~ ate-
nuante/agravante/eximente** (DER) ex-

tenuating/aggravating/exonerating circumstance.

circunstancial adj (accidental) chance (antes de sust).

circunvalar vt to go round.

cirio m (wax) candle; **montar un ~** to make a row.

cirrosis f inv cirrhosis.

ciruela f plum; **~ pasa** prune.

cirugía f surgery; **~ estética** o **plástica** cosmetic o plastic surgery.

cirujano, -na m y f surgeon.

cisco m 1. (carbón) slack; **hecho ~** fig shattered. 2. fam (alboroto) row, rumpus.

cisma m 1. (separación) schism. 2. (discordia) split.

cisne m swan.

cisterna f (de retrete) cistern.

cistitis f inv cystitis.

cita f 1. (entrevista) appointment; (de novios) date; **darse ~** to meet; **tener una ~** to have an appointment. 2. (referencia) quotation.

citación f (DER) summons (sg).

citar vt 1. (convocar) to make an appointment with. 2. (aludir) to mention; (textualmente) to quote. 3. (DER) to summons. ▶ **citarse** vpr: **~se (con alguien)** to arrange to meet (sb).

citología f 1. (análisis ginecológico) smear test. 2. (BIOL) cytology.

cítrico, -ca adj citric. ▶ **cítricos** mpl citrus fruits.

CiU (abrev de **Convergència i Unió**) f Catalan coalition party to the centre-right of the political spectrum.

ciudad f (localidad) city; (pequeña) town.

ciudadanía f 1. (nacionalidad) citizenship. 2. (población) citizens (pl).

ciudadano, -na m y f citizen.

Ciudad de México Mexico City.

cívico, -ca adj civic; (conducta) public-spirited.

civil ◆ adj lit & fig civil. ◆ m (no militar) civilian.

civilización f civilization.

civilizado, -da adj civilized.

civilizar vt to civilize.

civismo m 1. (urbanidad) community spirit. 2. (cortesía) civility, politeness.

cizaña f (BOT) darnel; **meter** o **sembrar ~** to sow discord.

cl (abrev de **centilitro**) cl.

clamar ◆ vt 1. (expresar) to exclaim. 2. (exigir) to cry out for. ◆ vi 1. (implorar) to appeal. 2. (protestar) to cry out.

clamor m clamour.

clamoroso, -sa adj 1. (rotundo)

resounding. 2. (vociferante) loud, clamorous.

clan m 1. (tribu, familia) clan. 2. (banda) faction.

clandestino, -na adj clandestine; (POLÍT) underground.

claqué m tap dancing.

claqueta f clapperboard.

clara → **claro**.

claraboya f skylight.

clarear v impers 1. (amanecer): **empezaba a ~** dawn was breaking. 2. (despejarse) to clear up. ▶ **clarearse** vpr (transparentarse) to be see-through.

claridad f 1. (transparencia) clearness, clarity. 2. (luz) light. 3. (franqueza) candidness. 4. (lucidez) clarity.

clarificar vt 1. (gen) to clarify; (misterio) to clear up. 2. (purificar) to refine.

clarín m (instrumento) bugle.

clarinete m (instrumento) clarinet.

clarividencia f farsightedness.

claro, -ra adj 1. (gen) clear; **~ está que ...** of course ...; **dejar algo ~** to make sthg clear; **a las claras** clearly; **pasar una noche en ~** to spend a sleepless night; **poner algo en ~** to get sthg clear, to clear sthg up; **sacar algo en ~ (de)** to make sthg out (from). 2. (luminoso) bright. 3. (color) light. 4. (diluido - té, café) weak. ▶ **claro** ◆ m 1. (en bosque) clearing; (en multitud) space, gap. 2. (METEOR) bright spell. ◆ adv clearly. ◆ interj ¡~! of course! ▶ **clara** f (de huevo) white.

clase f 1. (gen) class; **~ alta/media** upper/middle class; **~ obrera** o **trabajadora** working class; **~ preferente/turista** club/tourist class; **primera ~** first class. 2. (tipo) sort, kind; **toda ~ de** all sorts o kinds of. 3. (EDUC - asignatura, alumnos) class; (- aula) classroom; **dar ~s** (en un colegio) to teach; (en una universidad) to lecture; **~s particulares** private classes o lessons.

clásico, -ca ◆ adj 1. (de la Antigüedad) classical. 2. (ejemplar, prototípico) classic. 3. (peinado, estilo, música etc) classical. 4. (habitual) customary. 5. (peculiar): **~ de** typical of. ◆ m y f (persona) classic.

clasificación f classification; (DEP) (league) table.

clasificar vt to classify. ▶ **clasificarse** vpr (ganar acceso): **~se (para)** to qualify (for); (DEP) to get through (to).

clasista adj class-conscious; despec snobbish.

claudicar vi (ceder) to give in.

claustro m 1. (ARQUIT & RELIG) cloister.

2. (*de universidad*) senate.
claustrofobia *f* claustrophobia.
cláusula *f* clause.
clausura *f* **1.** (*acto solemne*) closing ceremony. **2.** (*cierre*) closing down.
clausurar *vt* **1.** (*acto*) to close, to conclude. **2.** (*local*) to close down.
clavadista *m y f* Amer diver.
clavado, -da *adj* **1.** (*en punto - hora*) on the dot. **2.** (*parecido*) almost identical; **ser ~ a alguien** to be the spitting image of sb.
clavar *vt* **1.** (*clavo, estaca etc*) to drive; (*cuchillo*) to thrust; (*chincheta, alfiler*) to stick. **2.** (*cartel, placa etc*) to nail, to fix. **3.** *fig* (*mirada, atención*) to fix, to rivet.
clave ◆ *adj inv* key. ◆ *m* (MÚS) harpsichord. ◆ *f* **1.** (*código*) code; **en ~** in code. **2.** *fig* (*solución*) key. **3.** (MÚS) clef. **4.** (INFORM) key.
clavel *m* carnation.
clavicémbalo *m* harpsichord.
clavicordio *m* clavichord.
clavícula *f* collar bone.
clavija *f* **1.** (ELECTR & TECN) pin; (*de auriculares, teléfono*) jack. **2.** (MÚS) peg.
clavo *m* **1.** (*pieza metálica*) nail; **agarrarse a un ~ ardiendo** to clutch at straws; **dar en el ~** to hit the nail on the head. **2.** (BOT & CULIN) clove. **3.** (MED) (*para huesos*) pin.
claxon (*pl* **cláxones**) *m* horn; **tocar el ~** to sound the horn.
clemencia *f* mercy, clemency.
clemente *adj* (*persona*) merciful.
cleptómano, -na *m y f* kleptomaniac.
clerical *adj* clerical.
clérigo *m* (*católico*) priest; (*anglicano*) clergyman.
clero *m* clergy.
cliché, clisé *m* **1.** (FOT) negative. **2.** (IMPRENTA) plate. **3.** *fig* (*tópico*) cliché.
cliente, -ta *m y f* (*de tienda, garaje, bar*) customer; (*de banco, abogado etc*) client; (*de hotel*) guest.
clientela *f* (*de tienda, garaje*) customers (*pl*); (*de banco, abogado etc*) clients (*pl*); (*de hotel*) guests (*pl*); (*de bar, restaurante*) clientele.
clima *m* lit & fig climate.
climatizado, -da *adj* air-conditioned.
climatizar *vt* to air-condition.
climatología *f* **1.** (*tiempo*) weather. **2.** (*ciencia*) climatology.
clímax *m inv* climax.
clínico, -ca *adj* clinical. ► **clínica** *f* clinic.

clip *m* (*para papel*) paper clip.
clisé = **cliché**.
clítoris *m inv* clitoris.
cloaca *f* sewer.
cloquear *vi* to cluck.
cloro *m* chlorine.
cloroformo *m* chloroform.
cloruro *m* chloride.
clown *m* clown.
club (*pl* **clubs** o **clubes**) *m* club; **~ de fans** fan club; **~ náutico** yacht club.
cm (*abrev de* **centímetro**) cm.
CNT (*abrev de* **Confederación Nacional del Trabajo**) *f* Spanish anarchist trade union federation created in 1911.
Co. (*abrev de* **compañía**) Co.
coacción *f* coercion.
coaccionar *vt* to coerce.
coagular *vt* (*gen*) to coagulate; (*sangre*) to clot; (*leche*) to curdle. ► **coagularse** *vpr* (*gen*) to coagulate; (*sangre*) to clot; (*leche*) to curdle.
coágulo *m* clot.
coalición *f* coalition.
coartada *f* alibi.
coartar *vt* to limit, to restrict.
coba *f* fam (*halago*) flattery; **dar ~ a alguien** (*hacer la pelota*) to suck up o crawl to sb; (*aplacar*) to soft-soap sb.
cobalto *m* cobalt.
cobarde ◆ *adj* cowardly. ◆ *m y f* coward.
cobardía *f* cowardice.
cobertizo *m* **1.** (*tejado adosado*) lean-to. **2.** (*barracón*) shed.
cobertura *f* **1.** (*gen*) cover. **2.** (*de un edificio*) covering. **3.** (PRENS) **~ informativa** news coverage.
cobija *f* Amer blanket.
cobijar *vt* **1.** (*albergar*) to house. **2.** (*proteger*) to shelter. ► **cobijarse** *vpr* to take shelter.
cobijo *m* shelter; **dar ~ a alguien** to give shelter to sb, to take sb in.
cobra *f* cobra.
cobrador, -ra *m y f* (*del autobús*) conductor (*f* conductress); (*de deudas, recibos*) collector.
cobrar ◆ *vt* **1.** (COM - *dinero*) to charge; (- *cheque*) to cash; (- *deuda*) to collect; **cantidades por ~** amounts due; **¿me cobra, por favor?** how much do I owe you? **2.** (*en el trabajo*) to earn. **3.** (*adquirir - importancia*) to get, to acquire; **~ fama** to become famous. **4.** (*sentir - cariño, afecto*) to start to feel. ◆ *vi* (*en el trabajo*) to get paid.

cobre m copper; **no tener un ~** Amer to be flat broke.

cobrizo, -za adj (color, piel) copper (antes de sust).

cobro m (de talón) cashing; (de pago) collection; **~ revertido** reverse charge.

coca f 1. (planta) coca. 2. fam (cocaína) coke.

Coca-Cola® f Coca-Cola®, Coke®.

cocaína f cocaine.

cocción f (gen) cooking; (en agua) boiling; (en horno) baking.

cóccix, coxis m inv coccyx.

cocear vi to kick.

cocer vt 1. (gen) to cook; (hervir) to boil; (en horno) to bake. 2. (cerámica, ladrillos) to fire. ▶ **cocerse** vpr fig (plan) to be afoot.

coche m 1. (automóvil) car, automobile Am; **~ de bomberos** fire engine; **~ de carreras** racing car; **~ celular** police van; **~ familiar** estate car. 2. (de tren) coach, carriage; **~ cama** sleeping car, sleeper; **~ restaurante** restaurant o dining car. 3. (de caballos) carriage. ▶ **coche bomba** m car bomb.

cochera f (para coches) garage; (de autobuses, tranvías) depot.

cochinilla f 1. (crustáceo) woodlouse. 2. (insecto) cochineal.

cochinillo m sucking pig.

cochino, -na ◆ adj 1. (persona) filthy. 2. (tiempo, dinero) lousy. ◆ m y f (animal - macho) pig; (- hembra) sow.

cocido m stew.

cociente m quotient.

cocina f 1. (habitación) kitchen. 2. (electrodoméstico) cooker, stove; **~ eléctrica/de gas** electric/gas cooker. 3. (arte) cooking; **~ española** Spanish cuisine o cooking; **libro/clase de ~** cookery book/class.

cocinar vt & vi to cook.

cocinero, -ra m y f cook.

cocker m cocker spaniel.

coco m (árbol) coconut palm; (fruto) coconut.

cocodrilo m crocodile.

cocotero m coconut palm.

cóctel, coctel m 1. (bebida, comida) cocktail. 2. (reunión) cocktail party. ▶ **cóctel molotov** m Molotov cocktail.

coctelera f cocktail shaker.

codazo m nudge, jab (with one's elbow); **abrirse paso a ~s** to elbow one's way through.

codearse vpr: **~se (con)** to rub shoulders (with).

codera f elbow patch.

codicia f (de riqueza) greed.

codiciar vt to covet.

codicioso, -sa adj greedy.

codificar vt 1. (ley) to codify. 2. (un mensaje) to encode. 3. (INFORM) to code.

código m (gen & INFORM) code; **~ postal/territorial** post/area code; **~ de barras/de señales** bar/signal code; **~ de circulación** highway code; **~ civil/penal** civil/penal code; **~ máquina** machine code.

codillo m (de jamón) shoulder.

codo m (en brazo, tubería) elbow; **estaba de ~s sobre la mesa** she was leaning (with her elbows) on the table.

codorniz f quail.

COE (abrev de **Comité Olímpico Español**) m SOC.

coeficiente m 1. (gen) coefficient. 2. (índice) rate.

coercer vt to restrict, to constrain.

coetáneo, -a adj, m y f contemporary.

coexistir vi to coexist.

cofia f (de enfermera, camarera) cap; (de monja) coif.

cofradía f 1. (religiosa) brotherhood (f sisterhood). 2. (no religiosa) guild.

cofre m 1. (arca) chest, trunk. 2. (para joyas) jewel box.

coger ◆ vt 1. (asir, agarrar) to take. 2. (atrapar - ladrón, pez, pájaro) to catch. 3. (alcanzar - persona, vehículo) to catch up with. 4. (recoger - frutos, flores) to pick. 5. (quedarse con - propina, empleo, piso) to take. 6. (quitar): **~ algo (a alguien)** to take sth (from sb). 7. (tren, autobús) to take, to catch. 8. (contraer - gripe, resfriado) to catch, to get. 9. (sentir - manía, odio, afecto) to start to feel; **~ cariño/miedo a** to become fond/scared of. 10. (oír) to catch; (entender) to get. 11. (sorprender, encontrar): **~ a alguien haciendo algo** to catch sb doing sthg. 12. (sintonizar - canal, emisora) to get, to receive. 13. Amer vulg (fornicar) to screw. ◆ vi (dirigirse): **~ a la derecha/la izquierda** to turn right/left. ▶ **cogerse** vpr 1. (agarrarse): **~se de** o **a algo** to cling to o clutch sthg. 2. (pillarse): **~se los dedos/la falda en la puerta** to catch one's fingers/skirt in the door.

cogida f (de torero) goring.

cognac = **coñá**.

cogollo m 1. (de lechuga) heart. 2. (brote - de árbol, planta) shoot.

cogorza f fam: **agarrarse una ~** to get smashed, to get blind drunk.

cogote m nape, back of the neck.

cohabitar vi to cohabit, to live together.

cohecho m bribery.

coherencia f (de razonamiento) coherence.

coherente adj coherent.

cohesión f cohesion.

cohete m rocket.

cohibido, -da adj inhibited.

cohibir vt to inhibit. ► **cohibirse** vpr to become inhibited.

COI (abrev de **Comité Olímpico Internacional**) m IOC.

coima f Amer fam bribe.

coincidencia f coincidence.

coincidir vi 1. (superficies, versiones, gustos) to coincide. 2. (personas - encontrarse) to meet; (- estar de acuerdo) to agree.

coito m (sexual) intercourse.

coja → coger.

cojear vi 1. (persona) to limp. 2. (mueble) to wobble.

cojera f (acción) limp; (estado) lameness.

cojín m cushion.

cojinete m (en eje) bearing; (en un riel de ferrocarril) chair.

cojo, -ja ◆ v → coger. ◆ adj 1. (persona) lame. 2. (mueble) wobbly. ◆ m y f cripple.

cojón m (gen pl) vulg ball. ► **cojones** interj vulg: ¡cojones! (enfado) for fuck's sake!

cojonudo, -da adj vulg bloody brilliant.

cojudo, -da adj Amer mfam bloody stupid.

col f cabbage; ~ **de Bruselas** Brussels sprout.

cola f 1. (de animal, avión) tail. 2. (fila) queue Br, line Am; **hacer** ~ to queue (up) Br, to stand in line Am. 3. (pegamento) glue. 4. (de clase, lista) bottom; (de desfile) end. 5. (peinado): ~ **(de caballo)** pony tail.

colaboración f 1. (gen) collaboration. 2. (de prensa) contribution, article.

colaborador, -ra m y f 1. (gen) collaborator. 2. (de prensa) contributor.

colaborar vi 1. (ayudar) to collaborate; ~ **con** to collaborate o work with. 2. (en prensa): ~ **en** o **con** to write for. 3. (contribuir) to contribute.

colación f loc: **sacar** o **traer algo a** ~ (tema) to bring sthg up.

colado, -da adj 1. (líquido) strained. 2. (enamorado): **estar** ~ **por alguien** fam to have a crush on sb. ► **colada** f (ropa) laundry; **hacer la** ~ to do the washing.

colador m (para líquidos) strainer, sieve; (para verdura) colander.

colapsar ◆ vt to bring to a halt, to stop. ◆ vi to come o grind to a halt.

colapso m 1. (MED) collapse, breakdown. 2. (de actividad) stoppage; (de tráfico) traffic jam, hold-up.

colar ◆ vt (verdura, té) to strain; (café) to filter. ◆ vi (pasar por bueno): **esto no colará** this won't wash. ► **colarse** vpr 1. (líquido): ~**se por** to seep through. 2. (persona) to slip, to sneak; (en una cola) to jump the queue Br o line Am; ~**se en una fiesta** to gatecrash a party.

colateral adj (lateral) on either side.

colcha f bedspread.

colchón m (de cama) mattress; ~ **inflable** air bed.

colchoneta f (para playa) beach mat; (en gimnasio) mat.

cole m fam school.

colear vi (animal) to wag its tail.

colección f lit & fig collection.

coleccionable ◆ adj collectable. ◆ m special supplement in serialized form.

coleccionar vt to collect.

coleccionista m y f collector.

colecta f collection.

colectividad f community.

colectivo, -va adj collective. ► **colectivo** m group.

colector, -ra m y f (persona) collector. ► **colector** m 1. (sumidero) sewer; ~ **de basuras** chute. 2. (MEC) (de motor) manifold.

colega m y f 1. (compañero profesional) colleague. 2. (homólogo) counterpart, opposite number. 3. fam (amigo) mate.

colegiado, -da adj who belongs to a professional association. ► **colegiado** m (DEP) referee.

colegial, -la m y f schoolboy (f schoolgirl).

colegio m 1. (escuela) school. 2. (de profesionales): ~ **(profesional)** professional association. ► **colegio electoral** m (lugar) polling station; (votantes) ward. ► **colegio mayor** m hall of residence.

cólera ◆ m (MED) cholera. ◆ f (ira) anger, rage; **montar en** ~ to get angry.

colérico, -ca adj (carácter) bad-tempered.

colesterol m cholesterol.

coleta f pigtail.

coletilla f postscript.

colgado, -da adj 1. (cuadro, jamón etc):

~ **(de)** hanging (from). **2.** (*teléfono*) on the hook.

colgador *m* hanger, coathanger.

colgante ◆ *adj* hanging. ◆ *m* pendant.

colgar ◆ *vt* **1.** (*suspender, ahorcar*) to hang; ~ **el teléfono** to hang up. **2.** (*imputar*): ~ **algo a alguien** to blame sthg on sb. ◆ *vi* **1.** (*pender*): ~ **(de)** to hang (from). **2.** (*hablando por teléfono*) to hang up.

colibrí *m* hummingbird.

cólico *m* stomachache.

coliflor *f* cauliflower.

colilla *f* (cigarette) butt o stub.

colimba *f* Amer fam military service.

colina *f* hill.

colindante *adj* neighbouring, adjacent.

colisión *f* (*de automóviles*) collision, crash; (*de ideas, intereses*) clash.

colisionar *vi* (*coche*): ~ **(contra)** to collide (with), to crash (into).

collar *m* **1.** (*de personas*) necklace. **2.** (*para animales*) collar.

collarín *m* surgical collar.

colmado, -da *adj*: ~ **(de)** full to the brim (with). ▶ **colmado** *m* grocer's (shop).

colmar *vt* **1.** (*recipiente*) to fill (to the brim). **2.** *fig* (*aspiración, deseo*) to fulfil.

colmena *f* beehive.

colmillo *m* **1.** (*de persona*) eye-tooth. **2.** (*de perro*) fang; (*de elefante*) tusk.

colmo *m* height; **para ~ de desgracias** to crown it all; **es el ~ de la locura** it's sheer madness; **¡eres el ~!** *fam* you're the limit!; **¡eso es el ~!** *fam* that's the last straw!

colocación *f* **1.** (*acción*) placing, positioning; (*situación*) place, position. **2.** (*empleo*) position, job.

colocado, -da *adj* **1.** (*gen*) placed; **estar muy bien ~** to have a very good job. **2.** *fam* (*borracho*) legless; (*drogado*) high, stoned.

colocar *vt* **1.** (*en su sitio*) to place, to put. **2.** (*en un empleo*) to find a job for. **3.** (*invertir*) to place, to invest. ▶ **colocarse** *vpr* **1.** (*en un trabajo*) to get a job. **2.** *fam* (*emborracharse*) to get legless; (*drogarse*) to get high o stoned.

colofón *m* (*remate, fin*) climax.

Colombia Colombia.

colombiano, -na *adj, m y f* Colombian.

colon *m* colon.

colonia *f* **1.** (*gen*) colony. **2.** (*perfume*) eau de cologne. **3.** Amer (*barrio*) district;

~ **proletaria** shanty town.

colonial *adj* colonial.

colonización *f* colonization.

colonizador, -ra *m y f* colonist.

colonizar *vt* to colonize.

colono *m* settler, colonist.

coloquial *adj* colloquial.

coloquio *m* **1.** (*conversación*) conversation. **2.** (*debate*) discussion, debate.

color *m* (*gen*) colour; ~ **rojo** red; ~ **azul** blue; **¿de qué ~?** what colour?; **de ~** (*persona*) coloured; **en ~** (*foto, televisor*) colour.

colorado, -da *adj* (*color*) red; **ponerse ~** to blush, to go red.

colorante *m* colouring.

colorear *vt* to colour (in).

colorete *m* rouge, blusher.

colorido *m* colours (*pl*).

colosal *adj* **1.** (*estatura, tamaño*) colossal. **2.** (*extraordinario*) great, enormous.

coloso *m* **1.** (*estatua*) colossus. **2.** *fig* (*cosa, persona*) giant.

columna *f* **1.** (*gen*) column. **2.** *fig* (*pilar*) pillar. ▶ **columna vertebral** *f* spinal column.

columnista *m y f* columnist.

columpiar *vt* to swing. ▶ **columpiarse** *vpr* to swing.

columpio *m* swing.

colza *f* (BOT) rape.

coma ◆ *m* (MED) coma; **en ~** in a coma. ◆ *f* **1.** (GRAM) comma. **2.** (MAT) ≃ decimal point.

comadreja *f* weasel.

comadrona *f* midwife.

comandancia *f* **1.** (*rango*) command. **2.** (*edificio*) command headquarters.

comandante *m* (MIL - *rango*) major; (- *de un puesto*) commander, commandant.

comandar *vt* (MIL) to command.

comando *m* (MIL) commando.

comarca *f* region, area.

comba *f* **1.** (*juego*) skipping; **jugar a la ~** to skip. **2.** (*cuerda*) skipping rope.

combar *vt* to bend. ▶ **combarse** *vpr* (*gen*) to bend; (*madera*) to warp; (*pared*) to bulge.

combate *m* (*gen*) fight; (*batalla*) battle.

combatiente *m y f* combatant, fighter.

combatir ◆ *vi*: ~ **(contra)** to fight (against). ◆ *vt* to combat, to fight.

combativo, -va *adj* combative.

combi *m* (*frigorífico*) fridge-freezer.

combinación *f* **1.** (*gen*) combination. **2.** (*de bebidas*) cocktail. **3.** (*prenda*) slip. **4.** (*de medios de transporte*) connections (*pl*).

combinado m 1. (*bebida*) cocktail. 2. (DEP) combined team. 3. Amer (*radiograma*) radiogram.

combinar vt 1. (*gen*) to combine. 2. (*bebidas*) to mix. 3. (*colores*) to match.

combustible ◆ adj combustible. ◆ m fuel.

combustión f combustion.

comecocos m inv fam (*para convencer*): **este panfleto es un ~** this pamphlet is designed to brainwash you.

comedia f comedy; *fig* (*engaño*) farce.

comediante, -ta m y f actor (f actress); *fig* (*farsante*) fraud.

comedido, -da adj moderate.

comedirse vpr to be restrained.

comedor m (*habitación - de casa*) dining room; (*- de fábrica*) canteen.

comensal m y f fellow diner.

comentar vt (*opinar sobre*) to comment on; (*hablar de*) to discuss.

comentario m 1. (*observación*) comment, remark. 2. (*crítica*) commentary. ▶ **comentarios** mpl (*murmuraciones*) gossip (U).

comentarista m y f commentator.

comenzar ◆ vt to start, to begin; ~ **a hacer algo** to start doing o to do sthg; ~ **diciendo que ...** to start o begin by saying that ... ◆ vi to start, to begin.

comer ◆ vi (*ingerir alimentos - gen*) to eat; (*- al mediodía*) to have lunch. ◆ vt 1. (*alimentos*) to eat. 2. (*en juegos de tablero*) to take, to capture. 3. *fig* (*consumir*) to eat up. ▶ **comerse** vpr 1. (*alimentos*) to eat. 2. (*desgastar - recursos*) to eat up; (*- metal*) to corrode. 3. (*en juegos de tablero*) to take, to capture. 4. Amer vulg (*fornicar*): **~se a** to fuck.

comercial adj commercial.

comercializar vt to market.

comerciante m y f tradesman (f tradeswoman); (*tendero*) shopkeeper.

comerciar vi to trade, to do business.

comercio m 1. (*de productos*) trade; **~ exterior/interior** foreign/domestic trade; **~ justo** fair trade; **libre ~** free trade. 2. (*actividad*) business, commerce. 3. (*tienda*) shop.

comestible adj edible, eatable. ▶ **comestibles** mpl (*gen*) food (U); (*en una tienda*) groceries.

cometa ◆ m (ASTRON) comet. ◆ f kite.

cometer vt (*crimen*) to commit; (*error*) to make.

cometido m 1. (*objetivo*) mission, task. 2. (*deber*) duty.

comezón f (*picor*) itch, itching (U).

cómic (*pl* cómics), **comic** (*pl* comics) m (*adult*) comic.

comicios mpl elections.

cómico, -ca ◆ adj 1. (*de la comedia*) comedy (*antes de sust*), comic. 2. (*gracioso*) comic, comical. ◆ m y f (*actor de teatro*) actor (f actress); (*humorista*) comedian (f comedienne), comic.

comida f 1. (*alimento*) food (U); **~ rápida** fast food. 2. (*almuerzo, cena etc*) meal. 3. (*al mediodía*) lunch.

comidilla f fam: **ser/convertirse en la ~ del pueblo** to be/to become the talk of the town.

comienzo m start, beginning; **a ~s de los años 50** in the early 1950s; **dar ~** to start, to begin.

comillas fpl inverted commas, quotation marks; **entre ~** in inverted commas.

comilona f fam (*festín*) blow-out.

comino m (*planta*) cumin, cummin; **me importa un ~** I don't give a damn.

comisaría f police station, precinct Am.

comisario, -ria m y f 1. **~ (de policía)** police superintendent. 2. (*delegado*) commissioner.

comisión f 1. (*de un delito*) perpetration. 2. (COM) commission; (*trabajar*) **a ~** (to work) on a commission basis. 3. (*delegación*) commission, committee; **~ investigadora** committee of inquiry; **~ permanente** standing commission.

comisura f corner (*of mouth, eyes*).

comité m committee.

comitiva f retinue.

como ◆ adv 1. (*comparativo*): **tan ... ~ ...** as ... as ...; **es (tan) negro ~ el carbón** it's as black as coal; **ser ~ algo** to be like sthg; **vive ~ un rey** he lives like a king; **lo que dijo fue ~ para ruborizarse** his words were enough to make you blush. 2. (*de la manera que*) as; **lo he hecho ~ es debido** I did it as o the way it should be done; **me encanta ~ bailas** I love the way you dance. 3. (*según*) as; **~ te decía ayer ...** as I was telling you yesterday ...; (*por qué*) why; **¿~ no me dijiste?** why didn't you tell me? 4. (*en calidad de*) as; **trabaja ~ bombero** he works as a fireman; **dieron el dinero ~ anticipo** they gave the money as an advance. 5. (*aproximadamente*) about; **me quedan ~ mil pesetas** I've got about a thousand pesetas left; **tiene un sabor ~ a naranja** it tastes a bit like an orange. ◆ *conj* 1. (*ya que*) as, since; ~ no llegabas, nos fuimos as o since you didn't arrive, we left. 2. (*si*) if; ~ no me hagas caso, lo pasarás mal if you don't listen to me, there will be trouble. ▶ como que *loc conj* 1. (*que*) that; le pareció ~ que lloraban it seemed to him (that) they were crying. 2. (*expresa causa*) pareces cansado ~ ~ que he trabajado toda la noche you seem tired – well, I've been up all night working. ▶ como quiera *loc adv* (*de cualquier modo*) anyway, anyhow. ▶ como quiera que *loc conj* 1. (*de cualquier modo que*) whichever way, however; ~ quiera que sea whatever the case may be. 2. (*dado que*) since, given that. ▶ como si *loc conj* as if.

cómo *adv* 1. (*de qué modo, por qué motivo*) how; ¿~ lo has hecho? how did you do it?; ¿~ son? what are they like?; no sé ~ has podido decir eso I don't know how you could say that; ¿~ que no la has visto nunca? what do you mean you've never seen her?; ¿a ~ están los tomates? how much are the tomatoes?; ¿~? *fam* (¿*qué dices?*) sorry?, what? 2. (*exclamativo*) how; ¡~ pasan los años! how time flies!; ¡~ no! of course!; está lloviendo, ¡y ~! it isn't half raining! 3. (*por qué*) why; ¿~ no me lo dijiste? why didn't you tell me?

cómoda *f* chest of drawers.

comodidad *f* comfort, convenience (U); para su ~ for your convenience.

comodín *m* (*naipe*) joker.

cómodo, -da *adj* 1. (*gen*) comfortable. 2. (*útil*) convenient. 3. (*oportuno, fácil*) easy.

comoquiera *adv*: ~ que (*de cualquier manera que*) whichever way, however; (*dado que*) since, seeing as.

compa *m y f Amer fam* mate, buddy.

compact *m* compact disc player.

compactar *vt* to compress.

compact disk, compact disc *m* compact disc.

compacto, -ta *adj* compact.

compadecer *vt* to pity, to feel sorry for. ▶ compadecerse de *vpr* to pity, to feel sorry for.

compadre *m fam* (*amigo*) friend, mate.

compadrear *vi Amer* to brag, to boast.

compaginar *vt* (*combinar*) to reconcile. ▶ compaginarse *vpr*: ~se con to square with, to go together with.

compañerismo *m* comradeship.

compañero, -ra *m y f* 1. (*pareja, acompañante*) companion. 2. (*colega*) colleague; ~ de clase classmate; ~ de piso flatmate.

compañía *f* company; en ~ de accompanied by, in the company of; hacer ~ a alguien to keep sb company.

comparación *f* comparison; en ~ con in comparison with, compared to.

comparar *vt*: ~ algo (con) to compare sthg (to).

comparativo, -va *adj* comparative.

comparecer *vi* to appear.

comparsa ◆ *f* (*instrumento*) pair of compasses. 2. (MÚS - *periodo*) bar; (- *ritmo*) rhythm, beat; al ~ (de la música) in time (with the music); llevar el ~ to keep time; perder el ~ to lose the beat.

compasión *f* compassion, pity.

compasivo, -va *adj* compassionate.

compatibilizar *vt* to make compatible.

compatible *adj* (*gen* & INFORM) compatible.

compatriota *m y f* compatriot, fellow countryman (*f* fellow countrywoman).

compendiar *vt* (*cualidades, características*) to summarize; (*libro, historia*) to abridge.

compendio *m* 1. (*libro*) compendium. 2. *fig* (*síntesis*) epitome, essence.

compenetración *f* mutual understanding.

compenetrarse *vpr* to understand each other.

compensación *f* (*gen*) compensation; en ~ (por) in return (for).

compensar *vt* 1. (*valer la pena*) to make up for; no me compensa (perder tanto tiempo) it's not worth my while (wasting all that time). 2. (*indemnizar*): ~ a alguien (de o por) to compensate sb (for).

competencia *f* 1. (*entre personas, empresas*) competition. 2. (*incumbencia*) field, province. 3. (*aptitud, atribuciones*) competence.

competente *adj* competent; ~ en materia de responsible for.

competer ▶ competer a *vi* (*gen*) to be up to, to be the responsibility of;

(*una autoridad*) to come under the jurisdiction of.

competición f competition.

competidor, -ra m y f competitor.

competir vi: ~ **(con/por)** to compete (with/for).

competitividad f competitiveness.

competitivo, -va adj competitive.

compilar vt (*gen* & INFORM) to compile.

compinche m y f fam crony.

complacencia f pleasure, satisfaction.

complacer vt to please.

complaciente adj 1. (*amable*) obliging, helpful. 2. (*indulgente*) indulgent.

complejo, -ja adj complex. ► **complejo** m complex; ~ **industrial** industrial park.

complementar vt to complement. ► **complementarse** vpr to complement each other.

complementario, -ria adj complementary.

complemento m 1. (*añadido*) complement. 2. (GRAM) object, complement.

completamente adv completely, totally.

completar vt to complete.

completo, -ta adj 1. (*entero, perfecto*) complete; **por** ~ completely; **un deportista muy** ~ an all-round sportsman. 2. (*lleno*) full.

complexión f build.

complicación f 1. (*gen*) complication. 2. (*complejidad*) complexity.

complicado, -da adj 1. (*difícil*) complicated. 2. (*implicado*): ~ **(en)** involved (in).

complicar vt (*dificultar*) to complicate.

cómplice m y f accomplice.

complicidad f complicity.

complot, compló m plot, conspiracy.

componente m 1. (*gen* & ELECTR) component. 2. (*persona*) member.

componer vt 1. (*formar un todo, ser parte de*) to make up. 2. (*música, versos*) to compose. 3. (*arreglar - algo roto*) to repair. ► **componerse** vpr (*estar formado*): ~**se de** to be made up of.

comportamiento m behaviour.

comportar vt to involve, to entail. ► **comportarse** vpr to behave.

composición f composition.

compositor, -ra m y f composer.

compostura f 1. (*reparación*) repair. 2. (*de persona, rostro*) composure. 3. (*en comportamiento*) restraint.

compota f (CULIN) stewed fruit (U).

compra f purchase; **ir de** ~**s** to go shopping; **ir a** o **hacer la** ~ to do the shopping; ~ **a plazos** hire purchase.

comprador, -ra m y f (*gen*) buyer; (*en una tienda*) shopper, customer.

comprar vt 1. (*adquirir*) to buy, to purchase. 2. (*sobornar*) to buy (off).

compraventa f buying and selling, trading.

comprender vt 1. (*incluir*) to include, to comprise. 2. (*entender*) to understand. ► **comprenderse** vpr (*personas*) to understand each other.

comprensión f understanding.

comprensivo, -va adj understanding.

compresa f (*para menstruación*) sanitary towel Br, sanitary napkin Am.

comprimido, -da adj compressed. ► **comprimido** m pill, tablet.

comprimir vt to compress.

comprobante m (*documento*) supporting document, proof; (*recibo*) receipt.

comprobar vt (*averiguar*) to check; (*demostrar*) to prove.

comprometer vt 1. (*poner en peligro - éxito etc*) to jeopardize; (- *persona*) to compromise. 2. (*avergonzar*) to embarrass. ► **comprometerse** vpr 1. (*hacerse responsable*): ~**se (a hacer algo)** to commit o.s. (to doing sthg). 2. (*ideológicamente, moralmente*): ~**se (en algo)** to become involved in sthg.

comprometido, -da adj 1. (*con una idea*) committed. 2. (*difícil*) compromising, awkward.

compromiso m 1. (*obligación*) commitment, obligation; (*acuerdo*) agreement. 2. (*cita*) engagement; ~ **matrimonial** engagement. 3. (*dificultad*) compromising o difficult situation.

compuerta f sluice, floodgate.

compuesto, -ta ◆ pp → **componer**. ◆ adj (*formado*): ~ **de** composed of. ► **compuesto** m (GRAM & QUÍM) compound.

compungido, -da adj contrite.

computador m, **computadora** f computer.

computar vt (*calcular*) to calculate.

cómputo m calculation.

comulgar vi (RELIG) to take communion.

común adj 1. (*gen*) common; **por lo** ~ generally; **poco** ~ unusual. 2. (*compartido - amigo, interés*) mutual; (- *bienes, pastos*) communal. 3. (*ordinario - vino etc*) ordinary, average.

comuna f commune.

comunicación f 1. (gen) communication; **ponerse en ~ con alguien** to get in touch with sb. 2. (escrito oficial) communiqué; (informe) report. ▶ **comunicaciones** fpl communications.

comunicado, -da adj: **bien ~** (lugar) well-served, with good connections. ▶ **comunicado** m announcement, statement; **~ a la prensa** press release.

comunicar ◆ vt 1. (transmitir - sentimientos, ideas) to convey; (- movimiento, virus) to transmit. 2. (información): **~ algo a alguien** to inform sb of sthg, to tell sb sthg. ◆ vi 1. (hablar - gen) to communicate; (- al teléfono) to get through; (escribir) to get in touch. 2. (dos lugares): **~ con algo** to connect with sthg, to join sthg. 3. (el teléfono) to be engaged Br, to be busy Am; **está comunicando** the line's engaged. ▶ **comunicarse** vpr 1. (hablarse) to communicate (with each other). 2. (dos lugares) to be connected.

comunicativo, -va adj communicative.

comunidad f (gen) community; **~ autónoma** autonomous region; **Comunidad Económica Europea** European Economic Community.

COMUNIDAD AUTÓNOMA

In Spain, the 'comunidad autónoma' is a region consisting of one or more provinces which enjoys a degree of autonomy in administrative matters. There are 17 'comunidades autónomas': Andalusia, Aragon, the Principality of Asturias, the Balearic Islands, the Canary Islands, Cantabria, Castile and León, Castile and La Mancha, Catalonia, Extremadura, La Rioja, Madrid, Murcia, Navarre, Valencia, Galicia and the Basque Country.

---

comunión f lit & fig communion.

comunismo m communism.

comunista adj, m y f communist.

comunitario, -ria adj 1. (de la comunidad) community (antes de sust). 2. (de la CEE) Community (antes de sust), of the European Community.

con prep 1. (gen) with; **¿~ quién vas?** who are you going with?; **lo ha conseguido ~ su esfuerzo** he has achieved it through his own efforts; **una cartera ~ varios documentos** a briefcase containing several documents. 2. (a pesar de) in spite of; **~ todo** despite everything; **~ lo**

estudioso que es, le suspendieron for all his hard work, they still failed him. 3. (hacia): **para ~** towards; **es amable para ~ todos** she is friendly towards o with everyone. 4. (+ infin) (para introducir una condición) by (+ gerund); **~ hacerlo así** by doing it this way; **~ salir a las diez es suficiente** if we leave at ten, we'll have plenty of time. 5. (a condición de que): **~ (tal) que** (+ subjuntivo) as long as; **~ que llegue a tiempo me conformo** I don't mind as long as he arrives on time.

conato m attempt; **~ de robo** attempted robbery; **un ~ de incendio** the beginnings of a fire.

concatenar, concadenar vt to link together.

concavidad f (lugar) hollow.

cóncavo, -va adj concave.

concebir ◆ vt (plan, hijo) to conceive; (imaginar) to imagine. ◆ vi to conceive.

conceder vt 1. (dar) to grant; (premio) to award. 2. (asentir) to admit, to concede.

concejal, -la m y f (town) councillor.

concentración f 1. (gen) concentration. 2. (de gente) gathering.

concentrado m concentrate.

concentrar vt 1. (gen) to concentrate. 2. (reunir - gente) to bring together; (- tropas) to assemble. ▶ **concentrarse** vpr to concentrate.

concéntrico, -ca adj concentric.

concepción f conception.

concepto m 1. (idea) concept. 2. (opinión) opinion. 3. (motivo): **bajo ningún ~** under no circumstances; **en ~ de** by way of, as.

concernir v impers to concern; **en lo que concierne a** as regards; **por lo que a mí me concierne** as far as I'm concerned.

concertar ◆ vt (precio) to agree on; (cita) to arrange; (pacto) to reach. ◆ vi (concordar): **~ (con)** to tally (with), to fit in (with).

concertina f concertina.

concesión f 1. (de préstamo etc) granting; (de premio) awarding. 2. (COM & fig) concession.

concesionario, -ria m y f (persona con derecho exclusivo de venta) licensed dealer; (titular de una concesión) concessionaire, licensee.

concha f 1. (de los animales) shell. 2. (material) tortoiseshell.

conchabarse vpr fam: **~ (contra)** to gang up (on).

conciencia, consciencia f 1. (conocimiento) consciousness, awareness; **tener/tomar ~ de** to be/become aware of. 2. (moral, integridad) conscience; **a ~** conscientiously; **me remuerde la ~** I have a guilty conscience.

concienciar, concientizar Amer vt to make aware. ▶ **concienciarse** vpr to become aware.

concientizar Amer = **concienciar**.

concienzudo, -da adj conscientious.

concierto m 1. (actuación) concert. 2. (composición) concerto.

conciliar vt to reconcile; **~ el sueño** to get to sleep.

concilio m council.

concisión f conciseness.

conciso, -sa adj concise.

conciudadano, -na m y f fellow citizen.

cónclave, conclave m conclave.

concluir ◆ vt to conclude; **~ haciendo o por hacer algo** to end up doing sthg. ◆ vi to (come to an) end.

conclusión f conclusion; **llegar a una ~** to come to o to reach a conclusion; **en ~** in conclusion.

concluyente adj conclusive.

concordancia f (gen & GRAM) agreement.

concordar ◆ vt to reconcile. ◆ vi 1. (estar de acuerdo): **~ (con)** to agree o tally (with). 2. (GRAM): **~ (con)** to agree (with).

concordia f harmony.

concretar vt (precisar) to specify, to state exactly. ▶ **concretarse** vpr (materializarse) to take shape.

concreto, -ta adj specific, particular; **en ~** (en resumen) in short; (específicamente) specifically; **nada en ~** nothing definite. ▶ **concreto armado** m Amer concrete.

concurrencia f 1. (asistencia) attendance; (espectadores) crowd, audience. 2. (de sucesos) concurrence.

concurrido, -da adj (bar, calle) crowded; (espectáculo) well-attended.

concurrir vi 1. (reunirse): **~ a algo** to go to sthg, to attend sthg. 2. (participar): **~ a** (concurso) to take part in, to compete in; (examen) to sit Br, to take.

concursante m y f (en concurso) competitor, contestant; (en oposiciones) candidate.

concursar vi (competir) to compete; (en oposiciones) to be a candidate.

concurso m 1. (prueba - literaria, deportiva) competition, contest; (- de televisión) game show. 2. (para una obra) tender; **salir a ~** to be put out to tender. 3. (ayuda) cooperation.

condado m (territorio) county.

condal adj: **la Ciudad ~** Barcelona.

conde, -desa m y f count (f countess).

condecoración f (insignia) medal.

condecorar vt to decorate.

condena f sentence.

condenado, -da adj 1. (a una pena) convicted, sentenced; (a un sufrimiento) condemned. 2. fam (maldito) damned.

condenar vt 1. (declarar culpable) to convict. 2. (castigar): **~ a alguien a algo** to sentence sb to sthg. 3. (recriminar) to condemn.

condensar vt lit & fig to condense.

condescendencia f (benevolencia) graciousness; (altivez) condescension.

condescender vi: **~ a** (con amabilidad) to consent to, to accede to; (con desprecio) to deign to, to condescend to.

condescendiente adj obliging.

condición f 1. (gen) condition; **condiciones de un contrato** terms of a contract; **con una sola ~** on one condition. 2. (naturaleza) nature. 3. (clase social) social class. ▶ **condiciones** fpl 1. (aptitud) talent (U), ability (U). 2. (circunstancias) conditions; **condiciones atmosféricas/de vida** weather/living conditions. 3. (estado) condition (U); **estar en condiciones de o para hacer algo** (físicamente) to be in a fit state to do sthg; (por la situación) to be in a position to do sthg; **no estar en condiciones** (carne, pescado) be off.

condicional adj & m conditional.

condicionar vt 1. (hacer depender): **~ algo a algo** to make sthg dependent on sthg. 2. (determinar) to determine.

condimento m seasoning (U), condiment.

condolencia f condolence.

condolerse vpr: **~ (de)** to feel pity (for).

condón m condom.

cóndor m condor.

conducción f (de vehículo) driving.

conducir ◆ vt 1. (vehículo) to drive. 2. (dirigir - empresa) to manage, to run; (- ejército) to lead; (- asunto) to handle. 3. (a una persona a un lugar) to lead. ◆ vi 1. (en vehículo) to drive. 2. (a sitio, situación): **~ a** to lead to.

conducta f behaviour, conduct.

conducto m 1. (de fluido) pipe. 2. fig (vía) channel. 3. (ANAT) duct.

conductor, -ra m y f 1. (de vehículo) driver. 2. (FÍS) conductor.

conectar vt: ~ algo (a o con) to connect sthg (to o up to).

conejillo ▶ **conejillo de Indias** m guinea pig.

conejo, -ja m y f rabbit (f doe).

conexión f 1. (gen) connection. 2. (RADIO & TV) link-up; ~ vía satélite satellite link.

conexo, -xa adj related, connected.

confabular ▶ **confabularse** vpr: ~se (para) to plot o conspire (to).

confección f 1. (de ropa) tailoring, dressmaking. 2. (de comida) preparation, making; (de lista) drawing up.

confeccionar vt 1. (ropa) to make (up); (lista) to draw up. 2. (plato) to prepare; (bebida) to mix.

confederación f confederation.

conferencia f 1. (charla) lecture; dar una ~ to give a talk o lecture. 2. (reunión) conference. 3. (por teléfono) (long-distance) call.

conferir vt 1. ~ algo a alguien (honor, dignidad) to confer o bestow sthg upon sb; (responsabilidades) to give sthg to sb. 2. (cualidad) to give.

confesar vt (gen) to confess; (debilidad) to admit. ▶ **confesarse** vpr (RELIG): ~se (de algo) to confess (sthg).

confesión f 1. (gen) confession. 2. (credo) religion, (religious) persuasion.

confesionario m confessional.

confeti mpl confetti (U).

confiado, -da adj (seguro) confident; (crédulo) trusting.

confianza f 1. (seguridad): ~ (en) confidence (in); ~ en uno mismo self-confidence. 2. (fe) trust; de ~ trustworthy. 3. (familiaridad) familiarity; en ~ in confidence.

confiar vt 1. (secreto) to confide. 2. (responsabilidad, persona, asunto): ~ algo a alguien to entrust sthg to sb. ▶ **confiar** vi 1. (tener fe) to trust in. 2. (suponer): ~ en que to be confident that. ▶ **confiarse** vpr (despreocuparse) to be too sure (of o.s.).

confidencia f confidence, secret.

confidencial adj confidential.

confidente m y f 1. (amigo) confidant (f confidante). 2. (soplón) informer.

configurar vt (formar) to shape, to form.

confín m (gen pl) 1. (límite) border, boundary. 2. (extremo - del reino, universo) outer reaches (pl); en los confines de on the very edge of.

confinar vt 1. (detener): ~ (en) to confine (to). 2. (desterrar): ~ (en) to banish (to).

confirmación f (gen & RELIG) confirmation.

confirmar vt to confirm.

confiscar vt to confiscate.

confitado, -da adj candied; frutas confitadas crystallized fruit.

confite m sweet Br, candy Am.

confitería f 1. (tienda) sweetshop, confectioner's. 2. Amer (café) cafe.

confitura f preserve, jam.

conflagración f conflict, war.

conflictivo, -va adj (asunto) controversial; (situación) troubled; (trabajador) difficult.

conflicto m (gen) conflict; (de intereses, opiniones) clash; ~ laboral industrial dispute.

confluir vi 1. (corriente, cauce): ~ (en) to converge o meet (at). 2. (personas): ~ (en) to come together o to gather (in).

conformar vt (configurar) to shape. ▶ **conformarse con** vpr (suerte, destino) to resign o.s. to; (apañárselas con) to make do with; (contentarse con) to be satisfied with.

conforme ◆ adj 1. (acorde): ~ a in accordance with. 2. (de acuerdo): ~ (con) in agreement (with). 3. (contento): ~ (con) happy (with). ◆ adv (gen) as; ~ envejecía as he got older.

conformidad f (aprobación): ~ (con) approval (of).

conformista adj, m y f conformist.

confort (pl conforts) m comfort; 'todo ~' 'all mod cons'.

confortable adj comfortable.

confortar vt to console, to comfort.

confrontar vt 1. (enfrentar) to confront. 2. (comparar) to compare.

confundir vt 1. (trastocar): ~ una cosa con otra to mistake one thing for another; ~ dos cosas to get two things mixed up. 2. (liar) to confuse. 3. (mezclar) to mix up. ▶ **confundirse** vpr 1. (equivocarse) to make a mistake; ~se de piso to get the wrong flat. 2. (liarse) to get confused. 3. (mezclarse - colores, siluetas): ~se (en) to merge (into); (- personas): ~se entre la gente to lose o.s. in the crowd.

confusión f 1. (gen) confusion. 2. (error) mix-up.

confuso, -sa *adj* 1. (*incomprensible - estilo, explicación*) obscure. 2. (*poco claro - rumor*) muffled; (*- clamor, griterío*) confused; (*- contorno, forma*) blurred. 3. (*turbado*) confused, bewildered.

congelación *f* 1. (*de alimentos*) freezing. 2. (ECON) (*de precios, salarios*) freeze.

congelador *m* freezer.

congelados *mpl* frozen foods.

congelar *vt* (*gen &* ECON) to freeze. ▶ **congelarse** *vpr* to freeze.

congeniar *vi*: ~ **(con)** to get on (with).

congénito, -ta *adj* (*enfermedad*) congenital; (*talento*) innate.

congestión *f* congestion.

congestionar *vt* to block. ▶ **congestionarse** *vpr* 1. (AUTOM & MED) to become congested. 2. (*cara - de rabia etc*) to flush, to turn purple.

congoja *f* anguish.

congraciarse *vpr*: ~ **con alguien** to win sb over.

congratular *vt*: ~ **a alguien (por)** to congratulate sb (on).

congregación *f* congregation.

congregar *vt* to assemble.

congresista *m y f* 1. (*en un congreso*) delegate. 2. (*político*) congressman (*f* congresswoman).

congreso *m* 1. (*de una especialidad*) congress, conference. 2. (*asamblea nacional*): ~ **de diputados** (*en España*) lower house of Spanish Parliament; = House of Commons *Br*; = House of Representatives *Am*; **el Congreso** (*en Estados Unidos*) Congress.

congrio *m* conger eel.

congruente *adj* consistent, congruous.

conjetura *f* conjecture; **hacer ~s, hacerse una ~** to conjecture.

conjugación *f* (GRAM) conjugation.

conjugar *vt* 1. (GRAM) to conjugate. 2. (*opiniones*) to bring together, to combine; (*esfuerzos, ideas*) to pool.

conjunción *f* (ASTRON & GRAM) conjunction.

conjunto, -ta *adj* (*gen*) joint; (*hechos, acontecimientos*) combined. ▶ **conjunto** *m* 1. (*gen*) set, collection; **un ~ de circunstancias** a number of reasons. 2. (*de ropa*) outfit. 3. (MÚS *- de rock*) group, band; (*- de música clásica*) ensemble. 4. (*totalidad*) whole; **en ~** overall, as a whole. 5. (MAT) set.

conjurar ♦ *vi* (*conspirar*) to conspire, to plot. ♦ *vt* 1. (*exorcizar*) to exorcize. 2. (*evitar - un peligro*) to ward off, to avert.

conjuro *m* spell, incantation.

conllevar *vt* (*implicar*) to entail.

conmemoración *f* commemoration.

conmemorar *vt* to commemorate.

conmigo *pron pers* with me; ~ **mismo/ misma** with myself.

conmoción *f* 1. (*física o psíquica*) shock; ~ **cerebral** concussion. 2. *fig* (*trastorno, disturbio*) upheaval.

conmocionar *vt* 1. (*psíquicamente*) to shock. 2. (*físicamente*) to concuss.

conmovedor, -ra *adj* moving, touching.

conmover *vt* 1. (*emocionar*) to move, to touch. 2. (*sacudir*) to shake.

conmutador *m* 1. (ELECTR) switch. 2. *Amer* (*centralita*) switchboard.

connotación *f* connotation; **una ~ irónica** a hint of irony.

cono *m* cone.

conocedor, -ra *m y f*: ~ **(de)** (*gen*) expert (on); (*de vinos*) connoisseur (of).

conocer *vt* 1. (*gen*) to know; **darse a ~** to make o.s. known; ~ **bien un tema** to know a lot about a subject; ~ **alguien de vista** to know sb by sight; ~ **a alguien de oídas** to have heard of sb. 2. (*descubrir - lugar, país*) to get to know. 3. (*a una persona - por primera vez*) to meet. 4. (*reconocer*): ~ **a alguien (por algo)** to recognize sb (by sthg). ▶ **conocerse** *vpr* 1. (*a uno mismo*) to know o.s. 2. (*dos o más personas - por primera vez*) to meet, to get to know each other; (*- desde hace tiempo*) to know each other.

conocido, -da ♦ *adj* well-known. ♦ *m y f* acquaintance.

conocimiento *m* 1. (*gen*) knowledge. 2. (MED) (*sentido*) consciousness. ▶ **conocimientos** *mpl* knowledge (U); **tener muchos ~s** to be very knowledgeable.

conozca *etc* → **conocer**.

conque *conj* so; **¿~ te has cansado?** so you're tired, are you?

conquista *f* (*de tierras, persona*) conquest.

conquistador, -ra *m y f* 1. (*de tierras*) conqueror. 2. (HIST) conquistador.

conquistar *vt* (*tierras*) to conquer.

consabido, -da *adj* (*conocido*) wellknown; (*habitual*) usual.

consagrar *vt* 1. (RELIG) to consecrate. 2. (*dedicar*): ~ **algo a algo/alguien** (*tiempo, espacio*) to devote sthg to sthg/sb; (*monumento, lápida*) to dedicate sthg to sthg/sb. 3. (*acreditar, confirmar*) to confirm, to establish.

consciencia = conciencia.

consciente adj conscious; **ser ~ de** to be aware of; **estar ~** (físicamente) to be conscious.

consecución f (de un deseo) realization; (de un objetivo) attainment; (de un premio) winning.

consecuencia f (resultado) consequence; **a** o **como ~ de** as a consequence o result of.

consecuente adj (coherente) consistent.

consecutivo, -va adj consecutive.

conseguir vt (gen) to obtain, to get; (un objetivo) to achieve; **~ hacer algo** to manage to do sthg.

consejero, -ra m y f 1. (en asuntos personales) counsellor; (en asuntos técnicos) adviser, consultant. 2. (de un consejo de administración) member; (POLÍT) councillor.

consejo m 1. (advertencia) advice (U); **dar un ~** to give some advice. 2. (organismo) council; **~ de administración** board of directors. 3. (reunión) meeting. ▶ **consejo de guerra** m court martial. ▶ **consejo de ministros** m cabinet.

consenso m (acuerdo) consensus; (consentimiento) consent.

consentimiento m consent.

consentir ♦ vt 1. (tolerar) to allow, to permit. 2. (mimar) to spoil. ♦ vi: **~ en algo/en hacer algo** to agree to sthg/to do sthg.

conserje m y f (portero) porter; (encargado) caretaker.

conserjería f 1. (de un hotel) reception desk. 2. (de un edificio público o privado) porter's lodge.

conserva f: **~ de carne** tinned meat; **en ~** tinned, canned.

conservación f (gen) conservation; (de alimentos) preservation.

conservador, -ra ♦ adj (gen) conservative; (del partido conservador) Conservative. ♦ m y f 1. (por ideología) conservative; (miembro del partido conservador) Conservative. 2. (de museo) curator.

conservante m y f preservative.

conservar vt 1. (gen & CULIN) to preserve; (amistad) to keep up, to maintain; (salud) to look after; (calor) to retain. 2. (guardar - libros, cartas, secreto) to keep. ▶ **conservarse** vpr to keep; **se conserva bien** he's keeping well.

conservatorio m conservatoire.

considerable adj (gen) considerable;

(importante, eminente) notable.

consideración f 1. (valoración) consideration. 2. (respeto) respect; **tratar a alguien con ~** to be nice to sb; **en ~ a algo** in recognition of sthg. 3. (importancia): **de ~** serious.

considerado, -da adj (atento) considerate, thoughtful; (respetado) respected.

considerar vt 1. (valorar) to consider. 2. (juzgar, estimar) to think.

consigna f 1. (órdenes) instructions (pl). 2. (para el equipaje) left-luggage office.

consignar vt 1. (poner por escrito) to record, to write down. 2. (enviar - mercancía) to dispatch. 3. (equipaje) to deposit in the left-luggage office.

consigo pron pers with him/her, (pl) with them; (con usted) with you; (con uno mismo) with o.s.; **~ mismo/misma** with himself/herself; **hablar ~ mismo** to talk to o.s.

consiguiente adj consequent; **por ~** consequently, therefore.

consistencia f lit & fig consistency.

consistente adj 1. (sólido - material) solid. 2. (coherente - argumento) sound. 3. (compuesto): **~ en** consisting of.

consistir ▶ **consistir en** vi 1. (gen) to consist of. 2. (deberse a) to lie in, to be based on.

consola f 1. (mesa) console table. 2. (INFORM & TECN) console; **~ de videojuegos** video console.

consolación f consolation.

consolar vt to console.

consolidación f consolidation.

consolidar vt to consolidate.

consomé m consommé.

consonancia f harmony; **en ~ con** in keeping with.

consonante f consonant.

consorcio m consortium.

conspiración f plot, conspiracy.

conspirador, -ra m y f conspirator.

conspirar vi to conspire, to plot.

constancia f 1. (perseverancia - en una empresa) perseverance; (- en las ideas, opiniones) steadfastness. 2. (testimonio) record; **dejar ~ de algo** (registrar) to put sthg on record; (probar) to demonstrate sthg.

constante ♦ adj 1. (persona - en una empresa) persistent. 2. (acción) constant. ♦ f constant.

constar vi 1. (una información): **~ (en)** to appear (in), to figure (in); **~le a alguien** to be clear to sb; **me consta que** I am quite sure that; **que conste que ...** let it be clearly understood that ..., let there be no doubt that ...; **hacer ~** to put on record. **2.** (*estar constituido por*): **~ de** to consist of.

constatar *vt* (*observar*) to confirm; (*comprobar*) to check.

constelación *f* constellation.

consternación *f* consternation.

consternar *vt* to dismay.

constipado, -da *adj*: **estar ~** to have a cold. ▶ **constipado** *m* cold.

constiparse *vpr* to catch a cold.

constitución *f* constitution.

constitucional *adj* constitutional.

constituir *vt* **1.** (*componer*) to make up. **2.** (*ser*) to be. **3.** (*crear*) to set up.

constituyente *adj & m* constituent.

constreñir *vt* (*oprimir, limitar*) to restrict.

construcción *f* **1.** (*gen*) construction; **en ~** under construction. **2.** (*edificio*) building.

constructivo, -va *adj* constructive.

constructor, -ra *adj* building (*antes de sust*), construction (*antes de sust*). ▶ **constructor** *m* (*de edificios*) builder. ▶ **constructora** *f*: (**empresa**) **~a** construction company.

construir *vt* (*edificio, barco*) to build; (*aviones, coches*) to manufacture; (*frase, teoría*) to construct.

consuelo *m* consolation, solace.

cónsul, consulesa *m y f* consul.

consulado *m* (*oficina*) consulate; (*cargo*) consulship.

consulta *f* **1.** (*sobre un problema*) consultation; **hacer una ~ a alguien** to seek sb's advice. **2.** (*despacho de médico*) consulting room, surgery Br; **horas de ~** surgery hours.

consultar ◆ *vt* (*dato, fecha*) to look up; (*libro, persona*) to consult. ◆ *vi*: **~ con** to consult, to seek advice from.

consultor, -ra *m y f* consultant.

consultorio *m* **1.** (*de un médico*) consulting room, surgery Br. **2.** (*en periódico*) problem page; (*en radio*) programme answering listeners' questions. **3.** (*asesoría*) advice bureau.

consumar *vt* (*gen*) to complete; (*un crimen*) to perpetrate; (*el matrimonio*) to consummate.

consumición *f* **1.** (*acción*) consumption. **2.** (*bebida*) drink; (*comida*) food.

consumidor, -ra *m y f* (*gen*) consumer; (*en un bar, restaurante*) patron.

consumir ◆ *vt* **1.** (*gen*) to consume.

2. (*destruir - suj: fuego*) to destroy. ◆ *vi* to consume. ▶ **consumirse** *vpr* **1.** (*persona*) to waste away. **2.** (*fuego*) to burn out.

consumismo *m* consumerism.

consumo *m* consumption; **bienes/ sociedad de ~** consumer goods/society.

contabilidad *f* **1.** (*oficio*) accountancy. **2.** (*de persona, empresa*) bookkeeping, accounting; **llevar la ~** to do the accounts.

contable *m y f* accountant.

contactar ◆ *vi*: **~ con** to contact. ◆ *vt* Amer to contact.

contacto *m* **1.** (*gen*) contact; **perder el ~** to lose touch. **2.** (AUTOM) ignition.

contado, -da *adj* (*raro*) rare, infrequent; **contadas veces** very rarely. ▶ **al contado** *loc adv*: **pagar al ~** to pay (in) cash.

contador, -ra *m y f* Amer (*persona*) accountant. ▶ **contador** *m* (*aparato*) meter.

contagiar *vt* (*persona*) to infect; (*enfermedad*) to transmit. ▶ **contagiarse** *vpr* (*enfermedad, risa*) to be contagious; (*persona*) to become infected.

contagio *m* infection, contagion.

contagioso, -sa *adj* (*enfermedad*) contagious, infectious; (*risa etc*) infectious.

container = **contenedor**.

contaminación *f* (*gen*) contamination; (*del medio ambiente*) pollution.

contaminante *m* pollutant.

contaminar *vt* (*gen*) to contaminate; (*el medio ambiente*) to pollute.

contar ◆ *vt* **1.** (*enumerar, incluir*) to count. **2.** (*historia, chiste*) to tell. ◆ *vi* to count. ▶ **contar con** *vi* **1.** (*confiar en*) to count on. **2.** (*tener, poseer*) to have. **3.** (*tener en cuenta*) to take into account; **con esto no contaba** I hadn't reckoned with that.

contemplación *f* contemplation.

contemplar *vt* (*mirar, considerar*) to contemplate.

contemporáneo, -a *adj, m y f* contemporary.

contenedor, -ra *adj* containing. ▶ **contenedor, container** *m* (*gen*) container; (*para escombros*) skip; **~ de basura** large rubbish bin for collecting rubbish from blocks of flats etc.

contener *vt* **1.** (*encerrar*) to contain. **2.** (*detener, reprimir*) to restrain. ▶ **contenerse** *vpr* to restrain o.s.

contenido *m* (*gen*) contents (*pl*); (*de discurso, redacción*) content.

contentar *vt* to please, to keep happy. ▶ **contentarse** *vpr*: ~se con to make do with.

contento, -ta *adj* (*alegre*) happy; (*satisfecho*) content.

contestación *f* answer.

contestador ▶ **contestador (automático)** *m* answering machine.

contestar *vt* to answer, to reply.

contestatario, -ria *adj* anti-establishment.

contexto *m* context.

contienda *f* (*competición, combate*) contest; (*guerra*) conflict, war.

contigo *pron pers* with you; ~ mismo/misma with yourself.

contiguo, -gua *adj* adjacent.

continencia *f* self-restraint.

continental *adj* continental.

continente *m* (GEOGR) continent.

contingente ◆ *adj* unforeseeable. ◆ *m* 1. (*grupo*) contingent. 2. (COM) quota.

continuación *f* continuation; a ~ next, then.

continuar ◆ *vt* to continue, to carry on with. ◆ *vi* to continue, to go on; ~ haciendo algo to continue doing o to do sthg; **continúa lloviendo** it's still raining.

continuidad *f* (*en una sucesión*) continuity; (*permanencia*) continuation.

continuo, -nua *adj* 1. (*ininterrumpido*) continuous. 2. (*constante, perseverante*) continual.

contonearse *vpr* (*hombre*) to swagger; (*mujer*) to swing one's hips.

contorno *m* 1. (GEOGR) contour; (*línea*) outline. 2. (*gen pl*) (*vecindad*) neighbourhood; (*de una ciudad*) outskirts (*pl*).

contorsionarse *vpr* (*gen*) to do contortions; (*de dolor*) to writhe.

contra ◆ *prep* against; un jarabe ~ la tos a cough syrup; en ~ against; estar en ~ de algo to be opposed to sthg; en ~ de (*a diferencia de*) contrary to. ◆ *m*: **los pros y los ~s** the pros and cons.

contraataque *m* counterattack.

contrabajo *m* 1. (*instrumento*) double-bass. 2. (*voz, cantante*) low bass.

contrabandista *m y f* smuggler.

contrabando *m* (*acto*) smuggling; (*mercancías*) contraband; **pasar algo de ~** to smuggle sthg in; ~ **de armas** gunrunning.

contracción *f* contraction.

contrachapado, -da *adj* made of plywood. ▶ **contrachapado** *m* plywood.

contradecir *vt* to contradict.

contradicción *f* contradiction; **estar en ~ con** to be in (direct) contradiction to.

contradicho, -cha *pp* → contradecir.

contradictorio, -ria *adj* contradictory.

contraer *vt* 1. (*gen*) to contract. 2. (*costumbre, acento etc*) to acquire. 3. (*enfermedad*) to catch. ▶ **contraerse** *vpr* to contract.

contrafuerte *m* (ARQUIT) buttress.

contraindicación *f*: 'contraindicaciones: ...' 'not to be taken with ...'

contralor *m* Amer inspector of public spending.

contralto *m* (*voz*) contralto.

contraluz *m* back lighting; **a ~** against the light.

contramaestre *m* 1. (NÁUT) boatswain; (MIL) warrant officer. 2. (*capataz*) foreman.

contrapartida *f* compensation; **como ~** to make up for it.

contrapelo ▶ **a contrapelo** *loc adv* 1. (*acariciar*) the wrong way. 2. (*vivir, actuar*) against the grain.

contrapesar *vt* (*físicamente*) to counterbalance.

contrapeso *m* 1. (*en ascensores, poleas*) counterweight. 2. *fig* (*fuerza que iguala*) counterbalance.

contraponer *vt* (*oponer*): ~ **(a)** to set up (against). ▶ **contraponerse** *vpr* to oppose.

contraportada *f* (*de periódico, revista*) back page; (*de libro, disco*) back cover.

contraproducente *adj* counterproductive.

contrariar *vt* 1. (*contradecir*) to go against. 2. (*disgustar*) to upset.

contrariedad *f* 1. (*dificultad*) setback. 2. (*disgusto*) annoyance.

contrario, -ria *adj* 1. (*opuesto - dirección, sentido*) opposite; (*- parte*) opposing; (*- opinión*) contrary; **ser ~ a algo** to be opposed to sthg. 2. (*perjudicial*): ~ **a** contrary to. ▶ **contrario** *m* 1. (*rival*) opponent. 2. (*opuesto*) opposite; **al ~, por el ~** on the contrary; **de lo ~** otherwise; **todo lo ~** quite the contrary.

contrarreloj *adj inv*: **etapa ~** time trial.

contrarrestar *vt* (*neutralizar*) to counteract.

contrasentido *m* nonsense (U); **es un ~ hacer eso** it doesn't make sense to do that.

contraseña *f* password.

contrastar ♦ vi to contrast. ♦ vt
1. (*probar - hechos*) to check, to verify.
2. (*resistir*) to resist.

contraste *m* contrast.

contratar vt 1. (*obreros, personal, detective*) to hire; (*deportista*) to sign. 2. (*servicio, obra, mercancía*): ~ **algo a alguien** to contract for sthg with sb.

contratiempo *m* (*accidente*) mishap; (*dificultad*) setback.

contratista *m y f* contractor.

contrato *m* contract.

contraventana *f* shutter.

contribución *f* 1. (*gen*) contribution. 2. (*impuesto*) tax.

contribuir vi 1. (*gen*): ~ **(a)** to contribute (to); ~ **con algo para** to contribute sthg towards. 2. (*pagar impuestos*) to pay taxes.

contribuyente *m y f* taxpayer.

contrincante *m y f* rival, opponent.

control *m* 1. (*gen*) control; **bajo** ~ under control; **perder el** ~ to lose one's temper. 2. (*verificación*) examination, inspection; **(bajo)** ~ **médico** (under) medical supervision; ~ **antidoping** dope test. 3. (*puesto policial*) checkpoint.

controlador, -ra *m y f* (*gen* & INFORM) controller; ~ **aéreo** air traffic controller. ▶ **controlador** *m*: ~ **de disco** disk controller.

controlar vt 1. (*gen*) to control; (*cuentas*) to audit. 2. (*comprobar*) to check. 3. (*vigilar*) to keep an eye on. ▶ **controlarse** *vpr* to control o.s.

controversia *f* controversy.

contundente *adj* 1. (*arma, objeto*) blunt; (*golpe*) thudding. 2. *fig* (*razonamiento, argumento*) forceful.

contusión *f* bruise.

convalecencia *f* convalescence.

convaleciente *adj* convalescent.

convalidar vt (*estudios*) to recognize; (*asignaturas*) to validate.

convencer vt to convince; ~ **a alguien de algo** to convince sb of sthg. ▶ **convencerse** *vpr*: ~**se de** to become convinced of.

convencimiento *m* (*certeza*) conviction; (*acción*) convincing.

convención *f* convention.

convencional *adj* conventional.

conveniencia *f* 1. (*utilidad*) usefulness; (*oportunidad*) suitability. 2. (*interés*) convenience; **sólo mira su** ~ he only looks after his own interests.

conveniente *adj* (*útil*) useful; (*oportuno*) suitable, appropriate; (*lugar, hora*) convenient; (*aconsejable*) advisable; **sería** ~ **asistir** it would be a good idea to go.

convenio *m* agreement.

convenir vi 1. (*venir bien*) to be suitable; **conviene analizar la situación** it would be a good idea to analyse the situation; **no te conviene hacerlo** you shouldn't do it. 2. (*acordar*): ~ **en** to agree on.

convento *m* (*de monjas*) convent; (*de monjes*) monastery.

converger vi to converge.

conversación *f* conversation. ▶ **conversaciones** *fpl* (*negociaciones*) talks.

conversada *f* Amer chat.

conversar vi to talk, to converse.

conversión *f* conversion.

converso, -sa *adj* converted.

convertir vt 1. (RELIG) to convert. 2. (*transformar*): ~ **algo/a alguien en** to convert sthg/sb into, to turn sthg/sb into. ▶ **convertirse** *vpr* 1. (RELIG): ~**se (a)** to convert (to). 2. (*transformarse*): ~**se en** to become, to turn into.

convexo, -xa *adj* convex.

convicción *f* conviction; **tener la** ~ **de que** to be convinced that.

convicto, -ta *adj* convicted.

convidar vt (*invitar*) to invite.

convincente *adj* convincing.

convite *m* 1. (*invitación*) invitation. 2. (*fiesta*) banquet.

convivencia *f* living together.

convivir vi to live together; ~ **con** to live with.

convocar vt (*reunión*) to convene; (*huelga, elecciones*) to call.

convocatoria *f* 1. (*anuncio, escrito*) notice. 2. (*de examen*) diet.

convulsión *f* 1. (*de músculos*) convulsion. 2. (*política, social*) upheaval (U).

conyugal *adj* conjugal; **vida** ~ married life.

cónyuge *m y f* spouse; **los** ~**s** husband and wife.

coña, coñac (*pl* coñacs), **cognac** (*pl* cognacs) *m* brandy, cognac.

coñazo *m fam* pain, drag.

coño *vulg* ♦ *m* (*genital*) cunt. ♦ *interj* 1. (*enfado*): ¡~! for fuck's sake! 2. (*asombro*): ¡~! fucking hell!

cooperación *f* cooperation.

cooperar vi: ~ **(con alguien en algo)** to cooperate (with sb in sthg).

cooperativo, -va *adj* cooperative. ▶ **cooperativa** *f* cooperative.

coordinador, -ra ◆ adj coordinating. ◆ m y f coordinator.

coordinar vt 1. (movimientos, gestos) to coordinate. 2. (esfuerzos, medios) to combine, to pool.

copa f 1. (vaso) glass; **ir de ~s** to go out drinking; **¿quieres (tomar) una ~?** would you like (to have) a drink? 2. (de árbol) top. 3. (en deporte) cup. ▶ **copas** fpl (naipes) suit with pictures of goblets in Spanish playing cards.

COPE (abrev de **Cadena de Ondas Populares Españolas**) f private Spanish radio station.

Copenhague Copenhagen.

copete m (de ave) crest.

copia f (reproducción) copy; **~ de seguridad** (INFORM) backup.

copiar ◆ vt (gen) to copy; (al dictado) to take down. ◆ vi (en examen) to cheat, to copy.

copiloto m y f copilot.

copión, -ona m y f (imitador) copycat; (en examen) cheat.

copioso, -sa adj copious.

copla f 1. (canción) folksong, popular song. 2. (estrofa) verse, stanza.

copo m (de nieve, cereales) flake; **~s de avena** rolled oats.

copropietario, -ria m y f co-owner.

copular vi to copulate.

copulativo, -va adj copulative.

coquetear vi to flirt.

coqueto, -ta adj (persona - que flirtea) flirtatious, coquettish; (- que se arregla mucho) concerned with one's appearance.

coraje m 1. (valor) courage. 2. (rabia) anger; **me da mucho ~** it makes me furious.

coral ◆ adj choral. ◆ m coral. ◆ f 1. (coro) choir. 2. (composición) chorale.

Corán m: **el ~ the** Koran.

coraza f 1. (de soldado) cuirasse, armour. 2. (de tortuga) shell.

corazón m 1. (gen) heart; **de buen ~** kindhearted. 2. (de frutas) core. 3. → **dedo**.

corazonada f 1. (presentimiento) hunch. 2. (impulso) sudden impulse.

corbata f tie.

Córcega Corsica.

corchea f quaver.

corchete m 1. (broche) hook and eye. 2. (signo ortográfico) square bracket.

corcho m cork.

corcholata f Amer metal bottle top.

cordel m cord.

cordero, -ra m y f lit & fig lamb.

cordial adj cordial.

cordialidad f cordiality.

cordillera f mountain range; **la ~ Cantábrica** the Cantabrian Mountains.

cordón m 1. (gen & ANAT) cord; (de zapato) lace; **~ umbilical** umbilical cord. 2. (cable eléctrico) flex. 3. fig (para protección, vigilancia) cordon; **~ sanitario** cordon sanitaire. 4. Amer (de la acera) kerb.

cordura f (juicio) sanity; (sensatez) sense.

Corea: **~ del Norte/Sur** North/South Korea.

corear vt to chorus.

coreógrafo, -fa m y f choreographer.

corista ◆ m y f (en coro) chorus singer. ◆ f (en teatro de revista) chorus girl.

cornada f goring.

cornamenta f (de toro) horns (pl); (de ciervo) antlers (pl).

córner m corner (kick).

corneta f (instrumento) bugle.

cornisa f (ARQUIT) cornice.

coro m 1. (gen) choir; **contestar a ~** to answer all at once. 2. (de obra musical) chorus.

corona f 1. (gen) crown. 2. (de flores) garland; **~ fúnebre/de laurel** funeral/laurel wreath. 3. (de santos) halo.

coronación f (de monarca) coronation.

coronar vt 1. (persona) to crown. 2. fig (terminar) to complete; (culminar) to crown, to cap.

coronel m colonel.

coronilla f crown (of the head); **estar hasta la ~ (de)** to be sick and tired (of).

corpiño m bodice.

corporación f corporation.

corporal adj corporal.

corporativo, -va adj corporate.

corpulento, -ta adj corpulent.

corral m (gen) yard; (para cerdos, ovejas) pen.

correa f 1. (de bolso, reloj) strap; (de pantalón) belt; (de perro) lead, leash. 2. (TECN) belt; **~ del ventilador** fan belt.

corrección f 1. (de errores) correction; **~ de pruebas** proofreading. 2. (de exámenes) marking. 3. (de texto) revision. 4. (de comportamiento) correctness.

correctivo, -va adj corrective. ▶ **correctivo** m punishment.

correcto, -ta adj 1. (resultado, texto, respuesta) correct. 2. (persona) polite; (conducta) proper.

corredor, -ra ◆ adj running. ◆ m y f 1. (deportista) runner. 2. (intermediario): **~**

de bolsa stockbroker; **~ de comercio**
(COM) registered broker; **~ de fincas**
land agent. ▶ **corredor** m (*pasillo*) corridor.

corregir vt (*gen*) to correct; (*exámenes*)
to mark. ▶ **corregirse** vpr to change
for the better.

correlación f correlation.

correo m post, mail; **echar al ~** to post;
a vuelta de ~ by return (of post); **~ aéreo**
air mail; **~ certificado** registered post o
mail; **~ electrónico** electronic mail; **~
urgente** special delivery; **~ de voz** voice
mail. ▶ **Correos** m (*organismo*) the post
office.

correr ◆ vi 1. (*andar de prisa*) to run; **a
todo ~** at full speed o pelt; **(ella) corre
que se las pela** she runs like the wind.
2. (*conducir de prisa*) to drive fast.
3. (*pasar por - río*) to flow; (*- camino, agua
del grifo*) to run. 4. (*el tiempo, las horas*) to
pass, to go by. 5. (*propagarse - noticia etc*)
to spread. ◆ vt 1. (*recorrer - una distancia*)
to cover; **corrió los 100 metros** he ran
the 100 metres. 2. (*deslizar - mesa, silla*)
to move o pull up. 3. (*cortinas*) to draw;
~ el pestillo to bolt the door. 4. (*experimentar - aventuras, vicisitudes*) to have;
(*- riesgo*) to run. ▶ **correrse** vpr 1. (*desplazarse - persona*) to move over; (*- cosa*)
to slide. 2. (*pintura, colores*) to run.

correspondencia f 1. (*gen*) correspondence; **mantener ~ con alguien** to
correspond with sb.

corresponder vi 1. (*compensar*): **~ (con
algo) a alguien/algo** to repay sb/sthg
(with sthg). 2. (*pertenecer*) to belong.
3. (*coincidir*): **~ (a/con)** to correspond
(to/with). 4. (*tocar*): **~le a alguien hacer
algo** to be sb's responsibility to do
sthg. 5. (*a un sentimiento*) to reciprocate.
▶ **corresponderse** vpr 1. (*escribirse*) to
correspond. 2. (*amarse*) to love each
other.

correspondiente adj 1. (*gen*): **~ (a)**
corresponding (to). 2. (*respectivo*) respective.

corresponsal m y f (PRENS) correspondent.

corretear vi (*correr*) to run about.

corrido, -da adj (*avergonzado*) embarrassed. ▶ **corrida** f 1. (TAUROM) bull
fight. 2. (*acción de correr*) run. ▶ **de corrido** loc prep by heart; **recitar algo de ~**
to recite sthg parrot-fashion.

corriente ◆ adj 1. (*normal*) ordinary,
normal. 2. (*agua*) running. 3. (*mes, año,
cuenta*) current. ◆ f 1. (*de río, electricidad*)

current; **~ alterna/continua** alternating/
direct current. 2. (*de aire*) draught. 3. *fig*
(*tendencia*) trend, current; (*de opinión*)
tide. 4. loc: **ir contra ~** to go against the
tide. ◆ m: **estar al ~ de** to be up to date
with.

corro m (*círculo*) circle, ring; **en ~** in a
circle; **hacer ~** to form a circle.

corroborar vt to corroborate.

corroer vt (*gen*) to corrode; (GEOL) to
erode.

corromper vt 1. (*pudrir - madera*) to
rot; (*- alimentos*) to turn bad, to spoil.
2. (*pervertir*) to corrupt.

corrosivo, -va adj lit & fig corrosive.

corrupción f 1. (*gen*) corruption. 2. (*de
una substancia*) decay.

corrusco m hard crust.

corsario, -ria adj pirate (*antes de sust*).
▶ **corsario** m corsair, pirate.

corsé m corset.

cortacésped (*pl* **cortacéspedes**) m
lawnmower.

cortado, -da adj 1. (*labios, manos*)
chapped. 2. (*leche*) sour, off; (*salsa*) cur-
dled. 3. fam fig (*tímido*) inhibited;
quedarse ~ to be left speechless.
▶ **cortado** m (*café*) small coffee with just a
little milk.

cortafuego m firebreak.

cortante adj 1. (*afilado*) sharp. 2. fig
(*tajante - frase, estilo*) cutting; (*- viento*) biting; (*- frío*) bitter.

cortapisa f limitation, restriction.

cortar ◆ vt 1. (*seccionar - pelo, uñas*) to
cut; (*- papel*) to cut up; (*- ramas*) to cut
off; (*- árbol*) to cut down. 2. (*amputar*) to
amputate, to cut off. 3. (*tela, figura de
papel*) to cut out. 4. (*interrumpir - retirada,
luz, teléfono*) to cut off; (*- carretera*) to
block (off); (*- hemorragia*) to stop, to
staunch; (*- discurso, conversación*) to interrupt. 5. (*labios, piel*) to chap. ◆ vi 1. (*producir un corte*) to cut. 2. (*cesar una relación*)
to break o split up. ▶ **cortarse** vpr
1. (*herirse*) to cut o.s.; **~se el pelo** to have
a haircut. 2. (*alimento*) to curdle. 3. (*turbarse*) to become tongue-tied.

cortaúñas m inv nail clippers (*pl*).

corte ◆ m 1. (*raja*) cut; (*en pantalones,
camisa etc*) tear; **~ y confección** (*para
mujeres*) dressmaking; (*para hombres*) tailoring. 2. (*interrupción*): **~ de luz** power
cut. 3. (*sección*) section. 4. (*concepción,
estilo*) style. 5. fam (*vergüenza*) embarrassment; **dar ~ a alguien** to embarrass
sb. ◆ f (*palacio*) court. ▶ **Cortes** fpl
(POLÍT) the Spanish parliament.

cortejar vt to court.

cortejo m retinue; ~ **fúnebre** funeral cortège o procession.

cortés adj polite, courteous.

cortesía f courtesy; **de** ~ courtesy.

corteza f 1. (del árbol) bark. 2. (de pan) crust; (de queso, tocino, limón) rind; (de naranja etc) peel. 3. (terrestre) crust.

cortijo m (casa de campo) farmhouse; (finca) large farm.

cortina f (de tela) curtain; fig: ~ **de agua** sheet of water; ~ **de humo** smoke screen.

cortisona f cortisone.

corto, -ta adj 1. (gen) short. 2. (escaso - raciones) meagre; (- disparo) short of the target; ~ **de vista** short-sighted. 3. fig (bobo) dim, simple. 4. loc: **quedarse** ~ (al calcular) to underestimate; **decir que es bueno es quedarse** ~ it's an understatement to call it good.

cortocircuito m short circuit.

cortometraje m short (film).

cosa f 1. (gen) thing; **¿queréis alguna** ~? is there anything you want?; **no es gran** ~ it's not important, it's no big deal; **poca** ~ nothing much. 2. (asunto) matter. 3. (ocurrencia): **¡qué** ~**s tienes!** you do say some funny things! 4. loc: **hacer algo como quien no quiere la** ~ (disimuladamente) to do sthg as if one wasn't intending to; (sin querer) to do sthg almost without realizing it; **como si tal** ~ as if nothing had happened; **eso es** ~ **mía** that's my affair o business. ▶ **cosa de** loc adv about.

coscorrón m bump on the head.

cosecha f 1. (gen) harvest; **ser de la (propia)** ~ **de alguien** to be made up o invented by sb. 2. (del vino) vintage.

cosechar ◆ vt 1. (cultivar) to grow. 2. (recolectar) to harvest. ◆ vi to (bring in the) harvest.

cosechero, -ra m y f (de cereales) harvester; (de frutos) picker.

coser ◆ vt (con hilo) to sew; ~ **un botón** to sew on a button. ◆ vi to sew; **ser cosa de** ~ **y cantar** to be child's play o a piece of cake.

cosido m stitching.

cosmético, -ca adj cosmetic (antes de sust). ▶ **cosmético** m cosmetic. ▶ **cosmética** f cosmetics (U).

cosmopolita adj, m y f cosmopolitan.

cosmos m cosmos.

cosquillas fpl: **hacer** ~ to tickle; **tener** ~ to be ticklish.

costa f (GEOGR) coast. ▶ **a costa de** loc prep at the expense of; **lo hizo a** ~ **de grandes esfuerzos** he did it by dint of much effort. ▶ **a toda costa** loc prep at all costs.

costado m side.

costal m sack.

costanera f Amer seaside promenade.

costar ◆ vt 1. (dinero) to cost; **¿cuánto cuesta?** how much is it? 2. (tiempo) to take. ◆ vi (ser difícil): ~**le a alguien hacer algo** to be difficult for sb to do sthg.

Costa Rica Costa Rica.

costarricense, costarriqueño, -ña adj; m y f Costa Rican.

coste m (de producción) cost; (de un objeto) price; ~ **de la vida** cost of living.

costear vt (pagar) to pay for.

costeño, -ña, costero, -ra adj coastal.

costilla f 1. (de persona, barco) rib. 2. (de animal) cutlet. ▶ **costillas** fpl (CULIN - de cerdo) spare ribs.

costo m (de una mercancía) price; (de un producto, de la vida) cost.

costoso, -sa adj (operación, maquinaria) expensive.

costra f (de herida) scab.

costumbre f habit, custom; **coger/perder la** ~ **de hacer algo** to get into/out of the habit of doing sthg; **como de** ~ as usual.

costura f 1. (labor) sewing, needlework. 2. (puntadas) seam. 3. (oficio) dressmaking; **alta** ~ haute couture.

costurera f dressmaker, seamstress.

costurero m (caja) sewing box.

cota f 1. (altura) altitude, height above sea level. 2. fig (nivel) level, height.

cotarro m riotous gathering; **dirigir el** ~ to rule the roost.

cotejar vt to compare.

cotejo m comparison.

cotidiano, -na adj daily.

cotilla m y f fam gossip, busybody.

cotillear vi fam to gossip.

cotilleo m fam gossip, tittle-tattle.

cotillón m New Year's Eve party.

cotización f 1. (valor) price. 2. (en Bolsa) quotation, price.

cotizar vt 1. (valorar) to quote, to price. 2. (pagar) to pay. ▶ **cotizarse** vpr 1. (estimarse - persona) to be valued o prized. 2. ~**se a** (producto) to sell for, to fetch; (bonos, valores) to be quoted at.

coto m preserve; ~ **de caza** game preserve; **poner** ~ **a** to put a stop to.

cotorra f (ave) parrot.

COU (*abrev de* **curso de orientación universitaria**) *m one-year course which prepares pupils aged 17-18 for Spanish university entrance examinations.*

coxis = **cóccix**.

coyote *m* coyote.

coyuntura *f* 1. (*situación*) moment; **la ~ económica** the economic situation. 2. (ANAT) joint.

coz *f* kick.

crac (*pl* **cracs**), **crack** (*pl* **cracks**) *m* (FIN) crash.

crack (*pl* **cracks**) *m* 1. (FIN) → **crac**. 2. (*droga*) crack.

cráneo *m* cranium, skull.

crápula *m y f* libertine.

cráter *m* crater.

creación *f* creation.

creador, -ra ◆ *adj* creative. ◆ *m y f* creator.

crear *vt* 1. (*gen*) to create. 2. (*inventar*) to invent 2. (*fundar - una academia*) to found.

creatividad *f* creativity.

creativo, -va *adj* creative.

crecer *vi* 1. (*persona, planta*) to grow. 2. (*días, noches*) to grow longer. 3. (*río, marea*) to rise. 4. (*aumentar - animosidad etc*) to grow, to increase; (*- rumores*) to spread. ► **crecerse** *vpr* to become more self-confident.

creces ► **con creces** *adv* with interest.

crecido, -da *adj* (*cantidad*) large; (*hijo*) grown-up. ► **crecida** *f* spate, flood.

creciente *adj* (*gen*) growing; (*luna*) crescent.

crecimiento *m* (*gen*) growth; (*de precios*) rise.

credibilidad *f* credibility.

crédito *m* 1. (*préstamo*) loan; **a ~** on credit; **~ al consumo** (ECON) consumer credit. 2. (*plazo de préstamo*) credit. 3. (*confianza*) trust, belief; **digno de ~** trustworthy; **dar ~ a algo** to believe sthg. 4. (*en universidad*) credit.

credo *m* (*religioso*) creed.

crédulo, -la *adj* credulous.

creencia *f* belief.

creer *vt* 1. (*gen*) to believe. 2. (*suponer*) to think. ► **creer en** *vi* to believe in. ► **creerse** *vpr* (*considerarse*) to believe o.s. to be.

creíble *adj* credible, believable.

creído, -da *m y f* (*presumido*) conceited.

crema *f* 1. (*gen*) cream. 2. (*betún*) shoe polish. 3. (*licor*) crème. 4. (*dulce, postre*) custard.

cremallera *f* (*para cerrar*) zip (fastener).

crematorio, -ria *adj*: **horno ~** cremator. ► **crematorio** *m* crematorium.

cremoso, -sa *adj* creamy.

crepe [krep] *f* crepe.

crepitar *vi* to crackle.

crepúsculo *m* (*al amanecer*) first light; (*al anochecer*) twilight, dusk.

crespo, -pa *adj* tightly curled, frizzy.

cresta *f* 1. (*gen*) crest. 2. (*del gallo*) comb.

Creta Crete.

cretino, -na *m y f* cretin.

creyente *m y f* believer.

cría → **crío**.

criadero *m* (*de animales*) farm (*breeding place*); (*de árboles, plantas*) nursery.

criadillas *fpl* bull's testicles.

criado, -da *m y f* servant (*f* maid).

criador, -ra *m y f* (*de animales*) breeder; (*de vinos*) grower.

crianza *f* 1. (*de animales*) breeding. 2. (*del vino*) vintage. 3. (*educación*) breeding.

criar *vt* 1. (*amamantar - suj: mujer*) to breastfeed; (*- suj: animal*) to suckle. 2. (*animales*) to breed, to rear; (*flores, árboles*) to grow. 3. (*vino*) to mature, to make. 4. (*educar*) to bring up. ► **criarse** *vpr* (*crecer*) to grow up.

criatura *f* 1. (*niño*) child; (*bebé*) baby. 2. (*ser vivo*) creature.

criba *f* 1. (*tamiz*) sieve. 2. (*selección*) screening.

cricket = **criquet**.

crimen *m* crime.

criminal *adj, m y f* criminal.

crin *f* mane.

crío, cría *m y f* (*niño*) kid. ► **cría** *f* 1. (*hijo del animal*) young. 2. (*crianza - de animales*) breeding; (*- de plantas*) growing.

criollo, -lla *adj* 1. (*persona*) native to Latin America. 2. (*comida, lengua*) creole.

cripta *f* crypt.

criquet, cricket [ˈkriket] *m* cricket.

crisantemo *m* chrysanthemum.

crisis *f inv* (*gen*) crisis; **~ económica** recession; **~ nerviosa** nervous breakdown.

crisma *f fam* bonce, nut.

crismas, christmas *m inv* Christmas card.

crispar *vt* (*los nervios*) to set on edge; (*los músculos*) to tense; (*las manos*) to clench.

cristal m 1. (material) glass (U); (vidrio fino) crystal. 2. (en la ventana) (window) pane. 3. (MIN) crystal.

cristalera f (puerta) French window; (techo) glass roof; (armario) glass-fronted cabinet.

cristalino, -na adj crystalline. ▶ **cristalino** m crystalline lens.

cristalizar vt 1. (una sustancia) to crystallize. 2. fig (un asunto) to bring to a head. ▶ **cristalizarse** vpr to crystallize. ▶ **cristalizarse en** vpr fig to develop into.

cristiandad f Christianity.

cristianismo m Christianity.

cristiano, -na adj, m y f Christian.

cristo m crucifix. ▶ **Cristo** m Christ.

criterio m 1. (norma) criterion. 2. (juicio) taste. 3. (opinión) opinion.

crítica → **crítico**.

criticar vt 1. (enjuiciar - literatura, arte) to review. 2. (censurar) to criticize.

crítico, -ca ◆ adj critical. ◆ m y f (persona) critic. ▶ **crítica** f 1. (juicio - sobre arte, literatura) review. 2. (conjunto de críticos): **la** ~ the critics (pl). 3. (ataque) criticism.

criticón, -ona ◆ adj nit-picking. ◆ m y f nitpicker.

Croacia Croatia.

croar vi to croak.

croata ◆ adj Croatian. ◆ m y f Croat.

croissant [krwa'san] (pl **croissants**) m croissant.

crol m (DEP) crawl.

cromo m 1. (metal) chrome. 2. (estampa) transfer.

cromosoma m chromosome.

crónico, -ca adj chronic. ▶ **crónica** f 1. (de la historia) chronicle. 2. (de un periódico) column; (de la televisión) feature, programme.

cronista m y f (historiador) chronicler; (periodista) columnist.

cronología f chronology.

cronometrar vt to time.

cronómetro m (DEP) stopwatch; (TECN) chronometer.

croqueta f croquette.

croquis m inv sketch.

cross m inv (carrera) cross-country race; (deporte) cross-country (running).

cruce m 1. (de líneas) crossing, intersection; (de carreteras) crossroads. 2. (de animales) cross.

crucero m 1. (viaje) cruise. 2. (barco) cruiser. 3. (de iglesias) transept.

crucial adj crucial.

crucificar vt (en una cruz) to crucify.

crucifijo m crucifix.

crucifixión f crucifixion.

crucigrama m crossword (puzzle).

crudeza f 1. (gen) harshness. 2. (de descripción, imágenes) brutality.

crudo, -da adj 1. (natural) raw; (petróleo) crude. 2. (sin cocer completamente) undercooked. 3. (realidad, clima, tiempo) harsh; (novela) harshly realistic, hard-hitting. 4. (cruel) cruel. ▶ **crudo** m crude (oil).

cruel adj (gen) cruel.

crueldad f 1. (gen) cruelty; (del clima) harshness. 2. (acción cruel) act of cruelty.

cruento, -ta adj bloody.

crujido m (de madera) creak, creaking (U); (de hojas secas) crackle, crackling (U).

crujiente adj (madera) creaky; (hojas secas) rustling; (patatas fritas) crunchy.

crujir vi (madera) to creak; (patatas fritas, nieve) to crunch; (hojas secas) to crackle; (dientes) to grind.

cruz f 1. (gen) cross; ~ **gamada** swastika. 2. (de una moneda) tails (U). 3. fig (aflicción) burden. ▶ **Cruz Roja** f Red Cross.

cruza f Amer cross, crossbreed.

cruzado, -da adj 1. (cheque, piernas, brazos) crossed. 2. (un animal) crossbred. 3. (abrigo, chaqueta) double-breasted. ▶ **cruzada** f lit & fig crusade.

cruzar vt 1. (gen) to cross. 2. (unas palabras) to exchange. ▶ **cruzarse** vpr 1. (gen) to cross; ~**se de brazos** to fold one's arms. 2. (personas): ~**se con alguien** (parándose) to bump into sb; (pasando de largo) to pass sb.

cta. (abrev de **cuenta**) a/c.

cte. (abrev de **corriente**) inst.

CTNE (abrev de **Compañía Telefónica Nacional de España**) f Spanish state telephone company.

cuaderno m (gen) notebook; (en el colegio) exercise book. ▶ **cuaderno de bitácora** m logbook.

cuadra f 1. (de caballos) stable. 2. Amer (manzana) block.

cuadrado, -da adj (gen & MAT) square. ▶ **cuadrado** m square.

cuadragésimo, -ma núm fortieth.

cuadrar ◆ vi 1. (información, hechos): ~ (**con**) to square o agree (with). 2. (números, cuentas) to tally, to add up. ◆ vt (gen) to square. ▶ **cuadrarse** vpr (MIL) to stand to attention.

cuadrícula f grid.

cuadrilátero m 1. (GEOM) quadrilateral. 2. (DEP) ring.

cuadrilla f (de amigos, trabajadores) group; (de maleantes) gang.

cuadro m 1. (pintura) painting, picture. 2. (escena) scene, spectacle. 3. (descripción) portrait. 4. (cuadrado) square; (de flores) bed; a o de ~s check(ed) (antes de sust). 5. (equipo) team. 6. (gráfico) chart, diagram. 7. (de la bicicleta) frame. 8. (TEATR) scene.

cuádruple m quadruple.

cuajar ◆ vt 1. (solidificar - leche) to curdle; (- huevo) to set; (- sangre) to clot, to coagulate. 2. ~ **de** (llenar) to fill with; (cubrir) to cover with. ◆ vi 1. (lograrse - acuerdo) to be settled; (- negocio) to take off, to get going. 2. (ser aceptado - persona) to fit in; (- moda) to catch on. 3. (nieve) to settle. ▶ **cuajarse** vpr 1. (leche) to curdle; (sangre) to clot, to coagulate. 2. (llenarse) ~**se de** to fill (up) with.

cuajo m rennet. ▶ **de cuajo** loc adv: **arrancar de ~** (árbol) to uproot; (brazo etc) to tear right off.

cual pron relat: **el/la ~** etc (de persona) (sujeto) who; (complemento) whom; (de cosa) which; **lo ~** which; **conoció a una española, la ~ vivía en Buenos Aires** he met a Spanish girl who lived in Buenos Aires; **está muy enfadada, lo ~ es comprensible** she's very angry, which is understandable; **todo lo ~** all of which; **sea ~ sea** o **fuere su decisión** whatever his decision (may be).

cuál pron (interrogativo) what; (en concreto, especificando) which one; **¿~ es tu nombre?** what is your name?; **¿~ es la diferencia?** what's the difference?; **no sé ~es son mejores** I don't know which are best; **¿~ prefieres?** which one do you prefer?

cualesquiera pl → cualquiera.

cualidad f quality.

cualificado, -da adj skilled.

cualitativo, -va adj qualitative.

cualquiera (pl **cualesquiera**) ◆ adj (antes de sust: **cualquier**) any; **cualquier día vendré a visitarte** I'll drop by one of these days; **en cualquier momento** at any time; **en cualquier lugar** anywhere. ◆ pron anyone; ~ **te lo dirá** anyone will tell you; ~ **que** (persona) anyone who; (cosa) whatever; ~ **que sea la razón** whatever the reason (may be). ◆ m y f (don nadie) nobody.

cuan adv (todo lo que): **se desplomó ~ largo era** he fell flat on the ground.

cuán adv how.

cuando ◆ adv when; **de ~ en ~, de vez en ~** from time to time, now and again. ◆ conj 1. (de tiempo) when; ~ **llegue el verano iremos de viaje** when summer comes we'll go travelling. 2. (si) if; ~ **tú lo dices será verdad** it must be true if you say so. 3. (después de 'aun') (aunque): **no mentiría aun ~ le fuera en ello la vida** she wouldn't lie even if her life depended on it. ▶ **cuando más** loc adv at the most. ▶ **cuando menos** loc adv at least. ▶ **cuando quiera que** loc conj whenever.

cuándo adv when; **¿~ vas a venir?** when are you coming?; **quisiera saber ~ sale el tren** I'd like to know when o at what time the train leaves.

cuantía f (suma) quantity; (alcance) extent.

cuantificar vt to quantify.

cuantioso, -sa adj large, substantial.

cuantitativo, -va adj quantitative.

cuanto, -ta ◆ adj 1. (todo): **despilfarra ~ dinero gana** he squanders all the money he earns; **soporté todas cuantas críticas me hizo** I put up with every single criticism he made of me. 2. (antes de adv) (compara cantidades): **cuantas más mentiras digas, menos te creerán** the more you lie, the less people will believe you. ◆ pron relat (gen pl) (de personas) everyone who; (de cosas) everything (that); ~**s fueron alabaron el espectáculo** everyone who went said the show was excellent; **dio las gracias a todos ~s le ayudaron** he thanked everyone who helped him. ▶ **cuanto** ◆ pron relat (neutro) 1. (todo lo que) everything, as much as; **come ~ quieras** eat as much as you like; **comprendo ~ dice** I understand everything he says; **todo ~** everything. 2. (compara cantidades): ~ **más tiene, más se quiere** the more you have, the more you want. ◆ adv (compara cantidades): ~ **más muevo la pierna, más me duele** the more I move my leg, the more it hurts. ▶ **cuanto antes** loc adv as soon as possible. ▶ **en cuanto** ◆ loc conj (tan pronto como) as soon as; **en ~ acabe** as soon as I've finished. ◆ loc prep (en calidad de) as; **en ~ cabeza de familia** as head of the family. ▶ **en cuanto a** loc prep as regards, as for.

cuánto, -ta ◆ adj 1. (interrogativo) how much, (pl) how many; **¿cuántas manzanas tienes?** how many apples do you have?; **¿~ pan quieres?** how much bread do you want?; **no sé ~s hombres había** I don't know how many men were there. **2.** (*exclamativo*) what a lot of; **¡cuánta gente (había)!** what a lot of people (were there)! ◆ *pron* (*gen pl*) **1.** (*interrogativo*) how much, (*pl*) how many; **¿~s han venido?** how many came?; **dime cuántas quieres** tell me how many you want. **2.** (*exclamativo*): **¡~s quisieran conocerte!** there are so many people who would like to meet you! ▶ **cuánto** *pron* (*neutro*) **1.** (*interrogativo*) how much; **¿~ quieres?** how much do you want?; **me gustaría saber ~ te costarán** I'd like to know how much they'll cost you; **¿a ~ estámos?** *Amer* (*fecha*) what's the date today? **2.** (*exclamativo*) **¡~ han cambiado las cosas!** how things have changed!

cuarenta *núm* forty; **los (años) ~** the forties.

cuarentena *f* (*por epidemia*) quarantine.

cuaresma *f* Lent.

cuartear *vt* to cut o chop up.

cuartel *m* (MIL) barracks (*pl*); **~ general** headquarters (*pl*).

cuartelazo *m Amer* military uprising.

cuarteto *m* quartet.

cuarto, -ta *núm* fourth; **la cuarta parte** a quarter. ▶ **cuarto** *m* **1.** (*parte*) quarter; **un ~ de hora** a quarter of an hour; **son las dos y/menos ~** it's a quarter past/to two. **2.** (*habitación*) room; **~ de baño** bathroom; **~ de estar** living room. ▶ **cuarta** *f* (*palmo*) span.

cuarzo *m* quartz.

cuate *m y f inv Amer* (*amigo*) friend.

cuatro ◆ *núm* four; *ver también* **seis.** ◆ *adj fig* (*poco*) a few; **hace ~ días** a few days ago.

cuatrocientos, -tas *núm* four hundred; *ver también* **seis.**

cuba *f* barrel, cask; **estar como una ~** to be legless o blind drunk.

Cuba Cuba.

cubalibre *m* rum and coke.

cubano, -na *adj, m y f* Cuban.

cubertería *f* set of cutlery, cutlery (U).

cúbico, -ca *adj* cubic.

cubierto, -ta ◆ *pp* → **cubrir.** ◆ *adj* **1.** (*gen*): **~ (de)** covered (with); **estar a ~** (*protegido*) to be under cover; (*con saldo acreedor*) to be in the black; **ponerse a ~** to take cover. **2.** (*cielo*) overcast. ▶ **cubierto** *m* **1.** (*pieza de cubertería*) piece of cutlery. **2.** (*para cada persona*) place setting. ▶ **cubierta** *f* **1.** (*gen*)

cover. **2.** (*de neumático*) tyre. **3.** (*de barco*) deck.

cubilete *m* (*en juegos*) cup; (*molde*) mould.

cubito *m* (*de hielo*) ice cube.

cubo *m* **1.** (*recipiente*) bucket; **~ de la basura** rubbish bin. **2.** (GEOM & MAT) cube; **elevar al ~** to cube.

cubrecama *m* bedspread.

cubrir *vt* **1.** (*gen*) to cover. **2.** (*proteger*) to protect. **3.** (*disimular*) to cover up, to hide. **4.** (*puesto, vacante*) to fill. ▶ **cubrir de** *vt*: **~ de algo a alguien** to heap sthg on sb. ▶ **cubrirse** *vpr* **1.** (*taparse*): **~se (de)** to become covered (with). **2.** (*protegerse*): **~se (de)** to shelter (from). **3.** (*con sombrero*) to put one's hat on. **4.** (*con ropa*): **~se (con)** to cover o.s. (with). **5.** (*cielo*) to cloud over.

cucaracha *f* cockroach.

cuchara *f* (*para comer*) spoon.

cucharada *f* spoonful.

cucharadita *f* teaspoonful.

cucharilla *f* teaspoon.

cucharón *m* ladle.

cuchichear *vi* to whisper.

cuchilla *f* blade; **~ de afeitar** razor blade.

cuchillo *m* knife.

cuchitril *m* hovel.

cuclillas ▶ **en cuclillas** *loc adv* squatting; **ponerse en ~** to squat (down).

cuclillo *m* cuckoo.

cuco, -ca *adj fam* **1.** (*bonito*) pretty. **2.** (*astuto*) shrewd, canny. ▶ **cuco** *m* cuckoo.

cucurucho *m* **1.** (*de papel*) paper cone. **2.** (*para helado*) cornet, cone.

cuello *m* **1.** (*gen*) neck; **~ de botella** bottleneck. **2.** (*de prendas*) collar; **~ de o en pico** V-neck; **~ vuelto** o **de cisne** turtleneck.

cuenca *f* **1.** (*de río*) basin. **2.** (*del ojo*) (eye) socket. **3.** (*región minera*) coalfield.

cuenco *m* earthenware bowl.

cuenta *f* **1.** (*acción de contar*) count; **echar ~s** to reckon up; **llevar/perder la ~ de** to keep/lose count of; **~ atrás** countdown. **2.** (*cálculo*) sum. **3.** (BANCA & COM) account; **abonar algo en ~ a alguien** to credit sthg to sb's account; **~ de gastos** expenditure account; **pagar mil pesetas a ~** to pay a thousand pesetas down; **~ de ahorros** savings account; **~ bancaria** bank account; **~ corriente** current account; **~ de crédito** current account with an overdraft facility; **~ deudora** overdrawn account; **~ a plazo fijo**

deposit account. **4.** (*factura*) bill; **pasar la ~ to** send the bill; **~ por cobrar/pagar** account receivable/payable. **5.** (*bolita - de collar, rosario*) bead. **6.** *loc:* **a fin de ~s** in the end; **ajustarle a alguien las ~s** to settle an account o a score with sb; **caer en la ~ de algo** to realize sthg; **darse ~ de algo** to realize sthg; **más de la ~** too much; **por mi/tu** *etc* **~** on my/ your *etc* own; **tener en ~ algo** to bear sthg in mind.

cuentagotas *m inv* dropper; **a o con ~** in dribs and drabs.

cuentakilómetros *m inv* (*de distancia recorrida*) ≈ milometer; (*de velocidad*) speedometer.

cuentarrevoluciones *m inv* tachometer, rev counter.

cuento *m* **1.** (*fábula*) tale; **~ de hadas** fairy tale. **2.** (*narración*) short story. **3.** (*mentira, exageración*) story, lie; **~ chino** tall story. **4.** *loc:* **tener ~** to put it on.

cuerda *f* **1.** (*para atar - fina*) string; (*- más gruesa*) rope; **~ floja** tightrope. **2.** (*de instrumento*) string. **3.** (*de reloj*) spring; **dar ~ a** (*reloj*) to wind up. **4.** (GEOM) chord. ▶ **cuerdas vocales** *fpl* vocal cords.

cuerdo, -da *adj* **1.** (*sano de juicio*) sane. **2.** (*sensato*) sensible.

cuerno *m* (*gen*) horn; (*de ciervo*) antler.

cuero *m* **1.** (*piel de animal*) skin; (*piel curtida*) hide; **~ cabelludo** scalp; **en ~s, en ~s vivos** stark naked. **2.** (*material*) leather.

cuerpo *m* **1.** (*gen*) body; **a ~** without a coat on; **luchar ~ a ~** to fight hand-to-hand; **tomar ~** to take shape; **en ~ y alma** body and soul. **2.** (*tronco*) trunk. **3.** (*corporación consular, militar etc*) corps; **~ de bomberos** fire brigade; **~ diplomático** diplomatic corps.

cuervo *m* crow.

cuesta *f* slope; **~ arriba** uphill; **~ abajo** downhill; **a ~s** on one's back, over one's shoulders.

cuestión *f* **1.** (*pregunta*) question. **2.** (*problema*) problem. **3.** (*asunto*) matter, issue.

cuestionar *vt* to question.

cuestionario *m* questionnaire.

cueva *f* cave.

cuicos *mpl* Amer fam cops.

cuidado ◆ *m* care; **tener ~ con** to be careful with; **~s intensivos** intensive care (U); **eso me tiene o trae sin ~** I couldn't care less about that. ◆ *interj:* **¡~!** (be) careful!, look out!

cuidadoso, -sa *adj* careful.

cuidar *vt* (*gen*) to look after; (*estilo etc*) to take care over; (*detalles*) to pay attention to. ▶ **cuidar de** *vi* to look after; **cuida de que no lo haga** make sure she doesn't do it. ▶ **cuidarse** *vpr* to take care of o to look after o.s.; **~se de** to worry about.

culata *f* **1.** (*de arma*) butt. **2.** (*de motor*) cylinder head.

culebra *f* snake.

culebrón *m* (TV) soap opera.

culinario, -ria *adj* culinary.

culminación *f* culmination.

culminar ◆ *vt:* **~ (con)** to crown (with). ◆ *vi* to finish, to culminate.

culo *m fam* **1.** (*de personas*) backside, bum Br. **2.** (*de objetos*) bottom.

culpa *f* (*responsabilidad*) fault; **tener la ~ de algo** to be to blame for sthg; **echar la ~ a alguien (de)** to blame sb (for); **por ~ de** because of.

culpabilidad *f* guilt.

culpable ◆ *adj:* **~ (de)** guilty (of); **declararse ~** to plead guilty. ◆ *m y f* (DER) guilty party; **tú eres el ~** you're to blame.

culpar *vt:* **~ a alguien (de)** (*atribuir la culpa*) to blame sb (for); (*acusar*) to accuse sb (of).

cultivar *vt* (*tierra*) to farm, to cultivate; (*plantas*) to grow. ▶ **cultivarse** *vpr* (*persona*) to improve o.s.

cultivo *m* **1.** (*de tierra*) farming; (*de plantas*) growing, cultivation; **de ~** arable. **2.** (*cosecha*) crop.

culto, -ta ◆ *adj* (*persona*) cultured, educated; (*estilo*) refined; (*palabra*) literary. ▶ **culto** *m* **1.** (*devoción*) worship. **2.** (*religión*) cult.

cultura *f* **1.** (*de sociedad*) culture. **2.** (*sabiduría*) learning, knowledge.

cultural *adj* cultural.

culturismo *m* body-building.

cumbre *f* **1.** (*de montaña*) summit. **2.** *fig* (*punto culminante*) peak. **3.** (POLÍT) summit (conference).

cumpleaños *m inv* birthday.

cumplido, -da *adj* **1.** (*completo, lleno*) full, complete. **2.** (*cortés*) courteous. ▶ **cumplido** *m* compliment.

cumplidor, -ra *adj* reliable.

cumplimentar *vt* **1.** (*felicitar*) to congratulate. **2.** (*cumplir - orden*) to carry out; (*- contrato*) to fulfil.

cumplimiento *m* (*de un deber*) performance; (*de contrato, promesa*) fulfilment; (*de la ley*) observance; (*de órdenes*) carrying out; (*de condena*) completion; (*de plazo*) expiry.

cumplir ◆ *vt* 1. (*orden*) to carry out; (*promesa*) to keep; (*ley*) to observe; (*contrato*) to fulfil. 2. (*años*) to reach; **mañana cumplo los 20** I'm 20 o it's my 20th birthday tomorrow. 3. (*condena*) to serve; (*servicio militar*) to do. ◆ *vi* 1. (*plazo, garantía*) to expire. 2. (*realizar el deber*) to do one's duty; **~ con el deber** to do one's duty; **~ con la palabra** to keep one's word.

cúmulo *m* 1. (*de objetos*) pile. 2. *fig* (*de asuntos, acontecimientos*) series.

cuna *f* (*para dormir*) cot, cradle.

cundir *vi* 1. (*propagarse*) to spread. 2. (*dar de sí - comida, reservas, tiempo*) to go a long way.

cuneta *f* (*de una carretera*) ditch; (*de una calle*) gutter.

cuña *f* 1. (*pieza*) wedge. 2. (*de publicidad*) commercial break.

cuñado, -da *m y f* brother-in-law (*f* sister-in-law).

cuño *m* 1. (*troquel*) die. 2. (*sello, impresión*) stamp.

cuota *f* 1. (*contribución - a entidad, club*) membership fee, subscription. 2. (*cupo*) quota.

cupiera *etc* → **caber**.

cuplé *m* popular song.

cupo ◆ *v* → **caber**. ◆ *m* 1. (*cantidad máxima*) quota. 2. (*cantidad proporcional*) share; (*de una cosa racionada*) ration.

cupón *m* (*gen*) coupon; (*de lotería, rifa*) ticket.

cúpula *f* 1. (ARQUIT) dome, cupola. 2. *fig* (*mandos*) leaders (*pl*).

cura ◆ *m* priest. ◆ *f* 1. (*curación*) recovery. 2. (*tratamiento*) treatment, cure.

curación *f* 1. (*de un enfermo - recuperación*) recovery; (*- tratamiento*) treatment; (*de una herida*) healing. 2. (*de jamón*) curing.

curado, -da *adj* (*alimento*) cured; (*pieles*) tanned; **~ de espanto** unshockable.

curandero, -ra *m y f* quack.

curar ◆ *vt* 1. (*gen*) to cure. 2. (*herida*) to dress. 3. (*pieles*) to tan. ◆ *vi* (*enfermo*) to recover; (*herida*) to heal up. ▶ **curarse** *vpr* 1. (*sanar*): **~se (de)** to recover (from). 2. (*alimento*) to cure.

curiosear ◆ *vi* (*fisgonear*) to nose around; (*por una tienda*) to browse round. ◆ *vt* (*libros, revistas*) to browse through.

curiosidad *f* (*gen*) curiosity.

curioso, -sa ◆ *adj* 1. (*por saber, averiguar*) curious, inquisitive. 2. (*raro*) odd, strange. ◆ *m y f* onlooker.

curita *f* *Amer* sticking plaster.

currante *adj fam* hard-working.

currar, currelar *vi fam* to work.

curre = **curro**.

currelar = **currar**.

currículum (vitae) [ku'rrikulum ('bite)] (*pl* currícula (vitae) o **currículums**), **currículo** (*pl* currículos) *m* curriculum vitae.

curro, curre *m fam* work.

cursar *vt* 1. (*estudiar*) to study. 2. (*enviar*) to send. 3. (*dar - órdenes etc*) to give, to issue. 4. (*tramitar*) to submit.

cursi *adj fam* (*vestido, canción etc*) naff, tacky; (*modales, persona*) affected.

cursilería *f* (*cualidad*) tackiness.

cursillo *m* (*curso*) short course.

cursiva → **letra**.

curso *m* 1. (*año académico*) year. 2. (*asignatura*) course; **~ intensivo** crash course. 3. (*dirección - de río, acontecimientos*) course; (*- de la economía*) trend; **seguir su ~** to go on, to continue; **en ~** (*mes, año*) current; (*trabajo*) in progress.

cursor *m* (INFORM) cursor.

curtido, -da *adj* 1. (*piel, cuero*) tanned. 2. *fig* (*experimentado*) seasoned.

curtir *vt* 1. (*piel*) to tan. 2. *fig* (*persona*) to harden.

curva → **curvo**.

curvatura *f* curvature.

curvo, -va *adj* (*gen*) curved; (*doblado*) bent. ▶ **curva** *f* (*gen*) curve; (*en carretera*) bend; **~ de nivel** contour line.

cúspide *f* 1. (*de montaña*) summit, top. 2. *fig* (*apogeo*) peak. 3. (GEOM) apex.

custodia *f* 1. (*de cosas*) safekeeping. 2. (*de personas*) custody.

custodiar *vt* 1. (*vigilar*) to guard. 2. (*proteger*) to look after.

custodio *m* guard.

cutáneo, -a *adj* skin (*antes de sust*).

cutícula *f* cuticle.

cutis *m inv* skin, complexion.

cutre *adj fam* 1. (*de bajo precio, calidad*) cheap and nasty. 2. (*sórdido*) shabby. 3. (*tacaño*) tight, stingy.

cutter (*pl* cutters) *m* (artist's) scalpel (*with retractable blade*).

cuy *m Amer* guinea pig.

cuyo, -ya *adj* (*posesión - por parte de personas*) whose; (*- por parte de cosas*) of which, whose; **ésos son los amigos en cuya casa nos hospedamos** those are the friends in whose house we spent the night; **ese señor, ~ hijo conociste ayer** that man, whose son you met yesterday; **un equipo cuya principal estrella ...** a team, the star player of which o whose star player ...; **en ~ caso** in which case.

CV (abrev de **curriculum vitae**) m CV.

D

d, D f (letra) d, D.

D. abrev de **don**.

dactilar → **huella**.

dádiva f (regalo) gift; (donativo) donation.

dado, -da adj given; **en un momento ~** at a certain point; **ser ~ a** to be fond of. ▶ **dado** m dice, die. ▶ **dado que** loc conj since, seeing as.

daga f dagger.

dale interj ¡~! - ¡otra vez con lo mismo! there you go again!

dalia f dahlia.

dálmata adj, m y f (perro) Dalmatian.

daltónico, -ca adj colour-blind.

daltonismo m colour blindness.

dama f 1. (mujer) lady. 2. (en damas) king; (en ajedrez, naipes) queen. ▶ **damas** fpl (juego) draughts (U).

damisela f desus damsel.

damnificar vt (cosa) to damage; (persona) to harm, to injure.

danés, -esa ◆ adj Danish. ◆ m y f (persona) Dane. ▶ **danés** m (lengua) Danish.

danza f (gen) dancing; (baile) dance.

danzar vi 1. (bailar) to dance. 2. fig (ir de un sitio a otro) to run about.

dañar vt (vista, cosecha) to harm, to damage; (persona) to hurt; (pieza, objeto) to damage. ▶ **dañarse** vpr (persona) to hurt o.s.; (cosa) to become damaged.

dañino, -na adj harmful.

daño m 1. (dolor) pain, hurt; **hacer ~ a alguien** to hurt sb; **hacerse ~** to hurt o.s. 2. (perjuicio - a cosa) damage; (- a persona) harm; **~s y perjuicios** damages.

dar ◆ vt 1. (gen) to give; (baile, fiesta) to hold, to give; (naipes) to deal; **~ algo a alguien** to give sthg to sb, to give sb sthg. 2. (producir - gen) to give, to produce; (- frutos, flores) to bear; (- beneficios, intereses) to yield. 3. (suj: reloj) to strike; **el reloj ha dado las doce** the clock struck twelve. 4. (suministrar luz etc - por primera vez) to connect; (- tras un corte) to turn back on; (encender) to turn o switch on. 5. (CIN, TEATR & TV) to show; (concierto, interpretación) to give. 6. (mostrar - señales etc) to show. 7. (untar con) to apply; **~ barniz a una silla** to varnish a chair. 8. (provocar - gusto, escalofríos etc) to give; **me da vergüenza/pena** it makes me ashamed/sad; **me da risa** it makes me laugh; **me da miedo** it frightens me. 9. (expresa acción): **~ un grito** to give a cry; **~le un golpe/una puñalada** to hit/stab sb; **voy a ~ un paseo** I'm going (to go) for a walk. 10. (considerar): **~ algo por** to consider sthg as; **eso lo doy por hecho** I take that for granted; **~ a alguien por muerto** to give sb up for dead. ◆ vi 1. (repartir - en naipes) to deal. 2. (horas) to strike; **han dado las tres en el reloj** three o'clock struck. 3. (golpear): **le dieron en la cabeza** they hit him on the head; **la piedra dio contra el cristal** the stone hit the window. 4. (accionar): **~ a** (llave de paso) to turn; (botón, timbre) to press. 5. (estar orientado): **~ a** (suj: ventana, balcón) to look out onto, to overlook; (suj: pasillo, puerta) to lead to; (suj: casa, fachada) to face. 6. (encontrar): **~ con algo/alguien** to find sthg/sb; **he dado con la solución** I've hit upon the solution. 7. (proporcionar): **~ de beber/comer a alguien** to give sb something to drink/eat; **le da de mamar a su hijo** she breast-feeds her son. 8. loc: **~ de sí** (ropa, calzado) to give, to stretch. ▶ **darse** vpr 1. (suceder) to occur, to happen; **se da pocas veces** it rarely happens. 2. (entregarse): **~se a** (droga etc) to take to. 3. (golpearse): **~se contra** to bump into. 4. (tener aptitud): **se me da bien/mal el latín** I'm good/bad at Latin. 5. (considerarse): **~se por** to consider o.s. (to be); **~se por vencido** to give in. 6. loc: **dársela a alguien** (engañar) to take sb in; **se las da de listo** he makes out (that) he is clever.

dardo m dart.

dársena f dock.

datar vt to date. ▶ **datar de** vi to date from.

dátil m (BOT & CULIN) date.

dato m (gen) piece of information, fact; **~s** (gen) information; (INFORM) data; **~s personales** personal details.

dcha. (*abrev de* **derecha**) rt.

d. de JC., d.JC. (*abrev de* **después de Jesucristo**) AD.

de *prep* (*de* + *el* = **del**) 1. (*posesión, pertenencia*) of; **el coche ~ mi padre/mis padres** my father's/parents' car; **es ~ ella** it's hers; **la pata ~ la mesa** the table leg. 2. (*materia*) (made) of; **un vaso ~ plástico** a plastic cup; **un reloj ~ oro** a gold watch. 3. (*en descripciones*): **un vaso ~ agua** a glass of water; **~ fácil manejo** user-friendly; **la señora ~ verde** the lady in green; **el chico ~ la coleta** the boy with the ponytail; **he comprado las peras ~ 100 ptas el kilo** I bought the pears that were o at 100 pesetas a kilo; **un sello ~ 50 ptas** a 50 peseta stamp. 4. (*asunto*) about; **hablábamos ~ ti** we were talking about you; **libros ~ historia** history books. 5. (*uso*): **una bici ~ carreras** a racer; **ropa ~ deporte** sportswear. 6. (*en calidad de*) as; **trabaja ~ bombero** he works as a fireman. 7. (*tiempo - desde*) from; (*- durante*) in; **trabaja ~ nueve a cinco** she works from nine to five; **~ madrugada** early in the morning; **a las cuatro ~ la tarde** at four in the afternoon; **trabaja ~ noche y duerme ~ día** he works at night and sleeps during the day. 8. (*procedencia, distancia*) from; **salir ~ casa** to leave home; **soy ~ Bilbao** I'm from Bilbao. 9. (*causa, modo*) with; **morirse ~ hambre** to die of hunger; **llorar ~ alegría** to cry with joy; **~ una patada** with a kick; **~ una sola vez** in one go. 10. (*con superlativos*): **el mejor ~ todos** the best of all; **el más importante del mundo** the most important in the world. 11. (*en comparaciones*): **más/menos ~ ...** more/less than ... 12. (*antes de infin*) (*condición*) if; **~ querer ayudarme, lo haría** if she wanted to help me, she'd do it; **~ no ser por ti, me hubiese hundido** if it hadn't been for you, I wouldn't have made it. 13. (*después de adj y antes de sust*) (*enfatiza cualidad*): **el idiota ~ tu hermano** your stupid brother. 14. (*después de adj y antes de infin*): **es difícil ~ creer** it's hard to believe.

dé → **dar**.

deambular *vi* to wander (about).

debajo *adv* underneath; **~ de** underneath, under; **por ~ de lo normal** below normal.

debate *m* debate.

debatir *vt* to debate. ▶ **debatirse** *vpr* (*luchar*) to struggle.

debe *m* debit (side).

deber ◆ *vt* (*adeudar*) to owe; **~ algo a alguien** to owe sb sthg, to owe sthg to sb. ◆ *vi* 1. (*antes de infin*) (*expresa obligación*): **debo hacerlo** I have to do it, I must do it; **deberían abolir esa ley** they ought to o should abolish that law; **debes dominar tus impulsos** you must o should control your impulses. 2. (*expresa posibilidad*): **~ de: el tren debe de llegar alrededor de las diez** the train should arrive at about ten; **deben de ser las diez** it must be ten o'clock; **no debe de ser muy mayor** she can't be very old. ◆ *m* duty. ▶ **deberse a** *vpr* 1. (*ser consecuencia de*) to be due to. 2. (*dedicarse a*) to have a responsibility towards. ▶ **deberes** *mpl* (*trabajo escolar*) homework (U).

debidamente *adv* properly, correctly.

debido, -da *adj* (*justo, conveniente*) due, proper; **como es ~** properly. ▶ **debido a** *loc conj* (*a principio de frase*) owing to; (*en mitad de frase*) due to.

débil *adj* 1. (*persona - sin fuerzas*) weak. 2. (*voz, sonido*) faint; (*luz*) dim.

debilidad *f* (*gen*) weakness; **tener ~ por** to have a soft spot for.

debilitar *vt* to weaken. ▶ **debilitarse** *vpr* to become o grow weak.

debutar *vi* to make one's debut.

década *f* decade.

decadencia *f* (*gen*) decadence.

decadente *adj* decadent.

decaer *vi* (*gen*) to decline; (*enfermo*) to get weaker; (*salud*) to fail; (*entusiasmo*) to flag; (*restaurante etc*) to go downhill.

decaído, -da *adj* (*desalentado*) gloomy, downhearted; (*débil*) frail.

decaimiento *m* (*desaliento*) gloominess; (*decadencia*) decline; (*falta de fuerzas*) weakness.

decano, -na *m y f* (*de corporación, facultad*) dean.

decapitar *vt* to decapitate, to behead.

decena *f* ten; **una ~ de veces** about ten times.

decencia *f* 1. (*gen*) decency; (*en el vestir*) modesty. 2. (*dignidad*) dignity.

decenio *m* decade.

decente *adj* 1. (*gen*) decent. 2. (*en el comportamiento*) proper; (*en el vestir*) modest. 3. (*limpio*) clean.

decepción *f* disappointment.

decepcionar *vt* to disappoint.

decibelio *m* decibel.

decidido, -da *adj* determined.

decidir ◆ *vt* **1.** (*gen*) to decide; **~ hacer algo** to decide to do sthg. **2.** (*determinar*) to determine. ◆ *vi* to decide.
▶ **decidirse** *vpr* to decide, to make up one's mind; **~se a hacer algo** to decide to do sthg; **~se por** to decide on, to choose.

décima → **décimo**.

decimal *adj* (*sistema*) decimal.

décimo, -ma *núm* tenth; **la décima parte** a tenth. ▶ **décimo** *m* **1.** (*fracción*) tenth. **2.** (*en lotería*) tenth part of a lottery ticket. ▶ **décima** *f* (*en medidas*) tenth; **una décima de segundo** a tenth of a second.

decir *vt* **1.** (*gen*) to say; **~ que sí/no** to say yes/no; **¿cómo se dice 'estación' en inglés?** how do you say 'estación' in English?; **¿diga?, ¿dígame?** (*al teléfono*) hello? **2.** (*contar, ordenar*) to tell; **~ a alguien que haga algo** to tell sb to do sthg; **se dice que** they o people say (that); **~ la verdad** to tell the truth. **3.** *fig* (*revelar*) to tell, to show; **eso lo dice todo** that says it all. **4.** *loc:* **~ para sí** to say to o.s.; **es ~** that is, that's to say; **(o) mejor dicho** or rather; **querer ~** to mean; **¿qué quieres ~ con eso?** what do you mean by that?

decisión *f* **1.** (*dictamen, resolución*) decision; **tomar una ~** to make o take a decision. **2.** (*empeño, tesón*) determination; (*seguridad, resolución*) decisiveness.

decisivo, -va *adj* decisive.

declamar *vt* & *vi* to declaim, to recite.

declaración *f* (*gen*) statement; (*de amor, impuestos, guerra*) declaration; **prestar ~** to give evidence; **~ del impuesto sobre la renta** income tax return.

declarar ◆ *vt* (*gen*) to declare; (*afirmar*) to state, to say; **~ culpable/inocente a alguien** to find sb guilty/not guilty. ◆ *vi* (DER) to testify, to give evidence.
▶ **declararse** *vpr* **1.** (*incendio, epidemia*) to break out. **2.** (*confesar el amor*) to declare one's feelings o love. **3.** (*dar una opinión*): **~se a favor de algo** to say that one supports sthg; **~se en contra de algo** to say one is opposed to sthg; **~se culpable/inocente** to plead guilty/not guilty.

declinar ◆ *vt* (*gen* & GRAM) to decline; (*responsabilidad*) to disclaim. ◆ *vi* (*día, tarde*) to draw to a close; (*fiebre*) to subside; (*economía*) to decline.

declive *m* **1.** (*decadencia*) decline, fall; **en ~** in decline. **2.** (*pendiente*) slope.

decodificador = **descodificador**.

decoración *f* **1.** (*acción*) decoration; (*efecto*) décor. **2.** (*adorno*) decorations (*pl*).

decorado *m* (CIN & TEATR) set.

decorar *vt* to decorate.

decorativo, -va *adj* decorative.

decoro *m* (*pudor*) decency.

decoroso, -sa *adj* (*decente*) decent; (*correcto*) seemly, proper.

decrecer *vi* (*gen*) to decrease, to decline; (*caudal del río*) to go down.

decrépito, -ta *adj despec* (*viejo*) decrepit; (*civilización*) decadent, declining.

decretar *vt* to decree.

decreto *m* decree; **~ ley** decree, ≈ order in council Br.

dedal *m* thimble.

dedicación *f* dedication.

dedicar *vt* **1.** (*tiempo, dinero, energía*) to devote. **2.** (*libro, monumento*) to dedicate. ▶ **dedicarse a** *vpr* **1.** (*tener una profesión*): **¿a qué se dedica usted?** what do you do for a living?; **se dedica a la enseñanza** she works as a teacher. **2.** (*a una actividad, persona*) to spend time on; **los domingos me dedico al estudio** I spend Sundays studying.

dedicatoria *f* dedication.

dedo *m* **1.** (*de la mano*) finger; **dos ~s de whisky** two fingers of whisky; **~ anular/corazón** ring/middle finger; **~ gordo** o **pulgar** thumb; **~ índice/meñique** index/little finger. **2.** (*del pie*) toe. **3.** *loc:* **hacer ~** *fam* to hitchhike; **nombrar a alguien a ~** to handpick sb; **pillarse** o **cogerse los ~s** *fig* to get one's fingers burnt; **poner el ~ en la llaga** to put one's finger on it.

deducción *f* deduction.

deducir *vt* **1.** (*inferir*) to guess, to deduce. **2.** (*descontar*) to deduct.

defecar *vi* to defecate.

defecto *m* (*físico*) defect; (*moral*) fault; **~ de pronunciación** speech defect.
▶ **por defecto** *loc adv* by default.

defectuoso, -sa *adj* (*mercancía*) defective, faulty; (*trabajo*) inaccurate.

defender *vt* (*gen*) to defend; (*amigo etc*) to stand up for. ▶ **defenderse** *vpr* (*protegerse*): **~se (de)** to defend o.s. (against).

defensa ◆ *f* defence. ◆ *m* *y* *f* (DEP) defender; **~ central** centre-back.

defensivo, -va *adj* defensive. ▶ **defensiva** *f*: **ponerse/estar a la defensiva** to go/be on the defensive.

defensor, -ra ◆ *adj* → **abogado**. ◆ *m* *y* *f* (*gen*) defender; (*abogado*) counsel for the defence; (*adalid*) champion; **~ del**

pueblo ≃ ombudsman.

deferencia f deference.

deficiencia f (*defecto*) deficiency, shortcoming; (*insuficiencia*) lack.

deficiente adj (*defectuoso - gen*) deficient; ~ **en** lacking o deficient in; (*audición, vista*) defective. ▶ **deficiente (mental)** m y f mentally handicapped person.

déficit (*pl* **déficits**) m (ECON) deficit.

deficitario, -ria adj (*empresa, operación*) loss-making; (*balance*) negative.

definición f 1. (*gen*) definition. 2. (*en televisión*) resolution.

definir vt (*gen*) to define. ▶ **definirse** vpr to take a clear stance.

definitivamente adv 1. (*sin duda*) definitely. 2. (*para siempre*) for good.

definitivo, -va adj (*texto etc*) definitive; (*respuesta*) definite; **en definitiva** in short, anyway.

deforestación f deforestation.

deformación f (*de huesos, objetos etc*) deformation; (*de la verdad etc*) distortion; ~ **física** (physical) deformity; **tener ~ profesional** to be always acting as if one were still at work.

deformar vt 1. (*huesos, objetos etc*) to deform. 2. fig (*la verdad etc*) to distort. ▶ **deformarse** vpr to go out of shape.

deforme adj (*cuerpo*) deformed; (*imagen*) distorted; (*objeto*) misshapen.

defraudar vt 1. (*decepcionar*) to disappoint. 2. (*estafar*) to defraud; ~ **a Hacienda** to practise tax evasion.

defunción f decease, death.

degeneración f degeneration.

degenerado, -da adj, m y f degenerate.

degenerar vi: ~ (**en**) to degenerate (into).

deglutir vt & vi to swallow.

degollar vt (*cortar la garganta*) to cut o slit the throat of; (*decapitar*) to behead.

degradar vt 1. (*moralmente*) to degrade. 2. (*de un cargo*) to demote. ▶ **degradarse** vpr to degrade o lower o.s.

degustación f tasting (*of wines etc*).

degustar vt to taste (*wines etc*).

dehesa f meadow.

dejadez f neglect; (*en aspecto*) slovenliness.

dejado, -da adj careless; (*aspecto*) slovenly.

dejar ◆ vt 1. (*gen*) to leave; **deja esa pera en el plato** put that pear on the plate; **deja el abrigo en la percha** leave your coat on the hanger; ~ **a alguien en algún sitio** (*con el coche*) to drop sb off somewhere; **deja algo de café para mí** leave some coffee for me; ~ **algo/a alguien a alguien** (*encomendar*) to leave sthg/sb with sb. 2. (*prestar*): ~ **algo a alguien** to lend sb sthg, to lend sthg to sb. 3. (*abandonar - casa, trabajo, país*) to leave; (- *tabaco, estudios*) to give up; (- *familia*) to abandon; ~ **algo por imposible** to give sthg up as a lost cause; ~ **a alguien atrás** to leave sb behind. 4. (*permitir*): ~ **a alguien hacer algo** to let sb do sthg, to allow sb to do sthg; **sus gritos no me dejaron dormir** his cries prevented me from sleeping; **deja que tu hijo venga con nosotros** let your son come with us; ~ **correr algo** fig to let sthg be. 5. (*omitir*) to leave out; ~ **algo por** o **sin hacer** to fail to do sthg; **dejó lo más importante por resolver** he left the most important question unsolved. 6. (*esperar*): ~ **que** to wait until; **dejó que acabara de llover para salir** he waited until it had stopped raining before going out. 7. (*dar*) to give ◆ vi 1. (*parar*): ~ **de hacer algo** to stop doing sthg; **no deja de venir ni un solo día** he never fails to come. 2. (*expresando promesa*): **no** ~ **de** to be sure to; **¡no dejes de escribirme!** be sure to write to me! ▶ **dejarse** vpr 1. (*olvidar*): ~**se algo en algún sitio** to leave sthg somewhere. 2. (*permitir*): ~**se engañar** to allow o.s. to be taken in; ~**se llevar** to let o.s. go.

deje m (*acento*) accent.

dejo m (*acento*) accent.

del → **de**.

delantal m apron.

delante adv 1. (*en primer lugar, en la parte delantera*) in front; **el de ~** the one in front; **el asiento de ~** the seat in front. 2. (*enfrente*) opposite. 3. (*presente*) present. ▶ **delante de** loc prep in front of.

delantero, -ra ◆ adj front. ◆ m y f (DEP) forward; ~ **centro** centre forward. ▶ **delantera** f 1. (DEP) forwards (*pl*), attack. 2. loc: **coger** o **tomar la delantera** to take the lead; **coger** o **tomar la delantera a alguien** to beat sb to it; **llevar la delantera** to be in the lead.

delatar vt to denounce; fig (*suj: sonrisa, ojos etc*) to betray. ▶ **delatarse** vpr to give o.s. away.

delator, -ra m y f informer.

delegación f Amer (*comisaría*) police station, precinct Am.

delegado, -da m y f 1. (*gen*) delegate; **~ de curso** form monitor. 2. (COM) representative.

delegar vt: ~ **algo (en** o **a)** to delegate sthg (to).

deleite m delight.

deletrear vt to spell (out).

deleznable adj fig (malo - clima, libro, actuación) appalling; (- excusa, razón) contemptible.

delfin m (animal) dolphin.

delgado, -da adj (gen) thin; (esbelto) slim.

deliberación f deliberation.

deliberar vi to deliberate.

delicadeza f 1. (miramiento - con cosas) care; (- con personas) kindness, attentiveness. 2. (finura - de perfume, rostro) delicacy; (- de sensibilidad) sensitivity. 3. (de un asunto, situación) delicacy.

delicado, -da adj 1. (gen) delicate; (perfume, gusto) subtle; (paladar) refined. 2. (persona - sensible) sensitive; (- muy exigente) fussy; (- educado) polite; **estar ~ de salud** to be very weak.

delicia f delight.

delicioso, -sa adj (comida) delicious; (persona) lovely, delightful.

delimitar vt (finca etc) to set out the boundaries of; (funciones etc) to define.

delincuencia f crime; **~ juvenil** juvenile delinquency.

delincuente m y f criminal.

delineante m y f draughtsman (f draughtswoman).

delinquir vi to commit a crime.

delirante adj (gen) delirious.

delirar vi (un enfermo) to be delirious; (desbarrar) to talk nonsense.

delirio m (por la fiebre) delirium; (de un enfermo mental) ravings (pl); **~s de grandeza** delusions of grandeur.

delito m crime, offence.

delta ◆ m delta. ◆ f delta.

demacrado, -da adj gaunt.

demagogo, -ga m y f demagogue.

demanda f 1. (petición) request; (reivindicación) demand; **~ salarial** wage claim; **en ~ de** asking for. 2. (ECON) demand. 3. (DER) lawsuit; (por daños y perjuicios) claim; **presentar una ~ contra** to take legal action against.

demandante m y f plaintiff.

demandar vt 1. (DER): **~ a alguien (por)** to sue sb (for). 2. (pedir) to ask for.

demarcación f 1. (señalización) demarcation. 2. (territorio demarcado) area; (jurisdicción) district.

demás ◆ adj other; **los ~ invitados** the

other o remaining guests. ◆ pron: **lo ~** the rest; **todo lo ~** everything else; **los/las ~** the others, the rest; **por lo ~** apart from that, otherwise; **y ~** and so on.

demasiado, -da ◆ adj too much, (pl) too many; **demasiada comida** too much food; **~s niños** too many children. ◆ adv (gen) too much; (antes de adj o adv) too; **habla ~** she talks too much; **iba ~ rápido** he was going too fast.

demencia f madness, insanity.

demencial adj (disparatado) chaotic.

demente adj mad.

democracia f democracy.

demócrata ◆ adj democratic. ◆ m y f democrat.

democrático, -ca adj democratic.

demografía f demography.

demoler vt (edificio) to demolish, to pull down; fig to destroy.

demolición f demolition.

demonio m 1. lit & fig devil. 2. (para enfatizar): **¿qué/dónde ~s ...?** what/where the hell ...? ▶ **demonios** interj: **¡~s!** damn (it)!

demora f delay.

demorar vt to delay. ▶ **demorarse** vpr 1. (retrasarse) to be delayed. 2. (detenerse) to stop (somewhere).

demostración f 1. (gen) demonstration. 2. (de un teorema) proof. 3. (exhibición) display; (señal) sign; (prueba) proof.

demostrar vt 1. (hipótesis, teoría, verdad) to prove. 2. (alegría, impaciencia, dolor) to show. 3. (funcionamiento, procedimiento) to demonstrate, to show.

denegar vt to turn down, to reject.

denigrante adj (humillante) degrading; (insultante) insulting.

denigrar vt (humillar) to denigrate, to vilify; (insultar) to insult.

denominación f naming; **'~ de origen'** 'appellation d'origine'.

denominador m denominator.

denotar vt to indicate, to show.

densidad f (gen & INFORM) density; **~ de población** population density; **alta/doble ~** (INFORM) high/double density.

denso, -sa adj (gen) dense; (líquido) thick.

dentadura f teeth (pl); **~ postiza** false teeth (pl), dentures (pl).

dentera f: **dar ~ a alguien** to set sb's teeth on edge.

dentífrico, -ca adj tooth (antes de sust). ▶ **dentífrico** m toothpaste.

dentista m y f dentist.

dentro adv inside; **está ahí ~** it's in

there; **hacia/para ~** inwards; **por ~** (on the) inside; *fig* inside, deep down. ▶ **dentro de** *loc prep* in; **~ del coche** in o inside the car; **~ de poco/un año** in a while/a year; **~ de lo posible** as far as possible.

denuedo *m* (*valor*) courage; (*esfuerzo*) resolve.

denuncia *f* (*acusación*) accusation; (*condena*) denunciation; (*a la policía*) complaint; **presentar una ~ (contra)** to file a complaint (against).

denunciar *vt* to denounce; (*delito*) to report.

departamento *m* Amer (*piso*) flat Br, apartment Am.

dependencia *f* 1. (*de una persona*) dependence; (*de país, drogas, alcohol*) dependency. 2. (*departamento*) section; (*sucursal*) branch. ▶ **dependencias** *fpl* (*habitaciones*) rooms; (*edificios*) outbuildings.

depender *vi* to depend; **depende ...** it depends ... ▶ **depender de** *vi*: **~ de algo** to depend on sthg; **~ de alguien** to be dependent on sb; **depende de ti** it's up to you.

dependienta *f* shop assistant, saleswoman.

dependiente ♦ *adj* dependent. ♦ *m* shop assistant, salesman.

depilar *vt* (*gen*) to remove the hair from; (*cejas*) to pluck; (*con cera*) to wax.

depilatorio, -ria *adj* hair-removing. ▶ **depilatorio** *m* hair-remover.

deplorable *adj* (*suceso, comportamiento*) deplorable; (*aspecto*) sorry, pitiful.

deponer *vt* 1. (*abandonar - actitud*) to drop, to set aside; (*las armas*) to lay down. 2. (*destituir - ministro, secretario*) to remove from office; (*- líder, rey*) to depose.

deportar *vt* to deport.

deporte *m* sport; **hacer ~** to do o practise sports; **practicar un ~** to do a sport.

deportista *m y f* sportsman (*f* sportswoman).

deportivo, -va *adj* 1. (*revista, evento*) sports (*antes de sust*). 2. (*conducta, espíritu*) sportsmanlike. ▶ **deportivo** *m* sports car.

depositar *vt* 1. (*gen*) to place; **~ algo en alguien** (*confianza, ilusiones*) to place sthg in sb. 2. (*en el banco etc*) to deposit. ▶ **depositarse** *vpr* (*asentarse*) to settle.

depositario, -ria *m y f* 1. (*de dinero*) trustee. 2. (*de confianza etc*) repository. 3. (*de mercancías etc*) depositary.

depósito *m* 1. (*almacén - de mercancías*) store, warehouse; (*- de armas*) dump; **~ de cadáveres** morgue, mortuary. 2. (*recipiente*) tank. 3. (*de dinero*) deposit.

depravado, -da *adj* depraved.

depreciar *vt* to (cause to) depreciate. ▶ **depreciarse** *vpr* to depreciate.

depredador, -ra ♦ *adj* predatory. ♦ *m y f* predator.

depresión *f* (*gen*) depression; **~ nerviosa** nervous breakdown.

depresivo, -va ♦ *adj* (PSICOL) depressive; (*deprimente*) depressing. ♦ *m y f* depressive.

deprimido, -da *adj* depressed.

deprimir *vt* to depress. ▶ **deprimirse** *vpr* to get depressed.

deprisa, de prisa *adv* fast, quickly; **¡~!** quick!

depuración *f* 1. (*de agua, metal, gas*) purification. 2. *fig* (*de organismo, sociedad*) purge.

depurar *vt* 1. (*agua, metal, gas*) to purify. 2. *fig* (*organismo, sociedad*) to purge.

derecha → **derecho**.

derecho, -cha ♦ *adj* 1. (*diestro*) right. 2. (*vertical*) upright. 3. (*recto*) straight. ♦ *adv* 1. (*en posición vertical*) upright. 2. (*directamente*) straight. ▶ **derecho** ♦ *m* 1. (*leyes, estudio*) law; **~ civil/penal** civil/ criminal law. 2. (*prerrogativa*) right; **el ~ al voto** the right to vote; **¡no hay ~!** it's not fair!; **reservado el ~ de admisión** the management reserves the right of admission; **~s civiles/humanos** civil/ human rights. 3. (*de una tela, prenda*) right side; **del ~** right side out. ♦ *adv* (*recto*) straight on o ahead. ▶ **derecha** *f* 1. (*contrario de izquierda*) right, right-hand side; **a la derecha** to the right; **girar a la derecha** to turn right. 2. (POLÍT) right (wing); **ser de derechas** to be right-wing. ▶ **derechos** *mpl* (*tasas*) duties; (*profesionales*) fees; **~s de aduana** customs duty (U); **~s de inscripción** membership fee (*sg*); **~s de autor** (*potestad*) copyright (U); (*dinero*) royalties.

deriva *f* drift; **a la ~** adrift; **ir a la ~** to drift.

derivado, -da *adj* (GRAM) derived. ▶ **derivado** *m* 1. (*producto*) by-product. 2. (QUÍM) derivative.

derivar ♦ *vt* 1. (*desviar*) to divert. 2. (MAT) to derive. ♦ *vi* (*desviarse*) to change direction, to drift. ▶ **derivar de** *vi* 1. (*proceder*) to derive from. 2. (GRAM) to be derived from.

derogación *f* repeal.

derramamiento *m* spilling; ~ de sangre bloodshed.

derramar *vt* (*por accidente*) to spill; (*verter*) to pour; ~ lágrimas/sangre to shed tears/blood.

derrame *m* 1. (MED) discharge. 2. (*de líquido*) spilling; (*de sangre*) shedding.

derrapar *vi* to skid.

derretir *vt* (*gen*) to melt; (*nieve*) to thaw. ▶ **derretirse** *vpr* (*metal, mantequilla*) to melt; (*hielo, nieve*) to thaw.

derribar *vt* 1. (*construcción*) to knock down, to demolish. 2. (*hacer caer - árbol*) to fell; (*- avión*) to bring down. 3. (*gobierno, gobernante*) to overthrow.

derribo *m* (*material*) rubble.

derrocar *vt* (*gobierno*) to bring down, to overthrow; (*ministro*) to oust.

derrochar *vt* (*malgastar*) to squander, to waste.

derroche *m* (*malgaste*) waste, squandering.

derrota *f* (*fracaso*) defeat.

derrotar *vt* to defeat.

derrotero *m* (*camino*) direction; tomar diferentes ~s to follow a different course.

derrotista *adj, m y f* defeatist.

derruir *vt* to demolish.

derrumbamiento *m* 1. (*de puente, edificio - por accidente*) collapse; (*- intencionado*) demolition. 2. *fig* (*de imperio*) fall; (*empresa etc*) collapse.

derrumbar *vt* (*puente, edificio*) to demolish. ▶ **derrumbarse** *vpr* (*puente, edificio*) to collapse; (*techo*) to fall o cave in.

desabotonar *vt* to unbutton. ▶ **desabotonarse** *vpr* (*suj: persona*) to undo one's buttons; (*suj: ropa*) to come undone.

desabrochar *vt* to undo. ▶ **desabrocharse** *vpr* (*suj: persona*) to undo one's buttons; (*suj: ropa*) to come undone.

desacato *m* 1. (*gen*): ~ (a) lack of respect (for), disrespect (for). 2. (DER) contempt of court.

desacierto *m* (*error*) error.

desaconsejar *vt*: ~ algo (a alguien) to advise (sb) against sthg; ~ a alguien que haga algo to advise sb not to do sthg.

desacorde *adj* (*opiniones*) conflicting.

desacreditar *vt* to discredit.

desactivar *vt* to defuse.

desacuerdo *m* disagreement.

desafiante *adj* defiant.

desafiar *vt* 1. (*persona*) to challenge; ~ a alguien a algo/a que haga algo to challenge sb to sthg/to do sthg. 2. (*peligro*) to defy.

desafinar *vi* (MÚS) to be out of tune.

desafío *m* challenge.

desaforado, -da *adj* 1. (*excesivo - apetito*) uncontrolled. 2. (*furioso - grito*) furious, wild.

desafortunadamente *adv* unfortunately.

desafortunado, -da *adj* 1. (*gen*) unfortunate. 2. (*sin suerte*) unlucky.

desagradable *adj* unpleasant.

desagradar *vi* to displease; me desagrada su actitud I don't like her attitude.

desagradecido, -da *m y f* ungrateful person.

desagrado *m* displeasure; con ~ reluctantly.

desagraviar *vt*: ~ a alguien por algo (*por una ofensa*) to make amends to sb for sthg; (*por un perjuicio*) to compensate sb for sthg.

desagüe *m* (*vaciado*) drain; (*cañería*) drainpipe.

desaguisado *m* (*destrozo*) damage (U).

desahogado, -da *adj* 1. (*de espacio*) spacious. 2. (*de dinero*) well-off.

desahogar *vt* (*ira*) to vent; (*pena*) to relieve, to ease. ▶ **desahogarse** *vpr* 1. (*contar penas*) ~se con alguien to pour out one's woes o to tell one's troubles to sb. 2. (*desfogarse*) to let off steam.

desahogo *m* 1. (*moral*) relief. 2. (*de espacio*) space, room. 3. (*económico*) ease.

desahuciar *vt* 1. (*inquilino*) to evict. 2. (*enfermo*): ~ a alguien to give up all hope of saving sb.

desahucio *m* eviction.

desaire *m* snub, slight; hacer un ~ a alguien to snub sb.

desajuste *m* 1. (*de piezas*) misalignment; (*de máquina*) breakdown. 2. (*de declaraciones*) inconsistency; (*económico etc*) imbalance.

desalentar *vt* to discourage.

desaliento *m* dismay, dejection.

desaliñado, -da *adj* (*aspecto*) scruffy; (*pelo*) dishevelled.

desaliño *m* (*del aspecto*) scruffiness; (*del pelo*) dishevelment.

desalmado, -da *adj* heartless.

desalojar *vt* 1. (*por una emergencia - edificio, personas*) to evacuate. 2. (*por la fuerza - suj: policía, ejército*) to clear;

descafeinado

(- *inquilinos etc*) to evict. **3.** (*por propia voluntad*) to abandon, to move out of.

desamor m (*falta de afecto*) indifference, coldness; (*odio*) dislike.

desamparado, -da adj (*niño*) helpless; (*lugar*) desolate, forsaken.

desamparar vt to abandon.

desamparo m (*abandono*) abandonment; (*aflicción*) helplessness.

desangrar vt **1.** (*animal, persona*) to bleed. **2.** *fig* (*económicamente*) to bleed dry. ▶ **desangrarse** vpr to lose a lot of blood.

desanimado, -da adj (*persona*) downhearted.

desanimar vt to discourage. ▶ **desanimarse** vpr to get downhearted o discouraged.

desánimo m (*gen*) dejection; (*depresión*) depression.

desapacible adj unpleasant.

desaparecer vi **1.** (*gen*) to disappear. **2.** (*en guerra, accidente*) to go missing.

desaparecido, -da m y f missing person.

desaparición f disappearance.

desapego m indifference.

desapercibido, -da adj: **pasar ~** to go unnoticed.

desaprensivo, -va m y f unscrupulous person.

desaprobar vt (*gen*) to disapprove of; (*un plan etc*) to reject.

desaprovechar vt to waste.

desarmador m Amer screwdriver.

desarmar vt **1.** (*gen*) to disarm. **2.** (*desmontar*) to take apart, to dismantle.

desarme m (MIL & POLÍT) disarmament.

desarraigar vt **1.** (*vicio, costumbre*) to root out. **2.** (*persona, pueblo*) to banish, to drive (out).

desarraigo m (*de árbol*) uprooting; (*de vicio, costumbre*) rooting out; (*de persona, pueblo*) banishment.

desarreglar vt (*armario, pelo*) to mess up; (*planes, horario*) to upset.

desarreglo m (*de cuarto, persona*) untidiness; (*de vida*) disorder.

desarrollado, -da adj developed.

desarrollar vt **1.** (*mejorar - crecimiento, país*) to develop. **2.** (*exponer - teoría, tema, fórmula*) to expound. **3.** (*realizar - actividad, trabajo*) to carry out. ▶ **desarrollarse** vpr **1.** (*crecer, mejorar*) to develop. **2.** (*suceder - reunión*) to take place; (- *película*) to be set.

desarrollo m **1.** (*evolución*) development. **2.** (*crecimiento*) growth.

desarticular vt **1.** (*huesos*) to dislocate. **2.** *fig* (*organización, banda*) to break up; (*plan*) to foil.

desasosegar vt to make uneasy.

desasosiego m **1.** (*mal presentimiento*) unease. **2.** (*nerviosismo*) restlessness.

desastrado, -da adj (*desaseado*) scruffy; (*sucio*) dirty.

desastre m disaster; **su madre es un ~** her mother is hopeless.

desastroso, -sa adj disastrous.

desatar vt **1.** (*nudo, lazo*) to untie; (*paquete*) to undo; (*animal*) to unleash. **2.** *fig* (*tormenta, iras, pasión*) to unleash; (*entusiasmo*) to arouse; (*lengua*) to loosen. ▶ **desatarse** vpr **1.** (*nudo, lazo*) to come undone. **2.** *fig* (*desencadenarse - tormenta*) to break; (- *ira, cólera*) to erupt.

desatascar vt to unblock.

desatender vt **1.** (*obligación, persona*) to neglect. **2.** (*ruegos, consejos*) to ignore.

desatino m **1.** (*locura*) foolishness. **2.** (*desacierto*) foolish act.

desautorizar vt **1.** (*desmentir - noticia*) to deny. **2.** (*prohibir - manifestación, huelga*) to ban. **3.** (*desacreditar*) to discredit.

desavenencia f (*desacuerdo*) friction, tension; (*riña*) quarrel.

desavenirse vpr to fall out.

desayunar ◆ vi to have breakfast. ◆ vt to have for breakfast.

desayuno m breakfast.

desazón f unease, anxiety.

desazonar vt to worry.

desbancar vt *fig* (*ocupar el puesto de*) to oust, to replace.

desbandada f breaking up, scattering; **a la ~** in great disorder.

desbarajuste m disorder, confusion.

desbaratar vt to ruin, to wreck.

desbloquear vt (*cuenta*) to unfreeze; (*país*) to lift the blockade on; (*negociación*) to end the deadlock in.

desbocado, -da adj (*caballo*) runaway.

desbocarse vpr (*caballo*) to bolt.

desbordar vt **1.** (*cauce, ribera*) to overflow, to burst. **2.** (*límites, previsiones*) to exceed; (*paciencia*) to push beyond the limit. ▶ **desbordarse** vpr **1.** (*líquido*): **~se (de)** to overflow (from). **2.** (*río*) to overflow. **3.** *fig* (*sentimiento*) to erupt.

descabalgar vi to dismount.

descabellado, -da adj crazy.

descafeinado, -da adj (*sin cafeína*) decaffeinated. ▶ **descafeinado** m decaffeinated coffee.

descalabro *m* setback, damage (U).

descalificar *vt* 1. (*en una competición*) to disqualify. 2. (*desprestigiar*) to discredit.

descalzar *vt*: ~ **a alguien** to take sb's shoes off. ▶ **descalzarse** *vpr* to take off one's shoes.

descalzo, -za *adj* barefoot.

descaminado, -da *adj fig* (*equivocado*): **andar** o **ir** ~ to be on the wrong track.

descampado *m* open country.

descansar *vi* 1. (*reposar*) to rest. 2. (*dormir*) to sleep; **¡que descanses!** sleep well!

descansillo *m* landing.

descanso *m* 1. (*reposo*) rest; **tomarse un** ~ to take a rest; **día de** ~ day off. 2. (*pausa*) break; (CIN & TEATR) interval; (DEP) half-time. 3. *fig* (*alivio*) relief.

descapotable *adj* & *m* convertible.

descarado, -da *adj* 1. (*desvergonzado - persona*) cheeky, impertinent. 2. (*flagrante - intento etc*) barefaced.

descarga *f* 1. (*de mercancías*) unloading. 2. (*de electricidad*) shock. 3. (*disparo*) firing, shots (*pl*).

descargar *vt* 1. (*vaciar - mercancías, pistola*) to unload. 2. (*disparar - munición, arma, ráfaga*): ~ (**sobre**) to fire (at). 3. (ELECTR) to run down. ▶ **descargarse** *vpr* 1. (*desahogarse*): ~**se con alguien** to take it out on sb. 2. (ELECTR) to go flat.

descargo *m* 1. (*excusa*): ~ **a** argument against. 2. (DER) defence. 3. (COM - *de deuda*) discharge; (- *recibo*) receipt.

descarnado, -da *adj* 1. (*descripción*) brutal. 2. (*persona, animal*) scrawny.

descaro *m* cheek, impertinence.

descarriarse *vpr* 1. (*ovejas, ganado*) to stray. 2. *fig* (*pervertirse*) to go astray.

descarrilamiento *m* derailment.

descarrilar *vi* to be derailed.

descartar *vt* (*ayuda*) to refuse, to reject; (*posibilidad*) to rule out.

descendencia *f* 1. (*hijos*) offspring. 2. (*linaje*) lineage, descent.

descender *vi* 1. (*en estimación*) to go down; ~ **a segunda** to be relegated to the second division. 2. (*cantidad, valor, temperatura, nivel*) to fall, to drop. ▶ **descender de** *vi* 1. (*avión*) to get off. 2. (*linaje*) to be descended from.

descenso *m* 1. (*en el espacio*) descent. 2. (*de cantidad, valor, temperatura, nivel*) drop.

descentralizar *vt* to decentralize.

descentrar *vt* 1. (*sacar del centro*) to knock off-centre. 2. *fig* (*desconcentrar*) to distract.

descifrar *vt* 1. (*clave, mensaje*) to decipher. 2. (*motivos, intenciones*) to work out; (*misterio*) to solve; (*problemas*) to puzzle out.

descodificador, decodificador *m* decoder.

descolgar *vt* 1. (*una cosa colgada*) to take down. 2. (*teléfono*) to pick up. ▶ **descolgarse** *vpr* (*bajar*): ~**se (por algo)** to let oneself down o to slide down (sthg).

descolocar *vt* (*objeto*) to put out of place, to disturb.

descolorido, -da *adj* faded.

descompasado, -da *adj* excessive, uncontrollable.

descomponer *vt* 1. (*pudrir - fruta*) to rot; (- *cadáver*) to decompose. 2. (*dividir*) to break down; ~ **algo en** to break sthg down into. 3. (*desordenar*) to mess up. 4. (*estropear*) to damage. ▶ **descomponerse** *vpr* 1. (*pudrirse - fruta*) to rot; (- *cadáver*) to decompose. 2. *Amer* (*averiarse*) to break down.

descomposición *f* 1. (*de elementos*) decomposition. 2. (*putrefacción - de fruta*) rotting; (- *de cadáver*) decomposition. 3. (*alteración*) distortion. 4. (*diarrea*) diarrhoea.

descompostura *f* 1. (*falta de mesura*) lack of respect, rudeness. 2. *Amer* (*avería*) breakdown.

descompuesto, -ta ♦ *pp* → **descomponer.** ♦ *adj* 1. (*putrefacto - fruta*) rotten; (- *cadáver*) decomposed. 2. (*alterado - rostro*) distorted, twisted.

descomunal *adj* enormous.

desconcentrar *vt* to distract.

desconcertante *adj* disconcerting.

desconcertar *vt* to disconcert, to throw. ▶ **desconcertarse** *vpr* to be thrown o bewildered.

desconchado *m* (*de pintura*) peeling paint; (*de enyesado*) peeling plaster.

desconcierto *m* (*desorden*) disorder; (*desorientación, confusión*) confusion.

desconectar *vt* (*aparato*) to switch off; (*línea*) to disconnect; (*desenchufar*) to unplug.

desconfianza *f* distrust.

desconfiar ▶ **desconfiar de** *vi* 1. (*sospechar de*) to distrust. 2. (*no confiar en*) to have no faith in.

descongelar *vt* 1. (*producto*) to thaw; (*nevera*) to defrost. 2. *fig* (*precios*) to free; (*créditos, salarios*) to unfreeze.

descongestionar vt 1. (MED) to clear. 2. fig (calle, centro de ciudad) to make less congested; ~ **el tráfico** to reduce congestion.

desconocer vt (ignorar) not to know.

desconocido, -da ◆ adj (no conocido) unknown. ◆ m y f stranger.

desconocimiento m ignorance.

desconsiderado, -da adj thoughtless, inconsiderate.

desconsolar vt to distress.

desconsuelo m distress, grief.

descontado, -da adj discounted. ▶ **por descontado** loc adv obviously; **dar algo por ~** to take sthg for granted.

descontar vt 1. (una cantidad) to deduct. 2. (COM) to discount.

descontentar vt to upset.

descontento, -ta adj unhappy, dissatisfied. ▶ **descontento** m dissatisfaction.

desconvocar vt to cancel, to call off.

descorazonador, -ra adj discouraging.

descorazonar vt to discourage.

descorchar vt to uncork.

descorrer vt 1. (cortinas) to draw back. 2. (cerrojo, pestillo) to draw back.

descortés adj rude.

descoser vt to unstitch. ▶ **descoserse** vpr to come unstitched.

descosido, -da adj unstitched.

descoyuntar vt to dislocate.

descrédito m discredit; **ir en ~ de algo/alguien** to count against sthg/sb.

descreído, -da m y f non-believer.

descremado, -da adj skimmed.

describir vt to describe.

descripción f description.

descrito, -ta pp → describir.

descuartizar vt (persona) to quarter; (res) to carve up.

descubierto, -ta ◆ pp → descubrir. ◆ adj 1. (gen) uncovered; (coche) open. 2. (cielo) clear. 3. (sin sombrero) bareheaded. ▶ **descubierto** m (FIN - de empresa) deficit; (- de cuenta bancaria) overdraft. ▶ **al descubierto** loc adv 1. (al raso) in the open. 2. (BANCA) overdrawn.

descubridor, -ra m y f discoverer.

descubrimiento m 1. (de continentes, invenciones) discovery. 2. (de placa, busto) unveiling. 3. (de complots) uncovering; (de asesinos) detection.

descubrir vt 1. (gen) to discover; (petróleo) to strike; (complot) to uncover. 2. (destapar - estatua, placa) to unveil.

3. (vislumbrar) to spot, to spy. 4. (delatar) to give away. ▶ **descubrirse** vpr (quitarse el sombrero) to take one's hat off; ~**se ante algo** fig to take one's hat off to sthg.

descuento m discount; **hacer ~** to give a discount; **con ~** at a discount; **un ~ del 10%** 10% off.

descuidado, -da adj 1. (desaseado - persona, aspecto) untidy; (- jardín) neglected. 2. (negligente) careless. 3. (distraído) off one's guard.

descuidar ◆ vt (desatender) to neglect. ◆ vi (no preocuparse) not to worry; **descuida, que yo me encargo** don't worry, I'll take care of it. ▶ **descuidarse** vpr 1. (abandonarse) to neglect one's appearance. 2. (despistarse) not to be careful.

descuido m 1. (falta de aseo) carelessness. 2. (olvido) oversight; (error) slip.

desde prep 1. (tiempo) since; **no lo veo ~ el mes pasado/~ ayer** I haven't seen him since last month/yesterday; **~ ahora** from now on; **~ hace mucho/un mes** for ages/a month; **~ ... hasta ...** from ... until ...; **~ el lunes hasta el viernes** from Monday till Friday; **~ entonces** since then; **~ que** since; **~ que murió mi madre** since my mother died. 2. (espacio) from; **~ ... hasta ...** from ... to ...; **~ aquí hasta el centro** from here to the centre. ▶ **desde luego** loc adv 1. (por supuesto) of course. 2. (en tono de reproche) for goodness' sake!

desdecir ▶ **desdecirse** vpr to go back on one's word; **~se de** to go back on.

desdén m disdain, scorn.

desdeñar vt to scorn.

desdeñoso, -sa adj disdainful.

desdibujarse vpr to become blurred.

desdicha f (desgracia - situación) misery; (- suceso) misfortune.

desdichado, -da adj (decisión, situación) unfortunate; (persona - sin suerte) unlucky; (- sin felicidad) unhappy.

desdicho, -cha pp → desdecir.

desdoblar vt (servilleta, carta) to unfold; (alambre) to straighten out.

desear vt 1. (querer) to want; (anhelar) to wish; **¿qué desea?** (en tienda) what can I do for you?; **desearía estar allí** I wish I was there. 2. (sexualmente) to desire.

desecar vt to dry out. ▶ **desecarse** vpr to dry out.

desechable adj disposable.

desechar vt 1. (tirar - ropa, piezas) to throw out, to discard. 2. (rechazar

- *ayuda, oferta*) to refuse, to turn down. **3.** (*desestimar - idea*) to reject; (*- plan, proyecto*) to drop.

desecho *m* (*objeto usado*) unwanted object; (*ropa*) castoff; **material de ~** (*gen*) waste products (*pl*); (*metal*) scrap. ▶ **desechos** *mpl* (*basura*) rubbish (U); (*residuos*) waste products.

desembalar *vt* to unpack.

desembarazar *vt* to clear. ▶ **desembarazarse** *vpr*: **~se de** to get rid of.

desembarcar ◆ *vt* (*pasajeros*) to disembark; (*mercancías*) to unload. ◆ *vi* **1.** (*de barco, avión*) to disembark. **2.** Amer (*de autobús, tren*) to get off. ▶ **desembarcarse** *vpr* Amer to get off.

desembarco *m* **1.** (*de pasajeros*) disembarkation. **2.** (MIL) landing.

desembarque *m* (*de mercancías*) unloading.

desembocadura *f* (*de río*) mouth; (*de calle*) opening.

desembocar ▶ **desembocar en** *vi* **1.** (*río*) to flow into. **2.** (*asunto*) to result in.

desembolso *m* payment; **~ inicial** down payment.

desempaquetar *vt* (*paquete*) to unwrap; (*caja*) to unpack.

desempatar *vi* to decide the contest; **jugar para ~** to have a play-off.

desempate *m* final result; **partido de ~** decider.

desempeñar *vt* **1.** (*función, misión*) to carry out; (*cargo, puesto*) to hold. **2.** (*papel*) to play. **3.** (*joyas*) to redeem.

desempeño *m* **1.** (*de función*) carrying out. **2.** (*de papel*) performance. **3.** (*de objeto*) redemption.

desempleado, -da *adj* unemployed.

desempleo *m* unemployment.

desempolvar *vt* **1.** (*mueble, jarrón*) to dust. **2.** *fig* (*recuerdos*) to revive.

desencadenar *vt* **1.** (*preso, perro*) to unchain. **2.** *fig* (*suceso, polémica*) to give rise to; (*reacción, furia*) to trigger off. ▶ **desencadenarse** *vpr* **1.** (*pasiones, odios, conflicto*) to erupt; (*guerra*) to break out. **2.** (*viento*) to blow up; (*tormenta*) to burst; (*terremoto*) to strike.

desencajar *vt* **1.** (*mecanismo, piezas - sin querer*) to knock out of place; (*- intencionadamente*) to take apart. **2.** (*hueso*) to dislocate. ▶ **desencajarse** *vpr* **1.** (*piezas*) to come apart. **2.** (*rostro*) to distort, to become distorted.

desencanto *m* disappointment.

desenchufar *vt* (*quitar el enchufe*) to unplug; (*apagar*) to switch off.

desenfadado, -da *adj* (*persona, conducta*) relaxed, easy-going; (*comedia, programa de TV*) light-hearted; (*estilo*) light; (*en el vestir*) casual.

desenfado *m* (*seguridad en sí mismo*) self-assurance; (*desenvoltura*) ease; (*desparpajo*) uninhibited nature.

desenfocado, -da *adj* (*imagen*) out of focus; (*visión*) blurred.

desenfrenado, -da *adj* (*ritmo, baile*) frantic, frenzied; (*comportamiento*) uncontrolled; (*apetito*) insatiable.

desenfreno *m* **1.** (*gen*) lack of restraint. **2.** (*vicio*) debauchery.

desenfundar *vt* (*pistola*) to draw.

desenganchar *vt* **1.** (*vagón*) to uncouple. **2.** (*caballo*) to unhitch. **3.** (*pelo, jersey*) to free.

desengañar *vt* **1.** (*a una persona equivocada*): **~ a alguien** to reveal the truth to sb. **2.** (*a una persona esperanzada*) to disillusion.

desengaño *m* disappointment; **llevarse un ~ con alguien** to be disappointed in sb.

desenlace *m* denouement, ending.

desenmarañar *vt* **1.** (*ovillo, pelo*) to untangle. **2.** *fig* (*asunto*) to sort out; (*problema*) to resolve.

desenmascarar *vt* (*descubrir*) to unmask.

desenredar *vt* **1.** (*hilos, pelo*) to untangle. **2.** *fig* (*asunto*) to sort out; (*problema*) to resolve. ▶ **desenredarse** *vpr*: **~se (de algo)** to extricate oneself (from sthg).

desenrollar *vt* (*hilo, cinta*) to unwind; (*persiana*) to roll down; (*pergamino, papel*) to unroll.

desenroscar *vt* to unscrew.

desentenderse *vpr* to pretend not to hear/know *etc*.

desenterrar *vt* (*cadáver*) to disinter; (*tesoro, escultura*) to dig up.

desentonar *vi* **1.** (MÚS *- cantante*) to sing out of tune; (*- instrumento*) to be out of tune. **2.** (*color, cortinas, edificio*): **~ (con)** to clash (with).

desentumecer *vt* to stretch. ▶ **desentumecerse** *vpr* to loosen up.

desenvoltura *f* (*al moverse, comportarse*) ease; (*al hablar*) fluency.

desenvolver *vt* to unwrap. ▶ **desenvolverse** *vpr* **1.** (*asunto, proceso*) to progress; (*trama*) to unfold; (*entrevista*) to pass off. **2.** (*persona*) to cope, to manage.

desenvuelto, -ta ♦ *pp* → **desenvolver**. ♦ *adj* (*al moverse, comportarse*)
natural; (*al hablar*) fluent.
deseo *m* 1. (*pasión*) desire. 2. (*anhelo*)
wish; **buenos ~s** good intentions.
deseoso, -sa *adj*: **estar ~ de algo/
hacer algo** to long for sthg/to do sthg.
desequilibrado, -da *adj* 1. (*persona*)
unbalanced. 2. (*balanza, eje*) off-centre.
desequilibrio *m* (*mecánico*) lack of balance; (*mental*) mental instability.
desertar *vi* to desert.
desértico, -ca *adj* (*del desierto*) desert
(*antes de sust*); (*despoblado*) deserted.
desertización *f* (*del terreno*) desertifi-
cation; (*de la población*) depopulation.
desertor, -ra *m y f* deserter.
desesperación *f* (*falta de esperanza*)
despair, desperation; **con ~** in despair.
desesperado, -da *adj* (*persona, intento*) desperate; (*estado, situación*) hopeless; (*esfuerzo*) furious.
desesperante *adj* infuriating.
desesperar *vt* 1. (*quitar la esperanza*) to
drive to despair. 2. (*irritar, enojar*) to
exasperate, to drive mad. ▶ **desesperarse** *vpr* 1. (*perder la esperanza*) to be
driven to despair. 2. (*irritarse, enojarse*)
to get mad o exasperated.
desestabilizar *vt* to destabilize.
desestimar *vt* 1. (*rechazar*) to turn
down. 2. (*despreciar*) to turn one's nose
up at.
desfachatez *f fam* cheek.
desfalco *m* embezzlement.
desfallecer *vi* 1. (*debilitarse*) to be
exhausted; **~ de** to feel faint from.
2. (*desmayarse*) to faint.
desfasado, -da *adj* (*persona*) out of
touch; (*libro, moda*) out of date.
desfase *m* (*diferencia*) gap.
desfavorable *adj* unfavourable.
desfigurar *vt* 1. (*rostro, cuerpo*) to disfigure. 2. *fig* (*la verdad*) to distort.
desfiladero *m* narrow mountain pass.
desfilar *vi* (MIL) to parade.
desfile *m* (MIL) parade; (*de carrozas*)
procession.
desfogar *vt* to vent. ▶ **desfogarse**
vpr to let off steam.
desgajar *vt* (*página*) to tear out; (*rama*)
to break off; (*libro, periódico*) to rip up;
(*naranja*) to split into segments. ▶ **des-
gajarse** *vpr* (*rama*) to break off; (*hoja*) to
fall.
desgana *f* 1. (*falta de hambre*) lack of
appetite. 2. (*falta de ánimo*) lack of

enthusiasm; **con ~** unwillingly, reluctantly.
desganado, -da *adj* (*sin apetito*): **estar
~** to be off one's food.
desgarbado, -da *adj* clumsy, ungainly.
desgarrador, -ra *adj* harrowing.
desgarrar *vt* to rip; **~ el corazón** to
break one's heart.
desgarro *m* tear.
desgastar *vt* to wear out. ▶ **desgastarse** *vpr* to wear o.s. out.
desgaste *m* 1. (*de tela, muebles etc*) wear
and tear; (*de roca*) erosion; (*de pilas*) running down; (*de cuerdas*) fraying; (*de metal*)
corrosion. 2. (*de persona*) wear and tear;
(*de dirigentes*) losing one's touch.
desglosar *vt* to break down.
desglose *m* breakdown.
desgracia *f* 1. (*mala suerte*) misfortune; **por ~** unfortunately. 2. (*catástrofe*)
disaster; **~s personales** casualties; **es
una ~ que ...** it's a terrible shame that
... 3. *loc*: **caer en ~** to fall into disgrace.
desgraciadamente *adv* unfortunately.
desgraciado, -da *adj* 1. (*gen*) unfortunate. 2. (*sin suerte*) unlucky. 3. (*infeliz*)
unhappy.
desgravar *vt* to deduct from one's
tax bill.
desgreñado, -da *adj* dishevelled.
desguace *m* (*de coches*) scrapping; (*de
buques*) breaking.
deshabitado, -da *adj* uninhabited.
deshabituar *vt*: **~ a alguien (de)** to get
sb out of the habit (of).
deshacer *vt* 1. (*costura, nudo, paquete*) to
undo; (*maleta*) to unpack; (*tarta, castillo de
arena*) to destroy. 2. (*disolver - helado,
mantequilla*) to melt; (- *pastilla, terrón de
azúcar*) to dissolve. 3. (*poner fin a - contrato, negocio*) to cancel; (- *pacto, tratado*) to
break; (- *plan, intriga*) to foil; (- *organización*) to dissolve. 4. (*destruir - enemigo*)
to rout; (- *matrimonio*) to ruin. ▶ **deshacerse** *vpr* 1. (*desvanecerse*) to disappear. 2. *fig* (*librarse*): **~se de** to get rid of.
3. *fig*: **~se en algo (con o hacia alguien)**
(*cumplidos*) to lavish sthg (on sb); (*insultos*) to heap sthg (on sb).
desharrapado, -da *adj* ragged.
deshecho, -cha ♦ *pp* → **deshacer**.
♦ *adj* 1. (*costura, nudo, paquete*) undone;
(*cama*) unmade; (*maleta*) unpacked.
2. (*enemigo*) destroyed; (*tarta, matrimonio*) ruined. 3. (*derretido - pastilla, terrón de
azúcar*) dissolved; (- *helado, mantequilla*)

melted. **4.** (*afligido*) devastated. **5.** (*cansado*) tired out.

desheredar *vt* to disinherit.

deshidratar *vt* to dehydrate.

deshielo *m* thaw.

deshilachar *vt* to unravel. ▶ **deshilacharse** *vpr* to fray.

deshinchar *vt* **1.** (*globo, rueda*) to let down, to deflate. **2.** (*hinchazón*) to reduce the swelling in. ▶ **deshincharse** *vpr* (*globo, hinchazón*) to go down; (*neumático*) to go flat.

deshojar *vt* (*árbol*) to strip the leaves off; (*flor*) to pull the petals off; (*libro*) to pull the pages out of. ▶ **deshojarse** *vpr* (*árbol*) to shed its leaves; (*flor*) to drop its petals.

deshonesto, -ta *adj* (*sin honradez*) dishonest; (*sin pudor*) indecent.

deshonor *m*, **deshonra** *f* dishonour.

deshonrar *vt* to dishonour.

deshora ▶ **a deshora, a deshoras** *loc adv* (*en momento inoportuno*) at a bad time; (*en horas poco habituales*) at an unearthly hour.

deshuesar *vt* (*carne*) to bone; (*fruto*) to stone.

desidia *f* (*en el trabajo*) neglect; (*en el aspecto*) slovenliness.

desierto, -ta *adj* **1.** (*gen*) deserted. **2.** (*vacante - premio*) deferred. ▶ **desierto** *m* desert.

designación *f* **1.** (*nombre*) designation. **2.** (*nombramiento*) appointment.

designar *vt* **1.** (*nombrar*) to appoint. **2.** (*fijar, determinar*) to name, to fix.

designio *m* intention, plan.

desigual *adj* **1.** (*diferente*) different; (*terreno*) uneven. **2.** (*tiempo, persona, humor*) changeable; (*alumno, actuación*) inconsistent; (*lucha*) unevenly matched, unequal; (*tratamiento*) unfair, unequal.

desilusión *f* disappointment, disillusionment (U); **llevarse una ~** to be disappointed.

desilusionar *vt* (*desengañar*) to reveal the truth to; (*decepcionar*) to disappoint, to disillusion. ▶ **desilusionarse** *vpr* (*decepcionarse*) to be disappointed o disillusioned; (*desengañarse*) to realize the truth.

desinfección *f* disinfection.

desinfectar *vt* to disinfect.

desinflar *vt* (*quitar aire*) to deflate. ▶ **desinflarse** *vpr* (*perder aire - gen*) to go down; (*- neumático*) to go flat.

desinformar *vt* to misinform.

desintegración *f* **1.** (*de objetos*) disintegration. **2.** (*de grupos, organizaciones*) breaking up.

desintegrar *vt* **1.** (*objetos*) to disintegrate; (*átomo*) to split. **2.** (*grupos, organizaciones*) to break up.

desinterés *m* **1.** (*indiferencia*) disinterest. **2.** (*generosidad*) unselfishness.

desinteresado, -da *adj* unselfish.

desinteresarse *vpr*: **~ de** o **por algo** to lose interest in sthg.

desistir *vi*: **~ (de hacer algo)** to give up o to stop (doing sthg).

desleal *adj*: **~ (con)** disloyal (to); (*competencia*) unfair.

deslealtad *f* disloyalty.

desleír *vt* (*sólido*) to dissolve; (*líquido*) to dilute.

desligar *vt* **1.** (*desatar*) to untie. **2.** *fig* (*separar*): **~ algo (de)** to separate sthg (from). ▶ **desligarse** *vpr* (*desatarse*) to untie oneself. **2.** *fig* (*separarse*): **~se de** to become separated from; **~se de un grupo** to distance o.s. from a group.

deslindar *vt* **1.** (*limitar*) to mark out (the boundaries of). **2.** *fig* (*separar*) to define.

desliz *m* slip, error; **tener** o **cometer un ~** to slip up.

deslizar *vt* (*mano, objeto*): **~ algo en** to slip sthg into; **~ algo por algo** to slide sthg along sthg. ▶ **deslizarse** *vpr* (*resbalar*): **~se por** to slide along.

deslomar *vt* (*a golpes*) to thrash.

deslucido, -da *adj* **1.** (*sin brillo*) faded; (*plata*) tarnished. **2.** (*sin gracia - acto, ceremonia*) dull; (*- actuación*) lacklustre.

deslumbrar *vt* *lit & fig* to dazzle.

desmadrarse *vpr* *fam* to go wild.

desmadre *m* *fam* chaos.

desmán *m* **1.** (*con la bebida, comida etc*) excess. **2.** (*abuso de poder*) abuse (of power).

desmandarse *vpr* **1.** (*desobedecer*) to be disobedient. **2.** (*insubordinarse*) to get out of hand.

desmantelar *vt* (*casa, fábrica*) to clear out, to strip; (*organización*) to disband; (*arsenal, andamio*) to dismantle; (*barco*) to unrig.

desmaquillador *m* make-up remover.

desmayar *vi* to lose heart. ▶ **desmayarse** *vpr* to faint.

desmayo *m* (*físico*) fainting fit; **sufrir ~** to have fainting fits.

desmedido, -da *adj* excessive, disproportionate.

desmelenado, -da adj 1. (*persona*) reckless, wild. 2. (*cabello*) tousled.

desmembrar vt 1. (*trocear - cuerpo*) to dismember; (*- miembro, extremidad*) to cut off. 2. (*disgregar*) to break up.

desmemoriado, -da adj forgetful.

desmentir vt 1. (*negar*) to deny. 2. (*no corresponder*) to belie.

desmenuzar vt 1. (*trocear - pan, pastel, roca*) to crumble; (*- carne*) to chop up; (*- papel*) to tear up into little pieces. 2. *fig* (*examinar, analizar*) to scrutinize.

desmerecer ◆ vt to be unworthy of. ◆ vi to lose value; **~ (en algo) de alguien** to be inferior to sb (in sthg).

desmesurado, -da adj (*excesivo*) excessive, disproportionate; (*enorme*) enormous.

desmitificar vt to demythologize.

desmontar vt 1. (*desarmar - máquina*) to take apart o to pieces; (*- motor*) to strip down; (*- piezas*) to dismantle; (*- rueda*) to remove, to take off; (*- tienda de campaña*) to take down; (*- arma*) to uncock. 2. (*jinete - suj: caballo*) to unseat; (*- suj: persona*) to help down.

desmoralizar vt to demoralize.

desmoronar vt (*edificios, rocas*) to cause to crumble. ► **desmoronarse** vpr (*edificio, roca, ideales*) to crumble.

desnatado, -da adj skimmed.

desnaturalizado, -da adj (*sustancia*) adulterated; (*alcohol*) denatured.

desnivel m (*del terreno*) irregularity, unevenness (U).

desnivelar vt to make uneven; (*balanza*) to tip.

desnucar vt to break the neck of.

desnudar vt 1. (*persona*) to undress. 2. *fig* (*cosa*) to strip. ► **desnudarse** vpr to get undressed.

desnudez f (*de persona*) nakedness, nudity; (*de cosa*) bareness.

desnudo, -da adj 1. (*persona, cuerpo*) naked. 2. *fig* (*salón, hombro, árbol*) bare; (*verdad*) plain; (*paisaje*) barren. ► **desnudo** m nude.

desnutrición f malnutrition.

desobedecer vt to disobey.

desobediencia f disobedience.

desobediente adj disobedient.

desocupado, -da adj 1. (*persona - ocioso*) free, unoccupied; (*- sin empleo*) unemployed. 2. (*lugar*) vacant.

desocupar vt (*edificio*) to vacate; (*habitación, mesa*) to leave.

desodorante m deodorant.

desolación f 1. (*destrucción*) desola-

tion. 2. (*desconsuelo*) distress, grief.

desolar vt 1. (*destruir*) to devastate, to lay waste. 2. (*afligir*) to cause anguish to.

desorbitado, -da adj 1. (*gen*) disproportionate; (*precio*) exorbitant. 2. *loc*: **con los ojos ~s** pop-eyed.

desorden m 1. (*confusión*) disorder, chaos; (*falta de orden*) mess. 2. (*disturbio*) disturbance.

desordenado, -da adj (*habitación, persona*) untidy, messy; (*documentos, fichas*) jumbled (up).

desorganización f disorganization.

desorganizar vt to disrupt, to disorganize.

desorientar vt 1. (*en el espacio*) to disorientate, to mislead. 2. *fig* (*en la mente*) to confuse. ► **desorientarse** vpr to lose one's way o bearings.

despabilado, -da adj 1. (*despierto*) wide-awake. 2. (*listo*) smart, quick.

despabilar vt 1. (*despertar*) to wake up. 2. (*hacer más avispado*) to make streetwise. ► **despabilarse** vpr 1. (*despertarse*) to wake up. 2. (*darse prisa*) to hurry up.

despachar ◆ vt 1. (*mercancía*) to dispatch. 2. (*en tienda - cliente*) to serve; (*- entradas, bebidas etc*) to sell. 3. *fam fig* (*terminar - trabajo, discurso*) to finish off. 4. (*asunto, negocio*) to settle. 5. *Amer* (*facturar*) to check in. ◆ vi (*en una tienda*) to serve.

despacho m 1. (*oficina*) office; (*en casa*) study. 2. (*comunicación oficial*) dispatch. 3. (*venta*) sale; (*lugar de venta*): **~ de billetes/localidades** ticket/box office.

despacio adv slowly.

desparpajo m *fam* forwardness, self-assurance.

desparramar vt (*líquido*) to spill; (*objetos*) to spread, to scatter.

despecho m (*rencor, venganza*) spite; (*desengaño*) bitterness; **(hacer algo) por ~** (to do sthg) out of spite.

despectivo, -va adj 1. (*despreciativo*) contemptuous, scornful. 2. (GRAM) pejorative.

despedazar vt 1. (*físicamente*) to tear apart. 2. *fig* (*moralmente*) to shatter.

despedida f (*adiós*) farewell.

despedir vt 1. (*decir adiós*) to say goodbye to; **fuimos a ~le a la estación** we went to see him off at the station. 2. (*echar - de un empleo*) to dismiss, to sack; (*- de un club*) to throw out. 3. (*lanzar, arrojar*) to fling; **salir despedido de/**

por/hacia algo to fly out of/through/ towards sthg. **4.** *fig (difundir, desprender)* to give off. ► **despedirse** *vpr (gen):* ~se **(de)** to say goodbye (to); *(en carta):* **Se despide atentamente** Yours faithfully.

despegar ◆ *vt* to unstick. ◆ *vi (avión)* to take off. ► **despegarse** *vpr (etiqueta, pegatina, sello)* to come unstuck.

despegue *m* takeoff.

despeinar *vt (pelo)* to ruffle; ~ a **alguien** to mess up sb's hair. ► **despeinarse** *vpr* to mess up one's hair.

despejado, -da *adj* **1.** *(tiempo, día)* clear. **2.** *fig (persona, mente)* alert. **3.** *(espacio - ancho)* spacious; *(- sin estorbos)* clear, uncluttered.

despejar *vt (gen)* to clear. ► **despejarse** *vpr* **1.** *(persona - espabilarse)* to clear one's head; *(- despertarse)* to wake o.s. up. **2.** *(tiempo)* to clear up; *(cielo)* to clear.

despeje *m* (DEP) clearance.

despellejar *vt (animal)* to skin.

despensa *f* larder, pantry.

despeñadero *m* precipice.

despeñar *vt* to throw over a cliff. ► **despeñarse** *vpr* to fall over a cliff.

desperdiciar *vt (tiempo, comida)* to waste; *(dinero)* to squander; *(ocasión)* to throw away.

desperdicio *m* **1.** *(acción)* waste. **2.** *(residuo):* ~s scraps.

desperdigar *vt* to scatter, to disperse.

desperezarse *vpr* to stretch.

desperfecto *m (deterioro)* damage (U); *(defecto)* flaw, imperfection.

despertador *m* alarm clock.

despertar ◆ *vt* **1.** *(persona, animal)* to wake (up). **2.** *fig (reacción)* to arouse. **3.** *fig (recuerdo)* to revive, to awaken. ◆ *vi* to wake up. ◆ *m* awakening. ► **despertarse** *vpr* to wake up.

despiadado, -da *adj* pitiless, merciless.

despido *m* dismissal, sacking.

despierto, -ta *adj* **1.** *(sin dormir)* awake. **2.** *fig (espabilado, listo)* sharp.

despilfarrar *vt (dinero)* to squander; *(electricidad, agua etc)* to waste.

despilfarro *m (de dinero)* squandering; *(de energía, agua etc)* waste.

despiole *m* Amer fam rumpus, shindy.

despistado, -da *adj* absent-minded.

despistar *vt* **1.** *(dar esquinazo)* to throw off the scent. **2.** *fig (confundir)* to mislead. ► **despistarse** *vpr* **1.** *(perderse)* to

lose one's way, to get lost. **2.** *fig (distraerse)* to get confused.

despiste *m (distracción)* absent-mindedness; *(error)* mistake, slip.

desplante *m* rude remark.

desplazamiento *m* **1.** *(viaje)* journey; *(traslado)* move. **2.** (NÁUT) displacement.

desplazar *vt* **1.** *(trasladar)* to move. **2.** *fig (desbancar)* to take the place of; ~ a **alguien/algo de** to remove sb/sthg from. ► **desplazarse** *vpr (viajar)* to travel; *(moverse)* to move.

desplegar *vt* **1.** *(tela, periódico, mapa)* to unfold; *(alas)* to spread, to open; *(bandera)* to unfurl. **2.** *(cualidad)* to display. **3.** (MIL) to deploy.

despliegue *m* **1.** *(de cualidad)* display. **2.** (MIL) deployment.

desplomarse *vpr (gen)* to collapse; *(techo)* to fall in.

desplumar *vt* **1.** *(ave)* to pluck. **2.** *fig (estafar)* to fleece.

despoblado, -da *adj (deshabitado)* uninhabited.

despojar *vt:* ~ a **alguien de algo** to strip sb of sthg. ► **despojarse** *vpr:* ~se **de algo** *(bienes, alimentos)* to give sthg up; *(abrigo, chándal)* to take sthg off.

despojo *m (acción)* plundering. ► **despojos** *mpl* **1.** *(sobras, residuos)* leftovers. **2.** *(de animales)* offal (U).

desposar *vt* to marry. ► **desposarse** *vpr* to get married.

desposeer *vt:* ~ a **alguien de** to dispossess sb of.

déspota *m y f* despot.

despotricar *vi:* ~ **(contra)** to rant on (at).

despreciar *vt* **1.** *(desdeñar)* to scorn. **2.** *(rechazar)* to spurn.

desprecio *m* scorn, contempt.

desprender *vt* **1.** *(lo que estaba fijo)* to remove, to detach. **2.** *(olor, luz)* to give off. ► **desprenderse** *vpr* **1.** *(caerse, soltarse)* to come o fall off. **2.** *fig (deducirse):* **de sus palabras se desprende que ...** from his words it is clear o it can be seen that ... **3.** *(librarse):* ~se **de** to get rid of.

desprendimiento *m (separación)* detachment; ~ **de tierras** landslide.

despreocupado, -da *adj (libre de preocupaciones)* unworried, unconcerned; *(en el vestir)* casual.

despreocuparse ► **despreocuparse de** *vpr (asunto)* to stop worrying about.

desprestigiar vt to discredit.

desprevenido, -da adj unprepared; **coger** o **pillar ~ a alguien** to catch sb unawares, to take sb by surprise.

desproporcionado, -da adj disproportionate.

despropósito m stupid remark.

desprovisto, -ta adj: ~ **de** lacking in, devoid of.

después adv 1. (en el tiempo - más tarde) afterwards, later; (- entonces) then; (- justo lo siguiente) next; **poco ~** soon after; **años ~** years later; **ellos llegaron ~** they arrived later; **llamé primero y ~ entré** I knocked first and then I went in; **yo voy ~** it's my turn next. 2. (en el espacio) next, after; **¿qué viene ~?** what comes next o after?; **hay una farmacia y ~ está mi casa** there's a chemist's and then there's my house. 3. (en una lista) further down. ▶ **después de** loc prep after; **llegó ~ de ti** she arrived after you; **~ de él, nadie lo ha conseguido** since he did it, no one else has; **~ de hacer algo** after doing sthg. ▶ **después de todo** loc adv after all.

despuntar ◆ vt (romper) to break the point off; (desgastar) to blunt. ◆ vi 1. fig (persona) to excel. 2. (alba) to break; (día) to dawn.

desquiciar vt fig (desequilibrar) to derange; (sacar de quicio) to drive mad.

desquite m revenge.

destacamento m detachment.

destacar ◆ vt 1. (poner de relieve) to emphasize, to highlight; **cabe ~ que ...** it is important to point out that ... 2. (MIL) to detach, to detail. ◆ vi (sobresalir) to stand out. ▶ **destacarse** vpr: **~se (de/por)** to stand out (from/because of).

destajo m piecework; **trabajar a ~** (por trabajo hecho) to do piecework; fig (afanosamente) to work flat out.

destapar vt 1. (abrir - caja, botella) to open; (olla) to take the lid off; (descorchar) to uncork. 2. (descubrir) to uncover. ▶ **destaparse** vpr (desabrigarse) to lose the covers.

destartalado, -da adj (viejo, deteriorado) dilapidated; (desordenado) untidy.

destello m 1. (de luz, brillo) sparkle; (de estrella) twinkle. 2. fig (manifestación momentánea) glimmer.

destemplado, -da adj 1. (persona) out of sorts. 2. (tiempo, clima) unpleasant. 3. (carácter, actitud) irritable.

desteñir ◆ vt to fade, to bleach. ◆ vi to run, not to be colour fast.

desternillarse vpr: ~ **de risa** to split one's sides laughing o with laughter.

desterrar vt (persona) to banish, to exile.

destetar vt to wean.

destiempo ▶ **a destiempo** loc adv at the wrong time.

destierro m exile; **en el ~** in exile.

destilar vt (agua, petróleo) to distil.

destilería f distillery.

destinar vt 1. ~ **algo a** o **para** (cantidad, edificio) to set sthg aside for; (empleo, cargo) to assign sthg to; (carta) to address sthg to; (medidas, programa, publicación) to aim sthg at. 2. ~ **a alguien a** (cargo, empleo) to appoint sb to; (plaza, lugar) to post sb to.

destinatario, -ria m y f addressee.

destino m 1. (sino) destiny, fate. 2. (rumbo) destination; **(ir) con ~ a** (to be) bound for o going to; **un vuelo con ~ a ...** a flight to ... 3. (empleo, plaza) position, post. 4. (finalidad) function.

destitución f dismissal.

destituir vt to dismiss.

destornillador m screwdriver.

destornillar vt to unscrew.

destreza f skill, dexterity.

destrozar vt 1. (físicamente - romper) to smash; (- estropear) to ruin. 2. (moralmente - persona) to shatter, to devastate; (- vida) to ruin.

destrozo m damage (U); **ocasionar grandes ~s** to cause a lot of damage.

destrucción f destruction.

destruir vt 1. (gen) to destroy; (casa, argumento) to demolish. 2. (proyecto) to ruin, to wreck; (ilusión) to dash.

desuso m disuse; **caer en ~** to become obsolete, to fall into disuse.

desvaído, -da adj (color) pale, washed-out; (forma, contorno) blurred; (mirada) vague.

desvalido, -da adj needy, destitute.

desvalijar vt (casa) to burgle; (persona) to rob.

desván m attic, loft.

desvanecer vt 1. (humo, nubes) to dissipate. 2. (sospechas, temores) to dispel. ▶ **desvanecerse** vpr 1. (desmayarse) to faint. 2. (disiparse - humo, nubes) to clear, to disappear; (- sonido, sospechas, temores) to fade away.

desvanecimiento m (desmayo) fainting fit.

desvariar vi (delirar) to be delirious; (decir locuras) to talk nonsense, to rave.

desvarío m 1. (dicho) raving; (hecho) act of madness. 2. (delirio) delirium.

desvelar vt 1. (quitar el sueño) to keep awake. 2. (noticia, secreto etc) to reveal.
▶ **desvelarse por** vpr: ~se por hacer algo to make every effort to do sthg.

desvelo m (esfuerzo) effort.

desvencijado, -da adj (silla, mesa) rickety; (camión, coche) battered.

desventaja f disadvantage; **en ~** at a disadvantage.

desventura f misfortune.

desvergonzado, -da adj shameless.

desvergüenza f (atrevimiento, frescura) shamelessness.

desvestir vt to undress. ▶ **desvestirse** vpr to undress (o.s.).

desviación f 1. (de dirección, cauce, norma) deviation. 2. (en la carretera) diversion, detour.

desviar vt (río, carretera, tráfico) to divert; (dirección) to change; (golpe) to parry; (pelota, disparo) to deflect; (pregunta) to evade; (conversación) to change the direction of; (mirada, ojos) to avert.
▶ **desviarse** vpr (cambiar de dirección - conductor) to take a detour; (- avión, barco) to go off course; ~se de to turn off.

desvío m diversion, detour.

desvirtuar vt (gen) to detract from; (estropear) to spoil; (verdadero sentido) to distort.

desvivirse vpr (desvelarse): ~ (por alguien/algo) to do everything one can (for sb/sthg); ~ por hacer algo to bend over backwards to do sthg.

detallado, -da adj detailed, thorough.

detallar vt (historia, hechos) to detail, to give a rundown of; (cuenta, gastos) to itemize.

detalle m 1. (gen) detail; **con ~** in detail; **entrar en ~s** to go into detail. 2. (atención) kind gesture o thought; **tener un ~ con alguien** to be thoughtful o considerate to sb. ▶ **al detalle** loc adv (COM) retail.

detallista m y f (COM) retailer.

detectar vt to detect.

detective m y f detective.

detener vt 1. (arrestar) to arrest. 2. (parar) to stop; (retrasar) to hold up.
▶ **detenerse** vpr 1. (pararse) to stop. 2. (demorarse) to linger.

detenidamente adv carefully, thoroughly.

detenido, -da ◆ adj 1. (detallado) thorough. 2. (arrestado): **(estar) ~ (to be)** under arrest. ◆ m y f prisoner.

detenimiento ▶ **con detenimiento** loc adv carefully, thoroughly.

detergente m detergent.

deteriorar vt to damage, to spoil.
▶ **deteriorarse** vpr fig (empeorar) to deteriorate, to get worse.

deterioro m (daño) damage; (empeoramiento) deterioration.

determinación f 1. (fijación - de precio etc) settling, fixing. 2. (resolución) determination, resolution. 3. (decisión): **tomar una ~** to take a decision.

determinado, -da adj 1. (concreto) specific; (en particular) particular. 2. (resuelto) determined. 3. (GRAM) definite.

determinar vt 1. (fijar - fecha, precio) to settle, to fix. 2. (averiguar) to determine. 3. (motivar) to cause, to bring about. 4. (decidir) to decide; ~ hacer algo to decide to do sthg. ▶ **determinarse** vpr: ~se a hacer algo to make up one's mind to do sthg.

detestar vt to detest.

detonante m (explosivo) explosive.

detractor, -ra m y f detractor.

detrás adv 1. (en el espacio) behind; **tus amigos vienen ~** your friends are coming on behind; **el interruptor está ~** the switch is at the back. 2. (en el orden) then, afterwards; **Portugal y ~ Puerto Rico** Portugal and then Puerto Rico.
▶ **detrás de** loc prep (gen) behind.
▶ **por detrás** loc adv at the back; **hablar de alguien por ~** to talk about sb behind his/her back.

detrimento m damage; **en ~ de** to the detriment of.

detrito m (BIOL) detritus. ▶ **detritos** mpl (residuos) waste (U).

deuda f debt; **~ pública** (ECON) national debt Br, public debt Am.

deudor, -ra ◆ adj (saldo) debit (antes de sust); (entidad) indebted. ◆ m y f debtor.

devaluación f devaluation.

devaluar vt to devalue.

devanar vt to wind.

devaneos mpl (amoríos) affairs; (coqueteos) flirting (U).

devastador, -ra adj devastating.

devastar vt to devastate.

devenir ◆ m transformation. ◆ vi (convertirse): ~ **en** to become, to turn into.

dibujo

devoción f: ~ (por) devotion (to).
devocionario m prayer book.
devolución f (gen) return; (de dinero) refund.
devolver ◆ vt 1. (restituir): ~ algo (a) (coche, dinero etc) to give sthg back (to); (producto defectuoso, carta) to return sthg (to). 2. (restablecer, colocar en su sitio): ~ algo a to return sthg to. 3. (favor, agravio) to pay back for; (visita) to return. 4. (vomitar) to bring o throw up. ◆ vi to throw up. ▸ **devolverse** vpr Amer to come back.
devorar vt lit & fig to devour.
devoto, -ta ◆ adj (piadoso) devout; ser ~ de to have a devotion for. ◆ m y f (admirador) devotee.
devuelto, -ta pp → devolver.
dg (abrev de decigramo) dg.
di etc 1. → dar. 2. → decir.
día m 1. (gen) day; me voy el ~ ocho I'm going on the eighth; ¿qué ~ es hoy? Amer, ¿a qué ~ estamos? what day is it today?; ¿qué tal ~ hace? what's the weather like today?; todos los ~s every day; ~ de los difuntos All Souls' Day; ~ de la Hispanidad Columbus Day; ~ de los inocentes 28th December, ≃ April Fools' Day; ~ de los muertos Amer All Souls' Day; ~ de Todos los Santos All Saints' Day; ~ del Trabajo Labour Day; ~ de pago payday; ~ festivo (public) holiday; ~ hábil o laborable o de trabajo working day; de ~ en ~ from day to day, day by day; del ~ fresh; hoy (en) ~ nowadays; todo el (santo) ~ all day long; el ~ de mañana in the future; al ~ siguiente on the following day; un ~ sí y otro no every other day; menú del ~ today's menu. 2. (luz) daytime, day; es de ~ it's daytime; hacer algo de ~ to do sthg in the daytime o during the day; ~ y noche day and night; en pleno ~, a plena luz del ~ in broad daylight. 3. loc: estar/ponerse al ~ (de) to be/get up to date (with); poner algo/a alguien al ~ to update sthg/sb; vivir al ~ to live from hand to mouth. ▸ **buen día** interj Amer: ¡buen ~! good morning! ▸ **buenos días** interj: ¡buenos ~! (gen) hello!; (por la mañana) good morning!

DÍA DE LOS INOCENTES
On 28 December, it is traditional for Spanish people to play tricks and practical jokes known as 'inocentadas' on each other, the most typical of which is to stick a paper doll to somebody's back without them realizing. It is also common for the media to run false stories aimed at duping the public.

DÍA DE LOS MUERTOS
In Mexico, 'Day of the Dead' is the name given to All Souls' Day. Officially, the Day of the Dead is 2 November, although the celebrations start on 1 November. Children dress up as skeletons, mummies, vampires etc, and the shops sell brightly-coloured sugar and chocolate skulls bearing the name of a dead person. These will form part of an offering to dead friends and relatives which may also include 'pan de muerto', a type of large, round cake coated in sugar.

diabético, -ca adj, m y f diabetic.
diablo m lit & fig devil; pobre ~ poor devil.
diablura f prank.
diabólico, -ca adj 1. (del diablo) diabolic. 2. fig (muy malo, difícil) diabolical.
diadema f (para el pelo) hairband.
diáfano, -na adj 1. (transparente) transparent, diaphanous. 2. fig (claro) clear.
diafragma m diaphragm.
diagnosticar vt to diagnose.
diagnóstico m diagnosis.
diagonal adj & f diagonal.
diagrama m diagram.
dial m dial.
dialecto m dialect.
dialogar vi: ~ (con) (hablar) to have a conversation (with), to talk (to); (negociar) to hold a dialogue o talks (with).
diálogo m (conversación) conversation; (LITER & POLÍT) dialogue.
diamante m (piedra preciosa) diamond.
diámetro m diameter.
diana f 1. (en blanco de tiro) bull's-eye, bull. 2. (en cuartel) reveille.
diapasón m tuning fork.
diapositiva f slide, transparency.
diario, -ria adj daily; a ~ every day; ropa de ~ everyday clothes. ▸ **diario** m 1. (periódico) newspaper, daily. 2. (relación día a día) diary; ~ de sesiones parliamentary report.
diarrea f diarrhoea.
dibujante m y f (gen) sketcher; (de dibujos animados) cartoonist; (de dibujo técnico) draughtsman (f draughtswoman).
dibujar vt & vi to draw, to sketch.
dibujo m 1. (gen) drawing; ~s animados cartoons; ~ artístico art; ~ lineal techni-

cal drawing. **2.** (*de tela, prenda etc*) pattern.

diccionario *m* dictionary.

dice → **decir**.

dicha *f* (*alegría*) joy.

dicho, -cha ◆ *pp* → **decir**. ◆ *adj* said, aforementioned; **~s hombres** the said men, these men; **lo ~** what I/we *etc* said; **o mejor ~** or rather; **~ y hecho** no sooner said than done. ▶ **dicho** *m* saying.

dichoso, -sa *adj* (*feliz*) happy; (*afortunado*) fortunate.

diciembre *m* December; *ver también* **septiembre**.

dicotomía *f* dichotomy.

dictado *m* dictation; **escribir al ~** to take dictation.

dictador, -ra *m y f* dictator.

dictadura *f* dictatorship.

dictáfono *m* Dictaphone®.

dictamen *m* (*opinión*) opinion, judgment; (*informe*) report.

dictar *vt* **1.** (*texto*) to dictate. **2.** (*emitir - sentencia, fallo*) to pronounce, to pass; (*- ley*) to enact; (*- decreto*) to issue.

didáctico, -ca *adj* didactic.

diecinueve *núm* nineteen; *ver también* **seis**.

dieciocho *núm* eighteen; *ver también* **seis**.

dieciséis *núm* sixteen; *ver también* **seis**.

diecisiete *núm* seventeen; *ver también* **seis**.

diente *m* tooth; **~ de leche** milk tooth; **armado hasta los ~s** armed to the teeth; **hablar entre ~s** to mumble, to mutter. ▶ **diente de ajo** *m* clove of garlic.

diera → **dar**.

diéresis *f inv* diaeresis.

dieron *etc* → **dar**.

diesel, diésel *adj* diesel.

diestro, -tra *adj* (*hábil*): **~ (en)** skilful (at); **a ~ y siniestro** *fig* left, right and centre, all over the place.

dieta *f* (MED) diet. ▶ **dietas** *fpl* (COM) expenses.

dietético, -ca *adj* dietetic, dietary. ▶ **dietética** *f* dietetics (U).

diez ◆ *núm* ten; *ver también* **seis**. ◆ *m* (*en la escuela*) A, top marks (*pl*).

difamar *vt* (*verbalmente*) to slander; (*por escrito*) to libel.

diferencia *f* difference.

diferenciar ◆ *vt*: **~ (de)** to distinguish (from). ◆ *vi*: **~ (entre)** to distinguish o differentiate (between). ▶ **diferenciarse** *vpr* (*diferir*): **~se (de/en)** to differ (from/in), to be different (from/in).

diferente ◆ *adj*: **~ (de o a)** different (from o to). ◆ *adv* differently.

diferido ▶ **en diferido** *loc adv* (TV) recorded.

diferir *vi* (*diferenciarse*) to differ.

difícil *adj* difficult; **~ de hacer** difficult to do; **es ~ que ganen** they are unlikely to win.

dificultad *f* **1.** (*calidad de difícil*) difficulty. **2.** (*obstáculo*) problem.

dificultar *vt* (*estorbar*) to hinder; (*obstruir*) to obstruct.

difuminar *vt* to blur.

difundir *vt* **1.** (*noticia, doctrina, epidemia*) to spread. **2.** (*luz, calor*) to diffuse; (*emisión radiofónica*) to broadcast. ▶ **difundirse** *vpr* **1.** (*noticia, doctrina, epidemia*) to spread. **2.** (*luz, calor*) to be diffused.

difunto, -ta *m y f*: **el ~** the deceased.

difusión *f* **1.** (*de cultura, noticia, doctrina*) dissemination. **2.** (*de programa*) broadcasting.

diga → **decir**.

digerir *vt* to digest; *fig* (*hechos*) to assimilate, to take in.

digestión *f* digestion.

digestivo, -va *adj* digestive.

digital *adj* (INFORM & TECN) digital.

dígito *m* digit.

dignarse *vpr*: **~ a** to deign to.

dignidad *f* (*cualidad*) dignity.

digno, -na *adj* **1.** (*noble - actitud, respuesta*) dignified; (*- persona*) honourable, noble. **2.** (*merecedor*): **~ de** worthy of; **~ de elogio** praiseworthy; **~ de mención/de ver** worth mentioning/seeing. **3.** (*adecuado*): **~ de** appropriate for, fitting for. **4.** (*decente - sueldo, actuación etc*) decent.

digo → **decir**.

digresión *f* digression.

dijera *etc* → **decir**.

dilapidar *vt* to squander, to waste.

dilatar *vt* **1.** (*extender*) to expand; (*partes del cuerpo*) to dilate. **2.** (*prolongar*) to prolong. **3.** (*demorar*) to delay.

dilema *m* dilemma.

diligencia *f* **1.** (*esmero, cuidado*) diligence. **2.** (*trámite, gestión*) business (U). **3.** (*vehículo*) stagecoach. ▶ **diligencias** *fpl* (DER) proceedings; **instruir ~s** to start proceedings.

diligente *adj* diligent.

diluir *vt* to dilute. ▶ **diluirse** *vpr* to dissolve.

diluvio *m* lit & *fig* flood.

dimensión *f* dimension; **las dimen-**

siones de la tragedia the extent of the tragedy.

diminutivo *m* diminutive.

diminuto, -ta *adj* tiny, minute.

dimisión *f* resignation; **presentar la ~** to hand in one's resignation.

dimitir *vi*: **~ (de)** to resign (from).

dimos → dar.

Dinamarca Denmark.

dinámico, -ca *adj* dynamic.

dinamismo *m* dynamism.

dinamita *f* dynamite.

dinamo, dínamo *f* dynamo.

dinastía *f* dynasty.

dineral *m fam* fortune.

dinero *m* money; **andar bien/mal de ~** to be well off for/short of money; **~ en metálico** cash; **~ negro** o **sucio** illegally obtained money.

dinosaurio *m* dinosaur.

dintel *m* (ARQUIT) lintel.

dio → dar.

diócesis *f* diocese.

dios, -sa *m y f* god (*f* goddess). ▶ **Dios** *m* God; **a la buena de Dios** any old how; **¡Dios mío!** good God!, (oh) my God!; **¡por Dios!** for God's sake!; **¡vaya por Dios!** for Heaven's sake!, honestly!

diploma *m* diploma.

diplomacia *f* (gen) diplomacy.

diplomado, -da *adj* qualified.

diplomático, -ca ◆ *adj lit & fig* diplomatic. ◆ *m y f* diplomat.

diptongo *m* diphthong.

diputación *f* (*corporación*) committee; **~ provincial** *governing body of each province of an autonomous region in Spain;* = county council Br.

diputado, -da *m y f* = Member of Parliament, MP Br, representative Am.

dique *m* 1. (*en río*) dike. 2. (*en puerto*) dock.

dirá → decir.

dirección *f* 1. (*sentido, rumbo*) direction; **calle de ~ única** one-way street; **en ~ a** towards, in the direction of. 2. (*domicilio*) address. 3. (*mando - de empresa, hospital*) management; (- *de partido*) leadership; (- *de colegio*) headship; (- *de periódico*) editorship; (- *de una película*) direction; (- *de una obra de teatro*) production; (- *de una orquesta*) conducting. 4. (*junta directiva*) management. 5. (*de un vehículo*) steering; **~ asistida** power steering. ▶ **Dirección** *f*: **Dirección General de Tráfico** *traffic department (part of the Ministry of the Interior).*

directivo, -va ◆ *adj* managerial. ◆ *m*

y f (*jefe*) manager. ▶ **directiva** *f* (*junta*) board (of directors).

directo, -ta *adj* 1. (gen) direct. 2. (*derecho*) straight. ▶ **directo** *adv* straight; **~ a** straight to. ▶ **directa** *f* (AUTOM) top gear. ▶ **en directo** *loc adv* live.

director, -ra *m y f* 1. (*de empresa*) director; (*de hotel, hospital*) manager (*f* manageress); (*de periódico*) editor; (*de cárcel*) governor. 2. (*de obra artística*): **~ de cine** film director; **~ de orquesta** conductor. 3. (*de colegio*) headmaster (*f* headmistress). 4. (*de tesis, trabajo de investigación*) supervisor; **~ técnico** (DEP) trainer.

directorio *m* (gen & INFORM) directory.

directriz *f* (GEOM) directrix. ▶ **directrices** *fpl* (*normas*) guidelines.

diría → decir.

dirigente *m y f* (*de partido político*) leader; (*de empresa*) manager.

dirigir *vt* 1. (*conducir - coche, barco*) to steer; (- *avión*) to pilot; *fig* (- *mirada*) to direct. 2. (*llevar - empresa, hotel, hospital*) to manage; (- *colegio, cárcel, periódico*) to run; (- *partido, revuelta*) to lead; (- *expedición*) to head. 3. (*película, obra de teatro*) to direct; (*orquesta*) to conduct. 4. (*carta, paquete*) to address. 5. (*guiar - persona*) to guide. 6. (*dedicar*): **~ algo a** to aim sthg at. ▶ **dirigirse** *vpr* 1. (*encaminarse*): **~se a** o **hacia** to head for. 2. (*hablar*): **~se a** to address, to speak to. 3. (*escribir*): **~se a** to write to.

discar *vt Amer* to dial.

discernir *vt* to discern, to distinguish.

disciplina *f* discipline.

discípulo, -la *m y f* disciple.

disco *m* 1. (ANAT, ASTRON & GEOM) disc. 2. (*de música*) record; **~ compacto** compact disc; **~ de larga duración** LP, long-playing record. 3. (*semáforo*) (traffic) light. 4. (DEP) discus. 5. (INFORM) disk; **~ duro/flexible** hard/floppy disk.

discografía *f* records previously released (*by an artist or group*).

disconforme *adj* in disagreement; **estar ~ con** to disagree with.

disconformidad *f* disagreement.

discontinuo, -nua *adj* (*esfuerzo*) intermittent; (*línea*) broken, dotted.

discordante *adj* (*sonidos*) discordant; (*opiniones*) clashing.

discordia *f* discord.

discoteca *f* (*local*) disco.

discreción *f* discretion. ▶ **a discreción** *loc adv* as much as one wants, freely.

discrecional adj (gen) optional; (parada) request (antes de sust).

discrepancia f (diferencia) difference, discrepancy; (desacuerdo) disagreement.

discrepar vi: ~ (de) (diferenciarse) to differ (from); (disentir) to disagree (with).

discreto, -ta adj 1. (prudente) discreet. 2. (cantidad) moderate, modest. 3. (normal - actuación) fair, reasonable.

discriminación f discrimination.

discriminar vt 1. (cosa): ~ algo de to discriminate o distinguish sthg from. 2. (persona, colectividad) to discriminate against.

disculpa f (pretexto) excuse; (excusa, perdón) apology; **dar ~s** to make excuses; **pedir ~s a alguien (por)** to apologize to sb (for).

disculpar ◆ vt to excuse; ~ a alguien (de o por algo) to forgive sb (for sthg); **¡disculpe!** (lo siento) I'm sorry!; (¡oiga!) exuse me! ▶ **disculparse** vpr: **~se (de o por algo)** to apologize (for sthg).

discurrir vi 1. (pasar - personas) to wander, to walk; (- tiempo, vida, sesión) to go by, to pass; (- río, tráfico) to flow. 2. (pensar) to think, to reflect.

discurso m speech.

discusión f (conversación) discussion; (pelea) argument.

discutible adj debatable.

discutir ◆ vi 1. (hablar) to discuss. 2. (pelear): ~ (de) to argue o quarrel (about). ◆ vt (hablar) to discuss; (contradecir) to dispute.

disecar vt (cadáver) to dissect; (animal) to stuff; (planta) to dry.

diseminar vt (semillas) to scatter; (ideas) to disseminate.

disentir vi: ~ (de/en) to disagree (with/on).

diseñar vt to design.

diseño m design; **ropa de ~** designer clothes; **~ asistido por ordenador** (INFORM) computer-aided design; **~ gráfico** graphic design.

disertación f (oral) lecture, discourse; (escrita) dissertation.

disfraz m (gen) disguise; (para baile, fiesta etc) fancy dress (U).

disfrazar vt to disguise. ▶ **disfrazarse** vpr to disguise o.s.; **~se de** to dress up as.

disfrutar ◆ vi 1. (sentir placer) to enjoy o.s. 2. (disponer de): ~ de algo to enjoy sthg. ◆ vt to enjoy.

disfrute m (goce) enjoyment.

disgregar vt 1. (multitud, manifestación) to disperse. 2. (roca, imperio, estado) to break up; (átomo) to split. ▶ **disgregarse** vpr 1. (multitud, manifestación) to disperse. 2. (roca, imperio, estado) to break up.

disgustar vt (suj: comentario, críticas, noticia) to upset. ▶ **disgustarse** vpr: **~se (con alguien/por algo)** (sentir enfado) to get upset (with sb/about sthg); (enemistarse) to fall out (with sb/over sthg).

disgusto m 1. (enfado) annoyance; (pesadumbre) sorrow; **dar un ~ a alguien** to upset sb; **llevarse un ~** to be upset. 2. (pelea): **tener un ~ con alguien** to have a quarrel with sb.

disidente m y f (político) dissident; (religioso) dissenter.

disimular ◆ vt to hide, to conceal. ◆ vi to pretend.

disimulo m pretence, concealment.

disipar vt 1. (dudas, sospechas) to dispel; (ilusiones) to shatter. 2. (fortuna, herencia) to squander, to throw away. ▶ **disiparse** vpr 1. (dudas, sospechas) to be dispelled; (ilusiones) to be shattered. 2. (niebla, humo, vapor) to vanish.

diskette = disquete.

dislexia f dyslexia.

dislocar vt to dislocate. ▶ **dislocarse** vpr to dislocate.

disminución f decrease, drop.

disminuido, -da adj handicapped.

disminuir ◆ vt to reduce, to decrease. ◆ vi (gen) to decrease; (precios, temperatura) to drop, to fall; (vista, memoria) to fail; (días) to get shorter; (beneficios) to fall off.

disolución f 1. (en un líquido) dissolving. 2. (de matrimonio, sociedad, partido) dissolution. 3. (mezcla) solution.

disolvente adj & m solvent.

disolver vt 1. (gen) to dissolve. 2. (reunión, manifestación, familia) to break up. ▶ **disolverse** vpr 1. (gen) to dissolve. 2. (reunión, manifestación, familia) to break up.

disparar ◆ vt to shoot; (pedrada) to throw. ◆ vi to shoot, to fire.

disparatado, -da adj absurd, crazy.

disparate m (comentario, acción) silly thing; (idea) crazy idea.

disparidad f difference, disparity.

disparo m shot.

dispensar vt 1. (disculpar) to excuse, to forgive. 2. (rendir): ~ algo (a alguien) (honores) to confer sthg (upon sb); (bienvenida, ayuda) to give sthg (to sb).

3. (*eximir*): ~ **a alguien de** to excuse o exempt sb from.
dispensario *m* dispensary.
dispersar *vt* **1.** (*esparcir - objetos*) to scatter. **2.** (*disolver - gentío*) to disperse; (*- manifestación*) to break up. ▶ **dispersarse** *vpr* to scatter.
dispersión *f* (*de objetos*) scattering.
disperso, -sa *adj* scattered.
disponer ◆ *vt* **1.** (*gen*) to arrange. **2.** (*cena, comida*) to lay on. **3.** (*decidir - suj: persona*) to decide; (*suj: ley*) to stipulate. ◆ *vi* **1.** (*poseer*): ~ **de** to have (at one's disposal). **2.** (*usar*): ~ **de** to make use of. ▶ **disponerse a** *vpr*: ~**se a hacer algo** to prepare o get ready to do sthg.
disponibilidad *f* (*gen*) availability.
disponible *adj* (*gen*) available; (*tiempo*) free, spare.
disposición *f* **1.** (*colocación*) arrangement, layout. **2.** (*orden*) order; (*de ley*) provision. **3.** (*uso*): **a ~ de** at the disposal of.
dispositivo *m* device; ~ **intrauterino** intrauterine device, IUD.
dispuesto, -ta *pp* → **disponer**. ◆ *adj* **1.** (*preparado*) ready; **estar ~ a hacer algo** to be prepared to do sthg. **2.** (*servicial*) willing.
disputa *f* dispute.
disputar *vt* **1.** (*cuestión, tema*) to argue about. **2.** (*trofeo, puesto*) to compete for; (*carrera, partido*) to compete in.
disquete, diskette [dis'ket̪e] *m* (INFORM) diskette, floppy disk.
disquetera *f* (INFORM) disk drive.
distancia *f* **1.** (*gen*) distance; **a ~ from** a distance; **mantener a ~ to** keep at a distance. **2.** (*en el tiempo*) gap, space.
distanciar *vt* (*gen*) to drive apart; (*rival*) to forge ahead of. ▶ **distanciarse** *vpr* (*alejarse - afectivamente*) to grow apart; (*- físicamente*) to distance o.s.
distante *adj* **1.** (*en el espacio*): ~ **(de)** far away (from). **2.** (*en el trato*) distant.
distar *vi* (*hallarse a*): **ese sitio dista varios kilómetros de aquí** that place is several kilometres away from here.
diste *etc* → **dar**.
distendido, -da *adj* (*informal*) relaxed, informal.
distensión *f* **1.** (*entre países*) détente; (*entre personas*) easing of tension. **2.** (MED) strain.
distinción *f* **1.** (*diferencia*) distinction; **a ~ de** in contrast to, unlike; **sin ~** alike. **2.** (*privilegio*) privilege. **3.** (*modales*) refinement.

distinguido, -da *adj* **1.** (*notable*) distinguished. **2.** (*elegante*) refined.
distinguir *vt* **1.** (*diferenciar*) to distinguish; ~ **algo de algo** to tell sthg from sthg. **2.** (*separar*) to pick out. **3.** (*caracterizar*) to characterize. ▶ **distinguirse** *vpr* (*destacarse*) to stand out.
distintivo, -va *adj* distinctive; (*señal*) distinguishing. ◆ **distintivo** *m* badge.
distinto, -ta *adj* (*diferente*) different. ▶ **distintos, -tas** *adj pl* (*varios*) various.
distorsión *f* (*de tobillo, rodilla*) sprain; (*de imágenes, sonidos, palabras*) distortion.
distracción *f* **1.** (*entretenimiento*) entertainment; (*pasatiempo*) hobby, pastime. **2.** (*despiste*) slip; (*falta de atención*) absent-mindedness.
distraer *vt* **1.** (*divertir*) to amuse, to entertain. **2.** (*despistar*) to distract. ▶ **distraerse** *vpr* **1.** (*divertirse*) to enjoy o.s.; (*pasar el tiempo*) to pass the time. **2.** (*despistarse*) to let one's mind wander.
distraído, -da *adj* **1.** (*entretenido*) amusing, entertaining. **2.** (*despistado*) absent-minded.
distribución *f* **1.** (*gen*) distribution; ~ **de premios** prizegiving. **2.** (*de correo, mercancías*) delivery. **3.** (*de casa, habitaciones*) layout.
distribuidor, -ra ◆ *adj* (*entidad*) wholesale; (*red*) supply (*antes de sust*). ◆ *m y f* (*persona*) deliveryman (*f* deliverywoman). ▶ **distribuidor** *m* (*aparato*) vending machine.
distribuir *vt* **1.** (*gen*) to distribute; (*carga, trabajo*) to spread; (*pastel, ganancias*) to divide up. **2.** (*correo, mercancías*) to deliver. **3.** (*casa, habitaciones*) to arrange.
distrito *m* district.
disturbio *m* disturbance; (*violento*) riot.
disuadir *vt*: ~ **(de)** to dissuade (from).
disuasión *f* deterrence.
disuasivo, -va *adj* deterrent.
disuelto, -ta *pp* → **disolver**.
DIU (*abrev de* **dispositivo intrauterino**) *m* IUD.
diurético, -ca *adj* & *m* diuretic.
diurno, -na *adj* (*gen*) daytime (*antes de sust*); (*planta, animal*) diurnal.
diva → **divo**.
divagar *vi* to digress.
diván *m* divan; (*de psiquiatra*) couch.
divergencia *f* **1.** (*de líneas*) divergence. **2.** (*de opinión*) difference of opinion.
divergir *vi* **1.** (*calles, líneas*) to diverge. **2.** *fig* (*opiniones*): ~ **(en)** to differ (on).

diversidad f diversity.
diversificar vt to diversify.
diversión f (entretenimiento) entertainment, amusement; (pasatiempo) pastime, hobby.
diverso, -sa adj (diferente) different.
▶ **diversos, -sas** adj pl (varios) several, various.
divertido, -da adj (entretenido - película, libro) entertaining; (- fiesta) enjoyable; (que hace reír) funny, amusing.
divertir vt to entertain, to amuse.
▶ **divertirse** vpr to enjoy o.s., to have a good time.
dividendo m (FIN & MAT) dividend.
dividir vt: ~ (en) to split up o divide (into); ~ entre (gen) to divide between; (MAT) to divide by.
divinidad f divinity, god.
divino, -na adj lit & fig divine.
divisa f 1. (gen pl) (moneda) foreign currency. 2. (distintivo) emblem.
divisar vt to spy, to make out.
división f (gen) division; (partición) splitting up.
divo, -va m y f (MÚS - mujer) diva, prima donna; (- hombre) opera singer.
divorciado, -da ◆ adj divorced. ◆ m y f divorcé (f divorcée).
divorciar vt lit & fig to divorce.
▶ **divorciarse** vpr to get divorced.
divorcio m (DER) divorce.
divulgar vt (noticia, secreto) to reveal; (rumor) to spread; (cultura, ciencia, doctrina) to popularize.
dizque adv Amer apparently.
DNI (abrev de **documento nacional de identidad**) m ID card.

DNI
All Spaniards over the age of 14 are required to have an identity card which they must carry at all times. The card has a photograph of the holder, their full name, date and place of birth, home address and tax number. Failure to present one's identity card when stopped by the police may result in a fine.

Dña abrev de **doña**.
do m (MÚS) C; (en solfeo) doh.
dobladillo m (de traje, vestido) hem; (de pantalón) turn-up Br, cuff Am.
doblado, -da adj 1. (papel, camisa) folded. 2. (voz, película) dubbed.
doblar ◆ vt 1. (duplicar) to double. 2. (plegar) to fold. 3. (torcer) to bend.

4. (esquina) to turn, to go round. 5. (voz, actor) to dub. ◆ vi 1. (girar) to turn. 2. (campanas) to toll. ▶ **doblarse** vpr (someterse): ~se a to give in to.
doble ◆ adj double; **tiene ~ número de habitantes** it has double o twice the number of inhabitants; **es ~ de ancho** it's twice as wide; **una frase de ~ sentido** a phrase with a double meaning. ◆ m y f (gen & CIN) double. ◆ m (duplo): **el ~** twice as much; **gana el ~ que yo** she earns twice as much as I do, she earns double what I do. ◆ adv double; **trabajar ~** to work twice as hard. ▶ **dobles** mpl (DEP) doubles.
doblegar vt (someter) to bend, to cause to give in. ▶ **doblegarse** vpr: ~se (ante) to give in o yield (to).
doblez m (pliegue) fold, crease.
doce núm twelve; ver también **seis**.
doceavo, -va núm twelfth.
docena f dozen; **a ~s** by the dozen.
docente adj teaching.
dócil adj obedient.
docto, -ta adj learned.
doctor, -ra m y f: ~ (en) doctor (of).
doctrina f doctrine.
documentación f (identificación personal) papers (pl).
documentado, -da adj (informado - película, informe) researched; (- persona) informed.
documental adj & m documentary.
documentar vt 1. (evidenciar) to document. 2. (informar) to brief. ▶ **documentarse** vpr to do research.
documento m 1. (escrito) document; ~ **nacional de identidad** identity card. 2. (testimonio) record.
dogma m dogma.
dogmático, -ca adj dogmatic.
dólar m dollar.
dolencia f pain.
doler vi to hurt; **me duele la pierna** my leg hurts; **¿te duele?** does it hurt?; **me duele la garganta/la cabeza** I have a sore throat/a headache. ▶ **dolerse** vpr: ~se de o por algo (quejarse) to complain about sthg; (arrepentirse) to be sorry about sthg.
dolido, -da adj hurt.
dolor m 1. (físico) pain; **siento un ~ en el brazo** I have a pain in my arm; (tener) ~ **de cabeza** (to have a) headache; ~ **de estómago** stomachache; ~ **de muelas** toothache. 2. (moral) grief, sorrow.
dolorido, -da adj (físicamente) sore; (moralmente) grieving, sorrowing.

doloroso, -sa adj (*físicamente*) painful; (*moralmente*) distressing.

domador, -ra m y f (*de caballos*) breaker; (*de leones*) tamer.

domar vt (*gen*) to tame; (*caballo*) to break in; *fig* (*personas*) to control.

domesticar vt *lit & fig* to tame.

doméstico, -ca adj domestic.

domiciliación f: ~ (*bancaria*) standing order, direct debit (U).

domiciliar vt (*pago*) to pay by direct debit o standing order.

domicilio m 1. (*vivienda*) residence, home; **servicio a** ~ home delivery; **venta a** ~ door-to-door selling. 2. (*dirección*) address; **sin** ~ **fijo** of no fixed abode; ~ **social** head office.

dominante adj 1. (*nación, religión, tendencia*) dominant; (*vientos*) prevailing. 2. (*persona*) domineering.

dominar ◆ vt 1. (*controlar - país, territorio*) to dominate, to rule (over); (*- pasión, nervios, caballo*) to control; (*- situación*) to be in control of; (*- incendio*) to bring under control; (*- rebelión*) to put down. 2. (*divisar*) to overlook. 3. (*conocer - técnica, tema*) to master; (*- lengua*) to be fluent in. ◆ vi (*predominar*) to predominate. ▶ **dominarse** vpr to control o.s.

domingo m Sunday; *ver también* **sábado**.

dominguero, -ra m y f Sunday tripper/driver *etc*.

Dominica Dominica.

dominical adj Sunday (*antes de sust*).

dominicano, -na adj, m y f Dominican.

dominico, -ca adj, m y f Dominican.

dominio m 1. (*dominación, posesión*): ~ (**sobre**) control (over). 2. (*autoridad*) authority, power. 3. *fig* (*territorio*) domain; (*ámbito*) realm. 4. (*conocimiento - de arte, técnica*) mastery; (*- de idiomas*) command.

dominó m 1. (*juego*) dominoes (U). 2. (*fichas*) set of dominoes.

don m 1. (*tratamiento*): ~ **Luis García** (*gen*) Mr Luis García; (*en cartas*) Luis García Esquire; ~ **Luis** *not translated in modern English or translated as 'Mr' + surname, if known.* 2. (*habilidad*) gift; **el** ~ **de la palabra** the gift of the gab.

donaire m (*al expresarse*) wit; (*al andar etc*) grace.

donante m y f donor; ~ **de sangre** blood donor.

donar vt to donate.

donativo m donation.

doncella f maid.

donde ◆ adv where; **el bolso está** ~ **lo dejaste** the bag is where you left it; **puedes marcharte** ~ **quieras** you can go wherever you want; **hasta** ~ as far as, up to where; **por** ~ wherever. ◆ pron where; **la casa** ~ **nací** the house where I was born; **la ciudad de** ~ **viene** the town (where) she comes from, the town from which she comes. ▶ **de donde** loc adv (*de lo cual*) from which.

dónde adv (*interrogativo*) where; **¿~ está el niño?** where's the child?; **no sé** ~ **se habrá metido** I don't know where she can be; **¿a** ~ **vas?** where are you going?; **¿de** ~ **eres?** where are you from?; **¿hacia** ~ **vas?** where are you heading?; **¿por** ~**?** whereabouts?; **¿por** ~ **se va al teatro?** how do you get to the theatre from here?

dondequiera ▶ **dondequiera que** adv wherever.

doña f: ~ **Luisa García** Mrs Luisa García; ~ **Luisa** *not translated in modern English or translated as 'Mrs' + surname, if known.*

dopado, -da adj having taken performance-enhancing drugs.

dopar vt to dope.

doping ['dopin] m doping.

doquier ▶ **por doquier** loc adv everywhere.

dorado, -da adj *lit & fig* golden. ▶ **dorada** f (*pez*) gilthead.

dorar vt 1. (*cubrir con oro*) to gild. 2. (*alimento*) to brown.

dormilón, -ona *fam* m y f (*persona*) sleepyhead.

dormir ◆ vt (*niño, animal*) to put to bed; ~ **la siesta** to have an afternoon nap. ◆ vi to sleep. ▶ **dormirse** vpr 1. (*persona*) to fall asleep. 2. (*brazo, mano*) to go to sleep.

dormitar vi to doze.

dormitorio m (*de casa*) bedroom; (*de colegio*) dormitory.

dorsal ◆ adj dorsal. ◆ m number (*on player's back*).

dorso m back; **al** ~**, en el** ~ on the back; **'véase al** ~**'** 'see overleaf'.

dos núm two; **cada** ~ **por tres** every five minutes; *ver también* **seis**.

doscientos, -tas núm two hundred; *ver también* **seis**.

dosificar vt *fig* (*fuerzas, palabras*) to use sparingly.

dosis f inv *lit & fig* dose.

dossier [do'sjer] *m inv* dossier, file.

dotación *f* 1. (*de dinero, armas, medios*) amount granted. 2. (*personal*) personnel; (*tripulantes*) crew; (*patrulla*) squad.

dotado, -da *adj* gifted; **~ de** (*persona*) blessed with; (*edificio, instalación, aparato*) equipped with.

dotar *vt* 1. (*proveer*): **~ algo de** to provide sthg with. 2. *fig* (*suj: la naturaleza*): **~ a algo/alguien de** to endow sthg/sb with.

dote *f* (*en boda*) dowry. ► **dotes** *fpl* (*dones*) qualities; **tener ~s para algo** to have a talent for sthg.

doy → **dar**.

Dr. (*abrev de* **doctor**) Dr.

Dra. (*abrev de* **doctora**) Dr.

dragar *vt* to dredge.

dragón *m* dragon.

drama *m* (*gen*) drama; (*obra*) play.

dramático, -ca *adj* dramatic.

dramatizar *vt* to dramatize.

dramaturgo, -ga *m y f* playwright, dramatist.

drástico, -ca *adj* drastic.

drenar *vt* to drain.

driblar *vt* (DEP) to dribble.

droga *f* drug; **la ~** drugs (*pl*).

drogadicto, -ta *m y f* drug addict.

drogar *vt* to drug. ► **drogarse** *vpr* to take drugs.

droguería *f* shop selling paint, cleaning materials etc.

dromedario *m* dromedary.

dto. *abrev de* **descuento**.

dual *adj* dual.

Dublín Dublin.

ducha *f* shower; **tomar o darse una ~** to have o take a shower.

duchar *vt* to shower. ► **ducharse** *vpr* to have a shower.

duda *f* doubt; **poner algo en ~** to call sthg into question; **salir de ~s** to set one's mind at rest; **sin ~** doubtless; **no cabe ~** there is no doubt about it.

dudar ◆ *vi* 1. (*desconfiar*): **~ de algo/ alguien** to have one's doubts about sthg/sb. 2. (*no estar seguro*): **~ sobre algo** to be unsure about sthg. 3. (*vacilar*) to hesitate; **~ entre hacer una cosa u otra** to be unsure whether to do one thing or another. ◆ *vt* to doubt; **dudo que venga** I doubt whether he'll come.

dudoso, -sa *adj* 1. (*improbable*): **ser ~ (que)** to be doubtful (whether), to be unlikely (that). 2. (*vacilante*) hesitant, indecisive. 3. (*sospechoso*) suspect.

duelo *m* 1. (*combate*) duel. 2. (*sentimiento*) grief, sorrow.

duende *m* (*personaje*) imp, goblin.

dueño, -ña *m y f* (*gen*) owner; (*de piso etc*) landlord (*f* landlady).

duerma *etc* → **dormir**.

dulce ◆ *adj* 1. (*gen*) sweet. 2. (*agua*) fresh. 3. (*mirada*) tender. ◆ *m* (*caramelo, postre*) sweet; (*pastel*) cake, pastry.

dulcificar *vt* (*endulzar*) to sweeten.

dulzura *f* (*gen*) sweetness.

duna *f* dune.

dúo *m* 1. (MÚS) duet. 2. (*pareja*) duo; **a ~** together.

duodécimo, -ma *núm* twelfth.

dúplex, duplex *m inv* (*piso*) duplex.

duplicado, -da *adj* in duplicate. ► **duplicado** *m*: **(por) ~** (in) duplicate.

duplicar *vt* 1. (*cantidad*) to double. 2. (*documento*) to duplicate. ► **duplicarse** *vpr* to double.

duque, -sa *m y f* duke (*f* duchess).

duración *f* length.

duradero, -ra *adj* (*gen*) lasting; (*ropa, zapatos*) hard-wearing.

durante *prep* during; **le escribí ~ las vacaciones** I wrote to him during the holidays; **estuve escribiendo ~ una hora** I was writing for an hour; **~ toda la semana** all week.

durar *vi* (*gen*) to last; (*permanecer, subsistir*) to remain, to stay; (*ropa*) to wear well; **aún dura la fiesta** the party's still going on.

durazno *m* Amer peach.

dureza *f* 1. (*de objeto, metal etc*) hardness. 2. (*de clima, persona*) harshness.

durmiera *etc* → **dormir**.

duro, -ra *adj* 1. (*gen*) hard; (*carne*) tough. 2. (*resistente*) tough. 3. (*palabras, clima*) harsh. ► **duro** ◆ *m* (*moneda*) five-peseta piece. ◆ *adv* hard.

d/v (*abrev de* **días vista**): **15 ~** within 15 days.

e¹, E *f* (*letra*) e, E.

e² *conj* (*en lugar de 'y' ante palabras que empiecen por 'i' o 'hi'*) and.

EA (*abrev de* **Eusko Alkartasuna**) *f* Basque nationalist political party.

ebanista m y f cabinet-maker.
ébano m ebony.
ebrio, ebria adj (borracho) drunk.
Ebro m: **el ~** the Ebro.
ebullición f boiling.
eccema m eczema.
echar ♦ vt 1. (tirar) to throw; (red) to cast. 2. (añadir): **~ algo (a o en algo)** (vino etc) to pour sthg (into sthg); (sal, azúcar etc) to add sthg (to sthg). 3. (carta, postal) to post. 4. (humo, vapor, chispas) to give off, to emit. 5. (hojas, flores) to shoot. 6. (expulsar): **~ a alguien (de)** to throw sb out (of). 7. (despedir): **~ a alguien (de)** to sack Br o fire sb (from). 8. (accionar): **~ la llave/el cerrojo** to lock/bolt the door; **~ el freno** to brake, to put the brakes on. 9. (acostar) to lie (down). 10. fam (en televisión, cine) to show; **¿qué echan esta noche en la tele?** what's on telly tonight? 11. loc: **~ abajo** (edificio) to pull down, to demolish; (gobierno) to bring down; (proyecto) to ruin; **~ a perder** (vestido, alimentos, plan) to ruin; (ocasión) to waste; **~ de menos** to miss. ♦ vi (empezar): **~ a hacer algo** to begin to do sthg, to start doing sthg; **~ a correr** to break into a run; **~ a llorar** to burst into tears; **~ a reír** to burst out laughing. ▶ **echarse** vpr 1. (acostarse) to lie down. 2. (apartarse): **~se (a un lado)** to move (aside); **~se atrás** fig to back out. 3. loc: **~se a perder** (comida) to go off, to spoil; (plan) to fall through.
echarpe m shawl.
eclesiástico, -ca adj ecclesiastical.
eclipsar vt lit & fig to eclipse.
eclipse m eclipse.
eco m (gen) echo; **hacerse ~ de** to report; **tener ~** to arouse interest.
ecología f ecology.
ecológico, -ca adj (gen) ecological; (alimentos) organic.
ecologista ♦ adj environmental, ecological. ♦ m y f environmentalist.
economato m company cooperative shop.
economía f 1. (gen) economy; **~ sumergida** black economy o market. 2. (estudio) economics (U); **~ familiar** home economics. 3. (ahorro) saving.
económico, -ca adj 1. (problema, doctrina etc) economic. 2. (barato) cheap, low-cost. 3. (que gasta poco - motor etc) economical; (- persona) thrifty.
economista m y f economist.
economizar vt lit & fig to save.
ecosistema m ecosystem.

ecoturismo m ecotourism.
ecu (abrev de **unidad de cuenta europea**) m ecu.
ecuación f equation.
ecuador m equator.
Ecuador Ecuador.
ecuánime adj 1. (en el ánimo) level-headed. 2. (en el juicio) impartial.
ecuatoriano, -na adj, m y f Ecuadorian, Ecuadoran.
ecuestre adj equestrian.
edad f age; **¿qué ~ tienes?** how old are you?; **tiene 25 años de ~** she's 25 (years old); **una persona de ~** an elderly person; **~ escolar** school age; **Edad Media** Middle Ages (pl); **~ del pavo** awkward age; **la tercera ~** (ancianos) senior citizens (pl).
edén m (RELIG) Eden; fig paradise.
edición f 1. (acción – IMPRENTA) publication; (– INFORM, RADIO & TV) editing. 2. (ejemplares) edition.
edicto m edict.
edificante adj (conducta) exemplary; (libro, discurso) edifying.
edificar vt (construir) to build.
edificio m building.
edil m (town) councillor.
Edimburgo Edinburgh.
editar vt 1. (libro, periódico) to publish; (disco) to release. 2. (INFORM, RADIO & TV) to edit.
editor, -ra ♦ adj publishing (antes de sust). ♦ m y f 1. (de libro, periódico) publisher. 2. (RADIO & TV) editor.
editorial ♦ adj publishing (antes de sust). ♦ m editorial, leader. ♦ f publisher, publishing house.
edredón m duvet, eiderdown.
educación f 1. (enseñanza) education. 2. (modales) good manners (pl); **¡qué poca ~!** how rude!; **mala ~** bad manners (pl).
educado, -da adj polite, well-mannered; **mal ~** rude, ill-mannered.
educador, -ra m y f teacher.
educar vt 1. (enseñar) to educate. 2. (criar) to bring up. 3. (cuerpo, voz, oído) to train.
edulcorante m sweetener.
edulcorar vt to sweeten.
EE (abrev de **Euskadiko Ezquerra**) m Basque political party to the left of the political spectrum.
EE UU (abrev de **Estados Unidos**) mpl USA.
efectivamente adv (en respuestas) precisely, exactly.

efectividad f effectiveness.

efectivo, -va adj 1. (útil) effective. 2. (real) actual, true; **hacer ~** (gen) to carry out; (promesa) to keep; (dinero, crédito) to pay; (cheque) to cash. ▶ **efectivo** m (dinero) cash; **en ~** in cash. ▶ **efectivos** mpl (personal) forces.

efecto m 1. (gen) effect; **~ invernadero** greenhouse effect; **~ óptico** optical illusion; **~s sonoros/visuales** sound/ visual effects; **~s especiales** special effects; **~s secundarios** side effects. 2. (finalidad) aim, purpose; **a tal ~** to that end; **a ~s o para los ~s de algo** as far as sthg is concerned. 3. (impresión) impression; **producir buen/mal ~** to make a good/bad impression. 4. (de balón, bola) spin; **dar ~ a** to put spin on. 5. (COM) (documento) bill. ▶ **efectos personales** mpl personal possessions o effects. ▶ **en efecto** loc adv indeed.

efectuar vt (gen) to carry out; (compra, pago, viaje) to make; (cambio) to make, to bring about. ▶ **efectuarse** vpr to take place.

efeméride f (suceso) major event; (conmemoración) anniversary.

efervescencia f (de líquido) effervescence; (de bebida) fizziness.

efervescente adj (bebida) fizzy.

eficacia f (eficiencia) efficiency; (efectividad) effectiveness, efficacy.

eficaz adj 1. (eficiente) efficient. 2. (efectivo) effective.

eficiencia f efficiency.

eficiente adj efficient.

efímero, -ra adj ephemeral.

efusión f (cordialidad) effusiveness.

efusivo, -va adj effusive.

EGB (abrev de educación general básica) f Spanish primary education system for pupils aged 6-14.

egipcio, -cia adj, m y f Egyptian.

Egipto Egypt.

egocéntrico, -ca adj egocentric.

egoísmo m selfishness, egoism.

egoísta ◆ adj egoistic, selfish. ◆ m y f egoist, selfish person.

ególatra ◆ adj egotistical. ◆ m y f egotist.

egresado, -da m y f Amer 1. (de escuela) student who has completed a course. 2. (de universidad) graduate.

egresar vi Amer 1. (de escuela) to leave school after graduation. 2. (de universidad) to graduate.

egreso m Amer 1. (de escuela) comple-

tion of course. 2. (de universidad) graduation.

eh interj: **¡~!** hey!

ej. abrev de **ejemplar**.

eje m 1. (de rueda) axle; (de máquina) shaft. 2. (GEOM) axis. 3. fig (idea central) central idea, basis.

ejecución f 1. (realización) carrying out. 2. (de condenado) execution. 3. (de concierto) performance, rendition.

ejecutar vt 1. (realizar) to carry out. 2. (condenado) to execute. 3. (concierto) to perform. 4. (INFORM) (programa) to run.

ejecutivo, -va ◆ adj executive. ◆ m y f (persona) executive. ▶ **ejecutivo** m (POLÍT): **el ~** the government.

ejem interj: **¡~!** (expresa duda) um!; (expresa ironía) ahem!

ejemplar ◆ adj exemplary. ◆ m (de libro) copy; (de revista) issue; (de moneda) example; (de especie, raza) specimen.

ejemplificar vt to exemplify.

ejemplo m example; **por ~** for example; **predicar con el ~** to practise what one preaches.

ejercer ◆ vt 1. (profesión) to practise; (cargo) to hold. 2. (poder, derecho) to exercise; (influencia, dominio) to exert; **~ presión sobre** to put pressure on. ◆ vi to practise (one's profession); **~ de** to practise o work as.

ejercicio m 1. (gen) exercise; **hacer ~** to (do) exercise. 2. (de profesión) practising; (de cargo, funciones) carrying out. 3. (de poder, derecho) exercising. 4. (MIL) drill. 5. (ECON): **~ económico/fiscal** financial/ tax year.

ejercitar vt (derecho) to exercise. ▶ **ejercitarse** vpr: **~se (en)** to train (in).

ejército m (MIL & fig) army.

ejote m Amer green bean.

el, la (mpl **los**, fpl **las**) art (**el** antes de sustantivo femenino que empiece por 'a' o 'ha' tónica; a + el = **al**; de + el = **del**) 1. (gen) the; (en sentido genérico) no se traduce; **~ coche** the car; **la casa** the house; **los niños** the children; **~ agua/hacha/ águila** the water/axe/eagle; **fui a recoger a los niños** I went to pick up the children; **los niños imitan a los adultos** children copy adults. 2. (con sustantivo abstracto) no se traduce; **~ amor** love; **la vida** life. 3. (indica posesión, pertenencia): **se partió la pierna** he broke his leg; **se quitó los zapatos** she took her shoes off; **tiene ~ pelo oscuro** he has dark hair. 4. (con días de la semana): **vuelven ~ sábado** they're coming back on Saturday.

5. (*con nombres propios geográficos*) the; ~ **Sena** the (River) Seine; ~ **Everest** (Mount) Everest; **la España de la postguerra** post-war Spain. **6.** (*con complemento de nombre, especificativo*): ~ **de** the one; **he perdido ~ tren, cogeré ~ de las nueve** I've missed the train, I'll get the nine o'clock one; ~ **de azul** the one in blue. **7.** (*con complemento de nombre, posesivo*): **mi hermano y ~ de Juan** my brother and Juan's. **8.** (*antes de frase*): ~ **que** (*cosa*) the one, whichever; (*persona*) whoever; **coge ~ que quieras** take whichever you like; ~ **que más corra** whoever runs fastest. **9.** (*antes de adjetivo*): **prefiero ~ rojo al azul** I prefer the red one to the blue one.

él, ella *pron pers* **1.** (*sujeto, predicado - persona*) he (*f* she); (- *animal, cosa*) it; **mi hermana es ella** she's the one who is my sister. **2.** (*después de prep*) (*complemento*) him (*f* her); **voy a ir de vacaciones con ella** I'm going on holiday with her; **díselo a ella** tell her it. **3.** (*posesivo*): **de ~** his; **de ella** hers.

elaborar *vt* (*producto*) to make, to produce; (*idea*) to work out; (*plan, informe*) to draw up.

elasticidad *f* (*gen*) elasticity.

elástico, -ca *adj* (*gen*) elastic. ▶ **elástico** *m* (*cinta*) elastic.

elección *f* **1.** (*nombramiento*) election. **2.** (*opción*) choice. ▶ **elecciones** *fpl* (POLÍT) election (*sg*).

electo, -ta *adj* elect; **el presidente ~** the president elect.

elector, -ra *m y f* voter, elector.

electorado *m* electorate.

electoral *adj* electoral.

electricidad *f* electricity.

electricista *m y f* electrician.

eléctrico, -ca *adj* electric.

electrificar *vt* to electrify.

electrizar *vt fig* (*exaltar*) to electrify.

electrocutar *vt* to electrocute.

electrodoméstico *m* (*gen pl*) electrical household appliance.

electromagnético, -ca *adj* electromagnetic.

electrón *m* electron.

electrónico, -ca *adj* (*de la electrónica*) electronic. ▶ **electrónica** *f* electronics (U).

elefante, -ta *m y f* elephant.

elegancia *f* elegance.

elegante *adj* **1.** (*persona, traje, estilo*) elegant. **2.** (*conducta, actitud, respuesta*) dignified.

elegantoso, -sa *adj Amer* elegant.

elegía *f* elegy.

elegir *vt* **1.** (*escoger*) to choose, to select. **2.** (*por votación*) to elect.

elemental *adj* **1.** (*básico*) basic, elementary. **2.** (*obvio*) obvious.

elemento *m* **1.** (*gen*) element. **2.** (*factor*) factor. **3.** (*persona - en equipo, colectivo*) individual.

elenco *m* (*reparto*) cast.

elepé *m LP* (*record*).

elevación *f* **1.** (*de pesos, objetos etc*) lifting; (*de nivel, altura, precios*) rise. **2.** (*de terreno*) elevation, rise.

elevado, -da *adj* (*alto*) high; *fig* (*sublime*) lofty.

elevador *m* **1.** (*montacargas*) hoist. **2.** *Amer* (*ascensor*) lift *Br*, elevator *Am*.

elevalunas *m inv* window winder.

elevar *vt* **1.** (*gen & MAT*) to raise; (*peso, objeto*) to lift. **2.** (*ascender*): ~ **a alguien (a)** to elevate sb (to). ▶ **elevarse** *vpr* (*gen*) to rise; (*edificio, montaña*) to rise up; ~**se a** (*altura*) to reach; (*gastos, daños*) to amount o come to.

elidir *vt* to elide.

eliminar *vt* (*gen*) to eliminate; (*contaminación, enfermedad*) to get rid of.

eliminatorio, -ria *adj* qualifying (*antes de sust*). ▶ **eliminatoria** *f* (*gen*) qualifying round; (*en atletismo*) heat.

elipse *f* ellipse.

élite, elite *f* elite.

elitista *adj, m y f* elitist.

elixir, elíxir *m* **1.** (FARM): ~ **bucal** mouthwash. **2.** *fig* (*remedio milagroso*) elixir.

ella → **él**.

ellas → **ellos**.

ello *pron pers* (*neutro*) it; **no nos llevamos bien, pero ~ no nos impide formar un buen equipo** we don't get on very well, but it o that doesn't stop us making a good team; **no quiero hablar de ~** I don't want to talk about it; **por ~** for that reason.

ellos, ellas *pron pers* **1.** (*sujeto, predicado*) they; **los invitados son ~** they are the guests, it is they who are the guests. **2.** (*después de prep*) (*complemento*) them; **me voy al bar con ellas** I'm going with them to the bar; **díselo a ~** tell them it. **3.** (*posesivo*): **de ~/ellas** theirs.

elocuencia *f* eloquence.

elocuente *adj* eloquent; **se hizo un silencio ~** the silence said it all.

elogiar *vt* to praise.

elogio *m* praise.

elote *m Amer* (*mazorca*) corncob.

El Salvador El Salvador.

elucidar *vt* to elucidate.

elucubración *f* 1. (*reflexión*) reflection, meditation. 2. *despec* (*divagación*) mental meandering.

elucubrar *vt* 1. (*reflexionar*) to reflect o meditate upon. 2. *despec* (*divagar*) to theorize about.

eludir *vt* (*gen*) to avoid; (*perseguidores*) to escape.

emanar ▶ **emanar de** *vi* to emanate from.

emancipación *f* (*de mujeres, esclavos*) emancipation; (*de menores de edad*) coming of age; (*de países*) obtaining of independence.

emancipar *vt* (*gen*) to emancipate; (*países*) to grant independence (to). ▶ **emanciparse** *vpr* to free o.s., to become independent.

embadurnar *vt*: ~ **algo (de)** to smear sthg (with).

embajada *f* (*edificio*) embassy.

embajador, -ra *m y f* ambassador.

embalaje *m* (*acción*) packing.

embalar *vt* to wrap up, to pack. ▶ **embalarse** *vpr* (*acelerar - corredor*) to race away; (*- vehículo*) to pick up speed.

embalsamar *vt* to embalm.

embalse *m* reservoir.

embarazada ◆ *adj f* pregnant; **dejar ~ a alguien** to get sb pregnant; **quedarse ~** to get pregnant. ◆ *f* pregnant woman.

embarazar *vt* 1. (*impedir*) to restrict. 2. (*cohibir*) to inhibit.

embarazo *m* 1. (*preñez*) pregnancy. 2. (*timidez*) embarrassment. 3. (*impedimento*) obstacle.

embarazoso, -sa *adj* awkward, embarrassing.

embarcación *f* (*barco*) craft, boat.

embarcadero *m* jetty.

embarcar ◆ *vt* (*personas*) to board; (*mercancías*) to ship. ◆ *vi* to board. ▶ **embarcarse** *vpr* (*para viajar*) to board.

embargar *vt* 1. (DER) to seize. 2. (*suj: emoción etc*) to overcome.

embargo *m* 1. (DER) seizure. 2. (ECON) embargo. ▶ **sin embargo** *loc adv* however, nevertheless.

embarque *m* (*de personas*) boarding; (*de mercancías*) embarkation.

embarrancar *vi* to run aground.

embarullar *vt fam* to mess up. ▶ **embarullarse** *vpr fam* to get into a muddle.

embaucar *vt* to swindle, to deceive.

embeber *vt* to soak up. ▶ **embeberse** *vpr*: ~**se (en algo)** (*ensimismarse*) to become absorbed (in sthg); *fig* (*emparparse*) to immerse o.s. (in sthg).

embellecer *vt* to adorn, to embellish.

embestida *f* (*gen*) attack; (*de toro*) charge.

embestir *vt* (*gen*) to attack, to assail; (*suj: toro*) to charge.

emblema *m* 1. (*divisa, distintivo*) emblem, badge. 2. (*símbolo*) symbol.

embobar *vt* to captivate.

embocadura *f* (*de instrumento*) mouthpiece.

embolia *f* clot, embolism.

émbolo *m* (AUTOM) piston.

embolsarse *vpr* (*ganar*) to earn.

embonar *vt Amer fam* to suit.

emborrachar *vt* to make drunk. ▶ **emborracharse** *vpr* to get drunk.

emborronar *vt* (*garabatear*) to scribble on; (*manchar*) to smudge.

emboscada *f lit & fig* ambush.

embotellado, -da *adj* bottled.

embotellamiento *m* (*de tráfico*) traffic jam.

embotellar *vt* (*líquido*) to bottle.

embozar *vt* 1. (*conducto*) to block. 2. (*rostro*) to cover (up). ▶ **embozarse** *vpr* 1. (*conducto*) to get blocked (up). 2. (*persona*) to cover one's face.

embragar *vi* to engage the clutch.

embrague *m* clutch.

embriagar *vt* 1. (*extasiar*) to intoxicate. 2. (*emborrachar*) to make drunk. ▶ **embriagarse** *vpr* (*emborracharse*): ~**se (con)** to get drunk (on).

embriaguez *f* 1. (*borrachera*) drunkenness. 2. (*éxtasis*) intoxication.

embrión *m* embryo.

embrionario, -ria *adj fig* (*inicial*) embryonic.

embrollo *m* 1. (*de hilos*) tangle. 2. *fig* (*lío*) mess; (*mentira*) lie.

embromado, -da *adj Amer fam* tricky.

embrujar *vt lit & fig* to bewitch.

embrujo *m* (*maleficio*) curse, spell; *fig* (*de ciudad, ojos*) charm, magic.

embrutecer *vt* to brutalize. ▶ **embrutecerse** *vpr* to become brutalized.

embuchado, -da *adj*: carne embuchada cured cold meat.

embudo *m* funnel.

embuste *m* lie.

embustero, -ra ◆ *adj* lying. ◆ *m y f* liar.

embute *m Amer fam* bribe.

embutido m (comida) cold cured meat.

embutir vt lit & fig to stuff.

emergencia f 1. (urgencia) emergency; **en caso de ~** in case of emergency. 2. (brote) emergence.

emerger vi (salir del agua) to emerge; (aparecer) to come into view, to appear.

emigración f (de personas) emigration; (de aves) migration.

emigrante adj, m y f emigrant.

emigrar vi (persona) to emigrate; (ave) to migrate.

eminencia f (persona) leading light. ▶ **Eminencia** f: **Su Eminencia** His Eminence.

eminente adj (distinguido) eminent.

emirato m emirate.

Emiratos Árabes Unidos mpl: **los ~** United Arab Emirates.

emisión f 1. (de energía, rayos etc) emission. 2. (de bonos, sellos, monedas) issue. 3. (RADIO & TV - transmisión) broadcasting; (- programa) programme, broadcast.

emisor, -ra adj transmitting (antes de sust). ▶ **emisora** f radio station.

emitir ◆ vt 1. (rayos, calor, sonidos) to emit. 2. (moneda, sellos, bonos) to issue. 3. (expresar - juicio, opinión) to express; (- fallo) to pronounce. 4. (RADIO & TV) to broadcast. ◆ vi to broadcast.

emoción f 1. (conmoción, sentimiento) emotion. 2. (expectación) excitement; **¡qué ~!** how exciting!

emocionado, -da adj 1. (conmovido) moved. 2. (excitado) excited.

emocionante adj 1. (conmovedor) moving, touching. 2. (apasionante) exciting, thrilling.

emocionar vt 1. (conmover) to move. 2. (excitar, apasionar) to thrill, to excite. ▶ **emocionarse** vpr 1. (conmoverse) to be moved. 2. (excitarse, apasionarse) to get excited.

emotivo, -va adj (persona) emotional; (escena, palabras) moving.

empachar vt to give indigestion to. ▶ **empacharse** vpr (hartarse) to stuff o.s.; (sufrir indigestión) to get indigestion.

empacho m (indigestión) upset stomach, indigestion.

empadronar vt = to register on the electoral roll. ▶ **empadronarse** vpr = to register on the electoral roll.

empalagoso, -sa adj sickly, cloying.

empalizada f (cerca) fence; (MIL) stockade.

empalmar ◆ vt (tubos, cables) to connect, to join. ◆ vi 1. (autocares, trenes) to connect. 2. (carreteras) to link o join (up).

empalme m 1. (entre cables, tubos) joint, connection. 2. (de líneas férreas, carreteras) junction.

empanada f pasty.

empanadilla f small pasty.

empanar vt (CULIN) to coat in breadcrumbs.

empantanar vt to flood. ▶ **empantanarse** vpr 1. (inundarse) to be flooded o waterlogged. 2. fig (atascarse) to get bogged down.

empañar vt 1. (cristal) to mist o steam up. 2. fig (reputación) to tarnish. ▶ **empañarse** vpr to mist o steam up.

empapar vt 1. (humedecer) to soak. 2. (absorber) to soak up. ▶ **empaparse** vpr (persona, traje) to get soaked.

empapelar vt (pared) to paper.

empaquetar vt to pack, to package.

emparedado, -da adj confined. ▶ **emparedado** m sandwich.

emparedar vt to lock away.

emparejar vt (aparejar - personas) to pair off; (- zapatos etc) to match (up).

emparentar vi: **~ con** to marry into.

empastar vt to fill.

empaste m filling.

empatar vi (DEP) to draw; (en elecciones etc) to tie; **~ a cero** to draw nil-nil.

empate m (resultado) draw; **un ~ a cero/dos** a goalless/two-all draw.

empedernido, -da adj (bebedor, fumador) heavy; (criminal, jugador) hardened.

empedrado m paving.

empedrar vt to pave.

empeine m (de pie, zapato) instep.

empeñado, -da adj 1. (en préstamo) in pawn. 2. (obstinado) determined; **estar ~ en hacer algo** to be determined to do sthg.

empeñar vt (joyas etc) to pawn. ▶ **empeñarse** vpr 1. (obstinarse) to insist; **~se en hacer algo** (obstinarse) to insist on doing sthg; (persistir) to persist in doing sthg. 2. (endeudarse) to get into debt.

empeño m 1. (de joyas etc) pawning; **casa de ~s** pawnshop. 2. (obstinación) determination; **tener ~ en hacer algo** to be determined to do sthg.

empeorar vi to get worse, to deteriorate.

empequeñecer vt (quitar importancia)

to diminish; (*en una comparación*) to overshadow, to dwarf.

emperador, emperatriz *m y f* emperor (*f* empress). ► **emperador** *m* (*pez*) swordfish.

emperifollar *vt fam* to doll o tart up.

emperrarse *vpr*: ~ **(en hacer algo)** to insist (on doing sthg).

empezar ♦ *vt* to begin, to start. ♦ *vi*: ~ **(a hacer algo)** to begin o start (to do sthg); ~ **(por hacer algo)** to begin o start (by doing sthg); **para** ~ to begin o start with.

empinado, -da *adj* steep.

empinar *vt* (*levantar*) to raise. ► **empinarse** *vpr* 1. (*animal*) to stand up on its hind legs. 2. (*persona*) to stand on tiptoe.

empírico, -ca *adj* empirical.

emplasto *m* (FARM) poultice.

emplazamiento *m* (*ubicación*) location.

emplazar *vt* 1. (*situar*) to locate; (MIL) to position. 2. (*citar*) to summon; (DER) to summons.

empleado, -da *m y f* (*gen*) employee; (*de banco, administración, oficina*) clerk.

emplear *vt* 1. (*usar - objetos, materiales etc*) to use; (- *tiempo*) to spend; ~ **algo en hacer algo** to use sthg to do sthg. 2. (*contratar*) to employ. ► **emplearse** *vpr* 1. (*colocarse*) to find a job. 2. (*usarse*) to be used.

empleo *m* 1. (*uso*) use. 2. (*trabajo*) employment; (*puesto*) job; **estar sin** ~ to be out of work.

emplomadura *f* Amer (*diente*) filling.

empobrecer *vt* to impoverish. ► **empobrecerse** *vpr* to get poorer.

empollar ♦ *vt* 1. (*huevo*) to incubate. 2. *fam* (*estudiar*) to swot up on. ♦ *vi fam* to swot.

empollón, -ona *fam m y f* swot.

empolvarse *vpr* to powder one's face.

empotrado, -da *adj* fitted, built-in.

empotrar *vt* to fit, to build in.

emprendedor, -ra *adj* enterprising.

emprender *vt* (*trabajo*) to start; (*viaje, marcha*) to set off on; ~ **vuelo** to fly off.

empresa *f* 1. (*sociedad*) company; **la pequeña y mediana** ~ small and medium-sized businesses. 2. (*dirección*) management. 3. (*acción*) enterprise, undertaking.

empresarial *adj* management (*antes de sust*). ► **empresariales** *fpl* business studies.

empresario, -ria *m y f* (*patrono*) employer; (*hombre, mujer de negocios*) businessman (*f* businesswoman); (*de teatro*) impresario.

empréstito *m* debenture loan.

empujar *vt* to push; ~ **a alguien a que haga algo** to push sb into doing sthg.

empuje *m* 1. (*presión*) pressure. 2. (*energía*) energy, drive.

empujón *m* (*empellón*) shove, push; **abrirse paso a empujones** to shove o push one's way through.

empuñadura *f* handle; (*de espada*) hilt.

empuñar *vt* to take hold of, to grasp.

emulsión *f* emulsion.

en *prep* 1. (*lugar - en el interior de*) in; (- *sobre la superficie de*) on; (- *en un punto concreto de*) at; **viven** ~ **la capital** they live in the capital; **tiene el dinero** ~ **el banco** he keeps his money in the bank; ~ **la mesa/el plato** on the table/plate; ~ **casa/el trabajo** at home/work. 2. (*dirección*) into; **el avión cayó** ~ **el mar** the plane fell into the sea; **entraron** ~ **la habitación** they came into the room. 3. (*tiempo - mes, año etc*) in; (- *día*) on; **nació** ~ **1940/mayo** he was born in 1940/May; ~ **aquel día** on that day; ~ **Nochebuena** on Christmas Eve; ~ **Navidades** at Christmas; ~ **aquella época** at that time, in those days; ~ **un par de días** in a couple of days. 4. (*medio de transporte*) by; **ir** ~ **tren/coche/avión/ barco** to go by train/car/plane/boat. 5. (*modo*) in; ~ **voz baja** in a low voice; **lo dijo** ~ **inglés** she said it in English; **pagar** ~ **libras** to pay in pounds; **la inflación aumentó** ~ **un 10%** inflation increased by 10%; **todo se lo gasta** ~ **ropa** he spends everything on clothes. 6. (*precio*) in; **las ganancias se calculan** ~ **millones** profits are calculated in millions; **te lo dejo en 5.000** I'll let you have it for 5,000. 7. (*tema*) **es un experto** ~ **la materia** he's an expert on the subject; **es doctor** ~ **medicina** he's a doctor of medicine. 8. (*causa*) from; **lo detecté** ~ **su forma de hablar** I could tell from the way he was speaking. 9. (*materia*) in, made of; ~ **seda** in silk. 10. (*cualidad*) in terms of; **le supera** ~ **inteligencia** she is more intelligent than he is.

enagua *f* (*gen pl*) petticoat.

enajenación *f*, **enajenamiento** *m* (*locura*) insanity; (*éxtasis*) rapture.

enajenar *vt* 1. (*volver loco*) to drive

mad; (*extasiar*) to enrapture. **2.** (*propiedad*) to alienate.

enaltecer *vt* to praise.

enamoradizo, -za *adj* who falls in love easily.

enamorado, -da ◆ *adj*: ~ (de) in love (with). ◆ *m y f* lover.

enamorar *vt* to win the heart of. ▶ **enamorarse** *vpr*: ~se (de) to fall in love (with).

enano, -na *adj, m y f* dwarf.

enarbolar *vt* (*bandera*) to raise, to hoist; (*pancarta*) to hold up; (*arma*) to brandish.

enardecer *vt* (*gen*) to inflame; (*persona, multitud*) to fill with enthusiasm.

encabezamiento *m* (*de carta, escrito*) heading; (*de artículo periodístico*) headline; (*preámbulo*) foreword.

encabezar *vt* **1.** (*artículo de periódico*) to headline; (*libro*) to write the foreword for. **2.** (*lista, carta*) to head. **3.** (*marcha, expedición*) to lead.

encabritarse *vpr* **1.** (*caballo, moto*) to rear up. **2.** *fam* (*persona*) to get shirty.

encadenar *vt* **1.** (*atar*) to chain (up). **2.** (*enlazar*) to link (together).

encajar ◆ *vt* **1.** (*meter ajustando*): ~ (en) to fit (into). **2.** (*meter con fuerza*): ~ (en) to push (into). **3.** (*hueso dislocado*) to set. **4.** (*recibir - golpe, noticia, críticas*) to take. ◆ *vi* **1.** (*piezas, objetos*) to fit. **2.** (*hechos, declaraciones, datos*): ~ (con) to square (with), to match.

encaje *m* (*tejido*) lace.

encalar *vt* to whitewash.

encallar *vi* (*barco*) to run aground.

encaminar *vt* **1.** (*persona, pasos*) to direct. **2.** (*medidas, leyes, actividades*) to aim; **encaminado a** aimed at. ▶ **encaminarse** *vpr*: ~se a/hacia to set off for/towards.

encandilar *vt* to dazzle.

encantado, -da *adj* **1.** (*contento*) delighted; ~ de conocerle pleased to meet you. **2.** (*hechizado - casa, lugar*) haunted; (- *persona*) bewitched.

encantador, -ra *adj* delightful, charming.

encantar ◆ *vi* (*gustar*): ~le a alguien algo/hacer algo to love sthg/doing sthg; **me encantan las orquídeas** I love orchids. ◆ *vt* (*embrujar*) to cast a spell on; (*cautivar*) to charm.

encanto *m* **1.** (*atractivo*) charm; **ser un ~** to be a treasure o a delight. **2.** (*hechizo*) spell.

encapotado, -da *adj* overcast.

encapotarse *vpr* to cloud over.

encapricharse *vpr* (*obstinarse*): ~ con algo/hacer algo to set one's mind on sthg/doing sthg.

encapuchado, -da *adj* hooded.

encaramar *vt* to lift up. ▶ **encaramarse** *vpr*: ~se (a o en) to climb up (onto).

encarar *vt* (*hacer frente a*) to confront, to face up to. ▶ **encararse** *vpr* (*enfrentarse*): ~se a o con to stand up to.

encarcelar *vt* to imprison.

encarecer *vt* (*productos, precios*) to make more expensive. ▶ **encarecerse** *vpr* to become more expensive.

encarecidamente *adv* earnestly.

encarecimiento *m* (*de producto, coste*) increase in price.

encargado, -da ◆ *adj*: ~ (de) responsible (for), in charge (of). ◆ *m y f* (*gen*) person in charge; (COM) manager (*f* manageress).

encargar *vt* **1.** (*poner al cargo*): ~ a alguien de algo to put sb in charge of sthg; ~ a alguien que haga algo to tell sb to do sthg. **2.** (*pedir*) to order. ▶ **encargarse** *vpr* (*ocuparse*): ~se de to take charge of; **yo me encargaré de eso** I'll take care of o see to that.

encargo *m* **1.** (*pedido*) order; **por ~** to order. **2.** (*recado*) errand. **3.** (*tarea*) task, assignment.

encariñarse *vpr*: ~ con to become fond of.

encarnación *f* (*personificación - cosa*) embodiment; (- *persona*) personification.

encarnado, -da *adj* **1.** (*personificado*) incarnate. **2.** (*color*) red.

encarnizado, -da *adj* bloody, bitter.

encarnizarse *vpr*: ~ con (*presa*) to fall upon; (*prisionero, enemigo*) to treat savagely.

encarrilar *vt* *fig* (*negocio, situación*) to put on the right track.

encasillar *vt* (*clasificar*) to pigeonhole; (TEATR) to typecast.

encasquetar *vt* **1.** (*imponer*): ~ algo a alguien (*idea, teoría*) to drum sthg into sb; (*discurso, lección*) to force sb to sit through sthg. **2.** (*sombrero*) to pull on.

encasquillarse *vpr* to get jammed.

encauzar *vt* **1.** (*corriente*) to channel. **2.** (*orientar*) to direct.

encendedor *m* lighter.

encender *vt* **1.** (*vela, cigarro, chimenea*) to light. **2.** (*aparato*) to switch on. **3.** *fig* (*avivar - entusiasmo, ira*) to arouse;

(- *pasión, discusión*) to inflame. ▶ **encen-derse** *vpr* 1. (*fuego, gas*) to ignite; (*luz, estufa*) to come on. 2. *fig* (*ojos*) to light up; (*persona, rostro*) to go red, to blush; (*de ira*) to flare up.

encendido, -da *adj* (*luz, colilla*) burning; **la luz está encendida** the light is on. ▶ **encendido** *m* (AUTOM) ignition.

encerado, -da *adj* waxed, polished. ▶ **encerado** *m* (*pizarra*) blackboard.

encerar *vt* to wax, to polish.

encerrar *vt* 1. (*recluir - gen*) to shut (up o in); (- *con llave*) to lock (up o in); (- *en la cárcel*) to lock away o up. 2. (*contener*) to contain. ▶ **encerrarse** *vpr* (*gen*) to shut o.s. away; (*con llave*) to lock o.s. away.

encestar *vt & vi* to score (*in basketball*).

enceste *m* basket.

encharcar *vt* to waterlog. ▶ **enchar-carse** *vpr* 1. (*terreno*) to become waterlogged. 2. (*pulmones*) to become flooded.

enchilarse *vpr* Amer fam to get angry.

enchufado, -da *adj fam*: **estar ~** to get where one is through connections.

enchufar *vt* 1. (*aparato*) to plug in. 2. *fam* (*a una persona*) to pull strings for.

enchufe *m* 1. (ELECTR - *macho*) plug; (- *hembra*) socket. 2. *fam* (*recomendación*) connections (*pl*); **obtener algo por ~** to get sthg by pulling strings o through one's connections.

encía *f* gum.

encíclica *f* encyclical.

enciclopedia *f* encyclopedia.

encierro *m* (*protesta*) sit-in.

encima *adv* 1. (*arriba*) on top; **yo vivo ~** I live upstairs; **por ~** (*superficialmente*) superficially. 2. (*además*) on top of that. 3. (*sobre sí*): **lleva un abrigo ~** she has a coat on; **¿llevas dinero ~?** have you got any money on you? ▶ **encima de** *loc prep* 1. (*en lugar superior que*) above; **vivo ~ de tu casa** I live upstairs from you. 2. (*sobre, en*) on (top of); **el pan está ~ de la mesa** the bread is on (top of) the table. 3. (*además*) on top of. ▶ **por encima de** *loc prep* 1. (*gen*) over; **vive por ~ de sus posibilidades** he lives beyond his means. 2. *fig* (*más que*) more than; **por ~ de todo** more than anything else.

encina *f* holm oak.

encinta *adj f* pregnant.

enclave *m* enclave.

enclenque *adj* sickly, frail.

encoger ◆ *vt* 1. (*ropa*) to shrink.

2. (*miembro, músculo*) to contract. ◆ *vi* to shrink. ▶ **encogerse** *vpr* 1. (*ropa*) to shrink; (*músculos etc*) to contract; **~se de hombros** to shrug one's shoulders. 2. *fig* (*apocarse*) to cringe.

encolar *vt* (*silla etc*) to glue; (*pared*) to size, to paste.

encolerizar *vt* to infuriate, to enrage. ▶ **encolerizarse** *vpr* to get angry.

encomendar *vt* to entrust. ▶ **enco-mendarse** *vpr*: **~se a** (*persona*) to entrust o.s. to; (*Dios, santos*) to put one's trust in.

encomienda *f* 1. (*encargo*) assignment, mission. 2. Amer (*paquete*) parcel.

encontrado, -da *adj* conflicting.

encontrar *vt* 1. (*gen*) to find. 2. (*dificul-tades*) to encounter. 3. (*persona*) to meet, to come across. ▶ **encontrarse** *vpr* 1. (*hallarse*) to be; **se encuentra en París** she's in Paris. 2. (*coincidir*): **~se** (**con alguien**) to meet (sb); **me encontré con Juan** I ran into o met Juan. 3. *fig* (*de ánimo*) to feel. 4. (*chocar*) to collide.

encorvar *vt* to bend. ▶ **encorvarse** *vpr* to bend down o over.

encrespar *vt* 1. (*pelo*) to curl; (*mar*) to make choppy o rough. 2. (*irritar*) to irritate. ▶ **encresparse** *vpr* 1. (*mar*) to get rough. 2. (*persona*) to get irritated.

encrucijada *f lit & fig* crossroads (*sg*).

encuadernación *f* binding.

encuadernador, -ra *m y f* bookbinder.

encuadernar *vt* to bind.

encuadrar *vt* 1. (*enmarcar - cuadro, tema*) to frame. 2. (*encerrar*) to contain. 3. (*encajar*) to fit.

encubierto, -ta ◆ *pp* → **encubrir**. ◆ *adj* (*intento*) covert; (*insulto, significado*) hidden.

encubridor, -ra *m y f*: **~ (de)** accessory (to).

encubrir *vt* (*delito*) to conceal; (*persona*) to harbour.

encuentro *m* 1. (*acción*) meeting, encounter. 2. (DEP) game, match. 3. (*hallazgo*) find.

encuesta *f* 1. (*de opinión*) survey, opinion poll. 2. (*investigación*) investigation, inquiry.

encuestador, -ra *m y f* pollster.

encuestar *vt* to poll.

endeble *adj* (*persona, argumento*) weak, feeble; (*objeto*) fragile.

endémico, -ca *adj* (MED & *fig*) endemic.

endemoniado, -da *adj* 1. *fam fig*

(*molesto - niño*) wicked; (*- trabajo*) very tricky. **2.** (*desagradable*) terrible, foul. **3.** (*poseído*) possessed (of the devil).

endenantes *adv* Amer *fam* before.

enderezar *vt* **1.** (*poner derecho*) to straighten. **2.** (*poner vertical*) to put upright. **3.** *fig* (*corregir*) to set right. ▶ **enderezarse** *vpr* (*sentado*) to sit up straight; (*de pie*) to stand up straight.

endeudamiento *m* debt.

endeudarse *vpr* to get into debt.

endiablado, -da *adj* (*persona*) wicked; (*tiempo, genio*) foul; (*problema, crucigrama*) fiendishly difficult.

endibia = **endivia**.

endiñar *vt fam:* ~ **algo a alguien** (*golpe*) to land o deal sb sthg; (*trabajo, tarea*) to lumber sb with sthg.

endivia, endibia *f* endive.

endomingado, -da *adj fam* dolled-up.

endosar *vt* **1.** *fig* (*tarea, trabajo*): ~ **algo a alguien** to lumber sb with sthg. **2.** (COM) to endorse.

endulzar *vt* (*con azúcar*) to sweeten; *fig* (*con dulzura*) to ease.

endurecer *vt* **1.** (*gen*) to harden. **2.** (*fortalecer*) to strengthen.

enemigo, -ga ◆ *adj* enemy (*antes de sust*); **ser** ~ **de algo** to hate sthg. ◆ *m y f* enemy.

enemistad *f* enmity.

enemistar *vt* to make enemies of. ▶ **enemistarse** *vpr:* ~**se (con)** to fall out (with).

energético, -ca *adj* energy (*antes de sust*).

energía *f* **1.** (*gen*) energy; ~ **atómica** o **nuclear** nuclear power; ~ **eólica/hidráulica** wind/water power; ~ **solar** solar energy o power. **2.** (*fuerza*) strength.

enérgico, -ca *adj* (*gen*) energetic; (*carácter*) forceful; (*gesto, medida*) vigorous; (*decisión, postura*) emphatic.

energúmeno, -na *m y f fig* madman (*f* madwoman).

enero *m* January; *ver también* **septiembre**.

enervar *vt* **1.** (*debilitar*) to sap, to weaken. **2.** (*poner nervioso*) to exasperate.

enésimo, -ma *adj* **1.** (MAT) n[th]. **2.** *fig* umpteenth; **por enésima vez** for the umpteenth time.

enfadado, -da *adj* angry.

enfadar *vt* to anger. ▶ **enfadarse** *vpr:* ~**se (con)** to get angry (with).

enfado *m* anger.

énfasis *m inv* emphasis; **poner** ~ **en algo** to emphasize sthg.

enfático, -ca *adj* emphatic.

enfatizar *vt* to emphasize, to stress.

enfermar ◆ *vt* (*causar enfermedad*) to make ill. ◆ *vi* to fall ill; ~ **del pecho** to develop a chest complaint.

enfermedad *f* (*física*) illness; ~ **infecciosa/venérea** infectious/venereal disease.

enfermera → **enfermero**.

enfermería *f* **1.** (*de colegio, fábrica*) sick bay, infirmary. **2.** (*profesión*) nursing.

enfermero, -ra *m y f* male nurse (*f* nurse).

enfermizo, -za *adj lit & fig* unhealthy.

enfermo, -ma ◆ *adj* ill, sick. ◆ *m y f* (*gen*) invalid, sick person; (*en el hospital*) patient.

enfilar *vt* **1.** (*ir por - camino*) to go o head straight along. **2.** (*apuntar - arma*) to aim.

enflaquecer *vi* to grow thin.

enfocar *vt* **1.** (*imagen, objetivo*) to focus. **2.** (*suj: luz, foco*) to shine on. **3.** *fig* (*tema, asunto*) to approach, to look at.

enfoque *m* **1.** (*de una imagen*) focus. **2.** *fig* (*de un asunto*) approach, angle.

enfrascar *vt* to bottle. ▶ **enfrascarse en** *vpr* (*riña*) to get embroiled in; (*lectura, conversación*) to become engrossed in.

enfrentar *vt* **1.** (*hacer frente*) to confront, to face. **2.** (*poner frente a frente*) to bring face to face. ▶ **enfrentarse** *vpr* **1.** (*luchar, encontrarse*) to meet, to clash. **2.** (*oponerse*): ~**se con alguien** to confront sb.

enfrente *adv* **1.** (*delante*) opposite; **la tienda de** ~ the shop across the road; ~ **de** opposite, facing. **2.** (*en contra*): **tiene a todos** ~ everyone's against her.

enfriamiento *m* **1.** (*catarro*) cold. **2.** (*acción*) cooling.

enfriar *vt lit & fig* to cool. ▶ **enfriarse** *vpr* **1.** (*líquido, pasión, amistad*) to cool down. **2.** (*quedarse demasiado frío*) to go cold. **3.** (MED) to catch a cold.

enfundar *vt* (*espada*) to sheathe; (*pistola*) to put away.

enfurecer *vt* to infuriate, to madden. ▶ **enfurecerse** *vpr* (*gen*) to get furious.

enfurruñarse *vpr fam* to sulk.

engalanar *vt* to decorate. ▶ **engalanarse** *vpr* to dress up.

enganchar *vt* **1.** (*agarrar - vagones*) to couple; (*- remolque, caballos*) to hitch up; (*- pez*) to hook. **2.** (*colgar de un gancho*) to hang up. ▶ **engancharse** vpr 1. (prenderse): **~se algo con algo** to catch sthg on sthg. 2. (alistarse) to enlist, to join up. 3. (hacerse adicto): **~se (a)** to get hooked (on).

enganche m 1. (de trenes) coupling. 2. (gancho) hook. 3. (reclutamiento) enlistment. 4. Amer (depósito) deposit.

engañar vt 1. (gen) to deceive; **engaña a su marido** she cheats on her husband. 2. (estafar) to cheat, to swindle. ▶ **engañarse** vpr 1. (hacerse ilusiones) to delude o.s. 2. (equivocarse) to be wrong.

engaño m (gen) deceit; (estafa) swindle.

engañoso, -sa adj (persona, palabras) deceitful; (aspecto, apariencia) deceptive.

engarzar vt 1. (encadenar - abalorios) to thread; (- perlas) to string. 2. (enlazar - palabras) to string together.

engatusar vt fam to get round; **~ a alguien para que haga algo** to coax o cajole sb into doing sthg.

engendrar vt 1. (procrear) to give birth to. 2. fig (originar) to give rise to.

engendro m 1. (obra de mala calidad) monstrosity. 2. (ser deforme) freak; (niño) malformed child.

englobar vt to bring together.

engomar vt (pegar) to stick, to glue.

engordar ◆ vt 1. to fatten up. 2. fig (aumentar) to swell. ◆ vi to put on weight.

engorroso, -sa adj bothersome.

engranaje m 1. (piezas - de reloj, piñón) cogs (pl); (AUTOM) gears (pl). 2. (aparato - político, burocrático) machinery.

engrandecer vt 1. fig (enaltecer) to exalt. 2. (aumentar) to increase, to enlarge.

engrasar vt (gen) to lubricate; (bisagra, mecanismo) to oil; (eje, bandeja) to grease.

engreído, -da adj conceited, full of one's own importance.

engrosar vt fig (aumentar) to swell.

engullir vt to gobble up.

enhebrar vt (gen) to thread; (perlas) to string.

enhorabuena ◆ f congratulations (pl). ◆ adv: **¡~ (por ...)!** congratulations (on ...)!

enigma m enigma.

enigmático, -ca adj enigmatic.

enjabonar vt (con jabón) to soap.

enjambre m lit & fig swarm.

enjaular vt (en jaula) to cage; fam fig (en prisión) to jail, to lock up.

enjuagar vt to rinse.

enjuague m rinse.

enjugar vt 1. (secar) to dry, to wipe away. 2. fig (pagar - deuda) to pay off; (- déficit) to cancel out.

enjuiciar vt 1. (DER) to try. 2. (opinar) to judge.

enjuto, -ta adj (delgado) lean.

enlace m 1. (acción) link. 2. (persona) go-between; **~ sindical** shop steward. 3. (casamiento): **~ (matrimonial)** marriage. 4. (de trenes) connection; **estación de ~** junction; **vía de ~** crossover.

enlatar vt to can, to tin.

enlazar ◆ vt: **~ algo a** (atar) to tie sthg up to; (trabar, relacionar) to link o connect sthg with. ◆ vi: **~ en** (trenes) to connect at.

enloquecer ◆ vt 1. (volver loco) to drive mad. 2. fig (gustar mucho) to drive wild o crazy. ◆ vi to go mad.

enlutado, -da adj in mourning.

enmarañar vt 1. (enredar) to tangle (up). 2. (complicar) to complicate. ▶ **enmarañarse** vpr 1. (enredarse) to become tangled. 2. (complicarse) to become confused o complicated.

enmarcar vt to frame.

enmascarado, -da adj masked.

enmascarar vt (rostro) to mask; fig (encubrir) to disguise.

enmendar vt (error) to correct; (ley, dictamen) to amend; (comportamiento) to mend; (daño, perjuicio) to redress. ▶ **enmendarse** vpr to mend one's ways.

enmienda f 1. (en un texto) corrections (pl). 2. (POLÍT) amendment.

enmohecer vt (gen) to turn mouldy; (metal) to rust. ▶ **enmohecerse** vpr (gen) to grow mouldy; (metal, conocimientos) to go rusty.

enmoquetar vt to carpet.

enmudecer ◆ vt to silence. ◆ vi (callarse) to fall silent, to go quiet; (perder el habla) to be struck dumb.

ennegrecer vt (gen) to blacken; (suj: nubes) to darken. ▶ **ennegrecerse** vpr (gen) to become blackened; (nublarse) to darken, to grow dark.

ennoblecer vt 1. fig (dignificar) to lend distinction to. 2. (dar un título a) to ennoble.

enojar vt (enfadar) to anger; (molestar) to annoy. ▶ **enojarse** vpr: **~se (con)** (enfadarse) to get angry (with); (molestarse) to get annoyed (with).

enojo m (enfado) anger; (molestia) annoyance.

enojoso, -sa adj (molesto) annoying; (delicado, espinoso) awkward.

enorgullecer vt to fill with pride. ► **enorgullecerse de** vpr to be proud of.

enorme adj (en tamaño) enormous, huge; (en gravedad) monstrous.

enormidad f (de tamaño) enormity, hugeness.

enrarecer vt 1. (contaminar) to pollute. 2. (rarificar) to rarefy. ► **enrarecerse** vpr 1. (contaminarse) to become polluted. 2. (rarificarse) to become rarefied. 3. fig (situación, ambiente) to become tense.

enredadera f creeper.

enredar vt 1. (madeja, pelo) to tangle up; (situación, asunto) to complicate, to confuse. 2. fig (implicar): ~ **a alguien (en)** to embroil sb (in), to involve sb (in). ► **enredarse** vpr (plantas) to climb; (madeja, pelo) to get tangled up; (situación, asunto) to become confused.

enredo m 1. (maraña) tangle, knot. 2. (lío) mess, complicated affair; (asunto ilícito) shady affair. 3. (amoroso) (love) affair.

enrejado m 1. (barrotes - de balcón, verja) railings (pl); (- de jaula, celda, ventana) bars (pl). 2. (de cañas) trellis.

enrevesado, -da adj complex, complicated.

enriquecer vt 1. (hacer rico) to make rich. 2. fig (engrandecer) to enrich. ► **enriquecerse** vpr to get rich.

enrojecer ♦ vt (gen) to redden; (rostro, mejillas) to cause to blush. ♦ vi (por calor) to flush; (por turbación) to blush. ► **enrojecerse** vpr (por calor) to flush; (por turbación) to blush.

enrolar vt to enlist. ► **enrolarse en** vpr (la marina) to enlist in; (un buque) to sign up for.

enrollar vt 1. (arrollar) to roll up. 2. fam (gustar): **me enrolla mucho** I love it, I think it's great.

enroscar vt 1. (atornillar) to screw in. 2. (enrollar) to roll up; (cuerpo, cola) to curl up.

ensaimada f cake made of sweet coiled pastry.

ensalada f (de lechuga etc) salad.

ensaladilla f: ~ **rusa** Russian salad.

ensalzar vt to praise.

ensambladura f, **ensamblaje** m (acción) assembly; (pieza) joint.

ensanchar vt (orificio, calle) to widen; (ropa) to let out; (ciudad) to expand.

ensanche m 1. (de calle etc) widening.

2. (en la ciudad) new suburb.

ensangrentar vt to cover with blood.

ensañarse vpr: ~ **con** to torment, to treat cruelly.

ensartar vt 1. (perlas) to string; (aguja) to thread. 2. (atravesar - torero) to gore; (puñal) to plunge, to bury.

ensayar vt 1. (gen) to test. 2. (TEATR) to rehearse.

ensayista m y f essayist.

ensayo m 1. (TEATR) rehearsal; ~ **general** dress rehearsal. 2. (prueba) test. 3. (LITER) essay. 4. (en rugby) try.

enseguida adv (inmediatamente) immediately, at once; (pronto) very soon; **llegará** ~ he'll be here any minute now.

ensenada f cove, inlet.

enseñanza f (gen) education; (instrucción) teaching; ~ **primaria/media** primary/secondary education.

enseñar vt 1. (instruir, aleccionar) to teach; ~ **a alguien a hacer algo** to teach sb (how) to do sthg. 2. (mostrar) to show.

enseres mpl 1. (efectos personales) belongings. 2. (utensilios) equipment (U).

ensillar vt to saddle up.

ensimismarse vpr (enfrascarse) to become absorbed; (abstraerse) to be lost in thought.

ensombrecer vt lit & fig to cast a shadow over. ► **ensombrecerse** vpr to darken.

ensoñación f daydream.

ensopar vt Amer to soak.

ensordecer ♦ vt (suj: sonido) to deafen. ♦ vi to go deaf.

ensortijar vt to curl.

ensuciar vt to (make) dirty; fig (desprestigiar) to sully, to tarnish. ► **ensuciarse** vpr to get dirty.

ensueño m lit & fig dream; **de** ~ dream (antes de sust), ideal.

entablado m (armazón) wooden platform; (suelo) floorboards (pl).

entablar vt (iniciar - conversación, amistad) to strike up.

entallar vt 1. (prenda) to cut, to tailor. 2. (madera) to carve, to sculpt.

entarimado m (plataforma) wooden platform; (suelo) floorboards (pl).

ente m 1. (ser) being. 2. (corporación) body, organization; ~ **público** (gen) state-owned body o institution; (televisión) Spanish state broadcasting company.

entender ♦ vt 1. (gen) to understand.

2. (*darse cuenta*) to realize. 3. (*oír*) to hear. 4. (*juzgar*) to think; **yo no lo entiendo así** I don't see it that way. ◆ *vi* 1. (*comprender*) to understand. 2. (*saber*): **~ de** o **en algo** to be an expert on sthg; **~ poco/algo de** to know very little/a little about. ◆ *m*: **a mí ~ ...** the way I see it ... ▶ **entenderse** *vpr* 1. (*comprenderse - uno mismo*) to know what one means; (*- dos personas*) to understand each other. 2. (*llevarse bien*) to get on. 3. (*ponerse de acuerdo*) to reach an agreement. 4. (*comunicarse*) to communicate (with each other).

entendido, -da *m y f*: **~ (en)** expert (on). ▶ **entendido** *interj*: **¡~!** all right!, okay!

entendimiento *m* (*comprensión*) understanding; (*juicio*) judgment; (*inteligencia*) mind, intellect.

enterado, -da *adj*: **~ (en)** well-informed (about); **estar ~ de algo** to be aware of sthg; **no darse por ~** to turn a deaf ear.

enterar *vt*: **~ a alguien de algo** to inform sb about sthg. ▶ **enterarse** *vpr* 1. (*descubrir*): **~se (de)** to find out (about). 2. *fam* (*comprender*) to get it, to understand. 3. (*darse cuenta*): **~se (de algo)** to realize (sthg).

entereza *f* (*serenidad*) composure; (*honradez*) integrity; (*firmeza*) firmness.

enternecer *vt* to move, to touch. ▶ **enternecerse** *vpr* to be moved.

entero, -ra *adj* 1. (*completo*) whole, entire. 2. (*sereno*) composed. 3. (*honrado*) upright, honest.

enterrador, -ra *m y f* gravedigger.

enterrar *vt* (*gen*) to bury.

entibiar *vt* 1. (*enfriar*) to cool. 2. (*templar*) to warm. ▶ **entibiarse** *vpr* (*sentimiento*) to cool.

entidad *f* 1. (*corporación*) body; (*empresa*) firm, company. 2. (FILOSOFÍA) entity. 3. (*importancia*) importance.

entierro *m* (*acción*) burial; (*ceremonia*) funeral.

entlo. *abrev de* **entresuelo**.

entoldado *m* (*toldo*) awning; (*para fiestas, bailes*) marquee.

entomólogo, -ga *m y f* entomologist.

entonación *f* intonation.

entonar *vt* 1. (*cantar*) to sing. 2. (*tonificar*) to pick up. ◆ *vi* 1. (*al cantar*) to sing in tune. 2. (*armonizar*): **~ (con algo)** to match (sthg).

entonces ◆ *adv* then; **desde ~** since

then; **en** o **por aquel ~** at that time. ◆ *interj*: **¡~!** well, then!

entornar *vt* to half-close.

entorno *m* environment, surroundings (*pl*).

entorpecer *vt* 1. (*debilitar - movimientos*) to hinder; (*- mente*) to cloud. 2. (*dificultar*) to obstruct, to hinder.

entrada *f* 1. (*acción*) entry; (*llegada*) arrival; **'prohibida la ~'** 'no entry'. 2. (*lugar*) entrance; (*puerta*) doorway. 3. (TECN) inlet, intake. 4. (*en espectáculos - billete*) ticket; (*- recaudación*) receipts (*pl*), takings (*pl*); **~ libre** admission free; **sacar una ~** to buy a ticket. 5. (*público*) audience; (DEP) attendance. 6. (*pago inicial*) down payment. 7. (*en contabilidad*) income. 8. (*plato*) starter, first course. 9. (*en la frente*): **tener ~s** to have a receding hairline. 10. (*en un diccionario*) entry. 11. (*principio*): **de ~** right from the beginning o the word go.

entrante ◆ *adj* (*año, mes*) coming; (*presidente, gobierno*) incoming. ◆ *m* 1. (*plato*) starter. 2. (*hueco*) recess.

entraña *f* (*gen pl*) 1. (*víscera*) entrails (*pl*), insides (*pl*). 2. *fig* (*centro, esencia*) heart.

entrañable *adj* intimate.

entrañar *vt* to involve.

entrar ◆ *vi* 1. (*introducirse - viniendo*) to enter, to come in; (*- yendo*) to enter, to go in; **~ en algo** to enter sthg, to come/go into sthg; **entré por la ventana** I got in through the window. 2. (*penetrar - clavo etc*) to go in; **~ en algo** to go into sthg. 3. (*caber*): **~ (en)** to fit (in); **este anillo no te entra** this ring won't fit you. 4. (*incorporarse*): **~ (en algo)** (*colegio, empresa*) to start (at sthg); (*club, partido político*) to join (sthg); **~ de** (*botones etc*) to start off as. 5. (*estado físico o de ánimo*): **le entraron ganas de hablar** he suddenly felt like talking; **me está entrando frío** I'm getting cold; **me entró mucha pena** I was filled with pity. 6. (*periodo de tiempo*) to start; **~ en** (*edad, vejez*) to reach; (*año nuevo*) to enter. 7. (*cantidad*): **¿cuántos entran en un kilo?** how many do you get to the kilo? 8. (*concepto, asignatura etc*): **no le entra la geometría** he can't get the hang of geometry. 9. (AUTOM) to engage. ◆ *vt* (*introducir*) to bring in.

entre *prep* 1. (*gen*) between; **~ nosotros** (*en confianza*) between you and me, between ourselves; **~ una cosa y otra** what with one thing and another. 2. (*en medio de muchos*) among, amongst; **esta-**

ba ~ los asistentes she was among those present; **~ sí** amongst themselves; **discutían ~ sí** they were arguing with each other.

entreabierto, -ta *pp* → **entreabrir**.

entreabrir *vt* to half-open.

entreacto *m* interval.

entrecejo *m* space between the brows; **fruncir el ~** to frown.

entrecortado, -da *adj* (*voz, habla*) faltering; (*respiración*) laboured; (*señal, sonido*) intermittent.

entrecot, entrecote *m* entrecôte.

entredicho *m*: **estar en ~** to be in doubt; **poner en ~** to question, to call into question.

entrega *f* 1. (*gen*) handing over; (*de pedido, paquete*) delivery; (*de premios*) presentation; **~ a domicilio** home delivery. 2. (*dedicación*): **~ (a)** devotion (to). 3. (*fascículo*) instalment.

entregar *vt* (*gen*) to hand over; (*pedido, paquete*) to deliver; (*examen, informe*) to hand in; (*persona*) to turn over. ▶ **entregarse** *vpr* (*rendirse - soldado, ejército*) to surrender; (*- criminal*) to turn o.s. in. ▶ **entregarse a** *vpr* 1. (*persona, trabajo*) to devote o.s. to. 2. (*vicio, pasión*) to give o.s. over to.

entreguerras ▶ **de entreguerras** *loc adj* between the wars.

entrelazar *vt* to interlace, to interlink.

entremés *m* (CULIN) (*gen pl*) hors d'œuvres.

entremeter *vt* to insert, to put in. ▶ **entremeterse** *vpr* (*inmiscuirse*): **~se (en)** to meddle (in).

entremezclar *vt* to mix up. ▶ **entremezclarse** *vpr* to mix.

entrenador, -ra *m y f* coach, trainer; (*seleccionador*) manager.

entrenamiento *m* 1. (*preparación*) training. 2. (*sesión*) training session.

entrenar *vt & vi* to train. ▶ **entrenarse** *vpr* to train.

entrepierna *f* crotch.

entresacar *vt* to pick out.

entresijos *mpl* ins and outs.

entresuelo *m* mezzanine.

entretanto *adv* meanwhile.

entretención *f* Amer entertainment.

entretener *vt* 1. (*despistar*) to distract. 2. (*retrasar*) to hold up, to keep. 3. (*divertir*) to entertain. ▶ **entretenerse** *vpr* 1. (*despistarse*) to get distracted. 2. (*divertirse*) to amuse o.s. 3. (*retrasarse*) to be held up.

entretenido, -da *adj* entertaining, enjoyable.

entretenimiento *m* 1. (*acción*) entertainment. 2. (*pasatiempo*) pastime.

entrever *vt* (*vislumbrar*) to barely make out; (*por un instante*) to glimpse.

entrevero *m* Amer tangle, mess.

entrevista *f* interview.

entrevistar *vt* to interview. ▶ **entrevistarse** *vpr*: **~se (con)** to have a meeting (with).

entrevisto, -ta *pp* → **entrever**.

entristecer *vt* to make sad. ▶ **entristecerse** *vpr* to become sad.

entrometerse *vpr*: **~ (en)** to interfere (in).

entrometido, -da *m y f* meddler.

entroncar *vi* 1. (*trenes etc*) to connect. 2. *fig* (*relacionarse*): **~ (con)** to be related (to).

entuerto *m* wrong, injustice.

entumecer *vt* to numb. ▶ **entumecerse** *vpr* to become numb.

entumecido, -da *adj* numb.

enturbiar *vt* lit & fig to cloud. ▶ **enturbiarse** *vpr* lit & fig to become cloudy.

entusiasmar *vt* 1. (*animar*) to fill with enthusiasm. 2. (*gustar*): **le entusiasma la música** he loves music. ▶ **entusiasmarse** *vpr*: **~se (con)** to get excited (about).

entusiasmo *m* enthusiasm.

entusiasta ◆ *adj* enthusiastic. ◆ *m y f* enthusiast.

enumeración *f* enumeration, listing.

enumerar *vt* to enumerate, to list.

enunciar *vt* to formulate, to enunciate.

envainar *vt* to sheathe.

envalentonar *vt* to urge on, to fill with courage. ▶ **envalentonarse** *vpr* to become daring.

envanecer *vt* to make vain. ▶ **envanecerse** *vpr* to become vain.

envasado *m* (*en botellas*) bottling; (*en latas*) canning; (*en paquetes*) packing.

envasar *vt* (*gen*) to pack; (*en latas*) to can; (*en botellas*) to bottle.

envase *m* 1. (*envasado - en botellas*) bottling; (*- en latas*) canning; (*- en paquetes*) packing, packaging. 2. (*recipiente*) container; (*botella*) bottle; **~ desechable** disposable container; **~ sin retorno** non-returnable bottle.

envejecer ◆ *vi* (*hacerse viejo*) to grow old; (*parecer viejo*) to age. ◆ *vt* to age.

envejecimiento *m* ageing.

envenenamiento m poisoning.

envenenar vt to poison.

envergadura f 1. (importancia) size, extent; (complejidad) complexity; **una reforma de gran ~** a wide-ranging reform. 2. (anchura) span.

envés m reverse (side), back; (de tela) wrong side.

enviado, -da m y f (POLÍT) envoy; (PRENS) correspondent.

enviar vt to send.

enviciar vt to addict, to get hooked. ▶ **enviciarse** vpr to become addicted.

envidia f envy; **tener ~ de** to envy.

envidiar vt to envy.

envidioso, -sa adj envious.

envilecer vt to debase.

envío m 1. (COM) dispatch; (de correo) delivery; (de víveres, mercancías) consignment. 2. (paquete) package.

envite m (en el juego) raise.

enviudar vi to be widowed.

envoltorio m, **envoltura** f wrapper, wrapping.

envolver vt 1. (embalar) to wrap (up). 2. (enrollar) to wind. 3. (implicar): **~ a alguien en** to involve sb in.

envuelto, -ta pp → envolver.

enyesar vt 1. (MED) to put in plaster. 2. (CONSTR) to plaster.

enzarzar vt to entangle, to embroil. ▶ **enzarzarse** vpr: ~se **en** to get entangled o embroiled in.

enzima f enzyme.

e.p.d. (abrev de en paz descanse) RIP.

épica → épico.

épico, -ca adj epic. ▶ **épica** f epic.

epidemia f epidemic.

epígrafe m heading.

epilepsia f epilepsy.

epílogo m epilogue.

episodio m (gen) episode.

epístola f culto (carta) epistle; (RELIG) Epistle.

epitafio m epitaph.

epíteto m epithet.

época f period; (estación) season; (de la historia) epoch, age; **de ~** period (antes de sust); **en aquella ~** at that time.

epopeya f 1. (gen) epic. 2. fig (hazaña) feat.

equidad f fairness.

equidistante adj equidistant.

equilibrado, -da adj 1. (gen) balanced. 2. (sensato) sensible.

equilibrar vt to balance.

equilibrio m balance; **mantenerse/perder el ~** to keep/lose one's balance;

hacer ~s fig to perform a balancing act.

equilibrista m y f (trapecista) trapeze artist; (funambulista) tightrope walker.

equino, -na adj equine.

equinoccio m equinox.

equipaje m luggage Br, baggage Am; **hacer el ~** to pack; **~ de mano** hand luggage.

equipar vt: **~ (de)** (gen) to equip (with); (ropa) to fit out (with).

equiparar vt to compare. ▶ **equipararse** vpr to be compared.

equipo m 1. (equipamiento) equipment. 2. (personas, jugadores) team; **~ de rescate** rescue team. 3. (de música) system; **~ de sonido** sound system.

equis adj X; **un número ~ de personas** x number of people.

equitación f (arte) equestrianism; (actividad) horse riding.

equitativo, -va adj fair, even-handed.

equivalente adj & m equivalent.

equivaler ▶ **equivaler a** vi to be equivalent to; fig (significar) to amount to.

equivocación f mistake; **por ~** by mistake.

equivocado, -da adj (número, respuesta) wrong; **estar ~** (persona) to be wrong o mistaken.

equivocar vt to choose wrongly; **~ algo con algo** to mistake sthg for sthg. ▶ **equivocarse** vpr to be wrong; ~se **en** to make a mistake in; **se equivocó de nombre** he got the wrong name.

equívoco, -ca adj 1. (ambiguo) ambiguous, equivocal. 2. (sospechoso) suspicious. ▶ **equívoco** m misunderstanding.

era ♦ v → ser. ♦ f (periodo) era.

erario m funds (pl).

erección f erection.

erecto, -ta adj erect.

eres → ser.

erguir vt to raise. ▶ **erguirse** vpr to rise up.

erigir vt (construir) to erect, to build.

erizado, -da adj (de punta) on end; (con púas o espinas) spiky.

erizar vt to cause to stand on end. ▶ **erizarse** vpr (pelo) to stand on end; (persona) to stiffen.

erizo m 1. (mamífero) hedgehog. 2. (pez) globefish; **~ de mar** sea urchin.

ermita f (capilla) chapel; (de ermitaño) hermitage.

erosión f erosion.

erosionar vt to erode. ▶ **erosionarse** vpr to erode.

erótico, -ca adj erotic.

erotismo m eroticism.

erradicación f eradication.

erradicar vt to eradicate.

errante adj wandering.

errar ◆ vt (vocación, camino) to choose wrongly; (disparo, golpe) to miss. ◆ vi 1. (vagar) to wander. 2. (equivocarse) to make a mistake. 3. (al disparar) to miss.

errata f misprint.

erróneo, -a adj mistaken.

error m mistake, error; **estar en un ~** to be mistaken; **salvo ~ u omisión** errors and omissions excepted; **~ de imprenta** misprint.

ertzaintza [er'tʃaintʃa] f Basque regional police force.

eructar vi to belch.

eructo m belch.

erudito, -ta adj erudite.

erupción f 1. (GEOL) eruption; **en ~** erupting. 2. (MED) rash.

es → ser.

esa → ese².

ésa → ése.

esbelto, -ta adj slender, slim.

esbozar vt to sketch, to outline; (sonrisa) to give a hint of.

esbozo m sketch, outline.

escabechado, -da adj (CULIN) marinated.

escabeche m (CULIN) marinade.

escabroso, -sa adj 1. (abrupto) rough. 2. (obsceno) risqué. 3. (espinoso) awkward, thorny.

escabullirse vpr (desaparecer): **~ (de)** to slip away (from).

escacharrar vt fam to knacker.

escafandra f diving suit.

escala f 1. (gen) scale; (de colores) range; **a ~** (gráfica) to scale; **a ~ mundial** fig on a worldwide scale; **a gran ~** on a large scale. 2. (en un viaje) stopover; **hacer ~** to stop over.

escalada f 1. (de montaña) climb. 2. (de violencia, precios) escalation, rise.

escalador, -ra m y f (alpinista) climber.

escalafón m scale, ladder.

escalar vt to climb.

escaldar vt to scald.

escalera f 1. (gen) stairs (pl), staircase; (escala) ladder; **~ mecánica** o **automática** escalator; **~ de caracol** spiral staircase. 2. (en naipes) run.

escalfar vt to poach.

escalinata f staircase.

escalofriante adj spine-chilling.

escalofrío m (gen pl) shiver; **dar ~s a alguien** to give sb the shivers.

escalón m step; fig grade.

escalonar vt 1. (gen) to spread out. 2. (terreno) to terrace.

escalope m escalope.

escama f 1. (de peces, reptiles) scale. 2. (de jabón, en la piel) flake.

escamar vt fam fig (mosquear) to make suspicious.

escamotear vt: **~ algo a alguien** (estafar) to do o swindle sb out of sthg; (hurtar) to rob sb of sthg.

escampar v impers to stop raining.

escandalizar vt to scandalize, to shock. ▶ **escandalizarse** vpr to be shocked.

escándalo m 1. (inmoralidad) scandal; (indignación) outrage. 2. (alboroto) uproar; **armar un ~** to kick up a fuss.

escandaloso, -sa adj 1. (inmoral) outrageous. 2. (ruidoso) very noisy.

Escandinavia Scandinavia.

escandinavo, -va adj, m y f Scandinavian.

escáner (pl **escáners**) m (INFORM & MED) scanner.

escaño m 1. (cargo) seat (in parliament). 2. (asiento) bench (in parliament).

escapada f 1. (huida) escape, flight; (DEP) breakaway. 2. (viaje) quick trip.

escapar vi (huir): **~ (de)** to get away o escape (from). ▶ **escaparse** vpr 1. (huir): **~se (de)** to get away o escape (from); **~se de casa** to run away from home. 2. (salir - gas, agua etc) to leak.

escaparate m (shop) window.

escapatoria f (fuga) escape; **no tener ~** to have no way out.

escape m (de gas etc) leak; (de coche) exhaust; **a ~** in a rush, at high speed.

escaquearse vpr fam to duck out; **~ de algo/de hacer algo** to worm one's way out of sthg/doing sthg.

escarabajo m beetle.

escaramuza f (MIL & fig) skirmish.

escarbar vt to scratch, to scrape.

escarcha f frost.

escarlata adj & m scarlet.

escarlatina f scarlet fever.

escarmentar vi to learn (one's lesson).

escarmiento m lesson; **servir de ~** to serve as a lesson.

escarnio m mockery, ridicule.

escarola f endive.

escarpado, -da adj (inclinado) steep; (abrupto) craggy.

escasear vi to be scarce.

escasez f (insuficiencia) shortage, scarcity; (pobreza) poverty.

escaso, -sa adj 1. (insuficiente - conocimientos, recursos) limited, scant; (- tiempo) short; (- cantidad, número) low; (- víveres, trabajo) scarce; (- visibilidad, luz) poor; **andar ~ de** to be short of. 2. (casi completo): **un metro ~** barely a metre.

escatimar vt (gastos, comida) to be sparing with, to skimp on; (esfuerzo, energías) to use as little as possible; **no ~ gastos** to spare no expense.

escay, skai m Leatherette®.

escayola f (CONSTR) plaster of Paris; (MED) plaster.

escena f 1. (gen) scene; **hacer una ~** to make a scene. 2. (escenario) stage; **poner en ~** to stage.

escenario m 1. (tablas, escena) stage; (CIN & TEATR) (lugar de la acción) setting. 2. fig (de suceso) scene.

escenificar vt (novela) to dramatize; (obra de teatro) to stage.

escenografía f set design.

escepticismo m scepticism.

escéptico, -ca ◆ adj (incrédulo) sceptical. ◆ m y f sceptic.

escindir vt to split. ► **escindirse** vpr: ~se (en) to split (into).

escisión f (del átomo) splitting; (de partido político) split.

esclarecer vt to clear up, to shed light on.

esclava → **esclavo**.

esclavitud f lit & fig slavery.

esclavizar vt lit & fig to enslave.

esclavo, -va m y f lit & fig (persona) slave.

esclerosis f inv (MED) sclerosis.

esclusa f (de canal) lock; (compuerta) floodgate.

escoba f broom.

escocedura f (sensación) stinging.

escocer vi lit & fig to sting.

escocés, -esa ◆ adj (gen) Scottish; (whisky) Scotch; (tejido) tartan, plaid. ◆ m y f (persona) Scot, Scotsman (f Scotswoman); **los escoceses** the Scottish, the Scots. ► **escocés** m (lengua) Scots (U).

Escocia Scotland.

escoger vt to choose.

escogido, -da adj (elegido) selected, chosen; (selecto) choice, select.

escolar ◆ adj school (antes de sust). ◆ m

y f pupil, schoolboy (f schoolgirl).

escolarizar vt to provide with schools.

escollo m 1. (en el mar) reef. 2. fig stumbling block.

escolta f escort.

escoltar vt to escort.

escombros mpl rubble (U), debris (U).

esconder vt to hide, to conceal. ► **esconderse** vpr: ~se (de) to hide (from).

escondido, -da adj (lugar) secluded. ► **a escondidas** loc adv in secret.

escondite m 1. (lugar) hiding place. 2. (juego) hide-and-seek.

escondrijo m hiding place.

escopeta f shotgun; ~ **de aire comprimido** air gun; ~ **de cañones recortados** sawn-off shotgun.

escoria f fig dregs (pl), scum.

Escorpio, Escorpión ◆ m (zodiaco) Scorpio. ◆ m y f (persona) Scorpio.

escorpión m scorpion. ► **Escorpión** = **Escorpio**.

escotado, -da adj low-cut.

escote m (de prendas) neckline; (de persona) neck; **pagar a ~** to go Dutch.

escotilla f hatch, hatchway.

escozor m stinging.

escribiente m y f clerk.

escribir vt & vi to write. ► **escribirse** vpr 1. (personas) to write to one another. 2. (palabras): **se escribe con 'h'** it is spelt with an 'h'.

escrito, -ta ◆ pp → **escribir**. ◆ adj written; **por ~** in writing. ► **escrito** m (gen) text; (documento) document; (obra literaria) writing, work.

escritor, -ra m y f writer.

escritorio m (mueble) desk, bureau.

escritura f 1. (arte) writing. 2. (sistema de signos) script. 3. (DER) deed.

escrúpulo m 1. (duda, recelo) scruple. 2. (minuciosidad) scrupulousness, great care. 3. (aprensión) qualm; **le da ~** he has qualms about it.

escrupuloso, -sa adj 1. (gen) scrupulous. 2. (aprensivo) particular, fussy.

escrutar vt (con la mirada) to scrutinize, to examine; (votos) to count.

escrutinio m count (of votes).

escuadra f 1. (GEOM) square. 2. (de buques) squadron. 3. (de soldados) squad.

escuadrilla f squadron.

escuadrón m squadron; ~ **de la muerte** death squad.

escuálido, -da adj culto emaciated.

escucha f listening-in, monitoring; **estar** o **permanecer a la ~** to listen in; **~s telefónicas** telephone tapping (U).

escuchar ◆ vt 1. (gen) to listen to. 2. Amer (oír) to hear. ◆ vi to listen.

escudería f team (in motor racing).

escudo m 1. (arma) shield. 2. (moneda) escudo. 3. (emblema) coat of arms.

escudriñar vt (examinar) to scrutinize, to examine; (otear) to search.

escuela f school; **~ normal** teacher training college; **~ privada** private school, public school Br; **~ pública** state school; **~ universitaria** university which awards degrees after three years of study.

escueto, -ta adj (sucinto) concise; (sobrio) plain, unadorned.

escuincle, -cla m y f Amer nipper, kid.

esculpir vt to sculpt, to carve.

escultor, -ra m y f sculptor (f sculptress).

escultura f sculpture.

escupidera f spittoon.

escupir ◆ vi to spit. ◆ vt (suj: persona, animal) to spit out; (suj: volcán, chimenea etc) to belch out.

escupitajo m gob, spit.

escurreplatos m inv dish rack.

escurridizo, -za adj lit & fig slippery.

escurridor m colander.

escurrir ◆ vt (gen) to drain; (ropa) to wring out; (en lavadora) to spin-dry. ◆ vi (gotear) to drip. ▶ **escurrirse** vpr (resbalarse) to slip.

ese¹ f (figura) zigzag; **hacer ~s** (en carretera) to zigzag; (al andar) to stagger about.

ese² (pl **esos**), **esa** adj demos 1. (gen) that, (pl) those. 2. (después de sust) fam despectivo that, (pl) those; **el hombre ~ no me inspira confianza** I don't trust that guy.

ése (pl **ésos**), **ésa** pron demos 1. (gen) that one, (pl) those ones. 2. (mencionado antes) the former. 3. fam despectivo: **fue el que me pegó** that's the guy who hit me. 4. loc: **¡a ~!** stop that man!; **ni por ésas** not even then; **no me lo vendió ni por ésas** even then he wouldn't sell me it.

esencia f essence.

esencial adj essential; **lo ~** the fundamental thing.

esfera f 1. (gen) sphere. 2. (de reloj) face. 3. (círculo social) circle.

esférico, -ca adj spherical.

esfinge f sphinx.

esforzar vt (voz) to strain. ▶ **es-**

forzarse vpr to make an effort; **~se en** o **por hacer algo** to try very hard to do sthg, to do one's best to do sthg.

esfuerzo m effort; **sin ~** effortlessly.

esfumarse vpr (esperanzas, posibilidades) to fade away; (persona) to vanish.

esgrima f fencing.

esgrimir vt 1. (arma) to brandish, to wield. 2. (argumento, hecho, idea) to use, to employ.

esguince m sprain.

eslabón m link.

eslip (pl **eslips**) m briefs (pl).

eslogan (pl **eslóganes**) m slogan.

eslora f (NÁUT) length.

eslovaco, -ca adj, m y f Slovak, Slovakian. ▶ **eslovaco** m (lengua) Slovak.

Eslovaquia Slovakia.

esmaltar vt to enamel.

esmalte m (sustancia - en dientes, cerámica etc) enamel; (- de uñas) (nail) varnish o polish.

esmerado, -da adj (persona) painstaking, careful; (trabajo) polished.

esmeralda f emerald.

esmerarse vpr: **~se (en algo/hacer algo)** (esforzarse) to take great pains (over sthg/doing sthg).

esmeril vt (pulir) to polish with emery.

esmero m great care.

esmoquin (pl **esmóquines**) m dinner jacket Br, tuxedo Am.

esnifar vt fam to sniff (drugs).

esnob (pl **esnobs**) m y f person who wants to be trendy.

eso pron demos (neutro) that; **~ es la Torre Eiffel** that's the Eiffel Tower; **~ es lo que yo pienso** that's just what I think; **~ que propones es irrealizable** what you're proposing is impossible; **~ de vivir solo no me gusta** I don't like the idea of living on my own; **¡~, ~!** that's right!, yes!; **¡~ es!** that's it; **¿cómo es ~?, ¿y ~?** (¿por qué?) how come?; **para ~ es mejor no ir** if that's all it is, you might as well not go; **por ~ vine** that's why I came. ▶ **a eso de** loc prep (at) about o around. ▶ **en eso** loc adv at that very moment. ▶ **y eso que** loc conj even though.

esófago m oesophagus.

esos, esas → **ese**.

ésos, ésas → **ése**.

esotérico, -ca adj esoteric.

espabilar vt 1. (despertar) to wake up. 2. (avispar): **~ a alguien** to sharpen sb's wits. ▶ **espabilarse** vpr 1. (despertarse) to wake up, to brighten up. **2.** (*darse prisa*) to get a move on. **3.** (*avisparse*) to sharpen one's wits.

espacial *adj* space (*antes de sust*).

espaciar *vt* to space out.

espacio *m* **1.** (*gen*) space; **no tengo mucho ~** I don't have much room; **a doble ~** double-spaced; **por ~ de** over a period of; **~ aéreo** air space. **2.** (RADIO & TV) programme.

espacioso, -sa *adj* spacious.

espada *f* (*arma*) sword; **estar entre la ~ y la pared** to be between the devil and the deep blue sea. ▶ **espadas** *fpl* (*naipes*) = spades.

espagueti *m* spaghetti (U).

espalda *f* **1.** (*gen*) back; **de ~s a alguien** with one's back turned on sb; **tumbarse de ~s** to lie on one's back; **cubrirse las ~s** to cover o.s.; **hablar de alguien a sus ~s** to talk about sb behind their back; **volver la ~ a alguien** to turn one's back on sb. **2.** (*en natación*) backstroke.

espantadizo, -za *adj* nervous, easily frightened.

espantajo *m* (*persona fea*) fright, sight.

espantapájaros *m inv* scarecrow.

espantar *vt* **1.** (*ahuyentar*) to frighten o scare away. **2.** (*asustar*) to frighten, to scare. ▶ **espantarse** *vpr* to get frightened o scared.

espanto *m* fright; **¡qué ~!** how terrible!

espantoso, -sa *adj* **1.** (*terrorífico*) horrific. **2.** (*enorme*) terrible. **3.** (*feísimo*) frightful, horrible.

España Spain.

español, -la ◆ *adj* Spanish. ◆ *m y f* (*persona*) Spaniard. ▶ **español** *m* (*lengua*) Spanish.

esparadrapo *m* (sticking) plaster, Band-Aid® Am.

esparcido, -da *adj* scattered.

esparcir *vt* (*gen*) to spread; (*semillas, papeles, objetos*) to scatter. ▶ **esparcirse** *vpr* to spread (out).

espárrago *m* asparagus (U).

esparto *m* esparto (grass).

espasmo *m* spasm.

espasmódico, -ca *adj* spasmodic.

espatarrarse *vpr fam* to sprawl (with one's legs wide open).

espátula *f* (CULIN & MED) spatula; (ARTE) palette knife; (CONSTR) bricklayer's trowel; (*de empapelador*) stripping knife.

especia *f* spice.

especial *adj* **1.** (*gen*) special; **~ para** specially for; **en ~** especially, particu-

larly; **¿alguno en ~?** any one in particular? **2.** (*peculiar - carácter, gusto, persona*) peculiar, strange.

especialmente *adv* especially.

especialidad *f* speciality, specialty Am.

especialista *m y f* **1.** (*experto*): **~ (en)** specialist (in). **2.** (CIN) stuntman (*f* stuntwoman).

especializado, -da *adj*: **~ en** specialized (in).

especializar *vt* to specialize.

especialmente *adv* especially.

especie *f* **1.** (BIOL) species (*sg*). **2.** (*clase*) kind, sort; **pagar en ~ o ~s** to pay in kind.

especificar *vt* to specify.

específico, -ca *adj* specific.

espécimen (*pl* **especímenes**) *m* specimen.

espectacular *adj* spectacular.

espectáculo *m* **1.** (*diversión*) entertainment. **2.** (*función*) show, performance. **3.** (*imagen, escena*) spectacle, sight.

espectador *m y f* (TV) viewer; (CIN & TEATR) member of the audience; (DEP) spectator; (*de suceso, discusión*) onlooker.

espectro *m* **1.** (*fantasma*) spectre, ghost. **2.** (FÍS & MED) spectrum.

especulación *f* speculation.

especular *vi*: **~ (sobre)** to speculate (about); **~ en** (COM) to speculate on.

espejismo *m* mirage; *fig* illusion.

espejo *m lit* & *fig* mirror.

espeleología *f* potholing.

espeluznante *adj* hair-raising, lurid.

espera *f* (*acción*) wait; **en ~ de, a la ~ de** waiting for, awaiting.

esperanza *f* (*deseo, ganas*) hope; (*confianza, expectativas*) expectation; **perder la ~** to lose hope; **tener ~ de hacer algo** to hope to be able to do sthg; **~ de vida** life expectancy.

esperanzar *vt* to give hope to, to encourage.

esperar ◆ *vt* **1.** (*aguardar*) to wait for. **2.** (*tener esperanza de*): **~ que** to hope that; **espero que sí** I hope so; **~ hacer algo** to hope to do sthg. **3.** (*tener confianza en*) to expect; **~ que** to expect (that); **~ algo de alguien** to expect sthg from sb, to hope for sthg from sb. ◆ *vi* **1.** (*aguardar*) to wait. **2.** (*ser inevitable*) to await; **como era de ~** as was to be expected. ▶ **esperarse** *vpr* **1.** (*imaginarse, figurarse*) to expect. **2.** (*aguardar*) to wait.

esperma ◆ *m o f* (BIOL) sperm. ◆ *f Amer* (*vela*) candle.

esperpento *m* (*persona*) grotesque sight; (*cosa*) piece of nonsense.

espesar *vt & vi* to thicken.

espeso, -sa *adj* (*gen*) thick; (*bosque, niebla*) dense; (*nieve*) deep.

espesor *m* 1. (*grosor*) thickness; **tiene 2 metros de ~** it's 2 metres thick. 2. (*densidad - de niebla, bosque*) density; (- *de nieve*) depth.

espesura *f* 1. (*vegetación*) thicket. 2. (*grosor*) thickness; (*densidad*) density.

espía *m y f* spy.

espiar *vt* to spy on.

espiga *f* 1. (*de trigo etc*) ear. 2. (*en telas*) herringbone. 3. (*pieza - de madera*) peg; (- *de hierro*) pin.

espigado, -da *adj* (*persona*) tall and slim.

espigón *m* breakwater.

espina *f* (*de pez*) bone; (*de planta*) thorn; **me da mala ~** it makes me uneasy, there's something fishy about it; **tener una ~ clavada** to bear a great burden.
► **espina dorsal** *f* spine.

espinaca *f* (*gen pl*) spinach (U).

espinazo *m* spine, backbone.

espinilla *f* 1. (*hueso*) shin, shinbone. 2. (*grano*) blackhead.

espinoso, -sa *adj lit & fig* thorny.

espionaje *m* espionage.

espiral *f lit & fig* spiral; **en ~** (*escalera, forma*) spiral.

espirar *vi & vt* to exhale, to breathe out.

espiritista *adj* spiritualist.

espíritu *m* (*gen*) spirit; (RELIG) soul.
► **Espíritu Santo** *m* Holy Ghost.

espiritual *adj & m* spiritual.

espléndido, -da *adj* 1. (*magnífico*) splendid, magnificent. 2. (*generoso*) generous, lavish.

esplendor *m* 1. (*magnificencia*) splendour. 2. (*apogeo*) greatness.

espliego *m* lavender.

espoleta *f* (*de proyectil*) fuse.

espolvorear *vt* to dust, to sprinkle.

esponja *f* sponge.

esponjoso, -sa *adj* spongy.

espontaneidad *f* spontaneity.

espontáneo, -a *adj* spontaneous.

esporádico, -ca *adj* sporadic.

esport *adj inv*: **(de) ~** sports (*antes de sust*).

esposa → **esposo**.

esposar *vt* to handcuff.

esposo, -sa *m y f* (*persona*) husband (*f* wife). ► **esposas** *fpl* (*objeto*) handcuffs.

espot (*pl* **espots**) *m* advertising spot, commercial.

espray (*pl* **esprays**) *m* spray.

esprint (*pl* **esprints**) *m* sprint.

espuela *f* (*gen*) spur.

espuma *f* 1. (*gen*) foam; (*de cerveza*) head; (*de jabón*) lather; (*de olas*) surf; (*de un caldo*) scum. 2. (*para pelo*) (*styling*) mousse.

espumadera *f* skimmer.

espumoso, -sa *adj* (*gen*) foamy, frothy; (*vino*) sparkling; (*jabón*) lathery.

esputo *m* (*gen*) spittle; (MED) sputum.

esqueje *m* cutting.

esquela *f* obituary.

esqueleto *m* (*de persona*) skeleton.

esquema *m* (*gráfico*) diagram; (*resumen*) outline.

esquemático, -ca *adj* schematic.

esquí (*pl* **esquíes** o **esquís**) *m* 1. (*instrumento*) ski. 2. (*deporte*) skiing; **~ náutico** o **acuático** water-skiing.

esquiador, -ra *m y f* skier.

esquiar *vi* to ski.

esquilar *vt* to shear.

esquimal *adj, m y f* Eskimo.

esquina *f* corner; **a la vuelta de la ~** just round the corner; **doblar la ~** to turn the corner.

esquinazo *m* corner; **dar (el) ~ a alguien** to give sb the slip.

esquirol *m fam* blackleg, scab.

esquivar *vt* (*gen*) to avoid; (*golpe*) to dodge.

esquivo, -va *adj* shy.

esquizofrenia *f* schizophrenia.

esta → **este²**.

ésta → **éste**.

estabilidad *f* stability.

estabilizar *vt* to stabilize. ► **estabilizarse** *vpr* to stabilize.

estable *adj* 1. (*firme*) stable. 2. (*permanente - huésped*) permanent; (- *cliente*) regular.

establecer *vt* 1. (*gen*) to establish; (*récord*) to set. 2. (*negocio, campamento*) to set up. 3. (*inmigrantes etc*) to settle. ► **establecerse** *vpr* 1. (*instalarse*) to settle. 2. (*poner un negocio*) to set up a business.

establecimiento *m* 1. (*gen*) establishment; (*de récord*) setting. 2. (*de negocio, colonia*) setting up.

establo *m* cowshed.

estaca *f* 1. (*para clavar, delimitar*) stake; (*de tienda de campaña*) peg. 2. (*garrote*) cudgel.

estación *f* 1. (*gen & INFORM*) station; **~ de autocares/de tren** coach/railway station; ~ **de esquí** ski resort; ~ **de gasolina** petrol station; ~ **de servicio** service station; ~ **de trabajo** workstation; ~ **meteorológica** weather station. **2.** (*del año, temporada*) season.

estacionamiento m (AUTOM) parking; ~ **indebido** parking offence.

estacionar vt (AUTOM) to park.

estacionario, -ria adj (*gen*) stationary; (ECON) stagnant.

estadio m **1.** (DEP) stadium. **2.** (*fase*) stage.

estadista m y f statesman (f stateswoman).

estadístico, -ca adj statistical. ▶ **estadística** f **1.** (*ciencia*) statistics (U). **2.** (*datos*) statistics (pl).

estado m state; **su ~ es grave** his condition is serious; **estar en buen/mal ~** (*coche, terreno etc*) to be in good/bad condition; (*alimento, bebida*) to be fresh/off; ~ **de ánimo** state of mind; ~ **civil** marital status; ~ **de bienestar** welfare state; ~ **de excepción** o **emergencia** state of emergency; ~ **de salud** (state of) health; **estar en ~** (de esperanza o buena esperanza) to be expecting. ▶ **Estado** m (*gobierno*) State; **Estado Mayor** (MIL) general staff. ▶ **Estados Unidos (de América)** United States (of America).

estadounidense ◆ adj United States (*antes de sust*). ◆ m y f United States citizen.

estafa f (*gen*) swindle; (COM) fraud.

estafador, -ra m y f swindler.

estafar vt (*gen*) to swindle; (COM) to defraud.

estafeta f sub-post office.

estallar vi **1.** (*reventar - bomba*) to explode; (*- neumático*) to burst. **2.** fig (*guerra, epidemia etc*) to break out.

estallido m **1.** (*de bomba*) explosion; (*de trueno*) crash; (*de látigo*) crack. **2.** fig (de guerra etc) outbreak.

Estambul Istanbul.

estamento m stratum, class.

estampa f **1.** (*imagen, tarjeta*) print. **2.** (*aspecto*) appearance.

estampado, -da adj printed. ▶ **estampado** m (*dibujo*) (cotton) print.

estampar vt **1.** (*imprimir - gen*) to print; (*- metal*) to stamp. **2.** (*escribir*): ~ **la firma** to sign one's name.

estampida f stampede.

estampido m report, bang.

estampilla f **1.** (*para marcar*) rubber stamp. **2.** Amer (*de correos*) stamp.

estancado, -da adj (*agua*) stagnant;

(*situación, proyecto*) at a standstill.

estancarse vpr (*líquido*) to stagnate; (*situación*) to come to a standstill.

estancia f **1.** (*tiempo*) stay. **2.** (*habitación*) room. **3.** Amer (*hacienda*) ranch, large farm.

estanciero m Amer ranch owner.

estanco, -ca adj watertight. ▶ **estanco** m tobacconist's.

estándar (pl **estándares**) adj & m standard.

estandarizar vt to standardize.

estandarte m standard, banner.

estanque m **1.** (*alberca*) pond; (*para riego*) reservoir. **2.** Amer (*depósito*) tank (of petrol).

estanquero m y f tobacconist.

estante m shelf.

estantería f (*gen*) shelves (pl), shelving (U); (*para libros*) bookcase.

estaño m tin.

estar ◆ vi **1.** (*hallarse*) to be; **¿dónde está la llave?** where is the key?; **¿está María?** is Maria in?; **no está** she's not in. **2.** (*con fechas*): **¿a qué estamos hoy?** what's the date today?; **hoy estamos a martes/a 15 de julio** today is Tuesday/the 15th of July; **estábamos en octubre** it was October. **3.** (*quedarse*) to stay, to be; **estaré un par de horas y me iré** I'll stay a couple of hours and then I'll go. **4.** (*antes de 'a'*) (*expresa valores, grados*): **estamos a veinte grados** it's twenty degrees here; **el dólar está a 95 pesetas** the dollar is at 95 pesetas; **están a 100 ptas el kilo** they're 100 pesetas a kilo. **5.** (*hallarse listo*) to be ready; **¿aún no está ese trabajo?** is that piece of work still not ready? **6.** (*servir*): ~ **para** to be (there) for; **para eso están los amigos** that's what friends are for. **7.** (*antes de gerundio*) (*expresa duración*) to be; **están golpeando la puerta** they're banging on the door. **8.** (*antes de 'sin' + infin*) (*expresa negación*): **estoy sin dormir desde ayer** I haven't slept since yesterday; **está sin acabar** it's not finished. **9.** (*faltar*): **eso está aún por escribir** that has yet to be written. **10.** (*hallarse a punto de*): ~ **por hacer algo** to be on the verge of doing sthg. **11.** (*expresa disposición*): ~ **para algo** to be in the mood for sthg. ◆ v copulativo **1.** (*antes de adj*) (*expresa cualidad, estado*) to be; **los pasteles están ricos** the cakes are delicious; **esta calle está sucia** this street is dirty. **2.** (*antes de 'con' o 'sin' + sust*) (*expresa estado*) to be; **estamos sin agua** we have no water, we're without water. **3.** (*expresa situación, acción*): ~ **de**: ~ **de camarero** to work as a waiter, to be a waiter; ~ **de vacaciones** to be on holiday; ~ **de viaje** to be on a trip; ~ **de mudanza** to be (in the process of) moving. **4.** (*expresa permanencia*): ~ **en uso** to be in use; ~ **en guardia** to be on guard. **5.** (*expresa apoyo, predilección*): ~ **por** to be in favour of. **6.** (*expresa ocupación*): ~ **como** to be; **está como cajera** she's a checkout girl. **7.** (*consistir*): ~ **en** to be, to lie in; **el problema está en la fecha** the problem is the date. **8.** (*sentar - ropa*): **este traje te está bien** this suit looks good on you. **9.** (*antes de 'que' + verbo*) (*expresa actitud*): **está que muerde porque ha suspendido** he's furious because he failed. ▶ **estarse** *vpr* (*permanecer*) to stay; **te puedes ~ con nosotros unos días** you can stay o spend a few days with us.

estárter (*pl* **estárters**) *m* starter.

estatal *adj* state (*antes de sust*).

estático, -ca *adj* (*inmóvil*) stock-still.

estatua *f* statue.

estatura *f* height.

estatus *m inv* status.

estatutario, -ria *adj* statutory.

estatuto *m* (*gen*) statute; (*de empresa*) article (of association); (*de ciudad*) by-law.

este¹ ◆ *adj* (*posición, parte*) east, eastern; (*dirección, viento*) easterly. ◆ *m* east; **los países del ~** the Eastern bloc countries.

este² (*pl* **estos**), **esta** *adj demos* **1.** (*gen*) this, (*pl*) these; **esta camisa** this shirt; ~ **año** this year. **2.** *fam despectivo* that, (*pl*) those; **no soporto a la niña esta** I can't stand that girl.

éste (*pl* **éstos**), **ésta** *pron demos* **1.** (*gen*) this one, (*pl*) these (ones); **dame otro boli**; ~ **no funciona** give me another pen; this one doesn't work; **aquellos cuadros no están mal, aunque éstos me gustan más** those paintings aren't bad, but I like these (ones) better; **ésta ha sido la semana más feliz de mi vida** this has been the happiest week of my life. **2.** (*recién mencionado*) the latter; **entraron Juan y Pedro, ~ con un abrigo verde** Juan and Pedro came in, the latter wearing a green coat. **3.** *fam despectivo*: ~ **es el que me pegó** this is the guy who hit me. ▶ **en éstas** *loc adv fam* just then, at that very moment.

estela *f* **1.** (*de barco*) wake; (*de avión, estrella fugaz*) trail. **2.** *fig* (*rastro*) trail.

estelar *adj* **1.** (ASTRON) stellar. **2.** (CIN & TEATR) star (*antes de sust*).

estepa *f* steppe.

estera *f* (*tejido*) matting; (*alfombrilla*) mat.

estéreo *adj inv & m* stereo.

estereofónico, -ca *adj* stereo.

estereotipo *m* stereotype.

estéril *adj* **1.** (*persona, terreno, imaginación*) sterile. **2.** *fig* (*inútil*) futile.

esterilizar *vt* to sterilize.

esterlina → **libra**.

esternón *m* breastbone, sternum.

esteroides *mpl* steroids.

esteta *m y f* aesthete.

estética → **estético**.

esteticista, esthéticienne [esteti-'θjen] *f* beautician.

estético, -ca *adj* aesthetic. ▶ **estética** *f* (FILOSOFÍA) aesthetics (U).

esthéticienne = **esteticista**.

estiércol *m* (*excrementos*) dung; (*abono*) manure.

estigma *m fig* (*deshonor*) stigma.

estilarse *vpr fam* to be in (fashion).

estilo *m* **1.** (*gen*) style; ~ **de vida** lifestyle. **2.** (*en natación*) stroke. **3.** (GRAM) speech; ~ **directo/indirecto** direct/indirect speech. **4.** *loc*: **algo por el ~** something of the sort.

estilográfica *f* fountain pen.

estima *f* esteem, respect.

estimación *f* **1.** (*aprecio*) esteem, respect. **2.** (*valoración*) valuation. **3.** (*en impuestos*) assessment.

estimado, -da *adj* (*querido*) esteemed, respected; **Estimado señor** Dear Sir.

estimar *vt* **1.** (*valorar - gen*) to value; (*- valor*) to estimate. **2.** (*apreciar*) to think highly of. **3.** (*creer*) to consider.

estimulante ◆ *adj* (*que excita*) stimulating. ◆ *m* stimulant.

estimular *vt* **1.** (*animar*) to encourage. **2.** (*excitar*) to stimulate.

estímulo *m* **1.** (*aliciente*) incentive; (*ánimo*) encouragement. **2.** (*de un órgano*) stimulus.

estío *m culto* summer.

estipendio *m* stipend, remuneration.

estipulación *f* **1.** (*acuerdo*) agreement. **2.** (DER) stipulation.

estipular *vt* to stipulate.

estirado, -da *adj* (*persona - altanero*) haughty; (*- adusto*) uptight.

estirar ◆ *vt* **1.** (*alargar - gen*) to stretch; (*- el cuello*) to crane. **2.** (*desarrugar*) to straighten. **3.** *fig* (*el dinero etc*) to make last; (*discurso, tema*) to spin out. ◆ *vi*: ~

(de) to pull. ► **estirarse** vpr 1. (*desperezarse*) to stretch. 2. (*tumbarse*) to stretch out.

estirón m (*acción*) tug, pull.

estirpe f stock, lineage.

estival adj summer (*antes de sust*).

esto pron demos (*neutro*) this thing; ~ **es tu regalo de cumpleaños** this is your birthday present; ~ **que acabas de decir no tiene sentido** what you just said doesn't make sense; ~ **de trabajar de noche no me gusta** I don't like this business of working at night; ~ **es** that is (to say). ► **en esto** loc adv just then, at that very moment.

estoc (*pl* **estocs**) m stock.

Estocolmo Stockholm.

estofa f: **de baja ~** (*gente*) low-class; (*cosas*) poor-quality.

estofado m stew.

estofar vt (CULIN) to stew.

estoicismo m stoicism.

estoico, -ca adj stoic, stoical.

estomacal adj (*dolencia*) stomach (*antes de sust*); (*bebida*) digestive.

estómago m stomach.

Estonia Estonia.

estop = stop.

estorbar ◆ vt (*obstaculizar*) to hinder; (*molestar*) to bother. ◆ vi (*estar en medio*) to be in the way.

estorbo m (*obstáculo*) hindrance; (*molestia*) nuisance.

estornudar vi to sneeze.

estos, -tas → **este²**.

éstos, -tas → **éste**.

estoy → **estar**.

estrabismo m squint.

estrado m platform.

estrafalario, -ria adj outlandish, eccentric.

estragón m tarragon.

estragos mpl: **causar** o **hacer ~ en** (*físicos*) to wreak havoc with; (*morales*) to destroy, to ruin.

estrambótico, -ca adj outlandish.

estrangulador, -ra m y f strangler.

estrangular vt (*ahogar*) to strangle; (MED) to strangulate.

estraperlo m black market; **de ~** black market (*antes de sust*).

estratagema f (MIL) stratagem; fig (*astucia*) artifice, trick.

estrategia f strategy.

estratégico, -ca adj strategic.

estrato m (GEOL & fig) stratum.

estrechar vt 1. (*hacer estrecho - gen*) to narrow; (- *ropa*) to take in. 2. fig (*rela-*

ciones) to make closer. 3. (*apretar*) to squeeze, to hug; ~ **la mano a alguien** to shake sb's hand. ► **estrecharse** vpr (*hacerse estrecho*) to narrow.

estrechez f 1. (*falta de anchura*) narrowness; (*falta de espacio*) lack of space; (*de ropa*) tightness; ~ **de miras** narrowmindedness. 2. fig (*falta de dinero*) hardship; **pasar estrecheces** to be hard up. 3. (*intimidad*) closeness.

estrecho, -cha adj 1. (*no ancho - gen*) narrow; (- *ropa*) tight; (- *habitación*) cramped; ~ **de miras** narrow-minded. 2. fig (*íntimo*) close. ► **estrecho** m (GEOGR) strait.

estrella f (*gen*) star; fig (*destino*) fate; ~ **fugaz** shooting star. ► **estrella de mar** f starfish.

estrellado, -da adj 1. (*con estrellas*) starry. 2. (*por la forma*) star-shaped.

estrellar vt (*arrojar*) to smash. ► **estrellarse** vpr (*chocar*): ~**se** (**contra**) (*gen*) to smash (against); (*avión, coche*) to crash (into).

estrellón m Amer crash.

estremecer vt to shake. ► **estremecerse** vpr: ~**se** (**de**) (*horror, miedo*) to tremble o shudder (with); (*frío*) to shiver (with).

estremecimiento m (*de miedo*) shudder; (*de frío*) shiver.

estrenar vt 1. (*gen*) to use for the first time; (*ropa*) to wear for the first time; (*piso*) to move into. 2. (CIN) to release; (TEATR) to premiere. ► **estrenarse** vpr (*persona*) to make one's debut, to start.

estreno m (*de espectáculo*) premiere, first night; (*de cosa*) first use; (*en un empleo*) debut.

estreñido, -da adj constipated.

estreñimiento m constipation.

estrépito m (*ruido*) racket, din; fig (*ostentación*) fanfare.

estrepitoso, -sa adj 1. (*gen*) noisy; (*aplausos*) deafening. 2. (*derrota*) resounding; (*fracaso*) spectacular.

estrés m inv stress.

estresado, -da adj stressed.

estría f (*gen*) groove; (*en la piel*) stretch mark.

estribación f (*gen pl*) foothills (*pl*).

estribar ► **estribar en** vi to be based on, to lie in.

estribillo m (MÚS) chorus; (LITER) refrain.

estribo m 1. (*de montura*) stirrup. 2. (*de coche, tren*) step. 3. loc: **perder los ~s** to fly off the handle.

estribor *m* starboard.

estricto, -ta *adj* strict.

estridente *adj* 1. (*ruido*) strident, shrill. 2. (*color*) garish, loud.

estrofa *f* stanza, verse.

estropajo *m* scourer.

estropeado, -da *adj* (*averiado, roto*) broken; (*dañado*) damaged.

estropear *vt* 1. (*averiar*) to break. 2. (*dañar*) to damage. 3. (*echar a perder*) to ruin, to spoil. ► **estropearse** *vpr* 1. (*máquina*) to break down. 2. (*comida*) to go off, to spoil; (*piel*) to get damaged. 3. (*plan*) to fall through.

estropicio *m*: **hacer** o **causar un ~** to wreak havoc.

estructura *f* structure.

estruendo *m* 1. (*estrépito*) din, roar; (*de trueno*) crash. 2. (*alboroto*) uproar, tumult.

estrujar *vt* 1. (*limón*) to squeeze; (*trapo, ropa*) to wring (out); (*papel*) to screw up; (*caja*) to crush. 2. (*abrazar - persona, mano*) to squeeze. 3. *fig* (*sacar partido*) to bleed dry.

estuario *m* estuary.

estuche *m* 1. (*caja*) case; (*de joyas*) jewellery box. 2. (*utensilios*) set.

estuco *m* stucco.

estudiante *m y f* student.

estudiantil *adj* student (*antes de sust*).

estudiar ◆ *vt* (*gen*) to study. ◆ *vi* to study; **~ para médico** to be studying to be a doctor.

estudio *m* 1. (*gen*) study; **estar en ~** to be under consideration; **~ de mercado** (*técnica*) market research; (*investigación*) market survey. 2. (*oficina*) study; (*de fotógrafo, pintor*) studio. 3. (*apartamento*) studio apartment. 4. (*gen pl*) (CIN, RADIO & TV) studio. ► **estudios** *mpl* (*serie de cursos*) studies; (*educación*) education (U); **~s primarios/secundarios** primary/secondary education.

estudioso, -sa *adj* studious.

estufa *f* 1. (*calentador*) heater, fire. 2. *Amer* (*cocina*) cooker.

estupefaciente *m* narcotic, drug.

estupefacto, -ta *adj* astonished.

estupendamente *adv* wonderfully; **estoy ~** I feel wonderful.

estupendo, -da *adj* great, fantastic. ► **estupendo** *interj*: **¡~!** great!

estupidez *f* stupidity; **decir/hacer una ~** to say/do sthg stupid.

estúpido, -da *adj* stupid.

estupor *m* astonishment.

esturión *m* sturgeon.

estuviera *etc* → **estar**.

esvástica *f* swastika.

ETA (*abrev de* **Euskadi ta Askatasuna**) *f* ETA, *terrorist Basque separatist organization.*

etapa *f* stage; **por ~s** in stages.

etarra *m y f* member of ETA.

ETB (*abrev de* **Euskal Telebista**) *f* Basque *television network.*

etc. (*abrev de* **etcétera**) etc.

etcétera *adv* etcetera.

etéreo, -a *adj fig* ethereal.

eternidad *f* eternity; **hace una ~ que no la veo** *fam* it's ages since I last saw her.

eterno, -na *adj* eternal; *fam* (*larguísimo*) never-ending, interminable.

ético, -ca *adj* ethical. ► **ética** *f* (*moralidad*) ethics (*pl*).

etílico, -ca *adj* (QUÍM) ethyl (*antes de sust*); **intoxicación etílica** alcohol poisoning.

etimología *f* etymology.

Etiopía Ethiopia.

etiqueta *f* 1. (*gen &* INFORM) label. 2. (*ceremonial*) etiquette; **de ~** formal.

etiquetar *vt lit & fig* to label; **~ a alguien de algo** to label sb sthg.

etnia *f* ethnic group.

étnico, -ca *adj* ethnic.

EUA (*abrev de* **Estados Unidos de América**) *mpl* USA.

eucalipto *m* eucalyptus.

eucaristía *f*: **la ~** the Eucharist.

eufemismo *m* euphemism.

euforia *f* euphoria, elation.

eufórico, -ca *adj* euphoric, elated.

eunuco *m* eunuch.

euro *m* (*unidad monetaria*) euro.

eurocheque *m* eurocheque *Br*, eurocheck *Am*.

eurócrata *adj, m y f* Eurocrat.

eurodiputado, -da *m y f* Euro-M.P., M.E.P.

Europa Europe.

europarlamentario, -ria *m y f* Euro-M.P., M.E.P.

europeo, -a *adj, m y f* European.

Euskadi the Basque Country.

euskara, euskera *m* Basque.

eutanasia *f* euthanasia.

evacuación *f* evacuation.

evacuar *vt* (*gen*) to evacuate; (*vientre*) to empty, to void.

evadir *vt* to evade; (*respuesta, peligro*) to avoid. ► **evadirse** *vpr*: **~se (de)** to escape (from).

evaluación *f* 1. (*gen*) evaluation. 2. (EDUC - *examen*) assessment.

evaluar vt to evaluate, to assess.

evangélico, -ca adj, m y f evangelical.

evangelio m (RELIG) gospel.

evaporar vt to evaporate. ▶ **evaporarse** vpr (líquido etc) to evaporate.

evasión f 1. (huida) escape. 2. (de dinero): ~ **de capitales** o **divisas** capital flight; ~ **fiscal** tax evasion. 3. fig (entretenimiento) amusement, recreation; (escapismo) escapism; **de** ~ escapist.

evasivo, -va adj evasive. ▶ **evasiva** f evasive answer.

evento m event.

eventual adj 1. (no fijo - trabajador) temporary, casual; (- gastos) incidental. 2. (posible) possible.

eventualidad f 1. (temporalidad) temporariness. 2. (hecho incierto) eventuality; (posibilidad) possibility.

Everest m: **el** ~ (Mount) Everest.

evidencia f 1. (prueba) evidence, proof. 2. (claridad) obviousness; **poner algo en** ~ to demonstrate sthg; **poner a alguien en** ~ to show sb up.

evidenciar vt to show, to demonstrate. ▶ **evidenciarse** vpr to be obvious o evident.

evidente adj evident, obvious.

evitar vt (gen) to avoid; (desastre, accidente) to avert; ~ **que alguien haga algo** to prevent sb from doing sthg.

evocación f recollection, evocation.

evocar vt (recordar) to evoke.

evolución f 1. (gen) evolution; (de enfermedad) development, progress. 2. (MIL) manoeuvre.

evolucionar vi 1. (gen) to evolve; (enfermedad) to develop, to progress; (cambiar) to change. 2. (MIL) to carry out manoeuvres.

ex prep ex; **el** ~ **presidente** the ex-president, the former president.

exacerbar vt 1. (agudizar) to exacerbate, to aggravate. 2. (irritar) to irritate, to infuriate.

exactitud f accuracy, precision; (puntualidad) punctuality.

exacto, -ta adj 1. (justo - cálculo, medida) exact; **tres metros** ~**s** exactly three metres. 2. (preciso) accurate, precise; (correcto) correct, right. 3. (idéntico): ~ **(a)** identical to, exactly the same (as). ▶ **exacto** interj: ¡~! exactly!, precisely!

exageración f exaggeration; **este precio es una** ~ this price is over the top.

exagerado, -da adj (gen) exaggerated; (persona) overly dramatic; (precio)

exorbitant; (gesto) flamboyant.

exagerar vt & vi to exaggerate.

exaltado, -da adj (jubiloso) elated; (acalorado - persona) worked up; (- discusión) heated; (excitable) hotheaded.

exaltar vt 1. (elevar) to promote, to raise. 2. (glorificar) to exalt. ▶ **exaltarse** vpr to get excited o worked up.

examen m 1. (ejercicio) exam, examination; **presentarse a un** ~ to sit an exam; ~ **de conducir** driving test; ~ **final/oral** final/oral (exam); ~ **parcial** = end-of-term exam. 2. (indagación) consideration, examination.

examinar vt to examine. ▶ **examinarse** vpr to sit o take an exam.

exánime adj 1. (muerto) dead. 2. (desmayado) lifeless.

exasperar vt to exasperate. ▶ **exasperarse** vpr to get exasperated.

excavación f (lugar) dig, excavation.

excavar vt (gen) to dig; (en arqueología) to excavate.

excedencia f leave (of absence); (EDUC) sabbatical.

excedente ◆ adj (producción etc) surplus. ◆ m (COM) surplus.

exceder vt to exceed, to surpass. ▶ **excederse** vpr 1. (pasarse de la raya): ~**se (en)** to go too far o overstep the mark (in). 2. (rebasar el límite): **se excede en el peso** it's too heavy.

excelencia f (cualidad) excellence; **por** ~ par excellence. ▶ **Su Excelencia** m y f His Excellency (f Her Excellency).

excelente adj excellent.

excelentísimo, -ma adj most excellent.

excentricidad f eccentricity.

excéntrico, -ca adj, m y f eccentric.

excepción f exception; **a** o **con** ~ **de** with the exception of, except for. ▶ **de excepción** loc adj exceptional.

excepcional adj exceptional.

excepto adv except (for).

exceptuar vt: ~ **(de)** (excluir) to exclude (from); (eximir) to exempt (from); **exceptuando a ...** excluding ...

excesivo, -va adj excessive.

exceso m (demasía) excess; ~ **de equipaje** excess baggage; ~ **de peso** (obesidad) excess weight.

excitación f (nerviosismo) agitation; (por enfado, sexo) arousal.

excitado, -da adj (nervioso) agitated; (por enfado, sexo) aroused.

excitante m stimulant.

excitar vt 1. (inquietar) to upset, to agitate. **2.** (*estimular - sentidos*) to stimulate; (*- apetito*) to whet; (*- pasión, curiosidad, persona*) to arouse. ▶ **excitarse** *vpr* (*alterarse*) to get worked up o excited.

exclamación *f* (*interjección*) exclamation; (*grito*) cry.

exclamar *vt & vi* to exclaim, to shout out.

excluir *vt* to exclude; (*hipótesis, opción*) to rule out; (*hacer imposible*) to preclude; **~ a alguien de algo** to exclude sb from sthg.

exclusión *f* exclusion.

exclusivo, -va *adj* exclusive. ▶ **exclusiva** *f* **1.** (PRENS) exclusive. **2.** (COM) exclusive o sole right.

Excma. *abrev de* **Excelentísima.**

Excmo. *abrev de* **Excelentísimo.**

excombatiente *m y f* ex-serviceman (*f* ex-servicewoman) Br, war veteran Am.

excomulgar *vt* to excommunicate.

excomunión *f* excommunication.

excremento *m* (*gen pl*) excrement (U).

exculpar *vt* to exonerate; (DER) to acquit.

excursión *f* (*viaje*) excursion, trip; **ir de ~** to go on an outing o a trip.

excursionista *m y f* (*en la ciudad*) sightseer, tripper; (*en el campo*) rambler; (*en la montaña*) hiker.

excusa *f* **1.** (*gen*) excuse. **2.** (*petición de perdón*) apology; **presentar uno sus ~s** to apologize, to make one's excuses.

excusar *vt* (*disculpar a*) to excuse; (*disculparse por*) to apologize for. ▶ **excusarse** *vpr* to apologize.

exento, -ta *adj* exempt; **~ de** (*sin*) free from, without; (*eximido de*) exempt from.

exequias *fpl* funeral (*sg*), funeral rites.

exhalación *f* (*emanación*) exhalation, vapour; (*suspiro*) breath.

exhalar *vt* **1.** (*aire*) to exhale, to breathe out; (*suspiros*) to heave. **2.** (*olor*) to give off. **3.** (*quejas*) to utter.

exhaustivo, -va *adj* exhaustive.

exhausto, -ta *adj* exhausted.

exhibición *f* **1.** (*demostración*) show, display. **2.** (*deportiva, artística etc*) exhibition. **3.** (*de películas*) showing.

exhibir *vt* **1.** (*exponer - cuadros, fotografías*) to exhibit; (*- modelos*) to show; (*- productos*) to display. **2.** (*lucir - joyas, cualidades etc*) to show off. **3.** (*película*) to show, to screen.

exhortación *f* exhortation.

exhortar *vt*: **~ a alguien a** to exhort sb to.

exigencia *f* **1.** (*obligación*) demand, requirement. **2.** (*capricho*) fussiness (U).

exigente *adj* demanding.

exigir *vt* **1.** (*gen*) to demand; **~ algo de** o **a alguien** to demand sthg from sb. **2.** (*requerir, necesitar*) to require.

exiguo, -gua *adj* (*escaso*) meagre, paltry; (*pequeño*) minute.

exiliado, -da ◆ *adj* exiled, in exile. ◆ *m y f* exile.

exiliar *vt* to exile. ▶ **exiliarse** *vpr* to go into exile.

exilio *m* exile.

eximir *vt*: **~ (de)** to exempt (from).

existencia *f* existence. ▶ **existencias** *fpl* (COM) stock (U).

existir *vi* to exist; **existe mucha pobreza** there is a lot of poverty.

éxito *m* **1.** (*gen*) success; **con ~** successfully; **tener ~** to be successful. **2.** (*libro*) bestseller; (*canción*) hit.

exitoso, -sa *adj* successful.

éxodo *m* exodus.

exorbitante *adj* exorbitant.

exorcista *m y f* exorcist.

exorcizar *vt* to exorcize.

exótico, -ca *adj* exotic.

expandir *vt* to spread; (FÍS) to expand. ▶ **expandirse** *vpr* to spread; (FÍS) to expand.

expansión *f* **1.** (FÍS) expansion. **2.** (ECON) growth; **en ~** expanding. **3.** (*recreo*) relaxation, amusement.

expansionarse *vpr* **1.** (*desahogarse*): **~ (con)** to open one's heart (to). **2.** (*divertirse*) to relax, to let off steam. **3.** (*desarrollarse*) to expand.

expansivo, -va *adj* **1.** (*gen*) expansive. **2.** *fig* (*persona*) open, frank.

expatriar *vt* to expatriate; (*exiliar*) to exile. ▶ **expatriarse** *vpr* to emigrate; (*exiliarse*) to go into exile.

expectación *f* expectancy, anticipation.

expectativa *f* (*espera*) expectation; (*esperanza*) hope; (*perspectiva*) prospect; **estar a la ~** to wait and see; **estar a la ~ de** (*atento*) to be on the lookout for; (*a la espera*) to be hoping for; **~ de vida** life expectancy.

expedición *f* (*viaje, grupo*) expedition.

expediente *m* **1.** (*documentación*) documents (*pl*); (*ficha*) file. **2.** (*historial*) record; **~ académico** academic record. **3.** (*investigación*) inquiry; **abrir ~ a alguien** (*castigar*) to take disciplinary action against sb; (*investigar*) to start proceedings against sb.

expedir vt (carta, pedido) to send, to dispatch; (pasaporte, decreto) to issue; (contrato, documento) to draw up.

expedito, -ta adj clear, free.

expeler vt (humo - suj: persona) to blow out; (- suj: chimenea, tubo de escape) to emit; (- suj: extractor, volcán) to expel.

expendedor, -ra m y f dealer; (de lotería) seller, vendor.

expendeduría f (de tabaco) tobacconist's Br, cigar store Am.

expensas fpl (gastos) expenses, costs. ▶ **a expensas de** loc prep at the expense of.

experiencia f (gen) experience; **por (propia) ~** from (one's own) experience.

experimentado, -da adj (persona) experienced; (método) tried and tested.

experimentar vt 1. (gen) to experience; (derrota, pérdidas) to suffer. 2. (probar) to test; (hacer experimentos con) to experiment with o on.

experimento m experiment.

experto, -ta adj, m y f expert.

expiar vt to atone for, to expiate.

expirar vi to expire.

explanada f (llanura) flat o level ground (U).

explayar vt to extend. ▶ **explayarse** vpr 1. (divertirse) to amuse o.s., to enjoy o.s. 2. (hablar mucho) to talk at length. 3. (desahogarse): **~se (con)** to pour out one's heart (to).

explicación f explanation.

explicar vt (gen) to explain; (teoría) to expound. ▶ **explicarse** vpr 1. (comprender) to understand; **no me lo explico** I can't understand it. 2. (dar explicaciones) to explain o.s. 3. (expresarse) to make o.s. understood.

explícito, -ta adj explicit.

exploración f (gen & MED) exploration.

explorador, -ra m y f explorer; (scout) boy scout (f girl guide).

explorar vt 1. (gen) to explore; (MIL) to scout. 2. (MED) to examine; (internamente) to explore, to probe.

explosión f lit & fig explosion; **hacer ~** to explode.

explosivo, -va adj (gen) explosive. ▶ **explosivo** m explosive.

explotación f 1. (acción) exploitation; (de fábrica etc) running; (de yacimiento minero) mining; (agrícola) farming; (de petróleo) drilling. 2. (instalaciones): **~ agrícola** farm.

explotar ◆ vt 1. (gen) to exploit.

2. (fábrica) to run, to operate; (terreno) to farm; (mina) to work. ◆ vi to explode.

expoliar vt to pillage, to plunder.

exponer vt 1. (gen) to expose. 2. (teoría) to expound; (ideas, propuesta) to set out, to explain. 3. (cuadro, obra) to exhibit, to show; (objetos en vitrinas) to display. 4. (vida, prestigio) to risk. ▶ **exponerse** vpr (arriesgarse): **~se (a)** (gen) to run the risk (of); (a la muerte) to expose o.s. (to).

exportación f 1. (acción) export. 2. (mercancías) exports (pl).

exportar vt (COM & INFORM) to export.

exposición f 1. (gen & FOT) exposure. 2. (de arte etc) exhibition; (de objetos en vitrina) display; **~ universal** world fair. 3. (de teoría) exposition; (de ideas, propuesta) setting out, explanation.

expositor, -ra m y f (de arte) exhibitor; (de teoría) exponent.

exprés ◆ adj 1. (tren) express. 2. (café) espresso. ◆ m = **expreso**.

expresado, -da adj (mencionado) abovementioned.

expresamente adv (a propósito) expressly; (explícitamente) explicitly.

expresar vt to express; (suj: rostro) to show.

expresión f expression.

expresivo, -va adj expressive; (cariñoso) affectionate.

expreso, -sa adj (explícito) specific; (deliberado) express; (claro) clear. ▶ **expreso** ◆ m 1. (tren) express train. 2. (café) espresso. ◆ adv on purpose, expressly.

exprimidor m squeezer.

exprimir vt (fruta) to squeeze; (zumo) to squeeze out.

expropiar vt to expropriate.

expuesto, -ta ◆ pp → **exponer**. ◆ adj 1. (dicho) stated, expressed. 2. (desprotegido): **~ (a)** exposed (to). 3. (arriesgado) dangerous, risky. 4. (exhibido) on display.

expulsar vt 1. (persona - de clase, local, asociación) to throw out; (- de colegio) to expel. 2. (DEP) to send off. 3. (humo) to emit, to give off.

expulsión f (gen) expulsion; (de clase, local, asociación) throwing-out; (DEP) sending-off.

exquisitez f (cualidad) exquisiteness.

exquisito, -ta adj exquisite; (comida) delicious, sublime.

extasiarse vpr: **~ (ante o con)** to go into ecstasies (over).

éxtasis m inv ecstasy.

extender vt **1.** (desplegar - tela, plano, alas) to spread (out); (- brazos, piernas) to stretch out. **2.** (esparcir - mantequilla) to spread; (- pintura) to smear; (- objetos etc) to spread out. **3.** (ampliar - castigo, influencia etc) to extend. **4.** (documento) to draw up; (cheque) to make out; (pasaporte, certificado) to issue. ▶ **extenderse** vpr **1.** (ocupar): ~se (por) to stretch o extend across. **2.** (hablar mucho): ~se (en) to enlarge o expand (on). **3.** (durar) to extend, to last. **4.** (difundirse): ~se (por) to spread (across). **5.** (tenderse) to stretch out.

extensión f **1.** (superficie - de terreno etc) area, expanse. **2.** (amplitud - de país etc) size; (- de conocimientos) extent. **3.** (duración) duration, length. **4.** (sentido - de concepto, palabra) range of meaning; **en toda la ~ de la palabra** in every sense of the word. **5.** (INFORM & TELECOM) extension.

extensivo, -va adj extensive.

extenso, -sa adj extensive; (país) vast; (libro, película) long.

extenuar vt to exhaust completely.

exterior ♦ adj **1.** (de fuera) outside, external; (capa) outer, exterior. **2.** (visible) outward. **3.** (extranjero) foreign. ♦ m **1.** (superficie) outside; **en el ~** outside. **2.** (extranjero) foreign countries (pl); **en el ~** abroad. **3.** (aspecto) appearance. ▶ **exteriores** mpl (CIN) outside shots; **rodar en ~es** to film on location.

exteriorizar vt to show, to reveal.

exterminar vt (aniquilar) to exterminate.

exterminio m extermination.

externo, -na adj **1.** (gen) external; (parte, capa) outer; (influencia) outside; (signo, aspecto) outward. **2.** (alumno) day (antes de sust).

extinción f (gen) extinction; (de esperanzas) loss.

extinguir vt (incendio) to put out, to extinguish; (raza) to wipe out; (afecto, entusiasmo) to put an end to. ▶ **extinguirse** vpr (fuego, luz) to go out; (animal, raza) to become extinct; (ruido) to die out; (afecto) to die.

extinto, -ta adj extinguished; (animal, volcán) extinct.

extintor m fire extinguisher.

extirpar vt (tumor) to remove; (muela) to extract; fig to eradicate.

extorsión f **1.** (molestia) trouble, bother. **2.** (DER) extortion.

extorsionista m y f extortionist.

extra ♦ adj **1.** (adicional) extra. **2.** (de gran calidad) top quality, superior. ♦ m y f (CIN) extra. ♦ m (gasto etc) extra. ♦ f → **paga**.

extracción f **1.** (gen) extraction. **2.** (en sorteos) draw. **3.** (de carbón) mining.

extracto m **1.** (resumen) summary, résumé; **~ de cuentas** statement (of account). **2.** (concentrado) extract.

extraditar vt to extradite.

extraer vt: ~ (de) (gen) to extract (from); (sangre) to draw (from); (carbón) to mine (from); (conclusiones) to come to o draw (from).

extralimitarse vpr fig to go too far.

extranjero, -ra ♦ adj foreign. ♦ m y f (persona) foreigner. ▶ **extranjero** m (territorio) foreign countries (pl); **estar en el/ir al ~** to be/go abroad.

extrañar vt **1.** (sorprender) to surprise; **me extraña (que digas esto)** I'm surprised (that you should say that). **2.** (echar de menos) to miss. ▶ **extrañarse de** vpr (sorprenderse de) to be surprised at.

extrañeza f (sorpresa) surprise.

extraño, -ña ♦ adj **1.** (gen) strange. **2.** (ajeno) detached, uninvolved. **3.** (MED) foreign. ♦ m y f stranger.

extraoficial adj unofficial.

extraordinario, -ria adj **1.** (gen) extraordinary. **2.** (gastos) additional; (edición, suplemento) special. ▶ **extraordinario** m **1.** (PRENS) special edition. **2.** → **paga**.

extraparlamentario, -ria adj non-parliamentary.

extrapolar vt to generalize about.

extrarradio m outskirts (pl), suburbs (pl).

extraterrestre adj, m y f extraterrestrial.

extravagancia f eccentricity.

extravagante adj eccentric, outlandish.

extravertido, -da = **extrovertido**.

extraviado, -da adj (perdido) lost; (animal) stray.

extraviar vt **1.** (objeto) to lose, to mislay. **2.** (excursionista) to mislead. ▶ **extraviarse** vpr **1.** (persona) to get lost. **2.** (objeto) to go missing.

extravío m (pérdida) loss, mislaying.

extremado, -da adj extreme.

extremar vt to go to extremes with. ▶ **extremarse** vpr to take great pains o care.

extremaunción f extreme unction.
extremidad f (extremo) end. ▶ **extremidades** fpl (ANAT) extremities.
extremista adj, m y f extremist.
extremo, -ma adj (gen) extreme; (en el espacio) far, furthest. ▶ **extremo** m 1. (punta) end. 2. (límite) extreme; **en último** ~ as a last resort. 3. (DEP): ~ **derecho/izquierdo** outside right/left.
extrovertido, -da, extravertido, -da adj, m y f extrovert.
exuberancia f exuberance.
exuberante adj exuberant.
exudar vt to exude, to ooze.
exultante adj exultant.
eyaculación f ejaculation.
eyacular vi to ejaculate.

F

f, F f (letra) f, F. ▶ **23 F** m 23rd February, day of the failed coup d'état in Spain in 1981.
f. 1. (abrev de **factura**) inv. 2. (abrev de folio) f.
fa m (MÚS) F; (en solfeo) fa.
fabada f Asturian stew made of beans, pork sausage and bacon.
fábrica f (establecimiento) factory; ~ **de papel** paper mill.
fabricación f manufacture; **de** ~ **casera** home-made; ~ **en serie** mass production.
fabricante m y f manufacturer.
fabricar vt 1. (producir) to manufacture, to make. 2. (construir) to build, to construct. 3. fig (inventar) to fabricate, to make up.
fábula f (LITER) fable; (leyenda) legend.
fabuloso, -sa adj 1. (ficticio) mythical. 2. (muy bueno) fabulous, fantastic.
facción f (POLÍT) faction. ▶ **facciones** fpl (rasgos) features.
faceta f facet.
facha f 1. (aspecto) appearance, look. 2. (mamarracho) mess; **vas hecho una** ~ you look a mess.
fachada f (ARQUIT) façade.
facial adj facial.
fácil adj 1. (gen) easy; ~ **de hacer** easy to do. 2. (probable) likely.

facilidad f 1. (simplicidad) ease, easiness. 2. (aptitud) aptitude, facility; **tener** ~ **para algo** to have a gift for sthg. ▶ **facilidades** fpl (comodidades) facilities; ~**es de pago** easy (payment) terms.
facilitar vt 1. (simplificar) to facilitate, to make easy; (posibilitar) to make possible. 2. (proporcionar) to provide.
facón m Amer sheath knife.
facsímil, facsímile m facsimile.
factible adj feasible.
fáctico, -ca → **poder**.
factor m (gen) factor.
factoría f (fábrica) factory.
factótum (pl factotums) m y f factotum.
factura f 1. (por mercancías, trabajo realizado) invoice. 2. (de gas, teléfono) bill; (en tienda, hotel) bill.
facturación f 1. (ventas) turnover Br, net revenue Am. 2. (de equipaje - en aeropuerto) checking-in; (- en estación) registration; **mostrador de** ~ check-in desk.
facturar vt 1. (cobrar): ~**le a alguien algo** to invoice o bill sb for sthg. 2. (vender) to turn over. 3. (equipaje - en aeropuerto) to check in; (- en estación) to register.
facultad f 1. (gen) faculty. 2. (poder) power, right.
facultativo, -va ◆ adj 1. (voluntario) optional. 2. (médico) medical. ◆ m y f doctor.
faena f (tarea) task, work (U); **hacer una** ~ **a alguien** fig to play a dirty trick on sb.
faenar vi to fish.
fagot m (instrumento) bassoon.
faisán m pheasant.
faja f 1. (prenda de mujer, terapéutica) corset; (banda) sash, cummerbund. 2. (de terreno - pequeña) strip; (- grande) belt.
fajo m (de billetes, papel) wad; (de leña, cañas) bundle.
falacia f deceit, trick.
falaz adj false.
falda f 1. (prenda) skirt; ~ **escocesa** kilt; ~ **pantalón** culottes (pl). 2. (de montaña) slope, mountainside.
faldón m (de ropa) tail; (de cortina, mesa camilla) folds (pl).
falla f (gen & GEOL) fault. ▶ **fallas** fpl (fiesta) celebrations in Valencia during which cardboard figures are burnt.

FALLAS

Valencia is famous for the festival known as 'las Fallas'. Throughout the year, people prepare grotesque papier-mâché giants ('ninots') which are decorated with ornaments called 'fallas'. These are displayed in the streets and squares of Valencia from 16–19 March, and a jury decides which will be spared from being burned in the 'cremà' at midnight on 19 March.

---

fallar ◆ vt 1. (sentenciar) to pass sentence on; (premio) to award. 2. (equivocar - respuesta) to get wrong; (- tiro) to miss. ◆ vi 1. (equivocarse) to get it wrong; (no acertar) to miss. 2. (fracasar, flaquear) to fail; (- plan) to go wrong. 3. (decepcionar): ~le a alguien to let sb down. 4. (sentenciar): ~ a favor/en contra de to find in favour of/against.

fallecer vi to pass away, to die.

fallecimiento m decease, death.

fallo m 1. (error) mistake; (DEP) miss. 2. (sentencia - de juez, jurado) verdict.

fallutería f Amer fam hypocrisy.

falo m phallus.

falsear vt (hechos, historia) to falsify, to distort; (moneda, firma) to forge.

falsedad f 1. (falta de verdad, autenticidad) falseness. 2. (mentira) falsehood.

falsete m falsetto.

falsificar vt to forge.

falso, -sa adj 1. (rumor, excusa etc) false, untrue. 2. (dinero, firma, cuadro) forged; (joyas) fake; **jurar en ~** to commit perjury. 3. (hipócrita) deceitful.

falta f 1. (carencia) lack; **hacer ~** to be necessary; **me hace ~ suerte** I need some luck; **por ~ de** for want o lack of. 2. (escasez) shortage. 3. (ausencia) absence; **echar en ~ algo/a alguien** (notar la ausencia de) to notice that sthg/sb is missing; (echar de menos) to miss sthg/sb. 4. (imperfección) fault; (error) mistake; **~ de educación** bad manners (pl); **~ de ortografía** spelling mistake. 5. (DEP) foul; (en tenis) fault. 6. (DER) offence. ▶ **a falta de** loc prep in the absence of. ▶ **sin falta** loc adv without fail.

faltar vi 1. (no haber) to be lacking, to be needed; **falta aire** there's not enough air; **falta sal** it needs a bit of salt. 2. (estar ausente) to be absent o missing; **falta Elena** Elena is missing. 3. (carecer): **le faltan las fuerzas** he lacks o doesn't have the strength. 4. (hacer falta) to be necessary; **me falta tiempo** I need time. 5. (quedar): **falta un mes para las vacaciones** there's a month to go till

the holidays; **sólo te falta firmar** all you have to do is sign; **¿cuánto falta para Leeds?** how much further is it to Leeds?; **falta mucho por hacer** there is still a lot to be done; **falta poco para que llegue** it won't be long till he arrives. 6. loc: **¡no faltaba o faltaría más!** (asentimiento) of course!; (rechazo) that tops it all!, that's a bit much! ▶ **faltar a** vi 1. (palabra, promesa) to break, not to keep; (deber, obligación) to neglect. 2. (cita, trabajo) not to turn up at; **¡no faltes (a la cita)!** I don't miss it!, be there! 3. (no respetar) to be disrespectful towards; **~ a alguien en algo** to offend sb in sthg.

falto, -ta adj: **~ de** lacking in, short of.

fama f 1. (renombre) fame. 2. (reputación) reputation.

famélico, -ca adj starving, famished.

familia f family; **en ~** in private.

familiar ◆ adj 1. (de familia) family (antes de sust). 2. (en el trato - agradable) friendly; (- en demasía) overly familiar. 3. (lenguaje, estilo) informal. 4. (conocido) familiar. ◆ m y f relative, relation.

familiaridad f familiarity.

familiarizar vt: **~ (con)** to familiarize (with). ▶ **familiarizarse** vpr: **~se con** (estudiar) to familiarize o.s. with; (acostumbrarse a) to get used to.

famoso, -sa adj famous.

fanático, -ca ◆ adj fanatical. ◆ m y f (gen) fanatic; (DEP) fan.

fanatismo m fanaticism.

fanfarria f 1. fam (jactancia) bragging. 2. (de música) fanfare; (banda) brass band.

fanfarrón, -ona adj boastful.

fango m mud.

fantasear vi to fantasize.

fantasía f (imaginación) imagination; (cosa imaginada) fantasy; **de ~** (ropa) fancy; (bisutería) imitation.

fantasma ◆ m (espectro) ghost, phantom. ◆ m y f fam (fanfarrón) show-off.

fantástico, -ca adj fantastic.

fantoche m 1. (títere) puppet. 2. (mamarracho) (ridiculous) sight.

fardo m bundle.

farfullar vt & vi to gabble, to splutter.

faringitis f inv sore throat.

farmacéutico, -ca ◆ adj pharmaceutical. ◆ m y f chemist, pharmacist.

farmacia f (establecimiento) chemist's (shop) Br, pharmacy, drugstore Am; **~ de turno o de guardia** duty chemist's.

fármaco m medicine, drug.

faro m 1. (para barcos) lighthouse. 2. (de coche) headlight, headlamp; ~ antiniebla foglamp.

farol m (farola) street lamp o light; (linterna) lantern, lamp.

farola f (farol) street lamp o light; (poste) lamppost.

farsa f lit & fig farce.

farsante adj deceitful.

fascículo m part, instalment (of serialization).

fascinante adj fascinating.

fascinar ◆ vt to fascinate. ◆ vi: ~le a alguien algo/hacer algo to love sthg/doing sthg; me fascina viajar I love travelling.

fascismo m fascism.

fascista adj, m y f fascist.

fase f phase.

fastidiado, -da adj (de salud) ill; ando ~ del estómago I've got a bad stomach.

fastidiar vt 1. (estropear - fiesta etc) to spoil, to ruin; (- máquina, objeto etc) to break. 2. (molestar) to annoy, to bother. ▶ **fastidiarse** vpr 1. (estropearse - fiesta etc) to be ruined; (- máquina) to break down. 2. (aguantarse) to put up with it.

fastidio m 1. (molestia) nuisance, bother. 2. (enfado) annoyance.

fastidioso, -sa adj (molesto) annoying.

fastuoso, -sa adj lavish, sumptuous.

fatal ◆ adj 1. (mortal) fatal. 2. (muy malo) terrible, dreadful. 3. (inevitable) inevitable. ◆ adv terribly; sentirse ~ to feel terrible.

fatalidad f 1. (destino) fate, destiny. 2. (desgracia) misfortune.

fatalismo m fatalism.

fatídico, -ca adj fateful, ominous.

fatiga f (cansancio) tiredness, fatigue. ▶ **fatigas** fpl (penas) hardships.

fatigar vt to tire, to weary. ▶ **fatigarse** vpr to get tired.

fatigoso, -sa adj tiring, fatiguing.

fatuo, -tua adj 1. (necio) fatuous, foolish. 2. (engreído) conceited.

fauna f fauna.

favor m favour; **a ~ de** in favour of; **hacerle un ~ a alguien** (ayudar a) to do sb a favour; fam fig (acostarse con) to go to bed with sb; **pedir un ~ a alguien** to ask sb a favour; **tener a o en su ~ a alguien** to enjoy sb's support. ▶ **por favor** loc adv please.

favorable adj favourable; **ser ~ a algo** to be in favour of sthg.

favorecer vt 1. (gen) to favour; (ayudar) to help, to assist. 2. (sentar bien) to suit.

favoritismo m favouritism.

favorito, -ta adj, m y f favourite.

fax m inv 1. (aparato) fax (machine); **mandar algo por ~** to fax sthg. 2. (documento) fax.

fayuquero m Amer dealer in contraband.

faz f culto 1. (cara) countenance, face. 2. (del mundo, de la tierra) face.

fe f 1. (gen) faith; **hacer algo de buena ~** to do sthg in good faith. 2. (documento) certificate; **~ de erratas** errata (pl). 3. loc: **dar ~ de que** to testify that.

fealdad f (de rostro etc) ugliness.

febrero m February; ver también septiembre.

febril adj feverish; fig (actividad) hectic.

fecha f (gen) date; (momento actual) current date; **hasta la ~** to date, so far; **~ de caducidad** (de alimentos) sell-by date; (de carné, pasaporte) expiry date; (de medicamento) 'use before' date; **~ tope** o **límite** deadline.

fechar vt to date.

fechoría f bad deed, misdemeanour.

fécula f starch (in food).

fecundación f fertilization; **~ artificial** artificial insemination; **~ in vitro** in vitro fertilization.

fecundar vt 1. (fertilizar) to fertilize. 2. (hacer productivo) to make fertile.

fecundo, -da adj (gen) fertile; (artista) prolific.

federación f federation.

federal adj, m y f federal.

federar vt to federate. ▶ **federarse** vpr 1. (formar federación) to become o form a federation. 2. (ingresar en federación) to join a federation.

feedback ['fidbak] (pl **feedbacks**) m feedback.

fehaciente adj irrefutable.

felicidad f happiness. ▶ **felicidades** fpl (gen) best wishes; **¡~es!** (en cumpleaños) happy birthday!; (enhorabuena) congratulations!

felicitación f 1. (acción): **felicitaciones** congratulations. 2. (postal) greetings card.

felicitar vt to congratulate.

feligrés, -esa m y f parishioner.

felino, -na adj feline.

feliz adj 1. (gen) happy. 2. (afortunado) lucky. 3. (oportuno) timely.

felpa f (de seda) plush; (de algodón) towelling.

felpudo m doormat.

femenino, -na adj (gen) feminine; (BOT & ZOOL) female. ▸ **femenino** m (GRAM) feminine.

fémina f woman, female.

feminismo m feminism.

feminista adj, m y f feminist.

fémur (pl **fémures**) m femur, thighbone.

fénix m inv (ave) phoenix.

fenomenal adj (magnífico) wonderful, marvellous; ¡lo pasé ~! I had a great time!

fenómeno ◆ m (gen) phenomenon. ◆ adv fam brilliantly, fantastically; **pasarlo** ~ to have a great time. ◆ interj: ¡~! great!, terrific!

feo, -a adj 1. (persona) ugly. 2. (aspecto, herida, conducta) nasty; **es** ~ **escupir** it's rude to spit.

féretro m coffin.

feria f 1. (gen) fair; ~ **(de muestras)** trade fair. 2. (fiesta popular) festival.

FERIA DE ABRIL

The 'feria de abril' in Seville is Spain's most famous festival. People gather in an open-air compound to look at the hundreds of stalls and to drink, talk and dance the 'sevillanas'. At the same time, the first bullfights of the season are held in Seville's bullrings.

---

fermentación f fermentation.

fermentar vt & vi to ferment.

ferocidad f ferocity, fierceness.

feroz adj 1. (animal, bestia) fierce, ferocious. 2. fig (criminal, asesino) cruel, savage. 3. fig (dolor, angustia) terrible.

férreo, -a adj lit & fig iron (antes de sust).

ferretería f ironmonger's (shop) Br, hardware store.

ferrocarril m (sistema, medio) railway, railroad Am; (tren) train; **por** ~ by train.

ferroviario, -ria adj railway (antes de sust) Br, rail (antes de sust), railroad (antes de sust) Am.

ferry m ferry.

fértil adj lit & fig fertile.

fertilidad f lit & fig fertility.

fertilizante m fertilizer.

fertilizar vt to fertilize.

ferviente adj fervent.

fervor m fervour.

festejar vt (celebrar) to celebrate.

festejo m (fiesta) party. ▸ **festejos** mpl (fiestas) public festivities.

festín m banquet, feast.

festival m festival.

FESTIVALES

The most important theatre festivals in Spain are the 'Festival Internacional de Teatro de Mérida', the 'Fira de Teatre al carrer de Tàrrega' and the 'Sitges Teatre Internacional'. Film festivals are usually held in September and October, the most important being the 'Festival Internacional de Cine de San Sebastián', the 'Semana Internacional de Cine de Valladolid (SEMINCI)', the 'Festival de Cinema Fantàstic de Sitges' and the 'Festival de Cine Iberoamericano de Huelva'.

---

festividad f festivity.

festivo, -va adj 1. (de fiesta) festive; **día** ~ (public) holiday. 2. (alegre) cheerful, jolly; (chistoso) funny, witty.

fetiche m fetish.

fétido, -da adj fetid, foul-smelling.

feto m foetus.

feudal adj feudal.

FF AA (abrev de **Fuerzas Armadas**) fpl Spanish armed forces.

fiable adj (máquina) reliable; (persona) trustworthy.

fiador, -ra m y f guarantor, surety; **salir** ~ **por** to vouch for.

fiambre m (comida) cold meat Br, cold cut Am.

fiambrera f lunch o sandwich box.

fianza f 1. (depósito) deposit. 2. (DER) bail; **bajo** ~ on bail. 3. (garantía) security, bond.

fiar ◆ vt (COM) to sell on credit. ◆ vi (COM) to sell on credit; **ser de** ~ fig to be trustworthy. ▸ **fiarse** vpr: ¡no te fíes! don't be too sure (about it)!; ~se de algo/alguien to trust sthg/sb.

fiasco m fiasco.

FIBA (abrev de **Federación Internacional de Baloncesto Amateur**) f IABF.

fibra f (gen) fibre; (de madera) grain; ~ de vidrio fibreglass.

ficción f (gen) fiction.

ficha f 1. (tarjeta) (index) card; (con detalles personales) file, record card. 2. (de guardarropa, aparcamiento) ticket. 3. (de teléfono) token. 4. (de juego - gen) counter; (en ajedrez) piece; (en un casino) chip. 5. (INFORM) card.

fichaje m (DEP) (contratación) signing (up); (importe) transfer fee.

fichar ◆ vt 1. (archivar) to note down

on an index card, to file. **2.** (*suj: policía*) to put on police files o records. **3.** (DEP) to sign up. ◆ *vi* **1.** (*suj: trabajador - al entrar*) to clock in; (*- al salir*) to clock out. **2.** (DEP): **~ (por)** to sign up (for).
fichero *m* (INFORM) file.
ficticio, -cia *adj* (*imaginario*) fictitious.
ficus *m inv* rubber plant.
fidedigno, -na *adj* reliable.
fidelidad *f* **1.** (*lealtad*) loyalty; (*de cónyuge, perro*) faithfulness. **2.** (*precisión*) accuracy; **alta ~** high fidelity.
fideo *m* noodle.
fiebre *f* fever; **tener ~** to have a temperature; **~ del heno** hay fever.
fiel *adj* **1.** (*leal - amigo, seguidor*) loyal; (*- cónyuge, perro*) faithful. **2.** (*preciso*) accurate. ▶ **fieles** *mpl* (RELIG): **los ~es** the faithful.
fieltro *m* felt.
fiero, -ra *adj* savage, ferocious. ▶ **fiera** *f* (*animal*) wild animal.
fierro *m* Amer **1.** (*hierro*) iron. **2.** (*navaja*) penknife.
fiesta *f* **1.** (*reunión*) party; (*de pueblo etc*) (local) festivities (*pl*); **~ mayor** local celebrations for the festival of a town's patron saint. **2.** (*día*) public holiday; **ser ~** to be a public holiday; **hacer ~** to be on holiday. ▶ **fiestas** *fpl* (*vacaciones*) holidays.

FIESTA MAYOR

All Spain's towns and villages hold a 'fiesta mayor', which consists of celebrations and cultural activities in honour of their patron saint. Dances are usually held every evening of the fiesta, which may last from a weekend up to 10 days.

FIESTAS PATRIAS

This is the name given to the national celebrations held across all of Spanish-speaking America to mark the day on which each country gained independence from Spain. The independence day celebrations usually last two days.

figura *f* **1.** (*gen*) figure; (*forma*) shape. **2.** (*en naipes*) picture card.
figuraciones *fpl* imaginings.
figurado, -da *adj* figurative.
figurar ◆ *vi* **1.** (*aparecer*): **~ (en)** to appear (in), to figure (in). **2.** (*ser importante*) to be prominent o important. ◆ *vt* **1.** (*representar*) to represent. **2.** (*simular*) to feign, to simulate. ▶ **figurarse** *vpr* (*imaginarse*) to imagine; **ya me lo figuraba yo** I thought as much.

fijación *f* **1.** (*gen* & FOT) fixing. **2.** (*obsesión*) fixation.
fijador *m* (*líquido*) fixative; **~ de pelo** (*crema*) hair gel; (*espray*) hair spray.
fijar *vt* **1.** (*gen*) to fix; (*asegurar*) to fasten; (*cartel*) to stick up; (*sello*) to stick on. **2.** (*significado*) to establish; **~ el domicilio** to take up residence; **~ la mirada/la atención en** to fix one's gaze/attention on. ▶ **fijarse** *vpr* to pay attention; **~se en algo** (*darse cuenta*) to notice sthg; (*prestar atención*) to pay attention to sthg.
fijo, -ja *adj* **1.** (*gen*) fixed; (*sujeto*) secure. **2.** (*cliente*) regular. **3.** (*fecha*) definite. **4.** (*empleado, trabajo*) permanent.
fila *f* (*hilera - gen*) line; (*- de asientos*) row; (*cola*) queue Br, line Am; **en ~, en ~ india** in line, in single file; **hacer ~** to queue; **ponerse en ~** to line up. ▶ **filas** *fpl* (MIL) ranks; **cerrar ~s** *fig* to close ranks.
filántropo, -pa *m y f* philanthropist.
filarmónico, -ca *adj* philharmonic.
filatelia *f* philately.
filete *m* (CULIN - *grueso*) (fillet) steak; (*- delgado*) fillet; (*solomillo*) sirloin.
filiación *f* (POLÍT) affiliation.
filial ◆ *adj* **1.** (*de hijo*) filial. **2.** (*de empresa*) subsidiary. ◆ *f* subsidiary.
filigrana *f* (*en orfebrería*) filigree.
Filipinas *fpl*: **(las) ~** the Philippines (*sg*).
filipino, -na *adj, m y f* Filipino. ▶ **filipino** *m* (*lengua*) Filipino.
film = **filme**.
filmar *vt* to film, to shoot.
filme (*pl* **filmes**), **film** (*pl* **films**) *m* film Br, movie Am.
filmoteca *f* (*archivo*) film library; (*sala de cine*) film institute.
filo *m* (*cutting*) edge; **de doble ~, de dos ~s** *lit* & *fig* double-edged. ▶ **al filo de** *loc prep* just before.
filología *f* **1.** (*ciencia*) philology. **2.** (*carrera*) language and literature.
filón *m* **1.** (*de carbón etc*) seam. **2.** *fig* (*mina*) gold mine.
filoso, -sa, filudo, -da *adj* Amer sharp.
filosofía *f* (*ciencia*) philosophy.
filósofo, -fa *m y f* philosopher.
filtración *f* **1.** (*de agua*) filtration. **2.** *fig* (*de noticia etc*) leak.
filtrar *vt* **1.** (*tamizar*) to filter. **2.** *fig* (*datos, noticia*) to leak. ▶ **filtrarse** *vpr* **1.** (*penetrar*): **~se (por)** to filter o seep (through). **2.** *fig* (*datos, noticia*) to be leaked.

filtro m 1. (gen) filter; (de cigarrillo) filter, filter tip. 2. (pócima) philtre.

filudo, -da = filoso.

fin m 1. (final) end; **dar** o **poner ~ a algo** to put an end to sthg; **tocar a su ~** to come to a close; **~ de semana** weekend; **a ~es de** at the end of; **al** o **por ~** at last, finally; **a ~ de cuentas** after all; **al ~ y al cabo** after all. 2. (objetivo) aim, goal. ▶ **a fin de** loc conj in order to. ▶ **en fin** loc adv anyway.

final ◆ adj final, end (antes de sust). ◆ m end; **~ feliz** happy ending; **a ~es de** at the end of; **al ~** (en conclusión) in the end. ◆ f final.

finalidad f aim, purpose.

finalista m y f finalist.

finalizar ◆ vt to finish, to complete. ◆ vi: **~ (con)** to end o finish (in).

financiación f financing.

financiar vt to finance.

financiero, -ra ◆ adj financial. ◆ m y f (persona) financier. ▶ **financiera** f (firma) finance company.

financista m y f Amer financier.

finanzas fpl finance (U).

finca f 1. (inmueble) property; (casa de campo) country residence. 2. (hacienda) farm.

fingir ◆ vt to feign. ◆ vi to pretend.

finiquito m settlement.

finito, -ta adj finite.

finlandés, -esa ◆ adj Finnish. ◆ m y f (persona) Finn. ▶ **finlandés** m (lengua) Finnish.

Finlandia Finland.

fino, -na adj 1. (gen) fine; (delgado) thin; (cintura) slim. 2. (cortés) refined. 3. (agudo - oído, olfato) sharp, keen; (- gusto, humor, ironía) refined. ▶ **fino** m dry sherry.

finura f (gen) fineness; (delgadez) thinness; (cortesía) refinement; (de oído, olfato) sharpness, keenness; (de gusto, humor, ironía) refinement.

firma f 1. (rúbrica) signature; (acción) signing. 2. (empresa) firm.

firmamento m firmament.

firmar vt to sign.

firme adj 1. (gen) firm; (mueble, andamio, edificio) stable. 2. (argumento, base) solid. 3. (carácter, actitud, paso) resolute.

firmeza f 1. (gen) firmness; (de mueble, edificio) stability. 2. (de argumento) solidity. 3. (de carácter, actitud) resolution.

fiscal ◆ adj tax (antes de sust), fiscal. ◆ m y f public prosecutor Br, district attorney Am.

fisco m treasury, exchequer.

fisgar, fisgonear vi (gen) to pry; (escuchando) to eavesdrop.

fisgón, -ona m y f nosy parker.

fisgonear = fisgar.

físicamente adv physically.

físico, -ca ◆ adj physical. ◆ m y f (persona) physicist. ▶ **físico** m (complexión) physique. ▶ **física** f (ciencia) physics (U).

fisiológico, -ca adj physiological.

fisionomía, fisonomía f features (pl), appearance.

fisioterapeuta m y f physiotherapist.

fisonomía = fisionomía.

fisura f (grieta) fissure.

flacidez, flaccidez f flabbiness.

flácido, -da, fláccido, -da adj flaccid, flabby.

flaco, -ca adj thin, skinny.

flagelar vt to flagellate.

flagrante adj flagrant.

flamante adj (vistoso) resplendent; (nuevo) brand-new.

flambear vt to flambé.

flamenco, -ca ◆ adj 1. (MÚS) flamenco (antes de sust). 2. (de Flandes) Flemish. ◆ m y f (de Flandes) Fleming. ▶ **flamenco** m 1. (ave) flamingo. 2. (lengua) Flemish. 3. (MÚS) flamenco.

flan m crème caramel; **estar hecho** o **como un ~** to shake like a jelly, to be a bundle of nerves.

flanco m flank.

flanquear vt to flank.

flaquear vi to weaken; fig to flag.

flaqueza f weakness.

flash [flaʃ] (pl flashes) m 1. (FOT) flash. 2. (informativo) newsflash.

flato m: **tener ~** to have a stitch.

flatulento, -ta adj flatulent.

flauta f flute; **~ dulce** recorder; **de la gran ~** Amer fig tremendous. ◆ interj: **¡(la gran) ~!** Amer good grief!, good heavens!

flecha f (gen) arrow; (ARQUIT) spire.

flechazo m fam fig (amoroso): **fue un ~** it was love at first sight.

fleco m (adorno) fringe.

flema f phlegm.

flemático, -ca adj (tranquilo) phlegmatic.

flemón m gumboil.

flequillo m fringe.

flete m 1. (precio) freightage. 2. (carga) cargo, freight.

flexible adj flexible.

flexo m adjustable table lamp o light.

flipar *fam vi* 1. (*disfrutar*) to have a wild time. 2. (*asombrarse*) to be gobsmacked. 3. (*con una droga*) to be stoned o high.

flirtear *vi* to flirt.

flojear *vi* (*decaer - piernas, fuerzas etc*) to weaken; (*- memoria*) to be failing; (*- película, libro*) to flag; (*- calor, trabajo*) to ease off; (*- ventas*) to fall off.

flojera *f* lethargy, feeling of weakness.

flojo, -ja *adj* 1. (*suelto*) loose. 2. (*débil - persona, bebida*) weak; (*- sonido*) faint; (*- tela*) thin; (*- salud*) poor; (*- viento*) light. 3. (*inactivo - mercado, negocio*) slack.

flor *f* 1. (BOT) flower; **echar ~es a alguien** to pay sb compliments. 2. (*lo mejor*): **la ~ (y nata)** the crème de la crème, the cream. ► **a flor de** *loc adv*: **a ~ de agua/tierra** at water/ground level.

flora *f* flora.

florecer *vi* to flower; *fig* to flourish.

floreciente *adj fig* flourishing.

florero *m* vase.

florido, -da *adj* (*con flores*) flowery; (*estilo, lenguaje*) florid.

florista *m y f* florist.

floristería *f* florist's (shop).

flota *f* fleet.

flotación *f* (*gen & ECON*) flotation.

flotador *m* 1. (*para nadar*) rubber ring. 2. (*de caña de pescar*) float.

flotar *vi* (*gen & ECON*) to float; (*banderas*) to flutter.

flote ► **a flote** *loc adv* afloat; **salir a ~** *fig* to get back on one's feet.

flotilla *f* flotilla.

fluctuar *vi* (*variar*) to fluctuate.

fluidez *f* 1. (*gen*) fluidity; (*del tráfico*) free flow; (*de relaciones*) smoothness. 2. *fig* (*en el lenguaje*) fluency.

fluido, -da *adj* 1. (*gen*) fluid; (*tráfico*) free-flowing. 2. (*relaciones*) smooth. 3. *fig* (*lenguaje*) fluent. ► **fluido** *m* fluid; **~ eléctrico** electric current o power.

fluir *vi* to flow.

flujo *m* flow; **~ de caja** cash flow.

flúor *m* fluorine.

fluorescente *m* strip light.

fluvial *adj* river (*antes de sust*).

FM (*abrev de frecuencia modulada*) *f* FM.

FMI (*abrev de Fondo Monetario Internacional*) *m* IMF.

fobia *f* phobia.

foca *f* seal.

foco *m* 1. *fig* (*centro*) centre, focus. 2. (*lámpara - para un punto*) spotlight; (*- para una zona*) floodlight. 3. (FÍS & GEOM) focus. 4. *Amer* (*bombilla*) light bulb.

fofo, -fa *adj* flabby.

fogata *f* bonfire, fire.

fogón *m* (*para cocinar*) stove.

fogoso, -sa *adj* passionate.

fogueo *m*: **de ~** blank.

foie-gras [fwa'xras] *m* (pâté de) foie-gras.

folclore, folclor, folklor *m* folklore.

folio *m* (*hoja*) leaf, sheet; (*tamaño*) folio.

folklor = **folclore**.

follaje *m* foliage.

folletín *m* (*dramón*) melodrama.

folleto *m* (*turístico, publicitario*) brochure; (*explicativo, de instrucciones*) leaflet.

follón *m fam* 1. (*discusión*) row; **se armó ~** there was an almighty row. 2. (*lío*) mess; **¡vaya ~!** what a mess!

fomentar *vt* to encourage, to foster.

fomento *m* encouragement, fostering.

fonda *f* boarding house.

fondear ◆ *vi* to anchor. ◆ *vt* (*sondear*) to sound; (*registrar - barco*) to search.

fondo *m* 1. (*de recipiente, mar, piscina*) bottom; **tocar ~** (*embarcación*) to scrape along the sea/river bed; *fig* to hit rock bottom; **doble ~** false bottom. 2. (*de habitación etc*) back; **al ~ de** (*calle, pasillo*) at the end of; (*sala*) at the back of. 3. (*dimensión*) depth. 4. (*de tela, cuadro, foto*) background; **al ~** in the background. 5. (*de asunto, tema*) heart, bottom. 6. (ECON) fund; **a ~ perdido** non-returnable; **~ común** kitty; **~ de amortización/de inversión/de pensiones** (ECON) sinking/investment/pension fund. 7. (*de biblioteca, archivo*) catalogue, collection. 8. (DEP) stamina. 9. *Amer* (*combinación*) petticoat. ► **fondos** *mpl* (ECON) (*capital*) funds; **recaudar ~s** to raise funds. ► **a fondo** ◆ *loc adv* thoroughly. ◆ *loc adj* thorough. ► **en el fondo** *loc adv* 1. (*en lo más íntimo*) deep down. 2. (*en lo esencial*) basically.

fonético, -ca *adj* phonetic. ► **fonética** *f* (*ciencia*) phonetics (U).

fontanería *f* plumbing.

fontanero, -ra *m y f* plumber.

football = **fútbol**.

footing ['futin] *m* jogging; **hacer ~** to go jogging.

forajido, -da *m y f* outlaw.

foráneo, -a *adj* foreign.

forastero, -ra *m y f* stranger.

forcejear *vi* to struggle.

fórceps *m inv* forceps.

forense ◆ *adj* forensic. ◆ *m y f* pathologist.

forestal adj forest (antes de sust).

forja f (fragua) forge; (forjadura) forging.

forjar vt 1. (metal) to forge. 2. fig (inventarse) to invent; (crear) to build up. ► **forjarse** vpr fig (labrarse) to carve out for o.s.

forma f 1. (gen) shape, form; **en ~ de** in the shape of; **guardar las ~s** to keep up appearances. 2. (manera) way, manner; **de cualquier ~, de todas ~s** anyway, in any case; **de esta ~** in this way; **de ~ que** in such a way that, so that. 3. (ARTE & LITER) form. 4. (condición física) fitness; **estar en ~** to be fit. ► **formas** fpl 1. (silueta) figure (sg). 2. (modales) social conventions.

formación f 1. (gen & MIL) formation. 2. (educación) training; **~ profesional** vocational training. 3. (conjunto) grouping.

formal adj 1. (gen) formal. 2. (que se porta bien) well-behaved, good. 3. (de confianza) reliable. 4. (serio) serious.

formalidad f 1. (gen) formality. 2. (educación) (good) manners (pl). 3. (fiabilidad) reliability. 4. (seriedad) seriousness.

formalizar vt to formalize.

formar ◆ vt 1. (gen) to form. 2. (educar) to train, to educate. ◆ vi (MIL) to fall in. ► **formarse** vpr 1. (gen) to form. 2. (educarse) to be trained o educated.

formatear vt (INFORM) to format.

formato m (gen & INFORM) format.

formica® f Formica®.

formidable adj (enorme) tremendous; (extraordinario) amazing, fantastic.

fórmula f formula; **~ uno** formula one.

formular vt (plan, política) to formulate; (queja) to lodge, to make.

formulario m form.

fornido, -da adj well-built.

foro m 1. (tribunal) court (of law). 2. (TEATR) back of the stage. 3. (debate) forum.

forofo, -fa m y f fam fan, supporter.

forraje m fodder.

forrar vt: **~ (de)** (libro) to cover (with); (ropa) to line (with); (asiento) to upholster (with).

forro m (de libro) cover; (de ropa) lining; (de asiento) upholstery.

fortalecer vt to strengthen.

fortaleza f 1. (gen) strength. 2. (recinto) fortress.

fortificación f fortification.

fortuito, -ta adj chance (antes de sust).

fortuna f 1. (suerte) (good) luck; **por ~** fortunately, luckily. 2. (destino) fortune, fate. 3. (riqueza) fortune.

forúnculo, furúnculo m boil.

forzado, -da adj forced.

forzar vt 1. (gen) to force; **~ la vista** to strain one's eyes. 2. (violar) to rape.

forzoso, -sa adj (obligatorio) obligatory, compulsory; (inevitable) inevitable; (necesario) necessary.

forzudo, -da adj strong.

fosa f 1. (sepultura) grave. 2. (ANAT) cavity; **~s nasales** nostrils. 3. (hoyo) pit; **~ marina** ocean trough.

fosfato m phosphate.

fosforescente adj phosphorescent.

fósforo m 1. (QUÍM) phosphorus. 2. (cerilla) match.

fósil m (CIENCIA) fossil.

foso m (hoyo) ditch; (de fortaleza) moat; (de garaje) pit; (DEP & TEATR) pit.

foto f photo.

fotocomponer vt (IMPRENTA) to typeset.

fotocopia f (objeto) photocopy.

fotocopiadora f photocopier.

fotocopiar vt to photocopy.

fotoeléctrico, -ca adj photoelectric.

fotogénico, -ca adj photogenic.

fotografía f 1. (arte) photography. 2. (objeto) photograph.

fotografiar vt to photograph.

fotógrafo, -fa m y f photographer.

fotomatón m passport photo machine.

fotonovela f photo story.

fotorrobot (pl **fotorrobots**) f Identikit®.

fotosíntesis f inv photosynthesis.

FP (abrev de **formación profesional**) f vocationally orientated secondary education in Spain for pupils aged 14-18.

fra. (abrev de **factura**) inv.

frac (pl **fracs**) m tails (pl), dress coat.

fracasar vi to fail, to be unsuccessful.

fracaso m failure; **todo fue un ~** the whole thing was a disaster.

fracción f 1. (gen) fraction. 2. (POLÍT) faction.

fraccionario, -ria adj fractional; **moneda fraccionaria** small change.

fractura f fracture.

fragancia f fragrance.

fraganti ► **in fraganti** loc adv: **coger a alguien in ~** to catch sb red-handed o in the act.

fragata f frigate.

frágil adj (objeto) fragile; (persona) frail.

fragilidad f (de objeto) fragility; (de persona) frailty.

fragmentar vt (romper) to fragment; (dividir) to divide.

fragmento m fragment, piece; (de obra) excerpt.

fragor m (de batalla) clamour; (de trueno) crash.

fragua f forge.

fraguar ♦ vt 1. (forjar) to forge. 2. fig (idear) to think up. ♦ vi to set, to harden. ▶ **fraguarse** vpr to be in the offing.

fraile m friar.

frambuesa f raspberry.

francés, -esa ♦ adj French. ♦ m y f Frenchman (f Frenchwoman); **los franceses** the French. ▶ **francés** m (lengua) French.

Francia France.

francmasonería f Freemasonry.

franco, -ca adj 1. (sincero) frank, open; (directo) frank. 2. (sin obstáculos, gastos) free. ▶ **franco** m (moneda) franc.

francotirador, -ra m y f (MIL) sniper.

franela f flannel.

franja f strip; (en bandera, uniforme) stripe.

franquear vt 1. (paso, camino) to clear. 2. (río, montaña etc) to negotiate, to cross. 3. (correo) to frank.

franqueo m postage.

franqueza f (sinceridad) frankness.

franquicia f exemption.

franquismo m: **el ~** (régimen) the Franco regime; (doctrina) Franco's doctrine.

frasco m small bottle.

frase f 1. (oración) sentence. 2. (locución) expression; **~ hecha** (modismo) set phrase; (tópico) cliché.

fraternidad, fraternización f brotherhood, fraternity.

fraterno, -na adj brotherly, fraternal.

fraude m fraud; **~ fiscal** tax evasion.

fraudulento, -ta adj fraudulent.

fray m brother.

frazada f Amer blanket; **~ eléctrica** electric blanket.

frecuencia f frequency; **con ~** often; **~ modulada, modulación de ~** frequency modulation.

frecuentar vt (lugar) to frequent; (persona) to see, to visit.

frecuente adj (reiterado) frequent; (habitual) common.

fregadero m (kitchen) sink.

fregado, -da adj Amer fam troublesome, annoying.

fregar vt 1. (limpiar) to wash; **~ los platos** to do the washing-up. 2. (frotar) scrub. 3. Amer fam (molestar) to bother, to pester.

fregona f 1. despec (criada) skivvy. 2. (utensilio) mop.

freidora f (gen) deep fat fryer; (para patatas fritas) chip pan.

freír vt (CULIN) to fry.

frenar ♦ vt 1. (AUTOM) to brake. 2. (contener) to check. ♦ vi to stop; (AUTOM) to brake.

frenazo m 1. (AUTOM): **dar un ~** to brake hard. 2. fig (parón) sudden stop.

frenesí (pl frenesíes) m frenzy.

frenético, -ca adj 1. (colérico) furious, mad. 2. (enloquecido) frenzied, frantic.

freno m 1. (AUTOM) brake. 2. (de caballerías) bit. 3. fig (contención) check; **poner ~ a** to put a stop to.

frenopático, -ca adj psychiatric.

frente ♦ f forehead; **~ a ~** face to face. ♦ m front; **estar al ~ (de)** to be at the head (of); **hacer ~ a** to face up to; **~ frío** cold front. ▶ **de frente** loc adv 1. (hacia delante) forwards. 2. (uno contra otro) head on. ▶ **frente a** loc prep 1. (enfrente de) opposite. 2. (con relación a) towards.

fresa f (planta, fruto) strawberry.

fresco, -ca ♦ adj 1. (gen) fresh; (temperatura) cool; (pintura, tinta) wet. 2. (caradura) cheeky. ♦ m y f (caradura) cheeky person. ▶ **fresco** m 1. (ARTE) fresco; **al ~** in fresco. 2. (frescor) coolness; **hace ~** it's chilly; **tomar el ~** to get a breath of fresh air.

frescor m coolness, freshness.

frescura f 1. (gen) freshness. 2. (descaro) cheek, nerve.

fresno m ash (tree).

fresón m large strawberry.

frialdad f lit & fig coldness.

fricción f (gen) friction; (friega) rub, massage.

friega f massage.

frigidez f frigidity.

frigorífico, -ca adj (camión) refrigerator (antes de sust); (cámara) cold. ▶ **frigorífico** m refrigerator, fridge Br, icebox Am.

frijol, frijol m Amer bean.

frío, -a adj (gen) cold; (inmutable) cool; **dejar a alguien ~** to leave sb cold. ▶ **frío** m cold; **hacer un ~ que pela** to be freezing cold; **tener ~** to be cold; **coger a alguien en ~** fig to catch sb on the hop.

friolento, -ta adj Amer sensitive to the cold.

friolero, -ra *adj* sensitive to the cold.

frisar *vt* to be getting on for (*a certain age*).

frito, -ta ◆ *pp* → **freír**. ◆ *adj* 1. (*alimento*) fried. 2. *fam fig* (*persona - harta*) fed up (to the back teeth); (- *dormida*) flaked out, asleep. ▶ **frito** *m* (*gen pl*) fried food (U).

frívolo, -la *adj* frivolous.

frondoso, -sa *adj* leafy.

frontal *adj* frontal.

frontera *f* border, frontier; *fig* (*límite*) bounds (*pl*).

fronterizo, -za *adj* border (*antes de sust*).

frontispicio *m* 1. (*de edificio - remate*) pediment. 2. (*de libro*) frontispiece.

frontón *m* (*deporte*) pelota; (*cancha*) pelota court.

frotar *vt* to rub. ▶ **frotarse** *vpr*: ~se las manos to rub one's hands.

fructífero, -ra *adj* fruitful.

frugal *adj* frugal.

fruncir *vt* 1. (*labios*) to purse; ~ el ceño to frown. 2. (*tela*) to gather.

fruslería *f* triviality, trifle.

frustración *f* frustration.

frustrar *vt* (*persona*) to frustrate. ▶ **frustrarse** *vpr* 1. (*persona*) to get frustrated. 2. (*ilusiones*) to be thwarted; (*proyecto*) to fail.

fruta *f* fruit.

frutal *m* fruit tree.

frutería *f* fruit shop.

frutero, -ra *m y f* (*persona*) fruiterer. ▶ **frutero** *m* (*recipiente*) fruit bowl.

frutilla *f* *Amer* strawberry.

fruto *m* 1. (*naranja, plátano etc*) fruit; (*nuez, avellana etc*) nut; ~s secos dried fruit and nuts. 2. (*resultado*) fruit; dar ~ to bear fruit; sacar ~ a o de algo to profit from sthg.

fucsia *f* (*planta*) fuchsia.

fue 1. → **ir**. 2. → **ser**.

fuego *m* 1. (*gen & MIL*) fire; (*de cocina, fogón*) ring, burner; a ~ lento/vivo (CULIN) over a low/high heat; pegar ~ a algo to set sthg on fire, to set fire to sthg; pedir/dar ~ to ask for/give a light; ¿tiene ~? have you got a light?; ~s artificiales fireworks. 2. (*apasionamiento*) passion, ardour.

fuelle *m* (*gen*) bellows (*pl*).

fuente *f* 1. (*manantial*) spring. 2. (*construcción*) fountain. 3. (*bandeja*) (serving) dish. 4. *fig* (*origen*) source; ~s oficiales official sources.

fuera ◆ *v* 1. → **ir**. 2. → **ser**. ◆ *adv* 1. (*en el exterior*) outside; le echó ~ she threw him out; hacia ~ outwards; por ~ (on the) outside. 2. (*en otro lugar*) away; (*en el extranjero*) abroad; estar ~ de casa to be away from home; de ~ (*extranjero*) from abroad. 3. *fig* (*alejado*): ~ de (*alcance, peligro*) out of; (*cálculos, competencia*) outside; estar ~ de sí to be beside o.s. (with rage). 4. (DEP): ~ de juego offside. ◆ *interj*: ¡~! (*gen*) (get) out!; (*en el teatro*) (get) off! ▶ **fuera de** *loc prep* (*excepto*) except for, apart from. ▶ **fuera de serie** *adj* exceptional.

fueraborda *m inv* outboard motor o engine.

fuero *m* 1. (*ley local*) (*gen pl*) ancient regional law still existing in some parts of Spain. 2. (*jurisdicción*) code of laws.

fuerte ◆ *adj* 1. (*gen*) strong. 2. (*carácter*) unpleasant. 3. (*frío, dolor, color*) intense; (*lluvia*) heavy; (*ruido*) loud; (*golpe, pelea*) hard. 4. (*comida, salsa*) rich. 5. (*nudo*) tight. ◆ *adv* 1. (*intensamente - gen*) hard; (- *abrazar, agarrar*) tight. 2. (*abundantemente*) a lot. 3. (*en voz alta*) loudly. ◆ *m* 1. (*fortificación*) fort. 2. (*punto fuerte*) strong point, forte.

fuerza *f* 1. (*gen*) strength; (*violencia*) force; (*de sonido*) loudness; (*de dolor*) intensity; por ~ of necessity; tener ~s para to have the strength to; ~ mayor (DER) force majeure; (*en seguros*) act of God; no llegué por un caso de ~ mayor I didn't make it due to circumstances beyond my control; ~ de voluntad willpower; a ~ de by dint of; a la ~ (*contra la voluntad*) by force; (*por necesidad*) of necessity; por la ~ by force. 2. (FÍS & MIL) force; ~s armadas armed forces; ~s del orden público police (*pl*). 3. (ELECTR) power. ▶ **fuerzas** *fpl* (*grupo*) forces.

fuese 1. → **ir**. 2. → **ser**.

fuga *f* 1. (*huida*) escape. 2. (*escape*) leak. 3. (MÚS) fugue.

fugarse *vpr* to escape; ~ de casa to run away from home; ~ con alguien to run off with sb.

fugaz *adj* fleeting.

fugitivo, -va *m y f* fugitive.

fui → **ir**.

fulano, -na *m y f* what's his/her name, so-and-so. ▶ **fulana** *f* (*prostituta*) tart, whore.

fulgor *m* shining; (*de disparo*) flash.

fulminante *adj* *fig* (*despido, muerte*) sudden; (*enfermedad*) devastating; (*mirada*) withering.

fulminar vt (suj: enfermedad) to strike down; ~ a alguien con la mirada to look daggers at sb.

fumador, -ra m y f smoker; ~ pasivo passive smoker; no ~ nonsmoker.

fumar vt & vi to smoke.

fumigar vt to fumigate.

función f 1. (gen) function; (trabajo) duty; director en funciones acting director; entrar en funciones to take up one's duties. 2. (CIN & TEATR) show. ▶ en función de loc prep depending on.

funcional adj functional.

funcionamiento m operation, functioning; poner algo en ~ to start sthg (working).

funcionar vi to work; ~ con gasolina to run on petrol; 'no funciona' 'out of order'.

funcionario, -ria m y f civil servant.

funda f (de sofá, máquina de escribir) cover; (de almohada) case; (de disco) sleeve; (de pistola) sheath.

fundación f foundation.

fundador, -ra m y f founder.

fundamental adj fundamental.

fundamentar vt 1. fig (basar) to base. 2. (CONSTR) to lay the foundations of. ▶ **fundamentarse en** vpr fig (basarse) to be based o founded on.

fundamento m 1. (base) foundation, basis. 2. (razón) reason, grounds (pl); sin ~ unfounded, groundless.

fundar vt 1. (crear) to found. 2. (basar): ~ (en) to base (on). ▶ **fundarse** vpr (basarse): ~se (en) to be based (on).

fundición f 1. (fusión - de vidrio) melting; (- de metal) smelting. 2. (taller) foundry.

fundir vt 1. (METAL - plomo) to melt; (- hierro) to smelt. 2. (ELECTR) to fuse; (bombilla, fusible) to blow. 3. (COM & fig) to merge. ▶ **fundirse** vpr 1. (ELECTR) to blow. 2. (derretirse) to melt. 3. (COM & fig) to merge.

fúnebre adj funeral (antes de sust).

funeral m (gen pl) funeral.

funerario, -ria adj funeral (antes de sust). ▶ **funeraria** f undertaker's Br, mortician's Am.

funesto, -ta adj fateful, disastrous.

fungir vi Amer to act, to serve.

funicular m 1. (por tierra) funicular. 2. (por aire) cable car.

furgón m (AUTOM) van; (FERROC) wagon.

furgoneta f van.

furia f fury.

furioso, -sa adj furious.

furor m 1. (enfado) fury, rage. 2. loc: hacer ~ to be all the rage.

furtivo, -va adj (mirada, sonrisa) furtive.

furúnculo = forúnculo.

fusible m fuse.

fusil m rifle.

fusilar vt (ejecutar) to execute by firing squad, to shoot.

fusión f 1. (agrupación) merging. 2. (de empresas, bancos) merger. 3. (derretimiento) melting. 4. (FÍS) fusion.

fusionar vt 1. (gen & ECON) to merge. 2. (FÍS) to fuse. ▶ **fusionarse** vpr (ECON) to merge.

fusta f riding crop.

fustán m Amer petticoat.

fuste m shaft.

fútbol, football ['fudbol] m football; ~ sala indoor five-a-side.

futbolín m table football.

futbolista m y f footballer.

fútil adj trivial.

futilidad f triviality.

futón m futon.

futuro, -ra adj future. ▶ **futuro** m (gen & GRAM) future. ▶ **futuros** mpl (ECON) futures.

futurología f futurology.

g¹, G f (letra) g, G.

g² (abrev de gramo) g.

gabacho, -cha fam despec m y f Frog, pejorative term referring to a French person.

gabán m overcoat.

gabardina f (prenda) raincoat, mac.

gabinete m 1. (gobierno) cabinet. 2. (despacho) office. 3. (sala) study.

gacela f gazelle.

gaceta f gazette.

gachas fpl (CULIN) (corn) porridge (U).

gacho, -cha adj drooping.

gafas fpl glasses; ~ graduales prescription glasses; ~ de sol sunglasses.

gafe ◆ adj jinxed. ◆ m y f jinxed person.

gaita f (instrumento) bagpipes (pl).

gajes mpl: ~ del oficio occupational hazards.

gajo m (*trozo de fruta*) segment.

gala f 1. (*fiesta*) gala; **ropa/uniforme de gala** (*ropa*) full dress/uniform; **cena de gala** black tie dinner, formal dinner. 2. (*ropa*): **galas** finery (U), best clothes. 3. (*actuación*) show. 4. *loc:* **hacer gala de algo** (*preciarse*) to be proud of sthg; (*exhibir*) to demonstrate sthg.

galán m (TEATR) leading man, lead.

galante adj gallant.

galantear vt to court, to woo.

galantería f 1. (*cualidad*) politeness. 2. (*acción*) gallantry, compliment.

galápago m turtle.

galardón m award, prize.

galaxia f galaxy.

galera f galley.

galería f 1. (*gen*) gallery; (*pasillo*) passage; (*corredor descubierto*) balcony. 2. *fig* (*vulgo*) masses (*pl*). ▶ **galerías (comerciales)** fpl shopping arcade (*sg*).

Gales: (**el país de**) ~ Wales.

galés, -esa ♦ adj Welsh. ♦ m y f Welshman m (f Welshwoman); **los galeses** the Welsh. ▶ **galés** m (*lengua*) Welsh.

galgo m greyhound.

galimatías m inv (*lenguaje*) gibberish (U); (*lío*) jumble.

gallardía f 1. (*valentía*) bravery. 2. (*elegancia*) elegance.

gallego, -ga adj, m y f Galician. ▶ **gallego** m (*lengua*) Galician.

galleta f (CULIN) biscuit.

gallina ♦ f (*ave*) hen; **la ~ ciega** blind man's buff. ♦ m y f fam (*persona*) chicken, coward.

gallinero m 1. (*corral*) henhouse. 2. fam (TEATR) gods (*sg*).

gallo m 1. (*ave*) cock, cockerel; **en menos que canta un ~** fam in no time at all. 2. (*al cantar*) false note; (*al hablar*) squeak. 3. (*pez*) John Dory.

galo, -la ♦ adj (HIST) Gallic; (*francés*) French. ♦ m y f (*persona*) Gaul.

galón m 1. (*adorno*) braid; (MIL) stripe. 2. (*medida*) gallon.

galopar vi to gallop.

galope m gallop; **al ~** at a gallop; **a ~ tendido** at full gallop.

galpón m Amer shed.

gama f (*gen*) range; (MÚS) scale.

gamba f prawn.

gamberro, -rra ♦ adj loutish. ♦ m y f vandal; (*en fútbol etc*) hooligan.

gamo m fallow deer.

gamonal m Amer village chief.

gamuza f 1. (*tejido*) chamois (leather); (*trapo*) duster; esp Amer (*ante*) suede. 2. (*animal*) chamois.

gana f 1. (*afán*): ~ (**de**) desire o wish (to); **de buena ~** willingly; **de mala ~** unwillingly; **me da/no me da la ~ hacerlo** I damn well feel like/don't damn well feel like doing it. 2. (*apetito*) appetite. ▶ **ganas** fpl (*deseo*): **tener ~s de algo/hacer algo, sentir ~s de algo/hacer algo** to feel like sthg/doing sthg; **quedarse con ~s de hacer algo** not to manage to do sthg; **no tengo ~s de que me pongan una multa** I don't fancy getting a fine; **tenerle ~s a alguien** to have it in for sb.

ganadería f 1. (*actividad*) livestock farming, stockbreeding. 2. (*ganado*) livestock.

ganadero, -ra m y f livestock farmer, stockbreeder.

ganado m livestock, stock; **~ porcino** pigs (*pl*); **~ vacuno** cattle (*pl*).

ganador, -ra ♦ adj winning. ♦ m y f winner.

ganancia f (*rendimiento*) profit; (*ingreso*) earnings (*pl*); **~s y pérdidas** profit and loss; **~ líquida** net profit.

ganancial → **bien**.

ganar ♦ vt 1. (*gen*) to win; (*sueldo, dinero*) to earn; (*peso, tiempo, terreno*) to gain. 2. (*derrotar*) to beat. 3. (*aventajar*): **~ a alguien en algo** to be better than sb as regards sthg. 4. (*cima etc*) to reach. 5. (*ciudad etc*) to take, to capture. ♦ vi 1. (*vencer*) to win. 2. (*lograr dinero*) to earn money. 3. (*mejorar*): **~ en algo** to gain in sthg. ▶ **ganarse** vpr 1. (*conquistar - simpatía, respeto*) to earn; (*- persona*) to win over. 2. (*merecer*) to deserve.

ganchillo m (*aguja*) crochet hook; (*labor*) crochet; **hacer ~** to crochet.

gancho m 1. (*gen*) hook; (*de percha*) peg. 2. (*cómplice - de timador*) decoy; (*- de vendedor*) person who attracts buyers. 3. fam (*atractivo*) sex appeal.

gandul, -la fam ♦ adj lazy. ♦ m y f lazybones, layabout.

ganga f fam snip, bargain.

gangrena f gangrene.

gángster (*pl* **gángsters**) m gangster.

ganso, -sa m y f 1. (*ave - hembra*) goose; (*- macho*) gander. 2. fam (*persona*) idiot, fool.

garabatear vi & vt to scribble.

garabato m scribble.

garaje m garage.

garante m y f guarantor; **salir ~** to act as guarantor.

garantía f 1. (gen) guarantee; **de ~** reliable, dependable; **ser ~ de algo** to guarantee sthg; **~s constitucionales** constitutional rights. 2. (fianza) surety.

garantizar vt 1. (gen) to guarantee; **~ algo a alguien** to assure sb of sthg. 2. (avalar) to vouch for.

garbanzo m chickpea.

garbeo m fam stroll; **dar un ~** to go for o take a stroll.

garbo m (de persona) grace; (de escritura) stylishness, style.

garete m: **ir o irse al ~** fam to come adrift.

garfio m hook.

gargajo m phlegm.

garganta f 1. (ANAT) throat. 2. (desfiladero) gorge.

gargantilla f choker, necklace.

gárgara f (gen pl) gargle, gargling (U); **hacer ~s** to gargle; **mandar a alguien a hacer ~s** fam to send sb packing; **¡vete a hacer ~s!** fam get lost!

gárgola f gargoyle.

garita f (gen) cabin; (de conserje) porter's lodge; (MIL) sentry box.

garito m despec (casa de juego) gambling den; (establecimiento) dive.

garra f (de animal) claw; (de ave de rapiña) talon; despec (de persona) paw, hand; **caer en las ~s de alguien** to fall into sb's clutches; **tener ~** (persona) to have charisma; (novela, canción etc) to be gripping.

garrafa f carafe.

garrafal adj monumental, enormous.

garrapata f tick.

garrapiñar vt (fruta) to candy; (almendras etc) to coat with sugar.

garrote m 1. (palo) club, stick. 2. (instrumento) garrotte.

garúa f Amer drizzle.

garza f heron; **~ real** grey heron.

gas m gas; **~ ciudad/natural** town/natural gas; **~ butano** butane (gas); **~ lacrimógeno** tear gas. ▶ **gases** mpl (en el estómago) wind (U). ▶ **a todo gas** loc adv flat out.

gasa f gauze.

gaseoducto m gas pipeline.

gaseoso, -sa adj gaseous; (bebida) fizzy. ▶ **gaseosa** f lemonade.

gasóleo m diesel oil.

gasolina f petrol Br, gas Am; **poner ~** to fill up (with petrol).

gasolinera f petrol station Br, gas station Am.

gastado, -da adj (prenda, pieza etc) worn; (frase, tema) hackneyed; (persona) broken, burnt out.

gastar ◆ vt 1. (consumir - dinero, tiempo) to spend; (- gasolina, electricidad) to use (up); (- ropa, zapatos) to wear out. 2. fig (usar - gen) to use; (- ropa) to wear; (- número de zapatos) to take; **~ una broma (a alguien)** to play a joke (on sb). 3. (malgastar) to waste. ◆ vi (despilfarrar) to spend (money). ▶ **gastarse** vpr 1. (deteriorarse) to wear out. 2. (terminarse) to run out.

gasto m (acción de gastar) outlay, expenditure; (cosa que pagar) expense; (de energía, gasolina) consumption; (despilfarro) waste; **cubrir ~s** to cover costs, to break even; **~ público** public expenditure; **~s fijos** (COM) fixed charges o costs; (en una casa) overheads; **~s generales** overheads; **~s de mantenimiento** maintenance costs; **~s de representación** entertainment allowance (sg).

gastritis f inv gastritis.

gastronomía f gastronomy.

gastrónomo, -ma m y f gourmet.

gatas ▶ **a gatas** loc adv on all fours.

gatear vi to crawl.

gatillo m trigger.

gato, -ta m y f cat; **dar ~ por liebre a alguien** to swindle o cheat sb; **buscar tres pies al ~** to overcomplicate matters; **aquí hay ~ encerrado** there's something fishy going on here. ▶ **gato** m (AUTOM) jack.

gauchada f Amer favour.

gaucho m gaucho.

gavilán m sparrowhawk.

gavilla f sheaf.

gaviota f seagull.

gay adj inv, m y f gay (homosexual).

gazmoño, -ña adj sanctimonious.

gazpacho m gazpacho, Andalusian soup made from tomatoes, peppers, cucumbers and bread, served chilled.

géiser, géyser (pl **géyseres**) m geyser.

gel m gel.

gelatina f (de carne) gelatine; (de fruta) jelly.

gema f gem.

gemelo, -la ◆ adj twin (antes de sust). ◆ m y f (persona) twin. ▶ **gemelo** m (músculo) calf. ▶ **gemelos** mpl 1. (de camisa) cufflinks. 2. (prismáticos) binoculars; (para teatro) opera glasses.

gemido m (de persona) moan, groan; (de animal) whine.

Géminis ♦ *m* (*zodiaco*) Gemini. ♦ *m y f* (*persona*) Gemini.

gemir *vi* 1. (*persona*) to moan, to groan; (*animal*) to whine. 2. (*viento*) to howl.

gene, gen *m* gene.

genealogía *f* genealogy.

generación *f* generation.

generador, -ra *adj* generating. ▶ **generador** *m* generator.

general ♦ *adj* 1. (*gen*) general; **por lo ~, en ~** in general, generally. 2. (*usual*) usual. ♦ *m* (MIL) general; **~ de brigada** brigadier Br, brigadier general Am; **~ de división** major general.

generalidad *f* 1. (*mayoría*) majority. 2. (*vaguedad*) generalization.

generalísimo *m* supreme commander, generalissimo.

Generalitat [ʒenerali'tat] *f* Generalitat, *autonomous government of Catalonia or Valencia.*

generalizar ♦ *vt* to spread, to make widespread. ♦ *vi* to generalize. ▶ **generalizarse** *vpr* to become widespread.

generalmente *adv* generally.

generar *vt* (*gen*) to generate; (*engendrar*) to create.

genérico, -ca *adj* (*común*) generic.

género *m* 1. (*clase*) kind, type. 2. (GRAM) gender. 3. (LITER) genre. 4. (BIOL) genus; **el ~ humano** the human race. 5. (*productos*) merchandise, goods (*pl*). 6. (*tejido*) cloth, material.

generosidad *f* generosity.

generoso, -sa *adj* generous.

genético, -ca *adj* genetic. ▶ **genética** *f* genetics (U).

genial *adj* 1. (*autor, compositor etc*) of genius. 2. *fig* (*estupendo*) brilliant, great.

genio *m* 1. (*talento*) genius. 2. (*carácter*) nature, disposition. 3. (*mal carácter*) bad temper; **estar de/tener mal ~** to be in a mood/bad-tempered. 4. (*ser sobrenatural*) genie.

genital *adj* genital. ▶ **genitales** *mpl* genitals.

genocidio *m* genocide.

gente *f* 1. (*gen*) people (*pl*); **~ bien** well-to-do people; **~ menuda** kids (*pl*). 2. *fam* (*familia*) folks (*pl*).

gentileza *f* courtesy, kindness.

gentío *m* crowd.

gentuza *f* riffraff.

genuflexión *f* genuflection.

genuino, -na *adj* genuine.

GEO (*abrev de* **Grupo Especial de Operaciones**) *m specially trained police force,*

≃ SAS Br, ≃ SWAT Am.

geografía *f* geography; *fig:* **varios puntos de la ~ nacional** several parts of the country.

geógrafo, -fa *m y f* geographer.

geología *f* geology.

geólogo, -ga *m y f* geologist.

geometría *f* geometry.

geranio *m* geranium.

gerencia *f* (*gen*) management.

gerente *m y f* manager, director.

geriatría *f* geriatrics (U).

germen *m lit & fig* germ.

germinar *vi lit & fig* to germinate.

gerundio *m* gerund.

gestar *vi* to gestate. ▶ **gestarse** *vpr:* **se estaba gestando un cambio sin precedentes** the seeds of an unprecedented change had been sown.

gesticulación *f* gesticulation; (*de cara*) face-pulling.

gesticular *vi* to gesticulate; (*con la cara*) to pull faces.

gestión *f* 1. (*diligencia*) step, thing that has to be done; **tengo que hacer unas gestiones** I have a few things to do. 2. (*administración*) management.

gestionar *vt* 1. (*tramitar*) to negotiate. 2. (*administrar*) to manage.

gesto *m* 1. (*gen*) gesture. 2. (*mueca*) face, grimace; **hacer un ~** to pull a face.

gestor, -ra ♦ *adj* managing (*antes de sust*). ♦ *m y f person who carries out dealings with public bodies on behalf of private customers or companies, combining the role of solicitor and accountant.*

géyser = **géiser**.

ghetto = **gueto**.

giba *f* (*de camello*) hump.

Gibraltar Gibraltar.

gibraltareño, -ña *adj, m y f* Gibraltarian.

gigabyte [xiɣa'βait] *m* (INFORM) gigabyte.

gigante, -ta *m y f* giant. ▶ **gigante** *adj* gigantic.

gigantesco, -ca *adj* gigantic, huge.

gil, -la *m y f* Amer fam twit, idiot.

gilipollada, jilipollada *f fam:* **hacer/decir una ~** to do/say sthg bloody stupid.

gilipollas, jilipollas *fam* ♦ *adj inv* daft, dumb Am. ♦ *m y f inv* prat.

gimnasia *f* (*deporte*) gymnastics (U); (*ejercicio*) gymnastics (*pl*).

gimnasio *m* gymnasium.

gimnasta *m y f* gymnast.

gimotear *vi* to whine, to whimper.

gin [jin] ▶ **gin tonic** m gin and tonic.
ginebra f gin.
Ginebra Geneva.
ginecología f gynaecology.
ginecólogo, -ga m y f gynaecologist.
gira f tour.
girar ♦ vi 1. (dar vueltas, torcer) to turn; (rápidamente) to spin. 2. fig (centrarse): ~ en torno a o alrededor de to revolve o be centred around. ♦ vt 1. (hacer dar vueltas) to turn; (rápidamente) to spin. 2. (COM) to draw. 3. (dinero - por correo, telégrafo) to transfer, to remit.
girasol m sunflower.
giratorio, -ria adj revolving; (silla) swivel (antes de sust).
giro m 1. (gen) turn. 2. (postal, telegráfico) money order; ~ postal postal order. 3. (de letras, órdenes de pago) draft. 4. (expresión) turn of phrase.
gis m Amer chalk.
gitano, -na m y f gypsy.
glacial adj glacial; (viento, acogida) icy.
glaciar ♦ adj glacial. ♦ m glacier.
gladiolo, gladíolo m gladiolus.
glándula f gland.
glicerina f glycerine.
global adj global, overall.
globo m 1. (Tierra) globe, earth. 2. (aeróstato, juguete) balloon. 3. (esfera) sphere.
glóbulo m (MED) corpuscle; ~ blanco/ rojo white/red corpuscle.
gloria f 1. (gen) glory. 2. (placer) delight.
glorieta f 1. (de casa, jardín) arbour. 2. (plaza - redonda) circus, roundabout Br, traffic circle Am.
glorificar vt to glorify.
glorioso, -sa adj (importante) glorious.
glosa f marginal note.
glosar vt 1. (anotar) to annotate. 2. (comentar) to comment on.
glosario m glossary.
glotón, -ona ♦ adj gluttonous, greedy. ♦ m y f glutton.
glúcido m carbohydrate.
glucosa f glucose.
gluten m gluten.
gnomo, nomo m gnome.
gobernador, -ra m y f governor.
gobernanta f cleaning and laundry staff manageress.
gobernante ♦ adj ruling (antes de sust). ♦ m y f ruler, leader.
gobernar vt 1. (gen) to govern, to rule; (casa, negocio) to run, to manage. 2. (barco) to steer; (avión) to fly.

gobierno m 1. (gen) government. 2. (administración, gestión) running, management. 3. (control) control.
goce m pleasure.
godo, -da ♦ adj Gothic. ♦ m y f (HIST) Goth.
gol (pl goles) m goal.
goleador, -ra m y f goalscorer.
golear vt to score a lot of goals against, to thrash.
golf m golf.
golfear vi fam (vaguear) to loaf around.
golfista m y f golfer.
golfo, -fa m y f (gamberro) lout; (vago) layabout. ▶ **golfo** m (GEOGR) gulf, bay. ▶ **Golfo Pérsico** m: el Golfo Pérsico the Persian Gulf.
golondrina f (ave) swallow.
golosina f (dulce) sweet; (exquisitez) titbit, delicacy.
goloso, -sa adj sweet-toothed.
golpe m 1. (gen) blow; (bofetada) smack; (con puño) punch; (en puerta etc) knock; (en tenis, golf) shot; (entre coches) bump, collision; a ~s by force; fig in fits and starts; un ~ bajo (DEP & fig) a blow below the belt; ~ de castigo (en rugby) penalty (kick); ~ franco free kick. 2. (disgusto) blow. 3. (atraco) raid, job, heist Am. 4. (POLÍT): ~ (de Estado) coup (d'état). 5. loc: no dar o pegar ~ not to lift a finger, not to do a stroke of work. ▶ **de golpe** loc adv suddenly. ▶ **de un golpe** loc adv at one fell swoop, all at once. ▶ **golpe de gracia** m coup de grâce. ▶ **golpe de suerte** m stroke of luck. ▶ **golpe de vista** m glance; al primer ~ de vista at a glance.
golpear vt & vi (gen) to hit, to strike; (puerta) to bang; (con puño) to punch.
golpista m y f person involved in military coup.
golpiza f Amer beating.
goma f 1. (sustancia viscosa, pegajosa) gum; ~ arábiga gum arabic; ~ de mascar chewing gum; ~ de pegar glue, gum. 2. (tira elástica) rubber band, elastic band Br; ~ elástica elastic. 3. (caucho) rubber; ~ espuma foam rubber; ~ de borrar rubber Br, eraser Am. ▶ **Goma 2** f plastic explosive.
gomina f hair gel.
gong m inv gong.
gordinflón, -ona m y f fatty.
gordo, -da ♦ adj 1. (persona) fat; me cae ~ I can't stand him. 2. (grueso) thick. 3. (grande) big. 4. (grave) big, serious. ♦ m y f 1. (persona obesa) fat man (f fat

woman); **armar la gorda** *fig* to kick up a row o stink. **2.** *Amer* (*querido*) sweetheart, darling. ► **gordo** *m* (*en lotería*) first prize, jackpot; **el ~** *first prize in the Spanish national lottery.*

EL GORDO

This is the name given to first prize in the Spanish National Lottery, especially the one in the Christmas draw, where all the winning numbers are sung out by children on national radio.

gordura *f* fatness.
gorgorito *m* warble.
gorila *m* **1.** (ZOOL) gorilla. **2.** *fig* (*guardaespaldas*) bodyguard. **3.** *fig* (*en discoteca etc*) bouncer.
gorjear *vi* to chirp, to twitter.
gorra *f* (peaked) cap; **de ~** for free; **vivir de ~** to scrounge.
gorrear = **gorronear**.
gorrinada *f* (*guarrada - acción*) disgusting behaviour (U); (*- lugar*) pigsty.
gorrión *m* sparrow.
gorro *m* (*gen*) cap; (*de niño*) bonnet.
gorrón, -ona *fam m y f* sponger.
gorronear, gorrear *vt & vi fam* to sponge, to scrounge.
gota *f* **1.** (*gen*) drop; (*de sudor*) bead; **caer cuatro ~s** to spit (with rain); **ni ~** anything; **no se veía ni ~** you couldn't see a thing; **sudar la ~ gorda** to sweat blood, to work very hard. **2.** *fig* (*de aire*) breath; (*de sensatez etc*) ounce. **3.** (MED) gout. ► **gota a gota** *m* (MED) intravenous drip. ► **gota fría** *f* (METEOR) *cold front that remains in one place for some time, causing continuous heavy rain.*
gotear ♦ *vi* (*líquido*) to drip; (*techo, depósito etc*) to leak; *fig* to trickle through. ♦ *v impers* (*chispear*) to spit, to drizzle.
gotera *f* (*filtración*) leak.
gótico, -ca *adj* Gothic.
gourmet = **gurmet**.
gozada *f fam* absolute delight.
gozar *vi* to enjoy o.s.; **~ de algo** to enjoy sthg; **~ con** to take delight in.
gozne *m* hinge.
gozo *m* joy, pleasure.
gr *abrev de* **grado**.
grabación *f* recording.
grabado *m* **1.** (*gen*) engraving; (*en madera*) carving. **2.** (*en papel - acción*) printing; (*- lámina*) print.
grabar *vt* **1.** (*gen*) to engrave; (*en madera*) to carve; (*en papel*) to print. **2.** (*sonido, cinta*) to record. ► **grabarse**

en *vpr fig*: **grabársele a alguien en la memoria** to become engraved on sb's mind.
gracia *f* **1.** (*humor, comicidad*) humour; **hacer ~ a alguien** to amuse sb; **no me hizo ~** I didn't find it funny; **tener ~** (*ser divertido*) to be funny; **tiene ~** (*es curioso*) it's funny; **caer en ~** to be liked. **2.** (*arte, habilidad*) skill, natural ability. **3.** (*encanto*) grace, elegance. **4.** (*chiste*) joke. ► **gracias** *fpl* thank you, thanks; **~s a** thanks to; **dar las ~s a alguien (por)** to thank sb (for); **muchas ~s** thank you, thanks very much.
gracioso, -sa ♦ *adj* **1.** (*divertido*) funny, amusing. **2.** (*curioso*) funny; **es ~ que ...** it's funny how ... ♦ *m y f* (TEATR) fool, clown.
grada *f* **1.** (*peldaño*) step. **2.** (TEATR) row. ► **gradas** *fpl* (DEP) terraces.
gradación *f* (*escalonamiento*) scale.
gradería *f*, **graderío** *m* (TEATR) rows (*pl*); (DEP) terraces (*pl*).
grado *m* **1.** (*gen*) degree. **2.** (*fase*) stage, level; (*índice, nivel*) extent, level; **en ~ sumo** greatly. **3.** (*rango - gen*) grade; (MIL) rank. **4.** (EDUC) year, class, grade *Am*. **5.** (*voluntad*): **hacer algo de buen/mal ~** to do sthg willingly/unwillingly.
graduación *f* **1.** (*acción*) grading; (*de la vista*) eye-test. **2.** (EDUC) graduation. **3.** (*de bebidas*) strength, = proof. **4.** (MIL) rank.
graduado, -da *m y f* (*persona*) graduate. ► **graduado** *m* (*título - gen*) certificate; **~ escolar** *qualification received on completing primary school.*

GRADUADO ESCOLAR

This is the qualification received on successful completion of primary education in Spain. It is needed in order to go to secondary school and is also one of the requirements for people over the age of 25 who wish to go to university.

gradual *adj* gradual.
graduar *vt* **1.** (*medir*) to gauge, to measure; (*regular*) to regulate; (*vista*) to test. **2.** (*escalonar*) to stagger; (*publicación*) to serialize. **3.** (EDUC) to confer a degree on. **4.** (MIL) to commission. ► **graduarse** *vpr*: **~se (en)** to graduate (in).
grafía *f* written symbol.
gráfico, -ca *adj* graphic. ► **gráfico** *m* (*gráfica*) graph, chart; (*dibujo*) diagram. ► **gráfica** *f* graph, chart.

gragea f (MED) pill, tablet.

grajo m rook.

gral. (abrev de **general**) gen.

gramática → **gramático**.

gramatical adj grammatical.

gramático, -ca adj grammatical.
▶ **gramática** f (disciplina, libro) grammar.

gramo m gram.

gramófono m gramophone.

gramola f gramophone.

gran = **grande**.

granada f 1. (fruta) pomegranate.
2. (proyectil) grenade.

granate ◆ m garnet. ◆ adj inv deep red.

Gran Bretaña f Great Britain.

grande ◆ adj (antes de sust: **gran**) 1. (de tamaño) big, large; (de altura) tall; (de intensidad, importancia) great; **este traje me está ~** this suit is too big for me. 2. fig & irón (enojoso) just great, a bit rich. 3. loc: **pasarlo en ~** fam to have a great time. ◆ m (noble) grandee. ▶ **grandes** mpl (adultos) grown-ups. ▶ **a lo grande** loc adv in style.

grandeza f 1. (de tamaño) (great) size. 2. (de sentimientos) generosity. 3. (importancia) greatness.

grandioso, -sa adj grand, splendid.

grandullón, -ona m y f big boy (f big girl).

granel ▶ **a granel** loc adv (sin envase - gen) loose; (- en gran cantidad) in bulk.

granero m granary.

granito m granite.

granizada f (METEOR) hailstorm.

granizado m iced drink.

granizar v impers to hail.

granizo m hail.

granja f farm.

granjearse vpr to gain, to earn.

granjero, -ra m y f farmer.

grano m 1. (semilla - de cereales) grain; **~ de café** coffee bean; **~ de pimienta** peppercorn. 2. (partícula) grain. 3. (en la piel) spot, pimple. 4. loc: **ir al ~** to get to the point.

granuja m y f (pillo) rogue, scoundrel; (canalla) trickster, swindler.

granulado, -da adj granulated.

grapa f (para papeles etc) staple; (para heridas) stitch, (wire) suture.

grapadora f stapler.

grapar vt to staple.

GRAPO (abrev de **Grupos de Resistencia Antifascista Primero de Octubre**) mpl former left-wing Spanish terrorist group.

grasa → **graso**.

grasiento, -ta adj greasy.

graso, -sa adj (gen) greasy; (con alto contenido en grasas) fatty. ▶ **grasa** f 1. (en comestibles) fat; (de cerdo) lard. 2. (lubricante) grease, oil. 3. (suciedad) grease.

gratén m gratin; **al ~** au gratin.

gratificación f 1. (moral) reward. 2. (monetaria) bonus.

gratificante adj rewarding.

gratificar vt (complacer) to reward; (retribuir) to give a bonus to; (dar propina) to tip.

gratinado, -da adj au gratin.

gratis adv (sin dinero) free, for nothing; (sin esfuerzo) for nothing.

gratitud f gratitude.

grato, -ta adj pleasant; **nos es ~ comunicarle que ...** we are pleased to inform you that ...

gratuito, -ta adj 1. (sin dinero) free. 2. (arbitrario) gratuitous; (infundado) unfair, uncalled for.

grava f gravel.

gravamen m 1. (impuesto) tax. 2. (obligación moral) burden.

gravar vt (con impuestos) to tax.

grave adj 1. (gen) serious; (estilo) formal; **estar ~** to be seriously ill. 2. (sonido, voz) low, deep.

gravedad f 1. (cualidad de grave) seriousness. 2. (FÍS) gravity.

gravilla f gravel.

gravitar vi to gravitate; fig (pender): **~ sobre** to hang o loom over.

graznar vi (cuervo) to caw; (ganso) to honk; (pato) to quack; fig (persona) to squawk.

graznido m (de cuervo) caw, cawing (U); (de ganso) honk, honking (U); (de pato) quack, quacking (U); fig (de personas) squawk, squawking (U).

Grecia Greece.

gremio m (sindicato) (trade) union; (profesión) profession, trade; (HIST) guild.

greña f (gen pl) tangle of hair.

gres m stoneware.

gresca f row.

griego, -ga adj, m y f Greek. ▶ **griego** m (lengua) Greek.

grieta f crack; (entre montañas) crevice; (que deja pasar luz) chink.

grifería f taps (pl), plumbing.

grifo m (llave) tap Br, faucet Am.

grillado, -da adj fam crazy, loopy.

grillete m shackle.

grillo m cricket.

grima f (dentera): **dar ~** to set one's teeth on edge.

gringo, -ga adj, m y f gringo.

gripa f Amer flu.

gripe f flu.

gris ◆ adj grey; fig (triste) gloomy, miserable. ◆ m grey.

gritar ◆ vi (hablar alto) to shout; (chillar) to scream, to yell. ◆ vt: **~ (algo) a alguien** to shout (sthg) at sb.

griterío m screaming, shouting.

grito m (gen) shout; (de dolor, miedo) cry, scream; (de sorpresa, de animal) cry; **dar o pegar un ~** to shout o scream (out); **a ~ limpio o pelado** at the top of one's voice; **pedir algo a ~s** fig to be crying out for sthg; **poner el ~ en el cielo** to hit the roof; **ser el último ~** to be the latest fashion o craze, to be the in thing.

Groenlandia Greenland.

grogui adj lit & fig groggy.

grosella f redcurrant; **~ negra** blackcurrant; **~ silvestre** gooseberry.

grosería f (cualidad) rudeness; (acción) rude thing; (palabrota) swear word.

grosero, -ra adj 1. (maleducado) rude, crude. 2. (tosco) coarse, rough.

grosor m thickness.

grosso ► **a grosso modo** loc adv roughly.

grotesco, -ca adj grotesque.

grúa f 1. (CONSTR) crane. 2. (AUTOM) breakdown truck.

grueso, -sa adj 1. (espeso) thick. 2. (corpulento) thickset; (obeso) fat. 3. (grande) large, big. 4. (mar) stormy. ► **grueso** m (grosor) thickness.

grulla f crane.

grumete m cabin boy.

grumo m (gen) lump; (de sangre) clot.

gruñido m 1. (gen) growl; (del cerdo) grunt. 2. fig (de personas) grumble.

gruñir vi 1. (gen) to growl; (cerdo) to grunt. 2. fig (personas) to grumble.

gruñón, -ona fam adj grumpy.

grupa f hindquarters.

grupo m (gen) group; (de árboles) cluster; (TECN) unit, set; **en ~** in a group; **~ electrógeno** generator. ► **grupo sanguíneo** m blood group.

gruta f grotto.

guacal m Amer 1. (calabaza) pumpkin. 2. (jaula) cage.

guachada f Amer fam mean trick.

guachimán m Amer night watchman.

guacho, -cha m y f Amer fam illegitimate child.

Guadalquivir m: **el ~** the Guadalquivir.

guadaña f scythe.

guagua f Amer 1. (autobús) bus. 2. (niño) baby.

guajolote m Amer turkey.

guampa f Amer horn.

guanajo m Amer turkey.

guantazo m fam slap.

guante m glove; **echarle el ~ a algo** to get hold of sthg, to get one's hands on sthg.

guantera f glove compartment.

guapo, -pa adj (gen) good-looking; (hombre) handsome; (mujer) pretty.

guarango, -ga adj Amer coarse, vulgar.

guarda ◆ m y f (vigilante) guard, keeper; **~ jurado** security guard. ◆ f 1. (tutela) guardianship. 2. (de libros) flyleaf.

guardabarros m inv mudguard Br, fender Am.

guardabosque m y f forest ranger.

guardacoches m y f inv parking attendant.

guardacostas m inv (barco) coastguard boat.

guardaespaldas m y f inv bodyguard.

guardameta m y f goalkeeper.

guardapolvo m overalls (pl).

guardar vt 1. (gen) to keep; (en su sitio) to put away. 2. (vigilar) to keep watch over; (proteger) to guard. 3. (reservar, ahorrar): **~ algo (a o para alguien)** to save sthg (for sb). 4. (cumplir - ley) to observe; (- secreto, promesa) to keep. ► **guardarse de** vpr: **~se de hacer algo** (evitar) to avoid doing sthg; (abstenerse de) to be careful not to do sthg.

guardarropa m (gen) wardrobe; (de cine, discoteca etc) cloakroom.

guardarropía f (TEATR) wardrobe.

guardería f nursery; (en el lugar de trabajo) crèche.

guardia ◆ f 1. (gen) guard; (vigilancia) watch, guard; **montar (la) ~** to mount guard; **~ municipal** urban police. 2. (turno) duty; **estar de ~** to be on duty. ◆ m y f (policía) policeman (f policewoman); **~ de tráfico** traffic warden. ► **Guardia Civil** f: **la Guardia Civil** the Civil Guard, military-style Spanish security force who police rural areas, highways and borders.

guardián, -ana m y f (de persona) guardian; (de cosa) watchman, keeper.

guarecer vt: **~ (de)** to protect o shelter

(from). ▶ **guarecerse** *vpr*: **~se (de)** to shelter (from).

guarida *f* lair; *fig* hideout.

guarnición *f* 1. (CULIN) garnish. 2. (MIL) garrison.

guarrería *f* 1. (*suciedad*) filth, muck. 2. (*acción*) filthy thing.

guarro, -rra ◆ *adj* filthy. ◆ *m y f* 1. (*animal*) pig. 2. *fam* (*persona*) filthy o dirty pig.

guarura *m Amer fam* bodyguard.

guasa *f fam* (*gracia*) humour; (*ironía*) irony; **estar de ~** to be joking.

guasearse *vpr fam*: **~ (de)** to take the mickey (out of).

guasón, -ona *m y f* joker, tease.

Guatemala 1. (*país*) Guatemala. 2. (*ciudad*) Guatemala City.

guatemalteco, -ca, guatemaltés, -esa *adj, m y f* Guatemalan.

guau *m* woof.

guay *adj fam* cool, neat.

guayín *m Amer fam* van.

gubernativo, -va *adj* government (*antes de sust*).

guepardo *m* cheetah.

güero, -ra *adj Amer fam* blond (*f* blonde).

guerra *f* war; (*referido al tipo de conflicto*) warfare; (*pugna*) struggle, conflict; (*de intereses, ideas*) conflict; **declarar la ~** to declare war; **en ~** at war; **~ civil/mundial** civil/world war; **~ fría** cold war; **~ de guerrillas** guerrilla warfare; **dar ~** to be a pain, to be annoying.

guerrear *vi* to (wage) war.

guerrero, -ra ◆ *adj* warlike. ◆ *m y f* (*luchador*) warrior.

guerrilla *f* (*grupo*) guerrilla group.

guerrillero, -ra *m y f* guerrilla.

gueto, ghetto ['geto] *m* ghetto.

güevón *m Amer vulg* bloody idiot.

guía ◆ *m y f* (*persona*) guide; **~ turístico** tourist guide. ◆ *f* 1. (*indicación*) guidance. 2. (*libro*) guide (book); **~ de ferrocarriles** train timetable; **~ telefónica** telephone book o directory.

guiar *vt* 1. (*indicar dirección*) to guide, to lead; (*aconsejar*) to guide, to direct. 2. (AUTOM) to drive; (NÁUT) to steer. ▶ **guiarse** *vpr*: **~se por algo** to be guided by o to follow sthg.

guijarro *m* pebble.

guillotina *f* guillotine.

guinda *f* morello cherry.

guindilla *f* chilli (pepper).

guiñapo *m* (*persona*) (physical) wreck.

guiño *m* wink.

guiñol *m* puppet theatre.

guión *m* 1. (CIN & TV) script. 2. (GRAM) (*signo*) hyphen.

guionista *m y f* scriptwriter.

guiri *fam despec m y f* foreigner.

guirigay *m fam* (*jaleo*) racket.

guirlache *m brittle sweet made of roasted almonds o hazelnuts and toffee.*

guirnalda *f* garland.

guisa *f* way; **a ~ de** by way of.

guisado *m* stew.

guisante *m* pea.

guisar *vt & vi* to cook. ▶ **guisarse** *vpr fig* to be cooking, to be going on.

guiso *m* dish.

güisqui, whisky *m* whisky.

guitarra *f* guitar.

guitarrista *m y f* guitarist.

gula *f* gluttony.

gurí, -isa *m y f Amer fam* kid, child.

gurmet, gourmet [gur'met] *m y f* gourmet.

guru, gurú *m* guru.

gusanillo *m fam*: **el ~ de la conciencia** conscience; **entrarle a uno el ~ de los videojuegos** to be bitten by the videogame bug; **matar el ~** (*bebiendo*) to have a drink on an empty stomach; (*comiendo*) to have a snack between meals; **sentir un ~ en el estómago** to have butterflies (in one's stomach).

gusano *m lit & fig* worm.

gustar ◆ *vi* (*agradar*) to be pleasing; **me gusta esa chica/ir al cine** I like that girl/going to the cinema; **me gustan las novelas** I like novels; **me gustaría conocerla** I'd like to meet her; **como guste** as you wish. ◆ *vt* to taste, to try.

gustazo *m fam* great pleasure.

gusto *m* 1. (*gen*) taste; (*sabor*) taste, flavour; **de buen/mal ~** in good/bad taste; **tener buen/mal ~** to have good/bad taste. 2. (*placer*) pleasure; **con mucho ~** gladly, with pleasure; **da ~ estar aquí** it's a real pleasure to be here; **mucho o tanto ~** pleased to meet you; **tomar ~ a algo** to take a liking to sthg. ▶ **a gusto** *loc adv*: **hacer algo a ~** (*de buena gana*) to do sthg willingly o gladly; (*cómodamente*) to do sthg comfortably; **estar a ~** to be comfortable o at ease.

gustoso, -sa *adj* 1. (*sabroso*) tasty. 2. (*con placer*): **hacer algo ~** to do sthg gladly o willingly.

gutural *adj* guttural.

Guyana *f* Guyana.

Guyana francesa *f*: **la ~** French Guyana.

H

h¹, H f (letra) h, H; **por h o por b** fig for one reason or another.

h², h. (abrev de hora) hr, h.

ha ◆ v → **haber**. ◆ (abrev de hectárea) ha.

haba f broad bean.

habano, -na adj Havanan. ▶ **habano** m Havana cigar.

haber ◆ vaux 1. (en tiempos compuestos) to have; **lo he/había hecho** I have/had done it; **los niños ya han comido** the children have already eaten; **en el estreno ha habido mucha gente** there were a lot of people at the premiere. 2. (expresa reproche): **~ venido antes** you could have come a bit earlier; **¡~lo dicho!** why didn't you say so? 3. (expresa obligación): **~ de hacer algo** to have to do sth; **has de estudiar más** you have to study more. ◆ v impers 1. (existir, estar): **hay** there is/are; **hay mucha gente en la calle** there are a lot of people in the street; **había/hubo muchos problemas** there were many problems; **habrá dos mil** (expresa futuro) there will be two thousand; (expresa hipótesis) there must be two thousand. 2. (expresa obligación): **~ que hacer algo** to have to do sth; **hay que hacer más ejercicio** one o you should do more exercise; **habrá que soportar su mal humor** we'll have to put up with his bad mood. 3. loc: **algo habrá** there must be something in it; **allá se las haya** that's his/her/your etc problem; **habérselas con alguien** to face o confront sb; **¡hay que ver!** well I never!; **no hay de qué** don't mention it; **¿qué hay?** fam (saludo) how are you doing? ◆ m 1. (bienes) assets (pl). 2. (en cuentas, contabilidad) credit (side). ▶ **haberes** mpl (sueldo) remuneration (U).

habichuela f bean.

hábil adj 1. (diestro) skilful; (inteligente) clever. 2. (utilizable - lugar) suitable, fit. 3. (DER): **días ~es** working days.

habilidad f (capacidad) ability; (destreza) skill; (inteligencia) cleverness; **tener ~ para algo** to be good at sth.

habilitar vt 1. (acondicionar) to fit out, to equip. 2. (autorizar) to authorize.

habiloso, -sa adj Amer shrewd, astute.

habitación f (gen) room; (dormitorio) bedroom; **~ doble** (con cama de matrimonio) double room; (con dos camas) twin room; **~ individual o simple** single room.

habitante m (de ciudad, país) inhabitant; (de barrio) resident.

habitar ◆ vi to live. ◆ vt to live in, to inhabit.

hábitat (pl hábitats) m (gen) habitat.

hábito m habit; **tener el ~ de hacer algo** to be in the habit of doing sth.

habitual adj habitual; (cliente, lector) regular.

habituar vt: **~ a alguien a** to accustom sb to. ▶ **habituarse** vpr: **~se a** (gen) to get used o accustomed to; (drogas etc) to become addicted to.

habla f (el) 1. (idioma) language; (dialecto) dialect; **de ~ hispana o española** Spanish-speaking. 2. (facultad) speech; **quedarse sin ~** to be left speechless. 3. (LING) discourse. 4. (al teléfono): **estar al ~ con alguien** to be on the line to sb.

hablador, -ra adj talkative.

habladurías fpl (rumores) rumours; (chismes) gossip (U).

hablante ◆ adj speaking. ◆ m y f speaker.

hablar ◆ vi: **~ (con)** to talk (to), to speak (to); **~ de** to talk about; **~ bien/mal de** to speak well/badly of; **~ en voz alta/baja** to speak loudly/softly; **¡ni ~!** no way! ◆ vt 1. (idioma) to speak. 2. (asunto): **~ algo (con)** to discuss sth (with). ▶ **hablarse** vpr to speak (to each other); **no ~se** not to be speaking, not to be on speaking terms; **'se habla inglés'** 'English spoken'.

habrá etc → **haber**.

hacendado, -da m y f landowner.

hacer ◆ vt 1. (elaborar, crear, cocinar) to make; **~ un vestido/planes** to make a dress/plans; **~ un poema/una sinfonía** to write a poem/symphony; **para ~ la carne ...** to cook the meat ... 2. (construir) to build; **han hecho un edificio nuevo** they've put up a new building. 3. (generar) to produce; **el árbol hace sombra** the tree gives shade; **la carretera hace una curva** there's a bend in the road. 4. (movimientos, sonidos, gestos) to make; **le hice señas** I signalled to her; **el reloj hace tic-tac** the clock goes ticktock; **~ ruido** to make a noise. 5. (obtener - fotocopia) to make; (- retrato) to paint; (- fotografía) to take. 6. (rea-

lizar - trabajo, estudios) to do; (- *viaje*) to make; (- *comunión*) to take; **hoy hace guardia** she's on duty today; **estoy haciendo segundo** I'm in my second year. 7. (*practicar - gen*) to do; (- *tenis, fútbol*) to play; **debes ~ deporte** you should start doing some sport. 8. (*arreglar - casa, colada*) to do; (- *cama*) to make. 9. (*transformar en*): **~ a alguien feliz** to make sb happy; **la guerra no le hizo un hombre** the war didn't make him (into) a man; **hizo pedazos el papel** he tore the paper to pieces; **~ de algo/alguien algo** to make sth/sb into sth; **hizo de ella una buena cantante** he made a good singer of her. 10. (*comportarse como*): **~ el tonto** to act the fool; **~ el vándalo** to act like a hooligan. 11. (*causar*): **~ daño a alguien** to hurt sb; **me hizo gracia** I thought it was funny. 12. (CIN & TEATR) to play; **hace el papel de la hija del rey** she plays (the part of) the king's daughter. 13. (*ser causa de*): **~ que alguien haga algo** to make sb do sth; **me hizo reír** it made me laugh; **has hecho que se enfadara** you've made him angry. 14. (*mandar*): **~ que se haga algo** to have sth done; **voy a ~ teñir este traje** I'm going to have the dress dyed. ◆ *vi* 1. (*actuar*): **~ de** (CIN & TEATR) to play; (*trabajar*) to act as. 2. (*aparentar*): **~ como si** to act as if; **haz como que no te importa** act as if you don't care. 3. (*procurar, intentar*): **~ por hacer algo** to try to do sth; **haré por verle esta noche** I'll try to see him tonight. 4. *loc*: **¿hace?** all right? ◆ *v impers* 1. (*tiempo meteorológico*): **hace frío/calor/sol/viento** it's cold/hot/sunny/windy; **hace un día precioso** it's a beautiful day. 2. (*tiempo transcurrido*): **hace diez años** ten years ago; **hace mucho/poco** a long time/not long ago; **hace tiempo que no la veo** I haven't seen her for a long while; **hace un mes que llegué** it's a month since I arrived; **no la veo desde hace un año** I haven't seen her for a year; **¿cuánto tiempo hace que esperas?** how long have you been waiting (for)? ▶ **hacerse** *vpr* 1. (*formarse*) to form. 2. (*desarrollarse, crecer*) to grow. 3. (*guisarse, cocerse*) to cook. 4. (*convertirse*) to become; **~se musulmán** to become a Moslem. 5. (*crearse en la mente*): **~se ilusiones** to get one's hopes up; **~se una idea de algo** to imagine what sth is like. 6. (*mostrarse*): **se hace el gracioso/el simpático** he tries to act the comedian/the nice guy; **~se el dis-**

traído to pretend to be miles away. 7. (+ *infin*): **~se entender** to make o.s. understood; **~se pasar por** to pass o.s. off as.

hacha *f* (*el*) axe.

hachís, hash [xaʃ] *m* hashish.

hacia *prep* 1. (*dirección, tendencia, sentimiento*) towards; **~ aquí/allí** this/that way; **~ abajo** downwards; **~ arriba** upwards; **~ atrás** backwards; **~ adelante** forwards. 2. (*tiempo*) around, about; **~ las diez** around o about ten o'clock.

hacienda *f* 1. (*finca*) country estate o property. 2. (*bienes*) property; **~ pública** public purse. ▶ **Hacienda** *f*: **Ministerio de Hacienda** the Treasury.

hada *f* (*el*) fairy.

haga *etc* → **hacer**.

Haití Haiti.

hala *interj*: **¡~!** (*para dar ánimo, prisa*) come on!; (*para expresar incredulidad*) no!, you're joking!; (*para expresar admiración, sorpresa*) wow!

halagador, -ra *adj* flattering.

halagar *vt* to flatter.

halago *m* flattery.

halagüeño, -ña *adj* (*prometedor*) promising, encouraging.

halcón *m* 1. (ZOOL) falcon, hawk. 2. *Amer fam* (*matón*) government-paid killer.

hálito *m* (*aliento*) breath.

halitosis *f inv* bad breath.

hall [xol] (*pl* **halls**) *m* foyer.

hallar *vt* (*gen*) to find; (*averiguar*) to find out. ▶ **hallarse** *vpr* 1. (*en un lugar - persona*) to be, to find o.s.; (- *casa etc*) to be (situated). 2. (*en una situación*) to be; **~se enfermo** to be ill.

hallazgo *m* 1. (*descubrimiento*) discovery. 2. (*objeto*) find.

halo *m* (*de astros, santos*) halo; (*de objetos, personas*) aura.

halógeno, -na *adj* (QUÍM) halogenous; (*faro*) halogen (*antes de sust*).

halterofilia *f* weightlifting.

hamaca *f* 1. (*para colgar*) hammock. 2. (*tumbona - silla*) deckchair; (- *canapé*) sunlounger.

hambre *f* 1. (*apetito*) hunger; (*inanición*) starvation; **tener ~** to be hungry; **matar el ~** to satisfy one's hunger. 2. (*epidemia*) famine. 3. *fig* (*deseo*): **~ de** hunger o thirst for.

hambriento, -ta *adj* starving.

hamburguesa *f* hamburger.

hampa *f* (*el*) underworld.

hámster ['xamster] (*pl* **hámsters**) *m* hamster.

hendidura

hándicap ['xandikap] (*pl* **hándicaps**) *m* handicap.

hará *etc* → **hacer**.

haraganear *vi* to laze about.

harapiento, -ta *adj* ragged, tattered.

harapo *m* rag, tatter.

hardware ['xarwar] *m* (INFORM) hardware.

harén *m* harem.

harina *f* flour.

harinoso, -sa *adj* floury; (*manzana*) mealy.

hartar *vt* **1.** (*atiborrar*) to stuff (full). **2.** (*fastidiar*): **~ a alguien** to annoy sb, to get on sb's nerves. ▶ **hartarse** *vpr* **1.** (*atiborrarse*) to stuff *o* gorge o.s. **2.** (*cansarse*): **~se (de)** to get fed up (with). **3.** (*no parar*): **~se de algo** to do sthg non-stop.

hartazgo, hartón *m* fill; **darse un ~ (de)** to have one's fill (of).

harto, -ta *adj* **1.** (*de comida*) full. **2.** (*cansado*): **~ (de)** tired (of), fed up (with). ▶ **harto** *adv* somewhat, rather.

hartón = **hartazgo**.

hash = **hachís**.

hasta ◆ *prep* **1.** (*en el espacio*) as far as, up to; **desde aquí ~ allí** from here to there; **¿~ dónde va este tren?** where does this train go? **2.** (*en el tiempo*) until, till; **~ ahora** (*up*) until now, so far; **~ el final** right up until the end; **~ luego** *o* **pronto** *o* **la vista** see you (later). **3.** (*con cantidades*) up to. ◆ *adv* (*incluso*) even. ▶ **hasta que** *loc conj* until, till.

hastiar *vt* (*aburrir*) to bore; (*asquear*) to sicken, to disgust. ▶ **hastiarse de** *vpr* to tire of.

hastío *m* (*tedio*) boredom (U); (*repugnancia*) disgust.

hatillo *m* bundle of clothes.

hay → **haber**.

haya ◆ *v* → **haber**. ◆ *f* (*árbol*) beech (tree); (*madera*) beech (wood).

haz ◆ *v* → **hacer**. ◆ *m* **1.** (*de leña*) bundle; (*de cereales*) sheaf. **2.** (*de luz*) beam.

hazaña *f* feat, exploit.

hazmerreír *m* laughing stock.

HB (*abrev de* **Herri Batasuna**) *f* political wing of ETA.

he → **haber**.

hebilla *f* buckle.

hebra *f* (*de hilo*) thread; (*de judías, puerros*) string; (*de tabaco*) strand (of tobacco).

hebreo, -a *adj*, *m y f* Hebrew. ▶ **hebreo** *m* (*lengua*) Hebrew.

hechicero, -ra *m y f* wizard (*f* witch), sorcerer (*f* sorceress).

hechizar *vt* to cast a spell on; *fig* to bewitch, to captivate.

hechizo *m* **1.** (*maleficio*) spell. **2.** *fig* (*encanto*) magic, charm.

hecho, -cha ◆ *pp* → **hacer**. ◆ *adj* **1.** (*acabado - persona*) mature; **estás ~ un artista** you've become quite an artist; **una mujer hecha y derecha** a fully-grown woman. **2.** (*carne*) done; **quiero el filete muy/poco ~** I'd like the steak well done/rare. ▶ **hecho** *m* **1.** (*obra*) action, deed. **2.** (*suceso*) event. **3.** (*realidad, dato*) fact. ▶ **de hecho** *loc adv* in fact, actually.

hechura *f* **1.** (*de traje*) cut. **2.** (*forma*) shape.

hectárea *f* hectare.

heder *vi* (*apestar*) to stink, to reek.

hediondo, -da *adj* (*pestilente*) stinking.

hedor *m* stink, stench.

hegemonía *f* (*gen*) dominance; (POLÍT) hegemony.

helada → **helado**.

heladera *f* Amer fridge Br, icebox Am.

heladería *f* (*tienda*) ice-cream parlour; (*puesto*) ice-cream stall.

helado, -da *adj* **1.** (*hecho hielo - agua*) frozen; (*- lago*) frozen over. **2.** (*muy frío - manos, agua*) freezing. ▶ **helado** *m* ice-cream. ▶ **helada** *f* frost.

helar ◆ *vt* (*líquido*) to freeze. ◆ *v impers*: **ayer heló** there was a frost last night. ▶ **helarse** *vpr* to freeze; (*plantas*) to be frostbitten.

helecho *m* fern, bracken.

hélice *f* **1.** (TECN) propeller. **2.** (*espiral*) spiral.

helicóptero *m* helicopter.

helio *m* helium.

Helsinki Helsinki.

hematoma *m* bruise, haematoma (MED).

hembra *f* **1.** (BIOL) female; (*mujer*) woman; (*niña*) girl. **2.** (*del enchufe*) socket.

hemiciclo *m* (*en el parlamento*) floor.

hemisferio *m* hemisphere.

hemofilia *f* haemophilia.

hemorragia *f* haemorrhage; **~ nasal** nosebleed.

hemorroides *fpl* haemorrhoids, piles.

henchir *vt* to fill (up).

hender, hendir *vt* (*carne, piel*) to carve open, to cleave; (*piedra, madera*) to crack open; (*aire, agua*) to cut *o* slice through.

hendidura *f* (*en carne, piel*) cut, split;

(*en piedra, madera*) crack.
hendir = **hender**.
heno *m* hay.
hepatitis *f inv* hepatitis.
herbicida *m* weedkiller.
herbolario, -ria *m y f* (*persona*) herbalist.
hercio, hertz ['erθjo] *m* hertz.
heredar *vt*: ~ (**de**) to inherit (from).
heredero, -ra *m y f* heir (*f* heiress).
hereditario, -ria *adj* hereditary.
hereje *m y f* heretic.
herejía *f* heresy.
herencia *f* (*de bienes*) inheritance; (*de características*) legacy; (BIOL) heredity.
herido, -da ◆ *adj* (*gen*) injured; (*en lucha, atentado*) wounded; (*sentimentalmente*) hurt, wounded. ◆ *m y f* (*gen*) injured person; (*en lucha, atentado*) wounded person; **no hubo ~s** there were no casualties; **los ~s** the wounded. ▶ **herida** *f* (*lesión*) injury; (*en lucha, atentado*) wound.
herir *vt* 1. (*físicamente*) to injure; (*en lucha, atentado*) to wound; (*vista*) to hurt; (*oído*) to pierce. 2. (*sentimentalmente*) to hurt.
hermanado, -da *adj* (*gen*) united, joined; (*ciudades*) twinned.
hermanar *vt* (*ciudades*) to twin.
hermanastro, -tra *m y f* stepbrother (*f* stepsister).
hermandad *f* (*asociación*) association; (RELIG - *de hombres*) brotherhood; (- *de mujeres*) sisterhood.
hermano, -na *m y f* brother (*f* sister).
hermético, -ca *adj* 1. (*al aire*) airtight, hermetic; (*al agua*) watertight, hermetic. 2. *fig* (*persona*) inscrutable.
hermoso, -sa *adj* (*gen*) beautiful, lovely; (*hombre*) handsome; (*excelente*) wonderful.
hermosura *f* (*gen*) beauty; (*de hombre*) handsomeness.
hernia *f* hernia, rupture.
herniarse *vpr* (MED) to rupture o.s.
héroe *m* hero.
heroico, -ca *adj* heroic.
heroína *f* 1. (*mujer*) heroine. 2. (*droga*) heroin.
heroinómano, -na *m y f* heroin addict.
heroísmo *m* heroism.
herpes *m inv* herpes (U).
herradura *f* horseshoe.
herramienta *f* tool.
herrería *f* (*taller*) smithy, forge.
herrero *m* blacksmith, smith.

herrumbre *f* (*óxido*) rust.
hertz = **hercio**.
hervidero *m* 1. (*de pasiones, intrigas*) hotbed. 2. (*de gente - muchedumbre*) swarm, throng; (- *sitio*) place throbbing o swarming with people.
hervir ◆ *vt* to boil. ◆ *vi* 1. (*líquido*) to boil. 2. *fig* (*lugar*): ~ **de** to swarm with.
hervor *m* boiling; **dar un ~ a algo** to blanch sthg.
heterodoxo, -xa *adj* unorthodox.
heterogéneo, -a *adj* heterogeneous.
heterosexual *adj, m y f* heterosexual.
hexágono *m* hexagon.
hez *f lit & fig* dregs (*pl*). ▶ **heces** *fpl* (*excrementos*) faeces.
hibernar *vi* to hibernate.
híbrido, -da *adj lit & fig* hybrid. ▶ **híbrido** *m* (*animal, planta*) hybrid.
hice *etc* → **hacer**.
hidalgo, -ga *m y f* nobleman (*f* noblewoman).
hidratante *m* moisturizing cream.
hidratar *vt* (*piel*) to moisturize; (QUÍM) to hydrate.
hidrato *m*: ~ **de carbono** carbohydrate.
hidráulico, -ca *adj* hydraulic.
hidroavión *m* seaplane.
hidroeléctrico, -ca *adj* hydroelectric.
hidrógeno *m* hydrogen.
hidroplano *m* (*barco*) hydrofoil.
hiedra *f* ivy.
hiel *f* 1. (*bilis*) bile. 2. *fig* (*mala intención*) spleen, bitterness.
hielo *m* 1. (*gen*) ice; **romper el ~** *fig* to break the ice. 2. (*helada*) frost.
hiena *f* hyena.
hierático, -ca *adj* solemn.
hierba, yerba *f* 1. (*planta*) herb; **mala ~** weed. 2. (*césped*) grass. 3. *fam* (*droga*) grass.
hierbabuena *f* mint.
hierro *m* (*metal*) iron; **de ~** (*severo*) iron (*antes de sust*); ~ **forjado** wrought iron; ~ **fundido** cast iron.
hígado *m* liver.
higiene *f* hygiene.
higiénico, -ca *adj* hygienic.
higienizar *vt* to sterilize.
higo *m* fig; ~ **chumbo** prickly pear; **de ~s a brevas** once in a blue moon.
higuera *f* fig tree.
hijastro, -tra *m y f* stepson (*f* stepdaughter).
hijo, -ja *m y f* (*descendiente*) son (*f* daughter); ~ **de papá** *fam* daddy's boy; ~ **único** only child. ▶ **hijo** *m* (*hijo o hija*)

child. ▶ **hijos** *mpl* children.
hilacha *f* loose thread.
hilada *f* row.
hilar *vt* (*hilo, tela*) to spin; (*ideas, planes*) to think up.
hilaridad *f* hilarity.
hilatura *f* spinning.
hilera *f* row.
hilo *m* **1.** (*fibra, hebra*) thread; **colgar** o **pender de un ~** to be hanging by a thread; **mover los ~s** to pull some strings. **2.** (*tejido*) linen. **3.** (*de metal, teléfono*) wire. **4.** (*de agua, sangre*) trickle. **5.** (MÚS): **~ musical**® piped music. **6.** *fig* (*de pensamiento*) train; (*de discurso, conversación*) thread; **perder el ~** to lose the thread; **seguir el ~** to follow (the thread).
hilvanar *vt* **1.** (*ropa*) to tack *Br*, to baste *Am*. **2.** *fig* (*coordinar - ideas*) to piece together.
Himalaya *m*: **el ~** the Himalayas (*pl*).
himno *m* hymn; **~ nacional** national anthem.
hincapié *m*: **hacer ~ en** (*insistir*) to insist on; (*subrayar*) to emphasize.
hincar *vt*: **~ algo en** to stick sthg into.
▶ **hincarse** *vpr*: **~se de rodillas** to fall to one's knees.
hincha *m y f* (*seguidor*) fan.
hinchado, -da *adj* **1.** (*rueda, globo*) inflated; (*cara, tobillo*) swollen. **2.** *fig* (*persona*) bigheaded, conceited; (*lenguaje, estilo*) bombastic.
hinchar *vt lit & fig* to blow up. ▶ **hincharse** *vpr* **1.** (*pierna, mano*) to swell (up). **2.** *fig* (*de comida*): **~se (a)** to stuff o.s. (with). ▶ **hincharse a** *vpr* (*no parar de*): **~se a hacer algo** to do sthg a lot.
hinchazón *f* swelling.
hindú (*pl* **hindúes**) *adj, m y f* **1.** (*de la India*) Indian. **2.** (RELIG) Hindu.
hinduismo *m* Hinduism.
hinojo *m* fennel.
hipar *vi* to hiccup, to have hiccups.
hiper *m fam* hypermarket.
hiperactivo, -va *adj* hyperactive.
hipérbola *f* hyperbola.
hipermercado *m* hypermarket.
hipertensión *f* high blood pressure.
hípico, -ca *adj* (*de las carreras*) horseracing (*antes de sust*); (*de la equitación*) showjumping (*antes de sust*). ▶ **hípica** *f* (*carreras de caballos*) horseracing; (*equitación*) showjumping.
hipnosis *f inv* hypnosis.
hipnótico, -ca *adj* hypnotic.
hipnotismo *m* hypnotism.
hipnotizador, -ra *adj* hypnotic; *fig*

spellbinding, mesmerizing.
hipnotizar *vt* to hypnotize; *fig* to mesmerize.
hipo *m* hiccups (*pl*); **tener ~** to have (the) hiccups; **quitar el ~ a uno** *fig* to take one's breath away.
hipocondriaco, -ca *adj, m y f* hypochondriac.
hipocresía *f* hypocrisy.
hipócrita ♦ *adj* hypocritical. ♦ *m y f* hypocrite.
hipodérmico, -ca *adj* hypodermic.
hipódromo *m* racecourse, racetrack.
hipopótamo *m* hippopotamus.
hipoteca *f* mortgage.
hipotecar *vt* (*bienes*) to mortgage.
hipotecario, -ria *adj* mortgage (*antes de sust*).
hipotenusa *f* hypotenuse.
hipótesis *f inv* hypothesis.
hipotético, -ca *adj* hypothetical.
hippy, hippie ['xipi] (*pl* **hippies**) *adj, m y f* hippy.
hiriente *adj* (*palabras*) hurtful, cutting.
hirsuto, -ta *adj* (*cabello*) wiry; (*brazo, pecho*) hairy.
hispánico, -ca *adj, m y f* Hispanic, Spanish-speaking.
hispanidad *f* (*cultura*) Spanishness; (*pueblos*) Spanish-speaking world.
hispano, -na ♦ *adj* (*español*) Spanish; (*hispanoamericano*) Spanish-American; (*en Estados Unidos*) Hispanic. ♦ *m y f* (*español*) Spaniard; (*estadounidense*) Hispanic.
hispanoamericano, -na ♦ *adj* Spanish-American. ♦ *m y f* Spanish American.
hispanohablante ♦ *adj* Spanish-speaking. ♦ *m y f* Spanish speaker.
histeria *f* (MED & *fig*) hysteria.
histérico, -ca *adj* (MED & *fig*) hysterical; **ponerse ~** to get hysterical.
histerismo *m* (MED & *fig*) hysteria.
historia *f* **1.** (*gen*) history; **~ del arte** art history; **pasar a la ~** to go down in history. **2.** (*narración, chisme*) story; **dejarse de ~s** to stop beating about the bush.
historiador, -ra *m y f* historian.
historial *m* (*gen*) record; (*profesional*) curriculum vitae, résumé *Am*; **~ médico** o **clínico** medical o case history.
histórico, -ca *adj* **1.** (*de la historia*) historical. **2.** (*verídico*) factual. **3.** (*importante*) historic.
historieta *f* **1.** (*chiste*) funny story, anecdote. **2.** (*tira cómica*) comic strip, cartoon.

hito *m* lit & fig milestone.

hizo → **hacer**.

hmnos. (*abrev de* **hermanos**) bros.

hobby ['xoβi] (*pl* **hobbies**) *m* hobby.

hocico *m* (*de perro*) muzzle; (*de gato*) nose; (*de cerdo*) snout.

hockey ['xokei] *m* hockey; **~ sobre hielo/patines** ice/roller hockey; **~ sobre hierba** (field) hockey.

hogar *m* 1. (*de chimenea*) fireplace; (*de horno, cocina*) grate. 2. (*domicilio*) home. 3. (*familia*) family.

hogareño, -ña *adj* (*gen*) family (*antes de sust*); (*amante del hogar*) home-loving.

hogaza *f* large loaf.

hoguera *f* bonfire; **morir en la ~** to be burned at the stake.

hoja *f* 1. (*de plantas*) leaf; (*de flor*) petal; (*de hierba*) blade. 2. (*de papel*) sheet (of paper); (*de libro*) page. 3. (*de cuchillo*) blade; **~ de afeitar** razor blade. 4. (*de puertas, ventanas*) leaf. ▶ **hoja de cálculo** *f* (INFORM) spreadsheet.

hojalata *f* tinplate.

hojaldre *m* puff pastry.

hojarasca *f* 1. (*hojas secas*) (dead) leaves (*pl*); (*frondosidad*) tangle of leaves. 2. *fig* (*paja*) rubbish.

hojear *vt* to leaf through.

hola *interj*: **¡~!** hello!

Holanda Holland.

holandés, -esa ◆ *adj* Dutch. ◆ *m y f* (*persona*) Dutchman (*f* Dutchwoman). ▶ **holandés** *m* (*lengua*) Dutch. ▶ **holandesa** *f* (*papel*) piece of paper measuring 22 x 28cm.

holding ['xoldin] (*pl* **holdings**) *m* holding company.

holgado, -da *adj* 1. (*ropa*) baggy, loose-fitting; (*habitación, espacio*) roomy. 2. (*victoria, situación económica*) comfortable.

holgar *vi* (*sobrar*) to be unnecessary; **huelga decir que ...** needless to say ...

holgazán, -ana ◆ *adj* idle, good-for-nothing. ◆ *m y f* good-for-nothing.

holgazanear *vi* to laze about.

holgura *f* 1. (*anchura - de espacio*) room; (*- de ropa*) bagginess, looseness; (*- entre piezas*) play, give. 2. (*bienestar*) comfort, affluence.

hollar *vt* to tread (on).

hollín *m* soot.

holocausto *m* holocaust.

hombre ◆ *m* man; **el ~** (*la humanidad*) man, mankind; **el ~ de la calle** o **de a pie** the man in the street; **~ de las cavernas**

caveman; **~ de negocios** businessman; **~ de palabra** man of his word; **un pobre ~** a nobody; **¡pobre ~!** poor chap Br o guy!; **de ~ a ~** man to man. ◆ *interj*: **¡~! ¡qué alegría verte!** (hey,) how nice to see you! ▶ **hombre orquesta** (*pl* **hombres orquesta**) *m* one-man band. ▶ **hombre rana** (*pl* **hombres rana**) *m* frogman.

hombrera *f* (*de traje, vestido*) shoulder pad; (*de uniforme*) epaulette.

hombría *f* manliness.

hombro *m* shoulder; **a ~s** over one's shoulders; **encogerse de ~s** to shrug one's shoulders; **arrimar el ~** *fig* to lend a hand.

hombruno, -na *adj* mannish.

homenaje *m* (*gen*) tribute; (*al soberano*) homage; **partido (de) ~** testimonial (match); **en ~ de** o **a** in honour of, as a tribute to; **rendir ~ a** to pay tribute to.

homenajeado, -da *m y f* guest of honour.

homenajear *vt* to pay tribute to.

homeopatía *f* homeopathy.

homicida ◆ *adj* (*mirada etc*) murderous; **arma ~** murder weapon. ◆ *m y f* murderer.

homicidio *m* homicide, murder.

homilía *f* homily, sermon.

homogeneizar *vt* to homogenize.

homogéneo, -a *adj* homogenous.

homologar *vt* 1. (*equiparar*): **~ (con)** to bring into line (with), to make comparable (with). 2. (*dar por válido - producto*) to authorize officially; (*- récord*) to confirm officially.

homólogo, -ga ◆ *adj* (*semejante*) equivalent. ◆ *m y f* counterpart.

homosexual *adj, m y f* homosexual.

hondo, -da *adj* 1. lit & fig (*gen*) deep; **lo ~** the depths (*pl*); **calar ~ en** to strike a chord with; **en lo más ~ de** in the depths of. 2. → **cante**. ▶ **honda** *f* sling.

hondonada *f* hollow.

hondura *f* depth.

Honduras Honduras.

hondureño, -ña *adj, m y f* Honduran.

honestidad *f* (*honradez*) honesty; (*decencia*) modesty, decency; (*justicia*) fairness.

honesto, -ta *adj* (*honrado*) honest; (*decente*) modest, decent; (*justo*) fair.

hongo *m* 1. (*planta - comestible*) mushroom; (*- no comestible*) toadstool. 2. (*enfermedad*) fungus.

honor *m* honour; **hacer ~ a** to live up to; **en ~ a la verdad** to be (quite) honest. ▶ **honores** mpl (ceremonial) honours.

honorable adj honourable.

honrar vt to honour.

honorario, -ria adj honorary. ▶ **honorarios** mpl fees.

honorífico, -ca adj honorific.

honra f honour; **¡y a mucha ~!** and proud of it! ▶ **honras fúnebres** fpl funeral (sg).

honradez f honesty.

honrado, -da adj honest.

honrar vt to honour. ▶ **honrarse** vpr: **~se (con algo/de hacer algo)** to be honoured (by sthg/to do sthg).

honroso, -sa adj 1. (que da honra) honorary. 2. (respetable) honourable, respectable.

hora f 1. (del día) hour; **a primera ~** first thing in the morning; **a última ~** (al final del día) at the end of the day; (en el último momento) at the last moment; **dar la ~** to strike the hour; **de última ~** (noticia) latest, up-to-the-minute; (preparativos) last-minute; **'última ~'** 'stop press'; **(pagar) por ~s** (to pay) by the hour; **~s de oficina/trabajo** office/working hours; **~ oficial** official time; **~ punta** rush hour; **~s extraordinarias** overtime (U); **~s de visita** visiting times; **media ~** half an hour. 2. (momento determinado) time; **¿a qué ~ sale?** what time o when does it leave?; **es ~ de irse** it's time to go; **a la ~** on time; **en su ~** when the time comes, at the appropriate time; **¿qué ~ es?** what time is it? 3. (cita) appointment; **pedir/dar ~** to ask for/give an appointment; **tener ~ en/con** to have an appointment at/with. 4. loc: **a altas ~s de la noche** in the small hours; **en mala ~** unluckily; **la ~ de la verdad** the moment of truth; **¡ya era ~!** and about time too!

horadar vt to pierce; (con máquina) to bore through.

horario, -ria adj time (antes de sust). ▶ **horario** m timetable; **~ comercial/laboral** opening/working hours (pl); **~ intensivo** working day without a long break for lunch; **~ de visitas** visiting hours (pl).

horca f 1. (patíbulo) gallows (pl). 2. (AGR) pitchfork.

horcajadas ▶ **a horcajadas** loc adv astride.

horchata f cold drink made from ground tiger nuts or almonds, milk and sugar.

horizontal adj horizontal.

horizonte m horizon.

horma f (gen) mould, pattern; (para arreglar zapatos) last; (para conservar zapatos) shoe tree; (de sombrero) hat block.

hormiga f ant.

hormigón m concrete; **~ armado** reinforced concrete.

hormigueo m pins and needles (pl).

hormiguero ♦ adj → **oso**. ♦ m ants' nest.

hormona f hormone.

hornada f lit & fig batch.

hornear vt to bake.

hornillo m (para cocinar) camping o portable stove; (de laboratorio) small furnace.

horno m (CULIN) oven; (TECN) furnace; (de cerámica, ladrillos) kiln; **al ~** baked; **alto ~** blast furnace; **altos ~s** (factoría) iron and steelworks; **~ eléctrico** electric oven; **~ microondas** microwave (oven).

horóscopo m 1. (signo zodiacal) star sign. 2. (predicción) horoscope.

horquilla f (para el pelo) hairpin.

horrendo, -da adj (gen) horrendous; (muy malo) terrible, awful.

horrible adj (gen) horrible; (muy malo) terrible, awful.

horripilante adj (terrorífico) horrifying, spine-chilling.

horripilar vt to terrify.

horror m 1. (miedo) terror, horror; **¡qué ~!** how awful! 2. (gen pl) (atrocidad) atrocity.

horrorizado, -da adj terrified, horrified.

horrorizar vt to terrify, to horrify. ▶ **horrorizarse** vpr to be terrified o horrified.

horroroso, -sa adj 1. (gen) awful. 2. (muy feo) horrible, hideous.

hortaliza f (garden) vegetable.

hortelano, -na m y f market gardener.

hortensia f hydrangea.

hortera fam adj tasteless, tacky.

horticultura f horticulture.

hosco, -ca adj (persona) sullen, gruff; (lugar) grim, gloomy.

hospedar vt to put up. ▶ **hospedarse** vpr to stay.

hospicio m (para niños) children's home; (para pobres) poorhouse.

hospital m hospital.

hospitalario, -ria adj (acogedor) hospitable.

hospitalidad f hospitality.

hospitalizar vt to hospitalize, to take o send to hospital.

hosquedad f sullenness, gruffness.

hostal m guesthouse.

hostelería f 1. (industria) hotel and catering business. 2. (profesión, curso) hospitality, hotel and catering management.

hostería f small hotel, guesthouse.

hostia f 1. (RELIG) host. 2. vulg (bofetada) bash, punch. 3. vulg (accidente) smash-up. ▶ **hostias** interj vulg: ¡~s! bloody hell!, damn it!

hostiar vt vulg to bash.

hostigar vt 1. (acosar) to pester, to bother. 2. (MIL) to harass.

hostil adj hostile.

hostilidad f (sentimiento) hostility. ▶ **hostilidades** fpl (MIL) hostilities.

hotel m hotel.

hotelero, -ra adj hotel (antes de sust).

hoy adv 1. (en este día) today; **de ~ en adelante** from now on. 2. (en la actualidad) nowadays, today; ~ **día**, ~ **en día**, ~ **por ~** these days, nowadays.

hoyo m (gen) hole, pit; (de golf) hole.

hoyuelo m dimple.

hoz f sickle; **la ~ y el martillo** the hammer and sickle.

huacal m Amer 1. (jaula) cage. 2. (cajón) drawer.

hubiera etc → **haber**.

hucha f moneybox.

hueco, -ca adj 1. (vacío) hollow. 2. (sonido) resonant, hollow. 3. (sin ideas) empty. ▶ **hueco** m 1. (cavidad - gen) hole; (- en pared) recess. 2. (tiempo libre) spare moment. 3. (espacio libre) space, gap; (de escalera) well; (de ascensor) shaft.

huela etc → **oler**.

huelga f strike; **estar/declararse en ~** to be/to go on strike; ~ **de brazos caídos** o **cruzados** sit-down (strike); ~ **de celo** work-to-rule; ~ **de hambre** hunger strike; ~ **general** general strike; ~ **salvaje** wildcat strike.

huelguista m y f striker.

huella f 1. (de persona) footprint; (de animal, rueda) track; ~ **digital** o **dactilar** fingerprint. 2. fig (vestigio) trace. 3. fig (impresión profunda) mark; **dejar ~** to leave one's mark.

huérfano, -na adj, m y f orphan.

huerta f (huerto) market garden Br, truck farm Am.

huerto m (de hortalizas) vegetable garden; (de frutales) orchard.

hueso m 1. (del cuerpo) bone; **ser un ~ duro de roer** to be a hard nut to crack. 2. (de fruto) stone Br, pit Am. 3. Amer fam

(enchufe) contacts (pl), influence.

huésped, -da m y f guest.

huesudo, -da adj bony.

hueva f roe.

huevada f Amer vulg bollocks (U), crap.

huevo m 1. (de animales) egg; ~ **a la copa** o **tibio** Amer boiled egg; ~ **escalfado/frito** poached/fried egg; ~ **pasado por agua/duro** soft-boiled/hard-boiled egg; ~s **revueltos** scrambled eggs. 2. (gen pl) vulg (testículos) balls (pl); **costar un ~** (ser caro) to cost a packet o bomb; (ser difícil) to be bloody hard.

huevón m Amer vulg stupid bastard.

huida f escape, flight.

huidizo, -za adj shy, elusive.

huir vi 1. (escapar): ~ **(de)** (gen) to flee (from); (de cárcel etc) to escape (from); ~ **del país** to flee the country. 2. (evitar): ~ **de algo** to avoid sthg, to keep away from sthg.

hule m oilskin.

humanidad f humanity. ▶ **humanidades** fpl (letras) humanities.

humanitario, -ria adj humanitarian.

humanizar vt to humanize.

humano, -na adj 1. (del hombre) human. 2. (compasivo) humane. ▶ **humano** m human being; **los ~s** mankind (U).

humareda f cloud of smoke.

humear vi (salir humo) to (give off) smoke; (salir vapor) to steam.

humedad f 1. (gen) dampness; (en pared, techo) damp; (de algo chorreando) wetness; (de piel, ojos etc) moistness. 2. (de atmósfera etc) humidity.

humedecer vt to moisten. ▶ **humedecerse** vpr to become moist; ~se **los labios** to moisten one's lips.

húmedo, -da adj 1. (gen) damp; (chorreando) wet; (piel, ojos etc) moist. 2. (aire, clima, atmósfera) humid.

humidificar vt to humidify.

humildad f humility.

humilde adj 1. (modesto) humble. 2. (pobre) poor.

humillación f humiliation.

humillado, -da adj humiliated.

humillante adj humiliating.

humillar vt to humiliate. ▶ **humillarse** vpr to humble o.s.

humo m (gen) smoke; (vapor) steam; (de coches etc) fumes (pl). ▶ **humos** mpl fig (aires) airs; **bajarle a alguien los ~s** fig to take sb down a peg or two.

humor m 1. (estado de ánimo) mood;

(*carácter*) temperament; **estar de buen/ mal ~** to be in a good/bad mood. **2.** (*gracia*) humour; **un programa de ~** a comedy programme; **~ negro** black humour. **3.** (*ganas*) mood; **no estoy de ~** I'm not in the mood.

humorismo *m* humour; (TEATR & TV) comedy.

humorista *m y f* humorist; (TEATR & TV) comedian (*f* comedienne).

humorístico, -ca *adj* humorous.

hundimiento *m* **1.** (*naufragio*) sinking. **2.** (*ruina*) collapse.

hundir *vt* **1.** (*gen*) to sink; **~ algo en el agua** to put sthg underwater. **2.** *fig* (*afligir*) to devastate, to destroy. **3.** *fig* (*hacer fracasar*) to ruin. ► **hundirse** *vpr* **1.** (*sumergirse*) to sink; (*intencionadamente*) to dive. **2.** (*derrumbarse*) to collapse; (*techo*) to cave in. **3.** *fig* (*fracasar*) to be ruined.

húngaro, -ra *adj, m y f* Hungarian. ► **húngaro** *m* (*lengua*) Hungarian.

Hungría Hungary.

huracán *m* hurricane.

huraño, -ña *adj* unsociable.

hurgar *vi*: **~ (en)** (*gen*) to rummage around (in); (*con el dedo, un palo*) to poke around (in). ► **hurgarse** *vpr*: **~se la nariz** to pick one's nose; **~se los bolsillos** to rummage around in one's pockets.

hurgonear *vt* to poke.

hurón *m* (ZOOL) ferret.

hurra *interj*: **¡~!** hurray!

hurtadillas ► **a hurtadillas** *loc adv* on the sly, stealthily.

hurtar *vt* to steal.

hurto *m* theft.

husmear ◆ *vt* (*olfatear*) to sniff out, to scent. ◆ *vi* (*curiosear*) to nose around.

huso *m* spindle; (*en máquina*) bobbin.

huy *interj*: **¡~!** (*dolor*) ouch!; (*sorpresa*) gosh!

I

i, I *f* (*letra*) i, I.

IAE (*abrev de Impuesto sobre Actividades Económicas*) *m Spanish tax paid by professionals and shop owners.*

iba → **ir.**

ibérico, -ca *adj* Iberian.

ibero, -ra *adj, m y f* Iberian. ► **ibero, ibero** *m* (*lengua*) Iberian.

iberoamericano, -na *adj, m y f* Latin American.

iceberg (*pl* **icebergs**) *m* iceberg.

Icona (*abrev de Instituto Nacional para la Conservación de la Naturaleza*) *m Spanish national institute for conservation,* ≃ NCC *Br.*

icono *m* icon.

iconoclasta *m y f* iconoclast.

id → **ir.**

ida *f* outward journey; **(billete de) ~ y vuelta** return (ticket).

idea *f* **1.** (*gen*) idea; (*propósito*) intention; **con la ~ de** with the idea o intention of; **~ fija** obsession; **no tener ni ~ (de)** not to have a clue (about). **2.** (*opinión*) impression; **cambiar de ~** to change one's mind.

ideal *adj* & *m* ideal.

idealista ◆ *adj* idealistic. ◆ *m y f* idealist.

idealizar *vt* to idealize.

idear *vt* **1.** (*planear*) to think up, to devise. **2.** (*inventar*) to invent.

ideario *m* ideology.

ídem *pron* ditto.

idéntico, -ca *adj*: **~ (a)** identical (to).

identidad *f* (*gen*) identity.

identificación *f* identification.

identificar *vt* to identify. ► **identificarse** *vpr*: **~se (con)** to identify (with).

ideología *f* ideology.

idílico, -ca *adj* idyllic.

idilio *m* love affair.

idioma *m* language.

idiosincrasia *f* individual character.

idiota ◆ *adj despec* (*tonto*) stupid. ◆ *m y f* idiot.

idiotez *f* (*tontería*) stupid thing, stupidity (U).

ido, ida *adj* mad, touched.

idolatrar *vt* to worship; *fig* to idolize.

ídolo *m* idol.

idóneo, -a *adj*: **~ (para)** suitable (for).

iglesia *f* church.

iglú (*pl* **iglúes**) *m* igloo.

ignorancia *f* ignorance.

ignorante ◆ *adj* ignorant. ◆ *m y f* ignoramus.

ignorar *vt* **1.** (*desconocer*) not to know, to be ignorant of. **2.** (*no tener en cuenta*) to ignore.

igual ◆ *adj* **1.** (*idéntico*): **~ (que)** the same (as); **llevan jerseys ~es** they're wearing the same jumper; **son ~es** they're the same. **2.** (*parecido*): **~ (que)**

similar (to). **3.** (*equivalente*): ~ **(a)** equal (to). **4.** (*liso*) even. **5.** (*constante - velocidad*) constant; (*- clima, temperatura*) even. **6.** (MAT): **A más B es ~ a C** A plus B equals C. ◆ *m y f* equal; **sin ~** without equal, unrivalled. ◆ *adv* **1.** (*de la misma manera*) the same; **yo pienso ~** I think the same, I think so too; **al ~ que** just like; **por ~** equally. **2.** (*posiblemente*) perhaps; **~ llueve** it could well rain. **3.** (DEP): **van ~es** the scores are level. **4.** *loc*: **dar** o **ser ~ a alguien** to be all the same to sb; **es** o **da ~** it doesn't matter, it doesn't make any difference.

igualado, -da *adj* level.

igualar *vt* **1.** (*gen*) to make equal; (DEP) to equalize; **~ algo a** o **con** to equate sthg with. **2.** (*persona*) to be equal to; **nadie le iguala en generosidad** nobody is as generous as he is. **3.** (*terreno*) to level; (*superficie*) to smooth. ▶ **igualarse** *vpr* **1.** (*gen*) to be equal. **2.** (*a otra persona*): **~se a** o **con alguien** to treat sb as an equal.

igualdad *f* **1.** (*equivalencia*) equality; **en ~ de condiciones** on equal terms; **~ de oportunidades** equal opportunities (*pl*). **2.** (*identidad*) sameness.

igualitario, -ria *adj* egalitarian.

igualmente *adv* **1.** (*también*) also, likewise. **2.** (*fórmula de cortesía*) the same to you, likewise.

iguana *f* iguana.

ikurriña *f* Basque national flag.

ilegal *adj* illegal.

ilegible *adj* illegible.

ilegítimo, -ma *adj* illegitimate.

ileso, -sa *adj* unhurt, unharmed; **salir** o **resultar ~** to escape unharmed.

ilícito, -ta *adj* illicit.

ilimitado, -da *adj* unlimited, limitless.

iluminación *f* **1.** (*gen*) lighting; (*acción*) illumination. **2.** (RELIG) enlightenment.

iluminar *vt* (*gen*) to illuminate, to light up. ▶ **iluminarse** *vpr* to light up.

ilusión *f* **1.** (*esperanza - gen*) hope; (*- infundada*) delusion, illusion; **hacerse** o **forjarse ilusiones** to build up one's hopes. **2.** (*emoción*) thrill, excitement (U); **¡qué ~!** how exciting!; **me hace mucha ~** I'm really looking forward to it. **3.** (*espejismo*) illusion.

ilusionar *vt* **1.** (*esperanzar*): **~ a alguien (con algo)** to build up sb's hopes (about sthg). **2.** (*emocionar*) to excite, to thrill. ▶ **ilusionarse** *vpr* (*emocionarse*): **~se (con)** to get excited (about).

ilusionista *m y f* conjurer.

iluso, -sa *adj* gullible.

ilusorio, -ria *adj* illusory; (*promesa*) empty.

ilustración *f* **1.** (*estampa*) illustration. **2.** (*cultura*) learning. ▶ **Ilustración** *f* (HIST): **la Ilustración** the Enlightenment.

ilustrado, -da *adj* **1.** (*publicación*) illustrated. **2.** (*persona*) learned. **3.** (HIST) enlightened.

ilustrar *vt* **1.** (*explicar*) to illustrate, to explain. **2.** (*publicación*) to illustrate.

ilustre *adj* (*gen*) illustrious, distinguished.

imagen *f* (*gen*) image; (TV) picture; **ser la viva ~ de alguien** to be the spitting image of sb.

imaginación *f* **1.** (*facultad*) imagination; **pasar por la ~ de alguien** to occur to sb, to cross sb's mind. **2.** (*gen pl*) (*idea falsa*) delusion.

imaginar *vt* **1.** (*gen*) to imagine. **2.** (*idear*) to think up, to invent. ▶ **imaginarse** *vpr* to imagine; **¡imagínate!** just think o imagine!; **me imagino que sí** I suppose so.

imaginario, -ria *adj* imaginary.

imaginativo, -va *adj* imaginative.

imán *m* (*para atraer*) magnet.

imbécil ◆ *adj* stupid. ◆ *m y f* idiot.

imbecilidad *f* stupidity; **decir/hacer una ~** to say/do sthg stupid.

imborrable *adj fig* indelible; (*recuerdo*) unforgettable.

imbuir *vt*: **~ (de)** to imbue (with).

imitación *f* imitation; (*de humorista*) impersonation; **a ~ de** in imitation of; **piel de ~** imitation leather.

imitador, -ra *m y f* imitator; (*humorista*) impersonator.

imitar *vt* (*gen*) to imitate, to copy; (*a personajes famosos*) to impersonate; (*producto, material*) to simulate.

impaciencia *f* impatience.

impacientar *vt* to make impatient. ▶ **impacientarse** *vpr* to grow impatient.

impaciente *adj* impatient; **~ por hacer algo** impatient o anxious to do sthg.

impactar ◆ *vt* (*suj: noticia*) to have an impact on. ◆ *vi* (*bala*) to hit.

impacto *m* **1.** (*gen*) impact; (*de bala*) hit. **2.** (*señal*) (impact) mark; **~s de bala** bullethole.

impagado, -da *adj* unpaid.

impar *adj* (MAT) odd.

imparable *adj* unstoppable.

imparcial *adj* impartial.

impartir vt to give.

impase, impasse [im'pas] m impasse.

impasible adj impassive.

impávido, -da adj (valeroso) fearless, courageous; (impasible) impassive.

impecable adj impeccable, faultless.

impedido, -da adj disabled; **estar ~ de un brazo** to have the use of only one arm.

impedimento m (gen) obstacle; (contra un matrimonio) impediment.

impedir vt 1. (imposibilitar) to prevent; **~ a alguien hacer algo** to prevent sb from doing sth. 2. (dificultar) to hinder, to obstruct.

impenetrable adj lit & fig impenetrable.

impensable adj unthinkable.

imperante adj prevailing.

imperar vi to prevail.

imperativo, -va adj 1. (gen & GRAM) imperative. 2. (autoritario) imperious. ► **imperativo** m (gen & GRAM) imperative.

imperceptible adj imperceptible.

imperdible m safety pin.

imperdonable adj unforgivable.

imperfección f 1. (cualidad) imperfection. 2. (defecto) flaw, defect.

imperfecto, -ta adj (gen) imperfect; (defectuoso) faulty, defective. ► **imperfecto** m (GRAM) imperfect.

imperial adj imperial.

imperialismo m imperialism.

impericia f lack of skill; (inexperiencia) inexperience.

imperio m 1. (territorio) empire. 2. (dominio) rule.

imperioso, -sa adj 1. (autoritario) imperious. 2. (apremiante) urgent.

impermeable ◆ adj waterproof. ◆ m raincoat, mac Br.

impersonal adj impersonal.

impertinencia f 1. (gen) impertinence. 2. (comentario) impertinent remark.

impertinente adj impertinent.

imperturbable adj imperturbable.

ímpetu m 1. (brusquedad) force. 2. (energía) energy. 3. (FÍS) impetus.

impetuoso, -sa adj 1. (olas, viento, ataque) violent. 2. fig (persona) impulsive, impetuous.

impío, -a adj godless, impious.

implacable adj implacable, relentless.

implantar vt 1. (establecer) to intro-

duce. 2. (MED) to insert. ► **implantarse** vpr (establecerse) to be introduced.

implicación f 1. (participación) involvement. 2. (gen pl) (consecuencia) implication.

implicar vt 1. (involucrar): **~ (en)** to involve (in); (DER) to implicate (in). 2. (significar) to mean. ► **implicarse** vpr (DER) to incriminate o.s.; **~se en** to become involved in.

implícito, -ta adj implicit.

implorar vt to implore.

imponente adj 1. (impresionante) imposing, impressive. 2. (estupendo) sensational, terrific.

imponer ◆ vt 1. **~ algo (a alguien)** (gen) to impose sth (on sb); (respeto) to command sth (from sb). 2. (moda) to set; (costumbre) to introduce. ◆ vi to be imposing. ► **imponerse** vpr 1. (hacerse respetar) to command respect, to show authority. 2. (prevalecer) to prevail. 3. (ser necesario) to be necessary. 4. (DEP) to win, to prevail.

impopular adj unpopular.

importación f (acción) importing; (artículo) import.

importador, -ra m y f importer.

importancia f importance; **dar ~ a algo** to attach importance to sth; **quitar ~ a algo** to play sth down; **darse ~** to give o.s. airs, to show off.

importante adj 1. (gen) important; (lesión) serious. 2. (cantidad) considerable.

importar ◆ vt 1. (gen & INFORM) to import. 2. (suj: factura, coste) to amount to, to come to. ◆ vi 1. (preocupar) to matter; **no me importa** I don't care, it doesn't matter to me; **¿y a ti qué te importa?** what's it got to do with you? 2. (en preguntas) to mind; **¿le importa que me siente?** do you mind if I sit down?; **¿te importaría acompañarme?** would you mind coming with me? ◆ v impers to matter; **no importa** it doesn't matter.

importe m (gen) price, cost; (de factura) total.

importunar vt to bother, to pester.

importuno, -na = **inoportuno**.

imposibilidad f impossibility; **su ~ para contestar la pregunta** his inability to answer the question.

imposibilitado, -da adj disabled; **estar ~ para hacer algo** to be unable to do sth.

imposibilitar vt: **~ a alguien para hacer algo** to make it impossible for sb to do sthg, to prevent sb from doing sthg.

imposible adj 1. (irrealizable) impossible. 2. (insoportable) unbearable, impossible.

imposición f 1. (obligación) imposition. 2. (impuesto) tax. 3. (BANCA) deposit.

impostor, -ra m y f (suplantador) impostor.

impotencia f impotence.

impotente adj impotent.

impracticable adj 1. (irrealizable) impracticable. 2. (intransitable) impassable.

imprecisión f imprecision, vagueness (U).

impreciso, -sa adj imprecise, vague.

impredecible adj unforeseeable; (variable) unpredictable.

impregnar vt: ~ (de) to impregnate (with). ▶ **impregnarse** vpr: ~se (de) to become impregnated (with).

imprenta f 1. (arte) printing. 2. (máquina) (printing) press. 3. (establecimiento) printing house.

imprescindible adj indispensable, essential.

impresentable adj unpresentable.

impresión f 1. (gen) impression; (sensación física) feeling; **causar (una) buena/mala ~** to make a good/bad impression; **dar la ~ de** to give the impression of; **tener la ~ de que** to have the impression that. 2. (huella) imprint; ~ **digital** o **dactilar** fingerprint. 3. (IMPRENTA - acción) printing; (- edición) edition.

impresionable adj impressionable.

impresionante adj impressive; (error) enormous.

impresionar ◆ vt 1. (maravillar) to impress. 2. (conmocionar) to move. 3. (horrorizar) to shock. 4. (FOT) to expose. ◆ vi (maravillar) to make an impression. ▶ **impresionarse** vpr 1. (maravillarse) to be impressed. 2. (conmocionarse) to be moved. 3. (horrorizarse) to be shocked.

impreso, -sa ◆ pp → **imprimir**. ◆ adj printed. ▶ **impreso** m 1. (texto) printed matter (U). 2. (formulario) form.

impresor, -ra m y f (persona) printer. ▶ **impresora** f (INFORM) printer; **impresora láser/térmica** laser/thermal printer; **impresora de matriz** o **de agujas** dot-matrix printer; **impresora de chorro de tinta** ink-jet printer.

imprevisible adj unforeseeable; (variable) unpredictable.

imprevisto, -ta adj unexpected. ▶ **imprevisto** m (hecho): **salvo ~s** barring accidents.

imprimir vt 1. (gen) to print; (huella, paso) to leave. 2. fig (transmitir): ~ **algo a** to impart o bring sthg to.

improbable adj improbable, unlikely.

improcedente adj 1. (inoportuno) inappropriate. 2. (DER) inadmissible.

improperio m insult.

impropio, -pia adj: ~ **(de)** improper (for), unbecoming (to).

improvisado, -da adj (gen) improvised; (discurso, truco) impromptu; (comentario) ad-lib; (cama etc) makeshift.

improvisar ◆ vt (gen) to improvise; (comida) to rustle up; ~ **una cama** to make (up) a makeshift bed. ◆ vi (gen) to improvise; (MÚS) to extemporize.

improviso ▶ **de improviso** loc adv unexpectedly, suddenly; **coger a alguien de** ~ to catch sb unawares.

imprudencia f (en los actos) carelessness (U); (en los comentarios) indiscretion.

imprudente adj (en los actos) careless, rash; (en los comentarios) indiscreet.

impúdico, -ca adj immodest, indecent.

impuesto, -ta pp → **imponer**. ▶ **impuesto** m tax; ~ **sobre el valor añadido** value-added tax; ~ **sobre la renta** ≃ income tax.

impugnar vt to contest, to challenge.

impulsar vt 1. (empujar) to propel, to drive. 2. (incitar): ~ **a alguien (a algo/a hacer algo)** to drive sb (to sthg/to do sthg). 3. (promocionar) to stimulate.

impulsivo, -va adj impulsive.

impulso m 1. (progreso) stimulus, boost. 2. (fuerza) momentum. 3. (motivación) impulse, urge.

impulsor, -ra m y f dynamic force.

impune adj unpunished.

impunidad f impunity.

impuntual adj unpunctual.

impureza f (gen pl) impurity.

impuro, -ra adj lit & fig impure.

imputación f accusation.

imputar vt (atribuir): ~ **algo a alguien** (delito) to accuse sb of sthg; (fracaso, error) to attribute sthg to sb.

in → **fraganti**, **vitro**.

inabarcable adj unmanageable.

inacabable adj interminable, endless.

inaccesible adj inaccessible.

inaceptable *adj* unacceptable.

inactividad *f* inactivity.

inactivo, -va *adj* inactive.

inadaptado, -da *adj* maladjusted.

inadecuado, -da *adj* (*inapropiado*) unsuitable, inappropriate.

inadmisible *adj* inadmissible.

inadvertido, -da *adj* unnoticed; **pasar ~** to go unnoticed.

inagotable *adj* inexhaustible.

inaguantable *adj* unbearable.

inalámbrico, -ca *adj* cordless.

inalcanzable *adj* unattainable.

inalterable *adj* 1. (*gen*) unalterable; (*salud*) stable; (*amistad*) undying. 2. (*color*) fast. 3. (*rostro, carácter*) impassive. 4. (*resultado, marcador*) unchanged.

inamovible *adj* immovable, fixed.

inanición *f* starvation.

inanimado, -da *adj* inanimate.

inánime *adj* lifeless.

inapreciable *adj* 1. (*incalculable*) invaluable. 2. (*insignificante*) imperceptible.

inapropiado, -da *adj* inappropriate.

inaudito, -ta *adj* unheard-of.

inauguración *f* inauguration, opening.

inaugurar *vt* to inaugurate, to open.

inca *adj, m y f* Inca.

incalculable *adj* incalculable.

incalificable *adj* unspeakable.

incandescente *adj* incandescent.

incansable *adj* untiring, tireless.

incapacidad *f* 1. (*imposibilidad*) inability. 2. (*inaptitud*) incompetence. 3. (DER) incapacity.

incapacitado, -da *adj* (DER - *gen*) disqualified; (- *para testar*) incapacitated; (- *para trabajar*) unfit.

incapacitar *vt*: **~ (para)** (*gen*) to disqualify (from); (*para trabajar etc*) to render unfit (for).

incapaz *adj* 1. (*gen*): **~ de** incapable of. 2. (*sin talento*): **~ para** incompetent at, no good at. 3. (DER) incompetent.

incautación *f* seizure, confiscation.

incautarse ▶ incautarse de *vpr* (DER) to seize, to confiscate.

incauto, -ta *adj* gullible.

incendiar *vt* to set fire to. ▶ **incendiarse** *vpr* to catch fire.

incendiario, -ria ◆ *adj* 1. (*bomba etc*) incendiary. 2. *fig* (*artículo, libro etc*) inflammatory. ◆ *m y f* arsonist.

incendio *m* fire; **~ provocado** arson.

incentivo *m* incentive.

incertidumbre *f* uncertainty.

incesto *m* incest.

incidencia *f* 1. (*repercusión*) impact, effect. 2. (*suceso*) event.

incidente *m* incident.

incidir ▶ incidir en *vi* 1. (*incurrir en*) to fall into, to lapse into. 2. (*insistir en*) to focus on. 3. (*influir en*) to have an impact on, to affect.

incienso *m* incense.

incierto, -ta *adj* 1. (*dudoso*) uncertain. 2. (*falso*) untrue.

incineración *f* (*de cadáver*) cremation; (*de basura*) incineration.

incinerar *vt* (*cadáver*) to cremate; (*basura*) to incinerate.

incipiente *adj* incipient; (*estado, etapa*) early.

incisión *f* incision.

incisivo, -va *adj* 1. (*instrumento*) sharp, cutting. 2. *fig* (*mordaz*) incisive.

inciso, -sa *adj* cut. ▶ **inciso** *m* passing remark.

incitante *adj* (*instigador*) inciting; (*provocativo*) provocative.

incitar *vt*: **~ a alguien a algo** (*violencia, rebelión etc*) to incite sb to sthg; **~ a alguien a la fuga/venganza** to urge sb to flee/avenge himself; **~ a alguien a hacer algo** (*rebelarse etc*) to incite sb to do sthg; (*fugarse, vengarse*) to urge sb to do sthg.

inclemencia *f* harshness, inclemency.

inclinación *f* 1. (*desviación*) slant, inclination; (*de terreno*) slope. 2. *fig* (*afición*): **~ (a o por)** penchant o propensity (for). 3. (*cariño*): **~ hacia alguien** fondness towards sb. 4. (*saludo*) bow.

inclinar *vt* 1. (*doblar*) to bend; (*ladear*) to tilt. 2. (*cabeza*) to bow. ▶ **inclinarse** *vpr* 1. (*doblarse*) to lean. 2. (*para saludar*): **~se (ante)** to bow (before). ▶ **inclinarse a** *vi* (*tender a*) to be o feel inclined to. ▶ **inclinarse por** *vi* (*preferir*) to favour, to lean towards.

incluir *vt* (*gen*) to include; (*adjuntar - en cartas*) to enclose.

inclusive *adv* inclusive.

incluso, -sa *adj* enclosed. ▶ **incluso** *adv & prep even*.

incógnito, -ta *adj* unknown. ▶ **incógnita** *f* 1. (MAT) unknown quantity. 2. (*misterio*) mystery. ▶ **de incógnito** *loc adv* incognito.

incoherencia *f* 1. (*cualidad*) incoherence. 2. (*comentario*) nonsensical remark.

incoherente *adj* 1. (*inconexo*) incoherent. 2. (*inconsecuente*) inconsistent.

incoloro, -ra adj lit & fig colourless.

incomodar vt 1. (causar molestia) to bother, to inconvenience. 2. (enfadar) to annoy. ▶ **incomodarse** vpr (enfadarse): **~se (por)** to get annoyed (about).

incomodidad f 1. (de silla etc) uncomfortableness. 2. (de situación, persona) awkwardness.

incómodo, -da adj 1. (silla etc) uncomfortable. 2. (situación, persona) awkward, uncomfortable.

incomparable adj incomparable.

incompatible adj: **~ (con)** incompatible (with).

incompetencia f incompetence.

incompetente adj incompetent.

incompleto, -ta adj 1. (gen) incomplete. 2. (inacabado) unfinished.

incomprendido, -da adj misunderstood.

incomprensible adj incomprehensible.

incomprensión f lack of understanding.

incomprensivo, -va adj unsympathetic.

incomunicado, -da adj 1. (gen) isolated. 2. (por la nieve etc) cut off. 3. (preso) in solitary confinement.

inconcebible adj inconceivable.

inconcluso, -sa adj unfinished.

incondicional ◆ adj unconditional; (ayuda) wholehearted; (seguidor) staunch. ◆ m y f staunch supporter.

inconexo, -xa adj (gen) unconnected; (pensamiento, texto) disjointed.

inconformista adj, m y f nonconformist.

inconfundible adj unmistakable; (prueba) irrefutable.

incongruente adj incongruous.

inconsciencia f 1. (gen) unconsciousness. 2. fig (falta de juicio) thoughtlessness.

inconsciente adj 1. (gen) unconscious. 2. fig (irreflexivo) thoughtless.

inconsecuente adj inconsistent.

inconsistente adj (tela, pared etc) flimsy; (salsa) runny; (argumento, discurso etc) lacking in substance.

inconstancia f 1. (en el trabajo, la conducta) unreliability; (en las relaciones) fickleness. 2. (de opinión, ideas) changeability.

inconstante adj 1. (en el trabajo, la conducta) unreliable; (en las relaciones) fickle. 2. (de opinión, ideas) changeable.

inconstitucional adj unconstitutional.

incontable adj (innumerable) countless.

incontestable adj indisputable.

incontinencia f (MED) incontinence.

incontrolable adj uncontrollable.

inconveniencia f 1. (inoportunidad) inappropriateness. 2. (comentario) tactless remark; (acto) mistake.

inconveniente ◆ adj 1. (inoportuno) inappropriate. 2. (descortés) rude. ◆ m 1. (dificultad) obstacle, problem. 2. (desventaja) drawback.

incordiar vt fam to bother, to pester.

incorporación f: **~ (a)** (gen) incorporation (into); (a un puesto) induction (into).

incorporar vt 1. (añadir): **~ (a)** (gen) to incorporate (into); (CULIN) to mix (into). 2. (levantar) to sit up. ▶ **incorporarse** vpr 1. (empezar): **~se (a)** (equipo) to join; (trabajo) to start. 2. (levantarse) to sit up.

incorrección f 1. (inexactitud) incorrectness; (error gramatical) mistake. 2. (descortesía) lack of courtesy, rudeness (U).

incorrecto, -ta adj 1. (equivocado) incorrect, wrong. 2. (descortés) rude, impolite.

incorregible adj incorrigible.

incredulidad f incredulity.

incrédulo, -la adj sceptical, incredulous; (RELIG) unbelieving.

increíble adj 1. (difícil de creer) unconvincing. 2. fig (extraordinario) incredible. 3. fig (inconcebible) unbelievable.

incrementar vt to increase. ▶ **incrementarse** vpr to increase.

incremento m increase; (de temperatura) rise.

increpar vt 1. (reprender) to reprimand. 2. (insultar) to abuse, insult.

incriminar vt to accuse.

incruento, -ta adj bloodless.

incrustar vt 1. (TECN) to inlay; (en joyería) to set. 2. fam fig (empotrar): **~ algo en algo** to sink sthg into sthg. ▶ **incrustarse** vpr (cal etc) to become encrusted.

incubar vt 1. (huevo) to incubate. 2. (enfermedad) to be sickening for.

inculcar vt: **~ algo a alguien** to instil sthg into sb.

inculpar vt: **~ a alguien (de)** (gen) to accuse sb (of); (DER) to charge sb (with).

inculto, -ta ◆ adj (persona) uneducated. ◆ m y f ignoramus.

incumbencia f: **es/no es de nuestra ~**

it is/isn't a matter for us, it falls/doesn't fall within our area of responsibility.

incumbir ► **incumbir a** *vi*: ~ **a alguien** to be a matter for sb; **esto no te incumbe** this is none of your business.

incumplimiento *m* (*de deber*) failure to fulfil; (*de orden, ley*) non-compliance; (*de promesa*) failure to keep; ~ **de contrato** breach of contract.

incumplir *vt* (*deber*) to fail to fulfil, to neglect; (*orden, ley*) to fail to comply with; (*promesa*) to break; (*contrato*) to breach.

incurable *adj* incurable.

incurrir ► **incurrir en** *vi* **1.** (*delito, falta*) to commit; (*error*) to make. **2.** (*desprecio etc*) to incur.

incursión *f* incursion.

indagación *f* investigation, inquiry.

indagar ◆ *vt* to investigate, to inquire into. ◆ *vi* to investigate, to inquire.

indecencia *f* **1.** (*cualidad*) indecency. **2.** (*acción*) outrage, crime.

indecente *adj* **1.** (*impúdico*) indecent. **2.** (*indigno*) miserable, wretched.

indecible *adj* (*alegría*) indescribable; (*dolor*) unspeakable.

indecisión *f* indecisiveness.

indeciso, -sa *adj* **1.** (*persona - inseguro*) indecisive; (*- que está dudoso*) undecided. **2.** (*pregunta, respuesta*) hesitant; (*resultado*) undecided.

indefenso, -sa *adj* defenceless.

indefinido, -da *adj* **1.** (*ilimitado*) indefinite; (*contrato*) open-ended. **2.** (*impreciso*) vague. **3.** (GRAM) indefinite.

indeleble *adj* culto indelible.

indemne *adj* unhurt, unharmed.

indemnización *f* (*gen*) compensation, indemnity; (*por despido*) severance pay.

indemnizar *vt*: ~ **a alguien (por)** to compensate sb (for).

independencia *f* independence; **con** ~ **de** independently of.

independiente *adj* **1.** (*gen*) independent. **2.** (*aparte*) separate.

independizar *vt* to grant independence to. ► **independizarse** *vpr*: ~**se (de)** to become independent (of).

indeseable *adj* undesirable.

indeterminación *f* indecisiveness.

indeterminado, -da *adj* **1.** (*sin determinar*) indeterminate; **por tiempo** ~ indefinitely. **2.** (*impreciso*) vague.

indexar *vt* (INFORM) to index.

India: **(la)** ~ India.

indiano, -na *m y f* **1.** (*indígena*) (Latin American) Indian. **2.** (*emigrante*) Spanish emigrant to Latin America who returned to Spain having made his fortune.

indicación *f* **1.** (*señal, gesto*) sign, signal. **2.** (*gen pl*) (*instrucción*) instruction; (*para llegar a un sitio*) directions (*pl*). **3.** (*nota, corrección*) note.

indicado, -da *adj* suitable, appropriate.

indicador, -ra *adj* indicating (*antes de sust*). ► **indicador** *m* (*gen*) indicator; (TECN) gauge, meter.

indicar *vt* (*señalar*) to indicate; (*suj: aguja etc*) to read.

indicativo, -va *adj* indicative. ► **indicativo** *m* **1.** (GRAM) indicative. **2.** (*de número de teléfono*) dialling code.

índice *m* **1.** (*gen*) index; (*proporción*) level, rate; ~ **de natalidad** birth rate; ~ **de precios al consumo** retail price index. **2.** (*señal*) sign, indicator. **3.** (*catálogo*) catalogue. **4.** (*dedo*) index finger.

indicio *m* sign; (*pista*) clue; (*cantidad pequeña*) trace.

índico *m*: **el (océano)** ~ the Indian Ocean.

indiferencia *f* indifference.

indiferente *adj* indifferent; **me es** ~ (*me da igual*) I don't mind, it's all the same to me; (*no me interesa*) I'm not interested in it.

indígena ◆ *adj* indigenous, native. ◆ *m y f* native.

indigencia *f* culto destitution.

indigente *adj* destitute.

indigestarse *vpr* to get indigestion.

indigestión *f* indigestion.

indigesto, -ta *adj* indigestible; *fam fig* (*pesado*) stodgy, heavy.

indignación *f* indignation.

indignar *vt* to anger. ► **indignarse** *vpr*: ~**se (por)** to get angry o indignant (about).

indigno, -na *adj* **1.** (*gen*): ~ **(de)** unworthy (of). **2.** (*impropio*) not fitting, wrong. **3.** (*vergonzoso*) contemptible.

indio, -dia ◆ *adj* Indian. ◆ *m y f* Indian; **hacer el** ~ to play the fool.

indirecto, -ta *adj* indirect. ► **indirecta** *f* hint; **lanzar una indirecta a alguien** to drop a hint to sb.

indisciplina *f* indiscipline.

indiscreción *f* **1.** (*cualidad*) indiscretion. **2.** (*comentario*) indiscreet remark.

indiscreto, -ta *adj* indiscreet.

indiscriminado, -da *adj* indiscriminate.

indiscutible *adj* (*gen*) indisputable; (*poder*) undisputed.

indispensable *adj* indispensable.

indisponer *vt* 1. (*enfermar*) to make ill, to upset. 2. (*enemistar*) to set at odds.

indisposición *f* (*malestar*) indisposition.

indispuesto, -ta ♦ *pp* → **indisponer**. ♦ *adj* indisposed, unwell.

indistinto, -ta *adj* 1. (*indiferente*): **es ~** it doesn't matter, it makes no difference. 2. (*cuenta, cartilla*) joint. 3. (*perfil, figura*) indistinct, blurred.

individual *adj* 1. (*gen*) individual; (*habitación, cama*) single; (*despacho*) personal. 2. (*prueba, competición*) singles (*antes de sust*). ▶ **individuales** *mpl* (DEP) singles.

individualizar *vi* to single people out.

individuo, -dua *m y f* person; *despec* individual.

indocumentado, -da *adj* 1. (*sin documentación*) without identity papers. 2. (*ignorante*) ignorant.

índole *f* (*naturaleza*) nature; (*tipo*) type, kind.

indolencia *f* indolence, laziness.

indoloro, -ra *adj* painless.

indómito, -ta *adj* 1. (*animal*) untameable. 2. (*carácter*) rebellious; (*pueblo*) unruly.

Indonesia Indonesia.

inducir *vt* (*incitar*): **~ a alguien a algo/a hacer algo** to lead sb into sthg/into doing sthg; **~ a error** to mislead.

inductor, -ra *adj* instigating.

indudable *adj* undoubted; **es ~ que ...** there is no doubt that ...

indulgencia *f* indulgence.

indultar *vt* to pardon.

indulto *m* pardon.

indumentaria *f* attire.

industria *f* (*gen*) industry.

industrial ♦ *adj* industrial. ♦ *m y f* industrialist.

industrializar *vt* to industrialize.

inédito, -ta *adj* 1. (*no publicado*) unpublished. 2. (*sorprendente*) unprecedented.

INEF (*abrev de* **Instituto Nacional de Educación Física**) *m Spanish university for training physical education teachers.*

inefable *adj* ineffable, inexpressible.

ineficaz *adj* 1. (*de bajo rendimiento*) inefficient. 2. (*de baja efectividad*) ineffective.

ineficiente *adj* 1. (*de bajo rendimiento*) inefficient. 2. (*de baja efectividad*) ineffective.

ineludible *adj* unavoidable.

INEM (*abrev de* **Instituto Nacional de Empleo**) *m Spanish department of employment.*

inenarrable *adj* spectacular.

ineptitud *f* ineptitude.

inepto, -ta *adj* inept.

inequívoco, -ca *adj* (*apoyo, resultado*) unequivocal; (*señal, voz*) unmistakeable.

inercia *f* lit & fig inertia.

inerme *adj* (*sin armas*) unarmed; (*sin defensa*) defenceless.

inerte *adj* 1. (*materia*) inert. 2. (*cuerpo, cadáver*) lifeless.

inesperado, -da *adj* unexpected.

inestable *adj* lit & fig unstable.

inevitable *adj* inevitable.

inexacto, -ta *adj* 1. (*impreciso*) inaccurate. 2. (*erróneo*) incorrect, wrong.

inexistente *adj* nonexistent.

inexperiencia *f* inexperience.

inexperto, -ta *adj* 1. (*falto de experiencia*) inexperienced. 2. (*falto de habilidad*) unskilful.

inexpresivo, -va *adj* expressionless.

infalible *adj* infallible.

infame *adj* vile, base.

infamia *f* (*deshonra*) infamy, disgrace.

infancia *f* (*periodo*) childhood; **primera ~** infancy.

infante, -ta *m y f* 1. (*niño*) infant. 2. (*hijo del rey*) infante (*f* infanta), prince (*f* princess).

infantería *f* infantry.

infantil *adj* 1. (*para niños*) children's; (*de niños*) child (*antes de sust*). 2. fig (*inmaduro*) infantile, childish.

infarto *m*: **~ (de miocardio)** heart attack.

infatigable *adj* indefatigable, tireless.

infección *f* infection.

infeccioso, -sa *adj* infectious.

infectar *vt* to infect. ▶ **infectarse** *vpr* to become infected.

infecundo, -da *adj* (*tierra*) infertile.

infeliz *adj* 1. (*desgraciado*) unhappy. 2. fig (*ingenuo*) gullible.

inferior ♦ *adj*: **~ (a)** (*en espacio, cantidad*) lower (than); (*en calidad*) inferior (to); **una cifra ~ a 100** a figure under o below 100. ♦ *m y f* inferior.

inferioridad *f* inferiority.

inferir *vt* 1. (*deducir*): **~ (de)** to deduce (from), to infer (from). 2. (*ocasionar - herida*) to inflict; (*- mal*) to cause.

infernal adj lit & fig infernal.
infestar vt to infest; (suj: carteles, propaganda etc) to be plastered across.
infidelidad f (conyugal) infidelity; (a la patria, un amigo) disloyalty.
infiel ◆ adj 1. (desleal - cónyuge) unfaithful; (- amigo) disloyal. 2. (inexacto) inaccurate, unfaithful. ◆ m y f (RELIG) infidel.
infiernillo m portable stove.
infierno m lit & fig hell; ¡vete al ~! go to hell!
infiltrado, -da m y f infiltrator.
infiltrar vt (inyectar) to inject. ► **infiltrarse en** vpr to infiltrate.
ínfimo, -ma adj (calidad, categoría) extremely low; (precio) giveaway; (importancia) minimal.
infinidad f: una ~ de an infinite number of; fig masses of; **en ~ de ocasiones** on countless occasions.
infinitivo m infinitive.
infinito, -ta adj lit & fig infinite. ► **infinito** m infinity.
inflación f (ECON) inflation.
inflamable adj inflammable.
inflamación f (MED) inflammation.
inflamar vt (MED & fig) to inflame. ► **inflamarse** vpr (hincharse) to become inflamed.
inflamatorio, -ria adj inflammatory.
inflar vt 1. (soplando) to blow up, to inflate; (con bomba) to pump up. 2. fig (exagerar) to blow up, to exaggerate. ► **inflarse** vpr: ~se (de) (hartarse) to stuff o.s. (with).
inflexible adj lit & fig inflexible.
inflexión f inflection.
infligir vt to inflict; (castigo) to impose.
influencia f influence.
influenciar vt to influence.
influir ◆ vt to influence. ◆ vi to have influence; ~ en to influence.
influjo m influence.
influyente adj influential.
información f 1. (conocimiento) information. 2. (PRENS - noticias) news (U); (- noticia) report, piece of news; (- sección) section, news (U); ~ **meteorológica** weather report o forecast. 3. (oficina) information office; (mostrador) information desk. 4. (TELECOM) directory enquiries (pl) Br, directory assistance Am.
informal adj 1. (desenfadado) informal. 2. (irresponsable) unreliable.
informante m y f informant.
informar ◆ vt: ~ a alguien (de) to

inform o tell sb (about). ◆ vi to inform; (PRENS) to report. ► **informarse** vpr to find out (details); ~se de to find out about.
informático, -ca ◆ adj computer (antes de sust). ◆ m y f (persona) computer expert. ► **informática** f (ciencia) information technology, computing.
informativo, -va adj 1. (instructivo, esclarecedor) informative. 2. (que da noticias) news (antes de sust); (que da información) information (antes de sust). ► **informativo** m news (bulletin).
informatizar vt to computerize.
informe ◆ adj shapeless. ◆ m 1. (gen) report. 2. (DER) plea. ► **informes** mpl (gen) information (U); (sobre comportamiento) report (sg); (para un empleo) references.
infortunio m misfortune, bad luck (U).
infracción f infringement; (de circulación) offence.
infraestructura f (de organización) infrastructure.
infrahumano, -na adj subhuman.
infranqueable adj impassable; fig insurmountable.
infrarrojo, -ja adj infrared.
infravalorar vt to undervalue, to underestimate.
infringir vt (quebrantar) to infringe, to break.
infundado, -da adj unfounded.
infundir vt: ~ algo a alguien to fill sb with sthg, to inspire sthg in sb; ~ **miedo** to inspire fear.
infusión f infusion; ~ **de manzanilla** camomile tea.
ingeniar vt to invent, to devise. ► **ingeniarse** vpr: **ingeniárselas** to manage, to engineer it; **ingeniárselas para hacer algo** to manage o contrive to do sthg.
ingeniería f engineering.
ingeniero, -ra m y f engineer; ~ **de caminos, canales y puertos** civil engineer.
ingenio m 1. (inteligencia) ingenuity. 2. (agudeza) wit. 3. (máquina) device.
ingenioso, -sa adj (inteligente) ingenious, clever; (agudo) witty.
ingenuidad f ingenuousness, naivety.
ingenuo, -nua adj ingenuous, naive.
ingerencia = **injerencia**.
ingerir vt to consume, to ingest.
Inglaterra England.

ingle f groin.

inglés, -esa ◆ adj English. ◆ m y f (persona) Englishman (f Englishwoman); **los ingleses** the English. ▶ **inglés** m (lengua) English.

ingratitud f ingratitude.

ingrato, -ta adj ungrateful; (trabajo) thankless.

ingrávido, -da adj weightless.

ingrediente m ingredient.

ingresar ◆ vt (BANCA) to deposit, to pay in. ◆ vi: ~ **(en)** (asociación, ejército) to join; (hospital) to be admitted (to); (convento, universidad) to enter; ~ **cadáver** to be dead on arrival.

ingreso m 1. (gen) entry; (en asociación, ejército) joining; (en hospital, universidad) admission. 2. (BANCA) deposit. ▶ **ingresos** mpl 1. (sueldo etc) income (U). 2. (recaudación) revenue (U).

inhabilitar vt to disqualify.

inhabitable adj uninhabitable.

inhabitado, -da adj uninhabited.

inhalador m inhaler.

inhalar vt to inhale.

inherente adj: ~ **(a)** inherent (in).

inhibir vt to inhibit. ▶ **inhibirse de** vpr (gen) to keep out of, to stay away from; (responsabilidades) to shirk.

inhóspito, -ta adj inhospitable.

inhumano, -na adj (despiadado) inhuman; (desconsiderado) inhumane.

INI (abrev de **Instituto Nacional de Industria**) m Spanish governmental organization that promotes industry.

iniciación f 1. (gen) initiation. 2. (de suceso, curso) start, beginning.

inicial adj & f initial.

inicializar vt (INFORM) to initialize.

iniciar vt (gen) to start, to begin; (debate, discusión) to start off.

iniciativa f initiative.

inicio m start, beginning.

inigualable adj unrivalled.

ininteligible adj unintelligible.

ininterrumpido, -da adj uninterrupted.

injerencia, ingerencia f interference, meddling.

injerir vt to introduce, to insert. ▶ **injerirse** vpr (entrometerse): ~**se (en)** to interfere (in), to meddle (in).

injertar vt to graft.

injerto m graft.

injuria f (insulto) insult, abuse (U); (agravio) offence; (DER) slander.

injuriar vt (insultar) to insult, to abuse; (agraviar) to offend; (DER) to slander.

injurioso, -sa adj insulting, abusive; (DER) slanderous.

injusticia f injustice.

injustificado, -da adj unjustified.

injusto, -ta adj unfair, unjust.

inmadurez f immaturity.

inmaduro, -ra adj (persona) immature.

inmediaciones fpl (de localidad) surrounding area (sg); (de lugar, casa) vicinity (sg).

inmediatamente adv immediately.

inmediato, -ta adj 1. (gen) immediate; **de** ~ immediately. 2. (contiguo) next, adjoining.

inmejorable adj unbeatable.

inmensidad f (grandeza) immensity.

inmenso, -sa adj (gen) immense.

inmersión f immersion; (de submarinista) dive.

inmerso, -sa adj: ~ **(en)** immersed (in).

inmigración f immigration.

inmigrante m y f immigrant.

inmigrar vi to immigrate.

inminente adj imminent, impending.

inmiscuirse vpr: ~ **(en)** to interfere o meddle (in).

inmobiliario, -ria adj property (antes de sust), real estate Am (antes de sust). ▶ **inmobiliaria** f (agencia) estate agency Br, real estate agent Am.

inmoral adj immoral.

inmortal adj immortal.

inmortalizar vt to immortalize.

inmóvil adj motionless, still; (coche, tren) stationary.

inmovilizar vt to immobilize.

inmueble ◆ adj: **bienes** ~**s** real estate (U). ◆ m (edificio) building.

inmundicia f (suciedad) filth, filthiness; (basura) rubbish.

inmundo, -da adj filthy, dirty.

inmune adj (MED) immune.

inmunidad f immunity.

inmunizar vt to immunize.

inmutar vt to upset, to perturb. ▶ **inmutarse** vpr to get upset, to be perturbed; **ni se inmutó** he didn't bat an eyelid.

innato, -ta adj innate.

innecesario, -ria adj unnecessary.

innoble adj ignoble.

innovación f innovation.

innovador, -ra ◆ adj innovative. ◆ m y f innovator.

innovar vt (método, técnica) to improve on.

innumerable *adj* countless, innumerable.

inocencia *f* innocence.

inocentada *f* practical joke, trick.

inocente *adj* 1. (*gen*) innocent. 2. (*ingenuo - persona*) naive, innocent. 3. (*sin maldad - persona*) harmless.

inodoro, -ra *adj* odourless. ▶ **inodoro** *m* toilet Br, washroom Am.

inofensivo, -va *adj* inoffensive, harmless.

inolvidable *adj* unforgettable.

inoperante *adj* ineffective.

inoportuno, -na, importuno, -na *adj* 1. (*en mal momento*) inopportune, untimely. 2. (*molesto*) inconvenient. 3. (*inadecuado*) inappropriate.

inoxidable *adj* rustproof; (*acero*) stainless.

inquebrantable *adj* unshakeable; (*lealtad*) unswerving.

inquietar *vt* to worry, to trouble. ▶ **inquietarse** *vpr* to worry.

inquieto, -ta *adj* 1. (*preocupado*): ~ (**por**) worried o anxious (about). 2. (*agitado, emprendedor*) restless.

inquietud *f* (*preocupación*) worry, anxiety.

inquilino, -na *m y f* tenant.

inquirir *vt culto* to inquire into, to investigate.

inquisición *f* (*indagación*) inquiry, investigation. ▶ **Inquisición** *f* (*tribunal*) Inquisition.

inquisidor, -ra *adj* inquisitive. ▶ **inquisidor** *m* inquisitor.

insaciable *adj* insatiable.

insalubre *adj culto* insalubrious, unhealthy.

Insalud (*abrev de* **Instituto Nacional de la Salud**) *m* ≈ NHS Br, ≈ Medicaid Am.

insatisfecho, -cha *adj* 1. (*descontento*) dissatisfied. 2. (*no saciado*) not full, unsatisfied.

inscribir *vt* 1. (*grabar*): ~ algo (**en**) to engrave o inscribe sthg (on). 2. (*apuntar*): ~ algo/a alguien (**en**) to register sthg/sb (on). ▶ **inscribirse** *vpr*: ~se (**en**) (*gen*) to enrol (on); (*asociación*) to enrol (with); (*concurso*) to enter.

inscripción *f* 1. (EDUC) registration, enrolment; (*en censo, registro*) registration; (*en partido etc*) enrolment; (*en concursos etc*) entry. 2. (*escrito*) inscription.

inscrito, -ta *pp* → **inscribir**.

insecticida *m* insecticide.

insecto *m* insect.

inseguridad *f* 1. (*falta de confianza*) insecurity. 2. (*duda*) uncertainty. 3. (*peligro*) lack of safety.

inseguro, -ra *adj* 1. (*sin confianza*) insecure. 2. (*dudoso*) uncertain. 3. (*peligroso*) unsafe.

inseminación *f* insemination; ~ artificial artificial insemination.

insensatez *f* foolishness; **hacer/decir una** ~ to do/say sthg foolish.

insensato, -ta ♦ *adj* foolish, senseless. ♦ *m y f* fool.

insensibilidad *f* (*emocional*) insensitivity; (*física*) numbness.

insensible *adj* 1. (*indiferente*): ~ (**a**) insensitive (to). 2. (*entumecido*) numb. 3. (*imperceptible*) imperceptible.

insertar *vt* (*gen & COMPUT*): ~ (**en**) to insert (into).

inservible *adj* useless, unserviceable.

insidioso, -sa *adj* malicious.

insigne *adj* distinguished, illustrious.

insignia *f* 1. (*distintivo*) badge; (MIL) insignia. 2. (*bandera*) flag, banner.

insignificante *adj* insignificant.

insinuar *vt*: ~ algo (**a**) to hint at o insinuate sthg (to). ▶ **insinuarse** *vpr* 1. (*amorosamente*): ~se (**a**) to make advances (to). 2. (*asomar*): ~se detrás de algo to peep out from behind sthg.

insípido, -da *adj lit & fig* insipid.

insistencia *f* insistence.

insistir *vi*: ~ (**en**) to insist (on).

insociable *adj* unsociable.

insolación *f* (MED) sunstroke (U).

insolencia *f* insolence; **hacer/decir una** ~ to do/say sthg insolent.

insolente *adj* (*descarado*) insolent; (*orgulloso*) haughty.

insolidario, -ria *adj* lacking in solidarity.

insólito, -ta *adj* very unusual.

insoluble *adj* insoluble.

insolvencia *f* insolvency.

insolvente *adj* insolvent.

insomnio *m* insomnia.

insondable *adj lit & fig* unfathomable.

insonorizar *vt* to soundproof.

insoportable *adj* unbearable, intolerable.

insostenible *adj* untenable.

inspección *f* inspection; (*policial*) search.

inspeccionar *vt* to inspect; (*suj: policía*) to search.

inspector, -ra *m y f* inspector; ~ **de aduanas** customs official; ~ **de Hacienda** tax inspector.

inspiración *f* 1. (*gen*) inspiration.

2. (*respiración*) inhalation, breath.
inspirar *vt* **1.** (*gen*) to inspire. **2.** (*respirar*) to inhale, to breathe in. ► **inspirarse** *vpr*: ~**se (en)** to be inspired (by).
instalación *f* **1.** (*gen*) installation; ~ **eléctrica** wiring. **2.** (*de gente*) settling. ► **instalaciones** *fpl* (*deportivas etc*) facilities.
instalar *vt* **1.** (*montar - antena etc*) to instal, to fit; (*- local, puesto etc*) to set up. **2.** (*situar - objeto*) to place; (*- gente*) to settle. ► **instalarse** *vpr* (*establecerse*): ~**se en** to settle (down) in; (*nueva casa*) to move into.
instancia *f* **1.** (*solicitud*) application (form). **2.** (*ruego*) request; **a ~s de** at the request o bidding of; **en última ~** as a last resort.
instantáneo, -a *adj* **1.** (*momentáneo*) momentary. **2.** (*rápido*) instantaneous. ► **instantánea** *f* snapshot, snap.
instante *m* moment; **a cada ~** all the time, constantly; **al ~** instantly, immediately; **en un ~** in a second.
instar *vt*: ~ **a alguien a que haga algo** to urge o press sb to do sthg.
instaurar *vt* to establish, to set up.
instigar *vt*: ~ **a alguien (a que haga algo)** to instigate sb (to do sthg); ~ **a algo** to incite to sthg.
instintivo, -va *adj* instinctive.
instinto *m* instinct; **por ~** instinctively.
institución *f* **1.** (*gen*) institution; **ser una ~** *fig* to be an institution. **2.** (*de ley, sistema*) introduction; (*de organismo*) establishment; (*de premio*) foundation.
instituir *vt* (*fundar - gobierno*) to establish; (*- premio, sociedad*) to found; (*- sistema, reglas*) to introduce.
instituto *m* **1.** (*corporación*) institute. **2.** (EDUC): ~ **(de Bachillerato o Enseñanza Media)** state secondary school; ~ **de Formación Profesional** ≃ technical college. ► **instituto de belleza** *m* beauty salon.
institutriz *f* governess.
instrucción *f* **1.** (*conocimientos*) education; (*docencia*) instruction. **2.** (DER - *investigación*) preliminary investigation; (*- curso del proceso*) proceedings (*pl*). ► **instrucciones** *fpl* (*de uso*) instructions.
instructivo, -va *adj* (*gen*) instructive; (*juguete, película*) educational.
instructor, -ra ♦ *adj* training. ♦ *m y f* (*gen*) instructor, teacher; (DEP) coach.
instruido, -da *adj* educated.
instruir *vt* (*enseñar*) to instruct.

instrumental *m* instruments (*pl*).
instrumentista *m y f* **1.** (MÚS) instrumentalist. **2.** (MED) surgeon's assistant.
instrumento *m* **1.** (MUS & *fig*) instrument. **2.** (*herramienta*) tool, instrument.
insubordinado, -da *adj* insubordinate.
insubordinar *vt* to incite to rebellion. ► **insubordinarse** *vpr* to rebel.
insubstancial = **insustancial**.
insuficiencia *f* **1.** (*escasez*) lack, shortage. **2.** (MED) failure.
insuficiente ♦ *adj* insufficient. ♦ *m* (*nota*) fail.
insufrible *adj* intolerable, insufferable.
insular *adj* insular, island (*antes de sust*).
insulina *f* insulin.
insulso, -sa *adj* lit & fig bland, insipid.
insultar *vt* to insult.
insulto *m* insult.
insumiso, -sa ♦ *adj* rebellious. ♦ *m y f* (*gen*) rebel; (MIL) *person who refuses to do military or community service*.
insuperable *adj* **1.** (*inmejorable*) unsurpassable. **2.** (*sin solución*) insurmountable, insuperable.
insurgente *adj* insurgent.
insurrección *f* insurrection, revolt.
insustancial, insubstancial *adj* insubstantial.
intachable *adj* irreproachable.
intacto, -ta *adj* untouched; *fig* intact.
integral *adj* **1.** (*total*) total, complete. **2.** (*sin refinar - pan, harina, pasta*) wholemeal; (*- arroz*) brown.
integrante ♦ *adj* integral, constituent; **estado ~ de la CE** member state of the EC. ♦ *m y f* member.
integrar *vt* **1.** (*gen* & MAT) to integrate. **2.** (*componer*) to make up. ► **integrarse** *vpr* to integrate.
integridad *f* (*gen*) integrity; (*totalidad*) wholeness.
íntegro, -gra *adj* **1.** (*completo*) whole, entire; (*versión etc*) unabridged. **2.** (*honrado*) honourable.
intelecto *m* intellect.
intelectual *adj, m y f* intellectual.
inteligencia *f* intelligence; ~ **artificial** (INFORM) artificial intelligence.
inteligente *adj* (*gen* & COMPUT) intelligent.
inteligible *adj* intelligible.
intemperie *f*: **a la ~** in the open air.
intempestivo, -va *adj* (*clima, comentario*) harsh; (*hora*) ungodly, unearthly; (*proposición, visita*) inopportune.

intención f intention; **tener la ~ de** to intend to; **buena/mala ~** good/bad intentions (pl).

intencionado, -da adj intentional, deliberate; **bien ~** (acción) well-meant; (persona) well-meaning; **mal ~** (acción) ill-meant; (persona) malevolent.

intensidad f (gen) intensity; (de lluvia) heaviness; (de luz, color) brightness; (de amor) passion, strength.

intensificar vt to intensify. ▶ **intensificarse** vpr to intensify.

intensivo, -va adj intensive.

intenso, -sa adj (gen) intense; (lluvia) heavy; (luz, color) bright; (amor) passionate, strong.

intentar vt: **~ (hacer algo)** to try (to do sthg).

intento m (tentativa) attempt; (intención) intention; **~ de golpe/robo** attempted coup/robbery.

interactivo, -va adj (INFORM) interactive.

intercalar vt to insert, to put in.

intercambiable adj interchangeable.

intercambiar vt (gen) to exchange; (lugares) to change.

intercambio m exchange; **~ comercial** trade.

interceder vi: **~ (por alguien)** to intercede (on sb's behalf).

interceptar vt 1. (detener) to intercept. 2. (obstruir) to block.

intercesión f intercession.

interés m 1. (gen & FIN) interest; **de ~** interesting; **tener ~ en** o **por** to be interested in; **tengo ~ en que venga pronto** it's in my interest that he should come soon; **intereses creados** vested interests. 2. (egoísmo) self-interest; **por ~** out of selfishness.

interesado, -da ◆ adj 1. (gen): **~ (en** o **por)** interested (in). 2. (egoísta) selfish, self-interested. ◆ m y f (deseoso) interested person; **los ~s** those interested.

interesante adj interesting.

interesar vi to interest; **le interesa el arte** she's interested in art. ▶ **interesarse** vpr: **~se (en** o **por)** to take an interest (in), to be interested (in); **se interesó por tu salud** she asked after your health.

interfaz f (INFORM) interface.

interferencia f interference.

interferir ◆ vt 1. (RADIO, TELECOM & TV) to jam. 2. (interponerse) to interfere with. ◆ vi: **~ (en)** to interfere (in).

interfono m intercom.

interino, -na ◆ adj (gen) temporary; (presidente, director etc) acting; (gobierno) interim. ◆ m y f (gen) stand-in; (médico, juez) locum; (profesor) supply teacher. ▶ **interina** f (asistenta) cleaning lady.

interior ◆ adj 1. (gen) inside, inner; (patio, jardín etc) interior, inside; (habitación, vida) inner. 2. (POLÍT) domestic. 3. (GEOGR) inland. ◆ m 1. (parte de dentro) inside, interior. 2. (GEOGR) interior. 3. (de una persona) inner self; **en mi ~** deep down.

interiorismo m interior design.

interiorizar vt to internalize; (sentimientos) to bottle up.

interjección f interjection.

interlocutor, -ra m y f interlocutor, speaker; **su ~** the person she was speaking to.

intermediario, -ria m y f (gen) intermediary; (COM) middleman; (en disputas) mediator.

intermedio, -dia adj 1. (etapa) intermediate, halfway; (calidad) average; (tamaño) medium. 2. (tiempo) intervening; (espacio) in between. ▶ **intermedio** m (gen & TEATR) interval; (CIN) intermission.

interminable adj endless, interminable.

intermitente ◆ adj intermittent. ◆ m indicator.

internacional adj international.

internado, -da adj (en manicomio) confined; (en colegio) boarding; (POLÍT) interned. ▶ **internado** m (colegio) boarding school.

internar vt: **~ (en)** (internado) to send to boarding school (at); (manicomio) to commit (to); (campo de concentración) to intern (in). ▶ **internarse** vpr: **~se (en)** (un lugar) to go o penetrate deep (into); (un tema) to become deeply involved (in).

internauta m y f Internet user.

Internet f: **(la red) ~** the Internet.

interno, -na ◆ adj 1. (gen) internal; (POLÍT) domestic. 2. (alumno) boarder. ◆ m y f 1. (alumno) boarder. 2. → **médico**. 3. (preso) prisoner, inmate.

interpelación f formal question.

interpolar vt to interpolate, to put in.

interponer vt 1. (gen) to interpose, to put in. 2. (DER) to lodge, to make. ▶ **interponerse** vpr to intervene.

interpretación f 1. (explicación) interpretation. 2. (artística) performance. 3. (traducción) interpreting.

interpretar vt 1. (gen) to interpret. 2. (artísticamente) to perform.

intérprete m y f 1. (traductor & INFORM) interpreter. 2. (artista) performer.

interpuesto, -ta pp → interponer.

interrogación f 1. (acción) questioning. 2. (signo) question mark.

interrogante m o f (incógnita) question mark.

interrogar vt (gen) to question; (con amenazas etc) to interrogate.

interrogatorio m (gen) questioning; (con amenazas) interrogation.

interrumpir vt 1. (gen) to interrupt. 2. (discurso, trabajo) to break off; (viaje, vacaciones) to cut short.

interrupción f 1. (gen) interruption. 2. (de discurso, trabajo) breaking-off; (de viaje, vacaciones) cutting-short.

interruptor m switch.

intersección f intersection.

interurbano, -na adj inter-city; (TELECOM) long-distance.

intervalo m 1. (gen & MÚS) interval; (de espacio) space, gap; **a ~s** at intervals. 2. (duración): **en el ~ de un mes** in the space of a month.

intervención f 1. (gen) intervention. 2. (discurso) speech; (interpelación) contribution. 3. (COM) auditing. 4. (MED) operation. 5. (TELECOM) tapping.

intervenir ♦ vi 1. (participar): **~ (en)** (gen) to take part (in); (pelea) to get involved (in); (discusión etc) to make a contribution (to). 2. (dar un discurso) to make a speech. 3. (interferir): **~ (en)** to intervene (in). 4. (MED) to operate. ♦ vt 1. (MED) to operate on. 2. (TELECOM) to tap. 3. (incautar) to seize. 4. (COM) to audit.

interventor, -ra m y f (COM) auditor.

interviú (pl **intervius**) f interview.

intestino, -na adj internecine. ▶ **intestino** m intestine.

intimar vi: **~ (con)** to become intimate o very friendly (with).

intimidad f 1. (vida privada) private life; (privacidad) privacy; **en la ~** in private. 2. (amistad) intimacy.

íntimo, -ma ♦ adj 1. (vida, fiesta) private; (ambiente, restaurante) intimate. 2. (relación, amistad) close. 3. (sentimiento etc) innermost. ♦ m y f close friend.

intolerable adj intolerable, unacceptable; (dolor, ruido) unbearable.

intolerancia f (actitud) intolerance.

intolerante adj intolerant.

intoxicación f poisoning (U); **~ ali-**

menticia food poisoning.

intoxicar vt to poison.

intranquilizar vt to worry. ▶ **intranquilizarse** vpr to get worried.

intranquilo, -la adj (preocupado) worried, anxious; (nervioso) restless.

intranscendente = **intrascendente**.

intransferible adj non-transferable.

intransigente adj intransigent.

intransitable adj impassable.

intrascendente, intranscendente adj insignificant, unimportant.

intrépido, -da adj intrepid.

intriga f 1. (curiosidad) curiosity; **de ~** suspense (antes de sust). 2. (maquinación) intrigue. 3. (trama) plot.

intrigante adj 1. (maquinador) scheming. 2. (interesante) intriguing.

intrigar vt & vi to intrigue.

intrincado, -da adj (problema etc) intricate.

intríngulis m inv fam (dificultad) snag, catch; (quid) crux.

intrínseco, -ca adj intrinsic.

introducción f: **~ (a)** introduction (to).

introducir vt 1. (meter - llave, carta etc) to put in, to insert. 2. (mercancías etc) to bring in, to introduce. 3. (dar a conocer): **~ a alguien en** to introduce sb to; **~ algo en** to introduce o bring sthg to. ▶ **introducirse** vpr: **~se en** to get into.

introductorio, -ria adj introductory.

intromisión f meddling, interfering.

introspectivo, -va adj introspective.

introvertido, -da ♦ adj introverted. ♦ m y f introvert.

intruso, -sa m y f intruder.

intuición f intuition.

intuir vt to know by intuition, to sense.

intuitivo, -va adj intuitive.

inundación f flood, flooding (U).

inundar vt to flood; fig to inundate. ▶ **inundarse** vpr to flood; **~se de** fig to be inundated o swamped with.

inusitado, -da adj uncommon, rare.

inútil adj 1. (gen) useless; (intento, esfuerzo) unsuccessful, vain. 2. (inválido) disabled.

inutilidad f (gen) uselessness; (falta de sentido) pointlessness.

inutilizar vt (gen) to make unusable; (máquinas, dispositivos) to disable.

invadir vt to invade; **le invade la tristeza** she's overcome by sadness.

invalidez f 1. (MED) disability; **~ permanente/temporal** permanent/temporary disability. 2. (DER) invalidity.

inválido, -da ◆ *adj* **1.** (MED) disabled. **2.** (DER) invalid. ◆ *m y f* invalid, disabled person; **los ~s** the disabled.

invariable *adj* invariable.

invasión *f* invasion.

invasor, -ra ◆ *adj* invading. ◆ *m y f* invader.

invención *f* invention.

inventar *vt* (*gen*) to invent; (*narración, falsedades*) to make up. ▶ **inventarse** *vpr* to make up.

inventario *m* inventory; **hacer el ~** (COM) to do the stocktaking.

inventiva *f* inventiveness.

invento *m* invention.

inventor, -ra *m y f* inventor.

invernadero, invernáculo *m* greenhouse.

invernar *vi* (*pasar el invierno*) to (spend the) winter; (*hibernar*) to hibernate.

inverosímil *adj* unlikely, improbable.

inversión *f* **1.** (*del orden*) inversion. **2.** (*de dinero, tiempo*) investment.

inverso, -sa *adj* opposite, inverse; **a la inversa** the other way round; **en orden ~** in reverse order.

inversor, -ra *m y f* (COM & FIN) investor.

invertebrado, -da *adj* **1.** (ZOOL) invertebrate. **2.** *fig* (*incoherente*) disjointed. ▶ **invertebrado** *m* invertebrate.

invertido, -da *adj* **1.** (*al revés*) reversed, inverted; (*sentido, dirección*) opposite. **2.** (*homosexual*) homosexual.

invertir *vt* **1.** (*gen*) to reverse; (*poner boca abajo*) to turn upside down. **2.** (*dinero, tiempo, esfuerzo*) to invest. **3.** (*tardar - tiempo*) to spend.

investidura *f* investiture.

investigación *f* **1.** (*estudio*) research; **~ y desarrollo** research and development. **2.** (*indagación*) investigation, inquiry.

investigador, -ra *m y f* **1.** (*estudioso*) researcher. **2.** (*detective*) investigator.

investigar ◆ *vt* **1.** (*estudiar*) to research. **2.** (*indagar*) to investigate. ◆ *vi* **1.** (*estudiar*) to do research. **2.** (*indagar*) to investigate.

investir *vt*: **~ a alguien con algo** to invest sb with sthg.

inveterado, -da *adj* deep-rooted.

inviable *adj* impractical, unviable.

invidente *m y f* blind o sightless person; **los ~s** the blind.

invierno *m* winter.

invisible *adj* invisible.

invitación *f* invitation.

invitado, -da *m y f* guest.

invitar ◆ *vt* **1.** (*convidar*): **~ a alguien (a algo/a hacer algo)** to invite sb (to sthg/to do sthg). **2.** (*pagar*): **os invito** it's my treat, this one's on me; **te invito a cenar fuera** I'll take you out for dinner. ◆ *vi* to pay; **invita la casa** it's on the house. ▶ **invitar a** *vi fig* (*incitar*): **~ a algo** to encourage sthg; **la lluvia invita a quedarse en casa** the rain makes you want to stay at home.

in vitro *loc adv* **1.** (*de probeta*) in vitro. **2.** → **fecundación**.

invocar *vt* to invoke.

involucrar *vt*: **~ a alguien (en)** to involve sb (in). ▶ **involucrarse** *vpr*: **~se (en)** to get involved (in).

involuntario, -ria *adj* (*espontáneo*) involuntary; (*sin querer*) unintentional.

inyección *f* injection.

inyectar *vt* to inject. ▶ **inyectarse** *vpr* (*drogas*) to take drugs intravenously; **~se algo** to inject o.s. with sthg.

iodo = **yodo**.

ion *m* ion.

IPC (*abrev de* **índice de precios al consumo**) *m* Spanish cost of living index, ≃ RPI Br.

ir *vi* **1.** (*gen*) to go; **~ hacia el sur/al cine** to go south/to the cinema; **~ en autobús/coche** to go by bus/car; **~ andando** to go on foot, to walk; **¡vamos!** let's go! **2.** (*expresa duración gradual*): **~ haciendo algo** to be (gradually) doing sthg; **va anocheciendo** it's getting dark; **voy mejorando mi estilo** I'm working on improving my style. **3.** (*expresa intención, opinión*): **~ a hacer algo** to be going to do sthg; **voy a decírselo a tu padre** I'm going to tell your father. **4.** (*cambiar*): **~ a mejor/peor** *etc* to get better/worse *etc*. **5.** (*funcionar*) to work; **la manivela va floja** the crank is loose; **la televisión no va** the television isn't working. **6.** (*desenvolverse*) to go; **le va bien en su nuevo trabajo** things are going well for him in his new job; **su negocio va mal** his business is going badly; **¿cómo te va?** how are you doing? **7.** (*vestir*): **~ en/con** to wear; **iba en camisa y con corbata** he was wearing a shirt and tie; **~ de azul/de uniforme** to be dressed in blue/in uniform. **8.** (*tener aspecto físico*) to look like; **iba hecho un pordiosero** he looked like a beggar. **9.** (*vacaciones, tratamiento*): **~le bien a alguien** to do sb good. **10.** (*ropa*): **~le (bien) a alguien** to suit sb; **~ con algo** to go with sthg. **11.** (*comen-*

tario, indirecta): ~ **con** o **por alguien** to be meant for sb, to be aimed at sb. **12.** *loc*: **fue y dijo que ...** he went and said that ...; **ni me va ni me viene** *fam* I don't care; **¡qué va!** you must be joking!; **ser el no va más** to be the ultimate. ▶ **ir de** *vi* **1.** (*película, novela*) to be about. **2.** *fig* (*persona*) to think o.s.; **va de listo** he thinks he's clever. ▶ **ir por** *vi* **1.** (*buscar*): ~ **por algo/alguien** to go and get sth/sb, to go and fetch sth/sb. **2.** (*alcanzar*): **va por el cuarto vaso de vino** he's already on his fourth glass of wine; **vamos por la mitad de la asignatura** we covered about half the subject. ▶ **irse** *vpr* **1.** (*marcharse*) to go, to leave; ~**se a** to go to; **¡vete!** go away! **2.** (*gastarse, desaparecer*) to go. **3.** *loc*: ~**se abajo** (*edificio*) to fall down; (*negocio*) to collapse; (*planes*) to fall through.

ira *f* anger, rage.

IRA (*abrev de* **Irish Republican Army**) *m* IRA.

iracundo, -da *adj* angry, irate; (*irascible*) irascible.

Irán: (**el**) ~ Iran.

iraní (*pl* **iraníes**) *adj, m y f* Iranian.

Iraq: (**el**) ~ Iraq.

iraquí (*pl* **iraquíes**) *adj, m y f* Iraqi.

irascible *adj* irascible.

iris *m inv* iris.

Irlanda Ireland.

irlandés, -esa ◆ *adj* Irish. ◆ *m y f* (*persona*) Irishman (*f* Irishwoman); **los irlandeses** the Irish. ▶ **irlandés** *m* (*lengua*) Irish.

ironía *f* irony.

irónico, -ca *adj* ironic, ironical.

ironizar ◆ *vt* to ridicule. ◆ *vi*: ~ (**sobre**) to be ironical (about).

IRPF (*abrev de* **Impuesto sobre la Renta de las Personas Físicas**) *m* Spanish personal income tax.

irracional *adj* irrational.

irradiar *vt lit & fig* to radiate.

irreal *adj* unreal.

irreconciliable *adj* irreconcilable.

irreconocible *adj* unrecognizable.

irrecuperable *adj* irretrievable.

irreflexión *f* rashness.

irreflexivo, -va *adj* rash.

irrefutable *adj* irrefutable.

irregular *adj* (*gen*) irregular; (*terreno, superficie*) uneven.

irrelevante *adj* irrelevant.

irremediable *adj* irremediable.

irreparable *adj* irreparable.

irresistible *adj* irresistible.

irresoluto, -ta *adj culto* irresolute.

irrespetuoso, -sa *adj* disrespectful.

irrespirable *adj* unbreathable.

irresponsable *adj* irresponsible.

irreverente *adj* irreverent.

irreversible *adj* irreversible.

irrevocable *adj* irrevocable.

irrigar *vt* to irrigate.

irrisorio, -ria *adj* **1.** (*excusa etc*) laughable, derisory. **2.** (*precio etc*) ridiculously low.

irritable *adj* irritable.

irritar *vt* to irritate. ▶ **irritarse** *vpr* **1.** (*enfadarse*) to get angry o annoyed. **2.** (*suj: piel etc*) to become irritated.

irrompible *adj* unbreakable.

irrupción *f* bursting in.

isla *f* island.

islam *m* Islam.

islamismo *m* Islam.

islandés, -esa ◆ *adj* Icelandic. ◆ *m y f* (*persona*) Icelander. ▶ **islandés** *m* (*lengua*) Icelandic.

Islandia Iceland.

isleño, -ña ◆ *adj* island (*antes de sust*). ◆ *m y f* islander.

islote *m* small, rocky island.

Israel Israel.

israelí (*pl* **israelíes**) *adj, m y f* Israeli.

istmo *m* isthmus.

Italia Italy.

italiano, -na *adj, m y f* Italian. ▶ **italiano** *m* (*lengua*) Italian.

itálico, -ca *adj* → **letra**.

itinerante *adj* itinerant; (*embajador*) roving.

itinerario *m* route, itinerary.

ITV (*abrev de* **inspección técnica de vehículos**) *f* annual technical inspection for motor vehicles of ten years or more, ≈ MOT *Br*.

IVA (*abrev de* **impuesto sobre el valor añadido**) *m* VAT.

izar *vt* to raise, to hoist.

izda (*abrev de* **izquierda**) L, I.

izquierda → **izquierdo**.

izquierdo, -da *adj* left. ▶ **izquierda** *f* **1.** (*lado*) left; **a la izquierda (de)** on o to the left (of); **girar a la izquierda** to turn left. **2.** (*mano*) left hand. **3.** (POLÍT) left (wing); **de izquierdas** left-wing.

J

j, J f (letra) j, J.

ja interj: ¡~! ha!

jabalí (pl jabalíes) m y f wild boar.

jabalina f (DEP) javelin.

jabón m soap; ~ **de afeitar/tocador** shaving/toilet soap.

jabonar vt to soap.

jabonera f soap dish.

jaca f (caballo pequeño) pony; (yegua) mare.

jacal m Amer hut.

jacinto m hyacinth.

jactarse vpr: ~ **(de)** to boast (about o of).

jacuzzi® [ja'kusi] (pl jacuzzis) m Jacuzzi®.

jadear vi to pant.

jadeo m panting.

jaguar (pl jaguars) m jaguar.

jaiba f Amer (cangrejo de río) crayfish.

jalea f jelly; ~ **real** royal jelly.

jalear vt to cheer on.

jaleo m 1. fam (alboroto) row, rumpus. 2. fam (lío) mess, confusion.

jalonar vt to stake o mark out; fig to mark.

Jamaica Jamaica.

jamás adv never; **no le he visto ~** I've never seen him; **la mejor película que ~ se haya hecho** the best film ever made; **~ de los jamases** never ever.

jamón m ham; ~ **(de) York** o **(en) dulce** boiled ham; ~ **serrano** cured ham, ≃ Parma ham.

Japón: **(el) ~** Japan.

japonés, -esa adj, m y f Japanese. ▸ **japonés** m (lengua) Japanese.

jaque m: ~ **mate** checkmate.

jaqueca f migraine.

jarabe m syrup; ~ **para la tos** cough mixture o syrup.

jarana f (juerga): **estar/irse de ~** to be/go out on the town.

jaranero, -ra adj fond of partying.

jardín m garden; ~ **botánico** botanical garden. ▸ **jardín de infancia** m kindergarten, nursery school.

jardinera → jardinero.

jardinería f gardening.

jardinero, -ra m y f gardener. ▸ **jar-**

dinera f flowerpot stand.

jarra f 1. (para servir) jug. 2. (para beber) tankard. ▸ **en jarras** loc adv (postura) hands on hips.

jarro m jug.

jarrón m vase.

jaspeado, -da adj mottled, speckled.

jauja f fam paradise.

jaula f cage.

jauría f pack of dogs.

jazmín m jasmine.

jazz [jas] m jazz.

JC (abrev de **Jesucristo**) JC.

je interj: ¡~! ha!

jeep [jip] (pl jeeps) m jeep.

jefa → jefe.

jefatura f 1. (cargo) leadership. 2. (organismo) headquarters, head office.

jefe, -fa m y f (gen) boss; (COM) manager (f manageress); (líder) leader; (de tribu, ejército) chief; (de departamento etc) head; **en ~** (MIL) in-chief; ~ **de cocina** chef; ~ **de estación** stationmaster; ~ **de Estado** head of state; ~ **de producción/ventas** production/sales manager; ~ **de redacción** editor-in-chief.

jengibre m ginger.

jeque m sheikh.

jerarquía f 1. (organización) hierarchy. 2. (persona) high-ranking person, leader.

jerárquico, -ca adj hierarchical.

jerez m sherry.

jerga f jargon; (argot) slang.

jeringuilla f syringe.

jeroglífico, -ca adj hieroglyphic. ▸ **jeroglífico** m 1. (inscripción) hieroglyphic. 2. (pasatiempo) rebus.

jerséi (pl jerséis), **jersey** (pl jerseys) m jumper, jersey.

Jerusalén Jerusalem.

jesuita adj & m Jesuit.

jesús interj: ¡~! (sorpresa) good heavens!; (tras estornudo) bless you!

jet [jet] (pl jets) ◆ m jet. ◆ → jet-set.

jeta m fam f (cara) mug, face; **tener (mucha) ~** to be a cheeky bugger.

jet-set ['jetset] f jet set.

Jibuti Djibouti.

jilguero m goldfinch.

jilipollada = gilipollada.

jilipollas = gilipollas.

jinete m y f rider; (yóquey) jockey.

jirafa f (ZOOL) giraffe.

jirón m (andrajo) shred, rag; **hecho jirones** in tatters.

jitomate m Amer tomato.

JJ OO (abrev de **juegos olímpicos**) mpl Olympic Games.

jockey ['jokei] = **yóquey**.

jocoso, -sa adj jocular.

joder vulg vi **1.** (copular) to fuck. **2.** (fastidiar) to be a pain in the arse; **¡no jodas!** (incredulidad) bollocks!, pull the other one!

jofaina f wash basin.

jolgorio m merrymaking.

jolín, jolines interj fam: **¡~!, ¡¡olines!** hell!, Christ!

jondo → **cante**.

jornada f **1.** (de trabajo): **~ (laboral)** working day; **~ intensiva** working day from 8 to 3 with only a short lunch break; **media ~** half day; **~ partida** typical Spanish working day from 9 to 1 and 4 to 7. **2.** (de viaje) day's journey. **3.** (DEP) round of matches, programme. ▶ **jornadas** fpl (conferencia) conference (sg).

jornal m day's wage.

jornalero, -ra m y f day labourer.

joroba f hump.

jorobado, -da ◆ adj (con joroba) hunchbacked. ◆ m y f hunchback.

jorongo m Amer **1.** (manta) blanket. **2.** (poncho) poncho.

jota f **1.** (baile) Aragonese folk song and dance. **2.** (loc): **no entender** o **saber ni ~** fam fig not to understand o know a thing.

joto m y f Amer fam despec queer Br, faggot Am.

joven ◆ adj young; **está muy ~ para la edad que tiene** she's very youthful for her age. ◆ m y f young man (f young woman); **los jóvenes** young people.

jovial adj jovial, cheerful.

joya f jewel; fig gem.

joyería f **1.** (tienda) jeweller's (shop). **2.** (arte, comercio) jewellery.

joyero, -ra m y f (persona) jeweller. ▶ **joyero** m (estuche) jewellery box.

Jr. (abrev de **junior**) Jr.

juanete m bunion.

jubilación f (retiro) retirement; **~ anticipada** early retirement.

jubilado, -da ◆ adj retired. ◆ m y f pensioner Br, senior citizen.

jubilar vt: **~ a alguien (de)** to pension sb off o retire sb (from). ▶ **jubilarse** vpr to retire.

jubileo m (RELIG) jubilee.

júbilo m jubilation, joy.

judía f bean; **~ blanca** haricot; **~ verde** green o French bean.

judicial adj judicial.

judío, -a ◆ adj Jewish. ◆ m y f Jew (f Jewess).

judo = **yudo**.

juega → **jugar**.

juego m **1.** (gen & DEP) game; (acción) play, playing; (con dinero) gambling; **estar/poner en ~** to be/put at stake; **~ de azar** game of chance; **~ de cartas** o **de naipes** card game; **~ de manos** conjuring trick; **~ de palabras** play on words, pun; **Juegos Olímpicos** Olympic Games; **~ sucio/limpio** foul/clean play; **descubrirle el ~ a alguien** to see through sb; **estar (en) fuera de ~** (DEP) to be offside; fig not to know what's going on. **2.** (conjunto de objetos) set; **~ de herramientas** tool kit; **~ de té/café** tea/coffee service; **hacer ~ (con)** to match.

juerga f fam rave-up; **irse/estar de ~** to go/be out on the town.

juerguista fam m y f reveller.

jueves m inv Thursday; **Jueves Santo** Maundy Thursday; ver también **sábado**.

juez m y f **1.** (DER) judge; **~ de paz** Justice of the Peace. **2.** (DEP - gen) judge; (- en atletismo) official; **~ de línea** (fútbol) linesman; (rugby) touch judge; **~ de salida** starter; **~ de silla** umpire.

jugada f **1.** (DEP) period of play; (en tenis, ping-pong) rally; (en fútbol, rugby etc) move; (en ajedrez etc) move; (en billar) shot. **2.** (treta) dirty trick; **hacer una mala ~ a alguien** to play a dirty trick on sb.

jugador, -ra m y f (gen) player; (de juego de azar) gambler.

jugar ◆ vi **1.** (gen) to play; **~ al ajedrez** to play chess; **~ en un equipo** to play for a team; **te toca ~** it's your turn o go. **2.** (con dinero): **~ (a)** to gamble (on); **~ (a la Bolsa)** to speculate (on the Stock Exchange). ◆ vt **1.** (gen) to play; (ficha, pieza) to move. **2.** (dinero): **~ algo (a algo)** to gamble sthg (on sthg). ▶ **jugarse** vpr **1.** (apostarse) to bet. **2.** (arriesgar) to risk. **3.** loc: **jugársela a alguien** to play a dirty trick on sb.

jugarreta f fam dirty trick.

juglar m minstrel.

jugo m **1.** (gen & ANAT) juice; (BOT) sap. **2.** (interés) meat, substance; **sacar ~ a algo/alguien** to get the most out of sthg/sb.

jugoso, -sa adj **1.** (con jugo) juicy. **2.** fig (picante) juicy; (sustancioso) meaty, substantial.

juguete m lit & fig toy; **de ~** toy (antes de sust).

juguetear *vi* to play (around); ~ **con algo** to toy with sthg.

juguetería *f* toy shop.

juguetón, -ona *adj* playful.

juicio *m* **1.** (DER) trial. **2.** (*sensatez*) (sound) judgement; (*cordura*) sanity, reason; **estar/no estar en su (sano)** ~ to be/not to be in one's right mind; **perder el** ~ to lose one's reason. **3.** (*opinión*) opinion; **a mi** ~ in my opinion. ▶ **Juicio Final** *m*: **el Juicio Final** the Last Judgement.

juicioso, -sa *adj* sensible, wise.

julio *m* **1.** (*mes*) July; *ver también* **septiembre. 2.** (FÍS) joule.

junco *m* **1.** (*planta*) rush, reed. **2.** (*embarcación*) junk.

jungla *f* jungle.

junio *m* June; *ver también* **septiembre.**

júnior (*pl* **juniors**) *adj* **1.** (DEP) under-21. **2.** (*hijo*) junior.

junta *f* **1.** (*gen*) committee; (*de empresa, examinadores*) board; ~ **directiva** board of directors; ~ **militar** military junta. **2.** (*reunión*) meeting. **3.** (*juntura*) joint; ~ **de culata** gasket.

juntar *vt* (*gen*) to put together; (*fondos*) to raise; (*personas*) to bring together. ▶ **juntarse** *vpr* **1.** (*reunirse - personas*) to get together; (- *ríos, caminos*) to meet. **2.** (*arrimarse*) to draw o move closer. **3.** (*convivir*) to live together.

junto, -ta ♦ *adj* **1.** (*gen*) together. **2.** (*próximo*) close together. ♦ *adv*: **todo** ~ (*ocurrir etc*) all at the same time; (*escribirse*) as one word. ▶ **junto a** *loc prep* **1.** (*al lado de*) next to. **2.** (*cerca de*) right by, near. ▶ **junto con** *loc prep* together with.

juntura *f* joint.

Júpiter *m* Jupiter.

jurado, -da *adj* **1.** (*declaración etc*) sworn. **2.** → **guarda.** ▶ **jurado** *m* **1.** (*tribunal*) jury. **2.** (*miembro*) member of the jury.

juramento *m* **1.** (*promesa*) oath. **2.** (*blasfemia*) oath, curse.

jurar ♦ *vt* to swear; (*constitución etc*) to pledge allegiance to; **te lo juro** I promise; ~ **por ... que** to swear by ... that. ♦ *vi* (*blasfemar*) to swear.

jurel *m* scad, horse mackerel.

jurídico, -ca *adj* legal.

jurisdicción *f* jurisdiction.

jurisdiccional *adj* jurisdictional; (*aguas*) territorial.

jurisprudencia *f* (*ciencia*) jurispru-

dence; (*casos previos*) case law.

jurista *m y f* jurist.

justa *f* (HIST) joust.

justamente *adv* **1.** (*con justicia*) justly. **2.** (*exactamente*) exactly.

justicia *f* **1.** (*gen*) justice; (*equidad*) fairness, justice; **hacer** ~ to do justice; **ser de** ~ to be only fair. **2.** (*organización*): **la** ~ the law.

justiciero, -ra *adj* righteous.

justificación *f* (*gen* & IMPRENTA) justification.

justificante *m* documentary evidence (U).

justificar *vt* **1.** (*gen* & IMPRENTA) to justify. **2.** (*excusar*): ~ **a alguien** to make excuses for sb. ▶ **justificarse** *vpr* (*suj: persona*) to justify o excuse o.s.

justo, -ta *adj* **1.** (*equitativo*) fair. **2.** (*merecido - recompensa, victoria*) deserved; (- *castigo*) just. **3.** (*exacto - medida, hora*) exact. **4.** (*idóneo*) right. **5.** (*apretado*) tight; **estar** o **venir** ~ to be a tight fit. ▶ **justo** *adv* just; ~ **ahora iba a llamarte** I was just about to ring you; ~ **en medio** right in the middle.

juvenil *adj* youthful; (DEP) youth (*antes de sust*).

juventud *f* **1.** (*edad*) youth. **2.** (*conjunto*) young people (*pl*).

juzgado *m* (*tribunal*) court; ~ **de guardia** court open during the night or at other times when ordinary courts are shut.

juzgar *vt* **1.** (*enjuiciar*) to judge; (DER) to try; ~ **mal a alguien** to misjudge sb; **a** ~ **por (como)** judging by (how). **2.** (*estimar*) to consider, to judge.

K

k, K *f* (*letra*) k, K.

kaki = **caqui.**

kárate, cárate *m* karate.

kart (*pl* **karts**) *m* go-kart.

Kenia Kenya.

ketchup ['ketʃup] *m* ketchup.

kg (*abrev de* **kilogramo**) kg.

kibutz [ki'βuθ] (*pl* **kibutzim**) *m* kibbutz.

kilo, quilo *m* (*peso*) kilo; **medio** ~ half a kilo.

kilogramo, quilogramo *m* kilogram.

kilometraje, quilometraje m ≃ mileage, distance in kilometres.

kilométrico, -ca, quilométrico, -ca adj (distancia) kilometric.

kilómetro, quilómetro m kilometre; ~ **cuadrado** square kilometre.

kilovatio, quilovatio m kilowatt.

kiosco = **quiosco**.

kiwi (pl **kiwis**) m (fruto) kiwi (fruit).

km (abrev de **kilómetro**) km.

km/h (abrev de **kilómetro por hora**) km/h.

KO (abrev de **knockout**) m KO.

kurdo, -da ◆ adj Kurdish. ◆ m y f Kurd.

Kuwait [ku'βait] Kuwait.

L

l¹, L f (letra) l, L.

l² (abrev de **litro**) l.

la¹ m (MÚS) A; (en solfeo) lah.

la² ◆ art → **el**. ◆ pron → **lo**.

laberinto m lit & fig labyrinth.

labia f fam smooth talk; **tener mucha ~** to have the gift of the gab.

labio m 1. (ANAT) lip. 2. (borde) edge.

labor f 1. (trabajo) work; (tarea) task; **~es domésticas** household chores; **ser de profesión sus ~es** to be a housewife. 2. (de costura) needlework.

laborable → **día**.

laboral adj labour; (semana, condiciones) working (antes de sust).

laboratorio m laboratory; **~ de idiomas o lenguas** language laboratory.

laborioso, -sa adj (difícil) laborious.

laborista ◆ adj Labour. ◆ m y f Labour Party supporter o member; **los ~s** Labour.

labrador, -ra m y f (agricultor) farmer; (trabajador) farm worker.

labranza f farming.

labrar vt 1. (campo - cultivar) to cultivate; (- arar) to plough. 2. (piedra, metal etc) to work. 3. fig (desgracia etc) to bring about; (porvenir, fortuna) to carve out. ▶ **labrarse** vpr (porvenir etc) to carve out for o.s.

labriego, -ga m y f farmworker.

laca f 1. (gen) lacquer; (para cuadros) lake. 2. (para el pelo) hairspray.

lacado, -da adj lacquered.

lacar vt to lacquer.

lacayo m footman; fig lackey.

lacerar vt to lacerate; fig to wound.

lacio, -cia adj 1. (cabello - liso) straight; (- sin fuerza) lank. 2. (planta) wilted. 3. fig (sin fuerza) limp.

lacón m shoulder of pork.

lacónico, -ca adj laconic.

lacra f scourge.

lacrar vt to seal with sealing wax.

lacre m sealing wax.

lacrimógeno, -na adj 1. (novela etc) weepy, tear-jerking. 2. → **gas**.

lacrimoso, -sa adj 1. (ojos etc) tearful. 2. (historia etc) weepy, tear-jerking.

lactancia f lactation; **~ materna** breastfeeding.

lactante m y f breast-fed baby.

lácteo, -a adj (gen) milk (antes de sust); (industria, productos) dairy.

ladear vt to tilt.

ladera f slope, mountainside.

ladino, -na adj crafty. ▶ **ladino** m (dialecto) Ladino.

lado m 1. (gen) side; **en el ~ de arriba/ abajo** on the top/bottom; **a ambos ~s** on both sides; **estoy de su ~** I'm on her side; **de ~** (torcido) crooked; **dormir de ~** to sleep on one's side; **por un ~** on the one hand; **por otro ~** on the other hand. 2. (lugar) place; **debe estar en otro ~** it must be somewhere else. 3. loc: **dar de ~ a alguien** to cold-shoulder sb; **dejar algo de ~ o a un ~** (prescindir) to leave sthg to one side. ▶ **al lado** loc adv (cerca) nearby. ▶ **al lado de** loc prep (junto a) beside, next to. ▶ **de al lado** loc adj next door; **la casa de al ~** the house next door.

ladrar vi lit & fig to bark.

ladrido m lit & fig bark, barking (U).

ladrillo m (CONSTR) brick.

ladrón, -ona m y f (persona) thief, robber. ▶ **ladrón** m (para varios enchufes) adapter.

lagartija f (small) lizard.

lagarto, -ta m y f (ZOOL) lizard.

lago m lake.

lágrima f tear; **llorar a ~ viva** to cry buckets.

lagrimal m corner of the eye.

laguna f 1. (lago pequeño) small lake; (en la costa) lagoon. 2. fig (en colección, memoria) gap; (en leyes, reglamento) loophole.

La Habana Havana.

La Haya The Hague.

laico, -ca adj lay, secular.

lama m lama.

lamber vt Amer fam to lick.

La Meca Mecca.

lamentable adj 1. (triste) terribly sad. 2. (malo) lamentable, deplorable.

lamentar vt to regret, to be sorry about; **lo lamento** I'm very sorry.

lamento m moan.

lamer vt to lick. ▶ **lamerse** vpr to lick o.s.

lamido, -da adj skinny. ▶ **lamido** m lick.

lámina f 1. (plancha) sheet; (placa) plate. 2. (rodaja) slice. 3. (plancha grabada) engraving. 4. (dibujo) plate.

laminar vt 1. (hacer láminas) to roll. 2. (cubrir con láminas) to laminate.

lámpara f 1. (aparato) lamp; ~ **de pie** standard lamp. 2. (bombilla) bulb. 3. (TECN) valve.

lamparón m grease stain.

lampiño, -ña adj (sin barba) beardless, hairless.

lamprea f lamprey.

lana ◆ f wool; **de** ~ woollen. ◆ m Amer fam dosh, dough.

lance m 1. (en juegos, deportes) incident; (acontecimiento) event. 2. (riña) dispute.

lanceta f Amer sting.

lancha f (embarcación - grande) launch; (- pequeña) boat; ~ **salvavidas** lifeboat.

lanero, -ra adj wool (antes de sust).

langosta f 1. (crustáceo) lobster. 2. (insecto) locust.

langostino m king prawn.

languidecer vi to languish; (conversación, entusiasmo) to flag.

languidez f (debilidad) listlessness; (falta de ánimo) disinterest.

lánguido, -da adj (débil) listless; (falto de ánimo) disinterested.

lanilla f 1. (pelillo) nap. 2. (tejido) flannel.

lanolina f lanolin.

lanza f (arma - arrojadiza) spear; (- en justas, torneos) lance.

lanzado, -da adj (atrevido) forward; (valeroso) fearless.

lanzagranadas m inv grenade launcher.

lanzamiento m 1. (de objeto) throwing; (de cohete) launching. 2. (DEP - con la mano) throw; (- con el pie) kick; (- en béisbol) pitch; ~ **de peso** shot put. 3. (de producto, artista) launch; (de disco) release.

lanzamisiles m inv rocket launcher.

lanzar vt 1. (gen) to throw; (con fuerza) to hurl, to fling; (de una patada) to kick; (bomba) to drop; (flecha, misil) to fire; (cohete) to launch. 2. (proferir) to let out; (acusación, insulto) to hurl; (suspiro) to heave. 3. (COM - producto, artista, periódico) to launch; (- disco) to release. ▶ **lanzarse** vpr 1. (tirarse) to throw o.s. 2. (abalanzarse): ~**se** (**sobre**) to throw o.s. (upon).

lapa f (ZOOL) limpet.

La Paz La Paz.

lapicera f Amer (bolígrafo) biro, pen.

lapicero m pencil.

lápida f memorial stone; ~ **mortuoria** tombstone.

lapidar vt to stone.

lapidario, -ria adj solemn.

lápiz (pl **lápices**) m pencil; ~ **de labios** lipstick; ~ **de ojos** eyeliner; ~ **óptico** (INFORM) light pen.

lapón, -ona adj, m y f Lapp. ▶ **lapón** m (lengua) Lapp.

lapso m space, interval.

lapsus m inv lapse, slip.

larga → **largo**.

largar vt 1. (aflojar) to pay out. 2. fam (dar, decir) to give; **le largué un bofetón** I gave him a smack. ▶ **largarse** vpr fam to clear off.

largavistas m inv Amer binoculars (pl).

largo, -ga adj 1. (en espacio, tiempo) long. 2. (alto) tall. 3. (sobrado): **media hora larga** a good half hour. ▶ **largo** ◆ m length; **a lo** ~ lengthways; **tiene dos metros de** ~ it's two metres long; **pasar de** ~ to pass by; **a lo** ~ **de** (en el espacio) along; (en el tiempo) throughout; **¡**~ **de aquí!** go away! ◆ adv at length; **y tendido** at great length. ▶ **larga** f: **a la larga** in the long run; **dar largas a algo** to put sthg off.

largometraje m feature film.

larguero m 1. (CONSTR) main beam. 2. (DEP) crossbar.

largura f length.

laringe f larynx.

laringitis f inv laryngitis.

larva f larva.

las ◆ art → **el**. ◆ pron → **lo**.

lasaña f lasagne, lasagna.

lascivo, -va adj lascivious, lewd.

láser ◆ adj inv → **rayo**. ◆ m inv laser.

lástex m inv Lastex®.

lástima f 1. (compasión) pity. 2. (pena) shame, pity; **da** ~ **ver gente así** it's sad to see people in that state; **¡qué** ~**!**

what a shame o pity!; **quedarse hecho una** ~ to be a sorry o pitiful sight.

lastimar vt to hurt. ► **lastimarse** vpr to hurt o.s.

lastimoso, -sa adj pitiful, woeful.

lastre m 1. (peso) ballast. 2. fig (estorbo) burden.

lata f 1. (envase) can, tin; (de bebidas) can; **en** ~ tinned, canned. 2. fam (fastidio) pain; **¡qué** ~! what a pain!; **dar la** ~ **a alguien** to pester sb.

latente adj latent.

lateral ◆ adj (del lado - gen) lateral; (- puerta, pared) side. ◆ m 1. (lado) side. 2. (DEP): ~ **derecho/izquierdo** right/left back.

latido m (del corazón) beat; (en dedo etc) throb, throbbing (U).

latifundio m large rural estate.

latigazo m 1. (golpe) lash. 2. (chasquido) crack (of the whip).

látigo m whip.

latín m Latin; **saber (mucho)** ~ fig to be sharp, to be on the ball.

latinajo m fam despec Latin word used in an attempt to sound academic.

latino, -na adj, m y f Latin.

latinoamericano, -na adj, m y f Latin American.

latir vi (suj: corazón) to beat.

latitud f (GEOGR) latitude. ► **latitudes** fpl (parajes) region (sg), area (sg).

latón m brass.

latoso, -sa fam adj tiresome.

laúd m lute.

laureado, -da adj prize-winning.

laurel m (BOT) laurel; (CULIN) bay leaf. ► **laureles** mpl (honores) laurels; **dormirse en los** ~**es** fig to rest on one's laurels.

lava f lava.

lavable adj washable.

lavabo m 1. (objeto) washbasin. 2. (habitación) lavatory Br, washroom Am.

lavadero m (en casa) laundry room; (público) washing place.

lavado m wash, washing (U); ~ **de cerebro** brainwashing.

lavadora f washing machine.

lavamanos m inv washbasin.

lavanda f lavender.

lavandería f laundry; (automática) launderette.

lavaplatos m inv (aparato) dishwasher.

lavar vt (limpiar) to wash; ~ **y marcar** shampoo and set. ► **lavarse** vpr (gen) to wash o.s.; (cara, manos, pelo) to wash; (dientes) to clean.

lavativa f enema.

lavavajillas m inv dishwasher.

laxante m (MED) laxative.

laxar vt (vientre) to loosen.

lazada f bow.

lazarillo m 1. (persona) blind person's guide. 2. → **perro**.

lazo m 1. (atadura) bow. 2. (trampa) snare; (de vaquero) lasso. 3. (gen pl) fig (vínculo) tie, bond.

Lda. abrev de **licenciada**.

Ldo. abrev de **licenciado**.

le pron pers 1. (complemento indirecto) (hombre) (to) him; (mujer) (to) her; (cosa) to it; (usted) to you; ~ **expliqué el motivo** I explained the reason to him/her; **tengo miedo** I'm afraid of him/her; **ya** ~ **dije lo que pasaría** (a usted) I told you what would happen. 2. (complemento directo) him; (usted) you. 3. → **se**.

leal adj: ~ **(a)** loyal (to).

lealtad f: ~ **(a)** loyalty (to).

leasing ['lisin] (pl **leasings**) m system of leasing whereby the lessee has the option of purchasing the property after a certain time.

lección f lesson; **dar a alguien una** ~ (como advertencia) to teach sb a lesson; (como ejemplo) to give sb a lesson.

lechal m sucking lamb.

leche f 1. (gen) milk; ~ **condensada/en polvo** condensed/powdered milk; ~ **descremada** o **desnatada** skimmed milk; ~ **merengada** drink made from milk, egg whites, sugar and cinnamon. 2. mfam (bofetada): **pegar una** ~ **a alguien** to belt o clobber sb. 3. mfam (malhumor) bloody awful mood; **estar de mala** ~ to be in a bloody awful mood; **tener mala** ~ to be a miserable git.

lechera → **lechero**.

lechería f dairy.

lechero, -ra ◆ adj milk (antes de sust), dairy. ◆ m y f (persona) milkman (f milkwoman). ► **lechera** f (para transportar) milk churn; (para beber) milk jug.

lecho m (gen) bed.

lechón m sucking pig.

lechuga f (planta) lettuce.

lechuza f (barn) owl.

lectivo, -va adj school (antes de sust).

lector, -ra m y f 1. (gen) reader. 2. (EDUC) language assistant. ► **lector** m (de microfilms etc) reader, scanner; ~ **óptico** optical scanner.

lectura f 1. (gen) reading. 2. (de tesis) viva voce. 3. (escrito) reading (matter) (U). 4. (de datos) scanning; ~ **óptica** optical scanning.

leer ◆ *vt* (*gen* & INFORM) to read. ◆ *vi* to read; ~ **de corrido** to read fluently.

legado *m* 1. (*herencia*) legacy. 2. (*representante - persona*) legate.

legajo *m* file.

legal *adj* 1. (*gen*) legal; (*hora*) standard. 2. *fam* (*persona*) honest, decent.

legalidad *f* legality.

legalizar *vt* (*gen*) to legalize.

legañas *fpl* sleep (U) (*in the eyes*).

legañoso, -sa *adj* full of sleep.

legar *vt* 1. (*gen*) to bequeath. 2. (*delegar*) to delegate.

legendario, -ria *adj* legendary.

legible *adj* legible.

legión *f* *lit* & *fig* legion.

legionario, -ria *adj* legionary. ▶ **legionario** *m* (HIST) legionary; (MIL) legionnaire.

legislación *f* (*leyes*) legislation.

legislar *vi* to legislate.

legislatura *f* (*periodo*) period of office.

legitimar *vt* 1. (*legalizar*) to legitimize. 2. (*certificar*) to authenticate.

legítimo, -ma *adj* (*gen*) legitimate; (*auténtico*) real, genuine; (*oro*) pure.

lego, -ga ◆ *adj* 1. (*gen*) lay. 2. (*ignorante*) ignorant. ◆ *m y f* (*gen*) layman (*f* laywoman).

legua *f* league; ~ **marina** marine league.

leguleyo, -ya *m y f despec* bad lawyer.

legumbre *f* (*gen pl*) pulse, pod vegetable.

lehendakari, lendakari [lenda-'kari] *m* president of the autonomous Basque government.

leído, -da *adj* (*persona*) well-read. ▶ **leída** *f* reading.

leitmotiv [leitmo'tif] (*pl* **leitmotivs**) *m* leitmotiv.

lejanía *f* distance.

lejano, -na *adj* distant; **no está ~** it's not far (away).

lejía *f* bleach.

lejos *adv* 1. (*en el espacio*) far (away); **¿está ~?** is it far?; **a lo ~** in the distance; **de** o **desde ~** from a distance. 2. (*en el pasado*) long ago; (*en el futuro*) far in the future; **eso queda ya ~** that happened a long time ago. ▶ **lejos de** ◆ *loc conj* far from; **~ de mejorar ...** far from getting better ... ◆ *loc prep* far (away) from.

lelo, -la ◆ *adj* stupid. ◆ *m y f* idiot.

lema *m* 1. (*norma*) motto; (*político, publicitario*) slogan. 2. (LING & MAT) lemma.

lencería *f* 1. (*ropa*) linen. 2. (*tienda*) draper's.

lendakari = **lehendakari**.

lengua *f* 1. (*gen*) tongue; ~ **de víbora** o **viperina** malicious tongue; **irse de la ~** to let the cat out of the bag; **morderse la ~** to bite one's tongue; **tirar a alguien de la ~** to draw sb out. 2. (*idioma, lenguaje*) language; ~ **materna** mother tongue.

lenguado *m* sole.

lenguaje *m* (*gen* & INFORM) language; ~ **cifrado** code; ~ **corporal** body language; ~ **gestual** gestures (*pl*); ~ **máquina** machine language; ~ **de programación** programming language; ~ **de los sordomudos** sign language.

lengüeta *f* (*gen* & MÚS) tongue.

lengüetazo *m*, **lengüetada** *f* lick.

lente *f* lens; **~s de contacto** contact lenses. ▶ **lentes** *mpl* (*gafas*) glasses.

lenteja *f* lentil.

lentejuela *f* sequin.

lentilla *f* (*gen pl*) contact lens.

lentitud *f* slowness; **con ~** slowly.

lento, -ta *adj* slow; (*veneno*) slow-working; (*agonía, enfermedad*) lingering.

leña *f* (*madera*) firewood; **echar ~ al fuego** to add fuel to the flames o fire.

leñador, -ra *m y f* woodcutter.

leño *m* (*de madera*) log; **dormir como un ~** to sleep like a log.

Leo ◆ *m* (*zodiaco*) Leo. ◆ *m y f* (*persona*) Leo.

león, -ona *m y f* lion (*f* lioness); *fig* fierce person; **no es tan fiero el ~ como lo pintan** *proverb* he/it *etc* is not as bad as he/it *etc* is made out to be. ▶ **león marino** *m* sea lion.

leonera *f* *fam fig* (*cuarto sucio*) pigsty.

leonino, -na *adj* (*contrato, condiciones*) one-sided.

leopardo *m* leopard.

leotardo *m* 1. (*gen pl*) (*medias*) stockings (*pl*), thick tights (*pl*). 2. (*de gimnasta etc*) leotard.

lépero, -ra *adj* *Amer fam* coarse, vulgar.

lepra *f* leprosy.

leproso, -sa *m y f* leper.

lerdo, -da *adj* (*idiota*) dim, slow-witted; (*torpe*) useless.

les *pron pers pl* 1. (*complemento indirecto*) (to) them; (*ustedes*) (to) you; **~ expliqué el motivo** I explained the reason to them; **~ tengo miedo** I'm afraid of them; **ya ~ dije lo que pasaría** (*a ustedes*) I told you what would happen. 2. (*complemento directo*) them; (*ustedes*) you. 3. → **se**.

lesbiano, -na *adj* lesbian. ▶ **lesbiana** *f* lesbian.

lesión f 1. (*herida*) injury. 2. (*DER*): ~ **grave** grievous bodily harm.

lesionado, -da ♦ adj injured. ♦ m y f injured person.

lesionar vt to injure; *fig* to damage, to harm. ▶ **lesionarse** vpr to injure o.s.

letal adj lethal.

letanía f (*gen pl*) *lit & fig* litany.

letargo m (*ZOOL*) hibernation.

Letonia Latvia.

letra f 1. (*signo*) letter. 2. (*caligrafía*) handwriting. 3. (*estilo*) script; (*IMPRENTA*) typeface; ~ **bastardilla** o **cursiva** o **itálica** italic type, italics (*pl*); ~ **de imprenta** o **molde** (*IMPRENTA*) print; (*en formularios etc*) block capitals (*pl*); ~ **mayúscula/minúscula** capital/small letter; ~ **negrita** o **negrilla** bold (face); **leer la** ~ **pequeña** *fig* to read the small print; **mandar cuatro** ~**s a alguien** to drop sb a line. 4. (*de una canción*) lyrics (*pl*). 5. (*COM*): ~ (**de cambio**) bill of exchange. ▶ **letras** fpl (*EDUC*) arts.

letrado, -da ♦ adj learned. ♦ m y f lawyer.

letrero m sign.

letrina f latrine.

leucemia f leukaemia.

leva f (*MIL*) levy.

levadura f yeast; ~ **de cerveza** brewer's yeast.

levantamiento m 1. (*sublevación*) uprising. 2. (*elevación*) raising; ~ **de pesas** (*DEP*) weightlifting. 3. (*supresión*) lifting, removal.

levantar vt 1. (*gen*) to raise; (*peso, capó, trampilla*) to lift; ~ **el ánimo** to cheer up; ~ **la vista** o **mirada** to look up. 2. (*separar - pintura, venda, tapa*) to remove. 3. (*recoger - campamento*) to strike; (*- tienda de campaña, puesto*) to take down; (*- mesa*) to clear. 4. (*encender - protestas, polémica*) to stir up; ~ **a alguien contra** to stir sb up against. 5. (*suspender - embargo, prohibición*) to lift; (*- pena, castigo*) to suspend; (*- sesión*) to adjourn. 6. (*redactar - acta, atestado*) to draw up. ▶ **levantarse** vpr 1. (*ponerse de pie*) to stand up. 2. (*de la cama*) to get up. 3. (*elevarse - avión etc*) to take off; (*- niebla*) to lift. 4. (*sublevarse*) to rise up. 5. (*empezar - viento, oleaje*) to get up; (*- tormenta*) to gather.

levante m 1. (*este*) east; (*región*) east coast. 2. (*viento*) east wind.

levar vt to weigh.

leve adj 1. (*gen*) light; (*olor, sabor, temblor*) slight. 2. (*pecado, falta, herida*) minor.

3. (*enfermedad*) mild, slight.

levedad f lightness; (*de temblor etc*) slightness; (*de pecado, falto, herida*) minor nature; (*de enfermedad*) mildness.

levita f frock coat.

levitar vi to levitate.

léxico, -ca adj lexical. ▶ **léxico** m (*vocabulario*) vocabulary.

lexicografía f lexicography.

lexicón m lexicon.

ley f 1. (*gen*) law; (*parlamentaria*) act; ~ **de incompatibilidades** act regulating which other positions may be held by people holding public office; **con todas las de la** ~ in due form, properly. 2. (*regla*) rule; ~ **del embudo** one law for o.s. and another for everyone else; ~ **de la oferta y de la demanda** law of supply and demand. 3. (*de un metal*): **de** ~ (*oro*) pure; (*plata*) sterling. ▶ **leyes** fpl (*derecho*) law (*sg*).

leyenda f (*narración*) legend.

liar vt 1. (*atar*) to tie up. 2. (*envolver - cigarrillo*) to roll; ~ **algo en** (*papel*) to wrap sthg up in; (*toalla etc*) to roll sthg up in. 3. (*involucrar*): ~ **a alguien (en)** to get sb mixed up (in). 4. (*complicar - asunto etc*) to confuse; **¡ya me has liado!** now you've really got me confused! ▶ **liarse** vpr 1. (*enredarse*) to get muddled up. 2. (*empezar*) to begin, to start.

Líbano m: **el** ~ the Lebanon.

libélula f dragonfly.

liberación f (*gen*) liberation; (*de preso*) release.

liberado, -da adj (*gen*) liberated; (*preso*) freed.

liberal adj, m y f liberal.

liberar vt (*gen*) to liberate; (*preso*) to free; ~ **de algo a alguien** to free sb from sthg. ▶ **liberarse** vpr to liberate o.s.; ~**se de algo** to free o liberate o.s. from sthg.

Liberia Liberia.

libertad f freedom, liberty; **dejar** o **poner a alguien en** ~ to set sb free, to release sb; **tener** ~ **para hacer algo** to be free to do sthg; **tomarse la** ~ **de hacer algo** to take the liberty of doing sthg; ~ **condicional** probation; ~ **de expresión** freedom of speech; ~ **de imprenta** o **prensa** freedom of the press.

libertar vt (*gen*) to liberate; (*preso*) to set free.

libertino, -na ♦ adj licentious. ♦ m y f libertine.

Libia Libya.

libido f libido.

libra f (*peso, moneda*) pound; ~ **esterlina**

pound sterling. ▶ **Libra** ◆ *m* (*zodiaco*) Libra. ◆ *m y f* (*persona*) Libran.

librador, -ra *m y f* drawer.

libramiento *m*, **libranza** *f* order of payment.

librar ◆ *vt* 1. (*eximir*): ~ **a alguien** (**de algo/de hacer algo**) (*gen*) to free sb (from sthg/from doing sthg); (*pagos, impuestos*) to exempt sb (from sthg/from doing sthg). 2. (*entablar - pelea, lucha*) to engage in; (*- batalla, combate*) to join, to wage. 3. (COM) to draw. ◆ *vi* (*no trabajar*) to be off work. ▶ **librarse** *vpr* 1. (*salvarse*): ~**se** (**de hacer algo**) to escape (from doing sthg); **de buena te libraste** you had a narrow escape. 2. (*deshacerse*): ~**se de algo/alguien** to get rid of sthg/sb.

libre *adj* 1. (*gen*) free; (*rato, tiempo*) spare; (*camino, vía*) clear; (*espacio, piso, lavabo*) empty, vacant; **200 metros** ~**s** 200 metres freestyle; ~ **de** (*gen*) free from; (*exento*) exempt from; ~ **de franqueo** post-free; ~ **de impuestos** tax-free; **ir por** ~ to go it alone. 2. (*alumno*) external; **estudiar por** ~ to be an external student.

librecambio *m* free trade.

librería *f* 1. (*tienda*) bookshop. 2. (*mueble*) bookcase.

librero, -ra ◆ *m y f* (*persona*) bookseller. ◆ *m* Amer (*mueble*) bookshelf.

libreta *f* 1. (*para escribir*) notebook. 2. (*del banco*): ~ (**de ahorros**) savings book.

libreto *m* 1. (MÚS) libretto. 2. Amer (CIN) script.

libro *m* (*gen &* COM) book; **llevar los** ~**s** to keep the books; ~ **de bolsillo** paperback; ~ **de consulta/cuentos** reference/story book; ~ **de escolaridad** school report; ~ **de familia** *document containing personal details of the members of a family*; ~ **de reclamaciones** complaints book; ~ **de registro (de entradas)** register; ~ **de texto** textbook.

Lic. *abrev de* **licenciado**.

licencia *f* 1. (*documento*) licence, permit; (*autorización*) permission; ~ **de armas/caza** gun/hunting licence; ~ **de obras** planning permission; ~ **poética** poetic licence. 2. (MIL) discharge. 3. (*confianza*) licence, freedom.

licenciado, -da *m y f* 1. (EDUC) graduate; ~ **en económicas** economics graduate. 2. (MIL) discharged soldier.

licenciar *vt* (MIL) to discharge. ▶ **licenciarse** *vpr* 1. (EDUC): ~**se** (**en**) to

graduate (in). 2. (MIL) to be discharged.

licenciatura *f* degree.

licencioso, -sa *adj* licentious.

liceo *m* (EDUC) lycée.

licitador, -ra *m y f* bidder.

lícito, -ta *adj* 1. (*legal*) lawful. 2. (*correcto*) right. 3. (*justo*) fair.

licor *m* liquor.

licuadora *f* liquidizer, blender.

licuar *vt* (CULIN) to liquidize.

líder ◆ *adj* leading. ◆ *m y f* leader.

liderar *vt* to lead.

liderato, **liderazgo** *m* 1. (*primer puesto*) lead; (*en liga*) first place. 2. (*dirección*) leadership.

lidia *f* 1. (*arte*) bullfighting. 2. (*corrida*) bullfight.

lidiar ◆ *vi* (*luchar*): ~ (**con**) to struggle (with). ◆ *vt* (TAUROM) to fight.

liebre *f* (ZOOL) hare.

Liechtenstein ['litʃenstein] Liechtenstein.

lienzo *m* 1. (*para pintar*) canvas. 2. (*cuadro*) painting.

lifting ['liftin] (*pl* **liftings**) *m* facelift.

liga *f* 1. (*gen*) league. 2. (*de medias*) suspender.

ligadura *f* 1. (MED & MÚS) ligature. 2. (*atadura*) bond, tie.

ligamento *m* (ANAT) ligament.

ligar ◆ *vt* (*gen &* CULIN) to bind; (*atar*) to tie (up). ◆ *vi* 1. (*coincidir*): ~ (**con**) to tally (with). 2. *fam* (*conquistar*): ~ (**con**) to get off (with).

ligazón *f* link, connection.

ligereza *f* 1. (*levedad - gen*) lightness. 2. (*agilidad*) agility. 3. (*irreflexión - cualidad*) rashness; (*- acto*) rash act.

ligero, -ra *adj* 1. (*gen*) light; (*dolor, rumor, descenso*) slight; (*traje, tela*) thin. 2. (*ágil*) agile, nimble. 3. (*rápido*) quick, swift. 4. (*irreflexivo*) flippant; **a la ligera** lightly; **juzgar a alguien a la ligera** to be quick to judge sb.

light [lait] *adj inv* (*comida*) low-calorie; (*refresco*) diet (*antes de sust*); (*cigarrillos*) light.

ligón, -ona *fam adj*: **es muy** ~ he's always getting off with sb or other.

liguero, -ra *adj* (DEP) league (*antes de sust*). ▶ **liguero** *m* suspender belt Br, garter belt Am.

lija *f* (*papel*) sandpaper.

lila ◆ *f* (*flor*) lilac. ◆ *adj inv & m* (*color*) lilac.

lima *f* 1. (*utensilio*) file; ~ **de uñas** nail file. 2. (BOT) lime.

Lima Lima.
limar vt 1. (*pulir*) to file down. 2. (*perfeccionar*) to polish.
limitación f 1. (*restricción*) limitation, limit. 2. (*distrito*) boundaries (pl).
limitado, -da adj 1. (*gen*) limited. 2. fig (*poco inteligente*) dim-witted.
limitar ◆ vt 1. (*gen*) to limit. 2. (*terreno*) to mark out. 3. (*atribuciones, derechos etc*) to set out, to define. ◆ vi: ~ (con) to border (on). ▶ **limitarse a** vpr to limit o.s. to.
límite ◆ adj inv 1. (*precio, velocidad, edad*) maximum. 2. (*situación*) extreme; (*caso*) borderline. ◆ m 1. (*tope*) limit; **dentro de un ~** within limits; **su pasión no tiene ~** her passion knows no bounds; **~ de velocidad** speed limit. 2. (*confín*) boundary.
limítrofe adj (*país, territorio*) bordering; (*terreno, finca*) neighbouring.
limón m lemon.
limonada f lemonade.
limonero, -ra adj lemon (*antes de sust*). ▶ **limonero** m lemon tree.
limosna f alms (pl); **pedir ~** to beg.
limpia f Amer cleaning.
limpiabotas m y f inv shoeshine, bootblack Br.
limpiacristales m inv window-cleaning fluid.
limpiamente adv 1. (*con destreza*) cleanly. 2. (*honradamente*) honestly.
limpiaparabrisas m inv windscreen wiper Br, windshield wiper Am.
limpiar vt 1. (*gen*) to clean; (*con trapo*) to wipe; (*mancha*) to wipe away; (*zapatos*) to polish. 2. fig (*desembarazar*): ~ **algo de algo** to clear sthg of sthg.
limpieza f 1. (*cualidad*) cleanliness. 2. (*acción*) cleaning; **~ en seco** dry cleaning. 3. fig (*destreza*) skill, cleanness. 4. fig (*honradez*) honesty.
limpio, -pia adj 1. (*gen*) clean; (*pulcro*) neat; (*cielo, imagen*) clear. 2. (*neto - sueldo etc*) net. 3. (*honrado*) honest; (*intenciones*) honourable; (*juego*) clean. 4. (*sin culpa*): **estar ~** to be in the clear. ▶ **limpio** adv cleanly, fair; **pasar a** o **poner en ~** to make a fair copy of; **sacar algo en ~ de** to make sthg out from.
linaje m lineage.
linaza f linseed.
lince m lynx; **ser un ~ para algo** to be very sharp at sthg.
linchar vt to lynch.
lindar ▶ **lindar con** vi 1. (*terreno*) to

adjoin, to be next to. 2. (*conceptos, ideas*) to border on.
linde m o f boundary.
lindero, -ra adj (*terreno*) adjoining. ▶ **lindero** m boundary.
lindo, -da adj (*bonito*) pretty, lovely; Amer (*agradable*) nice, pleasant; **de lo ~** a great deal.
línea f 1. (*gen*, DEP & TELECOM) line; **cortar la ~** (*telefónica*) to cut off the phone; **~ aérea** airline; **~ de conducta** course of action; **~ continua** (AUTOM) solid white line; **~ de puntos** dotted line. 2. (*de un coche etc*) lines (pl), shape. 3. (*silueta*) figure; **guardar la ~** to watch one's figure. 4. (*estilo*) style; **de ~ clásica** classical. 5. (*categoría*) class, category; **de primera ~** first-rate. 6. (INFORM): **en ~** on-line; **fuera de ~** off-line. 7. loc: **en ~s generales** in broad terms; **leer entre ~s** to read between the lines.
lingote m ingot.
lingüista m y f linguist.
lingüístico, -ca adj linguistic. ▶ **lingüística** f linguistics.
linier [li'njer] (pl **liniers**) m linesman.
linimento m liniment.
lino m 1. (*planta*) flax. 2. (*tejido*) linen.
linterna f 1. (*farol*) lantern, lamp. 2. (*de pilas*) torch Br, flashlight Am.
lío m 1. (*paquete*) bundle. 2. fam (*enredo*) mess; **hacerse un ~** to get muddled up; **meterse en ~s** to get into trouble. 3. fam (*jaleo*) racket, row. 4. fam (*amorío*) affair.
liposucción f liposuction.
liquen m lichen.
liquidación f 1. (*pago*) settlement, payment. 2. (*rebaja*) clearance sale. 3. (*fin*) liquidation.
liquidar vt 1. (*pagar - deuda*) to pay; (*- cuenta*) to settle. 2. (*rebajar*) to sell off. 3. (*malgastar*) to throw away. 4. (*acabar - asunto*) to settle; (*- negocio, sociedad*) to wind up.
líquido, -da adj 1. (*gen*) liquid. 2. (ECON) (*neto*) net. ▶ **líquido** m 1. (*gen*) liquid. 2. (ECON) liquid assets (pl). 3. (MED) fluid.
lira f 1. (MÚS) lyre. 2. (*moneda*) lira.
lírico, -ca adj (LITER) lyrical. ▶ **lírica** f lyric poetry.
lirio m iris.
lirón m (ZOOL) dormouse; **dormir como un ~** fig to sleep like a log.
lis f iris.
Lisboa Lisbon.
lisiado, -da ◆ adj crippled. ◆ m y f cripple.

lisiar vt to maim, to cripple.

liso, -sa ♦ adj 1. (llano) flat; (sin aspe-rezas) smooth; (pelo) straight; **los 400 metros ~s** the 400 metres; **lisa y llanamente** quite simply; **hablando lisa y llanamente** to put it plainly. 2. (no estampado) plain. ♦ m y f Amer coarse o rude person.

lisonja f flattering remark.

lisonjear vt to flatter.

lista f 1. (enumeración) list; **pasar ~** to call the register; **~ de boda/de espera/ de precios** wedding/waiting/price list. 2. (de tela, madera) strip; (de papel) slip; (de color) stripe. ▶ **lista de correos** f poste restante.

listado, -da adj striped.

listín ▶ **listín (de teléfonos)** m (tele-phone) directory.

listo, -ta adj 1. (inteligente, hábil) clever, bright; **dárselas de ~** to make o.s. out to be clever; **pasarse de ~** to be too clever by half; **ser más ~ que el hambre** to be nobody's fool. 2. (preparado) ready; **¿estáis ~s?** are you ready?; **estás o vas ~ (si crees que ...)** you've got another think coming (if you think that ...).

listón m lath; (DEP) bar.

litera f 1. (cama) bunk (bed); (de barco) berth; (de tren) couchette. 2. (vehículo) litter.

literal adj literal.

literario, -ria adj literary.

literato, -ta m y f writer.

literatura f literature.

litigar vi to go to law.

litigio m (DER) litigation (U); fig dis-pute; **en ~** in dispute.

litografía f 1. (arte) lithography. 2. (grabado) lithograph.

litoral ♦ adj coastal. ♦ m coast.

litro m litre.

Lituania Lithuania.

liturgia f liturgy.

liviano, -na adj 1. (ligero - blusa) thin; (- carga) light. 2. (sin importancia) slight.

lívido, -da adj 1. (pálido) very pale. 2. (amoratado) livid.

ll, Ll f (letra) ll, Ll.

llaga f lit & fig wound.

llagar vt to wound.

llama f 1. (de fuego, pasión) flame; **en ~s** ablaze. 2. (ZOOL) llama.

llamada f 1. (gen) call; (a la puerta) knock; (con timbre) ring. 2. (TELECOM) telephone call; **hacer una ~** to make a phone call; **~ urbana/interurbana/a cobro revertido** local/long-distance/ reverse-charge call.

llamado, -da adj so-called. ▶ **lla-mado** m Amer (de teléfono) call.

llamamiento m (apelación) appeal, call.

llamar ♦ vt 1. (gen) to call; (con gestos) to beckon. 2. (por teléfono) to phone, to call. 3. (convocar) to summon, to call; **~ (a filas)** (MIL) to call up. 4. (atraer) to attract, to call. ♦ vi 1. (a la puerta etc - con golpes) to knock; (- con timbre) to ring; **están llamando** there's somebody at the door. 2. (por teléfono) to phone. ▶ **llamarse** vpr (tener por nombre) to be called; **¿cómo te llamas?** what's your name?; **me llamo Pepe** my name's Pepe.

llamarada f (de fuego, ira etc) blaze.

llamativo, -va adj (color) bright, gaudy; (ropa) showy.

llamear vi to burn, to blaze.

llano, -na adj 1. (campo, superficie) flat. 2. (trato, persona) natural, straightfor-ward. 3. (pueblo, clase) ordinary. 4. (len-guaje, expresión) simple, plain. ▶ **llano** m (llanura) plain.

llanta f rim.

llanto m tears (pl), crying.

llanura f plain.

llave f 1. (gen) key; **bajo ~** under lock and key; **echar la ~** to lock up; **~ en mano** (vivienda) ready for immediate occupation; **~ de contacto** ignition key; **~ maestra** master key. 2. (del agua, gas) tap Br, faucet Am; (de la electricidad) switch; **cerrar la ~ de paso** to turn the water/gas off at the mains. 3. (he-rramienta) spanner; **~ inglesa** monkey wrench. 4. (de judo etc) hold, lock. 5. (signo ortográfico) curly bracket.

llavero m keyring.

llavín m latchkey.

llegada f 1. (gen) arrival. 2. (DEP) fin-ish.

llegar vi 1. (a un sitio): **~ (de)** to arrive (from); **~ a un hotel/una ciudad** to arrive at a hotel/in a city; **llegaré pronto** I'll be there early. 2. (un tiempo, la noche etc) to come. 3. (durar): **~ a o hasta** to last until. 4. (alcanzar): **~ a** to reach; **no llego al techo** I can't reach the ceiling; **~ hasta** to reach up to. 5. (ser suficiente): **~ (para)** to be enough (for). 6. (lograr): **~ a (ser) algo** to get to be sthg, to become sthg; **si llego a saberlo** if I get to know of it. ▶ **llegarse a** vpr to go round to.

llenar vt 1. (ocupar): **~ algo (de)** (vaso, hoyo, habitación) to fill sthg (with); (pared, suelo) to cover sthg (with). 2. (satisfacer) to satisfy. **3.** (*rellenar - impreso*) to fill in o out. **4.** (*colmar*): **~ a alguien de** to fill sb with. ▶ **llenarse** *vpr* **1.** (*ocuparse*) to fill up. **2.** (*saciarse*) to be full. **3.** (*cubrirse*): **~se de** to become covered in.

lleno, -na *adj* **1.** (*gen*) full; (*cubierto*) covered; **~ de** (*gen*) full of; (*manchas, pósters*) covered in. **2.** *fam* (*regordete*) chubby. ▶ **de lleno** *loc adv* full in the face; **acertó de ~** he was bang on target.

llevadero, -ra *adj* bearable.

llevar ◆ *vt* **1.** (*gen*) to carry. **2.** (*acompañar, coger y depositar*) to take; **~ algo/a alguien a** to take sthg/sb to; **me llevó en coche** he drove me there. **3.** (*prenda, objeto personal*) to wear; **llevo gafas** I wear glasses; **no llevo dinero** I haven't got any money on me. **4.** (*caballo, coche etc*) to handle. **5.** (*conducir*): **~ a alguien a algo** to lead sb to sthg; **~ a alguien a hacer algo** to lead o cause sb to do sthg. **6.** (*ocuparse de, dirigir*) to be in charge of; (*casa, negocio*) to run; **lleva la contabilidad** she keeps the books. **7.** (*hacer - de alguna manera*): **lleva muy bien sus estudios** he's doing very well in his studies. **8.** (*tener - de alguna manera*) to have; **~ el pelo largo** to have long hair; **llevas las manos sucias** your hands are dirty. **9.** (*soportar*) to deal o cope with. **10.** (*mantener*) to keep; **~ el paso** to keep in step. **11.** (*pasarse - tiempo*): **lleva tres semanas sin venir** she hasn't come for three weeks now, it's three weeks since she came last. **12.** (*ocupar - tiempo*) to take; **me llevó un día hacer este guiso** it took me a day to make this dish. **13.** (*sobrepasar en*): **te llevo seis puntos** I'm six points ahead of you; **me lleva dos centímetros** he's two centimetres taller than me. **14.** *loc*: **~ consigo** (*implicar*) to lead to, to bring about; **~ las de perder** to be heading for defeat. ◆ *vi* **1.** (*conducir*): **~ a** to lead to; **esta carretera lleva al norte** this road leads north. **2.** (*antes de participio*) (*haber*): **llevo leída media novela** I'm halfway through the novel; **llevo dicho esto mismo docenas de veces** I've said the same thing time and again. **3.** (*antes de gerundio*) (*estar*): **~ mucho tiempo haciendo algo** to have been doing sthg for a long time. ▶ **llevarse** *vpr* **1.** (*coger*) to take, to steal. **2.** (*conseguir*) to get; **se ha llevado el premio** she has carried off the prize; **yo me llevo siempre las culpas** I always get the blame. **3.** (*recibir - susto, sorpresa etc*) to get, to receive; **me llevé**

un disgusto I was upset. **4.** (*entenderse*): **~se bien/mal (con alguien)** to get on well/badly (with sb). **5.** (*estar de moda*) to be in (fashion); **este año se lleva el verde** green is in this year. **6.** (MAT): **me llevo una** carry (the) one.

llorar *vi* (*con lágrimas*) to cry.

lloriquear *vi* to whine, to snivel.

lloro *m* crying (U), tears (*pl*).

llorón, -ona *m y f* crybaby.

lloroso, -sa *adj* tearful.

llover *v impers* to rain; **está lloviendo** it's raining.

llovizna *f* drizzle.

lloviznar *v impers* to drizzle.

lluvia *f* (METEOR) rain; **bajo la ~** in the rain; **~ ácida** acid rain; **~ radiactiva** (nuclear) fallout.

lluvioso, -sa *adj* rainy, wet.

lo, la (*mpl* los, *fpl* las) *pron pers* (*complemento directo*) (*cosa*) it; (*pl*) them; (*persona*) him (*f* her); (*pl*) them; (*usted*) you. ▶ **lo** ◆ *pron pers* (*neutro*) (*predicado*) it; **su hermana es muy guapa pero él no ~ es** his sister is very good-looking, but he isn't; **es muy bueno aunque no ~ parezca** it's very good, even if it doesn't look it. ◆ *art det* (*neutro*): **~ antiguo me gusta más que ~ moderno** I like old things better than modern things; **~ mejor/peor** the best/worst part; **no te imaginas ~ grande que era** you can't imagine how big it was. ▶ **lo de** *loc prep*: **¿y ~ de la fiesta?** what about the party, then?; **siento ~ de ayer** I'm sorry about yesterday. ▶ **lo que** *loc conj* what; **acepté ~ que me ofrecieron** I accepted what they offered me.

loa *f* **1.** (*gen*) praise. **2.** (LITER) eulogy.

loable *adj* praiseworthy.

loar *vt* to praise.

lobato = lobezno.

lobby ['loβi] (*pl* lobbies) *m* lobby, pressure group.

lobezno, lobato *m* wolf cub.

lobo, -ba *m y f* wolf. ▶ **lobo de mar** *m* (*marinero*) sea dog. ▶ **lobo marino** *m* (*foca*) seal.

lóbrego, -ga *adj* gloomy, murky.

lóbulo *m* lobe.

local ◆ *adj* local. ◆ *m* **1.** (*edificio*) premises (*pl*). **2.** (*sede*) headquarters (*pl*).

localidad *f* **1.** (*población*) place, town. **2.** (*asiento*) seat. **3.** (*entrada*) ticket; **'no hay ~es'** 'sold out'.

localizar *vt* **1.** (*encontrar*) to locate. **2.** (*circunscribir*) to localize.

loción f lotion.
loco, -ca ♦ adj 1. (gen) mad; **estar ~ de/por** to be mad with/about; **volverse ~ por** to be mad about; **~ de atar** o **remate** stark raving mad; **a lo ~** (sin pensar) hastily; (temerariamente) wildly. 2. (extraordinario - interés, ilusión) tremendous; (- amor, alegría) wild. ♦ m y f lit & fig madman (f madwoman), lunatic.
locomoción f transport; (de tren) locomotion.
locomotor, -ra o **-triz** adj locomotive. ► **locomotora** f engine, locomotive.
locuaz adj loquacious, talkative.
locución f phrase.
locura f 1. (demencia) madness. 2. (imprudencia) folly.
locutor, -ra m y f (de radio) announcer; (de televisión) presenter.
locutorio m 1. (TELECOM) phone box o booth. 2. (RADIO) studio.
lodo m lit & fig mud.
logaritmo m logarithm.
lógico, -ca adj logical; **es ~ que se enfade** it stands to reason that he should get angry. ► **lógica** f (ciencia) logic.
logístico, -ca adj logistic. ► **logística** f logistics (pl).
logopeda m y f speech therapist.
logotipo m logo.
logrado, -da adj (bien hecho) accomplished.
lograr vt (gen) to achieve; (puesto, beca, divorcio) to get, to obtain; (resultado) to obtain, to achieve; (perfección) to attain; (victoria, premio) to win; (deseo, aspiración) to fulfil; **~ hacer algo** to manage to do sthg; **~ que alguien haga algo** to manage to get sb to do sthg.
logro m achievement.
LOGSE (abrev de **Ley Orgánica de Ordenación General del Sistema Educativo**) f Spanish Education Act.
loma f hillock.
lombriz f earthworm, worm.
lomo m 1. (espalda) back. 2. (carne) loin. 3. (de libro) spine.
lona f canvas.
loncha f slice; (de beicon) rasher.
londinense ♦ adj London (antes de sust). ♦ m y f Londoner.
Londres London.
longaniza f type of spicy, cold pork sausage.
longitud f 1. (dimensión) length; **tiene medio metro de ~** it's half a metre long;

~ de onda wavelength. 2. (ASTRON & GEOGR) longitude.
lonja f 1. (loncha) slice. 2. (edificio) exchange; **~ de pescado** fish market.
loro, -ra m y f (animal) parrot.
los ♦ art → **el**. ♦ pron → **lo**.
losa f paving stone, flagstone; (de tumba) tombstone.
loseta f floor tile.
lote m 1. (parte) share. 2. (conjunto) batch, lot.
lotería f 1. (gen) lottery; **jugar a la ~** to play the lottery; **le tocó la ~** she won the lottery; **~ primitiva** twice-weekly state-run lottery. 2. (juego de mesa) lotto.

LOTERÍA PRIMITIVA
In this Spanish state-run lottery, participants try to guess a combination of six numbers between one and forty-nine. A ticket contains eight grids of forty-nine boxes, each grid being equivalent to one entry. The 'lotería primitiva' is drawn twice a week.

loto f fam (lotería) weekly state-run lottery.
loza f 1. (material) earthenware; (porcelana) china. 2. (objetos) crockery.
lozanía f (de persona) youthful vigour.
lozano, -na adj 1. (planta) lush. 2. (persona) youthfully vigorous.
Ltd., ltda. (abrev de limitada) Ltd.
lubina f sea bass.
lubricante, lubrificante ♦ adj lubricating. ♦ m lubricant.
lubricar, lubrificar vt to lubricate.
lucero m bright star.
lucha f fight; fig struggle; **~ libre** all-in wrestling.
luchar vi to fight; fig to struggle; **~ contra/por** to fight against/for.
lucidez f lucidity, clarity.
lúcido, -da adj lucid.
luciérnaga f glow-worm.
lucimiento m (de ceremonia etc) sparkle; (de actriz etc) brilliant performance.
lucir ♦ vi 1. (gen) to shine. 2. (llevar puesto) to wear. 3. Amer (parecer) to seem. ♦ vt (gen) to show off; (ropa) to sport. ► **lucirse** vpr 1. (destacar) **~se (en)** to shine (at). 2. fam fig & irón (quedar mal) to mess things up.
lucrativo, -va adj lucrative; **no ~** non profit-making.
lucro m profit, gain.
lucubrar vt to rack one's brains over.
lúdico, -ca adj (del juego) game (antes de sust); (ocioso) of enjoyment, of pleasure.

ludopatía f pathological addiction to gambling.

luego ◆ adv 1. (justo después) then, next; **primero aquí y ~ allí** first here and then there. 2. (más tarde) later; **hazlo ~** do it later. 3. Amer (pronto) soon. ◆ conj (así que) so, therefore. ▶ **luego luego** loc adv Amer right away.

lugar m 1. (gen) place; (localidad) place, town; (del crimen, accidente etc) scene; (para acampar, merendar etc) spot; **en primer ~** in the first place, firstly; **fuera de ~** out of place; **no hay ~ a duda** there's no room for doubt; **tener ~** to take place; **yo en tu ~** if I were you. 2. (motivo) cause, reason; **dar ~ a** to bring about, to cause. 3. (puesto) position. ▶ **en lugar de** loc prep instead of. ▶ **lugar común** m platitude.

lugareño, -ña m y f villager.

lúgubre adj gloomy, mournful.

lujo m luxury; fig profusion; **permitirse el ~ de algo/de hacer algo** to be able to afford sthg/to do sthg.

lujoso, -sa adj luxurious.

lujuria f lust.

lumbago m lumbago.

lumbre f (fuego) fire; **dar ~ a alguien** to give sb a light.

lumbrera f fam leading light.

luminoso, -sa adj (gen) bright; (fuente, energía) light (antes de sust).

luna f 1. (astro) moon; **~ llena/nueva** full/new moon. 2. (cristal) window (pane). 3. loc: **estar en la ~** to be miles away. ▶ **luna de miel** f honeymoon.

lunar ◆ adj lunar. ◆ m 1. (en la piel) mole, beauty spot. 2. (en telas) spot; **a o de ~es** spotted.

lunático, -ca m y f lunatic.

lunes m inv Monday; ver también **sábado**.

luneta f (de coche) windscreen; **~ térmica** demister.

lupa f magnifying glass.

lustrabotas m inv, **lustrador** m Amer bootblack.

lustrar vt to polish.

lustre m (brillo) shine.

lustro m five-year period.

lustroso, -sa adj shiny.

luto m mourning; **de ~** in mourning.

luxación f dislocation.

Luxemburgo Luxembourg.

luxemburgués, -esa ◆ adj Luxembourg (antes de sust). ◆ m y f Luxembourger.

luz f (gen) light; (electricidad) electricity; (destello) flash (of light); **apagar la ~** to switch off the light; **cortar la ~** to cut off the electricity supply; **dar o encender la ~** to switch on the light; **pagar (el recibo de) la ~** to pay the electricity (bill); **se ha ido la ~** the lights have gone out; **~ solar** sunlight; **a la ~ de** in the light of; **arrojar o sobre** to shed light on; **dar a (un niño)** to give birth (to a child); **sacar a la ~** to bring to light. ▶ **luces** fpl (AUTOM) lights; **poner las luces de carretera o largas** to put (one's headlights) on full beam; **luces de cruce o cortas** dipped headlights; **luces de posición o situación** sidelights.

lycra® f Lycra®.

M

m¹, M f (letra) m, M.

m² (abrev de metro) m.

macabro, -bra adj macabre.

macana f Amer fam (disparate) stupid thing.

macarra m fam (de prostitutas) pimp; (rufián) thug.

macarrón m (tubo) sheath (of cable). ▶ **macarrones** mpl (pasta) macaroni (U).

macedonia f salad; **~ de frutas** fruit salad.

macerar vt (CULIN) to soak, to macerate.

maceta f (tiesto) flowerpot.

macetero m flowerpot holder.

machaca m y f (currante) dogsbody.

machacar ◆ vt 1. (triturar) to crush. 2. fig (insistir) to keep going on about. ◆ vi fig: **~ (sobre)** to go on (about).

machete m machete.

machista adj, m y f male chauvinist.

macho ◆ adj 1. (BIOL) male. 2. fig (hombre) macho. ◆ m 1. (BIOL) male. 2. fig (hombre) he-man. 3. (TECN) male part; (de enchufe) pin. ◆ interj fam: **¡oye, ~!** oy, mate!

macizo, -za adj solid; **estar ~** (hombre) to be hunky; (mujer) to be gorgeous. ▶ **macizo** m 1. (GEOGR) massif. 2. (BOT): **~ de flores** flowerbed.

macro f (INFORM) macro.

mal

macrobiótico, -ca *adj* macrobiotic.
mácula *f* spot; *fig* blemish.
macuto *m* backpack.
madeja *f* hank, skein.
madera *f* 1. (*gen*) wood; (CONSTR) timber; (*tabla*) piece of wood; **de ~** wooden; **~ contrachapada** plywood. 2. *fig* (*disposición*) **tener ~ de algo** to have the makings of sthg.
madero *m* (*tabla*) log.
madrastra *f* stepmother.
madrazo *m* Amer hard blow.
madre *f* 1. (*gen*) mother; **~ adoptiva/de alquiler** foster/surrogate mother; **~ política** mother-in-law; **~ soltera** single mother; **~ superiora** mother superior; **me vale ~** Amer *fig* I couldn't care less. 2. (*poso*) dregs (*pl*). ▶ **madre mía** *interj* **¡~ mía!** Jesus!, Christ!
Madrid Madrid.
madriguera *f* (*gen & fig*) den; (*de conejo*) burrow.
madrileño, -ña *m y f* native/inhabitant of Madrid.
madrina *f* (*gen*) patroness; (*de boda*) bridesmaid; (*de bautizo*) godmother.
madroño *m* 1. (*árbol*) strawberry tree. 2. (*fruto*) strawberry-tree berry.
madrugada *f* 1. (*amanecer*) dawn. 2. (*noche*) early morning; **las tres de la ~** three in the morning.
madrugador, -ra *adj* early-rising.
madrugar *vi* to get up early; *fig* to be quick off the mark.
madurar ◆ *vt* 1. (*gen*) to mature; (*fruta, mies*) to ripen. 2. (*idea, proyecto etc*) to think through. ◆ *vi* (*gen*) to mature; (*fruta*) to ripen.
madurez *f* 1. (*cualidad - gen*) maturity; (*- de fruta, mies*) ripeness. 2. (*edad adulta*) adulthood.
maduro, -ra *adj* (*gen*) mature; (*fruta, mies*) ripe; **de edad madura** middle-aged.
maestra → **maestro**.
maestría *f* (*habilidad*) mastery, skill.
maestro, -tra ◆ *adj* 1. (*perfecto*) masterly. 2. (*principal*) main; (*llave*) master (*antes de sust*). ◆ *m y f* 1. (*profesor*) teacher. 2. (*sabio*) master; (*experto*) expert. 3. (MÚS) maestro. 4. (*director*): **~ de ceremonias** master of ceremonies; **~ de cocina** chef; **~ de obras** foreman; **~ de orquesta** conductor.
mafia *f* mafia.
mafioso, -sa *m y f* mafioso.
magdalena *f* fairy cake.
magia *f* magic.

mágico, -ca *adj* 1. (*con magia*) magic. 2. (*atractivo*) magical.
magisterio *m* 1. (*enseñanza*) teaching. 2. (*profesión*) teaching profession.
magistrado, -da *m y f* (*juez*) judge, magistrate.
magistral *adj* 1. (*de maestro*) magisterial. 2. (*genial*) masterly.
magistratura *f* 1. (*jueces*) magistrature. 2. (*tribunal*) tribunal; **~ de trabajo** industrial tribunal.
magnánimo, -ma *adj* magnanimous.
magnate *m* magnate; **~ del petróleo/ de la prensa** oil/press baron.
magnesia *f* magnesia.
magnesio *m* magnesium.
magnético, -ca *adj* lit & fig magnetic.
magnetizar *vt* to magnetize; *fig* to mesmerize.
magnetofónico, -ca *adj* (*cinta*) magnetic.
magnetófono *m* tape recorder.
magnicidio *m* assassination (*of somebody important*).
magnificencia *f* magnificence.
magnífico, -ca *adj* wonderful, magnificent.
magnitud *f* magnitude.
magnolia *f* magnolia.
mago, -ga *m y f* 1. (*prestidigitador*) magician. 2. (*en cuentos etc*) wizard.
magro, -gra *adj* 1. (*sin grasa*) lean. 2. (*pobre*) poor. ▶ **magro** *m* lean meat.
maguey *m* agave.
magulladura *f* bruise.
magullar *vt* to bruise.
mahometano, -na *adj*, *m y f* Muslim.
mahonesa = **mayonesa**.
maicena *f* cornflour Br, cornstarch Am.
maître ['metre] *m* head waiter.
maíz *m* maize Br, corn Am; **~ dulce** sweetcorn.
maja → **majo**.
majadero, -ra *m y f* idiot.
majareta *fam* ◆ *adj* nutty. ◆ *m y f* nutcase.
majestad *f* majesty. ▶ **Su Majestad** *f* His/Her Majesty.
majestuoso, -sa *adj* majestic.
majo, -ja *adj* 1. (*simpático*) nice. 2. (*bonito*) pretty.
mal ◆ *adj* → **malo**. ◆ *m* 1. (*perversión*): **el ~** evil. 2. (*daño*) harm, damage. 3. (*enfermedad*) sickness; **~ de altura** o **de montaña** altitude o mountain sickness; **~ de ojo** evil eye. 4. (*inconveniente*) bad thing;

un ~ **necesario** a necessary evil. ◆ adv **1.** (*incorrectamente*) wrong; **esto está ~ hecho** this has been done wrong; **has escrito ~ esta palabra** you've spelt that word wrong. **2.** (*inadecuadamente*) badly; **la fiesta salió ~** the party went off badly; **oigo/veo ~** I can't hear/see very well; **encontrarse ~** (*enfermo*) to feel ill; (*incómodo*) to feel uncomfortable; **oler ~** (*tener mal olor*) to smell bad; *fam* (*tener mal cariz*) to smell fishy; **saber ~** (*tener mal sabor*) to taste bad; **sentar ~ a alguien** (*ropa*) not to suit sb; (*comida*) to disagree with sb; (*comentario, actitud*) to upset sb; **tomar algo a ~** to take sthg the wrong way. **3.** (*difícilmente*) hardly; **puede saberlo si no se lo cuentas** he's hardly going to know it if you don't tell him. **4.** *loc:* **estar a ~ con alguien** to have fallen out with sb; **ir de ~ en peor** to go from bad to worse; **no estaría ~ que ...** it would be nice if ... ▶ **mal que** *loc conj* although, even though. ▶ **mal que bien** *loc adv* somehow or other.

malabarismo m *lit & fig* juggling (U).

malabarista m y f juggler.

malacostumbrado, -da adj spoiled.

malaria f malaria.

Malasia Malaysia.

malcriado, -da adj spoiled.

maldad f **1.** (*cualidad*) evil. **2.** (*acción*) evil thing.

maldecir ◆ vt to curse. ◆ vi to curse.

maldición f curse.

maldito, -ta adj **1.** (*embrujado*) cursed. **2.** *fam* (*para enfatizar*) damned; **¡maldita sea!** damn it!

maleable adj *lit & fig* malleable.

maleante m y f crook.

malecón m (*atracadero*) jetty.

maleducado, -da adj rude.

maleficio m curse.

malentendido m misunderstanding.

malestar m **1.** (*dolor*) upset, discomfort; **siento un ~ en el estómago** I've got an upset stomach; **sentir ~ general** to feel unwell. **2.** *fig* (*inquietud*) uneasiness, unrest.

maleta f suitcase; **hacer o preparar la ~** to pack (one's bags).

maletero m boot Br, trunk Am.

maletín m briefcase.

malévolo, -la adj malevolent, wicked.

maleza f (*arbustos*) undergrowth; (*malas hierbas*) weeds (*pl*).

malformación f malformation.

malgastar vt (*dinero, tiempo*) to waste; (*salud*) to ruin.

malhablado, -da adj foul-mouthed.

malhechor, -ra adj, m y f criminal.

malhumorado, -da adj bad-tempered; (*enfadado*) in a bad mood.

malicia f (*maldad*) wickedness, evil; (*mala intención*) malice.

malicioso, -sa adj (*malo*) wicked, evil; (*malintencionado*) malicious.

maligno, -na adj malignant.

malla f **1.** (*tejido*) mesh; ~ **de alambre** wire mesh. **2.** (*red*) net. **3.** *Amer* (*traje de baño*) swimsuit. ▶ **mallas** fpl **1.** (*de gimnasia*) leotard (*sg*); (*de ballet*) tights. **2.** (*de portería*) net (*sg*).

Mallorca Majorca.

malo, -la, **mal** (*compar* peor, *superl* el peor) adj (*antes de sust masc sg* **mal**) **1.** (*gen*) bad; (*calidad*) poor, bad; **hizo mal tiempo** the weather was bad; **lo ~ fue que ...** the problem was (that) ... **2.** (*malicioso*) wicked. **3.** (*enfermo*) ill, sick; **estar/ponerse ~** to be/fall ill. **4.** (*travieso*) naughty. ▶ **malo, -la** m y f (*de película etc*) villain, baddie. ▶ **malas** fpl: **estar de malas** to be in a bad mood; **por las malas** by force.

malograr vt to waste. ▶ **malograrse** vpr **1.** (*fracasar*) to fail. **2.** (*morir*) to die before one's time.

malparado, -da adj: **salir ~ de algo** to come out of sthg badly.

malpensado, -da adj malicious, evil-minded.

malsano, -na adj unhealthy.

malsonante adj rude.

malta m malt.

Malta Malta.

maltés, -esa adj, m y f Maltese.

maltratar vt **1.** (*pegar, insultar*) to ill-treat. **2.** (*estropear*) to damage.

maltrecho, -cha adj battered.

malva ◆ f (BOT) mallow. ◆ adj inv mauve. ◆ m (*color*) mauve.

malvado, -da adj evil, wicked.

malversación f: ~ (*de fondos*) embezzlement (of funds).

malversar vt to embezzle, to misappropriate.

Malvinas fpl: **las (islas) ~** the Falkland Islands, the Falklands.

malvivir vi to scrape together an existence.

mama f **1.** (*órgano - de mujer*) breast; (ZOOL) udder. **2.** *fam* (*madre*) mum.

mamá (*pl* **mamás**) f *fam* mum, mummy; ~ **grande** Amer fam grandma.

mamadera f Amer (baby's) bottle.
mamar ◆ vt 1. (suj: bebé) to suckle. 2. fig (aprender): **lo mamó desde pequeño** he was immersed in it as a child. ◆ vi to suckle.
mamarracho m (fantoche) mess.
mambo m mambo.
mamífero, -ra adj mammal. ► **mamífero** m mammal.
mamografía f (MED) 1. (técnica) breast scanning, mammography. 2. (resultado) breast scan.
mamotreto m 1. despec (libro) hefty tome. 2. (objeto grande) monstrosity.
mampara f screen.
manada f (ZOOL - gen) herd; (- de lobos) pack; (- de ovejas) flock; (- de leones) pride.
manager (pl managers) m manager.
Managua Managua.
manantial m spring; fig source.
manar vi lit & fig: ~ **(de)** to flow (from).
manazas adj inv clumsy.
mancha f 1. (gen) stain, spot; (de tinta) blot; (de color) spot, mark. 2. (ASTRON) spot. 3. fig (deshonra) blemish.
manchar vt 1. (ensuciar): ~ **algo (de o con)** (gen) to make sthg dirty (with); (con manchas) to stain sthg (with); (embo-rronar) to smudge sthg (with). 2. fig (deshonrar) to tarnish.
manchego, -ga adj of/relating to La Mancha. ► **manchego** m → **queso**.
mancillar vt to tarnish.
manco, -ca adj (sin una mano) one-handed; (sin manos) handless; (sin un brazo) one-armed; (sin brazos) armless.
mancomunidad f association.
mancorna, mancuerna f Amer cuff-link.
mandado, -da m y f (subordinado) underling. ► **mandado** m (recado) errand.
mandamás (pl mandamases) m y f bigwig.
mandamiento m 1. (orden - militar) order, command; (- judicial) writ. 2. (RELIG) commandment.
mandar ◆ vt 1. (dar órdenes) to order; ~ **a alguien hacer algo** to order sb to do sthg; ~ **hacer algo** to have sthg done. 2. (enviar) to send. 3. (dirigir, gobernar) to lead, to be in charge of; (país) to rule. ◆ vi 1. (gen) to be in charge; (jefe de estado) to rule. 2. despec (dar órdenes) to order people around. 3. loc: **¿mande?** fam eh?, you what?
mandarina f mandarin.

mandatario, -ria m y f representa-tive, agent.
mandato m 1. (gen) order, command. 2. (poderes de representación, disposición) mandate; ~ **judicial** warrant. 3. (POLÍT) term of office; (reinado) period of rule.
mandíbula f jaw.
mandil m (delantal) apron.
mando m 1. (poder) command, author-ity; **al ~ de** in charge of. 2. (periodo en poder) term of office. 3. (gen pl) (autori-dades) leadership (U); (MIL) command (U); ~**s intermedios** middle management (sg). 4. (dispositivo) control; ~ **automático/a distancia** automatic/remote control.
mandolina f mandolin.
mandón, -ona ◆ adj bossy. ◆ m y f bossy-boots.
manecilla f (del reloj) hand.
manejable adj (gen) manageable; (herramienta) easy to use.
manejar vt 1. (conocimientos, datos) to use, to marshal. 2. (máquina, mandos) to operate; (caballo, bicicleta) to handle; (arma) to wield. 3. (negocio etc) to man-age, to run; (gente) to handle. 4. Amer (conducir) to drive. ► **manejarse** vpr 1. (moverse) to move o get about. 2. (desenvolverse) to manage.
manejo m 1. (de máquina, mandos) operation; (de armas, herramientas) use; **de fácil ~** user-friendly. 2. (de conocimien-tos, datos) marshalling; (de idiomas) com-mand. 3. (de caballo, bicicleta) handling. 4. (de negocio etc) management, running. 5. (gen pl) fig (intriga) intrigue.
manera f way, manner; **a mi ~ de ver** the way I see it; **de cualquier ~** (sin cuida-do) any old how; (de todos modos) anyway, in any case; **de esta ~** in this way; **de ninguna ~, en ~ alguna** (refuerza negación) by no means, under no circumstances; (respuesta exclamativa) no way!, certainly not!; **de todas ~s** anyway; **en cierta ~** in a way; ~ **de ser** way of being, nature; **de ~ que** (para) so (that); **no hay ~** there is no way, it's impossible. ► **maneras** fpl (modales) manners.
manga f 1. (de prenda) sleeve; **de ~ corta/larga** short-/long-sleeved; **en ~s de camisa** in shirt sleeves. 2. (manguera) hosepipe. 3. (de pastelería) forcing o pip-ing bag. 4. (DEP) stage, round.
mangante fam m y f thief.
mango m 1. (asa) handle. 2. (árbol) mango tree; (fruta) mango.
mangonear vi fam 1. (entrometerse) to meddle. 2. (mandar) to be bossy.

3. (*manipular*) to fiddle about.

manguera f hosepipe; (*de bombero*) fire hose.

maní (*pl* -**es**) m *Amer* peanut.

manía f **1.** (*idea fija*) obsession. **2.** (*peculiaridad*) idiosyncrasy. **3.** (*mala costumbre*) bad habit. **4.** (*afición exagerada*) mania, craze. **5.** *fam* (*ojeriza*) dislike. **6.** (PSICOL) mania.

maniaco, -ca, maníaco, -ca ♦ *adj* manic. ♦ *m y f* maniac.

maniatar vt to tie the hands of.

maniático, -ca ♦ *adj* fussy. ♦ *m y f* fussy person; **es un ~ del fútbol** he's football-crazy.

manicomio m mental o psychiatric hospital *Br*, insane asylum *Am*.

manicuro, -ra m y f (*persona*) manicurist. ▶ **manicura** f (*técnica*) manicure.

manido, -da *adj* (*tema etc*) hackneyed.

manifestación f **1.** (*de alegría, dolor etc*) show, display; (*de opinión*) declaration, expression; (*indicio*) sign. **2.** (*por la calle*) demonstration.

manifestar vt **1.** (*alegría, dolor etc*) to show. **2.** (*opinión etc*) to express. ▶ **manifestarse** vpr **1.** (*por la calle*) to demonstrate. **2.** (*hacerse evidente*) to become clear o apparent.

manifiesto, -ta *adj* clear, evident; **poner de ~ algo** (*revelar*) to reveal sthg; (*hacer patente*) to make sthg clear. ▶ **manifiesto** m manifesto.

manillar m handlebars (*pl*).

maniobra f **1.** (*gen*) manoeuvre; **hacer ~s** to manoeuvre. **2.** *fig* (*treta*) trick.

maniobrar vi to manoeuvre.

manipulación f **1.** (*gen*) handling. **2.** (*engaño*) manipulation.

manipular vt **1.** (*manejar*) to handle. **2.** (*mangonear - información, resultados*) to manipulate; (*- negocios, asuntos*) to interfere in.

maniquí (*pl* maniquíes) ♦ m dummy. ♦ m y f (*modelo*) model.

manirroto, -ta ♦ *adj* extravagant. ♦ m y f spendthrift.

manitas m y f *inv* handy person.

manito, mano m *Amer fam* mate, chum.

manivela f crank.

manjar m delicious food (U).

mano f **1.** (*gen*) hand; **a ~** (*cerca*) to hand, handy; (*sin máquina*) by hand; **a ~ armada** armed; **dar o estrechar la ~ a alguien** to shake hands with sb; **darse o estrecharse la ~** to shake hands; **echar/ tender una ~** to give/offer a hand; **¡~s**

arriba!, ¡arriba las ~s! hands up!; **~ de obra** (*capacidad de trabajo*) labour; (*trabajadores*) workforce. **2.** (ZOOL - *gen*) forefoot; (*- de perro, gato*) (front) paw; (*- de cerdo*) (front) trotter. **3.** (*lado*): **a ~ derecha/izquierda** on the right/left. **4.** (*de pintura etc*) coat. **5.** (*influencia*) influence. **6.** (*partida de naipes*) game. **7.** *fig* (*serie, tanda*) series. **8.** *loc*: **bajo ~** secretly; **caer en ~s de alguien** to fall into sb's hands; **con las ~s cruzadas, ~ sobre ~** sitting around doing nothing; **coger a alguien con las ~s en la masa** to catch sb red-handed o in the act; **de primera ~** (*coche etc*) brand new; (*noticias etc*) first-hand; **de segunda ~** secondhand; **~ a ~** tête-à-tête; **¡~s a la obra!** let's get down to it!; **tener buena ~ para algo** to have a knack for sthg.

manojo m bunch.

manoletina f (*zapato*) type of open, low-heeled shoe, often with a bow.

manómetro m pressure gauge.

manopla f mitten.

manosear vt **1.** (*gen*) to handle roughly; (*papel, tela*) to rumple. **2.** (*persona*) to fondle.

manotazo m slap.

mansalva ▶ **a mansalva** *loc adv* (*en abundancia*) in abundance.

mansedumbre f (*gen*) calmness, gentleness; (*de animal*) tameness.

mansión f mansion.

manso, -sa *adj* **1.** (*apacible*) calm, gentle. **2.** (*domesticado*) tame.

manta f (*abrigo*) blanket; **liarse la ~ a la cabeza** *fig* to take the plunge.

manteca f fat; (*mantequilla*) butter; **~ de cacao** cocoa butter; **~ de cerdo** lard.

mantecado m **1.** (*pastel*) shortcake. **2.** (*helado*) ice-cream made of milk, eggs and sugar.

mantel m tablecloth.

mantener vt **1.** (*sustentar, aguantar*) to support. **2.** (*conservar*) to keep; (*en buen estado*) to maintain, to service. **3.** (*tener - relaciones, conversación*) to have. **4.** (*defender - opinión*) to stick to, to maintain; (*- candidatura*) to refuse to withdraw. ▶ **mantenerse** vpr **1.** (*sustentarse*) to subsist, to support o.s. **2.** (*permanecer, continuar*) to remain; (*edificio*) to remain standing; **~se aparte** (*en discusión*) to stay out of it.

mantenimiento m **1.** (*sustento*) sustenance. **2.** (*conservación*) upkeep, maintenance.

mantequilla f butter.

mantilla f 1. (*de mujer*) mantilla. 2. (*de bebé*) shawl.

manto m (*gen*) cloak.

mantón m shawl.

manual ◆ *adj* (*con las manos*) manual. ◆ *m* manual.

manubrio m crank.

manufacturar *vt* to manufacture.

manuscrito, -ta *adj* handwritten. ▶ **manuscrito** m manuscript.

manutención f 1. (*sustento*) support, maintenance. 2. (*alimento*) food.

manzana f 1. (*fruta*) apple. 2. (*grupo de casas*) block (of houses).

manzanilla f 1. (*planta*) camomile. 2. (*infusión*) camomile tea. 3. (*jerez*) manzanilla, dry, light sherry.

manzano m apple tree.

maña f 1. (*destreza*) skill. 2. (*astucia*) wits (*pl*), guile (U).

mañana ◆ f morning; **a las dos de la ~** at two in the morning. ◆ m: **el ~** tomorrow, the future. ◆ *adv* tomorrow; **¡hasta ~!** see you tomorrow!; **~ por la** ~ tomorrow morning; **pasado** ~ the day after tomorrow.

mañoso, -sa *adj* skilful.

mapa m map.

mapamundi m world map.

maqueta f 1. (*reproducción a escala*) (scale) model. 2. (*de libro*) dummy.

maquillaje m 1. (*producto*) make-up. 2. (*acción*) making-up.

maquillar *vt* (*pintar*) to make up. ▶ **maquillarse** *vpr* to make o.s. up.

máquina f 1. (*gen*) machine; **a toda ~** at full pelt; **escribir a ~** to type; **hecho a ~** machine-made; **~ de coser** sewing machine; **~ de escribir** typewriter; **~ fotográfica** camera; **~ tragaperras, ~ traganíqueles** Amer slot machine, fruit machine. 2. (*locomotora*) engine; **~ de vapor** steam engine. 3. (*mecanismo*) mechanism. 4. Amer (*coche*) car. 5. fig (*de estado, partido etc*) machinery (U).

maquinación f machination.

maquinal *adj* mechanical.

maquinar *vt* to machinate, to plot.

maquinaria f 1. (*gen*) machinery. 2. (*de reloj etc*) mechanism.

maquinilla f: **~ de afeitar** razor; **~ eléctrica** electric razor.

maquinista m y f (*de tren*) engine driver Br, engineer Am; (*de barco*) engineer.

mar m o f lit & fig sea; **alta ~** high seas (*pl*); **el ~ del Norte** the North Sea; **llover a ~es** to rain buckets; **la ~ de** really, very.

marabunta f fig (*muchedumbre*) crowd.

maraca f maraca.

maraña f 1. (*maleza*) thicket. 2. fig (*enredo*) tangle.

maratón m lit & fig marathon.

maravilla f 1. (*gen*) marvel, wonder; **es una ~** it's wonderful; **hacer ~s** to do o work wonders; **a las mil ~s, de ~** wonderfully; **venir de ~** to be just the thing o ticket. 2. (BOT) marigold.

maravillar *vt* to amaze. ▶ **maravillarse** *vpr*: **~se (con)** to be amazed (by).

maravilloso, -sa *adj* marvellous, wonderful.

marca f 1. (*señal*) mark; (*de rueda, animal*) track; (*en ganado*) brand; (*en papel*) watermark; (COM - *de tabaco, café etc*) brand; (- *de coche, ordenador etc*) make; **de ~** designer (*antes de sust*); **~ de fábrica** trademark; **~ registrada** registered trademark. 3. (*etiqueta*) label. 4. (DEP - *gen*) performance; (- *en carreras*) time; (- *plusmarca*) record.

marcado, -da *adj* (*gen*) marked. ▶ **marcado** m 1. (*señalado*) marking. 2. (*peinado*) set.

marcador, -ra *adj* marking. ▶ **marcador** m 1. (*tablero*) scoreboard. 2. (DEP - *defensor*) marker; (- *goleador*) scorer.

marcapasos m inv pacemaker.

marcar ◆ *vt* 1. (*gen*) to mark. 2. (*poner precio a*) to price. 3. (*indicar*) to indicate. 4. (*resaltar*) to emphasise. 5. (*número de teléfono*) to dial. 6. (*suj: termómetro, contador etc*) to read; (*suj: reloj*) to say. 7. (DEP - *tanto*) to score; (- *a un jugador*) to mark. 8. (*cabello*) to set. ◆ *vi* 1. (*dejar secuelas*) to leave a mark. 2. (DEP) (*anotar un tanto*) to score.

marcha f 1. (*partida*) departure. 2. (*ritmo*) speed; **en ~** (*motor*) running; (*plan*) underway; **poner en ~** (*gen*) to start; (*dispositivo, alarma*) to activate; **hacer algo sobre la ~** to do sthg as one goes along. 3. (AUTOM) gear; **~ atrás** reverse; **dar ~ atrás** (AUTOM) to reverse; fig to back out. 4. (MIL & POLÍT) march. 5. (MÚS) march. 6. (*transcurso*) course; (*progreso*) progress. 7. (DEP) walk. 8. fam (*animación*) liveliness, life; **hay mucha ~** there's a great atmosphere.

marchar *vi* 1. (*andar*) to walk. 2. (*partir*) to leave, to go. 3. (*funcionar*) to work. 4. (*desarrollarse*) to progress; **el negocio marcha** business is going well. ▶ **marcharse** *vpr* to leave, to go.

marchitar *vt* lit & fig to wither. ▶ **mar-**

chitarse vpr 1. (planta) to fade, to wither. 2. fig (persona) to languish.

marchito, -ta adj (planta) faded.

marcial adj martial.

marco m 1. (cerco) frame. 2. fig (ambiente, paisaje) setting. 3. (ámbito) framework. 4. (moneda) mark. 5. (portería) goalmouth.

marea f (del mar) tide; ~ **alta/baja** high/low tide; ~ **negra** oil slick.

mareado, -da adj: **estar** ~ (con náuseas) to feel sick; (al borde del desmayo) to feel dizzy.

marear vt 1. (provocar náuseas) to make sick; (en coche, avión etc) to make travelsick. 2. (aturdir) to make dizzy. 3. fam fig (fastidiar) to annoy. ▶ **marearse** vpr 1. (tener náuseas) to feel sick; (en coche, avión etc) to feel travelsick. 2. (estar aturdido) to get dizzy. 3. (emborracharse) to get drunk.

marejada f (mar rizada) heavy sea, swell.

maremoto m tidal wave.

mareo m 1. (náuseas) sickness; (en coches, aviones etc) travelsickness. 2. (aturdimiento) dizziness. 3. fam fig (fastidio) drag, pain.

marfil m ivory.

margarina f margarine.

margarita f 1. (BOT) daisy. 2. (IMPRENTA) daisy wheel.

margen m o f 1. (gen f) (de río) bank; (de camino) side. 2. (gen m) (de página) margin. 3. (gen m) (COM) margin. 4. (gen m) (límites) leeway; **dejar al** ~ to exclude; **estar al** ~ **de** to have nothing to do with; **mantenerse al** ~ **de** to keep out of; ~ **de error** margin of error. 5. (gen m) (ocasión): **dar** ~ **a alguien para hacer algo** to give sb the chance to do sthg.

marginación f exclusion.

marginado, -da ◆ adj excluded. ◆ m y f outcast.

maría f Amer fam migrant from country to urban areas.

mariachi m (orquesta) mariachi band.

MARIACHI

Mariachi bands are groups of Mexican musicians who wear traditional Mexican dress and play their music at local 'fiestas', in restaurants and in the streets. They are often hired for private functions such as birthdays or weddings.

marica m mfam despec queer, poof.
Maricastaña → tiemp_

maricón m mfam despec queer, poof.

marido m husband.

marihuana f marijuana.

marimacho m fam mannish woman; despec butch woman.

marina → **marino**.

marinero, -ra adj (gen) sea (antes de sust); (buque) seaworthy; (pueblo) seafaring. ▶ **marinero** m sailor.

marino, -na adj sea (antes de sust), marine. ▶ **marino** m sailor. ▶ **marina** f (MIL): ~ (**de guerra**) navy.

marioneta f (muñeco) marionette, puppet. ▶ **marionetas** fpl (teatro) puppet show (sg).

mariposa f 1. (insecto) butterfly. 2. (en natación) butterfly.

mariquita f (insecto) ladybird Br, ladybug Am.

marisco m seafood (U), shellfish (U).

marisma f salt marsh.

marisquería f seafood restaurant.

marítimo, -ma adj (del mar) maritime; (cercano al mar) seaside (antes de sust).

marketing ['marketin] m marketing.

mármol m marble.

marmota f marmot.

mar Muerto m: **el** ~ the Dead Sea.

mar Negro m: **el** ~ the Black Sea.

marqués, -esa m marquis (f marchioness).

marquesina f glass canopy; (parada de autobús) bus-shelter.

marrano, -na m y f 1. (animal) pig. 2. fam fig (sucio) (filthy) pig.

mar Rojo m: **el** ~ the Red Sea.

marrón adj & m brown.

marroquí (pl **marroquíes**) adj, m y f Moroccan.

Marruecos Morocco.

Marte m Mars.

martes m inv Tuesday; ~ **de Carnaval** Shrove Tuesday; ~ **y trece** ≃ Friday 13th; ver también **sábado**.

martillear, martillar vt to hammer.

martillo m hammer.

mártir m y f lit & fig martyr.

martirio m 1. (RELIG) martyrdom. 2. fig (sufrimiento) trial, torment.

martirizar vt 1. (torturar) to martyr. 2. fig (hacer sufrir) to torment.

marxismo m Marxism.

marxista adj, m y f Marxist.

marzo m March; ver también **septiembre**.

mas conj but.

más ◆ adv 1. (comparativo) more; Pepe es ~ **alto/ambicioso** Pepe is taller/more ambitious; **tener ~ hambre** to be hungrier o more hungry; **~ de/que** more than; **~ ... que ...** more ... than ...; **Juan es ~ alto que tú** Juan is taller than you; **de ~** (*de sobra*) left over; **hay 100 ptas de ~** there are 100 pesetas left over; **eso está de ~** that's not necessary. **2.** (*superlativo*): **el/la/lo ~** the most; **el ~ listo/ambicioso** the cleverest/most ambitious. **3.** (*en frases negativas*) any more; **no necesito ~** (**trabajo**) I don't need any more (work). **4.** (*con pron interrogativos e indefinidos*) else; **¿qué/quién ~?** what/who else?; **nadie ~ vino** nobody else came. **5.** (*indica suma*) plus; **dos ~ dos igual a cuatro** two plus two is four. **6.** (*indica intensidad*): **no le aguanto, ¡es ~ tonto!** I can't stand him, he's so stupid!; **¡qué día ~ bonito!** what a lovely day! **7.** (*indica preferencia*): **~ vale que nos vayamos a casa** it would be better for us to go home. **8.** *loc*: **el que ~ y el que menos** everyone; **es ~** indeed, what is more; **~ bien** rather; **~ o menos** more or less; **¿qué ~ da?** what difference does it make?; **sin ~** (**ni ~**) just like that. ◆ *m inv* (MAT) plus (sign); **tiene sus ~ y sus menos** it has its good points and its bad points. ▶ **por más que** *loc conj* however much; **por ~ que lo intente no lo conseguirá** however much o hard she tries, she'll never manage it.

masa *f* **1.** (*gen*) mass. **2.** (CULIN) dough. **3.** *Amer* (*pastelillo*) small cake. ▶ **masas** *fpl*: **las ~s** the masses.

masacre *f* massacre.

masaje *m* massage.

masajista *m* masseur (*f* masseuse).

mascar *vt & vi* to chew.

máscara *f* (*gen*) mask; **~ antigás** gas mask.

mascarilla *f* **1.** (MED) mask. **2.** (*cosmética*) face pack.

mascota *f* mascot.

masculino, -na *adj* **1.** (BIOL) male. **2.** (*varonil*) manly. **3.** (GRAM) masculine.

mascullar *vt* to mutter.

masificación *f* overcrowding.

masilla *f* putty.

masivo, -va *adj* **1.** (*en masa*) mass (*antes de sust*). **2.** (*enorme*) massive; **en forma masiva** on a massive scale.

masón, -ona ◆ *adj* masonic. ◆ *m y f* mason, freemason.

masoquista ◆ *adj* masochistic. ◆ *m y f* masochist.

máster (*pl* **masters**) *m* Master's (degree).

masticar *vt* (*mascar*) to chew.

mástil *m* **1.** (NÁUT) mast. **2.** (*palo*) pole. **3.** (MÚS) neck.

mastín *m* mastiff.

masturbación *f* masturbation.

masturbar *vt* to masturbate. ▶ **masturbarse** *vpr* to masturbate.

mata *f* (*arbusto*) bush, shrub; (*matojo*) tuft; **~s** scrub. ▶ **mata de pelo** *f* mop of hair.

matadero *m* abattoir, slaughterhouse.

matador, -ra *fam adj* (*cansado*) killing, exhausting. ▶ **matador** *m* matador.

matambre *m* *Amer* cold cooked meat.

matamoscas *m inv* (*pala*) flyswat; (*esprai*) flyspray.

matanza *f* (*masacre*) slaughter.

matar *vt* **1.** (*gen*) to kill; **~las callando** to be up to sthg on the quiet. **2.** (*apagar - sed*) to quench; (*- hambre*) to stay. ▶ **matarse** *vpr* **1.** (*morir*) to die. **2.** (*suicidarse, esforzarse*) to kill o.s.

matasellos *m y f inv* postmark.

mate ◆ *adj* matt. ◆ *m* **1.** (*en ajedrez*) mate, checkmate. **2.** (*en baloncesto*) dunk; (*en tenis*) smash. **3.** (BOT) (*bebida*) maté.

MATE

Maté is a herbal infusion from the southern part of South America. It is drunk from a small cup, also known as a maté, which is made from a small, hollowed-out gourd.

---

matemático, -ca ◆ *adj* mathematical. ◆ *m y f* (*científico*) mathematician. ▶ **matemáticas** *fpl* (*ciencia*) mathematics (U).

materia *f* **1.** (*sustancia, asunto*) matter. **2.** (*material*) material; **~ prima, primera ~** raw material. **3.** (*asignatura*) subject; **en ~ de** on the subject of, concerning.

material ◆ *adj* **1.** (*gen*) physical; (*daños, consecuencias*) material. **2.** (*real*) real, actual. ◆ *m* **1.** (*gen*) material. **2.** (*instrumentos*) equipment.

materialismo *m* materialism.

materialista ◆ *adj* materialistic. ◆ *m y f* materialist.

materializar *vt* **1.** (*idea, proyecto*) to realize. **2.** (*hacer tangible*) to produce. ▶ **materializarse** *vpr* to materialize.

maternal *adj* motherly, maternal.

maternidad *f* **1.** (*cualidad*) motherhood. **2.** (*hospital*) maternity hospital.

materno, -na adj maternal; (lengua) mother (antes de sust).

matinal adj morning (antes de sust).

matiz m 1. (variedad - de color, opinión) shade; (- de sentido) nuance, shade of meaning. 2. (atisbo) trace, hint.

matizar vt 1. (teñir): ~ (de) to tinge (with). 2. fig (distinguir - rasgos, aspectos) to distinguish; (- tema) to explain in detail. 3. fig (dar tono especial) to tinge. 4. (ARTE) to blend.

matojo m (mata) tuft; (arbusto) bush, shrub.

matón, -ona m y f fam bully.

matorral m thicket.

matraca f (instrumento) rattle.

matriarcado m matriarchy.

matrícula f 1. (inscripción) registration. 2. (documento) registration document. 3. (AUTOM) number plate. ▶ **matrícula de honor** f top marks (pl).

matricular vt to register. ▶ **matricularse** vpr to register.

matrimonial adj marital; (vida) married.

matrimonio m 1. (gen) marriage. 2. (pareja) married couple.

matriz ◆ f 1. (ANAT) womb. 2. (de talonario) (cheque) stub. 3. (molde) mould. 4. (MAT) matrix. ◆ adj (empresa) parent (antes de sust); (casa) head (antes de sust); (iglesia) mother (antes de sust).

matrona f 1. (madre) matron. 2. (comadrona) midwife.

matutino, -na adj morning (antes de sust).

maullar vi to miaow.

maxilar m jaw.

máxima → máximo.

máxime adv especially.

máximo, -ma ◆ superl → grande. ◆ adj maximum; (galardón, puntuación) highest. ▶ **máximo** m maximum; **al** ~ to the utmost; **llegar al** ~ to reach the limit; **como** ~ (a más tardar) at the latest; (como mucho) at the most. ▶ **máxima** f 1. (sentencia, principio) maxim. 2. (temperatura) high, highest temperature.

mayo m May; ver también **septiembre**.

mayonesa, mahonesa f mayonnaise.

mayor ◆ adj 1. (comparativo): ~ (que) (en tamaño) bigger (than); (en importancia etc) greater (than); (en edad) older (than); (en número) higher (than). 2. (superlativo): **el/la** ~ ... (en tamaño) the biggest ...; (en importancia etc) the greatest ...; (en edad) the oldest ...; (en

número) the highest ... 3. (adulto) grown-up; (anciano) elderly. 4. (principal) main, principal. 5. (MÚS): **en do** ~ in C major. 6. loc: **al por** ~ (COM) wholesale. ◆ m y f: **el/la** ~ (hijo, hermano) the eldest. ◆ m (MIL) major. ▶ **mayores** mpl 1. (adultos) grown-ups. 2. (antepasados) ancestors.

mayoral m (capataz) foreman.

mayordomo m butler.

mayoreo m Amer wholesale.

mayoría f majority; **la** ~ **de** most of; **la** ~ **de los españoles** most Spaniards; **en su** ~ in the main. ▶ **mayoría de edad** f: **llegar a la** ~ **de edad** to come of age.

mayorista m y f wholesaler.

mayoritario, -ria adj majority (antes de sust).

mayúscula → letra.

mayúsculo, -la adj tremendous, enormous.

maza f mace; (del bombo) drumstick.

mazapán m marzipan.

mazmorra f dungeon.

mazo m 1. (martillo) mallet. 2. (de mortero) pestle. 3. (conjunto - de naipes) balance (of the deck).

me pron pers 1. (complemento directo) me; **le gustaría verme** she'd like to see me. 2. (complemento indirecto) (to) me; ~ **lo dio** he gave it to me; ~ **tiene miedo** he's afraid of me. 3. (reflexivo) myself.

mear vi vulg to piss.

MEC (abrev de **Ministerio de Educación y Ciencia**) m Spanish ministry of education and science.

mecachis interj fam eufemismo: ¡~! sugar! Br, shoot! Am.

mecánico, -ca ◆ adj mechanical. ◆ m y f (persona) mechanic. ▶ **mecánica** f 1. (ciencia) mechanics (U). 2. (funcionamiento) mechanics (pl).

mecanismo m (estructura) mechanism.

mecanografía f typing.

mecanógrafo, -fa m y f typist.

mecapal m Amer porter's leather harness.

mecedora f rocking chair.

mecenas m y f inv patron.

mecer vt to rock. ▶ **mecerse** vpr to rock back and forth; (en columpio) to swing.

mecha f 1. (de vela) wick. 2. (de explosivos) fuse. 3. (de pelo) streak.

mechero m (cigarette) lighter.

mechón m (de pelo) lock; (de lana) tuft.

medalla f medal.

medallón m 1. (*joya*) medallion. 2. (*rodaja*) médaillon; ~ **de pescado** (*empanado*) fishcake.

media → **medio**.

mediación f mediation; **por ~ de** through.

mediado, -da adj (*medio lleno*) half-full; **mediada la película** halfway through the film. ▶ **a mediados de** loc prep in the middle of, halfway through.

mediana → **mediano**.

mediano, -na adj 1. (*intermedio - de tamaño*) medium; (- *de calidad*) average. 2. (*mediocre*) average, ordinary. ▶ **mediana** f 1. (GEOM) median. 2. (*de carretera*) central reservation.

medianoche (*pl medias*noches) f (*hora*) midnight; **a ~** at midnight.

mediante prep by means of.

mediar vi 1. (*llegar a la mitad*) to be halfway through; **mediaba julio** it was mid-July. 2. (*estar en medio - tiempo, distancia, espacio*): ~ **entre** to be between; **media un jardín/un kilómetro entre las dos casas** there is a garden/one kilometre between the two houses; **medió una semana** a week passed by. 3. (*intervenir*): ~ **(en/entre)** to mediate (in/ between). 4. (*interceder*): ~ **(en favor de o por)** to intercede (on behalf of o for).

mediatizar vt to determine.

medicación f medication.

medicamento m medicine.

medicar vt to give medicine to. ▶ **medicarse** vpr to take medicine.

medicina f medicine.

medicinal adj medicinal.

medición f measurement.

médico, -ca ◆ adj medical. ◆ m y f doctor; ~ **de cabecera** o **familia** family doctor, general practitioner; ~ **de guardia** duty doctor; ~ **interno** houseman Br, intern Am.

medida f 1. (*gen*) measure; (*medición*) measurement; **a (la) ~** (*gen*) custombuilt; (*ropa*) made-to-measure. 2. (*disposición*) measure, step; **tomar ~s** to take measures o steps. 3. (*moderación*) moderation. 4. (*grado*) extent, degree; **en cierta/gran ~** to some/a large extent; **en la ~ de lo posible** as far as possible; **a ~ que entraban** as they were coming in. ▶ **medidas** fpl (*del cuerpo*) measurements.

medieval adj medieval.

medievo, medioevo m Middle Ages (*pl*).

medio, -dia adj 1. (*gen*) half; **a ~**

camino (*en viaje*) halfway there; (*en trabajo etc*) halfway through; **media docena/ hora** half a dozen/an hour; ~ **pueblo estaba allí** half the town was there; **a media luz** in the half-light; **hacer algo a medias** to half-do sthg; **pagar a medias** to go halves, to share the cost; **un kilo y ~** one and a half kilos; **son (las dos) y media** it's half past (two). 2. (*intermedio - estatura, tamaño*) medium; (- *posición, punto*) middle. 3. (*de promedio - temperatura, velocidad*) average. ▶ **medio** ◆ adv half; ~ **borracho** half drunk; **a ~ hacer** half done. ◆ m 1. (*mitad*) half. 2. (*centro*) middle, centre; **en ~ (de)** in the middle (of); **estar por (en) ~** to be in the way; **quitar de en ~ a alguien** to get rid of sb, to get sb out of the way. 3. (*sistema, manera*) means, method; **por ~ de** by means of, through. 4. (*elemento físico*) environment; ~ **ambiente** environment. 5. (*ambiente social*) circle; **en ~s bien informados** in well-informed circles. 6. (DEP) midfielder. ▶ **medios** mpl (*recursos*) means, resources; **los ~s de comunicación** o **información** the media. ▶ **media** f 1. (*promedio*) average. 2. (*hora*): **al dar la media** on the half-hour. 3. (*gen pl*) (*pantis*) tights (*pl*); (*hasta el muslo*) stocking; (*calcetín*) sock. 4. (DEP) midfielders (*pl*).

medioambiental adj environmental.

mediocre adj mediocre, average.

mediodía (*pl mediodías*) m (*hora*) midday, noon; **al ~** at noon o midday.

medioevo = **medievo**.

mediofondo m middle-distance running.

medir vt 1. (*gen*) to measure; **¿cuánto mides?** how tall are you?; **mido 1,80** ≃ I'm 6 foot (tall); **mide diez metros** it's ten metres long. 2. (*pros, contras etc*) to weigh up. 3. (*palabras*) to weigh carefully.

meditación f meditation.

meditar ◆ vi: ~ **(sobre)** to meditate (on). ◆ vt 1. (*gen*) to meditate, to ponder. 2. (*planear*) to plan, to think through.

mediterráneo, -a adj Mediterranean. ▶ **Mediterráneo** m: **el (mar) Mediterráneo** the Mediterranean (Sea).

médium m y f inv medium.

médula f 1. (ANAT) (bone) marrow; ~ **espinal** spinal cord. 2. (*esencia*) core.

medusa f jellyfish.

megafonía f public-address system.

megáfono m megaphone.

mejicano, -na = mexicano.
Méjico = México.
mejilla f cheek.
mejillón m mussel.
mejor ◆ adj 1. (comparativo): ~ (que) better (than). 2. (superlativo): el/la ~ ... the best ... ◆ m y f: el/la ~ (de) the best (in); el ~ de todos the best of all; lo ~ fue que ... the best thing was that ... ◆ adv 1. (comparativo): ~ (que) better (than); ahora veo ~ I can see better now; es ~ que no vengas it would be better if you didn't come; estar ~ (no tan malo) to feel better; (recuperado) to be better. 2. (superlativo) best; el que la conoce ~ the one who knows her best. ▶ a lo mejor loc adv maybe, perhaps. ▶ mejor dicho loc adv (or) rather.
mejora f (progreso) improvement.
mejorar ◆ vt (gen) to improve; (enfermo) to make better. ◆ vi to improve, to get better. ▶ mejorarse vpr to improve, to get better; ¡qué te mejores! get well soon!
mejoría f improvement.
mejunje m lit & fig concoction.
melancolía f melancholy.
melancólico, -ca adj melancholic.
melaza f molasses (pl).
melena f 1. (de persona) long hair (U). 2. (de león) mane.
melenudo, -da despec adj with a mop of hair.
mellado, -da adj 1. (con hendiduras) nicked. 2. (sin dientes) gap-toothed.
mellizo, -za adj, m y f twin.
melocotón m peach.
melodía f melody, tune.
melódico, -ca adj melodic.
melodioso, -sa adj melodious.
melodrama m melodrama.
melómano, -na m y f music lover.
melón m (fruta) melon.
meloso, -sa adj 1. (como la miel) honey; fig sweet. 2. (empalagoso) sickly.
membrana f membrane.
membrete m letterhead.
membrillo m 1. (fruto) quince. 2. (dulce) quince jelly.
memorable adj memorable.
memorándum (pl memorándums o memorandos) m 1. (cuaderno) notebook. 2. (nota diplomática) memorandum.
memoria f 1. (gen & INFORM) memory; de ~ by heart; hacer ~ to try to remember; traer a la ~ to call to mind. 2. (recuerdo) remembrance. 3. (disertación) (academic) paper. 4. (informe): ~

(anual) (annual) report. ▶ memorias fpl (biografía) memoirs.
memorizar vt to memorize.
menaje m household goods and furnishings (pl); ~ de cocina kitchenware.
mención f mention.
mencionar vt to mention.
menda ◆ pron fam (el que habla) yours truly. ◆ m y f (uno cualquiera): vino un ~ y ... this bloke came along and ...
mendigar ◆ vt to beg for. ◆ vi to beg.
mendigo, -ga m y f beggar.
mendrugo m crust (of bread).
menear vt (mover - gen) to move; (- la cabeza) to shake; (- la cola) to wag; (- las caderas) to wiggle. ▶ menearse vpr 1. (moverse) to move (about); (agitarse) to shake; (oscilar) to sway. 2. (darse prisa, espabilarse) to get a move on.
menester m necessity. ▶ menesteres mpl (asuntos) business (U), matters (pl).
menestra f vegetable stew.
mengano, -na m y f so-and-so.
menguante adj (luna) waning.
menguar ◆ vi (disminuir) to decrease, to diminish; (luna) to wane. ◆ vt (disminuir) to lessen, to diminish.
menopausia f menopause.
menor ◆ adj 1. (comparativo): ~ (que) (de tamaño) smaller (than); (de edad) younger (than); (de importancia etc) less o lesser (than); (de número) lower (than). 2. (superlativo): el/la ~ ... (de tamaño) the smallest ...; (de edad) the youngest ...; (de importancia) the slightest ...; (de número) the lowest ... 3. (de poca importancia) minor; un problema ~ a minor problem. 4. (joven): ser ~ de edad (para votar, conducir etc) to be under age; (DER) to be a minor. 5. (MÚS): en do ~ in C minor. 6. loc: al por ~ (COM) retail. ◆ m y f 1. (superlativo): el/la ~ (hijo, hermano) the youngest. 2. (DER) (niño) minor.
Menorca Minorca.
menos ◆ adj inv 1. (comparativo) (cantidad) less; (número) fewer; ~ aire less air; ~ manzanas fewer apples; ~ ... que ... less/fewer ... than ...; tiene ~ experiencia que tú she has less experience than you; hace ~ calor que ayer it's not as hot as it was yesterday. 2. (superlativo) (cantidad) the least; (número) the fewest; el que compró ~ acciones the one who bought the fewest shares; lo que ~ tiempo llevó the thing that took the least time. 3. fam (peor): éste es ~ coche que el mío that car isn't as good as mine.

◆ adv 1. (*comparativo*) less; ~ **de/que** less than; **estás ~ gordo** you're not as fat. 2. (*superlativo*): **el/la/lo ~** the least; **él es el ~ indicado para criticar** he's the last person who should be criticizing; **ella es la ~ adecuada para el cargo** she's the least suitable person for the job; **es lo ~ que puedo hacer** it's the least I can do. 3. (*expresa resta*) minus; **tres ~ dos igual a uno** three minus two is one. 4. (*con las horas*) to; **son (las dos) ~ diez** it's ten to (two). 5. loc: **es lo de ~** that's the least of it; **hacer de ~ a alguien** to snub sb; **¡~ mal!** just as well!, thank God!; **no es para ~** not without (good) reason; **venir a ~** to go down in the world. ◆ m inv (MAT) minus (sign). ◆ prep (*excepto*) except (for); **todo ~ eso** anything but that. ▶ **al menos, por lo menos** loc adv at least. ▶ **a menos que** loc conj unless; **no iré a ~ que me acompañes** I won't go unless you come with me. ▶ **de menos** loc adj (*que falta*) missing; **hay 100 ptas de ~** there's 100 pesetas missing.

menoscabar vt (*fama, honra etc*) to damage; (*derechos, intereses, salud*) to harm; (*belleza, perfección*) to diminish.

menospreciar vt (*despreciar*) to scorn, to despise; (*infravalorar*) to undervalue.

mensaje m (*gen & INFORM*) message.

mensajero, -ra m y f (*gen*) messenger; (*de mensajería*) courier.

menstruación f menstruation.

menstruar vi to menstruate, to have a period.

mensual adj monthly; **5.000 ptas ~es** 5,000 pesetas a month.

mensualidad f 1. (*sueldo*) monthly salary. 2. (*pago*) monthly payment o instalment.

menta f mint.

mental adj mental.

mentalidad f mentality.

mentalizar vt to put into a frame of mind. ▶ **mentalizarse** vpr to get into a frame of mind.

mentar vt to mention.

mente f (*gen*) mind; **traer a la ~** to bring to mind.

mentecato, -ta m y f idiot.

mentir vi to lie.

mentira f lie; (*acción*) lying; **aunque parezca ~** strange as it may seem; **de ~** pretend, false; **parece ~ (que ...)** it hardly seems possible (that ...).

mentirijillas ▶ **de mentirijillas** fam ◆ loc adv (*en broma*) as a joke, in fun.

◆ loc adj (*falso*) pretend, make-believe.

mentiroso, -sa ◆ adj lying; (*engañoso*) deceptive. ◆ m y f liar.

mentón m chin.

menú (pl **menús**) m 1. (*lista*) menu; (*comida*) food; **~ del día** set meal. 2. (INFORM) menu.

menudencia f trifle, insignificant thing.

menudeo m Amer retailing.

menudillos mpl giblets.

menudo, -da adj 1. (*pequeño - objeto*) small; (- *persona*) slight. 2. (*insignificante*) trifling, insignificant. 3. (*antes de sust*) (*para enfatizar*) what!; **¡~ lío/gol!** what a mess/goal! ▶ **a menudo** loc adv often.

meñique → **dedo**.

meollo m core, heart.

mercader m y f trader.

mercadería f merchandise, goods (pl).

mercadillo m flea market.

mercado m market; **~ común** Common Market.

mercancía f merchandise (U), goods (pl). ▶ **mercancías** m inv (FERROC) goods train, freight train Am.

mercante adj merchant.

mercantil adj mercantile, commercial.

mercenario, -ria adj, m y f mercenary.

mercería f (*tienda*) haberdasher's (shop) Br, notions store Am.

mercurio m mercury.

Mercurio m Mercury.

merecedor, -ra adj: **~ de** worthy of.

merecer ◆ vt to deserve, to be worthy of; **la isla merece una visita** the island is worth a visit; **no merece la pena** it's not worth it. ◆ vi to be worthy.

merecido m: **recibir su ~** to get one's just deserts.

merendar ◆ vi to have tea (*as a light afternoon meal*). ◆ vt to have for tea.

merendero m open-air café or bar (*in the country or on the beach*).

merengue m 1. (CULIN) meringue. 2. (*baile*) merengue.

meridiano, -na adj 1. (*hora etc*) midday. 2. fig (*claro*) crystal-clear. ▶ **meridiano** m meridian.

merienda f tea (*as a light afternoon meal*); (*en el campo*) picnic.

mérito m 1. (*cualidad*) merit. 2. (*valor*) value, worth; **tiene mucho ~** it's no mean achievement; **de ~** worthy.

merluza f (*pez, pescado*) hake.

merma f decrease, reduction.

mermar ◆ *vi* to diminish, to lessen. ◆ *vt* to reduce, to diminish.

mermelada *f* jam; **~ de naranja** marmalade.

mero, -ra *adj* (*antes de sust*) mere. ► **mero** *m* grouper.

merodear *vi*: **~ (por)** to snoop o prowl (about).

mes *m* 1. (*del año*) month. 2. (*salario*) monthly salary.

mesa *f* 1. (*gen*) table; (*de oficina, despacho*) desk; **bendecir la ~** to say grace; **poner/quitar la ~** to set/clear the table; **~ camilla** *small round table under which a heater is placed*; **~ de mezclas** mixing desk; **~ plegable** folding table. 2. (*comité*) board, committee; (*en un debate etc*) panel; **~ directiva** executive board o committee. ► **mesa redonda** *f* (*coloquio*) round table.

mesero, -ra *m y f Amer* waiter *m* (*f* waitress).

meseta *f* plateau, tableland.

mesías *m fig* Messiah.

mesilla, mesita *f* small table; **~ de noche** bedside table.

mesón *m* 1. (HIST) inn. 2. (*bar-restaurante*) *old, country-style restaurant and bar*.

mestizo, -za ◆ *adj* (*persona*) of mixed race; (*animal, planta*) cross-bred. ◆ *m y f* person of mixed race.

mesura *f* 1. (*moderación*) moderation, restraint; **con ~** (*moderadamente*) in moderation. 2. (*cortesía*) courtesy.

meta *f* 1. (DEP - *llegada*) finishing line; (- *portería*) goal. 2. *fig* (*objetivo*) aim, goal.

metabolismo *m* metabolism.

metáfora *f* metaphor.

metal *m* 1. (*material*) metal. 2. (MÚS) brass.

metálico, -ca ◆ *adj* (*sonido, color*) metallic; (*objeto*) metal. ◆ *m*: **pagar en ~** to pay (in) cash.

metalizado, -da *adj* (*pintura*) metallic.

metalurgia *f* metallurgy.

metamorfosis *f inv lit & fig* metamorphosis.

metedura ► **metedura de pata** *f* clanger.

meteorito *m* meteorite.

meteoro *m* meteor.

meteorología *f* meteorology.

meteorológico, -ca *adj* meteorological.

meteorólogo, -ga *m y f* meteorolo-

gist; (RADIO & TV) weatherman (*f* weatherwoman).

meter *vt* 1. (*gen*) to put in; **~ algo/a alguien en algo** to put sthg/sb in sthg; **~ la llave en la cerradura** to get the key into the lock; **le metieron en la cárcel** they put him in prison; **~ dinero en el banco** to put money in the bank. 2. (*hacer participar*): **~ a alguien en algo** to get sb into sthg. 3. (*obligar a*): **~ a alguien a hacer algo** to make sb start doing sthg. 4. (*causar*): **~ prisa/miedo a alguien** to rush/scare sb; **~ ruido** to make a noise. 5. *fam* (*asestar*) to give; **le metió un puñetazo** he gave him a punch. 6. (*estrechar - prenda*) to take in; **~ el bajo de una falda** to take up a skirt. ► **meterse** *vpr* 1. (*entrar*) to get in; **~se en** to get into. 2. (*en frase interrogativa*) (*estar*) to get to; **¿dónde se ha metido ese chico?** where has that boy got to? 3. (*dedicarse*): **~se a** to become; **~se a torero** to become a bullfighter. 4. (*involucrarse*): **~se (en)** to get involved (in). 5. (*entrometerse*) to meddle; **se mete en todo** he never minds his own business; **~se por medio** to interfere. 6. (*empezar*): **~se a hacer algo** to get started on doing sthg. ► **meterse con** *vpr* 1. (*incordiar*) to hassle. 2. (*atacar*) to go for.

meterete, metete *adj Amer fam* meddling, meddlesome.

meticuloso, -sa *adj* meticulous.

metido, -da *adj* 1. (*envuelto*): **andar** o **estar ~ en** to be mixed up o involved in. 2. (*abundante*): **~ en años** elderly; **~ en carnes** plump.

metódico, -ca *adj* methodical.

método *m* 1. (*sistema*) method. 2. (EDUC) course.

metodología *f* methodology.

metomentodo *fam m y f* busybody.

metralla *f* shrapnel.

metralleta *f* submachine gun.

métrico, -ca *adj* (*del metro*) metric.

metro *m* 1. (*gen*) metre. 2. (*transporte*) underground *Br*, tube *Br*, subway *Am*. 3. (*cinta métrica*) tape measure.

metrópoli *f*, **metrópolis** *f inv* (*ciudad*) metropolis.

metropolitano, -na *adj* metropolitan.

mexicanismo, mejicanismo *m* Mexicanism.

mexicano, -na, mejicano, -na *adj, m y f* Mexican.

México, Méjico Mexico.

mezcla *f* 1. (*gen*) mixture; (*tejido*)

215 **mimbre**

blend; (*de una grabación*) mix. **2.** (*acción*) mixing.
mezclar *vt* **1.** (*gen*) to mix; (*combinar, armonizar*) to blend. **2.** (*confundir, desordenar*) to mix up. **3.** *fig* (*implicar*): ~ **a alguien en** to get sb mixed up in.
▶ **mezclarse** *vpr* **1.** (*gen*): ~**se** (*con*) to mix (with). **2.** (*esfumarse*): ~**se entre** to disappear o blend into. **3.** *fig* (*implicarse*): ~**se en** to get mixed up in.
mezquino, -na *adj* mean.
mezquita *f* mosque.
mg (*abrev de* **miligramo**) mg.
mi¹ *m* (MÚS) E; (*en solfeo*) mi.
mi² (*pl* **mis**) *adj poses* my; ~ **casa** my house; ~**s libros** my books.
mí *pron pers* (*después de prep*) **1.** (*gen*) me; **este trabajo no es para** ~ this job isn't for me; **no se fía de** ~ he doesn't trust me. **2.** (*reflexivo*) myself. **3.** *loc*: **¡a** ~ **qué!** so what?, why should I care?; **para** ~ (*yo creo*) as far as I'm concerned, in my opinion; **por** ~ as far as I'm concerned; **por** ~, **no hay inconveniente** it's fine by me.
mía → **mío.**
miaja *f* crumb; *fig* tiny bit.
miau *m* miaow.
michelines *mpl fam* spare tyre (*sg*).
mico *m fam* (*persona*) ugly devil.
micro ♦ *m fam* (*abrev de* **micrófono**) mike. ♦ *m o f Amer* bus.
microbio *m* germ, microbe.
microbús *m* minibus.
microfilm (*pl* **microfilms**), **microfilme** *m* microfilm.
micrófono *m* microphone.
microondas *m inv* microwave (oven).
microordenador *m* (INFORM) microcomputer.
microprocesador *m* (INFORM) microprocessor.
microscópico, -ca *adj* microscopic.
microscopio *m* microscope; ~ **electrónico** electron microscope.
miedo *m* fear; **dar** ~ to be frightening; **me da** ~ **conducir** I'm afraid o frightened of driving; **temblar de** ~ to tremble with fear; **tener** ~ **a** o **de** (*hacer algo*) to be afraid of (doing sthg); **de** ~ *fam fig* (*estupendo*) smashing.
miedoso, -sa *adj* fearful.
miel *f* honey.
miembro *m* **1.** (*gen*) member. **2.** (*extremidad*) limb, member; ~ (*viril*) penis.
mientras ♦ *conj* **1.** (*al tiempo que*) while; **leía** ~ **comía** she was reading while eating; ~ **más ando más sudo** the more I

walk, the more I sweat. **2.** (*hasta que*): ~ **no se pruebe lo contrario** until proved otherwise. **3.** (*por el contrario*): ~ (**que**) whereas, whilst. ♦ *adv*: ~ (**tanto**) meanwhile, in the meantime.
miércoles *m* Wednesday; ~ **de ceniza** Ash Wednesday; *ver también* **sábado.**
mierda *vulg f* **1.** (*excremento*) shit. **2.** (*suciedad*) filth, shit. **3.** (*cosa sin valor*): **es una** ~ it's (a load of) crap. **4.** *loc*: **¡vete a la** ~**!** go to hell!, piss off!
mies *f* (*cereal*) ripe corn. ▶ **mieses** *fpl* (*campo*) cornfields.
miga *f* (*de pan*) crumb. ▶ **migas** *fpl* (CULIN) fried breadcrumbs; **hacer buenas/malas** ~**s** *fam* to get on well/badly.
migración *f* migration.
migraña *f* migraine.
migrar *vi* to migrate.
migratorio, -ria *adj* migratory.
mijo *m* millet.
mil *núm* thousand; **dos** ~ two thousand; ~ **pesetas** a thousand pesetas; *ver también* **seis.**
milagro *m* miracle; **de** ~ miraculously.
milagroso, -sa *adj* miraculous; *fig* amazing.
milenario, -ria *adj* ancient. ▶ **milenario** *m* millennium.
milenio *m* millennium.
milésimo, -ma *núm* thousandth.
mili *f fam* military service; **hacer la** ~ to do one's military service.
milicia *f* **1.** (*profesión*) military (profession). **2.** (*grupo armado*) militia.
miliciano, -na *m y f* militiaman (*f* female soldier).
miligramo *m* milligram.
milímetro *m* millimetre.
militante *mf* militant, activist.
militar ♦ *adj* military. ♦ *m y f* soldier; **los** ~**es** the military. ♦ *vi*: ~ (**en**) to be active (in).
milla *f* mile; ~ (**marina**) nautical mile.
millar *m* thousand; **un** ~ **de personas** a thousand people.
millón *núm* million; **dos millones** two million; **un** ~ **de personas** a million people; **un** ~ **de cosas que hacer** a million things to do; **un** ~ **de gracias** thanks a million. ▶ **millones** *mpl* (*dineral*) a fortune (*sg*).
millonario, -ria *m y f* millionaire (*f* millionairess).
millonésimo, -ma *núm* millionth.
mimado, -da *adj* spoilt.
mimar *vt* to spoil, to pamper.
mimbre *m* wicker; **de** ~ wickerwork.

mímico, -ca adj mime (antes de sust).
► **mímica** f 1. (mimo) mime. 2. (lenguaje) sign language.

mimo m 1. (zalamería) mollycoddling. 2. (cariño) show of affection. 3. (TEATR) mime.

mimosa f (BOT) mimosa.

min (abrev de minuto) min.

mina f 1. (GEOL & MIL) mine; ~ **de carbón** coalmine. 2. fig (chollo) goldmine.

minar vt 1. (MIL) to mine. 2. fig (aminorar) to undermine.

mineral ◆ adj mineral. ◆ m 1. (GEOL) mineral. 2. (MIN) ore.

minería f 1. (técnica) mining. 2. (sector) mining industry.

minero, -ra ◆ adj mining (antes de sust); (producción, riqueza) mineral. ◆ m y f miner.

miniatura f miniature.

minicadena f midi system.

minifalda f mini skirt.

minifundio m smallholding.

minigolf (pl **minigolfs**) m (juego) crazy golf.

mínimo, -ma ◆ superl → **pequeño**. ◆ adj 1. (lo más bajo posible o necesario) minimum. 2. (lo más bajo temporalmente) lowest. 3. (muy pequeño - efecto, importancia etc) minimal, very small; (- protesta, ruido etc) slightest; **no tengo la más mínima idea** I haven't the slightest idea; **como** ~ at the very least; **en lo más** ~ in the slightest. ► **mínimo** m (límite) minimum. ► **mínima** f (METEOR) low, lowest temperature.

ministerio m 1. (POLÍT) ministry Br, department Am. 2. (RELIG) ministry. ► **Ministerio de Asuntos Exteriores** m ≃ Foreign Office Br, ≃ State Department Am. ► **Ministerio de Economía y Hacienda** m ≃ Treasury Br, ≃ Treasury Department Am. ► **Ministerio del Interior** m ≃ Home Office Br, ≃ Department of the Interior Am.

ministro, -tra m y f (POLÍT) minister Br, secretary Am; **primer** ~ prime minister.

minoría f minority; ~**s étnicas** ethnic minorities.

minorista ◆ adj retail. ◆ m y f retailer.

minoritario, -ria adj minority (antes de sust).

minucia f trifle, insignificant thing.

minucioso, -sa adj 1. (meticuloso) meticulous. 2. (detallado) highly detailed.

minúsculo, -la adj 1. (tamaño) tiny, minute. 2. (letra) small; (IMPRENTA) lower-case. ► **minúscula** f small letter; (IMPRENTA) lower-case letter.

minusvalía f (física) handicap, disability.

minusválido, -da ◆ adj disabled, handicapped. ◆ m y f disabled o handicapped person.

minuta f 1. (factura) fee. 2. (menú) menu.

minutero m minute hand.

minuto m minute.

mío, mía ◆ adj poses mine; **este libro es** ~ this book is mine; **un amigo** ~ a friend of mine; **no es asunto** ~ it's none of my business. ◆ pron poses: **el** ~ mine; **el** ~ **es rojo** mine is red; **esta es la mía** fam this is the chance I've been waiting for; **lo** ~ **es el teatro** (lo que me va) theatre is what I should be doing; **los** ~**s** fam (mi familia) my folks; (mi bando) my lot, my side.

miope adj shortsighted, myopic.

miopía f shortsightedness, myopia.

mira f sight; fig intention; **con** ~**s a** with a view to. ◆ interj: ¡~! look!

mirado, -da adj (prudente) careful; **bien** ~ (bien pensado) if you look at it closely. ► **mirada** f (gen) look; (rápida) glance; (de cariño, placer, admiración) gaze; **mirada fija** stare; **apartar la mirada** to look away; **dirigir** o **lanzar la mirada a** to glance at; **echar una mirada (a algo)** to glance o to have a quick look (at sthg); **fulminar con la mirada a alguien** to look daggers at sb; **levantar la mirada** to look up.

mirador m 1. (balcón) enclosed balcony. 2. (para ver un paisaje) viewpoint.

miramiento m circumspection; **andarse con** ~**s** to stand on ceremony; **sin** ~**s** just like that.

mirar ◆ vt 1. (gen) to look at; (observar) to watch; (fijamente) to stare at; ~ **algo de cerca/lejos** to look at sthg closely/from a distance; ~ **algo por encima** to glance over sthg, to have a quick look at sthg; ~ **a alguien bien/mal** to think highly/poorly of sb. 2. (fijarse en) to keep an eye on. 3. (examinar, averiguar) to check, to look through; **le miraron todas las maletas** they searched all her luggage; **mira si ha llegado la carta** go and see if the letter has arrived. 4. (considerar) to consider, to take a look at. ◆ vi 1. (gen) to look; (observar) to watch; (fijamente) to stare; **mira, yo creo que ...** look, I think that ... 2. (buscar) to check, to look; **he mirado en todas partes** I've looked everywhere. **3.** (*orientarse*): **~ a** to face. **4.** (*cuidar*): **~ por alguien/algo** to look after sb/sthg. ▶ **mirarse** *vpr* (*uno mismo*) to look at o.s.; **si bien se mira** *fig* if you really think about it.

mirilla *f* spyhole.

mirlo *m* blackbird.

mirón, -ona *fam m y f* **1.** (*espectador*) onlooker. **2.** (*curioso*) nosy parker. **3.** (*voyeur*) peeping Tom.

misa *f* mass; **ir a ~** to go to mass o church; *fam fig* to be gospel; **~ del gallo** midnight mass (*on Christmas Eve*).

misal *m* missal.

misántropo, -pa *m y f* misanthropist.

miscelánea *f* miscellany.

miserable ◆ *adj* **1.** (*pobre*) poor; (*vivienda*) wretched, squalid. **2.** (*penoso, insuficiente*) miserable. **3.** (*vil*) contemptible, base. **4.** (*tacaño*) mean. ◆ *m y f* (*ruin*) wretch, vile person.

miseria *f* **1.** (*pobreza*) poverty. **2.** (*desgracia*) misfortune. **3.** (*tacañería*) meanness. **4.** (*vileza*) baseness. **5.** (*poco dinero*) pittance.

misericordia *f* compassion; **pedir ~** to beg for mercy.

mísero, -ra *adj* (*pobre*) wretched; **ni un ~ ...** not even a measly o miserable ...

misil (*pl* **misiles**) *m* missile; **~ de crucero** cruise missile.

misión *f* **1.** (*gen*) mission; (*cometido*) task. **2.** (*expedición científica*) expedition.

misionero, -ra *adj, m y f* missionary.

misiva *f culto* missive.

mismo, -ma ◆ *adj* **1.** (*igual*) same; **el ~ piso** the same flat; **del ~ color que** the same colour as. **2.** (*para enfatizar*): **yo ~** I myself; **en este ~ cuarto** in this very room; **en su misma calle** right in the street where he lives; **por mí/ti ~** by myself/yourself; **¡tú ~!** it's up to you. ◆ *pron*: **el ~** the same; **el ~ que vi ayer** the same one I saw yesterday; **lo ~** the same (thing); **lo ~ que** the same as; **da o es lo ~** it doesn't matter, it doesn't make any difference; **me da lo ~** I don't care. ▶ **mismo** (*después de sust*) *adv* **1.** (*para enfatizar*): **lo vi desde mi casa ~** I saw it from my own house; **ahora/aquí ~** right now/here; **ayer ~** only yesterday; **por eso ~** precisely for that reason. **2.** (*por ejemplo*): **escoge uno cualquiera – este ~** choose any – this one, for instance.

misógino, -na *adj* misogynistic.

miss (*pl* **misses**) *f* beauty queen.

misterio *m* mystery.

misterioso, -sa *adj* mysterious.

mística → **místico**.

místico, -ca *adj* mystical. ▶ **mística** *f* (*práctica*) mysticism.

mitad *f* **1.** (*gen*) half; **a ~ de precio** at half price; **a ~ de camino** halfway there; **a ~ de película** halfway through the film; **a ~ de** (*of*); **la ~ del tiempo no está** half the time she's not in; **~ y ~** half and half. **2.** (*centro*) middle; **en ~ de** in the middle of; (**cortar algo**) **por la ~** (to cut sthg) in half.

mítico, -ca *adj* mythical.

mitigar *vt* **1.** (*gen*) to alleviate, to reduce; (*ánimos*) to calm; (*sed*) to slake; (*hambre*) to take the edge off; (*choque, golpe*) to soften; (*dudas, sospechas*) to allay. **2.** (*justificar*) to mitigate.

mitin (*pl* **mítines**) *m* rally, meeting.

mito *m* (*gen*) myth.

mitología *f* mythology.

mitote *m Amer fam* (*alboroto*) racket.

mixto, -ta *adj* mixed; (*comisión*) joint.

ml (*abrev de* **mililitro**) ml.

mm (*abrev de* **milímetro**) mm.

mobiliario *m* furniture.

mocasín *m* moccasin.

mochila *f* backpack.

mochuelo *m* little owl.

moción *f* motion.

moco *m fam* snot (U); (MED) mucus (U); **limpiarse los ~s** to wipe one's nose.

mocoso, -sa *m y f fam despec* brat.

moda *f* (*gen*) fashion; (*furor pasajero*) craze; **estar de ~** to be fashionable o in fashion; **estar pasado de ~** to be unfashionable o out of fashion.

modal *adj* modal. ▶ **modales** *mpl* manners.

modalidad *f* form, type; (DEP) discipline.

modelar *vt* to model; *fig* to shape.

modelo ◆ *adj* model. ◆ *m y f* model. ◆ *m* **1.** (*gen*) model. **2.** (*prenda de vestir*) number.

modem ['moðem] (*pl* **modems**) *m* (INFORM) modem; **~ fax** fax modem.

moderación *f* moderation.

moderado, -da *adj, m y f* moderate.

moderador, -ra *m y f* chair, chairperson.

moderar *vt* **1.** (*gen*) to moderate; (*velocidad*) to reduce. **2.** (*debate*) to chair. ▶ **moderarse** *vpr* to restrain o.s.

modernizar *vt* to modernize.

moderno, -na adj modern.
modestia f modesty.
modesto, -ta adj modest.
módico, -ca adj modest.
modificar vt 1. (variar) to alter. 2. (GRAM) to modify.
modista m y f 1. (diseñador) fashion designer. 2. (que cose) tailor (f dressmaker).
modisto m 1. (diseñador) fashion designer. 2. (sastre) tailor.
modo m (manera, forma) way, manner; a ~ de as, by way of; de ese ~ in that way; de ningún ~ in no way; de todos ~s in any case, anyway; de un ~ u otro one way or another; en cierto ~ in some ways; ~ de empleo instructions (pl) for use; de ~ que (de manera que) in such a way that; (así que) so. ► **modos** mpl (modales) manners; **buenos/malos** ~s good/bad manners.
modorra f fam drowsiness.
modoso, -sa adj (recatado) modest; (formal) well-behaved.
modular vt to modulate.
módulo m 1. (gen) module. 2. (de muebles) unit.
mofa f mockery.
mofarse vpr to scoff; ~ de to mock.
moflete m chubby cheek.
mogollón m mfam 1. (muchos): ~ de tons (pl) of, loads (pl) of. 2. (lío) row, commotion.
mohair [mo'er] m mohair.
moho m 1. (hongo) mould. 2. (herrumbre) rust.
mohoso, -sa adj 1. (con hongo) mouldy. 2. (oxidado) rusty.
moisés m inv Moses basket.
mojado, -da adj wet; (húmedo) damp.
mojar vt to wet; (humedecer) to dampen; (comida) to dunk. ► **mojarse** vpr (con agua) to get wet.
mojigato, -ta adj 1. (beato) prudish. 2. (con falsa humildad) sanctimonious.
mojón m (piedra) milestone; (poste) milepost.
molar mfam vi to be bloody gorgeous.
molcajete m Amer mortar.
molde m mould.
moldeado m 1. (del pelo) soft perm. 2. (de figura, cerámica) moulding.
moldear vt 1. (gen) to mould. 2. (modelar) to cast. 3. (cabello) to give a soft perm to.
mole m Amer chilli sauce made with chocolate.
molécula f molecule.

moler vt 1. (gen) to grind; (aceitunas) to press; (trigo) to mill. 2. fam fig (cansar) to wear out.
molestar vt 1. (perturbar) to bother; ¿le molesta que fume? do you mind if I smoke?; perdone que le moleste ... I'm sorry to bother you ... 2. (irritar) to annoy, to irritate. 3. (doler) to hurt. 4. (ofender) to offend. ► **molestarse** vpr 1. (incomodarse) to bother; ~se en hacer algo to bother to do sthg; ~se por alguien/algo to put o.s. out for sb/sthg. 2. (ofenderse): ~se (por algo) to take offence (at sthg).
molestia f 1. (incomodidad) nuisance; si no es demasiada ~ if it's not too much trouble. 2. (malestar) discomfort.
molesto, -ta adj 1. (incordiante) annoying; (visita) inconvenient. 2. (irritado): ~ (con) annoyed (with). 3. (con malestar) in discomfort.
molido, -da adj fam fig (cansado) worn out; estar ~ de to be worn out from.
molinero, -ra m y f miller.
molinillo m grinder.
molino m mill; ~ de viento windmill.
molla f (parte blanda) flesh.
molleja f gizzard.
mollera f fam (juicio) brains (pl).
molusco m mollusc.
momentáneo, -a adj (de un momento) momentary; (pasajero) temporary.
momento m (gen) moment; (periodo) time; llegó un ~ en que ... there came a time when ...; a cada ~ all the time; al ~ straightaway; de ~, por el ~ for the time being o moment; del ~ (actual) of the day; de un ~ a otro any minute now; desde el ~ (en) que ... (tiempo) from the moment that ...; (causa) seeing as ...
momia f mummy.
Mónaco Monaco.
monada f 1. (persona) little beauty. 2. (cosa) lovely thing. 3. (gracia) antic.
monaguillo m altar boy.
monarca m monarch.
monarquía f monarchy.
monárquico, -ca adj monarchic.
monasterio m (de monjes) monastery; (de monjas) convent.
Moncloa f: la ~ residence of the Spanish premier which by extension refers to the Spanish government.

LA MONCLOA

The Moncloa palace has been the official residence of the Spanish premier and the seat of the Spanish govern-

montón

ment since 1977. It is situated in the northwest of Madrid, near the Complutense university campus. It forms part of a complex of government buildings and has been rebuilt several times, most notably after the Spanish Civil War.

---

monda *f* (*acción*) peeling; (*piel*) peel; **ser la ~** *mfam* (*extraordinario*) to be amazing; (*gracioso*) to be a scream.

mondadientes *m inv* toothpick.

mondadura *f* (*piel*) peel.

mondar *vt* to peel. ▶ **mondarse** *vpr*: **~se** (**de risa**) *fam* to laugh one's head off.

moneda *f* 1. (*pieza*) coin; **ser ~ corriente** to be commonplace. 2. (*divisa*) currency.

monedero *m* purse; **~ electrónico** *smart card which can be used to pay for small purchases such as bread or a newspaper.*

monegasco, -ca *adj*, *m y f* Monegasque.

monetario, -ria *adj* monetary.

mongólico, -ca (MED) *m y f* Down's syndrome person.

mongolismo *m* Down's syndrome.

monigote *m* 1. (*muñeco*) rag o paper doll. 2. (*dibujo*) doodle. 3. *fig* (*persona*) puppet.

monitor, -ra *m y f* (*persona*) instructor. ▶ **monitor** *m* (INFORM & TECN) monitor.

monja *f* nun.

monje *m* monk.

mono, -na ◆ *adj* lovely. ◆ *m y f* (*animal*) monkey; **ser el último ~** to be bottom of the heap. ◆ **mono** *m* 1. (*prenda - con peto*) dungarees (*pl*); (*- con mangas*) overalls (*pl*). 2. *fam* (*abstinencia*) cold turkey.

monóculo *m* monocle.

monogamia *f* monogamy.

monografía *f* monograph.

monolingüe *adj* monolingual.

monólogo *m* monologue; (TEATR) soliloquy.

monopatín *m* skateboard.

monopolio *m* monopoly.

monopolizar *vt lit & fig* to monopolize.

monosílabo, -ba *adj* monosyllabic. ▶ **monosílabo** *m* monosyllable.

monotonía *f* (*uniformidad*) monotony.

monótono, -na *adj* monotonous.

monseñor *m* Monsignor.

monserga *f fam* drivel (U).

monstruo ◆ *adj inv* (*grande*) enormous, monster (*antes de sust*). ◆ *m* 1. (*gen*)

monster. 2. (*prodigio*) giant, marvel.

monstruosidad *f* 1. (*crueldad*) monstrosity, atrocity. 2. (*fealdad*) hideousness. 3. (*anomalía*) freak.

monstruoso, -sa *adj* 1. (*cruel*) monstrous. 2. (*feo*) hideous. 3. (*enorme*) huge, enormous. 4. (*deforme*) terribly deformed.

monta *f* 1. (*importancia*) importance; **de poca/mucha ~** of little/great importance. 2. (*en un caballo*) ride, riding (U).

montacargas *m inv* goods lift Br, freight elevator Am.

montaje *m* 1. (*de una máquina*) assembly. 2. (TEATR) staging. 3. (FOT) montage. 4. (CIN) editing. 5. (*farsa*) put-up job.

montante *m* 1. (*ventanuco*) fanlight. 2. (*importe*) total; **~s compensatorios** (COM) compensating duties.

montaña *f lit & fig* mountain; **ir de excursión a la ~** to go camping in the mountains; **~ rusa** roller coaster; **hacer una ~ de un grano de arena** to make a mountain out of a molehill.

montañero, -ra *m y f* mountaineer.

montañismo *m* mountaineering.

montañoso, -sa *adj* mountainous.

montar ◆ *vt* 1. (*ensamblar - máquina, estantería*) to assemble; (*- tienda de campaña, tenderete*) to put up. 2. (*encajar*): **~ algo en algo** to fit sthg into sthg. 3. (*organizar - negocio, piso*) to set up. 4. (*cabalgar*) to ride. 5. (*poner encima*): **~ a alguien en** to lift sb onto. 6. (CULIN - *nata*) to whip; (*- claras, yemas*) to beat. 7. (TEATR) to stage. 8. (CIN) to cut, to edit. ◆ *vi* 1. (*subir*) to get on; (*en un coche*) to get in; **~ en** (*gen*) to get onto; (*coche*) to get into; (*animal*) to mount. 2. (*ir montado*) to ride; **~ en bicicleta/a caballo** to ride a bicycle/a horse. ▶ **montarse** *vpr* (*gen*) to get on; (*en un coche*) to get in; (*en un animal*) to mount; **~se en** (*gen*) to get onto; (*coche*) to get into; (*animal*) to mount.

montaraz *adj* mountain (*antes de sust*).

monte *m* (*elevación*) mountain; (*terreno*) woodland; **~ bajo** scrub. ▶ **monte de piedad** *m* state pawnbroker's.

montepío *m* mutual aid society.

montés *adj* wild.

Montevideo Montevideo.

montículo *m* hillock.

monto *m* total.

montón *m* 1. (*pila*) heap, pile; **a o en ~** everything together o at once; **del ~** *fig* run-of-the-mill. 2. *fig* (*muchos*) loads; **un ~ de** loads of.

montura f 1. (*cabalgadura*) mount. 2. (*arreos*) harness; (*silla*) saddle. 3. (*soporte - de gafas*) frame.

monumental adj 1. (*ciudad, lugar*) famous for its monuments. 2. fig (*fracaso etc*) monumental.

monumento m monument.

monzón m monsoon.

moña f fam (*borrachera*): **coger una ~** to get smashed.

moño m bun (*of hair*); **estar hasta el ~ (de)** to be sick to death (of).

MOPU (*abrev de Ministerio de Obras Públicas y Urbanismo*) m Spanish ministry of public works and town planning.

moquear vi to have a runny nose.

moqueta f fitted carpet.

mora f 1. (*de la zarzamora*) blackberry. 2. (*del moral*) mulberry.

morada f culto dwelling.

morado, -da ◆ adj purple. ▶ **morado** m (*color*) purple.

moral ◆ adj moral. ◆ f 1. (*ética*) morality. 2. (*ánimo*) morale.

moraleja f moral.

moralizar vi to moralize.

morbo m fam (*placer malsano*) morbid pleasure.

morboso, -sa adj morbid.

morcilla f (CULIN) ≃ black pudding Br, ≃ blood sausage Am.

mordaz adj caustic, biting.

mordaza f gag.

mordedura f bite.

morder ◆ vt 1. (*con los dientes*) to bite. 2. (*gastar*) to eat into. ◆ vi to bite; **estar que muerde** to be hopping mad. ▶ **morderse** vpr: ~se **la lengua/las uñas** to bite one's tongue/nails.

mordida f Amer fam (*soborno*) bribe.

mordisco m bite.

mordisquear vt to nibble (at).

moreno, -na ◆ adj 1. (*pelo, piel*) dark; (*por el sol*) tanned; **ponerse ~** to get a tan. 2. (*pan, azúcar*) brown. ◆ m y f (*por el pelo*) dark-haired person; (*por la piel*) dark-skinned person.

morera f white mulberry.

moretón m bruise.

morfina f morphine.

moribundo, -da adj dying.

morir vi 1. (*gen*) to die. 2. (*río, calle*) to come out. 3. (*fuego*) to die down; (*luz*) to go out; (*día*) to come to a close. ▶ **morirse** vpr 1. (*fallecer*): ~se **(de)** to die (of). 2. fig (*sentir con fuerza*): ~se **de envidia/ira** to be burning with envy/rage; **me muero de ganas de ir a bailar** I'm dying to go dancing; **me muero de hambre/frío** I'm starving/freezing; ~se **por algo** to be dying for sthg; ~se **por alguien** to be crazy about sb.

mormón, -ona adj, m y f Mormon.

moro, -ra ◆ adj (HIST) Moorish. ◆ m y f 1. (HIST) Moor; ~s y cristianos traditional Spanish festival involving mock battle between Moors and Christians. 2. (*árabe*) Arab (N.B.: *the term 'moro' is considered to be racist*).

moroso, -sa (COM) ◆ adj defaulting. ◆ m y f defaulter, bad debtor.

morral m (MIL) haversack; (*de cazador*) gamebag.

morrear mfam vt & vi to snog.

morriña f (*por el país de uno*) homesickness; (*por el pasado*) nostalgia.

morro m 1. (*hocico*) snout. 2. fam (*de coche, avión*) nose.

morsa f walrus.

morse m (*en aposición inv*) Morse (code).

mortadela f Mortadella.

mortaja f shroud.

mortal ◆ adj mortal; (*caída, enfermedad*) fatal; (*aburrimiento, susto, enemigo*) deadly. ◆ m y f mortal.

mortalidad f mortality.

mortandad f mortality.

mortero m mortar.

mortífero, -ra adj deadly.

mortificar vt to mortify.

mortuorio, -ria adj death (*antes de sust*).

mosaico, -ca adj Mosaic. ▶ **mosaico** m mosaic.

mosca f fly; **por si las ~s** just in case; **¿qué ~ te ha picado?** what's up with you? ▶ **mosca muerta** m y f slyboots.

moscardón m (ZOOL) blowfly.

moscón m (ZOOL) bluebottle.

moscovita adj, m y f Muscovite.

Moscú Moscow.

mosquearse vpr fam (*enfadarse*) to get cross; (*sospechar*) to smell a rat.

mosquete m musket.

mosquetero m musketeer.

mosquitero m mosquito net.

mosquito m mosquito.

mosso d'Esquadra m member of the Catalan police force.

mostacho m moustache.

mostaza f mustard.

mosto m (*residuo*) must; (*zumo de uva*) grape juice.

mostrador m (*en tienda*) counter; (*en bar*) bar.

mostrar *vt* to show. ▶ **mostrarse** *vpr* to appear, to show o.s.; **se mostró muy interesado** he expressed great interest.

mota *f* (*de polvo*) speck; (*en una tela*) dot.

mote *m* nickname.

moteado, -da *adj* speckled; (*vestido*) dotted.

motel *m* motel.

motín *m* (*del pueblo*) uprising, riot; (*de las tropas*) mutiny.

motivación *f* motive, motivation (U).

motivar *vt* 1. (*causar*) to cause; (*impulsar*) to motivate. 2. (*razonar*) to explain, to justify.

motivo *m* 1. (*causa*) reason, cause; (*de crimen*) motive; **con ~ de** (*por causa de*) because of; (*para celebrar*) on the occasion of; (*con el fin de*) in order to; **sin ~** for no reason. 2. (ARTE, LITER & MÚS) motif.

moto *f* motorbike Br, motorcycle.

motocicleta *f* motorbike, motorcycle.

motociclismo *m* motorcycling.

motociclista *m y f* motorcyclist.

motocross *m* motocross.

motoneta *f* Amer scooter, moped.

motor (*f* **motora** o **motriz**) *adj* motor. ▶ **motor** *m* 1. (*aparato*) motor, engine. 2. (*fuerza*) dynamic force. ▶ **motora** *f* motorboat.

motorismo *m* motorcycling.

motorista *m y f* motorcyclist.

motriz → **motor**.

mountain bike ['maunten 'bike] *m* (DEP) mountain biking.

mousse [mus] *m inv* (CULIN) mousse.

movedizo, -za *adj* (*movible*) movable, easily moved.

mover *vt* 1. (*gen* & INFORM) to move; (*mecánicamente*) to drive. 2. (*cabeza - afirmativamente*) to nod; (*- negativamente*) to shake. 3. (*suscitar*) to provoke. 4. *fig* (*empujar*): **~ a alguien a algo/a hacer algo** to drive sb to sthg/to do sthg. ▶ **mover a** *vi* 1. (*incitar*) to incite to. 2. (*causar*) to provoke, to cause. ▶ **moverse** *vpr* 1. (*gen*) to move; (*en la cama*) to toss and turn. 2. (*darse prisa*) to get a move on.

movido, -da *adj* 1. (*debate, torneo*) lively; (*persona*) active, restless; (*jornada, viaje*) hectic. 2. (FOT) blurred, fuzzy. ▶ **movida** *f fam* (*ambiente*) scene; **la movida madrileña** the Madrid scene of the late 1970s.

móvil ◆ *adj* mobile, movable. ◆ *m* 1. (*motivo*) motive. 2. (*juguete*) mobile.

movilidad *f* mobility.

movilización *f* 1. (MIL) mobilization. 2. (*manifestación*) protest, demonstration.

movilizar *vt* to mobilize.

movimiento *m* 1. (*gen* & POLÍT) movement. 2. (FÍS & TECN) motion; **~ sísmico** earth tremor. 3. (*circulación - gen*) activity; (*- de personal, mercancías*) turnover; (*- de vehículos*) traffic; **~ de capital** cash flow. 4. (MÚS - *parte de la obra*) movement.

moviola *f* editing projector.

moza → **mozo**.

mozárabe ◆ *adj* Mozarabic, *Christian in the time of Moorish Spain.* ◆ *m* (*lengua*) Mozarabic.

mozo, -za ◆ *adj* (*joven*) young; (*soltero*) single. ◆ *m y f* young boy (*f* young girl), young lad (*f* young lass). ▶ **mozo** *m* 1. (*trabajador*) assistant (worker); **~ de estación** (station) porter. 2. (*recluta*) conscript. 3. *Amer* (*camarero*) waiter.

mu *m* (*mugido*) moo; **no decir ni ~** not to say a word.

mucamo, -ma *m y f Amer* servant.

muchacho, -cha *m y f* boy (*f* girl). ▶ **muchacha** *f* (*sirvienta*) maid.

muchedumbre *f* (*de gente*) crowd, throng; (*de cosas*) great number, masses (*pl*).

mucho, -cha ◆ *adj* 1. (*gran cantidad*) (*en sg*) a lot of; (*en pl*) many, a lot of; (*en interrogativas y negativas*) much, a lot of; **tengo ~ sueño** I'm very sleepy; **~s días** several days; **no tengo ~ tiempo** I haven't got much time. 2. (*en sg*) (*demasiado*): **hay ~ niño aquí** there are too many kids here. ◆ *pron* (*en sg*) a lot; (*en pl*) many, a lot; **tengo ~ que contarte** I have a lot to tell you; **¿queda dinero? – no ~** is there any money left? – not much o not a lot; **~s piensan igual** a lot of o many people think the same. ▶ **mucho** *adv* 1. (*gen*) a lot; **habla ~** he talks a lot; **me canso ~** I get really o very tired; **me gusta ~** I like it a lot o very much; **no me gusta ~** I don't like it much; **(no) ~ más tarde** (not) much later. 2. (*largo tiempo*): **hace ~ que no vienes** I haven't seen you for a long time; **¿vienes ~ por aquí?** do you come here often?; **¿dura ~ la obra?** is the play long?; **~ antes/después** long before/after. 3. *loc*: **como ~** at the most; **con ~** by far, easily; **ni ~ menos** by no means; **no está ni ~ menos decidido** it is by no means decided. ▶ **por mucho que** *loc conj* no matter how much, however much; **por ~ que insistas** no matter how much o however much you insist.

mucosidad f mucus.

muda f (*ropa interior*) change of underwear.

mudanza f 1. (*cambio*) change; (*de carácter*) fickleness; (*de plumas, piel*) moulting. 2. (*de casa*) move; **estar de ~** to be moving.

mudar ◆ vt 1. (*gen*) to change; (*casa*) to move; **cuando mude la voz** when his voice breaks. 2. (*piel, plumas*) to moult. ◆ vi (*cambiar*): **~ de** (*opinión, color*) to change; (*domicilio*) to move. ▶ **mudarse** vpr: **~se (de casa)** to move (house); **~se (de ropa)** to change.

mudéjar adj, m y f Mudejar.

mudo, -da adj 1. (*sin habla*) dumb. 2. (*callado*) silent, mute; **se quedó ~** he was left speechless. 3. (*sin sonido*) silent.

mueble ◆ m piece of furniture; **los ~s** the furniture (U); **~ bar** cocktail cabinet. ◆ adj → **bien**.

mueblería f furniture store.

mueca f (*gen*) face, expression; (*de dolor*) grimace.

muela f (*diente - gen*) tooth; (*- molar*) molar.

muelle m 1. (*de colchón, reloj*) spring. 2. (*en el puerto*) dock, quay; (*en el río*) wharf, pier.

muera → **morir**.

muérdago m mistletoe.

muermo m fam bore, drag; **tener ~** to be bored.

muerte f 1. (*gen*) death; **de mala ~** third-rate, lousy. 2. (*homicidio*) murder.

muerto, -ta ◆ pp → **morir**. ◆ adj (*gen*) dead; **estar ~ de miedo/frío** to be scared/freezing to death; **estar ~ de hambre** to be starving. ◆ m y f dead person; (*cadáver*) corpse; **hubo dos ~s** two people died; **hacer el ~** to float on one's back.

muesca f 1. (*concavidad*) notch, groove. 2. (*corte*) nick.

muestra f 1. (*pequeña cantidad*) sample. 2. (*señal*) sign, show; (*prueba*) proof; (*de cariño, aprecio*) token; **dar ~s de** to show signs of. 3. (*modelo*) model, pattern. 4. (*exposición*) show, exhibition.

muestrario m collection of samples.

muestreo m sample; (*acción*) sampling.

mugido m (*de vaca*) moo, mooing (U); (*de toro*) bellow, bellowing (U).

mugir vi (*vaca*) to moo; (*toro*) to bellow.

mugre f filth, muck.

mugriento, -ta adj filthy.

mujer f woman; (*cónyuge*) wife; **~ de la limpieza** cleaning lady; **~ de negocios** businesswoman.

mujeriego, -ga adj fond of the ladies. ▶ **mujeriego** m womanizer.

mujerzuela f despec loose woman.

mulato, -ta adj, m y f mulatto.

muleta f 1. (*para andar*) crutch; fig prop, support. 2. (TAUROM) muleta, red cape hanging from a stick used to tease the bull.

Mulhacén m: **el ~** Mulhacén.

mullido, -da adj soft, springy.

mulo, -la m y f (ZOOL) mule.

multa f fine; **poner una ~ a alguien** to fine sb.

multar vt to fine.

multicopista f duplicator.

multimedia adj inv (INFORM) multimedia.

multimillonario, -ria m y f multimillionaire.

multinacional adj & f multinational.

múltiple adj (*variado*) multiple. ▶ **múltiples** adj pl (*numerosos*) many, numerous.

multiplicación f multiplication.

multiplicar vt & vi to multiply. ▶ **multiplicarse** vpr 1. (*esforzarse*) to do lots of things at the same time. 2. (BIOL) to multiply.

múltiplo, -pla adj multiple. ▶ **múltiplo** m multiple.

multitud f (*de personas*) crowd; **una ~ de cosas** loads of o countless things.

multitudinario, -ria adj extremely crowded; (*manifestación*) mass (*antes de sust*).

multiuso adj inv multipurpose.

mundanal adj worldly.

mundano, -na adj 1. (*del mundo*) worldly, of the world. 2. (*de la vida social*) (high) society.

mundial ◆ adj (*política, economía, guerra*) world (*antes de sust*); (*tratado, organización, fama*) worldwide. ◆ m World Championships (pl); (*en fútbol*) World Cup.

mundo m 1. (*gen*) world; **el tercer ~** the Third World; **se le cayó el ~ encima** his world fell apart; **todo el ~** everyone, everybody; **venir al ~** to come into the world, to be born. 2. (*experiencia*): **hombre/mujer de ~** man/woman of the world.

munición f ammunition.

municipal ◆ adj town (*antes de sust*),

municipal; (*elecciones*) local; (*instalaciones*) public. ◆ *m y f* → **guardia**.

municipio *m* 1. (*corporación*) town council. 2. (*territorio*) town, municipality.

muñeco, -ca *m y f* (*juguete*) doll; (*marioneta*) puppet. ▶ **muñeco** *m* fig puppet. ▶ **muñeca** *f* 1. (ANAT) wrist. 2. Amer fam (*enchufe*): **tener ~** to have friends in high places. ▶ **muñeco de nieve** *m* snowman.

muñequera *f* wristband.

muñón *m* stump.

mural ◆ *adj* (*pintura*) mural; (*mapa*) wall. ◆ *m* mural.

muralla *f* (*de ciudad*) city wall, ramparts (*pl*); (*muro*) wall.

murciélago *m* bat.

murmullo *m* (*gen*) murmur, murmuring (U); (*de hojas*) rustle, rustling (U); (*de insectos*) buzz, buzzing (U).

murmuración *f* gossip (U).

murmurar ◆ *vt* to murmur. ◆ *vi* 1. (*susurrar - persona*) to murmur, to whisper; (- *agua, viento*) to murmur, to gurgle. 2. (*criticar*): **~ (de)** to gossip o backbite (about). 3. (*rezongar, quejarse*) to grumble.

muro *m* lit & fig wall.

mus *m* inv card game played in pairs with bidding and in which players communicate by signs.

musa *f* (*inspiración*) muse.

musaraña *f* (ZOOL) shrew; **mirar a las ~s** to stare into space o thin air.

muscular *adj* muscular.

musculatura *f* muscles (*pl*).

músculo *m* muscle.

musculoso, -sa *adj* muscular.

museo *m* museum; **~ de arte** art gallery.

musgo *m* moss.

música → **músico**.

músico, -ca ◆ *adj* musical. ◆ *m y f* (*persona*) musician. ▶ **música** *f* music; **música ambiental** background music.

musitar *vt* to mutter, to mumble.

muslo *m* thigh; (*de pollo*) drumstick.

mustio, -tia *adj* 1. (*flor, planta*) withered, wilted. 2. (*persona*) gloomy.

musulmán, -ana *adj, m y f* Muslim.

mutación *f* (*cambio*) sudden change; (BIOL) mutation.

mutante *adj, m y f* mutant.

mutar *vt* to mutate.

mutilado, -da *adj* mutilated.

mutilar *vt* (*gen*) to mutilate; (*estatua*) to deface.

mutismo *m* (*silencio*) silence.

mutua → **mutuo**.

mutualidad *f* (*asociación*) mutual benefit society.

mutuo, -tua *adj* mutual. ▶ **mutua** *f* mutual benefit society.

muy *adv* very; **~ bueno/cerca** very good/near; **~ de mañana** very early in the morning; **¡~ bien!** (*vale*) OK!, all right!; (*qué bien*) very good!, well done!; **eso es ~ de ella** that's just like her; **eso es ~ de los americanos** that's typically American; **¡el ~ idiota!** what an idiot!

N

n, N *f* (*letra*) n, N. ▶ **N** *m*: **el 20 N** 20th November, the date of Franco's death.

n/ *abrev de* **nuestro**.

nabo *m* turnip.

nácar *m* mother-of-pearl.

nacer *vi* 1. (*venir al mundo - niño, animal*) to be born; (- *planta*) to sprout; (- *pájaro*) to hatch (out); **~ de/en** to be born of/in; **~ para algo** to be born to be sthg; **ha nacido cantante** she's a born singer. 2. (*surgir - pelo*) to grow; (- *río*) to rise; (- *costumbre, actitud, duda*) to have its roots.

nacido, -da ◆ *adj* born. ◆ *m y f*: **los ~s hoy** those born today; **recién ~** newborn baby; **ser un mal ~** to be a wicked o vile person.

naciente *adj* 1. (*día*) dawning; (*sol*) rising. 2. (*gobierno, estado*) new, fledgling; (*interés*) growing.

nacimiento *m* 1. (*gen*) birth; (*de planta*) sprouting; **de ~** from birth. 2. (*de río*) source. 3. (*origen*) origin, beginning. 4. (*belén*) Nativity scene.

nación *f* (*gen*) nation; (*territorio*) country. ▶ **Naciones Unidas** *fpl* United Nations.

nacional *adj* national; (*mercado, vuelo*) domestic; (*asuntos*) home (*antes de sust*).

nacionalidad *f* nationality.

nacionalismo *m* nationalism.

nacionalista *adj, m y f* nationalist.

nacionalizar *vt* 1. (*banca, bienes*) to nationalize. 2. (*persona*) to naturalize. ▶ **nacionalizarse** *vpr* to become naturalized.

nada ♦ *pron* nothing; (*en negativas*) anything; **no he leído ~ de este autor** I haven't read anything by this author; **~ más** nothing else, nothing more; **no quiero ~ más** I don't want anything else; **no dijo ~ de ~** he didn't say anything at all; **de ~** (*respuesta a 'gracias'*) you're welcome, don't mention it; **como si ~** as if nothing had happened. **♦** *adv* **1.** (*en absoluto*) at all; **la película no me ha gustado ~** I didn't like the film at all; **no cuesta ~** it's no trouble at all. **2.** (*poco*) a little, a bit; **no hace ~ que salió** he left just a minute ago; **~ menos que** (*cosa*) no less than; (*persona*) none other than. **♦** *f:* **la ~** nothingness, the void. **▶ nada más** *loc conj* no sooner, as soon as; **~ más salir de casa se puso a llover** no sooner had I left the house than it started to rain, as soon as I left the house, it started to rain.

nadador, -ra *m y f* swimmer.

nadar *vi* (*gen*) to swim; (*flotar*) to float.

nadería *f* trifle, little thing.

nadie *pron* nobody, no one; **~ lo sabe** nobody knows; **no se lo dije a ~** I didn't tell anybody; **no ha llamado ~** nobody phoned.

nado ▶ a nado *loc adv* swimming.

naïf [na'if] *adj* naïve, primitivistic.

nailon, nilón, nylon® *m* nylon.

naipe *m* (playing) card. **▶ naipes** *mpl* cards.

nalga *f* buttock.

nana *f* (*canción*) lullaby.

naranja ♦ *adj inv* orange. **♦** *m* (*color*) orange. **♦** *f* (*fruto*) orange. **▶ media naranja** *f fam fig* other o better half.

naranjo *m* (*árbol*) orange tree.

narciso *m* (BOT) narcissus.

narcótico, -ca *adj* narcotic. **▶ narcótico** *m* narcotic; (*droga*) drug.

narcotizar *vt* to drug.

narcotraficante *m y f* drug trafficker.

narcotráfico *m* drug trafficking.

nardo *m* nard, spikenard.

narigudo, -da *adj* big-nosed.

nariz *f* **1.** (*órgano*) nose. **2.** (*orificio*) nostril. **3.** *fig* (*olfato*) sense of smell. **4.** *loc:* **estar hasta las narices (de algo)** to be fed up to the back teeth (with sthg); **meter las narices en algo** to poke o stick one's nose into sthg.

narración *f* **1.** (*cuento, relato*) narrative, story. **2.** (*acción*) narration.

narrador, -ra *m y f* narrator.

narrar *vt* (*contar*) to recount, to tell.

narrativo, -va *adj* narrative. **▶ narrativa** *f* narrative.

nasal *adj* nasal.

nata *f* **1.** (*gen & fig*) cream; **~ batida** o **montada** whipped cream. **2.** (*de leche hervida*) skin.

natación *f* swimming.

natal *adj* (*país*) native; (*ciudad, pueblo*) home (*antes de sust*).

natalicio *m* (*cumpleaños*) birthday.

natalidad *f* birth rate.

natillas *fpl* custard (U).

nativo, -va *adj, m y f* native.

nato, -ta *adj* (*gen*) born; (*cargo, título*) ex officio.

natural ♦ *adj* **1.** (*gen*) natural; (*flores, fruta, leche*) fresh; **al ~** (*persona*) in one's natural state; (*fruta*) in its own juice; **ser ~ en alguien** to be natural o normal for sb. **2.** (*nativo*) native; **ser ~ de** to come from. **♦** *m y f* (*nativo*) native. **♦** *m* (*talante*) nature, disposition.

naturaleza *f* **1.** (*gen*) nature; **por ~** by nature. **2.** (*complexión*) constitution.

naturalidad *f* naturalness; **con ~** naturally.

naturalizar *vt* to naturalize. **▶ naturalizarse** *vpr* to become naturalized.

naturista *m y f person favouring return to nature.*

naufragar *vi* (*barco*) to sink, to be wrecked; (*persona*) to be shipwrecked.

naufragio *m* (*de barco*) shipwreck.

náufrago, -ga *m y f castaway.*

náusea *f* (*gen pl*) nausea (U), sickness (U); **me da ~s** it makes me sick.

nauseabundo, -da *adj* nauseating.

náutico, -ca *adj* (*gen*) nautical; (DEP) water (*antes de sust*). **▶ náutica** *f* navigation, seamanship.

navaja *f* **1.** (*cuchillo - pequeño*) penknife; (*- más grande*) jackknife. **2.** (*molusco*) razor-shell.

navajero, -ra *m y f thug who carries a knife.*

naval *adj* naval.

Navarra Navarre.

navarro, -rra *adj, m y f* Navarrese.

nave *f* **1.** (*barco*) ship; **quemar las ~s** to burn one's boats o bridges. **2.** (*vehículo*) craft; **~ espacial** spaceship. **3.** (*de fábrica*) shop, plant; (*almacén*) warehouse. **4.** (*de iglesia*) nave.

navegación *f* navigation.

navegante *m y f* navigator.

navegar *vi & vt* (*barco*) to sail; (*avión*) to fly.

Navidad *f* **1.** (*día*) Christmas (Day).

2. (gen pl) (periodo) Christmas (time); **felices Navidades** Merry Christmas.

navideño, -ña adj Christmas (antes de sust).

naviero, -ra adj shipping. ► **naviero** m (armador) shipowner. ► **naviera** f (compañía) shipping company.

navío m large ship.

nazi adj, m y f Nazi.

nazismo m Nazism.

neblina f mist.

nebuloso, -sa adj **1.** (con nubes) cloudy; (de niebla) foggy. **2.** fig (idea, mirada) vague. ► **nebulosa** f (ASTRON) nebula.

necedad f **1.** (estupidez) stupidity, foolishness. **2.** (dicho, hecho) stupid o foolish thing; **decir ~es** to talk nonsense.

necesario, -ria adj necessary; **es ~ hacerlo** it needs to be done; **no es ~ que lo hagas** you don't need to do it; **si fuera ~** if need be.

neceser m toilet bag o case.

necesidad f **1.** (gen) need. **2.** (obligación) necessity; **por ~** out of necessity. **3.** (hambre) hunger. ► **necesidades** fpl: **hacer (uno) sus necesidades** eufemismo to answer the call of nature.

necesitado, -da ◆ adj needy. ◆ m y f needy o poor person; **los ~s** the poor.

necesitar vt to need; **necesito que me lo digas** I need you to tell me; **'se necesita piso'** 'flat wanted'. ► **necesitar de** vi to have need of.

necio, -cia adj stupid, foolish.

necrología f obituary; (lista de esquelas) obituary column.

néctar m nectar.

nectarina f nectarine.

nefasto, -ta adj (funesto) ill-fated; (dañino) bad, harmful; (pésimo) terrible, awful.

negación f **1.** (desmentido) denial. **2.** (negativa) refusal. **3.** (lo contrario) antithesis, negation. **4.** (GRAM) negative.

negado, -da adj useless.

negar vt **1.** (rechazar) to deny. **2.** (denegar) to refuse, to deny; **~le algo a alguien** to refuse o deny sb sthg. ► **negarse** vpr: **~se (a)** to refuse (to).

negativo, -va adj (gen) negative. ► **negativo** m (FOT) negative. ► **negativa** f **1.** (rechazo) refusal. **2.** (mentís) denial.

negligencia f negligence.

negligente adj negligent.

negociable adj negotiable.

negociación f negotiation.

negociante m y f (comerciante) businessman (f businesswoman).

negociar ◆ vi **1.** (comerciar) to do business; **~ con** to deal o trade with. **2.** (discutir) to negotiate. ◆ vt to negotiate.

negocio m **1.** (gen) business; **el mundo de los ~s** the business world. **2.** (transacción) deal, (business) transaction; **~ sucio** shady deal. **3.** (operación ventajosa) good deal, bargain; **hacer ~** to do well. **4.** (comercio) trade.

negra → **negro**.

negrero, -ra m y f **1.** (HIST) slave trader. **2.** fig (explotador) slave driver.

negrita, negrilla → **letra**.

negro, -gra ◆ adj **1.** (gen) black. **2.** (furioso) furious; **ponerse ~** to get mad o angry. **3.** (CIN): **cine ~** film noir. ◆ m y f black man (f black woman). ► **negro** m (color) black. ► **negra** f **1.** (MÚS) crotchet. **2.** loc: **tener la negra** to have bad luck.

negrura f blackness.

nene, -na m y f fam (niño) baby.

nenúfar m water lily.

neocelandés, -esa, neozelandés, -esa m y f New Zealander.

neologismo m neologism.

neón m (QUÍM) neon.

neoyorquino, -na ◆ adj New York (antes de sust), of/relating to New York. ◆ m y f New Yorker.

neozelandés, -esa = **neocelandés**.

Nepal: **el ~** Nepal.

Neptuno Neptune.

nervio m **1.** (ANAT) nerve. **2.** (de carne) sinew. **3.** (vigor) energy, vigour. ► **nervios** mpl (estado mental) nerves; **tener ~s** to be nervous; **poner los ~s de punta a alguien** to get on sb's nerves; **tener los ~s de punta** to be on edge.

nerviosismo m nervousness, nerves (pl).

nervioso, -sa adj **1.** (ANAT - sistema, enfermedad) nervous; (- tejido, célula, centro) nerve (antes de sust). **2.** (inquieto) nervous; **ponerse ~** to get nervous. **3.** (irritado) worked-up; **ponerse ~** to get uptight o worked up.

nervudo, -da adj sinewy.

neto, -ta adj **1.** (claro) clear, clean; (verdad) simple, plain. **2.** (peso, sueldo) net.

neumático, -ca adj pneumatic. ► **neumático** m tyre; **~ de repuesto** spare tyre.

neumonía f pneumonia.

neurálgico, -ca adj **1.** (MED) neuralgic. **2.** fig (importante) critical.

neurastenia f nervous exhaustion.
neurología f neurology.
neurólogo, -ga m y f neurologist.
neurona f neuron, nerve cell.
neurosis f inv neurosis.
neurótico, -ca adj, m y f neurotic.
neutral adj, m y f neutral.
neutralidad f neutrality.
neutralizar vt to neutralize.
neutro, -tra adj 1. (gen) neutral. 2. (BIOL & GRAM) neuter.
neutrón m neutron.
nevado, -da adj snowy. ▶ **nevada** f snowfall.
nevar v impers to snow.
nevera f fridge Br, icebox Am.
nevisca f snow flurry.
nexo m link, connection; (relación) relation, connection.
ni ◆ conj: ~ ... ~ ... neither ... nor ...; ~ mañana ~ pasado neither tomorrow nor the day after; no ... ~ ... neither ... nor ..., not ... or ... (either); no es alto ~ bajo he's neither tall nor short, he's not tall or short (either); no es rojo ~ verde ~ azul it's neither red nor green nor blue; ~ un/una ... not a single ...; no me quedaré ~ un minuto más I'm not staying a minute longer; ~ uno/una not a single one; no he aprobado ~ una I haven't passed a single one; ~ que as if; ¡~ que yo fuera tonto! as if I were that stupid! ◆ adv not even; anda tan atareado que ~ tiene tiempo para comer he's so busy he doesn't even have time to eat.
Nicaragua Nicaragua.
nicaragüense adj, m y f Nicaraguan.
nicho m niche.
nicotina f nicotine.
nidal m nest.
nido m (gen) nest.
niebla f (densa) fog; (neblina) mist; hay ~ it's foggy.
nieto, -ta m y f grandson (f granddaughter). ▶ **nietos** mpl grandchildren.
nieve f (METEOR) snow. ▶ **nieves** fpl (nevada) snows, snowfall (sg).
NIF (abrev de número de identificación fiscal) m ≃ National Insurance number Br, identification number for tax purposes.
Nilo m: el ~ the (river) Nile.
nilón = **nailon**.
nimiedad f 1. (cualidad) insignificance, triviality. 2. (dicho, hecho) trifle.
nimio, -mia adj insignificant, trivial.
ninfa f nymph.
ninfómana f nymphomaniac.

ninguno, -na ◆ adj (antes de sust masculino: **ningún**) no; **ninguna respuesta se dio** no answer was given; **no tengo ningún interés en hacerlo** I've no interest in doing it, I'm not at all interested in doing it; **no tengo ningún hijo/ninguna buena idea** I don't have any children/good ideas; **no tiene ninguna gracia** it's not funny. ◆ pron (cosa) none, not any; (persona) nobody, no one; ~ **funciona** none of them works; **no hay** ~ there aren't any, there are none; ~ **lo sabrá** no one o nobody will know; ~ **de** none of; ~ **de ellos** none of them; ~ **de los dos** neither of them.
niña → **niño**.
niñería f 1. (cualidad) childishness (U). 2. fig (tontería) silly o childish thing.
niñero, -ra adj fond of children. ▶ **niñera** f nanny.
niñez f (infancia) childhood.
niño, -ña ◆ adj young. ◆ m y f (crío) child, boy (f girl); (bebé) baby; **los ~s** the children; ~ **bien** despec spoilt brat; ~ **prodigio** child prodigy; **ser el ~ bonito de alguien** to be sb's pet o blue-eyed boy. ▶ **niña** f (del ojo) pupil; **la niña de los ojos** fig the apple of one's eye.
nipón, -ona adj, m y f Japanese.
níquel m nickel.
niquelar vt to nickel-plate.
niqui m T-shirt.
níspero m medlar.
nitidez f clarity; (de imágenes, colores) sharpness.
nítido, -da adj clear; (imágenes, colores) sharp.
nitrato m nitrate.
nitrógeno m nitrogen.
nivel m 1. (gen) level; (altura) height; **al** ~ **de** level with; **al** ~ **del mar** at sea level. 2. (grado) level, standard; **al mismo** ~ **(que)** on a level o par (with); **a** ~ **europeo** at a European level; ~ **de vida** standard of living.
nivelador, -ra adj levelling. ▶ **niveladora** f bulldozer.
nivelar vt 1. (allanar) to level. 2. (equilibrar) to even out; (FIN) to balance.
no ◆ adv 1. (expresa negación - gen) not; (- en respuestas) no; (- con sustantivos) non-; ~ **sé** I don't know; ~ **veo nada** I can't see anything; ~ **es fácil** it's not easy, it isn't easy; ~ **tiene dinero** he has no money, he hasn't got any money; **todavía** ~ not yet; ¿~ **vienes?** - ~, ~ **creo** aren't you coming? – no, I don't think so; ~ **fumadores** non-smokers; ~ **bien** as

soon as; ~ **ya** ... **sino que** ... not only ... but (also) ...; **¡a que ~ lo haces!** I bet you don't do it!; **¿cómo ~?** of course; **pues ~, eso sí que ~** certainly not; **¡que ~!** I said no! **2.** (*expresa duda, extrañeza*): **¿~ irás a venir?** you're not coming, are you?; **estamos de acuerdo, ¿~?** we're agreed then, are we?; **es español, ¿~?** he's Spanish, isn't he? ◆ *m* no.

n.º (*abrev de* **número**) no.

nobiliario, -ria *adj* noble.

noble *adj, m y f* noble; **los ~s** the nobility.

nobleza *f* nobility.

noche *f* night; (*atardecer*) evening; **ayer por la ~** last night; **esta ~** tonight; **hacer ~ en** to stay the night in; **hacerse de ~** to get dark; **por la ~, de ~** at night; **buenas ~s** (*despedida*) good night; (*saludo*) good evening; **de la ~ a la mañana** overnight.

Nochebuena *f* Christmas Eve.

nochero *m* Amer **1.** (*vigilante*) night watchman. **2.** (*mesita*) bedside table.

Nochevieja *f* New Year's Eve.

NOCHEVIEJA

New Year's Eve traditions in Spain include the dancing of the 'cotillón' to see out the old year and the eating of twelve grapes, one for each of the twelve chimes of midnight, which supposedly brings good luck for the coming year.

noción *f* (*concepto*) notion; **tener ~ (de)** to have an idea (of). ► **nociones** *fpl* (*conocimiento básico*): **tener nociones de** to have a smattering of.

nocivo, -va *adj* (*gen*) harmful; (*gas*) noxious.

noctámbulo, -la *m y f* night owl.

nocturno, -na *adj* **1.** (*club, tren, vuelo*) night (*antes de sust*); (*clase*) evening (*antes de sust*). **2.** (*animales, plantas*) nocturnal.

nodriza *f* wet nurse.

Noel → **papá.**

nogal *m* walnut.

nómada ◆ *adj* nomadic. ◆ *m y f* nomad.

nomás *adv* Amer: **esta ahí ~** it's just over there; **faltan dos semanas ~** there are only two weeks to go.

nombramiento *m* appointment.

nombrar *vt* **1.** (*citar*) to mention. **2.** (*designar*) to appoint.

nombre *m* **1.** (*gen*) name; **~ y apellidos** full name; **~ compuesto** compound name; **~ de pila** first o Christian name;

~ de soltera maiden name; **a ~ de** (*carta*) adressed to; (*cheque*) made out to; **en ~ de** on behalf of. **2.** (*fama*) reputation; **tener mucho ~** to be renowned o famous. **3.** (GRAM) noun; **~ común/propio** common/proper noun.

nomenclatura *f* nomenclature.

nómina *f* **1.** (*lista de empleados*) payroll. **2.** (*hoja de salario*) payslip.

nominal *adj* nominal.

nominar *vt* to nominate.

nomo, gnomo *m* gnome.

non *m* odd number. ► **nones** *adv* (*no*) no way.

nonagésimo, -ma *núm* ninetieth.

nordeste = **noreste.**

nórdico, -ca *adj* **1.** (*del norte*) northern, northerly. **2.** (*escandinavo*) Nordic.

noreste, nordeste ◆ *adj* (*posición, parte*) northeast, northeastern; (*dirección, viento*) northeasterly. ◆ *m* north-east.

noria *f* **1.** (*para agua*) water wheel. **2.** (*de feria*) big wheel Br, Ferris wheel.

norma *f* standard; (*regla*) rule; **es la ~ hacerlo así** it's usual to do it this way.

normal *adj* normal.

normalidad *f* normality.

normalizar *vt* **1.** (*volver normal*) to return to normal. **2.** (*estandarizar*) to standardize. ► **normalizarse** *vpr* to return to normal.

normalmente *adv* normally, usually.

normativo, -va *adj* normative. ► **normativa** *f* regulations (*pl*).

noroeste ◆ *adj* (*posición, parte*) northwest, northwestern; (*dirección, viento*) northwesterly. ◆ *m* northwest.

norte ◆ *adj* (*posición, parte*) north, northern; (*dirección, viento*) northerly. ◆ *m* **1.** (GEOGR) north. **2.** (*guía*) guide.

norteamericano, -na *adj, m y f* North American, American.

Noruega Norway.

noruego, -ga *adj, m y f* Norwegian. ► **noruego** *m* (*lengua*) Norwegian.

nos *pron pers* **1.** (*complemento directo*) us; **le gustaría vernos** she'd like to see us. **2.** (*complemento indirecto*) (to) us; **~ lo dio** he gave it to us; **~ tiene miedo** he's afraid of us. **3.** (*reflexivo*) ourselves. **4.** (*recíproco*) each other; **~ enamoramos** we fell in love (with each other).

nosocomio *m* Amer hospital.

nosotros, -tras *pron pers* **1.** (*sujeto*) we. **2.** (*predicado*): **somos ~** it's us. **3.** (*después de prep*) (*complemento*) us; **vente a comer con ~** come and eat with us; **no compramos nada para ~** we didn't buy anything for ourselves. **4.** loc: **entre ~** between you and me.

nostalgia f (del pasado) nostalgia; (de país, amigos) homesickness.

nota f **1.** (gen & MÚS) note; **tomar ~ de algo** (apuntar) to note sthg down; (fijarse) to take note of sthg; **~ dominante** prevailing mood. **2.** (EDUC) mark; **sacar** o **tener buenas ~s** to get good marks. **3.** (cuenta) bill. **4.** loc: **dar la ~** to make o.s. conspicuous.

notable ♦ adj remarkable, outstanding. ♦ m (EDUC) merit, second class.

notar vt **1.** (advertir) to notice; **te noto cansado** you look tired to me; **hacer ~ algo** to point sthg out. **2.** (sentir) to feel. ▶ **notarse** vpr to be apparent; **se nota que le gusta** you can tell she likes it.

notaría f (oficina) notary's office.

notario, -ria m y f notary (public).

noticia f news (U); **una ~** a piece of news; **¿tienes ~s suyas?** have you heard from him? ▶ **noticias** fpl: **las ~s** (RADIO & TV) the news.

notificación f notification.

notificar vt to notify, to inform.

notoriedad f (fama) fame.

notorio, -ria adj **1.** (evidente) obvious. **2.** (conocido) widely-known.

novato, -ta ♦ adj inexperienced. ♦ m y f novice, beginner.

novecientos, -tas núm nine hundred; ver también **seis**.

novedad f **1.** (cualidad - de nuevo) newness; (- de novedoso) novelty. **2.** (cambio) change. **3.** (noticia) news (U); **sin ~** without incident; (MIL) all quiet. ▶ **novedades** fpl (libros, discos) new releases; (moda) latest fashion (sg).

novedoso, -sa adj novel, new.

novel adj new, first-time.

novela f novel; **~ policíaca** detective story.

novelesco, -ca adj **1.** (de la novela) fictional. **2.** (fantástico) fantastic.

novelista m y f novelist.

noveno, -na núm ninth.

noventa núm ninety; **los (años) ~** the nineties; ver también **seis**.

noviazgo m engagement.

noviembre m November; ver también **septiembre**.

novillada f (TAUROM) bullfight with young bulls.

novillo, -lla m y f young bull or cow; **hacer ~s** fam to play truant Br, to play hooky Am.

novio, -via m y f **1.** (compañero)

boyfriend (f girlfriend). **2.** (prometido) fiancé (f fiancée). **3.** (recién casado) bridegroom (f bride); **los ~s** the newly-weds.

nubarrón m storm cloud.

nube f **1.** (gen) fig cloud; **poner algo/a alguien por las ~s** fig to praise sthg/sb to the skies; **por las ~s** (caro) sky-high, terribly expensive. **2.** (de personas, moscas) swarm.

nublado, -da adj **1.** (encapotado) cloudy, overcast. **2.** fig (turbado) clouded.

nublar vt lit & fig to cloud. ▶ **nublarse** vpr **1.** (suj: cielo) to cloud over. **2.** fig (turbarse, oscurecerse) to become clouded.

nubosidad f cloudiness, clouds (pl).

nuca f nape, back of the neck.

nuclear adj nuclear.

núcleo m **1.** (centro) nucleus; fig centre. **2.** (grupo) core.

nudillo m knuckle.

nudismo m nudism.

nudo m **1.** (gen) knot; **se le hizo un ~ en la garganta** she got a lump in her throat. **2.** (cruce) junction. **3.** fig (vínculo) tie, bond. **4.** fig (punto principal) crux.

nudoso, -sa adj knotty, gnarled.

nuera f daughter-in-law.

nuestro, -tra ♦ adj poses our; **~ coche** our car; **este libro es ~** this book is ours, this is our book; **un amigo ~** a friend of ours; **no es asunto ~** it's none of our business. ♦ pron poses: **el ~** ours; **el ~ es rojo** ours is red; **esta es la nuestra** fam this is the chance we have been waiting for; **lo ~ es el teatro** (lo que nos va) theatre is what we should be doing; **los ~s** fam (nuestra familia) our folks; (nuestro bando) our lot, our side.

nueva → nuevo.

Nueva York New York.

Nueva Zelanda New Zealand.

nueve núm nine; ver también **seis**.

nuevo, -va ♦ adj (gen) new; (patatas, legumbres) new, fresh; (vino) young; **ser ~ en** to be new to. ♦ m y f newcomer. ▶ **buena nueva** f good news (U). ▶ **de nuevo** loc adv again.

nuez f **1.** (BOT) (gen) nut; (de nogal) walnut. **2.** (ANAT) Adam's apple. ▶ **nuez moscada** f nutmeg.

nulidad f **1.** (no validez) nullity. **2.** (ineptitud) incompetence.

nulo, -la adj **1.** (sin validez) null and void. **2.** fam (incapacitado): **~ (para)** useless (at).

núm. (abrev de **número**) No.

oboe

numeración f 1. (*acción*) numbering. 2. (*sistema*) numerals (*pl*), numbers (*pl*).
numeral adj numeral.
numerar vt to number.
numérico, -ca adj numeric(al).
número m 1. (*gen*) number; ~ **de matrícula** (AUTOM) registration number; ~ **redondo** round number; **en ~s rojos** in the red; **hacer ~s** to reckon up. 2. (*tamaño, talla*) size. 3. (*de publicación*) issue; ~ **atrasado** back number. 4. (*de lotería*) ticket. 5. (*de un espectáculo*) turn, number; **montar el ~** fam to make o cause a scene.
numeroso, -sa adj numerous; **un grupo ~** a large group.
nunca adv (*en frases afirmativas*) never; (*en frases negativas*) ever; **casi ~ viene** he almost never comes, he hardly ever comes; **¿~ le has visto?** have you never seen her?, haven't you ever seen her?; **más que ~** more than ever; ~ **jamás** o **más** never more o again.
nuncio m nuncio.
nupcial adj wedding (*antes de sust*).
nupcias fpl wedding (*sg*), nuptials.
nutria f otter.
nutrición f nutrition.
nutrido, -da adj 1. (*alimentado*) nourished; **mal ~** undernourished. 2. (*numeroso*) large.
nutrir vt 1. (*alimentar*): ~ **(con o de)** to nourish o feed (with). 2. fig (*fomentar*) to feed, to nurture. 3. fig (*suministrar*): ~ **(de)** to supply (with). ► **nutrirse** vpr 1. (*gen*): ~**se de** o **con** to feed on. 2. fig (*proveerse*): ~**se de** o **con** to supply o provide o.s. with. **nutritivo, -va** adj nutritious.
nylon® ['nailon] = **nailon**.

ñ, Ñ f (*letra*) ñ, Ñ, 15th letter of the Spanish alphabet.
ñoñería, ñoñez f inanity, insipidness (U).
ñoño, -ña adj 1. (*remilgado*) squeamish; (*quejica*) whining. 2. (*soso*) dull, insipid.
ñudo Amer ► **al ñudo** loc adv in vain.

o¹, O f (*letra*) o, O.
o² conj ('u' *en vez de* 'o' *antes de palabras que empiezan por* 'o' u 'ho') conj or; ~ **...** ~ either ... or; ~ **sea (que)** in other words, that is.
o/ abrev de **orden**.
oasis m inv lit & fig oasis.
obcecar vt to blind. ► **obcecarse** vpr to become stubborn; ~**se en hacer algo** to insist on doing sthg.
obedecer ♦ vt: ~ **(a alguien)** to obey (sb). ♦ vi 1. (*acatar*) to obey. 2. (*someterse*): ~ **a** to respond to. 3. (*estar motivado*): ~ **a** to be due to.
obediencia f obedience.
obediente adj obedient.
obertura f overture.
obesidad f obesity.
obeso, -sa adj obese.
óbice m: **no ser ~ para** not to be an obstacle to.
obispo m bishop.
objeción f objection; **poner objeciones a** to raise objections to; **tener objeciones** to have objections; ~ **de conciencia** conscientious objection.
objetar vt to object to; **no tengo nada que ~** I have no objection.
objetivo, -va adj objective. ► **objetivo** m 1. (*finalidad*) objective, aim. 2. (MIL) target. 3. (FOT) lens.
objeto m 1. (*gen*) object; **ser ~ de** to be the object of; ~**s de valor** valuables; ~**s perdidos** lost property (U). 2. (*propósito*) purpose, object; **sin ~** (*inútilmente*) to no purpose, pointlessly; **al** o **con ~ de** (*para*) in order to.
objetor, -ra m y f objector; ~ **de conciencia** conscientious objector.
oblicuo, -cua adj (*inclinado*) oblique; (*mirada*) sidelong.
obligación f 1. (*gen*) obligation, duty; **por ~** out of a sense of duty. 2. (FIN) (*gen pl*) bond, security.
obligar vt: ~ **a alguien (a hacer algo)** to oblige o force sb (to do sthg). ► **obligarse** vpr: ~**se a hacer algo** to undertake to do sthg.
obligatorio, -ria adj obligatory, compulsory.
oboe m (*instrumento*) oboe.

obra f 1. (gen) work (U); **es ~ suya** it's his doing; **poner en ~** to put into effect; **~ de caridad** (institución) charity; **~s sociales** community work (U); **por ~ (y gracia) de** thanks to. 2. (ARTE) work (of art); (TEATR) play; (LITER) book; (MÚS) opus; **~ maestra** masterpiece; **~s completas** complete works. 3. (CONSTR) (lugar) building site; (reforma) alteration; **'~s'** (en carretera) 'roadworks'; **~s públicas** public works.

obrar ◆ vi 1. (actuar) to act. 2. (causar efecto) to work, to take effect. 3. (estar en poder): **~ en manos de** to be in the possession of. ◆ vt to work.

obrero, -ra ◆ adj (clase) working; (movimiento) labour (antes de sust). ◆ m y f (en fábrica) worker; (en obra) workman; **~ cualificado** skilled worker.

obscenidad f obscenity.

obsceno, -na adj obscene.

obscurecer = oscurecer.

obscuridad = oscuridad.

obscuro, -ra = oscuro.

obsequiar vt: **~ a alguien con algo** to present sb with sthg.

obsequio m gift, present.

observación f 1. (gen) observation. 2. (nota) note. 3. (cumplimiento) observance.

observador, -ra ◆ adj observant. ◆ m y f observer.

observar vt 1. (contemplar) to observe, to watch. 2. (advertir) to notice, to observe. 3. (acatar - ley, normas) to observe; (- conducta, costumbre) to follow. ▶ **observarse** vpr to be noticed.

observatorio m observatory.

obsesión f obsession.

obsesionar vt to obsess. ▶ **obsesionarse** vpr to be obsessed.

obsesivo, -va adj obsessive.

obseso, -sa ◆ adj obsessed. ◆ m y f obsessed o obsessive person.

obstaculizar vt to hinder, to hamper.

obstáculo m obstacle; **un ~ para** an obstacle to; **poner ~s a algo/alguien** to hinder sthg/sb.

obstante ▶ **no obstante** loc adv nevertheless, however.

obstetricia f obstetrics (U).

obstinado, -da adj (persistente) persistent; (terco) obstinate, stubborn.

obstinarse vpr to refuse to give way; **~ en** to persist in.

obstrucción f lit & fig obstruction.

obstruir vt 1. (bloquear) to block, to obstruct. 2. (obstaculizar) to obstruct, to

impede. ▶ **obstruirse** vpr to get blocked (up).

obtener vt (beca, cargo, puntos) to get; (premio, victoria) to win; (información) to obtain; (ganancias) to make; (satisfacción) to gain.

obturar vt to block.

obtuso, -sa adj 1. (sin punta) blunt. 2. fig (tonto) obtuse, stupid.

obús (pl obuses) m (proyectil) shell.

obviar vt to avoid, to get round.

obvio, -via adj obvious.

oca f (animal) goose.

ocasión f 1. (oportunidad) opportunity, chance. 2. (momento) moment, time; (vez) occasion; **en dos ocasiones** on two occasions; **en alguna ~** sometimes; **en cierta ~** once; **en otra ~** some other time. 3. (motivo): **con ~ de** on the occasion of. 4. (ganga) bargain; **de ~** (precio, artículos etc) bargain (antes de sust).

ocasional adj 1. (accidental) accidental. 2. (irregular) occasional.

ocasionar vt to cause.

ocaso m 1. (puesta del sol) sunset. 2. fig (decadencia) decline.

occidental adj western.

occidente m west. ▶ **Occidente** m (bloque de países) the West.

ocurrente adj witty.

OCDE (abrev de **Organización para la Cooperación y el Desarrollo Económico**) f OECD.

Oceanía Oceania.

océano m ocean; fig (inmensidad) sea, host.

ochenta núm eighty; **los (años) ~** the eighties; ver también **seis**.

ocho núm eight; **de aquí en ~ días** (en una semana) a week today; ver también **seis**.

ochocientos, -tas núm eight hundred; ver también **seis**.

ocio m (tiempo libre) leisure, spare time; (inactividad) idleness.

ocioso, -sa adj 1. (inactivo) idle. 2. (innecesario) unnecessary; (inútil) pointless.

ocre ◆ m ochre. ◆ adj inv ochre.

octágono, -na adj octagonal. ▶ **octágono** m octagon.

octano m octane.

octava → octavo.

octavilla f 1. (de propaganda política) pamphlet, leaflet. 2. (tamaño) octavo.

octavo, -va núm eighth. ▶ **octavo** m (parte) eighth. ▶ **octava** f (MÚS) octave.

octeto m (INFORM) byte.

octogenario, -ria *adj, m y f* octogenarian.

octogésimo, -ma *núm* eightieth.

octubre *m* October; *ver también* **septiembre**.

ocular *adj* eye (*antes de sust*).

oculista *m y f* ophthalmologist.

ocultar *vt* 1. (*gen*) to hide. 2. *fig* (*delito*) to cover up. ▶ **ocultarse** *vpr* to hide.

oculto, -ta *adj* hidden.

ocupación *f* 1. (*gen*) occupation; **~ ilegal de viviendas** squatting. 2. (*empleo*) job.

ocupado, -da *adj* 1. (*persona*) busy. 2. (*teléfono, lavabo etc*) engaged. 3. (*lugar - gen, por ejército*) occupied; (*plaza*) taken.

ocupante *m y f* occupant; **~ ilegal de viviendas** squatter.

ocupar *vt* 1. (*gen*) to occupy. 2. (*superficie, espacio*) to take up; (*habitación, piso*) to live in; (*mesa*) to sit at; (*sillón*) to sit in. 3. (*suj: actividad*) to take up. 4. (*cargo*) to hold. 5. (*dar trabajo a*) to find o provide work for. ▶ **ocuparse** *vpr* (*encargarse*) **~se de** (*gen*) to deal with; (*niños, enfermos, finanzas*) to look after.

ocurrencia *f* 1. (*idea*) bright idea. 2. (*dicho gracioso*) witty remark.

ocurrente *adj* witty.

ocurrir *vi* 1. (*acontecer*) to happen. 2. (*pasar, preocupar*): **¿qué le ocurre a Juan?** what's up with Juan? ▶ **ocurrirse** *vpr* (*venir a la cabeza*): **no se me ocurre ninguna solución** I can't think of a solution; **¡ni se te ocurra!** don't even think about it!; **se me ocurre que ...** it occurs to me that ...

odiar *vt & vi* to hate.

odio *m* hatred; **tener ~ a algo/alguien** to hate sthg/sb.

odioso, -sa *adj* hateful, horrible.

odontólogo, -ga *m y f* dentist, dental surgeon.

OEA (*abrev de* **Organización de Estados Americanos**) *f* OAS.

oeste ◆ *adj* (*posición, parte*) west, western; (*dirección, viento*) westerly. ◆ *m* west.

ofender *vt* (*injuriar*) to insult; (*suj: palabras*) to offend, to hurt. ▶ **ofenderse** *vpr*: **~se (por)** to take offence (at).

ofensa *f* 1. (*acción*): **~ (a)** offence (against). 2. (*injuria*) slight, insult.

ofensivo, -va *adj* offensive. ▶ **ofensiva** *f* offensive.

oferta *f* 1. (*gen*) offer; **'~s de trabajo'** 'situations vacant'. 2. (ECON) (*suministro*) supply; **la ~ y la demanda** supply and demand; **~ monetaria** money supply.

3. (*rebaja*) bargain, special offer; **de ~** bargain (*antes de sust*), on offer. 4. (FIN) (*proposición*) bid, tender; **~ pública de adquisición** (COM) takeover bid.

ofertar *vt* to offer.

office ['ofis] *m inv* scullery.

oficial, -la *m y f* (*obrero*) journeyman; (*aprendiz*) trainee. ▶ **oficial** ◆ *adj* oficial. ◆ *m* 1. (MIL) officer. 2. (*funcionario*) clerk.

oficialismo *m Amer* (*gobierno*): **el ~** the Government.

oficiar *vt* to officiate at.

oficina *f* office; **~ de correos** post office; **~ de empleo** job centre; **~ de turismo** tourist office.

oficinista *m y f* office worker.

oficio *m* 1. (*profesión manual*) trade; **de ~** by trade. 2. (*trabajo*) job. 3. (*experiencia*): **tener mucho ~** to be very experienced. 4. (RELIG) service.

oficioso, -sa *adj* unofficial.

ofimática *f* office automation.

ofrecer *vt* 1. (*gen*) to offer; (*una fiesta*) to give, to throw; **~le algo a alguien** to offer sb sthg. 2. (*un aspecto*) to present. ▶ **ofrecerse** *vpr* (*presentarse*) to offer, to volunteer; **~se a** o **para hacer algo** to offer to do sthg.

ofrecimiento *m* offer.

ofrenda *f* (RELIG) offering; *fig* (*por gratitud, amor*) gift.

ofrendar *vt* to offer up.

oftalmología *f* ophthalmology.

ofuscar *vt* 1. (*deslumbrar*) to dazzle. 2. (*turbar*) to blind. ▶ **ofuscarse** *vpr*: **~se (con)** to be blinded (by).

ogro *m* ogre.

oh *interj*: **¡~!** oh!

oídas ▶ **de oídas** *loc adv* by hearsay.

oído *m* 1. (*órgano*) ear; **de ~** by ear; **hacer ~s sordos** to turn a deaf ear. 2. (*sentido*) (sense of) hearing; **ser duro de ~** to be hard of hearing; **tener ~, tener buen ~** to have a good ear.

oír ◆ *vt* 1. (*gen*) to hear. 2. (*atender*) to listen to. ◆ *vi* to hear; **¡oiga, por favor!** excuse me!; **¡oye!** *fam* hey!

OIT (*abrev de* **Organización Internacional del Trabajo**) *f* ILO.

ojal *m* buttonhole.

ojalá *interj*: **¡~!** if only (that were so)!; **¡~ lo haga!** I hope she does it!; **¡~ fuera ya domingo!** I wish it were Sunday!

ojeada *f* glance, look; **echar una ~ a algo/alguien** to take a quick glance at sthg/sb, to take a quick look at sthg/sb.

ojear *vt* to have a look at.

ojera f (gen pl) bags (pl) under the eyes.
ojeriza f fam dislike; **tener ~ a alguien** to have it in for sb.
ojeroso, -sa adj haggard.
ojo ◆ m 1. (ANAT) eye; **~s saltones** popping eyes. 2. (agujero - de aguja) eye; (- de puente) span; **~ de la cerradura** keyhole. 3. loc: **a ~ (de buen cubero)** roughly, approximately; **andar con (mucho) ~** to be (very) careful; **comerse con los ~s a alguien** fam to drool over sb; **echar el ~ a algo** to have one's eye on sthg; **en un abrir y cerrar de ~s** in the twinkling of an eye; **mirar algo con buenos/malos ~s** to look favourably/unfavourably on sthg; **no pegar ~** not to get a wink of sleep; **tener (buen) ~** to have a good eye. ◆ interj: **¡~!** watch out!
OK, okey [o'kei] (abrev de all correct) interj OK.
okupa m y f mfam squatter.
ola f wave; **~ de calor** heatwave; **~ de frío** cold spell.
ole, olé interj: **¡~!** bravo!
oleada f 1. (del mar) swell. 2. fig (abundancia) wave.
oleaje m swell.
óleo m oil (painting).
oleoducto m oil pipeline.
oler ◆ vt to smell. ◆ vi 1. (despedir olor): **~ (a)** to smell (of). 2. fig (parecer): **~ a** to smack of. ▶ **olerse** vpr: **~se algo** fig to sense sthg.
olfatear vt 1. (olisquear) to sniff. 2. fig (barruntar) to smell, to sense. ▶ **olfatear en** vi (indagar) to pry into.
olfato m 1. (sentido) sense of smell. 2. fig (sagacidad) nose, instinct; **tener ~ para algo** to be a good judge of sthg.
oligarquía f oligarchy.
olimpiada, olimpíada f Olympic Games (pl); **las ~s** the Olympics.
olisquear vt to sniff (at).
oliva f olive.
olivar m olive grove.
olivera f olive tree.
olivo m olive tree.
olla f pot; **~ exprés o a presión** pressure cooker; **~ podrida** (CULIN) stew.
olmo m elm (tree).
olor m smell; **~ a** smell of.
oloroso, -sa adj fragrant. ▶ **oloroso** m oloroso (sherry).
OLP (abrev de Organización para la Liberación de Palestina) f PLO.
olvidadizo, -za adj forgetful.
olvidar vt 1. (gen) to forget. 2. (dejarse) to leave; **olvidé las llaves en la oficina I**

left my keys at the office. ▶ **olvidarse** vpr 1. (gen) to forget; **~se de algo/hacer algo** to forget sthg/to do sthg. 2. (dejarse) to leave.
olvido m 1. (de un nombre, hecho etc) forgetting; **caer en el ~** to fall into oblivion. 2. (descuido) oversight.
ombligo m (ANAT) navel.
omisión f omission.
omitir vt to omit.
ómnibus m inv omnibus; (FERROC) local train.
omnipotente adj omnipotent.
omnívoro, -ra adj omnivorous.
omoplato, omóplato m shoulderblade.
OMS (abrev de Organización Mundial de la Salud) f WHO.
once núm eleven; ver también **seis**.
ONCE (abrev de Organización Nacional de Ciegos Españoles) f Spanish association for the blind, famous for its national lottery.

ONCE

The ONCE is an independent organization which was originally set up to help the blind, although it now covers other disabled people as well. One of its main aims is to provide work for its members, and to this end it runs a daily national lottery, tickets for which are sold by the blind. The lottery is the ONCE's main source of income.

---

onceavo, -va núm eleventh.
onda f wave; **~ corta/larga/media** short/long/medium wave; **~ expansiva** shock wave; **estar en la ~** fam to be on the ball.
ondear vi to ripple.
ondulación f (acción) rippling.
ondulado, -da adj wavy.
ondular ◆ vi (agua) to ripple; (terreno) to undulate. ◆ vt to wave.
ONG (abrev de organización no gubernamental) f NGO.
ónice, ónix m o f onyx.
onomástico, -ca adj culto onomastic. ▶ **onomástica** f culto name day.
ONU (abrev de Organización de las Naciones Unidas) f UN.
onza f (unidad de peso) ounce.
OPA (abrev de oferta pública de adquisición) f takeover bid.
opaco, -ca adj opaque.
ópalo m opal.
opción f 1. (elección) option; **no hay ~** there is no alternative. 2. (derecho)

right; **dar ~ a** to give the right to; **tener ~ a** (*empleo, cargo*) to be eligible for.
opcional *adj* optional.
OPEP (*abrev de* **Organización de Países Exportadores de Petróleo**) *f* OPEC.
ópera *f* opera; **~ bufa** comic opera, opera buffa.
operación *f* 1. (*gen*) operation; **~ quirúrgica** (surgical) operation; **~ retorno** *police operation to assist return of holidaymakers to their city homes, minimizing traffic congestion and maximizing road safety.* 2. (COM) transaction.
operador, -ra *m y f* 1. (INFORM & TELE-COM) operator. 2. (*de la cámara*) camera-man; (*del proyector*) projectionist.
▶ **operador** *m* (MAT) operator.
▶ **operador turístico** *m* tour operator.
operar ◆ *vt* 1. (*enfermo*): **~ a alguien (de algo)** (*enfermedad*) to operate on sb (for sthg); **le operaron del hígado** they've operated on his liver. 2. (*cambio etc*) to bring about, to produce. ◆ *vi* 1. (*gen*) to operate. 2. (*actuar*) to act. 3. (COM & FIN) to deal. ▶ **operarse** *vpr* 1. (*enfermo*) to be operated on, to have an operation; **me voy a ~ del hígado** I'm going to have an operation on my liver. 2. (*cambio etc*) to occur.
operario, -ria *m y f* worker.
operativo, -va *adj* operative.
opereta *f* operetta.
opinar ◆ *vt* to believe, to think. ◆ *vi* to give one's opinion; **~ de algo/alguien, ~ sobre algo/alguien** to think about sthg/sb.
opinión *f* (*parecer*) opinion; **expresar o dar una ~** to give an opinion; **la ~ pública** public opinion.
opio *m* opium.
opíparo, -ra *adj* sumptuous.
oponente *m y f* opponent.
oponer *vt* 1. (*resistencia*) to put up. 2. (*argumento, razón*) to put forward, to give. ▶ **oponerse** *vpr* 1. (*no estar de acuerdo*) to be opposed; **~se a algo** (*desaprobar*) to oppose sthg; (*contradecir*) to contradict sthg; **me opongo a creerlo** I refuse to believe it. 2. (*obstaculizar*): **~se a** to impede.
oporto *m* port (wine).
oportunidad *f* (*ocasión*) opportunity, chance.
oportunismo *m* opportunism.
oportunista *m y f* opportunist.
oportuno, -na *adj* 1. (*pertinente*) appropriate. 2. (*propicio*) timely; **el momento ~** the right time.

oposición *f* 1. (*gen*) opposition. 2. (*resistencia*) resistance. 3. (*gen pl*) (*examen*) public entrance examination; **~ a profesor** public examination to be a teacher; **preparar oposiciones** to be studying for a public entrance examination.
opositar *vi*: **~ (a)** to sit a public entrance examination (for).
opositor, -ra *m y f* 1. (*a un cargo*) candidate in a public entrance examination. 2. (*oponente*) opponent.
opresión *f fig* (*represión*) oppression.
opresivo, -va *adj* oppressive.
opresor, -ra *m y f* oppressor.
oprimir *vt* 1. (*apretar - botón etc*) to press; (- *garganta, brazo etc*) to squeeze. 2. (*suj: zapatos, cinturón*) to pinch. 3. *fig* (*reprimir*) to oppress. 4. *fig* (*angustiar*) to weigh down on, to burden.
optar *vi* (*escoger*): **~ (por algo)** to choose (sthg); **~ por hacer algo** to choose to do sthg; **~ entre** to choose between.
optativo, -va *adj* optional.
óptico, -ca ◆ *adj* optic. ◆ *m y f* (*persona*) optician. ▶ **óptica** *f* 1. (FÍS) optics (U). 2. (*tienda*) optician's (shop). 3. *fig* (*punto de vista*) point of view.
optimismo *m* optimism.
optimista ◆ *adj* optimistic. ◆ *m y f* optimist.
óptimo, -ma ◆ *superl* → **bueno.** ◆ *adj* optimum.
opuesto, -ta ◆ *pp* → **oponer.** ◆ *adj* 1. (*contrario*) conflicting; **~ a** opposed o contrary to. 2. (*de enfrente*) opposite.
opulencia *f* (*riqueza*) opulence; (*abundancia*) abundance.
opulento, -ta *adj* (*rico*) opulent.
opus *m* (MÚS) opus. ▶ **Opus Dei** *m*: **el Opus Dei** the Opus Dei, *traditionalist religious organization, the members of which are usually professional people or public figures.*
oración *f* 1. (*rezo*) prayer. 2. (GRAM) sentence; **~ principal/subordinada** main/subordinate clause.
orador, -ra *m y f* speaker.
oral ◆ *adj* oral. ◆ *m* → **examen.**
órale *interj Amer fam*: **¡~!** come on!
orangután *m* orangutang.
orar *vi* to pray.
órbita *f* 1. (ASTRON) orbit. 2. (*de ojo*) eye socket.
orca *f* killer whale.
orden ◆ *m* 1. (*gen*) order; **en ~** (*bien colocado*) tidy, in its place; (*como debe ser*) in order; **por ~** in order; **las fuerzas del ~** the forces of law and order; **~ público**

law and order. **2.** (*tipo*) type, order; **problemas de ~ económico** economic problems. ◆ *f* order; **por ~ de** by order of; **estar a la ~ del día** to be the order of the day. ▶ **del orden de** *loc prep* around, approximately. ▶ **orden del día** *m* agenda.

ordenado, -da *adj* (*lugar, persona*) tidy.

ordenador *m* (INFORM) computer; **~ personal** personal computer; **~ portátil** laptop computer. ◆

ordenanza ◆ *m* (*de oficina*) messenger. ◆ *f* (*gen pl*) ordinance, law; **~s municipales** by-laws.

ordenar *vt* **1.** (*poner en orden - gen*) to arrange; (*- habitación, armario etc*) to tidy (up). **2.** (*mandar*) to order. **3.** (RELIG) to ordain. ▶ **ordenarse** *vpr* (RELIG) to be ordained.

ordeñar *vt* to milk.

ordinariez *f* commonness, coarseness; **decir/hacer una ~** to say/do sthg rude.

ordinario, -ria *adj* **1.** (*común*) ordinary, usual. **2.** (*vulgar*) common, coarse. **3.** (*no selecto*) unexceptional. **4.** (*no especial - presupuesto, correo*) daily; (*- tribunal*) of first instance.

orégano *m* oregano.

oreja *f* (ANAT) ear.

orfanato, orfelinato *m* orphanage.

orfandad *f* orphanhood; *fig* abandonment.

orfebre *m y f* (*de plata*) silversmith; (*de oro*) goldsmith.

orfebrería *f* (*obra - de plata*) silver work; (*- de oro*) gold work.

orfelinato = **orfanato**.

orgánico, -ca *adj* organic.

organigrama *m* (*gen &* INFORM) flowchart.

organillo *m* barrel organ.

organismo *m* **1.** (BIOL) organism. **2.** (ANAT) body. **3.** *fig* (*entidad*) organization, body.

organización *f* organization.

organizar *vt* to organize.

órgano *m* organ.

orgasmo *m* orgasm.

orgía *f* orgy.

orgullo *m* pride.

orgulloso, -sa *adj* proud.

orientación *f* **1.** (*dirección - acción*) guiding; (*- rumbo*) direction. **2.** (*posicionamiento - acción*) positioning; (*- lugar*) position. **3.** *fig* (*información*) guidance; **~ profesional** careers advice o guidance.

oriental ◆ *adj* (*gen*) eastern; (*del Lejano*

Oriente) oriental. ◆ *m y f* oriental.

orientar *vt* **1.** (*dirigir*) to direct; (*casa*) to build facing. **2.** *fig* (*medidas etc*): **~ hacia** to direct towards o at. **3.** *fig* (*aconsejar*) to give advice o guidance to. ▶ **orientarse** *vpr* **1.** (*dirigirse - foco etc*): **~se a** to point towards o at. **2.** (*encontrar el camino*) to get one's bearings. **3.** *fig* (*encaminarse*): **~se hacia** to be aiming at.

oriente *m* east. ▶ **Oriente** *m*: **el Oriente** the East, the Orient; **Oriente Medio/Próximo** Middle/Near East; **Lejano** o **Extremo Oriente** Far East.

orificio *m* hole; (TECN) opening.

origen *m* **1.** (*gen*) origin; (*ascendencia*) origins (*pl*), birth; **de ~ español** of Spanish origin; **en ~** at source. **2.** (*causa*) cause; **dar ~ a** to give rise to.

original ◆ *adj* **1.** (*gen*) original. **2.** (*raro*) eccentric, different. ◆ *m* original.

originalidad *f* **1.** (*gen*) originality. **2.** (*extravagancia*) eccentricity.

originar *vt* to cause. ▶ **originarse** *vpr* to be caused.

originario, -ria *adj* **1.** (*inicial, primitivo*) original. **2.** (*procedente*): **ser ~ de** (*costumbres etc*) to come from (originally); (*persona*) to be a native of.

orilla *f* **1.** (*ribera - de río*) bank; (*- de mar*) shore; **a ~s del mar** by the sea. **2.** (*borde*) edge. **3.** (*acera*) pavement.

orillar *vt* (*dificultad, obstáculo*) to skirt around.

orín *m* (*herrumbre*) rust. ▶ **orines** *mpl* (*orina*) urine (U).

orina *f* urine.

orinal *m* chamberpot.

orinar *vi &* *vt* to urinate. ▶ **orinarse** *vpr* to wet o.s.

oriundo, -da *adj*: **~ de** native of.

ornamentación *f* ornamentation.

ornamento *m* (*objeto*) ornament.

ornar *vt* to decorate, to adorn.

ornitología *f* ornithology.

oro *m* gold; *fig* riches (*pl*); **hacerse de ~** to make one's fortune; **pedir el ~ y el moro** to ask the earth. ▶ **oros** *mpl* (*naipes*) suit of Spanish cards bearing gold coins. ▶ **oro negro** *m* oil.

orografía *f* (*relieve*) terrain.

orquesta *f* **1.** (*músicos*) orchestra. **2.** (*lugar*) orchestra pit.

orquestar *vt* to orchestrate.

orquestina *f* dance band.

orquídea *f* orchid.

ortiga *f* (*stinging*) nettle.

ortodoxia *f* orthodoxy.

ortodoxo, -xa *adj* orthodox.

ortografía f spelling.
ortográfico, -ca adj spelling (antes de sust).
ortopedia f orthopaedics (U).
ortopédico, -ca adj orthopaedic.
ortopedista m y f orthopaedist.
oruga f caterpillar.
orujo m strong spirit made from grape pressings.
orzuelo m stye.
os pron pers **1.** (complemento directo) you; **me gustaría veros** I'd like to see you. **2.** (complemento indirecto) (to) you; **~ lo dio** he gave it to you; **~ tengo miedo** I'm afraid of you. **3.** (reflexivo) yourselves. **4.** (recíproco) each other; **~ enamorasteis** you fell in love (with each other).
osadía f **1.** (valor) boldness, daring. **2.** (descaro) audacity, cheek.
osado, -da adj **1.** (valeroso) daring, bold. **2.** (descarado) impudent, cheeky.
osamenta f skeleton.
osar vi to dare.
oscilación f **1.** (movimiento) swinging; (FÍS) oscillation. **2.** fig (variación) fluctuation.
oscilar vi **1.** (moverse) to swing; (FÍS) to oscillate. **2.** fig (variar) to fluctuate.
oscurecer ◆ vt **1.** (privar de luz) to darken. **2.** fig (mente) to confuse, to cloud. ◆ v impers (anochecer) to get dark. ▶ **oscurecerse** vpr to grow dark.
oscuridad f **1.** (falta de luz) darkness. **2.** (zona oscura): **en la ~** in the dark. **3.** fig (falta de claridad) obscurity.
oscuro, -ra adj **1.** (gen) dark; **a oscuras** in the dark. **2.** (nublado) overcast. **3.** fig (inusual) obscure. **4.** fig (intenciones, asunto) shady.
óseo, -a adj bone (antes de sust).
Oslo Oslo.
oso, osa m y f bear (f she-bear); **~ de felpa** o **peluche** teddy bear; **~ hormiguero** ant-eater; **~ panda** panda; **~ polar** polar bear.
ostensible adj evident, clear.
ostentación f ostentation, show.
ostentar vt (poseer) to hold, to have.
ostentoso, -sa adj ostentatious.
ostepata m y f osteopath.
ostra f oyster; **aburrirse como una ~** fam to be bored to death. ▶ **ostras** interj fam: **¡~s!** blimey!
OTAN (abrev de **Organización del Tratado del Atlántico Norte**) f NATO.
OTI (abrev de **Organización de Televisiones Iberoamericanas**) f association of all Spanish-speaking television networks.

otitis f inv inflammation of the ear.
otoñal adj autumn Br (antes de sust), autumnal Br, fall Am (antes de sust).
otoño m lit & fig autumn Br, fall Am.
otorgar vt to grant; (premio) to award, to present; (DER) to execute.
otorrino, -na m y f fam ear, nose and throat specialist.
otorrinolaringología f ear, nose and throat medicine.
otro, -tra ◆ adj **1.** (distinto) (sg) another, (pl) other; **~ chico** another boy; **el ~ chico** the other boy; **(los) ~s chicos** (the) other boys; **no hacer otra cosa que llorar** to do nothing but cry; **el ~ día** (pasado) the other day. **2.** (nuevo) another; **estamos ante ~ Dalí** this is another Dali; **~s tres goles** another three goals. ◆ pron (sg) another (one), (pl) others; **dame ~** give me another (one); **el ~** the other one; **(los) ~s** (the) others; **yo no lo hice, fue ~** it wasn't me, it was somebody else; **~ habría abandonado, pero no él** anyone else would have given up, but not him; **¡otra!** (en conciertos) encore!
output ['autput] (pl **outputs**) m (INFORM) output (U).
ovación f ovation.
ovacionar vt to give an ovation to.
oval adj oval.
ovalado, -da adj oval.
ovario m ovary.
oveja f sheep, ewe. ▶ **oveja negra** f black sheep.
ovillo m ball (of wool etc); **hacerse un ~** to curl up into a ball.
ovino, -na adj ovine, sheep (antes de sust).
ovni ['ofni] m (abrev de **objeto volador no identificado**) UFO.
ovulación f ovulation.
ovular ◆ adj ovular. ◆ vi to ovulate.
oxidación f rusting.
oxidar vt to rust; (QUÍM) to oxidize. ▶ **oxidarse** vpr to get rusty.
óxido m **1.** (QUÍM) oxide. **2.** (herrumbre) rust.
oxigenado, -da adj **1.** (QUÍM) oxygenated. **2.** (cabello) peroxide (antes de sust), bleached.
oxigenar vt (QUÍM) to oxygenate. ▶ **oxigenarse** vpr (airearse) to get a breath of fresh air.
oxígeno m oxygen.
oye → oír.
oyente m y f **1.** (RADIO) listener. **2.** (alumno) unregistered student.
ozono m ozone.

P

p, P f (letra) p, P.
p. 1. = **pág.** 2. abrev de **paseo.**
pabellón m 1. (edificio) pavilion. 2. (parte de un edificio) block, section. 3. (en parques, jardines) summerhouse. 4. (tienda de campaa) bell tent. 5. (bandera) flag.
pábilo m wick.
PAC (abrev de **política agrícola común**) f CAP.
pacer vi to graze.
pachá (pl pachaes) m pasha; **vivir como un ~ fam** to live like a lord.
pachanga f fam rowdy celebration.
pacharán m liqueur made from brandy and sloes.
pachorra f fam calmness.
pachucho, -cha adj fam off-colour.
paciencia f patience; **perder la ~** to lose one's patience.
paciente adj, m y f patient.
pacificación f pacification.
pacificar vt 1. (país) to pacify. 2. (ánimos) to calm.
pacífico, -ca adj (gen) peaceful; (persona) peaceable.
Pacífico m: **el (océano) ~** the Pacific (Ocean).
pacifismo m pacifism.
pacifista adj, m y f pacifist.
paco, -ca m y f Amer fam cop.
pacotilla f: **de ~** trashy, third-rate.
pactar ◆ vt to agree to. ◆ vi: **~ (con)** to strike a deal (with).
pacto m (gen) agreement, pact; (entre países) treaty.
paddle = **pádel.**
padecer ◆ vt to suffer, to endure; (enfermedad) to suffer from. ◆ vi to suffer; (enfermedad): **~ de** to suffer from.
padecimiento m suffering.
pádel, paddle m ball game for two or four players played with a small rubber bat on a two-walled court.
padrastro m 1. (pariente) stepfather. 2. (pellejo) hangnail.
padre ◆ m (gen & RELIG) father. ◆ adj inv fam incredible. ▶ **padres** mpl (padre y madre) parents.
padrenuestro (pl padrenuestros) m Lord's Prayer.

padrino m 1. (de bautismo) godfather; (de boda) best man. 2. (en duelos, torneos etc) second. 3. fig (protector) patron. ▶ **padrinos** mpl (padrino y madrina) godparents.
padrísimo adj Amer fam fantastic, great.
padrón m (censo) census; (para votar) electoral roll o register.
padrote m Amer fam pimp.
paella f paella.
paellera f large frying-pan or earthenware dish for cooking paella.
pág., p. (abrev de **página**) p.
paga f payment; (salario) salary, wages (pl); (de niño) pocket money; **~ extra** o **extraordinaria** bonus paid twice a year to Spanish workers.
pagadero, -ra adj payable; **~ a 90 días/a la entrega** payable within 90 days/on delivery.
pagano, -na adj, m y f pagan, heathen.
pagar ◆ vt (gen) to pay; (deuda) to pay off, to settle; (ronda, gastos, delito) to pay for; (ayuda, favor) to repay; **me las pagarás** fam you'll pay for this. ◆ vi to pay.
pagaré (pl pagarés) m (COM) promissory note, IOU; **~ del Tesoro** Treasury note.
página f page; **~ inicial** o **de inicio** (INFORM) home page; **las ~s amarillas** the Yellow Pages.
pago m payment; fig reward, payment; **en ~ de** (en recompensa por) as a reward for; (a cambio de) in return for; **~ anticipado/inicial** advance/down payment. ▶ **pagos** mpl (lugar): **por estos ~s** around here.
paila f Amer 1. (sartén) frying pan. 2. (huevos fritos) fried eggs (pl).
país m country; **~ natal** native land; **los ~es bálticos** the Baltic States.
paisaje m (gen) landscape; (vista panorámica) scenery (U), view.
paisano, -na m y f (del mismo país) compatriot. ▶ **paisano** m (civil) civilian; **de ~** (MIL) in civilian clothes; **de ~** (policía) in plain clothes.
Países Bajos mpl: **los ~** the Netherlands.
País Vasco m: **el ~** the Basque Country.
paja f 1. (gen) straw. 2. fig (relleno) waffle. 3. vulg (masturbación) wank.
pajar m straw loft.
pájara f fig crafty o sly woman.

pajarería *f* pet shop.

pajarita *f* (*corbata*) bow tie.

pájaro *m* (ZOOL) bird; ~ **bobo** penguin; ~ **carpintero** woodpecker; ~ **de mal agüero** bird of ill omen; **más vale ~ en mano que ciento volando** *proverb* a bird in the hand is worth two in the bush; **matar dos ~s de un tiro** to kill two birds with one stone; **tener ~s en la cabeza** to be scatterbrained o emptyheaded.

paje *m* page.

pajilla, pajita *f* (drinking) straw.

Pakistán, Paquistán Pakistan.

pala *f* 1. (*herramienta*) spade; (*para recoger*) shovel; (CULIN) slice; ~ **mecánica** o **excavadora** excavator, digger. 2. (*de frontón, ping-pong*) bat. 3. (*de remo, hélice*) blade.

palabra *f* 1. (*gen*) word; **de ~** by word of mouth; **no tener ~** to go back on one's word; **tomar** o **coger la ~ a alguien** to hold sb to their word; ~ **de honor** word of honour. 2. (*habla*) speech. 3. (*derecho de hablar*) right to speak; **dar la ~ a alguien** to give the floor to sb. 4. *loc:* **en una ~** in a word. ▶ **palabras** *fpl* (*discurso*) words.

palabrería *f fam* hot air.

palabrota *f* swearword; **decir ~s** to swear.

palacete *m* mansion, small palace.

palacio *m* palace; ~ **de congresos** conference centre.

PALACIO DE LA MONEDA
The Palacio de la Moneda is the official residence of the Chilean president and the seat of the Chilean government. It is here that the president holds Cabinet meetings and receives State visits.

PALACIO DE LA ZARZUELA
This is the current residence of the Spanish monarch and is situated in the El Pardo hills to the northwest of Madrid. It was built during the reign of Philip IV, who used it as a country retreat and a hunting lodge. A neoclassical building which consists of a single floor built around an interior courtyard, it was rebuilt in the 18th century and redecorated in the rococo style.

palada *f* 1. (*al cavar*) spadeful, shovelful. 2. (*de remo*) stroke.

paladar *m* palate.

paladear *vt* to savour.

palanca *f* (*barra, mando*) lever; ~ **de cambio** gear lever o stick, gearshift Am; ~ **de mando** joystick.

palangana *f* (*para fregar*) washing-up bowl; (*para lavarse*) wash bowl.

palco *m* box (*at theatre*).

Palestina Palestine.

palestino, -na *adj, m y f* Palestinian.

paleta *f* (*gen*) small shovel, small spade; (*llana*) trowel; (CULIN) slice; (ARTE) palette.

paletilla *f* shoulder blade.

paleto, -ta ◆ *adj* coarse, uncouth. ◆ *m y f* yokel, hick Am.

paliar *vt* 1. (*atenuar*) to ease, to relieve. 2. (*disculpar*) to excuse, to justify.

palidecer *vi* (*ponerse pálido*) to go o turn pale.

palidez *f* paleness.

pálido, -da *adj* pale; *fig* dull.

palillero *m* toothpick holder.

palillo *m* 1. (*mondadientes*) toothpick. 2. (*baqueta*) drumstick. 3. (*para comida china*) chopstick.

palique *m fam* chat, natter; **estar de ~** to have a chat o a natter.

paliza *f* 1. (*golpes*) beating; **dar** o **pegar una ~ a alguien** to beat sb up. 2. (*derrota*) thrashing. 3. (*esfuerzo*) hard grind.

palma *f* 1. (*de mano*) palm. 2. (*palmera*) palm (tree); (*hoja de palmera*) palm leaf. ▶ **palmas** *fpl* (*aplausos*) applause (U); **batir ~s** to clap (one's hands).

palmada *f* 1. (*golpe*) pat; (*más fuerte*) slap. 2. (*aplauso*) clap; ~**s** clapping (U).

palmar[1] *m* palm grove.

palmar[2] *fam vi* to kick the bucket.

palmarés *m* 1. (*historial*) record. 2. (*lista*) list, roll.

palmear *vi* to clap, to applaud.

palmera *f* (*árbol*) palm (tree); (*datilera*) date palm.

palmito *m* 1. (*árbol*) palmetto, fan palm. 2. (CULIN) palm heart.

palmo *m* handspan; *fig* small amount; ~ **a ~** bit by bit; **dejar a alguien con un ~ de narices** to let sb down.

palmotear *vi* to clap.

palo *m* 1. (*gen*) stick; (*de golf*) club; (*de portería*) post; (*de la escoba*) handle. 2. (*mástil*) mast. 3. (*golpe*) blow (*with a stick*). 4. (*de baraja*) suit. 5. *fig* (*pesadez*) bind, drag. 6. *loc:* **a ~ seco** (*gen*) without anything else; (*bebida*) neat.

paloma → **palomo**.

palomar *m* dovecote; (*grande*) pigeon shed.

palomilla f 1. (*insecto*) grain moth. 2. (*tornillo*) wing nut. 3. (*soporte*) bracket.
palomita f: ~s popcorn (U).
palomo, -ma m y f dove, pigeon; **paloma mensajera** carrier o homing pigeon.
palpable adj touchable, palpable; *fig* obvious, clear.
palpar ◆ vt 1. (*tocar*) to feel, to touch; (MED) to palpate. 2. *fig* (*percibir*) to feel. ◆ vi to feel around.
palpitación f beat, beating (U); (*con fuerza*) throb, throbbing (U). ▶ **palpitaciones** fpl (MED) palpitations.
palpitante adj 1. (*que palpita*) beating; (*con fuerza*) throbbing. 2. *fig* (*interesante - interés, deseo, cuestión*) burning.
palpitar vi (*latir*) to beat; (*con fuerza*) to throb.
palta f Amer avocado.
paludismo m malaria.
palurdo, -da m y f yokel, hick Am.
palustre adj marsh (*antes de sust*).
pamela f sun hat.
pampa f: **la ~** the pampas (pl).
pamplina f (*gen pl*) *fam* trifle, unimportant thing.
pan m 1. (*alimento*) bread; **~ de molde** o **inglés** sliced bread; **~ integral** wholemeal bread; **~ moreno** o **negro** (*integral*) brown bread; **~ rallado** breadcrumbs (pl). 2. (*hogaza*) loaf. 3. *loc*: **contigo ~ y cebolla** I'll go through thick and thin with you; **llamar al ~ ~ y al vino vino** to call a spade a spade; **ser ~ comido** to be a piece of cake; **ser el ~ nuestro de cada día** to be commonplace; **ser más bueno que el ~** to be kindness itself.
pana f corduroy.
panacea f *lit & fig* panacea.
panadería f bakery, baker's.
panadero, -ra m y f baker.
panal m honeycomb.
Panamá Panama.
panameño, -ña adj, m y f Panamanian.
pancarta f placard, banner.
panceta f bacon.
pancho, -cha adj *fam* calm, unruffled; **estar/quedarse tan ~** to be/remain perfectly calm.
páncreas m inv pancreas.
panda ◆ m → **oso**. ◆ f gang.
pandemónium (pl pandemóniums) m pandemonium.
pandereta f tambourine.
pandero m (MÚS) tambourine.
pandilla f gang.
panecillo m bread roll.

panegírico, -ca adj panegyrical. ▶ **panegírico** m panegyric.
panel m 1. (*gen*) panel. 2. (*pared, biombo*) screen. 3. (*tablero*) board.
panera f bread basket.
pánfilo, -la adj simple, foolish.
panfleto m pamphlet.
pánico m panic.
panificadora f (large) bakery.
panocha f ear, cob.
panorama m 1. (*vista*) panorama. 2. *fig* (*situación*) overall state; (*perspectiva*) outlook.
panorámico, -ca adj panoramic. ▶ **panorámica** f panorama.
pantaletas fpl Amer knickers.
pantalla f 1. (*gen & INFORM*) screen; **~ de cristal líquido** liquid crystal display; **la pequeña ~** the small screen, television. 2. (*de lámpara*) lampshade.
pantalón m (*gen pl*) trousers (pl), pants (pl) Am; **~ corto** shorts (pl); **~ tejano** o **vaquero** jeans (pl); **~ pitillo** drainpipe trousers (pl).
pantano m 1. (*ciénaga*) marsh; (*laguna*) swamp. 2. (*embalse*) reservoir.
pantanoso, -sa adj 1. (*cenagoso*) marshy, boggy. 2. *fig* (*difícil*) tricky.
panteón m pantheon; (*familiar*) mausoleum, vault.
pantera f panther.
pantimedias fpl Amer tights.
pantorrilla f calf.
pantufla f (*gen pl*) slipper.
panty (pl pantys) m tights (pl).
panza f belly.
panzada f *fam* (*hartura*) bellyful.
pañal m nappy Br, diaper Am; **estar en ~es** (*en sus inicios*) to be in its infancy; (*sin conocimientos*) not to have a clue.
pañería f (*producto*) drapery; (*tienda*) draper's (shop), dry-goods store Am.
paño m 1. (*tela*) cloth, material. 2. (*trapo*) cloth; (*para polvo*) duster; (*de cocina*) tea towel. 3. (*lienzo*) panel. ▶ **paños** mpl (*vestiduras*) drapes; **~s menores** underwear (U).
pañoleta f shawl, wrap.
pañuelo m (*de nariz*) handkerchief; (*para el cuello*) scarf; (*para la cabeza*) headscarf; **~ de papel** paper handkerchief, tissue.
papa f potato; **no saber ni ~** *fam* not to have a clue. ▶ **Papa** m Pope.
papá m *fam* dad, daddy, pop Am. ▶ **Papá Noel** m Father Christmas.
papachador, -ra adj Amer comforting.

papachar *vt Amer* to spoil.

papada *f* (*de persona*) double chin; (*de animal*) dewlap.

papagayo *m* parrot.

papalote *m Amer* (*cometa*) kite.

papamoscas *m inv* flycatcher.

papanatas *m y f inv fam* sucker.

papaya *f* (*fruta*) papaya, pawpaw.

papel *m* **1.** (*gen*) paper; (*hoja*) sheet of paper; ~ **celofán** Cellophane; ~ **continuo** (INFORM) continuous paper; ~ **de embalar** o **de embalaje** wrapping paper; ~ **de estaño** o **de aluminio** o **de plata** tin o aluminium foil; ~ **de fumar** cigarette paper; ~ **de lija** sandpaper; ~ **higiénico** toilet paper; ~ **madera** *Amer* cardboard; ~ **milimetrado** graph paper; ~ **pintado** wallpaper. **2.** (CIN, TEATR & *fig*) role, part; ~ **principal/secundario** main/minor part; **hacer buen/mal** ~ to do well/badly. **3.** (FIN) stocks and shares (*pl*); ~ **moneda** paper money. ▶ **papeles** *mpl* (*documentos*) papers.

papeleo *m* paperwork, red tape.

papelera → **papelero**.

papelería *f* stationer's (shop).

papelero, -ra *adj* paper (*antes de sust*). ▶ **papelera** *f* (*cesto - en oficina etc*) wastepaper basket o bin; (*- en la calle*) litter bin.

papeleta *f* **1.** (*boleto*) ticket, slip (of paper); (*de votación*) ballot paper. **2.** (EDUC) *slip of paper with university exam results.*

paperas *fpl* mumps.

papi *m fam* daddy, dad.

papilla *f* (*para niños*) baby food; **hecho** ~ (*cansado*) shattered; (*roto*) smashed to bits.

papiro *m* papyrus.

paquete *m* **1.** (*de libros, regalos etc*) parcel; ~ **bomba** parcel bomb; ~ **postal** parcel. **2.** (*de cigarrillos, klínex, folios etc*) pack, packet; (*de azúcar, arroz*) bag. **3.** (*de medidas*) package; ~ **turístico** package tour. **4.** (INFORM) package.

Paquistán = **Pakistán**.

par ◆ *adj* **1.** (MAT) even. **2.** (*igual*) equal. ◆ *m* **1.** (*pareja - de zapatos etc*) pair. **2.** (*dos - veces etc*) couple. **3.** (*número indeterminado*) few, couple; **un** ~ **de copas** a couple of o a few drinks. **4.** (*en golf*) par. **5.** (*noble*) peer. ▶ **a la par** *loc adv* **1.** (*simultáneamente*) at the same time. **2.** (*a igual nivel*) at the same level. ▶ **de par en par** *loc adj*: **abierto de** ~ **en** ~ wide open. ▶ **sin par** *loc adj* matchless.

para *prep* **1.** (*finalidad*) for; **es** ~ **ti** it's for you; **una mesa** ~ **el salón** a table for the living room; **esta agua no es buena** ~ **beber** this water isn't fit for drinking o to drink; **te lo repetiré** ~ **que te enteres** I'll repeat it so you understand; **¿** ~ **qué?** what for? **2.** (*motivación*) (in order) to; ~ **conseguir sus propósitos** in order to achieve his aims; **lo he hecho** ~ **agradarte** I did it to please you. **3.** (*dirección*) towards; **ir** ~ **casa** to head (for) home; **salir** ~ **el aeropuerto** to leave for the airport. **4.** (*tiempo*) for; **tiene que estar acabado** ~ **mañana** it has to be finished by o for tomorrow. **5.** (*comparación*): **está muy delgado** ~ **lo que come** he's very thin considering how much he eats; ~ **ser verano hace mucho frío** considering it's summer, it's very cold. **6.** (*después de adj y antes de infin*) (*inminencia, propósito*) to; **la comida está lista** ~ **servir** the meal is ready to be served; **el atleta está preparado** ~ **ganar** the athlete is ready to win. ▶ **para con** *loc prep* towards; **es buena** ~ **con los demás** she is kind towards other people.

parabién (*pl* **parabienes**) *m* congratulations (*pl*).

parábola *f* **1.** (*alegoría*) parable. **2.** (GEOM) parabola.

parabólico, -ca *adj* parabolic.

parabrisas *m inv* windscreen, windshield *Am*.

paracaídas *m inv* parachute.

paracaidista *m y f* parachutist; (MIL) paratrooper.

parachoques *m inv* (AUTOM) bumper, fender *Am*; (FERROC) buffer.

parada → **parado**.

paradero *m* **1.** (*de persona*) whereabouts (*pl*). **2.** *Amer* (*parada de autobús*) bus stop.

paradisiaco, -ca, paradisíaco, -ca *adj* heavenly.

parado, -da ◆ *adj* **1.** (*inmóvil - coche*) stationary, standing; (*- persona*) still, motionless; (*- fábrica, proyecto*) at a standstill. **2.** *fam* (*sin empleo*) unemployed. **3.** *loc*: **salir bien/mal** ~ **de algo** to come off well/badly out of sthg. ◆ *m y f fam* (*desempleado*) unemployed person; **los** ~**s** the unemployed. ▶ **parada** *f* **1.** (*detención*) stop, stopping (U). **2.** (DEP) save. **3.** (*de autobús*) (bus) stop; (*de taxis*) taxi rank; (*de metro*) (underground) station; **parada discrecional** request stop. **4.** (MIL) parade.

paradoja *f* paradox.

paradójico, -ca *adj* paradoxical, ironical.

parador *m* 1. (*mesón*) roadside inn. 2. (*hotel*): ~ **(nacional)** state-owned luxury hotel, usually a building of historic or artistic importance.

PARADOR NACIONAL

A 'parador nacional' is a building of artistic or historic interest which has been converted into a luxury four-star hotel and is run by the Spanish state. Although some may be found in cities, they are usually situated in the countryside, in places of outstanding natural beauty.

---

parafernalia *f* paraphernalia.

parafrasear *vt* to paraphrase.

paráfrasis *f inv* paraphrase.

paraguas *m inv* umbrella.

Paraguay **(el)** ~ Paraguay.

paraguayo, -ya *adj*, *m y f* Paraguayan.

paragüero *m* umbrella stand.

paraíso *m* (RELIG) Paradise; *fig* paradise.

paraje *m* spot, place.

paralelismo *m* 1. (GEOM) parallelism. 2. (*semejanza*) similarity, parallels (*pl*).

paralelo, -la *adj*: ~ **(a)** parallel (to). ► **paralelo** *m* (GEOGR) parallel. ► **paralela** *f* (GEOM) parallel (line).

parálisis *f inv* paralysis; ~ **cerebral** cerebral palsy.

paralítico, -ca *adj*, *m y f* paralytic.

paralizar *vt* to paralyse. ► **paralizarse** *vpr* to become paralysed; (*producción etc*) to come to a standstill.

parámetro *m* parameter.

páramo *m* moor, moorland (U); *fig* wilderness.

parangón *m* paragon; **sin** ~ unparalleled.

paranoia *f* paranoia.

paranormal *adj* paranormal.

parapente *m* parapente, paraskiing.

parapetarse *vpr lit & fig*: ~ **(tras)** to take refuge (behind).

parapeto *m* (*antepecho*) parapet; (*barandilla*) bannister; (*barricada*) barricade.

parapléjico, -ca *adj*, *m y f* paraplegic.

parapsicología *f* parapsychology.

parar ◆ *vi* 1. (*gen*) to stop; ~ **de hacer algo** to stop doing sthg; **sin** ~ non-stop. 2. (*alojarse*) to stay. 3. (*recaer*): ~ **en manos de alguien** to come into the possession of sb. 4. (*acabar*) to end up; **¿en qué parará este lío?** where will it all end? ◆ *vt* 1. (*gen*) to stop; (*golpe*) to parry. 2. (*preparar*) to prepare. 3. Amer (*levantar*) to raise. ► **pararse** *vpr* 1. (*detenerse*) to stop. 2. Amer (*ponerse de pie*) to stand up.

pararrayos *m inv* lightning conductor.

parásito, -ta *adj* (BIOL) parasitic. ► **parásito** *m* (BIOL & *fig*) parasite. ► **parásitos** *mpl* (*interferencias*) statics (*pl*).

parasol *m* parasol.

parcela *f* plot (of land).

parche *m* 1. (*gen*) patch. 2. (*chapuza - para salir del paso*) makeshift solution.

parchís *m inv* ludo.

parcial ◆ *adj* 1. (*no total*) partial. 2. (*no ecuánime*) biased. ◆ *m* (*examen*) end-of-term exam at university.

parcialidad *f* 1. (*tendenciosidad*) bias, partiality. 2. (*bando*) faction.

parco, -ca *adj* (*escaso*) meagre; (*cena*) frugal; (*explicación*) brief, concise.

pardillo, -lla ◆ *adj* 1. (*ingenuo*) naive. 2. (*palurdo*) countrified. ◆ *m y f* 1. (*ingenuo*) naive person. 2. (*palurdo*) bumpkin.

pardo, -da *adj* greyish-brown, dull brown.

parecer ◆ *m* 1. (*opinión*) opinion. 2. (*apariencia*): **de buen** ~ good-looking. ◆ *vi* (*antes de sust*) to look like; **parece un palacio** it looks like a palace. ◆ *v copulativo* to look, to seem; **pareces cansado** you look o seem tired. ◆ *v impers* 1. (*opinar*): **me parece que ...** I think o it seems to me that ...; **me parece que sí/no** I think/don't think so; **¿qué te parece?** what do you think (of it)? 2. (*tener aspecto de*): **parece que va a llover** it looks like it's going to rain; **parece que le gusta** it looks as if o it seems that she likes it; **eso parece** so it seems; **al** ~ apparently. ► **parecerse** *vpr*: ~**se (en)** to be alike (in); ~**se a alguien** (*físicamente*) to look like sb; (*en carácter*) to be like sb.

parecido, -da *adj* similar; **bien** ~ (*atractivo*) good-looking. ► **parecido** *m*: ~ **(con/entre)** resemblance (to/between).

pared *f* 1. (*gen*) wall; **las** ~**es oyen** walls have ears; **subirse por las** ~**es** to hit the roof. 2. (*de montaña*) side.

participar

paredón m (thick) wall; (de fusilamiento) (execution) wall.

parejo, -ja adj: ~ (a) similar (to).
► **pareja** f 1. (gen) pair; (de novios) couple; **pareja de hecho** common law heterosexual or homosexual relationship; **por parejas** in pairs. 2. (miembro del par - persona) partner; **la pareja de este calcetín** the other sock of this pair.

parentela f relations (pl), family.

parentesco m relationship.

paréntesis m inv 1. (signo) bracket; **entre ~** in brackets, in parentheses. 2. (intercalación) digression. 3. (interrupción) break.

paria m y f pariah.

parida f fam tripe (U), nonsense (U).

pariente, -ta m y f (familiar) relation, relative.

parir ♦ vi to give birth. ♦ vt to give birth to.

París Paris.

parking ['parkin] (pl **parkings**) m car park, parking lot Am.

parlamentar vi to negotiate.

parlamentario, -ria ♦ adj parliamentary. ♦ m y f member of parliament.

parlamento m (POLÍT) parliament.

parlanchín, -ina ♦ adj talkative. ♦ m y f chatterbox.

parlante adj talking.

parlotear vi fam to chatter.

paro m 1. (desempleo) unemployment. 2. (cesación - acción) shutdown; (- estado) stoppage; **~ cardíaco** cardiac arrest.

parodia f parody.

parodiar vt to parody.

parpadear vi 1. (pestañear) to blink. 2. (centellear) to flicker.

párpado m eyelid.

parque m 1. (gen) park; **~ acuático** waterpark; **~ de atracciones** amusement park; **~ nacional** national park; **~ tecnológico** science park; **(~) zoológico** zoo. 2. (vehículos) fleet; **~ de bomberos** fire station. 3. (para niños) playpen.

PARQUE NACIONAL

Spanish national parks are areas of natural beauty that are protected by the government. Although admission is free, there are strict regulations governing what visitors may do, to minimize the damage they may cause to the surroundings. The best-known national parks are the Coto de Doñana in Huelva, the Ordesa national park in Huesca and the Delta del Ebro park in Tarragona.

parqué (pl **parqués**), **parquet** [par- 'ke] (pl **parquets**) m parquet (floor).

parqueadero m Amer car park.

parquear vt Amer to park.

parquet = **parqué**.

parquímetro m parking meter.

parra f grapevine.

parrafada f earful, dull monologue.

párrafo m paragraph.

parranda f fam (juerga): **irse de ~** to go out on the town.

parrilla f (utensilio) grill; **a la ~** grilled.

parrillada f mixed grill.

párroco m parish priest.

parroquia f 1. (iglesia) parish church. 2. (jurisdicción) parish. 3. (clientela) clientele.

parroquiano, -na m y f 1. (feligrés) parishioner. 2. (cliente) customer.

parsimonia f deliberation; **con ~** unhurriedly.

parte ♦ m report; **dar ~ (a alguien de algo)** to report (sthg to sb); **~ facultativo o médico** medical report; **~ meteorológico** weather forecast. ♦ f (gen) part; (bando) side; (DER) party; **la mayor ~ de la gente** most people; **la mayor ~ del tiempo** most of the time; **la tercera ~ de** a third of; **en alguna ~** somewhere; **no lo veo por ninguna ~** I can't find it anywhere; **en ~** to a certain extent, partly; **estar/ponerse de ~ de alguien** to be on/to take sb's side; **por mí ~** for my part; **por ~ de padre/madre** on one's father's/mother's side; **por ~s** bit by bit; **por una ~ ... por la otra** ... on the one hand ... on the other (hand) ...; **tomar ~ en algo** to take part in sthg. ► **de parte de** loc prep on behalf of, for; **¿de ~ de (quién)?** (TELECOM) who is calling, please? ► **por otra parte** loc adv (además) what is more, besides.

partera f midwife.

parterre m flowerbed.

partición f (reparto) sharing out; (de territorio) partitioning.

participación f 1. (colaboración) participation. 2. (de lotería) share of a lottery ticket. 3. (comunicación) notice.

participante m y f participant.

participar ♦ vi (colaborar): **~ (en)** to take part o participate (in); (FIN) to have a share (in). ♦ vt: **~ algo a alguien** to notify sb of sthg.

partícipe ◆ *adj:* ~ **(de)** involved (in); **hacer ~ de algo a alguien** (*notificar*) to notify sb of sthg; (*compartir*) to share sthg with sb. ◆ *m y f* participant.

partícula *f* particle.

particular ◆ *adj* **1.** (*gen*) particular; **tiene su sabor ~** it has its own particular taste; **en ~** in particular. **2.** (*no público - domicilio, clases etc*) private. **3.** (*no corriente - habilidad etc*) uncommon. ◆ *m y f* (*persona*) member of the public. ◆ *m* (*asunto*) matter.

particularizar ◆ *vt* (*caracterizar*) to characterize. ◆ *vi* **1.** (*detallar*) to go into details. **2.** (*personalizar*): ~ **en alguien** to single sb out.

partida *f* **1.** (*marcha*) departure. **2.** (*en juego*) game. **3.** (*documento*) certificate; ~ **de defunción/matrimonio/nacimiento** death/marriage/birth certificate. **4.** (COM *- mercancía*) consignment; (*- entrada*) item, entry.

partidario, -ria ◆ *adj:* ~ **de** in favour of. ◆ *m y f* supporter.

partidista *adj* partisan, biased.

partido *m* **1.** (POLÍT) party. **2.** (DEP) match; ~ **amistoso** friendly (match). **3.** *loc:* **sacar ~ de** to make the most of; **tomar ~ por** to side with.

partir ◆ *vt* **1.** (*dividir*) to divide, to split. **2.** (*repartir*) to share out. **3.** (*romper*) to break open; (*cascar*) to crack; (*tronco, loncha etc*) to cut. ◆ *vi* **1.** (*marchar*) to leave, to set off. **2.** (*basarse*): ~ **de** to start from. ▶ **partirse** *vpr* **1.** (*romperse*) to split. **2.** (*rajarse*) to crack. ▶ **a partir de** *loc prep* starting from; **a ~ de aquí** from here on.

partitura *f* score.

parto *m* birth; **estar de** ~ to be in labour.

parvulario *m* nursery school, kindergarten.

pasa *f* (*fruta*) raisin; ~ **de Corinto** currant; ~ **de Esmirna** sultana.

pasable *adj* passable.

pasada → **pasado**.

pasadizo *m* passage.

pasado, -da *adj* **1.** (*gen*) past; ~ **un año** a year later; **lo ~, ~ está** let bygones be bygones. **2.** (*último*) last; **el año ~** last year. **3.** (*podrido*) off, bad. **4.** (*hecho - filete, carne*) well done. ▶ **pasado** *m* (*gen*) past; (GRAM) past (tense). ▶ **pasada** *f* (*con el trapo*) wipe; (*con la brocha*) coat. ▶ **de pasada** *loc adv* in passing. ▶ **mala pasada** *f* dirty trick.

pasador *m* **1.** (*cerrojo*) bolt. **2.** (*para el pelo*) slide.

pasaje *m* **1.** (*billete*) ticket, fare. **2.** (*pasajeros*) passengers (*pl*). **3.** (*calle*) passage. **4.** (*fragmento*) passage.

pasajero, -ra ◆ *adj* passing. ◆ *m y f* passenger.

pasamanos *m inv* (*de escalera interior*) bannister; (*de escalera exterior*) handrail.

pasamontañas *m inv* balaclava (helmet).

pasaporte *m* passport.

pasapuré *m*, **pasapurés** *m inv* food mill.

pasar ◆ *vt* **1.** (*gen*) to pass; (*noticia, aviso*) to pass on; **¿me pasas la sal?** would you pass me the salt?; ~ **algo por** (*filtrar*) to pass sthg through. **2.** (*cruzar*) to cross; ~ **la calle** to cross the road; **pasé el río a nado** I swam across the river. **3.** (*traspasar*) to pass through. **4.** (*trasladar*): ~ **algo a** to move sthg to. **5.** (*llevar adentro*) to show in; **el criado nos pasó al salón** the butler showed us into the living room. **6.** (*contagiar*): ~ **algo a alguien** to give sthg to sb, to infect sb with sthg; **me has pasado la tos** you've given me your cough. **7.** (*admitir - instancia etc*) to accept. **8.** (*consentir*): ~ **algo a alguien** to let sb get away with sthg. **9.** (*rebasar - en el espacio*) to go through; (*- en el tiempo*) to have been through; ~ **un semáforo en rojo** to go through a red light. **10.** (*emplear - tiempo*) to spend; **pasó dos años en Roma** he spent two years in Rome. **11.** (*padecer*) to go through, to suffer; **pasarlo mal** to have a hard time of it. **12.** (*sobrepasar*): **ya ha pasado los veinticinco** he's over twenty-five now; **mi hijo me pasa ya dos centímetros** my son is already two centimetres taller than me. **13.** (*adelantar - coche, contrincante etc*) to overtake. **14.** (CIN) to show. ◆ *vi* **1.** (*gen*) to pass, to go; **pasó por mi lado** he passed by my side; **el autobús pasa por mi casa** the bus goes past o passes in front of my house; **el Manzanares pasa por Madrid** the Manzanares goes o passes through Madrid; **he pasado por tu calle** I went down your street; ~ **de ... a ...** to go o pass from ... to ...; ~ **de largo** to go by. **2.** (*entrar*) to go/come in; **¡pase!** come in! **3.** (*poder entrar*): ~ **(por)** to go (through); **por ahí no pasa** it won't go through there. **4.** (*ir un momento*) to pop in; **pasaré por mi oficina/por tu casa** I'll pop into my office/round to your place. **5.** (*suceder*) to happen; **¿qué pasa aquí?** what's going on here?; **¿qué pasa?** what's the matter?; **pase lo que pase** whatever happens, come what may. **6.** (*terminarse*) to be over; **pasó la Navidad** Christmas is over. **7.** (*transcurrir*) to go by. **8.** (*cambiar - acción*): **~ a** to move on to; **pasemos a otra cosa** let's move on to something else. **9.** (*conformarse*): **~ (con/sin algo)** to make do (with/without sthg); **tendrá que ~ sin coche** she'll have to make do without a car. **10.** (*servir*) to be all right, to be usable; **puede ~** it'll do. **11.** *fam* (*prescindir*): **~ de algo/alguien** to want nothing to do with sthg/sb; **paso de política** I'm not into politics. **12.** (*tolerar*): **~ por algo** to put up with sthg. ▶ **pasarse** *vpr* **1.** (*acabarse*) to pass; **siéntate hasta que se te pase** sit down until you feel better. **2.** (*emplear - tiempo*) to spend, to pass; **se pasaron el día hablando** they spent all day talking. **3.** (*desaprovecharse*) to slip by; **se me pasó la oportunidad** I missed my chance. **4.** (*estropearse - comida*) to go off; (*- flores*) to fade. **5.** (*cambiar de bando*): **~se a** to go over to. **6.** (*omitir*) to miss out; **te has pasado una página** you've missed a page out. **7.** (*olvidarse*): **pasársele a alguien** to slip sb's mind; **se me pasó decírtelo** I forgot to mention it to you. **8.** (*no fijarse*): **pasársele a alguien** to escape sb's attention; **no se le pasa nada** he never misses a thing. **9.** (*excederse*): **~se de generoso/bueno** to be far too generous/kind. **10.** *fam* (*propasarse*) to go over the top; **te has pasado diciéndole eso** what you said went too far o was over the top. **11.** (*divertirse*): **¿qué tal te lo estás pasando?** how are you enjoying yourself?; **pasárselo bien/mal** to have a good/bad time.

pasarela *f* **1.** (*puente*) footbridge; (*para desembarcar*) gangway. **2.** (*en un desfile*) catwalk.

pasatiempo *m* (*hobby*) pastime, hobby.

Pascua *f* **1.** (*de los judíos*) Passover. **2.** (*de los cristianos*) Easter. ▶ **Pascuas** *fpl* (*Navidad*) Christmas (*sg*); **¡felices Pascuas!** Merry Christmas!; **de Pascuas a Ramos** once in a blue moon.

pase *m* **1.** (*gen*, DEP & TAUROM) pass. **2.** (*proyección*) showing, screening. **3.** (*desfile*) parade; **~ de modelos** fashion parade.

pasear ◆ *vi* to go for a walk. ◆ *vt* to

take for a walk; (*perro*) to walk; *fig* to show off, to parade.

paseo *m* **1.** (*acción - a pie*) walk; (*- en coche*) drive; (*- a caballo*) ride; (*- en barca*) row; **dar un ~** (*a pie*) to go for a walk o stroll. **2.** (*lugar*) avenue; **~ marítimo** promenade. **3.** *loc*: **mandar** o **enviar a alguien a ~** to send sb packing.

pasillo *m* corridor.

pasión *f* passion. ▶ **Pasión** *f* (RELIG) Passion.

pasivo, -va *adj* **1.** (*gen* & GRAM) passive. **2.** (*población etc*) inactive. ▶ **pasivo** *m* (COM) liabilities (*pl*).

pasmado, -da *adj* **1.** (*asombrado*) astonished, astounded. **2.** (*atontado*) stunned.

pasmar *vt* to astound. ▶ **pasmarse** *vpr* to be astounded.

pasmo *m* astonishment.

pasmoso, -sa *adj* astonishing.

paso *m* **1.** (*gen*) step; (*huella*) footprint. **2.** (*acción*) passing; (*cruce*) crossing; (*camino de acceso*) way through, thoroughfare; **abrir ~ a alguien** *lit* & *fig* to make way for sb; **ceder el ~ (a alguien)** to let sb past; (AUTOM) to give way (to sb); **'ceda el ~'** 'give way'; **'prohibido el ~'** 'no entry'; **~ elevado** flyover; **~ a nivel** level crossing; **~ peatonal** o **de peatones** pedestrian crossing; **~ de cebra** zebra crossing. **3.** (*forma de andar*) walk; (*ritmo*) pace. **4.** (GEOGR - *en montaña*) pass; (*- en el mar*) strait. **5.** (*gen pl*) (*gestión*) step; (*progreso*) advance; **dar los ~s necesarios** to take the necessary steps. **6.** *loc*: **a cada ~** every other minute; **está a dos o cuatro ~s** it's just down the road; **¡a este ~ ...!** *fig* at that rate ...!; **estar de ~** to be passing through; **~ a ~** step by step; **salir del ~** to get out of trouble. ▶ **de paso** *loc adv* in passing.

pasodoble *m* paso doble.

pasota *fam* ◆ *adj* apathetic. ◆ *m y f* dropout.

pasta *f* **1.** (*masa*) paste; (*de papel*) pulp; **~ dentífrica** toothpaste. **2.** (CULIN - *espaguetti etc*) pasta; (*- de pasteles*) pastry; (*- de pan*) dough. **3.** (*pastelillo*) pastry. **4.** *fam* (*dinero*) dough. **5.** (*encuadernación*): **en ~** hardback.

pastar *vi* to graze.

pastel *m* **1.** (CULIN - *dulce*) cake; (*- salado*) pie. **2.** (ARTE) pastel.

pastelería *f* **1.** (*establecimiento*) cake shop, patisserie. **2.** (*repostería*) pastries (*pl*).

pasteurizado [pasteuri'θaðo], **-da** adj pasteurized.

pastiche m pastiche.

pastilla f 1. (MED) pill, tablet. 2. (de jabón, chocolate) bar.

pasto m 1. (acción) grazing; (sitio) pasture. 2. (hierba) fodder. 3. loc: **ser ~ de las llamas** to go up in flames.

pastón m fam: **vale un ~** it costs a bomb.

pastor, -ra m y f (de ganado) shepherd (f shepherdess). ▶ **pastor** m 1. (sacerdote) minister. 2. → **perro**.

pastoso, -sa adj 1. (blando) pasty; (arroz) sticky. 2. (seco) dry.

pata f 1. (pierna) leg. 2. (pie - gen) foot; (- de perro, gato) paw; (- de vaca, caballo) hoof. 3. fam (de persona) leg; **a cuatro ~s** on all fours; **ir a la ~ coja** to hop. 4. (de mueble) leg; (de gafas) arm. 5. loc: **meter la ~** to put one's foot in it; **poner/estar ~s arriba** to turn/be upside down; **tener mala ~** to be unlucky. ▶ **patas** fpl Amer fam (poca vergüenza) cheek (U). ▶ **pata de gallo** f (en la cara) crow's feet (pl).

patada f kick; (en el suelo) stamp; **dar una ~ a** to kick; **tratar a alguien a ~s** to treat sb like dirt.

patalear vi to kick about; (en el suelo) to stamp one's feet.

pataleo m kicking (U); (en el suelo) stamping (U).

pataleta f tantrum.

patán m bumpkin.

patata f potato; **~s fritas** (de sartén) chips; (de bolsa) crisps.

paté m paté.

patear ◆ vt (dar un puntapié) to kick; (pisotear) to stamp on. ◆ vi (patalear) to stamp one's feet.

patentado, -da adj patent, patented.

patente ◆ adj obvious; (demostración, prueba) clear. ◆ f (de invento) patent.

paternal adj fatherly, paternal; fig paternal.

paternidad f fatherhood; (DER) paternity.

paterno, -na adj paternal.

patético, -ca adj pathetic, moving.

patetismo m pathos (U).

patidifuso, -sa adj fam stunned.

patilla f 1. (de pelo) sideboard, sideburn. 2. (de gafas) arm.

patín m 1. (calzado - de cuchilla) ice skate; (- de ruedas) roller skate. 2. (patinete) scooter. 3. (embarcación) pedal boat.

pátina f patina.

patinaje m skating.

patinar vi 1. (sobre hielo) to skate; (sobre ruedas) to roller-skate. 2. (resbalar - coche) to skid; (- persona) to slip. 3. fam fig (meter la pata) to put one's foot in it.

patinazo m 1. (de coche) skid; (de persona) slip. 2. fam fig (planchazo) blunder.

patinete m scooter.

patio m (gen) patio, courtyard; (de escuela) playground; (de cuartel) parade ground.

patitieso, -sa adj 1. (de frío) frozen stiff. 2. (de sorpresa) aghast, amazed.

pato, -ta m y f duck; **pagar el ~** to carry the can.

patológico, -ca adj pathological.

patoso, -sa adj fam clumsy.

patria → **patrio**.

patriarca m patriarch.

patrimonio m 1. (bienes - heredados) inheritance; (- propios) wealth; (económico) national wealth. 2. fig (de una colectividad) exclusive birthright.

patrio, -tria adj native. ▶ **patria** f native country.

patriota m y f patriot.

patriotismo m patriotism.

patrocinador, -ra m y f sponsor.

patrocinar vt to sponsor.

patrocinio m sponsorship.

patrón, -ona m y f 1. (de obreros) boss; (de criados) master (f mistress). 2. (de pensión etc) landlord (f landlady). 3. (santo) patron saint. ▶ **patrón** m 1. (de barco) skipper. 2. (en costura) pattern.

patronal ◆ adj (empresarial) management (antes de sust). ◆ f 1. (de empresa) management. 2. (de país) employers' organisation.

patronato m (gen) board; (con fines benéficos) trust.

patrono, -na m y f 1. (de empresa - encargado) boss; (- empresario) employer. 2. (santo) patron saint.

patrulla f patrol; **~ urbana** vigilante group.

patrullar vt & vi to patrol.

patuco m (gen pl) bootee.

paulatino, -na adj gradual.

pausa f pause, break; (MÚS) rest; **con ~** unhurriedly.

pausado, -da adj deliberate, slow.

pauta f 1. (gen) standard, model. 2. (en un papel) guideline.

pava → **pavo**.

pavimentación f (de una carretera) road surfacing; (de la acera) paving; (de un suelo) flooring.

pavimento *m* (*de carretera*) road surface; (*de acera*) paving; (*de suelo*) flooring.

pavo, -va *m y f* (*ave*) turkey; ~ **real** peacock (*f* peahen).

pavonearse *vpr despec*: ~ **(de)** to boast o brag (about).

pavor *m* terror.

paya *f Amer improvised poem accompanied by guitar.*

payasada *f* clowning (U); **hacer ~s** to clown around.

payaso, -sa *m y f* clown.

payo, -ya *m y f* non-gipsy.

paz *f* peace; (*tranquilidad*) peacefulness; **dejar a alguien en ~** to leave sb alone o in peace; **estar** o **quedar en ~** to be quits; **hacer las paces** to make (it) up; **que en ~ descanse, que descanse en ~** may he/she rest in peace.

PC *m* (*abrev de* **personal computer**) PC.

PD, PS (*abrev de posdata*) PS.

pdo. *abrev de pasado.*

peaje *m* toll.

peana *f* pedestal.

peatón *m* pedestrian.

peca *f* freckle.

pecado *m* sin.

pecador, -ra *m y f* sinner.

pecaminoso, -sa *adj* sinful.

pecar *vi* 1. (RELIG) to sin. 2. (*pasarse*): ~ **de confiado/generoso** to be overconfident/too generous.

pecera *f* fish tank; (*redonda*) fish bowl.

pecho *m* 1. (*gen*) chest; (*de mujer*) bosom. 2. (*mama*) breast; **dar el ~ a** to breastfeed. 3. *loc*: **a lo hecho, ~** it's no use crying over spilt milk; **tomarse algo a ~** to take sthg to heart.

pechuga *f* (*de ave*) breast (*meat*).

pecoso, -sa *adj* freckly.

pectoral *adj* (ANAT) pectoral, chest (*antes de sust*).

peculiar *adj* 1. (*característico*) typical, characteristic. 2. (*curioso*) peculiar.

peculiaridad *f* 1. (*cualidad*) uniqueness. 2. (*detalle*) particular feature o characteristic.

pedagogía *f* education, pedagogy.

pedagogo, -ga *m y f* educator; (*profesor*) teacher.

pedal *m* pedal.

pedalear *vi* to pedal.

pedante *adj* pompous.

pedantería *f* pomposity (U).

pedazo *m* piece, bit; **hacer ~s** to break to bits; *fig* to destroy.

pedernal *m* flint.

pedestal *m* pedestal, stand.

pedestre *adj* on foot.

pediatra *m y f* pediatrician.

pedicuro, -ra *m y f* chiropodist Br, podiatrist Am.

pedido *m* (COM) order; **hacer un ~** to place an order.

pedigrí, pedigree [peðiˈɣri] *m* pedigree.

pedir ♦ *vt* 1. (*gen*) to ask for; (*en comercios, restaurantes*) to order; ~ **a alguien que haga algo** to ask sb to do sthg; ~ **a alguien (en matrimonio)** to ask for sb's hand (in marriage); ~ **prestado algo a alguien** to borrow sthg from sb. 2. (*exigir*) to demand. 3. (*requerir*) to call for, to need. 4. (*poner precio*): ~ **(por)** to ask (for); **pide un millón por la moto** he's asking a million for the motorbike. ♦ *vi* (*mendigar*) to beg.

pedo *m vulg* (*ventosidad*) fart; **tirarse un ~** to fart.

pedrada *f* (*golpe*): **a ~s** by stoning.

pedregullo *m Amer* gravel.

pedrería *f* precious stones (*pl*).

pedrusco *m* rough stone.

peeling [ˈpilin] (*pl* **peelings**) *m* face mask o pack.

pega *f* (*obstáculo*) difficulty, hitch; **poner ~s (a)** to find problems (with).

pegadizo, -za *adj* 1. (*música*) catchy. 2. *fig* (*contagioso*) catching.

pegajoso, -sa *adj* sticky; *despec* clinging.

pegamento *m* glue.

pegar ♦ *vt* 1. (*adherir*) to stick; (*con pegamento*) to glue; (*póster, cartel*) to fix, to put up; (*botón*) to sew on. 2. (*arrimar*): ~ **algo a** to put o place sthg against. 3. (*golpear*) to hit. 4. (*propinar - bofetada, paliza etc*) to give; (*- golpe*) to deal. 5. (*contagiar*): ~ **algo a alguien** to give sb sthg, to pass sthg on to sb. ♦ *vi* 1. (*adherir*) to stick. 2. (*golpear*) to hit. 3. (*armonizar*) to go together, to match; ~ **con** to go with. 4. (*sol*) to beat down. ▶ **pegarse** *vpr* 1. (*adherirse*) to stick. 2. (*agredirse*) to fight. 3. (*golpearse*): **~se (un golpe) con algo** to hit o.s. against sthg. 4. *fig* (*contagiarse - enfermedad*) to be transmitted; **se me pegó su acento** I picked up his accent.

pegatina *f* sticker.

pegote *m fam* 1. (*masa pegajosa*) sticky mess. 2. (*chapucería*) botch.

peinado *m* hairdo; (*estilo, tipo*) hairstyle.

peinar *vt lit & fig* to comb. ▶ **peinarse** *vpr* to comb one's hair.

peine m comb.

peineta f comb worn in the back of the hair.

p.ej. (abrev de **por ejemplo**) e.g.

Pekín Peking, Beijing.

pela f fam peseta; **no tengo ~s** I'm skint.

peladilla f sugared almond.

pelado, -da adj 1. (cabeza) shorn. 2. (piel, cara etc) peeling; (fruta) peeled. 3. (habitación, monte, árbol) bare. 4. (número) exact, round; **saqué un aprobado ~** I passed, but only just. 5. fam (sin dinero) broke, skint.

pelaje m (de gato, oso, conejo) fur; (de perro, caballo) coat.

pelar vt 1. (persona) to cut the hair of. 2. (fruta, patatas) to peel; (guisantes, marisco) to shell. 3. (aves) to pluck; (conejos etc) to skin. ▶ **pelarse** vpr 1. (cortarse el pelo) to have one's hair cut. 2. (piel, espalda etc) to peel.

peldaño m step; (de escalera de mano) rung.

pelea f 1. (a golpes) fight. 2. (riña) row, quarrel.

pelear vi 1. (a golpes) to fight. 2. (a gritos) to have a row o quarrel. 3. (esforzarse) to struggle. ▶ **pelearse** vpr 1. (a golpes) to fight. 2. (a gritos) to have a row o quarrel.

pelele m fam despec (persona) puppet.

peletería f (tienda) fur shop, furrier's.

peliagudo, -da adj tricky.

pelícano, pelicano m pelican.

película f (gen) film; **~ muda/de terror** silent/horror film; **~ del Oeste** western; **de ~** amazing.

peligro m danger; **correr ~ (de)** to be in danger (of); **estar/poner en ~** to be/put at risk; **fuera de ~** out of danger; **¡~ de muerte!** danger!

peligroso, -sa adj dangerous.

pelín m fam mite, tiny bit.

pelirrojo, -ja ◆ adj ginger, red-headed. ◆ m y f redhead.

pellejo m (piel, vida) skin.

pellizcar vt (gen) to pinch.

pellizco m pinch.

pelma, pelmazo, -za fam despec ◆ adj annoying, tiresome. ◆ m y f bore, pain.

pelo m 1. (gen) hair. 2. (de oso, conejo, gato) fur; (de perro, caballo) coat. 3. (de una tela) nap. 4. loc: **con ~s y señales** with all the details; **no tener ~s en la lengua** not to mince one's words; **poner a alguien los ~s de punta** fam to make sb's hair stand on end; **por los ~s, por un ~** by the skin of one's teeth; **tomar el ~ a**

alguien fam to pull sb's leg. ▶ **a contra pelo** loc adv lit & fig against the grain.

pelota ◆ f 1. (gen & DEP) ball; **jugar a la ~** to play ball; **~ vasca** pelota; **hacer la ~ (a alguien)** fam to suck up (to sb). 2. fam (cabeza) nut. ◆ m y f (persona) crawler, creep.

pelotera f fam scrap, fight.

pelotón m (de soldados) squad; (de gente) crowd; (DEP) pack.

pelotudo, -da adj Amer fam stupid.

peluca f wig.

peluche m plush.

peludo, -da adj hairy.

peluquería f 1. (establecimiento) hairdresser's (shop). 2. (oficio) hairdressing.

peluquero, -ra m y f hairdresser.

peluquín m toupee.

pelusa f 1. (de tela) fluff. 2. (vello) down.

pelvis f inv pelvis.

pena f 1. (lástima) shame, pity; **¡qué ~!** what a shame o pity!; **dar ~** to inspire pity; **el pobre me da ~** I feel sorry for the poor chap. 2. (tristeza) sadness, sorrow. 3. (gen pl) (desgracia) problem, trouble. 4. (gen pl) (dificultad) struggle (U); **a duras ~s** with great difficulty. 5. (castigo) punishment; **~ capital** o **de muerte** death penalty. 6. Amer (vergüenza) shame, embarrassment; **me da ~** I'm ashamed of it. 7. loc: **(no) valer** o **merecer la ~** (not) to be worthwhile o worth it.

penacho m 1. (de pájaro) crest. 2. (adorno) plume.

penal ◆ adj criminal. ◆ m prison.

penalidad f (gen pl) suffering (U); hardship.

penalización f 1. (acción) penalization. 2. (sanción) penalty.

penalti, penalty m (DEP) penalty.

penar ◆ vt (castigar) to punish. ◆ vi (sufrir) to suffer.

pender vi 1. (colgar): **~ (de)** to hang (from). 2. fig (amenaza etc): **~ sobre** to hang over.

pendiente ◆ adj 1. (por resolver) pending; (deuda) outstanding; **estar ~ de** (atento a) to keep an eye on; (a la espera de) to be waiting for. 2. (asignatura) failed. ◆ m earring. ◆ f slope.

pendón, -ona m y f fam libertine.

péndulo m pendulum.

pene m penis.

penene m y f untenured teacher or lecturer.

penetración f 1. (gen) penetration. 2. (sagacidad) astuteness.

penetrante adj 1. (intenso - dolor)

acute; (- *olor*) sharp; (- *frío*) biting; (- *mirada*) penetrating; (- *voz, sonido etc*) piercing. **2.** (*sagaz*) sharp, penetrating.
penetrar ◆ *vi*: ~ **en** (*internarse en*) to enter; (*filtrarse por*) to get into, to penetrate; (*perforar*) to pierce; (*llegar a conocer*) to get to the bottom of. ◆ *vt* **1.** (*introducirse en - suj: arma, sonido etc*) to pierce, to penetrate; (- *suj: humedad, líquido*) to permeate; (- *suj: emoción, sentimiento*) to pierce. **2.** (*llegar a conocer - secreto etc*) to get to the bottom of. **3.** (*sexualmente*) to penetrate.
penicilina *f* penicillin.
península *f* peninsula.
peninsular *adj* peninsular.
penitencia *f* penance.
penitenciaría *f* penitentiary.
penoso, -sa *adj* **1.** (*trabajoso*) laborious. **2.** (*lamentable*) distressing; (*aspecto, espectáculo*) sorry.
pensador, -ra *m y f* thinker.
pensamiento *m* **1.** (*gen*) thought; (*mente*) mind; (*idea*) idea. **2.** (BOT) pansy.
pensar ◆ *vi*: ~ **en algo/en alguien/en hacer algo** to think about sthg/about sb/about doing sthg; ~ **sobre algo** to think about sthg; **piensa en un número/buen regalo** think of a number/good present; **dar que** ~ **a alguien** to give sb food for thought. ◆ *vt* **1.** (*reflexionar*) to think about o over. **2.** (*opinar, creer*) to think; ~ **algo de alguien/algo** to think sthg of sb/sthg; **pienso que no vendrá** I don't think she'll come. **3.** (*idear*) to think up. **4.** (*tener la intención de*): ~ **hacer algo** to intend to do sthg. ▶ **pensarse** *vpr*: ~**se algo** to think sthg over.
pensativo, -va *adj* pensive, thoughtful.
pensión *f* **1.** (*dinero*) pension. **2.** (*de huéspedes*) ≃ guest house; **media** ~ (*en hotel*) half board; **estar a media** ~ (*en colegio*) to have school dinners; ~ **completa** full board.
pensionista *m y f* (*jubilado*) pensioner.
pentágono *m* pentagon.
pentagrama *m* (MÚS) stave.
penúltimo, -ma *adj, m y f* penultimate, last but one.
penumbra *f* half-light.
penuria *f* **1.** (*pobreza*) penury, poverty. **2.** (*escasez*) paucity, dearth.
peña *f* **1.** (*roca*) crag, rock; (*monte*) cliff. **2.** (*grupo de amigos*) circle, group; (*club*) club; (*quinielística*) pool. **3.** Amer (*folklórica*) folk club.

peñasco *m* large crag o rock.
peñón *m* rock. ▶ **Peñón** *m*: **el Peñón (de Gibraltar)** the Rock (of Gibraltar).
peón *m* **1.** (*obrero*) unskilled labourer. **2.** (*en ajedrez*) pawn.
peonza *f* (spinning) top.
peor ◆ *adj* **1.** (*comparativo*): ~ **(que)** worse (than). **2.** (*superlativo*): **el/la** ~ ... the worst ... ◆ *pron*: **el/la** ~ **(de)** the worst (in); **el** ~ **de todos** the worst of all; **lo** ~ **fue que** ... the worst thing was that ... ◆ *adv* **1.** (*comparativo*): ~ **(que)** worse (than); **ahora veo** ~ I see worse now; **estar** ~ (*enfermo*) to get worse; **estoy** ~ (*de salud*) I feel worse. **2.** (*superlativo*) worst; **el que lo hizo** ~ the one who did it (the) worst.
pepinillo *m* gherkin.
pepino *m* (BOT) cucumber; **me importa un** ~ I couldn't care less.
pepita *f* **1.** (*de fruta*) pip. **2.** (*de oro*) nugget.
peppermint = **pipermín**.
pequeñez *f* **1.** (*gen*) smallness. **2.** *fig* (*insignificancia*) trifle.
pequeño, -ña ◆ *adj* small, little; (*hermano*) little; (*posibilidad*) slight; (*ingresos, cifras etc*) low. ◆ *m y f* (*benjamín*): **el** ~, **la pequeña** the youngest, the baby.
pequinés *m* (*perro*) Pekinese.
pera *f* **1.** (*fruta*) pear. **2.** (*para ducha etc*) (rubber) bulb. **3.** *loc*: **pedir** ~**s al olmo** to ask (for) the impossible; **ser la** ~ *fam* to be the limit.
peral *m* pear-tree.
percance *m* mishap.
percatarse *vpr*: ~ **(de algo)** to notice (sthg).
percebe *m* (*pez*) barnacle.
percepción *f* **1.** (*de los sentidos*) perception. **2.** (*cobro*) receipt, collection.
perceptible *adj* (*por los sentidos*) noticeable, perceptible.
percha *f* **1.** (*de armario*) (coat) hanger. **2.** (*de pared*) coat rack. **3.** (*de pie*) coat stand. **4.** (*para pájaros*) perch.
perchero *m* (*de pared*) coat rack; (*de pie*) coat stand.
percibir *vt* **1.** (*con los sentidos*) to perceive, to notice; (*por los oídos*) to hear; (*ver*) to see. **2.** (*cobrar*) to receive, to get.
percusión *f* percussion.
perdedor, -ra *m y f* loser.
perder ◆ *vt* **1.** (*gen*) to lose. **2.** (*desperdiciar*) to waste. **3.** (*tren, oportunidad*) to miss. ◆ *vi* **1.** (*salir derrotado*) to lose. **2.** *loc*: **echar algo a** ~ to spoil sthg; **echarse**

a ~ (*alimento*) to go off. ▶ **perderse** *vpr*
1. (*gen*) to get lost. 2. (*desaparecer*) to
disappear. 3. (*desperdiciarse*) to be wast-
ed. 4. (*desaprovechar*): **¡no te lo pierdas!**
don't miss it! 5. *fig* (*por los vicios*) to be
beyond salvation.

perdición *f* ruin, undoing.

pérdida *f* 1. (*gen*) loss; **no tiene ~** you
can't miss it. 2. (*de tiempo, dinero*) waste.
3. (*escape*) leak. ▶ **pérdidas** *fpl* 1. (FIN &
MIL) losses. 2. (*daños*) damage (U).

perdidamente *adv* hopelessly.

perdido, -da *adj* 1. (*extraviado*) lost;
(*animal, bala*) stray. 2. (*sucio*) filthy. 3.
fam (*de remate*) complete, utter. 4. *loc*:
estar ~ to be done for o lost.

perdigón *m* pellet.

perdiz *f* partridge.

perdón *m* pardon, forgiveness; **no
tener ~** to be unforgivable; **¡~!** sorry!

perdonar ◆ *vt* 1. (*gen*) to forgive; **~le
algo a alguien** to forgive sb for sthg;
¡perdone! (*para disculparse*) I'm sorry!;
(*para llamar la atención*) excuse me!; **perdone que le moleste** sorry to bother you.
2. (*eximir de - deuda, condena*): **~ algo a
alguien** to let sb off sthg; **~le la vida a
alguien** to spare sb their life.

perdonavidas *m y f inv fam* bully.

perdurable *adj* 1. (*que dura siempre*)
eternal. 2. (*que dura mucho*) long-lasting.

perdurar *vi* 1. (*durar mucho*) to
endure, to last. 2. (*persistir*) to persist.

perecedero, -ra *adj* 1. (*productos*)
perishable. 2. (*naturaleza*) transitory.

perecer *vi* to perish, to die.

peregrinación *f* (RELIG) pilgrimage;
fig (*a un lugar*) trek.

peregrinaje *m* (RELIG) pilgrimage; *fig*
(*a un lugar*) trek.

peregrino, -na ◆ *adj* 1. (*ave*) migratory. 2. *fig* (*extraño*) strange. ◆ *m y f* (*persona*) pilgrim.

perejil *m* parsley.

perenne *adj* 1. (BOT) perennial.
2. (*recuerdo*) enduring. 3. (*continuo*) constant.

pereza *f* idleness.

perezoso, -sa *adj* 1. (*vago*) lazy.
2. (*lento*) slow, sluggish.

perfección *f* perfection; **es de una
gran ~** it's exceptionally good.

perfeccionar *vt* 1. (*redondear*) to perfect. 2. (*mejorar*) to improve.

perfeccionista *adj, m y f* perfectionist.

perfecto, -ta *adj* perfect.

perfidia *f* perfidy, treachery.

perfil *m* 1. (*contorno*) outline, shape.
2. (*de cara, cuerpo*) profile; **de ~** in profile. 3. *fig* (*característica*) characteristic. 4.
fig (*retrato moral*) profile. 5. (GEOM) cross
section.

perfilar *vt* to outline. ▶ **perfilarse** *vpr*
1. (*destacarse*) to be outlined. 2. (*concretarse*) to shape up.

perforación *f* 1. (*gen* & MED) perforation. 2. (*taladro*) bore-hole.

perforar *vt* (*horadar*) to perforate;
(*agujero*) to drill; (INFORM) to punch.

perfume *m* perfume.

perfumería *f* 1. (*tienda, arte*) per-
fumery. 2. (*productos*) perfumes (*pl*).

pergamino *m* parchment.

pericia *f* skill.

periferia *f* periphery; (*alrededores*) outskirts (*pl*).

periférico, -ca *adj* peripheral; (*barrio*)
outlying.

perifollos *mpl fam* frills (and frip-
peries).

perífrasis *f inv*: **~ (verbal)** wordy explanation.

perilla *f* goatee; **venir de ~(s)** to be just
the right thing.

perímetro *m* perimeter.

periódico, -ca *adj* (*gen*) periodic.
▶ **periódico** *m* newspaper.

periodismo *m* journalism.

periodista *m y f* journalist.

periodo, período *m* period; (DEP)
half.

peripecia *f* incident, sudden change.

peripuesto, -ta *adj fam* dolled-up.

periquete *m*: **en un ~** *fam* in a jiffy.

periquito *m* parakeet.

periscopio *m* periscope.

peritar *vt* (*casa*) to value; (*coche*) to
assess the damage to.

perito *m* 1. (*experto*) expert; **~ agró-
nomo** agronomist. 2. (*ingeniero técnico*)
technician.

perjudicar *vt* to damage, to harm.

perjudicial *adj*: **~ (para)** harmful (to).

perjuicio *m* harm (U), damage (U).

perjurar *vi* (*jurar en falso*) to commit
perjury.

perla *f* pearl; *fig* (*maravilla*) gem, treasure; **de ~s** great, fine; **me viene de ~s** it's
just the right thing.

perlé *m* beading.

permanecer *vi* 1. (*en un lugar*) to stay.
2. (*en un estado*) to remain, to stay.

permanencia *f* 1. (*en un lugar*) staying, continued stay. 2. (*en un estado*)
continuation.

permanente ◆ *adj* permanent; (*comisión*) standing. ◆ *f* perm; **hacerse la** ~ to have a perm.

permeable *adj* permeable.

permisible *adj* permissible, acceptable.

permisivo, -va *adj* permissive.

permiso *m* **1.** (*autorización*) permission; **con** ~ if I may. **2.** (*documento*) licence, permit; ~ **de armas** gun licence; ~ **de conducir** driving licence Br, driver's license Am. **3.** (*vacaciones*) leave.

permitir *vt* to allow, to permit; ~ **a alguien hacer algo** to allow sb to do sthg; **¿me permite?** may I? ▶ **permitirse** *vpr* to allow o.s. (the luxury of); **no puedo permitírmelo** I can't afford it.

permuta, permutación *f* exchange.

pernicioso, -sa *adj* damaging, harmful.

pero ◆ *conj* but; **la casa es vieja** ~ **céntrica** the house may be old, but it's central; ~ **¿qué es tanto ruido?** what on earth is all this noise about? ◆ *m* snag, fault; **poner** ~**s a todo** to find fault with everything.

perol *m* casserole (dish).

perorata *f* long-winded speech.

perpendicular *adj* perpendicular; **ser** ~ **a algo** to be at right angles to sthg.

perpetrar *vt* to perpetrate, to commit.

perpetuar *vt* to perpetuate. ▶ **perpetuarse** *vpr* to last, to endure.

perpetuo, -tua *adj* **1.** (*gen*) perpetual. **2.** (*para toda la vida*) lifelong; (DER) life (*antes de sust*).

perplejo, -ja *adj* perplexed, bewildered.

perra *f* **1.** (*rabieta*) tantrum; **coger una** ~ to throw a tantrum. **2.** (*dinero*) penny; **estoy sin una** ~ I'm flat broke. **3.** → **perro**.

perrera → **perrero**.

perrería *f fam*: **hacer** ~**s a alguien** to play dirty tricks on sb.

perrero, -ra *m y f* (*persona*) dogcatcher. ▶ **perrera** *f* **1.** (*lugar*) kennels (*pl*). **2.** (*vehículo*) dogcatcher's van.

perro, -rra *m y f* (*animal*) dog (*f* bitch); ~ **callejero** stray dog; ~ **de caza** hunting dog; ~ **lazarillo** guide dog; ~ **lobo** alsatian; ~ **pastor** sheepdog; ~ **policía** police dog; **ser** ~ **viejo** to be an old hand. ▶ **perro caliente** *m* hot dog.

persecución *f* **1.** (*seguimiento*) pursuit. **2.** (*acoso*) persecution.

perseguir *vt* **1.** (*seguir, tratar de obtener*) to pursue. **2.** (*acosar*) to persecute. **3.** (*suj: mala suerte, problema etc*) to dog.

perseverante *adj* persistent.

perseverar *vi*: ~ (**en**) to persevere (with), to persist (in).

persiana *f* blind.

persistente *adj* persistent.

persistir *vi*: ~ (**en**) to persist (in).

persona *f* **1.** (*individuo*) person; **cien** ~**s** a hundred people; **en** ~ in person; **por** ~ per head; **ser buena** ~ to be nice; ~ **mayor** adult, grown-up. **2.** (DER) party. **3.** (GRAM) person.

personaje *m* **1.** (*persona importante*) important person, celebrity. **2.** (*de obra*) character.

personal ◆ *adj* (*gen*) personal; (*teléfono, dirección*) private, home (*antes de sust*). ◆ *m* (*trabajadores*) staff, personnel.

personalidad *f* **1.** (*características*) personality. **2.** (*identidad*) identity. **3.** (*persona importante*) important person, celebrity.

personalizar *vi* **1.** (*nombrar*) to name names. **2.** (*aludir*) to get personal.

personarse *vpr* to turn up.

personificar *vt* to personify.

perspectiva *f* **1.** (*gen*) perspective. **2.** (*paisaje*) view. **3.** (*futuro*) prospect; **en** ~ in prospect.

perspicacia *f* insight, perceptiveness.

perspicaz *adj* sharp, perceptive.

persuadir *vt* to persuade; ~ **a alguien para que haga algo** to persuade sb to do sthg. ▶ **persuadirse** *vpr* to convince o.s.; ~**se de algo** to become convinced of sthg.

persuasión *f* persuasion.

persuasivo, -va *adj* persuasive. ▶ **persuasiva** *f* persuasive power.

pertenecer *vi* **1.** (*gen*): ~ **a** to belong to. **2.** (*corresponder*) to be a matter for.

perteneciente *adj*: **ser** ~ **a** to belong to.

pertenencia *f* **1.** (*propiedad*) ownership. **2.** (*afiliación*) membership. ▶ **pertenencias** *fpl* (*enseres*) belongings.

pértiga *f* **1.** (*vara*) pole. **2.** (DEP) pole-vault.

pertinaz *adj* **1.** (*terco*) stubborn. **2.** (*persistente*) persistent.

pertinente *adj* **1.** (*adecuado*) appropriate. **2.** (*relativo*) relevant, pertinent.

pertrechos *mpl* **1.** (MIL) supplies and ammunition. **2.** *fig* (*utensilios*) gear (U).

perturbación f 1. (*desconcierto*) disquiet, unease. 2. (*disturbio*) disturbance; ~ **del orden público** breach of the peace. 3. (MED) mental imbalance.

perturbado, -da adj 1. (MED) disturbed. 2. (*desconcertado*) perturbed.

perturbador, -ra ◆ adj unsettling. ◆ m y f troublemaker.

perturbar vt 1. (*trastornar*) to disrupt. 2. (*inquietar*) to disturb, to unsettle. 3. (*enloquecer*) to perturb.

Perú : (el) ~ Peru.

peruano, -na adj, m y f Peruvian.

perversión f perversion.

perverso, -sa adj depraved.

pervertido, -da m y f pervert.

pervertir vt to corrupt. ▶ **pervertirse** vpr to be corrupted.

pesa f 1. (*gen*) weight. 2. (*gen pl*) (DEP) weights (*pl*).

pesadez f 1. (*peso*) weight. 2. (*sensación*) heaviness. 3. (*molestia, fastidio*) drag, pain. 4. (*aburrimiento*) ponderousness.

pesadilla f nightmare.

pesado, -da ◆ adj 1. (*gen*) heavy. 2. (*caluroso*) sultry. 3. (*lento*) ponderous, sluggish. 4. (*duro*) difficult, tough. 5. (*aburrido*) boring. 6. (*molesto*) annoying, tiresome; **¡qué ~ eres!** you're so annoying! ◆ m y f bore, pain.

pesadumbre f grief, sorrow.

pésame m sympathy, condolences (*pl*); **dar el ~** to offer one's condolences.

pesar ◆ m 1. (*tristeza*) grief. 2. (*arrepentimiento*) remorse. 3. *loc*: **a ~ mío** against my will. ◆ vt 1. (*determinar el peso de*) to weigh. 2. (*examinar*) to weigh up. ◆ vi 1. (*tener peso*) to weigh. 2. (*ser pesado*) to be heavy. 3. (*importar*) to play an important part. 4. (*entristecer*): **me pesa tener que decirte esto** I'm sorry to have to tell you this. ▶ **a pesar de** loc prep despite. ▶ **a pesar de que** loc conj in spite of the fact that.

pesca f 1. (*acción*) fishing; **ir de ~** to go fishing; **~ de bajura/altura** coastal/deep-sea fishing. 2. (*lo pescado*) catch.

pescadería f fishmonger's (shop).

pescadilla f whiting.

pescado m fish; **~ azul/blanco** blue/white fish.

pescador, -ra m y f fisherman (f fisherwoman).

pescar ◆ vt 1. (*peces*) to catch. 2. *fig* (*enfermedad*) to catch. 3. *fam fig* (*conseguir*) to get o.s., to land. 4. *fam fig* (*atrapar*) to catch. ◆ vi to fish, to go fishing.

pescuezo m neck.

pese ▶ pese a loc prep despite.

pesebre m 1. (*para los animales*) manger. 2. (*belén*) crib, Nativity scene.

pesero m Amer fixed-rate taxi service.

peseta f (*unidad*) peseta. ▶ **pesetas** fpl fig (*dinero*) money (U).

pesetero, -ra adj money-grubbing.

pesimismo m pessimism.

pesimista ◆ adj pessimistic. ◆ m y f pessimist.

pésimo, -ma ◆ superl → **malo**. ◆ adj terrible, awful.

peso m 1. (*gen*) weight; **tiene un kilo de ~** it weighs a kilo; **de ~** (*razones*) weighty; (*persona*) influential; **~ bruto/neto** gross/net weight; **~ muerto** dead weight. 2. (*moneda*) peso. 3. (*de atletismo*) shot. 4. (*balanza*) scales (*pl*).

pespunte m backstitch.

pesquero, -ra adj fishing. ▶ **pesquero** m fishing boat.

pesquisa f investigation, inquiry.

pestaña f (*de párpado*) eyelash; **quemarse las ~s** fig to burn the midnight oil.

pestañear vi to blink; **sin ~** (*con serenidad*) without batting an eyelid; (*con atención*) without losing concentration once.

peste f 1. (*enfermedad, plaga*) plague; **~ bubónica** bubonic plague. 2. *fam* (*mal olor*) stink, stench. 3. *loc*: **decir ~s de alguien** to heap abuse on sb.

pesticida m pesticide.

pestilencia f stench.

pestillo m (*cerrojo*) bolt; (*mecanismo, en verjas*) latch; **correr o echar el ~** to shoot the bolt.

petaca f 1. (*para cigarrillos*) cigarette case; (*para tabaco*) tobacco pouch. 2. (*para bebidas*) flask. 3. Amer (*maleta*) suitcase.

pétalo m petal.

petanca f game similar to bowls played in parks, on beach etc.

petardo m (*cohete*) firecracker.

petate m kit bag.

petición f 1. (*acción*) request; **a ~ de** at the request of. 2. (DER) (*escrito*) petition.

petiso, -sa adj Amer fam short.

peto m (*de prenda*) bib.

petrificar vt lit & fig to petrify.

petrodólar m petrodollar.

petróleo m oil, petroleum.

petrolero, -ra adj oil (*antes de sust*). ▶ **petrolero** m oil tanker.

petrolífero, -ra adj oil (antes de sust).

petulante adj opinionated.

peúco m (gen pl) bootee.

peyorativo, -va adj pejorative.

pez m fish; ~ **de río** freshwater fish; ~ **espada** swordfish; **estar ~ (en algo)** to have no idea (about sthg). ► **pez gordo** m fam fig big shot.

pezón m (de pecho) nipple.

pezuña f hoof.

piadoso, -sa adj 1. (compasivo) kind-hearted. 2. (religioso) pious.

pianista m y f pianist.

piano m piano.

pianola f pianola.

piar vi to cheep, to tweet.

PIB (abrev de **producto interior bruto**) m GDP.

pibe, -ba m y f Amer fam kid, boy (f girl).

pica f 1. (naipe) spade. 2. (lanza) pike; **poner una ~ en Flandes** to do the impossible. ► **picas** fpl (palo de baraja) spades.

picadero m (de caballos) riding school.

picadillo m (de carne) mince; (de verdura) chopped vegetables (pl).

picado, -da adj 1. (marcado - piel) pockmarked; (- fruta) bruised. 2. (agujereado) perforated; ~ **de polilla** moth-eaten. 3. (triturado - alimento) chopped; (- carne) minced; (- tabaco) cut. 4. (vino) sour. 5. (diente) decayed. 6. (mar) choppy. 7. fig (enfadado) annoyed.

picador, -ra m y f (TAUROM) picador.

picadora f mincer.

picadura f 1. (de mosquito, serpiente) bite; (de avispa, ortiga, escorpión) sting. 2. (tabaco) (cut) tobacco (U).

picante ◆ adj 1. (comida etc) spicy, hot. 2. fig (obsceno) saucy. ◆ m (comida) spicy food; (sabor) spiciness.

picantería f Amer cheap restaurant.

picapica → **polvo**.

picaporte m (aldaba) doorknocker; (barrita) latch.

picar ◆ vt 1. (suj: mosquito, serpiente) to bite; (suj: avispa, escorpión, ortiga) to sting. 2. (escocer) to itch; **me pican los ojos** my eyes are stinging. 3. (triturar - verdura) to chop; (- carne) to mince. 4. (suj: ave) to peck. 5. (aperitivo) to pick at. 6. (tierra, piedra, hielo) to hack at. 7. fig (enojar) to irritate. 8. fig (estimular - persona, caballo) to spur on; (- curiosidad) to prick. 9. (perforar - billete, ficha) to punch. ◆ vi 1. (alimento) to be spicy o hot. 2. (pez) to bite. 3. (escocer) to itch. 4. (ave) to peck.

5. (picotear) to nibble. 6. (sol) to burn. 7. (dejarse engañar) to take the bait. ► **picarse** vpr 1. (vino) to turn sour. 2. (mar) to get choppy. 3. (diente) to get a cavity. 4. (oxidarse) to go rusty. 5. fig (enfadarse) to get annoyed o cross.

picardía f 1. (astucia) craftiness. 2. (travesura) naughty trick, mischief (U). 3. (atrevimiento) brazenness.

picaresco, -ca adj mischievous, roguish. ► **picaresca** f 1. (LITER) picaresque literature. 2. (modo de vida) roguery.

pícaro, -ra m y f 1. (astuto) sly person, rogue. 2. (travieso) rascal. 3. (atrevido) brazen person.

picatoste m crouton.

pichi m pinafore (dress).

pichichi m (DEP) top scorer.

pichincha f Amer fam snip, bargain.

pichón m (ZOOL) young pigeon.

picnic (pl picnics) m picnic.

pico m 1. (de ave) beak. 2. (punta, saliente) corner. 3. (herramienta) pick, pickaxe. 4. (cumbre) peak. 5. (cantidad indeterminada): **cincuenta y ~** fifty-odd; **llegó a las cinco y ~** he got there just after five. 6. fam (boca) gob, mouth; **cerrar el ~** (callar) to shut up.

picor m (del calor) burning; (que irrita) itch.

picoso, -sa adj Amer spicy, hot.

picotear vt (suj: ave) to peck.

pida, pidiera etc → **pedir**.

pie m 1. (gen & ANAT) foot; **a ~** on foot; **estar de** o **en ~** to be on one's feet o standing; **ponerse de** o **en ~** to stand up; **de ~s a cabeza** fig from head to toe; **seguir en ~** (vigente) to be still valid; **en ~ de igualdad** on an equal footing; **en ~ de guerra** at war; ~ **de foto** caption. 2. (de micrófono, lámpara etc) stand; (de copa) stem. 3. loc: **al ~ de la letra** to the letter, word for word; **andar con ~s de plomo** to tread carefully; **buscarle (los) tres ~s al gato** to split hairs; **dar ~ a alguien para que haga algo** to give sb cause to do sthg; **no tener ni ~s ni cabeza** to make no sense at all; **pararle los ~s a alguien** to put sb in their place; **tener un ~ en la tumba** to have one foot in the grave.

piedad f 1. (compasión) pity; **tener ~ de** to take pity on. 2. (religiosidad) piety.

piedra f 1. (gen) stone; ~ **angular** lit & fig cornerstone; ~ **pómez** pumice stone; ~ **preciosa** precious stone. 2. (de mechero) flint.

piel f 1. (ANAT) skin; ~ **roja** redskin (N.B: *the term 'piel roja' is considered to be racist*); **dejar** o **jugarse la** ~ to risk one's neck. 2. (*cuero*) leather. 3. (*pelo*) fur. 4. (*cáscara*) skin, peel.

piensa *etc* → **pensar**.

pierda *etc* → **perder**.

pierna f leg; **estirar las ~s** to stretch one's legs.

pieza f 1. (*gen*) piece; (*de mecanismo*) part; ~ **de recambio** o **repuesto** spare part, extra Am; **dejar/quedarse de una** ~ to leave/be thunderstruck. 2. (*obra dramática*) play. 3. (*habitación*) room.

pifiar vt: ~**la** *fam* to put one's foot in it.

pigmento m pigment.

pijama m pyjamas (*pl*).

pila f 1. (*generador*) battery. 2. (*montón*) pile; **tiene una** ~ **de deudas** he's up to his neck in debt. 3. (*fregadero*) sink.

pilar m lit & fig pillar.

píldora f pill; (*anticonceptivo*): **la** ~ the pill; **dorar la** ~ to sugar the pill.

pileta f Amer swimming pool.

pillaje m pillage.

pillar ♦ vt 1. (*gen*) to catch. 2. (*chiste, explicación*) to get. 3. (*atropellar*) to knock down. ♦ vi (*hallarse*): **me pilla lejos** it's out of the way for me; **me pilla de camino** it's on my way. ▶ **pillarse** vpr (*dedos etc*) to catch.

pillo, -lla *fam* ♦ adj 1. (*travieso*) mischievous. 2. (*astuto*) crafty. ♦ m y f (*pícaro*) rascal.

pilotar vt (*avión*) to fly, to pilot; (*coche*) to drive; (*barco*) to steer.

piloto ♦ m y f (*gen*) pilot; (*de coche*) driver; ~ **automático** automatic pilot. ♦ m (*luz - de coche*) tail light; (*- de aparato*) pilot lamp. ♦ adj inv pilot (*antes de sust*).

piltrafa f (*gen pl*) scrap; *fam* (*persona débil*) wreck.

pimentón m paprika.

pimienta f pepper.

pimiento m (*fruto*) pepper, capsicum; (*planta*) pimiento, pepper plant; ~ **morrón** sweet pepper.

pimpollo m 1. (*de rama, planta*) shoot; (*de flor*) bud. 2. *fam fig* (*persona atractiva*) gorgeous person.

pinacoteca f art gallery.

pinar m pine wood o grove.

pinaza f pine needles (*pl*).

pincel m (*para pintar*) paintbrush; (*para maquillar etc*) brush.

pinchadiscos m y f inv disc jockey.

pinchar ♦ vt 1. (*punzar - gen*) to prick; (*- rueda*) to puncture; (*- globo, balón*) to burst. 2. (*penetrar*) to pierce. 3. (*fijar*): ~ **algo en la pared** to pin sthg to the wall. 4. *fam* (*teléfono*) to tap. 5. *fig* (*irritar*) to torment. 6. *fig* (*incitar*): ~ **a alguien para que haga algo** to urge sb to do sthg. ♦ vi 1. (*rueda*) to get a puncture. 2. (*barba*) to be prickly. ▶ **pincharse** vpr 1. (*punzarse - persona*) to prick o.s.; (*- rueda*) to get a puncture. 2. (*inyectarse*): ~**se** (*algo*) (*medicamento*) to inject o.s. (with sthg); *fam* (*droga*) to shoot up (with sthg).

pinchazo m 1. (*punzada*) prick. 2. (*marca*) needle mark. 3. (*de neumático, balón etc*) puncture, flat Am.

pinche ♦ m y f kitchen boy (f kitchen maid). ♦ adj Amer fam damned.

pinchito m (CULIN) 1. (*tapa*) aperitif on a stick. 2. (*pincho moruno*) shish kebab.

pincho m 1. (*punta*) (sharp) point. 2. (*espina - de planta*) prickle, thorn. 3. (CULIN) snack food on a stick; ~ **moruno** shish kebab.

pinga f Amer vulg prick, cock.

pingajo m fam despec rag.

pingo m fam despec (*pingajo*) rag.

ping-pong [pin'pon] m table-tennis.

pingüino m penguin.

pinitos mpl: **hacer** ~ lit & fig to take one's first steps.

pino m pine; **en el quinto** ~ in the middle of nowhere; **los Pinos** *official residence of the Mexican president*.

LOS PINOS

Los Pinos is the official residence of the Mexican president and the seat of the Mexican government. It is here that the president holds Cabinet meetings and receives State visits.

pinta → **pinto**.

pintado, -da adj 1. (*coloreado*) coloured; '**recién** ~' 'wet paint'. 2. (*maquillado*) made-up. 3. (*moteado*) speckled. ▶ **pintada** f (*escrito*) graffiti (U).

pintalabios m inv lipstick.

pintar ♦ vt to paint; ~ **algo de negro** to paint sthg black. ♦ vi 1. (*con pintura*) to paint. 2. (*significar, importar*) to count; **aquí no pinto nada** there's no place for me here; **¿qué pinto yo en este asunto?** where do I come in? ▶ **pintarse** vpr (*maquillarse*) to make o.s. up.

pinto, -ta adj speckled, spotted. ▶ **pinta** f 1. (*lunar*) spot. 2. *fig* (*aspecto*) appearance; **tener pinta de algo** to look o seem sthg; **tiene buena pinta** it looks good. **3.** (*unidad de medida*) pint. **4.** *Amer* (*pintada*) graffiti (U).

pintor, -ra *m y f* painter; *despec* dauber.

pintoresco, -ca *adj* picturesque; *fig* (*extravagante*) colourful.

pintura *f* **1.** (ARTE) painting; **~ a la acuarela** watercolour; **~ al óleo** oil painting; **no poder ver a alguien ni en ~** *fig* not to be able to stand the sight of sb. **2.** (*materia*) paint.

pinza *f* (*gen pl*) **1.** (*gen*) tweezers (*pl*); (*de tender ropa*) peg, clothespin *Am*. **2.** (*de animal*) pincer, claw. **3.** (*pliegue*) fold.

piña *f* **1.** (*del pino*) pine cone. **2.** (*ananás*) pineapple. **3.** *fig* (*conjunto de gente*) close-knit group.

piñata *f* *pot full of sweets*.

PIÑATA

This is an earthenware pot filled with sweets and small gifts which blindfolded children break open with a stick at birthday parties. In Latin America, a papier-mâché doll is used instead of a jar.

---

piñón *m* **1.** (*fruto*) pine nut. **2.** (*rueda dentada*) pinion.

pío, -a *adj* pious. ▶ **pío** *m* cheep, cheeping (U); (*de gallina*) cluck, clucking (U); **no decir ni ~** *fig* not to make a peep.

piojo *m* louse.

piola *adj* *Amer fam* **1.** (*astuto*) shrewd. **2.** (*estupendo*) fabulous.

pionero, -ra *m y f* pioneer.

pipa *f* **1.** (*para fumar*) pipe. **2.** (*pepita*) seed, pip; **~s (de girasol)** *sunflower seeds coated in salt*. **3.** *loc*: **pasarlo** *o* **pasárselo ~** to have a whale of a time.

pipermín, peppermint [piper'min] *m* peppermint liqueur.

pipí *m* *fam* wee-wee; **hacer ~** to have a wee-wee.

pique *m* **1.** (*enfado*) grudge. **2.** (*rivalidad*) rivalry. **3.** *loc*: **irse a ~** (*barco*) to sink; (*negocio*) to go under; (*plan*) to fail.

piquete *m* (*grupo*): **~ de ejecución** firing squad; **~ (de huelga)** picket.

pirado, -da *adj fam* crazy.

piragua *f* canoe.

piragüismo *m* canoeing.

pirámide *f* pyramid.

piraña *f* piranha.

pirarse *vpr fam* to clear off.

pirata ◆ *adj* pirate (*antes de sust*); (*disco*) bootleg. ◆ *m y f lit & fig* pirate; **~ informático** hacker.

piratear ◆ *vi* **1.** (*gen*) to be involved in piracy. **2.** (INFORM) to hack. ◆ *vt* (INFORM) to hack into.

pirenaico, -ca *adj* Pyrenean.

pírex, pyrex® *m* Pyrex®.

Pirineos *mpl*: **los ~** the Pyrenees.

piripi *adj fam* tipsy.

pirómano, -na *m y f* pyromaniac.

piropo *m fam* flirtatious remark, ≃ wolf whistle.

pirotecnia *f* pyrotechnics (U).

pirrarse *vpr fam*: **~ por algo/alguien** to be dead keen on sthg/sb.

pirueta *f* pirouette; **hacer ~s** *fig* (*esfuerzo*) to perform miracles.

piruleta *f* lollipop.

piruli (*pl* pirulis) *m* lollipop.

pis (*pl* pises) *m fam* pee.

pisada *f* **1.** (*acción*) footstep; **seguir las ~s de alguien** to follow in sb's footsteps. **2.** (*huella*) footprint.

pisapapeles *m inv* paperweight.

pisar *vt* **1.** (*con el pie*) to tread on; **~ fuerte** *fig* to be firing on all cylinders. **2.** (*uvas*) to tread. **3.** *fig* (*llegar a*) to set foot in. **4.** *fig* (*despreciar*) to trample on. **5.** *fig* (*anticiparse*): **~ un contrato a alguien** to beat sb to a contract; **~ una idea a alguien** to think of something before sb.

piscina *f* swimming pool.

Piscis ◆ *m* (*zodiaco*) Pisces. ◆ *m y f* (*persona*) Pisces.

piscolabis *m inv fam* snack.

piso *m* **1.** (*vivienda*) flat. **2.** (*planta*) floor. **3.** (*suelo - de carretera*) surface; (*- de edificio*) floor. **4.** (*capa*) layer.

pisotear *vt* **1.** (*con el pie*) to trample on. **2.** (*humillar*) to scorn.

pista *f* **1.** (*gen*) track; **~ de aterrizaje** runway; **~ de baile** dance floor; **~ de esquí** ski slope; **~ de hielo** ice rink; **~ de tenis** tennis court. **2.** *fig* (*indicio*) clue.

pistacho *m* pistachio.

pisto *m* ≃ ratatouille.

pistola *f* **1.** (*arma - con cilindro*) gun; (*- sin cilindro*) pistol. **2.** (*pulverizador*) spraygun; **pintar a ~** to spray-paint.

pistolero, -ra *m y f* (*persona*) gunman. ▶ **pistolera** *f* (*funda*) holster.

pistón *m* **1.** (MEC) piston. **2.** (MÚS - corneta) cornet; (*- llave*) key.

pitada *f Amer fam* drag, puff.

pitar ◆ *vt* **1.** (*arbitrar - partido*) to referee; (*- falta*) to blow for. **2.** (*abuchear*): **~ a alguien** to whistle at sb in disapproval. **3.** Amer fam (dar una calada a) to puff (on). ◆ vi **1.** (tocar el pito) to blow a whistle; (del coche) to toot one's horn. **2.** loc: **salir/irse pitando** to rush out/off.

pitido m whistle.

pitillera f cigarette case.

pitillo m (cigarrillo) cigarette.

pito m **1.** (silbato) whistle. **2.** (claxon) horn.

pitón m (cuerno) horn.

pitonisa f fortune-teller.

pitorrearse vpr fam: **~ (de)** to take the mickey (out of).

pitorro m spout.

pivote (pl **pivotes**), **pívot** (pl **pivots**) m y f (DEP) pivot.

pizarra f **1.** (roca, material) slate. **2.** (encerado) blackboard.

pizca f fam **1.** (gen) tiny bit; (de sal) pinch. **2.** Amer (cosecha) harvest, crop.

pizza ['pitsa] f pizza.

pizzería [pitse'ria] f pizzeria.

placa f **1.** (lámina) plate; (de madera) sheet; **~ solar** solar panel. **2.** (inscripción) plaque; (de policía) badge. **3.** (matrícula) number plate. **4.** (de cocina) ring. **5.** (ELECTRÓN) board. **6. ~ dental** dental plaque.

placaje m tackle.

placenta f placenta.

placentero, -ra adj pleasant.

placer m pleasure; **ha sido un ~ (conocerle)** it has been a pleasure meeting you.

plácido, -da adj (persona) placid; (día, vida, conversación) peaceful.

plafón m (ARQUIT) soffit.

plaga f **1.** (gen) plague; (AGR) blight; (animal) pest. **2.** (epidemia) epidemic.

plagado, -da adj: **~ (de)** infested (with).

plagar vt: **~ de** (propaganda etc) to swamp with; (moscas etc) to infest with.

plagiar vt (copiar) to plagiarize.

plagio m (copia) plagiarism.

plan m **1.** (proyecto, programa) plan. **2.** fam (ligue) date. **3.** fam (modo, forma): **lo dijo en ~ serio** he was serious about it; **¡vaya ~ de vida!** what a life!; **si te pones en ese ~ ...** if you're going to be like that about it ...

plana → **plano**.

plancha f **1.** (para planchar) iron. **2.** (para cocinar) grill; **a la ~** grilled. **3.** (placa) plate; (de madera) sheet. **4.** (IMPRENTA) plate.

planchado m ironing.

planchar vt to iron.

planeador m glider.

planear ◆ vt to plan. ◆ vi **1.** (hacer planes) to plan. **2.** (en el aire) to glide.

planeta m planet.

planicie f plain.

planificación f planning; **~ familiar** family planning.

planificar vt to plan.

planilla f Amer (formulario) form.

plano, -na adj flat. ▶ **plano** m **1.** (diseño, mapa) plan. **2.** (nivel, aspecto) level. **3.** (CIN) shot; **primer ~** close-up. **4.** (GEOM) plane. **5.** loc: **de ~** (golpear) right, directly; (negar) flatly. ▶ **plana** f (página) page; **en primera plana** on the front page.

planta f **1.** (BOT & IND) plant; **~ depuradora** purification plant. **2.** (piso) floor, storey; **~ baja** ground floor. **3.** (del pie) sole.

plantación f **1.** (terreno) plantation. **2.** (acción) planting.

plantado, -da adj standing, planted; **dejar ~ a alguien** fam (cortar la relación) to walk out on sb; (no acudir) to stand sb up; **ser bien ~** to be good-looking.

plantar vt **1.** (sembrar): **~ algo (de)** to plant sthg (with). **2.** (fijar - tienda de campaña) to pitch; (- poste) to put in. **3.** fam (asestar) to deal, to land. ▶ **plantarse** vpr **1.** (gen) to plant o.s. **2.** (en un sitio con rapidez): **~se en** to get to, to reach.

planteamiento m **1.** (exposición) raising, posing. **2.** (enfoque) approach.

plantear vt **1.** (exponer - problema) to pose; (- posibilidad, dificultad, duda) to raise. **2.** (enfocar) to approach. ▶ **plantearse** vpr: **~se algo** to consider sthg, to think about sthg.

plantel m fig (conjunto) group.

plantilla f **1.** (de empresa) staff. **2.** (suela interior) insole. **3.** (patrón) pattern, template.

plantón m: **dar un ~ a alguien** fam to stand sb up.

plañidero, -ra adj plaintive.

plañir vi to moan, to wail.

plasmar vt **1.** fig (reflejar) to give shape to. **2.** (modelar) to shape, to mould. ▶ **plasmarse** vpr to take shape.

plasta ◆ adj mfam: **ser ~** to be a pain. ◆ m y f mfam (pesado) pain, drag.

plástico, -ca adj (gen) plastic. ▶ **plástico** m (gen) plastic.

plastificar vt to plasticize.

plastilina® f = Plasticine®.

plata f **1.** (metal) silver; **~ de ley** sterling silver; **hablar en ~** fam to speak bluntly. **2.** (*objetos de plata*) silverware. **3.** Amer (*dinero*) money.

plataforma *f* **1.** (*gen*) platform. **2.** ~ **petrolífera** oil rig. **3.** *fig* (*punto de partida*) launching pad. **4.** (GEOL) shelf.

platal *m* Amer fam: **un** ~ a fortune.

plátano *m* **1.** (*fruta*) banana. **2.** (*árbol*) banana tree.

platea *f* stalls (*pl*).

plateado, -da *adj* **1.** (*con plata*) silver-plated. **2.** *fig* (*color*) silvery.

platería *f* (*tienda*) silversmith's (shop).

plática *f* (*charla*) talk, chat.

platicar *vi* to talk, to chat.

platillo *m* **1.** (*plato pequeño*) small plate; (*de taza*) saucer. **2.** (*de una balanza*) pan. **3.** (*gen pl*) (MÚS) cymbal. ▶ **platillo volante** *m* flying saucer.

platina *f* (*de microscopio*) slide.

platino *m* (*metal*) platinum. ▶ **platinos** *mpl* (AUTOM & MEC) contact points.

plato *m* **1.** (*recipiente*) plate, dish; **lavar los** ~**s** to do the washing-up; **pagar los** ~**s rotos** to carry the can. **2.** (*parte de una comida*) course; **primer** ~ first course, starter; **de primer** ~ for starters; **segundo** ~ second course, main course. **3.** (*comida*) dish; ~ **combinado** single-course meal which usually consists of meat or fish accompanied by chips and vegetables; ~ **principal** main course. **4.** (*de tocadiscos, microondas*) turntable.

plató *m* set.

platónico, -ca *adj* Platonic.

platudo, -da *adj* Amer fam loaded, rolling in it.

plausible *adj* **1.** (*admisible*) acceptable. **2.** (*posible*) plausible.

playa *f* **1.** (*en el mar*) beach; **ir a la** ~ **de vacaciones** to go on holiday to the seaside. **2.** Amer (*aparcamiento*): ~ **de estacionamiento** car park.

play-back ['pleiβak] (*pl* **play-backs**) *m*: **hacer** ~ to mime (the lyrics).

playero, -ra *adj* beach (*antes de sust*). ▶ **playeras** *fpl* **1.** (*de deporte*) tennis shoes. **2.** (*para la playa*) canvas shoes.

plaza *f* **1.** (*en una población*) square. **2.** (*sitio*) place. **3.** (*asiento*) seat; **de dos** ~**s** two-seater (*antes de sust*). **4.** (*puesto de trabajo*) position, job; ~ **vacante** vacancy. **5.** (*mercado*) market, marketplace. **6.** (TAUROM): ~ **(de toros)** bull-ring.

plazo *m* **1.** (*de tiempo*) period (of time); **en un** ~ **de un mes** within a month; **mañana termina el** ~ **de inscripción** the deadline for registration is tomorrow; **a corto/largo** ~ (*gen*) in the short/long

term; (ECON) short/long term. **2.** (*de dinero*) instalment; **a** ~**s** in instalments, on hire purchase.

plazoleta *f* small square.

plebe *f*: **la** ~ *lit & fig* the plebs.

plebeyo, -ya *adj* **1.** (HIST) plebeian. **2.** (*vulgar*) common.

plebiscito *m* plebiscite.

plegable *adj* collapsible, foldaway; (*chair*) folding.

plegar *vt* to fold; (*mesita, hamaca*) to fold away.

plegaria *f* prayer.

pleito *m* **1.** (DER) (*litigio*) legal action (U), lawsuit. **2.** (*disputa*) argument, quarrel.

plenario, -ria *adj* plenary.

plenilunio *m* full moon.

plenitud *f* **1.** (*totalidad*) completeness, fullness. **2.** (*abundancia*) abundance.

pleno, -na *adj* full, complete; (*derecho*) perfect; **en** ~ **día** in broad daylight; **en plena guerra** in the middle of the war; **le dio en plena cara** she hit him right in the face; **en** ~ **uso de sus facultades** in full command of his faculties; **en plena forma** on top form. ▶ **pleno** *m* (*reunión*) plenary meeting.

pletina *f* cassette deck.

pletórico, -ca *adj*: ~ **de** full of.

pliego *m* **1.** (*hoja*) sheet (of paper). **2.** (*carta, documento*) sealed document o letter; ~ **de condiciones** specifications (*pl*). **3.** (IMPRENTA) signature.

pliegue *m* **1.** (*gen & GEOL*) fold. **2.** (*en un plisado*) pleat.

plisado *m* pleating.

plomería *f* Amer plumber's.

plomero *m* Amer plumber.

plomizo, -za *adj* (*color*) leaden.

plomo *m* **1.** (*metal*) lead; **caer a** ~ to fall o drop like a stone. **2.** (*pieza de metal*) lead weight. **3.** (*fusible*) fuse.

pluma ◆ *f* **1.** (*de ave*) feather. **2.** (*para escribir*) (fountain) pen; (HIST) quill; ~ **estilográfica** fountain pen. ◆ *adj inv* (DEP) featherweight.

plum-cake [pluŋ'keik] (*pl* **plum-cakes**) *m* fruit cake.

plumero *m* feather duster; **vérsele a alguien el** ~ *fam* to see through sb.

plumier (*pl* **plumiers**) *m* pencil box.

plumilla *f* nib.

plumón *m* (*de ave*) down.

plural *adj & m* plural.

pluralidad *f* diversity.

pluralismo *m* pluralism.

pluralizar *vi* to generalize.

pluriempleo m: hacer ~ to have more than one job.

plus (pl pluses) m bonus.

pluscuamperfecto adj & m pluperfect.

plusmarca f record.

plusvalía f (ECON) appreciation, added value.

Plutón Pluto.

pluvial adj rain (antes de sust).

p.m. (abrev de post meridiem) p.m.

PM (abrev de policía militar) f MP.

PNB (abrev de producto nacional bruto) m GNP.

PNV (abrev de Partido Nacionalista Vasco) m Basque nationalist party.

población f 1. (ciudad) town, city; (pueblo) village. 2. (habitantes) population.

poblado, -da adj 1. (habitado) inhabited; una zona muy poblada a densely populated area. 2. fig (lleno) full; (barba, cejas) bushy. ▶ **poblado** m settlement.

poblador, -ra m y f settler.

poblar vt 1. (establecerse en) to settle, to populate. 2. fig (llenar): ~ (de) (plantas, árboles) to plant (with); (peces etc) to stock (with). 3. (habitar) to inhabit. ▶ **poblarse** vpr: ~se (de) to fill up (with).

pobre ◆ adj poor; ¡~ hombre! poor man!; ¡~ de mí! poor me! ◆ m y f 1. (gen) poor person; los ~s the poor; ¡el ~! poor thing! 2. (mendigo) beggar.

pobreza f (escasez) poverty; ~ de lack o scarcity of.

pochismo m Amer fam language mistake caused by English influence.

pocho, -cha adj 1. (persona) off-colour. 2. (fruta) over-ripe. 3. Amer fam (americanizado) Americanized.

pocilga f lit & fig pigsty.

pocillo m Amer small cup.

pócima f (poción) potion.

poción f potion.

poco, -ca ◆ adj little, not much, (pl) few, not many; poca agua not much water; de poca importancia of little importance; hay ~s árboles there aren't many trees; pocas personas lo saben few o not many people know it; tenemos ~ tiempo we don't have much time; hace ~ tiempo not long ago; dame unos ~ días give me a few days. ◆ pron little, not much, (pl) few, not many; queda ~ there's not much left; tengo muy ~s I don't have very many, I have very few; ~s hay que sepan tanto not many peo-

ple know so much; un ~ a bit; ¿me dejas un ~? can I have a bit?; un ~ de a bit of; un ~ de sentido común a bit of common sense; unos ~s a few. ▶ **poco** adv 1. (escasamente) not much; este niño come ~ this boy doesn't eat much; es ~ común it's not very common; es un ~ triste it's rather sad; por ~ almost, nearly. 2. (brevemente): tardaré muy ~ I won't be long; al ~ de ... shortly after ...; dentro de ~ soon, in a short time; hace ~ not long ago; a ~ (progresivamente) little by little; ¡~ a ~! (despacio) steady on!

podar vt to prune.

podenco m hound.

poder ◆ m 1. (gen) power; estar en/hacerse con el ~ to be in/to seize power; ~ adquisitivo purchasing power; tener ~ de convocatoria to be a crowd-puller; ~es fácticos the church, military and press. 2. (posesión): estar en ~ de alguien to be in sb's hands. 3. (gen pl) (autorización) power, authorization; dar ~es a alguien para que haga algo to authorize sb to do sthg; por ~es by proxy. ◆ vi 1. (tener facultad) can, to be able to; no puedo decírtelo I can't tell you, I'm unable to tell you. 2. (tener permiso) can, may; no puedo salir por la noche I'm not allowed to o I can't go out at night; ¿se puede fumar aquí? may I smoke here? 3. (ser capaz moralmente) can; no podemos portarnos así con él we can't treat him like that. 4. (tener posibilidad, ser posible) may, can; podías haber cogido el tren you could have caught the train; puede estallar la guerra war could o may break out; ¡hubiera podido invitarnos! (expresa enfado) she could o might have invited us! 5. loc: a o hasta más no ~ as much as can be; es avaro a más no ~ he's as miserly as can be; no ~ más (estar cansado) to be too tired to carry on; (estar harto de comer) to be full (up); (estar enfadado) to have had enough; ¿se puede? may I come in? ◆ v impers (ser posible) may; puede que llueva it may o might rain; ¿vendrás mañana? – puede will you come tomorrow? – I may do; puede ser perhaps, maybe. ◆ vt (ser más fuerte que) to be stronger than. ▶ **poder con** vi + prep 1. (enfermedad, rival) to be able to overcome. 2. (tarea, problema) to be able to cope with. 3. (soportar): no ~ con algo/alguien not to be able to stand sthg/sb; no puedo con la hipocresía I can't stand hypocrisy.

poderío m (poder) power.

poderoso, -sa *adj* powerful.

podio, podium *m* podium.

podólogo, -ga *m y f* chiropodist.

podrá → **poder**.

podrido, -da ◆ *pp* → **pudrir**. ◆ *adj* rotten.

poema *m* poem.

poesía *f* 1. (*género literario*) poetry. 2. (*poema*) poem.

poeta *m y f* poet.

poético, -ca *adj* poetic.

poetisa *f* female poet.

póker = **póquer**.

polaco, -ca *adj, m y f* Polish. ▶ **polaco** *m* (*lengua*) Polish.

polar *adj* polar.

polarizar *vt fig* (*miradas, atención, esfuerzo*) to concentrate. ▶ **polarizarse** *vpr* (*vida política, opinión pública*) to become polarized.

polaroid® *f inv* Polaroid®.

polca *f* polka.

polea *f* pulley.

polémico, -ca *adj* controversial. ▶ **polémica** *f* controversy.

polemizar *vi* to argue, to debate.

polen *m* pollen.

poleo *m* pennyroyal.

poli *fam* ◆ *m y f* cop. ◆ *f* cops (*pl*).

polichinela *m* 1. (*personaje*) Punchinello. 2. (*títere*) puppet, marionette.

policía ◆ *m y f* policeman (*f* policewoman). ◆ *f:* **la ~** the police.

policiaco, -ca, policíaco, -ca *adj* police (*antes de sust*); (*novela, película*) detective (*antes de sust*).

policial *adj* police (*antes de sust*).

polideportivo, -va *adj* multi-sport; (*gimnasio*) multi-use. ▶ **polideportivo** *m* sports centre.

poliéster *m inv* polyester.

polietileno *m* polythene Br, polyethylene Am.

polifacético, -ca *adj* multifaceted, versatile.

poligamia *f* polygamy.

polígamo, -ma *adj* polygamous.

polígloto, -ta, políglota, -ta *adj, m y f* polyglot.

polígono *m* 1. (GEOM) polygon. 2. (*terreno*): **~ industrial/residencial** industrial/housing estate; **~ de tiro** firing range.

polilla *f* moth.

poliomelitis, polio *f inv* polio.

polipiel *f* artificial skin.

Polisario (*abrev de* **Frente Popular para la Liberación de Sakiet el Hamra y Río de Oro**) *m:* **el (Frente) ~** the Polisario Front.

politécnico, -ca *adj* polytechnic. ▶ **politécnica** *f* polytechnic.

político, -ca *adj* 1. (*de gobierno*) political. 2. (*pariente*): **hermano ~** brother-in-law; **familia política** in-laws (*pl*). ▶ **político** *m* politician. ▶ **política** *f* 1. (*arte de gobernar*) politics (U). 2. (*modo de gobernar, táctica*) policy.

politizar *vt* to politicize. ▶ **politizarse** *vpr* to become politicized.

polivalente *adj* (*vacuna, suero*) polyvalent.

póliza *f* 1. (*de seguro*) (insurance) policy. 2. (*sello*) *stamp on a document showing that a certain tax has been paid.*

polizón *m* stowaway.

polla → **pollo**.

pollera *f* Amer skirt.

pollería *f* poultry shop.

pollito *m* chick.

pollo, -lla *m y f* (ZOOL) chick. ▶ **pollo** *m* (CULIN) chicken. ▶ **polla** *f vulg* cock, prick.

polo *m* 1. (*gen*) pole; **~ norte/sur** North/South Pole; **ser ~s opuestos** *fig* to be poles apart. 2. (ELECTR) terminal. 3. (*helado*) ice lolly. 4. (*jersey*) polo shirt. 5. (DEP) polo.

pololo, -la *m y f Amer fam* boyfriend (*f* girlfriend).

Polonia Poland.

poltrón, -ona *adj* lazy. ▶ **poltrona** *f* easy chair.

polución *f* (*contaminación*) pollution.

polvareda *f* dust cloud.

polvera *f* powder compact.

polvo *m* 1. (*en el aire*) dust; **limpiar** o **quitar el ~** to do the dusting. 2. (*de un producto*) powder; **en ~** powdered; **~s de talco** talcum powder; **~s picapica** itching powder; **estar hecho ~** *fam* to be knackered; **hacer ~ algo** to smash sthg. ▶ **polvos** *mpl* (*maquillaje*) powder (U); **ponerse ~s** to powder one's face.

pólvora *f* (*sustancia explosiva*) gunpowder; **correr como la ~** to spread like wildfire.

polvoriento, -ta *adj* (*superficie*) dusty; (*sustancia*) powdery.

polvorín *m* munitions dump.

polvorón *m crumbly sweet made from flour, butter and sugar.*

pomada *f* ointment.

pomelo *m* (*fruto*) grapefruit.

pómez → **piedra**.

pomo *m* knob.

pompa *f* 1. (*suntuosidad*) pomp. 2. (*ostentación*) show, ostentation. 3. **~ (de**

pompis

jabón) (soap) bubble. ▶ **pompas
fúnebres** *fpl* (*servicio*) undertaker's (*sg*).
pompis *m inv fam* bottom, backside.
pompón *m* pompom.
pomposo, -sa *adj* 1. (*suntuoso*) sumptuous; (*ostentoso*) showy. 2. (*lenguaje*)
pompous.
pómulo *m* (*hueso*) cheekbone.
ponchar *vt Amer* to puncture.
ponche *m* punch.
poncho *m* poncho.
ponderar *vt* 1. (*alabar*) to praise.
2. (*considerar*) to weigh up.
ponedero *m* nesting box.
ponedor, -ra *adj* egg-laying.
ponencia *f* (*conferencia*) lecture, paper;
(*informe*) report.
poner ◆ *vt* 1. (*gen*) to put; (*colocar*) to
place, to put. 2. (*vestir*): ~ **algo a alguien**
to put sthg on sb. 3. (*contribuir, invertir*)
to put in; ~ **dinero en el negocio** to put
money into the business; ~ **algo de mi/
tu etc parte** to do my/your *etc* bit.
4. (*hacer estar de cierta manera*): ~ **a alguien
en un aprieto/de mal humor** to put sb in
a difficult position/in a bad mood; **le
has puesto colorado** you've made him
blush. 5. (*calificar*): ~ **a alguien de algo** to
call sb sthg. 6. (*oponer*): ~ **obstáculos a
algo** to hinder sthg; ~ **pegas a algo** to
raise objections to sthg. 7. (*asignar
- precio, medida*) to fix, to settle; (- *multa,
tarea*) to give; **le pusieron Mario** they
called him Mario. 8. (TELECOM - *telegrama, fax*) to send; (- *conferencia*) to make;
¿me pones con él? can you put me
through to him? 9. (*conectar - televisión
etc*) to switch o put on; (- *despertador*) to
set; (- *instalación, gas*) to put in. 10. (CIN,
TEATR & TV) to show; **¿qué ponen en la
tele?** what's on the telly? 11. (*montar - negocio*) to set up; **ha puesto una
tienda** she has opened a shop. 12. (*decorar*) to do up; **han puesto su casa con
mucho lujo** they've done up their house
in real style. 13. (*suponer*) to suppose;
pongamos que sucedió así (let's) suppose that's what happened; **pon que
necesitemos cinco días** suppose we
need five days; **poniendo que todo salga
bien** assuming everything goes according to plan. 14. (*decir*) to say; **¿qué pone
ahí?** what does it say? 15. (*huevo*) to lay.
◆ *vi* (*ave*) to lay (eggs). ▶ **ponerse**
◆ *vpr* 1. (*colocarse*) to put o.s.; ~**se de pie**
to stand up; **ponte en la ventana** stand
by the window. 2. (*ropa, gafas, maquillaje*)
to put on. 3. (*estar de cierta manera*) to go,

to become; **se puso rojo de ira** he went
red with anger; **se puso colorado** he
blushed; **se puso muy guapa** she made
herself attractive. 4. (*iniciar*): ~**se a
hacer algo** to start doing sthg. 5. (*de
salud*): ~**se malo** o **enfermo** to fall ill; ~**se
bien** to get better. 6. (*llenarse*): ~**se de
algo** to get covered in sthg; **se puso de
barro hasta las rodillas** he got covered
in mud up to the knees. 7. (*suj: astro*) to
set. 8. (*llegar*): ~**se en** to get to. ◆ *v
impers Amer fam* (*parecer*): **se me pone que
...** it seems to me that ...
poney = **poni**.
pongo → **poner**.
poni, poney ['poni] *m* pony.
poniente *m* (*occidente*) West; (*viento*)
west wind.
pontífice *m* Pope, Pontiff.
pontón *m* pontoon.
pop *adj* pop.
popa *f* stern.
pope *m fam fig* (*pez gordo*) big shot.
popote *m Amer* drinking straw.
populacho *m despec* mob, masses (*pl*).
popular *adj* 1. (*del pueblo*) of the people; (*arte, música*) folk. 2. (*famoso*) popular.
popularidad *f* popularity.
popularizar *vt* to popularize.
▶ **popularizarse** *vpr* to become
popular.
popurrí *m* potpourri.
póquer, póker *m* (*juego*) poker.
por *prep* 1. (*causa*) because of; **se
enfadó ~ tu comportamiento** she got
angry because of your behaviour.
2. (*finalidad*) (*antes de infin*) (in order) to;
(*antes de sust, pron*) for; **lo hizo ~ complacerte** he did it to please you; **lo hice ~
ella** I did it for her. 3. (*medio, modo,
agente*) by; ~ **mensajero/fax** by courier/
fax; ~ **escrito** in writing; **lo cogieron ~ el
brazo** they took him by the arm; **el
récord fue batido ~ el atleta** the record
was broken by the athlete. 4. (*tiempo
aproximado*): **creo que la boda será ~ abril**
I think the wedding will be some time
in April. 5. (*tiempo concreto*): ~ **la
mañana/tarde** in the morning/afternoon; ~ **la noche** at night; **ayer salimos ~
la noche** we went out last night; ~ **unos
días** for a few days. 6. (*lugar - aproximadamente en*): **¿~ dónde vive?** whereabouts does he live?; **vive ~ las afueras**
he lives somewhere on the outskirts;
había papeles ~ el suelo there were
papers all over the floor. 7. (*lugar - a*

través de) through; **iba paseando ~ el bosque/la calle** she was walking through the forest/along the street; **pasar ~ la aduana** to go through customs. **8.** (*a cambio de, en lugar de*) for; **lo ha comprado ~ poco dinero** she bought it for very little; **cambió el coche ~ la moto** he exchanged his car for a motorbike; **él lo hará ~ mí** he'll do it for me. **9.** (*distribución*) per; **cien pesetas ~ unidad** a hundred pesetas each; **20 kms ~ hora** 20 km an o per hour. **10.** (MAT): **dos ~ dos igual a cuatro** two times two is four. **11.** (*en busca de*) for; **baja ~ tabaco** go down to the shops for some cigarettes; **a ~** for; **vino a ~ las entradas** she came for the tickets. **12.** (*concesión*): **~ más o mucho que lo intentes no lo conseguirás** however hard you try o try as you might, you'll never manage it; **no me cae bien, ~ (muy) simpático que te parezca** you may think he's nice, but I don't like him. ▶ **por qué** *pron* why; **¿~ qué lo dijo?** why did she say it?; **¿~ qué no vienes?** why don't you come?

porcelana *f* (*material*) porcelain, china.

porcentaje *m* percentage.

porche *m* (*soportal*) arcade; (*entrada*) porch.

porción *f* portion, piece.

pordiosero, -ra *m y f* beggar.

porfía *f* (*insistencia*) persistence; (*tozudez*) stubbornness.

porfiar *vi* **1.** (*disputar*) to argue obstinately. **2.** (*empeñarse*): **~ en** to be insistent on.

pormenor *m* (*gen pl*) detail.

porno *adj fam* porno.

pornografía *f* pornography.

pornográfico, -ca *adj* pornographic.

poro *m* pore.

poroso, -sa *adj* porous.

poroto *m* *Amer* bean; **~ verde** green o French bean.

porque *conj* **1.** (*debido a que*) because. **2.** (*para que*) so that, in order that.

porqué *m* reason; **el ~ de** the reason for.

porquería *f* **1.** (*suciedad*) filth. **2.** (*cosa de mala calidad*) rubbish (U).

porra *f* **1.** (*palo*) club; (*de policía*) truncheon. **2.** *loc*: **mandar a alguien a la ~** *fam* to tell sb to go to hell.

porrazo *m* (*golpe*) bang, blow; (*caída*) bump.

porro *m fam* (*de droga*) joint.

porrón *m* *glass wine jar used for drinking wine from its long spout.*

portaaviones = **portaviones**.

portada *f* **1.** (*de libro*) title page; (*de revista*) (front) cover; (*de periódico*) front page. **2.** (*de disco*) sleeve.

portador, -ra *m y f* carrier, bearer; **al ~** (COM) to the bearer.

portaequipajes *m inv* boot Br, trunk Am.

portafolios *m inv*, **portafolio** *m* (*carpeta*) file; (*maletín*) attaché case.

portal *m* (*entrada*) entrance hall; (*puerta*) main door.

portalámparas *m inv* socket.

portamonedas *m inv* purse.

portar *vt* to carry. ▶ **portarse** *vpr* to behave; **se ha portado bien conmigo** she has treated me well; **~se mal** to misbehave.

portátil *adj* portable.

portaviones, portaaviones *m inv* aircraft carrier.

portavoz *m y f* (*persona*) spokesman (*f* spokeswoman).

portazo *m*: **dar un ~** to slam the door.

porte *m* **1.** (*gen pl*) (*gasto de transporte*) carriage; **~ debido/pagado** (COM) carriage due/paid. **2.** (*transporte*) carriage, transport. **3.** (*aspecto*) bearing, demeanour.

portento *m* wonder, marvel.

portentoso, -sa *adj* wonderful, amazing.

portería *f* **1.** (*de casa, colegio*) caretaker's office o lodge; (*de hotel, ministerio*) porter's office o lodge. **2.** (DEP) goal, goalmouth.

portero, -ra *m y f* **1.** (*de casa, colegio*) caretaker; (*de hotel, ministerio*) porter; **~ automático** o **electrónico** o **eléctrico** entry-phone. **2.** (DEP) goalkeeper.

pórtico *m* **1.** (*fachada*) portico. **2.** (*arcada*) arcade.

portillo *m* (*puerta pequeña*) wicket gate.

portuario, -ria *adj* port (*antes de sust*), harbour (*antes de sust*); (*de los muelles*) dock (*antes de sust*); **trabajador ~** docker.

Portugal Portugal.

portugués, -esa *adj, m y f* Portuguese. ▶ **portugués** *m* (*lengua*) Portuguese.

porvenir *m* future.

pos ▶ **en pos de** *loc prep* **1.** (*detrás de*) behind. **2.** (*en busca de*) after.

posada *f* **1.** (*fonda*) inn, guest house. **2.** (*hospedaje*) lodging, accommodation.

posaderas *fpl fam* backside (*sg*), bottom (*sg*).

posar ◆ vt to put o lay down; (mano, mirada) to rest. ◆ vi to pose. ▶ **posarse** vpr 1. (gen) to settle. 2. (pájaro) to perch; (nave, helicóptero) to come down.

posavasos m inv coaster; (en pub) beer mat.

posdata, postdata f postscript.

pose f pose.

poseedor, -ra m y f owner; (de cargo, acciones, récord) holder.

poseer vt (ser dueño de) to own; (estar en poder de) to have, to possess.

poseído, -da adj: ~ por possessed by.

posesión f possession.

posesivo, -va adj possessive.

poseso, -sa m y f possessed person.

posgraduado, -da, postgraduado, -da adj, m y f postgraduate.

posguerra, postguerra f post-war period.

posibilidad f possibility, chance; **cabe la ~ de que ...** there is a chance that ...

posibilitar vt to make possible.

posible adj possible; **es ~ que llueva** it could rain; **dentro de lo ~, en lo ~** as far as possible; **de ser ~** if possible; **hacer (todo) lo ~** to do everything possible; **lo antes ~** as soon as possible.

posición f 1. (gen) position. 2. (categoría - social) status (U); (- económica) situation.

posicionarse vpr to take a position o stance.

positivo, -va adj (gen & ELECTR) positive.

poso m sediment; fig trace.

posponer vt 1. (relegar) to put behind, to relegate. 2. (aplazar) to postpone.

pospuesto, -ta pp → **posponer**.

posta ▶ **a posta** loc adv on purpose.

postal ◆ adj postal. ◆ f postcard.

postdata = **posdata**.

poste m post, pole; (DEP) post.

póster (pl posters) m poster.

postergar vt 1. (retrasar) to postpone. 2. (relegar) to put behind, to relegate.

posteridad f 1. (generación futura) posterity. 2. (futuro) posterity.

posterior adj 1. (en el espacio) rear, back. 2. (en el tiempo) subsequent, later; **~ a** subsequent to, after.

posteriori ▶ **a posteriori** loc adv later, afterwards.

posterioridad f: **con ~** later, subsequently.

postgraduado, -da = **posgraduado**.

postguerra = **posguerra**.

postigo m (contraventana) shutter.

postín m showiness; **darse ~** to show off; **de ~** posh.

postizo, -za adj (falso) false. ▶ **postizo** m hairpiece.

postor, -ra m y f bidder.

postrado, -da adj prostrate.

postre m dessert, pudding; **a la ~** fig in the end.

postrero, -ra adj (antes de sust masculino sg: **postrer**) culto last.

postrimerías fpl final stages.

postulado m postulate.

postular ◆ vt (exigir) to call for. ◆ vi (para colectas) to collect.

póstumo, -ma adj posthumous.

postura f 1. (posición) position, posture. 2. (actitud) attitude, stance.

potable adj (bebible) drinkable; **agua ~** drinking water.

potaje m (CULIN - guiso) vegetable stew; (- caldo) vegetable stock.

potasio m potassium.

pote m pot.

potencia f (gen, MAT & POLÍT) power; **tiene mucha ~** it's very powerful.

potencial ◆ adj (gen & FÍS) potential. ◆ m 1. (fuerza) power. 2. (posibilidades) potential. 3. (GRAM) conditional.

potenciar vt 1. (fomentar) to encourage, to promote. 2. (reforzar) to boost.

potente adj powerful.

potra → **potro**.

potrero m Amer field, pasture.

potro, -tra m y f (ZOOL) colt (f filly). ▶ **potro** m (DEP) vaulting horse.

pozo m well; (de mina) shaft.

p.p. 1. (abrev de **por poder**) pp. 2. (abrev de **porte pagado**) c/p.

PP (abrev de **Partido Popular**) m Spanish political party to the right of the political spectrum.

práctica → **práctico**.

practicante ◆ adj practising. ◆ m y f 1. (de deporte) practitioner; (de religión) practising member of a Church. 2. (MED) medical assistant.

practicar ◆ vt 1. (gen) to practise; (deporte) to play. 2. (realizar) to carry out, to perform. ◆ vi to practise.

práctico, -ca adj practical. ▶ **práctica** f 1. (gen) practice; (de un deporte) playing; **en la práctica** in practice. 2. (clase no teórica) practical.

pradera f large meadow, prairie.

prado m meadow. ▶ **Prado** m: **el**

(Museo del) Prado the Prado (Museum).
Praga Prague.
pragmático, -ca ◆ adj pragmatic.
◆ m y f (persona) pragmatist.
pral. abrev de **principal**.
praliné m praline.
preacuerdo m draft agreement.
preámbulo m (introducción - de libro)
foreword, preface; (- de congreso, conferencia) introduction.
precalentar vt 1. (CULIN) to pre-heat.
2. (DEP) to warm up.
precario, -ria adj precarious.
precaución f 1. (prudencia) caution,
care. 2. (medida) precaution; **tomar precauciones** to take precautions.
precaver vt to guard against. ► **precaverse** vpr to take precautions.
precavido, -da adj (prevenido) prudent; **es muy ~** he always comes prepared.
precedente ◆ adj previous, preceding. ◆ m precedent.
preceder vt to go before, to precede.
preceptivo, -va adj obligatory, compulsory. ► **preceptiva** f rules (pl).
precepto m precept.
preciado, -da adj valuable, prized.
preciar vt to appreciate. ► **preciarse** vpr to have self-respect; **~se de** to be proud of.
precintar vt to seal.
precinto m seal.
precio m lit & fig price; **a cualquier ~** at any price; **al ~ de** fig at the cost of; **~ de fábrica/de coste** factory/cost price; **~ de salida** starting price; **~ de venta (al público)** retail price.
preciosidad f (cosa bonita): **¡es una ~!** it's lovely o beautiful!
precioso, -sa adj 1. (valioso) precious.
2. (bonito) lovely, beautiful.
precipicio m precipice.
precipitación f 1. (apresuramiento) haste. 2. (lluvia): **~ (pluvial)** rainfall (U).
precipitado, -da adj hasty.
precipitar vt 1. (arrojar) to throw o hurl down. 2. (acelerar) to speed up.
► **precipitarse** vpr 1. (caer) to plunge (down). 2. (acelerarse - acontecimientos etc) to speed up. 3. (apresurarse): **~se (hacia)** to rush (towards). 4. (obrar irreflexivamente) to act rashly.
precisamente adv (justamente): **¡~!** exactly!, precisely!; **~ por eso** for that very reason; **~ tú lo sugeriste** in fact it was you who suggested it.
precisar vt 1. (determinar) to fix, to set;

(aclarar) to specify exactly. 2. (necesitar) to need, to require.
precisión f accuracy, precision.
preciso, -sa adj 1. (determinado, conciso) precise. 2. (necesario): **ser ~ para (algo/hacer algo)** to be necessary (for sthg/to do sthg); **es ~ que vengas** you must come.
precocinado, -da adj pre-cooked.
preconcebido, -da adj (idea) preconceived; (plan) drawn up in advance.
preconcebir vt to draw up in advance.
preconizar vt to recommend.
precoz adj (persona) precocious.
precursor, -ra m y f precursor.
predecesor, -ra m y f predecessor.
predecir vt to predict.
predestinado, -da adj: **~ (a)** predestined (to).
predestinar vt to predestine.
predeterminar vt to predetermine.
prédica f sermon.
predicado m (GRAM) predicate.
predicador, -ra m y f preacher.
predicar vt & vi to preach.
predicción f prediction; (del tiempo) forecast.
predicho, -cha pp → **predecir**.
predilección f: **~ (por)** preference (for).
predilecto, -ta adj favourite.
predisponer vt: **~ (a)** to predispose (to).
predisposición f 1. (aptitud): **~ para** aptitude for. 2. (tendencia): **~ a** a predisposition to.
predispuesto, -ta ◆ pp → **predisponer**. ◆ adj: **~ (a)** predisposed (to).
predominante adj predominant;
(viento, actitudes) prevailing.
predominar vi: **~ (sobre)** to predominate o prevail (over).
predominio m preponderance, predominance (U).
preelectoral adj pre-election (antes de sust).
preeminente adj preeminent.
preescolar adj nursery (antes de sust), preschool.
prefabricado, -da adj prefabricated.
prefabricar vt to prefabricate.
prefacio m preface.
preferencia f preference; **con o de ~** preferably; **tener ~** (AUTOM) to have right of way; **tener ~ por** to have a preference for.
preferente adj preferential.

preferentemente *adv* preferably.
preferible *adj*: ~ (a) preferable (to).
preferido, -da *adj* favourite.
preferir *vt*: ~ algo (a algo) to prefer sthg (to sthg).
prefijo *m* 1. (GRAM) prefix. 2. (TELECOM) (telephone) dialling code.
pregón *m* (*discurso*) speech; (*bando*) proclamation.
pregonar *vt* 1. (*bando etc*) to proclaim. 2. *fig* (*secreto*) to spread about.
pregunta *f* question; **hacer una ~** to ask a question.
preguntar ◆ *vt* to ask; ~ algo a alguien to ask sb sthg. ◆ *vi*: ~ por alguien to ask about o after sb; ~ por algo to enquire about sthg. ▶ **preguntarse** *vpr*: ~se (si) to wonder (whether).
prehistoria *f* prehistory.
prehistórico, -ca *adj* prehistoric.
prejuicio *m* prejudice.
preliminar ◆ *adj* preliminary. ◆ *m* (*gen pl*) preliminary.
preludio *m* (*gen & MÚS*) prelude.
prematrimonial *adj* premarital.
prematuro, -ra *adj* premature.
premeditación *f* premeditation.
premeditar *vt* to think out in advance.
premiar *vt* 1. (*recompensar*) to reward. 2. (*dar un premio a*) to give a prize to.
premier (*pl* **premiers**) *m* British prime minister.
premio *m* (*en competición*) prize; (*recompensa*) reward; ~ gordo first prize.
premisa *f* premise.
premonición *f* premonition.
premura *f* (*urgencia*) urgency.
prenatal *adj* prenatal, antenatal.
prenda *f* 1. (*vestido*) garment, article of clothing. 2. (*garantía*) pledge; dejar algo en ~ to leave sthg as a pledge. 3. (*de un juego*) forfeit. 4. *loc*: no soltar ~ not to say a word.
prendar *vt* to enchant.
prender ◆ *vt* 1. (*arrestar*) to arrest, to apprehend. 2. (*sujetar*) to fasten. 3. (*encender*) to light. 4. (*agarrar*) to grip. ◆ *vi* (*arder*) to catch (fire). ▶ **prenderse** *vpr* (*arder*) to catch fire.
prendido, -da *adj* caught.
prensa *f* 1. (*gen*) press; ~ del corazón romantic magazines (*pl*). 2. (*imprenta*) printing press.
prensar *vt* to press.
preñado, -da *adj* 1. (*mujer*) pregnant. 2. *fig* (*lleno*): ~ de full of.
preocupación *f* concern, worry.

preocupado, -da *adj*: ~ (por) worried o concerned (about).
preocupar *vt* 1. (*inquietar*) to worry. 2. (*importar*) to bother. ▶ **preocuparse** *vpr* 1. (*inquietarse*): ~se (por) to worry (about), to be worried (about). 2. (*encargarse*): ~se de algo to take care of sthg; ~se de hacer algo to see to it that sthg is done; ~se de que ... to make sure that ...
preparación *f* 1. (*gen*) preparation. 2. (*conocimientos*) training.
preparado, -da *adj* 1. (*dispuesto*) ready; (*de antemano*) prepared. 2. (CULIN) ready-cooked. ▶ **preparado** *m* (FARM) preparation.
preparar *vt* 1. (*gen*) to prepare; (*trampa*) to set, to lay; (*maletas*) to pack. 2. (*examen*) to prepare for. 3. (DEP) to train. ▶ **prepararse** *vpr*: ~se (para algo) to prepare o.s. o get ready (for sthg); ~se para hacer algo to prepare o get ready to do sthg.
preparativo, -va *adj* preparatory, preliminary. ▶ **preparativos** *mpl* preparations.
preparatoria *f* (*Amér*) pre-university course in Latin America.

PREPARATORIA

This is the name given to the three years of pre-university education in Latin America. Students usually begin the 'prepa' , as it is known colloquially, at the age of 16 and finish when they are 19.

preposición *f* preposition.
prepotente *adj* (*arrogante*) domineering.
prerrogativa *f* prerogative.
presa *f* 1. (*captura - de cazador*) catch; (*- de animal*) prey; hacer ~ en alguien to seize o grip sb; ser ~ de to be prey to; ser ~ del pánico to be panic-stricken. 2. (*dique*) dam.
presagiar *vt* (*felicidad, futuro*) to foretell; (*tormenta, problemas*) to warn of.
presagio *m* 1. (*premonición*) premonition. 2. (*señal*) omen.
presbítero *m* priest.
prescindir ▶ **prescindir de** *vi* 1. (*renunciar a*) to do without. 2. (*omitir*) to dispense with.
prescribir ◆ *vt* to prescribe. ◆ *vi* 1. (*ordenar*) to prescribe. 2. (DER) to expire.
prescripción *f* prescription.

prescrito, -ta pp → **prescribir**.

presencia f (asistencia, aspecto) presence; **en ~ de** in the presence of. ▶ **presencia de ánimo** f presence of mind.

presencial → **testigo**.

presenciar vt (asistir) to be present at; (ser testigo de) to witness.

presentación f 1. (gen) presentation. 2. (entre personas) introduction.

presentador, -ra m y f presenter.

presentar vt 1. (gen) to present; (dimisión) to tender; (tesis, pruebas, propuesta) to submit; (solicitud, recurso, denuncia) to lodge; (moción) to propose. 2. (ofrecer - disculpas, excusas) to make; (- respetos) to pay. 3. (persona, amigos etc) to introduce. 4. (tener - aspecto etc) to have, to show; **presenta difícil solución** it's going to be difficult to solve. 5. (proponer): **~ a alguien para** to propose sb for. ▶ **presentarse** vpr 1. (aparecer) to turn up. 2. (en juzgado, comisaría): **~se (en)** to report (to); **~se a un examen** to sit an exam. 3. (darse a conocer) to introduce o.s. 4. (para un cargo): **~se (a)** to stand o run (for). 5. (futuro) to appear, to look. 6. (problema etc) to arise.

presente ♦ adj 1. (gen) present; **aquí ~** here present; **tener ~** (recordar) to remember; (tener en cuenta) to bear in mind. 2. (en curso) current; **del ~ mes** of this month. ♦ m y f (escrito): **por la ~ le informo ...** I hereby inform you ... ♦ m 1. (gen & GRAM) present. 2. (regalo) gift, present. 3. (corriente): **el ~** (mes) the current month; (año) the current year.

presentimiento m presentiment, feeling.

presentir vt to foresee; **~ que algo va a pasar** to have a feeling that sthg is going to happen; **~ lo peor** to fear the worst.

preservar vt to protect.

preservativo, -va adj protective. ▶ **preservativo** m condom.

presidencia f (de nación) presidency; (de asamblea, empresa) chairmanship.

presidente, -ta m y f (de nación) president; (de asamblea, empresa) chairman (f chairwoman); **~ (del gobierno)** = prime minister.

presidiario, -ria m y f convict.

presidio m prison.

presidir vt 1. (ser presidente de) to preside over; (reunión) to chair. 2. (predominar) to dominate.

presión f pressure.

presionar vt 1. (apretar) to press. 2. fig (coaccionar) to pressurize.

preso, -sa m y f prisoner.

prestación f (de servicio - acción) provision; (- resultado) service. ▶ **prestaciones** fpl (de coche etc) performance features.

prestado, -da adj on loan; **dar ~ algo** to lend sthg; **pedir/tomar ~ algo** to borrow sthg.

prestamista m y f moneylender.

préstamo m (acción - de prestar) lending; (- de pedir prestado) borrowing. 2. (cantidad) loan.

prestar vt 1. (dejar - dinero etc) to lend, to loan. 2. (dar - ayuda etc) to give, to offer; (- servicio) to provide; (- atención) to pay; (- declaración, juramento) to make. ▶ **prestarse a** vpr 1. (ofrecerse a) to offer to. 2. (acceder a) to consent to. 3. (dar motivo a) to be open to.

presteza f promptness.

prestidigitador, -ra m y f conjuror.

prestigio m prestige.

prestigioso, -sa adj prestigious.

presto, -ta adj (dispuesto): **~ (a)** ready (to).

presumible adj probable, likely.

presumido, -da adj conceited, vain.

presumir ♦ vt (suponer) to presume. ♦ vi 1. (jactarse) to show off. 2. (ser vanidoso) to be conceited o vain.

presunción f 1. (suposición) presumption. 2. (vanidad) conceit, vanity.

presunto, -ta adj presumed, supposed; (criminal, robo etc) alleged.

presuntuoso, -sa adj (vanidoso) conceited; (pretencioso) pretentious.

presuponer vt to presuppose.

presupuesto, -ta pp → **presuponer**. ▶ **presupuesto** m 1. (cálculo) budget; (de costo) estimate. 2. (suposición) assumption.

prêt-à-porter [pretapor'te] (pl **prêts-à-porter**) m off-the-peg clothing.

pretencioso, -sa adj (persona) pretentious; (cosa) showy.

pretender vt 1. (intentar): **~ hacer algo** to try to do sthg. 2. (aspirar a): **~ hacer algo** to aspire o want to do sthg; **~ que alguien haga algo** to want sb to do sthg; **¿qué pretendes decir?** what do you mean? 3. (afirmar) to claim. 4. (cortejar) to court.

pretendido, -da adj supposed.

pretendiente ♦ m y f 1. (aspirante): **~ (a)** candidate (for). 2. (a un trono): **~ (a)**

pretender (to). ♦ *m* (*a una mujer*) suitor.
pretensión *f* **1.** (*intención*) aim, intention. **2.** (*aspiración*) aspiration. **3.** (*supuesto derecho*): ~ (**a** o **sobre**) claim (to). **4.** (*afirmación*) claim. **5.** (*gen pl*) (*exigencia*) demand.
pretérito, -ta *adj* past. ▶ **pretérito** *m* (GRAM) preterite, past.
pretexto *m* pretext, excuse.
prevalecer *vi*: ~ (**sobre**) to prevail (over).
prevaler *vi*: ~ (**sobre**) to prevail (over).
prevención *f* (*acción*) prevention; (*medida*) precaution.
prevenido, -da *adj* **1.** (*previsor*): **ser** ~ to be cautious. **2.** (*avisado, dispuesto*): **estar** ~ to be prepared.
prevenir *vt* **1.** (*evitar*) to prevent; **más vale** ~ **que curar** *proverb* prevention is better than cure *proverb*. **2.** (*avisar*) to warn. **3.** (*prever*) to foresee. **4.** (*predisponer*): ~ **a alguien contra algo/alguien** to prejudice sb against sthg/sb.
preventivo, -va *adj* (*medicina, prisión*) preventive; (*medida*) precautionary.
prever *vt* **1.** (*conjeturar*) to foresee. **2.** (*planear*) to plan. **3.** (*predecir*) to forecast.
previniera *etc* → **prevenir**.
previo, -via *adj* prior; ~ **pago de multa** on payment of a fine.
previó → **prever**.
previsible *adj* foreseeable.
previsión *f* **1.** (*predicción*) forecast. **2.** (*visión de futuro*) foresight.
previsor, -ra *adj* prudent, farsighted.
previsto, -ta ♦ *pp* → **prever**. ♦ *adj* (*conjeturado*) predicted; (*planeado*) planned.
prieto, -ta *adj* **1.** (*ceñido*) tight. **2.** *Amer fam* (*moreno*) dark-haired.
prima → **primo**.
primacía *f* primacy.
primar *vi*: ~ (**sobre**) to have priority (over).
primario, -ria *adj* primary; *fig* primitive.
primavera *f* (*estación*) spring.
primaveral *adj* spring (*antes de sust*).
primer, primera → **primero**.
primerizo, -za *m y f* (*principiante*) beginner.
primero, -ra ♦ *núm adj* (*antes de sust masculino sg*: **primer**) **1.** (*para ordenar*) first. **2.** (*en importancia*) main, basic; **lo** ~ the most important o main thing. ♦ *núm m y f* **1.** (*en orden*): **el** ~ the first one; **llegó el** ~ he came first; **es el** ~ **de**

la clase he's top of the class; **a ~s de mes** at the beginning of the month. **2.** (*mencionado antes*): **vinieron Pedro y Juan, el** ~ **con ...** Pedro and Juan arrived, the former with ... ▶ **primero** ♦ *adv* **1.** (*en primer lugar*) first. **2.** (*antes, todo menos*): ~ **morir que traicionarle** I'd rather die than betray him. ♦ *m* **1.** (*piso*) first floor. **2.** (*curso*) first year.
▶ **primera** *f* **1.** (AUTOM) first (gear). **2.** (AERON & FERROC) first class. **3.** (DEP) first division. **4.** *loc*: **de primera** first-class.
primicia *f* scoop, exclusive.
primitivo, -va *adj* **1.** (*gen*) primitive. **2.** (*original*) original.
primo, -ma *m y f* **1.** (*pariente*) cousin. **2.** *fam* (*tonto*) sucker; **hacer el** ~ to be taken for a ride. ▶ **prima** *f* **1.** (*paga extra*) bonus. **2.** (*de un seguro*) premium. ▶ **prima dona** *f* prima donna.
primogénito, -ta *adj, m y f* first-born.
primor *m* fine thing.
primordial *adj* fundamental.
primoroso, -sa *adj* **1.** (*delicado*) exquisite, fine. **2.** (*hábil*) skilful.
princesa *f* princess.
principado *m* principality.
principal *adj* main, principal; (*puerta*) front.
príncipe *m* prince.
principiante ♦ *adj* inexperienced. ♦ *m y f* novice.
principio *m* **1.** (*comienzo*) beginning, start; **a ~s de** at the beginning of; **en un** ~ at first. **2.** (*fundamento, ley*) principle; **en** ~ in principle; **por** ~ on principle. **3.** (*origen*) origin, source. **4.** (*elemento*) element. ▶ **principios** *mpl* **1.** (*reglas de conducta*) principles. **2.** (*nociones*) rudiments.
pringar *vt* **1.** (*ensuciar*) to make greasy. **2.** (*mojar*) to dip.
pringoso, -sa *adj* (*grasiento*) greasy; (*pegajoso*) sticky.
pringue *m* (*suciedad*) muck, dirt; (*grasa*) grease.
priori ▶ **a priori** *loc adv* in advance, a priori.
prioridad *f* priority; (AUTOM) right of way.
prioritario, -ria *adj* priority (*antes de sust*).
prisa *f* haste, hurry; **a** o **de** ~ quickly; **correr** ~ to be urgent; **darse** ~ to hurry (up); **meter** ~ **a alguien** to hurry o rush sb; **tener** ~ to be in a hurry.
prisión *f* **1.** (*cárcel*) prison. **2.** (*encarce-*

lamiento) imprisonment.

prisionero, -ra *m y f* prisoner.

prisma *m* 1. (FÍS & GEOM) prism. 2. *fig* (*perspectiva*) perspective.

prismático, -ca *adj* prismatic. ▶ **prismáticos** *mpl* binoculars.

privación *f* (*gen*) deprivation; (*de libertad*) loss.

privado, -da *adj* private; **en ~** in private.

privar *vt* 1. (*quitar*): **~ a alguien/algo de** to deprive sb/sthg of. 2. (*prohibir*): **~ a alguien de hacer algo** to forbid sb to do sthg. ▶ **privarse de** *vpr* to go without.

privativo, -va *adj* exclusive.

privilegiado, -da *adj* 1. (*favorecido*) privileged. 2. (*excepcional*) exceptional.

privilegiar *vt* (*persona*) to favour; (*intereses*) to put first.

privilegio *m* privilege.

pro ◆ *prep* for, supporting; **una asociación ~ derechos humanos** a human rights organization. ◆ *m* advantage; **los ~s y los contras** the pros and cons. ▶ **en pro de** *loc prep* for, in support of.

proa *f* (NÁUT) prow, bows (*pl*); (AERON) nose.

probabilidad *f* probability; (*oportunidad*) chance.

probable *adj* probable, likely; **es ~ que llueva** it'll probably rain.

probador *m* fitting room.

probar ◆ *vt* 1. (*demostrar, indicar*) to prove. 2. (*comprobar*) to test, to check. 3. (*experimentar*) to try. 4. (*degustar*) to taste, to try. ◆ *vi*: **~ a hacer algo** to try to do sthg. ▶ **probarse** *vpr* (*ropa*) to try on.

probeta *f* test tube.

problema *m* problem.

problemático, -ca *adj* problematic. ▶ **problemática** *f* problems (*pl*).

procedencia *f* 1. (*origen*) origin. 2. (*punto de partida*) point of departure; **con ~ de** (arriving) from.

procedente *adj* 1. (*originario*): **~ de** (*gen*) originating in; (AERON & FERROC) (arriving) from. 2. (*oportuno*) appropriate; (DER) right and proper.

proceder ◆ *m* conduct, behaviour. ◆ *vi* 1. (*originarse*): **~ de** to come from. 2. (*actuar*): **~ (con)** to act (with). 3. (*empezar*): **~ (a algo/a hacer algo)** to proceed (with sthg/to do sthg). 4. (*ser oportuno*) to be appropriate.

procedimiento *m* 1. (*método*) procedure, method. 2. (DER) proceedings (*pl*).

procesado, -da *m y f* accused, defendant.

procesador *m* (INFORM) processor; **~ de textos** word processor.

procesar *vt* 1. (DER) to prosecute. 2. (INFORM) to process.

procesión *f* (RELIG & *fig*) procession.

proceso *m* 1. (*gen*) process. 2. (*desarrollo, intervalo*) course. 3. (DER - *juicio*) trial; (- *causa*) lawsuit.

proclama *f* proclamation.

proclamar *vt* 1. (*nombrar*) to proclaim. 2. (*anunciar*) to declare. ▶ **proclamarse** *vpr* 1. (*nombrarse*) to proclaim o.s. 2. (*conseguir un título*): **~se campeón** to become champion.

proclive *adj*: **~ a** prone to.

procreación *f* procreation.

procrear *vi* to procreate.

procurador, -ra *m y f* (DER) attorney.

procurar *vt* 1. (*intentar*): **~ hacer algo** to try to do sthg; **~ que ...** to make sure that ... 2. (*proporcionar*) to get, to secure. ▶ **procurarse** *vpr* to get, to obtain (for o.s.).

prodigar *vt*: **~ algo a alguien** to lavish sthg on sb.

prodigio *m* (*suceso*) miracle; (*persona*) prodigy.

prodigioso, -sa *adj* 1. (*sobrenatural*) miraculous. 2. (*extraordinario*) wonderful.

pródigo, -ga *adj* (*generoso*) generous, lavish.

producción *f* 1. (*gen* & CIN) production; **~ en serie** (ECON) mass production. 2. (*productos*) products (*pl*).

producir *vt* 1. (*gen* & CIN) to produce. 2. (*causar*) to cause, to give rise to. 3. (*interés, fruto*) to yield, to bear. ▶ **producirse** *vpr* (*ocurrir*) to take place.

productividad *f* productivity.

productivo, -va *adj* productive; (*que da beneficio*) profitable.

producto *m* 1. (*gen* & MAT) product; (AGR) produce (U); **~ interior/nacional bruto** gross domestic/national product; **~ químico** chemical. 2. (*ganancia*) profit. 3. *fig* (*resultado*) result.

productor, -ra ◆ *adj* producing. ◆ *m y f* (CIN) (*persona*) producer. ▶ **productora** *f* (CIN) (*firma*) production company.

proeza *f* exploit, deed.

profanar *vt* to desecrate.

profano, -na ◆ *adj* 1. (*no sagrado*) profane, secular. 2. (*ignorante*) ignorant, uninitiated. ◆ *m y f* layman (*f* lay-woman).

profecía *f* (*predicción*) prophecy.

proferir *vt* to utter; (*insultos*) to hurl.

profesar *vt* 1. (*una religión*) to follow; (*una profesión*) to practise. 2. (*admiración etc*) to profess.

profesión *f* profession.

profesional *adj, m y f* professional.

profesionista *m y f Amer* professional.

profesor, -ra *m y f* (*gen*) teacher; (*de universidad*) lecturer; (*de autoescuela, esquí etc*) instructor.

profesorado *m* (*plantilla*) teaching staff, faculty *Am*; (*profesión*) teachers (*pl*), teaching profession.

profeta *m* prophet.

profetisa *f* prophetess.

profetizar *vt* to prophesy.

profiera *etc* → **proferir**.

prófugo, -ga *adj, m y f* fugitive.

profundidad *f lit & fig* depth; **tiene dos metros de ~** it's two metres deep.

profundizar ◆ *vt fig* to study in depth. ◆ *vi* to go into detail; **~ en** to study in depth.

profundo, -da *adj* 1. (*gen*) deep. 2. *fig* (*respeto, libro, pensamiento*) profound, deep; (*dolor*) intense.

profusión *f* profusion.

progenitor, -ra *m y f* father (*f* mother). ▶ **progenitores** *mpl* parents.

programa *m* 1. (*gen*) programme. 2. (*de actividades*) schedule, programme; (*de estudios*) syllabus. 3. (INFORM) program.

programación *f* 1. (INFORM) programming. 2. (TV) scheduling; **la ~ del lunes** Monday's programmes.

programador, -ra *m y f* (*persona*) programmer.

programar *vt* 1. (*vacaciones, reforma etc*) to plan. 2. (CIN & TV) to put on, to show. 3. (TECN) to programme; (INFORM) to program.

progre *fam m y f* progressive.

progresar *vi* to progress.

progresión *f* (*gen & MAT*) progression; (*mejora*) progress, advance.

progresista *adj, m y f* progressive.

progresivo, -va *adj* progressive.

progreso *m* progress; **hacer ~s** to make progress.

prohibición *f* ban, banning (U).

prohibido, -da *adj* prohibited, banned; **'~ aparcar/fumar'** 'no parking/smoking', 'parking/smoking prohibit-ed'; **'prohibida la entrada'** 'no entry'; **'dirección prohibida'** (AUTOM) 'no entry'.

prohibir *vt* 1. (*gen*) to forbid; **~ a alguien hacer algo** to forbid sb to do sthg; **'se prohíbe el paso'** 'no entry'. 2. (*por ley - de antemano*) to prohibit; (*- a posteriori*) to ban.

prohibitivo, -va *adj* prohibitive.

prójimo *m* fellow human being.

prole *f* offspring.

proletariado *m* proletariat.

proletario, -ria *adj, m y f* proletarian.

proliferación *f* proliferation.

proliferar *vi* to proliferate.

prolífico, -ca *adj* prolific.

prolijo, -ja *adj* (*extenso*) long-winded.

prólogo *m* (*de libro*) preface, foreword; (*de obra de teatro*) prologue; *fig* prelude.

prolongación *f* extension.

prolongado, -da *adj* long; *fig* (*dilata-do*) lengthy.

prolongar *vt* (*gen*) to extend; (*espera, visita, conversación*) to prolong; (*cuerda, tubo*) to lengthen.

promedio *m* average.

promesa *f* (*compromiso*) promise.

prometer ◆ *vt* to promise. ◆ *vi* (*tener futuro*) to show promise. ▶ **prome-terse** *vpr* to get engaged.

prometido, -da ◆ *m y f* fiancé (*f* fiancée). ◆ *adj* (*para casarse*) engaged.

prominente *adj* 1. (*abultado*) protrud-ing. 2. (*elevado, ilustre*) prominent.

promiscuo, -cua *adj* promiscuous.

promoción *f* 1. (*gen & DEP*) promo-tion. 2. (*curso*) class, year.

promocionar *vt* to promote.

promotor, -ra *m y f* promoter; (*de una rebelión*) instigator.

promover *vt* 1. (*iniciar - fundación etc*) to set up; (*- rebelión*) to stir up. 2. (*oca-sionar*) to cause. 3. (*ascender*): **~ a alguien a** to promote sb to.

promulgar *vt* (*ley*) to pass.

pronombre *m* pronoun.

pronosticar *vt* to predict, to forecast.

pronóstico *m* 1. (*predicción*) forecast. 2. (MED) prognosis; **de ~ grave** serious, in a serious condition.

pronto, -ta *adj* quick, fast; (*respuesta*) prompt, early; (*curación, tramitación*) speedy. ▶ **pronto** ◆ *adv* 1. (*rápidamente*) quickly; **tan ~ como** as soon as. 2. (*tem-prano*) early; **salimos ~** we left early. 3. (*dentro de poco*) soon; **¡hasta ~!** see you soon! ◆ *m fam* sudden impulse. ▶ **al pronto** *loc adv* at first. ▶ **de pronto** *loc adv* suddenly. ▶ **por lo pronto** *loc adv*

1. (*de momento*) for the time being. **2.** (*para empezar*) to start with.

pronunciación *f* pronunciation.

pronunciado, -da *adj* ~ (*facciones*) pronounced; (*curva*) sharp; (*pendiente, cuesta*) steep; (*nariz*) prominent.

pronunciamiento *m* **1.** (*sublevación*) uprising. **2.** (DER) pronouncement.

pronunciar *vt* **1.** (*decir - palabra*) to pronounce; (- *discurso*) to deliver, to make. **2.** (DER) to pass. ▶ **pronunciarse** *vpr* **1.** (*definirse*): ~**se** (**sobre**) to state an opinion (on). **2.** (*sublevarse*) to revolt.

propagación *f* **1.** (*gen*) spreading (U). **2.** (BIOL & FÍS) propagation.

propaganda *f* **1.** (*publicidad*) advertising (U). **2.** (*política, religiosa*) propaganda.

propagar *vt* (*gen*) to spread; (*razas, especies*) to propagate. ▶ **propagarse** *vpr* **1.** (*gen*) to spread. **2.** (BIOL & FÍS) to propagate.

propasarse *vpr*: ~ (**con algo**) to go too far (with sthg); ~ **con alguien** (*sexualmente*) to take liberties with sb.

propensión *f* propensity, tendency.

propenso, -sa *adj*: ~ **a algo/a hacer algo** prone to sthg/doing sthg.

propicio, -cia *adj* **1.** (*favorable*) propitious, favourable. **2.** (*adecuado*) suitable, appropriate.

propiedad *f* **1.** (*derecho*) ownership; (*bienes*) property; ~ **privada** private property; ~ **pública** public ownership. **2.** (*facultad*) property. **3.** (*exactitud*) accuracy; **usar una palabra con** ~ to use a word properly.

propietario, -ria *m y f* (*de bienes*) owner; (*de cargo*) holder.

propina *f* tip.

propinar *vt* (*paliza*) to give; (*golpe*) to deal.

propio, -pia *adj* **1.** (*gen*) own; **tiene coche** ~ she has a car of her own, she has her own car; **por tu** ~ **bien** for your own good. **2.** (*peculiar*): ~ **de** typical o characteristic of; **no es** ~ **de él** it's not like him. **3.** (*apropiado*): ~ (**para**) suitable o right (for). **4.** (*correcto*) proper, true. **5.** (*en persona*) himself (*f* herself); **el** ~ **compositor** the composer himself.

proponer *vt* to propose; (*candidato*) to put forward. ▶ **proponerse** *vpr*: ~**se hacer algo** to plan o intend to do sthg.

proporción *f* **1.** (*gen* & MAT) proportion. **2.** (*gen pl*) (*importancia*) extent, size. ▶ **proporciones** *fpl* (*tamaño*) size (*sg*).

proporcionado, -da *adj*: ~ (**a**) (*estatura, sueldo*) commensurate (with); (*medidas*) proportionate (to); **bien** ~ well-proportioned.

proporcionar *vt* **1.** (*ajustar*): ~ **algo a algo** to adapt sthg to sthg. **2.** (*facilitar*): ~ **algo a alguien** to provide sb with sthg. **3.** *fig* (*conferir*) to lend, to add.

proposición *f* (*propuesta*) proposal.

propósito *m* **1.** (*intención*) intention. **2.** (*objetivo*) purpose. ▶ **a propósito** ◆ *loc adj* (*adecuado*) suitable. ◆ *loc adv* **1.** (*adrede*) on purpose. **2.** (*por cierto*) by the way. ▶ **a propósito de** *loc prep* with regard to.

propuesta *f* proposal; (*de empleo*) offer.

propuesto, -ta *pp* → **proponer**.

propugnar *vt* to advocate, to support.

propulsar *vt* **1.** (*impeler*) to propel. **2.** *fig* (*promover*) to promote.

propulsión *f* propulsion; ~ **a chorro** jet propulsion.

propulsor, -ra *m y f* (*persona*) promoter. ▶ **propulsor** *m* **1.** (*dispositivo*) engine. **2.** (*combustible*) propellent.

propusiera *etc* → **proponer**.

prórroga *f* **1.** (*gen*) extension; (*de estudios, servicio militar*) deferment. **2.** (DEP) extra time.

prorrogar *vt* (*alargar*) to extend; (*aplazar*) to defer, to postpone.

prorrumpir *vi*: ~ **en** to burst into.

prosa *f* (LITER) prose.

proscrito, -ta ◆ *adj* (*prohibido*) banned. ◆ *m y f* **1.** (*desterrado*) exile. **2.** (*fuera de la ley*) outlaw.

proseguir ◆ *vt* to continue. ◆ *vi* to go on, to continue.

prosiga *etc* → **proseguir**.

prosiguiera *etc* → **proseguir**.

prospección *f* (*gen*) exploration; (*petrolífera, minera*) prospecting.

prospecto *m* leaflet; (COM & EDUC) prospectus.

prosperar *vi* (*mejorar*) to prosper.

prosperidad *f* **1.** (*mejora*) prosperity. **2.** (*éxito*) success.

próspero, -ra *adj* prosperous.

prostíbulo *m* brothel.

prostitución *f* (*gen*) prostitution.

prostituir *vt lit* & *fig* to prostitute. ▶ **prostituirse** *vpr* to become a prostitute.

prostituta *f* prostitute.

protagonista *m y f* (*gen*) main character, hero (*f* heroine); (TEATR) lead, leading role.

protagonizar vt 1. (obra, película) to play the lead in, to star in. 2. fig (crimen, hazaña) to be responsible for.

protección f protection.

proteccionismo m protectionism.

protector, -ra ◆ adj protective. ◆ m y f (persona) protector.

proteger vt (gen) to protect; ~ algo de algo to protect sthg from sthg. ▶ **protegerse** vpr 1. (refugiarse) to take cover o refuge. 2. (tomar precauciones): ~ de/contra to protect o.s. from/against.

protege-slips m inv panty pad o liner.

protegido, -da ◆ adj protected. ◆ m y f protégé (f protégée).

proteína f protein.

prótesis f inv (MED) prosthesis; (miembro) artificial limb.

protesta f protest; (DER) objection.

protestante adj, m y f Protestant.

protestar vi 1. (quejarse): ~ (por/contra) to protest (about/against); ¡protesto! (DER) objection! 2. (refunfuñar) to grumble.

protocolo m 1. (gen & INFORM) protocol. 2. (ceremonial) etiquette.

prototipo m 1. (modelo) archetype. 2. (primer ejemplar) prototype.

protuberancia f protuberance, bulge.

provecho m 1. (gen) benefit; buen ~ enjoy your meal!; de ~ (persona) worthy; sacar ~ de to make the most of, to take advantage of. 2. (rendimiento) good effect.

provechoso, -sa adj 1. (ventajoso) beneficial, advantageous. 2. (lucrativo) profitable.

proveedor, -ra m y f supplier.

proveer vt 1. (abastecer) to supply, to provide. 2. (puesto, cargo) to fill. ▶ **proveerse de** vpr 1. (ropa, víveres) to stock up on. 2. (medios, recursos) to arm o.s. with.

provenir vi: ~ de to come from.

proverbial adj proverbial.

proverbio m proverb.

providencia f (medida) measure.

providencial adj lit & fig providential.

proviene etc → provenir.

provincia f (división administrativa) province. ▶ **provincias** fpl (no la capital) the provinces.

provinciano, -na adj, m y f despec provincial.

proviniera etc → provenir.

provisión f 1. (gen pl) (suministro) sup-

ply, provision; (de una plaza) filling (U). 2. (disposición) measure.

provisional adj provisional.

provisto, -ta pp → proveer.

provocación f (hostigamiento) provocation.

provocar vt 1. (incitar) to incite. 2. (irritar) to provoke. 3. (ocasionar - gen) to cause. 4. (excitar sexualmente) to arouse. 5. Amer fig (apetecer): ¿te provoca hacerlo? do you feel like doing it?

provocativo, -va adj provocative.

próximamente adv soon, shortly; (CIN) coming soon.

proximidad f (cercanía) closeness, proximity. ▶ **proximidades** fpl 1. (de ciudad) surrounding area (sg). 2. (de lugar) vicinity (sg).

próximo, -ma adj 1. (cercano) near, close; (casa, ciudad) nearby; en fecha próxima shortly. 2. (siguiente) next; el ~ año next year.

proyección f 1. (gen & GEOM) projection. 2. (CIN) screening. 3. fig (trascendencia) importance.

proyectar vt 1. (dirigir - focos etc) to shine, to direct. 2. (mostrar - película) to screen; (- sombra) to cast; (- diapositivas) to show. 3. (planear - viaje, operación, edificio) to plan; (- puente, obra) to design. 4. (arrojar) to throw forwards.

proyectil m projectile, missile.

proyecto m 1. (intención) project. 2. (plan) plan. 3. (diseño - ARQUIT) design; (- IND & TECN) plan. 4. (borrador) draft; ~ de ley bill. 5. (EDUC): ~ fin de carrera design project forming part of doctoral thesis for architecture students etc; ~ de investigación (de un grupo) research project; (de una persona) dissertation.

proyector, -ra adj projecting. ▶ **proyector** m (de cine, diapositivas) projector.

prudencia f (cuidado) caution, care; (previsión, sensatez) prudence; (moderación) moderation; con ~ in moderation.

prudente adj 1. (cuidadoso) careful, cautious; (previsor, sensato) sensible. 2. (razonable) reasonable.

prueba ◆ v → probar. ◆ f 1. (demostración) proof; (DER) evidence, proof; no tengo ~s I have no proof. 2. (manifestación) sign, token. 3. (EDUC & MED) test; ~ de acceso entrance examination. 4. (comprobación) test; a o de ~ (trabajador) on trial; (producto comprado) on approval; es a ~ de agua/balas its

waterproof/bulletproof; **poner a ~** to (put to the) test. **5.** (DEP) event. **6.** (IMPRENTA) proof.
PS = PD.

pseudónimo *m* pseudonym.

psicoanálisis *m inv* psychoanalysis.

psicoanalista *m y f* psychoanalyst.

psicodélico, -ca *adj* psychedelic.

psicología *f lit & fig* psychology.

psicológico, -ca *adj* psychological.

psicólogo, -ga *m y f* psychologist.

psicópata *m y f* psychopath.

psicosis *f inv* psychosis.

psicosomático, -ca *adj* psychosomatic.

psiquiatra *m y f* psychiatrist.

psiquiátrico, -ca *adj* psychiatric.

psíquico, -ca *adj* psychic.

PSOE [pe'soe, soe] (*abrev de* **Partido Socialista Obrero Español**) *m* major Spanish political party to the centre-left of the political spectrum.

pta. (*abrev de* peseta) pta.

púa *f* **1.** (*de planta*) thorn; (*de erizo*) quill; (*de peine*) tooth; (*de tenedor*) prong. **2.** (MÚS) plectrum.

pub [paβ] (*pl* **pubs**) *m* upmarket pub, = wine bar.

pubertad *f* puberty.

pubis *m inv* pubes (*pl*).

publicación *f* publication.

publicar *vt* **1.** (*editar*) to publish. **2.** (*difundir*) to publicize; (*ley*) to pass; (*aviso*) to issue.

publicidad *f* **1.** (*difusión*) publicity; **dar ~ a algo** to publicize sthg. **2.** (COM) advertising; (TV) adverts (*pl*), commercials (*pl*).

publicitario, -ria *adj* advertising (*antes de sust*).

público, -ca *adj* public; **ser ~** (*conocido*) to be common knowledge; **en ~** in public. ▶ **público** *m* **1.** (CIN, TEATR & TV) audience; (DEP) crowd. **2.** (*comunidad*) public; **el gran ~** the (general) public.

publirreportaje *m* (*anuncio de televisión*) promotional film; (*en revista*) advertising spread.

puchero *m* **1.** (*perola*) cooking pot. **2.** (*comida*) stew. ▶ **pucheros** *mpl* (*gesto*) pout (*sg*); **hacer ~s** to pout.

pucho *m* Amer (*colilla*) cigarette butt.

pudding = pudin.

púdico, -ca *adj* modest.

pudiente *adj* wealthy.

pudiera *etc* → **poder.**

pudin (*pl* **púdines**), **pudding** ['puðiŋ] (*pl* **puddings**) *m* (plum) pudding.

pudor *m* **1.** (*recato*) (sense of) shame. **2.** (*timidez*) bashfulness.

pudoroso, -sa *adj* **1.** (*recatado*) modest. **2.** (*tímido*) bashful.

pudrir *vt* to rot. ▶ **pudrirse** *vpr* to rot.

puebla *etc* → **poblar.**

pueblerino, -na *adj* village (*antes de sust*); *despec* provincial.

pueblo *m* **1.** (*población - pequeña*) village; (*- grande*) town. **2.** (*nación*) people.

pueda *etc* → **poder.**

puente *m* **1.** (*gen*) bridge. **2.** (*días festivos*): **hacer ~** to take an extra day off between two public holidays. ▶ **puente aéreo** *m* (*civil*) air shuttle; (*militar*) airlift.

puenting *m* bungee-jumping.

puerco, -ca ◆ *adj* filthy. ◆ *m y f* (*animal*) pig (*f* sow).

puercoespín *m* porcupine.

puericultor, -ra *m y f* pediatrician.

pueril *adj fig* childish.

puerro *m* leek.

puerta *f* **1.** (*de casa*) door; (*de jardín, ciudad etc*) gate; **de ~ en ~** from door to door; **~ principal/trasera** front/back door. **2.** *fig* (*posibilidad*) gateway, opening. **3.** (DEP) goalmouth. **4.** *loc*: **a las ~s de** on the verge of; **a ~ cerrada** (*gen*) behind closed doors; (*juicio*) in camera.

puerto *m* **1.** (*de mar*) port; **~ deportivo** marina. **2.** (*de montaña*) pass. **3.** (INFORM) port. **4.** *fig* (*refugio*) haven.

Puerto Rico Puerto Rico.

pues *conj* **1.** (*dado que*) since, as. **2.** (*por lo tanto*) therefore, so; **creo, ~, que ...** so, I think that ... **3.** (*así que*) so; **querías verlo, ~ ahí está** you wanted to see it, so here it is. **4.** (*enfático*): **¡~ ya está!** well, that's it!; **¡~ claro!** but of course!

puesto, -ta ◆ *pp* → **poner.** ◆ *adj*: **ir muy ~** to be all dressed up. ▶ **puesto** *m* **1.** (*empleo*) post, position. **2.** (*en fila, clasificación etc*) place. **3.** (*tenderete*) stall, stand. **4.** (MIL) post; **~ de policía** police station; **~ de socorro** first-aid post. ▶ **puesta** *f* (*acción*): **puesta a punto** (*de una técnica*) perfecting; (*de un motor*) tuning; **puesta al día** updating; **puesta en escena** staging, production; **puesta en marcha** (*de máquina*) starting, start-up; (*de acuerdo, proyecto*) implementation. ▶ **puesta de sol** *f* sunset. ▶ **puesto que** *loc conj* since, as.

puf (*pl* **pufs**) *m* pouf, pouffe.

púgil *m* boxer.

pugna *f* fight, battle.

pugnar *vi fig* (*esforzarse*): **~ por** to struggle o fight (for).

puja f (en subasta - acción) bidding; (- cantidad) bid.

pujar ◆ vi (en subasta) to bid higher. ◆ vt to bid.

pulcro, -cra adj neat, tidy.

pulga f flea.

pulgada f inch.

pulgar → dedo.

pulgón m aphid.

pulimentar vt to polish.

pulir vt to polish. ▶ **pulirse** vpr (gastarse) to blow.

pulmón m lung.

pulmonía f pneumonia.

pulpa f pulp; (de fruta) flesh.

púlpito m pulpit.

pulpo m (animal) octopus.

pulque m Amer fermented maguey juice.

pulsación f 1. (del corazón) beat, beating (U). 2. (en máquina de escribir) keystroke.

pulsador m button, push button.

pulsar vt (botón, timbre etc) to press; (teclas de ordenador) to hit, to strike; (teclas de piano) to play; (cuerdas de guitarra) to pluck.

pulsera f bracelet.

pulso m 1. (latido) pulse; **tomar el ~ a algo/alguien** fig to sound sthg/sb out. 2. (firmeza): **tener buen ~** to have a steady hand; **a ~** unaided.

pulular vi to swarm.

pulverizador, -ra adj spray (antes de sust). ▶ **pulverizador** m spray.

pulverizar vt 1. (líquido) to spray. 2. (sólido) to reduce to dust; (TECN) to pulverize. 3. fig (aniquilar) to pulverize.

puma m puma.

punción f puncture.

punición f punishment.

punk [paŋk] (pl punks), **punki** adj, m y f punk.

punta f 1. (extremo - gen) point; (- de pan, pelo) end; (- de dedo, cuerno) tip; **sacar ~ a (un lápiz)** to sharpen (a pencil); **a ~ (de) pala** by the dozen o bucket. 2. (pizca) touch, bit; (de sal) pinch.

puntada f (pespunte) stitch.

puntal m (madero) prop; fig (apoyo) mainstay.

puntapié m kick.

puntear vt to pluck.

punteo m guitar solo.

puntera → puntero.

puntería f 1. (destreza) marksmanship. 2. (orientación) aim.

puntero, -ra ◆ adj leading. ◆ m y f

(líder) leader. ▶ **puntera** f (de zapato) toecap.

puntiagudo, -da adj pointed.

puntilla f point lace. ▶ **de puntillas** loc adv on tiptoe.

puntilloso, -sa adj 1. (susceptible) touchy. 2. (meticuloso) punctilious.

punto m 1. (gen) point; **~ débil/fuerte** weak/strong point; **~ de ebullición** o **hervor** boiling point; **~ de fusión** melting point; **~ culminante** high point; **~s a tratar** matters to be discussed; **poner ~ final a algo** to bring sthg to a close. 2. (signo ortográfico) dot; **~ y coma** semicolon; **~s suspensivos** suspension points; **dos ~s** colon. 3. (marca) spot, dot. 4. (lugar) spot, place; **~ de venta** (COM) point of sale. 5. (momento) point, moment; **estar a ~** to be ready; **estar a ~ de hacer algo** to be on the point of doing sthg. 6. (estado) state, condition; **llegar a un ~ en que ...** to reach the stage where ...; **poner a ~** (gen) to finetune; (motor) to tune. 7. (cláusula) clause. 8. (puntada - en costura, cirugía) stitch; **~ de cruz** cross-stitch; **hacer ~** to knit; **un jersey de ~** a knitted jumper. 9. (estilo de tejer) knitting; **~ de ganchillo** crochet. 10. (objetivo) target. ▶ **en punto** loc adv on the dot. ▶ **hasta cierto punto** loc adv to some extent, up to a point. ▶ **punto de partida** m starting point. ▶ **punto de vista** m point of view. ▶ **punto muerto** m 1. (AUTOM) neutral. 2. (en un proceso) deadlock; **estar en un ~ muerto** to be deadlocked.

puntuación f 1. (calificación) mark; (en concursos, competiciones) score. 2. (ortográfica) punctuation.

puntual adj 1. (en el tiempo) punctual. 2. (exacto, detallado) detailed. 3. (aislado) isolated, one-off.

puntualidad f 1. (en el tiempo) punctuality. 2. (exactitud) exactness.

puntualizar vt to specify, to clarify.

puntuar ◆ vt 1. (calificar) to mark; (DEP) to award marks to. 2. (escrito) to punctuate. ◆ vi 1. (calificar) to mark. 2. (entrar en el cómputo): **~ (para)** to count (towards).

punzada f 1. (pinchazo) prick. 2. (dolor intenso) stabbing pain (U); fig pang.

punzante adj 1. (que pincha) sharp. 2. (intenso) sharp. 3. (mordaz) caustic.

punzar vt 1. (pinchar) to prick. 2. (suj: dolor) to stab; fig (suj: actitud) to wound.

punzón m punch.

puñado m handful.

puño *m* dagger.
puñalada *f* stab; (*herida*) stab wound.
puñeta ◆ *f fam* (*tontería*): **mandar a alguien a hacer ~s** to tell sb to get lost. ◆ *interj fam*: **¡~!, ¡~s!** damn it!
puñetazo *m* punch.
puñetero, -ra *fam* ◆ *adj* **1.** (*persona*) damn. **2.** (*cosa*) tricky. ◆ *m y f* pain.
puño *m* **1.** (*mano cerrada*) fist; **de su ~ y letra** in his/her own handwriting. **2.** (*de manga*) cuff. **3.** (*empuñadura - de espada*) hilt; (*- de paraguas*) handle.
pupila *f* pupil.
pupilo, -la *m y f* (*discípulo*) pupil.
pupitre *m* desk.
puré *m* (CULIN) purée; (*sopa*) thick soup; **~ de patatas** mashed potatoes (*pl*).
pureza *f* purity.
purga *f fig* (*depuración*) purge.
purgante *adj* & *m* purgative.
purgar *vt lit* & *fig* to purge.
purgatorio *m* purgatory.
purificar *vt* to purify; (*mineral, metal*) to refine.
puritano, -na *adj, m y f* puritan.
puro, -ra *adj* **1.** (*gen*) pure; (*oro*) solid. **2.** (*cielo, atmósfera*) clear. **3.** (*conducta, persona*) decent, honourable. **4.** (*mero*) sheer; (*verdad*) plain; **por pura casualidad** by pure chance. ▶ **puro** *m* cigar.
púrpura ◆ *adj inv* purple. ◆ *m* purple.
purpúreo, -a *adj culto* purple.
pus *m* pus.
pusilánime *adj* cowardly.
puso → **poner**.
puta ◆ *adj* → **puto**. ◆ *f vulg* whore.
putear *vulg vt* (*fastidiar*) to piss off.
puto, -ta *adj vulg* (*maldito*) bloody. ▶ **puto** *m vulg* male prostitute.
putrefacción *f* rotting, putrefaction.
puzzle ['puθle], **puzle** *m* jigsaw puzzle.
PVP (*abrev de* **precio de venta al público**) *m* = RRP.
PYME (*abrev de* **Pequeña y Mediana Empresa**) *f* SME.
pyrex® = **pirex**.
pza. (*abrev de* **plaza**) Sq.

q, Q *f* (*letra*) q, Q.
q.e.p.d. (*abrev de* **que en paz descanse**) RIP.
que ◆ *pron relat* **1.** (*sujeto*) (*persona*) who, that; (*cosa*) that, which; **la mujer ~ me saluda** the woman (who o that is) waving to me; **el ~ me lo compró** the one who bought it from me; **la moto ~ me gusta** the motorbike (that) I like. **2.** (*complemento directo*) (*persona*) whom, that; (*cosa*) that, which; **el hombre ~ conociste ayer** the man (whom o that) you met yesterday; **ese coche es el ~ me quiero comprar** that car is the one (that o which) I want to buy. **3.** (*complemento indirecto*): **al/a la ~** (to) whom; **ese es el chico al ~ presté dinero** that's the boy to whom I lent some money. **4.** (*complemento circunstancial*): **la playa a la ~ fui** the beach where o to which I went; **la mujer con la ~ hablas** the woman to whom you are talking; **la mesa sobre la ~ escribes** the table on which you are writing. **5.** (*complemento de tiempo*): **(en) ~** when; **el día (en) ~ me fui** the day (when) I left. ◆ *conj* **1.** (*con oraciones de sujeto*) that; **es importante ~ me escuches** it's important that you listen to me. **2.** (*con oraciones de complemento directo*) that; **me ha confesado ~ me quiere** he has told me that he loves me. **3.** (*comparativo*) than; **es más rápido ~ tú** he's quicker than you; **antes morir ~ vivir la guerra** I'd rather die than live through a war. **4.** (*expresa causa*): **hemos de esperar, ~ todavía no es la hora** we'll have to wait, as it isn't time yet. **5.** (*expresa consecuencia*) that; **tanto me lo pidió ~ se lo di** he asked me for it so insistently that I gave it to him. **6.** (*expresa finalidad*) so (that); **ven aquí ~ te vea** come over here so (that) I can see you. **7.** (+ *subjuntivo*) (*expresa deseo*) that; **quiero ~ lo hagas** I want you to do it; **espero ~ te diviertas** I hope (that) you have fun. **8.** (*en oraciones exclamativas*): **¡~ te diviertas!** have fun!; **¡~ te doy un bofetón!** do that again and I'll slap you! **9.** (*en oraciones interrogativas*): **¿~ quiere venir?** pues que venga so she wants to come? then let her.

10. (*expresa disyunción*) or; **quieras ~ no, harás lo que yo mando** you'll do what I tell you, whether you like it or not. **11.** (*expresa hipótesis*) if; **~ no quieres hacerlo, pues no pasa nada** it doesn't matter if you don't want to do it. **12.** (*expresa reiteración*) and; **estaban charla ~ charla** they were talking and talking.

qué ◆ *adj* (*gen*) what; (*al elegir, al concretar*) which; **¿~ hora es?** what's the time?; **¿~ coche prefieres?** which car do you prefer?; **¿a ~ distancia?** how far away? ◆ *pron* (*interrogativo*) what; **¿~ te dijo?** what did he tell you?; **no sé ~ hacer** I don't know what to do; **¿~?** (*¿cómo?*) sorry?, pardon? ◆ *adv* **1.** (*exclamativo*) how; **¡~ horror!** how awful!; **¡~ tonto eres!** how stupid you are!, you're so stupid!; **¡~ casa más bonita!** what a lovely house!; **¡y ~!** so what? **2.** (*expresa gran cantidad*) **¡~ de ...!** what a lot of ...!; **¡~ de gente hay aquí!** what a lot of people there are here!

quebradero ▶ **quebradero de cabeza** *m* headache, problem.

quebradizo, -za *adj* **1.** (*frágil*) fragile, brittle. **2.** (*débil*) frail. **3.** (*voz*) weak.

quebrado, -da *adj* (*terreno*) rough, uneven; (*perfil*) rugged.

quebradura *f* (*grieta*) crack, fissure.

quebrantar *vt* **1.** (*incumplir - promesa, ley*) to break; (*- obligación*) to fail in. **2.** (*debilitar*) to weaken; (*moral, resistencia*) to break. ▶ **quebrantarse** *vpr* (*debilitarse*) to deteriorate.

quebranto *m* **1.** (*pérdida*) loss. **2.** (*debilitamiento*) weakening, debilitation.

quebrar ◆ *vt* (*romper*) to break. ◆ *vi* (FIN) to go bankrupt. ▶ **quebrarse** *vpr* **1.** (*romperse*) to break. **2.** (*voz*) to break, to falter. **3.** (*deslomarse*) to rupture o.s.

quechua *m* (*idioma*) Quechua.

quedar *vi* **1.** (*permanecer*) to remain, to stay. **2.** (*haber aún, faltar*) to be left, to remain; **¿queda azúcar?** is there any sugar left?; **nos quedan 100 pesetas** we have 100 pesetas left; **¿cuánto queda para León?** how much further is it to León?; **~ por hacer** to remain to be done; **queda por fregar el suelo** the floor has still to be cleaned. **3.** (*mostrarse*) **~ como** to come across as; **~ bien/mal con alguien** to make a good/bad impression (on sb). **4.** (*llegar a ser, resultar*) **el trabajo ha quedado perfecto** the job turned out perfectly; **el cuadro queda muy bien ahí** the picture looks great

there. **5.** (*acabar*) **~ en** to end in; **~ en nada** to come to nothing. **6.** (*sentar*) to look; **te queda un poco corto el traje** your suit is a bit too short; **~ bien/mal a alguien** to look good/bad on sb; **~ bien/mal con algo** to go well/badly with sth. **7.** (*citarse*) **~ (con alguien)** to arrange to meet (sb); **hemos quedado el lunes** we've arranged to meet on Monday. **8.** (*acordar*) **~ en algo/en hacer algo** to agree on sth/to do sth; **~ en que ...** to agree that ...; **¿en qué quedamos?** what's it to be, then? **9.** *fam* (*estar situado*) to be; **¿por dónde queda?** whereabouts is it? ▶ **quedarse** *vpr* **1.** (*permanecer - en un lugar*) to stay, to remain. **2.** (*terminar - en un estado*) **~se ciego/sordo** to go blind/deaf; **~se triste** to be o feel sad; **~se sin dinero** to be left penniless; **la pared se ha quedado limpia** the wall is clean now. **3.** (*comprar*) to take; **me quedo éste** I'll take this one. ▶ **quedarse con** *vpr* **1.** (*retener, guardarse*) to keep. **2.** (*preferir*) to go for, to prefer.

quedo, -da *adj* quiet, soft. ▶ **quedo** *adv* quietly, softly.

quehacer *m* (*gen pl*) task; **~es domésticos** housework (U).

queja *f* **1.** (*lamento*) moan, groan. **2.** (*protesta*) complaint.

quejarse *vpr* **1.** (*lamentar*) to groan, to cry out. **2.** (*protestar*) to complain; **~ de** to complain about.

quejica *despec adj* whining, whingeing.

quejido *m* cry, moan.

quejoso, -sa *adj*: **~ (de)** annoyed o upset (with).

quemado, -da *adj* **1.** (*gen*) burnt; (*por agua hirviendo*) scalded; (*por electricidad*) burnt-out; (*fusible*) blown. **2.** (*por sol*) sunburnt. **3.** *loc*: **estar ~** (*agotado*) to be burnt-out; (*harto*) to be fed up.

quemador *m* burner.

quemadura *f* (*por fuego*) burn; (*por agua hirviendo*) scald; (*del sol*) sunburn.

quemar ◆ *vt* **1.** (*gen*) to burn; (*suj: agua hirviendo*) to scald; (*suj: electricidad*) to blow. **2.** *fig* (*malgastar*) to fritter away. **3.** *fig* (*desgastar*) to burn out. **4.** *fig* (*hartar*) to make fed up. ◆ *vi* (*estar caliente*) to be (scalding) hot. ▶ **quemarse** *vpr* **1.** (*por fuego*) to burn down; (*por agua hirviendo*) to get scalded; (*por calor*) to burn; (*por electricidad*) to blow. **2.** (*por el sol*) to get burned. **3.** *fig* (*desgastarse*) to burn out. **4.** *fig* (*hartarse*) to get fed up.

quemarropa ▶ **a quemarropa** *loc adv* point-blank.

quemazón *f* burning; (*picor*) itch.

quena *f* bamboo or wooden flute.

quepa → **caber**.

querella *f* 1. (DER) (*acusación*) charge. 2. (*discordia*) dispute.

querer ♦ *vt* 1. (*gen*) to want; **quiero una bicicleta** I want a bicycle; **¿quieren ustedes algo más?** would you like anything else?; **~ que alguien haga algo** to want sb to do sthg; **quiero que lo hagas tú** I want you to do it; **~ que pase algo** to want sthg to happen; **queremos que las cosas te vayan bien** we want things to go well for you; **quisiera hacerlo, pero ...** I'd like to do it, but ... 2. (*amar*) to love. 3. (*en preguntas - con amabilidad*): **¿quiere decirle a su amigo que pase?** could you tell your friend to come in, please? 4. (*pedir - precio*): **~ algo (por)** to want sthg (for); **¿cuánto quieres por el coche?** how much do you want for the car? 5. *fig & irón* (*dar motivos para*): **tú lo que quieres es que te pegue** you're asking for a smack. 6. *loc*: **como quien no quiere la cosa** as if it were nothing; **quien bien te quiere te hará llorar** *proverb* you have to be cruel to be kind *proverb*. ♦ *vi* to want; **ven cuando quieras** come whenever you like o want; **no me voy porque no quiero** I'm not going because I don't want to; **queriendo** on purpose; **sin ~** accidentally; **~ decir** to mean; **¿qué quieres decir con eso?** what do you mean by that?; **~ es poder** where there's a will there's a way. ♦ *v impers* (*haber atisbos*): **parece que quiere llover** it looks like rain. ♦ *m* love. ▶ **quererse** *vpr* to love each other.

querido, -da ♦ *adj* dear. ♦ *m y f* lover; (*apelativo afectuoso*) darling.

queso *m* cheese; **~ de bola** Dutch cheese; **~ manchego** *hard mild yellow cheese made in La Mancha*; **~ rallado** grated cheese.

quibutz [ki'βuθ] (*pl* quibutzs), **kibutz** (*pl* kibutzim) *m* kibbutz.

quicio *m* jamb; **estar fuera de ~** *fig* to be out of kilter; **sacar de ~ a alguien** *fig* to drive sb mad.

quiebra *f* 1. (*ruina*) bankruptcy; (*en bolsa*) crash. 2. *fig* (*pérdida*) collapse.

quiebro *m* (*ademán*) swerve.

quien *pron* 1. (*relativo*) (*sujeto*) who; (*complemento*) whom; **fue mi hermano ~ me lo explicó** it was my brother who explained it to me; **era Pepe a ~ vi/de ~ no me fiaba** it was Pepe (whom) I saw/

didn't trust. 2. (*indefinido*): **~es quieran verlo que se acerquen** whoever wants to see it will have to come closer; **hay ~ lo niega** there are those who deny it. 3. *loc*: **~ más ~ menos** everyone.

quién *pron* (*interrogativo*) (*sujeto*) who; (*complemento*) who, whom; **¿~ es ese hombre?** who's that man?; **no sé ~ viene** I don't know who is coming; **¿a ~es has invitado?** who o whom have you invited?; **¿de ~ es?** whose is it?; **¿~ es?** (*en la puerta*) who is it?; (*al teléfono*) who's calling?

quienquiera (*pl* quienesquiera) *pron* whoever; **~ que venga** whoever comes.

quiera *etc* → **querer**.

quieto, -ta *adj* (*parado*) still; **¡estáte ~!** keep still!; **¡~ ahí!** don't move!

quietud *f* 1. (*inmovilidad*) stillness. 2. (*tranquilidad*) quietness.

quijada *f* jaw.

quijotesco, -ca *adj* quixotic.

quilate *m* carat.

quilla *f* (NÁUT) keel.

quilo *etc* = **kilo**.

quimbambas *fpl*: **irse a las ~** to go to the ends of the earth.

quimera *f* fantasy.

quimérico, -ca *adj* fanciful.

químico, -ca ♦ *adj* chemical. ♦ *m y f* (*científico*) chemist. ▶ **química** *f* (*ciencia*) chemistry.

quina *f* (*bebida*) quinine.

quincalla *f* trinket.

quince *núm* fifteen; **~ días** a fortnight; *ver también* **seis**.

quinceañero, -ra *m y f* teenager.

quinceavo, -va *núm* fifteenth.

quincena *f* fortnight.

quincenal *adj* fortnightly.

quincuagésimo, -ma *núm* fiftieth.

quiniela *f* (*boleto*) pools coupon. ▶ **quinielas** *fpl* (*apuestas*) (football) pools. ▶ **quiniela hípica** *f* sweepstake.

quinientos, -tas *núm* five hundred; *ver también* **seis**.

quinina *f* quinine.

quinqué *m* oil lamp.

quinquenio *m* (*periodo*) five-year period.

quinqui *m y f* *fam* delinquent.

quinta → **quinto**.

quinteto *m* quintet.

quinto, -ta ♦ *núm* fifth. ▶ **quinto** *m* 1. (*parte*) fifth. 2. (MIL) recruit. ▶ **quinta** *f* 1. (*finca*) country house. 2. (MIL) call-up year.

quintuplicar *vt* to increase fivefold.

▶ **quintuplicarse** *vpr* to increase five-fold.

quiosco, kiosco *m* kiosk; (*de periódicos*) newspaper stand; ~ **de música** bandstand.

quiosquero, -ra *m y f* owner of a newspaper stand.

quirófano *m* operating theatre.

quiromancia *f* palmistry, chiromancy.

quiromasaje *m* (*manual*) massage.

quirúrgico, -ca *adj* surgical.

quisiera *etc* → **querer**.

quisque *m*: **cada** o **todo** ~ every man Jack.

quisquilloso, -sa *adj* **1.** (*detallista*) pernickety. **2.** (*susceptible*) touchy.

quiste *m* cyst.

quitaesmalte *m* nail-polish remover.

quitaipón ▶ **de quitaipón** *loc adj* removable; (*capucha*) detachable.

quitamanchas *m inv* stain remover.

quitanieves *m inv* snow plough.

quitar *vt* **1.** (*gen*) to remove; (*ropa, zapatos etc*) to take off; ~**le algo a alguien** to take sthg away from sb; **de quita y pon** removable; (*capucha*) detachable. **2.** (*dolor, ansiedad*) to take away, to relieve; (*sed*) to quench. **3.** (*tiempo*) to take up. **4.** (*robar*) to take, to steal. **5.** (*impedir*): **esto no quita que sea un vago** that doesn't change the fact that he's a layabout. **6.** (*exceptuar*): **quitando el queso, me gusta todo** apart from cheese, I'll eat anything. **7.** (*desconectar*) to switch off. ▶ **quitarse** *vpr* **1.** (*apartarse*) to get out of the way. **2.** (*ropa*) to take off. **3.** (*suj: mancha*) to come out. **4.** *loc*: ~**se a alguien de encima** o **de en medio** to get rid of sb.

quitasol *m* sunshade Br, parasol.

quite *m* (DEP) parry; **estar al** ~ to be on hand to help.

Quito Quito.

quizá, quizás *adv* perhaps; ~ **llueva mañana** it might rain tomorrow; ~ **no lo creas** you may not believe it; ~ **sí** maybe; ~ **no** maybe not.

R

r, R *f* (*letra*) r, R.

rábano *m* radish; **me importa un** ~ I couldn't care less.

rabí *m* rabbi.

rabia *f* **1.** (*ira*) rage; **me da** ~ it makes me mad; **tenerle** ~ **a alguien** *fig* not to be able to stand sb. **2.** (*enfermedad*) rabies.

rabiar *vi* **1.** (*sufrir*) to writhe in pain. **2.** (*enfadarse*) to be furious. **3.** (*desear*): ~ **por algo/hacer algo** to be dying for sthg/to do sthg.

rabieta *f fam* tantrum.

rabillo *m* corner; **mirar algo con el** ~ **del ojo** to look at sthg out of the corner of one's eye.

rabioso, -sa *adj* **1.** (*furioso*) furious. **2.** (*excesivo*) terrible. **3.** (*enfermo de rabia*) rabid. **4.** (*chillón*) loud, gaudy.

rabo *m* **1.** (*de animal*) tail; ~ **de buey** oxtail. **2.** (*de hoja, fruto*) stem.

rácano, -na *fam adj* **1.** (*tacaño*) mean, stingy. **2.** (*gandul*) idle, lazy.

RACE (*abrev de* **Real Automóvil Club de España**) *m* Spanish automobile association, ≈ AA Br, ≈ AAA Am.

racha *f* **1.** (*ráfaga*) gust (of wind). **2.** (*época*) spell; (*serie*) string; **buena/mala** ~ good/bad patch; **a** ~**s** in fits and starts.

racial *adj* racial.

racimo *m* **1.** (*de frutos*) bunch. **2.** (*de flores*) raceme.

raciocinio *m* (*razón*) (power of) reason.

ración *f* **1.** (*porción*) portion, helping. **2.** (*en bar, restaurante*) large portion of a dish served as a snack.

racional *adj* rational.

racionalizar *vt* to rationalize.

racionar *vt* to ration.

racismo *m* racism.

racista *adj, m y f* racist.

radar (*pl* **radares**) *m* radar.

radiación *f* radiation.

radiactivo, -va, radioactivo, -va *adj* radioactive.

radiador *m* radiator.

radiante *adj* radiant.

radiar *vt* **1.** (*irradiar*) to radiate. **2.** (*por radio*) to broadcast.

radical *adj, m y f* radical.

radicalizarse *vpr* (*movimiento, partido*)

to become more radical o extreme; (*conflicto*) to intensify.

radicar *vi*: ~ **en** (*suj: problema etc*) to lie in; (*suj: población*) to be (situated) in. ▶ **radicarse** *vpr* (*establecerse*): ~**se (en)** to settle (in).

radio ♦ *m* 1. (ANAT & GEOM) radius. 2. (*de rueda*) spoke. 3. (QUÍM) radium. ♦ *f* radio; **oír algo por la ~** to hear sthg on the radio.

radioactivo, -va = **radiactivo**.

radioaficionado, -da *m y f* radio ham.

radiocasete *m* radio cassette (player).

radiocontrol *m* remote control.

radiodespertador *m* clock radio.

radiodifusión *f* broadcasting.

radioescucha *m y f inv* listener.

radiofónico, -ca *adj* radio (*antes de sust*).

radiografía *f* (*fotografía*) X-ray; (*ciencia*) radiography.

radionovela *f* radio soap opera.

radiorreloj *m* clock radio.

radiotaxi *m* taxi (with radio link).

radioteléfono *m* radiotelephone.

radioterapia *f* radiotherapy.

radioyente *m y f* listener.

RAE *abrev de* **Real Academia Española**.

raer *vt* to scrape (off).

ráfaga *f* (*de aire, viento*) gust; (*de disparos*) burst; (*de luces*) flash.

raído, -da *adj* threadbare; (*por los bordes*) frayed.

raigambre *f* (*tradición*) tradition.

rail, rail *m* rail.

raíz (*pl* raíces) *f* (*gen* & MAT) root; ~ **cuadrada/cúbica** square/cube root; **a ~ de** as a result of, following; **echar raíces** to put down roots.

raja *f* 1. (*porción*) slice. 2. (*grieta*) crack.

rajar *vt* 1. (*partir*) to crack; (*melón*) to slice. 2. *mfam* (*apuñalar*) to slash. ▶ **rajarse** *vpr* 1. (*partirse*) to crack. 2. *fam* (*echarse atrás*) to chicken out.

rajatabla ▶ **a rajatabla** *loc adv* to the letter, strictly.

ralentí *m* neutral.

rallado, -da *adj* grated. ▶ **rallado** *m* grating.

rallador *m* grater.

ralladura *f* (*gen pl*) grating.

rallar *vt* to grate.

rally ['rali] (*pl* rallys) *m* rally.

RAM (*abrev de* **random access memory**) *f* RAM.

rama *f* branch; **andarse por las ~s** *fam* to beat about the bush.

ramaje *m* branches (*pl*).

ramal *m* (*de carretera, ferrocarril*) branch.

ramalazo *m* 1. *fam* (*hecho que delata*) giveaway sign. 2. (*ataque*) fit.

rambla *f* (*avenida*) avenue, boulevard.

ramera *f* whore, hooker Am.

ramificación *f* 1. (*gen*) ramification. 2. (*de carretera, ferrocarril, ciencia*) branch.

ramificarse *vpr* 1. (*bifurcarse*) to branch out. 2. (*subdividirse*): ~ **(en)** to subdivide (into).

ramillete *m* bunch, bouquet.

ramo *m* 1. (*de flores*) bunch, bouquet. 2. (*rama*) branch; **el ~ de la construcción** the building industry.

rampa *f* 1. (*para subir y bajar*) ramp. 2. (*cuesta*) steep incline.

rana *f* frog.

ranchero, -ra *m y f* rancher. ▶ **ranchera** *f* 1. (MÚS) popular Mexican song. 2. (AUTOM) estate car.

rancho *m* 1. (*comida*) mess. 2. (*granja*) ranch. 3. *Amer* (*choza*) hut.

rancio, -cia *adj* 1. (*pasado*) rancid. 2. (*antiguo*) ancient. 3. (*añejo - vino*) mellow.

rango *m* 1. (*social*) standing. 2. (*jerárquico*) rank.

ranking ['raŋkin] (*pl* rankings) *m* ranking.

ranura *f* groove; (*de máquina tragaperras, cabina telefónica*) slot.

rapaces *fpl* → **rapaz**.

rapapolvo *m fam* ticking-off.

rapar *vt* (*barba, bigote*) to shave off; (*cabeza*) to shave; (*persona*) to shave the hair of.

rapaz, -za *m y f fam* lad (*f* lass). ▶ **rapaz** *adj* 1. (*que roba*) rapacious, greedy. 2. (ZOOL) → **ave**. ▶ **rapaces** *fpl* (ZOOL) birds of prey.

rape *m* angler fish; **cortar el pelo al ~ a alguien** to crop sb's hair.

rapé *m* (*en aposición inv*) snuff.

rápidamente *adv* quickly.

rapidez *f* speed.

rápido, -da *adj* quick, fast; (*coche*) fast; (*beneficio, decisión*) quick; (*aumento, crecimiento*) rapid. ▶ **rápido** ♦ *adv* quickly; **más** ~ quicker; **¡ven, ~!** come, quick! ♦ *m* (*tren*) express train. ▶ **rápidos** *mpl* (*de río*) rapids.

rapiña *f* 1. (*robo*) robbery with violence. 2. → **ave**.

rappel ['rapel] (*pl* rappels) *m* (DEP) abseiling; **hacer** ~ to abseil.

rapsodia *f* rhapsody.

raptar *vt* to abduct, to kidnap.

rapto *m* 1. (*secuestro*) abduction, kidnapping. **2.** (*ataque*) fit.

raqueta *f* (*para jugar - al tenis*) racquet; (*- al ping pong*) bat.

raquítico, -ca *adj* **1.** (MED) rachitic. **2.** (*insuficiente*) miserable.

rareza *f* **1.** (*poco común, extraño*) rarity. **2.** (*extravagancia*) eccentricity.

raro, -ra *adj* **1.** (*extraño*) strange; **rara vez** rarely, seldom. **2.** (*excepcional*) unusual, rare; (*visita*) infrequent. **3.** (*extravagante*) odd, eccentric. **4.** (*escaso*) rare; **rara vez** rarely, seldom.

ras *m*: **a ~ de** level with; **a ~ de tierra** at ground level; **volar a ~ de tierra** to fly low.

rasante *f* (*de carretera*) gradient.

rascacielos *m inv* skyscraper.

rascador *m* (*herramienta*) scraper.

rascar ♦ *vt* **1.** (*con uñas, clavo*) to scratch. **2.** (*con espátula*) to scrape (off); (*con cepillo*) to scrub. ♦ *vi* to be rough.
▶ **rascarse** *vpr* to scratch o.s.

rasera *f* fish slice.

rasgar *vt* to tear; (*sobre*) to tear open.

rasgo *m* **1.** (*característica*) trait, characteristic. **2.** (*trazo*) flourish, stroke.
▶ **rasgos** *mpl* **1.** (*del rostro*) features. **2.** (*letra*) handwriting (U). ▶ **a grandes rasgos** *loc adv* in general terms.

rasguear *vt* to strum.

rasguñar *vt* to scratch.

rasguño *m* scratch.

raso, -sa *adj* **1.** (*terreno*) flat. **2.** (*cuchara- da etc*) level. **3.** (*a poca altura*) low. **4.** (MIL): **soldado ~** private. ▶ **raso** *m* (*tela*) satin.

raspa *f* backbone (of fish).

raspadura *f* (*gen pl*) scraping; (*señal*) scratch.

raspar *vt* **1.** (*rascar*) to scrape (off). **2.** (*rasar*) to graze, to shave.

rasposo, -sa *adj* rough.

rastras ▶ **a rastras** *loc adv*: **llevar algo/a alguien a ~** *lit & fig* to drag sthg/ sb along.

rastreador, -ra *m y f* tracker.

rastrear *vt* (*seguir las huellas de*) to track.

rastrero, -ra *adj* despicable.

rastrillo *m* **1.** (*en jardinería*) rake. **2.** (*mercado*) flea market; (*benéfico*) jumble sale.

rastro *m* **1.** (*pista*) trail; **perder el ~ de alguien** to lose track of sb; **sin dejar ~** without trace. **2.** (*vestigio*) trace. **3.** (*mercado*) flea market.

RASTRO

A 'rastro' is a street market where antiques, second-hand and new goods are sold. The most famous 'rastro' is the one in Madrid, although they are to be found in most Spanish cities.

---

rastrojo *m* stubble.

rasurar *vt* to shave. ▶ **rasurarse** *vpr* to shave.

rata *f* rat.

ratero, -ra *m y f* petty thief.

ratificar *vt* to ratify. ▶ **ratificarse en** *vpr* to stand by.

rato *m* while; **estuvimos hablando mucho ~** we were talking for quite a while; **al poco ~ (de)** shortly after; **pasar el ~** to kill time; **pasar un mal ~** to have a hard time of it; **~s libres** spare time (U); **a ~s** at times.

ratón *m* (*gen &* INFORM) mouse.

ratonera *f* **1.** (*para ratas*) mousetrap. **2.** *fig* (*trampa*) trap.

raudal *m* **1.** (*de agua*) torrent. **2.** *fig* (*montón*) abundance; (*de lágrimas*) flood; (*de desgracias*) string; **a ~es** in abundance, by the bucket.

ravioli *m* (*gen pl*) ravioli (U).

raya *f* **1.** (*línea*) line; (*en tejido*) stripe; **a o de ~s** striped. **2.** (*del pelo*) parting; **hacerse la ~** to part one's hair. **3.** (*de pantalón*) crease. **4.** *fig* (*límite*) limit; **pasarse de la ~** to overstep the mark. **5.** (*señal - en disco, pintura etc*) scratch. **6.** (*pez*) ray. **7.** (*guión*) dash.

rayado, -da *adj* **1.** (*a rayas - tela*) striped; (*- papel*) ruled. **2.** (*estropeado*) scratched. ▶ **rayado** *m* (*rayas*) stripes (*pl*).

rayar ♦ *vt* **1.** (*marcar*) to scratch. **2.** (*trazar rayas*) to rule lines on. ♦ *vi* **1.** (*aproximarse*): **~ en algo** to border on sthg; **raya en los cuarenta** he's pushing forty. **2.** (*alba*) to break. ▶ **rayarse** *vpr* to get scratched.

rayo *m* **1.** (*de luz*) ray; **~ solar** sunbeam. **2.** (FÍS) beam, ray; **~ láser** laser beam; **~s infrarrojos/ultravioleta/uva** infrared/ ultraviolet/UVA rays; **~s X** X-rays; **caer como un ~** *fig* to be a bombshell. **3.** (METEOR) bolt of lightning; **~s** lightning (U).

rayón *m* rayon.

rayuela *f* Amer (*juego en que se salta a la pata coja*) hopscotch.

raza *f* **1.** (*humana*) race; **~ humana** human race. **2.** (*animal*) breed; **de ~** (*caballo*) thoroughbred; (*perro*) pedigree. **3.** Amer fam (*cara*) cheek, nerve.

razón *f* **1.** (*gen*) reason; **dar la ~ a alguien** to say that sb is right; **en ~ de o**

a in view of; **~ de ser** raison d'être; **tener ~ (en hacer algo)** to be right (to do sthg); **no tener ~** to be wrong; **y con ~** and quite rightly so. **2.** (*información*): **se vende piso: ~ aquí** flat for sale: enquire within; **dar ~ de** to give an account of. **3.** (MAT) ratio. ▶ **a razón de** *loc adv* at a rate of.

razonable *adj* reasonable.

razonamiento *m* reasoning (U).

razonar ♦ *vt* (*argumentar*) to reason out. ♦ *vi* (*pensar*) to reason.

re *m* (MÚS) D; (*en solfeo*) re.

reacción *f* reaction; **~ en cadena** chain reaction.

reaccionar *vi* to react.

reaccionario, -ria *adj, m y f* reactionary.

reacio, -cia *adj* stubborn; **ser ~ a o en hacer algo** to be reluctant to do sthg.

reactivación *f* revival.

reactor *m* **1.** (*propulsor*) reactor. **2.** (*avión*) jet (plane).

readmitir *vt* to accept o take back.

reafirmar *vt* to confirm. ▶ **reafirmarse** *vpr* to assert o.s.; **~se en algo** to become confirmed in sthg.

reajuste *m* **1.** (*cambio*) readjustment; **~ ministerial** cabinet reshuffle. **2.** (ECON - *de precios, impuestos*) increase; (- *de sector*) streamlining; (- *de salarios*) reduction; **~ de plantilla** redundancies (*pl*).

real *adj* **1.** (*verdadero*) real. **2.** (*de monarquía*) royal.

realce *m* **1.** (*esplendor*) glamour; **dar ~ a algo/alguien** to enhance sthg/sb. **2.** (*en pintura*) highlight.

realeza *f* (*monarcas*) royalty.

realidad *f* **1.** (*mundo real*) reality; **~ virtual** (INFORM) virtual reality. **2.** (*verdad*) truth; **en ~** actually, in fact.

realista ♦ *adj* realistic. ♦ *m y f* (ARTE) realist.

realización *f* **1.** (*ejecución*) carrying-out; (*de proyecto, medidas*) implementation; (*de sueños, deseos*) fulfilment. **2.** (*obra*) achievement. **3.** (CIN) production.

realizador, -ra *m y f* (CIN & TV) director.

realizar *vt* **1.** (*ejecutar - esfuerzo, viaje, inversión*) to make; (- *operación, experimento, trabajo*) to perform; (- *encargo*) to carry out; (- *plan, reformas*) to implement; (- *desfile*) to go on. **2.** (*hacer real - sueño, deseos*) to fulfil, to realize; (- *objetivo, ambición*) to achieve, to attain. **3.** (CIN) to produce. ▶ **realizarse** *vpr* **1.** (*en un*

trabajo) to find fulfilment. **2.** (*hacerse real - sueño, predicción, deseo*) to come true; (- *esperanza, ambición*) to be fulfilled. **3.** (*ejecutarse*) to be carried out.

realmente *adv* **1.** (*en verdad*) in fact, actually. **2.** (*muy*) really, very.

realquilado, -da *m y f* sub-tenant.

realquilar *vt* to sublet.

realzar *vt* **1.** (*resaltar*) to enhance. **2.** (*en pintura*) to highlight.

reanimar *vt* **1.** (*físicamente*) to revive. **2.** (*moralmente*) to cheer up. **3.** (MED) to resuscitate.

reanudar *vt* (*conversación, trabajo*) to resume; (*amistad*) to renew.

reaparición *f* reappearance.

rearme *m* rearmament.

reavivar *vt* to revive.

rebaja *f* **1.** (*acción*) reduction. **2.** (*descuento*) discount. ▶ **rebajas** *fpl* (COM) sales; **'grandes ~s'** 'massive reductions'; **estar de ~s** to have a sale on.

rebajado, -da *adj* **1.** (*precio*) reduced. **2.** (*humillado*) humiliated.

rebajar *vt* **1.** (*precio*) to reduce; **te rebajo 100 pesetas** I'll knock 100 pesetas off for you. **2.** (*persona*) to humiliate. **3.** (*intensidad*) to tone down. **4.** (*altura*) to lower. ▶ **rebajarse** *vpr* (*persona*) to humble o.s.; **~se a hacer algo** to lower o.s. o stoop to do sthg.

rebanada *f* slice.

rebañar *vt* to scrape clean.

rebaño *m* flock; (*de vacas*) herd.

rebasar *vt* to exceed, to surpass; (*agua*) to overflow; (AUTOM) to overtake.

rebatir *vt* to refute.

rebeca *f* cardigan.

rebelarse *vpr* to rebel.

rebelde ♦ *adj* **1.** (*sublevado*) rebel (*antes de sust*). **2.** (*desobediente*) rebellious. ♦ *m y f* (*sublevado, desobediente*) rebel.

rebeldía *f* **1.** (*cualidad*) rebelliousness. **2.** (*acción*) (act of) rebellion.

rebelión *f* rebellion.

rebenque *m* Amer (*látigo*) whip.

reblandecer *vt* to soften.

rebobinar *vt* to rewind.

rebosante *adj*: **~ (de)** brimming o overflowing (with).

rebosar ♦ *vt* to overflow with. ♦ *vi* to overflow; **~ de** to be overflowing with; *fig* (*persona*) to brim with.

rebotar *vi*: **~ (en)** to bounce (off), to rebound (off).

rebote *m* **1.** (*bote*) bounce, bouncing (U). **2.** (DEP) rebound; **de ~** on the rebound.

rebozado, -da adj (CULIN) coated in batter o breadcrumbs.

rebozar vt (CULIN) to coat in batter o breadcrumbs.

rebuscado, -da adj recherché, pretentious.

rebuznar vi to bray.

recabar vt (pedir) to ask for; (conseguir) to manage to get.

recadero, -ra m y f messenger.

recado m 1. (mensaje) message; **dejar (un) ~** to leave a message. 2. (encargo) errand; **hacer ~s** to run errands.

recaer vi 1. (enfermo) to have a relapse. 2. (ir a parar): **~ sobre** to fall on. 3. (reincidir): **~ en** to relapse into.

recaída f relapse.

recalcar vt to stress, to emphasize.

recalcitrante adj recalcitrant.

recalentar vt 1. (volver a calentar) to warm up. 2. (calentar demasiado) to overheat.

recámara f 1. (de arma de fuego) chamber. 2. Amer (dormitorio) bedroom.

recamarera f Amer maid.

recambio m spare (part); (para pluma) refill; **de ~** spare.

recapacitar vi to reflect, to think.

recapitulación f recap, recapitulation.

recargado, -da adj (estilo etc) overelaborate.

recargar vt 1. (volver a cargar - encendedor, recipiente) to refill; (- batería, pila) to recharge; (- fusil, camión) to reload. 2. (cargar demasiado) to overload. 3. (adornar en exceso) to overelaborate. 4. (cantidad): **~ 1.000 pesetas a alguien** to charge sb 1,000 pesetas extra. 5. (poner en exceso): **~ algo de algo** to put too much of sthg in sthg.

recargo m extra charge, surcharge.

recatado, -da adj (pudoroso) modest, demure.

recato m (pudor) modesty, demureness.

recauchutar vt to retread.

recaudación f 1. (acción) collection. 2. (cantidad) takings (pl); (DEP) gate.

recaudador, -ra m y f: **~ (de impuestos)** tax collector.

recaudar vt to collect.

recelar ◆ vt 1. (sospechar) to suspect. 2. (temer) to fear. ◆ vi: **~ de** to mistrust.

recelo m mistrust, suspicion.

receloso, -sa adj mistrustful, suspicious.

recepción f (gen) reception.

recepcionista m y f receptionist.

receptáculo m receptacle.

receptivo, -va adj receptive.

receptor, -ra m y f (persona) recipient. ▶ **receptor** m (aparato) receiver.

recesión f recession.

receta f 1. (CULIN & fig) recipe. 2. (MED) prescription.

rechazar vt 1. (gen & MED) to reject; (oferta) to turn down. 2. (repeler - a una persona) to push away; (MIL) to repel.

rechazo m 1. (gen & MED) rejection; (hacia una ley, un político) disapproval; **~ a hacer algo** refusal to do sthg. 2. (negación) denial.

rechinar vi 1. (puerta) to creak; (dientes) to grind; (frenos, ruedas) to screech; (metal) to clank. 2. (dando dentera) to grate.

rechistar vi to answer back.

rechoncho, -cha adj fam chubby.

rechupete ▶ **de rechupete** loc adv fam (gen) brilliant, great; (comida) scrumptious.

recibidor m entrance hall.

recibimiento m reception, welcome.

recibir ◆ vt 1. (gen) to receive; (clase, instrucción) to have. 2. (dar la bienvenida a) to welcome. 3. (ir a buscar) to meet. ◆ vi (atender visitas) to receive visitors.

recibo m receipt; **acusar ~ de** to acknowledge receipt of.

reciclaje m 1. (de residuos) recycling. 2. (de personas) retraining.

reciclar vt (residuos) to recycle.

recién adv recently, newly; **el ~ casado** the newly-wed; **los ~ llegados** the newcomers; **el ~ nacido** the newborn baby.

reciente adj 1. (acontecimiento etc) recent. 2. (pintura, pan etc) fresh.

recientemente adv recently.

recinto m (zona cercada) enclosure; (área) place, area; (alrededor de edificios) grounds (pl); **~ ferial** fairground (of trade fair).

recio, -cia adj 1. (persona) robust. 2. (voz) gravelly. 3. (objeto) solid. 4. (material, tela) tough, strong.

recipiente m container, receptacle.

reciprocidad f reciprocity.

recíproco, -ca adj mutual, reciprocal.

recital m 1. (de música clásica) recital; (de rock) concert. 2. (de lectura) reading.

recitar vt to recite.

reclamación f 1. (petición) claim, demand. 2. (queja) complaint.

reclamar ◆ vt (pedir, exigir) to demand, to ask for. ◆ vi (protestar): **~ (contra)** to

protest (against), to complain (about).
reclamo m 1. (para atraer) inducement. 2. (para cazar) decoy, lure.
reclinar vt: ~ **algo (sobre)** to lean sthg (on). ► **reclinarse** vpr to lean back.
recluir vt to shut o lock away. ► **recluirse** vpr to shut o.s. away.
reclusión f 1. (encarcelamiento) imprisonment. 2. fig (encierro) seclusion.
recluso, -sa m y f (preso) prisoner.
recluta m (obligatorio) conscript; (voluntario) recruit.
reclutamiento m (de soldados - obligatorio) conscription; (- voluntario) recruitment.
recobrar vt (gen) to recover; (conocimiento) to regain; (tiempo perdido) to make up for. ► **recobrarse** vpr: ~se **(de)** to recover (from).
recodo m bend.
recogedor m dustpan.
recoger vt 1. (coger) to pick up. 2. (reunir) to collect, to gather. 3. (ordenar, limpiar - mesa) to clear; (- habitación, cosas) to tidy o clear up. 4. (ir a buscar) to pick up, to fetch. 5. (albergar) to take in. 6. (cosechar) to gather, to harvest; (fruta) to pick. ► **recogerse** vpr 1. (a dormir, meditar) to retire. 2. (cabello) to put up.
recogido, -da adj 1. (lugar) withdrawn, secluded. 2. (cabello) tied back. ► **recogida** f 1. (gen) collection. 2. (cosecha) harvest, gathering; (de fruta) picking.
recolección f 1. (cosecha) harvest, gathering. 2. (recogida) collection.
recolector, -ra m y f 1. (gen) collector. 2. (de cosecha) harvester; (de fruta) picker.
recomendación f (gen pl) 1. (gen) recommendation. 2. (referencia) reference.
recomendado, -da m y f protégé (f protégée).
recomendar vt to recommend; ~ **a alguien que haga algo** to recommend that sb do sthg.
recompensa f reward; **en ~ por** in return for.
recompensar vt (premiar) to reward.
recomponer vt to repair, to mend.
recompuesto, -ta pp → **recomponer**.
reconciliación f reconciliation.
reconciliar vt to reconcile. ► **reconciliarse** vpr to be reconciled, to make up.
recóndito, -ta adj hidden, secret.
reconfortar vt 1. (anímicamente) to comfort. 2. (físicamente) to revitalize.

reconocer vt 1. (gen) to recognize. 2. (MED) to examine. 3. (terreno) to survey. ► **reconocerse** vpr 1. (identificarse) to recognize each other. 2. (confesarse): ~se **culpable** to admit one's guilt.
reconocido, -da adj 1. (admitido) recognized, acknowledged. 2. (agradecido) grateful.
reconocimiento m 1. (gen) recognition. 2. (agradecimiento) gratitude. 3. (MED) check-up, medical. 4. (MIL) reconnaissance.
reconquista f reconquest, recapture. ► **Reconquista** f: **la Reconquista** (HIST) the Reconquest of Spain, when the Christian Kings retook the country from the Muslims.
reconquistar vt to reconquer; fig to regain, to win back.
reconstruir vt 1. (edificio, país etc) to rebuild. 2. (suceso) to reconstruct.
reconversión f restructuring; ~ **industrial** rationalization of industry.
recopilación f (texto - de poemas, artículos) compilation, collection; (- de leyes) code.
recopilar vt 1. (recoger) to collect, to gather. 2. (escritos, leyes) to compile.
récord (pl **récords**) ◆ m record; **batir un ~** to break a record. ◆ adj inv record.
recordar ◆ vt 1. (acordarse de) to remember, to recall. 2. (traer a la memoria) to remind; **me recuerda a un amigo mío** he reminds me of a friend of mine. ◆ vi to remember; **si mal no recuerdo** as far as I can remember.
recordatorio m (aviso) reminder.
recordman [re'korðman] (pl **recordmen** o **recordmans**) m record holder.
recorrer vt 1. (atravesar - lugar, país) to travel through o across, to cross; (- ciudad) to go round. 2. (distancia) to cover. 3. fig (con la mirada) to look over.
recorrida f Amer trip.
recorrido m 1. (trayecto) route, path. 2. (viaje) journey. 3. (visita) tour.
recortado, -da adj 1. (cortado) cut. 2. (borde) jagged.
recortar vt 1. (cortar - lo que sobra) to cut off o away; (- figuras de un papel) to cut out. 2. (pelo, flequillo) to trim. 3. fig (reducir) to cut. ► **recortarse** vpr (figura etc) to stand out.
recorte m 1. (pieza cortada) cut, trimming; (de periódico, revista) cutting. 2. (reducción) cut, cutback.
recostar vt to lean (back). ► **recostarse** vpr to lie down.
recoveco m 1. (rincón) nook. 2. (curva)

bend. **3.** *fig* (*lo más oculto*): **los ~s del alma** the innermost recesses of the mind.

recreación *f* re-creation.

recrear *vt* **1.** (*volver a crear*) to recreate. **2.** (*entretener*) to amuse, to entertain. ▶ **recrearse** *vpr* **1.** (*entretenerse*) to amuse o.s., to entertain o.s. **2.** (*regodearse*) to take delight o pleasure.

recreativo, -va *adj* recreational.

recreo *m* **1.** (*entretenimiento*) recreation, amusement. **2.** (EDUC - *en primaria*) playtime; (*- en secundaria*) break.

recriminar *vt* to reproach.

recrudecer *vi* to get worse. ▶ **recrudecerse** *vpr* to get worse.

recta → **recto**.

rectángulo *m* rectangle.

rectificar *vt* **1.** (*error*) to rectify, to correct. **2.** (*conducta, actitud etc*) to improve. **3.** (*ajustar*) to put right.

rectitud *f* straightness; *fig* rectitude.

recto, -ta *adj* **1.** (*sin curvas, vertical*) straight. **2.** *fig* (*íntegro*) honourable. ▶ **recto** ◆ *m* (ANAT) rectum. ◆ *adv*: (**todo**) **~ straight on o ahead.** ▶ **recta** *f* straight line; **la recta final** *lit* & *fig* the home straight.

rector, -ra ◆ *adj* governing. ◆ *m y f* (*de universidad*) vice-chancellor Br, president Am. ▶ **rector** *m* (RELIG) rector.

recuadro *m* box.

recubrir *vt* (*gen*) to cover; (*con pintura, barniz*) to coat.

recuento *m* recount.

recuerdo *m* **1.** (*rememoración*) memory. **2.** (*objeto - de viaje*) souvenir; (*- de persona*) keepsake. ▶ **recuerdos** *mpl* (*saludos*) regards; **dale ~s de mi parte** give her my regards.

recular *vi* (*retroceder*) to go o move back.

recuperable *adj* (*gen*) recoverable; (*fiestas, horas de trabajo*) that can be made up later.

recuperación *f* **1.** (*de lo perdido, la salud, la economía*) recovery. **2.** (*fisioterapia*) physiotherapy.

recuperar *vt* (*lo perdido*) to recover; (*horas de trabajo*) to catch up; (*conocimiento*) to regain. ▶ **recuperarse** *vpr* **1.** (*enfermo*) to recuperate, to recover. **2.** (*de una crisis*) to recover; (*negocio*) to pick up; **~se de algo** to get over sthg.

recurrir *vi* **1.** (*buscar ayuda*): **~ a alguien** to turn to sb; **~ a algo** to resort to sthg. **2.** (DER) to appeal.

recurso *m* **1.** (*medio*) resort; **como último ~** as a last resort. **2.** (DER) appeal. ▶ **recursos** *mpl* (*fondos*) resources;

(*financieros*) means; **~s propios** (ECON) equities.

red *f* **1.** (*malla*) net; (*para cabello*) hairnet. **2.** (*sistema*) network, system; (*de electricidad, agua*) mains (*sg*); **~ viaria** road network o system. **3.** (*organización - de espionaje*) ring; (*- de tiendas*) chain. **4.** (INFORM) network.

Red (INFORM) *f*: **la ~** the Net; **navegar por la ~** to surf the Net.

redacción *f* **1.** (*acción - gen*) writing; (*- de periódico etc*) editing. **2.** (*estilo*) wording. **3.** (*equipo de redactores*) editorial team o staff. **4.** (*oficina*) editorial office. **5.** (EDUC) essay.

redactar *vt* to write (up); (*carta*) to draft.

redactor, -ra *m y f* (PRENS - *escritor*) writer; (*- editor*) editor; **~ jefe** editor-in-chief.

redada *f* *fig* (*de policía - en un solo lugar*) raid; (*- en varios lugares*) round-up.

redención *f* redemption.

redil *m* fold, pen.

redimir *vt* **1.** (*gen*) to redeem. **2.** (*librar*) to free, to exempt. ▶ **redimirse** *vpr* to redeem o.s.

rédito *m* interest (U), yield (U).

redoblar ◆ *vt* to redouble. ◆ *vi* to roll.

redomado, -da *adj* out-and-out.

redondear *vt* **1.** (*hacer redondo*) to make round. **2.** (*negocio, acuerdo*) to round off. **3.** (*cifra, precio*) to round up/down.

redondel *m* **1.** (*gen*) circle, ring. **2.** (TAUROM) bullring.

redondo, -da *adj* **1.** (*circular, esférico*) round; **a la redonda** around; **caerse ~** *fig* to collapse in a heap. **2.** (*perfecto*) excellent.

reducción *f* **1.** (*gen*) reduction. **2.** (*sometimiento*) suppression.

reducido, -da *adj* **1.** (*pequeño*) small. **2.** (*limitado*) limited. **3.** (*estrecho*) narrow.

reducir *vt* **1.** (*gen*) to reduce. **2.** (*someter - país, ciudad*) to suppress; (*- sublevados, atracadores*) to bring under control. **3.** (MAT) (*convertir*) to convert. ▶ **reducirse a** *vpr* **1.** (*limitarse a*) to be reduced to. **2.** (*equivaler a*) to boil o come down to.

reducto *m* **1.** (*fortificación*) redoubt. **2.** *fig* (*refugio*) stronghold, bastion.

redundancia *f* redundancy, superfluousness.

redundante *adj* redundant, superfluous.

redundar *vi*: **~ en algo** to have an

effect on sthg; **redunda en beneficio nuestro** it is to our advantage.

reeditar vt to bring out a new edition of; (reimprimir) to reprint.

reelección f re-election.

reembolsar, **rembolsar** vt (gastos) to reimburse; (fianza, dinero) to refund; (deuda) to repay.

reembolso, **rembolso** m (de gastos) reimbursement; (de fianza, dinero) refund; (de deuda) repayment; **contra ~** cash on delivery.

reemplazar, **remplazar** vt (gen & INFORM) to replace.

reemplazo, **remplazo** m 1. (gen & INFORM) replacement. 2. (MIL) call-up, draft.

reemprender vt to start again.

reencarnación f reincarnation.

reencuentro m reunion.

reestructurar vt to restructure.

refacción f Amer 1. (reparaciones) repairs (pl). 2. (recambios) spare parts (pl).

refaccionar vt Amer to repair, to fix.

refaccionaria f Amer repair workshop.

referencia f reference; **con ~ a** with reference to. ▶ **referencias** fpl (información) information (U).

referéndum (pl referéndums) m referendum.

referente adj: **~ a** concerning, relating to.

referir vt 1. (narrar) to tell, to recount. 2. (remitir): **~ a alguien a** to refer sb to. 3. (relacionar): **~ algo a** to relate sthg to. ▶ **referirse a** vpr to refer to; **¿a qué te refieres?** what do you mean?; **por lo que se refiere a ...** as far as … is concerned.

refilón ▶ **de refilón** loc adv 1. (de lado) sideways; **mirar algo de ~** to look at sthg out of the corner of one's eye. 2. fig (de pasada) briefly.

refinado, -da adj refined.

refinamiento m refinement.

refinar vt to refine.

refinería f refinery.

reflector m (ELECTR) spotlight; (MIL) searchlight.

reflejar vt lit & fig to reflect. ▶ **reflejarse** vpr lit & fig: **~se (en)** to be reflected (in).

reflejo, -ja adj (movimiento, dolor) reflex (antes de sust). ▶ **reflejo** m 1. (gen) reflection. 2. (destello) glint, gleam. 3. (ANAT) reflex. ▶ **reflejos** mpl (de peluquería) highlights.

reflexión f reflection; **con ~** on reflec-

tion; **sin previa ~** without thinking.

reflexionar vi to reflect, to think.

reflexivo, -va adj 1. (que piensa) thoughtful. 2. (GRAM) reflexive.

reflujo m ebb (tide).

reforma f 1. (modificación) reform; **~ agraria** agrarian reform. 2. (en local, casa etc) alterations (pl). ▶ **Reforma** f: **la Reforma** (RELIG) the Reformation.

reformar vt 1. (gen & RELIG) to reform. 2. (local, casa etc) to renovate. ▶ **reformarse** vpr to mend one's ways.

reformatorio m ~ youth custody centre Br, = borstal Br, reformatory Am; (de menores de 15 años) ~ remand home.

reforzar vt to reinforce.

refractario, -ria adj 1. (material) refractory. 2. (opuesto): **~ a** averse to.

refrán m proverb, saying.

refregar vt 1. (frotar) to scrub. 2. fig (reprochar): **~ algo a alguien** to reproach sb for sthg.

refrenar vt to curb, to restrain.

refrendar vt (aprobar) to approve.

refrescante adj refreshing.

refrescar ◆ vt 1. (gen) to refresh; (bebidas) to chill. 2. fig (conocimientos) to brush up. ◆ vi 1. (tiempo) to cool down. 2. (bebida) to be refreshing. ▶ **refrescarse** vpr 1. (tomar aire fresco) to get a breath of fresh air. 2. (beber algo) to have a drink. 3. (mojarse con agua fría) to splash o.s. down.

refresco m 1. (bebida) soft drink; **~s** refreshments. 2. (MIL): **de ~** new, fresh.

refriega f scuffle; (MIL) skirmish.

refrigeración f 1. (aire acondicionado) air-conditioning. 2. (de alimentos) refrigeration. 3. (de máquinas) cooling.

refrigerador, -ra adj cooling. ▶ **refrigerador** m (de alimentos) refrigerator, fridge Br, icebox Am.

refrigerar vt 1. (alimentos) to refrigerate. 2. (local) to air-condition. 3. (máquina) to cool.

refrigerio m snack.

refrito, -ta adj (demasiado frito) overfried; (frito de nuevo) re-fried. ▶ **refrito** m fig (cosa rehecha) rehash.

refuerzo m reinforcement.

refugiado, -da m y f refugee.

refugiar vt to give refuge to. ▶ **refugiarse** vpr to take refuge; **~se de algo** to shelter from sthg.

refugio m 1. (lugar) shelter, refuge; **~ atómico** nuclear bunker. 2. fig (amparo, consuelo) refuge, comfort.

refulgir *vi* to shine brightly.

refunfuñar *vi* to grumble.

refutar *vt* to refute.

regadera *f* 1. (*para regar*) watering can. 2. Amer (*chubasco*) shower.

regadío *m* irrigated land.

regalado, -da *adj* 1. (*muy barato*) dirt cheap. 2. (*agradable*) comfortable.

regalar *vt* 1. (*dar - de regalo*) to give (as a present); (- *gratis*) to give away. 2. (*agasajar*): ~ **a alguien con algo** to shower sb with sthg.

regaliz *m* liquorice.

regalo *m* 1. (*obsequio*) present, gift. 2. (*placer*) joy, delight.

regalón, -ona *adj* Amer *fam* spoilt.

regañadientes ▶ a regañadientes *loc adv fam* unwillingly, reluctantly.

regañar ◆ *vt* (*reprender*) to tell off. ◆ *vi* (*pelearse*) to fall out, to argue.

regañina *f* (*reprimenda*) ticking off.

regañón, -ona *adj* grumpy.

regar *vt* 1. (*con agua - planta*) to water; (- *calle*) to hose down. 2. (*suj: río*) to flow through.

regata *f* (NÁUT) regatta, boat race.

regatear ◆ *vt* 1. (*escatimar*) to be sparing with; **no ha regateado esfuerzos** he has spared no effort. 2. (*suj*) to beat, to dribble past. 3. (*precio*) to haggle over. ◆ *vi* 1. (*negociar el precio*) to bargain, to haggle. 2. (NÁUT) to race.

regateo *m* bargaining, haggling.

regazo *m* lap.

regeneración *f* regeneration; (*moral*) reform.

regenerar *vt* to regenerate; (*moralmente*) to reform.

regentar *vt* (*país*) to run, to govern; (*negocio*) to run, to manage; (*puesto*) to hold.

regente ◆ *adj* regent. ◆ *m y f* 1. (*de un país*) regent. 2. (*administrador - de tienda*) manager; (- *de colegio*) governor. 3. Amer (*alcalde*) mayor (*f* mayoress).

regidor, -ra *m y f* (TEATR) stage manager; (CIN & TV) assistant director.

régimen (*pl* **regímenes**) *m* 1. (*sistema político*) regime; **Antiguo ~** ancien régime. 2. (*normativa*) rules (*pl*). 3. (*dieta*) diet. 4. (*de vida, lluvias etc*) pattern.

regimiento *m* (MIL & *fig*) regiment.

regio, -gia *adj lit & fig* royal.

región *f* region; (MIL) district.

regir ◆ *vt* 1. (*reinar en*) to rule, to govern. 2. (*administrar*) to run, to manage. 3. *fig* (*determinar*) to govern, to deter-

mine. ◆ *vi* (*ley*) to be in force, to apply.

▶ regirse por *vpr* to trust in.

registrador, -ra *m y f* registrar.

registrar *vt* 1. (*inspeccionar - zona, piso*) to search; (- *persona*) to frisk. 2. (*nacimiento, temperatura etc*) to register, to record. 3. (*grabar*) to record. ▶ **registrarse** *vpr* 1. (*suceder*) to occur. 2. (*observarse*) to be recorded.

registro *m* 1. (*oficina*) registry (office); ~ **civil** registry (office). 2. (*libro*) register. 3. (*inspección*) search, searching (U). 4. (INFORM) record. 5. (LING & MÚS) register.

regla *f* 1. (*para medir*) ruler, rule. 2. (*norma*) rule; **en ~** in order; **por ~ general** as a rule. 3. (MAT) operation. 4. *fam* (*menstruación*) period.

reglamentación *f* (*acción*) regulation; (*reglas*) rules (*pl*), regulations (*pl*).

reglamentar *vt* to regulate.

reglamentario, -ria *adj* lawful; (*arma, balón*) regulation (*antes de sust*); (DER) statutory.

reglamento *m* regulations (*pl*), rules (*pl*).

reglar *vt* to regulate.

regocijar ▶ regocijarse *vpr*: ~**se (de o con)** to rejoice (in).

regocijo *m* joy, delight.

regodeo *m* delight, pleasure; (*malicioso*) (cruel) delight o pleasure.

regordete *adj* chubby.

regresar ◆ *vi* (*yendo*) to go back, to return; (*viniendo*) to come back, to return. ◆ *vt* Amer (*devolver*) to give back.

regresión *f* 1. (*de epidemia*) regression. 2. (*de exportaciones*) drop, decline.

regresivo, -va *adj* regressive.

regreso *m* return; **estar de ~** to be back.

reguero *m* (*de sangre, agua*) trickle; (*de harina etc*) trail; **correr como un ~ de pólvora** to spread like wildfire.

regulación *f* (*gen*) regulation; (*de nacimientos, tráfico*) control; (*de mecanismo*) adjustment.

regulador, -ra *adj* regulatory.

regular ◆ *adj* 1. (*gen*) regular; (*de tamaño*) medium; **de un modo ~** regularly. 2. (*mediocre*) average, fair. 3. (*normal*) normal, usual. ◆ *adv* all right; (*de salud*) so-so. ◆ *vt* (*gen*) to control, to regulate; (*mecanismo*) to adjust. ▶ **por lo regular** *loc adv* as a rule, generally.

regularidad *f* regularity; **con ~** regularly.

regularizar *vt* (*legalizar*) to regularize.

regusto *m* aftertaste; (*semejanza, aire*) flavour, hint.

rehabilitación *f* 1. (*de personas*) rehabilitation; (*en un puesto*) reinstatement. 2. (*de local*) restoration.

rehabilitar *vt* 1. (*personas*) to rehabilitate; (*en un puesto*) to reinstate. 2. (*local*) to restore.

rehacer *vt* 1. (*volver a hacer*) to redo, to do again. 2. (*reconstruir*) to rebuild. ▶ **rehacerse** *vpr* (*recuperarse*) to recuperate, to recover.

rehecho, -cha *pp* → **rehacer**.

rehén (*pl* **rehenes**) *m* hostage.

rehogar *vt* to fry over a low heat.

rehuir *vt* to avoid.

rehusar *vt & vi* to refuse.

Reikiavik Reykjavik.

reimpresión *f* (*tirada*) reprint; (*acción*) reprinting.

reina *f* (*monarca*) queen.

reinado *m* lit & fig reign.

reinante *adj* 1. (*monarquía, persona*) reigning, ruling. 2. (*viento*) prevailing; (*frío, calor*) current.

reinar *vi* lit & fig to reign.

reincidir *vi*: ~ **en** (*falta, error*) to relapse into, to fall back into; (*delito*) to repeat.

reincorporar *vt* to reincorporate. ▶ **reincorporarse** *vpr*: ~**se (a)** to rejoin.

reino *m* (CIENCIA & POLÍT) kingdom; fig realm.

Reino Unido: **el ~** the United Kingdom.

reintegrar *vt* 1. (*a un puesto*) to reinstate. 2. (*dinero*) to reimburse. ▶ **reintegrarse** *vpr*: ~**se (a)** to return (to).

reintegro *m* 1. (*de dinero*) reimbursement; (BANCA) withdrawal. 2. (*en lotería*) return of one's stake (*in lottery*).

reír ◆ *vi* to laugh. ◆ *vt* to laugh at. ▶ **reírse** *vpr*: ~**se (de)** to laugh (at).

reiterar *vt* to reiterate.

reiterativo, -va *adj* repetitious.

reivindicación *f* claim, demand.

reivindicar *vt* 1. (*derechos, salario etc*) to claim, to demand. 2. (*atentado*) to claim responsibility for.

reivindicativo, -va *adj*: **plataforma reivindicativa** (set of) demands; **jornada reivindicativa** day of protest.

reja *f* (*gen*) bars (*pl*); (*en el suelo*) grating; (*celosía*) grille.

rejego, -ga *adj* Amer fam (*terco*) stubborn.

rejilla *f* 1. (*enrejado*) grid, grating; (*de ventana*) grille; (*de cocina*) grill (on stove);

(*de horno*) gridiron. 2. (*para sillas, muebles*) wickerwork. 3. (*para equipaje*) luggage rack.

rejón *m* (TAUROM) type of 'banderilla' used by mounted bullfighter.

rejoneador, -ra *m y f* (TAUROM) bullfighter on horseback who uses the 'rejón'.

rejuntarse *vpr fam* to live together.

rejuvenecer *vt & vi* to rejuvenate.

relación *f* 1. (*nexo*) relation, connection; **con ~ a, en ~ con** in relation to; **~ precio-calidad** value for money. 2. (*comunicación, trato*) relations (*pl*), relationship; **relaciones diplomáticas/públicas** diplomatic/public relations. 3. (*lista*) list. 4. (*descripción*) account. 5. (*informe*) report. 6. (*gen pl*) (*noviazgo*) relationship. 7. (MAT) ratio. ▶ **relaciones** *fpl* (*contactos*) connections.

relacionar *vt* (*vincular*) to relate, to connect. ▶ **relacionarse** *vpr*: ~**se (con)** (*alternar*) to mix (with).

relajación *f* relaxation.

relajar *vt* to relax. ▶ **relajarse** *vpr* to relax.

relajo *m* Amer fam (*alboroto*) racket, din.

relamer *vt* to lick repeatedly. ▶ **relamerse** *vpr* 1. (*persona*) to lick one's lips. 2. (*animal*) to lick its chops.

relamido, -da *adj* prim and proper.

relámpago *m* (*descarga*) flash of lightning, lightning (U); (*destello*) flash.

relampaguear *vi* fig to flash.

relatar *vt* (*suceso*) to relate, to recount; (*historia*) to tell.

relatividad *f* relativity.

relativo, -va *adj* 1. (*gen*) relative. 2. (*escaso*) limited.

relato *m* (*exposición*) account, report; (*cuento*) tale.

relax *m inv* 1. (*relajación*) relaxation. 2. (*sección de periódico*) personal column.

relegar *vt*: ~ **(a)** to relegate (to); **~ algo al olvido** to banish sthg from one's mind.

relevante *adj* outstanding, important.

relevar *vt* 1. (*sustituir*) to relieve, to take over from. 2. (*destituir*): ~ **(de)** to dismiss (from), to relieve (of). 3. (*eximir*): ~ **(de)** to free (from). 4. (DEP - *en partidos*) to substitute; (- *en relevos*) to take over from.

relevo *m* 1. (MIL) relief, changing. 2. (DEP) (*acción*) relay. 3. *loc*: **tomar el ~** to take over. ▶ **relevos** *mpl* (DEP) (*carrera*) relay (race) (*sg*).

relieve *m* 1. (*gen*, ARTE & GEOGR) relief; **bajo ~** bas-relief. 2. (*importancia*) importance; **poner de ~** to underline (the importance of).

religión f religion.

religioso, -sa ♦ adj religious. ♦ m y f (*monje*) monk (f nun).

relinchar vi to neigh, to whinny.

reliquia f relic; (*familiar*) heirloom.

rellano m (*de escalera*) landing.

rellenar vt 1. (*volver a llenar*) to refill. 2. (*documento, formulario*) to fill in o out. 3. (*pollo, cojín etc*) to stuff; (*tarta, pastel*) to fill.

relleno, -na adj (*gen*) stuffed; (*tarta, pastel*) filled. ► **relleno** m (*de pollo*) stuffing; (*de pastel*) filling.

reloj m (*de pared*) clock; (*de pulsera*) watch; **~ de arena** hourglass; **~ de pulsera** watch, wristwatch; **hacer algo contra ~** to do sthg against the clock.

relojero, -ra m y f watchmaker.

reluciente adj shining, gleaming.

relucir vi lit & fig to shine; **sacar algo a ~** to bring sthg up, to mention sthg.

remachar vt 1. (*machacar*) to rivet. 2. fig (*recalcar*) to drive home, to stress.

remache m (*clavo*) rivet.

remanente m 1. (*de géneros*) surplus stock; (*de productos agrícolas*) surplus. 2. (*en cuenta bancaria*) balance.

remangar = **arremangar**.

remanso m still pool.

remar vi to row.

rematado, -da adj utter, complete.

rematar ♦ vt 1. (*acabar*) to finish. 2. (*matar - persona*) to finish off; (- *animal*) to put out of its misery. 3. (DEP) to shoot. 4. (*liquidar, vender*) to sell off cheaply. ♦ vi (*en fútbol*) to shoot; (*de cabeza*) to head at goal.

remate m 1. (*fin, colofón*) end. 2. (*en fútbol*) shot; (*de cabeza*) header at goal. ► **de remate** loc adv totally, completely.

rembolsar = **reembolsar**.

rembolso = **reembolso**.

remedar vt to imitate; (*por burla*) to ape.

remediar vt (*daño*) to remedy, to put right; (*problema*) to solve; (*peligro*) to avoid.

remedio m 1. (*solución*) solution, remedy; **como último ~** as a last resort; **no hay** o **queda más ~ que ...** there's nothing for it but ...; **no tener más ~** to have no alternative o choice; **sin ~** (*sin cura, solución*) hopeless; (*ineludiblemente*) inevitably. 2. (*consuelo*) consolation. 3. (*medicamento*) remedy, cure.

rememorar vt to remember, to recall.

remendar vt to mend, to darn.

remero, -ra m y f (*persona*) rower. ► **remera** f Amer (*prenda*) T-shirt.

remesa f (*de productos*) consignment; (*de dinero*) remittance.

remeter vt to tuck in.

remezón m Amer earth tremor.

remiendo m (*parche*) mend, darn.

remilgado, -da adj 1. (*afectado*) affected. 2. (*escrupuloso*) squeamish; (*con comida*) fussy.

remilgo m 1. (*afectación*) affectation. 2. (*escrupulosidad*) squeamishness; (*con comida*) fussiness.

reminiscencia f reminiscence; **tener ~s de** to be reminiscent of.

remiso, -sa adj: **ser ~ a hacer algo** to be reluctant to do sthg.

remite m sender's name and address.

remitente m y f sender.

remitir ♦ vt 1. (*enviar*) to send. 2. (*perdonar*) to forgive, to remit. 3. (*traspasar*): **~ algo a** to refer sthg to. ♦ vi 1. (*en texto*): **~ a** to refer to. 2. (*disminuir*) to subside. ► **remitirse a** vpr 1. (*atenerse a*) to abide by. 2. (*referirse a*) to refer to.

remo m 1. (*pala*) oar. 2. (*deporte*) rowing.

remoción f Amer dismissal, sacking.

remodelar vt (*gen*) to redesign; (*gobierno*) to reshuffle.

remojar vt (*humedecer*) to soak.

remojo m: **poner en ~** to leave to soak; **estar en ~** to be soaking.

remolacha f beetroot Br, beet Am; (*azucarera*) (sugar) beet.

remolcador, -ra adj (*coche*) tow (*antes de sust*); (*barco*) tug (*antes de sust*). ► **remolcador** m (*camión*) breakdown lorry; (*barco*) tug, tugboat.

remolcar vt (*coche*) to tow; (*barco*) to tug.

remolino m 1. (*de agua*) eddy, whirlpool; (*de viento*) whirlwind; (*de humo*) cloud, swirl. 2. (*de gente*) throng, mass. 3. (*de pelo*) cowlick.

remolón, -ona adj lazy.

remolque m 1. (*acción*) towing. 2. (*vehículo*) trailer.

remontar vt (*pendiente, río*) to go up; (*obstáculo*) to overcome; (*puestos*) to catch up. ► **remontarse** vpr 1. (*ave, avión*) to soar, to climb high. 2. (*gastos*): **~se a** to amount o come to. 3. fig (*datar*): **~se a** to go o date back to.

remorder vt fig: **~le a alguien** to fill sb with remorse.

remordimiento m remorse.

remoto, -ta adj remote; **no tengo ni la más remota idea** I haven't got the faintest idea.

remover vt 1. (agitar - sopa, café) to stir; (- ensalada) to toss; (- bote, frasco) to shake; (- tierra) to dig up. 2. (desplazar) to move, to shift. 3. (reavivar - recuerdos, pasado) to rake up. 4. Amer (despedir) to dismiss, to sack. ▶ **removerse** vpr to move about; (mar) to get rough.

remplazar = **reemplazar**.

remplazo = **reemplazo**.

remuneración f remuneration.

remunerar vt 1. (pagar) to remunerate. 2. (recompensar) to reward.

renacer vi 1. (gen) to be reborn; (flores, hojas) to grow again. 2. (alegría, esperanza) to return, to revive.

renacimiento m (gen) rebirth; (de flores, hojas) budding. ▶ **Renacimiento** m: **el Renacimiento** the Renaissance.

renacuajo m tadpole; fam fig tiddler.

renal adj renal, kidney (antes de sust).

rencilla f quarrel.

rencor m resentment, bitterness.

rencoroso, -sa adj resentful, bitter.

rendición f surrender.

rendido, -da adj 1. (agotado) exhausted. 2. (sumiso) submissive; (admirador) devoted.

rendija f crack, gap.

rendimiento m 1. (de inversión, negocio) yield, return; (de trabajador, fábrica) productivity; (de tierra, cosecha) yield. 2. (de motor) performance.

rendir ◆ vt 1. (cansar) to tire out. 2. (rentar) to yield. 3. (vencer) to defeat, to subdue. 4. (ofrecer) to give, to present; (pleitesía) to pay. ◆ vi (máquina) to perform well; (negocio) to be profitable; (fábrica, trabajador) to be productive. ▶ **rendirse** vpr 1. (entregarse) to surrender. 2. (ceder): **~se a** to give in to. 3. (desanimarse) to give in o up.

renegado, -da adj, m y f renegade.

renegar vi 1. (repudiar): **~ de** (RELIG) to renounce; (familia) to disown. 2. fam (gruñir) to grumble.

Renfe (abrev de Red Nacional de los Ferrocarriles Españoles) f Spanish state railway network.

renglón m line; (COM) item.

reno m reindeer.

renombrar vt (INFORM) to rename.

renombre m renown, fame.

renovación f (de carné, contrato) renewal; (de mobiliario, local) renovation.

renovar vt 1. (cambiar - mobiliario, local) to renovate; (- vestuario) to clear out; (- personal, plantilla) to shake out. 2. (rehacer - carné, contrato, ataques) to renew. 3. (restaurar) to restore. 4. (innovar) to rethink, to revolutionize; (POLÍT) to reform.

renquear vi to limp, to hobble; fig to struggle along.

renta f 1. (ingresos) income; **~ fija** fixed income; **~ per cápita** o **per habitante** per capita income. 2. (alquiler) rent. 3. (beneficios) return. 4. (intereses) interest.

rentable adj profitable.

rentar ◆ vt 1. (rendir) to produce, to yield. 2. Amer (alquilar) to rent. ◆ vi to be profitable.

rentista m y f person of independent means.

renuncia f (abandono) giving up; (dimisión) resignation.

renunciar vi 1. (abandonar) to give up. 2. (dimitir) to resign. ▶ **renunciar a** vi 1. (prescindir de) to give up; (plan, proyecto) to drop; **~ al tabaco** to give up o stop smoking. 2. (rechazar): **~ (a hacer algo)** to refuse (to do sthg).

reñido, -da adj 1. (enfadado): **~ (con)** on bad terms o at odds (with); **están ~s** they've fallen out. 2. (disputado) hardfought. 3. (incompatible): **estar ~ con** to be incompatible with.

reñir ◆ vt 1. (regañar) to tell off. 2. (disputar) to fight. ◆ vi (enfadarse) to argue, to fall out.

reo, -a m y f (culpado) offender, culprit; (acusado) accused, defendant.

reojo m: **mirar algo de ~** to look at sthg out of the corner of one's eye.

repantigarse vpr to sprawl out.

reparación f 1. (arreglo) repair, repairing (U); **en ~** under repair. 2. (compensación) reparation, redress.

reparador, -ra adj (descanso, sueño) refreshing.

reparar ◆ vt (coche etc) to repair, to fix; (error, daño etc) to make amends for; (fuerzas) to restore. ◆ vi (advertir): **~ en algo** to notice sthg; **no ~ en gastos** to spare no expense.

reparo m 1. (objeción) objection. 2. (apuro): **no tener ~s en** not to be afraid to.

repartición f (reparto) sharing out.

repartidor, -ra m y f (gen) distributor; (de butano, carbón) deliveryman (f deliverywoman); (de leche) milkman (f milk-lady); (*de periódicos*) paperboy (*f* papergirl).

repartir *vt* 1. (*dividir - gen*) to share out, to divide; (*- territorio, nación*) to partition. 2. (*distribuir - leche, periódicos, correo*) to deliver; (*- folletos*) to distribute; (*- naipes*) to deal (out). 3. (*asignar - trabajo, órdenes*) to give out, to allocate; (*- papeles*) to assign.

reparto *m* 1. (*división*) division, distribution; **~ de beneficios** (ECON) profit sharing; **~ de premios** prizegiving. 2. (*distribución - de leche, periódicos, correo*) delivery. 3. (*asignación*) allocation. 4. (CIN & TEATR) cast.

repasador *m* Amer tea towel.

repasar *vt* 1. (*revisar*) to go over; (*lección*) to revise. 2. (*zurcir*) to darn, to mend.

repaso *m* (*revisión*) revision; (*de ropa*) darning, mending; **curso de ~** refresher course.

repatriar *vt* to repatriate.

repecho *m* steep slope.

repelente *adj* 1. (*desagradable, repugnante*) repulsive. 2. (*ahuyentador*) repellent.

repeler *vt* 1. (*rechazar*) to repel. 2. (*repugnar*) to repulse, to disgust.

repelús *m*: **me da ~** it gives me the shivers.

repente *m* (*arrebato*) fit. ► **de repente** *loc adv* suddenly.

repentino, -na *adj* sudden.

repercusión *f* 1. (*impacto, resonancia*) impact. 2. (*consecuencia*) repercussion.

repercutir *vi fig* (*afectar*): **~ en** to have repercussions on.

repertorio *m* 1. (*obras*) repertoire. 2. *fig* (*serie*) selection.

repesca *f* 1. (EDUC) resit. 2. (DEP) repêchage.

repetición *f* repetition; (*de una jugada*) action replay.

repetidor, -ra *m y f* (EDUC) student repeating a year. ► **repetidor** *m* (ELECTR) repeater.

repetir ◆ *vt* to repeat; (*ataque*) to renew; (*en comida*) to have seconds of. ◆ *vi* 1. (*alumno*) to repeat a year. 2. (*sabor, alimento*): **~ (a alguien)** to repeat (on sb). 3. (*comensal*) to have seconds. ► **repetirse** *vpr* 1. (*fenómeno*) to recur. 2. (*persona*) to repeat o.s.

repicar *vi* (*campanas*) to ring; (*tambor*) to sound.

repique *m* peal, ringing (U).

repiqueteo *m* (*de campanas*) pealing;

(*de tambor*) beating; (*de timbre*) ringing; (*de lluvia, dedos*) drumming.

repisa *f* (*estante*) shelf; (*sobre chimenea*) mantelpiece.

replantear *vt* 1. (*reenfocar*) to reconsider, to restate. 2. (*volver a mencionar*) to bring up again.

replegar *vt* (*ocultar*) to retract. ► **replegarse** *vpr* (*retirarse*) to withdraw, to retreat.

repleto, -ta *adj*: **~ (de)** packed (with).

réplica *f* 1. (*respuesta*) reply. 2. (*copia*) replica.

replicar ◆ *vt* (*responder*) to answer; (*objetar*) to answer back, to retort. ◆ *vi* (*objetar*) to answer back.

repliegue *m* 1. (*retirada*) withdrawal, retreat. 2. (*pliegue*) fold.

repoblación *f* (*con gente*) repopulation; (*con peces*) restocking; **~ forestal** reafforestation.

repoblar *vt* (*con gente*) to repopulate; (*con peces*) to restock; (*con árboles*) to replant.

repollo *m* cabbage.

reponer *vt* 1. (*gen*) to replace. 2. (CIN & TEATR) to re-run, to put on again; (TV) to repeat. 3. (*replicar*): **~ que** to reply that.

reportaje *m* (RADIO & TV) report; (PRENS) article.

reportar *vt* 1. (*traer*) to bring. 2. Amer (*informar*) to report.

reporte *m* Amer report.

reportero, -ra, **repórter** *m y f* reporter.

reposado, -da *adj* relaxed, calm.

reposar *vi* 1. (*descansar*) to (have a) rest. 2. (*sedimentarse*) to stand.

reposera *f* Amer easy chair.

reposición *f* 1. (CIN) rerun; (TEATR) revival; (TV) repeat. 2. (*de existencias, pieza etc*) replacement.

reposo *m* (*descanso*) rest.

repostar ◆ *vi* (*coche*) to fill up; (*avión*) to refuel. ◆ *vt* 1. (*gasolina*) to fill up with. 2. (*provisiones*) to stock up on.

repostería *f* (*oficio, productos*) confectionery.

reprender *vt* (*a niños*) to tell off; (*a empleados*) to reprimand.

reprensión *f* (*a niños*) telling-off; (*a empleados*) reprimand.

represalia *f* (*gen pl*) reprisal; **tomar ~s** to retaliate, to take reprisals.

representación *f* 1. (*gen* & COM) representation; **en ~ de** on behalf of. 2. (TEATR) performance.

representante ◆ *adj* representative.
◆ *m y f* **1.** (*gen & COM*) representative.
2. (*de artista*) agent.

representar *vt* **1.** (*gen & COM*) to represent. **2.** (*aparentar*) to look; **representa unos 40 años** she looks about 40.
3. (*significar*) to mean; **representa el 50% del consumo interno** it accounts for 50% of domestic consumption. **4.** (*TEATR - función*) to perform; (*- papel*) to play.

representativo, -va *adj* **1.** (*simbolizador*): **ser ~ de** to represent. **2.** (*característico, relevante*): **~ (de)** representative (of).

represión *f* repression.

reprimenda *f* reprimand.

reprimir *vt* (*gen*) to suppress; (*minorías, disidentes*) to repress. ▶ **reprimirse** *vpr*: **~se (de hacer algo)** to restrain o.s. (from doing sthg).

reprobar *vt* to censure, to condemn.

reprochar *vt*: **~ algo a alguien** to reproach sb for sthg. ▶ **reprocharse** *vpr*: **~se algo (uno mismo)** to reproach o.s. for sthg.

reproche *m* reproach.

reproducción *f* reproduction.

reproducir *vt* (*gen & ARTE*) to reproduce; (*gestos*) to copy, to imitate.
▶ **reproducirse** *vpr* **1.** (*volver a suceder*) to recur. **2.** (*procrear*) to reproduce.

reproductor, -ra *adj* reproductive.

reptil *m* reptile.

república *f* republic.

República Checa *f* Czech Republic.

República Dominicana *f* Dominican Republic.

republicano, -na *adj, m y f* republican.

repudiar *vt* **1.** (*condenar*) to repudiate. **2.** (*rechazar*) to disown.

repuesto, -ta ◆ *pp* → **reponer**. ◆ *adj*: **~ (de)** recovered (from). ▶ **repuesto** *m* (*gen*) reserve; (*AUTOM*) spare part; **la rueda de ~** the spare wheel.

repugnancia *f* disgust.

repugnante *adj* disgusting.

repugnar *vt*: **me repugna ese olor/su actitud** I find that smell/her attitude disgusting; **me repugna hacerlo** I'm loathe to do it.

repujado, -da *adj* embossed.

repujar *vt* to emboss.

repulsa *f* (*censura*) condemnation.

repulsión *f* repulsion.

repulsivo, -va *adj* repulsive.

reputación *f* reputation; **tener mucha ~** to be very famous.

reputar *vt* to consider.

requemado, -da *adj* burnt.

requerimiento *m* **1.** (*demanda*) entreaty. **2.** (*DER - intimación*) writ, injunction; (*- aviso*) summons (*sg*).

requerir *vt* **1.** (*necesitar*) to require. **2.** (*ordenar*) to demand. **3.** (*pedir*): **~ a alguien (para) que haga algo** to ask sb to do sthg. **4.** (*DER*) to order. ▶ **requerirse** *vpr* (*ser necesario*) to be required o necessary.

requesón *m* cottage cheese.

requisa *f* (*requisición - MIL*) requisition; (*- en aduana*) seizure.

requisito *m* requirement; **~ previo** prerequisite.

res *f* beast, animal.

resabio *m* **1.** (*sabor*) nasty aftertaste. **2.** (*vicio*) persistent bad habit.

resaca *f* **1.** *fam* (*de borrachera*) hangover. **2.** (*de las olas*) undertow.

resalado, -da *adj fam* charming.

resaltar ◆ *vi* **1.** (*destacar*) to stand out. **2.** (*en edificios - decoración*) to stand out. ◆ *vt* (*destacar*) to highlight.

resarcir *vt*: **~ a alguien (de)** to compensate sb (for). ▶ **resarcirse** *vpr* to be compensated; **~se de** (*daño, pérdida*) to be compensated for; (*desengaño, derrota*) to make up for.

resbalada *f Amer fam* slip.

resbaladizo, -za *adj lit & fig* slippery.

resbalar *vi* **1.** (*caer*): **~ (con o sobre)** to slip (on). **2.** (*deslizarse*) to slide. **3.** (*estar resbaladizo*) to be slippery. ▶ **resbalarse** *vpr* to slip (over).

resbalón *m* slip.

rescatar *vt* **1.** (*liberar, salvar*) to rescue; (*pagando rescate*) to ransom. **2.** (*recuperar - herencia etc*) to recover.

rescate *m* **1.** (*liberación, salvación*) rescue. **2.** (*dinero*) ransom. **3.** (*recuperación*) recovery.

rescindir *vt* to rescind.

rescisión *f* cancellation.

rescoldo *m* ember; *fig* lingering feeling.

resecar *vt* (*piel*) to dry out. ▶ **resecarse** *vpr* **1.** (*piel*) to dry out. **2.** (*tierra*) to become parched.

reseco, -ca *adj* **1.** (*piel, garganta, pan*) very dry. **2.** (*tierra*) parched. **3.** (*flaco*) emaciated.

resentido, -da *adj* bitter, resentful; **estar ~ con alguien** to be really upset with sb.

resentimiento *m* resentment, bitterness.

resentirse vpr 1. (*debilitarse*) to be weakened; (*salud*) to deteriorate. 2. (*sentir molestias*): ~ **de** to be suffering from. 3. (*ofenderse*) to be offended.

reseña f (*de libro, concierto*) review; (*de partido, conferencia*) report.

reseñar vt 1. (*criticar - libro, concierto*) to review; (*- partido, conferencia*) to report on. 2. (*describir*) to describe.

reserva f 1. (*de hotel, avión etc*) reservation. 2. (*provisión*) reserves (*pl*); **tener algo de** ~ to keep sthg in reserve. 3. (*objeción*) reservation. 4. (*de indígenas*) reservation. 5. (*de animales*) reserve; ~ **natural** nature reserve. 6. (MIL) reserve. ▶ **reservas** fpl 1. (*energía acumulada*) energy reserves. 2. (*recursos*) resources.

reservado, -da adj 1. (*gen*) reserved. 2. (*tema, asunto*) confidential. ▶ **reservado** m (*en restaurante*) private room; (FERROC) reserved compartment.

reservar vt 1. (*habitación, asiento etc*) to reserve, to book. 2. (*guardar - dinero, pasteles etc*) to set aside; (*- sorpresa*) to keep. 3. (*callar - opinión, comentarios*) to reserve. ▶ **reservarse** vpr 1. (*esperar*): ~**se para** to save o.s. for. 2. (*guardar para sí - secreto*) to keep to o.s.; (*- dinero, derecho*) to retain (for o.s.).

resfriado, -da adj: **estar** ~ to have a cold. ▶ **resfriado** m cold.

resfriar vt to make cold. ▶ **resfriarse** vpr (*constiparse*) to catch a cold.

resfrío m Amer cold.

resguardar vt & vi: ~ **de** to protect against. ▶ **resguardarse** vpr: ~**se de** (*en un portal*) to shelter from; (*con abrigo, paraguas*) to protect o.s. against.

resguardo m 1. (*documento*) receipt. 2. (*protección*) protection.

residencia f 1. (*estancia*) stay. 2. (*localidad, domicilio*) residence. 3. (*establecimiento - de estudiantes*) hall of residence; (*- de ancianos*) old people's home; (*- de oficiales*) residence. 4. (*hospital*) hospital. 5. (*permiso para extranjeros*) residence permit.

residencial adj residential.

residente adj, m y f resident.

residir vi 1. (*vivir*) to reside. 2. (*radicar*): ~ **en** to lie in.

residuo m 1. (*gen pl*) (*material inservible*) waste; (QUÍM) residue; ~**s nucleares** nuclear waste (U). 2. (*restos*) leftovers (*pl*).

resignación f resignation.

resignarse vpr: ~ (**a hacer algo**) to

resign o.s. (to doing sthg).

resina f resin.

resistencia f 1. (*gen,* ELECTR & POLÍT) resistance; **ofrecer** ~ to put up resistance. 2. (*de puente, cimientos*) strength. 3. (*física - para correr etc*) stamina.

resistente adj (*gen*) tough, strong; ~ **al calor** heat-resistant.

resistir ◆ vt 1. (*dolor, peso, críticas*) to withstand. 2. (*tentación, impulso, deseo*) to resist. 3. (*tolerar*) to tolerate, to stand. ◆ vi 1. (*ejército, ciudad etc*): ~ (**a algo/a alguien**) to resist (sthg/sb). 2. (*corredor etc*) to keep going; ~ **a algo** to stand up to sthg, to withstand sthg. 3. (*mesa, dique etc*) to take the strain; ~ **a algo** to withstand sthg. 4. (*mostrarse firme - ante tentaciones etc*) to resist (it); ~ **a algo** to resist sthg. ▶ **resistirse** vpr: ~**se** (**a algo**) to resist (sthg); **me resisto a creerlo** I refuse to believe it; **se le resisten las matemáticas** she just can't get the hang of maths.

resma f ream.

resollar vi to gasp (for breath); (*jadear*) to pant.

resolución f 1. (*solución - de una crisis*) resolution; (*- de un crimen*) solution. 2. (*firmeza*) determination. 3. (*decisión*) decision; (DER) ruling. 4. (*de Naciones Unidas etc*) resolution.

resolver vt 1. (*solucionar - duda, crisis*) to resolve; (*- problema, caso*) to solve. 2. (*decidir*): ~ **hacer algo** to decide to do sthg. 3. (*partido, disputa, conflicto*) to settle. ▶ **resolverse** vpr 1. (*solucionarse - duda, crisis*) to be resolved; (*- problema, caso*) to be solved. 2. (*decidirse*): ~**se a hacer algo** to decide to do sthg.

resonancia f 1. (*gen &* FÍS) resonance (U). 2. fig (*importancia*) repercussions (*pl*).

resonante adj resounding; (FÍS) resonant; fig important.

resonar vi to resound, to echo.

resoplar vi (*de cansancio*) to pant; (*de enfado*) to snort.

resoplido m (*por cansancio*) pant; (*por enfado*) snort.

resorte m spring; fig means (*pl*); **tocar todos los** ~**s** to pull out all the stops.

respaldar vt to back, to support. ▶ **respaldarse** vpr fig (*apoyarse*): ~**se en** to fall back on.

respaldo m 1. (*de asiento*) back. 2. fig (*apoyo*) backing, support.

respectar v impers: **por lo que respecta a alguien/a algo, en lo que respecta a**

alguien/a algo as far as sb/sthg is concerned.

respectivo, -va adj respective; **en lo ~ a** with regard to.

respecto m: **al ~, a este ~** in this respect; **no sé nada al ~** I don't know anything about it; **(con) ~ a, ~ de** regarding.

respetable adj (venerable) respectable.

respetar vt (gen) to respect; (la palabra) to honour.

respeto m: **~ (a o por)** respect (for); **es una falta de ~** it shows a lack of respect; **por ~ a** out of consideration for.

respetuoso, -sa adj: **~ (con)** respectful (of).

respingo m (movimiento) start, jump.

respingón, -ona adj snub.

respiración f breathing; (MED) respiration.

respirar ◆ vt (aire) to breathe. ◆ vi to breathe; fig (sentir alivio) to breathe again; **sin ~** (sin descanso) without a break; (atentamente) with great attention.

respiratorio, -ria adj respiratory.

respiro m 1. (descanso) rest. 2. (alivio) relief, respite.

resplandecer vi 1. (brillar) to shine. 2. fig (destacar) to shine, to stand out.

resplandeciente adj shining; (sonrisa) beaming; (época) glittering; (vestimenta, color) resplendent.

resplandor m 1. (luz) brightness; (de fuego) glow. 2. (brillo) gleam.

responder ◆ vt to answer. ◆ vi 1. (contestar) **~ (a algo)** to answer (sthg). 2. (reaccionar) **~ (a)** to respond (to). 3. (responsabilizarse): **~ de algo/por alguien** to answer for sthg/for sb. 4. (replicar) to answer back.

respondón, -ona adj insolent.

responsabilidad f responsibility; (DER) liability; **tener la ~ de algo** to be responsible for sthg; **~ limitada** limited liability.

responsabilizar vt: **~ a alguien (de algo)** to hold sb responsible (for sthg). ▶ **responsabilizarse** vpr: **~se (de)** to accept responsibility (for).

responsable ◆ adj responsible; **~ de** responsible for. ◆ m y f 1. (culpable) person responsible. 2. (encargado) person in charge.

respuesta f 1. (gen) answer, reply; (en exámenes) answer; **en ~ a** in reply to. 2. fig (reacción) response.

resquebrajar vt to crack. ▶ **resquebrajarse** vpr to crack.

resquicio m 1. (abertura) chink; (grieta) crack. 2. fig (pizca) glimmer.

resta f (MAT) subtraction.

restablecer vt to reestablish, to restore. ▶ **restablecerse** vpr (curarse): **~se (de)** to recover (from).

restallar vt & vi (látigo) to crack; (lengua) to click.

restante adj remaining; **lo ~** the rest.

restar ◆ vt 1. (MAT) to subtract. 2. (disminuir): **~ importancia a algo/méritos a alguien** to play down the importance of sthg/sb's qualities. ◆ vi (faltar) to be left.

restauración f restoration.

restaurante m restaurant.

restaurar vt to restore.

restitución f return.

restituir vt (devolver - objeto) to return; (- salud) to restore.

resto m: **el ~** (gen) the rest; (MAT) the remainder. ▶ **restos** mpl 1. (sobras) leftovers. 2. (cadáver) remains. 3. (ruinas) ruins.

restregar vt to rub hard; (para limpiar) to scrub. ▶ **restregarse** vpr (frotarse) to rub.

restricción f restriction.

restrictivo, -va adj restrictive.

restringir vt to limit, to restrict.

resucitar ◆ vt (person) to bring back to life; (costumbre) to revive. ◆ vi (persona) to rise from the dead.

resuello m gasp, gasping (U); (jadeo) pant, panting (U).

resuelto, -ta ◆ pp → **resolver**. ◆ adj (decidido) determined.

resulta f: **de ~s de** as a result of.

resultado m result.

resultante adj & f resultant.

resultar ◆ vi 1. (acabar siendo): **~ (ser)** to turn out (to be); **resultó ileso** he was uninjured; **nuestro equipo resultó vencedor** our team came out on top. 2. (salir bien) to work (out), to be a success. 3. (originarse): **~ de** to result from. 4. (ser) to be; **resulta sorprendente** it's surprising; **me resultó imposible terminar antes** I was unable to finish earlier. 5. (venir a costar): **~ a** to come to, to cost. ◆ v impers (suceder): **~ que** to turn out that; **ahora resulta que no quiere alquilarlo** now it seems that she doesn't want to rent it.

resumen m summary; **en ~** in short.

resumir vt to summarize; (discurso) to sum up. ▶ **resumirse en** vpr 1. (sintetizarse en) to be able to be summed up in. **2.** (*reducirse a*) to boil down to.

resurgir *vi* to undergo a resurgence.

resurrección *f* resurrection.

retablo *m* altarpiece.

retaguardia *f* (*tropa*) rearguard; (*territorio*) rear.

retahíla *f* string, series.

retal *m* remnant.

retardar *vt* (*retrasar*) to delay; (*frenar*) to hold up, to slow down.

retazo *m* remnant; *fig* fragment.

rete *adv* Amer fam very.

retén *m* reserve.

retención *f* **1.** (*en el sueldo*) deduction. **2.** (*gen pl*) (*de tráfico*) hold-up.

retener *vt* **1.** (*detener*) to hold back; (*en comisaría*) to detain. **2.** (*contener - impulso, ira*) to hold back, to restrain. **3.** (*conservar*) to retain. **4.** (*quedarse con*) to hold on to, to keep. **5.** (*memorizar*) to remember. **6.** (*deducir del sueldo*) to deduct.

reticente *adj* (*reacio*) unwilling, reluctant.

retina *f* retina.

retintín *m* (*ironía*) sarcastic tone.

retirado, -da *adj* **1.** (*jubilado*) retired. **2.** (*solitario, alejado*) isolated, secluded. ▶ **retirada** *f* **1.** (MIL) retreat; **batirse en retirada** to beat a retreat. **2.** (*de fondos, moneda, carné*) withdrawal. **3.** (*de competición, actividad*) withdrawal.

retirar *vt* **1.** (*quitar - gen*) to remove; (*- dinero, moneda, carné*) to withdraw; (*- nieve*) to clear. **2.** (*jubilar - a deportista*) to force to retire; (*- a empleado*) to retire. **3.** (*retractarse de*) to take back. ▶ **retirarse** *vpr* **1.** (*gen*) to retire. **2.** (*de competición, elecciones*) to withdraw; (*de reunión*) to leave. **3.** (*de campo de batalla*) to retreat. **4.** (*apartarse*) to move away.

retiro *m* **1.** (*jubilación*) retirement; (*pensión*) pension. **2.** (*refugio, ejercicio*) retreat.

reto *m* challenge.

retocar *vt* to touch up; (*prenda de vestir*) to alter.

retoño *m* (BOT) sprout, shoot; *fig* offspring (U).

retoque *m* touching-up (U); (*de prenda de vestir*) alteration; **dar los últimos ~s a** to put the finishing touches to.

retorcer *vt* (*torcer - brazo, alambre*) to twist; (*- ropa, cuello*) to wring. ▶ **retorcerse** *vpr* (*contraerse*): **~se (de)** (*risa*) to double up (with); (*dolor*) to writhe about (in).

retorcido, -da *adj* **1.** (*torcido - brazo,*

alambre) twisted. **2.** *fig* (*rebuscado*) complicated.

retornable *adj* returnable; **no ~** non-returnable.

retornar *vt & vi* to return.

retorno *m* (*gen* & INFORM) return; **~ de carro** carriage return.

retortijón *m* (*gen pl*) stomach cramp.

retozar *vi* to frolic; (*amantes*) to romp about.

retractarse *vpr* (*de una promesa*) to go back on one's word; (*de una opinión*) to take back what one has said; **~ de** (*lo dicho*) to retract, to take back.

retraer *vt* (*encoger*) to retract. ▶ **retraerse** *vpr* **1.** (*encogerse*) to retract. **2.** (*retroceder*) to withdraw, to retreat.

retraído, -da *adj* withdrawn, retiring.

retransmisión *f* broadcast; **~ en directo/diferido** live/recorded broadcast.

retransmitir *vt* to broadcast.

retrasado, -da ♦ *adj* **1.** (*país, industria*) backward; (*reloj*) slow; (*tren*) late, delayed. **2.** (*en el pago, los estudios*) behind. **3.** (MED) retarded, backward. ♦ *m y f:* **~ (mental)** mentally retarded person.

retrasar *vt* **1.** (*aplazar*) to postpone. **2.** (*demorar*) to delay, to hold up. **3.** (*hacer más lento*) to slow down, to hold up. **4.** (*en el pago, los estudios*) to set back. **5.** (*reloj*) to put back. ▶ **retrasarse** *vpr* **1.** (*llegar tarde*) to be late; **el tren se retrasó** the train was delayed. **2.** (*quedarse atrás*) to fall behind. **3.** (*aplazarse*) to be put off. **4.** (*reloj*) to lose time.

retraso *m* **1.** (*por llegar tarde*) delay; **llegar con (15 minutos de) ~** to be (15 minutes) late. **2.** (*por sobrepasar una fecha*): **llevo en mi trabajo un ~ de 20 páginas** I'm 20 pages behind with my work. **3.** (*subdesarrollo*) backwardness. **4.** (MED) mental deficiency.

retratar *vt* **1.** (*fotografiar*) to photograph. **2.** (*dibujar*) to do a portrait of. **3.** *fig* (*describir*) to portray.

retrato *m* **1.** (*dibujo*) portrait; (*fotografía*) photograph; **~ robot** photofit picture; **ser el vivo ~ de alguien** to be the spitting image of sb. **2.** *fig* (*reflejo*) portrayal.

retrete *m* toilet.

retribución *f* (*pago*) payment; (*recompensa*) reward.

retribuir *vt* (*pagar*) to pay; (*recompensa*) to reward.

retro *adj* reactionary.

retroactivo, -va *adj* (*ley*) retroactive; (*pago*) backdated.

retroceder *vi* to go back; *fig* to back down.

retroceso *m* (*regresión - gen*) backward movement; (*- en negociaciones*) setback; (*- en la economía*) recession.

retrógrado, -da *adj, m y f* reactionary.

retroproyector *m* overhead projector.

retrospectivo, -va *adj* retrospective.

retrovisor *m* rear-view mirror.

retumbar *vi* (*resonar*) to resound.

reuma, reúma *m o f* rheumatism.

reumatismo *m* rheumatism.

reunión *f* meeting.

reunir *vt* 1. (*público, accionistas etc*) to bring together. 2. (*objetos, textos etc*) to collect, to bring together; (*fondos*) to raise. 3. (*requisitos*) to meet; (*cualidades*) to possess, to combine. ▶ **reunirse** *vpr* (*congregarse*) to meet, to get together.

revalidar *vt* to confirm.

revalorar = **revalorizar**.

revalorizar, revalorar *vt* 1. (*aumentar el valor*) to increase the value of; (*moneda*) to revalue. 2. (*restituir el valor*) to reassess in a favourable light. ▶ **revalorizarse** *vpr* (*aumentar de valor*) to appreciate; (*moneda*) to be revalued.

revancha *f* 1. (*venganza*) revenge. 2. (DEP) return match.

revelación *f* revelation.

revelado *m* (FOT) developing.

revelador, -ra *adj* (*aclarador*) revealing.

revelar *vt* 1. (*declarar*) to reveal. 2. (*evidenciar*) to show. 3. (FOT) to develop. ▶ **revelarse** *vpr*: ~se como to show o.s. to be.

revendedor, -ra *m y f* ticket tout.

reventa *f* resale; (*de entradas*) touting.

reventar ◆ *vt* 1. (*explotar*) to burst. 2. (*echar abajo*) to break down; (*con explosivos*) to blow up. ◆ *vi* (*explotar*) to burst. ▶ **reventarse** *vpr* (*explotar*) to explode; (*rueda*) to burst.

reventón *m* 1. (*pinchazo*) blowout, flat Am, puncture Br. 2. (*estallido*) burst.

reverberación *f* (*de sonido*) reverberation; (*de luz, calor*) reflection.

reverberar *vi* (*sonido*) to reverberate; (*luz, calor*) to reflect.

reverdecer *vi fig* (*amor*) to revive.

reverencia *f* 1. (*respeto*) reverence.

2. (*saludo - inclinación*) bow; (*- flexión de piernas*) curtsy.

reverenciar *vt* to revere.

reverendo, -da *adj* reverend. ▶ **reverendo** *m* reverend.

reverente *adj* reverent.

reversible *adj* reversible.

reverso *m* back, other side.

revertir *vi* 1. (*volver, devolver*) to revert. 2. (*resultar*): ~ en to result in; ~ en beneficio/perjuicio de to be to the advantage/detriment of.

revés *m* 1. (*parte opuesta - de papel, mano*) back; (*- de tela*) other o wrong side; **al** ~ (*en sentido contrario*) the wrong way round; (*en forma opuesta*) the other way round; **del** ~ (*lo de detrás, delante*) the wrong way round, back to front; (*lo de dentro, fuera*) inside out; (*lo de arriba, abajo*) upside down. 2. (*bofetada*) slap. 3. (DEP) backhand. 4. (*contratiempo*) setback.

revestimiento *m* covering.

revestir *vt* 1. (*recubrir*): ~ (de) (*gen*) to cover (with); (*pintura*) to coat (with); (*forro*) to line (with). 2. (*poseer - solemnidad, gravedad etc*) to take on, to have.

revisar *vt* 1. (*comprobar*) to check. 2. (*inspeccionar*) to inspect; (*cuentas*) to audit. 3. (*modificar*) to revise.

revisión *f* 1. (*repaso*) revision. 2. (*inspección*) inspection; ~ **de cuentas** audit; ~ **médica** check-up. 3. (*modificación*) amendment. 4. (AUTOM - *puesta a punto*) service; (*- anual*) ≈ MOT (test).

revisor, -ra *m y f* (*en tren*) ticket inspector; (*en autobús*) (bus) conductor.

revista *f* 1. (*publicación*) magazine; ~ **del corazón** gossip magazine. 2. (*sección de periódico*) section, review. 3. (*espectáculo teatral*) revue. 4. (*inspección*) inspection; **pasar** ~ **a** (MIL) to inspect; (*examinar*) to examine.

revistero *m* (*mueble*) magazine rack.

revivir ◆ *vi* to revive. ◆ *vt* (*recordar*) to revive memories of.

revocar *vt* (*gen*) to revoke.

revolcar *vt* to upend. ▶ **revolcarse** *vpr* to roll about.

revolotear *vi* to flutter (about).

revoltijo, revoltillo *m* jumble.

revoltoso, -sa ◆ *adj* rebellious. ◆ *m y f* troublemaker.

revolución *f* revolution.

revolucionar *vt* (*transformar*) to revolutionize.

revolucionario, -ria *adj, m y f* revolutionary.

revolver vt 1. (*dar vueltas*) to turn around; (*líquido*) to stir. 2. (*mezclar*) to mix; (*ensalada*) to toss. 3. (*desorganizar*) to mess up; (*cajones*) to turn out. 4. (*irritar*) to upset; **me revuelve el estómago o las tripas** it makes my stomach turn. ▶ **revolver en** vi (*cajones etc*) to rummage around in. ▶ **revolverse** vpr 1. (*volverse*) to turn around. 2. (*el mar*) to become rough; (*el tiempo*) to turn stormy.

revólver m revolver.

revuelo m (*agitación*) commotion; **armar un gran ~** to cause a great stir.

revuelto, -ta ◆ pp → **revolver**. ◆ adj 1. (*desordenado*) in a mess. 2. (*alborotado - época etc*) turbulent. 3. (*clima*) unsettled. 4. (*aguas*) choppy. ▶ **revuelto** m (CULIN) scrambled eggs (*pl*). ▶ **revuelta** f (*disturbio*) riot, revolt.

revulsivo, -va adj fig stimulating, revitalizing. ▶ **revulsivo** m fig kickstart.

rey m king. ▶ **Reyes** mpl: **los Reyes** the King and Queen; **(Día de) Reyes** Twelfth Night.

REYES

On 6 January, Spanish children traditionally receive presents supposedly brought by the Three Wise Men. The 'roscón de reyes' is a large ring-shaped bun eaten for dessert on this day, in which a bean and a small figure are hidden. Whoever gets the slice with the bean has to pay for the 'roscón', whilst the person who finds the figure is proclaimed 'king of the party'.

reyerta f fight, brawl.

rezagado, -da adj: **ir ~** to lag behind.

rezar vi 1. (*orar*) **~ (a)** to pray (to). 2. (*decir*) to read, to say. 3. (*corresponderse*): **~ con** to have to do with.

rezo m (*oración*) prayer.

rezumar ◆ vt 1. (*transpirar*) to ooze. 2. fig (*manifestar*) to be overflowing with. ◆ vi to ooze o seep out.

ría f estuary.

riachuelo m brook, stream.

riada f lit & fig flood.

ribera f (*del río*) bank; (*del mar*) shore.

ribete m edging (U), trimming (U); fig touch, nuance.

ricino m (*planta*) castor oil plant.

rico, -ca ◆ adj 1. (*gen*) rich. 2. (*abundante*): **~ (en)** rich (in). 3. (*sabroso*) delicious. 4. (*simpático*) cute. ◆ m y f rich person; **los ~s** the rich.

rictus m inv 1. (*de ironía*) smirk. 2. (*de desprecio*) sneer. 3. (*de dolor*) wince.

ridiculez f 1. (*payasada*) silly thing, nonsense (U). 2. (*nimiedad*) trifle; **cuesta una ~** it costs next to nothing.

ridiculizar vt to ridicule.

ridículo, -la adj ridiculous; (*precio, suma*) laughable, derisory. ▶ **ridículo** m ridicule; **hacer el ~** to make a fool of o.s.; **poner o dejar en ~ a alguien** to make sb look stupid; **quedar en ~** to look like a fool.

riego m (*de campo*) irrigation; (*de jardín*) watering.

riel m 1. (*de vía*) rail. 2. (*de cortina*) (curtain) rail.

rienda f (*de caballería*) rein; **dar ~ suelta a** fig to give free rein to. ▶ **riendas** fpl fig (*dirección*) reins.

riesgo m risk; **a todo ~** (*seguro, póliza*) comprehensive.

rifa f raffle.

rifar vt to raffle. ▶ **rifarse** vpr fig to fight over.

rifle m rifle.

rigidez f 1. (*de un cuerpo, objeto etc*) rigidity. 2. (*del rostro*) stoniness. 3. fig (*severidad*) strictness, harshness.

rígido, -da adj 1. (*cuerpo, objeto etc*) rigid. 2. (*rostro*) stony. 3. (*severo - normas etc*) harsh; (*- carácter*) inflexible.

rigor m 1. (*severidad*) strictness. 2. (*exactitud*) accuracy, rigour. 3. (*inclemencia*) harshness. ▶ **de rigor** loc adj essential.

riguroso, -sa adj 1. (*severo - profesor, jefe*) strict; (*- medidas, política*) tough. 2. (*exacto*) rigorous. 3. (*inclemente*) harsh.

rimar vt & vi to rhyme.

rimbombante adj (*estilo, frases*) pompous.

rímel, rimmel m mascara.

rincón m corner (inside).

rinconera f corner piece.

ring (*pl* rings) m (boxing) ring.

rinoceronte m rhinoceros.

riña f (*disputa*) quarrel; (*pelea*) fight.

riñón m kidney.

riñonera f (*pequeño bolso*) bum bag Br, fanny pack Am.

río m lit & fig river; **ir ~ arriba/abajo** to go upstream/downstream; **cuando el ~ suena, agua lleva** proverb there's no smoke without fire proverb.

rioja m Rioja (wine).

riojano, -na adj, m y f Riojan.

riqueza f 1. (*fortuna*) wealth. 2. (*abundancia*) richness.

risa f laugh, laughter (U); **me da ~** I find it funny; **¡qué ~!** how funny!; **de ~** funny.

risotada f guffaw.

ristra f lit & fig string.

ristre ▶ **en ristre** loc adv at the ready.

risueño, -ña adj (*alegre*) smiling.

ritmo m 1. (*gen*) rhythm; (*cardíaco*) beat. 2. (*velocidad*) pace.

rito m 1. (RELIG) rite. 2. (*costumbre*) ritual.

ritual adj & m ritual.

rival adj, m y f rival.

rivalidad f rivalry.

rivalizar vi: ~ (**con**) to compete (with).

rizado, -da adj 1. (*pelo*) curly. 2. (*mar*) choppy. ▶ **rizado** m (*en peluquería*): **hacerse un ~** to have one's hair curled.

rizar vt (*pelo*) to curl. ▶ **rizarse** vpr (*pelo*) to curl.

rizo, -za adj (*pelo*) curly. ▶ **rizo** m 1. (*de pelo*) curl. 2. (*del agua*) ripple. 3. (*de avión*) loop. 4. loc: **rizar el ~** to split hairs.

RNE (*abrev de* **Radio Nacional de España**) f Spanish national radio station.

roast-beef [ros'βif] (*pl* **roast-beefs**), **rosbif** (*pl* **rosbifs**) m roast beef.

robar vt 1. (*gen*) to steal; (*casa*) to burgle; ~ **a alguien** to rob sb. 2. (*en naipes*) to draw. 3. (*cobrar caro*) to rob.

roble m 1. (BOT) oak. 2. fig (*persona*) strong person.

robo m (*delito*) robbery, theft; (*en casa*) burglary.

robot (*pl* **robots**) m (*gen* & INFORM) robot.

robótica f robotics (U).

robustecer vt to strengthen. ▶ **robustecerse** vpr to get stronger.

robusto, -ta adj robust.

roca f rock.

rocalla f rubble.

roce m 1. (*rozamiento - gen*) rub, rubbing (U); (- *suave*) brush, brushing (U); (FÍS) friction. 2. (*desgaste*) wear. 3. (*rasguño - en piel*) graze; (- *en zapato, puerta*) scuffmark; (- *en metal*) scratch. 4. (*trato*) close contact. 5. (*desavenencia*) brush.

rociar vt (*arrojar gotas*) to sprinkle; (*con espray*) to spray.

rocío m dew.

rock, rock and roll m inv (*estilo*) rock; (*de los 50*) rock and roll.

rockero, -ra, roquero, -ra m y f 1. (*músico*) rock musician. 2. (*fan*) rock fan.

rocoso, -sa adj rocky.

rodaballo m turbot.

rodado, -da adj 1. (*piedra*) rounded. 2. (*tráfico*) road (*antes de sust*). 3. loc: **estar muy ~** (*persona*) to be very experienced; **venir ~ para** to be the perfect opportunity to.

rodaja f slice.

rodaje m 1. (*filmación*) shooting. 2. (*de motor*) running-in. 3. (*experiencia*) experience.

Ródano m: **el ~** the (River) Rhône.

rodapié m skirting board.

rodar ◆ vi 1. (*deslizar*) to roll. 2. (*circular*) to travel, to go. 3. (*caer*): ~ (**por**) to tumble (down). 4. (*ir de un lado a otro*) to go around. 5. (CIN) to shoot. ◆ vt 1. (CIN) to shoot. 2. (*automóvil*) to run in.

rodear vt 1. (*gen*) to surround; **le rodeó el cuello con los brazos** she put her arms around his neck. 2. (*dar la vuelta a*) to go around. 3. (*eludir*) to skirt around. ▶ **rodearse** vpr: ~**se de** to surround o.s. with.

rodeo m 1. (*camino largo*) detour; **dar un ~** to make a detour. 2. (*gen pl*) (*evasiva*) evasiveness (U); **andar** o **ir con ~s** to beat about the bush. 3. (*espectáculo*) rodeo.

rodilla f knee; **de ~s** on one's knees.

rodillera f (*protección*) knee pad.

rodillo m (*gen*) roller; (*para repostería*) rolling pin.

rodríguez m inv grass widower.

roedor, -ra adj (ZOOL) rodent (*antes de sust*). ▶ **roedor** m rodent.

roer vt 1. (*con dientes*) to gnaw (at). 2. fig (*gastar*) to eat away (at).

rogar vt (*implorar*) to beg; (*pedir*) to ask; ~ **a alguien que haga algo** to ask o beg sb to do sthg; **te ruego me perdone** I beg your pardon; **'se ruega silencio'** 'silence, please'.

rogativa f (*gen pl*) rogation.

rojizo, -za adj reddish.

rojo, -ja ◆ adj red; **ponerse ~** (*gen*) to turn red; (*ruborizarse*) to blush. ◆ m y f (POLÍT) red. ▶ **rojo** m (*color*) red; **al ~ vivo** (*en incandescencia*) red hot; fig heated.

rol (*pl* **roles**) m (*papel*) role.

rollizo, -za adj chubby, plump.

rollo m 1. (*cilindro*) roll; ~ **de primavera** (CULIN) spring roll. 2. (CIN) roll. 3. fam (*discurso*): **el ~ de costumbre** the same old story; **tener mucho ~** to witter on. 4. fam (*embuste*) tall story. 5. fam (*pelmazo, pesadez*) bore, drag.

ROM (*abrev de* **read-only memory**) *f* ROM.

Roma Rome.

romance *m* 1. (LING) Romance language. 2. (*idilio*) romance.

románico, -ca *adj* 1. (ARQUIT & ARTE) Romanesque. 2. (LING) Romance.

romano, -na *m y f* Roman.

romanticismo *m* 1. (ARTE & LITER) Romanticism. 2. (*sentimentalismo*) romanticism.

romántico, -ca *adj, m y f* 1. (ARTE & LITER) Romantic. 2. (*sentimental*) romantic.

rombo *m* 1. (GEOM) rhombus. 2. (IMPRENTA) lozenge.

romería *f* (*peregrinación*) pilgrimage.

romero, -ra *m y f* (*peregrino*) pilgrim. ▶ **romero** *m* (BOT) rosemary.

romo, -ma *adj* (*sin filo*) blunt.

rompecabezas *m inv* 1. (*juego*) jigsaw. 2. *fam* (*problema*) puzzle.

rompeolas *m inv* breakwater.

romper ◆ *vt* 1. (*gen*) to break; (*hacer añicos*) to smash; (*rasgar*) to tear. 2. (*desgastar*) to wear out. 3. (*interrumpir - monotonía, silencio, hábito*) to break; (*- hilo del discurso*) to break off; (*- tradición*) to put an end to. 4. (*terminar - relaciones etc*) to break off. ◆ *vi* 1. (*terminar una relación*): ~ **(con alguien)** to break o split up (with sb). 2. (*olas, el día*) to break; (*hostilidades*) to break out; **al ~ el alba** o **día** at daybreak. 3. (*empezar*): ~ **a hacer algo** to suddenly start doing sthg; ~ **a llorar** to burst into tears; ~ **a reír** to burst out laughing. ◆ **romperse** *vpr* (*partirse*) to break; (*rasgarse*) to tear; **se ha roto una pierna** he has broken a leg.

rompimiento *m* breaking; (*de relaciones*) breaking-off.

ron *m* rum.

roncar *vi* to snore.

roncha *f* red blotch.

ronco, -ca *adj* 1. (*afónico*) hoarse. 2. (*bronco*) harsh.

ronda *f* 1. (*de vigilancia, visitas*) rounds (*pl*); **hacer la ~** to do one's rounds. 2. *fam* (*de bebidas, en el juego etc*) round.

rondar ◆ *vt* 1. (*vigilar*) to patrol. 2. (*rayar - edad*) to be around. ◆ *vi* (*merodear*): ~ **(por)** to wander o hang around.

ronquera *f* hoarseness.

ronquido *m* snore, snoring (U).

ronronear *vi* to purr.

ronroneo *m* purr, purring (U).

roña ◆ *adj fam* (*tacaño*) stingy. ◆ *f* 1. (*suciedad*) filth, dirt. 2. (VETER) mange.

roñoso, -sa ◆ *adj* 1. (*sucio*) dirty. 2. (*tacaño*) mean. ◆ *m y f* miser.

ropa *f* clothes (*pl*); ~ **blanca** linen; ~ **de abrigo** warm clothes (*pl*); ~ **de cama** bed linen; ~ **hecha** ready-to-wear clothes; ~ **interior** underwear.

ropaje *m* robes (*pl*).

ropero *m* 1. (*armario*) wardrobe. 2. (*habitación*) walk-in wardrobe; (TEATR) cloakroom.

roquero = **rockero**.

rosa ◆ *f* (*flor*) rose; **estar (fresco) como una** ~ to be as fresh as a daisy. ◆ *m* (*color*) pink. ◆ *adj inv* (*color*) pink. ▶ **rosa de los vientos** *f* (NÁUT) compass.

rosado, -da *adj* pink. ▶ **rosado** *m* → **vino**.

rosal *m* (*arbusto*) rose bush.

rosario *m* 1. (RELIG) rosary; **rezar el** ~ to say one's rosary. 2. (*sarta*) string.

rosca *f* 1. (*de tornillo*) thread. 2. (*forma - de anillo*) ring; (*- espiral*) coil. 3. (CULIN) ring doughnut. 4. *loc*: **pasarse de** ~ (*persona*) to go over the top.

rosco *m* ring-shaped bread roll.

roscón *m* ring-shaped bread roll; ~ **de reyes** roll eaten on 6th January.

rosetón *m* (*ventana*) rose window.

rosquilla *f* ring doughnut.

rostro *m* face.

rotación *f* 1. (*giro*) rotation; ~ **de cultivos** crop rotation. 2. (*alternancia*) rota; **por** ~ in turn.

rotativo, -va *adj* rotary, revolving. ▶ **rotativo** *m* newspaper. ▶ **rotativa** *f* rotary press.

roto, -ta ◆ *pp* → **romper**. ◆ *adj* 1. (*gen*) broken; (*tela, papel*) torn. 2. *fig* (*deshecho - vida etc*) destroyed; (*- corazón*) broken. 3. *fig* (*exhausto*) shattered. ◆ *m y f* Amer (*trabajador*) worker. ▶ **roto** *m* (*en tela*) tear, rip.

rotonda *f* (*plaza*) circus.

rotoso, -sa *adj* Amer ragged.

rótula *f* kneecap.

rotulador *m* felt-tip pen; (*fluorescente*) marker pen.

rótulo *m* 1. (*letrero*) sign. 2. (*encabezamiento*) headline, title.

rotundo, -da *adj* 1. (*categórico - negativa, persona*) categorical; (*- lenguaje, estilo*) emphatic. 2. (*completo*) total.

rotura *f* (*gen*) break, breaking (U); (*de hueso*) fracture; (*en tela*) rip, hole; ~ **de ligamento** torn ligament.

roturar *vt* to plough.

roulotte [ru'lot], **rulot** *f* caravan Br, trailer Am.

rozadura *f* 1. (*señal*) scratch, scrape. 2. (*herida*) graze.

rozamiento *m* (*fricción*) rub, rubbing (U); (*FÍS*) friction (U).

rozar *vt* 1. (*gen*) to rub; (*suavemente*) to brush; (*suj: zapato*) to graze. 2. (*pasar cerca de*) to skim. ▶ **rozar con** *vi* 1. (*tocar*) to brush against. 2. *fig* (*relacionarse con*) to touch on. ▶ **rozarse** *vpr* 1. (*tocarse*) to touch. 2. (*pasar cerca*) to brush past each other. 3. (*herirse - rodilla etc*) to graze. 4. *fig* (*tener trato*): **~se con** to rub shoulders with.

Rte. *abrev de* **remitente**.

RTVE (*abrev de* **Radiotelevisión Española**) *f Spanish state broadcasting company*.

rubeola, rubéola *f* German measles (U).

rubí (*pl* **rubís** o **rubíes**) *m* ruby.

rubio, -bia ◆ *adj* 1. (*pelo, persona*) blond (*f* blonde), fair. 2. (*tabaco*) Virginia (*antes de sust*). 3. (*cerveza*) lager (*antes de sust*). ◆ *m y f* (*persona*) blond (*f* blonde).

rubor *m* 1. (*vergüenza*) embarrassment. 2. (*sonrojo*) blush.

ruborizar *vt* (*avergonzar*) to embarrass. ▶ **ruborizarse** *vpr* to blush.

rúbrica *f* 1. (*de firma*) flourish. 2. (*conclusión*) final flourish; **poner ~ a algo** to complete sthg.

rubricar *vt* 1. *fig* (*confirmar*) to confirm. 2. *fig* (*concluir*) to complete.

rucio, -cia *adj* (*gris*) grey. ▶ **rucio** *m* ass, donkey.

rudeza *f* 1. (*tosquedad*) roughness. 2. (*grosería*) coarseness.

rudimentario, -ria *adj* rudimentary.

rudimentos *mpl* rudiments.

rudo, -da *adj* 1. (*tosco*) rough. 2. (*brusco*) sharp, brusque. 3. (*grosero*) rude, coarse.

rueda *f* 1. (*pieza*) wheel; **~ delantera/trasera** front/rear wheel; **~ de repuesto** spare wheel; **ir sobre ~s** *fig* to go smoothly. 2. (*corro*) circle. ▶ **rueda de prensa** *f* press conference.

ruedo *m* (TAUROM) bullring.

ruega *etc* → **rogar**.

ruego *m* request; **~s y preguntas** any other business.

rufián *m* villain.

rugby *m* rugby.

rugido *m* (*gen*) roar; (*de persona*) bellow.

rugir *vi* (*gen*) to roar; (*persona*) to bellow.

rugoso, -sa *adj* 1. (*áspero - material, terreno*) rough. 2. (*con arrugas - rostro etc*)

wrinkled; (*- tejido*) crinkled.

ruido *m* 1. (*gen*) noise; (*sonido*) sound; **mucho ~ y pocas nueces** much ado about nothing. 2. *fig* (*escándalo*) row.

ruidoso, -sa *adj* 1. (*que hace ruido*) noisy. 2. *fig* (*escandaloso*) sensational.

ruin *adj* 1. (*vil*) low, contemptible. 2. (*avaro*) mean.

ruina *f* 1. (*gen*) ruin; **amenazar ~** (*edificio*) to be about to collapse; **estar en la ~** to be ruined. 2. (*destrucción*) destruction. 3. (*fracaso - persona*) wreck; **estar hecho una ~** to be a wreck. ▶ **ruinas** *fpl* (*históricas*) ruins.

ruindad *f* 1. (*cualidad*) baseness. 2. (*acto*) vile deed.

ruinoso, -sa *adj* 1. (*poco rentable*) ruinous. 2. (*edificio*) ramshackle.

ruiseñor *m* nightingale.

ruleta *f* roulette.

ruletero *m* Amer taxi driver.

rulo *m* (*para el pelo*) roller.

rulot = **roulotte**.

ruma *f* Amer heap, pile.

Rumania Romania.

rumano, -na *adj, m y f* Romanian. ▶ **rumano** *m* (*lengua*) Romanian.

rumba *f* rumba.

rumbo *m* 1. (*dirección*) direction, course; **ir con ~ a** to be heading for; **perder el ~** (*barco*) to go off course; *fig* (*persona*) to lose one's way. 2. *fig* (*camino*) path, direction.

rumiante *adj & m* ruminant.

rumiar ◆ *vt* (*suj: rumiante*) to chew; *fig* to chew over. ◆ *vi* (*masticar*) to ruminate, to chew the cud.

rumor *m* 1. (*ruido sordo*) murmur. 2. (*chisme*) rumour.

rumorearse *v impers*: **~ que ...** to be rumoured that …

runrún *m* 1. (*ruido confuso*) hum, humming (U). 2. (*chisme*) rumour.

rupestre *adj* cave (*antes de sust*).

ruptura *f* (*gen*) break; (*de relaciones, conversaciones*) breaking-off; (*de contrato*) breach.

rural *adj* rural.

Rusia Russia.

ruso, -sa *adj, m y f* Russian. ▶ **ruso** *m* (*lengua*) Russian.

rústico, -ca *adj* 1. (*del campo*) country (*antes de sust*). 2. (*tosco*) rough, coarse. ▶ **en rústica** *loc adj* paperback.

ruta *f* route; *fig* way, course.

rutina *f* (*gen* & INFORM) routine; **por ~** as a matter of course.

rutinario, -ria *adj* routine.

S

s¹, S f (letra) s, S. ▶ **S** (abrev de **san**) St.
s² (abrev de **segundo**) s.
s., sig. (abrev de **siguiente**) foll.
SA (abrev de **sociedad anónima**) f ≃ Ltd, ≃ PLC.
sábado m Saturday; **¿qué día es hoy? – (es)** what day is it (today)? – (it's) Saturday; **cada ~, todos los ~s** every Saturday; **cada dos ~s, un ~ sí y otro no** every other Saturday; **caer en ~** to be on a Saturday; **te llamo el ~** I'll call you on Saturday; **el próximo ~, el ~ que viene** next Saturday; **el ~ pasado** last Saturday; **el ~ por la mañana/tarde/noche** Saturday morning/afternoon/night; **en ~** on Saturdays; **nací en ~** I was born on a Saturday; **este ~** (pasado) last Saturday; (próximo) this (coming) Saturday; **¿trabajas los ~s?** do you work (on) Saturdays?; **trabajar un ~** to work on a Saturday; **un ~ cualquiera** on any Saturday.
sábana f sheet.
sabandija f fig (persona) worm.
sabañón m chilblain.
sabático, -ca adj (del sábado) Saturday (antes de sust).
saber ◆ m knowledge. ◆ vt 1. (conocer) to know; **ya lo sé** I know; **hacer ~ algo a alguien** to inform sb of sthg, to tell sb sthg. 2. (ser capaz de): **~ hacer algo** to know how to do sthg, to be able to do sthg; **sabe hablar inglés/montar en bici** she can speak English/ride a bike. 3. (enterarse) to learn, to find out; **lo supe ayer** I only found out yesterday. 4. (entender de) to know about; **sabe mucha física** he knows a lot about physics. ◆ vi 1. (tener sabor): **~ (a)** to taste (of); **~ bien/mal** to taste good/bad; **~ mal a alguien** fig to upset o annoy sb. 2. (entender): **~ de algo** to know about sthg. 3. (tener noticia): **~ de alguien** to hear from sb; **~ de algo** to learn of sthg. 4. (parecer): **eso me sabe a disculpa** that sounds like an excuse to me. 5. Amer fam (soler): **~ hacer algo** to be wont to do sthg. 6. loc: **que yo sepa** as far as I know. ▶ **saberse** vpr: **~se algo** to know sthg. ▶ **a saber** loc adv (es decir) namely.

sabido, -da adj: **como es (bien) ~** as everyone knows.
sabiduría f 1. (conocimientos) knowledge, learning. 2. (prudencia) wisdom.
sabiendas ▶ **a sabiendas** loc adv knowingly.
sabihondo, -da, sabiondo, -da adj, m y f know-all.
sabio, -bia adj 1. (sensato, inteligente) wise. 2. (docto) learned. 3. (amaestrado) trained.
sabiondo, -da = sabihondo.
sablazo m fam fig (de dinero) scrounging (U); **dar un ~ a alguien** to scrounge money off sb.
sable m sabre.
sablear vi fam to scrounge money.
sabor m 1. (gusto) taste, flavour; **tener ~ a algo** to taste of sthg; **dejar mal/buen ~ (de boca)** fig to leave a nasty taste in one's mouth/a warm feeling. 2. fig (estilo) flavour.
saborear vt lit & fig to savour.
sabotaje m sabotage.
sabotear vt to sabotage.
sabrá etc → saber.
sabroso, -sa adj 1. (gustoso) tasty. 2. fig (substancioso) tidy, considerable.
sabueso m 1. (perro) bloodhound. 2. fig (policía) sleuth.
saca f sack.
sacacorchos m inv corkscrew.
sacapuntas m inv pencil sharpener.
sacar ◆ vt 1. (poner fuera, hacer salir) to take out; (lengua) to stick out; **~ algo de** to take sthg out of; **nos sacaron algo de comer** they gave us something to eat. 2. (quitar): **~ algo (de)** to remove sthg (from). 3. (librar, salvar): **~ a alguien de** to get sb out of. 4. (obtener - carné, buenas notas) to get, to obtain; (- premio) to win; (- foto) to take; (- fotocopia) to make; (- dinero del banco) to withdraw. 5. (sonsacar): **~ algo a alguien** to get sthg out of sb. 6. (extraer - producto): **~ algo de** to extract sthg from. 7. (fabricar) to produce. 8. (crear - modelo, disco etc) to bring out. 9. (exteriorizar) to show. 10. (resolver - crucigrama etc) to do, to finish. 11. (deducir) to gather, to understand; (conclusión) to come to. 12. (mostrar) to show; **le sacaron en televisión** he was on television. 13. (comprar - entradas etc) to get, to buy. 14. (prenda - de ancho) to let out; (- de largo) to let down. 15. (aventajar): **sacó tres minutos a su rival** he was three minutes ahead of his rival. 16.

(DEP - *con la mano*) to throw in; (- *con la raqueta*) to serve. ◆ *vi* (DEP) to put the ball into play; (*con la raqueta*) to serve. ▶ **sacarse** *vpr* (*carné etc*) to get. ▶ **sacar adelante** *vt* 1. (*hijos*) to bring up. 2. (*negocio*) to make a go of.

sacarina *f* saccharine.

sacerdote, -tisa *m y f* (*pagano*) priest (*f* priestess). ▶ **sacerdote** *m* (*cristiano*) priest.

saciar *vt* (*satisfacer - sed*) to quench; (- *hambre*) to satisfy.

saco *m* 1. (*bolsa*) sack, bag; ~ **de dormir** sleeping bag. 2. Amer jacket. 3. *loc*: **entrar a** ~ **en** to sack, to pillage; **no echar algo en** ~ **roto** to take good note of sthg.

sacramento *m* sacrament.

sacrificar *vt* 1. (*gen*) to sacrifice. 2. (*animal - para consumo*) to slaughter.

sacrificio *m* lit & *fig* sacrifice.

sacrilegio *m* lit & *fig* sacrilege.

sacristán, -ana *m y f* sacristan, sexton.

sacristía *f* sacristy.

sacro, -cra *adj* (*sagrado*) holy, sacred.

sacudida *f* 1. (*gen*) shake; (*de la cabeza*) toss; (*de tren, coche*) jolt; ~ **eléctrica** electric shock. 2. (*terremoto*) tremor.

sacudir *vt* 1. (*agitar*) to shake. 2. (*golpear - alfombra etc*) to beat. 3. *fig* (*conmover*) to shake, to shock. 4. *fam fig* (*pegar*) to smack.

sádico, -ca ◆ *adj* sadistic. ◆ *m y f* sadist.

sadismo *m* sadism.

saeta *f* 1. (*flecha*) arrow. 2. (MÚS) *flamenco-style song sung on religious occasions.*

safari *m* (*expedición*) safari.

saga *f* saga.

sagacidad *f* astuteness.

sagaz *adj* astute, shrewd.

Sagitario ◆ *m* (*zodiaco*) Sagittarius. ◆ *m y f* (*persona*) Sagittarian.

sagrado, -da *adj* holy, sacred; *fig* sacred.

Sahara *m*: **el (desierto del)** ~ the Sahara (Desert).

sal *f* (CULIN & QUÍM) salt. ▶ **sales** *fpl* 1. (*para reanimar*) smelling salts. 2. (*para baño*) bath salts.

sala *f* 1. (*habitación - gen*) room; (- *de una casa*) lounge, living room; (- *de hospital*) ward; ~ **de espera** waiting room; ~ **de estar** lounge, living room; ~ **de partos** delivery room. 2. (*local - de conferencias, conciertos*) hall; (- *de cine, teatro*) audito-rium; ~ **de fiestas** dance hall. 3. (DER - *lugar*) court (room); (- *magistrados*) bench. 4. Amer (*aula*) classroom.

salado, -da *adj* 1. (*con sal*) salted; (*agua*) salt (*antes de sust*); (*con demasiada sal*) salty. 2. *fig* (*gracioso*) witty. 3. Amer unfortunate.

salamandra *f* (*animal*) salamander.

salami, salame *m* salami.

salar *vt* 1. (*para conservar*) to salt. 2. (*para cocinar*) to add salt to.

salarial *adj* wage (*antes de sust*).

salario *m* salary, wages (*pl*); (*semanal*) wage.

salchicha *f* sausage.

salchichón *m* ≃ salami.

saldar *vt* 1. (*pagar - cuenta*) to close; (- *deuda*) to settle. 2. *fig* (*poner fin a*) to settle. 3. (COM) to sell off. ▶ **saldarse** *vpr* (*acabar*): ~**se con** to produce; **la pelea se saldó con 11 heridos** 11 people were injured in the brawl.

saldo *m* 1. (*de cuenta*) balance; ~ **acreedor/deudor** credit/debit balance. 2. (*de deudas*) settlement. 3. (*gen pl*) (*restos de mercancías*) remnant; (*rebajas*) sale; **de** ~ bargain. 4. *fig* (*resultado*) balance.

saldrá *etc* → **salir**.

saledizo, -za *adj* projecting.

salero *m* 1. (*recipiente*) salt cellar. 2. *fig* (*gracia*) wit; (*donaire*) charm.

salga *etc* → **salir**.

salida *f* 1. (*acción de partir - gen*) leaving; (- *de tren, avión*) departure. 2. (DEP) start. 3. (*lugar*) exit, way out. 4. (*momento*): **quedamos a la** ~ **del trabajo** we agreed to meet after work. 5. (*viaje*) trip. 6. (*aparición - de sol, luna*) rise; (- *de revista, nuevo modelo*) appearance. 7. (COM - *posibilidades*) market, outlet; (- *producción*) output. 8. *fig* (*solución*) way out; **si no hay otra** ~ if there's no alternative. 9. *fig* (*futuro - de carreras etc*) opening, opportunity.

salido, -da *adj* 1. (*saliente*) projecting, sticking out; (*ojos*) bulging. 2. (*animal*) on heat. 3. *mfam* (*persona*) horny.

saliente ◆ *adj* (POLÍT) outgoing. ◆ *m* projection.

salino, -na *adj* saline.

salir *vi* 1. (*ir fuera*) to go out; (*venir fuera*) to come out; ~ **de** to go/come out of; **¿salimos al jardín?** shall we go out into the garden?; **¡sal aquí fuera!** come out here! 2. (*ser novios*): ~ **(con alguien)** to go out (with sb). 3. (*marcharse*): ~ **(de/para)** to leave (from/for). 4. (*desembocar - calle*): ~ **a** to open out onto. 5. (*resultar*) to turn out; **ha salido muy estudioso** he has turned out to be very studious; **¿qué salió en la votación?** what was the result of the vote?; **~ elegida actriz del año** to be voted actress of the year; **~ bien/mal** to turn out well/badly; **~ ganando/perdiendo** to come off well/badly. **6.** (*proceder*): **~ de** to come from; **el vino sale de la uva** wine comes from grapes. **7.** (*surgir - luna, estrellas, planta*) to come out; (*- sol*) to rise; (*- dientes*) to come through; **le ha salido un sarpullido en la espalda** her back has come out in a rash. **8.** (*aparecer - publicación, producto, traumas*) to come out; (*- moda, ley*) to come in; (*- en imagen, prensa, televisión*) to appear; **¡qué bien sales en la foto!** you look great in the photo!; **ha salido en los periódicos** it's in the papers; **~ de** (CIN & TEATR) to appear as. **9.** (*costar*): **(a o por)** to work out (at); **~ caro** (*de dinero*) to be expensive; (*por las consecuencias*) to be costly. **10.** (*parecerse*): **~ a alguien** to take after sb. **11.** (*en juegos*) to lead; **te toca ~ a ti** it's your lead. **12.** (*quitarse - manchas*) to come out. **13.** (*librarse*): **~ de** (*gen*) to get out of; (*problema*) to get round. **14.** (INFORM): **(de)** to quit, to exit. ► **salirse** *vpr* **1.** (*marcharse - de lugar, asociación etc*): **~se (de)** to leave. **2.** (*filtrarse*): **~se (por)** (*líquido, gas*) to leak o escape (through); (*humo, aroma*) to come out (through). **3.** (*rebosar*) to overflow; (*leche*) to boil over; **el río se salió del cauce** the river broke its banks. **4.** (*desviarse*): **~se (de)** to come off; **el coche se salió de la carretera** the car came off o left the road. **5.** *fig* (*escaparse*): **~se de** (*gen*) to deviate from; (*límites*) to go beyond; **~se del tema** to digress. **6.** *loc*: **~se con la suya** to get one's own way. ► **salir adelante** *vi* **1.** (*persona, empresa*) to get by. **2.** (*proyecto, propuesta, ley*) to be successful.

salitre *m* saltpetre.

saliva *f* saliva.

salivar *vi* to salivate.

salmo *m* psalm.

salmón ◆ *m* (*pez*) salmon. ◆ *adj & m inv* (*color*) salmon (pink).

salmonete *m* red mullet.

salmuera *f* brine.

salobre *adj* salty.

salón *m* **1.** (*habitación - en casa*) lounge, sitting room; (*- en residencia, edificio público*) reception hall. **2.** (*local - de sesiones etc*) hall; **~ de actos** assembly hall. **3.** (*feria*) show, exhibition. **4.** (*estable-*

cimiento) shop; **~ de belleza/masaje** beauty/massage parlour; **~ de té** tearoom.

salpicadera *f* Amer mudguard Br, fender Am.

salpicadero *m* dashboard.

salpicar *vt* (*rociar*) to splash.

salpimentar *vt* to season.

salpullido = sarpullido.

salsa *f* **1.** (CULIN - *gen*) sauce; (*- de carne*) gravy; **~ bechamel** o **besamel** bechamel o white sauce; **~ rosa** thousand island dressing; **en su propia ~** *fig* in one's element. **2.** *fig* (*interés*) spice. **3.** (MÚS) salsa.

salsera *f* gravy boat.

salsero, -ra *m y f* salsa singer.

saltamontes *m inv* grasshopper.

saltar ◆ *vt* **1.** (*obstáculo*) to jump (over). **2.** (*omitir*) to skip, to miss out. **3.** (*hacer estallar*) to blow up. ◆ *vi* **1.** (*gen*) to jump; (*al agua*) to dive; **~ a la comba** o **cuerda** to skip; **~ sobre alguien** (*abalanzarse*) to set upon sb; **~ de un tema a otro** to jump (around) from one subject to another. **2.** (*levantarse*) to jump up; **~ de la silla** to jump out of one's seat. **3.** (*salir para arriba - objeto*) to jump (up); (*- champán, aceite*) to spurt (out); (*- corcho, válvula*) to pop out. **4.** (*explotar*) to explode, to blow up. **5.** (*romperse*) to break. **6.** (*reaccionar violentamente*) to explode. ► **saltarse** *vpr* **1.** (*omitir*) to skip, to miss out. **2.** (*salir despedido*) to pop off. **3.** (*no respetar - cola, semáforo*) to jump; (*- ley, normas*) to break.

salteado, -da *adj* **1.** (CULIN) sautéed. **2.** (*espaciado*) unevenly spaced.

salteador, -ra *m y f*: **~ de caminos** highwayman.

saltear *vt* (CULIN) to sauté.

saltimbanqui *m y f* acrobat.

salto *m* **1.** (*gen* & DEP) jump; (*grande*) leap; (*al agua*) dive; **~ de altura/longitud** high/long jump. **2.** *fig* (*diferencia, omisión*) gap. **3.** *fig* (*progreso*) leap forward. ► **salto de agua** *m* waterfall. ► **salto de cama** *m* negligée.

saltón, -ona *adj* (*ojos*) bulging; (*dientes*) sticking out.

salubre *adj* healthy.

salud ◆ *f lit & fig* health; **estar bien/mal de ~** to be well/unwell; **beber** o **brindar a la ~ de alguien** to drink to sb's health. ◆ *interj*: **¡~!** (*para brindar*) cheers!; (*después de estornudar*) bless you!

saludable *adj* **1.** (*sano*) healthy. **2.** *fig* (*provechoso*) beneficial.

saludar vt to greet; (MIL) to salute; **saluda a Ana de mi parte** give my regards to Ana; **le saluda atentamente** yours faithfully. ► **saludarse** vpr to greet one another.

saludo m greeting; (MIL) salute; **Ana te manda ~s** (en cartas) Ana sends you her regards; (al teléfono) Ana says hello; **un ~ afectuoso** (en cartas) yours sincerely.

salva f (MIL) salvo; **una ~ de aplausos** fig a round of applause.

salvación f 1. (remedio): **no tener ~** to be beyond hope. 2. (rescate) rescue. 3. (RELIG) salvation.

salvado m bran.

salvador, -ra m y f (persona) saviour. ► **Salvador** m (GEOGR): **El Salvador** El Salvador.

salvadoreño, -ña adj, m y f Salvadoran.

salvaguardar vt to safeguard.

salvaje ◆ adj 1. (gen) wild. 2. (pueblo, tribu) savage. ◆ m y f 1. (primitivo) savage. 2. (bruto) maniac.

salvamanteles m inv (llano) table mat; (con pies) trivet.

salvamento m rescue, saving; **equipo de ~** rescue team.

salvar vt 1. (gen & INFORM) to save. 2. (rescatar) to rescue. 3. (superar - moralmente) to overcome; (- físicamente) to go over o around. 4. (recorrer) to cover. 5. (exceptuar): **salvando algunos detalles** except for a few details. ► **salvarse** vpr 1. (librarse) to escape. 2. (RELIG) to be saved.

salvavidas ◆ adj inv life (antes de sust). ◆ m (chaleco) lifejacket; (flotador) lifebelt.

salvedad f exception.

salvia f sage.

salvo, -va adj safe; **estar a ~** to be safe; **poner algo a ~** to put sthg in a safe place. ► **salvo** adv except; **~ que** unless.

salvoconducto m safe-conduct, pass.

san adj Saint; **~ José** Saint Joseph.

sanar ◆ vt (persona) to cure; (herida) to heal. ◆ vi (persona) to get better; (herida) to heal.

sanatorio m sanatorium, nursing home.

sanción f (castigo) punishment; (ECON) sanction.

sancionar vt (castigar) to punish.

sandalia f sandal.

sandez f silly thing, nonsense (U).

sandía f watermelon.

sándwich ['sanwitʃ] (pl **sándwiches**) m toasted sandwich.

saneamiento m 1. (limpieza) cleaning; (higienización) disinfection. 2. (fig) - de moneda etc) stabilization; (- de economía) putting back on a sound footing.

sanear vt 1. (higienizar - tierras) to drain; (- un edificio) to disinfect. 2. fig (FIN - moneda) to stabilize; (- economía) to put back on a sound footing.

sanfermines mpl festival held in Pamplona when bulls are run through the streets of the town.

SANFERMINES

Pamplona is famous for the 'sanfermines', a week-long festival starting on 7 July, in which bulls are let loose in the streets of the town and young men demonstrate their bravery by running in front of them on the way to the bullring, sometimes receiving fatal wounds in the process. Bullfights are held every afternoon of the festival.

---

sangrar ◆ vi to bleed. ◆ vt 1. (sacar sangre) to bleed. 2. (IMPRENTA) to indent.

sangre f blood; **no llegó la ~ al río** it didn't get too nasty. ► **sangre fría** f sangfroid; **a ~ fría** in cold blood.

sangría f 1. (bebida) sangria. 2. (MED) bloodletting. 3. fig (ruina) drain.

sangriento, -ta adj (ensangrentado, cruento) bloody.

sanguijuela f lit & fig leech.

sanguinario, -ria adj bloodthirsty.

sanguíneo, -a adj blood (antes de sust).

sanidad f 1. (salubridad) health, healthiness. 2. (servicio) public health; (ministerio) health department.

sanitario, -ria adj health (antes de sust). ► **sanitarios** mpl (instalación) bathroom fittings (pl).

San José San José.

sano, -na adj 1. (saludable) healthy; **~ y salvo** safe and sound. 2. (positivo - principios, persona etc) sound; (- ambiente, educación) wholesome. 3. (entero) intact.

San Salvador San Salvador.

santero, -ra adj pious.

Santiago (de Chile) Santiago.

santiamén ► **en un santiamén** loc adv fam in a flash.

santidad f saintliness, holiness.

santiguar vt to make the sign of the cross over. ▶ **santiguarse** vpr (persignarse) to cross o.s.

santo, -ta ♦ adj 1. (sagrado) holy. 2. (virtuoso) saintly. 3. fam fig (dichoso) damn; **todo el ~ día** all day long. ♦ m y f (RELIG) saint. ▶ **santo** m 1. (onomástica) saint's day. 2. loc: **¿a ~ de qué?** why on earth? ▶ **santo y seña** m (MIL) password.

SANTO

Catholic tradition dictates that each day of the year is dedicated to a particular saint. On the day in question, people with the same name as the saint celebrate by buying drinks for their friends and family and, in turn, they are given presents.

Santo Domingo Santo Domingo.

santuario m shrine; fig sanctuary.

saña f viciousness, malice.

sapo m toad.

saque m 1. (en fútbol): **~ de banda** throw-in; **~ inicial** o **de centro** kick-off; **~ de esquina/meta** corner/goal kick. 2. (en tenis etc) serve.

saquear vt 1. (rapiñar - ciudad) to sack; (- tienda etc) to loot. 2. fam (vaciar) to ransack.

saqueo m (de ciudad) sacking; (de tienda etc) looting.

sarampión m measles (U).

sarao m (fiesta) party.

sarcasmo m sarcasm.

sarcástico, -ca adj sarcastic.

sarcófago m sarcophagus.

sardana f traditional Catalan dance and music.

sardina f sardine; **como ~s en canasta** o **en lata** like sardines.

sardónico, -ca adj sardonic.

sargento m y f (MIL) = sergeant.

sarpullido, salpullido m rash.

sarro m (de dientes) tartar.

sarta f lit & fig string.

sartén f frying pan; **tener la ~ por el mango** to be in control.

sastre, -tra m y f tailor.

sastrería f (oficio) tailoring; (taller) tailor's (shop).

Satanás m Satan.

satélite ♦ m satellite. ♦ adj fig satellite (antes de sust).

satén m satin; (de algodón) sateen.

satinado, -da adj glossy.

sátira f satire.

satírico, -ca ♦ adj satirical. ♦ m y f satirist.

satirizar vt to satirize.

satisfacción f satisfaction.

satisfacer vt 1. (gen) to satisfy; (sed) to quench. 2. (deuda, pago) to pay, to settle. 3. (ofensa, daño) to redress. 4. (duda, pregunta) to answer. 5. (cumplir - requisitos, exigencias) to meet.

satisfactorio, -ria adj satisfactory.

satisfecho, -cha ♦ pp → **satisfacer**. ♦ adj (gen) satisfied; (contento) pleased, contented; **~ de sí mismo** self-satisfied; **darse por ~** to be satisfied.

saturar vt to saturate. ▶ **saturarse** vpr: **~se (de)** to become saturated (with).

saturnismo m lead poisoning.

Saturno Saturn.

sauce m willow; **~ llorón** weeping willow.

sauna f sauna.

savia f sap; fig vitality; **~ nueva** fig new blood.

saxo m (instrumento) sax.

saxofón, saxófono m (instrumento) saxophone.

saxófono = saxofón.

sazón f 1. (madurez) ripeness; **en ~** ripe. 2. (sabor) seasoning. ▶ **a la sazón** loc adv then, at that time.

sazonado, -da adj seasoned.

sazonar vt to season.

scanner [es'kaner] = escáner.

schilling = chelín.

scout [es'kaut] (pl scouts) m scout.

se pron pers 1. (reflexivo) (de personas) himself (f herself), (pl) themselves; (usted mismo) yourself, (pl) yourselves; (de cosas, animales) itself, (pl) themselves; **~ está lavando, está lavándo~** she is washing (herself); **~ lavó los dientes** she cleaned her teeth; **espero que ~ diviertan** I hope you enjoy yourselves; **el perro ~ lame** the dog is licking itself; **~ lame la herida** it's licking its wound; **~ levantaron y ~ fueron** they got up and left. 2. (reflexivo impersonal) oneself; **hay que afeitar~ todos los días** one has to shave every day, you have to shave every day. 3. (recíproco) each other, one another; **~ aman** they love each other; **~ escriben cartas** they write to each other. 4. (en construcción pasiva): **~ ha suspendido la reunión** the meeting has been cancelled; **'~ prohíbe fumar'** 'no smoking'; **'~ habla inglés'** 'English spoken'. 5. (impersonal): **en esta sociedad ya**

no ~ **respeta a los ancianos** in our society old people are no longer respected; ~ **dice que ...** it is said that ..., people say that ... 6. (*en vez de 'le' o 'les' antes de 'lo', 'la', 'los' o 'las'*) (*complemento indirecto*) (*gen*) to him (*f* to her), (*pl*) to them; (*de cosa, animal*) to it, (*pl*) to them; (*usted, ustedes*) to you; ~ **lo dio** he gave it to him/her *etc*; ~ **lo dije, pero no me hizo caso** I told her, but she didn't listen; **si usted quiere, yo ~ lo arreglo en un minuto** if you like, I'll sort it out for you in a minute.

sé 1. → **saber**. 2. → **ser**.

sebo *m* fat; (*para jabón, velas*) tallow.

secador *m* dryer; ~ **de pelo** hair-dryer.

secadora *f* clothes o tumble dryer.

secar *vt* 1. (*desecar*) to dry. 2. (*enjugar*) to wipe away; (*con fregona*) to mop up. ▶ **secarse** *vpr* (*gen*) to dry up; (*ropa, vajilla, suelo*) to dry.

sección *f* 1. (*gen & GEOM*) section. 2. (*departamento*) department.

seccionar *vt* 1. (*cortar*) to cut; (*TECN*) to section. 2. (*dividir*) to divide (up).

secesión *f* secession.

seco, -ca *adj* 1. (*gen*) dry; (*plantas, flores*) withered; (*higos, pasas*) dried; **lavar en ~** to dry-clean. 2. (*tajante*) brusque. 3. *loc* **parar en ~** to stop dead. ▶ **a secas** *loc adv* simply, just; **llámame Juan a secas** just call me Juan.

secretaría *f* 1. (*oficina, lugar*) secretary's office. 2. (*organismo*) secretariat.

secretariado *m* 1. (*EDUC*) secretarial skills (*pl*). 2. (*cargo*) post of secretary.

secretario, -ria *m y f* secretary.

secreto, -ta *adj* (*gen*) secret; (*tono*) confidential; **en ~** in secret. ▶ **secreto** *m* 1. (*gen*) secret. 2. (*sigilo*) secrecy.

secta *f* sect.

sector *m* 1. (*gen*) sector; (*grupo*) group; (*campo*) field. 2. (*zona*) area.

secuaz *m y f despec* minion.

secuela *f* consequence.

secuencia *f* sequence.

secuestrador, -ra *m y f* kidnapper.

secuestrar *vt* 1. (*raptar*) to kidnap. 2. (*avión*) to hijack. 3. (*embargar*) to seize.

secuestro *m* 1. (*rapto*) kidnapping. 2. (*de avión, barco*) hijack. 3. (*de bienes etc*) seizure, confiscation.

secular *adj* 1. (*seglar*) secular, lay. 2. (*centenario*) age-old.

secundar *vt* to support, to back (up); (*propuesta*) to second.

secundario, -ria *adj* secondary.

sed ◆ *v* → **ser**. ◆ *f* thirst; **tener ~** to be thirsty; ~ **de** *fig* thirst for.

seda *f* silk.

sedal *m* fishing line.

sedante ◆ *adj* (*MED*) sedative; (*música*) soothing. ◆ *m* sedative.

sede *f* 1. (*emplazamiento*) headquarters (*pl*); (*de gobierno*) seat; ~ **social** head office. 2. (*RELIG*) see. ▶ **Santa Sede** *f*: **la Santa Sede** the Holy See.

sedentario, -ria *adj* sedentary.

sedición *f* sedition.

sediento, -ta *adj* 1. (*de agua*) thirsty. 2. *fig* (*deseoso*): ~ **de** hungry for.

sedimentar *vt* to deposit. ▶ **sedimentarse** *vpr* (*líquido*) to settle.

sedimento *m* 1. (*poso*) sediment. 2. (*GEOL*) deposit. 3. *fig* (*huella*) residue.

sedoso, -sa *adj* silky.

seducción *f* 1. (*cualidad*) seductiveness. 2. (*acción - gen*) attraction, charm; (*- sexual*) seduction.

seducir *vt* 1. (*atraer*) to attract, to charm; (*sexualmente*) to seduce. 2. (*persuadir*): ~ **a alguien para que haga algo** to tempt sb to do sthg.

seductor, -ra ◆ *adj* (*gen*) charming; (*sexualmente*) seductive; (*persuasivo*) tempting. ◆ *m y f* seducer.

segador, -ra *m y f* (*agricultor*) reaper.

segar *vt* 1. (*AGR*) to reap. 2. (*cortar*) to cut off. 3. *fig* (*truncar*) to put an end to.

seglar *m* lay person.

segmento *m* 1. (*GEOM & ZOOL*) segment. 2. (*trozo*) piece.

segregación *f* 1. (*separación, discriminación*) segregation; ~ **racial** racial segregation. 2. (*secreción*) secretion.

segregar *vt* 1. (*separar, discriminar*) to segregate. 2. (*secretar*) to secrete.

seguidilla *f* 1. (*gen pl*) (*baile*) traditional Spanish dance. 2. (*cante*) mournful flamenco song.

seguido, -da *adj* 1. (*consecutivo*) consecutive; **diez años ~s** ten years in a row. 2. (*sin interrupción - gen*) one after the other; (*- línea, pitido etc*) continuous. ▶ **seguido** *adv* 1. (*inmediatamente después*) straight after. 2. (*en línea recta*) straight on. ▶ **en seguida** *loc adv* straight away, at once; **en seguida nos vamos** we're going in a minute.

seguidor, -ra *m y f* follower.

seguimiento *m* (*de noticia*) following; (*de clientes*) follow-up.

seguir ◆ *vt* 1. (*gen*) to follow. 2. (*perseguir*) to chase. 3. (*reanudar*) to continue, to resume. ◆ *vi* 1. (*sucederse*): ~ **a algo** to follow sthg; **a la tormenta siguió la lluvia** the storm was followed by rain. **2.** (*continuar*) to continue, to go on; **¡sigue! ¡no te pares!** go o carry on, don't stop!; **sigo trabajando en la fábrica** I'm still working at the factory; **debes ~ haciéndolo** you should keep on o carry on doing it; **sigo pensando que está mal** I still think it's wrong; **sigue enferma/en el hospital** she's still ill/at the hospital. ▶ **seguirse** *vpr* to follow; **~se de algo** to follow o be deduced from sthg; **de esto se sigue que estás equivocado** it therefore follows that you are wrong.

según ◆ *prep* **1.** (*de acuerdo con*) according to; **~ su opinión, ha sido un éxito** in his opinion o according to him, it was a success; **~ yo/tú** *etc* in my/your *etc* opinion. **2.** (*dependiendo de*) depending on; **~ la hora que sea** depending on the time. ◆ *adv* **1.** (*como*) (just) as; **todo permanecía ~ lo recordaba** everything was just as she remembered it; **actuó ~ se le recomendó** he did as he had been advised. **2.** (*a medida que*) as; **entrarás en forma ~ vayas entrenando** you'll get fit as you train. **3.** (*dependiendo*) **¿te gusta la música? – ~ –** do you like music? – it depends; **lo intentaré – esté de tiempo** I'll try to do it, depending on how much time I have. ▶ **según que** *loc adv* depending on whether. ▶ **según qué** *loc adj* certain; **~ qué días la clase es muy aburrida** some days the class is really boring.

segunda → **segundo**.

segundero *m* second hand.

segundo, -da ◆ *núm adj* second. ◆ *núm m y f* **1.** (*en orden*) **el ~** the second one; **llegó el ~** he came second. **2.** (*mencionado antes*) **vinieron Pedro y Juan, el ~ con ...** Pedro and Juan arrived, the latter with ... **3.** (*ayudante*) number two; **~ de abordo** (NÁUT) first mate. ▶ **segundo** *m* **1.** (*gen*) second. **2.** (*piso*) second floor. ▶ **segunda** *f* **1.** (AUTOM) second (gear). **2.** (AERON & FERROC) second class. **3.** (DEP) second division. ▶ **con segundas** *loc adv* with an ulterior motive.

seguramente *adv* probably; **~ iré, pero aún no lo sé** the chances are I'll go, but I'm not sure yet.

seguridad *f* **1.** (*fiabilidad, ausencia de peligro*) safety; (*protección, estabilidad*) security; **de ~** (*cinturón, cierre*) safety (*antes de sust*); (*puerta, guardia*) security (*antes de sust*); **~ vial** road safety. **2.** (*cer-*

tidumbre) certainty; **con ~** for sure, definitely. **3.** (*confianza*) confidence; **~ en sí mismo** self-confidence. ▶ **Seguridad Social** *f* Social Security.

seguro, -ra *adj* **1.** (*fiable, sin peligro*) safe; (*protegido, estable*) secure. **2.** (*infalible - prueba, negocio etc*) reliable. **3.** (*confiado*) sure; **estar ~ de algo** to be sure about sthg. **4.** (*indudable - nombramiento, fecha etc*) definite, certain; **tener por ~ que** to be sure that. ▶ **seguro** ◆ *m* **1.** (*contrato*) insurance (U); **~ a todo riesgo/a terceros** comprehensive/third party insurance; **~ de incendios/de vida** fire/life insurance; **~ de paro** o **de desempleo** unemployment benefit; **~ del coche** car insurance; **~ mutuo** joint insurance. **2.** (*dispositivo*) safety device; (*de armas*) safety catch. **3.** Amer (*imperdible*) safety pin. ◆ *adv* for sure, definitely; **~ vendrá** she's bound to come.

seis ◆ *núm adj inv* **1.** (*para contar*) six; **tiene ~ años** she's six (years old). **2.** (*para ordenar*) (number) six; **la página ~** page six. ◆ *núm m* **1.** (*número*) six; **el ~** number six; **doscientos ~** two hundred and six; **treinta y ~** thirty-six. **2.** (*en fechas*) sixth; **el ~ de agosto** the sixth of August. **3.** (*en direcciones*) **calle Mayor (número) ~** number six calle Mayor. **4.** (*en naipes*) six; **el ~ de diamantes** the six of diamonds; **echar** o **tirar un ~** to play a six. ◆ *núm mpl* **1.** (*referido a grupos*) **invité a diez y sólo vinieron ~** I invited ten and only six came along; **somos ~** there are six of us; **de ~ en ~** in sixes; **los ~** the six of them. **2.** (*en temperaturas*) **estamos a ~ bajo cero** the temperature is six below zero. **3.** (*en puntuaciones*) **empatar a ~** to draw six all; **~ a cero** six-nil. ◆ *núm fpl* (*hora*) **las ~** six o'clock; **son las ~** it's six o'clock.

seiscientos, -tas *núm* six hundred; *ver también* **seis**.

seísmo *m* earthquake.

selección *f* **1.** (*gen*) selection; (*de personal*) recruitment. **2.** (*equipo*) team; **~ nacional** national team.

seleccionador, -ra *m y f* **1.** (DEP) selector, ≃ manager. **2.** (*de personal*) recruiter.

seleccionar *vt* to pick, to select.

selectividad *f* (*examen*) university entrance examination.

SELECTIVIDAD

The 'selectividad' is a series of exams which take place over two days at the end of secondary education in Spain. The mark obtained in these exams is one of the factors which determines whether or not a student is admitted to his or her preferred field of study at university.

---

selectivo, -va *adj* selective.
selecto, -ta *adj* 1. (*excelente*) fine, excellent. 2. (*escogido*) exclusive, select.
self-service *m inv* self-service restaurant.
sellar *vt* 1. (*timbrar*) to stamp. 2. (*lacrar*) to seal.
sello *m* 1. (*gen*) stamp. 2. (*tampón*) rubber stamp. 3. (*lacre*) seal. 4. *fig* (*carácter*) hallmark.
selva *f* (*gen*) jungle; (*bosque*) forest; **la ~ amazónica** the Amazon rainforest.
semáforo *m* traffic lights (*pl*).
semana *f* week; **entre ~** during the week; **~ laboral** working week. ▶ **Semana Santa** *f* Easter; (RELIG) Holy Week.

SEMANA SANTA
Throughout Easter week in Spain, a number of processions take place. People line the streets and pray, as statues of Christ and the saints are carried past. The most famous procession is that of Seville.

---

semanal *adj* weekly.
semanario, -ria *adj* weekly. ▶ **semanario** *m* (*publicación semanal*) weekly.
semántico, -ca *adj* semantic. ▶ **semántica** *f* semantics (U).
semblante *m* countenance, face.
semblanza *f* portrait, profile.
sembrado, -da *adj fig* (*lleno*): **~ de** scattered o plagued with.
sembrar *vt* 1. (*plantar*) to sow. 2. *fig* (*llenar*) to scatter. 3. *fig* (*confusión, pánico etc*) to sow.
semejante ◆ *adj* 1. (*parecido*): **~ (a)** similar (to). 2. (*tal*) such; **jamás aceptaría ~ invitación** I would never accept such an invitation. ◆ *m* (*gen pl*) fellow (human) being.
semejanza *f* similarity.
semejar *vt* to resemble. ▶ **semejarse** *vpr* to be alike.
semen *m* semen.
semental *m* stud; (*caballo*) stallion.
semestral *adj* half-yearly, six-monthly.

semestre *m* period of six months, semester Am; **cada ~** every six months.
semidirecto ◆ *adj* express. ◆ *m* → **tren**.
semifinal *f* semifinal.
semilla *f* seed.
seminario *m* 1. (*escuela para sacerdotes*) seminary. 2. (EDUC - *curso, conferencia*) seminar; (- *departamento*) department.
sémola *f* semolina.
Sena *m*: **el ~** the (river) Seine.
senado *m* senate.
senador, -ra *m y f* senator.
sencillez *f* 1. (*facilidad*) simplicity. 2. (*modestia*) unaffectedness. 3. (*discreción*) plainness.
sencillo, -lla *adj* 1. (*fácil, sin lujo, llano*) simple. 2. (*campechano*) unaffected. 3. (*billete, unidad etc*) single. ▶ **sencillo** *m* 1. (*disco*) single. 2. *Amer fam* (*cambio*) loose change.
senda *f*, **sendero** *m* path.
senderismo *m* trekking.
sendos, -das *adj pl* each, respective; **llegaron los dos con ~ paquetes** they arrived each carrying a parcel.
Senegal: **(el) ~** Senegal.
senil *adj* senile.
senior (*pl* seniors) *adj & m* senior.
seno *m* 1. (*pecho*) breast. 2. (*pechera*) bosom; **en el ~ de** *fig* within. 3. (*útero*): **~ (materno)** womb. 4. *fig* (*amparo, cobijo*) refuge, shelter. 5. (ANAT) (*de la nariz*) sinus.
sensación *f* 1. (*percepción*) feeling, sensation. 2. (*efecto*) sensation. 3. (*premonición*) feeling; **tener la ~ de que** to have a feeling that.
sensacional *adj* sensational.
sensacionalista *adj* sensationalist.
sensatez *f* wisdom, common sense.
sensato, -ta *adj* sensible.
sensibilidad *f* 1. (*perceptibilidad*) feeling. 2. (*sentimentalismo*) sensitivity. 3. (*don especial*) feel. 4. (*de emulsión fotográfica, balanza etc*) sensitivity.
sensibilizar *vt* 1. (*concienciar*) to raise the awareness of. 2. (FOT) to sensitize.
sensible *adj* 1. (*gen*) sensitive. 2. (*evidente*) perceptible; (*pérdida*) significant.
sensiblero, -ra *adj despec* mushy, sloppy.
sensitivo, -va *adj* 1. (*de los sentidos*) sensory. 2. (*receptible*) sensitive.
sensor *m* sensor.
sensorial *adj* sensory.
sensual *adj* sensual.
sentado, -da *adj* 1. (*en asiento*) seat-

ed; **estar ~** to be sitting down. 2. (*establecido*): **dar algo por ~** to take sthg for granted; **dejar ~ que ...** to make it clear that ...

sentar ◆ *vt* 1. (*en asiento*) to seat, to sit. 2. (*establecer*) to establish. ◆ *vi* 1. (*ropa, color*) to suit. 2. (*comida*): **~ bien/mal a alguien** to agree/disagree with sb. 3. (*vacaciones, medicamento*): **~ bien a alguien** to do sb good. 4. (*comentario, consejo*): **le sentó mal** it upset her; **le sentó bien** she appreciated it. ▶ **sentarse** *vpr* to sit down.

sentencia *f* 1. (DER) sentence. 2. (*proverbio, máxima*) maxim.

sentenciar *vt* (DER): **~ (a alguien a algo)** to sentence (sb to sthg).

sentido, -da *adj* (*profundo*) heartfelt. ▶ **sentido** *m* 1. (*gen*) sense; **tener ~** to make sense; **~ común** common sense; **~ del humor** sense of humour; **sexto ~** sixth sense. 2. (*conocimiento*) consciousness; **perder/recobrar el ~** to lose/regain consciousness. 3. (*significado*) meaning, sense; **sin ~** (*ilógico*) meaningless; (*inútil, irrelevante*) pointless; **doble ~** double meaning. 4. (*dirección*) direction; **de ~ único** one-way.

sentimental *adj* sentimental.

sentimentaloide *adj* mushy, sloppy.

sentimiento *m* 1. (*gen*) feeling. 2. (*pena, aflicción*): **le acompaño en el ~** my deepest sympathy.

sentir ◆ *vt* 1. (*gen*) to feel. 2. (*lamentar*) to regret, to be sorry about; **siento que no puedas venir** I'm sorry you can't come; **lo siento (mucho)** I'm (really) sorry. 3. (*oír*) to hear. ◆ *vi* to feel; **sin ~** *fig* without noticing. ◆ *m* feelings (*pl*), sentiments (*pl*). ▶ **sentirse** *vpr* to feel; **me siento mareada** I feel sick.

seña *f* (*gesto, indicio, contraseña*) sign, signal. ▶ **señas** *fpl* 1. (*dirección*) address (*sg*); **~s personales** (personal) description (*sg*). 2. (*gesto, indicio*) signs; **dar ~s de algo** to show signs of sthg; **(hablar) por ~s** (to talk) in sign language; **hacer ~s (a alguien)** to signal (to sb). 3. (*detalle*) details; **para o por más ~s** to be precise.

señal *f* 1. (*gen* & TELECOM) signal; (*de teléfono*) tone; **~ de alarma/salida** alarm/starting signal. 2. (*indicio, símbolo*) sign; **dar ~es de vida** to show signs of life; **~ de la Cruz** sign of the Cross; **~ de tráfico** road sign; **en ~ de** as a mark o sign of. 3. (*marca, huella*) mark; **no dejó ni ~** she didn't leave a trace. 4. (*cicatriz*) scar, mark. 5. (*fianza*) deposit.

señalado, -da *adj* (*importante - fecha*) special; (*- personaje*) distinguished.

señalar *vt* 1. (*marcar, denotar*) to mark; (*hora, temperatura etc*) to indicate, to say. 2. (*indicar - con el dedo, con un comentario*) to point out. 3. (*fijar*) to set, to fix.

señalización *f* 1. (*conjunto de señales*) signs (*pl*). 2. (*colocación de señales*) signposting.

señalizar *vt* to signpost.

señor, -ra *adj* (*refinado*) noble, refined. ▶ **señor** *m* 1. (*tratamiento - antes de nombre, cargo*) Mr; (*- al dirigir la palabra*) Sir; **el ~ López** Mr López; **¡~ presidente!** Mr President!; **¿qué desea el ~?** what would you like, Sir?; **Muy ~ mío** (*en cartas*) Dear Sir. 2. (*hombre*) man. 3. (*caballero*) gentleman. 4. (*dueño*) owner. 5. (*amo - de criado*) master. ▶ **señora** *f* 1. (*tratamiento - antes de nombre, cargo*) Mrs; (*- al dirigir la palabra*) Madam; **la señora López** Mrs López; **¡señora presidenta!** Madam President!; **¿qué desea la señora?** what would you like, Madam?; **¡señoras y ~es! ...** Ladies and Gentlemen! ...; **Estimada señora** (*en cartas*) Dear Madam. 2. (*mujer*) lady. 3. (*dama*) lady. 4. (*dueña*) owner. 5. (*ama - de criado*) mistress. 6. (*esposa*) wife. ▶ **señores** *mpl* (*matrimonio*): **los ~es Ruiz** Mr & Mrs Ruiz. ▶ **Nuestra Señora** *f* (RELIG) Our Lady.

señoría *f* lordship (*f* ladyship).

señorial *adj* 1. (*casa, mansión, barrio*) grand. 2. (*aspecto, porte, actitud*) lordly.

señorío *m* 1. (*dominio*) dominion, rule. 2. (*distinción*) nobility.

señorito, -ta *adj fam despec* (*refinado*) lordly. ▶ **señorito** *m* 1. *desus* (*hijo del amo*) master. 2. *fam despec* (*niñato*) rich kid. ▶ **señorita** *f* 1. (*soltera, tratamiento*) Miss. 2. (*joven*) young lady. 3. (*maestra*): **la ~** miss, the teacher. 4. *desus* (*hija del amo*) mistress.

señuelo *m* 1. (*reclamo*) decoy. 2. *fig* (*trampa*) bait, lure.

sepa → **saber**.

separación *f* 1. (*gen*) separation. 2. (*espacio*) space, distance.

separado, -da *adj* 1. (*gen*) separate; **está muy ~ de la pared** it's too far away from the wall; **por ~** separately. 2. (*del cónyuge*) separated.

separar *vt* 1. (*gen*) to separate; **~ algo de** to separate sthg from. 2. (*desunir*) to take off, to remove. 3. (*apartar - silla etc*) to move away. 4. (*reservar*) to put aside. 5. (*destituir*): **~ de** to remove o dismiss from. ▶ **separarse** *vpr* **1.** (*apartarse*) to move apart. **2.** (*ir por distinto lugar*) to part company. **3.** (*matrimonio*): **~se** (**de alguien**) to separate (from sb). **4.** (*desprenderse*) to come away o off.

separatismo *m* separatism.

separo *m* Amer cell.

sepia *f* (*molusco*) cuttlefish.

septentrional *adj* northern.

septiembre, **setiembre** *m* September; **el 1 de ~** the 1st of September; **uno de los ~s más lluviosos de la última década** one of the rainiest Septembers in the last decade; **a principios/mediados/finales de ~** at the beginning/in the middle/at the end of September; **el pasado/próximo** (**mes de**) **~** last/next September; **en ~** in September; **en pleno ~** in mid-September; **este** (**mes de**) **~** (*pasado*) (this) last September; (*próximo*) next September, this coming September; **para ~** by September.

séptimo, -ma, **sétimo, -ma** *núm* seventh.

septuagésimo, -ma *núm* seventieth.

sepulcral *adj fig* (*profundo - voz, silencio*) lugubrious, gloomy.

sepulcro *m* tomb.

sepultar *vt* to bury.

sepultura *f* **1.** (*enterramiento*) burial. **2.** (*fosa*) grave.

sepulturero, -ra *m y f* gravedigger.

sequedad *f* **1.** (*falta de humedad*) dryness. **2.** *fig* (*antipatía*) brusqueness.

sequía *f* drought.

séquito *m* (*comitiva*) retinue, entourage.

ser ◆ *vaux* (*antes de participio forma la voz pasiva*) to be; **fue visto por un testigo** he was seen by a witness. ◆ *v copulativo* **1.** (*gen*) to be; **es alto/gracioso** he is tall/funny; **es azul/difícil** it's blue/difficult; **es un amigo/el dueño** he is a friend/the owner. **2.** (*empleo, dedicación*) to be; **soy abogado/actriz** I'm a lawyer/an actress; **son estudiantes** they're students. ◆ *vi* **1.** (*gen*) to be; **fue aquí** it was here; **lo importante es decidirse** the important thing is to reach a decision; **~ de** (*estar hecho de*) to be made of; (*provenir de*) to be from; (*ser propiedad de*) to belong to; (*formar parte de*) to be a member of; **¿de dónde eres?** where are you from?; **los juguetes son de mi hijo** the toys are my son's. **2.** (*con precios, horas, números*) to be; **¿cuánto es?** how much is it?; **son 300 pesetas** that'll be 300 pesetas; **¿qué** (**día**) **es hoy?** what day is it today?; **mañana será 15 de julio** tomorrow (it) will be the 15th of July; **¿qué hora es?** what time is it?, what's the time?; **son las tres** (**de la tarde**) it's three o'clock (in the afternoon), it's three (pm). **3.** (*servir, ser adecuado*): **~ para** to be for; **este trapo es para** (**limpiar**) **las ventanas** this cloth is for (cleaning) the windows; **este libro es para niños** this book is (meant) for children. **4.** (*uso partitivo*): **~ de los que ...** to be one of those (people) who ...; **ése es de los que están en huelga** he is one of those on strike. ◆ *v impers* **1.** (*expresa tiempo*) to be; **es muy tarde** it's rather late; **era de noche/de día** it was night/day. **2.** (*expresa necesidad, posibilidad*): **es de desear que ...** it is to be hoped that ...; **es de suponer que aparecerá** presumably, he'll turn up. **3.** (*expresa motivo*): **es que no vine porque estaba enfermo** the reason I didn't come is that I was ill. **4.** *loc*: **a no ~ que** unless; **como sea** somehow or other; **de no ~ por** had it not been for; **érase una vez, érase que se era** once upon a time; **no es para menos** not without reason; **o sea** that is (to say), I mean; **por si fuera poco** as if that wasn't enough. ◆ *m* (*ente*) being; **~ humano/vivo** human/living being.

SER (*abrev de* **Sociedad Española de Radiodifusión**) *f Spanish independent radio company.*

Serbia Serbia.

serenar *vt* (*calmar*) to calm. ▶ **serenarse** *vpr* **1.** (*calmarse*) to calm down. **2.** (*estabilizarse - tiempo*) to clear up; (*- aguas*) to grow calm.

serenata *f* (*mús*) serenade.

serenidad *f* **1.** (*tranquilidad*) calm. **2.** (*quietud*) tranquility.

sereno, -na *adj* calm. ▶ **sereno** *m* (*vigilante*) night watchman.

serial *m* serial.

serie *f* **1.** (*gen & TV*) series (*sg*); (*de hechos, sucesos*) chain; (*de mentiras*) string. **2.** (*de sellos, monedas*) set. **3.** *loc*: **ser un fuera de ~** to be unique. ▶ **de serie** *loc adj* (*equipamiento*) (fitted) as standard. ▶ **en serie** *loc adv* (*fabricación*): **fabricar en ~** to mass-produce.

seriedad *f* **1.** (*gravedad*) seriousness. **2.** (*responsabilidad*) sense of responsibility. **3.** (*formalidad - de persona*) reliability.

serio, -ria *adj* **1.** (*gen*) serious; **estar ~** to look serious. **2.** (*responsable, formal*) responsible. **3.** (*sobrio*) sober. ▶ **en serio** *loc adv* seriously; **lo digo en ~** I'm serious; **tomar(se) algo/a alguien en ~** to take sthg/sb seriously.

sermón m lit & fig sermon.
seropositivo, -va (MED) ◆ adj HIV-positive. ◆ m y f HIV-positive person.
serpentear vi 1. (río, camino) to wind. 2. (culebra) to wriggle.
serpentina f streamer.
serpiente f (culebra) snake; (LITER) serpent.
serranía f mountainous region.
serrano, -na adj 1. (de la sierra) mountain (antes de sust). 2. (jamón) cured.
serrar vt to saw (up).
serrín m sawdust.
serrucho m handsaw.
servicial adj attentive, helpful.
servicio m 1. (gen) service; ~ **de prensa/de urgencias** press/casualty department; ~ **de mesa** dinner service; ~ **militar** military service; ~ **de té** tea set. 2. (servidumbre) servants (pl). 3. (turno) duty. 4. (gen pl) (WC) toilet, lavatory. 5. (DEP) serve, service.
servidor, -ra m y f 1. (en cartas): **su seguro** ~ yours faithfully. 2. (yo) yours truly, me. ▶ **servidor** m (INFORM) server.
servidumbre f 1. (criados) servants (pl). 2. (dependencia) servitude.
servil adj servile.
servilleta f serviette, napkin.
servilletero m serviette o napkin ring.
servir ◆ vt to serve; **sírvanos dos cervezas** bring us two beers; **¿te sirvo más patatas?** would you like some more potatoes?; **¿en qué puedo ~le?** what can I do for you? ◆ vi 1. (gen) to serve; ~ **en el gobierno** to be a government minister. 2. (valer, ser útil) to serve, to be useful; **no sirve para estudiar** he's no good at studying; **de nada sirve que se lo digas** it's no use telling him; ~ **de algo** to serve as sthg. ▶ **servirse** vpr 1. (aprovecharse): ~**se de** to make use of; **sírvase llamar cuando quiera** please call whenever you want. 2. (comida, bebida) to help o.s.
sésamo m sesame.
sesenta núm sixty; **los (años)** ~ the sixties; ver también **seis**.
sesgo m 1. (oblicuidad) slant. 2. fig (rumbo) course, path.
sesión f 1. (reunión) meeting, session; (DER) sitting, session. 2. (proyección, representación) show, performance; ~ **continua** continuous showing; ~ **matinal** matinée; ~ **de tarde** afternoon matinée; ~ **de noche** evening showing. 3. (periodo) session.

seso m (gen pl) 1. (cerebro) brain. 2. (sensatez) brains (pl), sense; **sorber el** ~ o **los** ~**s a alguien** to brainwash sb.
sesudo, -da adj (inteligente) brainy.
set (pl sets) m (DEP) set.
seta f mushroom; ~ **venenosa** toadstool.
setecientos, -tas núm seven hundred; ver también **seis**.
setenta núm seventy; **los (años)** ~ the seventies; ver también **seis**.
setiembre = **septiembre**.
sétimo, -ma = **séptimo**.
seto m fence; ~ **vivo** hedge.
seudónimo = **pseudónimo**.
severidad f 1. (rigor) severity. 2. (intransigencia) strictness.
severo, -ra adj 1. (castigo) severe, harsh. 2. (persona) strict.
Sevilla Seville.
sevillano, -na adj, m y f Sevillian. ▶ **sevillanas** fpl Andalusian dance and song.
sexagésimo, -ma núm sixtieth.
sexi, sexy (pl sexys) adj sexy.
sexista adj, m y f sexist.
sexo m (gen) sex.
sexteto m (MÚS) sextet.
sexto, -ta ◆ núm adj sixth; **capítulo** ~ chapter six; **el** ~ **día** the sixth day; **en** ~ **lugar, en sexta posición** in sixth place; **la sexta parte** a sixth. ◆ núm m y f: **el** ~**, la sexta** (persona, cosa) the sixth; **llegar el** ~ to come sixth. ▶ **sexto** m 1. (parte) sixth. 2. (piso) sixth floor. 3. (EDUC): ~ **(de EGB)** year six of Spanish primary education system.
sexual adj (gen) sexual; (educación, vida) sex (antes de sust).
sexualidad f sexuality.
sexy = **sexi**.
sha [sa, ʃa] m shah.
shock = **choc**.
shorts [ʃorts] mpl shorts.
show [ʃou] (pl shows) m show.
si¹ (pl sis) m (MÚS) B; (en solfeo) ti.
si² conj 1. (condicional) if; ~ **viene el yo me voy** if he comes, then I'm going; ~ **hubieses venido te habrías divertido** if you had come, you would have enjoyed yourself. 2. (en oraciones interrogativas indirectas) if, whether; **ignoro** ~ **lo sabe** I don't know if o whether she knows. 3. (expresa protesta) but; **¡**~ **te dije que no lo hicieras!** but I told you not to do it!
sí (pl síes) ◆ adv 1. (afirmación) yes; **¿vendrás?** – ~, **iré** will you come? – yes, I will; **claro que** ~ of course; **creo que** ~ I think so; **¿están de acuerdo?** – **algunos** ~ do

they agree? – some do. **2.** (*uso enfático*): **~ que** really, certainly; **~ que me gusta** I really o certainly like it. **3.** *loc*: **no creo que puedas hacerlo** – **¡a que ~!** I don't think you can do it – I bet I can!; **porque ~** (*sin razón*) because (I/you *etc* felt like it); **¿~?** (*incredulidad*) really? ◆ *pron pers* **1.** (*reflexivo*) (*de personas*) himself (*f* herself), (*pl*) themselves; (*usted*) yourself, (*pl*) yourselves; (*de cosas, animales*) itself, (*pl*) themselves; **lo quiere todo para ~ (misma)** she wants everything for herself; **se acercó la silla hacia ~** he drew the chair nearer (himself); **de (por) ~** (*cosa*) in itself. **2.** (*reflexivo impersonal*) oneself; **cuando uno piensa en ~ mismo** when one thinks about oneself, when you think about yourself. ◆ *m* consent; **dar el ~** to give one's consent.

siamés, -esa *adj* Siamese. ▶ **siamés** *m* (*gato*) Siamese.

Siberia: (**la**) ~ Siberia.

Sicilia Sicily.

sicoanálisis *etc* = **psicoanálisis**.

sicodélico, -ca = **psicodélico**.

sicología *etc* = **psicología**.

sicópata = **psicópata**.

sicosis = **psicosis**.

sicosomático, -ca = **psicosomático**.

sida (*abrev de* **síndrome de inmunodeficiencia adquirida**) *m* AIDS.

siderurgia *f* iron and steel industry.

siderúrgico, -ca *adj* (IND) iron and steel (*antes de sust*).

sidra *f* cider.

siega *f* **1.** (*acción*) reaping, harvesting. **2.** (*época*) harvest (time).

siembra *f* **1.** (*acción*) sowing. **2.** (*época*) sowing time.

siempre *adv* **1.** (*gen*) always; **como ~** as usual; **de ~** usual; **lo de ~** the usual; **somos amigos de ~** we've always been friends; **es así desde ~** it has always been that way; **para ~, para ~ jamás** for ever and ever. **2.** *Amer* (*sin duda*) really. ▶ **siempre que** *loc conj* **1.** (*cada vez que*) whenever. **2.** (*con tal de que*) provided that, as long as. ▶ **siempre y cuando** *loc conj* provided that, as long as.

sien *f* temple.

sienta *etc* **1.** → **sentar**. **2.** → **sentir**.

sierra *f* **1.** (*herramienta*) saw. **2.** (*cordillera*) mountain range. **3.** (*región montañosa*) mountains (*pl*).

siervo, -va *m y f* **1.** (*esclavo*) serf. **2.** (RELIG) servant.

siesta *f* siesta, nap; **dormir** o **echarse la ~** to have an afternoon nap.

siete ◆ *núm* seven; *ver también* **seis**. ◆ *f Amer fig*: **de la gran ~** amazing; **¡la gran ~!** good heavens!

sífilis *f inv* syphilis.

sifón *m* **1.** (*agua carbónica*) soda (water). **2.** (*tubo*) siphon.

sig. = **s.**

sigilo *m* (*gen*) secrecy; (*al robar, escapar*) stealth.

sigiloso, -sa *adj* (*discreto*) secretive; (*al robar, escapar*) stealthy.

siglas *fpl* acronym.

siglo *m* **1.** (*cien años*) century; **el ~ XX** the 20th century. **2.** *fig* (*mucho tiempo*): **hace ~s que no la veo** I haven't seen her for ages.

signatura *f* **1.** (*en biblioteca*) catalogue number. **2.** (*firma*) signature.

significación *f* **1.** (*importancia*) significance. **2.** (*acepción*) meaning.

significado, -da *adj* important. ▶ **significado** *m* (*sentido*) meaning.

significar ◆ *vt* **1.** (*gen*) to mean. **2.** (*expresar*) to express. ◆ *vi* (*tener importancia*): **no significa nada para mí** it means nothing to me.

significativo, -va *adj* significant.

signo *m* **1.** (*gen*) sign; **~ de multiplicar/dividir** multiplication/division sign; **~ del zodiaco** sign of the zodiac. **2.** (*en la escritura*) mark; **~ de admiración/interrogación** exclamation/question mark. **3.** (*símbolo*) symbol.

sigo *etc* → **seguir**.

siguiente ◆ *adj* **1.** (*en el tiempo, espacio*) next. **2.** (*a continuación*) following. ◆ *m y f* **1.** (*el que sigue*): **el ~** the next one; **¡el ~!** next, please! **2.** (*lo que sigue*): **lo ~** the following.

sílaba *f* syllable.

silabear *vt* to spell out syllable by syllable.

silbar ◆ *vt* **1.** (*gen*) to whistle. **2.** (*abuchear*) to hiss. ◆ *vi* **1.** (*gen*) to whistle. **2.** (*abuchear*) to hiss. **3.** *fig* (*oídos*) to ring.

silbato *m* whistle.

silbido, silbo *m* **1.** (*gen*) whistle. **2.** (*para abuchear, del serpiente*) hiss, hissing (U).

silenciador *m* silencer.

silenciar *vt* to hush up, to keep quiet.

silencio *m* **1.** (*gen*) silence; **guardar ~ (sobre algo)** to keep silent (about sthg); **romper el ~** to break the silence. **2.** (MÚS) rest.

silencioso, -sa *adj* silent.

silicona *f* silicone.

silla *f* **1.**

chair; ~ **eléctrica** electric chair. 2. (de caballo): ~ **(de montar)** saddle.

sillín m saddle, seat.

sillón m armchair.

silueta f 1. (cuerpo) figure. 2. (contorno) outline. 3. (dibujo) silhouette.

silvestre adj wild.

simbólico, -ca adj symbolic.

simbolizar vt to symbolize.

símbolo m symbol.

simetría f symmetry.

simiente f culto seed.

símil m 1. (paralelismo) similarity, resemblance. 2. (LITER) simile.

similar adj: ~ **(a)** similar (to).

similitud f similarity.

simio, -mia m y f simian, ape.

simpatía f 1. (cordialidad) friendliness, warmth. 2. (cariño) affection; **coger ~ a alguien** to take a liking to sb; **tener ~ a, sentir ~ por** to like.

simpático, -ca adj 1. (gen) nice, likeable; (abierto, cordial) friendly. 2. (anécdota, comedia etc) amusing, entertaining. 3. (reunión, velada etc) pleasant, agreeable.

simpatizante m y f sympathizer.

simpatizar vi: ~ **(con)** (persona) to hit it off (with); (cosa) to sympathize (with).

simple ◆ adj 1. (gen) simple. 2. (fácil) easy, simple. 3. (único, sin componentes) single; **dame una ~ razón** give me one single reason. 4. (mero) mere; **por ~ estupidez** through sheer stupidity. ◆ m y f (persona) simpleton.

simplemente adv simply.

simpleza f 1. (de persona) simplemindedness. 2. (tontería) trifle.

simplicidad f simplicity.

simplificar vt to simplify.

simplista adj simplistic.

simposio, simposium m symposium.

simulacro m simulation; ~ **de combate** mock battle.

simular vt 1. (sentimiento, desmayo etc) to feign; **simuló que no me había visto** he pretended not to have seen me. 2. (combate, salvamento) to simulate.

simultáneo, -nea adj simultaneous.

sin prep without; ~ **alcohol** alcohol-free; **estoy ~ una peseta** I'm penniless; **ha escrito cinco libros ~** (contar) las novelas he has written five books, not counting his novels; **está ~ hacer** it hasn't been done yet; **estamos ~ vino** we're out of wine; ~ **que** (+ subjuntivo) without (+ ...); ~ **que nadie se enterara** without

anyone noticing. ▶ **sin embargo** conj however.

sinagoga f synagogue.

sincerarse vpr: ~ **(con alguien)** to open one's heart (to sb).

sinceridad f sincerity; (llaneza, franqueza) frankness; **con toda ~** in all honesty.

sincero, -ra adj sincere; (abierto, directo) frank; **para ser ~** to be honest.

síncope m blackout.

sincronizar vt 1. (regular) to synchronize. 2. (FÍS) to tune.

sindical adj (trade) union (antes de sust).

sindicalista m y f trade unionist.

sindicato m trade union, labor union Am.

síndrome m syndrome; ~ **de abstinencia** withdrawal symptoms (pl); ~ **de Down** Down's syndrome; ~ **tóxico** toxic syndrome caused by ingestion of adulterated rapeseed oil.

sinfín m vast number; **un ~ de problemas** no end of problems.

sinfonía f symphony.

sinfónico, -ca adj symphonic.

Singapur Singapore.

single ['singel] m single.

singular ◆ adj 1. (raro) peculiar, odd. 2. (único) unique. 3. (GRAM) singular. ◆ m (GRAM) singular; **en ~** in the singular.

singularidad f 1. (rareza, peculiaridad) peculiarity. 2. (exclusividad) uniqueness.

singularizar vt to distinguish, to single out. ▶ **singularizarse** vpr to stand out.

siniestro, -tra adj 1. (perverso) sinister. 2. (desgraciado) disastrous. ▶ **siniestro** m disaster; (accidente de coche) accident, crash; (incendio) fire.

sinnúmero m: **un ~ de** countless.

sino conj 1. (para contraponer) but; **no lo hizo él, ~ ella** he didn't do it, she did; **no sólo es listo, ~ también trabajador** he's not only clever but also hardworking. 2. (para exceptuar) except, but; **¿quién ~ tú lo haría?** who else but you would do it?; **no quiero ~ que se haga justicia** I only want justice to be done.

sinónimo, -ma adj synonymous. ▶ **sinónimo** m synonym.

sinopsis f inv synopsis.

síntesis f inv synthesis; **en ~** in short.

sintético, -ca adj (artificial) synthetic.

sintetizador, -ra adj synthesizing. ▶ **sintetizador** m synthesizer.

sintetizar vt 1. (resumir) to summarize.
2. (fabricar artificialmente) to synthesize.

sintiera etc → **sentir**.

síntoma m symptom.

sintonía f 1. (música) signature tune.
2. (conexión) tuning. 3. fig (compenetración)
harmony.

sintonizar ♦ vt (conectar) to tune in to.
♦ vi 1. (conectar): ~ (con) to tune in (to).
2. fig (compenetrarse): ~ **en algo (con
alguien)** to be on the same wavelength
(as sb) about sthg.

sinuoso, -sa adj 1. (camino) winding.
2. (movimiento) sinuous.

sinvergüenza m y f 1. (canalla) rogue.
2. (fresco, descarado) cheeky person.

sionismo m Zionism.

siquiatra = **psiquiatra**.

siquiátrico, -ca = **psiquiátrico**.

síquico, -ca = **psíquico**.

siquiera ♦ conj (aunque) even if; **ven ~
por pocos días** do come, even if it's only
for a few days. ♦ adv (por lo menos) at
least; **dime ~ tu nombre** (you could) at
least tell me your name. ► **ni (tan)
siquiera** loc conj not even; **ni (tan) ~ me
hablaron** they didn't even speak to me.

sirena f 1. (MITOL) mermaid, siren.
2. (señal) siren.

Siria Syria.

sirimiri m drizzle.

sirviente, -ta m y f servant.

sisa f (en costura) dart; (de manga) armhole.

sisear vt & vi to hiss.

sísmico, -ca adj seismic.

sistema m 1. (gen & INFORM) system; ~
monetario/nervioso/solar monetary/
nervous/solar system; ~ **experto/opera-
tivo** (INFORM) expert/operating system;
~ **dual** (TV) system enabling dubbed TV programmes to be heard in the original language;
~ **métrico (decimal)** metric (decimal)
system; ~ **monetario europeo** European
Monetary System; ~ **montañoso** mountain chain o range; ~ **periódico de los
elementos** periodic table of elements.
2. (método, orden) method. ► **por sistema** loc adv systematically.

Sistema Ibérico m: **el ~** the Iberian
mountain chain.

sistemático, -ca adj systematic.

sistematizar vt to systematize.

sitiar vt (cercar) to besiege.

sitio m 1. (lugar) place; **cambiar de ~
(con alguien)** to change places (with sb);
en otro ~ elsewhere. 2. (espacio) room,
space; **hacer ~ a alguien** to make room

for sb. 3. (cerco) siege. 4. (INFORM): ~
Web Web site.

situación f 1. (circunstancias) situation;
(legal, social) status. 2. (condición, estado)
state, condition. 3. (ubicación) location.

situado, -da adj 1. (acomodado) comfortably off. 2. (ubicado) located, situated.

situar vt 1. (colocar) to place, to put;
(edificio, ciudad) to site, to locate. 2. (en
clasificación) to place, to rank. 3. (localizar) to locate, to find. ► **situarse** vpr
1. (colocarse) to take up position. 2. (ubicarse) to be located. 3. (acomodarse,
establecerse) to get o.s. established.
4. (en clasificación) to be placed; **se sitúa
entre los mejores** he's (ranked) amongst
the best.

skai [es'kai] = **escay**.

ski [es'ki] = **esquí**.

SL (abrev de sociedad limitada) f ≃ Ltd.

slip [es'lip] = **eslip**.

slogan [es'loɣan] = **eslogan**.

SME (abrev de **sistema monetario
europeo**) m EMS.

smoking [es'mokin] = **esmoquin**.

s/n abrev de **sin número**.

snob = **esnob**.

so ♦ prep under; ~ **pretexto de** under
the pretext of. ♦ adv: **¡~ tonto!** you
idiot! ♦ interj: **¡~!** whoa!

sobaco m armpit.

sobado, -da adj 1. (cuello, puños etc)
worn, shabby; (libro) dog-eared. 2. fig
(argumento, excusa) hackneyed. ► **sobado** m (CULIN) shortcrust pastry.

sobar vt 1. (tocar) to finger, to paw. 2.
despec (acariciar, besar) to touch up.

soberanía f sovereignty.

soberano, -na ♦ adj 1. (independiente)
sovereign. 2. fig (grande) massive; (paliza) thorough; (belleza, calidad) unrivalled. ♦ m y f sovereign.

soberbio, -bia adj 1. (arrogante)
proud, arrogant. 2. (magnífico) superb.
► **soberbia** f 1. (arrogancia) pride, arrogance. 2. (magnificencia) grandeur.

sobornar vt to bribe.

soborno m 1. (acción) bribery. 2. (dinero, regalo) bribe.

sobra f excess, surplus; **de ~** (en exceso)
more than enough; (de más) superflu-
ous; **lo sabemos de ~** we know it only
too well. ► **sobras** fpl (de comida) leftovers.

sobrado, -da adj 1. (de sobra) more
than enough, plenty of. 2. (de dinero)
well off.

sobrante adj remaining.

sobrar vi 1. (quedar, restar) to be left over; **nos sobró comida** we had some food left over. 2. (haber de más) to be more than enough; **parece que van a ~ bocadillos** it looks like there are going to be too many sandwiches. 3. (estar de más) to be superfluous; **lo que dices sobra** that goes without saying.

sobrasada f Mallorcan spiced sausage.

sobre¹ m 1. (para cartas) envelope. 2. (para alimentos) sachet, packet.

sobre² prep 1. (encima de) on (top of); **el libro está ~ la mesa** the book is on (top of) the table. 2. (por encima de) over, above; **el pato vuela ~ el lago** the duck is flying over the lake. 3. (acerca de) about, on; **un libro ~ el amor** a book about o on love; **una conferencia ~ el desarme** a conference on disarmament. 4. (alrededor de) about; **llegarán ~ las diez** they'll arrive at about ten o'clock. 5. (acumulación) upon; **nos contó mentira ~ mentira** he told us lie upon lie o one lie after another. 6. (cerca de) upon; **la desgracia estaba ya ~ nosotros** the disaster was already upon us.

sobrecarga f 1. (exceso de carga) excess weight. 2. (saturación) overload.

sobrecargo m (COM) surcharge.

sobrecoger vt to startle. ▶ **sobrecogerse** vpr to be startled.

sobredosis f inv overdose.

sobreentender = **sobrentender**.

sobregiro m (COM) overdraft.

sobremesa f after-dinner period.

sobrenatural adj (extraordinario) supernatural.

sobrenombre m nickname.

sobrentender, **sobreentender** vt to understand, to deduce. ▶ **sobrentenderse** vpr to be inferred o implied.

sobrepasar vt 1. (exceder) to exceed. 2. (aventajar): ~ **a alguien** to overtake sb.

sobrepeso m excess weight.

sobreponer, **superponer** vt fig (anteponer): ~ **algo a algo** to put sthg before sthg. ▶ **sobreponerse** vpr: **~se a algo** to overcome sthg.

sobreproducción, **superproducción** f (ECON) overproduction (U).

sobrepuesto, -ta, **superpuesto, -ta** adj superimposed. ▶ **sobrepuesto, -ta** pp → **sobreponer**.

sobresaliente ◆ adj (destacado) outstanding. ◆ m (en escuela) excellent, ≃ A; (en universidad) ≃ first class.

sobresalir vi 1. (en tamaño) to jut out.

2. (en importancia) to stand out.

sobresaltar vt to startle. ▶ **sobresaltarse** vpr to be startled, to start.

sobresalto m start, fright.

sobrestimar vt to overestimate.

sobretodo m overcoat.

sobrevenir vi to happen, to ensue; **sobrevino la guerra** the war intervened.

sobreviviente = **superviviente**.

sobrevivir vi to survive.

sobrevolar vt to fly over.

sobriedad f 1. (moderación) restraint, moderation. 2. (no embriaguez) soberness.

sobrino, -na m y f nephew (f niece).

sobrio, -bria adj 1. (moderado) restrained. 2. (no excesivo) simple. 3. (austero, no borracho) sober.

socarrón, -ona adj sarcastic.

socavar vt (excavar por debajo) to dig under; fig (debilitar) to undermine.

socavón m 1. (hoyo) hollow; (en la carretera) pothole. 2. (MIN) gallery.

sociable adj sociable.

social adj 1. (gen) social. 2. (COM) company (antes de sust).

socialdemócrata m y f social democrat.

socialismo m socialism.

socialista adj, m y f socialist.

sociedad f 1. (gen) society; ~ **de consumo** consumer society; ~ **deportiva** sports club; ~ **literaria** literary society. 2. (COM) (empresa) company; ~ **anónima** public (limited) company Br, incorporated company Am; ~ **(de responsabilidad) limitada** private limited company.

socio, -cia m y f 1. (COM) partner. 2. (miembro) member.

sociología f sociology.

sociólogo, -ga m y f sociologist.

socorrer vt to help.

socorrismo m first aid; (en la playa) lifesaving.

socorrista m y f first aid worker; (en la playa) lifeguard.

socorro ◆ m help, assistance. ◆ interj: **¡~!** help!

soda f (bebida) soda water.

sodio m sodium.

soez adj vulgar, dirty.

sofá (pl **sofás**) m sofa, settee; ~ **cama** sofa bed.

Sofía Sofia.

sofisticación f sophistication.

sofisticado, -da adj sophisticated.

sofocar vt 1. (ahogar) to suffocate. 2. (incendio) to put out. 3. fig (rebelión) to

quell. **4.** *fig* (*avergonzar*) to mortify.
▶ **sofocarse** *vpr* **1.** (*ahogarse*) to suffocate. **2.** *fig* (*irritarse*): **~se (por)** to get hot under the collar (about).

sofoco *m* **1.** (*ahogo*) breathlessness (U); (*sonrojo, bochorno*) hot flush. **2.** *fig* (*vergüenza*) mortification. **3.** *fig* (*disgusto*): **llevarse un ~** to have a fit.

sofreír *vt* to fry lightly over a low heat.

sofrito, -ta *pp* → **sofreír**. ▶ **sofrito** *m* *fried tomato and onion sauce*.

software ['sofwer] *m* (INFORM) software.

soga *f* rope; (*para ahorcar*) noose.

sois → **ser**.

soja *f* soya.

sol *m* **1.** (*astro*) sun; **hace ~** it's sunny; **no dejar a alguien ni a ~ ni a sombra** not to give sb a moment's peace. **2.** (*rayos, luz*) sunshine, sun; **tomar el ~** to sunbathe. **3.** (MÚS) G; (*en solfeo*) so. **4.** (*moneda*) sol.

solamente *adv* (*gen*) only, just; (*exclusivamente*) solely; **vino ~ él** only he came.

solapa *f* **1.** (*de prenda*) lapel. **2.** (*de libro, sobre*) flap.

solapado, -da *adj* underhand, devious.

solar ◆ *adj* solar. ◆ *m* undeveloped plot (of land).

solario, solárium (*pl* solariums) *m* solarium.

solazar *vt* to amuse, to entertain.

soldada *f* pay.

soldado *m* soldier; **~ raso** private.

soldador, -ra *m y f* (*persona*) welder. ▶ **soldador** *m* (*aparato*) soldering iron.

soldar *vt* to solder, to weld.

soleado, -da *adj* sunny.

soledad *f* loneliness; *culto* solitude.

solemne *adj* **1.** (*con pompa*) formal. **2.** (*grave*) solemn. **3.** *fig* (*enorme*) utter.

solemnidad *f* **1.** (*suntuosidad*) pomp, solemnity. **2.** (*acto*) ceremony.

soler *vi*: **~ hacer algo** to do sth usually; **aquí suele llover mucho** it usually rains a lot here; **solíamos ir a la playa cada día** we used to go to the beach every day.

solera *f* **1.** (*tradición*) tradition. **2.** (*del vino*) sediment; **de ~** vintage.

solfeo *m* (MÚS) solfeggio, singing of scales.

solicitar *vt* **1.** (*pedir*) to request; (*un empleo*) to apply for; **~ algo a o de alguien** to request sthg of sb. **2.** (*persona*) to pursue; **estar muy solicitado** to be much sought after.

solícito, -ta *adj* solicitous, obliging.

solicitud *f* **1.** (*petición*) request. **2.** (*documento*) application. **3.** (*atención*) care.

solidaridad *f* solidarity.

solidario, -ria *adj* **1.** (*adherido*): **~ (con)** sympathetic (to). **2.** (*obligación, compromiso*) mutually binding.

solidez *f* (*física*) solidity.

solidificar *vt* to solidify. ▶ **solidificarse** *vpr* to solidify.

sólido, -da *adj* **1.** (*gen*) solid; (*cimientos, fundamento*) firm. **2.** (*argumento, conocimiento, idea*) sound; (*empresa, industria*) well-established. ▶ **sólido** *m* solid.

soliloquio *m* soliloquy.

solista ◆ *adj* solo. ◆ *m y f* soloist.

solitario, -ria ◆ *adj* **1.** (*sin compañía*) solitary. **2.** (*lugar*) lonely, deserted. ◆ *m y f* (*persona*) loner. ▶ **solitario** *m* (*juego*) patience.

sollozar *vi* to sob.

sollozo *m* sob.

solo, -la *adj* **1.** (*sin nadie*) alone; **se quedó ~ a temprana edad** he was on his own from an early age; **a solas** alone, by oneself. **2.** (*sin nada*) on its own; (*café*) black; (*whisky*) neat. **3.** (*único*) single, sole; **ni una sola gota** not a (single) drop; **dame una sola cosa** give me just one thing. **4.** (*solitario*) lonely. ▶ **solo** *m* (MÚS) solo.

sólo *adv* (*gen*) only, just; (*exclusivamente*) solely; **no ~ ... sino (también) ...** not only ... but (also) ...; **~ que ...** only ...

solomillo *m* sirloin.

soltar *vt* **1.** (*desasir*) to let go of. **2.** (*desatar - gen*) to unfasten; (- *nudo*) to untie; (- *hebilla, cordones*) to undo. **3.** (*dejar libre*) to release. **4.** (*desenrollar - cable etc*) to let o pay out. **5.** (*palabra, grito, suspiro etc*) to give; **no suelta ni un duro** you can't get a penny out of her. **6.** (*decir bruscamente*) to come out with. ▶ **soltarse** *vpr* **1.** (*desasirse*) to break free. **2.** (*desatarse*) to come undone. **3.** (*desprenderse*) to come off. **4.** (*perder timidez*) to let go.

soltero, -ra ◆ *adj* single, unmarried. ◆ *m y f* bachelor (*f* single woman).

solterón, -ona ◆ *adj* unmarried. ◆ *m y f* old bachelor (*f* spinster, old maid).

soltura *f* **1.** (*gen*) fluency. **2.** (*seguridad de sí mismo*) assurance.

soluble *adj* **1.** (*que se disuelve*) soluble. **2.** (*que se soluciona*) solvable.

solución *f* solution.

solucionar *vt* to solve; (*disputa*) to resolve.

solventar vt 1. (pagar) to settle. 2. (resolver) to resolve.

solvente adj 1. (económicamente) solvent. 2. fig (fuentes etc) reliable.

Somalia Somalia.

sombra f 1. (proyección - fenómeno) shadow; (- zona) shade; **dar ~ a** to cast a shadow over. 2. (en pintura) shade. 3. fig (anonimato) background; **permanecer en la ~** to stay out of the limelight. 4. (suerte): **buena/mala ~** good/bad luck. ▶ **sombras** fpl (oscuridad, inquietud) darkness (U).

sombrero m (prenda) hat.

sombrilla f sunshade, parasol; **me vale ~** Amer fig I couldn't care less.

sombrío, -bría adj 1. (oscuro) gloomy, dark. 2. fig (triste) sombre, gloomy.

somero, -ra adj superficial.

someter vt 1. (a rebeldes) to subdue. 2. (presentar): **~ algo a la aprobación de alguien** to submit sthg for sb's approval; **~ algo a votación** to put sthg to the vote. 3. (subordinar) to subordinate. 4. (a operación, interrogatorio etc): **~ a alguien a algo** to subject sb to sthg. ▶ **someterse** vpr 1. (rendirse) to surrender. 2. (conformarse): **~se a algo** to yield o bow to sthg. 3. (a operación, interrogatorio etc): **~se a algo** to undergo sthg.

somier (pl somieres) m (de muelles) bed springs (pl); (de tablas) slats (of bed).

somnífero, -ra adj somniferous. ▶ **somnífero** m sleeping pill.

somos → ser.

son ◆ v → ser. ◆ m 1. (sonido) sound. 2. (estilo) way; **en ~ de** in the manner of; **en ~ de paz** in peace.

sonajero m rattle.

sonambulismo m sleepwalking.

sonámbulo, -la m y f sleepwalker.

sonar¹ vi sonar.

sonar² vi 1. (gen) to sound; (así o tal) **como suena** literally, in so many words. 2. (timbre) to ring. 3. (hora): **sonaron las doce** the clock struck twelve. 4. (ser conocido, familiar) to be familiar; **me suena** it rings a bell; **no me suena su nombre** I don't remember hearing her name before. 5. (pronunciarse - letra) to be pronounced. 6. (rumorearse) to be rumoured. ▶ **sonarse** vpr to blow one's nose.

sonda f 1. (MED & TECN) probe. 2. (NÁUT) sounding line. 3. (MIN) drill, bore.

sondear vt 1. (indagar) to sound out. 2. (MIN - terreno) to test; (- roca) to drill.

sondeo m 1. (encuesta) (opinion) poll. 2. (MIN) drilling (U). 3. (NÁUT) sounding.

sonido m sound.

sonoro, -ra adj 1. (gen) sound (antes de sust); (película) talking. 2. (ruidoso, resonante, vibrante) resonant.

sonreír vi (reír levemente) to smile. ▶ **sonreírse** vpr to smile.

sonriente adj smiling.

sonrisa f smile.

sonrojar vt to cause to blush. ▶ **sonrojarse** vpr to blush.

sonrojo m blush, blushing (U).

sonrosado, -da adj rosy.

sonsacar vt: **~ algo a alguien** (conseguir) to wheedle sthg out of sb; (hacer decir) to extract sthg from sb; **~ a alguien** to pump sb for information.

sonso, -sa adj Amer fam silly.

soñador, -ra m y f dreamer.

soñar ◆ vt lit & fig: to dream; **¡ni ~lo!** not on your life! ◆ vi lit & fig: **~ (con)** to dream (about); **~ despierto** to daydream.

soñoliento, -ta adj sleepy, drowsy.

sopa f 1. (guiso) soup. 2. (de pan) sop, piece of soaked bread. ▶ **sopa de letras** f (juego) wordsearch.

sopapo m slap.

sopero, -ra adj soup (antes de sust). ▶ **sopero** m (plato) soup plate. ▶ **sopera** f (recipiente) soup tureen.

sopesar vt to try the weight of; fig to weigh up.

sopetón ▶ **de sopetón** loc adv suddenly, abruptly.

soplar ◆ vt 1. (vela, fuego) to blow out. 2. (ceniza, polvo) to blow off. 3. (globo etc) to blow up. 4. (vidrio) to blow. 5. fig (pregunta, examen) to prompt. ◆ vi (gen) to blow.

soplete m blowlamp.

soplido m blow, puff.

soplo m 1. (soplido) blow, puff. 2. (MED) murmur. 3. fam (chivatazo) tip-off.

soplón, -ona m y f fam grass.

soponcio m fam fainting fit.

sopor m drowsiness.

soporífero, -ra adj lit & fig soporific.

soportar vt 1. (sostener) to support. 2. (resistir, tolerar) to withstand; **¡no la soporto!** I can't stand her! 3. (sobrellevar) to endure.

soporte m 1. (apoyo) support. 2. (INFORM) medium; **~ físico** hardware; **~ lógico** software.

soprano m y f soprano.

sor f sister (RELIG).

sorber vt 1. (beber) to sip; (haciendo ruido) to slurp. 2. (absorber) to soak up. 3. (atraer) to draw o suck in.

sorbete m sorbet.

sorbo m (acción) gulp, swallow; (pequeño) sip; **beber a ~s** to sip.

sordera f deafness.

sórdido, -da adj 1. (miserable) squalid. 2. (obsceno, perverso) sordid.

sordo, -da ◆ adj 1. (que no oye) deaf. 2. (ruido, dolor) dull. ◆ m y f (persona) deaf person; **los ~s** the deaf.

sordomudo, -da ◆ adj deaf and dumb. ◆ m y f deaf-mute.

sorna f sarcasm.

sorprendente adj surprising.

sorprender vt 1. (asombrar) to surprise. 2. (atrapar): **~ a alguien (haciendo algo)** to catch sb (doing sthg). 3. (coger desprevenido) to catch unawares. ▶ **sorprenderse** vpr to be surprised.

sorprendido, -da adj surprised.

sorpresa f surprise; **de** o **por ~** by surprise.

sorpresivo, -va adj Amer unexpected.

sortear vt 1. (rifar) to raffle. 2. (echar a suertes) to draw lots for. 3. fig (esquivar) to dodge.

sorteo m 1. (lotería) draw. 2. (rifa) raffle.

sortija f ring.

sortilegio m (hechizo) spell.

SOS (abrev de save our souls) m SOS.

sosa f soda.

sosegado, -da adj calm.

sosegar vt to calm. ▶ **sosegarse** vpr to calm down.

soseras m y f inv fam dull person, bore.

sosias m inv double, lookalike.

sosiego m calm.

soslayo ▶ **de soslayo** loc adv (oblicuamente) sideways, obliquely; **mirar a alguien de ~** to look at sb out of the corner of one's eye.

soso, -sa adj 1. (sin sabor) bland, tasteless. 2. (sin sal): **la sopa está sosa** the soup needs salt. 3. (sin gracia) dull, insipid.

sospecha f suspicion; **despertar ~s** to arouse suspicion.

sospechar ◆ vt (creer, suponer) to suspect; **sospecho que no lo terminará** I doubt whether she'll finish it. ◆ vi: **~ de** to suspect.

sospechoso, -sa ◆ adj suspicious. ◆ m y f suspect.

sostén m 1. (apoyo) support. 2. (sustento) main support; (alimento) sustenance. 3. (sujetador) bra.

sostener vt 1. (sujetar) to support, to hold up. 2. (defender - idea, opinión, tesis) to defend; (- promesa, palabra) to stand by, to keep; **~ que ...** to maintain that ... 3. (tener - conversación) to hold, to have; (- correspondencia) to keep up. ▶ **sostenerse** vpr to hold o.s. up; (en pie) to stand up; (en el aire) to hang.

sostenido, -da adj 1. (persistente) sustained. 2. (MÚS) sharp.

sota f ≃ jack.

sotabarba f double chin.

sotana f cassock.

sótano m basement.

soterrar vt (enterrar) to bury; fig to hide.

soufflé [su'fle] (pl soufflés) m soufflé.

soul m (MÚS) soul (music).

soviético, -ca ◆ adj 1. (del soviet) soviet. 2. (de la URSS) Soviet. ◆ m y f Soviet.

soy → ser.

spaghetti [espa'ɣeti] = **espagueti**.

sport [es'port] = **esport**.

spot [es'pot] = **espot**.

spray [es'prai] = **espray**.

sprint [es'prin] = **esprint**.

squash [es'kwaʃ] m inv squash.

Sr. (abrev de señor) Mr.

Sra. (abrev de señora) Mrs.

Sres. (abrev de señores) Messrs.

Srta. (abrev de señorita) Miss.

s.s.s. (abrev de su seguro servidor) formula used in letters.

Sta. (abrev de santa) St.

standard [es'tandar] = **estándar**.

standarizar [estandari'θar] = **estandarizar**.

starter [es'tarter] = **estárter**.

status [es'tatus] = **estatus**.

stereo [es'tereo] = **estéreo**.

sterling [es'terlin] = **esterlina**.

Sto. (abrev de santo) St.

stock [es'tok] = **estoc**.

stop, estop [es'top] m 1. (AUTOM) stop sign. 2. (en telegrama) stop.

stress [es'tres] = **estrés**.

strip-tease [es'triptis] m inv striptease.

su (pl sus) adj poses (de él) his; (de ella) her; (de cosa, animal) its; (de uno) one's; (de ellos, ellas) their; (de usted, ustedes) your.

suave adj 1. (gen) soft. 2. (liso) smooth. 3. (sabor, olor, color) delicate. 4. (apacible - persona, carácter) gentle; (- clima) mild. **5.** (*fácil - cuesta, tarea, ritmo*) gentle; (*- dirección de un coche*) smooth.

suavidad *f* **1.** (*gen*) softness. **2.** (*lisura*) smoothness. **3.** (*de sabor, olor, color*) delicacy. **4.** (*de carácter*) gentleness. **5.** (*de clima*) mildness. **6.** (*de cuesta, tarea, ritmo*) gentleness; (*de la dirección de un coche*) smoothness.

suavizante *m* conditioner; **~ para la ropa** fabric conditioner.

suavizar *vt* **1.** (*gen*) to soften; (*ropa, cabello*) to condition. **2.** (*ascensión, conducción, tarea*) to ease; (*clima*) to make milder. **3.** (*sabor, olor, color*) to tone down. **4.** (*alisar*) to smooth.

subacuático, -ca *adj* subaquatic.

subalquilar *vt* to sublet.

subalterno, -na *m y f* (*empleado*) subordinate.

subasta *f* **1.** (*venta pública*) auction; **sacar algo a ~** to put sthg up for auction. **2.** (*contrata pública*) tender; **sacar algo a ~** to put sthg out to tender.

subastar *vt* to auction.

subcampeón, -ona *m y f* runner-up.

subconsciente *adj & m* subconscious.

subdesarrollado, -da *adj* underdeveloped.

subdesarrollo *m* underdevelopment.

subdirector, -ra *m y f* assistant manager.

subdirectorio *m* (INFORM) subdirectory.

súbdito, -ta *m y f* **1.** (*subordinado*) subject. **2.** (*ciudadano*) citizen, national.

subdivisión *f* subdivision.

subestimar *vt* to underestimate; (*infravalorar*) to underrate. ▶ **subestimarse** *vpr* to underrate o.s.

subido, -da *adj* **1.** (*intenso*) strong, intense. **2.** *fam* (*atrevido*) risqué. ▶ **subida** *f* **1.** (*cuesta*) hill. **2.** (*ascensión*) ascent, climb. **3.** (*aumento*) increase, rise.

subir ◆ *vi* **1.** (*a piso, azotea*) to go/come up; (*a montaña, cima*) to climb. **2.** (*aumentar - precio, temperatura*) to go up, to rise; (*- cauce, marea*) to rise. **3.** (*montar - en avión, barco*) to get on; (*- en coche*) to get in; **sube al coche** get into the car. **4.** (*cuenta, importe*): **~ a** to come o amount to. **5.** (*de categoría*) to be promoted. ◆ *vt* **1.** (*ascender - calle, escaleras*) to go/come up; (*- pendiente, montaña*) to climb. **2.** (*poner arriba*) to lift up; (*llevar arriba*) to take/bring up. **3.** (*aumentar - precio, peso*) to put up, to increase; (*- volumen de radio etc*) to turn

up. **4.** (*montar*): **~ algo/a alguien a** to lift sthg/sb onto. **5.** (*alzar - mano, bandera, voz*) to raise; (*- persiana*) to roll up; (*- ventanilla*) to wind up. ▶ **subirse** *vpr* **1.** (*ascender*): **~se a** (*árbol*) to climb up; (*mesa*) to climb onto; (*piso*) to go/come up to. **2.** (*montarse*): **~se a** (*tren, avión*) to get on, to board; (*caballo, bicicleta*) to mount; (*coche*) to get into; **el taxi paró y me subí** the taxi stopped and I got in. **3.** (*alzarse - pernera, mangas*) to roll up; (*- cremallera*) to do up; (*- pantalones, calcetines*) to pull up.

súbito, -ta *adj* sudden.

subjetivo, -va *adj* subjective.

sub júdice [suβ'djuðiθe] *adj* (DER) sub judice.

subjuntivo, -va *adj* subjunctive. ▶ **subjuntivo** *m* subjunctive.

sublevación *f*, **sublevamiento** *m* uprising.

sublevar *vt* **1.** (*amotinar*) to stir up. **2.** (*indignar*) to infuriate. ▶ **sublevarse** *vpr* (*amotinarse*) to rebel.

sublime *adj* sublime.

submarinismo *m* skin-diving.

submarinista *m y f* skin-diver.

submarino, -na *adj* underwater. ▶ **submarino** *m* submarine.

subnormal ◆ *adj* **1.** *ofensivo* (*minusválido*) subnormal. **2.** *fig & despec* (*imbécil*) moronic. ◆ *m y f fig & despec* (*imbécil*) moron.

suboficial *m* (MIL) non-commissioned officer.

subordinado, -da *adj, m y f* subordinate.

subordinar *vt* (*gen & GRAM*) to subordinate.

subproducto *m* by-product.

subrayar *vt lit & fig* to underline.

subsanar *vt* **1.** (*solucionar*) to resolve. **2.** (*corregir*) to correct.

subscribir = suscribir.

subscripción = suscripción.

subscriptor = suscriptor.

subsecretario, -ria *m y f* **1.** (*de secretario*) assistant secretary. **2.** (*de ministro*) undersecretary.

subsidiario, -ria *adj* (DER) ancillary.

subsidio *m* benefit, allowance; **~ de invalidez** disability allowance; **~ de paro** unemployment benefit.

subsiguiente *adj* subsequent.

subsistencia *f* **1.** (*vida*) subsistence. **2.** (*conservación*) continued existence. ▶ **subsistencias** *fpl* (*provisiones*) provisions.

subsistir vi 1. (*vivir*) to live, to exist. 2. (*sobrevivir*) to survive.
substancia = **sustancia**.
substancial = **sustancial**.
substancioso = **sustancioso**.
substantivo = **sustantivo**.
substitución = **sustitución**.
substituir = **sustituir**.
substituto = **sustituto**.
substracción = **sustracción**.
substraer = **sustraer**.
subsuelo m subsoil.
subte m Amer fam underground Br, subway Am.
subterráneo, -a adj subterranean, underground. ▶ **subterráneo** m underground tunnel.
subtítulo m (*gen* & CIN) subtitle.
suburbio m poor suburb.
subvención f subsidy.
subvencionar vt to subsidize.
subversión f subversion.
subversivo, -va adj subversive.
subyacer vi (*ocultarse*): ~ **bajo algo** to underlie sthg.
subyugar vt 1. (*someter*) to subjugate. 2. fig (*dominar*) to quell, to master. 3. fig (*atraer*) to captivate.
succionar vt (*suj: raíces*) to suck up; (*suj: bebé*) to suck.
sucedáneo, -a adj ersatz, substitute. ▶ **sucedáneo** m substitute.
suceder ◆ v impers (*ocurrir*) to happen; **suceda lo que suceda** whatever happens. ◆ vi (*venir después*): ~ **a** to come after, to follow; **a la guerra sucedieron años muy tristes** the war was followed by years of misery.
sucesión f (*gen*) succession.
sucesivamente adv successively; **y así** ~ and so on.
sucesivo, -va adj 1. (*consecutivo*) successive, consecutive. 2. (*siguiente*): **en días ~s les informaremos** we'll let you know over the next few days; **en lo** ~ in future.
suceso m 1. (*acontecimiento*) event. 2. (*gen pl*) (*hecho delictivo*) crime; (*incidente*) incident.
sucesor, -ra m y f successor.
suciedad f 1. (*cualidad*) dirtiness (U). 2. (*porquería*) dirt, filth (U).
sucinto, -ta adj (*conciso*) succinct.
sucio, -cia adj 1. (*gen*) dirty; (*al comer, trabajar*) messy; **en** ~ in rough. 2. (*juego*) dirty.
suculento, -ta adj tasty.
sucumbir vi 1. (*rendirse, ceder*): ~ **(a)** to

succumb (to). 2. (*fallecer*) to die.
sucursal f branch.
sudadera f (*prenda*) sweatshirt.
Sudáfrica, Suráfrica f South Africa.
sudafricano, -na, surafricano, -na adj, m y f South African.
Sudamérica, Suramérica f South America.
sudamericano, -na, suramericano, -na adj, m y f South American.
Sudán Sudan.
sudar vi (*gen*) to sweat.
sudeste, sureste ◆ adj (*posición, parte*) southeast, southeastern; (*dirección, viento*) southeasterly. ◆ m southeast.
sudoeste, suroeste ◆ adj (*posición, parte*) southwest, southwestern; (*dirección, viento*) southwesterly. ◆ m southwest.
sudor m (*gen*) sweat (U).
sudoroso, -sa adj sweaty.
Suecia Sweden.
sueco, -ca ◆ adj Swedish. ◆ m y f (*persona*) Swede. ▶ **sueco** m (*lengua*) Swedish.
suegro, -gra m y f father-in-law (f mother-in-law).
suela f sole.
sueldo m salary, wages (pl); (*semanal*) wage; **a** ~ (*asesino*) hired; (*empleado*) salaried.
suelo ◆ v → **soler**. ◆ m 1. (*pavimento - en interiores*) floor; (- *en el exterior*) ground. 2. (*terreno, territorio*) soil; (*para edificar*) land. 3. (*base*) bottom. 4. loc: **echar por el** ~ **un plan** to ruin a project; **estar por los** ~**s** (*persona, precio*) to be at rock bottom; (*productos*) to be dirt cheap; **poner** o **tirar por los** ~**s** to run down, to criticize.
suelto, -ta adj 1. (*gen*) loose; (*cordones*) undone; **¿tienes cinco duros** ~**s?** have you got 25 pesetas in loose change?; **andar** ~ (*en libertad*) to be free; (*en fuga*) to be at large; (*con diarrea*) to have diarrhoea. 2. (*separado*) separate; (*desparejado*) odd; **no los vendemos** ~**s** we don't sell them separately. 3. (*arroz*) fluffy. 4. (*lenguaje, estilo*) fluent. 5. (*desenvuelto*) comfortable. ▶ **suelto** m (*calderilla*) loose change.
suena etc → **sonar²**.
sueño m 1. (*ganas de dormir*) sleepiness; (*por medicamento etc*) drowsiness; **¡qué** ~**!** I'm really sleepy!; **tener** ~ to be sleepy; **¿tiene** o **le entra** Amer ~**?** are you tired? 2. (*estado*) sleep; **coger** o **conciliar**

el ~ to get to sleep. **3.** (*imagen mental, objetivo, quimera*) dream; **en ~s** in a dream.

suero *m* **1.** (MED) serum; **~ artificial** saline solution. **2.** (*de la leche*) whey.

suerte *f* **1.** (*azar*) chance; **la ~ está echada** the die is cast. **2.** (*fortuna*) luck; **por ~** luckily; **¡qué ~!** that was lucky!; **¡qué mala ~!** what bad luck!; **tener ~** to be lucky. **3.** (*destino*) fate. **4.** (*situación*) situation, lot. **5.** culto (*clase*) **toda ~ de** all manner of. **6.** culto (*manera*) manner, fashion; **de ~ que** in such a way that.

suéter (*pl* **suéteres**) *m* sweater.

suficiencia *f* **1.** (*capacidad*) proficiency. **2.** (*presunción*) smugness.

suficiente ◆ *adj* **1.** (*bastante*) enough, sufficient; (*medidas, esfuerzos*) adequate; **no llevo (dinero) ~** I don't have enough (money) on me; **no tienes la estatura ~** you're not tall enough. **2.** (*presuntuoso*) smug. ◆ *m* (*nota*) pass.

sufragar *vt* to defray.

sufragio *m* suffrage.

sufragista *m y f* suffragette.

sufrido, -da *adj* **1.** (*resignado*) patient, uncomplaining; (*durante mucho tiempo*) long-suffering. **2.** (*resistente - tela*) hard-wearing; (*- color*) that does not show the dirt.

sufrimiento *m* suffering.

sufrir ◆ *vt* **1.** (*gen*) to suffer; (*accidente*) to have. **2.** (*soportar*) to bear, to stand; **tengo que ~ sus manías** I have to put up with his idiosyncrasies. **3.** (*experimentar - cambios etc*) to undergo. ◆ *vi* (*padecer*) to suffer; **~ del estómago** *etc* to have a stomach *etc* complaint.

sugerencia *f* suggestion.

sugerente *adj* evocative.

sugerir *vt* **1.** (*proponer*) to suggest. **2.** (*evocar*) to evoke.

sugestión *f* suggestion.

sugestionar *vt* to influence.

sugestivo, -va *adj* attractive.

suich *m Amer* switch.

suicida ◆ *adj* suicidal. ◆ *m y f* (*por naturaleza*) suicidal person; (*suicidado*) person who has committed suicide.

suicidarse *vpr* to commit suicide.

suicidio *m* suicide.

Suiza Switzerland.

suizo, -za *adj, m y f* Swiss.

sujeción *f* **1.** (*atadura*) fastening. **2.** (*sometimiento*) subjection.

sujetador *m* bra.

sujetar *vt* **1.** (*agarrar*) to hold down. **2.** (*aguantar*) to fasten; (*papeles*) to fasten together. **3.** (*someter*) to subdue; (*a niños*) to control. ▶ **sujetarse** *vpr* **1.** (*agarrarse*) **~se a** to hold on to, to cling to. **2.** (*aguantarse*) to keep in place. **3.** (*someterse*) **~se a** to keep o stick to.

sujeto, -ta *adj* **1.** (*agarrado - objeto*) fastened. **2.** (*expuesto*) **~ a** subject to. ▶ **sujeto** *m* **1.** (GRAM) subject. **2.** (*individuo*) individual.

sulfato *m* sulphate.

sulfurar *vt* (*encolerizar*) to infuriate. ▶ **sulfurarse** *vpr* (*encolerizarse*) to get mad.

sultán *m* sultan.

sultana *f* sultana.

suma *f* **1.** (MAT - *acción*) addition; (*- resultado*) total. **2.** (*conjunto - de conocimientos, datos*) total, sum; (*- de dinero*) sum. **3.** (*resumen*) **en ~** in short.

sumamente *adv* extremely.

sumar *vt* **1.** (MAT) to add together; **tres y cinco suman ocho** three and five are o make eight. **2.** (*costar*) to come to. ▶ **sumarse** *vpr*: **~se (a)** to join (in).

sumario, -ria *adj* **1.** (*conciso*) brief. **2.** (DER) summary. ▶ **sumario** *m* **1.** (DER) indictment. **2.** (*resumen*) summary.

sumergible *adj* waterproof.

sumergir *vt* (*hundir*) to submerge; (*- con fuerza*) to plunge; (*bañar*) to dip. ▶ **sumergirse** *vpr* (*hundirse*) to submerge; (*- con fuerza*) to plunge.

sumidero *m* drain.

suministrador, -ra *m y f* supplier.

suministrar *vt* to supply; **~ algo a alguien** to supply sb with sthg.

suministro *m* (*gen*) supply; (*acto*) supplying.

sumir *vt*: **~ a alguien en** to plunge sb into. ▶ **sumirse en** *vpr* **1.** (*depresión, sueño etc*) to sink into. **2.** (*estudio, tema*) to immerse o.s. in.

sumisión *f* **1.** (*obediencia - acción*) submission; (*- cualidad*) submissiveness. **2.** (*rendición*) surrender.

sumiso, -sa *adj* submissive.

sumo, -ma *adj* **1.** (*supremo*) highest, supreme. **2.** (*gran*) extreme, great.

sunnita ◆ *adj* Sunni. ◆ *m y f* Sunnite.

suntuoso, -sa *adj* sumptuous.

supeditar *vt*: **~ a** to subordinate (to); **estar supeditado a** to be dependent on. ▶ **supeditarse** *vpr*: **~se a** to submit to.

súper ◆ *m fam* supermarket. ◆ *f*: (**gasolina**) **~** = four-star (petrol).

superable *adj* surmountable.
superar *vt* 1. (*gen*) to beat; (*récord*) to break; ~ **algo/a alguien en algo** to beat sthg/sb in sthg. 2. (*adelantar - corredor*) to overtake, to pass. 3. (*época, técnica*): **estar superado** to have been superseded. 4. (*resolver - dificultad etc*) to overcome. ► **superarse** *vpr* 1. (*mejorar*) to better o.s. 2. (*lucirse*) to excel o.s.
superávit *m inv* surplus.
superdotado, -da *m y f* extremely gifted person.
superficial *adj lit & fig* superficial.
superficie *f* 1. (*gen*) surface. 2. (*área*) area.
superfluo, -flua *adj* superfluous; (*gasto*) unnecessary.
superior, -ra (RELIG) *m y f* superior (*f* mother superior). ► **superior** ◆ *adj* 1. (*de arriba*) top. 2. (*mayor*): ~ **(a)** higher (than). 3. (*mejor*): ~ **(a)** superior (to). 4. (*excelente*) excellent. 5. (ANAT & GEOGR) upper. 6. (EDUC) higher. ◆ *m* (*gen pl*) (*jefe*) superior.
superioridad *f lit & fig* superiority.
superlativo, -va *adj* 1. (*belleza etc*) exceptional. 2. (GRAM) superlative.
supermercado *m* supermarket.
superpoblación *f* overpopulation.
superponer = **sobreponer**.
superpotencia *f* superpower.
superpuesto, -ta ◆ *adj* = **sobrepuesto**. ◆ *pp* → **superponer**.
supersónico, -ca *adj* supersonic.
superstición *f* superstition.
supersticioso, -sa *adj* superstitious.
supervisar *vt* to supervise.
supervisor, -ra *m y f* supervisor.
supervivencia *f* survival.
superviviente, **sobreviviente** ◆ *adj* surviving. ◆ *m y f* survivor.
supiera *etc* → **saber**.
suplementario, -ria *adj* supplementary, extra.
suplemento *m* 1. (*gen & PRENS*) supplement. 2. (*complemento*) attachment.
suplente *m y f* 1. (*gen*) stand-in. 2. (TEATR) understudy. 3. (DEP) substitute.
supletorio, -ria *adj* additional, extra. ► **supletorio** *m* (TELECOM) extension.
súplica *f* 1. (*ruego*) plea, entreaty. 2. (DER) petition.
suplicar *vt* (*rogar*): ~ **algo (a alguien)** to plead for sthg (with sb); ~ **a alguien que haga algo** to beg sb to do sthg.
suplicio *m lit & fig* torture.
suplir *vt* 1. (*sustituir*): ~ **algo/a alguien**

(con) to replace sthg/sb (with). 2. (*compensar*): ~ **algo (con)** to compensate for sthg (with).
supo → **saber**.
suponer ◆ *vt* 1. (*creer, presuponer*) to suppose. 2. (*implicar*) to involve, to entail. 3. (*significar*) to mean. 4. (*conjeturar*) to imagine; **lo suponía** I guessed as much; **te suponía mayor** I thought you were older. ◆ *m*: **ser un** ~ to be conjecture. ► **suponerse** *vpr* to suppose.
suposición *f* assumption.
supositorio *m* suppository.
supremacía *f* supremacy.
supremo, -ma *adj lit & fig* supreme.
supresión *f* 1. (*de ley, impuesto, derecho*) abolition; (*de sanciones, restricciones*) lifting. 2. (*de palabras, texto*) deletion. 3. (*de puestos de trabajo, proyectos*) axing.
suprimir *vt* 1. (*ley, impuesto, derecho*) to abolish; (*sanciones, restricciones*) to lift. 2. (*palabras, texto*) to delete. 3. (*puestos de trabajo, proyectos*) to axe.
supuesto, -ta ◆ *pp* → **suponer**. ◆ *adj* supposed; (*culpable, asesino*) alleged; (*nombre*) false; **por** ~ of course. ► **supuesto** *m* assumption; **en el** ~ **de que ...** assuming ...
supurar *vi* to fester.
sur ◆ *adj* (*posición, parte*) south, southern; (*dirección, viento*) southerly. ◆ *m* south.
Suráfrica = **Sudáfrica**.
surafricano = **sudafricano**.
Suramérica = **Sudamérica**.
suramericano = **sudamericano**.
surcar *vt* (*tierra*) to plough; (*aire, agua*) to cut o slice through.
surco *m* 1. (*zanja*) furrow. 2. (*señal - de disco*) groove; (*- de rueda*) rut. 3. (*arruga*) line, wrinkle.
sureño, -ña ◆ *adj* southern; (*viento*) southerly. ◆ *m y f* southerner.
sureste = **sudeste**.
surf, surfing *m* surfing.
surgir *vi* 1. (*brotar*) to spring forth. 2. (*aparecer*) to appear. 3. *fig* (*producirse*) to arise.
suroeste = **sudoeste**.
surrealista *adj, m y f* surrealist.
surtido, -da *adj* 1. (*variado*) assorted. 2. (*aprovisionado*): **bien** ~ well-stocked. ► **surtido** *m* 1. (*gama*) range. 2. (*caja surtida*) assortment.
surtidor *m* (*de gasolina*) pump; (*de un chorro*) spout.
surtir ◆ *vt* (*proveer*): ~ **a alguien (de)** to supply sb (with). ◆ *vi* (*brotar*): ~ **(de)** to

spout o spurt (from). ▶ **surtirse de** *vpr*
(*proveerse de*) to stock up on.
susceptible *adj* **1.** (*sensible*) oversensi-
tive. **2.** (*posible*): ~ **de** liable to.
suscitar *vt* to provoke; (*interés, dudas,
sospechas*) to arouse.
suscribir *vt* **1.** (*firmar*) to sign. **2.** (*ratificar*) to endorse. **3.** (COM) (*acciones*) to
subscribe for. ▶ **suscribirse** *vpr*
1. (PRENS) ~**se (a)** to subscribe (to).
2. (COM): ~**se a** to take out an option
on.
suscripción *f* subscription.
suscriptor, -ra *m y f* subscriber.
susodicho, -cha *adj* above-
mentioned.
suspender *vt* **1.** (*colgar*) to hang (up).
2. (EDUC) to fail. **3.** (*interrumpir*) to suspend; (*sesión*) to adjourn. **4.** (*aplazar*) to
postpone. **5.** (*de un cargo*) to suspend.
suspense *m* suspense.
suspensión *f* **1.** (*gen* & AUTOM) suspension. **2.** (*aplazamiento*) postponement; (*de reunión, sesión*) adjournment.
suspenso, -sa *adj* **1.** (*colgado*): ~ **de**
hanging from. **2.** (*no aprobado*): **estar ~** to
have failed. **3.** *fig* (*interrumpido*): **en ~**
pending. ▶ **suspenso** *m* failure.
suspensores *mpl* Amer braces.
suspicacia *f* suspicion.
suspicaz *adj* suspicious.
suspirar *vi* (*dar suspiros*) to sigh.
suspiro *m* (*aspiración*) sigh.
sustancia *f* **1.** (*gen*) substance; **sin ~**
lacking in substance. **2.** (*esencia*)
essence. **3.** (*de alimento*) nutritional
value.
sustancial *adj* substantial, significant.
sustancioso, -sa *adj* substantial.
sustantivo, -va *adj* (GRAM) noun
(*antes de sust*). ▶ **sustantivo** *m* (GRAM)
noun.
sustentar *vt* **1.** (*gen*) to support. **2.** *fig*
(*mantener - argumento, teoría*) to defend.
sustento *m* **1.** (*alimento*) sustenance;
(*mantenimiento*) livelihood; **es su único ~**
it's her only means of support. **2.**
(*apoyo, soporte*) support.
sustitución *f* (*cambio*) replacement.
sustituir *vt*: ~ **(por)** to replace (with).
sustituto, -ta *m y f* substitute,
replacement.
susto *m* fright.
sustracción *f* **1.** (*robo*) theft. **2.** (MAT)
subtraction.
sustraer *vt* **1.** (*robar*) to steal. **2.** (MAT)
to subtract. ▶ **sustraerse** *vpr*: ~**se a** o
de (*obligación, problema*) to avoid.

susurrar *vt* & *vi* to whisper.
susurro *m* whisper; *fig* murmur.
sutil *adj* (*gen*) subtle; (*velo, tejido*) delicate, thin; (*brisa*) gentle; (*hilo, línea*) fine.
sutileza *f* subtlety; (*de velo, tejido*) delicacy, thinness; (*de brisa*) gentleness; (*de
hilo, línea*) fineness.
sutura *f* suture.
suyo, -ya ◆ *adj poses* (*de él*) his; (*de ella*)
hers; (*de uno*) one's (own); (*de ellos, ellas*)
theirs; (*de usted, ustedes*) yours; **este libro
es ~** this book is his/hers *etc*; **un amigo ~**
a friend of his/hers *etc*; **no es asunto ~**
it's none of his/her *etc* business; **es muy
~** *fam fig* he/she is really selfish. ◆ *pron
poses* **1.** **el ~** (*de él*) his; (*de ella*) hers; (*de
cosa, animal*) its (own); (*de uno*) one's
own; (*de ellos, ellas*) theirs; (*de usted, ustedes*) yours. **2.** *loc*: **de ~** in itself; **hacer de
las suyas** to be up to his/her *etc* usual
tricks; **hacer ~** to make one's own; **lo ~
es el teatro** he/she *etc* should be on the
stage; **lo ~ sería volver** the proper thing
to do would be to go back; **los ~s** *fam*
(*su familia*) his/her *etc* folks; (*su bando*)
his/her *etc* lot.
svástica = **esvástica**.

T

t¹, T *f* (*letra*) t, T.
t² **1.** (*abrev de* **tonelada**) t. **2.** *abrev de*
tomo.
tabacalero, -ra *adj* tobacco (*antes de
sust*). ▶ **Tabacalera** *f* state tobacco monopoly in Spain.
tabaco *m* **1.** (*planta*) tobacco plant.
2. (*picadura*) tobacco. **3.** (*cigarrillos*) ciga-
rrettes (*pl*).
tábano *m* horsefly.
tabarra *f fam*: **dar la ~** to be a pest.
taberna *f* country-style bar, usually cheap.
tabernero, -ra *m y f* (*propietario*) landlord (*f* landlady); (*encargado*) barman (*f*
barmaid).
tabique *m* (*pared*) partition (wall).
tabla *f* **1.** (*plancha*) plank; ~ **de planchar**
ironing board. **2.** (*pliegue*) pleat. **3.** (*lista,
gráfico*) table. **4.** (NÁUT) (*de surf, vela etc*)
board. **5.** (ARTE) panel. ▶ **tablas** *fpl*
1. (*en ajedrez*): **quedar en** o **hacer ~s** to

end in stalemate. 2. (TEATR) stage (sg), boards.

tablado m (de teatro) stage; (de baile) dancefloor; (plataforma) platform.

tablao m flamenco show.

tablero m 1. (gen) board. 2. (en baloncesto) backboard. 3. ~ (de mandos) (de avión) instrument panel; (de coche) dashboard.

tableta f 1. (MED) tablet. 2. (de chocolate) bar.

tablón m plank; (en el techo) beam; ~ de anuncios notice board.

tabú (pl tabúes o tabús) adj & m taboo.

tabular vt & vi to tabulate.

taburete m stool.

tacaño, -ña adj mean, miserly.

tacha f 1. (defecto) flaw, fault; sin ~ faultless. 2. (clavo) tack.

tachar vt 1. (lo escrito) to cross out. 2. fig (acusar): ~ a alguien de mentiroso etc to accuse sb of being a liar etc.

tacho m Amer bucket.

tachón m 1. (tachadura) correction, crossing out. 2. (clavo) stud.

tachuela f tack.

tácito, -ta adj tacit; (norma, regla) unwritten.

taciturno, -na adj taciturn.

taco m 1. (tarugo) plug. 2. (cuña) wedge. 3. fam fig (palabrota) swearword. 4. (de billar) cue. 5. (de hojas, billetes de banco) wad; (de billetes de autobús, metro) book. 6. (de jamón, queso) hunk. 7. Amer (CULIN) taco. 8. Amer (tacón) heel.

tacón m heel.

táctico, -ca adj tactical. ► **táctica** f lit & fig tactics (pl).

tacto m 1. (sentido) sense of touch. 2. (textura) feel. 3. fig (delicadeza) tact.

tafetán m taffeta.

Tailandia Thailand.

taimado, -da adj crafty.

Taiwán [tai'wan] Taiwan.

tajada f 1. (rodaja) slice. 2. fig (parte) share; sacar ~ de algo to get sthg out of sthg.

tajante adj (categórico) categorical.

tajar vt to cut o slice up; (en dos) to slice in two.

tajo m 1. (corte) deep cut. 2. (acantilado) precipice.

Tajo m: el (río) ~ the (River) Tagus.

tal ◆ adj 1. (semejante, tan grande) such; ¡jamás se vio cosa ~! you've never seen such a thing!; lo dijo con ~ seguridad que ... he said it with such conviction that ...; dijo cosas ~es como ... he said such

things as ... 2. (sin especificar) such and such; a ~ hora at such and such a time. 3. (desconocido): un ~ Pérez a (certain) Mr Pérez. ◆ pron 1. (alguna cosa) such a thing. ◆ loc: que si ~ que si cual this, that and the other; ser ~ para cual to be two of a kind; ~ y cual, ~ y ~ this and that; y ~ (etcétera) and so on. ◆ adv: ¿qué ~? how's it going?, how are you doing?; déjalo ~ cual leave it just as it is. ► con tal de loc prep as long as, provided; con ~ de volver pronto ... as long as we're back early ... ► con tal (de) que loc conj as long as, provided. ► tal (y) como loc conj just as o like. ► tal que loc prep fam (como por ejemplo) like.

taladrador, -ra adj drilling. ► **taladradora** f drill.

taladrar vt to drill; fig (suj: sonido) to pierce.

taladro m 1. (taladradora) drill. 2. (agujero) drill hole.

talante m 1. (humor) mood; estar de buen ~ to be in good humour. 2. (carácter) character, disposition.

talar vt to fell.

talco m talc, talcum powder.

talego m 1. (talega) sack. 2. mfam (mil pesetas) 1000 peseta note.

talento m 1. (don natural) talent. 2. (inteligencia) intelligence.

talgo (abrev de tren articulado ligero de Goicoechea Oriol) m Spanish intercity highspeed train.

talismán m talisman.

talla f 1. (medida) size; ¿qué ~ usas? what size are you? 2. (estatura) height. 3. fig (capacidad) stature; dar la ~ to be up to it. 4. (ARTE - en madera) carving; (- en piedra) sculpture.

tallado, -da adj (madera) carved; (piedras preciosas) cut.

tallar vt 1. (esculpir - madera, piedra) to carve; (- piedra preciosa) to cut. 2. (medir) to measure (the height of).

tallarín m (gen pl) noodle.

talle m 1. (cintura) waist. 2. (figura, cuerpo) figure.

taller m 1. (gen) workshop. 2. (AUTOM) garage. 3. (ARTE) studio.

tallo m stem; (brote) sprout, shoot.

talón m 1. (gen & ANAT) heel; ~ de Aquiles fig Achilles' heel; pisarle a alguien los talones to be hot on sb's heels. 2. (cheque) cheque; (matriz) stub; ~ cruzado/devuelto/en blanco crossed/bounced/blank cheque; ~ bancario cashier's cheque Br, cashier's check Am.

talonario m (de cheques) cheque book; (de recibos) receipt book.

tamaño, -ña adj such; ¡cómo pudo decir tamaña estupidez! how could he say such a stupid thing! ▶ **tamaño** m size; **de gran ~** large; **de ~ natural** life-size.

tambalearse vpr 1. (bambolearse - persona) to stagger; (- mueble) to wobble; (- tren) to sway. 2. fig (gobierno, sistema) to totter.

también adv also, too; **yo ~** me too; **él ~ quiere ir** he wants to go too o as well; **~ a mí me gusta** I like it too, I also like it.

tambor m 1. (MÚS & TECN) drum; (de pistola) cylinder. 2. (ANAT) eardrum. 3. (AUTOM) brake drum.

Támesis m: **el (río) ~** the (River) Thames.

tamiz m (cedazo) sieve.

tamizar vt 1. (cribar) to sieve. 2. fig (seleccionar) to screen.

tampoco adv neither, not … either; **ella no va y tú ~** she's not going and neither are you, she's not going and you aren't either; **¿no lo sabías? – yo ~** didn't you know? – me neither o neither did I.

tampón m 1. (sello) stamp; (almohadilla) inkpad. 2. (para la menstruación) tampon.

tan adv 1. (mucho) so; **~ grande/deprisa** so big/quickly; **¡qué película ~ larga!** what a long film!; **~ … que …** so … that …; **~ es así que …** so much so that … 2. (en comparaciones): **~ … como …** as … as … ▶ **tan sólo** loc adv only.

tanda f 1. (grupo, lote) group, batch. 2. (serie) series; (de inyecciones) course. 3. (turno de trabajo) shift.

tándem (pl tándemes) m 1. (bicicleta) tandem. 2. (pareja) duo, pair.

tangente f tangent.

tangible adj tangible.

tango m tango.

tanque m 1. (MIL) tank. 2. (vehículo cisterna) tanker. 3. (depósito) tank.

tantear ◆ vt 1. (sopesar - peso, precio, cantidad) to try to guess; (- problema, posibilidades, ventajas) to weigh up. 2. (probar, sondear) to test (out). 3. (toro, contrincante etc) to size up. ◆ vi 1. (andar a tientas) to feel one's way. 2. (apuntar los tantos) to (keep) score.

tanteo m 1. (prueba, sondeo) testing out. 2. (de posibilidades, ventajas) weighing up. 3. (de contrincante, puntos débiles) siz-ing up. 4. (puntuación) score. ▶ **a tanteo** loc adv roughly.

tanto, -ta ◆ adj 1. (gran cantidad) so much, (pl) so many; **~ dinero** so much money, such a lot of money; **tanta gente** so many people; **tiene ~ entusiasmo/~s amigos que …** she has so much enthusiasm/so many friends that … 2. (cantidad indeterminada) so much, (pl) so many; **nos daban tantas pesetas al día** they used to give us so many pesetas per day; **cuarenta y ~s** forty-something, forty-odd; **nos conocimos en el sesenta y ~s** we met sometime in the Sixties. 3. (en comparaciones): **~ … como** as much … as, (pl) as many … as. ◆ pron 1. (gran cantidad) so much, (pl) so many; **¿cómo puedes tener ~s?** how can you have so many? 2. (cantidad indeterminada) so much, (pl) so many; **a ~s de agosto** on such and such a date in August. 3. (igual cantidad) as much, (pl) as many; **había mucha gente aquí, allí no había tanta** there were a lot of people here, but not as many there; **otro ~** as much again, the same again; **otro ~ le ocurrió a los demás** the same thing happened to the rest of them. 4. loc: **ser uno de ~s** to be nothing special. ◆ **tanto** ◆ m 1. (punto) point; (gol) goal; **marcar un ~** to score. 2. fig (ventaja) point; **apuntarse un ~ a favor** to earn o.s. a point in one's favour. 3. (cantidad indeterminada): **un ~** so much, a certain amount; **~ por ciento** percentage. 4. loc: **estar al ~ (de)** to be on the ball (about). ◆ adv 1. (mucho): **~ (que …)** (cantidad) so much (that …); (tiempo) so long (that …); **no bebas ~** don't drink so much; **~ mejor/peor** so much the better/worse; **~ más cuanto que …** all the more so because … 2. (en comparaciones): **~ como** as much as; **~ hombres como mujeres** both men and women; **~ si estoy como si no** whether I'm there or not. 3. loc: **¡y ~!** most certainly!, you bet! ▶ **tantas** fpl fam: **eran las tantas** it was very late. ▶ **en tanto (que)** loc conj while. ▶ **entre tanto** loc adv meanwhile. ▶ **por (lo) tanto** loc conj therefore, so. ▶ **tanto (es así) que** loc conj so much so that. ▶ **un tanto** loc adv (un poco) a bit, rather.

tañido m (de campana) ringing.

tapa f 1. (para cerrar) lid. 2. (CULIN) snack, tapa. 3. (portada - de libro) cover. 4. (de zapato) heel plate. 5. Amer (de botella) top; (de frasco) stopper.

tapadera f 1. (*para encubrir*) front. 2. (*tapa*) lid.

tapar vt 1. (*cerrar - ataúd, cofre*) to close (the lid of); (- *olla, caja*) to put the lid on; (- *botella*) to put the top on. 2. (*ocultar, cubrir*) to cover; (*no dejar ver*) to block out. 3. (*abrigar - en la cama*) to tuck in; (- *con ropa*) to wrap up. 4. (*encubrir*) to cover up. ► **taparse** vpr 1. (*cubrirse*) to cover (up). 2. (*abrigarse - con ropa*) to wrap up; (- *en la cama*) to tuck o.s. in.

taparrabos m inv 1. (*de hombre primitivo*) loincloth. 2. (*tanga*) tanga briefs (pl).

tapeo m: **ir de ~** to go out for 'tapas'.

tapete m (*paño*) runner; (*en mesa de billar, para cartas*) baize.

tapia f (*stone*) wall.

tapiar vt 1. (*obstruir*) to brick up. 2. (*cercar*) to wall in.

tapicería f 1. (*tela*) upholstery. 2. (*tienda - para muebles*) upholsterer's. 3. (*tapices*) tapestries (pl).

tapiz m (*para la pared*) tapestry; (*para el suelo*) carpet.

tapizado m 1. (*de mueble*) upholstery. 2. (*de pared*) tapestries (pl).

tapizar vt (*mueble*) to upholster.

tapón m 1. (*para tapar - botellas, frascos*) stopper; (- *de corcho*) cork; (- *de metal, plástico*) cap, top; (- *de bañera, lavabo*) plug. 2. (*atasco*) traffic jam. 3. (*en el oído - de cerumen*) wax (U) in the ear; (- *de algodón*) earplug. 4. (*en baloncesto*) block.

taponar vt (*cerrar - botella*) to put the top on; (- *lavadero*) to put the plug in; (- *salida*) to block; (- *tubería*) to stop up.

tapujo m subterfuge; **hacer algo con/sin ~s** to do sthg deceitfully/openly.

taquería f (*Amér*) taco bar.

taquigrafía f shorthand.

taquilla f 1. (*ventanilla - gen*) ticket office; (CIN & TEATR) box office.

2. (*armario*) locker. 3. (*recaudación*) takings (pl).

taquillero, -ra ◆ adj: **es un espectáculo ~** the show is a box-office hit. ◆ m y f ticket clerk.

taquimecanógrafo, -fa m y f shorthand typist.

tara f 1. (*defecto*) defect. 2. (*peso*) tare.

tarántula f tarantula.

tararear vt to hum.

tardanza f lateness.

tardar vi 1. (*llevar tiempo*) to take; **tardó un año en hacerlo** she took a year to do it; **¿cuánto tardarás (en hacerlo)?** how long will it take you (to do it)? 2. (*retrasarse*) to be late; (*ser lento*) to be slow; **~ en hacer algo** to take a long time to do sthg; **no tardaron en hacerlo** they were quick to do it; **a más ~** at the latest.

tarde ◆ f (*hasta las cinco*) afternoon; (*después de las cinco*) evening; **por la ~** (*hasta las cinco*) in the afternoon; (*después de las cinco*) in the evening; **buenas ~s** (*hasta las cinco*) good afternoon; (*después de las cinco*) good evening; **de ~ en ~** from time to time. ◆ adv (*gen*) late; (*en demasía*) too late; **ya es ~ para eso** it's too late for that now; **~ o temprano** sooner or later.

tardío, -a adj (*gen*) late; (*consejo, decisión*) belated.

tarea f (*gen*) task; (EDUC) homework; **~s domésticas** o **de la casa** housework (U).

tarifa f 1. (*precio*) charge; (COM) tariff; (*en transportes*) fare. 2. (*gen pl*) (*lista*) price list.

tarima f platform.

tarjeta f (*gen* & INFORM) card; **~ de crédito** credit card; **~ de embarque** boarding pass; **~ postal** postcard; **~ de visita** visiting o calling card.

tarot m tarot.

tarrina f terrine.

tarro m (*recipiente*) jar.

tarta f (*gen*) cake; (*plana, con base de pasta dura*) tart; (*plana, con base de bizcocho*) flan.

tartaleta f tartlet.

tartamudear vi to stammer, to stutter.

tartamudo, -da ◆ adj stammering. ◆ m y f stammerer.

tartana f fam (*coche viejo*) banger.

tártaro, -ra ◆ adj (*pueblo*) Tartar. ◆ m y f Tartar.

tartera f (*fiambrera*) lunch box.

tarugo m 1. fam (*necio*) blockhead.

2. (*de madera*) block of wood.
tasa *f* 1. (*índice*) rate; ~ **de mortalidad/**
natalidad death/birth rate. 2. (*impuesto*)
tax. 3. (EDUC) fee. 4. (*tasación*) valuation.
tasación *f* valuation.
tasar *vt* 1. (*valorar*) to value. 2. (*fijar*
precio) to fix a price for.
tasca *f* = pub.
tatarabuelo, -la *m y f* great-great-
grandfather (*f* -grandmother).
tatuaje *m* 1. (*dibujo*) tattoo. 2. (*acción*)
tattooing.
tatuar *vt* to tattoo.
taurino, -na *adj* bullfighting (*antes de*
sust).
tauro ◆ *m* (*zodiaco*) Taurus. ◆ *m y f* (*per-*
sona) Taurean.
tauromaquia *f* bullfighting.

TAUROMAQUIA

Bullfights begin with a procession in
which all the participants parade across
the bullring in traditional costume. The
fight itself is divided into three parts: in
the first part, the 'picador' goads the
bull with a lance; in the second, the
'banderillero' sticks barbed darts into it
and in the final part, the 'matador' per-
forms a series of passes before killing
the bull.

TAV (*abrev de* **tren de alta velocidad**) *m*
Spanish high-speed train.
taxativo, -va *adj* precise, exact.
taxi *m* taxi.
taxidermista *m y f* taxidermist.
taxímetro *m* taximeter.
taxista *m y f* taxi driver.
taza *f* 1. (*para beber*) cup. 2. (*de retrete*)
bowl.
tazón *m* bowl.
te *pron pers* 1. (*complemento directo*) you; **le**
gustaría verte she'd like to see you.
2. (*complemento indirecto*) (to) you; ~ **lo dio**
he gave it to you; ~ **tiene miedo** he's
afraid of you. 3. (*reflexivo*) yourself. 4.
fam (*valor impersonal*): **si ~ dejas pisar,**
estás perdido if you let people walk all
over you, you've had it.
té (*pl* **tés**) *m* tea.
tea *f* (*antorcha*) torch.
teatral *adj* 1. (*de teatro - gen*) theatre
(*antes de sust*). (*- grupo*) drama (*antes de*
sust). 2. (*exagerado*) theatrical.
teatro *m* 1. (*gen*) theatre. 2. *fig* (*fin-*
gimiento) playacting.
tebeo® *m* (children's) comic.
techo *m* 1. (*gen*) roof; (*dentro de casa*)

ceiling; ~ **deslizante** o **corredizo** (AUTOM)
sun roof; **bajo** ~ under cover. 2. *fig*
(*límite*) ceiling.
techumbre *f* roof.
tecla *f* (*gen*, INFORM & MÚS) key.
teclado *m* (*gen* & MÚS) keyboard.
teclear *vt* & *vi* (*en ordenador etc*) to type;
(*en piano*) to play.
técnico, -ca ◆ *adj* technical. ◆ *m y f* 1.
(*mecánico*) technician. 2. (*experto*) expert.
▶ **técnica** *f* 1. (*gen*) technique. 2. (*tec-*
nología) technology.
tecnicolor *m* Technicolor®.
tecnócrata *m y f* technocrat.
tecnología *f* technology; ~ **punta**
state-of-the-art technology.
tecnológico, -ca *adj* technological.
tecolote *m* Amer owl.
tedio *m* boredom, tedium.
tedioso, -sa *adj* tedious.
Tegucigalpa Tegucigalpa.
Teide *m*: **el** ~ (Mount) Teide.
teja *f* (*de tejado*) tile.
tejado *m* roof.
tejano, -na ◆ *adj* 1. (*de Texas*) Texan.
2. (*tela*) denim. ◆ *m y f* (*persona*) Texan.
▶ **tejanos** *mpl* (*pantalones*) jeans.
tejedor, -ra *m y f* weaver.
tejemaneje *m fam* 1. (*maquinación*)
intrigue. 2. (*ajetreo*) to-do, fuss.
tejer ◆ *vt* 1. (*gen*) to weave. 2. (*labor de*
punto) to knit. 3. (*telaraña*) to spin. ◆ *vi*
(*hacer ganchillo*) to crochet; (*hacer punto*)
to knit.
tejido *m* 1. (*tela*) fabric, material; (IND)
textile. 2. (ANAT) tissue.
tejo *m* 1. (*juego*) hopscotch. 2. (BOT)
yew.
tejón *m* badger.
tel., teléf. (*abrev de* **teléfono**) tel.
tela *f* 1. (*tejido*) material, cloth; (*retal*)
piece of material; ~ **de araña** cobweb;
~ **metálica** wire netting. 2. (ARTE) (*lienzo*)
canvas. 3. *fam* (*dinero*) dough. 4. *fam*
(*cosa complicada*): **tener (mucha)** ~ (*ser difí-*
cil) to be (very) tricky. 5. *loc*: **poner en** ~
de juicio to call into question.
telar *m* 1. (*máquina*) loom. 2. (*gen pl*)
(*fábrica*) textiles mill.
telaraña *f* spider's web, cobweb.
tele *f fam* telly.
telearrastre *m* ski-tow.
telecomedia *f* television comedy
programme.
telecomunicación *f* (*medio*) telecom-
munication. ▶ **telecomunicaciones**
fpl (*red*) telecommunications.
telediario *m* television news (U).

teledirigido, -da adj remote-controlled.

teléf. = tel.

telefax m inv telefax, fax.

teleférico m cable-car.

telefilme, telefilm (pl **telefilms**) m TV film.

telefonear vi to phone.

telefónico, -ca adj telephone (antes de sust). ▶ **Telefónica** f Spanish national telephone monopoly.

telefonista m y f telephonist.

teléfono m 1. (gen) telephone, phone; **hablar por ~** to be on the phone; **~ inalámbrico** o **móvil** cordless o mobile phone; **~ público** public phone. 2. (número de) **~** telephone number.

telegrafía f telegraphy.

telegráfico, -ca adj lit & fig telegraphic.

telégrafo m (medio, aparato) telegraph.

telegrama m telegram.

telejuego m television game show.

telele m: **le dio un ~** (desmayo) he had a fainting fit; (enfado) he had a fit.

telemando m remote control.

telemática f telematics (U).

telenovela f television soap opera.

telepatía f telepathy.

telescópico, -ca adj telescopic.

telescopio m telescope.

telesilla m chair lift.

telespectador, -ra m y f viewer.

telesquí m ski lift.

teletexto m Teletext®.

teletipo m 1. (aparato) teleprinter. 2. (texto) Teletype®.

teletrabajo m teleworking.

televenta f 1. (por teléfono) telesales (pl). 2. (por televisión) TV advertising in which a phone number is given for clients to contact.

televidente m y f viewer.

televisar vt to televise.

televisión f television.

televisivo, -va adj television (antes de sust).

televisor m television (set).

télex m inv telex.

telón m (de escenario - delante) curtain; (- detrás) backcloth; **~ de acero** fig Iron Curtain; **~ de fondo** fig backdrop.

telonero, -ra m y f (cantante) support artist; (grupo) support band.

tema m 1. (gen) subject. 2. (MÚS) theme.

temario m (de una asignatura) curriculum; (de oposiciones) list of topics; (de reunión, congreso) agenda.

temático, -ca adj thematic. ▶ **temática** f subject matter.

temblar vi 1. (tiritar): **~ (de)** (gen) to tremble (with); (de frío) to shiver (with). 2. (vibrar - suelo etc) to shudder, to shake.

temblor m shaking (U), trembling (U).

tembloroso, -sa adj trembling, shaky.

temer ◆ vt 1. (tener miedo de) to fear, to be afraid of. 2. (sospechar) to fear. ◆ vi to be afraid; **no temas** don't worry; **~ por** to fear for. ▶ **temerse** vpr: **~se que** to be afraid that; **me temo que no vendrá** I'm afraid she won't come.

temerario, -ria adj rash; (conducción) reckless.

temeridad f 1. (cualidad) recklessness. 2. (acción) folly (U), reckless act.

temeroso, -sa adj (receloso) fearful.

temible adj fearsome.

temor m: **~ (a o de)** fear (of).

temperamental adj 1. (cambiante) temperamental. 2. (impulsivo) impulsive.

temperamento m temperament.

temperatura f temperature.

tempestad f storm.

tempestuoso, -sa adj lit & fig stormy.

templado, -da adj 1. (tibio - agua, bebida, comida) lukewarm. 2. (GEOGR) (clima, zona) temperate. 3. (nervios) steady. 4. (persona, carácter) calm, composed. 5. (MÚS) in tune.

templanza f 1. (serenidad) composure. 2. (moderación) moderation. 3. (benignidad - del clima) mildness.

templar vt 1. (entibiar - lo frío) to warm (up); (- lo caliente) to cool down. 2. (calmar - nervios, ánimos) to calm; (- ira, pasiones) to restrain; (- voz) to soften. 3. (TECN) (metal etc) to temper. 4. (MÚS) to tune. 5. (tensar) to tighten (up). ▶ **templarse** vpr to warm up.

temple m 1. (serenidad) composure. 2. (TECN) tempering. 3. (ARTE) tempera.

templete m pavilion.

templo m (edificio - gen) temple; (- católico, protestante) church; (- judío) synagogue.

temporada f 1. (periodo concreto) season; (de exámenes) period; **de ~** (fruta, trabajo) seasonal; (en turismo) peak (antes de sust); **~ alta/baja** high/low season; **~ media** mid-season. 2. (periodo indefinido) (period of) time; **pasé una ~ en el extranjero** I spent some time abroad.

temporal ♦ adj 1. (provisional) temporary. 2. (ANAT & RELIG) temporal. ♦ m
(tormenta) storm.
temporero, -ra m y f casual labourer.
temporizador m timing device.
temprano, -na adj early. ▶ **temprano** adv early.
ten v → **tener.** ▶ **ten con ten** m fam
tact.
tenacidad f tenacity.
tenacillas fpl tongs; (para vello) tweezers; (para rizar el pelo) curling tongs.
tenaz adj (perseverante) tenacious.
tenaza f (gen pl) 1. (herramienta) pliers
(pl). 2. (pinzas) tongs (pl). 3. (ZOOL) pincer.
tendedero m 1. (armazón) clothes
horse; (cuerda) clothes line. 2. (lugar)
drying place.
tendencia f tendency, trend; ~ **a**
hacer algo tendency to do sthg.
tendenciosidad f tendentiousness.
tendencioso, -sa adj tendentious.
tender vt 1. (colgar - ropa) to hang out.
2. (tumbar) to lay (out). 3. (extender) to
stretch (out); (mantel) to spread.
4. (dar - cosa) to hand; (- mano) to hold
out, to offer. 5. (entre dos puntos - cable,
vía) to lay; (- puente) to build. 6. fig
(preparar - trampa etc) to lay. ▶ **tender a**
vi: ~ **a hacer algo** to tend to do something; ~ **a la depresión** to have a tendency to get depressed. ▶ **tenderse**
vpr to stretch out, to lie down.
tenderete m (presto) stall.
tendero, -ra m y f shopkeeper.
tendido, -da adj 1. (extendido, tumbado)
stretched out. 2. (colgado - ropa) hung
out, on the line. ▶ **tendido** m 1. (instalación - de cable) laying; ~ **eléctrico** electrical installation. 2. (TAUROM) front rows
(pl).
tendón m tendon.
tendrá etc → **tener.**
tenebroso, -sa adj dark, gloomy; fig
shady, sinister.
tenedor[1] m (utensilio) fork.
tenedor[2]**, -ra** m y f (poseedor) holder; ~
de libros (COM) bookkeeper.
teneduría f (COM) bookkeeping.
tenencia f possession; ~ **ilícita de
armas** illegal possession of arms.
tener ♦ vaux 1. (antes de participio)
(haber): **teníamos pensado ir al teatro** we
had thought of going to the theatre.
2. (antes de adj) (hacer estar): **me tuvo
despierto** it kept me awake; **eso la tiene
despistada** that has confused her.

3. (expresa obligación): ~ **que hacer algo** to
have to do sthg; **tiene que ser así** it has
to be this way. 4. (expresa propósito): **tenemos que ir a cenar un día** we ought to o
should go for dinner some time. ♦ vt
1. (gen) to have; **tengo un hermano** I
have o I've got a brother; ~ **fiebre** to
have a temperature; **tuvieron una pelea**
they had a fight; ~ **un niño** to have a
baby; **¡que tengan buen viaje!** have a
good journey!; **hoy tengo clase** I have to
go to school today. 2. (medida, años, sensación, cualidad) to be; **tiene 3 metros de
ancho** it's 3 metres wide; **¿cuántos años
tienes?** how old are you?; **tiene diez años**
she's ten (years old); ~ **hambre/miedo**
to be hungry/afraid; ~ **mal humor** to be
bad-tempered; **le tiene lástima** he feels
sorry for her. 3. (sujetar) to hold; **tenlo
por el asa** hold it by the handle.
4. (tomar): **ten el libro que me pediste**
here's the book you asked me for;
¡aquí tienes! here you are! 5. (recibir) to
get; **tuve un verdadero desengaño** I was
really disappointed; **tendrá una sorpresa** he'll get a surprise. 6. (valorar): **me
tienen por tonto** they think I'm stupid; ~
a alguien en mucho to think the world of
sb. 7. (guardar, contener) to keep. 8. loc:
no las tiene todas consigo he is not too
sure about it; ~ **a bien hacer algo** to be
kind enough to do sthg; ~ **que ver con
algo/alguien** (existir relación) to have
something to do with sthg/sb; (existir
semejanza) to be in the same league as
sthg/sb. ▶ **tenerse** vpr 1. (sostenerse):
~**se de pie** to stand upright. 2. (considerarse): **se tiene por listo** he thinks he's
clever.
tengo → **tener.**
tenia f tapeworm.
teniente m lieutenant.
tenis m inv tennis; ~ **de mesa** table tennis.
tenista m y f tennis player.
tenor m 1. (MÚS) tenor. 2. (estilo) tone.
▶ **a tenor de** loc prep in view of.
tensar vt to tauten; (arco) to draw.
tensión f 1. (gen) tension; ~ **nerviosa**
nervous tension. 2. (TECN) (estiramiento)
stress. 3. (MED): ~ **(arterial)** blood pressure; **tener la ~ alta/baja** to have high/
low blood pressure. 4. (ELECTR) voltage; **alta ~** high voltage.
tenso, -sa adj taut; fig tense.
tentación f (deseo) temptation; **caer en
la ~** to give in to temptation; **tener la ~
de** to be tempted to.

tentáculo m tentacle.

tentador, -ra adj tempting.

tentar vt 1. (palpar) to feel. 2. (atraer, incitar) to tempt.

tentativa f attempt; ~ **de asesinato** attempted murder.

tentempié (pl **tentempiés**) m snack.

tenue adj 1. (tela, hilo, lluvia) fine. 2. (luz, sonido, dolor) faint. 3. (relación) tenuous.

teñir vt 1. (ropa, pelo): ~ **algo (de rojo** etc) to dye sthg (red etc). 2. fig (matizar): ~ **algo (de)** to tinge sthg (with). ▶ **teñirse** vpr: ~**se (el pelo)** to dye one's hair.

teología f theology; ~ **de la liberación** liberation theology.

teólogo, -ga m y f theologian.

teorema m theorem.

teoría f theory; **en** ~ in theory.

teórico, -ca ◆ adj theoretical. ◆ m y f (persona) theorist. ▶ **teórica** f (teoría) theory (U).

teorizar vi to theorize.

tequila m o f tequila.

TER (abrev de **tren español rápido**) m Spanish high-speed train.

terapéutico, -ca adj therapeutic.

terapia f therapy; ~ **ocupacional/de grupo** occupational/group therapy.

tercer → tercero.

tercera → tercero.

tercermundista adj third-world (antes de sust).

tercero, -ra núm (antes de sust masculino sg: **tercer**) third. ▶ **tercero** m 1. (piso) third floor. 2. (curso) third year. 3. (mediador, parte interesada) third party. ▶ **tercera** f (AUTOM) third (gear).

terceto m (MÚS) trio.

terciar ◆ vt (poner en diagonal - gen) to place diagonally; (- sombrero) to tilt. ◆ vi 1. (mediar): ~ **(en)** to mediate (in). 2. (participar) to intervene, to take part. ▶ **terciarse** vpr to arise; **si se tercia** if the opportunity arises.

tercio m 1. (tercera parte) third. 2. (TAU-ROM) stage (of bullfight).

terciopelo m velvet.

terco, -ca adj stubborn.

tergal® m Tergal®.

tergiversar vt to distort, to twist.

termal adj thermal.

termas fpl (baños) hot baths, spa (sg).

térmico, -ca adj thermal.

terminación f 1. (finalización) completion. 2. (parte final) end. 3. (GRAM) ending.

terminal ◆ adj (gen) final; (enfermo) terminal. ◆ m (ELECTR & INFORM) terminal.

◆ f (de aeropuerto) terminal; (de autobuses) terminus.

terminante adj categorical; (prueba) conclusive.

terminar ◆ vt to finish. ◆ vi 1. (acabar) to end; (tren) to stop, to terminate; ~ **en** (objeto) to end in. 2. (ir a parar): ~ **(de/en)** to end up (as/in); ~ **por hacer algo** to end up doing sthg. ▶ **terminarse** vpr 1. (finalizarse) to finish. 2. (agotarse) to run out.

término m 1. (fin, extremo) end; **poner** ~ **a algo** to put a stop to sthg. 2. (territorio): ~ **(municipal)** district. 3. (plazo) period; **en el** ~ **de un mes** within (the space of) a month. 4. (lugar, posición) place; **en primer** ~ (ARTE & FOT) in the foreground; **en último** ~ (ARTE & FOT) in the background; fig (si es necesario) as a last resort; (en resumidas cuentas) in the final analysis. 5. (elemento) point; ~ **medio** (media) average; (compromiso) compromise; **por** ~ **medio** on average. 6. (LING & MAT) term; **en** ~**s generales** generally speaking. ▶ **términos** mpl (condiciones) terms; **los** ~**s del contrato** the terms of the contract.

terminología f terminology.

termo m Thermos® (flask).

termómetro m thermometer.

termostato m thermostat.

terna f (POLÍT) shortlist of three candidates.

ternasco f suckling lamb.

ternero, -ra m y f (animal) calf. ▶ **ternera** f (carne) veal.

ternilla f 1. (CULIN) gristle. 2. (ANAT) cartilage.

ternura f tenderness.

terquedad f stubbornness.

terracota f terracotta.

terrado m terrace roof.

terral, tierral m Amer dust cloud.

terraplén m embankment.

terráqueo, -a adj Earth (antes de sust), terrestrial.

terrateniente m y f landowner.

terraza f 1. (balcón) balcony. 2. (de café) terrace, patio. 3. (azotea) terrace roof. 4. (bancal) terrace.

terremoto m earthquake.

terrenal adj earthly.

terreno, -na adj earthly. ▶ **terreno** m 1. (suelo - gen) land; (- GEOL) terrain; (- AGR) soil. 2. (solar) plot (of land). 3. (DEP): ~ **(de juego)** field, pitch. 4. fig (ámbito) field.

terrestre adj 1. (del planeta) terrestrial. 2. (de la tierra) land (antes de sust).

terrible adj 1. (gen) terrible. 2. (ate-rrador) terrifying.

terrícola m y f earthling.

territorial adj territorial.

territorio m territory; **por todo el ~ nacional** across the country, nation-wide.

terrón m 1. (de tierra) clod of earth. 2. (de harina etc) lump.

terror m terror; (CIN) horror; **dar ~** to terrify.

terrorífico, -ca adj terrifying.

terrorismo m terrorism.

terrorista adj, m y f terrorist.

terroso, -sa adj 1. (parecido a la tierra) earthy. 2. (con tierra) muddy.

terso, -sa adj 1. (piel, superficie) smooth. 2. (aguas, mar) clear. 3. (estilo, lenguaje) polished.

tersura f 1. (de piel, superficie) smooth-ness. 2. (de aguas, mar) clarity.

tertulia f regular meeting of people for infor-mal discussion of a particular issue of common interest; **~ literaria** literary circle.

tesina f (undergraduate) dissertation.

tesis f inv thesis.

tesitura f (circunstancia) circumstances (pl).

tesón m 1. (tenacidad) tenacity, per-severance. 2. (firmeza) firmness.

tesorero, -ra m y f treasurer.

tesoro m 1. (botín) treasure. 2. (hacienda pública) treasury, exchequer. ▶ **Tesoro** m (ECON): **el Tesoro** the Treasury.

test (pl tests) m test.

testamentario, -ria ◆ adj testamen-tary. ◆ m y f executor.

testamento m will; **hacer ~** to write one's will. ▶ **Antiguo Testamento** m Old Testament. ▶ **Nuevo Testamento** m New Testament.

testar vi to make a will.

testarudo, -da adj stubborn.

testículo m testicle.

testificar ◆ vt to testify; fig to testify to. ◆ vi to testify, to give evidence.

testigo ◆ m y f (persona) witness; **~ de cargo/descargo** witness for the prose-cution/defence; **~ ocular** o **presencial** eyewitness. ◆ m (DEP) baton. ▶ **testi-go de Jehová** m y f Jehovah's Witness.

testimonial adj (documento, prueba etc) testimonial.

testimoniar vt to testify; fig to testify to.

testimonio m 1. (DER) testimony. 2. (prueba) proof; **como ~ de** as proof of; **dar ~ de** to prove.

teta f 1. fam (de mujer) tit. 2. (de animal) teat.

tétanos m inv tetanus.

tetera f teapot.

tetilla f 1. (de hombre, animal) nipple. 2. (de biberón) teat.

tetina f teat.

tetrapléjico, -ca adj, m y f quadri-plegic.

tétrico, -ca adj gloomy.

textil adj & m textile.

texto m 1. (gen) text. 2. (pasaje) pas-sage.

textual adj 1. (del texto) textual. 2. (exacto) exact.

textura f (de tela etc) texture.

tez f complexion.

ti pron pers (después de prep) 1. (gen) you; **siempre pienso en ~** I'm always thinking about you; **me acordaré de ~** I'll remember you. 2. (reflexivo) yourself; **sólo piensas en ~ (mismo)** you only think about yourself.

tía → tío.

tianguis m inv Amer open-air market.

Tibet m: **el ~** Tibet.

tibia f shinbone, tibia.

tibieza f (calidez) warmth; (falta de calor) lukewarmness.

tibio, -bia adj 1. (cálido) warm; (falto de calor) tepid, lukewarm. 2. fig (frío) luke-warm.

tiburón m (gen) shark.

tic m tic.

ticket = **tiquet.**

tictac m tick tock.

tiempo m 1. (gen) time; **al poco ~** soon afterwards; **a ~ (de hacer algo)** in time (to do sthg); **a un ~** at the same time; **con el ~** in time; **del ~** (fruta) of the sea-son; (bebida) at room temperature; **estar a o tener ~ de** to have time to; **fuera de ~** at the wrong moment; **ganar ~** to save time; **perder el ~** to waste time; **~ libre** o **de ocio** spare time; **a ~ parcial** o **partido** part-time; **en ~s de Maricastaña** donkey's years ago; **engañar** o **matar el ~** to kill time. 2. (periodo largo) long time; **con ~** in good time; **hace ~ que** it is a long time since; **hace no vive aquí** he hasn't lived here for some time; **tomarse uno su ~** to take one's time. 3. (edad) age; **¿qué ~ tiene?** how old is he? 4. (movimiento) movement; **motor de cuatro ~s** four-stroke engine. 5. (METEOR) weather; **hizo buen/mal ~** the weather was good/bad; **si el ~ lo permite** o **no lo impide** weather permitting; **hace un ~ de perros** it's a foul day. **6.** (DEP) half. **7.** (GRAM) tense. **8.** (MÚS - compás) time; (- ritmo) tempo.

tienda f **1.** (establecimiento) shop. **2.** (para acampar): **~ (de campaña)** tent.

tiene → **tener**.

tienta ▶ **a tientas** loc adv blindly; **andar a ~s** to grope along.

tierno, -na adj **1.** (blando, cariñoso) tender. **2.** (del día) fresh.

tierra f **1.** (gen) land; **~ adentro** inland; **~ firme** terra firma. **2.** (materia inorgánica) earth, soil; **un camino de ~** a dirt track. **3.** (suelo) ground; **caer a ~** to fall to the ground; **tomar ~** to touch down. **4.** (patria) homeland, native land. **5.** (ELECTR) earth Br, ground Am. ▶ **Tierra** f: **la Tierra** the Earth.

tierral = **terral**.

tieso, -sa adj **1.** (rígido) stiff. **2.** (erguido) erect. **3.** fig (engreído) haughty.

tiesto m flowerpot.

tifoideo, -a adj typhoid (antes de sust).

tifón m typhoon.

tifus m inv typhus.

tigre m tiger.

tigresa f tigress.

tijera f (gen pl) scissors (pl); (de jardinero, esquilador) shears (pl); **unas ~s** a pair of scissors/shears.

tijereta f (insecto) earwig.

tila f (infusión) lime blossom tea.

tildar vt: **~ a alguien de algo** to brand o call sb sthg.

tilde f **1.** (signo ortográfico) tilde. **2.** (acento gráfico) accent.

tiliches mpl Amer bits and pieces.

tilín m tinkle, tinkling (U); **me hace ~** fam I fancy him.

tilo m (árbol) linden o lime tree.

timar vt (estafar): **~ a alguien** to swindle sb; **~ algo a alguien** to swindle sb out of sthg.

timbal m (MÚS - de orquesta) kettledrum.

timbrar vt to stamp.

timbre m **1.** (aparato) bell; **tocar el ~** to ring the bell. **2.** (de voz, sonido) tone; (TECN) timbre. **3.** (sello - de documentos) stamp; (- de impuestos) seal.

timidez f shyness.

tímido, -da adj shy, timid.

timo m (estafa) swindle.

timón m **1.** (AERON & NÁUT) rudder. **2.** fig (gobierno) helm; **llevar el ~ de** to be at the helm of. **3.** Amer (volante) steering wheel.

timonel, timonero m (NÁUT) helmsman.

timorato, -ta adj (mojigato) prudish.

tímpano m (ANAT) eardrum.

tina f **1.** (tinaja) pitcher. **2.** (gran cuba) vat. **3.** (bañera) bathtub.

tinaja f (large) pitcher.

tinglado m **1.** (cobertizo) shed. **2.** (armazón) platform. **3.** fig (lío) fuss. **4.** fig (maquinación) plot.

tinieblas fpl darkness (U); fig confusion (U), uncertainty (U).

tino m **1.** (puntería) good aim. **2.** fig (habilidad) skill. **3.** fig (juicio) sense, good judgment.

tinta f ink; **~ china** Indian ink; **cargar o recargar las ~s** to exaggerate; **saberlo de buena ~** to have it on good authority; **sudar ~** to sweat blood. ▶ **medias tintas** fpl: **andarse con medias ~s** to be wishy-washy.

tinte m **1.** (sustancia) dye. **2.** (operación) dyeing. **3.** (tintorería) dry cleaner's. **4.** fig (tono) shade, tinge.

tintero m (frasco) ink pot; (en la mesa) inkwell.

tintinear vi to jingle, to tinkle.

tinto, -ta adj **1.** (teñido) dyed. **2.** (manchado) stained. **3.** (vino) red. ▶ **tinto** m (vino) red wine.

tintorera f blue shark.

tintorería f dry cleaner's.

tiña f (MED) ringworm.

tío, -a m y f **1.** (familiar) uncle (f aunt). **2.** fam (individuo) guy (f bird). **3.** mfam (apelativo) mate (f darling).

tiovivo m merry-go-round.

típico, -ca adj typical; (traje, restaurante etc) traditional; **~ de** typical of.

tipificar vt **1.** (gen & DER) to classify. **2.** (simbolizar) to typify.

tiple m y f (cantante) soprano.

tipo, -pa m y f mfam guy (f bird). ▶ **tipo** m **1.** (clase) type, sort; **todo ~ de** all sorts of. **2.** (cuerpo - de mujer) figure; (- de hombre) build. **3.** (ECON) rate; **~ de interés/cambio** interest/exchange rate. **4.** (IMPRENTA & ZOOL) type.

tipografía f **1.** (procedimiento) printing. **2.** (taller) printing works (sg).

tipográfico, -ca adj typographical.

tipógrafo, -fa m y f printer.

tíquet (pl **tíquets**), **ticket** ['tiket] (pl **tickets**) m ticket.

tiquismiquis ◆ adj inv fam (maniático) pernickety. ◆ m y f inv fam (maniático) fusspot. ◆ mpl **1.** (riñas) squabbles. **2.** (bagatelas) trifles.

TIR (*abrev de* **transport international routier**) *m* International Road Transport, ≃ HGV Br.

tira *f* 1. (*banda cortada*) strip. 2. (*de viñetas*) comic strip. 3. *loc:* **la ~ de** *fam* loads (*pl*) of.

tirabuzón *m* (*rizo*) curl.

tirachinas *m inv* catapult.

tiradero *m Amer* rubbish dump.

tirado, -da *adj* 1. *fam* (*barato*) dirt cheap. 2. *fam* (*fácil*) simple, dead easy; **estar ~** to be a cinch. 3. *loc:* **dejar ~ a alguien** to leave sb in the lurch. ▶ **tirada** *f* 1. (*lanzamiento*) throw. 2. (IMPRENTA - *número de ejemplares*) print run; (- *reimpresión*) reprint; (- *número de lectores*) circulation. 3. (*sucesión*) series. 4. (*distancia*): **de** o **en una tirada** in one go.

tirador, -ra *m y f* (*persona*) marksman. ▶ **tirador** *m* (*mango*) handle. ▶ **tiradores** *mpl Amer* (*tirantes*) braces.

Tirana Tirana.

tiranía *f* tyranny.

tirano, -na ◆ *adj* tyrannical. ◆ *m y f* tyrant.

tirante ◆ *adj* 1. (*estirado*) taut. 2. *fig* (*violento, tenso*) tense. ◆ *m* 1. (*de tela*) strap. 2. (ARQUIT) brace. ▶ **tirantes** *mpl* (*para pantalones*) braces Br, suspenders Am.

tirantez *f fig* tension.

tirar ◆ *vt* 1. (*lanzar*) to throw; **~ algo a alguien/algo** (*para hacer daño*) to throw sthg at sb/sthg; **tírame una manzana** throw me an apple. 2. (*dejar caer*) to drop; (*derramar*) to spill; (*volcar*) to knock over. 3. (*desechar, malgastar*) to throw away. 4. (*disparar*) to fire; (- *bomba*) to drop; (- *petardo, cohete*) to let off. 5. (*derribar*) to knock down. 6. (*jugar - carta*) to play; (- *dado*) to throw. 7. (DEP - *falta, penalti etc*) to take; (- *balón*) to pass. 8. (*imprimir*) to print. ◆ *vi* 1. (*estirar, arrastrar*): **~ (de algo)** to pull (sthg); **tira y afloja** give and take. 2. (*disparar*) to shoot. 3. *fam* (*atraer*) to have a pull; **me tira la vida del campo** I feel drawn towards life in the country. 4. (*cigarrillo, chimenea etc*) to draw. 5. (*dirigirse*) to go, to head. 6. *fam* (*apañárselas*) to get by; **ir tirando** to get by; **voy tirando** I'm O.K. 7. (*parecerse*): **tira a gris** it's greyish; **tira a su abuela** she takes after her grandmother; **tirando a** approaching. 8. (*tender*): **~ para algo** (*persona*) to have the makings of sthg; **este programa tira a (ser) hortera** this programme is a bit on the tacky side; **el tiempo tira a mejorar** the weather looks as if it's getting better. 9. (DEP - *con el pie*)

to kick; (- *con la mano*) to throw; (- *a meta, canasta etc*) to shoot. ▶ **tirarse** *vpr* 1. (*lanzarse*): **~se (a)** (*agua*) to dive (into); (*aire*) to jump (into); **~se sobre alguien** to jump on top of sb. 2. (*tumbarse*) to stretch out. 3. (*tiempo*) to spend.

tirita® *f* (sticking) plaster Br, ≃ Bandaid® Am.

tiritar *vi:* **~ (de)** to shiver (with).

tiro *m* 1. (*gen*) shot; **pegar un ~ a alguien** to shoot sb; **pegarse un ~** to shoot o.s.; **ni a ~s** never in a million years. 2. (*acción*) shooting; **~ al blanco** (*deporte*) target shooting; (*lugar*) shooting range; **~ con arco** archery. 3. (*huella, marca*) bullet mark; (*herida*) gunshot wound. 4. (*alcance*) range; **a ~ de** within the range of; **a ~ de piedra** a stone's throw away. 5. (*de chimenea, horno*) draw. 6. (*de caballos*) team.

tiroides *m inv* thyroid (gland).

tirón *m* 1. (*estirón*) pull. 2. (*robo*) bagsnatching. ▶ **de un tirón** *loc adv* in one go.

tirotear ◆ *vt* to fire at. ◆ *vi* to shoot.

tiroteo *m* (*tiros*) shooting; (*intercambio de disparos*) shootout.

tisana *f* herbal tea.

tisis *f inv* (MED) (pulmonary) tuberculosis.

titánico, -ca *adj* titanic.

títere *m lit & fig* (*gen*) puppet; (*de cuerdas*) marionette; **no dejar ~ con cabeza** (*destrozar*) to destroy everything in sight; (*criticar*) to spare nobody. ▶ **títeres** *mpl* (*guiñol*) puppet show (*sg*).

titilar, titilear *vi* (*estrella, luz*) to flicker.

titiritar *vi:* **~ (de)** to shiver (with).

titiritero, -ra *m y f* 1. (*de títeres*) puppeteer. 2. (*acróbata*) acrobat.

titubeante *adj* 1. (*actitud*) hesitant. 2. (*voz*) stuttering. 3. (*al andar*) tottering.

titubear *vi* 1. (*dudar*) to hesitate. 2. (*al hablar*) to stutter.

titubeo *m* (*gen pl*) 1. (*duda*) hesitation. 2. (*al hablar*) stutter, stuttering (U). 3. (*al andar*) tottering.

titulado, -da *m y f* (*diplomado*) holder of a qualification; (*licenciado*) graduate.

titular ◆ *adj* (*profesor, médico*) official. ◆ *m y f* (*poseedor*) holder. ◆ *m* (*gen pl*) (PRENS) headline. ◆ *vt* (*llamar*) to title, to call. ▶ **titularse** *vpr* 1. (*llamarse*) to be titled o called. 2. (*licenciarse*): **~se (en)** to graduate (in). 3. (*diplomarse*): **~se (en)** to obtain a qualification (in).

título *m* 1. (*gen*) title; **~ de propiedad**

title deed. 2. (*licenciatura*) **degree;** (*diploma*) diploma; **tiene muchos ~s** she has a lot of qualifications. **3.** *fig* (*derecho*) right; **a ~ de** as.

tiza *f* chalk; **una ~** a piece of chalk.

tiznar *vt* to blacken.

tizne *m o f* soot.

tizón *m* burning stick o log.

tlapalería *f* Amer ironmonger's (shop).

toalla *f* (*para secarse*) towel; **~ de ducha/ manos** bath/hand towel; **arrojar** o **tirar la ~** to throw in the towel.

toallero *m* towel rail.

tobillo *m* ankle.

tobogán *m* (*rampa*) slide; (*en parque de atracciones*) helter-skelter; (*en piscina*) flume.

toca *f* wimple.

tocadiscos *m inv* record player.

tocado, -da *adj* (*chiflado*) soft in the head. ► **tocado** *m* (*prenda*) headgear (U).

tocador *m* **1.** (*mueble*) dressing table. **2.** (*habitación - en lugar público*) powder room; (*- en casa*) boudoir.

tocar ◆ *vt* **1.** (*gen*) to touch; (*palpar*) to feel; (*suj: país, jardín*) to border on. **2.** (*instrumento, canción*) to play; (*bombo*) to bang; (*sirena, alarma*) to sound; (*campana, timbre*) to ring; **el reloj tocó las doce** the clock struck twelve. **3.** (*abordar - tema etc*) to touch on. **4.** *fig* (*conmover*) to touch; (*herir*) to wound. **5.** *fig* (*concernir*): **por lo que a mí me toca/a eso le toca** as far as I'm/that's concerned. ◆ *vi* **1.** (*entrar en contacto*) to touch. **2.** (*estar próximo*): **~ (con)** (*gen*) to be touching; (*país, jardín*) to border (on). **3.** (*llamar - a la puerta, ventana*) to knock. **4.** (*corresponder - en un reparto*): **~ a alguien** to be due to sb; **tocamos a mil cada uno** we're due a thousand each; **le tocó la mitad** he got half of it; **te toca a ti hacerlo** (*turno*) it's your turn to do it; (*responsabilidad*) it's up to you to do it. **5.** (*caer en suerte*): **me ha tocado la lotería** I've won the lottery; **le ha tocado sufrir mucho** he has had to suffer a lot. **6.** (*llegar el momento*): **nos toca pagar ahora** it's time (for us) to pay now. ► **tocarse** *vpr* to touch.

tocayo, -ya *m y f* namesake.

tocinería *f* pork butcher's (shop).

tocino *m* (*para cocinar*) lard; (*para comer*) fat (*of bacon*). ► **tocino de cielo** *m* (CULIN) dessert made of syrup and eggs.

todavía *adv* **1.** (*aún*) still; (*con negativo*) yet, still; **~ no lo he recibido** I still

haven't got it, I haven't got it yet; **~ ayer** as late as yesterday; **~ no** not yet. **2.** (*sin embargo*) still. **3.** (*incluso*) even.

todo, -da ◆ *adj* **1.** (*gen*) all; **~ el mundo** everybody; **~ el libro** the whole book, all (of) the book; **~ el día** all day. **2.** (*cada, cualquier*): **~s los días/lunes** every day/Monday; **~ español** every Spaniard, all Spaniards. **3.** (*para enfatizar*): **es ~ un hombre** he's every bit a man; **ya es toda una mujer** she's a big girl now; **fue ~ un éxito** it was a great success. ◆ *pron* **1.** (*todas las cosas*) everything, (*pl*) all of them; **lo vendio ~** he sold everything, he sold it all; **~s están rotos** they're all broken, all of them are broken; **ante ~** (*sobre todo*) above all; (*en primer lugar*) first of all; **con ~** despite everything; **sobre ~** above all; **está en ~** he/she always makes sure everything is just so. **2.** (*todas las personas*): **~s** everybody; **todas vinieron** everybody o they all came. ► **todo** ◆ *m* whole. ◆ *adv* completely, all. ► **del todo** *loc adv*: **no estoy del ~ contento** I'm not entirely happy; **no lo hace mal del ~** she doesn't do it at all badly. ► **todo terreno** *m* Jeep®.

todopoderoso, -sa *adj* almighty.

toffee ['tofi] (*pl* **toffees**) *m* coffee- flavoured toffee.

toga *f* **1.** (*manto*) toga. **2.** (*traje*) gown.

Togo Togo.

toldo *m* (*de tienda*) awning; (*de playa*) sunshade.

tolerancia *f* tolerance.

tolerante *adj* tolerant.

tolerar *vt* **1.** (*consentir, aceptar*) to toler- ate; **~ que alguien haga algo** to tolerate sb doing sthg. **2.** (*aguantar*) to stand.

toma *f* **1.** (*de biberón, papilla*) feed. **2.** (*de medicamento*) dose; (*de sangre*) sample. **3.** (*de ciudad etc*) capture. **4.** (*de agua, aire*) inlet; **~ de corriente** (ELECTR) socket. **5.** (CIN) (*de escena*) take. **6.** *loc*: **ser un ~ y daca** to be give and take. ► **toma de posesión** *f* **1.** (*de gobierno, presidente*) investiture. **2.** (*de cargo*) undertaking.

tomar ◆ *vt* **1.** (*gen*) to take; (*actitud, cos- tumbre*) to adopt. **2.** (*datos, información*) to take down. **3.** (*comida, bebida*) to have; **¿qué quieres ~?** what would you like (to drink/eat)? **4.** (*autobús, tren etc*) to catch; (*taxi*) to take. **5.** (*considerar, con- fundir*): **~ a alguien por algo/alguien** to take sb for sthg/sb. **6.** *loc*: **~la o ~las con alguien** *fam* to have it in for sb; **¡toma!** (*al dar algo*) here you are!; (*expresando sor-*

presa) well I never! ♦ *vi* (*encaminarse*) to go, to head. ▶ **tomarse** *vpr* 1. (*comida, bebida*) to have; (*medicina, drogas*) to take. 2. (*interpretar*) to take; **~se algo a mal/bien** to take sth badly/well.

tomate *m* (*fruto*) tomato.

tómbola *f* tombola.

tomillo *m* thyme.

tomo *m* (*volumen*) volume.

ton ▶ **sin ton ni son** *loc adv* for no apparent reason.

tonada *f* tune.

tonadilla *f* ditty.

tonalidad *f* (*de color*) tone.

tonel *m* (*recipiente*) barrel.

tonelada *f* tonne.

tonelaje *m* tonnage.

tónico, -ca *adj* 1. (*reconstituyente*) revitalizing. 2. (GRAM & MÚS) tonic. ▶ **tónico** *m* (*reconstituyente*) tonic. ▶ **tónica** *f* 1. (*tendencia*) trend. 2. (MÚS) tonic. 3. (*bebida*) tonic water.

tonificar *vt* (*músculos*) to tone up; (*suj: ducha, masaje, infusión*) to invigorate.

tono *m* 1. (*gen*) tone; **fuera de ~** out of place. 2. (MÚS - *tonalidad*) key; (- *altura*) pitch. 3. (*de color*) shade; **~ de piel** complexion.

tonsura *f* tonsure.

tontear *vi* (*hacer el tonto*) to fool about.

tontería *f* 1. (*estupidez*) stupid thing; **decir una ~** to talk nonsense; **hacer una ~** to do sthg foolish. 2. (*cosa sin importancia o valor*) trifle.

tonto, -ta ♦ *adj* silly, foolish. ♦ *m y f* idiot; **hacer el ~** to play the fool; **hacerse el ~** to act innocent. ▶ **a tontas y a locas** *loc adv* haphazardly.

top (*pl* **tops**) *m* (*prenda*) short top.

topacio *m* topaz.

topadora *f* Amer bulldozer.

topar *vi* (*encontrarse*): **~ con alguien** to bump into sb; **~ con algo** to come across sthg.

tope ♦ *adj inv* (*máximo*) top, maximum; (*fecha*) last. ♦ *m* 1. (*pieza*) block; (*para puerta*) doorstop. 2. (FERROC) buffer. 3. (*límite máximo*) limit; (*de plazo*) deadline. 4. (*freno*): **poner ~ a** to rein in, to curtail. 5. *loc*: **estar hasta los ~s** to be bursting at the seams. ▶ **a tope** *loc adv* 1. (*de velocidad, intensidad*) flat out. 2. *fam* (*lleno - lugar*) packed.

topetazo *m* bump.

tópico, -ca *adj* 1. (MED) topical. 2. (*manido*) clichéd. ▶ **tópico** *m* cliché.

topo *m* (ZOOL & *fig*) mole.

topógrafo, -fa *m y f* topographer.

topónimo *m* place name.

toque *m* 1. (*gen*) touch; **dar los (últimos) ~s a algo** to put the finishing touches to sthg. 2. (*aviso*) warning; **dar un ~ a alguien** (*llamar*) to call sb; (*amonestar*) to prod sb, to warn sb. 3. (*sonido - de campana*) chime, chiming (U); (- *de tambor*) beat, beating (U); (- *de sirena etc*) blast; **~ de diana** reveille; **~ de difuntos** death knell; **~ de queda** curfew.

toquetear *vt* (*manosear - cosa*) to fiddle with; (- *persona*) to fondle.

toquilla *f* shawl.

tórax *m inv* thorax.

torbellino *m* 1. (*remolino - de aire*) whirlwind; (- *de agua*) whirlpool; (- *de polvo*) dustcloud. 2. *fig* (*mezcla confusa*) spate.

torcedura *f* 1. (*torsión*) twist, twisting (U). 2. (*esguince*) sprain.

torcer ♦ *vt* 1. (*gen*) to twist; (*doblar*) to bend. 2. (*girar*) to turn. ♦ *vi* (*girar*) to turn. ▶ **torcerse** *vpr* 1. (*retorcerse*) to twist; (*doblarse*) to bend; **me tuerzo al andar/escribir** I can't walk/write in a straight line. 2. (*dislocarse*) to sprain. 3. (*ir mal - esperanzas, negocios, día*) to go wrong; (- *persona*) to go astray.

torcido, -da *adj* (*enroscado*) twisted; (*doblado*) bent; (*cuadro, corbata*) crooked.

tordo, -da *adj* dappled. ▶ **tordo** *m* (*pájaro*) thrush.

torear ♦ *vt* 1. (*lidiar*) to fight (*bulls*). 2. *fig* (*eludir*) to dodge. 3. *fig* (*burlarse de*): **~ a alguien** to mess sb about. ♦ *vi* (*lidiar*) to fight bulls.

toreo *m* bullfighting.

torero, -ra *m y f* (*persona*) bullfighter; **saltarse algo a la torera** *fig* to flout sthg. ▶ **torera** *f* (*prenda*) bolero (jacket).

tormenta *f lit* & *fig* storm.

tormento *m* torment.

tormentoso, -sa *adj* stormy; (*sueño*) troubled.

tornado *m* tornado.

tornar *culto* ♦ *vt* (*convertir*): **~ algo en (algo)** to turn sthg into (sthg). ♦ *vi* 1. (*regresar*) to return. 2. (*volver a hacer*): **~ a hacer algo** to do sthg again. ▶ **tornarse** *vpr* (*convertirse*): **~se (en)** to turn (into), to become.

torneado, -da *adj* (*cerámica*) turned.

torneo *m* tournament.

tornillo *m* screw; (*con tuerca*) bolt; **le falta un ~** *fam* he has a screw loose.

torniquete *m* (MED) tourniquet.

torno *m* 1. (*de alfarero*) (potter's) wheel. 2. (*para pesos*) winch. ▶ **en torno a** *loc* *prep* **1.** (*alrededor de*) around. **2.** (*acerca de*) about; **girar en ~ a** to be about.

toro *m* bull. ▶ **toros** *mpl* (*lidia*) bullfight (*sg*), bullfighting (U).

toronja *f* grapefruit.

torpe *adj* **1.** (*gen*) clumsy. **2.** (*necio*) slow, dim-witted.

torpedear *vt* to torpedo.

torpedero *m* torpedo boat.

torpedo *m* (*proyectil*) torpedo.

torpeza *f* **1.** (*gen*) clumsiness; **fue una ~ hacerlo/decirlo** it was a clumsy thing to do/say. **2.** (*falta de inteligencia*) slowness.

torre *f* **1.** (*construcción*) tower; (ELECTR) pylon; **~ (de apartamentos)** tower block; **~ de control** control tower; **~ de perforación** oil derrick. **2.** (*en ajedrez*) rook, castle. **3.** (MIL) turret.

torrefacto, -ta *adj* high-roast (*antes de sust*).

torrencial *adj* torrential.

torrente *m* torrent; **un ~ de** *fig* (*gente, palabras etc*) a stream o flood of; (*dinero, energía*) masses of.

torreta *f* **1.** (MIL) turret. **2.** (ELECTR) pylon.

torrezno *m* chunk of fried bacon.

tórrido, -da *adj* torrid.

torrija *f* French toast (U).

torsión *f* **1.** (*del cuerpo, brazo*) twist, twisting (U). **2.** (MEC) torsion.

torso *m culto* torso.

torta *f* **1.** (CULIN) cake. **2.** *fam* (*bofetada*) thump; **dar** o **pegar una ~ a alguien** to thump sb. ▶ **ni torta** *loc adv fam* not a thing.

tortazo *m* **1.** (*bofetada*) thump. **2.** (*accidente*) crash.

tortícolis *f inv* crick in the neck.

tortilla *f* **1.** (*de huevos*) omelette; **~ de patatas, ~ (a la) española** Spanish o potato omelette; **~ (a la) francesa** French o plain omelette. **2.** (*de maíz*) tortilla.

tórtola *f* turtledove.

tortolito, -ta *m y f* (*gen pl*) *fam* (*enamorado*) lovebird.

tortuga *f* (*terrestre*) tortoise; (*marina*) turtle; (*fluvial*) terrapin.

tortuoso, -sa *adj* **1.** (*sinuoso*) tortuous, winding. **2.** *fig* (*perverso*) devious.

tortura *f* torture.

torturar *vt* to torture.

tos *f* cough; **~ ferina = tosferina**.

tosco, -ca *adj* **1.** (*basto*) crude. **2.** *fig* (*ignorante*) coarse.

toser *vi* to cough.

tosferina, tos ferina *f* whooping cough.

tostado, -da *adj* **1.** (*pan, almendras*) toasted. **2.** (*color*) brownish. **3.** (*piel*) tanned. ▶ **tostada** *f* piece of toast.

tostador *m*, **tostadora** *f* toaster.

tostar *vt* **1.** (*dorar, calentar - pan, almendras*) to toast; (- *carne*) to brown. **2.** (*broncear*) to tan. ▶ **tostarse** *vpr* to get brown.

tostón *m fam fig* (*rollo, aburrimiento*) bore, drag.

total ♦ *adj* total. ♦ *m* **1.** (*suma*) total. **2.** (*totalidad, conjunto*) whole; **el ~ del grupo** the whole group; **en ~** in all. ♦ *adv* anyway; **~ que me marché** so anyway, I left.

totalidad *f* whole; **en su ~** as a whole.

totalitario, -ria *adj* totalitarian.

totalizar *vt* to amount to.

tóxico, -ca *adj* toxic, poisonous. ▶ **tóxico** *m* poison.

toxicómano, -na *m y f* drug addict.

toxina *f* toxin.

tozudo, -da *adj* stubborn.

traba *f fig* (*obstáculo*) obstacle; **poner ~s (a alguien)** to put obstacles in the way (of sb).

trabajador, -ra ♦ *adj* hard-working. ♦ *m y f* worker.

trabajar ♦ *vi* **1.** (*gen*) to work; **~ de/en** to work as/in; **~ en una empresa** to work for a firm. **2.** (CIN & TEATR) to act. ♦ *vt* **1.** (*hierro, barro, tierra*) to work; (*masa*) to knead. **2.** (*mejorar*) to work on o at.

trabajo *m* **1.** (*gen*) work; **hacer un buen ~** to do a good job; **~ intelectual/físico** mental/physical effort; **~ manual** manual labour; **~s manuales** (*en el colegio*) arts and crafts. **2.** (*empleo*) job; **no tener ~** to be out of work. **3.** (*estudio escrito*) essay. **4.** (POLÍT) labour. **5.** *fig* (*esfuerzo*) effort.

trabajoso, -sa *adj* **1.** (*difícil*) hard, difficult. **2.** (*molesto*) tiresome.

trabalenguas *m inv* tongue-twister.

trabar *vt* **1.** (*sujetar*) to fasten; (*a preso*) to shackle. **2.** (*unir*) to join. **3.** (*iniciar - conversación, amistad*) to strike up. **4.** (*obstaculizar*) to hinder. **5.** (CULIN) to thicken. ▶ **trabarse** *vpr* **1.** (*enredarse*) to get tangled. **2.** *loc*: **se le trabó la lengua** he got tongue-tied.

trabazón *f fig* (*conexión, enlace*) link, connection.

trabucar *vt* to mix up.

tracción *f* traction; **~ delantera/trasera** front-wheel/rear-wheel drive.

tractor, -ra *adj* tractive. ▶ **tractor** *m* tractor.

tradición f tradition.

tradicional adj traditional.

tradicionalismo m traditionalism; (POLÍT) conservatism.

traducción f translation.

traducir ◆ vt (a otro idioma) to translate. ◆ vi: ~ (de/a) to translate (from/into). ▶ **traducirse** vpr (a otro idioma): ~se (por) to be translated (by o as).

traductor, -ra m y f translator.

traer vt 1. (trasladar, provocar) to bring; (consecuencias) to carry, to have; ~ consigo (implicar) to mean, to lead to. 2. (llevar) to carry; ¿qué traes ahí? what have you got there? 3. (llevar adjunto, dentro) to have; trae un artículo interesante it has an interesting article in it. 4. (llevar puesto) to wear. ▶ **traerse** vpr: traérselas fam fig to be a real handful.

traficante m y f (de drogas, armas etc) trafficker.

traficar vi: ~ (en/con algo) to traffic (in sthg).

tráfico m (gen) traffic.

tragaluz m skylight.

traganíqueles f inv Amer fam → máquina.

tragaperras f inv slot machine.

tragar ◆ vt 1. (ingerir, creer) to swallow. 2. (absorber) to swallow up. 3. fig (soportar) to put up with. ◆ vi to swallow. ▶ **tragarse** vpr fig (soportarse): no se tragan they can't stand each other.

tragedia f tragedy.

trágico, -ca adj tragic.

trago m 1. (de líquido) mouthful; de un ~ in one gulp. 2. fam (copa) drink. 3. fam fig (disgusto): ser un ~ para alguien to be tough on sb.

tragón, -ona fam ◆ adj greedy. ◆ m y f pig, glutton.

traición f 1. (infidelidad) betrayal. 2. (DER) treason.

traicionar vt lit & fig (ser infiel) to betray.

traicionero, -ra adj (desleal) treacherous; (DER) treasonous.

traidor, -ra ◆ adj treacherous; (DER) treasonous. ◆ m y f traitor.

traiga etc → traer.

trailer ['trailer] (pl trailers) m 1. (CIN) trailer. 2. (AUTOM) articulated lorry.

traje m 1. (con chaqueta) suit; (de una pieza) dress; ~ de baño swimsuit; ~ de chaqueta woman's two-piece suit. 2. (regional, de época etc) costume; ~ de luces matador's outfit. 3. (ropa) clothes (pl); ~ de paisano (de militar) civilian clothes; (de policía) plain clothes.

trajeado, -da adj fam (arreglado) spruced up.

trajín m fam fig (ajetreo) bustle.

trajinar vi fam fig to bustle about.

trajo → traer.

trama f 1. (de hilos) weft. 2. fig (confabulación) intrigue. 3. (LITER) plot.

tramar vt 1. (hilo) to weave. 2. fam fig (planear) to plot; (complot) to hatch; estar tramando algo to be up to something.

tramitar vt 1. (suj: autoridades - pasaporte, permiso) to take the necessary steps to obtain; (- solicitud, dimisión) to process. 2. (suj: solicitante): ~ un permiso to be in the process of applying for a licence.

trámite m (gestión) formal step; de ~ routine, formal. ▶ **trámites** mpl 1. (proceso) procedure (sg). 2. (papeleo) paperwork (U).

tramo m 1. (espacio) section, stretch. 2. (de escalera) flight (of stairs).

tramoya f (TEATR) stage machinery (U).

trampa f 1. (para cazar) trap. 2. fig (engaño) trick; tender una ~ (a alguien) to set o lay a trap (for sb); hacer ~s to cheat. 3. fig (deuda) debt.

trampear vi fam (estafar) to swindle money.

trampilla f (en el suelo) trapdoor.

trampolín m (de piscina) diving board; (de esquí) ski jump; (en gimnasia) springboard.

tramposo, -sa ◆ adj (fullero) cheating. ◆ m y f (fullero) cheat.

tranca f 1. (de puerta o ventana) bar. 2. (arma) cudgel. 3. loc: a ~s y barrancas with great difficulty.

trance m 1. (apuro) difficult situation; estar en ~ de hacer algo to be about to do sthg; pasar por un mal ~ to go through a bad patch. 2. (estado hipnótico) trance.

tranquilidad f peacefulness, tranquillity; para mayor ~ to be on the safe side.

tranquilizante m (FARM) tranquilizer.

tranquilizar vt 1. (calmar) to calm (down). 2. (dar confianza) to reassure. ▶ **tranquilizarse** vpr 1. (calmarse) to calm down. 2. (ganar confianza) to feel reassured.

tranquillo m fam: coger el ~ a algo to get the knack of sthg.

tranquilo, -la adj 1. (sosegado - lugar,

música) peaceful; (*- persona*) relaxed; (*- tono de voz, mar*) calm; (*- viento*) gentle; **¡(tú) ~!** *fam* don't you worry! **2.** (*velada, charla, negocio*) quiet. **3.** (*mente*) untroubled; (*conciencia*) clear. **4.** (*despreocupado*) casual, laid-back.

transacción *f* (COM) transaction.

transar *vi* Amer to compromise.

transatlántico, -ca *adj* transatlantic.
▶ **transatlántico** *m* (NÁUT) (ocean) liner.

transbordador *m* **1.** (NÁUT) ferry. **2.** (AERON): **~ (espacial)** space shuttle.

transbordar ♦ *vt* to transfer. ♦ *vi* to change (*trains etc*).

transbordo *m*: **hacer ~** to change (*trains etc*).

transcendencia *f* importance; **tener una gran ~** to be deeply significant.

transcendental *adj* **1.** (*importante*) momentous. **2.** (*meditación*) transcendental.

transcendente *adj* momentous.

transcender *vi* **1.** (*extenderse*): **~ (a algo)** to spread (across sthg). **2.** (*filtrarse*) to be leaked. **3.** (*sobrepasar*): **~ de** to transcend, to go beyond.

transcribir *vt* (*escribir*) to transcribe.

transcurrir *vi* **1.** (*tiempo*) to pass, to go by. **2.** (*ocurrir*) to take place.

transcurso *m* **1.** (*paso de tiempo*) passing. **2.** (*período de tiempo*): **en el ~ de** in the course of.

transeúnte *m y f* (*paseante*) passer-by.

transexual *adj, m y f* transsexual.

transferencia *f* transfer.

transferir *vt* to transfer.

transfigurar *vt* to transfigure.

transformación *f* transformation.

transformador, -ra *adj* transforming. ▶ **transformador** *m* (ELECTRÓN) transformer.

transformar *vt* **1.** (*cambiar radicalmente*): **~ algo/a alguien (en)** to transform sthg/sb (into). **2.** (*convertir*): **~ algo (en)** to convert sthg (into). **3.** (*en rugby*) to convert. ▶ **transformarse** *vpr* **1.** (*cambiar radicalmente*) to be transformed. **2.** (*convertirse*): **~se en algo** to be converted into sthg.

tránsfuga *m y f* (POLÍT) defector.

transfusión *f* transfusion.

transgredir *vt* to transgress.

transgresor, -ra *m y f* transgressor.

transición *f* transition; **período de ~** transition period; **~ democrática** transition to democracy.

transido, -da *adj*: **~ (de)** stricken

(with); **~ de pena** grief-stricken.

transigir *vi* **1.** (*ceder*) to compromise. **2.** (*ser tolerante*) to be tolerant.

transistor *m* transistor.

transitar *vi* to go (along).

tránsito *m* **1.** (*circulación - gen*) movement; (*- de coches*) traffic. **2.** (*transporte*) transit.

transitorio, -ria *adj* (*gen*) transitory; (*residencia*) temporary; (*régimen, medida*) transitional, interim.

translúcido, -da *adj* translucent.

transmisión *f* **1.** (*gen* & AUTOM) transmission; (*de saludos, noticias*) passing on. **2.** (RADIO & TV) broadcast, broadcasting (U). **3.** (*de herencia, poderes etc*) transference.

transmisor, -ra *adj* transmission (*antes de sust*). ▶ **transmisor** *m* transmitter.

transmitir *vt* **1.** (*gen*) to transmit; (*saludos, noticias*) to pass on. **2.** (RADIO & TV) to broadcast. **3.** (*ceder*) to transfer.

transparencia *f* transparency.

transparentarse *vpr* (*tela*) to be see-through; (*vidrio, líquido*) to be transparent.

transparente *adj* (*gen*) transparent; (*tela*) see-through.

transpiración *f* perspiration; (BOT) transpiration.

transpirar *vi* to perspire; (BOT) to transpire.

transplantar *vt* to transplant.

transplante *m* transplant, transplanting (U).

transponer *vt* (*cambiar*) to switch. ▶ **transponerse** *vpr* (*adormecerse*) to doze off.

transportador *m* (*para medir ángulos*) protractor.

transportar *vt* **1.** (*llevar - gen*) to carry; (*- suj: vehículo*) to transport. **2.** (*embelesar*) to captivate. ▶ **transportarse** *vpr* (*embelesarse*) to go into raptures.

transporte *m* transport; **~ público o colectivo** public transport.

transportista *m y f* carrier.

transvase *m* **1.** (*de líquido*) decanting. **2.** (*de río*) transfer.

transversal *adj* transverse.

tranvía *m* tram, streetcar Am.

trapecio *m* (*de gimnasia*) trapeze.

trapecista *m y f* trapeze artist.

trapero, -ra *m y f* rag-and-bone man (*f* rag-and-bone woman).

trapío *m culto* (TAUROM) good bearing.

trapisonda *f fam* (*enredo*) scheme.

trapo *m* **1.** (*trozo de tela*) rag. **2.** (*gamuza, bayeta*) cloth; **poner a alguien como un ~** to tear sb to pieces. ► **trapos** *mpl fam* (*ropa*) clothes.

tráquea *f* windpipe, trachea (MED).

traquetear ◆ *vt* to shake. ◆ *vi* (*hacer ruido*) to rattle.

traqueteo *m* (*ruido*) rattling.

tras *prep* **1.** (*detrás de*) behind. **2.** (*después de, en pos de*) after; **uno ~ otro** one after the other; **andar ~ algo** to be after sthg.

trasatlántico, -ca = transatlántico.

trasbordador = transbordador.

trasbordar = transbordar.

trasbordo = transbordo.

trascendencia = transcendencia.

trascendental = transcendental.

trascendente = transcendente.

trascender = transcender.

trascribir = transcribir.

trascurrir = transcurrir.

trascurso = transcurso.

trasegar *vt* (*desordenar*) to rummage about amongst.

trasero, -ra *adj* back (*antes de sust*), rear (*antes de sust*). ► **trasero** *m fam* backside.

trasferencia = transferencia.

trasferir = transferir.

trasfigurar = transfigurar.

trasfondo *m* background; (*de palabras, intenciones*) undertone.

trasformación = transformación.

trasformador, -ra = transformador.

trasformar = transformar.

trásfuga = tránsfuga.

trasfusión = transfusión.

trasgredir = transgredir.

trasgresor, -ra = transgresor.

trashumante *adj* seasonally migratory.

trasiego *m* (*movimiento*) comings and goings (*pl*).

traslación *f* (ASTRON) passage.

trasladar *vt* **1.** (*desplazar*) to move. **2.** (*a empleado, funcionario*) to transfer. **3.** (*reunión, fecha*) to postpone. ► **trasladarse** *vpr* **1.** (*desplazarse*) to go. **2.** (*mudarse*) to move; **me traslado de piso** I'm moving flat.

traslado *m* **1.** (*de casa, empresa, muebles*) move, moving (U). **2.** (*de trabajo*) transfer. **3.** (*de personas*) movement.

traslúcido, -da = translúcido.

trasluz *m* reflected light; **al ~** against the light.

trasmisión = transmisión.

trasmisor, -ra = transmisor.

trasmitir = transmitir.

trasnochar *vi* to stay up late.

traspapelar *vt* (*papeles, documentos*) to mislay.

trasparencia = transparencia.

trasparentarse = transparentarse.

trasparente = transparente.

traspasar *vt* **1.** (*atravesar*) to go through, to pierce. **2.** (*cruzar*) to cross (over); (*puerta*) to pass through. **3.** (*suj: líquido*) to soak through. **4.** (*jugador*) to transfer. **5.** (*negocio*) to sell (as a going concern). **6.** *fig* (*exceder*) to go beyond.

traspaso *m* (*venta - de jugador*) transfer; (*- de negocio*) sale (as a going concern).

traspié (*pl* traspiés) *m* **1.** (*resbalón*) trip, stumble; **dar un ~** to trip up. **2.** *fig* (*error*) slip.

traspiración = transpiración.

traspirar = transpirar.

trasplantar = transplantar.

trasplante = transplante.

trasponer = transponer.

trasportar *etc* = transportar.

trasquilar *vt* (*esquilar*) to shear.

trastabillar *vi* Amer to stagger.

trastada *f* dirty trick; **hacer una ~ a alguien** to play a dirty trick on sb.

traste *m* **1.** (MÚS) fret. **2.** *loc:* **dar al ~ con algo** to ruin sthg; **irse al ~** to fall through.

trastero *m* junk room.

trastienda *f* backroom.

trasto *m* **1.** (*utensilio inútil*) piece of junk, junk (U). **2.** *fam fig* (*persona traviesa*) menace, nuisance. ► **trastos** *mpl fam* (*pertenencias, equipo*) things, stuff (U); **tirarse los ~s a la cabeza** to have a flaming row.

trastocar *vt* (*cambiar*) to turn upside down. ► **trastocarse** *vpr* (*enloquecer*) to go mad.

trastornado, -da *adj* disturbed, unbalanced.

trastornar *vt* **1.** (*volver loco*) to drive mad. **2.** (*inquietar*) to worry, to trouble. **3.** (*alterar*) to turn upside down; (*planes*) to disrupt. ► **trastornarse** *vpr* (*volverse loco*) to go mad.

trastorno *m* **1.** (*mental*) disorder; (*digestivo*) upset. **2.** (*alteración - por huelga, nevada*) disruption (U); (*- por guerra etc*) upheaval.

trastrocar *vt* (*cambiar de orden*) to switch o change round.

trasvase = transvase.

tratable adj easy-going, friendly.
tratado m 1. (convenio) treaty. 2. (escrito) treatise.
tratamiento m 1. (gen & MED) treatment. 2. (título) title, form of address. 3. (INFORM) processing; ~ **de datos/textos** data/word processing; ~ **por lotes** batch processing.
tratar ♦ vt 1. (gen & MED) to treat. 2. (discutir) to discuss. 3. (INFORM) to process. 4. (dirigirse a): ~ **a alguien de** (usted, tú etc) to address sb as. ♦ vi 1. (versar): ~ **de/sobre** to be about. 2. (tener relación): ~ **con alguien** to mix with sb, to have dealings with sb. 3. (intentar): ~ **de hacer algo** to try to do sthg. 4. (utilizar): ~ **con** to deal with, to use. 5. (comerciar): ~ **en** to deal in. ► **tratarse** vpr 1. (relacionarse): ~**se con** to mix with, to have dealings with. 2. (versar): ~**se de** to be about; **¿de qué se trata?** what's it about?
tratativas fpl Amer procedure (sg).
trato m 1. (comportamiento, conducto) treatment; **de ~ agradable** pleasant; **malos ~s** battering (U) (of child, wife). 2. (relación) dealings (pl). 3. (acuerdo) deal; **cerrar** o **hacer un ~** to do o make a deal; **¡~ hecho!** it's a deal! 4. (tratamiento) title, term of address.
trauma m trauma.
traumatólogo, -ga m y f traumatologist.
través ► **a través de** loc prep 1. (de un lado a otro de) across, over. 2. (por, por medio de) through. ► **de través** loc adv (transversalmente) crossways; (de lado) sideways.
travesaño m 1. (ARQUIT) crosspiece. 2. (DEP) crossbar.
travesía f 1. (viaje - por mar) voyage, crossing. 2. (calle) cross-street.
travestido, -da, travestí (pl travestís) m y f transvestite.
travesura f prank, mischief (U).
traviesa f 1. (FERROC) sleeper (on track). 2. (CONSTR) crossbeam.
travieso, -sa adj mischievous.
trayecto m 1. (distancia) distance; **final de ~** end of the line. 2. (viaje) journey, trip. 3. (ruta) route.
trayectoria f 1. (recorrido) trajectory. 2. fig (evolución) path.
traza f (aspecto) appearance (U), looks (pl).
trazado m 1. (trazo) outline, sketching. 2. (diseño) plan, design. 3. (recorrido) route.

trazar vt 1. (dibujar) to draw, to trace; (ruta) to plot. 2. (indicar, describir) to outline. 3. (idear) to draw up.
trazo m 1. (de dibujo, rostro) line. 2. (de letra) stroke.
trébol m (planta) clover. ► **tréboles** mpl (naipes) clubs.
trece núm thirteen; ver también **seis**.
treceavo, -va núm thirteenth.
trecho m (espacio) distance; (tiempo) time.
tregua f truce; fig respite.
treinta núm thirty; **los (años)** ~ the Thirties; ver también **seis**.
treintena f thirty.
tremendo, -da adj (enorme) tremendous, enormous. ► **tremenda** f: **tomar** o **tomarse algo a la tremenda** to take sthg hard.
trémulo, -la adj (voz) trembling; (luz) flickering.
tren m 1. (ferrocarril) train; ~ **de alta velocidad/largo recorrido** high-speed/ long-distance train; ~ **semidirecto** through train, a section of which becomes a stopping train; **estar como (para parar) un** ~ to be really gorgeous; **perder el** ~ fig to miss the boat. 2. (TECN) line; ~ **de aterrizaje** undercarriage; ~ **de lavado** car wash.
trenza f 1. (de pelo) plait. 2. (de fibras) braid.
trenzar vt 1. (pelo) to plait. 2. (fibras) to braid.
trepa m y f fam social climber.
trepador, -ra ♦ adj: **planta trepadora** creeper. ♦ m y f fam social climber.
trepar ♦ vt to climb. ♦ vi 1. (subir) to climb. 2. fam fig (medrar) to be a social climber.
trepidar vi to shake, to vibrate.
tres núm three; **ni a la de** ~ for anything in the world, no way; ver también **seis**. ► **tres cuartos** m inv (abrigo) three-quarter-length coat. ► **tres en raya** m noughts and crosses (U) Br, tick-tack-toe Am.
trescientos, -tas núm three hundred; ver también **seis**.
tresillo m (sofá) sofa; (sofá y dos sillones) three-piece suite.
treta f (engaño) trick.
triangular adj triangular.
triángulo m (GEOM & MÚS) triangle.
triates mpl Amer triplets.
tribu f tribe.
tribulación f tribulation.
tribuna f 1. (estrado) rostrum, plat-

form; (del jurado) jury box. **2.** (DEP - localidad) stand; (- graderío) grandstand. **3.** (PRENS): **~ de prensa** press box; **~ libre** open forum.

tribunal m **1.** (gen) court; **llevar a alguien/acudir a los ~es** to take sb/go to court. **2.** (de examen) board of examiners; (de concurso) panel.

tributable adj taxable.

tributar vt (homenaje) to pay; (respeto, admiración) to have.

tributo m **1.** (impuesto) tax. **2.** fig (precio) price. **3.** (homenaje) tribute.

triciclo m tricycle.

tricornio m three-cornered hat.

tricot m inv knitting (U).

tricotar vt & vi to knit.

tricotosa f knitting machine.

tridimensional adj three-dimensional.

trifulca f fam row, squabble.

trigésimo, -ma núm thirtieth.

trigo m wheat.

trigonometría f trigonometry.

trillado, -da adj fig trite.

trillar vt to thresh.

trillizo, -za m y f triplet.

trilogía f trilogy.

trimestral adj three-monthly, quarterly; (exámenes, notas) end-of-term (antes de sust).

trimestre m three months (pl), quarter; (en escuela, universidad) term.

trinar vi to chirp; **está que trina** fig she's fuming.

trincar fam ◆ vt (detener) to nick, to arrest. ◆ vi (beber) to guzzle.

trincha f strap.

trinchante m (tenedor) meat fork.

trinchar vt to carve.

trinchera f (MIL) trench.

trineo m (pequeño) sledge; (grande) sleigh.

Trinidad f: **la (Santísima) ~** the (Holy) Trinity.

Trinidad y Tobago Trinidad and Tobago.

trino m (de pájaros) chirp, chirping (U); (MÚS) trill.

trío m (gen) trio.

tripa f **1.** (intestino) gut, intestine. **2.** fam (barriga) gut, belly. ► **tripas** fpl fig (interior) insides.

triple ◆ adj triple. ◆ m: **el ~** three times as much; **el ~ de gente** three times as many people.

triplicado m second copy, triplicate.

triplicar vt to triple, to treble. ► **tri-**

plicarse vpr to triple, to treble.

trípode m tripod.

tripulación f crew.

tripulante m y f crew member.

tripular vt to man.

tris m: **estar en un ~ de** fig to be within a whisker of.

triste adj **1.** (gen) sad; (día, tiempo, paisaje) gloomy, dreary; **es ~ que** it's a shame o pity that. **2.** fig (color, vestido, luz) pale. **3.** (antes de sust) (humilde) poor; (sueldo) sorry, miserable.

tristeza f (gen) sadness; (de paisaje, día) gloominess, dreariness.

triturador m (de basura) waste-disposal unit; (de papeles) shredder.

triturar vt **1.** (moler, desmenuzar) to crush, to grind; (papel) to shred. **2.** (mascar) to chew.

triunfador, -ra m y f winner.

triunfal adj triumphant.

triunfar vi **1.** (vencer) to win, to triumph. **2.** (tener éxito) to succeed, to be successful.

triunfo m (gen) triumph; (en encuentro, elecciones) victory, win.

trivial adj trivial.

trivializar vt to trivialize.

trizas fpl piece (sg), bit (sg); **hacer ~ algo** (hacer añicos) to smash sthg to pieces; (desgarrar) to tear sthg to shreds; **estar hecho ~** (persona) to be shattered.

trocar vt **1.** (transformar): **~ algo (en algo)** to change sthg (into sthg). **2.** (intercambiar) to swap.

trocear vt to cut up (into pieces).

trocha f Amer path.

troche ► **a troche y moche** loc adv haphazardly.

trofeo m trophy.

troglodita m y f **1.** (cavernícola) cave dweller, troglodyte. **2.** fam (bárbaro, tosco) roughneck.

trola f fam fib, lie.

trolebús m trolleybus.

trombón m (MÚS - instrumento) trombone; (- músico) trombonist.

trombosis f inv thrombosis.

trompa f **1.** (MÚS) horn. **2.** (de elefante) trunk; (de oso hormiguero) snout. **3.** fam (borrachera): **coger o pillar una ~** to get plastered.

trompazo m bang.

trompear vt Amer fam to punch. ► **trompearse** vpr Amer fam to have a fight.

trompeta f trumpet.

trompetista m y f trumpeter.

trompicón m (tropezón) stumble; **a trompicones** in fits and starts.

trompo m spinning top.

tronado, -da adj fam (radio etc) old, broken-down. ► **tronada** f thunderstorm.

tronar v impers & vi to thunder. ► **tronarse** vpr Amer fam to shoot o.s.

tronchar vt (partir) to snap. ► **troncharse** vpr fam: **~se (de risa)** to split one's sides laughing.

tronco m (ANAT & BOT) trunk; (talado y sin ramas) log; **dormir como un ~, estar hecho un ~** to sleep like a log.

tronera f 1. (ARQUIT & HIST) embrasure. 2. (en billar) pocket.

trono m throne.

tropa f (gen pl) (MIL) troops (pl).

tropel m (de personas) mob, crowd.

tropero m Amer cowboy.

tropezar vi (con pie): **~ (con)** to trip o stumble (on). ► **tropezarse** vpr fam (encontrar) to bump into each other; **~se con alguien** to bump into sb. ► **tropezar con** vi (problema, persona) to run into, to come across.

tropezón m 1. (tropiezo) trip, stumble; **dar un ~** to trip up, to stumble. 2. fig (desacierto) slip-up. ► **tropezones** mpl (CULIN) small chunks of meat.

tropical adj tropical.

trópico m tropic.

tropiezo m 1. (tropezón) trip, stumble; **dar un ~** to trip up, to stumble. 2. fig (equivocación) slip-up. 3. (revés) setback.

troquel m (molde) mould, die.

trotamundos m y f inv globe-trotter.

trotar vi to trot; fam fig (andar mucho) to dash o run around.

trote m (de caballo) trot; **al ~** at a trot.

troupe [trup, 'trupe] (pl **troupes**) f troupe.

trovador m troubadour.

trozo m (gen) piece; (de obra, película) extract; **cortar algo a ~s** to cut sthg into pieces.

trucar vt to doctor; (motor) to soup up.

trucha f (pez) trout.

truco m 1. (trampa, engaño) trick. 2. (habilidad, técnica) knack; **coger el ~ to** get the knack; **~ publicitario** advertising gimmick.

truculento, -ta adj horrifying, terrifying.

trueno m (METEOR) clap of thunder, thunder (U).

trueque m 1. (COM & HIST) barter. 2. (intercambio) exchange, swap.

trufa f (hongo, bombón) truffle.

truhán, -ana m y f rogue, crook.

truncar vt (frustrar - vida, carrera) to cut short; (- planes, ilusiones) to spoil, to ruin.

trusa f Amer 1. (calzoncillos) underpants (pl). 2. (bragas) knickers (pl).

tu (pl **tus**) adj poses (antes de sust) your.

tú pron pers you; **es más alta que ~** she's taller than you; **de ~ a ~** (lucha) evenly matched; **hablar o tratar de ~ a alguien** to address sb as 'tú'.

tubérculo m tuber, root vegetable.

tuberculosis f inv tuberculosis.

tubería f 1. (cañerías) pipes (pl), pipework. 2. (tubo) pipe.

tubo m 1. (tubería) pipe; **~ de escape** (AUTOM) exhaust (pipe); **~ del desagüe** drainpipe. 2. (recipiente) tube; **~ de ensayo** test tube. 3. (ANAT) tract; **~ digestivo** digestive tract.

tuerca f nut.

tuerto, -ta adj (sin un ojo) one-eyed; (ciego de un ojo) blind in one eye.

tuétano m (ANAT) (bone) marrow.

tufillo m whiff.

tufo m (mal olor) stench.

tugurio m hovel.

tul m tulle.

tulipa f (tulipán) tulip.

tulipán m tulip.

tullido, -da ◆ adj crippled. ◆ m y f cripple, disabled person.

tumba f grave, tomb; **ser (como) una ~** to be as silent as the grave.

tumbar vt (derribar) to knock over o down. ► **tumbarse** vpr (acostarse) to lie down.

tumbo m jolt, jerk.

tumbona f (en la playa) deck chair; (en el jardín) (sun) lounger.

tumor m tumour.

tumulto m 1. (disturbio) riot, disturbance. 2. (alboroto) uproar, tumult.

tumultuoso, -sa adj 1. (conflictivo) tumultuous. 2. (turbulento) rough, stormy.

tuna f → **tuno**.

tunante, -ta m y f crook, scoundrel.

tunda f fam (paliza) thrashing.

túnel m tunnel. ► **túnel de lavado** m (AUTOM) car wash.

Túnez 1. (capital) Tunis. 2. (país) Tunisia.

túnica f tunic.

Tunicia Tunisia.

tuno, -na *m y f* rogue, scoundrel.
▶ **tuna** *f* group of student minstrels.

TUNA

A 'tuna' is a musical group made up of university students who wear black capes and coloured ribbons. They wander the streets playing music, singing and dancing, either for pleasure or to collect money.

tuntún ▶ **al tuntún** *loc adv* without thinking.

tupé *m* (*cabello*) quiff.

tupido, -da *adj* thick, dense.

turba *f* 1. (*combustible*) peat, turf. 2. (*muchedumbre*) mob.

turbación *f* 1. (*desconcierto*) upset, disturbance. 2. (*azoramiento*) embarrassment.

turbante *m* turban.

turbar *vt* 1. (*alterar*) to disturb. 2. (*emocionar*) to upset. 3. (*desconcertar*) to trouble, to disconcert. ▶ **turbarse** *vpr* (*emocionarse*) to get upset.

turbina *f* turbine.

turbio, -bia *adj* 1. (*agua etc*) cloudy. 2. (*vista*) blurred. 3. *fig* (*negocio etc*) shady. 4. *fig* (*época etc*) turbulent.

turbulencia *f* 1. (*de fluido*) turbulence. 2. (*alboroto*) uproar, clamour.

turbulento, -ta *adj* 1. (*gen*) turbulent. 2. (*revoltoso*) unruly, rebellious.

turco, -ca ◆ *adj* Turkish. ◆ *m y f* (*persona*) Turk. ▶ **turco** *m* (*lengua*) Turkish.

turismo *m* 1. (*gen*) tourism; **hacer ~ (por)** to go touring (round). 2. (AUTOM) private car.

turista *m y f* tourist.

turístico, -ca *adj* tourist (*antes de sust*).

turnarse *vpr*: **~ (con alguien)** to take turns (with sb).

turno *m* 1. (*tanda*) turn, go. 2. (*de trabajo*) shift; **~ de día/noche** day/night shift.

turquesa ◆ *f* (*mineral*) turquoise. ◆ *adj inv* (*color*) turquoise. ◆ *m* (*color*) turquoise.

Turquía Turkey.

turrón *m* Christmas sweet similar to marzipan or nougat, made with almonds and honey.

tururú *interj fam*: **¡~!** you must be joking!

tute *m* (*juego*) card game similar to whist.

tutear *vt* to address as 'tú'. ▶ **tutearse** *vpr* to address each other as 'tú'.

tutela *f* 1. (DER) guardianship. 2. (*cargo*): **~ (de)** responsibility (for); **bajo la ~ de** under the protection of.

tutelar ◆ *adj* (DER) tutelary. ◆ *vt* to act as guardian to.

tutor, -ra *m y f* 1. (DER) guardian. 2. (*profesor - privado*) tutor; (*- de un curso*) form teacher.

tutoría *f* (DER) guardianship.

tutú (*pl* **tutús**) *m* tutu.

tuviera *etc* → **tener**.

tuyo, -ya ◆ *adj poses* yours; **este libro es ~** this book is yours; **un amigo ~** a friend of yours; **no es asunto ~** it's none of your business. ◆ *pron poses*: **el ~** yours; **el ~ es rojo** yours is red; **ésta es la tuya** *fam* this is the chance you've been waiting for; **lo ~ es el teatro** (*lo que haces bien*) you should be on the stage; **los ~s** *fam* (*tu familia*) your folks; (*tu bando*) your lot.

TV (*abrev de* **televisión**) *f* TV.

TV3 (*abrev de* **Televisión de Cataluña, SA**) *f* Catalan television channel.

TVE (*abrev de* **Televisión Española**) *f* Spanish state television network.

TVG (*abrev de* **Televisión de Galicia**) *f* Galician television channel.

TVV (*abrev de* **Televisión Valenciana, SA**) *f* Valencian television channel.

U

u¹, U *f* (*letra*) u, U.

u² *conj* or; *ver también* **o²**.

ubicación *f* position, location.

ubicar *vt* to place, to position; (*edificio etc*) to locate. ▶ **ubicarse** *vpr* (*edificio etc*) to be situated.

ubre *f* udder.

Ucrania the Ukraine.

Ud., Vd. *abrev de* **usted**.

Uds., Vds. *abrev de* **ustedes**.

UEFA (*abrev de* **Unión de Asociaciones Europeas de Fútbol**) *f* UEFA.

ufanarse *vpr*: **~ de** to boast about.

ufano, -na *adj* 1. (*satisfecho*) proud, pleased. 2. (*engreído*) boastful, conceited.

Uganda Uganda.

UGT (*abrev de* **Unión General de los Trabajadores**) *f* major socialist Spanish trade union.

UHF (*abrev de* **ultra high frequency**) *f* UHF.

ujier (*pl* ujieres) *m* usher.

újule *interj* Amer: ¡~! wow!

úlcera *f* (MED) ulcer.

ulcerar *vt* to ulcerate. ► **ulcerarse** *vpr* (MED) to ulcerate.

ulterior *adj culto* (*en el tiempo*) subsequent, ulterior.

ulteriormente *adv culto* subsequently.

ultimador, -ra *m y f* Amer killer.

últimamente *adv* recently.

ultimar *vt* 1. (*gen*) to conclude, to complete. 2. Amer (*matar*) to kill.

ultimátum (*pl* ultimátums *o* ultimatos) *m* ultimatum.

último, -ma ♦ *adj* 1. (*gen*) last; **por ~** lastly, finally. 2. (*más reciente*) latest, most recent. 3. (*más remoto*) furthest, most remote. 4. (*más bajo*) bottom. 5. (*más alto*) top. 6. (*de más atrás*) back. 7. (*definitivo - decisión, oferta*) final. ♦ *m y f* 1. (*en fila, carrera etc*): **el ~** the last (one); **llegar el ~** to come last. 2. (*en comparaciones, enumeraciones*): **éste ~ ...** the latter ...

ultra *m y f* (POLÍT) right-wing extremist.

ultraderecha *f* extreme right (wing).

ultraizquierda *f* extreme left (wing).

ultrajar *vt* to insult, to offend.

ultraje *m* insult.

ultramar *m* overseas (*pl*); **de ~** overseas (*antes de sust*).

ultramarino, -na *adj* overseas (*antes de sust*). ► **ultramarinos** ♦ *mpl* (*comestibles*) groceries. ♦ *m inv* (*tienda*) grocer's (shop) (*sg*).

ultranza ► **a ultranza** *loc adv* 1. (*con decisión*) to the death. 2. (*acérrimamente*) out-and-out.

ultrasonido *m* ultrasound.

ultratumba *f*: **de ~** from beyond the grave.

ultravioleta *adj inv* ultraviolet.

ulular *vi* 1. (*viento, lobo*) to howl. 2. (*búho*) to hoot.

umbilical *adj* → **cordón**.

umbral *m* 1. (*de puerta*) doorway; *fig* (*comienzo*) threshold. 2. *fig* (*límite*) bounds (*pl*), realms (*pl*).

un, una ♦ *art* (*antes de sust femenino que empiece por 'a' o 'ha' tónica:* **un**) a, an (*ante sonido vocálico*); **~ hombre/coche** a man/car; **una mujer/mesa** a woman/table; **~ águila/hacha** an eagle/axe; **una hora** an hour. ♦ *adj* → **uno**.

unánime *adj* unanimous.

unanimidad *f* unanimity; **por ~** unanimously.

unción *f* unction.

undécimo, -ma *núm* eleventh.

UNED (*abrev de* **Universidad Nacional de Educación a Distancia**) *f* Spanish open university.

ungüento *m* ointment.

únicamente *adv* only, solely.

único, -ca *adj* 1. (*sólo*) only; **es lo ~ que quiero** it's all I want; **el ~ sobreviviente** the sole survivor. 2. (*excepcional*) unique. 3. (*precio, función, razón*) single.

unicornio *m* unicorn.

unidad *f* 1. (*gen*, MAT & MIL) unit; **25 pesetas la ~** 25 pesetas each; **~ central de proceso** (INFORM) central processing unit; **~ de disco** (INFORM) disk drive. 2. (*cohesión, acuerdo*) unity.

unido, -da *adj* united; (*familia, amigo*) close.

unifamiliar *adj* detached.

unificar *vt* 1. (*unir*) to unite, to join; (*países*) to unify. 2. (*uniformar*) to standardize.

uniformar *vt* 1. (*igualar*) to standardize. 2. (*poner uniforme*) to put into uniform.

uniforme ♦ *adj* uniform; (*superficie*) even. ♦ *m* uniform.

uniformidad *f* uniformity; (*de superficie*) evenness.

unión *f* 1. (*gen*) union; **en ~ de** together with. 2. (*suma, adherimiento*) joining together. 3. (TECN) join, joint.

unir *vt* 1. (*pedazos, habitaciones etc*) to join. 2. (*empresas, estados, facciones*) to unite. 3. (*comunicar - ciudades etc*) to link. 4. (*suj: amistad, circunstancias etc*) to bind. 5. (*casar*) to join, to marry. 6. (*combinar*) to combine. 7. (*mezclar*) to mix *o* blend in. ► **unirse** *vpr* 1. (*gen*) to join together, to unite; **~se a algo** to join sthg. 2. (*casarse*): **~se en matrimonio** to be joined in wedlock.

unisexo, unisex *adj inv* unisex.

unísono ► **al unísono** *loc adv* in unison.

unitario, -ria *adj* 1. (*de una unidad - estado, nación*) single; (*- precio*) unit (*antes de sust*). 2. (POLÍT) unitarian.

universal *adj* 1. (*gen*) universal. 2. (*mundial*) world (*antes de sust*).

universidad *f* university.

universitario, -ria ♦ *adj* university (*antes de sust*). ♦ *m y f* (*estudiante*) university student.

universo *m* 1. (ASTRON) universe. 2. *fig* (*mundo*) world.

unívoco, -ca *adj* univocal, unambiguous.

uno, una ◆ *adj (antes de sust masculino sg:* **un**) **1.** (*indefinido*) one; **un día volveré** one o some day I'll return; **había ~s coches mal aparcados** there were some badly parked cars; **había ~s 12 muchachos** there were about o some 12 boys there. **2.** (*numeral*) one; **un hombre, un voto** one man, one vote; **la fila ~** row one. ◆ *pron* **1.** (*indefinido*) one; **coge ~** take one; **~ de vosotros** one of you; **~s ... otros ...** some ... others ...; **~ a otro, ~s a otros** each other, one another; **~ y otro** both; **~s y otros** all of them. **2.** *fam* (*cierta persona*) someone, somebody; **hablé con ~ que te conoce** I spoke to someone who knows you; **me lo han contado ~s** certain people told me so. **3.** (*yo*) one; **~ ya no está para estos trotes** one isn't really up to this sort of thing any more; **~ mismo, una misma** oneself. **4.** *loc:* **a una** (*en armonía, a la vez*) together; **de ~ en ~, ~ a ~, ~ por ~** one by one; **juntar varias cosas en una** to combine several things into one; **lo ~ por lo otro** it all evens out in the end; **más de ~** many people; **una de dos** it's either one thing or the other; **~s cuantos** a few; **una y no más** once bitten, twice shy. ▶ **uno** *m* (*número*) (number) one; **el ~** number one; *ver también* **seis**. ▶ **una** *f* (*hora*): **la una** one o'clock.

untar *vt* **1.** (*pan, tostada*): **~ (con)** to spread (with); (*piel, cara etc*) to smear (with). **2.** (*máquina, bisagra etc*) to grease.

untuoso, -sa *adj* greasy, oily.

uña *f* **1.** (*de mano*) fingernail, nail; **ser ~ y carne** to be as thick as thieves. **2.** (*de pie*) toenail. **3.** (*garra*) claw.

UPG (*abrev de* **Unión del Pueblo Gallego**) *f* Galician nationalist party.

UPN (*abrev de* **Unión del Pueblo Navarro**) *f* Navarrese nationalist party.

uralita® *f* (CONSTR) *material made of asbestos and cement, usually corrugated and used mainly for roofing.*

uranio *m* uranium.

Urano Uranus.

urbanidad *f* politeness, courtesy.

urbanismo *m* town planning.

urbanización *f* **1.** (*acción*) urbanization. **2.** (*zona residencial*) (housing) estate.

urbanizar *vt* to develop, to urbanize.

urbano, -na *adj* urban, city (*antes de sust*).

urbe *f* large city.

urdir *vt* **1.** (*planear*) to plot, to forge. **2.** (*hilos*) to warp.

urgencia *f* **1.** (*cualidad*) urgency. **2.** (*necesidad*) urgent need; **en caso de ~** in case of emergency. ▶ **urgencias** *fpl* (MED) casualty (department) (*sg*).

urgente *adj* **1.** (*apremiante*) urgent. **2.** (*correo*) express.

urgir *vi* to be urgently necessary; **me urge hacerlo** I urgently need to do it.

urinario, -ria *adj* urinary. ▶ **urinario** *m* urinal, comfort station *Am*.

urna *f* **1.** (*vasija*) urn. **2.** (*caja de cristal*) glass case. **3.** (*para votar*) ballot box.

urraca *f* magpie.

URSS (*abrev de* **Unión de Repúblicas Socialistas Soviéticas**) *f* USSR.

urticaria *f* nettle rash.

Uruguay **(el) ~** Uruguay.

uruguayo, -ya *adj, m y f* Uruguayan.

usado, -da *adj* **1.** (*utilizado*) used; **muy ~** widely-used. **2.** (*gastado*) worn-out, worn.

usanza *f*: **a la vieja ~** in the old way o style.

usar *vt* **1.** (*gen*) to use. **2.** (*prenda*) to wear. ▶ **usarse** *vpr* **1.** (*emplearse*) to be used. **2.** (*estar de moda*) to be worn.

uso *m* **1.** (*gen*) use; **al ~** fashionable; **al ~ andaluz** in the Andalusian style. **2.** (*gen pl*) (*costumbre*) custom. **3.** (LING) usage. **4.** (*desgaste*) wear and tear.

usted *pron pers* **1.** (*tratamiento de respeto - sg*) you; (*- pl*): **~es** you (*pl*); **contesten ~es a las preguntas** please answer the questions; **me gustaría hablar con ~** I'd like to talk to you. **2.** (*tratamiento de respeto - posesivo*): **de ~/~es** yours.

usual *adj* usual.

usuario, -ria *m y f* user.

usufructo *m* (DER) usufruct, use.

usura *f* usury.

usurero, -ra *m y f* usurer.

usurpar *vt* to usurp.

utensilio *m* (*gen*) tool, implement; (CULIN) utensil; **~s de pesca** fishing tackle.

útero *m* womb, uterus (MED).

útil ◆ *adj* (*beneficioso, aprovechable*) useful. ◆ *m* (*gen pl*) (*herramienta*) tool; (AGR) implement.

utilidad *f* **1.** (*cualidad*) usefulness. **2.** (*beneficio*) profit.

utilitario, -ria *adj* (AUTOM) utility. ▶ **utilitario** *m* (AUTOM) utility car.

utilización *f* use.

utilizar *vt* (*gen*) to use.

utopía *f* utopia.

utópico, -ca *adj* utopian.

uva *f* grape; **estar de mala ~** to be in a bad mood; **tener mala ~** to be a nasty piece of work; **~s de la suerte** *grapes eaten for good luck as midnight chimes on New Year's Eve.*

UVI (*abrev de* **unidad de vigilancia intensiva**) *f* ICU.

uy *interj*: ¡~! ahh!, oh!

v, V ['uβe] *f* (*letra*) v, V. ▶ **v doble** *f* W.

v. = **vid.**

va → **ir.**

vaca *f* 1. (*animal*) cow. 2. (*carne*) beef.

vacaciones *fpl* holiday (*sg*), holidays Br, vacation (*sg*) Am; **estar/irse de ~** to be/go on holiday.

vacante ◆ *adj* vacant. ◆ *f* vacancy.

vaciar *vt* 1. (*gen*): **~ algo (de)** to empty sthg (of). 2. (*dejar hueco*) to hollow (out). 3. (ARTE) to cast, to mould.

vacilación *f* 1. (*duda*) hesitation; (*al elegir*) indecision. 2. (*oscilación*) swaying; (*de la luz*) flickering.

vacilante *adj* 1. (*gen*) hesitant; (*al elegir*) indecisive. 2. (*luz*) flickering; (*pulso*) irregular; (*paso*) swaying, unsteady.

vacilar *vi* 1. (*dudar*) to hesitate; (*al elegir*) to be indecisive. 2. (*voz, principios, régimen*) to falter. 3. (*fluctuar - luz*) to flicker; (*- pulso*) to be irregular. 4. (*tambalearse*) to wobble, to sway. 5. *fam* (*chulear*) to swank. 6. *fam* (*bromear*) to take the mickey.

vacilón, -ona *fam m y f* 1. (*chulo*) show-off. 2. (*bromista*) tease. ▶ **vacilón** *m* Amer *fam* (*fiesta*) party.

vacío, -a *adj* empty. ▶ **vacío** *m* 1. (FÍS) vacuum; **envasar al ~** to vacuum-pack. 2. (*abismo, carencia*) void. 3. (*hueco*) space, gap.

vacuna *f* vaccine.

vacunar *vt* to vaccinate.

vacuno, -na *adj* bovine.

vadear *vt* to ford; *fig* to overcome.

vado *m* 1. (*en acera*) lowered kerb; **'~ permanente'** 'keep clear'. 2. (*de río*) ford.

vagabundear *vi* (*vagar*): **~ (por)** to wander, to roam.

vagabundo, -da ◆ *adj* (*persona*) vagrant; (*perro*) stray. ◆ *m y f* tramp, bum Am.

vagancia *f* 1. (*holgazanería*) laziness, idleness. 2. (*vagabundeo*) vagrancy.

vagar *vi*: **~ (por)** to wander, to roam.

vagina *f* vagina.

vago, -ga *adj* 1. (*perezoso*) lazy, idle. 2. (*impreciso*) vague.

vagón *m* (*de pasajeros*) carriage; (*de mercancías*) wagon.

vagoneta *f* wagon.

vaguedad *f* 1. (*cualidad*) vagueness. 2. (*dicho*) vague remark.

vahído *m* blackout, fainting fit.

vaho *m* 1. (*vapor*) steam. 2. (*aliento*) breath.

vaina *f* 1. (*gen*) sheath. 2. (BOT - *envoltura*) pod. 3. Amer *fam* (*engreído*) pain in the neck.

vainilla *f* vanilla.

vaivén *m* 1. (*balanceo - de barco*) swaying, rocking; (*- de péndulo, columpio*) swinging. 2. (*altibajo*) ups-and-downs (*pl*).

vajilla *f* crockery; **una ~** a dinner service.

vale ◆ *m* 1. (*bono*) coupon, voucher. 2. (*entrada gratuita*) free ticket. 3. (*comprobante*) receipt. 4. (*pagaré*) I.O.U. ◆ *interj* → **valer**.

valedero, -ra *adj* valid.

valenciano, -na *adj, m y f* (*de Valencia*) Valencian.

valentía *f* (*valor*) bravery.

valer ◆ *vt* 1. (*costar - precio*) to cost; (*tener un valor de*) to be worth; **¿cuánto vale?** (*de precio*) how much does it cost?, how much is it? 2. (*suponer*) to earn. 3. (*merecer*) to deserve, to be worth. 4. (*equivaler*) to be equivalent o equal to. ◆ *vi* 1. (*merecer aprecio*) to be worthy; **hacerse ~** to show one's worth. 2. (*servir*): **~ para algo** to be for sthg; **eso aún vale** you can still use that; **¿para qué vale?** what's it for? 3. (*ser válido*) to be valid; (*en juegos*) to be allowed. 4. (*ayudar*) to help, to be of use. 5. (*tener calidad*) to be of worth; **no ~ nada** to be worthless o useless. 6. (*equivaler*): **~ por** to be worth. 7. *loc*: **más vale tarde que nunca** better late than never; **más vale que te calles/vayas** it would be better if you shut up/left; **¿vale?** okay?, all right?; **¡vale!** okay!, all right! ▶ **valerse** *vpr* 1. (*servirse*): **~se de algo/alguien** to use sthg/sb. 2. (*desenvolverse*): **~se (por sí mismo)** to manage on one's own.

valeroso, -sa *adj* brave, courageous.

valía *f* value, worth.

validar vt to validate.

validez f validity; **dar ~ a** to validate.

válido, -da adj valid.

valiente adj (valeroso) brave.

valija f 1. (maleta) case, suitcase; ~ **diplomática** diplomatic bag. 2. (de correos) mailbag.

valioso, -sa adj 1. (gen) valuable. 2. (intento, esfuerzo) worthy.

valla f 1. (cerca) fence. 2. (DEP) hurdle. ▶ **valla publicitaria** f billboard, hoarding.

vallar vt to put a fence round.

valle m valley.

valor m 1. (gen, MAT & MÚS) value; **joyas por ~ de ...** jewels worth ...; **sin ~** worthless. 2. (importancia) importance; **dar ~ a** to give or attach importance to; **quitar ~ a algo** to take away from sthg. 3. (valentía) bravery. ▶ **valores** mpl 1. (principios) values. 2. (FIN) securities, bonds; **~es en cartera** investments.

valoración f 1. (de precio, pérdidas) valuation. 2. (de mérito, cualidad, ventajas) evaluation, assessment.

valorar vt 1. (tasar, apreciar) to value. 2. (evaluar) to evaluate, to assess.

vals (pl **valses**) m waltz.

valuar vt to value.

válvula f valve. ▶ **válvula de escape** f fig means of letting off steam.

vampiresa f fam vamp, femme fatale.

vampiro m (personaje) vampire.

vanagloriarse vpr: ~ **(de)** to boast (about), to show off (about).

vandalismo m vandalism.

vanguardia f 1. (MIL) vanguard; **ir a la ~ de** fig to be at the forefront of. 2. (cultural) avant-garde, vanguard.

vanidad f 1. (orgullo) vanity. 2. (inutilidad) futility.

vanidoso, -sa adj vain, conceited.

vano, -na adj 1. (gen) vain; **en ~** in vain. 2. (vacío, superficial) shallow, superficial.

vapor m 1. (emanación) vapour; (de agua) steam; **al ~** (CULIN) steamed; **de ~** (máquina etc) steam (antes de sust); **~ de agua** (FÍS & QUÍM) water vapour. 2. (barco) steamship.

vaporizador m 1. (pulverizador) spray. 2. (para evaporar) vaporizer.

vaporoso, -sa adj 1. (con vapor - ducha, baño) steamy; (- cielo) hazy, misty. 2. (fino - tela etc) diaphanous.

vapulear vt to beat, to thrash; fig to slate.

vaquero, -ra ◆ adj cowboy (antes de sust). ◆ m y f (persona) cowboy (f cowgirl), cowherd. ▶ **vaqueros** mpl (pantalón) jeans.

vara f 1. (rama, palo) stick. 2. (de metal etc) rod. 3. (insignia) staff.

variable adj changeable, variable.

variación f variation; (del tiempo) change.

variado, -da adj varied; (galletas, bombones) assorted.

variante ◆ adj variant. ◆ f 1. (variación) variation; (versión) version. 2. (AUTOM) by-pass.

variar ◆ vt 1. (modificar) to alter, to change. 2. (dar variedad) to vary. ◆ vi (cambiar): **para ~ irón** (just) for a change.

varicela f chickenpox.

varicoso, -sa adj varicose.

variedad f variety. ▶ **variedades, varietés** fpl (TEATR) variety (U), music hall (U).

varilla f 1. (barra larga) rod, stick. 2. (tira larga - de abanico, paraguas) spoke, rib; (- de gafas) arm; (- de corsé) bone, stay.

vario, -ria adj (variado) varied, different; (pl) various, several. ▶ **varios, -rias** pron pl several.

variopinto, -ta adj diverse.

varita f wand; ~ **mágica** magic wand.

variz f (gen pl) varicose vein.

varón m (hombre) male, man; (chico) boy.

varonil adj masculine, male.

Varsovia Warsaw.

vasallo, -lla m y f (siervo) vassal.

vasco, -ca adj, m y f Basque. ▶ **vasco** m (lengua) Basque.

vascuence m (lengua) Basque.

vasectomía f vasectomy.

vaselina® f Vaseline®.

vasija f (de barro) earthenware vessel.

vaso m 1. (recipiente, contenido) glass; **un ~ de plástico** a plastic cup. 2. (ANAT) vessel; **~s sanguíneos** blood vessels.

vástago m 1. (descendiente) offspring (U). 2. (brote) shoot. 3. (varilla) rod.

vasto, -ta adj vast.

váter = wáter.

vaticinar vt to prophesy, to predict.

vatio, watio ['batio] m watt.

vaya ◆ v → **ir.** ◆ interj 1. (sorpresa): **¡~!** well! 2. (énfasis): **¡~ moto!** what a motorbike!

VB abrev de **visto bueno.**

Vd. = Ud.

Vda. abrev de **viuda.**

Vds. = Uds.

ve → **ir**.

véase → **ver**.

vecinal adj (camino, impuestos) local.

vecindad f 1. (vecindario) neighbourhood. 2. (alrededores) vicinity.

vecindario m (de barrio) neighbourhood; (de población) community, inhabitants (pl).

vecino, -na ◆ adj (cercano) neighbouring. ◆ m y f 1. (de la misma casa, calle) neighbour; (de un barrio) resident. 2. (de una localidad) inhabitant.

vector m vector.

veda f 1. (prohibición) ban (on hunting and fishing); **levantar la** ~ to open the season. 2. (periodo) close season.

vedado, -da adj prohibited. ▶ **vedado** m reserve.

vedar vt to prohibit.

vedette [be'ðet] (pl **vedettes**) f star.

vegetación f vegetation.

vegetal ◆ adj 1. (BIOL) vegetable, plant (antes de sust). 2. (sandwich) salad (antes de sust). ◆ m vegetable.

vegetar vi to vegetate.

vegetariano, -na adj, m y f vegetarian.

vehemencia f (pasión, entusiasmo) vehemence.

vehemente adj (apasionado, entusiasta) vehement.

vehículo m (gen) vehicle; (de infección) carrier.

veinte núm twenty; **los (años)** ~ the twenties; ver también **seis**.

veinteavo, -va núm twentieth.

veintena f 1. (veinte) twenty. 2. (aproximadamente): **una** ~ (de) about twenty.

vejación f, **vejamen** m humiliation.

vejestorio m despec old fogey.

vejez f old age.

vejiga f bladder; ~ **de la bilis** gall bladder.

vela f 1. (para dar luz) candle; **estar a dos** ~s not to have two halfpennies to rub together. 2. (de barco) sail. 3. (DEP) sailing. 4. (vigilia) vigil; **pasar la noche en** ~ (adrede) to stay awake all night; (desvelado) to have a sleepless night.

velada f evening.

velado, -da adj 1. (oculto) veiled, hidden. 2. (FOT) blurred.

velar ◆ vi 1. (cuidar): ~ **por** to look after, to watch over. 2. (no dormir) to stay awake. ◆ vt 1. (de noche - muerto) to keep a vigil over. 2. (ocultar) to mask, to veil. 3. (FOT) to blur. ▶ **velarse** vpr (FOT) to blur.

veleidad f 1. (inconstancia) fickleness. 2. (antojo, capricho) whim, caprice.

velero m sailing boat/ship.

veleta f weather vane.

vello m 1. (pelusilla) down. 2. (pelo) hair.

velloso, -sa adj hairy.

velo m lit & fig veil.

velocidad f 1. (gen) speed; (TECN) velocity; **a toda** ~ at full speed; **de alta** ~ high-speed; ~ **punta** top speed. 2. (AUTOM) (marcha) gear; **cambiar de** ~ to change gear.

velocímetro m speedometer.

velódromo m cycle track, velodrome.

veloz adj fast, quick.

ven → **venir**.

vena f 1. (gen, ANAT & MIN) vein. 2. (inspiración) inspiration. 3. (don) vein, streak; **tener** ~ **de algo** to have a gift for doing sthg.

venado m (ZOOL) deer; (CULIN) venison.

vencedor, -ra ◆ adj winning, victorious. ◆ m y f winner.

vencer ◆ vt 1. (ganar) to beat, to defeat. 2. (derrotar - suj: sueño, cansancio, emoción) to overcome. 3. (aventajar): ~ **a alguien a o en algo** to outdo sb at sthg. 4. (superar - miedo, obstáculos) to overcome; (- tentación) to resist. ◆ vi 1. (ganar) to win, to be victorious. 2. (caducar - garantía, contrato, plazo) to expire; (- deuda, pago) to fall due; (- bono) to mature. 3. (prevalecer) to prevail. ▶ **vencerse** vpr (estante etc) to give way, to collapse.

vencido, -da adj 1. (derrotado) defeated; **darse por** ~ to give up. 2. (caducado - garantía, contrato, plazo) expired; (- pago, deuda) due, payable.

vencimiento m (término - de garantía, contrato, plazo) expiry; (- de pago, deuda) falling due.

venda f bandage.

vendaje m bandaging.

vendar vt to bandage; ~ **los ojos a alguien** to blindfold sb.

vendaval m gale.

vendedor, -ra m y f (gen) seller; (en tienda) shop o sales assistant; (de coches, seguros) salesman (f saleswoman).

vender vt lit & fig to sell; ~ **algo a o por** to sell sthg for. ▶ **venderse** vpr 1. (ser vendido) to be sold o on sale; '**se vende**' 'for sale'. 2. (dejarse sobornar) to sell o.s., to be bribed.

vendimia f grape harvest.

vendrá etc → **venir**.

veneno m (gen) poison; (de serpiente, insecto) venom.

venenoso, -sa adj 1. (gen) poisonous. 2. fig (malintencionado) venomous.

venerable adj venerable.

venerar vt to venerate, to worship.

venéreo, -a adj venereal.

venezolano, -na adj, m y f Venezuelan.

Venezuela Venezuela.

venga interj: ¡~! come on!

venganza f vengeance, revenge.

vengar vt to avenge. ► **vengarse** vpr: ~se (de) to take revenge (on).

vengativo, -va adj vengeful, vindictive.

vengo → venir.

venia f 1. (permiso) permission. 2. (DER) (perdón) pardon.

venial adj petty, venial.

venida f 1. (llegada) arrival. 2. (regreso) return.

venidero, -ra adj coming, future.

venir ◆ vi 1. (gen) to come; ~ a/de hacer algo to come to do sthg/from doing sthg; ~ de algo (proceder, derivarse) to come from sthg; no me vengas con exigencias don't come to me making demands; el año que viene next year. 2. (llegar) to arrive; vino a las doce he arrived at twelve o'clock. 3. (hallarse) to be; su foto viene en primera página his photo is o appears on the front page; el texto viene en inglés the text is in English. 4. (acometer, sobrevenir): me viene sueño I'm getting sleepy; le vinieron ganas de reír he was seized by a desire to laugh; le vino una tremenda desgracia he suffered a great misfortune. 5. (ropa, calzado): ~ a alguien to fit sb; ¿qué tal te viene? does it fit all right?; el abrigo le viene pequeño the coat is too small for her. 6. (convenir): ~ bien/mal a alguien to suit/not to suit sb. 7. (aproximarse): viene a costar un millón it costs almost a million. 8. loc: ¿a qué viene esto? what do you mean by that?; ~ a menos (negocio) to go downhill; (persona) to go down in the world; ~ a parar en to end in; ~ a ser to amount to. ◆ vaux 1. (antes de gerundio) (haber estado): ~ haciendo algo to have been doing sthg. 2. (antes de participio) (estar): los cambios vienen motivados por la presión de la oposición the changes have resulted from pressure on the part of the opposition. ► **venirse** vpr

1. (volver): ~se (de) to come back o return (from). 2. loc: ~se abajo (techo, estante etc) to collapse; (ilusiones) to be dashed.

venta f 1. (acción) sale, selling; estar en ~ to be for sale; ~ al contado cash sale; ~ a plazos sale by instalments. 2. (gen pl) (cantidad) sales (pl).

ventaja f 1. (hecho favorable) advantage. 2. (en competición) lead; llevar ~ a alguien to have a lead over sb.

ventajoso, -sa adj advantageous.

ventana f (gen & INFORM) window.

ventanilla f 1. (de vehículo, sobre) window. 2. (taquilla) counter.

ventilación f ventilation.

ventilador m ventilator, fan.

ventilar vt 1. (airear) to air. 2. (resolver) to clear up. 3. (discutir) to air. ► **ventilarse** vpr (airearse) to air.

ventiscar, ventisquear v impers to blow a blizzard.

ventisquero m (nieve amontonada) snowdrift.

ventolera f (viento) gust of wind.

ventosa f (gen & ZOOL) sucker.

ventosidad f wind, flatulence.

ventoso, -sa adj windy.

ventrílocuo, -cua m y f ventriloquist.

ventura f 1. (suerte) luck; a la (buena) ~ (al azar) at random, haphazardly; (sin nada previsto) without planning o a fixed plan. 2. (casualidad) fate, fortune.

Venus Venus.

ver ◆ vi 1. (gen) to see. 2. loc: a ~ (veamos) let's see; ¿a ~? (mirando con interés) let me see; ¡a ~! (¡pues claro!) what do you expect?; (al empezar algo) right!; dejarse ~ (por un sitio) to show one's face (somewhere); eso está por ~ that remains to be seen; ya veremos we'll see. ◆ vt 1. (gen) to see; (mirar) to look at; (televisión, partido de fútbol) to watch; ¿ves algo? can you see anything?; he estado viendo tu trabajo I've been looking at your work; ya veo que estás de mal humor I can see you're in a bad mood; ¿ves lo que quiero decir? do you see what I mean?; ir a ~ lo que pasa to go and see what's going on; es una manera de ~ las cosas that's one way of looking at it; yo no lo veo tan mal I don't think it's that bad. 2. loc: eso habrá que ~lo that remains to be seen; ¡hay que ~ qué lista es! you wouldn't believe how clever she is!; no puedo ~le (ni en pintura) fam I can't stand him; si no lo veo, no lo creo you'll never believe it; ~ venir a

alguien to see what sb is up to. ◆ *m*: **estar de buen ~** to be good-looking. ▶ **verse** *vpr* 1. (*mirarse, imaginarse*) to see o.s.; **~se en el espejo** to see o.s. in the mirror. 2. (*percibirse*): **desde aquí se ve el mar** you can see the sea from here. 3. (*encontrarse*) to meet, to see each other; **hace mucho que no nos vemos** we haven't seen each other for a long time. 4. (*darse, suceder*) to be seen. 5. *loc*: **vérselas y deseárselas para hacer algo** to have a real struggle doing sthg. ▶ **véase** *vpr* (*en textos*) see. ▶ **por lo visto, por lo que se ve** *loc adv* apparently.

vera *f* 1. (*orilla - de río, lago*) bank; (*- de camino*) edge, side. 2. *fig* (*lado*) side; **a la ~ de** next to.

veracidad *f* truthfulness.

veraneante *m y f* holidaymaker, (summer) vacationer *Am*.

veranear *vi*: **~ en** to spend one's summer holidays in.

veraneo *m* summer holidays (*pl*); **de ~** holiday (*antes de sust*).

veraniego, -ga *adj* summer (*antes de sust*).

verano *m* summer.

veras *fpl* truth (U); **de ~** (*verdaderamente*) really; (*en serio*) seriously.

veraz *adj* truthful.

verbal *adj* verbal.

verbena *f* (*fiesta*) street party (*on the eve of certain saints' days*).

verbo *m* (GRAM) verb.

verdad *f* 1. (*gen*) truth; **a decir ~** to tell the truth. 2. (*principio aceptado*) fact. 3. *loc*: **no te gusta, ¿~?** you don't like it, do you?; **está bueno, ¿~?** it's good, isn't it? ▶ **verdades** *fpl* (*opinión sincera*) true thoughts; **cantarle o decirle a alguien cuatro ~es** *fig* to tell sb a few home truths. ▶ **de verdad** ◆ *loc adv* 1. (*en serio*) seriously. 2. (*realmente*) really. ◆ *loc adj* (*auténtico*) real.

verdadero, -ra *adj* 1. (*cierto, real*) true, real. 2. (*sin falsificar*) real, genuine. 3. (*enfático*) real; **fue un ~ lío** it was a real mess.

verde ◆ *adj* 1. (*gen*) green; **~ oliva** olive green; **poner ~ a alguien** to criticize sb. 2. (*fruta*) unripe, green. 3. *fig* (*obsceno*) blue, dirty. 4. *fig* (*inmaduro - proyecto etc*) in its early stages. ◆ *m* (*color*) green. ▶ **Verdes** *mpl* (*partido*): **los Verdes** the Greens.

verdor *m* 1. (*color*) greenness. 2. (*madurez*) lushness.

verdugo *m* 1. (*de preso*) executioner; (*que ahorca*) hangman. 2. (*pasamontañas*) balaclava helmet.

verdulería *f* greengrocer's (shop).

verdulero, -ra *m y f* (*tendero*) greengrocer.

verdura *f* vegetables (*pl*), greens (*pl*).

vereda *f* 1. (*senda*) path. 2. *Amer* (*acera*) pavement *Br*, sidewalk *Am*.

veredicto *m* verdict.

vergonzoso, -sa *adj* 1. (*deshonroso*) shameful. 2. (*tímido*) bashful.

vergüenza *f* 1. (*turbación*) embarrassment; **dar ~** to embarrass; **¡qué ~!** how embarrassing!; **sentir ~** to feel embarrassed. 2. (*timidez*) bashfulness. 3. (*remordimiento*) shame; **sentir ~** to feel ashamed. 4. (*dignidad*) pride, dignity. 5. (*deshonra, escándalo*) disgrace; **¡es una ~!** it's disgraceful!

verídico, -ca *adj* (*cierto*) true, truthful.

verificar *vt* 1. (*comprobar - verdad, autenticidad*) to check, to verify. 2. (*examinar - funcionamiento, buen estado*) to check, to test. 3. (*confirmar - fecha, cita*) to confirm. 4. (*llevar a cabo*) to carry out. ▶ **verificarse** *vpr* (*tener lugar*) to take place.

verja *f* 1. (*puerta*) iron gate. 2. (*valla*) railings (*pl*). 3. (*enrejado*) grille.

vermú (*pl* **vermús**), **vermut** (*pl* **vermuts**) *m* 1. (*bebida*) vermouth. 2. *Amer* (CIN & TEATR) matinee.

vernáculo, -la *adj* vernacular.

verosímil *adj* 1. (*creíble*) believable, credible. 2. (*probable*) likely, probable.

verruga *f* wart.

versado, -da *adj*: **~ (en)** versed (in).

versar *vi*: **~ sobre** to be about, to deal with.

versátil *adj* 1. (*voluble*) fickle. 2. (*considerado incorrecto*) (*polifacético*) versatile.

versículo *m* verse.

versión *f* (*gen*) version; (*en música pop*) cover version; **~ original** (CIN) original (version).

verso *m* 1. (*género*) verse. 2. (*unidad rítmica*) line (*of poetry*). 3. (*poema*) poem.

vértebra *f* vertebra.

vertebrado, -da *adj* vertebrate. ▶ **vertebrados** *mpl* (ZOOL) vertebrates.

vertedero *m* (*de basuras*) rubbish tip o dump; (*de agua*) overflow.

verter *vt* 1. (*derramar*) to spill. 2. (*vaciar - líquido*) to pour (out); (*- recipiente*) to empty. 3. (*tirar - basura, residuos*) to dump. **4.** *fig* (*decir*) to tell. ➤ **verterse** *vpr* (*derramarse*) to spill.

vertical ✦ *adj* (GEOM) vertical; (*derecho*) upright. ✦ *f* (GEOM) vertical.

vértice *m* (*gen*) vertex; (*de cono*) apex.

vertido *m* **1.** (*gen pl*) (*residuo*) waste (U). **2.** (*acción*) dumping.

vertiente *f* **1.** (*pendiente*) slope. **2.** *fig* (*aspecto*) side, aspect.

vertiginoso, -sa *adj* **1.** (*mareante*) dizzy. **2.** *fig* (*raudo*) giddy.

vértigo *m* (*enfermedad*) vertigo; (*mareo*) dizziness; **trepar me da ~** climbing makes me dizzy.

vesícula *f*: **~ biliar** gall bladder.

vespertino, -na *adj* evening (*antes de sust*).

vestíbulo *m* (*de casa*) (entrance) hall; (*de hotel, oficina*) lobby, foyer.

vestido, -da *adj* dressed. ➤ **vestido** *m* **1.** (*indumentaria*) clothes (*pl*). **2.** (*prenda femenina*) dress.

vestidura *f* (*gen pl*) clothes (*pl*); (RELIG) vestments (*pl*); **rasgarse las ~s** to make a fuss.

vestigio *m* vestige; *fig* sign, trace.

vestimenta *f* clothes (*pl*), wardrobe.

vestir ✦ *vt* **1.** (*gen*) to dress. **2.** (*llevar puesto*) to wear. **3.** (*cubrir*) to cover. **4.** *fig* (*encubrir*): **~ algo de** to invest sthg with. ✦ *vi* **1.** (*llevar ropa*) to dress. **2.** *fig* (*estar bien visto*) to be the done thing. ➤ **vestirse** *vpr* **1.** (*ponerse ropa*) to get dressed, to dress. **2.** (*adquirir ropa*): **~se en** to buy one's clothes at.

vestuario *m* **1.** (*vestimenta*) clothes (*pl*), wardrobe; (TEATR) costumes (*pl*). **2.** (*guardarropa*) cloakroom. **3.** (*para cambiarse*) changing room; (*de actores*) dressing room.

veta *f* **1.** (*filón*) vein, seam. **2.** (*faja, lista*) grain.

vetar *vt* to veto.

veterano, -na *adj, m y f* veteran.

veterinario, -ria ✦ *adj* veterinary. ✦ *m y f* (*persona*) vet, veterinary surgeon. ➤ **veterinaria** *f* (*ciencia*) veterinary science o medicine.

veto *m* veto; **poner ~ a algo** to veto sthg.

vetusto, -ta *adj culto* ancient, very old.

vez *f* **1.** (*gen*) time; **una ~** once; **dos veces** twice; **tres veces** three times; **¿has estado allí alguna ~?** have you ever been there?; **a la ~ (que)** at the same time (as); **cada ~ (que)** every time; **cada ~ más** more and more; **cada ~ menos** less and less; **cada ~ la veo más feliz**

she seems happier and happier; **de una ~** in one go; **de una ~ para siempre o por todas** once and for all; **muchas veces** often, a lot; **otra ~** again; **pocas veces, rara ~** rarely, seldom; **por última ~** for the last time; **una ~ más** once again; **una y otra ~** time and again; **érase una ~** once upon a time. **2.** (*turno*) turn. ➤ **a veces, algunas veces** *loc adv* sometimes, at times. ➤ **de vez en cuando** *loc adv* from time to time, now and again. ➤ **en vez de** *loc prep* instead of. ➤ **tal vez** *loc adv* perhaps, maybe. ➤ **una vez que** *loc conj* once, after.

VHF (*abrev de* **very high frequency**) *f* VHF.

VHS (*abrev de* **video home system**) *m* VHS.

vía ✦ *f* **1.** (*medio de transporte*) route; **por ~ aérea** (*gen*) by air; (*correo*) (by) airmail; **por ~ marítima** by sea; **por ~ terrestre** overland, by land; **~ de circunvalación** bypass; **~ fluvial** waterway. **2.** (*calzada, calle*) road; **~ pública** public thoroughfare. **3.** (FERROC - *raíl*) rails (*pl*), track; (- *andén*) platform; **~ férrea** (*ruta*) railway line. **4.** (*proceso*): **estar en ~s de** to be in the process of; **país en ~s de desarrollo** developing country; **una especie en ~s de extinción** an endangered species. **5.** (ANAT) tract. **6.** (*opción*) channel, path; **por ~ oficial/judicial** through official channels/the courts. **7.** (*camino*) way; **dar ~ libre** (*dejar paso*) to give way; (*dar libertad de acción*) to give a free rein. **8.** (DER) procedure. ✦ *prep* via. ➤ **Vía Láctea** *f* Milky Way.

viabilidad *f* viability.

viable *adj fig* (*posible*) viable.

viaducto *m* viaduct.

viajante *m y f* travelling salesperson.

viajar *vi* **1.** (*trasladarse, irse*): **~ (en)** to travel (by). **2.** (*circular*) to run.

viaje *m* **1.** (*gen*) journey, trip; (*en barco*) voyage; **¡buen ~!** have a good journey o trip!; **estar/ir de ~** to be/go away (on a trip); **hay 11 días de ~** it's an 11-day journey; **~ de ida** outward journey; **~ de ida y vuelta** return journey o trip; **~ de novios** honeymoon. **2.** *fig* (*recorrido*) trip. ➤ **viajes** *mpl* (*singladuras*) travels.

viajero, -ra ✦ *adj* (*persona*) travelling; (*ave*) migratory. ✦ *m y f* (*gen*) traveller; (*en transporte público*) passenger.

vial *adj* road (*antes de sust*).

viandante *m y f* **1.** (*peatón*) pedestrian. **2.** (*transeúnte*) passer-by.

viario, -ria *adj* road (*antes de sust*).
víbora *f* viper.
vibración *f* vibration.
vibrante *adj* 1. (*oscilante*) vibrating. 2. *fig* (*emocionante*) vibrant.
vibrar *vi* 1. (*oscilar*) to vibrate. 2. *fig* (*voz, rodillas etc*) to shake. 3. *fig* (*público*) to get excited.
vicaría *f* (*residencia*) vicarage.
vicario *m* vicar.
vicepresidente, -ta *m y f* (*de país, asociación*) vice-president; (*de comité, empresa*) vice-chairman.
viceversa *adv* vice versa.
viciado, -da *adj* (*maloliente*) foul; (*contaminado*) polluted.
viciar *vt* 1. (*pervertir*) to corrupt. 2. (*contaminar*) to pollute. 3. (*adulterar*) to adulterate. ▶ **viciarse** *vpr* 1. (*pervertirse*) to become o get corrupted; (*enviciarse*) to take to vice. 2. (*contaminarse*) to become polluted.
vicio *m* 1. (*mala costumbre*) bad habit, vice. 2. (*libertinaje*) vice. 3. (*defecto físico, de dicción etc*) defect.
vicioso, -sa ◆ *adj* 1. (*depravado*) depraved. 2. (*defectuoso*) defective. ◆ *m y f* (*depravado*) depraved person.
vicisitud *f* (*inestabilidad*) instability, changeability. ▶ **vicisitudes** *fpl* (*avatares*) vicissitudes, ups and downs.
víctima *f* victim; (*en accidente, guerra*) casualty; **ser ~ de** to be the victim of.
victoria *f* victory; **cantar ~** to claim victory.
victorioso, -sa *adj* victorious.
vid *f* vine.
vid., v. (*abrev de véase*) v., vid.
vida *f* life; **de por ~** for life; **en ~ de** during the life o lifetime of; **en mi/tu etc ~** never (in my/your etc life); **estar con ~** to be alive; **ganarse la ~** to earn a living; **pasar a mejor ~** to pass away; **perder la ~** to lose one's life; **quitar la ~ a alguien** to kill sb; **¡así es la ~!** that's life!; **darse o pegarse la gran ~, darse o pegarse la ~ padre** to live the life of Riley.
vidente *m y f* clairvoyant.
vídeo, video *m* 1. (*gen*) video; **grabar en ~** to videotape. 2. (*aparato filmador*) camcorder.
videocámara *f* camcorder.
videocasete *m* video, videocassette.
videoclip *m* (*pop*) video.
videoclub (*pl* **videoclubes**) *m* video club.
videojuego *m* video game.
videotexto *m*, **videotex** *m inv* (*por*

señal de televisión) teletext; (*por línea telefónica*) videotext, viewdata.
vidriero, -ra *m y f* 1. (*que fabrica cristales*) glass merchant o manufacturer. 2. (*que coloca cristales*) glazier. ▶ **vidriera** *f* (*puerta*) glass door; (*ventana*) glass window; (*en catedrales*) stained glass window.
vidrio *m* (*material*) glass.
vidrioso, -sa *adj* 1. *fig* (*tema, asunto*) thorny, delicate. 2. *fig* (*ojos*) glazed.
vieira *f* scallop.
viejo, -ja ◆ *adj* old; **hacerse ~** to get o grow old. ◆ *m y f* 1. (*anciano*) old man (*f* old lady); **los ~s** the elderly; **~ verde** dirty old man (*f* dirty old woman). 2. *fam* (*padres*) old man (*f* old girl); **mis ~s** my folks. 3. *Amer fam* (*amigo*) pal, mate. ▶ **Viejo de Pascua** *m Amer* Father Christmas.
Viena Vienna.
viene → **venir**.
vienés, -esa *adj, m y f* Viennese.
viento *m* 1. (*aire*) wind; **~ de costado** o **de lado** crosswind. 2. (*cuerda*) guy (rope). 3. *loc*: **contra ~ y marea** in spite of everything; **mis esperanzas se las llevó el ~** my hopes flew out of the window; **~ en popa** splendidly.
vientre *m* (ANAT) stomach.
viera → **ver**.
viernes *m inv* Friday; *ver también* **sábado**. ▶ **Viernes Santo** *m* (RELIG) Good Friday.
Vietnam Vietnam.
vietnamita *adj, m y f* Vietnamese.
viga *f* (*de madera*) beam, rafter; (*de metal*) girder.
vigencia *f* (*de ley etc*) validity; (*de costumbre*) use.
vigente *adj* (*ley etc*) in force; (*costumbre*) in use.
vigésimo, -ma *núm* twentieth.
vigía *m y f* lookout.
vigilancia *f* 1. (*cuidado*) vigilance, care. 2. (*vigilantes*) security guards (*pl*).
vigilante ◆ *adj* vigilant. ◆ *m y f* guard; **~ nocturno** night watchman.
vigilar ◆ *vt* (*enfermo*) to watch over; (*presos, banco*) to guard; (*niños, bolso*) to keep an eye on; (*proceso*) to oversee. ◆ *vi* to keep watch.
vigilia *f* (*vela*) wakefulness; **estar de ~** to be awake.
vigor *m* 1. (*gen*) vigour. 2. (*vigencia*): **entrar en ~** to come into force.
vigorizar *vt* (*fortalecer*) to fortify.
vigoroso, -sa *adj* (*gen*) vigorous; (*colorido*) strong.

vikingo, -ga adj, m y f Viking.

vil adj vile, despicable; (metal) base.

vileza f 1. (acción) vile o despicable act. 2. (cualidad) vileness.

villa f 1. (población) small town. 2. (casa) villa, country house.

villancico m (navideño) Christmas carol.

villano, -na m y f villain.

vilo ▶ en vilo loc adv 1. (suspendido) in the air, suspended. 2. (inquieto) on tenterhooks; **tener a alguien en ~** to keep sb in suspense.

vinagre m vinegar.

vinagrera f (vasija) vinegar bottle. ▶ **vinagreras** fpl (CULIN) (convoy) cruet (sg).

vinagreta f vinaigrette, French dressing.

vinculación f link, linking (U).

vincular vt 1. (enlazar) to link; (por obligación) to tie, to bind. 2. (DER) to entail.

vínculo m (lazo - entre hechos, países) link; (- personal, familiar) tie, bond.

vinícola adj (país, región) wine-producing (antes de sust); (industria) wine (antes de sust).

vinicultura f wine producing.

vino ♦ v → **venir. ♦** m wine; **~ blanco/tinto** white/red wine; **~ dulce/seco** sweet/dry wine; **~ rosado** rosé.

viña f vineyard.

viñedo m (large) vineyard.

viñeta f 1. (de tebeo) (individual) cartoon. 2. (de libro) vignette.

vio → ver.

viola f viola.

violación f 1. (de ley, derechos) violation, infringement. 2. (de persona) rape.

violador, -ra adj, m y f rapist.

violar vt 1. (ley, derechos, domicilio) to violate, to infringe. 2. (persona) to rape.

violencia f 1. (agresividad) violence. 2. (fuerza - de viento, pasiones) force. 3. (incomodidad) embarrassment, awkwardness.

violentar vt 1. (incomodar) to embarrass. 2. (forzar - domicilio) to break into. ▶ **violentarse** vpr (incomodarse) to feel awkward.

violento, -ta adj 1. (gen) violent; (goce) intense. 2. (incómodo) awkward.

violeta ♦ f (flor) violet. **♦** adj & m (color) violet.

violín m violin.

violón m double bass.

violonchelo, violoncelo m cello.

VIP (abrev de **very important person**) m y f VIP.

viperino, -na adj fig venomous.

viraje m 1. (giro & AUTOM) turn; (NÁUT) tack. 2. (curva) bend, curve. 3. fig (cambio) change of direction.

virar ♦ vt (girar) to turn (round); (NÁUT) to tack. **♦** vi (girar) to turn (round).

virgen ♦ adj (gen) virgin; (cinta) blank; (película) unused. **♦** m y f (persona) virgin. **♦** f (ARTE) Madonna. ▶ **Virgen** f: **la Virgen** (RELIG) the (Blessed) Virgin.

virgo m (virginidad) virginity. ▶ **Virgo ♦** m (zodiaco) Virgo. **♦** m y f (persona) Virgo.

virguería f fam gem.

viril adj virile, manly.

virilidad f virility.

virtual adj 1. (posible) possible, potential. 2. (casi real) virtual.

virtud f 1. (cualidad) virtue. 2. (poder) power; **tener la ~ de** to have the power o ability to. ▶ **en virtud de** loc prep by virtue of.

virtuoso, -sa ♦ adj (honrado) virtuous. **♦** m y f (genio) virtuoso.

viruela f 1. (enfermedad) smallpox. 2. (pústula) pockmark; **picado de ~s** pockmarked.

virulé ▶ a la virulé loc adj 1. (torcido) crooked. 2. (hinchado): **un ojo a la ~** a black eye.

virulencia f (MED & fig) virulence.

virus m inv (gen & INFORM) virus.

viruta f shaving.

visado m visa.

víscera f internal organ; **~s** entrails.

visceral adj (ANAT & fig) visceral; **un sentimiento/una reacción ~** a gut feeling/reaction.

viscoso, -sa adj (gen) viscous; (baboso) slimy. ▶ **viscosa** f (tejido) viscose.

visera f 1. (de gorra) peak. 2. (de casco, suelta) visor. 3. (de automóvil) sun visor.

visibilidad f visibility.

visible adj visible.

visigodo, -da m y f Visigoth.

visillo m (gen pl) net/lace curtain.

visión f 1. (sentido, lo que se ve) sight. 2. (alucinación, lucidez) vision; **ver visiones** to be seeing things. 3. (punto de vista) (point of) view.

visionar vt to view privately.

visionario, -ria adj, m y f visionary.

visita f 1. (gen) visit; (breve) call; **hacer una ~ a alguien** to visit sb, to pay sb a visit; **pasar ~** (MED) to see one's patients. **2.** (*visitante*) visitor; **tener ~** o **~s** to have visitors.

visitante *m y f* visitor.

visitar *vt* (*gen*) to visit; (*suj: médico*) to call on.

vislumbrar *vt* **1.** (*entrever*) to make out, to discern. **2.** (*adivinar*) to have an inkling of. ▶ **vislumbrarse** *vpr* **1.** (*entreverse*) to be barely visible. **2.** (*adivinarse*) to become a little clearer.

vislumbre *m o f lit & fig* glimmer.

viso *m* **1.** (*aspecto*): **tener ~s de** to seem; **tiene ~s de hacerse realidad** it could become a reality. **2.** (*reflejo - de tejido*) sheen; (*- de metal*) glint.

visón *m* mink.

víspera *f* (*día antes*) day before, eve; **en ~s de** on the eve of.

vista → **visto**.

vistazo *m* glance, quick look; **echar** o **dar un ~ a** to have a quick look at.

visto, -ta ◆ *pp* → **ver**. ◆ *adj*: **estar bien/mal ~** to be considered good/frowned upon. ▶ **vista** ◆ *v* → **vestir**. ◆ *f* **1.** (*sentido*) sight, eyesight; (*ojos*) eyes (*pl*). **2.** (*observación*) watching. **3.** (*mirada*) gaze; **fijar la vista en** to fix one's eyes on; **a primera** o **simple vista** (*aparentemente*) at first sight, on the face of it; **estar a la vista** (*visible*) to be visible; (*muy cerca*) to be staring one in the face. **4.** (*panorama*) view. **5.** (DER) hearing. **6.** *loc*: **conocer a alguien de vista** to know sb by sight; **hacer la vista gorda** to turn a blind eye; **¡hasta la vista!** see you!; **no perder de vista a alguien/algo** (*vigilar*) not to let sb/sthg out of one's sight; (*tener en cuenta*) not to lose sight of sb/sthg; **perder de vista** (*dejar de ver*) to lose sight of; (*perder contacto*) to lose touch with; **saltar a la vista** to be blindingly obvious. ▶ **vistas** *fpl* (*panorama*) view (*sg*); **con vistas al mar** with a sea view. ▶ **visto bueno** *m*: **el ~ bueno** the go-ahead; **'~ bueno'** 'approved'. ▶ **a la vista** *loc adv* (BANCA) at sight. ▶ **con vistas a** *loc prep* with a view to. ▶ **en vista de** *loc prep* in view of. ▶ **en vista de que** *loc conj* since, seeing as. ▶ **por lo visto** *loc adv* apparently. ▶ **visto que** *loc conj* seeing o given that.

vistoso, -sa *adj* eye-catching.

visual ◆ *adj* visual. ◆ *f* line of sight.

visualizar *vt* **1.** (*gen*) to visualize. **2.** (INFORM) to display.

vital *adj* (*gen*) vital; (*ciclo*) life (*antes de sust*); (*persona*) full of life, vivacious.

vitalicio, -cia *adj* for life, life (*antes de sust*).

vitalidad *f* vitality.

vitamina *f* vitamin.

vitaminado, -da *adj* vitamin-enriched.

vitamínico, -ca *adj* vitamin (*antes de sust*).

viticultor, -ra *m y f* wine grower.

viticultura *f* wine growing, viticulture.

vitorear *vt* to cheer.

vítreo, -a *adj* vitreous.

vitrina *f* (*en casa*) display cabinet; (*en tienda*) showcase, glass case.

vitro ▶ **in vitro** *loc adv* in vitro.

vituperar *vt* to criticize harshly.

viudedad *f* **1.** (*viudez - de mujer*) widowhood; (*- de hombre*) widowerhood. **2.** (**pensión de**) **~** widow's/widower's pension.

viudo, -da *m y f* widower (*f* widow).

viva ◆ *m* cheer. ◆ *interj*: **¡~!** hurrah!; **¡~ el rey!** long live the King!

vivac = **vivaque**.

vivacidad *f* liveliness.

vivales *m y f inv* crafty person.

vivamente *adv* **1.** (*relatar, describir*) vividly. **2.** (*afectar, emocionar*) deeply.

vivaque, vivac *m* bivouac.

vivaz *adj* (*despierto*) alert, sharp.

vivencia *f* (*gen pl*) experience.

víveres *mpl* provisions, supplies.

vivero *m* **1.** (*de plantas*) nursery. **2.** (*de peces*) fish farm; (*de moluscos*) bed.

viveza *f* **1.** (*de colorido, descripción*) vividness. **2.** (*de persona, discusión, ojos*) liveliness; (*de ingenio, inteligencia*) sharpness.

vívido, -da *adj* vivid.

vividor, -ra *m y f despec* scrounger.

vivienda *f* **1.** (*alojamiento*) housing, accommodation. **2.** (*morada*) dwelling.

viviente *adj* living.

vivir ◆ *vt* (*experimentar*) to experience, to live through. ◆ *vi* (*gen*) to live; (*estar vivo*) to be alive; (*en armonía*) to be happy; **~ para ver** who'd have thought it?

vivito *adj*: **~ y coleando** *fam* alive and kicking.

vivo, -va *adj* **1.** (*existente - ser, lengua etc*) living; **estar ~** (*persona, costumbre, recuerdo*) to be alive. **2.** (*dolor, deseo, olor*) intense; (*luz, color, tono*) bright. **3.** (*gestos, ojos, descripción*) lively, vivid. **4.** (*activo - ingenio, niño*) quick, sharp; (*- ciudad*) lively. **5.** (*genio*) quick, hot. ▶ **vivos** *mpl*: **los ~s** the living. ▶ **en vivo** *loc adv* (*en directo*) live.

Vizcaya Vizcaya; **Golfo de ~** Bay of Biscay.

vizconde, -desa *m y f* viscount (*f* viscountess).

vocablo *m* word, term.

vocabulario *m* 1. (*riqueza léxica*) vocabulary. 2. (*diccionario*) dictionary.

vocación *f* vocation, calling.

vocacional *adj* vocational.

vocal ◆ *adj* vocal. ◆ *f* vowel.

vocalizar *vi* to vocalize.

vocear ◆ *vt* 1. (*gritar*) to shout o call out. 2. (*llamar*) to shout o call to. 3. (*pregonar - mercancía*) to hawk. ◆ *vi* (*gritar*) to shout.

vociferar *vi* to shout.

vodka ['boθka] *m o f* vodka.

vol. (*abrev de volumen*) vol.

volador, -ra *adj* flying.

volandas ▶ **en volandas** *loc adv* in the air.

volante ◆ *adj* flying. ◆ *m* 1. (*para conducir*) (steering) wheel. 2. (*de tela*) frill, flounce. 3. (*del médico*) (referral) note. 4. (*en bádminton*) shuttlecock.

volar ◆ *vt* (*en guerras, atentados*) to blow up; (*caja fuerte, puerta*) to blow open; (*edificio en ruinas*) to demolish (*with explosives*); (MIN) to blast. ◆ *vi* 1. (*gen*) to fly; (*papeles etc*) to blow away; **~ a** (*una altura*) to fly at; (*un lugar*) to fly to; **echar(se) a ~** to fly away o off. 2. *fam* (*desaparecer*) to disappear, to vanish.

volátil *adj* (QUÍM & *fig*) volatile.

vol-au-vent = **volován**.

volcán *m* volcano.

volcánico, -ca *adj* volcanic.

volcar ◆ *vt* 1. (*tirar*) to knock over; (*carretilla*) to tip up. 2. (*vaciar*) to empty out. ◆ *vi* (*coche, camión*) to overturn; (*barco*) to capsize. ▶ **volcarse** *vpr* (*esforzarse*): **~se (con/en)** to bend over backwards (for/in).

volea *f* volley.

voleibol *m* volleyball.

voleo *m* volley; **a o al ~** (*arbitrariamente*) randomly, any old how.

volován (*pl* volovanes), **vol-au-vent** [bolo'βan] (*pl* **vol-au-vents**) *m* vol-auvent.

volquete *m* dumper truck, dump truck *Am*.

voltaje *m* voltage.

voltear *vt* 1. (*heno, crepe, torero*) to toss; (*tortilla - con plato*) to turn over; (*mesa, silla*) to turn upside-down. 2. *Amer* (*derribar*) to knock over. ▶ **voltearse** *vpr*

Amer 1. (*volverse*) to turn around. 2. (*volcarse*) to overturn.

voltereta *f* (*en el suelo*) handspring; (*en el aire*) somersault; **~ lateral** cartwheel.

voltio *m* volt.

voluble *adj* changeable, fickle.

volumen *m* 1. (*gen* & COM) volume; **~ de negocio o ventas** turnover. 2. (*espacio ocupado*) size, bulk.

voluminoso, -sa *adj* bulky.

voluntad *f* 1. (*determinación*) will, willpower; **~ de hierro** iron will. 2. (*intención*) intention; **buena ~** goodwill; **mala ~** ill will. 3. (*deseo*) wishes (*pl*), will; **contra la ~ de alguien** against sb's will. 4. (*albedrío*) free will; **a ~** (*cuanto se quiere*) as much as one likes; **por ~ propia** of one's own free will.

voluntariado *m* voluntary enlistment.

voluntario, -ria ◆ *adj* voluntary. ◆ *m y f* volunteer.

voluntarioso, -sa *adj* (*esforzado*) willing.

voluptuoso, -sa *adj* voluptuous.

volver ◆ *vt* 1. (*dar la vuelta a*) to turn round; (*lo de arriba abajo*) to turn over. 2. (*poner del revés - boca abajo*) to turn upside down; (- *lo de dentro fuera*) to turn inside out; (- *lo de detrás delante*) to turn back to front. 3. (*cabeza, ojos etc*) to turn. 4. (*convertir en*): **eso le volvió un delincuente** that turned him into a criminal. ◆ *vi* (*ir de vuelta*) to go back, to return; (*venir de vuelta*) to come back, to return; **yo allí no vuelvo** I'm not going back there; **vuelve, no te vayas** come back, don't go; **~ en sí** to come to. ▶ **volver a** *vi* (*reanudar*) to return to; **~ a hacer algo** (*hacer otra vez*) to do sthg again. ▶ **volverse** *vpr* 1. (*darse la vuelta, girar la cabeza*) to turn round. 2. (*ir de vuelta*) to go back, to return; (*venir de vuelta*) to come back, to return. 3. (*convertirse en*) to become; **~se loco/pálido** to go mad/pale. 4. *loc*: **~se atrás** (*de una afirmación, promesa*) to go back on one's word; (*de una decisión*) to back out; **~se (en) contra (de) alguien** to turn against sb.

vomitar ◆ *vt* (*devolver*) to vomit, to bring up. ◆ *vi* to vomit, to be sick.

vómito *m* (*substancia*) vomit (U).

voraz *adj* 1. (*persona, apetito*) voracious. 2. *fig* (*fuego, enfermedad*) raging.

vos *pron pers* (tú) you.

vosotros, -tras *pron pers* you (*pl*).

votación *f* vote, voting (U); **decidir algo por ~** to put sthg to the vote; **~ a mano alzada** show of hands.

votante *m y f* voter.

votar ◆ *vt* **1.** (*partido, candidato*) to vote for; (*ley*) to vote on. **2.** (*aprobar*) to pass, to approve (*by vote*). **◆** *vi* to vote; **~ por** (*emitir un voto por*) to vote for; *fig* (*estar a favor de*) to be in favour of; **~ por que ...** to vote (that) ...; **~ en blanco** to return a blank ballot paper.

voto *m* **1.** (*gen*) vote; **~ de confianza/censura** vote of confidence/no confidence. **2.** (RELIG) vow.

voy → ir.

vóytelas *interj Amer fam* good grief!

voz *f* **1.** (*gen & GRAM*) voice; **a media ~** in a low voice, under one's breath; **a ~ en cuello** o **grito** at the top of one's voice; **alzar** o **levantar la ~ a alguien** to raise one's voice to sb; **en ~ alta** aloud; **en ~ baja** softly, in a low voice; **~ en off** (CIN) voice-over; (TEATR) voice offstage. **2.** (*grito*) shout; **a voces** shouting; **dar voces** to shout. **3.** (*vocablo*) word. **4.** (*derecho a expresarse*) say, voice; **no tener ni ~ ni voto** to have no say in the matter. **5.** (*rumor*) rumour.

VPO (*abrev de* **vivienda de protección oficial**) *f* = council house/flat Br, = public housing unit Am.

vudú (*en aposición inv*) *m* voodoo.

vuelco *m* upset; **dar un ~** (*coche*) to overturn; (*relaciones*) to change completely; (*empresa*) to go to ruin; **me dio un ~ el corazón** my heart missed o skipped a beat.

vuelo *m* **1.** (*gen & AERON*) flight; **alzar** o **emprender** o **levantar el ~** (*despegar*) to take flight, to fly off; *fig* (*irse de casa*) to fly the nest; **coger algo al ~** (*en el aire*) to catch sthg in flight; *fig* (*rápido*) to catch on to sthg very quickly; **remontar el ~** to soar; **~ chárter/regular** charter/scheduled flight; **~ libre** hang gliding; **~ sin motor** gliding. **2.** (*de vestido*): **una falda de ~** a full skirt.

vuelta *f* **1.** (*gen*) turn; (*acción*) turning; **darse la ~** to turn round; **dar ~s (a algo)** (*girándolo*) to turn (sthg) round; **media ~** (MIL) about-turn; (AUTOM) U-turn. **2.** (DEP) lap; **~ (ciclista)** tour. **3.** (*regreso, devolución*) return; **a la ~** (*volviendo*) on the way back; (*al llegar*) on one's return; **estar de ~** to be back. **4.** (*paseo*): **dar una ~** to go for a walk. **5.** (*dinero sobrante*) change. **6.** (*ronda, turno*) round. **7.** (*parte opuesta*) back, other side; **a la ~ de la página** over the page. **8.** (*cambio, avatar*) change. **9.** *loc*: **a ~ de correo** by return of post; **dar la ~ a la tortilla** *fam* to turn the

tables; **dar una ~/dos** *etc* **~s de campana** (*coche*) to turn over once/twice *etc*; **darle ~s a algo** to turn sthg over in one's mind; **estar de ~ de algo** to be blasé about sthg; **no tiene ~ de hoja** there are no two ways about it.

vuelto, -ta ◆ *pp →* **volver. ◆** *adj* turned. **▶ vuelto** *m Amer* change.

vuestro, -tra ◆ *adj poses* your; **~ libro/amigo** your book/friend; **este libro es ~** this book is yours; **un amigo ~** a friend of yours; **no es asunto ~** it's none of your business. **◆** *pron poses*: **el ~** yours; **los ~s están en la mesa** yours are on the table; **lo ~ es el teatro** (*lo que hacéis bien*) you should be on the stage; **los ~s** *fam* (*vuestra familia*) your folks; (*vuestro bando*) your lot.

vulgar *adj* **1.** (*no refinado*) vulgar. **2.** (*corriente, ordinario*) ordinary, common.

vulgaridad *f* **1.** (*grosería*) vulgarity; **hacer/decir una ~** to do/say sthg vulgar. **2.** (*banalidad*) banality.

vulgarizar *vt* to popularize.

vulgo *m despec*: **el ~** (*plebe*) the masses (*pl*); (*no expertos*) the lay public (U).

vulnerable *adj* vulnerable.

vulnerar *vt* **1.** (*prestigio etc*) to harm, to damage. **2.** (*ley, pacto etc*) to violate, to break.

vulva *f* vulva.

VV *abrev de* **ustedes.**

w, W *f* (*letra*) w, W.

walkie-talkie ['walki'talki] (*pl* **walkie-talkies**) *m* walkie-talkie.

walkman® ['walman] (*pl* **walkmans**) *m* Walkman®.

Washington ['wafiŋton] Washington.

wáter ['bater] (*pl* **wáteres**), **váter** (*pl* **váteres**) *m* toilet.

waterpolo [water'polo] *m* water polo.

watio = **vatio.**

Web *f*: **la (World Wide) ~** the World Wide Web.

WC (*abrev de* **water closet**) *m* WC.

whisky ['wiski] = **güisqui.**

windsurf ['winsurf], **windsurfing** ['winsurfin] *m* windsurfing.

x, X f (letra) x, X. ▶ **X** m y f: **la señora X** Mrs X.
xenofobia f xenophobia.
xilofón, xilófono m xylophone.

y¹, Y f (letra) y, Y.

y² conj 1. (gen) and; **un ordenador ~ una impresora** a computer and a printer; **horas ~ horas de espera** hours and hours of waiting. 2. (pero) and yet; **sabía que no lo conseguiría ~ seguía intentándolo** she knew she wouldn't manage it and yet she kept on trying. 3. (en preguntas) what about; **¿~ tu mujer?** what about your wife?

ya ◆ adv 1. (en el pasado) already; **~ me lo habías contado** you had already told me; **~ en 1926** as long ago as 1926. 2. (ahora) now; (inmediatamente) at once; **hay que hacer algo ~** something has to be done now/at once; **bueno, yo ~ me voy** right, I'm off now; **~ no es así** it's no longer like that. 3. (en el futuro): **~ te llamaré** I'll give you a ring some time; **~ hablaremos** we'll talk later; **~ nos habremos ido** we'll already have gone; **~ verás** you'll (soon) see. 4. (refuerza al verbo): **~ entiendo/lo sé** I understand/know. ◆ conj (distributiva): **~ (sea) por ... ~ (sea) por ...** whether for ... or ... ◆ interj **¡~!** (expresa asentimiento) right!; (expresa comprensión) yes!; **¡~, ~!** irón sure!, yes, of course! ▶ **ya no** loc adv: **~ no ... sino** not only ..., but. ▶ **ya que** loc conj since; **~ que has venido, ayúdame con esto** since you're here, give me a hand with this.
yacer vi to lie.
yacimiento m 1. (minero) bed, deposit; **~ de petróleo** oilfield. 2. (arqueológico) site.
yanqui m y f 1. (HIST) Yankee. 2. fam (estadounidense) pejorative term referring to a person from the US, yank.
yate m yacht.
yegua f mare.
yema f 1. (de huevo) yolk. 2. (de planta) bud, shoot. 3. (de dedo) fingertip.
Yemen: (el) ~ Yemen.
yen (pl yenes) m yen.
yerba = hierba.
yerbatero m Amer healer.
yermo, -ma adj (estéril) barren.
yerno m son-in-law.
yeso m 1. (GEOL) gypsum. 2. (CONSTR) plaster. 3. (ARTE) gesso.
yeyé adj sixties.
yo pron pers 1. (sujeto) I; **~ me llamo Luis** I'm called Luis. 2. (predicado): **soy ~** it's me. 3. loc: **~ que tú/él** etc if I were you/him etc.
yodo, iodo m iodine.
yoga m yoga.
yogur (pl yogures), **yogurt** (pl yogurts) m yoghurt.
yonqui m y f fam junkie.
yóquey (pl yóqueys), **jockey** (pl jockeys) m jockey.
yoyó m yoyo.
yuca f 1. (BOT) yucca. 2. (CULIN) cassava.
yudo, judo ['juðo] m judo.
yugo m lit & fig yoke.
Yugoslavia Yugoslavia.
yugoslavo, -va ◆ adj Yugoslavian. ◆ m y f Yugoslav.
yugular adj & f jugular.
yunque m anvil.
yuppie (pl yuppies), **yupi** m y f yuppie.
yuxtaponer vt to juxtapose.
yuxtaposición f juxtaposition.
yuxtapuesto, -ta pp → yuxtaponer.

z, Z f (letra) z, Z.
zafio, -fia adj rough, uncouth.
zafiro m sapphire.
zaga f (DEP) defence; **a la ~** behind, at the back; **no irle a la ~ a alguien** to be every bit o just as good as sb.
zaguán m (entrance) hall.
Zaire Zaire.

zalamería f (gen pl) flattery (U).
zalamero, -ra m y f flatterer; despec smooth talker.
zamarra f sheepskin jacket.
zambo, -ba m y f knock-kneed person.
zambullir vt to dip, to submerge. ▶ **zambullirse** vpr: **~se (en)** (agua) to dive (into); (actividad) to immerse o.s. (in).
zampar fam vi to gobble. ▶ **zamparse** vpr to wolf down.
zampoña m panpipes (pl).
zanahoria f carrot.
zanca f (de ave) leg, shank.
zancada f stride.
zancadilla f trip; **poner una** o **la ~ a alguien** (hacer tropezar) to trip sb up; (engañar) to trick sb.
zancadillear vt (hacer tropezar) to trip up.
zanco m stilt.
zancudo, -da adj long-legged. ▶ **zancudo** m Amer mosquito.
zángano, -na m y f fam (persona) lazy oaf. ▶ **zángano** m (abeja) drone.
zanja f ditch.
zanjar vt (poner fin a) to put an end to; (resolver) to settle, to resolve.
zapallo m Amer courgette.
zapata f (de freno) shoe.
zapateado m type of flamenco music and dance.
zapatear vi to stamp one's feet.
zapatería f 1. (oficio) shoemaking. 2. (taller) shoemaker's. 3. (tienda) shoe shop.
zapatero, -ra m y f 1. (fabricante) shoemaker. 2. (reparador): **~ (de viejo** o **remendón)** cobbler. 3. (vendedor) shoe seller.
zapatilla f 1. (de baile) shoe, pump; (de estar en casa) slipper; (de deporte) sports shoe, trainer. 2. (de grifo) washer.
zapato m shoe.
zapping [ˈθapin] m inv channel-hopping; **hacer ~** to channel-hop.
zar, zarina m y f tsar (f tsarina), czar (f czarina).
zarandear vt 1. (cosa) to shake. 2. (persona) to jostle, to knock about.
zarcillo m (gen pl) earring.
zarpa f (de animal - uña) claw; (- mano) paw.
zarpar vi to weigh anchor, to set sail.
zarpazo m clawing (U).
zarza f bramble, blackberry bush.
zarzal m bramble patch.

zarzamora f blackberry.
zarzaparrilla f sarsaparilla.
zarzuela f (MÚS) zarzuela, Spanish light opera.
zas interj: **¡~!** wham!, bang!
zenit, cenit m lit & fig zenith.
zepelín (pl **zepelines**) m zeppelin.
zigzag (pl **zigzags** o **zigzagues**) m zigzag.
zigzaguear vi to zigzag.
zinc = **cinc**.
zíper m Amer zip.
zócalo m 1. (de pared) skirting board. 2. (de edificio, pedestal) plinth.
zoco m souk, Arabian market.
zodiaco, zodíaco m zodiac.
zombi, zombie m y f lit & fig zombie.
zona f zone, area; **~ azul** (AUTOM) restricted parking zone; **~ verde** (grande) park; (pequeño) lawn.

ZONA AZUL

In Spain, blue lines on the road surface indicate areas where parking meters are in operation. Parking in 'zonas azules' is free between certain hours; these times are displayed on the parking meters.

---

zoo m zoo.
zoología f zoology.
zoológico, -ca adj zoological. ▶ **zoológico** m zoo.
zoólogo, -ga m y f zoologist.
zopenco, -ca m y f nitwit.
zoquete ♦ m (calcetín) ankle sock. ♦ m y f (tonto) blockhead.
zorro, -rra m y f lit & fig fox. ▶ **zorro** m (piel) fox (fur).
zozobra f anxiety, worry.
zozobrar vi 1. (naufragar) to be shipwrecked. 2. fig (fracasar) to fall through.
zueco m clog.
zulo m hideout.
zulú (pl **zulúes**) adj, m y f Zulu.
zumbar vi (gen) to buzz; (máquinas) to whirr, to hum; **me zumban los oídos** my ears are buzzing.
zumbido m (gen) buzz, buzzing (U); (de máquinas) whirr, whirring (U).
zumo m juice.
zurcido m 1. (acción) darning. 2. (remiendo) darn.
zurcir vt to darn.
zurdo, -da adj (mano etc) left; (persona) left-handed. ▶ **zurda** f (mano) left hand.
zurrar vt (pegar) to beat, to thrash.
zutano, -na m y f so-and-so, what's-his-name (f what's-her-name).

A

a¹ (*pl* **as** OR **a's**), **A** (*pl* **As** OR **A's**) [eɪ] *n* (*letter*) a *f*, A *f*. ▶ **A** *n* **1.** (MUS) la *m*. **2.** (SCH) (*mark*) ≈ sobresaliente *m*.

a² [*stressed* eɪ, *unstressed* ə] (*before vowel or silent 'h': an* [*stressed* æn, *unstressed* ən]) *indef art* **1.** (*gen*) un (una); **a boy** un chico; **a table** una mesa; **an orange** una naranja; **an eagle** un águila; **a hundred/ thousand pounds** cien/mil libras. **2.** (*referring to occupation*): **to be a dentist/ teacher** ser dentista/maestra. **3.** (*to express prices, ratios etc*) por; **£10 a person** 10 libras por persona; **50 km an hour** 50 kms. por hora; **20p a kilo** 20 peniques el kilo; **twice a week/month** dos veces a la semana/al mes.

AA *n* **1.** (*abbr of* **Automobile Association**) asociación británica del automóvil, ≈ RACE *m*. **2.** (*abbr of* **Alcoholics Anonymous**) AA *mpl*.

AAA *n* (*abbr of* **American Automobile Association**) asociación estadounidense del automóvil, ≈ RACE *m*.

AB (*abbr of* **Bachelor of Arts**) *n Am* (*titular de una*) licenciatura de letras.

aback [ə'bæk] *adv*: **to be taken ~** quedarse atónito(ta) OR estupefacto (ta).

abandon [ə'bændən] ◆ *vt* abandonar. ◆ *n*: **with ~** con desenfreno.

abashed [ə'bæʃt] *adj* avergonzado (da).

abate [ə'beɪt] *vi* (*storm*) amainar; (*noise*) debilitarse; (*fear*) apaciguarse.

abattoir ['æbətwɑːr] *n* matadero *m*.

abbey ['æbɪ] *n* abadía *f*.

abbot ['æbət] *n* abad *m*.

abbreviate [ə'briːvɪeɪt] *vt* abreviar.

abbreviation [ə,briːvɪ'eɪʃn] *n* abreviatura *f*.

ABC *n lit & fig* abecé *m*.

abdicate ['æbdɪkeɪt] ◆ *vi* abdicar. ◆ *vt* (*responsibility*) abdicar de.

abdomen ['æbdəmen] *n* abdomen *m*.

abduct [əb'dʌkt] *vt* raptar.

aberration [,æbə'reɪʃn] *n* aberración *f*.

abet [ə'bet] *vt* → **aid**.

abeyance [ə'beɪəns] *n*: **in ~** (*custom*) en desuso; (*law*) en suspenso.

abhor [əb'hɔːr] *vt* aborrecer.

abide [ə'baɪd] *vt* soportar, aguantar. ▶ **abide by** *vt fus* (*law, ruling*) acatar; (*principles, own decision*) atenerse a.

ability [ə'bɪlətɪ] *n* **1.** (*capability*) capacidad *f*. **2.** (*skill*) dotes *fpl*.

abject ['æbdʒekt] *adj* **1.** (*poverty*) vil, indigente. **2.** (*person*) sumiso(sa); (*apology*) humillante.

ablaze [ə'bleɪz] *adj* (*on fire*) en llamas.

able ['eɪbl] *adj* **1.** (*capable*): **to be ~ to do sthg** poder hacer algo. **2.** (*skilful*) capaz, competente.

ably ['eɪblɪ] *adv* eficientemente.

abnormal [æb'nɔːml] *adj* anormal.

aboard [ə'bɔːd] ◆ *adv* a bordo. ◆ *prep* (*ship, plane*) a bordo de; (*bus, train*) en.

abode [ə'bəʊd] *n fml*: **of no fixed ~** sin domicilio fijo.

abolish [ə'bɒlɪʃ] *vt* abolir.

abolition [,æbə'lɪʃn] *n* abolición *f*.

abominable [ə'bɒmɪnəbl] *adj* abominable, deplorable.

aborigine [,æbə'rɪdʒənɪ] *n* aborigen *m y f* de Australia.

abort [ə'bɔːt] *vt* **1.** (*pregnancy, plan, project*) abortar; (*pregnant woman*) provocar el aborto a. **2.** (COMPUT) abortar.

abortion [ə'bɔːʃn] *n* aborto *m*; **to have an ~** abortar.

abortive [ə'bɔ:tɪv] *adj* frustrado(da).

abound [ə'baʊnd] *vi* 1. (*be plentiful*) abundar. 2. (*be full*): **to ~ with** OR **in** abundar en.

about [ə'baʊt] ◆ *adv* 1. (*approximately*) más o menos, como; **there were ~ fifty/ a hundred** había (como) unos cincuenta/cien o así; **at ~ five o'clock** a eso de las cinco. 2. (*referring to place*) por ahí; **to leave things lying ~** dejar las cosas por ahí; **to walk ~** ir andando por ahí; **to jump ~** dar saltos. 3. (*on the point of*): **to be ~ to do sthg** estar a punto de hacer algo. ◆ *prep* 1. (*relating to, concerning*) sobre, acerca de; **a film ~ Paris** una película sobre París; **what is it ~?** ¿de qué trata?; **there's something odd ~ that man** hay algo raro en ese hombre; **how ~ ...?** → **how**; **what ~ ...?** → **what**. 2. (*referring to place*) por; **to wander ~ the streets** vagar por las calles.

about-turn, about-face *n* (MIL) media vuelta *f*; *fig* cambio *m* radical.

above [ə'bʌv] ◆ *adv* 1. (*on top, higher up*) arriba; **the flat ~** el piso de arriba; **see ~** (*in text*) véase más arriba. 2. (*more, over*): **children aged five and ~** niños de cinco años en adelante. ◆ *prep* 1. (*on top of*) encima de. 2. (*higher up than, over*) por encima de. 3. (*more than, superior to*) por encima de; **children ~ the age of 15** niños mayores de 15 años. ▶ **above all** *adv* sobre todo.

aboveboard [ə,bʌv'bɔ:d] *adj* honrado (da), sin tapujos.

abrasive [ə'breɪsɪv] *adj* 1. (*substance*) abrasivo(va). 2. (*person*) mordaz.

abreast [ə'brest] ◆ *adv* hombro con hombro. ◆ *prep*: **to keep ~ of** mantenerse OR estar al día de.

abridged [ə'brɪdʒd] *adj* abreviado (da).

abroad [ə'brɔ:d] *adv* en el extranjero; **to go ~** ir al extranjero.

abrupt [ə'brʌpt] *adj* 1. (*sudden*) repentino(na). 2. (*brusque*) brusco(ca).

abscess ['æbsɪs] *n* absceso *m*.

abscond [əb'skɒnd] *vi*: **to ~ (with/from)** escaparse OR fugarse (con/de).

abseil ['æbseɪl] *vi*: **to ~ (down sthg)** descolgarse OR descender haciendo rappel (por algo).

absence ['æbsəns] *n* 1. (*of person*) ausencia *f*. 2. (*of thing*) falta *f*.

absent ['æbsənt] *adj* (*not present*) ausente; **to be ~ from** faltar a, ausentarse de.

absentee [,æbsən'ti:] *n* ausente *m y f*.

absent-minded [-'maɪndɪd] *adj* (*person*) despistado(da); (*behaviour*) distraído(da).

absolute ['æbsəlu:t] *adj* absoluto(ta).

absolutely ['æbsəlu:tlɪ] ◆ *adv* (*completely*) completamente, absolutamente. ◆ *excl* ¡desde luego!

absolve [əb'zɒlv] *vt*: **to ~ sb (from)** absolver a alguien (de).

absorb [əb'sɔ:b] *vt* (*gen*) absorber; **to be ~ed in sthg** *fig* estar absorto OR embebido en algo.

absorbent [əb'sɔ:bənt] *adj* absorbente.

absorption [əb'sɔ:pʃn] *n* (*of liquid*) absorción *f*.

abstain [əb'steɪn] *vi*: **to ~ (from)** abstenerse (de).

abstemious [æb'sti:mjəs] *adj* *fml* sobrio(bria), moderado(da).

abstention [əb'stenʃn] *n* abstención *f*.

abstract ['æbstrækt] ◆ *adj* abstracto (ta). ◆ *n* (*summary*) resumen *m*, sinopsis *f*.

absurd [əb'sɜ:d] *adj* absurdo(da).

ABTA ['æbtə] (*abbr of* **Association of British Travel Agents**) *n* asociación británica de agencias de viajes.

abundant [ə'bʌndənt] *adj* abundante.

abundantly [ə'bʌndəntlɪ] *adv* (*extremely*): **it's ~ clear** está clarísimo.

abuse [*n* ə'bju:s, *vb* ə'bju:z] ◆ *n* (U) 1. (*offensive remarks*) insultos *mpl*. 2. (*misuse, maltreatment*) abuso *m*. ◆ *vt* 1. (*insult*) insultar. 2. (*maltreat, misuse*) abusar de.

abusive [ə'bju:sɪv] *adj* (*person*) grosero (ra); (*behaviour, language*) insultante.

abysmal [ə'bɪzml] *adj* pésimo(ma), nefasto(ta).

abyss [ə'bɪs] *n* abismo *m*, sima *f*.

a/c (*abbr of* **account (current)**) c/c.

AC *n* (*abbr of* **alternating current**) CA *f*.

academic [,ækə'demɪk] ◆ *adj* 1. (*of college, university*) académico(ca). 2. (*studious*) estudioso(sa). 3. (*hypothetical*) teórico(ca). ◆ *n* (*university lecturer*) profesor *m* universitario, profesora *f* universitaria.

academy [ə'kædəmɪ] *n* academia *f*.

ACAS ['eɪkæs] (*abbr of* **Advisory, Conciliation and Arbitration Service**) *n* organización británica para el arbitraje en conflictos laborales, ≃ IMAC *m*.

accede [æk'si:d] *vi* 1. (*agree*): **to ~ to** acceder a. 2. (*monarch*): **to ~ to the throne** subir al trono.

accelerate [ək'seləreɪt] *vi* 1. (*car, driver*) acelerar. 2. (*inflation, growth*) dispararse.

acceleration [ək,selə'reɪʃn] n aceleración f.

accelerator [ək'seləreɪtər] n acelerador m.

accent ['æksent] n lit & fig acento m.

accept [ək'sept] vt 1. (gen) aceptar. 2. (difficult situation, problem) asimilar. 3. (defeat, blame, responsibility) asumir. 4. (agree): **to ~ that** admitir que. 5. (subj: machine - coins, tokens) admitir.

acceptable [ək'septəbl] adj aceptable.

acceptance [ək'septəns] n 1. (gen) aceptación f. 2. (of piece of work, article) aprobación f. 3. (of defeat, blame, responsibility) reconocimiento m. 4. (of person - as part of group etc) admisión f.

access ['ækses] n 1. (entry) acceso m. 2. (opportunity to use or see) libre acceso m; **to have ~** to tener acceso a.

accessible [ək'sesəbl] adj 1. (place) accesible. 2. (service, book, film) asequible.

accessory [ək'sesərɪ] n 1. (of car, vacuum cleaner) accesorio m. 2. (JUR) cómplice m y f. ► **accessories** npl complementos mpl.

accident ['æksɪdənt] n accidente m; **it was an ~** fue sin querer; **by ~** (by chance) por casualidad.

accidental [,æksɪ'dentl] adj accidental.

accidentally [,æksɪ'dentəlɪ] adv 1. (by chance) por casualidad. 2. (unintentionally) sin querer.

accident-prone adj propenso(sa) a los accidentes.

acclaim [ə'kleɪm] ♦ n (U) elogio m, alabanza f. ♦ vt elogiar, alabar.

acclimatize, -ise [ə'klaɪmətaɪz], **acclimate** Am ['æklɪmeɪt] vi: **to ~ (to)** aclimatarse (a).

accolade ['ækəleɪd] n (praise) elogio m, halago m; (award) galardón m.

accommodate [ə'kɒmədeɪt] vt 1. (provide room for people - subj: person) alojar; (- subj: building, place) albergar. 2. (oblige) complacer.

accommodating [ə'kɒmədeɪtɪŋ] adj complaciente, servicial.

accommodation [ə,kɒmə'deɪʃn] n Br, **accommodations** [ə,kɒmə'deɪʃnz] npl Am (lodging) alojamiento m.

accompany [ə'kʌmpənɪ] vt acompañar.

accomplice [ə'kʌmplɪs] n cómplice m y f.

accomplish [ə'kʌmplɪʃ] vt (achieve) conseguir, alcanzar.

accomplished [ə'kʌmplɪʃt] adj competente, experto(ta).

accomplishment [ə'kʌmplɪʃmənt] n 1. (action) realización f. 2. (achievement) logro m.

accord [ə'kɔːd] ♦ n: **to do sthg of one's own ~** hacer algo por propia voluntad. ♦ vt: **to ~ sb sthg**, **to ~ sthg to sb** conceder algo a alguien.

accordance [ə'kɔːdəns] n: **in ~ with** acorde con, conforme a.

according [ə'kɔːdɪŋ] ► **according to** prep 1. (as stated or shown by) según; **to go ~ to plan** ir según lo planeado. 2. (with regard to) de acuerdo con, conforme a.

accordingly [ə'kɔːdɪŋlɪ] adv 1. (appropriately) como corresponde. 2. (consequently) por lo tanto.

accordion [ə'kɔːdjən] n acordeón m.

accost [ə'kɒst] vt abordar.

account [ə'kaʊnt] n 1. (with bank, shop etc) cuenta f. 2. (report - spoken) relato m; (- written) informe m. 3. phr: **to take ~ of sthg**, **to take sthg into ~** tener en cuenta algo; **of no ~** indiferente, de poca importancia; **on no ~** bajo ningún pretexto OR concepto. ► **accounts** npl (of business) cuentas fpl. ► **by all accounts** adv a decir de todos, según todo el mundo. ► **on account of** prep debido a. ► **account for** vt fus 1. (explain) justificar. 2. (represent) representar.

accountable [ə'kaʊntəbl] adj (responsible): **~ (for)** responsable (de).

accountancy [ə'kaʊntənsɪ] n contabilidad f.

accountant [ə'kaʊntənt] n contable m y f, contador m, -ra f Amer.

accrue [ə'kruː] vi acumularse.

accumulate [ə'kjuːmjʊleɪt] ♦ vt acumular. ♦ vi (money, things) acumularse; (problems) amontonarse.

accuracy ['ækjʊrəsɪ] n 1. (of description, report) veracidad f. 2. (of weapon, marksman) precisión f; (of typing, figures) exactitud f.

accurate ['ækjʊrət] adj 1. (description, report) veraz. 2. (weapon, marksman, typist) preciso(sa); (figures, estimate) exacto(ta).

accurately ['ækjʊrətlɪ] adv 1. (truthfully) verazmente. 2. (precisely) con precisión.

accusation [,ækjuː'zeɪʃn] n 1. (charge) acusación f. 2. (JUR) denuncia f.

accuse [ə'kjuːz] vt: **to ~ sb of sthg/of doing sthg** acusar a alguien de algo/de hacer algo.

accused [ə'kjuːzd] (pl inv) n (JUR): **the ~** el acusado, la acusada.

accustomed [əˈkʌstəmd] *adj*: ~ **to** acostumbrado(da) a.

ace [eɪs] *n* (*playing card*) as *m*.

ache [eɪk] ◆ *n* (*pain*) dolor *m*. ◆ *vi* (*hurt*) doler; **my back ~s** me duele la espalda.

achieve [əˈtʃiːv] *vt* (*success, goal, fame*) alcanzar, lograr; (*ambition*) realizar.

achievement [əˈtʃiːvmənt] *n* **1.** (*accomplishment*) logro *m*, éxito *m*. **2.** (*act of achieving*) consecución *f*, realización *f*.

achiever [əˈtʃiːvər] *n*: **low ~** (*at school*) estudiante *m y f* de bajo rendimiento escolar.

Achilles' tendon [əˈkɪliːz-] *n* tendón *m* de Aquiles.

acid [ˈæsɪd] ◆ *adj* **1.** (CHEM) ácido(da). **2.** (*sharp-tasting*) agrio (agria). **3.** *fig* (*person, remark*) mordaz. ◆ *n* ácido *m*.

acid rain *n* lluvia *f* ácida.

acknowledge [əkˈnɒlɪdʒ] *vt* **1.** (*accept*) reconocer. **2.** (*greet*) saludar. **3.** (*letter etc*): **to ~ receipt of** acusar recibo de. **4.** (*recognize*): **to ~ sb as** reconocer OR considerar a alguien como.

acknowledg(e)ment [əkˈnɒlɪdʒ-mənt] *n* **1.** (*acceptance*) reconocimiento *m*. **2.** (*confirmation of receipt*) acuse *m* de recibo. ► **acknowledg(e)ments** *npl* agradecimientos *mpl*.

acne [ˈækni] *n* acné *m*.

acorn [ˈeɪkɔːn] *n* bellota *f*.

acoustic [əˈkuːstɪk] *adj* acústico(ca). ► **acoustics** *npl* acústica *f*.

acquaint [əˈkweɪnt] *vt* **1.** (*make familiar*): **to ~ sb with sthg** (*information*) poner a alguien al corriente de algo; (*method, technique*) familiarizar a alguien con algo. **2.** (*make known*): **to be ~ed with sb** conocer a alguien.

acquaintance [əˈkweɪntəns] *n* conocido *m*, -da *f*.

acquire [əˈkwaɪər] *vt* **1.** (*buy, adopt*) adquirir. **2.** (*obtain - information, document*) procurarse.

acquisitive [əˈkwɪzɪtɪv] *adj* consumista.

acquit [əˈkwɪt] *vt* **1.** (JUR): **to ~ sb of sthg** absolver a alguien de algo. **2.** (*perform*): **to ~ o.s. well/badly** hacer un buen/mal papel.

acquittal [əˈkwɪtl] *n* (JUR) absolución *f*.

acre [ˈeɪkər] *n* acre *m*.

acrid [ˈækrɪd] *adj* *lit & fig* acre.

acrimonious [ˌækrɪˈməʊnjəs] *adj* (*words*) áspero(ra); (*dispute*) enconado (da).

acrobat [ˈækrəbæt] *n* acróbata *m y f*.

acronym [ˈækrənɪm] *n* siglas *fpl*.

across [əˈkrɒs] ◆ *adv* **1.** (*from one side to the other*) de un lado a otro; **to walk/run ~** cruzar andando/corriendo. **2.** (*in measurements*): **the river is 2 km ~** el río tiene 2 kms de ancho. ◆ *prep* **1.** (*from one side to the other of*) a través de, de un lado a otro de; **to walk/run ~ the road** cruzar la carretera andando/corriendo. **2.** (*on the other side of*) al otro lado de. ► **across from** *prep* enfrente de.

acrylic [əˈkrɪlɪk] ◆ *adj* acrílico(ca). ◆ *n* acrílico *m*.

act [ækt] ◆ *n* **1.** (*action, deed*) acto *m*, acción *f*; **to be in the ~ of doing sthg** estar haciendo algo. **2.** (*pretence*) farsa *f*. **3.** (*in parliament*) ley *f*. **4.** (THEATRE - *part of play*) acto *m*; (- *routine, turn*) número *m*. ◆ *vi* **1.** (*gen*) actuar; **to ~ as** (*person*) hacer de; (*thing*) actuar como. **2.** (*behave*): **to ~ (as if/like)** comportarse (como si/como). **3.** *fig* (*pretend*) fingir. ◆ *vt* (*part - in play, film*) interpretar.

acting [ˈæktɪŋ] ◆ *adj* (*interim*) en funciones. ◆ *n* actuación *f*; **I like ~** me gusta actuar.

action [ˈækʃn] *n* **1.** (*gen & MIL*) acción *f*; **to take ~** tomar medidas; **in ~** (*person*) en acción; (*machine*) en funcionamiento; **out of ~** (*person*) fuera de combate; (*machine*) averiado(da). **2.** (*deed*) acto *m*, acción *f*. **3.** (JUR) demanda *f*.

action replay *n* repetición *f* (de la jugada).

activate [ˈæktɪveɪt] *vt* (*device*) activar; (*machine*) poner en funcionamiento.

active [ˈæktɪv] *adj* **1.** (*person, campaigner*) activo(va). **2.** (*encouragement etc*) enérgico(ca). **3.** (*volcano*) en actividad; (*bomb*) activado(da).

actively [ˈæktɪvli] *adv* (*encourage, discourage*) enérgicamente.

activist [ˈæktɪvɪst] *n* activista *m y f*.

activity [ækˈtɪvətɪ] *n* **1.** (*movement, action*) actividad *f*. **2.** (*pastime, hobby*) afición *f*.

actor [ˈæktər] *n* actor *m*.

actress [ˈæktrɪs] *n* actriz *f*.

actual [ˈæktʃʊəl] *adj* (*emphatic*): **the ~ cost is £10** el coste real es de 10 libras; **the ~ spot where it happened** el sitio mismo en que ocurrió.

actually [ˈæktʃʊəlɪ] *adv* **1.** (*really, in truth*): **do you ~ like him?** ¿de verdad que te gusta?; **no-one ~ saw her** en realidad, nadie la vio. **2.** (*by the way*): **~, I was there yesterday** pues yo estuve ayer por allí.

acumen [ˈækjʊmen] *n*: **business ~** vista *f* para los negocios.

acupuncture [ˈækjʊpʌŋktʃəʳ] n acupuntura f.

acute [əˈkjuːt] adj 1. (illness) agudo(da); (pain, danger) extremo(ma). 2. (perceptive - person) perspicaz. 3. (hearing, smell) muy fino(na).

ad [æd] (abbr of **advertisement**) n anuncio m.

AD (abbr of **Anno Domini**) d. C.

adamant [ˈædəmənt] adj: **to be ~ (that)** mostrarse inflexible (en que).

Adam's apple [ˈædəmz-] n bocado m OR nuez f de Adán.

adapt [əˈdæpt] ◆ vt adaptar. ◆ vi: **to ~ (to)** adaptarse OR amoldarse (a).

adaptable [əˈdæptəbl] adj (person) capaz de adaptarse.

adapter, adaptor [əˈdæptəʳ] n (ELEC - for several devices) ladrón m; (- for different socket) adaptador m.

add [æd] vt 1. (gen): **to ~ sthg (to sthg)** añadir algo (a algo). 2. (numbers) sumar.
► **add on** vt sep (to bill, total): **to ~ sthg on (to sthg)** añadir or incluir algo (en algo). ► **add to** vt fus aumentar, acrecentar. ► **add up** ◆ vt sep (numbers) sumar. ◆ vi inf (make sense): **it doesn't ~ up** no tiene sentido.

adder [ˈædəʳ] n víbora f.

addict [ˈædɪkt] n 1. (taking drugs) adicto m, -ta f; **drug ~** drogadicto m, -ta f, toxicómano m, -na f. 2. fig (fan) fanático m, -ca f.

addicted [əˈdɪktɪd] adj 1. (to drug): **~ (to)** adicto(ta) (a). 2. fig (to food, TV): **to be ~ (to)** ser un fanático de.

addiction [əˈdɪkʃn] n 1. (to drug): **~ (to)** adicción f (a). 2. fig (to food, TV): **~ (to)** vicio m (por).

addictive [əˈdɪktɪv] adj lit & fig adictivo (va).

addition [əˈdɪʃn] n 1. (MATH) suma f. 2. (extra thing) adición f. 3. (act of adding) incorporación f; **in ~** además; **in ~ to** además de.

additional [əˈdɪʃənl] adj adicional.

additive [ˈædɪtɪv] n aditivo m.

address [əˈdres] ◆ n 1. (of person, organization) dirección f, domicilio m. 2. (speech) discurso m. ◆ vt 1. (letter, parcel, remark): **to ~ sthg to** dirigir algo a. 2. (meeting, conference) dirigirse a. 3. (issue): **to ~ o.s. to sthg** enfrentarse a OR abordar algo.

address book n agenda f de direcciones.

adenoids [ˈædɪnɔɪdz] npl vegetaciones fpl (adenoideas).

adept [ˈædept] adj: **to be ~ (at sthg/at doing sthg)** ser experto(ta) (en algo/en hacer algo).

adequate [ˈædɪkwət] adj 1. (sufficient) suficiente. 2. (good enough) aceptable.

adhere [ədˈhɪəʳ] vi 1. (to surface, principle): **to ~ (to)** adherirse (a). 2. (to rule, decision): **to ~ to** respetar, observar.

adhesive [ədˈhiːsɪv] ◆ adj adhesivo (va), adherente. ◆ n adhesivo m.

adhesive tape n cinta f adhesiva.

adjacent [əˈdʒeɪsənt] adj: **~ (to)** adyacente OR contiguo(gua) (a).

adjective [ˈædʒɪktɪv] n adjetivo m.

adjoining [əˈdʒɔɪnɪŋ] ◆ adj (table) adyacente; (room) contiguo(gua). ◆ prep junto a.

adjourn [əˈdʒɜːn] ◆ vt (decision) aplazar; (session) levantar; (meeting) interrumpir. ◆ vi aplazarse, suspenderse.

adjudge [əˈdʒʌdʒ] vt declarar, juzgar.

adjudicate [əˈdʒuːdɪkeɪt] vi actuar como juez; **to ~ on OR upon sthg** emitir un fallo or un veredicto sobre algo.

adjust [əˈdʒʌst] ◆ vt (machine, setting) ajustar; (clothing) arreglarse. ◆ vi: **to ~ (to)** adaptarse OR amoldarse (a).

adjustable [əˈdʒʌstəbl] adj (machine, chair) regulable, graduable.

adjustment [əˈdʒʌstmənt] n 1. (modification) modificación f, reajuste m. 2. (U) (change in attitude): **~ (to)** adaptación f OR amoldamiento m (a).

ad lib [ˌædˈlɪb] ◆ adj (improvised) improvisado(da). ◆ adv (without preparation) improvisando; (without limit) a voluntad. ► **ad-lib** vi improvisar.

administer [ədˈmɪnɪstəʳ] vt (gen) administrar; (punishment) aplicar.

administration [ədˌmɪnɪˈstreɪʃn] n (gen) administración f; (of punishment) aplicación f.

administrative [ədˈmɪnɪstrətɪv] adj administrativo(va).

admirable [ˈædmərəbl] adj admirable.

admiral [ˈædmərəl] n almirante m.

admiration [ˌædməˈreɪʃn] n admiración f.

admire [ədˈmaɪəʳ] vt: **to ~ sb (for)** admirar a alguien (por).

admirer [ədˈmaɪərəʳ] n admirador m, -ra f.

admission [ədˈmɪʃn] n 1. (permission to enter) admisión f, ingreso m. 2. (cost of entrance) entrada f. 3. (of guilt, mistake) reconocimiento m.

admit [ədˈmɪt] ◆ vt 1. (acknowledge, confess): **to ~ (that)** admitir OR reconocer (que); **to ~ doing sthg** reconocer haber hecho algo; **to ~ defeat** *fig* darse por vencido. **2.** *(allow to enter or join)* admitir; **to be admitted to hospital** Br OR **to the hospital** Am ser ingresado en el hospital. ◆ *vi*: **to ~ to sthg** confesar algo:

admittance [əd'mɪtəns] *n*: **to gain ~ to** conseguir entrar en; **'no ~'** 'prohibido el paso'.

admittedly [əd'mɪtɪdlɪ] *adv* sin duda.

admonish [əd'mɒnɪʃ] *vt* amonestar.

ad nauseam [,æd'nɔːzɪæm] *adv* hasta la saciedad.

ado [ə'duː] *n*: **without further** OR **more ~** sin más preámbulos, sin mayor dilación.

adolescence [,ædə'lesns] *n* adolescencia *f*.

adolescent [,ædə'lesnt] ◆ *adj* **1.** *(teenage)* adolescente. **2.** *pej (immature)* pueril. ◆ *n (teenager)* adolescente *m y f*.

adopt [ə'dɒpt] *vt & vi* adoptar.

adoption [ə'dɒpʃn] *n* adopción *f*.

adore [ə'dɔːr] *vt* **1.** *(love deeply)* adorar. **2.** *(like very much)*: **I ~ chocolate** me encanta el chocolate.

adorn [ə'dɔːn] *vt* adornar.

adrenalin [ə'drenəlɪn] *n* adrenalina *f*.

Adriatic [,eɪdrɪ'ætɪk] *n*: **the ~ (Sea)** el (mar) Adriático.

adrift [ə'drɪft] ◆ *adj (boat)* a la deriva. ◆ *adv*: **to go ~** *fig* irse a la deriva.

adult ['ædʌlt] ◆ *adj* **1.** *(fully grown)* adulto(ta). **2.** *(mature)* maduro(ra). **3.** *(suitable for adults only)* para adultos OR mayores. ◆ *n* adulto *m*, -ta *f*.

adultery [ə'dʌltərɪ] *n* adulterio *m*.

advance [əd'vɑːns] ◆ *n* **1.** *(gen)* avance *m*. **2.** *(money)* anticipo *m*. ◆ *comp*: **~ notice** OR **warning** previo aviso *m*; **~ booking** reserva *f* anticipada. ◆ *vt* **1.** *(improve)* promover. **2.** *(bring forward in time)* adelantar. **3.** *(give in advance)*: **to ~ sb sthg** adelantarle a alguien algo. ◆ *vi* avanzar. ▶ **advances** *npl*: **to make ~s to sb** *(sexual)* hacerle proposiciones a alguien, insinuarse a alguien; *(business)* hacerle una propuesta a alguien. ▶ **in advance** *adv (pay)* por adelantado; *(book)* con antelación; *(know)* de antemano.

advanced [əd'vɑːnst] *adj* **1.** *(developed)* avanzado(da). **2.** *(student, pupil)* adelantado(da); *(studies)* superior.

advantage [əd'vɑːntɪdʒ] *n*: **~ (over)** ventaja *f* (sobre); **to be to one's ~** ir en beneficio de uno; **to take ~ of sthg** aprovechar algo; **to take ~ of sb** aprovecharse de alguien.

advent ['ædvənt] *n (arrival)* advenimiento *m*. ▶ **Advent** *n* (RELIG) Adviento *m*.

adventure [əd'ventʃər] *n* aventura *f*.

adventure playground *n* Br parque *m* infantil.

adventurous [əd'ventʃərəs] *adj* **1.** *(daring)* aventurero(ra). **2.** *(dangerous)* arriesgado(da).

adverb ['ædvɜːb] *n* adverbio *m*.

adverse ['ædvɜːs] *adj* adverso(sa).

advert ['ædvɜːt] Br = **advertisement**.

advertise ['ædvətaɪz] ◆ *vt* anunciar. ◆ *vi* anunciarse, poner un anuncio; **to ~ for** buscar *(mediante anuncio)*.

advertisement [əd'vɜːtɪsmənt] *n* anuncio *m*.

advertiser ['ædvətaɪzər] *n* anunciante *m y f*.

advertising ['ædvətaɪzɪŋ] *n* publicidad *f*.

advice [əd'vaɪs] *n* (U) consejos *mpl*; **to take sb's ~** seguir el consejo de alguien; **a piece of ~** un consejo; **to give sb ~** aconsejar a alguien.

advisable [əd'vaɪzəbl] *adj* aconsejable.

advise [əd'vaɪz] ◆ *vt* **1.** *(give advice to)*: **to ~ sb to do sthg** aconsejar a alguien que haga algo; **to ~ sb against sthg/against doing sthg** desaconsejar a alguien algo/que haga algo. **2.** *(professionally)*: **to ~ sb on sthg** asesorar a alguien en algo. **3.** *fml (inform)*: **to ~ sb (of sthg)** informar a alguien (de algo). ◆ *vi* **1.** *(give advice)*: **to ~ against sthg** desaconsejar algo; **to ~ against doing sthg** aconsejar no hacer algo. **2.** *(professionally)*: **to ~ on** asesorar en (materia de).

advisedly [əd'vaɪzədlɪ] *adv (deliberately)* deliberadamente; *(after careful consideration)* con conocimiento de causa.

adviser Br, **advisor** Am [əd'vaɪzər] *n* consejero *m*, -ra *f*, asesor *m*, -ra *f*.

advisory [əd'vaɪzərɪ] *adj (body)* consultivo(va), asesor(ra).

advocate [*n* 'ædvəkət, *vb* 'ædvəkeɪt] ◆ *n* **1.** (JUR) abogado *m*, -da *f*. **2.** *(supporter)* defensor *m*, -ra *f*. ◆ *vt* abogar por.

Aegean [iː'dʒiːən] *n*: **the ~ (Sea)** el mar Egeo.

aerial ['eərɪəl] ◆ *adj* aéreo(a). ◆ *n* Br *(antenna)* antena *f*.

aerobics [eə'rəubɪks] *n* (U) aerobic *m*.

aerodynamic [,eərəudaɪ'næmɪk] *adj* aerodinámico(ca).

aeroplane ['eərəpleɪn] n Br avión m.

aerosol ['eərəsɒl] n aerosol m.

aesthetic, esthetic Am [iːs'θetɪk] adj estético(ca).

afar [ə'fɑːʳ] adv: **from ~** desde lejos.

affable ['æfəbl] adj afable.

affair [ə'feəʳ] n 1. (event, do) acontecimiento m. 2. (concern, matter) asunto m. 3. (extra-marital relationship) aventura f (amorosa).

affect [ə'fekt] vt 1. (influence, move emotionally) afectar. 2. (put on) fingir.

affected [ə'fektɪd] adj (insincere) afectado(da).

affection [ə'fekʃn] n cariño m, afecto m.

affectionate [ə'fekʃnət] adj cariñoso (sa).

affirm [ə'fɜːm] vt afirmar.

affix [ə'fɪks] vt fijar, pegar.

afflict [ə'flɪkt] vt aquejar, afligir.

affluence ['æfluəns] n opulencia f.

affluent ['æfluənt] adj pudiente.

afford [ə'fɔːd] vt 1. (gen): **to be able to ~** poder permitirse (el lujo de); **we can't ~ to let this happen** no podemos permitirnos el lujo de dejar que esto ocurra. 2. (provide, give) brindar.

affront [ə'frʌnt] n afrenta f.

Afghanistan [æf'gænɪstæn] n Afganistán.

afield [ə'fiːld] adv: **far ~** lejos.

afloat [ə'fləʊt] adj lit & fig a flote.

afoot [ə'fʊt] adj (plan) en marcha; **there is a rumour ~ that** corre el rumor de que.

afraid [ə'freɪd] adj 1. (gen) asustado (da); **to be ~ of sb** tenerle miedo a alguien; **to be ~ of sthg** tener miedo de algo; **to be ~ of doing** OR **to do sthg** tener miedo de hacer algo. 2. (in apologies): **to be ~ that** temerse que; **I'm ~ so/not** me temo que sí/no.

afresh [ə'freʃ] adv de nuevo.

Africa ['æfrɪkə] n África.

African ['æfrɪkən] ◆ adj africano(na). ◆ n africano m, -na f.

African American n negro m americano, negra f americana.

aft [ɑːft] adv en popa.

after ['ɑːftəʳ] ◆ prep 1. (gen) después de; **~ all my efforts** después de todos mis esfuerzos; **~ you!** ¡usted primero!; **day ~ day** día tras día; **the day ~ tomorrow** pasado mañana; **the week ~ next** no la semana que viene sino la otra. 2. inf (in search of): **to be ~ sthg** buscar algo; **to be ~ sb** andar detrás de alguien.

3. (with the name of): **to be named ~ sb/sthg** llamarse así por alguien/algo. 4. (towards retreating person): **to run ~ sb** correr tras alguien. 5. Am (telling the time): **it's twenty ~ three** son las tres y veinte. ◆ adv más tarde, después. ◆ conj después (de) que; **~ you had done it** después de que lo hubieras hecho. ▶ **afters** npl Br inf postre m.
▶ **after all** adv 1. (in spite of everything) después de todo. 2. (it should be remembered) al fin y al cabo.

aftereffects ['ɑːftərɪˌfekts] npl secuelas fpl, efectos mpl secundarios.

afterlife ['ɑːftəlaɪf] (pl **-lives** [-laɪvz]) n más allá m, vida f de ultratumba.

aftermath ['ɑːftəmæθ] n (time) periodo m posterior; (situation) situación f posterior.

afternoon [ˌɑːftə'nuːn] n tarde f; **in the ~** por la tarde; **good ~** buenas tardes.

aftershave ['ɑːftəʃeɪv] n loción f para después del afeitado.

aftertaste ['ɑːftəteɪst] n 1. (of food, drink) resabio m. 2. fig (of unpleasant experience) mal sabor m de boca.

afterthought ['ɑːftəθɔːt] n idea f a posteriori.

afterward(s) ['ɑːftəwəd(z)] adv después, más tarde.

again [ə'gen] adv 1. (gen) otra vez, de nuevo; **never ~** nunca jamás; **he's well ~ now** ya está bien; **to do sthg ~** volver a hacer algo; **to say sthg ~** repetir algo; **~ and ~** una y otra vez; **all over ~** otra vez desde el principio; **time and ~** una y otra vez. 2. phr: **half as much ~** la mitad otra vez; **twice as much ~** dos veces lo mismo otra vez; **then** OR **there ~** por otro lado, por otra parte.

against [ə'genst] ◆ prep contra; **I'm ~ it** estoy (en) contra (de) ello; **to lean ~ sthg** apoyarse en algo; **(as) ~** a diferencia de. ◆ adv en contra.

age [eɪdʒ] (cont **ageing** OR **aging**) ◆ n 1. (gen) edad f; **to come of ~** hacerse mayor de edad; **to be under ~** ser menor (de edad); **what ~ are you?** ¿qué edad tienes? 2. (state of being old) vejez f. ◆ vt & vi envejecer. ▶ **ages** npl (long time): **~s ago** hace siglos; **I haven't seen her for ~s** hace siglos que no la veo.

aged [adj eɪdʒd, npl 'eɪdʒɪd] ◆ adj (of the stated age): **children ~ between 8 and 15** niños de entre 8 y 15 años de edad. ◆ npl: **the ~** los ancianos.

age group n (grupo m de) edad f.

agency ['eɪdʒənsɪ] n 1. (business) agencia *f*. **2.** (*organization, body*) organismo *m*, instituto *m*.

agenda [ə'dʒendə] *n* orden *m* del día.

agent ['eɪdʒənt] *n* **1.** (COMM) (*of company*) representante *m y f*; (*of actor*) agente *m y f*. **2.** (*substance*) agente *m*. **3.** (*secret agent*) agente *m* (secreto).

aggravate ['ægrəveɪt] *vt* **1.** (*make worse*) agravar, empeorar. **2.** (*annoy*) irritar.

aggregate ['ægrɪgət] ◆ *adj* global, total. ◆ *n* (*total*) conjunto *m*, total *m*.

aggressive [ə'gresɪv] *adj* **1.** (*belligerent - person*) agresivo(va). **2.** (*forceful - person, campaign*) audaz, emprendedor (ra).

aggrieved [ə'griːvd] *adj* ofendido (da).

aghast [ə'gɑːst] *adj*: ~ (**at**) horrorizado (da) (ante).

agile [Br 'ædʒaɪl, Am 'ædʒəl] *adj* ágil.

agitate ['ædʒɪteɪt] ◆ *vt* **1.** (*disturb, worry*) inquietar. **2.** (*shake about*) agitar. ◆ *vi* (*campaign*): **to** ~ **for/against** hacer campaña a favor de/en contra de.

AGM *n abbr of* **annual general meeting**.

agnostic [æg'nɒstɪk] ◆ *adj* agnóstico (ca). ◆ *n* agnóstico *m*, -ca *f*.

ago [ə'gəʊ] *adv*: **a long time/three days/three years** ~ hace mucho tiempo/tres días/tres años.

agog [ə'gɒg] *adj* ansioso(sa), expectante.

agonizing ['ægənaɪzɪŋ] *adj* angustioso (sa).

agony ['ægənɪ] *n* **1.** (*physical pain*) dolor *m* muy intenso; **to be in** ~ tener tremendos dolores. **2.** (*mental pain*) angustia *f*; **to be in** ~ estar angustiado.

agony aunt *n* Br *inf* consejera *f* sentimental.

agree [ə'griː] ◆ *vi* **1.** (*be of same opinion*): **to** ~ (**with sb about sthg**) estar de acuerdo (con alguien acerca de algo); **to** ~ **on sthg** ponerse de acuerdo en algo. **2.** (*consent*): **to** ~ (**to sthg**) acceder (a algo). **3.** (*approve*): **to** ~ **with sthg** estar de acuerdo con algo. **4.** (*be consistent*) concordar. **5.** (*food*): **to** ~ **with sb** sentarle bien a alguien. **6.** (GRAMM): **to** ~ (**with**) concordar (con). ◆ *vt* **1.** (*fix*) acordar, convenir. **2.** (*be of same opinion*): **to** ~ **that** estar de acuerdo en que. **3.** (*agree, consent*): **to** ~ **to do sthg** acordar hacer algo. **4.** (*concede*): **to** ~ (**that**) reconocer que.

agreeable [ə'griːəbl] *adj* **1.** (*pleasant*) agradable. **2.** (*willing*): **to be** ~ **to sthg/**

doing sthg estar conforme con algo/ hacer algo.

agreed [ə'griːd] ◆ *adj*: **to be** ~ **on sthg** estar de acuerdo sobre algo. ◆ *adv* (*admittedly*) de acuerdo que.

agreement [ə'griːmənt] *n* **1.** (*accord, settlement, contract*) acuerdo *m*; **to be in** ~ **with** estar de acuerdo con. **2.** (*consent*) aceptación *f*. **3.** (*consistency*) correspondencia *f*. **4.** (GRAMM) concordancia *f*.

agricultural [ˌægrɪ'kʌltʃərəl] *adj* agrícola.

agriculture ['ægrɪkʌltʃəʳ] *n* agricultura *f*.

aground [ə'graʊnd] *adv*: **to run** ~ encallar.

ahead [ə'hed] *adv* **1.** (*in front*) delante. **2.** (*forwards*) adelante, hacia delante; **go** ~**!** ¡por supuesto!; **right** OR **straight** ~ todo recto OR de frente. **3.** (*winning*): **to be** ~ (*in race*) ir en cabeza; (*in football, rugby etc*) ir ganando. **4.** (*in better position*) por delante; **to get** ~ (*be successful*) abrirse camino. **5.** (*in time*): **to look** OR **think** ~ mirar hacia el futuro. ▶ **ahead of** *prep* **1.** (*in front of*) frente a. **2.** (*beating*): **to be two points** ~ **of** llevar dos puntos de ventaja a. **3.** (*in better position than*) por delante de. **4.** (*in time*) con anterioridad a; ~ **of schedule** por delante de lo previsto.

aid [eɪd] ◆ *n* ayuda *f*; **medical** ~ asistencia *f* médica; **in** ~ **of** a beneficio de. ◆ *vt* **1.** (*help*) ayudar. **2.** (JUR): **to** ~ **and abet** ser cómplice de.

aide [eɪd] *n* (POL) ayudante *m y f*.

AIDS, Aids [eɪdz] (*abbr of* **acquired immune deficiency syndrome**) ◆ *n* SIDA *m*. ◆ *comp*: ~ **patient** sidoso *m*, -sa *f*.

ailing ['eɪlɪŋ] *adj* **1.** (*ill*) achacoso(sa). **2.** *fig* (*economy*) debilitado(da), renqueante.

ailment ['eɪlmənt] *n* achaque *m*, molestia *f*.

aim [eɪm] ◆ *n* **1.** (*objective*) objetivo *m*, intención *f*. **2.** (*in firing gun*) puntería *f*; **to take** ~ **at** apuntar a. ◆ *vt* **1.** (*weapon*): **to** ~ **sthg at** apuntar algo a. **2.** (*plan, action*): **to be** ~**ed at doing sthg** ir dirigido OR encaminado a hacer algo. **3.** (*campaign, publicity, criticism*): **to** ~ **sthg at sb** dirigir algo a alguien. ◆ *vi* **1.** (*point weapon*): **to** ~ (**at sthg**) apuntar (a algo). **2.** (*intend*): **to** ~ **at** OR **for sthg** apuntar a OR pretender algo; **to** ~ **to do sthg** aspirar a OR pretender hacer algo.

aimless ['eɪmlɪs] *adj* sin un objetivo claro.

ain't [eɪnt] *inf* = **am not, are not, is not, have not, has not**.

air [eəʳ] ◆ *n* **1.** (*gen*) aire *m*; **into the ~** al aire; **by ~** en avión; **(up) in the ~** *fig* en el aire. **2.** (RADIO & TV): **on the ~** en el aire. ◆ *comp* aéreo(a). ◆ *vt* **1.** (*clothes, sheets*) airear; (*cupboard, room*) ventilar. **2.** (*views, opinions*) expresar. **3.** Am (*broadcast*) emitir. ◆ *vi* (*clothes, sheets*) airearse; (*cupboard, room*) ventilarse.

airbag ['eəbæg] *n* (AUT) colchón que se infla automáticamente en caso de accidente para proteger a los pasajeros.

airbase ['eəbeɪs] *n* base *f* aérea.

airbed ['eəbed] *n* Br colchón *m* inflable.

airborne ['eəbɔːn] *adj* **1.** (*troops*) aerotransportado(da); (*attack*) aéreo(a). **2.** (*plane*) en el aire, en vuelo.

air-conditioned [-kən'dɪʃnd] *adj* climatizado(da), con aire acondicionado.

air-conditioning [-kən'dɪʃnɪŋ] *n* aire *m* acondicionado.

aircraft ['eəkrɑːft] (*pl inv*) *n* (*plane*) avión *m*; (*any flying machine*) aeronave *m*.

aircraft carrier *n* portaaviones *m inv*.

airfield ['eəfiːld] *n* campo *m* de aviación.

airforce ['eəfɔːs] *n*: **the ~** las fuerzas aéreas.

air freshener [-'freʃnəʳ] *n* ambientador *m*.

airgun ['eəgʌn] *n* pistola *f* de aire comprimido.

airhostess ['eə,həʊstɪs] *n* azafata *f*, aeromoza *f* Amer.

airlift ['eəlɪft] ◆ *n* puente *m* aéreo. ◆ *vt* transportar por avión.

airline ['eəlaɪn] *n* línea *f* aérea.

airliner ['eəlaɪnəʳ] *n* avión *m* (grande) de pasajeros.

airlock ['eəlɒk] *n* **1.** (*in tube, pipe*) bolsa *f* de aire. **2.** (*airtight chamber*) cámara *f* OR esclusa *f* de aire.

airmail ['eəmeɪl] *n*: **by ~** por correo aéreo.

airplane ['eəpleɪn] *n* Am avión *m*.

airport ['eəpɔːt] *n* aeropuerto *m*.

air raid *n* ataque *m* aéreo.

airsick ['eəsɪk] *adj*: **to be ~** marearse (en el avión).

airspace ['eəspeɪs] *n* espacio *m* aéreo.

air steward *n* auxiliar *m* de vuelo.

airstrip ['eəstrɪp] *n* pista *f* de aterrizaje.

air terminal *n* terminal *f* aérea.

airtight ['eətaɪt] *adj* hermético(ca).

air-traffic controller *n* controlador aéreo *m*, controladora aérea *f*.

airy ['eərɪ] *adj* **1.** (*room*) espacioso(sa) y bien ventilado(da). **2.** (*fanciful*) ilusorio (ria). **3.** (*nonchalant*) despreocupado (da).

aisle [aɪl] *n* **1.** (*in church*) nave *f* lateral. **2.** (*in plane, theatre, supermarket*) pasillo *m*.

ajar [ə'dʒɑːʳ] *adj* entreabierto(ta).

aka (*abbr of* **also known as**) alias.

akin [ə'kɪn] *adj*: **~ to sthg/to doing sthg** semejante a algo/a hacer algo.

alacrity [ə'lækrətɪ] *n* presteza *f*.

alarm [ə'lɑːm] ◆ *n* alarma *f*; **to raise** OR **sound the ~** dar la (voz de) alarma. ◆ *vt* alarmar, asustar.

alarm clock *n* despertador *m*.

alarming [ə'lɑːmɪŋ] *adj* alarmante.

alas [ə'læs] *excl literary* ¡ay!

Albania [æl'beɪnjə] *n* Albania.

Albanian [æl'beɪnjən] ◆ *adj* albanés (esa). ◆ *n* **1.** (*person*) albanés *m*, -esa *f*. **2.** (*language*) albanés *m*.

albeit [ɔːl'biːɪt] *conj fml* aunque, si bien.

album ['ælbəm] *n* **1.** (*of stamps, photos*) álbum *m*. **2.** (*record*) elepé *m*.

alcohol ['ælkəhɒl] *n* alcohol *m*.

alcoholic [,ælkə'hɒlɪk] ◆ *adj* alcohólico (ca). ◆ *n* alcohólico *m*, -ca *f*.

alcopop ['ælkəʊpɒp] *n* refresco gaseoso que contiene un cierto porcentaje de alcohol.

alcove ['ælkəʊv] *n* hueco *m*.

alderman ['ɔːldəmən] (*pl* **-men** [-mən]) *n* = concejal *m*, -la *f*.

ale [eɪl] *n* tipo de cerveza.

alert [ə'lɜːt] ◆ *adj* **1.** (*vigilant*) atento (ta). **2.** (*perceptive*) despierto(ta). **3.** (*aware*): **to be ~ to** ser consciente de. ◆ *n* (*gen* & MIL) alerta *f*; **on the ~** alerta. ◆ *vt* alertar; **to ~ sb to sthg** alertar a alguien de algo.

A level (*abbr of* **Advanced level**) *n* Br (SCH) nivel escolar necesario para acceder a la universidad.

alfresco [æl'freskəʊ] *adj* & *adv* al aire libre.

algae ['ældʒiː] *npl* algas *fpl*.

algebra ['ældʒɪbrə] *n* álgebra *f*.

Algeria [æl'dʒɪərɪə] *n* Argelia.

alias ['eɪlɪəs] (*pl* **-es**) ◆ *adv* alias. ◆ *n* alias *m*.

alibi ['ælɪbaɪ] *n* coartada *f*.

alien ['eɪljən] ◆ *adj* **1.** (*from outer space*) extraterrestre. **2.** (*unfamiliar*) extraño (ña), ajeno(na). ◆ *n* **1.** (*from outer space*) extraterrestre *m* y *f*. **2.** (JUR) (*foreigner*) extranjero *m*, -ra *f*.

alienate ['eɪljəneɪt] vt (make unsympathetic) ganarse la antipatía de.

alight [ə'laɪt] (pt & pp **-ed**) ♦ adj (on fire) ardiendo. ♦ vi fml 1. (land) posarse. 2. (get off): **to ~ from** apearse de.

align [ə'laɪn] vt (line up) alinear.

alike [ə'laɪk] ♦ adj parecido(da). ♦ adv de la misma forma; **to look ~** parecerse.

alimony ['ælɪmənɪ] n pensión f alimenticia.

alive [ə'laɪv] adj 1. (living) vivo(va). 2. (active, lively) lleno(na) de vida; **to come ~** (story, description) cobrar vida; (person, place) animarse.

alkali ['ælkəlaɪ] (pl **-s** OR **-ies**) n álcali m.

all [ɔːl] ♦ adj 1. (with sg noun) todo(da); **~ the drink** toda la bebida; **~ day** todo el día; **~ night** toda la noche; **~ the time** todo el tiempo OR el rato. 2. (with pl noun) todos(das); **~ the boxes** todas las cajas; **~ men** todos los hombres; **~ three died** los tres murieron. ♦ pron 1. (sg) (the whole amount) todo m, -da f; **she drank it ~**, **she drank ~ of it** se lo bebió todo. 2. (pl) (everybody, everything) todos mpl, -das fpl; **~ of them came**, **they ~ came** vinieron todos. 3. (with superl): **he's the cleverest of ~** es el más listo de todos; **the most amazing thing of ~** lo más impresionante de todo; **best/worst of ~ ...** lo mejor/peor de todo es que ...; **above ~** → above; **after ~** → after; **at ~** → at. ♦ adv 1. (entirely) completamente; **I'd forgotten ~ about that** me había olvidado completamente de eso; **~ alone** completamente solo(la). 2. (in sport, competitions): **the score is two ~** el resultado es de empate a dos. 3. (with compar): **to run ~ the faster** correr aun más rápido. ► **all but** adv casi. ► **all in all** adv en conjunto. ► **all that** adv: **she's not ~ that pretty** no es tan guapa. ► **in all** adv en total.

Allah ['ælə] n Alá m.

all-around Am = **all-round**.

allay [ə'leɪ] vt fml apaciguar, mitigar.

all clear n 1. (signal) señal f de cese de peligro. 2. fig (go-ahead) luz f verde.

allegation [,ælɪ'geɪʃn] n acusación f.

allege [ə'ledʒ] vt alegar; **to be ~d to have done/said** ser acusado de haber hecho/dicho.

allegedly [ə'ledʒɪdlɪ] adv presuntamente.

allegiance [ə'liːdʒəns] n fidelidad f.

allergic [ə'lɜːdʒɪk] adj lit & fig: **~ (to sthg)** alérgico(ca) (a algo).

allergy ['ælədʒɪ] n alergia f.

alleviate [ə'liːvɪeɪt] vt aliviar.

alley(way) ['ælɪ(weɪ)] n callejuela f.

alliance [ə'laɪəns] n alianza f.

allied ['ælaɪd] adj 1. (powers, troops) aliado(da). 2. (subjects) afín.

alligator ['ælɪgeɪtər] (pl inv OR **-s**) n caimán m.

all-important adj crucial.

all-in adj Br (inclusive) todo incluido. ► **all in** ♦ adj inf (tired) hecho(cha) polvo. ♦ adv (inclusive) todo incluido.

all-night adj (party etc) que dura toda la noche; (chemist, bar) abierto(ta) toda la noche.

allocate ['æləkeɪt] vt: **to ~ sthg to sb** (money, resources) destinar algo a alguien; (task, tickets, seats) asignar algo a alguien.

allot [ə'lɒt] vt (job, time) asignar; (money, resources) destinar.

allotment [ə'lɒtmənt] n 1. Br (garden) parcela municipal arrendada para su cultivo. 2. (share - of money, resources) asignación f; (- of time) espacio m (de tiempo) concedido.

all-out adj (effort) supremo(ma); (war) sin cuartel.

allow [ə'laʊ] vt 1. (permit) permitir, dejar; **to ~ sb to do sthg** permitir OR dejar a alguien hacer algo. 2. (set aside - money) destinar; (- time) dejar. 3. (officially accept - subj: person) conceder; (- subj: law) admitir. 4. (concede): **to ~ that** admitir OR reconocer que. ► **allow for** vt fus contar con.

allowance [ə'laʊəns] n 1. (money received - from government) subsidio m; (- from employer) dietas fpl. 2. Am (pocket money) paga f. 3. (FIN) desgravación f. 4. **to make ~s for sthg/sb** (forgive) disculpar algo/a alguien; (take into account) tener en cuenta algo/a alguien.

alloy ['ælɔɪ] n aleación f.

all right ♦ adv 1. (gen) bien. 2. inf (only just acceptably) (más o menos) bien. 3. inf (in answer - yes) vale, bueno. ♦ adj 1. (gen) bien. 2. inf (not bad): **it's ~, but ...** no está mal, pero ... 3. inf (OK): **sorry – that's ~** lo siento – no importa.

all-round Br, **all-around** Am adj (multi-skilled) polifacético(ca).

All Saints' Day n día m de Todos los Santos.

All Souls' Day n día m de (los) difuntos, día de los muertos Amer.

all-time adj de todos los tiempos.

allude [ə'luːd] vi: **to ~ to** aludir a.

alluring [əˈljʊərɪŋ] *adj* (*person*) atrayente; (*thing*) tentador(ra).

allusion [əˈluːʒn] *n* alusión *f*.

ally [ˈælaɪ] *n* aliado *m*, -da *f*.

almighty [ɔːlˈmaɪtɪ] *adj inf* (*very big*) descomunal.

almond [ˈɑːmənd] *n* (*nut*) almendra *f*.

almost [ˈɔːlməʊst] *adv* casi.

alms [ɑːmz] *npl dated* limosna *f*.

aloft [əˈlɒft] *adv* (*in the air*) en lo alto.

alone [əˈləʊn] ◆ *adj* solo(la); **to be ~ with** estar a solas con. ◆ *adv* 1. (*without others*) solo(la). 2. (*only*) sólo. 3. *phr*: **to leave sthg/sb ~** dejar algo/a alguien en paz. ▶ **let alone** *conj* y mucho menos.

along [əˈlɒŋ] ◆ *adv* 1. (*forward*) hacia delante; **to go** OR **walk ~** avanzar; **she was walking ~** iba andando. 2. (*to this or that place*): **to come ~** venir; **to go ~** ir. ◆ *prep* (*towards one end of, beside*) por, a lo largo de. ▶ **all along** *adv* todo el rato, siempre. ▶ **along with** *prep* junto con.

alongside [əˌlɒŋˈsaɪd] ◆ *prep* 1. (*next to*) junto a. 2. (*together with*) junto con. ◆ *adv*: **to come ~** ponerse a la misma altura.

aloof [əˈluːf] ◆ *adj* frío(a), distante. ◆ *adv* distante; **to remain ~ (from)** mantenerse a distancia (de).

aloud [əˈlaʊd] *adv* en alto, en voz alta.

alphabet [ˈælfəbet] *n* alfabeto *m*.

alphabetical [ˌælfəˈbetɪkl] *adj* alfabético(ca); **in ~ order** en OR por orden alfabético.

Alps [ælps] *npl*: **the ~** los Alpes.

already [ɔːlˈredɪ] *adv* ya.

alright [ɔːlˈraɪt] = **all right**.

Alsatian [ælˈseɪʃn] *n* (*dog*) pastor *m* alemán.

also [ˈɔːlsəʊ] *adv* también.

altar [ˈɔːltəʳ] *n* altar *m*.

alter [ˈɔːltəʳ] ◆ *vt* (*modify*) alterar, modificar. ◆ *vi* cambiar.

alteration [ˌɔːltəˈreɪʃn] *n* alteración *f*.

alternate [*adj* Br ɔːlˈtɜːnət, Am ˈɔːltərnət, *vb* ˈɔːltərneɪt] ◆ *adj* 1. (*by turns*) alternativo(va), alterno(na). 2. (*every other*): **on ~ days/weeks** cada dos días/semanas. ◆ *vi*: **to ~ (with/between)** alternar (con/entre).

alternating current [ˈɔːltəneɪtɪŋ-] *n* (ELEC) corriente *f* alterna.

alternative [ɔːlˈtɜːnətɪv] ◆ *adj* alternativo(va). ◆ *n* alternativa *f*, opción *f*; **to have no ~ (but to do sthg)** no tener más remedio (que hacer algo).

alternatively [ɔːlˈtɜːnətɪvlɪ] *adv* o bien, por otra parte.

alternator [ˈɔːltəneɪtəʳ] *n* (ELEC) alternador *m*.

although [ɔːlˈðəʊ] *conj* aunque.

altitude [ˈæltɪtjuːd] *n* altitud *f*.

alto [ˈæltəʊ] (*pl* **-s**) *n* (*male voice*) contralto *m*; (*female voice*) contralto *f*.

altogether [ˌɔːltəˈɡeðəʳ] *adv* 1. (*completely*) completamente; **not ~** no del todo. 2. (*considering all things*) en conjunto. 3. (*in total*) en total.

aluminium Br [ˌæljʊˈmɪnɪəm], **aluminum** Am [əˈluːmɪnəm] *n* aluminio *m*.

always [ˈɔːlweɪz] *adv* siempre.

am [æm] → **be**.

a.m. (*abbr of* **ante meridiem**): **at 3 ~** a las tres de la mañana.

AM (*abbr of* **amplitude modulation**) *n* AM *f*.

amalgamate [əˈmælɡəmeɪt] ◆ *vt* (*unite*) amalgamar. ◆ *vi* (*unite*) amalgamarse.

amass [əˈmæs] *vt* amasar.

amateur [ˈæmətəʳ] ◆ *adj* aficionado (da); *pej* chapucero(ra). ◆ *n* aficionado *m*, -da *f*; *pej* chapucero *m*, -ra *f*.

amateurish [ˌæməˈtɜːrɪʃ] *adj* chapucero(ra).

amaze [əˈmeɪz] *vt* asombrar.

amazed [əˈmeɪzd] *adj* asombrado(da).

amazement [əˈmeɪzmənt] *n* asombro *m*.

amazing [əˈmeɪzɪŋ] *adj* asombroso (sa).

Amazon [ˈæməzn] *n* 1. (*river*): **the ~** el Amazonas. 2. (*region*): **the ~ (Basin)** la cuenca amazónica; **the ~ rain forest** la selva amazónica.

ambassador [æmˈbæsədəʳ] *n* embajador *m*, -ra *f*.

amber [ˈæmbəʳ] ◆ *adj* 1. (*amber-coloured*) de color ámbar. 2. Br (*traffic light*) ámbar. ◆ *n* ámbar *m*.

ambiguous [æmˈbɪɡjʊəs] *adj* ambiguo (gua).

ambition [æmˈbɪʃn] *n* ambición *f*.

ambitious [æmˈbɪʃəs] *adj* ambicioso (sa).

amble [ˈæmbl] *vi* (*walk*) deambular, pasear.

ambulance [ˈæmbjʊləns] *n* ambulancia *f*.

ambush [ˈæmbʊʃ] ◆ *n* emboscada *f*. ◆ *vt* emboscar.

amenable [əˈmiːnəbl] *adj* razonable; **~ to** favorable a.

amend [əˈmend] *vt* (*law*) enmendar; (*text*) corregir. ▶ **amends** *npl*: **to make ~s for sthg** reparar algo.

amendment [ə'mendmənt] *n* (*change - to law*) enmienda *f*; (*- to text*) corrección *f*.

amenities [ə'mi:nətız] *npl* (*of town*) facilidades *fpl*; (*of building*) comodidades *fpl*.

America [ə'merıkə] *n* América.

American [ə'merıkn] ♦ *adj* americano (na). ♦ *n* (*person*) americano *m*, -na *f*.

American Indian *n* amerindio *m*, -dia *f*.

amiable ['eımjəbl] *adj* amable, agradable.

amicable ['æmıkəbl] *adj* amigable, amistoso(sa).

amid(st) [ə'mıd(st)] *prep fml* entre, en medio de.

amiss [ə'mıs] ♦ *adj* mal. ♦ *adv*: **to take sthg ~** tomarse algo a mal.

ammonia [ə'məunjə] *n* amoniaco *m*.

ammunition [ˌæmju'nıʃn] *n* (U) (MIL) municiones *fpl*.

amnesia [æm'ni:zjə] *n* amnesia *f*.

amnesty ['æmnəstı] *n* amnistía *f*.

amok [ə'mɒk] *adv*: **to run ~** enloquecer atacando a gente de forma indiscriminada.

among(st) [ə'mʌŋ(st)] *prep* entre.

amoral [ˌeı'mɒrəl] *adj* amoral.

amorous ['æmərəs] *adj* amoroso(sa).

amount [ə'maunt] *n* cantidad *f*.
▶ **amount to** *vt fus* **1.** (*total*) ascender a. **2.** (*be equivalent to*) venir a ser.

amp [æmp] *n abbr of* **ampere**.

ampere ['æmpeər] *n* amperio *m*.

amphibian [æm'fıbıən] *n* anfibio *m*.

ample ['æmpl] *adj* **1.** (*enough*) suficiente; (*more than enough*) sobrado(da). **2.** (*garment, room*) amplio(plia); (*stomach, bosom*) abundante.

amplifier ['æmplıfaıər] *n* amplificador *m*.

amputate ['æmpjuteıt] *vt & vi* amputar.

Amsterdam [ˌæmstə'dæm] *n* Amsterdam.

Amtrak ['æmtræk] *n organismo que regula y coordina las líneas férreas en Estados Unidos.*

amuck [ə'mʌk] = **amok**.

amuse [ə'mju:z] *vt* **1.** (*make laugh, smile*) divertir. **2.** (*entertain*) distraer.

amused [ə'mju:zd] *adj* **1.** (*person, look*) divertido(da); **I was not ~ at OR by that** no me hizo gracia eso. **2.** (*entertained*): **to keep o.s. ~** entretenerse, distraerse.

amusement [ə'mju:zmənt] *n* **1.** (*enjoyment*) regocijo *m*, diversión *f*. **2.** (*diversion, game*) atracción *f*.

amusement arcade *n* salón *m* de juegos.

amusement park *n* parque *m* de atracciones.

amusing [ə'mju:zıŋ] *adj* divertido (da).

an [*stressed* æn, *unstressed* ən] → **a²**.

anabolic steroid [ˌænə'bɒlık-] *n* esteroide *m* anabolizante.

anaemic Br, **anemic** Am [ə'ni:mık] *adj* (*ill*) anémico(ca).

anaesthetic Br, **anesthetic** Am [ˌænıs'θetık] *n* anestesia *f*; **local/general ~** anestesia local/general.

analogue, analog Am ['ænəlɒg] ♦ *adj* (*watch, clock*) analógico(ca). ♦ *n fml* equivalente *m*.

analogy [ə'nælədʒı] *n* analogía *f*.

analyse Br, **analyze** Am ['ænəlaız] *vt* analizar.

analysis [ə'næləsıs] (*pl* **analyses** [ə'næləsi:z]) *n* análisis *m inv*.

analyst ['ænəlıst] *n* **1.** (*gen*) analista *m y f*. **2.** (*psychoanalyst*) psicoanalista *m y f*.

analytic(al) [ˌænə'lıtık(l)] *adj* analítico (ca).

analyze Am = **analyse**.

anarchist ['ænəkıst] *n* anarquista *m y f*.

anarchy ['ænəkı] *n* anarquía *f*.

anathema [ə'næθəmə] *n*: **the idea is ~ to me** la idea me parece aberrante.

anatomy [ə'nætəmı] *n* anatomía *f*.

ANC (*abbr of* **African National Congress**) *n* ANC *m*.

ancestor ['ænsestər] *n lit & fig* antepasado *m*.

anchor ['æŋkər] ♦ *n* (NAUT) ancla *f*; **to drop ~** echar el ancla; **to weigh ~** levar anclas. ♦ *vt* **1.** (*secure*) sujetar. **2.** (TV) presentar. ♦ *vi* (NAUT) anclar.

anchovy ['æntʃəvı] (*pl inv* OR **-ies**) *n* (*salted*) anchoa *f*; (*fresh*) boquerón *m*.

ancient ['eınʃənt] *adj* **1.** (*gen*) antiguo (gua). **2.** *hum* (*very old*) vetusto(ta).

ancillary [æn'sılərı] *adj* auxiliar.

and [*strong form* ænd, *weak form* ənd, ən] *conj* **1.** (*gen*) y; (*before 'i' or 'hi'*) e; **faster ~ faster** cada vez más rápido; **it's nice ~ easy** es sencillito. **2.** (*in numbers*): **one hundred ~ eighty** ciento ochenta; **one ~ a half** uno y medio; **2 ~ 2 is 4** 2 y 2 son 4. **3.** (*to*): **try ~ come** intenta venir; **come ~ see the kids** ven a ver a los niños; **wait ~ see** espera a ver. ▶ **and so on, and so forth** *adv* etcétera, y cosas así.

Andalusia [ˌændə'lu:zıə] *n* Andalucía.

Andes ['ændi:z] *npl*: **the ~** los Andes.

Andorra [æn'dɔːrə] n Andorra.

anecdote ['ænɪkdəʊt] n anécdota f.

anemic Am = **anaemic**.

anesthetic etc Am = **anaesthetic** etc.

anew [ə'njuː] adv de nuevo, nuevamente.

angel ['eɪndʒəl] n (RELIG) ángel m.

anger ['æŋgəʳ] ◆ n ira f, furia f. ◆ vt enfurecer.

angina [æn'dʒaɪnə] n angina f de pecho.

angle ['æŋgl] n 1. (gen) ángulo m; **at an ~** (aslant) torcido. 2. (point of view) enfoque m.

angler ['æŋgləʳ] n pescador m, -ra f (con caña).

Anglican ['æŋglɪkən] ◆ adj anglicano (na). ◆ n anglicano m, -na f.

angling ['æŋglɪŋ] n pesca f con caña.

Anglo-Saxon [,æŋgləʊ'sæksn] ◆ adj anglosajón(ona). ◆ n 1. (person) anglosajón m, -ona f. 2. (language) anglosajón m.

angry ['æŋgrɪ] adj (person) enfadado (da); (letter, look, face) furioso(sa), airado (da); **to be ~ at** OR **with sb** estar enfadado con alguien; **to get ~ with sb** enfadarse con alguien.

anguish ['æŋgwɪʃ] n angustia f.

angular ['æŋgjʊləʳ] adj (face, body) anguloso(sa).

animal ['ænɪml] ◆ adj animal. ◆ n animal m; pej animal m y f.

animate ['ænɪmət] adj animado(da).

animated ['ænɪmeɪtɪd] adj animado (da).

aniseed ['ænɪsiːd] n anís m.

ankle ['æŋkl] ◆ n tobillo m. ◆ comp: **~ boots** botines mpl; **~ socks** calcetines mpl por el tobillo.

annex ['æneks] ◆ n edificio m anejo. ◆ vt anexionar.

annexe ['æneks] = **annex**.

annihilate [ə'naɪəleɪt] vt (destroy) aniquilar.

anniversary [,ænɪ'vɜːsərɪ] n aniversario m.

announce [ə'naʊns] vt anunciar.

announcement [ə'naʊnsmənt] n anuncio m.

announcer [ə'naʊnsəʳ] n: **radio/television ~** presentador m, -ra f OR locutor m, -ra f de radio/televisión.

annoy [ə'nɔɪ] vt fastidiar, molestar.

annoyance [ə'nɔɪəns] n molestia f.

annoyed [ə'nɔɪd] adj: **~ at sthg/with sb** molesto(ta) por algo/con alguien.

annoying [ə'nɔɪɪŋ] adj fastidioso(sa).

annual ['ænjʊəl] ◆ adj anual. ◆ n 1. (plant) planta f anual. 2. (book) anuario m.

annual general meeting n junta f general anual.

annul [ə'nʌl] vt anular.

annum ['ænəm] n: **per ~** al año.

anomaly [ə'nɒməlɪ] n anomalía f.

anonymous [ə'nɒnɪməs] adj anónimo (ma).

anorak ['ænəræk] n chubasquero m, anorak m.

anorexia (nervosa) [,ænə'reksɪə (nɜː'vəʊsə)] n anorexia f.

anorexic [,ænə'reksɪk] ◆ adj anoréxico (ca). ◆ n anoréxico m, -ca f.

another [ə'nʌðəʳ] ◆ adj otro(tra); **in ~ few minutes** en unos minutos más. ◆ pron otro m, -tra f; **one ~** uno tras otro, una tras otra; **one ~** el uno al otro, la una a la otra; **we love one ~** nos queremos.

answer ['ɑːnsəʳ] ◆ n respuesta f; **in ~ to** en respuesta a. ◆ vt 1. (reply to) responder a, contestar a. 2. (respond to): **to ~ the door** abrir la puerta; **to ~ the phone** coger OR contestar el teléfono. ◆ vi responder, contestar. ▶ **answer back** vt sep & vi replicar. ▶ **answer for** vt fus 1. (accept responsibility for) responder por. 2. (suffer consequences of) responder de.

answerable ['ɑːnsərəbl] adj: **~ (to sb/ for sthg)** responsable (ante alguien/de algo).

answering machine ['ɑːnsərɪŋ-] n contestador m automático.

ant [ænt] n hormiga f.

antagonism [æn'tægənɪzm] n antagonismo m.

antagonize, -ise [æn'tægənaɪz] vt provocar la hostilidad de.

Antarctic [æn'tɑːktɪk] ◆ adj antártico (ca). ◆ n: **the ~** el Antártico.

Antarctica [æn'tɑːktɪkə] n (la) Antártida.

antelope ['æntɪləʊp] (pl inv OR -s) n antílope m.

antenatal [,æntɪ'neɪtl] adj prenatal.

antenatal clinic n maternidad f.

antenna [æn'tenə] (pl sense 1 **-nae** [-niː], pl sense 2 **-s**) n 1. (of insect) antena f. 2. Am (aerial) antena f.

anthem ['ænθəm] n himno m.

anthology [æn'θɒlədʒɪ] n antología f.

antibiotic [,æntɪbaɪ'ɒtɪk] n antibiótico m.

antibody ['æntɪ,bɒdɪ] n anticuerpo m.

anticipate [æn'tɪsɪpeɪt] vt 1. (expect) prever. 2. (look forward to) esperar ansiosamente. 3. (competitor) adelantarse a.

anticipation [æn,tɪsɪ'peɪʃn] n expectación f; **in ~ of** en previsión de.

anticlimax [æntɪ'klaɪmæks] n anticlímax m.

anticlockwise [,æntɪ'klɒkwaɪz] Br adv en sentido contrario al de las agujas del reloj.

antics ['æntɪks] npl payasadas fpl.

anticyclone [,æntɪ'saɪkləʊn] n anticiclón m.

antidepressant [,æntɪdɪ'presnt] n antidepresivo m.

antidote ['æntɪdəʊt] n lit & fig: ~ **(to)** antídoto m (contra).

antifreeze ['æntɪfriːz] n anticongelante m.

antihistamine [,æntɪ'hɪstəmɪn] n antihistamínico m.

antipathy [æn'tɪpəθɪ] n: ~ **(to OR towards)** antipatía f (hacia OR por).

antiperspirant [,æntɪ'pɜːspərənt] n antitranspirante m.

antiquated ['æntɪkweɪtɪd] adj anticuado(da).

antique [æn'tiːk] ◆ adj (furniture, object) antiguo(gua). ◆ n antigüedad f.

antique shop n tienda f de antigüedades.

anti-Semitism [,æntɪ'semɪtɪzm] n antisemitismo m.

antiseptic [,æntɪ'septɪk] ◆ adj antiséptico(ca). ◆ n antiséptico m.

antisocial [,æntɪ'səʊʃl] adj 1. (against society) antisocial. 2. (unsociable) poco sociable.

antlers ['æntləz] npl cornamenta f.

anus ['eɪnəs] n ano m.

anvil ['ænvɪl] n yunque m.

anxiety [æŋ'zaɪətɪ] n 1. (worry) ansiedad f, inquietud f. 2. (cause of worry) preocupación f. 3. (keenness) afán m, ansia f.

anxious ['æŋkʃəs] adj 1. (worried) preocupado(da); **to be ~ about** estar preocupado por. 2. (keen): **to be ~ that/to do sthg** estar ansioso(sa) por que/por hacer algo.

any ['enɪ] ◆ adj 1. (with negative) ninguno (na); **I haven't read ~ books** no he leído ningún libro; **I haven't got ~ money** no tengo nada de dinero. 2. (some) alguna (una); **are there ~ cakes left?** ¿queda algún pastel?; **is there ~ milk left?** ¿queda algo de leche?; **have you got ~** money? ¿tienes dinero? 3. (no matter which) cualquier; ~ **box will do** cualquier caja vale; see also **case, day, moment, rate.** ◆ pron 1. (with negative) ninguno m, -na f; **I didn't get ~** a mí no me tocó ninguno. 2. (some) alguno m, -na f; **can ~ of you do it?** ¿sabe alguno de vosotros hacerlo?; **I need some matches, do you have ~?** necesito cerillas, ¿tienes? 3. (no matter which) cualquiera; **take ~ you like** coge cualquiera que te guste. ◆ adv 1. (with negative): **I can't see it ~ more** ya no lo veo; **he's not feeling ~ better** no se siente nada mejor; **I can't stand it ~ longer** no lo aguanto más. 2. (some, a little): **do you want ~ more potatoes?** ¿quieres más patatas?; **is that ~ better/different?** ¿es así mejor/diferente?

anybody ['enɪ,bɒdɪ] = **anyone.**

anyhow ['enɪhaʊ] adv 1. (in spite of that) de todos modos. 2. (carelessly) de cualquier manera. 3. (in any case) en cualquier caso.

anyone ['enɪwʌn] 1. (in negative sentences) nadie; **I don't know ~** no conozco a nadie. 2. (in questions) alguien. 3. (any person) cualquiera.

anyplace Am = **anywhere.**

anything ['enɪθɪŋ] pron 1. (in negative sentences) nada; **I don't want ~** no quiero nada. 2. (in questions) algo; **would you like ~ else?** ¿quiere algo más? 3. (any object, event) cualquier cosa.

anyway ['enɪweɪ] adv 1. (in any case) de todas formas OR maneras. 2. (in conversation) en cualquier caso.

anywhere ['enɪweə*], **anyplace** Am ['enɪpleɪs] adv 1. (in negative sentences) en ningún sitio; **I didn't go ~** no fui a ninguna parte. 2. (in questions) en algún sitio; **did you go ~?** ¿fuiste a algún sitio? 3. (any place) cualquier sitio; ~ **you like** donde quieras.

apart [ə'pɑːt] adv 1. (separated) aparte; **we're living ~** vivimos separados. 2. (aside) aparte; **joking ~** bromas aparte. ▶ **apart from** prep 1. (except for) salvo. 2. (as well as) aparte de.

apartheid [ə'pɑːtheɪt] n apartheid m.

apartment [ə'pɑːtmənt] n piso m, departamento m Amer.

apartment building n Am bloque m de pisos, bloque de departamentos Amer.

apathy ['æpəθɪ] n apatía f.

ape [eɪp] ◆ n simio m. ◆ vt pej imitar.

aperitif [əperə'tiːf] n aperitivo m.

aperture ['æpə,tʃʊəʳ] n abertura f.

apex ['eɪpeks] (pl -es OR apices) n (top) vértice m.

APEX ['eɪpeks] (abbr of advance purchase excursion) n Br (tarifa f) APEX f.

apices ['eɪpɪsiːz] pl → **apex**.

apiece [ə'piːs] adv cada uno(na).

apocalypse [ə'pɒkəlɪps] n apocalipsis m inv.

apologetic [ə,pɒlə'dʒetɪk] adj (tone, look) lleno(na) de disculpas; **to be ~ (about)** no hacer más que disculparse (por).

apologize, -ise [ə'pɒlədʒaɪz] vi: **to ~ (to sb for sthg)** disculparse (con alguien por algo).

apology [ə'pɒlədʒɪ] n disculpa f.

apostle [ə'pɒsl] n (RELIG) apóstol m.

apostrophe [ə'pɒstrəfɪ] n apóstrofo m.

appal, appall Am [ə'pɔːl] vt horrorizar.

appalling [ə'pɔːlɪŋ] adj 1. (shocking) horroroso(sa). 2. inf (very bad) fatal.

apparatus [,æpə'reɪtəs] (pl inv OR -es) n (gen & POL) aparato m.

apparel [ə'pærəl] n Am ropa f.

apparent [ə'pærənt] adj 1. (evident) evidente, patente. 2. (seeming) aparente.

apparently [ə'pærəntlɪ] adv 1. (it seems) por lo visto. 2. (seemingly) aparentemente.

appeal [ə'piːl] ◆ vi 1. (request): **to ~ (to sb for sthg)** solicitar (de alguien algo). 2. (to sb's honour, common sense): **to ~ to** apelar a. 3. (JUR): **to ~ (against)** apelar (contra). 4. (attract, interest): **to ~ (to)** atraer (a). ◆ n 1. (request) llamamiento m, súplica f; (fundraising campaign) campaña f para recaudar fondos. 2. (JUR) apelación f. 3. (charm, interest) atractivo m.

appealing [ə'piːlɪŋ] adj (attractive) atractivo(va).

appear [ə'pɪəʳ] vi 1. (gen) aparecer. 2. (seem): **to ~ (to be/to do sthg)** parecer (ser/hacer algo); **it would ~ that ...** parece que ... 3. (in play, film, on TV): **to ~ on TV/in a film** salir en televisión/en una película. 4. (JUR): **to ~ (before)** comparecer (ante).

appearance [ə'pɪərəns] n 1. (gen) aparición f; **to make an ~** aparecer. 2. (look - of person, place, object) aspecto m.

appease [ə'piːz] vt aplacar, apaciguar.

append [ə'pend] vt fml: **to ~ sthg (to sthg)** agregar algo (a algo).

appendices [ə'pendɪsiːz] pl → **appendix**.

appendicitis [ə,pendɪ'saɪtɪs] n (U) apendicitis f inv.

appendix [ə'pendɪks] (pl -dixes OR -dices) n (gen & MED) apéndice m.

appetite ['æpɪtaɪt] n 1. (for food) apetito m; **~ for** ganas fpl de. 2. fig (enthusiasm): **~ for** entusiasmo m OR ilusión f por.

appetizer, -iser ['æpɪtaɪzəʳ] n aperitivo m.

appetizing, -ising ['æpɪtaɪzɪŋ] adj (food) apetitoso(sa).

applaud [ə'plɔːd] vt & vi lit & fig aplaudir.

applause [ə'plɔːz] n (U) aplausos mpl.

apple ['æpl] n manzana f.

apple tree n manzano m.

appliance [ə'plaɪəns] n aparato m.

applicable [ə'plɪkəbl] adj: **to be ~ (to)** aplicarse (a).

applicant ['æplɪkənt] n: **~ (for)** solicitante m y f (de).

application [,æplɪ'keɪʃn] n 1. (gen) aplicación f. 2. (for job, college, club): **~ (for)** solicitud f (para). 3. (COMPUT): **(program)** aplicación f.

application form n impreso m de solicitud.

applied [ə'plaɪd] adj (science) aplicado (da).

apply [ə'plaɪ] ◆ vt (gen) aplicar; (brakes) echar. ◆ vi 1. (for work, grant) presentar una solicitud; **to ~ to sb for sthg** solicitar a alguien algo. 2. (be relevant) aplicarse; **to ~ to** concernir a.

appoint [ə'pɔɪnt] vt 1. (to job, position): **to ~ sb (to sthg)** nombrar a alguien (para algo); **to ~ sb as sthg** nombrar a alguien algo. 2. fml (time, place) señalar, fijar.

appointment [ə'pɔɪntmənt] n 1. (to job, position) nombramiento m. 2. (job, position) puesto m, cargo m. 3. (with businessman, lawyer) cita f; (with doctor, hairdresser) hora f; **to have an ~** (with businessman) tener una cita; (with doctor) tener hora; **to make an ~** concertar una cita.

apportion [ə'pɔːʃn] vt (money) repartir; (blame) adjudicar.

appraisal [ə'preɪzl] n evaluación f.

appreciable [ə'priːʃəbl] adj apreciable.

appreciate [ə'priːʃɪeɪt] ◆ vt 1. (value, like) apreciar. 2. (recognize, understand) darse cuenta de. 3. (be grateful for) agradecer. ◆ vi (FIN) encarecerse.

appreciation [ə,priːʃɪ'eɪʃn] n 1. (liking) aprecio m. 2. (recognition, understand-

ing) entendimiento *m*. **3.** (*gratitude*) agradecimiento *m*. **4.** (FIN) encarecimiento *m*.

appreciative [ə'pri:ʃjətɪv] *adj* (*person, remark*) agradecido(da); (*audience*) entendido(da).

apprehensive [ˌæprɪ'hensɪv] *adj* aprensivo(va).

apprentice [ə'prentɪs] *n* aprendiz *m*, -za *f*.

apprenticeship [ə'prentɪʃɪp] *n* aprendizaje *m*.

approach [ə'prəʊtʃ] ◆ *n* **1.** (*arrival*) llegada *f*. **2.** (*way in*) acceso *m*. **3.** (*method*) enfoque *m*. **4.** (*to person*): **to makes ~es to sb** hacerle propuestas a alguien. ◆ *vt* **1.** (*come near to*) acercarse a. **2.** (*ask*): **to ~ sb about sthg** hacer una propuesta or dirigirse a alguien acerca de algo. **3.** (*problem, situation*) abordar. **4.** (*level, speed*) aproximarse a. ◆ *vi* acercarse.

approachable [ə'prəʊtʃəbl] *adj* accesible.

appropriate [*adj* ə'prəʊprɪət, *vb* ə'prəʊprɪeɪt] ◆ *adj* apropiado(da). ◆ *vt* (JUR) (*take*) apropiarse de.

approval [ə'pru:vl] *n* **1.** (*admiration*) aprobación *f*. **2.** (*official sanctioning*) visto *m* bueno. **3.** (COMM): **on ~** a prueba.

approve [ə'pru:v] ◆ *vi* estar de acuerdo; **to ~ of sthg/sb** ver con buenos ojos algo/a alguien. ◆ *vt* aprobar.

approx. [ə'prɒks] (*abbr of* **approximately**) aprox.

approximate [ə'prɒksɪmət] *adj* aproximado(da).

approximately [ə'prɒksɪmətlɪ] *adv* aproximadamente.

apricot ['eɪprɪkɒt] *n* (*fruit*) albaricoque *m*, chabacano *m* Amer.

April ['eɪprəl] *n* abril *m*; *see also* **September**.

April Fools' Day *n* primero *m* de abril, ≃ Día *m* de los Santos Inocentes.

apron ['eɪprən] *n* (*clothing*) delantal *m*, mandil *m*.

apt [æpt] *adj* **1.** (*pertinent*) acertado(da). **2.** (*likely*): **~ to do sthg** propenso(sa) a hacer algo.

aptitude ['æptɪtju:d] *n* aptitud *f*.

aptly ['æptlɪ] *adv* apropiadamente.

aqualung ['ækwəlʌŋ] *n* escafandra *f* autónoma.

aquarium [ə'kweərɪəm] (*pl* **-riums** or **-ria** [-rɪə]) *n* acuario *m*.

Aquarius [ə'kweərɪəs] *n* Acuario *m*.

aquatic [ə'kwætɪk] *adj* acuático(ca).

aqueduct ['ækwɪdʌkt] *n* acueducto *m*.

Arab ['ærəb] ◆ *adj* árabe. ◆ *n* (*person*) árabe *m y f*.

Arabic ['ærəbɪk] ◆ *adj* árabe. ◆ *n* (*language*) árabe *m*.

Arabic numeral *n* número *m* arábigo.

arable ['ærəbl] *adj* cultivable.

arbitrary ['ɑ:bɪtrərɪ] *adj* (*random*) arbitrario(ria).

arbitration [ˌɑ:bɪ'treɪʃn] *n* arbitraje *m*.

arcade [ɑ:'keɪd] *n* **1.** (*shopping arcade*) galería *f* or centro *m* comercial. **2.** (*covered passage*) arcada *f*, galería *f*.

arch [ɑ:tʃ] ◆ *n* **1.** (ARCHIT) arco *m*. **2.** (*of foot*) puente *m*. ◆ *vt* arquear.

archaeological [ˌɑ:kɪə'lɒdʒɪkl] *adj* arqueológico(ca).

archaeologist [ˌɑ:kɪ'ɒlədʒɪst] *n* arqueólogo *m*, -ga *f*.

archaeology [ˌɑ:kɪ'ɒlədʒɪ] *n* arqueología *f*.

archaic [ɑ:'keɪɪk] *adj* arcaico(ca).

archbishop [ˌɑ:tʃ'bɪʃəp] *n* arzobispo *m*.

archenemy [ˌɑ:tʃ'enɪmɪ] *n* peor enemigo *m*, enemigo acérrimo.

archeology *etc* [ˌɑ:kɪ'ɒlədʒɪ] = **archaeology** *etc*.

archer ['ɑ:tʃər] *n* arquero *m*.

archery ['ɑ:tʃərɪ] *n* tiro *m* con arco.

archetypal [ˌɑ:kɪ'taɪpl] *adj* arquetípico(ca).

architect ['ɑ:kɪtekt] *n* **1.** (*of buildings*) arquitecto *m*, -ta *f*. **2.** *fig* (*of plan, event*) artífice *m y f*.

architectural [ɑ:kɪ'tektʃərəl] *adj* arquitectónico(ca).

architecture ['ɑ:kɪtektʃər] *n* (*gen &* COMPUT) arquitectura *f*.

archives ['ɑ:kaɪvz] *npl* (*of documents*) archivos *mpl*.

archway ['ɑ:tʃweɪ] *n* (*passage*) arcada *f*; (*entrance*) entrada *f* en forma de arco.

Arctic ['ɑ:ktɪk] ◆ *adj* (GEOGR) ártico(ca). ◆ *n*: **the ~** el Ártico.

ardent ['ɑ:dənt] *adj* ardoroso(sa), ferviente.

arduous ['ɑ:djʊəs] *adj* arduo(dua).

are [*weak form* ər, *strong form* ɑ:r] → **be**.

area ['eərɪə] *n* **1.** (*region, designated space*) zona *f*, área *f*; **in the ~** en la zona. **2.** *fig* (*approximate size, number*): **in the ~ of** del orden de, alrededor de. **3.** (*surface size*) superficie *f*, área *f*. **4.** (*of knowledge, interest*) campo *m*.

area code *n* prefijo *m* (telefónico).

arena [əˈriːnə] n 1. (SPORT) pabellón m.
2. fig (area of activity): **she entered the
political ~** saltó al ruedo político.
aren't [ɑːnt] = **are not**.
Argentina [ˌɑːdʒənˈtiːnə] n (la)
Argentina.
Argentine [ˈɑːdʒəntaɪn] adj argentino
(na).
Argentinian [ˌɑːdʒənˈtɪnɪən] ◆ adj ar-
gentino(na). ◆ n argentino m, -na f.
arguably [ˈɑːgjʊəblɪ] adv probablemente.
argue [ˈɑːgjuː] ◆ vi 1. (quarrel): **to ~
(with sb about sthg)** discutir (con alguien
de algo). 2. (reason): **to ~ (for/against)**
argumentar (a favor de/contra). ◆ vt: **to
~ that** argumentar que.
argument [ˈɑːgjʊmənt] n 1. (gen) discusión f; **to have an ~ (with)** tener una
discusión (con). 2. (reason) argumento
m.
argumentative [ˌɑːgjʊˈmentətɪv] adj
muy propenso(sa) a discutir.
arid [ˈærɪd] adj lit & fig árido(da).
Aries [ˈeəriːz] n Aries m.
arise [əˈraɪz] (pt **arose**, pp **arisen**
[əˈrɪzn]) vi (appear): **to ~ (from)** surgir
(de).
aristocrat [Br ˈærɪstəkræt, Am
əˈrɪstəkræt] n aristócrata m y f.
arithmetic [əˈrɪθmətɪk] n aritmética f.
ark [ɑːk] n arca f.
arm [ɑːm] ◆ n 1. (of person, chair) brazo
m; **~ in ~** del brazo; **to twist sb's ~** fig persuadir a alguien. 2. (of garment) manga f.
◆ vt armar. ▶ **arms** npl (weapons) armas
fpl.
armaments [ˈɑːməmənts] npl armamento m.
armchair [ˈɑːmtʃeər] n sillón m.
armed [ɑːmd] adj 1. (police, thieves)
armado(da). 2. fig (with information): **~
with** provisto(ta) de.
armed forces npl fuerzas fpl armadas.
armhole [ˈɑːmhəʊl] n sobaquera f,
sisa f.
armour Br, **armor** Am [ˈɑːmər] n
1. (for person) armadura f. 2. (for military
vehicle) blindaje m.
armoured car [ɑːməd-] n (MIL) carro
m blindado.
armoury Br, **armory** Am [ˈɑːmərɪ] n
arsenal m.
armpit [ˈɑːmpɪt] n sobaco m, axila f.
armrest [ˈɑːmrest] n brazo m.
arms control [ˈɑːmz-] n control m
armamentístico.
army [ˈɑːmɪ] n lit & fig ejército m.

A road n Br = carretera f nacional.
aroma [əˈrəʊmə] n aroma m.
arose [əˈrəʊz] pt → **arise**.
around [əˈraʊnd] ◆ adv 1. (about, round)
por ahí; **to walk/look ~** andar/mirar por
ahí. 2. (on all sides) alrededor. 3. (present,
available): **is John ~?** (there) ¿está John
por ahí?; (here) ¿está John por aquí?
4. (turn, look): **to turn ~** volverse; **to look
~** volver la cabeza. ◆ prep 1. (on all sides
of) alrededor de. 2. (about, round - place)
por. 3. (in the area of) cerca de.
4. (approximately) alrededor de.
arouse [əˈraʊz] vt (excite - feeling) levantar, despertar; (- person) excitar.
arrange [əˈreɪndʒ] vt 1. (flowers, books,
furniture) colocar. 2. (event, meeting, party)
organizar; **to ~ to do sthg** acordar hacer
algo; **to ~ sthg for sb** organizarle algo a
alguien. 3. (MUS) arreglar.
arrangement [əˈreɪndʒmənt] n
1. (agreement) acuerdo m; **to come to an ~**
llegar a un acuerdo. 2. (of flowers, furniture) disposición f. 3. (MUS) arreglo m.
▶ **arrangements** npl preparativos
mpl.
array [əˈreɪ] n (of objects) surtido m.
arrears [əˈrɪəz] npl (money owed) atrasos mpl; **in ~** (retrospectively) con retraso;
(late) atrasado en el pago.
arrest [əˈrest] ◆ n arresto m, detención f; **under ~** bajo arresto. ◆ vt 1. (subj:
police) detener. 2. (sb's attention) captar.
3. fml (stop) poner freno a.
arrival [əˈraɪvl] n llegada f; **late ~** (of
train, bus, mail) retraso m; **new ~** (person)
recién llegado m, recién llegada f;
(baby) recién nacido m, recién nacida f.
arrive [əˈraɪv] vi 1. (gen) llegar; **to ~ at**
(conclusion, decision) llegar a. 2. (baby)
nacer.
arrogant [ˈærəgənt] adj arrogante.
arrow [ˈærəʊ] n flecha f.
arse Br [ɑːs], **ass** Am [æs] n v inf (bottom) culo m.
arsenic [ˈɑːsnɪk] n arsénico m.
arson [ˈɑːsn] n incendio m premedita-
do.
art [ɑːt] n arte m. ▶ **arts** npl 1. (SCH &
UNIV) (humanities) letras fpl. 2. (fine arts):
the ~s las bellas artes.
artefact [ˈɑːtɪfækt] = **artifact**.
artery [ˈɑːtərɪ] n arteria f.
art gallery n (public) museo m (de
arte); (commercial) galería f (de arte).
arthritis [ɑːˈθraɪtɪs] n artritis f inv.
artichoke [ˈɑːtɪtʃəʊk] n alcachofa f.
article [ˈɑːtɪkl] n artículo m; **~ of cloth-**

ing prenda *f* de vestir.

articulate [*adj* ɑːˈtɪkjʊlət, *vb* ɑːˈtɪkjʊleɪt] ◆ *adj* (*person*) elocuente; (*speech*) claro(ra), bien articulado(da). ◆ *vt* (*express clearly*) expresar.

articulated lorry [ɑːˈtɪkjʊleɪtɪd-] *n Br* camión *m* articulado.

artifact [ˈɑːtɪfækt] *n* artefacto *m*.

artificial [ˌɑːtɪˈfɪʃl] *adj* artificial.

artillery [ɑːˈtɪlərɪ] *n* (*guns*) artillería *f*.

artist [ˈɑːtɪst] *n* artista *m y f*.

artiste [ɑːˈtiːst] *n* artista *m y f*.

artistic [ɑːˈtɪstɪk] *adj* 1. (*gen*) artístico (ca). 2. (*good at art*) con sensibilidad artística.

artistry [ˈɑːtɪstrɪ] *n* maestría *f*.

artless [ˈɑːtlɪs] *adj* ingenuo(nua).

as [unstressed əz, stressed æz] ◆ *conj* 1. (*referring to time - while*) mientras; (- *when*) cuando; **she told it to me ~ we walked along** me lo contó mientras paseábamos; **~ time goes by a medida que pasa el tiempo; she rang (just) ~ I was leaving** llamó justo cuando iba a salir. 2. (*referring to manner, way*) como; **do ~ I say** haz lo que te digo. 3. (*introducing a statement*) como; **~ you know, ...** como (ya) sabes, ... 4. (*because*) como, ya que. 5. *phr*: **~ it is** (ya) de por sí. ◆ *prep* como; **I'm speaking ~ a friend** te hablo como amigo; **she works ~ a nurse** trabaja de OR como enfermera; **~ a boy, I lived in Spain** de niño vivía en España; **it came ~ a shock** fue una gran sorpresa. ◆ *adv* (*in comparisons*): **~ ... ~** tan ... como; **~ tall ~ I am** tan alto como yo; **I've lived ~ long ~ she has** he vivido durante tanto tiempo como ella; **twice ~ big** el doble de grande; **it's just ~ fast** es igual de rápido; **~ much ~** tanto como; **~ many ~** tantos(tas) como; **~ much wine ~ you like** tanto vino como quieras. ▶ **as for, as to** *prep* en cuanto a. ▶ **as from, as of** *prep* a partir de. ▶ **as if, as though** *conj* como si. ▶ **as to** *prep* Br con respecto a.

a.s.a.p. (*abbr of as soon as possible*) a la mayor brevedad posible.

asbestos [æsˈbestəs] *n* asbesto *m*, amianto *m*.

ascend [əˈsend] ◆ *vt* subir. ◆ *vi* ascender.

ascendant [əˈsendənt] *n*: **in the ~** en auge.

ascent [əˈsent] *n* 1. (*climb*) ascensión *f*. 2. (*upward slope*) subida *f*, cuesta *f*. 3. *fig* (*progress*) ascenso *m*.

ascertain [ˌæsəˈteɪn] *vt* determinar.

ASCII [ˈæskɪ] (*abbr of American Standard Code for Information Interchange*) *n* ASCII *m*.

ascribe [əˈskraɪb] *vt*: **to ~ sthg to** atribuir algo a.

ash [æʃ] *n* 1. (*from cigarette, fire*) ceniza *f*. 2. (*tree*) fresno *m*.

ashamed [əˈʃeɪmd] *adj* avergonzado (da), apenado(da) *Amer*; **I'm ~ to do it** me avergüenza hacerlo; **to be ~ of** avergonzarse de, achuncharse de *Amer*.

ashen-faced [ˈæʃnˌfeɪst] *adj*: **to be ~** tener la cara pálida.

ashore [əˈʃɔːr] *adv* (*swim*) hasta la orilla; **to go ~** desembarcar.

ashtray [ˈæʃtreɪ] *n* cenicero *m*.

Ash Wednesday *n* miércoles *m inv* de ceniza.

Asia [Br ˈeɪʃə, Am ˈeɪʒə] *n* Asia.

Asian [Br ˈeɪʃn, Am ˈeɪʒn] ◆ *adj* asiático (ca). ◆ *n* asiático *m*, -ca *f*.

aside [əˈsaɪd] ◆ *adv* 1. (*to one side*) a un lado; **to move ~** apartarse; **to take sb ~** llevar a alguien aparte. 2. (*apart*) aparte; **~ from** aparte de. ◆ *n* 1. (*in play*) aparte *m*. 2. (*remark*) inciso *m*.

ask [ɑːsk] ◆ *vt* 1. (*question - person*): **to ~ (sb sthg)** preguntar (a alguien algo). 2. (*put - question*): **to ~ a question** hacer una pregunta. 3. (*request, demand*) pedir; **to ~ sb (to do sthg)** pedir a alguien (que haga algo); **to ~ sb for sthg** pedirle algo a alguien. 4. (*invite*) invitar. ◆ *vi* 1. (*question*) preguntar. 2. (*request*) pedir. ▶ **ask after** *vt fus* preguntar por. ▶ **ask for** *vt fus* 1. (*person*) preguntar por. 2. (*thing*) pedir.

askance [əˈskæns] *adv*: **to look ~ at sb** mirar a alguien con recelo.

askew [əˈskjuː] *adj* torcido(da).

asking price [ˈɑːskɪŋ-] *n* precio *m* inicial.

asleep [əˈsliːp] *adj* dormido(da); **to fall ~** quedarse dormido.

asparagus [əˈspærəgəs] *n* (U) (*plant*) espárrago *m*; (*shoots*) espárragos *mpl*.

aspect [ˈæspekt] *n* 1. (*of subject, plan*) aspecto *m*. 2. (*appearance*) cariz *m*, aspecto *m*. 3. (*of building*) orientación *f*.

aspersions [əˈspɜːʃnz] *npl*: **to cast ~ on sthg** poner en duda algo.

asphalt [ˈæsfælt] *n* asfalto *m*.

asphyxiate [əsˈfɪksieɪt] *vt* asfixiar.

aspiration [ˌæspəˈreɪʃn] *n* aspiración *f*.

aspire [əˈspaɪər] *vi*: **to ~ to** aspirar a.

aspirin [ˈæsprɪn] *n* aspirina *f*.

ass [æs] *n* 1. (*donkey*) asno *m*, -na *f*.

2. Br *inf* (*idiot*) burro *m*, -rra *f*. **3.** Am *v inf* = **arse**.

assail [əˈseɪl] *vt* (*attack*) atacar.

assailant [əˈseɪlənt] *n* agresor *m*, -ra *f*.

assassin [əˈsæsɪn] *n* asesino *m*, -na *f*.

assassinate [əˈsæsɪneɪt] *vt* asesinar.

assassination [ə,sæsɪˈneɪʃn] *n* asesinato *m*.

assault [əˈsɔːlt] ◆ *n* **1.** (MIL.): ~ (on) ataque *m* (contra). **2.** (*physical attack*): ~ (on sb) agresión *f* (contra alguien). ◆ *vt* (*physically*) asaltar, agredir; (*sexually*) abusar de.

assemble [əˈsembl] ◆ *vt* **1.** (*gather*) juntar, reunir. **2.** (*fit together*) montar. ◆ *vi* reunirse.

assembly [əˈsemblɪ] *n* **1.** (*meeting, law-making body*) asamblea *f*. **2.** (*gathering together*) reunión *f*. **3.** (*fitting together*) montaje *m*.

assembly line *n* cadena *f* de montaje.

assent [əˈsent] ◆ *n* consentimiento *m*. ◆ *vi*: to ~ (to) asentir (a).

assert [əˈsɜːt] *vt* **1.** (*fact, belief*) afirmar. **2.** (*authority*) imponer.

assertive [əˈsɜːtɪv] *adj* enérgico(ca).

assess [əˈses] *vt* evaluar.

assessment [əˈsesmənt] *n* **1.** (*evaluation*) evaluación *f*. **2.** (*calculation*) cálculo *m*.

assessor [əˈsesər] *n* tasador *m*, -ra *f*.

asset [ˈæset] *n* **1.** (*valuable quality - of person*) cualidad *f*; (- *of thing*) ventaja *f*. **2.** (*valuable person*) elemento *m* importante. ▶ **assets** *npl* (COMM) activo *m*, bienes *mpl*.

assign [əˈsaɪn] *vt* **1.** (*gen*): to ~ sthg (to sb) asignar OR encomendar algo (a alguien); to ~ sb to sthg asignar OR encomendar a alguien algo; to ~ sb to do sthg asignar OR encomendar a alguien que haga algo. **2.** (*designate for specific use, purpose*): to ~ sthg (to) destinar algo (a).

assignment [əˈsaɪnmənt] *n* **1.** (*task*) misión *f*; (SCH) trabajo *m*. **2.** (*act of assigning*) asignación *f*.

assimilate [əˈsɪmɪleɪt] *vt* **1.** (*learn*) asimilar. **2.** (*absorb*): to ~ sb (into) integrar a alguien (en).

assist [əˈsɪst] *vt*: to ~ sb (with sthg/in doing sthg) ayudar a alguien (con algo/a hacer algo).

assistance [əˈsɪstəns] *n* ayuda *f*, asistencia *f*; to be of ~ (to) ayudar (a).

assistant [əˈsɪstənt] ◆ *n* ayudante *m* y *f*; (shop) ~ dependiente *m*, -ta *f*. ◆ *comp* adjunto(ta); ~ manager director adjunto *m*, directora adjunta *f*.

associate [*adj* & *n* əˈsəʊʃɪət, *vb* əˈsəʊʃɪeɪt] ◆ *adj* asociado(da). ◆ *n* socio *m*, -cia *f*. ◆ *vt* asociar; to ~ sthg/sb with asociar algo/a alguien con; to be ~d with (organization, plan, opinion) estar relacionado con; (people) estar asociado con. ◆ *vi*: to ~ with sb relacionarse con alguien.

association [ə,səʊsɪˈeɪʃn] *n* **1.** (organization, act of associating) asociación *f*; in ~ with en colaboración con. **2.** (in mind) connotación *f*.

assorted [əˈsɔːtɪd] *adj* (of various types) variado(da).

assortment [əˈsɔːtmənt] *n* surtido *m*.

assume [əˈsjuːm] *vt* **1.** (suppose) suponer. **2.** (power, responsibility) asumir. **3.** (appearance, attitude) adoptar.

assumed name [əˈsjuːmd-] *n* nombre *m* falso.

assuming [əˈsjuːmɪŋ] *conj* suponiendo que.

assumption [əˈsʌmpʃn] *n* **1.** (supposition) suposición *f*. **2.** (of power) asunción *f*.

assurance [əˈʃʊərəns] *n* **1.** (promise) garantía *f*. **2.** (confidence) seguridad *f* de sí mismo. **3.** (insurance) seguro *m*.

assure [əˈʃʊər] *vt* asegurar, garantizar; to ~ sb of sthg garantizar a alguien algo; to be ~d of sthg tener algo garantizado.

assured [əˈʃʊəd] *adj* (confident) seguro (ra).

asterisk [ˈæstərɪsk] *n* asterisco *m*.

astern [əˈstɜːn] *adv* (NAUT) a popa.

asthma [ˈæsmə] *n* asma *f*.

asthmatic [æsˈmætɪk] *adj* asmático (ca).

astonish [əˈstɒnɪʃ] *vt* asombrar.

astonishment [əˈstɒnɪʃmənt] *n* asombro *m*.

astound [əˈstaʊnd] *vt* asombrar.

astray [əˈstreɪ] *adv*: to go ~ (become lost) extraviarse; to lead sb ~ (into bad ways) llevar a alguien por el mal camino.

astride [əˈstraɪd] ◆ *adv* a horcajadas. ◆ *prep* a horcajadas en.

astrology [əˈstrɒlədʒɪ] *n* astrología *f*.

astronaut [ˈæstrənɔːt] *n* astronauta *m* y *f*.

astronomical [,æstrəˈnɒmɪkl] *adj* astronómico(ca).

astronomy [əˈstrɒnəmɪ] *n* astronomía *f*.

astute [əˈstjuːt] *adj* astuto(ta).

asylum [əˈsaɪləm] *n* **1.** (mental hospital) manicomio *m*. **2.** (protection) asilo *m*.

at [unstressed ət, stressed æt] *prep* **1.** (indi-

cating place) en; ~ **my father's** en casa de mi padre; **standing ~ the window** de pie junto a la ventana; ~ **the bottom of the hill** al pie de la colina; ~ **school/ work/home** en la escuela/el trabajo/ casa. **2.** (*indicating direction*) a; **to look ~ sthg/sb** mirar algo/a alguien. **3.** (*indicating a particular time*) en; ~ **a more suitable time** en un momento más oportuno; ~ **midnight/noon/eleven o'clock** a medianoche/mediodía/las once; ~ **night** por la noche; ~ **Christmas/Easter** en Navidades/Semana Santa. **4.** (*indicating speed, rate, price*) a; ~ **100mph/high speed** a 100 millas por hora/gran velocidad; ~ **£50 (a pair)** a 50 libras (el par). **5.** (*indicating particular state, condition*): ~ **peace/ war** en paz/guerra; **she's ~ lunch** está comiendo. **6.** (*indicating a particular age*) a; ~ **52/your age** a los 52/tu edad. **7.** (*after adjectives*): **delighted ~** encantado con; **clever/experienced ~** listo/experimentado en; **puzzled/horrified ~** perplejo/horrorizado ante; **he's good/bad ~ sport** se le dan bien/mal los deportes. ▶ **at all** *adv* **1.** (*with negative*): **not ~ all** (*when thanked*) de nada; (*when answering a question*) en absoluto; **she's not ~ all happy** no está nada contenta. **2.** (*in the slightest*): **anything ~ all** will do cualquier cosa valdrá; **do you know her ~ all?** ¿la conoces (de algo)?

ate [Br et, Am eɪt] *pt* → **eat**.

atheist ['eɪθɪɪst] *n* ateo *m*, -a *f*.

Athens ['æθɪnz] *n* Atenas.

athlete ['æθliːt] *n* atleta *m y f*.

athletic [æθ'letɪk] *adj* atlético(ca). ▶ **athletics** *npl* atletismo *m*.

Atlantic [ət'læntɪk] ◆ *adj* atlántico(ca). ◆ *n*: **the ~ (Ocean)** el (océano) Atlántico.

atlas ['ætləs] *n* atlas *m inv*.

ATM (*abbr of* **automatic teller machine**) *n* cajero automático.

atmosphere ['ætmə,sfɪəʳ] *n* **1.** (*of planet*) atmósfera *f*. **2.** (*air in room, mood of place*) ambiente *m*, atmósfera *f*.

atmospheric [,ætməs'ferɪk] *adj* **1.** (*pressure, pollution*) atmosférico(ca). **2.** (*attractive, mysterious*) cautivador(ra).

atom ['ætəm] *n* (TECH) átomo *m*.

atom bomb *n* bomba *f* atómica.

atomic [ə'tɒmɪk] *adj* atómico(ca).

atomic bomb *n* = **atom bomb**.

atomizer, -iser ['ætəmaɪzəʳ] *n* atomizador *m*.

atone [ə'təʊn] *vi*: **to ~ for** reparar.

A to Z *n* guía *f* alfabética; (*map*) callejero *m*.

atrocious [ə'trəʊʃəs] *adj* (*very bad*) atroz.

atrocity [ə'trɒsətɪ] *n* (*terrible act*) atrocidad *f*.

attach [ə'tætʃ] *vt* **1.** (*with pin, clip*): **to ~ sthg (to)** sujetar algo (a); (*with string*) atar algo (a). **2.** (*importance, blame*): **to ~ sthg (to sthg)** atribuir algo (a algo).

attaché case [ə'tæʃeɪ-] *n* maletín *m*.

attached [ə'tætʃt] *adj* **1.** (*fastened on*): ~ **(to)** adjunto(ta) (a). **2.** (*fond*): ~ **to** encariñado(da) con.

attachment [ə'tætʃmənt] *n* **1.** (*device*) accesorio *m*. **2.** (*fondness*): ~ **(to)** cariño *m* (por).

attack [ə'tæk] ◆ *n*: ~ **(on)** ataque *m* (contra). ◆ *vt* **1.** (*gen*) atacar. **2.** (*job, problem*) acometer. ◆ *vi* atacar.

attacker [ə'tækəʳ] *n* atacante *m y f*.

attain [ə'teɪn] *vt* lograr, alcanzar.

attainment [ə'teɪnmənt] *n* logro *m*.

attempt [ə'tempt] ◆ *n*: ~ **(at sthg)** intento *m* (de algo); ~ **on sb's life** atentado *m*. ◆ *vt*: **to ~ sthg/to do sthg** intentar algo/hacer algo.

attend [ə'tend] ◆ *vt* asistir a. ◆ *vi* **1.** (*be present*) asistir. **2.** (*pay attention*): **to ~ (to)** atender (a). ▶ **attend to** *vt fus* **1.** (*matter*) ocuparse de. **2.** (*customer*) atender a; (*patient*) asistir a.

attendance [ə'tendəns] *n* asistencia *f*.

attendant [ə'tendənt] ◆ *adj* concomitante. ◆ *n* (*at museum*) vigilante *m y f*; (*at petrol station*) encargado *m*, -da *f*.

attention [ə'tenʃn] ◆ *n* (U) **1.** (*gen*) atención *f*; **to bring sthg to sb's ~**, **to draw sb's ~ to sthg** llamar la atención de alguien sobre algo; **to attract** OR **catch sb's ~** atraer OR captar la atención de alguien; **to pay/pay no ~ (to)** prestar/no prestar atención (a); **for the ~ of** (COMM) a la atención de. **2.** (*care*) asistencia *f*. ◆ *excl* (MIL) ¡firmes!

attentive [ə'tentɪv] *adj* atento(ta).

attic ['ætɪk] *n* desván *m*, entretecho *m* *Amer*.

attitude ['ætɪtjuːd] *n* **1.** (*way of thinking, acting*): ~ **(to** OR **towards)** actitud *f* (hacia). **2.** (*posture*) postura *f*.

attn. (*abbr of* **for the attention of**) a/a.

attorney [ə'tɜːnɪ] *n* *Am* abogado *m*, -da *f*.

attorney general (*pl* **attorneys general**) *n* fiscal *m* general del estado.

attract [ə'trækt] *vt* **1.** (*gen*) atraer. **2.** (*support, criticism*) atraerse, ganarse.

attraction [ə'trækʃn] *n* **1.** (*gen*): ~ **(to sb)** atracción *f* (hacia OR por alguien).

avenue

2. (attractiveness - of thing) atractivo m.
attractive [ə'træktɪv] adj atractivo(va).
attribute [vb ə'trɪbjuːt, n 'ætrɪbjuːt]
♦ vt: **to ~ sthg to** atribuir algo a. ♦ n
atributo m.
attrition [ə'trɪʃn] n desgaste m; **war of
~** guerra de desgaste.
aubergine ['əʊbəʒiːn] n Br berenjena
f.
auburn ['ɔːbən] adj castaño rojizo.
auction ['ɔːkʃn] ♦ n subasta f. ♦ vt
subastar.
auctioneer [,ɔːkʃə'nɪəʳ] n subastador
m, -ra f.
audacious [ɔː'deɪʃəs] adj (daring)
audaz; (cheeky) atrevido(da).
audible ['ɔːdəbl] adj audible.
audience ['ɔːdjəns] n **1.** (of play, film)
público m. **2.** (formal meeting, TV viewers)
audiencia f.
audiotypist ['ɔːdɪəʊˌtaɪpɪst] n
mecanógrafo m, -fa f por dictáfono.
audio-visual ['ɔːdɪəʊ-] adj audiovisual.
audit ['ɔːdɪt] ♦ n auditoría f. ♦ vt audi-
tar.
audition [ɔː'dɪʃn] n prueba f (a un
artista).
auditor ['ɔːdɪtəʳ] n auditor m, -ra f.
auditorium [,ɔːdɪ'tɔːrɪəm] (pl **-riums**
OR **-ria** [-rɪə]) n auditorio m.
augment [ɔːg'ment] vt acrecentar.
augur ['ɔːgəʳ] vi: **to ~ well/badly** traer
buenos/malos augurios.
August ['ɔːgəst] n agosto m; see also
September.
Auld Lang Syne [,ɔːldlæŋ'saɪn] n canción escocesa en alabanza de los viejos tiempos.
aunt [ɑːnt] n tía f.
auntie, aunty ['ɑːntɪ] n inf tita f.
au pair [,əʊ'peəʳ] n au pair f.
aura ['ɔːrə] n aura f, halo m.
aural ['ɔːrəl] adj auditivo(va).
auspices ['ɔːspɪsɪz] npl: **under the ~ of**
bajo los auspicios de.
auspicious [ɔː'spɪʃəs] adj prometedor
(ra).
Aussie ['ɒzɪ] n inf australiano m, -na f.
austere [ɒ'stɪəʳ] adj austero(ra).
austerity [ɒ'sterətɪ] n austeridad f.
Australia [ɒ'streɪljə] n Australia.
Australian [ɒ'streɪljən] ♦ adj aus-
traliano(na). ♦ n australiano m, -na f.
Austria ['ɒstrɪə] n Austria.
Austrian ['ɒstrɪən] ♦ adj austriaco(ca).
♦ n austriaco m, -ca f.
authentic [ɔː'θentɪk] adj auténtico(ca).
author ['ɔːθəʳ] n autor m, -ra f.

authoritarian [ɔːˌθɒrɪ'teərɪən] adj
autoritario(ria).
authoritative [ɔː'θɒrɪtətɪv] adj **1.** (person, voice) autoritario(ria). **2.** (study)
autorizado(da).
authority [ɔː'θɒrətɪ] n **1.** (gen) autoridad f; **to be an ~ on** ser una autoridad
en. **2.** (permission) autorización f.
► **authorities** npl: **the authorities** las
autoridades fpl.
authorize, -ise ['ɔːθəraɪz] vt: **to ~ (sb
to do sthg)** autorizar (a alguien a hacer
algo).
autistic [ɔː'tɪstɪk] adj autista.
auto ['ɔːtəʊ] (pl **-s**) n Am coche m, auto
m.
autobiography [,ɔːtəbaɪ'ɒgrəfɪ] n
autobiografía f.
autocratic [,ɔːtə'krætɪk] adj autocráti-
co(ca).
autofocus ['ɔːtəʊˌfəʊkəs] n (FOT) autofoco m.
autograph ['ɔːtəgrɑːf] ♦ n autógrafo
m. ♦ vt autografiar.
automate ['ɔːtəmeɪt] vt automatizar.
automatic [,ɔːtə'mætɪk] ♦ adj
automático(ca). ♦ n **1.** (car) coche m
automático. **2.** (gun) arma f automática.
3. (washing machine) lavadora f automática.
automatically [,ɔːtə'mætɪklɪ] adv
automáticamente.
automation [,ɔːtə'meɪʃn] n automatización f.
automobile ['ɔːtəməbiːl] n Am coche
m, automóvil m.
autonomous [ɔː'tɒnəməs] adj
autónomo(ma).
autonomy [ɔː'tɒnəmɪ] n autonomía f.
autopsy ['ɔːtɒpsɪ] n autopsia f.
autumn ['ɔːtəm] n otoño m.
auxiliary [ɔːg'zɪljərɪ] ♦ adj auxiliar.
♦ n (medical worker) auxiliar sanitario m,
auxiliar sanitaria f.
Av. (abbr of **avenue**) Av.
avail [ə'veɪl] ♦ n: **to no ~** en vano. ♦ vt:
to ~ o.s. of sthg aprovechar algo.
available [ə'veɪləbl] adj **1.** (product, service) disponible. **2.** (person) libre,
disponible.
avalanche ['ævəlɑːnʃ] n lit & fig
avalancha f, alud m.
avant-garde [,ævɒŋ'gɑːd] adj de vanguardia, vanguardista.
avarice ['ævərɪs] n avaricia f.
Ave. (abbr of **avenue**) Avda.
avenge [ə'vendʒ] vt vengar.
avenue ['ævənjuː] n **1.** (wide road)

avenida f. **2.** fig (method, means) vía f.

average ['ævərɪdʒ] ◆ adj **1.** (mean, typical) medio(dia). **2.** (mediocre) regular. ◆ n media f, promedio m; **on** ~ de media, por término medio. ◆ vt alcanzar un promedio de. ▶ **average out** vi: **to** ~ **out at** salir a una media de.

aversion [ə'vɜːʃn] n (dislike): ~ (**to**) aversión f (a).

avert [ə'vɜːt] vt **1.** (problem, accident) evitar, prevenir. **2.** (eyes, glance) apartar, desviar.

aviary ['eɪvjərɪ] n pajarera f.

avid ['ævɪd] adj: ~ (**for**) ávido(da) (de).

avocado [ˌævə'kɑːdəʊ] (pl **-s** OR **-es**) n: ~ (**pear**) aguacate m, palta f Amer.

avoid [ə'vɔɪd] vt: **to** ~ (**sthg/doing sthg**) evitar (algo/hacer algo).

avoidance [ə'vɔɪdəns] → **tax avoidance**.

await [ə'weɪt] vt esperar, aguardar.

awake [ə'weɪk] (pt awoke OR awaked, pp awoken) ◆ adj (not sleeping) despierto (ta). ◆ vt lit & fig despertar. ◆ vi lit & fig despertarse.

awakening [ə'weɪknɪŋ] n lit & fig despertar m.

award [ə'wɔːd] ◆ n **1.** (prize) premio m, galardón m. **2.** (compensation) indemnización f. ◆ vt: **to** ~ **sb sthg, to** ~ **sthg to sb** (prize) conceder OR otorgar algo a alguien; (compensation) adjudicar algo a alguien.

aware [ə'weər] adj **1.** (conscious): ~ **of** consciente de. **2.** (informed, sensitive) informado(da), al día; ~ **of sthg** al día de algo; **to be** ~ **that** estar informado de que.

awareness [ə'weənɪs] n conciencia f.

awash [ə'wɒʃ] adj lit & fig: ~ (**with**) inundado(da) (de).

away [ə'weɪ] ◆ adv **1.** (move, walk, drive): **to walk** ~ (**from**) marcharse (de); **to drive** ~ (**from**) alejarse (de) (en coche); **to turn** OR **look** ~ apartar la vista. **2.** (at a distance - in space, time): ~ **from** a distancia de; **4 miles** ~ a 4 millas de distancia; **the exam is two days** ~ faltan dos días para el examen. **3.** (not at home or office) fuera. **4.** (in safe place): **to put sthg** ~ poner algo en su sitio. **5.** (indicating removal or disappearance): **to fade** ~ desvanecerse; **to give sthg** ~ regalar algo; **to take sthg** ~ llevarse algo. **6.** (continuously): **he was working** ~ **when** ... estaba muy concentrado trabajando cuando ... ◆ adj (SPORT) visitante; ~ **game** partido m fuera de casa.

awe [ɔː] n sobrecogimiento m; **to be in** ~ **of sb** estar sometido a alguien.

awesome ['ɔːsəm] adj impresionante.

awful ['ɔːful] adj **1.** (terrible) terrible, espantoso(sa); **I feel** ~ me siento fatal. **2.** inf (very great) tremendo(da).

awfully ['ɔːflɪ] adv inf (very) tremendamente.

awhile [ə'waɪl] adv literary un rato.

awkward ['ɔːkwəd] adj **1.** (clumsy - movement) torpe; (- person) desgarbado(da). **2.** (embarrassed, embarrassing) incómodo(da). **3.** (unreasonable) difícil. **4.** (inconvenient) poco manejable.

awning ['ɔːnɪŋ] n toldo m.

awoke [ə'wəʊk] pt → **awake**.

awoken [ə'wəʊkn] pp → **awake**.

awry [ə'raɪ] ◆ adj torcido(da), ladeado(da). ◆ adv: **to go** ~ salir mal.

axe Br, **ax** Am [æks] ◆ n hacha f. ◆ vt (project, jobs) suprimir.

axes ['æksiːz] pl → **axis**.

axis ['æksɪs] (pl axes) n eje m.

axle ['æksl] n eje m.

aye [aɪ] ◆ adv sí. ◆ n sí m.

azalea [ə'zeɪljə] n azalea f.

Aztec ['æztek] ◆ adj azteca. ◆ n (person) azteca m y f.

B

b (pl **b's** OR **bs**), **B** (pl **B's** OR **Bs**) [biː] n (letter) b f, B f. ▶ **B** n **1.** (MUS) si m. **2.** (SCH) (mark) = bien m.

BA n (abbr of **Bachelor of Arts**) (titular de una) licenciatura de letras.

babble ['bæbl] vi (person) farfullar.

baboon [bə'buːn] n babuino m.

baby ['beɪbɪ] n **1.** (newborn child) bebé m; (infant) niño m. **2.** inf (term of affection) cariño m.

baby buggy n **1.** Br (foldable pushchair) sillita f de niño (con ruedas). **2.** Am = **baby carriage**.

baby carriage n Am cochecito m de niños.

baby food n papilla f.

baby-sit vi cuidar a niños.

baby-sitter [-'sɪtər] n canguro m y f.

bachelor ['bætʃələr] n soltero m.

Bachelor of Arts n = licenciado m,

-da f en Letras.

Bachelor of Science n ≃ licenciado m, -da f en Ciencias.

back [bæk] ◆ adv 1. (in position) atrás; **stand ~!** ¡échense para atrás!; **to push ~** empujar hacia atrás. 2. (to former position or state) de vuelta; **to come ~** volver; **to go ~** volver; **to look ~** volver la mirada; **to walk ~** volver andando; **to give sthg ~** devolver algo; **to be ~** (in fashion) estar de vuelta; **he has been there and ~** ha estado allí y ha vuelto; **I spent all day going ~ and forth** pasé todo el día yendo y viniendo. 3. (in time): **two weeks ~** hace dos semanas; **it dates ~ to 1960** data de 1960; **~ in March** allá en marzo. 4. (phone, write) de vuelta. ◆ n 1. (of person) espalda f; (of animal) lomo m; **behind sb's ~** a espaldas de alguien. 2. (of hand, cheque) dorso m; (of coin, page) reverso m; (of car, book, head) parte f trasera; (of chair) respaldo m; (of room, cupboard) fondo m. 3. (SPORT) (player) defensa m. ◆ adj (in compounds) 1. (at the back - door, legs, seat) trasero(ra); (- page) último(ma). 2. (overdue - pay, rent) atrasado(da). ◆ vt 1. (reverse) dar marcha atrás a. 2. (support) respaldar. 3. (bet on) apostar por. 4. (line with material) forrar. ◆ vi (drive backwards) ir marcha atrás; (walk backwards) ir hacia atrás. ► **back to back** adv (with backs facing) espalda con espalda. ► **back to front** adv al revés. ► **back down** vi echarse OR volverse atrás. ► **back out** vi echarse OR volverse atrás. ► **back up** ◆ vt sep 1. (support) apoyar. 2. (COMPUT) hacer un archivo de seguridad de. ◆ vi (reverse) ir marcha atrás.

backache ['bækeɪk] n dolor m de espalda.

backbencher [,bæk'bentʃər] n Br diputado sin cargo en el gabinete del gobierno o la oposición.

backbone ['bækbəʊn] n lit & fig columna f vertebral.

backcloth ['bækklɒθ] n Br = **backdrop**.

backdate [,bæk'deɪt] vt: **a pay rise ~d to March** un aumento de sueldo con efecto retroactivo desde marzo.

back door n puerta f trasera.

backdrop ['bækdrɒp] n lit & fig telón m de fondo.

backfire [,bæk'faɪər] vi 1. (motor vehicle) petardear. 2. (go wrong): **it ~d on him** le salió el tiro por la culata.

backgammon ['bæk,gæmən] n

backgammon m.

background ['bækgraʊnd] n 1. (in picture, view) fondo m; **in the ~** (of painting etc) al fondo; (out of the limelight) en la sombra. 2. (of event, situation) trasfondo m. 3. (upbringing) origen m; **family ~** antecedentes mpl familiares.

backhand ['bækhænd] n revés m.

backhanded ['bækhændɪd] adj fig equívoco(ca).

backhander ['bækhændər] n Br inf: **to give sb a ~** untarle la mano a alguien.

backing ['bækɪŋ] n 1. (support) apoyo m, respaldo m. 2. (lining) refuerzo m. 3. (MUS) acompañamiento m.

backlash ['bæklæʃ] n reacción f violenta.

backlog ['bæklɒg] n acumulación f.

back number n número m atrasado.

backpack ['bækpæk] n mochila f.

back pay n (U) atrasos mpl.

back seat n asiento m trasero OR de atrás.

backside [,bæk'saɪd] n inf trasero m.

backstage [,bæk'steɪdʒ] adv entre bastidores.

back street n Br callejuela f de barrio.

backstroke ['bækstrəʊk] n espalda f (en natación).

backup ['bækʌp] ◆ adj 1. (plan) de emergencia; (team) de apoyo. 2. (COMPUT) de seguridad. ◆ n 1. (support) apoyo m. 2. (COMPUT) copia f de seguridad.

backward ['bækwəd] ◆ adj 1. (movement, look) hacia atrás. 2. (country, person) atrasado(da). ◆ adv Am = **backwards**.

backwards ['bækwədz], **backward** Am adv 1. (move, go) hacia atrás; **~ and forwards** (movement) de un lado a otro. 2. (back to front) al OR del revés.

backwater ['bæk,wɔːtər] n fig páramo m, lugar m atrasado.

backyard [,bæk'jɑːd] n 1. Br (yard) patio m. 2. Am (garden) jardín m (trasero).

bacon ['beɪkən] n bacon m, tocino m.

bacteria [bæk'tɪərɪə] npl bacterias fpl.

bad [bæd] (compar **worse**, superl **worst**) ◆ adj 1. (gen) malo(la); **he's ~ at French** se le da mal el francés; **to go ~** (food) echarse a perder; **too ~!** ¡qué pena!; **it's not ~ (at all)** no está nada mal; **how are you? - not ~** ¿qué tal? - bien. 2. (illness) fuerte, grave. 3. (guilty): **to feel ~ about sthg** sentirse mal por algo. ◆ adv Am = **badly**.

badge [bædʒ] n 1. (for decoration - metal, plastic) chapa f; (sewn-on) insignia f. 2. (for identification) distintivo m.

badger ['bædʒə'] ◆ n tejón m. ◆ vt: to ~ sb (to do sthg) ponerse pesado(da) con alguien (para que haga algo).

badly ['bædlɪ] (compar worse, superl worst) adv 1. (not well) mal. 2. (seriously) gravemente; I'm ~ in need of help necesito ayuda urgentemente.

badly-off adj 1. (poor) apurado(da) de dinero. 2. (lacking): to be ~ for sthg estar OR andar mal de algo.

bad-mannered [-'mænəd] adj maleducado(da).

badminton ['bædmɪntən] n bádminton m.

bad-tempered [-'tempəd] adj 1. (by nature) de mal genio. 2. (in a bad mood) malhumorado(da).

baffle ['bæfl] vt desconcertar.

bag [bæg] ◆ n 1. (container, bagful) bolsa f; to pack one's ~s fig hacer las maletas. 2. (handbag) bolso m, cartera f Amer. ◆ vt Br inf (reserve) pedirse, reservarse. ► **bags** npl 1. (under eyes) ojeras fpl. 2. (lots): ~s of inf un montón de.

bagel ['beɪgəl] n bollo de pan en forma de rosca.

baggage ['bægɪdʒ] n (U) equipaje m.

baggage reclaim n recogida f de equipajes.

baggy ['bægɪ] adj holgado(da).

bagpipes ['bægpaɪps] npl gaita f.

baguette [bə'get] n barra f de pan.

Bahamas [bə'hɑːməz] npl: the ~ (las) Bahamas.

bail [beɪl] n (U) fianza f; on ~ bajo fianza. ► **bail out** ◆ vt sep 1. (pay bail for) obtener la libertad bajo fianza de. 2. (rescue) sacar de apuros. ◆ vi (from plane) tirarse en paracaídas.

bailiff ['beɪlɪf] n alguacil m.

bait [beɪt] ◆ n lit & fig cebo m. ◆ vt 1. (put bait on) cebar. 2. (tease, torment) hacer sufrir, cebarse con.

bake [beɪk] ◆ vt (food) cocer al horno. ◆ vi (food) cocerse al horno.

baked beans [beɪkt-] npl alubias fpl cocidas en salsa de tomate.

baked potato [beɪkt-] n patata f asada OR al horno.

baker ['beɪkə'] n panadero m; ~'s (shop) panadería f.

bakery ['beɪkərɪ] n panadería f.

baking ['beɪkɪŋ] n cocción f.

balaclava (helmet) [bælə'klɑːvə-] n pasamontañas m inv.

balance ['bæləns] ◆ n 1. (equilibrium) equilibrio m; to keep/lose one's ~ mantener/perder el equilibrio; it caught me off ~ me pilló desprevenido(da). 2. fig (counterweight) contrapunto m. 3. (of evidence etc) peso m. 4. (scales) balanza f. 5. (of account) saldo m. ◆ vt 1. (keep in balance) poner en equilibrio. 2. (compare) sopesar. 3. (in accounting): to ~ the books/a budget hacer que cuadren las cuentas/cuadre un presupuesto. ◆ vi 1. (maintain equilibrium) sostenerse en equilibrio. 2. (in accounting) cuadrar. ► **on balance** adv tras pensarlo detenidamente.

balanced diet ['bælənst-] n dieta f equilibrada.

balance of payments n balanza f de pagos.

balance of trade n balanza f comercial.

balance sheet n balance m.

balcony ['bælkənɪ] n 1. (on building - big) terraza f; (- small) balcón m. 2. (in theatre) anfiteatro m, galería f.

bald [bɔːld] adj 1. (without hair) calvo (va). 2. (without tread) desgastado(da). 3. fig (blunt) escueto(ta).

bale [beɪl] n bala f, fardo m. ► **bale out** vi Br 1. (remove water) achicar agua. 2. (from plane) tirarse en paracaídas.

Balearic Islands [bælɪˈærɪk-], **Balearics** [bælɪˈærɪks] npl: the ~ las Baleares.

baleful ['beɪlful] adj maligno(na).

balk [bɔːk] vi: to ~ (at doing sthg) resistirse (a hacer algo).

Balkans ['bɔːlkənz], **Balkan States** npl: the ~ los países balcánicos.

ball [bɔːl] n 1. (for tennis, cricket) pelota f; (for golf, billiards) bola f; (for football) balón m; to be on the ~ fig estar al tanto de todo. 2. (round shape) bola f. 3. (of foot) pulpejo m. 4. (dance) baile m. ► **balls** v inf ◆ npl (testicles) pelotas fpl. ◆ n (U) (nonsense) gilipolleces fpl.

ballad ['bæləd] n balada f.

ballast ['bæləst] n lastre m.

ball bearing n cojinete m de bolas.

ball boy n recogepelotas m inv.

ballerina [bælə'riːnə] n bailarina f.

ballet ['bæleɪ] n ballet m.

ballet dancer n bailarín m, -ina f.

ball game n Am (baseball match) partido m de béisbol.

balloon [bə'luːn] n 1. (toy) globo m. 2. (hot-air balloon) globo m (aerostático). 3. (in cartoon) bocadillo m.

ballot ['bælət] ◆ n (voting process) votación f. ◆ vt: **to ~ the members on an issue** someter un asunto a votación entre los miembros.

ballot box n (container) urna f.

ballot paper n voto m, papeleta f.

ball park n Am estadio m de béisbol.

ballpoint (pen) ['bɔ:lpɔint-] n bolígrafo m.

ballroom ['bɔ:lrum] n salón m de baile.

ballroom dancing n (U) baile m de salón.

balm [bɑ:m] n bálsamo m.

balmy ['bɑ:mi] adj apacible.

balsa ['bɒlsə], **balsawood** ['bɒlsə-wud] n balsa f.

balti ['bɔ:lti] n (pan) cacerola utilizada en la cocina india; (food) plato sazonado con especias y preparado en un 'balti'.

Baltic ['bɔ:ltik] ◆ adj báltico(ca). ◆ n: **the ~ (Sea)** el (mar) Báltico.

Baltic Republic n: **the ~s** las repúblicas bálticas.

bamboo [bæm'bu:] n bambú m.

bamboozle [bæm'bu:zl] vt inf camelar, engatusar.

ban [bæn] ◆ n: **~ (on)** prohibición f (de). ◆ vt: **to ~ sb (from doing sthg)** prohibir a alguien (hacer algo).

banal [bə'nɑ:l] adj pej banal.

banana [bə'nɑ:nə] n plátano m, banana f Amer.

band [bænd] n 1. (musical group - pop) grupo m; (- jazz, military) banda f. 2. (of thieves etc) banda f. 3. (strip) cinta f. 4. (stripe, range) franja f. ▶ **band together** vi juntarse.

bandage ['bændidʒ] ◆ n venda f. ◆ vt vendar.

Band-Aid® n ≃ tirita® f.

b and b, B and B n abbr of **bed and breakfast.**

bandit ['bændit] n bandido m, -da f.

bandstand ['bændstænd] n quiosco m de música.

bandwagon ['bændwægən] n: **to jump on the ~** subirse OR apuntarse al carro.

bandy ['bændi] adj de piernas arqueadas. ▶ **bandy about, bandy around** vt sep sacar a relucir.

bandy-legged [-,legd] adj de piernas arqueadas.

bang [bæŋ] ◆ n 1. (blow) golpe m. 2. (loud noise) estampido m, estruendo m. ◆ vt 1. (hit - drum, desk) golpear; (- knee, head) golpearse. 2. (slam) cerrar de golpe. ◆ vi golpear. ◆ adv (exactly): **~**

in the middle of justo en mitad de; **~ on** muy acertado(da). ▶ **bangs** npl Am flequillo m.

banger ['bæŋər] n Br 1. inf (sausage) salchicha f. 2. inf (old car) carraca f, cacharro m. 3. (firework) petardo m.

Bangladesh [,bæŋglə'deʃ] n Bangladesh.

bangle ['bæŋgl] n brazalete m.

banish ['bæniʃ] vt lit & fig desterrar.

banister ['bænistər] n, **banisters** ['bænistəz] npl barandilla f, pasamanos m inv.

bank [bæŋk] ◆ n 1. (gen & FIN) banco m. 2. (by river, lake) ribera f, orilla f. 3. (slope) loma f. 4. (of clouds etc) masa f. ◆ vi 1. (FIN): **to ~ with** tener una cuenta en. 2. (plane) ladearse. ▶ **bank on** vt fus contar con.

bank account n cuenta f bancaria.

bank balance n saldo m.

bank card n = **banker's card.**

bank charges npl comisiones fpl bancarias.

bank draft n giro m bancario.

banker ['bæŋkər] n banquero m, -ra f.

banker's card n Br tarjeta f de identificación bancaria.

bank holiday n Br día m festivo.

banking ['bæŋkiŋ] n banca f.

bank manager n director m, -ra f de banco.

bank note n billete m de banco.

bank rate n tipo m de interés bancario.

bankrupt ['bæŋkrʌpt] ◆ adj (financially) quebrado(da), en quiebra; **to go ~** quebrar. ◆ vt llevar a la quiebra.

bankruptcy ['bæŋkrəptsi] n quiebra f, bancarrota f; fig (of ideas) agotamiento m, falta f total.

bank statement n extracto m de cuenta.

banner ['bænər] n pancarta f.

bannister ['bænistər] n, **bannisters** ['bænistəz] npl = **banister(s).**

banquet ['bæŋkwit] n banquete m.

banter ['bæntər] n (U) bromas fpl.

bap [bæp] n Br bollo m de pan.

baptism ['bæptizm] n bautismo m.

baptize, -ise [Br bæp'taiz, Am 'bæptaiz] vt bautizar.

bar [bɑ:r] ◆ n 1. (of soap) pastilla f; (of chocolate) tableta f; (of gold) lingote m; (of wood) tabla f; (of metal) barra f; **to be behind ~s** estar entre rejas. 2. fig (obstacle) barrera f; (ban) prohibición f. 3. (drinking place) bar m. 4. (counter) barra *f.* **5.** (MUS) compás *m.* ✦ *vt* **1.** (*close with a bar*) atrancar. **2.** (*block*): **to ~ sb's way** impedir el paso a alguien. **3.** (*ban*): **to ~ sb (from doing sthg)** prohibir a alguien (hacer algo); **to ~ sb from somewhere** prohibir a alguien la entrada en un sitio. ✦ *prep* (*except*) menos, salvo; **~ none** sin excepción. ▶ **Bar** *n* (JUR): **the Bar** *Br* conjunto de los abogados que ejercen en tribunales superiores; *Am* la abogacía.

barbaric [bɑːˈbærɪk] *adj* bárbaro(ra).

barbecue [ˈbɑːbɪkjuː] *n* barbacoa *f.*

barbed wire [bɑːbd-] *n* alambre *m* de espino.

barber [ˈbɑːbəʳ] *n* barbero *m*; **~'s** barbería *f.*

barbiturate [bɑːˈbɪtjʊrət] *n* barbitúrico *m.*

bar code *n* código *m* de barras.

bare [beəʳ] ✦ *adj* **1.** (*without covering - legs, trees, hills*) desnudo(da); (*- feet*) descalzo(za). **2.** (*absolute, minimum*) esencial. **3.** (*empty*) vacío(a). ✦ *vt* descubrir; **to ~ one's teeth** enseñar los dientes.

bareback [ˈbeəbæk] *adj & adv* a pelo.

barefaced [ˈbeəfeɪst] *adj* descarado(da).

barefoot(ed) [ˌbeəˈfʊt(ɪd)] *adj & adv* descalzo(za).

barely [ˈbeəlɪ] *adv* (*scarcely*) apenas.

bargain [ˈbɑːgɪn] ✦ *n* **1.** (*agreement*) trato *m*, acuerdo *m*; **into the ~** por añadidura, además. **2.** (*good buy*) ganga *f.* ✦ *vi* **1.** (*negotiate*): **to ~ (with sb for sthg)** negociar (con alguien para obtener algo). **2.** (*haggle*): **to ~ (with sb over sthg)** regatear (algo con alguien). ▶ **bargain for, bargain on** *vt fus* contar con.

bargaining [ˈbɑːgɪnɪŋ] *n* **1.** (*negotiating*) negociación *f.* **2.** (*haggling*) regateo *m.*

barge [bɑːdʒ] ✦ *n* barcaza *f.* ✦ *vi inf*: **to ~ into** (*person*) chocarse con; (*room*) irrumpir en. ▶ **barge in** *vi inf*: **to ~ in (on)** (*conversation etc*) entrometerse (en).

baritone [ˈbærɪtəʊn] *n* barítono *m.*

bark [bɑːk] ✦ *n* **1.** (*of dog*) ladrido *m.* **2.** (*on tree*) corteza *f.* ✦ *vi*: **to ~ (at)** ladrar (a).

barley [ˈbɑːlɪ] *n* cebada *f.*

barley sugar *n Br* azúcar *m o f* cande.

barley water *n Br* hordiate *m.*

barmaid [ˈbɑːmeɪd] *n* camarera *f.*

barman [ˈbɑːmən] (*pl* **-men** [-mən]) *n* camarero *m*, barman *m.*

barn [bɑːn] *n* granero *m.*

barometer [bəˈrɒmɪtəʳ] *n* barómetro *m*; *fig* (*of public opinion etc*) piedra *f* de toque.

baron [ˈbærən] *n* barón *m.*

baroness [ˈbærənɪs] *n* baronesa *f.*

barrack [ˈbærək] *vt Br* abroncar. ▶ **barracks** *npl* cuartel *m.*

barrage [ˈbærɑːʒ] *n* **1.** (*of firing*) bombardeo *m*, fuego *m* intenso de artillería. **2.** (*of questions*) aluvión *m*, alud *m.* **3.** *Br* (*dam*) presa *f*, dique *m.*

barrel [ˈbærəl] *n* **1.** (*for beer, wine, oil*) barril *m.* **2.** (*of gun*) cañón *m.*

barren [ˈbærən] *adj* estéril.

barricade [ˌbærɪˈkeɪd] ✦ *n* barricada *f.* ✦ *vt* levantar barricadas en.

barrier [ˈbærɪəʳ] *n lit & fig* barrera *f.*

barring [ˈbɑːrɪŋ] *prep* salvo.

barrister [ˈbærɪstəʳ] *n Br* abogado *m*, -da *f* (*de tribunales superiores*).

barrow [ˈbærəʊ] *n* carrito *m.*

bartender [ˈbɑːtendəʳ] *n* camarero *m*, -ra *f.*

barter [ˈbɑːtəʳ] ✦ *n* trueque *m.* ✦ *vt*: **to ~ (sthg for sthg)** trocar (algo por algo).

base [beɪs] ✦ *n* base *f.* ✦ *vt* **1.** (*place, establish*) emplazar; **he's ~d in Paris** trabaja en París. **2.** (*use as starting point*): **to ~ sthg on OR upon** basar algo en. ✦ *adj pej* bajo(ja), vil.

baseball [ˈbeɪsbɔːl] *n* béisbol *m.*

baseball cap *n* gorra *f* de béisbol.

basement [ˈbeɪsmənt] *n* sótano *m.*

base rate *n* tipo *m* de interés base.

bases [ˈbeɪsiːz] *pl* → **basis**.

bash [bæʃ] *inf* ✦ *n* **1.** (*attempt*): **to have a ~ at sthg** intentar algo. **2.** (*party*) juerga *f.* ✦ *vt* (*hit - person, thing*) darle un porrazo a; (*- one's head, knee*) darse un porrazo en.

bashful [ˈbæʃfʊl] *adj* (*person*) vergonzoso(sa); (*smile*) tímido(da).

basic [ˈbeɪsɪk] *adj* básico(ca). ▶ **basics** *npl* **1.** (*rudiments*) principios *mpl* básicos. **2.** (*essentials*) lo imprescindible.

BASIC [ˈbeɪsɪk] (*abbr of* **Beginner's All-purpose Symbolic Instruction Code**) *n* BASIC *m.*

basically [ˈbeɪsɪklɪ] *adv* **1.** (*essentially*) esencialmente. **2.** (*really*) en resumen.

basil [ˈbæzl] *n* albahaca *f.*

basin [ˈbeɪsn] *n* **1.** *Br* (*bowl*) balde *m*, barreño *m.* **2.** (*wash basin*) lavabo *m.* **3.** (GEOGR) cuenca *f.*

basis [ˈbeɪsɪs] (*pl* **bases**) *n* base *f*; **on the ~ of** de acuerdo con, a partir de; **on a weekly/monthly ~** de forma semanal/mensual.

bask [bɑːsk] vi (sunbathe): **to ~ in the sun** tostarse al sol.

basket ['bɑːskɪt] n cesto m, cesta f.

basketball ['bɑːskɪtbɔːl] n baloncesto m.

Basque [bɑːsk] ◆ adj vasco(ca). ◆ n 1. (person) vasco m, -ca f. 2. (language) vascuence m, euskera m.

Basque Country [bɑːsk-] n: **the ~** el País Vasco, Euskadi.

bass [beɪs] ◆ adj bajo(ja). ◆ n 1. (singer, bass guitar) bajo m. 2. (double bass) contrabajo m.

bass drum [beɪs-] n bombo m.

bass guitar [beɪs-] n bajo m.

bassoon [bə'suːn] n fagot m.

bastard ['bɑːstəd] n 1. (illegitimate child) bastardo m, -da f. 2. v inf pej cabrón m, -ona f.

bastion ['bæstɪən] n bastión m.

bat [bæt] n 1. (animal) murciélago m. 2. (for cricket, baseball) bate m. 3. (for table-tennis) pala f, paleta f.

batch [bætʃ] n 1. (of letters etc) remesa f. 2. (of work) montón m, serie f. 3. (of products) lote m.

bated ['beɪtɪd] adj: **with ~ breath** con el aliento contenido.

bath [bɑːθ] ◆ n 1. (bathtub) bañera f, bañadera f Amer. 2. (act of washing) baño m, bañada f Amer; **to have** OR **take a ~** darse un baño, bañarse. ◆ vt bañar.
▶ **baths** npl Br (public swimming pool) piscina f municipal.

bathe [beɪð] ◆ vt (wound) lavar. ◆ vi bañarse.

bathing ['beɪðɪŋ] n (U) baños mpl.

bathing cap n gorro m de baño.

bathing costume, bathing suit n traje m de baño, bañador m, malla f Amer.

bathrobe ['bɑːθrəʊb] n 1. (made of towelling) albornoz m. 2. (dressing gown) batín m, bata f.

bathroom ['bɑːθrʊm] n 1. Br (room with bath) (cuarto m de) baño m. 2. Am (toilet) servicio m.

bath towel n toalla f de baño.

bathtub ['bɑːθtʌb] n bañera f.

baton ['bætən] n 1. (of conductor) batuta f. 2. (in relay race) testigo m. 3. Br (of policeman) porra f.

batsman ['bætsmən] n (pl -men [-mən]) n bateador m.

battalion [bə'tæljən] n batallón m.

batten ['bætn] n listón m (de madera).

batter ['bætər] ◆ n pasta f para rebozar. ◆ vt 1. (child, woman) pegar.

2. (door, ship) sacudir, golpear. ▶ **batter down** vt sep echar abajo.

battered ['bætəd] adj 1. (child, woman) maltratado(da). 2. (car, hat) abollado (da).

battery ['bætərɪ] n (of radio) pila f; (of car, guns) batería f.

battle ['bætl] ◆ n 1. (in war) batalla f. 2. (struggle): **~ (for/against/with)** lucha f (por/contra/con). ◆ vi: **to ~ (for/against/with)** luchar (por/contra/con).

battlefield ['bætlfiːld], **battleground** ['bætlgraʊnd] n lit & fig campo m de batalla.

battlements ['bætlmənts] npl almenas fpl.

battleship ['bætlʃɪp] n acorazado m.

bauble ['bɔːbl] n baratija f.

baulk [bɔːk] = **balk**.

bawdy ['bɔːdɪ] adj verde, picante.

bawl [bɔːl] vi 1. (shout) vociferar. 2. (cry) berrear.

bay [beɪ] ◆ n 1. (of coast) bahía f. 2. (for loading) zona f de carga y descarga. 3. (for parking) plaza f. 4. phr: **to keep sthg/sb at ~** mantener algo/a alguien a raya. ◆ vi aullar.

bay leaf n (hoja f de) laurel m.

bay window n ventana f salediza.

bazaar [bə'zɑːr] n 1. (market) bazar m. 2. Br (charity sale) mercadillo m benéfico.

B & B abbr of **bed and breakfast**.

BBC (abbr of **British Broadcasting Corporation**) n BBC f, compañía estatal británica de radiotelevisión.

BC (abbr of **before Christ**) a.C.

be [biː] (pt **was** OR **were**, pp **been**) ◆ aux vb 1. (in combination with present participle: to form cont tense) estar; **what is he doing?** ¿qué hace OR está haciendo?; **it's snowing** está nevando; **I'm leaving tomorrow** me voy mañana; **they've been promising it for years** han estado prometiéndolo durante años. 2. (in combination with pp: to form passive) ser; **to ~ loved** ser amado; **there was no one to ~ seen** no se veía a nadie; **ten people were killed** murieron diez personas. 3. (in question tags): **you're not going now, are you?** no irás a marcharte ya ¿no?; **the meal was delicious, wasn't it?** la comida fue deliciosa ¿verdad? 4. (followed by 'to' + infin): **I'm to be promoted** me van a ascender; **you're not to tell anyone** no debes decírselo a nadie. ◆ copulative vb 1. (with adj, n) (indicating innate quality, permanent condition) ser; (indicating state, temporary condition) estar; **snow is white** la nieve es blanca; **she's intelligent/tall** es inteligente/alta; **to ~ a doctor/plumber** ser médico/fontanero; **I'm Scottish** soy escocés; **1 and 1 are 2** 1 y 1 son 2; **your hands are cold** tus manos están frías; **I'm tired/angry** estoy cansado/enfadado; **he's in a difficult position** está en una situación difícil. **2.** (*referring to health*) estar; **she's ill/better** está enferma/mejor; **how are you?** ¿cómo estás? **3.** (*referring to age*): **how old are you?** ¿qué edad OR cuántos años tienes?; **I'm 20 (years old)** tengo 20 años. **4.** (*cost*) ser, costar; **how much is it?** ¿cuánto es?; **that will ~ £10, please** son 10 libras; **apples are only 20p a kilo today** hoy las manzanas están a tan sólo 20 peniques el kilo. ◆ *vi* **1.** (*exist*) ser, existir; **the worst prime minister that ever was** el peor primer ministro que jamás existió; **~ that as it may** aunque así sea; **there is/are** hay; **is there life on Mars?** ¿hay vida en Marte? **2.** (*referring to place*) estar; **Valencia is in Spain** Valencia está en España; **he will ~ here tomorrow** estará aquí mañana. **3.** (*referring to movement*) estar; **where have you been?** ¿dónde has estado? ◆ *impersonal vb* **1.** (*referring to time, dates*) ser; **it's two o'clock** son las dos; **it's the 17th of February** estamos a 17 de febrero. **2.** (*referring to distance*): **it's 3 km to the next town** hay 3 kms hasta el próximo pueblo. **3.** (*referring to the weather*): **it's hot/cold/windy** hace calor/frío/viento. **4.** (*for emphasis*) ser; **it's me** soy yo.

beach [biːtʃ] ◆ *n* playa *f*. ◆ *vt* varar.

beacon ['biːkən] *n* **1.** (*warning fire*) almenara *f*. **2.** (*lighthouse*) faro *m*, fanal *m*. **3.** (*radio beacon*) radiofaro *m*.

bead [biːd] *n* **1.** (*of wood, glass*) cuenta *f*, abalorio *m*. **2.** (*of sweat*) gota *f*.

beagle ['biːgl] *n* sabueso *m*.

beak [biːk] *n* pico *m*.

beaker ['biːkər] *n* taza *f* (*sin asa*).

beam [biːm] ◆ *n* **1.** (*of wood, concrete*) viga *f*. **2.** (*of light*) rayo *m*. ◆ *vt* transmitir. ◆ *vi* **1.** (*smile*) sonreír resplandeciente. **2.** (*shine*) resplandecer.

bean [biːn] *n* (CULIN) (*haricot*) judía *f*, poroto *m* *Amer*; (*of coffee*) grano *m*.

beanbag ['biːnbæg] *n* cojín grande relleno de polietileno.

beanshoot ['biːnʃuːt], **beansprout** ['biːnspraut] *n* brote *m* de soja.

bear [beər] (*pt* bore, *pp* borne) ◆ *n* (*animal*) oso *m*, -sa *f*. ◆ *vt* **1.** (*carry*) llevar. **2.** (*support*) soportar. **3.** (*responsibility*) cargar con. **4.** (*marks, signs*) llevar. **5.** (*endure*) aguantar. **6.** (*fruit, crop*) dar. **7.** (*feeling*) guardar, albergar. ◆ *vi*: **to ~ left** torcer OR doblar a la izquierda; **to bring pressure/influence to ~ on** ejercer presión/influencia sobre. ► **bear down** *vi*: **to ~ down on** echarse encima de. ► **bear out** *vt sep* corroborar. ► **bear up** *vi* resistir. ► **bear with** *vt fus* tener paciencia con.

beard [bɪəd] *n* barba *f*.

bearer ['beərər] *n* **1.** (*of stretcher, news, cheque*) portador *m*, -ra *f*. **2.** (*of passport*) titular *m* y *f*.

bearing ['beərɪŋ] *n* **1.** (*connection*): **~ (on)** relación *f* (con). **2.** (*deportment*) porte *m*. **3.** (*for shaft*) cojinete *m*. **4.** (*on compass*) rumbo *m*; **to get one's ~s** orientarse; **to lose one's ~s** desorientarse.

beast [biːst] *n lit & fig* bestia *f*.

beastly ['biːstlɪ] *adj dated* atroz.

beat [biːt] (*pt* beat, *pp* beaten) ◆ *n* **1.** (*of drum*) golpe *m*. **2.** (*of heart, pulse*) latido *m*. **3.** (MUS) (*rhythm*) ritmo *m*; (*individual unit of time*) golpe *m* (*de compás*). **4.** (*of policeman*) ronda *f*. ◆ *vt* **1.** (*hit - person*) pegar; (*- thing*) golpear. **2.** (*wings, eggs, butter*) batir. **3.** (*defeat*) ganar; **it ~s me** *inf* no me lo explico. **4.** (*be better than*) ser mucho mejor que. **5.** *phr*: **~ it!** *inf* ¡largo! ◆ *vi* **1.** (*rain*) golpear. **2.** (*heart, pulse*) latir. ► **beat off** *vt sep* repeler. ► **beat up** *vt sep inf* dar una paliza a.

beating ['biːtɪŋ] *n* **1.** (*hitting*) paliza *f*. **2.** (*defeat*) derrota *f*.

beautiful ['bjuːtɪful] *adj* **1.** (*person*) guapo(pa). **2.** (*thing, animal*) precioso (sa). **3.** *inf* (*very good - shot, weather*) espléndido(da).

beautifully ['bjuːtəflɪ] *adv* **1.** (*attractively*) bellamente. **2.** *inf* (*very well*) espléndidamente.

beauty ['bjuːtɪ] *n* belleza *f*.

beauty parlour *n* salón *f* de belleza.

beauty salon = **beauty parlour**.

beauty spot *n* **1.** (*picturesque place*) bello paraje *m*. **2.** (*on skin*) lunar *m*.

beaver ['biːvər] *n* castor *m*.

became [bɪˈkeɪm] *pt* → **become**.

because [bɪˈkɒz] *conj* porque. ► **because of** *prep* por, a causa de.

beck [bek] *n*: **to be at sb's ~ and call** estar siempre a disposición de alguien.

beckon ['bekən] ◆ *vt* (*signal to*) llamar (con un gesto). ◆ *vi* (*signal*): **to ~ to sb** llamar (con un gesto) a alguien.

become [bɪˈkʌm] (*pt* became, *pp*

become) *vi* hacerse; **to ~ happy** ponerse contento; **to ~ angry** enfadarse; **he became Prime Minister in 1991** en 1991 se convirtió en primer ministro.

becoming [bɪˈkʌmɪŋ] *adj* 1. (*attractive*) favorecedor(ra). 2. (*appropriate*) apropiado(da).

bed [bed] *n* 1. (*to sleep on*) cama *f*; **to go to ~** irse a la cama; **to make the ~** hacer la cama; **to go to ~ with** *euphemism* acostarse con. 2. (*flowerbed*) macizo *m*. 3. (*of sea*) fondo *m*; (*of river*) lecho *m*.

bed and breakfast *n* (*service*) cama *f* y desayuno; (*hotel*) pensión *f*.

bedclothes [ˈbedkləʊðz] *npl* ropa *f* de cama.

bedlam [ˈbedləm] *n* jaleo *m*, alboroto *m*.

bed linen *n* ropa *f* de cama.

bedraggled [bɪˈdrægld] *adj* mojado y sucio (mojada y sucia).

bedridden [ˈbed,rɪdn] *adj* postrado (da) en cama.

bedroom [ˈbedrʊm] *n* dormitorio *m*, recámara *f* *Amer*.

bedside [ˈbedsaɪd] *n* (*side of bed*) lado *m* de la cama; (*of ill person*) lecho *m*; **~ table** mesita *f* de noche.

bed-sit(ter) *n* Br *habitación alquilada con cama*.

bedsore [ˈbedsɔːʳ] *n* úlcera *f* por decúbito.

bedspread [ˈbedspred] *n* colcha *f*.

bedtime [ˈbedtaɪm] *n* hora *f* de dormir.

bee [biː] *n* abeja *f*.

beech [biːtʃ] *n* haya *f*.

beef [biːf] *n* carne *f* de vaca. ▶ **beef up** *vt sep inf* reforzar.

beefburger [ˈbiːf,bɜːgəʳ] *n* hamburguesa *f*.

Beefeater [ˈbiːf,iːtəʳ] *n* guardián de la Torre de Londres.

beefsteak [ˈbiːf,steɪk] *n* bistec *m*.

beehive [ˈbiːhaɪv] *n* (*for bees*) colmena *f*.

beeline [ˈbiːlaɪn] *n*: **to make a ~ for** *inf* irse derechito(ta) hacia.

been [biːn] *pp* → **be**.

beer [bɪəʳ] *n* cerveza *f*.

beet [biːt] *n* remolacha *f*.

beetle [ˈbiːtl] *n* escarabajo *m*.

beetroot [ˈbiːtruːt] *n* remolacha *f*.

before [bɪˈfɔːʳ] ♦ *adv* antes; **we went the year ~** fuimos el año anterior. ♦ *prep* 1. (*in time*) antes de; **they arrived ~ us** llegaron antes que nosotros. 2. (*in space - facing*) ante, frente a. ♦ *conj* antes de; **~ it's too late** antes de que sea

demasiado tarde.

beforehand [bɪˈfɔːhænd] *adv* con antelación, de antemano.

befriend [bɪˈfrend] *vt* hacer OR entablar amistad con.

beg [beg] ♦ *vt* 1. (*money, food*) mendigar, pedir. 2. (*favour, forgiveness*) suplicar; **to ~ sb to do sthg** rogar a alguien que haga algo; **to ~ sb for sthg** rogar algo a alguien. ♦ *vi* 1. (*for money, food*): **to ~ (for sthg)** pedir OR mendigar (algo). 2. (*for favour, forgiveness*): **to ~ (for sthg)** suplicar OR rogar (algo).

began [bɪˈgæn] *pt* → **begin**.

beggar [ˈbegəʳ] *n* mendigo *m*, -ga *f*.

begin [bɪˈgɪn] (*pt* **began**, *pp* **begun**, *cont* **-ning**) ♦ *vt*: **to ~ (doing** OR **to do sthg)** empezar OR comenzar (a hacer algo). ♦ *vi* empezar, comenzar; **to ~ with** para empezar, de entrada.

beginner [bɪˈgɪnəʳ] *n* principiante *m* y *f*.

beginning [bɪˈgɪnɪŋ] *n* comienzo *m*, principio *m*; **at the ~ of the month** a principios de mes.

begrudge [bɪˈgrʌdʒ] *vt* 1. (*envy*): **to ~ sb sthg** envidiar a alguien algo. 2. (*give, do unwillingly*): **to ~ doing sthg** hacer algo de mala gana OR a regañadientes.

begun [bɪˈgʌn] *pp* → **begin**.

behalf [bɪˈhɑːf] *n*: **on ~ of** Br, **in ~ of** Am en nombre OR en representación de.

behave [bɪˈheɪv] ♦ *vt*: **to ~ o.s.** portarse bien. ♦ *vi* 1. (*in a particular way*) comportarse, portarse. 2. (*in an acceptable way*) comportarse OR portarse bien.

behaviour Br, **behavior** Am [bɪˈheɪvjəʳ] *n* comportamiento *m*, conducta *f*.

behead [bɪˈhed] *vt* decapitar.

beheld [bɪˈheld] *pt & pp* → **behold**.

behind [bɪˈhaɪnd] ♦ *prep* 1. (*in space*) detrás de. 2. (*causing, responsible for*) detrás de. 3. (*in support of*): **we're ~ you** nosotros te apoyamos. 4. (*in time*): **to be ~ schedule** ir retrasado(da). 5. (*less successful than*) por detrás de. ♦ *adv* 1. (*in space*) detrás. 2. (*in time*): **to be ~ (with)** ir atrasado(da) (con). 3. (*less successful*) por detrás. ♦ *n inf* trasero *m*.

behold [bɪˈhəʊld] (*pt & pp* **beheld**) *vt literary* contemplar.

beige [beɪʒ] *adj* beige.

being [ˈbiːɪŋ] *n* 1. (*creature*) ser *m*. 2. (*state of existing*): **in ~** en vigor; **to come into ~** ver la luz, nacer.

belated [bɪˈleɪtɪd] *adj* tardío(a).

belch [beltʃ] ♦ *vt* arrojar. ♦ *vi* 1. (*per-*

son) eructar. **2.** (*smoke, fire*) brotar.

beleaguered [brˈliːgəd] *adj* **1.** (MIL) asediado(da). **2.** *fig* (*harassed*) atosigado (da).

Belgian [ˈbeldʒən] ◆ *adj* belga. ◆ *n* belga *m y f*.

Belgium [ˈbeldʒəm] *n* Bélgica.

Belgrade [ˌbelˈgreɪd] *n* Belgrado.

belie [brˈlaɪ] (*cont* **belying**) *vt* **1.** (*disprove*) desmentir. **2.** (*give false idea of*) encubrir.

belief [brˈliːf] *n* **1.** (*faith, principle*): **~ (in)** creencia *f* (en). **2.** (*opinion*) opinión *f*.

believe [brˈliːv] ◆ *vt* creer; **~ it or not** lo creas o no. ◆ *vi* (*know to exist, be good*): **to ~ in** creer en.

believer [brˈliːvər] *n* **1.** (*religious person*) creyente *m y f*. **2.** (*in idea, action*): **~ in** *sthg* partidario *m*, -ria *f* de algo.

belittle [brˈlɪtl] *vt* menospreciar.

bell [bel] *n* (*of church*) campana *f*; (*hand-bell, on door, bike*) timbre *m*.

belligerent [brˈlɪdʒərənt] *adj* **1.** (*at war*) beligerante. **2.** (*aggressive*) belicoso(sa).

bellow [ˈbeləʊ] *vi* **1.** (*person*) rugir. **2.** (*bull*) mugir, bramar.

bellows [ˈbeləʊz] *npl* fuelle *m*.

belly [ˈbelɪ] *n* **1.** (*of person*) barriga *f*. **2.** (*of animal*) vientre *m*.

bellyache [ˈbelɪeɪk] *inf* ◆ *n* dolor *m* de barriga. ◆ *vi* gruñir.

belly button *n inf* ombligo *m*.

belong [brˈlɒŋ] *vi* **1.** (*be property*): **to ~ to** pertenecer a. **2.** (*be member*): **to ~ to** ser miembro de. **3.** (*be situated in right place*): **where does this book ~?** ¿dónde va este libro?; **he felt he didn't ~ there** sintió que no encajaba allí.

belongings [brˈlɒŋɪŋz] *npl* pertenencias *fpl*.

beloved [brˈlʌvd] ◆ *adj* querido(da). ◆ *n* amado *m*, -da *f*.

below [brˈləʊ] ◆ *adv* **1.** (*gen*) abajo; **the flat ~** el piso de abajo. **2.** (*in text*) más abajo; **see ~** véase más abajo. ◆ *prep* **1.** (*lower than in position*) (por) debajo de, bajo. **2.** (*lower than in rank, number*) por debajo de.

belt [belt] ◆ *n* **1.** (*for clothing*) cinturón *m*. **2.** (TECH) (*wide*) cinta *f*; (*narrow*) correa *f*. **3.** (*of land, sea*) franja *f*. ◆ *vt inf* arrear. ◆ *vi Br inf* ir a toda mecha.

beltway [ˈbelt.weɪ] *n Am* carretera *f* de circunvalación.

bemused [brˈmjuːzd] *adj* atónito(ta).

bench [bentʃ] *n* **1.** (*seat*) banco *m*. **2.** (*in lab, workshop*) mesa *f* de trabajo. **3.** Br (POL) escaño *m*.

bend [bend] (*pt & pp* **bent**) ◆ *n* curva *f*;

round the ~ *inf* majareta. ◆ *vt* doblar. ◆ *vi* (*person*) agacharse; (*tree*) doblarse; **to ~ over backwards for** hacer todo lo humanamente posible por.

beneath [brˈniːθ] ◆ *adv* debajo. ◆ *prep* **1.** (*under*) bajo. **2.** (*unworthy of*) indigno (na) de.

benefactor [ˈbenɪfæktər] *n* benefactor *m*.

beneficial [ˌbenɪˈfɪʃl] *adj*: **~ (to)** beneficioso(sa) (para).

beneficiary [ˌbenɪˈfɪʃərɪ] *n* **1.** (JUR) (*of will*) beneficiario *m*, -ria *f*. **2.** (*of change in law, new rule*) beneficiado *m*, -da *f*.

benefit [ˈbenɪfɪt] ◆ *n* **1.** (*advantage*) ventaja *f*; **for the ~ of** en atención a; **to be to sb's ~, to be of ~ to sb** ir en beneficio de alguien. **2.** (ADMIN) (*allowance of money*) subsidio *m*. ◆ *vt* beneficiar. ◆ *vi*: **to ~ from** beneficiarse de.

Benelux [ˈbenɪlʌks] *n* (el) Benelux; **the ~ countries** los países del Benelux.

benevolent [brˈnevələnt] *adj* benevolente.

benign [brˈnaɪn] *adj* **1.** (*person*) bondadoso(sa). **2.** (MED) benigno(na).

bent [bent] ◆ *pt & pp* → **bend**. ◆ *adj* **1.** (*wire, bar*) torcido(da). **2.** (*person, body*) encorvado(da). **3.** Br inf (*dishonest*) corrupto(ta). **4.** (*determined*): **to be ~ on** *sthg/on doing sthg* estar empeñado(da) en algo/en hacer algo. ◆ *n* (*natural tendency*) inclinación *f*; **~ for** don *m* OR talento *m* para.

bequeath [brˈkwiːð] *vt lit & fig*: **to ~ sb** *sthg*, **to ~ sthg to sb** legar algo a alguien.

bequest [brˈkwest] *n* legado *m*.

berate [brˈreɪt] *vt* regañar.

bereaved [brˈriːvd] (*pl inv*) *n*: **the ~** la persona más allegada al difunto.

beret [ˈbereɪ] *n* boina *f*.

berk [bɜːk] *n Br inf* gilipollas *m y f inv*.

Berlin [bɜːˈlɪn] *n* Berlín.

berm [bɜːm] *n Am* arcén *m*.

Bermuda [bəˈmjuːdə] *n* las Bermudas.

Bern [bɜːn] *n* Berna.

berry [ˈberɪ] *n* baya *f*.

berserk [bəˈzɜːk] *adj*: **to go ~** ponerse hecho(cha) una fiera.

berth [bɜːθ] ◆ *n* **1.** (*in harbour*) amarradero *m*, atracadero *m*. **2.** (*in ship, train*) litera *f*. ◆ *vt & vi* atracar.

beseech [brˈsiːtʃ] (*pt & pp* **besought** OR **beseeched**) *vt literary*: **to ~ (sb to do sthg)** suplicar (a alguien que haga algo).

beset [brˈset] (*pt & pp* **beset**) ◆ *adj*: **~ with** OR **by** (*subj: person*) acosado(da) por; (subj: plan) plagado(da) de. ◆ vt acosar.

beside [bɪ'saɪd] prep **1.** (next to) al lado de, junto a. **2.** (compared with) comparado(da) con. **3.** phr: that's ~ the point eso no viene al caso; to be ~ o.s. with rage estar fuera de sí; to be ~ o.s. with joy estar loco(ca) de alegría.

besides [bɪ'saɪdz] ◆ adv además. ◆ prep aparte de.

besiege [bɪ'siːdʒ] vt lit & fig asediar.

besotted [bɪ'sɒtɪd] adj: ~ with borracho(cha) de.

besought [bɪ'sɔːt] pt & pp → beseech.

best [best] ◆ adj mejor. ◆ adv mejor; which did you like ~? ¿cuál te gustó más? ◆ n: to do one's ~ hacerlo lo mejor que uno puede; to make the ~ of sthg sacarle el mayor partido posible a algo; for the ~ para bien; all the ~ (ending letter) un abrazo; (saying goodbye) que te vaya bien. ▶ at best adv en el mejor de los casos.

best man n = padrino m de boda.

bestow [bɪ'stəʊ] vt fml: to ~ sthg on sb (gift) otorgar OR conceder algo a alguien; (praise) dirigir algo a alguien; (title) conferir algo a alguien.

best-seller n (book) best seller m, éxito m editorial.

bet [bet] (pt & pp bet OR -ted) ◆ n **1.** (gen): ~ (on) apuesta f (a). **2.** fig (prediction) predicción f. ◆ vt apostar. ◆ vi **1.** (gamble): to ~ (on) apostar (a). **2.** (predict): to ~ on sthg contar con (que pase) algo.

betray [bɪ'treɪ] vt **1.** (person, trust, principles) traicionar. **2.** (secret) revelar. **3.** (feeling) delatar.

betrayal [bɪ'treɪəl] n **1.** (of person, trust, principles) traición f. **2.** (of secret) revelación f.

better ['betər] ◆ adj (compar of good) mejor; to get ~ mejorar. ◆ adv (compar of well) **1.** (in quality) mejor. **2.** (more): I like it ~ me gusta más. **3.** (preferably): we had ~ be going más vale que nos vayamos ya. ◆ n (best one) mejor m y f; to get the ~ of sb poder con alguien. ◆ vt mejorar; to ~ o.s. mejorarse.

better off adj **1.** (financially) mejor de dinero. **2.** (in better situation): you'd be ~ going by bus sería mejor si vas en autobús.

betting ['betɪŋ] n (U) apuestas fpl.

betting shop n Br casa f de apuestas.

between [bɪ'twiːn] ◆ prep entre; closed ~ 1 and 2 cerrado de 1 a 2. ◆ adv: (in) ~ en medio, entremedio.

beverage ['bevərɪdʒ] n fml bebida f.

beware [bɪ'weər] vi: to ~ (of) tener cuidado (con).

bewildered [bɪ'wɪldəd] adj desconcertado(da).

bewitching [bɪ'wɪtʃɪŋ] adj hechizante.

beyond [bɪ'jɒnd] ◆ prep más allá de; ~ midnight pasada la medianoche; ~ my reach/responsibility fuera de mi alcance/competencia. ◆ adv más allá.

bias ['baɪəs] n **1.** (prejudice) prejuicio m. **2.** (tendency) tendencia f, inclinación f.

biased ['baɪəst] adj parcial; to be ~ towards/against tener prejuicios en favor/en contra de.

bib [bɪb] n (for baby) babero m.

Bible ['baɪbl] n: the ~ la Biblia.

bicarbonate of soda [baɪ'kɑːbənət-] n bicarbonato m.

biceps ['baɪseps] (pl inv) n bíceps m inv.

bicker ['bɪkər] vi reñir.

bicycle ['baɪsɪkl] n bicicleta f.

bicycle path n camino m para bicicletas.

bicycle pump n bomba f.

bid [bɪd] (pt & pp bid) ◆ n **1.** (attempt): ~ (for) intento m (de hacerse con). **2.** (at auction) puja f. **3.** (financial offer): ~ (for sthg) oferta f (para adquirir algo). ◆ vt (money) pujar. ◆ vi (at auction): to ~ (for) pujar (por).

bidder ['bɪdər] n postor m, -ra f.

bidding ['bɪdɪŋ] n (U) (at auction) puja f.

bide [baɪd] vt: to ~ one's time esperar el momento oportuno.

bifocals [ˌbaɪ'fəʊklz] npl gafas fpl bifocales.

big [bɪg] adj **1.** (large, important) grande; a ~ problem un gran problema; ~ problems grandes problemas. **2.** (older) mayor. **3.** (successful) popular.

bigamy ['bɪgəmɪ] n bigamia f.

big deal inf ◆ n: it's no ~ no tiene (la menor) importancia. ◆ excl ¡y a mí qué!

Big Dipper [-'dɪpər] n Br (rollercoaster) montaña f rusa.

bigheaded [ˌbɪg'hedɪd] adj inf pej creído(da).

bigot ['bɪgət] n fanático m, -ca f.

bigoted ['bɪgətɪd] adj fanático(ca).

bigotry ['bɪgətrɪ] n fanatismo m.

big time n inf: the ~ el éxito, la fama.

big toe n dedo m gordo (del pie).

big top n carpa f.

big wheel n Br (at fairground) noria f.

bike [baɪk] n inf (bicycle) bici f; (motorcycle) moto f.

bikeway [ˈbaɪkweɪ] n Am (lane) carril-bici m.

bikini [bɪˈkiːnɪ] n biquini m, bikini m.

bile [baɪl] n (fluid) bilis f.

bilingual [baɪˈlɪŋgwəl] adj bilingüe.

bill [bɪl] ◆ n 1. (statement of cost): ~ (for) (meal) cuenta f (de); (electricity, phone) factura f (de). 2. (in parliament) proyecto m de ley. 3. (of show, concert) programa m. 4. Am (banknote) billete m. 5. (poster): 'post OR stick no ~s' 'prohibido fijar carteles'. 6. (beak) pico m. ◆ vt (send a bill): to ~ sb for mandar la factura a alguien por.

billboard [ˈbɪlbɔːd] n cartelera f.

billet [ˈbɪlɪt] n acantonamiento m.

billfold [ˈbɪlfəʊld] n Am billetera f.

billiards [ˈbɪljədz] n billar m.

billion [ˈbɪljən] num 1. Am (thousand million) millar m de millones. 2. Br (million million) billón m.

Bill of Rights n: the ~ las diez primeras enmiendas de la Constitución estadounidense.

bimbo [ˈbɪmbəʊ] (pl -s OR -es) n inf pej niña f mona, mujer joven, guapa y poco inteligente.

bin [bɪn] n 1. Br (for rubbish) cubo m de la basura; (for paper) papelera f. 2. (for grain, coal) depósito m.

bind [baɪnd] (pt & pp bound) vt 1. (tie up) atar. 2. (unite - people) unir. 3. (bandage) vendar. 4. (book) encuadernar. 5. (constrain) obligar.

binder [ˈbaɪndəʳ] n (cover) carpeta f.

binding [ˈbaɪndɪŋ] ◆ adj obligatorio (ria). ◆ n (on book) encuadernación f.

binge [bɪndʒ] inf n: to go on a ~ irse de juerga.

bingo [ˈbɪŋgəʊ] n bingo m.

binoculars [bɪˈnɒkjʊləz] npl gemelos mpl, prismáticos mpl.

biochemistry [ˌbaɪəʊˈkemɪstrɪ] n bioquímica f.

biodegradable [ˌbaɪəʊdɪˈgreɪdəbl] adj biodegradable.

biography [baɪˈɒgrəfɪ] n biografía f.

biological [ˌbaɪəˈlɒdʒɪkl] adj biológico (ca).

biology [baɪˈɒlədʒɪ] n biología f.

birch [bɜːtʃ] n (tree) abedul m.

bird [bɜːd] n 1. (animal - large) ave f; (- small) pájaro m. 2. inf (woman) tía f.

birdie [ˈbɜːdɪ] n (in golf) birdie m.

bird's-eye view n vista f panorámica.

bird-watcher [-ˌwɒtʃəʳ] n observador m, -ra f de pájaros.

Biro® [ˈbaɪərəʊ] n bolígrafo m, lapicera f Amer.

birth [bɜːθ] n (gen) nacimiento m; (delivery) parto m; **to give ~ (to)** dar a luz (a).

birth certificate n partida f de nacimiento.

birth control n control m de natalidad.

birthday [ˈbɜːθdeɪ] n cumpleaños m inv.

birthmark [ˈbɜːθmɑːk] n antojo m.

birthrate [ˈbɜːθreɪt] n índice m de natalidad.

Biscay [ˈbɪskɪ] n: **the Bay of ~** el golfo de Vizcaya.

biscuit [ˈbɪskɪt] n (in UK) galleta f; (in US) tipo de bollo.

bisect [baɪˈsekt] vt dividir en dos.

bishop [ˈbɪʃəp] n 1. (in church) obispo m. 2. (in chess) alfil m.

bison [ˈbaɪsn] (pl inv OR -s) n bisonte m.

bit [bɪt] ◆ pt → **bite**. ◆ n 1. (piece) trozo m; **a ~ of** un poco de; **a ~ of news** una noticia; **~s and pieces** Br (objects) cosillas fpl; (possessions) bártulos mpl; **to take sthg to ~s** desmontar algo. 2. (amount): **a ~ of** un poco de; **quite a ~ of** bastante. 3. (short time): (for) **a ~** un rato. 4. (of drill) broca f. 5. (of bridle) bocado m, freno m. 6. (COMPUT) bit m. ▶ **a bit** adv un poco. ▶ **bit by bit** adv poco a poco.

bitch [bɪtʃ] ◆ n 1. (female dog) perra f. 2. v inf pej (unpleasant woman) bruja f. ◆ vi inf (talk unpleasantly): **to ~ about** poner a parir a.

bitchy [ˈbɪtʃɪ] adj inf: **to be ~** tener mala uva.

bite [baɪt] (pt bit, pp bitten) ◆ n 1. (by dog, person) mordisco m; (by insect, snake) picotazo m. 2. inf (food): **a ~ (to eat)** un bocado. 3. (wound - from dog) mordedura f; (- from insect, snake) picadura f. ◆ vt 1. (subj: person, animal) morder. 2. (subj: insect, snake) picar. ◆ vi 1. (animal, person): **to ~ (into sthg)** morder (algo); **to ~ off sthg** arrancar algo de un mordisco. 2. (insect, snake) picar. 3. (grip) agarrar.

biting [ˈbaɪtɪŋ] adj 1. (very cold) gélido (da), cortante. 2. (caustic) mordaz.

bitten [ˈbɪtn] pp → **bite**.

bitter [ˈbɪtəʳ] ◆ adj 1. (coffee, chocolate) amargo(ga); (lemon) agrio(gria). 2. (icy) gélido(da). 3. (causing pain) amargo(ga). 4. (acrimonious) enconado(da). 5. (resentful) amargado(da). ◆ n Br (beer) tipo de cerveza amarga.

bitter lemon n bíter m de limón.

bitterness [ˈbɪtənɪs] n 1. (of taste) amargor m. 2. (of wind, weather) gelidez f.

3. (*resentment*) resentimiento *m*.

bizarre [bɪˈzɑː^r] *adj* (*behaviour, appearance*) extravagante; (*machine, remark*) singular, extraordinario(ria).

blab [blæb] *vi inf* irse de la lengua.

black [blæk] ◆ *adj* **1.** (*gen*) negro(gra); **~ and blue** amoratado(da); **~ and white** (*films, photos*) en blanco y negro; (*clear-cut*) extremadamente nítido(da). **2.** (*without milk*) solo. **3.** (*angry*) furioso (sa). ◆ *n* **1.** (*colour*) negro *m*. **2.** (*person*) negro *m*, -gra *f*. **3.** *phr*: **in ~ and white** (*in writing*) por escrito; **to be in the ~** tener saldo positivo. ◆ *vt* Br (*boycott*) boicotear. ▶ **black out** *vi* desmayarse.

blackberry [ˈblækbərɪ] *n* mora *f*, zarzamora *f*.

blackbird [ˈblækbɜːd] *n* mirlo *m*.

blackboard [ˈblækbɔːd] *n* pizarra *f*.

blackcurrant [ˌblækˈkʌrənt] *n* grosella *f* negra, casis *m*.

blacken [ˈblækn] *vt* **1.** (*make dark*) ennegrecer. **2.** (*tarnish*) manchar.

black eye *n* ojo *m* morado.

blackhead [ˈblækhed] *n* barrillo *m*.

black ice *n* hielo transparente en el suelo.

blackleg [ˈblækleg] *n pej* esquirol *m*.

blacklist [ˈblæklɪst] *n* lista *f* negra.

blackmail [ˈblækmeɪl] ◆ *n lit & fig* chantaje *m*. ◆ *vt lit & fig* chantajear.

black market *n* mercado *m* negro.

blackout [ˈblækaʊt] *n* **1.** (*in wartime, power cut*) apagón *m*. **2.** (*of news*) censura *f*. **3.** (*fainting fit*) desmayo *m*.

black pudding *n* Br morcilla *f*.

Black Sea *n*: **the ~** el mar Negro.

black sheep *n* oveja *f* negra.

blacksmith [ˈblæksmɪθ] *n* herrero *m*.

black spot *n* punto *m* negro.

bladder [ˈblædə^r] *n* (ANAT) vejiga *f*.

blade [bleɪd] *n* **1.** (*of knife, saw*) hoja *f*. **2.** (*of propeller*) aleta *f*, paleta *f*. **3.** (*of grass*) brizna *f*, hoja *f*.

blame [bleɪm] ◆ *n* culpa *f*; **to take the ~ for** hacerse responsable de; **to be to ~ for** ser el culpable de. ◆ *vt* echar la culpa a, culpar; **to ~ sthg on sthg/sb, to ~ sthg/sb for sthg** culpar algo/a alguien de algo.

bland [blænd] *adj* soso(sa).

blank [blæŋk] ◆ *adj* **1.** (*wall*) liso(sa); (*sheet of paper*) en blanco. **2.** (*cassette*) virgen. **3.** *fig* (*look*) vacío(a). ◆ *n* **1.** (*empty space*) espacio *m* en blanco. **2.** (MIL) (*cartridge*) cartucho *m* de fogueo.

blank cheque *n* cheque *m* en blanco; *fig* carta *f* blanca.

blanket [ˈblæŋkɪt] *n* **1.** (*bed cover*) manta *f*, frazada *f* Amer. **2.** (*layer*) manto *m*.

blare [bleə^r] *vi* resonar, sonar.

blasé [Br ˈblɑːzeɪ, Am ˌblɑːˈzeɪ] *adj*: **to be ~ about** estar de vuelta de.

blasphemy [ˈblæsfəmɪ] *n* blasfemia *f*.

blast [blɑːst] ◆ *n* **1.** (*of bomb*) explosión *f*. **2.** (*of wind*) ráfaga *f*. ◆ *vt* (*hole, tunnel*) perforar (*con explosivos*). ◆ *excl* Br *inf* ¡maldita sea! ▶ **(at) full blast** *adv* a todo trapo.

blasted [ˈblɑːstɪd] *adj inf* maldito(ta).

blast-off *n* despegue *m*.

blatant [ˈbleɪtənt] *adj* descarado(da).

blaze [bleɪz] ◆ *n* **1.** (*fire*) incendio *m*. **2.** *fig* (*of colour*) explosión *f*; (*of light*) resplandor *m*; **a ~ of publicity** una ola de publicidad. ◆ *vi lit & fig* arder.

blazer [ˈbleɪzə^r] *n* chaqueta *f* de sport generalmente con la insignia de un equipo, colegio etc.

bleach [bliːtʃ] ◆ *n* lejía *f*. ◆ *vt* (*hair*) blanquear; (*clothes*) desteñir.

bleached [bliːtʃt] *adj* (*hair*) teñido(da) de rubio; (*jeans*) desteñido(da).

bleachers [ˈbliːtʃəz] *npl* Am (SPORT) graderío *m* descubierto.

bleak [bliːk] *adj* **1.** (*future*) negro(gra). **2.** (*place, person, face*) sombrío(a). **3.** (*weather*) desapacible.

bleary-eyed [ˌblɪərɪˈaɪd] *adj* con los ojos nublados.

bleat [bliːt] *vi* **1.** (*sheep*) balar. **2.** *fig* (*person*) gimotear.

bleed [bliːd] (*pt & pp* bled) ◆ *vt* (*radiator etc*) vaciar. ◆ *vi* sangrar.

bleeper [ˈbliːpə^r] *n* busca *m*.

blemish [ˈblemɪʃ] *n* (*mark*) señal *f*, marca *f*; *fig* mancha *f*.

blend [blend] ◆ *n lit & fig* mezcla *f*. ◆ *vt*: **to ~ (sthg with sthg)** mezclar (algo con algo). ◆ *vi*: **to ~ (with)** combinarse (con).

blender [ˈblendə^r] *n* licuadora *f*.

bless [bles] (*pt & pp* -ed OR blest) *vt* **1.** (RELIG) bendecir. **2.** *phr*: **~ you!** (*after sneezing*) ¡jesús!; (*thank you*) ¡gracias!

blessing [ˈblesɪŋ] *n* **1.** (RELIG) bendición *f*. **2.** *fig* (*good wishes*) aprobación *f*.

blest [blest] *pt & pp* → **bless**.

blew [bluː] *pt* → **blow**.

blight [blaɪt] *vt* malograr, arruinar.

blimey [ˈblaɪmɪ] *excl* Br *inf* ¡ostias!

blind [blaɪnd] ◆ *adj* **1.** (*unsighted, irrational*) ciego(ga). **2.** *fig* (*unaware*): **to be ~ to sthg** no ver algo. ◆ *n* (*for window*) persiana *f*. ◆ *npl*: **the ~** los ciegos. ◆ *vt* (*permanently*) dejar ciego(ga); (*temporarily*) cegar; **to ~ sb to sthg** *fig* no dejar a alguien ver algo.

blind alley *n lit & fig* callejón *m* sin salida.

blind corner *n* curva *f* sin visibilidad.

blind date *n* cita *f* a ciegas.

blinders ['blaɪndəz] *npl* Am anteojeras *fpl*.

blindfold ['blaɪndfəʊld] ♦ *adv* con los ojos vendados. ♦ *n* venda *f*. ♦ *vt* vendar los ojos a.

blindly ['blaɪndlɪ] *adv* 1. (*unable to see*) a ciegas. 2. *fig* (*guess*) a boleo; (*accept*) ciegamente.

blindness ['blaɪndnɪs] *n lit & fig:* ~ **(to)** ceguera *f* (ante).

blind spot *n* 1. (*when driving*) ángulo *m* muerto. 2. *fig* (*inability to understand*) punto *m* débil.

blink [blɪŋk] ♦ *vt* 1. (*eyes*): **to ~ one's eyes** parpadear. 2. Am (AUT): **to ~ one's lights** dar las luces (intermitentemente). ♦ *vi* parpadear.

blinkers ['blɪŋkəz] *npl* Br anteojeras *fpl*.

bliss [blɪs] *n* gloria *f*, dicha *f*.

blissful ['blɪsfʊl] *adj* dichoso(sa), feliz.

blister ['blɪstər] ♦ *n* ampolla *f*. ♦ *vi* ampollarse.

blithely ['blaɪðlɪ] *adv* alegremente.

blitz [blɪts] *n* (MIL) bombardeo *m* aéreo.

blizzard ['blɪzəd] *n* ventisca *f* (de nieve).

bloated ['bləʊtɪd] *adj* hinchado(da).

blob [blɒb] *n* 1. (*drop*) gota *f*. 2. (*indistinct shape*) bulto *m* borroso.

bloc [blɒk] *n* bloque *m*.

block [blɒk] ♦ *n* 1. (*gen*) bloque *m*. 2. Am (*of buildings*) manzana *f*, cuadra *f* Amer. 3. (*obstruction - physical or mental*) bloqueo *m*. ♦ *vt* 1. (*road*) cortar; (*pipe*) obstruir. 2. (*view*) tapar. 3. (*prevent*) bloquear, obstaculizar.

blockade [blɒ'keɪd] ♦ *n* bloqueo *m*. ♦ *vt* bloquear.

blockage ['blɒkɪdʒ] *n* obstrucción *f*.

blockbuster ['blɒkbʌstər] *n inf* (*book*) (gran) éxito *m* editorial; (*film*) (gran) éxito de taquilla.

block capitals *npl* mayúsculas *fpl* (*de imprenta*).

block letters *npl* mayúsculas *fpl* (*de imprenta*).

bloke [bləʊk] *n* Br *inf* tío *m*, tipo *m*.

blond [blɒnd] *adj* rubio(bia).

blonde [blɒnd] ♦ *adj* rubia. ♦ *n* (*woman*) rubia *f*.

blood [blʌd] *n* sangre *f*; **in cold ~** a sangre fría.

bloodbath ['blʌdbɑːθ, *pl* -bɑːðz] *n* matanza *f*, carnicería *f*.

blood cell *n* glóbulo *m*.

blood donor *n* donante *m y f* de sangre.

blood group *n* grupo *m* sanguíneo.

bloodhound ['blʌdhaʊnd] *n* sabueso *m*.

blood poisoning *n* septicemia *f*.

blood pressure *n* tensión *f* arterial; **to have high/low ~** tener la tensión alta/baja.

bloodshed ['blʌdʃed] *n* derramamiento *m* de sangre.

bloodshot ['blʌdʃɒt] *adj* inyectado (da) (de sangre).

bloodstream ['blʌdstriːm] *n* flujo *m* sanguíneo, sangre *f*.

blood test *n* análisis *m inv* de sangre.

bloodthirsty ['blʌd.θɜːstɪ] *adj* sediento(ta) de sangre.

blood transfusion *n* transfusión *f* de sangre.

bloody ['blʌdɪ] ♦ *adj* 1. (*war, conflict*) sangriento(ta). 2. (*face, hands*) ensangrentado(da). 3. Br *v inf* maldito(ta), pinche Amer. ♦ *adv* Br *v inf*: **he's ~ useless** es un puto inútil; **it's ~ brilliant** es de puta madre.

bloody-minded [-'maɪndɪd] *adj* Br *inf* puñetero(ra), que lleva la contraria.

bloom [bluːm] ♦ *n* flor *f*. ♦ *vi* florecer.

blooming ['bluːmɪŋ] ♦ *adj* Br *inf* (*to show annoyance*) condenado(da). ♦ *adv* Br *inf* condenadamente.

blossom ['blɒsəm] ♦ *n* flor *f*; **in ~** en flor. ♦ *vi lit & fig* florecer.

blot [blɒt] ♦ *n* (*of ink*) borrón *m*; *fig* mancha *f*. ♦ *vt* 1. (*paper*) emborronar. 2. (*ink*) secar. ► **blot out** *vt sep* (*gen*) cubrir, ocultar; (*memories*) borrar.

blotchy ['blɒtʃɪ] *adj* lleno(na) de marcas.

blotting paper ['blɒtɪŋ-] *n* (U) papel *m* secante.

blouse [blaʊz] *n* blusa *f*.

blow [bləʊ] (*pt* **blew**, *pp* **blown**) ♦ *vi* 1. (*gen*) soplar. 2. (*in wind*) salir volando, volar. 3. (*fuse*) fundirse. ♦ *vt* 1. (*subj: wind*) hacer volar. 2. (*whistle, horn*) tocar, hacer sonar. 3. (*bubbles*) hacer. 4. (*kiss*) mandar. 5. (*fuse*) fundir. 6. (*clear*): **to ~ one's nose** sonarse la nariz. 7. *inf* (*money*) ventilarse. ♦ *n* (*hit, shock*) golpe *m*. ► **blow out** ♦ *vt sep* apagar. ♦ *vi* 1. (*candle*) apagarse. 2. (*tyre*) reventar. ► **blow over** *vi* 1. (*storm*) amainar.

2. (*argument*) disiparse. ▶ **blow up**
◆ *vt sep* **1.** (*inflate*) inflar. **2.** (*destroy*)
volar. **3.** (*photograph*) ampliar. ◆ *vi* saltar
por los aires, estallar.

blow-dry *n* secado *m* (con secador).

blowlamp *Br* ['bləʊlæmp], **blowtorch** ['bləʊtɔːtʃ] *n* soplete *m*.

blown [bləʊn] *pp* → **blow**.

blowout ['bləʊaʊt] *n* (*of tyre*) pinchazo
m, reventón *m*.

blowtorch = **blowlamp**.

blubber ['blʌbəʳ] *vi pej* lloriquear.

bludgeon ['blʌdʒən] *vt* apalear.

blue [bluː] ◆ *adj* **1.** (*colour*) azul. **2.** *inf*
(*sad*) triste. **3.** (*pornographic - film*) equis
(*inv*), porno; (*- joke*) verde. ◆ *n* azul *m*;
out of the ~ en el momento menos pensado. ▶ **blues** *npl* **1.** (MUS) blues *m inv.*
2. *inf* (*sad feeling*) depre *f*.

bluebell ['bluːbel] *n* campanilla *f*.

blueberry ['bluːbərɪ] *n* arándano *m*.

bluebottle ['bluːˌbɒtl] *n* moscardón *m*,
moscón *m*.

blue cheese *n* queso *m* azul.

blue-collar *adj*: **~ worker** obrero *m*, -ra
f.

blue jeans *npl Am* vaqueros *mpl*,
tejanos *mpl*.

blueprint ['bluːprɪnt] *n* **1.** (CONSTR)
cianotipo *m*. **2.** *fig* (*description*) proyecto
m.

bluff [blʌf] ◆ *adj* brusco(ca). ◆ *n* (*deception*) fanfarronada *f*; **to call sb's ~** desafiar a alguien a que haga lo que dice.
◆ *vi* fanfarronear.

blunder ['blʌndəʳ] ◆ *n* metedura *f* de
pata. ◆ *vi* **1.** (*make mistake*) meter la
pata. **2.** (*move clumsily*) ir tropezando.

blunt [blʌnt] *adj* **1.** (*knife*) desafilado
(da). **2.** (*object*) romo(ma). **3.** (*forthright*)
directo(ta), franco(ca).

blur [blɜːʳ] ◆ *n* imagen *f* borrosa. ◆ *vt*
1. (*vision*) nublar. **2.** (*distinction*) des-
dibujar.

blurb [blɜːb] *n inf* texto publicitario en la
cubierta o solapa de un libro.

blurt [blɜːt] ▶ **blurt out** *vt sep* espetar,
decir de repente.

blush [blʌʃ] ◆ *n* rubor *m*. ◆ *vi*
ruborizarse.

blusher ['blʌʃəʳ] *n* colorete *m*.

blustery ['blʌstərɪ] *adj* borrascoso(sa).

BMX (*abbr of* **bicycle motorcross**) *n*
mountain-bike.

BO *n* (*abbr of* **body odour**) OC *m*.

boar [bɔːʳ] *n* **1.** (*male pig*) verraco *m*.
2. (*wild pig*) jabalí *m*.

board [bɔːd] ◆ *n* **1.** (*plank*) tabla *f*.

2. (*for notices*) tablón *m*. **3.** (*for games*)
tablero *m*. **4.** (*blackboard*) pizarra *f*.
5. (COMPUT) placa *f*. **6.** (*of company*): **~ (of
directors)** (junta *f*) directiva *f*. **7.** (*committee*) comité *m*, junta *f*. **8.** *Br* (*at hotel,
guesthouse*) pensión *f*; **~ and lodging**
comida y habitación; **full ~** pensión
completa; **half ~** media pensión. **9. on
~** (*ship, plane*) a bordo; (*bus, train*) dentro. **10.** *phr*: **above ~** en regla. ◆ *vt* (*ship,
plane*) embarcar en; (*train, bus*) subirse
a.

boarder ['bɔːdəʳ] *n* **1.** (*lodger*)
huésped *m* y *f*. **2.** (*at school*) interno *m*,
-na *f*.

boarding card ['bɔːdɪŋ-] *n* tarjeta *f*
de embarque.

boardinghouse ['bɔːdɪŋhaʊs, *pl*
-haʊzɪz] *n* casa *f* de huéspedes.

boarding school ['bɔːdɪŋ-] *n* internado *m*.

Board of Trade *n Br*: **the ~** ≃ el
Ministerio de Comercio.

boardroom ['bɔːdrʊm] *n* sala *f* de jun-
tas.

boast [bəʊst] ◆ *vt* disfrutar de. ◆ *vi*: **to
~ (about)** alardear OR jactarse (de).

boastful ['bəʊstfʊl] *adj* fanfarrón(ona).

boat [bəʊt] *n* (*large*) barco *m*; (*small*)
barca *f*; **by ~** en barco/barca.

boater ['bəʊtəʳ] *n* (*hat*) canotié *m*.

boatswain ['bəʊsn] *n* (NAUT) contramaestre *m*.

bob [bɒb] ◆ *n* **1.** (*hairstyle*) corte *m* de
chico. **2.** *Br inf dated* (*shilling*) chelín *m*.
3. - **bobsleigh.** ◆ *vi* (*boat*) balancearse.

bobbin ['bɒbɪn] *n* bobina *f*.

bobby ['bɒbɪ] *n Br inf* poli *m*.

bobsleigh ['bɒbsleɪ] *n* bobsleigh *m*.

bode [bəʊd] *vi literary*: **to ~ ill/well for**
traer malos/buenos presagios para.

bodily ['bɒdɪlɪ] ◆ *adj* corporal. ◆ *adv*: **to
lift/move sb ~** levantar/mover a alguien
por la fuerza.

body ['bɒdɪ] *n* **1.** (*gen*) cuerpo *m*.
2. (*corpse*) cadáver *m*. **3.** (*organization*)
entidad *f*; **a ~ of thought/opinion** una
corriente de pensamiento/opinión.
4. (*of car*) carrocería *f*; (*of plane*) fuselaje
m.

body building *n* culturismo *m*.

bodyguard ['bɒdɪgɑːd] *n* guardaespaldas *m inv*, guarura *m Amer*.

body odour *n* olor *m* corporal.

bodywork ['bɒdɪwɜːk] *n* carrocería *f*.

bog [bɒg] *n* **1.** (*marsh*) cenagal *m*. **2.** *Br
v inf* (*toilet*) meódromo *m*.

bogged down [ˌbɒgd-] *adj* **1.** (*in*

details, work): ~ **(in)** empantanado(da) (en). **2.** (*in mud, snow*): ~ **in** atascado(da) en.

boggle ['bɒgl] *vi*: **the mind ~s!** ¡me da vueltas la cabeza!, ¡es increíble!

bogus ['bəʊgəs] *adj* falso(sa).

boil [bɔɪl] ◆ *n* **1.** (MED) pústula *f*, grano *m*. **2.** (*boiling point*): **to bring sthg to the ~** poner algo a hervir; **to come to the ~** romper a hervir. ◆ *vt* **1.** (*water*) hervir. **2.** (*pan, kettle*) poner a hervir. **3.** (*food*) cocer. ◆ *vi* hervir. ▶ **boil down to** *vt fus* reducirse a. ▶ **boil over** *vi* **1.** (*liquid*) rebosar. **2.** *fig* (*feelings*) desbordarse.

boiled [bɔɪld] *adj* cocido(da); ~ **egg** huevo *m* pasado por agua; ~ **sweets** *Br* caramelos *mpl* (duros).

boiler ['bɔɪlər] *n* caldera *f*.

boiler suit *n Br* mono *m*.

boiling ['bɔɪlɪŋ] *adj inf* (*hot*): **I'm ~** estoy asado(da) de calor; **it's ~** hace un calor de muerte.

boiling point *n* punto *m* de ebullición OR de hervor.

boisterous ['bɔɪstərəs] *adj* ruidoso (sa), alborotador(ra).

bold [bəʊld] *adj* **1.** (*brave, daring*) audaz. **2.** (*lines, design*) marcado(da). **3.** (*colour*) vivo(va). **4.** (TYPO): ~ **type** OR **print** negrita *f*.

Bolivia [bə'lɪvɪə] *n* Bolivia.

Bolivian [bə'lɪvɪən] ◆ *adj* boliviano (na). ◆ *n* boliviano *m*, -na *f*.

bollard ['bɒlɑːd] *n* (*on road*) poste *m*.

bollocks ['bɒləks] *Br v inf npl* cojones *mpl*.

bolster ['bəʊlstər] *vt* reforzar. ▶ **bolster up** *vt fus* reforzar.

bolt [bəʊlt] ◆ *n* **1.** (*on door, window*) cerrojo *m*. **2.** (*type of screw*) tornillo *m*, perno *m*. ◆ *adv*: ~ **upright** muy derecho (cha). ◆ *vt* **1.** (*fasten together*) atornillar. **2.** (*door, window*) echar el cerrojo a. **3.** (*food*) tragarse. ◆ *vi* salir disparado (da).

bomb [bɒm] ◆ *n* bomba *f*. ◆ *vt* bombardear.

bombard [bɒm'bɑːd] *vt* (MIL & *fig*): **to ~ (with)** bombardear (a).

bombastic [bɒm'bæstɪk] *adj* grandilocuente, rimbombante.

bomb disposal squad *n* equipo *m* de artificieros.

bomber ['bɒmər] *n* **1.** (*plane*) bombardero *m*. **2.** (*person*) persona *f* que pone bombas.

bombing ['bɒmɪŋ] *n* bombardeo *m*.

bombshell ['bɒmʃel] *n fig* bombazo *m*.

bona fide ['bəʊnə'faɪdɪ] *adj* de buena fe.

bond [bɒnd] ◆ *n* **1.** (*between people*) lazo *m*, vínculo *m*. **2.** (*binding promise*) compromiso *m*. **3.** (FIN) bono *m*. ◆ *vt* (*glue*) adherir; *fig* (*people*) unir.

bondage ['bɒndɪdʒ] *n literary* (*servitude*) esclavitud *f*, vasallaje *m*.

bone [bəʊn] ◆ *n* (*gen*) hueso *m*; (*of fish*) raspa *f*, espina *f*. ◆ *vt* (*fish*) limpiar; (*meat*) deshuesar.

bone-dry *adj* bien seco(ca).

bone-idle *adj* haragán(ana), gandul (la).

bonfire ['bɒn,faɪər] *n* hoguera *f*.

bonfire night *n Br* noche del 5 de noviembre en que se encienden hogueras y fuegos artificiales.

Bonn [bɒn] *n* Bonn.

bonnet ['bɒnɪt] *n* **1.** *Br* (*of car*) capó *m*. **2.** (*hat*) toca *f*.

bonny ['bɒnɪ] *adj Scot* majo(ja).

bonus ['bəʊnəs] (*pl* **-es**) *n* (*extra money*) paga *f* extra, prima *f*; *fig* beneficio *m* adicional.

bony ['bəʊnɪ] *adj* **1.** (*person, hand*) huesudo(da). **2.** (*meat*) lleno(na) de huesos; (*fish*) espinoso(sa).

boo [buː] (*pl* **-s**) ◆ *excl* ¡bu! ◆ *n* abucheo *m*. ◆ *vt* & *vi* abuchear.

boob [buːb] *n inf* (*mistake*) metedura *f* de pata. ▶ **boobs** *npl Br v inf* (*woman's breasts*) tetas *fpl*.

booby trap ['buːbɪ-] *n* (*bomb*) bomba *f* camuflada.

book [bʊk] ◆ *n* **1.** (*for reading*) libro *m*. **2.** (*of stamps*) librillo *m*; (*of tickets, cheques*) talonario *m*; (*of matches*) cajetilla *f*. ◆ *vt* **1.** (*reserve*) reservar; **to be fully ~ed** estar completo. **2.** *inf* (*subj: police*) multar. **3.** *Br* (FTBL) amonestar. ◆ *vi* hacer reserva. ▶ **books** *npl* (COMM) libros *mpl*. ▶ **book up** *vt sep*: **to be ~ed up** estar completo.

bookcase ['bʊkkeɪs] *n* estantería *f*.

bookie ['bʊkɪ] *n inf* corredor *m*, -ra *f* de apuestas.

booking ['bʊkɪŋ] *n* **1.** (*reservation*) reserva *f*. **2.** *Br* (FTBL) amonestación *f*.

booking office *n* taquilla *f*.

bookkeeping ['bʊk,kiːpɪŋ] *n* contabilidad *f*.

booklet ['bʊklɪt] *n* folleto *m*.

bookmaker ['bʊk,meɪkər] *n* corredor *m*, -ra *f* de apuestas.

bookmark ['bʊkmɑːk] *n* separador *m*.

bookseller ['bʊk,selər] *n* librero *m*, -ra *f*.

bookshelf ['bʊkʃelf] (*pl* **-shelves**
[-ʃelvz]) *n* (*shelf*) estante *m*; (*bookcase*)
estantería *f*, librero *m* Amer.
bookshop Br ['bʊkʃɒp], **bookstore**
Am ['bʊkstɔːr] *n* librería *f*.
book token *n* vale *m* para comprar
libros.
boom [buːm] ◆ *n* **1.** (*loud noise*) estampido *m*. **2.** (*increase*) auge *m*, boom *m*.
3. (*for TV camera, microphone*) jirafa *f*. ◆ *vi*
1. (*make noise*) tronar. **2.** (ECON) estar en
auge.
boon [buːn] *n* ayuda *f*.
boost [buːst] ◆ *n* **1.** (*in profits, production*) incremento *m*. **2.** (*to popularity, spirits*) empujón *m*. ◆ *vt* **1.** (*increase*) incrementar. **2.** (*improve*) levantar.
booster ['buːstər] *n* (MED) inyección *f*
de revacunación.
boot [buːt] ◆ *n* **1.** (*item of footwear*) bota
f; (*ankle boot*) botín *m*. **2.** Br (*of car*)
maletero *m*, cajuela *f* Amer. ◆ *vt inf* dar
una patada a. ▶ **to boot** *adv* además.
▶ **boot out** *vt sep inf* echar, poner (de
patitas) en la calle.
booth [buːð] *n* **1.** (*at fair*) puesto *m*.
2. (*for phoning, voting*) cabina *f*.
booty ['buːtɪ] *n literary* botín *m*.
booze [buːz] *inf* ◆ *n* (U) bebida *f*, alcohol *m*. ◆ *vi* pimplar, empinar el codo.
bop [bɒp] *inf* ◆ *n* (*disco, dance*) baile *m*.
◆ *vi* bailar.
border ['bɔːdər] ◆ *n* **1.** (*between countries*) frontera *f*. **2.** (*edge*) borde *m*. **3.** (*in
garden*) arriate *m*. ◆ *vt* **1.** (*country*) limitar
con. **2.** (*edge*) bordear. ▶ **border on** *vt
fus* rayar en.
borderline ['bɔːdəlaɪn] ◆ *adj*: **a ~ case**
un caso dudoso. ◆ *n fig* límite *m*.
bore [bɔːr] ◆ *pt* → **bear**. ◆ *n* **1.** *pej* (*person*) pelmazo *m*, -za *f*; (*situation, event*)
rollo *m*, lata *f*. **2.** (*of gun*) calibre *m*. ◆ *vt*
1. (*not interest*) aburrir; **to ~ sb stiff** OR **to
tears** OR **to death** aburrir a alguien un
montón. **2.** (*drill*) horadar.
bored [bɔːd] *adj* aburrido(da); **to be ~
with sthg** estar harto de algo.
boredom ['bɔːdəm] *n* aburrimiento *m*.
boring ['bɔːrɪŋ] *adj* aburrido(da).
born [bɔːn] *adj* **1.** (*given life*) nacido(da);
to be ~ nacer. **2.** (*natural*) nato(ta).
borne [bɔːn] *pp* → **bear**.
borough ['bʌrə] *n* (*area of town*) distrito
m; (*town*) municipio *m*.
borrow ['bɒrəʊ] *vt*: **to ~ sthg from sb**
coger OR tomar algo prestado a
alguien; **can I ~ your bike?** ¿me prestas
tu bici?

Bosnia ['bɒznɪə] *n* Bosnia.
Bosnia-Herzegovina [-,hɜːtsəgə-
'viːnə] *n* Bosnia-Hercegovina.
Bosnian ['bɒznɪən] ◆ *adj* bosnio(nia).
◆ *n* bosnio *m*, -nia *f*.
bosom ['bʊzəm] *n* (*of woman*) busto *m*,
pecho *m*.
boss [bɒs] ◆ *n* jefe *m*, -fa *f*. ◆ *vt pej*
mangonear, dar órdenes a. ▶ **boss
about, boss around** *vt sep pej* mangonear, dar órdenes a.
bossy ['bɒsɪ] *adj* mandón(ona).
bosun ['bəʊsn] = **boatswain**.
botany ['bɒtənɪ] *n* botánica *f*.
botch [bɒtʃ] ▶ **botch up** *vt sep inf*
estropear, hacer chapuceramente.
both [bəʊθ] ◆ *adj* los dos, las dos,
ambos(bas). ◆ *pron*: **~ (of them)** los dos
(las dos), ambos *mpl*, -bas *fpl*; **~ of us
are coming** vamos los dos. ◆ *adv*: **she is
~ pretty and intelligent** es guapa e
inteligente.
bother ['bɒðər] ◆ *vt* **1.** (*worry*) preocupar; (*irritate*) fastidiar; **I/she can't be ~ed
to do it** no tengo/tiene ganas de hacer-
lo. **2.** (*pester*) molestar. ◆ *vi*: **to ~ (doing
OR to do sthg)** molestarse (en hacer
algo); **to ~ about** preocuparse por. ◆ *n*
(U) **1.** (*inconvenience*) problema *m*.
2. (*pest, nuisance*) molestia *f*.
bothered ['bɒðəd] *adj* preocupado
(da).
bottle ['bɒtl] ◆ *n* **1.** (*gen*) botella *f*.
2. (*of shampoo, medicine - plastic*) bote *m*;
(*- glass*) frasco *m*. **3.** (*for baby*) biberón
m. **4.** (U) Br *inf* (*courage*) agallas *fpl*. ◆ *vt*
(*wine*) embotellar. ▶ **bottle up** *vt sep*
reprimir, tragarse.
bottle bank *n* contenedor *m* de
vidrio (*para reciclaje*).
bottleneck ['bɒtlnek] *n* **1.** (*in traffic*)
embotellamiento *m*. **2.** (*in production*)
freno *m*.
bottle-opener *n* abrebotellas *m inv*.
bottom ['bɒtəm] ◆ *adj* **1.** (*lowest*) más
bajo(ja), de abajo del todo. **2.** (*least
successful*) peor. ◆ *n* **1.** (*lowest part - of
glass, bottle*) culo *m*; (*- of bag, mine, sea*)
fondo *m*; (*- of ladder, hill*) pie *m*; (*- of page,
list*) final *m*. **2.** (*farthest point*) final *m*,
fondo *m*. **3.** (*of class etc*) parte *f* más baja.
4. (*buttocks*) trasero *m*. **5.** (*root*): **to get to
the ~ of** llegar al fondo de. ▶ **bottom
out** *vi* tocar fondo.
bottom line *n fig*: **the ~ is ...** a fin de
cuentas ...
bough [baʊ] *n* rama *f*.
bought [bɔːt] *pt & pp* → **buy**.

boulder ['bəuldə^r] n canto m rodado.

bounce [bauns] ◆ vi 1. (gen) rebotar. 2. (person): **to ~ (on sthg)** dar botes (en algo). 3. inf (cheque) ser rechazado(da) por el banco. ◆ vt botar. ◆ n bote m.

bouncer ['baunsə^r] n inf matón m, gorila m (de un local).

bound [baund] ◆ pt & pp → **bind**. ◆ adj 1. (certain): **it's ~ to happen** seguro que va a pasar. 2. (obliged): **~ (by sthg/to do sthg)** obligado(da) (por algo/a hacer algo); **I'm ~ to say** OR **admit** tengo que decir OR admitir. 3. (for place): **to be ~ for** ir rumbo a. ◆ n salto m. ◆ vi ir dando saltos. ▶ **bounds** npl (limits) límites mpl; **out of ~s** (en) zona prohibida.

boundary ['baundəri] n (gen) límite m; (between countries) frontera f.

bouquet [bəu'kei] n (of flowers) ramo m.

bourbon ['bɜːbən] n bourbon m.

bourgeois ['bɔːʒwɑː] adj pej burgués (esa).

bout [baut] n 1. (attack) ataque m, acceso m. 2. (session) racha f. 3. (boxing match) pelea f, combate m.

bow¹ [bau] ◆ n 1. (act of bowing) reverencia f. 2. (of ship) proa f. ◆ vt inclinar. ◆ vi 1. (make a bow) inclinarse. 2. (defer): **to ~ to sthg** ceder OR doblegarse ante algo.

bow² [bəu] n 1. (weapon, musical instrument) arco m. 2. (knot) lazo m.

bowels ['bauəlz] npl lit & fig entrañas fpl.

bowl [bəul] ◆ n (gen) cuenco m, bol m; (for soup) tazón m; (for washing clothes) barreño m, balde m. ◆ vi lanzar la bola. ▶ **bowls** n (U) bochas fpl. ▶ **bowl over** vt sep 1. (knock over) atropellar. 2. fig (surprise, impress) dejar atónito(ta).

bow-legged [ˌbəu'legid] adj de piernas arqueadas, estevado(da).

bowler ['bəulə^r] n 1. (CRICKET) lanzador m. 2. **~ (hat)** bombín m, sombrero m hongo.

bowling ['bəulɪŋ] n (U) bolos mpl.

bowling alley n 1. (building) bolera f. 2. (alley) calle f.

bowling green n campo de césped para jugar a las bochas.

bow tie [bəu-] n pajarita f.

box [bɒks] ◆ n 1. (container, boxful) caja f; (for jewels) estuche m. 2. (THEATRE) palco m. 3. Br inf (television): **the ~** la caja tonta. ◆ vt (put in boxes) encajonar. ◆ vi boxear.

boxer ['bɒksə^r] n 1. (fighter) boxeador m, púgil m. 2. (dog) bóxer m.

boxer shorts npl calzón m (de boxeo).

boxing ['bɒksɪŋ] n boxeo m.

Boxing Day n fiesta nacional en Inglaterra y Gales el 26 de diciembre (salvo domingos) en que tradicionalmente se da el aguinaldo.

boxing glove n guante m de boxeo.

box office n taquilla f, boletería f Amer.

boxroom ['bɒksrum] n Br trastero m.

boy [bɔi] ◆ n 1. (male child) chico m, niño m, pibe m Amer. 2. inf (young man) chaval m. ◆ excl: **(oh) ~!** ¡jolín!, ¡vaya, vaya!

boycott ['bɔikɒt] ◆ n boicot m. ◆ vt boicotear.

boyfriend ['bɔifrend] n novio m.

boyish ['bɔiiʃ] adj (man) juvenil.

BR (abbr of **British Rail**) n ferrocarriles británicos, ≃ Renfe f.

bra [brɑː] n sujetador m.

brace [breis] ◆ n 1. (on teeth) aparato m corrector. 2. (pair) par m. ◆ vt (steady) tensar; **to ~ o.s. (for)** lit & fig prepararse (para). ▶ **braces** npl Br tirantes mpl, tiradores mpl Amer.

bracelet ['breislit] n brazalete m, pulsera f.

bracing ['breisiŋ] adj tonificante.

bracken ['brækn] n helecho m.

bracket ['brækit] ◆ n 1. (support) soporte m, palomilla f. 2. (parenthesis - round) paréntesis m inv; (- square) corchete m; **in ~s** entre paréntesis. 3. (group) sector m, banda f. ◆ vt (enclose in brackets) poner entre paréntesis.

brag [bræg] vi fanfarronear, jactarse.

braid [breid] ◆ n 1. (on uniform) galón m. 2. (hairstyle) trenza f. ◆ vt trenzar.

brain [brein] n lit & fig cerebro m. ▶ **brains** npl cerebro m, seso m.

brainchild ['breintʃaild] n inf invención f, idea f.

brainwash ['breinwɒʃ] vt lavar el cerebro a.

brainwave ['breinweiv] n idea f genial.

brainy ['breini] adj inf listo(ta).

brake [breik] ◆ n lit & fig freno m. ◆ vi frenar.

brake light n luz f de freno.

bramble ['bræmbl] n (bush) zarza f, zarzamora f; (fruit) mora f.

bran [bræn] n salvado m.

branch [brɑːntʃ] ◆ n 1. (of tree, of subject) rama f. 2. (of river) afluente m; (of railway) ramal m. 3. (of company, bank)

sucursal f. ◆ vi bifurcarse. ► **branch out** vi (person) ampliar horizontes; (firm) expandirse, diversificarse.

brand [brænd] ◆ n 1. (of product) marca f. 2. fig (type) tipo m, estilo m. 3. (mark) hierro m. ◆ vt 1. (cattle) marcar (con hierro). 2. fig (classify): **to ~ sb (as sthg)** tildar a alguien (de algo).

brandish ['brændɪʃ] vt (weapon) blandir; (letter etc) agitar.

brand name n marca f.

brand-new adj flamante.

brandy ['brændɪ] n coñac m.

brash [bræʃ] adj pej insolente.

brass [brɑːs] n 1. (metal) latón m. 2. (MUS): **the ~** el metal.

brass band n banda f de metal.

brassiere [Br 'bræsɪər, Am brəˈzɪr] n sostén m, sujetador m.

brat [bræt] n inf pej mocoso m, -sa f.

bravado [brəˈvɑːdəʊ] n bravuconería f.

brave [breɪv] ◆ adj valiente. ◆ vt (weather, storm) desafiar; (sb's anger) hacer frente a.

bravery ['breɪvərɪ] n valentía f.

brawl [brɔːl] n gresca f, reyerta f.

brawn [brɔːn] n (U) 1. (muscle) musculatura f, fuerza f física. 2. Br (meat) carne de cerdo en gelatina.

bray [breɪ] vi (donkey) rebuznar.

brazen ['breɪzn] adj (person) descarado (da); (lie) burdo(da). ► **brazen out** vt sep: **to ~ it out** echarle cara.

brazier ['breɪzjər] n brasero m.

Brazil [brəˈzɪl] n (el) Brasil.

Brazilian [brəˈzɪljən] ◆ adj brasileño (ña), brasilero(ra) Amer. ◆ n brasileño m, -ña f, brasilero m, -ra f Amer.

brazil nut n nuez f de Pará.

breach [briːtʃ] ◆ n 1. (act of disobedience) incumplimiento m; **~ of confidence** abuso m de confianza; **to be in ~ of sthg** incumplir algo; **~ of contract** incumplimiento de contrato. 2. (opening, gap) brecha f. 3. fig (in friendship, marriage) ruptura f. ◆ vt 1. (disobey) incumplir. 2. (make hole in) abrir (una) brecha en.

breach of the peace n alteración f del orden público.

bread [bred] n 1. (food) pan m; **~ and butter** (buttered bread) pan con mantequilla; fig (main income) sustento m diario. 2. inf (money) pasta f.

bread bin Br, **bread box** Am n panera f.

breadcrumbs ['bredkrʌmz] npl migas

fpl (de pan); (CULIN) pan m rallado.

breadline ['bredlaɪn] n: **to be on the ~** vivir en la miseria.

breadth [bretθ] n 1. (in measurements) anchura f. 2. fig (scope) amplitud f.

breadwinner ['bred,wɪnər] n cabeza m y f de familia.

break [breɪk] (pt broke, pp broken) ◆ n 1. (gap - in clouds) claro m; (- in transmission) corte m. 2. (fracture) fractura f. 3. (pause): **~ (from)** descanso m (de); **to have OR take a ~** tomarse un descanso. 4. (playtime) recreo m. 5. inf (chance) oportunidad f; **a lucky ~** un golpe de suerte. ◆ vt 1. (gen) romper; (arm, leg etc) romperse; **to ~ sb's hold** escaparse OR liberarse de alguien. 2. (machine) estropear. 3. (journey, contact) interrumpir. 4. (habit, health) acabar con; (strike) reventar. 5. (law, rule) violar; (appointment, word) faltar a. 6. (record) batir. 7. (tell): **to ~ the news (of sthg to sb)** dar la noticia (de algo a alguien). ◆ vi 1. (come to pieces) romperse. 2. (stop working) estropearse. 3. (pause) parar; (weather) cambiar. 4. (start - day) romper; (- storm) estallar. 5. (escape): **to ~ loose** OR **free** escaparse. 6. (voice) cambiar. 7. (news) divulgarse. 8. phr: **to ~ even** salir sin pérdidas ni beneficios. ► **break away** vi escaparse; **to ~ away (from)** (end connection) separarse (de); (POL) escindirse (de). ► **break down** ◆ vt sep 1. (destroy - gen) derribar; (- resistance) vencer. 2. (analyse) descomponer. ◆ vi 1. (collapse, disintegrate, fail) venirse abajo. 2. (stop working) estropearse. 3. (lose emotional control) perder el control. 4. (decompose) descomponerse. ► **break in** ◆ vi 1. (enter by force) entrar por la fuerza. 2. (interrupt): **to ~ in (on sthg/sb)** interrumpir (algo/a alguien). ◆ vt sep 1. (horse, shoes) domar. 2. (person) amoldar, poner al tanto. ► **break into** vt fus 1. (house, shop) entrar (por la fuerza) en; (box, safe) forzar. 2. (begin suddenly): **to ~ into song/a run** echarse a cantar/correr. ► **break off** ◆ vt sep 1. (detach) partir. 2. (end) romper; (holiday) interrumpir. ◆ vi 1. (become detached) partirse. 2. (stop talking) interrumpirse. ► **break out** vi 1. (fire, fighting, panic) desencadenarse; (war) estallar. 2. (escape): **to ~ out (of)** escapar (de). ► **break up** ◆ vt sep 1. (ice) hacer pedazos; (car) desguazar. 2. (relationship) romper; (talks) poner fin a; (fight, crowd) disolver. ◆ vi 1. (into *smaller pieces*) hacerse pedazos. **2.** (*relationship*) deshacerse; (*conference*) concluir; (*school, pupils*) terminar el curso; **to ~ up with sb** romper con alguien. **3.** (*crowd*) disolverse.

breakage ['breɪkɪdʒ] *n* rotura *f*.

breakdown ['breɪkdaʊn] *n* **1.** (*of car, train*) avería *f*; (*of talks, in communications*) ruptura *f*; (*of law and order*) colapso *m*. **2.** (*analysis*) desglose *m*.

breakfast ['brekfəst] *n* desayuno *m*.

breakfast television *n* Br programación *f* matinal de televisión.

break-in *n* robo *m* (*con allanamiento de morada*).

breaking ['breɪkɪŋ] *n*: **~ and entering** (JUR) allanamiento *m* de morada.

breakneck ['breɪknek] *adj*: **at ~ speed** a (una) velocidad de vértigo.

breakthrough ['breɪkθruː] *n* avance *m*.

breakup ['breɪkʌp] *n* ruptura *f*.

breast [brest] *n* **1.** (*of woman*) pecho *m*, seno *m*; (*of man*) pecho *m*. **2.** (*meat of bird*) pechuga *f*.

breast-feed *vt & vi* amamantar.

breaststroke ['breststrəʊk] *n* braza *f*.

breath [breθ] *n* respiración *f*, aliento *m*; **to take a deep ~** respirar hondo; **to get one's ~ back** recuperar el aliento; **to say sthg under one's ~** decir algo en voz baja; **out of ~** sin aliento.

breathalyse Br, **-yze** Am ['breθəlaɪz] *vt* hacer la prueba del alcohol a.

breathe [briːð] ◆ *vi* respirar. ◆ *vt* **1.** (*inhale*) respirar. **2.** (*exhale*) despedir. ▶ **breathe in** *vt sep & vi* aspirar. ▶ **breathe out** *vi* espirar.

breather ['briːðəʳ] *n inf* respiro *m*.

breathing ['briːðɪŋ] *n* respiración *f*.

breathless ['breθlɪs] *adj* **1.** (*out of breath*) jadeante. **2.** (*with excitement*) sin aliento (*a la emoción*).

breathtaking ['breθ,teɪkɪŋ] *adj* sobrecogedor(ra), impresionante.

breed [briːd] (*pt & pp* **bred** [bred]) ◆ *n* **1.** (*of animal*) raza *f*. *fig* (*sort*) generación *f*, especie *f*. ◆ *vt* (*animals*) criar; (*plants*) cultivar. ◆ *vi* procrear.

breeding ['briːdɪŋ] *n* **1.** (*of animals*) cría *f*; (*of plants*) cultivo *m*. **2.** (*manners*) educación *f*.

breeze [briːz] ◆ *n* brisa *f*. ◆ *vi*: **to ~ in/out** entrar/salir como si tal cosa.

breezy ['briːzɪ] *adj* **1.** (*windy*): **it's ~** hace aire. **2.** (*cheerful*) jovial, despreocupado(da).

brevity ['brevɪtɪ] *n* brevedad *f*.

brew [bruː] ◆ *vt* (*beer*) elaborar; (*tea, coffee*) preparar. ◆ *vi* **1.** (*tea*) reposar. **2.** (*trouble*) fraguarse.

brewer ['bruːəʳ] *n* cervecero *m*, -ra *f*.

brewery ['brʊərɪ] *n* fábrica *f* de cerveza.

bribe [braɪb] ◆ *n* soborno *m*. ◆ *vt*: **to ~ (sb to do sthg)** sobornar (a alguien para que haga algo).

bribery ['braɪbərɪ] *n* soborno *m*.

bric-a-brac ['brɪkəbræk] *n* baratijas *fpl*.

brick [brɪk] *n* ladrillo *m*.

bricklayer ['brɪk,leɪəʳ] *n* albañil *m*.

bridal ['braɪdl] *adj* nupcial; **~ dress** traje *m* de novia.

bride [braɪd] *n* novia *f*.

bridegroom ['braɪdgrʊm] *n* novio *m*.

bridesmaid ['braɪdzmeɪd] *n* dama *f* de honor.

bridge [brɪdʒ] ◆ *n* **1.** (*gen*) puente *m*. **2.** (*on ship*) puente *m* de mando. **3.** (*of nose*) caballete *m*. **4.** (*card game*) bridge *m*. ◆ *vt fig* (*gap*) llenar.

bridle ['braɪdl] *n* brida *f*.

bridle path *n* camino *m* de herradura.

brief [briːf] ◆ *adj* **1.** (*short, to the point*) breve; **in ~** en resumen. **2.** (*clothes*) corto(ta). ◆ *n* **1.** (JUR) (*statement*) sumario *m*, resumen *m*. **2.** Br (*instructions*) instrucciones *fpl*. ◆ *vt*: **to ~ sb (on)** informar a alguien (acerca de). ▶ **briefs** *npl* (*underpants*) calzoncillos *mpl*; (*knickers*) bragas *fpl*.

briefcase ['briːfkeɪs] *n* maletín *m*, portafolios *m inv*.

briefing ['briːfɪŋ] *n* (*meeting*) reunión *f* informativa; (*instructions*) instrucciones *fpl*.

briefly ['briːflɪ] *adv* **1.** (*for a short time*) brevemente. **2.** (*concisely*) en pocas palabras.

brigade [brɪ'geɪd] *n* brigada *f*.

brigadier [,brɪgə'dɪəʳ] *n* brigadier *m*, general *m* de brigada.

bright [braɪt] *adj* **1.** (*light*) brillante; (*day, room*) luminoso(sa); (*weather*) despejado(da). **2.** (*colour*) vivo(va), fuerte. **3.** (*lively - eyes*) brillante; (*- smile*) radiante. **4.** (*intelligent - person*) listo(ta); (*- idea*) genial. **5.** (*hopeful*) prometedor(ra).

brighten ['braɪtn] *vi* **1.** (*become lighter*) despejarse. **2.** (*become more cheerful*) alegrarse. ▶ **brighten up** ◆ *vt sep* animar, alegrar. ◆ *vi* **1.** (*become more cheerful*) animarse. **2.** (*weather*) despejarse.

brilliance ['brɪljəns] n 1. (cleverness) brillantez f. 2. (of colour, light) brillo m.

brilliant ['brɪljənt] adj 1. (clever) genial, fantástico(ca). 2. (colour) vivo(va). 3. (light, career, future) brillante. 4. inf (wonderful) fenomenal, genial.

Brillo pad® ['brɪləʊ-] n estropajo m (jabonoso) de aluminio.

brim [brɪm] ◆ n 1. (edge) borde m. 2. (of hat) ala f. ◆ vi lit & fig: **to ~ with** rebosar de.

brine [braɪn] n salmuera f.

bring [brɪŋ] (pt & pp **brought**) vt (gen) traer; **to ~ sthg to an end** poner fin a algo. ▶ **bring about** vt sep producir. ▶ **bring around** vt sep (make conscious) reanimar. ▶ **bring back** vt sep 1. (books etc) devolver; (person) traer de vuelta. 2. (memories) traer (a la memoria). 3. (practice, hanging) volver a introducir; (fashion) recuperar. ▶ **bring down** vt sep 1. (plane, bird) derribar; (government, tyrant) derrocar. 2. (prices) reducir. ▶ **bring forward** vt sep 1. (meeting, elections etc) adelantar. 2. (in bookkeeping) sumar a la siguiente columna. ▶ **bring in** vt sep 1. (introduce - law) implantar; (- bill) presentar. 2. (earn) ganar. ▶ **bring off** vt sep (plan) sacar adelante; (deal) cerrar. ▶ **bring out** vt sep 1. (new product, book) sacar. 2. (the worst etc in sb) revelar, despertar. ▶ **bring round, bring to** vt sep = bring around. ▶ **bring up** vt sep 1. (raise - children) criar. 2. (mention) sacar a relucir. 3. (vomit) devolver.

brink [brɪŋk] n: **on the ~ of** al borde de.

brisk [brɪsk] adj 1. (quick) rápido(da). 2. (busy) boyante, activo(va). 3. (efficient, confident - manner) enérgico(ca); (- person) eficaz.

bristle ['brɪsl] ◆ n (gen) cerda f; (of person) pelillo m. ◆ vi 1. (stand up) erizarse, ponerse de punta. 2. (react angrily): **to ~ (at)** enfadarse (por).

Brit [brɪt] n inf británico m, -ca f.

Britain ['brɪtn] n Gran Bretaña.

British ['brɪtɪʃ] ◆ adj británico(ca). ◆ npl: **the ~** los británicos.

British Council n: **the ~** el British Council.

British Isles npl: **the ~** las Islas Británicas.

British Rail n compañía ferroviaria británica, = Renfe f.

British Telecom [-'telɪkɒm] n principal empresa británica de telecomunicaciones,

= Telefónica f.

Briton ['brɪtn] n británico m, -ca f.

brittle ['brɪtl] adj quebradizo(za), frágil.

broach [brəʊtʃ] vt abordar.

B road n Br ~ carretera f comarcal.

broad [brɔːd] adj 1. (shoulders, river, street) ancho(cha); (grin) amplio(plia). 2. (range, interests) amplio(plia). 3. (description, outline) general. 4. (hint) claro(ra). 5. (accent) cerrado(da). 6. phr: **in ~ daylight** a plena luz del día.

broad bean n haba f.

broadcast ['brɔːdkɑːst] (pt & pp broadcast) ◆ n emisión f. ◆ vt emitir.

broaden ['brɔːdn] ◆ vt 1. (road, pavement) ensanchar. 2. (scope, appeal) ampliar. ◆ vi (river, road) ensancharse; (smile) hacerse más amplia.

broadly ['brɔːdlɪ] adv 1. (generally) en general. 2. (smile) abiertamente.

broadminded [,brɔːd'maɪndɪd] adj abierto(ta), liberal.

broadsheet ['brɔːdʃiːt] n periódico con hojas de gran tamaño.

broccoli ['brɒkəlɪ] n brécol m.

brochure ['brəʊʃə'] n folleto m.

broil [brɔɪl] vt Am asar a la parrilla.

broke [brəʊk] ◆ pt → **break**. ◆ adj inf sin blanca, sin un duro.

broken ['brəʊkn] ◆ pp → **break**. ◆ adj 1. (gen) roto(ta). 2. (not working) estropeado(da). 3. (interrupted - sleep) entrecortado(da); (- journey) discontinuo (nua). 4. (hesitant, inaccurate) macarrónico(ca).

broker ['brəʊkə'] n (of stock) corredor m; (of insurance) agente m y f.

brolly ['brɒlɪ] n Br inf paraguas m inv.

bronchitis [brɒŋ'kaɪtɪs] n (U) bronquitis f.

bronze [brɒnz] n (metal, sculpture) bronce m.

brooch [brəʊtʃ] n broche m, alfiler m.

brood [bruːd] ◆ n 1. (of animals) cría f, nidada f. 2. inf (of children) prole f. ◆ vi: **to ~ (over OR about)** dar vueltas (a).

brook [brʊk] n arroyo m.

broom [bruːm] n (brush) escoba f.

broomstick ['bruːmstɪk] n palo m de escoba.

Bros., bros. (abbr of **brothers**) Hnos.

broth [brɒθ] n caldo m.

brothel ['brɒθl] n burdel m.

brother ['brʌðə'] n (relative, monk) hermano m.

brother-in-law (pl **brothers-in-law**) n cuñado m.

brought [brɔːt] pt & pp → **bring**.

brow [brau] n 1. (forehead) frente f.
2. (eyebrow) ceja f. 3. (of hill) cima f.

brown [braun] ◆ adj 1. (gen) marrón;
(hair, eyes) castaño(ña). 2. (tanned) moreno
(na). ◆ n marrón m. ◆ vt (food) dorar.

Brownie (Guide) ['braunɪ-] n guía f
(7-10 años).

brown paper n (U) papel m de
embalar.

brown rice n arroz m integral.

brown sugar n azúcar m moreno.

browse [brauz] vi (person) echar un
ojo, mirar; **to ~ through** hojear.

bruise [bruːz] ◆ n cardenal m. ◆ vt
1. (person, arm) magullar; (fruit) estropear. 2. fig (feelings) herir.

brunch [brʌntʃ] n brunch m, combinación de desayuno y almuerzo que se toma
por la mañana tarde.

brunette [bruːˈnet] n morena f.

brunt [brʌnt] n: **to bear** OR **take the ~ of**
aguantar lo peor de.

brush [brʌʃ] ◆ n 1. (for hair, teeth) cepillo m; (for shaving, painting) brocha f; (of
artist) pincel m; (broom) escoba f.
2. (encounter) roce m. ◆ vt 1. (clean with
brush) cepillar. 2. (move with hand) quitar,
apartar. 3. (touch lightly) rozar. ▶ **brush
aside** vt sep rechazar. ▶ **brush off** vt sep
(dismiss) hacer caso omiso de. ▶ **brush
up** ◆ vt sep fig (revise) repasar. ◆ vi: **to ~
up on** repasar.

brushwood ['brʌʃwud] n leña f.

brusque [bruːsk] adj brusco(ca).

Brussels ['brʌslz] n Bruselas.

brussels sprout n col f de Bruselas.

brutal ['bruːtl] adj brutal.

brute [bruːt] ◆ adj bruto(ta). ◆ n
1. (large animal) bestia f, bruto m.
2. (bully) bestia m y f.

BSc (abbr of **Bachelor of Science**) n (titular
de una) licenciatura de ciencias.

BT n abbr of **British Telecom**.

bubble ['bʌbl] ◆ n (gen) burbuja f; (of
soap) pompa f. ◆ vi 1. (produce bubbles)
burbujear. 2. (make a bubbling sound)
borbotar.

bubble bath n espuma f de baño.

bubble gum n chicle m (de globo).

bubblejet printer ['bʌbldʒet-] n
(COMPUT) impresora f de inyección.

Bucharest [ˌbuːkəˈrest] n Bucarest.

buck [bʌk] (pl inv OR **-s**) ◆ n 1. (male animal) macho m. 2. inf (dollar) dólar m. 3.
inf (responsibility): **to pass the ~ to sb**
echarle el muerto a alguien. ◆ vt (subj:
horse) tirar. ◆ vi corcovear. ▶ **buck up**

inf ◆ vt sep (improve) mejorar; **~ your
ideas up** más vale que espabiles. ◆ vi
1. (hurry up) darse prisa. 2. (cheer up)
animarse.

bucket ['bʌkɪt] n (container, bucketful)
cubo m.

Buckingham Palace ['bʌkɪŋəm-] n
el palacio de Buckingham.

buckle ['bʌkl] ◆ n hebilla f. ◆ vt 1. (fasten) abrochar con hebilla. 2. (bend)
combar, torcer. ◆ vi (wheel) combarse,
torcerse; (knees) doblarse.

bud [bʌd] ◆ n (shoot) brote m; (flower)
capullo m. ◆ vi brotar, echar brotes.

Budapest [ˌbjuːdəˈpest] n Budapest.

Buddha ['budə] n Buda m.

Buddhism ['budɪzm] n budismo m.

budding ['bʌdɪŋ] adj en ciernes.

buddy ['bʌdɪ] n inf (friend) amiguete m,
-ta f, colega m y f.

budge [bʌdʒ] ◆ vt mover. ◆ vi (move)
moverse; (give in) ceder.

budgerigar ['bʌdʒərɪgɑːr] n periquito
m.

budget ['bʌdʒɪt] ◆ adj económico(ca).
◆ n presupuesto m. ▶ **budget for** vt
fus contar con.

budgie ['bʌdʒɪ] n inf periquito m.

buff [bʌf] ◆ adj color de ante. ◆ n inf
(expert) aficionado m, -da f.

buffalo ['bʌfələu] (pl inv OR **-s** OR **-es**) n
búfalo m.

buffer ['bʌfər] n 1. Br (for trains) tope
m. 2. (protection) defensa f, salvaguarda
f. 3. (COMPUT) memoria f intermedia.

buffet[1] [Br 'bufeɪ, Am bəˈfeɪ] n 1. (meal)
bufé m. 2. (cafeteria) cafetería f.

buffet[2] ['bʌfɪt] vt (physically) golpear.

buffet car ['bufeɪ-] n coche m restaurante (sólo mostrador).

bug [bʌg] ◆ n 1. (small insect) bicho m.
2. inf (germ) microbio m. 3. inf (listening
device) micrófono m oculto. 4. (COMPUT)
error m. 5. (enthusiasm) manía f. ◆ vt 1.
inf (spy on - room) poner un micrófono
oculto en; (- phone) pinchar. 2. inf
(annoy) fastidiar, jorobar.

bugger ['bʌgər] Br v inf n (unpleasant
person) cabrón m, -ona f. ▶ **bugger off**
vi v inf: **~ off!** ¡vete a tomar por culo!

buggy ['bʌgɪ] n 1. (carriage) calesa f.
2. (pushchair) sillita f de ruedas; Am
(pram) cochecito m de niño.

bugle ['bjuːgl] n corneta f, clarín m.

build [bɪld] (pt & pp **built**) ◆ vt 1. (construct) construir. 2. fig (form, create) crear.
◆ n complexión f, constitución f.
▶ **build (up)on** ◆ vt fus (further) desa-

rrollar. ◆ vt sep (base on) fundar en.
▶ **build up** ◆ vt sep 1. (business - establish) poner en pie; (- promote) fomentar. 2. (person) fortalecer. ◆ vi acumularse.

builder ['bɪldər] n constructor m, -ra f.

building ['bɪldɪŋ] n 1. (structure) edificio m. 2. (profession) construcción f.

building and loan association n Am ≃ caja f de ahorros.

building site n solar m (de construcción), obra f.

building society n Br ≃ caja f de ahorros.

buildup ['bɪldʌp] n (increase) acumulación f.

built [bɪlt] pt & pp → **build**.

built-in adj 1. (physically integral) empotrado(da). 2. (inherent) incorporado(da).

built-up adj urbanizado(da).

bulb [bʌlb] n 1. (for lamp) bombilla f. 2. (of plant) bulbo m.

Bulgaria [bʌl'geərɪə] n Bulgaria.

Bulgarian [bʌl'geərɪən] ◆ adj búlgaro (ra). ◆ n 1. (person) búlgaro m, -ra f. 2. (language) búlgaro m.

bulge [bʌldʒ] ◆ n (lump) protuberancia f, bulto m. ◆ vi: to ~ (with) rebosar (de), estar atestado(da) (de).

bulk [bʌlk] ◆ n 1. (mass) bulto m, volumen m. 2. (large quantity): in ~ a granel. 3. (majority, most of): the ~ of la mayor parte de. ◆ adj a granel.

bulky ['bʌlkɪ] adj abultado(da), voluminoso(sa).

bull [bʊl] n 1. (male cow) toro m. 2. (male animal) macho m.

bulldog ['bʊldɒg] n buldog m.

bulldozer ['bʊldəʊzər] n bulldozer m.

bullet ['bʊlɪt] n bala f.

bulletin ['bʊlətɪn] n 1. (news) boletín m; (medical report) parte m. 2. (regular publication) boletín m, gaceta f.

bullet-proof adj a prueba de balas.

bullfight ['bʊlfaɪt] n corrida f (de toros).

bullfighter ['bʊl,faɪtər] n torero m, -ra f.

bullfighting ['bʊl,faɪtɪŋ] n toreo m.

bullion ['bʊljən] n (U) lingotes mpl.

bullock ['bʊlək] n buey m, toro m castrado.

bullring ['bʊlrɪŋ] n plaza f (de toros).

bull's-eye n diana f.

bully ['bʊlɪ] ◆ n abusón m, matón m. ◆ vt abusar de, intimidar.

bum [bʌm] n 1. v inf (bottom) culo m. 2. Am inf pej (tramp) vagabundo m, -da f.

bumblebee ['bʌmblbiː] n abejorro m.

bump [bʌmp] ◆ n 1. (lump - on head) chichón m; (- on road) bache m. 2. (knock, blow, noise) golpe m. ◆ vt (car) chocar con OR contra; (head, knee) golpearse en, I ~ed my head on the door me di con la cabeza en la puerta.
▶ **bump into** vt fus (meet by chance) toparse con.

bumper ['bʌmpər] ◆ adj abundante; ~ edition edición especial. ◆ n 1. (AUT) parachoques m inv. 2. Am (RAIL) tope m.

bumptious ['bʌmpʃəs] adj pej engreído(da).

bumpy ['bʌmpɪ] adj 1. (road) lleno(na) de baches. 2. (ride, journey) con muchas sacudidas.

bun [bʌn] n 1. (cake, bread roll) bollo m. 2. (hairstyle) moño m.

bunch [bʌntʃ] ◆ n (of people) grupo m; (of flowers) ramo m; (of fruit) racimo m; (of keys) manojo m. ◆ vi agruparse.
▶ **bunches** npl (hairstyle) coletas fpl.

bundle ['bʌndl] ◆ n (of clothes) lío m, bulto m; (of notes, papers) fajo m; (of wood) haz m. ◆ vt (clothes) empaquetar de cualquier manera; (person) empujar.
▶ **bundle up** vt sep (put into bundles) liar, envolver.

bung [bʌŋ] ◆ n tapón m. ◆ vt Br inf 1. (throw) tirar. 2. (pass) alcanzar.

bungalow ['bʌŋgələʊ] n bungalow m.

bungle ['bʌŋgl] vt chapucear.

bunion ['bʌnjən] n juanete m.

bunk [bʌŋk] n (bed) litera f.

bunk bed n litera f.

bunker ['bʌŋkər] n 1. (shelter, in golf) bunker m. 2. (for coal) carbonera f.

bunny ['bʌnɪ] n: ~ (rabbit) conejito m, -ta f.

bunting ['bʌntɪŋ] n (U) (flags) banderitas fpl.

buoy [Br bɔɪ, Am 'buːɪ] n boya f.
▶ **buoy up** vt sep (encourage) alentar.

buoyant ['bɔɪənt] adj 1. (able to float) boyante. 2. (optimistic - gen) optimista; (- market) con tendencia alcista.

burden ['bɜːdn] ◆ n 1. (heavy load) carga f. 2. fig (heavy responsibility): ~ on carga f para. ◆ vt: to ~ sb with cargar a alguien con.

bureau ['bjʊərəʊ] (pl -x) n 1. (government department) departamento m. 2. (office) oficina f. 3. Br (desk) secreter m; Am (chest of drawers) cómoda f.

bureaucracy [bjʊə'rɒkrəsɪ] n burocracia f.

bureau de change [,bjʊərəʊdə-

'ʃɒndʒ] (pl **bureaux de change** [ˌbjuərəudə'ʃɒndʒ]) n casa f de cambio.

bureaux ['bjuərəuz] pl → **bureau**.

burger ['bɜːgəʳ] n hamburguesa f.

burglar ['bɜːgləʳ] n ladrón m, -ona f.

burglar alarm n alarma f antirrobo.

burglarize Am = **burgle**.

burglary ['bɜːgləri] n robo m (de una casa).

burgle ['bɜːgl], **burglarize** ['bɜːgləraiz] Am vt robar, desvalijar (una casa).

burial ['beriəl] n entierro m.

burly ['bɜːli] adj fornido(da).

Burma ['bɜːmə] n Birmania.

burn [bɜːn] (pt & pp **burnt** OR **-ed**) ♦ vt 1. (gen) quemar. 2. (injure - by heat, fire) quemarse. ♦ vi 1. (gen) arder. 2. (be alight) estar encendido(da). 3. (food) quemar. 4. (cause burning sensation) escocer. 5. (become sunburnt) quemarse. ♦ n quemadura f. ► **burn down** ♦ vt sep incendiar. ♦ vi (be destroyed by fire) incendiarse.

burner ['bɜːnəʳ] n quemador m.

Burns' Night n fiesta celebrada en Escocia el 25 de enero en honor del poeta escocés Robert Burns.

burnt [bɜːnt] pt & pp → **burn**.

burp [bɜːp] inf vi eructar.

burrow ['bʌrəu] ♦ n madriguera f. ♦ vi 1. (dig) escarbar (un agujero). 2. fig (in order to search) hurgar.

bursar ['bɜːsəʳ] n tesorero m, -ra f.

bursary ['bɜːsəri] n Br beca f.

burst [bɜːst] (pt & pp burst) ♦ vi 1. (gen) reventarse; (bag) romperse; (tyre) pincharse. 2. (explode) estallar. ♦ vt (gen) reventar; (tyre) pinchar. ♦ n (of gunfire, enthusiasm) estallido m; (of song) clamor m. ► **burst into** vt fus 1. (tears, song): to ~ into tears/song romper a llorar/cantar. 2. (flames) estallar en. ► **burst out** vi (begin suddenly): to ~ out laughing/crying echarse a reír/llorar.

bursting ['bɜːstiŋ] adj 1. (full) lleno (na) a estallar. 2. (with emotion): ~ with rebosando de. 3. (eager): to be ~ to do sthg estar deseando hacer algo.

bury ['beri] vt 1. (in ground) enterrar. 2. (hide - face, memory) ocultar.

bus [bʌs] n autobús m; by ~ en autobús.

bush [buʃ] n 1. (plant) arbusto m. 2. (open country): the ~ el campo abierto, el monte. 3. phr: to beat about the ~ andarse por las ramas.

bushy ['buʃi] adj poblado(da), espeso (sa).

business ['biznis] n 1. (U) (commerce, amount of trade) negocios mpl; to be away on ~ estar en viaje de negocios; to mean ~ inf ir en serio; to go out of ~ quebrar. 2. (company) negocio m, empresa f. 3. (concern, duty) oficio m, ocupación f; mind your own ~! inf ¡no te metas donde no te llaman! 4. (U) (affair, matter) asunto m.

business class n clase f preferente.

businesslike ['biznislaik] adj formal, práctico(ca).

businessman ['biznismæn] (pl -men [-men]) n empresario m, hombre m de negocios.

business trip n viaje m de negocios.

businesswoman ['biznis,wumən] (pl -women [-,wimin]) n empresaria f, mujer f de negocios.

busker ['bʌskəʳ] n Br músico m ambulante or callejero.

bus-shelter n marquesina f (de parada de autobús).

bus station n estación f de autobuses.

bus stop n parada f de autobús, paradero m Amer.

bust [bʌst] (pt & pp -ed OR bust) ♦ adj inf 1. (broken) fastidiado(da), roto(ta). 2. (bankrupt): to go ~ quebrar. ♦ n (bosom, statue) busto m. ♦ vt inf (break) fastidiar, estropear.

bustle ['bʌsl] ♦ n bullicio m. ♦ vi apresurarse.

busy ['bizi] ♦ adj 1. (active) activo(va). 2. (hectic - life, week) ajetreado(da); (- town, office) concurrido(da). 3. (occupied) ocupado(da); to be ~ doing sthg estar ocupado haciendo algo. ♦ vt: to ~ o.s. (doing sthg) ocuparse (haciendo algo).

busybody ['bizi,bɒdi] n pej entrometido m, -da f.

busy signal n Am (TELEC) señal f de comunicando.

but [bʌt] ♦ conj pero; we were poor ~ happy éramos pobres pero felices; she owns not one ~ two houses tiene no una sino dos casas. ♦ prep menos, excepto; everyone ~ Jane was there todos estaban allí, menos Jane; we've had nothing ~ bad weather no hemos tenido más que mal tiempo; he has no one ~ himself to blame la culpa no es de otro más que él OR sino de él. ♦ adv fml: had I known de haberlo sabido; we can ~ try por intentarlo que no quede. ► **but**

for *conj* de no ser por.

butcher ['butʃər] ◆ *n* **1.** (*occupation*) carnicero *m*, -ra *f*; **~'s (shop)** carnicería *f*. **2.** (*indiscriminate killer*) carnicero *m*, -ra *f*, asesino *m*, -na *f*. ◆ *vt* (*animal - for meat*) matar; *fig* (*kill indiscriminately*) hacer una carnicería con.

butler ['bʌtlər] *n* mayordomo *m*.

butt [bʌt] ◆ *n* **1.** (*of cigarette, cigar*) colilla *f*. **2.** (*of rifle*) culata *f*. **3.** (*for water*) tina *f*. **4.** (*target*) blanco *m*. ◆ *vt* topetar. ▶ **butt in** *vi* (*interrupt*): **to ~ in on sb** cortar a alguien; **to ~ in on sthg** entrometerse en algo.

butter ['bʌtər] ◆ *n* mantequilla *f*. ◆ *vt* untar con mantequilla.

buttercup ['bʌtəkʌp] *n* ranúnculo *m*.

butter dish *n* mantequera *f*.

butterfly ['bʌtəflaɪ] *n* **1.** (*insect*) mariposa *f*. **2.** (*swimming style*) (estilo *m*) mariposa *f*.

buttocks ['bʌtəks] *npl* nalgas *fpl*.

button ['bʌtn] ◆ *n* **1.** (*gen & *COMPUT) botón *m*. **2.** *Am* (*badge*) chapa *f*. ◆ *vt* = **button up.** ▶ **button up** *vt sep* abotonar, abrochar.

button mushroom *n* champiñón *m* pequeño.

buttress ['bʌtrɪs] *n* contrafuerte *m*.

buxom ['bʌksəm] *adj* (*woman*) maciza, pechugona.

buy [baɪ] (*pt & pp* bought) ◆ *vt lit & fig* comprar; **to ~ sthg from sb** comprar algo a alguien. ◆ *n* compra *f*. ▶ **buy up** *vt sep* acaparar.

buyer ['baɪər] *n* (*purchaser*) comprador *m*, -ra *f*.

buyout ['baɪaʊt] *n* adquisición de la mayoría de las acciones de una empresa.

buzz [bʌz] ◆ *n* (*of insect, machinery*) zumbido *m*; (*of conversation*) rumor *m*; **to give sb a ~** *inf* (*on phone*) dar un toque OR llamar a alguien. ◆ *vi* **1.** (*make noise*) zumbar. **2.** *fig* (*be active*): **to ~ (with)** bullir (de).

buzzer ['bʌzər] *n* timbre *m*.

buzzword ['bʌzwɜːd] *n inf* palabra *f* de moda.

by [baɪ] *prep* **1.** (*indicating cause, agent*) por; **caused/written ~** causado/escrito por; **a book ~ Joyce** un libro de Joyce. **2.** (*indicating means, method, manner*): **to travel ~ bus/train/plane/ship** viajar en autobús/tren/avión/barco; **to pay ~ cheque** pagar con cheque; **he got rich ~ buying land** se hizo rico comprando terrenos; **~ profession/trade** de profesión/oficio. **3.** (*beside, close to*); **~**

the sea junto al mar. **4.** (*past*) por delante de; **to walk ~ sb/sthg** pasear por delante de alguien/algo; **we drove ~ the castle** pasamos por el castillo (conduciendo). **5.** (*via, through*) por; **we entered ~ the back door** entramos por la puerta trasera. **6.** (*with time - at or before, during*) para; **I'll be there ~ eight** estaré allí para las ocho; **~ now** ya; **~ day/night** de día/noche. **7.** (*according to*) según; **~ law/my standards** según la ley/mis criterios. **8.** (*in division*) entre; (*in multiplication, measurements*) por; **divide 20 ~ 2** dividir 20 entre 2; **multiply 20 ~ 2** multiplicar 20 por 2; **twelve feet ~ ten** doce pies por diez. **9.** (*in quantities, amounts*) por; **~ the thousand** OR **thousands** por miles; **~ the day/hour** por día/horas; **prices were cut ~ 50%** los precios fueron rebajados (en) un 50%. **10.** (*indicating gradual change*): **day ~ day** día a OR tras día; **one ~ one** uno a uno. **11.** (*to explain a word or expression*): **what do you mean ~ 'all right'?** ¿qué quieres decir con 'bien'?; **what do you understand ~ the word 'subsidiarity'?** ¿qué entiendes por 'subsidiariedad'? **12.** *phr*: **(all) ~ oneself** solo(la); **did you do it all ~ yourself?** ¿lo hiciste tú solo?

bye(-bye) [baɪ(baɪ)] *excl inf* ¡hasta luego!

bye-election = **by-election.**

byelaw ['baɪlɔː] = **bylaw.**

by-election *n* elección *f* parcial.

bygone ['baɪgɒn] *adj* pasado(da). ▶ **bygones** *npl*: **let ~s be ~s** lo pasado, pasado está.

bylaw ['baɪlɔː] *n* reglamento *m* OR estatuto *m* local.

bypass ['baɪpɑːs] ◆ *n* **1.** (*road*) carretera *f* OR vía *f* de circunvalación. **2.** (MED): **~ (operation)** (operación *f* de) by-pass *m*. ◆ *vt* evitar.

by-product *n* **1.** (*product*) subproducto *m*. **2.** (*consequence*) consecuencia *f*.

bystander ['baɪ,stændər] *n* espectador *m*, -ra *f*.

byte [baɪt] *n* (COMPUT) byte *m*, octeto *m*.

byword ['baɪwɜːd] *n*: **~ (for)** símbolo *m* (de), equivalente *m* (a).

C

c¹ (pl **c's** OR **cs**), **C** (pl **C's** OR **Cs**) [siː] n (letter) c f, C f. ► **C** n 1. (MUS) do m. 2. (abbr of **celsius, centigrade**) C.

c² (abbr of **cent(s)**) cént.

c. (abbr of **circa**) h.

c/a (abbr of **current account**) c/c.

cab [kæb] n 1. (taxi) taxi m. 2. (of lorry) cabina f.

cabaret ['kæbəreɪ] n cabaret m.

cabbage ['kæbɪdʒ] n col f, repollo m.

cabin ['kæbɪn] n 1. (on ship) camarote m. 2. (in aircraft) cabina f. 3. (house) cabaña f.

cabin class n clase f económica OR de cámara.

cabinet ['kæbɪnɪt] n 1. (cupboard) armario m. 2. (POL) consejo m de ministros, gabinete m.

cable ['keɪbl] ◆ n 1. (rope, wire) cable m. 2. (telegram) cablegrama m. ◆ vt cablegrafiar.

cable car n teleférico m.

cable television, cable TV n televisión f por cable.

cache [kæʃ] n 1. (store) alijo m. 2. (COMPUT) memoria f de acceso rápido.

cackle ['kækl] vi 1. (hen) cacarear. 2. (person) reírse.

cactus ['kæktəs] (pl **-tuses** OR **-ti** [-taɪ]) n cactus m inv.

cadet [kə'det] n cadete m.

cadge [kædʒ] Br inf vt: **to ~ sthg (off** OR **from sb)** gorronear algo (a alguien).

caesarean (section) Br, **cesarean (section)** Am [sɪ'zeərɪən-] n cesárea f.

cafe, café ['kæfeɪ] n café m, cafetería f.

cafeteria [,kæfɪ'tɪərɪə] n (restaurante m) autoservicio m, cantina f.

caffeine ['kæfiːn] n cafeína f.

cage [keɪdʒ] n jaula f.

cagey ['keɪdʒɪ] (compar **-ier**, superl **-iest**) adj inf reservado(da).

cagoule [kə'guːl] n Br chubasquero m.

cajole [kə'dʒəʊl] vt: **to ~ sb (into doing sthg)** engatusar a alguien (para que haga algo).

cake [keɪk] n 1. (sweet food) pastel m, tarta f; **to be a piece of ~** inf ser pan comido. 2. (of fish, potato) medallón m

empanado. 3. (of soap) pastilla f.

caked [keɪkt] adj: **~ with mud** cubierto (ta) de barro seco.

calcium ['kælsɪəm] n calcio m.

calculate ['kælkjʊleɪt] vt 1. (work out) calcular. 2. (plan): **to be ~d to do sthg** estar pensado(da) para hacer algo.

calculating ['kælkjʊleɪtɪŋ] adj pej calculador(ra).

calculation [,kælkjʊ'leɪʃn] n cálculo m.

calculator ['kælkjʊleɪtər] n calculadora f.

calendar ['kælɪndər] n calendario m.

calendar month n mes m civil.

calendar year n año m civil.

calf [kɑːf] (pl **calves**) n 1. (young animal - of cow) ternero m, -ra f, becerro m, -rra f; (- of other animals) cría f. 2. (leather) piel f de becerro. 3. (of leg) pantorrilla f.

calibre, caliber Am ['kælɪbər] n 1. (quality) nivel m. 2. (size) calibre m.

California [,kælɪ'fɔːnjə] n California.

calipers Am = **callipers**.

call [kɔːl] ◆ n 1. (cry, attraction, vocation) llamada f; (cry of bird) reclamo m. 2. (visit) visita f; **to pay a ~ on sb** hacerle una visita a alguien. 3. (demand): **~ for** petición f de. 4. (summons): **on ~** de guardia. 5. (TELEC) llamada f. ◆ vt 1. (gen & TELEC) llamar; **I'm ~ed Joan** me llamo Joan; **what is it ~ed?** ¿cómo se llama?; **he ~ed my name** me llamó por el nombre; **we'll ~ it £10** dejémoslo en 10 libras. 2. (announce - flight) anunciar; (- strike, meeting, election) convocar. ◆ vi 1. (gen & TELEC) llamar; **who's ~ing?** ¿quién es? 2. (visit) pasar. ► **call back** ◆ vt sep 1. (on phone) volver a llamar. 2. (ask to return) hacer volver. ◆ vi 1. (on phone) volver a llamar. 2. (visit again) volver a pasarse. ► **call for** vt fus 1. (collect) ir a buscar. 2. (demand) pedir. ► **call in** vt sep 1. (send for) llamar. 2. (recall - product, banknotes) retirar; (- loan) exigir pago de. ► **call off** vt sep 1. (meeting, party) suspender; (strike) desconvocar. 2. (dog etc) llamar (para que no ataque). ► **call on** vt fus 1. (visit) visitar. 2. (ask): **to ~ on sb to do sthg** pedir a alguien que haga algo. ► **call out** ◆ vt sep 1. (order to help - troops) movilizar; (- police, firemen) hacer intervenir. 2. (cry out) gritar. ◆ vi gritar. ► **call round** vi pasarse. ► **call up** vt sep 1. (MIL) llamar a filas a. 2. (on telephone) llamar (por teléfono). 3. (COMPUT) hacer aparecer en pantalla.

call box n Br cabina f telefónica.

caller ['kɔːləʳ] n 1. (*visitor*) visita f. 2. (*on telephone*) persona f que llama.

call-in n Am (RADIO & TV) programa m a micrófono abierto.

calling ['kɔːlɪŋ] n 1. (*profession*) profesión f. 2. (*vocation*) vocación f.

calling card n Am tarjeta f de visita.

callipers Br, **calipers** Am ['kælɪpəz] npl 1. (MED) aparato m ortopédico. 2. (MATH) compás m de grueso.

callous ['kæləs] adj despiadado(da).

calm [kɑːm] ◆ adj 1. (*not worried or excited*) tranquilo(la). 2. (*evening, weather*) apacible. 3. (*water*) en calma. ◆ n calma f. ◆ vt calmar. ► **calm down** ◆ vt sep calmar. ◆ vi calmarse.

calmly ['kɑːmlɪ] adv con calma, tranquilamente.

Calor gas® ['kælə-] n Br (gas m) butano m.

calorie ['kælərɪ] n caloría f.

calves [kɑːvz] pl → **calf**.

camber ['kæmbəʳ] n bombeo m.

Cambodia [kæm'bəʊdjə] n Camboya.

camcorder ['kæm,kɔːdəʳ] n camcorder m, cámara f de vídeo con micrófono.

came [keɪm] pt → **come**.

camel ['kæml] n camello m.

cameo ['kæmɪəʊ] (pl -s) n 1. (*jewellery*) camafeo m. 2. (*in acting*) actuación breve y memorable; (*in writing*) excelente descripción.

camera ['kæmərə] n cámara f. ► **in camera** adv fml a puerta cerrada.

cameraman ['kæmərəmæn] (pl -men [-men]) n cámara m.

camouflage ['kæməflɑːʒ] ◆ n camuflaje m. ◆ vt camuflar.

camp [kæmp] ◆ n 1. (gen & MIL) campamento m. 2. (*temporary mass accommodation*) campo m. 3. (*faction*) bando m. ◆ vi acampar. ► **camp out** vi acampar (al aire libre).

campaign [kæm'peɪn] ◆ n campaña f. ◆ vi: **to ~ (for/against)** hacer campaña (a favor de/en contra de).

camp bed n cama f de campaña.

camper ['kæmpəʳ] n 1. (*person*) campista m y f. 2. **~ (van)** caravana f.

campground ['kæmpgraʊnd] n Am camping m.

camping ['kæmpɪŋ] n camping m.

camping site, campsite ['kæmpsaɪt] n camping m.

campus ['kæmpəs] (pl -es) n campus m inv, ciudad f universitaria.

can¹ [kæn] (pt & pp -ned, cont -ning) ◆ n (*for drink, food*) lata f, bote m; (*for oil, paint*) lata f. ◆ vt enlatar.

can² [*weak form* kən, *strong form* kæn] (pt & *conditional* **could**, *negative* **cannot** OR **can't**) modal vb 1. (*be able to*) poder; **~ you come to lunch?** ¿puedes venir a comer?; **~ you see/hear something?** ¿ves/oyes algo? 2. (*know how to*) saber; **I ~ speak French/play the piano** sé hablar francés/tocar el piano. 3. (*indicating permission, in polite requests*) poder; **you ~ use my car if you like** puedes utilizar mi coche si quieres; **~ I speak to John, please?** ¿puedo hablar con John, por favor? 4. (*indicating disbelief, puzzlement*): **you ~'t be serious** estás de broma ¿no?; **what ~ she have done with it?** ¿qué puede haber hecho con ello? 5. (*indicating possibility*) poder; **you could have done it** podrías haberlo hecho; **I could see you tomorrow** podríamos vernos mañana.

Canada ['kænədə] n (el) Canadá.

Canadian [kə'neɪdjən] ◆ adj canadiense. ◆ n (*person*) canadiense m y f.

canal [kə'næl] n canal m, acequia f Amer.

canary [kə'neərɪ] n canario m.

Canary Islands, Canaries [kə'neərɪz] npl: **the ~** las (islas) Canarias.

cancel ['kænsl] vt 1. (*call off*) cancelar, suspender. 2. (*invalidate - cheque, debt*) cancelar. ► **cancel out** vt sep anular.

cancellation [,kænsə'leɪʃn] n suspensión f.

cancer ['kænsəʳ] n (*disease*) cáncer m. ► **Cancer** n Cáncer m.

candelabra [,kændɪ'lɑːbrə] n candelabro m.

candid ['kændɪd] adj franco(ca).

candidate ['kændɪdət] n: **~ (for)** candidato m, -ta f (a).

candle ['kændl] n vela f.

candlelight ['kændllaɪt] n luz f de una vela.

candlelit ['kændllɪt] adj a la luz de las velas.

candlestick ['kændlstɪk] n candelero m.

candour Br, **candor** Am ['kændəʳ] n franqueza f, sinceridad f.

candy ['kændɪ] n 1. (U) (*confectionery*) golosinas fpl; **~ bar** chocolatina f. 2. (*sweet*) caramelo m.

candyfloss Br ['kændɪflɒs], **cotton candy** Am n azúcar m hilado, algodón m.

cane [keɪn] n 1. (U) (*for making furniture, supporting plant*) caña f, mimbre m. 2. (*walking stick*) bastón m. 3. (*for punishment*): **the ~** la vara.

canine ['keɪnaɪn] ♦ *adj* canino(na).
♦ *n*: ~ (**tooth**) (diente *m*) canino *m*,
colmillo *m*.

canister ['kænɪstər] *n* (*for tea*) bote *m*;
(*for film*) lata *f*; (*for gas*) bombona *f*;
smoke ~ bote de humo.

cannabis ['kænəbɪs] *n* canabis *m*.

canned [kænd] *adj* (*food, drink*) enlata-
do(da), en lata.

cannibal ['kænɪbl] *n* caníbal *m y f*.

cannon ['kænən] (*pl inv* OR **-s**) *n* cañón
m.

cannonball ['kænənbɔːl] *n* bala *f* de
cañón.

cannot ['kænɒt] *fml* → **can²**.

canny ['kænɪ] *adj* (*shrewd*) astuto(ta).

canoe [kə'nuː] *n* (*gen*) canoa *f*; (SPORT)
piragua *f*.

canoeing [kə'nuːɪŋ] *n* piragüismo *m*.

canon ['kænən] *n* 1. (*clergyman*) canónigo *m*. 2. (*general principle*) canon *m*.

can opener *n* abrelatas *m inv*.

canopy ['kænəpɪ] *n* (*over bed, seat*)
dosel *m*.

can't [kɑːnt] = **cannot**.

cantankerous [kæn'tæŋkərəs] *adj*
(*person*) refunfuñón(ona); (*behaviour*)
arisco(ca).

canteen [kæn'tiːn] *n* 1. (*restaurant*) cantina *f*. 2. (*set of cutlery*) (juego *m* de)
cubertería *f*.

canter ['kæntər] ♦ *n* medio galope *m*.
♦ *vi* ir a medio galope.

cantilever ['kæntɪliːvər] *n* voladizo *m*.

Cantonese [ˌkæntə'niːz] ♦ *adj* can-
tonés(esa). ♦ *n* 1. (*person*) cantonés *m*,
-esa *f*. 2. (*language*) cantonés *m*.

canvas ['kænvəs] *n* 1. (*cloth*) lona *f*.
2. (*for painting on, finished painting*) lienzo
m.

canvass ['kænvəs] ♦ *vt* 1. (POL) (*person*)
solicitar el voto a. 2. (*opinion*) pulsar.
♦ *vi* solicitar votos yendo de puerta en puerta.

canyon ['kænjən] *n* cañón *m*.

cap [kæp] ♦ *n* 1. (*hat - peaked*) gorra *f*;
(- *with no peak*) gorro *m*. 2. (*on bottle*)
tapón *m*; (*on jar*) tapa *f*; (*on pen*)
capuchón *m*. 3. Br (*contraceptive device*)
diafragma *m*. ♦ *vt* 1. (*top*): **to be capped
with** estar coronado(da) de. 2. (*outdo*):
to ~ **it all** para colmo.

capability [ˌkeɪpə'bɪlətɪ] *n* capacidad
f.

capable ['keɪpəbl] *adj* 1. (*able*): **to be** ~
of sthg/of doing sthg ser capaz de algo/
de hacer algo. 2. (*competent*) hábil.

capacity [kə'pæsɪtɪ] *n* 1. (*gen*): ~ (**for**)
capacidad *f* (de); **seating** ~ aforo *m*; ~

for doing OR **to do sthg** capacidad de
hacer algo. 2. (*position*) calidad *f*.

cape [keɪp] *n* 1. (GEOGR) cabo *m*.
2. (*cloak*) capa *f*.

caper ['keɪpər] *n* 1. (*food*) alcaparra *f*. 2.
inf (*escapade*) treta *f*.

capita → **per capita**.

capital ['kæpɪtl] ♦ *adj* 1. (*letter*) mayúscula. 2. (*punishable by death*) capital. ♦ *n*
1. (*of country, main centre*) capital *f*. 2. ~
(**letter**) mayúscula *f*. 3. (*money*) capital *m*;
to make ~ (**out**) **of** *fig* sacar partido de.

capital expenditure *n* (U) inversión
f de capital.

capital gains tax *n* impuesto *m*
sobre plusvalías.

capital goods *npl* bienes *mpl* de capital.

capitalism ['kæpɪtəlɪzm] *n* capitalismo *m*.

capitalist ['kæpɪtəlɪst] ♦ *adj* capitalista. ♦ *n* capitalista *m y f*.

capitalize, -ise ['kæpɪtəlaɪz] *vi*: **to** ~
on sthg capitalizar algo.

capital punishment *n* (U) pena *f*
capital.

Capitol Hill ['kæpɪtl-] *n* el Capitolio,
ubicación del Congreso estadounidense, en
Washington.

capitulate [kə'pɪtjʊleɪt] *vi*: **to** ~ (**to**)
capitular (ante).

Capricorn ['kæprɪkɔːn] *n* Capricornio
m.

capsize [kæp'saɪz] ♦ *vt* hacer volcar OR
zozobrar. ♦ *vi* volcar, zozobrar.

capsule ['kæpsjuːl] *n* cápsula *f*.

captain ['kæptɪn] *n* capitán *m*, -ana *f*.

caption ['kæpʃn] *n* (*under picture etc*)
leyenda *f*; (*heading*) encabezamiento *m*.

captivate ['kæptɪveɪt] *vt* cautivar.

captive ['kæptɪv] ♦ *adj* 1. (*imprisoned*)
en cautividad. 2. *fig* (*market*) asegurado
(da). ♦ *n* cautivo *m*, -va *f*.

captivity [kæp'tɪvətɪ] *n*: **in** ~ en cautividad, en cautiverio.

captor ['kæptər] *n* apresador *m*, -ra *f*.

capture ['kæptʃər] ♦ *vt* 1. (*gen* & COM-
PUT) capturar. 2. (*audience, share of market*)
hacerse con; (*city*) tomar. 3. (*scene, mood,*
attention) captar. ♦ *n* captura *f*.

car [kɑːr] ♦ *n* 1. (*motorcar*) coche *m*,
automóvil *m*, carro *m* Amer. 2. (*on train*)
vagón *m*. ♦ *comp* (*door, tyre etc*) del
coche; (*industry*) del automóvil; (*acci-*
dent) de automóvil.

carafe [kə'ræf] *n* garrafa *f*.

caramel ['kærəmel] *n* 1. (*burnt sugar*)
caramelo *m* (líquido), azúcar *m* quema-

do. **2.** (*sweet*) tofe *m*.

carat ['kærət] *n* Br quilate *m*.

caravan ['kærəvæn] *n* caravana *f*, casa *f* rodante Amer.

caravan site *n* Br camping *m* para caravanas OR roulottes.

carbohydrate [ˌkɑːbəʊˈhaɪdreɪt] *n* (CHEM) hidrato *m* de carbono. ▶ **carbohydrates** *npl* (*in food*) féculas *fpl*.

carbon ['kɑːbən] *n* (*element*) carbono *m*.

carbonated ['kɑːbəneɪtɪd] *adj* con gas.

carbon copy *n* (*document*) copia *f* en papel carbón; *fig* (*exact copy*) calco *m*.

carbon dioxide [-daɪˈɒksaɪd] *n* bióxido *m* OR dióxido *m* de carbono.

carbon monoxide [-mɒˈnɒksaɪd] *n* monóxido *m* de carbono.

carbon paper *n* (U) papel *m* carbón.

car-boot sale *n* venta de objetos usados colocados en el portaequipajes del coche.

carburettor Br, **carburetor** Am [ˌkɑːbəˈretəʳ] *n* carburador *m*.

carcass ['kɑːkəs] *n* (*gen*) cadáver *m* (de animal); (*of bird*) carcasa *f*; (*at butcher's*) canal *m*.

card [kɑːd] *n* **1.** (*playing card*) carta *f*, naipe *m*. **2.** (*for information, greetings, computers*) tarjeta *f*. **3.** (*postcard*) postal *f*. **4.** (*cardboard*) cartulina *f*. ▶ **cards** *npl* las cartas, los naipes. ▶ **on the cards** Br, **in the cards** Am *adv inf* más que probable.

cardboard ['kɑːdbɔːd] ◆ *n* (U) cartón *m*. ◆ *comp* de cartón.

cardboard box *n* caja *f* de cartón.

cardiac ['kɑːdɪæk] *adj* cardíaco(ca).

cardigan ['kɑːdɪgən] *n* rebeca *f*.

cardinal ['kɑːdɪnl] ◆ *adj* capital. ◆ *n* (RELIG) cardenal *m*.

card index *n* Br fichero *m*.

card table *n* mesita *f* plegable (*para jugar a cartas*).

care [keəʳ] ◆ *n* **1.** (*gen*) cuidado *m*; in sb's ~ al cargo OR cuidado de alguien; **to be in/be taken into** ~ estar/ser internado en un centro de protección de menores; **to take** ~ **of** (*look after*) cuidar de; (*deal with*) encargarse de; **take** ~! ¡nos vemos!, ¡cuídate!; **to take** ~ **(to do sthg)** tener cuidado (de hacer algo). **2.** (*cause of worry*) preocupación *f*. ◆ *vi* **1.** (*be concerned*): **to** ~ **(about)** preocuparse (de OR por). **2.** (*mind*): **I don't** ~ no me importa. ▶ **care of** *prep* al cuidado de, en casa de. ▶ **care for** *vt fus dated* (*like*): **I don't** ~ **for cheese** no me gusta el queso.

career [kəˈrɪəʳ] ◆ *n* carrera *f*. ◆ *vi* ir a

toda velocidad.

careers adviser *n* persona que aconseja sobre salidas profesionales.

carefree ['keəfriː] *adj* despreocupado (da).

careful ['keəfʊl] *adj* (*gen*) cuidadoso (sa); (*driver*) prudente; (*work*) esmerado (da); **(be)** ~! ¡cuidado!; **to be** ~ **with** ser mirado OR cuidadoso con; **to be** ~ **to do sthg** tener cuidado de hacer algo.

carefully ['keəflɪ] *adv* **1.** (*cautiously*) con cuidado, cuidadosamente. **2.** (*thoroughly*) detenidamente.

careless ['keəlɪs] *adj* **1.** (*inattentive*) descuidado(da). **2.** (*unconcerned*) despreocupado(da).

caress [kəˈres] ◆ *n* caricia *f*. ◆ *vt* acariciar.

caretaker ['keəˌteɪkəʳ] *n* Br conserje *m* y *f*.

car ferry *n* transbordador *m* de coches.

cargo ['kɑːgəʊ] (*pl* **-es** OR **-s**) *n* carga *f*, cargamento *m*.

car hire *n* Br alquiler *m* de coches.

Caribbean [Br kærɪˈbiːən, Am kəˈrɪbɪən] *n*: **the** ~ **(Sea)** el (mar) Caribe.

caring ['keərɪŋ] *adj* solícito(ta), dedicado(da).

carnage ['kɑːnɪdʒ] *n* carnicería *f*.

carnal ['kɑːnl] *adj literary* carnal.

carnation [kɑːˈneɪʃn] *n* clavel *m*.

carnival ['kɑːnɪvl] *n* carnaval *m*.

carnivorous [kɑːˈnɪvərəs] *adj* carnívoro(ra).

carol ['kærəl] *n* villancico *m*.

carousel [ˌkærəˈsel] *n* **1.** (*at fair*) tiovivo *m*. **2.** (*at airport*) cinta *f* transportadora.

carp [kɑːp] (*pl inv* OR **-s**) ◆ *n* carpa *f*. ◆ *vi*: **to** ~ **(about)** refunfuñar OR renegar (de).

car park *n* Br aparcamiento *m*, parqueadero *m* Amer.

carpenter ['kɑːpəntəʳ] *n* carpintero *m*, -ra *f*.

carpentry ['kɑːpəntrɪ] *n* carpintería *f*.

carpet ['kɑːpɪt] ◆ *n lit & fig* alfombra *f*; **fitted** ~ moqueta *f*. ◆ *vt* (*fit with carpet*) enmoquetar.

carpet slipper *n* zapatilla *f*.

carpet sweeper [-ˈswiːpəʳ] *n* cepillo *m* mecánico (de alfombras).

car phone *n* teléfono *m* de coche.

car rental *n* Am alquiler *m* de coches.

carriage ['kærɪdʒ] *n* **1.** (*horsedrawn vehicle*) carruaje *m*. **2.** Br (*railway coach*) vagón *m*. **3.** (*transport of goods*) transporte *m*; ~ **paid** OR **free** Br porte pagado. **4.** (*on typewriter*) carro *m*.

carriage return *n* retorno *m* de carro.

carriageway ['kærɪdʒweɪ] *n* Br carril *m*.

carrier ['kærɪər] *n* **1.** (COMM) transportista *m y f*. **2.** (*of disease*) portador *m*, -ra *f*. **3.** = **carrier bag**.

carrier bag *n* bolsa *f* (*de papel o plástico*).

carrot ['kærət] *n* **1.** (*vegetable*) zanahoria *f*. **2.** inf (*incentive*) aliciente *m*.

carry ['kærɪ] ◆ *vt* **1.** (*transport*) llevar. **2.** (*disease*) transmitir. **3.** (*involve*) acarrear, conllevar. **4.** (*motion, proposal*) aprobar. **5.** (*be pregnant with*) estar embarazada de. **6.** (MATH) llevarse. ◆ *vi* (*sound*) oírse. ► **carry away** *vt fus*: **to get carried away** exaltarse. ► **carry forward** *vt sep* llevar a la página siguiente; **carried forward** suma y sigue. ► **carry off** *vt sep* **1.** (*make a success of*) llevar a cabo. **2.** (*win*) llevarse. ► **carry on** ◆ *vt fus* **1.** (*continue*) continuar, seguir; **to ~ on doing sthg** continuar OR seguir haciendo algo. **2.** (*conversation*) sostener. ◆ *vi* **1.** (*continue*): **to ~ on (with)** continuar OR seguir (con). **2.** inf (*make a fuss*) exagerar la nota. ► **carry out** *vt fus* **1.** (*perform*) llevar a cabo. **2.** (*fulfil*) cumplir. ► **carry through** *vt sep* (*accomplish*) llevar a cabo.

carryall ['kærɪɔːl] *n* Am bolsa *f* de viaje.

carrycot ['kærɪkɒt] *n* moisés *m*.

carry-out *n* comida *f* para llevar.

carsick ['kɑːˌsɪk] *adj* mareado(da) (*al ir en coche*).

cart [kɑːt] ◆ *n* carro *m*, carreta *f*. ◆ *vt* inf acarrear.

carton ['kɑːtn] *n* **1.** (*strong cardboard box*) caja *f* de cartón. **2.** (*for liquids*) cartón *m*, envase *m*.

cartoon [kɑːˈtuːn] *n* **1.** (*satirical drawing*) chiste *m* (en viñeta). **2.** (*comic strip*) tira *f* cómica, historieta *f*. **3.** (*film*) dibujos *mpl* animados.

cartridge ['kɑːtrɪdʒ] *n* **1.** (*for gun, camera*) cartucho *m*. **2.** (*for pen*) recambio *m*.

cartwheel ['kɑːtwiːl] *n* voltereta *f* lateral.

carve [kɑːv] ◆ *vt* **1.** (*wood*) tallar; (*stone*) esculpir. **2.** (*meat*) trinchar. **3.** (*cut*) grabar. ◆ *vi* trinchar. ► **carve out** *vt sep* (*niche, place*) conquistar. ► **carve up** *vt sep* repartir.

carving ['kɑːvɪŋ] *n* **1.** (*art, work - wooden*) tallado *m*; (*- stone*) labrado *m*.

2. (*object - wooden*) talla *f*; (*- stone*) escultura *f*.

carving knife *n* cuchillo *m* de trinchar.

car wash *n* lavado *m* de coches.

case [keɪs] *n* **1.** (*gen*) caso *m*; **to be the ~** ser el caso; **in that/which ~** en ese/cuyo caso; **as OR whatever the ~ may be** según sea el caso; **in ~ of** en caso de. **2.** (*argument*) argumento *m*; **the ~ for/against (sthg)** los argumentos a favor/en contra (de algo). **3.** (JUR) (*trial, inquiry*) pleito *m*, causa *f*. **4.** (*container - of leather*) funda *f*; (*- of hard material*) estuche *m*. **5.** Br (*suitcase*) maleta *f*. ► **in any case** *adv* en cualquier caso. ► **in case** *conj & adv* por si acaso.

cash [kæʃ] ◆ *n* **1.** (*notes and coins*) (dinero *m*) efectivo *m*; **to pay (in) ~** pagar al contado OR en efectivo. **2.** inf (*money*) dinero *m*. **3.** (*payment*): **~ in advance** pago *m* al contado por adelantado; **~ on delivery** entrega *f* contra reembolso. ◆ *vt* cobrar, hacer efectivo. ► **cash in** *vi*: **to ~ in on** inf sacar partido de.

cash and carry *n* almacén *m* de venta al por mayor.

cashbook ['kæʃbʊk] *n* libro *m* de caja.

cash box *n* caja *f* con cerradura (para el dinero).

cash card *n* tarjeta *f* de cajero automático.

cash desk *n* Br caja *f*.

cash dispenser [-dɪˈspensər] *n* cajero *m* automático.

cashew (nut) ['kæʃuː-] *n* (nuez *f* de) anacardo *m*.

cashier [kæˈʃɪər] *n* cajero *m*, -ra *f*.

cash machine = **cash dispenser**.

cashmere [kæʃˈmɪər] *n* cachemira *f*.

cash register *n* caja *f* (registradora).

casing ['keɪsɪŋ] *n* revestimiento *m*.

casino [kəˈsiːnəʊ] (*pl* -s) *n* casino *m*.

cask [kɑːsk] *n* tonel *m*, barril *m*.

casket ['kɑːskɪt] *n* **1.** (*for jewels*) estuche *m*. **2.** Am (*coffin*) ataúd *m*.

casserole ['kæsərəʊl] *n* **1.** (*stew*) guiso *m*. **2.** (*pan*) cazuela *f*, cacerola *f*.

cassette [kæˈset] *n* cinta *f*, casete *f*.

cassette player *n* casete *m*, magnetófono *m*.

cassette recorder *n* casete *m*, magnetófono *m*.

cast [kɑːst] (*pt & pp* **cast**) ◆ *n* (*of play, film*) reparto *m*. ◆ *vt* **1.** (*look*) echar, lanzar; **to ~ doubt on sthg** poner algo en duda. **2.** (*light*) irradiar; (*shadow*) proyectar. **3.** (*throw*) arrojar, lanzar. **4.** (*choose for play*): **to ~ sb as** asignar a alguien el papel de. **5.** (*vote*) emitir. **6.** (*metal, statue*) fundir. ▶ **cast aside** vt sep (*person*) abandonar; (*idea*) rechazar. ▶ **cast off** vi (NAUT) soltar amarras.

castanets [ˌkæstəˈnets] npl castañuelas fpl.

castaway [ˈkɑːstəweɪ] n náufrago m, -ga f.

caste [kɑːst] n casta f.

caster [ˈkɑːstər] n (*wheel*) ruedecilla f.

caster sugar n Br azúcar m extrafino.

Castile [kæsˈtiːl], **Castilla** [kæsˈtiʎa] n Castilla.

casting vote [ˈkɑːstɪŋ-] n voto m de calidad.

cast iron n hierro m fundido.

castle [ˈkɑːsl] n **1.** (*building*) castillo m. **2.** (*in chess*) torre f.

castor [ˈkɑːstər] = **caster**.

castor oil n aceite m de ricino.

castor sugar = **caster sugar**.

castrate [kæsˈtreɪt] vt castrar.

casual [ˈkæʒʊəl] adj **1.** (*relaxed, indifferent*) despreocupado(da). **2.** pej (*offhand*) descuidado(da), informal. **3.** (*chance - visitor*) ocasional; (*- remark*) casual. **4.** (*informal*) de sport, informal. **5.** (*irregular - labourer etc*) eventual.

casually [ˈkæʒʊəlɪ] adv **1.** (*in a relaxed manner, indifferently*) con aire despreocupado. **2.** (*informally*) informalmente.

casualty [ˈkæʒjʊəltɪ] n **1.** (*gen*) víctima f. **2.** (U) (*ward*) urgencias fpl.

casualty department n unidad f de urgencias.

cat [kæt] n **1.** (*domestic*) gato m, -ta f. **2.** (*wild*) felino m.

Catalan [ˈkætəˌlæn] ◆ adj catalán(ana). ◆ n **1.** (*person*) catalán m, -ana f. **2.** (*language*) catalán m.

catalogue Br, **catalog** Am [ˈkætəlɒg] ◆ n **1.** (*of items*) catálogo m. **2.** fig (*list*) serie f, cadena f. ◆ vt **1.** (*make official list of*) catalogar. **2.** fig (*list*) enumerar.

Catalonia [ˌkætəˈləʊnɪə] n Cataluña.

Catalonian [ˌkætəˈləʊnɪən] ◆ adj catalán(ana). ◆ n (*person*) catalán m, -ana f.

catalyst [ˈkætəlɪst] n lit & fig catalizador m.

catalytic convertor [ˌkætəˈlɪtɪk kənˈvɜːtər] n catalizador m.

catapult [ˈkætəpʌlt] Br n **1.** (HIST) (*hand-held*) tirachinas m inv. **2.** (HIST) (*machine*) catapulta f.

cataract [ˈkætərækt] n (*in eye, water-*

fall) catarata f.

catarrh [kəˈtɑːr] n (U) catarro m.

catastrophe [kəˈtæstrəfɪ] n catástrofe f.

catch [kætʃ] (pt & pp **caught**) ◆ vt **1.** (*gen*) coger, agarrar Amer. **2.** (*fish*) pescar; (*stop - person*) parar. **3.** (*be in time for*): **to ~ the (last) post** Br llegar a la (última) recogida del correo. **4.** (*hear clearly*) entender, llegar a oír. **5.** (*interest, imagination*) despertar. **6.** (*see*): **to ~ sight** OR **a glimpse of** alcanzar a ver. **7.** (*hook - shirt etc*) engancharse; (*shut in door - finger*) pillarse. **8.** (*strike*) golpear. ◆ vi **1.** (*become hooked, get stuck*) engancharse. **2.** (*start to burn*) prenderse. ◆ n **1.** (*of ball etc*) parada f. **2.** (*of fish*) pesca f, captura f. **3.** (*fastener*) pestillo m. **4.** (*snag*) trampa f. ▶ **catch on** vi **1.** (*become popular*) hacerse popular. **2.** inf (*understand*): **to ~ on (to)** caer en la cuenta (de). ▶ **catch out** vt sep (*trick*) pillar en un error. ▶ **catch up** ◆ vt sep alcanzar. ◆ vi: **we'll soon ~ up** pronto nos pondremos a la misma altura; **to ~ up on** (*sleep*) recuperar; (*work, reading*) ponerse al día con. ▶ **catch up with** vt fus **1.** (*group etc*) alcanzar. **2.** (*criminal*) pillar, descubrir.

catching [ˈkætʃɪŋ] adj contagioso(sa).

catchment area [ˈkætʃmənt-] n Br zona f de captación.

catchphrase [ˈkætʃfreɪz] n muletilla f.

catchy [ˈkætʃɪ] adj pegadizo(za).

categorically [ˌkætɪˈgɒrɪklɪ] adv (*state*) categóricamente; (*deny*) rotundamente.

category [ˈkætəgərɪ] n categoría f.

cater [ˈkeɪtər] vi proveer comida. ▶ **cater for** vt fus Br (*tastes, needs*) atender a; (*social group*) estar destinado(da) a; **I hadn't ~ed for that** no había contado con eso. ▶ **cater to** vt fus complacer.

caterer [ˈkeɪtərər] n proveedor m, -ra f.

catering [ˈkeɪtərɪŋ] n (*at wedding etc*) servicio m de banquetes; (*trade*) hostelería f.

caterpillar [ˈkætəpɪlər] n oruga f.

caterpillar tracks npl (rodado m de) oruga f.

cathedral [kəˈθiːdrəl] n catedral f.

Catholic [ˈkæθlɪk] ◆ adj católico(ca). ◆ n católico m, -ca f. ▶ **catholic** adj diverso(sa).

Catseyes® [ˈkætsaɪz] npl Br catafaros mpl.

cattle [ˈkætl] npl ganado m (vacuno).

catty [ˈkætɪ] adj inf pej (*spiteful*)

rencoroso(sa).

catwalk ['kætwɔːk] n pasarela f.

caucus ['kɔːkəs] n (political group) comité m. ▶ **Caucus** n Am congreso de los principales partidos estadounidenses.

caught [kɔːt] pt & pp → **catch**.

cauliflower ['kɒlɪ̩flaʊəʳ] n coliflor f.

cause [kɔːz] ◆ n 1. (gen) causa f. 2. (grounds): ~ (for) motivo m (para); ~ for complaint motivo de queja; ~ to do sthg motivo para hacer algo. ◆ vt causar; to ~ sb to do sthg hacer que alguien haga algo.

caustic ['kɔːstɪk] adj 1. (CHEM) cáustico(ca). 2. (comment) mordaz, hiriente.

caution ['kɔːʃn] ◆ n 1. (U) (care) precaución f, cautela f. 2. (warning) advertencia f. ◆ vt 1. (warn - against danger) prevenir; (- against behaving rudely etc) advertir. 2. Br (subj: policeman): to ~ sb (for) amonestar a alguien (por).

cautious ['kɔːʃəs] adj prudente, precavido(da).

cavalier [̩kævə'lɪəʳ] adj arrogante, desdeñoso(sa).

cavalry ['kævlrɪ] n caballería f.

cave [keɪv] n cueva f. ▶ **cave in** vi (roof, ceiling) hundirse.

caveman ['keɪvmæn] (pl **-men** [-men]) n cavernícola m y f.

caviar(e) ['kævɪɑːʳ] n caviar m.

cavity ['kævətɪ] n 1. (in object, structure) cavidad f. 2. (in tooth) caries f inv.

cavort [kə'vɔːt] vi retozar, brincar.

CB n abbr of **citizens' band**.

CBI abbr of **Confederation of British Industry**.

cc ◆ n (abbr of **cubic centimetre**) cc. ◆ (abbr of **carbon copy**) cc.

CD n (abbr of **compact disc**) CD m.

CD player n reproductor m de CD.

CD-ROM [̩siːdiː'rɒm] (abbr of **compact disc read only memory**) n CD-ROM m.

cease [siːs] fml ◆ vt cesar; to ~ doing OR to do sthg dejar de hacer algo. ◆ vi cesar.

cease-fire n alto m el fuego.

ceaseless ['siːslɪs] adj fml incesante.

cedar (tree) ['siːdəʳ-] n cedro m.

ceiling ['siːlɪŋ] n 1. (of room) techo m. 2. (limit) tope m, límite m.

celebrate ['selɪbreɪt] ◆ vt celebrar. ◆ vi divertirse.

celebrated ['selɪbreɪtɪd] adj célebre.

celebration [̩selɪ'breɪʃn] n 1. (U) (activity, feeling) celebración f. 2. (event) fiesta f, festejo m.

celebrity [sɪ'lebrətɪ] n celebridad f.

celery ['selərɪ] n apio m.

celibate ['selɪbət] adj célibe.

cell [sel] n 1. (BIOL, COMPUT & POL) célula f. 2. (prisoner's, nun's or monk's room) celda f.

cellar ['seləʳ] n 1. (basement) sótano m. 2. (stock of wine) bodega f.

cello ['tʃeləʊ] (pl **-s**) n violoncelo m.

Cellophane® ['seləfeɪn] n celofán® m.

Celsius ['selsɪəs] adj centígrado(da); **20 degrees** ~ 20 grados centígrados.

Celt [kelt] n celta m y f.

Celtic ['keltɪk] ◆ adj celta. ◆ n celta m.

cement [sɪ'ment] ◆ n 1. (for concrete) cemento m. 2. (glue) cola f. ◆ vt 1. (glue) encolar. 2. (agreement, relationship) cimentar, fortalecer.

cement mixer n hormigonera f.

cemetery ['semɪtrɪ] n cementerio m.

censor ['sensəʳ] ◆ n censor m, -ra f. ◆ vt censurar.

censorship ['sensəʃɪp] n censura f.

censure ['senʃəʳ] vt censurar.

census ['sensəs] (pl **-uses**) n censo m.

cent [sent] n centavo m.

centenary Br [sen'tiːnərɪ], **centennial** Am [sen'tenjəl] n centenario m.

center Am = **centre**.

centigrade ['sentɪgreɪd] adj centígrado(da); **20 degrees** ~ 20 grados centígrados.

centilitre Br, **centiliter** Am ['sentɪ̩liːtəʳ] n centilitro m.

centimetre Br, **centimeter** Am ['sentɪ̩miːtəʳ] n centímetro m.

centipede ['sentɪpiːd] n ciempiés m inv.

central ['sentrəl] adj 1. (gen) central; **in** ~ **Spain** en el centro de España. 2. (easily reached) céntrico(ca).

Central America n Centroamérica.

central heating n calefacción f central.

centralize, -ise ['sentrəlaɪz] vt centralizar.

central locking [-'lɒkɪŋ] n cierre m centralizado.

central reservation n Br mediana f.

centre Br, **center** Am ['sentəʳ] ◆ n centro m; **the** ~ (POL) el centro. ◆ adj 1. (middle) central. 2. (POL) centrista. ◆ vt centrar.

centre back n defensa m y f central.

centre forward n delantero m, -ra f centro (inv).

centre half = **centre back**.

century ['sentʃʊrɪ] n siglo m.

ceramic [sɪ'ræmɪk] adj de cerámica,

cerámico(ca). ▶ **ceramics** n cerámica f.

cereal ['sɪərɪəl] n 1. (crop) cereal m. 2. (breakfast food) cereales mpl.

ceremonial [ˌserɪ'məʊnjəl] adj ceremonial.

ceremony ['serɪmənɪ] n ceremonia f; **to stand on ~** andarse con cumplidos OR ceremonias.

certain ['sɜːtn] adj 1. (gen) seguro(ra); he's ~ **to be late** (es) seguro que llega tarde; **to be ~ (of)** estar seguro (de); **to make ~ (of)** asegurarse (de); **for ~** seguro, con toda seguridad. 2. (particular, some) cierto(ta); **to a ~ extent** hasta cierto punto. 3. (named person): **a ~ ...** un (una) tal ...

certainly ['sɜːtnlɪ] adv desde luego; ~ **not!** ¡claro que no!

certainty ['sɜːtntɪ] n seguridad f.

certificate [sə'tɪfɪkət] n (gen) certificado m; (SCH & UNIV) diploma m, título m; (of birth, death) partida f.

certified ['sɜːtɪfaɪd] adj (document) certificado(da); (person) diplomado(da).

certified mail n Am correo m certificado.

certified public accountant n Am contable diplomado m, contable diplomada f.

certify ['sɜːtɪfaɪ] vt 1. (declare true) certificar. 2. (declare insane) declarar demente.

cervical [sə'vaɪkl] adj cervical.

cervical smear n citología f, frotis f cervical.

cervix ['sɜːvɪks] (pl -ices [-ɪsiːz]) n (of womb) cuello m del útero.

cesarean (section) = **caesarean (section).**

cesspit ['sespɪt], **cesspool** ['sespuːl] n pozo m negro.

cf. (abbr of confer) cf., cfr.

CFC (abbr of chlorofluorocarbon) n CFC m.

Chad [tʃæd] n el Chad.

chafe [tʃeɪf] vt (rub) rozar.

chaffinch ['tʃæfɪntʃ] n pinzón m.

chain [tʃeɪn] ◆ n cadena f; ~ **of events** serie f OR cadena f de acontecimientos. ◆ vt (person, object) encadenar.

chain reaction n reacción f en cadena.

chain saw n sierra f (mecánica) continua OR de cinta.

chain-smoke vi fumar un cigarrillo tras otro.

chain store n grandes almacenes mpl.

chair [tʃeəʳ] ◆ n 1. (gen) silla f; (armchair) sillón m. 2. (university post) cátedra f. 3. (of meeting) presidencia f. ◆ vt presidir.

chair lift n telesilla m.

chairman ['tʃeəmən] (pl -men [-mən]) n presidente m.

chairperson ['tʃeə,pɜːsn] (pl -s) n presidente m, -ta f.

chalet ['ʃæleɪ] n chalé m, chalet m.

chalk [tʃɔːk] n 1. (type of rock) creta f. 2. (for drawing) tiza f, gis m Amer.

chalkboard ['tʃɔːkbɔːd] n Am pizarra f.

challenge ['tʃælɪndʒ] ◆ n desafío m, reto m. ◆ vt 1. (to fight, competition): **to ~ sb (to sthg/to do sthg)** desafiar a alguien (a algo/a que haga algo). 2. (question) poner en tela de juicio.

challenging ['tʃælɪndʒɪŋ] adj 1. (task, job) estimulante, que supone un reto. 2. (look, tone of voice) desafiante.

chamber ['tʃeɪmbəʳ] n (room) cámara f.

chambermaid ['tʃeɪmbəmeɪd] n (at hotel) camarera f.

chamber music n música f de cámara.

chamber of commerce n cámara f de comercio.

chameleon [kə'miːljən] n camaleón m.

champagne [ˌʃæm'peɪn] n champán m.

champion ['tʃæmpjən] n 1. (of competition) campeón m, -ona f. 2. (of cause) defensor m, -ra f.

championship ['tʃæmpjənʃɪp] n campeonato m.

chance [tʃɑːns] ◆ n 1. (luck) azar m, suerte f; **by ~** por casualidad. 2. (likelihood) posibilidad f; **not to stand a ~ (of)** no tener ninguna posibilidad (de); **by any ~** por casualidad, acaso. 3. (opportunity) oportunidad f. 4. (risk) riesgo m; **to take a ~ (on)** correr un riesgo OR arriesgarse (con). ◆ adj fortuito(ta), casual. ◆ vt arriesgar; **to ~ it** arriesgarse.

chancellor ['tʃɑːnsələʳ] n 1. (chief minister) canciller m. 2. (UNIV) ≃ rector m, -ra f.

Chancellor of the Exchequer n Br Ministro m, -tra f de Economía y Hacienda.

chandelier [ˌʃændə'lɪəʳ] n (lámpara f de) araña f.

change [tʃeɪndʒ] ◆ n 1. (gen) cambio m; ~ **of clothes** muda f; **for a ~** para variar. 2. (from payment) vuelta f, cambio *m,* vuelto *m* Amer. **3.** (*coins*) suelto *m,* calderilla *f.* **4.** (*money in exchange*): **have you got ~ for £5?** ¿tienes cambio de 5 libras? ◆ *vt* **1.** (*gen*) cambiar; **to ~ sthg into** transformar algo en; **to ~ pounds into francs** cambiar libras en francos; **to ~ direction** cambiar de rumbo; **to ~ one's mind** cambiar de idea OR opinión. **2.** (*goods in shop*) descambiar. **3.** (*switch - job, gear, train*) cambiar de; **to ~ one's clothes** cambiarse de ropa. ◆ *vi* **1.** (*alter*) cambiar; **to ~ into sthg** transformarse en algo. **2.** (*change clothes*) cambiarse. **3.** (*change trains, buses*) hacer transbordo. ▶ **change over** *vi* (*convert*): **to ~ over to** cambiar a.

changeable ['tʃeɪndʒəbl] *adj* variable.

change machine *n* máquina *f* de cambio.

changeover ['tʃeɪndʒ,əʊvə'] *n*: **~ (to)** cambio *m* (a).

changing ['tʃeɪndʒɪŋ] *adj* cambiante.

changing room *n* vestuario *m.*

channel ['tʃænl] ◆ *n* canal *m.* ◆ *vt lit & fig* canalizar. ▶ **Channel** *n*: **the (English) Channel** el Canal de la Mancha. ▶ **channels** *npl* (*procedure*) conductos *mpl,* medios *mpl.*

Channel Islands *npl*: **the ~** las islas del canal de la Mancha.

Channel tunnel *n*: **the ~** el túnel del Canal de la Mancha.

chant [tʃɑːnt] ◆ *n* **1.** (RELIG) canto *m.* **2.** (*repeated words*) soniquete *m.* ◆ *vt* **1.** (RELIG) cantar. **2.** (*words*) corear.

chaos ['keɪɒs] *n* caos *m.*

chaotic [keɪ'ɒtɪk] *adj* caótico(ca).

chap [tʃæp] *n Br* (*cleaner*) chico *m,* tío *m.*

chapel ['tʃæpl] *n* capilla *f.*

chaperon(e) ['ʃæpərəʊn] ◆ *n* carabina *f,* acompañanta *f.* ◆ *vt* acompañar.

chaplain ['tʃæplɪn] *n* capellán *m.*

chapped [tʃæpt] *adj* agrietado(da).

chapter ['tʃæptə'] *n lit & fig* capítulo *m.*

char [tʃɑː'] ◆ *n Br* (*cleaner*) mujer *f* de la limpieza. ◆ *vt* (*burn*) carbonizar, calcinar.

character ['kærəktə'] *n* **1.** (*nature, quality, letter*) carácter *m.* **2.** (*in film, book, play*) personaje *m.* **3.** *inf* (*person of stated kind*) tipo *m.* **4.** *inf* (*person with strong personality*): **to be a ~** ser todo un carácter.

characteristic [,kærəktə'rɪstɪk] ◆ *adj* característico(ca). ◆ *n* característica *f.*

characterize, -ise ['kærəktəraɪz] *vt* **1.** (*typify*) caracterizar. **2.** (*portray*): **to ~ sthg as** definir algo como.

charade [ʃə'rɑːd] *n* farsa *f.* ▶ **cha-**

rades *n* (U) charadas *fpl.*

charcoal ['tʃɑːkəʊl] *n* (*for barbecue etc*) carbón *m* (vegetal); (*for drawing*) carboncillo *m.*

charge [tʃɑːdʒ] ◆ *n* **1.** (*cost*) precio *m,* coste *m;* **free of ~** gratis. **2.** (JUR) cargo *m,* acusación *f.* **3.** (*responsibility*): **to have ~ of sthg** tener algo al cargo de uno; **to take ~ (of)** hacerse cargo (de); **to be in ~** ser el encargado (la encargada); **in ~ of** encargado(da) de. **4.** (ELEC) carga *f.* **5.** (MIL) (*of cavalry*) carga *f.* ◆ *vt* **1.** (*customer, sum*) cobrar; **to ~ sthg to sb** cargar algo en la cuenta de alguien. **2.** (*suspect, criminal*): **to ~ sb (with)** acusar a alguien (de). **3.** (*attack*) cargar contra. **4.** (*battery*) cargar. ◆ *vi* (*rush*) cargar; **to ~ in/out** entrar/salir en tromba.

charge card *n* tarjeta de crédito de un establecimiento comercial.

charger ['tʃɑːdʒə'] *n* (*for batteries*) cargador *m.*

chariot ['tʃærɪət] *n* carro *m,* cuadriga *f.*

charisma [kə'rɪzmə] *n* carisma *m.*

charitable ['tʃærətəbl] *adj* **1.** (*person, remark*) caritativo(va). **2.** (*organization*) benéfico(ca).

charity ['tʃærətɪ] *n* **1.** (*kindness, money*) caridad *f.* **2.** (*organization*) institución *f* benéfica.

charm [tʃɑːm] ◆ *n* **1.** (*appeal, attractiveness*) encanto *m.* **2.** (*spell*) hechizo *m.* **3.** (*on bracelet*) dije *m,* amuleto *m.* ◆ *vt* dejar encantado(da).

charming ['tʃɑːmɪŋ] *adj* encantador (ra).

chart [tʃɑːt] ◆ *n* **1.** (*diagram*) gráfico *m.* **2.** (*map*) carta *f.* ◆ *vt* **1.** (*plot, map*) representar en un mapa. **2.** *fig* (*record*) trazar. ▶ **charts** *npl*: **the ~s** la lista de éxitos.

charter ['tʃɑːtə'] ◆ *n* (*document*) carta *f.* ◆ *comp* chárter (*inv*). ◆ *vt* (*plane, boat*) fletar.

chartered accountant ['tʃɑːtəd-] *n Br* contable colegiado *m,* contable colegiada *f.*

charter flight *n* vuelo *m* chárter.

chase [tʃeɪs] ◆ *n* (*pursuit*) persecución *f.* ◆ *vt* **1.** (*pursue*) perseguir. **2.** (*drive away*) ahuyentar. **3.** (*money, jobs*) ir detrás de.

chasm ['kæzm] *n* (*deep crack*) sima *f; fig* (*divide*) abismo *m.*

chassis ['ʃæsɪ] (*pl inv*) *n* (*of vehicle*) chasis *m inv.*

chaste [tʃeɪst] *adj* casto(ta).

chat [tʃæt] ◆ *n* charla *f.* ◆ *vi* charlar. ▶ **chat up** *vt sep Br inf* ligar con.

chew

chat show n Br programa m de entrevistas.

chatter ['tʃætər] ◆ n 1. (of person) cháchara f. 2. (of bird) gorjeo m; (of monkey) chillidos mpl. ◆ vi 1. (person) parlotear. 2. (teeth) castañetear.

chatterbox ['tʃætəbɒks] n inf parlanchín m, -ina f.

chatty ['tʃætɪ] adj 1. (person) dicharachero(ra). 2. (letter) informal.

chauffeur ['ʃəʊfər] n chófer m y f.

chauvinist ['ʃəʊvɪnɪst] n 1. (sexist) sexista m y f; **male ~** machista m. 2. (nationalist) chovinista m y f.

cheap [tʃiːp] ◆ adj 1. (inexpensive) barato(ta). 2. (low - quality) de mala calidad. 3. (vulgar - joke etc) de mal gusto. ◆ adv barato.

cheapen ['tʃiːpn] vt (degrade) rebajar.

cheaply ['tʃiːplɪ] adv barato.

cheat [tʃiːt] ◆ n tramposo m, -sa f. ◆ vt timar, estafar; **to ~ sb out of sthg** estafar algo a alguien. ◆ vi (in exam) copiar; (at cards) hacer trampas.

check [tʃek] ◆ n 1. (inspection, test): **~ (on)** inspección f OR comprobación f (de); **to keep a ~ on** llevar un control de. 2. (restraint): **~ (on)** restricción f (en). 3. Am (cheque) cheque m. 4. Am (bill) cuenta f. 5. (pattern) cuadros mpl. ◆ vt 1. (test, verify) comprobar; (inspect) inspeccionar. 2. (restrain, stop) refrenar. ◆ vi comprobar; **to ~ (for/on sthg)** comprobar (algo). ▶ **check in** ◆ vt sep (luggage, coat) facturar. ◆ vi 1. (at hotel) inscribirse, registrarse. 2. (at airport) facturar. ▶ **check out** ◆ vt sep 1. (luggage, coat) recoger. 2. (investigate) comprobar. ◆ vi (from hotel) dejar el hotel. ▶ **check up** vi: **to ~ up (on)** informarse (acerca de).

checkbook Am = **chequebook**.

checked [tʃekt] adj a cuadros.

checkered Am = **chequered**.

checkers ['tʃekəz] n Am (U) damas fpl.

check-in n facturación f de equipajes.

checking account ['tʃekɪŋ-] n Am cuenta f corriente.

checkmate ['tʃekmeɪt] n jaque m mate.

checkout ['tʃekaʊt] n caja f.

checkpoint ['tʃekpɔɪnt] n control m.

checkup ['tʃekʌp] n chequeo m, reconocimiento m médico.

Cheddar (cheese) ['tʃedər-] n (queso m) cheddar m.

cheek [tʃiːk] n 1. (of face) mejilla f. 2. inf (impudence) cara f, descaro m.

cheekbone ['tʃiːkbəʊn] n pómulo m.

cheeky ['tʃiːkɪ] adj descarado(da).

cheer [tʃɪər] ◆ n (shout) aclamación f; **~s** vítores mpl. ◆ vt 1. (shout approval, encouragement at) aclamar. 2. (gladden) animar. ◆ vi gritar con entusiasmo. ▶ **cheers** excl (when drinking) ¡salud!; inf (thank you) ¡gracias!; inf (goodbye) ¡hasta luego! ▶ **cheer up** ◆ vt sep animar. ◆ vi animarse.

cheerful ['tʃɪəfʊl] adj (gen) alegre.

cheerio [,tʃɪərɪ'əʊ] excl inf ¡hasta luego!

cheese [tʃiːz] n queso m.

cheeseboard ['tʃiːzbɔːd] n tabla f de quesos.

cheeseburger ['tʃiːz,bɜːgər] n hamburguesa f de queso.

cheesecake ['tʃiːzkeɪk] n pastel m OR tarta f de queso.

cheetah ['tʃiːtə] n guepardo m, onza f.

chef [ʃef] n chef m, jefe m de cocina.

chemical ['kemɪkl] ◆ adj químico(ca). ◆ n sustancia f química.

chemist ['kemɪst] n 1. Br (pharmacist) farmacéutico m, -ca f; **~'s (shop)** farmacia f. 2. (scientist) químico m, -ca f.

chemistry ['kemɪstrɪ] n (science) química f.

cheque Br, **check** Am [tʃek] n cheque m, talón m.

chequebook Br, **checkbook** Am ['tʃekbʊk] n talonario m de cheques, chequera f Amer.

cheque card n Br tarjeta f de identificación bancaria.

chequered Br ['tʃekəd], **checkered** Am ['tʃekerd] adj 1. (patterned) a cuadros. 2. (varied) lleno(na) de altibajos.

cherish ['tʃerɪʃ] vt 1. (hope, memory) abrigar. 2. (privilege, right) apreciar. 3. (person, thing) tener mucho cariño a.

cherry ['tʃerɪ] n (fruit) cereza f; **~ (tree)** cerezo m.

chess [tʃes] n ajedrez m.

chessboard ['tʃesbɔːd] n tablero m de ajedrez.

chessman ['tʃesmæn] (pl **-men** [-men]) n pieza f.

chest [tʃest] n 1. (ANAT) pecho m. 2. (box, trunk - gen) arca f, cofre m; (- for tools) caja f.

chestnut ['tʃesnʌt] ◆ adj (colour) castaño(ña). ◆ n (nut) castaña f; **~ (tree)** castaño m.

chest of drawers (pl **chests of drawers**) n cómoda f.

chew [tʃuː] vt 1. (food) masticar.

2. (*nails*) morderse; (*carpet*) morder.
▶ **chew up** *vt sep* (*food*) masticar; (*slippers*) mordisquear.
chewing gum ['tʃuːɪŋ-] *n* chicle *m*.
chic [ʃiːk] *adj* chic (*inv*), elegante.
chick [tʃɪk] *n* (*baby bird*) polluelo *m*.
chicken ['tʃɪkɪn] *n* **1.** (*bird*) gallina *f*. **2.** (*food*) pollo *m*. **3.** *inf* (*coward*) gallina *m y f*. ▶ **chicken out** *vi inf*: **to ~ out (of sthg/of doing sthg)** rajarse (a la hora de algo/de hacer algo).
chickenpox ['tʃɪkɪnpɒks] *n* varicela *f*.
chickpea ['tʃɪkpiː] *n* garbanzo *m*.
chicory ['tʃɪkərɪ] *n* achicoria *f*.
chief [tʃiːf] ◆ *adj* principal. ◆ *n* jefe *m*, -fa *f*.
chief executive *n* (*head of company*) director *m*, -ra *f* general.
chiefly ['tʃiːflɪ] *adv* **1.** (*mainly*) principalmente. **2.** (*especially, above all*) por encima de todo.
chiffon ['ʃɪfɒn] *n* gasa *f*.
chilblain ['tʃɪlbleɪn] *n* sabañón *m*.
child [tʃaɪld] (*pl* **children**) *n* **1.** (*boy, girl*) niño *m*, -ña *f*. **2.** (*son, daughter*) hijo *m*, -ja *f*.
child benefit *n* (U) *Br* subsidio pagado a todas las familias por cada hijo.
childbirth ['tʃaɪldbɜːθ] *n* (U) parto *m*.
childhood ['tʃaɪldhʊd] *n* infancia *f*.
childish ['tʃaɪldɪʃ] *adj pej* infantil.
childlike ['tʃaɪldlaɪk] *adj* (*person*) como un niño; (*smile, trust*) de niño.
childminder ['tʃaɪld,maɪndəʳ] *n Br* niñera *f* (*durante el día*).
childproof ['tʃaɪldpruːf] *adj* a prueba de niños.
children ['tʃɪldrən] *pl* → **child**.
children's home *n* hogar *m* infantil.
Chile ['tʃɪlɪ] *n* Chile.
Chilean ['tʃɪlɪən] ◆ *adj* chileno(na). ◆ *n* chileno *m*, -na *f*.
chili ['tʃɪlɪ] = **chilli**.
chill [tʃɪl] ◆ *n* **1.** (*illness*) resfriado *m*. **2.** (*in temperature*): **there's a ~ in the air** hace un poco de fresco. ◆ *vt* **1.** (*drink, food*) (dejar) enfriar. **2.** (*person - with cold*) enfriar; (*- with fear*) hacer sentir escalofríos.
chilli ['tʃɪlɪ] (*pl* **-ies**) *n* guindilla *f*, chile *m*, ají *m Amer*.
chilling ['tʃɪlɪŋ] *adj* **1.** (*very cold*) helado (da). **2.** (*frightening*) escalofriante.
chilly ['tʃɪlɪ] *adj* frío(a).
chime [tʃaɪm] ◆ *n* campanada *f*. ◆ *vi* (*bell*) repicar; (*clock*) sonar.
chimney ['tʃɪmnɪ] *n* chimenea *f*.
chimneypot ['tʃɪmnɪpɒt] *n* cañón *m*

de chimenea.
chimneysweep ['tʃɪmnɪswiːp] *n* deshollinador *m*, -ra *f*.
chimp [tʃɪmp], **chimpanzee** [,tʃɪmpən'ziː] *n* chimpancé *m y f*.
chin [tʃɪn] *n* barbilla *f*.
china ['tʃaɪnə] *n* porcelana *f*, loza *f*.
China ['tʃaɪnə] *n* la China.
Chinese [,tʃaɪ'niːz] ◆ *adj* chino(na). ◆ *n* **1.** (*person*) chino *m*, -na *f*. **2.** (*language*) chino *m*. ◆ *npl*: **the ~** los chinos.
Chinese leaves *npl Br* (hojas *fpl* de) col *f* china.
chink [tʃɪŋk] ◆ *n* **1.** (*narrow opening*) grieta *f*; (*of light*) resquicio *m*. **2.** (*sound*) tintineo *m*. ◆ *vi* tintinear.
chip [tʃɪp] ◆ *n* **1.** *Br* (*fried potato chip*) patata *f* frita; *Am* (*potato crisp*) patata *f* frita (*de bolsa o de churrería*). **2.** (*fragment - gen*) pedacito *m*; (*- of wood*) viruta *f*; (*- of stone*) lasca *f*. **3.** (*flaw - in cup, glass*) desportilladura *f*. **4.** (COMPUT) chip *m*. **5.** (*token*) ficha *f*. ◆ *vt* (*damage*) desportillar. ▶ **chip in** *inf vi* **1.** (*pay money*) poner dinero. **2.** (*interrupt*) interrumpir. ▶ **chip off** *vt sep* desconchar.
chipboard ['tʃɪpbɔːd] *n* aglomerado *m*.
chip shop *n Br* tienda en la que se vende pescado y patatas fritas.
chiropodist [kɪ'rɒpədɪst] *n* podólogo *m*, -ga *f*, pedicuro *m*, -ra *f*.
chirp [tʃɜːp] *vi* (*bird*) piar; (*insect*) chirriar.
chirpy ['tʃɜːpɪ] *adj inf* alegre.
chisel ['tʃɪzl] *n* (*for wood*) formón *m*, escoplo *m*; (*for stone*) cincel *m*.
chit [tʃɪt] *n* (*note*) nota *f* firmada.
chitchat ['tʃɪtʃæt] *n* (U) *inf* cotilleos *mpl*.
chivalry ['ʃɪvlrɪ] *n* **1.** *literary* (*of knights*) caballería *f*. **2.** (*good manners*) caballerosidad *f*.
chives [tʃaɪvz] *npl* cebollana *f*.
chlorine ['klɔːriːn] *n* cloro *m*.
choc-ice ['tʃɒkaɪs] *n Br* helado *m* cubierto de chocolate.
chock [tʃɒk] *n* cuña *f*, calzo *m*.
chock-a-block, chock-full *adj inf*: **~ (with)** hasta los topes (de).
chocolate ['tʃɒkələt] ◆ *n* **1.** (*food, drink*) chocolate *m*. **2.** (*sweet*) bombón *m*. ◆ *comp* de chocolate.
choice [tʃɔɪs] ◆ *n* **1.** (*gen*) elección *f*; **to have no ~ but to do sthg** no tener más remedio que hacer algo. **2.** (*person chosen*) preferido *m*, -da *f*; (*thing chosen*) alternativa *f* preferida. **3.** (*variety, selec-*

tion) surtido *m.* ◆ *adj* de primera calidad.

choir ['kwaɪəʳ] *n* coro *m.*

choirboy ['kwaɪəbɔɪ] *n* niño *m* de coro.

choke [tʃəʊk] ◆ *n* (AUT) estárter *m.* ◆ *vt* 1. (*subj: person, fumes*) asfixiar; (*subj: fishbone etc*) hacer atragantarse. 2. (*block - pipes, gutter*) atascar. ◆ *vi* (*on fishbone etc*) atragantarse; (*to death*) asfixiarse.

cholera ['kɒlərə] *n* cólera *m.*

choose [tʃuːz] (*pt* chose, *pp* chosen) ◆ *vt* 1. (*select*) elegir, escoger. 2. (*decide*): **to ~ to do sthg** decidir hacer algo; **do whatever you ~** haz lo que quieras. ◆ *vi* elegir, escoger.

choos(e)y ['tʃuːzɪ] (*compar* -ier, *superl* -iest) *adj* (*gen*) quisquilloso(sa); (*about food*) exigente, remilgado(da).

chop [tʃɒp] ◆ *n* 1. (CULIN) chuleta *f.* 2. (*blow - with axe*) hachazo *m.* ◆ *vt* 1. (*cut up*) cortar. 2. *phr*: **to ~ and change** cambiar cada dos por tres. ► **chops** *npl inf* morros *mpl*, jeta *f.* ► **chop down** *vt sep* talar. ► **chop up** *vt sep* (*vegetables, meat*) picar; (*wood*) cortar.

chopper ['tʃɒpəʳ] *n* 1. (*for wood*) hacha *f*; (*for meat*) cuchillo *m* de carnicero. 2. *inf* (*helicopter*) helicóptero *m.*

choppy ['tʃɒpɪ] *adj* picado(da).

chopsticks ['tʃɒpstɪks] *npl* palillos *mpl.*

chord [kɔːd] *n* (MUS) acorde *m.*

chore [tʃɔːʳ] *n* tarea *f*, faena *f.*

chortle ['tʃɔːtl] *vi* reírse con satisfacción.

chorus ['kɔːrəs] *n* 1. (*part of song, refrain*) estribillo *m.* 2. (*choir, group of singers or dancers*) coro *m.*

chose [tʃəʊz] *pt* → choose.

chosen ['tʃəʊzn] *pp* → choose.

Christ [kraɪst] *n* Cristo *m.*

christen ['krɪsn] *vt* bautizar.

christening ['krɪsnɪŋ] *n* bautizo *m.*

Christian ['krɪstʃən] ◆ *adj* cristiano(na). ◆ *n* cristiano *m*, -na *f.*

Christianity [,krɪstɪ'ænətɪ] *n* cristianismo *m.*

Christian name *n* nombre *m* de pila.

Christmas ['krɪsməs] *n* Navidad *f*; **happy** OR **merry ~!** ¡Felices Navidades!

Christmas card *n* crismas *m inv.*

Christmas Day *n* día *m* de Navidad.

Christmas Eve *n* Nochebuena *f.*

Christmas pudding *n* Br pudín de frutas que se come caliente el día de Navidad.

Christmas tree *n* árbol *m* de Navidad.

chrome [krəʊm], **chromium** ['krəʊmɪəm] ◆ *n* cromo *m.* ◆ *comp* cromado(da).

chronic ['krɒnɪk] *adj* 1. (*illness, unemployment*) crónico(ca). 2. (*liar, alcoholic*) empedernido(da).

chronicle ['krɒnɪkl] *n* crónica *f.*

chronological [,krɒnə'lɒdʒɪkl] *adj* cronológico(ca).

chrysanthemum [krɪ'sænθəməm] (*pl* -s) *n* crisantemo *m.*

chubby ['tʃʌbɪ] *adj* (*person, hands*) rechoncho(cha); (*cheeks*) mofletudo(da).

chuck [tʃʌk] *vt inf* 1. (*throw*) tirar, arrojar; **to ~ sb out** echar a alguien. 2. (*job, girlfriend*) dejar. ► **chuck away, chuck out** *vt sep inf* tirar.

chuckle ['tʃʌkl] *vi* reírse entre dientes.

chug [tʃʌg] *vi* (*train*) traquetear; (*car*) resoplar.

chum [tʃʌm] *n inf* (*gen*) amiguete *m*, -ta *f*, manito *m* Amer; (*at school*) compañero *m*, -ra *f.*

chunk [tʃʌŋk] *n* (*piece*) trozo *m.*

church [tʃɜːtʃ] *n* iglesia *f*; **to go to ~** ir a misa.

Church of England *n*: **the ~** la Iglesia Anglicana.

churchyard ['tʃɜːtʃjɑːd] *n* cementerio *m*, camposanto *m.*

churlish ['tʃɜːlɪʃ] *adj* descortés.

churn [tʃɜːn] ◆ *n* 1. (*for making butter*) mantequera *f.* 2. (*for transporting milk*) lechera *f.* ◆ *vt* (*stir up*) agitar. ► **churn out** *vt sep inf* hacer como churros OR en cantidades industriales.

chute [ʃuːt] *n* (*for water*) vertedor *m*; (*slide*) tobogán *m*; (*for waste*) rampa *f.*

chutney ['tʃʌtnɪ] *n* salsa agridulce y picante de fruta y semillas.

CIA (*abbr of* Central Intelligence Agency) *n* CIA *f.*

CID (*abbr of* Criminal Investigation Department) *n* Br ≃ Brigada *f* de Policía Judicial.

cider ['saɪdəʳ] *n* sidra *f.*

cigar [sɪ'gɑːʳ] *n* puro *m.*

cigarette [,sɪgə'ret] *n* cigarrillo *m.*

cigarette paper *n* papel *m* de fumar.

cinch [sɪntʃ] *n inf*: **it's a ~** está tirado, es pan comido.

cinder ['sɪndəʳ] *n* ceniza *f.*

Cinderella [,sɪndə'relə] *n* Cenicienta *f.*

cine-camera ['sɪnɪ-] *n* cámara *f* cinematográfica.

cine-film ['sɪnɪ-] *n* película *f* cinematográfica.

cinema ['sɪnəmə] *n* cine *m*, biógrafo *m* Amer.

cinnamon ['sɪnəmən] *n* canela *f*.

cipher ['saɪfər] *n* (*secret writing system*) código *m*, cifra *f*.

circa ['sɜːkə] *prep* hacia.

circle ['sɜːkl] ◆ *n* 1. (*gen*) círculo *m*; **to go round in ~s** darle (mil) vueltas al mismo tema. 2. (*in theatre*) anfiteatro *m*; (*in cinema*) entresuelo *m*. ◆ *vt* 1. (*draw a circle round*) rodear con un círculo. 2. (*move round*) describir círculos alrededor de. ◆ *vi* dar vueltas.

circuit ['sɜːkɪt] *n* 1. (*gen*) circuito *m*. 2. (*of track*) vuelta *f*.

circuitous [sə'kjuːɪtəs] *adj* tortuoso (sa).

circular ['sɜːkjʊlər] ◆ *adj* (*gen*) circular. ◆ *n* circular *f*.

circulate ['sɜːkjʊleɪt] ◆ *vi* 1. (*gen*) circular. 2. (*socialize*) alternar. ◆ *vt* (*rumour, document*) hacer circular.

circulation [,sɜːkjʊ'leɪʃn] *n* 1. (*of blood, money*) circulación *f*. 2. (*of magazine, newspaper*) tirada *f*.

circumcise ['sɜːkəmsaɪz] *vt* circuncidar.

circumference [sə'kʌmfərəns] *n* circunferencia *f*.

circumspect ['sɜːkəmspekt] *adj* circunspecto(ta).

circumstances ['sɜːkəmstənsɪz] *npl* circunstancias *fpl*; **under** OR **in no ~s** bajo ningún concepto; **in** OR **under the ~** dadas las circunstancias.

circumvent [,sɜːkəm'vent] *vt fml* burlar.

circus ['sɜːkəs] *n* 1. (*for entertainment*) circo *m*. 2. (*in place names*) glorieta *f*.

CIS (*abbr of* **Commonwealth of Independent States**) *n* CEI *f*.

cistern ['sɪstən] *n* 1. Br (*in roof*) depósito *m* de agua. 2. (*in toilet*) cisterna *f*.

cite [saɪt] *vt* citar.

citizen ['sɪtɪzn] *n* ciudadano *m*, -na *f*.

Citizens' Advice Bureau *n* oficina británica de información y asistencia al ciudadano.

Citizens' Band *n* banda de radio reservada para radioaficionados y conductores.

citizenship ['sɪtɪznʃɪp] *n* ciudadanía *f*.

citrus fruit ['sɪtrəs-] *n* cítrico *m*.

city ['sɪtɪ] *n* ciudad *f*. ▶ **City** *n* Br: **the City** la City, *centro financiero de Londres*.

city centre *n* centro *m* de la ciudad.

city hall *n* Am ayuntamiento *m*.

city technology college *n* Br *centro de formación profesional financiado por la industria*.

civic ['sɪvɪk] *adj* 1. (*leader, event*) público (ca). 2. (*duty, pride*) cívico(ca).

civic centre *n* Br *zona de la ciudad donde se encuentran los edificios públicos*.

civil ['sɪvl] *adj* 1. (*involving ordinary citizens*) civil. 2. (*polite*) cortés.

civil engineering *n* ingeniería *f* civil.

civilian [sɪ'vɪljən] ◆ *n* civil *m y f*. ◆ *comp* (*organization*) civil; (*clothes*) de paisano.

civilization [,sɪvɪlaɪ'zeɪʃn] *n* civilización *f*.

civilized ['sɪvɪlaɪzd] *adj* civilizado(da).

civil law *n* derecho *m* civil.

civil liberties *npl* libertades *fpl* civiles.

civil rights *npl* derechos *mpl* civiles.

civil servant *n* funcionario *m*, -ria *f*.

civil service *n* administración *f* pública.

civil war *n* guerra *f* civil.

clad [klæd] *adj literary*: **~ in** vestido(da) de.

claim [kleɪm] ◆ *n* 1. (*for pay, insurance, expenses*) reclamación *f*. 2. (*of right*) reivindicación *f*; **to lay ~ to sthg** reclamar algo. 3. (*assertion*) afirmación *f*. ◆ *vt* 1. (*allowance, expenses, lost property*) reclamar. 2. (*responsibility, credit*) atribuirse. 3. (*maintain*): **to ~ (that)** mantener que. ◆ *vi*: **to ~ on one's insurance** reclamar al seguro; **to ~ for sthg** reclamar algo.

claimant ['kleɪmənt] *n* (*to throne*) pretendiente *m y f*; (*of unemployment benefit*) solicitante *m y f*; (JUR) demandante *m y f*.

clairvoyant [kleə'vɔɪənt] *n* clarividente *m y f*.

clam [klæm] *n* almeja *f*.

clamber ['klæmbər] *vi* trepar.

clammy ['klæmɪ] *adj* (*hands*) húmedo (da), pegajoso(sa); (*weather*) bochornoso (sa).

clamour Br, **clamor** Am ['klæmər] ◆ *n* (U) 1. (*noise*) clamor *m*. 2. (*demand*): **~ (for)** exigencias *fpl* OR demandas *fpl* (de). ◆ *vi*: **to ~ for sthg** exigir a voces algo.

clamp [klæmp] ◆ *n* (*gen*) abrazadera *f*; (*for car wheel*) cepo *m*. ◆ *vt* 1. (*with clamp*) sujetar (con abrazadera). 2. (*with wheel clamp*) poner un cepo a. ▶ **clamp down** *vi*: **to ~ down on** poner freno a.

clan [klæn] *n* clan *m*.

clandestine [klæn'destɪn] *adj* clandestino(na).

clang [klæŋ] *vi* hacer un ruido metálico.

clap [klæp] ◆ *vt*: **to ~ one's hands** dar palmadas. ◆ *vi* aplaudir.

clapping ['klæpɪŋ] *n* (U) aplausos *mpl*.

claret ['klærət] *n* burdeos *m inv*.

clarify ['klærɪfaɪ] *vt* aclarar.

clarinet [,klærə'net] *n* clarinete *m*.

clarity ['klærətɪ] *n* claridad *f*.

clash [klæʃ] ◆ *n* **1.** (*difference - of interests*) conflicto *m*; (*- of personalities*) choque *m*. **2.** (*fight, disagreement*): **~ (with)** conflicto *m* (con). **3.** (*noise*) estruendo *m*. ◆ *vi* **1.** (*fight, disagree*): **to ~ (with)** enfrentarse (con). **2.** (*opinions, policies*) estar en desacuerdo. **3.** (*date, event*): **to ~ (with)** coincidir (con). **4.** (*colour*): **to ~ (with)** desentonar (con).

clasp [klɑːsp] ◆ *n* (*on necklace, bracelet*) broche *m*; (*on belt*) cierre *m*. ◆ *vt* (*person*) abrazar (agarrando); (*thing*) agarrar.

class [klɑːs] ◆ *n* **1.** (*gen*) clase *f*. **2.** (*category*) clase *f*, tipo *m*. ◆ *vt*: **to ~ sb (as)** clasificar a alguien (de).

classic ['klæsɪk] ◆ *adj* (*typical*) clásico (ca). ◆ *n* clásico *m*.

classical ['klæsɪkl] *adj* clásico(ca).

classified ['klæsɪfaɪd] *adj* (*secret*) reservado(da), secreto(ta).

classified ad *n* anuncio *m* por palabras.

classify ['klæsɪfaɪ] *vt* clasificar.

classmate ['klɑːsmeɪt] *n* compañero *m*, -ra *f* de clase.

classroom ['klɑːsrʊm] *n* aula *f*, clase *f*.

classy ['klɑːsɪ] *adj inf* con clase.

clatter ['klætər] *n* (*gen*) estrépito *m*; (*of pots, pans, dishes*) ruido *m* (de cacharros); (*of hooves*) chacoloteo *m*.

clause [klɔːz] *n* **1.** (*in legal document*) cláusula *f*. **2.** (GRAMM) oración *f*.

claw [klɔː] ◆ *n* **1.** (*of animal, bird*) garra *f*; (*of cat*) uña *f*. **2.** (*of crab, lobster*) pinza *f*. ◆ *vi*: **to ~ at sthg** (*cat*) arañar algo; (*person*) intentar agarrarse a algo.

clay [kleɪ] *n* arcilla *f*.

clean [kliːn] ◆ *adj* **1.** (*gen*) limpio(pia). **2.** (*page*) en blanco. **3.** (*record, reputation*) impecable; (*driving licence*) sin multas. **4.** (*joke*) inocente. **5.** (*outline*) nítido (da); (*movement*) suelto(ta). ◆ *vt & vi* limpiar. ► **clean out** *vt sep* **1.** (*clear out*) limpiar el interior de. **2.** *inf* (*take everything from*): **they ~ed us out** (los ladrones) nos limpiaron la casa. ► **clean up** *vt sep* (*clear up*) ordenar, limpiar; **to ~ o.s. up** asearse.

cleaner ['kliːnər] *n* **1.** (*person*)

limpiador *m*, -ra *f*. **2.** (*substance*) producto *m* de limpieza.

cleaning ['kliːnɪŋ] *n* limpieza *f*.

cleanliness ['klenlɪnɪs] *n* limpieza *f*.

cleanse [klenz] *vt* (*gen*) limpiar; (*soul*) purificar; **to ~ sthg/sb of sthg** limpiar algo/a alguien de algo.

cleanser ['klenzər] *n* crema *f* OR loción *f* limpiadora.

clean-shaven [-'ʃeɪvn] *adj* (*never growing a beard*) barbilampiño(ña); (*recently shaved*) bien afeitado(da).

clear [klɪər] ◆ *adj* **1.** (*gen*) claro(ra); (*day, road, view*) despejado(da); **to make sthg ~ (to)** dejar algo claro (a); **it's ~ that ...** está claro que ...; **are you ~ about it?** ¿lo entiendes?; **to make o.s. ~** explicarse con claridad. **2.** (*transparent*) transparente. **3.** (*free of blemishes - skin*) terso(sa). **4.** (*free - time*) libre. **5.** (*complete - day, week*) entero(ra); (*- profit, wages*) neto(ta). ◆ *adv* (*out of the way*): **stand ~!** ¡aléjate!; **to jump/step ~** saltar/dar un paso para hacerse a un lado. ◆ *vt* **1.** (*remove objects, obstacles from*) despejar; (*pipe*) desatascar; **to ~ sthg of sthg** quitar algo de algo; **to ~ a space** hacer sitio; **to ~ the table** quitar la mesa. **2.** (*remove*) quitar. **3.** (*jump*) saltar. **4.** (*pay*) liquidar. **5.** (*authorize*) aprobar. **6.** (*prove not guilty*) declarar inocente; **to be ~ed of sthg** salir absuelto de algo. ◆ *vi* despejarse. ► **clear away** *vt sep* poner en su sitio. ► **clear off** *vi* Br *inf* largarse. ► **clear out** *vt sep* limpiar a fondo. ► **clear up** ◆ *vt sep* **1.** (*room, mess*) limpiar; (*toys, books*) ordenar. **2.** (*mystery, disagreement*) aclarar, resolver. ◆ *vi* **1.** (*weather*) despejarse; (*infection*) desaparecer. **2.** (*tidy up*) ordenar, recoger.

clearance ['klɪərəns] *n* **1.** (*removal - of rubbish, litter*) despeje *m*, limpieza *f*; (*of slums, houses*) eliminación *f*. **2.** (*permission*) autorización *f*, permiso *m*. **3.** (*free space*) distancia *f* de seguridad.

clear-cut *adj* (*issue, plan*) bien definido (da); (*division*) nítido(da).

clearing ['klɪərɪŋ] *n* claro *m*.

clearing bank *n* Br banco asociado a la cámara de compensación.

clearly ['klɪəlɪ] *adv* **1.** (*gen*) claramente. **2.** (*plainly*) obviamente.

clearway ['klɪəweɪ] *n* Br carretera donde no se puede parar.

cleavage ['kliːvɪdʒ] *n* (*between breasts*) escote *m*.

cleaver ['kliːvər] *n* cuchillo *m* OR

cuchilla f de carnicero.

clef [klef] n clave f.

cleft [kleft] n grieta f.

clench [klentʃ] vt apretar.

clergy ['klɜːdʒɪ] npl: **the ~** el clero.

clergyman ['klɜːdʒɪmən] (pl **-men** [-mən]) n clérigo m.

clerical ['klerɪkl] adj 1. (in office) de oficina. 2. (in church) clerical.

clerk [Br klɑːk, Am klɜːrk] n 1. (in office) oficinista m y f. 2. (in court) secretario m. 3. Am (shop assistant) dependiente m, -ta f.

clever ['klevər] adj 1. (intelligent) listo (ta), inteligente. 2. (idea, invention) ingenioso(sa); (with hands) hábil.

cliché ['kliːʃeɪ] n cliché m.

click [klɪk] ◆ vt chasquear. ◆ vi 1. (heels) sonar con un taconazo; (camera) hacer clic. 2. inf (fall into place): **suddenly, it ~ed (with me)** de pronto, caí en la cuenta.

client ['klaɪənt] n cliente m, -ta f.

cliff [klɪf] n (on coast) acantilado m; (inland) precipicio m.

climate ['klaɪmɪt] n (weather) clima m; fig (atmosphere) ambiente m.

climax ['klaɪmæks] n (culmination) clímax m, culminación f.

climb [klaɪm] ◆ n escalada f. ◆ vt (stairs, ladder) subir; (tree) trepar a; (mountain) escalar. ◆ vi 1. (clamber): **to ~ over sthg** trepar por algo; **to ~ into sthg** subirse a algo. 2. (plant) trepar; (road, plane) subir. 3. (increase) subir.

climb-down n rectificación f.

climber ['klaɪmər] n (mountaineer) escalador m, -ra f.

climbing ['klaɪmɪŋ] n montañismo m.

clinch [klɪntʃ] vt (deal) cerrar.

cling [klɪŋ] (pt & pp clung) vi 1. (hold tightly): **to ~ (to)** agarrarse (a). 2. (clothes, person): **to ~ (to sb)** pegarse (a alguien).

clingfilm ['klɪŋfɪlm] n Br film m de plástico adherente.

clinic ['klɪnɪk] n clínica f.

clinical ['klɪnɪkl] adj 1. (MED) clínico (ca). 2. (cold) frío(a).

clink [klɪŋk] vi tintinear.

clip [klɪp] ◆ n 1. (for paper) clip m; (for hair) horquilla f; (on earring) cierre m. 2. (of film) fragmento m, secuencias fpl. ◆ vt 1. (fasten) sujetar. 2. (cut - lawn, newspaper cutting) recortar; (punch - tickets) picar.

clipboard ['klɪpbɔːd] n tabloncillo m con pinza sujetapapeles.

clippers ['klɪpəz] npl (for nails) cor-

taúñas m inv; (for hair) maquinilla f para cortar el pelo; (for hedges, grass) tijeras fpl de podar.

clipping ['klɪpɪŋ] n 1. (from newspaper) recorte m. 2. (of nails) corte m.

clique [kliːk] n pej camarilla f.

cloak [kləʊk] n (garment) capa f, manto m.

cloakroom ['kləʊkrʊm] n 1. (for clothes) guardarropa m. 2. Br (toilets) servicios mpl.

clock [klɒk] n 1. (timepiece) reloj m; **round the ~** día y noche, las 24 horas. 2. (mileometer) cuentakilómetros m inv. ▶ **clock in, clock on** vi Br fichar (a la entrada). ▶ **clock off, clock out** vi Br fichar (a la salida).

clockwise ['klɒkwaɪz] adj & adv en el sentido de las agujas del reloj.

clockwork ['klɒkwɜːk] comp de cuerda.

clog [klɒg] vt atascar, obstruir. ▶ **clogs** npl zuecos mpl. ▶ **clog up** ◆ vt sep (drain, pipe) atascar; (eyes, nose) congestionar. ◆ vi atascarse.

close¹ [kləʊs] ◆ adj 1. (near) cercano (na); **~ to** cerca de; **~ to tears/laughter** a punto de llorar/reír; **~ up, ~ to** de cerca; **~ by, ~ at hand** muy cerca; **it was a ~ shave** OR **thing** OR **call** nos libramos por los pelos. 2. (relationship, friend) íntimo (ma); **to be ~ to sb** estar muy unido(da) a alguien. 3. (relative, family) cercano (na); (resemblance) grande; (link, tie, co-operation) estrecho(cha). 4. (questioning) minucioso(sa); (examination) detallado (da); (look) de cerca; (watch) estrecho (cha). 5. (room, air) cargado(da); (weather) bochornoso(sa). 6. (contest, race) reñido(da); (result) apretado(da). ◆ adv cerca. ▶ **close on, close to** prep (almost) cerca de.

close² [kləʊz] ◆ vt 1. (gen) cerrar. 2. (meeting) clausurar; (discussion, speech) terminar. ◆ vi cerrarse. ◆ n final m. ▶ **close down** ◆ vt sep cerrar (definitivamente). ◆ vi (factory etc) cerrarse (definitivamente).

closed [kləʊzd] adj cerrado(da).

close-knit [,kləʊs-] adj muy unido(da).

closely ['kləʊslɪ] adv 1. (of connection, relation etc) estrechamente; **to be ~ involved in sthg** estar muy metido en algo; (of resemblance) fielmente. 2. (carefully) atentamente.

closet ['klɒzɪt] ◆ adj inf en secreto. ◆ n Am armario m.

close-up ['kləʊs-] n primer plano m.

closing time n hora f de cierre.

closure ['kləʊʒəʳ] n cierre m.

clot [klɒt] ◆ n 1. (in blood) coágulo m; (in liquid) grumo m. 2. Br inf (fool) bobo m, -ba f. ◆ vi (blood) coagularse.

cloth [klɒθ] n 1. (U) (fabric) tela f. 2. (piece of cloth) trapo m.

clothe [kləʊð] vt fml vestir.

clothes [kləʊðz] npl ropa f; **to put one's ~ on** vestirse; **to take one's ~ off** quitarse la ropa.

clothes brush n cepillo m para la ropa.

clothesline ['kləʊðzlaɪn] n cuerda f para tender la ropa.

clothes peg Br, **clothespin** Am ['kləʊðzpɪn] n pinza f (para la ropa).

clothing ['kləʊðɪŋ] n ropa f.

cloud [klaʊd] n nube f. ▶ **cloud over** vi lit & fig nublarse.

cloudy ['klaʊdɪ] adj 1. (overcast) nublado(da). 2. (murky) turbio(bia).

clout [klaʊt] inf n 1. (blow) tortazo m. 2. (U) (influence) influencia f.

clove [kləʊv] n: **a ~ of garlic** un diente de ajo. ▶ **cloves** npl (spice) clavos mpl.

clover ['kləʊvəʳ] n trébol m.

clown [klaʊn] ◆ n (performer) payaso m. ◆ vi hacer payasadas.

cloying ['klɔɪɪŋ] adj empalagoso(sa).

club [klʌb] ◆ n 1. (organization, place) club m. 2. (weapon) porra f, garrote m. 3. (golf) ~ palo m de golf. ◆ vt apalear, aporrear. ▶ **clubs** npl (cards) tréboles mpl. ▶ **club together** vi Br recolectar dinero.

club car n Am (RAIL) vagón m restaurante.

clubhouse ['klʌbhaʊs, pl -haʊzɪz] n (for golfers) (edificio m del) club m.

cluck [klʌk] vi (hen) cloquear.

clue [kluː] n 1. (in crime) pista f; **not to have a ~ (about)** no tener ni idea (de). 2. (in crossword) pregunta f, clave f.

clued-up [kluːd-] adj Br inf al tanto.

clump [klʌmp] n (of bushes) mata f; (of trees, flowers) grupo m.

clumsy ['klʌmzɪ] adj 1. (ungraceful) torpe. 2. (unwieldy) difícil de manejar. 3. (tactless) torpe, sin tacto.

clung [klʌŋ] pt & pt → **cling**.

cluster ['klʌstəʳ] ◆ n (group) grupo m; (of grapes) racimo m. ◆ vi agruparse.

clutch [klʌtʃ] ◆ n (AUT) embrague m. ◆ vt (hand) estrechar; (arm, baby) agarrar. ◆ vi: **to ~ at sthg** tratar de agarrarse a algo.

clutter ['klʌtəʳ] ◆ n desorden m. ◆ vt

cubrir desordenadamente.

cm (abbr of **centimetre**) cm.

CND (abbr of **Campaign for Nuclear Disarmament**) n organización británica contra el armamento nuclear.

c/o (abbr of **care of**) c/d.

Co. 1. (abbr of **Company**) Cía. 2. abbr of **County**.

coach [kəʊtʃ] ◆ n 1. (bus) autocar m. 2. (RAIL) coche m, vagón m. 3. (horse-drawn) carruaje m. 4. (SPORT) entrenador m, -ra f. 5. (tutor) profesor m, -ra f particular. ◆ vt 1. (SPORT) entrenar. 2. (tutor) dar clases particulares a.

coaching ['kəʊtʃɪŋ] n (U) 1. (SPORT) entrenamiento m. 2. (tutoring) clases fpl particulares.

coal [kəʊl] n carbón m.

coalfield ['kəʊlfiːld] n cuenca f minera.

coalition [ˌkəʊə'lɪʃn] n coalición f.

coalman ['kəʊlmæn] (pl **-men** [-men]) n Br carbonero m.

coalmine ['kəʊlmaɪn] n mina f de carbón.

coarse [kɔːs] adj 1. (skin, hair, sandpaper) áspero(ra); (fabric) basto(ta). 2. (person, joke) ordinario(ria).

coast [kəʊst] ◆ n costa f. ◆ vi 1. (in car) ir en punto muerto. 2. (progress easily) ir holgadamente OR sin esfuerzos.

coastal ['kəʊstl] adj costero(ra).

coaster ['kəʊstəʳ] n (small mat) posavasos m inv.

coastguard ['kəʊstgɑːd] n (person) guardacostas m y f inv.

coastline ['kəʊstlaɪn] n litoral m.

coat [kəʊt] ◆ n 1. (garment) abrigo m. 2. (of animal) pelo m, pelaje m. 3. (layer) capa f. ◆ vt: **to ~ sthg (with)** cubrir algo (de).

coat hanger n percha f.

coating ['kəʊtɪŋ] n (of dust etc) capa f; (of chocolate, silver) baño m.

coat of arms (pl **coats of arms**) n escudo m de armas.

coax [kəʊks] vt: **to ~ sb (to do OR into doing sthg)** engatusar a alguien (para que haga algo).

cob [kɒb] → **corn**.

cobbled ['kɒbld] adj adoquinado(da).

cobbler ['kɒbləʳ] n zapatero (remendón) m, zapatera (remendona) f.

cobbles ['kɒblz], **cobblestones** ['kɒblstəʊnz] npl adoquines mpl.

cobweb ['kɒbweb] n telaraña f.

Coca-Cola® [ˌkəʊkə'kəʊlə] n Coca-Cola® f.

cocaine [kəʊˈkeɪn] n cocaína f.
cock [kɒk] ◆ n 1. (male chicken) gallo m.
2. (male bird) macho m. ◆ vt 1. (gun)
amartillar. 2. (head) ladear. ▶ **cock up**
vt sep Br v inf jorobar.
cockerel [ˈkɒkrəl] n gallo m joven.
cockeyed [ˈkɒkaɪd] adj inf 1. (lopsided)
torcido(da). 2. (foolish) disparatado
(da).
cockle [ˈkɒkl] n berberecho m.
Cockney [ˈkɒknɪ] (pl **Cockneys**) n
1. (person) cockney m y f, persona procedente del este de Londres. 2. (dialect, accent)
cockney m, dialecto del este de Londres.
cockpit [ˈkɒkpɪt] n (in plane) cabina f.
cockroach [ˈkɒkrəʊtʃ] n cucaracha f.
cocksure [ˌkɒkˈʃʊəʳ] adj presuntuoso
(sa).
cocktail [ˈkɒkteɪl] n cóctel m.
cock-up n v inf chapuza f, pifia f.
cocky [ˈkɒkɪ] adj inf chulo(la), chuleta.
cocoa [ˈkəʊkəʊ] n 1. (powder) cacao m.
2. (drink) chocolate m.
coconut [ˈkəʊkənʌt] n coco m.
cod [kɒd] (pl inv OR **-s**) n bacalao m.
COD (abbr of **cash on delivery**) contra
reembolso, = CAE.
code [kəʊd] ◆ n 1. (gen) código m.
2. (for telephone) prefijo m. ◆ vt (encode)
codificar, cifrar.
cod-liver oil n aceite m de hígado de
bacalao.
coed [ˌkəʊˈed] adj (abbr of **coeducational**)
mixto(ta).
coerce [kəʊˈɜːs] vt: to ~ sb (into doing
sthg) coaccionar a alguien (para que
haga algo).
coffee [ˈkɒfɪ] n café m.
coffee bar n Br cafetería f.
coffee break n pausa para descansar en
el trabajo por la mañana y por la tarde.
coffee morning n Br reunión matinal,
generalmente benéfica, en la que se sirve café.
coffeepot [ˈkɒfɪpɒt] n cafetera f.
coffee shop n 1. Br (shop) cafetería f.
2. Am (restaurant) café m.
coffee table n mesita f baja (de
salón).
coffin [ˈkɒfɪn] n ataúd m.
cog [kɒg] n (tooth on wheel) diente m;
(wheel) rueda f dentada.
cognac [ˈkɒnjæk] n coñac m.
coherent [kəʊˈhɪərənt] adj coherente.
cohesive [kəʊˈhiːsɪv] adj unido(da).
coil [kɔɪl] ◆ n 1. (of rope, wire) rollo m; (of
hair) tirabuzón m; (of smoke) espiral f.
2. (ELEC) bobina f. 3. Br (contraceptive
device) DIU m, espiral m. ◆ vi enrollarse,

enroscarse. ◆ vt enrollar, enroscar.
▶ **coil up** vt sep enrollar.
coin [kɔɪn] ◆ n moneda f. ◆ vt (invent)
acuñar, inventar.
coinage [ˈkɔɪnɪdʒ] n (currency) moneda
f.
coin-box n Br teléfono m público.
coincide [ˌkəʊɪnˈsaɪd] vi: to ~ (with)
coincidir (con).
coincidence [kəʊˈɪnsɪdəns] n coincidencia f.
coincidental [kəʊˌɪnsɪˈdentl] adj for-
tuito(ta).
coke [kəʊk] n (fuel) coque m.
Coke® [kəʊk] n Coca-Cola® f.
cola [ˈkəʊlə] n (bebida f de) cola f.
colander [ˈkʌləndəʳ] n colador m,
escurridor m.
cold [kəʊld] ◆ adj frío(a); it's ~ hace frío;
my hands are ~ tengo las manos frías;
I'm ~ tengo frío; to get ~ enfriarse. ◆ n
1. (illness) resfriado m, constipado m; to
catch (a) ~ resfriarse, coger un resfriado. 2. (low temperature) frío m.
cold-blooded [-ˈblʌdɪd] adj 1. (animal)
de sangre fría. 2. (person) despiadado
(da); (killing) a sangre fría.
cold sore n calentura f, pupa f.
cold war n: the ~ la guerra fría.
coleslaw [ˈkəʊlslɔː] n ensalada de col,
zanahoria, cebolla y mayonesa.
colic [ˈkɒlɪk] n cólico m.
collaborate [kəˈlæbəreɪt] vi: to ~ (with)
colaborar (con).
collapse [kəˈlæps] ◆ n 1. (of building)
derrumbamiento m; (of roof)
hundimiento m. 2. (of marriage, system)
fracaso m; (of government, currency) caída
f; (of empire) derrumbamiento m.
3. (MED) colapso m. ◆ vi 1. (building, person) derrumbarse; (roof) hundirse; to ~
with laughter partirse de risa. 2. (plan,
business) venirse abajo. 3. (MED) sufrir
un colapso.
collapsible [kəˈlæpsəbl] adj plegable.
collar [ˈkɒləʳ] n 1. (on clothes) cuello m.
2. (for dog) collar m. 3. (TECH) collar m.
collarbone [ˈkɒləbəʊn] n clavícula f.
collate [kəˈleɪt] vt 1. (compare) cotejar.
2. (put in order) poner en orden.
collateral [kɒˈlætərəl] n garantía f sub-
sidiaria, seguridad f colateral.
colleague [ˈkɒliːg] n colega m y f.
collect [kəˈlekt] ◆ vt 1. (gather together)
reunir, juntar; to ~ o.s. recobrar el
dominio de sí mismo. 2. (as a hobby)
coleccionar. 3. (go to get - person, parcel)
recoger. 4. (money, taxes) recaudar. ◆ vi

1. (*gather*) congregarse, reunirse. **2.** (*accumulate*) acumularse. **3.** (*for charity, gift*) hacer una colecta. ◆ *adv* Am (TELEC): **to call (sb) ~** llamar (a alguien) a cobro revertido.

collection [kə'lekʃn] *n* **1.** (*of stamps, art etc*) colección *f*. **2.** (*of poems, stories etc*) recopilación *f*. **3.** (*of rubbish, mail*) recogida *f*; (*of taxes*) recaudación *f*. **4.** (*of money*) colecta *f*.

collective [kə'lektɪv] ◆ *adj* colectivo (va). ◆ *n* colectivo *m*.

collector [kə'lektər] *n* **1.** (*as a hobby*) coleccionista *m y f*. **2.** (*of taxes*) recaudador *m*, -ra *f*. **3.** (*of debts, rent*) cobrador *m*, -ra *f*.

college ['kɒlɪdʒ] *n* **1.** (*for further education*) instituto *m*, escuela *f*. **2.** (*of university*) *colegio universitario que forma parte de ciertas universidades*. **3.** (*organized body*) colegio *m*.

college of education *n escuela de formación de profesores de enseñanza primaria y secundaria*.

collide [kə'laɪd] *vi*: **to ~ (with)** (*gen*) chocar (con); (*vehicles*) colisionar OR chocar (con).

collie ['kɒlɪ] *n* collie *m*.

colliery ['kɒljərɪ] *n* mina *f* de carbón.

collision [kə'lɪʒn] *n lit & fig*: **~ (with/between)** choque *m* (con/entre), colisión *f* (con/entre).

colloquial [kə'ləʊkwɪəl] *adj* coloquial.

collude [kə'luːd] *vi*: **to ~ with** estar en connivencia con.

Colombia [kə'lɒmbɪə] *n* Colombia.

Colombian [kə'lɒmbɪən] ◆ *adj* colombiano(na). ◆ *n* colombiano *m*, -na *f*.

colon ['kəʊlən] *n* **1.** (ANAT) colon *m*. **2.** (*punctuation mark*) dos puntos *mpl*.

colonel ['kɜːnl] *n* coronel *m y f*.

colonial [kə'ləʊnjəl] *adj* colonial.

colonize, -ise ['kɒlənaɪz] *vt* colonizar.

colony ['kɒlənɪ] *n* colonia *f*.

color *etc* Am = **colour** *etc*.

colossal [kə'lɒsl] *adj* colosal.

colour Br, **color** Am ['kʌlər] ◆ *n* color *m*; **in ~** en color. ◆ *adj* en color. ◆ *vt* **1.** (*give colour to*) dar color a; (*with pen, crayon*) colorear. **2.** (*dye*) teñir. **3.** (*affect*) influenciar. ◆ *vi* (*blush*) ruborizarse.

colour bar *n* discriminación *f* racial.

colour-blind *adj* daltónico(ca).

coloured Br, **colored** Am ['kʌləd] *adj* **1.** (*pens, sheets etc*) de colores. **2.** (*with stated colour*): **maroon-~** de color granate; **brightly-~** de vivos colores. **3.** (*person - black*) de color.

colourful Br, **colorful** Am ['kʌləfʊl] *adj* **1.** (*brightly coloured*) de vivos colores. **2.** (*story*) animado(da). **3.** (*person*) pintoresco(ca).

colouring Br, **coloring** Am ['kʌlərɪŋ] *n* **1.** (*dye*) colorante *m*. **2.** (*complexion, hair*) tez *f*. **3.** (*of animal's skin*) color *m*.

colour scheme *n* combinación *f* de colores.

colt [kəʊlt] *n* potro *m*.

column ['kɒləm] *n* **1.** (*gen*) columna *f*. **2.** (*of people, vehicles*) hilera *f*.

columnist ['kɒləmnɪst] *n* columnista *m y f*.

coma ['kəʊmə] *n* coma *m*.

comb [kəʊm] ◆ *n* peine *m*. ◆ *vt lit & fig* peinar.

combat ['kɒmbæt] ◆ *n* combate *m*. ◆ *vt* combatir.

combination [ˌkɒmbɪ'neɪʃn] *n* combinación *f*.

combine [*vb* kəm'baɪn, *n* 'kɒmbaɪn] ◆ *vt*: **to ~ sthg (with)** combinar algo (con). ◆ *vi* combinarse. ◆ *n* **1.** (*group*) grupo *m*. **2.** = **combine harvester**.

combine harvester [-'hɑːvɪstər] *n* cosechadora *f*.

come [kʌm] (*pt* came, *pp* come) *vi* **1.** (*move*) venir; (*arrive*) llegar; **the news came as a shock** la noticia constituyó un duro golpe; **coming!** ¡ahora voy! **2.** (*reach*): **to ~ up/down to** llegar hasta. **3.** (*happen*) pasar; **~ what may** pase lo que pase. **4.** (*become*): **to ~ true** hacerse realidad; **to ~ unstuck** despegarse; **my shoelaces have ~ undone** se me han desatado los cordones. **5.** (*begin gradually*): **to ~ to do sthg** llegar a hacer algo. **6.** (*be placed in order*): **to ~ first/last in a race** llegar el primero/el último en una carrera; **she came second in the exam** quedó segunda en el examen; **P ~s before Q** la P viene antes de la Q. ▶ **to come** *adv*: **in (the) days/years to ~** en días/años venideros. ▶ **come about** *vi* (*happen*) pasar, ocurrir. ▶ **come across** *vt fus* (*find*) cruzarse con. ▶ **come along** *vi* **1.** (*arrive by chance - opportunity*) surgir; (*- bus*) aparecer, llegar. **2.** (*improve*) ir; **the project is coming along nicely** el proyecto va muy bien. ▶ **come apart** *vi* deshacerse. ▶ **come back** *vi* **1.** (*in talk, writing*): **to ~ back to sthg** volver a algo. **2.** (*memory*): **to ~ back to sb** volverle a la memoria a alguien. ▶ **come by** *vt fus* (*get, obtain*) conseguir. ▶ **come down** *vi* **1.** (*decrease*) bajar. **2.** (*descend - plane, parachutist*) aterrizar;

(- *rain*) caer. ► **come down to** *vt fus* reducirse a. ► **come down with** *vt fus* coger, agarrar (*enfermedad*). ► **come forward** *vi* presentarse. ► **come from** *vt fus* (*noise etc*) venir de; (*person*) ser de. ► **come in** *vi* 1. (*enter*) entrar, pasar; ~ **in!** ¡pase! 2. (*arrive - train, letters, donations*) llegar. ► **come in for** *vt fus* (*criticism etc*) recibir, llevarse. ► **come into** *vt fus* 1. (*inherit*) heredar. 2. (*begin to be*): **to ~ into being** nacer, ver la luz. ► **come off** *vi* 1. (*button*) descoserse; (*label*) despegarse; (*lid*) soltarse; (*stain*) quitarse. 2. (*plan, joke*) salir bien. 3. *phr*: ~ **off it!** *inf* ¡venga ya! ► **come on** *vi* 1. (*start*) empezar. 2. (*start working - lights, heating*) encenderse. 3. (*progress, improve*) ir; **it's coming on nicely** va muy bien. 4. *phr*: ~ **on!** (*expressing encouragement, urging haste*) ¡vamos!; (*expressing disbelief*) ¡venga ya! ► **come out** *vi* 1. (*become known*) salir a la luz. 2. (*appear - product, book, sun*) salir; (- *film*) estrenarse. 3. (*go on strike*) ponerse en huelga. ► **come over** *vt fus* (*subj: feeling*) sobrevenir; **I don't know what has ~ over her** no sé qué le pasa. ► **come round** *vi* 1. (*change opinion*): **to ~ round (to sthg)** terminar por aceptar (algo). 2. (*regain consciousness*) volver en sí. ► **come through** *vt fus* (*difficult situation, period*) pasar por; (*operation, war*) sobrevivir a. ► **come to** ♦ *vt fus* 1. (*reach*): **to ~ to an end** tocar a su fin; **to ~ to a decision** alcanzar una decisión. 2. (*amount to*) ascender a. ♦ *vi* (*regain consciousness*) volver en sí. ► **come under** *vt fus* 1. (*be governed by*) estar bajo. 2. (*suffer*): **to ~ under attack** ser víctima de críticas. ► **come up** *vi* 1. (*name, topic, opportunity*) surgir. 2. (*be imminent*) estar al llegar. 3. (*sun, moon*) salir. ► **come up against** *vt fus* tropezarse OR toparse con. ► **come up with** *vt fus* (*idea*) salir con; (*solution*) encontrar.

comeback ['kʌmbæk] *n* (*return*) reaparición *f*; **to make a ~** (*fashion*) volver a ponerse de moda; (*actor*) hacer una reaparición.

comedian [kə'miːdjən] *n* cómico *m*.

comedown ['kʌmdaʊn] *n inf* desilusión *f*, decepción *f*.

comedy ['kɒmədɪ] *n* comedia *f*.

comet ['kɒmɪt] *n* cometa *m*.

come-uppance [ˌkʌm'ʌpəns] *n*: **to get one's ~** *inf* llevarse uno su merecido.

comfort ['kʌmfət] ♦ *n* 1. (*gen*) comodi-

dad *f*. 2. (*solace*) consuelo *m*. ♦ *vt* consolar, confortar.

comfortable ['kʌmftəbl] *adj* 1. (*gen*) cómodo(da). 2. (*financially secure*) acomodado(da). 3. (*victory, job, belief*) fácil; (*lead, majority*) amplio(plia).

comfortably ['kʌmftəblɪ] *adv* 1. (*sit, sleep*) cómodamente. 2. (*without financial difficulty*) sin aprietos. 3. (*easily*) fácilmente.

comfort station *n* Am euphemism aseos *mpl* públicos.

comic ['kɒmɪk] ♦ *adj* cómico(ca). ♦ *n* 1. (*comedian*) cómico *m*, -ca *f*. 2. (*magazine - for children*) tebeo *m*; (- *for adults*) cómic *m*.

comical ['kɒmɪkl] *adj* cómico(ca).

comic strip *n* tira *f* cómica.

coming ['kʌmɪŋ] ♦ *adj* (*future*) próximo (ma). ♦ *n*: ~**s and goings** idas *fpl* y venidas.

comma ['kɒmə] *n* coma *f*.

command [kə'mɑːnd] ♦ *n* 1. (*order*) orden *f*. 2. (U) (*control*) mando *m*. 3. (*of language, skill*) dominio *m*. 4. (COMPUT) comando *m*. ♦ *vt* 1. (*order*): **to ~ sb (to do sthg)** ordenar OR mandar a alguien (que haga algo). 2. (MIL) (*control*) comandar. 3. (*deserve - respect, attention*) hacerse acreedor(ra) de.

commandeer [ˌkɒmən'dɪəʳ] *vt* requisar.

commander [kə'mɑːndəʳ] *n* 1. (*in army*) comandante *m* y *f*. 2. (*in navy*) capitán *m*, -ana *f* de fragata.

commandment [kə'mɑːndmənt] *n* (RELIG) mandamiento *m*.

commando [kə'mɑːndəʊ] (*pl* -**s** OR -**es**) *n* comando *m*.

commemorate [kə'meməreɪt] *vt* conmemorar.

commemoration [kəˌmemə'reɪʃn] *n* conmemoración *f*.

commence [kə'mens] *fml* ♦ *vt*: **to ~ (doing sthg)** comenzar OR empezar (a hacer algo). ♦ *vi* comenzar, empezar.

commend [kə'mend] *vt* 1. (*praise*) alabar. 2. (*recommend*): **to ~ sthg (to)** recomendar algo (a).

commensurate [kə'menʃərət] *adj fml*: ~ **with** acorde OR en proporción con.

comment ['kɒment] ♦ *n* comentario *m*; **no ~** sin comentarios. ♦ *vi* comentar; **to ~ on** hacer comentarios sobre.

commentary ['kɒməntrɪ] *n* comentario *m*.

commentator ['kɒmənteɪtəʳ] *n* comentarista *m* y *f*.

commerce ['kɒmɜːs] *n* (U) comercio *m*.

commercial [kə'mɜːʃl] ◆ *adj* comercial. ◆ *n* anuncio *m* (*televisivo o radiofónico*).

commercial break *n* pausa *f* para la publicidad.

commiserate [kə'mızəreıt] *vi*: **to ~ (with)** compadecerse (de).

commission [kə'mıʃn] ◆ *n* **1**. (*money, investigative body*) comisión *f*. **2**. (*piece of work*) encargo *m*. ◆ *vt* encargar; **to ~ sb (to do sthg)** encargar a alguien (que haga algo).

commissionaire [kə,mıʃə'neər] *n* Br portero *m* (uniformado).

commissioner [kə'mıʃnər] *n* comisario *m*, -ria *f*.

commit [kə'mıt] *vt* **1**. (*crime, sin etc*) cometer. **2**. (*pledge - money, resources*) destinar; **to ~ o.s. (to)** comprometerse (a). **3**. (*consign - to mental hospital*) ingresar; **to ~ sthg to memory** aprender algo de memoria.

commitment [kə'mıtmənt] *n* compromiso *m*.

committee [kə'mıtı] *n* comisión *f*, comité *m*.

commodity [kə'mɒdətı] *n* mercancía *f*, producto *m*.

common ['kɒmən] ◆ *adj* **1**. (*gen*): **~ (to)** común (a). **2**. (*ordinary - man, woman*) corriente, de la calle. **3**. Br pej (*vulgar*) vulgar, ordinario(ria). ◆ *n* campo *m* común. ▶ **in common** *adv* en común.

common law *n* derecho *m* consuetudinario. ▶ **common-law** *adj* (*wife, husband*) de hecho.

commonly ['kɒmənlı] *adv* generalmente, comúnmente.

Common Market *n*: **the ~** el Mercado Común.

commonplace ['kɒmənpleıs] *adj* corriente, común.

common room *n* sala *f* de estudiantes.

Commons ['kɒmənz] *npl* Br: **the ~** (la Cámara de) los Comunes.

common sense *n* sentido *m* común.

Commonwealth ['kɒmənwelθ] *n*: **the ~** la Commonwealth.

Commonwealth of Independent States *n*: **the ~** la Comunidad de Estados Independientes.

commotion [kə'məʊʃn] *n* alboroto *m*.

communal ['kɒmjʊnl] *adj* comunal.

commune [*n* 'kɒmjuːn, *vb* kə'mjuːn] ◆ *n* comuna *f*. ◆ *vi*: **to ~ with** estar en comunión OR comulgar con.

communicate [kə'mjuːnıkeıt] ◆ *vt* transmitir, comunicar. ◆ *vi*: **to ~ (with)** comunicarse (con).

communication [kə,mjuːnı'keıʃn] *n* **1**. (*contact*) comunicación *f*. **2**. (*letter, phone call*) comunicado *m*.

communication cord *n* Br alarma *f* (*de un tren o metro*).

communion [kə'mjuːnjən] *n* (*communication*) comunión *f*. ▶ **Communion** *n* (U) (RELIG) comunión *f*.

communiqué [kə'mjuːnıkeı] *n* comunicado *m* oficial.

Communism ['kɒmjʊnızm] *n* comunismo *m*.

Communist ['kɒmjʊnıst] ◆ *adj* comunista. ◆ *n* comunista *m* y *f*.

community [kə'mjuːnətı] *n* comunidad *f*.

community centre *n* centro *m* social.

community charge *n* Br impuesto municipal pagado por todos los adultos, = contribución *f* urbana.

commutation ticket [,kɒmjuː'teıʃn-] *n* Am billete *m* de abono.

commute [kə'mjuːt] ◆ *vt* (JUR) conmutar. ◆ *vi* (*to work*) viajar diariamente al lugar de trabajo, esp en tren.

commuter [kə'mjuːtər] *n* persona que viaja diariamente al lugar de trabajo, esp en tren.

compact [*adj* kəm'pækt, *n* 'kɒmpækt] ◆ *adj* (*small and neat*) compacto(ta). ◆ *n* **1**. (*for face powder*) polvera *f*. **2**. Am (*car*) utilitario *m*.

compact disc *n* compact disc *m*.

compact disc player *n* compact *m* (disc), reproductor *m* de discos compactos.

companion [kəm'pænjən] *n* compañero *m*, -ra *f*.

companionship [kəm'pænjənʃıp] *n* compañerismo *m*.

company ['kʌmpənı] *n* (*gen*) compañía *f*; (*business*) empresa *f*, compañía *f*; **to keep sb ~** hacer compañía a alguien; **to part ~ (with)** separarse (de).

company secretary *n* ejecutivo de una empresa encargado de llevar las cuentas, asuntos legales etc.

comparable ['kɒmprəbl] *adj*: **~ (to OR with)** comparable (a).

comparative [kəm'pærətıv] *adj* **1**. (*relative*) relativo(va). **2**. (*study*) comparado(da). **3**. (GRAMM) comparativo(va).

comparatively [kəm'pærətɪvlɪ] adv
relativamente.

compare [kəm'peə^r] ♦ vt: **to ~ sthg/sb
(with), to ~ sthg/sb (to)** comparar algo/a
alguien (con); **~d with** OR **to** (as opposed
to) comparado con; (in comparison with)
en comparación con. ♦ vi: **to ~ (with)**
compararse (con).

comparison [kəm'pærɪsn] n comparación f; **in ~ (with** OR **to)** en comparación
(con).

compartment [kəm'pɑ:tmənt] n
1. (container) compartimento m. 2. (RAIL)
departamento m, compartimento m.

compass ['kʌmpəs] n (magnetic) brújula f. ▶ **compasses** npl compás m.

compassion [kəm'pæʃn] n compasión
f.

compassionate [kəm'pæʃənət] adj
compasivo(va).

compatible [kəm'pætəbl] adj: **~ (with)**
compatible (con).

compel [kəm'pel] vt (force) obligar; **to ~
sb to do sthg** forzar OR obligar a alguien
a hacer algo.

compelling [kəm'pelɪŋ] adj (forceful)
convincente.

compensate ['kompenseɪt] ♦ vt: **to ~
sb for sthg** (financially) compensar OR
indemnizar a alguien por algo. ♦ vi: **to
~ for sthg** compensar algo.

compensation [,kompen'seɪʃn] n
1. (money): **~ (for)** indemnización f (por).
2. (way of compensating): **~ (for)** compensación f (por).

compete [kəm'pi:t] vi 1. (gen): **to ~
(for/in)** competir (por/en); **to ~ (with** OR
against) competir (con). 2. (be in conflict)
rivalizar.

competence ['kompɪtəns] n (proficiency) competencia f, aptitud f.

competent ['kompɪtənt] adj competente, capaz.

competition [,kompɪ'tɪʃn] n 1. (rivalry)
competencia f. 2. (race, sporting event)
competición f. 3. (contest) concurso m.

competitive [kəm'petətɪv] adj 1. (person, spirit) competidor(ra). 2. (match,
exam, prices) competitivo(va).

competitor [kəm'petɪtə^r] n competidor m, -ra f.

compile [kəm'paɪl] vt recopilar.

complacency [kəm'pleɪsnsɪ] n
autosatisfacción f, autocomplacencia f.

complacent [kəm'pleɪsnt] adj autocomplaciente.

complain [kəm'pleɪn] vi 1. (moan): **to ~
(about)** quejarse (de). 2. (MED): **to ~ of**
sthg sufrir algo.

complaint [kəm'pleɪnt] n 1. (gen)
queja f. 2. (MED) dolencia f.

complement [n 'komplɪmənt, vb
'komplɪ,ment] ♦ n 1. (gen & GRAMM)
complemento m. 2. (number): **a full ~ of**
la totalidad de. ♦ vt complementar.

complementary [,komplɪ'mentərɪ]
adj complementario(ria).

complete [kəm'pli:t] ♦ adj 1. (total)
total. 2. (lacking nothing) completo(ta);
bathroom ~ with shower baño con
ducha. 3. (finished) terminado(da). ♦ vt
1. (make whole - collection) completar;
(- disappointment, amazement) colmar.
2. (finish) terminar. 3. (form) rellenar.

completely [kəm'pli:tlɪ] adv completamente.

completion [kəm'pli:ʃn] n finalización
f, terminación f.

complex ['kompleks] ♦ adj complejo
(ja). ♦ n complejo m.

complexion [kəm'plekʃn] n (of face)
tez f, cutis m inv.

compliance [kəm'plaɪəns] n (obedience):
~ (with) acatamiento m (de).

complicate ['komplɪkeɪt] vt complicar.

complicated ['komplɪkeɪtɪd] adj complicado(da).

complication [,komplɪ'keɪʃn] n complicación f.

compliment [n 'komplɪmənt, vb
'komplɪment] ♦ n cumplido m. ♦ vt: **to ~
sb (on)** felicitar a alguien (por). ▶ **compliments** npl fml saludos mpl.

complimentary [,komplɪ'mentərɪ] adj
1. (remark) elogioso(sa); (person) halagador(ra). 2. (drink, seats) gratis (inv).

complimentary ticket n entrada f
gratuita.

comply [kəm'plaɪ] vi: **to ~ with sthg**
(standards) cumplir (con) algo; (request)
acceder a algo; (law) acatar algo.

component [kəm'pəunənt] n (gen) elemento m; (TECH) pieza f.

compose [kəm'pəuz] vt 1. (constitute)
componer; **to be ~d of** estar compuesto
OR componerse de. 2. (music, poem, letter) componer. 3. (calm): **to ~ o.s.** calmarse.

composed [kəm'pəuzd] adj tranquilo
(la).

composer [kəm'pəuzə^r] n compositor
m, -ra f.

composition [,kompə'zɪʃn] n 1. (gen)
composición f. 2. (essay) redacción f.

compost [Br 'kompost, Am 'kompəust]
n abono m.

composure [kəmˈpəʊʒəʳ] n calma f.
compound [ˈkɒmpaʊnd] n 1. (gen & CHEM) compuesto m. 2. (enclosed area) recinto m.
compound fracture n fractura f complicada.
comprehend [ˌkɒmprɪˈhend] vt comprender.
comprehension [ˌkɒmprɪˈhenʃn] n comprensión f.
comprehensive [ˌkɒmprɪˈhensɪv] ◆ adj 1. (wide-ranging) amplio(plia). 2. (insurance) a todo riesgo. ◆ n Br = **comprehensive school.**
comprehensive school n instituto de enseñanza media no selectiva en Gran Bretaña.
compress [kəmˈpres] vt 1. (squeeze, press) comprimir. 2. (shorten) reducir.
comprise [kəmˈpraɪz] vt 1. (consist of) comprender. 2. (form) constituir.
compromise [ˈkɒmprəmaɪz] ◆ n arreglo m, término m medio. ◆ vt comprometer. ◆ vi llegar a un arreglo, transigir.
compulsion [kəmˈpʌlʃn] n 1. (strong desire) ganas fpl irrefrenables. 2. (U) (force) obligación f.
compulsive [kəmˈpʌlsɪv] adj 1. (gambler) empedernido(da); (liar) compulsivo(va). 2. (fascinating, compelling) absorbente.
compulsory [kəmˈpʌlsərɪ] adj (gen) obligatorio(ria); (retirement) forzoso(sa).
computer [kəmˈpjuːtəʳ] n ordenador m.
computer game n videojuego m.
computerized [kəmˈpjuːtəraɪzd] adj informatizado(da), computerizado (da).
computing [kəmˈpjuːtɪŋ], **computer science** n informática f.
comrade [ˈkɒmreɪd] n camarada m y f.
con [kɒn] inf ◆ n (trick) timo m. ◆ vt timar, estafar; **to ~ sb out of sthg** timarle algo a alguien; **to ~ sb into doing sthg** engañar a alguien para que haga algo.
concave [ˌkɒnˈkeɪv] adj concavo(va).
conceal [kənˈsiːl] vt (object, substance, information) ocultar; (feelings) disimular; **to ~ sthg from sb** ocultarle algo a alguien.
concede [kənˈsiːd] ◆ vt (defeat, a point) admitir, reconocer. ◆ vi (gen) ceder; (in sports, chess) rendirse.
conceit [kənˈsiːt] n vanidad f.
conceited [kənˈsiːtɪd] adj engreído (da).

conceive [kənˈsiːv] ◆ vt concebir. ◆ vi 1. (MED) concebir. 2. (imagine): **to ~ of sthg** imaginarse algo.
concentrate [ˈkɒnsəntreɪt] ◆ vt concentrar. ◆ vi: **to ~ (on)** concentrarse (en).
concentration [ˌkɒnsənˈtreɪʃn] n concentración f.
concentration camp n campo m de concentración.
concept [ˈkɒnsept] n concepto m.
concern [kənˈsɜːn] ◆ n 1. (worry, anxiety) preocupación f. 2. (company) negocio m, empresa f. ◆ vt 1. (worry) preocupar; **to be ~ed about** preocuparse por. 2. (involve) concernir; **to be ~ed with** (subj: person) estar involucrado en; **to ~ o.s. with sthg** preocuparse de OR por algo; **as far as ... is ~ed** por lo que a ... respecta.
concerning [kənˈsɜːnɪŋ] prep sobre, acerca de.
concert [ˈkɒnsət] n concierto m.
concerted [kənˈsɜːtɪd] adj conjunto (ta).
concert hall n sala f de conciertos.
concertina [ˌkɒnsəˈtiːnə] n concertina f.
concerto [kənˈtʃeətəʊ] (pl -s) n concierto m.
concession [kənˈseʃn] n 1. (allowance, franchise) concesión f. 2. (special price) descuento m, rebaja f; (reduced ticket) entrada f de descuento.
conciliatory [kənˈsɪliətrɪ] adj conciliador(ra).
concise [kənˈsaɪs] adj conciso(sa).
conclude [kənˈkluːd] ◆ vt 1. (bring to an end) concluir, terminar. 2. (deduce): **to ~ (that)** concluir que. 3. (agreement) llegar a; (business deal) cerrar; (treaty) firmar. ◆ vi terminar, concluir.
conclusion [kənˈkluːʒn] n 1. (decision) conclusión f. 2. (ending) final m. 3. (of business deal) cierre m; (of treaty) firma f; (of agreement) alcance m.
conclusive [kənˈkluːsɪv] adj concluyente, irrebatible.
concoct [kənˈkɒkt] vt 1. (excuse, story) ingeniar. 2. (food) confeccionar; (drink) preparar.
concoction [kənˈkɒkʃn] n (drink) brebaje m; (food) mezcla f.
concourse [ˈkɒŋkɔːs] n (of station etc) vestíbulo m.
concrete [ˈkɒŋkriːt] ◆ adj (definite, real) concreto(ta). ◆ n hormigón m, concreto m Amer. ◆ comp (made of concrete) de hormigón.

concur [kən'kɜːʳ] vi (agree): **to ~ (with)** estar de acuerdo OR coincidir (con).

concurrently [kən'kʌrəntlɪ] adv simultáneamente, al mismo tiempo.

concussion [kən'kʌʃn] n conmoción f cerebral.

condemn [kən'dem] vt 1. (gen): **to ~ sb (for/to)** condenar a alguien (por/a). 2. (building) declarar en ruinas.

condensation [ˌkɒnden'seɪʃn] n (on glass) vaho m.

condense [kən'dens] ◆ vt condensar. ◆ vi condensarse.

condensed milk [kən'denst-] n leche f condensada.

condescending [ˌkɒndɪ'sendɪŋ] adj altanero(ra), altivo(va).

condiment ['kɒndɪmənt] n fml condimento m.

condition [kən'dɪʃn] ◆ n 1. (state) estado m; **in good/bad ~** en buen/mal estado; **to be out of ~** no estar en forma. 2. (MED) (disease, complaint) afección f. 3. (provision) condición f; **on ~ that** a condición de que; **on one ~** con una condición. ◆ vt (gen) condicionar.

conditional [kən'dɪʃənl] adj condicional; **to be ~ on** OR **upon** depender de.

conditioner [kən'dɪʃnəʳ] n suavizante m.

condolences [kən'dəʊlənsɪz] npl pésame m; **to offer one's ~** dar uno su más sentido pésame.

condom ['kɒndəm] n condón m.

condominium [ˌkɒndə'mɪnɪəm] n Am 1. (apartment) piso m, apartamento m. 2. (apartment block) bloque m de pisos OR apartamentos.

condone [kən'dəʊn] vt perdonar.

conducive [kən'djuːsɪv] adj: **~ to** favorable para.

conduct [n 'kɒndʌkt, vb kən'dʌkt] ◆ n 1. (behaviour) conducta f. 2. (carrying out) dirección f. ◆ vt 1. (carry out) dirigir, llevar a cabo. 2. (behave): **to ~ o.s. well/badly** comportarse bien/mal. 3. (MUS) dirigir. 4. (PHYSICS) conducir.

conducted tour [kən'dʌktɪd-] n excursión f con guía.

conductor [kən'dʌktəʳ] n 1. (of orchestra, choir) director m, -ra f. 2. (on bus) cobrador m. 3. Am (on train) revisor m, -ra f.

conductress [kən'dʌktrɪs] n cobradora f.

cone [kəʊn] n 1. (shape) cono m. 2. (for ice cream) cucurucho m. 3. (from tree) piña f.

confectioner [kən'fekʃnəʳ] n confitero m, -ra f; **~'s (shop)** confitería f.

confectionery [kən'fekʃnərɪ] n (U) dulces mpl, golosinas fpl.

confederation [kənˌfedə'reɪʃn] n confederación f.

Confederation of British Industry n: **the ~** organización patronal británica, = **la CEOE.**

confer [kən'fɜːʳ] ◆ vt fml: **to ~ sthg (on)** otorgar OR conferir algo (a). ◆ vi: **to ~ (with)** consultar (con).

conference ['kɒnfərəns] n congreso m, conferencia f.

confess [kən'fes] ◆ vt confesar. ◆ vi 1. (to crime) confesarse; **to ~ to sthg** confesar algo. 2. (admit): **to ~ to sthg** admitir algo.

confession [kən'feʃn] n confesión f.

confetti [kən'fetɪ] n confeti m.

confide [kən'faɪd] vi: **to ~ (in)** confiar (en).

confidence ['kɒnfɪdəns] n 1. (self-assurance) confianza f OR seguridad f (en sí mismo/misma). 2. (trust) confianza f. 3. (secrecy): **in ~** en secreto. 4. (secret) intimidad f, secreto m.

confidence trick n timo m, estafa f.

confident ['kɒnfɪdənt] adj 1. (self-assured - person) seguro de sí mismo (segura de sí misma); (- smile, attitude) confiado(da). 2. (sure): **~ (of)** seguro(ra) (de).

confidential [ˌkɒnfɪ'denʃl] adj (gen) confidencial; (person) de confianza.

confine [kən'faɪn] vt 1. (limit, restrict) limitar, restringir; **to be ~d to** limitarse a. 2. (shut up) recluir, encerrar.

confined [kən'faɪnd] adj reducido(da).

confinement [kən'faɪnmənt] n (imprisonment) reclusión f.

confines ['kɒnfaɪnz] npl confines mpl.

confirm [kən'fɜːm] vt confirmar.

confirmation [ˌkɒnfə'meɪʃn] n confirmación f.

confirmed [kən'fɜːmd] adj (non-smoker) inveterado(da); (bachelor) empedernido.

confiscate ['kɒnfɪskeɪt] vt confiscar.

conflict [n 'kɒnflɪkt, vb kən'flɪkt] ◆ n conflicto m. ◆ vi: **to ~ (with)** estar en desacuerdo (con).

conflicting [kən'flɪktɪŋ] adj contrapuesto(ta).

conform [kən'fɔːm] vi 1. (behave as expected) amoldarse a las normas sociales. 2. (be in accordance): **to ~ (to** OR **with)** (expectations) corresponder (a);

(*rules*) ajustarse (a).

confound [kən'faʊnd] *vt* (*confuse, defeat*) confundir, desconcertar.

confront [kən'frʌnt] *vt* 1. (*problem, task*) hacer frente a. 2. (*subj: problem, task*) presentarse a. 3. (*enemy etc*) enfrentarse con. 4. (*challenge*): **to ~ sb (with)** poner a alguien cara a cara (con).

confrontation [ˌkɒnfrʌn'teɪʃn] *n* enfrentamiento *m*, confrontación *f*.

confuse [kən'fjuːz] *vt* 1. (*bewilder*) desconcertar. 2. (*mix up*): **to ~ (with)** confundir (con). 3. (*complicate, make less clear*) complicar.

confused [kən'fjuːzd] *adj* 1. (*not clear*) confuso(sa). 2. (*bewildered*) desconcertado(da).

confusing [kən'fjuːzɪŋ] *adj* confuso (sa).

confusion [kən'fjuːʒn] *n* 1. (*gen*) confusión *f*. 2. (*of person*) desconcierto *m*.

congeal [kən'dʒiːl] *vi* coagularse.

congenial [kən'dʒiːnjəl] *adj* ameno (na), agradable.

congested [kən'dʒestɪd] *adj* 1. (*area*) superpoblado(da); (*road*) congestionado(da). 2. (MED) congestionado(da).

congestion [kən'dʒestʃn] (U) *n* 1. (*of traffic*) retención *f*, congestión *f*. 2. (MED) congestión *f*.

conglomerate [kən'glɒmərət] *n* (COMM) conglomerado *m*.

congratulate [kən'grætʃʊleɪt] *vt*: **to ~ sb (on)** felicitar a alguien (por).

congratulations [kən,grætʃʊ'leɪʃənz] ◆ *npl* felicitaciones *fpl*. ◆ *excl* ¡enhorabuena!

congregate ['kɒŋgrɪgeɪt] *vi* (*people*) congregarse; (*animals*) juntarse.

congregation [ˌkɒŋgrɪ'geɪʃn] *n* (RELIG) feligreses *mpl*.

congress ['kɒŋgres] *n* congreso *m*. ► **Congress** *n* (*in US*): **(the) Congress** el Congreso.

congressman ['kɒŋgresmən] (*pl* -men [-mən]) *n* miembro *m* del Congreso.

conifer ['kɒnɪfəʳ] *n* conífera *f*.

conjugate ['kɒndʒʊgeɪt] *vt* conjugar.

conjugation [ˌkɒndʒʊ'geɪʃn] *n* conjugación *f*.

conjunction [kən'dʒʌŋkʃn] *n* 1. (GRAMM) conjunción *f*. 2. (*combination*): **in ~ with** juntamente con.

conjunctivitis [kən,dʒʌŋktɪ'vaɪtɪs] *n* conjuntivitis *f inv*.

conjure ['kʌndʒəʳ] *vi* hacer juegos de manos. ► **conjure up** *vt sep* (*evoke*) evocar.

conjurer ['kʌndʒərəʳ] *n* prestidigitador *m*, -ra *f*.

conk [kɒŋk] *n inf* (*nose*) napia *f*. ► **conk out** *vi inf* escacharrarse.

conker ['kɒŋkəʳ] *n* Br castaña *f* (*del castaño de Indias*).

conman ['kɒnmæn] (*pl* -men [-men]) *n* estafador *m*, timador *m*.

connect [kə'nekt] ◆ *vt* 1. (*join*): **to ~ sthg (to)** unir algo (con). 2. (*on telephone*): **I'll ~ you now** ahora le paso OR pongo. 3. (*associate*): **to ~ sthg/sb (with)** asociar algo/a alguien (con). 4. (ELEC): **to ~ sthg to** conectar algo a. ◆ *vi* (*train, plane, bus*): **to ~ (with)** enlazar (con).

connected [kə'nektɪd] *adj* (*related*): **~ (with)** relacionado(da) (con).

connection [kə'nekʃn] *n* 1. (*gen & ELEC*): **~ (between/with)** conexión *f* (entre/con); **in ~ with** con relación OR respecto a. 2. (*plane, train, bus*) enlace *m*. 3. (*professional acquaintance*) contacto *m*; **to have good ~s** tener mucho enchufe.

connive [kə'naɪv] *vi* 1. (*plot*): **to ~ (with)** confabularse (con). 2. (*allow to happen*): **to ~ at sthg** hacer la vista gorda con algo.

connoisseur [ˌkɒnə'sɜːʳ] *n* entendido *m*, -da *f*, experto *m*, -ta *f*.

conquer ['kɒŋkəʳ] *vt* 1. (*take by force*) conquistar. 2. (*gain control of, overcome*) doblegar, vencer.

conqueror ['kɒŋkərəʳ] *n* conquistador *m*, -ra *f*.

conquest ['kɒŋkwest] *n* conquista *f*.

cons [kɒnz] *npl* 1. Br *inf*: **all mod ~** con todas las comodidades. 2. → **pro.**

conscience ['kɒnʃəns] *n* conciencia *f*.

conscientious [ˌkɒnʃɪ'enʃəs] *adj* concienzudo(da).

conscious ['kɒnʃəs] *adj* 1. (*gen*) consciente; **to be ~ of** ser consciente de. 2. (*intentional*) deliberado(da).

consciousness ['kɒnʃəsnɪs] *n* 1. (*gen*) conciencia *f*. 2. (*state of being awake*) conocimiento *m*; **to lose/regain ~** perder/recobrar el conocimiento.

conscript ['kɒnskrɪpt] *n* recluta *m y f*.

conscription [kən'skrɪpʃn] *n* servicio *m* militar obligatorio.

consecutive [kən'sekjʊtɪv] *adj* consecutivo(va); **on three ~ days** tres días seguidos.

consent [kən'sent] ◆ *n* (U) 1. (*permission*) consentimiento *m*. 2. (*agreement*) acuerdo *m*. ◆ *vi*: **to ~ (to)** consentir (en).

consequence ['kɒnsɪkwəns] *n*
1. (*result*) consecuencia *f*; **in ~** por consiguiente. **2.** (*importance*) importancia *f*.
consequently ['kɒnsɪkwəntlɪ] *adv* por consiguiente.
conservation [ˌkɒnsə'veɪʃn] *n* conservación *f*.
conservative [kən'sɜːvətɪv] *adj* **1.** (*not modern*) conservador(ra). **2.** (*estimate, guess*) moderado(da). ▶ **Conservative** (POL) ◆ *adj* conservador(ra). ◆ *n* conservador *m*, -ra *f*.
Conservative Party *n*: **the ~** el partido Conservador británico.
conservatory [kən'sɜːvətrɪ] *n* pequeña habitación acristalada aneja a la casa.
conserve [*n* 'kɒnsɜːv, *vb* kən'sɜːv] ◆ *n* compota *f*. ◆ *vt* (*energy, supplies*) ahorrar; (*nature, wildlife*) conservar.
consider [kən'sɪdər] *vt* **1.** (*gen*) considerar; **to ~ doing sthg** pensar si hacer algo. **2.** (*take into account*) tener en cuenta; **all things ~ed** teniéndolo todo en cuenta.
considerable [kən'sɪdrəbl] *adj* considerable.
considerably [kən'sɪdrəblɪ] *adv* considerablemente, sustancialmente.
considerate [kən'sɪdərət] *adj* considerado(da).
consideration [kənˌsɪdə'reɪʃn] *n* consideración *f*; **to take sthg into ~** tomar OR tener algo en cuenta.
considering [kən'sɪdərɪŋ] ◆ *prep* habida cuenta de. ◆ *conj* después de todo.
consign [kən'saɪn] *vt*: **to ~ sthg/sb to** relegar algo/a alguien a.
consignment [kən'saɪnmənt] *n* remesa *f*.
consist [kən'sɪst] ▶ **consist in** *vt fus* consistir en, basarse en. ▶ **consist of** *vt fus* consistir en, constar de.
consistency [kən'sɪstənsɪ] *n* **1.** (*coherence - of behaviour, policy*) consecuencia *f*, coherencia *f*; (*of work*) regularidad *f*. **2.** (*texture*) consistencia *f*.
consistent [kən'sɪstənt] *adj* **1.** (*regular*) constante. **2.** (*coherent*): **~ (with)** consecuente (con).
consolation [ˌkɒnsə'leɪʃn] *n* consuelo *m*.
console [*n* 'kɒnsəʊl, *vt* kən'səʊl] ◆ *n* consola *f*. ◆ *vt* consolar.
consolidation [kənˌsɒlɪ'deɪʃn] *n* (*strengthening*) consolidación *f*.
consonant ['kɒnsənənt] *n* consonante *f*.
consortium [kən'sɔːtjəm] (*pl* **-tiums** OR

-tia [-tjə]) *n* consorcio *m*.
conspicuous [kən'spɪkjʊəs] *adj* (*building*) visible; (*colour*) llamativo(va).
conspiracy [kən'spɪrəsɪ] *n* conspiración *f*.
conspire [kən'spaɪər] ◆ *vt*: **to ~ to do sthg** conspirar para hacer algo. ◆ *vi* **1.** (*plan secretly*): **to ~ (against/with)** conspirar (contra/con). **2.** (*combine*) confabularse.
constable ['kʌnstəbl] *n* policía *m* y *f*.
constabulary [kən'stæbjʊlərɪ] *n* policía *f* (*de una zona determinada*).
constant ['kɒnstənt] *adj* (*gen*) constante.
constantly ['kɒnstəntlɪ] *adv* (*forever*) constantemente.
consternation [ˌkɒnstə'neɪʃn] *n* consternación *f*.
constipated ['kɒnstɪpeɪtɪd] *adj* estreñido(da).
constipation [ˌkɒnstɪ'peɪʃn] *n* estreñimiento *m*.
constituency [kən'stɪtjʊənsɪ] *n* (*area*) distrito *m* electoral.
constituent [kən'stɪtjʊənt] *n* **1.** (*voter*) votante *m* y *f*. **2.** (*element*) componente *m*, constituyente *m*.
constitute ['kɒnstɪtjuːt] *vt* constituir.
constitution [ˌkɒnstɪ'tjuːʃn] *n* constitución *f*.
constraint [kən'streɪnt] *n* **1.** (*restriction*): **~ (on)** limitación *f* (de). **2.** (*self-control*) autocontrol *m*. **3.** (*coercion*) coacción *f*.
construct [kən'strʌkt] *vt lit & fig* construir.
construction [kən'strʌkʃn] ◆ *n* construcción *f*. ◆ *comp*: **~ company** (empresa *f*) constructora *f*; **~ industry** (industria *f* OR sector *m* de la) construcción *f*; **~ site** obra *f*.
constructive [kən'strʌktɪv] *adj* constructivo(va).
construe [kən'struː] *vt fml*: **to ~ sthg as** interpretar algo como.
consul ['kɒnsəl] *n* cónsul *m* y *f*.
consulate ['kɒnsjʊlət] *n* consulado *m*.
consult [kən'sʌlt] ◆ *vt* consultar. ◆ *vi*: **to ~ with sb** consultar a OR con alguien.
consultant [kən'sʌltənt] *n* **1.** (*expert*) asesor *m*, -ra *f*. **2.** Br (*hospital doctor*) (médico) especialista *m*, (médica) especialista *f*.
consultation [ˌkɒnsəl'teɪʃn] *n* **1.** (*gen*) consulta *f*. **2.** (*discussion*) discusión *f*.
consulting room [kən'sʌltɪŋ-] *n* consultorio *m*, consulta *f*.

consume [kən'sju:m] *vt lit & fig* consumir.

consumer [kən'sju:mə^r] *n* consumidor *m*, -ra *f*.

consumer goods *npl* bienes *mpl* de consumo.

consumer society *n* sociedad *f* de consumo.

consummate [*adj* kən'sʌmət, *vb* 'kɒnsəmeɪt] ◆ *adj* 1. (*skill, ease*) absoluto (ta). 2. (*liar, politician, snob*) consumado (da). ◆ *vt* (*marriage*) consumar.

consumption [kən'sʌmpʃn] *n* (*use*) consumo *m*.

contact ['kɒntækt] ◆ *n* contacto *m*; **in ~ (with)** en contacto (con); **to lose ~ with** perder (el) contacto con; **to make ~ with** ponerse en contacto con. ◆ *vt* ponerse en contacto con, contactar con.

contact lens *n* lentilla *f*, lente *f* de contacto.

contagious [kən'teɪdʒəs] *adj* contagioso(sa).

contain [kən'teɪn] *vt* contener; **to ~ o.s.** contenerse.

container [kən'teɪnə^r] *n* 1. (*box, bottle etc*) recipiente *m*, envase *m*. 2. (*for transporting goods*) contenedor *m*.

contaminate [kən'tæmɪneɪt] *vt* contaminar.

cont'd *abbr of* **continued**.

contemplate ['kɒntempleɪt] ◆ *vt* 1. (*consider*) considerar, pensar en. 2. *fml* (*look at*) contemplar. ◆ *vi* reflexionar.

contemporary [kən'tempərərɪ] ◆ *adj* contemporáneo(a). ◆ *n* contemporáneo *m*, -a *f*.

contempt [kən'tempt] *n* 1. (*scorn*): **~ (for)** desprecio *m* OR desdén *m* (por). 2. (JUR) desacato *m*.

contemptuous [kən'temptʃʊəs] *adj* despreciativo(va); **to be ~ of sthg** despreciar algo.

contend [kən'tend] ◆ *vi* 1. (*deal*): **to ~ with** enfrentarse a. 2. (*compete*): **to ~ for/against** competir por/contra. ◆ *vt fml*: **to ~ that** sostener OR afirmar que.

contender [kən'tendə^r] *n* (*gen*) contendiente *m* y *f*; (*for title*) aspirante *m* y *f*.

content [*n* 'kɒntent, *adj* & *vb* kən'tent] ◆ *adj*: **~ (with)** contento(ta) OR satisfecho(cha) (con); **to be ~ to do sthg** contentarse con hacer algo. ◆ *n* contenido *m*. ◆ *vt*: **to ~ o.s. with sthg/with doing sthg** contentarse con algo/con hacer algo. ▶ **contents** *npl* contenido *m*.

contented [kən'tentɪd] *adj* satisfecho(cha), contento(ta).

contention [kən'tenʃn] *n fml* 1. (*argument, assertion*) argumento *m*. 2. (U) (*disagreement*) disputas *fpl*. 3. (*competition*): **to be in ~** entrar en liza.

contest [*n* 'kɒntest, *vb* kən'test] ◆ *n* 1. (*competition*) competición *f*, concurso *m*. 2. (*for power, control*) lucha *f*. ◆ *vt* 1. (*seat, election*) presentarse como candidato(ta) a. 2. (*dispute - statement*) disputar; (*- decision*) impugnar.

contestant [kən'testənt] *n* (*in quiz show*) concursante *m* y *f*; (*in race*) participante *m* y *f*; (*in boxing match*) contrincante *m* y *f*.

context ['kɒntekst] *n* contexto *m*.

continent ['kɒntɪnənt] *n* continente *m*. ▶ **Continent** *n* Br: **the Continent** la Europa continental.

continental [,kɒntɪ'nentl] *adj* 1. (GEOGR) continental. 2. (*European*) de la Europa continental.

continental breakfast *n* desayuno *m* continental.

continental quilt *n* Br edredón *m*.

contingency [kən'tɪndʒənsɪ] *n* contingencia *f*.

contingency plan *n* plan *m* de emergencia.

continual [kən'tɪnjʊəl] *adj* continuo (nua), constante.

continually [kən'tɪnjʊəlɪ] *adv* continuamente, constantemente.

continuation [kən,tɪnjʊ'eɪʃn] *n* continuación *f*.

continue [kən'tɪnju:] ◆ *vt*: **to ~ (doing OR to do sthg)** continuar (haciendo algo); **to be ~d** continuará. ◆ *vi*: **to ~ (with sthg)** continuar (con algo).

continuous [kən'tɪnjʊəs] *adj* continuo (nua).

continuously [kən'tɪnjʊəslɪ] *adv* continuamente, ininterrumpidamente.

contort [kən'tɔ:t] *vt* retorcer.

contortion [kən'tɔ:ʃn] *n* contorsión *f*.

contour ['kɒn,tʊə^r] *n* 1. (*outline*) contorno *m*. 2. (*on map*) curva *f* de nivel.

contraband ['kɒntrəbænd] ◆ *adj* de contrabando. ◆ *n* contrabando *m*.

contraception [,kɒntrə'sepʃn] *n* anticoncepción *f*.

contraceptive [,kɒntrə'septɪv] ◆ *adj* anticonceptivo(va). ◆ *n* anticonceptivo *m*.

contract [*n* 'kɒntrækt, *vb* kən'trækt] ◆ *n* contrato *m*. ◆ *vt* 1. (*through legal agreement*): **to ~ sb (to do sthg)** contratar a alguien (para hacer algo); **to ~ to do sthg** comprometerse a hacer algo (por contrato). 2. *fml* (*illness, disease*) contraer.

◆ *vi* (*decrease in size, length*) contraerse.
contraction [kən'trækʃn] *n* contracción *f*.
contractor [kən'træktər] *n* contratista *m* y *f*.
contradict [ˌkɒntrə'dɪkt] *vt* contradecir.
contradiction [ˌkɒntrə'dɪkʃn] *n* contradicción *f*.
contraflow ['kɒntrəfləʊ] *n* estrechamiento (*de la autopista*) a una carretera de dos direcciones.
contraption [kən'træpʃn] *n* chisme *m*, artilugio *m*.
contrary ['kɒntrərɪ, *adj sense 2* kən'treərɪ] ◆ *adj* 1. (*opposite*) contrario(ria); ~ **to** en contra de. 2. (*awkward*) obstinado(da). ◆ *n*: **the** ~ lo contrario; **on the** ~ al contrario. ▶ **contrary to** *prep* en contra de.
contrast [*n* 'kɒntrɑːst, *vb* kən'trɑːst] ◆ *n*: ~ (**between** OR **with**) contraste *m* (entre); **by** OR **in** ~ en cambio; **in** ~ **with** OR **to** a diferencia de. ◆ *vt*: **to** ~ **sthg with** contrastar algo con. ◆ *vi*: **to** ~ (**with**) contrastar (con).
contravene [ˌkɒntrə'viːn] *vt* contravenir.
contribute [kən'trɪbjuːt] ◆ *vt* (*give*) contribuir, aportar. ◆ *vi* 1. (*gen*): **to** ~ (**to**) contribuir (a). 2. (*write material*): **to** ~ **to** colaborar con.
contribution [ˌkɒntrɪ'bjuːʃn] *n* 1. (*gen*): ~ (**to**) contribución *f* (a). 2. (*article*) colaboración *f*.
contributor [kən'trɪbjutər] *n* 1. (*of money*) contribuyente *m* y *f*. 2. (*to magazine, newspaper*) colaborador *m*, -ra *f*.
contrive [kən'traɪv] *fml vt* 1. (*engineer*) maquinar, idear. 2. (*manage*): **to** ~ **to do sthg** lograr hacer algo.
contrived [kən'traɪvd] *adj* inverosímil.
control [kən'trəʊl] ◆ *n* 1. (*gen & COMPUT*) control *m*; (*on spending*) restricción *f*; **in** ~ **of** al mando de; **to be in** ~ **of the situation** dominar la situación; **out of/under** ~ fuera de/bajo control. 2. (*of emotions*) dominio *m*. ◆ *vt* 1. (*gen*) controlar; **to** ~ **o.s.** dominarse, controlarse. 2. (*operate - machine, plane*) manejar; (*- central heating*) regular. ▶ **controls** *npl* (*of machine, vehicle*) controles *mpl*.
controller [kən'trəʊlər] *n* (*FIN*) interventor *m*, -ra *f*; (*RADIO & TV*) director *m*, -ra *f*.
control panel *n* tablero *m* de instrumentos OR de mandos.
control tower *n* torre *f* de control.

controversial [ˌkɒntrə'vɜːʃl] *adj* polémico(ca).
controversy ['kɒntrəvɜːsɪ, *Br* kən'trɒvəsɪ] *n* controversia *f*, polémica *f*.
convalesce [ˌkɒnvə'les] *vi* convalecer.
convene [kən'viːn] ◆ *vt* convocar. ◆ *vi* reunirse.
convenience [kən'viːnjəns] *n* comodidad *f*; **do it at your** ~ hágalo cuando le venga bien.
convenience store *n Am* tienda *f* que abre hasta tarde.
convenient [kən'viːnjənt] *adj* 1. (*suitable*) conveniente; **is Monday** ~? ¿te viene bien el lunes? 2. (*handy - size*) práctico(ca); (*- position*) adecuado(da); ~ **for** (*well-situated*) bien situado para.
convent ['kɒnvənt] *n* convento *m*.
convention [kən'venʃn] *n* convención *f*.
conventional [kən'venʃənl] *adj* convencional.
converge [kən'vɜːdʒ] *vi lit & fig*: **to** ~ (**on**) converger (en).
conversant [kən'vɜːsənt] *adj fml*: ~ **with** familiarizado(da) con.
conversation [ˌkɒnvə'seɪʃn] *n* conversación *f*.
conversational [ˌkɒnvə'seɪʃənl] *adj* coloquial.
converse [*n* 'kɒnvɜːs, *vb* kən'vɜːs] ◆ *n*: **the** ~ lo contrario OR opuesto. ◆ *vi fml*: **to** ~ (**with**) conversar (con).
conversely [kən'vɜːslɪ] *adv fml* a la inversa.
conversion [kən'vɜːʃn] *n* (*gen & RELIG*) conversión *f*.
convert [*vb* kən'vɜːt, *n* 'kɒnvɜːt] ◆ *vt* 1. (*gen*): **to** ~ **sthg** (**to** OR **into**) convertir algo (en). 2. (*change belief of*): **to** ~ **sb** (**to**) convertir a alguien (a). ◆ *n* converso *m*, -sa *f*.
convertible [kən'vɜːtəbl] ◆ *adj* 1. (*sofa*): ~ **sofa** sofá-cama *m*. 2. (*currency*) convertible. 3. (*car*) descapotable. ◆ *n* (*coche m*) descapotable *m*.
convex [kɒn'veks] *adj* convexo(xa).
convey [kən'veɪ] *vt* 1. *fml* (*transport*) transportar. 2. (*express*): **to** ~ **sthg** (**to**) expresar OR transmitir algo (a).
conveyer belt [kən'veɪər-] *n* cinta *f* transportadora.
convict [*n* 'kɒnvɪkt, *vb* kən'vɪkt] ◆ *n* presidiario *m*, -ria *f*. ◆ *vt*: **to** ~ **sb of** condenar a alguien por.
conviction [kən'vɪkʃn] *n* 1. (*belief, fervour*) convicción *f*. 2. (*JUR*) condena *f*.
convince [kən'vɪns] *vt*: **to** ~ **sb** (**of sthg/**

to do sthg) convencer a alguien (de algo/para que haga algo).

convincing [kənˈvɪnsɪŋ] *adj* convincente.

convoluted [ˈkɒnvəluːtɪd] *adj* (*tortuous*) retorcido(da).

convoy [ˈkɒnvɔɪ] *n* convoy *m*.

convulse [kənˈvʌls] *vt*: **to be ~d with** (*pain*) retorcerse de; (*laughter*) troncharse de.

convulsion [kənˈvʌlʃn] *n* (MED) convulsión *f*.

coo [kuː] *vi* arrullar.

cook [kʊk] ◆ *n* cocinero *m*, -ra *f*. ◆ *vt* 1. (*gen*) cocinar, guisar; (*prepare*) preparar. 2. (*in oven*) asar, hacer en el horno. ◆ *vi* 1. (*prepare food*) cocinar, guisar. 2. (*in oven*) cocerse. ► **cook up** *vt sep* (*plan, deal*) tramar, urdir; (*excuse*) inventarse.

cookbook [ˈkʊkˌbʊk] = **cookery book**.

cooker [ˈkʊkər] *n* cocina *f* (*aparato*).

cookery [ˈkʊkərɪ] *n* cocina *f* (*arte*).

cookery book *n* libro *m* de cocina.

cookie [ˈkʊkɪ] *n* Am galleta *f*.

cooking [ˈkʊkɪŋ] *n* (*food*) cocina *f*.

cool [kuːl] ◆ *adj* 1. (*not warm*) fresco (ca). 2. (*calm*) tranquilo(la). 3. (*unfriendly*) frío(a). 4. *inf* (*hip*) guay, chachi. ◆ *vt* refrescar. ◆ *vi* (*become less warm*) enfriarse. ◆ *n*: **to keep/lose one's ~** mantener/perder la calma. ► **cool down** *vi* 1. (*become less warm*) enfriarse. 2. (*become less angry*) calmarse.

cool box *n* nevera *f* portátil.

coop [kuːp] *n* gallinero *m*. ► **coop up** *vt sep inf* encerrar.

Co-op [ˈkəʊˌɒp] (*abbr of* co-operative society) *n* Coop. *f*.

cooperate [kəʊˈɒpəreɪt] *vi*: **to ~ (with)** cooperar (con).

cooperation [kəʊˌɒpəˈreɪʃn] *n* (U) cooperación *f*.

cooperative [kəʊˈɒpərətɪv] ◆ *adj* 1. (*helpful*) servicial. 2. (*collective*) cooperativo(va). ◆ *n* cooperativa *f*.

coordinate [*n* kəʊˈɔːdɪnət, *vt* kəʊˈɔːdɪneɪt] ◆ *n* coordenada *f*. ◆ *vt* coordinar. ► **coordinates** *npl* (*clothes*) conjunto *m*.

coordination [kəʊˌɔːdɪˈneɪʃn] *n* coordinación *f*.

cop [kɒp] *n inf* poli *m*, paco *m* Amer.

cope [kəʊp] *vi* arreglárselas; **to ~ with** (*work*) poder con; (*problem, situation*) hacer frente a.

Copenhagen [ˌkəʊpənˈheɪgən] *n*

Copenhague.

copier [ˈkɒpɪər] *n* fotocopiadora *f*.

cop-out *n inf* escaqueo *m*.

copper [ˈkɒpər] *n* 1. (*metal*) cobre *m*. 2. Br *inf* (*policeman*) poli *m*.

coppice [ˈkɒpɪs], **copse** [kɒps] *n* bosquecillo *m*.

copy [ˈkɒpɪ] ◆ *n* 1. (*imitation, duplicate*) copia *f*. 2. (*of book, magazine*) ejemplar *m*. ◆ *vt* 1. (*imitate*) copiar. 2. (*photocopy*) fotocopiar.

copyright [ˈkɒpɪraɪt] *n* (U) derechos *mpl* de autor.

coral [ˈkɒrəl] *n* coral *m*.

cord [kɔːd] *n* 1. (*string*) cuerda *f*; (*for tying clothes*) cordón *m*. 2. (*wire*) cable *m*, cordón *m*. 3. (*fabric*) pana *f*. ► **cords** *npl* pantalones *mpl* de pana.

cordial [ˈkɔːdjəl] ◆ *adj* cordial, afectuoso(sa). ◆ *n* bebida *de frutas concentrada*.

cordon [ˈkɔːdn] *n* cordón *m*. ► **cordon off** *vt sep* acordonar.

corduroy [ˈkɔːdərɔɪ] *n* pana *f*.

core [kɔːr] ◆ *n* 1. (*of fruit*) corazón *m*. 2. (*of Earth, nuclear reactor, group*) núcleo *m*. 3. (*of issue, matter*) meollo *m*. ◆ *vt* quitar el corazón de.

Corfu [kɔːˈfuː] *n* Corfú.

corgi [ˈkɔːgɪ] (*pl* -s) *n* perro *m* galés.

coriander [ˌkɒrɪˈændər] *n* cilantro *m*.

cork [kɔːk] *n* corcho *m*.

corkscrew [ˈkɔːkskruː] *n* sacacorchos *m inv*.

corn [kɔːn] *n* 1. Br (*wheat, barley, oats*) cereal *m*. 2. Am (*maize*) maíz *m*, choclo *m* Amer; **~ on the cob** mazorca *f*. 3. (*callus*) callo *m*.

cornea [ˈkɔːnɪə] (*pl* -s) *n* córnea *f*.

corned beef [kɔːnd-] *n* carne de vaca cocinada y enlatada.

corner [ˈkɔːnər] ◆ *n* 1. (*angle - on outside*) esquina *f*; (*- on inside*) rincón *m*. 2. (*bend - in street, road*) curva *f*; **just around the ~** a la vuelta de la esquina. 3. (*faraway place*) rincón *m*. 4. (*in football*) córner *m*. ◆ *vt* 1. (*trap*) arrinconar. 2. (*monopolize*) acaparar.

corner shop *n* tienda pequeña de barrio que vende comida, artículos de limpieza etc.

cornerstone [ˈkɔːnəstəʊn] *n fig* piedra *f* angular.

cornet [ˈkɔːnɪt] *n* 1. (*instrument*) corneta *f*. 2. Br (*ice-cream cone*) cucurucho *m*.

cornflakes [ˈkɔːnfleɪks] *npl* copos *mpl* de maíz, cornflakes *mpl*.

cornflour Br [ˈkɔːnflaʊər], **cornstarch** Am [ˈkɔːnstɑːtʃ] *n* harina *f* de maíz, maicena *f*.

Cornwall ['kɔːnwɔːl] n Cornualles.

corny ['kɔːnɪ] adj inf trillado(da).

coronary ['kɒrənrɪ], **coronary thrombosis** [-θrɒm'bəʊsɪs] (pl coronary thromboses [-θrɒm'bəʊsiːz]) n trombosis f inv coronaria.

coronation [,kɒrə'neɪʃn] n coronación f.

coroner ['kɒrənər] n = juez m y f de instrucción.

Corp. (abbr of corporation) Corp.

corporal ['kɔːpərəl] n cabo m y f.

corporal punishment n castigo m corporal.

corporate ['kɔːpərət] adj 1. (business) corporativo(va). 2. (collective) colectivo (va).

corporation [,kɔːpə'reɪʃn] n 1. (council) ayuntamiento m. 2. (large company) = sociedad f mercantil.

corps [kɔːr] (pl inv) n cuerpo m.

corpse [kɔːps] n cadáver m.

correct [kə'rekt] ◆ adj 1. (accurate - time, amount, forecast) exacto(ta); (- answer) correcto(ta). 2. (socially acceptable) correcto(ta). 3. (appropriate, required) apropiado(da). ◆ vt corregir.

correction [kə'rekʃn] n corrección f.

correctly [kə'rektlɪ] adv 1. (gen) correctamente. 2. (appropriately, as required) apropiadamente.

correlation [,kɒrə'leɪʃn] n: ~ **(between)** correlación f (entre).

correspond [,kɒrɪ'spɒnd] vi 1. (correlate): to ~ **(with** OR **to)** corresponder (con OR a). 2. (match): to ~ **(with** OR **to)** coincidir (con). 3. (write letters): to ~ **(with)** cartearse (con).

correspondence [,kɒrɪ'spɒndəns] n: ~ **(with/between)** correspondencia f (con/entre).

correspondence course n curso m por correspondencia.

correspondent [,kɒrɪ'spɒndənt] n (reporter) corresponsal m y f.

corridor ['kɒrɪdɔːr] n pasillo m.

corroborate [kə'rɒbəreɪt] vt corroborar.

corrode [kə'rəud] ◆ vt corroer. ◆ vi corroerse.

corrosion [kə'rəʊʒn] n corrosión f.

corrugated ['kɒrəgeɪtɪd] adj ondulado(da).

corrugated iron n chapa f ondulada.

corrupt [kə'rʌpt] ◆ adj (gen & COMPUT) corrupto(ta). ◆ vt corromper; to ~ a minor pervertir a un menor.

corruption [kə'rʌpʃn] n corrupción f.

corset ['kɔːsɪt] n corsé m, faja f.

Corsica ['kɔːsɪkə] n Córcega.

cortege, cortège [kɔː'teɪʒ] n cortejo m.

cosh [kɒʃ] ◆ n porra f. ◆ vt aporrear.

cosmetic [kɒz'metɪk] ◆ n cosmético m. ◆ adj fig superficial.

cosmopolitan [kɒzmə'pɒlɪtn] adj cosmopolita.

cosset ['kɒsɪt] vt mimar.

cost [kɒst] (pt & pp cost OR -ed) ◆ n 1. (price) coste m, precio m. 2. fig (loss, damage) coste m, coste m; **at the ~ of** a costa de; **at all ~s** a toda costa. ◆ vt 1. (gen) costar; **it ~ us £20/a lot of effort** nos costó 20 libras/mucho esfuerzo; **how much does it ~?** ¿cuánto cuesta OR vale? 2. (estimate) presupuestar, preparar un presupuesto de. ▶ **costs** npl (JUR) litisexpensas fpl.

co-star ['kəu-] n coprotagonista m y f.

Costa Rica [,kɒstə'riːkə] n Costa Rica.

Costa Rican [,kɒstə'riːkən] ◆ adj costarricense. ◆ n costarricense m y f.

cost-effective adj rentable.

costing ['kɒstɪŋ] n cálculo m del coste.

costly ['kɒstlɪ] adj costoso(sa).

cost of living n: **the ~** el coste de la vida.

cost price n precio m de coste.

costume ['kɒstjuːm] n 1. (gen) traje m. 2. (swimming costume) traje m de baño.

costume jewellery n (U) bisutería f.

cosy Br, **cozy** Am ['kəʊzɪ] ◆ adj 1. (warm and comfortable - room) acogedor (ra). 2. (intimate) agradable, amigable. ◆ n funda f para tetera.

cot [kɒt] n 1. Br (for child) cuna f. 2. Am (folding bed) cama f plegable.

cottage ['kɒtɪdʒ] n casa f de campo, chalé m.

cottage cheese n requesón m.

cottage pie n Br pastel de carne picada con una capa de puré de patatas.

cotton ['kɒtn] n 1. (fabric) algodón m. 2. (thread) hilo m (de algodón). ▶ **cotton on** vi inf: to ~ **on (to)** caer en la cuenta (de).

cotton candy n Am azúcar m hilado, algodón m.

cotton wool n algodón m (hidrófilo).

couch [kautʃ] ◆ n 1. (sofa) sofá m, diván m. 2. (in doctor's surgery) camilla f. ◆ vt: to ~ **sthg** in formular algo en.

couchette [kuː'ʃet] n Br litera f.

cough [kɒf] ◆ n tos f. ◆ vi toser.

cough mixture n Br jarabe m para la tos.

cough sweet n Br caramelo m para la tos.

cough syrup = **cough mixture**.

could [kʊd] pt → **can²**.

couldn't ['kʊdnt] = **could not**.

could've ['kʊdəv] = **could have**.

council ['kaʊnsl] n 1. (of a town) ayuntamiento m; (of a county) = diputación f. 2. (group, organization) consejo m. 3. (meeting) junta f, consejo m.

council estate n urbanización de viviendas de protección oficial.

council house n Br = casa f de protección oficial.

councillor ['kaʊnsələ'] n concejal m y f.

council tax n Br impuesto municipal basado en el valor de la propiedad, = contribución f urbana.

counsel ['kaʊnsəl] n 1. (U) fml (advice) consejo m. 2. (lawyer) abogado m, -da f.

counsellor Br, **counselor** Am ['kaʊnsələ'] n 1. (gen) consejero m, -ra f. 2. Am (lawyer) abogado m, -da f.

count [kaʊnt] ◆ n 1. (total) total m; (of votes) recuento m; **to keep/lose ~ of** llevar/perder la cuenta de. 2. (aristocrat) conde m. ◆ vt 1. (add up) contar; (total, cost) calcular. 2. (consider): **to ~ sb as** considerar a alguien como. 3. (include) incluir, contar. ◆ vi contar; **to ~ (up) to** contar hasta; **to ~ for** valer. ▶ **count against** vt fus perjudicar. ▶ **count (up)on** vt fus contar con. ▶ **count up** vt fus contar.

countdown ['kaʊntdaʊn] n cuenta f atrás.

counter ['kaʊntə'] ◆ n 1. (in shop) mostrador m; (in bank) ventanilla f. 2. (in board game) ficha f. ◆ vt: **to ~ sthg with** responder a algo mediante; **to ~ sthg by doing sthg** contrarrestar algo haciendo algo. ▶ **counter to** adv contrario a.

counteract [ˌkaʊntə'rækt] vt contrarrestar.

counterattack [ˌkaʊntərə'tæk] ◆ n contraataque m. ◆ vt & vi contraatacar.

counterclockwise [ˌkaʊntə'klɒkwaɪz] adv Am en sentido opuesto a las agujas del reloj.

counterfeit ['kaʊntəfɪt] ◆ adj falsificado(da). ◆ vt falsificar.

counterfoil ['kaʊntəfɔɪl] n matriz f.

countermand [ˌkaʊntə'mɑːnd] vt revocar.

counterpart ['kaʊntəpɑːt] n homólogo m, -ga f.

counterproductive [ˌkaʊntəprə-'dʌktɪv] adj contraproducente.

countess ['kaʊntɪs] n condesa f.

countless ['kaʊntlɪs] adj innumerable.

country ['kʌntrɪ] n 1. (nation) país m. 2. (population): **the ~** el pueblo. 3. (countryside): **the ~** el campo. 4. (terrain) terreno m. ◆ comp campestre.

country dancing n (U) baile m tradicional.

country house n casa f de campo.

countryman ['kʌntrɪmən] (pl -men [-mən]) n (from same country) compatriota m.

country park n Br parque natural abierto al público.

countryside ['kʌntrɪsaɪd] n (land) campo m; (landscape) paisaje m.

county ['kaʊntɪ] n condado m.

county council n Br organismo que gobierna un condado, = diputación f provincial.

coup [kuː] n 1. (rebellion): **~ (d'état)** golpe m (de estado). 2. (masterstroke) éxito m.

couple ['kʌpl] ◆ n 1. (two people in relationship) pareja f. 2. (two objects, people): **a ~ (of)** un par (de). 3. (a few - objects, people): **a ~ (of)** un par (de), unos(nas). ◆ vt (join): **to ~ sthg (to)** enganchar algo (con).

coupon ['kuːpɒn] n (gen) cupón m; (for pools) boleto m.

courage ['kʌrɪdʒ] n valor m.

courageous [kə'reɪdʒəs] adj valiente.

courgette [kɔː'ʒet] n Br calabacín m.

courier ['kʊrɪə'] n 1. (on holiday) guía m y f. 2. (to deliver letters, packages) mensajero m, -ra f.

course [kɔːs] n 1. (gen) curso m; (of lectures) ciclo m; (UNIV) carrera f; **~ of treatment** (MED) tratamiento m; **off ~** fuera de su rumbo; **~ (of action)** medida f; **in the ~ of** a lo largo de. 2. (of meal) plato m. 3. (SPORT) (for golf) campo m (de golf); (for horse racing) hipódromo m. ▶ **of course** adv 1. (inevitably, not surprisingly) naturalmente. 2. (certainly) claro; **of ~ not** claro que no.

coursebook ['kɔːsbʊk] n libro m de texto.

coursework ['kɔːswɜːk] n (U) trabajo m realizado durante el curso.

court [kɔːt] ◆ n 1. (place of trial, judge, jury etc) tribunal m; **to take sb to ~** llevar a alguien a juicio. 2. (SPORT) cancha f, pista f. 3. (of king, queen etc) corte f. ◆ vi dated (go out together) cortejarse.

courteous ['kɜːtjəs] adj cortés.

courtesy ['kɜːtɪsɪ] ◆ n cortesía f.
◆ comp de cortesía. ▶ (by) courtesy of prep (the author) con permiso de; (a company) por cortesía OR gentileza de.

courthouse ['kɔːthaus, pl -hauzɪz] n Am palacio m de justicia.

courtier ['kɔːtjəʳ] n cortesano m.

court-martial (pl court-martials OR courts-martial) n consejo m de guerra.

courtroom ['kɔːtrum] n sala f del tribunal.

courtyard ['kɔːtjɑːd] n patio m.

cousin ['kʌzn] n primo m, -ma f.

cove [kəuv] n cala f, ensenada f.

covenant ['kʌvənənt] n 1. (of money) compromiso escrito para el pago regular de una contribución esp con fines caritativos. 2. (agreement) convenio m.

Covent Garden [ˌkɒvənt-] n famosa galería comercial londinense donde se dan cita todo tipo de artistas callejeros.

cover ['kʌvəʳ] ◆ n 1. (covering) cubierta f; (lid) tapa f; (for seat, typewriter) funda f. 2. (of book) tapa f, cubierta f; (of magazine - at the front) portada f; (- at the back) contraportada f. 3. (protection, shelter) refugio m; to take ~ (from weather, gunfire): refugiarse; under ~ (from weather) a cubierto. 4. (concealment) tapadera f; under ~ of al amparo OR abrigo de. 5. (insurance) cobertura f. 6. (blanket) manta f. ◆ vt 1. (gen): to ~ sthg (with) cubrir algo (de); (with lid) tapar algo (con). 2. (insure): to ~ sb (against) cubrir OR asegurar a alguien (contra). 3. (include) abarcar. 4. (report on) informar sobre. 5. (discuss, deal with) abarcar. ▶ cover up vt sep 1. (place sthg over) tapar. 2. (conceal) encubrir.

coverage ['kʌvərɪdʒ] n (of news) reportaje m, cobertura f informativa.

cover charge n precio m del cubierto.

covering ['kʌvərɪŋ] n 1. (for floor etc) cubierta f. 2. (of snow, dust) capa f.

covering letter Br, **cover letter** Am n (with CV) carta f de presentación; (with parcel, letter) nota f aclaratoria.

cover note n Br póliza f provisional.

covert ['kʌvət] adj (operation) encubierto(ta), secreto(ta); (glance) furtivo(va).

cover-up n encubrimiento m.

covet ['kʌvɪt] vt codiciar.

cow [kau] ◆ n 1. (female type of cattle) vaca f. 2. (female elephant, whale, seal) hembra f. 3. Br inf pej (woman) bruja f, foca f. ◆ vt acobardar, intimidar.

coward ['kauəd] n cobarde m y f.

cowardly ['kauədlɪ] adj cobarde.

cowboy ['kaubɔɪ] n (cattlehand) vaquero m, tropero m Amer.

cower ['kauəʳ] vi encogerse.

cox [kɒks], **coxswain** ['kɒksən] n timonel m y f.

coy [kɔɪ] adj gazmoño(ña) (afectada).

cozy Am = **cosy**.

crab [kræb] n cangrejo m.

crab apple n manzana f silvestre.

crack [kræk] ◆ n 1. (split - in wood, ground) grieta f; (- in glass, pottery) raja f. 2. (gap) rendija f. 3. (sharp noise - of whip) chasquido m; (- of twigs) crujido m. 4. inf (attempt): to have a ~ at sthg intentar algo. 5. drugs sl (cocaine) crack m. ◆ adj de primera. ◆ vt 1. (cause to split) romper, partir. 2. (egg, nut) cascar. 3. (whip etc) chasquear. 4. (bang - head) golpearse. 5. (solve) dar con la clave de. 6. inf (make - joke) contar. ◆ vi 1. (split - skin, wood, ground) agrietarse; (- pottery, glass) partirse. 2. (break down) hundirse. 3. (make sharp noise - whip) chasquear; (- twigs) crujir. 4. Br inf (act quickly): to get ~ing ponerse manos a la obra. ▶ crack down vi: to ~ down (on) tomar medidas severas (contra). ▶ crack up vi venirse abajo.

cracker ['krækəʳ] n 1. (biscuit) galleta f (salada). 2. Br (for Christmas) tubo con sorpresa típico de Navidades.

crackers ['krækəz] adj Br inf majara.

crackle ['krækl] vi (fire) crujir, chasquear; (radio) sonar con interferencias.

cradle ['kreɪdl] ◆ n (baby's bed, birthplace) cuna f. ◆ vt acunar, mecer.

craft [krɑːft] (pl sense 2 inv) n 1. (trade) oficio m; (skill) arte m. 2. (boat) embarcación f.

craftsman ['krɑːftsmən] (pl -men [-mən]) n artesano m.

craftsmanship ['krɑːftsmənʃɪp] n (U) 1. (skill) destreza f, habilidad f. 2. (skilled work) artesanía f.

craftsmen pl → **craftsman**.

crafty ['krɑːftɪ] adj astuto(ta).

crag [kræg] n peñasco m.

cram [kræm] ◆ vt 1. (push - books, clothes) embutir; (people) apiñar. 2. (overfill): to ~ sthg with atiborrar OR atestar algo de; to be crammed (with) estar repleto(ta) (de). ◆ vi empollar.

cramp [kræmp] n calambre m; stomach ~s retortijones mpl de vientre.

cranberry ['krænbərɪ] n arándano m (agrio).

crane [kreɪn] n 1. (machine) grúa f.
2. (bird) grulla f.

crank [kræŋk] ◆ n 1. (TECH) manivela f.
2. inf (eccentric) majareta m y f. ◆ vt (wind)
girar.

crankshaft ['kræŋkʃɑːft] n cigüeñal
m.

cranny ['krænɪ] → **nook**.

crap [kræp] n (U) v inf mierda f.

crash [kræʃ] ◆ n 1. (accident) choque m.
2. (loud noise) estruendo m. 3. (FIN) crac
m. ◆ vt estrellar. ◆ vi 1. (collide - two vehicles) chocar; (one vehicle - into wall etc)
estrellarse; **to ~ into** sthg chocar OR
estrellarse contra algo. 2. (FIN) quebrar. 3. (COMPUT) bloquearse.

crash course n cursillo m intensivo
de introducción, curso m acelerado.

crash helmet n casco m protector.

crash-land vi realizar un aterrizaje
forzoso.

crass [kræs] adj burdo(da); **a ~ error** un
craso error.

crate [kreɪt] n caja f (para embalaje o
transporte).

crater ['kreɪtər] n 1. (hole in ground)
socavón m. 2. (of volcano, on the moon)
cráter m.

cravat [krə'væt] n pañuelo m (de
hombre).

crave [kreɪv] ◆ vt ansiar. ◆ vi: **to ~ for**
sthg ansiar algo.

crawl [krɔːl] ◆ vi 1. (baby) andar a
gatas. 2. (insect, person) arrastrarse.
3. (move slowly, with difficulty) avanzar
lentamente. 4. inf (grovel): **to ~ (to)** arrastrarse (ante). ◆ n (swimming stroke): **the ~**
el crol.

crayfish ['kreɪfɪʃ] (pl inv OR **-es**) n (freshwater) cangrejo m de río; (spiny lobster)
langosta f.

crayon ['kreɪɒn] n lápiz m de cera.

craze [kreɪz] n moda f.

crazy ['kreɪzɪ] adj inf 1. (mad - person)
loco(ca). (- idea) disparatado(da).
2. (enthusiastic): **to be ~ about** estar loco
(ca) por.

creak [kriːk] vi (floorboard, bed) crujir;
(door, hinge) chirriar.

cream [kriːm] ◆ adj (in colour) (color)
crema (inv). ◆ n 1. (food) nata f. 2. (cosmetic, mixture for food) crema f. 3. (colour)
(color m) crema m. 4. (elite): **the ~** la flor
y nata, la crema.

cream cake n Br pastel m de nata.

cream cheese n queso m cremoso OR
blanco.

cream cracker n Br galleta sin azúcar

que generalmente se come con queso.

cream tea n Br merienda de té con bollos,
nata y mermelada.

crease [kriːs] ◆ n (deliberate - in shirt)
pliegue m; (- in trousers) raya f; (accidental) arruga f. ◆ vt arrugar. ◆ vi (gen) arrugarse; (forehead) fruncirse.

create [kriː'eɪt] vt (gen) crear; (interest)
producir.

creation [kriː'eɪʃn] n creación f.

creative [kriː'eɪtɪv] adj (gen) creativo
(va); (energy) creador(ra); **~ writing**
redacciones fpl.

creature ['kriːtʃər] n criatura f.

crèche [kreʃ] n Br guardería f (infantil).

credence ['kriːdns] n: **to give** OR **lend ~**
to dar crédito a.

credentials [krɪ'denʃlz] npl creden-
ciales fpl.

credibility [ˌkredə'bɪlətɪ] n credibilidad f.

credit ['kredɪt] ◆ n 1. (financial aid)
crédito m; **in ~** con saldo acreedor OR
positivo; **on ~** a crédito. 2. (U) (praise)
reconocimiento m; **to give sb ~ for**
reconocer a alguien el mérito de.
3. (SCH & UNIV) crédito m. 4. (money cred-
ited) saldo m acreedor OR positivo. ◆ vt
1. (FIN) (add) abonar; **we'll ~ your**
account le abonaremos en su cuenta. 2.
inf (believe) creer. 3. (give the credit to): **to ~**
sb with atribuir a alguien el mérito de.
▶ **credits** npl (on film) títulos mpl.

credit card n tarjeta f de crédito.

credit note n pagaré m.

creditor ['kredɪtər] n acreedor m, -ra f.

creed [kriːd] n credo m.

creek [kriːk] n 1. (inlet) cala f. 2. Am
(stream) riachuelo m.

creep [kriːp] (pt & pp **crept**) ◆ vi
1. (insect) arrastrarse; (traffic etc) avanzar
lentamente. 2. (person) deslizarse,
andar con sigilo. 3. inf (grovel): **to ~ (to**
sb) hacer la pelota (a alguien). ◆ n inf
(person) pelotillero m, -ra f. ▶ **creeps**
npl: **to give sb the ~s** inf ponerle a
alguien la piel de gallina.

creeper ['kriːpər] n enredadera f.

creepy ['kriːpɪ] adj inf horripilante.

creepy-crawly [-'krɔːlɪ] (pl **-ies**) n inf
bicho m.

cremate [krɪ'meɪt] vt incinerar.

crematorium Br [ˌkremə'tɔːrɪəm] (pl
-riums OR **-ria** [-rɪə]), **crematory** Am
['kremətrɪ] n (horno m) crematorio m.

crepe [kreɪp] n 1. (cloth) crespón m.
2. (rubber) crepé m. 3. (thin pancake)
crepe f.

crepe bandage n Br venda f de gasa.

crepe paper n (U) papel m seda.

crept [krept] pt & pp → **creep**.

crescendo [krɪ'ʃendəʊ] (pl -s) n crescendo m.

crescent ['kresnt] n 1. (shape) media luna f. 2. (street) calle en forma de arco.

cress [kres] n berro m.

crest [krest] n 1. (on bird's head, of wave) cresta f. 2. (of hill) cima f, cumbre f. 3. (on coat of arms) blasón m.

crestfallen ['krest,fɔːln] adj alicaído (da).

Crete [kriːt] n Creta.

cretin ['kretɪn] n inf (idiot) cretino m, -na f.

Creutzfeldt-Jakob disease [,krɔɪtsfelt'jækɒb-] n enfermedad f de Creutzfeldt-Jakob.

crevasse [krɪ'væs] n grieta f, fisura f.

crevice ['krevɪs] n grieta f, hendidura f.

crew [kruː] n 1. (of ship, plane) tripulación f. 2. (on film set etc) equipo m.

crew cut n rapado m, corte m al cero.

crew-neck(ed) [-nek(t)] adj con cuello redondo.

crib [krɪb] ◆ n (cot) cuna f. ◆ vt inf: **to ~ sthg off** OR **from sb** copiar algo de alguien.

crick [krɪk] n (in neck) tortícolis f.

cricket ['krɪkɪt] n 1. (game) críquet m. 2. (insect) grillo m.

crime [kraɪm] ◆ n 1. (criminal behaviour - serious) criminalidad f; (- less serious) delincuencia f. 2. (serious offence) crimen m; (less serious offence) delito m. 3. (immoral act) crimen m. ◆ comp: ~ **novel** novela f policíaca.

criminal ['krɪmɪnl] ◆ adj 1. (JUR) (act, behaviour) criminal, delictivo(va); (law) penal; (lawyer) criminalista. 2. inf (shameful) criminal. ◆ n (serious) criminal m y f; (less serious) delincuente m y f.

crimson ['krɪmzn] ◆ adj (in colour) carmesí. ◆ n carmesí m.

cringe [krɪndʒ] vi 1. (out of fear) encogerse. 2. inf (with embarrassment): **to ~ (at)** encogerse de vergüenza (ante).

crinkle ['krɪŋkl] vt arrugar.

cripple ['krɪpl] ◆ n dated & offensive tullido m, -da f. ◆ vt 1. (MED) dejar inválido (da). 2. (country, industry) paralizar; (ship, plane) dejar inutilizado(da).

crisis ['kraɪsɪs] (pl crises ['kraɪsiːz]) n crisis f inv.

crisp [krɪsp] adj 1. (pastry, bacon, snow) crujiente; (banknote, vegetables, weather)

fresco(ca). 2. (brisk) directo(ta). ▶ **crisps** npl patatas fpl fritas (de bolsa).

crisscross ['krɪskrɒs] adj entrecruzado (da).

criterion [kraɪ'tɪərɪən] (pl -ria [-rɪə] OR -rions) n criterio m.

critic ['krɪtɪk] n crítico m, -ca f.

critical ['krɪtɪkl] adj (gen) crítico(ca); (illness) grave; **to be ~ of** criticar a.

critically ['krɪtɪklɪ] adv (gen) críticamente; (ill) gravemente.

criticism ['krɪtɪsɪzm] n crítica f.

criticize, -ise ['krɪtɪsaɪz] vt & vi criticar.

croak [krəʊk] vi 1. (frog) croar; (raven) graznar. 2. (person) ronquear.

Croat ['krəʊæt], **Croatian** [krəʊ'eɪʃn] ◆ adj croata. ◆ n 1. (person) croata m y f. 2. (language) croata m.

Croatia [krəʊ'eɪʃə] n Croacia.

Croatian = **Croat**.

crochet ['krəʊʃeɪ] n ganchillo m.

crockery ['krɒkərɪ] n loza f, vajilla f.

crocodile ['krɒkədaɪl] (pl inv OR -s) n cocodrilo m.

crocus ['krəʊkəs] (pl -es) n azafrán m.

croft [krɒft] n Br granja o terreno pequeño que pertenece a una familia y les proporciona sustento.

crony ['krəʊnɪ] n inf amiguete m, -ta f, amigote m.

crook [krʊk] n 1. (criminal) ratero m, -ra f. 2. inf (dishonest person) ladrón m, -ona f, sinvergüenza m y f. 3. (shepherd's staff) cayado m.

crooked ['krʊkɪd] adj 1. (back) encorvado(da); (path) sinuoso(sa). 2. (teeth, tie) torcido(da). 3. inf (dishonest - person, policeman) corrupto(ta).

crop [krɒp] ◆ n 1. (kind of plant) cultivo m. 2. (harvested produce) cosecha f. 3. (whip) fusta f. ◆ vt (cut short) cortar (muy corto). ▶ **crop up** vi surgir, salir.

croquette [krɒ'ket] n croqueta f.

cross [krɒs] ◆ adj enfadado(da); **to get ~ (with)** enfadarse con. ◆ n 1. (gen) cruz f. 2. (hybrid) cruce m; **a ~ between** (combination) una mezcla de. ◆ vt 1. (gen & FIN) cruzar. 2. (face - subj: expression) reflejarse en. 3. (RELIG): **to ~ o.s.** santiguarse. ◆ vi (intersect) cruzarse. ▶ **cross off, cross out** vt sep tachar.

crossbar ['krɒsbɑːr] n 1. (on goal) travesaño m. 2. (on bicycle) barra f.

cross-Channel adj (ferry) que hace la travesía del Canal de la Mancha; (route) a través del Canal de la Mancha.

cross-country ◆ adj & adv a campo traviesa. ◆ n cross m.

cross-examine vt interrogar (para comprobar veracidad).

cross-eyed ['krɒsaɪd] adj bizco(ca).

crossfire ['krɒs,faɪəʳ] n fuego m cruzado.

crossing ['krɒsɪŋ] n **1.** (on road) cruce m, paso m de peatones; (on railway line) paso a nivel. **2.** (sea journey) travesía f.

cross-legged ['krɒslegd] adv con las piernas cruzadas.

cross-purposes npl: **to be at ~ with** sufrir un malentendido con.

cross-reference n remisión f, referencia f.

crossroads ['krɒsrəʊdz] (pl inv) n cruce m.

cross-section n **1.** (drawing) sección f transversal. **2.** (sample) muestra f representativa.

crosswalk ['krɒswɔːk] n Am paso m de peatones.

crosswind ['krɒswɪnd] n viento m de costado.

crosswise ['krɒswaɪz] adv en diagonal.

crossword (puzzle) ['krɒswɜːd-] n crucigrama m.

crotch [krɒtʃ] n entrepierna f.

crotchety ['krɒtʃɪtɪ] adj Br inf refunfuñón(ona).

crouch [kraʊtʃ] vi (gen) agacharse; (ready to spring) agazaparse.

crow [krəʊ] ◆ n corneja f. ◆ vi **1.** (cock) cantar. **2.** inf (gloat) darse pisto.

crowbar ['krəʊbɑːʳ] n palanca f.

crowd [kraʊd] ◆ n **1.** (mass of people) multitud f, muchedumbre f; (at football match etc) público m. **2.** (particular group) gente f. ◆ vi agolparse, apiñarse. ◆ vt **1.** (room, theatre etc) llenar. **2.** (people) meter, apiñar.

crowded ['kraʊdɪd] adj: ~ (with) repleto(ta) OR atestado(da) (de).

crown [kraʊn] ◆ n **1.** (of royalty, on tooth) corona f. **2.** (of hat) copa f; (of head) coronilla f; (of hill) cumbre f, cima f. ◆ vt (gen) coronar. ▶ **Crown** n: **the Crown** (monarchy) la corona.

crown jewels npl joyas fpl de la corona.

crown prince n príncipe m heredero.

crow's feet npl patas fpl de gallo.

crucial ['kruːʃl] adj crucial.

crucifix ['kruːsɪfɪks] n crucifijo m.

Crucifixion [,kruːsɪ'fɪkʃn] n: **the ~** la crucifixión.

crude [kruːd] adj **1.** (rubber, oil, joke) crudo(da). **2.** (person, behaviour) basto

(ta). **3.** (drawing, sketch) tosco(ca).

crude oil n crudo m.

cruel ['kruəl] adj (gen) cruel; (winter) crudo(da).

cruelty ['kruəltɪ] n (U) crueldad f.

cruet ['kruːɪt] n vinagreras fpl.

cruise [kruːz] ◆ n crucero m. ◆ vi **1.** (sail) hacer un crucero. **2.** (drive, fly) ir a velocidad de crucero.

cruiser ['kruːzəʳ] n **1.** (warship) crucero m. **2.** (cabin cruiser) yate m (para cruceros).

crumb [krʌm] n **1.** (of food) miga f, migaja f. **2.** (of information) pizca f.

crumble ['krʌmbl] ◆ n compota de fruta con una pasta seca por encima. ◆ vt desmigajar. ◆ vi **1.** (building, cliff) desmoronarse; (plaster) caerse. **2.** fig (relationship, hopes) venirse abajo.

crumbly ['krʌmblɪ] adj que se desmigaja con facilidad.

crumpet ['krʌmpɪt] n (food) bollo que se come tostado.

crumple ['krʌmpl] vt (dress, suit) arrugar; (letter) estrujar.

crunch [krʌntʃ] ◆ n crujido m. ◆ vt **1.** (with teeth) ronzar. **2.** (underfoot) hacer crujir.

crunchy ['krʌntʃɪ] adj crujiente.

crusade [kruː'seɪd] n lit & fig cruzada f.

crush [krʌʃ] ◆ n **1.** (crowd) gentío m. **2.** inf (infatuation): **to have a ~ on sb** estar colado(da) OR loco(ca) por alguien. ◆ vt **1.** (squash) aplastar. **2.** (grind - garlic, grain) triturar; (- ice) picar; (- grapes) exprimir. **3.** (destroy) demoler.

crust [krʌst] n **1.** (on bread) corteza f. **2.** (on pie) pasta f (dura). **3.** (of snow, earth) corteza f.

crutch [krʌtʃ] n **1.** (stick) muleta f; fig (support) apoyo m. **2.** (crotch) entrepierna f.

crux [krʌks] n: **the ~ of the matter** el quid de la cuestión.

cry [kraɪ] ◆ n **1.** (weep) llorera f. **2.** (shout) grito m. ◆ vi **1.** (weep) llorar. **2.** (shout) gritar. ▶ **cry off** vi volverse atrás.

crystal ['krɪstl] n cristal m.

crystal clear adj **1.** (transparent) cristalino(na). **2.** (clearly stated) claro(ra) como el agua.

CSE (abbr of **Certificate of Secondary Education**) n antiguo título de enseñanza secundaria en Gran Bretaña para alumnos de bajo rendimiento escolar.

CTC n abbr of **city technology college**.

cub [kʌb] n **1.** (young animal) cachorro

m. **2.** (*boy scout*) boy scout de entre 8 y 11 años.

Cuba ['kju:bə] *n* Cuba.

Cuban ['kju:bən] ◆ *adj* cubano(na). ◆ *n* (*person*) cubano *m*, -na *f*.

cubbyhole ['kʌbɪhəʊl] *n* (*room*) cuchitril *m*; (*cupboard*) armario *m*.

cube [kju:b] ◆ *n* (*gen*) cubo *m*; (*of sugar*) terrón *m*. ◆ *vt* (MATH) elevar al cubo.

cubic ['kju:bɪk] *adj* cúbico(ca).

cubicle ['kju:bɪkl] *n* (*at swimming pool*) caseta *f*; (*in shop*) probador *m*.

Cub Scout *n* boy scout de entre 8 y 11 años.

cuckoo ['kʊku:] *n* cuco *m*, cuclillo *m*.

cuckoo clock *n* reloj *m* de cuco.

cucumber ['kju:kʌmbər] *n* pepino *m*.

cuddle ['kʌdl] ◆ *n* abrazo *m*. ◆ *vt* abrazar. ◆ *vi* abrazarse.

cuddly toy ['kʌdlɪ-] *n* muñeco *m* de peluche.

cue [kju:] *n* **1.** (RADIO, THEATRE & TV) entrada *f*; **on ~** justo en aquel instante. **2.** *fig* (*stimulus, signal*) señal *f*. **3.** (*in snooker, pool*) taco *m*.

cuff [kʌf] *n* **1.** (*of sleeve*) puño *m*; **off the ~** improvisado(da), sacado(da) de la manga. **2.** Am (*of trouser leg*) vuelta *f*. **3.** (*blow*) cachete *m*.

cuff link *n* gemelo *m*, collera *f* Amer.

cuisine [kwɪ'zi:n] *n* cocina *f*.

cul-de-sac ['kʌldəsæk] *n* callejón *m* sin salida.

cull [kʌl] *vt* **1.** (*animals*) eliminar. **2.** *fml* (*information, facts*) recoger.

culminate ['kʌlmɪneɪt] *vi*: **to ~ in** culminar en.

culmination [,kʌlmɪ'neɪʃn] *n* culminación *f*.

culottes [kju:'lɒts] *npl* falda *f* pantalón.

culpable ['kʌlpəbl] *adj fml*: **~ (of)** culpable (de); **~ homicide** homicidio *m* involuntario.

culprit ['kʌlprɪt] *n* culpable *m y f*.

cult [kʌlt] ◆ *n* (RELIG) culto *m*. ◆ *comp* de culto.

cultivate ['kʌltɪveɪt] *vt* **1.** (*gen*) cultivar. **2.** (*get to know - person*) hacer amistad con.

cultivated ['kʌltɪveɪtɪd] *adj* **1.** (*cultured*) culto(ta). **2.** (*land*) cultivado(da).

cultivation [,kʌltɪ'veɪʃn] *n* (U) cultivo *m*.

cultural ['kʌltʃərəl] *adj* cultural.

culture ['kʌltʃər] *n* **1.** (*gen*) cultura *f*. **2.** (*of bacteria*) cultivo *m*.

cultured ['kʌltʃəd] *adj* culto(ta).

cumbersome ['kʌmbəsəm] *adj* **1.** (*par-*

cel*) abultado(da); (*machinery*) aparatoso (sa). **2.** (*system*) torpe.

cunning ['kʌnɪŋ] ◆ *adj* (*gen*) astuto(ta); (*device, idea*) ingenioso(sa). ◆ *n* (U) astucia *f*.

cup [kʌp] ◆ *n* **1.** (*gen*) taza *f*. **2.** (*prize, of bra*) copa *f*. ◆ *vt* ahuecar.

cupboard ['kʌbəd] *n* armario *m*.

Cup Final *n*: **the ~** ≈ la final de la Copa.

cup tie *n* Br partido *m* de copa.

curate ['kjʊərət] *n* coadjutor *m*, -ra *f*.

curator [,kjʊə'reɪtər] *n* conservador *m*, -ra *f*, director *m*, -ra *f*.

curb [kɜ:b] ◆ *n* **1.** (*control*): **~ (on)** control *m* OR restricción *f* (de); **to put a ~ on sthg** poner freno a algo. **2.** Am (*in road*) bordillo *m*. ◆ *vt* controlar, contener.

curdle ['kɜ:dl] *vi* (*milk*) cuajarse; *fig* (*blood*) helarse.

cure [kjʊər] ◆ *n* **1.** (MED): **~ (for)** cura *f* (para). **2.** (*solution*): **~ (for)** remedio *m* (a). ◆ *vt* **1.** (MED) curar. **2.** (*problem, inflation*) remediar. **3.** (*food, tobacco*) curar; (*leather*) curtir.

cure-all *n* panacea *f*.

curfew ['kɜ:fju:] *n* toque *m* de queda.

curio ['kjʊərɪəʊ] (*pl* **-s**) *n* curiosidad *f*.

curiosity [,kjʊərɪ'ɒsɪtɪ] *n* curiosidad *f*.

curious ['kjʊərɪəs] *adj* curioso(sa); **to be ~ about** sentir curiosidad por.

curl [kɜ:l] ◆ *n* (*of hair*) rizo *m*. ◆ *vt* **1.** (*hair*) rizar. **2.** (*twist*) enroscar. ◆ *vi* **1.** (*hair*) rizarse. **2.** (*paper*) abarquillarse. ▶ **curl up** *vi* (*person, animal*) acurrucarse; (*leaf, paper*) abarquillarse.

curler ['kɜ:lər] *n* rulo *m*.

curling tongs *npl* tenacillas *fpl* de rizar.

curly ['kɜ:lɪ] *adj* (*hair*) rizado(da); (*pig's tail*) enroscado(da).

currant ['kʌrənt] *n* (*dried grape*) pasa *f* de Corinto.

currency ['kʌrənsɪ] *n* **1.** (FIN) moneda *f*; **foreign ~** divisa *f*. **2.** *fml* (*acceptability*): **to gain ~** ganar aceptación.

current ['kʌrənt] ◆ *adj* (*price, method, girlfriend*) actual; (*year*) en curso; (*issue*) último(ma); (*ideas, expressions, customs*) corriente. ◆ *n* corriente *f*.

current account *n* Br cuenta *f* corriente.

current affairs *npl* temas *mpl* de actualidad, actualidades *fpl*.

currently ['kʌrəntlɪ] *adv* actualmente.

curriculum [kə'rɪkjələm] (*pl* **-lums** OR **-la** [-lə]) *n* (*course of study*) temario *m*, plan *m* de estudios.

curriculum vitae [-'vi:taɪ] (*pl* **curricula vitae**) *n* currículum *m* (vitae).

curry ['kʌrɪ] *n* curry *m*.

curse [kɜ:s] ◆ *n* 1. (*evil charm*) maldición *f*. 2. (*swearword*) taco *m*, palabrota *f*. ◆ *vt* maldecir. ◆ *vi* (*swear*) soltar tacos.

cursor ['kɜ:sər] *n* (COMPUT) cursor *m*.

cursory ['kɜ:sərɪ] *adj* superficial.

curt [kɜ:t] *adj* brusco(ca), seco(ca).

curtail [kɜ:'teɪl] *vt* 1. (*visit*) acortar. 2. (*expenditure*) reducir; (*rights*) restringir.

curtain ['kɜ:tn] *n* 1. (*gen*) cortina *f*. 2. (*in theatre*) telón *m*.

curts(e)y ['kɜ:tsɪ] (*pt & pp* **curtsied**) ◆ *n* reverencia *f* (*de mujer*). ◆ *vi* hacer una reverencia (*una mujer*).

curve [kɜ:v] ◆ *n* curva *f*. ◆ *vi* (*river*) hacer una curva; (*surface*) curvarse.

cushion ['kʊʃn] ◆ *n* 1. (*for sitting on*) cojín *m*. 2. (*protective layer*) colchón *m*. ◆ *vt lit & fig* amortiguar.

cushy ['kʊʃɪ] *adj inf* cómodo(da); **a ~ job** OR **number** un chollo (de trabajo).

custard ['kʌstəd] *n* (U) (*sauce*) natillas *fpl*.

custodian [kʌ'stəʊdjən] *n* (*of building, museum*) conservador *m*, -ra *f*.

custody ['kʌstədɪ] *n* custodia *f*; **to take sb into ~** detener a alguien; **in ~** bajo custodia.

custom ['kʌstəm] *n* 1. (*tradition, habit*) costumbre *f*. 2. (U) *fml* (*trade*) clientela *f*. ▶ **customs** *n* (*place*) aduana *f*.

customary ['kʌstəmrɪ] *adj* acostumbrado(da), habitual.

customer ['kʌstəmər] *n* 1. (*client*) cliente *m* y *f*. 2. *inf* (*person*) tipo *m*.

customize, -ise ['kʌstəmaɪz] *vt* personalizar.

Customs and Excise *n* (U) *Br* oficina *del gobierno británico encargada de la recaudación de derechos arancelarios.*

customs duty *n* (U) derechos *mpl* de aduana, aranceles *mpl*.

customs officer *n* empleado *m*, -da *f* de aduana.

cut [kʌt] (*pt & pp* **cut**) ◆ *n* 1. (*gen*) corte *m*. 2. (*reduction*): **~ (in)** reducción *f* (de). 3. *inf* (*share*) parte *f*. ◆ *vt* 1. (*gen*) cortar; (*one's finger etc*) cortarse. 2. (*spending, staff etc*) reducir, recortar. 3. *inf* (*lecture*) fumarse. ▶ **cut back** *vt sep* 1. (*plant*) podar. 2. (*expenditure, budget*) recortar. ▶ **cut down** ◆ *vt sep* 1. (*chop down*) cortar, talar. 2. (*reduce*) reducir. ◆ *vi*: **to ~ down on smoking** OR **cigarettes** fumar menos. ▶ **cut in** *vi* 1. (*interrupt*): **to ~ in**

(on sb) cortar OR interrumpir (a alguien). 2. (*in car*) colarse. ▶ **cut off** *vt sep* 1. (*gen*) cortar. 2. (*separate*): **to be ~ off (from)** (*person*) estar aislado(da) (de); (*town, village*) quedarse incomunicado (da) (de). ▶ **cut out** *vt sep* 1. (*remove*) recortar. 2. (*dress, pattern etc*) cortar. 3. (*stop*): **to ~ out smoking** OR **cigarettes** dejar de fumar; **~ it out!** *inf* ¡basta ya! 4. (*exclude - light etc*) eliminar; **to ~ sb out of one's will** desheredar a alguien. ▶ **cut up** *vt sep* (*chop up*) cortar, desmenuzar.

cutback ['kʌtbæk] *n*: **~ (in)** recorte *m* OR reducción *f* (en).

cute [kju:t] *adj* (*appealing*) mono(na), lindo(da).

cuticle ['kju:tɪkl] *n* cutícula *f*.

cutlery ['kʌtlərɪ] *n* (U) cubertería *f*.

cutlet ['kʌtlɪt] *n* chuleta *f*.

cutout ['kʌtaʊt] *n* 1. (*on machine*) cortacircuitos *m inv*. 2. (*shape*) recorte *m*.

cut-price, cut-rate *Am adj* de oferta.

cutthroat ['kʌtθrəʊt] *adj* (*ruthless*) encarnizado(da).

cutting ['kʌtɪŋ] ◆ *adj* (*sarcastic*) cortante, mordaz. ◆ *n* 1. (*of plant*) esqueje *m*. 2. (*from newspaper*) recorte *m*. 3. *Br* (*for road, railway*) desmonte *m*.

CV (*abbr of* **curriculum vitae**) *n* CV *m*.

cwt. *abbr of* **hundredweight**.

cyanide ['saɪənaɪd] *n* cianuro *m*.

cybercafe ['saɪbə,kæfeɪ] *n* cybercafé *m*.

cybernetics [,saɪbə'netɪks] *n* (U) cibernética *f*.

cyberspace ['saɪbəspeɪs] *n* cyberespacio *m*.

cycle ['saɪkl] ◆ *n* 1. (*series of events, poems, songs*) ciclo *m*. 2. (*bicycle*) bicicleta *f*. ◆ *comp*: **~ path** camino *m* para bicicletas. ◆ *vi* ir en bicicleta.

cycling ['saɪklɪŋ] *n* ciclismo *m*; **to go ~** ir en bicicleta.

cyclist ['saɪklɪst] *n* ciclista *m* y *f*.

cygnet ['sɪgnɪt] *n* pollo *m* de cisne.

cylinder ['sɪlɪndər] *n* 1. (*shape, engine component*) cilindro *m*. 2. (*container - for gas*) bombona *f*.

cymbals ['sɪmblz] *npl* platillos *mpl*.

cynic ['sɪnɪk] *n* cínico *m*, -ca *f*.

cynical ['sɪnɪkl] *adj* cínico(ca).

cynicism ['sɪnɪsɪzm] *n* cinismo *m*.

cypress ['saɪprəs] *n* ciprés *m*.

Cypriot ['sɪprɪət] ◆ *adj* chipriota. ◆ *n* chipriota *m* y *f*.

Cyprus ['saɪprəs] *n* Chipre.

cyst [sɪst] n quiste m.
cystitis [sɪs'taɪtɪs] n cistitis f inv.
czar [zɑːʳ] n zar m.
Czech [tʃek] ♦ adj checo(ca). ♦ n
1. (person) checo m, -ca f. 2. (language)
checo m.
Czechoslovak [ˌtʃekə'sləuvæk] =
Czechoslovakian.
Czechoslovakia [ˌtʃekəslə'vækɪə] n
Checoslovaquia.
Czechoslovakian [ˌtʃekəslə'vækɪən]
♦ adj checoslovaco(ca). ♦ n (person)
checoslovaco m, -ca f.

D

d (pl **d's** OR **ds**), **D** (pl **D's** OR **Ds**) [diː] n
(letter) d f, D f. ▶ **D** n (MUS) re m.
DA n abbr of **district attorney.**
dab [dæb] ♦ n (small amount) toque m,
pizca f; (of powder) pizca f. ♦ vt 1. (skin,
wound) dar ligeros toques en. 2. (cream,
ointment): **to ~ sthg on** OR **onto** aplicar
algo sobre.
dabble ['dæbl] vi: **to ~ (in)** pasar el
tiempo OR entretenerse (con).
dachshund ['dækshund] n perro m
salchicha.
dad [dæd], **daddy** ['dædɪ] n inf papá
m.
daddy longlegs [-'lɒŋlegz] (pl inv) n
típula f.
daffodil ['dæfədɪl] n narciso m.
daft [dɑːft] adj Br inf tonto(ta).
dagger ['dægəʳ] n daga f, puñal m.
daily ['deɪlɪ] ♦ adj diario(ria). ♦ adv
diariamente; **twice ~** dos veces al día.
♦ n (newspaper) diario m.
dainty ['deɪntɪ] adj delicado(da), fino
(na).
dairy ['deərɪ] n 1. (on farm) vaquería f.
2. (shop) lechería f.
dairy farm n granja f (de productos
lácteos).
dairy products npl productos mpl
lácteos.
dais ['deɪɪs] n tarima f, estrado m.
daisy ['deɪzɪ] n margarita f.
daisy wheel n margarita f (de máquina
de escribir).
dale [deɪl] n valle m.

dam [dæm] ♦ n (across river) presa f.
♦ vt represar.
damage ['dæmɪdʒ] ♦ n 1. (physical
harm): **~ (to)** daño m (a). 2. (harmful
effect): **~ (to)** perjuicio m (a). ♦ vt dañar.
▶ **damages** npl (JUR) daños mpl y perjuicios.
damn [dæm] ♦ adj inf maldito(ta).
♦ adv inf tela de, muy. ♦ n inf: **I don't
give** OR **care a ~ (about it)** me importa un
bledo. ♦ vt 1. (RELIG) (condemn) condenar. 2. v inf (curse): **~ it!** ¡maldita sea!
damned [dæmd] inf ♦ adj maldito(ta);
I'm ~ if ... que me maten si ...; **well I'll
be** OR **I'm ~!** ¡ostras! ♦ adv tela de, muy.
damning ['dæmɪŋ] adj compromete-
dor(ra).
damp [dæmp] ♦ adj húmedo(da). ♦ n
humedad f. ♦ vt (make wet) humedecer.
dampen ['dæmpən] vt 1. (make wet)
humedecer. 2. fig (emotion) apagar.
damson ['dæmzn] n (ciruela f) da-
mascena f.
dance [dɑːns] ♦ n baile m. ♦ vi 1. (to
music) bailar. 2. (move quickly and lightly)
agitarse, moverse.
dancer ['dɑːnsəʳ] n bailarín m, -ina f.
dancing ['dɑːnsɪŋ] n (U) baile m.
dandelion ['dændɪlaɪən] n diente m
de león.
dandruff ['dændrʌf] n caspa f.
Dane [deɪn] n danés m, -esa f.
danger ['deɪndʒəʳ] n: **~ (to)** peligro m
(para); **in/out of ~** en/fuera de peligro;
to be in ~ of doing sthg correr el riesgo
de hacer algo.
dangerous ['deɪndʒərəs] adj peligroso
(sa).
dangle ['dæŋgl] ♦ vt colgar; fig: **to ~
sthg before sb** poner los dientes largos
a alguien con algo. ♦ vi colgar, pender.
Danish ['deɪnɪʃ] ♦ adj danés(esa). ♦ n
1. (language) danés m. 2. Am = **Danish
pastry.** ♦ npl (people): **the ~** los daneses.
Danish pastry n pastel de hojaldre con
crema o manzana o almendras etc.
dank [dæŋk] adj húmedo(da) e insalubre.
dapper ['dæpəʳ] adj pulcro(cra).
dappled ['dæpld] adj 1. (light) motea-
do(da). 2. (horse) rodado(da).
dare [deəʳ] ♦ vt 1. (be brave enough): **to ~
to do sthg** atreverse a hacer algo, osar
hacer algo. 2. (challenge): **to ~ sb to do
sthg** desafiar a alguien a hacer algo.
3. phr: **I ~ say (...)** supongo OR me imagino (que ...). ♦ vi atreverse, osar;
how ~ you! ¿cómo te atreves? ♦ n

desafío m, reto m.

daredevil ['deə,devl] n temerario m, -ria f.

daring ['deərɪŋ] ◆ adj atrevido(da), audaz. ◆ n audacia f.

dark [dɑːk] ◆ adj 1. (night, colour, hair) oscuro(ra). 2. (person, skin) moreno(na). 3. (thoughts, days, mood) sombrío(a), triste. 4. (look, comment, side of character etc) siniestro(tra). ◆ n 1. (darkness): **the ~** la oscuridad; **to be in the ~ about sthg** estar a oscuras sobre algo. 2. (night): **before/after ~** antes/después del anochecer.

darken ['dɑːkn] ◆ vt oscurecer. ◆ vi (become darker) oscurecerse.

dark glasses npl gafas fpl oscuras.

darkness ['dɑːknɪs] n oscuridad f.

darkroom ['dɑːkrʊm] n (PHOT) cuarto m oscuro.

darling ['dɑːlɪŋ] ◆ adj (dear) querido (da). ◆ n 1. (loved person) encanto m. 2. inf (addressing any woman) maja f.

darn [dɑːn] ◆ adj inf maldito(ta), condenado(da). ◆ adv inf tela de, muy. ◆ vt zurcir. ◆ excl inf ¡maldita sea!

dart [dɑːt] ◆ n (arrow) dardo m. ◆ vi precipitarse. ▶ **darts** n (U) (game) dardos mpl.

dartboard ['dɑːtbɔːd] n blanco m, diana f.

dash [dæʃ] ◆ n 1. (of liquid, colour) gotas fpl, chorrito m. 2. (in punctuation) guión m. 3. (rush): **to make a ~ for sthg** salir disparado hacia algo. ◆ vt 1. literary (throw) arrojar. 2. (hopes) frustrar, malograr. ◆ vi ir de prisa.

dashboard ['dæʃbɔːd] n salpicadero m.

dashing ['dæʃɪŋ] adj gallardo(da).

data ['deɪtə] n (U) datos mpl.

database ['deɪtəbeɪs] n (COMPUT) base f de datos.

data processing n proceso m de datos.

date [deɪt] ◆ n 1. (in time) fecha f; **to ~** hasta la fecha. 2. (appointment) cita f. 3. Am (person) pareja f (con la que se sale). 4. (fruit) dátil m. ◆ vt 1. (establish the date of) datar. 2. (mark with the date) fechar. 3. Am (go out with) salir con.

dated ['deɪtɪd] adj anticuado(da).

date of birth n fecha f de nacimiento.

daub [dɔːb] vt: **to ~ sthg with** embadurnar algo con.

daughter ['dɔːtər] n hija f.

daughter-in-law (pl daughters-in-

law) n nuera f.

daunting ['dɔːntɪŋ] adj amedrantador (ra).

dawdle ['dɔːdl] vi remolonear.

dawn [dɔːn] ◆ n 1. (of day) amanecer m, alba f. 2. (of era, period) albores mpl. ◆ vi (day) amanecer. ▶ **dawn (up)on** vt fus: **it ~ed on me that ...** caí en la cuenta de que ...

day [deɪ] n 1. (gen) día m; **the ~ before/after** el día anterior/siguiente; **the ~ before yesterday** anteayer; **the ~ after tomorrow** pasado mañana; **any ~ now** cualquier día de estos; **one OR some ~, one of these ~s** uno de estos días; **to make sb's ~** dar un alegrón a alguien. 2. (period in history): **in my/your etc ~** en mis/tus etc tiempos; **in those ~s** en aquellos tiempos. ▶ **days** adv de día.

daybreak ['deɪbreɪk] n amanecer m, alba f; **at ~** al amanecer.

daycentre ['deɪsentər] n Br (centro estatal diurno donde se da) acogida y cuidado a niños, ancianos, minusválidos etc.

daydream ['deɪdriːm] ◆ n sueño m, ilusión f. ◆ vi soñar despierto(ta).

daylight ['deɪlaɪt] n 1. (light) luz f del día. 2. (dawn) amanecer m.

day off (pl days off) n día m libre.

day return n Br billete m de ida y vuelta para un día.

daytime ['deɪtaɪm] ◆ n (U) día m. ◆ comp de día, diurno(na).

day-to-day adj cotidiano(na).

day trip n excursión f (de un día).

daze [deɪz] ◆ n: **in a ~** aturdido(da). ◆ vt lit & fig aturdir.

dazzle ['dæzl] vt lit & fig deslumbrar.

DC ◆ n (abbr of direct current) CC f. ◆ abbr of District of Columbia.

D-day ['diːdeɪ] n el día D.

DEA (abbr of Drug Enforcement Administration) n organismo estadounidense para la lucha contra la droga.

deacon ['diːkn] n diácono m.

deactivate [,diːˈæktɪveɪt] vt desactivar.

dead [ded] ◆ adj 1. (person, animal, plant) muerto(ta); **to shoot sb ~** matar a alguien a tiros. 2. (numb - leg, arm) entumecido(da). 3. (telephone) cortado (da); (car battery) descargado(da). 4. (silence) absoluto(ta). 5. (lifeless - town, party) sin vida. ◆ adv 1. (directly, precisely) justo. 2. (completely) totalmente, completamente; **'~ slow'** 'al paso'. 3. inf (very) la mar de, muy. 4. (suddenly): **to stop ~** parar en seco. ◆ npl: **the**

~ los muertos.

deaden ['dedn] vt atenuar.

dead end n lit & fig callejón m sin salida.

dead heat n empate m.

deadline ['dedlaɪn] n plazo m, fecha f tope.

deadlock ['dedlɒk] n punto m muerto.

dead loss n inf 1. (person) inútil m y f. 2. (thing) inutilidad f.

deadly ['dedlɪ] ◆ adj 1. (gen) mortal. 2. (accuracy) absoluto(ta). ◆ adv (boring) mortalmente, terriblemente; (serious) totalmente.

deadpan ['dedpæn] adj inexpresivo (va), serio(ria).

deaf [def] ◆ adj (unable to hear) sordo (da). ◆ npl: **the ~** los sordos.

deaf-aid n Br audífono m.

deaf-and-dumb adj sordomudo(da).

deafen ['defn] vt ensordecer.

deaf-mute n sordomudo m, -da f.

deafness ['defnɪs] n sordera f.

deal [di:l] (pt & pp dealt) ◆ n 1. (quantity): **a good** OR **great ~ (of)** mucho. 2. (business agreement) trato m, transacción f; **to do** OR **strike a ~ with sb** hacer un trato con alguien. 3. inf (treatment) trato m; **big ~!** ¡vaya cosa! ◆ vt 1. (strike): **to ~ sb/sthg a blow, to ~ a blow to sb/sthg** lit & fig asestar un golpe a alguien/algo. 2. (cards) repartir, dar. ◆ vi 1. (in cards) repartir, dar. 2. (in drugs) traficar con droga. ▶ **deal in** vt fus (COMM) comerciar en. ▶ **deal out** vt sep repartir. ▶ **deal with** vt fus 1. (handle - situation, problem) hacer frente a, resolver; (- customer) tratar con. 2. (be about) tratar de. 3. (be faced with) enfrentarse a.

dealer ['di:lər] n 1. (trader) comerciante m y f. 2. (in cards) repartidor m, -ra f.

dealing ['di:lɪŋ] n comercio m. ▶ **dealings** npl (personal) trato m; (in business) tratos mpl.

dealt [delt] pt & pp → **deal**.

dean [di:n] n 1. (of university) = decano m, -na fpl. 2. (of church) deán m.

dear [dɪər] ◆ adj 1. (loved) querido(da); **~ to sb** preciado(da) para alguien. 2. (expensive) caro(ra). 3. (in letter): **Dear Sir** Estimado señor, Muy señor mío; **Dear Madam** Estimada señora. ◆ n querido m, -da f. ◆ excl: **oh ~!** ¡vaya por Dios!

dearly ['dɪəlɪ] adv (love, wish) profundamente.

death [deθ] n muerte f; **to frighten sb to ~** dar un susto de muerte a alguien; **to be sick to ~ of sthg/of doing sthg** estar hasta las narices de algo/de hacer algo.

death certificate n partida f OR certificado m de defunción.

death duty Br, **death tax** Am n impuesto m de sucesiones.

deathly ['deθlɪ] ◆ adj sepulcral. ◆ adv: **he was ~ pale** estaba pálido como un muerto.

death penalty n pena f de muerte.

death rate n índice m OR tasa f de mortalidad.

death tax Am = **death duty**.

death trap n inf trampa f mortal, sitio m peligroso.

debar [di:'ba:r] vt: **to ~ sb from somewhere/from doing sthg** privar a alguien del acceso a algún lugar/de hacer algo.

debase [dɪ'beɪs] vt: **to ~ o.s.** rebajarse.

debate [dɪ'beɪt] ◆ n debate m; **that's open to ~** eso está por ver. ◆ vt 1. (issue) discutir, debatir. 2. (what to do): **to ~ (whether to do sthg)** pensarse (si hacer algo). ◆ vi discutir, debatir.

debating society [dɪ'beɪtɪŋ-] n asociación de debates especialmente universitaria.

debauchery [dɪ'bɔːtʃərɪ] n depravación f, libertinaje m.

debit ['debɪt] ◆ n debe m, débito m. ◆ vt: **to ~ sb** OR **sb's account with an amount, to ~ an amount to sb** adeudar OR cargar una cantidad en la cuenta de alguien.

debit note n pagaré m.

debris ['deɪbriː] n (U) (of building) escombros mpl; (of aircraft) restos mpl.

debt [det] n deuda f; **to be in ~ (to sb)** tener una deuda (con alguien).

debt collector n cobrador m, -ra f de morosos.

debtor ['detər] n deudor m, -ra f.

debug [,di:'bʌg] vt (COMPUT) suprimir fallos de.

debunk [,di:'bʌŋk] vt desmentir.

debut ['deɪbjuː] n debut m.

decade ['dekeɪd] n década f.

decadent ['dekədənt] adj decadente.

decaffeinated [dɪ'kæfɪneɪtɪd] adj descafeinado(da).

decamp [dɪ'kæmp] vi inf escabullirse.

decanter [dɪ'kæntər] n licorera f.

decathlon [dɪ'kæθlɒn] n decatlón m.

decay [dɪ'keɪ] ◆ n (U) 1. (of tooth) caries f; (of body, plant) descomposición f. 2. fig (of building) deterioro m; (of soci-

ety) degradación *f.* ◆ *vi* **1.** (*tooth*) picarse; (*body, plant*) pudrirse. **2.** *fig* (*building*) deteriorarse; (*society*) degradarse.

deceased [dɪ'siːst] (*pl inv*) *fml n*: **the ~** el difunto (la difunta).

deceit [dɪ'siːt] *n* engaño *m.*

deceitful [dɪ'siːtful] *adj* (*person, smile*) embustero(ra); (*behaviour*) falso(sa).

deceive [dɪ'siːv] *vt* engañar; **to ~ o.s.** engañarse (a uno mismo/una misma).

December [dɪ'sembər] *n* diciembre *m*; *see also* **September**.

decency ['diːsnsɪ] *n* **1.** (*respectability*) decencia *f.* **2.** (*consideration*): **to have the ~ to do sthg** tener la delicadeza de hacer algo.

decent ['diːsnt] *adj* **1.** (*gen*) decente. **2.** (*considerate*): **that's very ~ of you** es muy amable de tu parte.

deception [dɪ'sepʃn] *n* engaño *m.*

deceptive [dɪ'septɪv] *adj* engañoso (sa).

decide [dɪ'saɪd] ◆ *vt* **1.** (*gen*): **to ~ (to do sthg)** decidir (hacer algo); **to ~ (that)** decidir que. **2.** (*person*) hacer decidirse. **3.** (*issue, case*). resolver. ◆ *vi* decidir. ▶ **decide (up)on** *vt fus* decidirse por.

decided [dɪ'saɪdɪd] *adj* **1.** (*advantage, improvement*) indudable. **2.** (*person*) decidido(da); (*opinion*) categórico(ca).

decidedly [dɪ'saɪdɪdlɪ] *adv* **1.** (*clearly*) decididamente. **2.** (*resolutely*) con decisión.

deciduous [dɪ'sɪdjuəs] *adj* de hoja caduca.

decimal ['desɪml] ◆ *adj* decimal. ◆ *n* (número *m*) decimal *m.*

decimal point *n* coma *f* decimal.

decimate ['desɪmeɪt] *vt* diezmar.

decipher [dɪ'saɪfər] *vt* descifrar.

decision [dɪ'sɪʒn] *n* decisión *f*; **to make a ~** tomar una decisión.

decisive [dɪ'saɪsɪv] *adj* **1.** (*person*) decidido(da). **2.** (*factor, event*) decisivo(va).

deck [dek] *n* **1.** (*of ship*) cubierta *f*; (*of bus*) piso *m.* **2.** (*of cards*) baraja *f.* **3.** *Am* (*of house*) entarimado *m* (*junto a una casa*).

deckchair ['dektʃeər] *n* tumbona *f.*

declaration [,deklə'reɪʃn] *n* declaración *f.*

Declaration of Independence *n*: **the ~** la declaración de independencia estadounidense de 1776.

declare [dɪ'kleər] *vt* declarar.

decline [dɪ'klaɪn] ◆ *n* declive *m*; **in ~** en decadencia; **on the ~** en declive. ◆ *vt* (*offer*) declinar; (*request*) denegar; **to**

~ to do sthg rehusar hacer algo. ◆ *vi* **1.** (*deteriorate*) disminuir. **2.** (*refuse*) negarse.

decode [,diː'kəʊd] *vt* descodificar.

decompose [,diːkəm'pəʊz] *vi* descomponerse.

decongestant [,diːkən'dʒestənt] *n* decongestivo *m.*

décor ['deɪkɔːr] *n* decoración *f.*

decorate ['dekəreɪt] *vt* **1.** (*make pretty*): **to ~ sthg (with)** decorar algo (de). **2.** (*with paint*) pintar; (*with wallpaper*) empapelar. **3.** (*with medal*) condecorar.

decoration [,dekə'reɪʃn] *n* **1.** (*gen*) decoración *f.* **2.** (*ornament*) adorno *m.* **3.** (*medal*) condecoración *f.*

decorator ['dekəreɪtər] *n* (*painter*) pintor *m*, -ra *f*; (*paperhanger*) empapelador *m*, -ra *f.*

decorum [dɪ'kɔːrəm] *n* decoro *m.*

decoy [*n* 'diːkɔɪ, *vb* dɪ'kɔɪ] ◆ *n* señuelo *m.* ◆ *vt* desviar (*mediante señuelo*).

decrease [*n* 'diːkriːs, *vb* dɪ'kriːs] ◆ *n*: **~ (in)** disminución *f* (en). ◆ *vt & vi* disminuir.

decree [dɪ'kriː] ◆ *n* **1.** (*order, decision*) decreto *m.* **2.** *Am* (*judgment*) sentencia *f*, fallo *m.* ◆ *vt* decretar.

decree nisi [-'naɪsaɪ] (*pl* **decrees nisi**) *n* Br (JUR) sentencia *f* provisional de divorcio.

decrepit [dɪ'krepɪt] *adj* decrépito(ta).

dedicate ['dedɪkeɪt] *vt* dedicar; **to ~ o.s. to sthg** consagrarse OR dedicarse a algo.

dedication [,dedɪ'keɪʃn] *n* **1.** (*commitment*) dedicación *f.* **2.** (*in book*) dedicatoria *f.*

deduce [dɪ'djuːs] *vt*: **to ~ (sthg from sthg)** deducir (algo de algo).

deduct [dɪ'dʌkt] *vt*: **to ~ (from)** deducir (de), descontar (de).

deduction [dɪ'dʌkʃn] *n* deducción *f.*

deed [diːd] *n* **1.** (*action*) acción *f*, obra *f.* **2.** (JUR) escritura *f.*

deem [diːm] *vt fml* estimar.

deep [diːp] ◆ *adj* **1.** (*gen*) profundo (da); **to be 10 feet ~** tener 10 pies de profundidad. **2.** (*sigh, breath*) hondo (da). **3.** (*colour*) intenso(sa). **4.** (*sound, voice*) grave. ◆ *adv* hondo; **~ down OR inside** por dentro.

deepen ['diːpn] ◆ *vt* (*hole, channel*) ahondar. ◆ *vi* **1.** (*river, sea*) ahondarse. **2.** (*crisis, recession*) agudizarse; (*emotion, darkness*) hacerse más intenso(sa).

deep freeze *n* congelador *m.*

deep fry *vt* freír (con mucho aceite).

deeply ['diːplɪ] *adv* (*gen*) profunda-

mente; (dig, breathe, sigh) hondo.
deep-sea adj: ~ **diving** buceo m de
profundidad.
deer [dɪəʳ] (pl inv) n ciervo m.
deface [dɪ'feɪs] vt pintarrajear.
defamatory [dɪ'fæmətrɪ] adj fml
difamatorio(ria).
default [dɪ'fɔːlt] ◆ n 1. (on payment,
agreement) incumplimiento m; (failure to
attend) incomparecencia f; **by ~** (win)
por incomparecencia. 2. (COMPUT): ~
(value) valor m de ajuste (por defecto).
◆ vi incumplir un compromiso.
defeat [dɪ'fiːt] ◆ n derrota f; **to admit ~**
darse por vencido(da). ◆ vt (team, opponent) derrotar; (motion) rechazar; (plans)
frustrar.
defeatist [dɪ'fiːtɪst] adj derrotista.
defect [n 'diːfekt, vb dɪ'fekt] ◆ n (fault)
defecto m. ◆ vi (POL): **to ~ to the other
side** pasarse al otro bando.
defective [dɪ'fektɪv] adj defectuoso
(sa).
defence Br, **defense** Am [dɪ'fens] n
defensa f.
defenceless Br, **defenseless** Am
[dɪ'fenslɪs] adj indefenso(sa).
defend [dɪ'fend] vt defender.
defendant [dɪ'fendənt] n acusado m,
-da f.
defender [dɪ'fendəʳ] n 1. (gen) defensor m, -ra f. 2. (SPORT) defensa m y f.
defense Am = **defence**.
defenseless Am = **defenceless**.
defensive [dɪ'fensɪv] ◆ adj 1. (weapons,
tactics) defensivo(va). 2. (person) receloso
(sa). ◆ n: **on the ~** a la defensiva.
defer [dɪ'fɜːʳ] ◆ vt deferir, aplazar.
◆ vi: **to ~ to sb** deferir con OR a alguien.
deferential [,defə'renʃl] adj deferente.
defiance [dɪ'faɪəns] n desafío m; **in ~
of** en desafío de, a despecho de.
defiant [dɪ'faɪənt] adj desafiante.
deficiency [dɪ'fɪʃnsɪ] n 1. (lack)
escasez f. 2. (inadequacy) deficiencia f.
deficient [dɪ'fɪʃnt] adj 1. (lacking): **to be
~ in** ser deficitario(ria) en, estar
falto(ta) de. 2. (inadequate) deficiente.
deficit ['defɪsɪt] n déficit m inv.
defile [dɪ'faɪl] vt (desecrate) profanar; fig
(mind, purity) corromper.
define [dɪ'faɪn] vt definir.
definite ['defɪnɪt] adj 1. (plan, date,
answer) definitivo(va). 2. (improvement,
difference) indudable. 3. (confident - person) tajante; **I am quite ~ (about it)** estoy
totalmente seguro (de ello).
definitely ['defɪnɪtlɪ] adv 1. (without

doubt) sin duda. 2. (for emphasis) desde
luego, con (toda) seguridad.
definition [defɪ'nɪʃn] n 1. (gen) definición f; **by ~** por definición. 2. (clarity)
nitidez f.
deflate [dɪ'fleɪt] ◆ vt (balloon) desinflar; fig (person) bajar los humos a. ◆ vi
desinflarse.
deflation [dɪ'fleɪʃn] n (ECON) deflación
f.
deflect [dɪ'flekt] vt (gen) desviar; (criticism) soslayar.
defogger [,diː'fɒgəʳ] n Am (AUT) dispositivo m antivaho, luneta f térmica.
deformed [dɪ'fɔːmd] adj deforme.
defraud [dɪ'frɔːd] vt defraudar, estafar.
defrost [,diː'frɒst] ◆ vt 1. (gen) descongelar. 2. Am (AUT) (demist) desempañar.
◆ vi descongelarse.
deft [deft] adj habilidoso(sa), diestro
(tra).
defunct [dɪ'fʌŋkt] adj (plan) desecha-
do(da); (body, organization) desapareci-
do(da).
defuse [,diː'fjuːz] vt Br 1. (bomb)
desactivar. 2. (situation) neutralizar.
defy [dɪ'faɪ] vt 1. (disobey - person, authority) desafiar, desobedecer; (law, rule)
violar. 2. (challenge): **to ~ sb to do sthg**
retar OR desafiar a alguien a hacer algo.
3. (description, analysis) hacer imposible;
(attempts, efforts) hacer inútil.
degenerate [adj dɪ'dʒenərət, vb dɪ-
'dʒenəreɪt] ◆ adj degenerado(da). ◆ vi:
to ~ (into) degenerar (en).
degrading [dɪ'greɪdɪŋ] adj denigrante.
degree [dɪ'griː] n 1. (unit of measurement, amount) grado m; **by ~s** poco a
poco. 2. (qualification) título m universitario, ≃ licenciatura f; **to have/take a ~
(in sthg)** tener/hacer una licenciatura
(en algo).
dehydrated [,diːhaɪ'dreɪtɪd] adj
deshidratado(da).
de-ice [diː'aɪs] vt descongelar.
deign [deɪn] vt: **to ~ to do sthg** dignarse
a hacer algo.
deity ['diːɪtɪ] n deidad f.
dejected [dɪ'dʒektɪd] adj abatido(da).
delay [dɪ'leɪ] ◆ n retraso m. ◆ vt
retrasar; **to ~ starting sthg** retrasar el
comienzo de algo. ◆ vi: **to ~ (in doing
sthg)** retrasarse (en hacer algo).
delayed [dɪ'leɪd] adj: **to be ~** (person)
retrasarse; (train) ir con retraso.
delectable [dɪ'lektəbl] adj 1. (food)

deleitable. **2.** (*person*) apetecible.

delegate [*n* 'delɪgət, *vb* 'delɪgeɪt] ◆ *n* delegado *m*, -da *f*. ◆ *vt*: **to ~ sthg (to sb)** delegar algo (en alguien); **to ~ sb to do sthg** delegar a alguien para hacer algo.

delegation [ˌdelɪ'geɪʃn] *n* delegación *f*.

delete [dɪ'liːt] *vt* (*gen* & COMPUT) borrar.

deli [delɪ] *n inf abbr of* **delicatessen**.

deliberate [*adj* dɪ'lɪbərət, *vb* dɪ'lɪbəreɪt] ◆ *adj* **1.** (*intentional*) deliberado(da). **2.** (*slow*) pausado(da). ◆ *vi fml* deliberar.

deliberately [dɪ'lɪbərətlɪ] *adv* **1.** (*on purpose*) adrede. **2.** (*slowly*) pausadamente.

delicacy ['delɪkəsɪ] *n* **1.** (*gracefulness, tact*) delicadeza *f*. **2.** (*food*) exquisitez *f*, manjar *m*.

delicate ['delɪkət] *adj* **1.** (*gen*) delicado (da). **2.** (*subtle - colour, taste*) suave, sutil. **3.** (*tactful*) prudente; (*instrument*) sensible.

delicatessen [ˌdelɪkə'tesn] *n* = charcutería *f*, = (tienda *f* de) ultramarinos *m inv*.

delicious [dɪ'lɪʃəs] *adj* delicioso(sa).

delight [dɪ'laɪt] ◆ *n* (*great pleasure*) gozo *m*, regocijo *m*; **to take ~ in doing sthg** disfrutar haciendo algo. ◆ *vt* encantar. ◆ *vi*: **to ~ in sthg/in doing sthg** disfrutar con algo/haciendo algo.

delighted [dɪ'laɪtɪd] *adj* encantado (da), muy contento(ta); **~ by** OR **with** encantado con; **to be ~ to do sthg/that** estar encantado de hacer algo/de que; **I'd be ~ (to come)** me encantaría (ir).

delightful [dɪ'laɪtfʊl] *adj* (*gen*) encantador(ra); (*meal*) delicioso(sa); (*view*) muy agradable.

delinquent [dɪ'lɪŋkwənt] ◆ *adj* (*behaviour*) delictivo(va); (*child*) delincuente. ◆ *n* delincuente *m y f*.

delirious [dɪ'lɪrɪəs] *adj* (*with fever*) delirante; *fig* (*ecstatic*) enfervorizado(da).

deliver [dɪ'lɪvər] *vt* **1.** (*distribute*) repartir; (*hand over*) entregar; **to ~ sthg to sb** entregar algo a alguien. **2.** (*give - speech, verdict, lecture*) pronunciar; (*- message*) entregar; (*- warning, ultimatum*) lanzar; (*- blow, kick*) asestar. **3.** (*baby*) traer al mundo. **4.** *fml* (*free*) liberar, libertar. **5.** Am (POL) (*votes*) captar.

delivery [dɪ'lɪvərɪ] *n* **1.** (*distribution*) reparto *m*; (*handing over*) entrega *f*. **2.** (*goods delivered*) partida *f*. **3.** (*way of speaking*) (estilo *m* de) discurso *m*. **4.** (*birth*) parto *m*.

delude [dɪ'luːd] *vt* engañar; **to ~ o.s.** engañarse (a uno mismo/una misma).

deluge ['deljuːdʒ] *n* (*flood*) diluvio *m*; *fig* (*huge number*) aluvión *m*.

delusion [dɪ'luːʒn] *n* espejismo *m*, engaño *m*.

de luxe [də'lʌks] *adj* de lujo.

delve [delv] *vi*: **to ~ (into)** (*bag, cupboard*) hurgar (en); *fig* (*mystery*) profundizar (en).

demand [dɪ'mɑːnd] ◆ *n* **1.** (*claim, firm request*) exigencia *f*, reclamación *f*; **on ~** a petición. **2.** (*need*): **~ for** demanda *f* de; **in ~** solicitado(da). ◆ *vt* (*gen*) exigir; (*pay rise*) reclamar, demandar; **to ~ to do sthg** exigir hacer algo.

demanding [dɪ'mɑːndɪŋ] *adj* **1.** (*exhausting*) que exige mucho esfuerzo. **2.** (*not easily satisfied*) exigente.

demean [dɪ'miːn] *vt*: **to ~ o.s.** humillarse, rebajarse.

demeaning [dɪ'miːnɪŋ] *adj* denigrante.

demeanour Br, **demeanor** Am [dɪ'miːnər] *n* (U) *fml* proceder *m*, comportamiento *m*.

demented [dɪ'mentɪd] *adj* demente.

demise [dɪ'maɪz] *n fml* **1.** (*death*) defunción *f*. **2.** (*end*) hundimiento *m*.

demister [ˌdiː'mɪstər] *n* Br (AUT) dispositivo *m* antivaho, luneta *f* térmica.

demo ['deməʊ] (*abbr of* **demonstration**) *n inf* mani *f*.

democracy [dɪ'mɒkrəsɪ] *n* democracia *f*.

democrat ['deməkræt] *n* demócrata *m y f*. ▶ **Democrat** *n* Am demócrata *m y f*.

democratic [deməˈkrætɪk] *adj* democrático(ca). ▶ **Democratic** *adj* Am demócrata.

Democratic Party *n* Am Partido *m* Demócrata (de Estados Unidos).

demolish [dɪ'mɒlɪʃ] *vt* (*building*) demoler; (*argument, myth*) destrozar.

demonstrate ['demənstreɪt] ◆ *vt* **1.** (*prove*) demostrar. **2.** (*show*) hacer una demostración de. ◆ *vi* manifestarse.

demonstration [demən'streɪʃn] *n* **1.** (*of machine, product*) demostración *f*. **2.** (*public meeting*) manifestación *f*.

demonstrator ['demənstreɪtər] *n* **1.** (*in march*) manifestante *m y f*. **2.** (*of machine, product*) *persona que hace demostraciones*.

demoralized [dɪ'mɒrəlaɪzd] *adj* desmoralizado(da).

demote [ˌdiː'məʊt] *vt* descender de categoría.

demure [dɪˈmjʊəʳ] adj recatado(da).

den [den] n (lair) guarida f.

denial [dɪˈnaɪəl] n 1. (refutation) negación f, rechazo m. 2. (refusal) denegación f.

denier [ˈdenɪəʳ] n denier m.

denigrate [ˈdenɪɡreɪt] vt fml desacreditar.

denim [ˈdenɪm] n tela f vaquera.
▶ **denims** npl (pantalones mpl) vaqueros mpl.

denim jacket n cazadora f vaquera.

Denmark [ˈdenmɑːk] n Dinamarca.

denomination [dɪˌnɒmɪˈneɪʃn] n 1. (religious group) confesión f. 2. (of money) valor m.

denounce [dɪˈnaʊns] vt denunciar.

dense [dens] adj 1. (gen) denso(sa); (trees) tupido(da). 2. inf (stupid) bruto (ta).

density [ˈdensətɪ] n densidad f.

dent [dent] ◆ n (on car) abolladura f; (in wall) melladura f. ◆ vt (car) abollar; (wall) mellar.

dental [ˈdentl] adj dental.

dental floss n hilo m or seda f dental.

dental surgeon n odontólogo m, -ga f.

dentist [ˈdentɪst] n dentista m y f; to go to the ~'s ir al dentista.

dentures [ˈdentʃəz] npl dentadura f postiza.

deny [dɪˈnaɪ] vt 1. (refute) negar, rechazar; to ~ doing sthg negar haber hecho algo. 2. fml (refuse): to ~ sb sthg denegar algo a alguien.

deodorant [diːˈəʊdərənt] n desodorante m.

depart [dɪˈpɑːt] vi fml 1. (leave): to ~ (from) salir (de); this train will ~ from Platform 2 este tren efectuará su salida de la vía 2. 2. (differ): to ~ from sthg apartarse de algo.

department [dɪˈpɑːtmənt] n 1. (gen) departamento m. 2. (in government) ministerio m.

department store n grandes almacenes mpl.

departure [dɪˈpɑːtʃəʳ] n 1. (of train, plane) salida f; (of person) marcha f. 2. (change): ~ (from) abandono m (de); a new ~ un nuevo enfoque.

departure lounge n (in airport) sala f de embarque; (in coach station) vestíbulo m de salidas.

depend [dɪˈpend] vi: to ~ on depender de; you can ~ on me puedes confiar en mí; it ~s depende; ~ing on según.

dependable [dɪˈpendəbl] adj fiable.

dependant [dɪˈpendənt] n persona dependiente del cabeza de familia.

dependent [dɪˈpendənt] adj 1. (gen): to be ~ (on) depender (de). 2. (addicted) adicto(ta).

depict [dɪˈpɪkt] vt 1. (in picture) retratar. 2. (describe): to ~ sthg/sb as sthg describir algo/a alguien como algo.

deplete [dɪˈpliːt] vt mermar, reducir.

deplorable [dɪˈplɔːrəbl] adj deplorable.

deplore [dɪˈplɔːʳ] vt deplorar.

deploy [dɪˈplɔɪ] vt desplegar.

depopulation [diːˌpɒpjʊˈleɪʃn] n despoblación f.

deport [dɪˈpɔːt] vt deportar.

depose [dɪˈpəʊz] vt deponer.

deposit [dɪˈpɒzɪt] ◆ n 1. (GEOL) yacimiento m. 2. (sediment) poso m, sedimento m. 3. (payment into bank) ingreso m. 4. (down payment - on house, car) entrada f; (- on hotel room) señal f, adelanto m; (- on hired goods) fianza f; (- on bottle) dinero m del envase OR casco. ◆ vt 1. (put down) depositar. 2. (in bank) ingresar.

deposit account n Br cuenta f de ahorro a plazo fijo.

depot [ˈdepəʊ] n 1. (storage facility) almacén m; (for buses) cochera f. 2. Am (bus or train terminus) terminal f.

depreciate [dɪˈpriːʃɪeɪt] vi depreciarse.

depress [dɪˈpres] vt 1. (person) deprimir. 2. (economy) desactivar. 3. (price, share value) reducir.

depressed [dɪˈprest] adj deprimido (da).

depressing [dɪˈpresɪŋ] adj deprimente.

depression [dɪˈpreʃn] n 1. (gen & ECON) depresión f. 2. fml (in pillow) hueco m.

deprivation [ˌdeprɪˈveɪʃn] n 1. (poverty) miseria f. 2. (lack) privación f.

deprive [dɪˈpraɪv] vt: to ~ sb of sthg privar a alguien de algo.

depth [depθ] n profundidad f; in ~ a fondo; he was out of his ~ with that job ese trabajo le venía grande. ▶ **depths** npl: in the ~s of winter en pleno invierno; to be in the ~s of despair estar en un abismo de desesperación.

deputation [ˌdepjʊˈteɪʃn] n delegación f.

deputize, -ise [ˈdepjʊtaɪz] vi: to ~ (for) actuar en representación (de).

deputy [ˈdepjʊtɪ] ◆ adj: ~ head subdirector *m*, -ra *f*; **~ chairman/president** vicepresidente *m*. ◆ *n* **1.** (*second-in-command*) asistente *m* y *f*, suplente *m* y *f*. **2.** Am (*deputy sheriff*) ayudante *m* y *f* del sheriff.

derail [dɪ'reɪl] *vt & vi* (*train*) descarrilar.

deranged [dɪ'reɪndʒd] *adj* perturbado (da), trastornado(da).

derby [Br 'dɑːbɪ, Am 'dɜːbɪ] *n* **1.** (*sports event*) derby *m* (local). **2.** Am (*hat*) sombrero *m* hongo.

deregulate [,diː'regjʊleɪt] *vt* liberalizar.

derelict ['derəlɪkt] *adj* abandonado (da).

deride [dɪ'raɪd] *vt* mofarse de.

derisory [də'raɪzərɪ] *adj* **1.** (*puny, trivial*) irrisorio(ria). **2.** (*derisive*) burlón (ona).

derivative [dɪ'rɪvətɪv] *n* derivado *m*.

derive [dɪ'raɪv] ◆ *vt* **1.** (*draw, gain*): **to ~ sthg from sthg** encontrar algo en algo. **2.** (*come*): **to be ~d from** derivar de. ◆ *vi*: **to ~ from** derivar de.

derogatory [dɪ'rɒgətrɪ] *adj* despectivo(va).

derrick ['derɪk] *n* **1.** (*crane*) grúa *f*. **2.** (*over oil well*) torre *f* de perforación.

derv [dɜːv] *n* Br gasóleo *m*, gasoil *m*.

descend [dɪ'send] ◆ *vt* fml (*go down*) descender por. ◆ *vi* **1.** fml (*go down*) descender. **2.** (*subj: silence, gloom*): **to ~ (on sthg/sb)** invadir (algo/a alguien). **3.** (*stoop*): **to ~ to sthg/to doing sthg** rebajarse a algo/a hacer algo.

descendant [dɪ'sendənt] *n* descendiente *m* y *f*.

descended [dɪ'sendɪd] *adj*: **to be ~ from** ser descendiente de, descender de.

descent [dɪ'sent] *n* **1.** (*downwards movement*) descenso *m*, bajada *f*. **2.** (*origin*) ascendencia *f*.

describe [dɪ'skraɪb] *vt* describir.

description [dɪ'skrɪpʃn] *n* **1.** (*account*) descripción *f*. **2.** (*type*): **of all ~s** de todas clases.

desecrate ['desɪkreɪt] *vt* profanar.

desert [*n* 'dezət, *vb* dɪ'zɜːt] ◆ *n* (GEOGR) desierto *m*. ◆ *vt* abandonar. ◆ *vi* (MIL) desertar.

deserted [dɪ'zɜːtɪd] *adj* abandonado (da).

deserter [dɪ'zɜːtər] *n* desertor *m*, -ra *f*.

desert island ['dezət-] *n* isla *f* desierta.

deserve [dɪ'zɜːv] *vt* merecer.

deserving [dɪ'zɜːvɪŋ] *adj* encomiable.

design [dɪ'zaɪn] ◆ *n* **1.** (*gen*) diseño *m*; (*of garment*) corte *m*. **2.** (*pattern*) dibujo *m*. **3.** fml (*intention*) designio *m*; **by ~** adrede; **to have ~s on** tener las miras puestas en. ◆ *vt* **1.** (*draw plans for*) diseñar. **2.** (*plan, prepare*) concebir.

designate [*adj* 'dezɪgnət, *vb* 'dezɪgneɪt] ◆ *adj* designado(da). ◆ *vt* designar.

designation [,dezɪg'neɪʃn] *n* (*appointment*) designación *f*.

designer [dɪ'zaɪnər] ◆ *adj* (*clothes*) de diseño; (*glasses*) de marca. ◆ *n* (*gen*) diseñador *m*, -ra *f*; (THEATRE) escenógrafo *m*, -fa *f*.

desirable [dɪ'zaɪərəbl] *adj* **1.** fml (*appropriate*) deseable, conveniente. **2.** (*attractive*) atractivo(va), apetecible.

desire [dɪ'zaɪər] ◆ *n*: **~ (for sthg/to do sthg)** deseo *m* (de algo/de hacer algo). ◆ *vt* desear.

desk [desk] *n* **1.** (*gen*) mesa *f*, escritorio *m*; (*in school*) pupitre *m*. **2.** (*service area*): **information ~** (mostrador *m* de) información *f*.

desktop publishing *n* (COMPUT) autoedición *f* de textos.

desolate ['desələt] *adj* (*place, person*) desolado(da); (*feeling*) desolador(ra).

despair [dɪ'speər] ◆ *n* desesperación *f*. ◆ *vi* desesperarse; **to ~ of sb** desesperarse con alguien; **to ~ of sthg/doing sthg** desesperar de algo/hacer algo.

despairing [dɪ'speərɪŋ] *adj* desesperado(da).

despatch [dɪ'spætʃ] = **dispatch**.

desperate ['desprət] *adj* desesperado (da); **to be ~ for sthg** necesitar desesperadamente algo.

desperately ['desprətlɪ] *adv* **1.** (*want, fight, love*) desesperadamente. **2.** (*ill*) gravemente; (*poor, unhappy, shy*) tremendamente.

desperation [,despə'reɪʃn] *n* desesperación *f*; **in ~** con desesperación.

despicable [dɪ'spɪkəbl] *adj* despreciable.

despise [dɪ'spaɪz] *vt* despreciar.

despite [dɪ'spaɪt] *prep* a pesar de, pese a.

despondent [dɪ'spɒndənt] *adj* descorazonado(da).

dessert [dɪ'zɜːt] *n* postre *m*.

dessertspoon [dɪ'zɜːtspuːn] *n* (*spoon*) cuchara *f* de postre.

destination [,destɪ'neɪʃn] *n* destino *m*.

destined ['destɪnd] *adj* **1.** (*fated, intended*): **~ for sthg/to do sthg** destinado(da) a algo/a hacer algo. **2.** (*bound*): **~ for**

rumbo a, con destino a.

destiny ['destını] n destino m.

destitute ['destıtjuːt] adj indigente.

destroy [dı'strɔɪ] vt 1. (ruin) destruir. 2. (put down) matar, sacrificar.

destruction [dı'strʌkʃn] n destrucción f.

detach [dı'tætʃ] vt 1. (pull off): to ~ sthg (from) quitar OR separar algo (de). 2. (disassociate): to ~ o.s. from sthg distanciarse de algo.

detachable [dı'tætʃəbl] adj (handle etc) de quita y pon; (collar) postizo(za).

detached [dı'tætʃt] adj (unemotional) objetivo(va).

detached house n casa f OR chalet m individual.

detachment [dı'tætʃmənt] n 1. (aloofness) distanciamiento m. 2. (MIL) destacamento m.

detail ['diːteıl] ◆ n 1. (small point) detalle m, pormenor m. 2. (U) (facts, points) detalles mpl; to go into ~ entrar en detalles; in ~ con detalle. 3. (MIL) destacamento m. ◆ vt (list) detallar. ▶ **details** npl (gen) información f; (personal) datos mpl.

detailed ['diːteıld] adj detallado(da).

detain [dı'teın] vt (gen) retener; (in police station) detener.

detect [dı'tekt] vt (gen) detectar; (difference) notar, percibir.

detection [dı'tekʃn] (U) n 1. (gen) detección f. 2. (of crime) investigación f; (of drugs) descubrimiento m.

detective [dı'tektıv] n (private) detective m y f; (policeman) agente m y f.

detective novel n novela f policíaca.

détente [deı'tɒnt] n (POL) distensión f.

detention [dı'tenʃn] n 1. (of suspect, criminal) detención f, arresto m. 2. (at school) castigo de permanecer en la escuela después de clase.

deter [dı'tɜːʳ] vt: to ~ sb (from doing sthg) disuadir a alguien (de hacer algo).

detergent [dı'tɜːdʒənt] n detergente m.

deteriorate [dı'tıərıəreıt] vi (health, economy) deteriorarse; (weather) empeorar.

determination [dı,tɜːmı'neıʃn] n determinación f.

determine [dı'tɜːmın] vt determinar.

determined [dı'tɜːmınd] adj decidido (da); ~ to do sthg decidido OR resuelto a hacer algo.

deterrent [dı'terənt] n fuerza f disua-

soria; **nuclear** ~ armas fpl nucleares disuasorias.

detest [dı'test] vt detestar.

detonate ['detəneıt] vt & vi detonar.

detour ['diːtʊəʳ] n desviación f, desvío m; **to make a** ~ dar un rodeo.

detract [dı'trækt] vi: to ~ from sthg (gen) mermar algo, aminorar algo; (achievement) restar importancia a algo.

detriment ['detrımənt] n: to the ~ of en detrimento de.

detrimental [,detrı'mentl] adj perjudicial.

deuce [djuːs] n (U) (TENNIS) deuce m, iguales mpl (a cuarenta).

devaluation [,diːvæljʊ'eıʃn] n devaluación f.

devastated ['devəsteıtıd] adj (area, city) asolado(da); fig (person) desolado (da).

devastating ['devəsteıtıŋ] adj 1. (destructive - hurricane etc) devastador (ra). 2. (effective - remark, argument) abrumador(ra). 3. (upsetting - news, experience) desolador(ra). 4. (attractive) imponente, irresistible.

develop [dı'veləp] ◆ vt 1. (land) urbanizar. 2. (illness) contraer, coger; (habit) adquirir; **to** ~ **a fault** fallar, estropearse. 3. (product) elaborar. 4. (idea, argument, resources) desarrollar. 5. (PHOT) revelar. ◆ vi 1. (grow) desarrollarse. 2. (appear) presentarse, darse.

developing country [dı'veləpıŋ-] n país m en vías de desarrollo.

development [dı'veləpmənt] (U) n 1. (growth) desarrollo m. 2. (of design, product) elaboración f. 3. (developed land) urbanización f. 4. (new event) (nuevo) acontecimiento m. 5. (advance - in science etc) avance m.

deviate ['diːvıeıt] vi: to ~ from sthg apartarse OR desviarse de algo.

device [dı'vaıs] n dispositivo m, mecanismo m.

devil ['devl] n diablo m, demonio m; **poor** ~ pobre diablo; **you lucky** ~! ¡vaya suerte que tienes!; **who/where/why the** ~ **...?** ¿quién/dónde/por qué demonios ...? ▶ **Devil** n (Satan): **the Devil** el Diablo.

devious ['diːvjəs] adj 1. (person, scheme) malévolo(la), retorcido(da); (means) dudoso(sa). 2. (route) sinuoso(sa).

devise [dı'vaız] vt (instrument, system) diseñar; (plan) trazar.

devoid [dı'vɔıd] adj fml: ~ of desprovisto(ta) de.

dig

devolution [ˌdiːvəˈluːʃn] n (POL) = autonomía f, = traspaso m de competencias.

devote [dɪˈvəʊt] vt: **to ~ sthg to** dedicar OR consagrar algo a.

devoted [dɪˈvəʊtɪd] adj (person) leal; **to be ~ to sb** tener veneración por alguien.

devotee [ˌdevəˈtiː] n (fan) devoto m, -ta f, admirador m, -ra f.

devotion [dɪˈvəʊʃn] (U) n 1. (commitment): ~ **(to)** dedicación f (a). 2. (RELIG) devoción f.

devour [dɪˈvaʊəʳ] vt literary lit & fig devorar.

devout [dɪˈvaʊt] adj (RELIG) devoto(ta).

dew [djuː] n rocío m.

dexterity [dekˈsterətɪ] n destreza f.

diabetes [ˌdaɪəˈbiːtiːz] n diabetes f inv.

diabetic [ˌdaɪəˈbetɪk] ◆ adj (person) diabético(ca). ◆ n diabético m, -ca f.

diabolic(al) [ˌdaɪəˈbɒlɪk(l)] adj inf (very bad) demencial, pésimo(ma).

diagnose [ˈdaɪəgnəʊz] vt (MED) diagnosticar.

diagnosis [ˌdaɪəgˈnəʊsɪs] (pl -oses [-əʊsiːz]) n (MED) (verdict) diagnóstico m; (science, activity) diagnosis f inv.

diagonal [daɪˈægənl] ◆ adj diagonal. ◆ n diagonal f.

diagram [ˈdaɪəgræm] n diagrama m, dibujo m esquemático.

dial [ˈdaɪəl] ◆ n 1. (of watch, clock, meter) esfera f. 2. (of telephone, radio) dial m. ◆ vt (number) marcar.

dialect [ˈdaɪəlekt] n dialecto m.

dialling code [ˈdaɪəlɪŋ-] n Br prefijo m (telefónico), indicativo m.

dialling tone Br [ˈdaɪəlɪŋ-], **dial tone** Am n señal f de llamada.

dialogue Br, **dialog** Am [ˈdaɪəlɒg] n diálogo m.

dial tone Am = **dialling tone**.

dialysis [daɪˈælɪsɪs] n diálisis f inv.

diameter [daɪˈæmɪtəʳ] n diámetro m.

diamond [ˈdaɪəmənd] n 1. (gem, playing card) diamante m. 2. (shape) rombo m. ▶ **diamonds** npl diamantes mpl.

diaper [ˈdaɪpəʳ] n Am pañal m.

diaphragm [ˈdaɪəfræm] n diafragma m.

diarrh(o)ea [ˌdaɪəˈrɪə] n diarrea f.

diary [ˈdaɪərɪ] n 1. (appointment book) agenda f. 2. (journal) diario m.

dice [daɪs] (pl inv) ◆ n dado m. ◆ vt cortar en cuadraditos.

dictate [dɪkˈteɪt] vt: **to ~ sthg (to sb)** dictar algo (a alguien).

dictation [dɪkˈteɪʃn] n dictado m; **to take** OR **do ~** escribir al dictado.

dictator [dɪkˈteɪtəʳ] n dictador m, -ra f.

dictatorship [dɪkˈteɪtəʃɪp] n dictadura f.

dictionary [ˈdɪkʃənrɪ] n diccionario m.

did [dɪd] pt → **do**.

diddle [ˈdɪdl] vt inf timar.

didn't [ˈdɪdnt] = **did not**.

die [daɪ] (pl **dice**, pt & pp **died**, cont **dying**) ◆ vi 1. (gen) morir, morirse; **to be dying** estar muriéndose OR agonizando; **to be dying for sthg/to do sthg** morirse por algo/por hacer algo. 2. literary (feeling) extinguirse. ◆ n (dice) dado m. ▶ **die away** vi desvanecerse. ▶ **die down** vi (wind) amainar; (sound) apaciguarse; (fire) remitir; (excitement, fuss) calmarse. ▶ **die out** vi extinguirse.

diehard [ˈdaɪhɑːd] n reaccionario m, -ria f.

diesel [ˈdiːzl] n 1. (vehicle) vehículo m diesel. 2. (fuel) gasóleo m, gasoil m.

diesel engine n (AUT) motor m diesel; (RAIL) locomotora f diesel.

diesel fuel, diesel oil n gasóleo m.

diet [ˈdaɪət] ◆ n 1. (eating pattern) dieta f. 2. (to lose weight) régimen m; **to be on a ~** estar a régimen. ◆ comp (low-calorie) light (inv). ◆ vi estar a régimen.

differ [ˈdɪfəʳ] vi 1. (be different) diferir, ser diferente; **to ~ from sthg** distinguirse OR diferir de algo. 2. (disagree): **to ~ with sb (about sthg)** disentir OR discrepar de alguien (en algo).

difference [ˈdɪfrəns] n diferencia f; **it doesn't make any ~** da lo mismo.

different [ˈdɪfrənt] adj: ~ **(from)** diferente OR distinto(ta) (de).

differentiate [ˌdɪfəˈrenʃɪeɪt] ◆ vt: **to ~ (sthg from sthg)** diferenciar OR distinguir (algo de algo). ◆ vi: **to ~ between** diferenciar OR distinguir entre.

difficult [ˈdɪfɪkəlt] adj difícil.

difficulty [ˈdɪfɪkəltɪ] n dificultad f; **to have ~ in doing sthg** tener dificultad en OR para hacer algo.

diffident [ˈdɪfɪdənt] adj retraído(da).

diffuse [dɪˈfjuːz] vt difundir.

dig [dɪg] (pt & pp **dug**) ◆ vt 1. (hole - with spade) cavar; (- with hands, paws) escarbar. 2. (garden) cavar en; (mine) excavar. 3. (press): **to ~ sthg into** clavar OR hundir algo en. ◆ vi 1. (with spade) cavar; (with hands, paws) escarbar. 2. (press): **to ~ into** clavarse OR hundirse en. ◆ n 1. fig (unkind remark) pulla f. 2. (ARCHEOL) excavación f. ▶ **dig out** vt sep inf (*find - letter*) desempolvar; (*- information*) extraer. ▶ **dig up** *vt sep* (*gen*) desenterrar; (*tree*) arrancar.

digest [*n* 'daɪdʒest, *vb* dɪ'dʒest] ◆ *n* compendio *m*. ◆ *vt lit & fig* digerir.

digestion [dɪ'dʒestʃn] *n* digestión *f*.

digestive biscuit [dɪ'dʒestɪv-] *n* Br galleta hecha con harina integral.

digit ['dɪdʒɪt] *n* 1. (*figure*) dígito *m*. 2. (*finger, toe*) dedo *m*.

digital ['dɪdʒɪtl] *adj* digital.

dignified ['dɪgnɪfaɪd] *adj* (*gen*) solemne; (*behaviour*) ceremonioso(sa).

dignity ['dɪgnətɪ] *n* dignidad *f*.

digress [daɪ'gres] *vi* apartarse del tema; **to ~ from** apartarse OR desviarse de.

digs [dɪgz] *npl* Br *inf* alojamiento *m*; **to live in ~** vivir de patrona.

dike [daɪk] *n* (*wall, bank*) dique *m*.

dilapidated [dɪ'læpɪdeɪtɪd] *adj* destartalado(da), derruido(da).

dilate [daɪ'leɪt] *vi* dilatarse.

dilemma [dɪ'lemə] *n* dilema *m*.

diligent ['dɪlɪdʒənt] *adj* diligente.

dilute [daɪ'luːt] *vt* diluir; (*wine, beer*) aguar.

dim [dɪm] ◆ *adj* 1. (*light*) tenue; (*room*) sombrío(a). 2. (*outline, figure*) difuso(sa). 3. (*eyesight*) nublado(da). 4. (*memory*) vago(ga). 5. *inf* (*stupid*) tonto(ta), torpe. ◆ *vt* atenuar. ◆ *vi* (*light*) atenuarse.

dime [daɪm] *n* Am *moneda de diez centavos*.

dimension [dɪ'menʃn] *n* dimensión *f*.

diminish [dɪ'mɪnɪʃ] *vt & vi* disminuir.

diminutive [dɪ'mɪnjʊtɪv] *fml* ◆ *adj* diminuto(ta). ◆ *n* (GRAMM) diminutivo *m*.

dimmer ['dɪmər], **dimmer switch** *n* potenciómetro *m*.

dimmers ['dɪməz] *npl* Am (*dipped headlights*) luces *fpl* cortas OR de cruce; (*parking lights*) luces de posición OR situación.

dimmer switch = **dimmer**.

dimple ['dɪmpl] *n* hoyuelo *m*.

din [dɪn] *n inf* estrépito *m*.

dine [daɪn] *vi fml* cenar. ▶ **dine out** *vi* cenar fuera.

diner ['daɪnər] *n* 1. (*person*) comensal *m* y *f* (*en cena*). 2. Am (*restaurant - cheap*) restaurante *m* barato; (*- on the road*) ≃ restaurante *m* OR parador *m* de carretera.

dinghy ['dɪŋgɪ] *n* bote *m*.

dingy ['dɪndʒɪ] *adj* (*room, street*) lóbrego (ga); (*clothes, carpet*) deslustrado(da).

dining car ['daɪnɪŋ-] *n* vagón *m* restaurante.

dining room ['daɪnɪŋ-] *n* comedor *m*.

dinner ['dɪnər] *n* 1. (*evening meal*) cena *f*; (*midday meal*) comida *f*, almuerzo *m*; **to have ~** (*at lunchtime*) almorzar; (*in evening*) cenar. 2. (*formal event*) cena *f* de gala, banquete *m*.

dinner jacket *n* esmoquin *m*.

dinner party *n* cena *f* (*de amigos en casa*).

dinnertime ['dɪnətaɪm] *n* (*in the evening*) la hora de la cena; (*at midday*) la hora del almuerzo OR de la comida.

dinosaur ['daɪnəsɔːr] *n* (*reptile*) dinosaurio *m*.

dint [dɪnt] *n fml*: **by ~ of** a base de.

dip [dɪp] ◆ *n* 1. (*in road, ground*) pendiente *f*, declive *m*. 2. (*sauce*) salsa *f*. 3. (*swim*) chapuzón *m*; **to go for/take a ~** ir a darse/darse un chapuzón. ◆ *vt* 1. (*into liquid*): **to ~ sthg in** OR **into sthg** mojar algo en algo. 2. Br (*headlights*): **to ~ one's lights** poner las luces de cruce. ◆ *vi* descender suavemente.

diploma [dɪ'pləʊmə] (*pl* -s) *n* diploma *m*.

diplomacy [dɪ'pləʊməsɪ] *n* diplomacia *f*.

diplomat ['dɪpləmæt] *n* 1. (*official*) diplomático *m*, -ca *f*. 2. (*tactful person*) persona *f* diplomática.

diplomatic [ˌdɪplə'mætɪk] *adj* diplomático(ca).

dipstick ['dɪpstɪk] *n* (AUT) varilla *f* (para medir el nivel) del aceite.

dire ['daɪər] *adj* (*consequences*) grave; (*warning*) estremecedor(ra); (*need, poverty*) extremo(ma).

direct [dɪ'rekt] ◆ *adj* directo(ta). ◆ *vt* 1. (*gen*): **to ~ sthg at sb** dirigir algo a alguien. 2. (*person to place*): **to ~ sb (to)** indicar a alguien el camino (a). 3. (*order*): **to ~ sb to do sthg** mandar a alguien hacer algo. ◆ *adv* directamente.

direct current *n* corriente *f* continua.

direct debit *n* Br domiciliación *f* (de pago).

direction [dɪ'rekʃn] *n* dirección *f*; **sense of ~** sentido *m* de la orientación. ▶ **directions** *npl* 1. (*instructions to place*) señas *fpl*, indicaciones *fpl*. 2. (*instructions for use*) modo *m* de empleo.

directly [dɪ'rektlɪ] *adv* 1. (*gen*) directamente. 2. (*immediately*) inmediatamente. 3. (*very soon*) pronto, en breve.

director [dɪ'rektər] *n* director *m*, -ra *f*.

directory [dɪ'rektərɪ] *n* 1. (*gen*) guía *f*

(alfabética). **2.** (COMPUT) directorio *m*.

directory enquiries *n* Br (servicio *m* de) información *f* telefónica.

dire straits *npl*: **in ~** en serios aprietos.

dirt [dɜ:t] *n* (U) **1.** (*mud*, *dust*) suciedad *f*. **2.** (*earth*) tierra *f*.

dirt cheap *inf* ◆ *adj* tirado(da) de precio. ◆ *adv* a precio de ganga.

dirty ['dɜ:tɪ] ◆ *adj* **1.** (*gen*) sucio(cia). **2.** (*joke*) verde; (*film*) pornográfico(ca); (*book*, *language*) obsceno(na). ◆ *vt* ensuciar.

disability [,dɪsə'bɪlətɪ] *n* minusvalía *f*.

disabled [dɪs'eɪbld] ◆ *adj* (*person*) minusválido(da). ◆ *npl*: **the ~** los minusválidos.

disadvantage [,dɪsəd'vɑ:ntɪdʒ] *n* desventaja *f*; **to be at a ~** estar en desventaja.

disagree [,dɪsə'gri:] *vi* **1.** (*have different opinions*): **to ~ (with)** no estar de acuerdo (con). **2.** (*differ*) contradecirse, no concordar. **3.** (*subj*: *food*, *drink*): **to ~ with sb** sentar mal a alguien.

disagreeable [,dɪsə'gri:əbl] *adj* desagradable.

disagreement [,dɪsə'gri:mənt] *n* **1.** (*fact of disagreeing*) desacuerdo *m*. **2.** (*argument*) discusión *f*.

disallow [,dɪsə'laʊ] *vt* **1.** *fml* (*appeal*, *claim*) rechazar. **2.** (*goal*) anular.

disappear [,dɪsə'pɪər] *vi* desaparecer.

disappearance [,dɪsə'pɪərəns] *n* desaparición *f*.

disappoint [,dɪsə'pɔɪnt] *vt* (*person*) decepcionar; (*expectations*, *hopes*) defraudar.

disappointed [,dɪsə'pɔɪntɪd] *adj* **1.** (*person*): **~ (in OR with sthg)** decepcionado(da) (con algo). **2.** (*expectations*, *hopes*) defraudado(da).

disappointing [,dɪsə'pɔɪntɪŋ] *adj* decepcionante.

disappointment [,dɪsə'pɔɪntmənt] *n* decepción *f*, desilusión *f*.

disapproval [,dɪsə'pru:vl] *n* desaprobación *f*.

disapprove [,dɪsə'pru:v] *vi*: **to ~ (of sthg/sb)** censurar (algo/a alguien).

disarm [dɪs'ɑ:m] ◆ *vt* *lit* & *fig* desarmar. ◆ *vi* desarmarse.

disarmament [dɪs'ɑ:məmənt] *n* desarme *m*.

disarray [,dɪsə'reɪ] *n*: **in ~** (*clothes*, *hair*) en desorden; (*army*, *political party*) sumido(da) en el desconcierto.

disaster [dɪ'zɑ:stər] *n* desastre *m*.

disastrous [dɪ'zɑ:strəs] *adj* desastroso (sa).

disband [dɪs'bænd] ◆ *vt* disolver, disgregar. ◆ *vi* disolverse, disgregarse.

disbelief [,dɪsbɪ'li:f] *n*: **in OR with ~** con incredulidad.

disc Br, **disk** Am [dɪsk] *n* disco *m*.

discard [dɪ'skɑ:d] *vt* (*old clothes etc*) desechar; (*possibility*) descartar.

discern [dɪ'sɜ:n] *vt* **1.** (*gen*) discernir; (*improvement*) percibir. **2.** (*figure*, *outline*) distinguir.

discerning [dɪ'sɜ:nɪŋ] *adj* refinado (da); (*audience*) entendido(da).

discharge [*n* 'dɪstʃɑːdʒ, *vb* dɪs'tʃɑːdʒ] ◆ *n* **1.** (*of patient*) alta *f*; (*of prisoner*, *defendant*) puesta *f* en libertad; (*of soldier*) licencia *f*. **2.** (*of gas*, *smoke*) emisión *f*; (*of sewage*) vertido *m*. **3.** (MED - *from wound*) supuración *f*. **4.** (ELEC) descarga *f*. ◆ *vt* **1.** (*patient*) dar de alta; (*prisoner*, *defendant*) poner en libertad; (*soldier*) licenciar. **2.** *fml* (*duty etc*) cumplir. **3.** (*gas*, *smoke*) despedir; (*sewage*) verter; (*cargo*) descargar. **4.** (*debt*) saldar.

disciple [dɪ'saɪpl] *n* **1.** (*follower*) discípulo *m*, -la *f*. **2.** (RELIG) discípulo *m*.

discipline ['dɪsɪplɪn] ◆ *n* disciplina *f*. ◆ *vt* **1.** (*control*) disciplinar. **2.** (*punish*) castigar.

disc jockey *n* pinchadiscos *m y f inv*.

disclaim [dɪs'kleɪm] *vt* *fml* negar.

disclose [dɪs'kləʊz] *vt* desvelar, revelar.

disclosure [dɪs'kləʊʒər] *n* revelación *f*.

disco ['dɪskəʊ] (*pl* **-s**) (*abbr of* **discotheque**) *n* (*place*) discoteca *f*; (*event*) baile *m*.

discomfort [dɪs'kʌmfət] *n* incomodidad *f*.

disconcert [,dɪskən'sɜ:t] *vt* desconcertar.

disconnect [,dɪskə'nekt] *vt* **1.** (*detach*) quitar, separar. **2.** (*from gas*, *electricity - appliance*) desconectar; (- *house*, *subscriber*) cortar el suministro a. **3.** (*on phone - person*) cortar la línea a.

disconsolate [dɪs'kɒnsələt] *adj* desconsolado(da).

discontent [,dɪskən'tent] *n*: **~ (with)** descontento *m* (con).

discontented [,dɪskən'tentɪd] *adj* descontento(ta).

discontinue [,dɪskən'tɪnju:] *vt* interrumpir.

discord ['dɪskɔːd] *n* **1.** (*disagreement*) discordia *f*. **2.** (MUS) disonancia *f*.

discotheque ['dɪskəʊtek] *n* discoteca *f*.

discount [*n* 'dɪskaʊnt, *vb* Br dɪs'kaʊnt, Am 'dɪskaʊnt] ◆ *n* descuento *m.* ◆ *vt* (*report, claim*) descartar.

discourage [dɪ'skʌrɪdʒ] *vt* **1.** (*dispirit*) desanimar. **2.** (*deter*) desaconsejar; **to ~ sb from doing sthg** disuadir a alguien de hacer algo.

discover [dɪ'skʌvəʳ] *vt* descubrir.

discoverer [dɪ'skʌvərəʳ] *n* descubridor *m*, -ra *f.*

discovery [dɪ'skʌvərɪ] *n* descubrimiento *m.*

discredit [dɪs'kredɪt] ◆ *n* descrédito *m.* ◆ *vt* **1.** (*person, organization*) desacreditar. **2.** (*idea, report*) refutar.

discreet [dɪ'skriːt] *adj* discreto(ta).

discrepancy [dɪ'skrepənsɪ] *n*: **~ (in/between)** desigualdad *f* (en/entre).

discretion [dɪ'skreʃn] (U) *n* **1.** (*tact*) discreción *f.* **2.** (*judgment*) capacidad *f* de decisión; **at the ~ of** a voluntad de.

discriminate [dɪ'skrɪmɪneɪt] *vi* **1.** (*distinguish*): **to ~ (between)** discriminar OR distinguir (entre). **2.** (*treat unfairly*): **to ~ against sb** discriminar a alguien.

discriminating [dɪ'skrɪmɪneɪtɪŋ] *adj* refinado(da); (*audience*) entendido(da).

discrimination [dɪ,skrɪmɪ'neɪʃn] *n* **1.** (*prejudice*): **~ (against)** discriminación *f* (hacia). **2.** (*judgment*) (buen) gusto *m.*

discus ['dɪskəs] (*pl* **-es**) *n* disco *m* (*en atletismo*).

discuss [dɪ'skʌs] *vt* **1.** (*gen*): **to ~ sthg (with sb)** discutir algo (con alguien). **2.** (*subj: book, lecture*) tratar de.

discussion [dɪ'skʌʃn] *n* discusión *f.*

disdain [dɪs'deɪn] *fml* ◆ *n*: **~ (for)** desdén *m* OR desprecio *m* (hacia). ◆ *vt* desdeñar, despreciar.

disease [dɪ'ziːz] *n lit & fig* enfermedad *f.*

disembark [,dɪsɪm'bɑːk] *vi* desembarcar.

disenchanted [,dɪsɪn'tʃɑːntɪd] *adj*: **~ (with)** desencantado(da) (con).

disengage [,dɪsɪn'geɪdʒ] *vt* **1.** (*release*): **to ~ sthg (from)** soltar OR desenganchar algo (de). **2.** (TECH) (*gears*) quitar; (*clutch*) soltar.

disfavour Br, **disfavor** Am [dɪs-'feɪvəʳ] *n* **1.** (*disapproval*) desaprobación *f.* **2.** (*state of being disapproved of*) desgracia *f.*

disfigure [dɪs'fɪgəʳ] *vt* desfigurar.

disgrace [dɪs'greɪs] ◆ *n* vergüenza *f*; **he's a ~ to his family** es una deshonra para su familia; **to be in ~** (*minister, offi-*)cial) estar desprestigiado(da); (*child, pet*) estar castigado(da). ◆ *vt* deshonrar.

disgraceful [dɪs'greɪsfʊl] *adj* vergonzoso(sa).

disgruntled [dɪs'grʌntld] *adj* disgustado(da).

disguise [dɪs'gaɪz] ◆ *n* disfraz *m*; **in ~** (*policeman, personality*) de incógnito. ◆ *vt* disfrazar.

disgust [dɪs'gʌst] ◆ *n*: **~ (at)** (*physical*) asco *m* (hacia); (*moral*) indignación *f* (ante). ◆ *vt* (*physically*) asquear; (*morally*) indignar.

disgusting [dɪs'gʌstɪŋ] *adj* (*physically*) asqueroso(sa); (*morally*) indignante.

dish [dɪʃ] *n* **1.** (*container*) fuente *f.* **2.** (*course*) plato *m.* **3.** Am (*plate*) plato *m.* ▶ **dishes** *npl* platos *mpl*; **to do** OR **wash the ~es** fregar (los platos). ▶ **dish out** *vt sep inf* repartir. ▶ **dish up** *vt sep inf* servir.

dish aerial Br, **dish antenna** Am *n* (antena *f*) parabólica *f.*

dishcloth ['dɪʃklɒθ] *n* trapo *m* de fregar los platos.

disheartened [dɪs'hɑːtnd] *adj* descorazonado(da).

dishevelled Br, **disheveled** Am [dɪ-'ʃevəld] *adj* desaliñado(da); (*hair*) despeinado(da).

dishonest [dɪs'ɒnɪst] *adj* deshonesto(ta), nada honrado(da).

dishonor *etc* Am = **dishonour** *etc.*

dishonour Br, **dishonor** Am [dɪs-'ɒnəʳ] *fml* ◆ *n* deshonra *f.* ◆ *vt* deshonrar.

dishonourable Br, **dishonorable** Am [dɪs'ɒnərəbl] *adj* deshonroso(sa).

dish soap *n* Am detergente *m* para vajillas.

dish towel *n* Am paño *m* de cocina.

dishwasher ['dɪʃ,wɒʃəʳ] *n* (*machine*) lavavajillas *m inv.*

disillusioned [,dɪsɪ'luːʒnd] *adj* desilusionado(da).

disincentive [,dɪsɪn'sentɪv] *n* freno *m*, traba *f.*

disinclined [,dɪsɪn'klaɪnd] *adj*: **to be ~ to do sthg** ser reacio(cia) a hacer algo.

disinfect [,dɪsɪn'fekt] *vt* desinfectar.

disinfectant [,dɪsɪn'fektənt] *n* desinfectante *m.*

disintegrate [dɪs'ɪntɪgreɪt] *vi lit & fig* desintegrarse.

disinterested [,dɪs'ɪntrəstɪd] *adj* **1.** (*objective*) desinteresado(da). **2.** *inf* (*uninterested*): **~ (in)** indiferente (a).

disjointed [dɪs'dʒɔɪntɪd] *adj* deslabazado(da).

disk [dɪsk] *n* 1. (COMPUT) disquete *m*. 2. Am = **disc**.

disk drive Br, **diskette drive** Am *n* (COMPUT) disquetera *f*.

diskette [dɪsk'et] *n* disquete *m*.

diskette drive Am = **disk drive**.

dislike [dɪs'laɪk] ♦ *n* 1. (*feeling*): ~ (**for**) (*things*) aversión *f* (a); (*people*) antipatía *f* (por); **to take a ~ to** cogerle manía a. 2. (*person, thing not liked*) fobia *f*. ♦ *vt* (*thing*) tener aversión a; (*person*) tener antipatía a.

dislocate ['dɪsləkeɪt] *vt* (MED) dislocar.

dislodge [dɪs'lɒdʒ] *vt*: **to ~ sthg/sb** (**from**) desalojar algo/a alguien (de).

disloyal [ˌdɪs'lɔɪəl] *adj*: ~ (**to**) desleal (a).

dismal ['dɪzml] *adj* 1. (*weather, future*) sombrío(a); (*place, atmosphere*) deprimente. 2. (*attempt, failure*) lamentable.

dismantle [dɪs'mæntl] *vt* (*machine*) desmontar; (*organization*) desmantelar.

dismay [dɪs'meɪ] ♦ *n* (U) consternación *f*. ♦ *vt* consternar.

dismiss [dɪs'mɪs] *vt* 1. (*refuse to take seriously*) desechar. 2. (*from job*): **to ~ sb** (**from**) despedir a alguien (de). 3. (*allow to leave*) dar permiso para irse a.

dismissal [dɪs'mɪsl] *n* (*from job*) despido *m*.

dismount [ˌdɪs'maʊnt] *vi*: **to ~ (from sthg)** desmontar (de algo).

disobedience [ˌdɪsə'biːdjəns] *n* desobediencia *f*.

disobedient [ˌdɪsə'biːdjənt] *adj*: ~ (**to**) desobediente (con).

disobey [ˌdɪsə'beɪ] *vt* & *vi* desobedecer.

disorder [dɪs'ɔːdər] *n* 1. (*disarray*): **in ~** en desorden. 2. (U) (*rioting*) disturbios *mpl*. 3. (MED) (*physical*) afección *f*, dolencia *f*; (*mental*) trastorno *m*.

disorderly [dɪs'ɔːdəlɪ] *adj* 1. (*untidy*) desordenado(da). 2. (*unruly - behaviour*) incontrolado(da).

disorganized, -ised [dɪs'ɔːgənaɪzd] *adj* desorganizado(da).

disorientated Br [dɪs'ɔːrɪənteɪtɪd], **disoriented** Am [dɪs'ɔːrɪəntɪd] *adj* desorientado(da).

disown [dɪs'əʊn] *vt* renegar de.

disparaging [dɪs'pærɪdʒɪŋ] *adj* menospreciativo(va).

dispassionate [dɪs'pæʃnət] *adj* desapasionado(da).

dispatch [dɪs'pætʃ] ♦ *n* despacho *m*.

♦ *vt* (*goods, parcel*) expedir; (*message, messenger, troops*) enviar.

dispel [dɪ'spel] *vt* disipar.

dispensary [dɪ'spensərɪ] *n* dispensario *m*.

dispense [dɪ'spens] *vt* 1. (*advice*) ofrecer; (*justice*) administrar. 2. (*drugs, medicine*) despachar, dispensar. ▶ **dispense with** *vt fus* prescindir de.

dispensing chemist Br, **dispensing pharmacist** Am [dɪ'spensɪŋ-] *n* farmacéutico *m*, -ca *f*.

disperse [dɪ'spɜːs] ♦ *vt* dispersar. ♦ *vi* dispersarse.

dispirited [dɪ'spɪrɪtɪd] *adj* desanimado (da).

displace [dɪs'pleɪs] *vt* (*supplant*) reemplazar, sustituir.

display [dɪ'spleɪ] ♦ *n* 1. (*arrangement - in shop window*) escaparate *m*; (- *in museum*) exposición *f*; (- *on stall, pavement*) muestrario *m*. 2. (*demonstration, public event*) demostración *f*. 3. (COMPUT) visualización *f*. ♦ *vt* 1. (*arrange*) exponer. 2. (*show*) demostrar.

displease [dɪs'pliːz] *vt* (*annoy*) disgustar; (*anger*) enfadar.

displeasure [dɪs'pleʒər] *n* (*annoyance*) disgusto *m*; (*anger*) enfado *m*.

disposable [dɪ'spəʊzəbl] *adj* desechable; ~ **income** ingresos *mpl* disponibles.

disposal [dɪ'spəʊzl] *n* 1. (*removal*) eliminación *f*. 2. (*availability*): **at sb's ~** a la disposición de alguien.

dispose [dɪ'spəʊz] ▶ **dispose of** *vt fus* (*rubbish*) deshacerse de; (*problem*) quitarse de encima OR de en medio.

disposed [dɪ'spəʊzd] *adj* 1. (*willing*): **to be ~ to do sthg** estar dispuesto(ta) a hacer algo. 2. (*friendly*): **to be well ~ to** OR **towards sb** tener buena disposición hacia alguien.

disposition [ˌdɪspə'zɪʃn] *n* (*temperament*) carácter *m*.

disproportionate [dɪsprə'pɔːʃnət] *adj*: ~ (**to**) desproporcionado(da) (a).

disprove [ˌdɪs'pruːv] *vt* refutar.

dispute [dɪ'spjuːt] ♦ *n* 1. (*quarrel*) disputa *f*. 2. (U) (*disagreement*) conflicto *m*, desacuerdo *m*. 3. (INDUSTRY) conflicto *m* laboral. ♦ *vt* cuestionar.

disqualify [ˌdɪs'kwɒlɪfaɪ] *vt* 1. (*subj: authority, illness etc*): **to ~ sb** (**from doing sthg**) incapacitar a alguien (para hacer algo). 2. (SPORT) descalificar. 3. Br (*from driving*) retirar el permiso de conducir a.

disquiet [dɪs'kwaɪət] n inquietud f.

disregard [ˌdɪsrɪ'gɑːd] ◆ n: ~ **(for)** indiferencia f (a), despreocupación f (por). ◆ vt hacer caso omiso de.

disrepair [ˌdɪsrɪ'peər] n: **in a state of** ~ en mal estado.

disreputable [dɪs'repjʊtəbl] adj (person, company) de mala fama; (behaviour) vergonzante.

disrepute [ˌdɪsrɪ'pjuːt] n: **to bring sthg into** ~ desprestigiar OR desacreditar algo.

disrupt [dɪs'rʌpt] vt (meeting) interrumpir; (transport system) trastornar, perturbar; (class) revolucionar, enredar en.

disruption [dɪs'rʌpʃn] n (of meeting) interrupción f; (of transport system) trastorno m, desbarajuste m.

dissatisfaction ['dɪsˌsætɪs'fækʃn] n descontento m.

dissatisfied [ˌdɪs'sætɪsfaɪd] adj: ~ **(with)** insatisfecho(cha) OR descontento (ta) (con).

dissect [dɪ'sekt] vt (MED) disecar; fig (study) analizar minuciosamente.

disseminate [dɪ'semɪneɪt] vt difundir.

dissent [dɪ'sent] ◆ n (gen) disconformidad f, disentimiento m; (SPORT): **he was booked for** ~ le amonestaron por protestar. ◆ vi: **to** ~ **(from)** disentir (de).

dissertation [ˌdɪsə'teɪʃn] n tesina f.

disservice [ˌdɪs'sɜːvɪs] n: **to do sb a** ~ hacer un flaco servicio a alguien.

dissident ['dɪsɪdənt] n disidente m y f.

dissimilar [ˌdɪ'sɪmɪlər] adj: ~ **(to)** distinto(ta) (de).

dissipate ['dɪsɪpeɪt] vt 1. (heat) disipar. 2. (efforts, money) desperdiciar.

dissociate [dɪ'səʊʃɪeɪt] vt disociar.

dissolute ['dɪsəluːt] adj disoluto(ta).

dissolve [dɪ'zɒlv] ◆ vt disolver. ◆ vi 1. (substance) disolverse. 2. fig (disappear) desvanecerse, desaparecer.

dissuade [dɪ'sweɪd] vt: **to** ~ **sb (from doing sthg)** disuadir a alguien (de hacer algo).

distance ['dɪstəns] n distancia f; **at a** ~ a distancia; **from a** ~ desde lejos; **in the** ~ a lo lejos.

distant ['dɪstənt] adj 1. (place, time, relative) lejano(na); ~ **from** distante de. 2. (person, manner) frío(a), distante.

distaste [dɪs'teɪst] n: ~ **(for)** desagrado m (por).

distasteful [dɪs'teɪstfʊl] adj desagradable.

distended [dɪ'stendɪd] adj dilatado (da).

distil Br, **distill** Am [dɪ'stɪl] vt (liquid) destilar.

distillery [dɪ'stɪlərɪ] n destilería f.

distinct [dɪ'stɪŋkt] adj 1. (different): ~ **(from)** distinto(ta) (de); **as** ~ **from** a diferencia de. 2. (clear - improvement) notable, visible; (- possibility) claro(ra).

distinction [dɪ'stɪŋkʃn] n 1. (difference, excellence) distinción f; **to draw** OR **make a** ~ **between** hacer una distinción entre. 2. (in exam result) sobresaliente m.

distinctive [dɪ'stɪŋktɪv] adj característico(ca), particular.

distinguish [dɪ'stɪŋgwɪʃ] vt (gen): **to** ~ **sthg (from)** distinguir algo (de).

distinguished [dɪ'stɪŋgwɪʃt] adj distinguido(da).

distinguishing [dɪ'stɪŋgwɪʃɪŋ] adj distintivo(va).

distort [dɪ'stɔːt] vt 1. (shape, face) deformar; (sound) distorsionar. 2. (truth, facts) tergiversar.

distract [dɪ'strækt] vt (person, attention): **to** ~ **sb (from)** distraer a alguien (de).

distracted [dɪ'stræktɪd] adj distraído (da).

distraction [dɪ'strækʃn] n (interruption, diversion) distracción f.

distraught [dɪ'strɔːt] adj muy turbado (da).

distress [dɪ'stres] ◆ n 1. (anxiety) angustia f; (pain) dolor m. 2. (danger, difficulty) peligro m. ◆ vt afligir, apenar.

distressed [dɪ'strest] adj angustiado(da).

distressing [dɪ'stresɪŋ] adj angustioso (sa), doloroso(sa).

distribute [dɪ'strɪbjuːt] vt (gen) distribuir, repartir.

distribution [ˌdɪstrɪ'bjuːʃn] n (gen) distribución f.

distributor [dɪ'strɪbjʊtər] n 1. (COMM) distribuidor m, -ra f. 2. (AUT) delco® m.

district ['dɪstrɪkt] n 1. (area - of country) zona f, región f; (- of town) barrio m. 2. (administrative area) distrito m.

district attorney n Am fiscal m y f (del distrito).

district council n Br (ADMIN) ≃ municipio m.

district nurse n Br enfermera encargada de atender a domicilio a los pacientes de una zona.

distrust [dɪs'trʌst] ◆ n desconfianza f. ◆ vt desconfiar de.

disturb [dɪ'stɜːb] vt 1. (interrupt - person) molestar; (- concentration) perturbar. 2. (upset, worry) inquietar. 3. (alter - sur-

face, arrangement) alterar; (*- papers*) desordenar.

disturbance [dɪˈstɜːbəns] *n* 1. (*fight*) tumulto *m*. 2. (*interruption*) interrupción *f*. 3. (*of mind, emotions*) trastorno *m*.

disturbed [dɪˈstɜːbd] *adj* 1. (*upset, ill*) trastornado(da). 2. (*worried*) inquieto (ta).

disturbing [dɪˈstɜːbɪŋ] *adj* inquietante.

disuse [ˌdɪsˈjuːs] *n*: **to fall into ~** (*regulation*) caer en desuso; (*building, mine*) verse paulatinamente abandonado (da).

disused [ˌdɪsˈjuːzd] *adj* abandonado (da).

ditch [dɪtʃ] ◆ *n* (*gen*) zanja *f*; (*by road*) cuneta *f*. ◆ *vt inf* 1. (*end relationship with*) romper con. 2. (*get rid of*) deshacerse de.

dither [ˈdɪðəʳ] *vi* vacilar.

ditto [ˈdɪtəʊ] *adv* ídem, lo mismo.

diuretic [ˌdaɪjʊˈretɪk] *n* diurético *m*.

dive [daɪv] (Br *pt & pp* **-d**, Am *pt* **-d** OR **dove**, *pp* **-d**) ◆ *vi* 1. (*into water - person*) zambullirse; (*- submarine, bird, fish*) sumergirse. 2. (*with breathing apparatus*) bucear. 3. (*through air - person*) lanzarse; (*- plane*) caer en picado. 4. (*into bag, cupboard*): **to ~ into** meter la mano en. ◆ *n* 1. (*of person - into water*) zambullida *f*. 2. (*of submarine*) inmersión *f*. 3. (*of person - through air*) salto *m*; (*- in football etc*) estirada *f*. 4. (*of plane*) picado *m*. 5. *inf pej* (*bar, restaurant*) garito *m*, antro *m*.

diver [ˈdaɪvəʳ] *n* (*underwater*) buceador *m*, -ra *f*; (*professional*) buzo *m*; (*from diving board*) saltador *m*, -ra *f* (de trampolín).

diverge [daɪˈvɜːdʒ] *vi* 1. (*gen*): **to ~ (from)** divergir (de). 2. (*disagree*) discrepar.

diversify [daɪˈvɜːsɪfaɪ] ◆ *vt* diversificar. ◆ *vi* diversificarse.

diversion [daɪˈvɜːʃn] *n* 1. (*distraction*) distracción *f*. 2. (*of traffic, river, funds*) desvío *m*.

diversity [daɪˈvɜːsətɪ] *n* diversidad *f*.

divert [daɪˈvɜːt] *vt* 1. (*traffic, river, funds*) desviar. 2. (*person, attention*) distraer.

divide [dɪˈvaɪd] ◆ *vt*: **to ~ sthg (between** OR **among)** dividir algo (entre); **to ~ sthg into** dividir algo en; **to ~ sthg by** dividir algo entre OR por; **~ 3 into 89** divide 89 entre 3. ◆ *vi* 1. (*river, road, wall*) bifurcarse. 2. (*group*) dividirse.

dividend [ˈdɪvɪdend] *n* (FIN) dividendo *m*; (*profit*) beneficio *m*.

divine [dɪˈvaɪn] *adj* divino(na).

diving [ˈdaɪvɪŋ] (U) *n* 1. (*into water*) salto *m*. 2. (*with breathing apparatus*) buceo *m*.

divingboard [ˈdaɪvɪŋbɔːd] *n* trampolín *m*.

divinity [dɪˈvɪnətɪ] *n* 1. (*godliness, deity*) divinidad *f*. 2. (*study*) teología *f*.

division [dɪˈvɪʒn] *n* 1. (*gen*) división *f*. 2. (*of labour, responsibility*) repartición *f*.

divorce [dɪˈvɔːs] ◆ *n* divorcio *m*. ◆ *vt* (*husband, wife*) divorciarse de.

divorced [dɪˈvɔːst] *adj* divorciado(da).

divorcee [dɪvɔːˈsiː] *n* divorciado *m*, -da *f*.

divulge [daɪˈvʌldʒ] *vt* divulgar, revelar.

DIY *abbr of* **do-it-yourself**.

dizzy [ˈdɪzɪ] *adj* 1. (*because of illness etc*) mareado(da). 2. (*because of heights*): **to feel ~** sentir vértigo.

DJ *n abbr of* **disc jockey**.

DNA (*abbr of* **deoxyribonucleic acid**) *n* ADN *m*.

do [duː] (*pt* **did**, *pp* **done**, *pl* **dos** OR **do's**) ◆ *aux vb* 1. (*in negatives*): **don't leave it there** no lo dejes ahí. 2. (*in questions*): **what did he want?** ¿qué quería?; **~ you think she'll come?** ¿crees que vendrá? 3. (*referring back to previous verb*): **~ you think so? - yes, I ~** ¿tú crees? - sí; **she reads more than I ~** lee más que yo; **so ~ I/they** yo/ellos también. 4. (*in question tags*): **you know her, don't you?** la conoces ¿no?; **so you think you can dance, ~ you?** así que te crees que sabes bailar ¿no? 5. (*for emphasis*): **I did tell you but you've forgotten** sí que te lo dije, pero te has olvidado; **~ come in** ¡pase, por favor! ◆ *vt* 1. (*gen*) hacer; **to ~ the cooking/cleaning** hacer la comida/limpieza; **to ~ one's hair** peinarse; **to ~ one's teeth** lavarse los dientes; **he did his duty** cumplió con su deber; **what can I ~ for you?** ¿en qué puedo servirle?; **what can we ~?** ¿qué le vamos a hacer? 2. (*referring to job*): **what ~ you ~?** ¿a qué te dedicas? 3. (*study*) hacer; **I did physics at school** hice física en la escuela. 4. (*travel at a particular speed*) ir a; **the car can ~ 110 mph** el coche puede ir a 110 millas por hora. 5. (*be good enough for*): **will that ~ you?** ¿te vale eso? ◆ *vi* 1. (*gen*) hacer; **~ as she says** haz lo que te dice; **they're ~ing really well** les va muy bien; **he could ~ better** lo podría hacer mejor; **how did you ~ in the exam?** ¿qué tal te salió el examen? 2. (*be good enough, sufficient*) servir, valer; **this kind of behaviour won't ~** ese tipo

de comportamiento no es aceptable;
that will ~ (nicely) con eso vale; that will
~! (showing annoyance) ¡basta ya! 3. phr:
how ~ you ~ (greeting) ¿cómo está
usted?; (answer) mucho gusto. ◆ n
(party) fiesta f. ▶ dos npl: ~s and don'ts
normas fpl de conducta. ▶ do away
with vt fus (disease, poverty) acabar con;
(law, reforms) suprimir. ▶ do down vt
sep inf: to ~ sb down menospreciar
a alguien. ▶ do up vt sep 1.
(fasten - shoelaces, tie) atar; (- coat, buttons)
abrochar; ~ your shoes up átate los zapatos. 2. (decorate) renovar, redecorar.
3. (wrap up) envolver. ▶ do with vt fus
1. (need): I could ~ with a drink/new car
no me vendría mal una copa/un coche
nuevo. 2. (have connection with): that has
nothing to ~ with it eso no tiene nada
que ver (con ello). ▶ do without ◆ vt
fus pasar sin; I can ~ without your sarcasm podrías ahorrarte tu sarcasmo.
◆ vi apañárselas.
Doberman ['dəʊbəmən] (pl -s) n: ~
(pinscher) doberman m.
docile [Br 'dəʊsaɪl, Am 'dɒsəl] adj dócil.
dock [dɒk] ◆ n 1. (in harbour) dársena f,
muelle m. 2. (in court) banquillo m (de
los acusados). ◆ vi atracar.
docker ['dɒkər] n estibador m.
docklands ['dɒkləndz] npl Br muelles
mpl.
dockyard ['dɒkjɑːd] n astillero m.
doctor ['dɒktər] ◆ n 1. (of medicine)
médico m, -ca f; to go to the ~'s ir al
médico. 2. (holder of PhD) doctor m, -ra f.
◆ vt 1. (results, text) amañar. 2. (food,
drink) adulterar.
doctorate ['dɒktərət], **doctor's
degree** n doctorado m.
doctrine ['dɒktrɪn] n doctrina f.
document ['dɒkjʊmənt] n documento
m.
documentary [,dɒkjʊ'mentərɪ] ◆ adj
documental. ◆ n documental m.
dodge [dɒdʒ] ◆ n inf (fraud) artimaña f.
◆ vt esquivar. ◆ vi echarse a un lado.
dodgy ['dɒdʒɪ] adj Br inf (business, plan)
arriesgado(da), comprometido(da);
(chair, brakes) poco fiable.
doe [dəʊ] n 1. (female deer) gama f.
2. (female rabbit) coneja f.
does [weak form dəz, strong form dʌz] →
do.
doesn't ['dʌznt] = does not.
dog [dɒg] ◆ n 1. (animal) perro m. 2.
Am (hot dog) perrito m caliente. ◆ vt
1. (subj: person) seguir. 2. (subj: problems,

bad luck) perseguir.
dog collar n 1. (of dog) collar m de
perro. 2. (of priest) alzacuello m.
dog-eared [-ɪəd] adj manoseado(da).
dogged ['dɒgɪd] adj tenaz.
dogsbody ['dɒgz,bɒdɪ] n Br inf último
mono m, burro m de carga.
doing ['duːɪŋ] n: this is all your ~ tú
eres responsable por esto. ▶ doings
npl actividades fpl.
do-it-yourself n bricolaje m.
doldrums ['dɒldrəmz] npl fig: to be in
the ~ (trade) estar estancado(da); (person) estar abatido(da).
dole [dəʊl] n (subsidio m de) paro m;
to be on the ~ estar parado(da). ▶ dole
out vt sep distribuir, repartir.
doleful ['dəʊlfʊl] adj lastimero(ra).
doll [dɒl] n (toy) muñeca f.
dollar ['dɒlər] n dólar m.
dolphin ['dɒlfɪn] n delfín m.
domain [də'meɪn] n 1. (sphere of interest)
campo m, ámbito m. 2. (land) dominios
mpl.
dome [dəʊm] n (roof) cúpula f; (ceiling)
bóveda f.
domestic [də'mestɪk] ◆ adj 1. (internal - policy, flight) nacional. 2. (chores,
water supply, animal) doméstico(ca).
3. (home-loving) hogareño(ña), casero
(ra). ◆ n criado m, -da f.
domestic appliance n electrodoméstico m.
dominant ['dɒmɪnənt] adj dominante.
dominate ['dɒmɪneɪt] vt dominar.
domineering [,dɒmɪ'nɪərɪŋ] adj dominante, tiránico(ca).
dominion [də'mɪnjən] n 1. (U) (power)
dominio m. 2. (land) dominios mpl.
domino ['dɒmɪnəʊ] (pl -es) n dominó
m. ▶ dominoes npl dominó m.
don [dɒn] n Br (UNIV) profesor m, -ra f
de universidad.
donate [də'neɪt] vt donar.
done [dʌn] ◆ pp → do. ◆ adj 1. (finished)
listo(ta). 2. (cooked) hecho(cha); well-~
muy hecho. ◆ adv (to conclude deal): ~!
¡(trato) hecho!
donkey ['dɒŋkɪ] (pl donkeys) n burro
m, -rra f.
donor ['dəʊnər] n donante m y f.
donor card n carné m de donante.
don't [dəʊnt] = do not.
doodle ['duːdl] vi garabatear.
doom [duːm] n perdición f, fatalidad f.
doomed [duːmd] adj (plan, mission)
condenado(da) al fracaso; to be ~
to sthg/to do sthg estar condenado a

algo/a hacer algo.
door [dɔːʳ] n 1. (gen) puerta f. 2. (door-way) entrada f.
doorbell ['dɔːbel] n timbre m (de la puerta).
doorknob ['dɔːnɒb] n pomo m.
doorman ['dɔːmən] (pl -men [-mən]) n portero m.
doormat ['dɔːmæt] n (mat) felpudo m.
doorstep ['dɔːstep] n peldaño m de la puerta.
doorway ['dɔːweɪ] n entrada f, portal m.
dope [dəʊp] ◆ n inf 1. drugs sl (cannabis) maría f. 2. (for athlete, horse) estimulante m. 3. (fool) bobo m, -ba f. ◆ vt drogar, dopar.
dopey ['dəʊpɪ] (compar -ier, superl -iest) adj inf 1. (groggy) atontado(da), grogui. 2. (stupid) imbécil.
dormant ['dɔːmənt] adj (volcano) inactivo(va).
dormitory ['dɔːmətrɪ] n dormitorio m.
Dormobile® ['dɔːmə,biːl] n combi m.
DOS [dɒs] (abbr of **disk operating system**) n DOS m.
dose [dəʊs] n lit & fig dosis f inv.
dosser ['dɒsəʳ] n Br inf gandul m, -la f.
dosshouse ['dɒshaʊs, pl -haʊzɪz] n Br inf pensión f de mala muerte.
dot [dɒt] ◆ n punto m; **on the ~** en punto. ◆ vt salpicar.
dote [dəʊt] ▶ **dote (up)on** vt fus adorar.
dot-matrix printer n (COMPUT) impresora f matricial de agujas.
double ['dʌbl] ◆ adj 1. (gen) doble. 2. (repeated) repetido(da); **~ three eight two** treinta y tres, ochenta y dos. ◆ adv 1. (twice) doble; **~ the amount** el doble. 2. (in two-fold) en dos; **to bend ~** doblarse, agacharse. ◆ n 1. (twice as much) el doble. 2. (drink) doble m. 3. (lookalike) doble m y f. ◆ vt doblar. ◆ vi (increase twofold) doblarse. ▶ **doubles** npl (TENNIS) (partido m de) dobles mpl.
double-barrelled Br, **double-barreled** Am [-'bærəld] adj 1. (shotgun) de dos cañones. 2. (name) con dos apellidos unidos con guión.
double bass [-beɪs] n contrabajo m.
double bed n cama f de matrimonio.
double-breasted [-'brestɪd] adj cruzado(da).
double-check vt & vi verificar dos veces.
double chin n papada f.

double cream n nata f enriquecida.
double-cross vt traicionar, timar.
double-decker [-'dekəʳ] n autobús m de dos pisos.
double-dutch n Br hum: **it's ~ to me** me suena a chino.
double-glazing [-'gleɪzɪŋ] n doble acristalamiento m.
double room n habitación f doble.
double vision n vista f doble.
doubly ['dʌblɪ] adv doblemente.
doubt [daʊt] ◆ n duda f; **there is no ~ that** no hay OR cabe duda de que; **without (a) ~** sin duda (alguna); **to be in ~ about sthg** estar dudando acerca de algo; **to cast ~ on** poner en duda; **no ~** sin duda. ◆ vt 1. (not trust) dudar de. 2. (consider unlikely) dudar; **to ~ whether** OR **if** dudar que.
doubtful ['daʊtfʊl] adj 1. (gen) dudoso (sa). 2. (unsure) incierto(ta); **to be ~ about** OR **of** tener dudas acerca de.
doubtless ['daʊtlɪs] adv sin duda.
dough [dəʊ] n (U) 1. (for baking) masa f, pasta f. 2. v inf (money) pasta f.
doughnut ['dəʊnʌt] n (without hole) buñuelo m; (with hole) dónut® m.
douse [daʊs] vt 1. (put out) apagar. 2. (drench) mojar, empapar.
dove¹ [dʌv] n paloma f.
dove² [dəʊv] Am pt → **dive**.
dovetail ['dʌvteɪl] vt & vi encajar.
dowdy ['daʊdɪ] adj poco elegante.
down [daʊn] ◆ adv 1. (downwards) (hacia) abajo; **to fall ~** caer; **to bend ~** agacharse; **~ here/there** aquí/allí abajo. 2. (along): **I'm going ~ the pub** voy a acercarme al pub. 3. (southwards) hacia el sur; **we're going ~ to Brighton** vamos a bajar a Brighton. 4. (lower in amount): **prices are coming ~** van bajando los precios. 5. (including): **~ to the last detail** hasta el último detalle. 6. (as deposit): **to pay £5 ~** pagar 5 libras ahora (y el resto después). ◆ prep 1. (downwards): **they ran ~ the hill** corrieron cuesta abajo; **he walked ~ the stairs** bajó la escalera; **rain poured ~ the window** la lluvia resbalaba por la ventana. 2. (along): **she was walking ~ the street** iba andando por la calle. ◆ adj 1. inf (depressed) deprimido(da). 2. (not in operation): **the computer is ~ again** el ordenador se ha estropeado otra vez. ◆ n (feathers) plumón m; (hair) pelusa f, vello m. ◆ vt 1. (knock over) derribar. 2. (swallow) beberse de un trago. ▶ **downs** npl Br montes del sur de Inglaterra. ▶ **down with** excl: **~ with the**

King! ¡abajo el rey!
down-and-out n vagabundo m, -da f.

down-at-heel adj desastrado(da).

downbeat ['daʊnbiːt] adj inf pesimista.

downcast ['daʊnkɑːst] adj fml (sad) alicaído(da), triste.

downfall ['daʊnfɔːl] n (U) ruina f, caída f.

downhearted [,daʊn'hɑːtɪd] adj desanimado(da).

downhill [,daʊn'hɪl] ◆ adj cuesta abajo. ◆ adv 1. (downwards) cuesta abajo. 2. (worse) en declive. ◆ n (SKIING) descenso m.

Downing Street ['daʊnɪŋ-] n calle londinense donde se encuentran las residencias del Primer Ministro y el ministro de Finanzas; por extensión el gobierno británico.

down payment n entrada f.

downpour ['daʊnpɔːr] n chaparrón m.

downright ['daʊnraɪt] ◆ adj patente, manifiesto(ta). ◆ adv completamente.

downstairs [,daʊn'steəz] ◆ adj de abajo. ◆ adv abajo; **to come/go ~** bajar (la escalera).

downstream [,daʊn'striːm] adv río OR aguas abajo.

down-to-earth adj realista.

downtown [,daʊn'taʊn] ◆ adj céntrico (ca), del centro (de la ciudad). ◆ adv (live) en el centro; (go) al centro.

downturn ['daʊntɜːn] n: ~ (in) descenso m (en).

down under adv en/a Australia o Nueva Zelanda.

downward ['daʊnwəd] ◆ adj 1. (towards ground) hacia abajo. 2. (decreasing) descendente. ◆ adv Am = **downwards**.

downwards ['daʊnwədz] adv (gen) hacia abajo; **face ~** boca abajo.

dowry ['daʊərɪ] n dote f.

doze [dəʊz] ◆ n sueñecito m; **to have a ~** echar una cabezada. ◆ vi dormitar. ▶ **doze off** vi quedarse adormilado (da).

dozen ['dʌzn] ◆ num adj: **a ~ eggs** una docena de huevos. ◆ n docena f; **50p a ~** 50 peniques la docena. ▶ **dozens** npl inf: **~s of** montones mpl OR miles mpl de.

dozy ['dəʊzɪ] adj 1. (sleepy) soñoliento (ta), amodorrado(da). 2. Br inf (stupid) tonto(ta).

Dr. 1. (abbr of **Drive**) c/. 2. (abbr of **Doctor**) Dr.

drab [dræb] adj (colour) apagado(da); (building, clothes) sobrio(bria); (lives) monótono(na).

draft [drɑːft] ◆ n 1. (early version) borrador m. 2. (money order) letra f de cambio, giro m. 3. Am (MIL): **the ~** la llamada a filas. 4. Am = **draught**. ◆ vt 1. (write) redactar, hacer un borrador de. 2. Am (MIL) llamar a filas. 3. (transfer - staff etc) transferir.

draftsman Am = **draughtsman**.

drafty Am = **draughty**.

drag [dræg] ◆ vt 1. (gen) arrastrar. 2. (lake, river) dragar. ◆ vi 1. (dress, coat) arrastrarse. 2. (time, play) ir muy despacio. ◆ n inf 1. (bore - thing) rollo m; (- person) pesado m, -da f. 2. (on cigarette) calada f. 3. (cross-dressing): **in ~** vestido de mujer. ▶ **drag on** vi ser interminable.

dragon ['drægən] n 1. (beast) dragón m. 2. inf (woman) bruja f.

dragonfly ['drægnflaɪ] n libélula f.

drain [dreɪn] ◆ n (for water) desagüe m; (for sewage) alcantarilla f; (grating) sumidero m. ◆ vt 1. (marsh, field) drenar; (vegetables) escurrir. 2. (energy, resources) agotar. 3. (drink, glass) apurar. ◆ vi 1. (dishes) escurrirse. 2. (colour, blood, tension) desaparecer poco a poco.

drainage ['dreɪnɪdʒ] n 1. (pipes, ditches) alcantarillado m. 2. (of land) drenaje m.

draining board Br ['dreɪnɪŋ-], **drainboard** Am ['dreɪnbɔːrd] n escurridero m.

drainpipe ['dreɪnpaɪp] n tubo m de desagüe.

dram [dræm] n trago m.

drama ['drɑːmə] n 1. (gen) drama m. 2. (subject) teatro m.

dramatic [drə'mætɪk] adj 1. (concerned with theatre) dramático(ca). 2. (gesture, escape, improvement) espectacular.

dramatist ['dræmətɪst] n dramaturgo m, -ga f.

dramatize, -ise ['dræmətaɪz] vt 1. (rewrite as play) adaptar, escenificar. 2. pej (make exciting) dramatizar, exagerar.

drank [dræŋk] pt → **drink**.

drape [dreɪp] vt: **to ~ sthg over sthg** cubrir algo con algo; **~d with** OR **in** cubierto con. ▶ **drapes** npl Am cortinas fpl.

draper ['dreɪpər] n pañero m, -ra f.

drastic ['dræstɪk] adj 1. (extreme, urgent) drástico(ca). 2. (noticeable) radical.

draught Br, **draft** Am [drɑːft] n 1. (air current) corriente f de aire. 2. **on ~** (beer) de barril. ▶ **draughts** n Br damas fpl.

draught beer n Br cerveza f de barril.
draughtboard ['drɑːftbɔːd] n Br tablero m de damas.
draughtsman Br (pl -men [-mən]), **draftsman** Am (pl -men [-mən]) ['drɑːftsmən] n delineante m y f.
draughty Br, **drafty** Am ['drɑːftɪ] adj que tiene corrientes de aire.
draw [drɔː] (pt **drew**, pp **drawn**) ◆ vt 1. (sketch) dibujar; (line, circle) trazar. 2. (pull - cart etc) tirar de; **she drew the comb through her hair** se pasó el peine por el cabello. 3. (curtains - open) descorrer; (- close) correr. 4. (gun, sword) sacar. 5. (conclusion) llegar a. 6. (distinction, comparison) señalar. 7. (attract - criticism, praise, person) atraer; **to ~ sb's attention to sthg** llamar la atención de alguien hacia algo. ◆ vi 1. (sketch) dibujar. 2. (move) moverse; **to ~ away** alejarse; **to ~ closer** acercarse. 3. (SPORT): **to ~ (with)** empatar (con). ◆ n 1. (SPORT) empate m. 2. (lottery) sorteo m. ▶ **draw out** vt sep 1. (encourage to talk) hacer hablar. 2. (prolong) prolongar. 3. (money) sacar. ▶ **draw up** ◆ vt sep (draft) preparar, redactar. ◆ vi (stop) pararse.
drawback ['drɔːbæk] n inconveniente m, desventaja f.
drawbridge ['drɔːbrɪdʒ] n puente m levadizo.
drawer [drɔːʳ] n (in desk, chest) cajón m.
drawing ['drɔːɪŋ] n dibujo m.
drawing board n tablero m de delineante.
drawing pin n Br chincheta f.
drawing room n salón m.
drawl [drɔːl] n manera lenta y poco clara de hablar, alargando las vocales.
drawn [drɔːn] pp → draw.
dread [dred] ◆ n pavor m. ◆ vt: **to ~ (doing sthg)** temer (hacer algo).
dreadful ['dredful] adj 1. (very unpleasant - pain, weather) terrible. 2. (poor - play, English) horrible, fatal. 3. (for emphasis - waste, bore) espantoso(sa).
dreadfully ['dredfulɪ] adv terriblemente.
dream [driːm] (pt & pp **-ed** OR **dreamt**) ◆ n lit & fig sueño m; **bad ~** pesadilla f. ◆ adj ideal. ◆ vt: **to ~ (that)** soñar que. ◆ vi lit & fig: **to ~ of doing sthg** soñar con hacer algo; **to ~ (of OR about)** soñar (con); **I wouldn't ~ of it** ¡ni hablar!, ¡de ninguna manera! ▶ **dream up** vt sep inventar, idear.
dreamt [dremt] pp → dream.

dreamy ['driːmɪ] adj 1. (distracted) soñador(ra). 2. (peaceful, dreamlike) de ensueño.
dreary ['drɪərɪ] adj 1. (weather, day) triste. 2. (job, life) monótono(na), aburrido(da); (persona) gris.
dredge [dredʒ] vt dragar. ▶ **dredge up** vt sep 1. (with dredger) extraer (del agua) con draga. 2. fig (from past) sacar a (la) luz.
dregs [dregz] npl 1. (of liquid) sedimento m. 2. fig (of society) hez f.
drench [drentʃ] vt empapar; **~ed to the skin** calado hasta los huesos.
dress [dres] ◆ n 1. (woman's garment) vestido m. 2. (U) (clothing) traje m. ◆ vt 1. (clothe) vestir; **to be ~ed in** ir vestido de; **to be ~ed** estar vestido; **to get ~ed** vestirse. 2. (bandage) vendar. 3. (CULIN) aliñar. ◆ vi 1. (put on clothing) vestirse. 2. (wear clothes) vestir; **to ~ well/badly** vestir bien/mal.
dress circle n piso m principal.
dresser ['dresəʳ] n 1. (for dishes) aparador m. 2. Am (chest of drawers) cómoda f.
dressing ['dresɪŋ] n 1. (bandage) vendaje m. 2. (for salad) aliño m. 3. Am (for turkey etc) relleno m.
dressing gown n bata f.
dressing room n (THEATRE) camerino m; (SPORT) vestuario m.
dressing table n tocador m.
dressmaker ['dres,meɪkəʳ] n costurero m, -ra f, modisto m, -ta f.
dressmaking ['dres,meɪkɪŋ] n costura f.
dress rehearsal n ensayo m general.
dressy ['dresɪ] adj elegante.
drew [druː] pt → draw.
dribble ['drɪbl] ◆ n 1. (saliva) baba f. 2. (trickle) hilo m. ◆ vt (SPORT) (ball) regatear. ◆ vi 1. (drool) babear. 2. (spill) gotear, caer gota a gota.
dried [draɪd] adj (gen) seco(ca); (milk, eggs) en polvo.
dried fruit n (U) fruta f pasa.
drier ['draɪəʳ] = dryer.
drift [drɪft] ◆ n 1. (trend, movement) movimiento m, tendencia f; (of current) flujo m. 2. (meaning) significado m, sentido m. 3. (mass - of snow) ventisquero m; (- of sand, leaves) montículo m. ◆ vi 1. (boat) ir a la deriva. 2. (snow, sand, leaves) amontonarse.
driftwood ['drɪftwud] n madera f de deriva.
drill [drɪl] ◆ n 1. (tool - gen) taladro m;

(- *bit*) broca *f*; (- *dentist's*) fresa *f*; (- *in mine, oilfield*) perforadora *f*. **2.** (*exercise - for fire, battle*) simulacro *m*. ◆ *vt* **1.** (*tooth, wood, oil well*) perforar. **2.** (*instruct - people, pupils*) adiestrar, entrenar; (- *soldiers*) instruir. ◆ *vi*: **to ~ into/for** perforar en/en busca de.

drink [drɪŋk] (*pt* **drank**, *pp* **drunk**) ◆ *n* **1.** (*gen*) bebida *f*; **a ~ of water** un trago de agua. **2.** (*alcoholic beverage*) copa *f*; **would you like a ~?** ¿quieres tomar algo (de beber)?; **to have a ~** tomar algo, tomar una copa. ◆ *vt* beber. ◆ *vi* beber.

drink-driving Br, **drunk-driving** Am *n* conducción *f* en estado de embriaguez.

drinker ['drɪŋkəʳ] *n* **1.** (*of alcohol*) bebedor *m*, -ra *f*. **2.** (*of tea, coffee*): **tea/coffee ~** persona que bebe té/café.

drinking water ['drɪŋkɪŋ-] *n* agua *f* potable.

drip [drɪp] ◆ *n* **1.** (*drop*) gota *f*; (*drops*) goteo *m*. **2.** (MED) gota a gota *m inv*. ◆ *vi* (*liquid, tap, nose*) gotear.

drip-dry *adj* de lava y pon.

drive [draɪv] (*pt* **drove**, *pp* **driven**) ◆ *n* **1.** (*outing*) paseo *m* (en coche); **to go for a ~** ir a dar una vuelta en coche. **2.** (*journey*) viaje *m* (en coche); **it's a two-hour ~ (away)** está a dos horas en coche. **3.** (*urge*) instinto *m*. **4.** (*campaign*) campaña *f*. **5.** (*energy*) vigor *m*, energía *f*. **6.** (*road to house*) camino *m* (de entrada). **7.** (SPORT) drive *m*. **8.** (COMPUT) unidad *f* de disco. ◆ *vt* **1.** (*vehicle*) conducir, manejar Amer. **2.** (*passenger*) llevar (en coche). **3.** (*fuel, power*) impulsar. **4.** (*force to move - gen*) arrastrar; (- *cattle*) arrear. **5.** (*motivate*) motivar. **6.** (*force*): **to ~ sb to do sthg** conducir OR llevar a alguien a hacer algo; **to ~ sb to despair** hacer desesperar a alguien; **to ~ sb mad** OR **crazy** volver loco a alguien. **7.** (*hammer*) clavar. ◆ *vi* (AUT) conducir; **I don't ~** no sé conducir.

drivel ['drɪvl] *n inf* (U) tonterías *fpl*.

driven ['drɪvn] *pp* → **drive**.

driver ['draɪvəʳ] *n* (*gen*) conductor *m*, -ra *f*; (RAIL) maquinista *m y f*; (*of racing car*) piloto *m y f*.

driver's license Am = **driving licence**.

drive shaft *n* (eje *m* de) transmisión *f*.

driveway ['draɪvweɪ] *n* camino *m* de entrada.

driving ['draɪvɪŋ] ◆ *adj* (*rain*) torrencial; (*wind*) huracanado(da). ◆ *n* (U) conducción *f*, el conducir.

driving instructor *n* instructor *m*, -ra *f* de conducción.

driving lesson *n* clase *f* de conducir OR conducción.

driving licence Br, **driver's license** Am *n* carné *m* OR permiso *m* de conducir.

driving mirror *n* retrovisor *m*.

driving school *n* autoescuela *f*.

driving test *n* examen *m* de conducir.

drizzle ['drɪzl] ◆ *n* llovizna *f*. ◆ *v impers* lloviznar.

droll [drəʊl] *adj* gracioso(sa).

drone [drəʊn] *n* **1.** (*hum*) zumbido *m*. **2.** (*bee*) zángano *m*.

drool [druːl] *vi* **1.** (*dribble*) babear. **2.** *fig* (*admire*): **to ~ over** caérsele la baba con.

droop [druːp] *vi* (*shoulders*) encorvarse; (*eyelids*) cerrarse; (*head*) inclinarse; (*flower*) marchitarse.

drop [drɒp] ◆ *n* **1.** (*of liquid, milk, whisky*) gota *f*. **2.** (*sweet*) pastilla *f*. **3.** (*decrease*): **~ (in)** (*price*) caída *f* (de); (*temperature*) descenso *m* (de); (*demand, income*) disminución *f* (en). **4.** (*distance down*) caída *f*. ◆ *vt* **1.** (*let fall - gen*) dejar caer; (- *bomb*) lanzar. **2.** (*decrease*) reducir. **3.** (*voice*) bajar. **4.** (*abandon - subject, course*) dejar; (- *charges*) retirar; (- *person, lover*) abandonar; (- *player*) excluir, no seleccionar. **5.** (*utter - hint, remark*) lanzar, soltar. **6.** (*write - letter, postcard*) poner, escribir. ◆ *vi* **1.** (*fall down*) caer; **to ~ to one's knees** arrodillarse; **we walked until we dropped** estuvimos andando hasta no poder más. **2.** (*fall away - ground*) ceder. **3.** (*decrease - temperature, price, voice*) bajar; (- *attendance, demand, unemployment*) disminuir; (- *wind*) amainar. ▶ **drops** *npl* (MED) gotas *fpl*. ▶ **drop in** *vi inf*: **to ~ in on** pasarse por casa de. ▶ **drop off** ◆ *vt sep* (*person, letter*) dejar. ◆ *vi* **1.** (*fall asleep*) quedarse dormido(da). **2.** (*grow less*) bajar. ▶ **drop out** *vi*: **to ~ out (of** **from)** (*school, college*) dejar de asistir (a); (*competition*) retirarse (de).

dropout ['drɒpaʊt] *n* (*from society*) marginado *m*, -da *f*; (*from university*) persona *f* que ha dejado los estudios.

droppings ['drɒpɪŋz] *npl* excremento *m* (de animales).

drought [draʊt] *n* sequía *f*.

drove [drəʊv] *pt* → **drive**.

drown [draʊn] ◆ *vt* (*kill*) ahogar. ◆ *vi* ahogarse.

drowsy ['draʊzɪ] *adj* (*person*) somnoliento(ta).

drudgery ['drʌdʒərɪ] n trabajo pesado y monótono.

drug [drʌg] ◆ n 1. (medicine) medicamento m. 2. (narcotic) droga f; **to be on OR take ~s** drogarse. ◆ vt 1. (person) drogar. 2. (food, drink) echar droga a.

drug abuse n consumo m de drogas.

drug addict n drogadicto m, -ta f.

druggist ['drʌgɪst] n Am farmacéutico m, -ca f.

drugstore ['drʌgstɔːr] n Am farmacia f (que también vende productos de perfumería etc).

drum [drʌm] ◆ n 1. (instrument) tambor m; ~s batería f. 2. (container, cylinder) bidón m. ◆ vt (fingers) tamborilear con. ◆ vi (rain, hoofs) golpetear. ▶ **drum up** vt sep intentar conseguir.

drummer ['drʌmər] n (in orchestra) tambor m y f; (in pop group) batería m y f.

drumstick ['drʌmstɪk] n 1. (for drum) palillo m. 2. (food) muslo m.

drunk [drʌŋk] ◆ pp → **drink**. ◆ adj (on alcohol) borracho(cha); **to get ~** emborracharse; **to be ~** estar borracho. ◆ n borracho m, -cha f.

drunkard ['drʌŋkəd] n borracho m, -cha f.

drunk-driving Am = **drink-driving**.

drunken ['drʌŋkn] adj 1. (person) borracho(cha). 2. (talk, steps, stupor) borracho(cha).

drunken driving = **drink-driving**.

dry [draɪ] ◆ adj 1. (gen) seco(ca). 2. (day) sin lluvia. 3. (earth, soil) árido (da). ◆ vt (gen) secar; (hands, hair) secarse; **to ~ o.s** secarse; **to ~ one's eyes** secarse las lágrimas. ◆ vi secarse. ▶ **dry up** ◆ vt sep secar. ◆ vi 1. (river, well) secarse. 2. (stop - supply) agotarse. 3. (stop speaking) cortarse. 4. (dry dishes) secar.

dry cleaner n: **~'s (shop)** tintorería f.

dryer ['draɪər] n (for clothes) secadora f.

dry land n tierra f firme.

dry rot n putrefacción f de la madera.

dry ski slope n pista f de esquí artificial.

DSS (abbr of Department of Social Security) n ministerio británico de la seguridad social.

DTI (abbr of Department of Trade and Industry) n ministerio británico de comercio e industria.

DTP (abbr of desktop publishing) n autoed. f.

dual ['djuːəl] adj doble.

dual carriageway n Br carretera de

dos sentidos y doble vía separados, ≃ autovía f.

dubbed [dʌbd] adj 1. (CINEMA) doblado(da). 2. (nicknamed) apodado(da).

dubious ['djuːbjəs] adj 1. (question-able - person, deal, reasons) sospechoso (sa); (- honour, distinction) paradójico(ca). 2. (uncertain, undecided) dudoso(sa); **to feel OR be ~ (about)** tener dudas (sobre).

Dublin ['dʌblɪn] n Dublín.

duchess ['dʌtʃɪs] n duquesa f.

duck [dʌk] ◆ n 1. (bird) pato m, -ta f. 2. (food) pato m. ◆ vt 1. (lower) agachar, bajar. 2. (try to avoid - duty) esquivar. ◆ vi (lower head) agacharse.

duckling ['dʌklɪŋ] n patito m.

duct [dʌkt] n conducto m.

dud [dʌd] ◆ adj (gen) falso(sa); (mine) que no estalla; (cheque) sin fondos. ◆ n persona o cosa inútil.

dude [djuːd] n Am inf (man) tío m.

due [djuː] ◆ adj 1. (expected) esperado (da); **it's ~ out in May** saldrá en mayo; **she's ~ back soon** tendría que volver dentro de poco; **the train's ~ in half an hour** el tren debe llegar dentro de media hora. 2. (appropriate) oportuno (na), debido(da); **with all ~ respect** sin ganas de ofender; **in ~ course** (at appro-priate time) a su debido tiempo; (eventu-ally) al final. 3. (owed, owing) pagadero (ra); **I'm ~ a bit of luck** ya sería hora que tuviera un poco de suerte; **to be ~ to** deberse a. ◆ n (deserts): **to give sb their ~** hacer justicia a alguien. ◆ adv: **~ north/south** derecho hacia el norte/sur. ▶ **dues** npl cuota f. ▶ **due to** prep debido a.

duel ['djuːəl] n duelo m.

duet [djuːˈet] n dúo m.

duffel bag ['dʌfl-] n morral m.

duffel coat ['dʌfl-] n trenca f.

duffle bag ['dʌfl-] = **duffel bag**.

duffle coat ['dʌfl-] = **duffel coat**.

dug [dʌg] pt & pp → **dig**.

duke [djuːk] n duque m.

dull [dʌl] ◆ adj 1. (boring) aburrido(da). 2. (listless) torpe. 3. (dim) apagado(da). 4. (cloudy) gris, triste. 5. (thud, boom, pain) sordo(da). ◆ vt (senses) embotar, entorpecer; (pain) aliviar; (pleasure, memory) enturbiar.

duly ['djuːlɪ] adv 1. (properly) debida-mente. 2. (as expected) como era de esperar.

dumb [dʌm] adj 1. (unable to speak) mudo(da); **to be struck ~** quedarse de una pieza. 2. inf (stupid) estúpido(da).

dumbfound [dʌm'faʊnd] *vt* dejar mudo(da) de asombro; **to be ~ed** quedar mudo de asombro.

dummy ['dʌmɪ] ◆ *adj* falso(sa). ◆ *n* **1.** (*of ventriloquist*) muñeco *m*; (*in shop window*) maniquí *m*. **2.** (*copy*) imitación *f*. **3.** Br (*for baby*) chupete *m*. **4.** (SPORT) amago *m*.

dump [dʌmp] ◆ *n* **1.** (*for rubbish*) basurero *m*, vertedero *m*. **2.** (*for ammunition*) depósito *m*. **3.** *inf* (*ugly place - house*) casucha *f*. ◆ *vt* **1.** (*put down - sand, load*) descargar; (- *bags, washing*) dejar. **2.** (*dispose of*) deshacerse de.

dumper (truck) Br ['dʌmpə-], **dump truck** Am *n* volquete *m*.

dumping ['dʌmpɪŋ] *n* vertido *m*; **'no ~'** 'prohibido verter basura'.

dumpling ['dʌmplɪŋ] *n* bola de masa que se guisa al vapor con carne y verduras.

dump truck Am = **dumper (truck)**.

dumpy ['dʌmpɪ] *adj inf* bajito y regordete (bajita y regordeta).

dunce [dʌns] *n* zoquete *m* y *f*.

dune [dju:n] *n* duna *f*.

dung [dʌŋ] *n* (*of animal*) excremento *m*; (*used as manure*) estiércol *m*.

dungarees [ˌdʌŋgə'ri:z] *npl* Br (*for work*) mono *m*; (*fashion garment*) pantalones *mpl* de peto.

dungeon ['dʌndʒən] *n* calabozo *m*.

duo ['dju:əʊ] *n* dúo *m*.

dupe [dju:p] ◆ *n* primo *m*, -ma *f*, inocente *m* y *f*. ◆ *vt*: **to ~ sb (into doing sthg)** embaucar a uno (a que haga algo).

duplex ['dju:pleks] *n* Am **1.** (*apartment*) dúplex *m*, piso *m* en que las habitaciones están distribuidas entre dos plantas. **2.** (*house*) casa *f* adosada.

duplicate [*adj* & *n* 'dju:plɪkət, *vb* 'dju:plɪkeɪt] ◆ *adj* duplicado(da). ◆ *n* copia *f*, duplicado *m*; **in ~** por duplicado. ◆ *vt* (*copy*) duplicar.

durable ['djʊərəbl] *adj* duradero(ra).

duration [dju'reɪʃn] *n* duración *f*; **for the ~ of** durante.

duress [dju'res] *n*: **under ~** por coacción *f*.

Durex® ['djʊəreks] *n* (*condom*) preservativo *m*, condón *m*.

during ['djʊərɪŋ] *prep* durante.

dusk [dʌsk] *n* crepúsculo *m*, anochecer *m*.

dust [dʌst] ◆ *n* polvo *m*. ◆ *vt* **1.** (*clean*) quitar el polvo a, limpiar. **2.** (*cover with powder*): **to ~ sthg (with)** espolvorear algo (con).

dustbin ['dʌstbɪn] *n* Br cubo *m* de la basura.

dustcart ['dʌstkɑːt] *n* Br camión *m* de la basura.

duster ['dʌstər] *n* (*cloth*) bayeta *f*, trapo *m* (de quitar el polvo).

dust jacket *n* sobrecubierta *f*.

dustman ['dʌstmən] (*pl* -**men** [-mən]) *n* Br basurero *m*.

dustpan ['dʌstpæn] *n* recogedor *m*.

dusty ['dʌstɪ] *adj* (*covered in dust*) polvoriento(ta).

Dutch [dʌtʃ] ◆ *adj* holandés(esa). ◆ *n* (*language*) holandés *m*. ◆ *npl*: **the ~** los holandeses.

Dutch elm disease *n* hongo que ataca a los olmos.

dutiful ['dju:tɪfʊl] *adj* obediente, sumiso(sa).

duty ['dju:tɪ] *n* **1.** (U) (*moral, legal responsibility*) deber *m*; **to do one's ~** cumplir uno con su deber. **2.** (*work*) servicio *m*; **to be on/off ~** estar/no estar de servicio. **3.** (*tax*) impuesto *m*. ▶ **duties** *npl* tareas *fpl*.

duty-free *adj* libre de impuestos.

duvet ['du:veɪ] *n* Br edredón *m*.

duvet cover *n* Br funda *f* del edredón.

dwarf [dwɔ:f] (*pl* -**s** OR **dwarves** [dwɔ:vz]) ◆ *n* enano *m*, -na *f*. ◆ *vt* achicar, empequeñecer.

dwell [dwel] (*pt* & *pp* -**ed** OR **dwelt**) *vi* literary morar, habitar. ▶ **dwell on** *vt fus* darle vueltas a.

dwelling ['dwelɪŋ] *n* literary morada *f*.

dwelt [dwelt] *pt* & *pp* → **dwell**.

dwindle ['dwɪndl] *vi* ir disminuyendo.

dye [daɪ] ◆ *n* tinte *m*. ◆ *vt* teñir.

dying ['daɪɪŋ] ◆ *cont* → **die**. ◆ *adj* **1.** (*person, animal*) moribundo(da). **2.** (*activity, practice*) en vías de desaparición.

dyke [daɪk] = **dike**.

dynamic [daɪ'næmɪk] *adj* dinámico (ca).

dynamite ['daɪnəmaɪt] *n lit* & *fig* dinamita *f*.

dynamo ['daɪnəməʊ] (*pl* -**s**) *n* dinamo *f*.

dynasty [Br 'dɪnəstɪ, Am 'daɪnəstɪ] *n* dinastía *f*.

dyslexia [dɪs'leksɪə] *n* dislexia *f*.

dyslexic [dɪs'leksɪk] *adj* disléxico(ca).

E

e (pl **e's** OR **es**), **E** (pl **E's** OR **Es**) [i:] n (letter) e f, E f. ▶ **E** n 1. (MUS) mi m. 2. (abbr of **east**) E m.

each [i:tʃ] ◆ adj cada. ◆ pron cada uno m, una f; **one** ~ uno cada uno; ~ **of us/ the boys** cada uno de nosotros/los niños; **two of** ~ dos de cada (uno); ~ **other** el uno al otro; **they kissed** ~ **other** se besaron; **we know** ~ **other** nos conocemos.

eager ['i:gər] adj (pupil) entusiasta; (smile, expression) de entusiasmo; **to be** ~ **for sthg/to do sthg** ansiar algo/hacer algo, desear vivamente algo/hacer algo.

eagle ['i:gl] n águila f.

ear [ɪər] n 1. (of person, animal) oreja f. 2. (of corn) espiga f.

earache ['ɪəreɪk] n dolor m de oídos.

eardrum ['ɪədrʌm] n tímpano m.

earl [ɜ:l] n conde m.

earlier ['ɜ:lɪər] ◆ adj anterior. ◆ adv antes; ~ **on** antes.

earliest ['ɜ:lɪəst] ◆ adj primero(ra). ◆ n: **at the** ~ como muy pronto.

earlobe ['ɪələub] n lóbulo m (de la oreja).

early ['ɜ:lɪ] ◆ adj 1. (before expected time, in day) temprano(na); **she was** ~ llegó temprano OR con adelanto; **I'll take an** ~ **lunch** almorzaré pronto OR temprano; **to get up** ~ madrugar. 2. (at beginning): ~ **morning** la madrugada; **in the** ~ **1950s** a principios de los años 50. ◆ adv 1. (before expected time) temprano, pronto; **we got up** ~ nos levantamos temprano; **it arrived ten minutes** ~ llegó con diez minutos de adelanto. 2. (at beginning): **as** ~ **as 1920** ya en 1920; ~ **this morning** esta mañana temprano; ~ **in the year** a principios de año; ~ **on** temprano.

early retirement n jubilación f anticipada.

earmark ['ɪəmɑ:k] vt: **to be** ~**ed for** estar destinado(da) a.

earn [ɜ:n] vt 1. (be paid) ganar. 2. (generate - subj: business, product) generar. 3. fig (gain - respect, praise) ganarse.

earnest ['ɜ:nɪst] adj (gen) serio(ria); (wish) sincero(ra). ▶ **in earnest** adv (seriously) en serio.

earnings ['ɜ:nɪŋz] npl ingresos mpl.

earphones ['ɪəfəunz] npl auriculares mpl.

earplugs ['ɪəplʌgz] npl tapones mpl para los oídos.

earring ['ɪərɪŋ] n pendiente m.

earshot ['ɪəʃɒt] n: **within/out of** ~ al alcance/fuera del alcance del oído.

earth [ɜ:θ] ◆ n 1. (gen) tierra f; **how/ what/where/why on** ~ **...?** ¿cómo/qué/ dónde/por qué demonios ...? 2. (in electric plug, appliance) toma f de tierra. ◆ vt Br: **to be** ~**ed** estar conectado(da) a tierra.

earthenware ['ɜ:θnweər] n loza f.

earthquake ['ɜ:θkweɪk] n terremoto m.

earthworm ['ɜ:θwɜ:m] n lombriz f (de tierra).

earthy ['ɜ:θɪ] adj 1. (rather crude) natural, desinhibido(da). 2. (of, like earth) terroso(sa).

earwig ['ɪəwɪg] n tijereta f.

ease [i:z] ◆ n (U) 1. (lack of difficulty) facilidad f; **with** ~ con facilidad. 2. (comfort) comodidad f; **at** ~ cómodo(da); **ill at** ~ incómodo(da). ◆ vt 1. (pain, grief) calmar, aliviar; (problems, tension) atenuar. 2. (move carefully): **to** ~ **sthg open** abrir algo con cuidado; **to** ~ **o.s. out of sthg** levantarse despacio de algo. ◆ vi (problem) atenuarse; (pain) calmarse; (rain) amainar; (grip) relajarse. ▶ **ease off** vi (problem) atenuarse; (pain) calmarse; (rain) amainar. ▶ **ease up** vi 1. inf (treat less severely): **to** ~ **up on sb** no ser muy duro(ra) con alguien. 2. (rain) amainar. 3. (relax - person) tomarse las cosas con más calma.

easel ['i:zl] n caballete m.

easily ['i:zɪlɪ] adv 1. (without difficulty) fácilmente. 2. (without doubt) sin lugar a dudas. 3. (in a relaxed manner) tranquilamente, relajadamente.

east [i:st] ◆ n 1. (direction) este m. 2. (region): **the** ~ el este. ◆ adj oriental; (wind) del este. ◆ adv: ~ **(of)** al este (de). ▶ **East** n: **the East** (POL) el Este; (Asia) el Oriente.

East End n: **the** ~ el este de Londres.

Easter ['i:stər] n Semana f Santa.

Easter egg n huevo m de Pascua.

easterly ['i:stəlɪ] adj del este.

eastern ['i:stən] adj del este, oriental. ▶ **Eastern** adj (gen & POL) del Este; (from Asia) oriental.

East German ◆ adj de Alemania Oriental. ◆ n (person) alemán m, -ana f oriental.

East Germany n: (the former) ~ (la antigua) Alemania Oriental.

eastward ['i:stwəd] ◆ adj hacia el este. ◆ adv = **eastwards**.

eastwards ['i:stwədz] adv hacia el este.

easy ['i:zɪ] adj 1. (not difficult) fácil. 2. (life, time) cómodo(da). 3. (manner) relajado(da).

easy chair n (armchair) sillón m.

easygoing [,i:zɪ'gəʊɪŋ] adj (person) tolerante; (manner) relajado(da).

eat [i:t] (pt ate, pp eaten) vt & vi comer. ▶ eat away, eat into vt sep 1. (corrode) corroer. 2. (deplete) mermar.

eaten ['i:tn] pp → eat.

eau de cologne [,əʊdəkə'ləʊn] n (agua f de) colonia f.

eaves ['i:vz] npl alero m.

eavesdrop ['i:vzdrɒp] vi: to ~ (on) escuchar secretamente (a).

ebb [eb] ◆ n reflujo m. ◆ vi (tide, sea) bajar.

ebony ['ebənɪ] n ébano m.

EC (abbr of European Community) n CE f.

eccentric [ɪk'sentrɪk] ◆ adj excéntrico (ca). ◆ n excéntrico m, -ca f.

echo ['ekəʊ] (pl -es) ◆ n lit & fig eco m. ◆ vt (words) repetir; (opinion) hacerse eco de. ◆ vi resonar.

eclipse [ɪ'klɪps] ◆ n lit & fig eclipse m. ◆ vt fig eclipsar.

ecological [,i:kə'lɒdʒɪkl] adj 1. (pattern, balance, impact) ecológico(ca). 2. (group, movement, person) ecologista.

ecology [ɪ'kɒlədʒɪ] n ecología f.

economic [,i:kə'nɒmɪk] adj 1. (of money, industry) económico(ca). 2. (profitable) rentable.

economical [,i:kə'nɒmɪkl] adj económico(ca).

economics [,i:kə'nɒmɪks] ◆ n (U) economía f. ◆ npl (of plan, business) aspecto m económico.

economize, -ise ['ɪkɒnəmaɪz] vi: to ~ (on) economizar (en).

economy [ɪ'kɒnəmɪ] n economía f.

economy class n clase f económica OR turista.

ecotourism [,i:kəʊ'tʊərɪzm] n ecoturismo m, turismo m verde.

ecstasy ['ekstəsɪ] n éxtasis m inv.

ecstatic [ek'stætɪk] adj extático(ca).

ECU, Ecu ['ekju:] (abbr of European

Currency Unit) n ECU m, ecu m.

Ecuador ['ekwədɔ:r] n (el) Ecuador.

Ecuadoran [,ekwə'dɔ:rən], **Ecuadorian** [,ekwə'dɔ:rɪən] ◆ adj ecuatoriano (na). ◆ n ecuatoriano m, -na f.

eczema ['eksɪmə] n eczema m.

Eden ['i:dn] n: (the Garden of) ~ (el jardín del) Edén m.

edge [edʒ] ◆ n 1. (of cliff, table, garden) borde m; to be on the ~ of estar al borde de. 2. (of coin) canto m; (of knife) filo m. 3. (advantage): to have an ~ over OR the ~ on llevar ventaja a. ◆ vi: to ~ away/closer ir alejándose/acercándose poco a poco. ▶ on edge adj con los nervios de punta.

edgeways ['edʒweɪz], **edgewise** ['edʒwaɪz] adv de lado.

edgy ['edʒɪ] adj nervioso(sa).

edible ['edɪbl] adj comestible.

edict ['i:dɪkt] n edicto m.

Edinburgh ['edɪnbrə] n Edimburgo.

edit ['edɪt] vt 1. (correct - text) corregir, revisar. 2. (select material for - book) recopilar. 3. (CINEMA, RADIO & TV) montar. 4. (run - newspaper, magazine) dirigir.

edition [ɪ'dɪʃn] n edición f.

editor ['edɪtər] n 1. (of newspaper, magazine) director m, -ra f. 2. (of section of newspaper, programme, text) redactor m, -ra f. 3. (compiler - of book) autor m, -ra f de la edición. 4. (CINEMA, RADIO & TV) montador m, -ra f.

editorial [,edɪ'tɔ:rɪəl] ◆ adj editorial; ~ staff redacción f. ◆ n editorial m.

educate ['edʒukeɪt] vt 1. (at school, college) educar. 2. (inform) informar.

education [,edʒu'keɪʃn] n (U) 1. (activity, sector) enseñanza f. 2. (process or result of teaching) educación f.

educational [,edʒu'keɪʃənl] adj educativo(va); (establishment) docente.

EEC (abbr of European Economic Community) n CEE f.

eel [i:l] n anguila f.

eerie ['ɪərɪ] adj espeluznante.

efface [ɪ'feɪs] vt borrar.

effect [ɪ'fekt] ◆ n efecto m; to have an ~ on tener OR surtir efecto en; to take ~ (law, rule) entrar en vigor; (drug) hacer efecto; to put sthg into ~ hacer entrar algo en vigor; words to that ~ palabras por el estilo. ◆ vt efectuar, llevar a cabo. ▶ effects npl: (special) ~s efectos mpl especiales.

effective [ɪ'fektɪv] adj 1. (successful) eficaz. 2. (actual, real) efectivo(va). 3. (law, *ceasefire*) operativo(va).

effectively [ɪ'fektɪvlɪ] *adv* 1. (*well, successfully*) eficazmente. 2. (*in fact*) de hecho.

effectiveness [ɪ'fektɪvnɪs] *n* eficacia *f*.

effeminate [ɪ'femɪnət] *adj pej* afeminado(da).

effervescent [,efə'vesənt] *adj* efervescente.

efficiency [ɪ'fɪʃənsɪ] *n* (*gen*) eficiencia *f*; (*of machine*) rendimiento *m*.

efficient [ɪ'fɪʃənt] *adj* (*gen*) eficiente; (*machine*) de buen rendimiento.

effluent ['efluənt] *n* aguas *fpl* residuales.

effort ['efət] *n* 1. (*gen*) esfuerzo *m*; **to be worth the ~** merecer la pena; **to make the ~ to do sthg** hacer el esfuerzo de hacer algo; **to make an/no ~ to do sthg** hacer un esfuerzo/no hacer ningún esfuerzo por hacer algo. 2. *inf* (*result of trying*) tentativa *f*.

effortless ['efətlɪs] *adj* sin gran esfuerzo.

effusive [ɪ'fjuːsɪv] *adj* efusivo(va).

e.g. (*abbr of exempli gratia*) *adv* p. ej.

egg [eg] *n* (*gen*) huevo *m*. ► **egg on** *vt sep* incitar.

eggcup ['egkʌp] *n* huevera *f*.

eggplant ['egplɑːnt] *n Am* berenjena *f*.

eggshell ['egʃel] *n* cáscara *f* de huevo.

egg white *n* clara *f* (de huevo).

egg yolk [-jəʊk] *n* yema *f* (de huevo).

ego ['iːgəʊ] (*pl* -s) *n* (*opinion of self*) amor *m* propio, ego *m*.

egoism ['iːgəʊɪzm] *n* egoísmo *m*.

egoistic [,iːgəʊ'ɪstɪk] *adj* egoísta.

egotistic(al) [,iːgə'tɪstɪk(l)] *adj* egotista.

Egypt ['iːdʒɪpt] *n* Egipto.

Egyptian [ɪ'dʒɪpʃn] ◆ *adj* egipcio(cia). ◆ *n* (*person*) egipcio *m*, -cia *f*.

eiderdown ['aɪdədaʊn] *n* edredón *m*.

eight [eɪt] *num* ocho; *see also* **six**.

eighteen [,eɪ'tiːn] *num* dieciocho; *see also* **six**.

eighth [eɪtθ] *num* octavo(va); *see also* **sixth**.

eighty ['eɪtɪ] *num* ochenta; *see also* **sixty**.

Eire ['eərə] *n* Eire.

either ['aɪðəʳ, 'iːðəʳ] ◆ *adj* 1. (*one or the other*) cualquiera de los dos; **she couldn't find ~ jumper** no podía encontrar ninguno de los dos jerseys; **~ way** de cualquiera de las formas. 2. (*each*) cada; **on ~ side** a ambos lados. ◆ *pron*: **~ (of them)** cualquiera (de ellos (ellas));

I don't like ~ (of them) no me gusta ninguno de ellos (ninguna de ellas). ◆ *adv* (*in negatives*) tampoco; **she can't and I can't ~** ella no puede y yo tampoco. ◆ *conj*: **~ ... or** o ... o; **~ you or me** o tú o yo; **I don't like ~ him or his wife** no me gusta ni él ni su mujer (tampoco).

eject [ɪ'dʒekt] *vt* 1. (*object*) expulsar, despedir. 2. (*person*): **to ~ sb (from)** expulsar a alguien (de).

eke [iːk] ► **eke out** *vt sep* alargar *fig*, estirar *fig*.

elaborate [*adj* ɪ'læbrət, *vb* ɪ'læbəreɪt] ◆ *adj* (*ceremony*) complicado(da); (*carving*) trabajado(da); (*explanation, plan*) detallado(da). ◆ *vi*: **to ~ on sthg** ampliar algo, explicar algo con más detalle.

elapse [ɪ'læps] *vi* transcurrir.

elastic [ɪ'læstɪk] ◆ *adj* 1. (*gen*) elástico (ca). 2. *fig* (*flexible*) flexible. ◆ *n* elástico *m*.

elasticated [ɪ'læstɪkeɪtɪd] *adj* elástico (ca).

elastic band *n Br* gomita *f*.

elated [ɪ'leɪtɪd] *adj* eufórico(ca).

elbow ['elbəʊ] *n* codo *m*.

elder ['eldəʳ] ◆ *adj* mayor. ◆ *n* 1. (*older person*) mayor *m* y *f*. 2. (*of tribe, church*) anciano *m*. 3. **~** (*tree*) saúco *m*.

elderly ['eldəlɪ] ◆ *adj* mayor, anciano (na). ◆ *npl*: **the ~** los ancianos.

eldest ['eldɪst] *adj* mayor.

elect [ɪ'lekt] ◆ *adj* electo(ta); **the president ~** el presidente electo. ◆ *vt* 1. (*by voting*) elegir; **to ~ sb (as) sthg** elegir a alguien (como) algo. 2. *fml* (*choose*): **to ~ to do sthg** optar por OR decidir hacer algo.

election [ɪ'lekʃn] *n* elección *f*; **to have** OR **hold an ~** celebrar (unas) elecciones.

electioneering [ɪ,lekʃə'nɪərɪŋ] *n usu pej* electoralismo *m*.

elector [ɪ'lektəʳ] *n* elector *m*, -ra *f*.

electorate [ɪ'lektərət] *n*: **the ~** el electorado.

electric [ɪ'lektrɪk] *adj* (*gen*) eléctrico (ca). ► **electrics** *npl Br inf* sistema *m* eléctrico.

electrical [ɪ'lektrɪkl] *adj* eléctrico(ca).

electrical shock *Am* = **electric shock**.

electric blanket *n* manta *f* eléctrica.

electric cooker *n* cocina *f* eléctrica.

electric fire *n* estufa *f* eléctrica.

electrician [,ɪlek'trɪʃn] *n* electricista *m* y *f*.

electricity [,ɪlek'trɪsətɪ] *n* electricidad *f*.

electric shock Br, **electrical shock** Am *n* descarga *f* eléctrica.

electrify [ɪ'lektrɪfaɪ] *vt* 1. (*rail line*) electrificar. 2. *fig* (*excite*) electrizar.

electrocute [ɪ'lektrəkjuːt] *vt*: **to ~ o.s., to be ~d** electrocutarse.

electrolysis [ˌɪlek'trɒləsɪs] *n* electrólisis *f inv*.

electron [ɪ'lektrɒn] *n* electrón *m*.

electronic [ˌɪlek'trɒnɪk] *adj* electrónico (ca). ▶ **electronics** ♦ *n* (U) (*technology*) electrónica *f*. ♦ *npl* (*equipment*) sistema *m* electrónico.

electronic data processing *n* proceso *m* electrónico de datos.

electronic mail *n* (COMPUT) correo *m* electrónico.

elegant ['elɪgənt] *adj* elegante.

element ['elɪmənt] *n* 1. (*gen*) elemento *m*. 2. (*amount, proportion*) toque *m*. 3. (*in heater, kettle*) resistencia *f*. ▶ **elements** *npl* 1. (*basics*) elementos *mpl*. 2. (*weather*): **the ~s** los elementos.

elementary [ˌelɪ'mentərɪ] *adj* elemental; **~ education** enseñanza *f* primaria.

elementary school *n* Am escuela *f* primaria.

elephant ['elɪfənt] (*pl inv* OR **-s**) *n* elefante *m*.

elevate ['elɪveɪt] *vt*: **to ~ sthg/sb (to** OR **into)** elevar algo/a alguien (a la categoría de).

elevator ['elɪveɪtər] *n* Am ascensor *m*, elevador *m* Amer.

eleven [ɪ'levn] *num* once *m*; *see also* **six**.

elevenses [ɪ'levnzɪz] *n* (U) Br tentempié *m* que se toma sobre las once.

eleventh [ɪ'levnθ] *num* undécimo(ma); *see also* **sixth**.

elicit [ɪ'lɪsɪt] *vt fml* 1. (*response, reaction*): **to ~ sthg (from sb)** provocar algo (en alguien). 2. (*information*): **to ~ sthg (from sb)** sacar algo (a alguien).

eligible ['elɪdʒəbl] *adj* (*suitable, qualified*) elegible; **to be ~ for sthg/to do sthg** reunir los requisitos para algo/para hacer algo.

eliminate [ɪ'lɪmɪneɪt] *vt* eliminar; **to be ~d from sthg** ser eliminado(da) de algo.

elite [ɪ'liːt] ♦ *adj* selecto(ta). ♦ *n* élite *f*.

elitist [ɪ'liːtɪst] *adj pej* elitista.

elk [elk] (*pl inv* OR **-s**) *n* alce *m*.

elm [elm] *n*: **~ (tree)** olmo *m*.

elocution [ˌelə'kjuːʃn] *n* dicción *f*.

elongated ['iːlɒŋgeɪtɪd] *adj* alargado (da).

elope [ɪ'ləup] *vi*: **to ~ (with)** fugarse (con).

eloquent ['eləkwənt] *adj* elocuente.

El Salvador [ˌel'sælvədɔːr] *n* El Salvador.

else [els] *adv*: **anything ~?** ¿algo más?; **I don't need anything ~** no necesito nada más; **everyone ~** todos los demás (todas las demás); **everywhere ~** en/a todas las otras partes; **little ~** poco más; **nothing/nobody ~** nada/nadie más; **someone/something ~** otra persona/cosa; **somewhere ~** en/a otra parte; **who ~?** ¿quién si no?; **what ~?** ¿qué más?; **where ~?** ¿en/a qué otro sitio? ▶ **or else** *conj* (*or if not*) si no, de lo contrario.

elsewhere [els'weər] *adv* a/en otra parte.

elude [ɪ'luːd] *vt* (*gen*) escaparse de, eludir a; (*blow*) esquivar.

elusive [ɪ'luːsɪv] *adj* (*person, success*) esquivo(va); (*quality*) difícil de encontrar.

emaciated [ɪ'meɪʃɪeɪtɪd] *adj* demacrado(da).

E-mail (*abbr of* **electronic mail**) *n* (COMPUT) correo *m* electrónico.

emanate ['eməneɪt] *fml vi*: **to ~ from** emanar de.

emancipate [ɪ'mænsɪpeɪt] *vt*: **to ~ sb (from)** emancipar a alguien (de).

embankment [ɪm'bæŋkmənt] *n* 1. (RAIL) terraplén *m*. 2. (*of river*) dique *m*.

embark [ɪm'baːk] *vi*: **to ~ on** *lit & fig* embarcarse en.

embarkation [ˌembaː'keɪʃn] *n* (*gen*) embarque *m*; (*of troops*) embarco *m*.

embarrass [ɪm'bærəs] *vt* 1. (*gen*) avergonzar; **it ~es me** me da vergüenza. 2. (*financially*) poner en un aprieto.

embarrassed [ɪm'bærəst] *adj* avergonzado(da), violento(ta).

embarrassing [ɪm'bærəsɪŋ] *adj* embarazoso(sa), violento(ta); **how ~!** ¡qué vergüenza!

embarrassment [ɪm'bærəsmənt] *n* (*feeling*) vergüenza *f*, pena *f* Amer.

embassy ['embəsɪ] *n* embajada *f*.

embedded [ɪm'bedɪd] *adj* (*buried*): **~ (in)** incrustado(da) (en).

embellish [ɪm'belɪʃ] *vt*: **to ~ sthg (with)** adornar OR embellecer algo (con).

embers ['embəz] *npl* rescoldos *mpl*.

embezzle [ɪm'bezl] *vt* malversar.

embittered [ɪm'bɪtəd] *adj* amargado (da), resentido(da).

emblem ['embləm] *n* emblema *m*.

embody [ɪm'bɒdɪ] *vt* personificar, encarnar; **to be embodied in sthg** estar plasmado en algo.

embossed [ɪm'bɒst] *adj* 1. (*heading, design*): ~ (**on**) (*paper*) estampado(da) (en); (*leather, metal*) repujado(da) (en). 2. (*paper*): ~ (**with**) estampado(da) (con). 3. (*leather, metal*): ~ (**with**) repujado(da) (con).

embrace [ɪm'breɪs] ◆ *n* abrazo *m*. ◆ *vt* 1. (*hug*) abrazar, dar un abrazo a. 2. *fml* (*convert to*) convertirse a. 3. *fml* (*include*) abarcar. ◆ *vi* abrazarse.

embroider [ɪm'brɔɪdər] *vt* 1. (SEWING) bordar. 2. *pej* (*embellish*) adornar.

embroidery [ɪm'brɔɪdərɪ] *n* (U) bordado *m*.

embroil [ɪm'brɔɪl] *vt*: **to get/be ~ed (in)** enredarse/estar enredado (en).

embryo ['embrɪəʊ] (*pl* **-s**) *n* embrión *m*.

emerald ['emərəld] ◆ *adj* (*colour*) esmeralda *m inv*. ◆ *n* (*stone*) esmeralda *f*.

emerge [ɪ'mɜ:dʒ] ◆ *vi* 1. (*gen*): **to ~ (from)** salir (de). 2. (*come into existence, become known*) surgir, emerger. ◆ *vt*: **it ~d that ...** resultó que ...

emergence [ɪ'mɜ:dʒəns] *n* surgimiento *m*, aparición *f*.

emergency [ɪ'mɜ:dʒənsɪ] ◆ *adj* (*case, exit, services*) de emergencia; (*ward*) de urgencia; (*supplies*) de reserva; (*meeting*) extraordinario(ria). ◆ *n* emergencia *f*.

emergency exit *n* salida *f* de emergencia.

emergency landing *n* aterrizaje *m* forzoso.

emergency services *npl* servicios *mpl* de urgencia.

emery board ['emərɪ-] *n* lima *f* de uñas.

emigrant ['emɪgrənt] *n* emigrante *m y f*.

emigrate ['emɪgreɪt] *vi*: **to ~ (to/from)** emigrar (a/de).

eminent ['emɪnənt] *adj* eminente.

emission [ɪ'mɪʃn] *n* emisión *f*.

emit [ɪ'mɪt] *vt* (*gen*) emitir; (*smell, smoke*) despedir.

emotion [ɪ'məʊʃn] *n* emoción *f*.

emotional [ɪ'məʊʃənl] *adj* 1. (*gen*) emotivo(va). 2. (*needs, problems*) emocional.

emperor ['empərər] *n* emperador *m*.

emphasis ['emfəsɪs] (*pl* **-ases** [-əsi:z]) *n*: ~ (**on**) énfasis *m inv* (en); **to lay** OR **place ~ on** poner énfasis en, hacer hincapié en.

emphasize, -ise ['emfəsaɪz] *vt* (*word,*

syllable) acentuar; (*point, fact, feature*) subrayar, hacer hincapié en; **to ~ that ...** poner de relieve OR subrayar que ...

emphatic [ɪm'fætɪk] *adj* (*forceful*) rotundo(da), categórico(ca).

emphatically [ɪm'fætɪklɪ] *adv* 1. (*with emphasis*) rotundamente, enfáticamente. 2. (*certainly*) ciertamente.

empire ['empaɪər] *n* imperio *m*.

employ [ɪm'plɔɪ] *vt* 1. (*give work to*) emplear; **to be ~ed as** estar empleado de. 2. *fml* (*use*) utilizar, emplear; **to ~ sthg as sthg/to do sthg** utilizar algo de algo/para hacer algo.

employee [ɪm'plɔɪi:] *n* empleado *m*, -da *f*.

employer [ɪm'plɔɪər] *n* patrono *m*, -na *f*, empresario *m*, -ria *f*.

employment [ɪm'plɔɪmənt] *n* empleo *m*; **to be in ~** tener trabajo.

employment agency *n* agencia *f* de trabajo.

empower [ɪm'paʊər] *vt fml*: **to be ~ed to do sthg** estar autorizado(da) a OR para hacer algo.

empress ['emprɪs] *n* emperatriz *f*.

empty ['emptɪ] ◆ *adj* 1. (*gen*) vacío(a); (*town*) desierto(ta). 2. *pej* (*words, threat, promise*) vano(na). ◆ *vt* vaciar; **to ~ sthg into sthg** vaciar algo en algo. ◆ *vi* vaciarse. ◆ *n inf* casco *m*.

empty-handed [-'hændɪd] *adv* con las manos vacías.

EMS (*abbr of* **European Monetary System**) *n* SME *m*.

emulate ['emjʊleɪt] *vt* emular.

emulsion [ɪ'mʌlʃn] *n*: ~ (**paint**) pintura *f* mate.

enable [ɪ'neɪbl] *vt*: **to ~ sb to do sthg** permitir a alguien hacer algo.

enact [ɪ'nækt] *vt* 1. (JUR) promulgar. 2. (*act*) representar.

enamel [ɪ'næml] *n* 1. (*gen*) esmalte *m*. 2. (*paint*) pintura *f* de esmalte.

encampment [ɪn'kæmpmənt] *n* campamento *m*.

encapsulate [ɪn'kæpsjʊleɪt] *vt*: **to ~ sthg (in)** sintetizar algo (en).

encase [ɪn'keɪs] *vt*: **~d in** encajonado (da) en.

enchanted [ɪn'tʃɑ:ntɪd] *adj*: ~ (**by** OR **with**) encantado(da) (con).

enchanting [ɪn'tʃɑ:ntɪŋ] *adj* encantador(ra).

encircle [ɪn'sɜ:kl] *vt* rodear.

enclose [ɪn'kləʊz] *vt* 1. (*surround, contain*) rodear; **~d by** OR **with** rodeado de; **an ~d space** un espacio cerrado. 2. (*put* *in envelope*) adjuntar; **please find ~d ...** envío adjunto ...

enclosure [ɪn'kləʊʒəʳ] n 1. (*place*) recinto m (vallado). 2. (*in letter*) anexo m.

encompass [ɪn'kʌmpəs] vt fml (*include*) abarcar.

encore ['ɒŋkɔːʳ] ♦ n bis m. ♦ excl ¡otra!

encounter [ɪn'kaʊntəʳ] ♦ n encuentro m. ♦ vt fml encontrarse con.

encourage [ɪn'kʌrɪdʒ] vt 1. (*give confidence to*): **to ~ sb (to do sthg)** animar a alguien (a hacer algo). 2. (*foster*) fomentar.

encouragement [ɪn'kʌrɪdʒmənt] n aliento m; (*of industry*) fomento m.

encroach [ɪn'krəʊtʃ] vi: **to ~ on** OR **upon** (*rights, territory*) usurpar; (*privacy, time*) invadir.

encyclop(a)edia [ɪn,saɪklə'piːdjə] n enciclopedia f.

end [end] ♦ n 1. (*last part, finish*) fin m, final m; **at the ~ of May/1992** a finales de mayo/1992; **at an ~** terminando; **to bring sthg to an ~** poner fin a algo; **to come to an ~** llegar a su fin, terminarse; **'the ~'** (*in films*) 'FIN'; **to put an ~ to sthg** poner fin a algo; **in the ~** (*finally*) finalmente, por fin. 2. (*of two-ended thing*) extremo m, punta f; (*of phone line*) lado m; **~ to ~** extremo con extremo; **cigarette ~** colilla f. 3. fml (*purpose*) fin m. ♦ vt: **to ~ sthg (with)** terminar algo (con). ♦ vi (*finish*) acabarse, terminarse; **to ~ in/with** acabar en/con, terminar en/con. ▶ **on end** adv 1. (*upright - hair*) de punta; (*- object*) de pie. 2. (*continuously*): **for days on ~** día tras día. ▶ **end up** vi acabar, terminar; **to ~ up doing sthg** acabar por hacer algo/haciendo algo; **to ~ up in** ir a parar a.

endanger [ɪn'deɪndʒəʳ] vt poner en peligro.

endearing [ɪn'dɪərɪŋ] adj simpático (ca).

endeavour Br, **endeavor** Am [ɪn'devəʳ] fml ♦ n esfuerzo m. ♦ vt: **to ~ to do sthg** procurar hacer algo.

ending ['endɪŋ] n final m, desenlace m.

endive ['endaɪv] n 1. (*salad vegetable*) endibia f. 2. (*chicory*) achicoria f.

endless ['endlɪs] adj (*gen*) interminable; (*patience, resources*) inagotable.

endorse [ɪn'dɔːs] vt 1. (*approve*) apoyar, respaldar. 2. (*cheque*) endosar.

endorsement [ɪn'dɔːsmənt] n 1. (*approval*) apoyo m, respaldo m. 2. Br

(*on driving licence*) nota de sanción que consta en el carnet de conducir.

endow [ɪn'daʊ] vt 1. fml (*equip*): **to be ~ed with** estar dotado(da) de. 2. (*donate money to*) donar fondos a.

endurance [ɪn'djʊərəns] n resistencia f.

endure [ɪn'djʊəʳ] ♦ vt soportar, aguantar. ♦ vi fml perdurar.

endways Br ['endweɪz], **endwise** Am ['endwaɪz] adv 1. (*not sideways*) de frente. 2. (*with ends touching*) extremo con extremo.

enemy ['enɪmɪ] n enemigo m, -ga f.

energetic [,enə'dʒetɪk] adj 1. (*lively, physically taxing*) enérgico(ca). 2. (*enthusiastic*) activo(va), vigoroso(sa).

energy ['enədʒɪ] n energía f.

enforce [ɪn'fɔːs] vt (*law*) hacer cumplir, aplicar; (*standards*) imponer.

enforced [ɪn'fɔːst] adj forzoso(sa).

engage [ɪn'geɪdʒ] ♦ vt 1. (*attract*) atraer. 2. (TECH - *clutch*) pisar; (- *gear*) meter. 3. fml (*employ*) contratar; **to be ~d in** OR **on** dedicarse a. ♦ vi (*be involved*): **to ~ in** (*gen*) meterse en, dedicarse a; (*conversation*) entablar.

engaged [ɪn'geɪdʒd] adj 1. (*to be married*): **~ (to)** prometido(da) (con); **to get ~** prometerse. 2. (*busy, in use*) ocupado (da); **~ in sthg** ocupado en algo. 3. (TELEC) comunicando.

engaged tone n Br señal f de comunicando.

engagement [ɪn'geɪdʒmənt] n 1. (*to be married*) compromiso m; (*period*) noviazgo m. 2. (*appointment*) cita f.

engagement ring n anillo m de compromiso.

engaging [ɪn'geɪdʒɪŋ] adj atractivo (va).

engender [ɪn'dʒendəʳ] vt fml engendrar.

engine ['endʒɪn] n 1. (*of vehicle*) motor m. 2. (RAIL) locomotora f, máquina f.

engine driver n Br maquinista m y f.

engineer [,endʒɪ'nɪəʳ] ♦ n 1. (*gen*) ingeniero m, -ra f. 2. Am (*engine driver*) maquinista m y f. ♦ vt 1. (*construct*) construir. 2. (*contrive*) tramar.

engineering [,endʒɪ'nɪərɪŋ] n ingeniería f.

England ['ɪŋglənd] n Inglaterra f.

English ['ɪŋglɪʃ] ♦ adj inglés(esa). ♦ n (*language*) inglés m. ♦ npl (*people*): **the ~** los ingleses.

English breakfast n desayuno m inglés.

English Channel *n*: **the ~** el canal de la Mancha.

Englishman ['ɪŋglɪʃmən] (*pl* **-men** [-mən]) *n* inglés *m*.

Englishwoman ['ɪŋglɪʃˌwʊmən] (*pl* **-women** [-ˌwɪmɪn]) *n* inglesa *f*.

engrave [ɪn'greɪv] *vt lit & fig*: **to ~ sthg (on)** grabar algo (en).

engraving [ɪn'greɪvɪŋ] *n* grabado *m*.

engrossed [ɪn'grəʊst] *adj*: **to be ~ (in)** estar absorto(ta) (en).

engulf [ɪn'gʌlf] *vt*: **to be ~ed in** (*flames etc*) verse devorado(da) por; (*fear, despair*) verse sumido(da) en.

enhance [ɪn'hɑːns] *vt* (*gen*) aumentar; (*status, position*) elevar; (*beauty*) realzar.

enjoy [ɪn'dʒɔɪ] *vt* **1.** (*like*) disfrutar de; **did you ~ the film/book?** ¿te gustó la película/el libro?; **she ~s reading** le gusta leer; **~ your meal!** ¡que aproveche!; **to ~ o.s.** pasarlo bien, divertirse. **2.** *fml* (*possess*) gozar OR disfrutar de.

enjoyable [ɪn'dʒɔɪəbl] *adj* agradable.

enjoyment [ɪn'dʒɔɪmənt] *n* (*pleasure*) placer *m*.

enlarge [ɪn'lɑːdʒ] *vt* (*gen & PHOT*) ampliar. ▶ **enlarge (up)on** *vt fus* ampliar.

enlargement [ɪn'lɑːdʒmənt] *n* (*gen & PHOT*) ampliación *f*.

enlighten [ɪn'laɪtn] *vt fml* iluminar.

enlightened [ɪn'laɪtnd] *adj* amplio (plia) de miras.

enlightenment [ɪn'laɪtnmənt] *n* (U) aclaración *f*. ▶ **Enlightenment** *n*: **the Enlightenment** la Ilustración.

enlist [ɪn'lɪst] ♦ *vt* **1.** (*person*) alistar, reclutar. **2.** (*support*) obtener. ♦ *vi* (MIL): **to ~ (in)** alistarse (en).

enmity ['enmɪtɪ] *n* enemistad *f*.

enormity [ɪ'nɔːmətɪ] *n* (*extent*) enormidad *f*.

enormous [ɪ'nɔːməs] *adj* enorme.

enough [ɪ'nʌf] ♦ *adj* bastante, suficiente. ♦ *pron* bastante; **more than ~** más que suficiente; **that's ~** (*sufficient*) ya está bien; **to have had ~ (of)** (*expressing annoyance*) estar harto (de). ♦ *adv* bastante, suficientemente; **I was stupid ~ to believe him** fui lo bastante tonto como para creerle; **he was good ~ to lend me his car** *fml* tuvo la bondad de dejarme su coche; **strangely ~** curiosamente.

enquire [ɪn'kwaɪə^r] *vi* (*ask for information*) informarse; **to ~ about sthg** informarse de algo; **to ~ when/how/**

whether/if ... preguntar cuándo/cómo/si ... ▶ **enquire into** *vt fus* investigar.

enquiry [ɪn'kwaɪərɪ] *n* **1.** (*question*) pregunta *f*; **'Enquiries'** 'Información'. **2.** (*investigation*) investigación *f*.

enraged [ɪn'reɪdʒd] *adj* enfurecido (da).

enrol *Br*, **enroll** *Am* [ɪn'rəʊl] ♦ *vt* matricular. ♦ *vi*: **to ~ (on)** matricularse (en).

en route [ˌɒn'ruːt] *adv*: **~ (from/to)** en el camino (de/a).

ensign ['ensaɪn] *n* **1.** (*flag*) bandera *f*. **2.** *Am* (*sailor*) ≃ alférez *m* de fragata.

ensue [ɪn'sjuː] *vi fml* originarse; (*war*) sobrevenir.

ensure [ɪn'ʃʊə^r] *vt*: **to ~ (that)** asegurar que.

ENT (*abbr of* **Ear, Nose & Throat**) *n* otorrinolaringología *f*.

entail [ɪn'teɪl] *vt* (*involve*) conllevar, suponer.

enter ['entə^r] ♦ *vt* **1.** (*gen*) entrar en. **2.** (*join - profession, parliament*) ingresar en; (*- university*) matricularse en; (*- army, navy*) alistarse en. **3.** (*become involved in - politics etc*) meterse en; (*- race, examination etc*) presentarse a. **4.** (*register*): **to ~ sthg/sb for sthg** inscribir algo/a alguien en algo. **5.** (*write down*) apuntar. **6.** (*appear in*) presentarse OR aparecer en. **7.** (COMPUT) dar entrada a. ♦ *vi* **1.** (*come or go in*) entrar. **2.** (*participate*): **to ~ (for)** presentarse (a algo). ▶ **enter into** *vt fus* entrar en; (*agreement*) comprometerse a.

enter key *n* (COMPUT) tecla *f* de entrada.

enterprise ['entəpraɪz] *n* empresa *f*.

enterprise zone *n* zona del Reino Unido donde se fomenta la actividad industrial y empresarial.

enterprising ['entəpraɪzɪŋ] *adj* emprendedor(ra).

entertain [ˌentə'teɪn] *vt* **1.** (*amuse*) divertir, entretener. **2.** (*invite*) recibir (en casa). **3.** *fml* (*idea, proposal*) considerar.

entertainer [ˌentə'teɪnə^r] *n* artista *m y f*.

entertaining [ˌentə'teɪnɪŋ] *adj* divertido(da), entretenido(da).

entertainment [ˌentə'teɪnmənt] *n* **1.** (U) (*amusement*) diversión *f*. **2.** (*show*) espectáculo *m*.

enthral, enthrall *Am* [ɪn'θrɔːl] *vt* embelesar.

enthusiasm [ɪn'θjuːzɪæzm] *n* **1.** (*passion, eagerness*): **~ (for)** entusiasmo *m* (por). **2.** (*interest*) pasión *f*, interés *m*.

enthusiast [ɪn'θjuːzɪæst] *n* entusiasta *m y f*.

enthusiastic [ɪn,θjuːzɪ'æstɪk] *adj* (*person*) entusiasta; (*cry, response*) entusiástico(ca).

entice [ɪn'taɪs] *vt* seducir, atraer.

entire [ɪn'taɪə^r] *adj* entero(ra); **the ~ evening** toda la noche.

entirely [ɪn'taɪəlɪ] *adv* enteramente; **I'm not ~ sure** no estoy del todo seguro.

entirety [ɪn'taɪrətɪ] *n fml*: **in its ~** en su totalidad.

entitle [ɪn'taɪtl] *vt* (*allow*): **to ~ sb to sthg** dar a alguien derecho a algo; **to ~ sb to do sthg** autorizar a alguien a hacer algo.

entitled [ɪn'taɪtld] *adj* **1.** (*allowed*): **to be ~ to sthg/to do sthg** tener derecho a algo/a hacer algo. **2.** (*having the title*) titulado(da).

entourage [,ɒntʊ'rɑːʒ] *n* séquito *m*.

entrails ['entreɪlz] *npl* entrañas *fpl*.

entrance [*n* 'entrəns, *vb* ɪn'trɑːns] ◆ *n*: **~ (to)** entrada *f* (a OR de); **to gain ~ to** *fml* (*building*) lograr acceso a; (*society, university*) lograr el ingreso en. ◆ *vt* encantar, hechizar.

entrance examination *n* examen *m* de ingreso.

entrance fee *n* (precio *m* de) entrada *f*.

entrant ['entrənt] *n* participante *m y f*.

entreat [ɪn'triːt] *vt*: **to ~ sb (to do sthg)** suplicar OR rogar a alguien (que haga algo).

entrenched [ɪn'trentʃt] *adj* (*firm*) arraigado(da).

entrepreneur [,ɒntrəprə'nɜː^r] *n* empresario *m*, -ria *f*.

entrust [ɪn'trʌst] *vt*: **to ~ sthg to sb, to ~ sb with sthg** confiar algo a alguien.

entry ['entrɪ] *n* **1.** (*gen*): **~ (into)** entrada *f* (en); **no ~** se prohibe la entrada, prohibido el paso. **2.** *fig* (*joining - of group, society*) ingreso *m*. **3.** (*in competition*) participante *m y f*. **4.** (*in diary*) anotación *f*; (*in ledger*) partida *f*.

entry form *n* boleto *m* OR impreso *m* de inscripción.

entry phone *n* Br portero *m* automático.

envelop [ɪn'veləp] *vt*: **to ~ sthg/sb in** envolver algo/a alguien en.

envelope ['envələup] *n* sobre *m*.

envious ['enviəs] *adj* (*person*) envidioso(sa); (*look*) de envidia.

environment [ɪn'vaɪərənmənt] *n* **1.** (*surroundings*) entorno *m*. **2.** (*natural world*): **the ~** el medio ambiente.

environmental [ɪn,vaɪərən'mentl] *adj* medioambiental; **~ pollution** contaminación *f* del medio ambiente.

environmentalist [ɪn,vaɪərən'mentəlɪst] *n* ecologista *m y f*.

environmentally [ɪn,vaɪərən'mentəlɪ] *adv* ecológicamente; **~ friendly** ecológico(ca).

envisage [ɪn'vɪzɪdʒ], **envision** Am [ɪn'vɪʒn] *vt* prever.

envoy ['envɔɪ] *n* enviado *m*, -da *f*.

envy ['envɪ] ◆ *n* envidia *f*. ◆ *vt*: **to ~ (sb sthg)** envidiar (algo a alguien).

epic ['epɪk] ◆ *adj* épico(ca). ◆ *n* epopeya *f*.

epidemic [,epɪ'demɪk] *n* epidemia *f*.

epileptic [,epɪ'leptɪk] ◆ *adj* epiléptico (ca). ◆ *n* epiléptico *m*, -ca *f*.

episode ['epɪsəud] *n* **1.** (*event*) episodio *m*. **2.** (*of story, TV series*) capítulo *m*.

epistle [ɪ'pɪsl] *n* epístola *f*.

epitaph ['epɪtɑːf] *n* epitafio *m*.

epitome [ɪ'pɪtəmɪ] *n*: **the ~ of** (*person*) la personificación de; (*thing*) el vivo ejemplo de.

epitomize, -ise [ɪ'pɪtəmaɪz] *vt* (*subj: person*) personificar; (*subj: thing*) representar el paradigma de.

epoch ['iːpɒk] *n* época *f*.

equable ['ekwəbl] *adj* (*calm, reasonable*) ecuánime.

equal ['iːkwəl] ◆ *adj* igual; **~ to** (*sum*) igual a; **to be ~ to** (*task etc*) estar a la altura de. ◆ *n* igual *m y f*. ◆ *vt* **1.** (MATH) ser igual a. **2.** (*person, quality*) igualar.

equality [iː'kwɒlətɪ] *n* igualdad *f*.

equalize, -ise ['iːkwəlaɪz] *vi* (SPORT) empatar.

equalizer ['iːkwəlaɪzə^r] *n* (SPORT) (gol *m* de la) igualada *f*.

equally ['iːkwəlɪ] *adv* **1.** (*gen*) igualmente; **~ important** igual de importante. **2.** (*share, divide*) a partes iguales, por igual.

equal opportunities *npl* igualdad *f* de oportunidades.

equanimity [,ekwə'nɪmətɪ] *n* ecuanimidad *f*.

equate [ɪ'kweɪt] *vt*: **to ~ sthg with** equiparar algo con.

equation [ɪ'kweɪʒn] *n* ecuación *f*.

equator [ɪ'kweɪtə^r] *n*: **the ~** el ecuador.

equilibrium [,iːkwɪ'lɪbrɪəm] *n* equilibrio *m*.

equip [ɪ'kwɪp] *vt* **1.** (*provide with equipment*): **to ~ sthg (with)** equipar algo (con); **to ~ sb (with)** proveer a alguien (de). **2.** (*prepare*): **to be equipped for** estar bien dotado(da) para.

equipment [ɪˈkwɪpmənt] *n* (U) equipo *m.*

equitable [ˈekwɪtəbl] *adj* equitativo (va).

equities [ˈekwətɪz] *npl* (ST EX) acciones *fpl* ordinarias.

equivalent [ɪˈkwɪvələnt] ◆ *adj* equivalente; **to be ~ to** equivaler a. ◆ *n* equivalente *m.*

equivocal [ɪˈkwɪvəkl] *adj* equívoco (ca).

er [ɜːʳ] *excl* ¡ejem!

era [ˈɪərə] (*pl* **-s**) *n* era *f*, época *f.*

eradicate [ɪˈrædɪkeɪt] *vt* erradicar.

erase [ɪˈreɪz] *vt lit & fig* borrar.

eraser [ɪˈreɪzəʳ] *n* goma *f* de borrar.

erect [ɪˈrekt] ◆ *adj* (*person, posture*) erguido(da). ◆ *vt* **1.** (*building, statue*) erigir, levantar. **2.** (*tent*) montar.

erection [ɪˈrekʃn] *n* **1.** (U) (*of building, statue*) construcción *f.* **2.** (*erect penis*) erección *f.*

ERM (*abbr of* **Exchange Rate Mechanism**) *n* mecanismo de tipos de cambio del SME.

ermine [ˈɜːmɪn] *n* armiño *m.*

erode [ɪˈrəʊd] *vt* **1.** (*rock, soil*) erosionar; (*metal*) desgastar. **2.** (*confidence, rights*) mermar.

erosion [ɪˈrəʊʒn] *n* **1.** (*of rock, soil*) erosión *f*; (*of metal*) desgaste *m.* **2.** (*of confidence, rights*) merma *f.*

erotic [ɪˈrɒtɪk] *adj* erótico(ca).

err [ɜːʳ] *vi* equivocarse, errar.

errand [ˈerənd] *n* recado *m*, mandado *m.*

erratic [ɪˈrætɪk] *adj* irregular.

error [ˈerəʳ] *n* error *m*; **spelling ~** falta *f* de ortografía; **in ~** por equivocación.

erupt [ɪˈrʌpt] *vi* (*volcano*) entrar en erupción; *fig* (*violence, war*) estallar.

eruption [ɪˈrʌpʃn] *n* **1.** (*of volcano*) erupción *f.* **2.** (*of violence, war*) estallido *m.*

escalate [ˈeskəleɪt] *vi* **1.** (*conflict*) intensificarse. **2.** (*costs*) ascender.

escalator [ˈeskəleɪtəʳ] *n* escalera *f* mecánica.

escapade [ˌeskəˈpeɪd] *n* aventura *f.*

escape [ɪˈskeɪp] ◆ *n* **1.** (*gen*) fuga *f.* **2.** (*leakage of gas, water*) escape *m.* ◆ *vt* **1.** (*avoid*) escapar a, eludir. **2.** (*subj: fact, name*): **her name ~s me** ahora mismo no caigo en su nombre. ◆ *vi* **1.** (*gen*): **to ~ (from)** escaparse (de). **2.** (*survive*) escapar.

escapism [ɪˈskeɪpɪzm] *n* (U) evasión *f.*

escort [*n* ˈeskɔːt, *vb* ɪˈskɔːt] ◆ *n* **1.** (*guard*) escolta *f.* **2.** (*companion*) acompañante *m y f.* ◆ *vt* escoltar; **to ~ sb home** acompañar a alguien a casa.

Eskimo [ˈeskɪməʊ] (*pl* **-s**) *n* (*person*) esquimal *m y f.*

espadrille [ˌespəˈdrɪl] *n* alpargata *f.*

especially [ɪˈspeʃəlɪ] *adv* **1.** (*in particular*) sobre todo. **2.** (*more than usually, specifically*) especialmente.

espionage [ˈespɪəˌnɑːʒ] *n* espionaje *m.*

esplanade [ˌespləˈneɪd] *n* paseo *m* marítimo.

Esquire [ɪˈskwaɪəʳ] *n* Sr. Don; **B. Jones ~** Sr. Don B. Jones.

essay [ˈeseɪ] *n* **1.** (SCH) redacción *f*; (UNIV) trabajo *m.* **2.** (LITERATURE) ensayo *m.*

essence [ˈesns] *n* esencia *f.*

essential [ɪˈsenʃl] *adj* **1.** (*absolutely necessary*): **~ (to OR for)** esencial OR indispensable (para). **2.** (*basic*) fundamental, esencial. ▶ **essentials** *npl* **1.** (*basic commodities*) lo indispensable. **2.** (*most important elements*) elementos *mpl* esenciales.

essentially [ɪˈsenʃəlɪ] *adv* (*basically*) esencialmente.

establish [ɪˈstæblɪʃ] *vt* **1.** (*gen*) establecer. **2.** (*facts, cause*) verificar.

establishment [ɪˈstæblɪʃmənt] *n* establecimiento *m.* ▶ **Establishment** *n*: **the Establishment** el sistema.

estate [ɪˈsteɪt] *n* **1.** (*land, property*) finca *f.* **2.** (*housing*) **~** urbanización *f.* **3.** (*industrial*) **~** polígono *m* industrial. **4.** (JUR) (*inheritance*) herencia *f.*

estate agency *n* Br agencia *f* inmobiliaria.

estate agent *n* Br agente inmobiliario *m*, agente inmobiliaria *f.*

estate car *n* Br ranchera *f.*

esteem [ɪˈstiːm] ◆ *n* estima *f*, consideración *f.* ◆ *vt* estimar, apreciar.

esthetic *etc* Am = **aesthetic** *etc.*

estimate [*n* ˈestɪmət, *vb* ˈestɪmeɪt] ◆ *n* **1.** (*calculation, judgment*) cálculo *m*, estimación *f.* **2.** (*written quote*) presupuesto *m.* ◆ *vt* estimar.

estimation [ˌestɪˈmeɪʃn] *n* **1.** (*opinion*) juicio *m.* **2.** (*calculation*) cálculo *m.*

Estonia [eˈstəʊnɪə] *n* Estonia.

estranged [ɪˈstreɪndʒd] *adj* (*husband, wife*) separado(da); **his ~ son** su hijo con el que no se habla.

estuary [ˈestjʊərɪ] *n* estuario *m.*

etc. (*abbr of* **etcetera**) etc.

etching ['etʃɪŋ] *n* aguafuerte *m o f*.

eternal [ɪ'tɜːnl] *adj* (*gen*) eterno(na); *fig* (*complaints, whining*) perpetuo(tua).

eternity [ɪ'tɜːnətɪ] *n* eternidad *f*.

ethic ['eθɪk] *n* ética *f*. ▶ **ethics** ◆ *n* (U) (*study*) ética *f*. ◆ *npl* (*morals*) moralidad *f*.

ethical ['eθɪkl] *adj* ético(ca).

Ethiopia [ˌiːθɪ'əʊpɪə] *n* Etiopía.

ethnic ['eθnɪk] *adj* **1.** (*traditions, groups, conflict*) étnico(ca). **2.** (*food*) típico de una cultura distinta a la occidental.

ethos ['iːθɒs] *n* código *m* de valores.

etiquette ['etɪket] *n* etiqueta *f*.

EU (*abbr of* **European Union**) *n* UE *f*.

euphemism ['juːfəmɪzm] *n* eufemismo *m*.

euphoria [juː'fɔːrɪə] *n* euforia *f*.

Eurocheque ['jʊərəʊˌtʃek] *n* eurocheque *m*.

Euro MP *n* eurodiputado *m*, -da *f*.

Europe ['jʊərəp] *n* Europa *f*.

European [ˌjʊərə'piːən] ◆ *adj* europeo (a). ◆ *n* europeo *m*, -a *f*.

European Community *n*: **the ~** la Comunidad Europea.

European Monetary System *n*: **the ~** el Sistema Monetario Europeo.

European Parliament *n*: **the ~** el Parlamento Europeo.

European Union *n*: **the ~** la Unión Europea.

euthanasia [ˌjuːθə'neɪzjə] *n* eutanasia *f*.

evacuate [ɪ'vækjʊeɪt] *vt* evacuar.

evade [ɪ'veɪd] *vt* eludir.

evaluate [ɪ'væljʊeɪt] *vt* evaluar.

evaporate [ɪ'væpəreɪt] *vi* (*liquid*) evaporarse; *fig* (*feeling*) desvanecerse.

evaporated milk [ɪ'væpəreɪtɪd-] *n* leche *f* evaporada.

evasion [ɪ'veɪʒn] *n* **1.** (*of responsibility, payment etc*) evasión *f*. **2.** (*lie*) evasiva *f*.

evasive [ɪ'veɪsɪv] *adj* evasivo(va).

eve [iːv] *n*: **on the ~ of** en la víspera de.

even ['iːvn] ◆ *adj* **1.** (*regular*) uniforme, constante. **2.** (*calm*) sosegado(da). **3.** (*flat, level*) llano(na), liso(sa). **4.** (*equal - contest, teams*) igualado(da); (*- chance*) igual; **to get ~ with** ajustarle las cuentas a. **5.** (*number*) par. ◆ *adv* **1.** (*gen*) incluso, hasta; **~ now/then** incluso ahora/entonces; **not ~** ni siquiera. **2.** (*in comparisons*) aun; **~ more** aun más. ▶ **even if** *conj* aunque, así *Amer*. ▶ **even so** *conj* aun así. ▶ **even though** *conj* aunque. ▶ **even out** *vi* igualarse.

evening ['iːvnɪŋ] *n* **1.** (*end of day - early part*) tarde *f*; (*- later part*) noche *f*. **2.** (*event, entertainment*) velada *f*. ▶ **evenings** *adv* (*early*) por la tarde; (*late*) por la noche.

evening class *n* clase *f* nocturna.

evening dress *n* **1.** (*worn by man*) traje *m* de etiqueta. **2.** (*worn by woman*) traje *m* de noche.

event [ɪ'vent] *n* **1.** (*happening*) acontecimiento *m*, suceso *m*; **in the ~ of** en caso de; **in the ~ that it rains** (en) caso de que llueva. **2.** (SPORT) prueba *f*. ▶ **in any event** *adv* en todo caso. ▶ **in the event** *adv* Br al final.

eventful [ɪ'ventfʊl] *adj* accidentado (da).

eventual [ɪ'ventʃʊəl] *adj* final.

eventuality [ɪˌventʃʊ'ælətɪ] *n* eventualidad *f*.

eventually [ɪ'ventʃʊəlɪ] *adv* finalmente.

ever ['evər] *adv* **1.** (*at any time*) alguna vez; **have you ~ done it?** ¿lo has hecho alguna vez?; **hardly ~** casi nunca. **2.** (*all the time*) siempre; **as ~** como siempre; **for ~** para siempre. **3.** (*for emphasis*): **~ so** muy; **~ such a mess** un lío tan grande; **why/how ~ did you do it?** ¿por qué/cómo diablos lo hiciste?; **what ~ can it be?** ¿qué diablos puede ser? ▶ **ever since** ◆ *adv* desde entonces. ◆ *conj* desde que. ◆ *prep* desde.

evergreen ['evəɡriːn] ◆ *adj* de hoja perenne. ◆ *n* árbol *m* de hoja perenne.

everlasting [ˌevə'lɑːstɪŋ] *adj* eterno (na).

every ['evrɪ] *adj* cada; **~ day** cada día, todos los días. ▶ **every now and then, every so often** *adv* de vez en cuando. ▶ **every other** *adj*: **~ other day** un día sí y otro no, cada dos días.

everybody ['evrɪˌbɒdɪ] = **everyone**.

everyday ['evrɪdeɪ] *adj* diario(ria), cotidiano(na).

everyone ['evrɪwʌn] *pron* todo el mundo, todos(das).

everyplace *Am* = **everywhere**.

everything ['evrɪθɪŋ] *pron* todo; **money isn't ~** el dinero no lo es todo.

everywhere ['evrɪweər], **everyplace** *Am* ['evrɪˌpleɪs] *adv* en *or* por todas partes; (*with verbs of motion*) a todas partes.

evict [ɪ'vɪkt] *vt*: **to ~ sb from** desahuciar a alguien de.

evidence ['evɪdəns] (U) *n* **1.** (*proof*) prueba *f*. **2.** (JUR) (*of witness*) declaración

f; **to give ~** dar testimonio.
evident ['evɪdənt] adj evidente, manifiesto(ta).
evidently ['evɪdəntlɪ] adv 1. (seemingly) por lo visto, al parecer. 2. (obviously) evidentemente, obviamente.
evil ['iːvl] ◆ adj (person) malo(la), malvado(da); (torture, practice) perverso(sa), vil. ◆ n 1. (evil quality) maldad f. 2. (evil thing) mal m.
evocative [ɪ'vɒkətɪv] adj evocador (ra).
evoke [ɪ'vəuk] vt 1. (memory, emotion) evocar. 2. (response) producir.
evolution [ˌiːvə'luːʃn] n 1. (BIOL) evolución f. 2. (development) desarrollo m.
evolve [ɪ'vɒlv] ◆ vt desarrollar. ◆ vi 1. (BIOL): **to ~ (into/from)** evolucionar (en/de). 2. (develop) desarrollarse.
ewe [juː] n oveja f.
ex- [eks] prefix ex-.
exacerbate [ɪg'zæsəbeɪt] vt exacerbar.
exact [ɪg'zækt] ◆ adj exacto(ta); **to be ~** para ser exacto. ◆ vt: **to ~ sthg (from)** exigir algo (de).
exacting [ɪg'zæktɪŋ] adj 1. (job, work) arduo(dua). 2. (standards) severo(ra); (person) exigente.
exactly [ɪg'zæktlɪ] ◆ adv (precisely) exactamente; **it's ~ ten o'clock** son las diez en punto. ◆ excl ¡exacto!
exaggerate [ɪg'zædʒəreɪt] vt & vi exagerar.
exaggeration [ɪgˌzædʒə'reɪʃn] n exageración f.
exalted [ɪg'zɔːltɪd] adj (person, position) elevado(da).
exam [ɪg'zæm] (abbr of **examination**) n examen m; **to take** OR **sit an ~** presentarse a un examen.
examination [ɪgˌzæmɪ'neɪʃn] n 1. = **exam**. 2. (inspection) inspección f, examen m. 3. (MED) reconocimiento m. 4. (consideration) estudio m.
examine [ɪg'zæmɪn] vt 1. (gen) examinar. 2. (MED) reconocer. 3. (consider - idea, proposal) estudiar, considerar. 4. (JUR) interrogar.
examiner [ɪg'zæmɪnər] n examinador m, -ra f.
example [ɪg'zɑːmpl] n ejemplo m; **for ~** por ejemplo.
exasperate [ɪg'zæspəreɪt] vt exasperar.
exasperation [ɪgˌzæspə'reɪʃn] n exasperación f, irritación f.

excavate ['ekskəveɪt] vt excavar.
exceed [ɪk'siːd] vt 1. (amount, number) exceder, pasar. 2. (limit, expectations) rebasar.
exceedingly [ɪk'siːdɪŋlɪ] adv extremadamente.
excel [ɪk'sel] vi: **to ~ (in** OR **at)** sobresalir (en); **to ~ o.s.** Br lucirse.
excellence ['eksələns] n excelencia f.
excellent ['eksələnt] adj excelente.
except [ɪk'sept] ◆ prep & conj: **~ (for)** excepto, salvo. ◆ vt: **to ~ sb (from)** exceptuar OR excluir a alguien (de).
excepting [ɪk'septɪŋ] prep & conj = **except**.
exception [ɪk'sepʃn] n 1. (exclusion): **~ (to)** excepción f (a); **with the ~ of** a excepción de. 2. (offence): **to take ~ to** ofenderse por.
exceptional [ɪk'sepʃənl] adj excepcional.
excerpt ['eksɜːpt] n: **~ (from)** extracto m (de).
excess [ɪk'ses, before nouns 'ekses] ◆ adj excedente. ◆ n exceso m.
excess baggage n exceso m de equipaje.
excess fare n Br suplemento m.
excessive [ɪk'sesɪv] adj excesivo(va).
exchange [ɪks'tʃeɪndʒ] ◆ n 1. (gen) intercambio m; **in ~ (for)** a cambio (de). 2. (FIN) cambio m. 3. (TELEC): (telephone) **~** central f telefónica. 4. fml (conversation): **a heated ~** una acalorada discusión. ◆ vt (swap) intercambiar, cambiar; **to ~ sthg for sthg** cambiar algo por algo; **to ~ sthg with sb** intercambiar algo con alguien.
exchange rate n (FIN) tipo m de cambio.
Exchequer [ɪks'tʃekər] n Br: **the ~** ≃ Hacienda.
excise ['eksaɪz] n (U) impuestos mpl sobre el consumo interior.
excite [ɪk'saɪt] vt 1. (person) emocionar. 2. (suspicion, interest) despertar.
excited [ɪk'saɪtɪd] adj emocionado(da).
excitement [ɪk'saɪtmənt] n emoción f.
exciting [ɪk'saɪtɪŋ] adj emocionante.
exclaim [ɪk'skleɪm] ◆ vt exclamar. ◆ vi: **to ~ (at)** exclamar (ante).
exclamation [ˌeksklə'meɪʃn] n exclamación f.
exclamation mark Br, **exclamation point** Am n signo m de admiración.
exclude [ɪk'skluːd] vt: **to ~ sthg/sb**

(from) excluir algo/a alguien (de).

excluding [ɪk'skluːdɪŋ] *prep* excepto, con excepción de.

exclusive [ɪk'skluːsɪv] ◆ *adj* **1.** *(high-class)* selecto(ta). **2.** *(sole)* exclusivo(va). ◆ *n (news story)* exclusiva *f*.
▶ **exclusive of** *prep* excluyendo.

excrement ['ekskrɪmənt] *n* excremento *m*.

excruciating [ɪk'skruːʃɪeɪtɪŋ] *adj* insoportable.

excursion [ɪk'skɜːʃn] *n* excursión *f*.

excuse [*n* ɪk'skjuːs, *vb* ɪk'skjuːz] ◆ *n* excusa *f*; **to make an ~** dar una excusa, excusarse. ◆ *vt* **1.** *(gen)*: **to ~ sb (for sthg/ for doing sthg)** perdonar a alguien (por algo/por haber hecho algo). **2.** *(let off)*: **to ~ sb (from)** dispensar a alguien (de). **3.** *phr*: **~ me** *(to attract attention)* oiga (por favor); *(when coming past)* ¿me deja pasar?; *(apologizing)* perdone; *Am (pardon me?)* ¿perdón?, ¿cómo?

ex-directory *adj Br* que no figura en la guía telefónica.

execute ['eksɪkjuːt] *vt (gen & COMPUT)* ejecutar.

execution [,eksɪ'kjuːʃn] *n* ejecución *f*.

executioner [,eksɪ'kjuːʃnə^r] *n* verdugo *m*.

executive [ɪg'zekjutɪv] ◆ *adj (decision-making)* ejecutivo(va). ◆ *n* **1.** *(person)* ejecutivo *m*, -va *f*. **2.** *(committee)* ejecutiva *f*, órgano *m* ejecutivo.

executive director *n* director ejecutivo *m*, directora ejecutiva *f*.

executor [ɪg'zekjutə^r] *n* albacea *m*.

exemplify [ɪg'zemplɪfaɪ] *vt* ejemplificar.

exempt [ɪg'zempt] ◆ *adj*: **~ (from)** exento(ta) (de). ◆ *vt*: **to ~ sthg/sb (from)** eximir algo/a alguien (de).

exercise ['eksəsaɪz] ◆ *n* **1.** *(gen)* ejercicio *m*. **2.** *(MIL)* maniobra *f*. ◆ *vt* **1.** *(dog)* llevar de paseo; *(horse)* entrenar. **2.** *fml (power, right)* ejercer; *(caution, restraint)* mostrar. ◆ *vi* hacer ejercicio.

exercise book *n* cuaderno *m* de ejercicios.

exert [ɪg'zɜːt] *vt* ejercer; **to ~ o.s.** esforzarse.

exertion [ɪg'zɜːʃn] *n* esfuerzo *m*.

exhale [eks'heɪl] ◆ *vt* exhalar, despedir. ◆ *vi* espirar.

exhaust [ɪg'zɔːst] ◆ *n* (U) *(fumes)* gases *mpl* de combustión; **~ (pipe)** tubo *m* de escape. ◆ *vt* agotar.

exhausted [ɪg'zɔːstɪd] *adj (person)* agotado(da).

exhausting [ɪg'zɔːstɪŋ] *adj* agotador(ra).

exhaustion [ɪg'zɔːstʃn] *n* agotamiento *m*.

exhaustive [ɪg'zɔːstɪv] *adj* exhaustivo(va).

exhibit [ɪg'zɪbɪt] ◆ *n* **1.** *(ART)* objeto *m* expuesto. **2.** *(JUR)* prueba *f* (instrumental). ◆ *vt* **1.** *fml (feeling)* mostrar, manifestar. **2.** *(ART)* exponer.

exhibition [,eksɪ'bɪʃn] *n* **1.** *(ART)* exposición *f*. **2.** *(of feeling)* manifestación *f*.

exhilarating [ɪg'zɪləreɪtɪŋ] *adj* estimulante.

exile ['eksaɪl] ◆ *n* **1.** *(condition)* exilio *m*; **in ~** en el exilio. **2.** *(person)* exiliado *m*, -da *f*. ◆ *vt*: **to ~ sb (from/to)** exiliar a alguien (de/a).

exist [ɪg'zɪst] *vi* existir.

existence [ɪg'zɪstəns] *n* existencia *f*; **to be in ~** existir; **to come into ~** nacer.

existing [ɪg'zɪstɪŋ] *adj* existente, actual.

exit ['eksɪt] ◆ *n* salida *f*. ◆ *vi fml* salir; *(THEATRE)* hacer mutis.

exodus ['eksədəs] *n* éxodo *m*.

exonerate [ɪg'zɒnəreɪt] *vt*: **to ~ sb (from)** exonerar a alguien (de).

exorbitant [ɪg'zɔːbɪtənt] *adj (cost)* excesivo(va); *(demand, price)* exorbitante.

exotic [ɪg'zɒtɪk] *adj* exótico(ca).

expand [ɪk'spænd] ◆ *vt* extender, ampliar. ◆ *vi* extenderse, ampliarse; *(materials, fluids)* expandirse, dilatarse.
▶ **expand (up)on** *vt fus* desarrollar.

expanse [ɪk'spæns] *n* extensión *f*.

expansion [ɪk'spænʃn] *n* expansión *f*.

expect [ɪk'spekt] ◆ *vt* **1.** *(gen)* esperar; **to ~ sb to do sthg** esperar que alguien haga algo; **to ~ sthg (from sb)** esperar algo (de alguien); **as ~ed** como era de esperar. **2.** *(suppose)* imaginar, suponer; **I ~ so** supongo que sí. ◆ *vi* **1.** *(anticipate)*: **to ~ to do sthg** esperar hacer algo. **2.** *(be pregnant)*: **to be ~ing** estar embarazada OR en estado.

expectancy → life expectancy.

expectant [ɪk'spektənt] *adj* expectante.

expectant mother *n* futura madre *f*.

expectation [,ekspek'teɪʃn] *n* esperanza *f*; **against all ~** OR **~s, contrary to all ~** OR **~s** contrariamente a lo que se esperaba; **to live up to/fall short of sb's ~s** estar/no estar a la altura de lo esperado.

expedient [ɪk'spiːdjənt] *fml* ◆ *adj* conveniente. ◆ *n* recurso *m*.

expedition [ˌekspɪ'dɪʃn] n 1. (journey) expedición f. 2. (outing) salida f.

expel [ɪk'spel] vt 1. (person): **to ~ sb (from)** expulsar a alguien (de). 2. (gas, liquid): **to ~ sthg (from)** expeler algo (de).

expend [ɪk'spend] vt: **to ~ sthg (on)** emplear algo (en).

expendable [ɪk'spendəbl] adj reemplazable.

expenditure [ɪk'spendɪtʃər] n (U) gasto m.

expense [ɪk'spens] n (U) gasto m; **at the ~ of** (sacrificing) a costa de; **at sb's ~** lit & fig a costa de alguien. ▶ **expenses** npl (COMM) gastos mpl.

expense account n cuenta f de gastos.

expensive [ɪk'spensɪv] adj caro(ra).

experience [ɪk'spɪərɪəns] ◆ n experiencia f. ◆ vt experimentar.

experienced [ɪk'spɪərɪənst] adj: **~ (at OR in)** experimentado(da) (en).

experiment [ɪk'sperɪmənt] ◆ n experimento m. ◆ vi: **to ~ (with/on)** experimentar (con), hacer experimentos (con).

expert ['ekspɜːt] ◆ adj: **~ (at sthg/at doing sthg)** experto(ta) (en algo/en hacer algo). ◆ n experto m, -ta f.

expertise [ˌekspɜː'tiːz] n (U) competencia f, aptitud f.

expire [ɪk'spaɪər] vi (licence, membership) caducar; (lease) vencer.

expiry [ɪk'spaɪərɪ] n (of licence) caducación f; (of lease) vencimiento m.

explain [ɪk'spleɪn] ◆ vt: **to ~ sthg (to sb)** explicar algo (a alguien). ◆ vi explicar; **to ~ sb about sthg** explicarle algo a alguien.

explanation [ˌeksplə'neɪʃn] n: **~ (for)** explicación f (de).

explicit [ɪk'splɪsɪt] adj explícito(ta).

explode [ɪk'spləud] ◆ vt (bomb) hacer explotar; (building etc) volar; fig (theory) reventar. ◆ vi lit & fig estallar.

exploit [n 'eksplɔɪt, vb ɪk'splɔɪt] ◆ n proeza f, hazaña f. ◆ vt explotar.

exploitation [ˌeksplɔɪ'teɪʃn] n (U) explotación f.

exploration [ˌeksplə'reɪʃn] n exploración f.

explore [ɪk'splɔːr] vt & vi lit & fig explorar.

explorer [ɪk'splɔːrər] n explorador m, -ra f.

explosion [ɪk'spləuʒn] n explosión f.

explosive [ɪk'spləusɪv] ◆ adj explosivo(va). ◆ n explosivo m.

exponent [ɪk'spəunənt] n 1. (supporter) partidario m, -ria f. 2. (expert) experto m, -ta f.

export [n & comp 'ekspɔːt, vb ɪk'spɔːt] ◆ n 1. (act) exportación f. 2. (exported product) artículo m de exportación. ◆ comp de exportación. ◆ vt exportar.

exporter [ek'spɔːtər] n exportador m, -ra f.

expose [ɪk'spəuz] vt lit & fig descubrir; **to be ~d to sthg** estar OR verse expuesto a algo.

exposed [ɪk'spəuzd] adj (land, house, position) expuesto(ta), al descubierto.

exposure [ɪk'spəuʒər] n 1. (to light, radiation) exposición f. 2. (MED) hipotermia f. 3. (PHOT) (time) (tiempo m de) exposición f; (photograph) fotografía f. 4. (publicity) publicidad f.

exposure meter n fotómetro m.

expound [ɪk'spaund] vt fml exponer.

express [ɪk'spres] ◆ adj 1. Br (letter, delivery) urgente. 2. (train, coach) rápido (da). 3. fml (specific) expreso(sa). ◆ adv urgente. ◆ n (train) expreso m. ◆ vt expresar; **to ~ o.s.** expresarse.

expression [ɪk'spreʃn] n expresión f.

expressive [ɪk'spresɪv] adj (full of feeling) expresivo(va).

expressly [ɪk'preslɪ] adv (specifically) expresamente.

expressway [ɪk'spreswei] n Am autopista f.

exquisite [ɪk'skwɪzɪt] adj exquisito (ta).

ext., extn. (abbr of extension) ext.

extend [ɪk'stend] ◆ vt 1. (gen) extender; (house) ampliar; (road, railway) prolongar; (visa) prorrogar. 2. (offer - welcome, help) brindar; (- credit) conceder. ◆ vi 1. (become longer) extenderse. 2. (from surface, object) sobresalir.

extension [ɪk'stenʃn] n 1. (gen & TELEC) extensión f. 2. (to building) ampliación f. 3. (of visit) prolongación f; (of deadline, visa) prórroga f. 4. (ELEC): **~ (lead)** alargador m.

extension cable n alargador m.

extensive [ɪk'stensɪv] adj (gen) extenso(sa); (changes) profundo(da); (negotiations) amplio(plia).

extensively [ɪk'stensɪvlɪ] adv extensamente.

extent [ɪk'stent] n 1. (size) extensión f. 2. (of problem, damage) alcance m. 3. (degree): **to what ~ ...?** ¿hasta qué punto ...?; **to the ~ that** (in that, in so far as) en la medida en que; (to the point *where*) hasta tal punto que; **to some/a certain ~** hasta cierto punto; **to a large** OR **great ~** en gran medida.

extenuating circumstances [ɪk-'stenjueɪtɪŋ-] *npl* circunstancias *fpl* atenuantes.

exterior [ɪk'stɪərɪər] ◆ *adj* exterior. ◆ *n* exterior *m*.

exterminate [ɪk'stɜːmɪneɪt] *vt* exterminar.

external [ɪk'stɜːnl] *adj* externo(na).

extinct [ɪk'stɪŋkt] *adj* extinto(ta).

extinguish [ɪk'stɪŋgwɪʃ] *vt fml* (*gen*) extinguir; (*cigarette*) apagar.

extinguisher [ɪk'stɪŋgwɪʃər] *n* extintor *m*.

extn. = **ext**.

extol, extoll Am [ɪk'stəul] *vt* (*merits, values*) ensalzar.

extort [ɪk'stɔːt] *vt*: **to ~ sthg from sb** (*confession, promise*) arrancar algo a alguien; (*money*) sacar algo a alguien.

extortionate [ɪk'stɔːʃnət] *adj* desorbitado(da), exorbitante.

extra ['ekstrə] ◆ *adj* (*additional*) extra (*inv*), adicional; (*spare*) de más; **take ~ care** pon sumo cuidado. ◆ *n* **1.** (*addition*) extra *m*. **2.** (*additional charge*) suplemento *m*. **3.** (CINEMA & THEATRE) extra *m* y *f*. ◆ *adv* extra; **to pay/charge ~** pagar/cobrar un suplemento.

extra- ['ekstrə] *prefix* extra-.

extract [*n* 'ekstrækt, *vb* ɪk'strækt] ◆ *n* **1.** (*from book, piece of music*) fragmento *m*. **2.** (CHEM) extracto *m*. ◆ *vt*: **to ~ sthg (from)** (*gen*) extraer algo (de); (*confession*) arrancar algo (de).

extradite ['ekstrədaɪt] *vt*: **to ~ sb (from/to)** extraditar OR extradir a alguien (de/a).

extramarital [ˌekstrə'mærɪtl] *adj* fuera del matrimonio.

extramural [ˌekstrə'mjuərəl] *adj* (UNIV) *fuera de la universidad pero organizado por ella.*

extraordinary [ɪk'strɔːdnrɪ] *adj* extraordinario(ria).

extraordinary general meeting *n* junta *f* (general) extraordinaria.

extravagance [ɪk'strævəgəns] *n* **1.** (U) (*excessive spending*) derroche *m*, despilfarro *m*. **2.** (*luxury*) extravagancia *f*.

extravagant [ɪk'strævəgənt] *adj* **1.** (*wasteful*) derrochador(ra). **2.** (*expensive*) caro(ra). **3.** (*exaggerated*) extravagante.

extreme [ɪk'striːm] ◆ *adj* extremo

(ma). ◆ *n* (*furthest limit*) extremo *m*.

extremely [ɪk'striːmlɪ] *adv* (*very*) sumamente, extremadamente.

extremist [ɪk'striːmɪst] ◆ *adj* extremista. ◆ *n* extremista *m* y *f*.

extricate ['ekstrɪkeɪt] *vt*: **to ~ sthg from** lograr sacar algo de; **to ~ o.s. from** lograr salirse de.

extrovert ['ekstrəvɜːt] ◆ *adj* extrovertido(da). ◆ *n* extrovertido *m*, -da *f*.

exultant [ɪg'zʌltənt] *adj* jubiloso(sa).

eye [aɪ] (*cont* **eyeing** OR **eying**) ◆ *n* ojo *m*; **to cast** OR **run one's ~ over sthg** echar un ojo OR un vistazo a algo; **to have one's ~ on sthg** echar el ojo a algo; **to keep one's ~s open for, to keep an ~ out for** estar atento a; **to keep an ~ on sthg** echar un ojo a algo, controlar algo. ◆ *vt* mirar.

eyeball ['aɪbɔːl] *n* globo *m* ocular.

eyebath ['aɪbɑːθ] *n* lavaojos *m inv*.

eyebrow ['aɪbrau] *n* ceja *f*.

eyebrow pencil *n* lápiz *m* de cejas.

eyedrops ['aɪdrɒps] *npl* colirio *m*.

eyelash ['aɪlæʃ] *n* pestaña *f*.

eyelid ['aɪlɪd] *n* párpado *m*.

eyeliner ['aɪˌlaɪnər] *n* lápiz *m* de ojos.

eye-opener *n inf* (*revelation*) revelación *f*; (*surprise*) sorpresa *f*.

eye shadow *n* sombra *f* de ojos.

eyesight ['aɪsaɪt] *n* vista *f*.

eyesore ['aɪsɔːr] *n* monstruosidad *f*.

eyestrain ['aɪstreɪn] *n* vista *f* cansada.

eyewitness [ˌaɪ'wɪtnɪs] *n* testigo *m* y *f* ocular.

F

f (*pl* **f's** OR **fs**), **F** (*pl* **F's** OR **Fs**) [ef] *n* (*letter*) f *f*, F *f*. ▶ **F** ◆ *n* (MUS) fa *m*. ◆ *adj* (*abbr of* Fahrenheit) F.

fable ['feɪbl] *n* (*traditional story*) fábula *f*.

fabric ['fæbrɪk] *n* **1.** (*cloth*) tela *f*, tejido *m*. **2.** (*of building, society*) estructura *f*.

fabrication [ˌfæbrɪ'keɪʃn] *n* **1.** (*lying, lie*) invención *f*. **2.** (*manufacture*) fabricación *f*.

fabulous ['fæbjuləs] *adj inf* (*excellent*) fabuloso(sa).

facade [fə'sɑːd] *n* fachada *f*.

face [feɪs] ◆ *n* **1.** (*of person*) cara *f*, rostro

m; ~ **to** ~ cara a cara; **to lose** ~ quedar mal; **to save** ~ salvar las apariencias; **to say sthg to sb's** ~ decir algo a alguien en su cara. **2.** (*expression*) semblante *m*; **to make** OR **pull a** ~ hacer muecas. **3.** (*of cliff, mountain, coin*) cara *f*; (*of building*) fachada *f*. **4.** (*of clock, watch*) esfera *f*. **5.** (*appearance, nature*) aspecto *m*. **6.** (*surface*) superficie *f*; **on the** ~ **of it** a primera vista. ◆ *vt* **1.** (*point towards*) mirar a. **2.** (*confront, accept, deal with*) hacer frente a. **3.** *inf* (*cope with*) aguantar, soportar. ◆ *vi*: **to** ~ **forwards/south** mirar hacia delante/al sur. ▶ **face down** *adv* boca abajo. ▶ **face up** *adv* boca arriba. ▶ **in the face of** *prep* (*in spite of*) a pesar de. ▶ **face up to** *vt fus* hacer frente a.

facecloth ['feɪsklɒθ] *n* Br toallita *f* (*para lavarse*).

face cream *n* crema *f* facial.

face-lift *n* (*on face*) lifting *m*; *fig* (*on building etc*) lavado *m* de cara.

face powder *n* (U) polvos *mpl* para la cara.

face-saving [-'seɪvɪŋ] *adj* para salvar las apariencias.

facet ['fæsɪt] *n* faceta *f*.

facetious [fə'siːʃəs] *adj* guasón(ona).

face value *n* (*of coin, stamp*) valor *m* nominal; **to take sthg at** ~ tomarse algo literalmente.

facility [fə'sɪlətɪ] *n* **1.** (*ability*): **to have a** ~ **for sthg** tener facilidad para algo. **2.** (*feature*) dispositivo *m*. ▶ **facilities** *npl* (*amenities*) instalaciones *fpl*; (*services*) servicios *mpl*.

facing ['feɪsɪŋ] *adj* opuesto(ta).

facsimile [fæk'sɪmɪlɪ] *n* facsímil *m*.

fact [fækt] *n* **1.** (*piece of information*) dato *m*; (*established truth*) hecho *m*; **to know sthg for a** ~ saber algo a ciencia cierta. **2.** (U) (*truth*) realidad *f*. ▶ **in fact** *conj* & *adv* de hecho, en realidad.

fact of life *n* hecho *m* ineludible. ▶ **facts of life** *npl euphemism*: **to tell sb** (**about**) **the facts of life** contar a alguien cómo nacen los niños.

factor ['fæktər] *n* factor *m*.

factory ['fæktərɪ] *n* fábrica *f*.

fact sheet *n* Br hoja *f* informativa.

factual ['fæktʃʊəl] *adj* basado(da) en hechos reales.

faculty ['fækltɪ] *n* **1.** (*gen*) facultad *f*. **2.** Am (*in college*): **the** ~ el profesorado.

fad [fæd] *n* (*of person*) capricho *m*; (*of society*) moda *f* pasajera.

fade [feɪd] ◆ *vt* descolorar, desteñir. ◆ *vi* **1.** (*jeans, curtains, paint*) descolo-

rarse, desteñirse; (*flower*) marchitarse. **2.** (*light, sound, smile*) irse apagando. **3.** (*memory, feeling, interest*) desvanecerse.

faeces Br, **feces** Am ['fiːsiːz] *npl* heces *fpl*.

fag [fæg] *n inf* **1.** Br (*cigarette*) pitillo *m*. **2.** Am *pej* (*homosexual*) marica *m*.

Fahrenheit ['færənhaɪt] *adj* Fahrenheit (*inv*).

fail [feɪl] ◆ *vt* **1.** (*exam, test, candidate*) suspender. **2.** (*not succeed*): **to** ~ **to do sthg** no lograr hacer algo. **3.** (*neglect*): **to** ~ **to do sthg** no hacer algo. **4.** (*let down*) fallar. ◆ *vi* **1.** (*not succeed*) fracasar. **2.** (*not pass exam*) suspender. **3.** (*stop functioning*) fallar. **4.** (*weaken*) debilitarse.

failing ['feɪlɪŋ] ◆ *n* (*weakness*) fallo *m*. ◆ *prep* a falta de; ~ **that** en su defecto.

failure ['feɪljər] *n* **1.** (*lack of success, unsuccessful thing*) fracaso *m*. **2.** (*person*) fracasado *m*, -da *f*. **3.** (*in exam*) suspenso *m*. **4.** (*act of neglecting*): **her** ~ **to do it** el que no lo hiciera. **5.** (*breakdown, malfunction*) avería *f*, fallo *m*.

faint [feɪnt] ◆ *adj* **1.** (*weak, vague*) débil; (*outline*) impreciso(sa); (*memory, longing*) vago(ga); (*trace, hint, smell*) leve. **2.** (*chance*) reducido(da). **3.** (*dizzy*) mareado(da). ◆ *vi* desmayarse.

fair [feər] ◆ *adj* **1.** (*just*) justo(ta); **it's not** ~! ¡no hay derecho! **2.** (*quite large*) considerable. **3.** (*quite good*) bastante bueno(na). **4.** (*hair*) rubio(bia). **5.** (*skin, complexion*) blanco(ca), claro(ra). **6.** (*weather*) bueno(na). ◆ *n* **1.** Br (*funfair*) parque *m* de atracciones. **2.** (*trade fair*) feria *f*. ◆ *adv* (*fairly*) limpio. ▶ **fair enough** *adv* Br *inf* vale.

fair-haired [-'heəd] *adj* rubio(bia).

fairly ['feəlɪ] *adv* **1.** (*moderately*) bastante. **2.** (*justly*) justamente.

fairness ['feənɪs] *n* (*justness*) justicia *f*.

fair play *n* juego *m* limpio.

fairy ['feərɪ] *n* hada *f*.

fairy tale *n* cuento *m* de hadas.

faith [feɪθ] *n* fe *f*.

faithful ['feɪθfʊl] ◆ *adj* fiel. ◆ *npl* (RELIG): **the** ~ los fieles.

faithfully ['feɪθfʊlɪ] *adv* fielmente; **Yours** ~ Br (*in letter*) le saluda atentamente.

fake [feɪk] ◆ *adj* falso(sa). ◆ *n* **1.** (*object, painting*) falsificación *f*. **2.** (*person*) impostor *m*, -ra *f*. ◆ *vt* **1.** (*results, signature*) falsificar. **2.** (*illness, emotions*) fingir. ◆ *vi* (*pretend*) fingir.

falcon ['fɔːlkən] *n* halcón *m*.

Falkland Islands ['fɔːklənd-], **Falk-**

lands ['fɔːkləndz] *npl*: **the ~** las (Islas) Malvinas.

fall [fɔːl] (*pt* **fell**, *pp* **fallen**) ◆ *vi* 1. (*gen*) caer; **he fell off the chair** se cayó de la silla; **to ~ to bits** OR **pieces** hacerse pedazos; **to ~ flat** *fig* no causar el efecto deseado. 2. (*decrease*) bajar. 3. (*become*): **to ~ ill** ponerse enfermo(ma); **to ~ asleep** dormirse; **to ~ in love** enamorarse. ◆ *n* 1. (*gen*) caída *f*. 2. (*of snow*) nevada *f*. 3. (MIL - *of city*) derrota *f*. 4. (*decrease*): **~ (in)** descenso *m* (de). 5. *Am* (*autumn*) otoño *m*. ▶ **falls** *npl* cataratas *fpl*. ▶ **fall apart** *vi* (*book, chair*) romperse; *fig* (*country, person*) desmoronarse. ▶ **fall back** *vi* (*person, crowd*) echarse atrás, retroceder. ▶ **fall back on** *vt fus* (*resort to*) recurrir a. ▶ **fall behind** *vi* 1. (*in race*) quedarse atrás. 2. (*with rent, work*) retrasarse. ▶ **fall for** *vt fus* 1. *inf* (*fall in love with*) enamorarse de. 2. (*trick, lie*) tragarse. ▶ **fall in** *vi* 1. (*roof, ceiling*) desplomarse, hundirse. 2. (MIL) formar filas. ▶ **fall off** *vi* 1. (*branch, handle*) desprenderse. 2. (*demand, numbers*) disminuir. ▶ **fall out** *vi* 1. (*hair, tooth*): **his hair is ~ing out** se le está cayendo el pelo. 2. (*friends*) pelearse, discutir. 3. (MIL) romper filas. ▶ **fall over** *vi* (*person, chair etc*) caerse. ▶ **fall through** *vi* (*plan, deal*) fracasar.

fallacy ['fæləsɪ] *n* concepto *m* erróneo, error *m*.

fallen ['fɔːln] *pp* → **fall**.

fallible ['fæləbl] *adj* falible.

fallout ['fɔːlaut] *n* (*radiation*) lluvia *f* radiactiva.

fallout shelter *n* refugio *m* atómico.

fallow ['fæləu] *adj* en barbecho.

false [fɔːls] *adj* (*gen*) falso(sa); (*eyelashes, nose*) postizo(za).

false alarm *n* falsa alarma *f*.

false teeth *npl* dentadura *f* postiza.

falsify ['fɔːlsɪfaɪ] *vt* (*facts, accounts*) falsificar.

falter ['fɔːltər] *vi* vacilar.

fame [feɪm] *n* fama *f*.

familiar [fə'mɪljər] *adj* 1. (*known*) familiar, conocido(da). 2. (*conversant*): **~ with** familiarizado(da) con. 3. *pej* (*too informal - tone, manner*) demasiado amistoso(sa).

familiarity [fə,mɪlɪˈærətɪ] *n* (U) (*knowledge*): **~ with** conocimiento *m* de.

familiarize, -ise [fə'mɪljəraɪz] *vt*: **to ~ o.s./sb with sthg** familiarizarse/familiarizar a alguien con algo.

family ['fæmlɪ] *n* familia *f*.

family credit *n* (U) *Br* ≃ prestación *f* OR ayuda *f* familiar.

family doctor *n* médico *m* de cabecera.

family planning *n* planificación *f* familiar.

famine ['fæmɪn] *n* hambruna *f*.

famished ['fæmɪʃt] *adj inf* (*very hungry*) muerto(ta) de hambre, famélico(ca).

famous ['feɪməs] *adj*: **~ (for)** famoso (sa) (por).

famously ['feɪməslɪ] *adv dated*: **to get on** OR **along ~ (with sb)** llevarse de maravilla (con alguien).

fan [fæn] ◆ *n* 1. (*of paper, silk*) abanico *m*. 2. (*electric or mechanical*) ventilador *m*. 3. (*enthusiast*) fan *m y f*, admirador *m*, -ra *f*; (FTBL) hincha *m y f*. ◆ *vt* 1. (*cool*) abanicar. 2. (*stimulate - fire, feelings*) avivar. ▶ **fan out** *vi* desplegarse en abanico.

fanatic [fə'nætɪk] *n* fanático *m*, -ca *f*.

fan belt *n* correa *f* del ventilador.

fanciful ['fænsɪful] *adj* (*odd*) rocambolesco(ca).

fancy ['fænsɪ] ◆ *vt* 1. *inf* (*feel like*): **I ~ a cup of tea/going to the cinema** me apetece una taza de té/ir al cine. 2. *inf* (*desire*): **do you ~ her?** ¿te gusta?, ¿te mola? 3. (*imagine*): **~ that!** ¡imagínate! 4. *dated* (*think*) creer. ◆ *n* (*desire, liking*) capricho *m*; **to take a ~ to** encapricharse con. ◆ *adj* 1. (*elaborate*) elaborado(da). 2. (*expensive*) de lujo, caro(ra); (*prices*) exorbitante.

fancy dress *n* (U) disfraz *m*.

fancy-dress party *n* fiesta *f* de disfraces.

fanfare ['fænfeər] *n* fanfarria *f*.

fang [fæŋ] *n* colmillo *m*.

fan heater *n* convector *m*.

fanny ['fænɪ] *n Am inf* (*buttocks*) nalgas *fpl*.

fantasize, -ise ['fæntəsaɪz] *vi* fantasear; **to ~ about sthg/about doing sthg** soñar con algo/con hacer algo.

fantastic [fæn'tæstɪk] *adj* (*gen*) fantástico(ca).

fantasy ['fæntəsɪ] *n* fantasía *f*.

fantasy football *n* ≃ la liga fantástica®.

fao (*abbr of* **for the attention of**) a/a.

far [fɑːr] (*compar* **farther** OR **further**, *superl* **farthest** OR **furthest**) ◆ *adv* 1. (*in distance, time*) lejos; **is it ~?** ¿está lejos?; **how ~ is it?** ¿a qué distancia está?; **how ~ is it to Prague?** ¿cuánto hay de aquí a Praga?; **~ away** OR **off** (*a long way away, a* *long time away*) lejos; **so** ~ por ahora, hasta ahora; ~ **and wide** por todas partes; **as** ~ **as** hasta. **2.** (*in degree or extent*): ~ **more/better/stronger** mucho más/mejor/más fuerte, **how** ~ **have you got?** ¿hasta dónde has llegado?; **as** ~ **as I know** que yo sepa; **as** ~ **as I'm concerned** por or en lo que a mí respecta; **as** ~ **as possible** en (la medida de) lo posible; ~ **and away, by** ~ con mucho; ~ **from it** en absoluto, todo lo contrario; **so** ~ hasta un cierto punto. ◆ *adj* (*extreme*) extremo(ma).

faraway ['fɑːrəweɪ] *adj* **1.** (*land etc*) lejano(na). **2.** (*look, expression*) ausente.

farce [fɑːs] *n lit & fig* farsa *f*.

farcical ['fɑːsɪkl] *adj* absurdo(da).

fare [feəʳ] *n* **1.** (*payment*) (precio *m* del) billete *m*; (*in taxi*) tarifa *f*; (*passenger*) cliente *m y f* (*de taxi*). **2.** (U) *fml* (*food*) comida *f*.

Far East *n*: **the** ~ el Extremo Oriente.

farewell [ˌfeəˈwel] ◆ *n* adiós *m*, despedida *f*. ◆ *excl literary* ¡vaya con Dios!

farm [fɑːm] ◆ *n* granja *f*, chacra *f Amer.* ◆ *vt* (*land*) cultivar; (*livestock*) criar.

farmer ['fɑːməʳ] *n* agricultor *m*, -ra *f*, granjero *m*, -ra *f*, chacarero *m*, -ra *f Amer.*

farmhand ['fɑːmhænd] *n* peón *m*.

farmhouse ['fɑːmhaʊs, *pl* -haʊzɪz] *n* granja *f*, caserío *m*.

farming ['fɑːmɪŋ] (U) *n* **1.** (AGR) (*industry*) agricultura *f*. **2.** (*act - of crops*) cultivo *m*; (*- of animals*) cría *f*, crianza *f*.

farm labourer = **farmhand**.

farmland ['fɑːmlænd] *n* (U) tierras *fpl* de labranza.

farmstead ['fɑːmsted] *n Am* granja *f*.

farm worker = **farmhand**.

farmyard ['fɑːmjɑːd] *n* corral *m*.

far-reaching [-'riːtʃɪŋ] *adj* trascendental, de amplio alcance.

farsighted [ˌfɑːˈsaɪtɪd] *adj* **1.** (*gen*) con visión de futuro. **2.** *Am* (*long-sighted*) présbita.

fart [fɑːt] *v inf* ◆ *n* (*flatulence*) pedo *m*. ◆ *vi* tirarse un pedo.

farther ['fɑːðəʳ] *compar* → **far**.

farthest ['fɑːðəst] *superl* → **far**.

fascinate ['fæsɪneɪt] *vt* fascinar.

fascinating ['fæsɪneɪtɪŋ] *adj* fascinante.

fascination [ˌfæsɪˈneɪʃn] *n* fascinación *f*.

fascism ['fæʃɪzm] *n* fascismo *m*.

fashion ['fæʃn] ◆ *n* **1.** (*clothing, style, vogue*) moda *f*; **in/out of** ~ de/pasado de moda. **2.** (*manner*) manera *f*. ◆ *vt fml*

elaborar; *fig* forjar.

fashionable ['fæʃnəbl] *adj* de moda.

fashion show *n* pase *m* or desfile *m* de modelos.

fast [fɑːst] ◆ *adj* **1.** (*rapid*) rápido(da). **2.** (*clock, watch*) que adelanta. **3.** (*dye, colour*) que no destiñe. ◆ *adv* **1.** (*rapidly*) de prisa, rápidamente. **2.** (*firmly*): **stuck** ~ bien pegado(da); ~ **asleep** profundamente dormido. ◆ *n* ayuno *m*. ◆ *vi* ayunar.

fasten ['fɑːsn] *vt* **1.** (*gen*) sujetar; (*clothes, belt*) abrochar; **he** ~**ed his coat** se abrochó el abrigo. **2.** (*attach*): **to** ~ **sthg to sthg** fijar algo a algo.

fastener ['fɑːsnəʳ] *n* cierre *m*, broche *m*; (*zip*) cremallera *f*.

fastening ['fɑːsnɪŋ] *n* (*of door, window*) cerrojo *m*, pestillo *m*.

fast food *n* (U) comida *f* rápida.

fastidious [fəˈstɪdɪəs] *adj* (*fussy*) quisquilloso(sa).

fat [fæt] ◆ *adj* **1.** (*gen*) gordo(da); **to get** ~ engordar. **2.** (*meat*) con mucha grasa. **3.** (*book, package*) grueso(sa). ◆ *n* **1.** (*gen*) grasa *f*. **2.** (*for cooking*) manteca *f*.

fatal ['feɪtl] *adj* **1.** (*serious*) fatal, funesto (ta). **2.** (*mortal*) mortal.

fatality [fəˈtælətɪ] *n* (*accident victim*) víctima *f* mortal, muerto *m*.

fate [feɪt] *n* **1.** (*destiny*) destino *m*; **to tempt** ~ tentar a la suerte. **2.** (*result, end*) final *m*, suerte *f*.

fateful ['feɪtfʊl] *adj* fatídico(ca).

father ['fɑːðəʳ] *n lit & fig* padre *m*.

Father Christmas *n Br* Papá *m* Noel.

father-in-law (*pl* **father-in-laws** or **fathers-in-law**) *n* suegro *m*.

fatherly ['fɑːðəlɪ] *adj* paternal.

fathom ['fæðəm] ◆ *n* braza *f*. ◆ *vt*: **to** ~ **sthg/sb (out)** llegar a comprender algo/ a alguien.

fatigue [fəˈtiːg] *n* fatiga *f*.

fatten ['fætn] *vt* engordar.

fattening ['fætnɪŋ] *adj* que engorda.

fatty ['fætɪ] ◆ *adj* graso(sa). ◆ *n inf pej* gordinflón *m*, -ona *f*.

fatuous ['fætjʊəs] *adj* necio(cia).

faucet ['fɔːsɪt] *n Am* grifo *m*.

fault [fɔːlt] ◆ *n* **1.** (*responsibility*) culpa *f*; **to be at** ~ tener la culpa. **2.** (*mistake, imperfection*) defecto *m*; **to find** ~ **with** encontrar defectos a. **3.** (GEOL) falla *f*. **4.** (*in tennis*) falta *f*. ◆ *vt*: **to** ~ **sb (on sthg)** criticar a alguien (en algo).

faultless ['fɔːltlɪs] *adj* impecable.

faulty ['fɔːltɪ] *adj* (*machine, system*)

defectuoso(sa); (*reasoning, logic*) imperfecto(ta).

fauna ['fɔːnə] *n* fauna *f*.

faux pas ['fəʊ'pɑː] (*pl inv*) *n* plancha *f*.

favour Br, **favor** Am ['feɪvər] ◆ *n* (*gen*) favor *m*; **in sb's ~** a favor de alguien; **to be in/out of ~ (with)** ser/dejar de ser popular (con); **to do sb a ~** hacerle un favor a alguien. ◆ *vt* 1. (*prefer*) decantarse por, preferir. 2. (*treat better, help*) favorecer. ▶ **in favour** *adv* (*in agreement*) a favor. ▶ **in favour of** *prep* 1. (*in preference to*) en favor de. 2. (*in agreement with*): **to be in ~ of sthg/of doing sthg** estar a favor de algo/de hacer algo.

favourable Br, **favorable** Am ['feɪvrəbl] *adj* (*positive*) favorable.

favourite Br, **favorite** Am ['feɪvrɪt] ◆ *adj* favorito(ta). ◆ *n* favorito *m*, -ta *f*.

favouritism Br, **favoritism** Am ['feɪvrɪtɪzm] *n* favoritismo *m*.

fawn [fɔːn] ◆ *adj* pajizo(za), beige (*inv*). ◆ *n* (*animal*) cervato *m*, cervatillo *m*. ◆ *vi*: **to ~ on sb** adular a alguien.

fax [fæks] ◆ *n* fax *m*. ◆ *vt* 1. (*send fax to*) mandar un fax a. 2. (*send by fax*) enviar por fax.

fax machine *n* fax *m*.

FBI (*abbr of* **Federal Bureau of Investigation**) *n* FBI *m*.

fear [fɪər] ◆ *n* 1. (*gen*) miedo *m*, temor *m*; **for ~ of** por miedo a. 2. (*risk*) peligro *m*. ◆ *vt* 1. (*be afraid of*) temer. 2. (*anticipate*) temerse; **to ~ (that)** ... temerse que ...

fearful ['fɪəful] *adj* 1. *fml* (*frightened*) temeroso(sa). 2. (*frightening*) terrible.

fearless ['fɪəlɪs] *adj* intrépido(da).

feasible ['fiːzəbl] *adj* factible, viable.

feast [fiːst] ◆ *n* (*meal*) banquete *m*, festín *m*. ◆ *vi*: **to ~ on** OR **off sthg** darse un banquete a base de algo.

feat [fiːt] *n* hazaña *f*.

feather ['feðər] *n* pluma *f*.

feature ['fiːtʃər] ◆ *n* 1. (*characteristic*) característica *f*. 2. (*of face*) rasgo *m*. 3. (GEOGR) accidente *m* geográfico. 4. (*article*) artículo *m* de fondo. 5. (RADIO & TV) (*programme*) programa *m* especial. 6. (CINEMA) = **feature film**. ◆ *vt* (*subj: film*) tener como protagonista a; (*subj: exhibition*) tener como atracción principal a. ◆ *vi*: **to ~ (in)** aparecer OR figurar (en).

feature film *n* largometraje *m*.

February ['februəri] *n* febrero *m*; *see also* **September**.

feces Am = **faeces**.

fed [fed] *pt* & *pp* → **feed**.

federal ['fedrəl] *adj* federal.

federation [,fedə'reɪʃn] *n* federación *f*.

fed up *adj*: **~ (with)** harto(ta) (de).

fee [fiː] *n* (*to lawyer, doctor etc*) honorarios *mpl*; **membership ~** cuota *f* de socio; **entrance ~** entrada *f*; **school ~s** (precio *m* de) matrícula *f*.

feeble ['fiːbl] *adj* 1. (*weak*) débil. 2. (*poor, silly*) pobre, flojo(ja).

feed [fiːd] (*pt* & *pp* **fed**) ◆ *vt* 1. (*gen*) alimentar; (*animal*) dar de comer a. 2. (*put, insert*): **to ~ sthg into sthg** introducir algo en algo. ◆ *vi* comer. ◆ *n* 1. (*meal*) comida *f*. 2. (*animal food*) pienso *m*.

feedback ['fiːdbæk] *n* (U) 1. (*reaction*) reacciones *fpl*. 2. (COMPUT & ELEC) realimentación *f*; (*on guitar etc*) feedback *m*.

feeding bottle ['fiːdɪŋ-] *n* Br biberón *m*.

feel [fiːl] (*pt* & *pp* **felt**) ◆ *vt* 1. (*touch*) tocar. 2. (*sense, notice, experience*) sentir; **I felt myself blushing** noté que me ponía colorado. 3. (*believe*) creer; **to ~ (that)** creer OR pensar que. 4. *phr*: **not to ~ o.s.** no encontrarse bien. ◆ *vi* 1. (*have sensation*): **to ~ hot/cold/sleepy** tener calor/frío/sueño. 2. (*have emotion*): **to ~ safe/happy** sentirse seguro/feliz. 3. (*seem*) parecer (al tacto). 4. (*by touch*): **to ~ for sthg** buscar algo a tientas. 5. (*be in mood*): **do you ~ like a drink/eating out?** ¿te apetece beber algo/comer fuera? ◆ *n* 1. (*sensation, touch*) tacto *m*, sensación *f*. 2. (*atmosphere*) atmósfera *f*.

feeler ['fiːlər] *n* antena *f*.

feeling ['fiːlɪŋ] *n* 1. (*emotion*) sentimiento *m*. 2. (*sensation*) sensación *f*. 3. (*intuition*) presentimiento *m*; **I have a** OR **get the ~ (that)** ... me da la sensación de que ... 4. (*understanding*) apreciación *f*, entendimiento *m*. ▶ **feelings** *npl* sentimientos *mpl*.

feet [fiːt] *pl* → **foot**.

feign [feɪn] *vt fml* fingir, aparentar.

fell [fel] ◆ *pt* → **fall**. ◆ *vt* (*tree*) talar. ▶ **fells** *npl* (GEOGR) monte *m*.

fellow ['feləʊ] ◆ *adj*: **~ students/prisoners** compañeros de clase/celda. ◆ *n* 1. *dated* (*man*) tipo *m*. 2. (*comrade, peer*) camarada *m* y *f*. 3. (*of society*) miembro *m*. 4. (*of college*) miembro *m* del claustro de profesores.

fellowship ['feləʊʃɪp] *n* 1. (*comradeship*) camaradería *f*. 2. (*society*) aso-

ciación f. **3.** (of society or college) pertenencia f.

felony ['felənɪ] n (JUR) delito m grave.

felt [felt] ◆ pt & pp → **feel**. ◆ n (U) fieltro m.

felt-tip pen n rotulador m.

female ['fiːmeɪl] ◆ adj (animal, plant, connector) hembra; (figure, sex) femenino (na). ◆ n **1.** (female animal) hembra f. **2.** (woman) mujer f.

feminine ['femɪnɪn] ◆ adj femenino (na). ◆ n (GRAMM) femenino m.

feminist ['femɪnɪst] n feminista m y f.

fence [fens] ◆ n valla f. ◆ vt cercar.

fencing ['fensɪŋ] n (SPORT) esgrima f.

fend [fend] vi: **to ~ for o.s.** valerse por sí mismo. ▶ **fend off** vt sep (blows) defenderse de, desviar; (questions, reporters) eludir.

fender ['fendər] n **1.** (round fireplace) guardafuego m. **2.** (on boat) defensa f. **3.** Am (on car) guardabarros m inv.

ferment [n 'fɜːment, vb fə'ment] ◆ n (unrest) agitación f. ◆ vi fermentar.

fern [fɜːn] n helecho m.

ferocious [fə'rəʊʃəs] adj feroz.

ferret ['ferɪt] n hurón m. ▶ **ferret about, ferret around** vi inf rebuscar.

ferris wheel ['ferɪs-] n noria f.

ferry ['ferɪ] ◆ n (large, for cars) transbordador m, ferry m; (small) barca f. ◆ vt llevar, transportar.

ferryboat ['ferɪbəʊt] n = **ferry**.

fertile ['fɜːtaɪl] adj fértil.

fertilizer ['fɜːtɪlaɪzər] n abono m.

fervent ['fɜːvənt] adj ferviente.

fester ['festər] vi enconarse.

festival ['festəvl] n **1.** (event, celebration) festival m. **2.** (holiday) día m festivo.

festive ['festɪv] adj festivo(va).

festive season n: **the ~** las Navidades.

festivities [fes'tɪvətɪz] npl festividades fpl.

festoon [fe'stuːn] vt engalanar.

fetch [fetʃ] vt **1.** (go and get) ir a buscar. **2.** inf (raise - money) venderse por.

fetching ['fetʃɪŋ] adj atractivo(va).

fete, fête [feɪt] n fiesta f benéfica.

fetish ['fetɪʃ] n **1.** (object of sexual obsession) fetiche m. **2.** (mania) obsesión f, manía f.

fetus ['fiːtəs] = **foetus**.

feud [fjuːd] ◆ n enfrentamiento m duradero. ◆ vi pelearse.

feudal ['fjuːdl] adj feudal.

fever ['fiːvər] n lit & fig fiebre f; **to have a ~** tener fiebre.

feverish ['fiːvərɪʃ] adj lit & fig febril.

few [fjuː] ◆ adj pocos(cas); **a ~** algunos(nas); **a ~ more potatoes** algunas patatas más; **quite a ~, a good ~** bastantes; **~ and far between** escasos, contados. ◆ pron pocos mpl, -cas fpl; **a ~ (of them)** algunos mpl, -nas fpl.

fewer ['fjuːər] ◆ adj menos. ◆ pron menos.

fewest ['fjuːəst] adj menos.

fiancé [fɪ'ɒnseɪ] n prometido m.

fiancée [fɪ'ɒnseɪ] n prometida f.

fiasco [fɪ'æskəʊ] (Br pl **-s**, Am pl **-es**) n fiasco m.

fib [fɪb] n inf bola f, trola f.

fibre Br, **fiber** Am ['faɪbər] n fibra f.

fibreglass Br, **fiberglass** Am ['faɪbəglɑːs] n (U) fibra f de vidrio.

fickle ['fɪkl] adj voluble.

fiction ['fɪkʃn] n **1.** (stories) (literatura f de) ficción f. **2.** (fabrication) ficción f.

fictional ['fɪkʃənl] adj **1.** (literary) novelesco(ca). **2.** (invented) ficticio(cia).

fictitious [fɪk'tɪʃəs] adj (false) ficticio (cia).

fiddle ['fɪdl] ◆ n **1.** (violin) violín m. **2.** Br inf (fraud) timo m. ◆ vt Br inf falsear. ◆ vi (play around): **to ~ (with sthg)** juguetear (con algo).

fiddly ['fɪdlɪ] adj Br (job) delicado(da); (gadget) intrincado(da).

fidget ['fɪdʒɪt] vi no estarse quieto(ta).

field [fiːld] n (gen & COMPUT) campo m; **in the ~** sobre el terreno.

field day n: **to have a ~** disfrutar de lo lindo.

field glasses npl prismáticos mpl.

field marshal n mariscal m de campo.

field trip n excursión f para hacer trabajo de campo.

fieldwork ['fiːldwɜːk] n (U) trabajo m de campo.

fiend [fiːnd] n (cruel person) malvado m, -da f.

fiendish ['fiːndɪʃ] adj **1.** (evil) malévolo (la). **2.** inf (very difficult) endiablado(da).

fierce [fɪəs] adj (gen) feroz; (temper) endiablado(da); (loyalty) ferviente; (heat) asfixiante.

fiery ['faɪərɪ] adj **1.** (burning) ardiente. **2.** (volatile - temper) endiablado(da); (- speech) encendido(da); (- person) apasionado(da).

fifteen [fɪf'tiːn] num quince; see also **six**.

fifth [fɪfθ] num quinto(ta); see also **sixth**.

fifty ['fɪftɪ] num cincuenta; see also **sixty**.

fifty-fifty ◆ *adj* al cincuenta por ciento; **a ~ chance** unas posibilidades de cincuenta por ciento. ◆ *adv*: **to go ~** ir a medias.

fig [fɪg] *n* higo *m*.

fight [faɪt] (*pt & pp* **fought**) ◆ *n* pelea *f*; (*fig*) lucha *f*; **to have a ~ (with)** pelearse (con); **to put up a ~** oponer resistencia. ◆ *vt* (*gen*) luchar contra; (*battle, campaign*) librar; (*war*) luchar en. ◆ *vi* **1.** (*in punch-up*) pelearse; (*in war*) luchar. **2.** *fig* (*battle, struggle*): **to ~ (for/against)** luchar (por/contra). **3.** (*argue*): **to ~ (about** OR **over)** pelearse OR discutir (por). ▶ **fight back** ◆ *vt fus* reprimir, contener. ◆ *vi* defenderse.

fighter ['faɪtə^r] *n* **1.** (*plane*) caza *m*. **2.** (*soldier*) combatiente *m y f*. **3.** (*combative person*) luchador *m*, -ra *f*.

fighting ['faɪtɪŋ] *n* (U) (*punch-up*) pelea *f*; (*on streets, terraces*) peleas *fpl*; (*in war*) combate *m*.

figment ['fɪgmənt] *n*: **a ~ of sb's imagination** un producto de la imaginación de alguien.

figurative ['fɪgərətɪv] *adj* figurado (da).

figure [Br 'fɪgə^r, Am 'fɪgjər] ◆ *n* **1.** (*statistic, number*) cifra *f*; **to be in single/double ~s** no sobrepasar/sobrepasar la decena. **2.** (*shape of person, personality*) figura *f*. **3.** (*diagram*) gráfico *m*, diagrama *m*. ◆ *vt* (*suppose*) figurarse, suponer. ◆ *vi* (*feature*) figurar. ▶ **figure out** *vt sep* (*reason, motives*) figurarse; (*problem etc*) resolver.

figurehead ['fɪgəhed] *n* (*leader without real power*) testaferro *m*.

figure of speech *n* forma *f* de hablar.

Fiji ['fiːdʒiː] *n* Fiyi.

file [faɪl] ◆ *n* **1.** (*folder*) carpeta *f*. **2.** (*report*) expediente *m*; **on ~, on the ~s** archivado. **3.** (COMPUT) fichero *m*. **4.** (*tool*) lima *f*. **5.** (*line*): **in single ~** en fila india. ◆ *vt* **1.** (*put in file*) archivar. **2.** (JUR) presentar. **3.** (*shape, smoothe*) limar. ◆ *vi* (*walk in single file*) ir en fila.

filet Am = **fillet**.

filing cabinet ['faɪlɪŋ-] *n* archivo *m*, fichero *m*.

Filipino [ˌfɪlɪ'piːnəʊ] (*pl* **-s**) ◆ *adj* filipino(na). ◆ *n* filipino *m*, -na *f*.

fill [fɪl] ◆ *vt* **1.** (*gen*): **to ~ sthg (with)** llenar algo (de). **2.** (*gap, hole, crack*) rellenar; (*tooth*) empastar. **3.** (*need, vacancy etc*) cubrir. ◆ *n*: **to eat one's ~** comer hasta hartarse. ▶ **fill in** ◆ *vt sep* **1.** (*complete*) rellenar. **2.** (*inform*): **to ~ sb in (on**

poner a alguien al corriente (de). ◆ *vi* (*substitute*): **to ~ in (for sb)** sustituir (a alguien). ▶ **fill out** *vt sep* (*complete*) rellenar. ▶ **fill up** ◆ *vt sep* llenar (hasta arriba). ◆ *vi* llenarse.

fillet Br, **filet** Am ['fɪlɪt] *n* filete *m*.

fillet steak *n* filete *m* (de carne).

filling ['fɪlɪŋ] ◆ *adj* (*satisfying*) que llena mucho. ◆ *n* **1.** (*in tooth*) empaste *m*. **2.** (*in cake, sandwich*) relleno *m*.

filling station *n* estación *f* de servicio.

film [fɪlm] ◆ *n* **1.** (*gen*) película *f*. **2.** (U) (*footage*) escenas *fpl* filmadas. ◆ *vt & vi* filmar, rodar.

film star *n* estrella *f* de cine.

Filofax® ['faɪləʊfæks] *n* agenda *f* (de hojas recambiables).

filter ['fɪltə^r] ◆ *n* filtro *m*. ◆ *vt* (*purify*) filtrar.

filter coffee *n* café *m* de filtro.

filter lane *n* Br carril *m* de giro.

filter-tipped [-'tɪpt] *adj* con filtro.

filth [fɪlθ] *n* (U) **1.** (*dirt*) suciedad *f*. **2.** (*obscenity*) obscenidades *fpl*.

filthy ['fɪlθɪ] *adj* **1.** (*very dirty*) mugriento(ta), sucísimo(ma). **2.** (*obscene*) obsceno(na).

fin [fɪn] *n* (*on fish*) aleta *f*.

final ['faɪnl] ◆ *adj* **1.** (*last*) último(ma). **2.** (*at end*) final. **3.** (*definitive*) definitivo(va). ◆ *n* final *f*. ▶ **finals** *npl* (UNIV) exámenes *mpl* finales.

finale [fɪ'nɑːlɪ] *n* final *m*.

finalize, -ise ['faɪnəlaɪz] *vt* ultimar.

finally ['faɪnəlɪ] *adv* **1.** (*at last*) por fin. **2.** (*lastly*) finalmente, por último.

finance [*n* 'faɪnæns, *vb* faɪ'næns] ◆ *n* (U) **1.** (*money*) fondos *mpl*. **2.** (*money management*) finanzas *fpl*. ◆ *vt* financiar. ▶ **finances** *npl* finanzas *fpl*.

financial [fɪ'nænʃl] *adj* financiero(ra).

find [faɪnd] (*pt & pp* **found**) ◆ *vt* **1.** (*gen*) encontrar. **2.** (*realize - fact*) darse cuenta de, descubrir. **3.** (JUR): **to be found guilty/not guilty (of)** ser declarado(da) culpable/inocente (de). ◆ *n* hallazgo *m*, descubrimiento *m*. ▶ **find out** ◆ *vi* informarse. ◆ *vt fus* **1.** (*fact*) averiguar. **2.** (*truth*) descubrir. ◆ *vt sep* (*person*) descubrir.

findings ['faɪndɪŋz] *npl* conclusiones *fpl*.

fine [faɪn] ◆ *adj* **1.** (*excellent*) excelente. **2.** (*perfectly satisfactory*): **it's/that's ~** está bien, perfecto; **how are you? – fine thanks** ¿qué tal? – muy bien. **3.** (*weather*) bueno(na); **it will be ~ tomorrow**

mañana hará buen día. **4.** (*thin, smooth*) fino(na). **5.** (*minute - detail, distinction*) sutil; (- *adjustment, tuning*) milimétrico (ca). ◆ *adv* (*very well*) muy bien. ◆ *n* multa *f.* ◆ *vt* multar.

fine arts *npl* bellas artes *fpl.*

finery ['faɪnrɪ] *n* (U) galas *fpl.*

finesse [fɪ'nes] *n* finura *f*, delicadeza *f.*

fine-tune *vt* poner a punto.

finger ['fɪŋgəʳ] ◆ *n* dedo *m.* ◆ *vt* acariciar con los dedos.

fingernail ['fɪŋgəneɪl] *n* uña *f* (*de las manos*).

fingerprint ['fɪŋgəprɪnt] *n* huella *f* dactilar OR digital.

fingertip ['fɪŋgətɪp] *n* punta *f* OR yema *f* del dedo.

finicky ['fɪnɪkɪ] *adj pej* (*person*) melindroso(sa); (*task*) delicado(da).

finish ['fɪnɪʃ] ◆ *n* **1.** (*end*) final *m.* **2.** (*surface texture*) acabado *m.* ◆ *vt:* **to ~ sthg/doing sthg** acabar algo/de hacer algo, terminar algo/de hacer algo. ◆ *vi* acabar, terminar. ▶ **finish off** *vt sep* acabar OR terminar del todo. ▶ **finish up** *vi* acabar, terminar.

finishing line ['fɪnɪʃɪŋ-] *n* línea *f* de meta.

finishing school ['fɪnɪʃɪŋ-] *n* colegio privado donde se prepara a las alumnas de clase alta para entrar en sociedad.

finite ['faɪnaɪt] *adj* **1.** (*limited*) finito(ta). **2.** (GRAMM) conjugado(da).

Finland ['fɪnlənd] *n* Finlandia *f.*

Finn [fɪn] *n* (*person*) finlandés *m*, -esa *f.*

Finnish ['fɪnɪʃ] ◆ *adj* finlandés(esa). ◆ *n* (*language*) finlandés *m.*

fir [fɜːʳ] *n* abeto *m.*

fire ['faɪəʳ] ◆ *n* **1.** (*gen*) fuego *m*; **on ~** en llamas; **to catch ~** incendiarse; **to open ~ (on sb)** abrir fuego (contra alguien); **to set ~ to** prender fuego a. **2.** (*blaze*) incendio *m.* **3.** Br (*heater*): **(electric/gas) ~** estufa *f* (eléctrica/de gas). ◆ *vt* **1.** (*shoot*) disparar. **2.** (*dismiss*) despedir. ◆ *vi:* **to ~ (on OR at)** disparar (contra).

fire alarm *n* alarma *f* antiincendios.

firearm ['faɪərɑːm] *n* arma *f* de fuego.

firebomb ['faɪəbɒm] *n* bomba *f* incendiaria.

fire brigade Br, **fire department** Am *n* cuerpo *m* de bomberos.

fire door *n* puerta *f* cortafuegos.

fire engine *n* coche *m* de bomberos.

fire escape *n* escalera *f* de incendios.

fire extinguisher *n* extintor *m* (de incendios).

fireguard ['faɪəgɑːd] *n* pantalla *f* (de chimenea).

firelighter ['faɪəlaɪtəʳ] *n* enciende-fuegos *m inv*, tea *f.*

fireman ['faɪəmən] (*pl* **-men** [-mən]) *n* bombero *m.*

fireplace ['faɪəpleɪs] *n* chimenea *f.*

fireproof ['faɪəpruːf] *adj* incombustible.

fireside ['faɪəsaɪd] *n:* **by the ~** al calor de la chimenea.

fire station *n* parque *m* de bomberos.

firewood ['faɪəwʊd] *n* leña *f.*

firework ['faɪəwɜːk] *n* fuego *m* de artificio. ▶ **fireworks** *npl* fuegos *mpl* artificiales OR de artificio.

firing ['faɪərɪŋ] *n* (U) (MIL) disparos *mpl.*

firing squad *n* pelotón *m* de ejecución OR fusilamiento.

firm [fɜːm] ◆ *adj* **1.** (*gen*) firme; **to stand ~** mantenerse firme. **2.** (FIN) (*steady*) estable. ◆ *n* firma *f*, empresa *f.*

first [fɜːst] ◆ *adj* primero(ra); **for the ~ time** por primera vez; **~ thing (in the morning)** a primera hora (de la mañana). ◆ *adv* **1.** (*gen*) primero; **~ of all** en primer lugar. **2.** (*for the first time*) por primera vez. ◆ *n* **1.** (*person*) primero *m*, -ra *f.* **2.** (*unprecedented event*) acontecimiento *m* sin precedentes. **3.** Br (UNIV) = sobresaliente *m.* ▶ **at first** *adv* al principio. ▶ **at first hand** *adv* de primera mano.

first aid *n* (U) primeros auxilios *mpl.*

first-aid kit *n* botiquín *m* de primeros auxilios.

first-class *adj* **1.** (*excellent*) de primera. **2.** (*letter, ticket*) de primera clase.

first floor *n* **1.** Br (*above ground level*) primer piso *m.* **2.** Am (*at ground level*) planta *f* baja.

firsthand [,fɜːst'hænd] ◆ *adj* de primera mano. ◆ *adv* directamente.

first lady *n* primera dama *f.*

firstly ['fɜːstlɪ] *adv* en primer lugar.

first name *n* nombre *m* de pila.

first-rate *adj* de primera.

firtree ['fɜːtriː] = **fir.**

fish [fɪʃ] (*pl inv*) ◆ *n* **1.** (*animal*) pez *m.* **2.** (U) (*food*) pescado *m.* ◆ *vt* pescar en. ◆ *vi* (*for fish*): **to ~ (for sthg)** pescar (algo).

fish and chips *npl* pescado *m* frito con patatas fritas.

fish and chip shop *n* Br tienda *f* de pescado frito con patatas fritas.

fishbowl ['fɪʃbəʊl] *n* pecera *f.*

fishcake ['fɪʃkeɪk] *n* pastelillo *m* de pescado.

fisherman ['fɪʃəmən] (pl -men [-mən]) n pescador m.

fish farm n piscifactoría f.

fish fingers Br, **fish sticks** Am npl palitos mpl de pescado.

fishing ['fɪʃɪŋ] n pesca f; **to go ~** ir de pesca.

fishing boat n barco m pesquero.

fishing line n sedal m.

fishing rod n caña f de pescar.

fishmonger ['fɪʃˌmʌŋgər] n pescadero m, -ra f; **~'s (shop)** pescadería f.

fish sticks Am = **fish fingers**.

fishy ['fɪʃɪ] adj 1. (smell, taste) a pescado. 2. (suspicious) sospechoso(sa).

fist [fɪst] n puño m.

fit [fɪt] ◆ adj 1. (suitable): **~ (for sthg/to do sthg)** apto(ta) (para algo/para hacer algo); **do as you think ~** haz lo que te parezca conveniente. 2. (healthy) en forma; **to keep ~** mantenerse en forma. ◆ n 1. (of clothes, shoes etc): **it's a good ~** le/te etc sienta OR va bien. 2. (bout, seizure) ataque m; **he had a ~** lit & fig le dio un ataque; **in ~s and starts** a trompicones. ◆ vt 1. (be correct size for) sentar bien a, ir bien a. 2. (place): **to ~ sthg into** encajar algo en. 3. (provide): **to ~ sthg with** equipar algo con; **to have an alarm fitted** poner una alarma. 4. (be suitable for) corresponder a. ◆ vi 1. (clothes, shoes) estar bien de talla. 2. (part - when assembling etc): **this bit ~s in here** esta pieza encaja aquí. 3. (have enough room) caber. ▶ **fit in** ◆ vt sep (accommodate) hacer un hueco a. ◆ vi 1. (subj: person): **to ~ in (with)** adaptarse a. 2. (be compatible): **it doesn't ~ in with our plans** no encaja con nuestros planes.

fitful ['fɪtful] adj irregular, intermitente.

fitment ['fɪtmənt] n mueble m.

fitness ['fɪtnɪs] (U) n 1. (health) buen estado m físico. 2. (suitability): **~ (for)** idoneidad f (para).

fitted carpet ['fɪtəd-] n moqueta f.

fitted kitchen ['fɪtəd-] n Br cocina f de módulos.

fitter ['fɪtər] n (mechanic) (mecánico m) ajustador m.

fitting ['fɪtɪŋ] ◆ adj fml conveniente, adecuado(da). ◆ n 1. (part) accesorio m. 2. (for clothing) prueba f. ▶ **fittings** npl accesorios mpl.

fitting room n probador m.

five [faɪv] num cinco; see also **six**.

fiver ['faɪvər] n Br inf (billete de) cinco libras.

fix [fɪks] ◆ vt 1. (gen) fijar; **to ~ sthg (to)** fijar algo (a). 2. (repair) arreglar, refaccionar Amer. 3. inf (rig) amañar. 4. (prepare - food, drink) preparar. ◆ n 1. inf (difficult situation): **to be in a ~** estar en un aprieto. 2. drugs sl dosis f inv. ▶ **fix up** vt sep 1. (provide): **to ~ sb up with** proveer a alguien de. 2. (arrange) organizar, preparar.

fixation [fɪk'seɪʃn] n: **~ (on OR about)** fijación f (con).

fixed [fɪkst] adj fijo(ja).

fixture ['fɪkstʃər] n 1. (furniture) instalación f fija. 2. (permanent feature) rasgo m característico. 3. (sports event) encuentro m.

fizz [fɪz] vi burbujear.

fizzle ['fɪzl] ▶ **fizzle out** vi (firework, fire) apagarse; fig disiparse.

fizzy ['fɪzɪ] adj gaseoso(sa).

flabbergasted ['flæbəgɑːstɪd] adj pasmado(da), boquiabierto(ta).

flabby ['flæbɪ] adj fofo(fa), gordo(da).

flag [flæg] ◆ n (banner) bandera f. ◆ vi decaer. ▶ **flag down** vt sep: **to ~ sb down** hacer señales a alguien para que se detenga.

flagpole ['flægpəul] n asta f (de bandera).

flagrant ['fleɪgrənt] adj flagrante.

flagstone ['flægstəun] n losa f.

flair [fleər] n don m.

flak [flæk] n (U) 1. (gunfire) fuego m antiaéreo. 2. inf (criticism) críticas fpl.

flake [fleɪk] ◆ n (of skin) escama f; (of snow) copo m; (of paint) desconchón m. ◆ vi (skin) descamarse; (paint, plaster) descascarillarse, desconcharse.

flamboyant [flæm'bɔɪənt] adj 1. (person, behaviour) extravagante. 2. (clothes, design) vistoso(sa).

flame [fleɪm] n llama f; **in ~s** en llamas.

flamingo [flə'mɪŋgəu] (pl -s OR -es) n flamenco m.

flammable ['flæməbl] adj inflamable.

flan [flæn] n tarta f (de fruta etc).

flank [flæŋk] ◆ n 1. (of animal) costado m, ijada f. 2. (of army) flanco m. ◆ vt: **to be ~ed by** estar flanqueado(da) por.

flannel ['flænl] n 1. (fabric) franela f. 2. Br (facecloth) toallita f (de baño para lavarse).

flap [flæp] ◆ n (of skin) colgajo m; (of pocket, book, envelope) solapa f. ◆ vt agitar; (wings) batir. ◆ vi (flag, skirt) ondear; (wings) aletear.

flapjack ['flæpdʒæk] n 1. Br (biscuit)

torta f de avena. **2.** Am (pancake) torta f, crepe f.

flare [fleəʳ] ◆ n (signal) bengala f. ◆ vi **1.** (burn brightly): **to ~ (up)** llamear. **2.** (intensify): **to ~ (up)** cstallar. ▶ **flares** npl Br pantalones mpl de campana.

flash [flæʃ] ◆ n **1.** (of light) destello m; (of lightning) relámpago m, refucilo m Amer. **2.** (PHOT) flash m. **3.** (of genius, inspiration etc) momento m; (of anger) acceso m; **in a ~** en un instante. ◆ vt **1.** (shine in specified direction) dirigir; (switch on briefly) encender intermitentemente. **2.** (send out) lanzar. **3.** (show - picture, image) mostrar; (- information, news) emitir. ◆ vi **1.** (light) destellar. **2.** (eyes) brillar. **3.** (rush): **to ~ by** OR **past** pasar como un rayo.

flashback ['flæʃbæk] n flashback m.

flashbulb ['flæʃbʌlb] n flash m.

flashgun ['flæʃgʌn] n disparador m de flash.

flashlight ['flæʃlaɪt] n (torch) linterna f eléctrica.

flashy ['flæʃɪ] adj inf chulo(la); pej ostentoso(sa).

flask [flɑːsk] n **1.** (thermos flask) termo m. **2.** (used in chemistry) matraz m. **3.** (hip flask) petaca f.

flat [flæt] ◆ adj **1.** (surface, ground) llano (na); (feet) plano. **2.** (shoes) bajo(ja). **3.** (tyre) desinflado(da). **4.** (refusal, denial) rotundo(da). **5.** (business, trade) flojo(ja); (voice, tone) monótono(na); (colour) soso(sa); (performance, writing) desangelado(da). **6.** (MUS) (lower than correct note) desafinado(da); (lower than stated note) bemol (inv). **7.** (fare, price) único(ca). **8.** (beer, lemonade) muerto(ta). **9.** (battery) descargado(da). ◆ adv **1.** (level): **to lie ~** estar totalmente extendido; **to fall ~** (person) caerse de bruces. **2.** (of time): **in five minutes ~** en cinco minutos justos. ◆ n **1.** (apartment) piso m, departamento m Amer. **2.** (MUS) bemol m. ▶ **flat out** adv a toda velocidad.

flatly ['flætlɪ] adv **1.** (refuse, deny) de plano, terminantemente. **2.** (speak, perform) monótonamente.

flatmate ['flætmeɪt] n Br compañero m, -ra f de piso.

flat rate n tarifa f única.

flatten ['flætn] vt **1.** (surface, paper, bumps) allanar, aplanar; (paper) alisar. **2.** (building, city) arrasar. ▶ **flatten out** ◆ vi allanarse, nivelarse. ◆ vt sep allanar.

flatter ['flætəʳ] vt **1.** (subj: person, report) adular, halagar. **2.** (subj: clothes, colour, photograph) favorecer.

flattering ['flætərɪŋ] adj **1.** (remark, interest) halagador(ra). **2.** (clothes, colour, photograph) favorecedor(ra).

flattery ['flætərɪ] n (U) halagos mpl.

flaunt [flɔːnt] vt ostentar, hacer gala de.

flavour Br, **flavor** Am ['fleɪvəʳ] ◆ n **1.** (taste) sabor m. **2.** fig (atmosphere) aire m, toque m. ◆ vt condimentar.

flavouring Br, **flavoring** Am ['fleɪvərɪŋ] n (U) condimento m.

flaw [flɔː] n (fault) desperfecto m.

flawless ['flɔːlɪs] adj impecable.

flax [flæks] n lino m.

flea [fliː] n pulga f.

flea market n rastro m.

fleck [flek] n mota f.

fled [fled] pt & pp → **flee.**

flee [fliː] (pt & pp fled) ◆ vt huir de. ◆ vi: **to ~ (from/to)** huir (de/a).

fleece [fliːs] ◆ n vellón m. ◆ vt inf (cheat) desplumar.

fleet [fliːt] n **1.** (of ships) flota f. **2.** (of cars, buses) parque m (móvil).

fleeting ['fliːtɪŋ] adj fugaz.

Fleet Street n calle londinense que antiguamente fue el centro de la prensa inglesa y cuyo nombre todavía se utiliza para referirse a ésta.

Flemish ['flemɪʃ] ◆ adj flamenco(ca). ◆ n (language) flamenco m. ◆ npl: **the ~** los flamencos.

flesh [fleʃ] n **1.** (of body) carne f; **in the ~** en persona. **2.** (of fruit, vegetable) pulpa f.

flesh wound n herida f superficial.

flew [fluː] pt → **fly.**

flex [fleks] ◆ n (ELEC) cable m, cordón m. ◆ vt flexionar.

flexible ['fleksəbl] adj flexible.

flexitime ['fleksɪtaɪm] n (U) horario m flexible.

flick [flɪk] ◆ n **1.** (of whip, towel) golpe m rápido. **2.** (with finger) toba f. ◆ vt (switch) apretar, pulsar. ▶ **flick through** vt fus hojear rápidamente.

flicker ['flɪkəʳ] vi (eyes) parpadear; (flame) vacilar.

flick knife n Br navaja f automática.

flight [flaɪt] n **1.** (gen) vuelo m. **2.** (of steps, stairs) tramo m. **3.** (of birds) bandada f. **4.** (escape) huida f, fuga f.

flight attendant n auxiliar m de vuelo, azafata f.

flight crew n tripulación f de vuelo.

flight deck n **1.** (of aircraft carrier)

cubierta f de vuelo. **2.** (*of plane*) cabina f del piloto.

flight recorder n registrador m de vuelo.

flimsy ['flɪmzɪ] adj **1.** (*dress, material*) muy ligero(ra). **2.** (*structure*) débil, poco sólido(da). **3.** (*excuse*) flojo(ja).

flinch [flɪntʃ] vi **1.** (*shudder*) estremecerse; **without ~ing** sin pestañear. **2.** (*be reluctant*): **to ~ (from sthg/from doing sthg)** retroceder (ante algo/ante hacer algo); **without ~ing** sin inmutarse.

fling [flɪŋ] (*pt & pp* **flung**) ◆ n (*affair*) aventura f amorosa. ◆ vt arrojar.

flint [flɪnt] n **1.** (*rock*) sílex m. **2.** (*in lighter*) piedra f.

flip [flɪp] ◆ vt **1.** (*turn*) dar la vuelta a; **to ~ sthg open** abrir algo de golpe. **2.** (*switch*) pulsar. ◆ n (*of coin*) papirotazo m.

flip-flop n (*shoe*) chancleta f.

flippant ['flɪpənt] adj frívolo(la).

flipper ['flɪpər] n aleta f.

flirt [flɜːt] ◆ n coqueto m, -ta f. ◆ vi (*with person*): **to ~ (with)** flirtear OR coquetear (con).

flirtatious [flɜːˈteɪʃəs] adj coqueto(ta).

flit [flɪt] vi (*bird*) revolotear.

float [fləʊt] ◆ n **1.** (*for fishing line*) corcho m. **2.** (*buoyant object*) flotador m. **3.** (*in procession*) carroza f. **4.** (*supply of change*) cambio m. ◆ vt (*on water*) hacer flotar. ◆ vi flotar.

flock [flɒk] n **1.** (*of sheep*) rebaño m; (*of birds*) bandada f. **2.** fig (*of people*) multitud f, tropel m.

flog [flɒg] vt **1.** (*whip*) azotar. **2.** Br inf (*sell*) vender.

flood [flʌd] ◆ n **1.** (*of water*) inundación f. **2.** (*of letters, people*) aluvión m, riada f. ◆ vt lit & fig: **to ~ sthg (with)** inundar algo (de).

flooding ['flʌdɪŋ] n (U) inundación f.

floodlight ['flʌdlaɪt] n foco m.

floor [flɔːr] ◆ n **1.** (*of room, forest*) suelo m; (*of club, disco*) pista f. **2.** (*of sea, valley*) fondo m. **3.** (*of building*) piso m, planta f. **4.** (*at meeting, debate*): **to give/have the ~** dar/tener la palabra. ◆ vt **1.** (*knock down*) derribar. **2.** (*baffle*) desconcertar, dejar perplejo(ja).

floorboard ['flɔːbɔːd] n tabla f (del suelo).

floor show n espectáculo m de cabaret.

flop [flɒp] n inf (*failure*) fracaso m.

floppy ['flɒpɪ] adj caído(da), flojo(ja).

floppy (disk) n disco m flexible.

flora ['flɔːrə] n flora f.

florid ['flɒrɪd] adj **1.** (*red*) rojizo(za). **2.** (*extravagant*) florido(da).

florist ['flɒrɪst] n florista m y f; **~'s (shop)** floristería f.

flotsam ['flɒtsəm] n (U): **~ and jetsam** restos mpl del naufragio; fig desechos mpl de la humanidad.

flounce [flaʊns] ◆ n (SEWING) volante m. ◆ vi: **to ~ out** salir airadamente.

flounder ['flaʊndər] vi **1.** (*move with difficulty*) debatirse. **2.** (*when speaking*) titubear.

flour ['flaʊər] n harina f.

flourish ['flʌrɪʃ] ◆ vi florecer. ◆ vt agitar. ◆ n: **to do sthg with a ~** hacer algo con una floritura.

flout [flaʊt] vt incumplir, no obedecer.

flow [fləʊ] ◆ n (*gen*) flujo m; (*of opinion*) corriente f. ◆ vi **1.** (*gen*) fluir, correr. **2.** (*hair, clothes*) ondear.

flow chart, flow diagram n organigrama m, cuadro m sinóptico.

flower ['flaʊər] ◆ n lit & fig flor f. ◆ vi lit & fig florecer.

flowerbed ['flaʊəbed] n arriate m.

flowerpot ['flaʊəpɒt] n tiesto m.

flowery ['flaʊərɪ] adj **1.** (*patterned*) de flores, floreado(da). **2.** pej (*elaborate*) florido(da). **3.** (*sweet-smelling*) con olor a flores.

flown [fləʊn] pp → **fly**.

flu [fluː] n gripe f.

fluctuate ['flʌktʃʊeɪt] vi fluctuar.

fluency ['fluːənsɪ] n soltura f, fluidez f.

fluent ['fluːənt] adj **1.** (*in foreign language*): **to be ~ in French, to speak ~ French** dominar el francés. **2.** (*style*) elocuente, fluido(da).

fluff [flʌf] n pelusa f.

fluffy ['flʌfɪ] adj (*jumper*) de pelusa; (*toy*) de peluche.

fluid ['fluːɪd] ◆ n fluido m, líquido m. ◆ adj **1.** (*flowing*) fluido(da). **2.** (*situation, opinion*) incierto(ta).

fluid ounce n = 0,03 litre, onza f líquida.

fluke [fluːk] n inf chiripa f; **by a ~** por OR de chiripa.

flummox ['flʌməks] vt Br inf desconcertar, confundir.

flung [flʌŋ] pt & pp → **fling**.

flunk [flʌŋk] vt & vi inf catear.

fluorescent [flʊəˈresnt] adj fluorescente.

fluoride ['flʊəraɪd] n fluoruro m.

flurry ['flʌrɪ] n **1.** (*shower*) ráfaga f. **2.** (*burst*) frenesí m.

flush [flʌʃ] ◆ adj (level): ~ **with** nivelado (da) con. ◆ n 1. (of lavatory) cadena f. 2. (blush) rubor m. 3. (sudden feeling) arrebato m. ◆ vt 1. (toilet) tirar de la cadena de. 2. (force out of hiding): **to ~ sb out** hacer salir a alguien. ◆ vi (blush) ruborizarse.

flushed [flʌʃt] adj 1. (red-faced) encendido(da). 2. (excited): ~ **(with)** enardecido(da) (por).

flustered ['flʌstəd] adj aturullado(da).

flute [fluːt] n (MUS) flauta f.

flutter ['flʌtər] ◆ n 1. (of wings) aleteo m; (of eyelashes) pestañeo m. 2. inf (of excitement) arranque m. ◆ vi 1. (bird) aletear. 2. (flag, dress) ondear.

flux [flʌks] n (change): **to be in a state of ~** cambiar constantemente.

fly [flaɪ] (pt flew, pp flown) ◆ n 1. (insect) mosca f. 2. (in trousers) bragueta f. ◆ vt 1. (plane) pilotar; (kite, model aircraft) hacer volar. 2. (passengers, supplies) transportar en avión. 3. (flag) ondear. ◆ vi 1. (bird, plane, person) volar. 2. (pilot a plane) pilotar. 3. (travel by plane) ir en avión. 4. (flag) ondear. ▶ **fly away** vi irse volando.

fly-fishing n pesca f con mosca.

flying ['flaɪɪŋ] ◆ adj (able to fly) volador (ra), volante. ◆ n: **I hate/love ~** odio/me encanta ir en avión; **her hobby is ~** es aficionada a la aviación.

flying colours npl: **to pass (sthg) with ~** salir airoso(sa) (de algo).

flying picket n piquete de apoyo proveniente de otra fábrica o sindicato.

flying saucer n platillo m volante.

flying squad n brigada f volante.

flying start n: **to get off to a ~** empezar con muy buen pie.

flying visit n visita f relámpago.

flyover ['flaɪ,əʊvər] n Br paso m elevado.

flysheet ['flaɪʃiːt] n doble techo m.

fly spray n matamoscas m inv (en aerosol).

FM (abbr of frequency modulation) FM f.

foal [fəʊl] n potro m.

foam [fəʊm] ◆ n 1. (bubbles) espuma f. 2. ~ **(rubber)** gomaespuma f. ◆ vi hacer espuma.

fob [fɒb] ▶ **fob off** vt sep: **to ~ sb off (with sthg)** dar largas a alguien (con algo); **to ~ sthg off on sb** endosar a alguien algo.

focal point ['fəʊkl-] n punto m focal OR central.

focus ['fəʊkəs] (pl -cuses OR -ci [-saɪ])

◆ n (gen) foco m; **in ~** enfocado; **out of ~** desenfocado. ◆ vt 1. (eyes, lens, rays) enfocar. 2. (attention) fijar, centrar. ◆ vi 1. (eyes, lens): **to ~ (on sthg)** enfocar (algo). 2. (attention): **to ~ on sthg** centrarse en algo.

fodder ['fɒdər] n forraje m.

foe [fəʊ] n literary enemigo m, -ga f.

foetus ['fiːtəs] n feto m.

fog [fɒg] n niebla f.

foggy ['fɒgɪ] adj (misty) brumoso(sa); (day) de niebla.

foghorn ['fɒghɔːn] n sirena f (de niebla).

fog lamp n faro m antiniebla.

foible ['fɔɪbl] n manía f.

foil [fɔɪl] ◆ n (U) (metal sheet) papel m aluminio OR de plata. ◆ vt frustrar.

fold [fəʊld] ◆ vt (sheet, blanket) doblar; (chair, pram) plegar; **to ~ one's arms** cruzar los brazos. ◆ vi 1. (table, chair etc) plegarse. 2. inf (collapse) venirse abajo. ◆ n 1. (in material, paper) pliegue m. 2. (for animals) redil m. ▶ **fold up** ◆ vt sep 1. (bend) doblar. 2. (close up) plegar. ◆ vi 1. (bend) doblarse. 2. (close up) plegarse. 3. (collapse) venirse abajo.

folder ['fəʊldər] n (gen) carpeta f.

folding ['fəʊldɪŋ] adj plegable; (ladder) de tijera.

foliage ['fəʊlɪdʒ] n follaje m.

folk [fəʊk] ◆ adj popular. ◆ npl (people) gente f. ◆ n (MUS) música f folklórica OR popular. ▶ **folks** npl inf (relatives) familia f.

folklore ['fəʊklɔːr] n folklore m.

folk music n música f folklórica OR popular.

folk song n canción f popular.

follow ['fɒləʊ] ◆ vt 1. (gen) seguir. 2. (understand) comprender. ◆ vi 1. (gen) seguir. 2. (be logical) ser lógico(ca); **it ~s that** se deduce que. 3. (understand) comprender. ▶ **follow up** vt sep examinar en más detalle; **to ~ sthg up with** proseguir algo con.

follower ['fɒləʊər] n partidario m, -ria f.

following ['fɒləʊɪŋ] ◆ adj siguiente. ◆ n partidarios mpl; (of team) afición f. ◆ prep tras.

folly ['fɒlɪ] n (U) (foolishness) locura f.

fond [fɒnd] adj 1. (affectionate) afectuoso(sa), cariñoso(sa). 2. (having a liking): **to be ~ of sb** tener cariño a alguien; **to be ~ of sthg/of doing sthg** ser aficionado(da) a algo/a hacer algo.

fondle ['fɒndl] vt acariciar.

font [fɒnt] n 1. (in church) pila f bautismal. 2. (COMPUT): **hard/printer/**

screen ~ grupo m de caracteres impreso/de impresora/de pantalla.

food [fu:d] n comida f.

food mixer n batidora f eléctrica.

food poisoning [-'pɔɪznɪŋ] n intoxicación f alimenticia.

food processor [-ˌprəʊsesə^r] n robot m de cocina.

foodstuffs ['fu:dstʌfs] npl comestibles mpl.

fool [fu:l] ◆ n 1. (idiot) tonto m, -ta f, imbécil m y f. 2. Br (dessert) mousse de fruta con nata. ◆ vt (deceive) engañar; (joke with) tomar el pelo a; **to ~ sb into doing sthg** embaucar a alguien para que haga algo. ◆ vi bromear. ▶ **fool about, fool around** vi 1. (behave foolishly): **to ~ about (with sthg)** hacer el tonto (con algo). 2. (be unfaithful): **to ~ about (with sb)** tontear (con alguien).

foolhardy ['fu:lˌhɑːdɪ] adj temerario (ria).

foolish ['fu:lɪʃ] adj tonto(ta).

foolproof ['fu:lpru:f] adj infalible.

foot [fʊt] (pl sense 1 feet, pl sense 2 inv OR feet) ◆ n 1. (gen) pie m; (of bird, animal) pata f; **to be on one's feet** estar de pie; **to get to one's feet** levantarse; **on ~** a pie, andando; **to put one's ~ in it** meter la pata; **to put one's feet up** descansar (con los pies en alto). 2. (unit of measurement) = 30,48 cm, pie m. ◆ vt inf: **to ~ the bill (for sthg)** pagar la cuenta (de algo).

footage ['fʊtɪdʒ] n (U) secuencias fpl.

football ['fʊtbɔːl] n 1. (game - soccer) fútbol m; (- American football) fútbol m americano. 2. (ball) balón m.

footballer ['fʊtbɔːlə^r] n Br futbolista m y f.

football ground n Br campo m de fútbol.

football player = **footballer**.

footbrake ['fʊtbreɪk] n freno m de pedal.

footbridge ['fʊtbrɪdʒ] n paso m elevado, pasarela f.

foothills ['fʊthɪlz] npl estribaciones fpl.

foothold ['fʊthəʊld] n punto m de apoyo para el pie.

footing ['fʊtɪŋ] n 1. (foothold) equilibrio m; **to lose one's ~** perder el equilibrio. 2. (basis) nivel m; **on an equal ~ (with)** en pie de igualdad (con).

footlights ['fʊtlaɪts] npl candilejas fpl.

footnote ['fʊtnəʊt] n nota f a pie de página.

footpath ['fʊtpɑːθ, pl -pɑːðz] n senda f.

footprint ['fʊtprɪnt] n huella f, pisada f.

footstep ['fʊtstep] n 1. (sound) paso m. 2. (footprint) pisada f.

footwear ['fʊtweə^r] n calzado m.

for [fɔː^r] ◆ prep 1. (indicating intention, destination, purpose) para; **this is ~ you** esto es para ti; **I'm going ~ the paper** voy (a) por el periódico; **the plane ~ Paris** (gen) el avión para OR de París; (in airport announcements) el avión con destino a París; **it's time ~ bed** es hora de irse a la cama; **we did it ~ a laugh** OR **~ fun** lo hicimos de broma OR por divertirnos; **to go ~ a walk** ir a dar un paseo; **what's it ~?** ¿para qué es OR sirve? 2. (representing, on behalf of) por; **the MP ~ Barnsley** el diputado por Barnsley; **let me do it ~ you** deja que lo haga por ti; **he plays ~ England** juega en la selección inglesa; **to work ~** trabajar para. 3. (because of) por; **a prize ~ bravery** un premio a la valentía; **to jump ~ joy** dar saltos de alegría; **~ fear of failing** por miedo a fracasar. 4. (with regard to) para; **it's not ~ me to say** no me toca a mí decidir; **he looks young ~ his age** aparenta ser más joven de lo que es. 5. (indicating amount of time, space) para; **there's no time/room ~ it** no hay tiempo/sitio para eso. 6. (indicating period of time - during) durante; (- by, in time for) para; **she cried ~ two hours** estuvo llorando durante dos horas; **I've lived here ~ three years** llevo tres años viviendo aquí, he vivido aquí (durante) tres años; **I've worked here ~ years** trabajo aquí desde hace años; **I'll do it ~ tomorrow** lo tendré hecho para mañana. 7. (indicating distance) en; **there were roadworks ~ 50 miles** había obras en 50 millas; **we walked ~ miles** andamos millas y millas. 8. (indicating particular occasion) para; **I got it ~ my birthday** me lo regalaron para OR por mi cumpleaños; **~ the first time** por vez primera. 9. (indicating amount of money, price) por; **I bought/sold it ~ £10** lo compré/vendí por 10 libras; **they're 50p ~ ten** son a 50 peniques cada diez. 10. (in favour of, in support of) a favor de, por; **to vote ~ sthg/sb** votar por algo/a alguien; **to be all ~ sthg** estar completamente a favor de algo. 11. (in ratios) por. 12. (indicating meaning): **P ~ Peter** P de Pedro; **what's the Greek ~ 'mother'?** ¿cómo se dice 'madre' en griego? ◆ conj fml (as, since) ya que. ▶ **for all** ◆ prep 1. (in spite of) a pesar de; **~ all your moaning** a pesar de lo mucho que te quejas. 2. (considering *how little*) para; ~ **all the good it has done me** para lo que me ha servido. ♦ *conj:* ~ **all I care, she could be dead** por mí, como si se muere; ~ **all I know** por lo que yo sé, que yo sepa.

forage ['fɒrɪdʒ] *vi* (*search*): **to ~ (for sthg)** buscar (algo).

foray ['fɒreɪ] *n lit & fig:* ~ **(into)** incursión *f* (en).

forbad [fə'bæd], **forbade** [fə'beɪd] *pt* → **forbid**.

forbid [fə'bɪd] (*pt* -**bade** OR -**bad**, *pp* **forbid** OR -**bidden**) *vt:* **to ~ sb (to do sthg)** prohibir a alguien (hacer algo).

forbidden [fə'bɪdn] *adj* prohibido(da).

forbidding [fə'bɪdɪŋ] *adj* (*building, landscape*) inhóspito(ta); (*person, expression*) severo(ra), austero(ra).

force [fɔːs] ♦ *n* fuerza *f;* **sales ~** personal *m* de ventas; **security ~s** fuerzas *fpl* de seguridad; **by ~** a la fuerza; **to be in/come into ~** estar/entrar en vigor; **in ~** (*in large numbers*) en masa, en gran número. ♦ *vt* forzar; **to ~ sb to do sthg** (*gen*) forzar a alguien a hacer algo; (*subj: event, circumstances*) obligar a alguien a hacer algo. ▶ **forces** *npl:* **the ~s** las fuerzas armadas; **to join ~s (with)** unirse (con).

force-feed *vt* alimentar a la fuerza.

forceful ['fɔːsful] *adj* (*person, impression*) fuerte; (*support, recommendation*) enérgico(ca); (*speech, idea, argument*) contundente.

forceps ['fɔːseps] *npl* fórceps *m inv.*

forcibly ['fɔːsəblɪ] *adv* 1. (*using physical force*) por la fuerza. 2. (*remind*) vivamente; (*express, argue, recommend*) enérgicamente.

ford [fɔːd] *n* vado *m.*

fore [fɔːr] *n:* **to come to the ~** empezar a destacar, emerger.

forearm ['fɔːrɑːm] *n* antebrazo *m.*

foreboding [fɔː'bəudɪŋ] *n* 1. (*presentiment*) presagio *m.* 2. (*apprehension*) miedo *m.*

forecast ['fɔːkɑːst] (*pt & pp* **forecast** OR -**ed**) ♦ *n* (*prediction*) predicción *f,* previsión *f;* (*of weather*) pronóstico *m.* ♦ *vt* (*predict*) predecir; (*weather*) pronosticar.

foreclose [fɔː'kləuz] ♦ *vi:* **to ~ on sb** privar a alguien del derecho a redimir su hipoteca. ♦ *vt* ejecutar.

forecourt ['fɔːkɔːt] *n* patio *m.*

forefinger ['fɔːfɪŋgər] *n* (dedo *m*) índice *m.*

forefront ['fɔːfrʌnt] *n:* **in** OR **at the ~ of**

en OR **a la vanguardia de.**

forego [fɔː'gəu] = **forgo.**

foregone conclusion ['fɔːgɒn-] *n:* **it's a ~** es un resultado inevitable.

foreground ['fɔːgraund] *n* primer plano *m.*

forehand ['fɔːhænd] *n* (*stroke*) golpe *m* natural, drive *m.*

forehead ['fɔːhed] *n* frente *f.*

foreign ['fɒrən] *adj* 1. (*from abroad*) extranjero(ra). 2. (*external - policy*) exterior; (- *correspondent, holiday*) en el extranjero. 3. (*unwanted, harmful*) extraño(ña). 4. (*alien, untypical*): ~ **(to sb/sthg)** ajeno (na) (a alguien/algo).

foreign affairs *npl* asuntos *mpl* exteriores.

foreign currency *n* (U) divisa *f.*

foreigner ['fɒrənər] *n* extranjero *m,* -ra *f.*

foreign minister *n* ministro *m,* -tra *f* de asuntos exteriores.

Foreign Office *n* Br: **the ~** el Ministerio de Asuntos Exteriores británico.

Foreign Secretary *n* Br Ministro *m,* -tra *f* de Asuntos Exteriores.

foreleg ['fɔːleg] *n* pata *f* delantera.

foreman ['fɔːmən] (*pl* -**men** [-mən]) *n* 1. (*of workers*) capataz *m.* 2. (*of jury*) presidente *m.*

foremost ['fɔːməust] ♦ *adj* primero (ra). ♦ *adv:* **first and ~** ante todo.

forensic [fə'rensɪk] *adj* forense.

forensic science *n* ciencia *f* forense.

forerunner [fɔː'rʌnər] *n* (*precursor*) precursor *m,* -ra *f.*

foresee [fɔː'siː] (*pt* -**saw** [-sɔː], *pp* -**seen**) *vt* prever.

foreseeable [fɔː'siːəbl] *adj* previsible; **for/in the ~ future** en un futuro próximo.

foreseen [fɔː'siːn] *pp* → **foresee.**

foreshadow [fɔː'ʃædəu] *vt* presagiar.

foresight ['fɔːsaɪt] *n* (U) previsión *f.*

forest ['fɒrɪst] *n* bosque *m.*

forestall [fɔː'stɔːl] *vt* anticiparse a.

forestry ['fɒrɪstrɪ] *n* silvicultura *f.*

foretaste ['fɔːteɪst] *n* anticipo *m.*

foretell [fɔː'tel] (*pt & pp* -**told**) *vt* predecir.

forever [fə'revər] *adv* 1. (*eternally*) para siempre. 2. *inf* (*incessantly*) siempre, continuamente.

forewarn [fɔː'wɔːn] *vt* prevenir.

foreword ['fɔːwɜːd] *n* prefacio *m.*

forfeit ['fɔːfɪt] ♦ *n* precio *m;* (*in game*) prenda *f.* ♦ *vt* renunciar a, perder.

forgave [fə'geɪv] *pt* → **forgive.**

forge [fɔːdʒ] ◆ *n* fragua *f.* ◆ *vt* **1.** (*gen*) fraguar. **2.** (*falsify*) falsificar. ▶ **forge ahead** *vi* hacer grandes progresos.

forger ['fɔːdʒə^r] *n* falsificador *m*, -ra *f.*

forgery ['fɔːdʒərɪ] *n* falsificación *f.*

forget [fə'get] (*pt* -**got**, *pp* -**gotten**) ◆ *vt*: **to ~** (**to do sthg**) olvidar (hacer algo). ◆ *vi*: **to ~** (**about sthg**) olvidarse (de algo).

forgetful [fə'getful] *adj* olvidadizo (za).

forget-me-not *n* nomeolvides *m inv.*

forgive [fə'gɪv] (*pt* -**gave**, *pp* -**given**) *vt*: **to ~ sb** (**for sthg/for doing sthg**) perdonar a alguien (algo/por haber hecho algo).

forgiveness [fə'gɪvnɪs] *n* perdón *m.*

forgo [fɔː'gəʊ] (*pt* -**went**, *pp* -**gone** [-'gɒn]) *vt* sacrificar, renunciar a.

forgot [fə'gɒt] *pt* → **forget**.

forgotten [fə'gɒtn] *pp* → **forget**.

fork [fɔːk] ◆ *n* **1.** (*for food*) tenedor *m.* **2.** (*for gardening*) horca *f.* **3.** (*in road etc*) bifurcación *f.* ◆ *vi* bifurcarse. ▶ **fork out** *inf vi*: **to ~ out for sthg** soltar pelas para algo.

forklift truck ['fɔːklɪft-] *n* carretilla *f* elevadora.

forlorn [fə'lɔːn] *adj* **1.** (*person, expression*) consternado(da). **2.** (*place, landscape*) desolado(da). **3.** (*hope, attempt*) desesperado(da).

form [fɔːm] ◆ *n* **1.** (*shape, type*) forma *f*; **in the ~ of** en forma de. **2.** (*fitness*): **on ~** Br, **in ~** Am en forma; **off ~** en baja forma. **3.** (*document*) impreso *m*, formulario *m.* **4.** (*figure - of person*) figura *f.* **5.** Br (*class*) clase *f.* ◆ *vt* formar; (*plan*) concebir; (*impression, idea*) formarse. ◆ *vi* formarse.

formal ['fɔːml] *adj* **1.** (*gen*) formal; (*education*) convencional. **2.** (*clothes, wedding, party*) de etiqueta.

formality [fɔː'mælətɪ] *n* formalidad *f.*

format ['fɔːmæt] ◆ *n* (*gen* & COMPUT) formato *m*; (*of meeting*) plan *m.* ◆ *vt* (COMPUT) formatear.

formation [fɔː'meɪʃn] *n* formación *f*; (*of ideas, plans*) creación *f.*

formative ['fɔːmətɪv] *adj* formativo (va).

former ['fɔːmə^r] ◆ *adj* **1.** (*previous*) antiguo(gua); **in ~ times** antiguamente. **2.** (*first of two*) primero(ra). ◆ *n*: **the ~** el primero (la primera) /los primeros (las primeras).

formerly ['fɔːməlɪ] *adv* antiguamente.

formidable ['fɔːmɪdəbl] *adj* **1.** (*frightening*) imponente, temible. **2.** (*impres-*sive) formidable.

formula ['fɔːmjʊlə] (*pl* -**as** OR -**ae** [-iː]) *n* fórmula *f.*

formulate ['fɔːmjʊleɪt] *vt* formular.

forsake [fə'seɪk] (*pt* **forsook**, *pp* **forsaken**) *vt literary* abandonar.

forsaken [fə'seɪkn] *adj* abandonado (da).

forsook [fə'sʊk] *pt* → **forsake**.

fort [fɔːt] *n* fuerte *m*, fortaleza *f.*

forte ['fɔːtɪ] *n* fuerte *m.*

forth [fɔːθ] *adv literary* **1.** (*outwards, onwards*) hacia adelante. **2.** (*into future*): **from that day ~** desde aquel día en adelante.

forthcoming [fɔːθ'kʌmɪŋ] *adj* **1.** (*election, book, events*) próximo(ma). **2.** (*person*) abierto(ta), amable.

forthright ['fɔːθraɪt] *adj* (*person, manner, opinions*) directo(ta), franco(ca); (*opposition*) rotundo(da).

forthwith [,fɔːθ'wɪθ] *adv fml* inmediatamente.

fortified wine ['fɔːtɪfaɪd-] *n* vino *m* licoroso.

fortify ['fɔːtɪfaɪ] *vt* **1.** (MIL) fortificar. **2.** (*person, resolve*) fortalecer.

fortnight ['fɔːtnaɪt] *n* quincena *f.*

fortnightly ['fɔːt,naɪtlɪ] ◆ *adj* quincenal. ◆ *adv* quincenalmente.

fortress ['fɔːtrɪs] *n* fortaleza *f.*

fortunate ['fɔːtʃnət] *adj* afortunado (da).

fortunately ['fɔːtʃnətlɪ] *adv* afortunadamente.

fortune ['fɔːtʃuːn] *n* **1.** (*money, luck*) fortuna *f.* **2.** (*future*): **to tell sb's ~** decir a alguien la buenaventura.

fortune-teller [-,telə^r] *n* adivino *m*, -na *f.*

forty ['fɔːtɪ] *num* cuarenta; *see also* **sixty**.

forum ['fɔːrəm] (*pl* -**s**) *n lit & fig* foro *m.*

forward ['fɔːwəd] ◆ *adj* **1.** (*towards front - movement*) hacia adelante; (*near front - position etc*) delantero(ra). **2.** (*towards future*): **~ planning** planificación *f* anticipada. **3.** (*advanced*): **we're (no) further ~** (no) hemos adelantado (nada). **4.** (*impudent*) atrevido(da). ◆ *adv* **1.** (*ahead*) hacia adelante; **to go** OR **move ~** avanzar. **2.** (*in time*): **to bring sthg ~** adelantar algo. ◆ *n* (SPORT) delantero *m*, -ra *f.* ◆ *vt* (*send on*) remitir; **'please ~'** 'remítase al destinatario'.

forwarding address ['fɔːwədɪŋ-] *n* nueva dirección *f* para reenvío de correo.

forwards ['fɔːwədz] *adv* = **forward**.
forwent [fɔː'went] *pt* → **forgo**.
fossil ['fɒsl] *n* fósil *m*.
foster ['fɒstər] *vt* 1. (*child*) acoger.
2. (*idea, arts, relations*) promover.
foster child *n* menor *m* y *f* en régimen de acogimiento familiar.
foster parents *npl* familia *f* de acogida.
fought [fɔːt] *pt* & *pp* → **fight**.
foul [faʊl] ◆ *adj* 1. (*unclean - smell*) fétido(da); (- *taste*) asqueroso(sa); (- *water, language*) sucio(cia). 2. (*very unpleasant*) horrible. ◆ *n* falta *f*. ◆ *vt* 1. (*make dirty*) ensuciar. 2. (SPORT) cometer una falta contra.
found [faʊnd] ◆ *pt* & *pp* → **find**. ◆ *vt*: **to ~ sthg (on)** fundar algo (en).
foundation [faʊn'deɪʃn] *n* 1. (*organization, act of establishing*) fundación *f*. 2. (*basis*) fundamento *m*, base *f*. 3. (*make-up*): **~ (cream)** crema *f* base. ▶ **foundations** *npl* (CONSTR) cimientos *mpl*.
founder ['faʊndər] ◆ *n* fundador *m*, -ra *f*. ◆ *vi lit* & *fig* hundirse, irse a pique.
foundry ['faʊndrɪ] *n* fundición *f*.
fountain ['faʊntɪn] *n* 1. (*structure*) fuente *f*. 2. (*jet*) chorro *m*.
fountain pen *n* (pluma *f*) estilográfica *f*.
four [fɔːr] *num* cuatro *m*; **on all ~s** a gatas; *see also* **six**.
four-letter word *n* palabrota *f*, taco *m*.
four-poster (bed) *n* cama *f* de columnas.
foursome ['fɔːsəm] *n* grupo *m* de cuatro personas.
fourteen [ˌfɔː'tiːn] *num* catorce; *see also* **six**.
fourth [fɔːθ] *num* cuarto(ta); *see also* **sixth**.
Fourth of July *n*: **the ~** el cuatro de julio, día de la independencia estadounidense.
four-wheel drive *n* tracción *f* a cuatro ruedas.
fowl [faʊl] (*pl inv* OR **-s**) *n* ave *f* de corral.
fox [fɒks] ◆ *n* zorro *m*. ◆ *vt* (*perplex*) dejar perplejo(ja).
foxglove ['fɒksglʌv] *n* dedalera *f*.
foyer ['fɔɪeɪ] *n* vestíbulo *m*.
fracas ['frækɑː; Am 'freɪkəs] (Br *pl inv*, Am *pl* **fracases**) *n fml* riña *f*, gresca *f*.
fraction ['frækʃn] *n* 1. (MATH) quebrado *m*, fracción *f*. 2. (*small part*) fracción *f*.
fractionally ['frækʃnəlɪ] *adv* ligeramente.

fracture ['fræktʃər] ◆ *n* fractura *f*. ◆ *vt* fracturar.
fragile ['frædʒaɪl] *adj* frágil.
fragment ['frægmənt] *n* (*of glass, text*) fragmento *m*; (*of paper, plastic*) trozo *m*.
fragrance ['freɪgrəns] *n* fragancia *f*.
fragrant ['freɪgrənt] *adj* fragante.
frail [freɪl] *adj* frágil.
frame [freɪm] ◆ *n* 1. (*of picture, door*) marco *m*; (*of glasses*) montura *f*; (*of chair, bed*) armadura *f*; (*of bicycle*) cuadro *m*; (*of boat*) armazón *m* o *f*. 2. (*physique*) cuerpo *m*. ◆ *vt* 1. (*put in a frame*) enmarcar. 2. (*express*) formular, expresar. 3. *inf* (*set up*) tender una trampa a, amañar la culpabilidad de.
frame of mind *n* estado *m* de ánimo.
framework ['freɪmwɜːk] *n* 1. (*physical structure*) armazón *m* o *f*, esqueleto *m*. 2. (*basis*) marco *m*.
France [frɑːns] *n* Francia.
franchise ['fræntʃaɪz] *n* 1. (POL) sufragio *m*, derecho *m* de voto. 2. (COMM) concesión *f*, licencia *f* exclusiva.
frank [fræŋk] ◆ *adj* franco(ca). ◆ *vt* franquear.
frankly ['fræŋklɪ] *adv* francamente.
frantic ['fræntɪk] *adj* frenético(ca).
fraternity [frə'tɜːnətɪ] *n* 1. *fml* (*community*) cofradía *f*. 2. (*in American university*) club *m* de estudiantes. 3. (U) *fml* (*friendship*) fraternidad *f*.
fraternize, -ise ['frætənaɪz] *vi*: **to ~ (with)** fraternizar (con).
fraud [frɔːd] *n* 1. (U) (*deceit*) fraude *m*. 2. *pej* (*impostor*) farsante *m* y *f*.
fraught [frɔːt] *adj* 1. (*full*): **~ with** lleno (na) OR cargado(da) de. 2. Br (*frantic*) tenso(sa).
fray [freɪ] ◆ *vt fig* (*temper, nerves*) crispar, poner de punta. ◆ *vi* 1. (*sleeve, cuff*) deshilacharse. 2. *fig* (*temper, nerves*) crisparse. ◆ *n literary*: **to enter the ~** saltar a la palestra.
frayed [freɪd] *adj* (*sleeve, cuff*) deshilachado(da).
freak [friːk] ◆ *adj* imprevisible. ◆ *n* 1. (*strange creature - in appearance*) monstruo *m*; (- *in behaviour*) estrafalario *m*, -ria *f*. 2. (*unusual event*) anormalidad *f*. 3. *inf* (*fanatic*): **film/fitness ~** fanático *m*, -ca *f* del cine/ejercicio. ▶ **freak out** *vi inf* flipar, alucinar.
freckle ['frekl] *n* peca *f*.
free [friː] (*compar* **freer**, *superl* **freest**, *pt* & *pp* **freed**) ◆ *adj* 1. (*gen*): **~ (from** OR **of)**

libre (de); **to be ~ to do sthg** ser libre de hacer algo; **feel ~!** ¡adelante!, ¡cómo no!; **to set ~** liberar. **2.** (*not paid for*) gratis (*inv*), gratuito(ta); **~ of charge** gratis (*inv*). **3.** (*unattached*) suelto(ta). **4.** (*generous*): **to be ~ with sthg** no regatear algo. ◆ *adv* **1.** (*without payment*): **(for) ~** gratis. **2.** (*unrestricted*) libremente. **3.** (*loose*): **to pull/cut sthg ~** soltar algo tirando/cortando. ◆ *vt* **1.** (*release*) liberar, libertar; **to ~ sb of sthg** librar a alguien de algo. **2.** (*make available*) dejar libre. **3.** (*extricate - person*) rescatar; (*- one's arm, oneself*) soltar.

freedom ['fri:dəm] *n* libertad *f*; **~ from** indemnidad *f* ante or de.

freefone ['fri:fəʊn] *n* (U) Br teléfono *m* or número *m* gratuito.

free-for-all *n* refriega *f*.

free gift *n* obsequio *m*.

freehand ['fri:hænd] *adj & adv* a pulso.

freehold ['fri:həʊld] *n* propiedad *f* absoluta.

free house *n* bar no controlado por una compañía cervecera.

free kick *n* tiro *m* libre.

freelance ['fri:lɑ:ns] ◆ *adj* autónomo (ma). ◆ *adv* por libre. ◆ *n* (*trabajador m*, *-ra f*) autónomo *m*, *-ma f*.

freely ['fri:lɪ] *adv* **1.** (*readily - admit, confess*) sin reparos; (*- available*) fácilmente. **2.** (*openly*) abiertamente, francamente. **3.** (*without restrictions*) libremente. **4.** (*generously*) liberalmente.

Freemason ['fri:,meɪsn] *n* francmasón *m*, *-ona f*.

freephone ['fri:fəʊn] *n* = **freefone**.

freepost ['fri:pəʊst] *n* franqueo *m* pagado.

free-range *adj* de granja.

freestyle ['fri:staɪl] *n* (*in swimming*) estilo *m* libre.

free trade *n* libre cambio *m*.

freeway ['fri:weɪ] *n* Am autopista *f*.

freewheel [,fri:'wi:l] *vi* (*on bicycle*) andar sin pedalear; (*in car*) ir en punto muerto.

free will *n* libre albedrío *m*; **to do sthg of one's own ~** hacer algo por voluntad propia.

freeze [fri:z] (*pt* **froze**, *pp* **frozen**) ◆ *vt* **1.** (*gen*) helar. **2.** (*food, wages, prices*) congelar. **3.** (*assets*) bloquear. ◆ *vi* (*gen*) helarse. ◆ *v impers* (METEOR) helar. ◆ *n* **1.** (*cold weather*) helada *f*. **2.** (*of wages, prices*) congelación *f*.

freeze-dried [-'draɪd] *adj* liofilizado (da).

freezer ['fri:zər] *n* congelador *m*.

freezing ['fri:zɪŋ] ◆ *adj* helado(da); **it's ~ in here** hace un frío espantoso aquí. ◆ *n* = **freezing point**.

freezing point *n* punto *m* de congelación.

freight [freɪt] *n* (U) (*goods*) mercancías *fpl*, flete *m*.

freight train *n* (tren *m* de) mercancías *m inv*.

French [frentʃ] ◆ *adj* francés(esa). ◆ *n* (*language*) francés *m*. ◆ *npl*: **the ~** los franceses.

French bean *n* judía *f* verde.

French bread *n* (U) pan *m* de barra.

French dressing *n* (*in UK*) (*vinaigrette*) vinagreta *f*; (*in US*) = salsa *f* rosa.

French fries *npl* patatas *fpl* fritas.

Frenchman ['frentʃmən] (*pl* **-men** [-mən]) *n* francés *m*.

French stick *n* Br barra *f* de pan.

French windows *npl* puertaventanas *fpl*.

Frenchwoman ['frentʃ,wʊmən] (*pl* **-women** [-,wɪmɪn]) *n* francesa *f*.

frenetic [frə'netɪk] *adj* frenético(ca).

frenzy ['frenzɪ] *n* frenesí *m*.

frequency ['fri:kwənsɪ] *n* frecuencia *f*.

frequent [*adj* 'fri:kwənt, *vb* frɪ'kwent] ◆ *adj* frecuente. ◆ *vt* frecuentar.

frequently ['fri:kwəntlɪ] *adv* a menudo.

fresh [freʃ] *adj* **1.** (*gen*) fresco(ca); (*flavour, taste*) refrescante. **2.** (*bread*) del día. **3.** (*not canned*) natural. **4.** (*water*) dulce. **5.** (*pot of tea, fighting, approach*) nuevo(va). **6.** (*bright and pleasant*) alegre.

freshen ['freʃn] ◆ *vt* (*air*) refrescar. ◆ *vi* (*wind*) soplar más fuerte. ▶ **freshen up** *vi* (*person*) refrescarse, lavarse.

fresher ['freʃər] *n* Br *inf* estudiante *m* y *f* de primer año.

freshly ['freʃlɪ] *adv* recién.

freshman ['freʃmən] (*pl* **-men** [-mən]) *n* estudiante *m* y *f* de primer año.

freshness ['freʃnɪs] *n* (U) **1.** (*of food*) buen estado *m*. **2.** (*originality*) novedad *f*, originalidad *f*. **3.** (*brightness*) pulcritud *f*. **4.** (*refreshing quality*) frescor *m*. **5.** (*energy*) vigor *m*.

freshwater ['freʃ,wɔ:tər] *adj* de agua dulce.

fret [fret] *vi* preocuparse.

friar ['fraɪər] *n* fraile *m*.

friction ['frɪkʃn] *n* fricción *f*.

Friday ['fraɪdɪ] *n* viernes *m inv*; *see also* **Saturday**.

fridge [frɪdʒ] *n* nevera *f*.

fridge-freezer n Br nevera f congeladora.

fried [fraɪd] adj frito(ta).

friend [frend] n (close acquaintance) amigo m, -ga f; **to be ~s with sb** ser amigo de alguien; **to make ~s (with)** hacerse amigo (de), trabar amistad (con).

friendly ['frendlɪ] adj **1.** (person) amable, simpático(ca); (attitude, manner, welcome) amistoso(sa); **to be ~ with sb** ser amigo de alguien. **2.** (nation) amigo (ga). **3.** (argument, game) amistoso(sa).

friendship ['frendʃɪp] n amistad f.

fries [fraɪz] = French fries.

frieze [friːz] n friso m.

fright [fraɪt] n **1.** (fear) miedo m; **to take ~** espantarse, asustarse. **2.** (shock) susto m; **to give sb a ~** darle un susto a alguien.

frighten ['fraɪtn] vt asustar.

frightened ['fraɪtnd] adj asustado (da); **to be ~ of sthg/of doing sthg** tener miedo a algo/a hacer algo.

frightening ['fraɪtnɪŋ] adj aterrador (ra), espantoso(sa).

frightful ['fraɪtful] adj dated terrible.

frigid ['frɪdʒɪd] adj (sexually) frígido (da).

frill [frɪl] n **1.** (decoration) volante m. **2.** inf (extra) adorno m.

fringe [frɪndʒ] ◆ n **1.** (decoration) flecos mpl. **2.** Br (of hair) flequillo m. **3.** (edge) periferia f. **4.** (extreme) margen m. ◆ vt (edge) bordear.

fringe benefit n beneficio m complementario.

frisk [frɪsk] vt cachear, registrar.

frisky ['frɪskɪ] adj inf retozón(ona), juguetón(ona).

fritter ['frɪtər] n buñuelo m. ▶ **fritter away** vt sep: **to ~ money/time away on sthg** malgastar dinero/tiempo en algo.

frivolous ['frɪvələs] adj frívolo(la).

frizzy ['frɪzɪ] adj crespo(pa), ensortijado(da).

fro [frəʊ] adv → **to**.

frock [frɒk] n dated vestido m.

frog [frɒg] n (animal) rana f.

frogman ['frɒgmən] (pl -men) n hombre-rana m.

frogmen ['frɒgmən] pl → **frogman**.

frolic ['frɒlɪk] (pt & pp -ked, cont -king) vi retozar, triscar.

from [weak form frəm, strong form frɒm] prep **1.** (indicating source, origin, removal) de; **where are you ~?** ¿de dónde eres?; **I got a letter ~ her today** hoy me ha lle-

gado una carta suya; **a flight ~ Paris** un vuelo de París; **to translate ~ Spanish into English** traducir del español al inglés; **he's not back ~ work yet** no ha vuelto del trabajo aún; **to take sthg away ~ sb** quitarle algo a alguien. **2.** (indicating a deduction): **take 15 (away) ~ 19** quita 15 a 19; **to deduct sthg ~ sthg** deducir OR descontar algo de algo. **3.** (indicating escape, separation) de; **he ran away ~ home** huyó de casa. **4.** (indicating position) desde; **seen ~ above/below** visto desde arriba/abajo; **a light bulb hung ~ the ceiling** una bombilla colgaba del techo. **5.** (indicating distance) de; **it's 60 km ~ here** está a 60 kms. de aquí. **6.** (indicating material object is made out of) de; **it's made ~ wood/plastic** está hecho de madera/plástico. **7.** (starting at a particular time) desde; **closed ~ 1 pm to 2 pm** cerrado de 13h a 14h; **~ the moment I saw him** desde el momento en que lo vi. **8.** (indicating difference, change) de; **to be different ~** ser diferente de; **~ ... to** de ... a; **the price went up ~ £100 to £150** el precio subió de 100 a 150 libras. **9.** (because of, as a result of) de; **to die ~ cold** morir de frío; **to suffer ~ cold/ hunger** padecer frío/hambre. **10.** (on the evidence of) por; **to speak ~ personal experience** hablar por propia experiencia. **11.** (indicating lowest amount): **prices range ~ £5 to £500** los precios oscilan entre 5 y 500 libras; **it could take anything ~ 15 to 20 weeks** podría llevar de 15 a 20 semanas.

front [frʌnt] ◆ n **1.** (gen) parte f delantera; (of house) fachada f. **2.** (METEOR, MIL & POL) frente m. **3.** (on coast): **(sea) ~** paseo m marítimo. **4.** (outward appearance) fachada f. ◆ adj (gen) delantero(ra); (page) primero(ra). ▶ **in front** adv **1.** (further forward) delante. **2.** (winning) en cabeza. ▶ **in front of** prep delante de.

frontbench [ˌfrʌnt'bentʃ] n Br en la Cámara de los Comunes, cada una de las dos filas de escaños ocupadas respectivamente por los ministros del Gobierno y los principales líderes de la oposición mayoritaria.

front door n puerta f principal.

frontier ['frʌn,tɪər, Am frʌn'tɪər] n lit & fig frontera f.

front man n **1.** (of group) portavoz m y f. **2.** (of programme) presentador m.

front room n sala f de estar.

front-runner n favorito m, -ta f.

front-wheel drive n (vehicle) vehículo *m* de tracción delantera.

frost [frɒst] *n* **1.** (*layer of ice*) escarcha *f*. **2.** (*weather*) helada *f*.

frostbite ['frɒstbaɪt] *n* (U) congelación *f* (MED).

frosted ['frɒstɪd] *adj* **1.** (*glass*) esmerilado(da). **2.** Am (CULIN) escarchado(da).

frosty ['frɒstɪ] *adj* **1.** (*very cold*) de helada. **2.** (*covered with frost*) escarchado(da). **3.** *fig* (*unfriendly*) glacial.

froth [frɒθ] ◆ *n* espuma *f*. ◆ *vi* hacer espuma.

frown [fraʊn] *vi* fruncir el ceño. ▶ **frown (up)on** *vt fus* desaprobar.

froze [frəʊz] *pt* → **freeze**.

frozen [frəʊzn] ◆ *pp* → **freeze**. ◆ *adj* **1.** (*gen*) helado(da). **2.** (*preserved*) congelado(da).

frugal ['fruːgl] *adj* frugal.

fruit [fruːt] (*pl inv* OR **fruits**) *n* **1.** (*food*) fruta *f*. **2.** (*result*) fruto *m*.

fruitcake ['fruːtkeɪk] *n* pastel *m* de frutas.

fruiterer ['fruːtərər] *n* Br frutero *m*, -ra *f*; ~'s (*shop*) frutería *f*.

fruitful ['fruːtfʊl] *adj* (*successful*) fructífero(ra).

fruition [fruːˈɪʃn] *n*: **to come to** ~ (*plan*) realizarse; (*hope*) cumplirse.

fruit juice *n* zumo *m* de fruta.

fruitless ['fruːtlɪs] *adj* infructuoso(sa).

fruit machine *n* Br máquina *f* tragaperras.

fruit salad *n* macedonia *f* (de frutas).

frumpy ['frʌmpɪ] *adj* chapado(da) a la antigua.

frustrate [frʌˈstreɪt] *vt* frustrar.

frustrated [frʌˈstreɪtɪd] *adj* frustrado(da).

frustration [frʌˈstreɪʃn] *n* frustración *f*.

fry [fraɪ] ◆ *vt* (*food*) freír. ◆ *vi* (*food*) freírse.

frying pan ['fraɪɪŋ-] *n* sartén *f*.

ft. *abbr of* **foot, feet**.

fuck [fʌk] *vt & vi vulg* joder, follar, chingar *Amer*. ▶ **fuck off** *vi vulg*: ~ **off!** ¡vete a tomar por culo!

fudge [fʌdʒ] *n* (U) (*sweet*) dulce de azúcar, leche y mantequilla.

fuel [fjʊəl] ◆ *n* combustible *m*. ◆ *vt* **1.** (*supply with fuel*) alimentar. **2.** (*increase*) agravar.

fuel tank *n* depósito *m* de gasolina.

fugitive ['fjuːdʒətɪv] *n* fugitivo *m*, -va *f*.

fulfil, fulfill Am [fʊlˈfɪl] *vt* (*promise, duty, threat*) cumplir; (*hope, ambition*) realizar, satisfacer; (*obligation*) cumplir

con; (*role*) desempeñar; (*requirement*) satisfacer.

fulfilment, fulfillment Am [fʊlˈfɪlmənt] *n* **1.** (*satisfaction*) satisfacción *f*, realización *f* (de uno mismo). **2.** (*of promise, duty, threat*) cumplimiento *m*; (*of hope, ambition*) realización *f*; (*of role*) desempeño *m*; (*of requirement*) satisfacción *f*.

full [fʊl] ◆ *adj* **1.** (*filled*): ~ (**of**) lleno(na) (de); **I'm** ~! (*after meal*) ¡no puedo más! **2.** (*complete - recovery, employment, control*) pleno(na); (- *name, price, fare*) completo (ta); (- *explanation, information*) detallado (da); (- *member, professor*) numerario(ria). **3.** (*maximum - volume, power etc*) máximo (ma). **4.** (*plump*) grueso(sa). **5.** (*wide*) holgado(da), amplio(plia). ◆ *adv* (*very*): **to know sthg** ~ **well** saber algo perfectamente. ◆ *n*: **in** ~ íntegramente.

full-blown [-ˈbləʊn] *adj* (*gen*) auténtico (ca); (AIDS) desarrollado(da).

full board *n* pensión *f* completa.

full-fledged Am = **fully-fledged**.

full moon *n* luna *f* llena.

full-scale *adj* **1.** (*life-size*) de tamaño natural. **2.** (*complete*) a gran escala.

full stop *n* punto *m*.

full time *n* Br (SPORT) final *m* del (tiempo reglamentario del) partido. ▶ **full-time** ◆ *adj* de jornada completa. ◆ *adv* a tiempo completo.

full up *adj* lleno(na).

fully ['fʊlɪ] *adv* **1.** (*completely*) completamente. **2.** (*thoroughly*) detalladamente.

fully-fledged Br, **full-fledged** Am [-ˈfledʒd] *adj* *fig* hecho(cha) y derecho (cha); (*member*) de pleno derecho.

fulsome ['fʊlsəm] *adj* exagerado(da).

fumble ['fʌmbl] *vi* hurgar; **to** ~ **for sthg** (*for key, light switch*) buscar algo a tientas; (*for words*) buscar algo titubeando.

fume [fjuːm] *vi* (*with anger*) rabiar. ▶ **fumes** *npl* humo *m*.

fumigate ['fjuːmɪgeɪt] *vt* fumigar.

fun [fʌn] *n* (U) **1.** (*pleasure, amusement*) diversión *f*; **to have** ~ divertirse, pasarlo bien; **have** ~! ¡que te diviertas!; **for** ~, **for the** ~ **of it** por diversión. **2.** (*playfulness*): **he's full of** ~ le encanta todo lo que sea diversión. **3.** (*at sb else's expense*): **to make** ~ **of sb**, **to poke** ~ **at sb** reírse OR burlarse de alguien.

function ['fʌŋkʃn] ◆ *n* **1.** (*gen* & MATH) función *f*. **2.** (*way of working*) funcionamiento *m*. **3.** (*formal social event*) acto *m*, ceremonia *f*. ◆ *vi* funcionar; **to** ~ **as** hacer de, actuar como.

gal.

functional [ˈfʌŋkʃnəl] *adj* 1. (*practical*) funcional. 2. (*operational*) en funcionamiento.

fund [fʌnd] ◆ *n* fondo *m*. ◆ *vt* financiar. ▶ **funds** *npl* fondos *mpl*.

fundamental [ˌfʌndəˈmentl] *adj*: ~ (**to**) fundamental (para).

funding [ˈfʌndɪŋ] *n* financiación *f*.

funeral [ˈfjuːnərəl] *n* funeral *m*.

funeral parlour *n* funeraria *f*.

funfair [ˈfʌnfeər] *n* parque *m* de atracciones.

fungus [ˈfʌŋgəs] (*pl* **-gi** [-gaɪ] OR **-guses**) *n* hongo *m*.

funnel [ˈfʌnl] *n* 1. (*for pouring*) embudo *m*. 2. (*on ship*) chimenea *f*.

funny [ˈfʌnɪ] *adj* 1. (*amusing*) divertido (da), gracioso(sa). 2. (*odd*) raro(ra). 3. (*ill*) pachucho(cha).

fur [fɜːr] *n* 1. (*on animal*) pelaje *m*, pelo *m*. 2. (*garment*) (prenda *f* de) piel *f*.

fur coat *n* abrigo *m* de piel OR pieles.

furious [ˈfjʊərɪəs] *adj* 1. (*very angry*) furioso(sa). 2. (*frantic*) frenético(ca).

furlong [ˈfɜːlɒŋ] *n* 201,17 *metros*.

furnace [ˈfɜːnɪs] *n* horno *m*.

furnish [ˈfɜːnɪʃ] *vt* 1. (*fit out*) amueblar. 2. *fml* (*provide - goods, explanation*) proveer; (*- proof*) aducir; **to ~ sb with sthg** proporcionar algo a alguien.

furnished [ˈfɜːnɪʃt] *adj* amueblado(da).

furnishings [ˈfɜːnɪʃɪŋz] *npl* mobiliario *m*.

furniture [ˈfɜːnɪtʃər] *n* (U) muebles *mpl*, mobiliario *m*; **a piece of ~** un mueble.

furrow [ˈfʌrəʊ] *n lit & fig* surco *m*.

furry [ˈfɜːrɪ] *adj* peludo(da).

further [ˈfɜːðər] ◆ *compar* → **far**. ◆ *adv* 1. (*in distance*) más lejos; **how much ~ is it?** ¿cuánto queda (de camino)?; **~ on** más adelante. 2. (*in degree, extent, time*) más; **~ on/back** más adelante/atrás. 3. (*in addition*) además. ◆ *adj* otro(tra); **until ~ notice** hasta nuevo aviso. ◆ *vt* promover, fomentar.

further education *n Br estudios postescolares no universitarios.*

furthermore [ˌfɜːðəˈmɔːr] *adv* lo que es más.

furthest [ˈfɜːðɪst] ◆ *superl* → **far**. ◆ *adj* 1. (*in distance*) más lejano(na). 2. (*greatest - in degree, extent*) extremo(ma). ◆ *adv* 1. (*in distance*) más lejos. 2. (*to greatest degree, extent*) más.

furtive [ˈfɜːtɪv] *adj* furtivo(va).

fury [ˈfjʊərɪ] *n* furia *f*.

fuse *esp Br*, **fuze** *Am* [fjuːz] ◆ *n* 1.

(ELEC) fusible *m*, plomo *m*. 2. (*of bomb, firework*) mecha *f*. ◆ *vt* fundir. ◆ *vi* (*gen & ELEC*) fundirse.

fuse-box *n* caja *f* de fusibles.

fused [fjuːzd] *adj* (*fitted with a fuse*) con fusible.

fuselage [ˈfjuːzəlɑːʒ] *n* fuselaje *m*.

fuss [fʌs] ◆ *n* (U) 1. (*excitement, anxiety*) jaleo *m*; **to make a ~** armar un escándalo. 2. (*complaints*) protestas *fpl*. ◆ *vi* apurarse, angustiarse.

fussy [ˈfʌsɪ] *adj* 1. (*fastidious*) quisquilloso(sa). 2. (*over-decorated*) recargado (da).

futile [ˈfjuːtaɪl] *adj* inútil, vano(na).

futon [ˈfuːtɒn] *n* futón *m*.

future [ˈfjuːtʃər] ◆ *n* futuro *m*; **in ~** de ahora en adelante; **in the ~** en el futuro; **~ (tense)** futuro *m*. ◆ *adj* futuro(ra).

fuze *Am* = **fuse**.

fuzzy [ˈfʌzɪ] *adj* 1. (*hair*) rizado(da), ensortijado(da). 2. (*photo, image*) borroso(sa).

G

g¹ (*pl* **g's** OR **gs**), **G** (*pl* **G's** OR **Gs**) [dʒiː] *n* (*letter*) g *f*, G *f*. ▶ **G** *n* 1. (MUS) sol *m*. 2. (*abbr of* **good**) B.

g² *n* (*abbr of* **gram**) g. *m*.

gab [gæb] *n* → **gift**.

gabble [ˈgæbl] ◆ *vt & vi* farfullar, balbucir. ◆ *n* farfulleo *m*.

gable [ˈgeɪbl] *n* aguilón *m*.

gadget [ˈgædʒɪt] *n* artilugio *m*.

Gaelic [ˈgeɪlɪk] *n* (*language*) gaélico *m*.

gaffe [gæf] *n* metedura *f* de pata.

gag [gæg] ◆ *n* 1. (*for mouth*) mordaza *f*. 2. *inf* (*joke*) chiste *m*. ◆ *vt* amordazar.

gage *Am* = **gauge**.

gaiety [ˈgeɪətɪ] *n* alegría *f*, regocijo *m*.

gaily [ˈgeɪlɪ] *adv* alegremente.

gain [geɪn] ◆ *n* 1. (*profit*) beneficio *m*, ganancia *f*. 2. (*improvement*) mejora *f*. ◆ *vt* (*gen*) ganar. ◆ *vi* 1. (*advance*): **to ~ in sthg** ganar algo. 2. (*benefit*): **to ~ (from** OR **by)** beneficiarse (de). 3. (*watch, clock*) adelantarse. ▶ **gain on** *vt fus* ganar terreno a.

gait [geɪt] *n* forma *f* de andar.

gal. *abbr of* **gallon**.

gala ['gɑːlə] n (celebration) fiesta f.

galaxy ['gæləksɪ] n galaxia f.

gale [geɪl] n vendaval m.

gall [gɔːl] n (nerve): **to have the ~ to do sthg** tener el descaro de hacer algo.

gallant [sense 1 'gælənt, sense 2 gə'lænt, 'gælænt] adj 1. (courageous) valiente, valeroso(sa). 2. (polite to women) galante.

gall bladder n vesícula f biliar.

gallery ['gælərɪ] n 1. (for art) galería f. 2. (in courtroom, parliament) tribuna f. 3. (in theatre) paraíso m.

galley ['gælɪ] (pl galleys) n 1. (ship) galera f. 2. (kitchen) cocina f.

galling ['gɔːlɪŋ] adj indignante.

gallivant [,gælɪ'vænt] vi inf andar por ahí holgazaneando.

gallon ['gælən] n = 4,546 litros, galón m.

gallop ['gæləp] ♦ n galope m. ♦ vi lit & fig galopar.

gallows ['gæləʊz] (pl inv) n horca f.

gallstone ['gɔːlstəʊn] n cálculo m biliar.

galore [gə'lɔːr] adj en abundancia.

galvanize, -ise ['gælvənaɪz] vt 1. (TECH) galvanizar. 2. (impel): **to ~ sb into action** impulsar a alguien a la acción.

gambit ['gæmbɪt] n táctica f.

gamble ['gæmbl] ♦ n (calculated risk) riesgo m, empresa f arriesgada. ♦ vi 1. (bet) jugar; **to ~ on** (race etc) apostar a; (stock exchange) jugar a. 2. (take risk): **to ~ on** contar de antemano con que.

gambler ['gæmblər] n jugador m, -ra f.

gambling ['gæmblɪŋ] n (U) juego m.

game [geɪm] ♦ n 1. (gen) juego m. 2. (of football, rugby etc) partido m; (of snooker, chess, cards) partida f. 3. (hunted animals) caza f. ♦ adj 1. (brave) valiente. 2. (willing): **~ (for sthg/to do sthg)** dispuesto(ta) (a algo/a hacer algo). ▶ **games** ♦ n (U) (at school) deportes mpl. ♦ npl (sporting contest) juegos mpl.

gamekeeper ['geɪm,kiːpər] n guarda m de caza.

game reserve n coto m de caza.

gammon ['gæmən] n jamón m.

gamut ['gæmət] n gama f.

gang [gæŋ] n 1. (of criminals) banda f. 2. (of young people) pandilla f. ▶ **gang up** vi inf: **to ~ up (on sb)** confabularse (contra alguien).

gangland ['gæŋlænd] n (U) bajos fondos mpl, mundo m del hampa.

gangrene ['gæŋgriːn] n gangrena f.

gangster ['gæŋstər] n gángster m.

gangway ['gæŋweɪ] n Br (aisle) pasillo m.

gantry ['gæntrɪ] n pórtico m (para grúas).

gaol [dʒeɪl] Br = **jail**.

gap [gæp] n 1. (empty space) hueco m; (in traffic, trees, clouds) claro m; (in text) espacio m en blanco. 2. (interval) intervalo m. 3. fig (in knowledge, report) laguna f. 4. fig (great difference) desfase m.

gape [geɪp] vi 1. (person) mirar boquiabierto(ta). 2. (hole, wound) estar muy abierto(ta).

gaping ['geɪpɪŋ] adj 1. (open-mouthed) boquiabierto(ta). 2. (wide-open) abierto(ta).

garage [Br 'gærɑːʒ, 'gærɪdʒ, Am gə'rɑːʒ] n 1. (for keeping car) garaje m. 2. Br (for fuel) gasolinera f. 3. (for car repair) taller m. 4. Br (for selling cars) concesionario m de automóviles.

garbage ['gɑːbɪdʒ] n (U) 1. (refuse) basura f. 2. inf (nonsense) tonterías fpl.

garbage can n Am cubo m de la basura.

garbage truck n Am camión m de la basura.

garbled ['gɑːbld] adj confuso(sa).

garden ['gɑːdn] n jardín m.

garden centre n centro m de jardinería.

gardener ['gɑːdnər] n jardinero m, -ra f.

gardening ['gɑːdnɪŋ] n jardinería f.

gargle ['gɑːgl] vi hacer gárgaras.

gargoyle ['gɑːgɔɪl] n gárgola f.

garish ['geərɪʃ] adj chillón(ona).

garland ['gɑːlənd] n guirnalda f.

garlic ['gɑːlɪk] n ajo m.

garlic bread n pan m de ajo.

garment ['gɑːmənt] n prenda f (de vestir).

garnish ['gɑːnɪʃ] vt guarnecer.

garrison ['gærɪsn] n guarnición f.

garrulous ['gærələs] adj parlanchín (ina).

garter ['gɑːtər] n 1. (band round leg) liga f. 2. Am (suspender) portaligas m inv.

gas [gæs] (pl -es OR -ses) ♦ n 1. (CHEM) gas m. 2. Am (petrol) gasolina f. ♦ vt asfixiar con gas.

gas cooker n Br cocina f de gas.

gas cylinder n bombona f de gas.

gas fire n Br estufa f de gas.

gas gauge n Am indicador m del nivel de gasolina.

gash [gæʃ] ♦ n raja f. ♦ vt rajar.

gasket ['gæskɪt] n junta f.

gasman ['gæsmæn] (pl -men [-men]) n

hombre *m* del gas.

gas mask *n* máscara *f* antigás.

gas meter *n* contador *m* del gas.

gasoline ['gæsəliːn] *n Am* gasolina *f*.

gasp [gɑːsp] ◆ *n* resuello *m*. ◆ *vi* 1. (*breathe quickly*) resollar, jadear. 2. (*in shock, surprise*) ahogar un grito.

gas pedal *n Am* acelerador *m*.

gas station *n Am* gasolinera *f*, grifo *m Amer*.

gas stove = **gas cooker**.

gas tank *n Am* depósito *m* de gasolina.

gas tap *n* llave *f* del gas.

gastroenteritis ['gæstrəʊ,entə'raɪtɪs] *n* (U) gastroenteritis *f inv*.

gastronomy [gæs'trɒnəmɪ] *n* gastronomía *f*.

gasworks ['gæswɜːks] (*pl inv*) *n* fábrica *f* de gas.

gate [geɪt] *n* 1. (*gen*) puerta *f*; (*metal*) verja *f*. 2. (SPORT) (*takings*) taquilla *f*; (*attendance*) entrada *f*.

gâteau ['gætəʊ] (*pl* -x [-z]) *n Br* tarta *f* (con nata).

gatecrash ['geɪtkræʃ] *vi inf* colarse de gorra.

gateway ['geɪtweɪ] *n* (*entrance*) puerta *f*, pórtico *m*.

gather ['gæðər] ◆ *vt* 1. (*collect*) recoger; **to ~ together** reunir. 2. (*increase - speed, strength*) ganar, cobrar. 3. (*understand*): **to ~ (that)** sacar en conclusión algo. 4. (*cloth*) fruncir. ◆ *vi* (*people, animals*) reunirse; (*clouds*) acumularse.

gathering ['gæðərɪŋ] *n* (*meeting*) reunión *f*.

gauche [gəʊʃ] *adj* torpe.

gaudy ['gɔːdɪ] *adj* chillón(ona), llamativo(va).

gauge, gage *Am* [geɪdʒ] ◆ *n* 1. (*for fuel, temperature*) indicador *m*; (*for width of tube, wire*) calibrador *m*. 2. (*calibre*) calibre *m*. 3. (RAIL) ancho *m* de vía. ◆ *vt lit & fig* calibrar.

gaunt [gɔːnt] *adj* 1. (*person, face*) enjuto(ta). 2. (*building, landscape*) adusto(ta).

gauntlet ['gɔːntlɪt] *n* guante *m*; **to run the ~ of** sthg exponerse a algo; **to throw down the ~ (to sb)** arrojar el guante (a alguien).

gauze [gɔːz] *n* gasa *f*.

gave [geɪv] *pt* → **give**.

gawky ['gɔːkɪ] *adj* desgarbado(da).

gawp [gɔːp] *vi*: **to ~ (at sthg/sb)** mirar boquiabierto(ta) (algo/a alguien).

gay [geɪ] ◆ *adj* 1. (*homosexual*) gay, homosexual. 2. (*cheerful, lively, bright*) alegre. ◆ *n* gay *m* y *f*.

gaze [geɪz] ◆ *n* mirada *f* fija. ◆ *vi*: **to ~ (at sthg/sb)** mirar fijamente (algo/a alguien).

gazelle [gə'zel] (*pl inv* OR **-s**) *n* gacela *f*.

gazetteer [,gæzɪ'tɪər] *n* índice *m* geográfico.

gazump [gə'zʌmp] *vt Br inf*: **to ~ sb** acordar vender una casa a alguien y luego vendérsela a otro a un precio más alto.

GB (*abbr of* **Great Britain**) *n* GB *f*.

GCE (*abbr of* **General Certificate of Education**) *n* 1. (O level) antiguo examen final de enseñanza secundaria en Gran Bretaña para alumnos de buen rendimiento escolar. 2. = **A level**.

GCSE (*abbr of* **General Certificate of Secondary Education**) *n* examen final de enseñanza secundaria en Gran Bretaña.

GDP (*abbr of* **gross domestic product**) *n* PIB *m*.

gear [gɪər] ◆ *n* 1. (*mechanism*) engranaje *m*. 2. (*speed - of car, bicycle*) marcha *f*; **in ~** con una marcha metida; **out of ~** en punto muerto. 3. (U) (*equipment, clothes*) equipo *m*. ◆ *vt*: **to ~ sthg to** orientar OR encaminar algo hacia. ▶ **gear up** *vi*: **to ~ up for sthg/to do sthg** hacer preparativos para algo/para hacer algo.

gearbox ['gɪəbɒks] *n* caja *f* de cambios.

gear lever, gear stick *Br*, **gear shift** *Am n* palanca *f* de cambios.

gear wheel *n* rueda *f* dentada.

geese [giːs] *pl* → **goose**.

gel [dʒel] ◆ *n* (*for shower*) gel *m*; (*for hair*) gomina *f*. ◆ *vi* 1. (*thicken*) aglutinarse. 2. (*plan*) cuajar; (*idea, thought*) tomar forma.

gelatin ['dʒelətɪn], **gelatine** [,dʒelə'tiːn] *n* gelatina *f*.

gelignite ['dʒelɪgnaɪt] *n* gelignita *f*.

gem [dʒem] *n lit & fig* joya *f*.

Gemini ['dʒemɪnaɪ] *n* Géminis *m inv*.

gender ['dʒendər] *n* género *m*.

gene [dʒiːn] *n* gene *m*, gen *m*.

general ['dʒenərəl] ◆ *adj* general. ◆ *n* general *m*. ▶ **in general** *adv* 1. (*as a whole*) en general. 2. (*usually*) por lo general.

general anaesthetic *n* anestesia *f* general.

general delivery *n Am* lista *f* de correos.

general election *n* elecciones *fpl* generales.

generalization [,dʒenərəlaɪ'zeɪʃn] *n* generalización *f*.

general knowledge n cultura f general.

generally ['dʒenərəlı] adv en general.

general practitioner n médico m, -ca f de cabecera.

general public n: the ~ el gran público.

generate ['dʒenəreıt] vt generar.

generation [,dʒenə'reıʃn] n generación f.

generator ['dʒenəreıtər] n generador m.

generosity [,dʒenə'rɒsətı] n generosidad f.

generous ['dʒenərəs] adj generoso (sa); (cut of clothes) amplio(plia).

genetic [dʒı'netık] adj genético(ca). ▶ **genetics** n (U) genética f.

Geneva [dʒı'ni:və] n Ginebra.

genial ['dʒi:njəl] adj cordial, afable.

genitals ['dʒenıtlz] npl genitales mpl.

genius ['dʒi:njəs] (pl -es) n genio m.

gent [dʒent] n inf caballero m. ▶ **gents** n Br (toilets) servicio m de caballeros.

genteel [dʒen'ti:l] adj fino(na), refinado(da).

gentle ['dʒentl] adj 1. (kind) tierno(na), dulce. 2. (breeze, movement, slope) suave. 3. (scolding) ligero(ra); (hint) sutil.

gentleman ['dʒentlmən] (pl -men [-mən]) n 1. (well-behaved man) caballero m. 2. (man) señor m, caballero m.

gently ['dʒentlı] adv 1. (kindly) dulcemente. 2. (softly, smoothly) suavemente. 3. (carefully) con cuidado.

gentry ['dʒentrı] n alta burguesía f.

genuine ['dʒenjuın] adj 1. (real) auténtico(ca). 2. (sincere) sincero(ra).

geography [dʒı'ɒgrəfı] n geografía f.

geology [dʒı'ɒlədʒı] n geología f.

geometric(al) [,dʒıə'metrık(l)] adj geométrico(ca).

geometry [dʒı'ɒmətrı] n geometría f.

geranium [dʒı'reınjəm] (pl -s) n geranio m.

gerbil ['dʒɜ:bıl] n jerbo m, gerbo m.

geriatric [,dʒerı'ætrık] adj 1. (of old people) geriátrico(ca). 2. pej (very old, inefficient) anticuado(da).

germ [dʒɜ:m] n (BIOL & fig) germen m; (MED) microbio m.

German ['dʒɜ:mən] ◆ adj alemán (ana). ◆ n 1. (person) alemán m, -ana f. 2. (language) alemán m.

German measles n rubéola f.

Germany ['dʒɜ:mənı] n Alemania.

germinate ['dʒɜ:mıneıt] vt & vi lit & fig germinar.

gerund ['dʒerənd] n gerundio m.

gesticulate [dʒes'tıkjuleıt] vi gesticular.

gesture ['dʒestʃər] ◆ n gesto m. ◆ vi: to ~ to OR towards sb hacer gestos a alguien.

get [get] (Br pt & pp got, Am pt got, pp gotten) ◆ vt 1. (cause to do): to ~ sb to do sthg hacer que alguien haga algo; I'll ~ my sister to help le pediré a mi hermana que ayude. 2. (cause to be done): to ~ sthg done mandar hacer algo; have you got the car fixed yet? ¿te han arreglado ya el coche? 3. (cause to become): to ~ sthg ready preparar algo; to ~ sb pregnant dejar a alguien preñada. 4. (cause to move): can you ~ it through the gap? ¿puedes meterlo por el hueco?; to ~ sthg/sb out of sthg conseguir sacar algo/ a alguien de algo. 5. (bring, fetch) traer; can I ~ you something to eat/drink? ¿te traigo algo de comer/beber?; I'll ~ my coat voy a por el abrigo; could you ~ me the boss, please? (when phoning) póngame con el jefe. 6. (obtain) conseguir; she got top marks sacó las mejores notas. 7. (receive) recibir; what did you ~ for your birthday? ¿qué te regalaron para tu cumpleaños?; she ~s a good salary gana un buen sueldo. 8. (experience - a sensation): do you ~ the feeling he doesn't like us? ¿no te da la sensación de que no le gustamos? 9. (catch - bus, criminal, illness) coger, agarrar Amer; I've got a cold estoy resfriado; he got cancer contrajo cáncer. 10. (understand) entender; I don't ~ it inf no me aclaro, no lo entiendo; he didn't seem to ~ the point no pareció captar el sentido. 11. inf (annoy) poner negro (gra). 12. (find): you ~ a lot of artists here hay mucho artista por aquí; see also have. ◆ vi 1. (become) ponerse; to ~ angry/pale ponerse furioso/pálido; to ~ ready prepararse; to ~ dressed vestirse; I'm getting cold/bored me estoy enfriando/aburriendo; it's getting late se está haciendo tarde. 2. (arrive) llegar; how do I ~ there? ¿cómo se llega (allí)?; I only got back yesterday regresé justo ayer. 3. (eventually succeed): to ~ to do sthg llegar a hacer algo; did you ~ to see him? ¿conseguiste verlo? 4. (progress) llegar; how far have you got? ¿cuánto llevas?, ¿hasta dónde has llegado?; now we're getting somewhere ahora sí que vamos por buen camino; we're getting nowhere así no llegamos a ninguna parte. ◆ *aux vb*: **to ~ excited** emocionarse; **someone could ~ hurt** alguien podría resultar herido; **I got beaten up** me zurraron; **let's ~ going** or **moving** vamos a ponernos en marcha. ▶ **get about, get around** *vi* 1. (*move from place to place*) salir a menudo. 2. (*circulate - news etc*) difundirse; *see also* **get around.** ▶ **get along** *vi* 1. (*manage*) arreglárselas. 2. (*progress*): **how are you getting along?** ¿cómo te va? 3. (*have a good relationship*): **to ~ along (with sb)** llevarse bien (con alguien). ▶ **get around, get round** ◆ *vt fus* (*overcome - problem*) solventar; (- *obstacle*) sortear. ◆ *vi* 1. (*circulate - news etc*) difundirse. 2. (*eventually do*): **to ~ around to (doing) sthg** sacar tiempo para (hacer) algo; *see also* **get about.** ▶ **get at** *vt fus* 1. (*reach*) llegar a, alcanzar. 2. (*imply*) referirse a. 3. *inf* (*criticize*): **stop getting at me!** ¡deja ya de meterte conmigo! ▶ **get away** *vi* 1. (*leave*) salir, irse. 2. (*go on holiday*): **I really need to ~ away** necesito unas buenas vacaciones. 3. (*escape*) escaparse. ▶ **get away with** *vt fus* salir impune de; **she lets him ~ away with everything** ella se lo consiente todo. ▶ **get back** ◆ *vt sep* (*recover, regain*) recuperar. ◆ *vi* (*move away*) echarse atrás, apartarse. ▶ **get back to** *vt fus* 1. (*return to previous state, activity*) volver a; **to ~ back to sleep/normal** volver a dormirse/a la normalidad. 2. *inf* (*phone back*): **I'll ~ back to you later** te llamo de vuelta más tarde. ▶ **get by** *vi* apañárselas, apañarse. ▶ **get down** *vt sep* 1. (*depress*) deprimir. 2. (*fetch from higher level*) bajar. ▶ **get down to** *vt fus*: **to ~ down to doing sthg** ponerse a hacer algo. ▶ **get in** *vi* 1. (*enter*) entrar. 2. (*arrive*) llegar. ▶ **get into** *vt fus* 1. (*car*) subir a. 2. (*become involved in*) meterse en. 3. (*enter into a particular situation, state*): **to ~ into a panic** or **state** ponerse nerviosísimo; **to ~ into trouble** meterse en líos; **to ~ into the habit of doing sthg** adquirir el hábito or coger la costumbre de hacer algo. 4. (*be accepted as a student at*): **she managed to ~ into Oxford** consiguió entrar en Oxford. ▶ **get off** ◆ *vt sep* (*remove*) quitar. ◆ *vt fus* 1. (*go away from*) irse or salirse de; **~ off my land!** ¡fuera de mis tierras! 2. (*train, bus, etc*) bajarse de. ◆ *vi* 1. (*leave bus, train*) bajarse, desembarcarse *Amer*. 2. (*escape punishment*) escaparse; **he got off lightly** salió bien

librado. 3. (*depart*) irse, salir. ▶ **get off with** *vt fus* Br *inf* ligar con. ▶ **get on** ◆ *vt fus* (*bus, train, horse*) subirse a, montarse en. ◆ *vi* 1. (*enter bus, train*) subirse, montarse. 2. (*have good relationship*) llevarse bien. 3. (*progress*): **how are you getting on?** ¿cómo te va? 4. (*proceed*): **to ~ on with sthg** seguir or continuar con algo. 5. (*be successful professionally*) triunfar. ▶ **get out** ◆ *vt sep* (*remove - object, prisoner*) sacar; (- *stain etc*) quitar; **she got a pen out of her bag** sacó un bolígrafo del bolso. ◆ *vi* 1. (*leave car, bus, train*) bajarse. 2. (*become known - news*) difundirse, filtrarse. ▶ **get out of** *vt fus* 1. (*car etc*) bajar de. 2. (*escape from*) escapar or huir de. 3. (*avoid*): **to ~ out of (doing) sthg** librarse de (hacer) algo. ▶ **get over** *vt fus* 1. (*recover from*) recuperarse de. 2. (*overcome*) superar. 3. (*communicate*) hacer comprender. ▶ **get round = get around.** ▶ **get through** ◆ *vt fus* 1. (*job, task*) terminar. 2. (*exam*) aprobar. 3. (*food, drink*) consumir. 4. (*unpleasant situation*) sobrevivir a. ◆ *vi* 1. (*make oneself understood*): **to ~ through (to sb)** hacerse comprender (por alguien). 2. (TELEC) conseguir comunicar. ▶ **get to** *vt fus inf* (*annoy*) fastidiar, molestar. ▶ **get together** ◆ *vt sep* (*organize - project, demonstration*) organizar, montar; (- *team*) juntar; (- *report*) preparar. ◆ *vi* juntarse, reunirse. ▶ **get up** ◆ *vi* levantarse. ◆ *vt fus* (*organize - petition etc*) preparar, organizar. ▶ **get up to** *vt fus inf* hacer, montar.

getaway ['getəweɪ] *n* fuga *f*, huida *f*; **to make one's ~** darse a la fuga.

get-together *n inf* reunión *f*.

geyser ['giːzər] *n* 1. (*hot spring*) géiser *m*. 2. Br (*water heater*) calentador *m* de agua.

Ghana ['gɑːnə] *n* Ghana.

ghastly ['gɑːstlɪ] *adj* 1. *inf* (*very bad, unpleasant*) horrible, espantoso(sa). 2. (*horrifying*) horripilante. 3. (*ill*) fatal.

gherkin ['gɜːkɪn] *n* pepinillo *m*.

ghetto ['getəʊ] *n* (*pl* -s or -es) gueto *m*.

ghetto blaster [-'blɑːstər] *n inf* radiocasete portátil de gran tamaño y potencia.

ghost [gəʊst] *n* (*spirit*) fantasma *m*.

giant ['dʒaɪənt] ◆ *adj* gigantesco(ca). ◆ *n* gigante *m*.

gibberish ['dʒɪbərɪʃ] *n* galimatías *m inv*.

gibe [dʒaɪb] ◆ *n* pulla *f*, sarcasmo *m*. ◆ *vi*: **to ~ (at)** mofarse (de).

giblets ['dʒɪblɪts] *npl* menudillos *mpl*.

Gibraltar [dʒɪˈbrɔːltəʳ] n Gibraltar; **the Rock of ~** el Peñón.

giddy [ˈgɪdɪ] adj (dizzy) mareado(da).

gift [gɪft] n 1. (present) regalo m, obsequio m. 2. (talent) don m; **to have a ~ for sthg/for doing sthg** tener un don especial para algo/para hacer algo; **to have the ~ of the gab** tener un pico de oro.

gift certificate Am = **gift token**.

gifted [ˈgɪftɪd] adj 1. (talented) dotado (da). 2. (extremely intelligent) superdotado(da).

gift token, gift voucher n Br vale m OR cupón m para regalo.

gig [gɪg] n inf (concert) concierto m.

gigabyte [ˈgaɪgəbaɪt] n (COMPUT) gigaocteto m.

gigantic [dʒaɪˈgæntɪk] adj gigantesco (ca).

giggle [ˈgɪgl] ◆ n 1. (laugh) risita f, risa f tonta. 2. Br inf (fun): **it's a real ~** es la mar de divertido; **to do sthg for a ~** hacer algo por puro cachondeo. ◆ vi (laugh) tener la risa tonta.

gilded [ˈgɪldɪd] = **gilt**.

gill [dʒɪl] n (unit of measurement) = 0,142 litros.

gills [gɪlz] npl (of fish) agallas fpl.

gilt [gɪlt] ◆ adj dorado(da). ◆ n dorado m.

gilt-edged adj (FIN) de máxima garantía.

gimmick [ˈgɪmɪk] n pej artilugio m innecesario; **advertising ~** reclamo m publicitario.

gin [dʒɪn] n ginebra f; **~ and tonic** gintonic m.

ginger [ˈdʒɪndʒəʳ] ◆ adj Br (hair) bermejo(ja); (cat) de color bermejo. ◆ n jengibre m.

ginger ale n (mixer) ginger-ale m.

ginger beer n (slightly alcoholic) refresco m de jengibre.

gingerbread [ˈdʒɪndʒəbred] n 1. (cake) pan m de jengibre. 2. (biscuit) galleta f de jengibre.

ginger-haired [-ˈheəd] adj pelirrojo (ja).

gingerly [ˈdʒɪndʒəlɪ] adv con mucho tiento.

gipsy [ˈdʒɪpsɪ] ◆ adj gitano(na). ◆ n Br gitano m, -na f.

giraffe [dʒɪˈrɑːf] (pl inv OR -s) n jirafa f.

girder [ˈgɜːdəʳ] n viga f.

girdle [ˈgɜːdl] n (corset) faja f.

girl [gɜːl] n 1. (child) niña f. 2. (young woman) chica f, muchacha f. 3. (daughter) niña f, chica f. 4. inf (female friend): **the ~s**

las amigas, las chicas.

girlfriend [ˈgɜːlfrend] n 1. (female lover) novia f. 2. (female friend) amiga f.

girl guide Br, **girl scout** Am n (individual) exploradora f.

giro [ˈdʒaɪrəʊ] (pl -s) n Br 1. (U) (system) giro m. 2. ~ (cheque) cheque m para giro bancario.

girth [gɜːθ] n 1. (circumference) circunferencia f. 2. (of horse) cincha f.

gist [dʒɪst] n: **the ~ of** lo esencial de; **to get the ~ (of sthg)** entender el sentido (de algo).

give [gɪv] (pt gave, pp given) ◆ vt 1. (gen) dar; (time, effort) dedicar; (attention) prestar; **to ~ sb/sthg sthg, to ~ sthg to sb/sthg** dar algo a alguien/algo. 2. (as present): **to ~ sb sthg, to ~ sthg to sb** regalar algo a alguien. 3. (hand over): **to ~ sb sthg, to ~ sthg to sb** entregar OR dar algo a alguien. ◆ vi (collapse, break) romperse, ceder. ▶ **give or take** prep más o menos; **in half an hour ~ or take five minutes** en más o menos media hora. ▶ **give away** vt sep 1. (as present) regalar. 2. (reveal) revelar, descubrir. ▶ **give back** vt sep (return) devolver, regresar Amer. ▶ **give in** vi 1. (admit defeat) rendirse, darse por vencido(da). 2. (agree unwillingly): **to ~ in to sthg** ceder ante algo. ▶ **give off** vt fus (produce, emit) despedir. ▶ **give out** ◆ vt sep (distribute) repartir, distribuir. ◆ vi (supply, strength) agotarse, acabarse; (legs, machine) fallar. ▶ **give up** ◆ vt sep 1. (stop) abandonar; **to ~ up chocolate** dejar de comer chocolate. 2. (job) dimitir de, renunciar a. 3. (surrender): **to ~ o.s. up (to sb)** rendirse (a alguien). ◆ vi rendirse, darse por vencido(da).

given [ˈgɪvn] ◆ adj 1. (set, fixed) dado (da). 2. (prone): **to be ~ to sthg/to doing sthg** ser dado(da) a algo/a hacer algo. ◆ prep (taking into account) dado(da); **~ that** dado que.

given name n nombre m de pila.

glacier [ˈglæsjəʳ] n glaciar m.

glad [glæd] adj 1. (happy, pleased) alegre, contento(ta); **to be ~ about/that** alegrarse de/de que. 2. (willing): **to be ~ to do sthg** tener gusto en hacer algo. 3. (grateful): **to be ~ of sthg** agradecer algo.

gladly [ˈglædlɪ] adv 1. (happily, eagerly) alegremente. 2. (willingly) con mucho gusto.

glamor Am = **glamour**.

glamorous [ˈglæmərəs] adj atractivo

(va), lleno(na) de encanto.

glamour Br, **glamor** Am ['glæmər] n encanto m, atractivo m.

glance [glɑ:ns] ♦ n 1. (quick look) mirada f, vistazo m; **at a ~** de un vistazo; **at first ~** a primera vista. ♦ vi (look quickly): **to ~ at sb** lanzar una mirada a alguien; **to ~ at sthg** echar una ojeada OR un vistazo a algo. ▶ **glance off** vt fus rebotar en.

glancing ['glɑ:nsɪŋ] adj oblicuo(cua).

gland [glænd] n glándula f.

glandular fever ['glændjʊlər-] n mononucleosis f inv infecciosa.

glare [gleər] ♦ n 1. (scowl) mirada f asesina. 2. (blaze, dazzle) destello m, deslumbramiento m. 3. (U) fig (of publicity) foco m. ♦ vi 1. (scowl): **to ~ (at sthg/ sb)** mirar con furia (algo/a alguien). 2. (blaze, dazzle) deslumbrar.

glaring ['gleərɪŋ] adj 1. (very obvious) evidente. 2. (blazing, dazzling) deslumbrante.

glasnost ['glæznɒst] n glasnost f.

glass [glɑ:s] ♦ n 1. (material) vidrio m, cristal m. 2. (drinking vessel, glassful) vaso m; (with stem) copa f. ♦ comp de vidrio, de cristal. ▶ **glasses** npl (spectacles) gafas fpl.

glassware ['glɑ:sweər] n (U) cristalería f.

glassy ['glɑ:sɪ] adj 1. (smooth, shiny) cristalino(na). 2. (blank, lifeless) vidrioso (sa).

glaze [gleɪz] ♦ n (on pottery) vidriado m; (on food) glaseado m. ♦ vt (pottery) vidriar; (food) glasear; (window) acristalar.

glazier ['gleɪzjər] n vidriero m, -ra f.

gleam [gli:m] ♦ n destello m; (of hope) rayo m. ♦ vi relucir.

gleaming ['gli:mɪŋ] adj reluciente.

glean [gli:n] vt (gather) recoger.

glee [gli:] n (U) (joy, delight) alegría f, regocijo m.

glen [glen] n Scot cañada f.

glib [glɪb] adj pej de mucha labia.

glide [glaɪd] vi 1. (move smoothly) deslizarse. 2. (fly) planear.

glider ['glaɪdər] n (plane) planeador m.

gliding ['glaɪdɪŋ] n (sport) vuelo m sin motor.

glimmer ['glɪmər] n 1. (faint light) luz f tenue. 2. fig (trace, sign) atisbo m; (of hope) rayo m.

glimpse [glɪmps] ♦ n 1. (look, sight) vislumbre f. 2. (idea, perception) asomo m, atisbo m. ♦ vt entrever, vislumbrar.

glint [glɪnt] ♦ n 1. (flash) destello m.

2. (in eyes) fulgor m. ♦ vi destellar.

glisten ['glɪsn] vi relucir, brillar.

glitter ['glɪtər] vi relucir, brillar.

gloat [gləʊt] vi: **to ~ (over sthg)** regodearse (con algo).

global ['gləʊbl] adj (worldwide) mundial.

global warming [-'wɔ:mɪŋ] n calentamiento m mundial.

globe [gləʊb] n 1. (gen) globo m. 2. (spherical map) globo m (terráqueo).

gloom [glu:m] n (U) 1. (darkness) penumbra f. 2. (unhappiness) pesimismo m, melancolía f.

gloomy ['glu:mɪ] adj 1. (dark, cloudy) oscuro(ra). 2. (unhappy) melancólico (ca). 3. (without hope - report, forecast) pesimista; (- situation, prospects) desalentador(ra).

glorious ['glɔ:rɪəs] adj magnífico(ca).

glory ['glɔ:rɪ] n 1. (gen) gloria f. 2. (beauty, splendour) esplendor m. ▶ **glory in** vt fus (relish) disfrutar de, regocijarse con.

gloss [glɒs] n 1. (shine) lustre m, brillo m. 2. ~ **(paint)** pintura f esmalte. ▶ **gloss over** vt fus tocar muy por encima.

glossary ['glɒsərɪ] n glosario m.

glossy ['glɒsɪ] adj 1. (smooth, shiny) lustroso(sa). 2. (on shiny paper) de papel satinado.

glove [glʌv] n guante m.

glove compartment n guantera f.

glow [gləʊ] ♦ n (light) fulgor m. ♦ vi (gen) brillar.

glower ['glauər] vi: **to ~ (at sthg/sb)** mirar con furia (algo/a alguien).

glucose ['glu:kəʊs] n glucosa f.

glue [glu:] (cont glueing OR gluing) ♦ n (paste) pegamento m; (for glueing wood, metal etc) cola f. ♦ vt (paste) pegar (con pegamento); (wood, metal etc) encolar.

glum [glʌm] adj (unhappy) sombrío(a).

glut [glʌt] n superabundancia f.

glutton ['glʌtn] n (greedy person) glotón m, -ona f; **to be a ~ for punishment** ser un masoquista.

gnarled [nɑ:ld] adj nudoso(sa).

gnash [næʃ] vt: **to ~ one's teeth** hacer rechinar los dientes.

gnat [næt] n mosquito m.

gnaw [nɔ:] vt (chew) roer; **to ~ (away) at sb** corroer a alguien.

gnome [nəʊm] n gnomo m.

GNP (abbr of **gross national product**) n PNB m.

go [gəʊ] (pt **went**, pp **gone**, pl **goes**) ♦ vi 1. (move, travel, attend) ir; **where are you**

~ing? ¿dónde vas?; **he's gone to Portugal** se ha ido a Portugal; **we went by bus/train** fuimos en autobús/tren; **to ~ and do sthg** ir a hacer algo; **where does this path ~?** ¿a dónde lleva este camino?; **to ~ swimming/shopping** ir a nadar/de compras; **to ~ for a walk/run** ir a dar un paseo/a correr; **to ~ to church/school** ir a misa/la escuela. **2.** (*depart - person*) irse, marcharse; (*- bus*) salir; **I must ~, I have to ~** tengo que irme; **it's time we went** es hora de irse OR marcharse; **let's ~!** ¡vámonos! **3.** (*pass - time*) pasar. **4.** (*progress*) ir; **to ~ well/badly** ir bien/mal; **how's it ~ing?** *inf* (*how are you?*) ¿qué tal? **5.** (*belong, fit*) ir; **the plates ~ in the cupboard** los platos van en el armario; **it won't ~ into the suitcase** no cabe en la maleta. **6.** (*become*) ponerse; **to ~ grey** ponerse gris; **to ~ mad** volverse loco; **to ~ blind** quedarse ciego. **7.** (*indicating intention, certainty, expectation*): **to be ~ing to do sthg** ir a hacer algo; **he said he was ~ing to be late** dijo que llegaría tarde; **it's ~ing to rain/snow** va a llover/nevar. **8.** (*match, be compatible*): **to ~ (with)** ir bien (con); **this blouse goes well with the skirt** esta blusa va muy bien or hace juego con la falda. **9.** (*function, work*) funcionar. **10.** (*bell, alarm*) sonar. **11.** (*stop working*) estropearse; **the fuse must have gone** han debido de saltar los plomos. **12.** (*deteriorate*): **her sight/hearing is ~ing** está perdiendo la vista/el oído. **13.** (*be disposed of*): **he'll have to ~** habrá que despedirle; **everything must ~!** ¡gran liquidación! **14.** *inf* (*expressing irritation, surprise*): **now what's he gone and done?** ¿qué leches ha hecho ahora? **15.** (*in division*): **three into two won't ~** dos entre tres no cabe. ◆ *n* **1.** (*turn*) turno *m*; **it's my ~** me toca a mí. **2.** *inf* (*attempt*): **to have a ~ at sthg** intentar OR probar algo. **3.** *phr*: **to have a ~ at sb** *inf* echar una bronca a alguien; **to be on the ~** *inf* no parar, estar muy liado. ▶ **to go** *adv* (*remaining*): **there are only three days to ~** sólo quedan tres días. ▶ **go about** ◆ *vt fus* **1.** (*perform*) hacer, realizar; **to ~ about one's business** ocuparse uno de sus asuntos. **2.** (*tackle*): **to ~ about doing sthg** apañárselas para hacer algo; **how do you intend ~ing about it?** ¿cómo piensas hacerlo? ◆ *vi* = **go around**. ▶ **go ahead** *vi* **1.** (*begin*): **to ~ ahead (with sthg)** seguir adelante (con algo); **~ ahead!** ¡adelante! **2.** (*take place*) cele-

brarse. ▶ **go along** *vi* (*proceed*): **as you ~ along** a medida que lo vayas haciendo. ▶ **go along with** *vt fus* estar de acuerdo con. ▶ **go around** *vi* **1.** (*associate*): **to ~ around with sb** juntarse con alguien. **2.** (*joke, illness, story*) correr (por ahí). ▶ **go back on** *vt fus* (*one's word, promise*) faltar a. ▶ **go back to** *vt fus* **1.** (*return to activity*) continuar OR seguir con; **to ~ back to sleep** volver a dormir. **2.** (*date from*) remontarse a. ▶ **go by** ◆ *vi* (*time*) pasar. ◆ *vt fus* **1.** (*be guided by*) guiarse por. **2.** (*judge from*): **~ing by her voice, I'd say she was French** a juzgar por su voz yo diría que es francesa. ▶ **go down** ◆ *vi* **1.** (*get lower - prices etc*) bajar. **2.** (*be accepted*): **to ~ down well/badly** tener una buena/mala acogida. **3.** (*sun*) ponerse. **4.** (*tyre, balloon*) deshincharse. ◆ *vt fus* bajar. ▶ **go for** *vt fus* **1.** (*choose*) decidirse por. **2.** (*be attracted to*): **I don't really ~ for men like him** no me gustan mucho los hombres como él. **3.** (*attack*) lanzarse sobre, atacar. **4.** (*try to obtain - record, job*) ir a por. ▶ **go in** *vi* entrar. ▶ **go in for** *vt fus* **1.** (*competition, exam*) presentarse a. **2.** *inf* (*enjoy*): **I don't really ~ in for classical music** no me va la música clásica. ▶ **go into** *vt fus* **1.** (*investigate*) investigar. **2.** (*take up as a profession*) dedicarse a. ▶ **go off** ◆ *vi* **1.** (*explode - bomb*) estallar; (*- gun*) dispararse. **2.** (*alarm*) sonar. **3.** (*go bad - food*) estropearse; (*- milk*) cortarse. **4.** (*lights, heating*) apagarse. **5.** (*happen*): **to ~ off (well/badly)** salir (bien/mal). ◆ *vt fus inf* (*lose interest in*) perder el gusto a OR el interés en. ▶ **go on** ◆ *vi* **1.** (*take place*) pasar, ocurrir. **2.** (*continue*): **to ~ on (doing sthg)** seguir (haciendo algo). **3.** (*proceed to further activity*): **to ~ on to sthg/to do sthg** pasar a algo/a hacer algo. **4.** (*heating etc*) encenderse. **5.** (*talk for too long*): **to ~ on (about)** no parar de hablar (de). ◆ *vt fus* (*be guided by*) guiarse por. ◆ *excl* ¡venga!, ¡vamos! ▶ **go on at** *vt fus* (*nag*) dar la lata a. ▶ **go out** *vi* **1.** (*leave house*) salir; **to ~ out for a meal** cenar fuera. **2.** (*as friends or lovers*): **to ~ out (with sb)** salir (con alguien). **3.** (*light, fire, cigarette*) apagarse. ▶ **go over** *vt fus* **1.** (*examine*) repasar. **2.** (*repeat*) repetir. ▶ **go round** *vi* (*revolve*) girar, dar vueltas; *see also* **go around**. ▶ **go through** *vt fus* **1.** (*experience*) pasar por, experimentar. **2.** (*study, search through*) registrar; **she went through his pockets** le miró en los bolsillos.

▶ **go through with** *vt fus* llevar a cabo. ▶ **go towards** *vt fus* contribuir a. ▶ **go under** *vi lit & fig* hundirse. ▶ **go up** ◆ *vi* 1. (*rise - prices, temperature, balloon*) subir. 2. (*be built*) levantarse, construirse. ◆ *vt fus* subir. ▶ **go without** ◆ *vt fus* prescindir de. ◆ *vi* apañárselas.

goad [gəʊd] *vt* (*provoke*) aguijonear, incitar.

go-ahead ◆ *adj* (*dynamic*) dinámico (ca). ◆ *n* (U) (*permission*) luz *f* verde.

goal [gəʊl] *n* 1. (SPORT) (*area between goalposts*) portería *f*, arco *m* Amer; (*point scored*) gol *m*. 2. (*aim*) objetivo *m*, meta *f*.

goalkeeper ['gəʊl,kiːpəʳ] *n* portero *m*, -ra *f*, arquero *m*, -ra *f* Amer.

goalmouth ['gəʊlmaʊθ, *pl* -maʊðz] *n* portería *f*, meta *f*, arco *m* Amer.

goalpost ['gəʊlpəʊst] *n* poste *m* (de la portería).

goat [gəʊt] *n* (*animal*) cabra *f*.

gob [gɒb] *v inf n* Br (*mouth*) pico *m*.

gobble ['gɒbl] *vt* (*food*) engullir, tragar. ▶ **gobble down, gobble up** *vt sep* engullir, tragar.

go-between *n* intermediario *m*, -ria *f*.

gobsmacked ['gɒbsmækt] *adj* Br *inf* alucinado(da), flipado(da).

go-cart = **go-kart**.

god [gɒd] *n* dios *m*. ▶ **God** ◆ *n* Dios *m*; **God knows** sabe Dios; **for God's sake** ¡por el amor de Dios!; **thank God** ¡gracias a Dios! ◆ *excl*: (my) **God!** ¡Dios (mío)!

godchild ['gɒdtʃaɪld] (*pl* -children [-,tʃɪldrən]) *n* ahijado *m*, -da *f*.

goddaughter ['gɒd,dɔːtəʳ] *n* ahijada *f*.

goddess ['gɒdɪs] *n* diosa *f*.

godfather ['gɒd,fɑːðəʳ] *n* padrino *m*.

godforsaken ['gɒdfə,seɪkn] *adj* dejado(da) de la mano de Dios.

godmother ['gɒd,mʌðəʳ] *n* madrina *f*.

godsend ['gɒdsend] *n*: **to be a ~** venir como agua de mayo.

godson ['gɒdsʌn] *n* ahijado *m*.

goes [gəʊz] → **go**.

goggles ['gɒglz] *npl* (*for swimming*) gafas *fpl* submarinas; (*for skiing*) gafas de esquí; (*for welding*) gafas de protección.

going ['gəʊɪŋ] ◆ *adj* 1. Br (*available*) disponible. 2. (*rate*) actual. ◆ *n* (U) 1. (*rate of advance*) marcha *f*. 2. (*conditions*) condiciones *fpl*.

go-kart [-kɑːt] *n* kart *m*.

gold [gəʊld] ◆ *adj* (*gold-coloured*) dorado(da). ◆ *n* (*gen*) oro *m*. ◆ *comp* (*made of gold*) de oro.

golden ['gəʊldən] *adj* 1. (*made of gold*) de oro. 2. (*gold-coloured*) dorado(da).

goldfish ['gəʊldfɪʃ] (*pl inv*) *n* pez *m* de colores.

gold leaf *n* pan *m* de oro.

gold medal *n* medalla *f* de oro.

goldmine ['gəʊldmaɪn] *n lit & fig* mina *f* de oro.

gold-plated [-'pleɪtɪd] *adj* chapado (da) en oro.

goldsmith ['gəʊldsmɪθ] *n* orfebre *m* y *f*.

golf [gɒlf] *n* golf *m*.

golf ball *n* 1. (*for golf*) pelota *f* de golf. 2. (*for typewriter*) esfera *f* impresora.

golf club *n* 1. (*society, place*) club *m* de golf. 2. (*stick*) palo *m* de golf.

golf course *n* campo *m* de golf.

golfer ['gɒlfəʳ] *n* golfista *m* y *f*.

gone [gɒn] ◆ *pp* → **go**. ◆ *adj*: **those days are ~** esos tiempos ya pasaron. ◆ *prep* (*past*): **it was ~ six already** ya eran las seis pasadas.

gong [gɒŋ] *n* gong *m*.

good [gʊd] (*compar* **better**, *superl* **best**) ◆ *adj* 1. (*gen*) bueno(na); **it's ~ to see you** me alegro de verte; **she's ~ at it** se le da bien; **to be ~ with** saber manejárselas con; **she's ~ with her hands** es muy mañosa; **it's ~ for you** es bueno, es beneficioso; **to feel ~** sentirse fenomenal; **it's ~ that ...** está bien que ...; **to look ~** (*attractive*) estar muy guapo; (*appetizing, promising*) tener buena pinta; **~ looks** atractivo *m*; **be ~!** ¡sé bueno!, ¡pórtate bien!; **~!** ¡muy bien!, ¡estupendo! 2. (*kind*) amable; **to be ~ to sb** ser amable con alguien; **to be ~ enough to do sthg** ser tan amable de hacer algo. ◆ *n* 1. (U) (*benefit*) bien *m*; **it will do him ~** le hará bien. 2. (*use*) beneficio *m*, provecho *m*; **what's the ~ of ...?** ¿de qué OR para qué sirve ...?; **it's no ~** no sirve para nada. 3. (*morally correct behaviour*) el bien; **to be up to no ~** estar tramando algo malo. ▶ **goods** *npl* 1. (COM - *for sale*) productos *mpl*; (- *when transported*) mercancías *fpl*. 2. (ECON) bienes *mpl*. ▶ **as good as** *adv* casi, prácticamente; **it's as ~ as new** está como nuevo. ▶ **for good** *adv* (*forever*) para siempre. ▶ **good afternoon** *excl* ¡buenas tardes! ▶ **good evening** *excl* (*in the evening*) ¡buenas tardes!; (*at night*) ¡buenas noches! ▶ **good morning** *excl*

¡buenos días!, ¡buen día! *Amer.*
▶ **good night** *excl* ¡buenas noches!
goodbye [ˌgʊd'baɪ] ◆ *excl* ¡adiós! ◆ *n* adiós *m*.
Good Friday *n* Viernes *m* Santo.
good-humoured [-'hjuːməd] *adj* jovial.
good-looking [-'lʊkɪŋ] *adj* (*person*) guapo(pa).
good-natured [-'neɪtʃəd] *adj* bondadoso(sa).
goodness ['gʊdnɪs] ◆ *n* (U) 1. (*kindness*) bondad *f*. 2. (*nutritive quality*) alimento *m*. ◆ *excl*: (**my**) **~!** ¡Dios mío!; **for ~' sake!** ¡por Dios!; **thank ~** ¡gracias a Dios!
goods train [gʊdz-] *n Br* mercancías *m inv.*
goodwill [ˌgʊd'wɪl] *n* 1. (*kind feelings*) buena voluntad *f*. 2. (COMM) fondo *m* de comercio.
goody ['gʊdɪ] *n inf* bueno *m*, -na *f*.
goose [guːs] (*pl* **geese**) *n* (*bird*) ganso *m*, oca *f*.
gooseberry ['gʊzbərɪ] *n* (*fruit*) grosella *f* silvestre, uva *f* espina.
gooseflesh ['guːsfleʃ] *n*, **goose pimples** *Br*, **goosebumps** *Am* ['guːsbʌmps] *npl* carne *f* de gallina.
gore [gɔːʳ] ◆ *n literary* (*blood*) sangre *f* (derramada). ◆ *vt* cornear.
gorge [gɔːdʒ] ◆ *n* cañón *m*. ◆ *vt*: **to ~ o.s. on** OR **with** atracarse de.
gorgeous ['gɔːdʒəs] *adj* 1. (*lovely*) magnífico(ca), espléndido(da). 2. *inf* (*good-looking*): **to be ~** estar como un tren.
gorilla [gə'rɪlə] *n* gorila *m y f*.
gormless ['gɔːmlɪs] *adj Br inf* memo (ma), lerdo(da).
gorse [gɔːs] *n* (U) tojo *m*.
gory ['gɔːrɪ] *adj* (*death, scene*) sangriento (ta); (*details, film*) escabroso(sa).
gosh [gɒʃ] *excl inf* ¡joroba!, ¡caray!
go-slow *n Br* huelga *f* de celo.
gospel ['gɒspl] *n* (*doctrine*) evangelio *m*.
▶ **Gospel** *n* (*in Bible*) Evangelio *m*.
gossip ['gɒsɪp] ◆ *n* 1. (*conversation*) cotilleo *m*. 2. (*person*) cotilla *m y f*, chismoso *m*, -sa *f*. ◆ *vi* cotillear.
gossip column *n* ecos *mpl* de sociedad.
got [gɒt] *pt & pp* → **get**.
gotten ['gɒtn] *pp Am* → **get**.
goulash ['guːlæʃ] *n* gulasch *m*.
gourmet ['gʊəmeɪ] ◆ *n* gastrónomo *m*, -ma *f*. ◆ *comp* para/de gastrónomos.
gout [gaʊt] *n* gota *f*.

govern ['gʌvən] ◆ *vt* 1. (POL) gobernar. 2. (*control*) dictar. ◆ *vi* (POL) gobernar.
governess ['gʌvənɪs] *n* institutriz *f*.
government ['gʌvnmənt] ◆ *n* gobierno *m*. ◆ *comp* gubernamental.
governor ['gʌvənəʳ] *n* 1. (POL) gobernador *m*, -ra *f*. 2. (*of school, bank, prison*) director *m*, -ra *f*.
gown [gaʊn] *n* 1. (*dress*) vestido *m*, traje *m*. 2. (*of judge etc*) toga *f*.
GP (*abbr of* **general practitioner**) *n* médico de cabecera.
grab [græb] ◆ *vt* 1. (*snatch away*) arrebatar; (*grip*) agarrar, asir. 2. *inf* (*appeal to*) seducir. ◆ *vi*: **to ~ at sthg** intentar agarrar algo.
grace [greɪs] ◆ *n* 1. (U) (*elegance*) elegancia *f*, gracia *f*. 2. (U) (*delay*) prórroga *f*. 3. (*prayer*): **to say ~** bendecir la mesa. ◆ *vt fml* 1. (*honour*) honrar. 2. (*decorate*) adornar, embellecer.
graceful ['greɪsfʊl] *adj* 1. (*beautiful*) elegante. 2. (*gracious*) cortés.
gracious ['greɪʃəs] ◆ *adj* 1. (*polite*) cortés. 2. (*elegant*) elegante. ◆ *excl*: (**good**) **~!** ¡Dios mío!
grade [greɪd] ◆ *n* 1. (*level, quality*) clase *f*, calidad *f*. 2. *Am* (*class*) curso *m*, clase *f*. 3. (*mark*) nota *f*. ◆ *vt* 1. (*classify*) clasificar. 2. (*mark, assess*) calificar.
grade crossing *n Am* paso *m* a nivel.
grade school *n Am* escuela *f* primaria.
gradient ['greɪdjənt] *n* pendiente *f*.
gradual ['grædʒʊəl] *adj* gradual.
gradually ['grædʒʊəlɪ] *adv* gradualmente.
graduate [*n* 'grædʒʊət, *vb* 'grædʒʊeɪt] ◆ *n* 1. (*person with a degree*) licenciado *m*, -da *f*, egresado *m*, -da *f Amer.* 2. *Am* (*of high school*) ≈ bachiller *m y f*. ◆ *vi* 1. (*with a degree*): **to ~ (from)** licenciarse (por), egresar (de) *Amer.* 2. *Am* (*from high school*): **to ~ (from)** ≈ obtener el título de bachiller (en).
graduation [ˌgrædʒʊ'eɪʃn] *n* graduación *f*, egreso *m Amer.*
graffiti [grə'fiːtɪ] *n* (U) pintadas *fpl*.
graft [grɑːft] ◆ *n* 1. (BOT & MED) injerto *m*. 2. *Br inf* (*hard work*) curro *m* muy duro. 3. *Am inf* (*corruption*) chanchullos *mpl*. ◆ *vt* (BOT & MED): **to ~ sthg (onto sthg)** injertar algo (en algo).
grain [greɪn] *n* 1. (*seed, granule*) grano *m*. 2. (U) (*crop*) cereales *mpl*. 3. *fig* (*small amount*) pizca *f*. 4. (*pattern*) veta *f*.
gram [græm] *n* gramo *m*.
grammar ['græməʳ] *n* gramática *f*.

grammar school n (in UK) colegio subvencionado para mayores de once años con un programa de asignaturas tradicional; (in US) escuela f primaria.

grammatical [grə'mætɪkl] adj 1. (of grammar) gramatical. 2. (correct) (gramaticalmente) correcto(ta).

gramme [græm] Br = gram.

gramophone ['græməfəʊn] n dated gramófono m.

gran [græn] n Br inf abuelita f, yaya f.

grand [grænd] ◆ adj 1. (impressive) grandioso(sa), monumental. 2. (ambitious) ambicioso(sa). 3. (important) distinguido(da). 4. inf dated (excellent) fenomenal. ◆ n inf (thousand pounds or dollars): **a ~** mil libras/dólares; **five ~** cinco mil libras/dólares.

grandchild ['græntʃaɪld] (pl -children [-,tʃɪldrən]) n nieto m, -ta f.

grand(d)ad ['grændæd] n inf abuelito m, yayo m.

granddaughter ['græn,dɔːtər] n nieta f.

grandeur ['grændʒər] n 1. (splendour) grandiosidad f. 2. (status) grandeza f.

grandfather ['grænd,fɑːðər] n abuelo m.

grandma ['grænmɑː] n inf abuelita f, yaya f, mamá f grande Amer.

grandmother ['græn,mʌðər] n abuela f.

grandpa ['grænpɑː] n inf abuelito m, yayo m, papá m grande Amer.

grandparents ['græn,peərənts] npl abuelos mpl.

grand piano n piano m de cola.

grand slam n (SPORT) (in tennis) gran slam m; (in rugby) gran chelem f.

grandson ['grænsʌn] n nieto m.

grandstand ['grændstænd] n tribuna f.

grand total n (total number) cantidad f total; (total sum, cost) importe m total.

granite ['grænɪt] n granito m.

granny ['grænɪ] n inf abuelita f, yaya f.

grant [grɑːnt] ◆ n subvención f; (for study) beca f. ◆ vt fml 1. (gen) conceder; **to take sthg/sb for ~ed** no apreciar algo/a alguien en lo que vale; **it is taken for ~ed that ...** se da por sentado que ... 2. (admit - truth, logic) admitir, aceptar.

granulated sugar ['grænjʊleɪtɪd-] n azúcar m granulado.

granule ['grænjuːl] n gránulo m.

grape [greɪp] n uva f.

grapefruit ['greɪpfruːt] (pl inv OR -s) n pomelo m.

grapevine ['greɪpvaɪn] n 1. (plant) vid f; (against wall) parra f. 2. (information channel): **I heard on the ~ that ...** me ha dicho un pajarito que ...

graph [grɑːf] n gráfica f.

graphic ['græfɪk] adj lit & fig gráfico (ca). ▶ **graphics** npl (pictures) ilustraciones fpl; **computer ~s** gráficos mpl.

graphite ['græfaɪt] n grafito m.

graph paper n (U) papel m cuadriculado.

grapple ['græpl] ▶ **grapple with** vt fus 1. (person) forcejear con. 2. (problem) esforzarse por resolver.

grasp [grɑːsp] ◆ n 1. (grip) agarre m, asimiento m. 2. (understanding) comprensión f; **to have a good ~ of sthg** dominar algo. ◆ vt 1. (grip, seize) agarrar, asir. 2. (understand) comprender. 3. (opportunity) aprovechar.

grasping ['grɑːspɪŋ] adj pej avaro(ra).

grass [grɑːs] ◆ n 1. (plant) hierba f; (lawn) césped m; (pasture) pasto m; **'keep off the ~'** prohibido pisar el césped'. 2. drugs sl (marijuana) hierba f, maría f. ◆ vi Br crime sl: **to ~ (on sb)** chivarse (de alguien).

grasshopper ['grɑːs,hɒpər] n saltamontes m inv.

grass roots ◆ npl bases fpl. ◆ comp de base.

grass snake n culebra f.

grate [greɪt] ◆ n parrilla f, rejilla f. ◆ vt rallar. ◆ vi rechinar, chirriar.

grateful ['greɪtfʊl] adj (gen) agradecido(da); (smile, letter) de agradecimiento; **to be ~ to sb (for sthg)** estar agradecido a alguien (por algo); **I'm very ~ to you** te lo agradezco mucho.

grater ['greɪtər] n rallador m.

gratify ['grætɪfaɪ] vt 1. (please - person): **to be gratified** estar satisfecho. 2. (satisfy - wish) satisfacer.

grating ['greɪtɪŋ] ◆ adj chirriante. ◆ n (grille) reja f, enrejado m.

gratitude ['grætɪtjuːd] n (U): **~ (to sb for)** agradecimiento m OR gratitud f (a alguien por).

gratuitous [grə'tjuːɪtəs] adj fml gratuito(ta).

grave [greɪv] ◆ adj grave. ◆ n sepultura f, tumba f.

gravel ['grævl] n grava f, gravilla f.

gravestone ['greɪvstəʊn] n lápida f (sepulcral).

graveyard ['greɪvjɑːd] n cementerio m.

gravity ['grævətɪ] n gravedad f.

gravy ['greɪvɪ] n (U) (meat juice) salsa f OR jugo m de carne.

gray Am = **grey**.

graze [greɪz] ◆ vt 1. (feed on) pacer OR pastar en. 2. (skin, knee etc) rasguñar. 3. (touch lightly) rozar. ◆ vi pacer, pastar. ◆ n rasguño m.

grease [griːs] ◆ n grasa f. ◆ vt engrasar.

greaseproof paper [ˌgriːspruːf-] n (U) Br papel m de cera (para envolver).

greasy ['griːzɪ] adj grasiento(ta); (inherently) graso(sa).

great [greɪt] ◆ adj 1. (gen) grande; (heat) intenso(sa); ~ **big** enorme. 2. inf (splendid) estupendo(da), fenomenal; **we had a ~ time** lo pasamos en grande; **~!** ¡estupendo! ◆ n grande m y f.

Great Britain n Gran Bretaña.

greatcoat ['greɪtkəʊt] n gabán m.

Great Dane n gran danés m.

great-grandchild n bisnieto m, -ta f.

great-grandfather n bisabuelo m.

great-grandmother n bisabuela f.

greatly ['greɪtlɪ] adv enormemente.

greatness ['greɪtnɪs] n grandeza f.

Greece [griːs] n Grecia.

greed [griːd] n (U): ~ **(for)** (food) glotonería f (con); (money) codicia f (de); (power) ambición f (de).

greedy ['griːdɪ] adj 1. (for food) glotón (ona). 2. (for money, power): ~ **for** codicioso(sa) OR ávido(da) de.

Greek [griːk] ◆ adj griego(ga). ◆ n 1. (person) griego m, -ga f. 2. (language) griego m.

green [griːn] ◆ adj 1. (gen) verde. 2. inf (pale) pálido(da). 3. inf (inexperienced) novato(ta). ◆ n 1. (colour) verde m. 2. (in village) terreno m comunal. 3. (in golf) green m. ▶ **Green** n (POL) verde m y f, ecologista m y f; **the Greens** los verdes. ▶ **greens** npl (vegetables) verduras fpl.

greenback ['griːnbæk] n Am inf billete de banco americano.

green belt n Br cinturón m verde.

green card n 1. Br (for vehicle) seguro que cubre a conductores en el extranjero. 2. Am (work permit) permiso m de trabajo (en Estados Unidos).

greenery ['griːnərɪ] n vegetación f.

greenfly ['griːnflaɪ] (pl inv OR -ies) n pulgón m.

greengage ['griːngeɪdʒ] n ciruela f claudia.

greengrocer ['griːnˌgrəʊsəʳ] n verdulero m, -ra f; **~'s (shop)** verdulería f.

greenhouse ['griːnhaʊs, pl -haʊzɪz] n invernadero m.

greenhouse effect n: **the ~** el efecto invernadero.

Greenland ['griːnlənd] n Groenlandia.

green salad n ensalada f verde.

greet [griːt] vt 1. (say hello to) saludar. 2. (receive) recibir.

greeting ['griːtɪŋ] n saludo m; (welcome) recibimiento m. ▶ **greetings** npl: **Christmas/birthday ~s!** ¡feliz navidad/cumpleaños!; **~s from ...** recuerdos de ...

greetings card Br ['griːtɪŋz-], **greeting card** Am n tarjeta f de felicitación.

grenade [grə'neɪd] n: **(hand) ~** granada f (de mano).

grew [gruː] pt → **grow**.

grey Br, **gray** Am [greɪ] ◆ adj lit & fig gris; **to go ~** (grey-haired) echar canas, encanecer. ◆ n gris m.

grey-haired [-'heəd] adj canoso(sa).

greyhound ['greɪhaʊnd] n galgo m.

grid [grɪd] n 1. (grating) reja f, enrejado m. 2. (system of squares) cuadrícula f.

griddle ['grɪdl] n plancha f.

gridlock ['grɪdlɒk] n Am embotellamiento m, atasco m.

grief [griːf] n (U) 1. (sorrow) dolor m, pesar m. 2. inf (trouble) problemas mpl. 3. phr: **to come to ~** (person) sufrir un percance; (plans) irse al traste; **good ~!** ¡madre mía!

grievance ['griːvns] n (motivo m de) queja f.

grieve [griːv] vi: **to ~ (for)** llorar (por).

grievous ['griːvəs] adj fml grave.

grievous bodily harm n (U) lesiones fpl graves.

grill [grɪl] ◆ n 1. (of cooker) parrilla f. 2. (food) parrillada f. ◆ vt 1. (CULIN) asar a la parrilla. 2. inf (interrogate) someter a un duro interrogatorio.

grille [grɪl] n (on radiator, machine) rejilla f; (on window, door) reja f.

grim [grɪm] adj 1. (expression) adusto (ta); (determination) inexorable. 2. (place, facts, prospects) descorazonador(ra), lúgubre.

grimace [grɪ'meɪs] ◆ n mueca f. ◆ vi hacer una mueca.

grime [graɪm] n mugre f.

grimy ['graɪmɪ] adj mugriento(ta).

grin [grɪn] ◆ n sonrisa f (abierta). ◆ vi: **to ~ (at)** sonreír (a).

grind [graɪnd] (pt & pp **ground**) ◆ vt (crush) moler. ◆ vi (scrape) rechinar,

chirriar. ◆ n (*hard, boring work*) rutina f.
▶ **grind down** vt sep (*oppress*) oprimir,
acogotar. ▶ **grind up** vt sep pulverizar.
grinder ['graɪndər] n molinillo m.

grip [grɪp] ◆ n 1. (*grasp, hold*): **to have a
~ (on sthg/sb)** tener (algo/a alguien)
bien agarrado. 2. (*control, domination*): **~
on** control m de, dominio m de; **to get to
~s with** llegar a controlar; **to get a ~ on
o.s.** calmarse, controlarse. 3. (*adhesion*)
sujeción f, adherencia f. 4. (*handle*)
asidero m. 5. (*bag*) bolsa f de viaje. ◆ vt
1. (*grasp*) agarrar, asir; (*hand*) apretar;
(*weapon*) empuñar. 2. (*seize*) apoderarse
de.

gripe [graɪp] inf ◆ n (*complaint*) queja f.
◆ vi: **to ~ (about)** quejarse (de).

gripping ['grɪpɪŋ] adj apasionante.

grisly ['grɪzlɪ] adj (*horrible, macabre*)
espeluznante.

gristle ['grɪsl] n cartílago m, ternilla f.

grit [grɪt] ◆ n 1. (*stones*) grava f; (*sand,
dust*) arena f. 2. inf (*courage*) valor m. ◆ vt
cubrir de arena (*las calles*).

gritty ['grɪtɪ] adj inf (*brave*) valiente.

groan [grəʊn] ◆ n gemido m. ◆ vi
1. (*moan*) gemir. 2. (*creak*) crujir.

grocer ['grəʊsər] n tendero m, -ra f,
abarrotero m, -ra f Amer; **~'s (shop)** tienda f de comestibles OR ultramarinos,
abarrotería f Amer.

groceries ['grəʊsərɪz] npl (*foods*)
comestibles mpl, abarrotes mpl Amer.

grocery ['grəʊsərɪ] n (*shop*) tienda f de
comestibles OR ultramarinos, abarrotería f Amer.

groggy ['grɒgɪ] adj atontado(da),
mareado(da).

groin [grɔɪn] n ingle f.

groom [gruːm] ◆ n 1. (*of horses*) mozo
m de cuadra. 2. (*bridegroom*) novio m.
◆ vt 1. (*brush*) cepillar, almohazar.
2. (*prepare*): **to ~ sb (for sthg)** preparar a
alguien (para algo).

groove [gruːv] n (*deep line*) ranura f; (*in
record*) surco m.

grope [grəʊp] ◆ vt 1. (*fondle*) meter
mano a. 2. (*try to find*): **to ~ one's way**
andar a tientas. ◆ vi: **to ~ (about) for sthg**
(*object*) buscar algo a tientas; (*solution,
remedy*) buscar algo a ciegas.

gross [grəʊs] (pl inv OR **-es**) ◆ adj
1. (*total*) bruto(ta). 2. fml (*serious, inexcusable*) grave. 3. (*coarse, vulgar*) basto(ta),
vulgar. 4. inf (*obese*) obeso(sa). ◆ n gruesa f. ◆ vt ganar en bruto.

grossly ['grəʊslɪ] adv (*seriously*)
enormemente.

grotesque [grəʊˈtesk] adj grotesco
(ca).

grotto ['grɒtəʊ] (pl **-es** OR **-s**) n gruta f.

grotty ['grɒtɪ] adj Br inf asqueroso(sa).

ground [graʊnd] ◆ pt & pp → **grind**.
◆ n 1. (*surface of earth*) suelo m, tierra f;
above/below ~ sobre/bajo tierra; **on the
~** en el suelo. 2. (*area of land*) terreno m;
(SPORT) campo m, terreno m de juego.
3. (*subject area*) campo m. 4. (*advantage*):
to gain/lose ~ ganar/perder terreno.
◆ vt 1. (*base*): **to be ~ed on** OR **in sthg**
basarse en algo. 2. (*aircraft, pilot*) hacer
permanecer en tierra. 3. Am inf (*child*)
castigar sin salir. 4. Am (ELEC): **to be
~ed** estar conectado(da) a tierra.
▶ **grounds** npl 1. (*reason*): **~s (for sthg/
for doing sthg**) motivos mpl (para algo/
para hacer algo); **on the ~s that**
aduciendo que, debido a que.
2. (*around building*) jardines mpl. 3. (*of
coffee*) poso m.

ground crew n personal m de tierra.

ground floor n planta f baja; **~ flat**
(piso m) bajo m.

grounding ['graʊndɪŋ] n: **~ (in)** base f
(de), conocimientos mpl básicos (de).

groundless ['graʊndlɪs] adj infundado
(da).

groundsheet ['graʊndʃiːt] n lona f
impermeable (*para camping etc*).

ground staff n 1. (*at sports ground*)
personal m al cargo de las instalaciones. 2. Br = **ground crew**.

groundwork ['graʊndwɜːk] n (U) trabajo m preliminar.

group [gruːp] ◆ n grupo m. ◆ vt agrupar. ◆ vi: **to ~ (together)** agruparse.

groupie ['gruːpɪ] n inf groupie f.

grouse [graʊs] (pl inv OR **-s**) ◆ n (*bird*)
urogallo m. ◆ vi inf quejarse.

grove [grəʊv] n (*of trees*) arboleda f.

grovel ['grɒvl] vi lit & fig: **to ~ (to)** arrastrarse (ante).

grow [grəʊ] (pt **grew**, pp **grown**) ◆ vi
1. (*gen*) crecer. 2. (*become*) volverse,
ponerse; **to ~ dark** oscurecer; **to ~ old**
envejecer. ◆ vt 1. (*plants*) cultivar.
2. (*hair, beard*) dejarse crecer. ▶ **grow
on** vt fus inf gustar cada vez más.
▶ **grow out of** vt fus 1. (*become too big
for*): **he has grown out of his clothes** se le
ha quedado pequeña la ropa.
2. (*lose - habit etc*) perder. ▶ **grow up** vi
crecer; **~ up!** ¡no seas niño!

grower ['grəʊər] n cultivador m, -ra f.

growl [graʊl] vi (*dog, person*) gruñir;
(*lion, engine*) rugir.

grown [grəʊn] ♦ pp → **grow**. ♦ adj crecido(da), adulto(ta).

grown-up n persona f mayor.

growth [grəʊθ] n 1. (gen): **(of OR in)** crecimiento m (de). 2. (MED) tumor m.

grub [grʌb] n 1. (insect) larva f, gusano m. 2. inf (food) manduca f, papeo m.

grubby ['grʌbɪ] adj sucio(cia), mugriento(ta).

grudge [grʌdʒ] ♦ n rencor m; **to bear sb a ~, to bear a ~ against sb** guardar rencor a alguien. ♦ vt: **to ~ sb sthg** conceder algo a alguien a regañadientes; **to ~ doing sthg** hacer algo a regañadientes.

gruelling Br, **grueling** Am ['grʊəlɪŋ] adj agotador(ra).

gruesome ['gruːsəm] adj horripilante.

gruff [grʌf] adj 1. (hoarse) bronco(ca). 2. (rough, unfriendly) hosco(ca).

grumble ['grʌmbl] vi 1. (complain) quejarse, refunfuñar; **to ~ about sthg** quejarse de algo, refunfuñar por algo. 2. (stomach) gruñir, hacer ruido.

grumpy ['grʌmpɪ] adj inf gruñón(ona).

grunt [grʌnt] vi gruñir.

G-string n taparrabos m inv, tanga m.

guarantee [ˌgærən'tiː] ♦ n garantía f. ♦ vt garantizar.

guard [gɑːd] ♦ n 1. (person) guardia m y f. 2. (group of guards, operation) guardia f; **to be on/stand ~** estar de/hacer guardia; **to catch sb off ~** coger a alguien desprevenido. 3. Br (RAIL) jefe m de tren. 4. (protective device - for body) protector m; (- for machine) cubierta f protectora. ♦ vt 1. (protect, hide) guardar. 2. (prevent from escaping) vigilar.

guard dog n perro m guardián.

guarded ['gɑːdɪd] adj cauteloso(sa).

guardian ['gɑːdjən] n 1. (of child) tutor m, -ra f. 2. (protector) guardián m, -ana f, protector m, -ra f.

guardrail ['gɑːdreɪl] n Am (on road) pretil m.

guard's van n Br furgón m de cola.

Guatemala [ˌgwɑːtə'mɑːlə] n Guatemala.

Guatemalan [ˌgwɑːtə'mɑːlən] ♦ adj guatemalteco(ca). ♦ n guatemalteco m, -ca f.

guerilla [gə'rɪlə] = **guerrilla**.

Guernsey ['gɜːnzɪ] n (place) Guernsey.

guerrilla [gə'rɪlə] n guerrillero m, -ra f.

guerrilla warfare n (U) guerra f de guerrillas.

guess [ges] ♦ n suposición f, conjetura f; **to take a ~** intentar adivinar. ♦ vt

adivinar; **~ what?** ¿sabes qué? ♦ vi 1. (conjecture) suponer, conjeturar; **to ~ at sthg** tratar de adivinar algo. 2. (suppose): **I ~ (so)** supongo OR me imagino que sí.

guesswork ['geswɜːk] n (U) conjeturas fpl, suposiciones fpl.

guest [gest] n 1. (at home) invitado m, -da f. 2. (at hotel) huésped m y f.

guesthouse ['gesthaʊs, pl -haʊzɪz] n casa f de huéspedes.

guestroom ['gestrʊm] n cuarto m de los huéspedes.

guffaw [gʌ'fɔː] ♦ n carcajada f. ♦ vi reírse a carcajadas.

guidance ['gaɪdəns] n (U) 1. (help) orientación f. 2. (leadership) dirección f.

guide [gaɪd] ♦ n 1. (person) guía m y f. 2. (book) guía f. ♦ vt 1. (show by leading) guiar. 2. (control) conducir, dirigir. 3. (influence): **to be ~d by** guiarse por. ▶ **Guide** n = Girl Guide.

guide book n guía f.

guide dog n perro m lazarillo.

guidelines ['gaɪdlaɪnz] npl directrices fpl.

guild [gɪld] n 1. (HISTORY) gremio m. 2. (association) corporación f.

guile [gaɪl] n (U) literary astucia f.

guillotine ['gɪlətiːn] n (gen) guillotina f.

guilt [gɪlt] n 1. (remorse) culpa f. 2. (JUR) culpabilidad f.

guilty ['gɪltɪ] adj (gen): **~ (of)** culpable (de); **to be found ~/not ~** ser declarado culpable/inocente.

guinea pig ['gɪnɪ-] n lit & fig conejillo m de Indias.

guise [gaɪz] n fml apariencia f.

guitar [gɪ'tɑːʳ] n guitarra f.

guitarist [gɪ'tɑːrɪst] n guitarrista m y f.

gulf [gʌlf] n 1. (sea) golfo m. 2. (chasm) sima f, abismo m. 3. (big difference): **(between)** abismo m (entre). ▶ **Gulf** n: **the Gulf** el Golfo.

gull [gʌl] n gaviota f.

gullet ['gʌlɪt] n esófago m.

gullible ['gʌləbl] adj crédulo(la).

gully ['gʌlɪ] n barranco m.

gulp [gʌlp] ♦ n trago m. ♦ vt (liquid) tragarse; (food) engullir. ♦ vi tragar saliva. ▶ **gulp down** vt sep (liquid) tragarse; (food) engullir.

gum [gʌm] ♦ n 1. (chewing gum) chicle m. 2. (adhesive) cola f, pegamento m. 3. (ANAT) encía f. ♦ vt pegar, engomar.

gumboots ['gʌmbuːts] npl Br botas fpl de agua OR de goma.

hail

gun [gʌn] n 1. (*pistol*) pistola f; (*rifle*) escopeta f, fusil m. 2. (*tool*) pistola f.
▶ **gun down** vt sep abatir (a tiros).

gunboat ['gʌnbəut] n cañonero m.

gunfire ['gʌnfaɪəʳ] n (U) disparos mpl, tiroteo m.

gunman ['gʌnmən] (pl -men [-mən]) n pistolero m.

gunpoint ['gʌnpɔɪnt] n: at ~ a punta de pistola.

gunpowder ['gʌn,paudəʳ] n pólvora f.

gunshot ['gʌnʃɒt] n tiro m, disparo m.

gunsmith ['gʌnsmɪθ] n armero m.

gurgle ['gɜːgl] vi 1. (*water*) gorgotear. 2. (*baby*) gorjear.

guru ['guruː] n lit & fig gurú m.

gush [gʌʃ] ♦ n chorro m. ♦ vi 1. (*flow out*) chorrear, manar. 2. pej (*enthuse*) ser muy efusivo(va).

gusset ['gʌsɪt] n escudete m.

gust [gʌst] n ráfaga f, racha f.

gusto ['gʌstəu] n: with ~ con deleite.

gut [gʌt] ♦ n 1. (MED) intestino m. 2. (*strong thread*) sedal m. ♦ vt 1. (*animal*) destripar. 2. (*building etc*) destruir el interior de. ▶ **guts** npl inf 1. (*intestines*) tripas fpl; to hate sb's ~s odiar a alguien a muerte. 2. (*courage*) agallas fpl.

gutter ['gʌtəʳ] n 1. (*ditch*) cuneta f. 2. (*on roof*) canalón m.

gutter press n pej prensa f amarilla OR sensacionalista.

guy [gaɪ] n 1. inf (*man*) tipo m, tío m, chavo m Amer. 2. Br (*dummy*) muñeco que se quema en Gran Bretaña la noche de Guy Fawkes.

Guy Fawkes' Night n fiesta que se celebra el 5 de noviembre en Gran Bretaña en que se encienden hogueras y se lanzan fuegos artificiales.

guy rope n viento m, cuerda f (de tienda de campaña).

guzzle ['gʌzl] ♦ vt zamparse. ♦ vi zampar.

gym [dʒɪm] n inf 1. (*gymnasium*) gimnasio m. 2. (*exercises*) gimnasia f.

gymnasium [dʒɪm'neɪzjəm] (pl -siums OR -sia [-zjə]) n gimnasio m.

gymnast ['dʒɪmnæst] n gimnasta m y f.

gymnastics [dʒɪm'næstɪks] n (U) gimnasia f.

gym shoes npl zapatillas fpl de gimnasia.

gymslip ['dʒɪm,slɪp] n Br bata f de colegio.

gynaecologist Br, **gynecologist** Am

[,gaɪnə'kɒlədʒɪst] n ginecólogo m, -ga f.

gynaecology Br, **gynecology** Am [,gaɪnə'kɒlədʒɪ] n ginecología f.

gypsy ['dʒɪpsɪ] = **gipsy**.

gyrate [dʒaɪ'reɪt] vi girar.

H

h (pl h's OR hs), **H** (pl H's OR Hs) [eɪtʃ] n (*letter*) h f, H f.

haberdashery ['hæbədæʃərɪ] n mercería f.

habit ['hæbɪt] n 1. (*custom*) costumbre f, hábito m; to make a ~ of doing sthg tener por costumbre hacer algo. 2. (*garment*) hábito m.

habitat ['hæbɪtæt] n hábitat m.

habitual [hə'bɪtʃuəl] adj 1. (*usual*) habitual, acostumbrado(da). 2. (*smoker, gambler*) empedernido(da).

hack [hæk] ♦ n pej (*writer*) escritorzuelo m, -la f; (*journalist*) gacetillero m, -ra f. ♦ vt (*cut*) cortar en tajos, acuchillar. ▶ **hack into** vt fus piratear.

hacker ['hækəʳ] n: (*computer*) ~ pirata m informático, pirata f informática.

hackneyed ['hæknɪd] adj pej trillado (da), gastado(da).

hacksaw ['hæksɔː] n sierra f para metales.

had [weak form həd, strong form hæd] pt & pp → **have**.

haddock ['hædək] (pl inv) n eglefino m.

hadn't ['hædnt] = **had not**.

haemophiliac [,hiːmə'fɪlɪæk] = **hemophiliac**.

haemorrhage ['hemərɪdʒ] = **hemorrhage**.

haemorrhoids ['hemərɔɪdz] = **hemorrhoids**.

haggard ['hægəd] adj ojeroso(sa).

haggis ['hægɪs] n plato típico escocés hecho con las asaduras del cordero.

haggle ['hægl] vi: to ~ (with sb over OR about sthg) regatear (algo con alguien).

Hague [heɪg] n: The ~ La Haya.

hail [heɪl] ♦ n 1. (METEOR) granizo m, pedrisco m. 2. fig (*large number*) lluvia f. ♦ vt 1. (*call*) llamar. 2. (*acclaim*): to ~ sb as sthg aclamar a alguien algo; to ~ sthg as sthg ensalzar algo catalogándolo de algo. ◆ *v impers* granizar.

hailstone ['heɪlstəʊn] *n* granizo *m*, piedra *f*.

hair [heəʳ] *n* **1.** (U) (*gen*) pelo *m*; **to do one's ~** arreglarse el pelo. **2.** (*on person's skin*) vello *m*.

hairbrush ['heəbrʌʃ] *n* cepillo *m* para el pelo.

haircut ['heəkʌt] *n* corte *m* de pelo.

hairdo ['heəduː] (*pl* **-s**) *n inf* peinado *m*.

hairdresser ['heə,dresəʳ] *n* peluquero *m*, -ra *f*; **~'s (salon)** peluquería *f*.

hairdryer ['heə,draɪəʳ] *n* secador *m* (de pelo).

hair gel *n* gomina *f*.

hairgrip ['heəgrɪp] *n Br* horquilla *f*.

hairpin ['heəpɪn] *n* horquilla *f* de moño.

hairpin bend *n* curva *f* muy cerrada.

hair-raising [-,reɪzɪŋ] *adj* espeluznante.

hair remover [-rɪ,muːvəʳ] *n* depilatorio *m*.

hair slide *n Br* pasador *m*.

hairspray ['heəspreɪ] *n* laca *f* (para el pelo).

hairstyle ['heəstaɪl] *n* peinado *m*.

hairy ['heərɪ] *adj* **1.** (*covered in hair*) peludo(da). **2.** *inf* (*scary*) espeluznante, espantoso(sa).

Haiti ['heɪtɪ] *n* Haití.

hake [heɪk] (*pl inv* OR **-s**) *n* merluza *f*.

half [*Br* hɑːf, *Am* hæf] (*pl senses 1 and 3* **halves**, *pl senses 2 and 4* **halves** OR **halfs**) ◆ *adj* medio(dia); **~ a dozen/mile** media docena/milla; **~ an hour** media hora. ◆ *adv* **1.** (*gen*): **~ full/open** lleno/abierto por la mitad; **~ and ~** mitad y mitad. **2.** (*by half*): **~ as big (as)** la mitad de grande (que). **3.** (*in telling the time*): **~ past nine**, **~ after nine** *Am* las nueve y media; **it's ~ past** son y media. ◆ *n* **1.** (*one of two parts*) mitad *f*; **~ (of) the group** la mitad del grupo; **a pound/mile and a ~** una libra/milla y media; **in ~** por la mitad, en dos; **to go halves (with sb)** ir a medias (con alguien). **2.** (*fraction, halfback, child's ticket*) medio *m*. **3.** (*of sports match*) tiempo *m*, mitad *f*. **4.** (*of beer*) media pinta *f*. ◆ *pron* la mitad; **~ of it/them** la mitad.

halfback ['hɑːfbæk] *n* medio *m*.

half board *n* media pensión *f*.

half-breed ◆ *adj* mestizo(za). ◆ *n* mestizo *m*, -za *f* (*atención: el término 'half-breed' se considera racista*).

half-caste [-kɑːst] ◆ *adj* mestizo(za). ◆ *n* mestizo *m*, -za *f* (*atención: el término 'half-caste' se considera racista*).

half-hearted [-'hɑːtɪd] *adj* poco entusiasta.

half hour *n* media hora *f*.

half-mast *n*: **at ~** (*flag*) a media asta.

half moon *n* media luna *f*.

half note *n Am* (MUS) blanca *f*.

halfpenny ['heɪpnɪ] (*pl* **-pennies** OR **-pence**) *n* medio penique *m*.

half-price *adj* a mitad de precio.

half term *n Br breves vacaciones escolares a mitad de trimestre.*

half time *n* (U) descanso *m*.

halfway [hɑːf'weɪ] ◆ *adj* intermedio (dia). ◆ *adv* **1.** (*in space*): **I was ~ down the street** llevaba la mitad de la calle andada. **2.** (*in time*): **the film was ~ through** la película iba por la mitad.

halibut ['hælɪbət] (*pl inv* OR **-s**) *n* halibut *m*.

hall [hɔːl] *n* **1.** (*in house*) vestíbulo *m*. **2.** (*public building*) sala *f*. **3.** *Br* (UNIV) colegio *m* mayor. **4.** (*country house*) mansión *f*, casa *f* solariega.

hallmark ['hɔːlmɑːk] *n* **1.** (*typical feature*) sello *m* distintivo. **2.** (*on metal*) contraste *m*.

hallo [hə'ləʊ] = **hello**.

hall of residence (*pl* **halls of residence**) *n Br* residencia *f* universitaria, colegio *m* mayor.

Hallowe'en [,hæləʊ'iːn] *n fiesta celebrada la noche del 31 de octubre.*

hallucinate [hə'luːsɪneɪt] *vi* alucinar.

hallway ['hɔːlweɪ] *n* vestíbulo *m*.

halo ['heɪləʊ] (*pl* **-es** OR **-s**) *n* halo *m*, aureola *f*.

halt [hɔːlt] ◆ *n* (*stop*): **to come to a ~** (*vehicle*) pararse; (*activity*) interrumpirse; **to call a ~ to** poner fin a. ◆ *vt* (*person*) parar, detener; (*development, activity*) interrumpir. ◆ *vi* (*person, train*) pararse, detenerse; (*development, activity*) interrumpirse.

halterneck ['hɔːltənek] *adj* escotado (da) por detrás.

halve [*Br* hɑːv, *Am* hæv] *vt* **1.** (*reduce by half*) reducir a la mitad. **2.** (*divide*) partir en dos.

halves [*Br* hɑːvz, *Am* hævz] *pl* → **half**.

ham [hæm] ◆ *n* (*meat*) jamón *m*. ◆ *comp* de jamón.

hamburger ['hæmbɜːgəʳ] *n* **1.** (*burger*) hamburguesa *f*. **2.** (U) *Am* (*mince*) carne *f* picada.

hamlet ['hæmlɪt] *n* aldea *f*.

hammer ['hæməʳ] ◆ *n* (*gen* & SPORT) martillo *m*. ◆ *vt* **1.** (*with tool*) martillear.

2. (with fist) aporrear. **3.** inf (defeat) dar una paliza a. ◆ vi (with fist): **to ~ (on sthg)** aporrear (algo). ► **hammer out** vt fus (solution, agreement) alcanzar con esfuerzo.

hammock ['hæmək] n hamaca f, chinchorro m Amer.

hamper ['hæmpəʳ] ◆ n **1.** (for food) cesta f. **2.** Am (for laundry) cesto m de la ropa sucia. ◆ vt obstaculizar.

hamster ['hæmstəʳ] n hámster m.

hamstring ['hæmstrɪŋ] (pt & pp -**strung** [-strʌŋ]) n tendón m de la corva.

hand [hænd] ◆ n **1.** (gen) mano f; **to hold ~s** ir cogidos de la mano; **~ in ~** (people) (cogidos) de la mano; **by ~** a mano; **in the ~s of** en manos de; **to have sthg on one's ~s** tener uno algo en sus manos; **to get** OR **lay one's ~s on sthg** hacerse con algo; **to get** OR **lay one's ~s on sb** pillar a alguien; **to get out of ~** (situation) hacerse incontrolable; (person) desmandarse; **to give** OR **lend sb a ~ (with)** echar una mano a alguien (con); **to have one's ~s full** estar muy ocupado; **to have time in ~** tener tiempo de sobra; **to take sb in ~** hacerse cargo OR ocuparse de alguien; **to try one's ~ at sthg** intentar hacer algo. **2.** (influence) influencia f. **3.** (worker - on farm) bracero m, peón m; (- on ship) tripulante m. **4.** (of clock, watch) manecilla f, aguja f. **5.** (handwriting) letra f. ◆ vt: **to ~ sthg to sb, to ~ sb sthg** dar OR entregar algo a alguien. ► **(close) at hand** adv cerca. ► **on hand** adv al alcance de la mano. ► **on the other hand** conj por otra parte. ► **out of hand** adv (completely) terminantemente. ► **to hand** adv a mano. ► **hand down** vt sep (heirloom) pasar en herencia; (knowledge) transmitir. ► **hand in** vt sep entregar. ► **hand out** vt sep repartir, distribuir. ► **hand over** ◆ vt sep **1.** (baton, money) entregar. **2.** (responsibility, power) ceder. ◆ vi: **to ~ over (to)** dar paso a (a).

handbag ['hændbæg] n bolso m.

handball ['hændbɔːl] n balonmano m.

handbook ['hændbʊk] n manual m.

handbrake ['hændbreɪk] n freno m de mano.

handcuffs ['hændkʌfs] npl esposas fpl.

handful ['hændfʊl] n (gen) puñado m.

handgun ['hændgʌn] n pistola f.

handicap ['hændɪkæp] ◆ n **1.** (disability) incapacidad f, minusvalía f. **2.** (disadvantage) desventaja f, obstáculo m. **3.** (SPORT) hándicap m. ◆ vt estorbar.

handicapped ['hændɪkæpt] ◆ adj

minusválido(da). ◆ npl: **the ~** los minusválidos.

handicraft ['hændɪkrɑːft] n (skill) trabajos mpl manuales, artesanía f.

handiwork ['hændɪwɜːk] n (U) (doing, work) obra f.

handkerchief ['hæŋkətʃɪf] (pl -**chiefs** OR -**chieves** [-tʃiːvz]) n pañuelo m.

handle ['hændl] ◆ n (of door, window) pomo m; (of tool) mango m; (of suitcase, cup, jug) asa f. ◆ vt (gen) manejar; (order, complaint, application) encargarse de; (negotiations, takeover) conducir; (people) tratar.

handlebars ['hændlbɑːz] npl manillar m.

handler ['hændləʳ] n **1.** (of animal) guardián m, -ana f. **2.** (at airport): **(baggage) ~** mozo m de equipajes.

hand luggage n Br equipaje m de mano.

handmade [,hænd'meɪd] adj hecho (cha) a mano.

handout ['hændaʊt] n **1.** (gift) donativo m. **2.** (leaflet) hojas fpl (informativas).

handrail ['hændreɪl] n pasamano m.

handset ['hændset] n auricular m (de teléfono); **to lift/replace the ~** descolgar/colgar (el teléfono).

handshake ['hændʃeɪk] n apretón m de manos.

handsome ['hænsəm] adj **1.** (man) guapo, atractivo. **2.** (literary) (woman) bella. **3.** (reward, profit) considerable.

handstand ['hændstænd] n pino m.

handwriting ['hænd,raɪtɪŋ] n letra f, caligrafía f.

handy ['hændɪ] adj inf **1.** (useful) práctico(ca); **to come in ~** venir bien. **2.** (skilful) mañoso(sa). **3.** (near) a mano, cerca.

handyman ['hændɪmæn] (pl -**men** [-men]) n: **a good ~** un manitas.

hang [hæŋ] (pt & pp sense 1 **hung**, pt & pp sense 2 **hung** OR **hanged**) ◆ vt **1.** (fasten) colgar. **2.** (execute) ahorcar. ◆ vi **1.** (be fastened) colgar, pender. **2.** (be executed) ser ahorcado(da). ◆ n: **to get the ~ of sthg** inf coger el tranquillo a algo. ► **hang about, hang around** vi pasar el rato; **they didn't ~ about** se pusieron en marcha sin perder un minuto. ► **hang on** vi **1.** (keep hold): **to ~ on (to)** agarrarse (a). **2.** inf (continue waiting) esperar, aguardar. **3.** (persevere) resistir. ► **hang out** vi inf (spend time) moverse, pasar el rato. ► **hang round** = **hang about.** ► **hang up** ◆ vt sep colgar. ◆ vi colgar. ► **hang up on** vt fus colgar.

hangar ['hæŋə^r] n hangar m.
hanger ['hæŋə^r] n percha f.
hanger-on (pl **hangers-on**) n lapa f, moscón m, -ona f.
hang gliding n vuelo m con ala delta.
hangover ['hæŋ,əʊvə^r] n (from drinking) resaca f.
hang-up n inf complejo m.
hanker ['hæŋkə^r] ► **hanker after, hanker for** vt fus anhelar.
hankie, hanky ['hæŋkı] (abbr of **handkerchief**) n inf pañuelo m.
haphazard [,hæp'hæzəd] adj caótico (ca).
hapless ['hæplıs] adj literary desventurado(da), desgraciado(da).
happen ['hæpən] vi 1. (occur) pasar, ocurrir; **to ~ to sb** pasarle OR sucederle a alguien. 2. (chance): **I ~ed to be looking out of the window ...** dio la casualidad de que estaba mirando por la ventana ...; **do you ~ to have a pen on you?** ¿no tendrás un boli acaso OR por casualidad?; **as it ~s ...** da la casualidad de que ...
happening ['hæpənıŋ] n suceso m, acontecimiento m.
happily ['hæpılı] adv 1. (with pleasure) alegremente, felizmente. 2. (fortunately) afortunadamente.
happiness ['hæpınıs] n (state) felicidad f; (feeling) alegría f.
happy ['hæpı] adj 1. (gen) feliz, contento(ta); **~ Christmas/birthday!** ¡Feliz Navidad/cumpleaños!; **to be ~ with/about sthg** estar contento con algo. 2. (causing contentment) feliz, alegre. 3. (fortunate) feliz, oportuno(na). 4. (willing): **to be ~ to do sthg** estar más que dispuesto(ta) a hacer algo; **I'd be ~ to do it** yo lo haría con gusto.
happy-go-lucky adj despreocupado (da).
happy medium n término m medio.
harangue [hə'ræŋ] ♦ n arenga f. ♦ vt arengar.
harass ['hærəs] vt acosar.
harbour Br, **harbor** Am ['hɑ:bə^r] ♦ n puerto m. ♦ vt 1. (feeling) abrigar. 2. (person) dar refugio a, encubrir.
hard [hɑ:d] ♦ adj 1. (gen) duro(ra); (frost) fuerte; **to be ~ on sb/sthg** (subj: person) ser duro con alguien/algo; (subj: work, strain) perjudicar a alguien/algo; (subj: result) ser inmerecido para alguien/algo. 2. (difficult) difícil. 3. (forceful - push, kick etc) fuerte. 4. (fact,

news) concreto(ta). 5. Br (extreme): **~ left/right** extrema izquierda/derecha. ♦ adv 1. (try) mucho; (work, rain) intensamente; (listen) atentamente. 2. (push, kick) fuerte, con fuerza. 3. phr: **to be ~ pushed** OR **put** OR **pressed to do sthg** vérselas y deseárselas para hacer algo; **to feel ~ done by** sentirse tratado injustamente.
hardback ['hɑ:dbæk] n edición f en pasta dura OR en tela.
hardboard ['hɑ:dbɔ:d] n madera f conglomerada.
hard-boiled adj lit & fig duro(ra).
hard cash n dinero m contante y sonante.
hard copy n (COMPUT) copia f impresa.
hard disk n (COMPUT) disco m duro.
harden ['hɑ:dn] ♦ vt 1. (gen) endurecer. 2. (resolve, opinion) reforzar. ♦ vi 1. (gen) endurecerse. 2. (resolve, opinion) reforzarse.
hard-headed [-'hedıd] adj realista.
hard-hearted [-'hɑ:tıd] adj insensible.
hard labour n (U) trabajos mpl forzados.
hard-liner n partidario m, -ria f de la línea dura.
hardly ['hɑ:dlı] adv apenas; **~ ever/anything** casi nunca/nada; **I'm ~ a communist, am I?** ¡pues sí que tengo yo mucho que ver con el comunismo!
hardness ['hɑ:dnıs] n 1. (firmness) dureza f. 2. (difficulty) dificultad f.
hardship ['hɑ:dʃıp] n 1. (U) (difficult conditions) privaciones fpl. 2. (difficult circumstance) infortunio m.
hard shoulder n Br (AUT) arcén m.
hard up adj inf sin un duro; **to be ~ for sthg** andar escaso de algo.
hardware ['hɑ:dweə^r] (U) n 1. (tools, equipment) artículos mpl de ferretería. 2. (COMPUT) hardware m.
hardware shop n ferretería f.
hardwearing [,hɑ:d'weərıŋ] adj Br resistente, duradero(ra).
hardworking [,hɑ:d'wɜ:kıŋ] adj trabajador(ra).
hardy ['hɑ:dı] adj 1. (person, animal) fuerte, robusto(ta). 2. (plant) resistente.
hare [heə^r] n liebre f.
harebrained ['heə,breınd] adj inf atolondrado(da).
harelip [,heə'lıp] n labio m leporino.
haricot (bean) ['hærıkəʊ-] n judía f, alubia f.

Harley Street ['hɑːlɪ-] n calle londinense famosa por sus médicos especialistas.

harm [hɑːm] ◆ n daño m; **to do ~ to sthg/sb, to do sthg/sb ~** (physically) hacer daño a algo/alguien; fig perjudicar algo/a alguien; **to be out of ~'s way** estar a salvo. ◆ vt (gen) hacer daño a, dañar; (reputation, chances, interests) dañar.

harmful ['hɑːmful] adj: **~ (to)** perjudicial OR dañino(na) (para).

harmless ['hɑːmlɪs] adj inofensivo (va).

harmonica [hɑːˈmɒnɪkə] n armónica f.

harmonize, -ise ['hɑːmənaɪz] ◆ vi: **to ~ (with)** armonizar (con). ◆ vt armonizar.

harmony ['hɑːmənɪ] n armonía f.

harness ['hɑːnɪs] ◆ n (for horse) arreos mpl, guarniciones fpl. ◆ vt 1. (horse) enjaezar. 2. (use) aprovechar.

harp [hɑːp] n arpa f. ▶ **harp on** vi: **to ~ on (about sthg)** dar la matraca (con algo).

harpoon [hɑːˈpuːn] n arpón m.

harpsichord ['hɑːpsɪkɔːd] n clavicordio m.

harrowing ['hærəʊɪŋ] adj pavoroso (sa).

harsh [hɑːʃ] adj 1. (life, conditions, winter) duro(ra). 2. (punishment, decision, person) severo(ra). 3. (texture, taste, voice) áspero (ra); (light, sound) violento(ta).

harvest ['hɑːvɪst] ◆ n (gen) cosecha f, pizca f Amer; (of grapes) vendimia f. ◆ vt cosechar.

has [weak form həz, strong form hæz] 3rd person sg → **have**.

has-been n inf pej vieja gloria f.

hash [hæʃ] n 1. (meat) picadillo m (de carne). 2. inf (mess): **to make a ~ of sthg** hacer algo fatal.

hashish ['hæʃiːʃ] n hachís m.

hasn't ['hæznt] = has not.

hassle ['hæsl] inf ◆ n (U) (annoyance) rollo m, lío m. ◆ vt dar la lata a.

haste [heɪst] n prisa f; **to do sthg in ~** hacer algo de prisa y corriendo.

hasten ['heɪsn] fml ◆ vt acelerar. ◆ vi: **to ~ (to do sthg)** apresurarse (a hacer algo).

hastily ['heɪstɪlɪ] adv 1. (quickly) de prisa, precipitadamente. 2. (rashly) a la ligera, sin reflexionar.

hasty ['heɪstɪ] adj 1. (quick) apresurado (da), precipitado(da). 2. (rash) irreflexivo(va).

hat [hæt] n sombrero m.

hatch [hætʃ] ◆ vi 1. (chick) romper el cascarón, salir del huevo. 2. (egg)

romperse. ◆ vt 1. (chick, egg) incubar. 2. fig (scheme, plot) idear, tramar. ◆ n (for serving food) ventanilla f.

hatchback ['hætʃˌbæk] n coche m con puerta trasera.

hatchet ['hætʃɪt] n hacha f.

hatchway ['hætʃˌweɪ] n escotilla f.

hate [heɪt] ◆ n odio m. ◆ vt odiar; **to ~ doing sthg** odiar hacer algo.

hateful ['heɪtful] adj odioso(sa).

hatred ['heɪtrɪd] n odio m.

hat trick n (SPORT) tres tantos marcados por un jugador en el mismo partido.

haughty ['hɔːtɪ] adj altanero(ra), altivo(va).

haul [hɔːl] ◆ n 1. (of stolen goods) botín m; (of drugs) alijo m. 2. (distance): **long ~** largo camino m, largo trayecto m. ◆ vt (pull) tirar, arrastrar.

haulage ['hɔːlɪdʒ] n transporte m.

haulier Br ['hɔːlɪər], **hauler** Am ['hɔːlər] n transportista m y f.

haunch [hɔːntʃ] n 1. (of person) asentaderas fpl; **to squat on one's ~es** ponerse en cuclillas. 2. (of animal) pernil m.

haunt [hɔːnt] ◆ n sitio m favorito. ◆ vt 1. (subj: ghost) aparecer en. 2. (subj: memory, fear, problem) atormentar.

have [hæv] (pt & pp had) ◆ aux vb (to form perfect tenses) haber; **to ~ eaten** haber comido; **he hasn't gone yet, has he?** no se habrá ido ya ¿no?; **no, he hasn't (done it)** no, no lo ha hecho; **yes, he has (done it)** sí, lo ha hecho; **I was out of breath, having run all the way** estaba sin aliento después de haber corrido todo el camino. ◆ vt 1. (possess, receive): **to ~ (got)** tener; **I ~ no money, I haven't got any money** no tengo dinero; **he has big hands** tiene las manos grandes; **do you ~ a car?, ~ you got a car?** ¿tienes coche? 2. (experience, suffer) tener; **I had an accident** tuve un accidente; **to ~ a cold** tener un resfriado. 3. (referring to an action, instead of another verb): **to ~ a look** mirar, echar una mirada; **to ~ a swim** darse un baño, nadar; **to ~ breakfast** desayunar; **to ~ lunch** comer; **to ~ dinner** cenar; **to ~ a cigarette** fumarse un cigarro; **to ~ an operation** operarse. 4. (give birth to): **to ~ a baby** tener un niño. 5. (cause to be done): **to ~ sb do sthg** hacer que alguien haga algo; **to ~ sthg done** hacer que se haga algo; **to ~ one's hair cut** (ir a) cortarse el pelo. 6. (be treated in a certain way): **I had my car stolen** me robaron el coche. 7. inf (cheat): **you've been had** te han timado. 8. phr: **to ~ had**

it (*car, machine*) estar para el arrastre. ◆ *modal vb* (*be obliged*): **to ~ (got) to do sthg** tener que hacer algo; **do you ~ to go?, ~ you got to go?** ¿tienes que irte? ▶ **have on** *vt sep* **1.** (*be wearing*) llevar (puesto). **2.** (*tease*) tomar el pelo a. **3.** (*have to do*): **~ you got anything on on Friday?** ¿estás libre OR haces algo el viernes? ▶ **have out** *vt sep* **1.** (*have removed*): **to ~ one's tonsils out** operarse de las amígdalas. **2.** (*discuss frankly*): **to ~ it out with sb** poner las cuentas claras con alguien.

haven ['heɪvn] *n fig* refugio *m*, asilo *m*.

haven't ['hævnt] = **have not**.

haversack ['hævəsæk] *n* mochila *f*.

havoc ['hævək] *n* (U) caos *m*, estragos *mpl*; **to play ~ with sthg** causar estragos en algo.

Hawaii [hə'waɪiː] *n* Hawai.

hawk [hɔːk] *n* halcón *m*.

hawker ['hɔːkər] *n* vendedor *m*, -ra *f* ambulante.

hay [heɪ] *n* heno *m*.

hay fever *n* (U) fiebre *f* del heno.

haystack ['heɪˌstæk] *n* almiar *m*.

haywire ['heɪˌwaɪər] *adj inf*: **to go ~** (*person*) volverse majara; (*plan*) liarse, embrollarse; (*computer, TV etc*) changarse.

hazard ['hæzəd] ◆ *n* riesgo *m*, peligro *m*. ◆ *vt* (*guess, suggestion*) aventurar.

hazardous ['hæzədəs] *adj* arriesgado (da), peligroso(sa).

hazard warning lights *npl Br* luces *fpl* de emergencia.

haze [heɪz] *n* neblina *f*.

hazel ['heɪzl] *adj* color avellana (*inv*).

hazelnut ['heɪzlˌnʌt] *n* avellana *f*.

hazy ['heɪzɪ] *adj* **1.** (*misty*) neblinoso (sa). **2.** (*vague*) vago(ga), confuso(sa).

he [hiː] ◆ *pers pron* él; **~'s tall/happy** es alto/feliz; **HE can't do it** ÉL no puede hacerlo; **there ~ is** allí está. ◆ *comp*: **~-goat** macho cabrío *m*.

head [hed] ◆ *n* **1.** (ANAT & COMPUT) cabeza *f*; **a** OR **per ~** por persona, por cabeza; **to be soft in the ~** estar mal de la sesera; **to be off one's ~** *Br*, **to be out of one's ~** *Am* estar como una cabra; **it went to her ~** se le subió a la cabeza; **to keep/lose one's ~** no perder/perder la cabeza; **to laugh one's ~ off** reír a mandíbula batiente. **2.** (*mind, brain*) talento *m*, aptitud *f*; **she has a ~ for figures** se le dan bien las cuentas. **3.** (*top - gen*) cabeza *f*; (*- of bed*) cabecera *f*. **4.** (*of flower*) cabezuela *f*; (*of cabbage*)

cogollo *m*. **5.** (*leader*) jefe *m*, -fa *f*. **6.** (*head teacher*) director *m*, -ra *f* (de colegio). ◆ *vt* **1.** (*procession, convoy, list*) encabezar. **2.** (*organization, delegation*) dirigir. **3.** (FTBL) cabecear. ◆ *vi*: **to ~ north/for home** dirigirse hacia el norte/ a casa. ▶ **heads** *npl* (*on coin*) cara *f*; **~s or tails?** ¿cara o cruz? ▶ **head for** *vt fus* **1.** (*place*) dirigirse a. **2.** *fig* (*trouble, disaster*) ir camino a.

headache ['hedeɪk] *n* **1.** (MED) dolor *m* de cabeza. **2.** *fig* (*problem*) quebradero *m* de cabeza.

headband ['hedbænd] *n* cinta *f*, banda *f* (para el pelo).

head boy *n Br* (*at school*) alumno delegado principal que suele representar a sus condiscípulos en actos escolares.

headdress ['hedˌdres] *n* tocado *m*.

header ['hedər] *n* (FTBL) cabezazo *m*.

headfirst [ˌhed'fɜːst] *adv* de cabeza.

head girl *n Br* (*in school*) alumna delegada principal que suele representar a sus condiscípulas en actos escolares.

heading ['hedɪŋ] *n* encabezamiento *m*.

headlamp ['hedlæmp] *n Br* faro *m*.

headland ['hedlənd] *n* cabo *m*, promontorio *m*.

headlight ['hedlaɪt] *n* faro *m*.

headline ['hedlaɪn] *n* titular *m*.

headlong ['hedlɒŋ] *adv* **1.** (*headfirst*) de cabeza. **2.** (*quickly, unthinkingly*) precipitadamente.

headmaster [ˌhed'mɑːstər] *n* director *m* (de colegio).

headmistress [ˌhed'mɪstrɪs] *n* directora *f* (de colegio).

head office *n* oficina *f* central.

head-on ◆ *adj* de frente, frontal. ◆ *adv* de frente.

headphones ['hedfəʊnz] *npl* auriculares *mpl*.

headquarters [ˌhed'kwɔːtəz] *npl* (oficina *f*) central *f*, sede *f*; (MIL) cuartel *m* general.

headrest ['hedrest] *n* reposacabezas *m inv*.

headroom ['hedrʊm] *n* (U) (*in car*) espacio *m* entre la cabeza y el techo; (*below bridge*) altura *f* libre, gálibo *m*.

headscarf ['hedskɑːf] (*pl* **-scarves** [-skɑːvz] OR **-scarfs**) *n* pañuelo *m* (para la cabeza).

headset ['hedset] *n* auriculares *mpl* con micrófono.

head start *n*: **~ (on** OR **over)** ventaja *f* (con respecto a).

headstrong ['hedstrɒŋ] *adj* obstinado (da).

head waiter *n* maître *m*.

headway ['hedweɪ] *n*: **to make ~** avanzar, hacer progresos.

headwind ['hedwɪnd] *n* viento *m* de proa.

heady ['hedɪ] *adj* 1. (*exciting*) emocionante. 2. (*causing giddiness*) embriagador(ra).

heal [hiːl] ◆ *vt* 1. (*person*) curar, sanar; (*wound*) cicatrizar. 2. *fig* (*troubles, discord*) remediar. ◆ *vi* cicatrizar.

healing ['hiːlɪŋ] *n* curación *f*.

health [helθ] *n* 1. (*gen*) salud *f*; **to be in good/poor ~** estar bien/mal de salud. 2. *fig* (*of country, organization*) buen estado *m*.

health centre *n* centro *m* de salud.

health food *n* comida *f* dietética.

health food shop *n* tienda *f* de dietética.

health service *n* servicio *m* sanitario de la Seguridad Social, ≃ INSALUD *m*.

healthy ['helθɪ] *adj* 1. (*gen*) sano(na), saludable. 2. (*profit*) pingüe. 3. (*attitude, respect*) natural, sano(na).

heap [hiːp] ◆ *n* montón *m*, pila *f*. ◆ *vt* (*pile up*): **to ~ sthg (on OR onto sthg)** amontonar algo (sobre algo). ▶ **heaps** *npl inf* montones *fpl*.

hear [hɪəʳ] (*pt & pp* heard [hɜːd]) ◆ *vt* 1. (*gen*) oír; **I ~ (that)** me dicen que. 2. (JUR) ver. ◆ *vi* 1. (*gen*) oír; **have you heard about that job yet?** ¿sabes algo del trabajo ese?; **to ~ from sb** tener noticias de alguien. 2. *phr*: **to have heard of** haber oído hablar de; **I won't ~ of it!** ¡de eso ni hablar!

hearing ['hɪərɪŋ] *n* 1. (*sense*) oído *m*; **hard of ~** duro de oído. 2. (JUR) vista *f*.

hearing aid *n* audífono *m*.

hearsay ['hɪəseɪ] *n* (U) habladurías *fpl*.

hearse [hɜːs] *n* coche *m* fúnebre.

heart [hɑːt] *n* 1. (*gen*) corazón *m*; **from the ~** con toda sinceridad; **to break sb's ~** romper OR partir el corazón a alguien. 2. (*courage*): **I didn't have the ~ to tell her** no tuve valor para decírselo; **to lose ~** descorazonarse. 3. (*centre - of issue, problem*) quid *m*; (*- of city etc*) centro *m*; (*- of lettuce*) cogollo *m*. ▶ **hearts** *npl* corazones *mpl*. ▶ **at heart** *adv* en el fondo. ▶ **by heart** *adv* de memoria.

heartache ['hɑːteɪk] *n* congoja *f*.

heart attack *n* infarto *m*.

heartbeat ['hɑːtbiːt] *n* latido *m*.

heartbroken ['hɑːt,brəʊkn] *adj* desolado(da), abatido(da).

heartburn ['hɑːtbɜːn] *n* ardor *m* de estómago.

heart failure *n* paro *m* cardíaco.

heartfelt ['hɑːtfelt] *adj* sincero(ra), de todo corazón.

hearth [hɑːθ] *n* hogar *m*.

heartless ['hɑːtlɪs] *adj* cruel.

heartwarming ['hɑːt,wɔːmɪŋ] *adj* gratificante, grato(ta).

hearty ['hɑːtɪ] *adj* 1. (*laughter*) bonachón(ona); (*welcome, congratulations, thanks*) cordial; (*person*) fuertote(ta). 2. (*meal*) abundante; (*appetite*) bueno(na). 3. (*dislike, distrust*) profundo(da).

heat [hiːt] ◆ *n* 1. (*gen*) calor *m*. 2. (*specific temperature*) temperatura *f*. 3. *fig* (*pressure*) tensión *f*; **in the ~ of the moment** en el calor del momento. 4. (*eliminating round*) serie *f*, prueba *f* eliminatoria. 5. (ZOOL): **on** Br OR **in ~** en celo. ◆ *vt* calentar. ▶ **heat up** ◆ *vt sep* calentar. ◆ *vt* calentarse.

heated ['hiːtɪd] *adj* acalorado(da).

heater ['hiːtəʳ] *n* calentador *m*.

heath [hiːθ] *n* (*place*) brezal *m*.

heathen ['hiːðn] *n* pagano *m*, -na *f*.

heather ['heðəʳ] *n* brezo *m*.

heating ['hiːtɪŋ] *n* calefacción *f*.

heatstroke ['hiːtstrəʊk] *n* (U) insolación *f*.

heat wave *n* ola *f* de calor.

heave [hiːv] ◆ *vt* 1. (*pull*) tirar de, arrastrar; (*push*) empujar. 2. *inf* (*throw*) tirar. ◆ *vi* 1. (*pull*) tirar. 2. (*rise and fall - waves*) ondular; (*- chest*) palpitar.

heaven ['hevn] *n* (*Paradise*) cielo *m*. ▶ **heavens** *npl*: **the ~s** *literary* los cielos; **(good) ~s!** ¡cielos!

heavenly ['hevnlɪ] *adj inf dated* (*delightful*) divino(na).

heavily ['hevɪlɪ] *adv* 1. (*smoke, drink*) mucho; (*rain*) con fuerza; **~ in debt** con muchas deudas. 2. (*solidly*): **~ built** corpulento(ta). 3. (*breathe, sigh*) profundamente. 4. (*sit, move, fall*) pesadamente. 5. (*speak*) pesarosamente.

heavy ['hevɪ] *adj* 1. (*gen*) pesado(da); (*solid*) sólido(da); **~ build** corpulencia *f*; **how ~ is it?** ¿cuánto pesa? 2. (*traffic, rain, fighting*) intenso(sa); **to be a ~ smoker/drinker** ser un fumador/bebedor empedernido. 3. (*soil, mixture*) denso(sa). 4. (*blow*) duro(ra). 5. (*busy - schedule, day*) apretado(da). 6. (*work*) duro(ra). 7. (*weather, air, day*) cargado(da).

heavy cream n Am nata f para montar.

heavy goods vehicle n Br vehículo m (de transporte) pesado.

heavyweight ['heviweit] (SPORT) ◆ adj de los pesos pesados. ◆ n peso m pesado.

Hebrew ['hi:bru:] ◆ adj hebreo(a). ◆ n 1. (person) hebreo m, -a f. 2. (language) hebreo m.

Hebrides ['hebridi:z] npl: **the ~** las Hébridas.

heck [hek] excl: **what/where/why the ~ ...?** ¿qué/dónde/por qué demonios ...?; **a ~ of** a lot of la mar de.

heckle ['hekl] vt & vi interrumpir con exabruptos.

hectic ['hektik] adj ajetreado(da).

he'd [hi:d] = **he had, he would**.

hedge [hedʒ] ◆ n seto m. ◆ vi (prevaricate) contestar con evasivas.

hedgehog ['hedʒhɒg] n erizo m.

heed [hi:d] ◆ n: **to take ~ of sthg** tener algo en cuenta. ◆ vt fml tener en cuenta.

heedless ['hi:dlis] adj: **to be ~ of sthg** no hacer caso de algo.

heel [hi:l] n 1. (of foot) talón m. 2. (of shoe) tacón m, taco m Amer.

hefty ['hefti] adj inf 1. (person) fornido (da). 2. (salary, fee, fine) considerable, importante.

heifer ['hefər] n vaquilla f.

height [hait] n 1. (gen) altura f; (of person) estatura f; **5 metres in ~** 5 metros de altura; **what ~ is it/are you?** ¿cuánto mide/mides? 2. (zenith): **the ~ of** (gen) el punto álgido de; (ignorance, bad taste) el colmo de.

heighten ['haitn] ◆ vt intensificar, aumentar. ◆ vi intensificarse, aumentar.

heir [eər] n heredero m.

heiress ['eəris] n heredera f.

heirloom ['eəlu:m] n reliquia f de familia.

heist [haist] n inf golpe m, robo m.

held [held] pt & pp → **hold**.

helicopter ['helikɒptər] n helicóptero m.

helium ['hi:liəm] n helio m.

hell [hel] ◆ n infierno m; **what/where/ why the ~ ...?** inf ¿qué/dónde/por qué demonios ...?; **one** OR **a ~ of a nice guy** inf un tipo estupendo; **to do sthg for the ~ of it** inf hacer algo porque sí; **to give sb ~** inf hacérselas pasar canutas a alguien; **go to ~!** v inf ¡vete al infierno! ◆ excl inf ¡hostias!

he'll [hi:l] = **he will**.

hellish ['heliʃ] adj inf diabólico(ca).

hello [hə'ləu] excl 1. (as greeting) ¡hola!; (on phone - when answering) ¡diga!, ¡bueno! Amer; (- when calling) ¡oiga! 2. (to attract attention) ¡oiga!

helm [helm] n lit & fig timón m.

helmet ['helmit] n casco m.

help [help] ◆ n 1. (gen) ayuda f; **with the ~ of** con la ayuda de; **to be a ~** ser una ayuda; **to be of ~** ayudar. 2. (U) (emergency aid) socorro m, ayuda f. ◆ vt 1. (assist): **to ~ sb (to) do sthg/with sthg** ayudar a alguien (a hacer algo/con algo); **can I ~ you?** (in shop, bank) ¿en qué puedo servirle? 2. (avoid): **I can't ~ it/feeling sad** no puedo evitarlo/evitar que me dé pena. 3. (with food, drink): **to ~ o.s. (to sthg)** servirse (algo). ◆ vi: **to ~ (with)** ayudar (con). ◆ excl ¡socorro!, ¡auxilio! ▶ **help out** ◆ vt sep echar una mano a. ◆ vi echar una mano.

helper ['helpər] n 1. (gen) ayudante m y f. 2. Am (to do housework) mujer f OR señora f de la limpieza.

helpful ['helpful] adj 1. (willing to help) servicial, atento(ta). 2. (providing assistance) útil.

helping ['helpiŋ] n ración f; **would you like a second ~?** ¿quiere repetir?

helpless ['helplis] adj (child) indefenso (sa); (look, gesture) impotente.

helpline ['helplain] n servicio m telefónico de ayuda.

Helsinki ['helsiŋki] n Helsinki.

hem [hem] n dobladillo m. ▶ **hem in** vt sep rodear, cercar.

hemisphere ['hemi,sfiər] n (of earth) hemisferio m.

hemline ['hemlain] n bajo m (de falda etc).

hemophiliac [,hi:mə'filiæk] n hemofílico m, -ca f.

hemorrhage ['heməridʒ] n hemorragia f.

hemorrhoids ['hemərɔidz] npl hemorroides fpl.

hen [hen] n 1. (female chicken) gallina f. 2. (female bird) hembra f.

hence [hens] adv fml 1. (therefore) por lo tanto, así pues. 2. (from now): **five years ~** de aquí a cinco años.

henceforth [,hens'fɔ:θ] adv fml de ahora en adelante.

henchman ['hentʃmən] (pl **-men** [-mən]) n pej esbirro m.

henpecked ['henpekt] adj pej calzonazos (inv).

hepatitis [ˌhepə'taɪtɪs] *n* hepatitis *f inv.*

her [hɜːʳ] ◆ *pers pron* **1.** (*direct - unstressed*) la; (- *stressed*) ella; (*referring to ship, car etc*) lo; **I know ~ la** conozco; **I like ~ me** gusta; **it's ~** es ella; **if I were** OR **was ~** si (yo) fuera ella; **you can't expect** HER **to do it** no esperarás que ELLA lo haga; **fill ~ up!** (AUT) ¡llénemelo!, ¡lléneme el depósito! **2.** (*indirect - gen*) le; (- *with other third person pronouns*) se; **he sent ~ a letter** le mandó una carta; **we spoke to ~** hablamos con ella; **I gave it to ~** se lo di. **3.** (*after prep, in comparisons etc*) ella; **I'm shorter than ~** yo soy más bajo que ella. ◆ *poss adj* su, sus (*pl*); **~ coat** su abrigo; **~ children** sus niños; **~ name is Sarah** se llama Sarah; **it wasn't** HER **fault** no fue culpa suya OR su culpa; **she washed ~ hair** se lavó el pelo.

herald ['herəld] ◆ *vt fml* **1.** (*signify, usher in*) anunciar. **2.** (*proclaim*) proclamar. ◆ *n* **1.** (*messenger*) heraldo *m.* **2.** (*sign*) anuncio *m.*

herb [hɜːb] *n* hierba *f* (*aromática o medicinal*).

herd [hɜːd] ◆ *n* manada *f*, rebaño *m.* ◆ *vt fig* (*push*) conducir (en grupo) bruscamente.

here [hɪəʳ] *adv* aquí; **~ he is/they are** aquí está/están; **~ it is** aquí está; **~ is the book** aquí tienes el libro; **~ and there** aquí y allá; **~ are the keys** aquí tienes las llaves.

hereabouts Br ['hɪərəˌbaʊts], **hereabout** Am [ˌhɪərə'baʊt] *adv* por aquí.

hereafter [ˌhɪər'ɑːftəʳ] ◆ *adv fml* (*from now on*) de ahora en adelante; (*later on*) más tarde. ◆ *n*: **the ~** el más allá, la otra vida.

hereby [ˌhɪə'baɪ] *adv fml* **1.** (*in documents*) por la presente. **2.** (*when speaking*): **I ~ declare you the winner** desde este momento te declaro vencedor.

hereditary [hɪ'redɪtrɪ] *adj* hereditario (ria).

heresy ['herəsɪ] *n* (RELIG & *fig*) herejía *f.*

herewith [ˌhɪə'wɪð] *adv fml* (*with letter*): **please find ~ ...** le mando adjunto ...

heritage ['herɪtɪdʒ] *n* patrimonio *m.*

hermetically [hɜː'metɪklɪ] *adv*: **~ sealed** cerrado(da) herméticamente.

hermit ['hɜːmɪt] *n* ermitaño *m*, -ña *f.*

hernia ['hɜːnjə] *n* hernia *f* de hiato OR hiatal.

hero ['hɪərəʊ] (*pl* **-es**) *n* **1.** (*gen*) héroe *m.* **2.** (*idol*) ídolo *m.*

heroic [hɪ'rəʊɪk] *adj* heroico(ca).

heroin ['herəʊɪn] *n* heroína *f* (*droga*).

heroine ['herəʊɪn] *n* heroína *f.*

heron ['herən] (*pl inv* OR **-s**) *n* garza *f* real.

herring ['herɪŋ] (*pl inv* OR **-s**) *n* arenque *m.*

hers [hɜːz] *poss pron* suyo (suya); **that money is ~** ese dinero es suyo; **those keys are ~** esas llaves son suyas; **it wasn't his fault, it was** HERS no fue culpa de él sino de ella; **a friend of ~** un amigo suyo, un amigo de ella; **mine is good, but ~ is bad** el mío es bueno pero el suyo es malo.

herself [hɜː'self] *pron* **1.** (*reflexive*) se; (*after prep*) sí misma; **with ~** consigo misma. **2.** (*for emphasis*) ella misma; **she did it ~** lo hizo ella sola.

he's [hiːz] = **he is**, **he has.**

hesitant ['hezɪtənt] *adj* **1.** (*unsure of oneself*) indeciso(sa), inseguro(ra). **2.** (*faltering, slow to appear*) vacilante.

hesitate ['hezɪteɪt] *vi* vacilar, dudar; **to ~ to do sthg** dudar en hacer algo.

hesitation [ˌhezɪ'teɪʃn] *n* vacilación *f.*

heterogeneous [ˌhetərə'dʒiːnjəs] *adj fml* heterogéneo(a).

heterosexual [ˌhetərəʊ'sekʃʊəl] ◆ *adj* heterosexual. ◆ *n* heterosexual *m y f.*

het up [het-] *adj inf* nervioso(sa), hecho(cha) un manojo de nervios.

hey [heɪ] *excl* ¡eh!, ¡oye!

heyday ['heɪdeɪ] *n* apogeo *m*, auge *m.*

HGV *n abbr of* **heavy goods vehicle.**

hi [haɪ] *excl inf* (*hello*) ¡hola!

hiatus [haɪ'eɪtəs] (*pl* **-es**) *n fml* (*pause*) pausa *f.*

hibernate ['haɪbəneɪt] *vi* hibernar.

hiccough, hiccup ['hɪkʌp] ◆ *n* **1.** (*caused by wind*) hipo *m*; **to have ~s** tener hipo. **2.** *fig* (*difficulty*) contratiempo *m.* ◆ *vi* hipar.

hid [hɪd] *pt* → **hide.**

hidden ['hɪdn] ◆ *pp* → **hide.** ◆ *adj* oculto(ta).

hide [haɪd] (*pt* **hid**, *pp* **hidden**) ◆ *vt* **1.** (*conceal*) esconder, ocultar; **to ~ sthg (from sb)** esconder OR ocultar algo (a alguien). **2.** (*cover*) tapar, ocultar. ◆ *vi* esconderse. ◆ *n* **1.** (*animal skin*) piel *f.* **2.** (*for watching birds, animals*) puesto *m.*

hide-and-seek *n* escondite *m.*

hideaway ['haɪdəweɪ] *n inf* escondite *m.*

hideous ['hɪdɪəs] *adj* horrible.

hiding ['haɪdɪŋ] *n* **1.** (*concealment*): **in ~** escondido(da). **2.** *inf* (*beating*): **to give sb/get a (good) ~** darle a alguien/recibir una (buena) paliza.

hiding place n escondite m.

hierarchy ['haɪərɑːkɪ] n jerarquía f.

hi-fi ['haɪfaɪ] n equipo m de alta fidelidad.

high [haɪ] ♦ adj 1. (gen) alto(ta); (wind) fuerte; (altitude) grande; **it's 6 metres ~** tiene 6 metros de alto OR altura; **how ~ is it?** ¿cuánto mide?; **temperatures in the ~ 20s** temperaturas cercanas a los 30 grados. 2. (ideals, principles, tone) elevado(da). 3. (high-pitched) agudo(da). 4. drug sl flipado(da). ♦ adv alto; **he threw the ball ~ in the air** lanzó la bola muy alto. ♦ n (highest point) punto m álgido.

highbrow ['haɪbraʊ] adj culto(ta), intelectual.

high chair n trona f.

high-class adj (superior) de (alta) categoría.

High Court n Br tribunal m supremo.

higher ['haɪər] adj (exam, qualification) superior. ► **Higher** n: **Higher (Grade)** en Escocia, examen realizado al final de la enseñanza secundaria.

higher education n enseñanza f superior.

high-handed [-'hændɪd] adj déspotico(ca), arbitrario(ria).

high jump n salto m de altura.

Highland Games ['haɪlənd-] npl fiesta de deportes escoceses.

Highlands ['haɪləndz] npl: **the ~** (of Scotland) las Tierras Altas del Norte (de Escocia).

highlight ['haɪlaɪt] ♦ n (of event, occasion) punto m culminante. ♦ vt 1. (visually) subrayar, marcar. 2. (emphasize) destacar, resaltar. ► **highlights** npl (in hair) reflejos mpl.

highlighter (pen) ['haɪlaɪtər-] n rotulador m, marcador m.

highly ['haɪlɪ] adv 1. (very, extremely) muy, enormemente. 2. (in important position): **~ placed** en un puesto importante. 3. (favourably): **to think ~ of sb** tener a alguien en mucha estima.

highly-strung adj muy nervioso(sa).

Highness ['haɪnɪs] n: **His/Her/Your (Royal) ~** Su Alteza f (Real); **their (Royal) ~es** Sus Altezas (Reales).

high-pitched [-'pɪtʃt] adj agudo(da).

high point n (of occasion) momento m OR punto m culminante.

high-powered [-'paʊəd] adj 1. (powerful) de gran potencia. 2. (prestigious - activity, place) prestigioso(sa); (- person) de altos vuelos.

high-ranking [-'ræŋkɪŋ] adj (in army

etc) de alta graduación; (in government): **~ official** alto cargo m.

high-rise adj: **~ building** edificio de muchos pisos.

high school n ≃ instituto m de bachillerato.

high season n temporada f alta.

high street n Br calle f mayor OR principal.

high tech [-'tek] adj de alta tecnología.

high tide n (of sea) marea f alta.

highway ['haɪweɪ] n 1. Am (main road between cities) autopista f. 2. Br (any main road) carretera f.

Highway Code n Br: **the ~** el código de la circulación.

hijack ['haɪdʒæk] vt (aircraft) secuestrar.

hijacker ['haɪdʒækər] n secuestrador m, -ra f (de un avión).

hike [haɪk] ♦ n (long walk) caminata f. ♦ vi (go for walk) ir de excursión.

hiker ['haɪkər] n excursionista m y f.

hiking ['haɪkɪŋ] n excursionismo m; **to go ~** ir de excursión.

hilarious [hɪ'leərɪəs] adj desternillante.

hill [hɪl] n 1. (mound) colina f. 2. (slope) cuesta f.

hillside ['hɪlsaɪd] n ladera f.

hilly ['hɪlɪ] adj montañoso(sa).

hilt [hɪlt] n puño m, empuñadura f; **to support/defend sb to the ~** apoyar/defender a alguien sin reservas.

him [hɪm] pers pron 1. (direct - unstressed) lo, le; (- stressed) él; **I know ~** lo OR le conozco; **I like ~** me gusta; **it's ~** es él; **if I were** OR **was ~** si (yo) fuera él; **you can't expect HIM to do it** no esperarás que ÉL lo haga. 2. (indirect - gen) le; (- with other third person pronouns) se; **she sent ~ a letter** le mandó una carta; **we spoke to ~** hablamos con él; **I gave it to ~** se lo di. 3. (after prep, in comparisons etc) él; **I'm shorter than ~** yo soy más bajo que él.

Himalayas [ˌhɪmə'leɪəz] npl: **the ~** el Himalaya.

himself [hɪm'self] pron 1. (reflexive) se; (after prep) sí mismo; **with ~** consigo mismo. 2. (for emphasis) él mismo; **he did it ~** lo hizo él solo.

hind [haɪnd] (pl inv OR -s) ♦ adj trasero(ra), posterior. ♦ n cierva f.

hinder ['hɪndər] vt (gen) estorbar; (progress, talks, attempts) entorpecer.

Hindi ['hɪndɪ] n (language) hindi m.

hindrance ['hɪndrəns] n 1. (obstacle)

obstáculo *m*, impedimento *m*; (*person*) estorbo *m*. **2.** (U) (*delay*) interrupciones *fpl*, retrasos *mpl*.

hindsight [ˈhaɪndsaɪt] *n*: **with the benefit of ~** ahora que se sabe lo que pasó.

Hindu [ˈhɪnduː] (*pl* -s) ◆ *adj* hindú. ◆ *n* hindú *m y f*.

hinge [hɪndʒ] *n* (*on door, window*) bisagra *f*. ► **hinge (up)on** *vt fus* (*depend on*) depender de.

hint [hɪnt] ◆ *n* **1.** (*indication*) indirecta *f*; **to drop a ~** lanzar una indirecta. **2.** (*piece of advice*) consejo *m*. **3.** (*small amount, suggestion*) asomo *m*; (*of colour*) pizca *f*. ◆ *vi*: **to ~ at sthg** insinuar algo. ◆ *vt*: **to ~ that** insinuar que.

hip [hɪp] *n* (ANAT) cadera *f*.

hippie [ˈhɪpɪ] *n* hippy *m y f*.

hippopotamus [ˌhɪpəˈpɒtəməs] (*pl* -muses OR -mi [-maɪ]) *n* hipopótamo *m*.

hippy [ˈhɪpɪ] = **hippie**.

hire [ˈhaɪəʳ] ◆ *n* (U) (*of car, equipment*) alquiler *m*; **for ~** (*taxi*) libre; **boats for ~** se alquilan barcos. ◆ *vt* **1.** (*rent*) alquilar. **2.** (*employ*) contratar. ► **hire out** *vt sep* (*car, equipment*) alquilar; (*one's services*) ofrecer.

hire car *n* Br coche *m* de alquiler.

hire purchase *n* (U) Br compra *f* a plazos.

his [hɪz] ◆ *poss adj* su, sus (*pl*); **~ house** su casa; **~ children** sus niños; **~ name is Joe** se llama Joe; **it wasn't HIS fault** no fue culpa suya OR su culpa; **he washed ~ hair** se lavó el pelo. ◆ *poss pron* suyo (suya); **that money is ~** ese dinero es suyo; **those keys are ~** esas llaves son suyas; **it wasn't her fault, it was HIS** no fue culpa de ella sino de él; **a friend of ~** un amigo suyo, un amigo de él; **mine is good, but ~ is bad** el mío es bueno pero el suyo es malo.

Hispanic [hɪˈspænɪk] ◆ *adj* hispánico (ca). ◆ *n* hispano *m*, -na *f*.

hiss [hɪs] ◆ *n* **1.** (*of person*) bisbiseo *m*, siseo *m*. **2.** (*of steam, gas, snake*) silbido *m*. ◆ *vi* **1.** (*person*) bisbisear, sisear; (*to express disapproval*) ≃ silbar, ≃ pitar. **2.** (*steam, gas, snake*) silbar.

historic [hɪˈstɒrɪk] *adj* (*significant*) histórico(ca).

historical [hɪˈstɒrɪkəl] *adj* histórico (ca).

history [ˈhɪstərɪ] *n* **1.** (*gen*) historia *f*. **2.** (*past record*) historial *m*.

hit [hɪt] (*pt & pp* hit) ◆ *n* **1.** (*blow*) golpe *m*. **2.** (*successful strike*) impacto *m*. **3.** (*success*) éxito *m*. ◆ *comp* de éxito. ◆ *vt*

1. (*subj: person*) pegar, golpear. **2.** (*crash into*) chocar contra OR con. **3.** (*reach*) alcanzar, llegar a; (*bull's-eye*) dar en. **4.** (*affect badly*) afectar. **5.** *phr*: **to ~ it off (with sb)** hacer buenas migas (con alguien).

hit-and-miss = **hit-or-miss**.

hit-and-run *adj* (*driver*) que se da a la fuga después de causar un accidente.

hitch [hɪtʃ] ◆ *n* (*problem, snag*) obstáculo *m*, pega *f*. ◆ *vt* **1.** (*catch*): **to ~ a lift** conseguir que le lleven en coche a uno. **2.** (*fasten*): **to ~ sthg on OR onto sthg** enganchar algo a algo. ◆ *vi* (*hitchhike*) hacer autostop. ► **hitch up** *vt sep* (*clothes*) subirse.

hitchhike [ˈhɪtʃhaɪk] *vi* hacer autostop.

hitchhiker [ˈhɪtʃhaɪkəʳ] *n* autostopista *m y f*.

hi-tech [ˌhaɪˈtek] = **high tech**.

hitherto [ˌhɪðəˈtuː] *adv fml* hasta ahora.

hit-or-miss *adj* azaroso(sa).

HIV (*abbr of* **human immunodeficiency virus**) *n* VIH *m*, HIV *m*; **to be ~-positive** ser seropositivo.

hive [haɪv] *n* (*for bees*) colmena *f*; **a ~ of activity** un enjambre, un centro de actividad. ► **hive off** *vt sep* (*separate*) transferir.

HNC (*abbr of* **Higher National Certificate**) *n* diploma técnico en Gran Bretaña.

HND (*abbr of* **Higher National Diploma**) *n* diploma técnico superior en Gran Bretaña.

hoard [hɔːd] ◆ *n* (*store*) acopio *m*. ◆ *vt* (*collect, save*) acumular; (*food*) acaparar.

hoarding [ˈhɔːdɪŋ] *n* Br (*for advertisements, posters*) valla *f* publicitaria.

hoarfrost [ˈhɔːfrɒst] *n* escarcha *f*.

hoarse [hɔːs] *adj* **1.** (*voice*) ronco(ca). **2.** (*person*) afónico(ca).

hoax [həʊks] *n* engaño *m*; **~ call** falsa alarma telefónica.

hob [hɒb] *n* Br (*on cooker*) encimera *f*.

hobble [ˈhɒbl] *vi* (*limp*) cojear.

hobby [ˈhɒbɪ] *n* (*leisure activity*) hobby *m*, distracción *f* favorita.

hobbyhorse [ˈhɒbɪhɔːs] *n* **1.** (*toy*) caballo *m* de juguete. **2.** (*favourite topic*) caballo *m* de batalla.

hobo [ˈhəʊbəʊ] (*pl* -es OR -s) *n* Am (*tramp*) vagabundo *m*, -da *f*.

hockey [ˈhɒkɪ] *n* **1.** (*on grass*) hockey *m* sobre hierba. **2.** Am (*ice hockey*) hockey *m* sobre hielo.

hoe [həʊ] ◆ *n* azada *f*. ◆ *vt* azadonar.

hog [hɒg] ◆ *n* cerdo *m*; **to go the whole ~** *fig* ir a por todas. ◆ *vt inf* (*monopo-*

lize) acaparar.

Hogmanay ['hɒgmənei] *n* denominación escocesa de la Nochevieja.

hoist [hɔist] ◆ *n* (*pulley, crane*) grúa *f*; (*lift*) montacargas *m inv.* ◆ *vt* izar.

hold [həʊld] (*pt & pp* **held**) ◆ *vt* 1. (*have hold of*) tener cogido(da). 2. (*embrace*) abrazar. 3. (*keep in position, sustain, support*) sostener, aguantar. 4. (*as prisoner*) detener; **to ~ sb prisoner/hostage** tener a alguien como prisionero/rehén. 5. (*have, possess*) poseer. 6. (*contain - gen*) contener; (*- fears, promise etc*) guardar; (*- number of people*) tener cabida para. 7. (*conduct, stage - event*) celebrar; (*- conversation*) mantener. 8. *fml* (*consider*) considerar; **to ~ sb responsible for sthg** considerar a alguien responsable de algo. 9. (*on telephone*): **please ~ the line** no cuelgue por favor. 10. (*maintain - interest etc*) mantener. 11. (MIL) ocupar, tener. 12. *phr:* **~ it** OR **everything!** ¡para!, ¡espera!; **to ~ one's own** defenderse. ◆ *vi* 1. (*luck, weather*) continuar así; (*promise, offer*) seguir en pie; **to ~ still** OR **steady** estarse quieto. 2. (*on phone*) esperar. ◆ *n* 1. (*grasp, grip*): **to have a firm ~ on** sthg tener algo bien agarrado; **to take** OR **lay ~ of sthg** agarrar algo; **to get ~ of sthg** (*obtain*) hacerse con algo; **to get ~ of sb** (*find*) localizar a alguien. 2. (*of ship, aircraft*) bodega *f.* 3. (*control, influence*) dominio *m.* ▶ **hold back** *vt sep* 1. (*tears, anger*) contener, reprimir. 2. (*secret*) ocultar. ▶ **hold down** *vt sep* (*job*) conservar. ▶ **hold off** *vt sep* (*fend off*) mantener a distancia. ▶ **hold on** *vi* 1. (*wait*) esperar; (*on phone*) no colgar. 2. (*grip*): **to ~ on (to sthg)** agarrarse (a algo). ▶ **hold out** ◆ *vt sep* (*hand, arms*) extender, tender. ◆ *vi* 1. (*last*) durar. 2. (*resist*): **to ~ out (against sthg/sb)** resistir (ante algo/a alguien). ▶ **hold up** *vt sep* 1. (*raise*) levantar, alzar. 2. (*delay*) retrasar.

holdall ['həʊldɔːl] *n* Br bolsa *f* de viaje.

holder ['həʊldə*r*] *n* 1. (*container*) soporte *m*; (*for candle*) candelero *m*; (*for cigarette*) boquilla *f.* 2. (*owner*) titular *m y f*; (*of ticket, record, title*) poseedor *m*, -ra *f.*

holding ['həʊldɪŋ] *n* 1. (*investment*) participación *f*, acciones *fpl.* 2. (*farm*) propiedad *f*, terreno *m* de cultivo.

holdup ['həʊldʌp] *n* 1. (*robbery*) atraco *m* a mano armada. 2. (*delay*) retraso *m.*

hole [həʊl] *n* 1. (*gen*) agujero *m*; (*in ground, road etc*) hoyo *m.* 2. (*in golf*) hoyo *m.* 3. (*horrible place*) cuchitril *m.*

holiday ['hɒlidei] *n* 1. (*vacation*) vacaciones *fpl*; **to be/go on ~** estar/ir de vacaciones. 2. (*public holiday*) fiesta *f*, día *m* festivo.

holiday camp *n* Br colonia *f* veraniega.

holidaymaker ['hɒlidei,meikə*r*] *n* Br turista *m y f.*

holiday pay *n* Br sueldo *m* de vacaciones.

holiday resort *n* Br lugar *m* OR centro *m* de veraneo.

holistic [həʊ'listik] *adj* holístico(ca).

Holland ['hɒlənd] *n* Holanda.

holler ['hɒlə*r*] *vt & vi inf* gritar.

hollow ['hɒləʊ] ◆ *adj* 1. (*not solid*) hueco(ca). 2. (*cheeks, eyes*) hundido(da). 3. (*resonant*) sonoro(ra), resonante. 4. (*false, meaningless*) vano(na); (*laugh*) falso(sa). ◆ *n* hueco *m*; (*in ground*) depresión *f*, hondonada *f.* ▶ **hollow out** *vt sep* 1. (*make hollow*) dejar hueco. 2. (*make by hollowing*) hacer ahuecando.

holly ['hɒli] *n* acebo *m.*

holocaust ['hɒləkɔːst] *n* holocausto *m.* ▶ **Holocaust** *n:* **the Holocaust** el Holocausto.

holster ['həʊlstə*r*] *n* pistolera *f.*

holy ['həʊli] *adj* 1. (*sacred*) sagrado(da); (*water*) bendito(ta). 2. (*pure and good*) santo(ta).

Holy Ghost *n:* **the ~** el Espíritu Santo.

Holy Spirit *n:* **the ~** el Espíritu Santo.

homage ['hɒmidʒ] *n* (U) *fml* homenaje *m*; **to pay ~ to** rendir homenaje a.

home [həʊm] ◆ *n* 1. (*house, flat*) casa *f*; **to make one's ~ somewhere** establecerse en algún sitio. 2. (*own country*) tierra *f*; (*own city*) ciudad *f* natal. 3. (*family*) hogar *m*; **to leave ~** independizarse, irse de casa. 4. (*place of origin*) cuna *f.* 5. (*institution*) asilo *m.* ◆ *adj* 1. (*not foreign*) nacional. 2. (*in one's own home - cooking*) casero(ra); (*- life*) familiar; (*- improvements*) en la casa. 3. (SPORT) de casa. ◆ *adv* (*to one's house*) a casa; (*at one's house*) en casa. ▶ **at home** *adv* 1. (*in one's house, flat*) en casa. 2. (*comfortable*): **at ~ (with)** a gusto (con); **to make o.s. at ~** acomodarse. 3. (*in one's own country*) en mi país.

home address *n* domicilio *m* particular.

home brew *n* (U) (*beer*) cerveza *f* casera.

home computer *n* ordenador *m* personal.

Home Counties *npl:* **the ~** *los condados*

de los alrededores de Londres.

home economics n (U) economía f doméstica.

home help n Br asistente empleado por el ayuntamiento para ayudar en las tareas domésticas a enfermos y ancianos.

homeland ['həʊmlænd] n 1. (*country of birth*) tierra f natal, patria f. 2. (*in South Africa*) territorio donde se confina a la población negra.

homeless ['həʊmlɪs] adj sin hogar.

homely ['həʊmlɪ] adj 1. (*simple*) sencillo(lla). 2. (*unattractive*) feúcho(cha).

homemade [,həʊm'meɪd] adj (*clothes*) de fabricación casera; (*food*) casero(ra).

Home Office n Br: the ~ el Ministerio del Interior británico.

homeopathy [,həʊmɪ'ɒpəθɪ] n homeopatía f.

home page n (*on Internet*) página f inicial OR de inicio.

Home Secretary n Br: the ~ el Ministro del Interior británico.

homesick ['həʊmsɪk] adj nostálgico (ca); to be ~ tener morriña.

hometown ['həʊmtaʊn] n pueblo m/ ciudad f natal.

homeward ['həʊmwəd] ◆ adj de regreso OR vuelta (a casa). ◆ adv = **homewards**.

homewards ['həʊmwədz] adv hacia casa.

homework ['həʊmwɜːk] n (U) lit & fig deberes mpl.

homey, homy ['həʊmɪ] adj Am confortable, agradable.

homicide ['hɒmɪsaɪd] n fml homicidio m.

homoeopathy [,həʊmɪ'ɒpəθɪ] etc = **homeopathy** etc.

homogeneous [,hɒmə'dʒiːnjəs] adj homogéneo(a).

homosexual [,hɒmə'sekʃʊəl] ◆ adj homosexual. ◆ n homosexual m y f.

homy = **homey**.

Honduran [hɒn'djʊərən] ◆ adj hondureño(ña). ◆ n hondureño m, -ña f.

Honduras [hɒn'djʊərəs] n Honduras.

hone [həʊn] vt 1. (*sharpen*) afilar. 2. (*develop, refine*) afinar.

honest ['ɒnɪst] ◆ adj 1. (*trustworthy, legal*) honrado(da). 2. (*frank*) franco(ca), sincero(ra); to be ~ ... si he de serte franco ... ◆ adv = **honestly 2**.

honestly ['ɒnɪstlɪ] ◆ adv 1. (*truthfully*) honradamente. 2. (*expressing sincerity*) de verdad, en serio. ◆ excl (*expressing impatience, disapproval*) ¡será posible!

honesty ['ɒnɪstɪ] n honradez f.

honey ['hʌnɪ] n 1. (*food*) miel f. 2. (*form of address*) cielo m, mi vida f.

honeycomb ['hʌnɪkəʊm] n panal m.

honeymoon ['hʌnɪmuːn] n luna f de miel; fig periodo m idílico.

honeysuckle ['hʌnɪ,sʌkl] n madreselva f.

Hong Kong [,hɒŋ'kɒŋ] n Hong Kong.

honk [hɒŋk] ◆ vi 1. (*motorist*) tocar el claxon. 2. (*goose*) graznar. ◆ vt tocar.

honor Am etc = **honour** etc.

honorary [Br 'ɒnərərɪ, Am ɒnə'reərɪ] adj 1. (*given as an honour*) honorario(ria). 2. (*unpaid*) honorífico(ca).

honour Br, **honor** Am ['ɒnəʳ] ◆ n 1. (*gen*) honor m, honra f; in ~ of en honor de. 2. (*source of pride - person*) honra f. ◆ vt 1. (*promise, agreement*) cumplir; (*debt*) satisfacer; (*cheque*) pagar, aceptar. 2. fml (*bring honour to*) honrar. ▶ **honours** npl 1. (*tokens of respect*) honores mpl. 2. Br (UNIV): ~s degree licenciatura de cuatro años necesaria para acceder a un máster.

honourable Br, **honorable** Am ['ɒnrəbl] adj 1. (*proper*) honroso(sa). 2. (*morally upright*) honorable.

hood [hʊd] n 1. (*on cloak, jacket*) capucha f. 2. (*of pram, convertible car*) capota f; (*of cooker*) campana f. 3. Am (*car bonnet*) capó m.

hoodlum ['huːdləm] n Am inf matón m.

hoof [huːf, hʊf] (pl -s OR **hooves**) n (*of horse*) casco m; (*of cow etc*) pezuña f.

hook [hʊk] ◆ n 1. (*gen*) gancho m; off the ~ (*phone*) descolgado(da). 2. (*for catching fish*) anzuelo m. 3. (*fastener*) corchete m. ◆ vt 1. (*attach with hook*) enganchar. 2. (*fish*) pescar, coger. ▶ **hook up** vt sep: to ~ sthg up to sthg conectar algo a algo.

hooked [hʊkt] adj 1. (*nose*) aguileño (ña). 2. inf (*addicted*): to be ~ (on) estar enganchado(da) (a).

hook(e)y ['hʊkɪ] n Am inf: to play ~ hacer pellas OR novillos.

hooligan ['huːlɪgən] n gamberro m.

hoop [huːp] n aro m.

hooray [hʊ'reɪ] = **hurray**.

hoot [huːt] ◆ n 1. (*of owl*) grito m, ululato m. 2. (*of horn*) bocinazo m. ◆ vi 1. (*owl*) ulular. 2. (*horn*) sonar. ◆ vt tocar.

hooter ['huːtəʳ] n (*horn*) claxon m, bocina f.

Hoover® ['huːvəʳ] n Br aspiradora f. ▶ **hoover** vt pasar la aspiradora por.

hooves [huːvz] pl → **hoof**.

hop [hɒp] *vi* **1.** (*person*) saltar a la pata coja. **2.** (*bird etc*) dar saltitos. **3.** *inf* (*move nimbly*) ponerse de un brinco. ▶ **hops** *npl* lúpulo *m*.

hope [həʊp] ◆ *vi*: **to ~ (for sthg)** esperar (algo); **I ~ so/not** espero que sí/no. ◆ *vt*: **to ~ (that)** esperar que; **to ~ to do sthg** esperar hacer algo. ◆ *n* esperanza *f*; **in the ~ of** con la esperanza de.

hopeful ['həʊpfʊl] *adj* **1.** (*optimistic*) optimista; **to be ~ of sthg/of doing sthg** tener esperanzas de algo/hacer algo. **2.** (*promising*) prometedor(ra).

hopefully ['həʊpfəlɪ] *adv* **1.** (*in a hopeful way*) esperanzadamente. **2.** (*with luck*) con suerte.

hopeless ['həʊplɪs] *adj* **1.** (*despairing*) desesperado(da). **2.** (*impossible*) imposible. **3.** *inf* (*useless*) inútil.

hopelessly ['həʊplɪslɪ] *adv* **1.** (*despairingly*) desesperadamente. **2.** (*completely*) totalmente.

horizon [həˈraɪzn] *n* (*of sky*) horizonte *m*; **on the ~** en el horizonte; *fig* a la vuelta de la esquina.

horizontal [ˌhɒrɪˈzɒntl] *adj* horizontal.

hormone ['hɔːməʊn] *n* hormona *f*.

horn [hɔːn] *n* **1.** (*of animal*) cuerno *m*. **2.** (MUS) (*instrument*) trompa *f*. **3.** (*on car*) claxon *m*, bocina *f*; (*on ship*) sirena *f*.

hornet ['hɔːnɪt] *n* avispón *m*.

horny ['hɔːnɪ] *adj* **1.** (*scale, body, armour*) córneo(a); (*hand*) calloso(sa). **2.** *v inf* (*sexually excited*) cachondo(da), caliente.

horoscope ['hɒrəskəʊp] *n* horóscopo *m*.

horrendous [hɒˈrendəs] *adj* horrendo (da).

horrible ['hɒrəbl] *adj* horrible.

horrid ['hɒrɪd] *adj* (*person*) antipático (ca); (*idea, place*) horroroso(sa).

horrific [hɒˈrɪfɪk] *adj* horrendo(da).

horrify ['hɒrɪfaɪ] *vt* horrorizar.

horror ['hɒrər] *n* horror *m*.

horror film *n* película *f* de terror OR de miedo.

hors d'oeuvre [ɔːˈdɜːvr] (*pl* **hors d'oeuvres** [ɔːˈdɜːvr]) *n* entremeses *mpl*.

horse [hɔːs] *n* (*animal*) caballo *m*.

horseback ['hɔːsbæk] ◆ *adj*: **~ riding** equitación *f*. ◆ *n*: **on ~** a caballo.

horse chestnut *n* (*nut*) castaña *f* de Indias; **~ (tree)** castaño *m* de Indias.

horseman ['hɔːsmən] (*pl* **-men** [-mən]) *n* jinete *m*.

horsepower ['hɔːsˌpaʊər] *n* (U) caballos *mpl* de vapor.

horse racing *n* (U) carreras *fpl* de caballos.

horseradish ['hɔːsˌrædɪʃ] *n* rábano *m* silvestre.

horse riding *n* equitación *f*; **to go ~** montar a caballo.

horseshoe ['hɔːsʃuː] *n* herradura *f*.

horsewoman ['hɔːsˌwʊmən] (*pl* **-women** [-ˌwɪmɪn]) *n* amazona *f*.

horticulture ['hɔːtɪkʌltʃər] *n* horticultura *f*.

hose [həʊz] *n* (*hosepipe*) manguera *f*.

hosepipe ['həʊzpaɪp] = **hose**.

hosiery ['həʊzɪərɪ] *n* (U) medias *fpl* y calcetines.

hospice ['hɒspɪs] *n* hospicio *m*.

hospitable [hɒˈspɪtəbl] *adj* hospitalario(ria).

hospital ['hɒspɪtl] *n* hospital *m*.

hospitality [ˌhɒspɪˈtælətɪ] *n* hospitalidad *f*.

host [həʊst] ◆ *n* **1.** (*person, place, organization*) anfitrión *m*, -ona *f*. **2.** (*compere*) presentador *m*, -ra *f*. **3.** *literary* (*large number*): **a ~ of** una multitud de. **4.** (RELIG) hostia *f*. ◆ *vt* (*show*) presentar; (*event*) ser el anfitrión de.

hostage ['hɒstɪdʒ] *n* rehén *m*.

hostel ['hɒstl] *n* albergue *m*.

hostess ['həʊstes] *n* **1.** (*at party*) anfitriona *f*. **2.** (*in club etc*) chica *f* de alterne.

hostile [Br 'hɒstaɪl, Am 'hɒstl] *adj* **1.** (*antagonistic, enemy*): **~ (to)** hostil (hacia). **2.** (*unfavourable*) adverso(sa).

hostility [hɒˈstɪlətɪ] *n* (*antagonism*) hostilidad *f*. ▶ **hostilities** *npl* hostilidades *fpl*.

hot [hɒt] *adj* **1.** (*gen*) caliente; **I'm ~** tengo calor. **2.** (*weather, climate*) caluroso (sa); **it's (very) ~** hace (mucho) calor. **3.** (*spicy*) picante, picoso(sa) *Amer*. **4.** *inf* (*expert*): **~ on** OR **at** experto(ta) en. **5.** (*recent*) caliente, último(ma). **6.** (*temper*) vivo(va).

hot-air balloon *n* aeróstato *m*, globo *m*.

hotbed ['hɒtbed] *n* semillero *m*.

hot-cross bun *n* bollo a base de especias y pasas con una cruz dibujada en una cara que se come en Semana Santa.

hot dog *n* perrito *m* caliente.

hotel [həʊˈtel] *n* hotel *m*.

hot flush Br, **hot flash** Am *n* sofoco *m*.

hotfoot ['hɒtˌfʊt] *adv literary* presto.

hotheaded [ˌhɒtˈhedɪd] *adj* irreflexivo (va).

hothouse ['hɒthaʊs, *pl* -haʊzɪz] *n* (*greenhouse*) invernadero *m*.

hot line n teléfono m rojo.

hotly ['hɒtlɪ] adv 1. (passionately) acaloradamente. 2. (closely): **we were ~ pursued** nos pisaban los talones.

hotplate ['hɒtpleɪt] n calentador m, fuego m.

hot-tempered adj iracundo(da).

hot-water bottle n bolsa f de agua caliente.

hound [haund] ◆ n (dog) perro m de caza, sabueso m. ◆ vt 1. (persecute) acosar. 2. (drive): **to ~ sb out (of somewhere)** conseguir echar a alguien (de algún sitio) acosándolo.

hour ['auər] n 1. (gen) hora f; **half an ~** media hora; **70 miles per** OR **an ~** 70 millas por hora; **on the ~** a la hora en punto cada hora. 2. literary (important time) momento m. ► **hours** npl 1. (of business) horas fpl. 2. (of person - routine) horario m.

hourly ['auəlɪ] ◆ adj 1. (happening every hour) de hora en hora, cada hora. 2. (per hour) por hora. ◆ adv 1. (every hour) cada hora. 2. (per hour) por hora.

house [n & adj haus, pl 'hauzɪz, vb hauz] ◆ n 1. (gen) casa f; **it's on the ~** la casa invita, es cortesía de la casa. 2. (POL) cámara f. 3. (in theatre) audiencia f; **to bring the ~ down** inf ser un exitazo, ser muy aplaudido. ◆ vt (person, family) alojar; (department, library, office) albergar. ◆ adj 1. (within business) de la empresa. 2. (wine) de la casa.

house arrest n: **under ~** bajo arresto domiciliario.

houseboat ['hausbəut] n casa f flotante.

housebreaking ['haus,breɪkɪŋ] n allanamiento m de morada.

housecoat ['hauskəut] n bata f.

household ['haushəuld] ◆ adj 1. (domestic) doméstico(ca), de la casa. 2. (word, name) conocido(da) por todos. ◆ n hogar m, casa f.

housekeeper ['haus,ki:pər] n ama f de llaves.

housekeeping ['haus,ki:pɪŋ] n (U) 1. (work) quehaceres mpl domésticos. 2. **~ (money)** dinero m para los gastos de la casa.

house music n música f ácida OR house.

House of Commons n Br: **the ~** la Cámara de los Comunes.

House of Lords n Br: **the ~** la Cámara de los Lores.

House of Representatives n Am:

the ~ la Cámara de los Representantes.

houseplant ['hauspla:nt] n planta f interior.

Houses of Parliament n: **the ~** el Parlamento británico.

housewarming (party) ['haus,wɔːmɪŋ-] n fiesta f de inauguración de una casa.

housewife ['hauswaɪf] (pl -wives [-waɪvz]) n ama f de casa.

housework ['hauswɜːk] n (U) quehaceres mpl domésticos, tareas fpl domésticas.

housing ['hauzɪŋ] n (houses) vivienda f; (act of accommodating) alojamiento m.

housing association n Br cooperativa f de viviendas.

housing benefit n (U) subsidio estatal para ayudar con el pago del alquiler y otros gastos.

housing estate Br, **housing project** Am n urbanización generalmente de protección oficial, ≈ fraccionamiento m Amer.

hovel ['hɒvl] n casucha f, tugurio m.

hover ['hɒvər] vi (fly) cernerse.

hovercraft ['hɒvəkraːft] (pl inv OR -s) n aerodeslizador m.

how [hau] adv 1. (gen) cómo; **~ do you do it?** ¿cómo se hace?; **I found out ~ he did it** averigüé cómo lo hizo; **~ are you?** ¿cómo estás?; **~ do you do?** mucho gusto. 2. (referring to degree, amount): **~ high is it?** ¿cuánto mide de alto OR de altura?; **he asked ~ high it was** preguntó cuánto medía de alto; **~ expensive is it?** ¿cómo de caro es?, ¿es muy caro?; **~ long have you been waiting?** ¿cuánto llevas esperando?; **~ many people came?** ¿cuánta gente vino?; **~ old are you?** ¿qué edad OR cuántos años tienes? 3. (in exclamations) qué; **~ nice/awful!** ¡qué bonito/horrible!; **~ I hate doing it!** ¡cómo or cuánto odio tener que hacerlo! ► **how about** adv: **~ about a drink?** ¿qué tal una copa?; **~ about you?** ¿qué te parece?, ¿y tú? ► **how much** ◆ pron cuánto(ta); **~ much does it cost?** ¿cuánto cuesta? ◆ adj cuánto(ta); **~ much bread?** ¿cuánto pan?

however [hau'evər] ◆ adv 1. (nevertheless) sin embargo, no obstante. 2. (no matter how): **~ difficult it may be** por (muy) difícil que sea; **~ many times** OR **much I told her** por mucho que se lo dijera. 3. (how) cómo. ◆ conj comoquiera que; **~ you want** como quieras.

howl [haul] ◆ n 1. (of animal) aullido m.

2. (of person - in pain, anger) alarido m, grito m; (- in laughter) carcajada f. ◆ vi **1.** (animal) aullar. **2.** (person - in pain, anger) gritar; (- in laughter) reírse a carcajadas. **3.** (wind) bramar.

hp (abbr of **horsepower**) CV m, cv m.

HP n **1.** Br abbr of **hire purchase**. **2.** = **hp**.

HQ n abbr of **headquarters**.

HTML (abbr of **hypertext markup language**) n HTML m.

hub [hʌb] n **1.** (of wheel) cubo m. **2.** (of activity) centro m, eje m.

hubbub ['hʌbʌb] n alboroto m.

hubcap ['hʌbkæp] n tapacubos m inv.

huddle ['hʌdl] vi **1.** (crouch, curl up) acurrucarse. **2.** (cluster) apretarse unos contra otros, apiñarse.

hue [hju:] n (colour) tono m, matiz m.

huff [hʌf] n: **in a ~** enojado(da).

hug [hʌg] ◆ n abrazo m; **to give sb a ~** abrazar a alguien. ◆ vt **1.** (embrace, hold) abrazar. **2.** (stay close to) ceñirse OR ir pegado a.

huge [hju:dʒ] adj enorme.

hulk [hʌlk] n **1.** (of ship) casco m abandonado. **2.** (person) tiarrón m, -ona f.

hull [hʌl] n casco m.

hullo [hə'ləu] = **hello**.

hum [hʌm] ◆ vi **1.** (buzz) zumbar. **2.** (sing) canturrear, tararear. **3.** (be busy) bullir, hervir. ◆ vt tararear, canturrear.

human ['hju:mən] ◆ adj humano(na). ◆ n: **~ (being)** (ser m) humano m.

humane [hju:'meɪn] adj humano(na), humanitario(ria).

humanitarian [hju:,mænɪ'teərɪən] adj humanitario(ria).

humanity [hju:'mænətɪ] n humanidad f. ▶ **humanities** npl: **the humanities** las humanidades.

human race n: **the ~** la raza humana.

human rights npl derechos mpl humanos.

humble ['hʌmbl] ◆ adj humilde. ◆ vt fml humillar.

humbug ['hʌmbʌg] n **1.** (U) dated (hypocrisy) farsa f, hipocresía f. **2.** Br (sweet) caramelo m de menta.

humdrum ['hʌmdrʌm] adj rutinario (ria), aburrido(da).

humid ['hju:mɪd] adj húmedo(da).

humidity [hju:'mɪdətɪ] n humedad f.

humiliate [hju:'mɪlɪeɪt] vt humillar.

humiliation [hju:,mɪlɪ'eɪʃn] n humillación f.

humility [hju:'mɪlətɪ] n humildad f.

humor Am = **humour**.

humorous ['hju:mərəs] adj humorístico(ca).

humour Br, **humor** Am ['hju:mər] ◆ n **1.** (sense of fun, mood) humor m; **in good/ bad ~** de buen/mal humor. **2.** (funny side) gracia f. ◆ vt complacer.

hump [hʌmp] n **1.** (hill) montículo m. **2.** (on back) joroba f, giba f.

humpbacked bridge ['hʌmpbækt-] n puente m peraltado.

hunch [hʌntʃ] ◆ n inf presentimiento m. ◆ vt encorvar.

hunchback ['hʌntʃbæk] n jorobado m, -da f.

hunched [hʌntʃt] adj encorvado(da).

hundred ['hʌndrəd] num cien; **a** OR **one ~** cien; **a** OR **one ~ and eighty** ciento ochenta; see also **six**. ▶ **hundreds** npl centenares mpl.

hundredth ['hʌndrətθ] ◆ num adj centésimo(ma). ◆ num n (fraction) centésimo m; **a ~ of a second** una centésima; see also **sixth**.

hundredweight ['hʌndrədweɪt] n (in UK) = 50,8 kg; (in US) = 45,3 kg.

hung [hʌŋ] pt & pp = **hang**.

Hungarian [hʌŋ'geərɪən] ◆ adj húngaro(ra). ◆ n **1.** (person) húngaro m, -ra f. **2.** (language) húngaro m.

Hungary ['hʌŋgərɪ] n Hungría.

hunger ['hʌŋgər] n **1.** (for food) hambre f. **2.** literary (for change, knowledge etc) sed f. ▶ **hunger after, hunger for** vt fus literary anhelar, ansiar.

hunger strike n huelga f de hambre.

hung over adj inf: **to be ~** tener resaca.

hungry ['hʌŋgrɪ] adj (for food) hambriento(ta); **to be/go ~** tener/pasar hambre.

hung up adj inf: **to be ~ (on** OR **about)** estar neura (por culpa de).

hunk [hʌŋk] n **1.** (large piece) pedazo m, trozo m. **2.** inf (attractive man) tío m bueno, macizo m.

hunt [hʌnt] ◆ n **1.** (of animals, birds) caza f, cacería f. **2.** (for person, clue etc) busca f, búsqueda f. ◆ vi **1.** (for animals, birds) cazar. **2.** (for person, clue etc): **to ~ (for sthg)** buscar (algo). ◆ vt **1.** (animals, birds) cazar. **2.** (person) perseguir.

hunter ['hʌntər] n (of animals, birds) cazador m, -ra f.

hunting ['hʌntɪŋ] n **1.** (of animals) caza f; **to go ~** ir de caza OR cacería. **2.** Br (of foxes) caza f del zorro.

hurdle ['hɜ:dl] ◆ n **1.** (in race) valla f. **2.** (obstacle) obstáculo m. ◆ vt saltar.

hurl [hɜ:l] vt **1.** (throw) lanzar, arrojar.

2. (*shout*) proferir, soltar.
hurray [hʊ'reɪ] *excl* ¡hurra!
hurricane ['hʌrɪkən] *n* huracán *m*.
hurried ['hʌrɪd] *adj* (*hasty*) apresurado (da), precipitado(da).
hurriedly ['hʌrɪdlɪ] *adv* apresuradamente, precipitadamente.
hurry ['hʌrɪ] ♦ *vt* (*person*) meter prisa a; (*work, speech*) apresurar. ♦ *vi:* **to ~ (to do sthg)** apresurarse (a hacer algo). ♦ *n* prisa *f*; **to be in a ~** tener prisa; **to do sthg in a ~** hacer algo de prisa OR apresuradamente. ► **hurry up** *vi* darse prisa.
hurt [hɜːt] (*pt & pp* **hurt**) ♦ *vt* **1.** (*physically - person*) hacer daño a; (*- one's leg, arm*) hacerse daño en. **2.** (*emotionally*) herir. **3.** (*harm*) perjudicar. ♦ *vi* **1.** (*gen*) doler; **my head ~s** me duele la cabeza. **2.** (*cause physical pain, do harm*) hacer daño. ♦ *adj* **1.** (*injured*) herido(da). **2.** (*offended*) dolido(da).
hurtful ['hɜːtfʊl] *adj* hiriente.
hurtle ['hɜːtl] *vi:* **to ~ past** pasar como un rayo.
husband ['hʌzbənd] *n* marido *m*.
hush [hʌʃ] ♦ *n* silencio *m*. ♦ *excl* ¡silencio!, ¡a callar!
husk [hʌsk] *n* (*of seed, grain*) cáscara *f*.
husky ['hʌskɪ] ♦ *adj* (*hoarse*) ronco(ca). ♦ *n* (perro *m*) samoyedo *m*, perro *m* esquimal.
hustle ['hʌsl] ♦ *vt* (*hurry*) meter prisa a. ♦ *n:* **~ (and bustle)** bullicio *m*, ajetreo *m*.
hut [hʌt] *n* **1.** (*rough house*) cabaña *f*, choza *f*. **2.** (*shed*) cobertizo *m*.
hutch [hʌtʃ] *n* conejera *f*.
hyacinth ['haɪəsɪnθ] *n* jacinto *m*.
hydrant ['haɪdrənt] *n* boca *f* de riego; (*for fire*) boca *f* de incendio.
hydraulic [haɪ'drɔːlɪk] *adj* hidráulico (ca).
hydroelectric [ˌhaɪdrəʊ'lektrɪk] *adj* hidroeléctrico(ca).
hydrofoil ['haɪdrəfɔɪl] *n* embarcación *f* con hidroala.
hydrogen ['haɪdrədʒən] *n* hidrógeno *m*.
hyena [haɪ'iːnə] *n* hiena *f*.
hygiene ['haɪdʒiːn] *n* higiene *f*.
hygienic [haɪ'dʒiːnɪk] *adj* higiénico (ca).
hymn [hɪm] *n* himno *m*.
hype [haɪp] *n inf* bombo *m*, publicidad *f* exagerada.
hyperactive [ˌhaɪpər'æktɪv] *adj* hiper-activo(va).
hypermarket ['haɪpəˌmɑːkɪt] *n* hi-

permercado *m*.
hyphen ['haɪfn] *n* guión *m*.
hypnosis [hɪp'nəʊsɪs] *n* hipnosis *f inv*.
hypnotic [hɪp'nɒtɪk] *adj* hipnótico(ca).
hypnotize, -ise ['hɪpnətaɪz] *vt* hipnotizar.
hypochondriac [ˌhaɪpə'kɒndriæk] *n* hipocondríaco *m*, -ca *f*.
hypocrisy [hɪ'pɒkrəsɪ] *n* hipocresía *f*.
hypocrite ['hɪpəkrɪt] *n* hipócrita *m y f*.
hypocritical [ˌhɪpə'krɪtɪkl] *adj* hipócri-ta.
hypothesis [haɪ'pɒθɪsɪs] (*pl* **-theses** [-θɪsiːz]) *n* hipótesis *f inv*.
hypothetical [ˌhaɪpə'θetɪkl] *adj* hipotético(ca).
hysteria [hɪs'tɪərɪə] *n* histeria *f*.
hysterical [hɪs'terɪkl] *adj* **1.** (*frantic*) histérico(ca). **2.** *inf* (*very funny*) tronchante.
hysterics [hɪs'terɪks] *npl* **1.** (*panic, excitement*) histeria *f*, histerismo *m*. **2.** *inf* (*fits of laughter*): **to be in ~** troncharse OR partirse de risa.

I

i (*pl* **i's** OR **is**), **I** (*pl* **I's** OR **Is**) [aɪ] *n* (*letter*) i *f*, I *f*.
I [aɪ] *pers pron* yo; **I'm happy** soy feliz; **I'm leaving** me voy; **she and ~ were at college together** ella y yo fuimos juntos a la universidad; **it is ~** *fml* soy yo; **I can't do it** yo no puedo hacer esto.
ice [aɪs] ♦ *n* **1.** (*frozen water*) hielo *m*. **2.** Br (*ice cream*) helado *m*. **3.** (*on road*) hielo transparente en el suelo. ♦ *vt* glasear, alcorzar. ► **ice over, ice up** *vi* helarse.
iceberg ['aɪsbɜːg] *n* iceberg *m*.
iceberg lettuce *n* lechuga *f* iceberg.
icebox ['aɪsbɒks] *n* **1.** Br (*in refrigerator*) congelador *m*. **2.** Am (*refrigerator*) refrigerador *m*.
ice cream *n* helado *m*.
ice cube *n* cubito *m* de hielo.
ice hockey *n* hockey *m* sobre hielo.
Iceland ['aɪslənd] *n* Islandia.
Icelandic [aɪs'lændɪk] ♦ *adj* islandés (esa). ♦ *n* (*language*) islandés *m*.
ice lolly *n* Br polo *m*.
ice pick *n* pico *m* para el hielo.

ice rink n pista f de (patinaje sobre) hielo.

ice skate n patín m de cuchilla. ► **ice-skate** vi patinar sobre hielo.

ice-skating n patinaje m sobre hielo.

icicle ['aɪsɪkl] n carámbano m.

icing ['aɪsɪŋ] n glaseado m.

icing sugar n Br azúcar m glas.

icon ['aɪkɒn] n (COMPUT & RELIG) icono m.

icy ['aɪsɪ] adj 1. (gen) helado(da). 2. fig (unfriendly) glacial.

I'd [aɪd] = **I would, I had**.

ID n (U) (abbr of **identification**) ≃ DNI m.

idea [aɪ'dɪə] n 1. (gen) idea f; **to have no ~** no tener ni idea; **to get the ~** inf captar la idea, hacerse una idea. 2. (intuition, feeling) sensación f, impresión f; **to have an ~ (that)** ... tener la sensación de que ...

ideal [aɪ'dɪəl] ◆ adj: **~ (for)** ideal (para). ◆ n ideal m.

ideally [aɪ'dɪəlɪ] adv 1. (perfectly) idealmente; (suited) perfectamente. 2. (preferably) a ser posible.

identical [aɪ'dentɪkl] adj idéntico(ca).

identification [aɪ,dentɪfɪ'keɪʃn] n 1. (gen): **~ (with)** identificación f (con). 2. (documentation) documentación f.

identify [aɪ'dentɪfaɪ] ◆ vt identificar; **to ~ sb with sthg** relacionar a alguien con algo. ◆ vi: **to ~ with sb/sthg** identificarse con alguien/algo.

Identikit picture® [aɪ'dentɪkɪt-] n fotorrobot f.

identity [aɪ'dentətɪ] n identidad f.

identity card n carné m OR documento m de identidad, cédula f Amer.

identity parade n rueda f de identificación.

ideology [,aɪdɪ'ɒlədʒɪ] n ideología f.

idiom ['ɪdɪəm] n 1. (phrase) locución f, modismo m. 2. fml (style) lenguaje m.

idiomatic [,ɪdɪə'mætɪk] adj idiomático (ca).

idiosyncrasy [,ɪdɪə'sɪŋkrəsɪ] n rareza f, manía f.

idiot ['ɪdɪət] n (fool) idiota m y f.

idiotic [,ɪdɪ'ɒtɪk] adj idiota.

idle ['aɪdl] ◆ adj 1. (lazy) perezoso(sa), vago(ga). 2. (not working - machine, factory) parado(da); (- person) desocupado (da), sin trabajo. 3. (rumour) infundado (da); (threat, boast) vano(na); (curiosity) que no viene a cuento. ◆ vi estar en punto muerto. ► **idle away** vt sep desperdiciar.

idol ['aɪdl] n ídolo m.

idolize, -ise ['aɪdəlaɪz] vt idolatrar.

idyllic [ɪ'dɪlɪk] adj idílico(ca).

i.e. (abbr of **id est**) i.e.

if [ɪf] conj 1. (gen) si; **~ I were you** yo que tú, yo en tu lugar. 2. (though) aunque. ► **if not** conj por no decir. ► **if only** ◆ conj 1. (naming a reason) aunque sólo sea. 2. (expressing regret) si; **~ only I'd been quicker!** ¡ojalá hubiera sido más rápido! ◆ excl ¡ojalá!

igloo ['ɪgluː] (pl -s) n iglú m.

ignite [ɪg'naɪt] ◆ vt encender. ◆ vi encenderse.

ignition [ɪg'nɪʃn] n 1. (act of igniting) ignición f. 2. (in car) encendido m; **to switch on the ~** arrancar (el motor).

ignition key n llave f de contacto.

ignorance ['ɪgnərəns] n ignorancia f.

ignorant ['ɪgnərənt] adj 1. (uneducated, rude) ignorante. 2. fml (unaware): **to be ~ of sthg** ignorar algo.

ignore [ɪg'nɔːʳ] vt (take no notice of) no hacer caso de, ignorar.

iguana [ɪ'gwɑːnə] (pl inv OR -s) n iguana f.

ilk [ɪlk] n: **of that ~** (of that sort) de ese tipo.

ill [ɪl] ◆ adj 1. (unwell) enfermo(ma); **to feel ~** encontrarse mal; **to be taken** OR **to fall ~** caer OR ponerse enfermo. 2. (bad) malo(la). ◆ adv 1. (badly) mal. 2. fml (unfavourably): **to speak/think ~ of sb** hablar/pensar mal de alguien.

I'll [aɪl] = **I will, I shall**.

ill-advised [-əd'vaɪzd] adj (action) poco aconsejable; (person) imprudente.

ill at ease adj incómodo(da), violento (ta).

illegal [ɪ'liːgl] adj ilegal.

illegible [ɪ'ledʒəbl] adj ilegible.

illegitimate [,ɪlɪ'dʒɪtɪmət] adj ilegítimo(ma).

ill-equipped [-ɪ'kwɪpt] adj: **to be ~ to do sthg** estar mal preparado(da) para hacer algo.

ill-fated [-'feɪtɪd] adj desafortunado (da).

ill feeling n resentimiento m.

ill health n mala salud f.

illicit [ɪ'lɪsɪt] adj ilícito(ta).

illiteracy [ɪ'lɪtərəsɪ] n analfabetismo m.

illiterate [ɪ'lɪtərət] ◆ adj analfabeto (ta). ◆ n analfabeto m, -ta f.

illness ['ɪlnɪs] n enfermedad f.

illogical [ɪ'lɒdʒɪkl] adj ilógico(ca).

ill-suited adj: **~ (for)** poco adecuado (da) (para).

ill-timed [-'taɪmd] adj inoportuno(na).
ill-treat vt maltratar.
illuminate [ɪ'lu:mɪneɪt] vt 1. (light up) iluminar. 2. (explain) ilustrar, aclarar.
illumination [ɪ,lu:mɪ'neɪʃn] n (lighting) alumbrado m, iluminación f. ▶ **illuminations** npl Br iluminaciones fpl, alumbrado m decorativo.
illusion [ɪ'lu:ʒn] n 1. (gen) ilusión f; **to be under the ~ that** creer equivocadamente que. 2. (magic trick) truco m de ilusionismo.
illustrate ['ɪləstreɪt] vt ilustrar.
illustration [,ɪlə'streɪʃn] n ilustración f.
illustrious [ɪ'lʌstrɪəs] adj fml ilustre.
ill will n rencor m, animadversión f.
I'm [aɪm] = **I am**.
image ['ɪmɪdʒ] n imagen f.
imagery ['ɪmɪdʒrɪ] n (U) imágenes fpl.
imaginary [ɪ'mædʒɪnrɪ] adj imaginario (ria).
imagination [ɪ,mædʒɪ'neɪʃn] n imaginación f.
imaginative [ɪ'mædʒɪnətɪv] adj imaginativo(va).
imagine [ɪ'mædʒɪn] vt 1. (gen) imaginar; **~ never having to work!** ¡imagina que nunca tuvieras que trabajar!; **~ (that)!** ¡imagínate! 2. (suppose): **to ~ (that)** imaginarse que.
imbalance [,ɪm'bæləns] n desequilibrio m.
imbecile ['ɪmbɪsi:l] n imbécil m y f.
IMF (abbr of **International Monetary Fund**) n FMI m.
imitate ['ɪmɪteɪt] vt imitar.
imitation [,ɪmɪ'teɪʃn] ♦ n imitación f. ♦ adj de imitación.
immaculate [ɪ'mækjʊlət] adj 1. (clean and tidy) inmaculado(da); (taste) exquisito(ta). 2. (impeccable) impecable.
immaterial [,ɪmə'tɪərɪəl] adj (irrelevant, unimportant) irrelevante.
immature [,ɪmə'tjʊəʳ] adj inmaduro (ra); (animal) joven.
immediate [ɪ'mi:djət] adj 1. (gen) inmediato(ta); **in the ~ future** en el futuro más cercano. 2. (family) directo (ta).
immediately [ɪ'mi:djətlɪ] ♦ adv 1. (at once) inmediatamente. 2. (directly) directamente. ♦ conj en cuanto.
immense [ɪ'mens] adj inmenso(sa).
immerse [ɪ'mɜ:s] vt 1. (plunge): **to ~ sthg in sthg** sumergir algo en algo. 2. (involve): **to ~ o.s. in sthg** enfrascarse en algo.
immersion heater [ɪ'mɜ:ʃn-] n

calentador m de inmersión.
immigrant ['ɪmɪgrənt] n inmigrante m y f.
immigration [,ɪmɪ'greɪʃn] n inmigración f.
imminent ['ɪmɪnənt] adj inminente.
immobilize, -ise [ɪ'məʊbɪlaɪz] vt inmovilizar.
immoral [ɪ'mɒrəl] adj inmoral.
immortal [ɪ'mɔ:tl] adj inmortal.
immortalize, -ise [ɪ'mɔ:təlaɪz] vt inmortalizar.
immovable [ɪ'mu:vəbl] adj 1. (fixed) fijo(ja), inamovible. 2. (determined, decided) inconmovible, inflexible.
immune [ɪ'mju:n] adj 1. (gen & MED): **~ (to)** inmune (a). 2. (exempt): **~ (from)** exento(ta) (de).
immunity [ɪ'mju:nətɪ] n 1. (gen & MED): **~ (to)** inmunidad f (a). 2. (exemption): **~ (from)** exención f (de).
immunize, -ise ['ɪmju:naɪz] vt: **to ~ sb (against sthg)** inmunizar a alguien (contra algo).
imp [ɪmp] n 1. (creature) duendecillo m. 2. (naughty child) diablillo m.
impact [n 'ɪmpækt, vb ɪm'pækt] ♦ n impacto m; **to make an ~ on** OR **upon** causar impacto en. ♦ vt (influence) influenciar.
impair [ɪm'peəʳ] vt (sight, hearing) dañar, debilitar; (ability, efficiency) mermar; (movement) entorpecer.
impart [ɪm'pɑ:t] vt fml 1. (information): **to ~ sthg (to sb)** comunicar algo (a alguien). 2. (feeling, quality): **to ~ sthg (to sthg)** conferir algo (a algo).
impartial [ɪm'pɑ:ʃl] adj imparcial.
impassable [ɪm'pɑ:səbl] adj intransitable, impracticable.
impasse [æm'pɑ:s] n impasse m, callejón m sin salida.
impassive [ɪm'pæsɪv] adj impasible.
impatience [ɪm'peɪʃns] n impaciencia f.
impatient [ɪm'peɪʃnt] adj impaciente; **to be ~ to do sthg** estar impaciente por hacer algo; **to be ~ for sthg** esperar algo con impaciencia.
impeccable [ɪm'pekəbl] adj impecable.
impede [ɪm'pi:d] vt dificultar.
impediment [ɪm'pedɪmənt] n 1. (obstacle) impedimento m, obstáculo m. 2. (disability) defecto m.
impel [ɪm'pel] vt: **to ~ sb to do sthg** impulsar OR impeler a alguien a hacer algo.

impending [ɪmˈpendɪŋ] *adj* inminente.
imperative [ɪmˈperətɪv] ◆ *adj* (*essential*) apremiante. ◆ *n* imperativo *m*.
imperfect [ɪmˈpɜːfɪkt] ◆ *adj* (*not perfect*) imperfecto(ta). ◆ *n* (GRAMM): ~ (**tense**) (pretérito *m*) imperfecto *m*.
imperial [ɪmˈpɪərɪəl] *adj* 1. (*of an empire or emperor*) imperial. 2. (*system of measurement*): ~ **system** sistema anglosajón de medidas.
imperialism [ɪmˈpɪərɪəlɪzm] *n* imperialismo *m*.
impersonal [ɪmˈpɜːsnl] *adj* impersonal.
impersonate [ɪmˈpɜːsəneɪt] *vt* (*gen*) hacerse pasar por; (THEATRE) imitar.
impersonation [ɪmˌpɜːsəˈneɪʃn] *n* 1. (*pretending to be*): **charged with ~ of a policeman** acusado de hacerse pasar por policía. 2. (*impression*) imitación *f*; **to do ~s (of)** imitar (a), hacer imitaciones (de).
impertinent [ɪmˈpɜːtɪnənt] *adj* impertinente, insolente.
impervious [ɪmˈpɜːvjəs] *adj* (*not influenced*): ~ **to** insensible a.
impetuous [ɪmˈpetʃuəs] *adj* impetuoso(sa), irreflexivo(va).
impetus [ˈɪmpɪtəs] *n* (U) 1. (*momentum*) ímpetu *m*. 2. (*stimulus*) incentivo *m*, impulso *m*.
impinge [ɪmˈpɪndʒ] *vi*: **to ~ on sthg/sb** afectar algo/a alguien.
implant [*n* ˈɪmplɑːnt, *vb* ɪmˈplɑːnt] ◆ *n* injerto *m*. ◆ *vt* 1. (*fix - idea etc*): **to ~ sthg in** OR **into** inculcar algo en. 2. (MED): **to ~ sthg in** OR **into** implantar algo en.
implausible [ɪmˈplɔːzəbl] *adj* inverosímil.
implement [*n* ˈɪmplɪmənt, *vt* ˈɪmplɪment] ◆ *n* herramienta *f*. ◆ *vt* llevar a cabo, poner en práctica.
implication [ˌɪmplɪˈkeɪʃn] *n* 1. (*involvement*) implicación *f*. 2. (*inference*) consecuencia *f*; **by ~** de forma indirecta.
implicit [ɪmˈplɪsɪt] *adj* 1. (*gen*): ~ (**in**) implícito(ta) (en). 2. (*complete - belief*) absoluto(ta); (- *faith*) incondicional.
implore [ɪmˈplɔːr] *vt*: **to ~ sb (to do sthg)** suplicar a alguien (que haga algo).
imply [ɪmˈplaɪ] *vt* 1. (*suggest*) insinuar, dar a entender. 2. (*involve*) implicar, suponer.
impolite [ˌɪmpəˈlaɪt] *adj* maleducado(da), descortés.
import [*n* ˈɪmpɔːt, *vt* ɪmˈpɔːt] ◆ *n* 1. (*act of importing, product*) importación *f*. 2. *fml* (*meaning*) sentido *m*, significado *m*. ◆ *vt*

lit & fig importar.
importance [ɪmˈpɔːtns] *n* importancia *f*.
important [ɪmˈpɔːtnt] *adj*: ~ (**to**) importante (para); **it's not ~** no importa.
importer [ɪmˈpɔːtər] *n* importador *m*, -ra *f*.
impose [ɪmˈpəuz] ◆ *vt*: **to ~ sthg (on)** imponer algo (a). ◆ *vi*: **to ~ (on)** abusar (de), molestar (a).
imposing [ɪmˈpəuzɪŋ] *adj* imponente, impresionante.
imposition [ˌɪmpəˈzɪʃn] *n* 1. (*enforcement*) imposición *f*. 2. (*cause of trouble*) molestia *f*.
impossible [ɪmˈpɒsəbl] *adj* 1. (*gen*) imposible. 2. (*person, behaviour*) inaguantable, insufrible.
impostor, imposter Am [ɪmˈpɒstər] *n* impostor *m*, -ra *f*.
impotent [ˈɪmpətənt] *adj* impotente.
impound [ɪmˈpaund] *vt* incautarse.
impoverished [ɪmˈpɒvərɪʃt] *adj* (*country, people, imagination*) empobrecido(da).
impracticable [ɪmˈpræktɪkəbl] *adj* impracticable, irrealizable.
impractical [ɪmˈpræktɪkl] *adj* poco práctico(ca).
impregnable [ɪmˈpregnəbl] *adj lit & fig* inexpugnable, impenetrable.
impregnate [ˈɪmpregneɪt] *vt* 1. (*introduce substance into*): **to ~ sthg (with)** impregnar OR empapar algo (de). 2. *fml* (*fertilize*) fecundar.
impress [ɪmˈpres] *vt* 1. (*produce admiration in*) impresionar. 2. (*stress*): **to ~ sthg on sb** hacer comprender a alguien la importancia de algo.
impression [ɪmˈpreʃn] *n* 1. (*gen*) impresión *f*; **to make an ~** impresionar; **to make a good/bad ~** causar una buena/mala impresión; **to be under the ~ that** tener la impresión de que. 2. (*imitation*) imitación *f*.
impressive [ɪmˈpresɪv] *adj* impresionante.
imprint [ˈɪmprɪnt] *n* 1. (*mark*) huella *f*, impresión *f*. 2. (*publisher's name*) pie *m* de imprenta.
imprison [ɪmˈprɪzn] *vt* encarcelar.
improbable [ɪmˈprɒbəbl] *adj* (*event*) improbable; (*story, excuse*) inverosímil; (*clothes, hat*) estrafalario(ria); (*contraption*) extraño(ña).
impromptu [ɪmˈprɒmptjuː] *adj* improvisado(da).
improper [ɪmˈprɒpər] *adj* 1. (*unsuitable*)

impropio(pia). **2.** (*incorrect, illegal*) indebido(da). **3.** (*rude*) indecoroso(sa).

improve [ɪm'pruːv] ◆ *vi* mejorar, mejorarse; **to ~ on** OR **upon sthg** mejorar algo. ◆ *vt* mejorar.

improvement [ɪm'pruːvmənt] *n* **1.** (*gen*): **~ (in/on)** mejora *f* (en/con respecto a). **2.** (*to home*) reforma *f*.

improvise ['ɪmprəvaɪz] *vt & vi* improvisar.

impudent ['ɪmpjʊdənt] *adj* insolente.

impulse ['ɪmpʌls] *n* impulso *m*; **on ~** sin pensar.

impulsive [ɪm'pʌlsɪv] *adj* impulsivo (va), irreflexivo(va).

impunity [ɪm'pjuːnətɪ] *n*: **with ~** impunemente.

impurity [ɪm'pjʊərətɪ] *n* impureza *f*.

in [ɪn] ◆ *prep* **1.** (*indicating place, position*) en; **~ a box/the garden/the lake** en una caja/el jardín/el lago; **~ Paris/Belgium/the country** en París/Bélgica/el campo; **~ here/there** aquí/allí dentro. **2.** (*wearing*) con; **she was still ~ her nightclothes** todavía llevaba su vestido de noche. **3.** (*at a particular time*): **at four o'clock ~ the morning/afternoon** a las cuatro de la mañana/tarde; **~ the morning** por la mañana; **~ 1992/May/the spring** en 1992/mayo/primavera. **4.** (*within*) en; **he learned to type ~ two weeks** aprendió a escribir a máquina en dos semanas; **I'll be ready ~ five minutes** estoy listo en cinco minutos. **5.** (*during*) desde hace; **it's my first decent meal ~ weeks** es lo primero decente que como desde hace OR en semanas. **6.** (*indicating situation, circumstances*): **~ danger/difficulty** en peligro/dificultades; **~ the sun** al sol; **~ the rain** bajo la lluvia; **a rise ~ prices** un aumento de los precios. **7.** (*indicating manner, condition*) en; **~ a loud/soft voice** en voz alta/baja; **~ pencil/ink** a lápiz/bolígrafo. **8.** (*indicating emotional state*) con; **~ anger/joy** con enfado/alegría. **9.** (*specifying area of activity*): **advances ~ medicine** avances en la medicina; **he's ~ computers** está metido en informática. **10.** (*with numbers - showing quantity, age*): **~ large/small quantities** en grandes/pequeñas cantidades; **~ (their) thousands** a OR por millares; **she's ~ her sixties** andará por los sesenta. **11.** (*describing arrangement*): **~ a line/circle** en línea/círculo; **to stand ~ twos** estar en pares OR parejas. **12.** (*as regards*) en; **~ these matters** en estos temas; **two metres ~ length/width** dos metros de largo/

ancho; **a change ~ direction** un cambio de dirección. **13.** (*in ratios*): **one ~ ten** uno de cada diez; **five pence ~ the pound** cinco peniques por libra. **14.** (*after superl*) de; **the best ~ the world** el mejor del mundo. **15.** (+ *present participle*): **~ doing sthg** al hacer algo. ◆ *adv* **1.** (*inside*) dentro; **to jump ~** saltar adentro; **do come ~** pasa por favor. **2.** (*at home, work*): **is Judith ~?** ¿está Judith?; **I'm staying ~ tonight** esta noche no salgo. **3.** (*of train, boat, plane*): **is the train ~ yet?** ¿ha llegado el tren? **4.** (*of tide*): **the tide's ~** la marea está alta. **5.** *phr*: **you're ~ for a surprise** te vas a llevar una sorpresa; **to have it ~ for sb** tenerla tomada con alguien. ◆ *adj inf* de moda.

▶ **ins** *npl*: **the ~s and outs** los detalles, los pormenores.

in. *abbr of* **inch.**

inability [ˌɪnə'bɪlətɪ] *n*: **~ (to do sthg)** incapacidad *f* (de hacer algo).

inaccessible [ˌɪnək'sesəbl] *adj* inaccesible.

inaccurate [ɪn'ækjʊrət] *adj* incorrecto (ta), inexacto(ta).

inadequate [ɪn'ædɪkwət] *adj* **1.** (*insufficient*) insuficiente. **2.** (*person*) incapaz.

inadvertently [ˌɪnəd'vɜːtəntlɪ] *adv* sin querer, accidentalmente.

inadvisable [ˌɪnəd'vaɪzəbl] *adj* poco aconsejable.

inane [ɪ'neɪn] *adj* necio(cia).

inanimate [ɪn'ænɪmət] *adj* inanimado (da).

inappropriate [ˌɪnə'prəʊprɪət] *adj* (*remark, clothing*) impropio(pia); (*time*) inoportuno(na).

inarticulate [ˌɪnɑː'tɪkjʊlət] *adj* (*person*) incapaz de expresarse; (*speech, explanation*) mal pronunciado(da) OR expresado(da).

inasmuch [ˌɪnəz'mʌtʃ] ▶ **inasmuch as** *conj* en la medida en que.

inaudible [ɪ'nɔːdɪbl] *adj* inaudible.

inauguration [ɪˌnɔːgjʊ'reɪʃn] *n* **1.** (*of leader, president*) investidura *f*. **2.** (*of building, system*) inauguración *f*.

in-between *adj* intermedio(dia).

inborn [ˌɪn'bɔːn] *adj* innato(ta).

inbound ['ɪnbaʊnd] *adj Am* que se aproxima.

inbred [ˌɪn'bred] *adj* **1.** (*closely related*) endogámico(ca). **2.** (*inborn*) innato(ta).

inbuilt [ˌɪn'bɪlt] *adj* (*in person*) innato (ta); (*in thing*) inherente.

inc. (*abbr of* **inclusive**) inclus.

Inc. [ɪŋk] (*abbr of* **incorporated**) ≈ S.A.

incapable [ɪn'keɪpəbl] *adj* **1.** (*unable*): to be ~ of sthg/of doing sthg ser incapaz de algo/de hacer algo. **2.** (*useless*) incompetente.

incapacitated [,ɪnkə'pæsɪteɪtɪd] *adj* incapacitado(da).

incarcerate [ɪn'kɑːsəreɪt] *vt fml* encarcelar.

incarnation [,ɪnkɑː'neɪʃn] *n* **1.** (*personification*) personificación *f.* **2.** (*existence*) encarnación *f.*

incendiary device [ɪn'sendjərɪ-] *n* artefacto *m* incendiario.

incense [*n* 'ɪnsens, *vt* ɪn'sens] ◆ *n* incienso *m.* ◆ *vt* sulfurar, indignar.

incentive [ɪn'sentɪv] *n* incentivo *m.*

incentive scheme *n* plan *m* de incentivos.

inception [ɪn'sepʃn] *n fml* inicio *m.*

incessant [ɪn'sesnt] *adj* incesante, constante.

incessantly [ɪn'sesntlɪ] *adv* incesantemente, constantemente.

incest ['ɪnsest] *n* incesto *m.*

inch [ɪntʃ] ◆ *n* = 2,5 *cm*, pulgada *f.* ◆ *vi* avanzar poco a poco.

incidence ['ɪnsɪdəns] *n* (*of disease, theft*) índice *m.*

incident ['ɪnsɪdənt] *n* incidente *m*, suceso *m.*

incidental [,ɪnsɪ'dentl] *adj* accesorio (ria).

incidentally [,ɪnsɪ'dentəlɪ] *adv* por cierto, a propósito.

incinerate [ɪn'sɪnəreɪt] *vt* incinerar.

incipient [ɪn'sɪpɪənt] *adj fml* incipiente.

incisive [ɪn'saɪsɪv] *adj* (*comment, person*) incisivo(va); (*mind*) penetrante.

incite [ɪn'saɪt] *vt* incitar, provocar; to ~ sb to do sthg incitar a alguien a que haga algo.

inclination [,ɪnklɪ'neɪʃn] *n* **1.** (U) (*liking, preference*) inclinación *f*, propensión *f.* **2.** (*tendency*): ~ to do sthg tendencia *f* a hacer algo.

incline [*n* 'ɪnklaɪn, *vb* ɪn'klaɪn] ◆ *n* pendiente *f.* ◆ *vt* (*head*) inclinar, ladear.

inclined [ɪn'klaɪnd] *adj* **1.** (*tending*): to be ~ to sthg ser propenso OR tener tendencia a algo; to be ~ to do sthg tener tendencia a hacer algo. **2.** *fml* (*wanting*): to be ~ to do sthg estar dispuesto a hacer algo. **3.** (*sloping*) inclinado(da).

include [ɪn'kluːd] *vt* **1.** (*gen*) incluir. **2.** (*with letter*) adjuntar.

included [ɪn'kluːdɪd] *adj* incluido(da).

including [ɪn'kluːdɪŋ] *prep* inclusive; six died, ~ a child seis murieron, incluido un niño.

inclusive [ɪn'kluːsɪv] *adj* **1.** (*including everything*) inclusivo(va); one to nine ~ uno a nueve inclusive. **2.** (*including all costs*): ~ of VAT con el IVA incluido; £150 ~ 150 libras todo incluido.

incoherent [,ɪnkəʊ'hɪərənt] *adj* incoherente, ininteligible.

income ['ɪŋkʌm] *n* (*gen*) ingresos *mpl*; (*from property*) renta *f*; (*from investment*) réditos *mpl*.

income support *n* (U) *Br* subsidio para personas con muy bajos ingresos o desempleados sin derecho a subsidio de paro, ≈ salario *m* social.

income tax *n* impuesto *m* sobre la renta.

incompatible [,ɪnkəm'pætɪbl] *adj*: ~ (with) incompatible (con).

incompetent [ɪn'kɒmpɪtənt] *adj* incompetente, incapaz.

incomplete [,ɪnkəm'pliːt] *adj* incompleto(ta).

incomprehensible [ɪn,kɒmprɪ'hensəbl] *adj* incomprensible.

inconceivable [,ɪnkən'siːvəbl] *adj* inconcebible.

inconclusive [,ɪnkən'kluːsɪv] *adj* (*evidence, argument*) poco convincente; (*meeting, outcome*) sin conclusión clara.

incongruous [ɪn'kɒŋgrʊəs] *adj* incongruente.

inconsequential [,ɪnkɒnsɪ'kwenʃl] *adj* intranscendente, de poca importancia.

inconsiderable [,ɪnkən'sɪdərəbl] *adj*: not ~ nada insignificante OR despreciable.

inconsiderate [,ɪnkən'sɪdərət] *adj* desconsiderado(da).

inconsistency [,ɪnkən'sɪstənsɪ] *n* **1.** (*between theory and practice*) inconsecuencia *f*; (*between statements etc*) falta *f* de correspondencia. **2.** (*contradictory point*) contradicción *f.*

inconsistent [,ɪnkən'sɪstənt] *adj* **1.** (*translation, statement*): ~ (with) falto(ta) de correspondencia (con). **2.** (*group, government, person*) inconsecuente. **3.** (*erratic*) irregular, desigual.

inconspicuous [,ɪnkən'spɪkjʊəs] *adj* discreto(ta).

inconvenience [,ɪnkən'viːnjəns] ◆ *n* **1.** (*difficulty, discomfort*) molestia *f*, incomodidad *f.* **2.** (*inconvenient thing*) inconveniente *m.* ◆ *vt* incomodar.

inconvenient [,ɪnkən'viːnjənt] *adj* (*time*) inoportuno(na); (*position*) incómodo(da); that date is ~ esa fecha no me viene bien.

incorporate [ɪn'kɔːpəreɪt] vt 1. (integrate): **to ~ sthg/sb (in), to ~ sthg/sb (into)** incorporar algo/a alguien (en). 2. (include) incluir, comprender.

incorporated [ɪn'kɔːpəreɪtɪd] adj (COMM): **~ company** sociedad f anónima.

incorrect [ˌɪnkə'rekt] adj incorrecto (ta).

incorrigible [ɪn'kɒrɪdʒəbl] adj incorregible.

increase [n 'ɪnkriːs, vb ɪn'kriːs] ◆ n: **~ (in)** (gen) aumento m (de); (in price) subida f (de); **to be on the ~** ir en aumento. ◆ vt aumentar, incrementar. ◆ vi (gen) aumentar, aumentarse; (price) subir.

increasing [ɪn'kriːsɪŋ] adj creciente.

increasingly [ɪn'kriːsɪŋlɪ] adv cada vez más.

incredible [ɪn'kredəbl] adj increíble.

incredulous [ɪn'kredjʊləs] adj incrédulo(la).

increment ['ɪnkrɪmənt] n incremento m.

incriminating [ɪn'krɪmɪneɪtɪŋ] adj incriminatorio(ria).

incubator ['ɪnkjʊbeɪtər] n (for baby) incubadora f.

incumbent [ɪn'kʌmbənt] fml ◆ adj: **to be ~ on** OR **upon sb to do sthg** incumbir a alguien hacer algo. ◆ n titular m y f.

incur [ɪn'kɜːr] vt (wrath, criticism) incurrir en, atraerse; (loss) contraer; (expenses) incurrir en.

indebted [ɪn'detɪd] adj 1. (grateful): **~ (to)** agradecido(da) (a). 2. (owing money): **~ (to)** en deuda (con).

indecent [ɪn'diːsnt] adj 1. (improper) indecente. 2. (unreasonable, excessive) desmedido(da).

indecent assault n atentado m contra el pudor.

indecent exposure n exhibicionismo m.

indecisive [ˌɪndɪ'saɪsɪv] adj 1. (person) indeciso(sa). 2. (result) no decisivo(va).

indeed [ɪn'diːd] adv 1. (certainly) ciertamente, realmente; **are you coming? - ~ I am** ¿vienes tú? – por supuesto que sí. 2. (in fact) de hecho. 3. (for emphasis) realmente; **very big ~** grandísimo; **very few ~** poquísimos. 4. (to express surprise, disbelief): **~?** ¿ah sí?

indefinite [ɪn'defɪnɪt] adj 1. (time, number) indefinido(da). 2. (answer, opinion) impreciso(sa).

indefinitely [ɪn'defɪnətlɪ] adv 1. (for unfixed period) indefinidamente. 2. (im-

precisely) de forma imprecisa.

indemnity [ɪn'demnətɪ] n 1. (insurance) indemnidad f. 2. (compensation) indemnización f, compensación f.

indent [ɪn'dent] vt 1. (dent) mellar. 2. (text) sangrar.

independence [ˌɪndɪ'pendəns] n independencia f.

Independence Day n fiesta del 4 de julio en Estados Unidos en conmemoración de la Declaración de Independencia de este país en 1776.

independent [ˌɪndɪ'pendənt] adj: **~ (of)** independiente (de).

independent school n Br colegio m privado.

in-depth adj a fondo, exhaustivo(va).

indescribable [ˌɪndɪ'skraɪbəbl] adj indescriptible.

indestructible [ˌɪndɪ'strʌktəbl] adj indestructible.

index ['ɪndeks] (pl **-es** OR **indices**) n índice m.

index card n ficha f.

index finger n (dedo m) índice m.

index-linked [-lɪŋkt] adj ligado(da) al coste de la vida.

India ['ɪndjə] n (la) India.

Indian ['ɪndjən] ◆ adj 1. (from India) hindú, indio(dia). 2. (from the Americas) indio(dia). ◆ n 1. (from India) hindú m y f, indio m, -dia f. 2. (from the Americas) indio m, -dia f.

Indian Ocean n: **the ~** el océano Índico.

indicate ['ɪndɪkeɪt] ◆ vt indicar. ◆ vi (when driving): **to ~ left/right** indicar a la izquierda/derecha.

indication [ˌɪndɪ'keɪʃn] n 1. (suggestion, idea) indicación f. 2. (sign) indicio m.

indicative [ɪn'dɪkətɪv] ◆ adj: **~ of sthg** indicativo(va) de algo. ◆ n (GRAMM) indicativo m.

indicator ['ɪndɪkeɪtər] n 1. (sign) indicador m. 2. (on car) intermitente m.

indices ['ɪndɪsiːz] pl → **index**.

indict [ɪn'daɪt] vt: **to ~ sb (for)** acusar a alguien (de).

indictment [ɪn'daɪtmənt] n 1. (JUR) acusación f. 2. (criticism) crítica f severa.

indifference [ɪn'dɪfrəns] n indiferencia f.

indifferent [ɪn'dɪfrənt] adj 1. (uninterested): **~ (to)** indiferente (a). 2. (mediocre) ordinario(ria), mediocre.

indigenous [ɪn'dɪdʒɪnəs] adj indígena.

indigestion [ˌɪndɪ'dʒestʃn] n (U) indigestión f.

indignant [ɪn'dɪgnənt] *adj:* ~ **(at)** indignado(da) (por).

indignity [ɪn'dɪgnətɪ] *n* indignidad *f.*

indigo ['ɪndɪgəʊ] ◆ *adj* (color) añil. ◆ *n* añil *m.*

indirect [,ɪndɪ'rekt] *adj* indirecto(ta).

indiscreet [,ɪndɪ'skriːt] *adj* indiscreto (ta), imprudente.

indiscriminate [,ɪndɪ'skrɪmɪnət] *adj* indiscriminado(da).

indispensable [,ɪndɪ'spensəbl] *adj* indispensable, imprescindible.

indisputable [,ɪndɪ'spjuːtəbl] *adj* incuestionable.

indistinct [,ɪndɪ'stɪŋkt] *adj (memory)* confuso(sa); *(picture, marking)* borroso (sa).

indistinguishable [,ɪndɪ'stɪŋgwɪʃəbl] *adj:* ~ **(from)** indistinguible (de).

individual [,ɪndɪ'vɪdʒʊəl] ◆ *adj* **1.** *(gen)* individual. **2.** *(tuition)* particular. **3.** *(approach, style)* personal. ◆ *n* individuo *m.*

individually [,ɪndɪ'vɪdʒʊəlɪ] *adv (separately)* individualmente, por separado.

indoctrination [ɪn,dɒktrɪ'neɪʃn] *n* adoctrinamiento *m.*

Indonesia [,ɪndə'niːzjə] *n* Indonesia.

indoor ['ɪndɔːr] *adj (gen)* interior; *(shoes)* de andar por casa; *(plant)* de interior; *(sports)* en pista cubierta; ~ **swimming pool** piscina *f* cubierta.

indoors [ɪn'dɔːz] *adv (gen)* dentro; *(at home)* en casa.

induce [ɪn'djuːs] *vt* **1.** *(persuade):* **to ~ sb to do sthg** inducir OR persuadir a alguien a que haga algo. **2.** *(labour, sleep, anger)* provocar.

inducement [ɪn'djuːsmənt] *n (incentive)* incentivo *m,* aliciente *m.*

induction [ɪn'dʌkʃn] *n* **1.** *(into official position):* ~ **into** introducción *f* OR inducción *f* a. **2.** (ELEC & MED) inducción *f.* **3.** *(introduction to job)* introducción *f.*

induction course *n* cursillo *m* introductorio.

indulge [ɪn'dʌldʒ] ◆ *vt* **1.** *(whim, passion)* satisfacer. **2.** *(child, person)* consentir. ◆ *vi:* **to ~ in sthg** permitirse algo.

indulgence [ɪn'dʌldʒəns] *n* **1.** *(act of indulging)* indulgencia *f.* **2.** *(special treat)* gratificación *f,* vicio *m.*

indulgent [ɪn'dʌldʒənt] *adj* indulgente.

industrial [ɪn'dʌstrɪəl] *adj* industrial.

industrial action *n* huelga *f;* **to take ~** declararse en huelga.

industrial estate Br, **industrial**

park Am *n* polígono *m* industrial.

industrialist [ɪn'dʌstrɪəlɪst] *n* industrial *m y f.*

industrial park Am = **industrial estate.**

industrial relations *npl* relaciones *fpl* laborales.

industrial revolution *n* revolución *f* industrial.

industrious [ɪn'dʌstrɪəs] *adj* diligente, trabajador(ra).

industry ['ɪndəstrɪ] *n* **1.** *(gen)* industria *f.* **2.** *(hard work)* laboriosidad *f.*

inebriated [ɪ'niːbrɪeɪtɪd] *adj fml* ebrio (ebria).

inedible [ɪn'edɪbl] *adj* no comestible.

ineffective [,ɪnɪ'fektɪv] *adj* ineficaz, inútil.

ineffectual [,ɪnɪ'fektʃʊəl] *adj* ineficaz, inútil.

inefficiency [,ɪnɪ'fɪʃnsɪ] *n* ineficacia *f.*

inefficient [,ɪnɪ'fɪʃnt] *adj* ineficaz, ineficiente.

ineligible [ɪn'elɪdʒəbl] *adj:* ~ **(for)** inelegible (para).

inept [ɪ'nept] *adj* inepto(ta); ~ **at** incapaz para.

inequality [,ɪnɪ'kwɒlətɪ] *n* desigualdad *f.*

inert [ɪ'nɜːt] *adj* inerte.

inertia [ɪ'nɜːʃə] *n* inercia *f.*

inescapable [,ɪnɪ'skeɪpəbl] *adj* ineludible.

inevitable [ɪn'evɪtəbl] *adj* inevitable.

inevitably [ɪn'evɪtəblɪ] *adv* inevitablemente.

inexcusable [,ɪnɪk'skjuːzəbl] *adj* inexcusable, imperdonable.

inexhaustible [,ɪnɪg'zɔːstəbl] *adj* inagotable.

inexpensive [,ɪnɪk'spensɪv] *adj* barato (ta), económico(ca).

inexperienced [,ɪnɪk'spɪərɪənst] *adj* inexperto(ta).

inexplicable [,ɪnɪk'splɪkəbl] *adj* inexplicable.

infallible [ɪn'fæləbl] *adj* infalible.

infamous ['ɪnfəməs] *adj* infame.

infancy ['ɪnfənsɪ] *n* primera infancia *f.*

infant ['ɪnfənt] *n* **1.** *(baby)* bebé *m.* **2.** *(young child)* niño pequeño *m,* niña pequeña *f.*

infantry ['ɪnfəntrɪ] *n* infantería *f.*

infant school *n* Br colegio *m* preescolar.

infatuated [ɪn'fætjʊeɪtɪd] *adj:* ~ **(with)** encaprichado(da) (con).

infatuation [ɪn,fætjʊ'eɪʃn] *n:* ~ **(with)**

encaprichamiento *m* (con).

infect [ɪn'fekt] *vt* (*wound*) infectar; (*person*): **to ~ sb (with sthg)** contagiar a alguien (algo).

infection [ɪn'fekʃn] *n* **1.** (*disease*) infección *f*. **2.** (*spreading of germs*) contagio *m*.

infectious [ɪn'fekʃəs] *adj lit & fig* contagioso(sa).

infer [ɪn'fɜːʳ] *vt* **1.** (*deduce*): **to ~ (that)** deducir OR inferir que; **to ~ sthg (from sthg)** deducir OR inferir algo (de algo). **2.** *inf* (*imply*) insinuar, sugerir.

inferior [ɪn'fɪərɪəʳ] ◆ *adj*: **~ (to)** inferior (a). ◆ *n* (*in status*) inferior *m y f*.

inferiority [ɪn,fɪərɪ'ɒrətɪ] *n* inferioridad *f*.

inferiority complex *n* complejo *m* de inferioridad.

inferno [ɪn'fɜːnəʊ] (*pl* -s) *n* infierno *m*.

infertile [ɪn'fɜːtaɪl] *adj* estéril.

infested [ɪn'festɪd] *adj*: **~ with** infestado(da) de.

infighting ['ɪn,faɪtɪŋ] *n* (U) disputas *fpl* internas.

infiltrate ['ɪnfɪltreɪt] *vt* infiltrar.

infinite ['ɪnfɪnət] *adj* infinito(ta).

infinitive [ɪn'fɪnɪtɪv] *n* infinitivo *m*.

infinity [ɪn'fɪnətɪ] *n* **1.** (MATH) infinito *m*. **2.** (*incalculable number*): **an ~ (of)** infinidad *f* (de).

infirm [ɪn'fɜːm] ◆ *adj* achacoso(sa). ◆ *npl*: **the ~** los enfermos.

infirmary [ɪn'fɜːmərɪ] *n* **1.** (*hospital*) hospital *m*. **2.** (*room*) enfermería *f*.

infirmity [ɪn'fɜːmətɪ] *n* **1.** (*illness*) dolencia *f*. **2.** (*state*) enfermedad *f*.

inflamed [ɪn'fleɪmd] *adj* (MED) inflamado(da).

inflammable [ɪn'flæməbl] *adj* (*burning easily*) inflamable.

inflammation [,ɪnflə'meɪʃn] *n* (MED) inflamación *f*.

inflatable [ɪn'fleɪtəbl] *adj* inflable, hinchable.

inflate [ɪn'fleɪt] *vt* **1.** (*gen*) inflar, hinchar. **2.** (ECON) inflar.

inflation [ɪn'fleɪʃn] *n* (ECON) inflación *f*.

inflationary [ɪn'fleɪʃnrɪ] *adj* (ECON) inflacionario(ria), inflacionista.

inflict [ɪn'flɪkt] *vt*: **to ~ sthg on sb** infligir algo a alguien.

influence ['ɪnfluəns] ◆ *n*: **~ (on OR over sb)** influencia *f* (sobre alguien); **~ (on sthg)** influencia (en algo); **under the ~ of** (*person, group*) bajo la influencia de; (*alcohol, drugs*) bajo los efectos de. ◆ *vt* influenciar.

influential [,ɪnflʊ'enʃl] *adj* influyente.

influenza [,ɪnflʊ'enzə] *n fml* gripe *f*.

influx ['ɪnflʌks] *n* afluencia *f*.

inform [ɪn'fɔːm] *vt*: **to ~ sb (of/about sthg)** informar a alguien (de/sobre algo). ▶ **inform on** *vt fus* delatar.

informal [ɪn'fɔːml] *adj* informal; (*language*) familiar.

informant [ɪn'fɔːmənt] *n* **1.** (*informer*) delator *m*, -ra *f*. **2.** (*of researcher*) fuente *f* de información (*persona*).

information [,ɪnfə'meɪʃn] *n* (U): **~ (on OR about)** información *f* OR datos *mpl* (sobre); **a piece of ~** un dato; **for your ~** para tu información.

information desk *n* (mostrador *m* de) información *f*.

information technology *n* informática *f*.

informative [ɪn'fɔːmətɪv] *adj* informativo(va).

informer [ɪn'fɔːməʳ] *n* delator *m*, -ra *f*.

infrared [,ɪnfrə'red] *adj* infrarrojo(ja).

infrastructure ['ɪnfrə,strʌktʃəʳ] *n* infraestructura *f*.

infringe [ɪn'frɪndʒ] ◆ *vt* infringir, vulnerar. ◆ *vi*: **to ~ on sthg** infringir OR vulnerar algo.

infringement [ɪn'frɪndʒmənt] *n* violación *f*, transgresión *f*.

infuriating [ɪn'fjʊərɪeɪtɪŋ] *adj* exasperante.

ingenious [ɪn'dʒiːnjəs] *adj* ingenioso(sa), inventivo(va).

ingenuity [,ɪndʒɪ'njuːətɪ] *n* ingenio *m*, inventiva *f*.

ingenuous [ɪn'dʒenjʊəs] *adj fml* ingenuo(nua).

ingot ['ɪŋgət] *n* lingote *m*.

ingrained [,ɪn'greɪnd] *adj* **1.** (*ground in*) incrustado(da). **2.** (*deeply rooted*) arraigado(da).

ingratiating [ɪn'greɪʃɪeɪtɪŋ] *adj* obsequioso(sa), lisonjero(ra).

ingredient [ɪn'griːdjənt] *n* ingrediente *m*.

inhabit [ɪn'hæbɪt] *vt* habitar.

inhabitant [ɪn'hæbɪtənt] *n* habitante *m y f*.

inhale [ɪn'heɪl] ◆ *vt* inhalar. ◆ *vi* (*gen*) inspirar; (*smoker*) tragarse el humo.

inhaler [ɪn'heɪləʳ] *n* (MED) inhalador *m*.

inherent [ɪn'hɪərənt, ɪn'herənt] *adj*: **~ (in)** inherente (a).

inherently [ɪn'hɪərəntlɪ, ɪn'herəntlɪ] *adv* intrínsecamente.

inherit [ɪn'herɪt] ◆ *vt*: **to ~ sthg (from sb)** heredar algo (de alguien). ◆ *vi* heredar.

inheritance [ɪn'herɪtəns] n herencia f.
inhibit [ɪn'hɪbɪt] vt (restrict) impedir.
inhibition [ˌɪnhɪ'bɪʃn] n inhibición f.
inhospitable [ˌɪnhɒ'spɪtəbl] adj
1. (unwelcoming) inhospitalario(ria).
2. (harsh) inhóspito(ta).
in-house ◆ adj (journal, report) de circulación interna; (staff) de plantilla.
◆ adv en la oficina.
inhuman [ɪn'hju:mən] adj 1. (cruel)
inhumano(na). 2. (not human) infrahumano(na).
initial [ɪ'nɪʃl] ◆ adj inicial. ◆ vt poner
las iniciales a. ▸ **initials** npl (of person)
iniciales fpl.
initially [ɪ'nɪʃəlɪ] adv inicialmente.
initiate [ɪ'nɪʃɪeɪt] vt iniciar; **to ~ sb into**
sthg iniciar a alguien en algo.
initiative [ɪ'nɪʃətɪv] n iniciativa f.
inject [ɪn'dʒekt] vt (MED): **to ~ sb with**
sthg, **to ~ sthg into sb** inyectarle algo a
alguien.
injection [ɪn'dʒekʃn] n inyección f.
injunction [ɪn'dʒʌŋkʃn] n interdicto m.
injure ['ɪndʒə'] vt (gen) herir; (reputation)
dañar; (chances) perjudicar.
injured ['ɪndʒəd] adj (gen) herido(da);
(reputation) dañado(da).
injury ['ɪndʒərɪ] n 1. (U) (physical harm)
lesiones fpl. 2. (wound) lesión f. 3. (to
pride, reputation) agravio m.
injury time n (U) (tiempo m de) descuento m.
injustice [ɪn'dʒʌstɪs] n injusticia f; **to
do sb an ~** no hacerle justicia a alguien.
ink [ɪŋk] n tinta f.
ink-jet printer n (COMPUT) impresora
f de chorro de tinta.
inkling ['ɪŋklɪŋ] n: **to have an ~ of** sthg
tener una vaga idea de algo.
inlaid [ˌɪn'leɪd] adj incrustado(da); **~
with** (jewels) con incrustaciones de.
inland [adj 'ɪnlənd, adv ɪn'lænd] ◆ adj
interior. ◆ adv hacia el interior.
Inland Revenue n Br: **the ~** ≃
Hacienda f.
in-laws npl inf suegros mpl.
inlet ['ɪnlet] n 1. (stretch of water)
entrante m. 2. (way in) entrada f,
admisión f.
inmate ['ɪnmeɪt] n (of prison) preso m,
-sa f; (of mental hospital) interno m, -na f.
inn [ɪn] n fonda f; (pub) pub decorado a la
vieja usanza.
innate [ˌɪ'neɪt] adj innato(ta).
inner ['ɪnə'] adj 1. (gen) interior. 2. (feelings) íntimo(ma); (fears, doubts, meaning)
interno(na).

inner city n núcleo m urbano deprimido.
inner tube n cámara f (de aire).
innings ['ɪnɪŋz] (pl inv) n Br (in cricket)
entrada f, turno m.
innocence ['ɪnəsəns] n inocencia f.
innocent ['ɪnəsənt] ◆ adj: **~ (of)**
inocente (de). ◆ n (naive person)
inocente m y f. \
innocuous [ɪ'nɒkjʊəs] adj inocuo(cua).
innovation [ˌɪnə'veɪʃn] n innovación f.
innovative ['ɪnəvətɪv] adj innovador
(ra).
innuendo [ˌɪnju:'endəʊ] (pl **-es** OR **-s**) n
1. (individual remark) insinuación f, indirecta f. 2. (U) (style of speaking) insinuaciones fpl, indirectas fpl.
inoculate [ɪ'nɒkjʊleɪt] vt: **to ~ sb with**
sthg inocular algo a alguien.
inordinately [ɪ'nɔ:dɪnətlɪ] adv fml
desmesuradamente.
in-patient n paciente interno m,
paciente interna f.
input ['ɪnpʊt] (pt & pp input OR **-ted**) ◆ n
1. (contribution) aportación f, contribución f. 2. (COMPUT) entrada f. ◆ vt (COMPUT) entrar.
inquest ['ɪnkwest] n investigación f
judicial.
inquire [ɪn'kwaɪə'] ◆ vi (ask for information) informarse, pedir información; **to
~ about sthg** informarse de algo. ◆ vt: **to
~ when/if/how ...** preguntar cuándo/si/
cómo ... ▸ **inquire after** vt fus preguntar por. ▸ **inquire into** vt fus investigar.
inquiry [ɪn'kwaɪərɪ] n 1. (question) pregunta f; **'Inquiries'** 'Información'.
2. (investigation) investigación f.
inquiry desk n (mostrador m de)
información f.
inquisitive [ɪn'kwɪzətɪv] adj curioso(sa).
inroads ['ɪnrəʊdz] npl: **to make ~ into**
(savings, supplies) mermar; (market, enemy
territory) abrirse paso en.
insane [ɪn'seɪn] adj (mad) demente; fig
(jealousy, person) loco(ca).
insanity [ɪn'sænətɪ] n (madness)
demencia f; fig locura f.
insatiable [ɪn'seɪʃəbl] adj insaciable.
inscription [ɪn'skrɪpʃn] n 1. (engraved)
inscripción f. 2. (written) dedicatoria f.
inscrutable [ɪn'skru:təbl] adj inescrutable.
insect ['ɪnsekt] n insecto m.
insecticide [ɪn'sektɪsaɪd] n insecticida
m.
insect repellent n loción f antiinsectos.

insecure [ˌɪnsɪˈkjʊəʳ] adj 1. (not confident) inseguro(ra). 2. (not safe) poco seguro(ra).

insensible [ɪnˈsensəbl] adj 1. (unconscious) inconsciente. 2. (unaware): **to be ~ of** sthg no ser consciente de algo. 3. (unable to feel): **to be ~ to** sthg ser insensible a algo.

insensitive [ɪnˈsensətɪv] adj: **~ (to)** insensible (a).

inseparable [ɪnˈseprəbl] adj: **~ (from)** inseparable (de).

insert [vb ɪnˈsɜːt, n ˈɪnsɜːt] ◆ vt: **to ~ sthg (in OR into)** (hole) introducir algo (en); (text) insertar algo (en). ◆ n (PRESS) encarte m.

insertion [ɪnˈsɜːʃn] n inserción f.

in-service training n Br formación f en horas de trabajo.

inshore [adj ˈɪnʃɔːʳ, adv ɪnˈʃɔːʳ] ◆ adj costero(ra). ◆ adv hacia la orilla OR la costa.

inside [ɪnˈsaɪd] ◆ prep dentro de; **~ three months** en menos de tres meses. ◆ adv (be, remain) dentro; (go, move etc) hacia dentro; fig (feel, hurt etc) interiormente; **come ~!** ¡metéos dentro! ◆ adj interior. ◆ n interior m; **from the ~** desde dentro; **to overtake on the ~** (of road) adelantar por dentro; **~ out** (wrong way) al revés; **to know** sthg **~ out** conocer algo de arriba abajo OR al dedillo. ▶ **insides** npl inf tripas fpl. ▶ **inside of** prep Am (building, object) dentro de.

inside lane n (AUT) carril m de dentro.

insight [ˈɪnsaɪt] n 1. (U) (power of understanding) perspicacia f. 2. (understanding) idea f.

insignificant [ˌɪnsɪgˈnɪfɪkənt] adj insignificante.

insincere [ˌɪnsɪnˈsɪəʳ] adj insincero(ra).

insinuate [ɪnˈsɪnjʊeɪt] vt pej: **to ~ (that)** insinuar (que).

insipid [ɪnˈsɪpɪd] adj pej soso(sa), insípido(da).

insist [ɪnˈsɪst] ◆ vt: **to ~ that** insistir en que. ◆ vi: **to ~ on** sthg exigir algo; **to ~ (on doing** sthg) insistir (en hacer algo).

insistent [ɪnˈsɪstənt] adj 1. (determined) insistente; **to be ~ on** sthg insistir en algo. 2. (continual) persistente.

insofar [ˌɪnsəʊˈfɑːʳ] ▶ **insofar as** conj en la medida en que.

insole [ˈɪnsəʊl] n plantilla f.

insolent [ˈɪnsələnt] adj insolente.

insolvent [ɪnˈsɒlvənt] adj insolvente.

insomnia [ɪnˈsɒmnɪə] n insomnio m.

inspect [ɪnˈspekt] vt inspeccionar; (troops) pasar revista a.

inspection [ɪnˈspekʃn] n inspección f.

inspector [ɪnˈspektəʳ] n inspector m, -ra f; (on bus, train) revisor m, -ra f.

inspiration [ˌɪnspəˈreɪʃn] n 1. (gen) inspiración f. 2. (source of inspiration): **~ (for)** fuente f de inspiración (para).

inspire [ɪnˈspaɪəʳ] vt 1. (stimulate, encourage): **to ~ sb (to do** sthg) alentar OR animar a alguien (a hacer algo). 2. (fill): **to ~ sb with** sthg, **to ~** sthg **in sb** inspirar algo a alguien.

install Br, **instal** Am [ɪnˈstɔːl] vt (gen & COMPUT) instalar.

installation [ˌɪnstəˈleɪʃn] n (gen & COMPUT) instalación f.

installment Am = **instalment**.

installment plan n Am compra f a plazos.

instalment Br, **installment** Am [ɪnˈstɔːlmənt] n 1. (payment) plazo m; **in ~s** a plazos. 2. (TV & RADIO) episodio m; (of novel) entrega f.

instance [ˈɪnstəns] n (example, case) ejemplo m; **for ~** por ejemplo; **in this ~** en este caso.

instant [ˈɪnstənt] ◆ adj instantáneo(a). ◆ n (moment) instante m; **at that** OR **the same ~** en aquel mismo instante; **the ~ (that) ...** en cuanto ...; **this ~** ahora mismo.

instantly [ˈɪnstəntlɪ] adv en el acto.

instead [ɪnˈsted] adv en cambio. ▶ **instead of** prep en lugar de, en vez de.

instep [ˈɪnstep] n (of foot) empeine m.

instigate [ˈɪnstɪgeɪt] vt iniciar; **to ~ sb to do** sthg instigar a alguien a hacer algo.

instil Br, **instill** Am [ɪnˈstɪl] vt: **to ~** sthg **in** OR **into sb** inculcar OR infundir algo a alguien.

instinct [ˈɪnstɪŋkt] n instinto m; **my first ~ was ...** mi primer impulso fue ...

instinctive [ɪnˈstɪŋktɪv] adj instintivo (va).

institute [ˈɪnstɪtjuːt] ◆ n instituto m. ◆ vt (proceedings) iniciar, entablar; (system) instituir.

institution [ˌɪnstɪˈtjuːʃn] n 1. (gen) institución f. 2. (home - for children, old people) asilo m; (- for mentally-handicapped) hospital m psiquiátrico.

instruct [ɪnˈstrʌkt] vt 1. (tell, order): **to ~ sb to do** sthg mandar OR ordenar a alguien que haga algo. 2. (teach): **to ~ sb (in** sthg) instruir a alguien (en algo).

instruction [ɪnˈstrʌkʃn] n instrucción f.
▶ **instructions** npl (for use) instrucciones fpl.

instructor [ɪnˈstrʌktəʳ] n 1. (gen) instructor m. 2. (in skiing) monitor m. 3. (in driving) profesor m. 4. Am (SCH) profesor m, -ra f.

instrument [ˈɪnstrʊmənt] n instrumento m.

instrumental [ˌɪnstrʊˈmentl] adj (important, helpful): **to be ~ in sthg** jugar un papel fundamental en algo.

instrument panel n tablero m de instrumentos.

insubordinate [ˌɪnsəˈbɔːdɪnət] adj fml insubordinado(da).

insubstantial [ˌɪnsəbˈstænʃl] adj (frame, structure) endeble; (meal) poco sustancioso(sa).

insufficient [ˌɪnsəˈfɪʃnt] adj: **~ (for)** insuficiente (para).

insular [ˈɪnsjʊləʳ] adj estrecho(cha) de miras.

insulate [ˈɪnsjʊleɪt] vt aislar; **to ~ sb against OR from sthg** aislar a alguien de algo.

insulating tape [ˈɪnsjʊleɪtɪŋ-] n Br cinta f aislante.

insulation [ˌɪnsjʊˈleɪʃn] n (material, substance) aislamiento m.

insulin [ˈɪnsjʊlɪn] n insulina f.

insult [vt ɪnˈsʌlt, n ˈɪnsʌlt] ◆ vt (with words) insultar; (with actions) ofender. ◆ n (remark) insulto m; (action) ofensa f.

insuperable [ɪnˈsuːprəbl] adj fml insalvable, insuperable.

insurance [ɪnˈʃʊərəns] n 1. (against fire, accident, theft): **~ (against)** seguro m (contra). 2. fig (safeguard, protection): **~ (against)** prevención f (contra).

insurance policy n póliza f de seguros.

insure [ɪnˈʃʊəʳ] ◆ vt 1. (against fire, accident, theft): **to ~ sthg/sb (against)** asegurar algo/a alguien (contra). 2. Am (make certain) asegurar. ◆ vi (prevent): **to ~ (against)** prevenir OR prevenirse (contra).

insurer [ɪnˈʃʊərəʳ] n asegurador m, -ra f.

insurmountable [ˌɪnsəˈmaʊntəbl] adj fml infranqueable, insuperable.

intact [ɪnˈtækt] adj intacto(ta).

intake [ˈɪnteɪk] n 1. (of food, drink) ingestión f; (of air) inspiración f. 2. (in army) reclutamiento m; (in organization) número m de ingresos.

integral [ˈɪntɪgrəl] adj integrante; **to be ~ to** ser parte integrante de.

integrate [ˈɪntɪgreɪt] ◆ vi: **to ~ (with OR into)** integrarse (en). ◆ vt: **to ~ sthg/sb with sthg, to ~ sthg/sb into sthg** integrar algo/a alguien en algo.

integrity [ɪnˈtegrətɪ] n integridad f.

intellect [ˈɪntəlekt] n (mind, cleverness) intelecto m, inteligencia f.

intellectual [ˌɪntəˈlektjʊəl] ◆ adj intelectual. ◆ n intelectual m y f.

intelligence [ɪnˈtelɪdʒəns] n (U) 1. (ability to think) inteligencia f. 2. (information service) servicio m secreto OR de espionaje. 3. (information) información f secreta.

intelligent [ɪnˈtelɪdʒənt] adj (clever) inteligente.

intelligent card n tarjeta f inteligente.

intend [ɪnˈtend] vt pretender, proponerse; **to be ~ed for/as sthg** (project, book) estar pensado para/como algo; **to ~ doing OR to do sthg** tener la intención de OR pretender hacer algo; **later than I had ~ed** más tarde de lo que había pensado.

intended [ɪnˈtendɪd] adj pretendido(da).

intense [ɪnˈtens] adj 1. (extreme, profound) intenso(sa). 2. (serious - person) muy serio(ria).

intensely [ɪnˈtenslɪ] adv 1. (very - boring, irritating) enormemente. 2. (very much - suffer) intensamente; (- dislike) profundamente.

intensify [ɪnˈtensɪfaɪ] ◆ vt intensificar. ◆ vi intensificarse.

intensity [ɪnˈtensətɪ] n intensidad f.

intensive [ɪnˈtensɪv] adj (concentrated) intensivo(va).

intensive care n (U): **(in) ~** (bajo) cuidados mpl intensivos.

intent [ɪnˈtent] ◆ adj 1. (absorbed) atento(ta). 2. (determined): **to be ~ on OR upon doing sthg** estar empeñado(da) en hacer algo. ◆ n fml intención f; **to all ~s and purposes** para todos los efectos.

intention [ɪnˈtenʃn] n intención f.

intentional [ɪnˈtenʃənl] adj deliberado(da), intencionado(da).

intently [ɪnˈtentlɪ] adv atentamente.

interact [ˌɪntərˈækt] vi 1. (communicate, work together): **to ~ (with sb)** comunicarse (con alguien). 2. (react): **to ~ (with sthg)** interaccionar (con algo).

intercede [ˌɪntəˈsiːd] vi fml: **to ~ (with/for)** interceder (ante/por).

intercept [ˌɪntəˈsept] vt interceptar.

interchange [n 'ıntətʃeındʒ, vb ,ıntə-'tʃeındʒ] ◆ n 1. (exchange) intercambio m. 2. (on motorway) cruce m. ◆ vt intercambiar.

interchangeable [,ıntə'tʃeındʒəbl] adj: ~ (with) intercambiable (con).

intercity [,ıntə'sıtı] n red de trenes rápidos que conecta las principales ciudades británicas.

intercom ['ıntəkɒm] n (for block of flats) portero m automático; (within a building) interfono m.

intercourse ['ıntəkɔ:s] n (U): sexual ~ relaciones fpl sexuales, coito m.

interest ['ıntrəst] ◆ n 1. (gen & FIN): ~ (in) interés m (en OR por); that's of no ~ eso no tiene interés. 2. (hobby) afición f. ◆ vt interesar.

interested ['ıntrəstıd] adj interesado (da); to be ~ in sthg/in doing sthg estar interesado en algo/en hacer algo.

interesting ['ıntrəstıŋ] adj interesante.

interest rate n tipo m de interés.

interface ['ıntəfeıs] n (COMPUT) interfaz f.

interfere [,ıntə'fıər] vi 1. (meddle): to ~ (with OR in sthg) entrometerse OR interferir (en algo). 2. (damage) interferir; to ~ with sthg (career, routine) interferir en algo; (work, performance) interrumpir algo.

interference [,ıntə'fıərəns] n (U) 1. (meddling): ~ (with OR in) intromisión f OR interferencia f (en). 2. (on radio, TV, telephone) interferencia f.

interim ['ıntərım] ◆ adj (report) parcial; (measure) provisional; (government) interino(na). ◆ n: in the ~ entre tanto.

interior [ın'tıərıər] ◆ adj 1. (inner) interior. 2. (POL) (minister, department) del Interior. ◆ n interior m.

interior decorator, interior designer n diseñador m, -ra f de interiores.

interlock [,ıntə'lɒk] vi (fingers) entrelazarse; (cogs) engranar.

interloper ['ıntələʊpər] n intruso m, -sa f.

interlude ['ıntəlu:d] n 1. (pause) intervalo m. 2. (interval) intermedio m.

intermediary [,ıntə'mi:djərı] n intermediario m, -ria f.

intermediate [,ıntə'mi:djət] adj intermedio(dia).

interminable [ın'tɜ:mınəbl] adj interminable.

intermission [,ıntə'mıʃn] n (of film) descanso m; (of play, opera, ballet) entreacto m.

intermittent [,ıntə'mıtənt] adj intermitente.

intern [vb ın'tɜ:n, n 'ıntɜ:n] ◆ vt recluir, internar. ◆ n médico m interno residente.

internal [ın'tɜ:nl] adj 1. (gen) interno (na). 2. (within a country) interior, nacional; ~ flight vuelo m nacional.

internally [ın'tɜ:nəlı] adv 1. (gen) internamente. 2. (within a country) a nivel nacional.

Internal Revenue n Am: the ~ ≃ Hacienda f.

international [,ıntə'næʃənl] ◆ adj internacional. ◆ n Br (SPORT) 1. (match) encuentro m internacional. 2. (player) internacional m y f.

Internet ['ıntənet] n: the ~ Internet f.

interpret [ın'tɜ:prıt] ◆ vt interpretar. ◆ vi hacer de intérprete.

interpreter [ın'tɜ:prıtər] n (person) intérprete m y f.

interrelate [,ıntərı'leıt] vi: to ~ (with) interrelacionarse (con).

interrogate [ın'terəgeıt] vt (gen & COMPUT) interrogar.

interrogation [ın,terə'geıʃn] n interrogatorio m.

interrogation mark n Am signo m de interrogación.

interrogative [,ıntə'rɒgətıv] adj (GRAMM) interrogativo(va).

interrupt [,ıntə'rʌpt] vt & vi interrumpir.

interruption [,ıntə'rʌpʃn] n interrupción f.

intersect [,ıntə'sekt] ◆ vi cruzarse, cortarse. ◆ vt cruzar, cortar.

intersection [,ıntə'sekʃn] n (junction) intersección f, cruce m.

intersperse [,ıntə'spɜ:s] vt: to be ~d with OR by estar entremezclado con.

interstate (highway) ['ıntəsteıt-] n autopista f interestatal.

interval ['ıntəvl] n 1. (gen & MUS): ~ (between) intervalo m (entre); at ~s (now and again) a ratos; (regularly) a intervalos; at monthly/yearly ~s a intervalos de un mes/un año. 2. Br (at play, concert) intermedio m, descanso m.

intervene [,ıntə'vi:n] vi 1. (gen): to ~ (in) intervenir (en). 2. (prevent thing from happening) interponerse. 3. (pass) transcurrir.

intervention [,ıntə'venʃn] n intervención f.

interview ['ıntəvju:] ◆ n entrevista f.

◆ *vt* entrevistar.

interviewer ['ɪntəvjuːəʳ] *n* entrevistador *m*, -ra *f*.

intestine [ɪn'testɪn] *n* intestino *m*.

intimacy ['ɪntɪməsɪ] *n*: ~ (between/with) intimidad *f* (entre/con).

intimate [*adj* 'ɪntɪmət, *vb* 'ɪntɪmeɪt] ◆ *adj* 1. (*gen*) íntimo(ma). 2. (*knowledge*) profundo(da). ◆ *vt fml*: to ~ (that) dar a entender (que).

intimidate [ɪn'tɪmɪdeɪt] *vt* intimidar.

into ['ɪntʊ] *prep* 1. (*inside*) en; to put sthg ~ sthg meter algo en algo; to get ~ a car subir a un coche. 2. (*against*) con; to bump/crash ~ tropezar/chocar con. 3. (*referring to change in condition etc*): to turn OR develop ~ convertirse en; to translate sthg ~ Spanish traducir algo al español. 4. (*concerning*) en relación con; research ~ electronics investigación en torno a la electrónica. 5. (MATH): to divide 4 ~ 8 dividir 8 entre 4.

intolerable [ɪn'tɒlrəbl] *adj fml* (*position, conditions*) intolerable; (*boredom, pain*) inaguantable.

intolerance [ɪn'tɒlərəns] *n* intolerancia *f*.

intolerant [ɪn'tɒlərənt] *adj* intolerante.

intoxicated [ɪn'tɒksɪkeɪtɪd] *adj* 1. (*drunk*) embriagado(da). 2. *fig* (*excited*): ~ (by OR with) ebrio (ebria) (de).

intractable [ɪn'træktəbl] *adj fml* 1. (*stubborn*) intratable. 2. (*insoluble*) inextricable, insoluble.

intransitive [ɪn'trænzətɪv] *adj* intransitivo(va).

intravenous [ˌɪntrə'viːnəs] *adj* intravenoso(sa).

in-tray *n* bandeja para cartas y documentos recién llegados a la oficina.

intricate ['ɪntrɪkət] *adj* intrincado(da).

intrigue [ɪn'triːg] ◆ *n* intriga *f*. ◆ *vt* intrigar.

intriguing [ɪn'triːgɪŋ] *adj* intrigante.

intrinsic [ɪn'trɪnsɪk] *adj* intrínseco(ca).

introduce [ˌɪntrə'djuːs] *vt* 1. (*present - person, programme*) presentar; to ~ sb (to sb) presentar a alguien (a alguien); to ~ o.s. presentarse. 2. (*bring in*): to ~ sthg (to OR into) introducir algo (en). 3. (*show for first time*): to ~ sb to sthg iniciar a alguien en algo.

introduction [ˌɪntrə'dʌkʃn] *n* 1. (*gen*): ~ (to sthg) introducción *f* (a algo). 2. (*of people*): ~ (to sb) presentación *f* (a alguien).

introductory [ˌɪntrə'dʌktrɪ] *adj* (*chap-*

ter) introductorio(ria); (*remarks*) preliminar.

introvert ['ɪntrəvɜːt] *n* introvertido *m*, -da *f*.

introverted ['ɪntrəvɜːtɪd] *adj* introvertido(da).

intrude [ɪn'truːd] *vi*: to ~ (on OR upon sb) inmiscuirse (en los asuntos de alguien); to ~ (on OR upon sthg) inmiscuirse (en algo).

intruder [ɪn'truːdəʳ] *n* intruso *m*, -sa *f*.

intrusive [ɪn'truːsɪv] *adj* (*person*) entrometido(da); (*presence*) indeseado (da).

intuition [ˌɪntjuː'ɪʃn] *n* intuición *f*.

inundate ['ɪnʌndeɪt] *vt* 1. *fml* (*flood*) inundar. 2. (*overwhelm*) desbordar; to be ~d with verse desbordado por.

invade [ɪn'veɪd] *vt* invadir.

invalid [*adj* ɪn'vælɪd, *n* 'ɪnvəlɪd] ◆ *adj* 1. (*marriage, vote, ticket*) nulo(la). 2. (*argument, result*) que no es válido (da). ◆ *n* inválido *m*, -da *f*.

invaluable [ɪn'væljʊəbl] *adj*: ~ (to) (*information, advice*) inestimable (para); (*person*) valiosísimo(ma) (para).

invariably [ɪn'veərɪəblɪ] *adv* siempre, invariablemente.

invasion [ɪn'veɪʒn] *n* invasión *f*.

invent [ɪn'vent] *vt* inventar.

invention [ɪn'venʃn] *n* 1. (*gen*) invención *f*. 2. (*ability to invent*) inventiva *f*.

inventive [ɪn'ventɪv] *adj* (*person, mind*) inventivo(va); (*solution*) ingenioso(sa).

inventor [ɪn'ventəʳ] *n* inventor *m*, -ra *f*.

inventory ['ɪnvəntrɪ] *n* 1. (*list*) inventario *m*. 2. *Am* (*goods*) existencias *fpl*.

invert [ɪn'vɜːt] *vt fml* invertir.

inverted commas [ɪn'vɜːtɪd-] *npl Br* comillas *fpl*; in ~ entre comillas.

invest [ɪn'vest] ◆ *vt* (*money, time, energy*): to ~ sthg (in) invertir algo (en). ◆ *vi lit & fig*: to ~ (in) invertir (en).

investigate [ɪn'vestɪgeɪt] *vt & vi* investigar.

investigation [ɪnˌvestɪ'geɪʃn] *n* (*enquiry, examination*): ~ (into) investigación *f* (en).

investment [ɪn'vestmənt] *n* inversión *f*.

investor [ɪn'vestəʳ] *n* inversor *m*, -ra *f*.

inveterate [ɪn'vetərət] *adj* (*liar*) incorregible; (*reader, smoker*) empedernido (da).

invidious [ɪn'vɪdɪəs] *adj* (*task, role*) desagradable; (*comparison*) odioso(sa).

invigilate [ɪn'vɪdʒɪleɪt] *vt & vi Br* vigilar (en un examen).

invigorating [ɪn'vɪgəreɪtɪŋ] *adj (bath, walk)* vigorizante; *(experience)* estimulante.

invincible [ɪn'vɪnsɪbl] *adj* 1. *(unbeatable)* invencible. 2. *(unchangeable)* inalterable.

invisible [ɪn'vɪzɪbl] *adj* invisible.

invitation [ˌɪnvɪ'teɪʃn] *n* invitación *f.*

invite [ɪn'vaɪt] *vt:* to ~ sb (to sthg/to do sthg) invitar a alguien (a algo/a hacer algo).

inviting [ɪn'vaɪtɪŋ] *adj* tentador(ra).

invoice ['ɪnvɔɪs] ♦ *n* factura *f.* ♦ *vt* 1. *(send invoice to)* mandar la factura a. 2. *(prepare invoice for)* facturar.

invoke [ɪn'vəʊk] *vt fml (quote as justification)* acogerse a.

involuntary [ɪn'vɒləntrɪ] *adj* involuntario(ria).

involve [ɪn'vɒlv] *vt* 1. *(entail, require):* to ~ sthg/doing sthg conllevar algo/hacer algo; it ~s working weekends supone OR implica trabajar los fines de semana. 2. *(concern, affect)* afectar a. 3. *(make part of sthg):* to ~ sb (in) involucrar a alguien (en).

involved [ɪn'vɒlvd] *adj* 1. *(complex)* enrevesado(da). 2. *(participating):* to be ~ in estar metido(da) en. 3. *(in a relationship):* to be/get ~ with sb estar liado (da)/liarse con alguien.

involvement [ɪn'vɒlvmənt] *n* 1. ~ (in) *(crime)* implicación *f* (en); *(running sthg)* participación *f* (en). 2. *(concern, enthusiasm):* ~ (in) compromiso *m* (con).

inward ['ɪnwəd] ♦ *adj* 1. *(inner)* interno(na). 2. *(towards the inside)* hacia el interior. ♦ *adv* Am = **inwards.**

inwards ['ɪnwədz] *adv* hacia dentro.

iodine [Br 'aɪədiːn, Am 'aɪədaɪn] *n* yodo *m.*

iota [aɪ'əʊtə] *n* pizca *f*, ápice *m.*

IOU *(abbr of* **I owe you)** *n* pag. *m.*

IQ *(abbr of* **intelligence quotient)** *n* C.I. *m.*

IRA *n (abbr of* **Irish Republican Army)** IRA *m.*

Iran [ɪ'rɑːn] *n* (el) Irán.

Iranian [ɪ'reɪnjən] ♦ *adj* iraní. ♦ *n (person)* iraní *m y f.*

Iraq [ɪ'rɑːk] *n* (el) Irak.

Iraqi [ɪ'rɑːkɪ] ♦ *adj* iraquí. ♦ *n (person)* iraquí *m y f.*

irate [aɪ'reɪt] *adj* iracundo(da), airado (da).

Ireland ['aɪələnd] *n* Irlanda.

iris ['aɪərɪs] *(pl* -es) *n* 1. *(flower)* lirio *m.* 2. *(of eye)* iris *m inv.*

Irish ['aɪrɪʃ] ♦ *adj* irlandés(esa). ♦ *n (language)* irlandés *m.* ♦ *npl (people):* the ~ los irlandeses.

Irishman ['aɪrɪʃmən] *(pl* -men [-mən]) *n* irlandés *m.*

Irish Sea *n:* the ~ el mar de Irlanda.

Irishwoman ['aɪrɪʃˌwʊmən] *(pl* -women [-ˌwɪmɪn]) *n* irlandesa *f.*

irksome ['ɜːksəm] *adj* fastidioso(sa).

iron ['aɪən] ♦ *adj lit & fig* de hierro. ♦ *n* 1. *(metal)* hierro *m*, fierro *m Amer.* 2. *(for clothes)* plancha *f.* 3. *(golf club)* hierro *m.* ♦ *vt* planchar. ▶ **iron out** *vt sep fig (overcome)* resolver.

Iron Curtain *n:* the ~ el telón de acero.

ironic(al) [aɪ'rɒnɪk(l)] *adj* irónico(ca); how ~! ¡qué ironía!

ironing ['aɪənɪŋ] *n* 1. *(work)* planchado *m.* 2. *(clothes to be ironed)* ropa *f* para planchar.

ironing board *n* tabla *f* de planchar.

ironmonger ['aɪənˌmʌŋgəʳ] *n Br* ferretero *m*, -ra *f;* ~'s (shop) ferretería *f.*

irony ['aɪrənɪ] *n* ironía *f.*

irrational [ɪ'ræʃənl] *adj* irracional.

irreconcilable [ɪˌrekən'saɪləbl] *adj (completely different)* irreconciliable.

irregular [ɪ'regjʊləʳ] *adj (gen & GRAMM)* irregular.

irrelevant [ɪ'reləvənt] *adj* irrelevante, que no viene al caso.

irreparable [ɪ'repərəbl] *adj* irreparable.

irreplaceable [ˌɪrɪ'pleɪsəbl] *adj* irreemplazable, insustituible.

irrepressible [ˌɪrɪ'presəbl] *adj (enthusiasm)* irreprimible; *(person)* imparable.

irresistible [ˌɪrɪ'zɪstəbl] *adj* irresistible.

irrespective [ˌɪrɪ'spektɪv] ▶ **irrespective of** *prep* con independencia de.

irresponsible [ˌɪrɪ'spɒnsəbl] *adj* irresponsable.

irrigate ['ɪrɪgeɪt] *vt* regar, irrigar.

irrigation [ˌɪrɪ'geɪʃn] *n* riego *m.*

irritable ['ɪrɪtəbl] *adj* irritable.

irritate ['ɪrɪteɪt] *vt* irritar.

irritating ['ɪrɪteɪtɪŋ] *adj* irritante.

irritation [ɪrɪ'teɪʃn] *n* 1. *(anger, soreness)* irritación *f.* 2. *(cause of anger)* motivo *m* de irritación.

IRS *(abbr of* **Internal Revenue Service)** *n Am:* the ~ ≃ Hacienda *f.*

is [ɪz] → **be.**

Islam ['ɪzlɑːm] *n (religion)* islam *m.*

island ['aɪlənd] *n* 1. *(in water)* isla *f.* 2. *(in traffic)* isleta *f*, refugio *m.*

islander ['aɪləndəʳ] *n* isleño *m*, -ña *f.*

isle [aɪl] n (as part of name) isla f; literary (island) ínsula f.
Isle of Man n: the ~ la isla de Man.
Isle of Wight [-waɪt] n: the ~ la isla de Wight.
isn't ['ɪznt] = **is not**.
isobar ['aɪsəbɑːr] n isobara f.
isolate ['aɪsəleɪt] vt: to ~ sb (from) (physically) aislar a alguien (de); (socially) marginar a alguien (de).
isolated ['aɪsəleɪtɪd] adj aislado(da).
Israel ['ɪzreɪəl] n Israel.
Israeli [ɪz'reɪlɪ] ◆ adj israelí. ◆ n israelí m y f.
issue ['ɪʃuː] ◆ n 1. (important subject) cuestión f, tema m; at ~ en cuestión; to make an ~ of sthg darle demasiada importancia a algo. 2. (of newspaper, magazine) número m, edición f. 3. (of stamps, shares, banknotes) emisión f. ◆ vt 1. (decree) promulgar; (statement, warning) hacer público(ca). 2. (stamps, shares, banknotes) emitir. 3. (passport, document): to ~ sthg to sb, to ~ sb with sthg expedir algo a alguien.
isthmus ['ɪsməs] n istmo m.
it [ɪt] pron 1. (referring to specific thing or person - subj) él m, ella f; (- direct object) lo m, la f; (- indirect object) le; ~ is in my hand está en mi mano; did you find ~? ¿lo encontraste?; give ~ to me dámelo; he gave ~ a kick le dio una patada. 2. (with prepositions) él m, ella f; (- meaning 'this matter' etc) ello; as if his life depended on ~ como si le fuera la vida en ello; in ~ dentro; have you been to ~ before? ¿has estado antes?; on ~ encima; to talk about ~ hablar de él/ella/ello; under/beneath ~ debajo; beside ~ al lado; from/of ~ de él/ella/ello; over ~ por encima. 3. (impersonal use): ~ was raining llovía; ~ is cold today hace frío hoy; ~'s two o'clock son las dos; who is ~? - it's Mary/me ¿quién es? - soy Mary/yo; what day is ~? ¿a qué (día) estamos hoy?
IT n abbr of **information technology**.
Italian [ɪ'tæljən] ◆ adj italiano(na). ◆ n 1. (person) italiano m, -na f. 2. (language) italiano m.
italic [ɪ'tælɪk] adj cursiva. ▶ **italics** npl cursiva f.
Italy ['ɪtəlɪ] n Italia.
itch [ɪtʃ] ◆ n picor m, picazón f. ◆ vi 1. (be itchy - person) tener picazón; (- arm, leg etc) picar. 2. fig (be impatient): to be ~ing to do sthg estar deseando hacer algo.

itchy ['ɪtʃɪ] adj que pica.
it'd ['ɪtəd] = **it would, it had**.
item ['aɪtəm] n 1. (in collection) artículo m; (on list, agenda) asunto m, punto m. 2. (article in newspaper) artículo m; **news ~** noticia f.
itemize, -ise ['aɪtəmaɪz] vt detallar.
itinerary [aɪ'tɪnərərɪ] n itinerario m.
it'll [ɪtl] = **it will**.
its [ɪts] poss adj su, sus (pl); **the dog broke ~ leg** el perro se rompió la pata.
it's [ɪts] = **it is, it has**.
itself [ɪt'self] pron 1. (reflexive) se; (after prep) sí mismo(ma); **with ~** consigo mismo(ma). 2. (for emphasis): **the town ~ is lovely** el pueblo en sí es bonito; **in ~** en sí.
ITV (abbr of **Independent Television**) n ITV f, canal privado de televisión en Gran Bretaña.
I've [aɪv] = **I have**.
ivory ['aɪvərɪ] n marfil m.
ivy ['aɪvɪ] n hiedra f.
Ivy League n Am grupo de ocho prestigiosas universidades del este de los EEUU.

J

j (pl **j's** OR **js**), **J** (pl **J's** OR **Js**) [dʒeɪ] n (letter) j f, J f.
jab [dʒæb] ◆ n Br inf (injection) pinchazo m. ◆ vt: to ~ sthg into clavar algo en; to ~ sthg at apuntarle algo a.
jabber ['dʒæbər] vi charlotear.
jack [dʒæk] n 1. (device) gato m. 2. (playing card) ≃ sota f. ▶ **jack up** vt sep 1. (lift with a jack) levantar con gato. 2. (force up) subir.
jackal ['dʒækəl] n chacal m.
jackdaw ['dʒækdɔː] n grajilla f.
jacket ['dʒækɪt] n 1. (garment) chaqueta f, americana f, saco m Amer. 2. (potato skin) piel f. 3. (book cover) sobrecubierta f. 4. Am (of record) cubierta f.
jacket potato n patata f asada con piel.
jackhammer ['dʒæk,hæmər] n Am martillo m neumático.
jack knife n navaja f. ▶ **jack-knife** vi derrapar la parte delantera.
jack plug n (enchufe m de) clavija f.

jackpot ['dʒækpɒt] n (premio m) gordo m.

jaded ['dʒeɪdɪd] adj (tired) agotado(da); (bored) hastiado(da).

jagged ['dʒægɪd] adj dentado(da).

jail [dʒeɪl] ◆ n cárcel f. ◆ vt encarcelar.

jailer ['dʒeɪlər] n carcelero m, -ra f.

jam [dʒæm] ◆ n 1. (preserve) mermelada f. 2. (of traffic) embotellamiento m, atasco m. 3. inf (difficult situation): **to get into/be in a ~** meterse/estar en un apuro. ◆ vt 1. (place roughly) meter a la fuerza. 2. (fix) sujetar; **~ the door shut** atranca la puerta. 3. (pack tightly) apiñar. 4. (fill) abarrotar, atestar. 5. (TELEC) bloquear. 6. (cause to stick) atascar. 7. (RADIO) interferir. ◆ vi (stick) atascarse.

Jamaica [dʒəˈmeɪkə] n Jamaica.

jam-packed [-ˈpækt] adj inf a tope.

jangle ['dʒæŋgl] vi tintinear.

janitor ['dʒænɪtər] n Am & Scot conserje m, portero m.

January ['dʒænjʊərɪ] n enero m; see also **September**.

Japan [dʒəˈpæn] n (el) Japón.

Japanese [ˌdʒæpəˈniːz] (pl inv) ◆ adj japonés(esa). ◆ n (language) japonés m. ◆ npl: **the ~** los japoneses.

jar [dʒɑːr] ◆ n tarro m. ◆ vt (shake) sacudir. ◆ vi 1. (upset): **to ~ (on sb)** poner los nervios de punta (a alguien). 2. (clash - opinions) discordar; (- colours) desentonar.

jargon ['dʒɑːgən] n jerga f.

jaundice ['dʒɔːndɪs] n ictericia f.

jaundiced ['dʒɔːndɪst] adj fig (attitude, view) desencantado(da).

jaunt [dʒɔːnt] n excursión f.

jaunty ['dʒɔːntɪ] adj (hat, wave) airoso (sa); (person) vivaz, desenvuelto(ta).

javelin ['dʒævlɪn] n jabalina f.

jaw [dʒɔː] n (of person) mandíbula f; (of animal) quijada f.

jawbone ['dʒɔːbəʊn] n (of person) mandíbula f, maxilar m; (of animal) quijada f.

jay [dʒeɪ] n arrendajo m.

jaywalker ['dʒeɪwɔːkər] n peatón m imprudente.

jazz [dʒæz] n (MUS) jazz m. ▶ **jazz up** vt sep inf alegrar, avivar.

jazzy ['dʒæzɪ] adj (bright) llamativo(va).

jealous ['dʒeləs] adj 1. (envious): **to be ~ (of)** tener celos OR estar celoso(sa) (de). 2. (possessive): **to be ~ (of)** ser celoso(sa) (de).

jealousy ['dʒeləsɪ] n (U) celos mpl.

jeans [dʒiːnz] npl vaqueros mpl, tejanos mpl.

jeep [dʒiːp] n jeep m, campero m Amer.

jeer [dʒɪər] ◆ vt (boo) abuchear; (mock) mofarse de. ◆ vi: **to ~ (at sb)** (boo) abuchear (a alguien); (mock) mofarse (de alguien).

Jehovah's Witness [dʒɪˈhəʊvəz-] n testigo m y f de Jehová.

Jello® ['dʒeləʊ] n Am jalea f, gelatina f.

jelly ['dʒelɪ] n 1. (dessert) jalea f, gelatina f. 2. (jam) mermelada f.

jellyfish ['dʒelɪfɪʃ] (pl inv OR -es) n medusa f.

jeopardize, -ise ['dʒepədaɪz] vt poner en peligro, arriesgar.

jerk [dʒɜːk] ◆ n 1. (of head) movimiento m brusco; (of arm) tirón m; (of vehicle) sacudida f. 2. v inf (fool) idiota m y f, majadero m, -ra f. ◆ vi (person) saltar; (vehicle) dar sacudidas.

jersey ['dʒɜːzɪ] (pl **jerseys**) n (sweater) jersey m.

Jersey ['dʒɜːzɪ] n Jersey.

jest [dʒest] n: **in ~** en broma.

Jesus (Christ) ['dʒiːzəs-] n Jesús m, Jesucristo m.

jet [dʒet] n 1. (aircraft) reactor m. 2. (stream) chorro m. 3. (nozzle, outlet) boquilla f.

jet-black adj negro(gra) azabache.

jet engine n reactor m.

jetfoil ['dʒetfɔɪl] n hidroplano m.

jet lag n aturdimiento tras un largo viaje en avión.

jetsam ['dʒetsəm] → **flotsam**.

jettison ['dʒetɪsən] vt (cargo) deshacerse de; fig (ideas) desechar.

jetty ['dʒetɪ] n embarcadero m.

Jew [dʒuː] n judío m, -a f.

jewel ['dʒuːəl] n 1. (gemstone) piedra f preciosa. 2. (jewellery) joya f.

jeweller Br, **jeweler** Am ['dʒuːələr] n joyero m, -ra f; **~'s (shop)** joyería f.

jewellery Br, **jewelry** Am ['dʒuːəlrɪ] n (U) joyas fpl, alhajas fpl.

Jewess ['dʒuːɪs] n judía f.

Jewish ['dʒuːɪʃ] adj judío(a).

jib [dʒɪb] n 1. (beam) aguilón m. 2. (sail) foque m.

jibe [dʒaɪb] n pulla f, burla f.

jiffy ['dʒɪfɪ] n inf: **in a ~** en un santiamén.

Jiffy bag® n sobre m acolchado.

jig [dʒɪg] n giga f.

jigsaw (puzzle) ['dʒɪgsɔː-] n rompecabezas m inv, puzzle m.

jilt [dʒɪlt] vt dejar plantado(da).

jingle ['dʒɪŋgl] ◆ n (song) sintonía de anuncio publicitario. ◆ vi tintinear.

jinx [dʒɪŋks] n gafe m.

jitters ['dʒɪtəz] npl inf: **to have the ~** estar como un flan.

job [dʒɒb] n 1. (paid employment) trabajo m, empleo m. 2. (task) trabajo m. 3. (difficult task): **we had a ~ doing it** nos costó trabajo hacerlo. 4. (function) cometido m. 5. phr: **that's just the ~** Br inf eso me viene de perilla.

job centre n Br oficina f de empleo.

jobless ['dʒɒblɪs] adj desempleado(da).

jobsharing ['dʒɒbʃeərɪŋ] n (U) empleo m compartido.

jockey ['dʒɒkɪ] (pl -s) ◆ n jockey m, jinete m. ◆ vi: **to ~ for position** competir por colocarse en mejor posición.

jocular ['dʒɒkjʊlər] adj 1. (cheerful) bromista. 2. (funny) jocoso(sa).

jodhpurs ['dʒɒdpəz] npl pantalón m de montar.

jog [dʒɒg] ◆ n trote m; **to go for a ~** hacer footing. ◆ vt golpear ligeramente; **to ~ sb's memory** refrescar la memoria a alguien. ◆ vi hacer footing.

jogging ['dʒɒgɪŋ] n footing m.

john [dʒɒn] n Am inf (toilet) wáter m.

join [dʒɔɪn] ◆ n juntura f. ◆ vt 1. (unite) unir, juntar. 2. (get together with) reunirse con. 3. (become a member of - political party) afiliarse a; (- club) hacerse socio de; (- army) alistarse en. 4. (take part in) unirse a; **to ~ a queue** Br, **to ~ a line** Am meterse en la cola. ◆ vi 1. (rivers) confluir; (edges, pieces) unirse, juntarse. 2. (become a member - of political party) afiliarse; (- of club) hacerse socio; (- of army) alistarse. ▶ **join in** vt fus participar en. ◆ vi participar. ▶ **join up** vi (MIL) alistarse.

joiner ['dʒɔɪnər] n carpintero m.

joinery ['dʒɔɪnərɪ] n carpintería f.

joint [dʒɔɪnt] ◆ adj (responsibility) compartido(da); (effort) conjunto(ta); **~ owner** copropietario m, -ria f. ◆ n 1. (ANAT) articulación f. 2. (place where things are joined) juntura f. 3. Br (of meat - uncooked) corte m para asar; (- cooked) asado m. 4. inf pej (place) antro m. 5. drugs sl porro m.

joint account n cuenta f conjunta.

jointly ['dʒɔɪntlɪ] adv conjuntamente.

joist [dʒɔɪst] n vigueta f.

joke [dʒəʊk] ◆ n (funny story) chiste m; (funny action) broma f; **to play a ~ on sb** gastarle una broma a alguien; **it's no ~**

(not easy) no es (nada) fácil. ◆ vi bromear; **you're joking** estás de broma; **to ~ about sthg/with sb** bromear acerca de algo/con alguien.

joker ['dʒəʊkər] n 1. (person) bromista m y f. 2. (playing card) comodín m.

jolly ['dʒɒlɪ] ◆ adj (person, laugh) alegre; (time) divertido(da). ◆ adv Br inf muy.

jolt [dʒəʊlt] ◆ n lit & fig sacudida f. ◆ vt (jerk) sacudir, zarandear.

Jordan ['dʒɔːdn] n Jordania.

jostle ['dʒɒsl] ◆ vt empujar, dar empujones a. ◆ vi empujar, dar empujones.

jot [dʒɒt] n pizca f. ▶ **jot down** vt sep apuntar, anotar.

jotter ['dʒɒtər] n bloc m.

journal ['dʒɜːnl] n 1. (magazine) revista f, boletín m. 2. (diary) diario m.

journalism ['dʒɜːnəlɪzm] n periodismo m.

journalist ['dʒɜːnəlɪst] n periodista m y f.

journey ['dʒɜːnɪ] (pl -s) n viaje m.

jovial ['dʒəʊvjəl] adj jovial.

jowls [dʒaʊlz] npl carrillo m.

joy [dʒɔɪ] n 1. (happiness) alegría f, regocijo m. 2. (cause of joy) placer m.

joyful ['dʒɔɪfʊl] adj alegre.

joyous ['dʒɔɪəs] adj jubiloso(sa).

joyride ['dʒɔɪraɪd] (pt -rode, pp -ridden) vi darse una vuelta en un coche robado.

joystick ['dʒɔɪstɪk] n (of aircraft) palanca f de mando; (for video games, computers) joystick m.

JP n abbr of **Justice of the Peace.**

Jr. Am (abbr of **Junior**) jr.

jubilant ['dʒuːbɪlənt] adj (person) jubiloso(sa); (shout) alborozado(da).

jubilee ['dʒuːbɪliː] n aniversario m.

judge [dʒʌdʒ] ◆ n (gen & JUR) juez m y f. ◆ vt 1. (gen & JUR) juzgar. 2. (age, distance) calcular. ◆ vi juzgar; **to ~ from** OR **by, judging from** OR **by** a juzgar por.

judg(e)ment ['dʒʌdʒmənt] n 1. (JUR) fallo m, sentencia f. 2. (opinion) juicio m; **to pass ~ (on sb/sthg)** pronunciarse (sobre alguien/algo). 3. (ability to form opinion) juicio m.

judiciary [dʒuːˈdɪʃərɪ] n: **the ~** el poder judicial.

judicious [dʒuːˈdɪʃəs] adj juicioso(sa).

judo ['dʒuːdəʊ] n judo m.

jug [dʒʌg] n jarra f.

juggernaut ['dʒʌgənɔːt] n camión m grande.

juggle ['dʒʌgl] ◆ vt 1. (throw) hacer juegos malabares con. 2. (rearrange) jugar con. ◆ vi hacer juegos malabares.

juggler ['dʒʌɡləʳ] n malabarista m y f.
jugular (vein) ['dʒʌɡjʊləʳ-] n yugular f.
juice [dʒuːs] n 1. (from fruit, vegetables) zumo m, jugo m. 2. (from meat) jugo m.
juicy ['dʒuːsɪ] adj 1. (yen) jugoso(sa). 2. inf (scandalous) picante.
jukebox ['dʒuːkbɒks] n máquina f de discos.
July [dʒuːˈlaɪ] n julio m; see also **September**.
jumble ['dʒʌmbl] ◆ n (mixture) revoltijo m. ◆ vt: to ~ (up) revolver.
jumble sale n Br rastrillo m benéfico.
jumbo jet ['dʒʌmbəʊ-] n jumbo m.
jumbo-sized ['dʒʌmbəʊsaɪzd] adj gigante.
jump [dʒʌmp] ◆ n 1. (act of jumping) salto m. 2. (rapid increase) incremento m, salto m. ◆ vt 1. (cross by jumping) saltar. 2. inf (attack) asaltar. ◆ vi 1. (spring) saltar. 2. (make a sudden movement) sobresaltarse. 3. (increase rapidly) aumentar de golpe. ▶ **jump at** vt fus no dejar escapar.
jumper ['dʒʌmpəʳ] n 1. Br (pullover) jersey m. 2. Am (dress) pichi m.
jump leads npl cables mpl de empalme (de batería).
jump-start vt arrancar empujando.
jumpsuit ['dʒʌmpsuːt] n mono m.
jumpy ['dʒʌmpɪ] adj inquieto(ta).
junction ['dʒʌŋkʃn] n (of roads) cruce m; (of railway lines) empalme m.
June [dʒuːn] n junio m; see also **September**.
jungle ['dʒʌŋgl] n lit & fig selva f.
junior ['dʒuːnjəʳ] ◆ adj 1. (officer) subalterno(na); (partner, member) de menor antigüedad, júnior (inv). 2. Am (after name) júnior (inv), hijo(ja). ◆ n 1. (person of lower rank) subalterno m, -na f. 2. (younger person): he's my ~ soy mayor que él. 3. Am (SCH & UNIV) alumno de penúltimo año.
junior high school n Am ≈ instituto m de bachillerato (13-15 años).
junior school n Br ≈ escuela f primaria.
junk [dʒʌŋk] n inf (U) (unwanted things) trastos mpl.
junk food n (U) pej comida preparada poco nutritiva o saludable.
junkie ['dʒʌŋkɪ] n drugs sl yonqui m y f.
junk mail n (U) pej propaganda f (por correo).
junk shop n tienda f de objetos usados.
Jupiter ['dʒuːpɪtəʳ] n Júpiter m.

jurisdiction [ˌdʒʊərɪsˈdɪkʃn] n jurisdicción f.
juror ['dʒʊərəʳ] n jurado m.
jury ['dʒʊərɪ] n jurado m.
just [dʒʌst] ◆ adv 1. (recently): he has ~ left/moved acaba de salir/mudarse. 2. (at that moment): we were ~ leaving when ... justo íbamos a salir cuando ...; I'm ~ about to do it voy a hacerlo ahora; I couldn't do it ~ then no lo podía hacer en aquel momento; ~ as I was leaving justo en el momento en que salía. 3. (only, simply) sólo, solamente; '~ add water' 'añada un poco de agua'; ~ a minute OR moment OR second un momento. 4. (almost not) apenas; I (only) ~ did it conseguí hacerlo por muy poco. 5. (for emphasis): I ~ know it! ¡estoy seguro! 6. (exactly, precisely) exactamente; ~ what I need justo lo que necesito; ~ here/there aquí/allí mismo. 7. (in requests): could you ~ open your mouth? ¿podrías abrir la boca un momento, por favor? ◆ adj justo(ta). ▶ **just about** adv casi. ▶ **just as** adv: ~ as ... as tan ... como, igual de ... que. ▶ **just now** adv 1. (a short time ago) hace un momento. 2. (at this moment) justo ahora, ahora mismo.
justice ['dʒʌstɪs] n justicia f; to bring sb to ~ llevar a alguien ante los tribunales.
Justice of the Peace (pl Justices of the Peace) n juez m y f de paz.
justify ['dʒʌstɪfaɪ] vt: to ~ (sthg/doing sthg) justificar (algo/el haber hecho algo).
jut [dʒʌt] vi: to ~ (out) sobresalir.
juvenile ['dʒuːvənaɪl] ◆ adj 1. (JUR) juvenil. 2. (childish) infantil. ◆ n (JUR) menor m y f (de edad).
juxtapose [ˌdʒʌkstəˈpəʊz] vt: to ~ sthg (with) yuxtaponer algo (a).

K

k (pl **k's** OR **ks**), **K** (pl **K's** OR **Ks**) [keɪ] n (letter) k f, K f. ▶ **K** 1. (abbr of **kilobyte(s)**) K. 2. abbr of **thousand**.
kaleidoscope [kəˈlaɪdəskəʊp] n lit & fig caleidoscopio m.

kangaroo [ˌkæŋgəˈruː] n canguro m.
karat [ˈkærət] n Am quilate m.
karate [kəˈrɑːtɪ] n kárate m.
kayak [ˈkaɪæk] n kayac m.
KB n abbr of **kilobyte**.
kcal (abbr of **kilocalorie**) kcal.
kebab [kɪˈbæb] n pincho m moruno.
keel [kiːl] n quilla f; **on an even ~** en equilibrio estable.
keen [kiːn] adj 1. (enthusiastic) entusiasta; **to be ~ on sthg** ser aficionado(da) a algo; **she is ~ on you** tú le gustas; **to be ~ to do** OR **on doing sthg** tener ganas de hacer algo. 2. (intense - interest, desire) profundo(da); (- competition) reñido(da). 3. (sharp - sense of smell, hearing, vision) agudo(da); (- eye, ear) fino(na); (- mind) agudo.
keep [kiːp] (pt & pp **kept**) ◆ vt 1. (maintain in a particular place or state or position) mantener; **to ~ sb waiting/awake** tener a alguien esperando/despierto. 2. (retain) quedarse con; **~ the change** quédese con la vuelta. 3. (put aside, store) guardar. 4. (prevent): **to ~ sb/sthg from doing sthg** impedir a alguien/algo hacer algo. 5. (detain) detener; **to ~ sb waiting** hacer esperar a alguien. 6. (fulfil, observe - appointment) acudir a; (- promise, vow) cumplir. 7. (not disclose): **to ~ sthg from sb** ocultar algo a alguien; **to ~ sthg to o.s.** no contarle algo a nadie. 8. (in writing - record, account) llevar; (- diary) escribir; (- note) tomar. 9. (own - animals) criar; (- shop) tener. ◆ vi 1. (remain) mantenerse; **to ~ quiet** callarse. 2. (continue): **to ~ doing sthg** (repeatedly) no dejar de hacer algo; (without stopping) continuar OR seguir haciendo algo; **to ~ going** seguir adelante. 3. (continue in a particular direction) continuar, seguir; **to ~ left/right** circular por la izquierda/derecha. 4. (food) conservarse. 5. Br (be in a particular state of health) estar, andar. ◆ n (food, board etc): **to earn one's ~** ganarse el pan. ▶ **keeps** n: **for ~s** para siempre. ▶ **keep back** vt sep (information) ocultar; (money, salary) retener. ▶ **keep off** vt fus: **'~ off the grass'** 'no pisar la hierba'. ▶ **keep on** vi 1. (continue): **to ~ on doing sthg** (continue to do) continuar OR seguir haciendo algo; (do repeatedly) no dejar de hacer algo. 2. (talk incessantly): **to ~ on (about)** seguir dale que te pego (con). ▶ **keep out** ◆ vt sep no dejar pasar. ◆ vi: **'~ out'** 'prohibida la entrada'. ▶ **keep to** vt fus (follow) ceñirse a. ▶ **keep up** ◆ vt sep mantener. ◆ vi (maintain pace, level etc) mantener el ritmo; **to ~ up with sb/sthg** seguir el ritmo de alguien/algo.
keeper [ˈkiːpər] n guarda m y f.
keep-fit n (U) Br ejercicios mpl de mantenimiento.
keeping [ˈkiːpɪŋ] n 1. (care): **in sb's ~** al cuidado de alguien; **in safe ~** en lugar seguro. 2. (conformity, harmony): **in/out of ~ (with)** en armonía/desacuerdo (con).
keepsake [ˈkiːpseɪk] n recuerdo m.
keg [keg] n barrilete m.
kennel [ˈkenl] n 1. (for dog) caseta f del perro. 2. Am = **kennels**. ▶ **kennels** npl Br residencia f para perros.
Kenya [ˈkenjə] n Kenia.
Kenyan [ˈkenjən] ◆ adj keniano(na). ◆ n keniano m, -na f.
kept [kept] pt & pp → **keep**.
kerb [kɜːb] n Br bordillo m.
kernel [ˈkɜːnl] n (of nut, fruit) pepita f.
kerosene [ˈkerəsiːn] n queroseno m.
kestrel [ˈkestrəl] n cernícalo m.
ketchup [ˈketʃəp] n catsup m.
kettle [ˈketl] n tetera f para hervir.
key [kiː] ◆ n 1. (for lock) llave f. 2. (of typewriter, computer, piano) tecla f. 3. (explanatory list) clave f. 4. (solution, answer): **the ~ (to)** la clave (de). 5. (MUS) (scale of notes) tono m. ◆ adj clave (inv).
keyboard [ˈkiːbɔːd] n teclado m.
keyed up [kiːd-] adj nervioso(sa).
keyhole [ˈkiːhəʊl] n ojo m de la cerradura.
keynote [ˈkiːnəʊt] comp: **~ speech** discurso m que marca la tónica.
keypad [ˈkiːpæd] n teclado m (de teléfono, fax etc).
key ring n llavero m.
kg (abbr of **kilogram**) kg m.
khaki [ˈkɑːkɪ] ◆ adj caqui. ◆ n caqui m.
kick [kɪk] ◆ n 1. (from person) patada f, puntapié m; (from animal) coz f. 2. inf (excitement): **to get a ~ from sthg** disfrutar con algo. ◆ vt 1. (hit with foot) dar una patada OR un puntapié a. 2. inf (give up) dejar. ◆ vi (person) dar patadas; (animal) dar coces, cocear. ▶ **kick about, kick around** vi Br inf andar rondando por ahí. ▶ **kick off** vi (football) hacer el saque inicial. ▶ **kick out** vt sep inf echar, poner de patitas en la calle.
kid [kɪd] ◆ n 1. inf (child) crío m, -a f. 2. inf (young person) chico m, -ca f, chaval m, -la f. 3. (young goat) cabrito m. 4. (leather) cabritilla f. ◆ comp inf (brother, sister) menor. ◆ vt inf 1. (tease) tomar el pelo a. 2. (delude): **to ~ o.s.** hacerse ilusiones.

♦ vi inf: **to be kidding** estar de broma.
kidnap ['kɪdnæp] vt secuestrar, raptar,
plagiar Amer.
kidnapper Br, **kidnaper** Am
['kɪdnæpəʳ] n secuestrador m, -ra f, rap-
tor m, -ra f, plagiario m, -ria f Amer.
kidnapping Br, **kidnaping** Am
['kɪdnæpɪŋ] n secuestro m, rapto m, plagio m Amer.
kidney ['kɪdnɪ] (pl kidneys) n (ANAT &
CULIN) riñón m.
kidney bean n judía f pinta.
kill [kɪl] ♦ vt 1. (gen) matar. 2. fig (cause
to end, fail) poner fin a. 3. (occupy): **to ~
time** matar el tiempo. ♦ vi matar. ♦ n
1. (killing) matanza f. 2. (dead animal)
pieza f.
killer ['kɪləʳ] n (person, animal) asesino
m, -na f.
killing ['kɪlɪŋ] n asesinato m.
killjoy ['kɪldʒɔɪ] n aguafiestas m y f inv.
kiln [kɪln] n horno m.
kilo ['kiːləʊ] (pl -s) (abbr of kilogram) n
kilo m.
kilobyte ['kɪləbaɪt] n kilobyte m.
kilogram(me) ['kɪləgræm] n kilogramo m.
kilohertz ['kɪləhɜːtz] (pl inv) n kiloher-
cio m.
kilometre Br ['kɪlə,miːtəʳ], **kilo-
meter** Am [kɪ'lɒmɪtəʳ] n kilómetro m.
kilowatt ['kɪləwɒt] n kilovatio m.
kilt [kɪlt] n falda f escocesa.
kin [kɪn] → kith.
kind [kaɪnd] ♦ adj (person, gesture)
amable; (thought) considerado(da). ♦ n
tipo m, clase f; **a ~ of** una especie de; **~
of** Am inf un poco; **they're two of a ~** son
tal para cual; **in ~** (payment) en especie.
kindergarten ['kɪndə,gɑːtn] n jardín
m de infancia.
kind-hearted [-'hɑːtɪd] adj bonda-
doso(sa).
kindle ['kɪndl] vt 1. (fire) encender. 2.
fig (idea, feeling) despertar.
kindly ['kaɪndlɪ] ♦ adj amable, bonda-
doso(sa). ♦ adv 1. (gently, favourably)
amablemente. 2. (please): **will you ~ ...?**
¿sería tan amable de ...?
kindness ['kaɪndnɪs] n 1. (gentleness)
amabilidad f. 2. (helpful act) favor m.
kindred ['kɪndrɪd] adj (similar) afín; **~
spirit** alma f gemela.
king [kɪŋ] n rey m.
kingdom ['kɪŋdəm] n reino m.
kingfisher ['kɪŋ,fɪʃəʳ] n martín m
pescador.
king-size(d) [-saɪz(d)] adj (cigarette)

extra largo; (bed, pack) gigante.
kinky ['kɪŋkɪ] adj inf morboso(sa), per-
vertido(da).
kiosk ['kiːɒsk] n 1. (small shop) quiosco
m. 2. Br (telephone box) cabina f telefónica.
kip [kɪp] Br inf ♦ n sueñecito m. ♦ vi
dormir.
kipper ['kɪpəʳ] n arenque m ahumado.
kiss [kɪs] ♦ n beso m. ♦ vt besar. ♦ vi
besarse.
kiss of life n (to resuscitate sb): **the ~** la
respiración boca a boca.
kit [kɪt] n 1. (set) utensilios mpl, equipo
m. 2. Br (clothes) equipo m. 3. (to be
assembled) modelo m para armar, kit m.
kit bag n macuto m, petate m.
kitchen ['kɪtʃɪn] n cocina f.
kitchen sink n fregadero m.
kitchen unit n módulo m OR armario
m de cocina.
kite [kaɪt] n (toy) cometa f.
kith [kɪθ] n: **~ and kin** parientes mpl y
amigos.
kitten ['kɪtn] n gatito m.
kitty ['kɪtɪ] n (for bills, drinks) fondo m
común; (in card games) bote m, puesta f.
kiwi ['kiːwiː] n 1. (bird) kiwi m. 2. inf
(New Zealander) persona f de Nueva
Zelanda.
kiwi fruit n kiwi m.
km (abbr of kilometre) km.
km/h (abbr of kilometres per hour) km/
h.
knack [næk] n: **it's easy once you've got
the ~** es fácil cuando le coges el tranquillo; **he has the ~ of appearing at the
right moment** tiene el don de aparecer
en el momento adecuado.
knackered ['nækəd] adj Br inf hecho
(cha) polvo.
knapsack ['næpsæk] n mochila f.
knead [niːd] vt amasar.
knee [niː] n rodilla f.
kneecap ['niːkæp] n rótula f.
kneel [niːl] (Br pt & pp knelt, Am pt & pp
-ed OR knelt) vi arrodillarse. ► **kneel
down** vi arrodillarse.
knelt [nelt] pt & pp → kneel.
knew [njuː] pt → know.
knickers ['nɪkəz] npl 1. Br (underwear)
bragas fpl, calzonarios mpl Amer. 2. Am
(knickerbockers) bombachos mpl.
knick-knack ['nɪknæk] n baratija f.
knife [naɪf] (pl knives) ♦ n cuchillo m.
♦ vt acuchillar.
knight [naɪt] ♦ n 1. (HIST) caballero m.
2. (knighted man) hombre con el título de

'Sir'. **3.** (*in chess*) caballo *m*. ♦ *vt* conceder el título de 'Sir' a.

knighthood ['naɪthʊd] *n* **1.** (*present-day title*) título *m* de 'Sir'. **2.** (HIST) título *m* de caballero.

knit [nɪt] (*pt & pp* **knit** OR **-ted**) ♦ *vt* (*make with wool*) tejer, tricotar. ♦ *vi* **1.** (*with wool*) hacer punto, tricotar. **2.** (*join*) soldarse.

knitting ['nɪtɪŋ] *n* (U) **1.** (*activity*) labor *f* de punto. **2.** (*work produced*) punto *m*, calceta *f*.

knitting needle *n* aguja *f* de hacer punto.

knitwear ['nɪtweəʳ] *n* (U) género *m* OR ropa *f* de punto.

knives [naɪvz] *pl* → **knife**.

knob [nɒb] *n* **1.** (*on door, drawer, bedstead*) pomo *m*. **2.** (*on TV, radio etc*) botón *m*.

knock [nɒk] ♦ *n* **1.** (*hit*) golpe *m*. **2.** *inf* (*piece of bad luck*) revés *m*. ♦ *vt* **1.** (*hit hard*) golpear; **to ~ sb over** (*gen*) hacer caer a alguien; (AUT) atropellar a alguien; **to ~ sthg over** tirar OR volcar algo. **2.** (*make by hitting*) hacer, abrir. **3.** *inf* (*criticize*) poner por los suelos. ♦ *vi* **1.** (*on door*): **to ~ (at** OR **on)** llamar (a). **2.** (*car engine*) traquetear. ▶ **knock down** *vt sep* **1.** (*subj: car, driver*) atropellar. **2.** (*building*) derribar. ▶ **knock off** *vi inf* (*stop working*) parar de currar. ▶ **knock out** *vt sep* **1.** (*subj: person, punch*) dejar sin conocimiento; (*subj: drug*) dejar dormido a. **2.** (*eliminate from competition*) eliminar.

knocker ['nɒkəʳ] *n* (*on door*) aldaba *f*.

knock-kneed [-'niːd] *adj* patizambo (ba).

knock-on effect *n* Br reacción *f* en cadena.

knockout ['nɒkaʊt] *n* K.O. *m*.

knot [nɒt] ♦ *n* **1.** (*gen*) nudo *m*; **to tie/ untie a ~** hacer/deshacer un nudo. **2.** (*of people*) corrillo *m*. ♦ *vt* anudar.

knotty ['nɒtɪ] *adj* intrincado(da).

know [nəʊ] (*pt* **knew**, *pp* **known**) ♦ *vt* **1.** (*gen*): **to ~ (that)** saber (que); (*language*) saber hablar; **to ~ how to do sthg** saber hacer algo; **to get to ~ sthg** enterarse de algo; **to let sb ~ (about)** avisar a alguien (de). **2.** (*be familiar with - person, place*) conocer; **to get to ~ sb** llegar a conocer a alguien. ♦ *vi* **1.** (*have knowledge*) saber; **to ~ of** OR **about sthg** saber algo, estar enterado(da) de algo; **you ~** (*to emphasize*) ¿sabes?; (*to remind*) ¡ya sabes!, ¡sí hombre! **2.** (*be knowledgeable*): **to ~ about sthg** saber de algo. ♦ *n*: **to be in the ~** estar enterado(da).

know-all *n* Br sabelotodo *m y f*.

know-how *n* conocimientos *mpl*.

knowing ['nəʊɪŋ] *adj* cómplice.

knowingly ['nəʊɪŋlɪ] *adv* **1.** (*in knowing manner*) con complicidad. **2.** (*intentionally*) adrede.

know-it-all = **know-all**.

knowledge ['nɒlɪdʒ] *n* (U) conocimiento *m*; **to the best of my ~** por lo que yo sé.

knowledgeable ['nɒlɪdʒəbl] *adj* entendido(da).

known [nəʊn] *pp* → **know**.

knuckle ['nʌkl] *n* **1.** (ANAT) nudillo *m*. **2.** (*of meat*) jarrete *m*.

knuckle-duster *n* puño *m* americano.

koala (bear) [kəʊ'ɑːlə-] *n* koala *m*.

Koran [kɒ'rɑːn] *n*: **the ~** el Corán.

Korea [kə'rɪə] *n* Corea.

Korean [kə'rɪən] ♦ *adj* coreano(na). ♦ *n* **1.** (*person*) coreano *m*, -na *f*. **2.** (*language*) coreano *m*.

kosher ['kəʊʃəʳ] *adj* **1.** (*meat*) permitido por la religión judía. **2.** *inf* (*reputable*) limpio (pia), legal.

Koweit [kəʊ'weɪt] = **Kuwait**.

kung fu [ˌkʌŋ'fuː] *n* kung-fu *m*.

Kurd [kɜːd] *n* kurdo *m*, -da *f*.

Kuwait [kʊ'weɪt] *n* Kuwait.

l¹ (*pl* **l's** OR **ls**), **L** (*pl* **L's** OR **Ls**) [el] *n* (*letter*) l *f*, L *f*.

l² (*abbr of* **litre**) l.

lab [læb] *inf* = **laboratory**.

label ['leɪbl] ♦ *n* **1.** (*identification*) etiqueta *f*. **2.** (*of record*) sello *m* discográfico. ♦ *vt* **1.** (*fix label to*) etiquetar. **2.** *usu pej* (*describe*): **to ~ sb (as)** calificar OR etiquetar a alguien (de).

labor *etc* Am = **labour** *etc*.

laboratory [Br lə'bɒrətrɪ, Am 'læbrəˌtɔːrɪ] *n* laboratorio *m*.

laborious [lə'bɔːrɪəs] *adj* laborioso (sa).

labor union *n* Am sindicato *m*.

labour Br, **labor** Am ['leɪbəʳ] ♦ *n* **1.** (*hard work*) trabajo *m*. **2.** (*piece of work*) esfuerzo *m*. **3.** (*workers, work carried out*) mano f de obra. **4.** (*giving birth*) parto m. ♦ vi **1.** (*work hard*) trabajar (duro). **2.** (*work with difficulty*): **to ~ at** OR **over** trabajar duro en. ► **Labour** (POL) ♦ adj laborista. ♦ n Br (U) los laboristas.

laboured Br, **labored** Am ['leɪbəd] adj (*style*) trabajoso(sa); (*gait, breathing*) penoso(sa), fatigoso(sa).

labourer Br, **laborer** Am ['leɪbərəʳ] n obrero m, -ra f.

Labour Party n Br: **the ~** el partido Laborista.

Labrador ['læbrədɔːʳ] n (*dog*) (perro m de) terranova m, labrador m.

labyrinth ['læbərɪnθ] n laberinto m.

lace [leɪs] ♦ n **1.** (*fabric*) encaje m. **2.** (*shoelace*) cordón m. ♦ vt **1.** (*shoe, boot*) atar. **2.** (*drink, food*): **coffee ~d with brandy** café con unas gotas de coñac. ► **lace up** vt sep atar.

lack [læk] ♦ n falta f; **for** OR **through ~ of** por falta de; **no ~ of** abundancia de. ♦ vt carecer de. ♦ vi: **to be ~ing in** carecer de; **to be ~ing** faltar.

lackadaisical [ˌlækə'deɪzɪkl] adj pej apático(ca), desganado(da).

lacklustre Br, **lackluster** Am ['lækˌlʌstəʳ] adj pej soso(sa), apagado(da).

laconic [lə'kɒnɪk] adj lacónico(ca).

lacquer ['lækəʳ] n laca f.

lad [læd] n inf (*boy*) chaval m.

ladder ['lædəʳ] ♦ n **1.** (*for climbing*) escalera f. **2.** Br (*in tights*) carrera f. ♦ vt Br (*tights*) hacerse una carrera en.

laden ['leɪdn] adj: ~ **(with)** cargado(da) (de).

ladies Br ['leɪdɪz], **ladies' room** Am n lavabo m de señoras.

ladle ['leɪdl] ♦ n cucharón m. ♦ vt servir con cucharón.

lady ['leɪdɪ] ♦ n **1.** (*woman*) señora f. **2.** (*woman of high status*) dama f. ♦ comp mujer; ~ **doctor** doctora f. ► **Lady** n (*woman of noble rank*) lady f.

ladybird Br ['leɪdɪbɜːd], **ladybug** Am ['leɪdɪbʌg] n mariquita f.

lady-in-waiting [-'weɪtɪŋ] (*pl* **ladies-in-waiting**) n dama f de honor.

ladylike ['leɪdɪlaɪk] adj distinguido (da), elegante.

Ladyship ['leɪdɪʃɪp] n: **her/your ~** su señoría f.

lag [læg] ♦ vi **1.** (*move more slowly*): **to ~ (behind)** rezagarse. **2.** (*develop more slowly*): **to ~ (behind)** andar a la zaga. ♦ vt revestir. ♦ n (*timelag*) retraso m, demora f.

lager ['lɑːgəʳ] n cerveza f rubia.

lagoon [lə'guːn] n laguna f.

laid [leɪd] pt & pp → **lay**.

laid-back adj inf relajado(da).

lain [leɪn] pp → **lie**.

lair [leəʳ] n guarida f.

laity ['leɪətɪ] n (RELIG): **the ~** los seglares.

lake [leɪk] n lago m.

Lake District n: **the ~** el Distrito de los Lagos al noroeste de Inglaterra.

lamb [læm] n cordero m.

lambswool ['læmzwʊl] ♦ n lana f de cordero. ♦ comp de lana de cordero.

lame [leɪm] adj **1.** (*person, horse*) cojo (ja). **2.** (*excuse, argument*) pobre.

lament [lə'ment] ♦ n lamento m. ♦ vt lamentar.

lamentable ['læməntəbl] adj lamentable.

laminated ['læmɪneɪtɪd] adj laminado (da).

lamp [læmp] n lámpara f.

lampoon [læm'puːn] ♦ n pasquín m, sátira f. ♦ vt satirizar.

lamppost ['læmppəʊst] n farol m.

lampshade ['læmpʃeɪd] n pantalla f.

lance [lɑːns] ♦ n lanza f. ♦ vt abrir con lanceta.

lance corporal n cabo m interino, soldado m de primero.

land [lænd] ♦ n **1.** (*gen*) tierra f. **2.** (*property*) tierras fpl, finca f. ♦ vt **1.** (*unload*) desembarcar. **2.** (*catch - fish*) pescar. **3.** inf (*obtain*) conseguir, pillar. **4.** (*plane*) hacer aterrizar. **5.** inf (*place*): **to ~ sb in sthg** meter a alguien en algo; **to ~ sb with sb/sthg** cargar a alguien con alguien/algo. ♦ vi **1.** (*by plane*) aterrizar, tomar tierra. **2.** (*fall*) caer. **3.** (*from ship*) desembarcar. ► **land up** vi inf: **to ~ up (in)** acabar (en).

landing ['lændɪŋ] n **1.** (*of stairs*) rellano m. **2.** (*of aeroplane*) aterrizaje m. **3.** (*of person*) desembarco m.

landing card n tarjeta f de desembarque.

landing gear n (U) tren m de aterrizaje.

landing stage n desembarcadero m.

landing strip n pista f de aterrizaje.

landlady ['lændˌleɪdɪ] n casera f, patrona f.

landlord ['lændlɔːd] n **1.** (*of rented room or building*) dueño m, casero m. **2.** (*of pub*) patrón m.

landmark ['lændmɑːk] n **1.** (*prominent feature*) punto m de referencia. **2.** fig (*in history*) hito m.

landowner ['lænd,əunər] n terrateniente m y f.

landscape ['lændskeɪp] n paisaje m.

landslide ['lændslaɪd] n 1. (of earth, rocks) desprendimiento m de tierras. 2. (POL) victoria f arrolladora OR aplastante.

lane [leɪn] n 1. (road in country) camino m. 2. (road in town) callejuela f, callejón m. 3. (for traffic) carril m. 4. (in swimming pool, race track) calle f. 5. (for shipping, aircraft) ruta f.

language ['læŋgwɪdʒ] n 1. (gen) lengua f, idioma m. 2. (faculty or style of communication) lenguaje m.

language laboratory n laboratorio m de idiomas.

languid ['læŋgwɪd] adj lánguido(da).

languish ['læŋgwɪʃ] vi (in misery) languidecer; (in prison) pudrirse.

lank [læŋk] adj lacio(cia).

lanky ['læŋkɪ] adj larguirucho(cha).

lantern ['læntən] n farol m.

lap [læp] ♦ n 1. (of person) regazo m. 2. (of race) vuelta f. ♦ vt 1. (subj: animal) beber a lengüetadas. 2. (overtake in race) doblar. ♦ vi (water, waves) romper con suavidad.

lapel [lə'pel] n solapa f.

Lapland ['læplænd] n Laponia.

lapse [læps] ♦ n 1. (failing) fallo m, lapsus m inv. 2. (in behaviour) desliz m. 3. (of time) lapso m, periodo m. ♦ vi 1. (membership) caducar; (treatment, agreement) cumplir, expirar. 2. (standards, quality) bajar momentáneamente; (tradition) extinguirse. 3. (subj: person): **to ~ into** terminar cayendo en.

lap-top (computer) n (COMPUT) (pequeño) ordenador m portátil.

larceny ['lɑːsənɪ] n (U) latrocinio m.

lard [lɑːd] n manteca f de cerdo.

larder ['lɑːdər] n despensa f.

large [lɑːdʒ] adj (gen) grande; (family) numeroso(sa); (sum) importante. ► **at large** adv 1. (as a whole) en general. 2. (escaped prisoner, animal) suelto(ta). ► **by and large** adv en general.

largely ['lɑːdʒlɪ] adv (mostly) en gran parte; (chiefly) principalmente.

lark [lɑːk] n 1. (bird) alondra f. 2. inf (joke) broma f. ► **lark about** vi hacer el gamberro.

laryngitis [,lærɪn'dʒaɪtɪs] n (U) laringitis f inv.

larynx ['lærɪŋks] n laringe f.

lasagna, lasagne [lə'zænjə] n (U) lasaña f.

laser ['leɪzər] n láser m.

laser printer n (COMPUT) impresora f láser.

lash [læʃ] ♦ n 1. (eyelash) pestaña f. 2. (blow with whip) latigazo m. ♦ vt 1. lit & fig (whip) azotar. 2. (tie): **to ~ sthg (to)** amarrar algo (a). ► **lash out** vi 1. (physically): **to ~ out (at OR against sb)** soltar un golpe (a alguien). 2. Br inf (spend money): **to ~ out (on sthg)** derrochar el dinero (en algo).

lass [læs] n chavala f, muchacha f.

lasso [læ'suː] (pl -s) n lazo m.

last [lɑːst] ♦ adj último(ma); **~ month/Tuesday** el mes/martes pasado; **~ but one** penúltimo(ma); **~ but two** antepenúltimo(ma); **~ night** anoche. ♦ adv 1. (most recently) por última vez. 2. (finally, in final position) en último lugar; **he arrived ~** llegó el último. ♦ pron: **the year/Saturday before ~** ni el año/sábado pasado, sino el anterior; **the ~ but one** el penúltimo (la penúltima); **the night before ~** anteanoche; **the time before ~** la vez anterior a la pasada; **to leave sthg till ~** dejar algo para lo último. ♦ n: **the ~ I saw/heard of him** la última vez que lo vi/que oí de él. ♦ vi durar; (food) conservarse. ► **at (long) last** adv por fin.

last-ditch adj último(ma), desesperado(da).

lasting ['lɑːstɪŋ] adj (peace, effect) duradero(ra); (mistrust) profundo(da).

lastly ['lɑːstlɪ] adv 1. (to conclude) por último. 2. (at the end) al final.

last-minute adj de última hora.

latch [lætʃ] n pestillo m. ► **latch onto** vt fus inf (person) pegarse OR engancharse a; (idea) pillar.

late [leɪt] ♦ adj 1. (not on time) con retraso; **to be ~ (for)** llegar tarde (a). 2. (near end of): **in the ~ afternoon** al final de la tarde; **in ~ December** a finales de diciembre. 3. (later than normal) tardío (a); **we had a ~ breakfast** desayunamos tarde. 4. (former): **the ~ president** el expresidente. 5. (dead) difunto(ta). ♦ adv 1. (gen) tarde. 2. (near end of period): **in the day** al final del día; **~ in August** a finales de agosto. ► **of late** adv últimamente.

latecomer ['leɪt,kʌmər] n persona f que llega tarde.

lately ['leɪtlɪ] adv últimamente.

latent ['leɪtənt] adj latente.

later ['leɪtər] ♦ adj 1. (date, edition) posterior. 2. (near end of): **in the ~ 15th cen-**

tury a finales del siglo XV. ◆ adv (at a later time): ~ **(on)** más tarde.

lateral ['lætərəl] adj lateral.

latest ['leɪtɪst] ◆ adj (most recent) último (ma). ◆ n: **at the ~** a más tardar, como muy tarde.

lathe [leɪð] n torno m.

lather ['lɑːðər] ◆ n espuma f (de jabón). ◆ vt enjabonar.

Latin ['lætɪn] ◆ adj 1. (temperament, blood) latino(na). 2. (studies) de latín. ◆ n (language) latín m.

Latin America n América f Latina, Latinoamérica f.

Latin American ◆ adj latinoamericano(na). ◆ n (person) latinoamericano m, -na f.

latitude ['lætɪtjuːd] n (GEOGR) latitud f.

latter ['lætər] ◆ adj 1. (near to end) último(ma). 2. (second) segundo(da). ◆ n: **the ~** éste m, -ta f.

latterly ['lætəlɪ] adv últimamente.

lattice ['lætɪs] n enrejado m, celosía f.

Latvia ['lætvɪə] n Letonia.

laudable ['lɔːdəbl] adj loable.

laugh [lɑːf] ◆ n 1. (sound) risa f. 2. inf (fun, joke): **to have a ~** reírse un rato; **to do sthg for ~s** OR **a ~** hacer algo para divertirse OR en cachondeo. ◆ vi reírse.
► **laugh at** vt fus (mock) reírse de.
► **laugh off** vt sep (dismiss) restar importancia a, tomarse a risa.

laughable ['lɑːfəbl] adj pej (absurd) ridículo(la), risible.

laughingstock ['lɑːfɪŋstɒk] n hazmerreír m.

laughter ['lɑːftər] n (U) risa f.

launch [lɔːntʃ] ◆ n 1. (of boat, ship) botadura f. 2. (of rocket, missile, product) lanzamiento m; (of book) publicación f. 3. (boat) lancha f. ◆ vt 1. (boat, ship) botar. 2. (missile, attack, product) lanzar; (book) publicar, sacar. 3. (strike) convocar; (company) fundar.

launch(ing) pad ['lɔːntʃ(ɪŋ)-] n plataforma f de lanzamiento.

launder ['lɔːndər] vt 1. (wash) lavar. 2. inf (money) blanquear.

laund(e)rette [lɔːn'dret], **Laundromat®** Am ['lɔːndrəmæt] n lavandería f (automática).

laundry ['lɔːndrɪ] n 1. (clothes - about to be washed) colada f, ropa f sucia; (- newly washed) ropa f limpia. 2. (business, room) lavandería f.

laureate ['lɔːrɪət] → **poet laureate**.

lava ['lɑːvə] n lava f.

lavatory ['lævətrɪ] n 1. (receptacle)

water m. 2. (room) servicio m.

lavender ['lævəndər] n 1. (plant) lavanda f. 2. (colour) color m lavanda.

lavish ['lævɪʃ] ◆ adj 1. (person) pródigo (ga); (gifts, portions) muy generoso(sa); **to be ~ with** (praise, attention) ser pródigo en; (money) ser desprendido(da) con. 2. (sumptuous) espléndido(da), suntuoso(sa). ◆ vt: **to ~ sthg on** (praise, care) prodigar algo a; (time, money) gastar algo en.

law [lɔː] n 1. (gen) ley f; **against the ~** contra la ley; **to break the ~** infringir OR violar la ley; **~ and order** el orden público. 2. (set of rules, study, profession) derecho m.

law-abiding [-ə,baɪdɪŋ] adj observante de la ley.

law court n tribunal m de justicia.

lawful ['lɔːful] adj fml legal, lícito(ta).

lawn [lɔːn] n (grass) césped m.

lawnmower ['lɔːn,məʊər] n cortacésped m o f.

lawn tennis n tenis m sobre hierba.

law school n facultad f de derecho.

lawsuit ['lɔːsuːt] n pleito m.

lawyer ['lɔːjər] n abogado m, -da f.

lax [læks] adj (discipline, morals) relajado (da); (person) negligente.

laxative ['læksətɪv] n laxante m.

lay [leɪ] (pt & pp **laid**) ◆ pt → **lie**. ◆ vt 1. (put, place) colocar, poner. 2. (prepare - plans) hacer; **to ~ the table** poner la mesa. 3. (put in position - bricks) poner; (- cable, trap) tender; (- foundations) echar. 4. (egg) poner. 5. (blame, curse) echar. ◆ adj 1. (not clerical) laico(ca). 2. (untrained, unqualified) lego(ga).
► **lay aside** vt sep 1. (store for future - food) guardar; (- money) ahorrar. 2. (put away) dejar a un lado.
► **lay down** vt sep 1. (set out) imponer, dictar. 2. (put down - arms) deponer, entregar; (- tools) dejar.
► **lay off** ◆ vt sep (make redundant) despedir. ◆ vt fus inf 1. (leave in peace) dejar en paz. 2. (stop, give up): **to ~ off (doing sthg)** dejar de (hacer algo).
► **lay on** vt sep Br (provide, supply) proveer.
► **lay out** vt sep 1. (arrange, spread out) disponer. 2. (plan, design) diseñar el trazado de.

layabout ['leɪəbaʊt] n Br inf holgazán m, -ana f, gandul m, -la f.

lay-by (pl **lay-bys**) n Br área f de descanso.

layer ['leɪər] n 1. (of substance, material) capa f. 2. fig (level) nivel m.

layman ['leɪmən] (pl **-men** [-mən]) n

1. (*untrained, unqualified person*) lego *m*, -ga *f*. 2. (RELIG) laico *m*, -ca *f*.

layout ['leɪaʊt] *n* (*of building, garden*) trazado *m*, diseño *m*; (*of text*) presentación *f*, composición *f*.

laze [leɪz] *vi*: **to ~ (about** OR **around)** gandulear, holgazanear.

lazy ['leɪzɪ] *adj* 1. (*person*) perezoso (sa), vago(ga). 2. (*stroll, gesture*) lento (ta); (*afternoon*) ocioso(sa).

lazybones ['leɪzɪbəʊnz] (*pl inv*) *n* gandul *m*, -la *f*.

lb (*abbr of* **pound**) lb.

LCD *n abbr of* **liquid crystal display**.

lead¹ [liːd] (*pt & pp* led) ◆ *n* 1. (*winning position*) delantera *f*; **to be in** OR **have the ~** llevar la delantera. 2. (*amount ahead*): **to have a ~ of ...** llevar una ventaja de ... 3. (*initiative, example*) iniciativa *f*, ejemplo *m*; **to take the ~** (*do sthg first*) tomar la delantera. 4. (THEATRE): **(to play) the ~** (*hacer*) el papel principal. 5. (*clue*) pista *f*. 6. (*for dog*) correa *f*. 7. (*wire, cable*) cable *m*. ◆ *adj* (*singer, actor*) principal; (*story in newspaper*) más destacado(da). ◆ *vt* 1. (*be in front of*) encabezar. 2. (*take, guide, direct*) conducir. 3. (*be in charge of, take the lead in*) estar al frente de, dirigir. 4. (*life*) llevar. 5. (*cause*): **to ~ sb to do sthg** llevar a alguien a hacer algo. ◆ *vi* 1. (*go*): **to ~ (to)** conducir OR llevar (a). 2. (*give access to*): **to ~ (to** OR **into)** dar a (*a*). 3. (*be winning*) ir en cabeza. 4. (*result in*): **to ~ to** conducir a. ▶ **lead up to** *vt fus* 1. (*build up to*) conducir a, preceder. 2. (*plan to introduce*) apuntar a.

lead² [led] *n* 1. (*metal*) plomo *m*. 2. (*in pencil*) mina *f*.

leaded ['ledɪd] *adj* 1. (*petrol*) con plomo. 2. (*window*) emplomado(da).

leader ['liːdə'] *n* 1. (*of party etc, in competition*) líder *m* y *f*. 2. Br (*in newspaper*) editorial *m*, artículo *m* de fondo.

leadership ['liːdəʃɪp] *n* (U) 1. (*people in charge*): **the ~** los líderes. 2. (*position of leader*) liderazgo *m*. 3. (*qualities of leader*) dotes *fpl* de mando.

lead-free [led-] *adj* sin plomo.

leading ['liːdɪŋ] *adj* 1. (*major - athlete, writer*) destacado(da). 2. (*at front*) que va en cabeza.

leading lady *n* primera actriz *f*.

leading light *n* cerebro *m*, cabeza *f* pensante.

leading man *n* primer actor *m*.

leaf [liːf] (*pl* leaves) *n* 1. (*of tree, book*) hoja *f*. 2. (*of table*) hoja *f* abatible.

▶ **leaf through** *vt fus* hojear.

leaflet ['liːflɪt] *n* (*small brochure*) folleto *m*; (*piece of paper*) octavilla *f*.

league [liːg] *n* (*gen & SPORT*) liga *f*; **to be in ~ with** (*work with*) estar confabulado con.

leak [liːk] ◆ *n* 1. (*hole - in tank, bucket*) agujero *m*; (*- in roof*) gotera *f*. 2. (*escape*) escape *m*, fuga *f*. 3. (*disclosure*) filtración *f*. ◆ *vt* (*make known*) filtrar. ◆ *vi* 1. (*bucket*) tener un agujero; (*roof*) tener goteras. 2. (*water, gas*) salirse, escaparse; **to ~ (out) from** salirse de. ▶ **leak out** *vi* 1. (*liquid*) escaparse. 2. *fig* (*secret, information*) trascender.

leakage ['liːkɪdʒ] *n* fuga *f*, escape *m*.

lean [liːn] (*pt & pp* leant OR -ed) ◆ *adj* 1. (*person*) delgado(da). 2. (*meat*) magro (gra), sin grasa. 3. (*winter, year*) de escasez. ◆ *vt* (*support, prop*): **to ~ sthg against** apoyar algo contra. ◆ *vi* 1. (*bend, slope*) inclinarse. 2. (*rest*): **to ~ on/against** apoyarse en/contra.

leaning ['liːnɪŋ] *n*: **~ (towards)** inclinación *f* (hacia or por).

leant [lent] *pt & pp* → **lean**.

lean-to (*pl* lean-tos) *n* cobertizo *m*.

leap [liːp] (*pt & pp* leapt OR -ed) ◆ *n* salto *m*. ◆ *vi* 1. (*gen*) saltar; (*prices*) dispararse.

leapfrog ['liːpfrɒg] ◆ *n* pídola *f*. ◆ *vt* saltar.

leapt [lept] *pt & pp* → **leap**.

leap year *n* año *m* bisiesto.

learn [lɜːn] (*pt & pp* -ed OR learnt) ◆ *vt* 1. (*acquire knowledge of, memorize*) aprender; **to ~ (how) to do sthg** aprender a hacer algo. 2. (*hear*): **to ~ (that)** enterarse de (que). ◆ *vi* 1. (*acquire knowledge*) aprender. 2. (*hear*): **to ~ (of** OR **about)** enterarse (de).

learned ['lɜːnɪd] *adj* erudito(ta).

learner ['lɜːnə'] *n* principiante *m* y *f*.

learner (driver) *n* conductor *m* principiante OR en prácticas.

learning ['lɜːnɪŋ] *n* saber *m*, erudición *f*.

learnt [lɜːnt] *pt & pp* → **learn**.

lease [liːs] ◆ *n* (JUR) contrato *m* de arrendamiento, arriendo *m*. ◆ *vt* arrendar; **to ~ sthg from/to sb** arrendar algo de/a alguien.

leasehold ['liːshəʊld] ◆ *adj* arrendado (da). ◆ *adv* en arriendo.

leash [liːʃ] *n* (*for dog*) correa *f*.

least [liːst] (*superl of* little) ◆ *adj* (*smallest in amount, degree*) menor; **he earns the ~ money** es el que menos dinero gana.

♦ *pron* (*smallest amount*): **the** ~ lo menos; **it's the** ~ (**that**) **he can do** es lo menos que puede hacer; **not in the** ~ en absoluto; **to say the** ~ por no decir otra cosa. ♦ *adv* (*to the smallest amount, degree*) menos. ▶ **at least** *adv* por lo menos. ▶ **least of all** *adv* y menos (todavía). ▶ **not least** *adv fml* en especial.

leather ['leðə^r] ♦ *n* cuero *m*, piel *f*. ♦ *comp* (*jacket, trousers*) de cuero; (*shoes, bag*) de piel.

leave [liːv] (*pt & pp* **left**) ♦ *vt* **1.** (*gen*) dejar; **he left it to her to decide** dejó que ella decidiera; **to** ~ **sb alone** dejar a alguien en paz. **2.** (*go away from - house, room*) salir de; (- *wife, home*) abandonar. **3.** (*do not take, forget*) dejarse. **4.** (*bequeath*): **to** ~ **sb sthg**, **to** ~ **sthg to sb** dejarle algo a alguien. ♦ *vi* (*bus, train, plane*) salir; (*person*) irse, marcharse. ♦ *n* (*time off*) permiso *m*; **to be on** ~ estar de permiso. ▶ **leave behind** *vt sep* **1.** (*abandon*) dejar. **2.** (*forget*) dejarse. ▶ **leave out** *vt sep* excluir.

leave of absence *n* excedencia *f*.

leaves [liːvz] *pl* → **leaf**.

Lebanon ['lebənən] *n*: (**the**) ~ (el) Líbano.

lecherous ['letʃərəs] *adj* lascivo(va).

lecture ['lektʃə^r] ♦ *n* **1.** (*talk - at university*) clase *f*; (- *at conference*) conferencia *f*. **2.** (*criticism, reprimand*) sermón *m*. ♦ *vt* (*scold*) echar un sermón a. ♦ *vi* (*give talk*): **to** ~ (**on/in**) (*at university*) dar una clase (de/en); (*at conference*) dar una conferencia (sobre/en).

lecturer ['lektʃərə^r] *n* profesor *m*, -ra *f* de universidad.

led [led] *pt & pp* → **lead**.

ledge [ledʒ] *n* **1.** (*of window*) alféizar *m*. **2.** (*of mountain*) saliente *m*.

ledger ['ledʒə^r] *n* libro *m* mayor.

leech [liːtʃ] *n lit & fig* sanguijuela *f*.

leek [liːk] *n* puerro *m*.

leer [lɪə^r] *vi*: **to** ~ **at sb** mirar lascivamente a alguien.

leeway ['liːweɪ] *n* (*room to manoeuvre*) libertad *f* (de acción OR movimientos).

left [left] ♦ *adj* **1.** (*remaining*): **there's no wine** ~ no queda vino. **2.** (*not right*) izquierdo(da). ♦ *adv* a la izquierda. ♦ *n*: **on** OR **to the** ~ a la izquierda. ▶ **Left** *n* (POL): **the Left** la izquierda.

left-hand *adj* izquierdo(da); **the** ~ **side** el lado izquierdo, la izquierda.

left-hand drive *adj* con el volante a la izquierda.

left-handed [-'hændɪd] *adj* **1.** (*person*)

zurdo(da). **2.** (*implement*) para zurdos.

left luggage (office) *n Br* consigna *f*.

leftover ['leftəuvə^r] *adj* sobrante. ▶ **leftovers** *npl* sobras *fpl*.

left wing *n* (POL) izquierda *f*. ▶ **left-wing** *adj* izquierdista.

leg [leg] *n* **1.** (*of person*) pierna *f*; **to pull sb's** ~ tomarle el pelo a alguien. **2.** (*of animal*) pata *f*. **3.** (*of trousers*) pernera *f*, pierna *f*. **4.** (CULIN) (*of lamb, pork*) pierna *f*; (*of chicken*) muslo *m*. **5.** (*of furniture*) pata *f*. **6.** (*of journey*) etapa *f*; (*of tournament*) fase *f*, manga *f*.

legacy ['legəsɪ] *n lit & fig* legado *m*.

legal ['liːgl] *adj* **1.** (*concerning the law*) jurídico(ca), legal. **2.** (*lawful*) legal, lícito(ta).

legalize, -ise ['liːgəlaɪz] *vt* legalizar.

legal tender *n* moneda *f* de curso legal.

legend ['ledʒənd] *n lit & fig* leyenda *f*.

leggings ['legɪŋz] *npl* mallas *fpl*.

legible ['ledʒəbl] *adj* legible.

legislation [,ledʒɪs'leɪʃn] *n* legislación *f*.

legislature ['ledʒɪsleɪtʃə^r] *n* legislatura *f*.

legitimate [lɪ'dʒɪtɪmət] *adj* legítimo(ma).

legless ['leglɪs] *adj Br inf* (*drunk*) trompa, como una cuba.

legroom ['legrum] *n* (U) sitio *m* para las piernas.

leg-warmers [-,wɔːməz] *npl* calentadores *mpl*.

leisure [Br 'leʒə^r, Am 'liːʒər] *n* ocio *m*, tiempo *m* libre; **do it at your** ~ hazlo cuando tengas tiempo.

leisure centre *n* centro *m* deportivo y cultural.

leisurely [Br 'leʒəlɪ, Am 'liːʒərlɪ] ♦ *adj* lento(ta). ♦ *adv* con calma, sin prisa.

leisure time *n* tiempo *m* libre, ocio *m*.

lemon ['lemən] *n* (*fruit*) limón *m*.

lemonade [,lemə'neɪd] *n* **1.** *Br* (*fizzy drink*) gaseosa *f*. **2.** (*made with fresh lemons*) limonada *f*.

lemon juice *n* zumo *m* de limón.

lemon sole *n* platija *f*.

lemon squeezer [-'skwiːzə^r] *n* exprimidor *m*, exprimelimones *m inv*.

lemon tea *n* té *m* con limón.

lend [lend] (*pt & pp* **lent**) *vt* **1.** (*loan*) prestar, dejar; **to** ~ **sb sthg**, **to** ~ **sthg to sb** prestarle algo a alguien. **2.** (*offer*): **to** ~ **sthg** (**to sb**) prestar algo (a alguien); **to** ~ **itself to sthg** prestarse a algo. **3.** (*add*): **to** ~ **sthg to** prestar algo a.

lending rate ['lendɪŋ-] *n* tipo *m* de interés (en un crédito).

length [leŋθ] *n* 1. (*measurement*) longitud *f*, largo *m*; **what ~ is it?** ¿cuánto mide de largo?; **in ~** de largo. 2. (*whole distance, size*) extensión *f*. 3. (*of swimming pool*) largo *m*. 4. (*piece - of string, wood*) trozo *m* alargado; (*- of cloth*) largo *m*. 5. (*duration*) duración *f*. 6. *phr*: **to go to great ~s to do sthg** hacer lo imposible para hacer algo. ▶ **at length** *adv* 1. (*eventually*) por fin. 2. (*in detail - speak*) largo y tendido; (*- discuss*) con detenimiento.

lengthen ['leŋθən] ◆ *vt* alargar. ◆ *vi* alargarse.

lengthways ['leŋθweɪz] *adv* a lo largo.

lengthy ['leŋθɪ] *adj* (*stay, visit*) extenso (sa); (*discussions, speech*) prolongado(da).

lenient ['li:njənt] *adj* indulgente.

lens [lenz] *n* 1. (*in glasses*) lente *f*; (*in camera*) objetivo *m*. 2. (*contact lens*) lentilla *f*, lente *f* de contacto.

lent [lent] *pt & pp* → **lend**.

Lent [lent] *n* Cuaresma *f*.

lentil ['lentɪl] *n* lenteja *f*.

Leo ['li:əʊ] *n* Leo *m*.

leopard ['lepəd] *n* leopardo *m*.

leotard ['li:ətɑ:d] *n* malla *f*.

leper ['lepər] *n* leproso *m*, -sa *f*.

leprosy ['leprəsɪ] *n* lepra *f*.

lesbian ['lezbɪən] *n* lesbiana *f*.

less [les] (*compar of* **little**) ◆ *adj* menos; **~ ... than menos ...** que; **~ and ~** cada vez menos. ◆ *pron* menos; **the ~ you work, the ~ you earn** cuanto menos trabajas, menos ganas; **it costs ~ than you think** cuesta menos de lo que piensas; **no ~ than** nada menos que. ◆ *adv* menos; **~ than five** menos de cinco; **~ and ~** cada vez menos. ◆ *prep* (*minus*) menos.

lessen ['lesn] ◆ *vt* aminorar, reducir. ◆ *vi* aminorarse, reducirse.

lesser ['lesər] *adj* menor; **to a ~ extent** OR **degree** en menor grado.

lesson ['lesn] *n* 1. (*class*) clase *f*. 2. (*warning experience*) lección *f*.

lest [lest] *conj fml* para que no; **~ we forget** no sea que nos olvidemos.

let [let] (*pt & pp* **let**) *vt* 1. (*allow*): **to ~ sb do sthg** dejar a alguien hacer algo; **to ~ sthg happen** dejar que algo ocurra; **to ~ sb know sthg** avisar a alguien de algo; **to ~ go of sthg/sb** soltar algo/a alguien; **to ~ sthg/sb go** (*release*) liberar a algo/alguien, soltar a algo/alguien. 2. (*in verb forms*): **~'s eat!** ¡a comer!; **~'s go!** ¡vamos!; **~'s see** veamos; **~ him wait!**

¡déjale que espere! 3. (*rent out - house, room*) alquilar; (*- land*) arrendar; **'to ~' 'se alquila'.** ▶ **let alone** *adv* ni mucho menos. ▶ **let down** *vt sep* 1. (*deflate*) desinflar. 2. (*disappoint*) fallar, defraudar. ▶ **let in** *vt sep* 1. (*admit*) dejar entrar. 2. (*leak*) dejar pasar. ▶ **let off** *vt sep* 1. (*excuse*): **to ~ sb off sthg** eximir a alguien de algo. 2. (*not punish*) perdonar. 3. (*cause to explode - bomb*) hacer estallar; (*- gun*) disparar. ▶ **let on** *vi*: **don't ~ on!** ¡no cuentes nada! ▶ **let out** *vt sep* 1. (*allow to go out*) dejar salir. 2. (*emit - sound*) soltar. ▶ **let up** *vi* 1. (*heat, rain*) cesar. 2. (*person*) parar.

letdown ['letdaʊn] *n inf* chasco *m*.

lethal ['li:θl] *adj* letal, mortífero(ra).

lethargic [lə'θɑ:dʒɪk] *adj* (*mood*) letárgico(ca); (*person*) aletargado(da).

let's [lets] = **let us**.

letter ['letər] *n* 1. (*written message*) carta *f*. 2. (*of alphabet*) letra *f*.

letter bomb *n* carta *f* bomba.

letterbox ['letəbɒks] *n Br* buzón *m*.

letter of credit *n* carta *f* de crédito.

lettuce ['letɪs] *n* lechuga *f*.

letup ['letʌp] *n* tregua *f*, respiro *m*.

leuk(a)emia [lu:'ki:mɪə] *n* leucemia *f*.

level ['levl] ◆ *adj* 1. (*equal in speed, score*) igualado(da); (*equal in height*) nivelado (da); **to be ~ (with sthg)** estar al mismo nivel (que algo). 2. (*flat - floor, field*) liso (sa), llano(na). ◆ *n* 1. (*gen*) nivel *m*. 2. *phr*: **to be on the ~** *inf* ir en serio. 3. *Am* (*spirit level*) nivel *m* de burbuja de aire. ◆ *vt* 1. (*make flat*) allanar. 2. (*demolish - building*) derribar; (*- forest*) arrasar. ▶ **level off, level out** *vi* 1. (*stabilize, slow down*) estabilizarse. 2. (*ground*) nivelarse; (*plane*) enderezarse. ▶ **level with** *vt fus inf* ser sincero(ra) con.

level crossing *n Br* paso *m* a nivel.

level-headed [-'hedɪd] *adj* sensato (ta).

lever [*Br* 'li:vər, *Am* 'levər] *n* 1. (*handle, bar*) palanca *f*. 2. *fig* (*tactic*) resorte *m*.

leverage [*Br* 'li:vərɪdʒ, *Am* 'levərɪdʒ] *n* (U) 1. (*force*) fuerza *f* de apalanque. 2. *fig* (*influence*) influencia *f*.

levy ['levɪ] ◆ *n*: **~ (on)** (*financial contribution*) contribución *f* (a OR para); (*tax*) recaudación *f* OR impuesto *m* (sobre). ◆ *vt* recaudar.

lewd [lju:d] *adj* (*person, look*) lascivo (va); (*behaviour, song*) obsceno(na); (*joke*) verde.

liability [,laɪə'bɪlətɪ] *n* 1. (*hindrance*) estorbo *m*. 2. (*legal responsibility*): **~ (for)**

responsabilidad *f* (de OR por). ▶ **liabilities** *npl* (FIN) pasivo *m*.

liable ['laɪəbl] *adj* **1.** (*likely*): **that's ~ to happen** eso pueda que ocurra. **2.** (*prone*): **to be ~ to** ser propenso(sa) a. **3.** (*legally responsible*): **to be ~ (for)** ser responsable (de).

liaise [lɪ'eɪz] *vi*: **to ~ (with)** estar en contacto (con).

liaison [lɪ'eɪzɒn] *n* (*contact, co-operation*): **~ (with/between)** relación *f* (con/entre), enlace *m* (con/entre).

liar ['laɪə^r] *n* mentiroso *m*, -sa *f*.

libel ['laɪbl] ◆ *n* libelo *m*. ◆ *vt* publicar un libelo contra.

liberal ['lɪbərəl] ◆ *adj* **1.** (*tolerant*) liberal. **2.** (*generous*) generoso(sa). ◆ *n* liberal *m* y *f*. ▶ **Liberal** (POL) ◆ *adj* liberal. ◆ *n* (miembro *m* del partido) liberal *m* y *f*.

Liberal Democrat ◆ *adj* demócrata liberal. ◆ *n* (miembro *m* del partido) demócrata liberal *m* y *f*.

liberate ['lɪbəreɪt] *vt* liberar.

liberation [,lɪbə'reɪʃn] *n* liberación *f*.

liberty ['lɪbətɪ] *n* libertad *f*; **at ~** en libertad; **to be at ~ to do sthg** ser libre de hacer algo; **to take liberties (with sb)** tomarse demasiadas libertades (con alguien).

Libra ['liːbrə] *n* Libra *f*.

librarian [laɪ'breərɪən] *n* bibliotecario *m*, -ria *f*.

library ['laɪbrərɪ] (*pl* **-ies**) *n* (*public institution*) biblioteca *f*.

libretto [lɪ'bretəʊ] (*pl* **-s**) *n* libreto *m*.

Libya ['lɪbɪə] *n* Libia *f*.

lice [laɪs] *pl* → **louse**.

licence ['laɪsəns] ◆ *n* permiso *m*, licencia *f*. ◆ *vt* Am = **license**.

license ['laɪsəns] ◆ *vt* (*person, organization*) dar licencia a; (*activity*) autorizar. ◆ *n* Am = **licence**.

licensed ['laɪsənst] *adj* **1.** (*person*): **to be ~ to do sthg** estar autorizado(da) para hacer algo. **2.** (*object*) registrado(da), con licencia. **3.** Br (*premises*) autorizado(da) a vender alcohol.

license plate *n* Am (placa *f* de) matrícula *f*.

lick [lɪk] ◆ *n inf* (*small amount*): **a ~ of paint** una mano de pintura. ◆ *vt lit & fig* lamer.

licorice ['lɪkərɪs] = **liquorice**.

lid [lɪd] *n* **1.** (*cover*) tapa *f*, tapadera *f*. **2.** (*eyelid*) párpado *m*.

lie [laɪ] (*pt sense* 1 **lied**, *pt senses* 2-5 **lay**, *pp sense* 1 **lied**, *pp senses* 2-5 **lain**, *cont all*

senses **lying**) ◆ *n* mentira *f*; **to tell ~s** contar mentiras, mentir. ◆ *vi* **1.** (*tell lie*) mentir; **to ~ to sb** mentirle a alguien. **2.** (*be horizontal, lie down*) tumbarse, echarse; (*be buried*) yacer; **to be lying** estar tumbado(da). **3.** (*be situated*) hallarse. **4.** (*be - solution, attraction*) hallarse, encontrarse. **5.** *phr*: **to ~ low** permanecer escondido(da). ▶ **lie about**, **lie around** *vi* estar OR andar tirado (da). ▶ **lie down** *vi* tumbarse, echarse. ▶ **lie in** *vi* Br quedarse en la cama hasta tarde.

Liechtenstein ['lɪktən,staɪn] *n* Liechtenstein.

lie-down *n* Br siesta *f*.

lie-in *n* Br: **to have a ~** quedarse en la cama hasta tarde.

lieu [ljuː, luː] ▶ **in lieu** *adv*: **in ~ of** en lugar de.

lieutenant [Br lef'tenənt, Am luː'tenənt] *n* teniente *m*.

life [laɪf] (*pl* **lives**) *n* (*gen*) vida *f*; **that's ~!** ¡así es la vida!; **for ~** de por vida, para toda la vida; **to come to ~** (*thing*) cobrar vida; (*person*) reanimarse de pronto; **to scare the ~ out of sb** pegarle a alguien un susto de muerte.

life assurance = **life insurance**.

life belt *n* flotador *m*, salvavidas *m inv*.

lifeboat ['laɪfbəʊt] *n* (*on a ship*) bote *m* salvavidas; (*on shore*) lancha *f* de salvamento.

life buoy *n* flotador *m*, salvavidas *m inv*.

life expectancy [-ɪk'spektənsɪ] *n* expectativa *f* de vida.

lifeguard ['laɪfgɑːd] *n* socorrista *m* y *f*.

life imprisonment [-ɪm'prɪznmənt] *n* cadena *f* perpetua.

life insurance *n* (U) seguro *m* de vida.

life jacket *n* chaleco *m* salvavidas.

lifeless ['laɪflɪs] *adj* **1.** (*dead*) sin vida. **2.** (*listless*) insulso(sa).

lifelike ['laɪflaɪk] *adj* realista, natural.

lifeline ['laɪflaɪn] *n* **1.** (*rope*) cuerda *f* OR cable *m* (de salvamento). **2.** (*something vital for survival*) cordón *m* umbilical.

lifelong ['laɪflɒŋ] *adj* de toda la vida.

life preserver [-prɪ,zɜːvə^r] *n* Am salvavidas *m inv*.

life raft *n* balsa *f* salvavidas.

lifesaver ['laɪf,seɪvə^r] *n* (*person*) socorrista *m* y *f*.

life sentence *n* (condena *f* a) cadena *f* perpetua.

life-size(d) [-saız(d)] *adj* (de) tamaño natural.

lifespan ['laıfspæn] *n* (*of person, animal, plant*) vida *f*.

lifestyle ['laıfstaıl] *n* estilo *m* OR modo *m* de vida.

life-support system *n* aparato *m* de respiración artificial.

lifetime ['laıftaım] *n* vida *f*.

lift [lıft] ◆ *n* 1. (*ride - in car etc*): **to give sb a ~ (somewhere)** acercar OR llevar a alguien (a algún sitio). 2. *Br* (*elevator*) ascensor *m*, elevador *m* *Amer*. ◆ *vt* 1. (*gen*) levantar; **to ~ sthg down** bajar algo. 2. (*plagiarize*) copiar. ◆ *vi* (*disappear - mist*) despejarse.

lift-off *n* despegue *m*.

light [laıt] (*pt* & *pp* **lit** OR **-ed**) ◆ *adj* 1. (*gen*) ligero(ra); (*rain*) fino(na); (*traffic*) escaso(sa). 2. (*not strenuous - duties, responsibilities*) simple; (*- work*) suave; (*- punishment*) leve. 3. (*bright*) luminoso(sa), lleno(na) de luz; **it's growing ~** se hace de día. 4. (*pale - colour*) claro(ra). ◆ *n* 1. (*brightness, source of light*) luz *f*. 2. (*for cigarette, pipe*) fuego *m*, lumbre *f*; **have you got a ~?** ¿tienes fuego? 3. (*perspective*): **in the ~ of** *Br*, **in ~ of** *Am* a la luz de. 4. *phr*: **to come to ~** salir a la luz (pública); **to set ~ to** prender fuego a. ◆ *vt* 1. (*ignite*) encender. 2. (*illuminate*) iluminar. ◆ *adv* con poco equipaje. ▶ **light up** ◆ *vt sep* (*illuminate*) iluminar. ◆ *vi* 1. (*look happy*) iluminarse, encenderse. 2. *inf* (*start smoking*) ponerse a fumar.

light bulb *n* bombilla *f*, foco *m* *Amer*.

lighten ['laıtn] ◆ *vt* 1. (*make brighter - room*) iluminar. 2. (*make less heavy*) aligerar. ◆ *vi* (*brighten*) aclararse.

lighter ['laıtər] *n* (*cigarette lighter*) encendedor *m*, mechero *m*.

light-headed [-'hedıd] *adj* mareado(da).

light-hearted [-'hɑːtıd] *adj* 1. (*cheerful*) alegre. 2. (*amusing*) frívolo(la).

lighthouse ['laıthaus, *pl* -hauzız] *n* faro *m*.

lighting ['laıtıŋ] *n* iluminación *f*; **street ~** alumbrado *m* público.

lightly ['laıtlı] *adv* 1. (*gently*) suavemente. 2. (*slightly*) ligeramente. 3. (*frivolously*) a la ligera.

light meter *n* fotómetro *m*.

lightning ['laıtnıŋ] *n* (U) relámpago *m*.

lightweight ['laıtweıt] ◆ *adj* (*object*) ligero(ra). ◆ *n* (*boxer*) peso *m* ligero.

likable ['laıkəbl] *adj* simpático(ca).

like [laık] ◆ *prep* 1. (*gen*) como; (*in questions or indirect questions*) cómo; **what did it taste ~?** ¿a qué sabía?; **what did it look ~?** ¿cómo era?; **tell me what it's ~** dime cómo es; **something ~ £100** algo así como cien libras; **something ~ that** algo así, algo por el estilo. 2. (*in the same way as*) como, igual que; **~ this/that** así. 3. (*typical of*) propio(pia) OR típico(ca) de. ◆ *vt* 1. (*find pleasant, approve of*): **I ~ it/them** me gusta/gustan; **I ~ cheese** me gusta el queso; **he ~s doing** OR **to do sthg** (a él) le gusta hacer algo. 2. (*want*) querer; **I don't ~ to bother her** no quiero molestarla; **would you ~ some more?** ¿quieres un poco más?; **I'd ~ to come tomorrow** querría OR me gustaría venir mañana; **I'd ~ you to come to dinner** me gustaría que vinieras a cenar; (*in shops, restaurants*): **I'd ~ a kilo of apples/the soup** póngame un kilo de manzanas/la sopa. ◆ *n*: **the ~ of sb/sthg** alguien/algo del estilo. ▶ **likes** *npl* (*things one likes*) gustos *mpl*, preferencias *fpl*.

likeable ['laıkəbl] = **likable**.

likelihood ['laıklıhud] *n* (U) probabilidad *f*.

likely ['laıklı] *adj* 1. (*probable*) probable; **rain is ~** es probable que llueva; **he's ~ to come** es probable que venga. 2. (*suitable*) indicado(da).

liken ['laıkn] *vt*: **to ~ sthg/sb to** comparar algo/a alguien con.

likeness ['laıknıs] *n* 1. (*resemblance*): **~ (to)** parecido *m* (con). 2. (*portrait*) retrato *m*.

likewise ['laıkwaız] *adv* (*similarly*) de la misma forma; **to do ~** hacer lo mismo.

liking ['laıkıŋ] *n*: **to have a ~ for sthg** tener afición *f* por OR a algo; **to take a ~ to sb** tomar OR coger cariño *m* a alguien; **to be to sb's ~** ser del gusto de alguien; **for my/his** *etc* **~** para mi/su *etc* gusto.

lilac ['laılək] ◆ *adj* (*colour*) lila. ◆ *n* 1. (*tree*) lila *f*. 2. (*colour*) lila *m*.

Lilo® ['laıləu] (*pl* -s) *n* *Br* colchoneta *f*, colchón *m* hinchable.

lily ['lılı] *n* lirio *m*, azucena *f*.

lily of the valley (*pl* **lilies of the valley**) *n* lirio *m* de los valles.

limb [lım] *n* 1. (*of body*) miembro *m*, extremidad *f*. 2. (*of tree*) rama *f*.

limber ['lımbər] ▶ **limber up** *vi* desentumecerse.

limbo ['lımbəu] (*pl* -s) *n* (U) (*uncertain state*): **to be in ~** estar en un estado de incertidumbre.

lime [laım] *n* 1. (*fruit*) lima *f*. 2. (*drink*):

~ **(juice)** lima f. **3.** (CHEM) cal f.
limelight ['laɪmlaɪt] n: **in the ~** en (el) candelero.
limerick ['lɪmərɪk] n copla humorística de cinco versos.
limestone ['laɪmstəʊn] n (U) (piedra f) caliza f.
limey ['laɪmɪ] (pl **limeys**) n Am inf término peyorativo que designa a un inglés.
limit ['lɪmɪt] ◆ n **1.** (gen) límite m. **2.** (test of patience): **you're the ~!** inf ¡eres el colmo! **3.** phr: **off ~s** en zona prohibida; **within ~s** dentro de un límite. ◆ vt limitar, restringir.
limitation [,lɪmɪ'teɪʃn] n limitación f.
limited ['lɪmɪtɪd] adj (restricted) limitado (da); **to be ~ to** estar limitado a.
limited (liability) company n sociedad f limitada.
limousine ['lɪməziːn] n limusina f.
limp [lɪmp] ◆ adj flojo(ja). ◆ vi cojear.
limpet ['lɪmpɪt] n lapa f.
line [laɪn] ◆ n **1.** (gen) línea f. **2.** (row) fila f. **3.** (queue) cola f; **to stand** OR **wait in ~** hacer cola. **4.** (course - direction) línea f; (- of action) camino m; **what's his ~ of business?** ¿a qué negocios se dedica? **5.** (length - of rope) cuerda f; (- for fishing) sedal m; (- of wire) hilo m. **6.** (TELEC): **(telephone) ~** línea f (telefónica); **hold the ~, please** no cuelgue, por favor; **the ~ is busy** está comunicando; **it's a bad ~** hay interferencias. **7.** (on page) línea f, renglón m; (of poem, song) verso m; (letter): **to drop sb a ~** inf mandar unas letras a alguien. **8.** (system of transport): **(railway) ~** (track) vía f (férrea); (route) línea f (férrea). **9.** (wrinkle) arruga f. **10.** (borderline) límite m. **11.** (COMM) línea f. **12.** phr: **to draw the ~ at sthg** no pasar por algo, negarse a algo. ◆ vt (coat, curtains) forrar; (drawer) cubrir el interior de. ► **out of line** adv: **to be out of ~** estar fuera de lugar. ► **line up** ◆ vt sep **1.** (make into a row or queue) alinear. **2.** (arrange) programar, organizar. ◆ vi (form a queue) alinearse.
lined [laɪnd] adj **1.** (of paper) de rayas. **2.** (wrinkled) arrugado(da).
linen ['lɪnɪn] n **1.** (cloth) lino m. **2.** (tablecloths, sheets) ropa f blanca OR de hilo; **bed ~** ropa f de cama.
liner ['laɪnər] n (ship) transatlántico m.
linesman ['laɪnzmən] (pl **-men** [-mən]) n juez m y f de línea.
lineup ['laɪnʌp] n **1.** (of players, competitors) alineación f. **2.** Am (identification parade) rueda f de identificación.

linger ['lɪŋgər] vi **1.** (remain - over activity) entretenerse; (- in a place) rezagarse. **2.** (persist) persistir.
lingerie ['lænʒərɪ] n ropa f interior femenina.
lingo ['lɪŋgəʊ] (pl **-es**) n inf (foreign language) idioma m; (jargon) jerga f.
linguist ['lɪŋgwɪst] n **1.** (someone good at languages) persona f con facilidad para las lenguas. **2.** (student or teacher of linguistics) lingüista m y f.
linguistics [lɪŋ'gwɪstɪks] n (U) lingüística f.
lining ['laɪnɪŋ] n **1.** (gen & AUT) forro m. **2.** (of stomach, nose) paredes fpl interiores.
link [lɪŋk] ◆ n **1.** (of chain) eslabón m. **2.** (connection) conexión f, enlace m; **~s (between/with)** lazos mpl (entre/con), vínculos mpl (entre/con). ◆ vt **1.** (connect - cities) comunicar; (- computers) conectar; (- facts) relacionar; **to ~ sthg with** OR **to** relacionar OR asociar algo con. **2.** (join - arms) enlazar. ► **link up** vt sep: **to ~ sthg up (with)** conectar algo (con).
links [lɪŋks] (pl inv) n campo m de golf.
lino ['laɪnəʊ], **linoleum** [lɪ'nəʊljəm] n linóleo m.
lintel ['lɪntl] n dintel m.
lion ['laɪən] n león m.
lioness ['laɪənes] n leona f.
lip [lɪp] n **1.** (of mouth) labio m. **2.** (of cup) borde m; (of jug) pico m.
lip-read vi leer en los labios.
lip salve [-sælv] n Br vaselina® f, cacao m.
lip service n: **to pay ~ to sthg** hablar en favor de algo sin hacer nada al respeto.
lipstick ['lɪpstɪk] n **1.** (container) lápiz m OR barra f de labios. **2.** (substance) carmín m, lápiz m de labios.
liqueur [lɪ'kjʊər] n licor m.
liquid ['lɪkwɪd] ◆ adj líquido(da). ◆ n líquido m.
liquidation [,lɪkwɪ'deɪʃn] n liquidación f.
liquid crystal display n pantalla f de cristal líquido.
liquidize, -ise ['lɪkwɪdaɪz] vt Br licuar.
liquidizer ['lɪkwɪdaɪzər] n Br licuadora f.
liquor ['lɪkər] n (U) alcohol m, bebida f alcohólica.
liquorice ['lɪkərɪʃ, 'lɪkərɪs] n (U) regaliz m.
liquor store n Am tienda donde se venden

bebidas alcohólicas para llevar.
Lisbon ['lɪzbən] *n* Lisboa.
lisp [lɪsp] ◆ *n* ceceo *m*. ◆ *vi* cecear.
list [lɪst] ◆ *n* lista *f*. ◆ *vt* 1. (*in writing*) hacer una lista de. 2. (*in speech*) enumerar. ◆ *vi* (NAUT) escorar.
listed building [,lɪstɪd-] *n* Br edificio declarado de interés histórico y artístico.
listen ['lɪsn] *vi* 1. (*give attention*): **to ~ (to sthg/sb)** escuchar (algo/a alguien); **to ~ for** estar atento a. 2. (*heed advice*): **to ~ (to sb/sthg)** hacer caso (a alguien/de algo); **to ~ to reason** atender a razones.
listener ['lɪsnər] *n* 1. (*person listening*) oyente *m* y *f*. 2. (*to radio*) radioyente *m* y *f*.
listless ['lɪstlɪs] *adj* apático(ca).
lit [lɪt] *pt* & *pp* → **light**.
litany ['lɪtənɪ] (*pl* **-ies**) *n* lit & fig letanía *f*.
liter Am = **litre**.
literacy ['lɪtərəsɪ] *n* alfabetización *f*.
literal ['lɪtərəl] *adj* literal.
literally ['lɪtərəlɪ] *adv* literalmente; **to take sthg ~** tomarse algo al pie de la letra.
literary ['lɪtərərɪ] *adj* 1. (*gen*) literario (ria). 2. (*person*) literato(ta).
literate ['lɪtərət] *adj* 1. (*able to read and write*) alfabetizado(da). 2. (*well-read*) culto(ta), instruido(da).
literature ['lɪtrətʃər] *n* 1. (*novels, plays, poetry*) literatura *f*. 2. (*books on a particular subject*) publicaciones *fpl*. 3. (*printed information*) documentación *f*.
lithe [laɪð] *adj* ágil.
Lithuania [,lɪθju'eɪnɪə] *n* Lituania.
litigation [,lɪtɪ'geɪʃn] *n* fml litigio *m*.
litre Br, **liter** Am ['liːtər] *n* litro *m*.
litter ['lɪtər] ◆ *n* 1. (*waste material*) basura *f*. 2. (*newborn animals*) camada *f*. ◆ *vt*: **papers ~ed the floor** los papeles estaban esparcidos por el suelo.
litterbin ['lɪtə,bɪn] *n* Br papelera *f*.
little ['lɪtl] (*compar sense 3* **less**, *superl sense 3* **least**) ◆ *adj* 1. (*small in size, younger*) pequeño(ña). 2. (*short in length*) corto (ta); **a ~ while** un ratito. 3. (*not much*) poco(ca); **he speaks ~ English** habla poco inglés; **he speaks a ~ English** habla un poco de inglés. ◆ *pron*: **I understood very ~** entendí muy poco; **a ~** un poco; **a ~ (bit)** un poco; **give me a ~ (bit)** dame un poco. ◆ *adv* poco; **~ by ~** poco a poco.
little finger *n* dedo *m* meñique.
live¹ [lɪv] ◆ *vi* (*gen*) vivir. ◆ *vt* llevar; **to ~ a quiet life** llevar una vida tranquila.

▶ **live down** *vt sep* lograr hacer olvidar.
▶ **live off** *vt fus* (*savings, land*) vivir de; (*people*) vivir a costa de. ▶ **live on** ◆ *vt fus* 1. (*survive on*) vivir con OR de. 2. (*eat*) vivir de. ◆ *vi* (*memory, feeling*) permanecer, perdurar. ▶ **live together** *vi* vivir juntos. ▶ **live up to** *vt fus* estar a la altura de. ▶ **live with** *vt fus* 1. (*live in same house as*) vivir con. 2. (*accept - situation, problem*) aceptar.
live² [laɪv] *adj* 1. (*living*) vivo(va). 2. (*burning*) encendido(da). 3. (*unexploded*) sin explotar. 4. (ELEC) cargado (da). 5. (*performance*) en directo.
livelihood ['laɪvlɪhʊd] *n* sustento *m*, medio *m* de vida.
lively ['laɪvlɪ] *adj* 1. (*person, debate, time*) animado(da). 2. (*mind*) agudo(da), perspicaz. 3. (*colours*) vivo(va), llamativo(va).
liven ['laɪvn] ▶ **liven up** ◆ *vt sep* animar. ◆ *vi* animarse.
liver ['lɪvər] *n* hígado *m*.
livery ['lɪvərɪ] *n* (*of servant*) librea *f*; (*of company*) uniforme *m*.
lives [laɪvz] *pl* → **life**.
livestock ['laɪvstɒk] *n* ganado *m*.
livid ['lɪvɪd] *adj* 1. (*angry*) furioso(sa). 2. (*blue-grey*) lívido(da).
living ['lɪvɪŋ] ◆ *adj* (*relatives, language*) vivo(va); (*artist etc*) contemporáneo(a). ◆ *n* 1. (*means of earning money*): **what do you do for a ~?** ¿cómo te ganas la vida? 2. (*lifestyle*) vida *f*.
living conditions *npl* condiciones *fpl* de vida.
living room *n* cuarto *m* de estar, salón *m*.
living standards *npl* nivel *m* de vida.
living wage *n* salario *m* OR sueldo *m* mínimo.
lizard ['lɪzəd] *n* (*small*) lagartija *f*; (*big*) lagarto *m*.
llama ['lɑːmə] (*pl inv* OR **-s**) *n* llama *f*.
load [ləʊd] ◆ *n* 1. (*something carried*) carga *f*. 2. (*amount of work*): **a heavy/light ~** mucho/poco trabajo. 3. (*large amount*): **~s of** inf montones OR un montón de; **it was a ~ of rubbish** inf fue una porquería. ◆ *vt* 1. (*gen* & COMPUT): **to ~ sthg/sb (with)** cargar algo/a alguien (de). 2. (*camera, video recorder*): **he ~ed the camera with a film** cargó la cámara con una película. ▶ **load up** *vt sep* & *vi* cargar.
loaded ['ləʊdɪd] *adj* 1. (*question, statement*) con doble sentido OR intención. 2. inf (*rich*) forrado(da).

loading bay ['ləʊdɪŋ-] n zona f de carga y descarga.

loaf [ləʊf] (pl **loaves**) n (of bread) (barra f de) pan m.

loafer ['ləʊfər] n (shoe) mocasín m.

loan [ləʊn] ◆ n (something lent) préstamo m; **on ~** prestado(da). ◆ vt prestar; **to ~ sthg to sb, to ~ sb sthg** prestar algo a alguien.

loath [ləʊθ] adj: **to be ~ to do sthg** ser reacio(cia) a hacer algo.

loathe [ləʊð] vt: **to ~ (doing sthg)** aborrecer OR detestar (hacer algo).

loathsome ['ləʊðsəm] adj (smell) repugnante; (person, behaviour) odioso (sa).

loaves [ləʊvz] pl → **loaf**.

lob [lɒb] n (TENNIS) lob m.

lobby ['lɒbɪ] ◆ n 1. (hall) vestíbulo m. 2. (pressure group) grupo m de presión, lobby m. ◆ vt ejercer presión (política) sobre.

lobe [ləʊb] n lóbulo m.

lobster ['lɒbstər] n langosta f.

local ['ləʊkl] ◆ adj local. ◆ n inf 1. (person): **the ~s** (in village) los lugareños; (in town) los vecinos del lugar. 2. Br (pub) bar m del barrio. 3. Am (bus, train) omnibús m.

local authority n Br autoridad f local.

local call n llamada f local.

local government n gobierno m municipal.

locality [ləʊ'kælətɪ] n localidad f.

locally ['ləʊkəlɪ] adv 1. (on local basis) en el lugar. 2. (nearby) por la zona.

locate [Br ləʊ'keɪt, Am 'ləʊkeɪt] vt 1. (find) localizar. 2. (situate) ubicar.

location [ləʊ'keɪʃn] n 1. (place) localización f, situación f. 2. (CINEMA): **on ~** en exteriores.

loch [lɒk, lɒx] n Scot lago m.

lock [lɒk] ◆ n 1. (of door) cerradura f; (of bicycle) candado m. 2. (on canal) esclusa f. 3. (AUT) (steering lock) ángulo m de giro. 4. literary (of hair) mechón m. ◆ vt 1. (with key) cerrar con llave; (with padlock) cerrar con candado. 2. (keep safely) poner bajo llave. 3. (immobilize) bloquear. ◆ vi 1. (with key) cerrarse con llave; (with padlock) cerrarse con candado. 2. (become immobilized) bloquearse. ▶ **lock in** vt sep encerrar. ▶ **lock out** vt sep 1. (accidentally) dejar fuera al cerrar accidentalmente la puerta; **to ~ o.s. out** quedarse fuera (por olvidarse la llave dentro). 2. (deliberately) dejar fuera a. ▶ **lock up** vt sep

locker ['lɒkər] n taquilla f, armario m.

locker room n Am vestuario m con taquillas.

locket ['lɒkɪt] n guardapelo m.

locksmith ['lɒksmɪθ] n cerrajero m, -ra f.

locomotive ['ləʊkə,məʊtɪv] n locomotora f.

locum ['ləʊkəm] (pl **-s**) n interino m, -na f.

locust ['ləʊkəst] n langosta f.

lodge [lɒdʒ] ◆ n 1. (caretaker's etc room) portería f. 2. (of manor house) casa f del guarda. 3. (of freemasons) logia f. 4. (for hunting) refugio m de caza. ◆ vi 1. (stay): **to ~ (with sb)** alojarse (con alguien). 2. (become stuck) alojarse. ◆ vt fml (register) presentar.

lodger ['lɒdʒər] n huésped m y f.

lodging ['lɒdʒɪŋ] → **board**. ▶ **lodgings** npl habitación f (alquilada).

loft [lɒft] n (in house) desván m, entretecho m Amer; (for hay) pajar m.

lofty ['lɒftɪ] adj 1. (noble) noble, elevado(da). 2. pej (haughty) arrogante, altanero(ra). 3. literary (high) elevado (da).

log [lɒg] ◆ n 1. (of wood) tronco m. 2. (written record - of ship) diario m de a bordo; (- of plane) diario m de vuelo. ◆ vt anotar. ▶ **log in** vi (COMPUT) entrar (en el sistema). ▶ **log out** vi (COMPUT) salir (del sistema).

logbook ['lɒgbʊk] n 1. (of ship) diario m de a bordo; (of plane) diario m de vuelo. 2. (of car) documentación f.

loggerheads ['lɒgəhedz] n: **to be at ~** estar a matar.

logic ['lɒdʒɪk] n lógica f.

logical ['lɒdʒɪkl] adj lógico(ca).

logistics [lə'dʒɪstɪks] ◆ n (U) logística f. ◆ npl logística f.

logo ['ləʊgəʊ] (pl **-s**) n logotipo m.

loin [lɔɪn] n lomo m.

loiter ['lɔɪtər] vi (for bad purpose) merodear; (hang around) vagar.

loll [lɒl] vi 1. (sit, lie about) repantigarse. 2. (hang down) colgar.

lollipop ['lɒlɪpɒp] n pirulí m.

lollipop lady n Br mujer encargada de parar el tráfico en un paso de cebra para que crucen los niños.

lollipop man n Br hombre encargado de parar el tráfico en un paso de cebra para que crucen los niños.

lolly ['lɒlɪ] *n inf* **1.** (*lollipop*) pirulí *m*. **2.** Br (*ice lolly*) polo *m*.

London ['lʌndən] *n* Londres.

Londoner ['lʌndənəʳ] *n* londinense *m y f*.

lone [ləʊn] *adj* solitario(ria).

loneliness ['ləʊnlɪnɪs] *n* soledad *f*.

lonely ['ləʊnlɪ] *adj* **1.** (*person*) solo(la). **2.** (*time, childhood*) solitario(ria). **3.** (*place*) solitario(ria), aislado(da).

lonesome ['ləʊnsəm] *adj Am inf* **1.** (*person*) solo(la). **2.** (*place*) solitario(ria).

long [lɒŋ] ◆ *adj* largo(ga); **two days ~** de dos días de duración; **the table is 5m ~** la mesa mide OR tiene 5m de largo; **the journey is 50km ~** el viaje es de 50 km; **the book is 500 pages ~** el libro tiene 500 páginas. ◆ *adv* mucho tiempo; **how ~ will it take?** ¿cuánto se tarda?; **how ~ will you be?** ¿cuánto tardarás?; **how ~ have you been waiting?** ¿cuánto tiempo llevas esperando?; **how ~ is the journey?** ¿cuánto hay de viaje?; **I'm no ~er young** ya no soy joven; **I can't wait any ~er** no puedo esperar más; **so ~** *inf* hasta luego OR pronto; **before ~** pronto; **for ~** mucho tiempo. ◆ *vt*: **to ~ to do sthg** desear ardientemente hacer algo. ▶ **as long as, so long as** *conj* mientras; **as ~ as you do it, so will I** siempre y cuando tú lo hagas, yo también lo haré. ▶ **long for** *vt fus* desear ardientemente.

long-distance *adj* (*runner*) de fondo; (*lorry driver*) para distancias grandes.

long-distance call *n* conferencia *f* (telefónica).

longhand ['lɒŋhænd] *n* escritura *f* a mano.

long-haul *adj* de larga distancia.

longing ['lɒŋɪŋ] ◆ *adj* anhelante. ◆ *n* **1.** (*desire*) anhelo *m*, deseo *m*; (*nostalgia*) nostalgia *f*, añoranza *f*. **2.** (*strong wish*): **(a) ~ (for)** (un) ansia *f* (de).

longitude ['lɒndʒɪtjuːd] *n* longitud *f*.

long jump *n* salto *m* de longitud.

long-life *adj* de larga duración.

long-playing record [-'pleɪɪŋ-] *n* disco *m* de larga duración.

long-range *adj* **1.** (*missile, bomber*) de largo alcance. **2.** (*plan, forecast*) a largo plazo.

long shot *n* posibilidad *f* remota.

longsighted [lɒŋ'saɪtɪd] *adj* présbita.

long-sleeved *adj* de manga larga.

long-standing *adj* antiguo(gua).

longsuffering [lɒŋ'sʌfərɪŋ] *adj* sufrido(da).

long term *n*: **in the ~** a largo plazo.

long wave *n* (U) onda *f* larga.

long weekend *n* puente *m*.

longwinded [lɒŋ'wɪndɪd] *adj* prolijo (ja).

loo [luː] (*pl* -s) *n Br inf* wáter *m*.

look [lʊk] ◆ *n* **1.** (*with eyes*) mirada *f*; **to give sb a ~** dirigir la mirada hacia OR a alguien; **to take** OR **have a ~ (at sthg)** echar una mirada OR ojeada (a algo). **2.** (*search*): **to have a ~ (for sthg)** buscar (algo). **3.** (*appearance*) aspecto *m*; **by the ~** OR **~s of it, it has been here for ages** parece que hace años que está aquí. ◆ *vi* **1.** (*with eyes*): **to ~ (at sthg/sb)** mirar (algo/a alguien). **2.** (*search*): **to ~ (for sthg/sb)** buscar (algo/a alguien). **3.** (*building, window*): **to ~ (out) onto** dar a. **4.** (*have stated appearance*) verse; (*seem*) parecer; **it ~s like rain** OR **as if it will rain** parece que va a llover; **she ~s like her mother** se parece a su madre. ◆ *vt* **1.** (*look at*) mirar. **2.** (*appear*): **to ~ one's age** representar la edad que se tiene. ▶ **looks** *npl* belleza *f*. ▶ **look after** *vt fus* **1.** (*take care of*) cuidar. **2.** (*be responsible for*) encargarse de. ▶ **look at** *vt fus* **1.** (*see, glance at*) mirar; (*examine*) examinar. **2.** (*judge*) estudiar. ▶ **look down on** *vt fus* (*condescend to*) despreciar. ▶ **look for** *vt fus* buscar. ▶ **look forward to** *vt fus* esperar (con ilusión). ▶ **look into** *vt fus* (*problem, possibility*) estudiar; (*issue*) investigar. ▶ **look on** *vi* mirar, observar. ▶ **look out** *vi* tener cuidado; **~ out!** ¡cuidado! ▶ **look out for** *vt fus* estar atento(ta) a. ▶ **look round** ◆ *vt fus* (*shop*) echar un vistazo; (*castle, town*) visitar. ◆ *vi* volver la cabeza. ▶ **look to** *vt fus* **1.** (*depend on*) recurrir a. **2.** (*think about*) pensar en. ▶ **look up** ◆ *vt sep* **1.** (*in book*) buscar. **2.** (*visit - person*) ir a ver OR visitar. ◆ *vi* (*improve*) mejorar. ▶ **look up to** *vt fus* respetar, admirar.

lookout ['lʊkaʊt] *n* **1.** (*place*) puesto *m* de observación. **2.** (*person*) centinela *m y f*. **3.** (*search*): **to be on the ~ for** estar al acecho de.

loom [luːm] ◆ *n* telar *m*. ◆ *vi* **1.** (*rise up*) surgir OR aparecer amenazante. **2.** *fig* (*be imminent*) ser inminente. ▶ **loom up** *vi* divisarse sombríamente.

loony ['luːnɪ] *inf* ◆ *adj* majara. ◆ *n* majara *m y f*.

loop [luːp] *n* **1.** (*shape*) lazo *m*. **2.** (COMPUT) bucle *m*.

loophole ['luːphəʊl] *n* laguna *f*.

loose [lu:s] *adj* 1. (*not firmly fixed*) flojo (ja). 2. (*unattached - paper, sweets, hair*) suelto(ta). 3. (*clothes, fit*) holgado(da). 4. *dated* (*promiscuous*) promiscuo(cua). 5. (*inexact - translation*) impreciso(sa).

loose change *n* (dinero *m*) suelto *m*.

loose end *n*: **to be at a ~** Br, **to be at ~s** Am estar desocupado(da).

loosely ['lu:slɪ] *adv* 1. (*not firmly*) holgadamente, sin apretar. 2. (*inexactly*) vagamente.

loosen ['lu:sn] *vt* aflojar. ► **loosen up** *vi* 1. (*before game, race*) desentumecerse. 2. *inf* (*relax*) relajarse.

loot [lu:t] ◆ *n* botín *m*. ◆ *vt* saquear.

looting ['lu:tɪŋ] *n* saqueo *m*.

lop [lɒp] *vt* podar. ► **lop off** *vt sep* cortar.

lop-sided [-'saɪdɪd] *adj* 1. (*uneven*) ladeado(da), torcido(da). 2. *fig* (*biased*) desequilibrado(da).

lord [lɔ:d] *n* Br (*man of noble rank*) noble *m*. ► **Lord** *n* 1. (RELIG): **the Lord** (*God*) el Señor; **good Lord!** Br ¡Dios mío! 2. (*in titles*) lord *m*; (*as form of address*): **my Lord** (*bishop*) su Ilustrísima; (*judge*) su Señoría. ► **Lords** *npl* Br (POL): **the Lords** la Cámara de los Lores.

lordly ['lɔ:dlɪ] *adj* (*noble*) señorial.

Lordship ['lɔ:dʃɪp] *n*: **your/his ~** su Señoría *f*.

lore [lɔ:ʳ] *n* (U) saber *m* OR tradición *f* popular.

lorry ['lɒrɪ] *n* Br camión *m*.

lorry driver *n* Br camionero *m*, -ra *f*.

lose [lu:z] (*pt & pp* **lost**) ◆ *vt* (*gen*) perder; (*subj: clock, watch*) atrasarse; **to ~ sight of sthg/sb** *lit & fig* perder de vista algo/a alguien; **to ~ one's way** perderse. ◆ *vi* (*fail to win*) perder.

loser ['lu:zəʳ] *n* 1. (*of competition*) perdedor *m*, -ra *f*. 2. *inf pej* (*unsuccessful person*) desgraciado *m*, -da *f*.

loss [lɒs] *n* 1. (*gen*) pérdida *f*; **to make a ~** sufrir pérdidas. 2. (*failure to win*) derrota *f*. 3. *phr*: **to be at a ~ to explain sthg** no saber cómo explicar algo.

lost [lɒst] ◆ *pt & pp* → **lose**. ◆ *adj* 1. (*unable to find way*) perdido(da); **to get ~** perderse; **get ~!** *inf* ¡vete a la porra! 2. (*that cannot be found*) extraviado(da), perdido(da).

lost-and-found office *n* Am oficina *f* de objetos perdidos.

lost property office *n* Br oficina *f* de objetos perdidos.

lot [lɒt] *n* 1. (*large amount*): **a ~ of**, **~s of** mucho(cha); **a ~ of people** mucha gente, muchas personas; **a ~ of problems** muchos problemas; **the ~** todo. 2. (*group, set*) grupo *m*. 3. (*destiny*) destino *m*, suerte *f*. 4. Am (*of land*) terreno *m*; (*car park*) aparcamiento *m*. 5. (*at auction*) partida *f*, lote *m*. 6. *phr*: **to draw ~s** echar a suerte. ► **a lot** *adv* mucho.

lotion ['ləʊʃn] *n* loción *f*.

lottery ['lɒtərɪ] *n* lotería *f*.

loud [laʊd] ◆ *adj* 1. (*voice, music*) alto (ta); (*bang*) fuerte; (*person*) ruidoso(sa). 2. (*emphatic*): **to be ~ in one's criticism of** ser enérgico(ca) en la crítica de. 3. (*too bright*) chillón(ona). ◆ *adv* fuerte; **out ~** en voz alta.

loudhailer [,laʊd'heɪləʳ] *n* Br megáfono *m*.

loudly ['laʊdlɪ] *adv* 1. (*shout*) a voz en grito; (*talk*) en voz alta. 2. (*gaudily*) con colores chillones OR llamativos.

loudspeaker [,laʊd'spi:kəʳ] *n* altavoz *m*.

lounge [laʊndʒ] ◆ *n* 1. (*in house*) salón *m*. 2. (*in airport*) sala *f* de espera. ◆ *vi* repantigarse.

lounge bar *n* Br salón-bar *m*.

louse [laʊs] (*pl* **lice**) *n* (*insect*) piojo *m*.

lousy ['laʊzɪ] *adj inf* (*poor quality*) fatal, pésimo(ma).

lout [laʊt] *n* gamberro *m*.

louvre Br, **louver** Am ['lu:vəʳ] *n* persiana *f*.

lovable ['lʌvəbl] *adj* adorable.

love [lʌv] ◆ *n* 1. (*gen*) amor *m*; **give her my ~** dale un abrazo de mi parte; **~ from** (*at end of letter*) un abrazo de; **to be in ~ (with)** estar enamorado(da) (de); **to fall in ~** enamorarse; **to make ~** hacer el amor. 2. (*liking, interest*) pasión *f*; **a ~ of** OR **for** una pasión por. 3. *inf* (*form of address*) cariño *m* y *f*. 4. (TENNIS): **30 ~** 30 a nada. ◆ *vt* 1. (*feel affection for*) amar, querer. 2. (*like*): **I ~ football** me encanta el fútbol; **I ~ going to** OR **to go to the theatre** me encanta ir al teatro.

love affair *n* aventura *f* amorosa.

love life *n* vida *f* amorosa.

lovely ['lʌvlɪ] *adj* 1. (*beautiful - person*) encantador(ra); (- *dress, place*) precioso (sa). 2. (*pleasant*) estupendo(da).

lover ['lʌvəʳ] *n* 1. (*sexual partner*) amante *m* y *f*. 2. (*enthusiast*) amante *m* y *f*, apasionado *m*, -da *f*.

love song *n* canción *f* de amor.

loving ['lʌvɪŋ] *adj* cariñoso(sa).

low [ləʊ] ◆ *adj* 1. (*gen*) bajo(ja); **in the ~ twenties** 20 y algo; **a ~ trick** una mala jugada. 2. (*little remaining*) escaso(sa).

3. (*unfavourable - opinion*) malo(la); (*- esteem*) poco(ca). **4.** (*dim*) tenue. **5.** (*dress, neckline*) escotado(da). **6.** (*depressed*) deprimido(da). ◆ *adv* **1.** (*gen*) bajo; **morale is very ~** la moral está por los suelos; **~ paid** mal pagado. **2.** (*speak*) en voz baja. ◆ *n* **1.** (*low point*) punto *m* más bajo. **2.** (METEOR) área *f* de bajas presiones.

low-calorie *adj* light (*inv*), bajo(ja) en calorías.

low-cut *adj* escotado(da).

lower ['ləʊə^r] ◆ *adj* inferior. ◆ *vt* **1.** (*gen*) bajar; (*flag*) arriar. **2.** (*reduce*) reducir.

low-fat *adj* bajo(ja) en grasas.

low-key *adj* discreto(ta).

lowly ['ləʊlɪ] *adj* humilde.

low-lying *adj* bajo(ja).

loyal ['lɔɪəl] *adj* leal, fiel.

loyalty ['lɔɪəltɪ] *n* lealtad *f*.

lozenge ['lɒzɪndʒ] *n* **1.** (*tablet*) tableta *f*, pastilla *f*. **2.** (*shape*) rombo *m*.

LP (*abbr of* **long-playing record**) *n* LP *m*.

L-plate *n* Br placa *f* L (de prácticas).

Ltd, ltd (*abbr of* **limited**) S.L.

lubricant ['lu:brɪkənt] *n* lubricante *m*.

lubricate ['lu:brɪkeɪt] *vt* lubricar, engrasar.

lucid ['lu:sɪd] *adj* **1.** (*clear*) claro(ra). **2.** (*not confused*) lúcido(da).

luck [lʌk] *n* suerte *f*; **good/bad ~** (*good, bad fortune*) buena/mala suerte; **good ~!** (*said to express best wishes*) ¡buena suerte!; **bad** OR **hard ~!** ¡mala suerte!; **to be in** ~ estar de suerte; **with (any) ~** con un poco de suerte.

luckily ['lʌkɪlɪ] *adv* afortunadamente.

lucky ['lʌkɪ] *adj* **1.** (*fortunate - person*) afortunado(da); (*- event*) oportuno(na). **2.** (*bringing good luck*) que trae buena suerte.

lucrative ['lu:krətɪv] *adj* lucrativo(va).

ludicrous ['lu:dɪkrəs] *adj* absurdo(da).

lug [lʌg] *vt inf* arrastrar, tirar con dificultad.

luggage ['lʌgɪdʒ] *n* Br equipaje *m*.

luggage rack *n* Br (*of car*) baca *f*, portaequipajes *m inv*; (*in train*) redecilla *f*.

lukewarm ['lu:kwɔ:m] *adj* **1.** (*tepid*) tibio(bia), templado(da). **2.** (*unenthusiastic*) indiferente, desapasionado(da).

lull [lʌl] ◆ *n*: **~ (in)** (*activity*) respiro *m* OR pausa *f* (en); (*fighting*) tregua *f* (en). ◆ *vt*: **to ~ sb into a false sense of security** infundir una sensación de falsa seguridad a alguien; **to ~ sb to sleep** adormecer OR hacer dormir a alguien.

lullaby ['lʌləbaɪ] *n* nana *f*, canción *f* de cuna.

lumber ['lʌmbə^r] *n* (U) **1.** Am (*timber*) maderos *mpl*. **2.** Br (*bric-a-brac*) trastos *mpl*. ▶ **lumber with** *vt sep* Br *inf*: **to ~ sb with sthg** cargar a alguien con algo.

lumberjack ['lʌmbədʒæk] *n* leñador *m*, -ra *f*.

luminous ['lu:mɪnəs] *adj* luminoso(sa).

lump [lʌmp] ◆ *n* **1.** (*of coal, earth*) trozo *m*; (*of sugar*) terrón *m*; (*in sauce*) grumo *m*. **2.** (*on body*) bulto *m*. **3.** *fig* (*in throat*) nudo *m*. ◆ *vt*: **to ~ sthg together** (*things*) amontonar algo; (*people, beliefs*) agrupar OR juntar algo.

lump sum *n* suma *f* OR cantidad *f* global.

lumpy ['lʌmpɪ] (*compar* -ier, *superl* -iest) *adj* (*sauce*) grumoso(sa); (*mattress*) lleno(na) de bultos.

lunacy ['lu:nəsɪ] *n* locura *f*.

lunar ['lu:nə^r] *adj* lunar.

lunatic ['lu:nətɪk] *n* **1.** *pej* (*fool*) idiota *m* y *f*. **2.** (*insane person*) loco *m*, -ca *f*.

lunch [lʌntʃ] ◆ *n* comida *f*, almuerzo *m*. ◆ *vi* almorzar, comer.

luncheon ['lʌntʃən] *n fml* comida *f*, almuerzo *m*.

luncheon meat *n* carne de cerdo en lata troceada.

luncheon voucher *n* Br vale *m* del almuerzo.

lunch hour *n* hora *f* del almuerzo.

lunchtime ['lʌntʃtaɪm] *n* hora *f* del almuerzo.

lung [lʌŋ] *n* pulmón *m*.

lunge [lʌndʒ] *vi* lanzarse, abalanzarse; **to ~ at sb** arremeter contra alguien.

lurch [lɜ:tʃ] ◆ *n* (*of boat*) bandazo *m*; (*of person*) tumbo *m*; **to leave sb in the ~** dejar a alguien en la estacada. ◆ *vi* (*boat*) dar bandazos; (*person*) tambalearse.

lure [ljʊə^r] ◆ *n* atracción *f*. ◆ *vt* atraer OR convencer con engaños.

lurid ['ljʊərɪd] *adj* **1.** (*brightly coloured*) chillón(ona). **2.** (*shockingly unpleasant*) espeluznante.

lurk [lɜ:k] *vi* **1.** (*person*) estar al acecho. **2.** (*memory, danger, fear*) ocultarse.

luscious ['lʌʃəs] *adj lit* & *fig* apetitoso(sa).

lush [lʌʃ] *adj* (*luxuriant*) exuberante.

lust [lʌst] *n* **1.** (*sexual desire*) lujuria *f*. **2.** (*strong desire*): **~ for sthg** ansia *f* de algo. ▶ **lust after, lust for** *vt fus* **1.** (*desire - wealth, success*) codiciar. **2.** (*desire sexually*) desear.

lusty ['lʌstɪ] *adj* vigoroso(sa), fuerte.

Luxembourg ['lʌksəm,bɜːg] *n* Luxemburgo.

luxuriant [lʌg'ʒʊərɪənt] *adj* exuberante.

luxurious [lʌg'ʒʊərɪəs] *adj* **1.** (*expensive*) lujoso(sa). **2.** (*pleasurable*) voluptuoso (sa).

luxury ['lʌkʃərɪ] ◆ *n* lujo *m*. ◆ *comp* de lujo.

LW (*abbr of* **long wave**) *n* OL *f*.

Lycra® ['laɪkrə] *n* lycra® *f*.

lying ['laɪɪŋ] ◆ *adj* mentiroso(sa), falso (sa). ◆ *n* (U) mentira *f*.

lynch [lɪntʃ] *vt* linchar.

lyric ['lɪrɪk] *adj* lírico(ca).

lyrical ['lɪrɪkl] *adj* (*poetic*) lírico(ca).

lyrics ['lɪrɪks] *npl* letra *f*.

m¹ (*pl* **m's** OR **ms**), **M** (*pl* **M's** OR **Ms**) [em] *n* (*letter*) m *f*, M *f*. ► **M** *abbr of* **motorway**.

m² **1.** (*abbr of* **metre**) m. **2.** (*abbr of* **million**) m. **3.** *abbr of* **mile**.

MA *n abbr of* **Master of Arts**.

mac [mæk] (*abbr of* **mackintosh**) *n* Br *inf* (*coat*) impermeable *m*.

macaroni [,mækə'rəʊnɪ] *n* (U) macarrones *mpl*.

mace [meɪs] *n* **1.** (*ornamental rod*) maza *f*. **2.** (*spice*) macis *f inv*.

machine [mə'ʃiːn] ◆ *n* **1.** (*power-driven device*) máquina *f*. **2.** (*organization*) aparato *m*. ◆ *vt* **1.** (SEWING) coser a máquina. **2.** (TECH) hacer con una máquina.

machinegun [mə'ʃiːngʌn] *n* ametralladora *f*.

machine language *n* (COMPUT) lenguaje *m* máquina.

machinery [mə'ʃiːnərɪ] *n lit & fig* maquinaria *f*.

macho ['mætʃəʊ] *adj inf* macho.

mackerel ['mækrəl] (*pl inv* OR **-s**) *n* caballa *f*.

mackintosh ['mækɪntɒʃ] *n* Br impermeable *m*.

mad [mæd] *adj* **1.** (*gen*) loco(ca); (*attempt, idea*) disparatado(da); **to be ~ about** sb/sthg estar loco(ca) por alguien/algo; **to go ~** volverse loco.

2. (*furious*) furioso(sa). **3.** (*hectic*) desenfrenado(da).

Madagascar [,mædə'gæskəʳ] *n* Madagascar.

madam ['mædəm] *n* señora *f*.

madcap ['mædkæp] *adj* descabellado (da).

madden ['mædn] *vt* volver loco(ca).

made [meɪd] *pt & pp* → **make**.

Madeira [mə'dɪərə] *n* **1.** (*wine*) madeira *m*, madera *m*. **2.** (GEOGR) Madeira.

made-to-measure *adj* hecho(cha) a la medida.

made-up *adj* **1.** (*with make-up - face, person*) maquillado(da); (*- lips, eyes*) pintado(da). **2.** (*invented*) inventado(da).

madly ['mædlɪ] *adv* (*frantically*) enloquecidamente; **~ in love** locamente enamorado.

madman ['mædmən] (*pl* **-men** [-mən]) *n* loco *m*.

madness ['mædnɪs] *n* locura *f*.

Madrid [mə'drɪd] *n* Madrid.

Mafia ['mæfɪə] *n*: **the ~** la mafia.

magazine [,mægə'ziːn] *n* **1.** (*periodical*) revista *f*. **2.** (*news programme*) magazín *m*. **3.** (*on a gun*) recámara *f*.

maggot ['mægət] *n* gusano *m*, cresa *f*.

magic ['mædʒɪk] ◆ *adj* (*gen*) mágico (ca). ◆ *n* magia *f*.

magical ['mædʒɪkl] *adj lit & fig* mágico (ca).

magician [mə'dʒɪʃn] *n* **1.** (*conjuror*) prestidigitador *m*, -ra *f*. **2.** (*wizard*) mago *m*.

magistrate ['mædʒɪstreɪt] *n* magistrado *m*, -da *f*.

magistrates' court *n* Br juzgado *m* de primera instancia.

magnanimous [mæg'nænɪməs] *adj* magnánimo(ma).

magnate ['mægneɪt] *n* magnate *m*.

magnesium [mæg'niːzɪəm] *n* magnesio *m*.

magnet ['mægnɪt] *n* imán *m*.

magnetic [mæg'netɪk] *adj* **1.** (*attracting iron*) magnético(ca). **2.** *fig* (*appealingly forceful*) atrayente, carismático(ca).

magnetic tape *n* cinta *f* magnetofónica.

magnificent [mæg'nɪfɪsənt] *adj* (*building, splendour*) grandioso(sa); (*idea, book, game*) magnífico(ca).

magnify ['mægnɪfaɪ] *vt* **1.** (*in vision*) aumentar. **2.** (*in the mind*) exagerar.

magnifying glass ['mægnɪfaɪɪŋ-] *n* lupa *f*.

magnitude ['mægnɪtjuːd] n magnitud f.

magpie ['mægpaɪ] n urraca f.

mahogany [mə'hɒgənɪ] n 1. (wood) caoba f. 2. (colour) caoba m.

maid [meɪd] n (in hotel) camarera f; (domestic) criada f.

maiden ['meɪdn] ◆ adj inaugural. ◆ n literary doncella f.

maiden aunt n tía f soltera.

maiden name n nombre m de soltera.

mail [meɪl] ◆ n 1. (letters, parcels received) correspondencia f. 2. (system) correo m; **by ~** por correo. ◆ vt (send) mandar por correo; (put in mail box) echar al buzón.

mailbox ['meɪlbɒks] n Am buzón m.

mailing list ['meɪlɪŋ-] n lista f de distribución de publicidad OR información.

mailman ['meɪlmən] (pl **-men** [-mən]) n Am cartero m.

mail order n pedido m por correo.

mailshot ['meɪlʃɒt] n folleto m de publicidad (por correo).

maim [meɪm] vt mutilar.

main [meɪn] ◆ adj principal. ◆ n (pipe) tubería f principal; (wire) cable m principal. ▶ **mains** npl: **the ~s** (gas, water) la tubería principal; (electricity) la red eléctrica. ▶ **in the main** adv por lo general.

main course n plato m fuerte.

mainframe (computer) ['meɪnfreɪm-] n unidad f central.

mainland ['meɪnlənd] ◆ adj continental; **~ Spain** la Península. ◆ n: **the ~** el continente.

mainly ['meɪnlɪ] adv principalmente.

main road n carretera f principal.

mainstay ['meɪnsteɪ] n fundamento m.

mainstream ['meɪnstriːm] ◆ adj (gen) predominante; (taste) corriente; (political party) convencional. ◆ n: **the ~** la tendencia general.

maintain [meɪn'teɪn] vt 1. (gen) mantener. 2. (support, provide for) sostener. 3. (assert): **to ~ (that)** sostener que.

maintenance ['meɪntənəns] n 1. (gen) mantenimiento m. 2. (money) pensión f alimenticia.

maize [meɪz] n maíz m.

majestic [mə'dʒestɪk] adj majestuoso (sa).

majesty ['mædʒəstɪ] n (grandeur) majestad f. ▶ **Majesty** n: **His/Her/Your Majesty** Su Majestad.

major ['meɪdʒəʳ] ◆ adj 1. (important)

principal. 2. (MUS) mayor. ◆ n (MIL) comandante m.

Majorca [mə'jɔːkə, mə'dʒɔːkə] n Mallorca.

majority [mə'dʒɒrətɪ] n mayoría f.

make [meɪk] (pt & pp **made**) ◆ vt 1. (produce) hacer; **she ~s her own clothes** se hace su propia ropa. 2. (perform - action) hacer; **to ~ a speech** pronunciar OR dar un discurso; **to ~ a decision** tomar una decisión; **to ~ a mistake** cometer un error. 3. (cause to be, cause to do) hacer; **it ~s me sick** me pone enfermo; **it made him angry** hizo que se enfadara; **you made me jump!** ¡vaya susto que me has dado!; **to ~ sb happy** hacer a alguien feliz; **to ~ sb sad** entristecer a alguien. 4. (force): **to ~ sb do sthg** hacer que alguien haga algo, obligar a alguien a hacer algo. 5. (construct): **to be made of sthg** estar hecho(cha) de algo; **made in Spain** fabricado en España. 6. (add up to) hacer, ser; **2 and 2 ~ 4** 2 y 2 hacen OR son 4. 7. (calculate) calcular; **I ~ it 50/six o'clock** calculo que serán 50/ las seis; **what time do you ~ it?** ¿qué hora es? 8. (earn) ganar; **to ~ a profit** obtener beneficios; **to ~ a loss** sufrir pérdidas. 9. (have the right qualities for) ser; **she'd ~ a good doctor** seguro que sería una buena doctora. 10. (reach) llegar a. 11. (gain - friend, enemy) hacer; **to ~ friends with sb** hacerse amigo de alguien. 12. phr: **to ~ it** (arrive in time) conseguir llegar a tiempo; (be a success) alcanzar el éxito; (be able to attend) venir/ ir; **to ~ do with sthg** apañarse OR arreglarse con algo. ◆ n (brand) marca f. ▶ **make for** vt fus 1. (move towards) dirigirse a OR hacia. 2. (contribute to) contribuir a. ▶ **make of** vt sep 1. (understand) entender; **what do you ~ of this word?** ¿qué entiendes tú por esta palabra? 2. (have opinion of) opinar de. ▶ **make off** vi darse a la fuga. ▶ **make out** vt sep 1. inf (see) distinguir; (hear) entender, oír. 2. inf (understand - word, number) descifrar; (- person, attitude) comprender. 3. (fill out - form) rellenar; (- cheque, receipt) extender; (- list) hacer. ▶ **make up** ◆ vt sep 1. (compose, constitute) componer, constituir. 2. (invent) inventar. 3. (apply cosmetics to) maquillar. 4. (prepare - parcel, prescription, bed) preparar. 5. (make complete - amount) completar; (- difference) cubrir. ◆ vi (become friends again) hacer las paces, reconciliarse. ▶ **make up**

for vt fus compensar. ▶ **make up to** vt sep: **to ~ it up to sb (for sthg)** recompensar a alguien (por algo).

make-believe n invención f.

maker ['meɪkəʳ] n (of film, programme) creador m, -ra f; (of product) fabricante m y f.

makeshift ['meɪkʃɪft] adj (temporary) provisional; (improvised) improvisado (da).

make-up n 1. (cosmetics) maquillaje m; ~ **remover** loción f OR leche f desmaquilladora. 2. (person's character) carácter m. 3. (structure) estructura f; (of team) composición f.

making ['meɪkɪŋ] n (of product) fabricación f; (of film) rodaje m; (of decision) toma f; **this is history in the ~** esto pasará a la historia; **your problems are of your own ~** tus problemas te los has buscado tú mismo; **to have the ~s of** tener madera de.

malaise [mə'leɪz] n fml malestar m.

malaria [mə'leərɪə] n malaria f.

Malaya [mə'leɪə] n Malaya.

Malaysia [mə'leɪzɪə] n Malaisia.

male [meɪl] ♦ adj 1. (animal) macho. 2. (human) masculino(na), varón. 3. (concerning men) masculino(na). ♦ n 1. (animal) macho m. 2. (human) varón m.

male nurse n enfermero m.

malevolent [mə'levələnt] adj malévolo(la).

malfunction [mæl'fʌŋkʃn] ♦ n funcionamiento m defectuoso. ♦ vi funcionar mal.

malice ['mælɪs] n malicia f.

malicious [mə'lɪʃəs] adj malicioso(sa).

malign [mə'laɪn] ♦ adj maligno(na), perjudicial. ♦ vt fml difamar.

malignant [mə'lɪgnənt] adj 1. fml (full of hate) malvado(da). 2. (MED) maligno (na).

mall [mɔːl] n: **(shopping)** ~ centro m comercial peatonal.

mallet ['mælɪt] n mazo m.

malnutrition [,mælnjuː'trɪʃn] n malnutrición f.

malpractice [,mæl'præktɪs] n (U) (JUR) negligencia f.

malt [mɔːlt] n 1. (grain) malta f. 2. (whisky) whisky m de malta.

Malta ['mɔːltə] n Malta.

mammal ['mæml] n mamífero m.

mammoth ['mæməθ] ♦ adj descomunal. ♦ n mamut m.

man [mæn] (pl **men**) ♦ n hombre m; **the ~ in the street** el hombre de la calle, el ciudadano de a pie. ♦ vt (gen) manejar; (ship, plane) tripular; **manned 24 hours a day** (telephone) en servicio las 24 horas del día.

manage ['mænɪdʒ] ♦ vi 1. (cope) poder. 2. (survive) apañárselas. ♦ vt 1. (succeed): **to ~ to do sthg** conseguir hacer algo. 2. (company) dirigir, llevar; (money) administrar, manejar; (pop star) representar; (time) organizar. 3. (cope with) poder con; **can you ~ that box?** ¿puedes con la caja?

manageable ['mænɪdʒəbl] adj (task) factible, posible; (children) dominable; (inflation, rate) controlable.

management ['mænɪdʒmənt] n 1. (control, running) gestión f. 2. (people in control) dirección f.

manager ['mænɪdʒəʳ] n 1. (of company) director m, -ra f; (of shop) jefe m, -fa f; (of pop star) manager m y f. 2. (SPORT) ≃ entrenador m, -ra f.

manageress [,mænɪdʒə'res] n Br (of company) directora f; (of shop) jefa f.

managerial [,mænɪ'dʒɪərɪəl] adj directivo(va).

managing director ['mænɪdʒɪŋ-] n director m, -ra f gerente.

mandarin ['mændərɪn] n (fruit) mandarina f.

mandate ['mændeɪt] n 1. (elected right or authority) mandato m. 2. (task) misión f.

mandatory ['mændətrɪ] adj obligatorio(ria).

mane [meɪn] n (of horse) crin f; (of lion) melena f.

maneuver Am = **manoeuvre**.

manfully ['mænfʊlɪ] adv valientemente.

mangle ['mæŋgl] vt (crush) aplastar; (tear to pieces) despedazar.

mango ['mæŋgəʊ] (pl -es OR -s) n mango m.

mangy ['meɪndʒɪ] adj sarnoso(sa).

manhandle ['mæn,hændl] vt (person) maltratar.

manhole ['mænhəʊl] n boca f (del alcantarillado).

manhood ['mænhʊd] n 1. (state) virilidad f. 2. (time) edad f viril OR adulta.

manhour ['mæn,aʊəʳ] n hora f de trabajo (realizada por una persona).

mania ['meɪnjə] n 1. (excessive liking): ~ **(for)** manía f (por). 2. (PSYCH) manía f.

maniac ['meɪnɪæk] n 1. (madman) maníaco m, -ca f. 2. (fanatic) fanático m, -ca f.

manic ['mænɪk] *adj* maníaco(ca).

manicure ['mænɪˌkjʊəʳ] *n* manicura *f*.

manifest ['mænɪfest] *fml* ◆ *adj* manifiesto(ta). ◆ *vt* manifestar.

manifesto [ˌmænɪ'festəʊ] (*pl* **-s** OR **-es**) *n* manifiesto *m*.

manipulate [mə'nɪpjʊleɪt] *vt* **1.** (*control for personal benefit*) manipular. **2.** (*machine*) manejar; (*controls, lever*) accionar.

mankind [mæn'kaɪnd] *n* la humanidad, el género humano.

manly ['mænlɪ] *adj* varonil, viril.

man-made *adj* (*environment, problem, disaster*) producido(da) por el hombre; (*fibre*) artificial.

manner ['mænəʳ] *n* **1.** (*method*) manera *f*, forma *f*. **2.** (*bearing, attitude*) comportamiento *m*. **3.** *esp literary* (*type, sort*) tipo *m*, clase *f*. ▶ **manners** *npl* modales *mpl*; **it's good/bad ~s to do sthg** es de buena/mala educación hacer algo.

mannerism ['mænərɪzm] *n* costumbre *f* (típica de uno).

mannish ['mænɪʃ] *adj* (*woman*) hombruno(na).

manoeuvre Br, **maneuver** Am [mə'nuːvəʳ] ◆ *n* lit & fig maniobra *f*. ◆ *vt* maniobrar. ◆ *vi* maniobrar.

manor ['mænəʳ] *n* (*house*) casa *f* solariega.

manpower ['mænˌpaʊəʳ] *n* (*manual workers*) mano *f* de obra; (*white-collar workers*) personal *m*.

mansion ['mænʃn] *n* (*manor*) casa *f* solariega; (*big house*) casa grande.

manslaughter ['mænˌslɔːtəʳ] *n* homicidio *m* involuntario.

mantelpiece ['mæntlpiːs] *n* repisa *f* (de la chimenea).

manual ['mænjʊəl] ◆ *adj* manual. ◆ *n* manual *m*.

manual worker *n* obrero *m*, -ra *f*.

manufacture [ˌmænjʊ'fæktʃəʳ] ◆ *n* fabricación *f*. ◆ *vt* (*make*) fabricar.

manufacturer [ˌmænjʊ'fæktʃərəʳ] *n* fabricante *m* y *f*.

manure [mə'njʊəʳ] *n* estiércol *m*.

manuscript ['mænjʊskrɪpt] *n* **1.** (*gen*) manuscrito *m*. **2.** (*in exam*) hoja *f* de examen.

many ['menɪ] (*compar* **more**, *superl* **most**) ◆ *adj* muchos(chas); **~ people** muchas personas, mucha gente; **how ~?** ¿cuántos(tas)?; **I wonder how ~ people went** me pregunto cuánta gente fue; **too ~** demasiados(das); **there weren't too ~ students** no había muchos estudiantes; **as ~ ... as** tantos(tas) ... como; **so ~ tan-**

tos(tas); **I've never seen so ~ people** nunca había visto tanta gente; **a good** OR **great ~** muchísimos(mas). ◆ *pron* muchos(chas).

map [mæp] *n* mapa *m*. ▶ **map out** *vt sep* planear, planificar.

maple ['meɪpl] *n* arce *m*.

mar [mɑːʳ] *vt* deslucir.

marathon ['mærəθn] *n* maratón *m*.

marauder [mə'rɔːdəʳ] *n* merodeador *m*, -ra *f*.

marble ['mɑːbl] *n* **1.** (*stone*) mármol *m*. **2.** (*for game*) canica *f*, bolita *f* Amer.

march [mɑːtʃ] ◆ *n* **1.** (MIL) marcha *f*. **2.** (*of demonstrators*) manifestación *f*. **3.** (*steady progress*) avance *m*, progreso *m*. ◆ *vi* **1.** (*in formation*) marchar. **2.** (*in protest*) manifestarse. **3.** (*speedily*): **to ~ up to sb** abordar a alguien decididamente. ◆ *vt* llevar por la fuerza.

March [mɑːtʃ] *n* marzo *m*; *see also* **September**.

marcher ['mɑːtʃəʳ] *n* (*protester*) manifestante *m* y *f*.

mare [meəʳ] *n* yegua *f*.

margarine [ˌmɑːdʒə'riːn, ˌmɑːgə'riːn] *n* margarina *f*.

marge [mɑːdʒ] *n inf* margarina *f*.

margin ['mɑːdʒɪn] *n* (*gen*) margen *m*.

marginal ['mɑːdʒɪnl] *adj* **1.** (*unimportant*) marginal. **2.** Br (POL.): **~ seat** OR **constituency** escaño vulnerable a ser perdido en las elecciones por tener una mayoría escasa.

marginally ['mɑːdʒɪnəlɪ] *adv* ligeramente.

marigold ['mærɪgəʊld] *n* caléndula *f*.

marihuana, marijuana [ˌmærɪ'wɑːnə] *n* marihuana *f*.

marine [mə'riːn] ◆ *adj* marino(na). ◆ *n* soldado *m* de infantería de marina.

marionette [ˌmærɪə'net] *n* marioneta *f*, títere *m*.

marital ['mærɪtl] *adj* matrimonial.

marital status *n* estado *m* civil.

maritime ['mærɪtaɪm] *adj* marítimo(ma).

mark [mɑːk] ◆ *n* **1.** (*stain*) mancha *f*. **2.** (*written symbol - on paper*) marca *f*; (*- in the sand*) señal *f*. **3.** (*in exam*) nota *f*; **to get good ~s** sacar buenas notas. **4.** (*stage, level*): **once past the halfway ~** una vez llegado a medio camino. **5.** (*sign - of respect*) señal *f*; (*- of illness, old age*) huella *f*. **6.** (*currency*) marco *m*. ◆ *vt* **1.** (*stain*) manchar. **2.** (*label - with initials etc*) señalar. **3.** (*exam, essay*) puntuar, calificar. **4.** (*identify - place*) señalar; (*- beginning, end*) marcar. **5.** (*commemorate*) con-

memorar. **6.** (*characterize*) caracterizar.
▶ **mark off** *vt sep* (*cross off*) tachar.

marked [mɑ:kt] *adj* (*improvement*) notable; (*difference*) acusado(da).

marker ['mɑ:kə'] *n* (*sign*) señal *f.*

marker pen *n* rotulador *m.*

market ['mɑ:kɪt] ◆ *n* mercado *m.* ◆ *vt* comercializar.

market garden *n* (*small*) huerto *m*; (*large*) huerta *f.*

marketing ['mɑ:kɪtɪŋ] *n* marketing *m.*

marketplace ['mɑ:kɪtpleɪs] *n lit & fig* mercado *m.*

market research *n* estudio *m* de mercados.

market value *n* valor *m* actual OR en venta.

marking ['mɑ:kɪŋ] *n* (*of exams etc*) corrección *f.* ▶ **markings** *npl* (*of flower, animal*) pintas *fpl*; (*on road*) señales *fpl.*

marksman ['mɑ:ksmən] (*pl* **-men** [-mən]) *n* tirador *m.*

marmalade ['mɑ:məleɪd] *n* mermelada *f* (*de cítricos*).

maroon [mə'ru:n] *adj* granate.

marooned [mə'ru:nd] *adj* incomunicado(da), aislado(da).

marquee [mɑ:'ki:] *n* carpa *f*, toldo *m* grande.

marriage ['mærɪdʒ] *n* **1.** (*act*) boda *f.* **2.** (*state, institution*) matrimonio *m.*

marriage bureau *n* Br agencia *f* matrimonial.

marriage certificate *n* certificado *m* de matrimonio.

marriage guidance *n* asesoría *f* matrimonial.

married ['mærɪd] *adj* **1.** (*wedded*) casado(da). **2.** (*of marriage*) matrimonial.

marrow ['mærəu] *n* **1.** Br (*vegetable*) calabacín *m* grande. **2.** (*in bones*) médula *f.*

marry ['mærɪ] ◆ *vt* casar; **to get married** casarse. ◆ *vi* casarse.

Mars [mɑ:z] *n* Marte *m.*

marsh [mɑ:ʃ] *n* **1.** (*area of land*) zona *f* pantanosa. **2.** (*type of land*) pantano *m.*

marshal ['mɑ:ʃl] ◆ *n* **1.** (MIL) mariscal *m.* **2.** (*steward*) oficial *m y f*, miembro *m y f* del servicio de orden. **3.** Am (*officer*) jefe *m*, -fa *f* de policía. ◆ *vt* (*people*) dirigir, conducir; (*thoughts*) ordenar.

marshy ['mɑ:ʃɪ] *adj* pantanoso(sa).

martial arts [,mɑ:ʃl-] *npl* artes *fpl* marciales.

martial law [,mɑ:ʃl-] *n* ley *f* marcial.

martyr ['mɑ:tə'] *n* mártir *m y f.*

martyrdom ['mɑ:tədəm] *n* martirio *m.*

marvel ['mɑ:vl] ◆ *n* maravilla *f.* ◆ *vi*: **to ~ (at)** maravillarse OR asombrarse (ante).

marvellous Br, **marvelous** Am ['mɑ:vələs] *adj* maravilloso(sa).

Marxism ['mɑ:ksɪzm] *n* marxismo *m.*

Marxist ['mɑ:ksɪst] ◆ *adj* marxista. ◆ *n* marxista *m y f.*

marzipan ['mɑ:zɪpæn] *n* mazapán *m.*

mascara [mæs'kɑ:rə] *n* rímel *m.*

masculine ['mæskjulɪn] *adj* (*gen*) masculino(na); (*woman, appearance*) hombruno(na).

mash [mæʃ] *vt* triturar.

mashed potatoes [mæʃt-] *npl* puré *m* de patatas.

mask [mɑ:sk] ◆ *n lit & fig* máscara *f.* ◆ *vt* **1.** (*to hide*) enmascarar. **2.** (*cover up*) ocultar, disfrazar.

masochist ['mæsəkɪst] *n* masoquista *m y f.*

mason ['meɪsn] *n* **1.** (*stonemason*) cantero *m.* **2.** (*freemason*) masón *m.*

masonry ['meɪsnrɪ] *n* (*stones*) albañilería *f.*

masquerade [,mæskə'reɪd] *vi*: **to ~ as** hacerse pasar por.

mass [mæs] ◆ *n* **1.** (*gen*) masa *f.* **2.** (*large amount*) cantidad *f*, montón *m.* ◆ *adj* (*unemployment*) masivo(va); (*communication*) de masas. ◆ *vi* agruparse, concentrarse. ▶ **Mass** *n* (*religious ceremony*) misa *f.* ▶ **masses** *npl* **1.** *inf* (*lots*) montones *mpl.* **2.** (*workers*): **the ~es** las masas.

massacre ['mæsəkə'] ◆ *n* matanza *f*, masacre *f.* ◆ *vt* masacrar.

massage [Br 'mæsɑ:ʒ, Am mə'sɑ:ʒ] ◆ *n* masaje *m.* ◆ *vt* dar masajes a.

massive ['mæsɪv] *adj* (*gen*) enorme; (*majority*) aplastante.

mass media *n or npl*: **the ~** los medios de comunicación de masas.

mass production *n* producción *f* OR fabricación *f* en serie.

mast [mɑ:st] *n* **1.** (*on boat*) mástil *m.* **2.** (RADIO & TV) poste *m*, torre *f.*

master ['mɑ:stə'] ◆ *n* **1.** (*of people, animals*) amo *m*, dueño *m*; (*of house*) señor *m.* **2.** *fig* (*of situation*) dueño *m*, -ña *f.* **3.** Br (*teacher - primary school*) maestro *m*; (*- secondary school*) profesor *m.* ◆ *adj* maestro (tra). ◆ *vt* **1.** (*situation*) dominar, controlar; (*difficulty*) superar. **2.** (*technique etc*) dominar.

master key *n* llave *f* maestra.

masterly ['mɑ:stəlɪ] *adj* magistral.

mastermind ['mɑ:stəmaɪnd] ◆ *n* cerebro *m.* ◆ *vt* ser el cerebro de, dirigir.

Master of Arts (pl **Masters of Arts**) n
1. (degree) maestría f OR máster m en
Letras. 2. (person) licenciado m, -da f
con maestría en Letras.

Master of Science (pl **Masters of
Science**) n 1. (degree) maestría f OR
máster m en Ciencias. 2. (person) licenciado m, -da f con maestría en
Ciencias.

masterpiece ['mɑːstəpiːs] n lit & fig
obra f maestra.

master's degree n máster m.

mastery ['mɑːstərɪ] n dominio m.

mat [mæt] n 1. (beer mat) posavasos m
inv; (tablemat) salvamanteles m inv.
2. (doormat) felpudo m; (rug) alfombrilla
f.

match [mætʃ] ◆ n 1. (game) partido m.
2. (for lighting) cerilla f. 3. (equal): **to be
no ~ for** no poder competir con. ◆ vt
1. (be the same as) coincidir con. 2. (pair
off): **to ~ sthg (to)** emparejar algo (con).
3. (be equal with) competir con. 4. (go well
with) hacer juego con. ◆ vi 1. (be the
same) coincidir. 2. (go together well) hacer
juego.

matchbox ['mætʃbɒks] n caja f de cerillas.

matching ['mætʃɪŋ] adj a juego, que
combina bien.

mate [meɪt] ◆ n 1. inf (friend) amigo m,
-ga f, compañero m, -ra f. 2. Br inf (term
of address) colega m y f. 3. (of animal)
macho m, hembra f. 4. (NAUT): **(first) ~**
(primer) oficial m. ◆ vi (animals): **to ~
(with)** aparearse (con).

material [mə'tɪərɪəl] ◆ adj 1. (physical)
material. 2. (important) sustancial. ◆ n
1. (substance) material m. 2. (type of substance) materia f. 3. (fabric) tela f, tejido
m. 4. (type of fabric) tejido m. 5. (U) (ideas,
information) información f, documentación f. ▶ **materials** npl: **building
~s** materiales mpl de construcción; **writing ~s** objetos mpl de escritorio; **cleaning ~s** productos mpl de limpieza.

materialistic [mə,tɪərɪə'lɪstɪk] adj
materialista.

maternal [mə'tɜːnl] adj (gen) maternal;
(grandparent) materno(na).

maternity [mə'tɜːnətɪ] n maternidad
f.

maternity dress n vestido m pre-
mamá.

maternity hospital n hospital m de
maternidad.

math Am = **maths**.

mathematical [,mæθə'mætɪkl] adj

matemático(ca).

mathematics [,mæθə'mætɪks] n (U)
matemáticas fpl.

maths Br [mæθs], **math** Am [mæθ]
(abbr of **mathematics**) inf n (U) mates fpl.

matinée ['mætɪneɪ] n (at cinema)
primera sesión f; (at theatre) función f de
tarde.

mating season ['meɪtɪŋ-] n época f
de celo.

matrices ['meɪtrɪsiːz] pl → **matrix**.

matriculation [mə,trɪkjʊ'leɪʃn] n
matrícula f.

matrimonial [,mætrɪ'məʊnjəl] adj
matrimonial.

matrimony ['mætrɪmənɪ] n (U) matrimonio m.

matrix ['meɪtrɪks] (pl **matrices** OR **-es**) n
matriz f.

matron ['meɪtrən] n 1. Br (in hospital)
enfermera f jefa. 2. (in school) ama f de
llaves.

matronly ['meɪtrənlɪ] adj euphemism
corpulenta y de edad madura.

matt Br, **matte** Am [mæt] adj mate.

matted ['mætɪd] adj enmarañado(da).

matter ['mætər] ◆ n 1. (question, situation) asunto m; **that's another** OR **a different ~** es otra cuestión OR cosa; **as a ~ of
course** automáticamente; **to make ~s
worse** para colmo de desgracias; **a ~ of
opinion** una cuestión de opiniones.
2. (trouble, cause of pain): **what's the ~ (with
it/her)?** ¿qué (le) pasa?; **something's the
~ with my car** algo le pasa a mi coche.
3. (PHYSICS) materia f. 4. (U) (material)
material m. ◆ vi (be important) importar;
it doesn't ~ no importa. ▶ **as a matter
of fact** adv en realidad. ▶ **for that
matter** adv de hecho. ▶ **no matter**
adv: **no ~ how hard I try** por mucho que
lo intente; **no ~ what he does** haga lo
que haga; **we must win, no ~ what** tenemos que ganar como sea.

Matterhorn ['mætə,hɔːn] n: **the ~** el
monte Cervino.

matter-of-fact adj pragmático(ca).

mattress ['mætrɪs] n colchón m.

mature [mə'tjʊər] ◆ adj (person, wine)
maduro(ra); (cheese) curado(da). ◆ vi
madurar.

mature student n Br (UNIV) estudiante m y f en edad adulta.

maul [mɔːl] vt (savage) herir gravemente.

mauve [məʊv] adj malva.

max. [mæks] (abbr of **maximum**) máx.

maxim ['mæksɪm] (pl **-s**) n máxima f.

maximum ['mæksɪməm] (*pl* **maxima** OR **-s**) ◆ *adj* máximo(ma). ◆ *n* máximo *m*.

may [meɪ] *modal vb* poder; **the coast ~ be seen** se puede ver la costa; **you ~ like it** puede OR es posible que te guste; **I ~ come, I ~ not** puede que venga, puede que no; **it ~ be done in two different ways** puede hacerse de dos maneras (distintas); **~ I come in?** ¿se puede (pasar)?; **~ I?** ¿me permite?; **it ~ be cheap, but it's good** puede que sea barato, pero es bueno; **~ all your dreams come true!** ¡que todos tus sueños se hagan realidad!; **be that as it ~** aunque así sea; **come what ~** pase lo que pase; *see also* **might**.

May [meɪ] *n* mayo *m*; *see also* **September**.

maybe ['meɪbiː] *adv* **1.** (*perhaps*) quizás, tal vez; **~ she'll come** tal vez venga. **2.** (*approximately*) más o menos.

May Day *n* Br día *m* del Trabajo.

mayhem ['meɪhem] *n* alboroto *m*.

mayonnaise [,meɪə'neɪz] *n* mayonesa *f*.

mayor [meəʳ] *n* alcalde *m*, -esa *f*.

mayoress ['meərɪs] *n* alcaldesa *f*.

maze [meɪz] *n lit* & *fig* laberinto *m*.

MB (*abbr of* **megabyte**) MB *m*.

MD *n abbr of* **managing director**.

me [miː] *pers pron* **1.** (*direct, indirect*) me; **can you see/hear ~?** ¿me ves/oyes?; **it's ~** soy yo; **they spoke to ~** hablaron conmigo; **she gave it to ~** me lo dio; **give it to ~!** ¡dámelo! **2.** (*stressed*): **you can't expect ME to do it** no esperarás que yo lo haga. **3.** (*after prep*) mí; **they went with/without ~** fueron conmigo/sin mí. **4.** (*in comparisons*) yo; **she's shorter than ~** (ella) es más baja que yo.

meadow ['medəʊ] *n* prado *m*, pradera *f*.

meagre Br, **meager** Am ['miːgəʳ] *adj* miserable, escaso(sa).

meal [miːl] *n* comida *f*.

mealtime ['miːltaɪm] *n* hora *f* de la comida.

mean [miːn] (*pt* & *pp* **meant**) ◆ *vt* **1.** (*signify*) significar, querer decir; **it ~s nothing to me** no significa nada para mí. **2.** (*have in mind*) querer decir, referirse a; **what do you ~?** ¿qué quieres decir?; **to ~ to do sthg** tener la intención de OR querer hacer algo; **to be meant for** estar destinado(da) a; **to be meant to do sthg** deber hacer algo; **that's not meant to be there** esto no debería estar allí; **it was meant to be a joke** era solamente una broma; **to ~ well** tener buenas intenciones. **3.** (*be serious about*): **I ~ it** hablo OR lo digo en serio. **4.** (*be important, matter*) significar. **5.** (*entail*) suponer, implicar. **6.** *phr*: **I ~** quiero decir, o sea. ◆ *adj* **1.** (*miserly*) tacaño(ña). **2.** (*unkind*) mezquino(na), malo(la); **to be ~ to sb** ser malo con alguien. **3.** (*average*) medio(dia). ◆ *n* (*average*) promedio *m*, media *f*; *see also* **means**.

meander [mɪ'ændəʳ] *vi* **1.** (*river, road*) serpentear. **2.** (*walk aimlessly*) vagar; (*write, speak aimlessly*) divagar.

meaning ['miːnɪŋ] *n* **1.** (*sense - of a word etc*) significado *m*. **2.** (*significance*) intención *f*, sentido *m*. **3.** (*purpose, point*) propósito *m*, razón *f* de ser.

meaningful ['miːnɪŋfʊl] *adj* **1.** (*expressive*) significativo(va). **2.** (*profound*) profundo(da).

meaningless ['miːnɪŋlɪs] *adj* **1.** (*without meaning, purpose*) sin sentido. **2.** (*irrelevant, unimportant*) irrelevante.

means [miːnz] ◆ *n* (*method, way*) medio *m*; **we have no ~ of doing it** no tenemos manera de hacerlo; **by ~ of** por medio de. ◆ *npl* (*money*) recursos *mpl*. ▶ **by all means** *adv* por supuesto. ▶ **by no means** *adv fml* en absoluto.

meant [ment] *pt* & *pp* → **mean**.

meantime ['miːn,taɪm] *n*: **in the ~** mientras tanto.

meanwhile ['miːn,waɪl] *adv* mientras tanto, entre tanto.

measles ['miːzlz] *n*: **(the) ~** sarampión *m*.

measly ['miːzlɪ] *adj inf* raquítico(ca).

measure ['meʒəʳ] ◆ *n* **1.** (*step, action*) medida *f*. **2.** (*of alcohol*) medida *f*. **3.** (*indication, sign*): **a ~ of** una muestra de. ◆ *vt* (*object*) medir; (*damage, impact etc*) determinar, juzgar. ◆ *vi* medir.

measurement ['meʒəmənt] *n* medida *f*.

meat [miːt] *n* carne *f*; **cold ~** fiambre *m*.

meatball ['miːtbɔːl] *n* albóndiga *f*.

meat pie *n* Br pastel *m* de carne.

meaty ['miːtɪ] *adj fig* sustancioso(sa).

Mecca ['mekə] *n* (GEOGR) La Meca; *fig* meca *f*.

mechanic [mɪ'kænɪk] *n* mecánico *m*, -ca *f*. ▶ **mechanics** ◆ *n* (U) (*study*) mecánica *f*. ◆ *npl fig* mecanismos *mpl*.

mechanical [mɪ'kænɪkl] *adj* (*worked by machinery, routine*) mecánico(ca).

mechanism ['mekənɪzm] *n lit* & *fig* mecanismo *m*.

medal ['medl] n medalla f.

medallion [mɪ'dæljən] n medallón m.

meddle ['medl] vi: **to ~ (in)** entrometerse OR interferir (en); **to ~ with** sthg manosear algo.

media ['miːdjə] ◆ pl → **medium**. ◆ n or npl: **the ~** los medios de comunicación.

mediaeval [,medr'iːvl] = **medieval**.

median ['miːdjən] ◆ adj mediano(na). ◆ n Am (of road) mediana f.

mediate ['miːdɪeɪt] vi: **to ~ (for/between)** mediar (por/entre).

mediator ['miːdɪeɪtər] n mediador m, -ra f.

Medicaid ['medɪkeɪd] n Am sistema estatal de ayuda médica.

medical ['medɪkl] ◆ adj médico(ca). ◆ n reconocimiento m médico.

Medicare ['medɪkeər] n Am ayuda médica estatal para ancianos.

medicated ['medɪkeɪtɪd] adj medicinal.

medicine ['medsɪn] n 1. (treatment of illness) medicina f; **Doctor of Medicine** (UNIV) doctor m, -ra f en medicina. 2. (substance) medicina f, medicamento m.

medieval [,medr'iːvl] adj medieval.

mediocre [,miːdr'əʊkər] adj mediocre.

meditate ['medɪteɪt] vi: **to ~ (on** OR **upon)** meditar OR reflexionar (sobre).

meditation [,medr'teɪʃn] n meditación f.

Mediterranean [,medɪtə'reɪnjən] ◆ n (sea): **the ~ (Sea)** el (mar) Mediterráneo. ◆ adj mediterráneo(a).

medium ['miːdjəm] (pl sense 1 **media**, pl sense 2 **mediums**) ◆ adj mediano(na). ◆ n 1. (way of communicating) medio m. 2. (spiritualist) médium m y f.

medium-sized [-saɪzd] adj de tamaño mediano.

medium wave n onda f media.

medley ['medlɪ] (pl **medleys**) n 1. (mixture) mezcla f. 2. (selection of music) popurrí m.

meek [miːk] adj sumiso(sa), dócil.

meet [miːt] (pt & pp **met**) ◆ vt 1. (by chance) encontrarse con; (for first time, come across) conocer; (by arrangement, for a purpose) reunirse con. 2. (go to meet - person) ir/venir a buscar. 3. (need, demand) satisfacer. 4. (deal with - problem, challenge) hacer frente a. 5. (costs, debts) pagar. 6. (experience - problem, situation) encontrarse con. 7. (hit, touch) darse OR chocar contra. 8. (join) juntarse OR unirse con. ◆ vi 1. (by chance) encon-

trarse; (by arrangement) verse; (for a purpose) reunirse. 2. (get to know sb) conocerse. 3. (hit in collision) chocar; (touch) tocar. 4. (eyes) cruzarse. 5. (join - roads etc) juntarse. ◆ n Am (meeting) encuentro m. ▶ **meet up** vi: **to ~ up (with sb)** quedarse en verse (con alguien). ▶ **meet with** vt fus 1. (refusal, disappointment) recibir; **to ~ with success** tener éxito; **to ~ with failure** fracasar. 2. Am (by arrangement) reunirse con.

meeting ['miːtɪŋ] n 1. (for discussions, business) reunión f. 2. (by chance, in sport) encuentro m; (by arrangement) cita f; (formal) entrevista f.

megabyte ['megəbaɪt] n (COMPUT) megaocteto m.

megaphone ['megəfəʊn] n megáfono m.

melancholy ['melənkəlɪ] ◆ adj melancólico(ca). ◆ n melancolía f.

mellow ['meləʊ] ◆ adj (sound, colour, light) suave; (wine) añejo(ja). ◆ vi suavizarse; (person) ablandarse.

melody ['melədɪ] n melodía f.

melon ['melən] n melón m.

melt [melt] ◆ vt 1. (make liquid) derretir. 2. fig (soften) ablandar. ◆ vi 1. (become liquid) derretirse. 2. fig (soften) ablandarse. 3. (disappear): **to ~ away** (savings) esfumarse; (anger) desvanecerse. ▶ **melt down** vt sep fundir.

meltdown ['meltdaʊn] n 1. (act of melting) fusión f. 2. (incident) fuga f radiactiva.

melting pot ['meltɪŋ-] n fig crisol m.

member ['membər] n 1. (of social group) miembro m y f. 2. (of party, union) afiliado m, -da f, miembro m y f; (of organization, club) socio m, -cia f.

Member of Congress (pl **Members of Congress**) n miembro m y f del Congreso (de los Estados Unidos).

Member of Parliament (pl **Members of Parliament**) n Br diputado m, -da f (del parlamento británico).

membership ['membəʃɪp] n 1. (of party, union) afiliación f; (of club) calidad f de miembro OR socio. 2. (number of members) número m de socios. 3. (people themselves): **the ~** (of organization) los miembros; (of club) los socios.

membership card n carnet m de socio, -cia f.

memento [mɪ'mentəʊ] (pl **-s**) n recuerdo m.

memo ['meməʊ] (pl **-s**) n memorándum m.

metal

memoirs ['memwɑːz] *npl* memorias *fpl.*

memorandum [ˌmeməˈrændəm] (*pl* **-da** [-də] OR **-dums**) *n fml* memorándum *m.*

memorial [mɪˈmɔːrɪəl] ♦ *adj* conmemorativo(va). ♦ *n* monumento *m* conmemorativo.

memorize, -ise ['meməraɪz] *vt* memorizar, aprender de memoria.

memory ['meməri] *n* **1.** (*faculty, of computer*) memoria *f.* **2.** (*thing or things remembered*) recuerdo *m*; **from ~** de memoria.

men [men] *pl* → **man.**

menace ['menəs] ♦ *n* **1.** (*threat*) amenaza *f*; (*danger*) peligro *m.* **2.** *inf* (*nuisance, pest*) pesadez *f.* ♦ *vt* amenazar.

menacing ['menəsɪŋ] *adj* amenazador (ra).

mend [mend] ♦ *n inf:* **to be on the ~** ir recuperándose. ♦ *vt* (*shoes, toy*) arreglar; (*socks*) zurcir; (*clothes*) remendar.

menial ['miːnjəl] *adj* servil, bajo(ja).

meningitis [ˌmenɪnˈdʒaɪtɪs] *n* (U) meningitis *f.*

menopause ['menəpɔːz] *n:* **the ~** la menopausia.

men's room *n* Am: **the ~** los servicios de caballeros.

menstruation [ˌmenstrʊˈeɪʃn] *n* menstruación *f.*

menswear ['menzweər] *n* ropa *f* de caballeros.

mental ['mentl] *adj* mental.

mental hospital *n* hospital *m* psiquiátrico.

mentality [menˈtælətɪ] *n* mentalidad *f.*

mentally handicapped ['mentəlɪ-] *npl:* **the ~** los disminuidos psíquicos.

mention ['menʃn] ♦ *vt:* **to ~ sthg (to)** mencionar algo (a); **not to ~** sin mencionar; **don't ~ it!** ¡de nada!, ¡no hay de qué! ♦ *n* mención *f.*

menu ['menjuː] *n* **1.** (*in restaurant*) carta *f.* **2.** (COMPUT) menú *m.*

meow Am = **miaow.**

MEP (*abbr of* **Member of the European Parliament**) *n* eurodiputado *m,* -da *f.*

mercenary ['mɜːsɪnrɪ] ♦ *adj* mercenario(ria). ♦ *n* mercenario *m,* -ria *f.*

merchandise ['mɜːtʃəndaɪz] *n* (U) mercancías *fpl,* géneros *mpl.*

merchant ['mɜːtʃənt] ♦ *adj* (*seaman, ship*) mercante. ♦ *n* comerciante *m y f.*

merchant bank *n* Br banco *m* comercial.

merchant navy Br, **merchant**

marine Am *n* marina *f* mercante.

merciful ['mɜːsɪfʊl] *adj* **1.** (*showing mercy*) compasivo(va). **2.** (*fortunate*) afortunado(da).

merciless ['mɜːsɪlɪs] *adj* despiadado (da).

mercury ['mɜːkjʊrɪ] *n* mercurio *m.*

Mercury ['mɜːkjʊrɪ] *n* Mercurio *m.*

mercy ['mɜːsɪ] *n* **1.** (*kindness, pity*) compasión *f,* misericordia *f*; **at the ~ of** *fig* a merced de. **2.** (*blessing*) suerte *f.*

mere [mɪər] *adj* simple, mero(ra); **she's a ~ child** no es más que una niña.

merely ['mɪəlɪ] *adv* simplemente, sólo.

merge [mɜːdʒ] ♦ *vt* **1.** (*gen*) mezclar. **2.** (COMM & COMPUT) fusionar. ♦ *vi* **1.** (*join, combine*): **to ~ (with)** (*company*) fusionarse (con); (*roads, branches*) unirse OR convergir (con). **2.** (*blend - colours*) fundirse; **to ~ into** confundirse con.

merger ['mɜːdʒər] *n* fusión *f.*

meringue [məˈræŋ] *n* merengue *m.*

merit ['merɪt] ♦ *n* mérito *m.* ♦ *vt* merecer, ser digno(na) de. ► **merits** *npl* ventajas *fpl.*

mermaid ['mɜːmeɪd] *n* sirena *f.*

merry ['merɪ] *adj* **1.** *literary* (*gen*) alegre. **2.** (*party*) animado(da); **Merry Christmas!** ¡feliz Navidad! **3.** *inf* (*tipsy*) achispado(da).

merry-go-round *n* tiovivo *m.*

mesh [meʃ] ♦ *n* malla *f.* ♦ *vi* encajar.

mesmerize, -ise ['mezməraɪz] *vt:* **to be ~d (by)** estar fascinado(da) (por).

mess [mes] *n* **1.** (*untidy state*) desorden *m.* **2.** (*muddle, problematic situation*) lío *m.* **3.** (MIL) (*room*) comedor *m*; (*food*) rancho *m.* ► **mess about, mess around** *inf* ♦ *vt sep* fastidiar. ♦ *vi* **1.** (*waste time*) pasar el rato; (*fool around*) hacer el tonto. **2.** (*interfere*): **to ~ about with sthg** manosear algo. ► **mess up** *vt sep inf* **1.** (*clothes*) ensuciar; (*room*) desordenar. **2.** (*plan, evening*) echar a perder.

message ['mesɪdʒ] *n* **1.** (*piece of information*) recado *m,* mensaje *m*; **to leave a ~** dejar (un) recado OR mensaje. **2.** (*of book etc*) mensaje *m.*

messenger ['mesɪndʒər] *n* mensajero *m,* -ra *f.*

Messrs, Messrs. ['mesəz] (*abbr of* **messieurs**) Sres.

messy ['mesɪ] *adj* (*dirty*) sucio(cia), desordenado(da).

met [met] *pt* & *pp* → **meet.**

metal ['metl] ♦ *n* metal *m.* ♦ *comp* de metal, metálico(ca).

metallic [mɪ'tælɪk] *adj* 1. (*gen*) metáli-co(ca). 2. (*paint, finish*) metalizado(da).

metalwork ['metəlwɜːk] *n* (*craft*) metalistería *f*.

metaphor ['metəfəʳ] *n* metáfora *f*.

mete [miːt] ▶ **mete out** *vt sep*: **to ~ sthg out to sb** imponer algo a alguien.

meteor ['miːtɪəʳ] *n* bólido *m*.

meteorology [,miːtjə'rɒlədʒɪ] *n* meteorología *f*.

meter ['miːtəʳ] *n* 1. (*device*) contador *m*. 2. Am = **metre**.

method ['meθəd] *n* método *m*.

methodical [mɪ'θɒdɪkl] *adj* metódico(ca).

Methodist ['meθədɪst] ◆ *adj* metodista. ◆ *n* metodista *m* y *f*.

meths [meθs] *n* Br *inf* alcohol *m* metilado OR desnaturalizado.

methylated spirits ['meθɪleɪtɪd-] *n* alcohol *m* metilado OR desnaturalizado.

meticulous [mɪ'tɪkjʊləs] *adj* meticuloso(sa), minucioso(sa).

metre Br, **meter** Am ['miːtəʳ] *n* metro *m*.

metric ['metrɪk] *adj* métrico(ca).

metronome ['metrənəʊm] *n* metrónomo *m*.

metropolitan [,metrə'pɒlɪtn] *adj* (*of a metropolis*) metropolitano(na).

Metropolitan Police *npl* policía *de Londres*.

mettle ['metl] *n*: **to be on one's ~** estar dispuesto(ta) a hacer lo mejor posible; **to show** OR **prove one's ~** mostrar el valor de uno.

mew [mjuː] = **miaow**.

mews [mjuːz] (*pl inv*) *n* Br callejuela de antiguas caballerizas convertidas en viviendas de lujo.

Mexican ['meksɪkn] ◆ *adj* mejicano (na). ◆ *n* mejicano *m*, -na *f*.

Mexico ['meksɪkəʊ] *n* Méjico *m*.

MI5 (*abbr of* **Military Intelligence 5**) *n* organismo británico de contraespionaje.

MI6 (*abbr of* **Military Intelligence 6**) *n* organismo británico de espionaje.

miaow Br [miː'aʊ], **meow** Am [mɪ'aʊ] ◆ *n* maullido *m*. ◆ *vi* maullar.

mice [maɪs] *pl* → **mouse**.

mickey ['mɪkɪ] *n*: **to take the ~ out of sb** Br *inf* tomar el pelo a alguien.

microchip ['maɪkrəʊtʃɪp] *n* (COMPUT) microchip *m*.

microcomputer [,maɪkrəʊkəm-'pjuːtəʳ] *n* microordenador *m*.

microfilm ['maɪkrəʊfɪlm] *n* microfilm *m*.

microphone ['maɪkrəfəʊn] *n* micrófono *m*.

microscope ['maɪkrəskəʊp] *n* microscopio *m*.

microscopic [,maɪkrə'skɒpɪk] *adj lit & fig* microscópico(ca).

microwave (oven) ['maɪkrəweɪv-] *n* (horno *m*) microondas *m inv*.

mid- [mɪd] *prefix* medio(dia); (in) **~morning** a media mañana; (in) **~August** a mediados de agosto; (in) **~winter** en pleno invierno; **she's in her ~twenties** tiene unos 25 años.

midair [mɪd'eəʳ] *n*: **in ~** en el aire.

midday ['mɪddeɪ] *n* mediodía *m*.

middle ['mɪdl] ◆ *adj* (*gen*) del medio. ◆ *n* 1. (*of room, town etc*) medio *m*, centro *m*; **in the ~ of the month/the 19th century** a mediados del mes/del siglo XIX; **to be in the ~ of doing sthg** estar haciendo algo; **in the ~ of the night** en plena noche. 2. (*waist*) cintura *f*.

middle-aged *adj* de mediana edad.

Middle Ages *npl*: **the ~** la Edad Media.

middle-class *adj* de clase media.

middle classes *npl*: **the ~** la clase media.

Middle East *n*: **the ~** el Oriente Medio.

middleman ['mɪdlmæn] (*pl* **-men** [-men]) *n* intermediario *m*.

middle name *n* segundo nombre *m* (*en un nombre compuesto*).

middleweight ['mɪdlweɪt] *n* peso *m* medio.

middling ['mɪdlɪŋ] *adj* regular, mediano(na).

Mideast [,mɪd'iːst] *n* Am: **the ~** el Oriente Medio.

midfield [,mɪd'fiːld] *n* (FTBL) medio campo *m*.

midge [mɪdʒ] *n* (tipo *m* de) mosquito *m*.

midget ['mɪdʒɪt] *n* enano *m*, -na *f*.

midi system ['mɪdɪ-] *n* minicadena *f*.

Midlands ['mɪdləndz] *npl*: **the ~** la región central de Inglaterra.

midnight ['mɪdnaɪt] *n* medianoche *f*.

midriff ['mɪdrɪf] *n* diafragma *m*.

midst [mɪdst] *n* 1. (*in space*): **in the ~ of** *literary* en medio de. 2. (*in time*): **in the ~ of** en medio de.

midsummer ['mɪd,sʌməʳ] *n* pleno verano *m*.

Midsummer Day *n* Día *m* de San Juan (24 *de junio*).

midway [,mɪd'weɪ] *adv* 1. (*in space*): ~ **(between)** a medio camino (entre). 2. (*in time*): ~ **(through)** a la mitad (dc).

midweek [*adj* mɪd'wi:k, *adv* 'mɪdwi:k] ◆ *adj* de entre semana. ◆ *adv* entre semana.

midwife ['mɪdwaɪf] (*pl* **-wives** [-waɪvz]) *n* comadrona *f*.

midwifery ['mɪd,wɪfərɪ] *n* obstetricia *f*.

might [maɪt] ◆ *modal vb* 1. (*expressing possibility*): he ~ be armed podría estar armado; I ~ do it puede que OR quizás lo haga; we ~ have been killed, had we not been careful si no hubiéramos tenido cuidado, podríamos haber muerto. 2. (*expressing suggestion*): you ~ have told me! ¡podrías habérmelo dicho!; it ~ be better to wait quizás sea mejor esperar. 3. *fml* (*asking permission*): he asked if he ~ leave the room pidió permiso para salir. 4. (*expressing concession*): you ~ well be right, but ... puede que tengas razón, pero ... 5. *phr*: I ~ have known OR guessed podría haberlo sospechado. ◆ *n* (U) fuerza *f*, poder *m*.

mighty ['maɪtɪ] ◆ *adj* (*strong*) fuerte; (*powerful*) poderoso(sa). ◆ *adv* muy.

migraine ['mi:greɪn, 'maɪgreɪn] *n* jaqueca *f*.

migrant ['maɪgrənt] ◆ *adj* 1. (*bird, animal*) migratorio(ria). 2. (*workers*) emigrante. ◆ *n* (*person*) emigrante *m y f*.

migrate [*Br* maɪ'greɪt, *Am* 'maɪgreɪt] *vi* emigrar.

mike [maɪk] (*abbr of* **microphone**) *n inf* micro *m*.

mild [maɪld] *adj* 1. (*taste, disinfectant, wind*) suave; (*effect, surprise, illness*) leve. 2. (*person, nature*) apacible; (*tone of voice*) sereno(na). 3. (*climate*) templado(da).

mildew ['mɪldju:] *n* (*gen*) moho *m*; (*on plants*) añublo *m*.

mildly ['maɪldlɪ] *adv* 1. (*gen*) ligeramente, levemente; **to put it** ~ por no decir más. 2. (*talk*) suavemente.

mile [maɪl] *n* milla *f*; **to be ~s away** *fig* estar en la luna.

mileage ['maɪlɪdʒ] *n* distancia *f* en millas.

mileometer [maɪ'lɒmɪtər] *n* cuentamillas *m inv*, = cuentakilómetros *m inv*.

milestone ['maɪlstəʊn] *n* 1. (*marker stone*) mojón *m*. 2. *fig* (*event*) hito *m*.

militant ['mɪlɪtənt] ◆ *adj* militante. ◆ *n* militante *m y f*.

military ['mɪlɪtrɪ] ◆ *adj* militar. ◆ *n*: the

~ los militares.

militia [mɪ'lɪʃə] *n* milicia *f*.

milk [mɪlk] ◆ *n* lcchc *f*. ◆ *vt* 1. (*cow etc*) ordeñar. 2. (*use to own ends*) sacar todo el jugo a; **they ~ed him for every penny he had** le chuparon hasta el último centavo.

milk chocolate *n* chocolate *m* con leche.

milkman ['mɪlkmən] (*pl* **-men** [-mən]) *n* lechero *m*.

milk shake *n* batido *m*.

milky ['mɪlkɪ] *adj* 1. *Br* (*with milk*) con mucha leche. 2. (*pale white*) lechoso(sa).

Milky Way *n*: **the** ~ la Vía Láctea.

mill [mɪl] ◆ *n* 1. (*flour-mill*) molino *m*. 2. (*factory*) fábrica *f*. 3. (*grinder*) molinillo *m*. ◆ *vt* moler. ▶ **mill about, mill around** *vi* arremolinarse.

millennium [mɪ'lenɪəm] (*pl* **-nnia** [-nɪə]) *n* milenio *m*.

miller ['mɪlər] *n* molinero *m*, -ra *f*.

millet ['mɪlɪt] *n* mijo *m*.

milligram(me) ['mɪlɪgræm] *n* miligramo *m*.

millimetre *Br*, **millimeter** *Am* ['mɪlɪ,mi:tər] *n* milímetro *m*.

millinery ['mɪlɪnrɪ] *n* sombrerería *f* (de señoras).

million ['mɪljən] *n* millón *m*; **a ~, ~s of** *fig* millones de.

millionaire [,mɪljə'neər] *n* millonario *m*.

millstone ['mɪlstəʊn] *n* piedra *f* de molino, muela *f*.

milometer [maɪ'lɒmɪtər] = **mileometer**.

mime [maɪm] ◆ *n* (*acting*) mímica *f*. ◆ *vt* describir con gestos. ◆ *vi* hacer mímica.

mimic ['mɪmɪk] (*pt & pp* **-ked**, *cont* **-king**) ◆ *n* imitador *m*, -ra *f*. ◆ *vt* imitar.

mimicry ['mɪmɪkrɪ] *n* imitación *f*.

min. [mɪn] 1. (*abbr of* **minute**) min. 2. (*abbr of* **minimum**) mín.

mince [mɪns] ◆ *n* *Br* carne *f* picada. ◆ *vt* picar. ◆ *vi* andar dando pasitos.

mincemeat ['mɪnsmi:t] *n* 1. (*fruit*) mezcla de fruta confitada y especias. 2. *Am* (*minced meat*) carne *f* picada.

mince pie *n* pastelillo *m* de fruta confitada.

mincer ['mɪnsər] *n* máquina *f* de picar carne.

mind [maɪnd] ◆ *n* 1. (*gen*) mente *f*; **state of** ~ estado *m* de ánimo, estado OR tono *m* de ánimo; **to cross sb's** ~ pasársele a alguien por la cabeza; **to have sthg on one's** ~ estar preocupado por algo; **to keep an open** ~

tener una actitud abierta; **to take sb's ~ off sthg** hacer olvidar algo a alguien; **to make one's ~ up** decidirse. **2.** (*attention*) atención *f*; **to put one's ~ to sthg** poner empeño en algo. **3.** (*opinion*): **to change one's ~** cambiar de opinión; **to my ~** en mi opinión; **to be in two ~s about sthg** no estar seguro(ra) de algo; **to speak one's ~** hablar sin rodeos. **4.** (*memory*) memoria *f*; **to bear sthg in ~** tener presente algo. **5.** (*intention*): **to have sthg in ~** tener algo en mente; **to have a ~ to do sthg** estar pensando en hacer algo. ◆ *vi* (*be bothered*): **do you ~?** ¿te importa?; **I don't ~ ...** no me importa ...; **never ~** (*don't worry*) no te preocupes; (*it's not important*) no importa. ◆ *vt* **1.** (*be bothered about, dislike*): **do you ~ if I leave?** ¿te molesta si me voy?; **I don't ~ waiting** no me importa esperar; **I wouldn't ~ a ...** no me vendría mal un ... **2.** (*pay attention to*) tener cuidado con. **3.** (*take care of*) cuidar. ▶ **mind you** *adv*: **he's a bit deaf; ~ you, he is old** está un poco sordo; te advierto que es ya mayor.

minder ['maɪndər] *n* Br *inf* (*bodyguard*) guardaespaldas *m y f*.

mindful ['maɪndfʊl] *adj*: **~ of** consciente de.

mindless ['maɪndlɪs] *adj* **1.** (*stupid*) absurdo(da), sin sentido. **2.** (*not requiring thought*) aburrido(da).

mine¹ [maɪn] *poss pron* mío (mía); **that money is ~** ese dinero es mío; **his car hit ~** su coche chocó contra el mío; **it wasn't your fault, it was** MINE la culpa no fue tuya sino MÍA; **a friend of ~** un amigo mío.

mine² [maɪn] ◆ *n* mina *f*. ◆ *vt* **1.** (*excavate - coal*) extraer. **2.** (*lay mines in*) minar.

minefield ['maɪnfiːld] *n lit & fig* campo *m* de minas.

miner ['maɪnər] *n* minero *m*, -ra *f*.

mineral ['mɪnərəl] ◆ *adj* mineral. ◆ *n* mineral *m*.

mineral water *n* agua *f* mineral.

minesweeper ['maɪnˌswiːpər] *n* dragaminas *m inv*.

mingle ['mɪŋgl] *vi* **1.** (*combine*): **to ~ (with)** mezclarse (con). **2.** (*socially*): **to ~ (with)** alternar (con).

miniature ['mɪnətʃər] ◆ *adj* en miniatura. ◆ *n* **1.** (*painting*) miniatura *f*. **2.** (*of alcohol*) botellín de licor en miniatura.

minibus ['mɪnɪbʌs] (*pl* -es) *n* microbús *m*.

minicab ['mɪnɪkæb] *n* Br taxi que se puede pedir por teléfono, pero no se puede parar en la calle.

minima ['mɪnɪmə] *pl* → **minimum**.

minimal ['mɪnɪml] *adj* mínimo(ma).

minimum ['mɪnɪməm] (*pl* -mums OR -ma) ◆ *adj* mínimo(ma). ◆ *n* mínimo *m*.

mining ['maɪnɪŋ] ◆ *n* minería *f*. ◆ *adj* minero(ra).

miniskirt ['mɪnɪskɜːt] *n* minifalda *f*.

minister ['mɪnɪstər] *n* **1.** (POL): **~ (for)** ministro *m*, -tra *f* (de). **2.** (RELIG) pastor *m*, -ra *f*. ▶ **minister to** *vt fus* atender a.

ministerial [ˌmɪnɪ'stɪərɪəl] *adj* ministerial.

minister of state *n*: **~ (for)** ministro *m*, -tra *f* de estado (para).

ministry ['mɪnɪstrɪ] *n* **1.** (POL) ministerio *m*. **2.** (RELIG): **the ~** el clero.

mink [mɪŋk] (*pl inv*) *n* visón *m*.

minnow ['mɪnəʊ] *n* pececillo *m* (de agua dulce).

minor ['maɪnər] ◆ *adj* menor. ◆ *n* menor *m y f* (de edad).

Minorca [mɪ'nɔːkə] *n* Menorca *f*.

minority [maɪ'nɒrətɪ] *n* minoría *f*.

mint [mɪnt] ◆ *n* **1.** (*herb*) menta *f*, hierbabuena *f*. **2.** (*peppermint*) pastilla *f* de menta. **3.** (*for coins*): **the ~** la Casa de la Moneda; **in ~ condition** en perfecto estado, como nuevo(va). ◆ *vt* acuñar.

minus ['maɪnəs] (*pl* -es) ◆ *prep* **1.** (MATH) (*less*): **4 ~ 2 is 2** 4 menos 2 es 2. **2.** (*in temperatures*): **it's ~ 5°C** estamos a 5° bajo cero. ◆ *n* **1.** (MATH) signo *m* (de) menos. **2.** (*disadvantage*) pega *f*, desventaja *f*.

minus sign *n* signo *m* (de) menos.

minute¹ ['mɪnɪt] *n* minuto *m*; **at any ~** en cualquier momento; **this ~** ahora mismo. ▶ **minutes** *npl* acta *f*; **to take ~s** levantar OR tomar acta.

minute² [maɪ'njuːt] *adj* diminuto(ta).

miracle ['mɪrəkl] *n lit & fig* milagro *m*.

miraculous [mɪ'rækjʊləs] *adj* milagroso(sa).

mirage [mɪ'rɑːʒ] *n lit & fig* espejismo *m*.

mire [maɪər] *n* fango *m*, lodo *m*.

mirror ['mɪrər] ◆ *n* espejo *m*. ◆ *vt* reflejar.

mirth [mɜːθ] *n* risa *f*.

misadventure [ˌmɪsəd'ventʃər] *n* desgracia *f*; **death by ~** (JUR) muerte *f* accidental.

misapprehension ['mɪsˌæprɪ'henʃn] *n* **1.** (*misunderstanding*) malentendido *m*. **2.** (*mistaken belief*) creencia *f* errónea.

misappropriation ['mɪsəˌprəʊprɪ'eɪʃn] *n*: **~ (of)** malversación *f* (de).

misbehave [ˌmɪsbɪ'heɪv] vi portarse mal.

miscalculate [ˌmɪs'kælkjʊleɪt] vt & vi calcular mal.

miscarriage [ˌmɪs'kærɪdʒ] n (at birth) aborto m (natural).

miscarriage of justice n error m judicial.

miscellaneous [ˌmɪsə'leɪnjəs] adj diverso(sa).

mischief ['mɪstʃɪf] n (U) 1. (playfulness) picardía f. 2. (naughty behaviour) travesuras fpl. 3. (harm) daño m.

mischievous ['mɪstʃɪvəs] adj 1. (playful) lleno(na) de picardía. 2. (naughty) travieso(sa).

misconception [ˌmɪskən'sepʃn] n concepto m erróneo.

misconduct [ˌmɪs'kɒndʌkt] n mala conducta f.

misconstrue [ˌmɪskən'struː] vt fml malinterpretar.

miscount [ˌmɪs'kaʊnt] vt & vi contar mal.

misdeed [ˌmɪs'diːd] n literary fechoría f.

misdemeanour Br, **misdemeanor** Am [ˌmɪsdɪ'miːnəʳ] n fml delito m menor.

miser ['maɪzəʳ] n avaro m, -ra f.

miserable ['mɪzrəbl] adj 1. (unhappy) infeliz, triste. 2. (wretched, poor) miserable. 3. (weather) horrible. 4. (pathetic) lamentable.

miserly ['maɪzəlɪ] adj miserable, mezquino(na).

misery ['mɪzərɪ] n 1. (unhappiness) desdicha f. 2. (wretchedness) miseria f.

misfire [ˌmɪs'faɪəʳ] vi 1. (car engine) no arrancar. 2. (plan) fracasar.

misfit ['mɪsfɪt] n inadaptado m, -da f.

misfortune [mɪs'fɔːtʃuːn] n 1. (bad luck) mala suerte f. 2. (piece of bad luck) desgracia f, infortunio m.

misgivings [mɪs'ɡɪvɪŋz] npl recelos mpl.

misguided [ˌmɪs'ɡaɪdɪd] adj (person) descaminado(da); (attempt) equivocado(da).

mishandle [ˌmɪs'hændl] vt 1. (person, animal) maltratar. 2. (affair) llevar mal.

mishap ['mɪshæp] n contratiempo m.

misinform [ˌmɪsɪn'fɔːm] vt desinformar.

misinterpret [ˌmɪsɪn'tɜːprɪt] vt malinterpretar.

misjudge [ˌmɪs'dʒʌdʒ] vt 1. (guess wrongly) calcular mal. 2. (appraise wrongly) juzgar mal.

mislay [ˌmɪs'leɪ] (pt & pp -laid) vt extraviar, perder.

mislead [ˌmɪs'liːd] (pt & pp -led) vt engañar.

misleading [ˌmɪs'liːdɪŋ] adj engañoso (sa).

misled [ˌmɪs'led] pt & pp → **mislead**.

misnomer [ˌmɪs'nəʊməʳ] n término m equivocado.

misplace [ˌmɪs'pleɪs] vt extraviar.

misprint ['mɪsprɪnt] n errata f, error m de imprenta.

miss [mɪs] ◆ vt 1. (fail to see - TV programme, film) perderse; (- error, person in crowd) no ver. 2. (shot) fallar; (ball) no dar a. 3. (feel absence of) echar de menos OR en falta. 4. (opportunity) perder, dejar pasar; (turning) pasarse. 5. (train, bus) perder. 6. (appointment) faltar a. 7. (avoid) evitar. ◆ vi fallar. ◆ n: **to give sthg a ~ inf** pasar de algo. ▶ **miss out** ◆ vt sep pasar por alto. ◆ vi: **to ~ out (on sthg)** perderse (algo).

Miss [mɪs] n señorita f.

misshapen [ˌmɪs'ʃeɪpn] adj deforme.

missile [Br 'mɪsaɪl, Am 'mɪsəl] n 1. (weapon) misil m. 2. (thrown object) proyectil m.

missing ['mɪsɪŋ] adj 1. (lost) perdido (da), extraviado(da). 2. (not present) que falta; **to be ~** faltar.

mission ['mɪʃn] n misión f.

missionary ['mɪʃənrɪ] n misionero m, -ra f.

misspend [ˌmɪs'spend] (pt & pp -spent) vt malgastar.

mist [mɪst] n (gen) neblina f; (at sea) bruma f. ▶ **mist over, mist up** vi (windows, spectacles) empañarse; (eyes) llenarse de lágrimas.

mistake [mɪ'steɪk] (pt -took, pp -taken) ◆ n error m; **to make a ~** equivocarse, cometer un error; **by ~** por error. ◆ vt 1. (misunderstand) entender mal. 2. (fail to recognize): **to ~ sthg/sb for** confundir algo/a alguien con.

mistaken [mɪ'steɪkn] ◆ pp → **mistake**. ◆ adj equivocado(da); **to be ~ about sb/sthg** estar equivocado respecto a alguien/algo.

mister ['mɪstəʳ] n inf amigo m. ▶ **Mister** n señor m.

mistletoe ['mɪsltəʊ] n muérdago m.

mistook [mɪ'stʊk] pt → **mistake**.

mistreat [ˌmɪs'triːt] vt maltratar.

mistress ['mɪstrɪs] n 1. (woman in control) señora f. 2. (female lover) amante f. 3. Br (school teacher - primary) maestra f; (- secondary) profesora f.

mistrust [,mɪs'trʌst] ◆ n desconfianza f, recelo m. ◆ vt desconfiar de.

misty ['mɪstɪ] adj (gen) neblinoso(sa); (at sea) brumoso(sa).

misunderstand [,mɪsʌndə'stænd] (pt & pp -**stood**) vt & vi entender OR comprender mal.

misunderstanding [,mɪsʌndə-'stændɪŋ] n malentendido m.

misunderstood [,mɪsʌndə'stʊd] pt & pp → **misunderstand**.

misuse [n ,mɪs'juːs, vb ,mɪs'juːz] ◆ n uso m indebido. ◆ vt hacer uso indebido de.

miter Am = mitre.

mitigate ['mɪtɪgeɪt] vt fml mitigar.

mitre Br, **miter** Am ['maɪtər] n (hat) mitra f.

mitt [mɪt] n manopla f.

mitten ['mɪtn] n manopla f.

mix [mɪks] ◆ vt: to ~ sthg (with) mezclar algo (con). ◆ vi 1. (substances) mezclarse; (activities) ir bien juntos(tas). 2. (socially): to ~ with alternar OR salir con. ◆ n mezcla f. ► **mix up** vt sep 1. (confuse) confundir. 2. (disorder) mezclar.

mixed [mɪkst] adj 1. (of different kinds) surtido(da), variado(da). 2. (of different sexes) mixto(ta).

mixed-ability adj Br de varios niveles.

mixed grill n parrillada f mixta.

mixed up adj 1. (confused) confuso(sa). 2. (involved): ~ in (fight, crime) involucrado(da) en.

mixer ['mɪksər] n 1. (for food) batidora f; (for cement) hormigonera f. 2. (non-alcoholic drink) bebida no alcohólica para mezclar con bebidas alcohólicas.

mixture ['mɪkstʃər] n (gen) mezcla f; (of sweets) surtido m.

mix-up n inf lío m, confusión f.

mm (abbr of millimetre) mm.

moan [məʊn] ◆ n (of pain, sadness) gemido m. ◆ vi 1. (in pain, sadness) gemir. 2. inf (complain): to ~ (about) quejarse (de).

moat [məʊt] n foso m.

mob [mɒb] ◆ n muchedumbre f. ◆ vt asediar.

mobile ['məʊbaɪl] ◆ adj (able to move) móvil. ◆ n móvil m.

mobile home n caravana f.

mobile phone n (teléfono m) móvil m, celular m Amer.

mobilize, -ise ['məʊbɪlaɪz] vt movilizar.

mock [mɒk] ◆ adj fingido(da); ~ (**exam**) simulacro m de examen. ◆ vt burlarse de. ◆ vi burlarse.

mockery ['mɒkərɪ] n burla f.

mod cons [,mɒd-] (abbr of modern conveniences) npl Br inf: **all** ~ con todas las comodidades.

mode [məʊd] n modo m.

model ['mɒdl] ◆ n 1. (gen) modelo m. 2. (small copy) maqueta f. 3. (for painter, in fashion) modelo m y f. ◆ adj 1. (exemplary) modelo (inv). 2. (reduced-scale) en miniatura. ◆ vt 1. (shape) modelar. 2. (wear) lucir (en pase de modelos). 3. (copy): to ~ o.s. on sb tener a alguien como modelo. ◆ vi trabajar de modelo.

modem ['məʊdem] n (COMPUT) módem m.

moderate [adj & n 'mɒdərət, vb 'mɒdəreɪt] ◆ adj moderado(da). ◆ n (POL) moderado m, -da f. ◆ vt moderar. ◆ vi moderarse.

moderation [,mɒdə'reɪʃn] n moderación f; **in** ~ con moderación.

modern ['mɒdən] adj moderno(na).

modernize, -ise ['mɒdənaɪz] ◆ vt modernizar. ◆ vi modernizarse.

modern languages npl lenguas fpl modernas.

modest ['mɒdɪst] adj 1. (gen) modesto(ta). 2. (improvement) ligero(ra); (price) módico(ca).

modesty ['mɒdɪstɪ] n modestia f.

modicum ['mɒdɪkəm] n fml: **a** ~ **of** un mínimo de.

modify ['mɒdɪfaɪ] vt modificar.

module ['mɒdjuːl] n módulo m.

mogul ['məʊgl] n magnate m y f.

mohair ['məʊheər] n mohair m.

moist [mɔɪst] adj húmedo(da).

moisten ['mɔɪsn] vt humedecer.

moisture ['mɔɪstʃər] n humedad f.

moisturizer ['mɔɪstʃəraɪzər] n (crema f) hidratante m.

molar ['məʊlər] n muela f.

molasses [mə'læsɪz] n (U) melaza f.

mold etc Am = mould.

mole [məʊl] n 1. (animal, spy) topo m. 2. (spot) lunar m.

molecule ['mɒlɪkjuːl] n molécula f.

molest [mə'lest] vt 1. (attack sexually) acosar sexualmente. 2. (attack) atacar.

mollusc, mollusk Am ['mɒləsk] n molusco m.

mollycoddle ['mɒlɪ,kɒdl] vt inf mimar.

molt Am = moult.

molten ['məʊltn] adj fundido(da).

mom [mɒm] n Am inf mamá f.

moment ['məumənt] *n* momento *m*; **at any ~** de un momento a otro; **at the ~** en este momento; **for the ~** de momento

momentarily ['məuməntərɪlɪ] *adv* 1. (*for a short time*) momentáneamente. 2. Am (*soon*) pronto.

momentary ['məuməntrɪ] *adj* momentáneo(a).

momentous [mə'mentəs] *adj* trascendental.

momentum [mə'mentəm] *n* (U) 1. (PHYSICS) momento *m*. 2. *fig* (*speed, force*) ímpetu *m*, impulso *m*; **to gather ~** cobrar intensidad.

momma ['mɒmə], **mommy** ['mɒmɪ] *n* Am mamá *f*.

Monaco ['mɒnəkəu] *n* Mónaco.

monarch ['mɒnək] *n* monarca *m y f*.

monarchy ['mɒnəkɪ] *n* 1. (*gen*) monarquía *f*. 2. (*royal family*): **the ~** la familia real.

monastery ['mɒnəstrɪ] *n* monasterio *m*.

Monday ['mʌndɪ] *n* lunes *m inv; see also* **Saturday**.

monetary ['mʌnɪtrɪ] *adj* monetario (ria).

money ['mʌnɪ] *n* dinero *m*; **to make ~** hacer dinero; **to get one's ~'s worth** sacarle provecho al dinero de uno.

moneybox ['mʌnɪbɒks] *n* hucha *f*.

moneylender ['mʌnɪ,lendər] *n* prestamista *m y f*.

money order *n* giro *m* postal.

money-spinner [-,spɪnər] *n inf* mina *f* (de dinero).

mongol ['mɒŋgəl] *n dated & offensive* mongólico *m*, -ca *f*.

Mongolia [mɒŋ'gəulɪə] *n* Mongolia.

mongrel ['mʌŋgrəl] *n* perro *m* cruzado OR sin pedigrí.

monitor ['mɒnɪtər] ◆ *n* (*gen & COMPUT*) monitor *m*. ◆ *vt* 1. (*check*) controlar. 2. (*listen in to*) escuchar.

monk [mʌŋk] *n* monje *m*.

monkey ['mʌŋkɪ] (*pl* **monkeys**) *n* mono *m*.

monkey nut *n* cacahuete *m*.

monkey wrench *n* llave *f* inglesa.

mono ['mɒnəu] *adj* mono (*inv*).

monochrome ['mɒnəkrəum] *adj* monocromo(ma).

monocle ['mɒnəkl] *n* monóculo *m*.

monologue, monolog Am ['mɒnəlɒg] *n* monólogo *m*.

monopolize, -ise [mə'nɒpəlaɪz] *vt* monopolizar.

monopoly [mə'nɒpəlɪ] *n*: **~ (on** OR **of)** monopolio *m* (de).

monotone ['mɒnətəun] *n*: **in a ~** con voz monótona.

monotonous [mə'nɒtənəs] *adj* monótono(na).

monotony [mə'nɒtənɪ] *n* monotonía *f*.

monsoon [mɒn'su:n] *n* monzón *m*.

monster ['mɒnstər] *n* (*imaginary creature, cruel person*) monstruo *m*.

monstrosity [mɒn'strɒsətɪ] *n* monstruosidad *f*.

monstrous ['mɒnstrəs] *adj* 1. (*very unfair, frightening, ugly*) monstruoso(sa). 2. (*very large*) gigantesco(ca).

Mont Blanc [mõblã] *n* Mont Blanc.

month [mʌnθ] *n* mes *m*.

monthly ['mʌnθlɪ] ◆ *adj* mensual. ◆ *adv* mensualmente.

monument ['mɒnjumənt] *n* monumento *m*.

monumental [,mɒnju'mentl] *adj* 1. (*gen*) monumental. 2. (*error*) descomunal.

moo [mu:] (*pl* **-s**) *vi* mugir.

mood [mu:d] *n* (*of individual*) humor *m*; (*of public, voters*) disposición *f*; **in a (bad) ~** de mal humor; **in a good ~** de buen humor.

moody ['mu:dɪ] *adj pej* 1. (*changeable*) de humor variable. 2. (*bad-tempered*) malhumorado(da).

moon [mu:n] *n* luna *f*.

moonlight ['mu:nlaɪt] *n* luz *f* de la luna.

moonlighting ['mu:nlaɪtɪŋ] *n* pluriempleo *m*.

moonlit ['mu:nlɪt] *adj* (*night*) de luna; (*landscape*) iluminado(da) por la luna.

moor [mɔ:r] ◆ *n* páramo *m*. ◆ *vt* amarrar. ◆ *vi* echar las amarras.

Moor [mɔ:r] *n* moro *m*, -ra *f*.

Moorish ['mɔ:rɪʃ] *adj* moro(ra), morisco(ca).

moorland ['mɔ:lənd] *n* páramo *m*, brezal *m*.

moose [mu:s] (*pl inv*) *n* (*North American*) alce *m*.

mop [mɒp] ◆ *n* 1. (*for cleaning*) fregona *f*. 2. *inf* (*of hair*) pelambrera *f*. ◆ *vt* 1. (*clean with mop*) pasar la fregona por. 2. (*dry with cloth - sweat*) enjugar. ▶ **mop up** *vt sep* (*clean up*) limpiar.

mope [məup] *vi pej* estar deprimido (da).

moped ['məuped] *n* ciclomotor *m*, motoneta *f Amer*.

moral ['mɒrəl] ◆ *adj* moral. ◆ *n* (*lesson*)

moraleja f. ▶ **morals** npl (principles) moral f.

morale [mɒˈrɑːl] n (U) moral f.

morality [məˈrælətɪ] n 1. (gen) moralidad f. 2. (system of principles) moral f.

morass [məˈræs] n cenagal m.

morbid [ˈmɔːbɪd] adj morboso(sa).

more [mɔːr] ◆ adv 1. (with adjectives and adverbs) más; ~ **important (than)** más importante (que); ~ **quickly/often (than)** más rápido/a menudo (que). 2. (to a greater degree) más; **we were ~ hurt than angry** más que enfadados estábamos heridos. 3. (another time): **once/twice ~** una vez/dos veces más. ◆ adj más; ~ **food than drink** más comida que bebida; ~ **than 70 people died** más de 70 personas murieron; **have some ~ tea** toma un poco más de té; **I finished two ~ chapters today** acabé otros dos capítulos hoy. ◆ pron más; ~ **than five** más de cinco; **he's got ~ than I have** él tiene más que yo; **there's no ~ (left)** no queda nada (más); **(and) what's ~** (y lo que) es más. ▶ **any more** adv: **not ... any ~** ya no ... ▶ **more and more** adv, adj & pron cada vez más. ▶ **more or less** adv más o menos.

moreover [mɔːˈrəʊvər] adv fml además.

morgue [mɔːg] n depósito m de cadáveres.

Mormon [ˈmɔːmən] n mormón m, -ona f.

morning [ˈmɔːnɪŋ] n 1. (first part of day) mañana f; **in the ~** por la mañana; **six o'clock in the ~** las seis de la mañana. 2. (between midnight and dawn) madrugada f. 3. (tomorrow morning): **in the ~** mañana por la mañana. ▶ **mornings** adv Am por la mañana.

Moroccan [məˈrɒkən] ◆ adj marroquí. ◆ n marroquí m y f.

Morocco [məˈrɒkəʊ] n Marruecos.

moron [ˈmɔːrɒn] n inf imbécil m y f.

morose [məˈrəʊs] adj malhumorado(da).

morphine [ˈmɔːfiːn] n morfina f.

Morse (code) [mɔːs-] n (alfabeto m) Morse m.

morsel [ˈmɔːsl] n bocado m.

mortal [ˈmɔːtl] ◆ adj (gen) mortal. ◆ n mortal m y f.

mortality [mɔːˈtælətɪ] n mortalidad f.

mortar [ˈmɔːtər] n 1. (cement mixture) argamasa f. 2. (gun, bowl) mortero m.

mortgage [ˈmɔːgɪdʒ] ◆ n hipoteca f. ◆ vt hipotecar.

mortified [ˈmɔːtɪfaɪd] adj muerto(ta) de vergüenza.

mortuary [ˈmɔːtʃʊərɪ] n depósito m de cadáveres.

mosaic [məˈzeɪɪk] n mosaico m.

Moscow [ˈmɒskəʊ] n Moscú.

Moslem [ˈmɒzləm] = **Muslim**.

mosque [mɒsk] n mezquita f.

mosquito [məˈskiːtəʊ] (pl -es OR -s) n mosquito m, zancudo m Amer.

moss [mɒs] n musgo m.

most [məʊst] (superl of **many**) ◆ adj 1. (the majority of) la mayoría de; ~ **people** la mayoría de la gente. 2. (largest amount of): **(the) ~** más; **who has got (the) ~ money?** ¿quién es el que tiene más dinero? ◆ pron 1. (the majority): ~ **(of)** la mayoría (de); ~ **of the time** la mayor parte del tiempo. 2. (largest amount): **(the) ~** lo más, lo máximo; **at ~** como mucho, todo lo más. 3. phr: **to make the ~ of sthg** sacarle el mayor partido a algo. ◆ adv 1. (to the greatest extent): **(the) ~** el/la/lo más; **what I like ~** lo que más me gusta. 2. fml (very) muy; ~ **certainly** con toda seguridad. 3. Am (almost) casi.

mostly [ˈməʊstlɪ] adv (in the main part) principalmente; (usually) normalmente.

MOT (abbr of Ministry of Transport test) n ≈ ITV f.

motel [məʊˈtel] n motel m.

moth [mɒθ] n polilla f.

mothball [ˈmɒθbɔːl] n bola f de naftalina.

mother [ˈmʌðər] ◆ n madre f. ◆ vt usu pej (spoil) mimar.

motherhood [ˈmʌðəhʊd] n maternidad f.

mother-in-law (pl **mothers-in-law** OR **mother-in-laws**) n suegra f.

motherly [ˈmʌðəlɪ] adj maternal.

mother-of-pearl n nácar m.

mother-to-be (pl **mothers-to-be**) n futura madre f.

mother tongue n lengua f materna.

motif [məʊˈtiːf] n (ART & MUS) motivo m.

motion [ˈməʊʃn] ◆ n 1. (gen) movimiento m; **to set sthg in ~** poner algo en marcha. 2. (proposal) moción f. ◆ vt: **to ~ sb to do sthg** indicar a alguien con un gesto que haga algo. ◆ vi: **to ~ to sb** hacer una señal (con la mano) a alguien.

motionless [ˈməʊʃənlɪs] adj inmóvil.

motion picture n Am película f.

motivated [ˈməʊtɪveɪtɪd] adj motivado(da).

motivation [ˌməʊtɪˈveɪʃn] n motivación f.

motive [ˈməʊtɪv] n (gen) motivo m; (for crime) móvil m.

motley [ˈmɒtlɪ] adj pej variopinto(ta).

motor [ˈməʊtər] ◆ adj Br (industry, accident) automovilístico(ca); (mechanic) de automóviles. ◆ n motor m.

motorbike [ˈməʊtəbaɪk] n inf moto f.

motorboat [ˈməʊtəbəʊt] n lancha f motora.

motorcar [ˈməʊtəkɑːr] n automóvil m.

motorcycle [ˈməʊtəˌsaɪkl] n motocicleta f.

motorcyclist [ˈməʊtəˌsaɪklɪst] n motociclista m y f.

motoring [ˈməʊtərɪŋ] n dated automovilismo m.

motorist [ˈməʊtərɪst] n automovilista m y f, conductor m, -ra f.

motor racing n automovilismo m deportivo.

motor scooter n Vespa® f, escúter m.

motor vehicle n vehículo m de motor.

motorway [ˈməʊtəweɪ] n Br autopista f.

mottled [ˈmɒtld] adj moteado(da).

motto [ˈmɒtəʊ] (pl -s OR -es) n lema m.

mould, mold Am [məʊld] ◆ n 1. (growth) moho m. 2. (shape) molde m. ◆ vt lit & fig moldear.

moulding, molding Am [ˈməʊldɪŋ] n (decoration) moldura f.

mouldy, moldy Am [ˈməʊldɪ] adj mohoso(sa).

moult, molt Am [məʊlt] vi (bird) mudar la pluma; (dog) mudar el pelo.

mound [maʊnd] n 1. (small hill) montículo m. 2. (untidy pile) montón m.

mount [maʊnt] ◆ n 1. (gen) montura f; (for photograph) marco m; (for jewel) engaste m. 2. (mountain) monte m. ◆ vt 1. (horse, bike) subirse a, montar en. 2. (attack) lanzar. 3. (exhibition) montar. 4. (jewel) engastar; (photograph) enmarcar. ◆ vi (increase) aumentar.

mountain [ˈmaʊntɪn] n lit & fig montaña f.

mountain bike n bicicleta f de montaña.

mountaineer [ˌmaʊntɪˈnɪər] n montañero m, -ra f, andinista m y f Amer.

mountaineering [ˌmaʊntɪˈnɪərɪŋ] n montañismo m, andinismo m Amer.

mountainous [ˈmaʊntɪnəs] adj montañoso(sa).

mourn [mɔːn] ◆ vt (person) llorar por; (thing) lamentarse de. ◆ vi afligirse; to ~ for sb llorar la muerte de alguien.

mourner [ˈmɔːnər] n doliente m y f.

mournful [ˈmɔːnfʊl] adj (face, voice) afligido(da), lúgubre; (sound) lastimero (ra).

mourning [ˈmɔːnɪŋ] n luto m; in ~ de luto.

mouse [maʊs] (pl mice) n (ZOOL & COMPUT) ratón m.

mousetrap [ˈmaʊstræp] n ratonera f.

mousse [muːs] n 1. (food) mousse m. 2. (for hair) espuma f.

moustache Br [məˈstɑːʃ], **mustache** Am [ˈmʌstæʃ] n bigote m.

mouth [maʊθ] n (gen) boca f; (of river) desembocadura f.

mouthful [ˈmaʊθfʊl] n (of food) bocado m; (of drink) trago m.

mouthorgan [ˈmaʊθˌɔːgən] n armónica f.

mouthpiece [ˈmaʊθpiːs] n 1. (of telephone) micrófono m. 2. (of musical instrument) boquilla f. 3. (spokesperson) portavoz m y f.

mouthwash [ˈmaʊθwɒʃ] n elixir m bucal.

mouth-watering [-ˌwɔːtərɪŋ] adj muy apetitoso(sa).

movable [ˈmuːvəbl] adj movible.

move [muːv] ◆ n 1. (movement) movimiento m; to get a ~ on inf espabilarse, darse prisa. 2. (change - of house) mudanza f; (- of job) cambio m. 3. (in board game) jugada f. 4. (course of action) medida f. ◆ vt 1. (shift) mover. 2. (change - house) mudarse de; (- job) cambiar de. 3. (affect) conmover. 4. (in debate - motion) proponer. 5. (cause): to ~ sb to do sthg mover OR llevar a alguien a hacer algo. ◆ vi 1. (gen) moverse; (events) cambiar. 2. (change house) mudarse; (change job) cambiar de trabajo. ► **move about** vi 1. (fidget) ir de aquí para allá. 2. (travel) viajar. ► **move along** vi sep hacer circular. ◆ vi 1. (move towards front or back) hacerse a un lado. 2. (move away - crowd, car) circular. ► **move around** = move about. ► **move away** vi (leave) marcharse. ► **move in** vi 1. (to new house) instalarse. 2. (take control, attack) prepararse para el ataque. ► **move on** vi 1. (go away) reanudar la marcha. 2. (progress) avanzar. ► **move out** vi mudarse. ► **move over** vi hacer sitio. ► **move up** vi (on bench etc) hacer sitio.

moveable = movable.

movement ['muːvmənt] n 1. (gen) movimiento m. 2. (transportation) transporte m.

movie ['muːvɪ] n película f.

movie camera n cámara f cinematográfica.

moving ['muːvɪŋ] adj 1. (touching) conmovedor(ra). 2. (not fixed) móvil.

mow [məʊ] (pt -ed, pp -ed OR mown) vt (grass, lawn) cortar; (corn) segar. ► **mow down** vt sep acribillar.

mower ['məʊər] n cortacésped m o f.

mown [məʊn] pp → **mow**.

MP n 1. (abbr of Military Police) PM f. 2. Br abbr of **Member of Parliament**.

mpg (abbr of miles per gallon) millas/galón.

mph (abbr of miles per hour) mph.

Mr ['mɪstər] n Sr.; ~ **Jones** el Sr. Jones.

Mrs ['mɪsɪz] n Sra.; ~ **Jones** la Sra. Jones.

Ms [mɪz] n abreviatura utilizada delante de un apellido de mujer cuando no se quiere especificar si está casada o no.

MS, ms n abbr of **multiple sclerosis**.

MSc (abbr of Master of Science) n (titular de un) título postuniversitario de unos dos años de duración en el campo de las ciencias.

much [mʌtʃ] (compar **more**, superl **most**) ◆ adj mucho(cha); **there isn't ~ rice left** no queda mucho arroz; **as ~ time as ...** tanto tiempo como ...; **how ~ money?** ¿cuánto dinero?; **so ~** tanto(ta); **too ~** demasiado(da); **how ~ ...?** ¿cuánto? ...? ◆ pron: **have you got ~?** ¿tienes mucho?; **I don't see ~ of him** no lo veo mucho; **I don't think ~ of it** no me parece gran cosa; **as ~ as** tanto como; **too ~** demasiado; **how ~?** ¿cuánto?; **this isn't ~ of a party** esta fiesta no es nada del otro mundo; **so ~ for** tanto; **I thought as ~** ya me lo imaginaba. ◆ adv mucho; **I don't go out ~** no salgo mucho; ~ **too cold** demasiado frío; **so ~** tanto; **thank you very ~** muchas gracias; **as ~ as** tanto como; **he is not so ~ stupid as** lazy más que tonto es vago; **too ~** demasiado; **without so ~ as ...** sin siquiera ... ► **much as** conj: ~ **as (I like him)** por mucho OR más que (me guste).

muck [mʌk] n (U) inf 1. (dirt) mugre f, porquería f. 2. (manure) estiércol m. ► **muck about, muck around** vi Br inf hacer el indio OR tonto. ► **muck up** vt sep Br inf fastidiar.

mucky ['mʌkɪ] adj guarro(rra).

mucus ['mjuːkəs] n mucosidad f.

mud [mʌd] n barro m, lodo m.

muddle ['mʌdl] ◆ n 1. (disorder) desorden m. 2. (confusion) lío m, confusión f; **to be in a ~** estar hecho un lío. ◆ vt 1. (put into disorder) desordenar. 2. (confuse) liar, confundir. ► **muddle along** vi apañárselas más o menos. ► **muddle through** vi arreglárselas. ► **muddle up** vt sep (put into disorder) desordenar; (confuse) liar, confundir.

muddy ['mʌdɪ] adj (gen) lleno(na) de barro; (river) cenagoso(sa).

mudguard ['mʌdɡɑːd] n guardabarros m inv, tapabarro m Amer.

mudslinging ['mʌdˌslɪŋɪŋ] n (U) fig insultos mpl, improperios mpl.

muesli ['mjuːzlɪ] n Br muesli m.

muff [mʌf] ◆ n manguito m. ◆ vt inf (catch) fallar; (chance) dejar escapar.

muffin ['mʌfɪn] n 1. Br (bread roll) panecillo m. 2. Am (cake) especie de magdalena que se come caliente.

muffle ['mʌfl] vt (sound) amortiguar.

muffler ['mʌflər] n Am (for car) silenciador m.

mug [mʌɡ] ◆ n 1. (cup) taza f (alta). 2. inf (fool) primo m, -ma f. ◆ vt asaltar, atracar.

mugging ['mʌɡɪŋ] n (single attack) atraco m; (series of attacks) atracos mpl.

muggy ['mʌɡɪ] adj bochornoso(sa).

mule [mjuːl] n mula f.

mull [mʌl] ► **mull over** vt sep reflexionar sobre.

mulled [mʌld] adj: ~ **wine** vino caliente con azúcar y especias.

multicoloured Br, **multicolored** Am [ˌmʌltɪˈkʌləd] adj multicolor.

multigym ['mʌltɪdʒɪm] n multiestación f (de musculación).

multilateral [ˌmʌltɪˈlætərəl] adj multilateral.

multinational [ˌmʌltɪˈnæʃənl] n multinacional f.

multiple ['mʌltɪpl] ◆ adj múltiple. ◆ n múltiplo m.

multiple sclerosis [-sklɪˈrəʊsɪs] n esclerosis f inv múltiple.

multiplex cinema ['mʌltɪpleks-] n (cine m) multisalas m inv.

multiplication [ˌmʌltɪplɪˈkeɪʃn] n multiplicación f.

multiply ['mʌltɪplaɪ] ◆ vt multiplicar. ◆ vi (increase, breed) multiplicarse.

multistorey Br, **multistory** Am [ˌmʌltɪˈstɔːrɪ] adj de varias plantas.

multitude ['mʌltɪtjuːd] n multitud f.

mum [mʌm] Br inf ◆ n mamá f. ◆ adj: **to**

keep ~ no decir ni pío.

mumble ['mʌmbl] ♦ vt mascullar. ♦ vi musitar, hablar entre dientes.

mummy ['mʌmɪ] n 1. Br inf (mother) mamá f. 2. (preserved body) momia f.

mumps [mʌmps] n (U) paperas fpl.

munch [mʌntʃ] vt & vi masticar.

mundane [mʌn'deɪn] adj trivial.

municipal [mjuː'nɪsɪpl] adj municipal.

municipality [mjuːˌnɪsɪ'pælətɪ] n municipio m.

mural ['mjuːərəl] n mural m.

murder ['mɜːdər] ♦ n asesinato m. ♦ vt asesinar.

murderer ['mɜːdərər] n asesino m.

murderous ['mɜːdərəs] adj asesino (na).

murky ['mɜːkɪ] adj 1. (water, past) turbio(bia). 2. (night, street) sombrío(a), lúgubre.

murmur ['mɜːmər] ♦ n (low sound) murmullo m. ♦ vt & vi murmurar.

muscle ['mʌsl] n 1. (MED) músculo m. 2. fig (power) poder m. ► **muscle in** vi entrometerse.

muscular ['mʌskjʊlər] adj 1. (of muscles) muscular. 2. (strong) musculoso (sa).

muse [mjuːz] ♦ n musa f. ♦ vi meditar.

museum [mjuː'ziːəm] n museo m.

mushroom ['mʌʃrʊm] ♦ n (button) champiñón m; (field) seta f; (BOT) hongo m, callampa f Amer. ♦ vi extenderse rápidamente.

music ['mjuːzɪk] n música f.

musical ['mjuːzɪkl] ♦ adj 1. (gen) musical. 2. (talented in music) con talento para la música. ♦ n musical m.

musical instrument n instrumento m musical.

music centre n cadena f (musical).

music hall n Br teatro m de variedades OR de revista.

musician [mjuː'zɪʃn] n músico m, -ca f.

Muslim ['mʊzlɪm] ♦ adj musulmán (ana). ♦ n musulmán m, -ana f.

muslin ['mʌzlɪn] n muselina f.

mussel ['mʌsl] n mejillón m.

must [mʌst] ♦ aux vb 1. (have to, intend to) deber, tener que; **I ~ go** tengo que OR debo irme. 2. (as suggestion) tener que; **you ~ come and see us** tienes que venir a vernos. 3. (to express likelihood) deber (de); **it ~ be true** debe (de) ser verdad; **they ~ have known** deben de haberlo sabido. ♦ n inf: **a ~** algo imprescindible.

mustache Am = **moustache**.

mustard ['mʌstəd] n mostaza f.

muster ['mʌstər] vt reunir.

mustn't ['mʌsnt] = **must not**.

must've ['mʌstəv] = **must have**.

musty ['mʌstɪ] adj (room) que huele a cerrado; (book) que huele a viejo.

mute [mjuːt] ♦ adj mudo(da). ♦ n mudo m, -da f.

muted ['mjuːtɪd] adj 1. (not bright) apagado(da). 2. (subdued) contenido(da).

mutilate ['mjuːtɪleɪt] vt mutilar.

mutiny ['mjuːtɪnɪ] ♦ n motín m. ♦ vi amotinarse.

mutter ['mʌtər] ♦ vt musitar, mascullar. ♦ vi murmurar.

mutton ['mʌtn] n (carne f de) carnero m.

mutual ['mjuːtʃʊəl] adj 1. (reciprocal) mutuo(tua). 2. (common) común.

mutually ['mjuːtʃʊəlɪ] adv mutuamente.

muzzle ['mʌzl] ♦ n 1. (animal's nose and jaws) hocico m, morro m. 2. (wire guard) bozal m. 3. (of gun) boca f. ♦ vt (put muzzle on) poner bozal a.

MW (abbr of medium wave) OM f.

my [maɪ] poss adj 1. (gen) mi, mis (pl); **~ house/sister** mi casa/hermana; **~ children** mis hijos; **~ name is Sarah** me llamo Sarah; **it wasn't MY fault** no fue culpa mía OR mi culpa; **I washed ~ hair** me lavé el pelo. 2. (in titles): **~ Lord** milord; **~ Lady** milady.

myriad ['mɪrɪəd] adj literary innumerables.

myself [maɪ'self] pron 1. (reflexive) me; (after prep) mí mismo(ma); **with ~** conmigo mismo. 2. (for emphasis) yo mismo (ma); **I did it ~** lo hice yo solo(la).

mysterious [mɪ'stɪərɪəs] adj misterioso(sa).

mystery ['mɪstərɪ] n misterio m.

mystical ['mɪstɪkl] adj místico(ca).

mystified ['mɪstɪfaɪd] adj desconcertado(da), perplejo(ja).

mystifying ['mɪstɪfaɪɪŋ] adj desconcertante.

mystique [mɪ'stiːk] n misterio m.

myth [mɪθ] n mito m.

mythical ['mɪθɪkl] adj 1. (imaginary) mítico(ca). 2. (untrue) falso(sa).

mythology [mɪ'θɒlədʒɪ] n (collection of myths) mitología f.

N

n (*pl* **n's** OR **ns**), **N** (*pl* **N's** OR **Ns**) [en] *n* (*letter*) n f, N f. ▶ **N** (*abbr of* **north**) N.

n/a, N/A (*abbr of* **not applicable**) *no interesa*.

nab [næb] *vt inf* 1. (*arrest*) pillar, echar el guante a. 2. (*get quickly*) coger.

nag [næg] *vt* dar la lata a.

nagging ['nægɪŋ] *adj* 1. (*thought, doubt*) persistente. 2. (*person*) gruñón(ona).

nail [neɪl] ◆ *n* 1. (*for fastening*) clavo *m*. 2. (*of finger, toe*) uña *f*. ◆ *vt*: **to ~ sthg to sthg** clavar algo en OR a algo. ▶ **nail down** *vt sep* 1. (*fasten*) clavar. 2. (*person*): **I couldn't ~ him down** no pude hacerle concretar.

nailbrush ['neɪlbrʌʃ] *n* cepillo *m* de uñas.

nail file *n* lima *f* de uñas.

nail polish *n* esmalte *m* para las uñas.

nail scissors *npl* tijeras *fpl* para las uñas.

nail varnish *n* esmalte *m* para las uñas.

nail varnish remover [-rɪ'muːvəʳ] *n* quitaesmaltes *m inv*.

naive, naïve [naɪ'iːv] *adj* ingenuo (nua).

naked ['neɪkɪd] *adj* 1. (*gen*) desnudo (da); **~ flame** llama *f* sin protección. 2. (*blatant - hostility, greed*) abierto(ta); (*- facts*) sin tapujos. 3. (*unaided*): **with the ~ eye** a simple vista.

name [neɪm] ◆ *n* (*gen*) nombre *m*; (*surname*) apellido *m*; **what's your ~?** ¿cómo te llamas?; **my ~ is John** me llamo John; **by ~** por el nombre; **in sb's ~** a nombre de alguien; **in the ~ of** en nombre de; **to call sb ~s** llamar de todo a alguien. ◆ *vt* 1. (*christen*) poner nombre a; **to ~ sb after sb** Br, **to ~ sb for sb** Am poner a alguien el nombre de alguien. 2. (*identify*) nombrar. 3. (*date, price*) poner, decir. 4. (*appoint*) nombrar.

nameless ['neɪmlɪs] *adj* (*unknown - person, author*) anónimo(ma); (*- disease*) desconocido(da).

namely ['neɪmlɪ] *adv* a saber.

namesake ['neɪmseɪk] *n* tocayo *m*, -ya *f*.

nanny ['nænɪ] *n* niñera *f*.

nap [næp] ◆ *n* siesta *f*. ◆ *vi*: **we were caught napping** *inf* nos pilló desprevenidos.

nape [neɪp] *n*: **~ of the neck** nuca *f*.

napkin ['næpkɪn] *n* servilleta *f*.

nappy ['næpɪ] *n* Br pañal *m*.

nappy liner *n* parte desechable de un pañal de gasa.

narcissi [nɑː'sɪsaɪ] *pl* → **narcissus**.

narcissus [nɑː'sɪsəs] (*pl* **-cissuses** OR **-cissi**) *n* narciso *m*.

narcotic [nɑː'kɒtɪk] *n* narcótico *m*.

narrative ['nærətɪv] ◆ *adj* narrativo (va). ◆ *n* 1. (*account*) narración *f*. 2. (*art of narrating*) narrativa *f*.

narrator [Br nə'reɪtəʳ, Am 'næreɪtər] *n* narrador *m*, -ra *f*.

narrow ['nærəʊ] ◆ *adj* 1. (*not wide*) estrecho(cha). 2. (*limited*) estrecho(cha) de miras. 3. (*victory, defeat*) por un estrecho margen; (*escape, miss*) por muy poco. ◆ *vi* 1. (*become less wide*) estrecharse. 2. (*eyes*) entornarse. 3. (*gap*) reducirse. ▶ **narrow down** *vt sep* reducir.

narrowly ['nærəʊlɪ] *adv* (*barely*) por muy poco.

narrow-minded [-'maɪndɪd] *adj* estrecho(cha) de miras.

nasal ['neɪzl] *adj* nasal.

nasty ['nɑːstɪ] *adj* 1. (*unkind*) malintencionado(da). 2. (*smell, taste, feeling*) desagradable; (*weather*) horrible. 3. (*problem, decision*) peliagudo(da). 4. (*injury, disease*) doloroso(sa); (*fall*) malo(la).

nation ['neɪʃn] *n* nación *f*.

national ['næʃənl] ◆ *adj* nacional. ◆ *n* súbdito *m*, -ta *f*.

national anthem *n* himno *m* nacional.

national dress *n* traje *m* típico (de un país).

National Front *n*: **the ~** partido político minoritario de extrema derecha en Gran Bretaña.

National Health Service *n* Br: **the ~** organismo gestor de la salud pública, ≃ el Insalud.

National Insurance *n* Br ≃ Seguridad *f* Social.

nationalism ['næʃnəlɪzm] *n* nacionalismo *m*.

nationalist ['næʃnəlɪst] ◆ *adj* nacionalista. ◆ *n* nacionalista *m y f*.

nationality [ˌnæʃə'nælətɪ] *n* nacionalidad *f*.

nationalize, -ise ['næʃnəlaɪz] vt nacionalizar.

national park n parque m nacional.

national service n Br (MIL) servicio m militar.

National Trust n Br: the ~ organización británica encargada de la preservación de edificios históricos y lugares de interés, ≈ el Patrimonio Nacional.

nationwide ['neɪʃənwaɪd] ◆ adj a escala nacional. ◆ adv (travel) por todo el país; (be broadcast) a todo el país.

native ['neɪtɪv] ◆ adj 1. (country, area) natal. 2. (speaker) nativo(va); ~ language lengua f materna. 3. (plant, animal): ~ (to) originario(ria) (de). ◆ n natural m y f, nativo m, -va f.

Native American n indio americano m, india americana f.

Nativity [nə'tɪvətɪ] n: the ~ la Natividad.

NATO ['neɪtəʊ] (abbr of North Atlantic Treaty Organization) n OTAN f.

natural ['nætʃrəl] adj 1. (gen) natural. 2. (comedian, musician) nato(ta).

natural gas n gas m natural.

naturalize, -ise ['nætʃrəlaɪz] vt naturalizar; to be ~d naturalizarse.

naturally ['nætʃrəlɪ] adv 1. (as expected, understandably) naturalmente. 2. (unaffectedly) con naturalidad. 3. (instinctively) por naturaleza.

natural wastage n (U) reducción de plantilla por jubilación escalonada.

nature ['neɪtʃər] n 1. (gen) naturaleza f. 2. (disposition) modo m de ser, carácter m; by ~ por naturaleza.

nature reserve n reserva f natural.

naughty ['nɔːtɪ] adj 1. (badly behaved) travieso(sa), malo(la). 2. (rude) verde.

nausea ['nɔːsjə] n náusea f.

nauseam ['nɔːzɪæm] → ad nauseam.

nauseating ['nɔːsɪeɪtɪŋ] adj lit & fig nauseabundo(da).

nautical ['nɔːtɪkl] adj náutico(ca), marítimo(ma).

naval ['neɪvl] adj naval.

nave [neɪv] n nave f.

navel ['neɪvl] n ombligo m.

navigate ['nævɪgeɪt] ◆ vt 1. (steer) pilotar, gobernar. 2. (travel safely across) surcar, navegar por. ◆ vi (in plane, ship) dirigir, gobernar; (in car) guiar, dirigir.

navigation [,nævɪ'geɪʃn] n gobierno m.

navigator ['nævɪgeɪtər] n oficial m y f de navegación, navegante m y f.

navvy ['nævɪ] n Br inf peón m caminero.

navy ['neɪvɪ] ◆ n armada f. ◆ adj (in colour) azul marino (inv).

navy blue adj azul marino (inv).

Nazi ['nɑːtsɪ] (pl -s) ◆ adj nazi. ◆ n nazi m y f.

NB (abbr of nota bene) N.B.

near [nɪər] ◆ adj 1. (close in distance, time) cerca; in the ~ future en un futuro próximo. 2. (related) cercano(na), próximo(ma). 3. (almost happened): it was a ~ thing poco le faltó. ◆ adv 1. (close in distance, time) cerca; nowhere ~ ni de lejos, ni mucho menos; to draw OR come ~ acercarse. 2. (almost) casi. ◆ prep 1. (close in position): ~ (to) cerca de. 2. (close in time): ~ (to) casi; ~ the end casi al final; ~er the time cuando se acerque la fecha. 3. (on the point of): ~ (to) al borde de. 4. (similar to): ~ (to) cerca de. ◆ vt acercarse OR aproximarse a. ◆ vi acercarse, aproximarse.

nearby [nɪə'baɪ] ◆ adj cercano(na). ◆ adv cerca.

nearly ['nɪəlɪ] adv casi; I ~ fell por poco me caigo.

near miss n 1. (nearly a hit): to be a ~ fallar por poco. 2. (nearly a collision) incidente m aéreo (sin colisión).

nearside ['nɪəsaɪd] ◆ adj (right-hand drive) del lado izquierdo; (left-hand drive) del lado derecho. ◆ n (right-hand drive) lado m izquierdo; (left-hand drive) lado derecho.

nearsighted [,nɪə'saɪtɪd] adj Am miope, corto(ta) de vista.

neat [niːt] adj 1. (tidy, precise - gen) pulcro(cra); (- room, house) arreglado(da); (- handwriting) esmerado(da). 2. (smart) arreglado(da), pulcro(cra). 3. (skilful) hábil. 4. (undiluted) solo(la). 5. Am inf (very good) guay, de buten (inv).

neatly ['niːtlɪ] adv 1. (tidily, smartly) con pulcritud. 2. (skilfully) hábilmente.

nebulous ['nebjʊləs] adj fml nebuloso(sa).

necessarily [Br 'nesəsrəlɪ, ,nesə'serəlɪ] adv necesariamente.

necessary ['nesəsrɪ] adj 1. (required) necesario(ria). 2. (inevitable) inevitable.

necessity [nɪ'sesətɪ] n necesidad f; of ~ por fuerza, por necesidad. ▶ **necessities** npl artículos mpl de primera necesidad.

neck [nek] ◆ n (of person) cuello m; (of animal) pescuezo m, cuello. ◆ vi inf pegarse el lote.

necklace ['neklɪs] n collar m.

neckline ['neklaın] n escote m.

necktie ['nektaɪ] n Am corbata f.

nectarine ['nektərɪn] n nectarina f.

née [neɪ] adj de soltera.

need [niːd] ◆ n: ~ (for sthg/to do sthg) necesidad f (de algo/de hacer algo); **to be in** OR **to have ~ of sthg** necesitar algo; **there's no ~ for you to cry** no hace falta que llores; **if ~ be** si hace falta; **in ~** necesitado(da). ◆ vt 1. (require) necesitar; **I ~ a haircut** me hace falta un corte de pelo. 2. (be obliged): **to ~ to do sthg** tener que hacer algo. ◆ modal vb: **to ~ to do sthg** necesitar hacer algo; **~ we go?** ¿tenemos que irnos?; **it ~ not happen** no tiene por qué ser así.

needle ['niːdl] ◆ n aguja f. ◆ vt inf pinchar.

needless ['niːdlɪs] adj innecesario(ria); **~ to say ...** está de más decir que ...

needlework ['niːdlwɜːk] n 1. (embroidery) bordado m. 2. (U) (activity) costura f.

needn't ['niːdnt] = need not.

needy ['niːdɪ] adj necesitado(da).

negative ['negətɪv] ◆ adj negativo (va). ◆ n 1. (PHOT) negativo m. 2. (LING) negación f; **to answer in the ~** decir que no.

neglect [nɪ'glekt] ◆ n (of garden, work) descuido m; (of duty) incumplimiento m; **a state of ~** un estado de abandono. ◆ vt 1. (ignore) desatender. 2. (duty, work) no cumplir con; **to ~ to do sthg** dejar de hacer algo.

neglectful [nɪ'glektfʊl] adj descuidado(da), negligente.

negligee ['neglɪʒeɪ] n salto m de cama.

negligence ['neglɪdʒəns] n negligencia f.

negligible ['neglɪdʒəbl] adj insignificante.

negotiate [nɪ'gəʊʃɪeɪt] ◆ vt 1. (obtain through negotiation) negociar. 2. (obstacle) salvar, franquear; (hill) superar; (bend) tomar. ◆ vi: **to ~ (with sb for sthg)** negociar (con alguien algo).

negotiation [nɪ,gəʊʃɪ'eɪʃn] n negociación f. ▶ **negotiations** npl negociaciones fpl.

Negress ['niːgrɪs] n negra f.

Negro ['niːgrəʊ] (pl -es) ◆ adj negro (gra). ◆ n negro m, -gra f.

neigh [neɪ] vi relinchar.

neighbour Br, **neighbor** Am ['neɪbər] n vecino m, -na f.

neighbourhood Br, **neighbor-**

hood Am ['neɪbəhʊd] n 1. (of town) barrio m, vecindad f. 2. (approximate figure): **in the ~ of** alrededor de.

neighbouring Br, **neighboring** Am ['neɪbərɪŋ] adj vecino(na).

neighbourly Br, **neighborly** Am ['neɪbəlɪ] adj de buen vecino.

neither ['naɪðər, 'niːðər] ◆ adv: **I don't drink – me –** no bebo – yo tampoco; **the food was ~ good nor bad** la comida no era ni buena ni mala; **to be ~ here nor there** no tener nada que ver. ◆ pron ninguno(na); **~ of us/them** ninguno de nosotros/ellos. ◆ adj: **~ cup is blue** ninguna de las dos tazas es azul. ◆ conj: **~ ... nor ...** ni ... ni ...; **she could ~ eat nor sleep** no podía ni comer ni dormir.

neon ['niːɒn] n neón m.

neon light n lámpara f OR luz f de neón.

nephew ['nefjuː] n sobrino m.

Neptune ['neptjuːn] n Neptuno m.

nerve [nɜːv] n 1. (ANAT) nervio m. 2. (courage) valor m; **to keep one's ~** mantener la calma, no perder los nervios; **to lose one's ~** echarse atrás, perder el valor. 3. (cheek) cara f. ▶ **nerves** npl nervios mpl; **to get on sb's ~s** sacar de quicio OR poner los nervios de punta a alguien.

nerve-racking [-,rækɪŋ] adj crispante.

nervous ['nɜːvəs] adj 1. (ANAT & PSYCH) nervioso(sa). 2. (apprehensive) inquieto (ta), aprensivo(va).

nervous breakdown n crisis f inv nerviosa.

nest [nest] ◆ n nido m; **wasps' ~** avispero m; **~ of tables** mesas fpl nido. ◆ vi anidar.

nest egg n ahorros mpl.

nestle ['nesl] vi (settle snugly - in chair) arrellanarse; (- in bed) acurrucarse.

net [net] ◆ adj (weight, price, loss) neto (ta). ◆ n red f. ◆ vt 1. (catch) coger con red. 2. (acquire) embolsarse.

Net [net] n (COMPUT): **the ~** la Red; **to surf the ~** navegar por la Red.

netball ['netbɔːl] n deporte parecido al baloncesto femenino.

net curtains npl visillos mpl.

Netherlands ['neðələndz] npl: **the ~** los Países Bajos.

net revenue n Am facturación f.

nett [net] adj = net.

netting ['netɪŋ] n red f, malla f.

nettle ['netl] n ortiga f.

network ['netwɜːk] ♦ n 1. (gen & COMPUT) red f. 2. (RADIO & TV) (station) cadena f. ♦ vt (COMPUT) conectar a la red.

neurosis [ˌnjʊəˈrəʊsɪs] (pl -ses [-siːz]) n neurosis f inv.

neurotic [ˌnjʊəˈrɒtɪk] ♦ adj neurótico (ca). ♦ n neurótico m, -ca f.

neuter ['njuːtəʳ] ♦ adj neutro(tra). ♦ vt castrar.

neutral ['njuːtrəl] ♦ adj 1. (gen) neutro (tra); (shoe cream) incoloro(ra). 2. (non-allied) neutral. ♦ n (AUT) punto m muerto.

neutrality [njuːˈtrælətɪ] n neutralidad f.

neutralize, -ise ['njuːtrəlaɪz] vt neutralizar.

never ['nevəʳ] adv 1. (at no time) nunca, jamás; ~ ever nunca jamás; well I ~! ¡vaya!, ¡caramba! 2. inf (as negative) no; you ~ did! ¡no (me digas)!

never-ending adj inacabable.

nevertheless [ˌnevəðəˈles] adv sin embargo, no obstante.

new [adj njuː, n njuːz] adj nuevo(va); (baby) recién nacido (recién nacida); as good as ~ como nuevo. ▶ **news** n (U) noticias fpl; a piece of ~s una noticia; the ~s las noticias; that's ~s to me me coge de nuevas.

newborn ['njuːbɔːn] adj recién nacido (recién nacida).

newcomer ['njuːˌkʌməʳ] n: ~ (to) recién llegado m, recién llegada f (a).

newfangled [ˌnjuːˈfæŋgld] adj inf pej novedoso(sa).

new-found adj (gen) recién descubierto (recién descubierta); (friend) reciente.

newly ['njuːlɪ] adv recién.

newlyweds ['njuːlɪwedz] npl recién casados mpl.

new moon n luna f nueva.

news agency n agencia f de noticias.

newsagent Br ['njuːzeɪdʒənt], **newsdealer** Am ['njuːzdiːlər] n (person) vendedor m, -ra f de periódicos; ~'s (shop) = quiosco m de periódicos.

newscaster ['njuːzkɑːstəʳ] n presentador m, -ra f, locutor m, -ra f.

newsdealer Am = newsagent.

newsflash ['njuːzflæʃ] n flash m informativo, noticia f de última hora.

newsletter ['njuːzˌletəʳ] n boletín m, hoja f informativa.

newspaper ['njuːzˌpeɪpəʳ] n 1. (publication, company) periódico m, diario m. 2. (paper) papel m de periódico.

newsprint ['njuːzprɪnt] n papel m de periódico.

newsreader ['njuːzˌriːdəʳ] n presentador m, -ra f, locutor m, -ra f.

newsreel ['njuːzriːl] n noticiario m cinematográfico.

newsstand ['njuːzstænd] n puesto m de periódicos.

newt [njuːt] n tritón m.

new technology n nueva tecnología f.

new town n Br ciudad nueva construida por el gobierno.

New Year n Año m Nuevo; Happy ~! ¡Feliz Año Nuevo!

New Year's Day n día m de Año Nuevo.

New Year's Eve n Nochevieja f.

New York [-'jɔːk] n 1. (city): ~ (City) Nueva York. 2. (state): ~ (State) (el estado de) Nueva York.

New Zealand [-'ziːlənd] n Nueva Zelanda.

New Zealander [-'ziːləndəʳ] n neozelandés m, -esa f.

next [nekst] ♦ adj 1. (in time) próximo (ma); the ~ day el día siguiente; ~ Tuesday/year el martes/el año que viene; ~ week la semana próxima OR que viene; the ~ week los próximos siete días. 2. (in space - page etc) siguiente; (- room) de al lado. ♦ pron el siguiente (la siguiente); the day after ~ pasado mañana; the week after ~ la semana que viene no, la otra. ♦ adv 1. (afterwards) después. 2. (again) de nuevo. 3. (with superlatives): ~ best/biggest etc el segundo mejor/más grande etc. ♦ prep Am al lado de, junto a. ▶ **next to** prep al lado de, junto a; ~ to nothing casi nada.

next door adv (en la casa de) al lado. ▶ **next-door** adj: next-door neighbour vecino m, -na f de al lado.

next of kin n pariente más cercano m, pariente más cercana f.

NHS n abbr of National Health Service.

NI ♦ n abbr of National Insurance. ♦ abbr of Northern Ireland.

nib [nɪb] n plumilla f.

nibble ['nɪbl] vt mordisquear.

Nicaragua [ˌnɪkəˈrægjʊə] n Nicaragua.

Nicaraguan [ˌnɪkəˈrægjʊən] ♦ adj nicaragüense. ♦ n nicaragüense m y f.

nice [naɪs] adj 1. (attractive) bonito(ta); (good) bueno(na). 2. (kind) amable; (pleasant, friendly) agradable, simpático (ca), dije Amer; **to be ~ to sb** ser agradable con alguien.

nice-looking [-'lukɪŋ] *adj* (*person*) guapo(pa); (*car, room*) bonito(ta).

nicely ['naɪslɪ] *adv* **1.** (*well, attractively*) bien. **2.** (*politely*) educadamente, con educación. **3.** (*satisfactorily*) bien; **that will do** ~ esto irá de perlas.

niche [niːʃ] *n* **1.** (*in wall*) nicho *m*, hornacina *f*. **2.** (*in life*) buena posición *f*.

nick [nɪk] ♦ *n* **1.** (*cut*) cortecito *m*; (*notch*) muesca *f*. **2.** *phr*: **in the ~ of time** justo a tiempo. ♦ *vt* **1.** (*cut*) cortar; (*make notch in*) mellar. **2.** *Br inf* (*steal*) birlar.

nickel ['nɪkl] *n* **1.** (*metal*) níquel *m*. **2.** *Am* (*coin*) moneda *f* de cinco centavos.

nickname ['nɪkneɪm] ♦ *n* apodo *m*. ♦ *vt* apodar.

nicotine ['nɪkətiːn] *n* nicotina *f*.

niece [niːs] *n* sobrina *f*.

Nigeria [naɪ'dʒɪərɪə] *n* Nigeria.

Nigerian [naɪ'dʒɪərɪən] ♦ *adj* nigeriano(na). ♦ *n* nigeriano *m*, -na *f*.

niggle ['nɪgl] *vt Br* **1.** (*worry*) inquietar. **2.** (*criticize*) meterse con, criticar.

night [naɪt] *n* noche *f*; (*evening*) tarde *f*; **last ~** anoche, ayer por la noche; **at ~** por la noche, de noche; **to have an early/a late ~** irse a dormir pronto/tarde. ▶ **nights** *adv* **1.** *Am* (*at night*) por las noches. **2.** *Br* (*nightshift*): **to work ~s** hacer el turno de noche.

nightcap ['naɪtkæp] *n* (*drink*) bebida que se toma antes de ir a dormir.

nightclub ['naɪtklʌb] *n* club *m* nocturno.

nightdress ['naɪtdres] *n* camisón *m*.

nightfall ['naɪtfɔːl] *n* anochecer *m*.

nightgown ['naɪtgaʊn] *n* camisón *m*.

nightie ['naɪtɪ] *n inf* camisón *m*.

nightingale ['naɪtɪŋgeɪl] *n* ruiseñor *m*.

nightlife ['naɪtlaɪf] *n* vida *f* nocturna.

nightly ['naɪtlɪ] ♦ *adj* nocturno(na), de cada noche. ♦ *adv* cada noche.

nightmare ['naɪtmeəʳ] *n lit & fig* pesadilla *f*.

night porter *n* recepcionista *m y f* del turno de noche.

night school *n* (U) escuela *f* nocturna.

night shift *n* turno *m* de noche.

nightshirt ['naɪtʃɜːt] *n* camisa *f* de dormir (masculina).

nighttime ['naɪttaɪm] *n* noche *f*.

nil [nɪl] *n* **1.** (*nothing*) nada *f*. **2.** *Br* (SPORT) cero *m*.

Nile [naɪl] *n*: **the ~** el Nilo.

nimble ['nɪmbl] *adj* **1.** (*person, fingers*)

ágil. **2.** (*mind*) rápido(da).

nine [naɪn] *num* nueve; *see also* **six**.

nineteen [,naɪn'tiːn] *num* diecinueve; *see also* **six**.

ninety ['naɪntɪ] *num* noventa; *see also* **sixty**.

ninth [naɪnθ] *num* noveno(na); *see also* **sixth**.

nip [nɪp] ♦ *n* (*of drink*) trago *m*. ♦ *vt* (*pinch*) pellizcar; (*bite*) mordisquear.

nipple ['nɪpl] *n* **1.** (*of woman*) pezón *m*. **2.** (*of baby's bottle, man*) tetilla *f*.

nit [nɪt] *n* (*in hair*) liendre *f*.

nitpicking ['nɪtpɪkɪŋ] *n* (U) *inf* nimiedades *fpl*.

nitrogen ['naɪtrədʒən] *n* nitrógeno *m*.

nitty-gritty [,nɪtɪ'grɪtɪ] *n inf*: **to get down to the ~** ir al grano.

no [nəʊ] (*pl* -es ♦ *adv* (*gen*) no; **you're ~ better than me** tú no eres mejor que yo. ♦ *adj* no; **I have ~ time** no tengo tiempo; **that's ~ excuse** esa no es excusa que valga; **there are ~ taxis** no hay taxis; **he's ~ fool** no es ningún tonto; **she's ~ friend of mine** no es amiga mía; **'~ smoking/ parking/cameras'** 'prohibido fumar/ aparcar/hacer fotos'. ♦ *n* no *m*; **he/she won't take ~ for an answer** no acepta una respuesta negativa.

No., no. (*abbr of* **number**) n.º.

nobility [nə'bɪlətɪ] *n* nobleza *f*.

noble ['nəʊbl] ♦ *adj* noble. ♦ *n* noble *m y f*.

nobody ['nəʊbədɪ] ♦ *pron* nadie. ♦ *n pej* don nadie *m*.

nocturnal [nɒk'tɜːnl] *adj* nocturno(na).

nod [nɒd] ♦ *vt*: **to ~ one's head** (*in agreement*) asentir con la cabeza; (*as greeting*) saludar con la cabeza. ♦ *vi* **1.** (*in agreement*) asentir con la cabeza. **2.** (*to indicate sthg*) indicar con la cabeza. **3.** (*as greeting*) saludar con la cabeza. ▶ **nod off** *vi* dar cabezadas.

noise [nɔɪz] *n* ruido *m*; **to make a ~** armar oR hacer ruido.

noisy ['nɔɪzɪ] *adj* ruidoso(sa).

no-man's-land *n* tierra *f* de nadie.

nominal ['nɒmɪnl] *adj* nominal.

nominate ['nɒmɪneɪt] *vt* **1.** (*propose*): **to ~ sb (for oR as)** proponer a alguien (por oR como). **2.** (*appoint*): **to ~ sb (to sthg)** nombrar a alguien (algo).

nomination [,nɒmɪ'neɪʃn] *n* **1.** (*proposal*) nominación *f*. **2.** (*appointment*): **~ (to sthg)** nombramiento *m* (a algo).

nominee [,nɒmɪ'niː] *n* nominado *m*, -da *f*.

non- [nɒn] *prefix* no.

nonalcoholic [ˌnɒnælkə'hɒlɪk] *adj* sin alcohol.

nonaligned [ˌnɒnə'laɪnd] *adj* no alineado(da).

nonchalant [Br 'nɒnʃələnt, Am ˌnɒnʃə-'lɑːnt] *adj* despreocupado(da).

noncommittal [ˌnɒnkə'mɪtl] *adj* que no compromete a nada, evasivo(va).

nonconformist [ˌnɒnkən'fɔːmɪst] ◆ *adj* inconformista. ◆ *n* inconformista *m y f*.

nondescript [Br 'nɒndɪskrɪpt, Am ˌnɒndɪ'skrɪpt] *adj* anodino(na), soso(sa).

none [nʌn] ◆ *pron* 1. (*not any*) nada; **there is ~ left** no queda nada; **it's ~ of your business** no es asunto tuyo. 2. (*not one - object, person*) ninguno(na); **~ of us/ the books** ninguno de nosotros/de los libros; **I had ~** no tenía ninguno. ◆ *adv*: **I'm ~ the worse/better** no me ha perjudicado/ayudado en nada; **I'm ~ the wiser** no he entendido nada. ► **none too** *adv* no demasiado.

nonentity [nɒ'nentətɪ] *n* cero *m* a la izquierda.

nonetheless [ˌnʌnðə'les] *adv* sin embargo, no obstante.

non-event *n* fracaso *m*.

nonexistent [ˌnɒnɪg'zɪstənt] *adj* inexistente.

nonfiction [ˌnɒn'fɪkʃn] *n* no ficción *f*.

no-nonsense *adj* práctico(ca).

nonpayment [ˌnɒn'peɪmənt] *n* impago *m*.

nonplussed, nonplused Am [ˌnɒn-'plʌst] *adj* perplejo(ja).

nonreturnable [ˌnɒnrɪ'tɜːnəbl] *adj* no retornable, sin retorno.

nonsense ['nɒnsəns] ◆ *n* (U) 1. (*gen*) tonterías *fpl*, bobadas *fpl*; **it is ~ to suggest that ...** es absurdo sugerir que ...; **to make (a) ~ of sthg** dar al traste con algo. 2. (*incomprehensible words*) galimatías *m inv*. ◆ *excl* ¡tonterías!

nonsensical [nɒn'sensɪkl] *adj* disparatado(da), absurdo(da).

nonsmoker [ˌnɒn'sməʊkəʳ] *n* no fumador *m*, no fumadora *f*.

nonstick [ˌnɒn'stɪk] *adj* antiadherente.

nonstop [ˌnɒn'stɒp] ◆ *adj* (*activity, rain*) continuo(nua), incesante; (*flight*) sin escalas. ◆ *adv* sin parar.

noodles ['nuːdlz] *npl* fideos *mpl*.

nook [nʊk] *n* (*of room*): **every ~ and cranny** todos los recovecos.

noon [nuːn] *n* mediodía *m*.

no one *pron* = **nobody**.

noose [nuːs] *n* (*loop*) nudo *m* corredizo;

(*for hanging*) soga *f*.

no-place Am = **nowhere**.

nor [nɔːʳ] *conj* 1. → **neither**. 2. (*and not*) ni; **I don't smoke - ~ do I** no fumo - yo tampoco; **I don't know, ~ do I care** ni lo sé, ni me importa.

norm [nɔːm] *n* norma *f*; **the ~** lo normal.

normal ['nɔːml] *adj* normal.

normality [nɔː'mælɪtɪ], **normalcy** Am ['nɔːmlsɪ] *n* normalidad *f*.

normally ['nɔːməlɪ] *adv* normalmente.

north [nɔːθ] ◆ *n* 1. (*direction*) norte *m*. 2. (*region*): **the North** el norte. ◆ *adj* del norte; **North London** el norte de Londres. ◆ *adv*: **~ (of)** al norte (de).

North Africa *n* África del Norte.

North America *n* Norteamérica.

North American ◆ *adj* norteamericano(na). ◆ *n* norteamericano *m*, -na *f*.

northeast [ˌnɔːθ'iːst] ◆ *n* 1. (*direction*) nordeste *m*. 2. (*region*): **the Northeast** el nordeste. ◆ *adj* del nordeste. ◆ *adv*: **~ (of)** al nordeste (de).

northerly ['nɔːðəlɪ] *adj* del norte.

northern ['nɔːðən] *adj* del norte, norteño(ña).

Northern Ireland *n* Irlanda del Norte.

northernmost ['nɔːðənməʊst] *adj* más septentrional OR al norte.

North Korea *n* Corea del Norte.

North Pole *n*: **the ~** el Polo Norte.

North Sea *n*: **the ~** el Mar del Norte.

northward ['nɔːθwəd] ◆ *adj* hacia el norte. ◆ *adv* = **northwards**.

northwards ['nɔːθwədz] *adv* hacia el norte.

northwest [ˌnɔːθ'west] ◆ *n* 1. (*direction*) noroeste *m*. 2. (*region*): **the Northwest** el noroeste. ◆ *adj* del noroeste. ◆ *adv*: **~ (of)** al noroeste (de).

Norway ['nɔːweɪ] *n* Noruega.

Norwegian [nɔː'wiːdʒən] ◆ *adj* noruego(ga). ◆ *n* 1. (*person*) noruego *m*, -ga *f*. 2. (*language*) noruego *m*.

nose [nəʊz] *n* (*of person*) nariz *f*; (*of animal*) hocico *m*; (*of plane, car*) morro *m*; **to keep one's ~ out of sthg** no meter las narices en algo; **to look down one's ~ at sb/sthg** mirar por encima del hombro a alguien/algo; **to poke** OR **stick one's ~ in** *inf* meter las narices; **to turn up one's ~ at sthg** hacerle ascos a algo. ► **nose about, nose around** *vi* curiosear.

nosebleed ['nəʊzbliːd] *n* hemorragia *f* nasal.

nosedive ['nəʊzdaɪv] ◆ *n* (*of plane*) picado *m*. ◆ *vi lit & fig* bajar en picado.

nosey ['nǝʊzɪ] = **nosy**.

nostalgia [nɒ'stældʒǝ] n: ~ **(for)** nostalgia f (de).

nostril ['nɒstrǝl] n ventana f de la nariz.

nosy ['nǝʊzɪ] adj fisgón(ona), curioso (sa).

not [nɒt] adv no; **this is ~ the first time** no es la primera vez; **it's green, isn't it?** es verde, ¿no?; **I hope/think ~** espero/creo que no; **~ a chance** de ninguna manera; **~ even a ...** ni siquiera un (una) ...; **~ all** OR **every** no todos(das); **~ always** no siempre; **~ that ...** no es que ...; **~ at all** (no) en absoluto; (to acknowledge thanks) de nada.

notable ['nǝʊtǝbl] adj notable; **to be ~ for sthg** destacar por algo.

notably ['nǝʊtǝblɪ] adv 1. (in particular) especialmente. 2. (noticeably) marcadamente.

notary ['nǝʊtǝrɪ] n: ~ **(public)** notario m, -ria f.

notch [nɒtʃ] n (cut) muesca f.

note [nǝʊt] ◆ n 1. (gen) nota f; **to take ~ of sthg** tener algo presente. 2. (paper money) billete m. 3. (tone) tono m. ◆ vt 1. (observe) notar. 2. (mention) mencionar. ▶ **notes** npl (written record) apuntes mpl; (in book) notas fpl; **to take ~s** tomar apuntes. ▶ **note down** vt sep anotar, apuntar.

notebook ['nǝʊtbʊk] n 1. (for taking notes) libreta f, cuaderno m. 2. (COMPUT): ~ **(computer)** ordenador m portátil.

noted ['nǝʊtɪd] adj destacado(da); **to be ~ for** distinguirse por.

notepad ['nǝʊtpæd] n bloc m de notas.

notepaper ['nǝʊtpeɪpǝʳ] n papel m de escribir OR de cartas.

noteworthy ['nǝʊt,wɜːðɪ] adj digno (na) de mención.

nothing ['nʌθɪŋ] ◆ pron nada; **I've got ~ to do** no tengo nada que hacer; **for ~** (free) gratis; (for no purpose) en vano, en balde; **he's ~ if not generous** otra cosa no será pero desde luego generoso sí que es; **~ but** tan sólo; **there's ~ for it (but to do sthg)** Br no hay más remedio (que hacer algo). ◆ adv: **to be ~ like sb/sthg** no parecerse en nada a alguien/algo; **I'm ~ like finished** no he terminado ni mucho menos.

notice ['nǝʊtɪs] ◆ n 1. (on wall, door) letrero m, cartel m; (in newspaper) anuncio m. 2. (attention) atención f; **to take ~ (of)** hacer caso (de), prestar atención

(a). 3. (warning) aviso m; **at short ~** casi sin previo aviso; **until further ~** hasta nuevo aviso. 4. (at work): **to be given one's ~** ser despedido(da); **to hand in one's ~** presentar la dimisión. ◆ vt (sense, smell) notar; (see) fijarse en, ver; **to ~ sb doing sthg** fijarse en alguien que está haciendo algo.

noticeable ['nǝʊtɪsǝbl] adj notable.

notice board n tablón m de anuncios.

notify ['nǝʊtɪfaɪ] vt: **to ~ sb (of sthg)** notificar OR comunicar (algo) a alguien.

notion ['nǝʊʃn] n noción f. ▶ **notions** npl Am artículos mpl de mercería.

notorious [nǝʊ'tɔːrɪǝs] adj notorio (ria), célebre.

notwithstanding [,nɒtwɪθ'stændɪŋ] fml ◆ prep a pesar de. ◆ adv sin embargo.

nougat ['nuːgɑː] n dulce hecho a base de nueces y frutas.

nought [nɔːt] num cero.

noun [naʊn] n nombre m, sustantivo m.

nourish ['nʌrɪʃ] vt 1. (feed) nutrir. 2. (entertain) alimentar, albergar.

nourishing ['nʌrɪʃɪŋ] adj nutritivo(va).

nourishment ['nʌrɪʃmǝnt] n alimento m, sustento m.

novel ['nɒvl] ◆ adj original. ◆ n novela f.

novelist ['nɒvǝlɪst] n novelista m y f.

novelty ['nɒvltɪ] n 1. (gen) novedad f. 2. (cheap object) baratija f (poco útil).

November [nǝ'vembǝʳ] n noviembre m; see also **September**.

novice ['nɒvɪs] n 1. (inexperienced person) principiante m y f. 2. (RELIG) novicio m, -cia f.

now [naʊ] ◆ adv 1. (at this time, at once) ahora; **do it ~** hazlo ahora; **he's been away for two weeks ~** lleva dos semanas fuera; **any day ~** cualquier día de éstos; **any time ~** en cualquier momento; **for ~** por ahora, por el momento; **~ and then** OR **again** de vez en cuando. 2. (at a particular time in the past) entonces. 3. (to introduce statement) vamos a ver. ◆ conj: **~ (that)** ahora que, ya que. ◆ n ahora; **from ~ on** a partir de ahora; **they should be here by ~** ya deberían estar aquí; **up until ~** hasta ahora.

nowadays ['naʊǝdeɪz] adv hoy en día, actualmente.

nowhere Br ['nǝʊweǝʳ], **no-place** Am adv en ninguna parte; **~ else** en ninguna otra parte; **to be getting ~** no estar avanzando nada, no ir a ninguna parte; **(to be) ~ near (as ... as ...)** (no ser) ni mucho menos (tan ... como ...).

nozzle ['nɒzl] *n* boquilla *f*.

nuance [nju:'ɑ:ns] *n* matiz *m*.

nuclear ['nju:klɪər] *adj* nuclear.

nuclear bomb *n* bomba *f* atómica.

nuclear disarmament *n* desarme *m* nuclear.

nuclear energy *n* energía *f* nuclear.

nuclear power *n* energía *f* nuclear.

nuclear reactor *n* reactor *m* nuclear.

nucleus ['nju:klɪəs] (*pl* **-lei** [-lɪaɪ]) *n lit & fig* núcleo *m*.

nude [nju:d] ◆ *adj* desnudo(da). ◆ *n* (ART) desnudo *m*; **in the ~** desnudo(da), en cueros.

nudge [nʌdʒ] *vt* (*with elbow*) dar un codazo a.

nudist ['nju:dɪst] *n* nudista *m y f*.

nudity ['nju:dətɪ] *n* desnudez *f*.

nugget ['nʌgɪt] *n* (*of gold*) pepita *f*.

nuisance ['nju:sns] *n* (*thing*) fastidio *m*, molestia *f*; (*person*) pesado *m*; **to make a ~ of o.s.** dar la lata.

nuke [nju:k] *inf* ◆ *n* bomba *f* atómica. ◆ *vt* atacar con arma nuclear.

null [nʌl] *adj*: **~ and void** nulo(la) y sin efecto.

numb [nʌm] ◆ *adj* (*gen*) entumecido (da); (*leg, hand*) dormido(da); **to be ~ with cold** estar helado(da) de frío; **to be ~ with fear** estar paralizado(da) de miedo. ◆ *vt* entumecer.

number ['nʌmbər] ◆ *n* **1.** (*gen*) número *m*; **a ~ of** varios(rias); **any ~ of** la mar de. **2.** (*of car*) matrícula *f*. ◆ *vt* **1.** (*amount to*) ascender a. **2.** (*give a number to*) numerar. **3.** (*include*): **to be ~ed among** figurar entre.

number one ◆ *adj* principal, número uno. ◆ *n inf* (*oneself*) uno mismo (una misma).

numberplate ['nʌmbəpleɪt] *n* matrícula *f* (de vehículo).

Number Ten *n* el número 10 de Downing Street, residencia oficial del primer ministro británico.

numeral ['nju:mərəl] *n* número *m*, cifra *f*.

numerate ['nju:mərət] *adj Br* competente en aritmética.

numerical [nju:'merɪkl] *adj* numérico (ca).

numerous ['nju:mərəs] *adj* numeroso (sa).

nun [nʌn] *n* monja *f*.

nurse [nɜ:s] ◆ *n* (MED) enfermero *m*, -ra *f*; (*nanny*) niñera *f*. ◆ *vt* **1.** (*care for*) cuidar, atender. **2.** (*try to cure - a cold*) curarse. **3.** (*nourish*) abrigar. **4.** (*subj: mother*) amamantar.

nursery ['nɜ:sərɪ] *n* **1.** (*at home*) cuarto *m* de los niños; (*away from home*) guardería *f*. **2.** (*for plants*) semillero *m*, vivero *m*.

nursery rhyme *n* poema *m* OR canción *f* infantil.

nursery school *n* parvulario *m*.

nursery slopes *npl* pista *f* para principiantes.

nursing ['nɜ:sɪŋ] *n* (*profession*) enfermería *f*; (*of patient*) asistencia *f*, cuidado *m*.

nursing home *n* (*for old people*) clínica *f* de reposo (privada); (*for childbirth*) clínica *f* (privada) de maternidad.

nurture ['nɜ:tʃər] *vt* **1.** (*child, plant*) criar. **2.** (*plan, feelings*) alimentar.

nut [nʌt] *n* **1.** (*to eat*) nuez *f*. **2.** (*of metal*) tuerca *f*. **3.** *inf* (*mad person*) chiflado *m*, -da *f*. ► **nuts** *inf* ◆ *adj*: **to be ~s** estar chalado(da). ◆ *excl Am* ¡maldita sea!

nutcrackers ['nʌt,krækəz] *npl* cascanueces *m inv*.

nutmeg ['nʌtmeg] *n* nuez *f* moscada.

nutritious [nju:'trɪʃəs] *adj* nutritivo (va).

nutshell ['nʌtʃel] *n*: **in a ~** en una palabra.

nuzzle ['nʌzl] ◆ *vt* rozar con el hocico. ◆ *vi*: **to ~ (up) against** arrimarse a.

nylon ['naɪlɒn] ◆ *n* nylon *m*. ◆ *comp* de nylon.

o (*pl* **o's** OR **os**), **O** (*pl* **O's** OR **Os**) [əʊ] *n* **1.** (*letter*) o *f*, O *f*. **2.** (*zero*) cero *m*.

oak [əʊk] ◆ *n* roble *m*. ◆ *comp* de roble.

OAP *n abbr of* **old age pensioner**.

oar [ɔ:r] *n* remo *m*.

oasis [əʊ'eɪsɪs] (*pl* **oases** [əʊ'eɪsi:z]) *n lit & fig* oasis *m inv*.

oatcake ['əʊtkeɪk] *n* galleta *f* de avena.

oath [əʊθ] *n* **1.** (*promise*) juramento *m*;

on OR **under** ~ bajo juramento. **2.** (*swearword*) palabrota *f*.

oatmeal ['əʊtmiːl] *n* harina *f* de avena.

oats [əʊts] *npl* (*grain*) avena *f*.

obedience [ə'biːdjəns] *n*: ~ **(to sb)** obediencia *f* (a alguien).

obedient [ə'biːdjənt] *adj* obediente.

obese [əʊ'biːs] *adj fml* obeso(sa).

obey [ə'beɪ] *vt* & *vi* obedecer.

obituary [ə'bɪtjʊərɪ] *n* nota *f* necrológica, necrología *f*.

object [*n* 'ɒbdʒɪkt, *vb* ɒb'dʒekt] ◆ *n* **1.** (*gen*) objeto *m*. **2.** (*aim*) objeto *m*, propósito *m*. **3.** (GRAMM) complemento *m*. ◆ *vt* objetar. ◆ *vi*: **to ~ (to sthg/to doing sthg)** oponerse (a algo/a hacer algo).

objection [əb'dʒekʃn] *n* objeción *f*, reparo *m*; **to have no ~ (to sthg/to doing sthg)** no tener inconveniente (en algo/en hacer algo).

objectionable [əb'dʒekʃənəbl] *adj* (*person*) desagradable; (*behaviour*) censurable.

objective [əb'dʒektɪv] ◆ *adj* objetivo (va). ◆ *n* objetivo *m*.

obligation [ˌɒblɪ'geɪʃn] *n* **1.** (*compulsion*) obligación *f*; **to be under an ~ to do sthg** tener la obligación de hacer algo. **2.** (*duty*) deber *m*.

obligatory [ə'blɪgətrɪ] *adj* obligatorio (ria).

oblige [ə'blaɪdʒ] *vt* **1.** (*force*): **to ~ sb to do sthg** obligar a alguien a hacer algo. **2.** *fml* (*do a favour to*) hacer un favor a.

obliging [ə'blaɪdʒɪŋ] *adj* servicial, atento(ta).

oblique [ə'bliːk] ◆ *adj* **1.** (*indirect - reference*) indirecto(ta). **2.** (*slanting*) oblicuo (cua). ◆ *n* (TYPO) barra *f*.

obliterate [ə'blɪtəreɪt] *vt* arrasar.

oblivion [ə'blɪvɪən] *n* olvido *m*.

oblivious [ə'blɪvɪəs] *adj* inconsciente; **to be ~ to** OR **of sthg** no ser consciente de algo.

oblong ['ɒblɒŋ] ◆ *adj* rectangular, oblongo(ga). ◆ *n* rectángulo *m*.

obnoxious [əb'nɒkʃəs] *adj* detestable.

oboe ['əʊbəʊ] *n* oboe *m*.

obscene [əb'siːn] *adj* obsceno(na).

obscure [əb'skjʊər] ◆ *adj lit* & *fig* oscuro(ra). ◆ *vt* **1.** (*make difficult to understand*) oscurecer. **2.** (*hide*) esconder.

obsequious [əb'siːkwɪəs] *adj fml* & *pej* servil.

observance [əb'zɜːvəns] *n* observancia *f*, cumplimiento *m*.

observant [əb'zɜːvnt] *adj* observador (ra).

observation [ˌɒbzə'veɪʃn] *n* **1.** (*by police*) vigilancia *f*; (*by doctor*) observación *f*. **2.** (*comment*) comentario *m*.

observatory [əb'zɜːvətrɪ] *n* observatorio *m*.

observe [əb'zɜːv] *vt* **1.** (*gen*) observar. **2.** (*obey*) cumplir con, observar.

observer [əb'zɜːvər] *n* observador *m*, -ra *f*.

obsess [əb'ses] *vt* obsesionar; **to be ~ed by** OR **with** estar obsesionado con.

obsessive [əb'sesɪv] *adj* obsesivo(va).

obsolescent [ˌɒbsə'lesnt] *adj* obsolescente.

obsolete ['ɒbsəliːt] *adj* obsoleto(ta).

obstacle ['ɒbstəkl] *n* **1.** (*object*) obstáculo *m*. **2.** (*difficulty*) estorbo *m*.

obstetrics [ɒb'stetrɪks] *n* obstetricia *f*.

obstinate ['ɒbstənət] *adj* **1.** (*stubborn*) obstinado(da), terco(ca). **2.** (*persistent*) tenaz.

obstruct [əb'strʌkt] *vt* **1.** (*block*) obstruir, bloquear. **2.** (*hinder*) estorbar.

obstruction [əb'strʌkʃn] *n* (*gen*) obstrucción *f*; (*in road*) obstáculo *m*.

obtain [əb'teɪn] *vt* obtener, conseguir.

obtainable [əb'teɪnəbl] *adj* que se puede conseguir, asequible.

obtrusive [əb'truːsɪv] *adj* (*smell*) penetrante; (*colour*) chillón(ona); (*person*) entrometido(da).

obtuse [əb'tjuːs] *adj lit* & *fig* obtuso(sa).

obvious ['ɒbvɪəs] *adj* obvio(via), evidente.

obviously ['ɒbvɪəslɪ] *adv* **1.** (*of course*) evidentemente, obviamente; ~ **not** claro que no. **2.** (*clearly*) claramente.

occasion [ə'keɪʒn] *n* **1.** (*time*) vez *f*, ocasión *f*; **on one ~** una vez, en una ocasión; **on several ~s** varias veces, en varias ocasiones. **2.** (*important event*) acontecimiento *m*; **to rise to the ~** ponerse a la altura de las circunstancias. **3.** *fml* (*opportunity*) ocasión *f*.

occasional [ə'keɪʒənl] *adj* (*trip, drink*) poco frecuente, esporádico(ca); (*showers*) ocasional.

occasionally [ə'keɪʒnəlɪ] *adv* de vez en cuando.

occult [ɒ'kʌlt] *adj* oculto(ta).

occupant ['ɒkjʊpənt] *n* **1.** (*of building, room*) inquilino *m*, -na *f*. **2.** (*of chair, vehicle*) ocupante *m* y *f*.

occupation [ˌɒkjʊ'peɪʃn] *n* **1.** (*job*) empleo *m*, ocupación *f*. **2.** (*pastime*) pasatiempo *m*. **3.** (MIL) (*of country, build-*

ing) ocupación *f*.

occupational hazard [ɒkju-,peɪʃənl-] *n*: **~s** gajes *mpl* del oficio.

occupational therapy [ɒkju-,peɪʃənl-] *n* terapia *f* ocupacional.

occupier ['ɒkjupaɪəʳ] *n* inquilino *m*, -na *f*.

occupy ['ɒkjupaɪ] *vt* 1. (*gen*) ocupar. 2. (*live in*) habitar. 3. (*entertain*): **to ~ o.s.** entretenerse.

occur [əˈkɜːʳ] *vi* 1. (*happen*) ocurrir, suceder. 2. (*be present*) encontrarse. 3. (*thought, idea*): **to ~ to sb** ocurrírsele a alguien.

occurrence [əˈkʌrəns] *n* (*event*) acontecimiento *m*.

ocean ['əʊʃn] *n* océano *m*; Am (*sea*) mar *m* o *f*.

oceangoing ['əʊʃn,ɡəʊɪŋ] *adj* de alta mar.

ochre Br, **ocher** Am ['əʊkəʳ] *adj* ocre.

o'clock [əˈklɒk] *adv*: **it's one ~** es la una; **it's two/three ~** son las dos/las tres; **at one/two ~** a la una/las dos.

octave ['ɒktɪv] *n* octava *f*.

October [ɒkˈtəʊbəʳ] *n* octubre *m*; *see also* **September**.

octopus ['ɒktəpəs] (*pl* **-puses** OR **-pi** [-paɪ]) *n* pulpo *m*.

OD 1. *abbr of* **overdose**. 2. *abbr of* **overdrawn**.

odd [ɒd] *adj* 1. (*strange*) raro(ra), extraño(ña). 2. (*not part of pair*) sin pareja. 3. (*number*) impar. 4. *inf* (*leftover*) sobrante. 5. *inf* (*occasional*): **I play the ~ game** juego alguna que otra vez. 6. *inf* (*approximately*): **30 ~ years** 30 y tantos OR y pico años. ▶ **odds** *npl* 1. **the ~s** (*probability*) las probabilidades; (*in betting*) las apuestas; **the ~s are that ...** lo más probable es que ...; **against all ~s** contra viento y marea. 2. (*bits*): **~s and ends** chismes *mpl*, cosillas *fpl*. 3. *phr*: **to be at ~s with sb** estar reñido con alguien.

oddity ['ɒdɪtɪ] (*pl* **-ies**) *n* rareza *f*.

odd jobs *npl* chapuzas *fpl*.

oddly ['ɒdlɪ] *adv* extrañamente; **~ enough** aunque parezca mentira.

oddments ['ɒdmənts] *npl* retales *mpl*.

odds-on ['ɒdz-] *adj inf*: **the ~ favourite** el favorito indiscutible.

odometer [əʊˈdɒmɪtəʳ] *n* cuentakilómetros *m inv*.

odour Br, **odor** Am ['əʊdəʳ] *n* (*gen*) olor *m*; (*of perfume*) fragancia *f*.

of [*unstressed* əv, *stressed* ɒv] *prep* 1. (*gen*) de; **the cover ~ a book** la portada de un libro; **both ~ us** nosotros dos; **to die ~**

sthg morir de algo. 2. (*expressing quantity, referring to container*) de; **thousands ~ people** miles de personas; **a cup ~ coffee** un café, una taza de café. 3. (*indicating amount, age, time*) de; **a child ~ five** un niño de cinco (años); **an increase ~ 6%** un incremento del 6%; **the 12th ~ February** el 12 de febrero. 4. (*made from*) de; **a dress ~ silk** un vestido de seda. 5. (*with emotions, opinions*): **fear ~ ghosts** miedo a los fantasmas; **love ~ good food** amor por la buena mesa; **it was very kind ~ you** fue muy amable de or por tu parte.

off [ɒf] ◆ *adv* 1. (*away*): **to drive ~** alejarse conduciendo; **to turn ~ (the road)** salir de la carretera; **I'm ~!** ¡me voy! 2. (*at a distance - in time*): **it's two days ~** quedan dos días; **that's a long time ~** aún queda mucho para eso; (*- in space*): **it's ten miles ~** está a diez millas; **far ~** lejos. 3. (*so as to remove*): **to take ~** (*gen*) quitar; (*one's clothes*) quitarse; **to cut ~** cortar; **could you help me ~ with my coat?** ¿me ayudas a quitarme el abrigo? 4. (*so as to complete*): **to finish ~** terminar, acabar; **to kill ~** rematar. 5. (*not at work*) libre, de vacaciones; **a day ~** un día libre; **time ~** tiempo *m* libre. 6. (*so as to separate*): **to fence ~** vallar; **to wall ~** tapiar. 7. (*discounted*): **£10 ~** 10 libras de descuento. 8. (*having money*): **to be well/badly ~** andar bien/mal de dinero. ◆ *prep* 1. (*away from*): **to get ~** bajarse de algo; **to keep ~ sthg** mantenerse alejado de algo; **'keep ~ the grass'** 'prohibido pisar el césped'. 2. (*close to*): **just ~ the coast** muy cerca de la costa; **it's ~ Oxford Street** está al lado de Oxford Street. 3. (*removed from*): **to cut a slice ~ sthg** cortar un pedazo de algo; **take your hands ~ me!** ¡quítame las manos de encima! 4. (*not attending*): **to be ~ work/duty** no estar trabajando/de servicio. 5. *inf* (*no longer liking*): **she's ~ coffee/her food** no le apetece café/comer. 6. (*deducted from*): **there's 10% ~ the price** hay un 10% de rebaja sobre el precio. 7. *inf* (*from*): **I bought it ~ him** se lo compré a él. ◆ *adj* 1. (*gone bad - meat, cheese*) pasado(da), estropeado(da); (*- milk*) cortado(da). 2. (*not operating*) apagado(da). 3. (*cancelled*) suspendido (da).

offal ['ɒfl] *n* (U) asaduras *fpl*.

off-chance *n*: **on the ~** por si acaso.

off colour *adj* indispuesto(ta).

off duty *adj* fuera de servicio.

offence Br, **offense** Am [ə'fens] *n*
1. (*crime*) delito *m*. 2. (*cause of upset*)
ofensa *f*; **to take** ~ ofenderse.

offend [ə'fend] *vt* ofender.

offender [ə'fendə^r] *n* 1. (*criminal*)
delincuente *m y f*. 2. (*culprit*) culpable
m y f.

offense Am [*sense* 2 'ɒfens] *n* 1. =
offence. 2. (SPORT) ataque *m*.

offensive [ə'fensɪv] ◆ *adj* 1. (*remark,
behaviour*) ofensivo(va); (*smell*) repugnante. 2. (*aggressive*) atacante. ◆ *n* (MIL)
ofensiva *f*.

offer ['ɒfə^r] ◆ *n* oferta *f*; **on** ~ (*available*)
disponible; (*at a special price*) en oferta.
◆ *vt* ofrecer; **to** ~ **sthg to sb**, **to** ~ **sb sthg**
ofrecer algo a alguien; (*be willing*): **to** ~ **to
do sthg** ofrecerse a hacer algo. ◆ *vi*
ofrecerse.

offering ['ɒfərɪŋ] *n* 1. (*thing offered*)
ofrecimiento *m*; (*gift*) regalo *m*. 2. (*sacrifice*) ofrenda *f*.

off-guard *adj* desprevenido(da).

offhand [ˌɒf'hænd] ◆ *adj* brusco(ca),
descortés. ◆ *adv* de improviso.

office ['ɒfɪs] *n* 1. (*gen*) oficina *f*.
2. (*room*) despacho *m*, oficina *f*. 3. (*position of authority*) cargo *m*; **in** ~ (*political
party*) en el poder; (*person*) en el cargo;
to take ~ (*political party*) subir al poder;
(*person*) asumir el cargo.

office automation *n* ofimática *f*.

office block *n* bloque *m* de oficinas.

office hours *npl* horas *fpl* de oficina.

officer ['ɒfɪsə^r] *n* 1. (MIL) oficial *m y f*.
2. (*in organization*) director *m*, -ra *f*. 3. (*in
police force*) agente *m y f* de policía.

office worker *n* oficinista *m y f*.

official [ə'fɪʃl] ◆ *adj* oficial. ◆ *n* (*of
union*) delegado *m*, -da *f*; (*of government*)
funcionario *m*, -ria *f*.

officialdom [ə'fɪʃəldəm] *n* burocracia
f.

offing ['ɒfɪŋ] *n*: **to be in the** ~ estar al
caer OR a la vista.

off-licence *n* Br *tienda donde se venden
bebidas alcohólicas para llevar.*

off-line *adj* (COMPUT) desconectado(da).

off-peak *adj* (*electricity, phone call, travel*)
de tarifa reducida; (*period*) económico
(ca).

off-putting [-ˌpʊtɪŋ] *adj* repelente.

off season *n*: **the** ~ la temporada
baja.

offset ['ɒfset] (*pt & pp* **offset**) *vt* compensar, contrarrestar.

offshoot ['ɒfʃuːt] *n* retoño *m*.

offshore ['ɒfʃɔː^r] ◆ *adj* (*wind*) costero

(ra); (*fishing*) de bajura; (*oil rig*) maríti-
mo(ma); (*banking*) en bancos extranjeros. ◆ *adv* mar adentro; **two miles** ~ a
dos millas de la costa.

offside [ˌɒf'saɪd] ◆ *adj* 1. (*part of vehicle - right-hand drive*) izquierdo(da); (*- left-
hand drive*) derecho(cha). 2. (SPORT) fuera
de juego. ◆ *adv* (SPORT) fuera de juego.

offspring ['ɒfsprɪŋ] (*pl inv*) *n* 1. (*of people - child*) *fml or hum* descendiente *m y f*;
(*- children*) descendencia *f*. 2. (*of animals*)
crías *fpl*.

offstage [ˌɒf'steɪdʒ] *adj & adv* entre
bastidores.

off-the-cuff ◆ *adj* improvisado(da).
◆ *adv* improvisadamente.

off-the-peg *adj* Br confeccionado
(da).

off-the-record ◆ *adj* extraoficial.
◆ *adv* extraoficialmente.

off-white *adj* blancuzco(ca).

often ['ɒfn, 'ɒftn] *adv* (*many times*) a
menudo, con frecuencia; **how** ~ **do you
go?** ¿cada cuánto OR con qué frecuencia vas?; **I don't** ~ **see him** no lo veo
mucho. ▶ **as often as not** *adv* muchas
veces. ▶ **every so often** *adv* cada
cierto tiempo. ▶ **more often than
not** *adv* la mayoría de las veces.

ogle ['əʊgl] *vt pej* comerse con los ojos.

oh [əʊ] *excl* 1. (*to introduce comment*) ¡ah!;
~ **really?** ¿de verdad? 2. (*expressing joy,
surprise, fear*) ¡oh!; ~ **no!** ¡no!

oil [ɔɪl] ◆ *n* 1. (*gen*) aceite *m*. 2. (*petroleum*) petróleo *m*. ◆ *vt* engrasar.

oilcan ['ɔɪlkæn] *n* aceitera *f*.

oilfield ['ɔɪlfiːld] *n* yacimiento *m*
petrolífero.

oil filter *n* filtro *m* del aceite.

oil-fired [-ˌfaɪəd] *adj* de fuel-oil.

oil painting *n* (*pintura f al*) óleo *m*.

oilrig ['ɔɪlrɪg] *n* plataforma *f* petrolífera.

oilskins ['ɔɪlskɪnz] *npl* (*gen*) prenda *f*
de hule; (*coat*) impermeable *m*,
chubasquero *m*.

oil slick *n* marea *f* negra.

oil tanker *n* 1. (*ship*) petrolero *m*. 2.
(*lorry*) camión *m* cisterna.

oil well *n* pozo *m* petrolífero OR de
petróleo.

oily ['ɔɪlɪ] *adj* (*food*) aceitoso(sa); (*rag,
cloth*) grasiento(ta).

ointment ['ɔɪntmənt] *n* pomada *f*,
ungüento *m*.

OK (*pt & pp* **OKed**, *cont* **OKing**), **okay**
[ˌəʊ'keɪ] *inf* ◆ *adj*: **is it** ~ **with you?** ¿te
parece bien? ◆ *excl* 1. (*gen*) vale, de

acuerdo. **2.** (*to introduce new topic*) bien, vale. ◆ *vt* dar el visto bueno a.

old [əʊld] ◆ *adj* **1.** (*gen*) viejo(ja); **how ~ are you?** ¿cuántos años tienes?, ¿qué edad tienes?; **I'm 20 years ~** tengo 20 años. **2.** (*former*) antiguo(gua). ◆ *npl*: **the ~** los ancianos.

old age *n* vejez *f*.

old age pensioner *n* Br pensionista *m y f*, jubilado *m*, -da *f*.

Old Bailey [-'beɪlɪ] *n*: **the ~** el juzgado criminal central de Inglaterra.

old-fashioned [-'fæʃnd] *adj* **1.** (*outmoded*) pasado(da) de moda, anticuado (da). **2.** (*traditional*) tradicional.

old people's home *n* residencia *f* OR hogar *m* de ancianos.

O level *n* Br ≃ Bachillerato *m*, ≃ BUP *m*.

olive ['ɒlɪv] ◆ *adj* verde oliva. ◆ *n* (*fruit*) aceituna *f*, oliva *f*.

olive green *adj* verde oliva.

olive oil *n* aceite *m* de oliva.

Olympic [ə'lɪmpɪk] *adj* olímpico(ca). ▶ **Olympics** *npl*: **the ~s** los Juegos Olímpicos.

Olympic Games *npl*: **the ~** los Juegos Olímpicos.

ombudsman ['ɒmbʊdzmən] (*pl* **-men** [-mən]) *n* ≃ Defensor *m* del Pueblo.

omelet(te) ['ɒmlɪt] *n* tortilla *f*.

omen ['əʊmen] *n* presagio *m*, agüero *m*.

ominous ['ɒmɪnəs] *adj* siniestro(tra), de mal agüero.

omission [ə'mɪʃn] *n* **1.** (*thing left out*) olvido *m*, descuido *m*. **2.** (*act of omitting*) omisión *f*.

omit [ə'mɪt] *vt* omitir; (*name - from list*) pasar por alto; **to ~ to do sthg** olvidar hacer algo.

omnibus ['ɒmnɪbəs] *n* **1.** (*book*) antología *f*. **2.** Br (RADIO & TV) *programa que emite varios capítulos seguidos*.

on [ɒn] ◆ *prep* **1.** (*indicating position - gen*) en; (*- on top of*) sobre, en; **~ a chair** en OR sobre una silla; **~ the wall/ground** en la pared/el suelo; **he was lying ~ his side/ back** estaba tumbado de costado/de espaldas; **~ the left/right** a la izquierda/derecha; **I haven't got any money ~ me** no llevo nada de dinero encima. **2.** (*indicating means*): **it runs ~ diesel** funciona con diesel; **~ TV/the radio** en la tele/la radio; **she's ~ the telephone** está al teléfono; **he lives ~ fruit** vive (a base) de fruta; **to hurt o.s. ~ sthg** hacerse daño con algo. **3.** (*indicating mode of*

transport): **to travel ~ a bus/train/ship** viajar en autobús/tren/barco; **I was ~ the bus** iba en el autobús; **to get ~ a bus/train/ship** subirse a un autobús/ tren/barco; **~ foot** a pie. **4.** (*indicating time, activity*): **~ Thursday** el jueves; **~ my birthday** el día de mi cumpleaños; **~ the 10th of February** el 10 de febrero; **~ my return**, **~ returning** al volver; **~ business/holiday** de negocios/vacaciones. **5.** (*concerning*) sobre, acerca de; **a book ~ astronomy** un libro acerca de OR sobre astronomía. **6.** (*indicating influence*) en, sobre; **the impact ~ the environment** el impacto en OR sobre el medio ambiente. **7.** (*using, supported by*): **to be ~ social security** cobrar dinero de la seguridad social; **he's ~ tranquillizers** está tomando tranquilizantes; **to be ~ drugs** (*addicted*) drogarse. **8.** (*earning*): **she's ~ £25,000 a year** gana 25.000 libras al año. **9.** (*referring to musical instrument*) con; **~ the violin** con el violín; **~ the piano** al piano. **10.** *inf* (*paid by*): **the drinks are ~ me** yo pago las copas, a las copas invito yo. ◆ *adv* **1.** (*indicating covering, clothing*): **put the lid ~** pon la tapa; **what did she have ~?** ¿qué llevaba encima OR puesto?; **put your coat ~** ponte el abrigo. **2.** (*being shown*): **what's ~ at the cinema?** ¿qué echan OR ponen en el cine? **3.** (*working - machine*) funcionando; (*- radio, TV, light*) encendido; (*- tap*) abierto(ta); (*- brakes*) puesto(ta); **turn ~ the power** pulse el botón de encendido. **4.** (*indicating continuing action*): **he kept ~ walking** siguió caminando. **5.** (*forward*): **send my mail ~ (to me)** reenvíame el correo; **later ~** más tarde, después; **earlier ~** con anterioridad, antes. **6.** *inf* (*referring to behaviour*): **it's just not ~!** ¡es una pasada! ▶ **from ... on** *adv*: **from now ~** de ahora en adelante; **from that moment/time ~** desde aquel momento/aquella vez. ▶ **on and off** *adv* de vez en cuando. ▶ **on to, onto** *prep* (*only written as onto for senses 4 and 5*) **1.** (*to a position on top of*) encima de, sobre; **she jumped ~ to the chair** salto encima de OR sobre la silla. **2.** (*to a position on a vehicle*): **to get ~ to a bus/train/plane** subirse a un autobús/ tren/avión. **3.** (*to a position attached to*): **stick the photo ~ to the page** pega la foto a la hoja. **4.** (*aware of wrongdoing*): **to be onto sb** andar detrás de alguien. **5.** (*into contact with*): **get onto the factory** ponte en contacto con la fábrica.

once [wʌns] ♦ adv 1. (on one occasion) una vez; ~ **a week** una vez a la semana; ~ **again** OR **more** otra vez; **for** ~ por una vez; ~ **and for all** de una vez por todas; ~ **or twice** alguna que otra vez; ~ **in a while** de vez en cuando. 2. (previously) en otro tiempo, antiguamente; ~ **upon a time** érase una vez. ♦ conj una vez que; ~ **you have done it** una vez que lo hayas hecho. ▶ **at once** adv 1. (immediately) en seguida, inmediatamente. 2. (at the same time) a la vez, al mismo tiempo; **all at** ~ de repente, de golpe.

oncoming ['ɒn,kʌmɪŋ] adj (traffic) que viene en dirección contraria; (danger, event) venidero(ra).

one [wʌn] ♦ num (the number 1) un (una); **I only want** ~ sólo quiero uno; ~ **fifth** un quinto, una quinta parte; ~ **of my friends** uno de mis amigos; **on page a hundred and** ~ en la página ciento uno; (number) ~ el uno. ♦ adj 1. (only) único(ca); **it's her** ~ **ambition** es su única ambición. 2. (indefinite): ~ **of these days** un día de éstos. ♦ pron 1. (referring to a particular thing or person) uno (una); **I want the red** ~ yo quiero el rojo; **the** ~ **with the blond hair** la del pelo rubio; **which** ~ **do you want?** ¿cuál quieres?; **this** ~ éste (ésta); **that** ~ ése (ésa); **she's the** ~ **I told you about** es (ésa) de la que te hablé. 2. fml (you, anyone) uno (una); **to do** ~'s **duty** cumplir uno con su deber. ▶ **for one** adv: **I for** ~ **remain unconvinced** yo, por lo menos OR por mi parte, sigo poco convencido.

one-armed bandit n (máquina f) tragaperras f inv.

one-man adj individual, en solitario.

one-man band n (musician) hombre m orquesta.

one-off inf ♦ adj único(ca). ♦ n caso m excepcional.

one-on-one Am = **one-to-one**.

one-parent family n familia f monoparental.

oneself [wʌn'self] pron 1. (reflexive, after prep) uno mismo (una misma); **to buy presents for** ~ hacerse regalos a sí mismo. 2. (for emphasis): **by** ~ (without help) solo(la).

one-sided [-'saɪdɪd] adj 1. (unequal) desigual. 2. (biased) parcial.

one-to-one Br, **one-on-one** Am adj (relationship, discussion) entre dos; (tuition) individual.

one-upmanship [,wʌn'ʌpmənʃɪp] n habilidad para ganar ventaja sin hacer trampas.

one-way adj 1. (street) de dirección única. 2. (ticket) de ida.

ongoing ['ɒn,gəʊɪŋ] adj actual, en curso.

onion ['ʌnjən] n cebolla f.

online ['ɒnlaɪn] adj & adv (COMPUT) en línea.

onlooker ['ɒn,lʊkər] n espectador m, -ra f.

only ['əʊnlɪ] ♦ adj único(ca); **an** ~ **child** hijo único. ♦ adv (exclusively) sólo, solamente; **I was** ~ **too willing to help** estaba encantado de poder ayudar; **I** ~ **wish I could!** ¡ojalá pudiera!; **it's** ~ **natural** es completamente normal; **not** ~ ... **but** no sólo ... sino; ~ **just** apenas. ♦ conj sólo OR solamente que; **I would go,** ~ **I'm too tired** iría, lo que pasa es que estoy muy cansado.

onset ['ɒnset] n comienzo m.

onshore ['ɒnʃɔːr] adj (wind) procedente del mar; (oil production) en tierra firme.

onslaught ['ɒnslɔːt] n lit & fig acometida f.

onto [unstressed before consonant 'ɒntə, unstressed before vowel 'ɒntʊ, stressed 'ɒntuː] = **on to**.

onus ['əʊnəs] n responsabilidad f.

onward ['ɒnwəd] ♦ adj (in time) progresivo(va); (in space) hacia delante. ♦ adv = **onwards**.

onwards ['ɒnwədz] adv (in space) adelante, hacia delante; (in time): **from now/then** ~ de ahora/allí en adelante.

ooze [uːz] ♦ vt fig rebosar. ♦ vi: ~ **(from** OR **out of)** rezumar (de); **to** ~ **with sthg** fig rebosar OR irradiar algo.

opaque [əʊ'peɪk] adj 1. (not transparent) opaco(ca). 2. fig (obscure) oscuro(ra).

OPEC ['əʊpek] (abbr of **Organization of Petroleum Exporting Countries**) n OPEP f.

open ['əʊpn] ♦ adj 1. (gen) abierto(ta); (curtains) descorrido(da); (view, road) despejado(da). 2. (receptive): **to be** ~ **to** (ideas, suggestions) estar abierto a; (blame, criticism, question) prestarse a. 3. (frank) sincero(ra), franco(ca). 4. (uncovered - car) descubierto(ta). 5. (available - subj: choice, chance): **to be** ~ **to sb** estar disponible para alguien. ♦ n: **in the** ~ (fresh air) al aire libre; **to bring sthg out into the** ~ sacar a luz algo. ♦ vt 1. (gen) abrir; **to** ~ **fire** abrir fuego. 2. (inaugurate - public area, event) inaugurar. ♦ vi 1. (door, flower) abrirse. 2. (shop, office) abrir. 3. (event, play) dar comienzo.

▶ **open on to** vt fus dar a. ▶ **open up** ◆ vt sep abrir. ◆ vi **1.** (become available) surgir. **2.** (unlock door) abrir.

opener ['əupnə^r] n (gen) abridor m; (for tins) abrelatas m inv; (for bottles) abrebotellas m inv.

opening ['əupnɪŋ] ◆ adj inicial. ◆ n **1.** (beginning) comienzo m, principio m. **2.** (gap - in fence) abertura f. **3.** (opportunity) oportunidad f. **4.** (job vacancy) puesto m vacante.

opening hours npl horario m (de apertura).

openly ['əupənlɪ] adv abiertamente.

open-minded [-'maɪndɪd] adj sin prejuicios.

open-plan adj de plan abierto, sin tabiques.

Open University n Br: the ~ ≃ la Universidad Nacional de Educación a Distancia.

opera ['ɒpərə] n ópera f.

opera house n teatro m de la ópera.

operate ['ɒpəreɪt] ◆ vt **1.** (machine) hacer funcionar. **2.** (business, system) dirigir. ◆ vi **1.** (carry out trade, business) operar, actuar. **2.** (function) funcionar. **3.** (MED): **to ~ (on sb/sthg)** operar (a alguien/de algo).

operating theatre Br, **operating room** Am ['ɒpəreɪtɪŋ-] n quirófano m.

operation [,ɒpə'reɪʃn] n **1.** (planned activity - police, rescue, business) operación f; (- military) maniobra f. **2.** (running - of business) administración f. **3.** (functioning - of machine) funcionamiento m; **to be in ~** (machine) funcionar; (law) estar en vigor. **4.** (MED) operación f, intervención f quirúrgica; **to have an ~ (for/on)** operarse (de).

operational [,ɒpə'reɪʃənl] adj (ready for use) operacional, en estado de funcionamiento.

operative ['ɒprətɪv] ◆ adj en vigor, vigente. ◆ n operario m, -ria f.

operator ['ɒpəreɪtə^r] n **1.** (TELEC) operador m, -ra f, telefonista m y f. **2.** (employee) operario m, -ria f. **3.** (person in charge - of business) encargado m, -da f.

opinion [ə'pɪnjən] n opinión f; **to be of the ~ that** opinar OR creer que; **in my ~** a mi juicio, en mi opinión.

opinionated [ə'pɪnjəneɪtɪd] adj pej terco(ca).

opinion poll n sondeo m, encuesta f.

opponent [ə'pəunənt] n **1.** (POL) adversario m, -ria f. **2.** (SPORT) contrincante m y f.

opportune ['ɒpətjuːn] adj oportuno (na).

opportunist [,ɒpə'tjuːnɪst] n oportunista m y f.

opportunity [,ɒpə'tjuːnətɪ] n oportunidad f, ocasión f; **to take the ~ to do** OR **of doing sthg** aprovechar la ocasión de OR para hacer algo.

oppose [ə'pəuz] vt oponerse a.

opposed [ə'pəuzd] adj opuesto(ta); **to be ~ to** oponerse a; **as ~ to** en vez de, en lugar de; **I like beer as ~ to wine** me gusta la cerveza y no el vino.

opposing [ə'pəuzɪŋ] adj opuesto(ta), contrario(ria).

opposite ['ɒpəzɪt] ◆ adj **1.** (facing - side, house) de enfrente. **2.** (very different): ~ **(to)** opuesto(ta) OR contrario(ria) (a). ◆ adv enfrente. ◆ prep enfrente de. ◆ n contrario m.

opposite number n homólogo m, -ga f.

opposition [,ɒpə'zɪʃn] n **1.** (gen) oposición f. **2.** (opposing team) oponentes mpl y fpl. ▶ **Opposition** n Br (POL): **the Opposition** la oposición.

oppress [ə'pres] vt **1.** (persecute) oprimir. **2.** (depress) agobiar, deprimir.

oppressive [ə'presɪv] adj **1.** (unjust) tiránico(ca), opresivo(va). **2.** (stifling) agobiante, sofocante. **3.** (causing unease) opresivo(va), agobiante.

opt [ɒpt] ◆ vt: **to ~ to do sthg** optar por OR elegir hacer algo. ◆ vi: **to ~ for sthg** optar por OR elegir algo. ▶ **opt in** vi: **to ~ in (to sthg)** optar por participar (en algo). ▶ **opt out** vi: **to ~ out (of sthg)** decidir no tomar parte (en algo).

optical ['ɒptɪkl] adj óptico(ca).

optician [ɒp'tɪʃn] n óptico m, -ca f; **~'s (shop)** la óptica.

optimist ['ɒptɪmɪst] n optimista m y f.

optimistic [,ɒptɪ'mɪstɪk] adj optimista.

optimum ['ɒptɪməm] adj óptimo(ma).

option ['ɒpʃn] n opción f; **to have the ~ to do** OR **of doing sthg** tener la opción de OR la posibilidad de hacer algo.

optional ['ɒpʃənl] adj facultativo(va), optativo(va); ~ **extra** extra m opcional.

or [ɔː^r] conj **1.** (gen) o; (before 'o' or 'ho') u; ~ **(else)** o de lo contrario, si no. **2.** (after negative): **he cannot read ~ write** no sabe ni leer ni escribir.

oral ['ɔːrəl] ◆ adj **1.** (spoken) oral. **2.** (relating to the mouth) bucal. ◆ n examen m oral.

orally ['ɔːrəlɪ] adv **1.** (in spoken form) oralmente. **2.** (via the mouth) por vía oral.

orange ['ɒrɪndʒ] ◆ *adj* naranja (*inv*). ◆ *n* (*fruit*) naranja *f*.

orator ['ɒrətəʳ] *n* orador *m*, -ra *f*.

orbit ['ɔːbɪt] ◆ *n* órbita *f*. ◆ *vt* girar alrededor de.

orchard ['ɔːtʃəd] *n* huerto *m*.

orchestra ['ɔːkɪstrə] *n* orquesta *f*.

orchestral [ɔːr'kestrəl] *adj* orquestal.

orchid ['ɔːkɪd] *n* orquídea *f*.

ordain [ɔːr'deɪn] *vt* **1.** *fml* (*decree*) decretar, ordenar. **2.** (RELIG): **to be ~ed** ordenarse (sacerdote).

ordeal [ɔːr'diːl] *n* calvario *m*, experiencia *f* terrible.

order ['ɔːdəʳ] ◆ *n* **1.** (*instruction*) orden *f*; **to be under ~s to do sthg** tener órdenes de hacer algo. **2.** (COMM) (*request*) pedido *m*; **to ~ por** encargo. **3.** (*sequence, discipline, system*) orden *m*; **in ~** en orden; **in ~ of importance** por orden de importancia. **4.** (*fitness for use*): **in working ~** en funcionamiento; **'out of ~'** 'no funciona'; **to be out of ~** (*not working*) estar estropeado(da); (*incorrect behaviour*) ser improcedente; **in ~** (*correct*) en regla. **5.** (RELIG) orden *f*. **6.** *Am* (*portion*) ración *f*. ◆ *vt* **1.** (*command*): **to ~ sb (to do sthg)** ordenar a alguien (que haga algo); **to ~ that** ordenar que. **2.** (*request - drink, taxi*) pedir. **3.** (COM) encargar. ▶ **in the order of** Br, **on the order of** Am *prep* del orden de. ▶ **in order that** *conj* para que. ▶ **in order to** *conj* para. ▶ **order about, order around** *vt sep* mangonear.

order form *n* hoja *f* de pedido.

orderly ['ɔːdəlɪ] ◆ *adj* (*person, crowd*) obediente; (*room*) ordenado(da), en orden. ◆ *n* (*in hospital*) auxiliar *m* y *f* sanitario.

ordinarily ['ɔːdənrəlɪ] *adv* de ordinario.

ordinary ['ɔːdənrɪ] ◆ *adj* **1.** (*normal*) corriente, normal. **2.** *pej* (*unexceptional*) mediocre, ordinario(ria). ◆ *n*: **out of the ~** fuera de lo común.

ordnance ['ɔːdnəns] *n* (U) **1.** (*military supplies*) pertrechos *mpl* de guerra. **2.** (*artillery*) artillería *f*.

ore [ɔːʳ] *n* mineral *m*.

oregano [ˌɒrɪ'gɑːnəʊ] *n* orégano *m*.

organ ['ɔːgən] *n* órgano *m*.

organic [ɔːr'gænɪk] *adj* orgánico(ca).

organization [ˌɔːgənaɪ'zeɪʃn] *n* organización *f*.

organize, -ise ['ɔːgənaɪz] *vt* organizar.

organizer ['ɔːgənaɪzəʳ] *n* organizador *m*, -ra *f*.

orgasm ['ɔːgæzm] *n* orgasmo *m*.

orgy ['ɔːdʒɪ] *n* lit & fig orgía *f*.

Orient ['ɔːrɪənt] *n*: **the ~** el Oriente.

oriental [ˌɔːrɪ'entl] ◆ *adj* oriental. ◆ *n* oriental *m* y *f* (*atención: el término 'oriental' se considera racista*).

orienteering [ˌɔːrɪən'tɪərɪŋ] *n* deporte *m* de orientación, orienteering *m*.

origami [ˌɒrɪ'gɑːmɪ] *n* papiroflexia *f*.

origin ['ɒrɪdʒɪn] *n* origen *m*; **country of ~** país *m* de origen. ▶ **origins** *npl* origen *m*.

original [ə'rɪdʒənl] ◆ *adj* original; **the ~ owner** el primer propietario. ◆ *n* original *m*.

originally [ə'rɪdʒənəlɪ] *adv* (*at first*) originariamente; (*with originality*) originalmente.

originate [ə'rɪdʒəneɪt] ◆ *vt* originar, producir. ◆ *vi*: **to ~ (in)** nacer OR surgir (de); **to ~ from** nacer OR surgir de.

Orkney Islands ['ɔːknɪ-], **Orkneys** ['ɔːknɪz] *npl*: **the ~** las Orcadas.

ornament ['ɔːnəmənt] *n* adorno *m*.

ornamental [ˌɔːnə'mentl] *adj* ornamental, decorativo(va).

ornate [ɔːr'neɪt] *adj* (*style*) recargado (da); (*decoration, vase*) muy vistoso(sa).

ornithology [ˌɔːnɪ'θɒlədʒɪ] *n* ornitología *f*.

orphan ['ɔːfn] ◆ *n* huérfano *m*, -na *f*. ◆ *vt*: **to be ~ed** quedarse huérfano.

orphanage ['ɔːfənɪdʒ] *n* orfelinato *m*.

orthodox ['ɔːθədɒks] *adj* ortodoxo (xa).

orthopaedic [ˌɔːθə'piːdɪk] *adj* ortopédico(ca).

orthopedic [ˌɔːθə'piːdɪk] *etc* = **orthopaedic** *etc*.

oscillate ['ɒsɪleɪt] *vi* lit & fig: **to ~ (between)** oscilar (entre).

Oslo ['ɒzləʊ] *n* Oslo.

ostensible [ɒ'stensəbl] *adj* aparente.

ostentatious [ˌɒstən'teɪʃəs] *adj* **1.** (*lifestyle, wealth*) ostentoso(sa). **2.** (*person*) ostentativo(va). **3.** (*behaviour*) ostensible.

osteopath ['ɒstɪəpæθ] *n* osteópata *m* y *f*.

ostracize, -ise ['ɒstrəsaɪz] *vt* (*colleague etc*) marginar, hacer el vacío a; (POL) condenar al ostracismo.

ostrich ['ɒstrɪtʃ] *n* avestruz *m*.

other ['ʌðəʳ] ◆ *adj* otro (otra); **the ~ one** el otro (la otra); **the ~ day** el otro día. ◆ *pron* **1.** (*different one*): **~s** otros (otras).

2. (*remaining, alternative one*): **the ~** el otro (la otra); **the ~s** los otros (las otras), los demás (las demás); **one after the ~** uno tras otro; **one or ~** uno u otro; **to be none ~ than** no ser otro(tra) sino. ▶ **something or other** *pron* una cosa u otra. ▶ **somehow or other** *adv* de una u otra forma. ▶ **other than** *conj* excepto, salvo.

otherwise [ˈʌðəwaɪz] ♦ *adv* **1.** (*or else*) si no. **2.** (*apart from that*) por lo demás. **3.** (*differently*) de otra manera; **deliberately or ~** adrede o no. ♦ *conj* sino, de lo contrario.

otter [ˈɒtəʳ] *n* nutria *f*.

ouch [aʊtʃ] *excl* ¡ay!

ought [ɔːt] *aux vb* deber; **you ~ to go/ to be nicer** deberías irte/ser más amable; **she ~ to pass the exam** tiene probabilidades de aprobar el examen.

ounce [aʊns] *n* (*unit of measurement*) = 28,35g, = onza *f*.

our [ˈaʊəʳ] *poss adj* nuestro(tra), nuestros(tras) (*pl*); **~ money** nuestro dinero; **~ house** nuestra casa; **~ children** nuestros hijos; **it wasn't our fault** no fue culpa nuestra OR nuestra culpa; **we washed ~ hair** nos lavamos el pelo.

ours [ˈaʊəz] *poss pron* nuestro(tra); **that money is ~** ese dinero es nuestro; **those keys are ~** esas llaves son nuestras; **it wasn't their fault, it was OURS** no fue culpa de ellos sino de nosotros; **a friend of ~** un amigo nuestro; **their car hit ~** suyo coche chocó contra el nuestro.

ourselves [aʊəˈselvz] *pron pl* **1.** (*reflexive*) nos *mpl* y *fpl*; (*after prep*) nosotros *mpl*, nosotras *fpl*. **2.** (*for emphasis*) nosotros mismos *mpl*, nosotras mismas *fpl*; **we did it by ~** lo hicimos por nosotros solos.

oust [aʊst] *vt fml*: **to ~ sb (from)** (*job*) desbancar a alguien (de); (*land*) desalojar a alguien (de).

out [aʊt] *adv* **1.** (*not inside, out of doors*) fuera; **we all went ~** todos salimos fuera; **I'm going ~ for a walk** voy a salir a dar un paseo; **they ran ~** salieron corriendo; **he poured the water ~** sirvió el agua; **~ here/there** aquí/allí fuera. **2.** (*away from home, office*) fuera; **John's ~ at the moment** John está fuera ahora mismo. **3.** (*extinguished*) apagado(da); **the fire went ~** el fuego se apagó. **4.** (*of tides*): **the tide had gone ~** la marea estaba baja. **5.** (*out of fashion*) pasado(da) de moda. **6.** (*published, released - book*) publicado(da); **they've a new record ~** han

sacado un nuevo disco. **7.** (*in flower*) en flor. **8.** *inf* (*on strike*) en huelga. **9.** (*determined*): **to be ~ to do sthg** estar decidido (da) a hacer algo. ▶ **out of** *prep* **1.** (*away from, outside*) fuera de; **to go ~ of the room** salir de la habitación. **2.** (*indicating cause*) por; **~ of spite/love** por rencor/ amor. **3.** (*indicating origin, source*) de; **a page ~ of a book** una página de un libro. **4.** (*without*) sin; **we're ~ of sugar** estamos sin azúcar, se nos ha acabado el azúcar. **5.** (*made from*) de; **it's made ~ of plastic** está hecho de plástico. **6.** (*sheltered from*) a resguardo de. **7.** (*to indicate proportion*): **one ~ of ten people** una de cada diez personas; **ten ~ of ten** (*mark*) diez de OR sobre diez.

out-and-out *adj* (*disgrace, lie*) infame; (*liar, crook*) redomado(da).

outback [ˈaʊtbæk] *n*: **the ~** los llanos del interior de Australia.

outboard (motor) [ˈaʊtbɔːd-] *n* (motor *m*) fueraborda *m*.

outbreak [ˈaʊtbreɪk] *n* (*of war*) comienzo *m*; (*of crime*) ola *f*; (*of illness*) epidemia *f*; (*of spots*) erupción *f*.

outburst [ˈaʊtbɜːst] *n* **1.** (*sudden expression of emotion*) explosión *f*, arranque *m*. **2.** (*sudden occurrence*) estallido *m*.

outcast [ˈaʊtkɑːst] *n* marginado *m*, -da *f*, paria *m* y *f*.

outcome [ˈaʊtkʌm] *n* resultado *m*.

outcrop [ˈaʊtkrɒp] *n* afloramiento *m*.

outcry [ˈaʊtkraɪ] *n* protestas *fpl*.

outdated [ˌaʊtˈdeɪtɪd] *adj* anticuado (da), pasado(da) de moda.

outdid [ˌaʊtˈdɪd] *pt* → outdo.

outdo [ˌaʊtˈduː] (*pt* -did, *pp* -done [-dʌn]) *vt* aventajar, superar.

outdoor [ˈaʊtdɔːʳ] *adj* (*life, swimming pool*) al aire libre; (*clothes*) de calle.

outdoors [aʊtˈdɔːz] *adv* al aire libre.

outer [ˈaʊtəʳ] *adj* exterior, externo(na).

outer space *n* espacio *m* exterior.

outfit [ˈaʊtfɪt] *n* **1.** (*clothes*) conjunto *m*, traje *m*. **2.** *inf* (*organization*) equipo *m*.

outfitters [ˈaʊtˌfɪtəz] *n dated* tienda *f* de confección.

outgoing [ˈaʊtˌgəʊɪŋ] *adj* **1.** (*chairman*) saliente. **2.** (*sociable*) extrovertido(da). ▶ **outgoings** *npl* Br gastos *mpl*.

outgrow [ˌaʊtˈgrəʊ] (*pt* -grew, *pp* -grown) *vt* **1.** (*grow too big for*): **he has ~n his shirts** las camisas se le han quedado pequeñas. **2.** (*grow too old for*) ser demasiado mayor para.

outhouse [ˈaʊthaʊs, *pl* -haʊzɪz] *n* dependencia *f*.

outing ['aʊtɪŋ] n (trip) excursión f.

outlandish [aʊt'lændɪʃ] adj estrafalario(ria).

outlaw ['aʊtlɔː] ◆ n proscrito m, -ta f. ◆ vt (make illegal) ilegalizar.

outlay ['aʊtleɪ] n desembolso m.

outlet ['aʊtlet] n 1. (for emotions) salida f. 2. (for water) desagüe m; (for gas) salida f. 3. (shop) punto m de venta. 4. Am (ELEC) toma f de corriente.

outline ['aʊtlaɪn] ◆ n 1. (brief description) esbozo m, resumen m; **in ~** en líneas generales. 2. (silhouette) contorno m. ◆ vt (describe briefly) esbozar, resumir.

outlive [,aʊt'lɪv] vt (subj: person) sobrevivir a.

outlook ['aʊtlʊk] n 1. (attitude, disposition) enfoque m, actitud f. 2. (prospect) perspectiva f (de futuro).

outlying ['aʊt,laɪŋ] adj (remote) lejano (na), remoto(ta); (on edge of town) periférico(ca).

outmoded [,aʊt'məʊdɪd] adj anticuado(da), pasado(da) de moda.

outnumber [,aʊt'nʌmbər] vt exceder en número.

out-of-date adj 1. (clothes, belief) anticuado(da), pasado(da) de moda. 2. (passport, season ticket) caducado(da).

out of doors adv al aire libre.

out-of-the-way adj (far away) remoto (ta); (unusual) poco común.

outpatient ['aʊt,peɪʃnt] n paciente externo m, paciente externa f.

outpost ['aʊtpəʊst] n puesto m avanzado.

output ['aʊtpʊt] n 1. (production) producción f, rendimiento m. 2. (COMPUT - printing out) salida f; (- printout) impresión f.

outrage ['aʊtreɪdʒ] ◆ n 1. (anger) indignación f. 2. (atrocity) atrocidad f, escándalo m. ◆ vt ultrajar, atropellar.

outrageous [aʊt'reɪdʒəs] adj 1. (offensive, shocking) indignante, escandaloso (sa). 2. (very unusual) extravagante.

outright [adj 'aʊtraɪt, adv ,aʊt'raɪt] ◆ adj 1. (categoric) categórico(ca). 2. (total - disaster) completo(ta); (- victory, winner) indiscutible. ◆ adv 1. (ask) abiertamente; (deny) categóricamente. 2. (win, ban) totalmente; (be killed) en el acto.

outset ['aʊtset] n: **at the ~** al principio; **from the ~** desde el principio.

outside [adv ,aʊt'saɪd, adj, prep & n 'aʊtsaɪd] ◆ adj 1. (gen) exterior. 2. (opinion, criticism) independiente. 3. (chance) remoto(ta). ◆ adv fuera; **to go/run/look** ~ ir/correr/mirar fuera. ◆ prep fuera de; **we live half an hour ~ London** vivimos a media hora de Londres. ◆ n (exterior) exterior m. ▶ **outside of** prep Am (apart from) aparte de.

outside lane n carril m de adelantamiento.

outside line n línea f exterior.

outsider [,aʊt'saɪdər] n 1. (stranger) forastero m, -ra f. 2. (in horse race) caballo que no es uno de los favoritos.

outsize ['aʊtsaɪz] adj 1. (bigger than usual) enorme. 2. (clothes) de talla muy grande.

outskirts ['aʊtskɜːts] npl: **the ~** las afueras.

outspoken [,aʊt'spəʊkn] adj franco (ca).

outstanding [,aʊt'stændɪŋ] adj 1. (excellent) destacado(da). 2. (not paid, unfinished) pendiente.

outstay [,aʊt'steɪ] vt: **to ~ one's welcome** quedarse más tiempo de lo debido.

outstretched [,aʊt'stretʃt] adj extendido(da).

outstrip [,aʊt'strɪp] vt lit & fig aventajar, dejar atrás.

out-tray n cubeta o bandeja de asuntos ya resueltos.

outward ['aʊtwəd] ◆ adj 1. (journey) de ida. 2. (composure, sympathy) aparente. 3. (sign, proof) visible, exterior. ◆ adv Am = **outwards**.

outwardly ['aʊtwədlɪ] adv (apparently) aparentemente, de cara al exterior.

outwards Br ['aʊtwədz], **outward** Am adv hacia fuera.

outweigh [,aʊt'weɪ] vt pesar más que.

outwit [,aʊt'wɪt] vt ser más listo(ta) que.

oval ['əʊvl] ◆ adj oval, ovalado(da). ◆ n óvalo m.

Oval Office n: **the ~** el Despacho Oval, oficina que tiene el presidente de Estados Unidos en la Casa Blanca.

ovary ['əʊvərɪ] n ovario m.

ovation [əʊ'veɪʃn] n ovación f; **a standing ~** una ovación de gala (con el público en pie).

oven ['ʌvn] n horno m.

ovenproof ['ʌvnpruːf] adj refractario (ria).

over ['əʊvər] ◆ prep 1. (directly above, on top of) encima de; **a fog hung ~ the river** una espesa niebla flotaba sobre el río; **put your coat ~ the chair** pon el abrigo encima de la silla. 2. (to cover) sobre;

she wore a veil ~ her face un velo le cubría el rostro. **3.** (on other side of) al otro lado de; **he lives ~ the road** vive enfrente. **4.** (across surface of) por encima de; **they sailed ~ the ocean** cruzaron el océano en barco. **5.** (more than) más de; **~ and above** además de. **6.** (senior to) por encima de. **7.** (with regard to) por; **a fight ~ a woman** una pelea por una mujer. **8.** (during) durante; **~ the weekend** (en) el fin de semana. ◆ adv **1.** (short distance away): **~ here** aquí; **~ there** allí. **2.** (across): **to cross ~** cruzar; **to go ~** ir. **3.** (down): **to fall ~** caerse; **to push ~** empujar, tirar. **4.** (round): **to turn sthg ~** dar la vuelta a algo; **to roll ~** darse la vuelta. **5.** (more) más. **6.** (remaining): **to be (left) ~** quedar, sobrar. **7.** (at sb's house): **invite them ~** invítalos a casa. **8.** (RADIO): **~ (and out)!** ¡cambio (y cierro)! **9.** (involving repetitions): **(all) ~ again** otra vez desde el principio; **~ and ~ (again)** una y otra vez. ◆ adj (finished) terminado(da). ▶ **all over** ◆ prep por todo(da). ◆ adv (everywhere) por todas partes. ◆ adj (finished) terminado(da).

overall [adj & n 'əʊvərɔːl, adv ˌəʊvər'ɔːl] ◆ adj (general) global, total. ◆ adv en conjunto. ◆ n **1.** (gen) guardapolvo m. **2.** Am (for work) mono m. ▶ **overalls** npl **1.** (for work) mono m. **2.** Am (dungarees) pantalones mpl de peto.

overawe [ˌəʊvər'ɔː] vt intimidar.

overbalance [ˌəʊvə'bæləns] vi perder el equilibrio.

overbearing [ˌəʊvə'beərɪŋ] adj pej despótico(ca).

overboard ['əʊvəbɔːd] adv: **to fall ~** caer al agua OR por la borda.

overbook [ˌəʊvə'bʊk] vi hacer overbooking.

overcame [ˌəʊvə'keɪm] pt → **overcome**.

overcast ['əʊvəkɑːst] adj cubierto(ta), nublado(da).

overcharge [ˌəʊvə'tʃɑːdʒ] vt: **to ~ sb (for sthg)** cobrar a alguien en exceso (por algo).

overcoat ['əʊvəkəʊt] n abrigo m.

overcome [ˌəʊvə'kʌm] (pt **-came**, pp **-come**) vt **1.** (deal with) vencer, superar. **2.** (overwhelm): **to be ~ (by OR with)** (fear, grief, emotion) estar abrumado(da) (por); (smoke, fumes) estar asfixiado(da) (por).

overcrowded [ˌəʊvə'kraʊdɪd] adj (room) atestado(da) de gente; (country) superpoblado(da).

overcrowding [ˌəʊvə'kraʊdɪŋ] n (of country) superpoblación f; (of prison) hacinamiento m.

overdo [ˌəʊvə'duː] (pt **-did** [-dɪd], pp **-done**) vt **1.** pej (exaggerate) exagerar. **2.** (do too much): **to ~ one's work/the walking** trabajar/andar demasiado. **3.** (overcook) hacer demasiado.

overdone [ˌəʊvə'dʌn] ◆ pp → **overdo**. ◆ adj muy hecho(cha).

overdose ['əʊvədəʊs] sobredosis f inv.

overdraft ['əʊvədrɑːft] n (sum owed) saldo m deudor; (loan arranged) (giro m OR crédito m en) descubierto m.

overdrawn [ˌəʊvə'drɔːn] adj: **to be ~** tener un saldo deudor.

overdue [ˌəʊvə'djuː] adj **1.** (late): **to be ~** (train) ir con retraso; (library book) estar con el plazo de préstamo caducado; **I'm ~ (for) a bit of luck** va siendo hora de tener un poco de suerte. **2.** (awaited): **(long) ~** (largamente) esperado(da), ansiado(da). **3.** (unpaid) vencido(da) y sin pagar.

overestimate [ˌəʊvər'estɪmeɪt] vt sobreestimar.

overflow [vb ˌəʊvə'fləʊ, n 'əʊvəfləʊ] ◆ vi **1.** (spill over) rebosar; (river) desbordarse. **2.** (go beyond limits): **to ~ (into)** rebosar (hacia). **3.** (be very full): **to be ~ing (with)** rebosar (de). ◆ n (pipe) cañería f de desagüe.

overgrown [ˌəʊvə'grəʊn] adj cubierto(ta) de matojos.

overhaul [n 'əʊvəhɔːl, vb ˌəʊvə'hɔːl] ◆ n **1.** (of car, machine) revisión f. **2.** (of method, system) repaso m general. ◆ vt revisar.

overhead [adv ˌəʊvə'hed, adj & n 'əʊvəhed] ◆ adj aéreo(a). ◆ adv por lo alto, por encima. ◆ n Am (U) gastos mpl generales. ▶ **overheads** npl gastos mpl generales.

overhead projector n retroproyector m.

overhear [ˌəʊvə'hɪər] (pt & pp **-heard** [-hɜːd]) vt oír por casualidad.

overheat [ˌəʊvə'hiːt] vi recalentarse.

overjoyed [ˌəʊvə'dʒɔɪd] adj: **to be ~ (at sthg)** estar encantado(da) (con algo).

overkill ['əʊvəkɪl] n exageración f, exceso m.

overladen [ˌəʊvə'leɪdn] pp → **overload**.

overland ['əʊvəlænd] ◆ adj terrestre. ◆ adv por tierra.

overlap [ˌəʊvə'læp] vi **1.** (cover each other) superponerse. **2.** (be similar): **to ~**

(with sthg**)** coincidir en parte (en algo).

overleaf [ˌəʊvə'liːf] adv al dorso.

overload [ˌəʊvə'ləʊd] (pp **-loaded** OR **-laden**) vt sobrecargar.

overlook [ˌəʊvə'lʊk] vt 1. (look over) mirar OR dar a. 2. (disregard, miss) pasar por alto. 3. (forgive) perdonar.

overnight [adj 'əʊvənaɪt, adv ˌəʊvə'naɪt] ◆ adj 1. (for all of night) de noche, nocturno(na). 2. (for a night's stay - clothes) para una noche. 3. (very sudden) súbito(ta). ◆ adv 1. (for all of night) durante la noche. 2. (very suddenly) de la noche a la mañana.

overpass ['əʊvəpɑːs] n Am paso m elevado.

overpower [ˌəʊvə'paʊəʳ] vt 1. (in fight) vencer, subyugar. 2. fig (overwhelm) sobreponerse a, vencer.

overpowering [ˌəʊvə'paʊərɪŋ] adj arrollador(ra), abrumador(ra).

overran [ˌəʊvə'ræn] pt → overrun.

overrated [ˌəʊvə'reɪtɪd] adj sobreestimado(da).

override [ˌəʊvə'raɪd] (pt **-rode**, pp **-ridden**) vt 1. (be more important than) predominar sobre. 2. (overrule) desautorizar.

overriding [ˌəʊvə'raɪdɪŋ] adj predominante.

overrode [ˌəʊvə'rəʊd] pt → override.

overrule [ˌəʊvə'ruːl] vt (person) desautorizar; (decision) anular; (request) denegar.

overrun [ˌəʊvə'rʌn] (pt **-ran**, pp **-run**) ◆ vt 1. (MIL) (enemy, army) apabullar, arrasar; (country) ocupar, invadir. 2. fig (cover): **to be ~ with** estar invadido(da) de. ◆ vi rebasar el tiempo previsto.

oversaw [ˌəʊvə'sɔː] pt → oversee.

overseas [adj 'əʊvəsiːz, adv ˌəʊvə'siːz] ◆ adj 1. (in or to foreign countries - market) exterior; (- sales, aid) al extranjero; (- network, branches) en el extranjero. 2. (from abroad) extranjero(ra). ◆ adv (go, travel) al extranjero; (study, live) en el extranjero.

oversee [ˌəʊvə'siː] (pt **-saw**, pp **-seen** [-'siːn]) vt supervisar.

overseer ['əʊvəˌsiːəʳ] n supervisor m, -ra f.

overshadow [ˌəʊvə'ʃædəʊ] vt 1. (be more important than): **to be ~ed by** ser eclipsado(da) por. 2. (mar): **to be ~ed by** sthg ser ensombrecido(da) por algo.

overshoot [ˌəʊvə'ʃuːt] (pt & pp **-shot**) vt (go past) pasarse.

oversight ['əʊvəsaɪt] n descuido m.

oversleep [ˌəʊvə'sliːp] (pt & pp **-slept** [-'slept]) vi no despertarse a tiempo, quedarse dormido(da).

overspill ['əʊvəspɪl] n exceso m de población.

overstep [ˌəʊvə'step] vt pasar de; **to ~ the mark** pasarse de la raya.

overt ['əʊvɜːt] adj abierto(ta), evidente.

overtake [ˌəʊvə'teɪk] (pt **-took**, pp **-taken** [-'teɪkn]) vt 1. (AUT) adelantar. 2. (subj: event) coger de improviso.

overthrow [ˌəʊvə'θrəʊ] (pt **-threw**, pp **-thrown**) vt (oust) derrocar.

overtime ['əʊvətaɪm] ◆ n (U) 1. (extra work) horas fpl extra. 2. Am (SPORT) (tiempo m de) descuento m. ◆ adv: **to work ~** trabajar horas extra.

overtones ['əʊvətəʊnz] npl matiz m.

overtook [ˌəʊvə'tʊk] pt → overtake.

overture ['əʊvəˌtjʊəʳ] n (MUS) obertura f.

overturn [ˌəʊvə'tɜːn] ◆ vt 1. (turn over) volcar. 2. (overrule) rechazar. 3. (overthrow) derrocar, derrumbar. ◆ vi (vehicle) volcar; (boat) zozobrar.

overweight [ˌəʊvə'weɪt] adj grueso(sa), gordo(da).

overwhelm [ˌəʊvə'welm] vt 1. (make helpless) abrumar. 2. (defeat) aplastar.

overwhelming [ˌəʊvə'welmɪŋ] adj 1. (despair, kindness) abrumador(ra). 2. (defeat, majority) aplastante.

overwork [ˌəʊvə'wɜːk] ◆ n trabajo m excesivo. ◆ vt (give too much work to) hacer trabajar demasiado.

overwrought [ˌəʊvə'rɔːt] adj fml nerviosísimo(ma), sobreexcitado(da).

owe [əʊ] vt: **to ~ sthg to sb, to ~ sb sthg** deber algo a alguien.

owing ['əʊɪŋ] adj que se debe.
▶ **owing to** prep debido a.

owl [aʊl] n búho m, lechuza f.

own [əʊn] ◆ adj: **my/your/his** etc ~ **car** mi/tu/su etc propio coche. ◆ pron: **my ~** el mío (la mía); **his/her ~** el suyo (la suya); **a house of my/his ~** mi/su propia casa; **on one's ~** solo(la); **to get one's ~ back** inf tomarse la revancha, desquitarse. ◆ vt poseer, tener.
▶ **own up** vi: **to ~ up (to** sthg**)** confesar (algo).

owner ['əʊnəʳ] n propietario m, -ria f.

ownership ['əʊnəʃɪp] n propiedad f.

ox [ɒks] (pl oxen) n buey m.

Oxbridge ['ɒksbrɪdʒ] n (U) las universidades de Oxford y Cambridge.

oxen ['ɒksn] pl → ox.

oxtail soup [ˈɒksteɪl-] n sopa f de rabo de buey.

oxygen [ˈɒksɪdʒən] n oxígeno m.

oxygen mask n máscara f de oxígeno.

oxygen tent n tienda f de oxígeno.

oyster [ˈɔɪstəʳ] n ostra f.

oz. abbr of **ounce**.

ozone [ˈəʊzəʊn] n ozono m.

ozone-friendly adj que no daña a la capa de ozono.

ozone layer n capa f de ozono.

P

p¹ (pl **p's** OR **ps**), **P** (pl **P's** OR **Ps**) [piː] n (letter) p f, P f.

p² 1. (abbr of **page**) p. 2. abbr of **penny, pence**.

pa [paː] n inf papá m.

p.a. (abbr of **per annum**) p.a.

PA n 1. Br abbr of **personal assistant**. 2. abbr of **public-address system**.

pace [peɪs] ◆ n paso m, ritmo m; **to keep ~ (with sthg)** (change, events) mantenerse al corriente (de algo); **to keep ~ (with sb)** llevar el mismo paso (que alguien). ◆ vi: **to ~ (up and down)** pasearse de un lado a otro.

pacemaker [ˈpeɪsˌmeɪkəʳ] n 1. (MED) marcapasos m inv. 2. (in race) liebre f.

Pacific [pəˈsɪfɪk] ◆ adj del Pacífico. ◆ n: **the ~ (Ocean)** el (océano) Pacífico.

pacifier [ˈpæsɪfaɪəʳ] n Am (for child) chupete m.

pacifist [ˈpæsɪfɪst] n pacifista m y f.

pacify [ˈpæsɪfaɪ] vt (person, mob) calmar, apaciguar.

pack [pæk] ◆ n 1. (bundle) lío m, fardo m; (rucksack) mochila f. 2. (packet) paquete m. 3. (of cards) baraja f. 4. (of dogs) jauría f; (of wolves) manada f; (of people) banda f. ◆ vt 1. (for journey - bags, suitcase) hacer; (- clothes, etc) meter (en la maleta). 2. (put in parcel) empaquetar; (put in container) envasar. 3. (fill) llenar, abarrotar; **to be ~ed into** estar apretujados dentro de. ◆ vi hacer las maletas. ▶ **pack in** inf ◆ vt sep Br (stop) dejar; **~ it in!** ¡déjalo!, ¡ya basta! ◆ vi parar. ▶ **pack off** vt sep inf enviar, mandar.

package [ˈpækɪdʒ] ◆ n (gen & COMPUT) paquete m. ◆ vt (wrap up) envasar.

package deal n convenio m OR acuerdo m global.

package tour n vacaciones fpl con todo incluido.

packaging [ˈpækɪdʒɪŋ] n (wrapping) envasado m.

packed [pækt] adj: ~ **(with)** repleto(ta) (de).

packed lunch n Br almuerzo preparado de antemano que se lleva uno al colegio, la oficina etc.

packed-out adj Br inf a tope.

packet [ˈpækɪt] n (gen) paquete m; (of crisps, sweets) bolsa f.

packing [ˈpækɪŋ] n 1. (protective material) embalaje m. 2. (for journey): **to do the ~** hacer el equipaje.

packing case n cajón m de embalaje.

pact [pækt] n pacto m.

pad [pæd] ◆ n 1. (of material) almohadillado m. 2. (of paper) bloc m. 3. (SPACE): (launch) ~ plataforma f de lanzamiento). 4. inf dated (home) casa f. ◆ vt acolchar, rellenar. ◆ vi (walk softly) andar con suavidad.

padding [ˈpædɪŋ] n (U) 1. (in jacket, chair) relleno m. 2. (in speech) paja f.

paddle [ˈpædl] ◆ n 1. (for canoe, dinghy) pala f, canalete m. 2. (walk in sea) paseo m por la orilla. ◆ vt remar. ◆ vi 1. (in canoe) remar. 2. (person - in sea) pasear por la orilla.

paddle boat, paddle steamer n vapor m de paletas OR ruedas.

paddling pool [ˈpædlɪŋ-] n Br 1. (in park) estanque m para chapotear. 2. (inflatable) piscina f inflable.

paddock [ˈpædək] n 1. (small field) potrero m, corral m. 2. (at racecourse) paddock m.

paddy field [ˈpædɪ-] n arrozal m.

padlock [ˈpædlɒk] ◆ n candado m. ◆ vt cerrar con candado.

paediatrics [ˌpiːdɪˈætrɪks] = **pediatrics**.

pagan [ˈpeɪgən] ◆ adj pagano(na). ◆ n pagano m, -na f.

page [peɪdʒ] ◆ n página f. ◆ vt (in hotel, airport) llamar por megafonía.

pageant [ˈpædʒənt] n desfile m.

pageantry [ˈpædʒəntrɪ] n boato m.

paid [peɪd] ◆ pt & pp → **pay**. ◆ adj (holiday, leave) pagado(da); (work, staff) remunerado(da).

pail [peɪl] n cubo m.

pain [peɪn] n 1. (ache) dolor m; **to be in ~** dolerse, sufrir dolor. 2. (mental suffering) pena f, sufrimiento m. 3. inf (annoyance - person) pesado m, -da f; (- thing) pesadez f. ▶ **pains** npl (effort, care) esfuerzos mpl; **to be at ~s to do sthg** afanarse por hacer algo; **to take ~s to do sthg** esforzarse en hacer algo.

pained [peɪnd] adj apenado(da).

painful [ˈpeɪnfʊl] adj (back, eyes) dolorido(da); (injury, exercise, memory) doloroso(sa).

painfully [ˈpeɪnfʊlɪ] adv 1. (causing pain) dolorosamente. 2. (extremely) terriblemente.

painkiller [ˈpeɪnˌkɪləʳ] n analgésico m.

painless [ˈpeɪnlɪs] adj 1. (physically) indoloro(ra). 2. (emotionally) sin complicaciones.

painstaking [ˈpeɪnzˌteɪkɪŋ] adj meticuloso(sa), minucioso(sa).

paint [peɪnt] ◆ n pintura f. ◆ vt pintar; **to ~ the ceiling white** pintar el techo de blanco.

paintbrush [ˈpeɪntbrʌʃ] n 1. (ART) pincel m. 2. (of decorator) brocha f.

painter [ˈpeɪntəʳ] n pintor m, -ra f.

painting [ˈpeɪntɪŋ] n 1. (picture) cuadro m, pintura f. 2. (U) (art form, trade) pintura f.

paint stripper n quitapinturas f inv.

paintwork [ˈpeɪntwɜːk] n (U) pintura f.

pair [peəʳ] n 1. (of shoes, socks, wings) par m; (of aces) pareja f. 2. (two-part object): **a ~ of scissors** unas tijeras; **a ~ of trousers** unos pantalones. 3. (couple - of people) pareja f.

pajamas [pəˈdʒɑːməz] = **pyjamas**.

Pakistan [Br ˌpɑːkɪˈstɑːn, Am ˌpækɪˈstæn] n (el) Paquistán.

Pakistani [Br ˌpɑːkɪˈstɑːnɪ, Am ˌpækɪˈstænɪ] ◆ adj paquistaní. ◆ n paquistaní m y f.

pal [pæl] n inf (friend) amiguete m, -ta f, colega m y f.

palace [ˈpælɪs] n palacio m.

palatable [ˈpælətəbl] adj 1. (pleasant to taste) sabroso(sa). 2. (acceptable) aceptable.

palate [ˈpælət] n paladar m.

palaver [pəˈlɑːvəʳ] n inf (fuss) follón m.

pale [peɪl] ◆ adj 1. (colour, clothes, paint) claro(ra); (light) tenue. 2. (person) pálido(da). ◆ vi palidecer.

Palestine [ˈpælɪˌstaɪn] n Palestina.

Palestinian [ˌpælɪˈstɪnɪən] ◆ adj palestino(na). ◆ n (person) palestino m, -na f.

palette [ˈpælət] n paleta f.

palings [ˈpeɪlɪŋz] npl empalizada f.

pall [pɔːl] ◆ n 1. (of smoke) nube f, cortina f. 2. Am (coffin) féretro m. ◆ vi hacerse pesado(da).

pallet [ˈpælɪt] n plataforma f de carga.

pallor [ˈpæləʳ] n literary palidez f.

palm [pɑːm] n 1. (tree) palmera f. 2. (of hand) palma f. ▶ **palm off** vt sep inf: **to ~ sthg off on sb** endosar OR encasquetar algo a alguien; **to ~ sb off with** despachar a alguien con.

Palm Sunday n Domingo m de Ramos.

palm tree n palmera f.

palpable [ˈpælpəbl] adj palpable.

paltry [ˈpɔːltrɪ] adj mísero(ra).

pamper [ˈpæmpəʳ] vt mimar.

pamphlet [ˈpæmflɪt] n (political) panfleto m; (publicity, information) folleto m.

pan [pæn] ◆ n 1. (saucepan) cazuela f, cacerola f; (frying pan) sartén f. 2. Am (for bread, cakes etc) molde m. ◆ vt inf (criticize) poner por los suelos. ◆ vi (CINEMA) tomar vistas panorámicas.

panacea [ˌpænəˈsɪə] n: **a ~ (for)** la panacea (de).

Panama [ˌpænəˈmɑː] n Panamá.

Panama Canal n: **the ~** el canal de Panamá.

panama (hat) n panamá m.

pancake [ˈpænkeɪk] n torta f, crepe f.

Pancake Day n Br ≃ Martes m inv de Carnaval.

panda [ˈpændə] (pl inv OR -s) n panda m.

Panda car n Br coche m patrulla.

pandemonium [ˌpændɪˈməʊnjəm] n pandemónium m, jaleo m.

pander [ˈpændəʳ] vi: **to ~ to** complacer a.

pane [peɪn] n (hoja f de) cristal m.

panel [ˈpænl] n 1. (group of people) equipo m; (in debates) mesa f. 2. (of a material) panel m. 3. (of a machine) tablero m, panel m.

panelling Br, **paneling** Am [ˈpænəlɪŋ] n (U) (on a ceiling) artesonado m; (on a wall) paneles mpl.

pang [pæŋ] n punzada f.

panic [ˈpænɪk] (pt & pp -ked, cont -king) ◆ n pánico m. ◆ vi aterrarse.

panicky [ˈpænɪkɪ] adj (person) aterrado(da), nervioso(sa); (feeling) de pánico.

panic-stricken adj preso(sa) OR víctima del pánico.

panorama [ˌpænəˈrɑːmə] n panorama m, vista f.

pansy ['pænzɪ] n 1. (flower) pensamiento m. 2. pej inf (man) marica m.

pant [pænt] vi jadear.

panther ['pænθər] (pl inv OR -s) n pantera f.

panties ['pæntɪz] npl inf bragas fpl.

pantihose ['pæntɪhəʊz] = **panty hose**.

pantomime ['pæntəmaɪm] n Br obra musical humorística para niños celebrada en Navidad.

pantry ['pæntrɪ] n despensa f.

pants [pænts] npl 1. Br (underpants) calzoncillos mpl. 2. Am (trousers) pantalones mpl.

panty hose ['pæntɪ-] npl Am medias fpl.

papa [Br pə'pɑː, Am 'pæpə] n papá m.

paper ['peɪpər] ◆ n 1. (U) (material) papel m; **piece of ~** (sheet) hoja f de papel; (scrap) trozo m de papel; **on ~** (written down) por escrito; (in theory) sobre el papel. 2. (newspaper) periódico m. 3. (in exam) examen m. 4. (essay - gen) estudio m, ensayo m; (- for conference) ponencia f. ◆ adj (made of paper) de papel. ◆ vt empapelar. ▶ **papers** npl (official documents) documentación f.

paperback ['peɪpəbæk] n libro m en rústica.

paper clip n clip m.

paper handkerchief n pañuelo m de papel, klínex® m inv.

paper knife n abrecartas m inv.

paper shop n Br quiosco m de periódicos.

paperweight ['peɪpəweɪt] n pisapapeles m inv.

paperwork ['peɪpəwɜːk] n papeleo m.

papier-mâché [,pæpjeɪ'mæʃeɪ] n cartón m piedra.

paprika ['pæprɪkə] n pimentón m.

par [pɑːr] n 1. (parity): **on a ~ with** al mismo nivel que. 2. (GOLF) par m. 3. (good health): **below** OR **under ~** pachucho(cha).

parable ['pærəbl] n parábola f.

parachute ['pærəʃuːt] n paracaídas m inv.

parade [pə'reɪd] ◆ n (procession) desfile m. ◆ vt 1. (soldiers) hacer desfilar; (criminals, captives) pasear. 2. fig (flaunt) hacer alarde de. ◆ vi desfilar.

paradise ['pærədaɪs] n fig paraíso m.

paradox ['pærədɒks] n paradoja f.

paradoxically [,pærə'dɒksɪklɪ] adv paradójicamente.

paraffin ['pærəfɪn] n parafina f.

paragon ['pærəgən] n dechado m.

paragraph ['pærəgrɑːf] n párrafo m.

Paraguay ['pærəgwaɪ] n (el) Paraguay.

Paraguayan [,pærə'gwaɪən] ◆ adj paraguayo(ya). ◆ n paraguayo m, -ya f.

parallel ['pærəlel] ◆ adj: ~ **(to** OR **with)** paralelo(la) (a). ◆ n 1. (parallel line, surface) paralela f. 2. (something, someone similar): **to have no ~** no tener precedente. 3. (similarity) semejanza f. 4. (GEOGR) paralelo m.

paralyse Br, **-yze** Am ['pærəlaɪz] vt lit & fig paralizar.

paralysis [pə'rælɪsɪs] (pl **-lyses** [-lɪsiːz]) n parálisis f inv.

paramedic [,pærə'medɪk] n auxiliar sanitario m, auxiliar sanitaria f.

parameter [pə'ræmɪtər] n parámetro m.

paramount ['pærəmaʊnt] adj vital, fundamental; **of ~ importance** de suma importancia.

paranoid ['pærənɔɪd] adj paranoico (ca).

paraphernalia [,pærəfə'neɪljə] n parafernalia f.

parasite ['pærəsaɪt] n parásito m, -ta f.

parasol ['pærəsɒl] n sombrilla f.

paratrooper ['pærətruːpər] n paracaidista m y f (del ejército).

parcel ['pɑːsl] n paquete m. ▶ **parcel up** vt sep empaquetar.

parcel post n (servicio m de) paquete m postal.

parched [pɑːtʃt] adj 1. (throat, mouth) seco(ca); (lips) quemado(da). 2. inf (very thirsty) seco(ca).

parchment ['pɑːtʃmənt] n (paper) pergamino m.

pardon ['pɑːdn] ◆ n 1. (JUR) perdón m, indulto m. 2. (forgiveness) perdón m; **I beg your ~?** (showing surprise, asking for repetition) ¿perdón?, ¿cómo (dice)?; **I beg your ~** (to apologize) le ruego me disculpe, perdón. ◆ vt 1. (forgive): **to ~ sb (for sthg)** perdonar a alguien (por algo); **~?** ¿perdón?, ¿cómo (dice)?; **~ me** (touching sb accidentally, belching) discúlpeme, perdón; (excuse me) con permiso. 2. (JUR) indultar.

parent ['peərənt] n (father) padre m; (mother) madre f. ▶ **parents** npl padres mpl.

parental [pə'rentl] adj (paternal) paterno(na); (maternal) materno(na).

parenthesis [pə'renθɪsɪs] (pl **-theses**

[-θɪsɪːz]) n paréntesis m inv.

Paris ['pærɪs] n París.

parish ['pærɪʃ] n 1. (of church) parroquia f. 2. Br (area of local government) municipio m.

parity ['pærətɪ] n: ~ (with/between) igualdad f (con/entre).

park [pɑːk] ◆ n parque m. ◆ vt & vi aparcar, parquear Amer.

parking ['pɑːkɪŋ] n aparcamiento m; 'no ~' 'prohibido aparcar'.

parking lot n Am aparcamiento m (al aire libre).

parking meter n parquímetro m.

parking ticket n multa f por aparcamiento indebido.

parlance ['pɑːləns] n: in common/legal etc ~ en el habla común/legal etc, en el lenguaje común/legal etc.

parliament ['pɑːləmənt] n 1. (assembly, institution) parlamento m. 2. (session) legislatura f.

parliamentary [,pɑːlə'mentərɪ] adj parlamentario(ria).

parlour Br, **parlor** Am ['pɑːləʳ] n dated salón m.

parochial [pə'rəukjəl] adj pej de miras estrechas.

parody ['pærədɪ] ◆ n parodia f. ◆ vt parodiar.

parole [pə'rəul] n libertad f condicional (bajo palabra); on ~ en libertad condicional.

parquet ['pɑːkeɪ] n parqué m.

parrot ['pærət] n loro m, -ra f, papagayo m.

parry ['pærɪ] vt (blow) parar; (attack) desviar.

parsimonious [,pɑːsɪ'məunjəs] adj fml & pej mezquino(na), tacaño(ña).

parsley ['pɑːslɪ] n perejil m.

parsnip ['pɑːsnɪp] n chirivía f.

parson ['pɑːsn] n párroco m.

part [pɑːt] ◆ n 1. (gen) parte f; for the most ~ en su mayoría. 2. (component) pieza f. 3. (THEATRE) papel m. 4. (involvement): ~ (in) participación f (en); to play an important ~ (in) desempeñar OR jugar un papel importante (en); to take ~ (in) tomar parte (en); for my/his ~ por mi/su parte. 5. Am (hair parting) raya f. ◆ adv en parte. ◆ vt 1. (lips, curtains) abrir. 2. (hair) peinar con raya. ◆ vi 1. (leave one another) separarse. 2. (separate - lips, curtains) abrirse. ▶ **parts** npl (place) pagos mpl. ▶ **part with** vt fus separarse de.

part exchange n sistema de pagar parte

de algo con un artículo usado; in ~ como parte del pago.

partial ['pɑːʃl] adj 1. (incomplete, biased) parcial. 2. (fond): ~ to amigo(ga) de, aficionado(da) a.

participant [pɑː'tɪsɪpənt] n participante m y f.

participate [pɑː'tɪsɪpeɪt] vi: to ~ (in) participar (en).

participation [pɑː,tɪsɪ'peɪʃn] n participación f.

participle ['pɑːtɪsɪpl] n participio m.

particle ['pɑːtɪkl] n partícula f.

particular [pə'tɪkjuləʳ] adj 1. (specific, unique) especial, en concreto OR particular. 2. (extra, greater) especial. 3. (difficult) exigente. ▶ **particulars** npl (of person) datos mpl; (of thing) detalles mpl. ▶ **in particular** adv en particular.

particularly [pə'tɪkjuləlɪ] adv especialmente.

parting ['pɑːtɪŋ] n 1. (separation) despedida f. 2. Br (in hair) raya f.

partisan [,pɑːtɪ'zæn] ◆ adj partidista. ◆ n (freedom fighter) partisano m, -na f.

partition [pɑː'tɪʃn] ◆ n 1. (wall) tabique m; (screen) separación f. 2. (of a country) división f. ◆ vt 1. (room) dividir con tabiques. 2. (country) dividir.

partly ['pɑːtlɪ] adv en parte.

partner ['pɑːtnəʳ] n 1. (spouse, lover) pareja f. 2. (in an activity) compañero m, -ra f. 3. (in a business) socio m, -cia f. 4. (ally) colega m y f.

partnership ['pɑːtnəʃɪp] n 1. (relationship) asociación f. 2. (business) sociedad f.

partridge ['pɑːtrɪdʒ] n perdiz f.

part-time ◆ adj a tiempo parcial. ◆ adv a tiempo parcial.

party ['pɑːtɪ] n 1. (POL) partido m. 2. (social gathering) fiesta f. 3. (group) grupo m. 4. (JUR) parte f.

party line n 1. (POL) línea f (política) del partido. 2. (TELEC) línea f (telefónica) compartida.

pass [pɑːs] ◆ n 1. (SPORT) pase m. 2. (document, permit) pase m; travel ~ tarjeta f OR abono m de transportes. 3. Br (successful result) aprobado m. 4. (route between mountains) vía f, desfiladero m. 5. phr: to make a ~ at sb intentar ligar con alguien. ◆ vt 1. (gen) pasar; to ~ sthg (to sb), to ~ (sb) sthg pasar or pasarle algo (a alguien). 2. (move past - thing) pasar por (delante de); (- person) pasar delante de; to ~ sb in the street cruzarse con alguien. 3. (AUT) adelantar. 4.

(*exceed*) sobrepasar. **5.** (*exam, candidate, law*) aprobar; **to ~ sthg fit (for)** dar algo por bueno (para). **6.** (*opinion, judgement*) formular; (*sentence*) dictar. ◆ *vi* **1.** (*gen*) pasar. **2.** (AUT) adelantar. **3.** (*in exam*) pasar, aprobar. **4.** (*occur*) transcurrir. ▶ **pass as** *vt fus* pasar por. ▶ **pass away** *vi* fallecer. ▶ **pass by** ◆ *vt sep* (*subj: people*) hacer caso omiso a; (*subj: events, life*) pasar desapercibido(da) a. ◆ *vi* pasar cerca. ▶ **pass for** *vt fus* = **pass as.** ▶ **pass on** ◆ *vt sep*: **to ~ sthg on (to)** pasar algo (a). ◆ *vi* **1.** (*move on*) continuar. **2.** = **pass away.** ▶ **pass out** *vi* **1.** (*faint*) desmayarse. **2.** Br (MIL) graduarse. ▶ **pass over** *vt fus* pasar por alto. ▶ **pass up** *vt sep* dejar pasar OR escapar.

passable ['pɑːsəbl] *adj* **1.** (*satisfactory*) pasable. **2.** (*not blocked*) transitable.

passage ['pæsɪdʒ] *n* **1.** (*corridor - between houses*) pasadizo *m*, pasaje *m*; (*- between rooms*) pasillo *m*. **2.** (*clear path*) paso *m*, hueco *m*. **3.** (MED) conducto *m*, tubo *m*. **4.** (*of music, speech*) pasaje *m*. **5.** *fml* (*of vehicle, person, time*) paso *m*. **6.** (*sea journey*) travesía *f*.

passageway ['pæsɪdʒweɪ] *n* (*between houses*) pasadizo *m*, pasaje *m*; (*between rooms*) pasillo *m*.

passbook ['pɑːsbʊk] *n* = cartilla *f* OR libreta *f* de banco.

passenger ['pæsɪndʒə^r] *n* pasajero *m*, -ra *f*.

passerby [ˌpɑːsəˈbaɪ] (*pl* **passersby** [ˌpɑːsəzˈbaɪ]) *n* transeúnte *m y f*.

passing ['pɑːsɪŋ] ◆ *adj* (*fad*) pasajero (ra); (*remark*) de pasada. ◆ *n* transcurso *m*. ▶ **in passing** *adv* de pasada.

passion ['pæʃn] *n*: **~ (for)** pasión *f* (por).

passionate ['pæʃənət] *adj* apasionado (da).

passive ['pæsɪv] *adj* pasivo(va).

Passover ['pɑːsˌəʊvə^r] *n*: **(the) ~** (la) Pascua judía.

passport ['pɑːspɔːt] *n* pasaporte *m*.

passport control *n* control *m* de pasaportes.

password ['pɑːswɜːd] *n* (*gen* & COMPUT) contraseña *f*.

past [pɑːst] ◆ *adj* **1.** (*former*) anterior. **2.** (*most recent*) pasado(da); **over the ~ week** durante la última semana. **3.** (*finished*) terminado(da). ◆ *adv* **1.** (*telling the time*): **it's ten ~** son y diez. **2.** (*beyond, in front*) por delante; **to walk/run ~** pasar andando/corriendo. ◆ *n* **1.** (*time*): **the ~**

el pasado. **2.** (*personal history*) pasado *m*. ◆ *prep* **1.** (*telling the time*): **it's five/half/ a quarter ~ ten** son las diez y cinco/ media/cuarto. **2.** (*alongside, in front of*) por delante de. **3.** (*beyond*) más allá de; **it's ~ the bank** está pasado el banco.

pasta ['pæstə] *n* (U) pasta *f*.

paste [peɪst] ◆ *n* **1.** (*smooth mixture*) pasta *f*. **2.** (*food*) paté *m*, pasta *f*. **3.** (*glue*) engrudo *m*. ◆ *vt* (*labels, stamps*) pegar; (*surface*) engomar, engrudar.

pastel ['pæstl] ◆ *adj* pastel (inv). ◆ *n* (ART) (*crayon*) pastel *m*.

pasteurize, -ise ['pɑːstʃəraɪz] *vt* pasteurizar.

pastille ['pæstɪl] *n* pastilla *f*.

pastime ['pɑːstaɪm] *n* pasatiempo *m*.

pastor ['pɑːstə^r] *n* pastor *m* (RELIG).

past participle *n* participio *m* pasado.

pastry ['peɪstrɪ] *n* **1.** (*mixture*) pasta *f*. **2.** (*cake*) pastel *m*.

past tense *n*: **the ~** el pasado.

pasture ['pɑːstʃə^r] *n* pasto *m*.

pasty¹ ['peɪstɪ] *adj* pálido(da).

pasty² ['pæstɪ] *n* Br empanada *f*.

pat [pæt] ◆ *n* (*of butter etc*) porción *f*. ◆ *vt* (*gen*) golpear ligeramente; (*dog*) acariciar; (*back, hand*) dar palmaditas a.

patch [pætʃ] ◆ *n* **1.** (*for mending*) remiendo *m*; (*to cover eye*) parche *m*. **2.** (*part of surface*) área *f*. **3.** (*area of land*) bancal *m*, parcela *f*. **4.** (*period of time*) periodo *m*. ◆ *vt* remendar. ▶ **patch up** *vt sep* **1.** (*mend*) reparar. **2.** (*resolve - quarrel*) resolver.

patchwork ['pætʃwɜːk] *adj* de trozos de distintos colores y formas.

patchy ['pætʃɪ] *adj* **1.** (*uneven - fog, sunshine*) irregular; (*- colour*) desigual. **2.** (*incomplete*) deficiente, incompleto (ta). **3.** (*good in parts*) irregular.

pâté ['pæteɪ] *n* paté *m*.

patent [Br 'peɪtənt, Am 'pætənt] ◆ *adj* (*obvious*) patente, evidente. ◆ *n* patente *f*. ◆ *vt* patentar.

patent leather *n* charol *m*.

paternal [pəˈtɜːnl] *adj* (*love, attitude*) paternal; (*grandmother, grandfather*) paterno(na).

paternity [pəˈtɜːnətɪ] *n* paternidad *f*.

path [pɑːθ, *pl* pɑːðz] *n* **1.** (*track, way ahead*) camino *m*. **2.** (*trajectory - of bullet*) trayectoria *f*; (*- of flight*) rumbo *m*. **3.** (*course of action*) curso *m*.

pathetic [pəˈθetɪk] *adj* **1.** (*causing pity*) patético(ca), lastimoso(sa). **2.** (*attempt, person*) inútil; (*actor, film*) malísimo(ma).

pathological [ˌpæθə'lɒdʒɪkl] *adj* patológico(ca).

pathology [pə'θɒlədʒɪ] *n* patología *f*.

pathos ['peɪθɒs] *n* patetismo *m*.

pathway ['pɑːθweɪ] *n* camino *m*, sendero *m*.

patience ['peɪʃns] *n* **1.** (*quality*) paciencia *f*. **2.** (*card game*) solitario *m*.

patient ['peɪʃnt] ♦ *adj* paciente. ♦ *n* paciente *m* y *f*.

patio ['pætɪəʊ] (*pl* **-s**) *n* patio *m*.

patriotic [Br ˌpætrɪ'ɒtɪk, Am ˌpeɪtrɪ-'ɒtɪk] *adj* patriótico(ca).

patrol [pə'trəʊl] ♦ *n* patrulla *f*. ♦ *vt* patrullar.

patrol car *n* coche *m* patrulla.

patrolman [pə'trəʊlmən] (*pl* **-men** [-mən]) *n* Am policía *m*, guardia *m*.

patron ['peɪtrən] *n* **1.** (*of arts*) mecenas *m* y *f inv*. **2.** Br (*of charity, campaign*) patrocinador *m*, -ra *f*. **3.** *fml* (*customer*) cliente *m* y *f*.

patronize, -ise ['pætrənaɪz] *vt* **1.** *pej* (*talk down to*) tratar con aire paternalista OR condescendiente. **2.** *fml* (*back financially*) patrocinar.

patronizing ['pætrənaɪzɪŋ] *adj pej* paternalista, condescendiente.

patter ['pætər] ♦ *n* **1.** (*of raindrops*) repiqueteo *m*; (*of feet*) pasitos *mpl*. **2.** (*sales talk*) charlatanería *f*. ♦ *vi* (*dog, feet*) corretear; (*rain*) repiquetear.

pattern ['pætən] *n* **1.** (*design*) dibujo *m*, diseño *m*. **2.** (*of life, work*) estructura *f*; (*of illness, events*) desarrollo *m*, evolución *f*. **3.** (*for sewing, knitting*) patrón *m*. **4.** (*model*) modelo *m*.

paunch [pɔːntʃ] *n* barriga *f*, panza *f*.

pauper ['pɔːpər] *n* indigente *m* y *f*.

pause [pɔːz] ♦ *n* pausa *f*. ♦ *vi* **1.** (*stop speaking*) hacer una pausa. **2.** (*stop moving, doing sthg*) detenerse.

pave [peɪv] *vt* pavimentar; **to ~ the way for** preparar el terreno para.

pavement ['peɪvmənt] *n* **1.** Br (*at side of road*) acera *f*, andén *m* Amer. **2.** Am (*roadway*) calzada *f*.

pavilion [pə'vɪljən] *n* **1.** Br (*at sports field*) vestuarios *mpl*. **2.** (*at exhibition*) pabellón *m*.

paving ['peɪvɪŋ] *n* (U) pavimento *m*.

paving stone *n* losa *f*.

paw [pɔː] *n* (*foot*) pata *f*; (*claw*) zarpa *f*.

pawn [pɔːn] ♦ *n* **1.** (*chesspiece*) peón *m*. **2.** (*unimportant person*) marioneta *f*. ♦ *vt* empeñar.

pawnbroker ['pɔːnˌbrəʊkər] *n* prestamista *m* y *f*.

pawnshop ['pɔːnʃɒp] *n* monte *m* de piedad.

pay [peɪ] (*pt* & *pp* **paid**) ♦ *vt* **1.** (*gen*) pagar; **to ~ sb for sthg** pagar a alguien por algo; **he paid £20 for it** pagó 20 libras por ello. **2.** Br (*put into bank account*): **to ~ sthg into** ingresar algo en. **3.** (*be profitable to*) ser rentable a. **4.** (*compliment, visit*) hacer; (*respects*) ofrecer; (*attention*) prestar; (*homage*) rendir. ♦ *vi* **1.** (*gen*) pagar; **to ~ dearly for sthg** pagar caro (por) algo. **2.** (*be profitable*) ser rentable. ♦ *n* paga *f*. ▶ **pay back** *vt sep* **1.** (*money*) devolver, reembolsar. **2.** (*revenge oneself*): **to ~ sb back (for sthg)** hacer pagar a alguien (por algo). ▶ **pay for** *vt fus* pagar. ▶ **pay off** ♦ *vt sep* **1.** (*repay - debt*) liquidar, saldar. **2.** (*dismiss*) despedir con indemnización. **3.** (*bribe*) comprar, pagar. ♦ *vi* salir bien, tener éxito. ▶ **pay up** *vi* pagar.

payable ['peɪəbl] *adj* **1.** (*to be paid*) pagadero(ra). **2.** (*on cheque*): **~ to** a favor de.

paycheck ['peɪtʃek] *n* Am paga *f*.

payday ['peɪdeɪ] *n* día *m* de paga.

payee [peɪ'iː] *n* beneficiario *m*, -ria *f*.

pay envelope *n* Am sobre *m* de paga.

payment ['peɪmənt] *n* pago *m*.

pay packet *n* Br **1.** (*envelope*) sobre *m* de paga. **2.** (*wages*) paga *f*.

pay phone, pay station Am *n* teléfono *m* público.

payroll ['peɪrəʊl] *n* nómina *f*.

payslip ['peɪslɪp] *n* Br hoja *f* de paga.

pay station Am = **pay phone**.

pc (*abbr of* **per cent**) p.c.

PC 1. (*abbr of* **personal computer**) PC *m*. **2.** *abbr of* **police constable**.

PE (*abbr of* **physical education**) *n* EF *f*.

pea [piː] *n* guisante *m*, arveja *f* Amer.

peace [piːs] *n* **1.** (*gen*) paz *f*. **2.** (*quiet*) calma *f*, tranquilidad *f*. **3.** (*freedom from disagreement*) orden *m*; **to make (one's) ~ (with)** hacer las paces (con).

peaceable ['piːsəbl] *adj* (*not aggressive*) pacífico(ca).

peaceful ['piːsful] *adj* **1.** (*quiet, calm*) tranquilo(la). **2.** (*not aggressive*) pacífico (ca).

peacetime ['piːstaɪm] *n* (U) tiempos *mpl* de paz.

peach [piːtʃ] ♦ *adj* (*in colour*) de color melocotón. ♦ *n* **1.** (*fruit*) melocotón *m*. **2.** (*colour*) color *m* melocotón.

peacock ['piːkɒk] *n* pavo *m* real.

penance

peak [pi:k] ◆ *n* **1.** (*mountain top*) pico *m*, cima *f*. **2.** (*highest point*) apogeo *m*. **3.** (*of cap*) visera *f*. ◆ *adj* (*season*) alto(ta); (*condition*) perfecto(ta). ◆ *vi* alcanzar el máximo.

peaked [pi:kt] *adj* con visera.

peak hour *n* hora *f* punta.

peak period *n* (*of electricity etc*) periodo *m* de tarifa máxima; (*of traffic*) horas *fpl* punta.

peak rate *n* tarifa *f* máxima.

peal [pi:l] ◆ *n* (*of bells*) repique *m*; ~ (**of laughter**) carcajada *f*. ◆ *vi* repicar.

peanut ['pi:nʌt] *n* cacahuete *m*, maní *m* Amer.

peanut butter *n* manteca *f* de cacahuete.

pear [peər] *n* pera *f*.

pearl [pɜ:l] *n* perla *f*.

peasant ['peznt] *n* (*in countryside*) campesino *m*, -na *f*.

peat [pi:t] *n* turba *f*.

pebble ['pebl] *n* guijarro *m*.

peck [pek] ◆ *n* **1.** (*with beak*) picotazo *m*. **2.** (*kiss*) besito *m*. ◆ *vt* (*with beak*) picotear. ◆ *vi* picotear.

pecking order ['pekɪŋ-] *n* jerarquía *f*.

peckish ['pekɪʃ] *adj* Br *inf*: **to feel** ~ estar algo hambriento(ta).

peculiar [pɪ'kju:ljər] *adj* **1.** (*odd*) singular, extraño(ña). **2.** (*slightly ill*) raro(ra), indispuesto(ta). **3.** (*characteristic*): **to be** ~ **to** ser propio(pia) de.

peculiarity [pɪˌkju:lɪ'ærətɪ] *n* **1.** (*eccentricity*) extravagancia *f*. **2.** (*characteristic*) peculiaridad *f*.

pedal ['pedl] ◆ *n* pedal *m*. ◆ *vi* pedalear.

pedal bin *n* cubo *m* de basura con pedal.

pedantic [pɪ'dæntɪk] *adj pej* puntilloso (sa).

peddle ['pedl] *vt* (*drugs*) traficar con; (*wares*) vender de puerta en puerta.

pedestal ['pedɪstl] *n* pedestal *m*.

pedestrian [pɪ'destrɪən] ◆ *adj pej* mediocre. ◆ *n* peatón *m*.

pedestrian crossing *n* Br paso *m* de peatones.

pedestrian precinct Br, **pedestrian zone** Am *n* zona *f* peatonal.

pediatrics [ˌpi:dɪ'ætrɪks] *n* pediatría *f*.

pedigree ['pedɪgri:] ◆ *adj* de raza. ◆ *n* **1.** (*of animal*) pedigrí *m*. **2.** (*of person*) linaje *m*.

pedlar Br, **peddler** Am ['pedlər] *n* vendedor *m*, -ra *f* ambulante.

pee [pi:] *inf* ◆ *n* pis *m*. ◆ *vi* mear.

peek [pi:k] *inf* ◆ *n* mirada *f*, ojeada *f*. ◆ *vi* mirar a hurtadillas.

peel [pi:l] ◆ *n* (*gen*) piel *f*; (*of orange, lemon*) corteza *f*; (*once removed*) mondaduras *fpl*. ◆ *vt* pelar, mondar. ◆ *vi* (*walls, paint*) desconcharse; (*wallpaper*) despegarse; (*skin, nose*) pelarse.

peelings ['pi:lɪŋz] *npl* peladuras *fpl*.

peep [pi:p] ◆ *n* **1.** (*look*) mirada *f* furtiva, ojeada *f*. **2.** *inf* (*sound*) pío *m*. ◆ *vi* (*look*) mirar furtivamente. ▶ **peep out** *vi* asomar.

peephole ['pi:phəʊl] *n* mirilla *f*.

peer [pɪər] ◆ *n* **1.** (*noble*) par *m*. **2.** (*equal*) igual *m*. ◆ *vi* mirar con atención.

peerage ['pɪərɪdʒ] *n* **1.** (*rank*) rango *m* de par. **2.** (*group*): **the** ~ la nobleza.

peer group *n* grupo generacional o social.

peeved [pi:vd] *adj inf* disgustado(da).

peevish ['pi:vɪʃ] *adj* malhumorado (da).

peg [peg] *n* **1.** (*hook*) gancho *m*. **2.** (*for washing line*) pinza *f*. **3.** (*on tent*) estaca *f*.

pejorative [pɪ'dʒɒrətɪv] *adj* peyorativo(va), despectivo(va).

pekinese [ˌpi:kə'ni:z], **pekingese** [ˌpi:kɪŋ'i:z] (*pl inv* OR **-s**) *n* (*dog*) pequinés *m*.

Peking [pi:'kɪŋ] *n* Pekín.

pelican ['pelɪkən] (*pl inv* OR **-s**) *n* pelícano *m*.

pelican crossing *n* Br paso de peatones con semáforo accionado por el usuario.

pellet ['pelɪt] *n* **1.** (*small ball*) bolita *f*. **2.** (*for gun*) perdigón *m*.

pelmet ['pelmɪt] *n* Br galería *f*.

pelt [pelt] ◆ *n* (*animal skin*) piel *f*. ◆ *vt*: **to** ~ **sb with sthg** acribillar a alguien con algo, arrojar algo a alguien. ◆ *vi* **1.** (*rain*) llover a cántaros. **2.** (*run very fast*) correr a toda pastilla.

pelvis ['pelvɪs] (*pl* **-vises** OR **-ves** [-vi:z]) *n* pelvis *f*.

pen [pen] ◆ *n* **1.** (*ballpoint*) bolígrafo *m*, lapicera *f* Amer; (*fountain pen*) pluma *f*; (*felt-tip*) rotulador *m*. **2.** (*enclosure*) redil *m*, corral *m*. ◆ *vt* (*enclose*) encerrar.

penal ['pi:nl] *adj* penal.

penalize, -ise ['pi:nəlaɪz] *vt* (*gen*) penalizar; (SPORT) penalizar, castigar.

penalty ['penltɪ] *n* **1.** (*punishment*) pena *f*; **to pay the** ~ (**for sthg**) *fig* pagar las consecuencias (de algo). **2.** (*fine*) multa *f*. **3.** (SPORT) penalty *m*; ~ (**kick**) (FTBL) penalty *m*; (RUGBY) golpe *m* de castigo.

penance ['penəns] *n* penitencia *f*.

pence [pens] Br pl → **penny**.

penchant [Br 'pãʃã, Am 'pentʃənt] n: **to have a ~ for** tener debilidad por.

pencil ['pensl] n lápiz m, lapicero m; **in ~** a lápiz.

pencil case n estuche m, plumero m.

pencil sharpener n sacapuntas m inv.

pendant ['pendənt] n (jewel on chain) colgante m.

pending ['pendɪŋ] fml ♦ adj 1. (about to happen) inminente. 2. (waiting to be dealt with) pendiente. ♦ prep a la espera de.

pendulum ['pendjuləm] (pl -s) n (of clock) péndulo m.

penetrate ['penɪtreɪt] vt 1. (barrier) atravesar; (jungle, crowd) penetrar en. 2. (infiltrate - organization) infiltrarse en.

pen friend n amigo m, -ga f por correspondencia.

penguin ['peŋgwɪn] n pingüino m.

penicillin [,penɪ'sɪlɪn] n penicilina f.

peninsula [pə'nɪnsjulə] (pl -s) n península f.

penis ['piːnɪs] (pl **penises** ['piːnɪsɪz]) n pene m.

penitentiary [,penɪ'tenʃərɪ] n Am penitenciaría f.

penknife ['pennaɪf] (pl -knives [-naɪvz]) n navaja f.

pen name n seudónimo m.

pennant ['penənt] n banderín m.

penniless ['penɪlɪs] adj sin dinero.

penny ['penɪ] (pl sense 1 -ies, pl sense 2 pence) n 1. (coin) Br penique m; Am centavo m. 2. Br (value) penique m.

pen pal n inf amigo m, -ga f por correspondencia.

pension ['penʃn] n 1. Br (gen) pensión f. 2. (disability pension) subsidio m.

pensioner ['penʃənər] n Br: **(old-age) ~** pensionista m y f.

pensive ['pensɪv] adj pensativo(va).

pentagon ['pentəgən] n pentágono m. ▶ **Pentagon** n Am: **the Pentagon** el Pentágono, sede del ministerio de Defensa estadounidense.

Pentecost ['pentɪkɒst] n Pentecostés m.

penthouse ['penthaus, pl -hauzɪz] n ático m.

pent up ['pent-] adj reprimido(da).

penultimate [pe'nʌltɪmət] adj penúltimo(ma).

people ['piːpl] ♦ n (nation, race) pueblo m. ♦ npl 1. (gen) gente f; (individuals) personas fpl; **a table for eight ~** una mesa para ocho personas; **~ say that ...** dice la gente que ... 2. (inhabitants) habitantes mpl. 3. (POL): **the ~** el pueblo. ♦ vt: **to be ~d by** OR **with** estar poblado(da) de.

pep [pep] n inf vitalidad f. ▶ **pep up** vt sep animar.

pepper ['pepər] n 1. (spice) pimienta f. 2. (vegetable) pimiento m.

pepperbox Am = **pepper pot**.

peppermint ['pepəmɪnt] n 1. (sweet) pastilla f de menta. 2. (herb) menta f.

pepper pot Br, **pepperbox** Am ['pepəbɒks] n pimentero m.

pep talk n inf palabras fpl de ánimo.

per [pɜːr] prep (expressing rate, ratio) por; **~ hour/kilo/person** por hora/kilo/persona; **~ day** al día; **as ~ instructions** de acuerdo con OR según las instrucciones.

per annum adv al OR por año.

per capita [pə'kæpɪtə] ♦ adj per cápita. ♦ adv por cabeza.

perceive [pə'siːv] vt 1. (notice) percibir, apreciar. 2. (understand, realize) advertir, apreciar. 3. (see): **to ~ sthg/sb as** ver algo/a alguien como.

per cent adv por ciento.

percentage [pə'sentɪdʒ] n porcentaje m.

perception [pə'sepʃn] n 1. (act of seeing) percepción f. 2. (insight) perspicacia f. 3. (opinion) idea f.

perceptive [pə'septɪv] adj perspicaz.

perch [pɜːtʃ] ♦ n 1. (for bird) percha f, vara f. 2. (fish) perca f. ♦ vi: **to ~ (on)** (bird) posarse (en); (person) sentarse (en).

percolator ['pɜːkəleɪtər] n percolador m.

percussion [pə'kʌʃn] n (MUS) percusión f.

perennial [pə'renjəl] ♦ adj (gen & BOT) perenne. ♦ n (BOT) planta f perenne.

perfect [adj & n 'pɜːfɪkt, vb pə'fekt] ♦ adj perfecto(ta); **he's a ~ stranger to me** me es completamente desconocido. ♦ n (GRAMM): **the ~ (tense)** el perfecto. ♦ vt perfeccionar.

perfection [pə'fekʃn] n perfección f; **to ~ a la perfección.

perfectionist [pə'fekʃənɪst] n perfeccionista m y f.

perfectly ['pɜːfɪktlɪ] adv 1. (for emphasis) absolutamente; **~ well** perfectamente bien. 2. (to perfection) perfectamente.

perforate ['pɜːfəreɪt] vt perforar.

perforation [,pɜːfə'reɪʃn] n (in paper)

perforación f.

perform [pə'fɔ:m] ♦ vt 1. (carry out) llevar a cabo, realizar. 2. (music, dance) interpretar; (play) representar. ♦ vi 1. (function - car, machine) funcionar; (- person, team) desenvolverse. 2. (in front of audience) actuar.

performance [pə'fɔ:məns] n 1. (carrying out) realización f. 2. (show) representación f. 3. (of actor, singer etc) interpretación f, actuación f. 4. (of car, engine) rendimiento m.

performer [pə'fɔ:mər] n (actor, singer etc) intérprete m y f.

perfume ['pɜ:fju:m] n perfume m.

perfunctory [pə'fʌŋktəri] adj superficial.

perhaps [pə'hæps] adv 1. (maybe) quizás, quizá; ~ she'll do it quizás ella lo haga; ~ so/not tal vez sí/no. 2. (in polite requests, suggestions, remarks): ~ you could help? ¿te importaría ayudar?; ~ you should start again ¿por qué no empiezas de nuevo?

peril ['peril] n literary peligro m.

perimeter [pə'rimitər] n perímetro m.

period ['piəriəd] ♦ n 1. (of time) período m, periodo m. 2. (HISTORY) época f. 3. (SCH) clase f, hora f. 4. (menstruation) período m. 5. Am (full stop) punto m. ♦ comp de época.

periodic [,piəri'ɒdik] adj periódico (ca).

periodical [,piəri'ɒdikl] ♦ adj = **periodic**. ♦ n (magazine) revista f.

peripheral [pə'rifərəl] ♦ adj 1. (of little importance) marginal. 2. (at edge) periférico(ca). ♦ n (COMPUT) periférico m.

perish ['periʃ] vi 1. (die) perecer. 2. (decay) deteriorarse.

perishable ['periʃəbl] adj perecedero (ra). ► **perishables** npl productos mpl perecederos.

perjury ['pɜ:dʒəri] n (JUR) perjurio m.

perk [pɜ:k] n inf extra m, beneficio m adicional. ► **perk up** vi animarse.

perky ['pɜ:ki] adj inf alegre, animado (da).

perm [pɜ:m] n permanente f.

permanent ['pɜ:mənənt] ♦ adj 1. (gen) permanente; (job, address) fijo(ja). 2. (continuous, constant) constante. ♦ n Am (perm) permanente f.

permeate ['pɜ:mieit] vt impregnar.

permissible [pə'misəbl] adj permisible.

permission [pə'miʃn] n: ~ (to do sthg) permiso m (para hacer algo).

permissive [pə'misiv] adj permisivo (va).

permit [vb pə'mit, n 'pɜ:mit] ♦ vt permitir; **to ~ sb sthg/to do sthg** permitir a alguien algo/hacer algo. ♦ n permiso m.

pernicious [pə'niʃəs] adj fml pernicioso(sa).

pernickety [pə'nikəti] adj inf quisquilloso(sa).

perpendicular [,pɜ:pən'dikjulər] ♦ adj 1. (MATH): ~ **(to)** perpendicular (a). 2. (upright) vertical. ♦ n (MATH) perpendicular f.

perpetrate ['pɜ:pitreit] vt fml perpetrar.

perpetrator ['pɜ:pitreitər] n fml perpetrador m, -ra f, autor m, -ra f.

perpetual [pə'petʃuəl] adj 1. pej (constant) constante. 2. (everlasting) perpetuo(tua).

perplex [pə'pleks] vt dejar perplejo (ja).

perplexing [pə'pleksiŋ] adj desconcertante.

persecute ['pɜ:sikju:t] vt perseguir.

perseverance [,pɜ:si'viərəns] n perseverancia f.

persevere [,pɜ:si'viər] vi: **to ~ (with sthg/in doing sthg)** perseverar (en algo/en hacer algo).

Persian ['pɜ:ʃn] adj persa.

persist [pə'sist] vi 1. (problem, rain) persistir. 2. (person): **to ~ in doing sthg** empeñarse en hacer algo.

persistence [pə'sistəns] n 1. (continuation) persistencia f. 2. (determination) perseverancia f.

persistent [pə'sistənt] adj 1. (constant) continuo(nua). 2. (determined) persistente.

person ['pɜ:sn] (pl people OR persons fml) n 1. (man, woman) persona f; **in ~** en persona. 2. (body): **about one's ~** en su cuerpo.

personable ['pɜ:snəbl] adj agradable.

personal ['pɜ:sənl] adj 1. (gen) personal. 2. (private - life, problem) privado (da). 3. pej (rude) ofensivo(va); **to be ~** hacer alusiones personales.

personal assistant n asistente m, -ta f personal.

personal column n sección f de asuntos personales.

personal computer n ordenador m personal.

personality [,pɜ:sə'næləti] n personalidad f.

personally ['pɜːsnəlɪ] *adv* personalmente; **to take sthg ~** tomarse algo como algo personal.

personal organizer *n* agenda *f* (personal).

personal property *n* (U) bienes *mpl* muebles.

personal stereo *n* walkman® *m inv*.

personify [pə'sɒnɪfaɪ] *vt* personificar.

personnel [,pɜːsə'nel] ◆ *n* (U) (*department*) personal *m*. ◆ *npl* (*staff*) personal *m*.

perspective [pə'spektɪv] *n* perspectiva *f*.

Perspex® ['pɜːspeks] *n* Br ≃ plexiglás® *m*.

perspiration [,pɜːspə'reɪʃn] *n* transpiración *f*.

persuade [pə'sweɪd] *vt*: **to ~ sb (of sthg/to do sthg)** persuadir a alguien (de algo/a hacer algo); **to ~ sb that** convencer a alguien (de) que.

persuasion [pə'sweɪʒn] *n* **1.** (*act of persuading*) persuasión *f*. **2.** (*belief*) creencia *f*.

persuasive [pə'sweɪsɪv] *adj* persuasivo(va).

pert [pɜːt] *adj* vivaracho(cha).

pertain [pə'teɪn] *vi fml*: **~ing to** relacionado(da) con.

pertinent ['pɜːtɪnənt] *adj* pertinente.

perturb [pə'tɜːb] *vt fml* perturbar.

Peru [pə'ruː] *n* (el) Perú.

peruse [pə'ruːz] *vt* (*read carefully*) leer detenidamente; (*browse through*) leer por encima.

Peruvian [pə'ruːvjən] ◆ *adj* peruano(na). ◆ *n* (*person*) peruano *m*, -na *f*.

pervade [pə'veɪd] *vt* impregnar.

perverse [pə'vɜːs] *adj* (*delight, enjoyment*) perverso(sa); (*contrary*) puñetero(ra).

perversion [Br pə'vɜːʃn, Am pə'vɜːrʒn] *n* **1.** (*sexual deviation*) perversión *f*. **2.** (*of justice, truth*) tergiversación *f*.

pervert [*n* 'pɜːvɜːt, *vb* pə'vɜːt] ◆ *n* pervertido *m*, -da *f*. ◆ *vt* **1.** (*course of justice*) tergiversar. **2.** (*corrupt sexually*) pervertir.

pessimist ['pesɪmɪst] *n* pesimista *m y f*.

pessimistic [,pesɪ'mɪstɪk] *adj* pesimista.

pest [pest] *n* **1.** (*insect*) insecto *m* nocivo; (*animal*) animal *m* nocivo. **2.** *inf* (*annoying person*) pesado *m*, -da *f*; (*annoying thing*) lata *f*.

pester ['pestər] *vt* dar la lata a.

pet [pet] ◆ *adj* (*subject, theory*) preferido

(da); **~ hate** gran fobia *f*. ◆ *n* **1.** (*domestic animal*) animal *m* doméstico. **2.** (*favourite person*) preferido *m*, -da *f*. ◆ *vt* acariciar. ◆ *vi* besuquearse.

petal ['petl] *n* pétalo *m*.

peter ['piːtər] ▶ **peter out** *vi* (*supplies, interest*) agotarse; (*path*) desaparecer.

petite [pə'tiːt] *adj* (*woman*) chiquita.

petition [pɪ'tɪʃn] ◆ *n* petición *f*. ◆ *vi* (JUR): **to ~ for divorce** pedir el divorcio.

petrified ['petrɪfaɪd] *adj* (*terrified*) petrificado(da).

petrol ['petrəl] *n* Br gasolina *f*, nafta *f* Amer.

petrol bomb *n* Br bomba *f* de gasolina.

petrol can *n* Br lata *f* de gasolina.

petroleum [pɪ'trəʊljəm] *n* petróleo *m*.

petrol pump *n* Br surtidor *m* de gasolina, bomba *f* Amer.

petrol station *n* Br gasolinera *f*, grifo *m* Amer.

petrol tank *n* Br depósito *m* de gasolina.

petticoat ['petɪkəʊt] *n* (*underskirt*) enaguas *fpl*; (*full-length*) combinación *f*.

petty ['petɪ] *adj* **1.** (*small-minded*) mezquino(na). **2.** (*trivial*) insignificante.

petty cash *n* dinero *m* para gastos menores.

petty officer *n* sargento *m* de la marina.

petulant ['petjʊlənt] *adj* cascarrabias (*inv*).

pew [pjuː] *n* banco *m*.

pewter ['pjuːtər] *n* peltre *m*.

phantom ['fæntəm] ◆ *adj* ilusorio(ria). ◆ *n* (*ghost*) fantasma *m*.

pharmaceutical [,fɑːmə'sjuːtɪkl] *adj* farmacéutico(ca).

pharmacist ['fɑːməsɪst] *n* farmacéutico *m*, -ca *f*.

pharmacy ['fɑːməsɪ] *n* (*shop*) farmacia *f*.

phase [feɪz] ◆ *n* fase *f*. ◆ *vt* escalonar. ▶ **phase in** *vt sep* introducir progresivamente. ▶ **phase out** *vt sep* retirar progresivamente.

PhD (*abbr of* **Doctor of Philosophy**) *n* (*titular de un*) doctorado en el campo de las humanidades.

pheasant ['feznt] (*pl inv OR* **-s**) *n* faisán *m*.

phenomena [fɪ'nɒmɪnə] *pl* → **phenomenon**.

phenomenal [fɪ'nɒmɪnl] *adj* fenomenal.

phenomenon [fɪ'nɒmɪnən] (*pl* **-mena**)

n lit & fig fenómeno *m*.
phial ['faɪəl] *n* frasco *m* (pequeño).
philanthropist   [fɪ'lænθrəpɪst]   *n*
filantrópico *m*, -ca *f*.
philately [fɪ'lætəlɪ] *n* filatelia *f*.
Philippine ['fɪlɪpiːn] *adj* filipino(na).
► **Philippines** *npl*: **the ~s** las Filipinas.
philosopher [fɪ'lɒsəfəʳ] *n* filósofo *m*,
-fa *f*.
philosophical [ˌfɪlə'sɒfɪkl] *adj* filosófi-
co(ca).
philosophy [fɪ'lɒsəfɪ] *n* filosofía *f*.
phlegm [flem] *n* (*mucus*) flema *f*.
phlegmatic [fleg'mætɪk] *adj* flemático
(ca).
phobia ['fəʊbjə] *n* fobia *f*.
phone [fəʊn] ◆ *n* teléfono *m*; **to be on
the ~** (*speaking*) estar al teléfono; Br (*connected to network*) tener teléfono. ◆ *vt & vi*
telefonear, llamar. ► **phone up** *vt sep &
vi* llamar.
phone book *n* guía *f* telefónica.
phone booth *n* teléfono *m* público.
phone box *n* Br cabina *f* telefónica.
phone call *n* llamada *f* telefónica; **to
make a ~** hacer una llamada.
phonecard ['fəʊnkɑːd] *n* tarjeta *f* telefónica.
phone-in *n* (RADIO & TV) programa *m* a
micrófono abierto.
phone number *n* número *m* de teléfono.
phonetics [fə'netɪks] *n* (U) fonética *f*.
phoney Br, **phony** Am ['fəʊnɪ] (*compar -ier, superl -iest*) ◆ *adj inf* falso(sa).
◆ *n* farsante *m y f*.
phosphorus ['fɒsfərəs] *n* fósforo *m*.
photo ['fəʊtəʊ] *n* foto *f*; **to take a ~ (of)**
sacar una foto (de).
photocopier [ˌfəʊtəʊ'kɒpɪəʳ] *n* fotocopiadora *f*.
photocopy ['fəʊtəʊˌkɒpɪ] ◆ *n* fotocopia *f*. ◆ *vt* fotocopiar.
photograph ['fəʊtəgrɑːf] ◆ *n* fotografía *f*; **to take a ~ (of)** sacar una
fotografía (de). ◆ *vt* fotografiar.
photographer [fə'tɒgrəfəʳ] *n* fotógrafo *m*, -fa *f*.
photography [fə'tɒgrəfɪ] *n* (U) fotografía *f*.
phrasal verb ['freɪzl-] *n* verbo *m* con
preposición.
phrase [freɪz] ◆ *n* **1.** (*group of words*)
locución *f*, frase *f*. **2.** (*expression*) expresión *f*. ◆ *vt* (*apology, refusal*) expresar;
(*letter*) redactar.
phrasebook ['freɪzbʊk] *n* libro *m* de
frases.

physical ['fɪzɪkl] ◆ *adj* físico(ca). ◆ *n*
(*examination*) examen *m* médico.
physical education *n* educación *f*
física.
physically ['fɪzɪklɪ] *adv* físicamente.
physically handicapped *npl*: **the ~**
los minusválidos.
physician [fɪ'zɪʃn] *n* médico *m y f*.
physicist ['fɪzɪsɪst] *n* físico *m*, -ca *f*.
physics ['fɪzɪks] *n* (U) física *f*.
physiotherapy   [ˌfɪzɪəʊ'θerəpɪ]   *n*
fisioterapia *f*.
physique [fɪ'ziːk] *n* físico *m*.
pianist ['pɪənɪst] *n* pianista *m y f*.
piano [pɪ'ænəʊ] (*pl* -s) *n* (*instrument*)
piano *m*.
piccolo ['pɪkələʊ] (*pl* -s) *n* flautín *m*.
pick [pɪk] ◆ *n* **1.** (*tool*) piqueta *f*.
2. (*selection*): **take your ~** escoge el que
quieras. **3.** (*best*): **the ~ of** lo mejor de.
◆ *vt* **1.** (*team, winner*) seleccionar; (*time,
book, dress*) elegir. **2.** (*fruit, flowers*) coger.
3. (*remove - hairs etc*): **to ~ sthg off sthg**
quitar algo de algo. **4.** (*nose*) hurgarse;
(*teeth*) mondarse. **5.** (*provoke*): **to ~ a
fight/quarrel (with)** buscar pelea/bronca
(con). **6.** (*open - lock*)   forzar   (con
ganzúa). ► **pick on** *vt fus* meterse con.
► **pick out** *vt sep* **1.** (*recognize*) reconocer, identificar. **2.** (*select*) escoger.
► **pick up** ◆ *vt sep* **1.** (*gen*) recoger.
2. (*buy, acquire*) adquirir; **to ~ up speed**
(*car*) acelerar. **3.** (*learn - tips, language*)
aprender. **4.** *inf* (*approach*) ligar con.
5. (RADIO & TELEC) captar. **6.** (*start again*)
reanudar. ◆ *vi* **1.** (*improve*) mejorar.
2. (*start again*) proseguir.
pickaxe Br, **pickax** Am ['pɪkæks] *n*
piqueta *f*.
picket ['pɪkɪt] ◆ *n* piquete *m*. ◆ *vt* formar piquetes en.
picket line *n* piquete *m* (de huelga).
pickle ['pɪkl] ◆ *n* **1.** (*vinegar preserve*)
encurtido *m*; (*sweet vegetable sauce*) salsa
espesa agridulce con trozos de cebolla etc. **2.** *inf*
(*difficult situation*): **to be in a ~** estar en un
lío. ◆ *vt* encurtir.
pickpocket ['pɪkˌpɒkɪt] *n* carterista *m
y f*.
pick-up *n* **1.** (*of record player*) fonocap-
tor *m*. **2.** (*truck*) furgoneta *f*.
picnic ['pɪknɪk] (*pt & pp* -ked, *cont* -king)
◆ *n* comida *f* campestre, picnic *m*. ◆ *vi*
ir de merienda al campo.
pictorial [pɪk'tɔːrɪəl] *adj* ilustrado
(da).
picture ['pɪktʃəʳ] ◆ *n* **1.** (*painting*)
cuadro *m*; (*drawing*) dibujo *m*. **2.** (*photo-*

graph) foto *f*. **3.** (*on* TV) imagen *f*. **4.** (*cinema film*) película *f*. **5.** (*in mind*) idea *f*, imagen *f*. **6.** (*situation*) situación *f*. **7.** *phr*: **to get the ~** *inf* entenderlo; **to put sb in the ~** poner a alguien al corriente. ◆ *vt* **1.** (*in mind*) imaginarse. **2.** (*in media*): **to be ~d** aparecer en la foto. ► **pictures** *npl* Br: **the ~s** el cine.

picture book *n* libro *m* ilustrado.

picturesque [ˌpɪktʃə'resk] *adj* pintoresco(ca).

pie [paɪ] *n* (*sweet*) tarta *f* (*cubierta de hojaldre*); (*savoury*) empanada *f*, pastel *m*.

piece [piːs] *n* **1.** (*individual part or portion*) trozo *m*, pedazo *m*; **to come to ~s** deshacerse; **to take sthg to ~s** desmontar algo; **in ~s** en pedazos; **in one ~** (*intact*) intacto(ta); (*unharmed*) sano y salvo (sana y salva). **2.** (*with uncountable noun*) (*individual object*): **~ of furniture** mueble *m*; **~ of clothing** prenda *f* de vestir; **~ of advice** consejo *m*; **~ of news** noticia *f*; **~ of luck** golpe *m* de suerte. **3.** (*in board game*) pieza *f*. **4.** (*of journalism*) artículo *m*. **5.** (*coin*) moneda *f*. ► **piece together** *vt sep* (*discover*) componer.

piecemeal ['piːsmiːl] ◆ *adj* poco sistemático(ca). ◆ *adv* por etapas.

piecework ['piːswɜːk] *n* (U) trabajo *m* a destajo.

pie chart *n* gráfico *m* circular OR de sectores.

pier [pɪər] *n* **1.** Br (*at seaside*) paseo marítimo en un malecón. **2.** (*landing platform*) muelle *m*.

pierce [pɪəs] *vt* **1.** (*subj: bullet, needle*) perforar; **to have one's ears ~d** hacerse agujeros en las orejas. **2.** (*subj: voice, scream*) romper.

piercing ['pɪəsɪŋ] *adj* **1.** (*scream*) desgarrador(ra); (*sound, voice*) agudo(da). **2.** (*wind*) cortante. **3.** (*look, eyes*) penetrante.

piety ['paɪətɪ] *n* piedad *f*.

pig [pɪg] *n* **1.** (*animal*) cerdo *m*, puerco *m*, chancho *m* Amer. **2.** *inf pej* (*greedy eater*) tragón *m*, -ona *f*. **3.** *inf pej* (*unkind person*) cerdo *m*, -da *f*.

pigeon ['pɪdʒɪn] (*pl inv* OR **-s**) *n* paloma *f*.

pigeonhole ['pɪdʒɪnhəʊl] ◆ *n* (*compartment*) casilla *f*. ◆ *vt* (*classify*) encasillar.

piggybank ['pɪgɪbæŋk] *n* hucha *f* con forma de cerdito.

pigheaded [ˌpɪg'hedɪd] *adj* cabezota.

pigment ['pɪgmənt] *n* pigmento *m*.

pigpen Am = **pigsty**.

pigskin ['pɪgskɪn] *n* piel *f* de cerdo.

pigsty ['pɪgstaɪ], **pigpen** Am ['pɪgpen] *n lit & fig* pocilga *f*.

pigtail ['pɪgteɪl] *n* (*girl's*) trenza *f*; (*Chinese, bullfighter's*) coleta *f*.

pike [paɪk] (*pl sense* 1 *only inv* OR **-s**) *n* **1.** (*fish*) lucio *m*. **2.** (*weapon*) pica *f*.

pilchard ['pɪltʃəd] *n* sardina *f*.

pile [paɪl] ◆ *n* **1.** (*heap*) montón *m*; **a ~** OR **~s of** un montón de. **2.** (*neat stack*) pila *f*. **3.** (*of carpet, fabric*) pelo *m*. ◆ *vt* amontonar. ► **piles** *npl* (MED) almorranas *fpl*. ► **pile into** *vt fus inf* amontonarse OR meterse en. ► **pile up** ◆ *vt sep* amontonar. ◆ *vi* **1.** (*form a heap*) amontonarse. **2.** (*mount up*) acumularse.

pileup ['paɪlʌp] *n* accidente *m* en cadena.

pilfer ['pɪlfər] ◆ *vt* sisar. ◆ *vi*: **to ~ (from)** sisar (de).

pilgrim ['pɪlgrɪm] *n* peregrino *m*, -na *f*.

pilgrimage ['pɪlgrɪmɪdʒ] *n* peregrinación *f*.

pill [pɪl] *n* **1.** (MED) píldora *f*, pastilla *f*. **2.** (*contraceptive*): **the ~** la píldora (anticonceptiva); **to be on the ~** tomar la píldora.

pillage ['pɪlɪdʒ] *vt* saquear, pillar.

pillar ['pɪlər] *n lit & fig* pilar *m*.

pillar box *n* Br buzón *m*.

pillion ['pɪljən] *n*: **to ride ~** ir en el asiento trasero (*de una moto*).

pillow ['pɪləʊ] *n* **1.** (*for bed*) almohada *f*. **2.** Am (*on sofa, chair*) cojín *m*.

pillowcase ['pɪləʊkeɪs], **pillowslip** ['pɪləʊslɪp] *n* funda *f* de almohada.

pilot ['paɪlət] ◆ *n* **1.** (AERON & NAUT) piloto *m*. **2.** (TV) programa *m* piloto. ◆ *comp* piloto (*inv*), de prueba. ◆ *vt* (AERON & NAUT) pilotar.

pilot burner, pilot light *n* piloto *m*, luz *f* indicadora.

pilot study *n* estudio *m* piloto.

pimp [pɪmp] *n inf* chulo *m*, padrote *m* Amer.

pimple ['pɪmpl] *n* grano *m*.

pin [pɪn] ◆ *n* **1.** (*for sewing*) alfiler *m*; **~s and needles** hormigueo *m*. **2.** (*of plug*) polo *m*. **3.** (TECH) clavija *f*. ◆ *vt* **1.** (*fasten*): **to ~ sthg to** OR **on** (*notice*) clavar con alfileres algo en; (*medal, piece of cloth*) prender algo en. **2.** (*trap*): **to ~ sb against** OR **to** inmovilizar a alguien contra. **3.** (*apportion*): **to ~ sthg on** OR **upon sb** endosar algo a alguien. ► **pin down** *vt sep* **1.** (*identify*) determinar, identificar. **2.** (*force to make a decision*): **to ~ sb down (to)** obligar a alguien a comprometerse (a).

pinafore ['pɪnəfɔːʳ] n 1. (apron) delantal m. 2. Br (dress) pichi m.

pinball ['pɪnbɔːl] n millón m, flíper m.

pincers ['pɪnsəz] npl 1. (tool) tenazas fpl. 2. (front claws) pinzas fpl.

pinch [pɪntʃ] ◆ n 1. (nip) pellizco m. 2. (small quantity) pizca f. ◆ vt 1. (nip) pellizcar; (subj: shoes) apretar. 2. inf (steal) mangar. ▶ **at a pinch** Br, **in a pinch** Am adv si no hay más remedio.

pincushion ['pɪn.kuʃn] n acerico m.

pine [paɪn] ◆ n pino m. ◆ vi: **to ~ for** suspirar por. ▶ **pine away** vi morirse de pena.

pineapple ['paɪnæpl] n piña f, ananá m Amer.

pinetree ['paɪntriː] n pino m.

ping [pɪŋ] n (of bell) tilín m; (of metal) sonido m metálico.

Ping-Pong® [-pɒŋ] n ping-pong® m.

pink [pɪŋk] ◆ adj rosa. ◆ n 1. (colour) rosa m. 2. (flower) clavel m.

pinnacle ['pɪnəkl] n 1. (high point) cumbre f. 2. (mountain peak, spire) pináculo m, cima f.

pinpoint ['pɪnpɔɪnt] vt determinar, identificar.

pin-striped [-.straɪpt] adj a rayas.

pint [paɪnt] n 1. (unit of measurement) Br = 0,568 litros; Am = 0,473 litros, ≃ pinta f. 2. Br (beer): **they went out for a ~** salieron a tomar una caña.

pioneer [.paɪə'nɪəʳ] n pionero m, -ra f.

pious ['paɪəs] adj 1. (religious) piadoso (sa). 2. pej (sanctimonious) mojigato(ta).

pip [pɪp] n 1. (seed) pepita f. 2. Br (bleep) señal f.

pipe [paɪp] ◆ n 1. (for gas, water) tubería f. 2. (for smoking) pipa f. ◆ vt (transport via pipes) conducir por tuberías. ▶ **pipes** npl (MUS) gaita f. ▶ **pipe down** vi inf cerrar la boca. ▶ **pipe up** vi inf: **to ~ up with a suggestion** saltar con una sugerencia.

pipe cleaner n limpiapipas m inv.

pipe dream n sueño m imposible.

pipeline ['paɪplaɪn] n (for gas) gasoducto m; (for oil) oleoducto m; (for water) tuberías fpl.

piper ['paɪpəʳ] n gaitero m, -ra f.

piping hot ['paɪpɪŋ-] adj humeante, calentito(ta).

piquant ['piːkənt] adj 1. (food) picante. 2. (story) intrigante; (situation) que suscita un placer mordaz.

pique [piːk] n resentimiento m.

pirate ['paɪrət] ◆ adj (gen & COMPUT)

pirata. ◆ n (sailor) pirata m y f. ◆ vt piratear.

pirate radio n Br radio f pirata.

pirouette [.pɪru'et] n pirueta f.

Pisces ['paɪsiːz] n Piscis m inv.

piss [pɪs] vulg ◆ n (urine) meada f. ◆ vi mear.

pissed [pɪst] adj vulg 1. Br (drunk) pedo (inv). 2. Am (annoyed) irritado(da).

pissed off adj vulg: **to be** OR **to feel ~** estar cabreado(da).

pistol ['pɪstl] n pistola f.

piston ['pɪstən] n pistón m, émbolo m.

pit [pɪt] ◆ n 1. (large hole) hoyo m. 2. (small hole - in metal, glass) señal f, marca f; (- on face) picadura f. 3. (for orchestra) foso m de la orquesta. 4. (mine) mina f. 5. Am (of fruit) hueso m. ◆ vt: **to be pitted against** ser enfrentado (da) con. ▶ **pits** npl (in motor racing): **the ~s** el box.

pitch [pɪtʃ] ◆ n 1. (SPORT) campo m. 2. (MUS) tono m. 3. (level, degree) grado m, punto m. 4. (selling place) puesto m. 5. inf (sales talk) labia f de comerciante. ◆ vt 1. (throw) lanzar, arrojar. 2. (speech) dar un tono a; (price) establecer un precio para. 3. (tent) montar, poner. ◆ vi 1. (ball) tocar el suelo; **to ~ forwards** (person) precipitarse hacia delante. 2. (ship, plane) dar un bandazo.

pitch-black adj negro(gra) como boca de lobo.

pitched battle [.pɪtʃt-] n (HISTORY) batalla f campal; fig (bitter struggle) lucha f encarnizada.

pitcher ['pɪtʃəʳ] n Am (jug) cántaro m.

pitchfork ['pɪtʃfɔːk] n horca f.

piteous ['pɪtɪəs] adj lastimero(ra).

pitfall ['pɪtfɔːl] n peligro m, escollo m.

pith [pɪθ] n parte blanca de la piel de una fruta.

pithy ['pɪθɪ] adj conciso(sa) y contundente.

pitiful ['pɪtɪfʊl] adj (condition, excuse, effort) lamentable; (person, appearance) lastimoso(sa).

pitiless ['pɪtɪlɪs] adj (person) despiadado(da), cruel; (weather) deplorable.

pit stop n (in motor racing) parada f en boxes.

pittance ['pɪtəns] n miseria f.

pity ['pɪtɪ] ◆ n (compassion) compasión f; (shame) pena f, lástima f; **what a ~!** ¡qué pena!; **to take** OR **have ~ on** compadecerse de. ◆ vt compadecerse de, sentir pena por.

pivot ['pɪvət] n pivote m, eje m; fig eje m.

pizza ['pi:tsə] n pizza f.

placard ['plæka:d] n pancarta f.

placate [pləˈkeɪt] vt aplacar, apaciguar.

place [pleɪs] ◆ n 1. (gen) lugar m, sitio m; ~ of birth lugar de nacimiento. 2. (proper position) sitio m. 3. (suitable occasion, time) momento m. 4. (home) casa f. 5. (specific seat) asiento m; (THEATRE) localidad f. 6. (setting at table) cubierto m. 7. (on course, at university) plaza f. 8. (on committee, in team) puesto m. 9. (role, function) papel m; to have an important ~ in desempeñar un papel importante en. 10. (rank) lugar m, posición f. 11. (in book) página f; (in speech) momento m; to lose one's ~ no saber (uno) dónde estaba. 12. (MATH): decimal ~ punto m decimal. 13. (instance): in the first ~ (from the start) desde el principio; in the first ~ ... and in the second ~ ... (firstly, secondly) en primer lugar ... y en segundo lugar ... 14. phr: to take ~ tener lugar; to take the ~ of sustituir a. ◆ vt 1. (position, put) colocar, poner; to be well ~d to do sthg estar en buena posición para hacer algo. 2. (lay, apportion): to ~ pressure on ejercer presión sobre. 3. (identify): I recognize the face, but I can't ~ her me suena su cara, pero no sé de qué. 4. (bet, order etc) hacer. 5. (in horse racing): to be ~d llegar entre los tres primeros. ▶ all over the place adv por todas partes. ▶ in place adv 1. (in proper position) en su sitio. 2. (established, set up) en marcha OR funcionamiento. ▶ in place of prep en lugar de. ▶ out of place adv 1. (in wrong position): to be out of ~ no estar en su sitio. 2. (inappropriate, unsuitable) fuera de lugar.

place mat n mantel m individual.

placement ['pleɪsmənt] n colocación f.

placid ['plæsɪd] adj 1. (even-tempered) apacible. 2. (peaceful) tranquilo(la).

plagiarize, -ise ['pleɪdʒəraɪz] vt plagiar.

plague [pleɪg] ◆ n 1. (attack of disease) peste f. 2. (disease): (the) ~ la peste. 3. (of rats, insects) plaga f. ◆ vt: to ~ sb with (complaints, requests) acosar a alguien con; (questions) coser a alguien a; to be ~d by (ill health) estar acosado de; (doubts) estar atormentado de.

plaice [pleɪs] (pl inv) n platija f.

plaid [plæd] n tejido m escocés.

Plaid Cymru [ˌplaɪdˈkʌmri] n Br (POL) partido nacionalista galés.

plain [pleɪn] ◆ adj 1. (not patterned) liso (sa). 2. (simple - gen) sencillo(lla); (- yoghurt) natural. 3. (clear) evidente, claro(ra). 4. (speaking, statement) franco (ca). 5. (absolute - madness etc) total, auténtico(ca). 6. (not pretty) sin atractivo. ◆ adv inf completamente. ◆ n (GEOGR) llanura f, planicie f.

plain chocolate n Br chocolate m amargo.

plain-clothes adj vestido(da) de paisano.

plain flour n Br harina f (sin levadura).

plainly ['pleɪnlɪ] adv 1. (upset, angry) evidentemente. 2. (visible, audible) claramente. 3. (frankly) francamente. 4. (simply) sencillamente.

plaintiff ['pleɪntɪf] n demandante m y f.

plait [plæt] ◆ n trenza f. ◆ vt trenzar.

plan [plæn] ◆ n 1. (strategy) plan m, proyecto m; to go according to ~ salir según lo previsto. 2. (of story, essay) esquema m. 3. (of building etc) plano m. ◆ vt 1. (organize) planear, organizar. 2. (career, future) planificar; to ~ to do sthg tener la intención de hacer algo. 3. (design, devise) trazar un esquema OR boceto de. ◆ vi hacer planes OR proyectos. ▶ plans npl planes mpl; to have ~s for tener planes para. ▶ plan on vt fus: to ~ on doing sthg pensar hacer algo.

plane [pleɪn] ◆ adj plano(na). ◆ n 1. (aircraft) avión m. 2. (GEOM) (flat surface) plano m. 3. fig (level - intellectual) plano m. 4. (tool) cepillo m. 5. (tree) plátano m.

planet ['plænɪt] n planeta m.

plank [plæŋk] n (piece of wood) tablón m, tabla f.

planning ['plænɪŋ] n (gen) planificación f.

planning permission n permiso m de construcción OR de obras.

plant [plɑːnt] ◆ n 1. (BOT) planta f. 2. (factory) planta f, fábrica f. 3. (heavy machinery) maquinaria f. ◆ vt 1. (seed, tree, vegetable): to ~ sthg (in) plantar algo (en). 2. (field, garden): to ~ sthg with sembrar algo de. 3. (bomb, bug) colocar secretamente.

plantation [plænˈteɪʃn] n plantación f.

plaque [plɑːk] n placa f.

plaster ['plɑːstər] ◆ n 1. (for wall, ceiling) yeso m. 2. (for broken bones) escayola f. 3. Br (bandage) tirita® f,

esparadrapo *m.* ♦ *vt* **1.** (*put plaster on*)
enyesar. 2. (*cover*): **to ~ sthg (with)** cubrir
algo (de).

plaster cast *n* **1.** (*for broken bones*)
escayola *f.* **2.** (*model, statue*) vaciado *m*
en yeso.

plastered ['plɑːstəd] *adj inf* (*drunk*)
cocido(da).

plasterer ['plɑːstərər] *n* yesero *m*, -ra *f.*

plastic ['plæstɪk] ♦ *adj* (*made from plastic*) de plástico. ♦ *n* plástico *m.*

Plasticine® ['plæstɪsiːn] *n Br* plastili-
na® *f.*

plastic surgery *n* cirugía *f* plástica.

plate [pleɪt] ♦ *n* **1.** (*dish, plateful*) plato
m. **2.** (*on machinery, wall, door*) placa *f.* **3.**
(U) (*metal covering*): **gold/silver ~** chapa *f*
de oro/plata. **4.** (*photograph*) lámina *f.*
5. (*in dentistry*) dentadura *f* postiza.
♦ *vt*: **to be ~d (with)** estar chapado(da)
(en or de).

plateau ['plætəʊ] (*pl* **-s** OR **-x** [-z]) *n*
(*high, flat land*) meseta *f.*

plate glass *n* vidrio *m* cilindrado.

platform ['plætfɔːm] *n* **1.** (*gen*) plataforma *f*; (*stage*) estrado *m*; (*at meeting*) tribuna *f.* **2.** (RAIL) andén *m*; **~ 12** la vía 12.
3. (POL) programa *m* electoral.

platform ticket *n Br* billete *m* de
andén.

platinum ['plætɪnəm] *n* platino *m.*

platitude ['plætɪtjuːd] *n* tópico *m.*

platoon [plə'tuːn] *n* pelotón *m.*

platter ['plætər] *n* (*dish*) fuente *f.*

plausible ['plɔːzəbl] *adj* plausible,
admisible.

play [pleɪ] ♦ *n* **1.** (U) (*amusement*) juego
m. **2.** (*piece of drama*) obra *f.* **3.** (*game*): **~
on words** juego *m* de palabras. **4.** (TECH)
juego *m.* ♦ *vt* **1.** (*game, sport*) jugar a.
2. (*play game against*): **to ~ sb (at sthg)**
jugar contra alguien (a algo). **3.** (*perform
for amusement*): **to ~ a joke on** gastar una
broma a; **to ~ a dirty trick on** jugar una
mala pasada a. **4.** (*act - part, character*)
representar; **to ~ a part OR role in** *fig*
desempeñar un papel en; **to ~ the fool**
hacer OR hacerse el tonto. **5.** (*instrument, tune*) tocar; (*record, cassette*) poner.
6. *phr*: **to ~ it safe** actuar sobre seguro.
♦ *vi* **1.** (*gen*): **to ~ (with/against)** jugar
(con/contra); **to ~ for sb/a team** jugar
para alguien/con un equipo.
2. (MUS - *person*) tocar; (- *music*) sonar.
▶ **play along** *vi*: **to ~ along (with)**
seguir la corriente (a). ▶ **play down**
vt sep quitar importancia a. ▶ **play up**
♦ *vt sep* (*emphasize*) hacer resaltar. ♦ *vi*

(*machine, part of body, child*) dar guerra.

play-act *vi* fingir, hacer comedia.

playboy ['pleɪbɔɪ] *n* playboy *m.*

player ['pleɪər] *n* **1.** (*of sport, game*)
jugador *m*, -ra *f.* **2.** (MUS) intérprete *m* y
f. **3.** (THEATRE) actor *m*, actriz *f.*

playful ['pleɪfʊl] *adj* juguetón(ona).

playground ['pleɪgraʊnd] *n* patio *m*
de recreo.

playgroup ['pleɪgruːp] *n* jardín *m* de
infancia, guardería *f.*

playing card ['pleɪɪŋ-] *n* naipe *m*,
carta *f.*

playing field ['pleɪɪŋ-] *n* campo *m* de
juego.

playmate ['pleɪmeɪt] *n* compañero *m*,
-ra *f* de juego.

play-off *n* partido *m* de desempate.

playpen ['pleɪpen] *n* parque *m* (de
niños) (*tipo cuna*).

playschool ['pleɪskuːl] *n* jardín *m* de
infancia, guardería *f.*

plaything ['pleɪθɪŋ] *n lit & fig* juguete
m.

playtime ['pleɪtaɪm] *n* recreo *m.*

playwright ['pleɪraɪt] *n* dramaturgo
m, -ga *f.*

plc *abbr of* **public limited company**.

plea [pliː] *n* **1.** (*appeal*) súplica *f*, petición *f.* **2.** (JUR) declaración por parte del acusado de culpabilidad o inocencia.

plead [pliːd] (*pt & pp* **-ed** OR **pled**) ♦ *vt*
1. (JUR) (*one's cause*) defender; **to ~
guilty/not guilty** declararse culpable/
inocente. **2.** (*give as excuse*) pretender.
♦ *vi* **1.** (*beg*): **to ~ (with sb to do sthg)**
rogar OR implorar (a alguien que haga
algo); **to ~ for sthg** pedir algo. **2.** (JUR)
declarar.

pleasant ['pleznt] *adj* **1.** (*smell, taste,
view*) agradable; (*surprise, news*) grato(ta).
2. (*person, smile, face*) simpático(ca).

pleasantry ['plezntrɪ] *n*: **to exchange
pleasantries** intercambiar cumplidos.

please [pliːz] ♦ *vt* complacer, agradar;
he always ~s himself él siempre hace lo
que le da la gana; **~ yourself!** ¡como
quieras! ♦ *vi* **1.** (*give satisfaction*) satisfacer, agradar. **2.** (*think appropriate*): **to do
as one ~s** hacer como a uno le parezca.
♦ *adv* por favor.

pleased [pliːzd] *adj*: **to be ~ (about/
with)** estar contento(ta) (por/con); **~ to
meet you!** ¡encantado(da) de conocerle!, ¡mucho gusto!

pleasing ['pliːzɪŋ] *adj* agradable, grato
(ta).

pleasure ['pleʒər] *n* **1.** (*feeling of happi-*

ness) gusto *m*; **to take ~ in sthg** disfrutar haciendo algo. **2.** (*enjoyment*) diversión *f*. **3.** (*delight*) placer *m*; **it's a ~, my ~** no hay de qué.

pleat [pliːt] ◆ *n* pliegue *m*. ◆ *vt* plisar.

pled [pled] *pt & pp* → **plead**.

pledge [pledʒ] ◆ *n* **1.** (*promise*) promesa *f*. **2.** (*token*) señal *f*, prenda *f*. ◆ *vt* **1.** (*promise*) prometer. **2.** (*make promise*): **to ~ sb to sthg** hacer jurar a alguien algo; **to ~ o.s. to** comprometerse a. **3.** (*pawn*) empeñar.

plentiful ['plentɪfʊl] *adj* abundante.

plenty ['plentɪ] ◆ *n* (U) abundancia *f*. ◆ *pron*: **we've got ~** tenemos de sobra; **~ of** mucho(cha).

pliable ['plaɪəbl], **pliant** ['plaɪənt] *adj* flexible.

pliers ['plaɪəz] *npl* alicates *mpl*.

plight [plaɪt] *n* grave situación *f*.

plimsoll ['plɪmsəl] *n* Br playera *f*, zapato *m* de tenis.

plinth [plɪnθ] *n* (*for statue*) peana *f*; (*for pillar*) plinto *m*.

PLO (*abbr of* **Palestine Liberation Organization**) *n* OLP *f*.

plod [plɒd] *vi* **1.** (*walk slowly*) caminar con paso cansino. **2.** (*work slowly*) llevar a cabo un trabajo pesado.

plodder ['plɒdəʳ] *n pej* persona *f* mediocre pero voluntariosa (en el trabajo).

plonk [plɒŋk] *n* (U) Br *inf* (*wine*) vino *m* peleón. ▶ **plonk down** *vt sep inf* dejar caer.

plot [plɒt] ◆ *n* **1.** (*plan*) complot *m*, conspiración *f*. **2.** (*story*) argumento *m*, trama *f*. **3.** (*of land*) parcela *f*. ◆ *vt* **1.** (*plan*) tramar, urdir. **2.** (*on map, graph*) trazar. ◆ *vi*: **to ~ (to do sthg)** tramar (hacer algo); **to ~ against** conspirar contra.

plotter ['plɒtəʳ] *n* (*schemer*) conspirador *m*, -ra *f*.

plough Br, **plow** Am [plaʊ] ◆ *n* arado *m*. ◆ *vt* arar. ▶ **plough into** ◆ *vt sep* (*invest*) invertir. ◆ *vt fus* (*hit*) chocar contra.

ploughman's ['plaʊmənz] (*pl inv*) *n* Br: **~ (lunch)** queso, cebolletas y ensalada con pan.

plow *etc* Am = **plough** *etc*.

ploy [plɔɪ] *n* táctica *f*, estratagema *f*.

pluck [plʌk] ◆ *vt* **1.** (*fruit, flower*) coger. **2.** (*pull sharply*) arrancar. **3.** (*bird*) desplumar. **4.** (*eyebrows*) depilar. **5.** (*instrument*) puntear. ◆ *n dated* valor *m*. ▶ **pluck up** *vt fus*: **to ~ up the courage to**

do sthg armarse de valor para hacer algo.

plucky ['plʌkɪ] *adj dated* valiente.

plug [plʌg] ◆ *n* **1.** (ELEC) enchufe *m*, clavija *f*. **2.** (*for bath or sink*) tapón *m*. ◆ *vt* **1.** (*hole, leak*) tapar. **2.** *inf* (*mention favourably*) dar publicidad a. ▶ **plug in** *vt sep* enchufar.

plughole ['plʌghəʊl] *n* desagüe *m*.

plum [plʌm] ◆ *adj* **1.** (*colour*) de color ciruela. **2.** (*choice*): **~ job** chollo *m*. ◆ *n* (*fruit*) ciruela *f*.

plumb [plʌm] ◆ *adv* **1.** Br (*exactly*): **~ in the middle** justo en medio. **2.** Am (*completely*) completamente. ◆ *vt*: **to ~ the depths of** alcanzar las cotas más bajas de.

plumber ['plʌməʳ] *n* fontanero *m*, -ra *f*, gásfiter *m* Amer.

plumbing ['plʌmɪŋ] *n* (U) **1.** (*fittings*) tubería *f*. **2.** (*work*) fontanería *f*.

plume [pluːm] *n* **1.** (*feather*) pluma *f*. **2.** (*decoration, of smoke*) penacho *m*.

plummet ['plʌmɪt] *vi* caer en picado.

plump [plʌmp] *adj* regordete(ta). ▶ **plump for** *vt fus* optar OR decidirse por. ▶ **plump up** *vt sep* ahuecar.

plum pudding *n* budín *navideño con pasas*.

plunder ['plʌndəʳ] ◆ *n* **1.** (*stealing, raiding*) saqueo *m*, pillaje *m*. **2.** (*stolen goods*) botín *m*. ◆ *vt* saquear.

plunge [plʌndʒ] ◆ *n* (*fall, dive*) chapuzón *m*, zambullida *f*; **to take the ~** dar el paso decisivo. ◆ *vt* **1.** (*knife etc*): **to ~ sthg into** hundir algo en. **2.** (*into darkness, water*): **to ~ sthg into** sumergir algo en. ◆ *vi* **1.** (*fall, dive*) hundirse, zambullirse. **2.** (*decrease*) bajar vertiginosamente.

plunger ['plʌndʒəʳ] *n* (*for blocked pipes*) desatascador *m*.

pluperfect [ˌpluːˈpɜːfɪkt] *n*: **~ (tense)** (pretérito *m*) pluscuamperfecto *m*.

plural ['plʊərəl] ◆ *adj* (*gen*) plural. ◆ *n* plural *m*.

plus [plʌs] (*pl* -es OR -ses) ◆ *adj* (*or more*): **35-~** 35 o más. ◆ *n* **1.** (MATH) (*sign*) signo *m* más. **2.** *inf* (*bonus*) ventaja *f*. ◆ *prep* más. ◆ *conj* además.

plush [plʌʃ] *adj* lujoso(sa).

plus sign *n* signo *m* más.

Pluto ['pluːtəʊ] *n* (*planet*) Plutón *m*.

plutonium [pluːˈtəʊnɪəm] *n* plutonio *m*.

ply [plaɪ] ◆ *vt* **1.** (*trade*) ejercer. **2.** (*supply, provide*): **to ~ sb with sthg** (*questions*) acosar a alguien con algo; (*food, drink*) no parar de ofrecer a alguien algo. ◆ *vi* navegar.

plywood ['plaɪwʊd] n contrachapado m.

p.m., pm (abbr of post meridiem)· at 3 ~ a las tres de la tarde.

PM n abbr of prime minister.

PMT, PMS (abbr of premenstrual tension, premenstrual syndrome) n SPM m.

pneumatic [njuːˈmætɪk] adj (tyre, chair) neumático(ca).

pneumatic drill n martillo m neumático.

pneumonia [njuːˈməʊnjə] n (U) pulmonía f.

poach [pəʊtʃ] ◆ vt 1. (game) cazar en vedado; (fish) pescar en vedado. 2. (copy) plagiar. 3. (CULIN) (salmon) hervir; (egg) escalfar. ◆ vi (for game) cazar en vedado; (for fish) pescar en vedado.

poacher ['pəʊtʃər] n (hunter) cazador furtivo m, cazadora furtiva f; (fisherman) pescador furtivo m, pescadora furtiva f.

poaching ['pəʊtʃɪŋ] n (for game) caza f furtiva; (for fish) pesca f furtiva.

PO Box (abbr of Post Office Box) n apdo. m.

pocket ['pɒkɪt] ◆ n 1. (in clothes) bolsillo m; to be £10 out of ~ salir perdiendo 10 libras; to pick sb's ~ vaciar a alguien el bolsillo. 2. (in car door etc) bolsa f, bolsillo m. 3. (of resistance) foco m; (of air) bolsa f. ◆ vt 1. (place in pocket) meterse en el bolsillo. 2. (steal) birlar. ◆ adj de bolsillo.

pocketbook ['pɒkɪtbʊk] n 1. (notebook) libreta f. 2. Am (handbag) bolso m.

pocketknife ['pɒkɪtnaɪf] (pl -knives [-naɪvz]) n navaja f (de bolsillo).

pocket money n propina f, dinero m para gastar.

pockmark ['pɒkmɑːk] n marca f OR señal f (en la cara).

pod [pɒd] n (of plants) vaina f.

podgy ['pɒdʒɪ] adj inf gordinflón(ona).

podiatrist [pəˈdaɪətrɪst] n Am podólogo m, -ga f.

podium ['pəʊdɪəm] (pl -diums OR -dia [-dɪə]) n podio m.

poem ['pəʊɪm] n poema m, poesía f.

poet ['pəʊɪt] n poeta m y f.

poetic [pəʊˈetɪk] adj poético(ca).

poet laureate n poeta m laureado.

poetry ['pəʊɪtrɪ] n poesía f.

poignant ['pɔɪnjənt] adj patético(ca), conmovedor(ra).

point [pɔɪnt] ◆ n 1. (gen) punto m; at that ~ en aquel momento. 2. (tip) punta

f. 3. (detail, argument): to make a ~ hacer una observación; to have a ~ tener razón. 4. (main idea): the ~ is ... lo fundamental OR más importante es ...; to miss the ~ of no coger la idea de; to get OR come to the ~ ir al grano; it's beside the ~ no viene al caso. 5. (feature) cualidad f; weak/strong ~ punto m débil/fuerte. 6. (purpose) sentido m; what's the ~? ¿para qué?; there's no ~ in it no tiene sentido. 7. (decimal point) coma f; two ~ six dos coma seis. 8. Br (ELEC) toma f de corriente. ◆ phr: to make a ~ of doing sthg poner empeño en hacer algo. ◆ vt: to ~ a gun at sthg/sb apuntar a algo/alguien con una pistola; to ~ one's finger at sthg/sb señalar algo/a alguien con el dedo. ◆ vi 1. (indicate with finger): to ~ at sthg/sb, to ~ to sthg/sb señalar algo/a alguien con el dedo. 2. fig (suggest): everything ~s to her her guilt todo indica que ella es la culpable. ▶ **points** npl Br (RAIL) agujas fpl. ▶ **up to a point** adv hasta cierto punto. ▶ **on the point of** prep: to be on the ~ of doing sthg estar a punto de hacer algo. ▶ **point out** vt sep (person, object, fact) señalar, indicar; (mistake) hacer notar.

point-blank adv 1. (refuse, deny) categóricamente. 2. (at close range) a quemarropa.

pointed ['pɔɪntɪd] adj 1. (sharp, angular) en punta, puntiagudo(da). 2. (cutting, incisive) intencionado(da).

pointer ['pɔɪntər] n 1. (piece of advice) consejo m. 2. (needle) aguja f. 3. (COMPUT) puntero m.

pointless ['pɔɪntlɪs] adj sin sentido.

point of view (pl points of view) n 1. (opinion) punto m de vista. 2. (aspect, perspective) perspectiva f.

poise [pɔɪz] n (self-assurance) aplomo m, serenidad f; (elegance) elegancia f.

poised [pɔɪzd] adj 1. (ready): to be ~ to do sthg estar listo(ta) para hacer algo. 2. (calm and dignified) sereno(na).

poison ['pɔɪzn] ◆ n veneno m. ◆ vt (gen - intentionally) envenenar; (- unintentionally) intoxicar.

poisoning ['pɔɪznɪŋ] n (intentional) envenenamiento m; (unintentional) intoxicación f.

poisonous ['pɔɪznəs] adj 1. (substance, gas) tóxico(ca). 2. (snake) venenoso(sa).

poke [pəʊk] ◆ vt 1. (with finger, stick) empujar; (with elbow) dar un codazo a; (fire) atizar; to ~ sb in the eye meter el dedo en el ojo de alguien. 2. (push,

stuff): **to ~ sthg into** meter algo en. ◆ *vi*
(*protrude*): **to ~ out of sthg** sobresalir por
algo. ▶ **poke about, poke around** *vi*
inf fisgonear, hurgar.

poker ['pəukər] *n* 1. (*game*) póker *m*.
2. (*for fire*) atizador *m*.

poker-faced [-ˌfeɪst] *adj* con cara
inexpresiva.

poky ['pəukɪ] *adj pej*: **a ~ little room** un
cuartucho.

Poland ['pəulənd] *n* Polonia.

polar ['pəulər] *adj* polar.

Polaroid® ['pəulərɔɪd] *n* 1. (*camera*)
polaroid® *f*. 2. (*photograph*) fotografía *f*
polaroid.

pole [pəul] *n* 1. (*rod, post*) palo *m*; **telegraph ~ poste** *m* telegráfico. 2. (ELEC &
GEOGR) polo *m*.

Pole [pəul] *n* polaco *m*, -ca *f*.

pole vault *n*: **the ~** el salto con pértiga.

police [pə'liːs] ◆ *npl* (*police force*): **the ~** la
policía. ◆ *vt* mantener el orden en, vi-
gilar.

police car *n* coche *m* patrulla.

police constable *n* Br policía *m y f*.

police force *n* cuerpo *m* de policía.

policeman [pə'liːsmən] (*pl* **-men**
[-mən]) *n* policía *m*.

police officer *n* agente *m y f* de la
policía.

police record *n*: (**to have a**) **~** (tener)
antecedentes *mpl* policiales.

police station *n* comisaría *f* (de
policía).

policewoman [pə'liːsˌwumən] (*pl*
-women [-ˌwɪmɪn]) *n* (mujer *f*) policía *f*.

policy ['pɒləsɪ] *n* 1. (*plan, practice*) política *f*. 2. (*document, agreement*) póliza *f*.

polio ['pəulɪəu] *n* polio *f*.

polish ['pɒlɪʃ] ◆ *n* 1. (*for floor*) cera *f*;
(*for shoes*) betún *m*; (*for window*)
limpiacristales *m inv*; (*for nails*) esmalte
m. 2. (*shine*) brillo *m*, lustre *m*. 3. *fig*
(*refinement*) refinamiento *m*. ◆ *vt* (*floor*)
encerar; (*shoes, window, car*) limpiar; (*cutlery, silver, glasses*) sacar brillo a. ▶ **polish off** *vt sep inf* (*food*) zamparse; (*job*)
despachar.

Polish ['pəulɪʃ] ◆ *adj* polaco(ca). ◆ *n*
(*language*) polaco *m*. ◆ *npl*: **the ~** los
polacos *mpl*.

polished ['pɒlɪʃt] *adj* 1. (*person, manner*) refinado(da). 2. (*performance, speech*)
esmerado(da).

polite [pə'laɪt] *adj* educado(da),
cortés.

politic ['pɒlətɪk] *adj fml* oportuno

(na), conveniente.

political [pə'lɪtɪkl] *adj* (*concerning politics*) político(ca).

politically correct [pəˌlɪtɪklɪ-] *adj*
políticamente correcto(ta), *conforme a la
ética según la cual se sustituyen términos con-
siderados sexistas, racistas etc por otros consi-
derados aceptables*.

politician [ˌpɒlɪ'tɪʃn] *n* político *m*, -ca *f*.

politics ['pɒlətɪks] ◆ *n* (U) 1. (*gen*)
política *f*. 2. (*field of study*) ciencias *fpl*
políticas. ◆ *npl* 1. (*personal beliefs*) ideas
fpl políticas. 2. (*of a group, area*) política *f*.

polka ['pɒlkə] *n* polca *f*.

polka dot *n* lunar *m* (*en un vestido*).

poll [pəul] ◆ *n* (*vote*) votación *f*; (*of opinion*) encuesta *f*. ◆ *vt* 1. (*people*) sondear.
2. (*votes*) obtener. ▶ **polls** *npl*: **the ~s** los
comicios.

pollen ['pɒlən] *n* polen *m*.

polling booth ['pəulɪŋ-] *n* cabina *f*
electoral.

polling day ['pəulɪŋ-] *n* Br día *m* de
elecciones.

polling station ['pəulɪŋ-] *n* mesa *f* OR
centro *m* electoral.

pollutant [pə'luːtnt] *n* contaminante
m.

pollute [pə'luːt] *vt* contaminar.

pollution [pə'luːʃn] *n* (U) 1. (*process of
polluting*) contaminación *f*. 2. (*impurities*)
substancias *fpl* contaminantes.

polo ['pəuləu] *n* polo *m*.

polo neck Br *n* 1. (*neck*) cuello *m* alto.
2. (*jumper*) jersey *m* de cuello alto.

polyethylene Am = **polythene**.

Polynesia [ˌpɒlɪ'niːʒə] *n* Polinesia *f*.

polystyrene [ˌpɒlɪ'staɪriːn] *n* polies-
tireno *m*.

polytechnic [ˌpɒlɪ'teknɪk] *n* Br
politécnico *m*, escuela *f* politécnica.

polythene Br ['pɒlɪθiːn], **polyethylene** Am ['pɒlɪ'eθiliːn] *n* polietileno *m*.

polythene bag *n* Br bolsa *f* de plástico.

pomegranate ['pɒmɪˌgrænɪt] *n* granada *f*.

pomp [pɒmp] *n* pompa *f*.

pompom ['pɒmpɒm] *n* borla *f*, pompón *m*.

pompous ['pɒmpəs] *adj* 1. (*self-
important*) presumido(da). 2. (*style*)
pomposo(sa); (*building*) ostentoso(sa).

pond [pɒnd] *n* estanque *m*.

ponder ['pɒndər] *vt* considerar.

ponderous ['pɒndərəs] *adj* 1. (*speech,
book*) pesado(da). 2. (*action, walk*) len-
to(ta) y torpe.

pong [pɒŋ] *n* Br *inf* (olor *m* a) peste *f*.

pontoon [pɒn'tu:n] *n* 1. (*bridge*) pontón *m*. 2. Br (*game*) veintiuna *f*.

pony ['pəʊnɪ] *n* poni *m*.

ponytail ['pəʊnɪteɪl] *n* coleta *f* (de caballo).

pony-trekking [-,trekɪŋ] *n* (U) excursión *f* en poni.

poodle ['pu:dl] *n* caniche *m*.

pool [pu:l] ◆ *n* 1. (*of water, blood, ink*) charco *m*; (*pond*) estanque *m*. 2. (*swimming pool*) piscina *f*. 3. (*of light*) foco *m*. 4. (COMM) (*fund*) fondos *mpl* comunes. 5. (*of people, things*): **typing** ~ servicio *m* de mecanografía; **car** ~ parque *m* de automóviles. 6. (*game*) billar *m* americano. ◆ *vt* (*resources, funds*) juntar; (*knowledge*) poner en común. ▶ **pools** *npl* Br: **the ~s** las quinielas.

poor [pɔ:ʳ] ◆ *adj* 1. (*gen*) pobre; ~ **old John!** ¡el pobre de John! 2. (*quality, result*) malo(la). ◆ *npl*: **the** ~ los pobres.

poorly ['pɔ:lɪ] ◆ *adj* Br pachucho(cha). ◆ *adv* mal.

pop [pɒp] ◆ *n* 1. (*music*) (música *f*) pop *m*. 2. (U) *inf* (*fizzy drink*) gaseosa *f*. 3. *inf* (*father*) papá *m*. 4. (*sound*) pequeña explosión *f*. ◆ *vt* 1. (*balloon, bubble*) pinchar. 2. (*put quickly*): **to** ~ **sthg into** meter algo en. ◆ *vi* 1. (*balloon*) reventar; (*cork, button*) saltar. 2. (*eyes*) salirse de las órbitas. 3. (*go quickly*): **I'm just popping round to the shop** voy un momento a la tienda. ▶ **pop in** *vi* entrar un momento. ▶ **pop up** *vi* aparecer de repente.

pop concert *n* concierto *m* de música pop.

popcorn ['pɒpkɔ:n] *n* palomitas *fpl* (de maíz).

pope [pəʊp] *n* papa *m*.

pop group *n* grupo *m* (de música) pop.

poplar ['pɒpləʳ] *n* álamo *m*.

poppy ['pɒpɪ] *n* amapola *f*.

Popsicle® ['pɒpsɪkl] *n* Am polo *m*.

populace ['pɒpjʊləs] *n*: **the** ~ (*masses*) el populacho; (*people*) el pueblo.

popular ['pɒpjʊləʳ] *adj* 1. (*gen*) popular; (*person*) estimado(da). 2. (*belief, attitude, discontent*) generalizado(da). 3. (*newspaper, politics*) para las masas.

popularize, -ise ['pɒpjʊləraɪz] *vt* 1. (*make popular*) popularizar. 2. (*simplify*) vulgarizar.

populate ['pɒpjʊleɪt] *vt* poblar.

population [,pɒpjʊ'leɪʃn] *n* población *f*.

porcelain ['pɔ:səlɪn] *n* porcelana *f*.

porch [pɔ:tʃ] *n* 1. (*entrance*) porche *m*, pórtico *m*. 2. Am (*verandah*) terraza *f*.

porcupine ['pɔ:kjʊpaɪn] *n* puerco *m* espín.

pore [pɔ:ʳ] *n* poro *m*. ▶ **pore over** *vt fus* estudiar esmeradamente.

pork [pɔ:k] *n* carne *f* de cerdo.

pork pie *n* empanada *f* de carne de cerdo.

pornography [pɔ:'nɒgrəfɪ] *n* pornografía *f*.

porous ['pɔ:rəs] *adj* poroso(sa).

porridge ['pɒrɪdʒ] *n* papilla *f* OR gachas *fpl* de avena.

port [pɔ:t] *n* 1. (*coastal town, harbour*) puerto *m*. 2. (NAUT) (*left-hand side*) babor *m*. 3. (*drink*) oporto *m*. 4. (COMPUT) conexión *f*.

portable ['pɔ:təbl] *adj* portátil.

portent ['pɔ:tənt] *n literary* presagio *m*.

porter ['pɔ:təʳ] *n* 1. Br (*in block of flats*) portero *m*, -ra *f*; (*in public building, hotel*) conserje *m* y *f*. 2. (*for luggage*) mozo *m*.

portfolio [,pɔ:t'fəʊljəʊ] (*pl* **-s**) *n* 1. (ART, FIN & POL) cartera *f*. 2. (*sample of work*) carpeta *f*.

porthole ['pɔ:thəʊl] *n* portilla *f*.

portion ['pɔ:ʃn] *n* 1. (*part, section*) porción *f*. 2. (*of chips, vegetables etc*) ración *f*.

portly ['pɔ:tlɪ] *adj* corpulento(ta).

port of call *n* 1. (NAUT) puerto *m* de escala. 2. *fig* (*on journey*) escala *f*.

portrait ['pɔ:treɪt] *n* retrato *m*.

portray [pɔ:'treɪ] *vt* 1. (*represent - in a play, film*) representar. 2. (*describe*) describir. 3. (*paint*) retratar.

Portugal ['pɔ:tʃʊgl] *n* Portugal.

Portuguese [,pɔ:tʃʊ'gi:z] ◆ *adj* portugués(esa). ◆ *n* (*language*) portugués *m*. ◆ *npl*: **the** ~ los portugueses.

pose [pəʊz] ◆ *n* 1. (*position, stance*) postura *f*. 2. *pej* (*pretence, affectation*) pose *f*. ◆ *vt* 1. (*problem, threat*) presentar. 2. (*question*) formular. ◆ *vi* 1. (*model*) posar. 2. *pej* (*behave affectedly*) adoptar una pose. 3. (*pretend to be*): **to** ~ **as sb/ sthg** fingir ser alguien/algo.

posh [pɒʃ] *adj inf* 1. (*hotel, area etc*) de lujo, elegante. 2. Br (*person, accent*) afectado(da).

position [pə'zɪʃn] ◆ *n* 1. (*gen*) posición *f*. 2. (*right place*) sitio *m*, lugar *m*. 3. (*status*) rango *m*. 4. (*job*) puesto *m*. 5. (*in a race, competition*) lugar *m*. 6. (*state, situation*) situación *f*. 7. (*stance, opinion*): ~ **on** opinión *f* respecto a. ◆ *vt* colocar.

positive ['pɒzətɪv] adj 1. (gen) positivo (va). 2. (sure): **to be ~ (about)** estar seguro(ra) (de). 3. (optimistic, confident): **to be ~ (about)** ser optimista (respecto a). 4. (definite - action) decisivo(va); (- decision) categórico(ca). 5. (irrefutable - evidence, fact) irrefutable; (- proof) concluyente.

posse ['pɒsɪ] n Am 1. (to pursue criminal) grupo m de hombres a caballo. 2. (group) grupo m.

possess [pə'zes] vt 1. (gen) poseer. 2. (subj: emotion) adueñarse de.

possession [pə'zeʃn] n posesión f. ▶ **possessions** npl bienes mpl.

possessive [pə'zesɪv] adj 1. (gen) posesivo(va). 2. pej (selfish) egoísta.

possibility [,pɒsə'bɪlətɪ] n posibilidad f.

possible ['pɒsəbl] adj 1. (gen) posible; **as soon as ~** cuanto antes; **as much as ~** todo lo posible; **it's ~ that she'll come** es posible que venga. 2. (viable - plan etc) viable, factible.

possibly ['pɒsəblɪ] adv 1. (perhaps) posiblemente, quizás. 2. (within one's power): **could you ~ help me?** ¿te importaría ayudarme? 3. (to show surprise): **how could he ~ do that?** ¿cómo demonios pudo hacer eso? 4. (for emphasis): **I can't ~ do it** no puedo hacerlo de ninguna manera.

post [pəust] ◆ n 1. (service): **the ~** el correo; **by ~** por correo. 2. (U) (letters etc) cartas fpl. 3. (delivery) reparto m. 4. Br (collection) colecta f. 5. (pole) poste m. 6. (position, job) puesto m. 7. (MIL) puesto m. ◆ vt 1. (by mail) echar al correo. 2. (transfer) enviar, destinar.

postage ['pəustɪdʒ] n franqueo m, porte m; **~ and packing** gastos mpl de envío.

postal ['pəustl] adj postal.

postal order n giro m postal.

postbox ['pəustbɒks] n Br buzón m.

postcard ['pəustkɑːd] n postal f.

postcode ['pəustkəud] n Br código m postal.

postdate [,pəust'deɪt] vt poner posfecha a.

poster ['pəustər] n cartel m, póster m.

poste restante [,pəust'restɑːnt] n lista f de correos.

posterior [pɒ'stɪərɪər] n hum trasero m.

postgraduate [,pəust'grædʒuət] n posgraduado m, -da f.

posthumous ['pɒstjuməs] adj póstumo(ma).

postman ['pəustmən] (pl **-men** [-mən]) n cartero m.

postmark ['pəustmɑːk] n matasellos m inv.

postmaster ['pəust,mɑːstər] n administrador m de correos.

postmortem [,pəust'mɔːtəm] ◆ adj post-mórtem (inv). ◆ n (autopsy) autopsia f.

post office n 1. (organization): **the Post Office** ≃ Correos m inv. 2. (building) oficina f de correos.

post office box n apartado m de correos, casilla f postal Amer.

postpone [,pəust'pəun] vt posponer.

postscript ['pəustskrɪpt] n (additional message) posdata f; fig (additional information) nota f final.

posture ['pɒstʃər] n lit & fig postura f; **~ on sthg** postura hacia algo.

postwar [,pəust'wɔːr] adj de (la) posguerra.

posy ['pəuzɪ] n ramillete m.

pot [pɒt] ◆ n 1. (for cooking) olla f. 2. (for tea) tetera f; (for coffee) cafetera f. 3. (for paint) bote m; (for jam) tarro m. 4. (flowerpot) tiesto m, maceta f. 5. (U) inf (cannabis) maría f, hierba f. 6. phr: **to go to ~** ir al traste. ◆ vt plantar (en un tiesto).

potassium [pə'tæsɪəm] n potasio m.

potato [pə'teɪtəu] (pl **-es**) n patata f.

potato peeler [-,piːlər] n pelapatatas m inv.

potent ['pəutənt] adj 1. (powerful, influential) poderoso(sa). 2. (drink, drug) fuerte. 3. (sexually capable) potente.

potential [pə'tenʃl] ◆ adj potencial, posible. ◆ n (U) potencial m; **to have ~** tener posibilidades, prometer.

potentially [pə'tenʃəlɪ] adv en potencia.

pothole ['pɒthəul] n 1. (in road) bache m. 2. (underground) cueva f.

potholing ['pɒt,həulɪŋ] n Br espeleología f.

potion ['pəuʃn] n poción f.

potluck [,pɒt'lʌk] n: **to take ~** (gen) elegir a ojo; (at meal) conformarse con lo que haya.

potshot ['pɒt,ʃɒt] n: **to take a ~ (at sthg/sb)** disparar (a algo/alguien) sin apuntar.

potted ['pɒtɪd] adj 1. (plant) en tiesto. 2. (meat, fish) en conserva.

potter ['pɒtər] n alfarero m, -ra f. ▶ **potter about, potter around** vi Br entretenerse.

pottery ['pɒtərɪ] n 1. (gen) cerámica f, alfarería f. 2. (factory) fábrica f de cerámica.

potty ['pɒtɪ] Br inf ♦ adj (person) chalado(da). ♦ n orinal m.

pouch [pautʃ] n 1. (small bag) bolsa f pequeña; (for tobacco) petaca f. 2. (on animal's body) bolsa f (abdominal).

poultry ['pəultrɪ] ♦ n (meat) carne f de pollería. ♦ npl (birds) aves fpl de corral.

pounce [pauns] vi (leap): **to ~ (on** OR **upon)** abalanzarse (sobre).

pound [paund] ♦ n 1. (unit of money, weight) libra f. 2. (for cars) depósito m (de coches); (for dogs) perrera f. ♦ vt 1. (hammer on) golpear, aporrear. 2. (pulverize) machacar. ♦ vi 1. (hammer): **to ~ on sthg** golpear OR aporrear algo. 2. (beat, throb) palpitar.

pound sterling n libra f esterlina.

pour [pɔːr] ♦ vt (cause to flow): **to ~ sthg (into)** echar OR verter algo (en); **to ~ sb a drink, to ~ a drink for sb** servirle una copa a alguien. ♦ vi 1. (liquid) chorrear; (smoke) salir a borbotones. 2. fig (rush): **to ~ in/out** entrar/salir en manada. ♦ v impers (rain hard) llover a cántaros. ► **pour in** vi llegar a raudales. ► **pour out** vt sep 1. (empty) echar, vaciar. 2. (serve) servir.

pouring ['pɔːrɪŋ] adj (rain) torrencial.

pout [paut] vi (showing displeasure) hacer pucheros; (being provocative) hacer un gesto provocador con los labios.

poverty ['pɒvətɪ] n lit & fig pobreza f.

poverty-stricken adj necesitado (da).

powder ['paudər] ♦ n polvo m; (make-up) polvos mpl. ♦ vt poner polvos en; **to ~ o.s.** darse polvos, empolvarse.

powder compact n polvera f.

powdered ['paudəd] adj (in powder form) en polvo.

powder puff n borla f.

powder room n servicios mpl de señoras.

power ['pauər] ♦ n 1. (U) (authority, control) poder m; **to come to/take ~** llegar al/hacerse con el poder; **to be in ~** estar en el poder. 2. (ability) facultad f; **it isn't within my ~ to do it** no está dentro de mis posibilidades hacerlo. 3. (legal authority) autoridad f, competencia f. 4. (physical strength) fuerza f. 5. (energy - solar, steam etc) energía f. 6. (electricity) corriente f; **to turn the ~ on/ off** dar/cortar la corriente. 7. (powerful nation, person, group) potencia f.

♦ vt impulsar.

powerboat ['pauəbəut] n motora f.

power cut n apagón m.

power failure n corte m de corriente.

powerful ['pauəful] adj 1. (gen) poderoso(sa). 2. (blow, voice, drug) potente. 3. (speech, film) conmovedor(ra).

powerless ['pauəlɪs] adj 1. (helpless) impotente. 2. (unable): **to be ~ to do sthg** no poder hacer algo.

power point n Br toma f (de corriente).

power station n central f eléctrica.

power steering n dirección f asistida.

pp (abbr of per procurationem) p.p.

p & p abbr of **postage and packing**.

PR n 1. abbr of **proportional representation**. 2. abbr of **public relations**.

practicable ['præktɪkəbl] adj factible.

practical ['præktɪkl] ♦ adj 1. (gen) práctico(ca). 2. (skilled with hands) hábil, mañoso(sa). ♦ n práctica f.

practicality [,præktɪ'kælətɪ] n viabilidad f.

practical joke n broma f pesada.

practically ['præktɪklɪ] adv 1. (in a practical way) de manera práctica. 2. (almost) prácticamente, casi.

practice, practise Am ['præktɪs] n 1. (training, training session) práctica f; (SPORT) entrenamiento m; (MUS) ensayo m; **I'm out of ~** me falta práctica. 2. (reality): **to put sthg into ~** llevar algo a la práctica; **in ~** (in fact) en la práctica. 3. (habit, regular activity) costumbre f. 4. (of profession) ejercicio m. 5. (business - of doctor) consulta f; (- of lawyer) bufete m, despacho m.

practicing Am = **practising**.

practise, practice Am ['præktɪs] ♦ vt 1. (SPORT) entrenar; (MUS & THEATRE) ensayar. 2. (religion, economy, safe sex) practicar. 3. (medicine, law) ejercer. ♦ vi 1. (train - gen) practicar; (SPORT) entrenarse. 2. (as doctor) practicar; (as lawyer) ejercer.

practising, practicing Am ['præktɪsɪŋ] adj 1. (Catholic, Jew etc) practicante. 2. (doctor, lawyer) en ejercicio. 3. (homosexual) activo(va).

practitioner [præk'tɪʃnər] n: **medical ~** médico m, -ca f.

Prague [prɑːg] n Praga.

prairie ['preərɪ] n pradera f, prado m.

praise [preɪz] ♦ n (U) elogio m, alabanza f. ♦ vt elogiar, alabar.

praiseworthy ['preɪz,wɜːðɪ] *adj* encomiable.

pram [præm] *n* cochecito *m* de niño.

prance [prɑːns] *vi* 1. (*person*) ir dando
brincos. 2. (*horse*) hacer cabriolas.

prank [præŋk] *n* travesura *f*.

prawn [prɔːn] *n* gamba *f*.

pray [preɪ] *vi* rezar, orar; **to ~ to sb**
rogar a alguien; **to ~ for sthg/for sthg to
happen** *lit & fig* rogar algo/que pase
algo.

prayer [preər] *n* 1. (RELIG) oración *f*. 2.
fig (*strong hope*) ruego *m*, súplica *f*.

prayer book *n* misal *m*.

preach [priːtʃ] ◆ *vt* (*gen*) predicar; (*sermon*) dar. ◆ *vi* 1. (RELIG): **to ~ (to)**
predicar (a). 2. *pej* (*pontificate*): **to ~ (at)**
sermonear (a).

preacher ['priːtʃər] *n* predicador *m*,
-ra *f*.

precarious [prɪ'keərɪəs] *adj* precario
(ria).

precaution [prɪ'kɔːʃn] *n* precaución *f*.

precede [prɪ'siːd] *vt* preceder.

precedence ['presɪdəns] *n*: **to take ~
over** tener prioridad sobre.

precedent ['presɪdənt] *n* precedente
m.

precinct ['priːsɪŋkt] *n* 1. Br (*shopping
area*) zona *f* comercial. 2. Am (*district*)
distrito *m*. ▶ **precincts** *npl* recinto *m*.

precious ['preʃəs] *adj* 1. (*gen*) precioso
(sa). 2. (*memories, possessions*) preciado
(da). 3. (*affected*) afectado(da).

precipice ['presɪpɪs] *n* *lit & fig* precipicio *m*.

precipitate [prɪ'sɪpɪteɪt] *vt* *fml* precipitar.

precise [prɪ'saɪs] *adj* preciso(sa), exac-
to(ta).

precisely [prɪ'saɪslɪ] *adv* 1. (*with accuracy*) exactamente. 2. (*exactly, literally*)
precisamente. 3. (*as confirmation*): **~!**
¡eso es!

precision [prɪ'sɪʒn] *n* precisión *f*.

preclude [prɪ'kluːd] *vt* *fml* evitar,
impedir; (*possibility*) excluir; **to ~ sthg/sb
from doing sthg** impedir que algo/
alguien haga algo.

precocious [prɪ'kəʊʃəs] *adj* precoz.

preconceived [,priːkən'siːvd] *adj* pre-
concebido(da).

precondition [,priːkən'dɪʃn] *n* *fml*: **~
(for)** requisito *m* previo (para).

predator ['predətər] *n* depredador *m*,
-ra *f*; *fig* buitre *m* y *f*.

predecessor ['priːdɪsesər] *n* antecesor *m*, -ra *f*.

predicament [prɪ'dɪkəmənt] *n* apuro
m.

predict [prɪ'dɪkt] *vt* predecir, pronosticar.

predictable [prɪ'dɪktəbl] *adj* 1. (*result
etc*) previsible. 2. (*film, book, person*)
poco original.

prediction [prɪ'dɪkʃn] *n* pronóstico *m*.

predispose [,priːdɪs'pəʊz] *vt*: **to be ~d
to sthg/to do sthg** (*by nature*) estar pre-
dispuesto(ta) a algo/a hacer algo.

predominant [prɪ'dɒmɪnənt] *adj* predominante.

predominantly [prɪ'dɒmɪnəntlɪ] *adv*
fundamentalmente.

preempt [,priː'empt] *vt* (*make ineffective*)
adelantarse a.

preemptive [,priː'emptɪv] *adj* preven-
tivo(va).

preen [priːn] *vt* 1. (*subj: bird*) arreglar
(con el pico). 2. *fig* (*subj: person*): **to ~ o.s.**
acicalarse.

prefab ['priːfæb] *n* *inf* casa *f* prefabri-
cada.

preface ['prefɪs] *n*: **~ (to)** prólogo *m* OR
prefacio *m* (a).

prefect ['priːfekt] *n* Br (*pupil*) delegado *m*, -da *f* de curso.

prefer [prɪ'fɜːr] *vt*: **to ~ sthg (to)** preferir
algo (a); **to ~ to do sthg** preferir hacer
algo.

preferable ['prefrəbl] *adj*: **to be ~ (to)**
ser preferible (a).

preferably ['prefrəblɪ] *adv* preferentemente.

preference ['prefərəns] *n*: **~ (for)** preferencia *f* (por).

preferential [,prefə'renʃl] *adj* preferente.

prefix ['priːfɪks] *n* prefijo *m*.

pregnancy ['pregnənsɪ] *n* embarazo *m*.

pregnant ['pregnənt] *adj* (*carrying
unborn baby*) embarazada.

prehistoric [,priːhɪ'stɒrɪk] *adj* pre-
histórico(ca).

prejudice ['predʒʊdɪs] ◆ *n*: **~ (against)**
prejuicio *m* (contra); **~ in favour of** predisposición *f* a favor de. ◆ *vt* 1. (*bias*): **to
~ sb (in favour of/against)** predisponer a
alguien (a favor de/en contra de).
2. (*harm*) perjudicar.

prejudiced ['predʒʊdɪst] *adj* parcial; **to
be ~ in favour of/against** estar predispuesto a favor de/en contra de.

prejudicial [,predʒʊ'dɪʃl] *adj*: **~ (to)**
perjudicial (para).

preliminary [prɪ'lɪmɪnərɪ] *adj* preliminar.

prelude ['prelju:d] n (event)· ~ **(to)** preludio m (a).

premarital [,pri:'mærɪtl] adj prematrimonial.

premature ['premə,tjʊəʳ] adj prematuro(ra).

premeditated [,pri:'medɪteɪtɪd] adj premeditado(da).

premenstrual syndrome, premenstrual tension [pri:'menstruəl-] n síndrome m premenstrual.

premier ['premjəʳ] ◆ adj primero(ra). ◆ n primer ministro m, primera ministra f.

premiere ['premɪeəʳ] n estreno m.

premise ['premɪs] n premisa f. ▶ **premises** npl local m; **on the ~s** en el local.

premium ['pri:mjəm] n prima f; **at a ~** (above usual value) por encima de su valor; (in great demand) muy solicitado(da).

premium bond n Br boleto numerado emitido por el Estado que autoriza a participar en sorteos mensuales de dinero hasta su amortización.

premonition [,premə'nɪʃn] n premonición f.

preoccupied [pri:'ɒkjupaɪd] adj: ~ **(with)** preocupado(da) (por).

prep [prep] (abbr of **preparation**) n (U) Br inf tarea f, deberes mpl.

prepaid ['pri:peɪd] adj (post paid) porte pagado.

preparation [,prepə'reɪʃn] n (act of preparing) preparación f. ▶ **preparations** npl preparativos mpl; **to make ~s for** hacer los preparativos para.

preparatory [prɪ'pærətrɪ] adj preparatorio(ria), preliminar.

preparatory school n (in UK) colegio de pago para niños de 7 a 12 años; (in US) colegio privado que prepara a sus alumnos para estudios superiores.

prepare [prɪ'peəʳ] ◆ vt preparar. ◆ vi: **to ~ for sthg/to do sthg** prepararse para algo/para hacer algo.

prepared [prɪ'peəd] adj 1. (gen) preparado(da). 2. (willing): **to be ~ to do sthg** estar dispuesto(ta) a hacer algo.

preposition [,prepə'zɪʃn] n preposición f.

preposterous [prɪ'pɒstərəs] adj absurdo(da).

prep school n inf abbr of **preparatory school**.

prerequisite [,pri:'rekwɪzɪt] n: ~ **(for)**

requisito m (para).

prerogative [prɪ'rɒgətɪv] n prerrogativa f.

Presbyterian [,prezbɪ'tɪərɪən] ◆ adj presbiteriano(na). ◆ n presbiteriano m, -na f.

preschool [,pri:'sku:l] ◆ adj preescolar. ◆ n Am parvulario m.

prescribe [prɪ'skraɪb] vt 1. (MED) recetar. 2. (order) ordenar, mandar.

prescription [prɪ'skrɪpʃn] n receta f; **on ~** con receta médica.

presence ['prezns] n presencia f; **to be in sb's ~** OR **in the ~ of sb** estar en presencia de alguien.

presence of mind n aplomo m.

present [adj & n 'preznt, vb prɪ'zent] ◆ adj 1. (current) actual. 2. (in attendance) presente; **to be ~ at sthg** asistir a algo, estar presente en algo. ◆ n 1. (current time): **the ~** el presente; **at ~** actualmente. 2. (LING): ~ **(tense)** (tiempo m) presente m. 3. (gift) regalo m. ◆ vt 1. (gen) presentar; **to ~ sb with sthg, to ~ sthg to sb** (challenge, opportunity) representar algo para alguien; **to ~ sb to sb** presentar a alguien a alguien; **to ~ o.s.** (arrive) presentarse. 2. (give): **to ~ sb with sthg, to ~ sthg to sb** (as present) obsequiar algo a alguien; (at ceremony) entregar algo a alguien. 3. (play etc) representar.

presentable [prɪ'zentəbl] adj presentable; **to make o.s. ~** arreglarse.

presentation [,prezn'teɪʃn] n 1. (gen) presentación f. 2. (ceremony) entrega f. 3. (performance) representación f.

present day n: **the ~** el presente. ▶ **present-day** adj de hoy en día.

presenter [prɪ'zentəʳ] n Br presentador m, -ra f.

presently ['prezntlɪ] adv 1. (soon) dentro de poco. 2. (now) actualmente.

preservation [,prezə'veɪʃn] n preservación f, conservación f.

preservative [prɪ'zɜːvətɪv] n conservante m.

preserve [prɪ'zɜːv] ◆ vt conservar. ◆ n (jam) mermelada f. ▶ **preserves** npl (jam) mermelada f; (vegetables) conserva f.

preset [,pri:'set] (pt & pp preset) vt programar.

president ['prezɪdənt] n presidente m, -ta f.

presidential [,prezɪ'denʃl] adj presidencial.

press [pres] ◆ n 1. (push): **to give sthg a**

~ apretar algo. **2.** (*newspapers, reporters*): **the ~** la prensa. **3.** (*machine*) prensa *f*. ◆ *vt* **1.** (*gen*) apretar; **to ~ sthg against sthg** apretar algo contra algo. **2.** (*grapes, flowers*) prensar. **3.** (*iron*) planchar. **4.** (*urge*): **to ~ sb (to do sthg OR into doing sthg)** presionar a alguien (para que haga algo). **5.** (*pursue - claim*) insistir en. ◆ *vi* **1.** (*gen*): **to ~ (on sthg)** apretar (algo). **2.** (*crowd*): **to ~ forward** empujar hacia adelante. ► **press for** *vt fus* exigir, reclamar. ► **press on** *vi* (*continue*): **to ~ on (with)** proseguir (con).

press agency *n* agencia *f* de prensa.

press conference *n* rueda *f* de prensa.

pressed [prest] *adj*: **to be ~ (for time/money)** andar escaso(sa) (de tiempo/de dinero).

pressing ['presiŋ] *adj* apremiante.

press officer *n* jefe *m*, -fa *f* de prensa.

press release *n* comunicado *m* de prensa.

press-stud *n* Br automático *m*.

press-up *n* Br flexión *f*.

pressure ['preʃə^r] *n* presión *f*; **to put ~ on sb (to do sthg)** presionar a alguien (para que haga algo).

pressure cooker *n* olla *f* a presión.

pressure gauge *n* manómetro *m*.

pressure group *n* grupo *m* de presión.

pressurize, -ise ['preʃəraiz] *vt* **1.** (TECH) presurizar. **2.** Br (*force*): **to ~ sb to do OR into doing sthg** presionar a alguien para que haga algo.

prestige [pre'stiːʒ] *n* prestigio *m*.

presumably [prɪ'zjuːməblɪ] *adv*: **~ you've read it** supongo que los has leído.

presume [prɪ'zjuːm] *vt* suponer; **he is ~d dead** se supone que está muerto.

presumption [prɪ'zʌmpʃn] *n* **1.** (*assumption*) suposición *f*; (*of innocence*) presunción *f*. **2.** (U) (*audacity*) presunción *f*, osadía *f*.

presumptuous [prɪ'zʌmptʃuəs] *adj* presuntuoso(sa).

pretence, pretense Am [prɪ'tens] *n* fingimiento *m*, simulación *f*; **to make a ~ of doing sthg** fingir hacer algo; **under false ~s** con engaños, con falsos pretextos.

pretend [prɪ'tend] ◆ *vt*: **to ~ to do sthg** fingir hacer algo. ◆ *vi* fingir, simular.

pretense Am = **pretence**.

pretension [prɪ'tenʃn] *n* pretensión *f*.

pretentious [prɪ'tenʃəs] *adj* pretencioso(sa).

pretext ['priːtekst] *n* pretexto *m*; **on OR under the ~ that .../of doing sthg** con el pretexto de que .../de estar haciendo algo.

pretty ['prɪtɪ] ◆ *adj* bonito(ta). ◆ *adv* bastante; **~ much** más o menos; **~ well** (*almost*) casi.

prevail [prɪ'veɪl] *vi* **1.** (*be widespread*) predominar, imperar. **2.** (*triumph*): **to ~ (over)** prevalecer (sobre). **3.** (*persuade*): **to ~ on OR upon sb to do sthg** persuadir a alguien para que haga algo.

prevailing [prɪ'veɪlɪŋ] *adj* predominante.

prevalent ['prevələnt] *adj* predominante.

prevent [prɪ'vent] *vt* impedir; (*event, illness, accident*) evitar; **to ~ sthg (from) happening** impedir OR evitar que algo pase; **to ~ sb (from) doing sthg** impedir a alguien que haga algo.

preventive [prɪ'ventɪv] *adj* preventivo (va).

preview ['priːvjuː] *n* (*of film, exhibition*) preestreno *m*.

previous ['priːvjəs] *adj* previo(via), anterior; **the ~ week/president** la semana/el presidente anterior.

previously ['priːvjəslɪ] *adv* **1.** (*formerly*) anteriormente. **2.** (*before*): **two years ~** dos años antes.

prewar [ˌpriːˈwɔːr] *adj* de preguerra.

prey [preɪ] *n* presa *f*, víctima *f*. ► **prey on** *vt fus* **1.** (*live off*) cazar, alimentarse de. **2.** (*trouble*): **to ~ on sb's mind** atormentar a alguien.

price [prais] ◆ *n lit & fig* precio *m*; **to go up/down in ~** subir/bajar de precio; **at any ~** a toda costa, a cualquier precio; **at a ~** a un alto precio. ◆ *vt* poner precio a.

priceless ['praislis] *adj lit & fig* que no tiene precio, inestimable.

price list *n* lista *f* OR tarifa *f* de precios.

price tag *n* (*label*) etiqueta *f* (del precio).

pricey ['praisi] (*compar* **-ier**, *superl* **-iest**) *adj* caro(ra).

prick [prɪk] ◆ *n* **1.** (*wound*) pinchazo *m*. **2.** *vulg* (*penis*) polla *f*. **3.** *vulg* (*stupid person*) gilipollas *m y f inv*. ◆ *vt* **1.** (*gen*) pinchar. **2.** (*sting*) picar. ► **prick up** *vt fus*: **to ~ up one's ears** (*subj: animal*) levantar las orejas; (*subj: person*) aguzar el oído.

prickle ['prɪkl] ◆ *n* **1.** (*thorn*) espina *f*. **2.** (*sensation*) comezón *f*. ◆ *vi* picar.

prickly ['prɪklɪ] adj **1.** (thorny) espinoso (sa). **2.** fig (touchy) susceptible, enojadizo(za).

prickly heat n (U) sarpullido por causa del calor.

pride [praɪd] ◆ n orgullo m; **to take ~ in sthg/in doing sthg** enorgullecerse de algo/de hacer algo. ◆ vt: **to ~ o.s. on sthg** enorgullecerse de algo.

priest [priːst] n sacerdote m.

priestess ['priːstɪs] n sacerdotisa f.

priesthood ['priːsthʊd] n **1.** (position, office): **the ~** el sacerdocio. **2.** (priests collectively): **the ~** el clero.

prig [prɪg] n mojigato m, -ta f.

prim [prɪm] adj remilgado(da).

primarily ['praɪmərɪlɪ] adv principalmente.

primary ['praɪmərɪ] ◆ adj **1.** (main) principal. **2.** (SCH) primario(ria). ◆ n Am (POL) primaria f.

primary school n escuela f primaria.

primate ['praɪmeɪt] n **1.** (ZOOL) primate m. **2.** (RELIG) primado m.

prime [praɪm] ◆ adj **1.** (main) primero (ra), principal. **2.** (excellent) excelente; (quality) primero(ra). ◆ n: **in one's ~** en la flor de la vida. ◆ vt **1.** (inform): **to ~ sb about sthg** preparar a alguien a fondo para algo. **2.** (surface) preparar. **3.** (gun, pump) cebar.

prime minister n primer ministro m, primera ministra f.

primer ['praɪməʳ] n **1.** (paint) imprimación f. **2.** (textbook) cartilla f.

primeval [praɪ'miːvl] adj (ancient) primitivo(va).

primitive ['prɪmɪtɪv] adj (tribe, species etc) primitivo(va); (accommodation, sense of humour) rudimentario(ria).

primrose ['prɪmrəʊz] n primavera f, prímula f.

Primus stove® ['praɪməs-] n hornillo m de camping.

prince [prɪns] n príncipe m.

princess [prɪn'ses] n princesa f.

principal ['prɪnsəpl] ◆ adj principal. ◆ n (SCH) director m, -ra f.

principle ['prɪnsəpl] n **1.** (gen) principio m. **2.** (U) (integrity) principios mpl; **on ~, as a matter of ~** por principio. ▶ **in principle** adv en principio.

print [prɪnt] ◆ n **1.** (U) (type) caracteres mpl (de imprenta); **in ~** (available) disponible; (in printed characters) en letra impresa; **to be out of ~** estar agotado. **2.** (piece of artwork) grabado m. **3.** (reproduction) reproducción f. **4.** (photograph)

fotografía f. **5.** (fabric) estampado m. **6.** (mark - of foot etc) huella f. ◆ vt **1.** (TYPO) imprimir. **2.** (produce by printing - book, newspaper) tirar. **3.** (publish) publicar. **4.** (decorate - cloth etc) estampar. **5.** (write in block letters) escribir con letra de imprenta. ◆ vi imprimir. ▶ **print out** vt sep (COMPUT) imprimir.

printer ['prɪntəʳ] n **1.** (person) impresor m, -ra f; (firm) imprenta f. **2.** (machine) impresora f.

printing ['prɪntɪŋ] n **1.** (U) (act of printing) impresión f. **2.** (trade) imprenta f.

printout ['prɪntaʊt] n (COMPUT) salida f de impresora.

prior ['praɪəʳ] ◆ adj **1.** (previous) anterior, previo(via). **2.** (more important) preferente. ◆ n (monk) prior m. ▶ **prior to** prep antes de.

priority [praɪ'ɒrətɪ] n prioridad f; **to have OR take ~ (over)** tener prioridad (sobre).

prise [praɪz] vt: **to ~ sthg open/away** abrir/separar algo haciendo palanca.

prison ['prɪzn] n cárcel f, prisión f.

prisoner ['prɪznəʳ] n **1.** (convict) preso m, -sa f. **2.** (captive) prisionero m, -ra f.

prisoner of war (pl prisoners of war) n prisionero m, -ra f de guerra.

privacy [Br 'prɪvəsɪ, Am 'praɪvəsɪ] n intimidad f.

private ['praɪvɪt] ◆ adj **1.** (gen) privado (da); (class) particular; (telephone call, belongings) personal. **2.** (thoughts, plans) secreto(ta). **3.** (secluded) retirado(da). **4.** (unsociable - person) reservado(da). ◆ n **1.** (soldier) soldado m raso. **2. (to do sthg) in ~** (in secret) (hacer algo) en privado.

private enterprise n (U) empresa f privada.

private eye n detective privado m, -da f.

privately ['praɪvɪtlɪ] adv **1.** (not by the state) de forma privada; **~ owned** de propiedad privada. **2.** (confidentially) en privado.

private property n propiedad f privada.

private school n colegio m privado.

privatize, -ise ['praɪvɪtaɪz] vt privatizar.

privet ['prɪvɪt] n alheña f.

privilege ['prɪvɪlɪdʒ] n privilegio m.

privy ['prɪvɪ] adj: **to be ~ to sthg** estar enterado(da) de algo.

Privy Council n Br: **the ~** en Gran Bretaña, consejo privado que asesora al monarca.

prize [praɪz] ◆ *adj* de primera. ◆ *n* premio *m*. ◆ *vt*: **to be ~d** ser apreciado(da).
prize-giving [-ˌgɪvɪŋ] *n* Br entrega *f* de premios.
prizewinner ['praɪzˌwɪnəʳ] *n* premiado *m*, -da *f*.
pro [prəʊ] (*pl* **-s**) *n* **1.** *inf* (*professional*) profesional *m* y *f*. **2.** (*advantage*): **the ~s and cons** los pros y los contras.
probability [ˌprɒbə'bɪlətɪ] *n* probabilidad *f*.
probable ['prɒbəbl] *adj* probable.
probably ['prɒbəblɪ] *adv* probablemente.
probation [prə'beɪʃn] *n* **1.** (*of prisoner*) libertad *f* condicional; **to put sb on ~** poner a alguien en libertad condicional. **2.** (*trial period*) periodo *m* de prueba; **to be on ~** estar en periodo de prueba.
probe [prəʊb] ◆ *n* **1.** (*investigation*): **~ (into)** investigación *f* (sobre). **2.** (MED & SPACE) sonda *f*. ◆ *vt* **1.** (*investigate*) investigar. **2.** (*with tool*) sondar; (*with finger, stick*) hurgar en.
problem ['prɒbləm] *n* problema *m*; **no ~!** *inf* ¡por supuesto!, ¡desde luego!
procedure [prə'siːdʒəʳ] *n* procedimiento *m*.
proceed [*vb* prə'siːd, *npl* 'prəʊsiːdz] *vi* **1.** (*do subsequently*): **to ~ to do sthg** proceder a hacer algo. **2.** (*continue*): **to ~ (with sthg)** proseguir (con algo). **3.** *fml* (*advance*) avanzar. ▶ **proceeds** *npl* ganancias *fpl*, beneficios *mpl*.
proceedings [prə'siːdɪŋz] *npl* **1.** (*series of events*) acto *m*. **2.** (*legal action*) proceso *m*.
process ['prəʊses] ◆ *n* proceso *m*; **in the ~** en el intento; **to be in the ~ of doing sthg** estar en vías de hacer algo. ◆ *vt* **1.** (gen & COMPUT) procesar. **2.** (*application*) tramitar.
processing ['prəʊsesɪŋ] *n* **1.** (gen & COMPUT) procesamiento *m*. **2.** (*of applications etc*) tramitación *f*.
procession [prə'seʃn] *n* desfile *m*; (*religious*) procesión *f*.
proclaim [prə'kleɪm] *vt* (gen) proclamar; (*law*) promulgar.
procrastinate [prə'kræstɪneɪt] *vi* andarse con dilaciones.
procure [prə'kjʊəʳ] *vt* (*obtain*) obtener.
prod [prɒd] *vt* (*push, poke*) dar golpecitos a.
prodigal ['prɒdɪgl] *adj* (*son, daughter*) pródigo(ga).
prodigy ['prɒdɪdʒɪ] *n* (*person*) prodigio *m*.

produce [*n* 'prɒdjuːs, *vb* prə'djuːs] ◆ *n* (U) productos *mpl* agrícolas. ◆ *vt* **1.** (gen) producir; (*offspring, flowers*) engendrar. **2.** (*bring out*) mostrar, enseñar. **3.** (THEATRE) poner en escena.
producer [prə'djuːsəʳ] *n* **1.** (gen) productor *m*, -ra *f*. **2.** (THEATRE) director *m*, -ra *f* de escena.
product ['prɒdʌkt] *n* producto *m*.
production [prə'dʌkʃn] *n* **1.** (gen) producción *f*. **2.** (U) (THEATRE) puesta *f* en escena.
production line *n* cadena *f* de producción.
productive [prə'dʌktɪv] *adj* **1.** (*efficient*) productivo(va). **2.** (*rewarding*) provechoso(sa).
productivity [ˌprɒdʌk'tɪvətɪ] *n* productividad *f*.
profane [prə'feɪn] *adj* (*disrespectful*) obsceno(na).
profession [prə'feʃn] *n* profesión *f*; **by ~** de profesión.
professional [prə'feʃənl] ◆ *adj* profesional. ◆ *n* profesional *m* y *f*.
professor [prə'fesəʳ] *n* **1.** Br (*head of department*) catedrático *m*, -ca *f*. **2.** Am & Can (*lecturer*) profesor *m*, -ra *f* (de universidad).
proficiency [prə'fɪʃənsɪ] *n*: **~ (in)** competencia *f* (en).
profile ['prəʊfaɪl] *n* perfil *m*; **high ~** notoriedad *f*.
profit ['prɒfɪt] ◆ *n* **1.** (*financial gain*) beneficio *m*, ganancia *f*; **to make a ~** sacar un beneficio. **2.** (*advantage*) provecho *m*. ◆ *vi*: **to ~ (from OR by)** sacar provecho (de).
profitability [ˌprɒfɪtə'bɪlətɪ] *n* rentabilidad *f*.
profitable ['prɒfɪtəbl] *adj* **1.** (*making a profit*) rentable. **2.** (*beneficial*) provechoso(sa).
profiteering [ˌprɒfɪ'tɪərɪŋ] *n* especulación *f*.
profound [prə'faʊnd] *adj* profundo (da).
profusely [prə'fjuːslɪ] *adv* profusamente.
profusion [prə'fjuːʒn] *n* profusión *f*.
progeny ['prɒdʒənɪ] *n* progenie *f*.
prognosis [prɒg'nəʊsɪs] (*pl* **-noses** [-'nəʊsiːz]) *n* pronóstico *m*.
program ['prəʊgræm] (*pt* & *pp* **-med** OR **-ed**, *cont* **-ming** OR **-ing**) ◆ *n* **1.** (COMPUT) programa *m*. **2.** Am = **programme**. ◆ *vt* **1.** (COMPUT) programar. **2.** Am = **pro-**

gramme. ♦ *vi* (COMPUT) programar.

programer Am = **programmer**.

programme Br, **program** Am ['prəʊgræm] ♦ *n* programa *m*. ♦ *vt*: **to ~ sth (to do sth)** programar algo (para que haga algo).

programmer Br, **programer** Am ['prəʊgræmər] *n* (COMPUT) programador *m*, -ra *f*.

programming ['prəʊgræmɪŋ] *n* programación *f*.

progress [*n* 'prəʊgres, *vb* prə'gres] ♦ *n* 1. (*gen*) progreso *m*; **in ~** en curso; **to make ~** hacer progresos. 2. (*forward movement*) avance *m*. ♦ *vi* 1. (*gen*) progresar; (*pupil etc*) hacer progresos. 2. (*move forward*) avanzar.

progressive [prə'gresɪv] *adj* 1. (*enlightened*) progresista. 2. (*gradual*) progresivo(va).

prohibit [prə'hɪbɪt] *vt* prohibir; **to ~ sb from doing sth** prohibirle a alguien hacer algo.

project [*n* 'prɒdʒekt, *vb* prə'dʒekt] ♦ *n* 1. (*plan, idea*) proyecto *m*. 2. (SCH): **~ (on)** estudio *m* OR trabajo *m* (sobre). ♦ *vt* 1. (*gen*) proyectar. 2. (*estimate - statistic, costs*) estimar. 3. (*company, person*) dar una imagen de; (*image*) proyectar. ♦ *vi* proyectarse.

projectile [prə'dʒektaɪl] *n* proyectil *m*.

projection [prə'dʒekʃn] *n* 1. (*gen*) proyección *f*. 2. (*protrusion*) saliente *m*.

projector [prə'dʒektər] *n* proyector *m*.

proletariat [ˌprəʊlɪ'teərɪət] *n* proletariado *m*.

prolific [prə'lɪfɪk] *adj* prolífico(ca).

prologue, prolog Am ['prəʊlɒg] *n* prólogo *m*.

prolong [prə'lɒŋ] *vt* prolongar.

prom [prɒm] *n* 1. *abbr of* **promenade concert**. 2. (*abbr of* **promenade**) Br *inf* (*road by sea*) paseo *m* marítimo. 3. Am (*ball*) baile *m* de gala (en la escuela).

promenade [ˌprɒmə'nɑːd] *n* Br (*by sea*) paseo *m* marítimo.

promenade concert *n* Br concierto sinfónico en donde parte del público está de pie.

prominent ['prɒmɪnənt] *adj* 1. (*important*) destacado(da), importante. 2. (*noticeable*) prominente.

promiscuous [prɒ'mɪskjʊəs] *adj* promiscuo(cua).

promise ['prɒmɪs] ♦ *n* promesa *f*. ♦ *vt*: **to ~ (to do sth)** prometer (hacer algo); **to ~ sb sth** prometer a alguien algo. ♦ *vi*: **I ~** te lo prometo.

promising ['prɒmɪsɪŋ] *adj* prometedor (ra).

promontory ['prɒməntrɪ] *n* promontorio *m*.

promote [prə'məʊt] *vt* 1. (*foster*) fomentar, promover. 2. (*push, advertise*) promocionar. 3. (*in job*): **to ~ sb (to sth)** ascender a alguien (a algo). 4. (SPORT): **to be ~d** subir.

promoter [prə'məʊtər] *n* 1. (*organizer*) organizador *m*, -ra *f*. 2. (*supporter*) promotor *m*, -ra *f*.

promotion [prə'məʊʃn] *n* 1. (*in job*) ascenso *m*. 2. (*advertising*) promoción *f*. 3. (*campaign*) campaña *f* de promoción.

prompt [prɒmpt] ♦ *adj* rápido(da). ♦ *adv* en punto. ♦ *vt* 1. (*motivate*): **to ~ sb (to do sth)** inducir OR impulsar a alguien (a hacer algo). 2. (THEATRE) apuntar. ♦ *n* (THEATRE) (*line*) apunte *m*.

promptly ['prɒmptlɪ] *adv* 1. (*reply, react, pay*) inmediatamente, rápidamente. 2. (*arrive, leave*) puntualmente.

prone [prəʊn] *adj* 1. (*susceptible*): **to be ~ to sth/to do sth** ser propenso(sa) a algo/a hacer algo. 2. (*lying flat*) boca abajo.

prong [prɒŋ] *n* diente *m*, punta *f*.

pronoun ['prəʊnaʊn] *n* pronombre *m*.

pronounce [prə'naʊns] ♦ *vt* 1. (*gen*) pronunciar. 2. (*declare*) declarar. ♦ *vi*: **to ~ on sth** pronunciarse sobre algo.

pronounced [prə'naʊnst] *adj* pronunciado(da), marcado(da).

pronouncement [prə'naʊnsmənt] *n* declaración *f*.

pronunciation [prəˌnʌnsɪ'eɪʃn] *n* pronunciación *f*.

proof [pruːf] ♦ *n* 1. (*gen & TYPO*) prueba *f*. 2. (*of alcohol*): **to be 10% ~** tener 10 grados. ♦ *adj* (*secure*): **~ against** a prueba de.

prop [prɒp] ♦ *n* 1. (*physical support*) puntal *m*, apoyo *m*. 2. *fig* (*supporting thing, person*) sostén *m*. ♦ *vt*: **to ~ sth on OR against sth** apoyar algo contra algo. ▶ **props** *npl* accesorios *mpl*. ▶ **prop up** *vt sep* 1. (*physically support*) apuntalar. 2. *fig* (*sustain*) apoyar.

propaganda [ˌprɒpə'gændə] *n* propaganda *f*.

propel [prə'pel] *vt* propulsar, impulsar.

propeller [prə'pelər] *n* hélice *f*.

propelling pencil [prə'pelɪŋ-] *n* Br portaminas *m inv*.

propensity [prə'pensətɪ] *n fml*: **~ (for OR to sth)** propensión *f* (a algo).

proper ['prɒpər] *adj* 1. (*real*) de verdad. 2. (*correct - gen*) correcto(ta).

(- *time, place, equipment*) adecuado(da).

properly ['prɒpəlɪ] *adv* **1.** (*satisfactorily, correctly*) bien. **2.** (*decently*) correctamente.

proper noun *n* nombre *m* propio.

property ['prɒpətɪ] *n* **1.** (*gen*) propiedad *f*. **2.** (*estate*) finca *f*. **3.** *fml* (*house*) inmueble *m*.

property owner *n* propietario *m*, -ria *f* de un inmueble.

prophecy ['prɒfɪsɪ] *n* profecía *f*.

prophesy ['prɒfɪsaɪ] *vt* profetizar.

prophet ['prɒfɪt] *n* profeta *m* y *f*.

proportion [prə'pɔːʃn] *n* **1.** (*part*) parte *f*. **2.** (*ratio, comparison*) proporción *f*. **3.** (*correct relationship*): **out of ~** desproporcionado(da); **sense of ~** *fig* sentido *m* de la medida.

proportional [prə'pɔːʃənl] *adj*: **~ (to)** proporcional (a).

proportional representation *n* representación *f* proporcional.

proportionate [prə'pɔːʃnət] *adj*: **~ (to)** proporcional (a).

proposal [prə'pəuzl] *n* **1.** (*plan, suggestion*) propuesta *f*. **2.** (*offer of marriage*) proposición *f*.

propose [prə'pəuz] ♦ *vt* **1.** (*suggest*) proponer; (*motion*) presentar. **2.** (*intend*): **to ~ doing** OR **to do sthg** tener la intención de hacer algo. ♦ *vi* (*make offer of marriage*) declararse; **to ~ to sb** pedir la mano de alguien.

proposition [ˌprɒpə'zɪʃn] *n* (*suggestion*) propuesta *f*.

proprietor [prə'praɪətəʳ] *n* propietario *m*, -ria *f*.

propriety [prə'praɪətɪ] *n* (U) *fml* **1.** (*moral correctness*) propiedad *f*. **2.** (*rightness*) conveniencia *f*, oportunidad *f*.

pro rata [-'rɑːtə] *adj* & *adv* a prorrata.

prose [prəuz] *n* **1.** (U) (LITERATURE) prosa *f*. **2.** (SCH) traducción *f* inversa.

prosecute ['prɒsɪkjuːt] ♦ *vt* procesar, enjuiciar. ♦ *vi* **1.** (*bring a charge*) entablar una acción judicial. **2.** (*represent in court*) representar al demandante.

prosecution [ˌprɒsɪ'kjuːʃn] *n* **1.** (*gen*) procesamiento *m*. **2.** (*lawyers*): **the ~** la acusación.

prosecutor ['prɒsɪkjuːtəʳ] *n* fiscal *m* y *f*.

prospect [*n* 'prɒspekt, *vb* prə'spekt] ♦ *n* **1.** (*gen*) perspectiva *f*. **2.** (*possibility*) posibilidad *f*. ♦ *vi*: **to ~ (for)** hacer prospecciones (de). ▶ **prospects** *npl*: **~s (for)** perspectivas *fpl* (de).

prospecting [prə'spektɪŋ] *n* (U) prospecciones *fpl*.

prospective [prə'spektɪv] *adj* posible.

prospector [prə'spektəʳ] *n* prospector *m*, -ra *f*.

prospectus [prə'spektəs] (*pl* **-es**) *n* prospecto *m*, folleto *m* informativo.

prosper ['prɒspəʳ] *vi* prosperar.

prosperity [prɒ'sperətɪ] *n* prosperidad *f*.

prosperous ['prɒspərəs] *adj* próspero (ra).

prostitute ['prɒstɪtjuːt] *n* prostituta *f*.

prostrate ['prɒstreɪt] *adj* postrado (da).

protagonist [prə'tægənɪst] *n* **1.** *fml* (*supporter*) partidario *m*, -ria *f*. **2.** (*main character*) protagonista *m* y *f*.

protect [prə'tekt] *vt*: **to ~ sthg/sb (against/from)** proteger algo/a alguien (contra/de).

protection [prə'tekʃn] *n*: **~ (against/from)** protección *f* (contra/de).

protective [prə'tektɪv] *adj* protector (ra).

protégé ['prɒteʒeɪ] *n* protegido *m*.

protein ['prəutiːn] *n* proteína *f*.

protest [*n* 'prəutest, *vb* prə'test] ♦ *n* protesta *f*. ♦ *vt* **1.** (*state*) manifestar, aseverar. **2.** Am (*oppose*) protestar en contra de. ♦ *vi*: **to ~ (about/against/at)** protestar (por/en contra de/por).

Protestant ['prɒtɪstənt] ♦ *adj* protestante. ♦ *n* protestante *m* y *f*.

protester [prə'testəʳ] *n* manifestante *m* y *f*.

protest march *n* manifestación *f*.

protocol ['prəutəkɒl] *n* protocolo *m*.

prototype ['prəutətaɪp] *n* prototipo *m*.

protracted [prə'træktɪd] *adj* prolongado(da).

protrude [prə'truːd] *vi*: **to ~ (from)** sobresalir (de).

protuberance [prə'tjuːbərəns] *n* protuberancia *f*.

proud [praud] *adj* **1.** (*gen*): **~ (of)** orgulloso(sa) (de). **2.** *pej* (*arrogant*) soberbio (bia), arrogante.

prove [pruːv] (*pp* **-d** OR **proven**) *vt* **1.** (*show to be true*) probar, demostrar. **2.** (*show oneself to be*): **to ~ (to be) sthg** demostrar ser algo; **to ~ o.s.** demostrar (uno) sus cualidades.

proven ['pruːvn, 'prəuvn] ♦ *pp* → **prove**. ♦ *adj* probado(da).

proverb ['prɒvɜːb] *n* refrán *m*.

provide [prə'vaɪd] *vt* proporcionar, proveer; **to ~ sb with sthg** proporcionar a alguien algo; **to ~ sthg for sb** ofrecer algo a alguien. ▶ **provide for** vt fus **1.** (support) mantener. **2.** fml (make arrangements for) prevenir, tomar medidas para.

provided [prə'vaɪdɪd] ▶ **provided (that)** conj con tal (de) que.

providing [prə'vaɪdɪŋ] ▶ **providing (that)** conj = **provided**.

province ['prɒvɪns] n **1.** (part of country) provincia f. **2.** (speciality) campo m, competencia f.

provincial [prə'vɪnʃl] adj **1.** (of a province) provincial. **2.** pej (narrow-minded) provinciano(na).

provision [prə'vɪʒn] n **1.** (gen) suministro m. **2.** (U) (arrangement): **to make ~ for** (eventuality, future) tomar medidas para. **3.** (in agreement, law) disposición f. ▶ **provisions** npl (supplies) víveres mpl.

provisional [prə'vɪʒənl] adj provisional.

proviso [prə'vaɪzəʊ] (pl -s) n condición f; **with the ~ that ...** con la condición de que ...

provocative [prə'vɒkətɪv] adj **1.** (controversial) provocador(ra). **2.** (sexy) provocativo(va).

provoke [prə'vəʊk] vt provocar; **to ~ sb to do sthg** provocar a alguien a que haga algo.

prow [praʊ] n proa f.

prowess ['praʊɪs] n fml proezas fpl.

prowl [praʊl] ♦ n: **on the ~** merodeando. ♦ vt merodear por. ♦ vi merodear.

prowler ['praʊlə^r] n merodeador m, -ra f.

proxy ['prɒksɪ] n: **by ~** por poderes.

prudent ['pruːdnt] adj prudente.

prudish ['pruːdɪʃ] adj mojigato(ta).

prune [pruːn] ♦ n (fruit) ciruela f pasa. ♦ vt podar.

pry [praɪ] vi fisgonear; **to ~ into sthg** entrometerse en algo.

PS (abbr of postscript) n P.D.

psalm [sɑːm] n salmo m.

pseudonym ['sjuːdənɪm] n seudónimo m.

psyche ['saɪkɪ] n psique f.

psychiatric [,saɪkɪ'ætrɪk] adj psiquiátrico(ca).

psychiatrist [saɪ'kaɪətrɪst] n psiquiatra m y f.

psychiatry [saɪ'kaɪətrɪ] n psiquiatría f.

psychic ['saɪkɪk] adj **1.** (clairvoyant) clarividente. **2.** (mental) psíquico(ca).

psychoanalysis [,saɪkəʊə'næləsɪs] n psicoanálisis m inv.

psychoanalyst [,saɪkəʊ'ænəlɪst] n psicoanalista m y f.

psychological [,saɪkə'lɒdʒɪkl] adj psicológico(ca).

psychologist [saɪ'kɒlədʒɪst] n psicólogo m, -ga f.

psychology [saɪ'kɒlədʒɪ] n psicología f.

psychopath ['saɪkəpæθ] n psicópata m y f.

psychotic [saɪ'kɒtɪk] ♦ adj psicótico (ca). ♦ n psicótico m, -ca f.

pt 1. abbr of **pint**. **2.** abbr of **point**.

PTO (abbr of please turn over) sigue.

pub [pʌb] (abbr of public house) n pub m (británico).

puberty ['pjuːbətɪ] n pubertad f.

pubic ['pjuːbɪk] adj púbico(ca).

public ['pʌblɪk] ♦ adj público(ca). ♦ n público m; **in ~** en público; **the ~** el gran público.

public-address system n sistema m de megafonía.

publican ['pʌblɪkən] n Br patrón m, -ona f en un 'pub'.

publication [,pʌblɪ'keɪʃn] n publicación f.

public bar n Br en ciertos pubs y hoteles, bar de sencilla decoración con precios más bajos que los del 'saloon bar'.

public company n sociedad f anónima (con cotización en Bolsa).

public convenience n Br aseos mpl públicos.

public holiday n fiesta f nacional.

public house n Br fml pub m (británico).

publicity [pʌb'lɪsɪtɪ] n publicidad f.

publicize, -ise ['pʌblɪsaɪz] vt divulgar.

public limited company n sociedad f anónima (con cotización en Bolsa).

public opinion n (U) opinión f pública.

public prosecutor n fiscal m y f del Estado.

public relations ♦ n (U) relaciones fpl públicas. ♦ npl relaciones fpl públicas.

public school n **1.** Br (private school) colegio m privado. **2.** Am (state school) escuela f pública.

public-spirited adj con sentido cívico.

public transport n transporte m público.

publish ['pʌblɪʃ] vt **1.** (gen) publicar. **2.** (make known) hacer público(ca).

publisher ['pʌblɪʃər] n (person) editor m, -ra f; (firm) editorial f.

publishing ['pʌblɪʃɪŋ] n (U) industria f editorial.

pub lunch n almuerzo servido en un 'pub'.

pucker ['pʌkər] vt fruncir.

pudding ['pudɪŋ] n 1. (sweet) pudín m; (savoury) pastel m. 2. (U) Br (course) postre m.

puddle ['pʌdl] n charco m.

Puerto Rico [,pwɜːtəu'riːkəu] n Puerto Rico.

puff [pʌf] ◆ n 1. (of cigarette, pipe) calada f. 2. (gasp) jadeo m. 3. (of air) soplo m; (of smoke) bocanada f. ◆ vt dar caladas a. ◆ vi 1. (smoke): **to ~ at** OR **on** dar caladas a. 2. (pant) jadear. ▶ **puff out** vt sep (cheeks, chest) hinchar; (feathers) ahuecar.

puffed [pʌft] adj (swollen): **~ (up)** hinchado(da).

puffin ['pʌfɪn] n frailecillo m.

puff pastry, puff paste Am n hojaldre m.

puffy ['pʌfɪ] adj hinchado(da).

pugnacious [pʌg'neɪʃəs] adj fml pugnaz.

pull [pul] ◆ vt 1. (gen) tirar de; (trigger) apretar. 2. (tooth, cork) sacar, extraer. 3. (muscle) sufrir un tirón en. 4. (attract) atraer. 5. (gun) sacar y apuntar. ◆ vi tirar. ◆ n 1. (tug with hand) tirón m. 2. (U) (influence) influencia f. ▶ **pull apart** vt sep (machine etc) desmontar. ▶ **pull at** vt fus dar tirones de. ▶ **pull away** vi (from roadside) alejarse (de la acera). ▶ **pull down** vt sep (building) derribar. ▶ **pull in** vi (train) pararse (en el andén). ▶ **pull off** vt sep (succeed in) conseguir llevar a cabo. ▶ **pull out** ◆ vt sep retirar. ◆ vi 1. (vehicle) alejarse (de la acera). 2. (withdraw) retirarse. ▶ **pull over** vi (AUT) hacerse a un lado. ▶ **pull through** vi recobrarse. ▶ **pull together** vt sep: **to ~ o.s. together** calmarse, serenarse. ▶ **pull up** ◆ vt sep (move closer) acercar. ◆ vi parar, detenerse.

pulley ['pulɪ] (pl pulleys) n polea f.

pullover ['pul,əuvər] n jersey m.

pulp [pʌlp] n 1. (soft mass) papilla f. 2. (of fruit) pulpa f. 3. (of wood) pasta f de papel.

pulpit ['pulpɪt] n púlpito m.

pulsate [pʌl'seɪt] vi palpitar.

pulse [pʌls] ◆ n 1. (in body) pulso m. 2. (TECH) impulso m. ◆ vi latir. ▶ **pulses** npl (food) legumbres fpl.

puma ['pjuːmə] (pl inv OR -s) n puma m.

pumice (stone) ['pʌmɪs-] n piedra f pómez.

pummel ['pʌml] vt aporrear.

pump [pʌmp] ◆ n 1. (machine) bomba f. 2. (for petrol) surtidor m. ◆ vt (convey by pumping) bombear. ▶ **pumps** npl (shoes) zapatillas fpl de tenis.

pumpkin ['pʌmpkɪn] n calabaza f.

pun [pʌn] n juego m de palabras.

punch [pʌntʃ] ◆ n 1. (blow) puñetazo m. 2. (tool - for leather etc) punzón m; (- for tickets) máquina f para picar billetes. 3. (drink) ponche m. ◆ vt 1. (hit) dar un puñetazo a. 2. (ticket) picar. 3. (hole) perforar.

Punch-and-Judy show [-'dʒuːdɪ-] n teatro de guiñol para niños con personajes arquetípicos y representado normalmente en la playa.

punch(ed) card [pʌntʃ(t)-] n tarjeta f perforada.

punch line n remate m (de un chiste).

punch-up n Br inf pelea f.

punchy ['pʌntʃɪ] adj inf efectista, resultón(ona).

punctual ['pʌŋktʃuəl] adj puntual.

punctuation [,pʌŋktʃu'eɪʃn] n puntuación f.

punctuation mark n signo m de puntuación.

puncture ['pʌŋktʃər] ◆ n pinchazo m; (in skin) punción f. ◆ vt pinchar.

pundit ['pʌndɪt] n experto m, -ta f.

pungent ['pʌndʒənt] adj (strong-smelling) penetrante, fuerte.

punish ['pʌnɪʃ] vt: **to ~ sb (for sthg/for doing sthg)** castigar a alguien (por algo/por haber hecho algo).

punishing ['pʌnɪʃɪŋ] adj penoso(sa).

punishment ['pʌnɪʃmənt] n (for crime) castigo m.

punk [pʌŋk] ◆ adj punk. ◆ n 1. (music): **~ (rock)** punk m. 2. (person): **~ (rocker)** punki m y f. 3. Am inf (lout) gamberro m.

punt [pʌnt] n batea f.

punter ['pʌntər] n Br 1. (gambler) apostante m y f. 2. inf (customer) cliente m, -ta f, parroquiano m, -na f.

puny ['pjuːnɪ] adj (person, limbs) enclenque, raquítico(ca); (effort) penoso(sa), lamentable.

pup [pʌp] n 1. (young dog) cachorro m. 2. (young seal, otter) cría f.

pupil ['pjuːpl] n 1. (student) alumno m, -na f. 2. (follower) pupilo m, -la f. 3. (of eye) pupila f.

puppet ['pʌpɪt] n lit & fig títere m.

puppy ['pʌpɪ] n cachorro m, perrito m.

purchase ['pɜːtʃəs] *fml* ◆ *n* compra *f*, adquisición *f*. ◆ *vt* comprar, adquirir.

purchaser ['pɜːtʃəsər] *n* comprador *m*, -ra *f*.

purchasing power ['pɜːtʃəsɪŋ-] *n* poder *m* adquisitivo.

pure [pjʊər] *adj* puro(ra).

puree ['pjʊəreɪ] *n* puré *m*.

purely ['pjʊəlɪ] *adv* puramente.

purge [pɜːdʒ] ◆ *n* (POL) purga *f*. ◆ *vt*: to ~ sthg (of) purgar algo (de).

purify ['pjʊərɪfaɪ] *vt* purificar.

purist ['pjʊərɪst] *n* purista *m y f*.

puritan ['pjʊərɪtən] ◆ *adj* puritano (na). ◆ *n* puritano *m*, -na *f*.

purity ['pjʊərətɪ] *n* pureza *f*.

purl [pɜːl] *n* (U) punto *m* del revés.

purple ['pɜːpl] *adj* morado(da).

purport [pə'pɔːt] *vi fml*: to ~ to do/be sthg pretender hacer/ser algo.

purpose ['pɜːpəs] *n* (gen) propósito *m*; **it serves no ~** carece de sentido; **to no ~** en vano. ► **on purpose** *adv* a propósito, adrede.

purposeful ['pɜːpəsfʊl] *adj* resuelto (ta).

purr [pɜːr] *vi* 1. (cat, person) ronronear. 2. (engine, machine) zumbar.

purse [pɜːs] ◆ *n* 1. (for money) monedero *m*. 2. Am (handbag) bolso *m*. ◆ *vt* fruncir (con desagrado).

purser ['pɜːsər] *n* contador *m*, -ra *f*.

pursue [pə'sjuː] *vt* 1. (follow) perseguir. 2. *fml* (policy) llevar a cabo; (aim, pleasure etc) ir en pos de, buscar; (topic, question) profundizar en; (hobby, studies) dedicarse a.

pursuer [pə'sjuːər] *n* perseguidor *m*, -ra *f*.

pursuit [pə'sjuːt] *n* 1. (U) *fml* (attempt to achieve) búsqueda *f*. 2. (chase, in cycling) persecución *f*. 3. (occupation, activity) ocupación *f*; **leisure ~** pasatiempo *m*.

pus [pʌs] *n* pus *m*.

push [pʊʃ] ◆ *vt* 1. (shove) empujar; **to ~ sthg into sthg** meter algo en algo; **to ~ sthg open/shut** abrir/cerrar algo empujándolo. 2. (press - button) apretar, pulsar. 3. (encourage): **to ~ sb (to do sthg)** empujar a alguien (a hacer algo). 4. (force): **to ~ sb (into doing sthg)** obligar a alguien (a hacer algo). 5. *inf* (promote) promocionar. ◆ *vi* (press forward) empujar; (on button) apretar, pulsar. ◆ *n* lit & *fig* empujón *m*. ► **push around** *vt sep inf* mandonear. ► **push for** *vt fus* (demand) reclamar. ► **push in** *vi* (in queue) colarse. ► **push off** *vi inf*

largarse. ► **push on** *vi* seguir adelante sin parar. ► **push through** *vt sep* (law etc) conseguir que se apruebe.

pushchair ['pʊʃtʃeər] *n* Br silla *f* (de paseo).

pushed [pʊʃt] *adj inf*: **to be ~ for sthg** andar corto(ta) de algo; **to be hard ~ to do sthg** tenerlo difícil para hacer algo.

pusher ['pʊʃər] *n inf* camello *m*.

pushover ['pʊʃ,əʊvər] *n inf*: **it's a ~** está chupado.

push-up *n* flexión *f*.

pushy ['pʊʃɪ] *adj pej* agresivo(va), insistente.

puss [pʊs], **pussy (cat)** ['pʊsɪ-] *n inf* gatito *m*, minino *m*.

put [pʊt] (*pt & pp* **put**) *vt* 1. (gen) poner; **to ~ sthg into sthg** meter algo en algo. 2. (place exactly) colocar. 3. (send - to prison etc) meter; **to ~ the children to bed** acostar a los niños. 4. (express) expresar, formular. 5. (ask - question) hacer. 6. (estimate): **to ~ sthg at** calcular algo en. 7. (invest): **to ~ sthg into sthg** poner algo en algo, dedicar algo a algo. 8. (apply): **to ~ pressure on** presionar a. ► **put across** *vt sep* transmitir. ► **put away** *vt sep* (tidy away) poner en su sitio, guardar. ► **put back** *vt sep* 1. (replace) volver a poner en su sitio. 2. (postpone) aplazar. 3. (clock, watch) atrasar. ► **put by** *vt sep* ahorrar. ► **put down** *vt sep* 1. (lay down) dejar (encima de algún sitio). 2. (quell) sofocar, reprimir. 3. Br (animal) matar (a un animal que es viejo o está enfermo). 4. (write down) apuntar. ► **put down to** *vt sep* achacar a. ► **put forward** *vt sep* 1. (plan, theory, name) proponer; (proposal) someter. 2. (clock, meeting, event) adelantar. ► **put in** *vt sep* 1. (spend - time) dedicar. 2. (submit) presentar. ► **put off** *vt sep* 1. (postpone) posponer, aplazar. 2. (cause to wait) hacer esperar. 3. (discourage) disuadir. 4. (cause to dislike): **to ~ sb off sthg** hacerle pasar a alguien las ganas de algo. ► **put on** *vt sep* 1. (wear) ponerse. 2. (show, play) representar; (exhibition) hacer. 3. (gain): **to ~ on weight** engordar. 4. (radio, light) encender; **to ~ on the brakes** poner el freno, frenar. 5. (record, tape) poner. 6. (start cooking) empezar a hacer OR cocinar. 7. (bet) apostar por. 8. (add) añadir. 9. (feign - air, accent) fingir. ► **put out** *vt sep* 1. (place outside) sacar. 2. (issue - statement) hacer público. 3. (extinguish) apagar. 4. (switch off) quitar, apagar. 5. (prepare for use - clothes) sacar. **6.** (*extend - hand, leg*) extender; (*- tongue*) sacar. **7.** (*upset*): **to be ~ out** estar enfadado(da). **8.** (*inconvenience*) causar molestias a. ▶ **put through** *vt sep* (TELEC) (*call*) poner; **to ~ sb through to sb** poner a alguien con alguien. ▶ **put up** ◆ *vt sep* **1.** (*build*) construir. **2.** (*umbrella*) abrir; (*flag*) izar. **3.** (*poster*) fijar; (*painting*) colgar. **4.** (*provide - money*) poner. **5.** (*propose - candidate*) proponer. **6.** (*increase*) subir, aumentar. **7.** (*provide accommodation for*) alojar, hospedar. ◆ *vt fus* (*resistance*) ofrecer; **to ~ up a fight** resistir. ▶ **put up with** *vt fus* aguantar.

putrid ['pjuːtrɪd] *adj fml* putrefacto (ta).

putt [pʌt] *n* putt *m*, tiro *m* al hoyo.

putting green ['pʌtɪŋ-] *n* minigolf *m* (*sin obstáculos*).

putty ['pʌtɪ] *n* masilla *f*.

puzzle ['pʌzl] ◆ *n* **1.** (*toy, game*) rompecabezas *m inv*. **2.** (*mystery*) misterio *m*, enigma *m*. ◆ *vt* dejar perplejo, desconcertar. ◆ *vi*: **to ~ over sthg** romperse la cabeza con algo. ▶ **puzzle out** *vt sep* descifrar.

puzzling ['pʌzlɪŋ] *adj* desconcertante.

pyjamas [pə'dʒɑːməz] *npl* pijama *m*.

pylon ['paɪlən] *n* torre *f* (*de conducción eléctrica*).

pyramid ['pɪrəmɪd] *n* **1.** (*structure*) pirámide *f*. **2.** (*pile*) montón *m*, pila *f*.

Pyrenees [,pɪrə'niːz] *npl*: **the ~** los Pirineos.

Pyrex® ['paɪreks] *n* pírex® *m*.

python ['paɪθn] (*pl inv* OR **-s**) *n* pitón *m*.

Q

q (*pl* **q's** OR **qs**), **Q** (*pl* **Q's** OR **Qs**) [kjuː] *n* (*letter*) q *f*, Q *f*.

quack [kwæk] *n* **1.** (*noise*) graznido *m* (*de pato*). **2.** *inf* (*doctor*) matasanos *m inv*.

quad [kwɒd] *n abbr of* **quadrangle**.

quadrangle ['kwɒdræŋgl] *n* **1.** (*figure*) cuadrángulo *m*. **2.** (*courtyard*) patio *m*.

quadruple [kwɒ'druːpl] ◆ *vt* cuadruplicar. ◆ *vi* cuadruplicarse.

quadruplets ['kwɒdruplɪts] *npl* cuatrillizos *mpl*, -zas *fpl*.

quads [kwɒdz] *npl inf* cuatrillizos *mpl*, -zas *fpl*.

quagmire ['kwægmaɪər] *n* lodazal *m*.

quail [kweɪl] (*pl inv* OR **-s**) ◆ *n* codorniz *f*. ◆ *vi literary* amedrentarse.

quaint [kweɪnt] *adj* pintoresco(ca).

quake [kweɪk] ◆ *n inf* terremoto *m*. ◆ *vi* temblar, estremecerse.

Quaker ['kweɪkər] *n* cuáquero *m*, -ra *f*.

qualification [,kwɒlɪfɪ'keɪʃn] *n* **1.** (*examination, certificate*) título *m*. **2.** (*ability, skill*) aptitud *f*. **3.** (*qualifying statement*) modificación *f*.

qualified ['kwɒlɪfaɪd] *adj* **1.** (*trained*) cualificado(da). **2.** (*limited*) limitado(da).

qualify ['kwɒlɪfaɪ] ◆ *vt* **1.** (*modify*) modificar. **2.** (*entitle*): **to ~ sb to do sthg** capacitar a alguien para hacer algo. ◆ *vi* **1.** (*pass exams*) sacar el título. **2.** (*be entitled*): **to ~ (for)** tener derecho (a). **3.** (SPORT) clasificarse.

quality ['kwɒlətɪ] ◆ *n* **1.** (*standard*) calidad *f*. **2.** (*characteristic*) cualidad *f*. ◆ *comp* de calidad.

qualms [kwɑːmz] *npl* escrúpulos *mpl*.

quandary ['kwɒndərɪ] *n*: **to be in a ~ about** OR **over sthg** estar en un dilema sobre algo.

quantify ['kwɒntɪfaɪ] *vt* cuantificar.

quantity ['kwɒntətɪ] *n* cantidad *f*.

quantity surveyor *n* aparejador *m*, -ra *f*.

quarantine ['kwɒrəntiːn] *n* cuarentena *f*.

quark [kwɑːk] *n* (CULIN) *tipo de queso blando bajo en grasas.*

quarrel ['kwɒrəl] ◆ *n* pelea *f*, disputa *f*. ◆ *vi* pelearse, reñir; **to ~ with sb** pelearse con alguien; **to ~ with sthg** no estar de acuerdo con algo.

quarrelsome ['kwɒrəlsəm] *adj* pendenciero(ra).

quarry ['kwɒrɪ] *n* **1.** (*place*) cantera *f*. **2.** (*prey*) presa *f*.

quart [kwɔːt] *n* cuarto *m* de galón.

quarter ['kwɔːtər] *n* **1.** (*fraction*) cuarto *m*. **2.** (*in telling time*): **~ past two** Br, **~ after two** Am las dos y cuarto; **~ to two** Br, **~ of two** Am las dos menos cuarto. **3.** (*of year*) trimestre *m*. **4.** Am (*coin*) moneda *f* de 25 centavos. **5.** (*four ounces*) cuatro onzas *fpl*. **6.** (*area in town*) barrio *m*. **7.** (*group of people*) lugar *m*, parte *f*. ▶ **quarters** *npl* (*rooms*) residencia *f*, alojamiento *m*. ▶ **at close quarters** *adv* muy de cerca.

quarterfinal [,kwɔːtə'faɪnl] *n* cuarto *m* de final.

quarterly ['kwɔːtəlɪ] ◆ *adj* trimestral.

◆ *adv* trimestralmente. ◆ *n* trimestral *f*.

quartermaster [ˈkwɔːtəˌmɑːstəʳ] *n* oficial *m* de intendencia.

quartet [kwɔːˈtet] *n* cuarteto *m*.

quartz [kwɔːts] *n* cuarzo *m*.

quartz watch *n* reloj *m* de cuarzo.

quash [kwɒʃ] *vt* 1. (*reject*) anular, invalidar. 2. (*quell*) reprimir, sofocar.

quasi- [ˈkweizaɪ] *prefix* cuasi-.

quaver [ˈkweivəʳ] ◆ *n* (MUS) corchea *f*. ◆ *vi* temblar.

quay [kiː] *n* muelle *m*.

quayside [ˈkiːsaɪd] *n* muelle *m*.

queasy [ˈkwiːzɪ] *adj* mareado(da).

queen [kwiːn] *n* 1. (*gen*) reina *f*. 2. (*playing card*) dama *f*.

Queen Mother *n*: **the ~** la reina madre.

queer [kwɪəʳ] ◆ *adj* (*odd*) raro(ra), extraño(ña). ◆ *n inf pej* marica *m*.

quell [kwel] *vt* 1. (*rebellion*) sofocar, reprimir. 2. (*feelings*) dominar, contener.

quench [kwentʃ] *vt* apagar.

querulous [ˈkwerʊləs] *adj fml* quejumbroso(sa).

query [ˈkwɪərɪ] ◆ *n* pregunta *f*, duda *f*. ◆ *vt* poner en duda.

quest [kwest] *n literary*: **~ (for)** búsqueda *f* (de).

question [ˈkwestʃn] ◆ *n* 1. (*query, problem in exam*) pregunta *f*; **to ask (sb) a ~** hacer una pregunta (a alguien). 2. (*doubt*) duda *f*; **to call sthg into ~** poner algo en duda; **without ~** sin duda; **beyond ~** fuera de toda duda. 3. (*issue, matter*) cuestión *f*, asunto *m*. 4. *phr*: **there's no ~ of ...** es imposible que ... ◆ *vt* 1. (*interrogate*) interrogar. 2. (*express doubt about*) cuestionar. ▶ **in question** *adv*: **the matter in ~** el asunto en cuestión. ▶ **out of the question** *adv* imposible.

questionable [ˈkwestʃənəbl] *adj* (*gen*) cuestionable; (*taste*) dudoso(sa).

question mark *n* (signo *m* de) interrogación *f*.

questionnaire [ˌkwestʃəˈneəʳ] *n* cuestionario *m*.

queue [kjuː] Br ◆ *n* cola *f*. ◆ *vi*: **to ~ (up for sthg)** hacer cola (para algo).

quibble [ˈkwɪbl] *vi pej* quejarse por tonterías.

quiche [kiːʃ] *n* quiche *f*.

quick [kwɪk] ◆ *adj* 1. (*gen*) rápido(da); **be ~!** ¡date prisa! 2. (*clever - person*) espabilado(da); (*- wit*) agudo(da). 3. (*irritable*): **a ~ temper** un genio vivo. ◆ *adv* rápidamente.

quicken [ˈkwɪkn] ◆ *vt* apretar, acelerar. ◆ *vi* acelerarse, apresurarse.

quickly [ˈkwɪklɪ] *adv* 1. (*rapidly*) rápidamente, de prisa. 2. (*without delay*) rápidamente, en seguida.

quicksand [ˈkwɪksænd] *n* arenas *fpl* movedizas.

quick-witted [-ˈwɪtɪd] *adj* agudo(da).

quid [kwɪd] (*pl inv*) *n* Br *inf* libra *f* (esterlina).

quiet [ˈkwaɪət] ◆ *adj* 1. (*silent - gen*) silencioso(sa); (*- room, place*) tranquilo (la); **be ~!** ¡cállate!; **in a ~ voice** en voz baja; **to keep ~ about sthg** guardar silencio sobre algo. 2. (*not talkative*) callado (da). 3. (*tranquil, uneventful*) tranquilo (la). 4. (*unpublicized - wedding etc*) privado (da), íntimo(ma). ◆ *n* tranquilidad *f*, silencio *m*; **on the ~** a escondidas. ◆ *vt* Am tranquilizar. ▶ **quiet down** ◆ *vt sep* tranquilizar. ◆ *vi* tranquilizarse.

quieten [ˈkwaɪətn] *vt* tranquilizar. ▶ **quieten down** ◆ *vt sep* tranquilizar. ◆ *vi* tranquilizarse.

quietly [ˈkwaɪətlɪ] *adv* 1. (*without noise*) silenciosamente, sin hacer ruido; **to speak ~** hablar en voz baja. 2. (*without moving*) sin moverse. 3. (*without excitement*) tranquilamente. 4. (*without fuss*) discretamente.

quilt [kwɪlt] *n* edredón *m*.

quinine [kwɪˈniːn] *n* quinina *f*.

quins Br [kwɪnz], **quints** Am [kwɪnts] *npl inf* quintillizos *mpl*, -zas *fpl*.

quintet [kwɪnˈtet] *n* quinteto *m*.

quints Am = quins.

quintuplets [kwɪnˈtjuːplɪts] *npl* quintillizos *mpl*, -zas *fpl*.

quip [kwɪp] *n* ocurrencia *f*, salida *f*.

quirk [kwɜːk] *n* 1. (*habit*) manía *f*, rareza *f*. 2. (*strange event*) extraña coincidencia *f*.

quit [kwɪt] (Br *pt* & *pp* quit OR -ted, Am *pt* & *pp* quit) ◆ *vt* 1. (*resign from*) dejar, abandonar. 2. (*stop*): **to ~ doing sthg** dejar de hacer algo. ◆ *vi* (*resign*) dimitir.

quite [kwaɪt] *adv* 1. (*completely*) totalmente, completamente. 2. (*fairly*) bastante; **~ a lot of people** bastante gente. 3. (*after negative*): **it's not ~ big enough** no es todo lo grande que tendría que ser; **I don't ~ understand/know** no entiendo/ sé muy bien. 4. (*to emphasize*): **~ a ...** todo un (toda una) ... 5. (*to express agreement*): **~ (so)!** ¡efectivamente!, ¡desde luego!

quits [kwɪts] *adj inf*: **to be ~ (with sb)** estar en paz (con alguien); **to call it ~**

quedar en paz.

quiver ['kwɪvəʳ] ◆ n (for arrows) carcaj m. ◆ vi temblar, estremecerse.

quiz [kwɪz] (pl -zes) ◆ n 1. (gen) concurso m. 2. Am (SCH) control m. ◆ vt: to ~ sb (about) interrogar a alguien (sobre).

quizzical ['kwɪzɪkl] adj (smile) burlón (ona); (look, glance) interrogativo(va).

quota ['kwəʊtə] n cuota f.

quotation [kwəʊ'teɪʃn] n 1. (citation) cita f. 2. (COMM) presupuesto m.

quotation marks npl comillas fpl.

quote [kwəʊt] ◆ n 1. (citation) cita f. 2. (COMM) presupuesto m. ◆ vt 1. (cite) citar. 2. (figures, example, price) dar; he ~d £100 fijo un precio de 100 libras. ◆ vi 1. (cite): to ~ (from) citar (de). 2. (COMM): to ~ for dar un presupuesto por.

quotient ['kwəʊʃnt] n cociente m.

R

r (pl **r's** OR **rs**), **R** (pl **R's** OR **Rs**) [ɑːʳ] n (letter) r f, R f.

rabbi ['ræbaɪ] n rabino m.

rabbit ['ræbɪt] n conejo m.

rabbit hutch n conejera f.

rabble ['ræbl] n chusma f, populacho m.

rabies ['reɪbiːz] n rabia f.

RAC (abbr of **Royal Automobile Club**) n asociación británica del automóvil, ≃ RACE m.

race [reɪs] ◆ n 1. lit & fig (competition) carrera f. 2. (people, descent) raza f. ◆ vt 1. (compete against) competir con (corriendo); **they ~d each other to the door** echaron una carrera hasta la puerta. 2. (cars, pigeons) hacer carreras de; (horses) hacer correr. ◆ vi 1. (rush) ir corriendo. 2. (beat fast) acelerarse.

race car Am = **racing car**.

racecourse ['reɪskɔːs] n hipódromo m.

race driver Am = **racing driver**.

racehorse ['reɪshɔːs] n caballo m de carreras.

racetrack ['reɪstræk] n (for horses) hipódromo m; (for cars) autódromo m; (for runners) pista f (de carreras).

racial discrimination ['reɪʃl-] n discriminación f racial.

racing ['reɪsɪŋ] n carreras fpl; **motor ~** carreras de coches.

racing car Br, **race car** Am n coche m de carreras.

racing driver Br, **race driver** Am n piloto m y f de carreras.

racism ['reɪsɪzm] n racismo m.

racist ['reɪsɪst] ◆ adj racista. ◆ n racista m y f.

rack [ræk] ◆ n 1. (for plates) escurreplatos m inv; (for clothes) percha f; (for magazines) revistero m; (for bottles) botellero m. 2. (for luggage) portaequipajes m inv. ◆ vt: **to ~ one's brains** Br devanarse los sesos.

racket ['rækɪt] n 1. (noise) jaleo m, alboroto m. 2. (swindle) timo m. 3. (illegal activity) negocio m sucio. 4. (SPORT) raqueta f.

racquet ['rækɪt] n (SPORT) = **racket**.

racy ['reɪsɪ] adj entretenido(da) y picante.

radar ['reɪdɑːʳ] n radar m.

radial (tyre) ['reɪdjəl-] n neumático m radial.

radiant ['reɪdjənt] adj 1. (happy) radiante. 2. literary (brilliant) resplandeciente.

radiate ['reɪdɪeɪt] ◆ vt lit & fig irradiar. ◆ vi 1. (be emitted) ser irradiado(da). 2. (spread from centre) salir, extenderse.

radiation [,reɪdɪ'eɪʃn] n radiación f.

radiator ['reɪdɪeɪtəʳ] n radiador m.

radical ['rædɪkl] ◆ adj radical. ◆ n (POL) radical m y f.

radically ['rædɪklɪ] adv radicalmente.

radii ['reɪdɪaɪ] pl → **radius**.

radio ['reɪdɪəʊ] (pl -s) ◆ n radio f. ◆ comp de radio, radiofónico(ca).

radioactive [,reɪdɪəʊ'æktɪv] adj radiactivo(va).

radio alarm n radiodespertador m.

radio-controlled [-kən'trəʊld] adj teledirigido(da).

radiography [,reɪdɪ'ɒgrəfɪ] n radiografía f.

radiology [,reɪdɪ'ɒlədʒɪ] n radiología f.

radiotherapy [,reɪdɪəʊ'θerəpɪ] n radioterapia f.

radish ['rædɪʃ] n rábano m.

radius ['reɪdɪəs] (pl radii) n (gen & ANAT) radio m.

RAF [ɑːreɪ'ef, ræf] n abbr of **Royal Air Force**.

raffle ['ræfl] ◆ n rifa f, sorteo m. ◆ comp: ~ **ticket** boleto m. ◆ vt rifar.

raft [rɑːft] n (craft) balsa f.
rafter ['rɑːftər] n par m (de armadura de tejado).
rag [ræg] n 1. (piece of cloth) trapo m, harapo m. 2. pej (newspaper) periodicucho m. ▶ **rags** npl (clothes) trapos mpl.
rag-and-bone man n trapero m.
rag doll n muñeca f de trapo.
rage [reɪdʒ] ◆ n 1. (fury) rabia f, ira f. 2. inf (fashion): **it's all the ~** es la última moda. ◆ vi 1. (behave angrily) estar furioso(sa). 2. (subj: storm, sea) enfurecerse; (subj: disease) hacer estragos; (subj: argument, controversy) continuar con violencia.
ragged ['rægɪd] adj 1. (wearing torn clothes) andrajoso(sa), harapiento(ta). 2. (torn) hecho(cha) jirones.
rag week n Br semana en que los universitarios organizan actividades divertidas con fines benéficos.
raid [reɪd] ◆ n 1. (attack) incursión f. 2. (forced entry - by robbers) asalto m; (- by police) redada f. ◆ vt 1. (attack) atacar por sorpresa. 2. (subj: robbers) asaltar; (subj: police) hacer una redada en.
raider ['reɪdər] n 1. (attacker) invasor m, -ra f. 2. (thief) ladrón m, -ona f.
rail [reɪl] n 1. (on staircase) barandilla f. 2. (bar) barra f; **towel ~** toallero m. 3. (of railway line) carril m, riel m. 4. (U) (form of transport) ferrocarril m; **by ~** por ferrocarril.
railcard ['reɪlkɑːd] n Br tarjeta que permite algunos descuentos al viajar en tren.
railing ['reɪlɪŋ] n reja f.
railway Br ['reɪlweɪ], **railroad** Am ['reɪlrəʊd] n 1. (company) ferrocarril m. 2. (route) línea f de ferrocarril.
railway line n línea f de ferrocarril.
railwayman ['reɪlweɪmən] (pl **-men** [-mən]) n Br ferroviario m.
railway station n estación f de ferrocarril.
railway track n vía f férrea.
rain [reɪn] ◆ n lluvia f. ◆ v impers (METEOR) llover. ◆ vi caer.
rainbow ['reɪnbəʊ] n arco m iris.
rain check n Am: **I'll take a ~ (on that)** no lo quiero ahora, pero igual me apunto la próxima vez.
raincoat ['reɪnkəʊt] n impermeable m.
raindrop ['reɪndrɒp] n gota f de lluvia.
rainfall ['reɪnfɔːl] n pluviosidad f.
rain forest n bosque m tropical.
rainy ['reɪnɪ] adj lluvioso(sa).
raise [reɪz] ◆ vt 1. (lift up) levantar; **to**

~ o.s. levantarse. 2. (increase - level) aumentar; **to ~ one's voice** levantar la voz. 3. (improve) elevar. 4. (obtain - from donations) recaudar; (- by selling, borrowing) conseguir. 5. (memory, thoughts) traer; (doubts) levantar. 6. (bring up, breed) criar. 7. (crops) cultivar. 8. (mention) plantear. 9. (build) construir. ◆ n Am aumento m.
raisin ['reɪzn] n pasa f.
rake [reɪk] ◆ n 1. (implement) rastrillo m. 2. dated & literary (immoral man) libertino m. ◆ vt (smooth) rastrillar.
rally ['rælɪ] ◆ n 1. (meeting) mitin m, reunión f. 2. (car race) rally m. 3. (in tennis etc) peloteo m. ◆ vt reunir. ◆ vi 1. (come together) reunirse. 2. (recover) recuperarse. ▶ **rally round** ◆ vt fus formar una piña con. ◆ vi inf formar una piña.
ram [ræm] ◆ n carnero m. ◆ vt 1. (crash into) chocar con OR contra. 2. (force) embutir.
RAM [ræm] (abbr of random access memory) n (COMPUT) RAM f.
ramble ['ræmbl] ◆ n paseo m por el campo. ◆ vi 1. (walk) pasear. 2. (talk) divagar. ▶ **ramble on** vi divagar sin parar.
rambler ['ræmblər] n (walker) excursionista m y f.
rambling ['ræmblɪŋ] adj 1. (building, house) laberíntico(ca); (town) desparramado(da). 2. (speech, writing) confuso (sa), incoherente.
ramp [ræmp] n 1. (slope) rampa f. 2. (AUT) (in road) rompecoches m inv.
rampage [ræm'peɪdʒ] n: **to go on the ~** desbandarse.
rampant ['ræmpənt] adj desenfrenado(da).
ramparts ['ræmpɑːts] npl murallas fpl.
ramshackle ['ræm,ʃækl] adj destartalado(da).
ran [ræn] pt → **run**.
ranch [rɑːntʃ] n rancho m.
rancher ['rɑːntʃər] n ranchero m, -ra f.
rancid ['rænsɪd] adj rancio(cia).
rancour Br, **rancor** Am ['ræŋkər] n rencor m.
random ['rændəm] ◆ adj fortuito(ta), hecho(cha) al azar. ◆ n: **at ~** al azar.
random access memory n (COMPUT) memoria f de acceso aleatorio.
R and R (abbr of rest and recreation) n Am permiso militar.
randy ['rændɪ] adj inf cachondo(da), caliente.

rang [ræŋ] pt → **ring**.

range [reɪndʒ] ◆ n 1. (of missile, telescope) alcance m; (of ship, plane) autonomía f; **at close ~** de cerca. 2. (variety) variedad f, gama f. 3. (of prices, salaries) escala f. 4. (of mountains) sierra f, cordillera f. 5. (shooting area) campo m de tiro. 6. (of voice) registro m. ◆ vt alinear. ◆ vi 1. (vary): **to ~ from ... to ...**, **to ~ between ... and ...** oscilar OR fluctuar entre ... y ... 2. (deal with, include): **to ~ over sthg** comprender algo.

ranger ['reɪndʒər] n guardabosques m y f inv.

rank [ræŋk] ◆ adj 1. (utter, absolute - bad luck, outsider) absoluto(ta); (- disgrace, injustice) flagrante. 2. (foul) pestilente. ◆ n 1. (position, grade) grado m, graduación f. 2. (social class) clase f, categoría f; **the ~ and file** las bases (del partido). 3. (row) fila f. ◆ vt (class): **to be ~ed** estar clasificado(da). ◆ vi: **to ~ as** estar considerado(da) (como); **to ~ among** encontrarse entre. ▶ **ranks** npl 1. (MIL): **the ~s** los soldados rasos. 2. fig (members) filas fpl.

rankle ['ræŋkl] vi amargar, doler.

ransack ['rænsæk] vt (search) registrar a fondo; (plunder) saquear.

ransom ['rænsəm] n rescate m; **to hold sb to ~** fig hacer chantaje a alguien.

rant [rænt] vi despotricar.

rap [ræp] ◆ n 1. (knock) golpecito m. 2. (type of music) rap m. ◆ vt dar golpecitos en.

rape [reɪp] ◆ n 1. (crime) violación f. 2. (BOT) colza f. ◆ vt violar.

rapeseed ['reɪpsiːd] n semilla f de colza.

rapid ['ræpɪd] adj rápido(da). ▶ **rapids** npl rápidos mpl.

rapidly ['ræpɪdlɪ] adv rápidamente.

rapist ['reɪpɪst] n violador m, -ra f.

rapport [ræ'pɔːr] n compenetración f.

rapture ['ræptʃər] n arrobamiento m.

rapturous ['ræptʃərəs] adj muy entusiasta.

rare [reər] adj 1. (scarce) poco común, raro(ra). 2. (infrequent) poco frecuente, raro(ra). 3. (exceptional) raro(ra), excepcional. 4. (CULIN) poco hecho(cha).

rarely ['reəlɪ] adv raras veces.

raring ['reərɪŋ] adj: **to be ~ to go** estar ansioso(sa) por empezar.

rarity ['reərətɪ] n rareza f.

rascal ['rɑːskl] n pícaro m, -ra f.

rash [ræʃ] ◆ adj precipitado(da). ◆ n 1. (MED) erupción f (cutánea), sarpulli-

do m. 2. (spate) aluvión m.

rasher ['ræʃər] n loncha f.

rasp [rɑːsp] n (harsh sound) chirrido m.

raspberry ['rɑːzbərɪ] n (fruit) frambuesa f.

rat [ræt] n (animal) rata f.

rate [reɪt] ◆ n 1. (speed) velocidad f; **at this ~** a este paso. 2. (of birth, death) índice m; (of unemployment, inflation) tasa f. 3. (price) precio m, tarifa f; (of interest) tipo m. ◆ vt 1. (consider): **to ~ sthg/sb (as/among)** considerar algo/a alguien (como/entre). 2. (deserve) merecer. ▶ **rates** npl Br ≃ contribución f urbana. ▶ **at any rate** adv 1. (at least) al menos. 2. (anyway) de todos modos.

ratepayer ['reɪt,peɪər] n Br contribuyente m y f.

rather ['rɑːðər] adv 1. (to quite a large extent) bastante. 2. (to a limited extent) algo; **he's ~ like you** se parece (en) algo a ti. 3. (as preference): **I would ~ wait** preferiría esperar; **I'd ~ not** mejor que no. 4. (more exactly): **or ~ ...** o más bien ..., o mejor dicho ... 5. (on the contrary): **(but) ~ ...** (sino) más bien OR por el contrario ... ▶ **rather than** conj antes que.

ratify ['rætɪfaɪ] vt ratificar.

rating ['reɪtɪŋ] n (standing) clasificación f, posición f.

ratio ['reɪʃɪəʊ] (pl -s) n proporción f, relación f.

ration ['ræʃn] ◆ n ración f. ◆ vt racionar. ▶ **rations** npl víveres mpl.

rational ['ræʃənl] adj racional.

rationale [,ræʃə'nɑːl] n lógica f, razones fpl.

rationalize, -ise ['ræʃənəlaɪz] vt racionalizar.

rat race n mundo despiadada competitivo de los negocios.

rattle ['rætl] ◆ n 1. (of engine, metal) ruido m, traqueteo m; (of glass) tintineo m; (of typewriter) repiqueteo m. 2. (toy) sonajero m. ◆ vt 1. (make rattle) hacer sonar. 2. (unsettle) desconcertar. ◆ vi golpetear; (gunfire) tabletear.

rattlesnake ['rætlsneɪk], **rattler** Am ['rætlər] n serpiente f de cascabel.

raucous ['rɔːkəs] adj ronco(ca) y estridente.

ravage ['rævɪdʒ] vt estragar, asolar. ▶ **ravages** npl estragos mpl.

rave [reɪv] ◆ n Br inf (party) juerga f. ◆ vi 1. (talk angrily): **to ~ against sb/sthg** despotricar contra alguien/algo. 2. (talk enthusiastically): **to ~ about sthg** deshacerse en alabanzas sobre algo.

raven ['reɪvn] n cuervo m.

ravenous ['rævənəs] adj (person, animal) famélico(ca); (appetite) voraz.

ravine [rə'viːn] n barranco m.

raving ['reɪvɪŋ] adj (lunatic) de atar; (fantasy) delirante.

ravioli [ˌrævɪ'əʊlɪ] n (U) raviolis mpl.

ravishing ['rævɪʃɪŋ] adj (sight, beauty) de ensueño; (person) bellísimo(ma).

raw [rɔː] adj 1. (uncooked) crudo(da). 2. (untreated) en bruto. 3. (painful - wound) en carne viva. 4. (inexperienced) novato(ta). 5. (cold) crudo(da).

raw deal n: to get a ~ recibir un trato injusto.

raw material n materia f prima.

ray [reɪ] n rayo m; ~ of hope resquicio m de esperanza.

rayon ['reɪɒn] n rayón m.

raze [reɪz] vt arrasar.

razor ['reɪzəʳ] n (wet shaver) navaja f; (electric machine) maquinilla f de afeitar.

razor blade n hoja f de afeitar.

RC abbr of **Roman Catholic**.

Rd abbr of **road**.

R & D (abbr of **research and development**) n I + D f.

re [riː] prep Ref.

RE n (abbr of **religious education**) religión f.

reach [riːtʃ] ◆ n alcance m; he has a long ~ tiene los brazos largos; within (sb's) ~ (easily touched) al alcance (de alguien); (easily travelled) a poco distancia (de alguien); out of OR beyond sb's ~ fuera del alcance de alguien. ◆ vt 1. (gen) alcanzar, llegar a; to ~ an agreement/a decision llegar a un acuerdo/una decisión. 2. (arrive at - place etc) llegar a. 3. (get by stretching - object, shelf) alcanzar. 4. (contact) localizar. ◆ vi: to ~ out/across alargar la mano; to ~ down agacharse.

react [rɪ'ækt] vi 1. (respond): to ~ (to) reaccionar (a OR ante). 2. (rebel): to ~ against reaccionar en contra de. 3. (CHEM): to ~ with reaccionar con.

reaction [rɪ'ækʃn] n: ~ (to/against) reacción f (a/contra).

reactionary [rɪ'ækʃənrɪ] ◆ adj reaccionario(ria). ◆ n reaccionario m, -ria f.

reactor [rɪ'æktəʳ] n reactor m.

read [riːd] (pt & pp read [red]) ◆ vt 1. (gen) leer. 2. (subj: sign, words) poner, decir. 3. (interpret) interpretar. 4. (subj: thermometer, meter etc) marcar. 5. Br (UNIV) estudiar. ◆ vi 1. (person) leer. 2. (read aloud): to ~ (to sb) leerle (a alguien).

3. (piece of writing) leerse. ▶ **read out** vt sep leer en voz alta. ▶ **read up on** vt fus leer OR documentarse sobre.

readable ['riːdəbl] adj ameno(na), que se lee con agrado.

reader ['riːdəʳ] n (person who reads) lector m, -ra f.

readership ['riːdəʃɪp] n (total number of readers) lectores mpl.

readily ['redɪlɪ] adv 1. (willingly) de buena gana. 2. (easily) en seguida.

reading ['riːdɪŋ] n 1. (gen) lectura f. 2. (recital) recital m.

readjust [ˌriːə'dʒʌst] ◆ vt reajustar. ◆ vi: to ~ (to) volverse a adaptar (a).

readout ['riːdaʊt] n (COMPUT) texto m en pantalla.

ready ['redɪ] ◆ adj 1. (prepared) listo (ta), preparado(da); to be ~ for sthg/to do sthg estar listo para algo/para hacer algo. 2. (willing): to be ~ to do sthg estar dispuesto(ta) a hacer algo. 3. (in need of): to be ~ for sthg necesitar algo. 4. (likely): to be ~ to do sthg estar a punto de hacer algo. 5. (cash) contante; (smile) pronto(ta). ◆ vt preparar.

ready cash n dinero m contante.

ready-made adj (products) hecho (cha); (clothes) confeccionado(da).

ready money n dinero m contante.

ready-to-wear adj confeccionado (da).

reafforestation ['riːəˌfɒrɪ'steɪʃn] n repoblación f forestal.

real ['rɪəl] ◆ adj 1. (not imagined, actual) real; the ~ thing lo auténtico; for ~ de verdad; in ~ terms en términos reales. 2. (genuine, proper) auténtico(ca). ◆ adv Am muy.

real estate n propiedad f inmobiliaria.

realign [ˌriːə'laɪn] vt volver a alinear.

realism ['rɪəlɪzm] n realismo m.

realistic [ˌrɪə'lɪstɪk] adj realista.

reality [rɪ'ælətɪ] n realidad f.

realization [ˌrɪəlaɪ'zeɪʃn] n 1. (recognition) comprensión f. 2. (achievement) consecución f.

realize, -ise ['rɪəlaɪz] vt 1. (become aware of) darse cuenta de. 2. (produce, achieve, make profit of) realizar.

really ['rɪəlɪ] ◆ adv 1. (for emphasis) de verdad; ~ good buenísimo. 2. (actually, honestly) realmente. 3. (to sound less negative) en realidad. ◆ excl 1. (expressing doubt): ~? (in affirmatives) ¿ah sí?; (in negatives) ¿ah no? 2. (expressing surprise, disbelief): ~? ¿de verdad?

realm [relm] n 1. (field) campo m, esfera f. 2. (kingdom) reino m.

realtor ['rɪəltər] n Am agente inmobiliario m, agente inmobiliaria f.

reap [riːp] vt lit & fig cosechar.

reappear [ˌriːə'pɪər] vi reaparecer.

rear [rɪər] ◆ adj trasero(ra), de atrás. ◆ n (back) parte f de atrás; **to bring up the ~** cerrar la marcha. ◆ vt criar. ◆ vi: **to ~ (up)** encabritarse.

rearm [riːˈɑːm] vi rearmarse.

rearmost ['rɪəməʊst] adj último(ma).

rearrange [ˌriːəˈreɪndʒ] vt 1. (room, furniture) colocar de otro modo; (system, plans) reorganizar. 2. (meeting) volver a concertar.

rearview mirror ['rɪəvjuː-] n (espejo m) retrovisor m.

reason ['riːzn] ◆ n 1. (cause): **~ (for)** razón f (para); **for some ~** por alguna razón. 2. (justification): **to have ~ to do sthg** tener motivo para hacer algo. 3. (rationality) razón f, sensatez f; **it stands to ~** es razonable; **to listen to ~** avenirse a razones. ◆ vt & vi razonar. ▸ **reason with** vt fus razonar con.

reasonable ['riːznəbl] adj razonable.

reasonably ['riːznəblɪ] adv razonablemente.

reasoned ['riːznd] adj razonado(da).

reasoning ['riːznɪŋ] n razonamiento m.

reassess [ˌriːəˈses] vt reconsiderar.

reassurance [ˌriːəˈʃɔːrəns] n 1. (U) (comfort) palabras fpl tranquilizadoras. 2. (promise) promesa f, compromiso m.

reassure [ˌriːəˈʃɔːr] vt tranquilizar.

reassuring [ˌriːəˈʃɔːrɪŋ] adj tranquilizador(ra).

rebate ['riːbeɪt] n devolución f, bonificación f.

rebel [n 'rebl, vb rɪ'bel] ◆ n rebelde m y f. ◆ vi: **to ~ (against)** rebelarse (contra).

rebellion [rɪˈbeljən] n rebelión f.

rebellious [rɪˈbeljəs] adj rebelde.

rebound [n 'riːbaʊnd, vb ˌriːˈbaʊnd] ◆ n: **on the ~** (ball) de rebote m. ◆ vi (bounce back) rebotar.

rebuff [rɪˈbʌf] n desaire m, negativa f.

rebuild [ˌriːˈbɪld] (pt & pp **-built**) vt reconstruir.

rebuke [rɪˈbjuːk] ◆ n reprimenda f, reprobación f. ◆ vt: **to ~ sb (for)** reprender a alguien (por).

rebuttal [rɪˈbʌtl] n refutación f.

recalcitrant [rɪˈkælsɪtrənt] adj recalcitrante.

recall [rɪˈkɔːl] ◆ n (memory) memoria f.

◆ vt 1. (remember) recordar, acordarse de. 2. (ambassador) retirar.

recant [rɪˈkænt] vi (deny statement) retractarse; (deny religion) renegar de la fe.

recap ['riːkæp] inf ◆ n resumen m, recapitulación f. ◆ vt (summarize) recapitular, resumir. ◆ vi recapitular, resumir.

recapitulate [ˌriːkəˈpɪtjʊleɪt] vt & vi recapitular, resumir.

recd, rec'd (abbr of **received**) rbdo.

recede [rɪˈsiːd] vi 1. (person, car) alejarse; (coastline) retroceder. 2. fig (disappear) esfumarse.

receding [rɪˈsiːdɪŋ] adj (chin) medida hacia dentro; (forehead) hundida; **~ hairline** entradas fpl.

receipt [rɪˈsiːt] n recibo m; **to acknowledge ~** acusar recibo. ▸ **receipts** npl recaudación f.

receive [rɪˈsiːv] vt 1. (gen) recibir. 2. (reaction) tener; (injury, setback) sufrir. 3. (greet): **to be well/badly ~d** tener una buena/mala acogida.

receiver [rɪˈsiːvər] n 1. (of telephone) auricular m. 2. (radio, TV set) receptor m. 3. (criminal) perista m y f. 4. (FIN) síndico m, -ca f.

recent ['riːsnt] adj reciente.

recently ['riːsntlɪ] adv recientemente.

receptacle [rɪˈseptəkl] n receptáculo m.

reception [rɪˈsepʃn] n recepción f.

reception desk n recepción f.

receptionist [rɪˈsepʃənɪst] n recepcionista m y f.

recess ['riːses, Br rɪˈses] n 1. (vacation) periodo m vacacional; **to be in ~** estar clausurado(da). 2. (alcove) nicho m, hueco m. 3. Am (SCH) recreo m. ▸ **recesses** npl (of mind, heart) recovecos mpl; (of building) escondrijos mpl.

recession [rɪˈseʃn] n recesión f.

recharge [ˌriːˈtʃɑːdʒ] vt recargar.

recipe ['resɪpɪ] n (CULIN & fig) receta f.

recipient [rɪˈsɪpɪənt] n (of letter, cheque) destinatario m, -ria f.

reciprocal [rɪˈsɪprəkl] adj recíproco (ca).

recital [rɪˈsaɪtl] n recital m.

recite [rɪˈsaɪt] vt 1. (poem) recitar. 2. (list) enumerar.

reckless ['reklɪs] adj imprudente, temerario(ria).

reckon ['rekn] vt 1. inf (think): **to ~ (that)** pensar que, suponer que. 2. (consider, judge): **to be ~ed to be sthg** ser considerado(da) algo. **3.** (*calculate*) calcular. ▶ **reckon on** *vt fus* contar con. ▶ **reckon with** *vt fus* (*expect*) contar con.

reckoning ['rekənɪŋ] *n* (*calculation*) cálculo *m*.

reclaim [rɪ'kleɪm] *vt* **1.** (*claim back*) reclamar. **2.** (*recover*): **to ~ land from the sea** ganarle tierra al mar.

recline [rɪ'klaɪn] *vi* reclinarse.

reclining [rɪ'klaɪnɪŋ] *adj* reclinable.

recluse [rɪ'kluːs] *n* solitario *m*, -ria *f*.

recognition [ˌrekəg'nɪʃn] *n* reconocimiento *m*; **beyond** OR **out of all ~ de** modo irreconocible; **in ~ of** en reconocimiento a.

recognizable ['rekəgnaɪzəbl] *adj* reconocible.

recognize, -ise ['rekəgnaɪz] *vt* reconocer.

recoil [*vb* rɪ'kɔɪl, *n* 'riːkɔɪl] ◆ *vi* **1.** (*draw back*) retroceder, echarse atrás. **2.** *fig* (*shrink from*): **to ~ from** OR **at sthg** (*truth, bad news*) esquivar OR rehuir algo; (*idea, suggestion*) estremecerse ante algo. ◆ *n* (*of gun*) retroceso *m*.

recollect [ˌrekə'lekt] *vt* recordar.

recollection [ˌrekə'lekʃn] *n* recuerdo *m*.

recommend [ˌrekə'mend] *vt* recomendar.

recompense ['rekəmpens] ◆ *n*: **~ (for)** compensación *f* OR indemnización *f* (por). ◆ *vt*: **to ~ sb (for)** recompensar a alguien (por).

reconcile ['rekənsaɪl] *vt* **1.** (*find agreement between*) conciliar; **to ~ sthg with** hacer compatible algo con. **2.** (*make friendly again*) reconciliar. **3.** (*accept*): **to ~ o.s. to** resignarse a.

reconditioned [ˌriːkən'dɪʃnd] *adj* revisado(da), reparado(da).

reconnaissance [rɪ'kɒnɪsəns] *n* reconocimiento *m*.

reconnoitre Br, **reconnoiter** Am [ˌrekə'nɔɪtər] ◆ *vt* reconocer. ◆ *vi* hacer un reconocimiento.

reconsider [ˌriːkən'sɪdər] *vt & vi* reconsiderar.

reconstruct [ˌriːkən'strʌkt] *vt* (*building, crime*) reconstruir.

record [*n & adj* 'rekɔːd, *vb* rɪ'kɔːd] ◆ *n* **1.** (*of event, piece of information*) registro *m*, anotación *f*; (*of meeting*) actas *fpl*; **on ~** (*on file*) archivado; (*ever recorded*) de que se tiene constancia; **off the ~** confidencial. **2.** (*vinyl disc*) disco *m*. **3.** (*best achievement*) récord *m*. **4.** (*history*) historial *m*; **criminal ~** antecedentes *mpl* penales. ◆ *vt*

1. (*write down*) anotar, tomar nota de. **2.** (*put on tape*) grabar. ◆ *adj* récord (*inv*).

recorded delivery [rɪ'kɔːdɪd-] *n* correo *m* certificado.

recorder [rɪ'kɔːdər] *n* (*musical instrument*) flauta *f*.

record holder *n* plusmarquista *m y f*.

recording [rɪ'kɔːdɪŋ] *n* grabación *f*.

record player *n* tocadiscos *m inv*.

recount [*n* 'riːkaʊnt, *vt sense* 1 rɪ'kaʊnt, *sense* 2 ˌriː'kaʊnt] ◆ *n* recuento *m*. ◆ *vt* **1.** (*narrate*) narrar. **2.** (*count again*) volver a contar.

recoup [rɪ'kuːp] *vt* recuperar.

recourse [rɪ'kɔːs] *n fml*: **to have ~ to** recurrir a.

recover [rɪ'kʌvər] ◆ *vt* **1.** (*retrieve, recoup*) recuperar. **2.** (*regain - calm etc*) recobrar. ◆ *vi*: **to ~ (from)** recuperarse (de).

recovery [rɪ'kʌvərɪ] *n* recuperación *f*.

recreation [ˌrekrɪ'eɪʃn] *n* (*leisure*) esparcimiento *m*, recreo *m*.

recrimination [rɪˌkrɪmɪ'neɪʃn] *n* recriminación *f*.

recruit [rɪ'kruːt] ◆ *n* recluta *m y f*. ◆ *vt* **1.** (*gen*) reclutar; **to ~ sb (for sthg/to do sthg**) reclutar a alguien (para algo/para hacer algo). **2.** (*find, employ*) contratar. ◆ *vi* buscar empleados nuevos.

recruitment [rɪ'kruːtmənt] *n* (*gen*) reclutamiento *m*; (*of staff*) contratación *f*.

rectangle ['rek,tæŋgl] *n* rectángulo *m*.

rectangular [rek'tæŋgjʊlər] *adj* rectangular.

rectify ['rektɪfaɪ] *vt fml* rectificar.

rector ['rektər] *n* **1.** (*priest*) párroco *m*. **2.** *Scot* (*head - of school*) director *m*, -ra *f*; (*- of college, university*) rector *m*, -ra *f*.

rectory ['rektərɪ] *n* rectoría *f*.

recuperate [rɪ'kuːpəreɪt] *vi fml*: **to ~ (from)** recuperarse (de).

recur [rɪ'kɜːr] *vi* repetirse.

recurrence [rɪ'kʌrəns] *n fml* repetición *f*.

recurrent [rɪ'kʌrənt] *adj* que se repite.

recycle [ˌriː'saɪkl] *vt* reciclar.

red [red] ◆ *adj* rojo(ja); (*hair*) pelirrojo (ja). ◆ *n* (*colour*) rojo *m*; **to be in the ~** *inf* estar en números rojos.

red card *n* (FTBL): **to show sb the ~** mostrarle a alguien (la) tarjeta roja.

red carpet *n*: **to roll out the ~ for sb** recibir a alguien con todos los honores. ▶ **red-carpet** *adj*: **to give sb the red-carpet treatment** dispensar a alguien un gran recibimiento.

Red Cross n: **the ~** la Cruz Roja.
redcurrant ['redkʌrənt] n **1.** (fruit) grosella f. **2.** (bush) grosellero m.
redden ['redn] ◆ vt (make red) teñir de rojo. ◆ vi (flush) enrojecer.
redecorate [ˌriː'dekəreɪt] vt & vi volver a pintar (o empapelar).
redeem [rɪ'diːm] vt **1.** (save, rescue) salvar, rescatar. **2.** fml (at pawnbroker's) desempeñar.
redeeming [rɪ'diːmɪŋ] adj: **his only ~ feature** lo único que le salva.
redeploy [ˌriːdɪ'plɔɪ] vt reorganizar.
red-faced [-'feɪst] adj **1.** (flushed) rojo (ja), colorado(da). **2.** (with embarrassment) rojo(ja) de vergüenza.
red-haired [-'heəd] adj pelirrojo(ja).
red-handed [-'hændɪd] adj: **to catch sb ~** coger a alguien con las manos en la masa.
redhead ['redhed] n pelirrojo m, -ja f.
red herring n fig (unhelpful clue) pista f falsa; (means of distracting attention) ardid m para distraer la atención.
red-hot adj (metal, person, passion) al rojo (vivo); (zeal) fervoroso(sa).
redid [ˌriː'dɪd] pt → **redo**.
redirect [ˌriːdɪ'rekt] vt **1.** (retarget) redirigir. **2.** (send elsewhere) enviar a otro lugar. **3.** (forward) reexpedir.
rediscover [ˌriːdɪ'skʌvər] vt **1.** (re-experience) volver a descubrir. **2.** (make popular, famous again): **to be ~ed** ser descubierto(ta) de nuevo.
red light n (traffic signal) semáforo m rojo.
red-light district n barrio m chino.
redo [ˌriː'duː] (pt **-did**, pp **-done**) vt (do again) volver a hacer.
redolent ['redələnt] adj literary **1.** (reminiscent): **~ of** evocador(ra) de. **2.** (smelling): **~ of** con olor a.
redouble [ˌriː'dʌbl] vt: **to ~ one's efforts (to do sthg)** redoblar esfuerzos (para hacer algo).
redraft [ˌriː'drɑːft] vt volver a redactar.
redress [rɪ'dres] fml ◆ n (U) reparación f, desagravio m. ◆ vt: **to ~ the balance (between)** equilibrar la balanza (entre).
red tape n fig papeleo m.
reduce [rɪ'djuːs] ◆ vt reducir; **to be ~d to doing sthg** verse rebajado OR forzado a hacer algo; **to be ~d to** verse sumido OR hundido en. ◆ vi Am (diet) (intentar) adelgazar.
reduction [rɪ'dʌkʃn] n **1.** (gen): **~ (in)** reducción f (de). **2.** (COMM): **~ (of)** descuento m (de).

redundancy [rɪ'dʌndənsɪ] n **1.** Br (job loss) despido m. **2.** (unemployment) desempleo m.
redundant [rɪ'dʌndənt] adj **1.** Br (jobless): **to be made ~** perder el empleo. **2.** (not required - equipment, factory) innecesario(ria); (- comment) redundante.
reed [riːd] n **1.** (plant) carrizo m, cañavera f. **2.** (of musical instrument) lengüeta f.
reef [riːf] n arrecife m.
reek [riːk] vi: **to ~ (of)** apestar (a).
reel [riːl] ◆ n (of cotton, film, on fishing rod) carrete m. ◆ vi **1.** (stagger) tambalearse. **2.** (be stunned): **to ~ from sthg** quedarse atónito(ta) por algo. ▶ **reel in** vt sep sacar enrollando el carrete (en pesca). ▶ **reel off** vt sep recitar al corrido.
reenact [ˌriːɪ'nækt] vt representar de nuevo.
ref [ref] n **1.** (abbr of **referee**) inf (SPORT) árbitro m. **2.** (abbr of **reference**) (ADMIN) ref.
refectory [rɪ'fektərɪ] n refectorio m.
refer [rɪ'fɜːr] vt **1.** (send, direct): **to ~ sb to** (to place) enviar a alguien a; (to source of information) remitir a alguien a. **2.** (report, submit): **to ~ sthg to** remitir algo a. ▶ **refer to** vt fus **1.** (mention, speak about) referirse a. **2.** (consult) consultar.
referee [ˌrefə'riː] ◆ n **1.** (SPORT) árbitro m. **2.** Br (for job application) persona que recomienda a alguien para un trabajo. ◆ vt & vi (SPORT) arbitrar.
reference ['refrəns] n **1.** (mention, reference number): **to make ~ to** hacer referencia a; **with ~ to** fml con referencia a. **2.** (U) (for advice, information): **~ (to)** consulta f (a). **3.** (for job - letter) referencias fpl; (- person) persona que recomienda a alguien para un trabajo.
reference book n libro m de consulta.
reference number n número m de referencia.
referendum [ˌrefə'rendəm] (pl **-s** OR **-da** [-də]) n referéndum m.
refill [n 'riːfɪl, vb ˌriː'fɪl] ◆ n inf: **would you like a ~?** ¿te apetece otra copa? ◆ vt volver a llenar.
refine [rɪ'faɪn] vt **1.** (oil, food) refinar. **2.** (plan, speech) pulir.
refined [rɪ'faɪnd] adj **1.** (oil, food, person) refinado(da). **2.** (equipment, theory) perfeccionado(da).
refinement [rɪ'faɪnmənt] n **1.** (improve-

ment): ~ **(on)** mejora f (de). 2. (U) (gentility) refinamiento m.

reflect [rɪ'flekt] ♦ vt 1. (gen) reflejar. 2. (think, consider): to ~ **that** ... considerar que ... ♦ vi: to ~ **(on** OR **upon)** reflexionar (sobre).

reflection [rɪ'flekʃn] n 1. (gen) reflejo m. 2. (criticism): ~ **on** crítica f de. 3. (thinking) reflexión f; **on** ~ pensándolo bien.

reflector [rɪ'flektər] n reflector m.

reflex ['ri:fleks] n: ~ **(action)** (acto m) reflejo m.

reflexive [rɪ'fleksɪv] adj (GRAMM) reflexivo(va).

reforestation [rɪ:ˌfɒrɪ'steɪʃn] = **reafforestation.**

reform [rɪ'fɔ:m] ♦ n reforma f. ♦ vt reformar. ♦ vi reformarse.

Reformation [ˌrefə'meɪʃn] n: the ~ la Reforma.

reformatory [rɪ'fɔ:mətrɪ] n Am reformatorio m, centro m de menores.

reformer [rɪ'fɔ:mər] n reformador m, -ra f.

refrain [rɪ'freɪn] ♦ n (chorus) estribillo m. ♦ vi fml: to ~ **from doing sthg** abstenerse de hacer algo.

refresh [rɪ'freʃ] vt refrescar.

refreshed [rɪ'freʃt] adj descansado (da).

refresher course [rɪ'freʃər-] n cursillo m de reciclaje.

refreshing [rɪ'freʃɪŋ] adj (change, honesty, drink) refrescante; (sleep) vigorizante.

refreshments [rɪ'freʃmənts] npl refrigerio m.

refrigerator [rɪ'frɪdʒəreɪtər] n refrigerador m.

refuel [ˌri:'fjʊəl] ♦ vt llenar de carburante. ♦ vi repostar.

refuge ['refju:dʒ] n refugio m; **to seek** OR **take** ~ **(in)** fig buscar refugio (en).

refugee [ˌrefjʊ'dʒi:] n refugiado m, -da f.

refund [n 'ri:fʌnd, vb rɪ'fʌnd] ♦ n reembolso m. ♦ vt: to ~ **sthg to sb, to** ~ **sb sthg** reembolsar algo a alguien.

refurbish [ˌri:'fɜ:bɪʃ] vt (building) restaurar; (office, shop) renovar.

refusal [rɪ'fju:zl] n 1. (disagreement, saying no): ~ **(to do sthg)** negativa f (a hacer algo). 2. (withholding, denial) denegación f. 3. (non-acceptance): **to meet with** ~ ser rechazado(da).

refuse¹ [rɪ'fju:z] ♦ vt 1. (withhold, deny): to ~ **sb sthg, to** ~ **sthg to sb** denegar a alguien algo. 2. (decline, reject) rechazar. 3. (not agree, be completely unwilling): **to** ~ **to do sthg** negarse a hacer algo. ♦ vi negarse.

refuse² ['refju:s] n (rubbish) basura f.

refuse collection ['refju:s-] n recogida f de basuras.

refute [rɪ'fju:t] vt fml refutar.

regain [rɪ'geɪn] vt (leadership, first place) recuperar; (health, composure) recobrar.

regal ['ri:gl] adj regio(gia).

regalia [rɪ'geɪljə] n (U) fml ropaje m.

regard [rɪ'gɑ:d] ♦ n 1. fml (respect, esteem): ~ **(for)** estima f OR respeto m (por). 2. (aspect): **in this/that** ~ a este/ ese respecto. ♦ vt 1. (consider): to ~ **o.s. as sthg** considerarse algo; **to** ~ **sthg/sb as** considerar algo/a alguien como. 2. (look at, view): **to be highly** ~**ed** estar muy bien considerado. ▶ **regards** npl (in greetings) recuerdos mpl. ♦ **as regards** prep en cuanto a, por lo que se refiere a. ▶ **in regard to, with regard to** prep respecto a, en cuanto a.

regarding [rɪ'gɑ:dɪŋ] prep respecto a, en cuanto a.

regardless [rɪ'gɑ:dlɪs] adv a pesar de todo. ▶ **regardless of** prep sin tener en cuenta; ~ **of the cost** cueste lo que cueste.

regime [reɪ'ʒi:m] n régimen m.

regiment ['redʒɪmənt] n (MIL) regimiento m.

region ['ri:dʒən] n región f; **in the** ~ **of** alrededor de.

regional ['ri:dʒənl] adj regional.

register ['redʒɪstər] ♦ n (of electors etc) registro m; (at school) lista f. ♦ vt 1. (record - gen) registrar; (- car) matricular. 2. (express) mostrar, reflejar. ♦ vi 1. (be put on official list): **to** ~ **(as/for)** inscribirse (como/para). 2. (book in - at hotel) registrarse; (- at conference) inscribirse. 3. inf (be noticed): **I told him but it didn't seem to** ~ se lo dije, pero no pareció que lo captara.

registered ['redʒɪstəd] adj 1. (officially listed) inscrito(ta) oficialmente. 2. (letter, parcel) certificado(da).

registered trademark n marca f registrada.

registrar [ˌredʒɪ'strɑ:ʳ] n 1. (keeper of records) registrador m, -ra f oficial. 2. (UNIV) secretario m, -ria f general. 3. (doctor) médico m, -ca f de hospital.

registration [ˌredʒɪ'streɪʃn] n 1. (gen) registro m. 2. (AUT) = **registration number.**

registration number n número m de matrícula.

registry ['redʒɪstrɪ] n registro m.

registry office n registro m civil.

regret [rɪ'gret] ◆ n 1. fml (sorrow) pesar m. 2. (sad feeling): **I've no ~s about it** no lo lamento en absoluto. ◆ vt (be sorry about): **to ~ sthg/doing sthg** lamentar algo/haber hecho algo.

regretfully [rɪ'gretfulɪ] adv con pesar; **~, we have to announce ...** lamentamos tener que anunciar ...

regrettable [rɪ'gretəbl] adj fml lamentable.

regroup [,ri:'gru:p] vi reagruparse.

regular ['regjulər] ◆ adj 1. (gen) regular. 2. (customer) habitual, asiduo(dua). 3. (time, place) acostumbrado(da); (problem) usual, normal. 4. Am (pleasant) legal. ◆ n cliente m habitual.

regularly ['regjuləlɪ] adv 1. (gen) con regularidad. 2. (equally spaced) de manera uniforme.

regulate ['regjuleɪt] vt regular.

regulation [,regju'leɪʃn] n 1. (rule) regla f, norma f. 2. (U) (control) regulación f.

rehabilitate [,ri:ə'bɪlɪteɪt] vt rehabilitar.

rehearsal [rɪ'hɜ:sl] n ensayo m.

rehearse [rɪ'hɜ:s] vt ensayar.

reign [reɪn] lit & fig ◆ n reinado m. ◆ vi: **to ~ (over)** reinar (sobre).

reimburse [,ri:ɪm'bɜ:s] vt: **to ~ sb (for sthg)** reembolsar a alguien (algo).

rein [reɪn] n fig: **to give (a) free ~ to sb, to give sb free ~** dar rienda suelta a alguien. ▶ **reins** npl (for horse) riendas fpl.

reindeer ['reɪn,dɪər] (pl inv) n reno m.

reinforce [,ri:ɪn'fɔ:s] vt reforzar.

reinforced concrete [,ri:ɪn'fɔ:st-] n cemento m OR hormigón m armado.

reinforcement [,ri:ɪn'fɔ:smənt] n refuerzo m. ▶ **reinforcements** npl refuerzos mpl.

reinstate [,ri:ɪn'steɪt] vt 1. (give job back to) restituir OR reintegrar en su puesto a. 2. (bring back) restablecer.

reissue [ri:'ɪʃu:] vt (gen) reeditar, reimprimir; (film) reestrenar.

reiterate [ri:'ɪtəreɪt] vt fml reiterar.

reject [n 'ri:dʒekt, vb rɪ'dʒekt] ◆ n desecho m; **~s** artículos mpl defectuosos. ◆ vt rechazar.

rejection [rɪ'dʒekʃn] n rechazo m.

rejoice [rɪ'dʒɔɪs] vi: **to ~ (at OR in)** ale-

grarse OR regocijarse (con).

rejuvenate [rɪ'dʒu:vəneɪt] vt rejuvenecer.

rekindle [,ri:'kɪndl] vt fig reavivar.

relapse [rɪ'læps] ◆ n recaída f. ◆ vi: **to ~ into** volver a caer en.

relate [rɪ'leɪt] ◆ vt 1. (connect): **to ~ sthg (to)** relacionar algo (con). 2. (tell) contar, relatar. ◆ vi 1. (be connected): **to ~ to** estar relacionado(da) con. 2. (concern): **to ~ to** referirse a. 3. (empathize): **to ~ (to sb)** tener mucho en común (con alguien). ▶ **relating to** prep concerniente OR referente a.

related [rɪ'leɪtɪd] adj 1. (in same family) emparentado(da); **to be ~ to sb** ser pariente de alguien. 2. (connected) relacionado(da).

relation [rɪ'leɪʃn] n 1. (connection): **~ (to/between)** relación f (con/entre); **to bear no ~ to** no tener nada que ver con. 2. (family member) pariente m y f, familiar m y f. ▶ **relations** npl (family, race, industrial) relaciones fpl.

relationship [rɪ'leɪʃnʃɪp] n relación f; **a good ~** buenas relaciones.

relative ['relətɪv] ◆ adj relativo(va). ◆ n pariente m y f, familiar m y f. ▶ **relative to** prep fml con relación a.

relatively ['relətɪvlɪ] adv relativamente.

relax [rɪ'læks] ◆ vt 1. (gen) relajar. 2. (loosen - grip) aflojar. ◆ vi 1. (gen) relajarse. 2. (loosen) aflojarse.

relaxation [,ri:læk'seɪʃn] n 1. (recreation) relajación f, esparcimiento m. 2. (slackening - of discipline) relajación f.

relaxed [rɪ'lækst] adj (gen) relajado (da); (person) tranquilo(la); (atmosphere) desenfadado(da).

relaxing [rɪ'læksɪŋ] adj relajante.

relay ['ri:leɪ] ◆ n 1. (SPORT): **~ (race)** carrera f de relevos. 2. (RADIO & TV) retransmisión f. ◆ vt 1. (broadcast) retransmitir. 2. (repeat): **to ~ sthg (to)** transmitir algo (a).

release [rɪ'li:s] ◆ n 1. (setting free) puesta f en libertad, liberación f. 2. (relief) liberación f. 3. (statement) comunicado m. 4. (emitting - of gas) escape m; (- of heat, pressure) emisión f. 5. (thing issued - of film) estreno m; (- of record) grabación f. ◆ vt 1. (set free): **to ~ sb (from)** liberar a alguien (de). 2. (lift restriction on): **to ~ sb from** descargar OR liberar a alguien de. 3. (make available - funds, resources) entregar. 4. (let go - rope, reins, person) soltar; (- grip) aflojar; (- *brake, lever*) soltar; (- *mechanism, trigger*) **dispar**ar. 5. (*emit - gas, heat*) despedir. 6. (*issue - film*) estrenar; (- *record*) sacar.

relegate ['relɪgeɪt] vt 1. (*demote*): **to ~ sthg/sb (to)** relegar algo/a alguien (a). 2. Br (FTBL): **to be ~d** descender (*a una división inferior*).

relent [rɪ'lent] vi (*person*) ablandarse; (*wind, storm*) remitir, aminorar.

relentless [rɪ'lentlɪs] adj implacable.

relevant ['reləvənt] adj 1. (*connected*): ~ **(to)** relacionado(da) (con), pertinente (a). 2. (*important*): ~ **(to)** importante OR relevante (para). 3. (*appropriate*) pertinente, oportuno(na).

reliable [rɪ'laɪəbl] adj 1. (*dependable*) fiable. 2. (*information*) fidedigno(na).

reliably [rɪ'laɪəblɪ] adv 1. (*dependably*) sin fallar. 2. (*correctly*): **to be ~ informed about sthg** saber algo de fuentes fidedignas.

reliant [rɪ'laɪənt] adj: **to be ~ on sb/sthg** depender de alguien/de algo.

relic ['relɪk] n 1. (*gen*) reliquia f. 2. (*custom still in use*) vestigio m.

relief [rɪ'li:f] n 1. (*comfort*) alivio m. 2. (*for poor, refugees*) ayuda f (benéfica). 3. (U) Am (*social security*) subsidio m.

relieve [rɪ'li:v] vt 1. (*ease, lessen*) aliviar. 2. (*take away from*): **to ~ sb of sthg** liberar a alguien de algo.

religion [rɪ'lɪdʒn] n religión f.

religious [rɪ'lɪdʒəs] adj religioso(sa).

relinquish [rɪ'lɪŋkwɪʃ] vt (*power, claim*) renunciar a; (*hold*) soltar.

relish ['relɪʃ] ♦ n 1. (*enjoyment*): **with (great)** ~ con (gran) deleite. 2. (*pickle*) salsa rojiza agridulce con pepinillo etc. ♦ vt disfrutar con; **to ~ the thought** OR **idea** OR **prospect of doing sthg** disfrutar de antemano con la idea de hacer algo.

relocate [ˌri:ləʊ'keɪt] ♦ vt trasladar. ♦ vi trasladarse.

reluctance [rɪ'lʌktəns] n desgana f.

reluctant [rɪ'lʌktənt] adj reacio(cia); **to be ~ to do sthg** estar poco dispuesto a hacer algo.

reluctantly [rɪ'lʌktəntlɪ] adv con desgana.

rely [rɪ'laɪ] ► **rely on** vt fus 1. (*count on*) contar con; **to ~ on sb/sthg to do sthg** estar seguro de que alguien/algo hará algo. 2. (*be dependent on*): **to ~ on sb/sthg for sthg** depender de alguien/algo para algo.

remain [rɪ'meɪn] ♦ vt continuar como; **to ~ the same** continuar siendo igual.

♦ vi 1. (*stay*) quedarse, permanecer. 2. (*survive - custom, problem*) quedar, continuar. 3. (*be left*): **to ~ to be done/proved** quedar por hacer/probar. ► **remains** npl restos mpl.

remainder [rɪ'meɪndər] n 1. (*rest*): **the ~** el resto. 2. (MATH) resto m.

remaining [rɪ'meɪnɪŋ] adj restante.

remand [rɪ'mɑ:nd] (JUR) ♦ n: **on ~** detenido(da) en espera de juicio. ♦ vt: **to be ~ed in custody** estar bajo custodia.

remark [rɪ'mɑ:k] ♦ n (*comment*) comentario m. ♦ vt: **to ~ (that)** comentar que.

remarkable [rɪ'mɑ:kəbl] adj excepcional, extraordinario(ria).

remarry [ˌri:'mærɪ] vi volverse a casar.

remedial [rɪ'mi:djəl] adj 1. (SCH) (*class, teacher*) de refuerzo; (*pupil*) atrasado (da). 2. (*corrective*) correctivo(va).

remedy ['remədɪ] ♦ n lit & fig: ~ **(for)** remedio m (para). ♦ vt remediar.

remember [rɪ'membər] ♦ vt (*gen*) recordar, acordarse de; **to ~ to do sthg** acordarse de hacer algo; **to ~ doing sthg** recordar OR acordarse de haber hecho algo. ♦ vi (*gen*) recordar, acordarse.

remembrance [rɪ'membrəns] n fml: **in ~ of** en conmemoración de.

Remembrance Day n en Gran Bretaña, día en conmemoración por los caídos en las dos guerras mundiales.

remind [rɪ'maɪnd] vt: **to ~ sb (about sthg/to do sthg)** recordar a alguien (algo/que haga algo); **she ~s me of my sister** me recuerda a mi hermana.

reminder [rɪ'maɪndər] n 1. (*to jog memory*) recordatorio m, recuerdo m. 2. (*letter, note*) notificación f, aviso m.

reminisce [ˌremɪ'nɪs] vi: **to ~ (about sthg)** rememorar (algo).

reminiscent [ˌremɪ'nɪsnt] adj (*similar to*): ~ **of** evocador(ra) de.

remiss [rɪ'mɪs] adj negligente, remiso (sa); **it was ~ of me** fue una negligencia por mi parte.

remit[1] [rɪ'mɪt] vt (*money*) remitir.

remit[2] ['ri:mɪt] n (*responsibility*) misión f.

remittance [rɪ'mɪtns] n giro m.

remnant ['remnənt] n 1. (*remaining part*) resto m. 2. (*of cloth*) retal m.

remold Am = **remould**.

remorse [rɪ'mɔ:s] n (U) remordimiento m.

remorseful [rɪ'mɔ:sfʊl] adj lleno(na) de remordimiento.

remorseless [rɪ'mɔ:slɪs] adj 1. (*pitiless*)

despiadado(da). **2.** (*unstoppable*) implacable.

remote [rɪ'məʊt] *adj* **1.** (*place, time possibility*) remoto(ta). **2.** (*from reality etc*): ~ **(from)** apartado(da) OR alejado(da) (de).

remote control *n* mando m a distancia.

remotely [rɪ'məʊtlɪ] *adv* **1.** (*in the slightest*): **not** ~ ni remotamente, en lo más mínimo. **2.** (*far off*) muy lejos.

remould Br, **remold** Am ['riːməʊld] *n* neumático m recauchutado.

removable [rɪ'muːvəbl] *adj* (*detachable*) separable.

removal [rɪ'muːvl] *n* **1.** (U) (*act of removing*) separación f, extracción f; (*of threat, clause*) supresión f. **2.** Br (*change of house*) mudanza f.

removal van *n* Br camión m de mudanzas.

remove [rɪ'muːv] *vt* **1.** (*take away, clean away*): **to** ~ **sthg (from)** quitar algo (de). **2.** (*take off*) quitarse, sacarse. **3.** (*from a job, post*): **to** ~ **sb (from)** destituir a alguien (de). **4.** (*problem*) eliminar, resolver; (*suspicion*) disipar.

remuneration [rɪ,mjuːnə'reɪʃn] *n fml* remuneración f.

Renaissance [rə'neɪsəns] *n*: **the** ~ **el** Renacimiento.

render ['rendə^r] *vt* **1.** (*make*): **to** ~ **sthg useless** hacer OR volver algo inútil. **2.** (*give - help*) prestar, dar.

rendering ['rendərɪŋ] *n* interpretación f.

rendezvous ['rɒndɪvuː] (*pl inv*) *n* (*meeting*) cita f.

renegade ['renɪgeɪd] ♦ *adj* renegado (da). ♦ *n* renegado m, -da f.

renew [rɪ'njuː] *vt* **1.** (*attempt, attack*) reemprender. **2.** (*relationship*) reanudar, renovar. **3.** (*licence, contract*) renovar. **4.** (*strength, interest*) reavivar.

renewable [rɪ'njuːəbl] *adj* renovable.

renewal [rɪ'njuːəl] *n* **1.** (*of an activity*) reanudación f. **2.** (*of a contract, licence etc*) renovación f.

renounce [rɪ'naʊns] *vt* renunciar a.

renovate ['renəveɪt] *vt* reformar, renovar.

renown [rɪ'naʊn] *n* renombre m.

renowned [rɪ'naʊnd] *adj*: ~ **(for)** célebre (por).

rent [rent] ♦ *n* alquiler m. ♦ *vt* alquilar, rentar Amer.

rental ['rentl] ♦ *adj* de alquiler. ♦ *n* alquiler m.

renunciation [rɪ,nʌnsɪ'eɪʃn] *n* renuncia f.

reorganize, -ise [,riː'ɔːgənaɪz] *vt* reorganizar.

rep [rep] *n* **1.** *abbr of* **representative**. **2.** *abbr of* **repertory**.

repaid [riː'peɪd] *pt & pp* → **repay**.

repair [rɪ'peə^r] ♦ *n* reparación f, refacción f Amer; **in good/bad** ~ en buen/mal estado. ♦ *vt* reparar, refaccionar Amer.

repair kit *n* caja de herramientas de una bicicleta.

repartee [,repɑː'tiː] *n* intercambio m de réplicas ingeniosas.

repatriate [,riː'pætrɪeɪt] *vt* repatriar.

repay [riː'peɪ] (*pt & pp* **repaid**) *vt* devolver; **to** ~ **sb sthg, to** ~ **sthg to sb** devolver a alguien algo.

repayment [riː'peɪmənt] *n* **1.** (*act of paying back*) devolución f, reembolso m. **2.** (*sum*) pago m.

repeal [rɪ'piːl] ♦ *n* revocación f, abrogación f. ♦ *vt* revocar, abrogar.

repeat [rɪ'piːt] ♦ *vt* **1.** (*gen*) repetir. **2.** (*TV, radio programme*) volver a emitir. ♦ *n* reposición f.

repeatedly [rɪ'piːtɪdlɪ] *adv* repetidamente.

repel [rɪ'pel] *vt* (*disgust*) repeler.

repellent [rɪ'pelənt] ♦ *adj* repelente. ♦ *n* espray m anti-insectos.

repent [rɪ'pent] ♦ *vt* arrepentirse de. ♦ *vi*: **to** ~ **of** arrepentirse de.

repentance [rɪ'pentəns] *n* arrepentimiento m.

repercussions [,riːpə'kʌʃnz] *npl* repercusiones fpl.

repertoire ['repətwɑː^r] *n* repertorio m.

repertory ['repətrɪ] *n* repertorio m.

repetition [,repɪ'tɪʃn] *n* repetición f.

repetitious [,repɪ'tɪʃəs], **repetitive** [rɪ'petɪtɪv] *adj* repetitivo(va).

replace [rɪ'pleɪs] *vt* **1.** (*take the place of*) sustituir. **2.** (*change for something else*): **to** ~ **sthg (with)** cambiar algo (por). **3.** (*change for somebody else*): **to** ~ **sb (with)** sustituir a alguien (por). **4.** (*supply another*): **to** ~ **sthg** dar otro(tra). **5.** (*put back*) poner en su sitio.

replacement [rɪ'pleɪsmənt] *n* **1.** (*act of replacing*) sustitución f. **2.** (*something new*): ~ **(for)** sustituto m, -ta f (para). **3.** (*somebody new*): ~ **(for)** sustituto m, -ta f OR suplente m y f (de).

replay [*n* 'riːpleɪ, *vb* ,riː'pleɪ] ♦ *n* repetición f (*de un partido*). ♦ *vt* (*film, tape*) volver a poner.

replenish [rɪ'plenɪʃ] *vt fml*: **to** ~ **sthg**

(with) reaprovisionar OR reponer algo (de).

replica ['replɪkə] n réplica f.

reply [rɪ'plaɪ] ♦ n: ~ **(to)** respuesta f (a). ♦ vt responder, contestar. ♦ vi: **to ~ (to sb/sthg)** responder (a alguien/algo).

reply coupon n cupón m de respuesta.

report [rɪ'pɔːt] ♦ n 1. (gen) informe m; (PRESS & TV) reportaje m. 2. Br (SCH) boletín m de evaluación. ♦ vt 1. (say, make known): **to ~ that** informar que, reportar que Amer; **to ~ sthg (to)** informar de algo (a). 2. (complain about): **to ~ sb (to sb for sthg)** denunciar a alguien (a alguien por algo), reportar a alguien (a alguien por algo) Amer. ♦ vi 1. (give account): **to ~ on** informar sobre. 2. (present oneself): **to ~ to sb/for sthg** presentarse a alguien/para algo.

report card n boletín m de evaluación.

reportedly [rɪ'pɔːtɪdlɪ] adv según se afirma.

reporter [rɪ'pɔːtər] n reportero m, -ra f.

repose [rɪ'pəʊz] n literary reposo m.

repossess [ˌriːpə'zes] vt requisar la posesión de.

reprehensible [ˌreprɪ'hensəbl] adj fml reprensible.

represent [ˌreprɪ'zent] vt (gen) representar; (person, country) representar a.

representation [ˌreprɪzen'teɪʃn] n representación f. ▶ **representations** npl fml: **to make ~s** to presentar una queja a.

representative [ˌreprɪ'zentətɪv] ♦ adj: ~ **(of)** representativo(va) (de). ♦ n representante m y f.

repress [rɪ'pres] vt reprimir.

repression [rɪ'preʃn] n represión f.

reprieve [rɪ'priːv] n 1. (delay) tregua f. 2. (of death sentence) indulto m.

reprimand ['reprɪmɑːnd] ♦ n reprensión f. ♦ vt reprender.

reprisal [rɪ'praɪzl] n represalia f.

reproach [rɪ'prəʊtʃ] ♦ n reproche m. ♦ vt: **to ~ sb (for OR with sthg)** reprochar a alguien (algo).

reproachful [rɪ'prəʊtʃfʊl] adj de reproche.

reproduce [ˌriːprə'djuːs] ♦ vt reproducir. ♦ vi (BIOL) reproducirse.

reproduction [ˌriːprə'dʌkʃn] n reproducción f.

reproof [rɪ'pruːf] n 1. (words of blame) reprobación f. 2. (disapproval) reproche m.

reprove [rɪ'pruːv] vt: **to ~ sb (for)** reprobar a alguien (por).

reptile ['reptaɪl] n reptil m.

republic [rɪ'pʌblɪk] n república f.

republican [rɪ'pʌblɪkən] ♦ adj republicano(na). ♦ n republicano m, -na f. ▶ **Republican** ♦ adj 1. (in US) republicano(na); **the Republican Party** el partido republicano. 2. (in Northern Ireland) independentista. ♦ n 1. (in US) republicano m, -na f. 2. (in Northern Ireland) independentista m y f.

repudiate [rɪ'pjuːdɪeɪt] vt fml repudiar.

repulse [rɪ'pʌls] vt rechazar.

repulsive [rɪ'pʌlsɪv] adj repulsivo(va).

reputable ['repjʊtəbl] adj de buena fama OR reputación.

reputation [ˌrepjʊ'teɪʃn] n reputación f.

repute [rɪ'pjuːt] n fml: **of good/ill ~** de buena/mala fama.

reputed [rɪ'pjuːtɪd] adj reputado(da); **to be ~ to be/do sthg** tener fama de ser/hacer algo.

reputedly [rɪ'pjuːtɪdlɪ] adv según se dice.

request [rɪ'kwest] ♦ n: ~ **(for)** petición f (de); **on ~** a petición del interesado. ♦ vt solicitar, pedir; **to ~ sb to do sthg** rogar a alguien que haga algo.

request stop n Br parada f discrecional.

require [rɪ'kwaɪər] vt necesitar, requerir; **to ~ sb to do sthg** exigir a alguien que haga algo.

requirement [rɪ'kwaɪəmənt] n requisito m.

requisition [ˌrekwɪ'zɪʃn] vt requisar.

rerun ['riːrʌn] n 1. (film, programme) reposición f. 2. (repeated situation) repetición f.

resat [ˌriː'sæt] pt & pp → **resit**.

rescind [rɪ'sɪnd] vt (JUR) (contract) rescindir; (law) revocar.

rescue ['reskjuː] ♦ n rescate m. ♦ vt: **to ~ sb/sthg (from)** rescatar a alguien/algo (de).

rescuer ['reskjʊər] n rescatador m, -ra f.

research [ˌrɪ'sɜːtʃ] ♦ n (U): ~ **(on OR into)** investigación f (de OR sobre); ~ **and development** investigación y desarrollo. ♦ vt investigar.

researcher [rɪ'sɜːtʃər] n investigador m, -ra f.

resemblance [rɪ'zembləns] n parecido m, semejanza f.

resemble [rɪ'zembl] vt parecerse a.

resent [rɪ'zent] *vt* tomarse a mal.

resentful [rɪ'zentful] *adj* resentido (da).

resentment [rɪ'zentmənt] *n* resentimiento *m*.

reservation [ˌrezə'veɪʃn] *n* **1.** (*booking*) reserva *f*. **2.** (*uncertainty*): **without ~** sin reserva. **3.** Am (*for Native Americans*) reserva *f*. ▶ **reservations** *npl* (*doubts*) reservas *fpl*.

reserve [rɪ'zɜːv] ◆ *n* **1.** (*gen*) reserva *f*; **in ~** en reserva. **2.** (SPORT) suplente *m y f*. ◆ *vt* **1.** (*save, book*) reservar. **2.** (*retain*): **to ~ the right to do sthg** reservarse el derecho a hacer algo.

reserved [rɪ'zɜːvd] *adj* reservado(da).

reservoir ['rezəvwɑːr] *n* (*lake*) pantano *m*, embalse *m*.

reset [ˌriː'set] (*pt & pp* **reset**) *vt* (*clock*) poner en hora; (*meter, controls, computer*) reinicializar.

reshape [ˌriː'ʃeɪp] *vt* (*policy, thinking*) reformar, rehacer.

reshuffle [ˌriː'ʃʌfl] *n* remodelación *f*; **cabinet ~** remodelación del gabinete.

reside [rɪ'zaɪd] *vi fml* (*live*) residir.

residence ['rezɪdəns] *n* **1.** (*house*) residencia *f*. **2.** (*state of residing*): **to be in ~** (**at**) residir (a).

residence permit *n* permiso *m* de residencia.

resident ['rezɪdənt] ◆ *adj* **1.** (*settled, living*) residente. **2.** (*on-site, live-in*) que vive en su lugar de trabajo. ◆ *n* residente *m y f*.

residential [ˌrezɪ'denʃl] *adj* (*live-in*) en régimen de internado.

residential area *n* zona *f* residencial.

residue ['rezɪdjuː] *n* residuo *m*.

resign [rɪ'zaɪn] ◆ *vt* **1.** (*give up*) dimitir de, renunciar a. **2.** (*accept calmly*): **to ~ o.s. to sthg** resignarse a algo. ◆ *vi* (*quit*): **to ~ (from)** dimitir (de).

resignation [ˌrezɪg'neɪʃn] *n* **1.** (*from job*) dimisión *f*. **2.** (*calm acceptance*) resignación *f*.

resigned [rɪ'zaɪnd] *adj*: **~ to** resignado(da) (a).

resilient [rɪ'zɪlɪənt] *adj* (*person*) resistente, fuerte; (*rubber*) elástico(ca).

resin ['rezɪn] *n* resina *f*.

resist [rɪ'zɪst] *vt* **1.** (*refuse to accept*) resistir, oponerse a. **2.** (*fight against*) resistir a. **3.** (*refuse to give in to - temptation*) resistir.

resistance [rɪ'zɪstəns] *n*: **~ (to)** resistencia *f* (a).

resit [*n* 'riːsɪt, *vb* ˌriː'sɪt] (*pt & pp* **-sat**) Br ◆ *n* (examen *m* de) repesca *f*. ◆ *vt* volver a presentarse a.

resolute ['rezəluːt] *adj* resuelto(ta), determinado(da).

resolution [ˌrezə'luːʃn] *n* **1.** (*gen*) resolución *f*. **2.** (*vow, promise*) propósito *m*.

resolve [rɪ'zɒlv] ◆ *n* (U) resolución *f*. ◆ *vt* **1.** (*vow, promise*): **to ~ that** resolver que; **to ~ to do sthg** resolver hacer algo. **2.** (*solve*) resolver.

resort [rɪ'zɔːt] *n* **1.** (*for holidays*) lugar *m* de vacaciones. **2.** (*solution*): **as a** OR **in the last ~** como último recurso. ▶ **resort to** *vt fus* recurrir a.

resound [rɪ'zaʊnd] *vi* **1.** (*noise*) resonar. **2.** (*place*): **the room ~ed with laughter** la risa resonaba por la habitación.

resounding [rɪ'zaʊndɪŋ] *adj* **1.** (*loud - noise, knock*) retumbante; (- *crash*) estruendoso(sa). **2.** (*very great*) clamoroso (sa).

resource [rɪ'sɔːs] *n* recurso *m*.

resourceful [rɪ'sɔːsful] *adj* de recursos.

respect [rɪ'spekt] ◆ *n* **1.** (*gen*): **~ (for)** respeto *m* (por); **with ~** con respeto. **2.** (*aspect*) aspecto *m*; **in this ~** a este respecto; **in that ~** en cuanto a esto. ◆ *vt* (*admire*) respetar; **to ~ sb for sthg** respetar a alguien por algo. ▶ **respects** *npl*: **to pay one's ~s (to)** presentar uno sus respetos (a). ▶ **with respect to** *prep* con respecto a.

respectable [rɪ'spektəbl] *adj* respetable.

respectful [rɪ'spektful] *adj* respetuoso (sa).

respective [rɪ'spektɪv] *adj* respectivo (va).

respectively [rɪ'spektɪvlɪ] *adv* respectivamente.

respite ['respaɪt] *n* **1.** (*lull*) respiro *m*. **2.** (*delay*) aplazamiento *m*.

resplendent [rɪ'splendənt] *adj literary* resplandeciente.

respond [rɪ'spɒnd] *vi*: **to ~ (to)** responder (a); **to ~ by doing sthg** responder haciendo algo.

response [rɪ'spɒns] *n* respuesta *f*.

responsibility [rɪˌspɒnsə'bɪlətɪ] *n*: **~ (for)** responsabilidad *f* (de).

responsible [rɪ'spɒnsəbl] *adj* **1.** (*gen*) responsable; **~ (for)** responsable (de). **2.** (*answerable*): **~ to sb** responsable ante alguien. **3.** (*job, position*) de responsabilidad.

responsibly [rɪ'spɒnsəblɪ] *adv* de

manera responsable.

responsive [rɪ'spɒnsɪv] *adj* 1. (*quick to react*) que responde muy bien. 2. (*aware*): ~ **(to)** sensible OR perceptivo (va) (a).

rest [rest] ♦ *n* 1. (*remainder*): **the ~ (of)** el resto (de). 2. (*relaxation, break*) descanso *m*; **to have a ~** descansar. 3. (*support - for feet*) descanso *m*; (*- for head*) respaldo *m*. ♦ *vt* 1. (*relax - eyes, feet*) descansar. 2. (*support*) apoyar, descansar. ♦ *vi* 1. (*relax, be still*) descansar. 2. (*depend*): **to ~ on** OR **upon** depender de. 3. (*be supported*) apoyarse, descansar. 4. *phr*: **~ assured that ...** tenga la seguridad de que ...

restaurant ['restərɒnt] *n* restaurante *m*.

restaurant car *n* Br coche *m* OR vagón *m* restaurante.

restful ['restfʊl] *adj* tranquilo(la), apacible.

rest home *n* (*for the elderly*) asilo *m* de ancianos; (*for the sick*) casa *f* de reposo.

restive ['restɪv] *adj* inquieto(ta).

restless ['restlɪs] *adj* 1. (*bored, dissatisfied*) impaciente, desasosegado(da). 2. (*fidgety*) inquieto(ta), agitado(da). 3. (*sleepless*) en blanco, agitado(da).

restoration [,restə'reɪʃn] *n* restauración *f*.

restore [rɪ'stɔːr] *vt* 1. (*reestablish*) restablecer. 2. (*to a previous position or condition*): **to ~ sb to sthg** restaurar a alguien en algo; **to ~ sthg to sthg** volver a poner algo en algo. 3. (*renovate*) restaurar. 4. (*give back*) devolver.

restrain [rɪ'streɪn] *vt* controlar; **to ~ o.s. from doing sthg** contenerse para no hacer algo.

restrained [rɪ'streɪnd] *adj* comedido(da).

restraint [rɪ'streɪnt] *n* 1. (*rule, check*) restricción *f*. 2. (*control*) (U) control *m*.

restrict [rɪ'strɪkt] *vt* (*limit*) restringir, limitar; **to ~ sthg/sb to** restringir algo/a alguien a.

restriction [rɪ'strɪkʃn] *n* restricción *f*.

restrictive [rɪ'strɪktɪv] *adj* restrictivo(va).

rest room *n* Am aseos *mpl*.

result [rɪ'zʌlt] ♦ *n* resultado *m*; **as a ~** como resultado. ♦ *vi* 1. (*cause*): **to ~ (in sthg)** tener como resultado (algo). 2. (*be caused*): **to ~ (from)** resultar (de).

resume [rɪ'zjuːm] ♦ *vt* (*start again*) reanudar. ♦ *vi* volver a empezar.

résumé ['rezjuːmeɪ] *n* 1. (*summary*)

resumen *m*. 2. Am (*of career, qualifications*) currículum *m* (vitae).

resumption [rɪ'zʌmpʃn] *n* reanudación *f*.

resurgence [rɪ'sɜːdʒəns] *n* resurgimiento *m*.

resurrection [,rezə'rekʃn] *n* resurrección *f*.

resuscitate [rɪ'sʌsɪteɪt] *vt* resucitar.

retail ['riːteɪl] ♦ *n* venta *f* al por menor OR al detalle. ♦ *adv* al por menor.

retailer ['riːteɪlər] *n* minorista *m y f*, detallista *m y f*.

retail price *n* precio *m* de venta al público.

retain [rɪ'teɪn] *vt* retener.

retainer [rɪ'teɪnər] *n* (*fee*) anticipo *m*.

retaliate [rɪ'tælɪeɪt] *vi* desquitarse, tomar represalias.

retaliation [rɪ,tælɪ'eɪʃn] *n* (U) represalias *fpl*.

retarded [rɪ'tɑːdɪd] *adj* retrasado(da).

retch [retʃ] *vi* tener náuseas.

retentive [rɪ'tentɪv] *adj* retentivo(va).

reticent ['retɪsənt] *adj* reticente, reservado(da).

retina ['retɪnə] (*pl* **-nas** OR **-nae** [-niː]) *n* retina *f*.

retinue ['retɪnjuː] *n* séquito *m*.

retire [rɪ'taɪər] *vi* 1. (*from work*) jubilarse. 2. *fml* (*to another place, to bed*) retirarse.

retired [rɪ'taɪəd] *adj* jubilado(da).

retirement [rɪ'taɪəmənt] *n* jubilación *f*, retiro *m*.

retiring [rɪ'taɪərɪŋ] *adj* (*shy*) retraído(da).

retort [rɪ'tɔːt] ♦ *n* (*sharp reply*) réplica *f*. ♦ *vt*: **to ~ (that)** replicar (que).

retrace [rɪ'treɪs] *vt*: **to ~ one's steps** desandar lo andado.

retract [rɪ'trækt] ♦ *vt* 1. (*withdraw, take back*) retractarse de. 2. (*pull in - claws*) retraer. ♦ *vi* (*subj: claws*) meterse, retraerse; (*subj: wheels*) replegarse.

retrain [,riː'treɪn] *vt* reciclar.

retraining [,riː'treɪnɪŋ] *n* reciclaje *m*.

retread ['riːtred] *n* neumático *m* recauchutado.

retreat [rɪ'triːt] ♦ *n* 1. (MIL): ~ **(from)** retirada *f* (de). 2. (*peaceful place*) refugio *m*. ♦ *vi* (*move away*): **to ~ (from)** (*gen*) retirarse (de); (*from a person*) apartarse (de).

retribution [,retrɪ'bjuːʃn] *n* castigo *m* merecido.

retrieval [rɪ'triːvl] *n* (COMPUT) recuperación *f*.

retrieve [rɪ'triːv] *vt* 1. (*get back*) recobrar. 2. (COMPUT) recuperar. 3. (*rescue - situation*) salvar.

retriever [rɪ'triːvə^r] *n* perro *m* cobrador.

retrograde ['retrəgreɪd] *adj fml* (*gen*) retrógrado(da); (*step*) hacia atrás.

retrospect ['retrəspekt] *n*: **in ~** retrospectivamente, mirando hacia atrás.

retrospective [,retrə'spektɪv] *adj* 1. *fml* (*gen*) retrospectivo(va). 2. (*law, pay rise*) con efecto retroactivo.

return [rɪ'tɜːn] ◆ *n* 1. (U) (*arrival back*) vuelta *f*, regreso *m*. 2. Br (*ticket*) billete *m* de ida y vuelta. 3. (*profit*) ganancia *f*, rédito *m*. ◆ *vt* 1. (*book, visit, compliment*) devolver. 2. (*reciprocate*) corresponder a. 3. (*replace*) volver a poner en su sitio. 4. (JUR) (*verdict*) pronunciar. 5. (POL) (*candidate*) elegir. ◆ *vi*: **to ~ (from/to)** volver (de/a), regresar (de/a). ▶ **returns** *npl* 1. (COMM) réditos *mpl*. 2. *phr*: **many happy ~s (of the day)!** ¡y que cumplas muchos más! ▶ **in return** *adv* en recompensa. ▶ **in return for** *prep* en recompensa por.

return (key) *n* (COMPUT) tecla *f* de retorno de carro.

return ticket *n* Br billete *m* de ida y vuelta.

reunification [,riːjuːnɪfɪ'keɪʃn] *n* reunificación *f*.

reunion [,riː'juːnjən] *n* reunión *f*.

reunite [,riːjuː'naɪt] *vt* (*people*): **to be ~d with** volver a encontrarse OR verse con; (*factions, parts*) reunir.

rev [rev] *inf* ◆ *n* (*abbr of revolution*) revolución *f* (motriz). ◆ *vt*: **to ~ sthg (up)** acelerar algo. ◆ *vi*: **to ~ (up)** acelerar el motor.

revamp [,riː'væmp] *vt inf* renovar.

reveal [rɪ'viːl] *vt* revelar.

revealing [rɪ'viːlɪŋ] *adj* revelador(ra).

reveille [Br rɪ'vælɪ, Am 'revəlɪ] *n* toque *m* de diana.

revel ['revl] *vi*: **to ~ in** deleitarse en.

revelation [,revə'leɪʃn] *n* revelación *f*.

revenge [rɪ'vendʒ] *n* venganza *f*; **to take ~ (on sb)** vengarse (en alguien).

revenue ['revənjuː] *n* ingresos *mpl*.

reverberate [rɪ'vɜːbəreɪt] *vi* 1. (*reecho*) resonar, retumbar. 2. (*have repercussions*) repercutir.

reverberations [rɪ,vɜːbə'reɪʃnz] *npl* 1. (*echoes*) reverberación *f*. 2. (*repercussions*) repercusiones *fpl*.

revere [rɪ'vɪə^r] *vt fml* venerar.

reverence ['revərəns] *n fml* reverencia *f*.

Reverend ['revərənd] *n* reverendo *m*.

reverie ['revərɪ] *n fml* ensueño *m*.

reversal [rɪ'vɜːsl] *n* 1. (*turning around*) cambio *m* total. 2. (*ill fortune*) contratiempo *m*.

reverse [rɪ'vɜːs] ◆ *adj* inverso(sa). ◆ *n* 1. (AUT): **~ (gear)** marcha *f* atrás. 2. (*opposite*): **the ~** lo contrario. 3. (*opposite side, back*): **the ~** (*gen*) el revés; (*of coin*) el reverso; (*of piece of paper*) el dorso. ◆ *vt* 1. (AUT) dar marcha atrás a. 2. (*change usual order*) invertir. 3. (*change to opposite*) cambiar completamente. 4. Br (TELEC): **to ~ the charges** llamar a cobro revertido. ◆ *vi* (AUT) dar marcha atrás.

reverse-charge call *n* Br llamada *f* a cobro revertido.

reversing light [rɪ'vɜːsɪŋ-] *n* Br luz *f* de marcha atrás.

revert [rɪ'vɜːt] *vi*: **to ~ to** volver a.

review [rɪ'vjuː] ◆ *n* 1. (*examination*) revisión *f*, repaso *m*. 2. (*critique*) reseña *f*. ◆ *vt* 1. (*reexamine*) revisar. 2. (*consider*) reconsiderar. 3. (*write an article on*) reseñar. 4. Am (*study again*) repasar.

reviewer [rɪ'vjuːə^r] *n* crítico *m*, -ca *f*.

revile [rɪ'vaɪl] *vt literary* injuriar.

revise [rɪ'vaɪz] ◆ *vt* 1. (*reconsider*) revisar. 2. (*rewrite*) modificar, corregir. 3. Br (*study*) repasar. ◆ *vi* Br: **to ~ (for sthg)** repasar (para algo).

revision [rɪ'vɪʒn] *n* 1. (*alteration*) corrección *f*, modificación *f*. 2. Br (*study*) repaso *m*.

revitalize, -ise [,riː'vaɪtəlaɪz] *vt* revivificar.

revival [rɪ'vaɪvl] *n* reactivación *f*.

revive [rɪ'vaɪv] ◆ *vt* 1. (*person, plant*) resucitar; (*economy*) reactivar. 2. (*tradition, play, memories*) restablecer. ◆ *vi* reponerse.

revolt [rɪ'vəult] ◆ *n* rebelión *f*. ◆ *vt* repugnar. ◆ *vi*: **to ~ (against)** rebelarse OR sublevarse (contra).

revolting [rɪ'vəultɪŋ] *adj* repugnante, asqueroso(sa).

revolution [,revə'luːʃn] *n* revolución *f*.

revolutionary [revə'luːʃnərɪ] ◆ *adj* revolucionario(ria). ◆ *n* revolucionario *m*, -ria *f*.

revolve [rɪ'vɒlv] *vi* (*go round*) dar vueltas, girar.

revolver [rɪ'vɒlvə^r] *n* revólver *m*.

revolving [rɪ'vɒlvɪŋ] *adj* giratorio(ria).

revolving door *n* puerta *f* giratoria.

revue [rɪ'vjuː] *n* revista *f* (teatral).

revulsion [rɪ'vʌlʃn] n asco m, repugnancia f.

reward [rɪ'wɔːd] ◆ n recompensa f, premio m. ◆ vt: **to ~ sb (for/with)** recompensar a alguien (por/con).

rewarding [rɪ'wɔːdɪŋ] adj gratificador (ra).

rewind [,riː'waɪnd] (pt & pp **rewound**) vt rebobinar.

rewire [,riː'waɪəʳ] vt cambiar la instalación eléctrica de.

reword [,riː'wɜːd] vt expresar de otra forma.

rewound [,riː'waʊnd] pt & pp → **rewind**.

rewrite [,riː'raɪt] (pt **rewrote** [,riː'rəʊt], pp **rewritten** [,riː'rɪtn]) vt volver a escribir.

Reykjavik ['rekjəvɪk] n Reykjavik.

rhapsody ['ræpsədɪ] n (MUS) rapsodia f.

rhetoric ['retərɪk] n retórica f.

rhetorical question [rɪ'tɒrɪkl-] n pregunta f retórica (a la que no se espera contestación).

rheumatism ['ruːmətɪzm] n reumatismo m.

Rhine [raɪn] n: **the ~** el Rin.

rhino ['raɪnəʊ] (pl inv OR **-s**), **rhinoceros** [raɪ'nɒsərəs] (pl inv OR **-es**) n rinoceronte m.

rhododendron [,rəʊdə'dendrən] n rododendro m.

Rhône [rəʊn] n: **the (River) ~** el (río) Ródano.

rhubarb ['ruːbɑːb] n ruibarbo m.

rhyme [raɪm] ◆ n 1. (gen) rima f. 2. (poem) poesía f, versos mpl. ◆ vi: **to ~ (with)** rimar (con).

rhythm ['rɪðm] n ritmo m.

rib [rɪb] n 1. (ANAT) costilla f. 2. (of umbrella) varilla f.

ribbed [rɪbd] adj de canalé.

ribbon ['rɪbən] n cinta f.

rice [raɪs] n arroz m.

rice pudding n arroz m con leche.

rich [rɪtʃ] ◆ adj 1. (gen) rico(ca). 2. (full): **to be ~ in** abundar en. 3. (fertile) fértil. 4. (indigestible) pesado(da). ◆ npl: **the ~** los ricos. ► **riches** npl 1. (natural resources) riquezas fpl. 2. (wealth) riqueza f.

richly ['rɪtʃlɪ] adv 1. (well-rewarded) ricamente. 2. (plentifully) copiosamente.

richness ['rɪtʃnɪs] n 1. (gen) riqueza f. 2. (fertility) fertilidad f. 3. (indigestibility) pesadez f.

rickety ['rɪkətɪ] adj desvencijado(da).

rickshaw ['rɪkʃɔː] n jinrikisha f.

ricochet ['rɪkəʃeɪ] (pt & pp **-ed** OR **-ted**, cont **-ing** OR **-ting**) ◆ n rebote m. ◆ vi: **to ~ (off)** rebotar (de).

rid [rɪd] (pt **rid** OR **-ded**, pp **rid**) vt: **to ~ sthg/sb of** librar algo/a alguien de; **to get ~ of** deshacerse de.

ridden ['rɪdn] pp → **ride**.

riddle ['rɪdl] n 1. (verbal puzzle) acertijo m. 2. (mystery) enigma m.

riddled ['rɪdld] adj: **to be ~ with** estar plagado(da) de.

ride [raɪd] (pt **rode**, pp **ridden**) ◆ n paseo m; **to go for a ~** (on horseback) darse un paseo a caballo; (on bike) darse un paseo en bicicleta; (in car) darse una vuelta en coche; **to take sb for a ~** inf fig embaucar a alguien. ◆ vt 1. (horse) montar a. 2. (bicycle, motorbike) montar en; **he rode his bike to the station** fue a la estación en bici. 3. Am (bus, train) ir en; (elevator) subir/bajar en. 4. (distance) recorrer. ◆ vi 1. (on horseback) ir a caballo; **she rode over to see me** vino a verme a caballo. 2. (on bicycle) ir en bici; (on motorbike) ir en moto. 3. (in car): **we rode to London in a jeep** fuimos a Londres en jeep.

rider ['raɪdəʳ] n 1. (on horseback) jinete m, amazona f. 2. (on bicycle) ciclista m y f; (on motorbike) motorista m y f.

ridge [rɪdʒ] n 1. (on mountain) cresta f. 2. (on flat surface) rugosidad f.

ridicule ['rɪdɪkjuːl] ◆ n (U) burlas fpl. ◆ vt ridiculizar.

ridiculous [rɪ'dɪkjʊləs] adj ridículo(la).

riding ['raɪdɪŋ] n equitación f.

riding school n escuela f de equitación.

rife [raɪf] adj extendido(da); **to be ~ with** estar lleno de.

riffraff ['rɪfræf] n gentuza f.

rifle ['raɪfl] ◆ n rifle m, fusil m. ◆ vt desvalijar.

rifle range n campo m de tiro.

rift [rɪft] n 1. (GEOL) hendedura f, grieta f. 2. (quarrel) desavenencia f. 3. (POL): **~ between/in** escisión f entre/en.

rig [rɪg] ◆ n: (oil) **~** (onshore) torre f de perforación; (offshore) plataforma f petrolífera. ◆ vt (falsify) amañar, falsificar. ► **rig up** vt sep construir, armar.

rigging ['rɪgɪŋ] n cordaje m.

right [raɪt] ◆ adj 1. (correct) correcto (ta), bueno(na); **to be ~ (about)** tener razón (respecto a); **get it ~!** ¡hazlo bien!

2. (*satisfactory*) bien. **3.** (*morally correct, socially acceptable*) apropiado(da); **to be ~ to do sthg** hacer bien en hacer algo. **4.** (*uppermost*): **~ side** cara *f* anterior OR de arriba. **5.** (*on right-hand side*) derecho (cha). ◆ *n* **1.** (U) (*moral correctness*) bien *m*; **to be in the ~** tener razón. **2.** (*entitlement, claim*) derecho *m*; **by ~s** en justicia. **3.** (*right-hand side*) derecha *f*. ◆ *adv* **1.** (*correctly*) bien, correctamente. **2.** (*to right-hand side*) a la derecha. **3.** (*emphatic use*): **~ here** aquí mismo; **~ at the top** arriba del todo; **~ in the middle** justo en el medio. **4.** (*immediately*): **I'll be ~ back** ahora mismo vuelvo; **~ before/after (sthg)** justo antes/después (de algo); **~ now** ahora mismo, ahorita Amer; **~ away** en seguida. ◆ *vt* **1.** (*correct*) corregir, rectificar. **2.** (*make upright*) enderezar. ◆ *excl* ¡bien! ▶ **Right** *n* (POL): **the Right** la derecha.

right angle *n* ángulo *m* recto; **at ~s (to)** en ángulo recto (con).

righteous ['raɪtʃəs] *adj* (*anger*) justo (ta); (*person*) honrado(da).

rightful ['raɪtful] *adj* legítimo(ma).

right-hand *adj* derecho(cha); **the ~ side** el lado derecho, la derecha.

right-hand drive *adj* que se conduce por la derecha.

right-handed [-'hændɪd] *adj* diestro (tra).

right-hand man *n* brazo *m* derecho.

rightly ['raɪtlɪ] *adv* **1.** (*correctly*) correctamente. **2.** (*appropriately*) debidamente, bien. **3.** (*morally*) con razón.

right of way *n* **1.** (AUT) prioridad *f*. **2.** (*access*) derecho *m* de paso.

right-on *adj inf* esnob.

right wing *n*: **the ~** la derecha. ▶ **right-wing** *adj* derechista.

rigid ['rɪdʒɪd] *adj* **1.** (*stiff*) rígido(da). **2.** (*harsh, unbending*) inflexible.

rigmarole ['rɪgmərəʊl] *n inf pej* **1.** (*process*) ritual *m*. **2.** (*story*) galimatías *m inv*.

rigor Am = **rigour**.

rigorous ['rɪgərəs] *adj* riguroso(sa).

rigour Br, **rigor** Am ['rɪgər] *n* (*firmness*) rigor *m*, severidad *f*.

rile [raɪl] *vt* irritar, sacar de quicio.

rim [rɪm] *n* **1.** (*of container*) borde *m*. **2.** (*of spectacles*) montura *f*.

rind [raɪnd] *n* corteza *f*.

ring [rɪŋ] (*pt* **rang**, *pp* **rung** *vt* senses 1 & 2 & *vi*, *pt* & *pp* **ringed** *vt* senses 3 & 4 only) ◆ *n* **1.** (*telephone call*): **to give sb a ~** llamar a alguien (por teléfono). **2.** (*sound of doorbell*) timbrazo *m*. **3.** (*metal hoop*) aro *m*; (*for curtains*) anilla *f*. **4.** (*on finger*) anillo *m*. **5.** (*circle - of trees*) círculo *m*; (- *of people*) corro *m*. **6.** (*for boxing*) cuadrilátero *m*. **7.** (*illegal group*) cartel *m*. ◆ *vt* **1.** Br (*phone*) llamar por teléfono, telefonear. **2.** (*bell*) tocar. **3.** (*draw a circle round*) señalar con un círculo. **4.** (*surround*) rodear. ◆ *vi* **1.** Br (*phone*) llamar por teléfono, telefonear. **2.** (*bell*) sonar. **3.** (*to attract attention*): **to ~ (for)** llamar (para). **4.** (*resound*): **to ~ with** resonar con. ▶ **ring back** *vt sep* & *vi* Br volver a llamar. ▶ **ring off** *vi* Br colgar. ▶ **ring up** *vt sep* Br llamar (por teléfono).

ring binder *n* carpeta *f* de anillas.

ringing ['rɪŋɪŋ] *n* (*of bell*) repique *m*, tañido *m*; (*in ears*) zumbido *m*.

ringing tone *n* tono *m* de llamada.

ringleader ['rɪŋˌliːdər] *n* cabecilla *m* y *f*.

ringlet ['rɪŋlɪt] *n* rizo *m*, tirabuzón *m*.

ring road *n* Br carretera *f* de circunvalación.

rink [rɪŋk] *n* pista *f*.

rinse [rɪns] *vt* **1.** (*dishes, vegetables*) enjuagar; (*clothes*) aclarar. **2.** (*wash out*): **to ~ one's mouth out** enjuagarse la boca.

riot ['raɪət] ◆ *n* disturbio *m*; **to run ~** desbocarse. ◆ *vi* amotinarse.

rioter ['raɪətər] *n* amotinado *m*, -da *f*.

riotous ['raɪətəs] *adj* ruidoso(sa).

riot police *npl* brigada *f* antidisturbios.

rip [rɪp] ◆ *n* rasgón *m*. ◆ *vt* **1.** (*tear*) rasgar, desgarrar. **2.** (*remove violently*) quitar de un tirón. ◆ *vi* rasgarse, romperse.

RIP (*abbr of* **rest in peace**) RIP.

ripe [raɪp] *adj* maduro(ra); **to be ~ (for sthg)** estar listo (para algo).

ripen ['raɪpn] *vt* & *vi* madurar.

rip-off *n inf* estafa *f*.

ripple ['rɪpl] ◆ *n* **1.** (*in water*) onda *f*, rizo *m*. **2.** (*of laughter, applause*) murmullo *m*. ◆ *vt* rizar.

rise [raɪz] (*pt* **rose**, *pp* **risen** ['rɪzn]) ◆ *n* **1.** (*increase*) ascenso *m*. **2.** Br (*increase in salary*) aumento *m*. **3.** (*to fame etc*) subida *f*. **4.** *phr*: **to give ~ to sthg** dar origen a algo. ◆ *vi* **1.** (*gen*) elevarse. **2.** (*sun, moon*) salir. **3.** (*price, wage, temperature*) subir. **4.** (*stand up, get out of bed*) levantarse. **5.** (*street, ground*) subir. **6.** (*respond*): **to ~** to reaccionar ante. **7.** (*rebel*) sublevarse. **8.** (*move up in status*) ascender; **to ~ to power/fame** ascender al poder/a la gloria.

rising ['raɪzɪŋ] ◆ *adj* **1.** (*sloping upwards*)

ascendente. **2.** (*increasing*) creciente. **3.** (*increasingly successful*) prometedor (ra). ◆ *n* rebelión *f*.

risk [rɪsk] ◆ *n* (*gen*) riesgo *m*; (*danger*) peligro *m*; **to run the ~ of sthg/of doing sthg** correr el riesgo de algo/de hacer algo; **to take a ~** arriesgarse; **at your own ~** bajo tu cuenta y riesgo; **at ~** en peligro. ◆ *vt* **1.** (*put in danger*) arriesgar. **2.** (*take the chance of*): **to ~ doing sthg** exponerse a hacer algo.

risky ['rɪskɪ] *adj* peligroso(sa), arriesgado(da).

risqué ['riːskeɪ] *adj* subido(da) de tono.

rissole ['rɪsəʊl] *n* Br *especie de albóndiga de carne o verduras.*

rite [raɪt] *n* rito *m*.

ritual ['rɪtʃʊəl] ◆ *adj* ritual. ◆ *n* ritual *m*.

rival ['raɪvl] ◆ *adj* rival, opuesto(ta). ◆ *n* rival *m* y *f*, competidor *m*, -ra *f*. ◆ *vt* rivalizar OR competir con.

rivalry ['raɪvlrɪ] *n* rivalidad *f*, competencia *f*.

river ['rɪvəʳ] *n* río *m*.

river bank *n* orilla *f* OR margen *f* del río.

riverbed ['rɪvəbed] *n* cauce *m* OR lecho *m* del río.

riverside ['rɪvəsaɪd] *n*: **the ~** la ribera OR orilla del río.

rivet ['rɪvɪt] ◆ *n* remache *m*. ◆ *vt* **1.** (*fasten*) remachar. **2.** *fig* (*fascinate*): **to be ~ed by sthg** estar fascinado(da) con algo.

Riviera [,rɪvɪ'eərə] *n*: **the French ~** la Riviera francesa.

road [rəʊd] *n* (*minor*) camino *m*; (*major*) carretera *f*; (*street*) calle *f*; **to be on the ~ to** *fig* estar en camino de.

roadblock ['rəʊdblɒk] *n* control *m*.

road hog *n inf pej conductor rápido y negligente.*

road map *n* mapa *m* de carreteras.

road rage *n* arrebato de ira de un automovilista que puede conducirle en ocasiones a cometer una agresión.

road safety *n* seguridad *f* en carretera.

roadside ['rəʊdsaɪd] *n*: **the ~** el borde de la carretera.

road sign *n* señal *f* de carretera.

road tax *n* impuesto *m* de circulación.

roadway ['rəʊdweɪ] *n* calzada *f*.

road works *npl* obras *fpl* de carretera.

roadworthy ['rəʊd,wɜːðɪ] *adj* apto

(ta) para circular.

roam [rəʊm] ◆ *vt* vagar por. ◆ *vi* vagar.

roar [rɔːʳ] ◆ *vi* (*make a loud noise*) rugir, bramar; **to ~ with laughter** reírse a carcajadas. ◆ *vt* rugir, decir a voces. ◆ *n* **1.** (*of traffic*) fragor *m*. **2.** (*of lion, person*) rugido *m*.

roaring ['rɔːrɪŋ] *adj* **1.** (*loud*) clamoroso (sa). **2.** (*fire*) espectacular. **3.** (*as emphasis*): **to do a ~ trade** hacer un gran negocio.

roast [rəʊst] ◆ *adj* asado(da). ◆ *n* asado *m*. ◆ *vt* **1.** (*potatoes, meat*) asar. **2.** (*nuts, coffee beans*) tostar.

roast beef *n* rosbif *m*.

rob [rɒb] *vt* robar; **to ~ sb of sthg** *lit & fig* robar a alguien algo.

robber ['rɒbəʳ] *n* ladrón *m*, -ona *f*.

robbery ['rɒbərɪ] *n* robo *m*.

robe [rəʊb] *n* **1.** (*towelling*) albornoz *m*. **2.** (*of student*) toga *f*. **3.** (*of priest*) sotana *f*. **4.** Am (*dressing gown*) bata *f*.

robin ['rɒbɪn] *n* petirrojo *m*.

robot ['rəʊbɒt] *n* robot *m*.

robust [rəʊ'bʌst] *adj* robusto(ta), fuerte.

rock [rɒk] ◆ *n* **1.** (U) (*substance*) roca *f*. **2.** (*boulder*) peñasco *m*. **3.** Am (*pebble*) guijarro *m*. **4.** (*music*) rock *m*. **5.** Br (*sweet*) palo *m* de caramelo. ◆ *comp* de rock. ◆ *vt* (*cause to move*) mecer, balancear. ◆ *vi* mecerse. ▶ **Rock** *n inf* (*Gibraltar*): **the Rock** el Peñón. ▶ **on the rocks** *adv* **1.** (*drink*) con hielo. **2.** (*marriage, relationship*) que va mal.

rock and roll *n* rock and roll *m*.

rock bottom *n* el fondo; **to hit ~** tocar fondo. ▶ **rock-bottom** *adj*: **rock-bottom prices** precios muy bajos.

rockery ['rɒkərɪ] *n* jardín *m* de rocas.

rocket ['rɒkɪt] *n* cohete *m*.

rocket launcher [-,lɔːntʃəʳ] *n* lanzacohetes *m inv*.

rocking chair ['rɒkɪŋ-] *n* mecedora *f*.

rocking horse ['rɒkɪŋ-] *n* caballo *m* de balancín.

rock'n'roll [,rɒkən'rəʊl] = **rock and roll**.

rocky ['rɒkɪ] *adj* (*full of rocks*) rocoso (sa).

Rocky Mountains *npl*: **the ~** las montañas Rocosas.

rod [rɒd] *n* (*wooden*) vara *f*; (*metal*) barra *f*; (*for fishing*) caña *f*.

rode [rəʊd] *pt* → **ride**.

rodent ['rəʊdənt] *n* roedor *m*.

roe [rəʊ] *n* hueva *f*.

roe deer *n* corzo *m*.

rogue [rəʊg] n (*likeable rascal*) picaruelo m, -la f.

role [rəʊl] n (THEATRE & *fig*) papel m.

roll [rəʊl] ◆ n 1. (*gen*) rollo m; (*of paper, banknotes*) fajo m; (*of cloth*) pieza f. 2. (*of bread*) panecillo m. 3. (*list*) lista f; (*payroll*) nómina f. 4. (*of drums*) redoble m; (*of thunder*) retumbo m. ◆ vt 1. (*turn over*) hacer rodar. 2. (*roll up*) enrollar. 3. (*cigarette*) liar. ◆ vi 1. (*ball, barrel*) rodar. 2. (*vehicle*) ir, avanzar. 3. (*ship*) balancearse. 4. (*thunder*) retumbar; (*drum*) redoblar. ▶ **roll about, roll around** vi: **to ~ about** OR **around (on)** rodar (por). ▶ **roll in** vi inf llegar a raudales. ▶ **roll over** vi darse la vuelta. ▶ **roll up** ◆ vt sep 1. (*make into roll*) enrollar. 2. (*sleeves*) remangarse. ◆ vi 1. (*vehicle*) llegar. 2. inf (*person*) presentarse, aparecer.

roll call n: **to take a ~** pasar lista.

roller ['rəʊlər] n 1. (*cylinder*) rodillo m. 2. (*curler*) rulo m.

roller coaster n montaña f rusa.

roller skate n patín m de ruedas.

rolling ['rəʊlɪŋ] adj 1. (*undulating*) ondulante. 2. phr: **to be ~ in it** inf nadar en la abundancia.

rolling pin n rodillo m (de cocina).

rolling stock n material m rodante.

roll-on adj (*deodorant etc*) de bola.

ROM [rɒm] (*abbr of* **read only memory**) n ROM f.

Roman ['rəʊmən] ◆ adj romano(na). ◆ n romano m, -na f.

Roman Catholic ◆ adj católico (romano) (católica (romana)). ◆ n católico (romano) m, católica (romana) f.

romance [rəʊ'mæns] n 1. (*romantic quality*) lo romántico. 2. (*love affair*) amorío m. 3. (*in fiction - modern*) novela f romántica.

Romania [ruː'meɪnjə] n Rumanía.

Romanian [ruː'meɪnjən] ◆ adj rumano (na). ◆ n 1. (*person*) rumano m, -na f. 2. (*language*) rumano m.

Roman numerals npl números mpl romanos.

romantic [rəʊ'mæntɪk] adj romántico (ca).

Rome [rəʊm] n Roma.

romp [rɒmp] ◆ n retozo m, jugueteo m. ◆ vi retozar, juguetear.

rompers ['rɒmpəz] npl, **romper suit** ['rɒmpər-] n pelele m.

roof [ruːf] n 1. (*of building*) tejado m; (*of vehicle*) techo m; **to go through** OR **hit the ~** (*person*) subirse por las paredes. 2. (*of mouth*) paladar m.

roofing ['ruːfɪŋ] n techumbre f.

roof rack n baca f, portaequipajes m inv.

rooftop ['ruːftɒp] n tejado m.

rook [rʊk] n 1. (*bird*) grajo m. 2. (*chess piece*) torre f.

rookie ['rʊkɪ] n Am inf novato m, -ta f.

room [ruːm, rʊm] n 1. (*in house, building*) habitación f. 2. (*for conferences etc*) sala f. 3. (*bedroom*) habitación f, cuarto m. 4. (U) (*space*) sitio m, espacio m.

rooming house ['ruːmɪŋ-] n Am casa f de huéspedes, pensión f.

roommate ['ruːmmeɪt] n compañero m, -ra f de habitación.

room service n servicio m de habitación.

roomy ['ruːmɪ] adj espacioso(sa), amplio(plia).

roost [ruːst] n percha f, palo m.

rooster ['ruːstər] n gallo m.

root [ruːt] ◆ n lit & fig raíz f; **to take ~** lit & fig arraigar. ◆ vi (*pig etc*) hozar; (*person*) hurgar, escarbar. ▶ **roots** npl (*origins*) raíces fpl. ▶ **root for** vt fus Am inf apoyar a. ▶ **root out** vt sep (*eradicate*) desarraigar.

rope [rəʊp] ◆ n (*thin*) cuerda f; (*thick*) soga f; (NAUT) maroma f, cable m; **to know the ~s** saber de qué va el asunto. ◆ vt atar con cuerda. ▶ **rope in** vt sep inf arrastrar OR enganchar a.

rosary ['rəʊzərɪ] n rosario m.

rose [rəʊz] ◆ pt → **rise**. ◆ adj (*pink*) rosa, color de rosa. ◆ n (*flower*) rosa f.

rosé ['rəʊzeɪ] n rosado m.

rosebud ['rəʊzbʌd] n capullo m de rosa.

rose bush n rosal m.

rosemary ['rəʊzmərɪ] n romero m.

rosette [rəʊ'zet] n (*badge*) escarapela f.

roster ['rɒstər] n lista f.

rostrum ['rɒstrəm] (*pl* **-trums** OR **-tra** [-trə]) n tribuna f.

rosy ['rəʊzɪ] adj 1. (*pink*) sonrosado (da). 2. (*hopeful*) prometedor(ra).

rot [rɒt] ◆ n (U) 1. (*of wood, food*) podredumbre f; (*in society, organization*) decadencia f. 2. Br dated (*nonsense*) tonterías fpl. ◆ vt pudrir. ◆ vi pudrirse.

rota ['rəʊtə] n lista f (de turnos).

rotary ['rəʊtərɪ] ◆ adj giratorio(ria), rotativo(va). ◆ n Am (*roundabout*) glorieta f, cruce m de circulación giratoria.

rotate [rəʊ'teɪt] ◆ vt (*turn*) hacer girar, dar vueltas a. ◆ vi (*turn*) girar, dar vueltas.

rotation [rəʊˈteɪʃn] n (gen) rotación f.
rote [rəʊt] n: **by** ~ de memoria.
rotten [ˈrɒtn] adj 1. (decayed) podrido (da). 2. inf (poor-quality) malísimo(ma), fatal. 3. inf (unpleasant) despreciable. 4. inf (unwell): **to feel** ~ sentirse fatal OR muy mal.
rouge [ruːʒ] n colorete m.
rough [rʌf] ◆ adj 1. (not smooth - surface, skin) áspero(ra); (- ground, road) desigual. 2. (not gentle, brutal) bruto(ta). 3. (crude, not refined - person, manner) grosero(ra), tosco(ca); (- shelter) precario(ria); (- food, living conditions) simple. 4. (approximate - plan, sketch) a grandes rasgos; (- estimate, translation) aproximado(da). 5. (unpleasant) duro(ra), difícil. 6. (wind) violento(ta); (sea) picado(da); (weather, day) tormentoso(sa). 7. (harsh - wine, voice) áspero(ra). 8. (violent - area) peligroso(sa); (- person) violento(ta). ◆ adv: **to sleep** ~ dormir al raso. ◆ n 1. (GOLF): **the** ~ el rough. 2. (undetailed form): **in** ~ en borrador. ◆ vt phr: **to** ~ **it** vivir sin comodidades.
roughage [ˈrʌfɪdʒ] n (U) fibra f.
rough and ready adj tosco(ca).
roughcast [ˈrʌfkɑːst] n mortero m grueso.
roughen [ˈrʌfn] vt poner áspero(ra).
roughly [ˈrʌflɪ] adv 1. (approximately) más o menos. 2. (not gently) brutalmente. 3. (crudely) toscamente.
roulette [ruːˈlet] n ruleta f.
round [raʊnd] ◆ adj redondo(da). ◆ prep 1. (surrounding) alrededor de. 2. (near) cerca de; ~ **here** por aquí. 3. (all over - the world etc) por todo(da). 4. (in circular movement): ~ **(and ~)** alrededor de. 5. (in measurements): **she's 30 inches** ~ **the waist** mide 30 pulgadas de cintura. 6. (at or to the other side of): **they were waiting** ~ **the corner** esperaban a la vuelta de la esquina; **to drive** ~ **the corner** doblar la esquina; **to go** ~ **sthg** rodear algo. 7. (so as to avoid): **he drove** ~ **the pothole** condujo esquivando el bache. ◆ adv 1. (on all sides): **all** ~ por todos lados. 2. (near): ~ **about** alrededor, en las proximidades. 3. (all over): **to travel** ~ viajar por ahí. 4. (in circular movement): ~ **(and ~)** en redondo; **to go** OR **spin** ~ girar. 5. (in measurements): en redondo. 6. (to the other side) al otro lado; **to go** ~ dar un rodeo. 7. (at or to nearby place): **he came** ~ **to see us** vino a vernos. ◆ n 1. (of talks, drinks) ronda f; **a** ~ **of applause** una salva de aplausos.

2. (in championship) vuelta f. 3. (of doctor) visita f; (of milkman, postman) recorrido m. 4. (of ammunition) cartucho m. 5. (in boxing) asalto m. 6. (in golf) vuelta f. ◆ vt doblar. ▶ **rounds** npl (of doctor) visitas fpl; (of postman) recorrido m; **to do** OR **go the** ~**s** (joke, rumour) divulgarse; (illness) estar rodando. ▶ **round off** vt sep terminar. ▶ **round up** vt sep 1. (gather together) reunir. 2. (MATH) redondear.
roundabout [ˈraʊndəbaʊt] n Br 1. (on road) glorieta f, cruce m de circulación giratoria. 2. (at fairground) tiovivo m.
rounders [ˈraʊndəz] n Br juego parecido al béisbol.
roundly [ˈraʊndlɪ] adv rotundamente.
round-shouldered [-ˈʃəʊldəd] adj cargado(da) de espaldas.
round trip n viaje m de ida y vuelta.
roundup [ˈraʊndʌp] n (summary) resumen m.
rouse [raʊz] vt 1. fml (wake up) despertar. 2. (impel): **to** ~ **sb/o.s. to do sthg** animar a alguien/animarse a hacer algo. 3. (excite) excitar.
rousing [ˈraʊzɪŋ] adj (speech) conmovedor(ra); (cheer) entusiasta.
rout [raʊt] ◆ n derrota f aplastante. ◆ vt derrotar, aplastar.
route [ruːt] n (gen) ruta f; (of bus) línea f, recorrido m; (of ship) rumbo m.
route map n plano m (del camino).
routine [ruːˈtiːn] ◆ adj rutinario(ria). ◆ n rutina f.
roving [ˈrəʊvɪŋ] adj volante, itinerante.
row¹ [rəʊ] ◆ n 1. (line) fila f, hilera f. 2. (succession) serie f; **three in a** ~ tres seguidos. ◆ vt (boat) remar. ◆ vi remar.
row² [raʊ] ◆ n 1. (quarrel) pelea f, bronca f. 2. inf (noise) estruendo m, ruido m. ◆ vi (quarrel) reñir, pelearse.
rowboat [ˈrəʊbəʊt] n Am bote m de remos.
rowdy [ˈraʊdɪ] adj (noisy) ruidoso(sa); (quarrelsome) pendenciero(ra).
row house [rəʊ-] n Am casa f adosada.
rowing [ˈrəʊɪŋ] n remo m.
rowing boat n bote m de remo.
royal [ˈrɔɪəl] ◆ adj real. ◆ n inf miembro m de la familia real.
Royal Air Force n: **the** ~ las Fuerzas Aéreas de Gran Bretaña.
royal family n familia f real.
Royal Mail n Br: **the** ~ ≃ Correos m.
Royal Navy n: **the** ~ la Armada de Gran Bretaña.

royalty ['rɔɪəltɪ] *n* realeza *f*. ▶ **royalties** *npl* derechos *mpl* de autor.

rpm (*abbr of* **revolutions per minute**) r.p.m. *fpl*.

RSPCA (*abbr of* **Royal Society for the Prevention of Cruelty to Animals**) *n* sociedad británica protectora de animales, = SPA *f*.

RSVP (*abbr of* **répondez s'il vous plaît**) s.r.c.

Rt Hon (*abbr of* **Right Honourable**) su Sría.

rub [rʌb] ◆ *vt*: **to ~ sthg (against** OR **on)** frotar algo (en OR contra); **to ~ sthg on** OR **onto** frotar algo en; **to ~ sthg in** OR **into** frotar algo en; **to ~ sb up the wrong way** Br, **to ~ sb the wrong way** Am sacar a alguien de quicio. ◆ *vi*: **to ~ (against** sthg) rozar (algo); **to ~ (together)** rozarse. ▶ **rub off on** *vt fus* (*subj: quality*) influir en. ▶ **rub out** *vt sep* (*erase*) borrar.

rubber ['rʌbər] *n* 1. (*substance*) goma *f*, caucho *m*. 2. Br (*eraser*) goma *f* de borrar. 3. Am *inf* (*condom*) goma *f*. 4. (*in bridge*) partida *f*.

rubber band *n* gomita *f*, goma *f*.

rubber plant *n* ficus *m inv*.

rubber stamp *n* estampilla *f*. ▶ **rubber-stamp** *vt* aprobar oficialmente.

rubbish ['rʌbɪʃ] *n* (U) 1. (*refuse*) basura *f*. 2. *inf fig* (*worthless matter*) porquería *f*. 3. *inf* (*nonsense*) tonterías *fpl*.

rubbish bin *n* Br cubo *m* de la basura.

rubbish dump *n* Br vertedero *m*, basurero *m*.

rubble ['rʌbl] *n* (U) escombros *mpl*.

ruby ['ru:bɪ] *n* rubí *m*.

rucksack ['rʌksæk] *n* mochila *f*.

ructions ['rʌkʃnz] *npl inf* bronca *f*.

rudder ['rʌdər] *n* timón *m*.

ruddy ['rʌdɪ] *adj* 1. (*reddish*) rojizo(za). 2. Br *dated* (*for emphasis*) maldito(ta).

rude [ru:d] *adj* 1. (*impolite - person, manners, word*) grosero(ra), liso(sa) Amer; (*- joke*) verde. 2. (*shocking*) violento(ta), brusco(ca).

rudimentary [,ru:dɪ'mentərɪ] *adj* rudimentario(ria).

rueful ['ru:fʊl] *adj* arrepentido(da).

ruffian ['rʌfjən] *n* rufián *m*.

ruffle ['rʌfl] *vt* 1. (*hair*) despeinar; (*water*) agitar; (*feathers*) encrespar. 2. (*composure, nerves*) encrespar.

rug [rʌg] *n* 1. (*carpet*) alfombra *f*. 2. (*blanket*) manta *f* de viaje.

rugby ['rʌgbɪ] *n* rugby *m*.

rugged ['rʌgɪd] *adj* 1. (*wild, inhospitable*) escabroso(sa). 2. (*sturdy*) fuerte. 3. (*roughly handsome*) duro y atractivo (dura y atractiva).

rugger ['rʌgər] *n* Br *inf* rugby *m*.

ruin ['ru:ɪn] ◆ *n* ruina *f*. ◆ *vt* 1. (*destroy*) arruinar, estropear. 2. (*bankrupt*) arruinar. ▶ **in ruin(s)** *adv* en ruinas.

rule [ru:l] ◆ *n* 1. (*regulation, guideline*) regla *f*, norma *f*. 2. (*norm*): **the ~** la norma; **as a ~** por regla general. 3. (*government*) dominio *m*. 4. (*ruler*) regla *f*. ◆ *vt* 1. *fml* (*control*) regir. 2. (*govern*) gobernar. 3. (*decide*): **to ~ that** decidir OR ordenar que. ◆ *vi* 1. (*give decision*) decidir, fallar. 2. *fml* (*be paramount*) ser primordial. 3. (*govern*) gobernar. ▶ **rule out** *vt sep* descartar.

ruled [ru:ld] *adj* rayado(da).

ruler ['ru:lər] *n* 1. (*for measurement*) regla *f*. 2. (*monarch*) soberano *m*, -na *f*.

ruling ['ru:lɪŋ] ◆ *adj* en el poder. ◆ *n* fallo *m*, decisión *f*.

rum [rʌm] *n* ron *m*.

Rumania [ru:'meɪnjə] = **Romania**.

Rumanian [ru:'meɪnjən] = **Romanian**.

rumble ['rʌmbl] ◆ *n* (*gen*) estruendo *m*; (*of stomach*) ruido *m*. ◆ *vi* (*gen*) retumbar; (*stomach*) hacer ruido.

rummage ['rʌmɪdʒ] *vi* hurgar, rebuscar.

rumour Br, **rumor** Am ['ru:mər] *n* rumor *m*.

rumoured Br, **rumored** Am ['ru:məd] *adj*: **to be ~** rumorearse; **she is ~ to be very rich** se rumorea que es muy rica.

rump [rʌmp] *n* 1. (*of animal*) grupa *f*, ancas *fpl*. 2. *inf* (*of person*) trasero *m*.

rump steak *n* filete *m* de lomo.

rumpus ['rʌmpəs] *n inf* lío *m*, jaleo *m*.

run [rʌn] (*pt* ran, *pp* run) ◆ *n* 1. (*on foot*) carrera *f*; **to go for a ~** ir a correr; **on the ~** en fuga. 2. (*journey - in car*) paseo *m* OR vuelta *f* (en coche); (*- in plane, ship*) viaje *m*. 3. (*series - of wins, disasters*) serie *f*; (*- of luck*) racha *f*. 4. (THEATRE): **the play had a 6-week ~** la obra estuvo en cartelera 6 semanas. 5. (*great demand*): **~ on sthg** gran demanda de algo. 6. (*in tights*) carrera *f*. 7. (*in cricket, baseball*) carrera *f*. 8. (*for skiing etc*) pista *f*. 9. (*term*): **in the short/long ~** a corto/largo plazo. ◆ *vt* 1. (*on foot*) correr. 2. (*manage - business*) dirigir, administrar; (*- life, event*) organizar. 3. (*operate - computer program, machine, film*) poner. 4. (*have and use - car etc*) hacer funcionar. 5. (*open - tap*) abrir;

to ~ a bath llenar la bañera. **6.** (*publish*)
publicar. **7.** (*move*): **to ~ sthg along** OR
over pasar algo por. ◆ *vi* **1.** (*on foot*) correr. **2.** (*follow a direction*) seguir. **3.** (*in election*): **to ~ (for)** presentarse como
candidato(ta) (a). **4.** (*factory, machine*)
funcionar; (*engine*) estar encendido
(da); **to ~ on** OR **off sthg** funcionar con
algo; **to ~ smoothly** ir bien. **5.** (*bus, train*)
ir. **6.** (*flow*) correr. **7.** (*tap*) gotear; (*nose*)
moquear; (*eyes*) llorar. **8.** (*colour*)
desteñir. **9.** (*pass - gen*) pasar. **10.** (*continue to be*) seguir. **11.** (*remain valid*) ser
válido(da). ▶ **run across** *vt fus* (*meet*)
encontrarse con. ▶ **run away** *vi* (*flee*):
to ~ away (from) huir OR fugarse (de).
▶ **run down** ◆ *vt sep* **1.** (*run over*) atropellar. **2.** (*criticize*) hablar mal de.
3. (*allow to decline*) debilitar. ◆ *vi* (*battery*)
acabarse; (*clock*) pararse; (*project, business*) debilitarse. ▶ **run into** *vt fus*
1. (*problem*) encontrar; (*person*) tropezarse con. **2.** (*in vehicle*) chocar con.
▶ **run off** ◆ *vt sep* imprimir. ◆ *vi*: **to ~ off
(with)** fugarse (con). ▶ **run out** *vi*
1. (*become used up*) acabarse. **2.** (*expire*)
caducar. ▶ **run out of** *vt fus* quedarse
sin. ▶ **run over** *vt sep* atropellar. ▶ **run
through** *vt fus* **1.** (*be present in*) recorrer,
atravesar. **2.** (*practise*) ensayar. **3.** (*read
through*) echar un vistazo a. ▶ **run to** *vt
fus* (*amount to*) ascender a. ▶ **run up** *vt
fus* (*amass*) incurrir en. ▶ **run up
against** *vt fus* tropezar con.

runaway ['rʌnəweɪ] ◆ *adj* **1.** (*gen*)
fugitivo(va); (*horse*) desbocado(da);
(*train*) fuera de control; (*inflation*)
desenfrenado(da). **2.** (*victory*) fácil. ◆ *n*
fugitivo *m*, -va *f*.

rundown ['rʌndaʊn] *n* (*report*) informe
m, resumen *m*. ▶ **run-down** *adj*
1. (*dilapidated*) en ruinas. **2.** (*tired*) agotado(da).

rung [rʌŋ] ◆ *pp* → **ring**. ◆ *n lit & fig* peldaño *m*.

runner ['rʌnəʳ] *n* **1.** (*athlete*) corredor
m, -ra *f*. **2.** (*smuggler*) contrabandista *m y
f*. **3.** (*on skate*) cuchilla *f*; (*on sledge*) carril
m; (*of drawer, sliding seat*) carro *m*.

runner bean *n* Br judía *f* escarlata.

runner-up (*pl* **runners-up**) *n* subcampeón *m*, -ona *f*.

running ['rʌnɪŋ] ◆ *adj* **1.** (*continuous*)
continuo(nua). **2.** (*consecutive*) seguidos
(das). **3.** (*water*) corriente. ◆ *n* **1.** (*act of
running*) el correr; **to go ~** hacer footing.
2. (SPORT) carreras *fpl*. **3.** (*management*)
dirección *f*, organización *f*. **4.** (*operation*)

funcionamiento *m*. **5.** *phr*: **to be in/out of
the ~ (for sthg)** tener/no tener posibilidades (de algo).

runny ['rʌnɪ] *adj* **1.** (*food*) derretido
(da). **2.** (*nose*) que moquea; (*eyes*)
llorosos(as).

run-of-the-mill *adj* normal y corriente.

runt [rʌnt] *n* **1.** (*animal*) cría *f* más
pequeña y débil. **2.** *pej* (*person*)
renacuajo *m*.

run-up *n* **1.** (*preceding time*) periodo *m*
previo. **2.** (SPORT) carrerilla *f*.

runway ['rʌnweɪ] *n* pista *f*.

rupture ['rʌptʃəʳ] *n* (MED) hernia *f*.

rural ['rʊərəl] *adj* rural.

ruse [ruːz] *n* ardid *m*.

rush [rʌʃ] ◆ *n* **1.** (*hurry*) prisa *f*; **to be in
a ~** tener prisa. **2.** (*burst of activity*): **~ (for**
OR **on sthg)** avalancha *f* (en busca de
algo). **3.** (*busy period*) hora *f* punta.
4. (*surge - of air*) ráfaga *f*; (- *of water*) torrente *m*; (- *mental*) arrebato *m*; **to make
a ~ for sthg** ir en desbandada hacia
algo. ◆ *vt* **1.** (*hurry*) apresurar. **2.** (*send
quickly*) llevar rápidamente. ◆ *vi*
1. (*hurry*) ir de prisa, correr; **to ~ into
sthg** meterse de cabeza en algo.
2. (*surge*) precipitarse. ▶ **rushes** *npl*
(BOT) juncos *mpl*.

rush hour *n* hora *f* punta.

rusk [rʌsk] *n* galleta que se da a los niños
pequeños para que se acostumbran a masticar.

Russia ['rʌʃə] *n* Rusia.

Russian ['rʌʃn] ◆ *adj* ruso(sa). ◆ *n*
1. (*person*) ruso *m*, -sa *f*. **2.** (*language*)
ruso *m*.

rust [rʌst] ◆ *n* moho *m*, óxido *m*. ◆ *vi*
oxidarse.

rustic ['rʌstɪk] *adj* rústico(ca).

rustle ['rʌsl] ◆ *vt* **1.** (*paper*) hacer crujir.
2. Am (*cattle*) robar. ◆ *vi* (*wind, leaves*)
susurrar; (*paper*) crujir.

rusty ['rʌstɪ] *adj lit & fig* oxidado(da).

rut [rʌt] *n* (*track*) rodada *f*; **to get into/be
in a ~** *fig* caer/estar metido en una rutina.

ruthless ['ruːθlɪs] *adj* despiadado(da).

RV *n* Am (*abbr of* **recreational vehicle**)
casa-remolque *f*.

rye [raɪ] *n* (*grain*) centeno *m*.

rye bread *n* pan *m* de centeno.

S

s (pl **ss** OR **s's**), **S** (pl **Ss** OR **S's**) [es] n (letter) s f, S f. ▶ **S** (abbr of south) S.

Sabbath ['sæbəθ] n: **the ~** (for Christians) el domingo; (for Jews) el sábado.

sabbatical [sə'bætɪkl] n sabático m; **on ~** de sabático.

sabotage ['sæbətɑːʒ] ◆ n sabotaje m. ◆ vt sabotear.

saccharin(e) ['sækərɪn] n sacarina f.

sachet ['sæʃeɪ] n bolsita f.

sack [sæk] ◆ n 1. (bag) saco m. 2. Br inf (dismissal): **to get** OR **be given the ~** ser despedido(da). ◆ vt Br inf despedir.

sacking ['sækɪŋ] n (fabric) harpillera f.

sacred ['seɪkrɪd] adj lit & fig sagrado (da).

sacrifice ['sækrɪfaɪs] (RELIG & fig) ◆ n sacrificio m. ◆ vt sacrificar.

sacrilege ['sækrɪlɪdʒ] n (RELIG & fig) sacrilegio m.

sacrosanct ['sækrəʊsæŋkt] adj sacrosanto(ta).

sad [sæd] adj triste.

sadden ['sædn] vt entristecer.

saddle ['sædl] ◆ n 1. (for horse) silla f (de montar). 2. (of bicycle, motorcycle) sillín m, asiento m. ◆ vt 1. (horse) ensillar. 2. fig (burden): **to ~ sb with sthg** cargar a alguien con algo.

saddlebag ['sædlbæg] n alforja f.

sadistic [sə'dɪstɪk] adj sádico(ca).

sadly ['sædlɪ] adv tristemente.

sadness ['sædnɪs] n tristeza f.

s.a.e., sae n abbr of **stamped addressed envelope**.

safari [sə'fɑːrɪ] n safari m.

safe [seɪf] ◆ adj 1. (gen) seguro(ra); **~ and sound** sano y salvo (sana y salva). 2. (without harm) sin contratiempos. 3. (not causing disagreement): **it's ~ to say that ...** se puede afirmar con seguridad que ...; **to be on the ~ side** por mayor seguridad. 4. (reliable) digno(na) de confianza. ◆ n caja f (de caudales).

safe-conduct n salvoconducto m.

safe-deposit box n caja f de seguridad.

safeguard ['seɪfgɑːd] ◆ n salvaguardia f, protección f; **~ against sthg** protección contra algo. ◆ vt: **to ~ sthg/ sb (against sthg)** salvaguardar OR proteger algo/a alguien (contra algo).

safekeeping [,seɪf'kiːpɪŋ] n protección f.

safely ['seɪflɪ] adv 1. (with no danger) con seguridad. 2. (not in danger) seguramente. 3. (unharmed) sin novedad. 4. (for certain): **I can ~ say that** puedo decir con toda confianza que.

safe sex n sexo m sin riesgo.

safety ['seɪftɪ] n seguridad f.

safety belt n cinturón m de seguridad.

safety pin n imperdible m, seguro m Amer.

saffron ['sæfrən] n (spice) azafrán m.

sag [sæg] vi (sink downwards) hundirse, combarse.

sage [seɪdʒ] ◆ adj sabio(bia). ◆ n 1. (herb) salvia f. 2. (wise man) sabio m.

Sagittarius [,sædʒɪ'teərɪəs] n Sagitario m.

Sahara [sə'hɑːrə] n: **the ~ (Desert)** el (desierto del) Sáhara.

said [sed] pt & pp → **say**.

sail [seɪl] ◆ n 1. (of boat) vela f; **to set ~** zarpar. 2. (journey by boat) paseo m en barco de vela. ◆ vt 1. (boat, ship) gobernar. 2. (sea) cruzar. ◆ vi 1. (travel by boat) navegar. 2. (move - boat): **the ship ~ed across the ocean** el barco cruzó el océano. 3. (leave by boat) zarpar. ▶ **sail through** vt fus hacer con facilidad.

sailboat Am = **sailing boat**.

sailing ['seɪlɪŋ] n 1. (U) (SPORT) vela f. 2. (trip by ship) travesía f.

sailing boat Br, **sailboat** Am ['seɪlbəʊt] n barco m de vela.

sailing ship n (buque m) velero m.

sailor ['seɪlər] n marinero m, -ra f.

saint [seɪnt] n (RELIG & fig) santo m, -ta f.

saintly ['seɪntlɪ] adj santo(ta), piadoso (sa).

sake [seɪk] n: **for the ~ of** por (el bien de); **for God's** OR **heaven's ~** ¡por el amor de Dios!

salad ['sæləd] n ensalada f.

salad bowl n ensaladera f.

salad cream n Br salsa parecida a la mahonesa para aderezar la ensalada.

salad dressing n aliño m (para la ensalada).

salami [sə'lɑːmɪ] n salami m.

salary ['sælərɪ] n sueldo m.

sale [seɪl] n 1. (gen) venta f; **on ~** en venta; **(up) for ~** en venta; **'for ~'** 'se vende'. **2.** (*at reduced prices*) liquidación f, saldo m. ▶ **sales** *npl* **1.** (ECON) ventas *fpl*. **2.** (*at reduced prices*): **the ~s** las rebajas.

saleroom Br ['seɪlrʊm], **salesroom** Am ['seɪlzrʊm] *n* sala f de subastas.

sales assistant ['seɪlz-], **salesclerk** Am ['seɪlzklɜːrk] *n* dependiente m, -ta f.

salesman ['seɪlzmən] (*pl* **-men** [-mən]) *n* (*in shop*) dependiente m, vendedor m; (*travelling*) viajante m.

sales rep *n inf* representante m y f.

salesroom Am = **saleroom**.

saleswoman ['seɪlz,wʊmən] (*pl* **-women** [-,wɪmɪn]) *n* (*in shop*) dependienta f, vendedora f; (*travelling*) viajante f.

salient ['seɪljənt] *adj fml* sobresaliente.

saliva [sə'laɪvə] *n* saliva f.

sallow ['sæləʊ] *adj* cetrino(na).

salmon ['sæmən] (*pl inv* OR **-s**) *n* salmón m.

salmonella [,sælmə'nelə] *n* salmonelosis f inv.

salon ['sælɒn] *n* salón m.

saloon [sə'luːn] *n* **1.** Br (*car*) (coche m) utilitario m. **2.** Am (*bar*) bar m. **3.** Br (*in pub*): **~ (bar)** en ciertos pubs y hoteles, bar elegante con precios más altos que los del 'public bar'. **4.** (*in ship*) salón m.

salt [sɔːlt, sɒlt] ◆ *n* sal f. ◆ *vt* (*food*) salar; (*roads*) echar sal en (*las carreteras etc para evitar que se hielen*). ▶ **salt away** *vt sep inf* ahorrar.

salt cellar Br, **salt shaker** Am [-,ʃeɪkər] *n* salero m.

saltwater ['sɔːlt,wɔːtər] *adj* de agua salada.

salty ['sɔːltɪ] *adj* salado(da), salobre.

salutary ['sæljʊtrɪ] *adj* saludable.

salute [sə'luːt] ◆ *n* **1.** (*with hand*) saludo m. **2.** (MIL) (*firing of guns*) salva f, saludo m. ◆ *vt* **1.** (MIL) (*with hand*) saludar. **2.** (*acknowledge formally*) reconocer.

Salvadorean, Salvadorian [,sælvə'dɔːrɪən] ◆ *adj* salvadoreño(ña). ◆ *n* salvadoreño m, -ña f.

salvage ['sælvɪdʒ] ◆ *n* (U) **1.** (*rescue of ship*) salvamento m. **2.** (*property rescued*) objetos *mpl* recuperados OR rescatados. ◆ *vt lit & fig*: **to ~ sthg (from)** salvar algo (de).

salvation [sæl'veɪʃn] *n* salvación f.

Salvation Army *n*: **the ~** el Ejército de Salvación.

same [seɪm] ◆ *adj* mismo(ma); **the ~ colour as his** el mismo color que el suyo; **at the ~ time** (*simultaneously*) al mismo tiempo; (*yet*) aún así; **one and the ~** el mismo (la misma). ◆ *pron*: **the ~** el mismo (la misma); **she did the ~** hizo lo mismo; **the ingredients are the ~** los ingredientes son los mismos OR iguales; **I'll have the ~ (again)** tomaré lo mismo (que antes); **all** OR **just the ~** (*nevertheless, anyway*) de todos modos; **it's all the ~ to me** me da igual; **it's not the ~** no es lo mismo. ◆ *adv*: **the ~** lo mismo.

sample ['sɑːmpl] ◆ *n* muestra f. ◆ *vt* (*food, wine, attractions*) probar.

sanatorium (*pl* **-riums** OR **-ria** [-rɪə]), **sanitorium** Am (*pl* **-riums** OR **-ria** [-rɪə]) [,sænə'tɔːrɪəm] *n* sanatorio m.

sanctimonious [,sæŋktɪ'məʊnjəs] *adj pej* santurrón(ona).

sanction ['sæŋkʃn] ◆ *n* sanción f. ◆ *vt* sancionar.

sanctity ['sæŋktətɪ] *n* santidad f.

sanctuary ['sæŋktʃʊərɪ] *n* **1.** (*for birds, wildlife*) reserva f. **2.** (*refuge*) refugio m. **3.** (*holy place*) santuario m.

sand [sænd] ◆ *n* arena f. ◆ *vt* lijar.

sandal ['sændl] *n* sandalia f.

sandalwood ['sændlwʊd] *n* sándalo m.

sandbox Am = **sandpit**.

sandcastle ['sænd,kɑːsl] *n* castillo m de arena.

sand dune *n* duna f.

sandpaper ['sænd,peɪpər] ◆ *n* (U) papel m de lija. ◆ *vt* lijar.

sandpit Br ['sændpɪt], **sandbox** Am ['sændbɒks] *n* cuadro m de arena.

sandstone ['sændstəʊn] *n* piedra f arenisca.

sandwich ['sænwɪdʒ] ◆ *n* (*made with roll etc*) bocadillo m; (*made with sliced bread*) sandwich m frío. ◆ *vt fig* apretujar.

sandwich board *n* cartelón m (de hombre-anuncio).

sandwich course *n* Br curso universitario que incluye un cierto tiempo de experiencia profesional.

sandy ['sændɪ] *adj* **1.** (*covered in sand*) arenoso(sa). **2.** (*sand-coloured*) rojizo (za).

sane [seɪn] *adj* **1.** (*not mad*) cuerdo(da). **2.** (*sensible*) prudente, sensato(ta).

sang [sæŋ] *pt* → **sing**.

sanitary ['sænɪtrɪ] *adj* **1.** (*connected with health*) sanitario(ria). **2.** (*clean, hygienic*) higiénico(ca).

sanitary towel, sanitary napkin Am *n* (*disposable*) compresa f (higiénica); (*made of cloth*) paño m (higiénico).

sanitation [,sænɪ'teɪʃn] n sanidad f.
sanitorium Am = **sanatorium**.
sanity ['sænɪtɪ] n 1. (*saneness*) cordura f. 2. (*good sense*) sensatez f.
sank [sæŋk] pt → **sink**.
Santa (Claus) ['sæntə(,klauz)] n Papá m Noel.
sap [sæp] ◆ n (*of plant*) savia f. ◆ vt (*weaken*) minar.
sapling ['sæplɪŋ] n árbol m nuevo, arbolito m.
sapphire ['sæfaɪəʳ] n zafiro m.
Saragossa [,særə'gɒsə] n Zaragoza.
sarcastic [sɑːˈkæstɪk] adj sarcástico (ca).
sardine [sɑːˈdiːn] n sardina f.
sardonic [sɑːˈdɒnɪk] adj sardónico(ca).
SAS (*abbr of* **Special Air Service**) n unidad especial del ejército británico encargada de operaciones de sabotaje.
SASE n abbr of **self-addressed stamped envelope**.
sash [sæʃ] n faja f.
sat [sæt] pt & pp → **sit**.
SAT [sæt] n 1. (*abbr of* **Standard Assessment Test**) examen de aptitud que se realiza a los siete, once y catorce años en Inglaterra y Gales. 2. (*abbr of* **Scholastic Aptitude Test**) examen de ingreso a la universidad en Estados Unidos.
Satan ['seɪtn] n Satanás m.
satchel ['sætʃəl] n cartera f.
satellite ['sætəlaɪt] n lit & fig satélite m.
satellite TV n televisión f por satélite.
satin ['sætɪn] ◆ n satén m, raso m. ◆ comp de satén, de raso.
satire ['sætaɪəʳ] n sátira f.
satisfaction [,sætɪs'fækʃn] n satisfacción f.
satisfactory [,sætɪs'fæktərɪ] adj satisfactorio(ria).
satisfied ['sætɪsfaɪd] adj satisfecho (cha).
satisfy ['sætɪsfaɪ] vt 1. (*gen*) satisfacer. 2. (*convince*) convencer; **to ~ sb that** convencer a alguien (de) que.
satisfying ['sætɪsfaɪɪŋ] adj agradable, satisfactorio(ria).
satsuma [,sæt'suːmə] n satsuma f, tipo de mandarina.
saturate ['sætʃəreɪt] vt 1. (*drench*): **to ~ sth (with)** empapar algo (de). 2. (*fill completely*): **to ~ sth (with)** saturar algo (de).
Saturday ['sætədɪ] ◆ n sábado m; **what day is it? – it's ~** ¿a qué estamos hoy? – estamos a sábado; **on ~** el sábado; **on ~s** los sábados; **last ~** el sábado pasado; **this ~** este sábado, el sábado que viene; **next ~** el sábado de la semana que viene; **every ~** todos los sábados; **every other ~** cada dos sábados; **the ~ before** el sábado anterior; **the ~ after next** no este sábado sino el siguiente; **the ~ before last** hace dos sábados; **~ week, a week on ~** del sábado en ocho días. ◆ comp del sábado.
Saturn ['sætən] n Saturno m.
sauce [sɔːs] n (CULIN) salsa f.
saucepan ['sɔːspən] n (with two handles) cacerola f; (with one long handle) cazo m.
saucer ['sɔːsəʳ] n platillo m.
saucy ['sɔːsɪ] adj inf descarado(da), fresco(ca).
Saudi Arabia [,saʊdɪə'reɪbjə] n Arabia Saudí.
Saudi (Arabian) ['saʊdɪ-] ◆ adj saudí, saudita. ◆ n (person) saudí m y f, saudita m y f.
sauna ['sɔːnə] n sauna f.
saunter ['sɔːntəʳ] vi pasearse (tranquilamente).
sausage ['sɒsɪdʒ] n salchicha f.
sausage roll n Br salchicha envuelta en masa como de empanadilla.
sauté [Br 'səʊteɪ, Am səʊ'teɪ] (pt & pp **sautéed** OR **sautéd**) vt saltear.
savage ['sævɪdʒ] ◆ adj (cruel, fierce) feroz, salvaje. ◆ n pej salvaje m y f. ◆ vt 1. (subj: animal) embestir, atacar. 2. (subj: person) atacar con ferocidad.
save [seɪv] ◆ vt 1. (rescue) salvar, rescatar; **to ~ sb from sthg** salvar a alguien de algo. 2. (prevent waste of - time, money, energy) ahorrar; (- food, strength) guardar, reservar. 3. (set aside - money) ahorrar; (- food, strength) guardar, reservar. 4. (avoid) evitar; **to ~ sb from doing sthg** evitar a alguien (el) hacer algo. 5. (SPORT) parar. 6. (COMPUT) guardar. ◆ vi ahorrar. ◆ n (SPORT) parada f. ◆ prep fml: **~ (for)** excepto. ▶ **save up** vi ahorrar.
saving grace ['seɪvɪŋ-] n lo único positivo.
savings ['seɪvɪŋz] npl ahorros mpl.
savings account n Am cuenta f de ahorros.
savings and loan association n Am sociedad f de préstamos inmobiliarios.
savings bank n ≃ caja f de ahorros.
saviour Br, **savior** Am ['seɪvjəʳ] n salvador m, -ra f.
savour Br, **savor** Am ['seɪvəʳ] vt lit & fig saborear.

savoury Br, **savory** Am ['seɪvərɪ] ◆ adj 1. (not sweet) salado(da). 2. (respectable, pleasant) agradable. ◆ n comida f de aperitivo.

saw [sɔː] (Br pt -ed, pp sawn, Am pt & pp -ed) ◆ pt → **see**. ◆ n sierra f. ◆ vt serrar.

sawdust ['sɔːdʌst] n serrín m.

sawed-off shotgun Am = **sawn-off shotgun**.

sawmill ['sɔːmɪl] n aserradero m.

sawn [sɔːn] pp Br → **saw**.

sawn-off shotgun Br, **sawed-off shotgun** Am [sɔːd-] n arma f de cañones recortados.

saxophone ['sæksəfəʊn] n saxofón m.

say [seɪ] (pt & pp said) ◆ vt 1. (gen) decir; to ~ yes decir que sí; he's said to be good se dice que es bueno; let's ~ you were to win pongamos que ganaras; that goes without ~ing ni que decir tiene; it has a lot to be said for it tiene muy buenos puntos en su favor. 2. (indicate - clock, meter) marcar. ◆ n: to have a/no ~ in sthg tener/no tener voz y voto en algo; let me have my ~ déjame decir lo que pienso. ▶ that is to say adv es decir.

saying ['seɪɪŋ] n dicho m.

scab [skæb] n 1. (MED) costra f. 2. pej (non-striker) esquirol m.

scaffold ['skæfəʊld] n 1. (around building) andamio m. 2. (for execution) cadalso m.

scaffolding ['skæfəldɪŋ] n (U) andamios mpl, andamiaje m.

scald [skɔːld] vt escaldar.

scale [skeɪl] ◆ n 1. (gen) escala f. 2. (size, extent) tamaño m, escala f; to ~ a escala. 3. (of fish, snake) escama f. 4. Am = **scales**. ◆ vt 1. (climb) escalar. 2. (remove scales from) escamar. ▶ **scales** npl 1. (for weighing food) balanza f. 2. (for weighing person) báscula f. ▶ **scale down** vt fus reducir.

scale model n maqueta f.

scallop ['skɒləp] ◆ n (ZOOL) vieira f. ◆ vt (decorate edge of) festonear.

scalp [skælp] ◆ n cuero m cabelludo. ◆ vt escalpar.

scalpel ['skælpəl] n bisturí m.

scamper ['skæmpər] vi corretear.

scampi ['skæmpɪ] n (U): (breaded) ~ gambas fpl a la gabardina.

scan [skæn] ◆ n exploración f ultra-sónica. ◆ vt 1. (examine carefully) exami-nar. 2. (glance at) dar un vistazo a. 3. (ELECTRON & TV) registrar.

scandal ['skændl] n 1. (scandalous event, outrage) escándalo m. 2. (scandalous talk) habladurías fpl.

scandalize, -ise ['skændəlaɪz] vt escandalizar.

Scandinavia [ˌskændɪ'neɪvjə] n Escandinavia.

Scandinavian [ˌskændɪ'neɪvjən] ◆ adj escandinavo(va). ◆ n (person) escandi-navo m, -va f.

scant [skænt] adj escaso(sa).

scanty ['skæntɪ] adj (amount, resources) escaso(sa); (dress) ligero(ra); (meal) insuficiente.

scapegoat ['skeɪpgəʊt] n cabeza f de turco.

scar [skɑːr] n 1. (physical) cicatriz f. 2. fig (mental) señal f.

scarce ['skeəs] adj escaso(sa).

scarcely ['skeəslɪ] adv apenas; ~ any-one/ever casi nadie/nunca.

scarcity ['skeəsɪtɪ] n escasez f.

scare [skeər] ◆ n 1. (sudden fear) susto m, sobresalto m. 2. (public fear) temor m. ◆ vt asustar, sobresaltar. ▶ **scare away, scare off** vt sep ahuyentar.

scarecrow ['skeəkrəʊ] n espantapá-jaros m inv.

scared ['skeəd] adj 1. (frightened) asus-tado(da); to be ~ stiff OR to death estar muerto de miedo. 2. (worried): to be ~ that tener miedo que.

scarf [skɑːf] (pl -s OR scarves) n (for neck) bufanda f; (for head) pañuelo m de cabeza.

scarlet ['skɑːlət] adj color escarlata.

scarlet fever n escarlatina f.

scarves [skɑːvz] pl → **scarf**.

scathing ['skeɪðɪŋ] adj mordaz.

scatter ['skætər] ◆ vt esparcir, despa-rramar. ◆ vi dispersarse.

scatterbrained ['skætəbreɪnd] adj inf atolondrado(da).

scavenger ['skævɪndʒər] n 1. (animal) carroñero m, -ra f. 2. (person) persona f que rebusca en las basuras.

scenario [sɪ'nɑːrɪəʊ] (pl -s) n 1. (pos-sible situation) situación f hipotética. 2. (of film, play) resumen m del argu-mento.

scene [siːn] n 1. (gen) escena f; behind the ~s entre bastidores. 2. (painting of place) panorama m, paisaje m. 3. (loca-tion) sitio m. 4. (show of emotion) jaleo m, escándalo m. 5. phr: to set the ~ (for per-son) describir la escena; (for event) crear el ambiente propicio.

scenery ['siːnərɪ] n (U) 1. (of countryside) paisaje m. 2. (THEATRE) decorado m.

scenic ['si:nɪk] adj (view) pintoresco (ca); (tour) turístico(ca).

scent [sent] n 1. (smell - of flowers) fragancia f; (- of animal) rastro m. 2. fig (track) pista f. 3. (perfume) perfume m.

scepter Am = sceptre.

sceptic Br, **skeptic** Am ['skeptɪk] n escéptico m, -ca f.

sceptical Br, **skeptical** Am ['skeptɪkl] adj escéptico(ca); **to be ~ about** tener muchas dudas acerca de.

sceptre Br, **scepter** Am ['septər] n cetro m.

schedule [Br 'ʃedju:l, Am 'skedʒʊl] ◆ n 1. (plan) programa m, plan m; **on ~** sin retraso; **ahead of ~** con adelanto; **behind ~** con retraso. 2. (of prices, contents) lista f; (of times) horario m. ◆ vt: **to ~ sthg (for)** fijar algo (para).

scheduled flight [Br 'ʃedju:ld-, Am 'skedʒʊld-] n vuelo m regular.

scheme [ski:m] ◆ n 1. (plan) plano m, proyecto m. 2. pej (dishonest plan) intriga f. 3. (arrangement, decoration - of room) disposición f; (- of colours) combinación f. ◆ vi pej: **to ~ (to do sthg)** intrigar (para hacer algo).

scheming ['ski:mɪŋ] adj intrigante.

schism ['sɪzm, 'skɪzm] n cisma f.

schizophrenic [,skɪtsə'frenɪk] adj esquizofrénico(ca).

scholar ['skɒlər] n 1. (expert) erudito m, -ta f. 2. dated (student) alumno m, -na f.

scholarship ['skɒləʃɪp] n 1. (grant) beca f. 2. (learning) erudición f.

school [sku:l] n 1. (gen) colegio m, escuela f; (for driving, art) escuela f; (for medicine, law) facultad f. 2. Am (university) universidad f.

school age n edad f escolar.

schoolbook ['sku:lbʊk] n libro m de texto.

schoolboy ['sku:lbɔɪ] n colegial m.

schoolchild ['sku:ltʃaɪld] (pl -children [-tʃɪldrən]) n colegial m, -la f.

schooldays ['sku:ldeɪz] npl años mpl de colegio.

schoolgirl ['sku:lgɜ:l] n colegiala f.

schooling ['sku:lɪŋ] n educación f escolar.

school-leaver [-,li:vər] n Br joven que ha terminado la enseñanza obligatoria.

schoolmaster ['sku:l,mɑ:stər] n dated (at primary school) maestro m; (at secondary school) profesor m.

schoolmistress ['sku:l,mɪstrɪs] n dated (at primary school) maestra f; (at secondary

school) profesora f.

school of thought n corriente f de opinión.

schoolteacher ['sku:l,ti:tʃər] n (primary) maestro m, -tra f; (secondary) profesor m, -ra f.

school year n año m escolar.

schooner ['sku:nər] n 1. (ship) goleta f. 2. Br (sherry glass) copa f larga (para jerez).

sciatica [saɪ'ætɪkə] n ciática f.

science ['saɪəns] n ciencia f.

science fiction n ciencia f ficción.

scientific [,saɪən'tɪfɪk] adj científico (ca).

scientist ['saɪəntɪst] n científico m, -ca f.

scintillating ['sɪntɪleɪtɪŋ] adj brillante, chispeante.

scissors ['sɪzəz] npl tijeras fpl; **a pair of ~** unas tijeras.

sclerosis → multiple sclerosis.

scoff [skɒf] ◆ vt Br inf zamparse, tragarse. ◆ vi: **to ~ (at sb/sthg)** mofarse OR burlarse (de alguien/de algo).

scold [skəʊld] vt regañar, reñir.

scone [skɒn] n bollo tomado con té a la hora de la merienda.

scoop [sku:p] ◆ n 1. (utensil - for sugar) cucharita f plana; (- for ice cream) pinzas fpl (de helado); (- for flour) paleta f. 2. (PRESS) exclusiva f. ◆ vt 1. (with hands) recoger. 2. (with utensil) recoger con cucharilla. ▶ **scoop out** vt sep sacar con cuchara.

scooter ['sku:tər] n 1. (toy) patinete m. 2. (motorcycle) Vespa® f, motoneta f Amer.

scope [skəʊp] n (U) 1. (opportunity) posibilidades fpl. 2. (range) alcance m.

scorch [skɔ:tʃ] vt 1. (dress, meat) chamuscar; (face, skin) quemar. 2. (dry out) secar.

scorching ['skɔ:tʃɪŋ] adj inf abrasador (ra).

score [skɔ:r] ◆ n 1. (in test) calificación f, nota f; (in competition) puntuación f. 2. (SPORT) resultado m; **what's the ~?** ¿cómo van? 3. dated (twenty) veintena f. 4. (MUS) partitura f. 5. (subject): **on that ~** a ese respecto. ◆ vt 1. (SPORT) marcar. 2. (achieve - success, victory) obtener. 3. (cut) grabar. ◆ vi 1. (SPORT) marcar. 2. (in test etc) obtener una puntuación. ▶ **score out** vt sep Br tachar.

scoreboard ['skɔ:bɔ:d] n marcador m.

scorer ['skɔ:rər] n 1. (official) tanteador m, -ra f. 2. (player - in football) goleador *m*, -ra *f*; (- *in other sports*) marcador *m*, -ra *f*.

scorn [skɔ:n] ◆ *n* menosprecio *m*, desdén *m*. ◆ *vt* menospreciar, desdeñar.

scornful ['skɔ:nful] *adj* despectivo (va); **to be ~ of sthg** desdeñar algo.

Scorpio ['skɔ:pɪəʊ] (*pl* **-s**) *n* Escorpión *m*.

scorpion ['skɔ:pjən] *n* alacrán *m*.

Scot [skɒt] *n* escocés *m*, -esa *f*.

scotch [skɒtʃ] *vt* (*rumour*) desmentir; (*idea*) desechar.

Scotch [skɒtʃ] ◆ *adj* escocés(esa). ◆ *n* whisky *m* escocés.

Scotch (tape)® *n* Am cinta *f* adhesiva.

scot-free *adj inf*: **to get off ~** salir impune.

Scotland ['skɒtlənd] *n* Escocia.

Scots [skɒts] ◆ *adj* escocés(esa). ◆ *n* (*dialect*) escocés *m*.

Scotsman ['skɒtsmən] (*pl* **-men** [-mən]) *n* escocés *m*.

Scotswoman ['skɒtswʊmən] (*pl* **-women** [-,wɪmɪn]) *n* escocesa *f*.

Scottish ['skɒtɪʃ] *adj* escocés(esa).

Scottish National Party *n*: **the ~** el Partido Nacionalista Escocés.

scoundrel ['skaʊndrəl] *n* dated sinvergüenza *m*, canalla *m*.

scour [skaʊəʳ] *vt* **1.** (*clean*) fregar, restregar. **2.** (*search*) registrar, batir.

scourge [skɜ:dʒ] *n* **1.** (*cause of suffering*) azote *m*. **2.** (*critic*) castigador *m*, -ra *f*.

scout [skaʊt] *n* (MIL) explorador *m*. ► **Scout** *n* (*boy scout*) explorador *m*. ► **scout around** *vi*: **to ~ around (for)** explorar el terreno (en busca de).

scowl [skaʊl] *vi* fruncir el ceño; **to ~ at sb** mirar con ceño a alguien.

scrabble ['skræbl] *vi* **1.** (*scramble, scrape*) escarbar. **2.** (*feel around*): **to ~ around for sthg** hurgar en busca de algo.

Scrabble® ['skræbl] *n* Scrabble® *m*.

scraggy ['skrægɪ] *adj inf* flaco(ca).

scramble ['skræmbl] ◆ *n* (*rush*) pelea *f*. ◆ *vi* **1.** (*climb*) trepar. **2.** (*move clumsily*): **to ~ to one's feet** levantarse rápidamente y tambaleándose.

scrambled eggs ['skræmbld-] *npl* huevos *mpl* revueltos.

scrap [skræp] ◆ *n* **1.** (*small piece*) trozo *m*, pedazo *m*. **2.** (*metal*) chatarra *f*. **3.** *inf* (*fight, quarrel*) pelotera *f*. ◆ *vt* desechar, descartar. ► **scraps** *npl* (*food*) sobras *fpl*.

scrapbook ['skræpbʊk] *n* álbum *m* de recortes.

scrap dealer *n* chatarrero *m*, -ra *f*.

scrape [skreɪp] ◆ *n* **1.** (*noise*) chirrido *m*. **2.** dated (*difficult situation*) apuro *m*. ◆ *vt* **1.** (*remove*): **to ~ sthg off sthg** raspar algo de algo. **2.** (*vegetables*) raspar. **3.** (*car, bumper, glass*) rayar; (*knee, elbow, skin*) rasguñar. ◆ *vi* **1.** (*rub*): **to ~ against/on sthg** rozar contra/en algo. **2.** (*save money*) economizar. ► **scrape through** *vt fus* aprobar por los pelos.

scraper ['skreɪpəʳ] *n* raspador *m*.

scrap merchant *n* Br chatarrero *m*, -ra *f*.

scrap paper Br, **scratch paper** Am *n* (U) papel *m* usado.

scrapyard ['skræpjɑ:d] *n* (*gen*) depósito *m* de chatarra; (*for cars*) cementerio *m* de coches.

scratch [skrætʃ] ◆ *n* **1.** (*wound*) arañazo *m*, rasguño *m*. **2.** (*mark*) raya *f*, surco *m*. **3.** *phr*: **to do sthg from ~** hacer algo partiendo desde el principio; **to be up to ~** estar a la altura requerida. ◆ *vt* **1.** (*wound*) arañar, rasguñar. **2.** (*mark*) rayar. **3.** (*rub - head, leg*) rascar. ◆ *vi* (*rub*) rascarse.

scratch card *n* tarjeta con una zona que hay que rascar para ver si contiene premio.

scratch paper Am = **scrap paper**.

scrawl [skrɔ:l] ◆ *n* garabatos *mpl*. ◆ *vt* garabatear.

scrawny ['skrɔ:nɪ] *adj* flaco(ca).

scream [skri:m] ◆ *n* **1.** (*cry, shout*) grito *m*, chillido *m*. **2.** (*noise*) chirrido *m*. ◆ *vt* vociferar. ◆ *vi* (*person*) chillar.

scree [skri:] *n* montón de piedras desprendidas de la ladera de una montaña.

screech [skri:tʃ] ◆ *n* **1.** (*of person*) chillido *m*; (*of bird*) chirrido *m*. **2.** (*of car, tyres*) chirrido *m*, rechinar *m*. ◆ *vt* gritar. ◆ *vi* **1.** (*person, bird*) chillar. **2.** (*car, tyres*) chirriar, rechinar.

screen [skri:n] ◆ *n* **1.** (TV, CINEMA & COMPUT) pantalla *f*. **2.** (*panel*) biombo *m*. ◆ *vt* **1.** (*show in cinema*) proyectar. **2.** (*broadcast on TV*) emitir. **3.** (*shield*): **to ~ sthg/sb (from)** proteger algo/a alguien (de). **4.** (*candidate, patient*) examinar.

screening ['skri:nɪŋ] *n* **1.** (*of film*) proyección *f*. **2.** (*of TV programme*) emisión *f*. **3.** (*for security*) examen *m*. **4.** (MED) (*examination*) chequeo *m*.

screenplay ['skri:npleɪ] *n* guión *m*.

screw [skru:] ◆ *n* (*for fastening*) tornillo *m*. ◆ *vt* **1.** (*fix*): **to ~ sthg to** atornillar algo a. **2.** (*twist*) enroscar. **3.** *vulg* (*woman*) follar, coger Amer. ► **screw up** *vt sep* **1.** (*sheet of paper etc*) arrugar. **2.** (*eyes*) entornar; (*face*) arrugar. **3.** *v inf* (*ruin*) jorobar.

screwdriver ['skru:‚draɪvə^r] *n* destornillador *m*.

scribble ['skrɪbl] ♦ *n* garabato *m*. ♦ *vt & vi* garabatear.

script [skrɪpt] *n* **1.** (*of play, film etc*) guión *m*. **2.** (*system of writing*) escritura *f*. **3.** (*handwriting*) letra *f*.

Scriptures ['skrɪptʃəz] *npl*: **the ~** las Sagradas Escrituras.

scriptwriter ['skrɪpt‚raɪtə^r] *n* guionista *m y f*.

scroll [skrəʊl] ♦ *n* rollo *m* de pergamino/papel. ♦ *vt* (COMPUT) desplazar.

scrounge [skraʊndʒ] *vt inf* gorronear.

scrounger ['skraʊndʒə^r] *n inf* gorrón *m*, -ona *f*.

scrub [skrʌb] ♦ *n* **1.** (*rub*) restregón *m*. **2.** (*undergrowth*) maleza *f*. ♦ *vt* restregar.

scruff [skrʌf] *n*: **by the ~ of** the neck por el pescuezo.

scruffy ['skrʌfɪ] *adj* (*person*) dejado (da); (*clothes*) andrajoso(sa); (*room*) desordenado(da).

scrum(mage) ['skrʌm(ɪdʒ)] *n* (RUGBY) melé *f*.

scruples ['skru:plz] *npl* escrúpulos *mpl*.

scrutinize, -ise ['skru:tɪnaɪz] *vt* escudriñar.

scrutiny ['skru:tɪnɪ] *n* (U) escrutinio *m*, examen *m*.

scuff [skʌf] *vt* (*damage - shoes*) pelar; (*- furniture, floor*) rayar.

scuffle ['skʌfl] *n* refriega *f*, reyerta *f*.

scullery ['skʌlərɪ] *n* trascocina *f*.

sculptor ['skʌlptə^r] *n* escultor *m*, -ra *f*.

sculpture ['skʌlptʃə^r] *n* escultura *f*.

scum [skʌm] *n* **1.** (*froth*) espuma *f*. **2.** *v inf pej* (*worthless person*) escoria *f*.

scupper ['skʌpə^r] *vt* (NAUT & *fig*) hundir.

scurrilous ['skʌrələs] *adj fml* injurioso (sa), difamatorio(ria).

scurry ['skʌrɪ] *vi*: **to ~ off** OR **away** escabullirse.

scuttle ['skʌtl] ♦ *n* cubo *m* del carbón. ♦ *vi* (*rush*): **to ~ off** OR **away** escabullirse.

scythe [saɪð] *n* guadaña *f*.

SDLP (*abbr of* **Social Democratic and Labour Party**) *n* partido político norirlandés que defiende la integración pacífica en la república de Irlanda.

sea [si:] ♦ *n* **1.** (*not land*) mar *m o f*; **at ~** en el mar; **by ~** en barco; **by the ~** a orillas del mar; **out to ~** (*away from shore*) mar adentro; (*across the water*) hacia el mar. **2.** (*not ocean*) mar *m*. **3.** *phr*: **to be all**

at ~ estar totalmente perdido(da). ♦ *comp* de mar.

seabed ['si:bed] *n*: **the ~** el lecho marino.

seaboard ['si:bɔ:d] *n fml* litoral *m*.

sea breeze *n* brisa *f* marina.

seafood ['si:fu:d] *n* (U) mariscos *mpl*.

seafront ['si:frʌnt] *n* paseo *m* marítimo.

seagull ['si:gʌl] *n* gaviota *f*.

seal [si:l] (*pl inv* OR **-s**) ♦ *n* **1.** (*animal*) foca *f*. **2.** (*official mark*) sello *m*. **3.** (*on bottle, meter*) precinto *m*; (*on letter*) sello *m*. ♦ *vt* **1.** (*envelope*) sellar, cerrar. **2.** (*opening, tube, crack*) tapar, cerrar. ▶ **seal off** *vt sep* (*entrance, exit*) cerrar; (*area*) acordonar.

sea level *n* nivel *m* del mar.

sea lion (*pl inv* OR **-s**) *n* león *m* marítimo.

seam [si:m] *n* **1.** (SEWING) costura *f*. **2.** (*of coal*) veta *f*.

seaman ['si:mən] (*pl* **-men** [-mən]) *n* marinero *m*.

seamy ['si:mɪ] *adj* sórdido(da).

séance ['seɪɒns] *n* sesión *f* de espiritismo.

seaplane ['si:pleɪn] *n* hidroavión *m*.

seaport ['si:pɔ:t] *n* puerto *m* de mar.

search [sɜ:tʃ] ♦ *n* (*gen*) búsqueda *f*; (*of room, drawer*) registro *m*; (*of person*) cacheo *m*; **~ for sthg** búsqueda de algo; **in ~ of** en busca de. ♦ *vt* (*gen*) registrar; (*one's mind*) escudriñar; **to ~ sthg for sthg** buscar algo en algo. ♦ *vi*: **to ~ (for sthg/ sb)** buscar (algo/a alguien).

searching ['sɜ:tʃɪŋ] *adj* (*question*) agudo(da); (*look*) penetrante.

searchlight ['sɜ:tʃlaɪt] *n* reflector *m*.

search party *n* equipo *m* de búsqueda.

search warrant *n* mandamiento *m* de registro.

seashell ['si:ʃel] *n* concha *f* (marina).

seashore ['si:ʃɔ:^r] *n*: **the ~** la orilla del mar.

seasick ['si:sɪk] *adj* mareado(da).

seaside ['si:saɪd] *n*: **the ~** la playa.

seaside resort *n* lugar *m* de veraneo (en la playa).

season ['si:zn] ♦ *n* **1.** (*of year*) estación *f*. **2.** (*particular period*) época *f*. **3.** (*of holiday*) temporada *f*. **4.** (*of food*): **out of/in ~** fuera de/en temporada. **5.** (*of talks, films*) temporada *f*. ♦ *vt* sazonar.

seasonal ['si:zənl] *adj* (*work*) temporal; (*change*) estacional.

seasoned ['si:znd] *adj* (*experienced*)

veterano(na).

seasoning ['si:zniŋ] n condimento m.

season ticket n abono m.

seat [si:t] ◆ n 1. (gen) asiento m. 2. (of trousers, skirt) trasero m. 3. (POL) (in parliament) escaño m. ◆ vt 1. (sit down) sentar; **be ~ed!** ¡siéntese! 2. (subj: building, vehicle) tener cabida para.

seat belt n cinturón m de seguridad.

seating ['si:tiŋ] n (U) (capacity) asientos mpl.

seawater ['si:,wɔ:tər] n agua f de mar.

seaweed ['si:wi:d] n (U) alga f marina.

seaworthy ['si:,wɜ:ði] adj en condiciones de navegar.

sec. (abbr of second) seg.

secede [sɪ'si:d] vi fml: **to ~ (from sthg)** separarse (de algo).

secluded [sɪ'klu:dɪd] adj apartado(da).

seclusion [sɪ'klu:ʒn] n aislamiento m.

second ['sekənd] ◆ n 1. (gen) segundo m. 2. Br (UNIV) ≃ licenciatura f con notable. ◆ num segundo(da); see also **sixth**. ◆ vt secundar. ▶ **seconds** npl 1. (COMM) artículos mpl defectuosos. 2. (of food): **to have ~s** repetir (en una comida).

secondary ['sekəndrı] adj 1. (SCH - school) secundario(ria); (- education) medio(dia). 2. (less important): **to be ~** ser secundario(ria) a.

secondary school n escuela f de enseñanza media.

second-class ['sekənd-] adj 1. (gen) de segunda clase. 2. Br (UNIV) nota global de licenciatura equivalente a un notable o un aprobado alto.

second hand ['sekənd-] n (of clock) segundero m.

second-hand ['sekənd-] ◆ adj (goods, information) de segunda mano. ◆ adv (not new) de segunda mano.

secondly ['sekəndlı] adv en segundo lugar.

secondment [sɪ'kɒndmənt] n Br traslado m temporal.

second-rate ['sekənd-] adj pej de segunda categoría, mediocre.

second thought ['sekənd-] n: **to have ~s about sthg** tener dudas acerca de algo; **on ~s** Br, **on ~** Am pensándolo bien.

secrecy ['si:krəsı] n (U) secreto m.

secret ['si:krɪt] ◆ adj secreto(ta). ◆ n secreto m; **in ~** en secreto.

secretarial [,sekrə'teərıəl] adj (course, training) de secretariado; (staff) administrativo(va).

secretary [Br 'sekrətrı, Am 'sekrə,terı] n 1. (gen) secretario m, -ria f. 2. (POL) (minister) ministro m.

Secretary of State n 1. Br: **~ (for)** ministro m (de). 2. Am ministro m estadounidense de Asuntos Exteriores.

secretive ['si:krətıv] adj (person) reservado(da); (organization) secreto(ta).

secretly ['si:krɪtlı] adv (hope, think) secretamente; (tell) en secreto.

sect [sekt] n secta f.

sectarian [sek'teərıən] adj sectario (ria).

section ['sekʃn] n sección f.

sector ['sektər] n sector m.

secular ['sekjulər] adj (education, life) laico(ca), secular; (music) profano(na).

secure [sɪ'kjuər] ◆ adj (gen) seguro(ra). ◆ vt 1. (obtain) conseguir, obtener. 2. (make safe) proteger. 3. (fasten) cerrar bien.

security [sɪ'kjuərətı] n 1. seguridad f. 2. (for loan) garantía f. ▶ **securities** npl (FIN) valores mpl.

security guard n guardia m jurado OR de seguridad.

sedan [sɪ'dæn] n Am (coche m) utilitario m.

sedate [sɪ'deɪt] ◆ adj sosegado(da). ◆ vt sedar.

sedation [sɪ'deɪʃn] n (U) sedación f.

sedative ['sedətıv] n sedante m.

sediment ['sedımənt] n sedimento m.

seduce [sɪ'dju:s] vt: **to ~ sb (into doing sthg)** seducir a alguien (a hacer algo).

seductive [sɪ'dʌktıv] adj seductor(ra).

see [si:] (pt **saw**, pp **seen**) ◆ vt 1. (gen) ver. 2. (visit - friend, doctor) ir a ver, visitar; **~ you soon/later/tomorrow!** etc ¡hasta pronto/luego/mañana! etc; **~ you!** ¡hasta luego!; **~ below/p 10** véase más abajo/pág. 10. 3. (accompany - to door etc) acompañar. 4. (make sure): **to ~ (to it) that** ... encargarse de que ... ◆ vi (gen) ver; (understand) entender; **let's ~, let me ~** vamos a ver, veamos; **you ~ ...** verás, es que ...; **I ~** ya veo. ▶ **seeing as, seeing that** conj inf como. ▶ **see about** vt fus (arrange) encargarse de. ▶ **see off** vt sep 1. (say goodbye to) despedir. 2. Br (chase away) ahuyentar. ▶ **see through** vt fus (person) ver claramente las intenciones de. ▶ **see to** vt fus ocuparse de.

seed [si:d] n (of plant) semilla f. ▶ **seeds** npl fig (of doubt) semilla f; (of idea) germen m.

seedling ['si:dlıŋ] n plantón m.

seedy ['siːdɪ] *adj* (*room, area*) sórdido (da); (*person*) desaliñado(da).

seek [siːk] (*pt & pp* **sought**) *vt fml* **1.** (*look for, try to obtain*) buscar. **2.** (*ask for*) solicitar. **3.** (*try*): **to ~ to do sthg** procurar hacer algo.

seem [siːm] ◆ *vi* parecer; **it ~s (to be) good** parece (que es) bueno; **I can't ~ to do it** no puedo hacerlo (por mucho que lo intente). ◆ *v impers*: **it ~s (that)** parece que.

seemingly ['siːmɪŋlɪ] *adv* aparentemente.

seen [siːn] *pp* → **see**.

seep [siːp] *vi* rezumar, filtrarse.

seesaw ['siːsɔː] *n* balancín *m*.

seethe [siːð] *vi* **1.** (*person*) rabiar. **2.** (*place*): **to be seething with** estar a rebosar de.

see-through *adj* transparente.

segment ['segmənt] *n* **1.** (*proportion, section*) segmento *m*. **2.** (*of fruit*) gajo *m*.

segregate ['segrɪgeɪt] *vt* segregar.

Seine [seɪn] *n*: **the (River) ~** el (río) Sena.

seize [siːz] *vt* **1.** (*grab*) agarrar, coger. **2.** (*capture - control, power, town*) tomar, hacerse con. **3.** (*arrest*) detener. **4.** (*take advantage of*) aprovechar. ▶ **seize (up)on** *vt fus* valerse de. ▶ **seize up** *vi* agarrotarse.

seizure ['siːʒəʳ] *n* **1.** (MED) ataque *m*. **2.** (*taking, capturing*) toma *f*.

seldom ['seldəm] *adv* raramente.

select [sɪˈlekt] ◆ *adj* selecto(ta). ◆ *vt* (*gen*) elegir, escoger; (*team*) seleccionar.

selection [sɪˈlekʃn] *n* **1.** (*gen*) selección *f*. **2.** (*fact of being selected*) elección *f*. **3.** (*in shop*) surtido *m*.

selective [sɪˈlektɪv] *adj* selectivo(va).

self [self] (*pl* **selves**) *n* uno mismo *m*, una misma *f*; **the ~** el yo.

self-addressed stamped envelope [-ə,drest'stæmpt-] *n Am* sobre con sus señas y franqueo.

self-assured *adj* seguro de sí mismo (segura de sí misma).

self-catering *adj* sin pensión.

self-centred [-ˈsentəd] *adj* egocéntrico (ca).

self-confessed [-kənˈfest] *adj* confeso (sa).

self-confident *adj* (*person*) seguro de sí mismo (segura de sí misma); (*attitude, remark*) lleno(na) de seguridad.

self-conscious *adj* cohibido(da).

self-contained [-kənˈteɪnd] *adj* autosuficiente.

self-control *n* control *m* de sí mismo/ misma.

self-defence *n* defensa *f* propia; **in ~** en defensa propia.

self-discipline *n* autodisciplina *f*.

self-employed [-ɪmˈplɔɪd] *adj* autónomo(ma), que trabaja por cuenta propia.

self-esteem *n* amor *m* propio.

self-evident *adj* evidente, patente.

self-explanatory *adj* evidente.

self-government *n* autogobierno *m*.

self-important *adj pej* engreído(da).

self-indulgent *adj pej* que se permite excesos.

self-interest *n pej* (U) interés *m* propio.

selfish ['selfɪʃ] *adj* egoísta.

selfishness ['selfɪʃnɪs] *n* egoísmo *m*.

selfless ['selflɪs] *adj* desinteresado (da).

self-made *adj* que ha triunfado por su propio esfuerzo.

self-opinionated *adj pej* que siempre tiene que decir la suya.

self-pity *n pej* lástima *f* de uno mismo/ una misma.

self-portrait *n* autorretrato *m*.

self-possessed [-pəˈzest] *adj* dueño de sí mismo (dueña de sí misma).

self-raising flour Br [-ˌreɪzɪŋ-], **self-rising flour** Am *n* harina *f* con levadura.

self-reliant *adj* independiente.

self-respect *n* amor *m* propio.

self-respecting [-rɪsˈpektɪŋ] *adj* que se precie, digno(na).

self-restraint *n* dominio *m* de sí mismo/misma.

self-righteous *adj pej* santurrón(ona).

self-rising flour Am = **self-raising flour**.

self-sacrifice *n* abnegación *f*.

self-satisfied *adj pej* (*person*) satisfecho de sí mismo (satisfecha de sí misma); (*smile*) lleno(na) de suficiencia.

self-service *comp* de autoservicio.

self-sufficient *adj*: **~ (in)** autosuficiente (en).

self-taught *adj* autodidacta.

sell [sel] (*pt & pp* **sold**) ◆ *vt* **1.** (*gen*) vender; **to ~ sthg to sb**, **to ~ sb sthg** vender algo a alguien; **to ~ sthg for** vender algo por. **2.** (*encourage sale of*) hacer vender. ◆ *vi* **1.** (*exchange for money*) vender. **2.** (*be bought*): **to ~ (for OR at)** venderse (a). ▶ **sell off** *vt sep* liquidar. ▶ **sell out** ◆ *vt sep* (*performance*): **to have**

sold out estar agotado(da). ◆ vi
1. (shop): **to ~ out (of sthg)** agotar las
existencias (de algo) 2. (be disloyal, un-
principled) venderse.

sell-by date n Br fecha f de caducidad.

seller ['selər] n vendedor m, -ra f.

selling price ['selıŋ-] n precio m de
venta.

Sellotape® ['seləteıp] n Br celo® m,
cinta f adhesiva.

sell-out n (performance, match) lleno m.

selves [selvz] pl → self.

semaphore ['semǝfɔːr] n (U) semáforo m.

semblance ['semblǝns] n fml apariencia f.

semen ['siːmen] n semen m.

semester [sı'mestǝr] n semestre m.

semicircle ['semı,sɜːkl] n semicírculo
m.

semicolon [,semı'kǝulǝn] n punto m y
coma.

semidetached [,semıdı'tætʃt] ◆ adj
adosado(da). ◆ n Br casa f adosada (a
otra).

semifinal [,semı'faınl] n semifinal f.

seminar ['semınɑːr] n seminario m.

seminary ['semınǝrı] n (RELIG) seminario m.

semiskilled [,semı'skıld] adj semicua-
lificado(da).

semolina [,semǝ'liːnǝ] n sémola f.

Senate ['senıt] n (POL): **the (United
States) ~** el Senado (de los Estados
Unidos).

senator ['senǝtǝr] n senador m, -ra f.

send [send] (pt & pp **sent**) vt 1. (gen)
mandar; **to ~ sb sthg, to ~ sthg to sb**
mandar a alguien algo. 2. (tell to go,
arrange for attendance): **to ~ sb (to)** enviar
OR mandar a alguien (a). ▶ **send for** vt
fus (person) mandar llamar a. ▶ **send in**
vt sep mandar, enviar. ▶ **send off** vt sep
1. (by post) mandar (por correo).
2. (SPORT) expulsar. ▶ **send off for** vt
fus (goods, information) pedir, encargar.
▶ **send up** vt sep Br inf (imitate) parodiar.

sender ['sendǝr] n remitente m y f.

send-off n despedida f.

senile ['siːnaıl] adj senil.

senior ['siːnjǝr] ◆ adj 1. (highest-ranking)
superior, de rango superior. 2.
(higher-ranking): **~ to sb** superior a
alguien. 3. (SCH) (pupil) mayor; (class,
common room) de los mayores. ◆ n
1. (older person): **I'm five years his ~** le
llevo cinco años. 2. (SCH) mayor m y f.

senior citizen n ciudadano m, -na f
de la tercera edad.

sensation [sen'seıʃn] n sensación f.

sensational [sen'seıʃǝnl] adj (gen) sensacional.

sensationalist [sen'seıʃnǝlıst] adj pej
sensacionalista.

sense [sens] ◆ n 1. (faculty, meaning)
sentido m; **to make ~** (have meaning)
tener sentido. 2. (feeling - of guilt, terror)
sentimiento m; (- of urgency) sensación
f; (- of honour, duty) sentido m. 3. (natural
ability): **business ~** talento m para los
negocios; **~ of humour/style** sentido m
del humor/estilo. 4. (wisdom, reason)
juicio m, sentido m común; **to make ~**
(be sensible) ser sensato. ◆ vt sentir,
percibir; **to ~ (that)** percibir or sentir
que. ▶ **in a sense** adv en cierto sentido.

senseless ['senslıs] adj 1. (stupid) sin
sentido. 2. (unconscious) inconsciente.

sensibilities [,sensı'bılǝtız] npl (delicate
feelings) sensibilidad f.

sensible ['sensǝbl] adj (person, decision)
sensato(ta); (clothes) práctico(ca).

sensitive ['sensıtıv] adj 1. (understanding): **~ (to)** comprensivo(va) (hacia).
2. (easily hurt, touchy): **~ (to/about)** susceptible (a/acerca de). 3. (controversial)
delicado(da). 4. (easily damaged, tender):
~ (to) sensible (a). 5. (responsive - instrument) sensible.

sensual ['sensjʊǝl] adj sensual.

sensuous ['sensjʊǝs] adj sensual.

sent [sent] pt & pp → send.

sentence ['sentǝns] ◆ n 1. (group of
words) frase f, oración f. 2. (JUR) sentencia f. ◆ vt: **to ~ sb (to)** condenar a
alguien (a).

sentiment ['sentımǝnt] n 1. (feeling)
sentimiento m. 2. (opinion) opinión f.

sentimental [,sentı'mentl] adj sentimental.

sentry ['sentrı] n centinela m.

separate [adj & n 'seprǝt, vb 'sepǝreıt]
◆ adj 1. (not joined, apart): **~ (from)** sepa-
rado(da) (de). 2. (individual, distinct) dis-
tinto(ta). ◆ vt 1. (keep or move apart): **to ~
sthg/sb (from)** separar algo/a alguien
(de). 2. (distinguish): **to ~ sthg/sb from**
diferenciar algo/a alguien de.
3. (divide): **to ~ sthg/sb into** dividir algo/
a alguien en. ◆ vi 1. (gen): **to ~ (from)**
separarse (de). 2. (divide): **to ~ (into)**
dividirse (en). ▶ **separates** npl Br
piezas fpl (de vestir que combinan).

separately ['seprǝtlı] adv 1. (on one's

own) independientemente. **2.** (*one by one*) por separado.

separation [,sepə'reɪʃn] *n* separación *f*.

September [sep'tembər] *n* septiembre *m*, setiembre *m*; **1 ~ 1992** (*in letters etc*) 1 de septiembre de 1992; **by/in ~** para/en septiembre; **last/this/next ~** en septiembre del año pasado/de este año/del año que viene; **every ~** todos los años en septiembre; **during ~** en septiembre; **at the beginning/end of ~** a principios/finales de septiembre; **in the middle of ~** a mediados de septiembre.

septic ['septɪk] *adj* séptico(ca).

septic tank *n* fosa *f* séptica.

sequel ['si:kwəl] *n* **1.** (*book, film*): **~ (to)** continuación *f* (de). **2.** (*consequence*): **~ (to)** secuela *f* (de).

sequence ['si:kwəns] *n* **1.** (*series*) sucesión *f*. **2.** (*order, of film*) secuencia *f*.

Serb = **Serbian**.

Serbia ['sɜ:bjə] *n* Serbia.

Serbian ['sɜ:bjən], **Serb** [sɜ:b] ◆ *adj* serbio(bia). ◆ *n* **1.** (*person*) serbio *m*, -bia *f*. **2.** (*dialect*) serbio *m*.

serene [sɪ'ri:n] *adj* sereno(na).

sergeant ['sɑ:dʒənt] *n* **1.** (MIL) sargento *m*. **2.** (*in police*) = subinspector *m* de policía.

sergeant major *n* sargento *m* mayor.

serial ['sɪərɪəl] *n* serial *m*.

serial number *n* número *m* de serie.

series ['sɪəri:z] (*pl inv*) *n* serie *f*.

serious ['sɪərɪəs] *adj* **1.** (*gen*) serio(ria); **are you ~?** ¿hablas en serio? **2.** (*very bad*) grave.

seriously ['sɪərɪəslɪ] *adv* **1.** (*honestly*) en serio. **2.** (*very badly*) gravemente. **3.** (*in a considered, earnest, solemn manner*) seriamente. **4.** *phr*: **to take sthg/sb ~** tomar algo/a alguien en serio.

seriousness ['sɪərɪəsnɪs] *n* **1.** (*gravity*) gravedad *f*. **2.** (*solemnity*) seriedad *f*.

sermon ['sɜ:mən] *n* (RELIG & *pej*) sermón *m*.

serrated [sɪ'reɪtɪd] *adj* dentado(da).

servant ['sɜ:vənt] *n* sirviente *m*, -ta *f*.

serve [sɜ:v] ◆ *vt* **1.** (*work for*) servir. **2.** (*have effect*): **to ~ to do sthg** servir para hacer algo. **3.** (*fulfil*): **to ~ a purpose** cumplir un propósito. **4.** (*provide for*) abastecer. **5.** (*food, drink*): **to ~ sthg to sb, to ~ sb sthg** servir algo a alguien. **6.** (*in shop, bar etc*) despachar, servir. **7.** (JUR): **to ~ sb with sthg, to ~ sthg on sb** entregar a alguien algo. **8.** (*prison sentence*)

cumplir; (*apprenticeship*) hacer; (*term of office*) ejercer. **9.** (SPORT) servir, sacar. **10.** *phr*: **that ~s you right!** ¡bien merecido lo tienes! ◆ *vi* **1.** (*work, give food or drink*) servir. **2.** (*function*): **to ~ as** servir de. **3.** (*in shop, bar etc*) despachar. **4.** (SPORT) sacar. ◆ *n* saque *m*. ▶ **serve out, serve up** *vt sep* servir.

service ['sɜ:vɪs] ◆ *n* **1.** (*gen*) servicio *m*; **in ~** en funcionamiento; **out of ~** fuera de servicio. **2.** (*mechanical check*) revisión *f*. **3.** (RELIG) oficio *m*, servicio *m*. **4.** (*set - of plates etc*) servicio *m*, juego *m*. **5.** (SPORT) saque *m*. **6.** (*use*): **to be of ~ (to sb)** servir (a alguien). ◆ *vt* (*car, machine*) revisar. ▶ **services** *npl* **1.** (*on motorway*) área *f* de servicios. **2.** (*armed forces*): **the ~s** las fuerzas armadas. **3.** (*efforts, work*) servicios *mpl*.

serviceable ['sɜ:vɪsəbl] *adj* útil, práctico(ca).

service area *n* área *f* de servicios.

service charge *n* servicio *m*.

serviceman ['sɜ:vɪsmən] (*pl* -**men** [-mən]) *n* militar *m*.

service station *n* estación *f* de servicio.

serviette [,sɜ:vɪ'et] *n* servilleta *f*.

sesame ['sesəmɪ] *n* sésamo *m*.

session ['seʃn] *n* **1.** (*gen*) sesión *f*; **in ~** en sesión. **2.** Am (*school term*) trimestre *m*.

set [set] (*pt* & *pp* **set**) ◆ *adj* **1.** (*fixed - expression, amount*) fijo(ja); (*- pattern, method*) establecido(da). **2.** Br (SCH - *text etc*) asignado(da). **3.** (*ready, prepared*): **~ (for sthg/to do sthg)** listo(ta) (para algo/para hacer algo). **4.** (*determined*): **to be ~ on sthg/doing sthg** estar empeñado(da) en algo/hacer algo. ◆ *n* **1.** (*collection - gen*) juego *m*; (*- of stamps*) serie *f*. **2.** (TV, *radio*) aparato *m*. **3.** (THEATRE) decorado *m*; (CINEMA) plató *m*. **4.** (TENNIS) set *m*. ◆ *vt* **1.** (*position, place*) poner, colocar. **2.** (*fix, insert*): **to ~ sthg in** OR **into** montar algo en. **3.** (*cause to be or start*): **to ~ free** poner en libertad; **to ~ fire to** prender fuego a; **to ~ sthg in motion** poner algo en marcha. **4.** (*trap, table, essay*) poner. **5.** (*alarm, meter*) poner. **6.** (*time, wage*) fijar. **7.** (*example*) dar; (*precedent*) sentar; (*trend*) imponer, dictar. **8.** (*target*) fijar. **9.** (MED - *bones, leg*) componer. **10.** (*book, play, film*) situar, ambientar. ◆ *vi* **1.** (*sun*) ponerse. **2.** (*jelly*) cuajarse; (*glue, cement*) secarse. ▶ **set about** *vt fus* (*start - task*) comenzar; (*- problem*) atacar; **to ~ about doing**

sthg ponerse a hacer algo. ▸ **set aside** vt sep 1. (keep, save) reservar. 2. (dismiss - enmity, differences) dejar de lado. ▸ **set back** vt sep (delay) retrasar. ▸ **set off** ◆ vt sep 1. (initiate, cause) provocar. 2. (ignite - bomb) hacer estallar. ◆ vi ponerse en camino. ▸ **set out** ◆ vt sep 1. (arrange) disponer. 2. (explain) exponer. ◆ vi 1. (on journey) ponerse en camino. 2. (intend): **to ~ out to do sthg** proponerse a hacer algo. ▸ **set up** vt sep 1. (business) poner, montar; (committee, organization) crear; (procedure) establecer; (interview, meeting) organizar. 2. (statue, roadblock) levantar. 3. (prepare for use) preparar. 4. inf (frame) tender una trampa a.

setback ['setbæk] n revés m, contratiempo m.

set menu n menú m del día.

settee [se'ti:] n sofá m.

setting ['setɪŋ] n 1. (surroundings) escenario m. 2. (of dial, control) posición f.

settle ['setl] ◆ vt 1. (conclude, decide) resolver. 2. (pay) ajustar, saldar. 3. (calm - nerves) tranquilizar. ◆ vi 1. (stop travelling) instalarse. 2. (make o.s. comfortable) acomodarse. 3. (dust, sediment) depositarse. 4. (calm down - person) calmarse. ▸ **settle down** vi 1. (concentrate on): **to ~ down to doing sthg** ponerse a hacer algo. 2. (become respectable) sentar la cabeza. 3. (calm oneself) calmarse. ▸ **settle for** vt fus conformarse con. ▸ **settle in** vi (in new home) instalarse; (in new job) adaptarse. ▸ **settle on** vt fus (choose) decidirse por. ▸ **settle up** vi: **to ~ up (with sb)** ajustar las cuentas (con alguien).

settlement ['setlmənt] n 1. (agreement) acuerdo m. 2. (village) poblado m.

settler ['setlər] n colono m.

set-up n inf 1. (system, organization) sistema m. 2. (frame, trap) trampa f.

seven ['sevn] num siete; see also **six**.

seventeen [,sevn'ti:n] num diecisiete; see also **six**.

seventeenth [,sevn'ti:nθ] num decimoséptimo(ma); see also **sixth**.

seventh ['sevnθ] num séptimo(ma); see also **sixth**.

seventy ['sevntɪ] num setenta; see also **sixty**.

sever ['sevər] vt 1. (cut through) cortar. 2. (finish completely) romper.

several ['sevrəl] ◆ adj varios(rias). ◆ pron varios mpl, -rias fpl.

severance ['sevrəns] n fml ruptura f.

severance pay n despido m.

severe [sɪ'vɪər] adj (gen) severo(ra); (pain) fuerte, agudo(da).

severity [sɪ'verətɪ] n (gen) gravedad f; (of shortage, problem) severidad f.

Seville [sə'vɪl] n Sevilla.

sew [səʊ] (Br pp sewn, Am pp sewed OR sewn) vt & vi coser. ▸ **sew up** vt sep (cloth) coser.

sewage ['su:ɪdʒ] n (U) aguas fpl residuales.

sewer ['sʊər] n alcantarilla f, cloaca f.

sewing ['səʊɪŋ] n (U) 1. (activity) labor f de costura. 2. (items) costura f.

sewing machine n máquina f de coser.

sewn [səʊn] pp → **sew**.

sex [seks] n sexo m; **to have ~** tener relaciones sexuales.

sexist ['seksɪst] ◆ adj sexista. ◆ n sexista m y f.

sexual ['sekʃʊəl] adj sexual.

sexual harassment n acoso m sexual.

sexual intercourse n (U) relaciones fpl sexuales.

sexy ['seksɪ] adj inf sexi (inv).

shabby ['ʃæbɪ] adj 1. (clothes, briefcase) desastrado(da); (street) de aspecto abandonado. 2. (person) andrajoso(sa).

shack [ʃæk] n chabola f.

shackle ['ʃækl] vt (enchain) poner grilletes a. ▸ **shackles** npl (metal rings) grilletes mpl.

shade [ʃeɪd] ◆ n 1. (U) (shadow) sombra f. 2. (lampshade) pantalla f. 3. (of colour, meaning) matiz m. ◆ vt (from light) dar sombra a. ▸ **shades** npl inf (sunglasses) gafas fpl de sol.

shadow ['ʃædəʊ] n 1. (dark shape, form) sombra f. 2. (darkness) oscuridad f. 3. phr: **there's not a OR the ~ of a doubt** no hay la menor duda.

shadow cabinet n gobierno m en la sombra, directiva del principal partido de la oposición en Gran Bretaña.

shadowy ['ʃædəʊɪ] adj 1. (dark) sombrío(a). 2. (hard to see) vago(ga).

shady ['ʃeɪdɪ] adj 1. (sheltered from sun) sombreado(da). 2. inf (dishonest - businessman) sospechoso(sa); (- deal) turbio (bia).

shaft [ʃɑ:ft] n 1. (vertical passage) pozo m. 2. (rod - of propellor etc) eje m. 3. (of light) rayo m.

shaggy ['ʃægɪ] adj (dog) peludo(da).

shake [ʃeɪk] (pt shook, pp shaken ['ʃeɪkən]) ◆ vt 1. (move vigorously) sacudir; **to ~ sb's hand** dar OR estrechar la mano a alguien; **to ~ hands** darse OR estrecharse la mano; **to ~ one's head** (*in refusal*) negar con la cabeza; (*in disbelief*) mover la cabeza mostrando incredulidad. **2.** (*shock*) trastornar, conmocionar. ◆ *vi* temblar. ▶ **shake off** *vt sep* (*pursuer*) deshacerse de; (*cold*) quitarse de encima; (*illness*) superar.

shaken ['ʃeɪkn] *pp* → **shake**.

shaky ['ʃeɪkɪ] *adj* **1.** (*weak, nervous*) tembloroso(sa). **2.** (*unconfident, insecure - start*) incierto(ta); (*- argument*) poco sólido(da).

shall [*weak form* ʃəl, *strong form* ʃæl] *aux vb* **1.** (1st person sg & 1st person pl) (*to express future tense*): **we ~ be there tomorrow** mañana estaremos ahí; **I shan't be home till ten** no estaré en casa hasta las diez. **2.** (*esp* 1st person sg & 1st person pl) (*in questions*): **~ we go for a walk?** ¿vamos a dar una vuelta?; **~ I give her a ring?** ¿la llamo?; **I'll do that, ~ I?** hago esto, ¿vale? **3.** (*in orders*): **you ~ do as I tell you!** ¡harás lo que yo te diga!; **no one ~ leave until I say so** que nadie salga hasta que yo lo diga.

shallow ['ʃæləʊ] *adj* **1.** (*in size*) poco profundo(da). **2.** *pej* (*superficial*) superficial.

sham [ʃæm] ◆ *n* farsa *f*. ◆ *vi* fingir.

shambles ['ʃæmblz] *n* desbarajuste *m*, follón *m*.

shame [ʃeɪm] ◆ *n* **1.** (U) (*remorse*) vergüenza *f*, pena *f* Amer. **2.** (*dishonour*): **to bring ~ on** OR **upon sb** deshonrar a alguien. **3.** (*pity*): **what a ~!** ¡qué pena OR lástima!; **it's a ~** es una pena OR lástima. ◆ *vt* **1.** (*fill with shame*) avergonzar. **2.** (*force by making ashamed*): **to ~ sb into doing sthg** conseguir que alguien haga algo avergonzándole.

shamefaced [,ʃeɪm'feɪst] *adj* avergonzado(da).

shameful ['ʃeɪmfʊl] *adj* vergonzoso(sa).

shameless ['ʃeɪmlɪs] *adj* desvergonzado(da).

shampoo [ʃæm'puː] (*pl* **-s**) ◆ *n* (*liquid*) champú *m*. ◆ *vt* lavar (con champú).

shamrock ['ʃæmrɒk] *n* trébol *m*.

shandy ['ʃændɪ] *n* cerveza *f* con gaseosa, clara *f*.

shan't [ʃɑːnt] = **shall not**.

shantytown ['ʃæntɪtaʊn] *n* barrio *m* de chabolas, cantegril *m* Amer.

shape [ʃeɪp] ◆ *n* **1.** (*outer form*) forma *f*. **2.** (*definite form, silhouette*) figura *f*.

3. (*structure*) configuración *f*; **to take ~** tomar forma. **4.** (*form, health*): **to be in good/bad ~** (*person*) estar/no estar en forma; (*business etc*) estar en buen/mal estado. ◆ *vt* **1.** (*mould*): **to ~ sthg (into)** dar a algo forma (de). **2.** (*cause to develop*) desarrollar. ▶ **shape up** *vi* (*develop*) desarrollarse.

-shaped ['ʃeɪpt] *suffix*: **egg/star~** en forma de huevo/estrella.

shapeless ['ʃeɪplɪs] *adj* sin forma.

shapely ['ʃeɪplɪ] *adj* bien hecho(cha).

share [ʃeəᵣ] ◆ *n* **1.** (*portion*): **~ (of** OR **in)** parte *f* (de). **2.** (*contribution, quota*): **to have/do one's ~ of sthg** tener/hacer la parte que a uno le toca de algo. ◆ *vt* (*gen*): **to ~ sthg (with)** compartir algo (con). ◆ *vi* compartir. ▶ **shares** *npl* acciones *fpl*. ▶ **share out** *vt sep* repartir, distribuir.

shareholder ['ʃeə,həʊldəᵣ] *n* accionista *m y f*.

shark [ʃɑːk] (*pl inv* OR **-s**) *n* tiburón *m*; *fig* estafador *m*, -ra *f*.

sharp [ʃɑːp] ◆ *adj* **1.** (*not blunt*) afilado (da). **2.** (*well-defined - outline*) definido (da); (*- photograph*) nítido(da); (*- contrast*) marcado(da). **3.** (*intelligent, keen - person*) listo(ta); (*- eyesight*) penetrante; (*- hearing*) fino(na); (*- intelligence*) vivo(va). **4.** (*abrupt, sudden*) brusco(ca). **5.** (*quick, firm - blow*) seco(ca). **6.** (*angry, severe*) cortante. **7.** (*piercing, acute - sound, cry, pain*) agudo(da); (*- cold, wind*) penetrante. **8.** (*bitter*) ácido(da). **9.** (MUS) desafinado(da). ◆ *adv* **1.** (*punctually*) en punto. **2.** (*quickly, suddenly*) bruscamente. ◆ *n* (MUS) sostenido *m*.

sharpen ['ʃɑːpn] *vt* **1.** (*make sharp*) afilar; (*pencil*) sacar punta a. **2.** (*make keener, quicker, greater*) agudizar.

sharpener ['ʃɑːpnəᵣ] *n* (*for pencils*) sacapuntas *m inv*; (*for knives*) afilador *m*.

sharp-eyed [-'aɪd] *adj* perspicaz.

sharply ['ʃɑːplɪ] *adv* **1.** (*distinctly*) claramente. **2.** (*suddenly*) repentinamente. **3.** (*harshly*) duramente.

shat [ʃæt] *pt & pp* → **shit**.

shatter ['ʃætəᵣ] ◆ *vt* **1.** (*smash*) hacer añicos. **2.** (*hopes etc*) echar por tierra. ◆ *vi* hacerse añicos.

shattered ['ʃætəd] *adj* **1.** (*shocked, upset*) destrozado(da). **2.** Br inf (*very tired*) hecho(cha) polvo.

shave [ʃeɪv] ◆ *n* afeitado *m*; **to have a ~** afeitarse. ◆ *vt* **1.** (*face, body*) afeitar. **2.** (*cut pieces off*) raspar. ◆ *vi* afeitar.

shaver ['ʃeɪvəᵣ] *n* maquinilla *f* (de

afeitar) eléctrica.

shaving brush ['ʃeɪvɪŋ-] n brocha f
de afeitar.

shaving cream ['ʃeɪvɪŋ-] n crema f
de afeitar.

shaving foam ['ʃeɪvɪŋ-] n espuma f
de afeitar.

shavings ['ʃeɪvɪŋz] npl virutas fpl.

shawl [ʃɔːl] n chal m.

she [ʃiː] ◆ pers pron 1. (referring to woman,
girl, animal) ella; ~'s **tall** es alta; SHE can't
do it ella no puede hacerlo; there ~ is
allí está; if I were ~ or was ~ fml si (yo)
fuera ella. 2. (referring to boat, car, country): ~'s a **fine ship** es un buen barco.
◆ comp: ~-**elephant** elefanta f; ~ bear osa
f.

sheaf [ʃiːf] (pl **sheaves**) n 1. (of papers,
letters) fajo m. 2. (of corn, grain) gavilla f.

shear [ʃɪəʳ] (pp -ed OR shorn) vt (sheep)
esquilar. ► **shears** npl (for garden)
tijeras fpl de podar. ► **shear off** vi
romperse.

sheath [ʃiːθ] (pl -s) n 1. (covering for
knife) vaina f. 2. Br (condom) preservativo m.

sheaves [ʃiːvz] pl → sheaf.

shed [ʃed] (pt & pp shed) ◆ n cobertizo
m. ◆ vt 1. (skin) mudar de; (leaves)
despojarse de. 2. (discard) deshacerse
de. 3. (tears, blood) derramar.

she'd [weak form ʃɪd, strong form ʃiːd] =
she had, she would.

sheen [ʃiːn] n brillo m, lustre m.

sheep [ʃiːp] (pl inv) n (animal) oveja f;
fig (person) borrego m, cordero m.

sheepdog ['ʃiːpdɒg] n perro m pastor.

sheepish ['ʃiːpɪʃ] adj avergonzado
(da).

sheepskin ['ʃiːpskɪn] n piel f de
carnero.

sheer [ʃɪəʳ] adj 1. (absolute) puro(ra).
2. (very steep - cliff) escarpado(da);
(- drop) vertical. 3. (delicate) diáfano(na).

sheet [ʃiːt] n 1. (for bed) sábana f. 2. (of
paper) hoja f. 3. (of glass, metal, wood)
lámina f.

sheik(h) [ʃeɪk] n jeque m.

shelf [ʃelf] (pl shelves) n estante m.

shell [ʃel] ◆ n 1. (of egg, nut) cáscara f.
2. (of tortoise, crab) caparazón m.(of snail,
mussels) concha f. 3. (on beach) concha f.
4. (of building) esqueleto m; (of boat)
casco m; (of car) armazón m, chasis m
inv. 5. (MIL) (missile) proyectil m. ◆ vt
1. (peas) desvainar; (nuts, eggs) quitar la
cáscara a. 2. (MIL) (fire shells at) bombardear.

she'll [ʃiːl] = she will, she shall.

shellfish ['ʃelfɪʃ] (pl inv) n 1. (creature)
crustáceo m. 2. (U) (food) mariscos mpl.

shell suit n Br chandal m (de nailon).

shelter ['ʃeltəʳ] ◆ n (building, protection)
refugio m. ◆ vt 1. (protect): to be ~ed by/
from estar protegido(da) por/de.
2. (provide place to live for) dar asilo OR
cobijo a. 3. (hide) proteger, esconder.
◆ vi: to ~ from/in resguardarse de/en,
protegerse de/en.

sheltered ['ʃeltəd] adj (place, existence)
protegido(da).

shelve [ʃelv] vt dar carpetazo a.

shelves [ʃelvz] pl → shelf.

shepherd ['ʃepəd] ◆ n pastor m. ◆ vt
fig acompañar.

shepherd's pie ['ʃepədz-] n carne picada cubierta de puré de patatas.

sheriff ['ʃerɪf] n Am sheriff m.

sherry ['ʃerɪ] n jerez m.

she's [ʃiːz] = she is, she has.

Shetland ['ʃetlənd] n: (the) ~ (Islands)
las islas Shetland.

shield [ʃiːld] ◆ n (armour, sports trophy)
escudo m. ◆ vt: to ~ sb (from) proteger a
alguien (de).

shift [ʃɪft] ◆ n 1. (slight change) cambio
m. 2. (period of work, workers) turno m. ◆ vt
1. (furniture etc) cambiar de sitio,
mover. 2. (attitude, belief) cambiar de.
◆ vi 1. (person) moverse; (wind, opinion)
cambiar. 2. Am (AUT) cambiar de marcha.

shiftless ['ʃɪftlɪs] adj vago(ga).

shifty ['ʃɪftɪ] adj inf (person) con pinta
deshonesta; (behaviour) sospechoso
(sa); (look) huidizo(za).

shilling ['ʃɪlɪŋ] n chelín m.

shilly-shally ['ʃɪlɪˌʃælɪ] (pt & pp -ied) vi
titubear, vacilar.

shimmer ['ʃɪməʳ] vi rielar, brillar con
luz trémula.

shin [ʃɪn] n espinilla f.

shinbone ['ʃɪnbəʊn] n espinilla f.

shine [ʃaɪn] (pt & pp shone) ◆ n brillo
m. ◆ vt (torch, lamp) dirigir. ◆ vi (gen) brillar.

shingle ['ʃɪŋgl] n (U) (on beach) guija-
rros mpl. ► **shingles** n (U) herpes m inv.

ship [ʃɪp] n barco m, buque m. ◆ vt
enviar por barco.

shipbuilding ['ʃɪpˌbɪldɪŋ] n construcción f naval.

shipment ['ʃɪpmənt] n envío m.

shipper ['ʃɪpəʳ] n compañía f naviera.

shipping ['ʃɪpɪŋ] n (U) 1. (transport)
envío m, transporte m. 2. (ships) barcos

mpl, buques *mpl.*

shipshape ['ʃɪpʃeɪp] *adj* en orden.

shipwreck ['ʃɪprek] ◆ *n* 1. (*destruction of ship*) naufragio *m.* 2. (*wrecked ship*) barco *m* náufrago. ◆ *vt*: **to be ~ed** naufragar.

shipyard ['ʃɪpjɑːd] *n* astillero *m.*

shire [ʃaɪəʳ] *n* (*county*) condado *m.*

shirk [ʃɜːk] *vt* eludir.

shirt [ʃɜːt] *n* camisa *f.*

shirtsleeves ['ʃɜːtsliːvz] *npl*: **to be in (one's) ~** ir en mangas de camisa.

shit [ʃɪt] (*pt & pp* **shit** *-ted* OR **shat**) *vulg* ◆ *n* 1. (*excrement*) mierda *f.* 2. (U) (*nonsense*) gilipolleces *fpl.* ◆ *vi* cagar. ◆ *excl* ¡mierda!

shiver ['ʃɪvəʳ] ◆ *n* escalofrío *m.* ◆ *vi*: **to ~ (with)** (*fear*) temblar OR estremecerse (de); (*cold*) tiritar (de).

shoal [ʃəʊl] *n* banco *m.*

shock [ʃɒk] ◆ *n* 1. (*unpleasant surprise, reaction, emotional state*) susto *m*; **it came as a ~** fue un duro golpe. 2. (U) (MED): **to be suffering from ~** estar en un estado de choque. 3. (*impact*) choque *m.* 4. (*electric shock*) descarga *f* OR sacudida *f* (eléctrica). ◆ *vt* 1. (*upset*) conmocionar. 2. (*offend*) escandalizar.

shock absorber [-əb,zɔːbəʳ] *n* amortiguador *m.*

shocking ['ʃɒkɪŋ] *adj* 1. (*very bad*) pésimo(ma). 2. (*behaviour, film*) escandaloso (sa); (*price*) de escándalo.

shod [ʃɒd] ◆ *pt & pp* → **shoe.** ◆ *adj* calzado(da).

shoddy ['ʃɒdɪ] *adj* (*work*) chapucero (ra); (*goods*) de pacotilla; *fig* (*treatment*) vil, despreciable.

shoe [ʃuː] (*pt & pp* **shod** OR **shoed**) ◆ *n* zapato *m.* ◆ *vt* herrar.

shoebrush ['ʃuːbrʌʃ] *n* cepillo *m* para los zapatos.

shoehorn ['ʃuːhɔːn] *n* calzador *m.*

shoelace ['ʃuːleɪs] *n* cordón *m* del zapato.

shoe polish *n* betún *m.*

shoe shop *n* zapatería *f.*

shoestring ['ʃuːstrɪŋ] *n fig*: **on a ~** con cuatro cuartos, con muy poco dinero.

shone [ʃɒn] *pt & pp* → **shine.**

shoo [ʃuː] ◆ *vt* (*animal*) espantar, ahuyentar; (*person*) mandar a otra parte. ◆ *excl* ¡fuera!

shook [ʃʊk] *pt* → **shake.**

shoot [ʃuːt] (*pt & pp* **shot**) ◆ *n* 1. Br (*hunting expedition*) cacería *f.* 2. (*new growth*) brote *m*, retoño *m.* ◆ *vt* 1. (*fire gun at*) disparar contra, abalear *Amer*;

(*injure*) herir a tiros; (*kill*) matar a tiros; **to ~ o.s.** pegarse un tiro. 2. Br (*hunt*) cazar. 3. (*arrow*) disparar. 4. (CINEMA) rodar, filmar. ◆ *vi* 1. (*fire gun*): **to ~ (at)** disparar (contra). 2. Br (*hunt*) cazar. 3. (*move quickly*): **to ~ in/out/past** entrar/salir/pasar disparado(da). 4. (CINEMA) rodar, filmar. 5. (SPORT) chutar. ▶ **shoot down** *vt sep* 1. (*plane*) derribar. 2. (*person*) matar a tiros. ▶ **shoot up** *vi* 1. (*child, plant*) crecer rápidamente. 2. (*prices*) dispararse.

shooting ['ʃuːtɪŋ] *n* 1. (*killing*) asesinato *m* (a tiros). 2. (U) (*hunting*) caza *f*, cacería *f.*

shooting star *n* estrella *f* fugaz.

shop [ʃɒp] ◆ *n* 1. (*store*) tienda *f.* 2. (*workshop*) taller *m.* ◆ *vi* comprar; **to go shopping** ir de compras.

shop assistant *n* Br dependiente *m*, -ta *f.*

shop floor *n*: **the ~** el personal, los obreros.

shopkeeper ['ʃɒp,kiːpəʳ] *n* tendero *m*, -ra *f.*

shoplifting ['ʃɒp,lɪftɪŋ] *n* (U) robo *m* en una tienda.

shopper ['ʃɒpəʳ] *n* comprador *m*, -ra *f.*

shopping ['ʃɒpɪŋ] *n* (U) 1. (*purchases*) compras *fpl.* 2. (*act of shopping*) compra *f.*

shopping bag *n* bolsa *f* de la compra.

shopping centre Br, **shopping mall** Am, **shopping plaza** Am [-,plɑːzə] *n* centro *m* comercial.

shopsoiled Br ['ʃɒpsɔɪld], **shopworn** Am ['ʃɒpwɔːn] *adj* deteriorado (da).

shop steward *n* enlace *m y f* sindical.

shopwindow [,ʃɒp'wɪndəʊ] *n* escaparate *m.*

shopworn Am = **shopsoiled.**

shore [ʃɔːʳ] *n* 1. (*of sea, lake, river*) orilla *f.* 2. (*land*): **on ~** en tierra. ▶ **shore up** *vt sep* apuntalar.

shorn [ʃɔːn] ◆ *pp* → **shear.** ◆ *adj* (*grass, hair*) corto(ta); (*head*) rapado(da).

short [ʃɔːt] ◆ *adj* 1. (*gen*) corto(ta). 2. (*not tall*) bajo(ja). 3. (*curt*): **to be ~ (with sb)** ser seco(ca) (con alguien). 4. (*lacking*) escaso(sa); **to be ~ on sthg** no andar sobrado de algo; **to be ~ of** estar OR andar mal de algo. 5. (*be shorter form*): **to be ~ for** ser el diminutivo de. ◆ *adv* 1. (*out of*): **we are running ~ of water** se nos está acabando el agua. 2. (*suddenly, abruptly*): **to cut sthg ~** interrumpir algo antes de acabar; **to stop ~**

parar en seco OR de repente; **to bring OR pull sb up** ~ hacer a alguien parar en seco. ◆ *n* **1.** Br (*alcoholic drink*) licor *m*. **2.** (*film*) cortometraje *m*. ▶ **shorts** *npl* **1.** (*gen*) pantalones *mpl* cortos. **2.** Am (*underwear*) calzoncillos *mpl*. ▶ **for short** *adv* para abreviar. ▶ **in short** *adv* en resumen. ▶ **nothing short of** *prep*: **it was nothing ~ of madness/a disgrace** fue una auténtica locura/vergüenza. ▶ **short of** *prep* **1.** (*just before*) cerca de. **2.** (*without*): **~ of asking, I can't see how you'll find out** salvo que preguntes, no sé cómo lo vas a averiguar.

shortage [ˈʃɔːtɪdʒ] *n* falta *f*, escasez *f*.

shortbread [ˈʃɔːtbred] *n* especie de torta hecha de azúcar, harina y mantequilla.

short-change *vt* (*in shop*) dar mal el cambio a; *fig* (*reward unfairly*) estafar.

short circuit *n* cortocircuito *m*.

shortcomings [ˈʃɔːtˌkʌmɪŋz] *npl* defectos *mpl*.

shortcrust pastry [ˈʃɔːtkrʌst-] *n* pasta *f* quebrada.

short cut *n* **1.** (*quick way*) atajo *m*. **2.** (*quick method*) método *m* rápido.

shorten [ˈʃɔːtn] ◆ *vt* acortar. ◆ *vi* acortarse.

shortfall [ˈʃɔːtfɔːl] *n*: ~ **(in OR of)** déficit *m* (de).

shorthand [ˈʃɔːthænd] *n* (*writing system*) taquigrafía *f*.

shorthand typist *n* Br taquimecanógrafo *m*, -fa *f*.

short list *n* Br (*for job*) lista *f* de candidatos seleccionados; (*for prize*) relación *f* de finalistas.

shortly [ˈʃɔːtlɪ] *adv* (*soon*) dentro de poco; ~ **before/after** poco antes/después de.

shortsighted [ˌʃɔːtˈsaɪtɪd] *adj* (*myopic*) miope, corto(ta) de vista; *fig* (*lacking foresight*) corto de miras.

short-sleeved *adj* de manga corta.

short-staffed [-ˈstɑːft] *adj*: **to be ~** estar falto(ta) de personal.

short story *n* cuento *m*.

short-tempered [-ˈtempəd] *adj* de mal genio.

short-term *adj* a corto plazo.

short wave *n* (U) onda *f* corta.

shot [ʃɒt] ◆ *pt* & *pp* → **shoot.** ◆ *n* **1.** (*gunshot*) tiro *m*, disparo *m*; **like a ~** (*quickly*) en el acto. **2.** (*marksman*) tirador *m*, -ra *f*. **3.** (*in football*) chut *m*, tiro *m*; (*in golf, tennis*) golpe *m*. **4.** (*photograph*) foto *f*. **5.** (CINEMA) plano *m*, toma *f*. **6.** *inf* (*try, go*) intento *m*. **7.** (*injec-*

tion) inyección *f*.

shotgun [ˈʃɒtgʌn] *n* escopeta *f*.

should [ʃʊd] *aux vb* **1.** (*be desirable*): **we ~ leave now** deberíamos irnos ya con ahora. **2.** (*seeking advice, permission*): **~ I go too?** ¿voy yo también? **3.** (*as suggestion*): **I ~** deny everything yo lo negaría todo. **4.** (*indicating probability*): **she ~ be home soon** tiene que llegar a casa pronto. **5.** (*have been expected*): **they ~ have won the match** tendrían que OR deberían haber ganado el partido. **6.** (*indicating intention, wish*): **I ~ like to come with you** me gustaría ir contigo. **7.** (*as conditional*): **you ~ go if you were invited** tendrías que OR deberías ir si te han invitado. **8.** (*in 'that' clauses*): **we decided that you ~ do it** decidimos que lo hicieras tú. **9.** (*expressing uncertain opinion*): **I ~ think he's about 50 (years old)** yo diría que tiene unos 50 (años).

shoulder [ˈʃəʊldəʳ] ◆ *n* **1.** (*part of body, clothing*) hombro *m*. **2.** (CULIN) espaldilla *f*. ◆ *vt* (*accept - responsibility*) cargar con.

shoulder blade *n* omóplato *m*.

shoulder strap *n* **1.** (*on dress*) tirante *m*. **2.** (*on bag*) correa *f*, bandolera *f*.

shouldn't [ˈʃʊdnt] = **should not.**

should've [ˈʃʊdəv] = **should have.**

shout [ʃaʊt] ◆ *n* grito *m*. ◆ *vt* gritar. ◆ *vi*: **to ~ (at)** gritar (a). ▶ **shout down** *vt sep* acallar a gritos.

shouting [ˈʃaʊtɪŋ] *n* (U) gritos *mpl*.

shove [ʃʌv] ◆ *n*: **(to give sthg/sb) a ~** (dar a algo/a alguien) un empujón. ◆ *vt* empujar; **to ~ sthg/sb in** meter algo/a alguien a empujones; **to ~ sthg/sb out** sacar algo/a alguien a empujones. ▶ **shove off** *vi* (*go away*) *inf* largarse.

shovel [ˈʃʌvl] ◆ *n* pala *f*. ◆ *vt* remover con la pala OR a paletadas.

show [ʃəʊ] (*pp* **shown** OR **-ed**) ◆ *n* **1.** (*display, demonstration*) demostración *f*. **2.** (*piece of entertainment - at theatre*) espectáculo *m*; (*- on radio, TV*) programa *m*. **3.** (*performance*) función *f*. **4.** (*of dogs, flowers, art*) exposición *f*. ◆ *vt* **1.** (*gen*) mostrar; **to ~ sb sthg, to ~ sthg to sb** enseñar OR mostrar a alguien algo. **2.** (*escort*): **to ~ sb to sthg** llevar OR acompañar a alguien hasta algo. **3.** (*make visible, reveal*) dejar ver. **4.** (*indicate - increase, profit, loss*) arrojar, registrar. **5.** (*broadcast - film*) proyectar; (*- TV programme*) emitir. **6.** (*exhibit - paintings, products*) exponer. ◆ *vi* **1.** (*indicate, make clear*) indicar, mostrar. **2.** (*be visible*) verse. **3.** (*film*) proyectarse. ▶ **show off** ◆ *vt*

sep lucir, presumir de. ◆ *vi* presumir.
▶ **show up** ◆ *vt sep* poner en evidencia. ◆ *vi* **1.** (*stand out*) resaltar. **2.** (*turn up*) aparecer.

show business *n* (U) mundo *m* del espectáculo.

showdown ['ʃəudaun] *n*: **to have a ~ with** enfrentarse abiertamente a OR con.

shower ['ʃauəʳ] ◆ *n* **1.** (*device*) ducha *f*. **2.** (*wash*): **to have** OR **take a ~** ducharse. **3.** (*of rain*) chubasco *m*, chaparrón *m*. **4.** (*stream*) lluvia *f*. ◆ *vt* **1.** (*sprinkle*) rociar. **2.** (*bestow*): **to ~ sb with sthg, to ~ sthg on** OR **upon sb** (*present, compliments*) colmar a alguien de algo; (*insults*) acribillar a alguien a algo. ◆ *vi* ducharse.

shower cap *n* gorro *m* de baño.

showing ['ʃəuɪŋ] *n* (*of film*) pase *m*, proyección *f*; (*of paintings*) exposición *f*.

show jumping [-,dʒʌmpɪŋ] *n* concurso *m* hípico de salto.

shown [ʃəun] *pp* → **show**.

show-off *n inf* presumido *m*, -da *f*.

showpiece ['ʃəupiːs] *n* pieza *f* de mayor interés.

showroom ['ʃəurum] *n* salón *m* OR sala *f* de exposición.

shrank [ʃræŋk] *pt* → **shrink**.

shrapnel ['ʃræpnl] *n* metralla *f*.

shred [ʃred] ◆ *n* (*small piece - of material*) jirón *m*; (- *of paper*) pedacito *m*; *fig* (*scrap*) pizca *f*. ◆ *vt* (*paper*) hacer trizas; (*food*) rallar.

shredder ['ʃredəʳ] *n* (*for paper*) destructora *f*; (*for food*) rallador *m*.

shrewd [ʃruːd] *adj* astuto(ta).

shriek [ʃriːk] ◆ *n* chillido *m*, grito *m*. ◆ *vi*: **to ~** (**with** OR **in**) chillar (de).

shrill [ʃrɪl] *adj* (*high-pitched*) estridente, agudo(da).

shrimp [ʃrɪmp] *n* camarón *m*.

shrine [ʃraɪn] *n* santuario *m*.

shrink [ʃrɪŋk] (*pt* **shrank**, *pp* **shrunk**) ◆ *vt* encoger. ◆ *vi* **1.** (*become smaller*) encoger. **2.** *fig* (*contract, diminish*) disminuir. **3.** (*recoil*): **to ~ away from** retroceder OR arredrarse ante. **4.** (*be reluctant*): **to ~ from doing sthg** eludir algo.

shrinkage ['ʃrɪŋkɪdʒ] *n* (*loss in size*) encogimiento *m*; *fig* (*contraction*) reducción *f*.

shrink-wrap *vt* precintar o envasar con plástico termoretráctil.

shrivel ['ʃrɪvl] ◆ *vt*: **to ~** (**up**) secar, marchitar. ◆ *vi*: **to ~** (**up**) secarse, marchitarse.

shroud [ʃraud] ◆ *n* (*cloth*) mortaja *f*, sudario *m*. ◆ *vt*: **to be ~ed in sthg** estar envuelto(ta) en algo.

Shrove Tuesday ['ʃrəuv-] *n* martes *m inv* de carnaval.

shrub [ʃrʌb] *n* arbusto *m*.

shrubbery ['ʃrʌbəri] *n* (*zona f de*) arbustos *mpl*.

shrug [ʃrʌg] ◆ *vt*: **to ~ one's shoulders** encogerse de hombros. ◆ *vi* encogerse de hombros. ▶ **shrug off** *vt sep* quitar importancia a.

shrunk [ʃrʌŋk] *pp* → **shrink**.

shudder ['ʃʌdəʳ] *vi* (*tremble*): **to ~** (**with**) estremecerse (de).

shuffle ['ʃʌfl] ◆ *vt* **1.** (*feet*) arrastrar. **2.** (*cards*) barajar. ◆ *vi* (*walk by dragging feet*): **to ~ in/out/along** entrar/salir/andar arrastrando los pies.

shun [ʃʌn] *vt* rehuir, esquivar.

shunt [ʃʌnt] *vt* (RAIL) cambiar de vía; *fig* (*move*) llevar (de un sitio a otro).

shut [ʃʌt] (*pt* & *pp* **shut**) ◆ *adj* cerrado (da). ◆ *vt* cerrar. ◆ *vi* **1.** (*close*) cerrarse. **2.** (*close for business*) cerrar. ▶ **shut away** *vt sep* guardar bajo llave. ▶ **shut down** *vt sep* & *vi* cerrar. ▶ **shut out** *vt sep* (*person, cat*) dejar fuera a; (*light, noise*) no dejar entrar. ▶ **shut up** *inf* ◆ *vt sep* (*silence*) hacer callar. ◆ *vi* callarse.

shutter ['ʃʌtəʳ] *n* **1.** (*on window*) postigo *m*. **2.** (*in camera*) obturador *m*.

shuttle ['ʃʌtl] ◆ *adj*: **~ service** (*of planes*) puente *m* aéreo; (*of buses, trains*) servicio *m* regular. ◆ *n* (*plane*) avión *m* (de puente aéreo).

shuttlecock ['ʃʌtlkɒk] *n* volante *m*.

shy [ʃaɪ] ◆ *adj* (*timid*) tímido(da). ◆ *vi* espantarse.

Siberia [saɪ'bɪərɪə] *n* Siberia.

sibling ['sɪblɪŋ] *n* hermano *m*, -na *f*.

Sicily ['sɪsɪlɪ] *n* Sicilia.

sick [sɪk] *adj* **1.** (*ill*) enfermo(ma). **2.** (*nauseous*): **to feel ~** estar mareado (da). **3.** (*vomiting*): **to be ~** Br devolver, vomitar. **4.** (*fed up*): **to be ~ of sthg/of doing sthg** estar harto(ta) de algo/de hacer algo. **5.** (*offensive*) de mal gusto.

sickbay ['sɪkbeɪ] *n* enfermería *f*.

sicken ['sɪkn] ◆ *vt* poner enfermo(ma), asquear. ◆ *vi* Br: **to be ~ing for sthg** estar cogiendo algo.

sickening ['sɪknɪŋ] *adj* **1.** (*disgusting*) asqueroso(sa). **2.** (*infuriating*) exasperante.

sickle ['sɪkl] *n* hoz *f*.

sick leave *n* (U) baja *f* por enfermedad.

sickly ['sɪklɪ] *adj* **1.** (*unhealthy*) enfermizo(za). **2.** (*unpleasant*) nauseabundo(da).

sickness ['sɪknɪs] *n* **1.** (*illness*) enfermedad *f*. **2.** Br (U) (*nausea, vomiting*) mareo *m*.

sick pay *n* (U) paga *f* por enfermedad.

side [saɪd] ◆ *n* **1.** (*gen*) lado *m*; **at** OR **by one's ~** al lado de uno; **on every ~, on all ~s** por todos los lados; **from ~ to ~** de un lado a otro; **~ by ~** juntos, uno al lado de otro. **2.** (*of person*) costado *m*; (*of animal*) ijada *f*. **3.** (*edge*) lado *m*, borde *m*. **4.** (*of hill, valley*) falda *f*, ladera *f*. **5.** (*bank*) orilla *f*. **6.** (*page*) cara *f*. **7.** (*participant - in war, game*) lado *m*, bando *m*; (*- in sports match*) equipo *m*. **8.** (*viewpoint*) punto *m* de vista; **to take sb's ~** ponerse del lado OR de parte de alguien. **9.** (*aspect*) aspecto *m*; **to be on the safe ~** para estar seguro. ◆ *adj* lateral. ▶ **side with** *vt fus* ponerse de parte de.

sideboard ['saɪdbɔːd] *n* aparador *m*.

sideboards Br ['saɪdbɔːdz], **sideburns** Am ['saɪdbɜːnz] *npl* patillas *fpl*.

side effect *n* (MED & *fig*) efecto *m* secundario.

sidelight ['saɪdlaɪt] *n* luz *f* lateral.

sideline ['saɪdlaɪn] *n* **1.** (*extra business*) negocio *m* suplementario. **2.** (*on tennis court*) línea *f* lateral; (*on football pitch*) línea de banda.

sidelong ['saɪdlɒŋ] *adj* & *adv* de reojo OR soslayo.

sidesaddle ['saɪd,sædl] *adv*: **to ride ~** montar a sentadillas OR mujeriegas.

sideshow ['saɪdʃəu] *n* barraca *f* OR caseta *f* de feria.

sidestep ['saɪdstep] *vt* **1.** (*in football, rugby*) regatear. **2.** *fig* (*problem, question*) esquivar.

side street *n* calle *f* lateral.

sidetrack ['saɪdtræk] *vt*: **to be ~ed** desviarse OR salirse del tema.

sidewalk ['saɪdwɔːk] *n* Am acera *f*.

sideways ['saɪdweɪz] ◆ *adj* (*movement*) hacia un lado; (*glance*) de soslayo. ◆ *adv* (*move*) de lado; (*look*) de reojo.

siding ['saɪdɪŋ] *n* vía *f* muerta.

sidle ['saɪdl] ▶ **sidle up** *vi*: **to ~ up to** acercarse furtivamente a.

siege [siːdʒ] *n* **1.** (*by army*) sitio *m*, cerco *m*. **2.** (*by police*) cerco *m* policial.

sieve [sɪv] ◆ *n* (*utensil*) colador *m*. ◆ *vt* (*soup*) colar; (*flour, sugar*) tamizar.

sift [sɪft] ◆ *vt* **1.** (*sieve*) tamizar. **2.** *fig* (*examine carefully*) examinar cuidadosamente. ◆ *vi*: **to ~ through sthg** examinar

cuidadosamente algo.

sigh [saɪ] ◆ *n* suspiro *m*. ◆ *vi* suspirar.

sight [saɪt] ◆ *n* **1.** (*vision*) vista *f*. **2.** (*act of seeing*): **her first ~ of the sea** la primera vez que vio el mar; **in ~** a la vista; **to disappear out of ~** perderse de vista; **at first ~** a primera vista. **3.** (*something seen*) imagen *f*. **4.** (*on gun*) mira *f*. ◆ *vt* divisar, avistar. ▶ **sights** *npl* atracciones *fpl* turísticas.

sightseeing ['saɪt,siːɪŋ] *n* (U) recorrido *m* turístico.

sightseer ['saɪt,siːər] *n* turista *m y f*.

sign [saɪn] ◆ *n* **1.** (*written symbol*) signo *m*. **2.** (*gesture*) señal *f*. **3.** (*of pub, shop*) letrero *m*; (*on road*) señal *f*; (*notice*) cartel *m*. **4.** (*indication*) señal *f*. ◆ *vt* firmar. ▶ **sign on** *vi* **1.** (*enrol, register*): **to ~ on (for)** (*army*) alistarse (en); (*job*) firmar el contrato (de); (*course*) matricularse (en). **2.** (*register as unemployed*) firmar para cobrar el paro. ▶ **sign up** ◆ *vt sep* (*employee*) contratar; (*recruit*) alistar. ◆ *vi*: **to ~ up (for)** (*army*) alistarse (en); (*job*) firmar el contrato (de); (*course*) matricularse (en).

signal ['sɪgnl] ◆ *n* señal *f*. ◆ *vt* **1.** (*indicate*) indicar. **2.** (*tell*): **to ~ sb (to do sthg)** hacer señas a alguien (para que haga algo). ◆ *vi* **1.** (AUT) señalizar. **2.** (*indicate*): **to ~ to sb (to do sthg)** hacer señas a alguien (para que haga algo).

signalman ['sɪgnlmən] (*pl* **-men** [-mən]) *n* (RAIL) guardavía *m*.

signature ['sɪgnətʃər] *n* firma *f*.

signature tune *n* sintonía *f*.

signet ring ['sɪgnɪt-] *n* (anillo *m* de) sello *m*.

significance [sɪg'nɪfɪkəns] *n* trascendencia *f*, importancia *f*.

significant [sɪg'nɪfɪkənt] *adj* **1.** (*considerable, meaningful*) significativo(va). **2.** (*important*) trascendente.

signify ['sɪgnɪfaɪ] *vt* significar.

signpost ['saɪnpəust] *n* letrero *m* indicador.

Sikh [siːk] ◆ *adj* sij. ◆ *n* (*person*) sij *m y f*.

silence ['saɪləns] ◆ *n* silencio *m*. ◆ *vt* (*person, critic*) acallar; (*gun*) silenciar.

silencer ['saɪlənsər] *n* silenciador *m*.

silent ['saɪlənt] *adj* **1.** (*gen*) silencioso (sa). **2.** (*not revealing anything*): **to be ~ about** quedar en silencio respecto a. **3.** (CINEMA & LING) mudo(da).

silhouette [,sɪluː'et] *n* silueta *f*.

silicon chip [,sɪlɪkən-] *n* chip *m* de silicio.

silk [sɪlk] ◆ n seda f. ◆ comp de seda.

silky ['sɪlkɪ] adj (hair, dress, skin) sedoso (sa); (voice) aterciopelado(da).

sill [sɪl] n (of window) alféizar m.

silly ['sɪlɪ] adj estúpido(da).

silo ['saɪləʊ] (pl -s) n silo m.

silt [sɪlt] n cieno m, légamo m.

silver ['sɪlvər] ◆ adj (of colour) plateado (da). ◆ n (U) 1. (metal, silverware) plata f. 2. (coins) monedas fpl plateadas. ◆ comp de plata.

silver foil, silver paper n (U) papel m de plata.

silver-plated [-'pleɪtɪd] adj plateado (da).

silversmith ['sɪlvəsmɪθ] n platero m, -ra f.

silverware ['sɪlvəweər] n (U) 1. (dishes etc) plata f. 2. Am (cutlery) cubertería f de plata.

similar ['sɪmɪlər] adj: ~ (to) parecido (da) OR similar (a).

similarly ['sɪmɪləlɪ] adv (likewise) asimismo; (equally) igualmente.

simmer ['sɪmər] vt & vi hervir a fuego lento.

simpering ['sɪmpərɪŋ] adj (person) que sonríe con cara de tonto(ta); (smile) bobo(ba).

simple ['sɪmpl] adj 1. (gen) sencillo (lla). 2. dated (mentally retarded) simple. 3. (plain - fact) mero(ra); (- truth) puro (ra).

simple-minded [-'maɪndɪd] adj simple.

simplicity [sɪm'plɪsətɪ] n sencillez f.

simplify ['sɪmplɪfaɪ] vt simplificar.

simply ['sɪmplɪ] adv 1. (merely) sencillamente, simplemente. 2. (for emphasis): ~ dreadful/wonderful francamente terrible/maravilloso. 3. (in a simple way) de manera sencilla.

simulate ['sɪmjʊleɪt] vt simular.

simultaneous [Br ˌsɪmʊl'teɪnjəs, Am ˌsaɪməl'teɪnjəs] adj simultáneo(a).

sin [sɪn] ◆ n pecado m. ◆ vi: to ~ (against) pecar (contra).

since [sɪns] ◆ adv desde entonces. ◆ prep desde; he has worked here ~ 1975 trabaja aquí desde 1975. ◆ conj 1. (in time) desde que; it's ages ~ I saw you hace siglos que no te veo. 2. (because) ya que, puesto que.

sincere [sɪn'sɪər] adj sincero(ra).

sincerely [sɪn'sɪəlɪ] adv sinceramente; Yours ~ (at end of letter) Se despide atentamente.

sincerity [sɪn'serətɪ] n sinceridad f.

sinew ['sɪnjuː] n tendón m.

sinful ['sɪnfʊl] adj 1. (person) pecador (ra). 2. (thought, act) pecaminoso(sa).

sing [sɪŋ] (pt sang, pp sung) vt & vi cantar.

Singapore [ˌsɪŋə'pɔːr] n Singapur.

singe [sɪndʒ] vt chamuscar.

singer ['sɪŋər] n cantante m y f.

singing ['sɪŋɪŋ] n (U) canto m.

single ['sɪŋgl] ◆ adj 1. (only one) único (ca). 2. (individual): every ~ penny todos y cada uno de los peniques. 3. (unmarried) soltero(ra). 4. Br (one-way) de ida. ◆ n 1. Br (one-way ticket) billete m de ida. 2. (MUS) (record) sencillo m, single m. ► singles npl (TENNIS) (partido m) individual m. ► single out vt sep: to ~ sb out (for) escoger a alguien (para).

single bed n cama f individual.

single-breasted [-'brestɪd] adj recto (ta).

single cream n Br nata f líquida.

single file n: in ~ en fila india.

single-handed [-'hændɪd] adv sin ayuda.

single-minded [-'maɪndɪd] adj resuelto(ta).

single-parent family n familia f en la que falta uno de los padres.

single room n habitación f individual.

singlet ['sɪŋglɪt] n Br camiseta f sin mangas.

singular ['sɪŋgjʊlər] ◆ adj singular. ◆ n singular m.

sinister ['sɪnɪstər] adj siniestro(tra).

sink [sɪŋk] (pt sank, pp sunk) ◆ n 1. (in kitchen) fregadero m. 2. (in bathroom) lavabo m. ◆ vt 1. (cause to go under water) hundir. 2. (cause to penetrate): to ~ sthg into (knife, claws) clavar algo en; (teeth) hincar algo en. ◆ vi 1. (go down - ship, sun) hundirse. 2. (slump - person) hundirse. 3. (decrease) bajar. ► sink in vi hacer mella.

sink unit n fregadero m (con mueble debajo).

sinner ['sɪnər] n pecador m, -ra f.

sinus ['saɪnəs] (pl -es) n seno m.

sip [sɪp] ◆ n sorbo m. ◆ vt beber a sorbos.

siphon ['saɪfn] n sifón m. ► siphon off vt sep 1. (liquid) sacar con sifón. 2. fig (funds) desviar.

sir [sɜːr] n 1. (form of address) señor m. 2. (in titles): Sir Philip Holden Sir Philip Holden.

siren ['saɪərən] n (alarm) sirena f.

sirloin (steak) ['sɜːlɔɪn] n solomillo m.

sissy ['sɪsɪ] n inf mariquita m.

sister ['sɪstəʳ] n 1. (gen) hermana f. 2. Br (senior nurse) enfermera f jefe.

sister-in-law (pl sisters-in-law OR sister-in-laws) n cuñada f.

sit [sɪt] (pt & pp sat) ◆ vi 1. (be seated, sit down) sentarse. 2. (be member): **to ~ on** ser miembro de. 3. (be in session) reunirse. ◆ vt Br (exam) presentarse a. ▶ **sit about, sit around** vi estar sentado(da) sin hacer nada. ▶ **sit down** vi sentarse. ▶ **sit in on** vt fus estar presente en (sin tomar parte). ▶ **sit through** vt fus aguantar (hasta el final). ▶ **sit up** vi 1. (sit upright) incorporarse. 2. (stay up) quedarse levantado(da).

sitcom ['sɪtkɒm] n inf comedia f de situación.

site [saɪt] ◆ n (place) sitio m, lugar m; (of construction work) obra f. ◆ vt situar.

sit-in n sentada f.

sitting ['sɪtɪŋ] n 1. (serving of meal) turno m (para comer). 2. (session) sesión f.

sitting room n sala f de estar.

situated ['sɪtjʊeɪtɪd] adj (located): **to be ~** estar situado(da).

situation [ˌsɪtjʊ'eɪʃn] n 1. (gen) situación f. 2. (job) colocación f; **'Situations Vacant'** Br 'Ofertas de trabajo'.

six [sɪks] ◆ num adj seis (inv); **she's ~ (years old)** tiene seis años. ◆ num n 1. (the number six) seis m inv; **two hundred and ~** doscientos seis; **~ comes before seven** el seis va antes que el siete. 2. (in times): **it's ~ (thirty)** son las seis (y media); **we arrived at ~** llegamos a las seis. 3. (in addresses): **~ Peyton Place** Peyton Place número seis. 4. (in scores): **~-nil** seis a cero. ◆ num pron seis m y f; **there are ~ of us** somos seis.

sixteen [sɪks'tiːn] num dieciséis; see also **six**.

sixteenth [sɪks'tiːnθ] num decimosexto(ta); see also **sixth**.

sixth [sɪksθ] ◆ num adj sexto(ta). ◆ num adv sexto(ta). ◆ num pron sexto m, -ta f. ◆ n 1. (fraction): **a ~** OR **one ~ of** un sexto de, la sexta parte de. 2. (in dates): **the ~** el (día) seis; **the ~ of September** el seis de septiembre.

sixth form n Br (SCH) curso optativo de dos años de enseñanza secundaria con vistas al examen de ingreso a la universidad, ≈ COU m.

sixth form college n Br centro público para alumnos de 16 a 18 años donde se preparan para los 'A levels' o para exámenes de formación profesional.

sixty ['sɪkstɪ] num sesenta; see also **six**. ▶ **sixties** npl 1. (decade): **the sixties** los años sesenta. 2. (in ages): **to be in one's sixties** tener más de sesenta años.

size [saɪz] n 1. (gen) tamaño m. 2. (of clothes) talla f; (of shoes) número m. ▶ **size up** vt sep (situation) evaluar; (person) juzgar.

sizeable ['saɪzəbl] adj considerable.

sizzle ['sɪzl] vi chisporrotear.

skate [skeɪt] (pl sense 2 only inv OR -s) ◆ n 1. (ice skate, roller skate) patín m. 2. (fish) raya f. ◆ vi (on skates) patinar.

skateboard ['skeɪtbɔːd] n monopatín m.

skater ['skeɪtəʳ] n patinador m, -ra f.

skating ['skeɪtɪŋ] n patinaje m.

skating rink n pista f de patinaje.

skeleton ['skelɪtn] n (ANAT) esqueleto m.

skeleton key n llave f maestra.

skeleton staff n personal m mínimo.

skeptic etc Am = **sceptic** etc.

sketch [sketʃ] ◆ n 1. (drawing, brief outline) esbozo m, bosquejo m. 2. (humorous scene) sketch m. ◆ vt esbozar.

sketchbook ['sketʃbʊk] n cuaderno m de dibujo.

sketchpad ['sketʃpæd] n bloc m de dibujo.

sketchy ['sketʃɪ] adj incompleto(ta).

skewer ['skjʊəʳ] n brocheta f.

ski [skiː] (pt & pp skied, cont skiing) ◆ n esquí m. ◆ vi esquiar.

ski boots npl botas fpl de esquí.

skid [skɪd] ◆ n patinazo m. ◆ vi patinar.

skier ['skiːəʳ] n esquiador m, -ra f.

skies [skaɪz] pl ▶ **sky**.

skiing ['skiːɪŋ] n (U) esquí m.

ski jump n 1. (slope) pista f para saltos de esquí. 2. (event) saltos mpl de esquí.

skilful, skillful Am ['skɪlfʊl] adj hábil.

ski lift n telesilla m.

skill [skɪl] n 1. (U) (expertise) habilidad f, destreza f. 2. (craft, technique) técnica f.

skilled [skɪld] adj 1. (skilful) habilidoso (sa). 2. (trained) cualificado(da).

skillful etc Am = **skilful** etc.

skim [skɪm] ◆ vt 1. (remove - cream) desnatar. 2. (fly above) volar rozando. ◆ vi: **to ~ through sthg** hojear algo, leer algo por encima.

skim(med) milk [skɪm(d)-] n leche f desnatada.

skimp [skɪmp] ◆ vt (gen) escatimar;

(*work*) hacer de prisa y corriendo. ◆ *vi*:
to ~ on sthg (*gen*) escatimar algo; (*work*)
hacer algo de prisa y corriendo.

skimpy ['skɪmpɪ] *adj* (*clothes*) muy corto
y estrecho (muy corta y estrecha);
(*meal, facts*) escaso(sa).

skin [skɪn] ◆ *n* 1. (*gen*) piel *f*; (*on face*)
cutis *m*. 2. (*on milk, pudding*) nata *f*; (*on
paint*) capa *f*, película *f*. ◆ *vt* 1. (*animal*)
despellejar. 2. (*knee, elbow etc*) ras-
guñarse.

skin-deep *adj* superficial.

skin diving *n* buceo *m*, submarinismo *m* (sin traje ni escafandra).

skinny ['skɪnɪ] *adj inf* flaco(ca).

skin-tight *adj* muy ajustado(da).

skip [skɪp] ◆ *n* 1. (*little jump*) brinco *m*,
saltito *m*. 2. Br (*large container*) contenedor *m*, container *m*. ◆ *vt* saltarse. ◆ *vi*
1. (*move in little jumps*) ir dando brincos.
2. Br (*jump over rope*) saltar a la comba
OR cuerda.

ski pants *npl* pantalones *mpl* de
esquí.

ski pole *n* bastón *m* para esquiar.

skipper ['skɪpə^r] *n* (NAUT & SPORT)
capitán *m*, -ana *f*.

skipping rope ['skɪpɪŋ-] *n* Br comba
f, cuerda *f* de saltar.

skirmish ['skɜːmɪʃ] *n lit & fig* escaramuza *f*.

skirt [skɜːt] ◆ *n* falda *f*. ◆ *vt* 1. (*border*)
rodear, bordear. 2. (*go round - obstacle*)
sortear; (*- person, group*) esquivar.
3. (*avoid dealing with*) eludir. ▶ **skirt
round** *vt fus* 1. (*obstacle*) sortear. 2.
(*issue, problem*) evitar, eludir.

skit [skɪt] *n*: **~ (on)** parodia *f* (de).

skittle ['skɪtl] *n* Br bolo *m*. ▶ **skittles** *n*
(U) bolos *mpl*.

skive [skaɪv] *vi* Br inf: **to ~ (off)**
escaquearse.

skulk [skʌlk] *vi* esconderse.

skull [skʌl] *n* (*gen*) calavera *f*; (ANAT)
cráneo *m*.

skunk [skʌŋk] *n* mofeta *f*.

sky [skaɪ] *n* cielo *m*.

skylight ['skaɪlaɪt] *n* claraboya *f*, tragaluz *m*.

skyscraper ['skaɪˌskreɪpə^r] *n* rascacielos *m inv*.

slab [slæb] *n* (*of stone*) losa *f*; (*of cheese*)
pedazo *m*; (*of chocolate*) tableta *f*.

slack [slæk] ◆ *adj* 1. (*rope, cable*) flojo
(ja). 2. (*business*) inactivo(va). 3. (*person - careless*) descuidado(da). ◆ *n* (*in
rope*) parte *f* floja.

slacken ['slækn] ◆ *vt* (*speed, pace*)

reducir; (*rope*) aflojar. ◆ *vi* (*speed, pace*)
reducirse.

slag [slæg] *n* (*waste material*) escoria *f*.

slagheap ['slæghiːp] *n* escorial *m*.

slain [sleɪn] *pp* → **slay**.

slam [slæm] ◆ *vt* 1. (*shut*) cerrar de
golpe. 2. (*place with force*): **to ~ sthg on** OR
onto sthg dar un golpe con algo contra
algo violentamente. ◆ *vi* (*shut*) cerrarse
de golpe.

slander ['slɑːndə^r] ◆ *n* calumnia *f*,
difamación *f*. ◆ *vt* calumniar, difamar.

slang [slæŋ] *n* argot *m*, jerga *f*.

slant [slɑːnt] ◆ *n* 1. (*diagonal angle*)
inclinación *f*. 2. (*perspective*) enfoque *m*.
◆ *vi* inclinarse.

slanting ['slɑːntɪŋ] *adj* inclinado(da).

slap [slæp] ◆ *n* (*in face*) bofetada *f*; (*on
back*) palmada *f*. ◆ *vt* 1. (*person, face*)
abofetear; (*back*) dar una palmada a.
2. (*place with force*): **to ~ sthg on** OR **onto**
dar un golpe con algo contra. ◆ *adv inf*
(*directly*) de narices.

slapdash ['slæpdæʃ], **slaphappy**
['slæpˌhæpɪ] *adj inf* chapucero(ra).

slapstick ['slæpstɪk] *n* (U) payasadas
fpl.

slap-up *adj* Br inf: **~ meal** comilona *f*.

slash [slæʃ] ◆ *n* 1. (*long cut*) raja *f*, tajo
m. 2. (*oblique stroke*) barra *f* oblicua. ◆ *vt*
1. (*material*) rasgar; (*wrists*) cortar. 2. *inf*
(*prices etc*) recortar drásticamente.

slat [slæt] *n* tablilla *f*.

slate [sleɪt] ◆ *n* pizarra *f*. ◆ *vt* (*criticize*)
poner por los suelos.

slaughter ['slɔːtə^r] ◆ *n lit & fig* matanza *f*. ◆ *vt* matar.

slaughterhouse ['slɔːtəhaus, *pl*
-hauzɪz] *n* matadero *m*.

slave [sleɪv] ◆ *n* esclavo *m*, -va *f*. ◆ *vi*
(*work hard*): **to ~ (over)** trabajar como un
negro (en).

slavery ['sleɪvərɪ] *n lit & fig* esclavitud
f.

slay [sleɪ] (*pt* **slew**, *pp* **slain**) *vt literary*
asesinar, matar.

sleazy ['sliːzɪ] *adj* (*disreputable*) de mala
muerte.

sledge [sledʒ], **sled** Am [sled] *n* trineo
m.

sledgehammer ['sledʒˌhæmə^r] *n*
almádena *f*.

sleek [sliːk] *adj* 1. (*hair*) suave y brillante; (*fur*) lustroso(sa). 2. (*shape*) de
línea depurada.

sleep [sliːp] (*pt & pp* **slept**) ◆ *n* sueño *m*;
to go to ~ (*doze off*) dormirse. ◆ *vi*
dormir. ▶ **sleep in** *vi* levantarse tarde.

▶ **sleep with** *vt fus euphemism* acostarse con.

sleeper ['sli:pə'] *n* **1.** (*person*): **to be a heavy/light ~** tener el sueño profundo/ligero. **2.** (*sleeping compartment*) coche-cama *m*. **3.** (*train*) tren *m* nocturno (con literas). **4.** Br (*on railway track*) traviesa *f*.

sleeping bag ['sli:pɪŋ-] *n* saco *m* de dormir.

sleeping car ['sli:pɪŋ-] *n* coche-cama *m*.

sleeping pill ['sli:pɪŋ-] *n* pastilla *f* para dormir.

sleepless ['sli:plɪs] *adj* en blanco.

sleepwalk ['sli:pwɔ:k] *vi* (*be a sleepwalker*) ser somnámbulo(la); (*walk in one's sleep*) andar mientras uno duerme.

sleepy ['sli:pɪ] *adj* (*person*) soñoliento (ta).

sleet [sli:t] ◆ *n* aguanieve *f*. ◆ *v impers*: **it's ~ing** cae aguanieve.

sleeve [sli:v] *n* **1.** (*of garment*) manga *f*. **2.** (*for record*) cubierta *f*.

sleigh [sleɪ] *n* trineo *m*.

sleight of hand [,slaɪt-] *n* (U) *lit & fig* juego *m* de manos.

slender ['slendə'] *adj* **1.** (*thin*) esbelto (ta). **2.** (*scarce*) escaso(sa).

slept [slept] *pt & pp* → **sleep**.

slew [slu:] ◆ *pt* → **slay**. ◆ *vi* girar bruscamente.

slice [slaɪs] ◆ *n* **1.** (*of bread*) rebanada *f*; (*of cheese*) loncha *f*; (*of sausage*) raja *f*; (*of lemon*) rodaja *f*; (*of meat*) tajada *f*. **2.** (*of market, glory*) parte *f*. ◆ *vt* (*gen*) cortar; (*bread*) rebanar.

slick [slɪk] *adj* **1.** (*smooth, skilful*) logrado (da). **2.** *pej* (*superficial - talk*) aparentemente brillante; (- *person*) de labia fácil.

slide [slaɪd] (*pt & pp* **slid** [slɪd]) ◆ *n* **1.** (*decline*) descenso *m*. **2.** (PHOT) diapositiva *f*. **3.** (*in playground*) tobogán *m*. **4.** Br (*for hair*) pasador *m*. ◆ *vt* deslizar. ◆ *vi* **1.** (*slip*) resbalar. **2.** (*glide*) deslizarse. **3.** (*decline gradually*) caer.

sliding door [,slaɪdɪŋ-] *n* puerta *f* corredera.

sliding scale [,slaɪdɪŋ-] *n* escala *f* móvil.

slight [slaɪt] ◆ *adj* **1.** (*improvement, hesitation etc*) ligero(ra); (*wound*) superficial; **not in the ~est** *fml* en absoluto. **2.** (*slender*) menudo(da). ◆ *n* desaire *m*. ◆ *vt* menospreciar, desairar.

slightly ['slaɪtlɪ] *adv* (*to small extent*) ligeramente.

slim [slɪm] ◆ *adj* **1.** (*person, object*) del-

gado(da). **2.** (*chance, possibility*) remoto (ta). ◆ *vi* (*intentar*) adelgazar.

slime [slaɪm] *n* (*in pond etc*) lodo *m*, cieno *m*; (*of snail, slug*) baba *f*.

slimming ['slɪmɪŋ] *n* adelgazamiento *m*.

sling [slɪŋ] (*pt & pp* **slung**) ◆ *n* **1.** (*for injured arm*) cabestrillo *m*. **2.** (*for carrying things*) braga *f*, honda *f*. ◆ *vt* **1.** (*hang roughly*) colgar descuidadamente. **2.** *inf* (*throw*) tirar.

slip [slɪp] ◆ *n* **1.** (*mistake*) descuido *m*, desliz *m*; **a ~ of the pen/tongue** un lapsus. **2.** (*of paper - gen*) papelito *m*; (- *form*) hoja *f*. **3.** (*underskirt*) enaguas *fpl*. **4.** *phr*: **to give sb the ~** *inf* dar esquinazo a alguien. ◆ *vt*: **to ~ sthg into** meter algo rápidamente en; **to ~ into sthg, to ~ sthg on** (*clothes*) ponerse rápidamente algo. ◆ *vi* **1.** (*lose one's balance*) resbalar, patinar. **2.** (*slide*) escurrirse, resbalar. **3.** (*decline*) empeorar. ▶ **slip up** *vi* cometer un error (poco importante).

slipped disc [,slɪpt-] *n* hernia *f* discal.

slipper ['slɪpə'] *n* zapatilla *f*.

slippery ['slɪpərɪ] *adj* resbaladizo(za).

slip road *n* Br (*for joining motorway*) acceso *m*; (*for leaving motorway*) salida *f*.

slipshod ['slɪpʃɒd] *adj* chapucero(ra).

slip-up *n inf* fallo *m* poco importante.

slipway ['slɪpweɪ] *n* grada *f*.

slit [slɪt] (*pt & pp* **slit**) ◆ *n* ranura *f*, hendidura *f*. ◆ *vt* abrir, cortar (a lo largo).

slither ['slɪðə'] *vi* deslizarse.

sliver ['slɪvə'] *n* (*of glass*) esquirla *f*; (*of wood*) astilla *f*; (*of cheese, ham*) tajada *f* muy fina.

slob [slɒb] *n inf* guarro *m*, -rra *f*.

slog [slɒg] *inf* ◆ *n* (*work*) curro *m*, trabajo *m* pesado. ◆ *vi* (*work*): **to ~ (away) at** trabajar sin descanso en.

slogan ['sləugən] *n* eslogan *m*.

slop [slɒp] ◆ *vt* derramar. ◆ *vi* derramarse.

slope [sləup] ◆ *n* cuesta *f*, pendiente *f*. ◆ *vi* inclinarse.

sloping ['sləupɪŋ] *adj* (*gen*) inclinado (da); (*ground*) en pendiente.

sloppy ['slɒpɪ] *adj* (*person*) descuidado (da); (*work*) chapucero(ra); (*appearance*) dejado(da).

slot [slɒt] *n* **1.** (*opening - gen & COMPUT*) ranura *f*. **2.** (*groove*) muesca *f*. **3.** (*place in schedule*) espacio *m*.

slot machine *n* **1.** (*vending machine*) máquina *f* automática (*de bebidas, cigarrillos etc*). **2.** (*arcade machine*) máquina *f* tragaperras.

slouch [slaʊtʃ] vi ir con los hombros caídos.

Slovakia [sləˈvækɪə] n Eslovaquia.

slovenly [ˈslʌvnlɪ] adj (unkempt) desaliñado(da); (careless) descuidado(da).

slow [sləʊ] ◆ adj 1. (not fast) lento(ta). 2. (not prompt): **to be ~ to do sthg** tardar en hacer algo. 3. (clock etc) atrasado (da). 4. (not intelligent) corto(ta) (de alcances). ◆ vt aminorar, ralentizar. ◆ vi ir más despacio. ▶ **slow down, slow up** ◆ vt sep (growth) retrasar; (car) reducir la velocidad de. ◆ vi (walker) ir más despacio; (car) reducir la velocidad.

slowdown [ˈsləʊdaʊn] n ralentización f.

slowly [ˈsləʊlɪ] adv despacio, lentamente.

slow motion n: **in ~** a cámara lenta.

sludge [slʌdʒ] n (U) (mud) fango m, lodo m; (sewage) aguas fpl residuales.

slug [slʌg] n 1. (animal) babosa f. 2. Am inf (bullet) bala f.

sluggish [ˈslʌgɪʃ] adj (movement, activity) lento(ta); (feeling) aturdido(da).

sluice [slu:s] n (passage) canal m de desagüe; (gate) compuerta f.

slum [slʌm] n (area) barrio m bajo.

slumber [ˈslʌmbər] vi literary dormir.

slump [slʌmp] ◆ n 1. (decline): **~ (in)** bajón m (en). 2. (ECON) crisis f económica. ◆ vi 1. (fall in value) dar un bajón. 2. (fall heavily - person) desplomarse, dejarse caer.

slung [slʌŋ] pt & pp → **sling**.

slur [slɜ:r] ◆ n (insult) agravio m. ◆ vt mascullar.

slush [slʌʃ] n nieve f medio derretida.

slush fund, slush money Am n fondos utilizados para actividades corruptas.

slut [slʌt] n 1. inf (dirty or untidy woman) marrana f. 2. v inf (sexually immoral woman) ramera f.

sly [slaɪ] (compar **slyer** OR **slier**, superl **slyest** OR **sliest**) adj 1. (look, smile) furtivo (va). 2. (person) astuto(ta).

smack [smæk] ◆ n 1. (slap) cachete m. 2. (impact) golpe m. ◆ vt 1. (slap) pegar, dar un cachete a. 2. (place violently) tirar de golpe.

small [smɔ:l] adj (gen) pequeño(ña); (person) bajo(ja); (matter, attention) de poca importancia; (importance) poco (ca).

small ads [-ædz] npl Br anuncios mpl clasificados.

small change n cambio m, suelto m.

smallholder [ˈsmɔ:l,həʊldər] n Br minifundista m y f.

small hours npl primeras horas fpl de la madrugada.

smallpox [ˈsmɔ:lpɒks] n viruela f.

small print n: **the ~** la letra pequeña.

small talk n (U) conversación f trivial.

smarmy [ˈsmɑ:mɪ] adj cobista.

smart [smɑ:t] ◆ adj 1. (neat, stylish) elegante. 2. (clever) inteligente. 3. (fashionable, exclusive) elegante. 4. (quick, sharp) rápido(da). ◆ vi 1. (eyes, wound) escocer. 2. (person) sentir resquemor.

smarten [ˈsmɑ:tn] ▶ **smarten up** vt sep arreglar.

smash [smæʃ] ◆ n 1. (sound) estrépito m. 2. inf (car crash) accidente m. 3. (TENNIS) mate m, smash m. ◆ vt 1. (break into pieces) romper, hacer pedazos. 2. (hit, crash): **to ~ one's fist into sthg** dar un puñetazo en algo. 3. fig (defeat) aplastar. ◆ vi 1. (break into pieces) romperse, hacerse pedazos. 2. (crash, collide): **to ~ into sthg** chocar violentamente con algo.

smashing [ˈsmæʃɪŋ] adj inf fenomenal.

smattering [ˈsmætərɪŋ] n nociones fpl; **he has a ~ of Spanish** habla cuatro palabras de español.

smear [smɪər] ◆ n 1. (dirty mark) mancha f. 2. (MED) frotis m. 3. (slander) calumnia f, difamación f. ◆ vt 1. (smudge) manchar. 2. (spread): **to ~ sthg onto sthg** untar algo con algo. 3. (slander) calumniar, difamar.

smell [smel] (pt & pp **-ed** OR **smelt**) ◆ n 1. (odour) olor m. 2. (sense of smell) olfato m. ◆ vt lit & fig oler. ◆ vi 1. (gen) oler; **to ~ of/like** oler a/como; **to ~ good/bad** oler bien/mal. 2. (smell unpleasantly) apestar.

smelly [ˈsmelɪ] adj maloliente.

smelt [smelt] ◆ pt & pp → **smell**. ◆ vt fundir.

smile [smaɪl] ◆ n sonrisa f. ◆ vi sonreír.

smirk [smɜ:k] n sonrisa f desdeñosa.

smock [smɒk] n blusón m.

smog [smɒg] n niebla f baja, smog m.

smoke [sməʊk] ◆ n (gen) humo m. ◆ vt 1. (cigarette, cigar) fumar. 2. (fish, meat, cheese) ahumar. ◆ vi 1. (smoke tobacco) fumar. 2. (give off smoke) echar humo.

smoked [sməʊkt] adj ahumado(da).

smoker [ˈsməʊkər] n 1. (person) fumador m, -ra f. 2. (RAIL) (compartment) compartimiento m de fumadores.

smokescreen [ˈsməʊkskri:n] n fig cortina f de humo.

smoke shop n Am estanco m.

smoking ['sməʊkɪŋ] n: ~ **is bad for you** fumar es malo; **'no ~'** 'prohibido fumar'.

smoky ['sməʊkɪ] adj 1. (full of smoke) lleno(na) de humo. 2. (taste, colour) ahumado(da).

smolder Am = **smoulder**.

smooth [smuːð] ◆ adj 1. (surface) liso (sa); (skin) terso(sa). 2. (mixture) sin grumos. 3. (movement, taste) suave. 4. (flight, ride) tranquilo(la). 5. pej (person, manner) meloso(sa). 6. (trouble-free) sin problemas. ◆ vt alisar. ▶ **smooth out** vt sep alisar.

smother ['smʌðər] vt 1. (cover thickly): to ~ sthg in OR with cubrir algo de. 2. (kill) asfixiar. 3. (extinguish) sofocar, apagar. 4. fig (control) contener.

smoulder Br, **smolder** Am ['sməʊldər] vi 1. (fire) arder sin llama. 2. fig (person, feelings) arder.

smudge [smʌdʒ] ◆ n (dirty mark) mancha f; (ink blot) borrón m. ◆ vt (by blurring) emborronar; (by dirtying) manchar.

smug [smʌg] adj pej pagado(da) OR satisfecho(cha) de sí mismo(ma).

smuggle ['smʌgl] vt (across frontiers) pasar de contrabando.

smuggler ['smʌglər] n contrabandista m y f.

smuggling ['smʌglɪŋ] n (U) contrabando m.

smutty ['smʌtɪ] adj inf pej guarro(rra).

snack [snæk] n bocado m, piscolabis m inv.

snack bar n bar m, cafetería f.

snag [snæg] ◆ n (problem) pega f. ◆ vi: to ~ (on) engancharse (en).

snail [sneɪl] n caracol m.

snake [sneɪk] n (large) serpiente f; (small) culebra f.

snap [snæp] ◆ adj repentino(na). ◆ n 1. (act or sound) crujido m, chasquido m. 2. inf (photograph) foto f. ◆ vt 1. (break) partir (en dos). 2. (move with a snap): to ~ sthg open abrir algo de golpe. ◆ vi 1. (break) partirse (en dos). 2. (attempt to bite): to ~ at sthg/sb intentar morder algo/a alguien. 3. (speak sharply): to ~ (at sb) contestar bruscamente OR de mala manera a alguien. ▶ **snap up** vt sep no dejar escapar.

snap fastener n cierre m (en la ropa etc).

snappy ['snæpɪ] adj inf 1. (stylish) con estilo. 2. (quick) rápido(da); **make it ~!** ¡date prisa!

snapshot ['snæpʃɒt] n foto f.

snare [sneər] n trampa f.

snarl [snɑːl] vi gruñir.

snatch [snætʃ] ◆ n (of conversation, song) fragmento m. ◆ vt (grab) agarrar; **to ~ sthg from sb** arrancarle OR arrebatarle algo a alguien.

sneak [sniːk] (Am pt snuck) ◆ n Br inf acusica m y f, chivato m, -ta f. ◆ vt colar, pasar a escondidas. ◆ vi: **to ~ in/out** entrar/salir a escondidas.

sneakers ['sniːkəz] npl Am zapatos mpl de lona.

sneaky ['sniːkɪ] adj inf solapado(da).

sneer [snɪər] vi (smile unpleasantly) sonreír con desprecio.

sneeze [sniːz] vi estornudar.

snide [snaɪd] adj sarcástico(ca).

sniff [snɪf] ◆ vt 1. (smell) oler. 2. (drug) esnifar. ◆ vi (to clear nose) sorber por la nariz.

snigger ['snɪgər] ◆ n risa f disimulada. ◆ vi reírse por lo bajo.

snip [snɪp] ◆ n inf (bargain) ganga f. ◆ vt cortar con tijeras.

sniper ['snaɪpər] n francotirador m, -ra f.

snippet ['snɪpɪt] n retazo m.

snivel ['snɪvl] vi lloriquear.

snob [snɒb] n esnob m y f.

snobbish ['snɒbɪʃ], **snobby** ['snɒbɪ] adj esnob.

snooker ['snuːkər] n snooker m, juego parecido al billar.

snoop [snuːp] vi inf fisgonear.

snooty ['snuːtɪ] adj engreído(da).

snooze [snuːz] ◆ n cabezada f. ◆ vi dormitar.

snore [snɔːr] ◆ n ronquido m. ◆ vi roncar.

snoring ['snɔːrɪŋ] n (U) ronquidos mpl.

snorkel ['snɔːkl] n tubo m respiratorio.

snort [snɔːt] ◆ n resoplido m. ◆ vi resoplar.

snout [snaʊt] n hocico m.

snow [snəʊ] ◆ n nieve f. ◆ v impers nevar.

snowball ['snəʊbɔːl] ◆ n bola f de nieve. ◆ vi fig aumentar rápidamente.

snowbound ['snəʊbaʊnd] adj bloqueado(da) por la nieve.

snowdrift ['snəʊdrɪft] n montón m de nieve.

snowdrop ['snəʊdrɒp] n campanilla f blanca.

snowfall ['snəʊfɔːl] n nevada f.

snowflake ['snəʊfleɪk] n copo m de nieve.

snowman ['snəʊmæn] (pl -men [-men]) n muñeco m de nieve.

snowplough Br, **snowplow** Am ['snəʊplaʊ] n quitanieves m inv.

snowshoe ['snəʊʃuː] n raqueta f de nieve.

snowstorm ['snəʊstɔːm] n tormenta f de nieve.

SNP n abbr of **Scottish National Party**.

Snr, snr (abbr of **senior**) sén.

snub [snʌb] ◆ n desaire m. ◆ vt desairar.

snuck [snʌk] Am pt → **sneak**.

snuff [snʌf] n (tobacco) rapé m.

snug [snʌg] adj 1. (person) cómodo y calentito (cómoda y calentita); (feeling) de bienestar. 2. (place) acogedor(ra). 3. (close-fitting) ajustado(da).

snuggle ['snʌgl] vi: to ~ up to sb arrimarse a alguien acurrucándose.

so [səʊ] ◆ adv 1. (to such a degree) tan; ~ difficult (that) tan difícil (que); don't be ~ stupid! ¡no seas bobo!; I've never seen ~ much money/many cars en mi vida he visto tanto dinero/tantos coches. 2. (in referring back to previous statement, event etc): ~ what's the point then? entonces ¿qué sentido tiene?; ~ you knew already? ¿así que ya lo sabías?; I don't think ~ no creo, me parece que no; I'm afraid ~ me temo que sí; if ~ de ser así; is that ~? ¿es así? 3. (also) también; ~ can I y yo (también puedo); ~ do I y yo (también); she speaks French and ~ does her husband ella habla francés y su marido también. 4. (in such a way): (like) ~ así, de esta forma. 5. (in expressing agreement): ~ there is! ¡pues (sí que) es verdad!; ¡sí que lo hay, sí!; ~ I see ya lo veo. 6. (unspecified amount, limit): they pay us ~ much a week nos pagan tanto a la semana; it's not ~ much the money as the time involved no es tanto el dinero como el tiempo que conlleva; or ~ o así. ◆ conj 1. (with the result that, therefore) así que, por lo tanto. 2. (to introduce a statement) (bueno) pues; ~ what have you been up to? bueno, ¿y qué has estado haciendo?; ~ that's who she is! ¡anda! ¡o sea que ella!; ~ what? inf ¿y qué?; ~ there inf ¡(y si no te gusta,) te chinchas! ▶ and so on, and so forth adv y cosas por el estilo. ▶ so as conj para; we didn't knock ~ as not to disturb them no llamamos para no molestarlos. ▶ so that conj para que; he lied ~ that she would go free mintió para que ella saliera en libertad.

soak [səʊk] ◆ vt 1. (leave immersed) poner en remojo. 2. (wet thoroughly) empapar. ◆ vi 1. (become thoroughly wet): to leave sthg to ~, to let sthg ~ dejar algo en remojo. 2. (spread): to ~ into OR through sthg calar algo. ▶ soak up vt sep (liquid) absorber.

soaking ['səʊkɪŋ] adj empapado(da).

so-and-so n inf 1. (to replace a name) fulano m, -na f de tal. 2. (annoying person) hijo m, -ja f de tal.

soap [səʊp] n 1. (U) (for washing) jabón m. 2. (TV) culebrón m.

soap flakes npl escamas fpl de jabón.

soap opera n culebrón m.

soap powder n jabón m en polvo.

soapy ['səʊpɪ] adj (full of soap) jabonoso (sa).

soar [sɔːr] vi 1. (bird) remontar el vuelo. 2. (rise into the sky) elevarse. 3. (increase rapidly) alcanzar cotas muy altas.

sob [sɒb] ◆ n sollozo m. ◆ vi sollozar.

sober ['səʊbər] adj 1. (gen) sobrio(bria). 2. (serious) serio(ria). ▶ sober up vi pasársele a uno la borrachera.

sobering ['səʊbərɪŋ] adj que hace reflexionar.

so-called [-kɔːld] adj 1. (misleadingly named) mal llamado(da), supuesto(ta). 2. (widely known as) así llamado(da).

soccer ['sɒkər] n (U) fútbol m.

sociable ['səʊʃəbl] adj sociable.

social ['səʊʃl] adj social.

social club n local m social de una empresa.

socialism ['səʊʃəlɪzm] n socialismo m.

socialist ['səʊʃəlɪst] ◆ adj socialista. ◆ n socialista m y f.

socialize, -ise ['səʊʃəlaɪz] vi: to ~ (with) alternar (con).

social security n seguridad f social.

social services npl servicios mpl sociales.

social worker n asistente m, -ta f social.

society [sə'saɪətɪ] n 1. (gen) sociedad f. 2. (club, organization) sociedad f, asociación f.

sociology [,səʊsɪ'ɒlədʒɪ] n sociología f.

sock [sɒk] n calcetín m.

socket ['sɒkɪt] n 1. (ELEC) enchufe m. 2. (of eye) cuenca f; (of joint) glena f.

sod [sɒd] n 1. (of turf) tepe m. 2. v inf (person) cabroncete m.

soda ['səʊdə] n 1. (gen) soda f. 2. Am (fizzy drink) gaseosa f.

soda water n soda f.

sodden ['sɒdn] adj empapado(da).

sodium ['səʊdɪəm] n sodio m.

sofa ['səʊfə] n sofá m.

Sofia ['səʊfjə] n Sofía.

soft [sɒft] adj 1. (pliable, not stiff, not strict) blando(da). 2. (smooth, gentle, not bright) suave.

soft drink n refresco m.

soften ['sɒfn] ◆ vt suavizar. ◆ vi 1. (substance) ablandarse. 2. (expression) suavizarse.

softhearted [,sɒft'hɑːtɪd] adj de buen corazón.

softly ['sɒftlɪ] adv 1. (gently) con delicadeza. 2. (quietly, not brightly) suavemente. 3. (leniently) con indulgencia.

soft-spoken adj de voz suave.

software ['sɒftweər] n (COMPUT) software m.

soggy ['sɒgɪ] adj inf empapado(da).

soil [sɔɪl] ◆ n (earth) tierra f, suelo m. ◆ vt ensuciar.

soiled [sɔɪld] adj sucio(cia).

solace ['sɒləs] n literary consuelo m.

solar ['səʊlər] adj solar.

sold [səʊld] pt & pp → sell.

solder ['səʊldər] ◆ n (U) soldadura f. ◆ vt soldar.

soldier ['səʊldʒər] n soldado m.

sold-out adj agotado(da); **the theatre was ~** se agotaron las localidades.

sole [səʊl] (pl sense 2 only inv OR -s) ◆ adj 1. (only) único(ca). 2. (exclusive) exclusivo(va). ◆ n 1. (of foot) planta f; (of shoe) suela f. 2. (fish) lenguado m.

solely ['səʊllɪ] adv únicamente, única y exclusivamente.

solemn ['sɒləm] adj solemne.

solicit [sə'lɪsɪt] ◆ vt fml (request) solicitar. ◆ vi (prostitute) ofrecer sus servicios.

solicitor [sə'lɪsɪtər] n Br (JUR) abogado que lleva casos administrativos y legales, pero que no acude a los tribunales superiores.

solid ['sɒlɪd] ◆ adj 1. (gen) sólido(da). 2. (rock, wood, gold) macizo(za). 3. (reliable, respectable) serio(ria), formal. 4. (without interruption) sin interrupción. ◆ n sólido m.

solidarity [,sɒlɪ'dærətɪ] n solidaridad f.

solitaire [,sɒlɪ'teər] n 1. (jewel, board game) solitario m. 2. Am (card game) solitario m.

solitary ['sɒlɪtrɪ] adj solitario(ria).

solitary confinement n: **to be in ~** estar incomunicado(da) (en la cárcel).

solitude ['sɒlɪtjuːd] n soledad f.

solo ['səʊləʊ] (pl -s) ◆ adj & adv a solas. ◆ n solo m.

soloist ['səʊləʊɪst] n solista m y f.

soluble ['sɒljʊbl] adj soluble.

solution [sə'luːʃn] n: **~ (to)** solución f (a).

solve [sɒlv] vt resolver.

solvent ['sɒlvənt] ◆ adj (FIN) solvente. ◆ n disolvente m.

Somalia [sə'mɑːlɪə] n Somalia.

sombre Br, **somber** Am ['sɒmbər] adj sombrío(a).

some [sʌm] ◆ adj 1. (a certain amount, number of): **would you like ~ coffee?** ¿quieres café?; **give me ~ money** dame algo de dinero; **there are ~ good articles in it** tiene algunos artículos buenos; **I bought ~ socks** (one pair) me compré unos calcetines; (more than one pair) me compré calcetines. 2. (fairly large number or quantity of): **I've known him for ~ years** lo conozco desde hace bastantes años; **I had ~ difficulty getting here** me costó lo mío llegar aquí. 3. (contrastive use) (certain) algunos(as), ciertos(as); **~ jobs are better paid than others** algunos trabajos están mejor pagados que otros; **~ people say that ...** los hay que dicen que ... 4. (in imprecise statements) algún(una); **there must be ~ mistake** debe haber un OR algún error; **she married ~ writer or other** se casó con no sé qué escritor. 5. inf (very good) menudo(da); **that's ~ car he's got** ¡menudo coche tiene! ◆ pron 1. (a certain amount): **can I have ~?** (money, milk, coffee etc) ¿puedo coger un poco?; **~ of** parte de. 2. (a certain number) algunos(as); **can I have ~?** (books, potatoes etc) ¿puedo coger algunos?; **~** (of them) **left early** algunos se fueron temprano; **~ say he lied** hay quien dice que mintió. ◆ adv unos(as); **there were ~ 7,000 people there** habría unas 7.000 personas.

somebody ['sʌmbədɪ] pron alguien.

someday ['sʌmdeɪ] adv algún día.

somehow ['sʌmhaʊ], **someway** Am ['sʌmweɪ] adv 1. (by some action) de alguna manera. 2. (for some reason) por alguna razón.

someone ['sʌmwʌn] pron alguien; **~ or other** alguien, no sé quién.

someplace Am = **somewhere**.

somersault ['sʌməsɔːlt] n (in air) salto m mortal; (on ground) voltereta f.

something ['sʌmθɪŋ] ◆ pron algo; **or ~** inf o algo así. ◆ adv: **~ like, ~ in the region of** algo así como.

sometime ['sʌmtaɪm] adv en algún momento; **~ next week** durante la semana que viene.

sometimes ['sʌmtaɪmz] *adv* a veces.

someway Am = **somehow**.

somewhat ['sʌmwɒt] *adv fml* algo.

somewhere Br ['sʌmweəʳ], **someplace** Am ['sʌmpleɪs] *adv* **1.** (*unknown place - with verbs of position*) en alguna parte; (- *with verbs of movement*) a alguna parte; **it's ~ else** está en otra parte; **shall we go ~ else?** ¿nos vamos a otra parte? **2.** (*in approximations*): **~ between five and ten** entre cinco y diez; **~ around 20** alrededor de 20.

son [sʌn] *n* hijo *m*.

song [sɒŋ] *n* **1.** (*gen*) canción *f*. **2.** (*of bird*) canto *m*.

sonic ['sɒnɪk] *adj* sónico(ca).

son-in-law (*pl* **sons-in-law** OR **son-in-laws**) *n* yerno *m*.

sonnet ['sɒnɪt] *n* soneto *m*.

sonny ['sʌnɪ] *n inf* hijo *m*, chico *m*.

soon [su:n] *adv* pronto; **how ~ will it be ready?** ¿para cuándo estará listo?; **~ after** poco después; **as ~ as** tan pronto como; **as ~ as possible** cuanto antes.

sooner ['su:nəʳ] *adv* **1.** (*in time*) antes; **no ~ did he arrive than ...** apenas había llegado cuando ...; **~ or later** (más) tarde o (más) temprano; **the ~ the better** cuanto antes mejor. **2.** (*expressing preference*): **I'd ~ ...** preferiría ...

soot [sʊt] *n* hollín *m*.

soothe [su:ð] *vt* **1.** (*pain*) aliviar. **2.** (*nerves etc*) calmar.

sophisticated [sə'fɪstɪkeɪtɪd] *adj* (*gen*) sofisticado(da).

sophomore ['sɒfəmɔːʳ] *n* Am estudiante *m y f* del segundo curso.

soporific [,sɒpə'rɪfɪk] *adj* soporífico(ca).

sopping ['sɒpɪŋ] *adj*: **~ (wet)** chorreando.

soppy ['sɒpɪ] *adj inf pej* sentimentaloide.

soprano [sə'prɑːnəʊ] (*pl* **-s**) *n* soprano *f*.

sorbet ['sɔːbeɪ] *n* sorbete *m*.

sorcerer ['sɔːsərəʳ] *n* brujo *m*, -ja *f*.

sordid ['sɔːdɪd] *adj* **1.** (*immoral*) obsceno(na). **2.** (*dirty, unpleasant*) sórdido (da).

sore [sɔːʳ] ◆ *adj* **1.** (*painful*) dolorido (da); **to have a ~ throat** tener dolor de garganta. **2.** Am (*upset*) enfadado(da). ◆ *n* llaga *f*, úlcera *f*.

sorely ['sɔːlɪ] *adv literary* enormemente.

sorrow ['sɒrəʊ] *n* pesar *m*, pena *f*.

sorry ['sɒrɪ] ◆ *adj* **1.** (*expressing apology*): **to be ~ about sthg** sentir OR lamentar algo; **I'm ~ for what I did** siento lo que hice; **I'm ~** lo siento. **2.** (*expressing shame, disappointment*): **to be ~ that** sentir que; **we were ~ about his resignation** sentimos que dimitiera; **to be ~ for** arrepentirse de. **3.** (*expressing regret*): **I'm ~ to have to say that ...** siento tener que decir que ... **4.** (*expressing pity*): **to be** OR **feel ~ for sb** sentir lástima por alguien. **5.** (*expressing polite disagreement*): **I'm ~, but ...** perdón, pero ... **6.** (*poor, pitiable*) lamentable, penoso(sa). ◆ *excl* **1.** (*pardon*): **~?** ¿perdón? **2.** (*to correct oneself*): **a girl, ~, a woman** una chica, perdón, una mujer.

sort [sɔːt] ◆ *n* tipo *m*, clase *f*; **all ~s of** todo tipo de; **~ of** más o menos, así así; **a ~ of** una especie de. ◆ *vt* clasificar. ▶ **sort out** *vt sep* **1.** (*classify*) clasificar. **2.** (*solve*) solucionar, resolver.

sorting office ['sɔːtɪŋ-] *n* oficina de clasificación del correo.

SOS (*abbr of* **save our souls**) *n* SOS *m*.

so-so *adj & adv inf* así así.

soufflé ['suːfleɪ] *n* suflé *m*.

sought [sɔːt] *pt & pp* → **seek**.

soul [səʊl] *n* **1.** (*gen*) alma *f*. **2.** (*music*) música *f* soul.

soul-destroying [-dɪ,strɔɪɪŋ] *adj* desmoralizador(ra).

soulful ['səʊlfʊl] *adj* lleno(na) de sentimiento.

sound [saʊnd] ◆ *adj* **1.** (*healthy*) sano (na). **2.** (*sturdy*) sólido(da). **3.** (*reliable*) fiable, seguro(ra). ◆ *adv*: **to be ~ asleep** estar profundamente dormido(da). ◆ *n* **1.** (*gen*) sonido *m*. **2.** (*particular noise*) ruido *m*. **3.** (*impression*): **by the ~ of it** por lo que parece. ◆ *vt* (*bell etc*) hacer sonar, tocar. ◆ *vi* **1.** (*gen*) sonar. **2.** (*give impression*): **it ~s like fun** suena divertido. ▶ **sound out** *vt sep*: **to ~ sb out (on** OR **about)** sondear a alguien (sobre).

sound barrier *n* barrera *f* del sonido.

sound effects *npl* efectos *mpl* sonoros.

sounding ['saʊndɪŋ] *n* (NAUT) sondeo *m* marino.

soundly ['saʊndlɪ] *adv* **1.** (*severely - beat*) totalmente. **2.** (*deeply*) profundamente.

soundproof ['saʊndpruːf] *adj* insonorizado(da).

sound system *n* equipo *m* de sonido.

soundtrack ['saʊndtræk] *n* banda *f* sonora.

soup [su:p] *n* (*thick*) sopa *f*; (*clear*) caldo *m*.

soup plate *n* plato *m* hondo OR sopero.

soup spoon *n* cuchara *f* sopera.

sour [saʊəʳ] ♦ *adj* **1.** (*acidic*) ácido(da). **2.** (*milk, person, reply*) agrio(gria). ♦ *vt* agriar.

source [sɔːs] *n* **1.** (*gen*) fuente *f*. **2.** (*cause*) origen *m*.

sour grapes *n* (U) *inf*: it's ~! ¡están verdes!

south [saʊθ] ♦ *n* **1.** (*direction*) sur *m*. **2.** (*region*): **the South** el sur. ♦ *adj* del sur. ♦ *adv*: ~ (**of**) al sur (de).

South Africa *n*: (**the Republic of**) ~ (la república de) Suráfrica.

South African ♦ *adj* surafricano(na). ♦ *n* (*person*) surafricano *m*, -na *f*.

South America *n* Sudamérica.

South American ♦ *adj* sudamericano(na). ♦ *n* (*person*) sudamericano *m*, -na *f*.

southeast [ˌsaʊθ'iːst] ♦ *n* **1.** (*direction*) sudeste *m*. **2.** (*region*): **the Southeast** el sudeste. ♦ *adj* del sudeste. ♦ *adv*: ~ (**of**) hacia el sudeste (de).

southerly [ˈsʌðəlɪ] *adj* del sur.

southern [ˈsʌðən] *adj* del sur, sureño (ña).

South Korea *n* Corea del Sur.

South Pole *n*: **the** ~ el polo Sur.

southward [ˈsaʊθwəd] ♦ *adj* sur. ♦ *adv* = **southwards**.

southwards [ˈsaʊθwədz] *adv* hacia el sur.

southwest [ˌsaʊθ'west] ♦ *n* **1.** (*direction*) suroeste *m*. **2.** (*region*): **the Southwest** el suroeste. ♦ *adj* del suroeste. ♦ *adv*: ~ (**of**) hacia el suroeste (de).

souvenir [ˌsuːvəˈnɪəʳ] *n* recuerdo *m*.

sovereign [ˈsɒvrɪn] ♦ *adj* soberano (na). ♦ *n* **1.** (*ruler*) soberano *m*, -na *f*. **2.** (*coin*) soberano *m*.

soviet [ˈsəʊvɪət] *n* soviet *m*. ▶ **Soviet** ♦ *adj* soviético(ca). ♦ *n* (*person*) soviético *m*, -ca *f*.

Soviet Union *n*: **the (former)** ~ la (antigua) Unión Soviética.

sow[1] [səʊ] (*pt* **-ed**, *pp* **sown** OR **-ed**) *vt lit & fig* sembrar.

sow[2] [saʊ] *n* cerda *f*, puerca *f*.

sown [səʊn] *pp* → **sow**[1].

soya [ˈsɔɪə] *n* soja *f*.

soy(a) bean [ˈsɔɪ(ə)-] *n* semilla *f* de soja.

spa [spɑː] *n* balneario *m*.

space [speɪs] ♦ *n* espacio *m*. ♦ *comp* espacial. ♦ *vt* espaciar. ▶ **space out** *vt sep* (*arrange with spaces between*) espaciar.

spacecraft [ˈspeɪskrɑːft] (*pl inv*) *n* nave *f* espacial.

spaceman [ˈspeɪsmæn] (*pl* **-men** [-men]) *n inf* astronauta *m*.

spaceship [ˈspeɪsʃɪp] *n* nave *f* espacial.

space shuttle *n* transbordador *m* espacial.

spacesuit [ˈspeɪssuːt] *n* traje *m* espacial.

spacing [ˈspeɪsɪŋ] *n* (TYPO) espacio *m*.

spacious [ˈspeɪʃəs] *adj* espacioso(sa).

spade [speɪd] *n* (*tool*) pala *f*. ▶ **spades** *npl* picas *fpl*.

spaghetti [spəˈgetɪ] *n* (U) espaguetis *mpl*.

Spain [speɪn] *n* España *f*.

span [spæn] ♦ *pt* → **spin**. ♦ *n* **1.** (*in time*) lapso *m*, periodo *m*. **2.** (*range*) gama *f*. **3.** (*of wings*) envergadura *f*. **4.** (*of bridge, arch*) ojo *m*. ♦ *vt* **1.** (*in time*) abarcar. **2.** (*subj: bridge etc*) cruzar, atravesar.

Spaniard [ˈspænjəd] *n* español *m*, -la *f*.

spaniel [ˈspænjəl] *n* perro *m* de aguas.

Spanish [ˈspænɪʃ] ♦ *adj* español(la). ♦ *n* (*language*) español *m*, castellano *m*. ♦ *npl* (*people*): **the** ~ los españoles.

spank [spæŋk] *vt* zurrar.

spanner [ˈspænəʳ] *n* llave *f* inglesa.

spar [spɑːʳ] ♦ *n* palo *m*, verga *f*. ♦ *vi* (BOXING): **to** ~ (**with**) entrenarse (con).

spare [speəʳ] ♦ *adj* **1.** (*surplus*) de sobra. **2.** (*free - chair, time*) libre. ♦ *n* **1.** (*spare object*) (pieza *f* de) recambio *m*, repuesto *m*. **2.** *inf* (*part*) pieza *f* de recambio OR repuesto. ♦ *vt* **1.** (*time*) conceder; (*money*) dejar; **we can't** ~ **any time/money** no tenemos tiempo/dinero; **to** ~ de sobra. **2.** (*not harm - person, life*) perdonar; (*- company, city*) salvar. **3.** (*not use, not take*): **to** ~ **no expense/effort** no escatimar gastos/esfuerzos. **4.** (*save from*): **to** ~ **sb sthg** ahorrarle a alguien algo.

spare part *n* (AUT) pieza *f* de recambio OR repuesto.

spare time *n* tiempo *m* libre.

spare wheel *n* rueda *f* de recambio.

sparing [ˈspeərɪŋ] *adj*: ~ **with** OR **of** parco(ca) en.

sparingly [ˈspeərɪŋlɪ] *adv* con moderación.

spark [spɑːk] *n lit & fig* chispa *f*.

sparking plug [ˈspɑːkɪŋ-] Br = **spark plug**.

sparkle ['spɑːkl] ◆ n (U) (of diamond) destello m; (of eyes) brillo m. ◆ vi (star, jewels) centellear; (eyes) brillar.

sparkling wine ['spɑːklɪŋ-] n vino m espumoso.

spark plug n bujía f.

sparrow ['spærəʊ] n gorrión m.

sparse [spɑːs] adj escaso(sa).

spasm ['spæzm] n 1. (MED) (state) espasmo m. 2. (MED) (attack) acceso m.

spastic ['spæstɪk] n (MED) espástico m, -ca f.

spat [spæt] pt & pp → spit.

spate [speɪt] n cadena f, serie f.

spatter ['spætər] vt salpicar.

spawn [spɔːn] ◆ n (U) huevas fpl. ◆ vt fig engendrar. ◆ vi desovar, frezar.

speak [spiːk] (pt spoke, pp spoken) ◆ vt 1. (say) decir. 2. (language) hablar. ◆ vi hablar; **to ~ to** OR **with** hablar con; **to ~ to sb** (about) hablar con alguien (de); **to ~ about** hablar de; **to ~ to sb** (on sthg) (give speech) hablar ante alguien (sobre algo). ▶ **so to speak** adv por así decirlo. ▶ **speak for** vt fus (represent) hablar en nombre de. ▶ **speak up** vi 1. (speak out): **to ~ up for** salir en defensa de. 2. (speak louder) hablar más alto.

speaker ['spiːkər] n 1. (person talking) persona f que habla. 2. (person making a speech - at meal etc) orador m, -ra f; (- at conference) conferenciante m y f. 3. (of a language) hablante m y f. 4. (of radio) altavoz m.

speaking ['spiːkɪŋ] adv: **generally ~** en general; **legally ~** desde una perspectiva legal.

spear [spɪər] ◆ n (gen) lanza f; (for hunting) jabalina f. ◆ vt (animal) atravesar; (piece of food) pinchar.

spearhead ['spɪəhed] vt encabezar.

spec [spek] n Br inf: **to buy on ~** comprar sin garantías.

special ['speʃl] adj 1. (gen) especial. 2. (particular, individual) particular.

special delivery n correo m urgente.

specialist ['speʃəlɪst] ◆ adj (doctor) especialista; (literature) especializado (da). ◆ n especialista m y f.

speciality [ˌspeʃɪ'ælətɪ], **specialty** Am ['speʃltɪ] n especialidad f.

specialize, -ise ['speʃəlaɪz] vi: **to ~ (in)** especializarse (en).

specially ['speʃəlɪ] adv especialmente.

specialty Am = **speciality**.

species ['spiːʃiːz] (pl inv) n especie f.

specific [spə'sɪfɪk] adj 1. (particular)

determinado(da). 2. (precise) específico(ca). 3. (unique): **~ to** específico(ca) de.

specifically [spə'sɪfɪklɪ] adv 1. (particularly) expresamente. 2. (precisely) específicamente.

specify ['spesɪfaɪ] vt: **to ~ (that)** especificar (que).

specimen ['spesɪmən] n 1. (example) espécimen m, ejemplar m. 2. (sample) muestra f.

speck [spek] n 1. (small stain) manchita f. 2. (small particle) mota f.

speckled ['spekld] adj: **~ (with)** moteado(da) (de).

specs [speks] npl Br inf (glasses) gafas fpl.

spectacle ['spektəkl] n (gen) espectáculo m. ▶ **spectacles** npl Br gafas fpl.

spectacular [spek'tækjʊlər] adj espectacular.

spectator [spek'teɪtər] n espectador m, -ra f.

spectre Br, **specter** Am ['spektər] n lit & fig fantasma m.

spectrum ['spektrəm] (pl -tra [-trə]) n 1. (gen) espectro m. 2. fig (variety) gama f.

speculation [ˌspekjʊ'leɪʃn] n especulación f.

sped [sped] pt & pp → speed.

speech [spiːtʃ] n 1. (gen) habla f. 2. (formal talk) discurso m. 3. (THEATRE) parlamento m. 4. (manner of speaking) manera f de hablar. 5. (dialect) dialecto m, habla f.

speechless ['spiːtʃlɪs] adj: **to be ~ (with)** enmudecer (de).

speed [spiːd] (pt & pp -ed OR sped) ◆ n 1. (rate of movement) velocidad f; **at top ~** a toda velocidad. 2. (rapidity) rapidez f. ◆ vi 1. (move fast): **to ~ (along/away/by)** ir/alejarse/pasar a toda velocidad. 2. (AUT) (go too fast) conducir con exceso de velocidad. ▶ **speed up** ◆ vt sep (gen) acelerar; (person) meter prisa a. ◆ vi (gen) acelerarse; (person) darse prisa.

speedboat ['spiːdbəʊt] n lancha f motora.

speeding ['spiːdɪŋ] n (U) exceso m de velocidad.

speed limit n límite m de velocidad.

speedometer [spɪ'dɒmɪtər] n velocímetro m.

speedway ['spiːdweɪ] n 1. (U) (SPORT) carreras fpl de moto. 2. Am (road) autopista f.

speedy ['spiːdɪ] adj rápido(da).

spell [spel] (Br *pt & pp* **spelt** OR **-ed**, Am *pt & pp* **-ed**) ◆ *n* 1. (*of time*) temporada *f*; (*of weather*) racha *f*. 2. (*enchantment*) hechizo *m*; **to cast** OR **put a ~ on sb** hechizar a alguien. 3. (*magic words*) conjuro *m*. ◆ *vt* 1. (*form by writing*) deletrear. 2. *fig* (*signify*) significar. ◆ *vi* escribir correctamente. ▶ **spell out** *vt sep* 1. (*read aloud*) deletrear. 2. (*explain*): **to ~ sthg out (for** OR **to sb)** decir algo por las claras (a alguien).

spellbound ['spelbaund] *adj* hechizado(da), embelesado(da).

spelling ['spelɪŋ] *n* ortografía *f*; **~ mistake** falta *f* de ortografía.

spelt [spelt] Br *pt & pp* → **spell**.

spend [spend] (*pt & pp* **spent**) *vt* 1. (*gen*) gastar; **to ~ sthg on** gastar algo en. 2. (*time, life*) pasar.

spendthrift ['spendθrɪft] *n* derrochador *m*, -ra *f*.

spent [spent] ◆ *pt & pp* → **spend**. ◆ *adj* (*matches, ammunition*) usado(da); (*patience*) agotado(da).

sperm [spɜːm] (*pl inv* OR **-s**) *n* esperma *m*.

spew [spjuː] *vt* arrojar, escupir.

sphere [sfɪəʳ] *n* 1. (*gen*) esfera *f*. 2. (*of people*) círculo *m*.

spice [spaɪs] *n* (CULIN) especia *f*.

spick-and-span [,spɪkən'spæn] *adj* inmaculado(da).

spicy ['spaɪsɪ] *adj* (CULIN & *fig*) picante.

spider ['spaɪdəʳ] *n* araña *f*.

spike [spaɪk] *n* 1. (*on railing etc*) punta *f*; (*on wall*) clavo *m*. 2. (*on plant*) pincho *m*; (*of hair*) pelo *m* de punta.

spill [spɪl] (Br *pt & pp* **spilt** OR **-ed**, Am *pt & pp* **-ed**) ◆ *vt* derramar, verter. ◆ *vi* (*flow*) derramarse, verterse.

spilt [spɪlt] Br *pt & pp* → **spill**.

spin [spɪn] (*pt* **span** OR **spun**, *pp* **spun**) ◆ *n* 1. (*turn*) vuelta *f*. 2. (AERON) barrena *f*. 3. *inf* (*in car*) vuelta *f* ◆ *vt* 1. (*cause to rotate*) girar, dar vueltas a. 2. (*clothes, washing*) centrifugar. 3. (*wool, yarn*) hilar. ◆ *vi* (*rotate*) girar, dar vueltas. ▶ **spin out** *vt sep* (*story*) alargar, prolongar; (*money*) estirar.

spinach ['spɪnɪdʒ] *n* (U) espinacas *fpl*.

spinal column ['spaɪnl-] *n* columna *f* vertebral.

spinal cord ['spaɪnl-] *n* médula *f* espinal.

spindly ['spɪndlɪ] *adj* larguirucho(cha).

spin-dryer *n* Br centrifugadora *f*.

spine [spaɪn] *n* 1. (ANAT) espina *f* dorsal. 2. (*of book*) lomo *m*. 3. (*spike, prickle*) espina *f*, púa *f*.

spinning ['spɪnɪŋ] *n* hilado *m*.

spinning top *n* pconza *f*.

spin-off *n* (*by-product*) resultado *m* OR efecto *m* indirecto.

spinster ['spɪnstəʳ] *n* soltera *f*.

spiral ['spaɪərəl] ◆ *adj* en espiral. ◆ *n* (*curve*) espiral *f*. ◆ *vi* (*move in spiral curve*) moverse en espiral.

spiral staircase *n* escalera *f* de caracol.

spire [spaɪəʳ] *n* aguja *f*.

spirit ['spɪrɪt] *n* 1. (*gen*) espíritu *m*. 2. (*vigour*) vigor *m*, valor *m*. ▶ **spirits** *npl* 1. (*mood*) humor *m*; **to be in high/low ~s** estar exultante/alicaído. 2. (*alcohol*) licores *mpl*.

spirited ['spɪrɪtɪd] *adj* enérgico(ca).

spirit level *n* nivel *m* de burbuja de aire.

spiritual ['spɪrɪtʃʊəl] *adj* espiritual.

spit [spɪt] (Br *pt & pp* **spat**, Am *pt & pp* **spit**) ◆ *n* 1. (*saliva*) saliva *f*. 2. (*skewer*) asador *m*. ◆ *vi* escupir. ◆ *v impers* Br (*rain lightly*): **it's spitting** está chispeando.

spite [spaɪt] ◆ *n* rencor *m*. ◆ *vt* fastidiar, molestar. ▶ **in spite of** *prep* a pesar de.

spiteful ['spaɪtful] *adj* (*person, behaviour*) rencoroso(sa); (*action, remark*) malintencionado(da).

spittle ['spɪtl] *n* saliva *f*.

splash [splæʃ] ◆ *n* 1. (*sound*) chapoteo *m*. 2. (*of colour, light*) mancha *f*. ◆ *vt* salpicar. ◆ *vi* 1. (*person*): **to ~ about** OR **around** chapotear. 2. (*water, liquid*): **to ~ on** OR **against sthg** salpicar algo. ▶ **splash out** *vi inf*: **to ~ out (on sthg)** gastar un dineral (en algo).

spleen [spliːn] *n* (ANAT) bazo *m*; *fig* (*anger*) cólera *f*.

splendid ['splendɪd] *adj* 1. (*marvellous*) espléndido(da). 2. (*magnificent, beautiful*) magnífico(ca).

splint [splɪnt] *n* tablilla *f*.

splinter ['splɪntəʳ] ◆ *n* (*of wood*) astilla *f*; (*of glass, metal*) fragmento *m*. ◆ *vi* astillarse.

split [splɪt] (*pt & pp* **split**) ◆ *n* 1. (*crack - in wood*) grieta *f*; (*- in garment*) desgarrón *m*. 2. (*division*): **~ (in)** escisión *f* (en). 3. (*difference*): **~ (between)** diferencia *f* (entre). ◆ *vt* 1. (*tear*) desgarrar, rasgar; (*crack*) agrietar. 2. (*break in two*) partir. 3. (*party, organization*) escindir. 4. (*share*) repartir. ◆ *vi* 1. (*break up - road*) bifurcarse; (*- object*) partirse. 2. (*party,* *organization*) escindirse. **3.** (*wood*) agrietarse; (*fabric*) desgarrarse. ▶ **split up** ◆ *vi* separarse. ◆ *vt sep:* **to ~ sthg up (into)** dividir algo (en).

split second *n* fracción *f* de segundo.

splutter ['splʌtə^r] *vi* **1.** (*person*) balbucear. **2.** (*fire, oil*) chisporrotear.

spoil [spɔɪl] (*pt* & *pp* **-ed** OR **spoilt**) *vt* **1.** (*ruin*) estropear, echar a perder. **2.** (*child etc*) mimar. ▶ **spoils** *npl* botín *m.*

spoiled [spɔɪld] = **spoilt**.

spoilsport ['spɔɪlspɔːt] *n* aguafiestas *m y f inv.*

spoilt [spɔɪlt] ◆ *pt* & *pp* → **spoil**. ◆ *adj* mimado(da), consentido(da).

spoke [spəʊk] ◆ *pt* → **speak**. ◆ *n* radio *m.*

spoken ['spəʊkn] *pp* → **speak**.

spokesman ['spəʊksmən] (*pl* **-men** [-mən]) *n* portavoz *m.*

spokeswoman ['spəʊks,wʊmən] (*pl* **-women** [-,wɪmɪn]) *n* portavoz *f.*

sponge [spʌndʒ] ◆ *n* **1.** (*for cleaning, washing*) esponja *f.* **2.** (*cake*) bizcocho *m.* ◆ *vt* limpiar con una esponja. ◆ *vi inf:* **to ~ off** vivir a costa de.

sponge bag *n* Br neceser *m.*

sponge cake *n* bizcocho *m.*

sponsor ['spɒnsə^r] ◆ *n* patrocinador *m,* -ra *f.* ◆ *vt* **1.** (*gen*) patrocinar. **2.** (*support*) respaldar.

sponsored walk [,spɒnsəd-] *n* marcha *f* benéfica.

sponsorship ['spɒnsəʃɪp] *n* patrocinio *m.*

spontaneous [spɒn'teɪnjəs] *adj* espontáneo(a).

spooky ['spuːkɪ] *adj inf* escalofriante.

spool [spuːl] *n* (*gen* & COMPUT) bobina *f.*

spoon [spuːn] *n* **1.** (*piece of cutlery*) cuchara *f.* **2.** (*spoonful*) cucharada *f.*

spoon-feed *vt* (*feed with spoon*) dar de comer con cuchara a.

spoonful ['spuːnfʊl] (*pl* **-s** OR **spoonsful** ['spuːnzfʊl]) *n* cucharada *f.*

sporadic [spə'rædɪk] *adj* esporádico(ca).

sport [spɔːt] *n* **1.** (*game*) deporte *m.* **2.** *dated* (*cheerful person*) persona *f* amable.

sporting ['spɔːtɪŋ] *adj lit* & *fig* deportivo(va); **to give sb a ~ chance** dar a alguien la oportunidad de ganar.

sports car ['spɔːts-] *n* coche *m* deportivo.

sports jacket ['spɔːts-] *n* chaqueta *f* de esport.

sportsman ['spɔːtsmən] (*pl* **-men** [-mən]) *n* deportista *m.*

sportsmanship ['spɔːtsmənʃɪp] *n* deportividad *f.*

sportswear ['spɔːtsweə^r] *n* ropa *f* deportiva.

sportswoman ['spɔːts,wʊmən] (*pl* **-women** [-,wɪmɪn]) *n* deportista *f.*

sporty ['spɔːtɪ] *adj inf* (*fond of sports*) aficionado(da) a los deportes.

spot [spɒt] ◆ *n* **1.** (*stain*) mancha *f,* mota *f;* (*dot*) punto *m.* **2.** (*pimple*) grano *m.* **3.** (*drop*) gota *f.* **4.** *inf* (*bit, small amount*) pizca *f.* **5.** (*place*) lugar *m;* **on the ~** en el lugar; **to do sthg on the ~** hacer algo en el acto. **6.** (RADIO & TV) espacio *m.* ◆ *vt* (*notice*) notar, ver.

spot check *n* control *m* aleatorio.

spotless ['spɒtlɪs] *adj* (*thing*) inmaculado(da); (*reputation*) intachable.

spotlight ['spɒtlaɪt] *n* (*of car*) faro *m* auxiliar; (*in theatre, home*) foco *m,* reflector *m* de luz; **to be in the ~** *fig* ser el centro de atención.

spotted ['spɒtɪd] *adj* a OR de lunares.

spotty ['spɒtɪ] *adj* Br (*skin*) con granos.

spouse [spaʊs] *n* cónyuge *m y f.*

spout [spaʊt] ◆ *n* (*of kettle, teapot*) pitorro *m;* (*of jug*) pico *m;* (*of pipe*) caño *m.* ◆ *vi:* **to ~ from** OR **out of** (*liquid*) salir a chorros de; (*smoke, flames*) salir incesantemente de.

sprain [spreɪn] ◆ *n* torcedura *f.* ◆ *vt* torcerse.

sprang [spræŋ] *pt* → **spring**.

sprawl [sprɔːl] *vi* (*sit*) repantigarse, arrellanarse; (*lie*) echarse, tumbarse.

spray [spreɪ] ◆ *n* **1.** (*small drops - of liquid*) rociada *f;* (*- of sea*) espuma *f;* (*- of aerosol*) pulverización *f.* **2.** (*pressurized liquid*) líquido *m* pulverizado, espray *m.* **3.** (*can, container - gen*) atomizador *m;* (*- for garden*) pulverizador *m.* **4.** (*of flowers*) ramo *m.* ◆ *vt* rociar, vaporizar.

spread [spred] (*pt* & *pp* **spread**) ◆ *n* **1.** (*soft food*): **cheese ~** queso *m* para untar. **2.** (*of fire, disease*) propagación *f.* ◆ *vt* **1.** (*rug, tablecloth*) extender; (*map*) desplegar. **2.** (*legs, fingers etc*) estirar. **3.** (*butter, jam*) untar; (*glue*) repartir; **to ~ sthg over sthg** extender algo por algo. **4.** (*disease*) propagar; (*news*) difundir, diseminar. **5.** (*wealth, work*) repartir equitativamente. ◆ *vi* **1.** (*disease, fire, news*) extenderse, propagarse. **2.** (*gas, cloud*) esparcirse. ▶ **spread out** *vi* diseminarse, dispersarse.

spread-eagled [-,iːgld] *adj* despatarrado(da).

spreadsheet ['spredʃiːt] n (COMPUT) hoja f de cálculo electrónica.

spree [spriː] n jarana f.

sprightly ['spraɪtlɪ] adj animado(da).

spring [sprɪŋ] (pt **sprang**, pp **sprung**) ♦ n 1. (season) primavera f. 2. (coil) muelle m. 3. (jump) salto m. 4. (water source) manantial m, vertiente f Amer. ♦ vi 1. (jump) saltar. 2. (move suddenly) moverse de repente. ▶ **spring up** vi surgir de repente.

springboard ['sprɪŋbɔːd] n lit & fig trampolín m.

spring-clean vt limpiar a fondo.

spring onion n Br cebolleta f.

springtime ['sprɪŋtaɪm] n: **in (the)** ~ en primavera.

springy ['sprɪŋɪ] adj (carpet, mattress, grass) mullido(da); (rubber) elástico(ca).

sprinkle ['sprɪŋkl] vt rociar, salpicar; **to ~ sthg over OR on sthg, to ~ sthg with sthg** rociar algo sobre algo.

sprinkler ['sprɪŋklər] n aspersor m.

sprint [sprɪnt] ♦ n 1. (SPORT) esprint m. 2. (fast run) carrera f. ♦ vi (SPORT) esprintar; (run fast) correr a toda velocidad.

sprout [spraut] ♦ n 1. **(Brussels)** ~s coles fpl de Bruselas. 2. (shoot) brote m, retoño m. ♦ vt (subj: plant) echar. ♦ vi 1. (plants, vegetables) crecer. 2. (leaves, shoots) brotar.

spruce [spruːs] ♦ adj pulcro(cra). ♦ n picea f. ▶ **spruce up** vt sep arreglar.

sprung [sprʌŋ] pp → **spring**.

spry [spraɪ] adj ágil, activo(va).

spun [spʌn] pt & pp → **spin**.

spur [spɜːr] ♦ n 1. (incentive): ~ **(to sthg)** estímulo m (para conseguir algo). 2. (on rider's boot) espuela f. ♦ vt (encourage): **to ~ sb to do sthg** animar a alguien a hacer algo. ▶ **on the spur of the moment** adv sin pensarlo dos veces. ▶ **spur on** vt sep: **to ~ sb on** animar a alguien.

spurious ['spuərɪəs] adj falso(sa).

spurn [spɜːn] vt rechazar.

spurt [spɜːt] ♦ n 1. (of water) chorro m; (of flame) llamarada f. 2. (of activity, effort) arranque m. 3. (of speed) acelerón m. ♦ vi (gush): **to ~ (out of OR from)** (liquid) salir a chorros de; (flame) salir incesantemente de.

spy [spaɪ] ♦ n espía m y f. ♦ vt inf divisar. ♦ vi: **to ~ (on)** espiar (a), aguaitar (a) Amer.

spying ['spaɪɪŋ] n espionaje m.

Sq., sq. abbr of **square**.

squabble ['skwɒbl] ♦ n riña f. ♦ vi: **to ~ (about OR over)** reñir (por).

squad [skwɒd] n 1. (of police) brigada f. 2. (MIL) pelotón m. 3. (SPORT - of club) plantilla f, equipo m completo; (- of national team) seleccionado m.

squadron ['skwɒdrən] n (of planes) escuadrilla f; (of warships) escuadra f; (of soldiers) escuadrón m.

squalid ['skwɒlɪd] adj (filthy) miserable, sórdido(da).

squall [skwɔːl] n (storm) turbión m.

squalor ['skwɒlər] n (U) miseria f.

squander ['skwɒndər] vt (opportunity) desaprovechar; (money) despilfarrar; (resources) malgastar.

square [skweər] ♦ adj 1. (gen) cuadrado(da). 2. (not owing money): **we're ~ now** ya estamos en paz. ♦ n 1. (shape) cuadrado m. 2. (in town, city) plaza f. 3. inf (unfashionable person) carroza m y f. ♦ vt 1. (MATH) elevar al cuadrado. 2. (balance, reconcile): **how can you ~ that with your principles?** ¿cómo encajas esto con tus principios? ▶ **square up** vi (settle up): **to ~ up with** saldar cuentas con.

squarely ['skweəlɪ] adv (directly) justo, exactamente.

square meal n comida f satisfactoria.

squash [skwɒʃ] ♦ n 1. (game) squash m. 2. Br (drink) zumo m. 3. Am (vegetable) cucurbitácea f. ♦ vt (squeeze, flatten) aplastar.

squat [skwɒt] ♦ adj achaparrado(da). ♦ vi (crouch): **to ~ (down)** agacharse, ponerse en cuclillas.

squatter ['skwɒtər] n Br ocupante m y f ilegal, squatter m y f.

squawk [skwɔːk] n (of bird) graznido m.

squeak [skwiːk] n 1. (of animal) chillido m. 2. (of hinge) chirrido m.

squeal [skwiːl] vi 1. (person, animal) chillar, gritar. 2. (brakes) chirriar.

squeamish ['skwiːmɪʃ] adj aprensivo(va).

squeeze [skwiːz] ♦ n (pressure) apretón m. ♦ vt 1. (press firmly) apretar. 2. (force out - toothpaste) sacar (estrujando); (- juice) exprimir. 3. (cram): **to ~ sthg into sthg** (into place) conseguir meter algo en algo; (into time) arreglárselas para hacer algo en algo.

squelch [skweltʃ] vi: **to ~ through mud** cruzar el barro chapoteando.

squid [skwɪd] (pl inv OR -s) n 1. (ZOOL) calamar m. 2. (U) (food) calamares mpl.

squiggle ['skwɪgl] n garabato m.

squint [skwɪnt] ◆ *n* estrabismo *m*, bizquera *f*. ◆ *vi*: **to ~ at** mirar con los ojos entrecerrados.

squire ['skwaɪəʳ] *n* (*landowner*) terrateniente *m y f*.

squirm [skwɜːm] *vi* (*wriggle*) retorcerse.

squirrel [Br 'skwɪrəl, Am 'skwɜːrəl] *n* ardilla *f*.

squirt [skwɜːt] ◆ *vt* (*force out*) sacar a chorro de. ◆ *vi*: **to ~ out of** salir a chorro.

Sr *abbr of* **senior**.

Sri Lanka [ˌsriːˈlæŋkə] *n* Sri Lanka.

St 1. (*abbr of* **saint**) Sto. (Sta.). **2.** (*abbr of* **Street**) c/.

stab [stæb] ◆ *n* **1.** (*with knife*) puñalada *f*. **2.** *inf* (*attempt*): **to have a ~ (at sthg)** probar (a hacer algo). **3.** (*twinge*) punzada *f*. ◆ *vt* **1.** (*with knife*) apuñalar. **2.** (*jab*) pinchar.

stable ['steɪbl] ◆ *adj* **1.** (*unchanging*) estable. **2.** (*not moving*) fijo(ja). **3.** (MED) (*condition*) estacionario(ria); (*mental health*) equilibrado(da). ◆ *n* (*building*) cuadra *f*.

stack [stæk] ◆ *n* (*pile*) pila *m*. ◆ *vt* (*pile up*) apilar.

stadium ['steɪdjəm] (*pl* **-diums** OR **-dia** [-djə]) *n* estadio *m*.

staff [stɑːf] ◆ *n* (*employees*) empleados *mpl*, personal *m*. ◆ *vt*: **the shop is ~ed by women** la tienda está llevada por una plantilla de mujeres.

stag [stæg] (*pl inv* OR **-s**) *n* ciervo *m*, venado *m*.

stage [steɪdʒ] ◆ *n* **1.** (*part of process, phase*) etapa *f*. **2.** (*in theatre, hall*) escenario *m*, escena *f*. **3.** (*acting profession*): **the ~** el teatro. ◆ *vt* **1.** (THEATRE) representar. **2.** (*event, strike*) organizar.

stagecoach ['steɪdʒkəʊtʃ] *n* diligencia *f*.

stage fright *n* miedo *m* al público.

stage-manage *vt* **1.** (THEATRE) dirigir. **2.** *fig* (*orchestrate*) urdir, maquinar.

stagger ['stægəʳ] ◆ *vt* **1.** (*astound*) dejar atónito(ta). **2.** (*arrange at different times*) escalonar. ◆ *vi* tambalearse.

stagnant ['stægnənt] *adj lit & fig* estancado(da).

stagnate [stæg'neɪt] *vi* estancarse.

stag party *n* despedida *f* de soltero.

staid [steɪd] *adj* recatado y conservador (recatada y conservadora).

stain [steɪn] ◆ *n* mancha *f*. ◆ *vt* manchar.

stained glass [ˌsteɪnd-] *n* (U) vidrio *m* de color.

stainless steel [ˌsteɪnlɪs-] *n* acero *m* inoxidable.

stain remover [-rɪˌmuːvəʳ] *n* quitamanchas *m inv*.

stair [steəʳ] *n* peldaño *m*, escalón *m*. ▶ **stairs** *npl* escaleras *fpl*, escalera *f*.

staircase ['steəkeɪs] *n* escalera *f*.

stairway ['steəweɪ] *n* escalera *f*.

stairwell ['steəwel] *n* hueco *m* OR caja *f* de la escalera.

stake [steɪk] ◆ *n* **1.** (*share*): **to have a ~ in** tener intereses en. **2.** (*wooden post*) estaca *f*. **3.** (*in gambling*) apuesta *f*. ◆ *vt* **1.** (*risk*): **to ~ sthg (on** OR **upon**) arriesgar OR jugarse algo (en). **2.** (*in gambling*) apostar. ▶ **at stake** *adv*: **to be at ~** estar en juego.

stale [steɪl] *adj* (*bread*) duro(ra); (*food*) pasado(da); (*air*) viciado(da).

stalemate ['steɪlmeɪt] *n* **1.** (*deadlock*) punto *m* muerto. **2.** (CHESS) tablas *fpl*.

stalk [stɔːk] ◆ *n* **1.** (*of flower, plant*) tallo *m*. **2.** (*of leaf, fruit*) pecíolo *m*, rabillo *m*. ◆ *vt* (*hunt*) acechar, seguir sigilosamente. ◆ *vi*: **to ~ in/out** entrar/salir con paso airado.

stall [stɔːl] ◆ *n* (*in market, at exhibition*) puesto *m*, caseta *f*. ◆ *vt* (AUT) calar. ◆ *vi* **1.** (AUT) calarse. **2.** (*delay*) andar con evasivas. ▶ **stalls** *npl* Br platea *f*, patio *m* de butacas.

stallion ['stæljən] *n* semental *m*.

stalwart ['stɔːlwət] *n* partidario *m*, -ria *f* incondicional.

stamina ['stæmɪnə] *n* resistencia *f*.

stammer ['stæməʳ] ◆ *n* tartamudeo *m*. ◆ *vi* tartamudear.

stamp [stæmp] ◆ *n* **1.** (*gen*) sello *m*, estampilla *f* Amer. **2.** (*tool*) tampón *m*. ◆ *vt* **1.** (*mark by stamping*) timbrar. **2.** (*stomp*): **to ~ one's feet** patear. ◆ *vi* **1.** (*stomp*) patalear. **2.** (*tread heavily*): **to ~ on sthg** pisotear OR pisar algo.

stamp album *n* álbum *m* de sellos.

stamp-collecting [-kəˌlektɪŋ] *n* filatelia *f*.

stamped addressed envelope ['stæmptəˌdrest-] *n* Br sobre con sus señas y franqueo.

stampede [stæm'piːd] ◆ *n lit & fig* estampida *f*. ◆ *vi* salir de estampida.

stance [stæns] *n* **1.** (*way of standing*) postura *f*. **2.** (*attitude*): **~ (on)** postura *f* (ante).

stand [stænd] (*pt & pp* **stood**) ◆ *n* **1.** (*stall*) puesto *m*; (*selling newspapers*) quiosco *m*. **2.** (*supporting object*) soporte *m*; **coat ~** perchero *m*. **3.** (SPORT) tribuna *f*. **4.** (*act of defence*): **to make a ~** resistir al

enemigo. **5.** (*publicly stated view*) postura f. **6.** Am (JUR) estrado m. ◆ vt **1.** (*place upright*) colocar (verticalmente). **2.** (*withstand, tolerate*) soportar. ◆ vi **1.** (*be upright - person*) estar de pie; (*- object*) estar (*en posición vertical*). **2.** (*get to one's feet*) ponerse de pie, levantarse. **3.** (*liquid*) reposar. **4.** (*still be valid*) seguir vigente OR en pie. **5.** (*be in particular state*): **as things ~** tal como están las cosas. **6.** Br (POL) (*be a candidate*) presentarse; **to ~ for Parliament** presentarse para las elecciones al Parlamento. **7.** Am (AUT): **'no ~ing'** 'prohibido aparcar.'
▶ **stand back** vi echarse para atrás.
▶ **stand by** ◆ vt fus **1.** (*person*) seguir al lado de. **2.** (*promise, decision*) mantener. ◆ vi **1.** (*in readiness*): **to ~ by (for sthg/to do sthg)** estar preparado(da) (para algo/para hacer algo). **2.** (*remain inactive*) quedarse sin hacer nada. ▶ **stand down** vi (*resign*) retirarse. ▶ **stand for** vt fus **1.** (*signify*) significar. **2.** (*tolerate*) aguantar, tolerar. ▶ **stand in** vi: **to ~ in for sb** sustituir a alguien. ▶ **stand out** vi sobresalir, destacarse. ▶ **stand up** ◆ vt sep inf (*boyfriend etc*) dejar plantado (da). ◆ vi (*rise from seat*) levantarse. ▶ **stand up for** vt fus salir en defensa de. ▶ **stand up to** vt fus **1.** (*weather, heat etc*) resistir. **2.** (*person*) hacer frente a.
standard ['stændəd] ◆ adj **1.** (*normal*) corriente, estándar. **2.** (*accepted*) establecido(da). ◆ n **1.** (*acceptable level*) nivel m. **2.** (*point of reference - moral*) criterio m; (*- technical*) norma f. **3.** (*flag*) estandarte m. ▶ **standards** npl (*principles*) valores mpl morales.
standard lamp n Br lámpara f de pie.
standard of living (*pl* **standards of living**) n nivel m de vida.
standby ['stændbaɪ] (*pl* **standbys**) ◆ n recurso m; **on ~** preparado(da). ◆ comp: **~ ticket** billete m en lista de espera.
stand-in n (*stuntman*) doble m y f; (*temporary replacement*) sustituto m, -ta f.
standing ['stændɪŋ] ◆ adj (*permanent*) permanente. ◆ n **1.** (*reputation*) reputación f. **2.** (*duration*) duración f; **friends of 20 years'** ~ amigos desde hace 20 años.
standing order n domiciliación f de pago.
standing room n (U) (*on bus*) sitio m para estar de pie; (*at theatre, sports ground*) localidades fpl de pie.
standoffish [,stænd'ɒfɪʃ] adj distante.

standpoint ['stændpɔɪnt] n punto m de vista.
standstill ['stændstɪl] n: **at a ~** (*not moving*) parado(da); fig (*not active*) en un punto muerto; **to come to a ~** (*stop moving*) pararse; fig (*cease*) llegar a un punto muerto.
stank [stæŋk] pt → **stink**.
staple ['steɪpl] ◆ adj (*principal*) básico (ca), de primera necesidad. ◆ n **1.** (*item of stationery*) grapa f. **2.** (*principal commodity*) producto m básico OR de primera necesidad. ◆ vt grapar.
stapler ['steɪplər] n grapadora f.
star [stɑːr] ◆ n (*gen*) estrella f. ◆ comp estelar. ◆ vi: **to ~ (in)** hacer de protagonista en. ▶ **stars** npl horóscopo m.
starboard ['stɑːbəd] ◆ adj de estribor. ◆ n: **to ~** a estribor.
starch [stɑːtʃ] n **1.** (*gen*) almidón m. **2.** (*in potatoes etc*) fécula f.
stardom ['stɑːdəm] n estrellato m.
stare [steər] ◆ n mirada f fija. ◆ vi: **to ~ (at sthg/sb)** mirar fijamente (algo/a alguien).
stark [stɑːk] ◆ adj **1.** (*landscape, decoration, room*) austero(ra). **2.** (*harsh - reality*) crudo(da). ◆ adv: **~ naked** en cueros.
starling ['stɑːlɪŋ] n estornino m.
starry ['stɑːrɪ] adj estrellado(da).
starry-eyed [-'aɪd] adj (*optimism etc*) iluso(sa); (*lovers*) encandilado(da).
Stars and Stripes n: **the ~** la bandera de las barras y estrellas.
start [stɑːt] ◆ n **1.** (*beginning*) principio m, comienzo m; **at the ~ of the year** a principios de año. **2.** (*jerk, jump*) sobresalto m. **3.** (*starting place*) salida f. **4.** (*time advantage*) ventaja f. ◆ vt **1.** (*begin*) empezar, comenzar; **to ~ doing** OR **to do sthg** empezar a hacer algo. **2.** (*turn on - machine, engine*) poner en marcha; (*- vehicle*) arrancar. **3.** (*set up*) formar, crear; (*business*) montar. ◆ vi **1.** (*begin*) empezar, comenzar; **to ~ with sb/sthg** empezar por alguien/algo. **2.** (*machine, tape*) ponerse en marcha; (*vehicle*) arrancar. **3.** (*begin journey*) ponerse en camino. **4.** (*jerk, jump*) sobresaltarse. ▶ **start off** ◆ vt sep (*discussion, rumour*) desencadenar; (*meeting*) empezar; (*person*): **this should be enough to ~ you off** con esto tienes suficiente trabajo para empezar. ◆ vi **1.** (*begin*) empezar, comenzar. **2.** (*leave on journey*) salir, ponerse en camino. ▶ **start out** vi **1.** (*originally be*) empezar, comenzar. **2.** (*leave on journey*) salir, ponerse en

camino. ▶ **start up** ◆ vt sep **1.** (business) montar; (shop) poner; (association) crear. **2.** (car, engine) arrancar. ◆ vi **1.** (begin) empezar. **2.** (car, engine) arrancar.

starter ['stɑːtər] n **1.** Br (of meal) primer plato m, entrada f. **2.** (AUT) (motor m de) arranque m. **3.** (person participating in race) participante m y f.

starting point ['stɑːtɪŋ-] n lit & fig punto m de partida.

startle ['stɑːtl] vt asustar.

startling ['stɑːtlɪŋ] adj asombroso (sa).

starvation [stɑːˈveɪʃn] n hambre f, inanición f.

starve [stɑːv] ◆ vt (deprive of food) privar de comida. ◆ vi **1.** (have no food) pasar hambre. **2.** inf (be hungry): **I'm starving!** ¡me muero de hambre!

state [steɪt] ◆ n estado m; **not to be in a fit ~ to do sthg** no estar en condiciones de hacer algo; **to be in a ~** tener los nervios de punta. ◆ comp (ceremony) oficial, de Estado; (control, ownership) estatal. ◆ vt **1.** (gen) indicar; (reason, policy) plantear; (case) exponer. **2.** (time, date, amount) fijar. ▶ **State** n: **the State** el Estado. ▶ **States** npl: **the States** los Estados Unidos.

State Department n Am ≃ Ministerio m de Asuntos Exteriores.

stately ['steɪtlɪ] adj majestuoso(sa).

statement ['steɪtmənt] n **1.** (gen) declaración f. **2.** (from bank) extracto m OR estado m de cuenta.

state of mind (pl states of mind) n estado m de ánimo.

statesman ['steɪtsmən] (pl -men [-mən]) n estadista m.

static ['stætɪk] ◆ adj estático(ca). ◆ n (U) interferencias fpl, parásitos mpl.

static electricity n electricidad f estática.

station ['steɪʃn] ◆ n **1.** (gen) estación f. **2.** (RADIO) emisora f. **3.** (centre of activity) centro m, puesto m. **4.** fml (rank) rango m. ◆ vt **1.** (position) situar, colocar. **2.** (MIL) estacionar, apostar.

stationary ['steɪʃnərɪ] adj inmóvil.

stationer ['steɪʃnər] n papelero m, -ra f; **~'s** (shop) papelería f.

stationery ['steɪʃnərɪ] n (U) objetos mpl de escritorio.

stationmaster ['steɪʃn,mɑːstər] n jefe m de estación.

station wagon n Am ranchera f.

statistic [stəˈtɪstɪk] n estadística f. ▶ **statistics** n (U) estadística f.

statistical [stəˈtɪstɪkl] adj estadístico (ca).

statue ['stætʃuː] n estatua f.

stature ['stætʃər] n **1.** (height) estatura f, talla f. **2.** (importance) categoría f.

status ['steɪtəs] n (U) **1.** (position, condition) condición f, estado m. **2.** (prestige) prestigio m, estatus m inv.

status symbol n símbolo m de posición social.

statute ['stætʃuːt] n estatuto m.

statutory ['stætjʊtrɪ] adj reglamentario(ria).

staunch [stɔːntʃ] ◆ adj fiel, leal. ◆ vt restañar.

stave [steɪv] (pt & pp -d OR stove) n (MUS) pentagrama m. ▶ **stave off** vt sep (disaster, defeat) retrasar; (hunger, illness) aplacar temporalmente.

stay [steɪ] ◆ vi **1.** (not move away) quedarse, permanecer; **to ~ put** permanecer en el mismo sitio. **2.** (as visitor) alojarse. **3.** (continue, remain) permanecer. ◆ n estancia f. ▶ **stay in** vi quedarse en casa. ▶ **stay on** vi permanecer, quedarse. ▶ **stay out** vi (from home) quedarse fuera. ▶ **stay up** vi quedarse levantado(da).

staying power ['steɪɪŋ-] n resistencia f.

stead [sted] n: **to stand sb in good ~** servir de mucho a alguien.

steadfast ['stedfɑːst] adj (supporter) fiel; (gaze) fijo(ja); (resolve) inquebrantable.

steadily ['stedɪlɪ] adv **1.** (gradually) constantemente. **2.** (regularly - breathe, move) normalmente. **3.** (calmly - look) fijamente; (- speak) con tranquilidad.

steady ['stedɪ] ◆ adj **1.** (gradual) gradual. **2.** (regular, constant) constante, continuo(nua). **3.** (not shaking) firme. **4.** (voice) sereno(na); (stare) fijo(ja). **5.** (relationship) estable, serio(ria); (boyfriend, girlfriend) formal; **a ~ job** un trabajo fijo. **6.** (reliable, sensible) sensato(ta). ◆ vt **1.** (stop from shaking) mantener firme; **to ~ o.s.** dejar de temblar. **2.** (nerves, voice) dominar, controlar.

steak [steɪk] n **1.** (U) (meat) bistec m, filete m, bife m Amer. **2.** (piece of meat, fish) filete m.

steal [stiːl] (pt stole, pp stolen) ◆ vt (gen) robar; (idea) apropiarse de; **to ~ sthg from sb** robar algo a alguien. ◆ vi (move secretly) moverse sigilosamente.

stealthy ['stelθɪ] adj cauteloso(sa), sigiloso(sa).

steam [sti:m] ◆ n (U) vapor m, vaho m. ◆ vt (CULIN) cocer al vapor. ◆ vi (water, food) echar vapor. ► **steam up** ◆ vt sep (mist up) empañar. ◆ vi empañarse.

steamboat ['sti:mbəʊt] n buque m de vapor.

steam engine n máquina f de vapor.

steamer ['sti:mər] n (ship) buque m de vapor.

steamroller ['sti:m,rəʊlər] n apisonadora f.

steamy ['sti:mɪ] adj 1. (full of steam) lleno(na) de vaho. 2. inf (erotic) caliente, erótico(ca).

steel [sti:l] ◆ n acero m. ◆ comp de acero.

steelworks ['sti:lwɜ:ks] (pl inv) n fundición f de acero.

steep [sti:p] ◆ adj 1. (hill, road) empinado(da). 2. (considerable - increase, fall) considerable. 3. inf (expensive) muy caro (ra), abusivo(va). ◆ vt remojar.

steeple ['sti:pl] n aguja f (de un campanario).

steeplechase ['sti:pltʃeɪs] n carrera f de obstáculos.

steer ['stɪər] ◆ n buey m. ◆ vt 1. (vehicle) conducir. 2. (person, discussion etc) dirigir. ◆ vi: **the car ~s well** el coche se conduce bien; **to ~ clear of sthg/sb** evitar algo/a alguien.

steering ['stɪərɪŋ] n (U) dirección f.

steering wheel n volante m, timón m Amer.

stem [stem] ◆ n 1. (of plant) tallo m. 2. (of glass) pie m. 3. (of pipe) tubo m. 4. (GRAMM) raíz f. ◆ vt (flow) contener; (blood) restañar. ► **stem from** vt fus derivarse de.

stench [stentʃ] n hedor m.

stencil ['stensl] ◆ n plantilla f. ◆ vt estarcir.

stenographer [stə'nɒɡrəfər] n Am taquígrafo m, -fa f.

step [step] ◆ n 1. (gen) paso m; **~ by ~** paso a paso; **to be in/out of ~** llevar/no llevar el paso; fig estar/no estar al tanto. 2. (action) medida f. 3. (stair, rung) peldaño m. ◆ vi 1. (move foot) dar un paso; **he stepped off the bus** se bajó del autobús. 2. (tread): **to ~ on sthg** pisar algo; **to ~ in sthg** meter el pie en algo. ► **steps** npl 1. (stairs - indoors) escaleras fpl; (- outside) escalinata f. 2. Br (stepladder) escalera f de tijera. ► **step down** vi (leave job) renunciar. ► **step in** vi intervenir. ► **step up** vt sep aumentar.

stepbrother ['step,brʌðər] n hermanastro m.

stepdaughter ['step,dɔ:tər] n hijastra f.

stepfather ['step,fɑ:ðər] n padrastro m.

stepladder ['step,lædər] n escalera f de tijera.

stepmother ['step,mʌðər] n madrastra f.

stepping-stone ['stepɪŋ-] n (in river) pasadera f.

stepsister ['step,sɪstər] n hermanastra f.

stepson ['stepsʌn] n hijastro m.

stereo ['sterɪəʊ] (pl -s) ◆ adj estéreo (inv). ◆ n 1. (record player) equipo m estereofónico. 2. (stereo sound) estéreo m.

stereotype ['sterɪətaɪp] n estereotipo m.

sterile ['steraɪl] adj 1. (germ-free) esterilizado(da). 2. (unable to produce offspring) estéril.

sterilize, -ise ['sterəlaɪz] vt esterilizar.

sterling ['stɜ:lɪŋ] ◆ adj 1. (of British money) esterlina. 2. (excellent) excelente. ◆ n (U) libra f esterlina.

sterling silver n plata f de ley.

stern [stɜ:n] ◆ adj severo(ra). ◆ n popa f.

steroid ['stɪərɔɪd] n esteroide m.

stethoscope ['steθəskəʊp] n estetoscopio m.

stew [stju:] ◆ n estofado m, guisado m. ◆ vt (meat, vegetables) estofar, guisar; (fruit) hacer una compota de.

steward ['stjʊəd] n 1. (on plane) auxiliar m de vuelo; (on ship, train) camarero m. 2. Br (organizer) ayudante m y f de organización.

stewardess ['stjʊədɪs] n auxiliar f de vuelo, azafata f.

stick [stɪk] (pt & pp stuck) ◆ n 1. (of wood, for playing sport) palo m. 2. (of dynamite) cartucho m; (of liquorice, rock) barra f. 3. (walking stick) bastón m. ◆ vt 1. (push): **to ~ sthg in on into sthg** (knife, pin) clavar algo en algo; (finger) meter algo en algo. 2. (make adhere): **to ~ sthg (on or to sthg)** pegar algo (en algo). 3. inf (put) meter. 4. Br inf (tolerate) soportar, aguantar. ◆ vi 1. (adhere): **to ~ (to)** pegarse (a). 2. (jam) atrancarse. ► **stick out** ◆ vt sep 1. (make protrude) sacar. 2. (endure) aguantar. ◆ vi (protrude) sobresalir. ► **stick to** vt fus 1. (follow closely) seguir. 2. (principles) ser fiel a; (promise, agreement) cumplir con; (decision) atenerse a. ► **stick up** vi salir,

sobresalir. ▸ **stick up for** vt fus defender.

sticker ['stɪkə'] n (piece of paper) pegatina f.

sticking plaster ['stɪkɪŋ-] n esparadrapo m.

stickler ['stɪklə'] n: ~ for sthg maniático m, -ca f de algo.

stick shift n Am palanca f de cambios.

stick-up n inf atraco m a mano armada.

sticky ['stɪkɪ] adj 1. (tacky) pegajoso (sa). 2. (adhesive) adhesivo(va). 3. inf (awkward) engorroso(sa).

stiff [stɪf] ◆ adj 1. (inflexible) rígido(da). 2. (door, drawer) atascado(da). 3. (aching) agarrotado(da); to be ~ tener agujetas. 4. (formal - person, manner) estirado(da); (- smile) rígido(da). 5. (severe, intense) severo(ra). 6. (difficult - task) duro(ra). ◆ adv inf: bored/frozen ~ muerto(ta) de aburrimiento/frío.

stiffen ['stɪfn] vi 1. (become inflexible) endurecerse. 2. (bones) entumecerse; (muscles) agarrotarse. 3. (become more severe, intense) intensificarse.

stifle ['staɪfl] vt 1. (prevent from breathing) ahogar, sofocar. 2. (prevent from happening) reprimir.

stifling ['staɪflɪŋ] adj sofocante.

stigma ['stɪgmə] n estigma m.

stile [staɪl] n escalones mpl para pasar una valla.

stiletto heel [stɪ'letəu-] n Br tacón m fino OR de aguja.

still [stɪl] ◆ adv 1. (up to now, up to then, even now) todavía. 2. (to emphasize remaining amount) aún; I've ~ got two left aún me quedan dos. 3. (nevertheless, however) sin embargo, no obstante. 4. (with comparatives) aún. 5. (motionless) sin moverse. ◆ adj 1. (not moving) inmóvil. 2. (calm, quiet) tranquilo(la), sosegado (da). 3. (not windy) apacible. 4. (not fizzy) sin gas. ◆ n 1. (PHOT) vista f fija. 2. (for making alcohol) alambique m.

stillborn ['stɪlbɔːn] adj nacido muerto (nacida muerta).

still life (pl -s) n bodegón m, naturaleza f muerta.

stilted ['stɪltɪd] adj forzado(da).

stilts [stɪlts] npl 1. (for person) zancos mpl. 2. (for building) pilotes mpl.

stimulate ['stɪmjuleɪt] vt (gen) estimular; (interest) excitar.

stimulating ['stɪmjuleɪtɪŋ] adj (physically) estimulante; (mentally) interesante.

stimulus ['stɪmjuləs] (pl -li [-laɪ]) n estímulo m.

sting [stɪŋ] (pt & pp stung) ◆ n 1. (by bee) picadura f. 2. (of bee) aguijón m. 3. (sharp pain) escozor m. ◆ vt 1. (subj: bee, nettle) picar. 2. (cause sharp pain to) escocer. ◆ vi picar.

stingy ['stɪndʒɪ] adj inf tacaño(ña), roñoso(sa).

stink [stɪŋk] (pt stank OR stunk, pp stunk) ◆ n peste f, hedor m. ◆ vi (have unpleasant smell) apestar, heder.

stinking ['stɪŋkɪŋ] inf fig ◆ adj asqueroso(sa). ◆ adv increíblemente.

stint [stɪnt] ◆ n periodo m. ◆ vi: to ~ on sthg escatimar algo.

stipulate ['stɪpjuleɪt] vt estipular.

stir [stɜː'] ◆ n (public excitement) revuelo m. ◆ vt 1. (mix) remover. 2. (move gently) agitar, mover. 3. (move emotionally) conmover. ◆ vi (move gently) moverse, agitarse. ▸ **stir up** vt sep 1. (cause to rise) levantar. 2. (cause) provocar.

stirrup ['stɪrəp] n estribo m.

stitch [stɪtʃ] ◆ n 1. (SEWING) puntada f. 2. (in knitting) punto m. 3. (MED) punto m (de sutura). 4. (stomach pain): to have a ~ sentir pinchazos (en el estómago). ◆ vt 1. (SEWING) coser. 2. (MED) suturar.

stoat [stəut] n armiño m.

stock [stɒk] ◆ n 1. (supply) reserva f. 2. (U) (COMM) (reserves) existencias fpl; (selection) surtido m; in ~ en existencia, out of ~ agotado(da). 3. (FIN) (of company) capital m; ~s and shares acciones fpl, valores mpl. 4. (ancestry) linaje m, estirpe f. 5. (CULIN) caldo m. 6. (livestock) ganado m, ganadería f. 7. phr: to take ~ (of sthg) evaluar (algo). ◆ adj estereotipado(da). ◆ vt 1. (COMM) abastecer de, tener en el almacén. 2. (shelves) llenar; (lake) repoblar. ▸ **stock up** vi: to ~ up (with) abastecerse (de).

stockbroker ['stɒk,brəukə'] n corredor m, -ra f de bolsa.

stock cube n Br pastilla f de caldo.

stock exchange n bolsa f.

stockholder ['stɒk,həuldə'] n Am accionista m y f.

Stockholm ['stɒkhəum] n Estocolmo.

stocking ['stɒkɪŋ] n (for woman) media f.

stockist ['stɒkɪst] n Br distribuidor m, -ra f.

stock market n bolsa f, mercado m de valores.

stock phrase n frase f estereotipada.

stockpile ['stɒkpaɪl] ◆ n reservas fpl.

◆ *vt* almacenar, acumular.

stocktaking ['stɒk,teɪkɪŋ] *n* (U) inventario *m*, balance *m*.

stocky ['stɒkɪ] *adj* corpulento(ta), robusto(ta).

stodgy ['stɒdʒɪ] *adj* (*indigestible*) indigesto(ta).

stoical ['stəʊɪkl] *adj* estoico(ca).

stoke [stəʊk] *vt* (*fire*) avivar, alimentar.

stole [stəʊl] ◆ *pt* → **steal**. ◆ *n* estola *f*.

stolen ['stəʊln] *pp* → **steal**.

stolid ['stɒlɪd] *adj* impasible.

stomach ['stʌmək] ◆ *n* 1. (*organ*) estómago *m*. 2. (*abdomen*) vientre *m*. ◆ *vt* tragar, aguantar.

stomachache ['stʌməkeɪk] *n* dolor *m* de estómago.

stomach upset [-'ʌpset] *n* trastorno *m* gástrico.

stone [stəʊn] (*pl sense 4 only inv* OR **-s**) ◆ *n* 1. (*mineral*) piedra *f*. 2. (*jewel*) piedra *f* preciosa. 3. (*seed*) hueso *m*. 4. Br (*unit of measurement*) = 6,35 *kilos*. ◆ *comp* de piedra. ◆ *vt* apedrear.

stone-cold *adj* helado(da).

stonewashed ['stəʊnwɒʃt] *adj* lavado (da) a la piedra.

stonework ['stəʊnwɜ:k] *n* mampostería *f*.

stood [stʊd] *pt & pp* → **stand**.

stool [stu:l] *n* (*seat*) taburete *m*.

stoop [stu:p] ◆ *n* (*bent back*): **to walk with a ~** caminar encorvado(da). ◆ *vi* 1. (*bend*) inclinarse, agacharse. 2. (*hunch shoulders*) encorvarse.

stop [stɒp] ◆ *n* 1. (*gen*) parada *f*; **to put a ~ to sthg** poner fin a algo. 2. (*full stop*) punto *m*. ◆ *vt* 1. (*gen*) parar; **to ~ doing sthg** dejar de hacer algo. 2. (*prevent*) impedir; **to ~ sb/sthg from doing sthg** impedir que alguien/algo haga algo. 3. (*cause to stop moving*) detener. ◆ *vi* (*gen*) pararse; (*rain, music*) cesar. ► **stop off** *vi* hacer una parada. ► **stop up** *vt sep* (*block*) taponar, tapar.

stopgap ['stɒpgæp] *n* (*thing*) recurso *m* provisional; (*person*) sustituto *m*, -ta *f*.

stopover ['stɒp,əʊvər] *n* (*gen*) parada *f*; (*of plane*) escala *f*.

stoppage ['stɒpɪdʒ] *n* 1. (*strike*) paro *m*, huelga *f*. 2. Br (*deduction*) retención *f*.

stopper ['stɒpər] *n* tapón *m*.

stop press *n* noticias *fpl* de última hora.

stopwatch ['stɒpwɒtʃ] *n* cronómetro *m*.

storage ['stɔ:rɪdʒ] *n* almacenamiento *m*.

storage heater *n* Br calentador por almacenamiento térmico.

store [stɔ:r] ◆ *n* 1. (*shop*) tienda *f*. 2. (*supply*) provisión *f*, reserva *f*. 3. (*place of storage*) almacén *m*. ◆ *vt* 1. (*gen & COMPUT*) almacenar. 2. (*keep*) guardar. ► **store up** *vt sep* (*provisions, goods*) almacenar; (*information*) acumular.

storekeeper ['stɔ:,ki:pər] *n* Am tendero *m*, -ra *f*.

storeroom ['stɔ:rʊm] *n* (*gen*) almacén *m*; (*for food*) despensa *f*.

storey Br (*pl* **storeys**), **story** Am ['stɔ:rɪ] *n* planta *f*.

stork [stɔ:k] *n* cigüeña *f*.

storm [stɔ:m] ◆ *n* 1. (*bad weather*) tormenta *f*. 2. (*violent reaction*) torrente *m*. ◆ *vt* (MIL) asaltar. ◆ *vi* 1. (*go angrily*): **to ~ out** salir echando pestes. 2. (*say angrily*) vociferar.

stormy ['stɔ:mɪ] *adj* 1. (*weather*) tormentoso(sa). 2. (*meeting*) acalorado (da); (*relationship*) tempestuoso(sa).

story ['stɔ:rɪ] *n* 1. (*tale*) cuento *m*. 2. (*history*) historia *f*. 3. (*news article*) artículo *m*. 4. Am = **storey**.

storybook ['stɔ:rɪbʊk] *adj* de cuento.

storyteller ['stɔ:rɪ,telər] *n* (*teller of story*) narrador *m*, -ra *f*, cuentista *m* y *f*.

stout [staʊt] ◆ *adj* 1. (*rather fat*) corpulento(ta). 2. (*strong, solid*) fuerte, sólido (da). 3. (*resolute*) firme. ◆ *n* (U) cerveza *f* negra.

stove [stəʊv] ◆ *pt & pp* → **stave**. ◆ *n* (*for heating*) estufa *f*; (*for cooking*) cocina *f*.

stow [stəʊ] *vt*: **to ~ sthg (away)** guardar algo.

stowaway ['stəʊəweɪ] *n* polizón *m*.

straddle ['strædl] *vt* (*subj: person*) sentarse a horcajadas sobre.

straggle ['strægl] *vi* 1. (*sprawl*) desparramarse. 2. (*dawdle*) rezagarse.

straggler ['stræglər] *n* rezagado *m*, -da *f*.

straight [streɪt] ◆ *adj* 1. (*not bent*) recto (ta). 2. (*hair*) liso(sa). 3. (*honest, frank*) sincero(ra). 4. (*tidy*) arreglado(da). 5. (*choice, swap*) simple, fácil. 6. (*alcoholic drink*) solo(la). ◆ *adv* 1. (*in a straight line - horizontally*) directamente; (*- vertically*) recto(ta); **~ ahead** todo recto. 2. (*directly*) directamente; (*immediately*) inmediatamente. 3. (*frankly*) francamente. 4. (*tidy*) en orden. 5. (*undiluted*) solo(la). 6. *phr*: **let's get things ~** vamos a aclarar las cosas. ► **straight off** *adv* en el acto. ► **straight out** *adv* sin tapujos.

straightaway [ˌstreɪtə'weɪ] *adv* en seguida.

straighten ['streɪtn] *vt* **1.** (*tidy - room*) ordenar; (*- hair, dress*) poner bien. **2.** (*make straight - horizontally*) poner recto(ta); (*- vertically*) enderezar. ▶ **straighten out** *vt sep* (*mess*) arreglar; (*problem*) resolver.

straight face *n*: **to keep a ~** aguantar la risa.

straightforward [ˌstreɪt'fɔːwəd] *adj* **1.** (*easy*) sencillo(lla). **2.** (*frank - answer*) directo(ta); (*- person*) sincero(ra).

strain [streɪn] ◆ *n* **1.** (*weight*) peso *m*; (*pressure*) presión *f*. **2.** (*mental stress*) tensión *f* nerviosa. **3.** (*physical injury*) torcedura *f*. **4.** (*worry, difficulty*) esfuerzo *m*. ◆ *vt* **1.** (*overtax - budget*) estirar; (*- enthusiasm*) agotar. **2.** (*use hard*): **to ~ one's eyes/ears** aguzar la vista/el oído. **3.** (*injure - eyes*) cansar; (*- muscle, back*) torcerse. **4.** (*drain*) colar. ◆ *vi*: **to ~ to do sthg** esforzarse por hacer algo. ▶ **strains** *npl literary* (*of music*) acordes *mpl*.

strained [streɪnd] *adj* **1.** (*worried*) preocupado(da). **2.** (*unfriendly*) tirante, tenso(sa). **3.** (*insincere*) forzado(da).

strainer ['streɪnəʳ] *n* colador *m*.

strait [streɪt] *n* estrecho *m*. ▶ **straits** *npl*: **in dire** OR **desperate ~s** en un serio aprieto.

straitjacket ['streɪtˌdʒækɪt] *n* (*garment*) camisa *f* de fuerza.

straitlaced [ˌstreɪt'leɪst] *adj pej* mojigato(ta).

strand [strænd] *n* (*thin piece*) hebra *f*; **a ~ of hair** un pelo del cabello.

stranded ['strændɪd] *adj* (*ship*) varado(da); (*person*) colgado(da).

strange [streɪndʒ] *adj* **1.** (*unusual*) raro(ra), extraño(ña). **2.** (*unfamiliar*) extraño(ña), desconocido(da).

stranger ['streɪndʒəʳ] *n* **1.** (*unfamiliar person*) extraño *m*, -ña *f*, desconocido *m*, -da *f*. **2.** (*outsider*) forastero *m*, -ra *f*.

strangle ['stræŋgl] *vt* (*kill*) estrangular.

stranglehold ['stræŋglhəʊld] *n fig* (*strong influence*) dominio *m* absoluto.

strap [stræp] ◆ *n* **1.** (*of handbag, rifle*) bandolera *f*. **2.** (*of watch, case*) correa *f*; (*of dress, bra*) tirante *m*. ◆ *vt* (*fasten*) atar con correa.

strapping ['stræpɪŋ] *adj* robusto(ta).

Strasbourg ['stræzbɔːg] *n* Estrasburgo.

strategic [strə'tiːdʒɪk] *adj* estratégico(ca).

strategy ['strætɪdʒɪ] *n* estrategia *f*.

straw [strɔː] *n* **1.** (AGR) paja *f*. **2.** (*for drinking*) pajita *f*, paja *f*. **3.** *phr*: **the last ~** el colmo.

strawberry ['strɔːbəri] ◆ *n* fresa *f*, frutilla *f Amer*. ◆ *comp* de fresa.

stray [streɪ] ◆ *adj* **1.** (*animal - without owner*) callejero(ra); (*- lost*) extraviado (da). **2.** (*bullet*) perdido(da); (*example*) aislado(da). ◆ *vi* **1.** (*from path*) desviarse; (*from group*) extraviarse. **2.** (*thoughts, mind*) perderse.

streak [striːk] ◆ *n* **1.** (*of hair*) mechón *m*; (*of lightning*) rayo *m*; (*of grease*) raya *f*. **2.** (*in character*) vena *f*. ◆ *vi* (*move quickly*) ir como un rayo.

stream [striːm] ◆ *n* **1.** (*small river*) riachuelo *m*. **2.** (*of liquid, smoke*) chorro *m*; (*of light*) raudal *m*. **3.** (*current*) corriente *f*. **4.** (*of people, cars*) torrente *m*. **5.** (*continuous series*) sarta *f*, serie *f*. **6.** Br (SCH) grupo *m*. ◆ *vi* **1.** (*liquid, smoke, light*): **to ~ into** entrar a raudales en; **to ~ out of** brotar de. **2.** (*people, cars*): **to ~ into** entrar atropelladamente en; **to ~ out of** salir atropelladamente de. ◆ *vt* Br (SCH) agrupar de acuerdo con el rendimiento escolar.

streamer ['striːməʳ] *n* (*for party*) serpentina *f*.

streamlined ['striːmlaɪnd] *adj* **1.** (*aerodynamic*) aerodinámico(ca). **2.** (*efficient*) racional.

street [striːt] *n* calle *f*.

streetcar ['striːtkɑːʳ] *n Am* tranvía *m*.

street lamp, street light *n* farola *f*.

street plan *n* plano *m* (de la ciudad).

streetwise ['striːtwaɪz] *adj inf* espabilado(da).

strength [streŋθ] *n* **1.** (*physical or mental power*) fuerza *f*. **2.** (*power, influence*) poder *m*. **3.** (*quality*) punto *m* fuerte. **4.** (*solidity - of material structure*) solidez *f*. **5.** (*intensity - of feeling, smell, wind*) intensidad *f*; (*- of accent, wine*) fuerza *f*; (*- of drug*) potencia *f*. **6.** (*credibility, weight*) peso *m*, fuerza *f*.

strengthen ['streŋθn] *vt* **1.** (*gen*) fortalecer. **2.** (*reinforce - argument, bridge*) reforzar. **3.** (*intensify*) acentuar, intensificar. **4.** (*make closer*) estrechar.

strenuous ['strenjʊəs] *adj* agotador (ra).

stress [stres] ◆ *n* **1.** (*emphasis*): **~ (on)** hincapié *m* OR énfasis *m inv* (en). **2.** (*tension, anxiety*) estrés *m*. **3.** (*physical pressure*): **~ (on)** presión *f* (en). **4.** (LING) (*on word, syllable*) acento *m*. ◆ *vt* **1.** (*emphasize*) recalcar, subrayar. **2.** (LING) (*word,* *syllable)* acentuar.

stressed [strest] *adj (anxious)* estresado(da).

stressful ['stresful] *adj* estresante.

stretch [stretʃ] ◆ *n* 1. *(of land, water)* extensión *f*; *(of road, river)* tramo *m*, trecho *m*. 2. *(of time)* periodo *m*. ◆ *vt* 1. *(gen)* estirar. 2. *(overtax - person)* extender. 3. *(challenge)* hacer rendir al máximo. ◆ *vi (area)*: **to ~ over/from ... to** extenderse por/desde ... hasta. ► **stretch out** ◆ *vt sep (foot, leg)* estirar; *(hand, arm)* alargar. ◆ *vi* 1. *(lie down)* tumbarse. 2. *(reach out)* estirarse.

stretcher ['stretʃəʳ] *n* camilla *f*.

strew [struː] *(pp* strewn [struːn] OR **-ed)** *vt*: **to be strewn with** estar cubierto(ta) de.

stricken ['strɪkn] *adj*: **to be ~ by** OR **with** *(illness)* estar aquejado(da) de; *(grief)* estar afligido(da) por; *(doubts, horror)* estar atenazado(da) por.

strict [strɪkt] *adj* 1. *(gen)* estricto(ta). 2. *(precise)* exacto(ta), estricto(ta).

strictly ['strɪktlɪ] *adv* 1. *(severely)* severamente. 2. *(absolutely - prohibited)* terminantemente; *(- confidential)* absolutamente. 3. *(exactly)* exactamente; **~ speaking** en el sentido estricto de la palabra. 4. *(exclusively)* exclusivamente.

stride [straɪd] *(pt* strode, *pp* stridden ['strɪdn])* ◆ *n* zancada *f*. ◆ *vi* andar a zancadas.

strident ['straɪdnt] *adj* 1. *(harsh)* estridente. 2. *(vociferous)* exaltado(da).

strife [straɪf] *n (U) fml* conflictos *mpl*.

strike [straɪk] *(pt & pp* struck)* ◆ *n* 1. *(refusal to work etc)* huelga *f*; **to be (out) on ~** estar en huelga; **to go on ~** declararse en huelga. 2. (MIL) ataque *m*. 3. *(find)* descubrimiento *m*. ◆ *vt* 1. *fml (hit - deliberately)* golpear, pegar; *(- accidentally)* chocar contra. 2. *(subj: disaster, earthquake)* asolar; *(subj: lightning)* fulminar. 3. *(subj: thought, idea)* ocurrírsele a. 4. *(deal, bargain)* cerrar. 5. *(match)* encender. ◆ *vi* 1. *(stop working)* estar en huelga. 2. *fml (hit accidentally)*: **to ~ against** chocar contra. 3. *(hurricane, disaster)* sobrevenir; *(lightning)* caer. 4. *fml (attack)* atacar. 5. *(chime)* dar la hora; **the clock struck six** el reloj dio las seis. ► **strike down** *vt sep* fulminar. ► **strike out** *vt sep* tachar. ► **strike up** *vt fus* 1. *(friendship)* trabar; *(conversation)* entablar. 2. *(tune)* empezar a tocar.

striker ['straɪkəʳ] *n* 1. *(person on strike)*

huelguista *m y f*. 2. (FTBL) delantero *m*, -ra *f*.

striking ['straɪkɪŋ] *adj* 1. *(noticeable, unusual)* chocante, sorprendente. 2. *(attractive)* llamativo(va), atractivo(va).

string [strɪŋ] *(pt & pp* strung)* *n* 1. *(thin rope)* cuerda *f*; **a (piece of) ~** un cordón; **to pull ~s** utilizar uno sus influencias. 2. *(of beads, pearls)* sarta *f*. 3. *(series)* serie *f*, sucesión *f*. 4. *(of musical instrument)* cuerda *f*. ► **strings** *npl* (MUS): **the ~s** los instrumentos de cuerda. ► **string out** *vt fus*: **to be strung out** alinearse. ► **string together** *vt sep* enlazar.

string bean *n* judía *f* verde.

stringed instrument ['strɪŋd-] *n* instrumento *m* de cuerda.

stringent ['strɪndʒənt] *adj* estricto(ta), severo(ra).

strip [strɪp] ◆ *n* 1. *(narrow piece)* tira *f*. 2. *(narrow area)* franja *f*. 3. Br (SPORT) camiseta *f*, colores *mpl*. ◆ *vt* 1. *(undress)* desnudar. 2. *(paint, wallpaper)* quitar. ◆ *vi (undress)* desnudarse. ► **strip off** *vi* desnudarse.

strip cartoon *n* Br historieta *f*, tira *f* cómica.

stripe [straɪp] *n* 1. *(band of colour)* raya *f*, franja *f*. 2. *(sign of rank)* galón *m*.

striped [straɪpt] *adj* a OR de rayas.

strip lighting *n* alumbrado *m* fluorescente.

stripper ['strɪpəʳ] *n* 1. *(performer of striptease)* artista *m y f* de striptease. 2. *(for paint)* disolvente *m*.

striptease ['strɪptiːz] *n* striptease *m*.

strive [straɪv] *(pt* strove, *pp* striven ['strɪvn])* *vi fml*: **to ~ for sthg** luchar por algo; **to ~ to do sthg** esforzarse por hacer algo.

strode [strəʊd] *pt* → **stride**.

stroke [strəʊk] ◆ *n* 1. (MED) apoplejía *f*, derrame *m* cerebral. 2. *(of pen)* trazo *m*; *(of brush)* pincelada *f*. 3. *(style of swimming)* estilo *m*. 4. *(in tennis, golf etc)* golpe *m*. 5. *(of clock)* campanada *f*. 6. Br (TYPO) *(oblique)* barra *f*. 7. *(piece)*: **a ~ of genius** una genialidad; **a ~ of luck** un golpe de suerte; **at a ~** de una vez, de golpe. ◆ *vt* acariciar.

stroll [strəʊl] ◆ *n* paseo *m*. ◆ *vi* pasear.

stroller ['strəʊləʳ] *n* Am *(for baby)* sillita *f* (de niño).

strong [strɒŋ] *adj* 1. *(gen)* fuerte. 2. *(material, structure)* sólido(da), resistente. 3. *(feeling, belief)* profundo (da); *(opposition, denial)* firme; *(support)* acérrimo(ma); *(accent)* marcado(da).

4. (*discipline, policy*) estricto(ta). **5.** (*argument*) convincente. **6.** (*in numbers*): **the crowd was 2,000 ~** la multitud constaba de 2.000 personas. **7.** (*good, gifted*) **one's ~ point** el punto fuerte de uno. **8.** (*concentrated*) concentrado(da).

strongbox ['strɒŋbɒks] *n* caja *f* fuerte.

stronghold ['strɒŋhəʊld] *n* fig (*bastion*) bastión *m*, baluarte *m*.

strongly ['strɒŋlɪ] *adv* **1.** (*sturdily*) fuertemente. **2.** (*in degree*) intensamente. **3.** (*fervently*): **to support/oppose sthg ~** apoyar/oponerse a algo totalmente.

strong room *n* cámara *f* acorazada.

strove [strəʊv] *pt* → **strive**.

struck [strʌk] *pt & pp* → **strike**.

structure ['strʌktʃər] *n* **1.** (*arrangement*) estructura *f*. **2.** (*building*) construcción *f*.

struggle ['strʌgl] ◆ *n* **1.** (*great effort*): **~ (for sthg/to do sthg)** lucha *f* (por algo/por hacer algo). **2.** (*fight, tussle*) forcejeo *m*. ◆ *vi* **1.** (*make great effort*): **to ~ (for sthg/to do sthg)** luchar (por algo/por hacer algo). **2.** (*to free o.s.*): **to ~ free** forcejear para soltarse. **3.** (*move with difficulty*): **to ~ with sthg** llevar algo con dificultad.

strum [strʌm] *vt & vi* rasguear.

strung [strʌŋ] *pt & pp* → **string**.

strut [strʌt] ◆ *n* (CONSTR) puntal *m*. ◆ *vi* andar pavoneándose.

stub [stʌb] ◆ *n* **1.** (*of cigarette*) colilla *f*; (*of pencil*) cabo *m*. **2.** (*of ticket*) resguardo *m*; (*of cheque*) matriz *f*. ◆ *vt*: **to ~ one's toe on** darse con el pie en. ▶ **stub out** *vt sep* apagar.

stubble ['stʌbl] *n* **1.** (U) (*in field*) rastrojo *m*. **2.** (*on chin*) barba *f* incipiente OR de tres días.

stubborn ['stʌbən] *adj* (*person*) terco (ca), testarudo(da).

stuck [stʌk] ◆ *pt & pp* → **stick**. ◆ *adj* **1.** (*jammed - lid, window*) atascado(da). **2.** (*unable to progress*) atascado(da). **3.** (*stranded*) colgado(da). **4.** (*in a meeting, at home*) encerrado(da).

stuck-up *adj inf pej* engreído(da).

stud [stʌd] *n* **1.** (*metal decoration*) tachón *m*. **2.** (*earring*) pendiente *m*. **3.** Br (*on boot, shoe*) taco *m*. **4.** (*horse*) semental *m*.

studded ['stʌdɪd] *adj*: **~ (with)** tachonado(da) (con).

student ['stju:dnt] ◆ *n* **1.** (*at college, university*) estudiante *m* y *f*. **2.** (*scholar*) estudioso *m*, -sa *f*. ◆ *comp* estudiantil.

studio ['stju:dɪəʊ] (*pl* **-s**) *n* estudio *m*.

studio flat Br, **studio apartment** Am *n* estudio *m*.

studious ['stju:djəs] *adj* estudioso(sa).

studiously ['stju:djəslɪ] *adv* cuidadosamente.

study ['stʌdɪ] ◆ *n* estudio *m*. ◆ *vt* **1.** (*learn*) estudiar. **2.** (*examine - report, sb's face*) examinar, estudiar. ◆ *vi* estudiar. ▶ **studies** *npl* estudios *mpl*.

stuff [stʌf] ◆ *n* (U) *inf* **1.** (*things, belongings*) cosas *fpl*. **2.** (*substance*): **what's that ~ in your pocket?** ¿qué es eso que llevas en el bolsillo? ◆ *vt* **1.** (*push, put*) meter. **2.** (*fill, cram*): **to ~ sthg (with)** (*box, room*) llenar algo (de); (*pillow, doll*) rellenar algo (de). **3.** (CULIN) rellenar. **4.** *inf* (*with food*): **to ~ o.s. (with** OR **on)** atiborrarse OR hartarse (de).

stuffed [stʌft] *adj* **1.** (*filled, crammed*): **~ with** atestado(da) de. **2.** *inf* (*subj: person - with food*) lleno(na), inflado(da). **3.** (CULIN) relleno(na). **4.** (*preserved - animal*) disecado(da).

stuffing ['stʌfɪŋ] *n* (U) relleno *m*.

stuffy ['stʌfɪ] *adj* **1.** (*atmosphere*) cargado(da); (*room*) mal ventilado(da). **2.** (*old-fashioned*) retrógrado(da), carca.

stumble ['stʌmbl] *vi* (*trip*) tropezar. ▶ **stumble across, stumble on** *vt fus* (*thing*) dar con; (*person*) encontrarse con.

stumbling block ['stʌmblɪŋ-] *n* obstáculo *m*, escollo *m*.

stump [stʌmp] ◆ *n* (*of tree*) tocón *m*; (*of limb*) muñón *m*. ◆ *vt* (*subj: question, problem*) dejar perplejo(ja).

stun [stʌn] *vt lit & fig* aturdir.

stung [stʌŋ] *pt & pp* → **sting**.

stunk [stʌŋk] *pt & pp* → **stink**.

stunning ['stʌnɪŋ] *adj* **1.** (*very beautiful*) imponente. **2.** (*shocking*) pasmoso(sa).

stunt [stʌnt] ◆ *n* **1.** (*for publicity*) truco *m* publicitario. **2.** (CINEMA) escena *f* arriesgada OR peligrosa. ◆ *vt* atrofiar.

stunted ['stʌntɪd] *adj* esmirriado(da).

stunt man *n* especialista *m*, doble *m*.

stupefy ['stju:pɪfaɪ] *vt* **1.** (*tire, bore*) aturdir, atontar. **2.** (*surprise*) dejar estupefacto(ta).

stupendous [stju:'pendəs] *adj inf* (*wonderful*) estupendo(da); (*very large*) enorme.

stupid ['stju:pɪd] *adj* **1.** (*foolish*) estúpido(da). **2.** *inf* (*annoying*) puñetero(ra).

stupidity [stju:'pɪdətɪ] *n* (U) estupidez *f*.

sturdy ['stɜːdɪ] *adj* (*person, shoulders*) fuerte; (*furniture, bridge*) firme, sólido (da).

stutter ['stʌtər] *vi* tartamudear.

sty [staɪ] n (pigsty) pocilga f.
stye [staɪ] n orzuelo m.
style [staɪl] ◆ n 1. (characteristic manner) estilo m. 2. (U) (smartness, elegance) clase f. 3. (design) modelo m. ◆ vt (hair) peinar.
stylish ['staɪlɪʃ] adj elegante, con estilo.
stylist ['staɪlɪst] n (hairdresser) peluquero m, -ra f.
stylus ['staɪləs] (pl -es) n (on record player) aguja f.
suave [swɑːv] adj (well-mannered) afable, amable; (obsequious) zalamero(ra).
sub [sʌb] n inf (SPORT) (abbr of substitute) reserva m y f.
subconscious [,sʌb'kɒnʃəs] adj subconsciente.
subcontract [,sʌbkən'trækt] vt subcontratar.
subdivide [,sʌbdɪ'vaɪd] vt subdividir.
subdue [səb'djuː] vt 1. (enemy, nation) sojuzgar. 2. (feelings) contener.
subdued [səb'djuːd] adj 1. (person) apagado(da). 2. (colour, light) tenue.
subject [adj, n & prep 'sʌbdʒɪkt, vt səb-'dʒekt] ◆ adj (affected): ~ to (taxes, changes, law) sujeto(ta) a; (illness) proclive a. ◆ n 1. (topic) tema m. 2. (GRAMM) sujeto m. 3. (SCH & UNIV) asignatura f. 4. (citizen) súbdito m, -ta f. ◆ vt 1. (bring under control) someter, dominar. 2. (force to experience): to ~ sb to sthg someter a alguien a algo. ▶ subject to prep dependiendo de.
subjective [səb'dʒektɪv] adj subjetivo (va).
subject matter ['sʌbdʒekt-] n (U) tema m, contenido m.
subjunctive [səb'dʒʌŋktɪv] n (GRAMM): ~ (mood) (modo m) subjuntivo m.
sublet [,sʌb'let] (pt & pp sublet) vt & vi subarrendar.
sublime [sə'blaɪm] adj (wonderful) sublime.
submachine gun [,sʌbmə'ʃiːn-] n metralleta f.
submarine [,sʌbmə'riːn] n submarino m.
submerge [səb'mɜːdʒ] ◆ vt 1. (in water) sumergir. 2. fig (in activity): to ~ o.s. in sthg dedicarse de lleno a algo. ◆ vi sumergirse.
submission [səb'mɪʃn] n 1. (capitulation) sumisión f. 2. (presentation) presentación f.
submissive [səb'mɪsɪv] adj sumiso (sa).
submit [səb'mɪt] ◆ vt presentar. ◆ vi:

to ~ (to sb) rendirse (a alguien); to ~ (to sthg) someterse (a algo).
subnormal [,sʌb'nɔːml] adj subnormal.
subordinate [sə'bɔːdɪnət] ◆ adj fml (less important): ~ (to) subordinado(da) (a). ◆ n subordinado m, -da f.
subpoena [sə'piːnə] (JUR) ◆ n citación f. ◆ vt citar.
subscribe [səb'skraɪb] vi 1. (to magazine, newspaper): to ~ (to) suscribirse (a). 2. (to belief): to ~ to estar de acuerdo con.
subscriber [səb'skraɪbər] n 1. (to magazine, newspaper) suscriptor m, -ra f. 2. (to service) abonado m, -da f.
subscription [səb'skrɪpʃn] n (to magazine) suscripción f; (to service) abono m; (to society, club) cuota f.
subsequent ['sʌbsɪkwənt] adj subsiguiente, posterior.
subsequently ['sʌbsɪkwəntlɪ] adv posteriormente.
subservient [səb'sɜːvjənt] adj (servile): ~ (to sb) servil (ante alguien).
subside [səb'saɪd] vi 1. (anger) apaciguarse; (pain) calmarse; (grief) pasarse; (storm, wind) amainar. 2. (noise) apagarse. 3. (river) bajar, descender; (building, ground) hundirse.
subsidence [səb'saɪdns, 'sʌbsɪdns] n (CONSTR) hundimiento m.
subsidiary [səb'sɪdjərɪ] ◆ adj secundario(ria). ◆ n: ~ (company) filial f.
subsidize, -ise ['sʌbsɪdaɪz] vt subvencionar.
subsidy ['sʌbsɪdɪ] n subvención f.
substance ['sʌbstəns] n 1. (gen) sustancia f. 2. (essence) esencia f.
substantial [səb'stænʃl] adj 1. (large, considerable) sustancial, considerable; (meal) abundante. 2. (solid) sólido(da).
substantially [səb'stænʃəlɪ] adv 1. (quite a lot) sustancialmente, considerablemente. 2. (fundamentally) esencialmente; (for the most part) en gran parte.
substantiate [səb'stænʃɪeɪt] vt fml justificar.
substitute ['sʌbstɪtjuːt] ◆ n 1. (replacement): ~ (for) sustituto m, -ta f (de). 2. (SPORT) suplente m y f, reserva m y f. ◆ vt: to ~ sthg/sb for sustituir algo/a alguien por.
subtitle ['sʌb,taɪtl] n subtítulo m.
subtle ['sʌtl] adj 1. (gen) sutil; (taste, smell) delicado(da). 2. (plan, behaviour) ingenioso(sa).

subtlety ['sʌtltɪ] *n* **1.** (*gen*) sutileza *f*; (*of taste, smell*) delicadeza *f*. **2.** (*of plan, behaviour*) ingenio *m*.

subtract [səb'trækt] *vt*: **to ~ sthg (from)** restar algo (de).

subtraction [səb'trækʃn] *n* resta *f*.

suburb ['sʌbɜːb] *n* barrio *m* residencial. ▶ **suburbs** *npl*: **the ~s** las afueras.

suburban [sə'bɜːbn] *adj* **1.** (*of suburbs*) de los barrios residenciales. **2.** *pej* (*boring*) convencional, burgués(esa).

suburbia [sə'bɜːbɪə] *n* (U) barrios *mpl* residenciales.

subversive [səb'vɜːsɪv] ◆ *adj* subversivo(va). ◆ *n* subversivo *m*, -va *f*.

subway ['sʌbweɪ] *n* **1.** Br (*underground walkway*) paso *m* subterráneo. **2.** Am (*underground railway*) metro *m*.

succeed [sək'siːd] ◆ *vt* suceder a. ◆ *vi* **1.** (*gen*) tener éxito. **2.** (*achieve desired result*): **to ~ in sthg/in doing sthg** conseguir algo/hacer algo. **3.** (*plan, tactic*) salir bien. **4.** (*go far in life*) triunfar.

succeeding [sək'siːdɪŋ] *adj fml* sucesivo(va).

success [sək'ses] *n* **1.** (*gen*) éxito *m*; **to be a ~** tener éxito. **2.** (*in career, life*) triunfo *m*.

successful [sək'sesfʊl] *adj* (*gen*) de éxito; (*attempt*) logrado(da); (*politician*) popular.

succession [sək'seʃn] *n* sucesión *f*.

successive [sək'sesɪv] *adj* sucesivo (va).

succinct [sək'sɪŋkt] *adj* sucinto(ta).

succumb [sə'kʌm] *vi*: **to ~ (to)** sucumbir (a).

such [sʌtʃ] ◆ *adj* **1.** (*like that*) semejante, tal; **~ stupidity** tal OR semejante estupidez. **2.** (*like this*): **have you got ~ a thing as a tin opener?** ¿tendrías acaso un abrelatas?; **~ words as 'duty' and 'honour'** palabras (tales) como 'deber' y 'honour'. **3.** (*whatever*): **I've spent ~ money as I had** he gastado el poco dinero que tenía. **4.** (*so great, so serious*): **there are ~ differences that ...** las diferencias son tales que ...; **~ ... that** tal ... que. ◆ *adv* tan; **~ a lot of books** tantos libros; **~ nice people** una gente tan amable; **~ a good car** un coche tan bueno; **~ a long time** tanto tiempo. ◆ *pron*: **and ~ (like)** y otros similares OR por el estilo. ▶ **as ~** *pron* propiamente dicho(cha). ▶ **such and such** *adj*: **at ~ and ~ a time** a tal hora.

suck [sʌk] *vt* **1.** (*by mouth*) chupar. **2.** (*subj: machine*) aspirar.

sucker ['sʌkə'] *n* **1.** (*of animal*) ventosa *f*. **2.** *inf* (*gullible person*) primo *m*, -ma *f*, ingenuo *m*, -nua *f*.

suction ['sʌkʃn] *n* (*gen*) succión *f*; (*by machine*) aspiración *f*.

Sudan [suː'dɑːn] *n* (el) Sudán.

sudden ['sʌdn] *adj* (*quick*) repentino (na); (*unforeseen*) inesperado(da); **all of a ~** de repente.

suddenly ['sʌdnlɪ] *adv* de repente.

suds [sʌdz] *npl* espuma *f* del jabón.

sue [suː] *vt*: **to ~ sb (for)** demandar a alguien (por).

suede [sweɪd] *n* (*for jacket, shoes*) ante *m*, gamuza *f esp Amer*; (*for gloves*) cabritilla *f*.

suet ['suɪt] *n* sebo *m*.

suffer ['sʌfə'] ◆ *vt* sufrir. ◆ *vi* **1.** (*gen*) sufrir. **2.** (*experience negative effects*) salir perjudicado(da). **3.** (MED): **to ~ from** (*illness*) sufrir OR padecer de.

sufferer ['sʌfrə'] *n* enfermo *m*, -ma *f*.

suffering ['sʌfrɪŋ] *n* (*gen*) sufrimiento *m*; (*pain*) dolor *m*.

suffice [sə'faɪs] *vi fml* ser suficiente, bastar.

sufficient [sə'fɪʃnt] *adj fml* suficiente, bastante.

sufficiently [sə'fɪʃntlɪ] *adv fml* suficientemente, bastante.

suffocate ['sʌfəkeɪt] ◆ *vt* asfixiar, ahogar. ◆ *vi* asfixiarse, ahogarse.

suffrage ['sʌfrɪdʒ] *n* sufragio *m*.

suffuse [sə'fjuːz] *vt*: **~d with** bañado de.

sugar ['ʃʊgə'] ◆ *n* azúcar *m o f*. ◆ *vt* echar azúcar a.

sugar beet *n* remolacha *f* (azucarera).

sugarcane ['ʃʊgəkeɪn] *n* (U) caña *f* de azúcar.

sugary ['ʃʊgərɪ] *adj* (*high in sugar*) azucarado(da), dulce.

suggest [sə'dʒest] *vt* **1.** (*propose*) sugerir; **to ~ that sb do sthg** sugerir que alguien haga algo. **2.** (*imply*) insinuar.

suggestion [sə'dʒestʃn] *n* **1.** (*proposal*) sugerencia *f*. **2.** (*implication*) insinuación *f*.

suggestive [sə'dʒestɪv] *adj* (*implying sexual connotation*) provocativo(va), insinuante.

suicide ['suːɪsaɪd] *n lit & fig* suicidio *m*; **to commit ~** suicidarse.

suit [suːt] ◆ *n* **1.** (*clothes - for men*) traje *m*; (*- for women*) traje de chaqueta. **2.** (*in cards*) palo *m*. **3.** (JUR) pleito *m*. ◆ *vt* **1.** (*look attractive on*) favorecer, sentar bien a. **2.** (*be convenient or agreeable to*) convenir. **3.** (*be appropriate to*) ser ade-

cuado(da) para; **that job ~s you perfectly** ese trabajo te va de perlas.
suitable ['su:təbl] *adj* adecuado(da);
the most ~ person la persona más indicada.
suitably ['su:təblɪ] *adv* adecuada-
mente.
suitcase ['su:tkeɪs] *n* maleta *f*, petaca *f*
Amer.
suite [swi:t] *n* **1.** (*of rooms*) suite *f*. **2.** (*of
furniture*) juego *m*; **dining-room ~** come-
dor *m*.
suited ['su:tɪd] *adj*: **~ to/for** adecuado
(da) para; **the couple are ideally ~** for-
man una pareja perfecta.
suitor ['su:tər] *n dated* pretendiente *m*.
sulfur *Am* = **sulphur**.
sulk [sʌlk] *vi* estar de mal humor.
sulky ['sʌlkɪ] *adj* malhumorado(da).
sullen ['sʌlən] *adj* hosco(ca), antipático
(ca).
sulphur *Br*, **sulfur** *Am* ['sʌlfər] *n*
azufre *m*.
sultana [səl'tɑ:nə] *n Br* (*dried grape*)
pasa *f* de Esmirna.
sultry ['sʌltrɪ] *adj* (*hot*) bochornoso(sa),
sofocante.
sum [sʌm] *n* suma *f*. ▶ **sum up** *vt sep &
vi* (*summarize*) resumir.
summarize, -ise ['sʌməraɪz] *vt & vi*
resumir.
summary ['sʌmərɪ] *n* resumen *m*.
summer ['sʌmər] ◆ *n* verano *m*.
◆ *comp* de verano.
summerhouse ['sʌməhaus, *pl* -hauzɪz]
n cenador *m*.
summer school *n* escuela *f* de verano.
summertime ['sʌmətaɪm] *n*: **(the) ~**
(el) verano.
summit ['sʌmɪt] *n* **1.** (*mountain-top*)
cima *f*, cumbre *f*. **2.** (*meeting*) cumbre *f*.
summon ['sʌmən] *vt* (*person*) llamar;
(*meeting*) convocar. ▶ **summon up** *vt
sep* (*courage*) armarse de.
summons ['sʌmənz] (*pl* **summonses**)
(JUR) ◆ *n* citación *f*. ◆ *vt* citar.
sump [sʌmp] *n* cárter *m*.
sumptuous ['sʌmptʃuəs] *adj* suntuoso
(sa).
sun [sʌn] *n* sol *m*; **in the ~** al sol.
sunbathe ['sʌnbeɪð] *vi* tomar el sol.
sunbed ['sʌnbed] *n* camilla *f* de rayos
ultravioletas.
sunburn ['sʌnbɜ:n] *n* (U) quemadura *f*
de sol.
sunburned ['sʌnbɜ:nd], **sunburnt**
['sʌnbɜ:nt] *adj* quemado(da) por el sol.

Sunday ['sʌndɪ] *n* domingo *m*; **~ lunch**
*comida del domingo que generalmente consiste
en rosbif, patatas asadas etc*; *see also*
Saturday.
Sunday school *n* catequesis *f inv.*
sundial ['sʌndaɪəl] *n* reloj *m* de sol.
sundown ['sʌndaun] *n* anochecer *m*.
sundries ['sʌndrɪz] *npl fml* (*gen*) artículos *mpl* diversos; (FIN) gastos *mpl* diversos.
sundry ['sʌndrɪ] *adj fml* diversos(sas);
all and ~ todos sin excepción.
sunflower ['sʌn,flauər] *n* girasol *m*.
sung [sʌŋ] *pp* → **sing**.
sunglasses ['sʌn,glɑ:sɪz] *npl* gafas *fpl*
de sol.
sunk [sʌŋk] *pp* → **sink**.
sunlight ['sʌnlaɪt] *n* luz *f* del sol.
sunlit ['sʌnlɪt] *adj* iluminado(da) por el
sol.
sunny ['sʌnɪ] *adj* **1.** (*day*) de sol; (*room*)
soleado(da). **2.** (*cheerful*) alegre.
sunrise ['sʌnraɪz] *n* **1.** (U) (*time of day*)
amanecer *m*. **2.** (*event*) salida *f* del sol.
sunroof ['sʌnru:f] *n* (*on car*) techo *m*
corredizo; (*on building*) azotea *f*.
sunset ['sʌnset] *n* **1.** (U) (*time of day*)
anochecer *m*. **2.** (*event*) puesta *f* del sol.
sunshade ['sʌnʃeɪd] *n* sombrilla *f*.
sunshine ['sʌnʃaɪn] *n* (luz *f* del) sol *m*.
sunstroke ['sʌnstrəuk] *n* (U) insolación *f*.
suntan ['sʌntæn] ◆ *n* bronceado *m*.
◆ *comp* bronceador(ra).
suntrap ['sʌntræp] *n* lugar *m* muy
soleado.
super ['su:pər] *adj* **1.** *inf* (*wonderful*)
estupendo(da), fenomenal. **2.** (*better
than normal - size etc*) superior.
superannuation ['su:pə,rænju'eɪʃn] *n*
(U) jubilación *f*, pensión *f*.
superb [su:'pɜ:b] *adj* excelente, mag-
nífico(ca).
supercilious [,su:pə'sɪlɪəs] *adj* altane-
ro(ra).
superficial [,su:pə'fɪʃl] *adj* superficial.
superfluous [su:'pɜ:fluəs] *adj* super-
fluo(flua).
superhuman [,su:pə'hju:mən] *adj*
sobrehumano(na).
superimpose [,su:pərɪm'pəuz] *vt*: **to ~
sthg on** superponer OR sobreponer algo
a.
superintendent [,su:pərɪn'tendənt] *n*
1. *Br* (*of police*) = subjefe *m*, -fa *f* (de
policía). **2.** *fml* (*of department*) supervisor
m, -ra *f*.
superior [su:'pɪərɪər] ◆ *adj* **1.** (*gen*): **~**

(to) superior (a). **2.** pej (arrogant) altanero(ra), arrogante. ◆ n superior m y f.

superlative [suːˈpɜːlətɪv] ◆ adj (of the highest quality) supremo(ma). ◆ n (GRAMM) superlativo m.

supermarket [ˈsuːpəˌmɑːkɪt] n supermercado m.

supernatural [ˌsuːpəˈnætʃrəl] adj sobrenatural.

superpower [ˈsuːpəˌpaʊəʳ] n superpotencia f.

supersede [ˌsuːpəˈsiːd] vt suplantar.

supersonic [ˌsuːpəˈsɒnɪk] adj supersónico(ca).

superstitious [ˌsuːpəˈstɪʃəs] adj supersticioso(sa).

superstore [ˈsuːpəstɔːʳ] n hipermercado m.

supertanker [ˈsuːpəˌtæŋkəʳ] n superpetrolero m.

supervise [ˈsuːpəvaɪz] vt (person) vigilar; (activity) supervisar.

supervisor [ˈsuːpəvaɪzəʳ] n (gen) supervisor m, -ra f; (of thesis) director m, -ra f.

supper [ˈsʌpəʳ] n (evening meal) cena f; **to have ~** cenar.

supple [ˈsʌpl] adj flexible.

supplement [n ˈsʌplɪmənt, vb ˈsʌplɪment] ◆ n suplemento m. ◆ vt complementar.

supplementary [ˌsʌplɪˈmentərɪ] adj suplementario(ria).

supplementary benefit n Br subsidio m social.

supplier [səˈplaɪəʳ] n proveedor m, -ra f.

supply [səˈplaɪ] ◆ n **1.** (gen) suministro m; (of jokes etc) surtido m. **2.** (U) (ECON) oferta f. ◆ vt: **to ~ sthg (to)** suministrar OR proveer algo (a); **to ~ sb (with)** proveer a alguien (de). ▶ **supplies** npl (MIL) pertrechos mpl; (food) provisiones fpl; (for office etc) material m.

support [səˈpɔːt] ◆ n **1.** (U) (physical, moral, emotional) apoyo m. **2.** (U) (financial) ayuda f. **3.** (U) (intellectual) respaldo m. **4.** (TECH) soporte m. ◆ vt **1.** (physically) sostener. **2.** (emotionally, morally, intellectually) apoyar. **3.** (financially - oneself, one's family) mantener; (- company, organization) financiar. **4.** (SPORT) seguir.

supporter [səˈpɔːtəʳ] n **1.** (gen) partidario m, -ria f. **2.** (SPORT) hincha m y f.

suppose [səˈpəʊz] ◆ vt suponer. ◆ vi suponer; **I ~ (so)** supongo (que sí); **I ~ not** supongo que no.

supposed [səˈpəʊzd] adj **1.** (doubtful)

supuesto(ta). **2.** (intended): **he was ~ to be here at eight** debería haber estado aquí a las ocho. **3.** (reputed): **it's ~ to be very good** se supone OR se dice que es muy bueno.

supposedly [səˈpəʊzɪdlɪ] adv según cabe suponer.

supposing [səˈpəʊzɪŋ] conj: **~ your father found out?** ¿y si se entera tu padre?

suppress [səˈpres] vt **1.** (uprising) reprimir. **2.** (emotions) contener.

supreme [suˈpriːm] adj supremo(ma).

Supreme Court n: **the ~** (in US) el Tribunal Supremo (de los Estados Unidos).

surcharge [ˈsɜːtʃɑːdʒ] n: **~ (on)** recargo m (en).

sure [ʃʊəʳ] ◆ adj **1.** (gen) seguro(ra). **2.** (certain - of outcome): **to be ~ of** poder estar seguro(ra) de; **make ~ (that) you do it** asegúrate de que lo haces. **3.** (confident): **to be ~ of o.s.** estar seguro(ra) de uno mismo. ◆ adv **1.** inf (yes) por supuesto, pues claro. **2.** Am (really) realmente. ▶ **for sure** adv a ciencia cierta. ▶ **sure enough** adv efectivamente.

surely [ˈʃʊəlɪ] adv sin duda; **~ you remember him?** ¡no me digas que no te acuerdas de él!

surety [ˈʃʊərətɪ] n (U) fianza f.

surf [sɜːf] n espuma f (de las olas).

surface [ˈsɜːfɪs] ◆ n **1.** (gen) superficie f. **2.** fig (immediately visible part): **on the ~** a primera vista. ◆ vi (gen) salir a la superficie.

surface mail n correo m por vía terrestre/marítima.

surfboard [ˈsɜːfbɔːd] n plancha f OR tabla f de surf.

surfeit [ˈsɜːfɪt] n fml exceso m.

surfing [ˈsɜːfɪŋ] n surf m.

surge [sɜːdʒ] ◆ n **1.** (of waves, people) oleada f; (of electricity) sobrecarga f momentánea. **2.** (of emotion) arrebato m. **3.** (of interest, support, sales) aumento m súbito. ◆ vi (people, vehicles) avanzar en masa; (sea) encresparse.

surgeon [ˈsɜːdʒən] n cirujano m, -na f.

surgery [ˈsɜːdʒərɪ] n **1.** (U) (MED) (performing operations) cirugía f. **2.** Br (MED) (place) consultorio m; (consulting period) consulta f.

surgical [ˈsɜːdʒɪkl] adj (gen) quirúrgico(ca).

surgical spirit n Br alcohol m de 90°.

surly ['sɜːlɪ] adj hosco(ca), malhumorado(da).

surmount [sɜː'maunt] vt (overcome) superar, vencer.

surname ['sɜːneɪm] n apellido m.

surpass [sə'pɑːs] vt fml (exceed) superar, sobrepasar.

surplus ['sɜːpləs] ◆ adj excedente, sobrante. ◆ n (gen) excedente m, sobrante m; (in budget) superávit m.

surprise [sə'praɪz] ◆ n sorpresa f. ◆ vt sorprender.

surprised [sə'praɪzd] adj (person, expression) asombrado(da).

surprising [sə'praɪzɪŋ] adj sorprendente.

surrender [sə'rendər] ◆ n rendición f. ◆ vi lit & fig: to ~ (to) rendirse OR entregarse (a).

surreptitious [ˌsʌrəp'tɪʃəs] adj subrepticio(cia).

surrogate ['sʌrəgeɪt] ◆ adj sustitutorio(ria). ◆ n sustituto m, -ta f.

surrogate mother n madre f de alquiler.

surround [sə'raund] vt lit & fig rodear.

surrounding [sə'raundɪŋ] adj 1. (area, countryside) circundante. 2. (controversy, debate) relacionado(da).

surroundings [sə'raundɪŋz] npl (physical) alrededores mpl; (social) entorno m.

surveillance [sɜː'veɪləns] n vigilancia f.

survey [n 'sɜːveɪ, vb sə'veɪ] ◆ n 1. (of public opinion, population) encuesta f. 2. (of land) medición f; (of building) inspección f. ◆ vt 1. (contemplate) contemplar. 2. (investigate statistically) hacer un estudio de. 3. (examine - land) medir; (- building) inspeccionar.

surveyor [sə'veɪər] n (of property) perito m tasador de la propiedad; (of land) agrimensor m, -ra f.

survival [sə'vaɪvl] n (gen) supervivencia f.

survive [sə'vaɪv] ◆ vt sobrevivir a. ◆ vi (person) sobrevivir; (custom, project) perdurar.

survivor [sə'vaɪvər] n (person who escapes death) superviviente m y f.

susceptible [sə'septəbl] adj 1. (to pressure, flattery): ~ (to) sensible (a). 2. (MED): ~ (to) propenso(sa) (a).

suspect [adj & n 'sʌspekt, vb sə'spekt] ◆ adj sospechoso(sa). ◆ n sospechoso m, -sa f. ◆ vt 1. (distrust) sospechar. 2. (think likely) imaginar. 3. (consider guilty): to ~ sb (of) considerar a alguien sospechoso(sa) (de).

suspend [sə'spend] vt (gen) suspender; (payments, work) interrumpir; (schoolchild) expulsar temporalmente.

suspended sentence [sə'spendɪd-] n condena f condicional.

suspender belt [sə'spendər-] n Br liguero m.

suspenders [sə'spendəz] npl 1. Br (for stockings) ligas fpl. 2. Am (for trousers) tirantes mpl.

suspense [sə'spens] n (gen) incertidumbre f; (CINEMA) suspense m.

suspension [sə'spenʃn] n 1. (gen & AUT) suspensión f. 2. (from job, school) expulsión f temporal.

suspension bridge n puente m colgante.

suspicion [sə'spɪʃn] n 1. (gen) sospecha f; (distrust) recelo m. 2. (small amount) pizca f.

suspicious [sə'spɪʃəs] adj 1. (having suspicions) receloso(sa). 2. (causing suspicion) sospechoso(sa).

sustain [sə'steɪn] vt 1. (gen) sostener. 2. fml (injury, damage) sufrir.

sustenance ['sʌstɪnəns] n (U) fml sustento m.

SW (abbr of short wave) OC.

swab [swɒb] n (trozo m de) algodón m.

swagger ['swægər] vi pavonearse.

Swahili [swɑː'hiːlɪ] n (language) suahili m.

swallow ['swɒləu] ◆ n (bird) golondrina f. ◆ vt (food, drink) tragar.

swam [swæm] pt → swim.

swamp [swɒmp] ◆ n pantano m, ciénaga f. ◆ vt 1. (flood - boat) hundir; (- land) inundar. 2. (overwhelm): to ~ sthg (with) (office) inundar algo (de); to ~ sb (with) agobiar a alguien (con).

swan [swɒn] n cisne m.

swap [swɒp] vt 1. (of one thing): to ~ sthg (for/with) cambiar algo (por/con). 2. (of two things): to ~ sthg (over OR round) (hats, chairs) cambiarse algo. 3. fig (stories, experiences) intercambiar.

swarm [swɔːm] ◆ n (of bees) enjambre m; fig (of people) multitud f. ◆ vi 1. fig (people) ir en tropel. 2. fig (place): to be ~ing (with) estar abarrotado(da) (de).

swarthy ['swɔːðɪ] adj moreno(na).

swastika ['swɒstɪkə] n esvástica f, cruz f gamada.

swat [swɒt] vt aplastar.

sway [sweɪ] ◆ vt (influence) convencer. ◆ vi balancearse.

swear [sweər] (pt **swore**, pp **sworn**)

◆ *vt*: **to ~ (to do sthg)** jurar (hacer algo).
◆ *vi* **1.** (*state emphatically*) jurar. **2.** (*use swearwords*) decir tacos, jurar.

swearword ['sweəwɜ:d] *n* palabrota *f*.

sweat [swet] ◆ *n* (*perspiration*) sudor *m*.
◆ *vi* (*perspire*) sudar.

sweater ['swetər] *n* suéter *m*, jersey *m*.

sweatshirt ['swetʃɜ:t] *n* sudadera *f*.

sweaty ['sweti] *adj* (*skin*) sudoroso (sa); (*clothes*) sudado(da).

swede [swi:d] *n* Br nabo *m* sueco.

Swede [swi:d] *n* sueco *m*, -ca *f*.

Sweden ['swi:dn] *n* Suecia.

Swedish ['swi:dɪʃ] ◆ *adj* sueco(ca).
◆ *n* (*language*) sueco *m*. ◆ *npl*: **the ~** los suecos.

sweep [swi:p] (*pt* & *pp* **swept**) ◆ *n* **1.** (*movement - of broom*) barrido *m*; (- *of arm, hand*) movimiento *m* OR gesto *m* amplio. **2.** (*chimney sweep*) deshollinador *m*, -ra *f*. ◆ *vt* **1.** (*with brush*) barrer. **2.** (*with light-beam*) rastrear; (*with eyes*) recorrer. ◆ *vi* **1.** (*wind, rain*): **to ~ over** OR **across sthg** azotar algo. **2.** (*person*): **to ~ past** pasar como un rayo. ▶ **sweep away** *vt sep* (*destroy*) destruir completamente. ▶ **sweep up** *vt sep* & *vi* barrer.

sweeping ['swi:pɪŋ] *adj* **1.** (*effect, change*) radical. **2.** (*statement*) demasiado general. **3.** (*curve*) amplio(plia).

sweet [swi:t] ◆ *adj* **1.** (*gen*) dulce; (*sugary*) azucarado(da). **2.** (*feelings*) placentero(ra). **3.** (*smell - of flowers, air*) fragante, perfumado(da). **4.** (*sound*) melodioso(sa). **5.** (*character, person*) amable.
◆ *n* Br **1.** (*candy*) caramelo *m*, golosina *f*. **2.** (*dessert*) postre *m*.

sweet corn *n* maíz *m*.

sweeten ['swi:tn] *vt* endulzar.

sweetheart ['swi:thɑ:t] *n* **1.** (*term of endearment*) cariño *m*. **2.** (*boyfriend or girlfriend*) amor *m*, novio *m*, -via *f*.

sweetness ['swi:tnɪs] *n* **1.** (*gen*) dulzura *f*. **2.** (*of taste*) dulzor *m*.

sweet pea *n* guisante *m* de olor.

swell [swel] (*pp* **swollen** OR **-ed**) ◆ *vi* **1.** (*become larger*) hincharse. **2.** (*population, sound*) aumentar. ◆ *vt* (*numbers etc*) aumentar. ◆ *n* (*of sea*) oleaje *m*. ◆ *adj* Am *inf* estupendo(da).

swelling ['swelɪŋ] *n* hinchazón *f*.

sweltering ['sweltərɪŋ] *adj* **1.** (*weather*) abrasador(ra), sofocante. **2.** (*person*) achicharrado(da).

swept [swept] *pt* & *pp* → **sweep**.

swerve [swɜ:v] *vi* virar bruscamente.

swift [swift] ◆ *adj* **1.** (*fast*) rápido(da). **2.** (*prompt*) pronto(ta). ◆ *n* (*bird*) vencejo *m*.

swig [swig] *n inf* trago *m*.

swill [swil] ◆ *n* (*pig food*) bazofia *f*. ◆ *vt* Br (*wash*) enjuagar.

swim [swim] (*pt* **swam**, *pp* **swum**) ◆ *n* baño *m*; **to go for a ~** ir a nadar OR a darse un baño. ◆ *vi* **1.** (*in water*) nadar. **2.** (*head, room*) dar vueltas.

swimmer ['swimər] *n* nadador *m*, -ra *f*.

swimming ['swimɪŋ] *n* natación *f*.

swimming cap *n* gorro *m* de baño.

swimming costume *n* Br bañador *m*, traje *m* de baño.

swimming pool *n* piscina *f*, alberca *f* Amer.

swimming trunks *npl* bañador *m*.

swimsuit ['swimsu:t] *n* bañador *m*, traje *m* de baño.

swindle ['swindl] ◆ *n* estafa *f*, timo *m*. ◆ *vt* estafar, timar; **to ~ sb out of sthg** estafar a alguien algo.

swine [swain] *n inf pej* (*person*) cerdo *m*, -da *f*, canalla *m* y *f*.

swing [swiŋ] (*pt* & *pp* **swung**) ◆ *n* **1.** (*child's toy*) columpio *m*. **2.** (*change*) viraje *m*. **3.** (*sway*) meneo *m*, balanceo *m*. **4.** *phr*: **to be in full ~** estar en plena marcha. ◆ *vt* **1.** (*move back and forth*) balancear. **2.** (*move in a curve - car etc*) hacer virar bruscamente. ◆ *vi* **1.** (*move back and forth*) balancearse, oscilar. **2.** (*move in a curve*) girar. **3.** (*turn*): **to ~ (round)** volverse, girarse. **4.** (*change*) virar, cambiar.

swing bridge *n* puente *m* giratorio.

swing door *n* puerta *f* oscilante.

swingeing ['swindʒɪŋ] *adj* severo(ra).

swipe [swaip] ◆ *vt inf* (*steal*) birlar. ◆ *vi*: **to ~ at sthg** intentar golpear algo.

swirl [swɜ:l] *vi* arremolinarse.

swish [swiʃ] *vt* (*tail*) agitar, menear.

Swiss [swis] ◆ *adj* suizo(za). ◆ *n* (*person*) suizo *m*, -za *f*. ◆ *npl*: **the ~** los suizos.

switch [switʃ] ◆ *n* **1.** (*control device*) interruptor *m*. **2.** (*change*) cambio *m* completo, viraje *m*. ◆ *vt* **1.** (*change*) cambiar de. **2.** (*swap*) intercambiar. ▶ **switch off** *vt sep* (*light, radio etc*) apagar; (*engine*) parar. ▶ **switch on** *vt sep* (*light, radio etc*) encender; (*engine*) poner en marcha.

switchboard ['switʃbɔ:d] *n* centralita *f*, conmutador *m* Amer.

Switzerland ['switsələnd] *n* Suiza.

swivel ['swivl] ◆ *vt* hacer girar. ◆ *vi* girar.

swivel chair n silla f giratoria.
swollen ['swəʊln] ◆ pp → swell. ◆ adj
(ankle, leg etc) hinchado(da); (river) creci-
do(da).
swoop [swuːp] ◆ n (raid) redada f. ◆ vi
1. (move downwards) caer en picado.
2. (move quickly) atacar por sorpresa.
swop [swɒp] = swap.
sword [sɔːd] n espada f.
swordfish ['sɔːdfɪʃ] (pl inv OR -es) n
pez m espada.
swore [swɔːr] pt → swear.
sworn [swɔːn] ◆ pp → swear. ◆ adj
(JUR) jurado(da).
swot [swɒt] Br inf ◆ n pej empollón m,
-ona f. ◆ vi: to ~ (for) empollar (para).
swum [swʌm] pp → swim.
swung [swʌŋ] pt & pp → swing.
sycamore ['sɪkəmɔːr] n sicomoro m.
syllable ['sɪləbl] n sílaba f.
syllabus ['sɪləbəs] (pl -buses OR -bi
[-baɪ]) n programa m (de estudios).
symbol ['sɪmbl] n símbolo m.
symbolize, -ise ['sɪmbəlaɪz] vt simbolizar.
symmetry ['sɪmətrɪ] n simetría f.
sympathetic [ˌsɪmpə'θetɪk] adj
1. (understanding) comprensivo(va).
2. (willing to support) favorable; ~ to bien
dispuesto(ta) hacia.
sympathize, -ise ['sɪmpəθaɪz] vi
1. (feel sorry): to ~ (with) compadecerse
(de). 2. (understand): to ~ (with sthg)
comprender (algo). 3. (support): to ~
with sthg apoyar algo.
sympathizer, -iser ['sɪmpəθaɪzər] n
simpatizante m y f.
sympathy ['sɪmpəθɪ] n 1. (understanding): ~ (for) comprensión f (hacia); (compassion) compasión f (por). 2. (agreement)
solidaridad f. ► sympathies npl (to
bereaved person) pésame m.
symphony ['sɪmfənɪ] n sinfonía f.
symposium [sɪm'pəʊzjəm] (pl -siums
OR -sia [-zjə]) n fml simposio m.
symptom ['sɪmptəm] n lit & fig síntoma
m.
synagogue ['sɪnəgɒg] n sinagoga f.
syndicate ['sɪndɪkət] n sindicato m.
syndrome ['sɪndrəʊm] n síndrome m.
synonym ['sɪnənɪm] n: ~ (for OR of)
sinónimo m (de).
synopsis [sɪ'nɒpsɪs] (pl -ses [-siːz]) n
sinopsis f inv.
syntax ['sɪntæks] n sintaxis f inv.
synthesis ['sɪnθəsɪs] (pl -ses [-siːz]) n
síntesis f inv.
synthetic [sɪn'θetɪk] adj 1. (man-made)

sintético(ca). 2. pej (insincere) artificial.
syphilis ['sɪfɪlɪs] n sífilis f inv.
syphon ['saɪfn] = siphon.
Syria ['sɪrɪə] n Siria.
syringe [sɪ'rɪndʒ] n jeringa f, jeringuilla f.
syrup ['sɪrəp] n (U) 1. (CULIN) almíbar
m. 2. (MED) jarabe m.
system ['sɪstəm] n (gen) sistema m; (of
central heating etc) instalación f.
systematic [ˌsɪstə'mætɪk] adj sis-
temático(ca).
system disk n (COMPUT) disco m del
sistema.
systems analyst ['sɪstəmz-] n (COM-
PUT) analista m y f de sistemas.

T

t (pl t's OR ts), **T** (pl T's OR Ts) [tiː] n (letter)
t f, T f.
ta [tɑː] excl Br inf ¡gracias!
tab [tæb] n 1. (of cloth) etiqueta f. 2. (of
metal, card etc) lengüeta f. 3. Am (bill)
cuenta f. 4. phr: to keep ~s on sb vigilar
de cerca a alguien.
tabby ['tæbɪ] n: ~ (cat) gato m atigrado.
table ['teɪbl] ◆ n 1. (piece of furniture)
mesa f; (small) mesilla f. 2. (diagram)
tabla f. ◆ vt Br (propose) presentar.
tablecloth ['teɪblklɒθ] n mantel m.
table lamp n lámpara f de mesa.
tablemat ['teɪblmæt] n salvamanteles
m inv.
tablespoon ['teɪblspuːn] n 1. (spoon)
cuchara f grande (para servir). 2. (spoonful) cucharada f (grande).
tablet ['tæblɪt] n 1. (pill, piece of soap)
pastilla f. 2. (piece of stone) lápida f.
table tennis n tenis m de mesa.
table wine n vino m de mesa.
tabloid ['tæblɔɪd] n: the ~s los periódicos sensacionalistas; ~ (newspaper)
tabloide m.
tabulate ['tæbjʊleɪt] vt tabular.
tacit ['tæsɪt] adj fml tácito(ta).
taciturn ['tæsɪtɜːn] adj fml taciturno
(na).
tack [tæk] ◆ n 1. (nail) tachuela f. 2. fig
(course of action) táctica f. ◆ vt 1. (fasten
with nail) fijar con tachuelas. 2. (in

sewing) hilvanar. ♦ *vi* (NAUT) virar.
tackle ['tækl] ♦ *n* 1. (FTBL) entrada *f*.
2. (RUGBY) placaje *m*. 3. (U) (*equipment*)
equipo *m*, aparejos *mpl*. 4. (*for lifting*)
aparejo *m*. ♦ *vt* 1. (*deal with - job*)
emprender; (*- problem*) abordar. 2.
(FTBL) entrar. 3. (RUGBY) placar.
4. (*attack*) atacar, arremeter.
tacky ['tækɪ] *adj* 1. *inf* (*cheap and nasty*)
cutre; (*ostentatious and vulgar*) hortera.
2. (*sticky*) pegajoso(sa).
tact [tækt] *n* (U) tacto *m*, discreción *f*.
tactful ['tæktful] *adj* discreto(ta).
tactic ['tæktɪk] *n* táctica *f*. ▶ **tactics** *n*
(U) (MIL) táctica *f*.
tactical ['tæktɪkl] *adj* estratégico(ca);
(*weapons*) táctico(ca).
tactless ['tæktlɪs] *adj* indiscreto(ta).
tadpole ['tædpəʊl] *n* renacuajo *m*.
tag [tæg] *n* (*of cloth, paper*) etiqueta *f*.
▶ **tag along** *vi inf* pegarse, engancharse.
tail [teɪl] ♦ *n* (*gen*) cola *f*; (*of coat, shirt*)
faldón *m*. ♦ *vt inf* (*follow*) seguir de
cerca. ▶ **tails** *npl* 1. (*formal dress*) frac *m*.
2. (*side of coin*) cruz *f*. ▶ **tail off** *vi* (*voice*)
ir debilitándose; (*sound*) ir disminu-
yendo.
tailback ['teɪlbæk] *n* Br cola *f*.
tailcoat [ˌteɪl'kəʊt] *n* frac *m*.
tail end *n* parte *f* final.
tailgate ['teɪlgeɪt] *n* (*of hatchback car*)
portón *m*.
tailor ['teɪlər] ♦ *n* sastre *m*. ♦ *vt* adaptar.
tailor-made *adj* (hecho(cha)) a la
medida.
tailwind ['teɪlwɪnd] *n* viento *m* de
cola.
tainted ['teɪntɪd] *adj* 1. (*reputation*)
manchado(da). 2. Am (*food*) estropea-
do(da).
Taiwan [ˌtaɪ'wɑːn] *n* Taiwán.
take [teɪk] (*pt* **took**, *pp* **taken**) ♦ *vt*
1. (*gen*) tomar; **to ~ a photo** hacer OR
tomar una foto; **to ~ a walk** dar un
paseo; **to ~ a bath** bañarse; **to ~ a test**
hacer un examen; **to ~ offence** ofenderse. 2. (*bring, carry, accompany*) llevar.
3. (*steal*) quitar, robar. 4. (*buy*) coger,
quedarse con; (*rent*) alquilar. 5. (*receive*)
recibir. 6. (*take hold of*) coger; **to ~ sb
prisoner** capturar a alguien.
7. (*accept - offer, cheque, criticism*) aceptar;
(*- advice*) seguir; (*- responsibility, blame*)
asumir; **the machine only ~s 50p pieces**
la máquina sólo admite monedas de
50 peniques. 8. (*have room for - passen-*

gers, goods) tener cabida para.
9. (*bear - pain etc*) soportar, aguantar.
10. (*require - time, courage*) requerir;
(*- money*) costar; **it will ~ a week/three
hours** llevará una semana/tres horas.
11. (*travel by - means of transport, route*)
tomar, coger. 12. (*wear - shoes*) calzar;
(*- clothes*) usar. 13. (*consider*) considerar.
14. (*assume*): **I ~ it (that)** ... supongo que
... ♦ *n* (CINEMA) toma *f*. ▶ **take after** *vt
fus* parecerse a. ▶ **take apart** *vt sep*
(*dismantle*) desmontar. ▶ **take away** *vt
sep* 1. (*remove*) quitar. 2. (*deduct*) restar,
sustraer. ▶ **take back** *vt sep* 1. (*return*)
devolver. 2. (*accept - faulty goods*) aceptar la devolución de. 3. (*admit as wrong*)
retirar. ▶ **take down** *vt sep* 1. (*dismantle*) desmontar. 2. (*write down*) tomar
nota de. ▶ **take in** *vt sep* 1. (*deceive*)
engañar. 2. (*understand*) comprender,
asimilar. 3. (*include*) incluir, abarcar.
4. (*provide accommodation for*) acoger.
▶ **take off** ♦ *vt sep* 1. (*clothes, glasses*)
quitarse. 2. (*have as holiday*) tomarse. 3.
Br *inf* (*imitate*) imitar. ♦ *vi* 1. (*plane*)
despegar. 2. (*go away suddenly*) irse,
marcharse. ▶ **take on** *vt sep*
1. (*accept - work, job*) aceptar; (*- responsibility*) asumir. 2. (*employ*) emplear,
coger. 3. (*confront*) desafiar. ▶ **take out**
vt sep 1. (*from container, pocket*) sacar.
2. (*go out with*): **to ~ sb out** invitar a salir
a alguien. ▶ **take over** ♦ *vt sep* 1. (*company, business*) absorber, adquirir; (*country, government*) apoderarse de. 2. (*job*)
asumir. ♦ *vi* 1. (*take control*) tomar el
poder. 2. (*in job*) entrar en funciones.
▶ **take to** *vt fus* 1. (*feel a liking for - person*) coger cariño a; (*- activity*) aficionarse a. 2. (*begin*): **to ~ to doing sthg**
empezar a hacer algo. ▶ **take up** *vt sep*
1. (*begin*): **to ~ up singing** dedicarse a
cantar; (*job*) aceptar, tomar. 2. (*use
up - time, space*) ocupar; (*- effort*) requerir.
▶ **take up on** *vt sep* (*accept*): **to ~ sb up
on an offer** aceptar una oferta de
alguien.
takeaway Br ['teɪkəˌweɪ], **takeout**
Am ['teɪkaʊt] *n* (*food*) comida *f* para llevar.
taken ['teɪkn] *pp* → **take**.
takeoff ['teɪkɒf] *n* (*of plane*) despegue
m.
takeout Am = **takeaway**.
takeover ['teɪkˌəʊvər] *n* (*of company*)
adquisición *f*.
takings *npl* (*of shop*) venta *f*; (*of show*)
recaudación *f*.

talc [tælk], **talcum (powder)** ['tælkəm-] n talco m.

tale [teɪl] n 1. (fictional story) cuento m. 2. (anecdote) anécdota f.

talent ['tælənt] n: ~ **(for sthg)** talento m (para algo).

talented ['tæləntɪd] adj con talento.

talk [tɔːk] ◆ n 1. (conversation) conversación f. 2. (U) (gossip) habladurías fpl. 3. (lecture) charla f, conferencia f. ◆ vi 1. (gen) hablar; **to ~ to/of** hablar con/de; **to ~ on** OR **about** hablar acerca de OR sobre. 2. (gossip) chismorrear. ◆ vt hablar de. ▶ **talks** npl conversaciones fpl. ▶ **talk into** vt sep: **to ~ sb into doing sthg** convencer a alguien para que haga algo. ▶ **talk out of** vt sep: **to ~ sb out of doing sthg** disuadir a alguien de que haga algo. ▶ **talk over** vt sep discutir, hablar de.

talkative ['tɔːkətɪv] adj hablador(ra).

talk show n Am programa m de entrevistas.

tall [tɔːl] adj alto(ta); **she's 2 metres ~** mide 2 metros.

tall story n cuento m (increíble).

tally ['tælɪ] ◆ n cuenta f; **to keep a ~** llevar la cuenta. ◆ vi concordar.

talon ['tælən] n garra f.

tambourine [,tæmbə'riːn] n pandereta f.

tame [teɪm] ◆ adj 1. (domesticated) doméstico(ca). 2. pej (unexciting) soso (sa). ◆ vt 1. (domesticate) domesticar. 2. (bring under control) dominar.

tamper ['tæmpər] ▶ **tamper with** vt fus (lock) intentar forzar; (records, file) falsear; (machine) manipular.

tampon ['tæmpɒn] n tampón m.

tan [tæn] ◆ adj de color marrón claro. ◆ n bronceado m. ◆ vi broncearse.

tang [tæŋ] n (smell) olor m fuerte; (taste) sabor m fuerte.

tangent ['tændʒənt] n (GEOM) tangente f; **to go off at a ~** salirse por la tangente.

tangerine [,tændʒə'riːn] n mandarina f.

tangible ['tændʒəbl] adj tangible.

tangle ['tæŋgl] n (mass) maraña f; fig (mess) embrollo m, embrollo m.

tank [tæŋk] n 1. (container) depósito m, tanque m. 2. (MIL) tanque m, carro m de combate.

tanker ['tæŋkər] n 1. (ship - gen) barco m cisterna, tanque m; (- for oil) petrolero m. 2. (truck) camión m cisterna.

tanned [tænd] adj bronceado(da).

Tannoy® ['tænɔɪ] n (sistema m de) altavoces mpl.

tantalizing ['tæntəlaɪzɪŋ] adj tentador (ra).

tantamount ['tæntəmaʊnt] adj: ~ **to** equivalente a.

tantrum ['tæntrəm] (pl -s) n rabieta f.

Tanzania [,tænzə'nɪə] n Tanzania.

tap [tæp] ◆ n 1. (device) grifo m. 2. (light blow) golpecito m. ◆ vt 1. (hit) golpear ligeramente. 2. (strength, resources) utilizar. 3. (phone) intervenir.

tap dance n claqué m.

tape [teɪp] ◆ n 1. (cassette, magnetic tape, strip of cloth) cinta f. 2. (adhesive plastic) cinta f adhesiva. ◆ vt 1. (on tape recorder, video recorder) grabar. 2. (with adhesive tape) pegar con cinta adhesiva.

tape measure n cinta f métrica.

taper ['teɪpər] ◆ n (candle) vela f. ◆ vi afilarse.

tape recorder n magnetófono m.

tapestry ['tæpɪstrɪ] n 1. (piece of work) tapiz m. 2. (craft) tapicería f.

tar [tɑːr] n alquitrán m.

target ['tɑːgɪt] n 1. (of missile, goal, aim) objetivo m. 2. (in archery, shooting, of criticism) blanco m.

tariff ['tærɪf] n tarifa f.

Tarmac® ['tɑːmæk] n (material) alquitrán m. ▶ **tarmac** n (AERON): **the tarmac** la pista.

tarnish ['tɑːnɪʃ] vt (make dull) deslustrar; fig (damage) empañar, manchar.

tarpaulin [tɑː'pɔːlɪn] n lona f alquitranada.

tart [tɑːt] ◆ adj (bitter) agrio (agria). ◆ n 1. (sweet pastry) tarta f. 2. v inf (prostitute) furcia f, fulana f. ▶ **tart up** vt sep Br inf pej emperejilar.

tartan ['tɑːtn] ◆ n tartán m. ◆ comp de tartán.

tartar(e) sauce ['tɑːtər-] n salsa f tártara.

task [tɑːsk] n tarea f.

task force n (MIL) destacamento m de fuerzas.

tassel ['tæsl] n borla f.

taste [teɪst] ◆ n 1. (physical sense, discernment) gusto m; **in bad/good ~** de mal/buen gusto. 2. (flavour) sabor m. 3. (try): **have a ~** pruébalo. 4. fig (for success, fast cars etc): ~ **(for)** afición f (a), gusto m (por). 5. fig (experience) experiencia f. ◆ vt 1. (food) notar un sabor a. 2. (test, try) probar. 3. fig (experience) conocer. ◆ vi saber; **to ~ of** OR **like** saber a.

tasteful ['teɪstful] *adj* de buen gusto.

tasteless ['teɪstlɪs] *adj* 1. (*offensive, cheap and unattractive*) de mal gusto. 2. (*without flavour*) insípido(da), soso(sa).

tasty ['teɪstɪ] *adj* sabroso(sa).

tatters ['tætəz] *npl*: **in ~** (*clothes*) andrajoso(sa); *fig* (*confidence, reputation*) por los suelos.

tattoo [tə'tuː] (*pl* **-s**) ◆ *n* 1. (*design*) tatuaje *m*. 2. Br (*military display*) desfile *m* militar. ◆ *vt* tatuar.

tatty ['tætɪ] *adj* Br *inf pej* desastrado (da).

taught [tɔːt] *pt & pp* → **teach**.

taunt [tɔːnt] ◆ *vt* zaherir a. ◆ *n* pulla *f*.

Taurus ['tɔːrəs] *n* Tauro *m*.

taut [tɔːt] *adj* tenso(sa).

tawdry ['tɔːdrɪ] *adj pej* de oropel.

tax [tæks] ◆ *n* impuesto *m*. ◆ *vt* 1. (*goods, profits*) gravar. 2. (*business, person*) imponer contribuciones a. 3. (*strain, test*) poner a prueba.

taxable ['tæksəbl] *adj* imponible.

tax allowance *n* desgravación *f* fiscal.

taxation [tæk'seɪʃn] *n* (U) 1. (*system*) sistema *m* tributario. 2. (*amount*) impuestos *mpl*.

tax avoidance [-ə'vɔɪdəns] *n* evasión *f* fiscal.

tax collector *n* recaudador *m*, -ra *f* de impuestos.

tax disc *n* Br pegatina del impuesto de circulación.

tax evasion *n* fraude *m* fiscal, evasión *f* de impuestos.

tax-exempt Am = **tax-free**.

tax-free Br, **tax-exempt** Am *adj* exento(ta) de impuestos.

taxi ['tæksɪ] ◆ *n* taxi *m*. ◆ *vi* (*plane*) rodar por la pista.

taxi driver *n* taxista *m* y *f*.

tax inspector *n* = inspector *m*, -ra *f* de Hacienda.

taxi rank Br, **taxi stand** *n* parada *f* de taxis.

taxpayer ['tæks,peɪər] *n* contribuyente *m* y *f*.

tax relief *n* (U) desgravación *f* fiscal.

tax return *n* declaración *f* de renta.

TB *n abbr of* **tuberculosis**.

tea [tiː] *n* 1. (*drink, leaves*) té *m*. 2. Br (*afternoon snack*) té *m*, merienda *f*. 3. Br (*evening meal*) merienda cena *f*.

teabag ['tiːbæg] *n* bolsita *f* de té.

tea break *n* Br descanso *m* (*durante la jornada laboral*).

teach [tiːtʃ] (*pt & pp* **taught**) ◆ *vt* 1. (*give lessons to*) dar clases a; **to ~ sb sthg** enseñar algo a alguien; **to ~ sb to do sthg** enseñar a alguien a hacer algo. 2. (*give lessons in*) dar clases de. ◆ *vi* ser profesor(ra).

teacher ['tiːtʃər] *n* (*at primary school*) maestro *m*, -tra *f*; (*at secondary school*) profesor *m*, -ra *f*.

teachers college Am = **teacher training college**.

teacher training college Br, **teachers college** Am *n* escuela *f* normal.

teaching ['tiːtʃɪŋ] *n* enseñanza *f*.

tea cloth *n* Br 1. (*tablecloth*) mantel *m*. 2. (*tea towel*) paño *m* de cocina.

tea cosy Br, **tea cozy** Am *n* cubretetera *f*.

teacup ['tiːkʌp] *n* taza *f* de té.

teak [tiːk] *n* teca *f*.

team [tiːm] *n* equipo *m*.

teammate ['tiːmmeɪt] *n* compañero *m*, -ra *f* de equipo.

teamwork ['tiːmwɜːk] *n* (U) trabajo *m* en equipo.

teapot ['tiːpɒt] *n* tetera *f*.

tear¹ [tɪər] *n* lágrima *f*; **in ~s** llorando.

tear² [teər] (*pt* **tore**, *pp* **torn**) ◆ *vt* 1. (*rip*) rasgar, romper. 2. (*remove roughly*) arrancar. ◆ *vi* 1. (*rip*) romperse, rasgarse. 2. *inf* (*move quickly*) ir a toda pastilla. ◆ *n* rasgón *m*, desgarrón *m*. ▶ **tear apart** *vt sep* 1. (*rip up*) despedazar. 2. (*upset greatly*) desgarrar. ▶ **tear down** *vt sep* echar abajo. ▶ **tear up** *vt sep* hacer pedazos.

teardrop ['tɪədrɒp] *n* lágrima *f*.

tearful ['tɪəful] *adj* (*person*) lloroso(sa).

tear gas [tɪər-] *n* (U) gas *m* lacrimógeno.

tearoom ['tiːrʊm] *n* salón *m* de té.

tease [tiːz] *vt* (*mock*): **to ~ sb** (*about*) tomar el pelo a alguien (acerca de).

tea service, tea set *n* servicio *m* OR juego *m* de té.

teaspoon ['tiːspuːn] *n* 1. (*utensil*) cucharilla *f*. 2. (*amount*) cucharadita *f*.

teat [tiːt] *n* 1. (*of animal*) tetilla *f*. 2. (*of bottle*) tetina *f*.

teatime ['tiːtaɪm] *n* Br hora *f* del té.

tea towel *n* paño *m* de cocina.

technical ['teknɪkl] *adj* técnico(ca).

technical college *n* Br = centro *m* de formación profesional.

technicality [,teknɪ'kælətɪ] *n* detalle *m* técnico.

technically ['teknɪklɪ] *adv* 1. (*gen*) técnicamente. 2. (*theoretically*) teóricamente, en teoría.

technician [tek'nɪʃn] n técnico m, -ca f.

technique [tek'niːk] n técnica f.

technological [,teknə'lɒdʒɪkl] adj tecnológico(ca).

technology [tek'nɒlədʒɪ] n tecnología f.

teddy ['tedɪ] n: ~ **(bear)** oso m de peluche.

tedious ['tiːdjəs] adj tedioso(sa).

tee [tiː] n tee m.

teem [tiːm] vi 1. (rain) llover a cántaros. 2. (be busy): **to be ~ing with** estar inundado(da) de.

teenage ['tiːneɪdʒ] adj adolescente.

teenager ['tiːn,eɪdʒər] n adolescente m y f, quinceañero m, -ra f.

teens [tiːnz] npl adolescencia f.

tee shirt n camiseta f.

teeter ['tiːtər] vi lit & fig tambalearse.

teeth [tiːθ] pl → **tooth**.

teethe [tiːð] vi echar los dientes.

teething troubles ['tiːðɪŋ-] npl fig problemas mpl iniciales.

teetotaller Br, **teetotaler** Am [tiː-'təʊtlər] n abstemio m, -mia f.

TEFL ['tefl] (abbr of **teaching of English as a foreign language**) n enseñanza de inglés para extranjeros.

tel. (abbr of **telephone**) tfno.

telecommunications ['telɪkə,mjuːnɪ-'keɪʃnz] npl telecomunicaciones fpl.

telegram ['telɪgræm] n telegrama m.

telegraph ['telɪgrɑːf] n telégrafo m.

telegraph pole, telegraph post Br n poste m de telégrafos.

telepathy [tɪ'lepəθɪ] n telepatía f.

telephone ['telɪfəʊn] ◆ n teléfono m; **to be on the ~** Br (connected to network) tener teléfono; (speaking) estar al teléfono. ◆ vt & vi telefonear.

telephone book n guía f telefónica.

telephone booth n teléfono m público.

telephone box n Br cabina f (telefónica).

telephone call n llamada f telefónica.

telephone directory n guía f telefónica.

telephone number n número m de teléfono.

telephonist [tɪ'lefənɪst] n Br telefonista m y f.

telephoto lens [,telɪ'fəʊtəʊ-] n teleobjetivo m.

telescope ['telɪskəʊp] n telescopio m.

teletext ['telɪtekst] n teletexto m.

televise ['telɪvaɪz] vt televisar.

television ['telɪ,vɪʒn] n televisión f.

television set n televisor m, (aparato m de) televisión f.

telex ['teleks] ◆ n télex m. ◆ vt (message) transmitir por télex; (person) mandar un télex a.

tell [tel] (pt & pp **told**) ◆ vt 1. (gen) decir; **to ~ sb (that)** decir a alguien que; **to ~ sb sthg, to ~ sthg to sb** decir a alguien algo; **to ~ sb to do sthg** decir a alguien que haga algo. 2. (joke, story) contar. 3. (judge, recognize): **to ~ what sb is thinking** saber en qué está pensando alguien; **to ~ the time** decir la hora. ◆ vi (have effect) surtir efecto. ► **tell apart** vt sep distinguir. ► **tell off** vt sep reñir, reprender.

telling ['telɪŋ] adj 1. (speech, argument) efectivo(va). 2. (remark, incident) revelador(ra).

telltale ['telteɪl] ◆ adj revelador(ra). ◆ n chivato m, -ta f, acusica m y f.

telly ['telɪ] (abbr of **television**) n Br inf tele f.

temp [temp] ◆ n inf Br (abbr of **temporary (employee)**) secretario m eventual, secretaria f eventual (por horas). ◆ vi: **she's ~ing** está de secretaria eventual.

temper ['tempər] ◆ n 1. (state of mind, mood) humor m; **to lose one's ~** enfadarse, perder la paciencia. 2. (angry state): **to be in a ~** estar de mal humor. 3. (temperament) temperamento m. ◆ vt fml templar, suavizar.

temperament ['tempərəmənt] n temperamento m.

temperamental [,temprə'mentl] adj (volatile) temperamental.

temperate ['temprət] adj templado (da).

temperature ['temprətʃər] n temperatura f; **to have a ~** tener fiebre.

tempestuous [tem'pestjʊəs] adj lit & fig tempestuoso(sa).

template ['templɪt] n plantilla f.

temple ['templ] n 1. (RELIG) templo m. 2. (ANAT) sien f.

temporarily [,tempə'rerəlɪ] adv temporalmente, provisionalmente.

temporary ['tempərərɪ] adj (gen) temporal, provisional; (improvement, problem) pasajero(ra).

tempt [tempt] vt (entice): **to ~ sb (to do sthg)** tentar a alguien (a hacer algo).

temptation [temp'teɪʃn] n tentación f.

tempting ['temptɪŋ] adj tentador(ra).

ten [ten] num diez; see also **six**.

tenable ['tenəbl] adj (reasonable, credible) sostenible.

tenacious [tɪ'neɪʃəs] adj tenaz.

tenancy ['tenənsɪ] n (period - of house) alquiler m; (- of land) arrendamiento m.

tenant ['tenənt] n (of house) inquilino m, -na f; (of pub) arrendatario m, -ria f.

tend [tend] vt 1. (have tendency): **to ~ to do sthg** soler hacer algo, tender a hacer algo. 2. (look after) cuidar.

tendency ['tendənsɪ] n 1. (trend): **~ (for sb/sthg to do sthg)** tendencia f (de alguien/algo a hacer algo). 2. (leaning, inclination) inclinación f.

tender ['tendər] ◆ adj (gen) tierno(na); (sore) dolorido(da). ◆ n (COMM) propuesta f, oferta f. ◆ vt fml (resignation) presentar; (apology, suggestion) ofrecer.

tendon ['tendən] n tendón m.

tenement ['tenəmənt] n bloque de viviendas modestas.

Tenerife [,tenə'riːf] n Tenerife.

tenet ['tenɪt] n fml principio m.

tennis ['tenɪs] ◆ n tenis m. ◆ comp de tenis; **~ player** tenista m y f.

tennis ball n pelota f de tenis.

tennis court n pista f de tenis.

tennis racket n raqueta f de tenis.

tenor ['tenər] n (singer) tenor m.

tense [tens] ◆ adj tenso(sa). ◆ n tiempo m. ◆ vt tensar.

tension ['tenʃn] n tensión f.

tent [tent] n tienda f (de campaña), carpa f Amer.

tentacle ['tentəkl] n tentáculo m.

tentative ['tentətɪv] adj 1. (person) indeciso(sa); (step, handshake) vacilante. 2. (suggestion, conclusion etc) provisional.

tenterhooks ['tentəhuks] npl: **to be on ~** estar sobre ascuas.

tenth [tenθ] num décimo(ma); see also **sixth**.

tent peg n estaca f.

tent pole n mástil m de tienda.

tenuous ['tenjuəs] adj (argument) flojo (ja); (evidence, connection) débil, insignificante; (hold) ligero(ra).

tenure ['tenjər] n (U) fml 1. (of property) arrendamiento m. 2. (of job) ocupación f, ejercicio m.

tepid ['tepɪd] adj (liquid) tibio(bia).

term [tɜːm] ◆ n 1. (word, expression) término m. 2. (SCH & UNIV) trimestre m. 3. (POL) mandato m. 4. (period of time) periodo m; **in the long/short ~** a largo/ corto plazo. ◆ vt: **to ~ sthg sthg** calificar algo de algo. ▶ **terms** npl 1. (of contract, agreement) condiciones fpl. 2. (basis): **in**

international/real ~s en términos internacionales/reales; **to be on good ~s (with sb)** mantener buenas relaciones (con alguien); **to come to ~s with sthg** aceptar algo. ▶ **in terms of** prep por lo que se refiere a.

terminal ['tɜːmɪnl] ◆ adj (MED) incurable, terminal. ◆ n 1. (transport) terminal f. 2. (COMPUT) terminal m.

terminate ['tɜːmɪneɪt] ◆ vt fml (gen) poner fin a; (pregnancy) interrumpir. ◆ vi 1. (bus, train) finalizar el trayecto. 2. (contract) terminarse.

termini ['tɜːmɪnaɪ] pl → **terminus**.

terminus ['tɜːmɪnəs] (pl -ni OR -nuses) n (estación f) terminal f.

terrace ['terəs] n 1. (gen) terraza f. 2. Br (of houses) hilera f de casas adosadas. ▶ **terraces** npl (FTBL): **the ~s** las gradas.

terraced ['terəst] adj 1. (hillside) a terrazas. 2. (house, housing) adosado(da).

terraced house n Br casa f adosada.

terrain [te'reɪn] n terreno m.

terrible ['terəbl] adj 1. (crash, mess, shame) terrible, espantoso(sa). 2. (unwell, unhappy, very bad) fatal.

terribly ['terəblɪ] adv (sing, play, write) malísimamente; (injured, sorry, expensive) terriblemente.

terrier ['terɪər] n terrier m.

terrific [tə'rɪfɪk] adj 1. (wonderful) estupendo(da). 2. (enormous) enorme.

terrified ['terɪfaɪd] adj aterrorizado (da); **to be ~ (of)** tener terror a.

terrifying ['terɪfaɪɪŋ] adj aterrador(ra).

territory ['terətrɪ] n 1. (political area) territorio m. 2. (terrain) terreno m. 3. (area of knowledge) esfera f.

terror ['terər] n (fear) terror m.

terrorism ['terərɪzm] n terrorismo m.

terrorist ['terərɪst] n terrorista m y f.

terrorize, -ise ['terəraɪz] vt aterrorizar.

terse [tɜːs] adj seco(ca).

Terylene® ['terɪliːn] n terylene® m.

test [test] ◆ n 1. (trial) prueba f. 2. (examination) examen m, prueba f. 3. (MED) (of blood, urine) análisis m inv; (of eyes) revisión f. ◆ vt 1. (try out) probar, poner a prueba. 2. (examine) examinar; **to ~ sb on** examinar a alguien de.

testament ['testəmənt] n (will) testamento m.

test-drive vt someter a prueba de carretera.

testicles ['testɪklz] npl testículos mpl.

testify ['testɪfaɪ] ◆ vi 1. (JUR) prestar declaración. 2. (be proof): **to ~ to sthg** dar fe de OR atestiguar algo. ♦ *vt*: **to ~ that** declarar que.

testimony [Br 'tɛstɪmənɪ, Am 'tɛstəməʊnɪ] *n* (JUR) testimonio *m*, declaración *f*.

testing ['tɛstɪŋ] *adj* duro(ra).

test match *n* Br partido *m* internacional.

test pilot *n* piloto *m* y *f* de pruebas.

test tube *n* probeta *f*.

test-tube baby *n* bebé *m* y *f* probeta.

tetanus ['tɛtənəs] *n* tétanos *m inv*.

tether ['teðə^r] ♦ *vt* atar. ♦ *n*: **to be at the end of one's ~** estar uno que ya no puede más.

text [tekst] *n* **1.** (*gen*) texto *m*. **2.** (*textbook*) libro *m* de texto.

textbook ['tekstbʊk] *n* libro *m* de texto.

textile ['tekstaɪl] *n* textil *m*, tejido *m*.

texture ['tekstʃə^r] *n* textura *f*.

Thai [taɪ] ♦ *adj* tailandés(esa). ♦ *n* **1.** (*person*) tailandés *m*, -esa *f*. **2.** (*language*) tailandés *m*.

Thailand ['taɪlænd] *n* Tailandia.

Thames [temz] *n*: **the ~** el Támesis.

than [weak form ðən, strong form ðæn] ♦ *prep* que; **you're older ~ me** eres mayor que yo; **you're older ~ I thought** eres mayor de lo que pensaba. ♦ *conj* que; **I'd sooner read ~ sleep** prefiero leer que dormir; **no sooner did he arrive ~ she left** tan pronto llegó él, ella se fue; **more ~ three/once** más de tres/de una vez; **rather ~ stay, he chose to go** en vez de quedarse, prefirió irse.

thank [θæŋk] *vt*: **to ~ sb (for sthg)** dar las gracias a alguien (por algo), agradecer a alguien (algo); **~ God** OR **goodness** OR **heavens!** ¡gracias a Dios!, ¡menos mal! ► **thanks** ♦ *npl* agradecimiento *m*. ♦ *excl* ¡gracias! ► **thanks to** *prep* gracias a.

thankful ['θæŋkfʊl] *adj* **1.** (*relieved*) aliviado(da). **2.** (*grateful*): **~ (for)** agradecido(da) (por).

thankless ['θæŋklɪs] *adj* ingrato(ta).

thanksgiving ['θæŋks,gɪvɪŋ] *n* acción *f* de gracias. ► **Thanksgiving (Day)** *n* Día *m* de Acción de Gracias.

thank you *excl* ¡gracias!; **~ for** gracias por.

that [ðæt, weak form of pron and conj ðət] (*pl* **those**) ♦ *pron* **1.** (*demonstrative use: pl* '*those*') ése *m*, ésa *f*, ésos *mpl*, ésas *fpl*; (*indefinite*) eso; **~ sounds familiar** eso me resulta familiar; **who's ~?** (*who is it?*)

¿quién es?; **what's ~?** ¿qué es eso?; **~'s a shame** es una pena; **is ~ Maureen?** (*asking someone else*) ¿es ésa Maureen?; (*asking person in question*) ¿eres Maureen?; **do you like these or those?** ¿te gustan éstos o ésos? **2.** (*further away in distance, time*) aquél *m*, aquélla *f*, aquéllos *mpl*, aquéllas *fpl*; (*indefinite*) aquello; **~ was the life!** ¡aquello sí que era vida!; **all those who helped me** todos aquellos que me ayudaron. **3.** (*to introduce relative clauses*) que; **a path ~ led into the woods** un sendero que conducía al bosque; **everything ~ I have done** todo lo que he hecho; **the room ~ I sleep in** el cuarto donde OR en (el) que duermo; **the day ~ he arrived** el día en que llegó; **the firm ~ he's applying to** la empresa a la que solicita trabajo. ♦ *adj* (*demonstrative: pl* '*those*') ese (esa), esos (esas) (*pl*); (*further away in distance, time*) aquel (aquella), aquellos (aquellas) (*pl*); **those chocolates are delicious** esos bombones están exquisitos; **I'll have ~ book at the back** yo cogeré aquel libro del fondo; **later ~ day** más tarde ese/aquel mismo día. ♦ *adv* tan; **it wasn't ~ bad** no estuvo tan mal; **it doesn't cost ~ much** no cuesta tanto; **it was ~ big** fue así de grande. ♦ *conj* que; **he recommended ~ I phone you** aconsejó que te telefoneara; **it's time ~ we were leaving** deberíamos irnos ya, ya va siendo hora de irse. ► **that is** *adv* es decir, o sea.

thatched [θætʃt] *adj* con techo de paja.

that's [ðæts] = **that is**.

thaw [θɔː] ♦ *vt* (*snow, ice*) derretir; (*frozen food*) descongelar. ♦ *vi* (*snow, ice*) derretirse; (*frozen food*) descongelarse; *fig* (*people, relations*) distenderse. ♦ *n* deshielo *m*.

the [weak form ðə, before vowel ðɪ, strong form ðiː] *def art* **1.** (*gen*) el (la), (*pl*) los (las); (*before feminine nouns beginning with stressed* '*a*' *or* '*ha*' = **el**; '*a*' + '*el*' = **al**; '*de*' + '*el*' = **del**): **~ boat** el barco; **~ Queen** la reina; **~ men** los hombres; **~ women** las mujeres; **~ (cold) water** el agua (fría); **to ~ end of ~ world** al fin del mundo; **to play ~ piano** tocar el piano; **~ Joneses are coming to supper** los Jones vienen a cenar. **2.** (*with an adjective to form a noun*): **~ old/young** los viejos/jóvenes; **~ impossible** lo imposible. **3.** (*in dates*): **~ twelfth of May** el doce de mayo; **~ forties** los cuarenta. **4.** (*in comparisons*): **~**

more I see her, ~ less I like her cuanto más la veo, menos me gusta; **~ sooner ~ better** cuanto antes mejor. **5.** (*in titles*): **Catherine ~ Great** Catalina la Grande; **George ~ First** Jorge Primero.

theatre, theater Am ['θɪətər] *n* **1.** (*for plays etc*) teatro *m*. **2.** Br (*in hospital*) quirófano *m*. **3.** Am (*cinema*) cine *m*.

theatregoer, theatergoer Am ['θɪətə,gəʊər] *n* aficionado *m*, -da *f* al teatro.

theatrical [θɪ'ætrɪkl] *adj lit & fig* teatral.

theft [θeft] *n* (*more serious*) robo *m*; (*less serious*) hurto *m*.

their [ðeər] *poss adj* su, sus (*pl*); **~ house** su casa; **~ children** sus hijos; **it wasn't THEIR fault** no fue culpa suya *or* su culpa; **they washed ~ hair** se lavaron el pelo.

theirs [ðeəz] *poss pron* suyo (suya); **that money is ~** ese dinero es suyo; **our car hit ~** nuestro coche chocó contra el suyo; **it wasn't our fault, it was THEIRS** no fue culpa nuestra sino suya *or* de ellos; **a friend of ~** un amigo suyo *or* de ellos.

them [*weak form* ðəm, *strong form* ðem] *pers pron pl* **1.** (*direct*) los *mpl*, las *fpl*; **I know ~** los conozco; **I like ~** me gustan; **if I were** *or* **was ~** si (yo) fuera ellos. **2.** (*indirect - gen*) les *mpl y fpl*; (*- with other third person prons*) se *mpl y fpl*; **she sent ~ a letter** les mandó una carta; **we spoke to ~** hablamos con ellos; **I gave it to ~** se lo di (a ellos). **3.** (*stressed, after prep, in comparisons etc*) ellos *mpl*, ellas *fpl*; **you can't expect THEM to do it** no esperarás que ELLOS lo hagan; **with/without ~** con/sin ellos; **we're not as wealthy as ~** no somos tan ricos como ellos.

theme [θiːm] *n* **1.** (*gen*) tema *m*. **2.** (*signature tune*) sintonía *f*.

theme tune *n* tema *m* musical.

themselves [ðem'selvz] *pron* **1.** (*reflexive*) se; (*after preposition*) sí; **they enjoyed ~** se divirtieron. **2.** (*for emphasis*) ellos mismos *mpl*, ellas mismas *fpl*; **they did it ~** lo hicieron ellos mismos. **3.** (*alone*) solos(las); **they organized it (by) ~** lo organizaron ellas solas.

then [ðen] *adv* **1.** (*not now*) entonces. **2.** (*next, afterwards*) luego, después. **3.** (*in that case*) entonces; **all right ~** de acuerdo, pues. **4.** (*therefore*) entonces, por lo tanto. **5.** (*furthermore, also*) además.

theology [θɪ'ɒlədʒɪ] *n* teología *f*.

theoretical [θɪə'retɪkl] *adj* teórico(ca).

theorize, -ise ['θɪəraɪz] *vi*: **to ~** (**about sthg**) teorizar (sobre algo).

theory ['θɪərɪ] *n* teoría *f*; **in ~** en teoría.

therapist ['θerəpɪst] *n* terapeuta *m y f*.

therapy ['θerəpɪ] *n* terapia *f*.

there [ðeər] ◆ *pron* (*indicating existence*): **~ is/~ are** hay; **~'s someone at the door** hay alguien en la puerta; **~ must be some mistake** debe (de) haber un error; **~ are five of us** somos cinco. ◆ *adv* **1.** (*in existence, available*) ahí; **is anybody ~?** ¿hay alguien ahí?; **is John ~, please?** (*when telephoning*) ¿está John? **2.** (*referring to place - near speaker*) ahí; (*- further away*) allí, allá; **I'm going ~ next week** voy para allá *or* allí la semana que viene; **~ it is** ahí está; **over ~** por allí; **it's six miles ~ and back** hay seis millas entre ir y volver. ◆ *excl*: **~, I knew he'd turn up** ¡mira!, sabía que aparecería; **~, ~ (don't cry)** ¡venga, venga (no llores)! ▶ **there and then, then and there** *adv* en el acto.

thereabouts [,ðeərə'baʊts], **thereabout** Am [,ðeərə'baʊt] *adv*: **or ~** o por ahí.

thereafter [,ðeər'ɑːftər] *adv fml* después, a partir de entonces.

thereby [,ðeər'baɪ] *adv fml* de ese modo.

therefore ['ðeəfɔːr] *adv* por lo tanto.

there's [ðeəz] = **there is**.

thermal ['θɜːml] *adj* térmico(ca).

thermometer [θə'mɒmɪtər] *n* termómetro *m*.

Thermos (flask)® ['θɜːməs-] *n* termo *m*.

thermostat ['θɜːməstæt] *n* termostato *m*.

thesaurus [θɪ'sɔːrəs] (*pl* **-es**) *n* diccionario *m* de sinónimos y voces afines.

these [ðiːz] *pl* → **this**.

thesis ['θiːsɪs] (*pl* **theses** ['θiːsiːz]) *n* tesis *f inv*.

they [ðeɪ] *pers pron pl* **1.** (*gen*) ellos *mpl*, ellas *fpl*; **~'re pleased** (ellos) están satisfechos; **~'re pretty earrings** son unos pendientes bonitos; **THEY can't do it** ELLOS no pueden hacerlo; **there ~ are** allí están. **2.** (*unspecified people*): **~ say it's going to snow** dicen que va a nevar.

they'd [ðeɪd] = **they had, they would**.

they'll [ðeɪl] = **they shall, they will**.

they're [ðeər] = **they are**.

they've [ðeɪv] = **they have**.

thick [θɪk] ◆ *adj* **1.** (*not thin*) grueso(sa); **it's 3 cm ~** tiene 3 cm de grueso; **how ~ is it?** ¿qué espesor tiene? **2.** (*dense - hair, liquid, fog*) espeso(sa). **3.** *inf* (*stu-*

pid) necio(cia). ◆ *n*: **to be in the ~ of** estar en el centro OR meollo de.

thicken ['θɪkn] ◆ *vt* espesar. ◆ *vi* (*gen*) espesarse.

thicket ['θɪkɪt] *n* matorral *m*.

thickness ['θɪknɪs] *n* espesor *m*.

thickset [,θɪk'set] *adj* fornido(da).

thick-skinned [-'skɪnd] *adj* insensible.

thief [θi:f] (*pl* **thieves**) *n* ladrón *m*, -ona *f*.

thieve [θi:v] *vt* & *vi* robar, hurtar.

thieves [θi:vz] *pl* → **thief**.

thigh [θaɪ] *n* muslo *m*.

thimble ['θɪmbl] *n* dedal *m*.

thin [θɪn] *adj* **1.** (*not thick*) delgado(da), fino(na). **2.** (*skinny*) delgado(da), flaco (ca). **3.** (*watery*) claro(ra), aguado(da). **4.** (*sparse - crowd, vegetation, mist*) poco denso (poco densa); (- *hair*) ralo(la). ▶ **thin down** *vt sep* aclarar.

thing [θɪŋ] *n* **1.** (*gen*) cosa *f*; **the next ~ on the list** lo siguiente de la lista; **the (best) ~ to do would be ...** lo mejor sería ...; **the ~ is ...** el caso es que ... **2.** (*anything*): **not a ~** nada. **3.** (*person*): **poor ~!** ¡pobrecito *m*, -ta *f*! ▶ **things** *npl* **1.** (*clothes, possessions*) cosas *fpl*. **2.** *inf* (*life*): **how are ~s?** ¿qué tal (van las cosas)?

think [θɪŋk] (*pt* & *pp* **thought**) ◆ *vt* **1.** (*believe*): **to ~ (that)** creer OR pensar que; **I ~ so/not** creo que sí/no. **2.** (*have in mind*) pensar; **what are you ~ing?** ¿en qué piensas? **3.** (*imagine*) entender, hacerse una idea de; **I thought so** ya me lo imaginaba. **4.** (*in polite requests*) creer; **do you ~ you could help me?** ¿cree que podría ayudarme? ◆ *vi* **1.** (*use mind*) pensar. **2.** (*have stated opinion*): **what do you ~ of** OR **about his new film?** ¿qué piensas de su nueva película?; **to ~ a lot of sthg/sb** tener en mucha estima algo/a alguien. **3.** *phr*: **to ~ twice** pensárselo dos veces. ▶ **think about** *vt fus* pensar en; **I'll have to ~ about it** tendré que pensarlo; **to ~ about doing sthg** pensar en hacer algo. ▶ **think of** *vt fus* **1.** (*consider*): **to ~ of doing sthg** pensar en hacer algo. **2.** (*remember*) acordarse de. **3.** (*conceive*) pensar en; **how did you ~ of (doing) that?** ¿cómo se te ocurrió (hacer) esto? ▶ **think out, think through** *vt sep* (*plan*) elaborar; (*problem*) examinar. ▶ **think over** *vt sep* pensarse. ▶ **think up** *vt sep* idear.

think tank *n* grupo de expertos convocados por una organización para aconsejar sobre un tema determinado.

third [θɜ:d] ◆ *num adj* tercer(ra). ◆ *num n* **1.** (*fraction*) tercio *m*. **2.** (*in order*) tercero *m*, -ra *f*. **3.** (UNIV) ~ aprobado *m* (*en un título universitario*); *see also* **sixth**.

thirdly ['θɜ:dlɪ] *adv* en tercer lugar.

third party insurance *n* seguro *m* a terceros.

third-rate *adj pej* de poca categoría.

Third World *n*: **the ~** el Tercer Mundo.

thirst [θɜ:st] *n lit* & *fig*: **~ (for)** sed *f* (de).

thirsty ['θɜ:stɪ] *adj* (*parched*): **to be** OR **feel ~** tener sed.

thirteen [,θɜ:'ti:n] *num* trece; *see also* **six**.

thirty ['θɜ:tɪ] *num* treinta; *see also* **sixty**.

this [ðɪs] (*pl* **these**) ◆ *pron* (*gen*) éste *m*, ésta *f*, éstos *mpl*, éstas *fpl*; (*indefinite*) esto; **~ is/these are for you** esto es/ éstos son para tí; **~ can't be true** esto no puede ser cierto; **do you prefer these or those?** ¿prefieres éstos o aquéllos?; **~ is Daphne Logan** (*introducing another person*) ésta es OR te presento a Daphne Logan; (*introducing oneself on phone*) soy Daphne Logan; **what's ~?** ¿qué es eso? ◆ *adj* **1.** (*gen*) este (esta), estos (estas) (*pl*); **~ country** este país; **these thoughts** estos pensamientos; **I prefer ~ one** prefiero éste; **~ morning/week** esta mañana/semana; **~ Sunday/summer** este domingo/verano. **2.** *inf* (*a certain*) un (una); **there's ~ woman I know** hay una tía que conozco. ◆ *adv*: **it was ~ big** era así de grande; **you'll need about ~ much** te hará falta un tanto así.

thistle ['θɪsl] *n* cardo *m*.

thong [θɒŋ] *n* (*of leather*) correa *f*.

thorn [θɔ:n] *n* (*prickle*) espina *f*.

thorough ['θʌrə] *adj* **1.** (*investigation etc*) exhaustivo(va). **2.** (*person, work*) minucioso(sa).

thoroughbred ['θʌrəbred] *n* pura sangre *m y f*.

thoroughfare ['θʌrəfeər] *n fml* calle *f* mayor.

thoroughly ['θʌrəlɪ] *adv* **1.** (*fully, in detail*) a fondo. **2.** (*completely, utterly*) completamente.

those [ðəʊz] *pl* → **that**.

though [ðəʊ] ◆ *conj* aunque; **even ~** aunque; **as ~** como si. ◆ *adv* sin embargo.

thought [θɔ:t] ◆ *pt* & *pp* → **think**. ◆ *n* **1.** (*notion, idea*) idea *f*. **2.** (*act of thinking*): **after much ~** después de pensarlo mucho. **3.** (*philosophy, thinking*) pensamiento *m*. ▶ **thoughts** *npl* **1.** (*reflec-*

tions) reflexiones *fpl*. **2.** (*views*) opiniones *fpl*.

thoughtful ['θɔːtful] *adj* **1.** (*pensive*) pensativo(va). **2.** (*considerate*) considerado(da).

thoughtless ['θɔːtlɪs] *adj* desconsiderado(da).

thousand ['θaʊznd] *num* mil; **a** OR **one ~** mil; **two ~** dos mil; **~s of** miles de; *see also* **six**.

thousandth ['θaʊzntθ] ◆ *num adj* milésimo(ma). ◆ *num n* (*fraction*) milésima *f*; *see also* **sixth**.

thrash [θræʃ] *vt lit & fig* dar una paliza a. ▶ **thrash about, thrash around** *vi* agitarse violentamente. ▶ **thrash out** *vt sep* darle vueltas a, discutir.

thread [θred] ◆ *n* **1.** (*of cotton, argument*) hilo *m*. **2.** (*of screw*) rosca *f*, filete *m*. ◆ *vt* (*needle*) enhebrar.

threadbare ['θredbeəᵣ] *adj* raído(da).

threat [θret] *n*: **~ (to/of)** amenaza *f* (para/de).

threaten ['θretn] ◆ *vt* amenazar; **to ~ sb (with)** amenazar a alguien (con); **to ~ to do sthg** amenazar con hacer algo. ◆ *vi* amenazar.

three [θriː] *num* tres; *see also* **six**.

three-dimensional [-dɪ'menʃənl] *adj* tridimensional.

threefold ['θriːfəʊld] ◆ *adj* triple. ◆ *adv* tres veces.

three-piece *adj* de tres piezas; **~ suite** tresillo *m*.

three-ply *adj* (*wood*) de tres capas; (*rope, wool*) de tres hebras.

thresh [θreʃ] *vt* trillar.

threshold ['θreʃhəʊld] *n* **1.** (*doorway*) umbral *m*. **2.** (*level*) límite *m*.

threw [θruː] *pt* → **throw**.

thrifty ['θrɪftɪ] *adj* (*person*) ahorrativo (va), (*meal*) frugal.

thrill [θrɪl] ◆ *n* **1.** (*sudden feeling*) estremecimiento *m*. **2.** (*exciting experience*): **it was a ~ to see it** fue emocionante verlo. ◆ *vt* entusiasmar.

thrilled [θrɪld] *adj*: **~ (with sthg/to do sthg)** encantado(da) (de algo/de hacer algo).

thriller ['θrɪləᵣ] *n* novela *f*/película *f*/obra *f* de suspense.

thrilling ['θrɪlɪŋ] *adj* emocionante.

thrive [θraɪv] (*pt* **-d** OR **throve**) *vi* (*plant*) crecer mucho; (*person*) rebosar de salud; (*business*) prosperar.

thriving ['θraɪvɪŋ] *adj* (*plant*) que crece bien.

throat [θrəʊt] *n* garganta *f*.

throb [θrɒb] *vi* **1.** (*heart, pulse*) latir; (*head*) palpitar. **2.** (*engine, music*) vibrar, resonar.

throes [θrəʊz] *npl*: **to be in the ~ of** estar en medio de.

throne [θrəʊn] *n* trono *m*.

throng [θrɒŋ] ◆ *n* multitud *f*. ◆ *vt* llegar en tropel a.

throttle ['θrɒtl] ◆ *n* válvula *f* reguladora. ◆ *vt* (*strangle*) estrangular.

through [θruː] ◆ *adj* (*finished*): **to be ~ with sthg** haber terminado algo. ◆ *adv* **1.** (*in place*) de parte a parte, de un lado a otro; **they let us ~** nos dejaron pasar; **I read it ~** lo leí hasta el final. **2.** (*in time*) hasta el final. ◆ *prep* **1.** (*relating to place, position*) a través de; **to cut/travel ~ sthg** cortar/viajar por algo. **2.** (*during*) durante; **to go ~ an experience** pasar por una experiencia. **3.** (*because of*) a causa de, por. **4.** (*by means of*) gracias a, por medio de; **I got it ~ a friend** lo conseguí a través de un amigo. **5.** *Am* (*up to and including*): **Monday ~ Friday** de lunes a viernes. ▶ **through and through** *adv* de pies a cabeza.

throughout [θruː'aʊt] ◆ *prep* **1.** (*during*) a lo largo de, durante todo (durante toda). **2.** (*everywhere in*) por todo(da). ◆ *adv* **1.** (*all the time*) todo el tiempo. **2.** (*everywhere*) por todas partes.

throve [θrəʊv] *pt* → **thrive**.

throw [θrəʊ] (*pt* **threw**, *pp* **thrown**) ◆ *vt* **1.** (*gen*) tirar; (*ball, hammer, javelin*) lanzar. **2.** (*subj: horse*) derribar, desmontar. **3.** *fig* (*confuse*) desconcertar. ◆ *n* lanzamiento *m*, tiro *m*. ▶ **throw away** *vt sep* (*discard*) tirar; *fig* (*waste*) desperdiciar. ▶ **throw out** *vt sep* **1.** (*discard*) tirar. **2.** (*force to leave*) echar. ▶ **throw up** *vi inf* (*vomit*) vomitar.

throwaway ['θrəʊə,weɪ] *adj* **1.** (*bottle, product*) desechable. **2.** (*remark, gesture*) hecho(cha) como quien no quiere la cosa.

throw-in *n Br* (FTBL) saque *m* de banda.

thrown [θrəʊn] *pp* → **throw**.

thru [θruː] *Am inf* = **through**.

thrush [θrʌʃ] *n* **1.** (*bird*) tordo *m*. **2.** (MED) (*vaginal*) hongos *mpl* (vaginales).

thrust [θrʌst] (*pt & pp* **thrust**) ◆ *n* **1.** (*of sword*) estocada *f*; (*of knife*) cuchillada *f*; (*of troops*) arremetida *f*. **2.** (TECH) (*fuerza f de*) propulsión *f*. **3.** (*main meaning*) esencia *f*. ◆ *vt* (*shove*): **he ~ the knife into his enemy** hundió el cuchillo en el

cuerpo de su enemigo.
thud [θʌd] vi dar un golpe seco.
thug [θʌg] n matón m.
thumb [θʌm] ◆ n (of hand) pulgar m.
◆ vt inf (hitch): **to ~ a lift** hacer dedo.
▶ **thumb through** vt fus hojear.
thumbs down [,θʌmz-] n: **to get** OR **be given the ~** (plan) ser rechazado(da); (play) ser recibido(da) con descontento.
thumbs up [,θʌmz-] n: **we got** OR **were given the ~** nos dieron luz verde OR el visto bueno.
thumbtack [ˈθʌmtæk] n Am chincheta f.
thump [θʌmp] ◆ n 1. (blow) puñetazo m. 2. (thud) golpe m seco. ◆ vt (punch) dar un puñetazo a. ◆ vi (heart, head) latir con fuerza.
thunder [ˈθʌndər] ◆ n (U) 1. (METEOR) truenos mpl. 2. fig (loud sound) estruendo m. ◆ v impers (METEOR) tronar. ◆ vi (make loud sound) retumbar.
thunderbolt [ˈθʌndəbəult] n rayo m.
thunderclap [ˈθʌndəklæp] n trueno m.
thunderstorm [ˈθʌndəstɔːm] n tormenta f.
thundery [ˈθʌndərɪ] adj tormentoso(sa).
Thursday [ˈθɜːzdɪ] n jueves m inv; see also **Saturday**.
thus [ðʌs] adv fml 1. (therefore) por consiguiente, así que. 2. (in this way) así, de esta manera.
thwart [θwɔːt] vt frustrar.
thyme [taɪm] n tomillo m.
thyroid [ˈθaɪrɔɪd] n tiroides m inv.
tiara [tɪˈɑːrə] n tiara f.
Tibet [tɪˈbet] n (el) Tíbet.
tic [tɪk] n tic m.
tick [tɪk] ◆ n 1. (written mark) marca f OR señal f de visto bueno. 2. (sound) tictac m. ◆ vt marcar (con una señal). ◆ vi (make ticking sound) hacer tictac. ▶ **tick off** vt sep 1. (mark off) marcar (con una señal de visto bueno). 2. (tell off): **to ~ sb off (for sthg)** echar una bronca a alguien (por algo). ▶ **tick over** vi funcionar al ralentí.
ticket [ˈtɪkɪt] n 1. (for bus, train etc) billete m, boleto m Amer; (for cinema, football match) entrada f. 2. (for traffic offence) multa f.
ticket collector n Br revisor m, -ra f.
ticket inspector n Br revisor m, -ra f.
ticket machine n máquina f automática para la venta de billetes.
ticket office n taquilla f, boletería f Amer.

tickle [ˈtɪkl] vt 1. (touch lightly) hacer cosquillas a. 2. fig (amuse) divertir.
ticklish [ˈtɪklɪʃ] adj (sensitive to touch): **to be ~** tener cosquillas.
tidal [ˈtaɪdl] adj de la marea.
tidal wave n maremoto m.
tidbit Am = **titbit**.
tiddlywinks [ˈtɪdlɪwɪŋks], **tiddledywinks** Am [ˈtɪdldɪwɪŋks] n juego m de la pulga.
tide [taɪd] n 1. (of sea) marea f. 2. fig (of protest, feeling) oleada f.
tidy [ˈtaɪdɪ] ◆ adj 1. (room, desk etc) ordenado(da). 2. (person, dress, hair) arreglado(da). ◆ vt ordenar, arreglar.
▶ **tidy up** vt sep ordenar, arreglar.
tie [taɪ] (pt & pp **tied**, cont **tying**) ◆ n 1. (necktie) corbata f. 2. (string, cord) atadura f. 3. (bond, link) vínculo m, lazo m. 4. (SPORT) (draw) empate m. ◆ vt 1. (attach, fasten): **to ~ sthg (to** OR **onto sthg)** atar algo (a algo); **to ~ sthg round/with sthg** atar algo a/con algo. 2. (do up - shoelaces) atar; (- knot) hacer. 3. fig (link): **to be ~d to** estar ligado a. ◆ vi (draw): **to ~ (with)** empatar (con). ▶ **tie down** vt sep fig atar. ▶ **tie in with** vt fus concordar con. ▶ **tie up** vt sep 1. (gen) atar. 2. fig (money, resources) inmovilizar. 3. fig (link): **to be ~d up with** estar ligado (da) a.
tiebreak(er) [ˈtaɪbreɪk(ər)] n 1. (TENNIS) muerte f súbita, tiebreak m. 2. (in game, competition) pregunta adicional para romper un empate.
tiepin [ˈtaɪpɪn] n alfiler m de corbata.
tier [tɪər] n (of seats) hilera f; (of cake) piso m.
tiff [tɪf] n pelea f (de poca importancia).
tiger [ˈtaɪgər] n tigre m.
tight [taɪt] ◆ adj 1. (gen) apretado(da); (shoes) estrecho(cha). 2. (string, skin) tirante. 3. (budget) ajustado(da). 4. (rules, restrictions) riguroso(sa). 5. (corner, bend) cerrado(da). 6. (match, finish) reñido(da). 7. inf (drunk) cocido(da). 8. inf (miserly) agarrado(da). ◆ adv 1. (hold, squeeze) con fuerza; **to hold ~** agarrarse (fuerte); **to shut** OR **close sthg ~** cerrar algo bien. 2. (pull, stretch) de modo tirante. ▶ **tights** npl medias fpl.
tighten [ˈtaɪtn] ◆ vt 1. (hold, grip): **to ~ one's hold** OR **grip on sthg** coger con más fuerza algo. 2. (rope, chain) tensar. 3. (knot) apretar; (belt) apretarse. 4. (rules, system) intensificar. ◆ vi (rope, chain) tensarse.

tightfisted [,taɪt'fɪstɪd] *adj inf pej* agarrado(da).

tightly ['taɪtlɪ] *adv* **1.** (*hold, squeeze*) con fuerza; (*fasten*) bien. **2.** (*pack*) apretadamente.

tightrope ['taɪtrəup] *n* cuerda *f* floja.

tile [taɪl] *n* **1.** (*on roof*) teja *f*. **2.** (*on floor*) baldosa *f*; (*on wall*) azulejo *m*.

tiled [taɪld] *adj* (*roof*) tejado(da); (*floor*) embaldosado(da); (*wall*) alicatado(da).

till [tɪl] ◆ *prep* hasta; **~ now/then** hasta ahora/entonces. ◆ *conj* hasta que; **wait ~ he arrives** espera hasta que llegue. ◆ *n* caja *f* (registradora).

tiller ['tɪlər] *n* (NAUT) caña *f* del timón.

tilt [tɪlt] ◆ *vt* inclinar. ◆ *vi* inclinarse.

timber ['tɪmbər] *n* **1.** (U) (*wood*) madera *f* (*para la construcción*). **2.** (*beam - of ship*) cuaderna *f*; (*- of house*) viga *f*.

time [taɪm] ◆ *n* **1.** (*gen*) tiempo *m*; **ahead of ~** temprano; **in good ~** con tiempo; **on ~** puntualmente; **to take ~** llevar tiempo; **it's (about) ~ to ...** ya es hora de ...; **to have no ~ for** no poder con, no aguantar; **to pass the ~** pasar el rato; **to play for ~** intentar ganar tiempo; **to take one's ~ (doing sthg)** tomarse uno mucho tiempo (para hacer algo). **2.** (*as measured by clock*) hora *f*; **what ~ is it?, what's the ~?** ¿qué hora es?; **the ~ is three o'clock** son las tres; **in a week's/year's ~** dentro de una semana/un año. **3.** (*length of time*) rato *m*; **it was a long ~ before he came** pasó mucho tiempo antes de que viniera; **for a ~** durante un tiempo. **4.** (*point in time in past, era*) época *f*; **at that ~** en aquella época; **before my ~** antes de que yo naciera. **5.** (*occasion*) vez *f*; **three ~s a week** tres veces a la semana; **from ~ to ~** de vez en cuando; **~ after ~, ~ and again** una y otra vez. **6.** (*experience*) **we had a good/bad ~** lo pasamos bien/mal. **7.** (MUS) compás *m*. ◆ *vt* **1.** (*schedule*) programar. **2.** (*race, runner*) cronometrar. **3.** (*arrival, remark*) elegir el momento oportuno para. ▶ **times** ◆ *n*: **four ~s as much as me** cuatro veces más que yo. ◆ *prep* (MATH): **4 ~s 5** 4 por 5. ▶ **about time** *adv*: **it's about ~** ya va siendo hora. ▶ **at a time** *adv*: **for months at a ~** durante meses seguidos; **one at a ~** de uno en uno. ▶ **at times** *adv* a veces. ▶ **at the same time** *adv* al mismo tiempo. ▶ **for the time being** *adv* de momento. ▶ **in time** *adv* **1.** (*not late*): **in ~ (for)** a tiempo (para). **2.** (*eventually*) con el tiempo.

time bomb *n* (*bomb*) bomba *f* de relojería; *fig* (*dangerous situation*) bomba *f*.

time lag *n* intervalo *m*.

timeless ['taɪmlɪs] *adj* eterno(na).

time limit *n* plazo *m*.

timely ['taɪmlɪ] *adj* oportuno(na).

time off *n* tiempo *m* libre.

time out *n* Am (SPORT) tiempo *m* muerto.

timer ['taɪmər] *n* temporizador *m*.

time scale *n* tiempo *m* de ejecución.

time-share *n* Br multipropiedad *f*.

time switch *n* interruptor *m* de reloj.

timetable ['taɪm,teɪbl] *n* **1.** (*of buses, trains, school*) horario *m*. **2.** (*schedule of events*) programa *m*.

time zone *n* huso *m* horario.

timid ['tɪmɪd] *adj* tímido(da).

timing ['taɪmɪŋ] *n* (U) **1.** (*judgment*): **she made her comment with perfect ~** su comentario fue hecho en el momento más oportuno. **2.** (*scheduling*): **the ~ of the election is crucial** es crucial que las elecciones se celebren en el momento oportuno. **3.** (*measuring*) cronometraje *m*.

timpani ['tɪmpənɪ] *npl* timbales *mpl*.

tin [tɪn] *n* **1.** (*metal*) estaño *m*; **~ plate** hojalata *f*. **2.** Br (*can, container*) lata *f*.

tin can *n* lata *f*.

tinfoil ['tɪnfɔɪl] *n* (U) papel *m* de aluminio.

tinge [tɪndʒ] *n* **1.** (*of colour*) matiz *m*. **2.** (*of feeling*) ligera sensación *f*.

tinged [tɪndʒd] *adj*: **~ with** con un toque de.

tingle ['tɪŋgl] *vi*: **my feet are tingling** siento hormigueo en los pies.

tinker ['tɪŋkər] ◆ *n* Br pej (*gypsy*) gitano *m*, -na *f*. ◆ *vi* hacer chapuzas; **to ~ with** enredar con.

tinkle ['tɪŋkl] *vi* (*ring*) tintinear.

tinned [tɪnd] *adj* Br enlatado(da), en conserva.

tin opener *n* Br abrelatas *m inv*.

tinsel ['tɪnsl] *n* (U) oropel *m*.

tint [tɪnt] *n* tinte *m*, matiz *m*.

tinted ['tɪntɪd] *adj* (*glasses, windows*) tintado(da), ahumado(da).

tiny ['taɪnɪ] *adj* diminuto(ta), pequeñito(ta).

tip [tɪp] ◆ *n* **1.** (*end*) punta *f*. **2.** Br (*dump*) vertedero *m*. **3.** (*gratuity*) propina *f*. **4.** (*piece of advice*) consejo *m*. ◆ *vt* **1.** (*tilt*) inclinar, ladear. **2.** (*spill, pour*) vaciar, verter. **3.** (*give a gratuity to*) dar una propina a. ◆ *vi* **1.** (*tilt*) inclinarse, ladearse. **2.** (*spill*) derramarse. ▶ **tip**

over ◆ *vt sep* volcar. ◆ *vi* volcarse.

tip-off *n* información *f* (confidencial).

tipped [tɪpt] *adj* (*cigarette*) con filtro.

tipsy ['tɪpsɪ] *adj inf dated* piripi.

tiptoe ['tɪptəʊ] *n*: **on ~** de puntillas.

tip-top *adj inf dated* de primera.

tire ['taɪəʳ] ◆ *n Am* = **tyre**. ◆ *vt* cansar. ◆ *vi*: **to ~ (of)** cansarse (de).

tired ['taɪəd] *adj*: **~ (of sthg/of doing sthg)** cansado(da) (de algo/de hacer algo).

tireless ['taɪəlɪs] *adj* incansable.

tiresome ['taɪəsəm] *adj* pesado(da).

tiring ['taɪərɪŋ] *adj* cansado(da).

tissue ['tɪʃuː] *n* **1.** (*paper handkerchief*) pañuelo *m* de papel. **2.** (U) (BIOL) tejido *m*. **3.** (*paper*) papel *m* de seda.

tissue paper *n* (U) papel *m* de seda.

tit [tɪt] *n* **1.** (*bird*) herrerillo *m*. **2.** *vulg* (*breast*) teta *f*.

titbit *Br* ['tɪtbɪt], **tidbit** *Am* ['tɪdbɪt] *n* **1.** (*of food*) golosina *f*. **2.** *fig* (*of news*) noticia *f* breve e interesante.

tit for tat [-'tæt] *n*: **it's ~** donde las dan las toman.

titillate ['tɪtɪleɪt] *vt & vi* excitar.

title ['taɪtl] *n* título *m*.

title deed *n* título *m* de propiedad.

title role *n* papel *m* principal.

titter ['tɪtəʳ] *vi* reírse por lo bajo.

TM *abbr of* **trademark**.

to [*unstressed before consonant* tə, *unstressed before vowel* tu, *stressed* tuː] ◆ *prep* **1.** (*indicating place, direction*) a; **to go ~ Liverpool/Spain/school** ir a Liverpool/España/la escuela; **to go ~ the doctor's/John's** ir al médico/a casa de John; **the road ~ Glasgow** la carretera de Glasgow; **~ the left/right** a la izquierda/derecha; **~ the east/west** hacia el este/oeste. **2.** (*to express indirect object*) a; **to give sthg ~ sb** darle algo a alguien; **to talk ~ sb** hablar con alguien; **a threat ~ sb** una amenaza para alguien; **we were listening ~ the radio** escuchábamos la radio. **3.** (*as far as*) hasta, a; **to count ~ ten** contar hasta diez; **we work from nine ~ five** trabajamos de nueve a cinco. **4.** (*in expressions of time*): **it's ten/a quarter ~ three** son las tres menos diez/cuarto. **5.** (*per*) por; **40 miles ~ the gallon** un galón por cada 40 millas. **6.** (*of*) de; (*for*) para; **the key ~ the car** la llave del coche; **a letter ~ my daughter** una carta para OR a mi hija. **7.** (*indicating reaction, effect*): **~ my surprise** para sorpresa mía. **8.** (*in stating opinion*): **it seemed quite unnecessary ~ me/him** *etc* para mí/él *etc* aquello

parecía del todo innecesario. **9.** (*indicating state, process*): **to drive sb ~ drink** llevar a alguien a la bebida; **to lead ~ trouble** traer problemas. ◆ *adv* (*shut*): **push the door ~** cierra la puerta. ◆ *with infinitive* **1.** (*forming simple infinitive*): **~ walk** andar. **2.** (*following another verb*): **to begin ~ do sthg** empezar a hacer algo; **to try/want ~ do sthg** intentar/querer hacer algo; **to hate ~ do sthg** odiar tener que hacer algo. **3.** (*following an adjective*): **difficult ~ do** difícil de hacer; **ready ~ go** listos para marchar. **4.** (*indicating purpose*) para; **I'm doing it ~ help you** lo hago para ayudarte; **he came ~ see me** vino a verme. **5.** (*substituting for a relative clause*): **I have a lot ~ do** tengo mucho que hacer; **he told me ~ leave** me dijo que me fuera. **6.** (*to avoid repetition of infinitive*): **I meant to call him but I forgot ~** tenía intención de llamarle pero se me olvidó. **7.** (*in comments*): **~ be honest ...** para ser honesto ...; **~ sum up ...** para resumir ..., resumiendo ... ▶ **to and fro** *adv* de un lado para otro.

toad [təʊd] *n* sapo *m*.

toadstool ['təʊdstuːl] *n* seta *f* venenosa.

toast [təʊst] ◆ *n* **1.** (U) (*bread*) pan *m* tostado; **a slice of ~** una tostada. **2.** (*drink*) brindis *m*. ◆ *vt* **1.** (*bread*) tostar. **2.** (*person*) brindar por.

toasted sandwich [,təʊstɪd-] *n* sándwich *m* tostado.

toaster ['təʊstəʳ] *n* tostador *m*, -ra *f*.

tobacco [tə'bækəʊ] *n* tabaco *m*.

tobacconist [tə'bækənɪst] *n* estanquero *m*, -ra *f*; **~'s (shop)** estanco *m*.

toboggan [tə'bɒgən] *n* tobogán *m*, trineo *m*.

today [tə'deɪ] ◆ *n* **1.** (*this day*) hoy *m*. **2.** (*nowadays*) hoy (en día). ◆ *adv* **1.** (*this day*) hoy. **2.** (*nowadays*) hoy (en día).

toddler ['tɒdləʳ] *n* niño pequeño *m*, niña pequeña *f* (que empieza a andar).

toddy ['tɒdɪ] *n* ponche *m*.

to-do (*pl* **-s**) *n inf dated* jaleo *m*.

toe [təʊ] ◆ *n* **1.** (*of foot*) dedo *m* (del pie). **2.** (*of sock*) punta *f*; (*of shoe*) puntera *f*. ◆ *vt*: **to ~ the line** acatar las normas.

toenail ['təʊneɪl] *n* uña *f* del dedo del pie.

toffee ['tɒfɪ] *n* caramelo *m*.

toga ['təʊgə] *n* toga *f*.

together [tə'geðəʳ] *adv* **1.** (*gen*) juntos (tas); **all ~** todos juntos; **to stick ~** pegar; **to go (well) ~** combinar bien. **2.** (*at the same time*) a la vez, juntos(tas).

toil   356

▶ **together with** prep junto con.

toil [tɔɪl] fml ◆ n trabajo m duro. ◆ vi trabajar sin descanso.

toilet ['tɔɪlɪt] n (at home) wáter m, lavabo m; (in public place) servicios mpl, lavabo m; **to go to the ~** ir al wáter.

toilet bag n neceser m, bolsa f de aseo.

toilet paper n (U) papel m higiénico.

toiletries ['tɔɪlɪtrɪz] npl artículos mpl de tocador.

toilet roll n (roll) rollo m de papel higiénico.

toilet water n (agua f de) colonia f.

token ['təʊkn] ◆ adj simbólico(ca). ◆ n 1. (voucher) vale m; (disk) ficha f. 2. (symbol) muestra f, símbolo m. ▶ **by the same token** adv del mismo modo.

told [təʊld] pt & pp → **tell**.

tolerable ['tɒlərəbl] adj tolerable, pasable.

tolerance ['tɒlərəns] n tolerancia f.

tolerant ['tɒlərənt] adj tolerante.

tolerate ['tɒləreɪt] vt 1. (put up with) soportar, tolerar. 2. (permit) tolerar.

toll [təʊl] ◆ n 1. (number): **death ~** número m de víctimas. 2. (fee) peaje m. 3. phr: **to take its ~** hacer mella. ◆ vi tocar, doblar.

toll-free adv Am: **to call a number ~** llamar a un número gratis.

tomato [Br tə'mɑːtəʊ, Am tə'meɪtəʊ] (pl **-es**) n tomate m.

tomb [tuːm] n tumba f, sepulcro m.

tomboy ['tɒmbɔɪ] n niña f poco feminina.

tombstone ['tuːmstəʊn] n lápida f.

tomcat ['tɒmkæt] n gato m (macho).

tomorrow [tə'mɒrəʊ] ◆ n lit & fig mañana f; **the day after ~** pasado mañana; **~ night** mañana por la noche. ◆ adv mañana.

ton [tʌn] (pl inv OR **-s**) n 1. (imperial) Br = 1016 kg; Am = 907,2 kg, ≈ tonelada f. 2. (metric) = 1000 kg, tonelada f. ▶ **tons** npl inf: **~s (of)** un montón de.

tone [təʊn] n 1. (gen) tono m. 2. (on phone) señal f. ▶ **tone down** vt sep suavizar, moderar. ▶ **tone up** vt sep tonificar.

tone-deaf adj que no tiene (buen) oído.

tongs [tɒŋz] npl (for coal) tenazas fpl; (for sugar) pinzas fpl, tenacillas fpl.

tongue [tʌŋ] n 1. (gen) lengua f; **to hold one's ~** fig quedarse callado(da). 2. (of shoe) lengüeta f.

tongue-in-cheek adj: **it was only ~**

no iba en serio.

tongue-tied [-ˌtaɪd] adj incapaz de hablar (por timidez o nervios).

tongue twister [-ˌtwɪstər] n trabalenguas m inv.

tonic ['tɒnɪk] n 1. (gen) tónico m. 2. (tonic water) tónica f.

tonic water n agua f tónica.

tonight [tə'naɪt] ◆ n esta noche f. ◆ adv esta noche.

tonnage ['tʌnɪdʒ] n tonelaje m.

tonne [tʌn] (pl inv OR **-s**) n tonelada f métrica.

tonsil ['tɒnsl] n amígdala f.

tonsil(l)itis [ˌtɒnsɪ'laɪtɪs] n (U) amigdalitis f inv.

too [tuː] adv 1. (also) también. 2. (excessively) demasiado; **~ much** demasiado; **~ many things** demasiadas cosas; **it finished all** OR **only ~ soon** terminó demasiado pronto; **I'd be only ~ happy to help me** encantaría ayudarte; **not ~ ...** no muy ...

took [tʊk] pt → **take**.

tool [tuːl] n (implement) herramienta f; **garden ~s** útiles mpl del jardín.

tool box n caja f de herramientas.

tool kit n juego m de herramientas.

toot [tuːt] ◆ n bocinazo m. ◆ vi tocar la bocina.

tooth [tuːθ] (pl **teeth**) n (in mouth, of saw, gear wheel) diente m.

toothache ['tuːθeɪk] n dolor m de muelas.

toothbrush ['tuːθbrʌʃ] n cepillo m de dientes.

toothpaste ['tuːθpeɪst] n pasta f de dientes.

toothpick ['tuːθpɪk] n palillo m.

top [tɒp] ◆ adj 1. (highest - step, floor) de arriba; (- object on pile) de encima. 2. (most important, successful) importante; **she got the ~ mark** sacó la mejor nota. 3. (maximum) máximo(ma). ◆ n 1. (highest point) parte f superior OR de arriba; (of list) cabeza f, principio m; (of tree) copa f; (of hill, mountain) cumbre f, cima f; **on ~** encima; **at the ~ of one's voice** a voz en grito. 2. (lid, cap - of jar, box) tapa f; (- of bottle, tube) tapón m; (- of pen) capuchón m. 3. (upper side) superficie f. 4. (blouse) blusa f; (T-shirt) camiseta f; (of pyjamas) parte f de arriba. 5. (toy) peonza f. 6. (most important level) cúpula f. 7. (of league, table, scale) cabeza f. ◆ vt 1. (be first in) estar a la cabeza de. 2. (better) superar. 3. (exceed) exceder. ▶ **on top of** prep 1. (in space) encima

de. **2.** (*in addition to*) además de. ▶ **top up** Br, **top off** Am *vt sep* volver a llenar.
top floor *n* último piso *m*.
top hat *n* sombrero *m* de copa.
top-heavy *adj* demasiado pesado (da) en la parte de arriba.
topic ['tɒpɪk] *n* tema *m*, asunto *m*.
topical ['tɒpɪkl] *adj* actual.
topless ['tɒplɪs] *adj* en topless.
top-level *adj* de alto nivel.
topmost ['tɒpməʊst] *adj* más alto(ta).
topping ['tɒpɪŋ] *n* capa *f*; **with a ~ of cream** cubierto de nata.
topple ['tɒpl] ◆ *vt* (*government, pile*) derribar; (*president*) derrocar. ◆ *vi* venirse abajo.
top-secret *adj* sumamente secreto (sumamente secreta).
topspin ['tɒpspɪn] *n* (TENNIS) liftado *m*.
topsy-turvy [,tɒpsɪ'tɜːvɪ] ◆ *adj* (*messy*) patas arriba (*inv*). ◆ *adv* (*messily*) en desorden, de cualquier manera.
torch [tɔːtʃ] *n* **1.** Br (*electric*) linterna *f*. **2.** (*burning*) antorcha *f*.
tore [tɔːr] *pt* → **tear²**.
torment [*n* 'tɔːment, *vb* tɔː'ment] ◆ *n* tormento *m*. ◆ *vt* **1.** (*worry greatly*) atormentar. **2.** (*annoy*) fastidiar.
torn [tɔːn] *pp* → **tear²**.
tornado [tɔː'neɪdəʊ] (*pl* -es OR -s) *n* tornado *m*.
torpedo [tɔː'piːdəʊ] (*pl* -es) *n* torpedo *m*.
torrent ['tɒrənt] *n* torrente *m*.
torrid ['tɒrɪd] *adj* (*hot*) tórrido(da); *fig* (*passionate*) apasionado(da).
tortoise ['tɔːtəs] *n* tortuga *f* (de tierra).
tortoiseshell ['tɔːtəʃel] ◆ *adj*: **~ cat** gato *m* pardo atigrado. ◆ *n* (U) (*material*) carey *m*, concha *f*.
torture ['tɔːtʃər] ◆ *n* tortura *f*. ◆ *vt* torturar.
Tory ['tɔːrɪ] ◆ *adj* tory, del partido conservador (británico). ◆ *n* tory *m y f*, miembro *m* del partido conservador (británico).
toss [tɒs] ◆ *vt* **1.** (*throw carelessly*) tirar. **2.** (*move from side to side - head, boat*) sacudir. **3.** (*salad*) remover; (*pancake*) dar la vuelta en el aire. **4.** (*coin*): **to ~ a coin** echar a cara o cruz. ◆ *vi* (*move rapidly*): **to ~ and turn** dar vueltas (en la cama). ▶ **toss up** *vi* jugar a cara o cruz.
tot [tɒt] *n* **1.** *inf* (*small child*) nene *m*, nena *f*. **2.** (*of drink*) trago *m*.
total ['təʊtl] ◆ *adj* total. ◆ *n* total *m*. ◆ *vt* (*add up*) sumar. ◆ *vi* (*amount to*) ascender a.

totalitarian [,təʊtælɪ'teərɪən] *adj* totalitario(ria).
totally ['təʊtəlɪ] *adv* (*entirely*) totalmente.
totter ['tɒtər] *vi lit & fig* tambalearse.
touch [tʌtʃ] ◆ *n* **1.** (*sense, act of feeling*) tacto *m*. **2.** (*detail, skill, knack*) toque *m*. **3.** (*contact*): **to get/keep in ~ (with)** ponerse/mantenerse en contacto (con); **to lose ~ (with)** perder el contacto (con); **to be out of ~ with** no estar al tanto de. **4.** (SPORT): **in ~** fuera de banda. **5.** (*small amount*): **a ~** un poquito. ◆ *vt* **1.** (*gen*) tocar. **2.** (*emotionally*) conmover. ◆ *vi* (*be in contact*) tocarse. ▶ **touch down** *vi* (*plane*) aterrizar. ▶ **touch on** *vt fus* tratar por encima.
touch-and-go *adj* dudoso(sa), poco seguro (poco segura).
touchdown ['tʌtʃdaʊn] *n* **1.** (*of plane*) aterrizaje *m*. **2.** (*in American football*) ensayo *m*.
touched [tʌtʃt] *adj* (*grateful*) emocionado(da).
touching ['tʌtʃɪŋ] *adj* conmovedor(ra).
touchline ['tʌtʃlaɪn] *n* línea *f* de banda.
touchy ['tʌtʃɪ] *adj* **1.** (*person*): **~ (about)** susceptible (con). **2.** (*subject, question*) delicado(da).
tough [tʌf] *adj* **1.** (*resilient*) fuerte. **2.** (*hard-wearing*) resistente. **3.** (*meat, regulations, policies*) duro(ra). **4.** (*difficult to deal with*) difícil. **5.** (*rough - area*) peligroso(sa).
toughen ['tʌfn] *vt* endurecer.
toupee ['tuːpeɪ] *n* peluquín *m*.
tour [tʊər] ◆ *n* **1.** (*long journey*) viaje *m* largo. **2.** (*of pop group etc*) gira *f*. **3.** (*for sightseeing*) recorrido *m*, visita *f*. ◆ *vt* (*museum*) visitar; (*country*) recorrer, viajar por. ◆ *vi* estar de gira.
touring ['tʊərɪŋ] *n* viajes *mpl* turísticos.
tourism ['tʊərɪzm] *n* turismo *m*.
tourist ['tʊərɪst] *n* turista *m y f*.
tourist (information) office *n* oficina *f* de turismo.
tournament ['tɔːnəmənt] *n* torneo *m*.
tour operator *n* touroperador *m*.
tousle ['taʊzl] *vt* despeinar, alborotar.
tout [taʊt] ◆ *n* revendedor *m*, -ra *f*. ◆ *vt* revender. ◆ *vi*: **to ~ for sthg** solicitar algo.
tow [təʊ] ◆ *n*: **on ~** Br (*car*) a remolque. ◆ *vt* remolcar.
towards Br [tə'wɔːdz], **toward** Am [tə'wɔːd] *prep* **1.** (*gen*) hacia. **2.** (*for the*

purpose or benefit of) para.

towel ['tauəl] *n* toalla *f*.

towelling Br, **toweling** Am ['tauəlɪŋ] *n* (U) (tejido *m* de) toalla *f*.

towel rail *n* toallero *m*.

tower ['tauər] ◆ *n* torre *f*. ◆ *vi*: **to ~ (over sthg)** elevarse (por encima de algo).

tower block *n* Br bloque *m* (*de pisos u oficinas*).

towering ['tauərɪŋ] *adj* altísimo(ma).

town [taun] *n* 1. (*gen*) ciudad *f*; (*smaller*) pueblo *m*. 2. (*centre of town, city*) centro *m* de la ciudad; **to go out on the ~** irse de juerga; **to go to ~** *fig* (*to put in a lot of effort*) emplearse a fondo; (*spend a lot of money*) tirar la casa por la ventana.

town centre *n* centro *m* (de la ciudad).

town council *n* ayuntamiento *m*.

town hall *n* ayuntamiento *m*.

town plan *n* plano *m* de la ciudad.

town planning *n* (*study*) urbanismo *m*.

township ['taunʃɪp] *n* 1. (*in South Africa*) zona urbana asignada por el gobierno para la población negra. 2. (*in US*) ≃ municipio *m*.

towpath ['təupɑːθ, *pl* -pɑːðz] *n* camino *m* de sirga.

towrope ['təurəup] *n* cable *m* de remolque.

tow truck *n* Am (coche *m*) grúa *f*.

toxic ['tɒksɪk] *adj* tóxico(ca).

toy [tɔɪ] *n* juguete *m*. ▶ **toy with** *vt fus* (*idea*) acariciar; (*food, coin etc*) jugetear con.

toy shop *n* juguetería *f*.

trace [treɪs] ◆ *n* 1. (*evidence, remains*) rastro *m*, huella *f*. 2. (*small amount*) pizca *f*. ◆ *vt* 1. (*find*) localizar, encontrar. 2. (*follow progress of*) describir. 3. (*on paper*) calcar.

tracing paper ['treɪsɪŋ-] *n* (U) papel *m* de calcar.

track [træk] ◆ *n* 1. (*path*) sendero *m*. 2. (SPORT) pista *f*. 3. (RAIL) vía *f*. 4. (*mark, trace*) rastro *m*, huella *f*. 5. (*on record, tape*) canción *f*. 6. *phr*: **to keep/lose ~ of sb** no perder/perder la pista a alguien; **to be on the right/wrong ~** ir por el buen/mal camino. ◆ *vt* (*follow tracks of*) seguir la pista de. ▶ **track down** *vt sep* localizar.

track record *n* historial *m*.

tracksuit ['træksuːt] *n* chandal *m*.

tract [trækt] *n* 1. (*pamphlet*) artículo *m* breve. 2. (*of land, forest*) extensión *f*.

traction ['trækʃn] *n* tracción *f*; **to have one's leg in ~** tener la pierna escayolada en alto.

tractor ['træktər] *n* tractor *m*.

trade [treɪd] ◆ *n* 1. (U) (*commerce*) comercio *m*. 2. (*job*) oficio *m*; **by ~** de oficio. ◆ *vt* (*exchange*): **to ~ sthg (for)** cambiar algo (por). ◆ *vi* (COMM): **to ~ (with)** comerciar (con). ▶ **trade in** *vt sep* (*exchange*) dar como entrada.

trade fair *n* feria *f* de muestras.

trade-in *n* artículo usado que se entrega como entrada al comprar un artículo nuevo.

trademark ['treɪdmɑːk] *n* (COMM) marca *f* comercial.

trade name *n* (COMM) nombre *m* comercial.

trader ['treɪdər] *n* comerciante *m y f*.

tradesman ['treɪdzmən] (*pl* -men [-mən]) *n* (*trader*) comerciante *m*; (*shopkeeper*) tendero *m*.

trade(s) union *n* Br sindicato *m*.

Trades Union Congress *n* Br: **the ~** la asociación británica de sindicatos.

trade(s) unionist *n* Br sindicalista *m y f*.

trading ['treɪdɪŋ] *n* (U) comercio *m*.

trading estate *n* Br polígono *m* industrial.

tradition [trə'dɪʃn] *n* tradición *f*.

traditional [trə'dɪʃənl] *adj* tradicional.

traffic ['træfɪk] (*pt & pp* -ked, *cont* -king) ◆ *n* 1. (*vehicles*) tráfico *m*. 2. (*illegal trade*): **~ (in)** tráfico *m* (de). ◆ *vi*: **to ~ in** traficar con.

traffic circle *n* Am glorieta *f*.

traffic jam *n* embotellamiento *m*.

trafficker ['træfɪkər] *n*: **~ (in)** traficante *m y f* (de).

traffic lights *npl* semáforos *mpl*.

traffic warden *n* Br ≃ guardia *m y f* de tráfico.

tragedy ['trædʒədɪ] *n* tragedia *f*.

tragic ['trædʒɪk] *adj* trágico(ca).

trail [treɪl] ◆ *n* 1. (*path*) sendero *m*, camino *m*. 2. (*trace, track*) rastro *m*, huellas *fpl*. ◆ *vt* 1. (*drag*) arrastrar. 2. (*lose to*) ir por detrás de. ◆ *vi* 1. (*drag*) arrastrarse. 2. (*move slowly*) andar con desgana. 3. (*lose*) ir perdiendo. ▶ **trail away, trail off** *vi* apagarse.

trailer ['treɪlər] *n* 1. (*vehicle for luggage*) remolque *m*. 2. (*for living in*) roulotte *m*, caravana *f*. 3. (CINEMA) tráiler *m*.

train [treɪn] ◆ *n* 1. (RAIL) tren *m*. 2. (*of dress*) cola *f*. ◆ *vt* 1. (*teach*): **to ~ sb (to do sthg)** enseñar a alguien (a hacer algo); **to ~ sb in sthg** preparar a alguien para algo. **2.** (for job): **to ~ sb (as sthg)** formar OR preparar a alguien (como algo). **3.** (SPORT): **to ~ sb (for)** entrenar a alguien (para). **4.** (aim - gun) apuntar. ◆ vi **1.** (for job) estudiar; **to ~ as** formarse OR prepararse como. **2.** (SPORT): **to ~ (for)** entrenarse (para).

trained [treɪnd] adj cualificado(da).

trainee [treɪ'niː] n aprendiz m, -za f.

trainer ['treɪnə'] n **1.** (of animals) amaestrador m, -ra f. **2.** (SPORT) entrenador m, -ra f. ▶ **trainers** npl Br zapatillas fpl de deporte.

training ['treɪnɪŋ] n (U) **1.** (for job): **~ (in)** formación f OR preparación f (para). **2.** (SPORT) entrenamiento m.

training college n Br (gen) centro m de formación especializada; (for teachers) escuela f normal.

training shoes npl Br zapatillas fpl de deporte.

train of thought n hilo m del razonamiento.

traipse [treɪps] vi andar con desgana.

trait [treɪt] n rasgo m, característica f.

traitor ['treɪtə'] n: **~ (to)** traidor m, -ra f (a).

trajectory [trə'dʒektərɪ] n trayectoria f.

tram [træm], **tramcar** ['træmkɑː'] n Br tranvía m.

tramp [træmp] ◆ n **1.** (homeless person) vagabundo m, -da f. **2.** Am inf (woman) fulana f. ◆ vi andar pesadamente.

trample ['træmpl] vt pisar, pisotear.

trampoline ['træmpəliːn] n cama f elástica.

trance [trɑːns] n trance m.

tranquil ['træŋkwɪl] adj literary tranquilo(la), apacible.

tranquillity Br, **tranquility** Am [træŋ'kwɪlɪtɪ] n tranquilidad f.

tranquillizer Br, **tranquilizer** Am ['træŋkwɪlaɪzə'] n tranquilizante m.

transaction [træn'zækʃn] n transacción f.

transcend [træn'send] vt fml ir más allá de.

transcript ['trænskrɪpt] n transcripción f.

transfer [n 'trænsfɜː', vb træns'fɜː'] ◆ n **1.** (gen) transferencia f. **2.** (for job) traslado m. **3.** (SPORT) traspaso m. **4.** (design) calcomanía f. ◆ vt **1.** (from one place to another) trasladar. **2.** (from one person to another) transferir. ◆ vi (to different job etc): **he transferred to a different department** lo trasladaron a otro departamento.

transfix [træns'fɪks] vt (immobilize) paralizar.

transform [træns'fɔːm] vt: **to ~ sthg/sb (into)** transformar algo/a alguien (en).

transfusion [træns'fjuːʒn] n transfusión f.

transient ['trænzɪənt] adj fml (fleeting) transitorio(ria), pasajero(ra).

transistor [træn'zɪstə'] n transistor m.

transistor radio n dated transistor m.

transit ['trænsɪt] n: **in ~** de tránsito.

transition [træn'zɪʃn] n: **~ (from sthg to sthg)** transición f (de algo a algo).

transitive ['trænzɪtɪv] adj (GRAMM) transitivo(va).

transitory ['trænzɪtrɪ] adj transitorio (ria).

translate [træns'leɪt] vt (languages) traducir.

translation [træns'leɪʃn] n traducción f.

translator [træns'leɪtə'] n traductor m, -ra f.

transmission [trænz'mɪʃn] n transmisión f.

transmit [trænz'mɪt] vt transmitir.

transmitter [trænz'mɪtə'] n (ELECTRON) transmisor m.

transparency [trans'pærənsɪ] n transparencia f.

transparent [træns'pærənt] adj **1.** (see-through) transparente. **2.** (obvious) claro(ra).

transpire [træn'spaɪə'] fml ◆ vt: **it ~s that ...** resulta que ... ◆ vi (happen) ocurrir.

transplant ['trænsplɑːnt] n trasplante m.

transport [n 'trænspɔːt, vb træn'spɔːt] ◆ n transporte m. ◆ vt transportar.

transportation [,trænspɔː'teɪʃn] n transporte m.

transport cafe ['trænspɔːt-] n Br bar m de camioneros.

transpose [træns'pəuz] vt (change round) invertir.

trap [træp] ◆ n trampa f. ◆ vt **1.** (catch - animals, birds) coger con trampa. **2.** (trick) atrapar, engañar.

trapdoor [,træp'dɔː'] n (gen) trampilla f, trampa f; (THEATRE) escotillón m.

trapeze [trə'piːz] n trapecio m.

trappings ['træpɪŋz] npl atributos mpl.

trash [træʃ] n Am lit & fig basura f.

trashcan ['træʃkæn] n Am cubo m de la basura.

traumatic [trɔː'mætɪk] adj traumático (ca).

travel ['trævl] ◆ n (U) viajes mpl. ◆ vt (place) viajar por; (distance) recorrer. ◆ vi viajar.

travel agency n agencia f de viajes.

travel agent n empleado m, -da f de una agencia de viajes; ~'s agencia f de viajes.

traveller Br, **traveler** Am ['trævlər] (person on journey) viajero m, -ra f.

traveller's cheque n cheque m de viajero.

travelling Br, **traveling** Am ['trævliŋ] adj (theatre, showman) ambulante.

travelsick ['trævəlsik] adj que se marea al viajar.

travesty ['trævəsti] n burda parodia f.

trawler ['trɔːlər] n trainera f.

tray [treɪ] n bandeja f.

treacherous ['tretʃərəs] adj 1. (plan, action) traicionero(ra); (person) traidor (ra). 2. (dangerous) peligroso(sa).

treachery ['tretʃəri] n traición f.

treacle ['triːkl] n Br melaza f.

tread [tred] (pt **trod**, pp **trodden**) ◆ n 1. (on tyre, shoe) banda f. 2. (sound of walking) pasos mpl; (way of walking) modo m de andar. ◆ vi 1. (step): **to ~ on sthg** pisar algo. 2. (walk) andar.

treason ['triːzn] n traición f.

treasure ['treʒər] ◆ n lit & fig tesoro m. ◆ vt guardar como oro en paño.

treasurer ['treʒərər] n tesorero m, -ra f.

treasury ['treʒəri] n (room) habitación donde se guarda el tesoro de un castillo, de una catedral etc. ▶ **Treasury** n: **the Treasury** ≃ el Ministerio de Hacienda.

treat [triːt] ◆ vt 1. (gen) tratar; **to ~ sb as/like** tratar a alguien como. 2. (give sthg special): **to ~ sb (to)** invitar a alguien (a). ◆ n (something special) regalo m; **he took me out to dinner as a ~** me invitó a cenar.

treatise ['triːtis] n fml: ~ **(on)** tratado m (sobre).

treatment ['triːtmənt] n 1. (MED) tratamiento m. 2. (manner of dealing) trato m.

treaty ['triːti] n tratado m.

treble ['trebl] ◆ adj 1. (MUS) de tiple. 2. (with numbers) triple. ◆ n (MUS) (range, singer) tiple m. ◆ vt triplicar. ◆ vi triplicarse.

treble clef n clave f de sol.

tree [triː] n (BOT & COMPUT) árbol m.

treetop ['triːtɒp] n copa f (de árbol).

tree-trunk n tronco m (de árbol).

trek [trek] n viaje m largo y difícil.

trekking ['trekiŋ] n senderismo m.

trellis ['trelis] n enrejado m, espaldera f.

tremble ['trembl] vi temblar.

tremendous [tri'mendəs] adj 1. (impressive, large) enorme, tremendo(da). 2. inf (really good) estupendo(da).

tremor ['tremər] n 1. (of person, body, voice) estremecimiento m. 2. (small earthquake) temblor m.

trench [trentʃ] n 1. (narrow channel) zanja f. 2. (MIL) trinchera f.

trench coat n trinchera f.

trend [trend] n (tendency) tendencia f; (fashion) moda f.

trendy ['trendi] adj inf (person) moderno(na); (clothes) de moda.

trepidation [,trepi'deiʃn] n fml: **in** OR **with ~** con ansiedad OR agitación.

trespass ['trespəs] vi entrar ilegalmente; **'no ~ing'** 'prohibido el paso'.

trespasser ['trespəsər] n intruso m, -sa f.

trestle ['tresl] n caballete m.

trestle table n mesa f de caballete.

trial ['traɪəl] n 1. (JUR) juicio m, proceso m; **to be on ~ (for)** ser procesado(da) (por). 2. (test, experiment) prueba f; **on ~** de prueba; **by ~ and error** a base de probar. 3. (unpleasant experience) suplicio m, fastidio m.

triangle ['traɪæŋgl] n (GEOM & MUS) triángulo m.

tribe [traɪb] n tribu f.

tribunal [traɪ'bjuːnl] n tribunal m.

tributary ['tribjutri] n afluente m.

tribute ['tribjuːt] n 1. (credit) tributo m; **to be a ~ to** hacer honor a. 2. (U) (respect, admiration): **to pay ~ (to)** rendir homenaje (a).

trice [traɪs] n: **in a ~** en un dos por tres.

trick [trik] ◆ n 1. (to deceive) truco m; (to trap) trampa f; (joke) broma f; **to play a ~ on sb** gastarle una broma a alguien. 2. (in magic) juego m (de manos). 3. (knack) truco m; **that should do the ~** eso es lo que necesitamos. ◆ vt engañar; **to ~ sb into doing sthg** engañar a alguien para que haga algo.

trickery ['trikəri] n (U) engaño m.

trickle ['trikl] ◆ n (of liquid) hilo m. ◆ vi 1. (liquid) resbalar (formando un hilo). 2. (people, things): **to ~ in/out** llegar/salir poco a poco.

tricky ['triki] adj (difficult) difícil.

tricycle ['traisikl] n triciclo m.

tried [traɪd] adj: ~ **and tested** probado (da).

trifle ['traɪfl] n 1. Br (CULIN) postre de bizcocho con gelatina, crema, frutas y nata. 2. (unimportant thing) nadería f. ▶ **a trifle** adv fml un poco, ligeramente. ◆

trifling ['traɪflɪŋ] adj pej trivial.

trigger ['trɪgər] n (on gun) gatillo m. ▶ **trigger off** vt sep desencadenar.

trill [trɪl] n trino m.

trim [trɪm] ◆ adj 1. (neat and tidy) limpio y arreglado (limpia y arreglada). 2. (slim) esbelto(ta). ◆ n (of hair) recorte m. ◆ vt 1. (nails, moustache) recortar. 2. (decorate): **to ~ sthg (with)** adornar algo (con).

trimmings ['trɪmɪŋz] npl 1. (on clothing) adornos mpl. 2. (with food) guarnición f.

trinket ['trɪŋkɪt] n baratija f.

trio ['triːəʊ] (pl -s) n trío m.

trip [trɪp] ◆ n (gen & drugs sl) viaje m. ◆ vt (make stumble) hacer la zancadilla a. ◆ vi (stumble) tropezar; **to ~ over sthg** tropezar con algo. ▶ **trip up** vt sep (make stumble) hacer tropezar, hacer la zancadilla a.

tripe [traɪp] n (U) 1. (CULIN) callos mpl. 2. inf (nonsense) tonterías fpl.

triple ['trɪpl] ◆ adj triple. ◆ vt triplicar. ◆ vi triplicarse.

triple jump n: **the ~** el triple salto.

triplets ['trɪplɪts] npl trillizos mpl, -zas fpl.

triplicate ['trɪplɪkət] n: **in ~** por triplicado.

tripod ['traɪpɒd] n trípode m.

trite [traɪt] adj pej trillado(da).

triumph ['traɪəmf] ◆ n triunfo m. ◆ vi: **to ~ (over)** triunfar (sobre).

trivia ['trɪvɪə] n (U) trivialidades fpl.

trivial ['trɪvɪəl] adj pej trivial.

trod [trɒd] pt → **tread**.

trodden ['trɒdn] pp → **tread**.

trolley ['trɒlɪ] (pl **trolleys**) n 1. Br (for shopping, food, drinks) carrito m. 2. Am (tram) tranvía m.

trombone [trɒm'bəʊn] n trombón m.

troop [truːp] ◆ n (of people) grupo m, bandada f; (of animals) manada f. ◆ vi ir en grupo. ▶ **troops** npl tropas fpl.

trooper ['truːpər] n 1. (MIL) soldado m de caballería. 2. Am (policeman) miembro de la policía estatal.

trophy ['trəʊfɪ] n (SPORT) trofeo m.

tropical ['trɒpɪkl] adj tropical.

tropics ['trɒpɪks] npl: **the ~** el trópico.

trot [trɒt] ◆ n 1. (of horse) trote m. 2. (of person) paso m rápido. ◆ vi 1. (horse) tro-

tar. 2. (person) andar con pasos rápidos. ▶ **on the trot** adv inf: **three times on the ~** tres veces seguidas.

trouble ['trʌbl] ◆ n (U) 1. (bother) molestia f; (difficulty, main problem) problema m; **would it be too much ~ to ask you to ...?** ¿tendría inconveniente en ...?; **to be in ~** tener problemas; **to take the ~ to do sthg** tomarse la molestia de hacer algo. 2. (U) (pain) dolor m; (illness) enfermedad f. 3. (U) (violence, unpleasantness) problemas mpl. ◆ vt 1. (worry, upset) preocupar. 2. (disturb, give pain to) molestar. ▶ **troubles** npl 1. (problems, worries) problemas mpl. 2. (POL) conflicto m.

troubled ['trʌbld] adj 1. (worried, upset) preocupado(da). 2. (disturbed, problematic) agitado(da), turbulento(ta).

troublemaker ['trʌbl,meɪkər] n alborotador m, -ra f.

troubleshooter ['trʌbl,ʃuːtər] n (for machines) especialista en la localización y reparación de averías; (in organizations) persona contratada para resolver problemas.

troublesome ['trʌblsəm] adj molesto (ta).

trough [trɒf] n 1. (for drinking) abrevadero m; (for eating) comedero m. 2. (low point) punto m más bajo.

troupe [truːp] n compañía f.

trousers ['traʊzəz] npl pantalones mpl.

trousseau ['truːsəʊ] (pl **-x** [-z] OR **-s**) n ajuar m.

trout [traʊt] (pl inv OR **-s**) n trucha f.

trowel ['traʊəl] n 1. (for the garden) desplantador m. 2. (for cement, plaster) paleta f, palustre m.

truant ['truːənt] n (child) alumno m, -na f que hace novillos; **to play ~** hacer novillos.

truce [truːs] n: **~ (between)** tregua f (entre).

truck [trʌk] n 1. (lorry) camión m. 2. (RAIL) vagón m de mercancías.

truck driver n camionero m, -ra f.

trucker ['trʌkər] n Am camionero m, -ra f.

truck farm n Am puesto de verduras y frutas para la venta.

truculent ['trʌkjʊlənt] adj agresivo (va), pendenciero(ra).

trudge [trʌdʒ] vi caminar con dificultad.

true [truː] adj 1. (gen) verdadero(ra); **it's ~** es verdad; **to come ~** hacerse realidad. 2. (genuine) auténtico(ca); (friend) de verdad. 3. (exact) exacto(ta).

truffle | 362

truffle ['trʌfl] n trufa f.

truly ['truːlɪ] adv verdaderamente; **yours ~** le saluda atentamente.

trump [trʌmp] n triunfo m (en cartas).

trumped-up ['trʌmpt-] adj pej inventado(da).

trumpet ['trʌmpɪt] n trompeta f.

truncheon ['trʌntʃən] n porra f.

trundle ['trʌndl] vi rodar lentamente.

trunk [trʌŋk] n 1. (of tree, person) tronco m. 2. (of elephant) trompa f. 3. (box) baúl m. 4. Am (of car) maletero m, cajuela f Amer. ▶ **trunks** npl bañador m (de hombre).

trunk call n Br conferencia f, llamada f interurbana.

trunk road n = carretera f nacional.

truss [trʌs] n (MED) braguero m.

trust [trʌst] ◆ vt 1. (believe in) confiar en. 2. (have confidence in): **to ~ sb to do sthg** confiar en alguien para que haga algo. 3. (entrust): **to ~ sb with sthg** confiar algo a alguien. 4. (accept as safe, reliable) fiarse de. ◆ n 1. (U) (faith, responsibility): **~ (in)** confianza f (en). 2. (FIN) trust m; **in ~** en fideicomiso.

trusted ['trʌstɪd] adj de confianza.

trustee [trʌs'tiː] n (FIN & JUR) fidei-. comisario m, -ria f.

trust fund n fondo m de fideicomiso.

trusting ['trʌstɪŋ] adj confiado(da).

trustworthy ['trʌst,wɜːðɪ] adj digno (na) de confianza.

truth [truːθ] n verdad f; **in (all) ~** en verdad, verdaderamente.

truthful ['truːθfʊl] adj 1. (person) sincero(ra). 2. (story) verídico(ca).

try [traɪ] ◆ vt 1. (attempt) intentar; **to ~ to do sthg** tratar de OR intentar hacer algo. 2. (sample, test) probar. 3. (JUR) (case) ver; (criminal) juzgar, procesar. 4. (put to the test - person) acabar con la paciencia de; (- patience) acabar con. ◆ vi intentar; **to ~ for sthg** tratar de conseguir algo. ◆ n 1. (attempt) intento m, tentativa f. 2. (sample, test): **to give sthg a ~** probar algo. 3. (RUGBY) ensayo m. ▶ **try on** vt sep probarse. ▶ **try out** vt sep (car, machine) probar; (plan) poner a prueba.

trying ['traɪɪŋ] adj difícil, pesado(da).

T-shirt n camiseta f.

T-square n escuadra f en forma de T.

tub [tʌb] n 1. (container - small) bote m; (- large) tina f. 2. inf (bath) bañera f.

tubby ['tʌbɪ] adj inf regordete(ta).

tube [tjuːb] n 1. (cylinder, container) tubo m. 2. (ANAT) conducto m. 3. Br (RAIL) metro m; **by ~** en metro.

tuberculosis [tjuː,bɜːkjʊ'ləʊsɪs] n tuberculosis f.

tubing ['tjuːbɪŋ] n (U) tubos mpl.

tubular ['tjuːbjʊlər] adj tubular.

TUC n abbr of **Trades Union Congress**.

tuck [tʌk] vt (place neatly) meter. ▶ **tuck away** vt sep (money etc) guardar. ▶ **tuck in** ◆ vt sep 1. (person - in bed) arropar. 2. (clothes) meterse. ◆ vi inf comer con apetito. ▶ **tuck up** vt sep arropar.

tuck shop n Br confitería f (emplazada cerca de un colegio).

Tuesday ['tjuːzdɪ] n martes m inv; see also **Saturday**.

tuft [tʌft] n (of hair) mechón m; (of grass) manojo m.

tug [tʌg] ◆ n 1. (pull) tirón m. 2. (boat) remolcador m. ◆ vt tirar de. ◆ vi: **to ~ (at)** tirar (de).

tug-of-war n juego m de la cuerda (en el que dos equipos compiten tirando de ella).

tuition [tjuː'ɪʃn] n enseñanza f; **private ~** clases fpl particulares.

tulip ['tjuːlɪp] n tulipán m.

tumble ['tʌmbl] ◆ vi (person) caerse (rodando). ◆ n caída f. ▶ **tumble to** vt fus Br inf caerse en la cuenta de.

tumbledown ['tʌmbldaʊn] adj ruinoso(sa).

tumble-dryer [-,draɪər] n secadora f.

tumbler ['tʌmblər] n (glass) vaso m.

tummy ['tʌmɪ] n inf barriga f.

tumour Br, **tumor** Am ['tjuːmər] n tumor m.

tuna [Br 'tjuːnə, Am 'tuːnə] (pl inv OR **-s**) n atún m.

tune [tjuːn] ◆ n 1. (song, melody) melodía f. 2. (harmony): **in ~** (MUS) afinado(da); **out of ~** (MUS) desafinado(da); **to be out of/in ~ (with sb/sthg)** fig no avenirse/avenirse (con alguien/algo). ◆ vt 1. (MUS) afinar. 2. (RADIO & TV) sintonizar. 3. (engine) poner a punto. ▶ **tune in** vi (RADIO & TV): **to ~ in (to sthg)** sintonizar (algo). ▶ **tune up** vi (MUS) concertar OR afinar los instrumentos.

tuneful ['tjuːnfʊl] adj melodioso(sa).

tuner ['tjuːnər] n 1. (RADIO & TV) sintonizador m. 2. (MUS) afinador m, -ra f.

tunic ['tjuːnɪk] n túnica f.

tuning fork ['tjuːnɪŋ-] n diapasón m.

Tunisia [tjuː'nɪzɪə] n Túnez.

tunnel ['tʌnl] ◆ n túnel m. ◆ vi hacer un túnel.

turban ['tɜːbən] n turbante m.

turbine ['tɜːbaɪn] n turbina f.

turbocharged ['tɜːbəʊtʃɑːdʒd] *adj* provisto(ta) de turbina; (*car*) turbo (*inv*).

turbulence ['tɜːbjʊləns] *n* (U) *lit & fig* turbulencia *f*.

turbulent ['tɜːbjʊlənt] *adj lit & fig* turbulento(ta).

tureen [tə'riːn] *n* sopera *f*.

turf [tɜːf] (*pl* **-s** OR **turves**) ◆ *n* **1.** (*grass surface*) césped *m*. **2.** (*clod*) tepe *m*. ◆ *vt* encespedar. ▶ **turf out** *vt sep* Br *inf* (*person*) dar la patada a, echar; (*old clothes*) tirar.

turgid ['tɜːdʒɪd] *adj fml* (*over-solemn*) ampuloso(sa).

Turk [tɜːk] *n* turco *m*, -ca *f*.

turkey ['tɜːkɪ] (*pl* **turkeys**) *n* pavo *m*.

Turkey ['tɜːkɪ] *n* Turquía *f*.

Turkish ['tɜːkɪʃ] ◆ *adj* turco(ca). ◆ *n* (*language*) turco *m*. ◆ *npl* (*people*): **the ~** los turcos.

Turkish delight *n* rahat lokum *m*, *dulce de una sustancia gelatinosa, cubierto de azúcar glas.*

turmoil ['tɜːmɔɪl] *n* confusión *f*, alboroto *m*.

turn [tɜːn] ◆ *n* **1.** (*in road, river*) curva *f*. **2.** (*of knob, wheel*) vuelta *f*. **3.** (*change*) cambio *m*. **4.** (*in game*) turno *m*; **it's my ~** me toca a mí; **in ~** sucesivamente, uno tras otro. **5.** (*performance*) número *m*. **6.** (MED) ataque *m*. **7.** *phr*: **to do sb a good ~** hacerle un favor a alguien. ◆ *vt* **1.** (*chair, page, omelette*) dar la vuelta a. **2.** (*knob, wheel*) girar. **3.** (*corner*) doblar. **4.** (*thoughts, attention*): **to ~ sthg to** dirigir algo hacia. **5.** (*change*): **to ~ sthg into** convertir OR transformar algo en. **6.** (*cause to become*): **the cold ~ed his fingers blue** se le pusieron los dedos azules por el frío. **7.** (*become*): **it ~ed black** se volvió negro. ◆ *vi* **1.** (*car*) girar; (*road*) torcer; (*person*) volverse, darse la vuelta. **2.** (*wheel*) dar vueltas. **3.** (*turn page over*): **~ to page two** pasen a la página dos. **4.** (*thoughts, attention*): **to ~ to** dirigirse hacia. **5.** (*seek consolation*): **to ~ to sb/sthg** buscar consuelo en alguien/algo. **6.** (*change*): **to ~ into** convertirse OR transformarse en. **7.** (*go sour*) cortarse. ▶ **turn around** = **turn round**. ▶ **turn away** *vt sep* (*refuse entry to*) no dejar entrar. ▶ **turn back** ◆ *vt sep* (*person, vehicle*) hacer volver. ◆ *vi* volver, volverse. ▶ **turn down** *vt sep* **1.** (*offer, person*) rechazar. **2.** (*volume etc*) bajar. ▶ **turn in** *vi inf* (*go to bed*) irse a dormir. ▶ **turn off** ◆ *vt fus* (*road, path*) desviarse

de. ◆ *vt sep* (*radio, heater*) apagar; (*engine*) parar; (*gas, tap*) cerrar. ◆ *vi* (*leave road*) desviarse. ▶ **turn on** ◆ *vt sep* **1.** (*radio, TV, engine*) encender; (*gas, tap*) abrir. **2.** *inf* (*excite sexually*) poner cachondo(da). ◆ *vt fus* (*attack*) atacar. ▶ **turn out** ◆ *vt sep* **1.** (*extinguish*) apagar. **2.** (*empty - pockets, bag*) vaciar. ◆ *vt fus*: **to ~ out to be** resultar ser. ◆ *vi* **1.** (*end up*) salir. **2.** (*arrive*): **to ~ out (for)** venir OR presentarse (a). ▶ **turn over** ◆ *vt sep* **1.** (*turn upside down*) dar la vuelta a; (*page*) volver. **2.** (*consider*) darle vueltas a. **3.** Br (RADIO & TV) cambiar. **4.** (*hand over*): **to ~ sthg/sb over (to)** entregar algo/a alguien (a). ◆ *vi* **1.** (*roll over*) darse la vuelta. **2.** Br (RADIO & TV) cambiar de canal. ▶ **turn round** ◆ *vt sep* **1.** (*gen*) dar la vuelta a. **2.** (*knob, key*) hacer girar. ◆ *vi* (*person*) darse la vuelta, volverse. ▶ **turn up** ◆ *vt sep* (*volume, heating*) subir. ◆ *vi inf* aparecer.

turning ['tɜːnɪŋ] *n* (*road*) bocacalle *f*.

turning point *n* momento *m* decisivo.

turnip ['tɜːnɪp] *n* nabo *m*.

turnout ['tɜːnaʊt] *n* número *m* de asistentes, asistencia *f*.

turnover ['tɜːnˌəʊvər] *n* (U) **1.** (*of personnel*) movimiento *m* de personal. **2.** Br (FIN) volumen *m* de ventas, facturación *f*.

turnpike ['tɜːnpaɪk] *n* Am autopista *f* de peaje.

turnstile ['tɜːnstaɪl] *n* torniquete *m*.

turntable ['tɜːnˌteɪbl] *n* plato *m* giratorio.

turn-up *n* Br (*on trousers*) vuelta *f*; **a ~ for the books** *inf* una auténtica sorpresa.

turpentine ['tɜːpəntaɪn] *n* trementina *f*.

turquoise ['tɜːkwɔɪz] ◆ *adj* turquesa. ◆ *n* (*mineral, gem*) turquesa *f*.

turret ['tʌrɪt] *n* torreta *f*, torrecilla *f*.

turtle ['tɜːtl] (*pl inv* OR **-s**) *n* tortuga *f* (*marina*).

turtleneck ['tɜːtlnek] *n* (*sweater*) jersey *m* de cuello vuelto OR de cisne.

turves [tɜːvz] Br *pl* → **turf**.

tusk [tʌsk] *n* colmillo *m*.

tussle ['tʌsl] ◆ *n* lucha *f*, pelea *f*. ◆ *vi*: **to ~ (over)** pelearse (por).

tutor ['tjuːtər] *n* **1.** (*private*) profesor particular *m*, profesora particular *f*, tutor *m*, -ra *f*. **2.** (UNIV) profesor universitario *m*, profesora universitaria *f* (*de un grupo pequeño*).

tutorial [tjuː'tɔːrɪəl] *n* tutoría *f*, clase *f*

con grupo reducido.
tuxedo [tʌk'siːdəu] (*pl* **-s**) *n* esmoquin *m*.
TV (*abbr of* **television**) ◆ *n* televisión *f*; **on ~** en la televisión. ◆ *comp* de televisión.
twang [twæŋ] *n* 1. (*of guitar*) tañido *m*; (*of string, elastic*) sonido *m* vibrante. 2. (*accent*) gangueo *m*, acento *m* nasal.
tweed [twiːd] *n* tweed *m*.
tweezers ['twiːzəz] *npl* pinzas *fpl*.
twelfth [twelfθ] *num* duodécimo(ma); *see also* **sixth**.
twelve [twelv] *num* doce; *see also* **six**.
twentieth ['twentɪəθ] *num* vigésimo (ma); *see also* **sixth**.
twenty ['twentɪ] *num* veinte; *see also* **sixty**.
twice [twaɪs] ◆ *num adv* dos veces; **~ a week** dos veces por semana; **it costs ~ as much** cuesta el doble. ◆ *num adj* dos veces; **~ as big** el doble de grande.
twiddle ['twɪdl] ◆ *vt* dar vueltas a. ◆ *vi*: **to ~ with** juguetear con.
twig [twɪg] *n* ramita *f*.
twilight ['twaɪlaɪt] *n* crepúsculo *m*.
twin [twɪn] ◆ *adj* gemelo(la). ◆ *n* gemelo *m*, -la *f*.
twin-bedded [-'bedɪd] *adj* de dos camas.
twine [twaɪn] ◆ *n* (U) bramante *m*. ◆ *vt*: **to ~ sthg round sthg** enrollar algo en algo.
twinge [twɪndʒ] *n* (*of pain*) punzada *f*; (*of guilt*) remordimiento *m*.
twinkle ['twɪŋkl] *vi* 1. (*star*) centellear, parpadear. 2. (*eyes*) brillar.
twin room *n* habitación *f* con dos camas.
twin town *n* ciudad *f* hermanada.
twirl [twɜːl] ◆ *vt* dar vueltas a. ◆ *vi* dar vueltas rápidamente.
twist [twɪst] ◆ *n* 1. (*in road*) vuelta *f*, recodo *m*; (*in river*) meandro *m*. 2. (*of head, lid, knob*) giro *m*. 3. (*shape*) espiral *f*. 4. *fig* (*in plot*) giro *m* imprevisto. ◆ *vt* 1. (*cloth, rope*) retorcer; (*hair*) enroscar. 2. (*face etc*) torcer. 3. (*dial, lid*) dar vueltas a; (*head*) volver. 4. (*ankle, knee etc*) torcerse. 5. (*misquote*) tergiversar. ◆ *vi* 1. (*person*) retorcerse; (*road, river*) serpentear. 2. (*face*) contorsionarse; (*frame, rail*) torcerse. 3. (*turn - head, hand*) volverse.
twit [twɪt] *n* Br *inf* imbécil *m y f*.
twitch [twɪtʃ] ◆ *n* contorsión *f*; **nervous ~ tic** *m* (nervioso). ◆ *vi* contorsionarse.

two [tuː] *num* dos; **in ~** en dos; *see also* **six**.
two-door *adj* (*car*) de dos puertas.
twofaced [,tuː'feɪst] *adj pej* hipócrita.
twofold ['tuːfəuld] ◆ *adj* doble; **a ~ increase** un incremento del doble. ◆ *adv*: **to increase ~** duplicarse.
two-piece *adj* (*suit*) de dos piezas.
twosome ['tuːsəm] *n inf* pareja *f*.
two-way *adj* (*traffic*) en ambas direcciones; (*agreement, cooperation*) mutuo (tua).
tycoon [taɪ'kuːn] *n* magnate *m*.
type [taɪp] ◆ *n* 1. (*gen*) tipo *m*. 2. (U) (TYPO) tipo *m*, letra *f*. ◆ *vt* 1. (*on typewriter*) escribir a máquina, mecanografiar. 2. (*on computer*) escribir en el ordenador; **to ~ sthg into sthg** entrar algo en algo. ◆ *vi* escribir a máquina.
typecast ['taɪpkɑːst] (*pt & pp* **typecast**) *vt*: **to ~ sb (as)** encasillar a alguien (como).
typeface ['taɪpfeɪs] *n* tipo *m*, letra *f*.
typescript ['taɪpskrɪpt] *n* copia *f* mecanografiada.
typeset ['taɪpset] (*pt & pp* **typeset**) *vt* componer.
typewriter ['taɪp,raɪtər] *n* máquina *f* de escribir.
typhoid (fever) ['taɪfɔɪd-] *n* fiebre *f* tifoidea.
typhoon [taɪ'fuːn] *n* tifón *m*.
typical ['tɪpɪkl] *adj*: **~ (of)** típico(ca) (de).
typing ['taɪpɪŋ] *n* mecanografía *f*.
typist ['taɪpɪst] *n* mecanógrafo *m*, -fa *f*.
typography [taɪ'pɒgrəfɪ] *n* (*process, job*) tipografía *f*.
tyranny ['tɪrənɪ] *n* tiranía *f*.
tyrant ['taɪrənt] *n* tirano *m*, -na *f*.
tyre Br, **tire** Am ['taɪər] *n* neumático *m*.
tyre pressure *n* presión *f* de los neumáticos.

U

u (*pl* **u's** OR **us**), **U** (*pl* **U's** OR **Us**) [juː] *n* (*letter*) u *f*, U *f*.
U-bend *n* sifón *m*.
udder ['ʌdər] *n* ubre *f*.
UFO (*abbr of* **unidentified flying object**) *n* OVNI *m*.

Uganda [juːˈgændə] *n* Uganda.

ugh [ʌg] *excl* ¡puf!

ugly [ˈʌglɪ] *adj* **1.** (*unattractive*) feo(a). **2.** *fig* (*unpleasant*) desagradable.

UHF (*abbr of* **ultra-high frequency**) UHF.

UK (*abbr of* **United Kingdom**) *n* RU *m*; **the ~** el Reino Unido.

Ukraine [juːˈkreɪn] *n*: **the ~** Ucrania.

ulcer [ˈʌlsəʳ] *n* úlcera *f*.

ulcerated [ˈʌlsəreɪtɪd] *adj* ulceroso (sa).

Ulster [ˈʌlstəʳ] *n* (el) Úlster.

ulterior [ʌlˈtɪərɪəʳ] *adj*: **~ motive** motivo *m* oculto.

ultimata [ˌʌltɪˈmeɪtə] *pl* → **ultimatum**.

ultimate [ˈʌltɪmət] ◆ *adj* **1.** (*final, long-term*) final, definitivo(va). **2.** (*most powerful*) máximo(ma). ◆ *n*: **the ~ in** el colmo de.

ultimately [ˈʌltɪmətlɪ] *adv* finalmente, a la larga.

ultimatum [ˌʌltɪˈmeɪtəm] (*pl* **-s** OR **-ta**) *n* ultimátum *m*.

ultrasound [ˈʌltrəsaʊnd] *n* ultrasonido *m*.

ultraviolet [ˌʌltrəˈvaɪələt] *adj* ultravioleta.

umbilical cord [ʌmˈbɪlɪkl-] *n* cordón *m* umbilical.

umbrella [ʌmˈbrelə] ◆ *n* **1.** (*for rain*) paraguas *m inv*. **2.** (*on beach*) parasol *m*. ◆ *adj* que engloba a otros (otras).

umpire [ˈʌmpaɪəʳ] *n* árbitro *m*.

umpteen [ˌʌmpˈtiːn] *num adj inf*: **~ times** la tira de veces.

umpteenth [ˌʌmpˈtiːnθ] *num adj inf* enésimo(ma); **for the ~ time** por enésima vez.

UN (*abbr of* **United Nations**) *n*: **the ~** la ONU.

unabated [ˌʌnəˈbeɪtɪd] *adj* incesante.

unable [ʌnˈeɪbl] *adj*: **to be ~ to do sthg** no poder hacer algo.

unacceptable [ˌʌnəkˈseptəbl] *adj* inaceptable.

unaccompanied [ˌʌnəˈkʌmpənɪd] *adj* **1.** (*child*) que no va acompañado(da); (*luggage*) desatendido(da). **2.** (*song*) sin acompañamiento.

unaccountably [ˌʌnəˈkaʊntəblɪ] *adv* inexplicablemente.

unaccounted [ˌʌnəˈkaʊntɪd] *adj*: **12 people are ~ for** hay 12 personas aún sin localizar.

unaccustomed [ˌʌnəˈkʌstəmd] *adj* (*unused*): **to be ~ to** no estar acostumbrado(da) a.

unadulterated [ˌʌnəˈdʌltəreɪtɪd] *adj*

1. (*unspoilt*) sin adulterar. **2.** (*absolute*) completo(ta), absoluto(ta).

unanimous [juːˈnænɪməs] *adj* unánime.

unanimously [juːˈnænɪməslɪ] *adv* unánimemente.

unanswered [ˌʌnˈɑːnsəd] *adj* sin contestar.

unappetizing, -ising [ˌʌnˈæpɪtaɪzɪŋ] *adj* poco apetitoso(sa).

unarmed [ˌʌnˈɑːmd] *adj* desarmado (da).

unarmed combat *n* lucha *f* OR combate *m* a brazo partido.

unashamed [ˌʌnəˈʃeɪmd] *adj* descarado(da).

unassuming [ˌʌnəˈsjuːmɪŋ] *adj* sin pretensiones.

unattached [ˌʌnəˈtætʃt] *adj* **1.** (*not fastened, linked*) independiente; **~ to** que no está ligado a. **2.** (*without partner*) libre, sin compromiso.

unattended [ˌʌnəˈtendɪd] *adj* desatendido(da).

unattractive [ˌʌnəˈtræktɪv] *adj* poco atractivo(va).

unauthorized, -ised [ˌʌnˈɔːθəraɪzd] *adj* no autorizado(da).

unavailable [ˌʌnəˈveɪləbl] *adj* que no está disponible.

unavoidable [ˌʌnəˈvɔɪdəbl] *adj* inevitable, ineludible.

unaware [ˌʌnəˈweəʳ] *adj* inconsciente; **to be ~ of** no ser consciente de.

unawares [ˌʌnəˈweəz] *adv*: **to catch** OR **take sb ~** coger a alguien desprevenido (da).

unbalanced [ʌnˈbælənst] *adj* desequilibrado(da).

unbearable [ʌnˈbeərəbl] *adj* insoportable, inaguantable.

unbeatable [ˌʌnˈbiːtəbl] *adj* (*gen*) insuperable; (*prices, value*) inmejorable.

unbeknown(st) [ˌʌnbɪˈnaʊn(st)] *adv*: **~ to** sin conocimiento de.

unbelievable [ˌʌnbɪˈliːvəbl] *adj* increíble.

unbending [ʌnˈbendɪŋ] *adj* resoluto (ta).

unbia(s)sed [ʌnˈbaɪəst] *adj* imparcial.

unborn [ʌnˈbɔːn] *adj* (*child*) no nacido (da) aún.

unbreakable [ˌʌnˈbreɪkəbl] *adj* irrompible.

unbridled [ʌnˈbraɪdld] *adj* desmesurado(da), desenfrenado(da).

unbutton [ʌnˈbʌtn] *vt* desabrochar.

uncalled-for [ʌnˈkɔːld-] *adj* injusto

(ta), inmerecido(da).

uncanny [ʌn'kænɪ] adj extraño(ña).

unceasing [ʌn'si:sɪŋ] adj fml incesante.

unceremonious ['ʌn,serɪ'məunjəs] adj (curt) brusco(ca).

uncertain [ʌn's3:tn] adj (gen) incierto (ta); (undecided, hesitant) indeciso(sa); **in no ~ terms** de forma vehemente.

unchanged [ʌn'tʃeɪndʒd] adj sin alterar.

unchecked [ʌn'tʃekt] ◆ adj (unrestrained) desenfrenado(da). ◆ adv (unrestrained) libremente, sin restricciones.

uncivilized, -ised [ʌn'sɪvɪlaɪzd] adj (society) incivilizado(da); (person) inculto (ta).

uncle ['ʌŋkl] n tío m.

unclear [ʌn'klɪər] adj poco claro(ra); **to be ~ about sthg** no tener claro algo.

uncomfortable [ʌn'kʌmftəbl] adj 1. (gen) incómodo(da). 2. fig (fact, truth) inquietante, desagradable.

uncommon [ʌn'kɒmən] adj (rare) poco común, raro(ra).

uncompromising [ʌn'kɒmprəmaɪzɪŋ] adj inflexible, intransigente.

unconcerned [ʌnkən's3:nd] adj (not anxious) indiferente.

unconditional [ʌnkən'dɪʃənl] adj incondicional.

unconscious [ʌn'kɒnʃəs] ◆ adj inconsciente; **to be ~ of sthg** ser inconsciente de OR ignorar algo. ◆ n inconsciente m.

unconsciously [ʌn'kɒnʃəslɪ] adv inconscientemente.

uncontrollable [ʌnkən'trəuləbl] adj (gen) incontrolable; (desire, hatred) irrefrenable; (laughter) incontenible.

unconventional [ʌnkən'venʃənl] adj poco convencional.

unconvinced [ʌnkən'vɪnst] adj: **to remain ~** seguir sin convencerse.

uncouth [ʌn'ku:θ] adj grosero(ra).

uncover [ʌn'kʌvər] vt (gen) descubrir; (jar, tin etc) destapar.

undecided [ʌndɪ'saɪdɪd] adj 1. (person) indeciso(sa). 2. (issue) pendiente.

undeniable [ʌndɪ'naɪəbl] adj innegable.

under ['ʌndər] ◆ prep 1. (beneath) debajo de. 2. (with movement) bajo; **they walked ~ the bridge** pasaron por debajo del puente. 3. (subject to, undergoing, controlled by) bajo; **~ the circumstances** dadas las circunstancias; **~ discussion** en proceso de discusión; **he has 20 men ~ him** tiene 20 hombres a su cargo.

4. (less than) menos de. 5. (according to) según. 6. (in headings, classifications): **he filed it ~ 'D'** lo archivó en la 'D'. 7. (name, title): **~ an alias** bajo nombre supuesto. ◆ adv 1. (gen) debajo; **to go ~** (business) irse a pique. 2. (less): **children of 12 years and ~** niños menores de 13 años.

underage [ʌndər'eɪdʒ] adj (person) menor de edad; (sex, drinking) en menores de edad.

undercarriage ['ʌndə,kærɪdʒ] n tren m de aterrizaje.

undercharge [ʌndə'tʃɑ:dʒ] vt cobrar menos del precio estipulado a.

underclothes ['ʌndəkləuðz] npl ropa f interior.

undercoat ['ʌndəkəut] n (of paint) primera mano f OR capa f.

undercover ['ʌndə,kʌvər] adj secreto (ta).

undercurrent ['ʌndə,kʌrənt] n fig sentimiento m oculto.

undercut [ʌndə'kʌt] (pt & pp undercut) vt (in price) vender más barato que.

underdeveloped [ʌndədɪ'veləpt] adj subdesarrollado(da).

underdog ['ʌndədɒg] n: **the ~** el que lleva las de perder.

underdone [ʌndə'dʌn] adj poco hecho(cha).

underestimate [ʌndər'estɪmeɪt] vt subestimar.

underexposed [ʌndərɪk'spəuzd] adj (PHOT) subexpuesto(ta).

underfoot [ʌndə'fut] adv debajo de los pies; **it's wet ~** el suelo está mojado.

undergo [ʌndə'gəu] (pt -went, pp -gone) vt (pain, change, difficulties) sufrir, experimentar; (operation, examination) someterse a.

undergraduate [ʌndə'grædʒuət] n estudiante universitario no licenciado m, estudiante universitaria no licenciada f.

underground [adj & n 'ʌndəgraund, adv ʌndə'graund] ◆ adj 1. (below the ground) subterráneo(a). 2. fig (secret, illegal) clandestino(na). ◆ adv: **to go ~** pasar a la clandestinidad. ◆ n 1. Br (railway system) metro m. 2. (activist movement) movimiento m clandestino.

undergrowth ['ʌndəgrəuθ] n (U) maleza f.

underhand [ʌndə'hænd] adj turbio (bia), poco limpio(pia).

underline [ʌndə'laɪn] vt subrayar.

underlying [ˌʌndəˈlaɪɪŋ] *adj* subyacente.

undermine [ˌʌndəˈmaɪn] *vt fig* minar, socavar.

underneath [ˌʌndəˈniːθ] ◆ *prep* 1. (*beneath*) debajo de. 2. (*with movement*) bajo. ◆ *adv* (*under, below*) debajo. ◆ *adj inf* inferior, de abajo. ◆ *n* (*underside*): **the ~** la superficie inferior.

underpaid [ˈʌndəpeɪd] *adj* mal pagado(da).

underpants [ˈʌndəpænts] *npl* calzoncillos *mpl*.

underpass [ˈʌndəpɑːs] *n* paso *m* subterráneo.

underprivileged [ˌʌndəˈprɪvɪlɪdʒd] *adj* desvalido(da), desamparado(da).

underrated [ˌʌndəˈreɪtɪd] *adj* subestimado(da), infravalorado(da).

undershirt [ˈʌndəʃɜːt] *n Am* camiseta *f*.

underside [ˈʌndəsaɪd] *n*: **the ~** la superficie inferior.

underskirt [ˈʌndəskɜːt] *n* enaguas *fpl*.

understand [ˌʌndəˈstænd] (*pt & pp* **-stood**) ◆ *vt* 1. (*gen*) comprender, entender. 2. (*know all about*) entender de. 3. *fml* (*be informed*): **to ~ that** tener entendido que. ◆ *vi* comprender, entender.

understandable [ˌʌndəˈstændəbl] *adj* comprensible.

understanding [ˌʌndəˈstændɪŋ] ◆ *n* 1. (*knowledge*) entendimiento *m*, comprensión *f*. 2. (*sympathy*) comprensión *f* mutua. 3. (*informal agreement*) acuerdo *m*. ◆ *adj* comprensivo(va).

understatement [ˌʌndəˈsteɪtmənt] *n* 1. (*inadequate statement*) atenuación *f*; **it's an ~ to say he's fat** decir que es gordo es quedarse corto. 2. (U) (*quality of understating*): **he's a master of ~** puede quitarle importancia a cualquier cosa.

understood [ˌʌndəˈstʊd] *pt & pp* → **understand**.

understudy [ˈʌndəˌstʌdɪ] *n* suplente *m y f*.

undertake [ˌʌndəˈteɪk] (*pt* **-took**, *pp* **-taken**) *vt* 1. (*task*) emprender; (*responsibility, control*) asumir, tomar. 2. (*promise*): **to ~ to do sthg** comprometerse a hacer algo.

undertaker [ˈʌndəˌteɪkəʳ] *n* director *m*, -ra *f* de pompas fúnebres.

undertaking [ˌʌndəˈteɪkɪŋ] *n* 1. (*task*) tarea *f*, empresa *f*. 2. (*promise*) promesa *f*.

undertone [ˈʌndətəʊn] *n* 1. (*quiet voice*) voz *f* baja. 2. (*vague feeling*) matiz *m*.

undertook [ˌʌndəˈtʊk] *pt* → **undertake**.

underwater [ˌʌndəˈwɔːtəʳ] ◆ *adj* submarino(na). ◆ *adv* bajo el agua.

underwear [ˈʌndəweəʳ] *n* ropa *f* interior.

underwent [ˌʌndəˈwent] *pt* → **undergo**.

underworld [ˈʌndəˌwɜːld] *n* (*criminal society*): **the ~** el hampa, los bajos fondos.

underwriter [ˈʌndəˌraɪtəʳ] *n* asegurador *m*, -ra *f*.

undid [ˌʌnˈdɪd] *pt* → **undo**.

undies [ˈʌndɪz] *npl inf* paños *mpl* menores.

undisputed [ˌʌndɪˈspjuːtɪd] *adj* indiscutible.

undistinguished [ˌʌndɪˈstɪŋgwɪʃt] *adj* mediocre.

undo [ˌʌnˈduː] (*pt* **-did**, *pp* **-done**) *vt* 1. (*unfasten - knot*) desatar, desanudar; (- *button, clasp*) desabrochar; (- *parcel*) abrir. 2. (*nullify*) anular, deshacer.

undoing [ˌʌnˈduːɪŋ] *n* (U) *fml* ruina *f*, perdición *f*.

undone [ˌʌnˈdʌn] ◆ *pp* → **undo**. ◆ *adj* 1. (*coat*) desabrochado(da); (*shoes*) desatado(da). 2. *fml* (*not done*) por hacer.

undoubted [ʌnˈdaʊtɪd] *adj* indudable.

undoubtedly [ʌnˈdaʊtɪdlɪ] *adv fml* indudablemente, sin duda (alguna).

undress [ˌʌnˈdres] ◆ *vt* desnudar. ◆ *vi* desnudarse.

undue [ˌʌnˈdjuː] *adj fml* indebido(da).

undulate [ˈʌndjʊleɪt] *vi fml* ondular.

unduly [ˌʌnˈdjuːlɪ] *adv fml* indebidamente.

unearth [ʌnˈɜːθ] *vt* (*dig up*) desenterrar; *fig* (*discover*) descubrir.

unearthly [ʌnˈɜːθlɪ] *adj inf* (*hour*) intempestivo(va).

unease [ʌnˈiːz] *n* malestar *m*.

uneasy [ʌnˈiːzɪ] *adj* 1. (*person*) intranquilo(la), ansioso(sa); (*feeling*) incómodo(da). 2. (*peace*) inseguro(ra).

uneconomic [ˈʌnˌiːkəˈnɒmɪk] *adj* poco rentable.

uneducated [ˌʌnˈedjʊkeɪtɪd] *adj* ignorante, inculto(ta).

unemployed [ˌʌnɪmˈplɔɪd] ◆ *adj* parado(da), desempleado(da). ◆ *npl*: **the ~** los parados.

unemployment [ˌʌnɪmˈplɔɪmənt] *n* desempleo *m*, paro *m*.

unemployment benefit *Br*, **unemployment compensation** *Am n* subsidio *m* de desempleo OR paro.

unerring [ʌn'ɜːrɪŋ] adj infalible.

uneven [ʌn'iːvn] adj 1. (not flat - road) lleno(na) de baches; (- land) escabroso (sa). 2. (inconsistent, unfair) desigual.

unexpected [ʌnɪk'spektɪd] adj inesperado(da).

unexpectedly [ʌnɪk'spektɪdlɪ] adv inesperadamente.

unfailing [ʌn'feɪlɪŋ] adj indefectible.

unfair [ʌn'feər] adj injusto(ta).

unfaithful [ʌn'feɪθful] adj (sexually) infiel.

unfamiliar [ʌnfə'mɪljər] adj 1. (not well-known) desconocido(da). 2. (not acquainted): **to be ~ with sthg/sb** desconocer algo/a alguien.

unfashionable [ʌn'fæʃnəbl] adj (clothes, ideas) pasado(da) de moda; (area of town) poco popular.

unfasten [ʌn'fɑːsn] vt (garment, buttons) desabrochar; (rope, tie) desatar, soltar; (door) abrir.

unfavourable Br, **unfavorable** Am [ʌn'feɪvrəbl] adj desfavorable.

unfeeling [ʌn'fiːlɪŋ] adj insensible.

unfinished [ʌn'fɪnɪʃt] adj sin terminar.

unfit [ʌn'fɪt] adj 1. (injured) lesionado (da); (in poor shape) que no está en forma. 2. (not suitable - thing) impropio (pia); (- person): **~ to** incapaz de; **~ for** no apto para.

unfold [ʌn'fəʊld] ◆ vt 1. (open out) desplegar, desdoblar. 2. (explain) revelar. ◆ vi (become clear) revelarse.

unforeseen [ʌnfɔː'siːn] adj imprevisto(ta).

unforgettable [ʌnfə'getəbl] adj inolvidable.

unforgivable [ʌnfə'gɪvəbl] adj imperdonable.

unfortunate [ʌn'fɔːtʃnət] adj 1. (unlucky) desgraciado(da), desdichado (da). 2. (regrettable) inoportuno(na).

unfortunately [ʌn'fɔːtʃnətlɪ] adv desgraciadamente, desafortunadamente.

unfounded [ʌn'faʊndɪd] adj infundado(da).

unfriendly [ʌn'frendlɪ] adj poco amistoso(sa).

unfurnished [ʌn'fɜːnɪʃt] adj desamueblado(da).

ungainly [ʌn'geɪnlɪ] adj desgarbado (da).

ungodly [ʌn'gɒdlɪ] adj inf (hour) intempestivo(va).

ungrateful [ʌn'greɪtful] adj desagradecido(da), ingrato(ta).

unhappy [ʌn'hæpɪ] adj 1. (sad) triste; (wretched) desdichado(da), infeliz. 2. (uneasy): **to be ~ (with OR about)** estar inquieto(ta) (por). 3. fml (unfortunate) desafortunado(da).

unharmed [ʌn'hɑːmd] adj (person) ileso(sa); (thing) indemne.

unhealthy [ʌn'helθɪ] adj 1. (in bad health) enfermizo(za). 2. (causing bad health) insalubre. 3. fig (interest etc) morboso(sa).

unheard-of [ʌn'hɜːd-] adj 1. (unknown, completely absent) inaudito(ta). 2. (unprecedented) sin precedente.

unhook [ʌn'hʊk] vt 1. (unfasten hooks of) desabrochar. 2. (remove from hook) descolgar, desenganchar.

unhurt [ʌn'hɜːt] adj ileso(sa).

unhygienic [ʌnhaɪ'dʒiːnɪk] adj antihigiénico(ca).

unidentified flying object n objeto m volador no identificado.

unification [,juːnɪfɪ'keɪʃn] n unificación f.

uniform ['juːnɪfɔːm] ◆ adj uniforme, constante. ◆ n uniforme m.

unify ['juːnɪfaɪ] vt unificar, unir.

unilateral [,juːnɪ'lætərəl] adj unilateral.

unimportant [,ʌnɪm'pɔːtənt] adj sin importancia, insignificante.

uninhabited [,ʌnɪn'hæbɪtɪd] adj deshabitado(da).

uninjured [,ʌn'ɪndʒəd] adj ileso(sa).

unintelligent [,ʌnɪn'telɪdʒent] adj poco inteligente.

unintentional [,ʌnɪn'tenʃənl] adj involuntario(ria).

union ['juːnjən] ◆ n 1. (trade union) sindicato m. 2. (alliance) unión f, alianza f. ◆ comp sindical.

Union Jack n: **the ~** la bandera del Reino Unido.

unique [juː'niːk] adj 1. (gen) único(ca). 2. fml (peculiar, exclusive): **~ to** peculiar de.

unison ['juːnɪzn] n unísono m; **in ~** (simultaneously) al unísono.

unit ['juːnɪt] n 1. (gen) unidad f. 2. (piece of furniture) módulo m, elemento m.

unite [juː'naɪt] ◆ vt (gen) unir; (country) unificar. ◆ vi unirse, juntarse.

united [juː'naɪtɪd] adj unido(da).

United Kingdom n: **the ~** el Reino Unido.

United Nations n: **the ~** las Naciones Unidas.

United States n: **the ~ (of America)** los Estados Unidos (de América).

unit trust *n* Br fondo *m* de inversión mobiliaria.

unity ['ju:nətɪ] *n* (U) unidad *f*, unión *f*.

universal [ˌju:nɪ'vɜːsl] *adj* universal.

universe ['ju:nɪvɜːs] *n*: **the ~** el universo.

university [ˌju:nɪ'vɜːsətɪ] ◆ *n* universidad *f*. ◆ *comp* universitario(ria); **~ student** (estudiante) universitario *m*, (estudiante) universitaria *f*.

unjust [ˌʌn'dʒʌst] *adj* injusto(ta).

unkempt [ˌʌn'kempt] *adj* (*person*) desaseado(da); (*hair*) despeinado(da); (*clothes*) descuidado(da).

unkind [ʌn'kaɪnd] *adj* (*uncharitable*) poco amable, cruel.

unknown [ˌʌn'nəʊn] *adj* desconocido(da).

unlawful [ˌʌn'lɔːfʊl] *adj* ilegal, ilícito(ta).

unleaded [ˌʌn'ledɪd] *adj* sin plomo.

unleash [ˌʌn'liːʃ] *vt literary* desatar.

unless [ən'les] *conj* a menos que; **~ I say so** a menos que yo lo diga; **~ I'm mistaken** si no me equivoco.

unlike [ˌʌn'laɪk] *prep* **1.** (*different from*) distinto(ta) a, diferente a. **2.** (*differently from*) a diferencia de. **3.** (*not typical of*) poco característico(ca) de.

unlikely [ʌn'laɪklɪ] *adj* **1.** (*not probable*) poco probable. **2.** (*bizarre*) inverosímil.

unlisted [ʌn'lɪstɪd] *adj* Am (*phone number*) que no figura en la guía telefónica.

unload [ˌʌn'ləʊd] *vt* (*goods, car*) descargar.

unlock [ˌʌn'lɒk] *vt* abrir (con llave).

unlucky [ʌn'lʌkɪ] *adj* **1.** (*unfortunate*) desgraciado(da). **2.** (*number, colour etc*) de la mala suerte.

unmarried [ˌʌn'mærɪd] *adj* que no se ha casado.

unmistakable [ˌʌnmɪ'steɪkəbl] *adj* inconfundible.

unmitigated [ʌn'mɪtɪgeɪtɪd] *adj* absoluto(ta).

unnatural [ʌn'nætʃrəl] *adj* **1.** (*unusual, strange*) anormal. **2.** (*affected*) afectado(da).

unnecessary [ʌn'nesəsərɪ] *adj* innecesario(ria).

unnerving [ˌʌn'nɜːvɪŋ] *adj* desconcertante.

unnoticed [ˌʌn'nəʊtɪst] *adj* inadvertido(da), desapercibido(da).

unobtainable [ˌʌnəb'teɪnəbl] *adj* inasequible.

unobtrusive [ˌʌnəb'truːsɪv] *adj* discreto(ta).

unofficial [ˌʌnə'fɪʃl] *adj* extraoficial.

unorthodox [ˌʌn'ɔːθədɒks] *adj* poco ortodoxo(xa).

unpack [ˌʌn'pæk] ◆ *vt* **1.** (*box*) desempaquetar, desembalar; (*suitcases*) deshacer. **2.** (*clothes*) sacar (de la maleta). ◆ *vi* deshacer las maletas.

unpalatable [ʌn'pælətəbl] *adj* (*food*) incomible; (*drink*) imbebible; *fig* (*difficult to accept*) desagradable.

unparalleled [ʌn'pærəleld] *adj* incomparable, sin precedente.

unpleasant [ʌn'pleznt] *adj* **1.** (*disagreeable*) desagradable. **2.** (*unfriendly, rude - person*) antipático(ca); (*- remark*) mezquino(na).

unplug [ʌn'plʌg] *vt* desenchufar, desconectar.

unpopular [ʌn'pɒpjʊləʳ] *adj* poco popular.

unprecedented [ʌn'presɪdəntɪd] *adj* sin precedentes, inaudito(ta).

unpredictable [ˌʌnprɪ'dɪktəbl] *adj* imprevisible.

unprofessional [ˌʌnprə'feʃənl] *adj* poco profesional.

unpunctual [ʌn'pʌŋktʃʊəl] *adj* impuntual.

unqualified [ʌn'kwɒlɪfaɪd] *adj* **1.** (*not qualified*) sin título, no cualificado(da). **2.** (*total, complete*) incondicional.

unquestionable [ʌn'kwestʃənəbl] *adj* incuestionable, indiscutible.

unquestioning [ʌn'kwestʃənɪŋ] *adj* incondicional.

unravel [ʌn'rævl] *vt lit & fig* desenmarañar.

unreal [ˌʌn'rɪəl] *adj* irreal.

unrealistic [ˌʌnrɪə'lɪstɪk] *adj* (*person*) poco realista; (*idea, plan*) impracticable.

unreasonable [ʌn'riːznəbl] *adj* **1.** (*person, behaviour, decision*) poco razonable. **2.** (*demand, price*) excesivo(va).

unrelated [ˌʌnrɪ'leɪtɪd] *adj*: **to be ~ (to)** no tener conexión (con).

unrelenting [ˌʌnrɪ'lentɪŋ] *adj* implacable, inexorable.

unreliable [ˌʌnrɪ'laɪəbl] *adj* que no es de fiar.

unremitting [ˌʌnrɪ'mɪtɪŋ] *adj* incesante.

unrequited [ˌʌnrɪ'kwaɪtɪd] *adj* no correspondido(da).

unreserved [ˌʌnrɪ'zɜːvd] *adj* (*wholehearted*) incondicional, absoluto(ta).

unresolved [ˌʌnrɪ'zɒlvd] *adj* sin resolver, pendiente.

unrest [ˌʌn'rest] *n* (U) malestar *m*, inquietud *f*.

unrivalled Br, **unrivaled** Am [ʌn-ˈraɪvld] adj incomparable, sin par.

unroll [ˌʌnˈrəʊl] vt desenrollar.

unruly [ʌnˈruːlɪ] adj 1. (person, behaviour) revoltoso(sa). 2. (hair) rebelde.

unsafe [ˌʌnˈseɪf] adj (gen) inseguro(ra); (risky) arriesgado(da).

unsaid [ˌʌnˈsed] adj: **to leave sthg ~** dejar algo sin decir.

unsatisfactory [ˈʌnˌsætɪsˈfæktərɪ] adj insatisfactorio(ria).

unsavoury Br, **unsavory** Am [ˌʌnˈseɪvərɪ] adj desagradable.

unscathed [ˌʌnˈskeɪðd] adj ileso(sa).

unscrew [ˌʌnˈskruː] vt 1. (lid, top) abrir. 2. (sign, hinge) desatornillar.

unscrupulous [ʌnˈskruːpjʊləs] adj desaprensivo(va), poco escrupuloso (sa).

unseemly [ʌnˈsiːmlɪ] adj indecoroso (sa).

unselfish [ˌʌnˈselfɪʃ] adj altruista.

unsettle [ˌʌnˈsetl] vt perturbar.

unsettled [ˌʌnˈsetld] adj 1. (person) nervioso(sa), intranquilo(la). 2. (weather) variable. 3. (argument, matter, debt) pendiente. 4. (situation) inestable.

unshak(e)able [ʌnˈʃeɪkəbl] adj inquebrantable.

unshaven [ˌʌnˈʃeɪvn] adj sin afeitar.

unsightly [ʌnˈsaɪtlɪ] adj (building) feo (fea); (scar, bruise) desagradable.

unskilled [ˌʌnˈskɪld] adj (person) no cualificado(da); (work) no especializado(da).

unsociable [ʌnˈsəʊʃəbl] adj poco sociable.

unsocial [ʌnˈsəʊʃl] adj: **to work ~ hours** trabajar a horas intempestivas.

unsound [ˌʌnˈsaʊnd] adj 1. (conclusion, method) erróneo(a). 2. (building, structure) defectuoso(sa).

unspeakable [ʌnˈspiːkəbl] adj (crime) incalificable; (pain) indecible.

unstable [ˌʌnˈsteɪbl] adj inestable.

unsteady [ˌʌnˈstedɪ] adj (gen) inestable; (hands, voice) tembloroso(sa); (footsteps) vacilante.

unstoppable [ˌʌnˈstɒpəbl] adj irrefrenable.

unstuck [ˌʌnˈstʌk] adj: **to come ~** (notice, stamp, label) despegarse, desprenderse; fig (plan, system, person) fracasar.

unsuccessful [ˌʌnsəkˈsesfʊl] adj (person) fracasado(da); (attempt, meeting) infructuoso(sa); **to be ~** (person) fracasar.

unsuccessfully [ˌʌnsəkˈsesfʊlɪ] adv sin éxito, en vano.

unsuitable [ˌʌnˈsuːtəbl] adj inadecuado(da), inapropiado(da); **he is ~ for the job** no es la persona indicada para el trabajo; **I'm afraid 3 o'clock would be ~** lo siento, pero no me va bien a las 3.

unsure [ˌʌnˈʃɔːr] adj 1. (not confident): **to be ~ of o.s.** sentirse inseguro(ra). 2. (not certain): **to be ~ (about OR of)** no estar muy seguro (de).

unsuspecting [ˌʌnsəˈspektɪŋ] adj desprevenido(da), confiado(da).

unsympathetic [ˈʌnˌsɪmpəˈθetɪk] adj: **~ to** indiferente a.

untangle [ˌʌnˈtæŋgl] vt desenmarañar.

untapped [ˌʌnˈtæpt] adj sin explotar.

untenable [ˌʌnˈtenəbl] adj insostenible.

unthinkable [ʌnˈθɪŋkəbl] adj impensable, inconcebible.

untidy [ʌnˈtaɪdɪ] adj (room, desk) desordenado(da); (person, appearance) desaliñado(da).

untie [ˌʌnˈtaɪ] (cont untying) vt desatar.

until [ənˈtɪl] ◆ prep hasta; **~ now/then** hasta ahora/entonces. ◆ conj 1. (gen) hasta que. 2. (after negative): **don't leave ~ you've finished** no te vayas hasta que no hayas terminado.

untimely [ʌnˈtaɪmlɪ] adj 1. (premature) prematuro(ra). 2. (inappropriate) inoportuno(na).

untold [ˌʌnˈtəʊld] adj (incalculable, vast) incalculable; (suffering, joy) indecible.

untoward [ˌʌntəˈwɔːd] adj (event) adverso(sa); (behaviour) fuera de lugar.

untrue [ˌʌnˈtruː] adj (not true) falso(sa).

unused [sense 1 ˌʌnˈjuːzd, sense 2 ˌʌnˈjuːst] adj 1. (not previously used) nuevo (va), sin usar. 2. (unaccustomed): **to be ~ to sthg/to doing sthg** no estar acostumbrado(da) a algo/a hacer algo.

unusual [ʌnˈjuːʒl] adj (rare) insólito (ta), poco común.

unusually [ʌnˈjuːʒəlɪ] adv 1. (exceptionally) extraordinariamente. 2. (surprisingly) sorprendentemente.

unveil [ˌʌnˈveɪl] vt 1. (statue, plaque) descubrir. 2. fig (plans, policy) revelar.

unwanted [ˌʌnˈwɒntɪd] adj (clothes, furniture) superfluo(flua); (child, pregnancy) no deseado(da).

unwavering [ʌnˈweɪvərɪŋ] adj (determination, feeling) firme, inquebrantable; (concentration) constante; (gaze) fijo(ja).

unwelcome [ʌnˈwelkəm] adj inoportuno(na).

unwell [ˌʌnˈwel] adj: **to be/feel ~** estar/sentirse mal.

unwieldy [ʌn'wiːldɪ] adj 1. (object) abultado(da); (tool) poco manejable. 2. fig (system, organization) poco eficiente.

unwilling [ʌn'wɪlɪŋ] adj: **to be ~ to do sthg** no estar dispuesto a hacer algo.

unwind [ʌn'waɪnd] (pt & pp **unwound**) ◆ vt desenrollar. ◆ vi fig (person) relajarse.

unwise [ʌn'waɪz] adj imprudente.

unwitting [ʌn'wɪtɪŋ] adj fml inconsciente.

unworkable [ʌn'wɜːkəbl] adj impracticable.

unworthy [ʌn'wɜːðɪ] adj (undeserving): **to be ~ of** no ser digno(na) de.

unwound [ʌn'waʊnd] pt & pp → **unwind**.

unwrap [ʌn'ræp] vt (present) desenvolver; (parcel) desempaquetar.

unwritten law [ʌn'rɪtn-] n ley f no escrita.

up [ʌp] ◆ adv 1. (towards a higher position) hacia arriba; (in a higher position) arriba; **to throw sthg ~** lanzar algo hacia arriba; **she's ~ in her room** está arriba en su cuarto; **pick it ~!** ¡cógelo!, ¡agárralo! Amer; **we walked ~ to the top** subimos hasta arriba del todo; **prices are going ~** los precios están subiendo. 2. (into an upright position): **to stand ~** levantarse. 3. (northwards): **I'm going ~ to York next week** voy a subir a York la semana próxima; **~ north** en el norte. 4. (along a road or river) adelante; **their house is 100 metres further ~** su casa está 100 metros más adelante. ◆ prep 1. (towards a higher position): **we went ~ the mountain** subimos por la montaña; **I went ~ the stairs** subí las escaleras. 2. (in a higher position) en lo alto de; **~ a tree** en un árbol. 3. (at far end of) al final de; **they live ~ the road from us** viven al final de nuestra calle. 4. (against current of river): **~ the Amazon** Amazonas arriba. ◆ adj 1. (out of bed) levantado(da); **I was ~ at six today** hoy me levanté a las seis. 2. (at an end) terminado(da). 3. inf (wrong): **is something ~?** ¿pasa algo?, ¿algo va mal?; **what's ~?** ¿qué pasa? ◆ n: **~s and downs** altibajos mpl. ▶ **up and down** ◆ adv: **to jump ~ and down** saltar para arriba y para abajo; **to walk ~ and down** andar para un lado y para otro. ◆ prep: **we walked ~ and down the avenue** estuvimos caminando arriba y abajo de la avenida. ▶ **up to** prep 1. (indicating level) hasta; **it could take ~ to six weeks** podría tardar hasta seis semanas; **it's not ~ to**

standard no tiene el nivel necesario. 2. (well or able enough for): **to be ~ to doing sthg** sentirse con fuerzas (como) para hacer algo; **my French isn't ~ to much** mi francés no es gran cosa. 3. inf (secretly doing something): **what are you ~ to?** ¿qué andas tramando? 4. (indicating responsibility): **it's not ~ to me to decide** no depende de mí el decidir. ▶ **up to, up until** prep hasta.

up-and-coming adj prometedor(ra).

upbringing ['ʌp,brɪŋɪŋ] n educación f.

update [ʌp'deɪt] vt actualizar.

upheaval [ʌp'hiːvl] n trastorno m, agitación f.

upheld [ʌp'held] pt & pp → **uphold**.

uphill [ʌp'hɪl] ◆ adj (rising) empinado (da), cuesta arriba; fig (difficult) arduo (dua), difícil. ◆ adv cuesta arriba.

uphold [ʌp'həʊld] (pt & pp **-held**) vt sostener, apoyar.

upholstery [ʌp'həʊlstərɪ] n tapicería f.

upkeep ['ʌpkiːp] n mantenimiento m.

uplifting [ʌp'lɪftɪŋ] adj inspirador(ra).

up-market adj de clase superior.

upon [ə'pɒn] prep fml en, sobre; **~ entering the room** al entrar en el cuarto; **question ~ question** pregunta tras pregunta; **summer is ~ us** ya tenemos el verano encima.

upper ['ʌpər] ◆ adj superior. ◆ n (of shoe) pala f.

upper class n: **the ~** la clase alta. ▶ **upper-class** adj de clase alta.

upper hand n: **to have/gain the ~ (in)** llevar/empezar a llevar la ventaja (en).

uppermost ['ʌpəməʊst] adj 1. (highest) más alto(ta). 2. (most important): **to be ~ in one's mind** ser lo más importante para uno.

upright [adj senses 1 & 2 & adv ˌʌp'raɪt, adj sense 3 & n 'ʌpraɪt] ◆ adj 1. (erect - person, chair) derecho(cha). 2. (standing vertically - object) vertical. 3. fig (honest) recto(ta), honrado(da). ◆ adv erguidamente. ◆ n poste m.

uprising ['ʌp,raɪzɪŋ] n sublevación f.

uproar ['ʌprɔːr] n 1. (U) (commotion) alboroto m. 2. (protest) escándalo m.

uproot [ʌp'ruːt] vt 1. (person) desplazar, mudar. 2. (BOT) (plant) desarraigar.

upset [ʌp'set] (pt & pp **upset**) ◆ adj 1. (distressed) disgustado(da). 2. (MED): **to have an ~ stomach** sentirse mal del estómago. ◆ n: **to have a stomach ~** sentirse mal del estómago. ◆ vt 1. (dis-

tress) disgustar, perturbar. **2.** (*mess up*) dar al traste con. **3.** (*overturn, knock over*) volcar.

upshot [ˈʌpʃɒt] *n* resultado *m*.

upside down [ˌʌpsaɪd-] ♦ *adj* al revés. ♦ *adv* al revés; **to turn sthg ~** revolver algo, desordenar algo.

upstairs [ˌʌpˈsteəz] ♦ *adj* de arriba. ♦ *adv* arriba. ♦ *n* el piso de arriba.

upstart [ˈʌpstɑːt] *n* advenedizo *m*, -za *f*.

upstream [ˌʌpˈstriːm] *adv* río arriba.

upsurge [ˈʌpsɜːdʒ] *n*: **~ of** OR **in** aumento *m* considerable de.

uptake [ˈʌpteɪk] *n*: **to be quick on the ~** cogerlas al vuelo; **to be slow on the ~** ser un poco torpe.

uptight [ʌpˈtaɪt] *adj inf* tenso(sa), nervioso(sa).

up-to-date *adj* **1.** (*modern*) moderno (na). **2.** (*most recent*) actual, al día. **3.** (*informed*): **to keep ~ with** mantenerse al día de.

upturn [ˈʌptɜːn] *n*: **~ (in)** mejora *f* (de).

upward [ˈʌpwəd] ♦ *adj* hacia arriba. ♦ *adv* Am = **upwards**.

upwards [ˈʌpwədz] *adv* hacia arriba; **from 18 (years of age) ~** de 18 años en adelante. ▶ **upwards of** *prep* más de.

uranium [jʊˈreɪnjəm] *n* uranio *m*.

Uranus [ˈjʊərənəs] *n* Urano *m*.

urban [ˈɜːbən] *adj* urbano(na).

urbane [ɜːˈbeɪn] *adj* cortés, urbano(na).

urchin [ˈɜːtʃɪn] *n dated* pilluelo *m*, -la *f*.

Urdu [ˈʊəduː] *n* urdu *m*.

urge [ɜːdʒ] ♦ *n* impulso *m*, deseo *m*; **to have an ~ to do sthg** desear ardientemente hacer algo. ♦ *vt* **1.** (*try to persuade*): **to ~ sb to do sthg** instar a alguien a hacer algo. **2.** (*advocate*) recomendar encarecidamente.

urgency [ˈɜːdʒənsɪ] *n* (U) urgencia *f*.

urgent [ˈɜːdʒənt] *adj* **1.** (*pressing*) urgente. **2.** (*desperate*) apremiante.

urinal [ˌjʊəˈraɪnl] *n* (*place*) urinario *m*; (*vessel*) orinal *m*.

urinate [ˈjʊərɪneɪt] *vi* orinar.

urine [ˈjʊərɪn] *n* orina *f*.

urn [ɜːn] *n* **1.** (*for ashes*) urna *f*. **2.** (*for tea, coffee*) cilindro o barril con grifo para servir té o café en grandes cantidades.

Uruguay [ˈjʊərəgwaɪ] *n* Uruguay.

Uruguayan [ˌjʊərəˈgwaɪən] ♦ *adj* uruguayo(ya). ♦ *n* uruguayo *m*, -ya *f*.

us [ʌs] *pers pron* **1.** (*direct, indirect*) nos; **can you see/hear ~?** ¿puedes vernos/oírnos?; **it's ~** somos nosotros; **he sent ~ a letter** nos mandó una carta; **she gave it to ~** nos lo dio. **2.** (*stressed, after prep, in comparisons etc*) nosotros(tras); **you can't expect US to do it** no esperarás que lo hagamos NOSOTROS; **with/without ~** con/sin nosotros; **they are more wealthy than ~** son más ricos que nosotros; **all of ~** todos (nosotros); **some of ~** algunos de nosotros.

US (*abbr of* **United States**) *n* EEUU *mpl*.

USA *n* (*abbr of* **United States of America**) EEUU *mpl*.

usage [ˈjuːzɪdʒ] *n* uso *m*.

use [*n* & *aux vb* juːs, *vt* juːz] ♦ *n* uso *m*; **to be in ~** usarse; **to be out of ~** no usarse; **'out of ~'** 'no funciona'; **to make ~ of sthg** utilizar OR aprovechar algo; **to be of/no ~** ser útil/inútil; **what's the ~ (of doing sthg)?** ¿de qué sirve (hacer algo)? ♦ *aux vb* soler, acostumbrar; **he ~d to be fat** antes estaba gordo; **I ~d to go swimming** solía OR acostumbraba ir a nadar. ♦ *vt* **1.** (*utilize, employ*) usar, emplear. **2.** (*exploit*) usar, manejar. ▶ **use up** *vt sep* agotar.

used [*sense 1* juːzd, *sense 2* juːst] *adj* **1.** (*dirty, second-hand*) usado(da). **2.** (*accustomed*): **to be ~ to** estar acostumbrado (da) a; **to get ~ to** acostumbrarse a.

useful [ˈjuːsfʊl] *adj* **1.** (*handy*) útil. **2.** (*helpful - person*) valioso(sa).

useless [ˈjuːslɪs] *adj* **1.** (*gen*) inútil. **2.** *inf* (*hopeless*) incompetente.

user [ˈjuːzər] *n* usuario *m*, -ria *f*.

user-friendly *adj* (*gen* & COMPUT) fácil de utilizar.

usher [ˈʌʃər] ♦ *n* (*at wedding*) ujier *m*; (*at theatre, concert*) acomodador *m*, -ra *f*. ♦ *vt*: **to ~ sb in** hacer pasar a alguien; **to ~ sb out** acompañar a alguien hasta la puerta.

usherette [ˌʌʃəˈret] *n* acomodadora *f*.

USSR (*abbr of* **Union of Soviet Socialist Republics**) *n*: **the (former) ~** la (antigua) URSS.

usual [ˈjuːʒəl] *adj* habitual; **as ~** (*as normal*) como de costumbre; (*as often happens*) como siempre.

usually [ˈjuːʒəlɪ] *adv* por regla general.

usurp [juːˈzɜːp] *vt fml* usurpar.

utensil [juːˈtensl] *n* utensilio *m*.

uterus [ˈjuːtərəs] (*pl* **-ri** [-raɪ] OR **-ruses**) *n* útero *m*.

utility [juːˈtɪlətɪ] *n* **1.** (*gen* & COMPUT) utilidad *f*. **2.** (*public service*) servicio *m* público.

utility room *n* trascocina *f*.

utilize, -ise [ˈjuːtəlaɪz] *vt* utilizar.

utmost [ˈʌtməʊst] ♦ *adj* mayor, supremo(ma). ◆ *n*: **to do one's ~** hacer lo imposible; **to the ~** al máximo, a más no poder.

utter ['ʌtəʳ] ◆ *adj* puro(ra), completo (ta). ◆ *vt* (*word*) pronunciar; (*sound, cry*) emitir.

utterly ['ʌtəlɪ] *adv* completamente.

U-turn *n lit* & *fig* giro *m* de 180°.

v¹ (*pl* **v's** OR **vs**), **V** (*pl* **V's** OR **Vs**) [viː] *n* (*letter*) v *f*, V *f*

v² 1. (*abbr of verse*) v. 2. (*abbr of volt*) v. 3. (*abbr of vide*) (*cross-reference*) v. 4. *abbr of* **versus**.

vacancy ['veɪkənsɪ] *n* 1. (*job, position*) vacante *f*. 2. (*room available*) habitación *f* libre; **'no vacancies'** 'completo'.

vacant ['veɪkənt] *adj* 1. (*room, chair, toilet*) libre. 2. (*job, post*) vacante. 3. (*look, expression*) distraído(da).

vacant lot *n* terreno *m* disponible.

vacate [və'keɪt] *vt* 1. (*job, post*) dejar vacante. 2. (*room, seat, premises*) desocupar.

vacation [və'keɪʃn] *n* vacaciones *fpl*.

vacationer [və'keɪʃənəʳ] *n Am*: **summer ~** veraneante *m* y *f*.

vaccinate ['væksɪneɪt] *vt*: **to ~ sb (against sthg)** vacunar a alguien (de OR contra algo).

vaccine [Br 'væksiːn, Am væk'siːn] *n* vacuna *f*.

vacuum ['vækjʊəm] ◆ *n* 1. (TECH & *fig*) vacío *m*. 2. (*cleaner*) aspiradora *f*. ◆ *vt* pasar la aspiradora por.

vacuum cleaner *n* aspiradora *f*.

vacuum-packed *adj* envasado(da) al vacío.

vagina [və'dʒaɪnə] *n* vagina *f*.

vagrant ['veɪgrənt] *n* vagabundo *m*, -da *f*.

vague [veɪg] *adj* 1. (*imprecise*) vago(ga), impreciso(sa). 2. (*person*) poco claro (ra). 3. (*feeling*) leve. 4. (*evasive*) evasivo (va). 5. (*absent-minded*) distraído(da). 6. (*outline*) borroso(sa).

vaguely ['veɪglɪ] *adv* 1. (*imprecisely*) vagamente. 2. (*slightly, not very*) levemente.

vain [veɪn] *adj* 1. *pej* (*conceited*) vanidoso (sa). 2. (*futile*) vano(na). ▶ **in vain** *adv* en vano.

valentine card ['væləntaɪn-] *n* tarjeta *f* que se manda el Día de los Enamorados.

Valentine's Day ['væləntaɪnz-] *n*: **(St) ~** San Valentín *m*, Día *m* de los Enamorados.

valet ['væleɪ, 'væleɪt] *n* ayuda *m* de cámara.

valiant ['væljənt] *adj* valeroso(sa).

valid ['vælɪd] *adj* 1. (*argument, explanation*) válido(da). 2. (*ticket, driving licence*) valedero(ra).

valley ['vælɪ] (*pl* **valleys**) *n* valle *m*.

valour Br, **valor** Am ['væləʳ] *n* (U) *fml* & *literary* valor *m*.

valuable ['væljʊəbl] *adj* valioso(sa). ▶ **valuables** *npl* objetos *mpl* de valor.

valuation [,væljʊ'eɪʃn] *n* 1. (*pricing, estimated price*) valuación *f*. 2. (*opinion, judging of worth*) valoración *f*.

value ['væljuː] ◆ *n* valor *m*; **to be good ~** estar muy bien de precio; **to be ~ for money** estar muy bien de precio. ◆ *vt* 1. (*estimate price of*) valorar, tasar. 2. (*cherish*) apreciar. ▶ **values** *npl* (*morals*) valores *mpl* morales.

value-added tax [-ædɪd-] *n* impuesto *m* sobre el valor añadido.

valued ['væljuːd] *adj* apreciado(da).

valve [vælv] *n* (*in pipe, tube*) válvula *f*.

van [væn] *n* 1. (AUT) furgoneta *f*, camioneta *f*. 2. Br (RAIL) furgón *m*.

vandal ['vændl] *n* vándalo *m*, gamberro *m*, -rra *f*.

vandalism ['vændəlɪzm] *n* vandalismo *m*, gamberrismo *m*.

vandalize, -ise ['vændəlaɪz] *vt* destruir, destrozar.

vanguard ['vængɑːd] *n* vanguardia *f*; **in the ~ of** a la vanguardia de.

vanilla [və'nɪlə] *n* vainilla *f*.

vanish ['vænɪʃ] *vi* desaparecer.

vanity ['vænətɪ] *n pej* vanidad *f*.

vantagepoint ['vɑːntɪdʒ,pɔɪnt] *n* posición *f* ventajosa.

vapour Br, **vapor** Am ['veɪpəʳ] *n* (U) vapor *m*.

variable ['veərɪəbl] *adj* variable.

variance ['veərɪəns] *n fml*: **at ~ (with)** en desacuerdo (con).

variation [,veərɪ'eɪʃn] *n*: **~ (in/on)** variación *f* (en/sobre).

varicose veins ['værɪkəʊs-] *npl* varices *fpl*.

varied ['veərɪd] adj variado(da).

variety [və'raɪətɪ] n 1. (gen) variedad f; **for a ~ of reasons** por razones varias. 2. (U) (THEATRE) variedades fpl.

variety show n espectáculo m de variedades.

various ['veərɪəs] adj 1. (several) varios (rias). 2. (different) diversos(sas).

varnish ['vɑːnɪʃ] ◆ n barniz m. ◆ vt (with varnish) barnizar; (with nail varnish) pintar.

vary ['veərɪ] ◆ vt variar. ◆ vi: **to ~ (in/with)** variar (de/con).

vase [Br vɑːz, Am veɪz] n florero m.

Vaseline® ['væsəliːn] n vaselina® f.

vast [vɑːst] adj enorme, inmenso(sa).

vat [væt] n cuba f, tina f.

VAT [væt, viːeɪtiː] (abbr of **value added tax**) n IVA m.

Vatican ['vætɪkən] n: **the ~** el Vaticano.

vault [vɔːlt] ◆ n 1. (in bank) cámara f acorazada. 2. (in church) cripta f. 3. (roof) bóveda f. ◆ vt saltar. ◆ vi: **to ~ over sthg** saltar por encima de algo.

VCR (abbr of **video cassette recorder**) n vídeo m.

VD (abbr of **venereal disease**) n ETS f.

VDU (abbr of **visual display unit**) n monitor m.

veal [viːl] n (U) ternera f.

veer [vɪər] vi virar.

vegan ['viːgən] n vegetariano que no consume ningún producto que provenga de un animal, como huevos, leche etc.

vegetable ['vedʒtəbl] ◆ n 1. (BOT) vegetal m. 2. (food) hortaliza f, legumbre f; **~s** verduras fpl. ◆ adj vegetal.

vegetarian [,vedʒɪ'teərɪən] ◆ adj vegetariano(na). ◆ n vegetariano m, -na f.

vegetation [,vedʒɪ'teɪʃn] n vegetación f.

vehement ['viːəmənt] adj (person, denial) vehemente; (attack, gesture) violento(ta).

vehicle ['viːəkl] n (for transport) vehículo m.

veil [veɪl] n lit & fig velo m.

vein [veɪn] n 1. (ANAT & BOT) vena f. 2. (of mineral) filón m, veta f.

velocity [vɪ'lɒsətɪ] n velocidad f.

velvet ['velvɪt] n terciopelo m.

vendetta [ven'detə] n enemistad f mortal.

vending machine ['vendɪŋ-] n máquina f de venta.

vendor ['vendɔːr] n vendedor m, -ra f.

veneer [və'nɪər] n (of wood) chapa f; fig (appearance) apariencia f.

venereal disease [vɪ'nɪərɪəl-] n enfermedad f venérea.

venetian blind n persiana f veneciana.

Venezuela [,venɪz'weɪlə] n Venezuela.

Venezuelan [,venɪz'weɪlən] ◆ adj venezolano(na). ◆ n venezolano m, -na f.

vengeance ['vendʒəns] n venganza f; **with a ~** con creces.

venison ['venɪzn] n carne f de venado.

venom ['venəm] n (poison) veneno m; fig (spite) malevolencia f.

vent [vent] ◆ n (opening) abertura f de escape; (grille) rejilla f de ventilación; **to give ~ to sthg** dar rienda suelta a algo. ◆ vt: **to ~ sthg (on)** desahogar algo (contra).

ventilate ['ventɪleɪt] vt ventilar.

ventilator ['ventɪleɪtər] n ventilador m.

ventriloquist [ven'trɪləkwɪst] n ventrílocuo m, -cua f.

venture ['ventʃər] ◆ n empresa f. ◆ vt aventurar; **to ~ to do sthg** aventurarse a hacer algo. ◆ vi 1. (go somewhere dangerous): **she ~d outside** se atrevió a salir. 2. (take a risk): **to ~ into** lanzarse a.

venue ['venjuː] n lugar m (en que se celebra algo).

Venus ['viːnəs] n (planet) Venus m.

veranda(h) [və'rændə] n veranda f.

verb [vɜːb] n verbo m.

verbal ['vɜːbl] adj verbal.

verbatim [vɜː'beɪtɪm] ◆ adj literal. ◆ adv literalmente, palabra por palabra.

verbose [vɜː'bəus] adj fml (person) verboso(sa); (report) prolijo(ja).

verdict ['vɜːdɪkt] n 1. (JUR) veredicto m, fallo m. 2. (opinion): **~ (on)** juicio m OR opinión f (sobre).

verge [vɜːdʒ] n 1. (edge, side) borde m. 2. (brink): **on the ~ of sthg** al borde de algo; **on the ~ of doing sthg** a punto de hacer algo. ▶ **verge (up)on** vt fus rayar en.

verify ['verɪfaɪ] vt 1. (check) verificar, comprobar. 2. (confirm) confirmar.

veritable ['verɪtəbl] adj hum or fml verdadero(ra).

vermin ['vɜːmɪn] npl bichos mpl.

vermouth ['vɜːməθ] n vermut m.

versa → **vice versa**.

versatile ['vɜːsətaɪl] adj 1. (person) polifacético(ca). 2. (machine, tool) que tiene muchos usos.

verse [vɜːs] n 1. (U) (poetry) versos mpl, poesía f. 2. (stanza) estrofa f. 3. (in Bible) versículo m.

versed [vɜːst] adj: **well ~ in** versado (da) en.

version ['vɜːʃn] n versión f.

versus ['vɜːsəs] prep (SPORT) contra.

vertebra ['vɜːtɪbrə] (pl **-brae** [-briː]) n vértebra f.

vertical ['vɜːtɪkl] adj vertical.

vertigo ['vɜːtɪgəʊ] n vértigo m.

verve [vɜːv] n brío m, entusiasmo m.

very ['verɪ] ◆ adv 1. (as intensifier) muy; ~ **much** mucho. 2. (as euphemism): **not ~ often** OR **much** no mucho; **he's not ~ intelligent** no es muy inteligente; **is it good? – not ~** ¿es bueno? – no mucho. ◆ adj mismísimo(ma); **the ~ thing I was looking for** justo lo que estaba buscando; **the ~ thought makes me ill** sólo con pensarlo me pongo enfermo; **fighting for his ~ life** luchando por su propia vida; **the ~ best** el mejor (de todos); **at the ~ least** como muy poco; **a house of my ~ own** mi propia casa. ▶ **very well** adv muy bien; **you can't ~ well stop him now** es un poco tarde para impedírselo.

vessel ['vesl] n fml 1. (boat) nave f. 2. (container) vasija f, recipiente m.

vest [vest] n 1. Br (undershirt) camiseta f. 2. Am (waistcoat) chaleco m.

vested interest ['vestɪd-] n: ~ **(in)** intereses mpl creados (en).

vestibule ['vestɪbjuːl] n fml (entrance hall) vestíbulo m.

vestige ['vestɪdʒ] n fml vestigio m.

vestry ['vestrɪ] n sacristía f.

vet [vet] ◆ n Br (abbr of **veterinary surgeon**) veterinario m, -ria f. ◆ vt someter a una investigación.

veteran ['vetrən] n veterano m, -na f.

veterinarian [,vetərɪ'neərɪən] n Am veterinario m, -ria f.

veterinary surgeon ['vetərɪnrɪ-] n Br fml veterinario m, -ria f.

veto ['viːtəʊ] (pl **-es**) ◆ n veto m. ◆ vt vetar.

vex [veks] vt fml molestar.

vexed question [,vekst-] n manzana f de la discordia.

vg (abbr of **very good**) MB.

VHF (abbr of **very high frequency**) VHF.

VHS (abbr of **video home system**) n VHS m.

via ['vaɪə] prep 1. (travelling through) vía. 2. (by means of) a través de, por.

viable ['vaɪəbl] adj viable.

vibrate [vaɪ'breɪt] vi vibrar.

vicar ['vɪkər] n (in Church of England) párroco m; (in Roman Catholic Church) vicario m.

vicarage ['vɪkərɪdʒ] n casa f del párroco.

vicarious [vɪ'keərɪəs] adj indirecto(ta).

vice [vaɪs] n 1. (immorality, moral fault) vicio m. 2. (tool) torno m de banco.

vice-chairman n vicepresidente m.

vice-chancellor n (UNIV) rector m, -ra f.

vice-president n vicepresidente m, -ta f.

vice versa [,vaɪsɪ'vɜːsə] adv viceversa.

vicinity [vɪ'sɪnətɪ] n: **in the ~ (of)** cerca (de).

vicious ['vɪʃəs] adj (dog) furioso(sa); (person, ruler) cruel; (criticism, attack) despiadado(da).

vicious circle n círculo m vicioso.

victim ['vɪktɪm] n víctima f.

victimize, -ise ['vɪktɪmaɪz] vt (retaliate against) tomar represalias contra; (pick on) mortificar.

victor ['vɪktər] n literary vencedor m, -ra f.

victorious [vɪk'tɔːrɪəs] adj victorioso (sa).

victory ['vɪktərɪ] n: ~ **(over)** victoria f (sobre).

video ['vɪdɪəʊ] (pl **-s**) ◆ n 1. (recording, medium, machine) vídeo m. 2. (cassette) videocasete m. ◆ comp vídeo. ◆ vt 1. (using video recorder) grabar en vídeo. 2. (using camera) hacer un vídeo de.

video camera n videocámara f.

video cassette n videocasete m.

video game n videojuego m.

videorecorder ['vɪdɪəʊrɪ,kɔːdər] n vídeo m.

video shop n tienda f de vídeos.

videotape ['vɪdɪəʊteɪp] n videocinta f.

vie [vaɪ] (pt & pp **vied**, cont **vying**) vi: **to ~ (with sb for sthg/to do sthg)** competir (con alguien por algo/para hacer algo).

Vienna [vɪ'enə] n Viena.

Vietnam [Br ,vjet'næm, Am ,vjet'nɑːm] n (el) Vietnam.

Vietnamese [,vjetnə'miːz] ◆ adj vietnamita. ◆ n 1. (person) vietnamita m y f. 2. (language) vietnamita m.

view [vjuː] ◆ n 1. (opinion) parecer m, opinión f; **in my ~** en mi opinión. 2. (attitude): ~ **(of)** actitud f (frente a). 3. (scene) vista f, panorama m. 4. (field of vision) vista f; **to come into ~** aparecer. ◆ vt 1. (consider) ver, considerar. 2. fml (examine, look at - stars etc) observar;

(- *house*, *flat*) visitar, ver. ▶ **in view of**
prep en vista de. ▶ **with a view to** *conj*
con miras OR vistas a.

viewer ['vjuːə'] *n* **1.** (*person*) espectador *m*, -ra *f.* **2.** (*apparatus*) visionador *m*.

viewfinder ['vjuːˌfaɪndə'] *n* visor *m*.

viewpoint ['vjuːpɔɪnt] *n* **1.** (*opinion*)
punto *m* de vista. **2.** (*place*) mirador *m*.

vigil ['vɪdʒɪl] *n* **1.** (*watch*) vigilia *f.*
2. (RELIG) Vigilia *f.*

vigilante [ˌvɪdʒɪ'læntɪ] *n* *persona que
extraoficialmente patrulla un área para prote-
gerla, tomándose la justicia en sus manos.*

vigorous ['vɪgərəs] *adj* enérgico(ca).

vile [vaɪl] *adj* (*person*, *act*) vil, infame;
(*food*, *smell*) repugnante; (*mood*) de perros.

villa ['vɪlə] *n* (*in country*) villa *f*; (*in town*)
chalet *m*.

village ['vɪlɪdʒ] *n* aldea *f*, pueblecito
m.

villager ['vɪlɪdʒə'] *n* aldeano *m*, -na *f*.

villain ['vɪlən] *n* **1.** (*of film*, *book*) malo
m, -la *f.* **2.** *dated* (*criminal*) criminal *m y f.*

vinaigrette [ˌvɪnɪ'gret] *n* vinagreta *f.*

vindicate ['vɪndɪkeɪt] *vt* justificar.

vindictive [vɪn'dɪktɪv] *adj* vengativo
(va).

vine [vaɪn] *n* (*on ground*) vid *f*; (*climbing
plant*) parra *f.*

vinegar ['vɪnɪgə'] *n* vinagre *m*.

vineyard ['vɪnjəd] *n* viña *f*, viñedo *m*.

vintage ['vɪntɪdʒ] ◆ *adj* **1.** (*wine*) añejo
(ja). **2.** (*classic*) clásico(ca). ◆ *n* cosecha *f*
(*de vino*).

vintage wine *n* vino *m* añejo.

vinyl ['vaɪnɪl] *n* vinilo *m*.

viola [vɪ'əʊlə] *n* viola *f.*

violate ['vaɪəleɪt] *vt* **1.** (*law*, *treaty*,
rights) violar, infringir. **2.** (*peace*, *privacy*)
invadir.

violence ['vaɪələns] *n* violencia *f.*

violent ['vaɪələnt] *adj* **1.** (*gen*) violento
(ta). **2.** (*emotion*, *anger*) intenso(sa).

violet ['vaɪələt] ◆ *adj* violeta, violado
(da). ◆ *n* (*flower*) violeta *f.*

violin [ˌvaɪə'lɪn] *n* violín *m*.

violinist [ˌvaɪə'lɪnɪst] *n* violinista *m y f.*

VIP (*abbr of* **very important person**) *n*
celebridad *f.*

viper ['vaɪpə'] *n* víbora *f.*

virgin ['vɜːdʒɪn] ◆ *adj literary* (*spotless*)
virgen. ◆ *n* virgen *m y f.*

Virgo ['vɜːgəʊ] (*pl* -s) *n* Virgo *m*.

virile ['vɪraɪl] *adj* viril.

virtually ['vɜːtʃʊəlɪ] *adv* prácticamente.

virtual reality *n* realidad *f* virtual.

virtue ['vɜːtjuː] *n* **1.** (*morality*, *good quality*) virtud *f.* **2.** (*benefit*) ventaja *f.* ▶ **by
virtue of** *prep fml* en virtud de.

virtuous ['vɜːtʃʊəs] *adj* virtuoso(sa).

virus ['vaɪrəs] *n* (COMPUT & MED) virus
m.

visa ['viːzə] *n* visado *m*.

vis-à-vis [ˌviːzɑː'viː] *prep fml* con
relación a.

viscose ['vɪskəʊs] *n* viscosa *f.*

visibility [ˌvɪzɪ'bɪlətɪ] *n* visibilidad *f.*

visible ['vɪzəbl] *adj* visible.

vision ['vɪʒn] *n* **1.** (U) (*ability to see*)
visión *f*, vista *f.* **2.** *fig* (*foresight*) clarividencia *f.* **3.** (*impression*, *dream*) visión *f.*

visit ['vɪzɪt] ◆ *n* visita *f*; **on a ~** de visita. ◆ *vt* visitar.

visiting hours ['vɪzɪtɪŋ-] *npl* horas *fpl*
de visita.

visitor ['vɪzɪtə'] *n* **1.** (*to one's home*, *hospital*) visita *f.* **2.** (*to museum*, *town etc*) visitante *m y f.*

visitors' book *n* libro *m* de visitas.

visitor's passport *n* Br pasaporte *m*
provisional.

visor ['vaɪzə'] *n* visera *f.*

vista ['vɪstə] *n* (*view*) vista *f*, perspectiva *f*; *fig* (*wide range*) perspectiva *f.*

visual ['vɪʒʊəl] *adj* (*gen*) visual; (*of the
eyes*) ocular.

visual aids *npl* medios *mpl* visuales.

visual display unit *n* monitor *m*.

visualize, -ise ['vɪʒʊəlaɪz] *vt* visualizar; **to ~** (*sb*) **doing sthg** imaginar (a
alguien) haciendo algo.

vital ['vaɪtl] *adj* **1.** (*essential*) vital, esencial. **2.** (*full of life*) enérgico(ca).

vitally ['vaɪtəlɪ] *adv* sumamente.

vital statistics *npl inf* medidas *fpl* (*del
cuerpo de la mujer*).

vitamin [Br 'vɪtəmɪn, Am 'vaɪtəmɪn] *n*
vitamina *f.*

vivacious [vɪ'veɪʃəs] *adj* vivaz.

vivid ['vɪvɪd] *adj* **1.** (*colour*) vivo(va).
2. (*description*, *memory*) vívido(da).

vividly ['vɪvɪdlɪ] *adv* **1.** (*brightly*) con
colores muy vivos. **2.** (*clearly*) vívida-
mente.

vixen ['vɪksn] *n* zorra *f.*

VLF (*abbr of* **very low frequency**) VLF.

V-neck *n* (*sweater*) jersey *m* de cuello
de OR en pico.

vocabulary [və'kæbjʊlərɪ] *n* vocabulario *m*.

vocal ['vəʊkl] *adj* **1.** (*outspoken*) vociferante. **2.** (*of the voice*) vocal.

vocal cords *npl* cuerdas *fpl* vocales.

vocalist ['vəʊkəlɪst] *n* (*in orchestra*)

vocalista *m* y *f*; (*in pop group*) cantante *m* y *f*.

vocation [vəʊˈkeɪʃn] *n* vocación *f*.

vocational [vəʊˈkeɪʃənl] *adj* profesional.

vociferous [vəˈsɪfərəs] *adj fml* ruidoso (sa).

vodka [ˈvɒdkə] *n* (*drink*) vodka *m*.

vogue [vəʊg] *n* moda *f*; **in ~** en boga.

voice [vɔɪs] ◆ *n* voz *f*. ◆ *vt* (*opinion, emotion*) expresar.

voice mail *n* correo *m* de voz; **to send/receive ~** mandar/recibir un mensaje de correo de voz.

void [vɔɪd] ◆ *adj* **1.** (*invalid*) inválido (da); → **null**. **2.** *fml* (*empty*): **~ of** falto(ta) de. ◆ *n literary* vacío *m*.

volatile [*Br* ˈvɒlətaɪl, *Am* ˈvɒlətl] *adj* (*situation*) volátil; (*person*) voluble.

vol-au-vent [ˈvɒləʊvɒŋ] *n* volován *m*.

volcano [vɒlˈkeɪnəʊ] (*pl* **-es** OR **-s**) *n* volcán *m*.

volition [vəˈlɪʃn] *n fml*: **of one's own ~** por voluntad propia.

volley [ˈvɒlɪ] (*pl* **volleys**) ◆ *n* **1.** (*of gunfire*) ráfaga *f*. **2.** *fig* (*rapid succession*) torrente *m*. **3.** (SPORT) volea *f*. ◆ *vt* volear.

volleyball [ˈvɒlɪbɔːl] *n* voleibol *m*.

volt [vəʊlt] *n* voltio *m*.

voltage [ˈvəʊltɪdʒ] *n* voltaje *m*.

voluble [ˈvɒljʊbl] *adj fml* locuaz.

volume [ˈvɒljuːm] *n* (*gen* & COMPUT) volumen *m*.

voluntarily [*Br* ˈvɒləntrɪlɪ, *Am* ˌvɒlənˈterəlɪ] *adv* voluntariamente.

voluntary [ˈvɒləntrɪ] *adj* voluntario (ria); **~ organization** organización *f* benéfica.

volunteer [ˌvɒlənˈtɪər] ◆ *n* (*person who volunteers*) voluntario *m*, -ria *f*. ◆ *vt* **1.** (*offer of one's free will*): **to ~ to do sthg** ofrecerse para hacer algo. **2.** (*information, advice*) dar, ofrecer. ◆ *vi* **1.** (*freely offer one's services*): **to ~ (for)** ofrecerse (para). **2.** (MIL) alistarse.

vomit [ˈvɒmɪt] ◆ *n* vómito *m*. ◆ *vi* vomitar.

vote [vəʊt] ◆ *n* **1.** (*gen*) voto *m*; **~ for/ against** voto a favor de/en contra de. **2.** (*session, ballot, result*) votación *f*. **3.** (*votes cast*): **the ~** los votos. ◆ *vt* **1.** (*person, leader*) elegir. **2.** (*choose*): **to ~ to do sthg** votar hacer algo. ◆ *vi*: **to ~ (for/against)** votar (a favor de/en contra de).

vote of thanks (*pl* **votes of thanks**) *n* palabras *fpl* de agradecimiento.

voter [ˈvəʊtər] *n* votante *m* y *f*.

voting [ˈvəʊtɪŋ] *n* votación *f*.

vouch [vaʊtʃ] ► **vouch for** *vt fus* **1.** (*person*) responder por. **2.** (*character, accuracy*) dar fe de.

voucher [ˈvaʊtʃər] *n* vale *m*.

vow [vaʊ] ◆ *n* (RELIG) voto *m*; (*solemn promise*) promesa *f* solemne. ◆ *vt*: **to ~ to do sthg** jurar hacer algo; **to ~ that** jurar que.

vowel [ˈvaʊəl] *n* vocal *f*.

voyage [ˈvɔɪɪdʒ] *n* viaje *m*.

vs *abbr of* **versus**.

VSO (*abbr of* **Voluntary Service Overseas**) *n organización británica de voluntarios que ayuda a países en vías de desarrollo*.

vulgar [ˈvʌlgər] *adj* **1.** (*in bad taste*) ordinario(ria). **2.** (*offensive*) grosero(ra).

vulnerable [ˈvʌlnərəbl] *adj*: **~ (to)** vulnerable (a).

vulture [ˈvʌltʃər] *n lit* & *fig* buitre *m*.

w (*pl* **w's** OR **ws**), **W** (*pl* **W's** OR **Ws**) [ˈdʌbljuː] *n* (*letter*) w *f*, W *f*. ► **W 1.** (*abbr of* **west**) O. **2.** (*abbr of* **watt**) w.

wad [wɒd] *n* **1.** (*of paper*) taco *m*. **2.** (*of banknotes, documents*) fajo *m*. **3.** (*of cotton, cotton wool, tobacco*) bola *f*.

waddle [ˈwɒdl] *vi* anadear.

wade [weɪd] *vi* caminar por el agua. ► **wade through** *vt fus fig*: **he was wading through the documents** le costaba mucho leer los documentos.

wading pool [ˈweɪdɪŋ-] *n Am* piscina *f* para niños.

wafer [ˈweɪfər] *n* (*thin biscuit*) barquillo *m*.

waffle [ˈwɒfl] ◆ *n* **1.** (CULIN) gofre *m*. **2.** *Br inf* (*vague talk*) paja *f*. ◆ *vi* enrollarse.

waft [wɑːft, wɒft] *vi* flotar.

wag [wæg] ◆ *vt* menear. ◆ *vi* menearse.

wage [weɪdʒ] ◆ *n* (*gen*) salario *m*; (*daily*) jornal *m*. ◆ *vt*: **to ~ war** hacer la guerra. ► **wages** *npl* (*gen*) salario *m*; (*daily*) jornal *m*.

wage earner [-ˌɜːnər] *n* asalariado *m*, -da *f*.

wage packet *n Br* **1.** (*envelope*) sobre *m* de pago. **2.** *fig* (*pay*) paga *f*.

wager ['weɪdʒəʳ] n apuesta f.

waggle ['wægl] vt inf menear.

waggon ['wægən] Br = **wagon**.

wagon ['wægən] n 1. (horse-drawn vehicle) carro m. 2. Br (RAIL) vagón m.

wail [weɪl] ◆ n lamento m, gemido m. ◆ vi lamentarse, gemir.

waist [weɪst] n cintura f.

waistcoat ['weɪskəʊt] n chaleco m.

waistline ['weɪstlaɪn] n cintura f, talle m.

wait [weɪt] ◆ n espera f. ◆ vi: **to ~ (for sthg/sb)** esperar (algo/a alguien); **to be unable to ~ to do sthg** estar impaciente por hacer algo; **to ~ and see** esperar y ver lo que pasa. ▶ **wait for** vt fus esperar. ▶ **wait on** vt fus (serve food to) servir. ▶ **wait up** vi quedarse despierto(ta) esperando.

waiter ['weɪtəʳ] n camarero m.

waiting list ['weɪtɪŋ-] n lista f de espera.

waiting room ['weɪtɪŋ-] n sala f de espera.

waitress ['weɪtrɪs] n camarera f.

waive [weɪv] vt fml (rule) no aplicar.

wake [weɪk] (pt woke OR -d, pp woken OR -d) ◆ n (of ship, boat) estela f. ◆ vt despertar. ◆ vi despertarse. ▶ **wake up** ◆ vt sep despertar. ◆ vi (wake) despertarse.

waken ['weɪkən] fml ◆ vt despertar. ◆ vi despertarse.

Wales [weɪlz] n (el país de) Gales.

walk [wɔːk] ◆ n 1. (way of walking) andar m, paso m. 2. (journey on foot) paseo m; **to go for a ~** dar un paseo; **it's ten minutes' ~ away** está a diez minutos andando. ◆ vt 1. (dog) pasear. 2. (streets) andar por; (distance) recorrer, andar. ◆ vi 1. (move on foot) andar, caminar. 2. (for pleasure) pasear. ▶ **walk out** vi 1. (leave suddenly) salirse. 2. (go on strike) declararse en huelga. ▶ **walk out on** vt fus abandonar.

walker ['wɔːkəʳ] n caminante m y f, paseante m y f.

walkie-talkie [,wɔːkɪ'tɔːkɪ] n walkie-talki m.

walking ['wɔːkɪŋ] n (U) (for sport) marcha f; (for pleasure) andar m.

walking shoes npl zapatos mpl para caminar.

walking stick n bastón m.

Walkman® ['wɔːkmən] n walkman® m.

walk of life (pl walks of life) n: people from all walks of life gente de

toda condición.

walkout ['wɔːkaʊt] n huelga f.

walkover ['wɔːk,əʊvəʳ] n victoria f fácil.

walkway ['wɔːkweɪ] n (on ship, oilrig, machine) pasarela f; (between buildings) paso m.

wall [wɔːl] n 1. (inside building, of cell, stomach) pared f. 2. (outside) muro m.

wallchart ['wɔːltʃɑːt] n (gráfico m) mural m.

walled [wɔːld] adj amurallado(da).

wallet ['wɒlɪt] n cartera f, billetera f.

wallflower ['wɔːl,flaʊəʳ] n 1. (plant) alhelí m. 2. inf fig (person) persona tímida que queda al margen de una fiesta.

wallop ['wɒləp] vt inf (child) pegar una torta a; (ball) golpear fuerte.

wallow ['wɒləʊ] vi (in liquid) revolcarse.

wallpaper ['wɔːl,peɪpəʳ] ◆ n papel m de pared OR de empapelar. ◆ vt empapelar.

Wall Street n Wall Street f, zona financiera neoyorquina.

wally ['wɒlɪ] n Br inf imbécil m y f.

walnut ['wɔːlnʌt] n 1. (nut) nuez f. 2. (wood, tree) nogal m.

walrus ['wɔːlrəs] (pl inv OR -es) n morsa f.

waltz [wɔːls] ◆ n vals m. ◆ vi (dance) bailar el vals.

wan [wɒn] adj pálido(da).

wand [wɒnd] n varita f mágica.

wander ['wɒndəʳ] vi vagar; **my mind kept ~ing** se me iba la mente en otras cosas.

wane [weɪn] vi (influence, interest) disminuir, decrecer.

wangle ['wæŋgl] vt inf agenciarse.

want [wɒnt] ◆ n fml 1. (need) necesidad f. 2. (lack) falta f; **for ~ of** por OR a falta de. 3. (deprivation) indigencia f, miseria f. ◆ vt (desire) querer; **to ~ to do sthg** querer hacer algo; **to ~ sb to do sthg** querer que alguien haga algo.

wanted ['wɒntɪd] adj: **to be ~ (by the police)** ser buscado(da) (por la policía).

wanton ['wɒntən] adj fml gratuito(ta), sin motivo.

war [wɔːʳ] ◆ n lit & fig guerra f. ◆ vi estar en guerra.

ward [wɔːd] n 1. (in hospital) sala f. 2. Br (POL) distrito m electoral. 3. (JUR) pupilo m, -la f. ▶ **ward off** vt fus protegerse de.

warden ['wɔːdn] n 1. (of park) guarda m y f. 2. Br (of youth hostel, hall of residence) encargado *m*, -da *f*. **3.** (*of monument*) guardián *m*, -ana *f*. **4.** Am (*prison governor*) director *m*, -ra *f*.

warder ['wɔːdəʳ] *n* (*in prison*) carcelero *m*, -ra *f*.

wardrobe ['wɔːdrəʊb] *n* **1.** (*piece of furniture*) armario *m*, guardarropa *m*. **2.** (*collection of clothes*) guardarropa *m*, vestuario *m*.

warehouse ['weəhaʊs, *pl* -haʊzɪz] *n* almacén *m*.

wares [weəz] *npl literary* mercancías *fpl*.

warfare ['wɔːfeəʳ] *n* (U) guerra *f*.

warhead ['wɔːhed] *n* ojiva *f*, cabeza *f*.

warily ['weərəlɪ] *adv* con cautela.

warm [wɔːm] ◆ *adj* **1.** (*pleasantly hot - gen*) caliente; (- *weather, day*) caluroso(sa); (*lukewarm*) tibio(bia), templado(da); **it's/I'm** ~ hace/tengo calor. **2.** (*clothes etc*) que abriga. **3.** (*colour, sound*) cálido(da). **4.** (*friendly - person, atmosphere, smile*) afectuoso(sa); (- *congratulations*) efusivo(va). ◆ *vt* calentar. ▶ **warm up** *vt sep* calentar. ◆ *vi* (*gen*) entrar en calor; (*weather, room, engine*) calentarse.

warm-hearted [-'hɑːtɪd] *adj* afectuoso(sa).

warmly ['wɔːmlɪ] *adv* **1.** (*in warm clothes*): **to dress** ~ vestirse con ropa de abrigo. **2.** (*in a friendly way*) calurosamente.

warmth [wɔːmθ] *n* **1.** (*heat*) calor *m*. **2.** (*of clothes*) abrigo *m*. **3.** (*friendliness*) cordialidad *f*.

warn [wɔːn] *vt* prevenir, advertir; **to** ~ **sb of sthg** prevenir a alguien algo; **to** ~ **sb not to do sthg** advertir a alguien que no haga algo.

warning ['wɔːnɪŋ] *n* aviso *m*, advertencia *f*.

warning light *n* piloto *m*.

warning triangle *n* Br triángulo *m* de avería.

warp [wɔːp] ◆ *vt* **1.** (*wood*) alabear. **2.** (*personality*) torcer, deformar. ◆ *vi* alabearse.

warrant ['wɒrənt] ◆ *n* orden *f* OR mandamiento *m* judicial. ◆ *vt fml* merecer.

warranty ['wɒrəntɪ] *n* garantía *f*.

warren ['wɒrən] *n* zona *f* de conejos.

warrior ['wɒrɪəʳ] *n* guerrero *m*, -ra *f*.

Warsaw ['wɔːsɔː] *n* Varsovia; **the** ~ **Pact** el Pacto de Varsovia.

warship ['wɔːʃɪp] *n* buque *m* de guerra.

wart [wɔːt] *n* verruga *f*.

wartime ['wɔːtaɪm] *n* tiempos *mpl* de guerra.

wary ['weərɪ] *adj*: ~ **(of)** receloso(sa) (de).

was [*weak form* wəz, *strong form* wɒz] *pt* → **be**.

wash [wɒʃ] ◆ *n* **1.** (*act of washing*) lavado *m*. **2.** (*things to wash*) ropa sucia. **3.** (*from boat*) estela *f*. ◆ *vt* **1.** (*gen*) lavar; (*hands, face*) lavarse. **2.** (*carry - subj: waves etc*) arrastrar, llevarse. ◆ *vi* **1.** (*clean oneself*) lavarse. **2.** (*waves, oil*): **to** ~ **over sthg** bañar algo. ▶ **wash away** *vt sep* (*subj: water, waves*) llevarse, barrer. ▶ **wash up** ◆ *vt sep* Br (*dishes*) lavar, fregar. ◆ *vi* **1.** Br (*wash the dishes*) fregar OR lavar los platos. **2.** Am (*wash o.s.*) lavarse.

washable ['wɒʃəbl] *adj* lavable.

washbasin Br ['wɒʃˌbeɪsn], **washbowl** Am ['wɒʃbəʊl] *n* lavabo *m*.

washcloth ['wɒʃˌklɒθ] *n* Am toallita *f* para lavarse la cara.

washer ['wɒʃəʳ] *n* (TECH) arandela *f*.

washing ['wɒʃɪŋ] *n* (U) **1.** (*operation*) colada *f*. **2.** (*clothes - dirty*) ropa *f* sucia OR para lavar; (- *clean*) colada *f*.

washing line *n* tendedero *m*.

washing machine *n* lavadora *f*.

washing powder *n* Br detergente *m*, jabón *m* en polvo.

Washington ['wɒʃɪŋtən] *n* (*town*): ~ **D.C.** ciudad *f* de Washington.

washing-up *n* **1.** Br (*crockery, pans etc*) platos *mpl* para fregar. **2.** (*operation*) fregado *m*; **to do the** ~ fregar los platos.

washing-up liquid *n* Br detergente *m* para vajillas.

washout ['wɒʃaʊt] *n inf* desastre *m*.

washroom ['wɒʃrʊm] *n* Am aseos *mpl*.

wasn't [wɒznt] = **was not**.

wasp [wɒsp] *n* (*insect*) avispa *f*.

wastage ['weɪstɪdʒ] *n* desperdicio *m*.

waste [weɪst] ◆ *adj* (*land*) yermo(ma); (*material, fuel*) de desecho. ◆ *n* **1.** (*misuse, incomplete use*) desperdicio *m*, derroche *m*; **a** ~ **of time** una pérdida de tiempo. **2.** (U) (*refuse*) desperdicios *mpl*; (*chemical, toxic etc*) residuos *mpl*. ◆ *vt* (*time*) perder; (*money*) malgastar, derrochar; (*food, energy, opportunity*) desperdiciar. ▶ **wastes** *npl literary* yermos *mpl*.

wastebasket Am = **wastepaper basket**.

waste disposal unit *n* triturador *m* de basuras.

wasteful ['weɪstfʊl] *adj* derrochador (ra).

waste ground *n* (U) descampados *mpl*.

wastepaper basket [ˌweɪstˈpeɪpəʳ-], **wastepaper bin** [ˌweɪstˈpeɪpəʳ-], **wastebasket** Am ['weɪstˌbɑːskɪt] *n* papelera *f*.

watch [wɒtʃ] ◆ *n* **1.** (*timepiece*) reloj *m*. **2.** (*act of watching*): **to keep ~** estar de guardia; **to keep ~ on sthg/sb** vigilar algo/a alguien. **3.** (MIL) (*group of people*) guardia *f*. ◆ *vt* **1.** (*look at - gen*) mirar; (*- sunset*) contemplar; (*- football match,* TV) ver. **2.** (*spy on*) vigilar. **3.** (*be careful about*) tener cuidado con, vigilar. ◆ *vi* mirar, observar. ► **watch out** *vi* tener cuidado.

watchdog ['wɒtʃdɒg] *n* **1.** (*dog*) perro *m* guardián. **2.** *fig* (*organization*) comisión *f* de vigilancia.

watchful ['wɒtʃful] *adj* atento(ta).

watchmaker ['wɒtʃˌmeɪkəʳ] *n* relojero *m*, -ra *f*.

watchman ['wɒtʃmən] (*pl* **-men** [-mən]) *n* vigilante *m*.

water ['wɔːtəʳ] ◆ *n* (*gen*) agua *f*. ◆ *vt* regar. ◆ *vi* **1.** (*eyes*): **my eyes are ~ing** me lloran los ojos. **2.** (*mouth*): **my mouth is ~ing** se me hace la boca agua. ► **waters** *npl* aguas *fpl*. ► **water down** *vt sep* **1.** (*dilute*) diluir, aguar. **2.** *usu pej* (*moderate*) moderar.

water bottle *n* cantimplora *f*.

water closet *n* dated wáter *m*.

watercolour ['wɔːtəˌkʌləʳ] *n* acuarela *f*.

watercress ['wɔːtəkres] *n* berro *m*.

waterfall ['wɔːtəfɔːl] *n* cascada *f*, salto *m* de agua.

water heater *n* calentador *m* de agua.

waterhole ['wɔːtəhəʊl] *n* balsa *f* (donde acuden a beber los animales).

watering can ['wɔːtərɪŋ-] *n* regadera *f*.

water level *n* nivel *m* del agua.

water lily *n* nenúfar *m*.

waterline ['wɔːtəlaɪn] *n* (NAUT) línea *f* de flotación.

waterlogged ['wɔːtəlɒgd] *adj* inundado(da).

water main *n* cañería *f* principal.

watermark ['wɔːtəmɑːk] *n* **1.** (*in paper*) filigrana *f*. **2.** (*showing water level*) marca *f* del nivel del agua.

watermelon ['wɔːtəˌmelən] *n* sandía *f*.

water polo *n* water-polo *m*.

waterproof ['wɔːtəpruːf] ◆ *adj* imper-

meable. ◆ *n* impermeable *m*.

watershed ['wɔːtəʃed] *n fig* momento *m* decisivo.

water skiing *n* esquí *m* acuático.

water tank *n* reserva *f* de agua.

watertight ['wɔːtətaɪt] *adj* (*waterproof*) hermético(ca).

waterway ['wɔːtəweɪ] *n* vía *f* navegable.

waterworks ['wɔːtəwɜːks] (*pl inv*) *n* (*building*) central *f* de agua.

watery ['wɔːtərɪ] *adj* **1.** (*food*) soso(sa). **2.** (*pale*) desvaído (da).

watt [wɒt] *n* vatio *m*.

wave [weɪv] ◆ *n* **1.** (*of hand*) ademán *m* OR señal *f* (con la mano). **2.** (*of water*) ola *f*. **3.** (*of emotion, nausea, panic*) arranque *m*; (*of immigrants, crime etc*) oleada *f*. **4.** (*of light, sound, heat*) onda *f*. **5.** (*in hair*) ondulación *f*. ◆ *vt* **1.** (*move about as signal*) agitar. **2.** (*signal to*) hacer señales OR señas a. ◆ *vi* **1.** (*with hand - in greeting*) saludar con la mano; (*- to say goodbye*) decir adiós con la mano; **to ~ at** OR **to sb** saludar a alguien con la mano. **2.** (*flag*) ondear; (*trees*) agitarse.

wavelength ['weɪvleŋθ] *n* longitud *f* de onda; **to be on the same ~** *fig* estar en la misma onda.

waver ['weɪvəʳ] *vi* **1.** (*falter - resolution, confidence*) flaquear. **2.** (*hesitate*) dudar, vacilar. **3.** (*fluctuate*) oscilar.

wavy ['weɪvɪ] *adj* ondulado(da).

wax [wæks] ◆ *n* cera *f*. ◆ *vt* encerar.

wax paper *n* Am papel *m* de cera.

waxworks ['wækswɜːks] (*pl inv*) *n* museo *m* de cera.

way [weɪ] ◆ *n* **1.** (*manner, method*) manera *f*, modo *m*; **in the same ~** del mismo modo, igualmente; **this/that ~** así; **in a ~** en cierto modo; **to get** OR **have one's ~** salirse uno con la suya. **2.** (*route, path*) camino *m*; **to lose one's ~** perderse; **~ in** entrada *f*; **~ out** salida *f*; **it's out of my ~** no me pilla de camino; **it's out of the ~** (*place*) está algo aislado; **on the** OR **on one's ~** de camino; **I'm on my ~** voy de camino; **to be under ~** (*ship*) estar navegando; *fig* (*meeting*) estar en marcha; **to get under ~** (*ship*) zarpar; (*meeting*) ponerse en marcha; **to be in the ~** estar en medio; **to go out of one's ~ to do sthg** tomarse muchas molestias para hacer algo; **to keep out of the ~** mantenerse alejado; **to make ~ for** dar paso a. **3.** (*direction*) dirección *f*; **come this ~** ven por aquí; **go that ~** ve por ahí;

which ~ **do we go?** ¿hacia dónde vamos?; **the wrong ~ up** OR **round** al revés; **the right ~ up** OR **round** del derecho. **4.** (*distance*): **all the ~** todo el camino OR trayecto; **it's a long ~ away** está muy lejos; **we have a long ~ to go** queda mucho camino por recorrer. **5.** *phr:* **to give ~** (*under weight, pressure*) ceder; **'give ~'** Br' (AUT) 'ceda el paso'; **no ~!** ¡ni hablar! ♦ *adv inf* (*far*) mucho; **it's ~ too big** es tela de grande. ▶ **ways** *npl* (*customs, habits*) costumbres *fpl*, hábitos *mpl*. ▶ **by the way** *adv* por cierto.

waylay [,weɪˈleɪ] (*pt & pp* **-laid**) *vt* abordar.

wayward [ˈweɪwəd] *adj* (*person, behaviour*) incorregible.

WC (*abbr of* **water closet**) WC.

we [wiː] *pers pron* nosotros *mpl*, -tras *fpl*; **WE can't do it** NOSOTROS no podemos hacerlo; **as ~ say in France** como decimos en Francia; **~ British** nosotros los británicos.

weak [wiːk] *adj* **1.** (*gen*) débil. **2.** (*material, structure*) frágil. **3.** (*argument, tea etc*) flojo(ja). **4.** (*lacking knowledge, skill*): **to be ~ on sthg** estar flojo(ja) en algo.

weaken [ˈwiːkn] ♦ *vt* debilitar. ♦ *vi* **1.** (*become less determined*) ceder, flaquear. **2.** (*physically*) debilitarse.

weakling [ˈwiːklɪŋ] *n pej* enclenque *m y f*.

weakness [ˈwiːknɪs] *n* **1.** (*gen*) debilidad *f*. **2.** (*imperfect point*) defecto *m*.

wealth [welθ] *n* **1.** (*riches*) riqueza *f*. **2.** (*abundance*) profusión *f*.

wealthy [ˈwelθɪ] *adj* rico(ca).

wean [wiːn] *vt* (*from mother's milk*) destetar.

weapon [ˈwepən] *n* arma *f*.

weaponry [ˈwepənrɪ] *n* (U) armamento *m*.

wear [weər] (*pt* **wore**, *pp* **worn**) ♦ *n* (U) **1.** (*use*) uso *m*. **2.** (*damage*) desgaste *m*; **~ and tear** desgaste. **3.** (*type of clothes*) ropa *f*. ♦ *vt* **1.** (*clothes, hair*) llevar; (*shoes*) calzar; **to ~ red** vestirse de rojo. **2.** (*damage*) desgastar. ♦ *vi* **1.** (*deteriorate*) desgastarse. **2.** (*last*): **to ~ well/badly** durar mucho/poco. ▶ **wear away** ♦ *vt sep* desgastar. ♦ *vi* desgastarse. ▶ **wear down** *vt sep* **1.** (*reduce size of*) desgastar. **2.** (*weaken*) agotar. ▶ **wear off** *vi* desaparecer, disiparse. ▶ **wear out** ♦ *vt sep* **1.** (*shoes, clothes*) gastar. **2.** (*person*) agotar. ♦ *vi* gastarse.

weary [ˈwɪərɪ] *adj* fatigado(da), cansa-

do(da); **to be ~ of sthg/of doing sthg** estar cansado de algo/de hacer algo.

weasel [ˈwiːzl] *n* comadreja *f*.

weather [ˈweðər] ♦ *n* tiempo *m*; **to be under the ~** no encontrarse muy bien. ♦ *vt* (*crisis etc*) superar.

weather-beaten [-,biːtn] *adj* (*face, skin*) curtido(da).

weathercock [ˈweðəkɒk] *n* veleta *f*.

weather forecast *n* parte *m* meteorológico.

weatherman [ˈweðəmæn] (*pl* **-men** [-men]) *n* hombre *m* del tiempo.

weather vane [-veɪn] *n* veleta *f*.

weave [wiːv] (*pt* **wove**, *pp* **woven**) ♦ *vt* (*using loom*) tejer. ♦ *vi* (*move*): **to ~ through** colarse por entre.

weaver [ˈwiːvər] *n* tejedor *m*, -ra *f*.

web [web] *n* **1.** (*cobweb*) telaraña *f*. **2.** *fig* (*of lies etc*) urdimbre *f*.

Web site *n* sitio *m* Web.

wed [wed] (*pt & pp* **-ded** OR **wed**) *literary* ♦ *vt* desposar. ♦ *vi* desposarse.

we'd [wiːd] = **we had**, **we would**.

wedding [ˈwedɪŋ] *n* boda *f*, casamiento *m*.

wedding anniversary *n* aniversario *m* de boda.

wedding cake *n* tarta *f* nupcial.

wedding dress *n* traje *m* de novia.

wedding ring *n* anillo *m* de boda, argolla *f* Amer.

wedge [wedʒ] ♦ *n* **1.** (*for steadying or splitting*) cuña *f*. **2.** (*triangular slice*) porción *f*, trozo *m*. ♦ *vt*: **to ~ sthg open/shut** dejar algo abierto/cerrado con una cuña.

Wednesday [ˈwenzdɪ] *n* miércoles *m inv; see also* **Saturday**.

wee [wiː] ♦ *adj* Scot pequeño(ña). ♦ *n v inf* pipí *m*. ♦ *vi v inf* hacer pipí.

weed [wiːd] ♦ *n* **1.** (*wild plant*) mala hierba *f*. **2.** Br *inf* (*feeble person*) canijo *m*, -ja *f*. ♦ *vt* desherbar, escardar.

weedkiller [ˈwiːd,kɪlər] *n* herbicida *m*.

weedy [ˈwiːdɪ] *adj* Br *inf* (*feeble*) enclenque.

week [wiːk] *n* (*gen*) semana *f*.

weekday [ˈwiːkdeɪ] *n* día *m* laborable.

weekend [,wiːkˈend] *n* fin *m* de semana.

weekly [ˈwiːklɪ] ♦ *adj* semanal. ♦ *adv* semanalmente. ♦ *n* semanario *m*.

weep [wiːp] (*pt & pp* **wept**) ♦ *vt* derramar. ♦ *vi* llorar.

weeping willow [,wiːpɪŋ-] *n* sauce *m* llorón.

weigh [weɪ] vt 1. (gen) pesar. 2. (consider carefully) sopesar. ► **weigh down** vt sep 1. (physically) sobrecargar. 2. (mentally): **to be ~ed down by** OR **with** estar abrumado(da) de OR por. ► **weigh up** vt sep 1. (consider carefully) sopesar. 2. (size up) hacerse una idea de.

weight [weɪt] n 1. (gen) peso m; **to put on** OR **gain ~** engordar; **to lose ~** adelgazar; **to pull one's ~** poner (uno) de su parte. 2. (metal object) pesa f.

weighted ['weɪtɪd] adj: **to be ~ in favour of/against** inclinarse a favor/en contra de.

weighting ['weɪtɪŋ] n prima por vivir en una ciudad con alto coste de vida.

weightlifting ['weɪt,lɪftɪŋ] n levantamiento m de pesos, halterofilia f.

weighty ['weɪtɪ] adj (serious) de peso.

weir [wɪər] n presa f, dique m.

weird [wɪəd] adj raro(ra), extraño(ña).

welcome ['welkəm] ◆ adj 1. (guest) bienvenido(da). 2. (free): **you're ~ to come** si quieres, puedes venir. 3. (appreciated): **to be ~** ser de agradecer. 4. (in reply to thanks): **you're ~** de nada. ◆ n bienvenida f. ◆ vt 1. (receive) dar la bienvenida a. 2. (approve, support) recibir bien. ◆ excl ¡bienvenido(da)!

weld [weld] ◆ n soldadura f. ◆ vt soldar.

welfare ['welfeər] ◆ adj de asistencia social. ◆ n 1. (state of well-being) bienestar m. 2. Am (income support) subsidio m de la seguridad social.

welfare state n: **the ~** el Estado de bienestar.

well [wel] (compar **better**, superl **best**) ◆ adj bien; **to be ~** (healthy) estar bien (de salud); **to get ~** mejorarse; **all is ~** todo va bien; **(it's) just as ~** menos mal. ◆ adv 1. (satisfactorily, thoroughly) bien; **they were ~ beaten** fueron ampliamente derrotados; **to go ~** ir bien; **~ done!** ¡muy bien!; **~ and truly** completamente. 2. (definitely, certainly) claramente, definitivamente; **it was ~ worth it** sí que valió la pena. 3. (as emphasis): **you know perfectly ~ (that)** sabes de sobra (que). 4. (very possibly): **it could ~ rain** es muy posible que llueva. ◆ n pozo m. ◆ excl 1. (gen) bueno; **oh ~!** ¡en fin! 2. (in surprise) ¡vaya! ► **as well** adv 1. (in addition) también. 2. (with same result): **you may** OR **might as ~ (do it)** ¿y por qué no (lo haces)? ► **as well as** conj además de. ► **well up** vi brotar.

we'll [wiːl] = we shall, we will.

well-advised [-əd'vaɪzd] adj sensato (ta); **you would be ~ to do it** sería aconsejable que lo hicieras.

well-behaved [-bɪ'heɪvd] adj formal, bien educado(da).

wellbeing [,wel'biːɪŋ] n bienestar m.

well-built adj fornido(da).

well-done adj (thoroughly cooked) muy hecho(cha).

well-dressed [-'drest] adj bien vestido(da).

well-earned [-'ɜːnd] adj bien merecido(da).

well-heeled [-hiːld] adj inf ricachón (ona).

wellington boots ['welɪŋtən-], **wellingtons** ['welɪŋtənz] npl botas fpl de agua.

well-kept adj 1. (neat, tidy) bien cuidado(da). 2. (not revealed) bien guardado(da).

well-known adj conocido(da).

well-mannered [-'mænəd] adj de buenos modales.

well-meaning adj bienintencionado (da).

well-nigh [-naɪ] adv casi.

well-off adj 1. (rich) acomodado(da), rico(ca). 2. (well-provided): **to be ~ for sthg** tener bastante de algo.

well-read [-'red] adj instruido(da), culto(ta).

well-rounded [-'raundɪd] adj (varied) completo(ta).

well-timed adj oportuno(na).

well-to-do adj adinerado(da).

wellwisher ['wel,wɪʃər] n simpatizante m y f (que da muestras de apoyo).

Welsh [welʃ] ◆ adj galés(esa). ◆ n (language) galés m. ◆ npl: **the ~** los galeses.

Welshman ['welʃmən] (pl **-men** [-mən]) n galés m.

Welshwoman ['welʃ,wumən] (pl **-women** [-,wɪmɪn]) n galesa f.

went [went] pt → **go**.

wept [wept] pt & pp → **weep**.

were [wɜːr] pt → **be**.

we're [wɪər] = we are.

weren't [wɜːnt] = were not.

west [west] ◆ n 1. (direction) oeste m. 2. (region): **the West** el Oeste. ◆ adj del oeste. ◆ adv: **~ (of)** al oeste (de). ► **West** n (POL.) the West Occidente.

West Bank n: **the ~** Cisjordania.

West Country n Br: **the ~** el sudoeste de Inglaterra.

West End n Br: **the ~** zona central de

Londres, famosa por sus teatros, tiendas etc.
westerly ['westəlɪ] *adj* del oeste.
western ['westən] ♦ *adj* occidental.
♦ *n* (*book*) novela *f* del oeste; (*film*) película *f* del oeste, western *m*.
West German ♦ *adj* de la Alemania Occidental. ♦ *n* (*person*) alemán *m*, -ana *f* occidental.
West Germany *n*: (the former) ~ (la antigua) Alemania Occidental.
West Indian ♦ *adj* antillano(na). ♦ *n* (*person*) antillano *m*, -na *f*.
West Indies [-'ɪndɪːz] *npl*: the ~ las Antillas.
Westminster ['westmɪnstər] *n barrio londinense en que se encuentra el parlamento británico; por extensión éste.*
westward ['westwəd] ♦ *adj* hacia el oeste. ♦ *adv* = **westwards**.
westwards ['westwədz] *adv* hacia el oeste.
wet [wet] (*pt & pp* **wet** OR **-ted**) ♦ *adj* **1.** (*soaked*) mojado(da); (*damp*) húmedo (da). **2.** (*rainy*) lluvioso(sa). **3.** (*paint, cement*) fresco(ca). **4.** Br *inf pej* (*weak, feeble*) ñoño(ña). ♦ *n inf* (POL) político conservador moderado. ♦ *vt* (*soak*) mojar; (*dampen*) humedecer.
wet blanket *n inf pej* aguafiestas *m y f.*
wet suit *n* traje *m* de submarinista.
we've [wiːv] = **we have**.
whack [wæk] *n inf* (*hit*) castañazo *m.*
whale [weɪl] *n* (*animal*) ballena *f.*
wharf [wɔːf] (*pl* **-s** OR **wharves** [wɔːvz]) *n* muelle *m*, embarcadero *m.*
what [wɒt] ♦ *adj* **1.** (*in direct, indirect questions*) qué; ~ **shape is it?** ¿qué forma tiene?; **he asked me ~ shape it was** me preguntó qué forma tenía; ~ **colour is it?** ¿de qué color es? **2.** (*in exclamations*) qué; ~ **a surprise!** ¡qué sorpresa!; ~ **a stupid idea!** ¡qué idea más tonta! ♦ *pron* **1.** (*interrogative*) qué; ~ **are they doing?** ¿qué hacen?; ~ **are they talking about?** ¿de qué están hablando?; ~ **is it called?** ¿cómo se llama?; ~ **does it cost?** ¿cuánto cuesta?; ~ **is it like?** ¿cómo es?; ~**'s the Spanish for 'book'?** ¿cómo se dice 'book' en español?; ~ **about another drink/going out for a meal?** ¿qué tal otra copa/si salimos a comer?; ~ **about me?** ¿y yo qué?; ~ **if nobody comes?** ¿y si no viene nadie, qué? **2.** (*relative*) lo que; **I saw ~ happened/he did** yo vi lo que ocurrió/hizo; **I don't know ~ to do** no sé qué hacer. ♦ *excl* (*expressing disbelief*) ¿qué?; ~, **no milk!** ¿cómo?

¿que no hay leche?
whatever [wɒt'evər] ♦ *adj* cualquier; **eat ~ food you find** come lo que encuentres; **no chance** ~ ni la más remota posibilidad; **nothing** ~ nada en absoluto. ♦ *pron* **1.** (*no matter what*): **they may offer** ofrezcan lo que ofrezcan; ~ **you like** lo que (tú) quieras; ~ **happens** pase lo que pase. **2.** (*indicating surprise*): ~ **do you mean?** ¿qué diablos quieres decir? **3.** (*indicating ignorance*): ~ **that is** OR **may be** sea lo que sea eso; **or** ~ o lo que sea.
whatsoever [ˌwɒtsəʊ'evər] *adj*: **nothing** ~ nada en absoluto; **none** ~ ni uno.
wheat [wiːt] *n* trigo *m.*
wheedle ['wiːdl] *vt* decir con zalamería; **to ~ sb into doing sthg** camelar OR engatusar a alguien para que haga algo; **to ~ sthg out of sb** sonsacarle algo a alguien.
wheel [wiːl] ♦ *n* **1.** (*gen*) rueda *f.* **2.** (*steering wheel*) volante *m.* ♦ *vt* empujar (*algo sobre ruedas*). ♦ *vi* **1.** (*move in circle*) dar vueltas. **2.** (*turn round*): **to ~ round** darse la vuelta.
wheelbarrow ['wiːlˌbærəʊ] *n* carretilla *f.*
wheelchair ['wiːlˌtʃeər] *n* silla *f* de ruedas.
wheelclamp ['wiːlˌklæmp] *n* cepo *m.*
wheeze [wiːz] *vi* resollar.
whelk [welk] *n* buccino *m.*
when [wen] ♦ *adv* (*in direct, indirect question*) cuándo; ~ **does the plane arrive?** ¿cuándo llega el avión?; **he asked me** ~ **I would be in London** me preguntó cuándo estaría en Londres. ♦ *conj* cuando; **tell me** ~ **you've read it** avísame cuando lo hayas leído; **on the day** ~ **it happened** el día (en) que pasó; **you said it was black** ~ **it was actually white** dijiste que era negro cuando en realidad era blanco.
whenever [wen'evər] ♦ *conj* (*no matter when*) cuando; (*every time*) cada vez que; ~ **you like** cuando quieras. ♦ *adv* cuando sea.
where [weər] ♦ *adv* (*in direct, indirect questions*) dónde; ~ **do you live?** ¿dónde vives?; **do you know** ~ **he lives?** ¿sabes dónde vive?; ~ **are we going?** ¿adónde vamos?; **I don't know** ~ **to start** no sé por dónde empezar. ♦ *conj* (*referring to place, situation*) donde; **this is** ~ **...** es aquí donde ...; **go** ~ **you like** vete (a) donde quieras.
whereabouts [*adv* ˌweərə'baʊts, *n*

'weərəbaʊts] ♦ *adv* (por) dónde. ♦ *npl* paradero *m*.

whereas [weər'æz] *conj* mientras que.

whereby [weə'baɪ] *conj fml* por el/la cual.

whereupon [ˌweərə'pɒn] *conj fml* tras OR con lo cual.

wherever [weər'evər] ♦ *conj* (*no matter where*) dondequiera que; **~ you go** dondequiera que vayas; **sit ~ you like** siéntate donde quieras. ♦ *adv* **1.** (*no matter where*) en cualquier parte. **2.** (*indicating surprise*): **~ did you hear that?** ¿dónde diablos habrás oído eso?

wherewithal ['weəwɪðɔːl] *n fml*: **to have the ~ to do sthg** disponer de los medios para hacer algo.

whet [wet] *vt*: **to ~ sb's appetite (for sthg)** despertar el interés de alguien (por algo).

whether ['weðər] *conj* **1.** (*indicating choice, doubt*) si; **I doubt ~ she'll do it** dudo que lo haga. **2.** (*no matter if*): **~ I want to or not** tanto si quiero como si no.

which [wɪtʃ] ♦ *adj* **1.** (*in direct, indirect questions*) qué; **~ house is yours?** ¿cuál es tu casa?; **~ one?** ¿cuál?; **~ ones?** ¿cuáles? **2.** (*to refer back to*): **in ~ case** en cuyo caso. ♦ *pron* **1.** (*in direct, indirect questions*) cuál, cuáles (*pl*); **~ do you prefer?** ¿cuál prefieres?; **I can't decide ~ to have** no sé cuál coger. **2.** (*in relative clause replacing noun*) que; **the table, ~ was made of wood, ...** la mesa, que OR la cual era de madera, ...; **the world in ~ we live** el mundo en que OR en el cual vivimos. **3.** (*to refer back to a clause*) lo cual; **she denied it, ~ surprised me** lo negó, lo cual me sorprendió.

whichever [wɪtʃ'evər] ♦ *adj* **1.** (*no matter which*): **~ route you take** vayas por donde vayas. **2.** (*the one which*): **~ colour you prefer** el color que prefieras. ♦ *pron* el que (la que), los que (las que) (*pl*); **take ~ you like** coge el que quieras.

whiff [wɪf] *n* (*smell*) olorcillo *m*.

while [waɪl] ♦ *n* rato *m*; **it's a long ~ since I did that** hace mucho que no hago eso; **for a ~** un rato; **after a ~** después de un rato; **in a ~** dentro de poco; **once in a ~** de vez en cuando. ♦ *conj* **1.** (*during the time that*) mientras. **2.** (*whereas*) mientras que. **3.** (*although*) aunque. ▶ **while away** *vt sep* pasar.

whilst [waɪlst] *conj* = **while**.

whim [wɪm] *n* capricho *m*.

whimper ['wɪmpər] *vt & vi* gimotear.

whimsical ['wɪmzɪkl] *adj* (*idea, story*) fantasioso(sa); (*remark*) juguetón(ona).

whine [waɪn] *vi* (*child, dog*) gemir; (*siren*) ulular.

whinge [wɪndʒ] *vi* Br: **to ~ (about)** quejarse (de).

whip [wɪp] ♦ *n* **1.** (*for hitting*) látigo *m*; (*for horse*) fusta *f*. **2.** Br (POL) *miembro de un partido encargado de asegurar que otros miembros voten en el parlamento.* ♦ *vt* **1.** (*gen*) azotar. **2.** (*take quickly*): **to ~ sthg out/off** sacar/quitar algo rápidamente. **3.** (*whisk*) batir.

whipped cream [wɪpt-] *n* nata *f* montada.

whip-round *n* Br *inf*: **to have a ~** hacer una colecta.

whirl [wɜːl] ♦ *n fig* (*of activity, events*) torbellino *m*. ♦ *vt*: **to ~ sb/sthg round** hacer dar vueltas a alguien/algo. ♦ *vi* (*move around*) arremolinarse; (*dancers*) girar vertiginosamente.

whirlpool ['wɜːlpuːl] *n* remolino *m*.

whirlwind ['wɜːlwɪnd] *n* torbellino *m*.

whirr [wɜːr] *vi* zumbar.

whisk [wɪsk] ♦ *n* (CULIN) varilla *f*. ♦ *vt* **1.** (*move quickly*): **to ~ sthg away/out** llevarse/sacar algo rápidamente. **2.** (CULIN) batir.

whisker ['wɪskər] *n* (pelo *m* del) bigote *m*. ▶ **whiskers** *npl* (*of person*) patillas *fpl*; (*of cat*) bigotes *mpl*.

whisky Br, **whiskey** Am & Irish (*pl* **whiskeys**) ['wɪskɪ] *n* whisky *m*.

whisper ['wɪspər] ♦ *vt* susurrar. ♦ *vi* cuchichear.

whistle ['wɪsl] ♦ *n* **1.** (*sound*) silbido *m*, pitido *m*. **2.** (*device*) silbato *m*, pito *m*. ♦ *vt* silbar. ♦ *vi* (*person*) silbar, chiflar Amer; (*referee*) pitar; (*bird*) piar.

white [waɪt] ♦ *adj* **1.** (*gen*) blanco(ca). **2.** (*coffee, tea*) con leche. ♦ *n* **1.** (*colour*) blanco *m*. **2.** (*person*) blanco *m*, -ca *f*. **3.** (*of egg*) clara *f*. **4.** (*of eye*) blanco *m*.

white-collar *adj* de oficina; **~ worker** oficinista *m y f*.

white elephant *n fig* mamotreto *m* (*caro e inútil*).

Whitehall ['waɪthɔːl] *n* *calle londinense en que se encuentra la Administración británica; por extensión ésta.*

white-hot *adj* incandescente.

White House *n*: **the ~** la Casa Blanca.

white lie *n* mentira *f* piadosa.

whiteness ['waɪtnɪs] *n* blancura *f*.

white paper *n* (POL) libro *m* blanco.

white sauce *n* (salsa *f*) bechamel *f*.

white spirit *n* Br especie de aguarrás.

whitewash ['waɪtwɒʃ] ♦ *n* **1.** (U)

(*paint*) blanqueo *m*, lechada *f* (de cal).
2. *pej* (*cover-up*) encubrimiento *m*. ◆ *vt*
(*paint*) blanquear.

whiting ['waɪtɪŋ] (*pl inv* OR **-s**) *n*
pescadilla *f*.

Whitsun ['wɪtsn] *n* (*day*) Pentecostés
m.

whittle ['wɪtl] *vt* (*reduce*): **to ~ down** OR
away reducir gradualmente.

whiz, whizz [wɪz] *vi*: **to ~ past** OR **by**
pasar muy rápido OR zumbando.

whiz(z) kid *n inf* genio *m*, prodigio *m*.

who [huː] *pron* **1.** (*in direct, indirect questions*) quién, quiénes (*pl*); **~ are you?**
¿quién eres tú?; **~ did you see?** ¿a
quién viste?; **I didn't know ~ she was** no
sabía quién era. **2.** (*in relative clauses*)
que; **he's the doctor ~ treated me** es el
médico que me atendió; **those ~ are in
favour** los que están a favor.

who'd [huːd] = **who had, who
would**.

whodu(n)nit [ˌhuːˈdʌnɪt] *n inf* historia
f policíaca de misterio.

whoever [huːˈevəʳ] *pron* **1.** (*unknown
person*) quienquiera, (*pl*) quienesquiera; **~ finds it** quienquiera que lo
encuentre; **tell ~ you like** díselo a quien
quieras. **2.** (*indicating surprise, astonishment*): **~ can that be?** ¿quién podrá ser?
3. (*no matter who*): **come in, ~ you are**
pasa, seas quién seas.

whole [həʊl] ◆ *adj* **1.** (*entire, complete*)
entero(ra). **2.** (*for emphasis*): **a ~ lot taller**
muchísimo más alto; **a ~ new idea** una
idea totalmente nueva. ◆ *n* **1.** (*all*): **the
~ of the school/summer** el colegio/vera-
no entero. **2.** (*unit, complete thing*) todo
m. ▶ **as a whole** *adv* en conjunto.
▶ **on the whole** *adv* en general.

wholefood ['həʊlfuːd] *n Br* comida *f*
integral.

whole-hearted [-'hɑːtɪd] *adj* profun-
do(da).

wholemeal ['həʊlmiːl] *adj Br* integral.

wholesale ['həʊlseɪl] ◆ *adj* **1.** (COMM)
al por mayor. **2.** *pej* (*indiscriminate*) indis-
criminado(da). ◆ *adv* **1.** (COMM) al por
mayor. **2.** *pej* (*indiscriminately*) indiscri-
minadamente.

wholesaler ['həʊlˌseɪləʳ] *n* mayorista
m y f.

wholesome ['həʊlsəm] *adj* sano(na).

whole wheat *Am* = **wholemeal**.

who'll [huːl] = **who will**.

wholly ['həʊlɪ] *adv* completamente.

whom [huːm] *pron* **1.** (*in direct, indirect
questions*) *fml* quién, quiénes (*pl*); **from ~**

did you receive it? ¿de quién lo
recibiste?; **for/of/to ~** por/de/a quién.
2. (*in relative clauses*) que; **the man ~ I saw**
el hombre que vi; **the man to ~ I gave it**
el hombre al que se lo di; **several people came, none of ~ I knew** vinieron
varias personas, de las que no conocía
a ninguna.

whooping cough ['huːpɪŋ-] *n* tos *f*
ferina.

whopping ['wɒpɪŋ] *inf* ◆ *adj* enorme.
◆ *adv*: **a ~ great lorry/lie, a ~ big lorry/
lie** un camión/una mentira enorme.

whore [hɔːʳ] *n pej* zorra *f*, puta *f*.

who're ['huːəʳ] = **who are**.

whose [huːz] ◆ *pron* (*in direct, indirect
questions*) de quién, (*pl*) de quiénes; **~ is
this?** ¿de quién es esto?; **I wonder ~
they are** me pregunto de quién serán.
◆ *adj* **1.** (*in direct, indirect questions*) de
quién; **~ car is that?** ¿de quién es ese
coche? **2.** (*in relative clauses*) cuyo(ya),
cuyos(yas) (*pl*); **that's the boy ~ father's
an MP** ese es el chico cuyo padre es
diputado; **the woman ~ daughters are
twins** la mujer cuyas hijas son gemelas.

who's who [huːz-] *n* (*book*) Quién es
Quién *m*.

who've [huːv] = **who have**.

why [waɪ] ◆ *adv* por qué; **~ did you lie
to me?** ¿por qué me mentiste?; **~ don't
you all come?** ¿por qué no venís
todos?; **~ not?** ¿por qué no? ◆ *conj* por
qué; **I don't know ~ he said that** no sé
por qué dijo eso. ◆ *pron*: **there are several reasons ~ he left** hay varias razones
por las que se marchó; **that's ~ she did
it** por eso es por lo que lo hizo; **I don't
know the reason ~** no se por qué razón.
◆ *excl* ¡hombre!, ¡vaya! ▶ **why ever**
adv: **~ ever did you do that?** ¿por qué
diablos has hecho eso?

wick [wɪk] *n* mecha *f*.

wicked ['wɪkɪd] *adj* **1.** (*evil*) malvado
(da). **2.** (*mischievous, devilish*) travieso
(sa).

wicker ['wɪkəʳ] *adj* de mimbre.

wickerwork ['wɪkəwɜːk] *n* (U) artículos *mpl* de mimbre.

wicket ['wɪkɪt] *n* (CRICKET) (*stumps*)
palos *mpl*.

wide [waɪd] ◆ *adj* **1.** (*broad*) ancho
(cha); **it's 50 cm ~** tiene 50 cm de ancho.
2. (*range, choice etc*) amplio(plia). **3.** (*gap,
difference, implications*) grande, considerable. **4.** (*off-target*) desviado(da).
◆ *adv* **1.** (*broadly*): **to open/spread sthg ~**
abrir/desplegar algo completamente.

2. (*off target*): **to go** OR **be ~** salir desviado.

wide-angle lens *n* gran angular *m*.

wide-awake *adj* completamente despierto(ta).

widely ['waɪdlɪ] *adv* **1.** (*travel, read*) extensamente. **2.** (*believed, known, loved*) generalmente. **3.** (*differ, vary*) mucho.

widen ['waɪdn] *vt* (*gen*) ampliar; (*road, bridge*) ensanchar.

wide open *adj* **1.** (*window, door*) abierto(ta) de par en par. **2.** (*eyes*) completamente abierto(ta).

wide-ranging [-'reɪndʒɪŋ] *adj* (*changes, survey, consequences*) de gran alcance; (*discussion, interests*) de gran variedad; (*selection*) amplio(plia).

widespread ['waɪdspred] *adj* extendido(da), general.

widow ['wɪdəʊ] *n* (*woman*) viuda *f*.

widowed ['wɪdəʊd] *adj* viudo(da).

widower ['wɪdəʊəʳ] *n* viudo *m*.

width [wɪdθ] *n* **1.** (*breadth*) anchura *f*; **it's 50 cm in ~** tiene 50 cm de ancho. **2.** (*in swimming pool*) ancho *m*.

wield [wiːld] *vt* **1.** (*weapon*) esgrimir; (*implement*) manejar. **2.** (*power*) ejercer.

wife [waɪf] (*pl* **wives**) *n* mujer *f*, esposa *f*.

wig [wɪg] *n* peluca *f*.

wiggle ['wɪgl] *vt inf* menear; (*hips etc*) contonear.

wild [waɪld] *adj* **1.** (*gen*) salvaje; (*plant, flower*) silvestre; (*bull*) bravo(va). **2.** (*landscape, scenery*) agreste. **3.** (*weather, sea*) borrascoso(sa). **4.** (*crowd, laughter, applause*) frenético(ca). **5.** (*hair*) alborotado(da). **6.** (*hope, idea, plan*) descabellado(da). **7.** (*guess, exaggeration*) extravagante. ► **wilds** *npl*: **the ~s** las tierras remotas.

wilderness ['wɪldənɪs] *n* **1.** (*barren land*) yermo *m*, desierto *m*. **2.** (*overgrown land*) jungla *f*.

wild-goose chase *n inf* búsqueda *f* infructuosa.

wildlife ['waɪldlaɪf] *n* (U) fauna *f*.

wildly ['waɪldlɪ] *adv* **1.** (*enthusiastically*) frenéticamente. **2.** (*without discipline, inaccurately*) a lo loco. **3.** (*very*) extremadamente.

wilful *Br*, **willful** *Am* ['wɪlfʊl] *adj* **1.** (*stubborn*) que siempre se tiene que salir con la suya. **2.** (*deliberate*) deliberado(da).

will¹ [wɪl] ♦ *n* **1.** (*gen*) voluntad *f*. **2.** (*document*) testamento *m*. ♦ *vt*: **to ~ sth to happen** desear mucho que ocu-

rra algo; **to ~ sb to do sthg** desear mucho que alguien haga algo.

will² [wɪl] *modal vb* **1.** (*to express future tense*): **they say it ~ rain tomorrow** dicen que lloverá OR va a llover mañana; **when ~ we get paid?** ¿cuándo nos pagarán?; **~ they come? - yes, they ~** ¿vendrán? – sí. **2.** (*indicating willingness*): **~ you have some more tea?** ¿te apetece más té?; **I won't do it** no lo haré. **3.** (*in commands, requests*): **you ~ leave this house at once** vas a salir de esta casa ahora mismo; **close that window, ~ you?** cierra la ventana, ¿quieres?; **~ you be quiet!** ¿queréis hacer el favor de callaros? **4.** (*indicating possibility, what usually happens*): **the hall ~ hold up to 1,000 people** la sala tiene cabida para 1.000 personas. **5.** (*expressing an assumption*): **that'll be your father** ese va a ser OR será tu padre. **6.** (*indicating irritation*): **she ~ keep phoning me** ¡y venga a llamarme!

willful *Am* = **wilful**.

willing ['wɪlɪŋ] *adj* **1.** (*prepared*): **to be ~ (to do sthg)** estar dispuesto(ta) (a hacer algo). **2.** (*eager*) servicial.

willingly ['wɪlɪŋlɪ] *adv* de buena gana.

willow (tree) ['wɪləʊ-] *n* sauce *m*.

willpower ['wɪl,paʊəʳ] *n* fuerza *f* de voluntad.

willy-nilly [,wɪlɪ'nɪlɪ] *adv* pase lo que pase.

wilt [wɪlt] *vi* (*plant*) marchitarse; (*person*) desfallecer, extenuarse.

wily ['waɪlɪ] *adj* astuto(ta).

wimp [wɪmp] *n pej inf* blandengue *m* y *f*.

win [wɪn] (*pt & pp* **won**) ♦ *n* victoria *f*, triunfo *m*. ♦ *vt* ganar. ♦ *vi* ganar. ► **win over, win round** *vt sep* convencer.

wince [wɪns] *vi* hacer una mueca de dolor; **to ~ at/with sthg** estremecerse ante/de algo.

winch [wɪntʃ] *n* torno *m*.

wind¹ [wɪnd] ♦ *n* **1.** (METEOR) viento *m*. **2.** (*breath*) aliento *m*, resuello *m*. **3.** (U) (*in stomach*) gases *mpl*. ♦ *vt* (*knock breath out of*) dejar sin aliento.

wind² [waɪnd] (*pt & pp* **wound**) ♦ *vt* **1.** (*string, thread*) enrollar; **to ~ sthg around sthg** enrollar algo alrededor de algo. **2.** (*clock, watch*) dar cuerda a. ♦ *vi* serpentear. ► **wind down** ♦ *vt sep* **1.** (*car window*) bajar. **2.** (*business*) cerrar poco a poco. ♦ *vi* (*person*) relajarse, descansar. ► **wind up** ♦ *vt sep* **1.** (*finish - activity*) finalizar, concluir; (*business*) liquidar. **2.** (*clock, watch*) dar cuerda a. **3.** (*car window*) subir. **4.** Br inf (*annoy*) vacilar, tomar el pelo a. ◆ *vi inf* (*end up*) terminar, acabar.

windfall ['wɪndfɔːl] *n* (*unexpected gift*) dinero *m* llovido del cielo.

winding ['waɪndɪŋ] *adj* tortuoso(sa).

wind instrument [wɪnd-] *n* instrumento *m* de viento.

windmill ['wɪndmɪl] *n* (*building*) molino *m* de viento.

window ['wɪndəu] *n* **1.** (*gen & COMPUT*) ventana *f*. **2.** (*AUT*) ventanilla *f*. **3.** (*of shop*) escaparate *m*.

window box *n* jardinera *f* (de ventana).

window cleaner *n* limpiacristales *m* y *f inv*.

window ledge *n* alféizar *m*.

window pane *n* cristal *m* (de la ventana).

windowsill ['wɪndəusɪl] *n* alféizar *m*.

windpipe ['wɪndpaɪp] *n* tráquea *f*.

windscreen Br ['wɪndskriːn], **windshield** Am ['wɪndfiːld] *n* parabrisas *m inv*.

windscreen washer *n* lavaparabrisas *m inv*.

windscreen wiper *n* limpiaparabrisas *m inv*.

windshield Am *m* = **windscreen**.

windsurfing ['wɪnd,sɜːfɪŋ] *n* windsurf *m*.

windswept ['wɪndswept] *adj* (*scenery*) azotado(da) por el viento.

windy ['wɪndɪ] *adj* **1.** (*day, weather*) ventoso(sa), de mucho viento; (*place*) expuesto(ta) al viento; **it's ~** hace viento.

wine [waɪn] *n* vino *m*; **red/white ~** vino tinto/blanco.

wine bar *n* Br bar de cierta elegancia especializado en vinos que suele servir comidas.

wine cellar *n* bodega *f*.

wineglass ['waɪnglɑːs] *n* copa *f* OR vaso *m* (de vino).

wine list *n* lista *f* de vinos.

wine merchant *n* Br vinatero *m*, -ra *f*.

wine tasting [-,teɪstɪŋ] *n* cata *f* de vinos.

wine waiter *n* sommelier *m*.

wing [wɪŋ] *n* **1.** (*gen*) ala *f*. **2.** (*AUT*) guardabarros *m inv*. **3.** (*SPORT*) (*side of pitch*) banda *f*; (*winger*) extremo *m*. ► **wings** *npl* (*THEATRE*): **the ~s** los bastidores.

winger ['wɪŋər] *n* (*SPORT*) extremo *m*.

wing mirror *n* retrovisor *m*.

wink [wɪŋk] ◆ *n* guiño *m*. ◆ *vi* (*eye*): **to ~** (**at sb**) guiñar (a alguien).

winkle ['wɪŋkl] *n* bígaro *m*.

winner ['wɪnər] *n* ganador *m*, -ra *f*.

winning ['wɪnɪŋ] *adj* **1.** (*team, competitor*) vencedor(ra); (*goal, point*) de la victoria; (*ticket, number*) premiado(da). **2.** (*smile, ways*) atractivo(va). ► **winnings** *npl* ganancias *fpl*.

winning post *n* meta *f*.

winter ['wɪntər] ◆ *n* (U) invierno *m*. ◆ *comp* de invierno, invernal.

winter sports *npl* deportes *mpl* de invierno.

wintertime ['wɪntətaɪm] *n* (U) invierno *m*.

wint(e)ry ['wɪntrɪ] *adj* (*gen*) de invierno, invernal; (*showers*) con nieve.

wipe [waɪp] ◆ *n*: **give the table a ~** pásale un trapo a la mesa. ◆ *vt* (*rub to clean*) limpiar, pasar un trapo a; (*rub to dry*) secar. ► **wipe out** *vt sep* **1.** (*erase*) borrar. **2.** (*eradicate*) aniquilar. ► **wipe up** *vt sep* empapar, limpiar.

wire ['waɪər] ◆ *n* **1.** (*gen*) alambre *m*; (*ELEC*) cable *m*. **2.** (*telegram*) telegrama *m*. ◆ *vt* **1.** (*connect*): **to ~ sthg to sthg** conectar algo a algo. **2.** (*ELEC - house*) poner la instalación eléctrica de; (*- plug*) conectar el cable a. **3.** (*send telegram to*) enviar un telegrama a.

wireless ['waɪəlɪs] *n dated* radio *f*.

wiring ['waɪərɪŋ] *n* (U) instalación *f* eléctrica.

wiry ['waɪərɪ] *adj* **1.** (*hair*) estropajoso(sa). **2.** (*body, man*) nervudo(da).

wisdom ['wɪzdəm] *n* **1.** (*learning*) sabiduría *f*. **2.** (*good sense*) sensatez *f*.

wisdom tooth *n* muela *f* del juicio.

wise [waɪz] *adj* **1.** (*learned*) sabio(bia). **2.** (*sensible*) prudente.

wisecrack ['waɪzkræk] *n pej* broma *f*, chiste *m*.

wish [wɪʃ] ◆ *n*: **~** (**for sthg/to do sthg**) deseo *m* (de algo/de hacer algo). ◆ *vt*: **to ~ to do sthg** *fml* desear hacer algo; **to ~ sb sthg** desear a alguien algo; **I ~ (that) you had told me before!** ¡ojalá me lo hubieras dicho antes!; **I ~ (that) I were** OR **was rich** ojalá fuera rico. ◆ *vi* (*by magic*): **to ~ for sthg** pedir (como deseo) algo. ► **wishes** *npl*: (**with**) **best ~es** (*in letter*) muchos recuerdos.

wishful thinking [,wɪʃful-] *n* (U): **it's just ~** no son más que (vanas) ilusiones.

wishy-washy ['wɪʃɪ,wɒʃɪ] *adj inf pej* soso(sa), insípido(da).

wisp [wɪsp] n 1. (of hair) mechón m; (of grass) brizna f. 2. (cloud) nubecilla f; (of smoke) voluta f.

wistful ['wɪstful] adj melancólico(ca).

wit [wɪt] n 1. (humour) ingenio m, agudeza f. 2. (intelligence): **to have the ~ to do sthg** tener el buen juicio de hacer algo. ► **wits** npl: **to have** OR **keep one's ~s about one** mantenerse alerta.

witch [wɪtʃ] n bruja f.

with [wɪð] prep 1. (in company of) con; **we stayed ~ them for a week** estuvimos con ellos una semana; ~ **me** conmigo; ~ **you** contigo; ~ **himself/herself** consigo. 2. (indicating opposition) con; **to argue ~ sb** discutir con alguien. 3. (indicating means, manner, feelings) con; **I washed it ~ detergent** lo lavé con detergente; **he filled it ~ wine** lo llenó de vino; **covered ~ mud** cubierto de barro; **she was trembling ~ fear** temblaba de miedo. 4. (having - gen) con; **a man ~ a beard** un hombre con barba; **the woman ~ the black hair/big dog** la señora del pelo negro/perro grande. 5. (regarding) con; **he's very mean ~ money** es muy tacaño con el dinero; **the trouble ~ her is that ...** su problema es que ... 6. (because of) con; ~ **my luck, I'll probably lose** con la suerte que tengo seguro que pierdo. 7. (indicating understanding): **are you ~ me?** ¿me sigues? 8. (indicating support) con; **I'm ~ Dad on this** en eso estoy con papá.

withdraw [wɪð'drɔː] (pt **-drew**, pp **-drawn**) ◆ vt 1. (gen): **to ~ sthg (from)** retirar algo (de). 2. (money) sacar. ◆ vi: **to ~ (from/to)** retirarse (de/a).

withdrawal [wɪð'drɔːəl] n 1. (gen & MIL) retirada f. 2. (retraction) retractación f. 3. (FIN) reintegro m.

withdrawal symptoms npl síndrome m de abstinencia.

withdrawn [wɪð'drɔːn] ◆ pp → **withdraw**. ◆ adj (shy, quiet) reservado(da).

withdrew [wɪð'druː] pt → **withdraw**.

wither ['wɪðər] vi 1. (dry up) marchitarse. 2. (become weak) debilitarse.

withhold [wɪð'həʊld] (pt & pp **-held** [-'held]) vt (gen) retener; (consent, permission) negar.

within [wɪ'ðɪn] ◆ prep 1. (gen) dentro de; ~ **reach** al alcance de la mano. 2. (less than - distance) a menos de; (- time) en menos de; **it's ~ walking distance** se puede ir andando; ~ **the next six months** en los próximos seis meses; **it arrived ~ a week** llegó en una se-

mana. ◆ adv dentro.

without [wɪð'aʊt] ◆ prep sin; ~ **sthg/doing sthg** sin algo/hacer algo; **it happened ~ my realizing** pasó sin que me diera cuenta. ◆ adv: **to go** OR **do ~ sthg** pasar sin algo.

withstand [wɪð'stænd] (pt & pp **-stood** [-'stʊd]) vt resistir, aguantar.

witness ['wɪtnɪs] ◆ n 1. (person) testigo m y f. 2. (testimony): **to bear ~ to sthg** atestiguar algo, dar fe de algo. ◆ vt 1. (see) presenciar. 2. (countersign) firmar (como testigo).

witness box Br, **witness stand** Am n tribuna f (de los testigos).

witticism ['wɪtɪsɪzm] n ocurrencia f.

witty ['wɪtɪ] adj ingenioso(sa), ocurrente.

wives [waɪvz] pl → **wife**.

wizard ['wɪzəd] n 1. (magician) mago m (en cuentos). 2. (skilled person) genio m.

wobble ['wɒbl] vi (gen) tambalearse; (furniture) cojear; (legs) temblar.

woe [wəʊ] n literary aflicción f.

woke [wəʊk] pt → **wake**.

woken ['wəʊkn] pp → **wake**.

wolf [wʊlf] (pl **wolves**) n (ZOOL) lobo m.

wolves ['wʊlvz] pl → **wolf**.

woman ['wʊmən] (pl **women**) ◆ n 1. (female) mujer f. 2. (womanhood) la mujer. ◆ comp: ~ **doctor** médica f.

womanly ['wʊmənlɪ] adj femenino (na).

womb [wuːm] n matriz f, útero m.

women ['wɪmɪn] pl → **woman**.

women's lib [-'lɪb] n liberación f de la mujer.

women's liberation n liberación f de la mujer.

won [wʌn] pt & pp → **win**.

wonder ['wʌndər] ◆ n 1. (amazement) asombro m, admiración f. 2. (cause for surprise): **it's a ~ (that) ...** es un milagro que ...; **no** OR **little** OR **small ~ ...** no es de extrañar que ... 3. (amazing thing, person) maravilla f. ◆ vt 1. (speculate): **to ~ (if** OR **whether)** preguntarse (si). 2. (in polite requests): **I ~ if** OR **whether I could ask you a question?** ¿le importaría que le hiciera una pregunta? ◆ vi (speculate): **I was only ~ing** (preguntaba) sólo por curiosidad; **to ~ about sthg** preguntarse por algo.

wonderful ['wʌndəful] adj maravilloso(sa), estupendo(da).

wonderfully ['wʌndəfulɪ] adv 1. (very well) estupendamente. 2. (very) extremadamente.

won't [wəʊnt] = **will not**.

woo [wuː] vt **1**. literary (court) cortejar. **2**. (try to win over) granjearse el apoyo de.

wood [wʊd] n **1**. (timber) madera f; (for fire) leña f. **2**. (group of trees) bosque m. ▶ **woods** npl bosque m.

wooded ['wʊdɪd] adj arbolado(da).

wooden ['wʊdn] adj **1**. (of wood) de madera. **2**. pej (actor) envarado(da).

woodpecker ['wʊd,pekəʳ] n pájaro m carpintero.

woodwind ['wʊdwɪnd] n: **the ~** los instrumentos de viento de madera.

woodwork ['wʊdwɜːk] n carpintería f.

woodworm ['wʊdwɜːm] n carcoma f.

wool [wʊl] n lana f; **to pull the ~ over sb's eyes** inf fig dar a alguien gato por liebre.

woollen Br, **woolen** Am ['wʊlən] adj de lana. ▶ **woollens** npl géneros mpl de lana.

woolly ['wʊlɪ] adj **1**. (woollen) de lana. **2**. inf (fuzzy, unclear) confuso(sa).

word [wɜːd] ◆ n **1**. (LING) palabra f; **~ for ~** palabra por palabra; **in other ~s** en otras palabras; **in a ~** en una palabra; **too ... for ~s** de lo más ...; **she doesn't mince her ~s** no tiene pelos en la lengua; **to have a ~ with sb** hablar con alguien; **I couldn't get a ~ in edgeways** no pude meter baza. **2**. (U) (news) noticia f. **3**. (promise) palabra f; **to give sb one's ~** dar (uno) su palabra a alguien. ◆ vt redactar, expresar.

wording ['wɜːdɪŋ] n (U) términos mpl, forma f (de expresión).

word processing n (U) proceso m de textos.

word processor [-'prəʊsesəʳ] n procesador m de textos.

wordsearch ['wɜːdsɜːtʃ] n (puzzle) sopa f de letras.

wore [wɔːʳ] pt → **wear**.

work [wɜːk] ◆ n **1**. (U) (employment) trabajo m, empleo m; **to be out of ~** estar desempleado; **at ~** en el trabajo. **2**. (activity, tasks) trabajo m; **at ~** trabajando. **3**. (of art, literature etc) obra f. ◆ vt **1**. (employees, subordinates) hacer trabajar. **2**. (machine) manejar, operar. **3**. (wood, metal, land) trabajar. ◆ vi **1**. (person): **to ~ (on sthg)** trabajar (en algo). **2**. (machine, system, idea) funcionar. **3**. (drug) surtir efecto. **4**. (become by movement): **to ~ loose** soltarse; **to ~ free** desprenderse. ▶ **works** ◆ n (factory) fábrica f. ◆ npl (mechanism) mecanismo m. ▶ **work on** vt fus **1**. (pay attention to) trabajar en.

2. (take as basis) partir de. ▶ **work out** ◆ vt sep **1**. (plan, schedule) elaborar. **2**. (total, amount) calcular; (answer) dar con. ◆ vi **1**. (figure etc): **to ~ out at** salir a. **2**. (turn out) resolverse. **3**. (be successful) salir bien. **4**. (train, exercise) hacer ejercicio. ▶ **work up** vt sep **1**. (excite): **to ~ o.s. up into a frenzy** ponerse frenético(ca). **2**. (generate) despertar.

workable ['wɜːkəbl] adj factible, viable.

workaholic [,wɜːkə'hɒlɪk] n adicto m, -ta f al trabajo.

workday ['wɜːkdeɪ] n (not weekend) día m laborable.

worked up [,wɜːkt-] adj nervioso(sa).

worker ['wɜːkəʳ] n (person who works) trabajador m, -ra f; (manual worker) obrero m, -ra f.

workforce ['wɜːkfɔːs] n mano f de obra.

working ['wɜːkɪŋ] adj **1**. (in operation) funcionando. **2**. (having employment) empleado(da). **3**. (relating to work - gen) laboral; (- day) laborable. ▶ **workings** npl mecanismo m.

working class n: **the ~** la clase obrera. ▶ **working-class** adj obrero(ra).

working order n: **to be in (good) ~** funcionar (bien).

workload ['wɜːkləʊd] n cantidad f de trabajo.

workman ['wɜːkmən] (pl -men [-mən]) n obrero m.

workmanship ['wɜːkmənʃɪp] n artesanía f.

workmate ['wɜːkmeɪt] n compañero m, -ra f de trabajo, colega m y f.

work permit [-,pɜːmɪt] n permiso m de trabajo.

workplace ['wɜːkpleɪs] n lugar m de trabajo.

workshop ['wɜːkʃɒp] n taller m.

workstation ['wɜːk,steɪʃn] n (COMPUT) estación f de trabajo.

worktop ['wɜːktɒp] n Br mármol m, encimera f.

work-to-rule n Br huelga f de celo.

world [wɜːld] ◆ n mundo m; **the best in the ~** el mejor del mundo; **to think the ~ of sb** querer a alguien con locura; **a ~ of difference** una diferencia enorme. ◆ comp mundial.

world-class adj de primera categoría.

world-famous adj famoso(sa) en el mundo entero.

worldly ['wɜːldlɪ] adj literary mundano (na).

World War I

World War I *n* la Primera Guerra Mundial.

World War II *n* la Segunda Guerra Mundial.

worldwide ['wɜːldwaɪd] ◆ *adj* mundial. ◆ *adv* en todo el mundo.

World Wide Web *n*: **the ~** la (World Wide) Web.

worm [wɜːm] *n* (*animal*) gusano *m*; (*earthworm*) lombriz *f* (de tierra).

worn [wɔːn] ◆ *pp* → **wear**. ◆ *adj* 1. (*threadbare*) gastado(da). 2. (*tired*) ajado (da).

worn-out *adj* 1. (*old, threadbare*): **to be ~** estar ya para tirar. 2. (*tired*) agotado (da).

worried ['wʌrɪd] *adj* preocupado(da).

worry ['wʌrɪ] ◆ *n* preocupación *f*. ◆ *vt* (*trouble*) preocupar. ◆ *vi*: **to ~ (about)** preocuparse (por); **not to ~!** ¡no importa!

worrying ['wʌrɪɪŋ] *adj* preocupante.

worse [wɜːs] ◆ *adj* peor; **to get ~** empeorar. ◆ *adv* peor; **~ off** (*gen*) en peor situación; (*financially*) peor económicamente. ◆ *n*: **~ was to come** lo peor estaba aún por venir; **for the ~** para peor.

worsen ['wɜːsn] *vt & vi* empeorar.

worship ['wɜːʃɪp] ◆ *vt lit & fig* adorar. ◆ *n lit & fig*: **~ (of)** culto *m* (a), adoración *f* (por). ▶ **Worship** *n*: **Your/Her/His Worship** su señoría; **his Worship the Mayor** el Excelentísimo Señor alcalde.

worst [wɜːst] ◆ *adj* peor; **the ~ thing is** ... lo peor es que ... ◆ *adv* peor; **the ~ affected area** la región más afectada. ◆ *n*: **the ~** (*thing*) lo peor; (*person*) el peor *m*, la peor *f*; **if the ~ comes to the ~** en último extremo. ▶ **at (the) worst** *adv* en el peor de los casos.

worth [wɜːθ] ◆ *prep* 1. (*having the value of*): **it's ~ £50** vale 50 libras; **how much is it ~?** ¿cuánto vale? 2. (*deserving of*) digno(na) de; **the museum is ~ visiting** OR **a visit, it's ~ visiting the museum** el museo merece una visita. ◆ *n* 1. (*amount*): **£50,000 ~ of antiques** antigüedades por valor de 50.000 libras; **a month's ~ of groceries** provisiones para un mes. 2. *fml* (*value*) valor *m*.

worthless ['wɜːθlɪs] *adj* 1. (*object*) sin valor. 2. (*person*) despreciable.

worthwhile [ˌwɜːθ'waɪl] *adj* que vale la pena; (*cause*) noble, digno(na).

worthy ['wɜːðɪ] *adj* 1. (*gen*) digno(na). 2. (*good but unexciting*) encomiable.

would [wʊd] *modal vb* 1. (*in reported speech*): **she said she ~ come** dijo que vendría. 2. (*indicating likelihood*): **what ~ you do?** ¿qué harías?; **he ~ have resigned** habría dimitido. 3. (*indicating willingness*): **she ~n't go** no quiso/quería ir; **he ~ do anything for her** haría cualquier cosa por ella. 4. (*in polite questions*): **~ you like a drink?** ¿quieres beber algo?; **~ you mind closing the window?** ¿le importaría cerrar la ventana?; **help me shut this suitcase, ~ you?** ayúdame a cerrar esta maleta, ¿quieres? 5. (*indicating inevitability*): **he WOULD say that, ~n't he?** hombre, era de esperar que dijera eso, ¿no? 6. (*expressing opinions*): **I ~ have thought (that) it ~ be easy** hubiera pensado que sería fácil; **I ~ prefer** ... preferiría ...; **I ~ like** ... quisiera ..., quiero ... 7. (*giving advice*): **I ~ report it if I were you** yo en tu lugar lo denunciaría. 8. (*indicating habit*): **he ~ smoke a cigar after dinner** solía fumar un puro después de la cena; **she ~ often complain about the neighbours** se quejaba a menudo de los vecinos.

would-be *adj*: **a ~ author** un aspirante a literato.

wouldn't ['wʊdnt] = **would not**.

would've ['wʊdəv] = **would have**.

wound¹ [wuːnd] ◆ *n* herida *f*. ◆ *vt lit & fig* herir.

wound² [waʊnd] *pt & pp* → **wind**².

wove [wəʊv] *pt* → **weave**.

woven ['wəʊvn] *pp* → **weave**.

WP 1. *abbr of* **word processing**. 2. *abbr of* **word processor**.

wrangle ['ræŋgl] ◆ *n* disputa *f*. ◆ *vi*: **to ~ (with sb over sthg)** discutir OR pelearse (con alguien por algo).

wrap [ræp] ◆ *vt* 1. (*cover*) envolver; **to ~ sthg in sthg** envolver algo en algo; **to ~ sthg around** OR **round sthg** liar algo alrededor de algo. 2. (*encircle*): **he wrapped his hands around it** lo rodeó con sus manos. ◆ *n* (*garment*) echarpe *m*. ▶ **wrap up** ◆ *vt sep* (*cover*) envolver. ◆ *vi* (*put warm clothes on*): **~ up well** OR **warmly** abrígate bien.

wrapper ['ræpər] *n* envoltorio *m*.

wrapping ['ræpɪŋ] *n* envoltorio *m*.

wrapping paper *n* (U) papel *m* de envolver.

wrath [rɒθ] *n literary* ira *f*, cólera *f*.

wreak [riːk] *vt* causar; **to ~ havoc** hacer estragos; **to ~ revenge** OR **vengeance** tomar la revancha.

wreath [riːθ] *n* corona *f* (de flores).

wreck [rek] ◆ n 1. (of car, plane) restos mpl del siniestro; (of ship) restos del naufragio. 2. inf (person) guiñapo m. ◆ vt 1. (destroy) destrozar. 2. (NAUT) hacer naufragar; **to be ~ed** naufragar. 3. (spoil) dar al traste con; (health) acabar con.

wreckage ['rekɪdʒ] n (U) (of plane, car) restos mpl; (of building) escombros mpl.

wren [ren] n chochín m.

wrench [rentʃ] ◆ n 1. (tool) llave f inglesa. 2. (injury) torcedura f. ◆ vt 1. (pull violently): **to ~ sthg (off)** arrancar algo; **to ~ sthg open** abrir algo de un tirón. 2. (twist and injure) torcer.

wrestle ['resl] vi lit & fig: **to ~ (with)** luchar (con).

wrestler ['reslər] n luchador m, -ra f.

wrestling ['reslɪŋ] n lucha f libre.

wretch [retʃ] n desgraciado m, -da f.

wretched ['retʃɪd] adj 1. (miserable) miserable. 2. inf (damned) maldito(ta).

wriggle ['rɪgl] vi 1. (move about) menearse. 2. (twist) escurrirse, deslizarse.

wring [rɪŋ] (pt & pp wrung) vt 1. (wet clothes etc) estrujar, escurrir. 2. (neck) retorcer.

wringing ['rɪŋɪŋ] adj: **~ (wet)** empapado(da).

wrinkle ['rɪŋkl] ◆ n arruga f. ◆ vt arrugar. ◆ vi arrugarse.

wrist [rɪst] n muñeca f.

wristwatch ['rɪstwɒtʃ] n reloj m de pulsera.

writ [rɪt] n mandato m judicial.

write [raɪt] (pt wrote, pp written) ◆ vt 1. (gen & COMPUT) escribir. 2. Am (person) escribir a. ◆ vi (gen & COMPUT) escribir. ▶ **write back** vt sep & vi contestar. ▶ **write down** vt sep apuntar. ▶ **write into** vt sep incluir en. ▶ **write off** vt sep 1. (plan, hopes) abandonar. 2. (debt) cancelar, anular. 3. (person - as failure) considerar un fracaso. 4. Br inf (wreck) cargarse. ▶ **write up** vt sep redactar.

write-off n: **the car was a ~** el coche quedó totalmente destrozado.

writer ['raɪtər] n 1. (as profession) escritor m, -ra f. 2. (of letter, article, story) autor m, -ra f.

writhe [raɪð] vi retorcerse.

writing ['raɪtɪŋ] n 1. (U) (handwriting) letra f, caligrafía f. 2. (something written) escrito m; **in ~** por escrito. 3. (activity) escritura f.

writing paper n (U) papel m de carta.

written ['rɪtn] ◆ pp → write. ◆ adj 1. (not oral) escrito(ta). 2. (official) por escrito.

wrong [rɒŋ] ◆ adj 1. (not normal, not satisfactory) malo(la); **the clock's ~** el reloj anda mal; **what's ~?** ¿qué pasa?; **there's nothing ~ with me** no me pasa nada. 2. (not suitable, not correct) equivocado (da); (moment, time) inoportuno(na); **to be ~** equivocarse; **to be ~ to do sthg** cometer un error al hacer algo. 3. (morally bad) malo(la); **it's ~ to steal/lie** robar/mentir está mal; **what's ~ with being a communist?** ¿qué tiene de malo ser comunista? ◆ adv (incorrectly) mal; **to get sthg ~** entender mal algo; **to go ~** (make a mistake) cometer un error; (stop functioning) estropearse. ◆ n 1. (evil) mal m; **to be in the ~** haber hecho mal. 2. (injustice) injusticia f. ◆ vt ser injusto (ta) con, agraviar.

wrongful ['rɒŋful] adj (dismissal) improcedente; (arrest, imprisonment) ilegal.

wrongly ['rɒŋlɪ] adv equivocadamente.

wrong number n: sorry, **~** lo siento, se ha equivocado de número.

wrote [rəut] pt → write.

wrought iron [rɔːt-] n hierro m forjado.

wrung [rʌŋ] pt & pp → wring.

wry [raɪ] adj 1. (amused) irónico(ca). 2. (displeased) de asco.

WWW (abbr of World Wide Web) n WWW f.

XYZ

x (pl **x's** OR **xs**), **X** (pl **X's** OR **Xs**) [eks] n (letter) x f inv, X f inv.

xenophobia [ˌzenə'fəubjə] n xenofobia f.

Xmas ['eksməs] ◆ n Navidad f. ◆ comp de Navidad.

X-ray ◆ n 1. (ray) rayo m X. 2. (picture) radiografía f. ◆ vt examinar con rayos X, radiografiar.

xylophone ['zaɪləfəun] n xilofón m.

y (pl **y's** OR **ys**), **Y** (pl **Y's** OR **Ys**) [waɪ] n (letter) y f, Y f.

yacht [jɒt] n yate m; (for racing) balandro m.

yachting ['jɒtɪŋ] n balandrismo m.
yachtsman ['jɒtsmən] (pl -men
[-mən]) n balandrista m.
Yank [jæŋk] n inf término peyorativo que
designa a un estadounidense, yanqui m y f.
Yankee ['jæŋkɪ] n Br inf término peyorativo que designa a un estadounidense, yanqui
m y f.
yap [jæp] vi (dog) ladrar.
yard [jɑːd] n 1. (unit of measurement) =
91,44 cm, yarda f. 2. (walled area) patio m.
3. (shipyard) astillero m; **builder's/goods**
~ depósito m de materiales/de mercancías. 4. Am (attached to house) jardín
m.
yardstick ['jɑːdstɪk] n criterio m,
pauta f.
yarn [jɑːn] n (thread) hilo m, hilaza f.
yawn [jɔːn] ◆ n (when tired) bostezo m.
◆ vi 1. (when tired) bostezar. 2. (gap,
chasm) abrirse.
yd abbr of **yard**.
yeah [jeə] adv inf sí.
year [jɪər] n 1. (gen) año m; **he's 25 ~s
old** tiene 25 años; **all (the) ~ round** todo
el año. 2. (SCH) curso m; **he's in (his) first
~** está en primero. ▶ **years** npl (ages)
años mpl; **it's ~s since I last saw you** hace
siglos que no te veo.
yearly ['jɪəlɪ] ◆ adj anual. ◆ adv
1. (once a year) una vez al año. 2. (every
year) cada año.
yearn [jɜːn] vi: **to ~ for sthg/to do sthg**
ansiar algo/hacer algo.
yearning ['jɜːnɪŋ] n: ~ **(for sb/sthg)**
anhelo m (de alguien/algo).
yeast [jiːst] n levadura f.
yell [jel] ◆ n grito m, alarido m. ◆ vt &
vi vociferar.
yellow ['jeləʊ] ◆ adj (in colour) amarillo
(lla). ◆ n amarillo m.
yellow card n (FTBL) tarjeta f amarilla.
yelp [jelp] ◆ n aullido m. ◆ vi aullar.
yeoman of the guard ['jəʊmən-] (pl
yeomen of the guard ['jəʊmən-]) n
alabardero m de la Casa Real británica.
yes [jes] ◆ adv sí; **to say ~** decir que sí;
to say ~ to sthg consentir algo. ◆ n sí m.
yesterday ['jestədɪ] ◆ n ayer m. ◆ adv
ayer; ~ **afternoon** ayer por la tarde; **the
day before ~** anteayer.
yet [jet] ◆ adv 1. (gen) todavía, aún;
have you had lunch ~? ¿has comido ya?;
their worst defeat ~ la mayor derrota
que han sufrido hasta la fecha; **as ~** de
momento, hasta ahora; **not ~** todavía
OR aún no. 2. (even): ~ **another car** otro

coche más; ~ **again** otra vez más; ~
more aún más. ◆ conj pero, sin embargo.
yew [juː] n tejo m.
Yiddish ['jɪdɪʃ] ◆ adj yídish (inv). ◆ n
yídish m.
yield [jiːld] ◆ n 1. (AGR) cosecha f.
2. (FIN) rédito m. ◆ vt 1. (gen) producir,
dar. 2. (give up) ceder. ◆ vi 1. (shelf, lock
etc) ceder. 2. fml (person, enemy)
rendirse; **to ~ to sb/sthg** claudicar ante
alguien/algo. 3. Am (AUT) (give way): '~'
'ceda el paso'.
YMCA (abbr of **Young Men's Christian
Association**) n asociación internacional de
jóvenes cristianos.
yoga ['jəʊgə] n yoga m.
yoghourt, yoghurt, yogurt [Br
'jɒgət, Am 'jəʊgərt] n yogur m.
yoke [jəʊk] n lit & fig yugo m.
yolk [jəʊk] n yema f.
you [juː] pers pron 1. (subject - sg) tú, vos
(+ pl vb) Amer; (- formal use) usted; (- pl)
vosotros mpl, -tras fpl; (- formal use) ustedes (pl); ~'re **a good cook** eres/usted
es un buen cocinero; **are ~ French?**
¿eres/es usted francés?; ~ **idiot!** ¡imbécil!; **if I were** OR **was ~** si (yo) fuera tú/
usted, yo en tu/su lugar; **excuse me,
Madam, have ~ got the time?** perdone,
señora, ¿tiene usted hora?; **there ~ are**
(you've appeared) ¡ya estás/está usted
aquí!; (have this) ahí tienes/tiene; **that
jacket isn't really ~** esa chaqueta no te/
le pega. 2. (direct object - unstressed - sg)
te; (- pl) os; (- formal use) le m, la f; (- pl)
les mpl, las fpl; **I can see ~** te/os veo; **yes,
Madam, I understand ~** sí, señora, la
comprendo. 3. (direct object - stressed): **I
don't expect ~ to do it** no te voy a
pedir que TÚ lo hagas. 4. (indirect object -
sg) te; (- pl) os; (- formal use) le; (- pl) les;
she gave it to ~ te/os lo dio; **can I get ~ a
chair, sir?** ¿le traigo una silla, señor?
5. (after prep, in comparisons etc - sg) ti;
(- pl) vosotros mpl, -tras fpl; (- formal use)
usted; (- pl) ustedes; **we shall go with/
without ~** iremos contigo/sin ti, iremos
con/sin vosotros (pl); **I'm shorter than ~**
soy más bajo que tú/vosotros. 6. (anyone, one) uno; ~ **wouldn't have thought so**
uno no lo habría pensado; **exercise is
good for ~** el ejercicio es bueno.
you'd [juːd] = **you had, you would**.
you'll [juːl] = **you will**.
young [jʌŋ] ◆ adj (not old) joven. ◆ npl
1. (young people): **the ~** los jóvenes.
2. (baby animals) crías fpl.

younger ['jʌŋgəʳ] *adj* : **Pitt the ~** Pitt el joven, Pitt hijo.

youngster ['jʌŋstəʳ] *n* joven *m y f*.

your [jɔːʳ] *poss adj* **1.** (*everyday use - referring to one person*) tu; (- *referring to more than one person*) vuestro(tra); **~ dog** tu/vuestro perro; **~ children** tus niños; **what's ~ name?** ¿cómo te llamas?; **it wasn't YOUR fault** no fue culpa tuya/vuestra; **you didn't wash ~ hair** no te lavaste/os lavasteis el pelo. **2.** (*formal use*) su; **~ dog** su perro; **what are ~ names?** ¿cuáles son sus nombres? **3.** (*impersonal - one's*): **~ attitude changes as you get older** la actitud de uno cambia con la vejez; **it's good for ~ teeth/hair** es bueno para los dientes/el pelo; **~ average Englishman** el inglés medio.

you're [jɔːʳ] = **you are**.

yours [jɔːz] *poss pron* **1.** (*everyday use - referring to one person*) tuyo (tuya); (- *referring to more than one person*) vuestro (vuestra); **that money is ~** ese dinero es tuyo/vuestro; **those keys are ~** esas llaves son tuyas/vuestras; **my car hit ~** mi coche chocó contra el tuyo/el vuestro; **it wasn't her fault, it was YOURS** no fue culpa de ella sino TUYA/VUESTRA; **a friend of ~** un amigo tuyo/vuestro. **2.** (*formal use*) suyo (suya). ▶ **Yours** *adv* (*in letter*) un saludo; *see also* **faithfully, sincerely** *etc*.

yourself [jɔː'self] (*pl* **-selves** [-'selvz]) *pron* **1.** (*as reflexive - sg*) te; (- *pl*) os; (- *formal use*) se; **did you hurt ~?** ¿te hiciste/se hizo daño? **2.** (*after prep - sg*) ti mismo (ti misma); (- *pl*) vosotros mismos (vosotras mismas); (- *formal use*) usted mismo (usted misma); **with ~** contigo mismo/misma. **3.** (*for emphasis*): **you ~** tú mismo (tú misma); (*formal use*) usted mismo (ma); **you yourselves** vosotros mismos (vosotras mismas); (*formal use*) ustedes mismos(mas). **4.** (*without help*) solo(la); **did you do it (by) ~?** ¿lo hiciste solo?

youth [juːθ] *n* **1.** (*gen*) juventud *f*. **2.** (*boy, young man*) joven *m*.

youth club *n* club *m* juvenil.

youthful ['juːθfʊl] *adj* juvenil.

youth hostel *n* albergue *m* juvenil.

you've [juːv] = **you have**.

YTS (*abbr of* **Youth Training Scheme**) *n* programa gubernamental de promoción del empleo juvenil en Gran Bretaña.

Yugoslav = **Yugoslavian**.

Yugoslavia [ˌjuːgə'slɑːvɪə] *n* Yugoslavia.

Yugoslavian [ˌjuːgə'slɑːvɪən], **Yugoslav** [ˌjuːgə'slɑːv] ◆ *adj* yugoslavo(va). ◆ *n* yugoslavo *m*, -va *f*.

yuppie, yuppy ['jʌpɪ] (*abbr of* **young urban professional**) *n* yuppy *m y f*.

YWCA (*abbr of* **Young Women's Christian Association**) *n* asociación internacional de jóvenes cristianas.

z (*pl* **z's** OR **zs**), **Z** (*pl* **Z's** OR **Zs**) [Br zed, Am ziː] *n* (*letter*) z *f*, Z *f*.

Zambia ['zæmbɪə] *n* Zambia.

zany ['zeɪnɪ] *adj inf* (*humour, trick*) disparatado(da); (*person*) loco(ca).

zap [zæp] *vi inf* : **to ~ off (somewhere)** hacer una escapada (a algún sitio).

zeal [ziːl] *n fml* celo *m*.

zealous ['zeləs] *adj fml* entusiasta.

zebra [Br 'zebrə, Am 'ziːbrə] (*pl inv* OR **-s**) *n* cebra *f*.

zebra crossing *n* Br paso *m* cebra.

zenith [Br 'zenɪθ, Am 'ziːnəθ] *n* (ASTRON & *fig*) cenit *m*.

zero [Br 'zɪərəʊ, Am 'ziːrəʊ] (*pl inv* OR **-es**) ◆ *adj* cero (*inv*), nulo(la). ◆ *n* cero *m*; **below ~** bajo cero.

zest [zest] *n* (U) **1.** (*excitement, eagerness*) entusiasmo *m*. **2.** (*of orange, lemon*) cáscara *f*.

zigzag ['zɪgzæg] ◆ *n* zigzag *m*. ◆ *vi* zigzaguear.

Zimbabwe [zɪm'bɑːbwɪ] *n* Zimbabue.

zinc [zɪŋk] *n* cinc *m*, zinc *m*.

zip [zɪp] *n* Br (*fastener*) cremallera *f*, cierre *m* relámpago Amer. ▶ **zip up** *vt sep* cerrar la cremallera de.

zip code *n* Am código *m* postal.

zip fastener Br = **zip**.

zipper ['zɪpəʳ] *n* Am = **zip**.

zodiac ['zəʊdɪæk] *n*: **the ~** el zodiaco.

zone [zəʊn] *n* zona *f*.

zoo [zuː] *n* zoo *m*.

zoology [zəʊ'ɒlədʒɪ] *n* zoología *f*.

zoom [zuːm] *vi inf* (*move quickly*): **to ~ past** pasar zumbando.

zoom lens *n* zoom *m*.

zucchini [zuː'kiːnɪ] (*pl inv*) *n* Am calabacín *m*.